ISBN 978-0-260-70033-9
PIBN 10965019

FB &c Ltd, Dalton House, 60 Windsor Avenue, London, SW19 2RR.
Company number 08720141. Registered in England and Wales.

For support please visit www.forgottenbooks.com

National Reporter System.—State Series.

THE

NORTHEASTERN REPORTER,

VOLUME 70,

CONTAINING ALL THE CURRENT DECISIONS OF THE

SUPREME COURTS OF MASSACHUSETTS, OHIO, ILLINOIS, INDIANA, APPELLATE COURT OF INDIANA, AND THE COURT OF APPEALS OF NEW YORK.

PERMANENT EDITION.

MARCH 25—JUNE 17, 1904.

WITH TABLE OF NORTHEASTERN CASES IN WHICH REHEARINGS HAVE BEEN DENIED.

ST. PAUL:
WEST PUBLISHING CO.
1904.

JUDGES

OF THE

COURTS REPORTED DURING THE PERIOD COVERED BY THIS VOLUME.

ILLINOIS—Supreme Court.

JOHN P. HAND, CHIEF JUSTICE.[1]
JAMES B. RICKS, CHIEF JUSTICE.[2]

JUSTICES.

JAMES H. CARTWRIGHT.
CARROLL C. BOGGS.
JAMES B. RICKS.[2]
JACOB W. WILKIN.
BENJAMIN D. MAGRUDER.
GUY C. SCOTT.
JOHN P. HAND.[1]

10/2/46 Boston Law Book Co.

INDIANA—Supreme Court.[3]

JAMES H. JORDAN, CHIEF JUSTICE.

ASSOCIATE JUSTICES.

ALEXANDER DOWLING.
JOHN V. HADLEY.
LEANDER J. MONKS.
JOHN H. GILLETT.

INDIANA—Appellate Court.[3]

JAMES B. BLACK, CHIEF JUDGE.

ASSOCIATE JUDGES.

DANIEL W. COMSTOCK.
ULRIC Z. WILEY.
FRANK S. ROBY.
WOODFIN D. ROBINSON.
WILLIAM J. HENLEY.

Division No. 1.[3]

JAMES B. BLACK, CHIEF JUDGE.

ASSOCIATE JUDGES.

WOODFIN D. ROBINSON.
WILLIAM J. HENLEY.

Division No. 2.[3]

FRANK S. ROBY, PRESIDING JUDGE.

ASSOCIATE JUDGES.

DANIEL W. COMSTOCK.
ULRIC Z. WILEY.

MASSACHUSETTS—Supreme Judicial Court.

MARCUS P. KNOWLTON, CHIEF JUSTICE.

ASSOCIATE JUSTICES.

JAMES M. MORTON.
JOHN LATHROP.
JAMES M. BARKER.
JOHN WILKES HAMMOND.
WILLIAM CALEB LORING.
HENRY K. BRALEY.

[1] Ceased to be Chief Justice June 7, 1904.
[2] Became Chief Justice June 7, 1904.
[3] Beginning May Term, 1904.

NEW YORK—Court of Appeals.

ALTON B. PARKER, Chief Judge.

ASSOCIATE JUDGES.

JOHN C. GRAY.
DENIS O'BRIEN.
EDWARD T. BARTLETT.
ALBERT HAIGHT.
CELORA E. MARTIN.
IRVING G. VANN.
EDGAR M. CULLEN.
WILLIAM E. WERNER.

OHIO—Supreme Court.

JACOB F. BURKET, Chief Justice.[4]
WILLIAM T. SPEAR, Chief Justice.[5]

JUDGES.

WILLIAM T. SPEAR.[5]
WILLIAM Z. DAVIS.
JAMES L. PRICE.
JOHN A. SHAUCK.
WILLIAM B. CREW.
AUGUSTUS N. SUMMERS.[6]

[4] Retired February 9, 1904.
[5] Became Chief Justice February 9, 1904.
[6] Elected November, 1903, and took office February 9, 1904.

CASES REPORTED.

REHEARINGS DENIED.

[Cases in which rehearings have been denied, without the rendition of a written opinion, since the publication of the original opinions in previous volumes of this reporter.]

Bolton v. Clark (Ind. Sup.) 68 N. E. 283.
Branstrator v. Crow (Ind. Sup.) 69 N. E. 668.
Brown v. Central Bermudez Co. (Ind. Sup.) 69 N. E. 150.

Chicago, I. & L. R. Co. v. Cunningham (Ind. App.) 69 N. E. 304.
Chicago, I. & L. R. Co. v. Turner (Ind. App.) 69 N. E. 484.
Christ v. State (Ind. App.) 69 N. E. 269.
Consumers' Gas Trust Co. v. American Plate Glass Co. (Ind. Sup.) 68 N. E. 1020.
Coppes v. Union Nat. Savings Loan Ass'n (Ind. App.) 69 N. E. 702.

Edmunds Electric Const. Co. v. Mariotte (Ind. Sup.) 69 N. E. 396.

Fink v. Montgomery (Ind. Sup.) 68 N. E. 1010.

Griffin, In re (Ind. App.) 69 N. E. 192.

Hitchcock v. Cosper (Ind. App.) 69 N. E. 1029.

Indianapolis & G. Rapid Transit Co. v. Haines (Ind. App.) 69 N. E. 187.

Keiser v. Mills (Ind. Sup.) 69 N. E. 142.

Lake Erie & W. R. Co. v. Holland (Ind. Sup.) 69 N. E. 138.
Lux & Talbott Stone Co. v. Donaldson (Ind. Sup.) 68 N. E. 1014.

McKee v. Pendleton (Ind. Sup.) 69 N. E. 997.
Michigan City v. Phillips (Ind. App.) 69 N. E. 700.

Paul v. Baltimore & O. R. Co. (Ind. App.) 69 N. E. 1024.
Pittsburgh, C., C. & St. L. R. Co. v. McNeil (Ind. App.) 69 N. E. 471.
Pittsburgh, C., C. & St. L. R. Co. v. West (Ind. App.) 69 N. E. 1017.
Pittsburgh, C., C. & St. L. R. Co. v. Wolcott (Ind. Sup.) 69 N. E. 451.

Supreme Lodge K. H. v. Jones (Ind. App.) 69 N. E. 718.

Union Central Life Ins. Co. v. Loughmiller (Ind. App.) 69 N. E. 264.
Union Traction Co. of Indiana v. Vandercook (Ind. App.) 69 N. E. 486.
United States Express Co. v. Joyce (Ind. App.) 69 N. E. 1015.

Valparaiso City Water Co. v. Valparaiso (Ind. App.) 69 N. E. 1018.

Webb v. John Hancock Mut. Life Ins. Co. (Ind. Sup.) 69 N. E. 1006.
Weil v. Stone (Ind. App.) 69 N. E. 698.
Westervelt v. National Mfg. Co. (Ind. App.) 69 N. E. 169.
Williams v. Manley (Ind. App.) 69 N. E. 469.

THE
NORTHEASTERN REPORTER
VOLUME 70.

(177 N. Y. 408)

PEOPLE v. RODAWALD.

(Court of Appeals of New York. Feb. 16, 1904.)

MURDER — EVIDENCE — REPUTATION OF DECEASED—SELF-DEFENSE—INSTRUCTIONS.

1. Evidence *held* sufficient to warrant conviction of murder in the first degree.

2. On a trial for murder, it appeared that accused was disputing with a third party as to the ownership of certain posts, which such party asserted had been given to her by the section foreman of the railroad which owned them, and that defendant had attempted to move them, when deceased interfered. *Held*, that evidence of the foreman that he gave the posts to the woman was admissible to show some foundation for her claim.

3. On a trial for murder, opinion evidence is inadmissible to show whether the witness would have taken deceased into her family if she had known that he had been in prison.

4. On a trial for murder, evidence to show that deceased had been guilty of certain crimes, and a letter written by him to an acquaintance, referring to his criminal record, are inadmissible, where there is no evidence that defendant had heard of such convictions, though he knew that deceased had been in prison.

5. The general reputation of deceased for violence may be shown, where the defense on a trial for murder is a claim of self-defense, if defendant had knowledge of the same.

6. Evidence is inadmissible on a trial for murder to show specific acts of violence of which deceased had been guilty, not towards the defendant, or to his knowledge, but towards third persons or their property.

7. The record of a judgment in a criminal case is not conclusive when the question arises collaterally.

8. An instruction on a trial for murder that if defendant honestly believed himself to be in danger of great bodily harm from deceased, and in shooting him he acted on that belief, he was excusable, whether such danger actually existed or not, is improper, as there must not only be a reasonable ground to apprehend great personal injury, but imminent danger that the design will be accomplished.

9. Though an instruction as to self-defense was general in its nature, so that the jury may have misunderstood it, it is not ground for reversal, where counsel did not request further instructions.

Parker, C. J., and Martin and O'Brien, JJ., dissenting.

Appeal from Supreme Court, Trial Term, Cattaraugus County.

William Rodawald was convicted of murder in the first degree, and he appeals. Affirmed.

¶ 5. See Homicide, vol. 26, Cent. Dig. §§ 382, 398.

Thomas H. Dowd, for appellant. George W. Cole, Dist. Atty., for the People.

VANN, J. The homicide which is the subject of this appeal was committed in April, 1903. The defendant was indicted in May, convicted in June, and appealed to this court in July of the same year. The appeal was argued in January, 1904.

In the outskirts of the village of West Salamanca, Cattaraugus county, there is a public highway known as "South Street," running from Broad street, on the south bank of the Allegheny river, southerly to the Pennsylvania Railroad, a distance of 1,070 feet. On that street the homicide in question occurred, and on that street the deceased, the accused, and all the witnesses of the tragedy resided. On the west side, about 200 feet north of the railroad, the defendant lived, with his family, consisting of his wife and 3 children, Mary, Robert, and William, aged, respectively, 15, 13, and 12 years. Mrs. Keating, a widow with 6 children, ranging in age from 3 to 13 years, resided on the east side of the street, about 700 feet south of Broad street. Davis, a colored man, and his wife, also lived on the east side of the street, a few feet south of Mrs. Keating, and nearly opposite the defendant. No one else lived on that street, or within 1,000 feet of the scene of the homicide.

The defendant was born in Germany, and at the time of the fatal event was 49 years of age, and had lived in this country since 1889. He was in the German army for 3 years, and had worked as a bricklayer in Germany, and as a laborer in this country. A short time before he left Germany he was arrested for fighting during a strike, and after a trial was imprisoned for 9 months. After coming to this country he was arrested upon a peace warrant, but gave bail and was discharged. He was a temperate, industrious man, and was never charged with any other crime until the present accusation was brought against him. About 1887, during a strike in the brickyard where he was employed, he was struck on the head with a spade, and so seriously injured that he could not work at any employment which required him to bend over. For a while after that he sometimes fainted, on other occasions grew dizzy, and ever since he has been troubled with sick headache occasionally—oftener in warm weather than in cold. Except as stated, his health was good. He was somewhat excitable, and, under excitement, spoke and acted in a strange way.

The deceased, Jesse Frederick Bayer, was born in Amsterdam, N. Y., and was about 25 years old at the time of his death. He does not appear to have had a fixed place of abode for long at a time. He had been a circus performer, and he lived on the Indian reservation in Cattaraugus county for a while prior to the spring of 1902, when he enlisted in the United States navy. Why he was discharged does not appear, but in less than a year he returned to the reservation, and eight days before his death began to board with Mrs. Keating. During this period he worked in a bicycle factory in Salamanca, a little more than a mile from his boarding house. These two men had never met, but the defendant knew who Bayer was, and that he had been in State's Prison.

For several years prior to the homicide the defendant had been accustomed to get from the side of the railroad old posts and ties to use as fuel, and he claimed that this privilege had been given him by the section boss. Mrs. Keating also claimed the same privilege by permission from the same person, but he had no right to give the material away. On the day before the homicide, Mrs. Keating had drawn one load of old fence posts to her premises, and, with the help of her little boy, had piled up some more on the south side of the track, in the vicinity of the South street crossing; intending to draw them at her convenience. On the day of the homicide, Mrs. Rodawald had taken away some of the posts, but the defendant did not know it. At this time the defendant was working in a tannery at Salamanca, more than a mile from where he resided. On the 7th of April, 1903, after working during the day as usual, he stopped at 10 minutes of 6, and reached home between half past 6 and a quarter of 7. He at once put down his dinner pail, threw off his coat, called his two boys to bring the wheelbarrow, and started to get some posts; there being but four left at that time. They loaded the posts on the barrow, and wheeled them to the crossing, where it was necessary to unload in order to get over the rails; and the defendant, taking one of the posts on his shoulder, started for his house. On his way he passed by Davis, who was working in his garden. Davis said to him: "You are getting some wood," and the defendant answered: "Yes; I am getting some wood. Why don't you go and get some?" Davis replied: "I don't want any. That widow says it is her wood, and I don't want any of it." The defendant said: "It is just as much yours as it is hers. Why don't you go and get some?" But Davis said he would not get any. Mrs. Keating saw him carrying the post, and called to him, saying: "Mr. Rodawald, I wish you would please leave that wood alone. It was given to me." He shouted: "To hell mit you! Anybody can take this wood." As she stepped back into her house, Bayer came out, and went up to the railroad, where the rest of the posts were. Davis came out in the road and said: "I wouldn't take her wood. She is a poor woman. I wouldn't take her wood." But the defendant did not stop. After throwing down the fence post by his wood pile, he returned to the little boys, who in the meantime had run the wheelbarrow across the railroad tracks. Two of the posts were again loaded, and the defendant took the third and carried it to his house. The boys wheeled the loaded barrow a short distance, and stopped in a vacant lot a few feet west of the street, and about 125 feet from the defendant's house. At about this time, Bayer said to the defendant: "Now, mister, you oughtn't to take that wood from that woman. She is a widow woman, and you are a man, and you can get wood better than she can." Shaking his fist, the defendant said: "To hell mit you! To hell mit you! Go on mit you! Anybody can take this wood." On his way back to the wheelbarrow, after he had thrown the second post on the woodpile, the defendant saw Bayer throw the remaining posts off on the ground, and, shouting to his wife, said, "Go get my gun, get my revolver," but she did not go. He also said, "Shoot 'em, kill 'em," and was "shaking mad and swearing." He ran into his house by the back door, and came out with a revolver and a double-barreled shotgun. The revolver, of 32 caliber, could be cocked and discharged by a single pull on the trigger. It contained five ball cartridges, and both barrels of the shotgun were loaded, but it does not appear that the hammer of either barrel was cocked. As he came out of his house, he held the gun "up in the attitude of shooting." Mrs. Keating shouted to Bayer: "Come away, Jesse. If you don't he will shoot you." Davis said to the defendant: "Put down that gun. You are not going to shoot nobody here. There is nobody done anything to you. You put it down." The defendant said: "I will shoot 'em all. I will kill 'em"—and kept on going fast toward Bayer, who had gone from the wheelbarrow into the street, and was advancing rapidly toward the defendant. As the defendant spoke, he lowered his gun, shifted it to his left hand, drew the revolver from his hip pocket, and said, as one of the witnesses stated, "I will shoot you, you son of a ——." Bayer threw up both hands and said: "Don't shoot. Please don't shoot." But the defendant fired at close range. Bayer staggered back two or three steps from the highway, fell to the ground, and died "without a word or a groan." As the revolver went off, Bayer "ducked his head." The place where he fell was 17 feet from the nearest part of the foundation of an old building that had been burned, 25 feet from the wheelbarrow, and 101 feet from the front door of the defendant's house. Davis rushed up and said to the defendant, "You have killed this man," and called him a cowardly murderer. The defendant walked around the head of the deceased, and said, according to the statement of one witness, "If he no dead, me shoot him again." No other witness mentioned this fact. The defendant gave the shotgun to one of his sons, wheeled the two posts to his house, put away his revolver, put on his coat, and started for Salamanca. On his way he said to some witnesses for the prosecution that they need not arrest him, for he was going to arrest himself. He went to the office of a deputy sheriff, told him that he had shot a man, and in response to questions, said that the man was dead, that he shot him in the shoulder, and that he did not see him have a weapon of any kind or a knife. When asked what he shot him for, he said that it was over some wood that he got from the railroad company; that Bayer had pushed his wife away from the wheelbarrow, and shoved his little boys around; and that a man who would not take care of his wife and children was not much of a man. He was excited; spoke fast and in broken English.

These are the facts as the jury might have found them from the testimony of Mrs. Keating and her daughter Pearl, 11 years old, Mr. and Mrs. Davis, and the deputy sheriff, all of whom were called by the people, and all except the officer saw the homicide. They did not all testify to all of these facts, as some apparently observed acts that escaped the attention of others. There was some difference in their statements, especially in regard to what was said and when it was said, but as to what was done at the critical moment they were in substantial accord. The evidence showed traces of ill feeling between the Keating and Davis families, on the one hand, and the family of the defendant, on the other.

The surgeon who made the autopsy reached the body at about half-past 7. He found the height of the dead man, from measurement, to be 5 feet 8 inches, and estimated the weight at 135 pounds. The bullet entered the left temple at a point an inch and a half in front of the ear, and half an inch higher than the ear. The course of the wound was "backward, downward, and inward toward the middle line of the brain." The bullet penetrated 4½ inches, and went half an inch downward in going that distance.

The eyewitnesses of the homicide who were called by the defendant were himself, his wife, and the three children who lived at home. According to their version, the defendant, calling to the boys, told them to get the wheelbarrow, saying that he wanted some posts to make a calf pasture. While he was carrying one of the posts to the house, Bayer asked him if the section boss gave him those posts, and the defendant said, "Yes," when Bayer remarked, "All right, you can have them." Davis came out to the road and said, "That wood ain't yours," and the defendant replied, "I have got it so far, and I can have it now." Later, Bayer threw the rest of the posts off of the wheelbarrow, and Mrs. Rodawald tried to put them on again, when he caught her by the dress and shoved her, pushed the boys away, and ran the wheelbarrow against one of them. One of the boys denied that the defendant told his wife to go for the gun, but his other witnesses said he did, after first telling Bayer that, if he did not go away, he would get his gun. When the defendant came out of his house with the gun and went toward Bayer, he said to him that, if he did not go away from there, he would shoot him, and Bayer then left the wheelbarrow and walked toward Davis' house. Thereupon the defendant turned around and said, partly in German and partly in English: "Come in the house, and let the wood go to hell." As he said this he started toward his house, and Bayer, who was 12 or 15 feet away, with three fingers drew a knife from a pocket situated like a watch pocket in the front part of the pantaloons he had worn in the navy, opened it, and, holding it in his right hand, ran up behind the defendant, caught him by the back of the collar with his left hand, and raised the knife over his head. The defendant dropped his gun, and with his right hand seized Bayer by the right hand, and the revolver went off, and Bayer staggered, threw his hands in the air, and fell over backward. The defendant did not say that, if Bayer was not dead, he would shoot him again. He told his son Robert to take the gun in the house, piled the posts on the wheelbarrow, and wheeled it home. Two of these witnesses swore that, when the defendant started for his gun, Bayer had not taken hold of Mrs. Rodawald; but several of them said that, after the defendant came out with the gun, Bayer caught hold of her. Although they all saw the knife in Bayer's hands as he ran up behind the defendant, none of them warned him. The defendant, however, swore that he heard the children scream, and, turning partly around, saw Bayer holding the knife up high, in readiness to strike. The defendant also testified that when he dropped his gun and seized Bayer he had the revolver in the same hand with which he caught hold of Bayer's hand, and that in the struggle the revolver went off by accident. He did not intend to shoot any one when he went for his gun or at any time. He went for the gun because Mrs. Keating had a butcher knife and shouted, "Kill the sons of bitches," and he wanted to scare them away. He thought Bayer was going to strike him with the knife when he caught him by the hand. There was evidence that Mrs. Keating had a butcher knife, and Davis a revolver, when they were in the vicinity of the wheelbarrow, before the defendant went for his gun, but no attempt was made to use either, although Mrs. Keating said, "Kill the sons of bitches," and repeated it. The members of defendant's family did not look for the knife after all was over, but two days later his sons were playing ball, and, as they testified, found a knife in some dead grass by one of the stones in the foundation of the burned building, about 17 feet from where Bayer fell. It was a clasp knife, with the blade open, and was bright and free from rust, although rain had fallen several times since the homicide, and the knife had been exposed to dampness for more than 40 hours. One of the boys testified that Bayer had no coat on, or anything that covered the pocket from which he took the knife; but the surgeon who made the autopsy, as well as the coroner, who promptly viewed the body, said that it had a sweater on, which came down over all the pockets. The defendant swore that when he surrendered himself he told the officer that the man he shot came up behind him with a knife. Members of the defendant's family were examined by the district attorney, with the aid of a stenographer, the day after the homicide; and, while some of the statements made were inconsistent with their statements on the trial, still it was then said that Bayer had a knife, drew it, jumped and caught the defendant by the collar, and had hold of him when the revolver went off. The knife was found on the afternoon of the day when the defendant was examined before a magistrate in the forenoon. Mrs. Keating and her daughter, on their redirect examination, denied that the former had a butcher knife or any knife, or that she said what was attributed to her about killing. They never saw Bayer have a knife, and he did not have one in his hand that night and run up behind the defendant. Mr. and Mrs. Davis testified to the same effect, and said that Davis had no revolver, and had not owned one for over 18 years. Three witnesses swore that the defendant showed great excitement while a witness at a trial in Elmira in November, 1902; raising himself up from the chair, and saying several times to the attorney, who was sharply cross-examining him upon the subject of his arrest in Germany, "Who told you that? That's a lie," with variations. An officer, by order of the court, forced him to keep seated in his chair. These acts impressed those witnesses, who had never seen him before, as irrational. One of them, however, testified that the answers of the defendant, when separated from his actions, were not irrational, and other testimony was given to the same effect. The same acts impressed a physician, who observed them carefully through curiosity, as rational. A married daughter of the defendant testified that after he was struck on the head with a spade in Germany he was more excitable, more irritable, and less kind to the members of his family than before. No expert upon the subject of insanity was called by either side.

We have thus stated the leading facts as fully as space will permit. It is clear that the evidence presented a grave question of fact, depending to an unusual extent upon the credibility of witnesses, and requiring the judgment of a jury for its determination. No court is wise enough to decide who told the truth without seeing the witnesses. According to the evidence for the prosecution, although the actors in the tragedy were strangers, the defendant was the aggressor from the outset; acting with deliberation and without reasonable provocation. According to the evidence for the defendant, although he may have armed himself without adequate cause, he had given up the controversy over the wood, and had started for home, when he was attacked by the deceased with a dangerous weapon, and the revolver was fired in lawful defense of his person, or went off accidentally. A fearful mistake may have been made by the jury, yet justice cannot be administered without running that risk in almost every murder case that is tried.

The downward course of the bullet after it went through the skull may have been owing to mechanical deflection, or it may have been in the line of origin. If the former was the cause, the fact is without significance; and if the latter, it could be accounted for by the theory of either side. The ground on which the parties stood was level. If the deceased "ducked his head" as the revolver went off, or if the defendant, with the revolver in his hand, seized the hand of the deceased as it was held aloft in readiness to strike, the course of the bullet may have been straight from the muzzle of the revolver to the center of the brain. The story about finding the knife so long after the death, and so far from where the dead man fell, in view of its condition when found after prolonged exposure to dampness, seems improbable, yet members of the defendant's family on the day after the homicide, without consulting counsel or talking with the defendant, so far as appears, or with any one except a relative who called, told the district attorney that the deceased drew a knife and was in the act of attacking when he was shot. The deputy sheriff —apparently a fair and disinterested witness —said that defendant told him within an hour after the occurrence that the deceased had no knife, but the defendant swore directly the reverse. The use of a self-cocking revolver gives some support to the claim either that the killing was accidental, or that the defendant acted without deliberation; but if he shifted the shotgun to his left hand, and with his right drew the revolver from a pocket behind and fired at the deceased, it warrants the inference of deliberation and premeditation. If the deceased was running toward the defendant when he was shot, as the people claim, it may indicate an intention to seize and disarm, as Rodawald was then facing Bayer and advancing towards him with his gun up in readiness to shoot, but it does not support the theory of the defense that Bayer ran up from behind. It bears, however, upon the question of deliberation. The prompt surrender of the defendant to an officer of justice is a circumstance in his favor, but it also indicates that his mind was clear, and that he was controlled by reason and judgment.

There are no controlling circumstances to guide us through the labyrinth of contradiction. If a reasonable doubt existed as to the defendant's guilt, or as to the degree of his guilt, it was for the jury to find it. Even if we should reach a different conclusion, we must accept their verdict as rendered, for the Constitution and the law make their judgment supreme under such circumstances. People v. Kelly, 113 N. Y. 647, 21 N. E. 122; People v. Hoch, 150 N. Y. 291, 44 N. E. 976.

Four questions of law are presented for our consideration:

1. The defendant claims that the trial justice erred in allowing the section foreman of the Pennsylvania Railroad to testify, under objection and exception, that he gave the posts which were the cause of the trouble to Mrs. Keating, although he had no authority to give them away, as his orders were to burn them. Both the defendant and Mrs. Keating claimed the posts, but apparently neither had any right to them. As Mrs. Keating did not know that her title was defective, it was proper to show that her claim had some foundation, and that she was not stealing the property, but acting in good faith. She told the defendant that the posts belonged to her, and the people had the right to prove that an employé of the railroad company, in charge of the section from which they were taken, had assumed to give them to her. This was part of the history of the case, and threw some light on the conduct of the parties who claimed the wood.

2. During the cross-examination of Mrs. Keating, an effort was made by counsel for the defendant to show that Bayer told her that he had been in prison. Among other questions, the following was asked, "Did he [Bayer], at any time afterward, and during his lifetime, and before his death, had he ever told you that he had been in prison?" Soon after this question had been answered, the witness was asked, "Would it have made any difference with your taking him in your family, had you known he had served a term in State's Prison for robbery?" The court sustained the objection of the district attorney, and the defendant excepted. The question was improper, because it was hypothetical and called for an opinion upon a subject to which evidence by opinion does not apply. If the real object was to discredit or impeach, the question should have called for a fact, not an opinion. Any act or experience of the witness which reflected upon her character could, in the sound discretion of the court, be shown on her cross-examination, but what she thought she would do upon a state of facts not proved was clearly immaterial for any purpose.

3. The defendant offered in evidence certified copies of the following records: A judgment rendered by a court of special sessions held in Montgomery county on the 14th of January, 1889, convicting the deceased of petit larceny upon his plea of guilty, and sentencing him to the State Industrial School at the city of Rochester. A judgment of the county court of Cattaraugus county convicting the deceased, also upon a plea of guilty, of assault in the first degree, and sentencing him to imprisonment in State Prison for four years. The defendant also offered in evidence a letter written by the deceased, dated Norfolk, Va., June 19, 1902, in which he asked an acquaintance to aid in freeing him from his enlistment in the United States navy upon the ground that he was an ex-convict, and closing as follows: "Auburn record is four years for assault, 14 months for burglary. Also to Albany for U. S. offense; also State I. School you will know how to work it I guess now do this as a favor." No offer was made to show that the defendant had heard that the deceased had been convicted of any of these offenses. All this evidence was excluded upon the objection that it was not the proper method of proving the character of the deceased, that specific acts are incompetent, and that the proof should be limited to general reputation. An exception was taken to each ruling as it was made. The defendant was allowed to show, without objection, that the deceased had been in State Prison, and that his wife told him so, but no effort was made to prove that the nature of the offense for which he was thus punished was brought to the knowledge of the defendant. So far as he knew, the imprisonment might have been for bigamy, forgery, or some crime not involving violence. The general character of the deceased was immaterial, for the worst man has the right to live, the same as the best, and no one may attack another because his general reputation is bad. The law protects every one from unlawful violence, regardless of his character. Upon a trial for murder, however, the accused, after giving evidence tending to show that he acted in self-defense, may prove that the general reputation of the deceased was that of a quarrelsome, vindictive, or violent man, and that such reputation had come to his knowledge prior to the homicide. People v. Gaimari, 176 N. Y. 84, 95, 68 N. E. 112; People v. Lamb, *41 N. Y. 360, 366; Abbott v. People, 86 N. Y. 460; Eggler v. People, 56 N. Y. 642; Wharton's Criminal Law [2d Ed.] § 606; Wharton's Criminal Evidence [9th Ed.] § 69; Underhill's Criminal Evidence, § 324. Such evidence is not received to show that the deceased was the aggressor, for, if competent for that purpose, similar evidence could be

given as to the reputation of the defendant, as bearing on the probability that he was the aggressor. It is competent "only in cases where the killing took place under circumstances that afforded the slayer reasonable grounds to believe himself in peril, and then solely for the purpose of illustrating to the jury the motive which actuated him." People v. Lamb, *41 N. Y. 376. Fear founded on fact tends to rebut the presumption of malice. The character of the deceased with reference to violence, when known to the accused, enables him to judge of the danger, and aids the jury in deciding whether he acted in good faith, and upon the honest belief that his life was in peril. It shows the state of his mind as to the necessity of defending himself. It bears upon the question whether, in the language of the Penal Code, "there is reasonable ground to apprehend a design on the part of the person slain * * * to do some great personal injury to the slayer * * * and there is imminent danger of such design being accomplished." Section 205. When self-defense is an issue, threats of the deceased, even if unknown to the defendant, are admissible, as they tend to show the state of mind of the deceased, and that he was the aggressor. Stokes v. People, 53 N. Y. 164, 174, 13 Am. Rep. 492. People v. Taylor, 177 N. Y. 237, 69 N. E. 534. Evidence of general reputation for violence, however, is received, not to show the state of mind of the deceased, but of the accused—not to show who was in fact the aggressor, but whether the defendant had reasonable ground to believe that he was in danger of great personal injury. Hence it is obvious that, whatever the reputation of the deceased for violence may be, it can have no bearing on what the defendant apprehended, unless he knew it. If he knew that the deceased was reputed to be violent, it might raise in his mind a fear of danger, but not otherwise. We think the evidence of previous convictions was incompetent, because the defendant knew nothing about them, or about the nature of the offenses, so far as appears.

The evidence, moreover, was incompetent for another reason. The offer was not to prove the general reputation of the deceased for violence, but to show specific acts of which he had been guilty, not toward the defendant, or to his knowledge, but toward third persons, or their property. The rule is well settled that this is improper, not only because character is never established by proof of individual acts, but because each specific act shown would create a new issue. People v. Gaimari, 176 N. Y. 84, 95, 68 N. E. 112; People v. Druse, 103 N. Y. 655, 8 N. E. 733; Thomas v. People, 67 N. Y. 218, 225; Eggler v. People, 56 N. Y. 642; People v. Lamb, *41 N. Y. 360, 366. Eggler v. People is not fully reported, but we make the following extract from the statement of the reporter: "After general evidence had been given on behalf of the prisoner, tending to show that the deceased was disposed to be sullen and violent in temper when angry, and that when excited she was ungovernable and passionate, questions were asked tending to show particular instances of exhibitions of temper. These were excluded, under objection. Held, no error." In Thomas v. People, Judge Earl, writing for the court, said: "Upon the trial the prisoner was permitted to prove threats and acts of violence toward himself by the deceased, and also to prove that the general character of the deceased was bad; that he was very quarrelsome and vindictive. He offered to prove, also, that before he came to the prison the deceased was engaged in several fights with other parties, in each of which he used a knife, and cut his opponent, also his declarations about cutting people with razors, and that all these matters had been communicated to the prisoner. These offers were overruled, and this is now complained of as error. Even if the proof given of the general character of the deceased was competent upon the facts of this case, there is no authority for holding that proof of specific acts of violence upon other persons, no part of the res gestæ, and in no way connected with the prisoner, was competent." In People v. Druse, Judge Andrews, speaking for all the judges, said: "The rule is that, after evidence has been given by a defendant tending to show that the homicide was committed in self-defense, he may follow it by proof of the general reputation of the deceased for quarrelsomeness and violence. But a defendant is confined to proof of general reputation, and evidence of specific acts of violence toward third persons is inadmissible."

The defendant insists that a judgment record imports absolute verity, and that it cannot give rise to a new issue, because it cannot be contradicted. When, however, the question arises collaterally, the record of a judgment in a criminal case is not conclusive. In Sims v. Sims, 75 N. Y. 466, the defendant testified as a witness in his own behalf, and a record of his conviction in the state of Ohio for a felony was offered by the plaintiff and received in evidence for the purpose of impeaching him. He was thereupon asked by his counsel whether he was guilty of the offense of which he had been convicted, but the question was objected to and excluded. It was held that the ruling was erroneous, and the judgment was reversed.

4. At the close of the charge, to which no exception was taken, counsel for the defendant said that, while he recognized "the exceeding fairness and impartiality" of the charge, he wished to present two requests, one of which was charged, and the other, with the action of the court thereon, was as follows: "I ask your honor to charge the jury that if, at the time of the commission of the act charged in the indictment, if, in this case, at the time that Rodawald actually shot the revolver, the defendant honestly believed

himself to be in danger of great bodily harm from the deceased—from the man killed—and, in firing the shot charged in the indictment, the defendant acted upon that belief, then the defendant is excusable, whether in fact such danger actually existed or not." The court declined to charge "in that form," and remarked: "I leave my charge as I have made it on that subject." The defendant excepted. In the body of the charge the court said: "Homicide is excusable when committed by accident and misfortune, in lawfully correcting a child or a servant, or in doing any other lawful act by lawful means, with ordinary caution and without any unlawful intent. Homicide is also justifiable when committed either in the lawful defense of the slayer, or of his or her husband, wife, parent, child, brother, sister, master, or servant, or of any other person in his presence or company, when there is reasonable ground to apprehend a design on the part of the person slain to commit a felony, or to do some great personal injury to the slayer or to any such person, and there is imminent danger of such design being accomplished, or in the actual resistance of the attempt to commit a felony upon the slayer in his presence, or upon or in a dwelling or other place of abode in which he is. There is a further provision of law as follows: An act otherwise criminal is justifiable when it is done to protect the person committing it, or another whom he is bound to protect, from inevitable and irreparable personal injury, and the injury could only be prevented by the act; nothing more being done than is necessary to prevent the injury. * * * As regards the question of self-defense, I think I can render you no better service, and certainly can state it no clearer by any words of my own, than the words which are used in the Court of Appeals, where this question is referred to. It is said: 'Before a party can justify the taking of life in self-defense, he must show that there was reasonable grounds for believing he was in great peril, that the killing was necessary for his escape, and that no other safe means was open to him. When one believes himself about to be attacked by another and to receive great bodily injury, it is his duty to avoid the attack, if in his power to do so; and the right of attack, for the purpose of self-defense, does not arise until he has done everything in his power to avoid its necessity.' * * * It is contended, at least, that Bayer did attack Rodawald with the knife while Rodawald was on his way home, with his back turned, and that Rodawald grabbed Bayer's arm with one of his hands, and that he dropped the gun and took the revolover, and in some way that was discharged and Bayer was killed. It is contended on the part of Rodawald that he did not intend to shoot; that it was a mere accident, or, at all events, that, if it was not that, that he did no more than was necessary to protect his own life, and it was absolutely necessary to protect him from great bodily harm; and that what he did there he was justified in doing, as a matter of self-defense; and his counsel urges that, under the law as it is in this state, he had the right to do what he did. I have read the law in your hearing." The law does not justify homicide upon the theory of self-defense, so far as it is applicable to this case, unless two facts exist: (1) There must be reasonable ground to apprehend a design on the part of the person slain to do some great personal injury to the slayer; (2) there must be imminent danger of such design being accomplished. The question is not, merely, what did the accused believe? but, also, what did he have the right to believe? Whatever may be said as to the sufficiency of the request so far as the first requirement is concerned, there was no attempt to comply with the second. The element of imminent danger that the design would be accomplished was wholly wanting, and hence the exception raises no error. Pen. Code, § 205.

The defendant's counsel further urges that, so far as the charge related to self-defense—a subject of vital importance to his client—it consisted mainly of certain sections read from the Penal Code, and was so general that the jury may not have clearly understood it. There is some force in this criticism, for a statute framed to cover all cases may produce confusion where it is all read to the jury with no explanation, instead of the part only that applies to the case in hand, but no reversible error is presented. The counsel should have requested further instructions, which would doubtless have been given, or, if they had been refused, he could have been protected by an exception. As we have recently said: "Only errors raised by exception require a new trial, and it is only when we are satisfied that the verdict was against the weight of evidence, or against law, or that justice requires a new trial, that we are permitted to reverse whether an exception shall have been taken or not in the court below." People v. Tobin, 176 N. Y. 278, 288, 68 N. E. 359. A new trial should not be granted without substantial reasons, for a loose administration of the law against murder tends to cheapen human life.

The judgment of conviction should be affirmed.

O'BRIEN, J. (dissenting). The homicide of which the defendant was convicted was concededly the result of a quarrel between him and the deceased. The subject-matter of the quarrel was some old fence posts on the line of the railroad in the vicinity of which the parties lived. These posts were of no value except for firewood. The defendant claimed that they were given to him by some of the railroad officials, while a Mrs. Keating claimed they belonged to her for the same reason. The deceased had no interest whatever in the controversy, but he lived with Mrs. Keating and became, in some sense, the champion of her cause. The vital question in the case is upon the facts concerning the actions of the deceased and the defendant at the moment of the tragedy. The witnesses on either side did not possess a very high grade of intelligence. The defendant, his wife and children, testified, in substance, that, at the moment when the fatal shot was fired, the deceased was advancing toward the defendant in a hostile attitude, with a knife in his uplifted hand. On the part of the people, the witnesses were the friends and associates of the deceased; and they testified, substantially, that he had no knife, and made no hostile demonstrations toward the defendant. It is certain that a knife was found a day or two after the tragedy in the vicinity of the place where the killing occurred. It was claimed on the part of the people that this knife was placed there after the transaction for the purpose of furnishing evidence in the defendant's behalf. It is quite clear that the defendant himself had no opportunity to place it there, nor had he any opportunity to confer directly with his wife or children. So the people's theory must be that some of the children or the wife must have had the gift of foresight to such an extent that they placed the knife where it was found for the purpose of building upon that fact a theory for the defense of the accused. It is not absolutely impossible that that theory may be true, but, considering all the facts and circumstances of the case, and especially the age of the children, and their general intelligence, as well as that of their mother, it is difficult to believe. But the important fact is that there was a sharp conflict of evidence in the case as to what actually took place at the time of the homicide. On the one side, it is claimed that the defendant shot the deceased with deliberation and premeditation, without any cause and without any reason to fear any assault upon himself, although the deceased and the defendant, so far as it appears, never had any quarrel before, and no animosity existed between them. On the other hand, the claim is that the defendant fired the fatal shot when he saw the deceased advancing towards him with a knife in his uplifted hand, and under the fear and apprehension that his own life was imperiled. It is important, therefore, that every right secured to the defendant was awarded to him upon the trial; and, if there is any error in the rulings or decisions at the trial, then, clearly, the judgment ought to be reversed. I think there was such error, and it will be necessary to refer to the charge of the learned trial judge, or rather, to what took place after the charge.

The defendant's counsel, at the close of all the proceedings, including the charge, requested the court to charge as follows: "I ask your honor to charge the jury that if, at the time of the commission of the act charged in the indictment, if, in this case, at the time Rodawald actually shot the revolver, the defendant honestly believed himself to be in danger of great bodily harm from the deceased—from the man killed—and, in firing the shot charged in the indictment, the defendant acted upon that belief, then that the defendant is excusable, whether in fact such danger actually existed or not." This request was refused, and the defendant duly excepted. This ruling of the learned trial court is now defended by the learned district attorney in one way only, and that is that the request was not expressed in the precise language of the statute—that is to say, it omitted the language, "when there is a reasonable ground to apprehend a design," etc.; but the request embraced the condition that the defendant honestly believed that he was in great bodily harm, and that if, acting upon that belief, he fired the fatal shot, then he was excusable. I think that the request was substantially sufficient, within the scope and meaning of the statute. If the jury could find that what the defendant did was under an honest belief that his life was imperiled, or that he was in danger of great bodily harm, then, clearly, the defendant could not have been convicted of murder in the first degree, even if he could be convicted of some inferior grade of homicide. There was proof in the case, as already stated, which would justify the jury in finding that to be the fact; and the refusal of the learned trial court to give the instructions as presented was error, since the refusal to so charge amounted, in substance, to a direction that the jury could convict of murder in the first degree, even though satisfied of the truth of the facts embraced in the request. But some of my associates now think that the district attorney has not placed his justification of this ruling upon the proper ground, and that the ruling should now be upheld on the ground that it had already been given. The only reference to this subject to be found in the charge is the following: The learned trial court read to the jury all the statutes upon the subject of murder in its different degrees, and upon the subject of manslaughter, justifiable or excusable homicide. These statutes are all of considerable length, and it is too much to expect that the mere reading of the text is sufficient to inform the lay mind as to their application. The learned trial judge referred to the question now under consideration only by reading the statute, which is as follows: "Homicide is also justifiable when committed, either in the lawful defense of the slayer or of his or her husband, wife, parent, child, brother, sister, master or servant, or of any other person in his presence or company when there is reasonable ground to apprehend a design on the part of the person slain to commit a felony or to do some great personal injury to the slayer, or to any such person, and there is imminent danger of such design being accomplished." In no other way did the learned trial judge convey to the jury the idea embraced in the request.

There are only a few words in this statute which have any application to this case, and the proposition now is that the mere reading of the statute, with a great number of other statutes on the subject of homicide, must have conveyed to the minds of the jury the same idea that is embraced in the request; that is to say, the argument is that the jury must be deemed not only to have carried in their minds this vast mass of statutory verbiage, but was able to pick out of it the idea that applied to the case. The request was framed in simple terms, well calculated to convey to the jury the precise rule of law that applied to the evidence which they were about to consider. The mere reading in the presence of a jury of such a statute, without any explanation as to how and in what respect the statute applies to the case, is not a sufficient discharge of the duty of the trial court engaged in the trial of a capital offense. If the request had a foundation in the evidence, as it certainly had, then it should have been given to the jury for their guidance.

In Remsen v. People, 43 N. Y. 6, the defendant's counsel read to the court, in the presence of the jury, three propositions in writing, which he requested the court to charge. The recorder, addressing the counsel for the defendant, replied: "I charge your third proposition. The first and second, I decline to charge." And to this refusal there was an exception. The third request was this: "Third. That good character is a fact to be considered by the jury, like every other fact in the case, no matter what the other testimony in the case may be." The question in this court was whether the charge was sufficient, and Judge Allen, speaking for a unanimous court, said: "I doubt if the response of the judge to the request of the counsel for the prisoner to charge as stated in respect to the evidence of good character by the accused can be regarded as a part of the charge and instructions to the jury. It was a transaction between the counsel and the court, and constituted no part of the charge and instructions addressed to the jury." The full facts of that case are not reported in the volume cited, but they appear in the record of the case upon appeal just as here stated. Now, if the written request in that case, which was assented to and charged by the court, and in terms covered the whole question, and was concededly correct, did not control the case, as a part of the charge, how can it be said that the mere reading of a series of complicated statutes to the jury, followed by a refusal to charge a request which embodied the very pith and substance of the statute, and pointed out its application to the evidence, gave to the defendant all his rights upon the trial? The request was a very reasonable one. It applied to the case directly, and to the vital question involved, and, I think, should not have been refused. The law applicable to this feature of the case has been well stated by a modern author of the highest authority in these words: "The law of the case which the judge is to lay down to the jury is not the abstract law, such as a statute or a common-law definition of a crime, but the law's conclusions from the several, and perhaps varied, facts which the evidence tends to establish, viewed in connection with the pleadings. Therefore no abstract proposition, however correct, should be given in charge, not only because it would be confusing to the jury, who, being unused to legal disquisitions, would not know how to apply it, but also because its combination with the special facts might render it erroneous. In other words, the judge should state, not the general law of the subject, but the legal rules governing the facts in controversy—all of them, not a part only—as the evidence tends to prove them; and his words should be interpreted and judged of, not in any abstract way, but with reference to those facts. For the same language may be correct or erroneous according to the facts whereof it is spoken. Still, an abstract proposition possibly may, and sometimes does, fit the facts, in which case it is properly given. And it will not always be error to read extracts from reported decisions, or the words of the statute or of a text-book, accompanied by instructions adapting them to the particular case; yet it is not often advisable." Bishop's New Crim. Pro. vol. 1 (4th Ed.) § 978. The text quoted seems to be such a reasonable and sensible statement of the law concerning the duties of the court upon the trial of a capital case, and the legal rights of the defendant, that any reference to the numerous cases cited in the notes is unnecessary. It must be obvious to any one that the rule thus stated applies directly to this case. "It is not the words of the law, but the internal sense of it, that makes the law. The letter of the law is the body. The sense and reason of the law is the soul." So in this case it was not the statute or bare words of the law that should have been given to the jury, but the sense and meaning of the law, when applied to the facts in evidence—in other words, the conclusion which the law draws from the particular facts of the case. Even if the question is more doubtful than it appears to me to be, the defendant should receive the benefit of the doubt.

I think there should be a new trial in this case.

GRAY, BARTLETT, and WERNER, JJ., concur with VANN, J. PARKER, C. J., and MARTIN, J., concur with O'BRIEN,

Judgment of conviction affirmed.

(177 N. Y. 515)

PEOPLE ex rel. CONTINENTAL INS. CO. v. MILLER, State Comptroller.

(Court of Appeals of New York. Feb. 23, 1904.)

TAXATION—INSURANCE COMPANIES—GROSS PREMIUMS—REINSURANCE.

1. The gross amount of premiums received by domestic insurance companies for business done in a state, for the purposes of taxation, under Laws 1896, p. 859, c. 908, § 187, as amended by Laws 1901, p. 297, c. 118, § 1, imposing an annual state tax for the privilege of carrying on the business, and providing that the term "gross premiums" shall include such premiums as are collected from policies subsequently canceled, and from reinsurance, does not include premiums unearned and paid in advance, but refunded on cancellation of a policy.

2. Premiums paid for reinsurance by a domestic insurance company cannot be deducted from the gross receipts in determining the gross amount of business received or business done in the state by a domestic insurance company for purposes of taxation, under Laws 1896, p. 859, c. 908, § 187, as amended by Laws 1901, p. 297, c. 118, § 1.

Haight, J., dissenting.

Appeal from Supreme Court, Appellate Division, Third Department.

Certiorari by the people, on the relation of the Continental Insurance Company, against Nathan L. Miller, comptroller of the state of New York, to review refusal of defendant to revise a tax assessed against the relator. From an order of the Appellate Division (85 N. Y. Supp. 1142), confirming such order, relator appeals. Modified.

John S. Sheppard, Jr., for appellant. John Cunneen, Atty. Gen. (William H. Wood, on the brief), for respondent.

VANN, J. The relator, a domestic fire insurance corporation, is subject to taxation at the rate of 1 per cent. per annum on the gross amount of premiums received during the calendar year for business done in this state. Tax Law, § 187 (Laws 1896, p. 859, c. 908, as amended by Laws 1901, p. 297, c. 118, § 1). The comptroller, in computing the gross amount of its premiums for the year 1901, included the sum of $49,280.81 refunded to policy holders upon canceled policies, and refused to deduct the sum of $13,149.40 paid by the company for reinsurance. Upon due application made, he declined to readjust the tax by deducting either of the sums named, and a writ of certiorari, issued to review his determination, resulted in the affirmance thereof by the Appellate Division, one of the justices dissenting.

The questions presented require us to construe section 187 of the tax law, which, so far as applicable to the case in hand, is as follows: "An annual state tax for the privilege of exercising corporate franchises or for carrying on business in their corporate or organized capacity within this state equal to one per centum on the gross amount of premiums received during the preceding calendar year for business done in this state, whether such premiums were in the form of money, notes, credits, or any other substitute for money, shall be paid annually into the treasury of the state, on or before the first day of June by the following corporations: "(1) Every domestic insurance corporation, incorporated, organized or formed under, by, or pursuant to a general or special law. * * * (3) * * * The term 'gross premiums' as used in this article shall include, in addition to all other premiums, such premiums as are collected from policies subsequently canceled and from reinsurance. * * *" Laws 1901, p. 297, c. 118, § 1; Tax Law, Laws 1896, p. 859, c. 908, § 187. When the law was passed in 1896, as well as after it was amended in 1897, the last sentence above quoted did not appear, but in 1901 the section was revised and enlarged in many respects, and that sentence was then added. Laws 1896, p. 859, c. 908, § 187, as amended by Laws 1897, p. 630, c. 494, § 1.

Two questions are presented for decision: (1) Should unearned premiums, paid in advance, but refunded upon the cancellation of policies, be included in "the gross amount of premiums received * * * for business done"? (2) Should the sum paid by the relator to other companies for reinsuring its risks be deducted from such gross amount?

The tax under consideration is an annual tax imposed upon a corporation for the privilege of exercising its corporate franchises and carrying on business in a corporate capacity within this state. People ex rel. Mutual Trust Co. v. Miller, 177 N. Y. 51, 54, 69 N. E. 124. It is measured by business done during the calendar year ending on the 31st of December, and is payable on June 30th of the following year. Tax Law, Laws 1901, pp. 297, 298, c. 118, §§ 187, 189. As an aid to the comptroller in fixing the amount of the tax, each corporation subject to taxation under section 187 is required "on or before March 1st in each year" to make a written report "stating the entire amount of premiums received on business done thereby in this state during the year. * * *" Tax Law, § 189. The consideration for the tax is the insurance business done during an entire year, ascertained after the expiration of the year, and expressed in the gross amount of premiums received during the year. The gross premiums embrace, in addition to all others, such as are collected from policies subsequently canceled. Id. § 187. The statute does not expressly include in the gross premiums those received, but those collected from canceled policies. What is the business done through a canceled policy? It is the insurance made or indemnity furnished during the period that the policy is in force. That is the only business that a fire insurance company can do. Every fire insurance policy in this state, by its terms, is subject to cancellation, and in that event it is provided both by the policy and by statute that the unearned premium shall be refunded by the company.

Ins. Law, Laws 1892, p. 1981, c. 690, § 122. Thus a policy for a specified time continues in force no longer than both parties elect, for either may end it at will. If a policy is written for one year, but is canceled after it has run six months, the business done by means of that policy is insurance of the property affected for six months. That period covers the entire life of the policy, and the company furnishes no insurance after it has expired. It then ceases to do business, so far as that policy is concerned; and, if all its policies were canceled at the same time, it would cease to do business altogether.

What is the amount collected, within the meaning of the act, upon such a policy, assuming that the premium for one year was paid in advance, and that the proper proportion was refunded upon cancellation? The time of viewing the transaction, as is apparent from the time when the report to the comptroller is made and the tax fixed, is not the date of the policy, but the date of cancellation, when the contract ends and insurance ceases. As the tax is paid for business done, and the business done is insurance for six months, the amount collected is either the sum collected and retained, or else it includes something for business not done, or unrealized anticipations of business. While, in a certain sense, it may be said that payment of the premium in advance for one year involves insurance made for one year, notwithstanding the fact that according to its terms the policy is subsequently canceled, a majority of the court is of the opinion that this is inconsistent with the fair meaning of the words "business done," when looked back upon at the end of the year. The premium which represents business done is the amount that the company has the benefit of and furnishes an equivalent for. It is the money earned by the policy, for the rest is a liability. Ins. Law, Laws 1892, p. 1979, c. 690, § 118. When part of the premium is refunded, it is the same in effect as if it had never been paid. The contract is terminated pursuant to its provisions, and thereafter the company neither gives nor takes any benefit therefrom. It no longer does business or provides insurance through that policy. If all its policies should be canceled on the first of July and it should issue no others during the rest of the calendar year, it could not properly be said that it did any insurance business during that period. A tax upon the sum repaid would be arbitrary, for it would have no relation to the privilege of exercising the corporate franchise for which in express terms the tax is imposed. If two companies during the same year should each receive $100,000 in premiums, and one should refund half while the other refunded nothing on canceled policies, taxation of both in the same amount would violate the theory of the act, and trample upon the presumption that a tax is laid in return for some proportionate value received by the taxpayer. According to the construction that we have adopted, however, which impresses us as just and reasonable, the amount paid to the state would be in exact proportion to the value received by the corporation for the tax, and the object of the statute would thus be carried out in every respect. The company would have the benefit of doing the business and the state would have the revenue from all the business done.

It may be asked, why does the statute say "gross premiums" unless it means all premiums received, whether refunded or not? We think the use of the word "gross" was intended to include all premiums that remain in the treasury of the company, and to exclude any deductions for the commissions of agents or the expenses of doing business. The gross amount collected from canceled policies means the gross amount collected and retained by the company. The amount paid back is not collected for business done, but received for business expected to be done. The key to the construction of the statute is business done, for that is the basis of the tax. The state allows the corporation to do business, and taxes it for such business as it actually does, not for business attempted, but never completed. A canceled policy does not represent business done after the date of cancellation, for no business is done through that policy after that date. The exercise of the right to cancel interrupts the business being done by the policy and ipso facto renders the company liable to repay the unearned premium; and we think it would be unreasonable to hold that the sum refunded is, for the purposes of taxation under this statute, actually collected.

The Supreme Court of Illinois recently passed upon the meaning of similar words in a statute of that state (Hurd's Rev. St. 1899. c. 73, § 297), which imposed a tax of "two per cent. of the gross amount of premiums received by [the company] for business done * * * during the preceding calendar year." That learned court united in construing the act as follows: "There is no dispute as to the meaning of the word 'gross,' and it is conceded that it means the whole or entire amount of premiums received for business done in this state during the year. The word 'gross' is opposed to 'net,' and its ordinary meaning is the entire amount of the receipts of a business, while the net receipts are those remaining after deductions for the expenses and charges of conducting the business. * * * If it is true that a part of a premium unearned and returned to the insured is premium for business done, it is equally true that, if a whole premium were returned, and there was in fact no insurance, the money would be premium for business done. According to the argument which would include premiums returned on canceled policies, if an insurance company should issue a policy and receive a premium, and at once cancel the policy and return the premium, it would have done the amount of business represented by the policy, and the amount received would be a premium for insurance business done. We do not think the language used will bear that construction. The merchant would not think of including in the gross receipts of his business any sales of goods with the privilege of return on the part of the purchaser, where they are in fact returned. In such a case there is in the end no sale, and no business done, in any proper sense. So in the case of an insurance policy for a definite period with an agreement that it may run any portion of that period and then cease. If the policy is canceled, and the insurance ceases, there is no insurance business for the remaining portion of the period. * * * An insurance company would not be authorized to omit from its statement any part of premiums received merely on the ground that policies might be canceled in the future; but where they have been in fact canceled, and the money returned, the entire or gross premium receipts cannot, by any fair interpretation, include the moneys so returned. * * * The apparent purpose of the act is to levy a tax on gross income, and not upon money which is in no sense revenue to the insurance companies." The German Alliance Insurance Co. v. Van Cleave, 191 Ill. 410, 414, 61 N. E. 94, 96. We adopt this reasoning, and decide that the comptroller erred in including the amount refunded to policy holders upon canceled policies in the gross amount of premiums collected.

The second question involves the meaning of "reinsurance," as used by the Legislature in enacting that the term "gross premiums" shall include such "as are collected from policies subsequently canceled and from reinsurance." This means, as we read it, premiums collected by the relator from reinsuring the risks of other companies. Reinsurance is a contract by which one insurer insures the risks of another insurer. The statute is dealing with the gross premiums collected by an insurance company for business done; that is, for insurance furnished. It has to do with receipts, not with disbursements. It includes premiums collected from canceled policies and premiums collected from reinsurance, for the word "collected" applies to the latter subject with the same force as to the former. The act does not refer to what is paid out, for it permits no deduction even for expenses, but to what is paid in. A premium paid for reinsurance is an expense of the business, but a premium collected from reinsurance is part of the gross receipts from the corporate business, which is what the statute aims at. The original contract is not terminated as in the case of a canceled policy, but remains in force, and the liability of the first insurer to the insured is not affected by the reinsurance. Business is still done through that policy, and a profit is made therefrom, represented by the difference between the premium received and the premium paid. If a company should reinsure all its risks, it would still be doing an insurance business, and liable to taxation for the privilege of exercising its corporate franchise. The word "reinsurance," as used in the statute, in so far as it applies to the relator, refers to the premiums received by it for reinsuring the risks of other companies. The test here, the same as in the first question discussed, is the business done by the company in using the privilege for which the tax is imposed. When it causes its own risks to be reinsured by another company, it is not, so far as that act is concerned, doing an insurance business; but when it reinsures the risks of other companies it is doing an insurance business, and should, according to the statute, be taxed for the privilege. We think the comptroller did right in refusing to deduct from the gross amount of premiums received for business done the sum paid by the relator to other companies for reinsuring its risks.

The order appealed from should be modified in accordance with this opinion, and, as modified, affirmed, without costs in any court to either party.

PARKER, C. J., and GRAY, O'BRIEN, MARTIN, and CULLEN, JJ., concur. HAIGHT, J., dissents.

Ordered accordingly.

(208 Ill. 147)

GRACE & HYDE CO. v. PROBST.

(Supreme Court of Illinois. Feb. 17, 1904.)

MASTER AND SERVANT—PERSONAL INJURIES—EVIDENCE—SUFFICIENCY—DIRECTED VERDICT—LOAN OF SERVANT—FELLOW SERVANTS—WARNING OF DANGER—INSTRUCTIONS—APPEAL.

1. In an action by a servant for personal injuries, evidence examined, and *held* that it was not proved without controversy that plaintiff was loaned by his master to work for another at the time of his injury, but that the question was for the jury.

2. A general agent may be loaned or hired by his master to a third party for some special service, and as to that particular service he will become the servant of the third party; the test is whether, in the particular service, the servant continues liable to the direction and control of his master, or becomes subject to the party to whom he is loaned or hired.

3. Where plaintiff, while employed by defendant to work on the construction of a building, was directed to assist iron workers, and was injured while doing so, and the evidence was conflicting as to whether the iron workers, who were in the regular employ of another company, were loaned for a special purpose to defendant, or whether plaintiff was loaned by defendant to the iron workers for such special purpose, it was not error to refuse to direct a verdict for defendant on the ground that the injury was from the negligence of fellow servants.

4. Where a carpenter's helper, directed to assist iron workers, took hold of a heavy iron beam which they were lifting, supposing they were to carry it, and was injured by their dropping it in order to break it, the negligence

in failing to warn him of the danger was that of a master and not of the fellow servants.

5. On appeal from the Appellate to the Supreme Court, controverted questions of fact are to be regarded as settled finally by the judgment of affirmance by the Appellate Court.

6. Where, in an action by a servant for personal injuries, there was a conflict of evidence as to whether defendant or another was plaintiff's master at the time of the injury, instructions to find for defendant if the jury found as true certain facts tending to show that such other person was the master, but ignoring evidence tending to show that defendant was doing the work and had merely secured a loan of servants from such other person, were properly refused.

Appeal from Appellate Court, First District.

Action by William Probst against the Grace & Hyde Company for personal injuries alleged to have been received while in the defendant's employment. From a judgment of the Appellate Court affirming a judgment for plaintiff, defendant appeals. Affirmed.

F. J. Canty and J. C. M. Clow, for appellant. John F. Waters and Douthart & Brendecke, for appellee.

CARTWRIGHT, J. Appellee brought this suit in the superior court of Cook county against appellant, a corporation engaged in the contracting business, to recover damages for a personal injury suffered in its employ. The declaration consisted of a single count, which alleged that on January 8, 1900, plaintiff was in defendant's employ as a carpenter's helper; that, outside of the building where plaintiff was working, a gang of men were cutting and breaking beams of iron and steel by cutting by hand, and then raising the beams several feet and suddenly dropping them on a block; that said work was extremely dangerous, and was known by defendant to be so, but plaintiff was inexperienced in such work, and ignorant of the methods used; that defendant failed to instruct him as to the manner of performing the work, or to warn him of the attendant dangers, and ordered him to go out and assist said gang of men, and that plaintiff, while, in the exercise of ordinary care, assisting to lift one of the beams, and without any knowledge that it would be suddenly dropped, was injured by the men dropping the beam, in consequence of defendant's failure to so instruct and warn him. The plea was the general issue. Upon a trial there was a verdict for plaintiff for $5,000. Upon a motion for a new trial the court required a remittitur of $1,250, and, upon said sum being remitted, overruled the motion, and entered judgment for $3,750. The Appellate Court for the First District affirmed the judgment.

At the conclusion of the evidence defendant moved the court to direct a verdict in its favor. The motion was denied, and it is contended that the court erred in such denial. Upon that proposition counsel insists that the evidence showed beyond all controversy that, while plaintiff was a general servant of the defendant, he was loaned for the time being to the Brown-Ketcham Iron Works to assist in breaking the beam; that he thereby became the servant of the Brown-Ketcham Company for that particular work; and that whatever liability might exist on account of his injury is against the Brown-Ketcham Company, and not the defendant.

The evidence was, in substance, as follows: Defendant was a building contractor, and agreed with the Union Stockyards Company of Chicago to rebuild a very large building, known as the "Horse Pavilion," at the stockyards, which had been destroyed by fire. The contract was verbal, and was made during the fire. Defendant was to buy and pay for the material and labor, and furnish monthly statements to the stockyards company, which was to pay the defendant all moneys paid out in constructing the building, and 10 per cent. thereon for defendant's profit. The structural ironwork of the building was let to the Brown-Ketcham Iron Works, of Indianapolis, but it does not appear from the evidence just what said contract was, or who let it. As the work of construction progressed, iron beams were to be placed over the driveway entering the building. Two beams furnished for that purpose were too long, and it was in cutting and breaking one of them that plaintiff was injured. It does not clearly appear from the evidence whether the cutting and setting of these beams were in the Brown-Ketcham contract or not, but it does appear that defendant was proposing to do the work, and was prevented from cutting the beams by the steward of the labor union, and that a bill for the cutting and hoisting was rendered by the Brown-Ketcham Company to the defendant. The arrangement for cutting the beam was made between James R. Howie, a timekeeper of defendant, and John P. Hart, the foreman of the Brown-Ketcham Company. Hart testified that Howie came to him and told him that he had a couple of I-beams that he wanted cut, and Hart said: "I will give you a couple of men, provided the steward will allow me to, and they can go out and cut it, and then you can break it. Take some of the laborers, or some of your own men, if he will let you." Howie's testimony was that he asked Hart if he had any objections to having defendant's men cut and set the beams, and he told him he would have to go and see the steward, Quinn. The men belonged to a union, and under its rules none but iron workers could do ironwork. Quinn was appointed steward of the building, and was to see that the rules of the union were enforced. Howie thereupon went up into the building about 90 feet, where Quinn was, and asked him if he had any objections to defendant's men cutting and setting the iron beams. Quinn said he would not allow it under any circumstances; that all ironwork on the building must be done by iron men.

Howie went down and told Hart that Quinn would not allow any iron to be cut by any other than iron men, and Hart then sent two of the iron men, under his charge, out to cut the beams, which were lying outside the building. The method was to cut around the beam with a hand cutter, and then lift the beam and drop it across a steel rail or block to break it. Hart went out and measured the beam, and saw the men started to cut it at the proper place, and then went into the building. After the two iron men had cut around the beam, one of them went into the building to get men to help break it, and Hart said he would get him some men. Hart then went to Gleichart, defendant's carpenter foreman, and told him he wanted a few more men, and asked if he would let him have them. Gleichart told the men to go with Hart and do what he wanted. There were about 400 working on the building, and probably about 150 hammering at the same time. There was a great noise, and Gleichart testified that he did not know what Hart wanted the men for, while Hart testified that he told Gleichart they were ready to break the beam. Plaintiff had been in the employ of defendant three days as a carpenter's helper, and was carrying lumber and doing other work with the men who were sent out. In compliance with the order of Gleichart, several of defendant's men went out to the beam. One of the iron men told them that they were going to break the beam; that they would pick it up and drop it and break it. The men picked it up and dropped it, but it did not break. Then more men were called for, and they came, plaintiff being among them. He was the last one who reached the beam. It was partially raised, and no one told him what they were going to do with it. He supposed, from appearances, that they were picking it up to carry it. He took hold of the beam to help lift, and just then the other men dropped it. He held on, and it dropped on his leg and broke it.

One who is the general agent of another may be loaned or hired by his master to a third party for some special service, and as to that particular service he will become the servant of the third party. The master is the one who has the direction and control of the servant, and the test is whether, in the particular service, the servant continues liable to the direction and control of his master, or becomes subject to the party to whom he is loaned or hired. Consolidated Fireworks Co. v. Koehl, 190 Ill. 145, 60 N. E. 87. Plaintiff was in the employ of defendant, and so remained unless he was loaned to the Brown-Ketcham Company for the particular service of breaking the beam and became subject to the direction and control of the latter company in doing that work. The evidence was of such a nature that the court could not say, as a matter of law, that plaintiff was so loaned to the Brown-Ketcham Company. The testimony of defendant's timekeeper and of the foreman for the Brown-Ketcham Company tended to prove that the iron men were furnished to the defendant to cut the beam because Quinn, the stewart of the labor union, would not allow defendant's men to do that work, and the Brown-Ketcham Company rendered a bill to defendant for cutting and hoisting the beams. In view of this evidence it cannot be said that it was proved, without disute or controversy, that the plaintiff was loaned to the Brown-Ketcham Company.

The next proposition is that plaintiff was a fellow servant of the two iron men, and that the negligence in failing to advise plaintiff that the beam was about to be dropped was chargeable to the iron men, if anybody. The court could not direct a verdict on that ground without first finding, as a matter of law, that plaintiff had become the servant of the Brown-Ketcham Company by a loaning to them, and we have expressed our opinion on that subject. Furthermore, the negligence charged was negligence of the master, and not that of a fellow servant. While a master is not liable for a negligent injury by one fellow servant to another, he is responsible for his own negligence, which may consist in subjecting the servant to risks not within the employment and which he has no reason to expect. The servant is held to a knowledge of the ordinary hazards of his employment, but he does not contract to take upon himself a risk outside of his regular employment which he neither knows of nor has any reason to look for. In this case plaintiff was taken from his employment and sent to this work by order of defendant's foreman, under whom he worked. There can be no question but that his injury was due to the negligence of some one in failing to inform him how the work was to be done. The failure to notify him that the heavy 12-inch iron beam was going to be dropped was to expose him to an unknown danger not within his regular work. The court could neither say, as a matter of law, that plaintiff was a fellow servant of the two iron men, nor that there was no negligence on the part of the defendant.

It is next claimed that the defendant was only the servant of the stockyards company, managing its business, and was not liable on that ground. The evidence does not justify the claim, but tends to show that the defendant was an independent contractor, buying the material, employing the men, and doing the work for 10 per cent. of the cost of the building.

The other points are that the plaintiff was advised that he was going into the employ of the Brown-Ketcham Company temporarily; that he proceeded to do the work without any objection or inquiry what he was to do, and therefore assumed the risk, because the danger was apparent to his observation;

that if he did not know what the men were going to do with the beam it was his duty to inquire; and that the negligence charged was not the proximate cause of the injury. These were all controverted questions of fact, which have been finally settled by the judgment of the Appellate Court.

The evidence was not such as to justify the court in directing a verdict, and it was not error to overrule the motion.

It is also argued that the judgment should be reversed because of the refusal of the court to give instructions numbered 1, 2, 3, 4, 5, 6, and 26, as requested by the defendant. They were all of the same nature, and stated that if the jury believed, from the evidence, that certain facts existed, then, in law, the plaintiff was loaned to the Brown-Ketcham Company for the purpose of breaking the beam, and became the servant of that company, and defendant would not be liable for his injury. The state of facts recited in each instruction was, in substance, that the Brown-Ketcham Company undertook to cut the beam, and was engaged in cutting it by its men, and requested the defendant to assist in breaking it, and that defendant's men, including the plaintiff, were sent to render such assistance. In view of the evidence, we do not regard the hypothesis of fact as sufficient to establish, in law, a loaning of the plaintiff to the Brown-Ketcham Company. Some of the instructions would be as applicable to the loaning of the iron men to the defendant as the loaning of the plaintiff to the Brown-Ketcham Company. It was not disputed that the two iron men were cutting the iron beam and called for more men to assist in breaking it, and that defendant's men, including the plaintiff, were sent to their assistance, but there was also evidence fairly tending to prove that defandant proposed to do the work itself, and that the iron men were furnished to the defendant to cut the beam, preparatory to breaking it, on account of the rules of the labor union. This evidence could not be ignored in determining whether the Brown-Ketcham Company or defendant was plaintiff's master in doing the work, or in giving an instruction as to whether, in law, plaintiff was to be regarded as loaned to the Brown-Ketcham Company. Plaintiff did not know what he was sent to do, or that he was sent to work for Brown-Ketcham, or came under the control of a new master. The instructions were at least misleading. Some of the instructions stated the correct principle that where a servant is loaned to another for particular service he becomes, in the particular employment, the servant of the person to whom he is loaned, although he is the general servant of his employer; but as applied to the case each instruction omitted important qualifications, and they were all properly refused.

The judgment of the Appellate Court is affirmed. Judgment affirmed.

(208 Ill. 155)

CHICAGO & A. RY. CO. v. HOWELL.

(Supreme Court of Illinois. Feb. 17, 1904.)

MASTER AND SERVANT—INJURY—ASSUMPTION OF RISK—CONTRIBUTORY NEGLIGENCE—EVIDENCE—ADMISSIBILITY.

1. Where a railway switchman knew where a switch stand was located, and how its handle was operated, and had operated it, but had never stood there as cars passed, it was a question for the jury whether he assumed the risk of an injury by being knocked from a car as it passed the switch.

2. Any negligence of a switchman in attempting to uncouple cars in motion while the snow rendered footing uncertain was not the proximate cause of his injury from being knocked from a car, on which he was riding, by a switch stand near the track.

3. Where witnesses testified that box cars were purchased in series, and that all cars of a series were the same size, their testimony as to the measurements of cars of the same series as that on which a switchman was riding when injured by being struck by a switch stand as the car passed it, and as to the distance they would project over the rail, was admissible, though not confined to the particular car.

4. In an action for injuries to a switchman from being knocked from a car as it passed a switch stand, testimony as to the distance between the end of the switch handle and passing freight cars, not based on any measurements, but given on a hypothetical question, presuming the length of the connecting rod used with the switch stand and the width of the car, was properly stricken out.

5. Where a railway company showed that switch stands like the one which caused a switchman's injury had been in use for 20 years, it was proper to show on cross-examination that they were being replaced by others of a later pattern.

Appeal from Appellate Court, Fourth District; M. W. Schaffer, Judge.

Action by Harry D. Howell against the Chicago & Alton Railway Company. From a judgment of the Appellate Court (109 Ill. App. 546) affirming a judgment in favor of plaintiff, defendant appeals. Affirmed.

Appellee, on the morning of December 15, 1901, at about 4:20 o'clock, was injured while performing his duties in the switch yards of appellant at Venice, Ill., by one of appellant's cars. The car passed over his leg, necessitating its amputation below the knee. Appellee brought an action on the case in the circuit court of St. Clair county, and was, by the verdict of a jury, awarded $11,000 damages. The circuit court required him to remit $1,000 of this amount, and entered judgment for $10,000. The appellant appealed to the Appellate Court for the Fourth District, where the judgment of the trial court was affirmed, and it has prosecuted a further appeal to this court.

The negligence charged in the declaration is, in substance, that appellant failed to furnish a reasonably safe place for appellee in which to work. Appellant filed the general issue to the declaration. Appellee, on October 8, 1901, was employed by appellant as an extra switchman. From this time until the time of the injury he worked as a member of various switching crews as many days out of each week as appellant had work for him to do. These switching crews were composed of an engineer, fireman, foreman of the crew, and two switchmen. The switchmen's duties consisted in uncoupling cars from the train to which they were attached, riding on the cars so cut off from the train and controlling them by means of a brake until they reached the place at which they were to be left. Appellee had been engaged in switching for various roads five or six years before entering appellant's employ. In the lower end of the railroad yards of appellant at Venice was a switch controlled and operated by a handle on a switch stand at the side of the track. It regulated two tracks. When turned to regulate one track the handle was parallel with the track, and when turned to regulate the other it was turned toward the track. This handle was about 11 inches long. When turned toward the track, the end of the handle was 44½ inches from the rail of the track, and about 3 feet above the ground. The side of a box car of the width of the one plaintiff had hold of when the accident occurred, as shown by evidence in his behalf, projected over the rail 25½ inches, and the ladder on the side of the car a distance of 3 inches farther, so that there was a space of approximately 16 inches between the ladder of a car passing this switch and the handle of the switch stand when turned toward the track. On the morning of the injury the crew of which appellee was a member at that time was engaged in switching in the lower end of the yards, at and near this switch. Edwards, the other switchman of the crew, attempted to uncouple a car on the side farthest from the switch stand in question, but the lever which controlled the coupling mechanism failed to work, and he called to appellee, and told him it would have to be uncoupled from the other side. Appellee crossed the track, and caught hold of the ladder of the moving car with his left hand, and while trying to locate and operate the lever to uncouple the car the handle of the switch stand, which was at that time turned towards the track, either caught his coat or struck him on the body, and turned him around, and threw him under the wheels of the car, causing the injury complained of. Appellee had passed over this switch before while riding on top of cars, and had thrown the switch at least once, but the evidence does not show that he ever stood at the switch stand while cars passed, or that he knew, or had enjoyed an opportunity of knowing, how near the end of the handle, when thrown toward the track, would be to a passing freight car.

At the close of plaintiff's evidence, and again at the close of all the testimony in the case, appellant offered an instruction directing the jury to find the defendant not guilty, which instruction the court refused in both instances. The action of the court in refusing this instruction, in permitting witnesses to testify to the width of cars used by appellant without identifying such cars as the car which caused the injury, in permitting plaintiff to show by cross-examination that in many places a different kind of switch stand, of the latest pattern, was being substituted for the kind in use at the switch where plaintiff was injured, in refusing two instructions offered by appellant, and in giving appellant's first instruction, are all urged by appellant as errors necessitating a reversal of the cause by this court.

Chas. P. Wise, for appellant. Daniel McGlynn and M. W. Borders, for appellee.

SCOTT, J. (after stating the facts). Under the evidence in this case the court was warranted in submitting to the jury the question of defendant's negligence. Whether plaintiff can be said, as a matter of law, to have assumed the risk resulting from the proximity of the end of the switch-stand handle to the tracks is more difficult to determine. Appellee contends that this is solely a question of fact, and cannot be reviewed by this court. This is not always true. Where there is a contrariety of evidence on the question, it is a question of fact, and the judgment of the Appellate Court is final; but where there is no dispute in the evidence—where it is all harmonious and consistent—the question whether the plaintiff assumed the risk becomes one of law, and if, under such circumstances, it clearly appears that he did assume the risk, there being no evidence to the contrary, and the question, as here, is properly presented to this court, a judgment in his favor will be reversed by this court notwithstanding the adjudication of the Appellate Court. In this case, however, we are of opinion that the record is not in that condition. It is certain that Howell knew where the switch stand was located, and the manner in which the handle was operated, but we think that it cannot be held, as a matter of law, that he knew, or by the exercise of ordinary prudence should have known, of the danger resulting therefrom. He cannot, therefore, be said by this court to have assumed the risk. Consolidated Coal Co. v. Haenni, 146 Ill. 614, 35 N. E. 162; Union Show Case Co. v. Blindauer, 175 Ill. 325, 51 N. E. 709; Chicago & Eastern Illinois Railroad Co. v. Knapp, 176 Ill. 127, 52 N. E. 927; North Chicago Street Railroad Co. v. Dudgeon, 184 Ill. 477, 56 N. E. 796; Swift v. O'Neill, 187 Ill. 337, 58 N. E. 416. It appears that he had thrown the switch there at least once, but it does not appear that he ever stood on that side of the track while an engine or car passed, so that he would have had an opportunity to observe how dangerously close that switch handle, when turned towards the track, would be to a passing freight car. It is easy to see that he could go to the switch stand, throw the handle over toward the track, and pass on about the performance of his duties, without at any time being in a position where he would observe, or have his attention called to, the proximity of the handle to a passing freight car. He himself testified that he did not know, prior to the accident, how close these two objects would be to each other.

It is also urged that the plaintiff was guilty of negligence in attempting to uncouple the cars while they were in motion, for the reason that the snow rendered the footing uncertain and slippery, making it unsafe to uncouple the car while it was in motion. His negligence in this respect, if any, did not contribute to the injury.

Under these circumstances we cannot say that the evidence, with the reasonable inferences to be drawn therefrom, does not warrant the verdict. The instruction to find for the defendant was properly refused.

The car which ran over Howell was numbered 5,900. Two witnesses testified that appellant's box cars were purchased in different series, and that the cars of one series were all the same size; that this car was one of a series; and then testified to the measurements of cars of that series, and to the distance they would project over the rail. The objection is that the evidence should have been confined to the car appellee was beside when he came against the handle. The objection is not good. One question was whether the defendant was negligent, and in determining that question the jury had a right to take into consideration the proximity of the handle, when turned towards the track, to passing freight cars of the entire series. Moreover, the abstract does not show any objection whatever to the testimony of McCarthy, who testified in greatest detail in reference to these measurements.

The court properly struck out the evidence of the witness Webster, offered on behalf of appellant, in reference to the distance that intervened between the end of the switch handle, when turned toward the track, and passing freight cars, for the reason that it did not appear to be based upon any measurements whatever, but the testimony was merely upon a hypothetical question propounded by counsel for the appellant, presuming the length of the connecting rod used in conjunction with the switch stand and the width of the car. It was not a proper subject to be submitted upon a hypothesis.

Appellant showed by another witness that switch stands like the one in question had been in general use on railroads for the last 20 years. Appellee was properly permitted to show on cross-examination that they were now being replaced by others of a later pattern. This was germane to the examination in chief.

Objection is made to the first instruction given on the part of the plaintiff. As that instruction has been approved by this court in the recent case of City of La Salle v. Kostka, 190 Ill. 130, 60 N. E. 72, in which the same criticism was made as is now urged, we do not deem it necessary to enter upon any discussion of the point presented.

Complaint is also made of the refusal of the court to give two instructions asked by the defendant. These instructions would have advised the jury that the plaintiff assumed all the risks of his employment, and, if injured while in the performance of his duties, could not recover. Each amounted to an instruction to find for the defendant; each ignored the question of defendant's negligence, and was properly refused. The doctrine of assumed risk was accurately stated to the jury in the third and fourth instructions given on the part of the defendant.

The judgment of the Appellate Court will be affirmed. Judgment affirmed.

(208 Ill. 116)

MARQUETTE THIRD VEIN COAL CO. v. DIELIE.

(Supreme Court of Illinois. Feb. 17, 1904.)

MASTER AND SERVANT—MINOR—INJURY IN MINES — NEGLIGENCE — WILLFUL VIOLATION OF STATUTE—PLEADING—EVIDENCE — QUESTION FOR JURY.

1. In an action for injuries, a count for negligence was properly joined with a count for violation of the mines and miners act (Hurd's Rev. St. 1899, c. 93), in employing the plaintiff, a minor under 14 years old, in a mine, whereby he was injured; both counts being based on the same state of facts.

2. Where the evidence fairly tends to support the cause of action set out in the declaration, it is the court's duty to submit it to the jury.

3. Evidence *held* to tend fairly to support the causes of action for injuries to a minor from defendant's negligence, and from its violation of the mines and miners act (Hurd's Rev. St. 1899, c. 93) in employing a minor under 14 years old in a mine.

4. A count charging that the plaintiff was under 14 years old, and that the defendant had notice of that fact, and wrongfully and unlawfully employed him to work in a mine, sufficiently shows a willful violation of the mines and miners act (Hurd's Rev. St. 1899, c. 93), within the provision that a willful violation thereof shall give a right of action to the person injured against the mine owner.

5. Under Hurd's Rev. St. 1899, c. 93, prohibiting the employment of minors under 14 years old in mines, and giving a right of action against the mine owner for any injuries resulting from such employment, where it is shown that a minor under 14 years old was so employed, whether the violation of the act was willful and was the proximate cause of the injury are questions of fact for the jury, which are conclusively settled by the judgment of the Appellate Court if there is any evidence on which to base a finding.

6. Where one count of a declaration is for negligence, and the remaining counts for willful violation of a statute, a charge that if the plaintiff was injured by defendant's negligence, as charged in the declaration, the defendant should be found guilty, was not reversible error, though it was not confined to the first count, where an instruction was given, at defendant's request, that if the defendant was not guilty of the negligent acts alleged in the declaration there could be no recovery.

7. A question whether plaintiff was willing, if his attorneys consented to it, to be ex-

amined by the physicians of the defendant company as to his injuries, excluded on objection, formed no basis for an instruction that if the plaintiff, in open court, had refused to allow himself to be examined, the jury might consider such refusal in weighing the testimony as to his injuries.

8. In an action for injuries to a minor under 14 years old, employed in a mine, evidence that the defendant's manager had ordered him out of the mine some months before the accident, because of his being under age, was inadmissible.

9. Under Hurd's Rev. St. 1899, c. 93, § 22, providing that before any boy can be permitted to work in a mine he must produce an affidavit from his parent or guardian that he is 14 years of age, it is sufficient, in an action for injuries to a boy resulting from his employment in a mine, to show that he did not produce the affidavit, without showing that his stepfather did not do so.

Appeal from Appellate Court, Second District.

Action by Patrick Dielle, by his next friend, against the Marquette Third Vein Coal Company. From a judgment of the Appellate Court affirming a judgment in favor of plaintiff, defendant appeals. Affirmed.

Peck, Miller & Starr and Cairo A. Trimble, for appellant. O. H. Porter, Wood & Elmer, and Daniel Belasco, for appellee.

HAND, C. J. This is an action commenced in the circuit court of Bureau county by the appellee, a minor under the age of 14 years, by his next friend, against the appellant, to recover damages for a personal injury sustained by him while in the employ of the appellant as a "trapper" in its coal mine. The case was tried upon a declaration containing three counts. The first count charged the appellant with negligence in failing to provide appellee a safe place in which to work. The second count charged the appellant with a willful violation of the twenty-second section of the mines and miners act (Hurd's Rev. St. 1899, c. 93), in having employed and permitted appellee, a minor under the age of 14 years, to work in its mine, and without having produced to it, by him, an affidavit that he was 14 years of age, by means whereof he was injured. The last count charged that plaintiff was under 14 years of age; that the defendant was aware of that fact; and that he was carelessly, negligently, unlawfully, and wrongfully employed by the defendant to work in its mine: and that by reason of being permitted to work in said mine, and because of his youthful indiscretion, he was injured. The general issue was filed, and a trial resulted in a verdict and judgment in favor of appellee for the sum of $4,000, which judgment has been affirmed by the Appellate Court for the Second District, and a further appeal has been prosecuted to this court.

It is first contended that there is a misjoinder of causes of action in the several counts of the declaration, the position of the appellant being that an action for negligence at common law, in failing to furnish appellee a safe place in which to work, and an action for a willful violation of the mines and miners act by employing and permitting appellee, a minor under 14 years of age, to work in its mine, and without having produced to it, by him, an affidavit that he was 14 years of age, cannot be joined in the same declaration. The counts are based upon the same state of facts, and if the appellant is liable to appellee for damages for negligence as at common law, and also liable to him for damages by reason of a willful violation of the mines and miners act, no valid reason has been suggested why said causes of action may not be joined in different counts of the same declaration. To hold otherwise would be to hold that appellee must bring two actions against the appellant based upon the same state of facts, or abandon one of said causes of action.

The test by which to decide as to the joinder of counts—that is, what actions may be joined in separate counts of the same declaration—is thus stated in Chitty's Pleadings (volume 1, p. 200): "The result of the authorities is stated to be that 'when the same plea may be pleaded and the same judgment given on all the counts of the declaration, or whenever the counts are of the same nature and the same judgment is to be given on them all, though the pleas be different, as in the case of debt upon bond and on simple contract, they may be joined.'"

In Hays v. Borders, 1 Gilman, 46, on page 50, the rule is announced in substantially the same language. It is there said: "It is objected to the declaration that it is defective by reason of a misjoinder of counts and causes of action, in this: that it contains counts for a penalty founded on statute, and others for such damages as could have been recovered at common law. The result of authorities on the subject of the joinder of different forms of action is said to be that 'when the same plea may be pleaded and the same judgment given on all the counts of the declaration,' or 'wherever the causes of action are of the same nature and may properly be the subject of counts in the same species of action, they may be joined, otherwise they cannot.'"

In Brady v. Spurck, 27 Ill. 478, on page 482, the court, again speaking upon the subject through Mr. Justice Breese, said: "The rules of correct pleading allow several causes of action of the same nature to be joined in one count and a recovery had pro tanto. The defendant can plead specially to each cause of action. Godfrey v. Buckmaster, 1 Scam. 477. Different actions cannot be joined in the same declaration. The rule is that, when the same plea may be pleaded and the same judgment rendered on all the counts, they may be joined."

In Fairfield v. Burt, 11 Pick. 244, the court, through Mr. Chief Justice Shaw, on page 246 said: "It is further objected that a count on the statute for double damages cannot be joined with counts at common law for damage of like kind. It is difficult to perceive how, either upon principle or authority, this position can be maintained. The form of action is the same. The statute of 1812 (chapter 146, § 3), providing that the owner of a dog shall forfeit and pay double the damage done by such dog, further provides that it may be recovered by action of trespass. It only affects the rule for assessing damages. The plea is the same and the judgment is the same, and therefore the case comes within the rule regulating the joinder of causes of action."

It is the practice in this state to try personal injury cases under declarations the separate counts of which charge negligence and willful and wanton misconduct (Chicago Terminal Transfer Railroad Co. v. Gruss, 200 Ill. 195, 65 N. E. 693); and, although the rules of law as applied to the separate counts of such a declaration are not the same, it has never been thought for that reason such counts could not be joined in the same declaration. We are of the opinion there was no misjoinder of counts or causes of action in said declaration, but that the counts for negligence at common law and for a willful violation of the statute were properly joined in said declaration.

At the close of the plaintiff's evidence, and again at the close of all the evidence, the defendant asked the court to peremptorily instruct the jury to return a verdict in its favor, which the court declined to do. The evidence introduced on behalf of plaintiff fairly tended to show that he was a minor under the age of 14 years; that he was in the employ of the defendant as a "trapper," for which service he was paid one dollar per day; that it was his duty to open certain doors in an entry in the mine for cars drawn by mules to pass through, and to immediately close the doors after the cars had passed, and to keep them closed except when cars were passing, in order to prevent the escape of air which had been forced into the mine, and, when the cars were stalled in the vicinity of his doors, to assist the driver in starting the cars. He had charge of two doors, situated about 40 feet apart. On the 28th of April, 1902, a train of cars became stalled near appellee's doors. He went to the assistance of the driver, got behind the cars, and blocked the rear wheels when the mules stopped, to prevent the train from backing down the grade. When the train was started, to get to the doors and open them that the train might pass through, it was necessary for him to pass the cars when they were in motion. At a point between where the cars had stalled and his doors, a timber projected from the wall to within a few inches of the cars. He had passed the place frequently, but testified that he had not observed the proximity of the timber to the cars as they passed it. He was caught between the timber and the cars and seriously injured.

At the time appellee entered the employ of appellant he was under 13 years of age, and had been in its employ about 5 months at the time of the injury, and no affidavit was produced by him to the defendant or its mine manager, at the time he entered its employ, that he was 14 years of age. The statute is as follows: "No boy under the age of fourteen years, and no woman or girl of any age shall be permitted to do any manual labor in or about any mine, and before any boy can be permitted to work in any mine he must produce to the mine manager or operator thereof an affidavit from his parent or guardian or next of kin, sworn and subscribed to before a justice of the peace or notary public, that he, the said boy, is fourteen years of age." Hurd's Rev. St. 1899, c. 93, § 22. Section 33 of said act makes any willful neglect, refusal, or failure to do the things required to be done by any provision of the act on the part of a person required to do them, or any violation of any of the provisions or requirements of the act, a misdemeanor, punishable by fine or imprisonment. It also enacts: "For any injury to person or property, occasioned by any willful violations of this act, or willful failure to comply with any of its provisions, a right of action shall acrrue to the party injured, for any direct damages sustained thereby."

If the evidence fairly tends to support the cause of action set out in the declaration, it is the duty of the court to submit the case to the jury. We think the evidence found in this record fairly tended to support the several causes of action set out in the different counts of the declaration, and that the court did not err in refusing to take the case from the jury.

It is also urged that the last count of the declaration is insufficient, in that it does not charge a willful violation of the statute. The statute provides that a willful violation thereof, or a willful failure to comply with its provisions, shall give a right of action against the mine owner to a person injured, for any direct damages which the injured party may sustain by reason of such violation. The count charges the plaintiff was under 14 years of age; that the defendant had notice of that fact, yet it wrongfully and unlawfully employed plaintiff and permitted him to work in its mine, contrary to the statute, etc. A willful violation, within the meaning of the statute, signifies a conscious violation thereof. Odin Coal Co. v. Denman, 185 Ill. 413, 57 N. E. 192, 76 Am. St. Rep. 45; Donk Bros. Coal & Coke Co. v. Peton, 192 Ill. 41, 61 N. E. 330. The sufficiency of the count was not challenged by demurrer or otherwise, and we think the averment "wrongfully and unlawfully," found in the count, a sufficient averment of the conscious violation of the statute after verdict.

It is also said that it does not appear that

the violation of the statute by the appellant by its employing appellee, who was a minor under the age of 14 years, and without requiring him to produce to the appellant an affidavit that he was 14 years of age, was willful or the proximate cause of the injury. The statute makes it unlawful for a mine owner to employ or permit a boy under 14 years of age to perform manual labor in or about a mine, and further provides that before any boy can be permitted to work in a mine he must produce to the mine manager or operator an affidavit from his parent or guardian or next of kin that he is 14 years of age. The second count of the declaration alleged that appellee was under 14 years of age, and that no affidavit was produced by him that he was 14 years of age, to the defendant or its manager, at the time he entered the employ of the defendant, and the evidence tended to support the averment. The object sought to be accomplished by the statute was to prevent the employment of boys of immature years in the coal mines of this state, and we think, in case the statute is violated and a boy is injured while engaged in performing manual labor which he is employed or permitted to do in a mine, the statutory liability for damages has accrued, and in such case the questions of a willful violation of the statute and the proximate cause of the injury are questions of fact for the jury, which facts are conclusively settled by the judgment of the Appellate Court, if there is any evidence in the record upon which to base a finding. Pullman Palace Car Co. v. Laack, 143 Ill. 242, 32 N. E. 285, 18 L. R. A. 215; Swift & Co. v. Rutkowski, 182 Ill. 18, 54 N. E. 1038.

It is urged the court misdirected the jury on behalf of appellee. The court gave to the jury one or more instructions in which they were informed that if they believed plaintiff was injured in consequence of the negligence of the defendant, as charged in the declaration, they should find the defendant guilty. The instructions should have been confined to the first count of the declaration, as the right of recovery in the other two counts of the declaration is based upon the willful violation of the statute by the defendant, and not by reason of its negligence. But we do not think the giving of said instructions was reversible error. The court, at the instance of the defendant, in its fifth instruction informed the jury that before they considered the question of damages they should first determine whether the defendant was guilty of any of the negligent acts charged in the declaration, and if they found, from the evidence, the defendant was not guilty, there could be no recovery. The court having been induced by the defendant to commit the same error in the defendant's instructions which the appellant complains the court committed in plaintiff's instructions, this court will not reverse for such error. Consolidated Coal Co. of St. Louis v. Haenni, 146 Ill. 614, 35 N. E. 162. While appellee was not bound to prove negligence in order to fix a liability upon the defendant under the counts of the declaration other than the first, the word "negligence" was used in each of the counts, and, if the jury were misled by the instructions complained of, it seems apparent they were misled to the detriment of appellee rather than of appellant, as from said instructions the jury might have inferred that appellee could not recover under any of the counts of the declaration without proving negligence.

The jury were fully instructed as to the provisions of the statute against employing a boy under 14 years of age in a mine, and without requiring him to produce an affidavit that he was 14 years of age, and as to what would constitute a willful violation of the statute, and we think it clear the jury understood, from the instructions, they could not find the defendant guilty under the second and last counts of the declaration unless they found, from the evidence, the defendant had knowingly violated the statute by employing or permitting appellee to work in its mine when he was under 14 years of age and without his producing an affidavit that he was 14 years of age, and that he was injured while performing the manual service which he was employed to perform in the mine.

When plaintiff was on the witness stand the attorney for the defendant asked him, "Are you willing, if your lawyers consent to it, to be examined by the physicians of the defendant company here, as to your injuries?" An objection was sustained to the question upon the ground it was not proper cross-examination, and the court remarked, in ruling upon the question, "I do not suppose the boy could determine this; it ought not to be required of him; it ought to be the adults representing him to determine that." The defendant sought to base an instruction upon the question, the objection, and the ruling of the court, to the effect that if the jury believed, from the evidence, that plaintiff, in their presence, in open court, on the trial of the case, with the advice of his counsel, had refused to allow himself to be examined by the physicians of the defendant for the purpose of ascertaining the character of his injuries, they might consider the fact of such refusal in weighing the testimony as to the character of his injuries. There was nothing before the court upon which to predicate the instruction, and it was properly refused.

It is also urged that the court erred in refusing to permit the defendant to prove that its manager ordered appellee out of the mine some months before the injury, when he was working in the mine with his stepfather, because of his being under age. We do not see that there was any error in this. The most the testimony would have tended to prove would have been that the boy was under 14 years of age, and that the manager of the defendant, who afterwards put him to work as a "trapper," knew of that fact.

It is also argued that proof should have been submitted by the plaintiff that his stepfather did not produce to the defendant an affidavit that appellee was 14 years of age at the time he commenced to work in the mine. The statute provides that the minor shall produce the affidavit. Appellee testified an affidavit was not produced by him. That testimony fully met the requirement of the statute, and plaintiff was not required to go further. If an affidavit was presented by some one other than plaintiff, and the defendant was of the opinion such fact was material, it should have offered proof of the fact, and, in case the same was rejected, preserved an exception if it desired a ruling of this court upon the materiality of such testimony. This it failed to do.

We find no reversible error in this record. The judgment of the Appellate Court will therefore be affirmed.

Judgment affirmed.

(208 Ill. 128)

McDONALD et al. v. HOLDOM.

(Supreme Court of Illinois. Feb. 17, 1904.)

ADMINISTRATORS—ACCOUNTING—APPEAL—INTEREST—JUDGMENT—RES ADJUDICATA.

1. On the report of an administrator to collect, admitting a certain sum due and claiming certain disbursements, the court ordered him to pay the admitted amount, and ordered a hearing as to the allowance of disbursements, and on this hearing disallowed a certain sum, and charged him with interest thereon, and with interest on the principal sum admitted due, and ordered him to pay these sums in addition to that admitted. *Held* that, while ordinarily a plaintiff cannot recover the principal sum due in one action and recover interest in another, the administrator, by appealing from that part of the order disallowing disbursements and granting interest, severed the claims, and could not complain in a suit on the bond given on such appeal that in a suit on his official bond, pending the appeal, the plaintiff did not demand such interest.

2. On an appeal in the action on the bond of the administrator, the Supreme Court held that recovery could be had notwithstanding the pendency of the appeal from the order of disallowance and granting interest, and the Supreme Court on appeal also affirmed the order of disallowance and granting interest. *Held*, that the question as to the administrator's liability for such interest was res judicata, and could not be raised by motion in proceedings on the appeal bonds.

3. A court of law is powerless to cause the satisfaction of a judgment to be entered after the term at which it was rendered has expired, for matters which existed at the time the judgment was rendered, and which might have been pleaded and proven in bar of the action.

Appeal from Appellate Court, First District; Elbridge Hanecy, Judge.

Action by Jesse Holdom against Michael C. McDonald and others on an appeal bond. From a judgment of the Appellate Court (108 Ill. App. 449) reversing an order of the circuit court directing the clerk to satisfy the record of the judgment, defendants appeal. Affirmed.

It appears from the record that on December 1, 1894, Joseph Salomon was appointed by the probate court of Cook county administrator to collect of the estate of George Wincox, deceased; that on February 11, 1897, Jesse Holdom was appointed by said probate court administrator of said estate; that on March 4, 1897, Salomon filed his account as administrator to collect in said court, showing receipts $29,857.02, disbursements $5,030.65, balance on hand $24,826.37; that on January 28, 1898, objections were filed to said account, on which day the probate court entered an order reciting that it appeared from said account that Salomon admitted he had in his hands, belonging to the said estate, the sum of $24,826.37, which amount the court ordered him to pay to Holdom as administrator, and ordered the further hearing upon the objections to said account to be continued; that no appeal was prosecuted from said order; that on February 9, 1898, the probate court sustained objections to items contained in said account, aggregating the sum of $4,715, and charged Salomon interest on said sums of $24,826.37 and $4,715, aggregating the sum of $29,541.37, for one year, at 5 per cent. per annum—that is, from February 9, 1897, to February 9, 1898—which amounted to the sum of $1,477.06, on the ground that said Salomon had during that period used the money belonging to said estate in his own business, which interest, added to the amount of the items stricken from said account and for which said administrator to collect had been refused credit, amounted to the sum of $6,192.06, and ordered said Salomon to pay said amount to Holdom, as administrator, in addition to said sum of $24,826.37, which he had before that time been ordered to pay to Holdom, as administrator; that Salomon appealed from that part of the order which refused him credit in his account for the sum of $4,715, and which charged him with the sum of $1,477.06 as interest, to the circuit court of said county, where, on June 30, 1898, a judgment was rendered in that court for $6,249.25 against Salomon in favor of Holdom as administrator, that judgment being the same as that of the probate court, with the interest which had accrued upon the sum of $4,715 of disallowed items between the dates of the judgments in the probate and circuit courts; that Salomon appealed from that judgment to the Appellate Court (85 Ill. App. 613), and from a judgment of affirmance in that court to this court (186 Ill. 445, 57 N. E. 1073), where the judgment of the Appellate Court was affirmed; that after the decision of this court in that case two suits were brought by Holdom as administrator against Joseph Salomon and Michael C. McDonald as surety, one upon the appeal bond from the circuit court to the Appellate Court, and one upon the appeal bond from the Appellate Court to the Supreme Court; that on February 16, 1901, in the suit upon the appeal bond from the circuit to the Appellate Court, judgment was rendered in favor of Holdom, administrator, and against Salomon and McDonald, for $8,000 debt and $7,093.78 damages and costs, which judgment, on January 30, 1902, was affirmed by the Appellate Court (99 Ill. App. 656); that on January 23, 1902, in the suit upon the appeal bond from the Appellate Court to the Supreme Court, judgment was rendered in favor of Holdom, administrator, and against Salomon and McDonald, for $8,000 debt and $7,373.75 damages and costs, the difference in the two judgments being the amount of the interest which accrued upon the amount sued for between the dates of the respective judgments; that on May 2, 1898, Salomon having failed to pay to Holdom, administrator, the amount, to wit, $24,826.37, ordered to be paid to Holdom by the probate court on January 28, 1898, Holdom commenced suit in the circuit court of Cook county upon the bond of Joseph Salomon, as administrator to collect, against Joseph Salomon as principal and Moses Salomon and Michael C. McDonald as sureties, and recovered judgment for $60,000 debt and $29,791.64 damages and costs, said judgment being for the sum of $24,826.37 ordered paid by the probate court on January 28, 1898, and the statutory penalty of 20 per cent. on said amount; that an appeal from that judgment was prosecuted to the Appellate Court (89 Ill. App. 374), where it was held the sureties were not liable for said penalty, but that they were liable for interest at 5 per cent. on said sum of $24,826.37 from the date of demand by Holdom upon Joseph Salomon to July 8, 1899, which demand was found by the court to have been made on March 21, 1898, and which interest was found by the court to amount to $1,593.35, which, added to the sum of $24,826.37, equaled the sum of $26,419.72, and affirmed the judgment of the circuit court upon Holdom, administrator, consenting to a remittitur of the amount of said judgment in excess of $26,419.72, which judgment was affirmed by this court (191 Ill. 290, 61 N. E. 83); that, after the affirmance by this court of the judgment upon the bond of the administrator to collect, that judgment was paid in full, and thereafter the sum of $5,678.15 was paid to Holdom, administrator, by Salomon, to apply upon the judgments obtained upon said appeal bonds, which, it was claimed, fully satisfied the same, with the exception of $1,477.06 and interest thereon, charged to Joseph Salomon by the probate court in his account for wrongfully using the money of said estate in his own business from February 9, 1897, to February 9, 1898, and which amount and accrued interest were included in the circuit court judgment on the appeal from the judgment of the probate court, and a motion was made in the circuit court in each of the cases brought upon said appeal bonds that the court direct the clerk thereof to satisfy of record each of said judgments. Affidavits in support of the motion and counter affidavits were filed, and the court granted said motions, and ordered that said judgments be satisfied. Holdom, as administrator, sued out writs of error from the Appellate Court to reverse the orders entered in each of said cases, in which court the orders of the circuit court were reversed, and the cases were remanded, with directions to the circuit court to enter an order in each of said cases expunging from the judgment docket of that court the satisfaction of said judgments entered therein, respectively, pursuant to said orders of said circuit court. The two writs of error sued out from the Appellate Court to the circuit court were considered in the Appellate Court together, and but one opinion was filed in disposing of said writs. Separate appeals, however, have been prosecuted to this court, and this appeal involves the validity of the order satisfying the judgment entered in the circuit court upon the appeal bond from the Appellate to the Supreme Court.

Edward Maher and Robert F. Kolb, for appellants. Bulkley, Gray & More, for appellee.

HAND, C. J. It is apparent from the statement of facts preceding this opinion that the matter in dispute between the parties to this appeal is the right of the appellee to recover the amount of $1,477.06 as interest allowed the appellee by the judgment of the probate court on February 9, 1898, for the wrongful use of the money of the estate by Joseph Salomon in his own business from February 9, 1897, to February 9, 1898, and which amount was included, with accrued interest, in the circuit court judgment on appeal from the judgment of the probate court. The judgment of the circuit court having been affirmed by the Appellate and Supreme Courts, it would seem the right of the appellee to recover said interest had been settled in favor of the appellee beyond controversy. It is, however, contended by the appellants that the probate court had no right to separate the interest from the principal sum of $24,826.37, which was on January 28, 1898, ordered paid to Holdom as administrator, and afterwards, on February 9, 1898, to order the sum of $1,477.06, as interest on said principal sum and as interest upon the $4,715, to be paid to Holdom as administrator, and it is urged that when the appellee brought suit upon the bond of the administrator to collect, for the principal sum of $24,826.37, he abandoned his right to recover the interest which had been held to have accrued upon said principal sums prior to the date said principal sum of $24,826.37 was ordered paid to the appellee. We do not agree with that contention. While it is true that the plaintiff cannot ordinarily split a demand, and recover in one action the principal and in another the interest due upon the principal sum in the probate court, it is held, upon an accounting by an administrator, an appeal may be prosecuted from each item of the administrator's account. Morgan v. Morgan, 83 Ill. 134. In this case Joseph Salomon prosecuted the appeal from the order of the probate court, and thereby severed the item allowed for interest from the principal sum, and he, or his surety upon said appeal bond, cannot be heard to complain that the appellee did not sue for said principal sum and the interest thereon at the time he brought suit upon the bond of the administrator to collect, when, by the appeal of the administrator to collect from the judgment allowing said item of interest, he prevented the appellee from pursuing that course. When the suit upon the bond of the administrator to collect was here (191 Ill. 200, 61 N. E. 83), the converse of the position now taken by the appellants was then assumed by Joseph Salomon, and it was then contended by him that no recovery could be had in that case, for the reason that his appeal from the order of the probate court disallowing the items in his account to the amount of $4,715, and charging him with interest to the amount of $1,477.06, was then pending, and the amount for which he was liable upon said bond could not then be determined; but this court held that the pendency of said appeal did not constitute a valid reason for Salomon not paying to Holdom, as his successor in office, the portion of the estate which he admitted was in his hands and belonged to Holdom as administrator. It has heretofore been held by this court (186 Ill. 445, 57 N. E. 1073) that the item of $1,477.06 allowed for interest was properly charged to the account of Joseph Salomon. No claim is made that said interest has been paid by Joseph Salomon or released by the appellee. The question, therefore, of the liability of Joseph Salomon to pay said interest is res judicata, and cannot be inquired into collaterally, by motion or otherwise. When the liability of Joseph Salomon to pay the judgment for $6,249.25 of the circuit court, rendered upon the appeal from the judgment of the probate court, was finally decided by this court, and he failed to pay the same, he and his surety upon the appeal bond from the Appellate Court to this court became liable on said appeal bond to pay the judgment of the circuit court, and judgment having been rendered against the appellants upon said appeal bond for the amount of the judgment of the circuit court, which included said item of interest, that judgment was final and could only be discharged by the payment or release of said judgment. Furthermore, the term at which the judgment upon the appeal bond had been rendered having expired, the jurisdiction of the circuit court over said judgment, and its right to eliminate from said judgment the said item of $1,477.06 and the accrued interest thereon, had ceased. A court of law, when a judgment has been paid or discharged, may cause satisfaction of the judgment to be entered upon its record, but it is powerless to cause the satisfaction of a judgment to be entered, after the term at which it was rendered has expired, for matters which existed at the time the judgment was rendered, and which might have been pleaded and proven in bar of the action. All the matters sought to be reviewed by the motion made in the circuit court existed before the judgment sought to be satisfied was rendered, and the circuit court was without jurisdiction to enter the order of July 28, 1902, the effect of which was to change a judgment which had been rendered by said court at a former term.

The judgment of the Appellate Court will be affirmed. Judgment affirmed.

(208 Ill. 186)

WATSON v. FAGNER.

(Supreme Court of Illinois. Feb. 17, 1904.)

BANKER — DEPOSITOR'S MONEY — AGENCY TO LOAN—CONTRACT—VARIANCE AS TO DATE—ADMISSIBILITY OF EVIDENCE—SAFE BORROWER — SUFFICIENCY OF EVIDENCE — INSTRUCTIONS — RATIFICATION — DEGREE OF CARE—BANKRUPTCY OF BORROWER.

1. Where a depositor sues a banker on a parol contract to loan the depositor's money, alleging that it was made on a certain date, but the proof shows that the contract was made seven years earlier, the variance is immaterial.

2. Where a depositor sues a banker on an alleged contract to loan the depositor's money to responsible borrowers, care for and collect the loans, and reloan the money, plaintiff's evidence that it was defendant's custom to collect the principal and interest of plaintiff's notes and loan his money, and that defendant caused or permitted his cashier to indorse plaintiff's name on a note as a preliminary to its being put in judgment, is admissible.

3. Defendant's evidence that he performed like services for other persons with reference to papers left at the bank merely for safe-keeping is properly excluded as irrelevant.

4. Evidence in an action by a depositor against a banker for negligence in loaning plaintiff's money, whereby it was lost, examined, and *held* to sustain a finding that the person borrowing the money without security was not a safe, responsible, and conservative borrower.

5. In an action by a depositor against a banker for negligence in loaning the depositor's money, the court, at plaintiff's instance, gave two instructions, embodying all the facts necessary to sustain a recovery, but not noticing the two affirmative defenses of ratification and the extension of time to the borrower by plaintiff himself. In two instructions, however, given by the court of its own motion, the jury were told that if plaintiff ratified the loan in question defendant would not be responsible for anything done prior thereto, and that if plaintiff extended the time of payment or assumed the burden of collecting the note, and as a result thereof it was lost, defendant would not be liable. *Held*, that the instructions as a whole sufficiently covered the affirmative defenses.

6. A banker who agrees to loan a depositor's money to safe borrowers, and look after and collect the loans and reloan the money, is not

relieved of responsibility for the loss of a negligent loan by the fact that the depositor made no attempt to collect it.

7. A banker who acts as agent for his depositor in making loans, though without compensation, is bound to exercise ordinary care and diligence.

8. Where instructions given show, as a whole, that no recovery can be had on the first three counts of the declaration, it is not error to refuse instructions specifically telling the jury that fact.

9. In an action by a depositor against a banker for negligence in loaning the depositor's money in 1896 to a borrower who became bankrupt in 1899, the defendant requested an instruction that the fact that the borrower was insolvent when the bankruptcy proceedings were begun was not evidence that he was not a safe, responsible, and conservative borrower in 1896. It appeared that the borrower was in failing circumstances at and after the loan, and the bankruptcy was the culmination of this condition of affairs. *Held*, that the instruction was properly refused.

Appeal from Appellate Court, Third District.

Action by Christian Fagner against Daniel Watson. From a judgment of the Appellate Court, Third District (105 Ill. App. 52), affirming a judgment for the plaintiff, defendant appeals. Affirmed.

This suit was brought to the January term, 1901, of the circuit court of Vermilion county, and resulted in a verdict for $4,144.50 in favor of the plaintiff, Fagner, and after a remittitur of $373.80 had been entered and a motion for a new trial overruled judgment was entered against appellant, Watson, for $3,770.70. An appeal was taken by Watson to the Appellate Court for the Third District, where the judgment of the circuit court was affirmed, and a further appeal is prosecuted by Watson to this court. The first three counts of the declaration are common counts. The fourth count, after setting out that on June 1, 1900, the defendant was engaged in the banking business, and that plaintiff, at the request of defendant, deposited $5,000 with him, which defendant agreed to loan to safe, responsible, and conservative borrowers, and to use due diligence in collecting the same, charges that the defendant so carelessly and negligently loaned said sum that the same was wholly lost to the plaintiff, etc. An additional count, designated as the fifth count, was afterwards filed, which differs from the fourth count in that it charges that the defendant carelessly loaned said sum on August 23, 1896, to Dwiggins Bros., and took a note therefor, and that when said note matured did not use due diligence in collecting the same, whereby the same was lost to the plaintiff, etc. Defendant filed the general issue and one special plea, to which replications were filed.

The transaction out of which this suit arose was the loaning of $3,000 by Daniel Watson, for Christian Fagner, to Dwiggins Bros., who were in the mercantile business at Rossville, Ill. Appellant was engaged in the banking business at Rossville, and appellee in farming near that place, for some time prior to 1892. In the spring of 1892 appellee sold his personal property, and took sale notes payable at appellant's bank, and after the sale placed the notes in the bank, so that they could be paid there and the proceeds credited to the account of appellee. After leaving the notes at the bank appellee went to Dakota, where he stayed for a period of seven months. In the spring of 1893 appellee bought property in and moved to Hoopeston, Ill. The evidence of appellee tends to show that he went to appellant's bank to draw out money to pay for the property he had bought, and that Watson requested him not to take his business away from Watson's bank; that appellant wanted to loan out and collect Fagner's money, and said that he would do it in a safe way, so that appellee would have no trouble; that he represented that he (appellant) knew all the people in Rossville, and would loan appellee's money so that it would be perfectly safe, and that he would loan it on the best security. The evidence tends to show that from the time of this conversation appellant transacted all of appellee's business of collecting interest and principal of notes when due and reloaning the money; that appellee knew of some of the loans before they were made, but concerning others he was not consulted; that in 1895 appellee went to the bank, and appellant told him there was about $3,000 of his money in the bank, and asked him if he wanted to loan it; that appellant said a shoe factory and a building and loan association wanted some money; that he told appellant if they were good loans to let them have the money.

On August 23, 1896, appellant loaned to Charles Dwiggins and Howard L. Dwiggins, partners doing business under the name of Dwiggins Bros., $3,000, and took a judgment note, signed by them alone, for that amount, payable to C. Fagner one year after date. The evidence tends to show that appellee was not consulted about this loan; that his notes were kept in an envelope in the bank, and that he kept a list of the notes with him in a book; that in June or July, 1897, he took the envelope containing the notes home with him, and then for the first time learned of the loan to Dwiggins Bros. by finding their note in the envelope; that his book showed a loan of $3,000 to a shoe factory, but none to Dwiggins Bros.; that he kept the notes about a month, and then returned them to the bank, at which time he called appellant's attention to the Dwiggins loan, and asked him why it did not appear on his book; that appellant told him that the $3,000 appearing on his book to the shoe factory was the Dwiggins loan, and that the shoe factory never had any of appellee's money; that appellant further said that the Dwiggins note was just as good as any in the bank.

It further appears that in June, 1898, appellee told appellant that he wanted the

Dwiggins note collected, and appellant said that he would collect it; that in July, 1898, appellee sent his son-in-law to notify appellant to collect the note by January 2, 1899, and that the son-in-law in December, 1898, again visited appellant at his bank to see if the note had been collected; that on January 2, 1899, appellee went to the bank to draw out money to pay for a farm which his son-in-law had bought, and asked whether the note had been collected, and appellant replied that it had not; that appellee told him to collect it as soon as possible, which appellant agreed to do, but at the same time told appellee that he ought not to be in a hurry; that Dwiggins Bros. were all right, and that he ought to leave it, because it was a safe place.

In February, 1899, Ream, a stepson of Watson and cashier of the bank, took this note, together with two notes belonging to Watson, to a firm of attorneys in Danville. Ream indorsed Fagner's name on the note, and judgment by confession was taken on all the notes in one judgment in favor of Watson. Appellee testified that he knew nothing of these proceedings until he saw an account of the failure of Dwiggins Bros. in the papers, and that he never authorized any one to indorse the note for him.

In March, 1899, Dwiggins Bros. filed a petition in bankruptcy, and Watson filed a claim for the judgment against the bankrupts' estate, which paid a dividend of 25¾ per cent. to creditors. Watson tendered to appellee $903.73, which represented the dividend on that portion of the judgment covering the note to Fagner and interest, which tender was refused.

The evidence further shows that at the time of this loan to Dwiggins Bros. that firm was indebted to Watson at least $9,000, with several years' interest thereon, $6,000 of this amount having been loaned in 1890 or 1892, and $3,000 in October, 1889, which latter amount was secured by a mortgage upon the building in which Dwiggins Bros.' business was conducted. In 1898 this indebtedness to Watson had increased to $12,500, and in 1898 Dwiggins Bros. told Watson that they had an equity of only $4,000 or $5,000 in the business. On January 25, 1899, one of the Dwiggins Bros. deeded the real estate, covered by the mortgage above mentioned, to Watson in consideration of $5,000, he paying something over $800 in cash and satisfying the mortgage indebtedness with the remainder of the consideration.

H. M. Steely and J. B. Mann, for appellant. Penwell & Lindley and C. M. Briggs, for appellee.

SCOTT, J. (after stating the facts). The counts in the declaration setting up the express contracts aver that they were made on June 1, 1900. The evidence of the plaintiff shows the contract to have been made in the year 1898. The defendant, at the close of the plaintiff's testimony, moved to strike out the evidence in regard to this contract on account of this variance, and the action of the court in overruling that motion is assigned as error. A different rule prevails in this respect where the contract sued on is written from that which obtains where it is verbal. In assumpsit upon a parol contract, the day upon which it is made being alleged only for form, and where the time within which the contract is to be performed is not determined from that date, the plaintiff is at liberty to prove a contract express or implied, made at any time. Singer v. Hutchinson, 183 Ill. 606, 56 N. E. 388, 75 Am. St. Rep. 133; Frazer v. Smith, 60 Ill. 145; Searing v. Butler, 69 Ill. 575.

The case of Wabash Western Railway Co. v. Friedman, 146 Ill. 583, 30 N. E. 353, 34 N. E. 1111, is one in which the contract itself was not correctly described in the declaration. As counted upon there, the contract was to carry the plaintiff from Kirksville to Glenwood Junction, while the evidence showed a contract to carry the plaintiff from Moberly to Ottumwa, Kirksville and Glenwood Junction being intermediate stations between Moberly and Ottumwa, all on the line of the defendant. It will be observed that in the case at bar the date was no part of the contract, and the contract itself was not misdescribed. There was no error in overruling the motion.

It is assigned as error that the court improperly permitted the plaintiff to testify that Watson's custom was to collect the principal and interest of plaintiff's notes and loan his money, and improperly permitted plaintiff to show that Watson caused or permitted the indorsement of Fagner's name upon the back of the note before it was put in judgment. This evidence tended to show that Watson was complying with the contract as plaintiff claimed it existed, and therefore supported the latter's theory.

It is also urged that the court erroneously refused to permit the defendant to show that Watson performed like services for other persons with reference to papers that were left in the bank merely for safe-keeping. It is manifest that such testimony would not throw any light on the question as to whether such a contract existed between the parties hereto as appeared from the averments of the plaintiff's declaration. The evidence was properly excluded.

The exceptions taken to the action of the court in passing upon objections to other evidence offered are equally without merit, and concern matters of less importance.

It is argued with earnestness that there was no evidence tending to support the fourth count of the declaration, in so far as that count charges a failure to loan the money to safe, responsible, and conservative borrowers. We are unable to adopt this view. This loan was made on August 23, 1896, to

Dwiggins Bros., and no security was taken. It appears that at the time they were the owners of a stock of merchandise in a country village; that several years before they had purchased the stock with which they had been carrying on their business, and that for the purpose of making this purchase they had borrowed $6,000 from Watson, which still remained unpaid; that one of the brothers owned the building in which they carried on their business, and that Watson held a mortgage thereon for the sum of $3,000 (this building was sold in 1899 for $5,000); that no interest had been paid on the real estate loan for several years; and that Watson had begun the practice of carrying an overdraft against the firm at his bank. It does not appear that the firm owned any other property, and while it is true that the evidence does not warrant the conclusion that Dwiggins Bros. were insolvent in August, 1896, it does warrant a finding that they were not safe, responsible, and conservative borrowers, and to loan to them the sum of $3,000 for one year without security was not a compliance with the contract declared upon by the fourth count.

Where a banker takes upon himself the duty of loaning money deposited with him, and loans it to persons already largely indebted to the bank, who afterwards become insolvent, whereby the money of the depositor is lost, the act of the banker in making the loan is properly the subject of the closest scrutiny. In such case the suspicion will always arise that the money of the depositor was loaned with a view to carrying the borrower along until the money due the bank could be collected. Aside from the denial by Watson, and Ream, his cashier, that any contract was made with Fagner to loan his money and collect the principal and interest as they fell due, the defense was that, if such a contract existed, the loan to Dwiggins Bros. had been ratified by Fagner, and that Fagner himself, by an agreement with Howard Dwiggins, one of the makers of the note, had agreed that the note need not be paid until January 1, 1899, and had conveyed information of this agreement to Watson, and that Watson was thereby relieved from any duty to collect. The evidence was conflicting in reference to whether or not there had been any ratification and in reference to whether there had been an extension of the time of payment. Under these circumstances it is contended that the two defenses last suggested were not properly submitted to the jury.

The first and eighth instructions given on the part of the plaintiff both advised the jury what facts are necessary to make the defendant liable to the plaintiff, but contained no reference whatever to a defense founded upon ratification or extension of the time of payment. By these instructions the jury were told that if they found certain facts from the evidence the defendant was liable, and it is not contended that such facts would not establish the liability of the defendant. The complaint is that the instruction did not deal with the affirmative defenses. The court gave to the jury six instructions of its own motion. By the second the jury were instructed that if Fagner ratified the making of the loan Watson would not be responsible for anything done prior to the ratification. By the sixth of these instructions the jury were advised that if the plaintiff extended the time of payment or assumed the burden of collecting the note, and that as a result thereof the note was lost, in whole or in part, Watson would not be responsible. The first and eighth instructions given at the request of plaintiff, when read in connection with the second and sixth given by the court of its own motion, are unobjectionable. The four instructions taken together are a harmonious whole, and state with accuracy the law of defendant's liability upon the contract counted upon, and the law applicable to the alleged ratification and extension.

The defendant, on his part, by his nineteenth and twenty-second instructions, sought to have the jury advised that if Fagner extended the time of payment, and that such extension contributed to the loss of the money, Watson was not liable. In each of these instructions this proposition was coupled with the statement that, if the jury believed Fagner was negligent in allowing the note to run after it became due, Watson could not be held responsible. There was nothing in the evidence upon which to base this last direction to the jury. If the contract existed as Fagner claimed it did, then it was Watson's duty to collect the note when it matured, and the fact that Fagner merely failed to attempt the performance of a duty which rested upon the agent could not relieve the agent.

The defendant's fifth instruction is based on the theory that if Watson was a gratuitous bailee there would be liability for nothing except gross negligence. The court modified this instruction, and gave it as modified, instructing the jury that Watson would be liable for "carelessness or negligence in making the loan, or carelessness or negligence in failing to collect the same, which would amount to a want of ordinary care and diligence" on his part. The modification was properly made.

Where a banker acts as agent or trustee for his depositor, without compensation, in investing his money and collecting the same, he is bound to exercise ordinary care and diligence in the performance of the duties which he assumes, and a failure to observe such ordinary care and diligence will make him responsible for any loss resulting from such failure. Isham v. Post, 141 N. Y. 100, 35 N. E. 1084, 23 L. R. A. 90, 38 Am. St. Rep. 766; Watson v. Roth, 191 Ill. 382, 61 N. E. 65.

In the cases of Gray v. Merriam, 148 Ill. 179, 35 N. E. 810, 32 L. R. A. 769, 39 Am. St.

Rep. 172, and Preston v. Prather, 137 U. S. 604, 11 Sup. Ct. 162, 34 L. Ed. 788, the question of the liability of a bank as the gratuitous bailee of securities left as a special deposit was considered, and the conclusion reached that the bank was bound to exercise ordinary care and diligence. The reasoning followed in those two cases requires the exercise of the same degree of care and diligence where the duties assumed are the loaning of money deposited with the bank and the collection of the loans as they mature.

We have carefully considered the other objections urged to the giving and refusing of instructions, and are of the opinion that upon the whole the jury was fairly instructed. The defendant requested the giving of 26 instructions. The court gave 4 of these as requested, modified 2 others and gave them as modified, refused 20, and gave 6 of its own motion, while 9 were given on the part of the plaintiff. Three instructions were offered by the defendant for the purpose of telling the jury that no recovery could be had under the first, second, or third count of the declaration. The refusal of these instructions is complained of. No harm resulted from this action of the court, as it is apparent from the instructions given as a series that no recovery could be had except under the fourth or fifth count.

The defendant's seventh refused instruction was to the effect that the fact that Dwiggins Bros. were insolvent when the bankruptcy proceedings were begun was not evidence that they "were not safe, responsible, and conservative borrowers" on August 23, 1896. It appeared that they were in failing circumstances at and after the making of the loan in question. The bankruptcy was the culmination of this condition of affairs. The instruction was properly refused.

In so far as the other instructions refused correctly stated principles of law applicable to this case, the same principles were embodied in instructions given. The principal questions in this case were issues of fact, which have been settled against appellant by the judgment of the Appellate Court. The judgment of the Appellate Court will be affirmed. Judgment affirmed.

(208 Ill. 173)

MILLER et al. v. JOHN.

(Supreme Court of Illinois. Feb. 17, 1904.)

CONSPIRACY—CIVIL LIABILITY—MISREPRESENTATIONS INDUCING EXCHANGE OF LANDS—PLEADING—DECLARATION—MISJOINDER OF COUNTS—REVIEW—EVIDENCE—SUFFICIENCY—TRIAL—OPENING ARGUMENT—INSTRUCTIONS.

1. Where the testimony, though more or less conflicting, fairly tends to establish the allegations of the declaration, it must be accepted as sustaining plaintiff's cause of action, where considered on review of a judgment of affirmance by the Appellate Court.

2. The original count of a declaration alleged that plaintiff was induced to exchange his lands for other lands by the false and fraudulent statements of defendants as to the character and value of the land traded for, the nature of which was set out; and, it was alleged that they were false, and made knowingly and willingly for the purpose of misleading, deceiving, and defrauding plaintiff, and that the land was of little or no value, by means whereof plaintiff was damaged to a specified amount. A second count was substantially the same, except that it charged that defendants, combining and confederating, then and there represented to plaintiff, and so promised and agreed with him, that they would be his agents, and trade and exchange for him his farm for other farm lands of greater value, consisting, etc. *Held*, that both counts were in tort, for fraud and deceit, and hence there was no misjoinder.

3. It being impossible for the court to know in advance what testimony will become competent on the trial, no error can be predicated on a statement in the opening argument, where the court, on objection, warned the jury not to accept it as evidence.

4. In an action for conspiracy to cheat and defraud by false and fraudulent representations inducing an exchange of lands, evidence as to the amount paid by two of the defendants for services of a third party in the transaction, and as to a subsequent conveyance of a part of plaintiff's land to them, and their reconveyance to another, with the circumstances attending the latter sale, was competent to show the conspiracy.

5. After the introduction of competent evidence tending to prove a conspiracy, evidence of conversations between plaintiff and either of defendants relating to the transaction is competent and binding on the others, though they were not present.

6. No error can be predicated on an instruction which, when read with a preceding instruction to which it referred, stated the law correctly.

7. A person who recklessly makes false representations of a matter about which he has no knowledge, for the fraudulent purpose of inducing another to rely thereon, and to make a contract to do any act to the prejudice of such person, who does rely and act thereon, suffering injury thereby, is legally liable.

8. The fact that one of the defendants in an action for conspiracy to cheat and defraud by false representations was not present when any of the false representations were made to plaintiff, and did not himself make such statements, would not absolve him from liability if he knew that they had been made, and assisted in the transaction, or approved the same.

9. All who aid, advise, or assist in the commission of a wrongful act by another, or who approve of it after it is done, if done for their benefit, are liable in the same manner as they would be if they had done the same wrongful act themselves.

10. An instruction which simply advised the jury as to the elements to be considered in determining the preponderance of the evidence, and, after enumerating such elements, directed them to determine the same from all the evidence, facts, and circumstances shown on the trial, was proper.

11. No error can be predicated on the refusal of instructions where no special reasons for giving them are pointed out, and it appears that the jury were otherwise sufficiently and properly instructed.

Appeal from Appellate Court, Second District.

Action by Chalkly John against Joseph T. Miller and others. A judgment for plaintiff was affirmed by the Appellate Court, and defendants appeal. Affirmed.

¶ 7. See Fraud, vol. 23, Cent. Dig. § 5.

C. L. & C. E. Sheldon and J. E. McPherran, for appellants. C. C. Johnson and C. C. McMahon, for appellee.

WILKIN, J. The appellee, Chalkly John, brought an action for fraud and deceit against the three appellants, Joseph T. Miller, Frank P. Stabler, and Frank W. Walzer, in the circuit court of Whiteside county. Upon a trial by jury, all the defendants were found guilty, and the plaintiff's damages assessed at $5,440. Upon the argument of a motion for new trial, at the suggestion of the trial court, $940 was remitted, and judgment entered for $4,500. On appeal to the Appellate Court for the Second District, that judgment has been affirmed, and appellants again appeal.

The original count of the declaration alleges that the plaintiff owned 160 acres of land in Whiteside county, known as the "Jordan Farm," of the value of $80 per acre, and also 160 acres in the state of Kansas, worth $7 per acre, all of which he was induced by the defendants, by false and fraudulent representations, to exchange and trade for 320 acres in Barron county, Wis. The false and fraudulent statements are charged to be that the Wisconsin land belonged to an estate to which there were a large number of heirs; that the owners could not agree, because each one wanted this particular tract; that the rest of the estate had been divided, and that the owners had agreed to sell this to an outside party in order to make it satisfactory, and that it could be had at a great bargain; that there was a good log house and a good log barn on the land; that it was all fenced; that about 40 or 50 acres were cleared and seeded down in timothy, and the balance was covered with good timber, such as would make good lumber; that the part north of the cleared land would make 800 or 900 cords of wood, worth $5 per cord in that locality; that the owners had been offered $1,600 for the timber on the stump on that part north of the cleared land; that the owners asked $8,000 for the 320 acres, and the land was cheap at $25 per acre; that the land lay as nice as his Jordan farm, and was not broken or stony; and that, if the owners would trade it to him for his Jordan farm, he would have the best of the bargain. It is also averred that the plaintiff, not having seen the Wisconsin land, but relying and confiding in the statements and representations of the defendants, bargained with them to exchange his Jordan farm and his Kansas 160 acres for the Wisconsin land, and executed deeds to the defendants for the same. All of the representations of the defendants respecting the Wisconsin land are charged to be false, made knowingly and willfully for the purpose of misleading, deceiving, and defrauding plaintiff, and that the Wisconsin land was of little or no value, by means whereof the plaintiff is damaged to the amount of $8,000. The second count is substantially the same as the first, except that it charges that "defendants, combining and confederating, then and there represented to the plaintiff, and so promised and agreed with the plaintiff, that they (the defendants) would, as the plaintiff's agents, trade and exchange for the plaintiff his said farm for other farm lands of greater value, consisting of three hundred and twenty acres of land in the state of Wisconsin," and then and there falsely and fraudulently made the representations, in substance, set out in the first count of the declaration. A general demurrer was filed to the original count, and overruled. Afterwards a similar demurrer was filed to the second count, which was also overruled, and the defendants thereupon filed a plea of not guilty, and the case proceeded to trial.

The Appellate Court, after stating the issues as above, in the discussion of the question whether the evidence supported the verdict of the jury, set forth in extenso the facts, but it will not be necessary to repeat them here. See opinion of Appellate Court in — Ill. App. —.

The testimony produced upon the trial is voluminous and more or less conflicting, but it at least fairly tends to establish the allegations of the declaration, and, in view of the judgment of affirmance in the Appellate Court, must, for the purposes of our decision, be accepted as sustaining plaintiff's cause of action.

The first assigned error of law urged as a ground of reversal is that the two counts of the declaration are misjoined, being inconsistent with each other, and the measure of damages being different on the allegations of each of them. The contention is based on the assumption that the second count is a count on a contract of agency or in assumpsit. This is a misapprehension. Both counts are in tort, and seek to recover damages for fraud and deceit. The Appellate Court, in its opinion, properly disposes of the question on the authorities cited by it.

It is also insisted by appellants that the trial court erred in permitting counsel for the appellee, in his opening to the jury, to state that the defendant Walzer had cheated and swindled John in a former Kansas land deal. Upon the objection made by counsel for the defendants, the court stated that it could not then determine whether such evidence would be admissible or not, and told the jury that they should bear in mind that statements of counsel were not evidence for their consideration, and that the case was to be tried upon the evidence admitted by the court, and nothing else. In opening statements by counsel to juries, the trial court is necessarily compelled to rely largely upon the integrity and fairness of the attorney; it being impossible for it to know in advance what testimony will or will not become pertinent and competent upon the trial. The court could at that stage of the trial do no more than it did: that is, warn the jury not to accept the statement as evidence. From an examination of the record, we are further of the opinion that the statement was in no sense improper, but was justified by the subsequently developed facts in the case.

The ruling of the trial court on the admission of evidence is next assigned and urged as reversible error. There are several objections, but they all involve the same legal principle, and may therefore be considered together. The plaintiff was permitted to detail a conversation between himself and Walzer in the absence of the other defendants, in which Walzer made certain statements relative to the Wisconsin land, which were to the effect that plaintiff had been cheated in the Kansas land deal, and he wanted to make it up to him in the trade then being negotiated; also a conversation between himself, Miller, and Walzer when Stabler was not present. Testimony was also admitted, over the defendants' objection, as to the amount paid one Prock for his services in Wisconsin by Miller and Stabler, and concerning the conveyance of the Jordan farm by Pettis to Stabler and Miller, his quitclaim deed to them, and their conveyance afterwards to one Newman, together with the facts and circumstances attending the sale to Newman. Appellants claim that this evidence was incompetent, and tended to prejudice the jury against them. The theory of plaintiff's case is that the defendants had entered into a conspiracy to cheat and defraud him. Such a conspiracy might be proved by the facts and circumstances surrounding the parties to the transaction or trade, and, after the introduction of competent testimony tending to prove it, each of the parties connected therewith would become responsible not only for his own acts and words, but for those of each of the parties with whom he acted. The rule is that, in order to render one responsible for a false representation, it is not necessary that he should have made the representation himself. If a person authorizes or causes a representation to be made, he is as fully responsible as if he made it himself; and, if two or more persons act in concert or conspire to commit a fraud upon another, each is responsible for the false and fraudulent representations of the others within the scope of the conspiracy. 14 Am. & Eng. Ency. of Law (2d Ed.) 155, and authorities in note 6. The evidence as to the amount paid Prock, and that concerning the sale and conveyance of the Jordan farm to Miller and Stabler, and by them to Newman, were circumstances competent to be shown as tending to establish the conspiracy; and conversations between either of them and the plaintiff, even in the absence of the others, were competent and binding upon all of them. The trial court committed no error in admitting the several items of evidence objected to.

It is again insisted that the trial court erred in giving the first, fifth, seventh, eighth, and eleventh instructions on behalf of the plaintiff. It is said the first told the jury that they should allow such damages to the plaintiff as they thought him entitled to, without any reference to the evidence, and that, in assessing the damages, they should confine themselves to the difference in value between the Wisconsin land at the time of the exchange or trade, and the value at that time if it had been as represented by the defendants. We do not think this is a fair interpretation of the instruction. As a matter of fact, this instruction, which is numbered 1 in the record, was the second instruction given by the court for plaintiff, and expressly refers to the one which just precedes it. The two instructions, read together, stated the law correctly. The so-called first was in no sense, when considered with the preceding one, capable of the construction sought to be placed upon it.

It is insisted that the fifth, seventh, and eighth should have been refused, on the ground that there was no evidence before the jury upon which to base them. The fifth is to the effect that if a person recklessly makes false representations of a matter about which he has no knowledge, for the fraudulent purpose of inducing another to rely upon his statements, and to make a contract or to do an act to the prejudice of such person, who does rely and act upon such representations, suffering injury thereby, the party making the representation is legally liable. The seventh informed the jury that, although Stabler was not present when any of the false representations were made to plaintiff, if they were made, or did not himself make such statements, but knew that they had been made, and assisted in the transaction or approved the same, he would be equally chargeable with the other defendants. The eighth told the jury that all who aid, command, advise, or assist in the commission of a wrongful act by another, or who approve of it after it is done, if done for their benefit, are liable in the same manner as they would be if they had done the same wrongful act themselves. We are of the opinion that each of these instructions not only laid down correct principles of law applicable to this case, but that there is sufficient evidence in the record upon which to base them. There was no error in giving them.

The eleventh instruction given on behalf of the plaintiff simply advised the jury as to the elements which they might take into consideration in determining the preponderance of the evidence, and, after enumerating those elements, directed that, from all the evidence, facts, and circumstances shown on the trial, they should determine on which side is the preponderance. We are unable to see any substantial objection to it. It has frequently been approved, in substance, at least, by this court.

Complaint is also made of the refusal of the trial court to give the ninth, tenth, eleventh, twelfth, and fourteenth instructions asked on behalf of the defendants, but no special reasons are pointed out why they, or either of them, should have been given; and, on a consideration of the whole record, we think the trial court sufficiently and properly instructed the jury as to the law of the case by the instructions given, and committed no error in refusing the five above mentioned.

That plaintiff below was outrageously overreached in the transaction between himself and these parties admits of no doubt. Whether he was guilty of such omission of duty to protect himself, and whether the false and fraudulent representations were made in such manner as to make all three of the defendants jointly liable, were questions of fact, depending upon conflicting testimony; and, they having been settled adversely to the appellants by the trial and appellate courts, there is no substantial merit in the grounds of reversal here urged.

The judgment of the Appellate Court will be affirmed. Judgment affirmed.

(208 Ill. 98)

BENHAM v. BENHAM.

(Supreme Court of Illinois. Feb. 17, 1904.)

PRACTICE—ABSTRACT ON APPEAL—FURNISHING ADDITIONAL ABSTRACT—DIVORCE—ALIMONY—TRIAL COURT'S DISCRETION.

1. Where, on appeal in divorce, it appeared to the Appellate Court that appellant's abstract was imperfect, appellee should have been allowed to file an additional abstract, the cost to be charged to appellant; and, if appellee was financially unable to do so, appellant should have been ruled to furnish a complete abstract, or furnish appellee with sufficient money with which she could file it.

2. In divorce, the amount of alimony and solicitor's fees are within the sound discretion of the chancellor, which will not be disturbed unless abused.

Appeal from Appellate Court, First District.

Suit by Matilda C. Benham against Raymond S. Benham for divorce. From a decree of the Appellate Court (107 Ill. App. 424) affirming a decree in favor of complainant, defendant appeals. Affirmed.

Joseph W. Latimer and Milford J. Thompson, for appellant. Frank F. Douglass (A. B. Jenks, of counsel), for appellee.

WILKIN, J. Appellee filed her bill for divorce against appellant, charging cruelty. Appellant, in his cross-bill, charged appellee with adultery. Answers were filed to the bill and cross-bill, denying the material allegations contained therein. Upon a hearing in open court before the chancellor, a jury having been waived, a decree of divorce was granted to appellee, and the cross-bill of appellant was dismissed. The decree gave appellee the care and custody of their minor child, together with $75 per month as alimony and $1,000 as solicitor's fees. This decree was affirmed by the Appellate Court for the First District, and the case is now brought to this court.

There are several errors assigned by appellant, but they all resolve themselves into the one question whether or not the decree is sustained by the evidence. The record is very voluminous, containing about 2,000 pages of typewritten matter, and the abstract contains 366 pages.

It is claimed by appellee that the abstract as filed in the Appellate Court is incomplete and unfair, omitting much material evidence offered by appellee. The Appellate Court, in passing upon that question, after an examination of a number of instances cited by appellee in which she claimed the abstract to be so imperfect, and, as it stated, comparing the abstract with the record, held that appellee's position was justifiable, and that court seems to have affirmed the decree below upon that ground. The same abstract has been filed in this court, and the same objection is here renewed. The proper practice in the Appellate Court would have been to allow appellee to file an additional abstract, the cost to be charged to the appellant; and, if she was financially unable to do so, as claimed by her, then appellant should have been ruled to furnish a complete abstract, or pay to appellee sufficient money with which she could file the same. Treating the case, however, as submitted in this court on the abstract filed, we have examined it and some parts of the record, and reached the conclusion that the decree of the circuit court should be affirmed. The evidence is in hopeless conflict, and cannot be reconciled, and no good purpose would be served by our attempting to analyze or discuss it. There is no end of crimination and recrimination by the parties as to the conduct of each other, and the details of some of the testimony is most disgusting. Neither party would be benefited or vindicated by a reiteration of it here, and we content ourselves with the simple statement that, in our view, the chancellor was justified in his finding and decree in favor of the appellee. The testimony was heard by him in open court, and he could better judge of the weight and credit to be given to the several witnesses than we can.

Objection is further made on behalf of appellant to the amount of alimony and solicitor's fees allowed appellee. These matters were within the sound legal discretion of the chancellor, and, considering all the evidence, the relation of the parties, and their condition in life, we see no good reason for holding that the discretion has been abused.

The judgment of the Appellate Court will accordingly be affirmed. Judgment affirmed.

¶ 2. See Divorce, vol. 17, Cent. Dig. § 770.

(208 Ill. 166)

LARSEN v. THURINGIA AMERICAN INS. CO.

(Supreme Court of Illinois. Feb. 17, 1904.)

FIRE INSURANCE—CANCELLATION OF POLICY AND REPLACING INSURANCE—AGENTS—UNAUTHORIZED ACTS—RATIFICATION—ELECTION—CONSIDERATION.

1. An agent, who attended to plaintiff's insurance, insured his machine shop in three different companies, including defendant, which was entitled to cancel its policy on five days' notice. Two days before a fire the agent received a notice of cancellation from defendant, stating that the holder could have until 12 o'clock to replace the insurance elsewhere, which the agent did on receipt of the notice, and at their first meeting after the fire informed plaintiff of the notice and what he had done. Plaintiff said it made no difference to him so he got his insurance. Thereafter, at the agent's request, he delivered to him defendant's policy, and received in lieu thereof the one issued to replace it. All the policies, including defendant's, provided that the loss should be prorated in the proportion that the amount insured bore to the whole insurance, and in adjusting the loss it was contended that defendant's policy at the time of the fire was still subsisting. To this plaintiff assented, and agreed to the proportion charged defendant, which was not represented, and did not agree thereto. Plaintiff accepted payments from the other companies on that basis. *Held*, that defendant was not liable though the agent acted without authority in canceling defendant's policy and replacing the insurance, for plaintiff could and did ratify his acts with a full knowledge at the time of all of the facts necessary to bind him, whether he then knew or not that defendant's policy would have to be taken into account in adjusting the loss.

2. Even if the agent acted for defendant, plaintiff, after being fully and fairly informed as to the facts, was put to his election as to whether he would rely on defendant's policy or take the one issued to replace it, and, having accepted the latter, and received payment thereon according to his agreement with the adjusters, he could not claim a want of consideration for the surrender of defendant's policy, and that defendant was not relieved from liability.

Appeal from Appellate Court, First District.

Action by Ivert Larsen against the Thuringia American Insurance Company. A judgment for defendant was affirmed by the Appellate Court (108 Ill. App. 420), and plaintiff appeals. Affirmed.

Bulkley, Gray & More (Fred L. Divine, of counsel), for appellant. Lackner, Butz & Miller, for appellee.

RICKS, J. This is an appeal from a judgment of the Appellate Court for the First District affirming a judgment of the circuit court of Cook county for costs in favor of appellee in a suit brought by appellant against appellee in an action of assumpsit on an insurance policy. The cause is here upon a certificate of importance. Trial was had before a jury in the court below, and at the close of the evidence the court directed the jury to find the issues for the defendant, which was done, and judgment for costs entered upon the verdict. No other instructions were offered, and no questions of law are raised except as to the propriety of the court giving the instruction directing a verdict.

Appellant is a machinist doing business in the city of Chicago, and owning a machine shop on Market street, in that city. One N. J. Bennett was an insurance agent and solicitor, who sought and received business not only for companies that he represented, but procured insurance in companies that he did not represent. On the 19th day of January, 1899, appellant called upon Mr. Bennett, and directed him to write or have written $2,500 insurance upon his (appellant's) machine shop. Appellant did not direct what companies the insurance should be placed with, nor was anything said at the time as to the number of policies, or the amount of each, that should be written. The evidence discloses that Bennett had for some time had the insurance business of appellant, and was acquainted with him and his building upon which insurance was sought; and on or about the same day that the request for the insurance was made Bennett either wrote or procured for and delivered to appellant three policies—one in the Merchants' Insurance Company for $1,000, one in the North German Insurance Company for $1,000, and one in appellee company for $500. On the morning of February 23, 1899, the property insured was partially destroyed by fire, and by all the companies, except appellee, that were interested, the loss was adjusted at $1,981.80, and the amount of the loss is not questioned by appellee. Of the loss $360.33 was not paid, and for that this suit was brought.

The only question is as to the liability of appellee under the policy issued by it. The policy contained a condition or provision for cancellation, by the terms of which it might be canceled at any time at the request of the insured or by the company by giving five days' notice of such cancellation. If canceled by the company upon notice, the company was only to have the pro rata premium for the time it carried the risk. On the 21st day of February, Bennett, the agent, received from appellee a notice that it had elected to cancel its policy, and that the holder would be allowed until the 21st day of February, 1899, at 12 o'clock, to replace the insurance elsewhere. Upon receipt of this notice, Bennett, the agent, replaced the insurance to the amount of $500, being the same amount as appellee's policy, in the North British & Mercantile Insurance Company, paying the premium therefor out of the rebate from the Thuringia policy, as the evidence tends to show, or, at all events, without charging any premium to appellant. The policy in the North British and Mercantile Company was kept by Bennett until after the fire, as he did not see appellant from the time he received the notice until the day of and after the fire. At their first meeting after the fire Bennett told appellant of receiving the notice from appellee and of the cancellation of its policy, and that he (Bennett) had placed the insurance with the North British & Mercantile Company, and appellant testifies that he then said it did not make any difference to him, just so he got his $2,500 of insurance. After the fire appellant engaged the firm of Peckham, Flagg & Peckham, who were insurance adjusters, to represent him in the matter of his policies, and Mr. Luthur N. Flagg, of said firm, did take charge of appellant's policies, and represented him. After Flagg had received the policies of appellant, and before the adjustment, they together met Bennett, who explained to both Flagg and appellant the transaction of the cancellation of the policy issued by appellee and of the replacing of that insurance in the North British & Mercantile Company, and thereupon requested that appellant deliver up to him (Bennett) the policy issued by appellee, and receive in lieu thereof the one issued by the North British & Mercantile Company, to which appellant assented, and which was done. After receiving this policy, Flagg, representing appellant, and adjusters representing the Merchants, the North German, and the North British & Mercantile Insurance Companies, met, and agreed that the extent of appellant's loss was $1,981.80, as above stated; but it there appeared that each of the policies there represented contained the provision: "This company shall not be liable under this policy for a greater proportion of any loss on the described property, or for loss by and expense of removal from premises endangered by fire, than the amount hereby insured shall bear to the whole insurance, whether valid or not, or by solvent or insolvent insurers, covering such property." Those companies represented at the adjustment insisted that at the time of the fire appellee's policy was still a subsisting policy, and that the above provision of their policies (and there was the same provision in appellee's policy) was broad enough to require that in prorating the loss among the companies the policy held by appellee must be taken into consideration, and the basis of the insurance fixed at $3,000 instead of $2,500. To this contention appellant assented, and the proportion that it was agreed between appellant and the adjusters that should be charged to appellee's policy was $300.33. As we have said, appellee was not represented at the adjustment, and did not agree to the basis fixed there.

The facts as above set forth are undisputed, and the only question remaining is as to the liability of appellee under them. The appellee contends that it is not liable upon two grounds: First, that appellant could and did ratify the acts of Bennett after being fully informed as to them; and, secondly, that, if Bennett was not the agent of appellant, but was the agent of appellee, and by its direction canceled its policy and procured other insurance in the place of it, appellant was fully and fairly informed as to the entire transaction, and he was put to his election whether he would rely upon the policy issued by appellee, or whether he would take the policy issued by the North British & Mercantile Company in lieu thereof, and that he did elect to and did receive the latter policy; and the evidence shows, and it is undisputed, that appellant received from the North British & Mercantile Company the proportion of the loss that it was agreed at the adjustment should be paid by it. Appellant's contention is that Bennett was not his agent for the purpose of canceling or consenting to the cancellation of appellee's policy, and did not represent him when he replaced the insurance covered by appellee's policy in the policy of the North British & Mercantile Company, and that, as he had no knowledge of the transaction until after the fire and the loss had been incurred, it did not lie in his power then to ratify any agreement by which appellee would be released from a liability that had become fixed and substitute another therefor, and that appellant received no consideration for such agreement, if it was made. It is not claimed by appellant that he was at any time to have more than $2,500 insurance upon his property. The North British & Mercantile Company at no time denied its liability, but acknowledged the same and paid according to the adjustment. We can see no reason, and none has been pointed out, why appellant could not ratify the acts of Bennett if they were not authorized at the time they were done, if he was fully and fairly informed as to such acts, and why such ratification would not and ought not to be binding upon him. The general rule seems to be that one may ratify that which is done by another if he could have himself done the same thing in the first instance. 1 Am. & Eng. Ency. of Law (2d Ed.) 1184; Zottman v. San Francisco, 20 Cal. 96, 81 Am. Dec. 96. It is said that "ratification, as it relates to the law of agency, is the express or implied adoption of the acts of another by one for whom the other assumes to be acting, but without authority; and this results as effectually to establish the duties, rights, and liabilities of an agency as if the acts ratified had been fully authorized in the beginning." 1 Am. & Eng. Ency. of Law (2d Ed.) 1181.

Appellant does not contend that he was not fully advised as to all the facts relating to the cancellation of appellee's policy and the issuance of the policy to replace the same, which was received by him; but counsel now urge that he would not have accepted the same had he known that in the adjustment of his loss appellee's policy must be taken into account in determining the whole amount of insurance. We are not called upon to determine whether, as a matter of law, the insurance companies at that adjustment had the right to make the insistence that the insurance should be prorated upon the basis of $8,-000 insurance instead of $2,500. If they did have that right, it was not due to any newly discovered or undisclosed fact between Bennett and appellant at the time appellant accepted the policy in the North British & Mercantile Company and surrendered the policy issued by appellee, because all the policies that appellant had, including that of appellee and the one that he received in lieu thereof, contained the provision relied upon by the adjusters for the other companies, and their right to such insistence, and the duty of appellant to yield to the same in the adjustment of his loss, was a question of law, and not a question of fact.

It is a familiar principle that, though one may be entitled to be invested with all the facts pertaining to a transaction before he can be bound, it is not incumbent on the part of those who claim he is so bound to explain to him the legal effect of the transaction, and certainly not of other transactions ancillary thereto and growing out of and arising from the subject-matter thereof. Without the agreement of the appellant to accept the North British & Mercantile Company's policy in lieu of the policy held from appellee, it may be well doubted if appellee's liability would have been released or affected by anything that had transpired up to that time, and also, without the surrender of appellee's policy by appellant as a condition and consideration for the receiving of the policy of the North British & Mercantile Company, it may well be doubted if that company could have been held liable for any part of the loss; but it would seem that when appellant was fully advised as to the transaction, and assented thereto, and delivered up his policy in the appellee company, and received the policy in the North British & Mercantile Company, and received payment on that policy according to his agreement with the adjusters, it cannot lie in him now to say that there was no consideration for the surrender of the policy issued by appellee, and that appellee is not relieved from liability by that transaction.

Counsel for appellant urge that the case of Hartford Fire Ins. Co. v. McKenzie, 70 Ill. App. 615, is in point, and, in effect, holds that under the circumstances of this case there could be no ratification of the acts of Bennett, the agent. We are unable to adopt the view of that case as urged by appellant. There the notice of cancellation was, as here, given to the agent, and the agent started to write, or began to write, a policy in the Hartford Company on the same property. He did not, however, do so, but he did go through the process of making charges on his books against the insured for the new policy, and credited the insurance company with the same. Before the policy was issued, and before the insured had any knowledge of such policy, his property was destroyed, and he elected to surrender, or agreed to the cancellation of, the first policy, and the acceptance of the second; but the Hartford Company, whose policy was the second, denied liability, denied the authority of its agent to take the risk, which was extrahazardous, and had been refused by several companies, without its knowledge, and denied liability upon the further ground that its policy provided that it should be void if there was any other insurance, and it was held in that case that, as the first policy was not released at the time of the loss or the cancellation consented to by the insured, it was subsisting insurance, and avoided the Hartford policy.

We regard the case of Arnfeld & Son v. Assurance Co., 172 Pa. 605, 34 Atl. 580, as very similar in its facts to the facts of the case at bar, and the reasoning of that case very cogent, and in support of the views we entertain.

We think upon both grounds—that of ratification and election—under the facts disclosed by this record appellant was bound by the bargain he had advisedly made, and that the judgments of the circuit and Appellate Courts are right, and the judgment of the Appellate Court is affirmed. Judgment affirmed.

(208 Ill. 108)

VAN DER AA v. VAN DRUNEN et al.

(Supreme Court of Illinois. Feb. 17, 1904.)

DEEDS—DELIVERY—EVIDENCE—SUFFICIENCY—EQUITY—REVIEW.

1. On an issue as to whether there had been manual delivery of a deed, evidence *held* sufficient to sustain a finding that there was no delivery.

2. On appeal in a chancery case the findings of the chancellor on the facts will not be disturbed unless clearly erroneous.

3. On an issue as to whether there had been delivery of a deed, the certificate of acknowledgment indorsed thereon is of no weight as evidence, it being conceded that no delivery was made at the time of acknowledgment.

Appeal from Circuit Court, Cook County; Frank Baker, Judge.

Suit by Naatje Van der Aa against Johanna Van Drunen and others. From a decree in favor of defendants, complainant appeals. Affirmed.

John C. Trainor and Charles J. Trainor, for appellant. I. T. Greenacre, for certain appellees. Rogers & Mahoney, for Lizzie Van der Aa, insane. F. R. De Young, pro se.

RICKS, J. This is an appeal from a decree of the circuit court of Cook county dismissing complainant's bill in a suit filed in that court in March, 1901, by appellant, Naatje Van der Aa, widow of Gerritt Van der Aa. By said bill complainant sought to have vacated several deeds made by the defendants, the daughters and sons-in-law of complainant, to certain property described therein; to obtain a release of parts of said property from certain incumbrances thereon; to have decree to complainant money paid by her to defendants as rent; and for an order requiring defendants to return to complainant a certain warranty deed alleged to have been made to her by said Gerritt Van der Aa conveying the property in question, and for other general relief.

Appellant, by her bill, sets forth facts substantially as follows: That her husband, Gerritt Van der Aa, owned four pieces of land (describing the same) in Cook county; that three of the pieces are contiguous, and aggregate 64.72 acres, and the remaining piece is separate, and contains about 30 acres; that said husband died March 28, 1898, leaving six daughters, his only children, the principal appellees here; that in May, 1897, her husband, by warranty deed, conveyed said lands to complainant, but the deed was never recorded; that in August, 1898, she gave this deed to the husband of one of these daughters; that he kept it, and was appointed administrator of her husband's estate, and in February, 1899, inventoried the lands in the probate court; that she paid rent in 1899 and 1900; that December 8, 1900, these heirs partitioned the land among themselves by deeds which were recorded, and that two of them incumbered their respective parts, and got her to join in the incumbrances. Lizzie Van der Aa, one of the defendants, a daughter of complainant, having been adjudged insane, her conservator filed an answer for her, denying the allegations of the bill, and calling for strict proof of the matters therein alleged. F. R. De Young, another of the defendants, answered pro se, claiming to have acted only as an attorney for the administrator, and disclaiming all interest in the property except as trustee in a certain trust deed, and insisted upon the legal defenses interposed by the main defendants. The other 10 defendants, being the daughters and sons-in-law of complainant, answered, denying the allegations of complainant's bill and asserting their ownership of the property in question as the heirs of Gerritt Van der Aa, deceased. The case was tried before the chancellor upon evidence, oral and documentary, introduced in open court, and resulted in the chancellor dismissing complainant's bill for want of equity, which action of the court below, upon appeal to this court, appellant assigns as error, and insists that the decree of the chancellor dismissing her bill was not warranted by the evidence, and should by this court be reversed, and the relief prayed for by her be granted.

On this appeal there is practically no question of law presented, the only substantial controversy being as to whether the evidence is sufficient to sustain the decree rendered. The parties to this suit all live in South Holland, in Cook county—a Dutch settlement on the outskirts of Chicago. In 1866 Gerritt Van der Aa married a Mrs. Gouwens, the present appellant, who was then a widow with two children—one, John J. Gouwens, a witness in her favor in this case; and the other a daughter, who died in 1881, leaving as her only heir Peter Peerbolte, also a witness of appellant. Six children, all daughters, were born to Mr. and Mrs. Van der Aa. The daughters, except Lizzie, insane, were at the time of this suit married, and all, with the husbands, are defendants to the bill. The children of the complainant by her first marriage, during childhood, also constituted part of the family of the complainant and her second husband. In 1897 Gerritt Van der Aa, being somewhat advanced in years, was considering some plan by which he could so arrange his affairs that after his death his estate might be settled without the interposition of any court, and the cost of administration be thus saved to his heirs. He consulted with friends (not lawyers) as to how this purpose might be accomplished, and finally one Peter De Young, a police magistrate and notary public, seems to have informed Mr. Van der Aa that he could arrange his matters as he desired, and he prepared the deed in question, and on May 31, 1897, Mr. Van der Aa, before said De Young, executed and acknowledged the same. Concerning this deed the testimony is conflicting. Appellant contends that it was properly executed, acknowledged, and delivered, and $1 given as a consideration therefor. She, being incompetent to testify as to what took place prior to the death of her husband, the maker of the deed, offered Peter Peerbolte, above mentioned, as a witness, who, it is claimed, is the only eyewitness to the delivery of the deed by Gerritt Van der Aa to complainant. This witness testified that he and Van der Aa had been to Roseland, and on their way home stopped and got the deed, which had been previously prepared, other title deeds having been taken to the scrivener previously for ascertainment of the proper data; that on the way home he saw the deed; that the word "Naatje," complainant's first or given name, was then in the body of the deed; that after arriving at home and going into the house he saw Van dér Aa deliver the deed to complainant; that he told her she would have to give him $1 as consideration, which she did. In corroboration of this testimony, John J. Gouwens, also above mentioned, testified that Van der Aa, the grantor, told him of his intentions to make the deed to complainant, and that, after the deed was made, he told witness that he had deeded his property to his wife, the complainant. Mary Gouwens, wife of the above-mentioned witness, also testified to conversations with Van der Aa similar to those testified to by her husband. On the contrary, Peter De Young, the notary who took the acknowledgment, testified that Gerritt Van der Aa consulted him about the disposition of his property, stating that he wanted to divide his property before his death so as to save the cost of administration; that the witness then told him that he could draw a deed so that it would not be any good while he (the grantor) lived, but would spring into life after he died; that he drew up the deed in question, leaving out the first or given name of the grantee, his purpose and intention being that with the deed so drawn it would not be effective until returned and the omitted name inserted, which arrangement was approved by Mr. Van der Aa, who stated he would take the deed home, and change it afterwards, when his mind was fully made up as to what he desired to do, but that he was not ready then; that he wanted to remain "boss" as long as he lived. The witness further stated that four or five days before Van der Aa died young Peerbolte came after him to go to Van der Aa's house, which witness did, and found there a family meeting of the daughters and sons-in-law; that witness told Van der Aa that he had brought along the blank deeds, supposing that Van der Aa desired him to make out deeds to the various children for the several tracts of land to be given them in accordance with the previous suggestions and conversations had between witness and Van der Aa; that Van der Aa stated to witness he wanted to divide his land among his children, and preparations were made to that end, but because of some hitch in the grantor's plans, occasioned by Peerbolte and John J. Gouwens, the matter was not consummated. Witness further stated that the next time he saw the deed in question was about two months after the death of Gerritt Van der Aa, when Peter Peerbolte brought the deed to him at his house, and stated that the "old lady" wanted the deed fixed up, and that witness then filled in the name "Naatje," which had been lacking. Witness further stated that it was the distinct intention of Gerritt Van der Aa, as expressed to him, that he was having the deed made so that, in case he did not further distribute his land before he died, it would be in such shape that after his death his wife might distribute it among his children; that it was the understanding of both the witness and Van der Aa that omitting the first name of the grantee destroyed the validity of the instrument until the same was inserted.

As to the family meeting that took place four or five days prior to the death of Gerritt Van der Aa, and the purpose of it, the daughters and sons-in-law who were present testified in corroboration of the witness Peter De Young. Catharine De Young, daughter of Peter De Young, corroborated her father as to the circumstance of the deed being returned and the filling in of the name "Naatje." The original deed was, by order of the court below, transmitted to this court for inspection. The given name "Naatje" quite clearly appears to have been written with different ink and pen from any other part of the deed, which fact tends to corroborate appellee's contention that the deed was left incomplete when made, and tends to contradict appellant's son and main witness. Peerbolte denied returning the deed for the insertion of complainant's name, having stated that it was originally placed in the deed. On the part of complainant it was also denied that the family meeting spoken of was for the purpose stated by defendants, but, on the other hand, it was for the purpose of the deceased stating to his children and their husbands the fact that he had deeded the land to his wife, and that she understood the disposition he wished her to make of it. Seven different witnesses testified that the complainant stated to them that she did not know of the deed until after the death of her husband, when she found it in a trunk; one of the witnesses being attorney F. R. De Young. It further appears from the evidence that complainant, some time after the death of Gerritt Van der Aa, gave the deed to two persons—Michael Van der Aa, a brother-in-law of Gerritt Van der Aa, and John J. Gouwens, her son by a former husband—to have recorded, but each of these parties failed (as they stated, because they did not have time) to record the same. Gerritt Pon, of the firm of Tenniga Bros. & Pon, real estate agents, testified that in the spring of 1898 complainant, and, as he thought, in company with John J. Gouwens, came to his office, and asked his advice about the deed, and that, after hearing her statement, he told her he did not think the deed was good, but directed her to apply to the Security Title & Trust Company for further information. The evidence further discloses that matters remained in an unchanged and unsettled condition until one Kirkert, who had a claim against the deceased, began to take steps to have it settled, and his attorney, F. R. De Young, one of the defendants, informed appellant that it would be necessary to have the estate administered on, and, if she did not select some one to act for that purpose, the creditor might institute such proceeding. Finally, Bastian Van Drunen, one of the sons-in-law and one of the defendants, was appointed administrator—as stated by defendants, at the request of appellant; but this she denies. After the probate of the estate was entered upon, appellant received and receipted for her award, retained homestead, and rented the land, retaining one-third of the rent as her dower, and accounting for the balance to the heirs. Certain claims having been allowed against the estate, and there being a deficiency of personal assets to meet the same, according to defendants it was arranged that a fund be raised by the daughters to meet this demand, and accordingly those who had not the money mortgaged their portions to raise the required amount. In order to carry out this plan, the partition of the land was made among the several heirs subject to the dower rights of appellant, and then those who had to borrow mortgaged the portions so set off to them, appellant joining in said incumbrances. Appellant, it is claimed, also went with her daughter Lizzie, who was single, to procure the loan necessary for her contribution.

We might go on and enumerate other circumstances disclosed by the evidence tending to show the deed in question was not legally delivered, and tending to support the decree rendered in the court below, but we think enough has already been set forth, notwithstanding the contradictory evidence of appellant, to show that unmistakably the decree is not manifestly against the weight of the evidence, and, in our judgment, the decided weight of the evidence is in its favor.

Appellant insists that Peter Peerbolte was the only eyewitness to the alleged delivery of the deed, and, as he testified to such delivery, and there being no direct evidence to the contrary on that particular point, the fact of such delivery is conclusively established. We think the conflicting statements made by this witness, as shown by the record, but which we have not taken the space to enumerate; the overwhelming evidence by which he is in many particulars contradicted; and the great weight of the evidence to the effect that the complainant admitted to various persons that she never saw the deed until after the grantor's death, when she found it in an old trunk; and her subsequent acts, which are entirely consistent with defendants' theory of the case, but which, if complainant's position be true, her alleged illiteracy can hardly explain—all taken together, are more than sufficient to overcome the statement of complainant's witness as to the delivery of the deed.

On the whole record we do not see how the chancellor could have found otherwise than he did; but, even if we were in doubt as to the correctness of the conclusions reached by the trial court as to the facts established by the evidence, according to the well-established rule of this court we would not be justified in setting aside the decree, unless, from a review of the record, we were able to say that the decree of the chancellor was clearly and palpably erroneous. This case was tried before the chancellor, and, as we have so often said, and as is patent to every one, the trial judge, in cases of this kind, has opportunities for correctly weighing the evidence and arriving at the truth far superior to our own, which fact this court is bound to take into consideration and give due weight thereto when called upon to review a decree. Dowie v. Driscoll, 203 Ill. 480, 68 N. E. 56; Duncan v. Duncan, 203 Ill. 461, 67 N. E. 763; Hardy v. Dyas, 203 Ill. 211, 67 N. E. 852; Fabrice v. Von der Brelie, 190 Ill. 460, 60 N. E. 835; Van Vleet v. De Witt, 200 Ill. 153, 65 N. E. 677; Springer v. Chicago Real Estate Loan Co., 202 Ill. 17, 66 N. E. 850; Garden City Sand Co. v. Gettins, 200 Ill. 268, 65 N. E. 664; Coari v. Olsen, 91 Ill. 273.

The certificate of acknowledgment indorsed on the deed here in question can have no weight as evidence of a delivery, since it is conceded by appellant that at the time of said acknowledgment no delivery was made.

The decree of the circuit court of Cook county is affirmed. Decree affirmed.

(185 Mass. 186)

ELDREDGE v. NORFOLK COUNTY COM'RS.

(Supreme Judicial Court of Massachusetts. Suffolk. Feb. 26, 1904.)

EMINENT DOMAIN—LAYING OUT ROADS—POWER OF COUNTY COMMISSIONERS—ROAD OVER RAILWAY LAND.

1. Under Pub. St. 1882, c. 189, § 20 (Rev. Laws, c. 195, § 18), providing that a party desiring to have a private way laid out shall file a petition with the county commissioners, and section 25, providing that, when the premises are situated entirely in one town, the petition may be made to the selectmen, where the premises are entirely within one town the petition may be made to the county commissioners or the selectmen at the option of the petitioner.

2. Under Pub. St. 1882, c. 189, §§ 19-22 (Rev. Laws, c. 195, §§ 17-20), providing for the laying out of roads on petition to the county commissioners, a road can be laid out over land of a railroad company outside of the line of its road, and within a location acquired for railroad purposes under St. 1895, p. 402, c. 356 (Rev. Laws, c. 111, §§ 92-96).

Case Reserved from Supreme Judicial Court, Suffolk County; Henry K. Braley, Judge.

Petition by one Eldredge for a writ of certiorari to quash the proceedings of the county commissioners of Norfolk in laying out a private way. Case reserved from Supreme Judicial Court, Suffolk county. Petition dismissed.

Frank T. Benner, George L. Clarke, and Walter Soren, for petitioner. Robert W. Nason, Thomas W. Proctor, and Thomas F. Hunt, for respondents.

KNOWLTON, C. J. The respondents, acting officially under Pub. St. 1882, c. 189, §§ 19-22, laid out a private way, on the application of one McNeil, to give access to his quarry. The petitioner asks for a writ of certiorari to quash their proceedings, on the ground, first, that, inasmuch as the premises are situated entirely in one town, the application should have been to the selectmen, under section 25; and, secondly, that, since the way passes for a considerable distance over land owned by the Old Colony Railroad Company, and located by the corporation under St. 1895, p. 402, c. 356, the respondents had no jurisdiction to lay it out.

Section 20 of the chapter first mentioned provides that a party desiring to make such improvements "shall file a petition with the county commissioners," etc., while section 25 says that, when the premises mentioned in section 19 are situated entirely in one town or city, "the petition may be made to the

¶ 2. See Eminent Domain, vol. 18, Cent. Dig. § 108.

selectmen or mayor and aldermen thereof," etc. The petitioner contends that in this last section the word "may" means "must." If the different parts of the statute had all been originally enacted at one time, there would be considerable ground for the petitioner's contention. But the sections from 19 to 24 of this chapter were first passed as St. 1855, p. 574, c. 104, and have subsequently appeared as Gen. St. 1860, c. 148, §§ 19-24; Pub. St. 1882, c. 189, §§ 19-24; Rev. Laws, c. 195, §§ 17-22. Under the original act, jurisdiction was given to the county commissioners alone. By St. 1857, p. 637, c. 292, permission was given to commence proceedings before the selectmen or mayor and aldermen when the premises were situated entirely in one town or city, and this provision has since appeared without material change in Gen. St. 1860, c. 148, §§ 25-28; Pub. St. 1882, c. 189, §§ 25-28; and Rev. Laws, c. 195, §§ 23-25. The terms of this additional act were plainly permissive, and not mandatory, and they leave the original act with no limitation of the powers conferred by it. The subsequent provisions were not intended to change the existing legislation, and the application in the present case might be made to the county commissioners or to the selectmen, at the option of the applicant.

The next question is whether a way can be laid out under this statute over land of a railroad company outside of the location of the line of its road, five rods in width, but within a location for railroad purposes, under St. 1895, p. 402, c. 356 (Rev. Laws, c. 111, §§ 92-96). It is a general rule that land acquired under the right of eminent domain for a public use cannot be appropriated to a different public use which is inconsistent with that to which it was first appropriated, unless the intention of the Legislature so to appropriate it is plainly expressed. Old Colony Railroad Company v. Framingham Water Company, 153 Mass. 561, 27 N. E. 662, 13 L. R. A. 332; Boston & Albany Railroad Company v. Cambridge, 166 Mass. 224, 44 N. E. 140. But where the new use is not necessarily inconsistent with the old one, authority to take for the new use may be inferred from slight indications of intention. Boston v. Brookline, 156 Mass. 172, 30 N. E. 611; Old Colony Railroad Company v. Framingham Water Company, ubi supra. In Boston v. Brookline it was held that the town of Brookline, under the general laws, might lay out a way over land taken and held by the city of Boston for the line of its aqueduct. The doctrines stated in that case and the cases there cited fully cover the case at bar.

The law has long recognized the right of the public to lay out ways across railroads. Gen. St. 1860, c. 63, § 57; Pub. St. 1892, c. 112, § 125; Rev. Laws, c. 111, § 130; Boston & Albany Railroad Company v. Boston, 140 Mass. 87, 2 N. E. 943. Under all these statutes the county commissioners have been the tribunal to determine when and how this right of the public should be exercised. The reason for permitting its exercise over lands which are located by the company outside of the line of the railroad for incidental uses, and which are subject to taxation because these uses are not so strictly public as that of the railroad itself, are stronger than the reasons for permitting ways across railroads.

This statute authorizing such improvements has stood without limitation for nearly 50 years. It contains ample provisions for compensation for those whose property is damaged by proceedings under it. We are of opinion that it gives authority to lay out a way over land located for railroad purposes outside of the location of the railroad itself.

Petition dismissed.

(185 Mass. 183)

KEEFE v. LEXINGTON & B. ST. RY. CO.

(Supreme Judicial Court of Massachusetts. Middlesex. Feb. 26, 1904.)

STREET RAILWAYS—LIMITATION OF FARE—VALIDITY—AUTHORITY OF SELECTMEN.

1. Under Pub. St. 1882, c. 113, § 43 (Rev. Laws, c. 112, § 69), providing that a street railway company may establish the rates of fare, subject to its charter and the statutes, and in view of the course of legislation (Pub. St. 1882, c. 113, §§ 44, 45; St. 1898, pp. 747, 748, c. 578, §§ 23, 26; St. 1901, p. 113, c. 180) relating to limitations and revision of rates of fare, St. 1898, p. 743, c. 578, § 13, providing that the selectmen of a town, in granting a location to a street railway company, may impose such conditions as the public interest may require, does not authorize them to impose a limitation on the rates of fare the company may charge.

2. The acceptance by a street railway company of a location granted by a town does not make valid conditions in the grant as to fares, which the town could not legally impose, nor does it make a contract as to fares between the company and the town.

Appeal from Superior Court, Middlesex County.

Action by one Keefe against the Lexington & Boston Street Railway Company. From a judgment in favor of defendant, plaintiff appeals. Affirmed.

Alexander Wilson, for appellant. Coolidge & Hight, for appellee.

KNOWLTON, C. J. The plaintiff seeks to recover five cents, paid under protest for his fare, demanded by the conductor on one of the defendant's cars. The defendant corporation was organized under the laws of this commonwealth, after St. 1898, p. 737, c. 578, went into effect. The selectmen of the town of Concord and the selectmen of the town of Bedford, in granting the defendant a location in their respective towns, prescribed conditions as to the fares that might be charged for the transportation of passengers within the limits of the town. The plaintiff contends that the fare charged and collected in his case was in violation of these conditions. The first and most important question before us is whether such a condition could be imposed legally by a board of selectmen in granting a location. Under St. 1898, p. 743, c. 578, § 13, the board of aldermen of a city or the selectmen of a town in granting a location to a street railway company may prescribe the manner in which the "tracks shall be laid, and the kind of rails, poles, wires and other appliances which shall be used, and they may also impose such other terms, conditions and obligations in addition to those applying to all street railways under the general provisions of law, as the public interest may, in their judgment, require." The question is whether a condition may be imposed regulating and restricting the fares to be charged. The statute contains other provisions in regard to fares. By Pub. St. 1882, c. 113, § 43, which was in force when the defendant corporation was organized (Rev. Laws, c. 112, § 69), the directors of a street railway company "may establish the rates of fare on all passengers and property conveyed or transported in its cars, subject, however, to the limitations named in its charter, or hereinafter set forth." Section 44 provided for a revision and regulation of the fares by the railroad commissioners, and section 45 provided that nothing contained in the two preceding sections should authorize the company or the board to raise the rate of fare above the rate established by agreement, made as a condition of location or otherwise, between the company or its directors and the mayor and aldermen of a city or the selectmen of a town, except by a mutual arrangement with the parties. This section recognizes the validity of such agreements under the former statute. But this and the next preceding section were repealed by St. 1898, p. 748, c. 578, § 26, leaving the section as to the authority of the directors to stand with no limitations upon their right. A new section in regard to the revision of the fares by the railroad commissioners was enacted, which is St. 1898, p. 747, c. 578, § 23. Under this last section "the fares shall not, without the consent of the company, be reduced below the average rate of fare charged for similar service by other street railway companies, which, in the judgment of the board of railroad commissioners, are operated under substantially similar conditions." This statute gives to the directors primarily the right to fix and regulate fares. It then makes their action subject to revision by the railroad commissioners, who are to act, according to the terms of the section, upon broad considerations of public policy. The conditions which may be imposed in granting a location are of a different character, and do not include those for which special provision is made in other parts of the statute. See Newcomb v. Norfolk Western Street Railway Company, 179 Mass. 449, 61 N. E. 42. With street railways extending long distances and passing through numerous cities and towns, it would be unwise and inexpedient to permit each town to fix the fares within its boundaries as a condition of granting a location. The purpose of the Legislature to prescribe broad and general provisions for the regulation of fares is further emphasized by St. 1901, p. 113, c. 180 (Rev. Laws, c. 112, § 73), which puts street railways upon precisely the same ground as railroads as to provisions relative to changes and regulations of their fares.

The acceptance by the defendant of the locations granted by these towns did not make valid these conditions as to fares which the towns could not legally impose, nor did it make a contract as to fares between the corporation and the selectmen or the town. The defendant might, therefore, at least prescribe for its passengers the payment of any fare which was reasonable. It is not contended that the fare collected of the plaintiff was more than was reasonable, or more than the company was accustomed to collect from other passengers who were traveling as he was. Indeed, it is contended by the defendant that it has complied with the terms prescribed by these towns, according to a proper understanding of them, certainly according to its own understanding of them, and that the charge complained of by the plaintiff was for a through passenger, to whom these conditions were not intended to apply. We need not consider this contention particularly, as we deem it unimportant. The plaintiff, in his brief, does not contend that he is entitled to recover, except upon the ground that the conditions imposed as to fares were binding upon the defendant.

Judgment affirmed.

(185 Mass. 91)

CRONAN v. CITY OF WOBURN.

(Supreme Judicial Court of Massachusetts. Middlesex. Feb. 26, 1904.)

DEFECTIVE HIGHWAY—NOTICE OF INJURY—DECLARATION—AMENDMENT—DEMURRER.

1. A notice served on the city of W. stated that C. received injuries by reason of the neglect and carelessness of the city and of employés of it, who neglected to guard an excavation which the city and its employés had made at the corner of E. and M. streets; that C. on a certain day, while crossing M. street, on account of said neglect of the city and its servants, fell into an unguarded excavation on a certain corner of said streets, on the edge of the sidewalk of M. street; that, by reason of said carelessness in leaving said excavation unguarded, C. was injured. *Held*, that while open to the criticism that in part it refers to the carelessness of certain employés of the city, who neglected to guard the excavation, as a separate ground of liability, yet, taken together, its fair construction is that plaintiff was injured by reason of a defect in a way, negligently caused by an excavation which the city and its employés had made.

2. There being no surprise at the trial, and the merits of the case having been tried, allowance of an amendment of the declaration will be treated as made before verdict, when permission to amend was given, though the amendment was in fact made and allowed after verdict.

3. A declaration for injury from a defect in a street need not aver the city was obliged to keep

the street in repair, this being a statutory obligation of which the court will take judicial notice.

4. The averment in the declaration that owing to the neglect and carelessness of defendant city, or its employés, plaintiff fell into an unlighted and unguarded excavation which defendant or its employés had made in the street, if deemed ambiguous, as stating an alternative liability, should be demurred to; such defect is not available, at the trial on the merits, under a general denial.

Exceptions from Superior Court, Middlesex County; Robt. R. Bishop, Judge.

Action by Daniel Cronan against the city of Woburn. Verdict for plaintiff. Defendant excepted. Exceptions overruled.

The declaration filed in the case is as follows:

"And the plaintiff says on Tuesday, the 8th day of October, 1901, at or about 7:30 o'clock in the evening, while in the exercise of due care, he attempted to cross Main street, a public street in the city of Woburn, when, owing to the neglect and carelessness of the city of Woburn or its employés he fell into an unlighted and unguarded excavation which the defendant or its employés had made on the southeast corner of said Main street and Eaton avenue, a public street, on the westerly side of the sidewalk on Main street, at or near the corner of said streets, which the defendants had carelessly left unlighted, unfenced, and unguarded; that the plaintiff knew nothing of said excavation, and, while attempting to cross said street at said point, fell into said excavation, and thereby received great and severe bodily and mental injuries, which said injuries are permanent. And he further says that on account of said fall he has suffered great and severe pain and mental anguish, and has suffered great loss in not being able to attend to his customary work, and has been put to great expense for necessary nurses, medical care and attendants, and medicine. He further says that on the 26th day of October, he caused a written notice to be served upon John H. Finn, city clerk of the city of Woburn, stating the time, place, and cause of said injuries, and that he should look to the city for compensation for the damages he had thereby sustained."

A notice was served on J. H. Finn, city clerk of the city of Woburn, which read as follows: "Boston, Oct. 29, 1901. John H. Finn, City Clerk of the City of Woburn. I, Thomas Weston, for and in behalf of Daniel Cronan of Woburn, in the County of Middlesex and Commonwealth of Massachusetts, hereby give you notice that the said Daniel Cronan received serious injuries by reason of the neglect and carelessness of the city of Woburn and by certain persons to me unknown, employed by the city of Woburn who neglected to guard by fence, lights or otherwise, an excavation which the said city and its employés had made at the corner of Eaton Avenue and Main Street, in that part of Woburn known as Central Square. The said Daniel Cronan, on Tuesday, the 8th day of October, 1901, at or about half past seven in the evening while crossing Main Street, on account of the said neglect of the city of Woburn and its servants, fell into an unguarded excavation which was situated on the southeast corner of said Main Street and Eaton Avenue, on the westerly edge of the sidewalk on said Main Street at or near said corner; that, by reason of said carelessness in leaving said excavation unfenced, unlighted, and unguarded, said Daniel Cronan was greatly injured, and he hereby gives you notice that he will claim damages for the said injuries he has sustained. Thomas Weston, for and in behalf of Daniel Cronan."

Weston & Weston, for plaintiff. Francis P. Curran, for defendant.

BRALEY, J. This was an action of tort for injuries received by reason of a defect in a public highway within the municipal limits of the city of Woburn, and which it was required to keep in suitable repair for the use of travelers. A verdict having been returned for the plaintiff, the case is here on exceptions by the defendant.

We treat all exceptions not argued as waived; and it is now contended that the notice given, and the declaration itself, are not sufficient in law to sustain the verdict. While the notice given to the defendant may be open to a refined criticism that in part it refers to the carelessness of certain persons employed by the city, and who neglected to properly guard the excavation in the street into which the plaintiff fell, as a possible separate ground of liability, yet, taken together, the fair construction is that the plaintiff was injured by reason of a defect in a way negligently caused by an excavation "which the said city and its employés had made at the corner of Eaton Avenue and Main Street, in that part of Woburn known as Central Square." It is not suggested that the defendant was misled by the notice, as it was fully informed of the cause of action, and the case was tried solely upon the issue of such a defect, and submitted to the jury under appropriate instructions. When this question was raised at the trial, at the close of all the evidence the plaintiff was given leave to amend his declaration at any time before final judgment, in order to support the action for the cause for which it was intended to be brought. And after verdict, and before judgment, under the exception of the defendant, an amendment was accordingly made and allowed. The evidence shows that the cause of action relied on was the defect in the way, caused by the negligence of the defendant, and the defendant now makes no claim that the alleged defect in pleading was not cured by the amendment.

As there was no surprise at the trial, and the merits of the case were fully tried upon the understanding that the city was to be held liable only if the way proved to be defective by reason of its negligence, the allowance of the amendment for the purposes of justice may be treated, in legal effect, as if made before verdict, and at the time when permission to amend was given. If, originally, the exception that there was a variance between the allegations and the evidence offered to sustain them was well taken, it became worthless after the amendment was allowed. It no longer stated a legal defense, but raised only an academic question. Rev. Laws, c. 173, § 48; Keller v. Webb, 126 Mass. 393, 394; Whitney v. Houghton, 127 Mass. 527–529; Denham et al. v. Bryant, 139 Mass. 110–112, 28 N. E. 691; United States Nat'l Bank v. Venner, 172 Mass. 449–451, 52 N. E. 543; King v. Howes, 181 Mass. 445, 446, 63 N. E. 1062. But the original declaration set out a good cause of action against the defendant for a defect in the way caused by its negligence.

It was not necessary to aver that the city was obliged to keep the street in repair, as this is a statutory obligation, of which the court is bound to take judicial notice. Pub. St. 1882, c. 52, §§ 1, 18; Read v. Chelmsford, 16 Pick. 128, 130.

If the phrase "the defendant or its employés" was deemed ambiguous as stating a possible alternative liability, such a defect is to be pointed out by demurrer. It is not legally available at a trial on the merits, for the purpose of defense, by a defendant whose answer is a general denial.

Exceptions overruled.

(185 Mass. 205)

BRADFORD v. METCALF.

SAME v. STONE.

(Supreme Judicial Court of Massachusetts. Suffolk. Feb. 27, 1904.)

TIDE-WATER FLATS — RIGHT TO FILL — PAYMENT FOR DISPLACEMENT OF TIDE WATERS.

1. Acts 1852, p. 72, c. 105, and Acts 1855, p. 917, c. 481, gave to a corporation the right to fill certain tide-water flats, and by various statutes extension of time was allowed the corporation for completing its work. After defendants had had possession for 40 years of part of the flats, in accordance with an agreement and votes of the corporation, and as against the corporation had a title by disseisin, as well as a strong equitable right, to the upland, to which the rights to such part of the flats were appurtenant, and, though they had not, perhaps, a title to these rights which was technically perfect, such rights had long been treated as existing in connection with their ownership of the upland, it was provided by St. 1893, p. 972, c. 334, § 1, that the time theretofore allowed by the laws for the completion of the improvements by the proprietors of such lands and flats was, with the rights and subject to the requirements of such laws, extended for 10 years. *Held*, that the statute of 1893 was an extension of the right to fill defendants' flats without paying for the displacement of tide water, in accordance with the rights granted the corporation; so that they were outside Pub. St. 1882, c. 19, § 14, which would otherwise require them to pay for such displacement.

Appeal from Superior Court, Suffolk County.

Two actions on agreed facts, both by Edward S. Bradford, treasurer of the commonwealth of Massachusetts, one against Albert Metcalf, the other against Joseph Stone, to recover compensation for tide-water displacements. From judgments for defendants, plaintiff appeals. Affirmed.

Frederick H. Nash, for appellant. Charles F. Jenney and Sumner Robinson, for appellees.

KNOWLTON, C. J. These two cases present the same questions, and they may be considered together. Each of the defendants filled certain flats in the harbor, near the channel of Mystic river, under a license from the harbor and land commissioners, issued in accordance with the provisions of Pub. St. 1882, c. 19, §§ 12, 13. The treasurer of the commonwealth brought these suits to recover the money due for the displacement of tide water caused by the filling, and the agreed facts show that he is entitled to recover, unless the defendants had a right to fill the flats without payment, under certain special statutes which relate to the improvements to be made in the harbor by the Mystic River Corporation. The licenses were granted without prejudice to the rights of either of the parties.

The first of these statutes was the act of 1852, p. 72, c. 105, which incorporated the Mystic River Corporation, whose members were to be the city of Charlestown, and such other proprietors of land and flats situated in Charlestown, bounding on the southerly side of Mystic river between Johnson's Wharf and Chelsea Bridge, as should vote to accept the act at a meeting called for that purpose. Among these corporators were the predecessors in title of the defendants. The statute gave the corporation the right to fill flats and make improvements within certain specified lines, upon the condition that the regulation and control of certain other designated flats belonging to individuals and corporations should be surrendered to the commonwealth before any construction authorized by the act should be commenced. This act was duly accepted, and a code of by-laws was adopted, and officers were chosen in accordance with its provisions. A by-law provided that the value of the grant should be "estimated and fixed by the directors, and the amount thereof distributed among the grantees, according to their several interests in the same." By St. 1855, p. 917, c. 481, this statute was repealed, except that part of it which incorporated the company, and a new grant was made which gave authority to fill the same flats and others, with additional rights and upon additional and changed conditions. The act was not to take effect unless accepted by the corporation within 90 days, but it was duly accepted.

Previously to the year 1852 there had been

attempts to obtain legislation, which had not resulted satisfactorily, and, in anticipation of the application for the grant contained in St. 1852, p. 72, c. 105, parties interested, owners and representatives of estates bordering on Mystic river, entered into an agreement, under seal, whereby they undertook to bind themselves in regard to the distribution and use of the benefits to be obtained by the act of incorporation, giving to the owners of a certain part of the shore the benefits of the grant opposite their respective estates, to be divided among them in proportion to their ownership of the shore. A similar arrangement was made in regard to the owners of estates on another part of the shore. The benefits upon another part were to be the property of all the owners who were parties to the contract to be divided among them in proportion to the length of their respective estates upon the line of the river bank between Malden Bridge and Chelsea Bridge. It was also agreed that they should all waive all claims for damages, and that the required excavations opposite estates whose owners were to hold in severalty were to be made by the respective owners, and all others by the whole company.

It is plain that this contract did not bind the corporation afterwards created. It could not affect in any way the legal rights of the corporation or of its members in their action, as corporators in the exercise of rights given them by the statute. The corporation could not even ratify the agreement in terms, for at the time of the agreement there was no corporation in existence for which any one could assume to make such a contract. Abbott v. Hapgood, 150 Mass. 248, 22 N. E. 907, 5 L. R. A. 586, 15 Am. St. Rep. 193; In re Northumberland Avenue Hotel Company, 33 Ch. D. 16; Howard v. Patent Irony, 38 Ch. D. 156; In re Empress Engineering Company, 16 Ch. D. 125; Melhado v. Porto Alegre Railway Company, L. R. 9 C. P. 503. But, as to matters within the powers of the corporation under its charter, it could enter into a new contract of a similar character. After the passage of St. 1855, p. 917, c. 481, the directors employed an engineer to designate the lines of the corporate property, and appointed a committee to ascertain the interest of the different members of the corporation in it. The report of the committee showed that the preliminary agreement between the associates had been examined, estimates by an engineer had been made, and a valuation put upon the flats, and they had been divided among the different classes of owners according to the agreement. The report was adopted, and all shore owners received certificates of stock in accordance with the original plan. "It thereby appears that the middle shore owners [among whom were the defendants' predecessors in title], by reason of the terms of the agreement of January 16, 1852, having received the grant opposite their estates in severalty, received a less interest in the corporate property on account thereof. * * * From 1852 to the present time the middle and upper shore owners from time to time have filled, some to the outer line, and some to a less extent, each his own flats, acting by virtue of said acts, and have held possession of said flats in accordance with the agreement of January, 1852, and said votes of said corporation."

The time allowed to the corporation to complete their improvements was extended from time to time by the Legislature, until everything was done that pertained to that portion of the property which was not connected with the estates set off to individual stockholders in severalty. See St. 1859, p. 230, c. 19; St. 1867, p. 580, c. 150; St. 1878, p. 11, c. 5; St. 1887, p. 908, c. 278; St. 1889, p. 800, c. 25; St. 1891, p. 810, c. 240. By St. 1887, p. 908, c. 278, the Mystic River Corporation was authorized to transfer its property, rights, privileges, and franchises to the Boston & Lowell Railroad Company, subject to all the conditions, limitations, and obligations which then pertained to the ownership of the Mystic River Corporation, and the property has since been held by the Boston & Lowell Railroad Company and the Boston & Maine Railroad.

The effect of the attempt of the corporation to give the benefits of its grant on a part of the shore to individual members of the corporation, to be held in severalty, if considered by itself alone, is very questionable. It would seem as if the directors treated the preliminary agreement as binding upon the corporation and its officers and members. Action in intended execution of the agreement as a contract binding on the corporation would be of no effect. No conveyances were made from the corporation to anybody at that time, and the only title of these defendants and others owning the shore near their lands rests upon the action of the corporation in accepting the report of the committee and treating them as owners in severalty of their land and of a part of the benefits granted by the charter. Probably it was in the power of the corporation to sell and convey parts of its property, with the appurtenant rights, subject to the conditions imposed by its charter; although it hardly could relieve itself of the effect of these conditions, and its obligations, upon its title to the remainder of the property. Its right to make such sales was recognized by St. 1884, p. 151, c. 183. The defendants and their predecessors in title having been in possession of this property, claiming it and its appurtenant rights and privileges, from 1855 to 1893, the Legislature, by St. 1893, p. 972, c. 334, § 1, made this provision: "The time heretofore allowed for the completion of the improvements by the proprietors of the lands, wharves and flats laying between Johnson's Wharf and Elm street on Mystic river, by the laws of this commonwealth, is, with the rights and subject to the requirements of such laws, extended ten years from the passage hereof."

This is an express recognition of the rights of these defendants and others, acquired by virtue of St. 1852, p. 72, c. 105, and St. 1855, p. 917, c. 481, and the action of the corporation and the shore owners under them. It may be assumed in favor of the plaintiff that if these defendants had no rights whatever, legal or equitable, in the privileges granted by these acts, this later statute did not create such rights. Salters v. Tobias, 3 Paige, 338; Van Norman v. Jackson, Circuit Judge, 45 Mich. 204, 7 N. W. 796; Bingham v. Winona Company, 8 Minn. 441 (Gil. 390). As against the commonwealth, after the passage of St. 1867, p. 676, c. 275 (Rev. Laws, c. 202, § 30), a title by disseisin could not be acquired in property below high-water mark. See Nichols v. Boston, 98 Mass. 39, 93 Am. Dec. 132. But these rights had been granted by the commonwealth to the Mystic River Corporation, had been attached to the lands, and had been held by the defendants and their predecessors as their own property, under a claim of right for more than 40 years, without interference by the corporation. As against this corporation, property rights could be acquired by disseisin and adverse possession. Under these circumstances the Legislature might well treat the grant as in force against the commonwealth, and treat the defendants as the rightful owners of the benefits, as against the Mystic River Corporation. We are of opinion that St. 1893, p. 972, c. 334, was an extension of the right to fill the defendants' lands without paying for the displacement of tide water, which was originally granted to the Mystic River Corporation, and that this extension, granted in terms to the defendants and others who were in possession, inured to their benefit in such a way as to leave them outside of Pub. St. 1882, c. 19, § 14. Even though they had not a title to these rights which was technically perfect, the rights had long been treated as existing in connection with their ownership of their land, and, as against the corporation, they had a title by disseisin to the upland to which the rights were appurtenant. There were also strong equitable considerations in support of their claim of ownership. At least this last act of the Legislature should be treated as a release and a grant to them, by implication, of all rights which the commonwealth might assert as to their filling these flats under authority of the earlier statutes, and subject to the requirements of those statutes.

Judgments affirmed.

(185 Mass. 222)

GERRISH v. HAYES.

(Supreme Judicial Court of Massachusetts. Suffolk. Feb. 27, 1904.)

APPEAL—SUFFICIENCY OF DECLARATION—EXCEPTION IN TRIAL COURT.

1. Where the defendant excepted to a ruling as to the declaration, but asked for no ruling on the declaration as amended, and, in his opening to the jury, stated that a question of fact was his only defense, he cannot maintain in the appellate court that the declaration as amended sets forth no cause of action.

Exceptions from Superior Court, Suffolk County; Edward J. Pierce, Judge.

Action by John H. Gerrish against Michael C. Hayes. Judgment for plaintiff, and defendant excepts. Exceptions overruled.

W. F. Prime and W. C. Cogswell, for plaintiff. Michael C. Hayes, in pro. per.

LATHROP, J. While the defendant excepted to the refusal of the judge to rule that the declaration did not set forth any cause of action, he asked for no ruling on the declaration as amended, and, in his opening to the jury, stated that a question of fact was his only defense. On this question the jury found in favor of the plaintiff. In his brief the defendant contends that the declaration, as amended, sets forth no cause of action. We are of opinion that this defense is not open to him.

The exceptions are frivolous, and are overruled, with double costs. So ordered.

(185 Mass. 227)

COLBERT v. MOORE et al.

(Supreme Judicial Court of Massachusetts. Middlesex. Feb. 27, 1904.)

NOTE—BONA FIDE HOLDER—EVIDENCE—DECREE IN EQUITY—APPEAL—REVIEW.

1. While the decree of a judge in equity on questions of fact will be reviewed on appeal, his decision will not be reversed unless it is plainly wrong.

2. Evidence *held* to show that the signatures on a note and mortgage were not forged.

Appeal from Superior Court, Middlesex County.

Bill in equity by John D. Colbert against Michael J. Moore and others. From a judgment in favor of defendants Grace E. Stults and another, complainant appeals. Affirmed.

Francis A. Campbell, for appellant. James R. Murphy, for appellees.

LATHROP, J. This is a bill in equity against Michael J. Moore, Grace E. Stults, and Mabel M. Stults, to have a mortgage deed and note, purporting to be signed by the plaintiff, declared null and void, on the ground that the signatures thereto were forgeries. The justice of the superior court who heard the case entered a decree which ordered the bill to be taken for confessed against Moore, who did not appear, and recited that the mortgage and note were executed and given by the petitioner to Michael J. Moore without fraud or deceit on the part of Moore, and that the other defendants were bona fide holders of the mortgage, and ordered that the bill be dismissed, as against them, with a single bill of costs. The bill comes before us on the plaintiff's appeal, with a full report of the evidence taken in open court at the hearing.

The appeal brings before the court questions of fact as well as questions of law, and it is the duty of the court to examine the evidence, and to decide the case according to its judgment; giving due weight to the finding of the justice. Goodell v. Goodell, 173 Mass. 140, 146, 53 N. E. 275. It is, however, true that, upon an appeal from a decree of a judge in equity upon questions of fact arising on oral testimony heard before him, his decision will not be reversed unless it is plainly wrong. Dickinson v. Todd, 172 Mass. 183, 51 N. E. 976, and cases cited. In the case before us there was evidence on which the judge properly could find for the defendants other than Moore. They were the assignees of the mortgage, and there can be no doubt, on the evidence, that they were bona fide holders of the mortgage and note, for a valuable consideration.

The only question upon which any doubt can be raised is whether the signatures of the plaintiff to the mortgage and note were forged. On his direct examination, the plaintiff testified that each signature was forged. On cross-examination he admitted with reluctance that his signature to the mortgage was genuine, and the only reason he gave for disputing the genuineness of the signature to the note was that it was blurred. This seems to us a very insufficient reason. The evidence showed that at the time the mortgage was given he was the debtor of Moore, and he refused to produce his books of accounts and papers, although it appeared that he kept his accounts in a methodical manner. The mortgage and note were produced at the trial in the superior court, and at the argument before us. It seemed to us that there was no difference in the two signatures.

On the whole case, we are of opinion that the decree should be affirmed. So ordered.

(185 Mass. 165)

CUSHMAN v. ARNOLD et al.

(Supreme Judicial Court of Massachusetts. Suffolk. Feb. 27, 1904.)

WILLS—CONSTRUCTION—VESTING OF REMAINDER.

1. A will, after making a number of specific legacies, provided that, if any residue remained after paying the legacies, it should be converted into money, and divided among said legatees in proportion to their legacies. The codicil gave to one of said legatees the use of a house for life on condition of her occupying it, and provided that "at her decease, * * * said house * * * shall fall into the rest and residue of my estate and be disposed of as is by said will provided for the disposal of said rest and residue." *Held*, that the remainder, after the life estate in the house, vested at testator's death, so that the life tenant was one of the remaindermen.

Case Reserved from Supreme Judicial Court, Suffolk County; John W. Hammond, Judge.

Bill by Cushman, administrator, against Arnold and others, for instructions. The case was reserved for the full court. Decree directed.

Alphonso A. Wyman, for John F. Aldrich. Danl. L. Smith, for A. A. Haskell. Frank Gaylord Cook, for Helen M. Albee. G. Philip Wardner, for Edwd. Devlin.

BRALEY, J. The testatrix, Mary J. Aldrich, died May 13, 1891, leaving a will and codicil, which were duly admitted to probate. Apparently Sarah Aldrich, mother of the testatrix, to whom all the rest and residue of the estate was given, did not survive her, and the property was divided among a large number of legatees, who are specifically named, and for whom the further provisions were made that, if any residue remained after paying all the pecuniary legacies in full, it should be converted into money, and divided among "said legatees in proportion to the amount of their several legacies hereinbefore named." The estate so left was of sufficient value not only to pay all these legacies in full, but to leave a large amount for distribution under the residuary clause of the will. Cushman v. Albee, 183 Mass. 108 66 N. E. 590. All the estate has been distributed except the house and land in Newbury street, which was given by the codicil to Sarah Ferris for life. She is now dead. And the question raised is whether the proceeds to be derived from a conversion of this property into money in accordance with the provisions of the will and codicil is to be distributed and apportioned as of the date of the death of the testatrix or that of the life tenant.

The will and codicil are to be construed together, and form one instrument for the purpose of ascertaining her intention as to the disposition of her estate. Lyman v. Coolidge, 176 Mass. 7, 9, 56 N. E. 831; Bassett v. Nickerson, 184 Mass. 169, 68 N. E. 25. Except so far as she gave to Sarah Ferris, who by a subsequent marriage became Sarah Ferris Devlin, the use for life of the family residence under certain conditions, the provisions of the will were not affected or modified by the codicil. Nothing is shown in the case to take it out of the ordinary rule that a remainder after a life estate must be held to have vested at the death of the testatrix, unless from the terms of the will it was clearly her intention that it should not vest, except upon the happening of the event, on which final distribution is to be made. Peck v. Carlton, 154 Mass. 231, 233, 28 N. E. 166; Marsh v. Hoyt, 161 Mass. 459, 461, 37 N. E. 454; Cook v. Hayward, 172 Mass. 195, 196, 51 N. E. 1075. Not only was a life estate given to her, but the life tenant was also made one of the legatees in the will, and is within the class among whom the residue of the entire estate is to be divided. This clause of the will is, in legal effect, the same as if each legatee had been again named, and his or her proportionate share of the residue stated. Shaw v. Eckley, 169 Mass. 119, 121, 47

N. E. 609. In other words, she was given a fractional interest in a remainder, which was subject to the life estate given her by the codicil. But, if this part of the estate was not to be divided until her death, while the life estate would not be affected, she could not be personally benefited by such distribution; but the conditions upon which the life estate was to be enjoyed were that she should reside in the house, keep it in good repair, pay all taxes assessed thereon, and make it her permanent home. If it was abandoned by her as a permanent home, then, as well as at her decease, final distribution was to be made of this part of the estate. Mrs. Devlin might have chosen not to occupy the house, the life interest in which is stated to be given to her in addition to the provision made for her benefit in the will; or after occupancy she might choose to make her home elsewhere. In either event, distribution would immediately follow. There is nothing inconsistent or repugnant in the gift of a life estate with a remainder to a life tenant, even though such remainder can never come into the possession of the remainderman. Chesman v. Cummings, 142 Mass. 65, 70, 7 N. E. 13; Rotch v. Rotch, 173 Mass. 125, 130, 53 N. E. 268. And this fact is not enough to change the time when the remainder must be held to have become vested. No words of contingency are used, as if she had said the distribution should be among the legatees then surviving, or such as shall be alive at the death of the life tenant; and no intention appears in her scheme for the distribution of her estate as a whole to make other than a present bequest to the legatees named. Neither does the language used create two classes of legatees—those who are to take at her death, and those who, if they survive, would take at the death of the life tenant. Blanchard v. Blanchard, 1 Allen, 223. The codicil provides "and at her decease * * * said house * * * shall fall into the rest and residue of my estate, and be disposed of as is by said will provided for the disposal of said rest and residue." The words "at her decease" are not susceptible of any stronger meaning than if she had said that this part of her estate should then become the property of the legatees for the purpose of possession and enjoyment, and to which they already had the legal title. These words do not state a contingency on which their interest was to vest, but merely designate the time when the class called "said legatees" would be entitled to possession of the respective portion of each in the proceeds of the sale. The death of Sarah Ferris Devlin was the time fixed when this part of the estate of the testatrix was to be converted into money and distributed to those whose right to receive any portion of it had already vested at the date of the death of the testatrix. White v. Curtis, 12 Gray, 54; Abbott v. Bradstreet, 3 Allen, 587; Gibbens v. Gibbens, 140 Mass. 102, 3 N. E. 1, 54 Am. Rep. 453; Loring v. Carnes, 148 Mass. 223, 19 N. E. 343; Pollock v. Farnham, 156 Mass. 388, 31 N. E. 298; Harding v. Harding, 174 Mass. 268, 54 N. E. 549. When the petitioner has converted this house into money according to the terms of the will of Mary J. Aldrich, the net proceeds are to be distributed among the legatees named therein as of the date of her death, and in the proportion that the specific pecuniary legacy given to each bears to the whole sum of the residue to be divided; the heir or legatee of any deceased legatee named in the will to take his or her portion, and Edward Devlin, trustee under the will of Sarah Ferris Devlin, is to receive the share given to her.

Decree accordingly.

(185 Mass. 196)

STEARNS et al. v. BEMIS et al.

(Supreme Judicial Court of Massachusetts. Suffolk. Feb. 26, 1904.)

WILLS—WIDOW'S ELECTION—CONDITIONAL CHARACTER.

1. Under Rev. Laws, c. 135, § 16, providing that the surviving husband, except in certain cases, or the widow of the deceased, within a year after probate of a will, may file in the registry of probate a writing, waiving any provisions that may have been made for him or for her, or claiming the portion of the estate he or she would have taken if deceased had died intestate, whereupon he or she shall take such portion of the deceased's property, a widow's election, conditioned on the construction and legal effect to be given to the will, is insufficient.

Case Reserved from Supreme Judicial Court, Suffolk County; James M. Morton, Judge.

Action by Stearns and others, executors and trustees under the will of John H. Bemis, against Leslie Lepington Bemis and others. Case reserved for the Supreme Court. Decree rendered.

Boyd B. Jones and Frederick P. Cabot, for Leslie L. Bemis, widow. William H. White, for Leonora Bemis and George Fisher Bemis.

KNOWLTON, C. J. This is a bill brought by executors and trustees under the will of John W. Bemis, late of Boston, deceased, for instructions as to their duties. The testator left a large estate, most of which he gave to trustees for the benefit of his widow and minor children, with remainder over to other relatives in case his children should die leaving no issue surviving them. The widow, within one year after the probate of the will, filed in the probate court a writing signed by her, in which she recited the death of the testator and the provisions of the will in her favor and in favor of her children, and then proceeded as follows: "Therefore the said Leslie Lepington Bemis, as stated in this writing, as a whole waives and declines to accept the provisions made in the said will for her, and claims such portion of the estate of the deceased as she would have taken if the deceased had died intestate; that is, she claims such portion to the extent of ten thousand dollars absolutely, and, in addition thereto, the income during her life of the excess of her share of such estate above ten thousand dollars, if, under the terms of said will, and by reason of its provisions and operation, and by reason of the laws of the commonwealth, upon this waiver, declination, and claim, her said two children forthwith become entitled to the net income of the remaining fund left in trust by the will, even though said Leslie is still living and unmarried. The said Leslie does not waive and decline the provisions made in said will for her, and does not claim such portion of the estate of the deceased as she would have taken had deceased died intestate, as hereinbefore set forth, but expressly accepts the provisions made in said will for her if said will by its terms, or by reason of its provisions and operation, and by reason of the laws of the commonwealth, does not entitle her two said children or their guardian to the net income of said trust fund forthwith, though the said Leslie is living and unmarried, she, the said Leslie, having made this waiver, declination, and claim; or, if said will by its terms, or by reason of its provisions and operation and by reason of the laws of the commonwealth, postpones payment of such income to said children or their guardian until the death or remarriage of said Leslie, she, the said Leslie, having made this waiver, declination and claim." The plaintiffs are in doubt, and ask the instructions of the court whether the construction of the will should be such as to give this writing effect as a waiver by the widow of the provisions for her benefit. The counsel for the widow in their brief say: "Furthermore, the question presented to the widow under the statutes and by the will, in view of the decisions of this court by divided opinions hereinafter discussed, was not free from difficulty. A widow should not necessarily be compelled to make an election absolute in form, at her peril, upon a question concerning which the members of this court may differ." Rev. Laws, c. 135, § 16, is in part as follows: "The surviving husband, except as provided in section thirty-six of chapter one hundred fifty-three, or the widow of a deceased person, at any time within one year after the probate of the will of such deceased, may file in the registry of probate a writing signed by him or by her, waiving any provisions that may have been made in it for him or for her, or claiming such portion of the estate of the deceased as he or she would have taken if the deceased had died intestate; and he or she shall thereupon take such portion of the property of the deceased, real and personal, that he or she would have taken if the deceased had died intestate," etc. Then follow certain exceptions, which are not now material.

We meet at the outset the question whether such a waiver, to take effect, must be absolute, or whether it may be contingent upon the decision that may afterwards be made of a doubtful question of law. We deem it pretty plain that a person contemplating such a waiver must determine for himself, in view of the facts as they are and the law as it is, whether he will waive the provisions of the will or not, and make a statement in writing accordingly; otherwise great uncertainty might be introduced into the settlement of estates of deceased persons. Parties interested as heirs or devisees or legatees would be troubled with doubts created by the surviving husband or widow in regard to their legal rights in reference to a condition whose existence was due to the filing of the writing. Embarrassments would arise, as in the present case, such that executors or trustees would not know how to perform their official duties without a decision and instructions from the court. It might happen that, if executors or trustees did not find it necessary to bring a suit to determine the legal questions raised by the filing of the paper, other persons interested in the estate might be left for years without knowledge whether the writing filed was or was not a waiver of the provisions of the will, for there might be cases where the questions raised would concern the interests in remainder of those who would not, for a long time, be in a position to bring a suit to determine their rights. The surviving husband or widow is in as good a position to know the legal effect of a waiver as any one. If the law is plain in regard to the questions raised by a waiver, he ought to determine whether to file an effectual waiver. If the law is doubtful, he ought to resolve the doubt as well as possible for himself, and not to create a condition which gives rise to uncertainty, and then decline to act definitely until a suit has been brought by others, and the doubt dispelled by a decision of the court. The statute permits the filing of a waiver at any time within a year after the probate of the will. It contemplates a writing whose meaning is clear, and whose effect is to waive the provisions of the will. It assumes that the executors will then know whether the estate is to be settled according to the provisions of the will or according to the law applicable when a waiver has been filed. Upon the contention of the widow in this case, a writing may be filed which will suspend the settlement of the estate, and leave everybody uncertain for a long time whether there is or is not a waiver. The writing filed in the present case does not purport to be an absolute waiver. It is a claim of a right to file a writing which shall leave undetermined the question whether the widow will waive the provisions of the will until it shall be decided what the law applicable to this will would be if an absolute waiver were filed. The filing of this writing was therefore of no effect.

As there was no waiver of the provisions of the will, we understand that there are no further questions upon which the plaintiffs need the instructions of the court.

Decree accordingly.

(185 Mass. 247)

KEEFE v. NORFOLK SUBURBAN ST. RY. CO. et al.

(Supreme Judicial Court of Massachusetts. Suffolk. Feb. 27, 1904.)

PERSONAL INJURY—RELEASE—FRAUD—EVIDENCE—OBJECTION NOT MADE BELOW—DAMAGES.

1. Plaintiff, after testifying, in regard to a release signed by her, that defendant's agent gave her an order on a physician, and then handed her the paper to sign, saying to her, "Sign that slip of paper, so that I can show it to the company, so they can see I have sent you to a doctor," and that she signed it without seeing anything on it, and without knowing that she was making a settlement, may testify that just after she signed the paper the agent told her to come to him after she was well, and he would settle all her claims; this having a bearing, at least, on her claim of fraud.

2. The objection that witness' answer was not responsive may not be made for the first time on appeal.

3. Evidence, in an action for personal injury to a woman 40 years old, *held* sufficient, as to the likelihood of her climacteric occurring before she should fully recover, to take to the jury the question of its being an element of damages.

Exceptions from Superior Court, Suffolk County; Robert O. Harris, Judge.

Action by Nellie Keefe against the Norfolk Suburban Street Railway Company and another for personal injuries. Verdict for plaintiff, and defendant excepted. Exceptions overruled.

Defendant introduced a paper purporting to be a release to the Norfolk Suburban Street Railway Company (which was absorbed by the West Roxbury & Roslindale Street Railway Company, the defendant in this case) of all claims and demands against the Norfolk Suburban Street Railway Company by reason of the accident for which the plaintiff sued. The plaintiff acknowledged that the signature upon the paper was hers, but stated that the paper was blank when she signed it, and that there was no writing or printing upon it. She testified that she rode on another car to the mill where she worked, where she remained all day; that on the afternoon of the accident an agent of the railroad called for her at the mill; that she learned after meeting him that he was giving money to other girls who had been on the car and claimed injury, but that she did not know whether she learned it before meeting him or not; that she was sent down into the office of the mill, where she talked with him and told him she was injured. She testified that he then suggested her having a doctor, and she told him she had a family physician, to wit, Dr. Hodgdon; that thereupon he gave her an order upon Dr. Hodgdon for medical treatment, a copy of which order is annexed to this bill of exceptions, marked "B"; that thereupon he handed her a paper upon which she saw neither printing nor a seal, and asked her to sign it; that he did not read the paper to her; that when she signed the paper and received the order on the doctor she did not know that she was making a settlement of the case; that he said to her, after giving her the order on the doctor, and presenting the paper to her, "Sign that slip of paper, so that I can show it to the company, so they can see I have sent you to a doctor;" that thereupon she signed the paper. Plaintiff further testified: "After I signed the note he told me when I was all better to come down to Quincy, and he gave me his name and address, but I have forgotten it. He said he would settle all my claims. I have never been able to get that far, and I have never seen him since. He knew where I lived, but he never came to me."

James E. Cotter and Thomas F. McAnarney, for plaintiff. Henry F. Hurlburt and Damon E. Hall, for defendant.

HAMMOND, J. 1. We think no error of law appears in the admission of the statements made to the plaintiff by McAloon in the same conversation in which she alleges she was fraudulently induced to sign the release, although they were made after she had signed it. While it may be true that they could not have formed any part of the statements which induced her to sign, yet they were a part of the conversation during which the paper was signed, and had a bearing, at least, upon her good faith in pressing the claim of fraud, and to meet the argument likely to be made by the defendant that this claim was an afterthought on her part. It is argued by the defendant that this part of the plaintiff's testimony was not responsive to the question put to her. It was certainly responsive to the question as originally put, and the colloquy between the two counsel does not show that her counsel ever withdrew that question; but, however that may be, the point that the answer was not responsive to the question was not then taken by the defendant, and it is manifest that the court understood, and properly, that the objection of the defendant was based solely upon the ground that the testimony was not admissible. The objection that it was not responsive cannot now be of avail to the defendant.

2. At the time of the trial the plaintiff was 39 years and 11 months old, and her contention was that, if she should reach her climacteric before she had fully recovered, her suffering might be prolonged as one of the results of the accident. The defendant contended that upon the evidence the possibility that the plaintiff would reach her climacteric before her full recovery from the accident was so remote that it should not be consid-

ered by the jury as an element of damage, and at the close of the evidence asked the court so to rule. The court declined to rule as requested, and submitted this question to the jury, with instructions to which we do not understand the defendant to object, except so far as inconsistent with the ruling requested. While the evidence tended to show that the average age of married women at the time of the climacteric is about 45 or 46 years, and of unmarried women a year or two earlier, yet it tended also to show that sometimes it occurred when the woman was only 30 years of age, and sometimes not until after she was 55; and the physician who attended the plaintiff testified that she was at the age when the change of life might come, and "if that should come at the age of 40, as it often does with unmarried women, it might prolong her nervous condition and keep her from rapidly recovering her health." An expert physician called by the plaintiff testified that she was getting better now, and that it was "only a question of time when she will get well, provided the climacteric does not come on very soon"; that this period in the case of an unmarried woman "is liable to come at 40 years of age." Another expert called by the plaintiff testified that, "if the change of life should develop within the course of the next two years, I think that that would have a tendency to delay the recovery very much." It is true that there was much testimony to show that, after all, the chances seemed to be against the occurrence of the climacteric until after full recovery; still, in view of all the evidence, it cannot be said as matter of law that the likelihood that the climacteric would not occur until after full recovery from the effects of the accident was so remote as to call for the instruction requested by the defendant. The whole question was one of fact for the jury. The remaining exceptions, having been waived, are not considered.

Exceptions overruled.

(185 Mass. 223)

CLARK v. LEE.

(Supreme Judicial Court of Massachusetts. Norfolk. Feb. 27, 1904.)

DEEDS—RESTRICTIVE COVENANTS—CONSTRUCTION.

1. A deed to plaintiff's grantor, whereby it was provided that no dwelling or other house or building, or any part thereof or projection therefrom, should be built on defendant's remaining land, within a certain distance of the premises conveyed, and that not more than one house, and no house except a single, detached dwelling house, should be erected thereon, restricted defendant only in reference to the house to be built on the land, and did not prevent the building of a wall by him, even though it should extend from the house into the restricted space.

¶ 1. See Covenants, vol. 14, Cent. Dig. § 50; Deeds, vol. 16, Cent. Dig. § 542.

Case reserved from Supreme Judicial Court, Norfolk County; Jas. M. Morton, Judge.

Bill for injunction by one Clark against one Lee. Case reserved from the Supreme Judicial Court. Bill dismissed.

Roger F. Sturgis, for plaintiff. William H. White, for defendant.

LATHROP, J. In the defendant's deed to the plaintiff's grantor, it was provided that on the defendant's remaining land, lying southerly of the land conveyed, no dwelling or other house or building, or any part thereof or projection therefrom, should be built thereon within 65 feet of the easterly line of Walnut street, or within 15 feet of the southerly line of the premises conveyed, and that not more than one house, and no house except a single, detached dwelling house, should be erected thereon. We regret that we have not been furnished with a copy of the deed, which should have been annexed to the bill, so that the exact language could be given; but we have stated the substance of the language used, as we gather it from the bill and answer. It is admitted that the defendant has built his house in conformity with the language of the deed, and the only complaint is that he has erected certain walls on his land, which it is said are in conflict with his covenant not to build, or are contrary to the restriction imposed by him on his remaining land.

We are of opinion that the covenant or restriction applies only to the house to be built upon the land, and not to a wall, even if the wall extends from the house into the restricted space. Such a wall as was here built, extending from the house, cannot be deemed to be "any part of or projection" from the house. These words evidently refer to bay windows or porches, or things of that nature. That a wall cannot be held to come within the term "building" is, in our opinion, conclusively settled by the cases in this commonwealth. Thus in Truesdell v. Gay, 13 Gray, 311, it was said by Mr. Justice Bigelow: "The word 'building' cannot be held to include every species of erection on land, such as fences, gates, or other like structure. Taken in its broadest sense, it can mean only an erection intended for use and occupation as a habitation, or for some purpose of trade, manufacture, ornament, or use, constituting a fabric or edifice, such as a house, a store, a church, a shed." See, also, Nowell v. Boston Academy of Notre Dame, 130 Mass. 209, which seems to us conclusive of this case.

Bill dismissed.

(185 Mass. 190)

In re MAYOR, ETC., OF CITY OF TAUNTON.

(Supreme Judicial Court of Massachusetts. Bristol. Feb. 26, 1904.)

RAILROADS—GRADE CROSSINGS—ABOLITION—DIFFERENT STREETS—ALTERATION OF TRAVEL—EXPENSE—APPORTIONMENT.

1. St. 1901, p. 145, c. 205, authorized the E. T. Street Railway Company to intervene in certain proceedings for the abolition of a grade crossing on M. avenue, in the city of T., and provided that the proceedings under the petitions relative to the crossings on such avenue and R. street should be independent of the proceedings as to all others, and that if the abolition of the crossings was necessary the commissioners might require the railway company to pay such part of the total cost of the abolition of the crossing on M. avenue as they should find to be just and equitable. The commissioners directed that the grade crossings be abolished, and the abolition of the one on R. street was effected by discontinuing that part of the street which crossed the railroad and constructing a new street connecting with M. avenue, so that the travel might cross the railroad on the bridge constructed at such avenue. *Held*, that the railroad commissioners were entitled to treat the changing of R. street as a part of the changes on M. avenue, in determining the measure of the expense to be borne by the railway company.

Appeal from Superior Court, Bristol County.

Proceeding by the mayor and aldermen of the city of Taunton for the abolition of certain grade crossings. From an auditor's order assessing the cost of the abolition of a crossing of another street as a part of the assessment of the cost of the abolition of a crossing on a street known as "Middleboro Avenue," which was affirmed on exceptions by the superior court, the East Taunton Street Railway Company appeals. Affirmed.

F. A. Farnham, for Old Colony R. Co. and New York, N. H. & H. R. Co. Arthur M. Alger, for East Taunton St. Ry. Co.

KNOWLTON, C. J. Petitions were pending in the superior court for the abolition of a large number of grade crossings in the city of Taunton, and, among them, those on Middleboro avenue and Richmond street. The East Taunton Street Railway had a location on Middleboro avenue, and by St. 1901, p. 145, c. 205, it was authorized to intervene in the proceedings in court, and thereupon to construct and maintain for a time its railway across the track of the Old Colony Railroad Company at Chace's Crossing, at the same level therewith, subject to restrictions and regulations to be prescribed by the railroad commissioners. It was also provided that the proceedings under the petitions relative to the crossings on Middleboro avenue and Richmond street should be had independently of the proceedings as to the others, and that, if the commissioners should decide that the abolition of this crossing was necessary, the street railway company should pay such part of the total actual cost of the abolition of the grade crossing on Middleboro avenue as they should find to be just and equitable, and should prescribe in their report. The commissioners ordered the abolition of these crossings, and prescribed in detail how the change on Middleboro avenue should be made. They determined that it was just and equitable that the railroad company should pay 25 per cent. of this cost, and so prescribed in their report. The grade crossing on Richmond street was abolished by discontinuing that part of the street which crossed the railroad, and constructing a new way as a substitute for the other, which came into Middleboro avenue at a point that made it convenient to cross the railroad on the bridge constructed over the railroad on Middleboro avenue. The auditor appointed under the statute made his report, and the East Taunton Street Railway Company filed exceptions thereto, which were overruled by the superior court. The case is before us upon the appeal of the railway company from the decree overruling the exceptions and confirming the report.

The exceptions are, in substance, to the auditor's including, as a part of the cost of the abolition of the grade crossings on Middleboro avenue, the entire cost of the bridge and masonry for the overhead crossing, and of the grading for the approaches, the land damages, and other incidental expenses of effecting the change on that avenue. The contention of the railway company is that, inasmuch as no bridge was needed on Richmond street, because Richmond street was changed so as to enter Middleboro avenue at a point which brought the travel upon it across the railroad over the Middleboro Avenue Bridge, only half of the cost of this bridge should be treated as chargeable upon Middleboro avenue, and that the other half should be charged upon Richmond street. This subject is covered by the statute and the action of the commissioners. They were authorized to prescribe the manner of making the changes, and to apportion the cost. All the expenses included by the auditor were incurred in making the changes on Middleboro avenue which the commissioners prescribed in detail. In apportioning the cost between the street railway company and the others, they treated all these changes as belonging to Middleboro avenue, as they had a right to do, and they made their order as to the percentages to be paid on this basis. The auditor has followed exactly their order, made under the authority of the statute. The street railway company has no reason to complain because the expenses of the change on Richmond street were small. This resulted from the fact that proper changes on Middleboro avenue made it unnecessary to construct a bridge on Richmond street.

Decree affirmed.

(185 Mass. 251)

HOUGHTON et al. v. FURBUSH.

(Supreme Judicial Court of Massachusetts. Suffolk. Feb. 27, 1904.)

CONTRACT TO PURCHASE BOOKS—BREACH—MEASURE OF DAMAGE—EXCEPTION—WAIVER.

1. A failure to argue an exception to the allowance of an amendment to a declaration is a waiver thereof.

2. The measure of damage in an action for breach of contract in refusing to take books which the defendant had ordered of publishers is the difference between the market value at the time and place of delivery and the contract price.

Exceptions from Superior Court, Suffolk County; Edgar J. Sherman, Judge.

Action by Albert E. Houghton and others against Caroline C. Furbush. Judgment for plaintiffs, and defendant brings exceptions. Exceptions overruled.

Samuel W. Forrest, for plaintiffs. Dana Malone, for defendant.

HAMMOND, J. The original declaration contained three counts—the first being on an account annexed, apparently as for goods sold and delivered; the second being for balance due the plaintiffs on an accounting together; and the third being for interest. The answer contained a general denial, and set up fraud on the part of the plaintiffs. Upon these pleadings the case went to trial. At the close of the evidence the defendant asked the court to rule, in substance, that upon the whole evidence the plaintiffs could not recover, and that "the action should have been for damages for the breach of a special contract." The defendant also requested certain rulings as to the rule of damages and as to fraud. In this state of things the case was argued and submitted to the judge sitting without a jury. Subsequently, without announcing any final decision, the judge notified the counsel for the plaintiffs that, in his opinion, it was doubtful if the action could be maintained upon the declaration. The counsel for the plaintiffs then moved for leave to amend his declaration by adding thereto a count for breach of contract in refusing to take the books which the defendant had ordered. After a hearing this motion was granted, and the defendant excepted. The court "found for the plaintiffs on the amended declaration in the sum of five hundred and sixty-one dollars as damages for the breach of the contract." The defendant excepted to the rulings of the court and to the refusal to give the rulings requested.

The exception to the allowance of the amendment is not argued, and therefore, in view of its nature, we consider it waived.

The record discloses no evidence to establish the defense of fraud. The contract, when made, was binding upon the defendant, and it does not appear that by rescission or otherwise she has been released from it. She must be held, therefore, and the only remaining questions relate to the assessment of damages. Upon this question the defendant requested the court to rule (1) that the plaintiffs could recover only nominal damages; (2) that they could recover "only the actual expense made before the order was countermanded"; and, further (3) that "the measure of damages is the difference between the market value at the time and place of delivery and the contract price, and, no evidence having been introduced of that difference, the court can award nominal damages only." A short but decisive answer to the first two requests is that they each exclude from the amount of damages the item of profit which the plaintiffs would have made from the contract. They were therefore properly refused. The last ruling requested was given so far as it stated the rule of damage. So far, therefore, as respected the rule of damage, the defendant has no ground for complaint as to the manner in which the court dealt with her requests. The counsel for the defendant has addressed an argument to us in support of the proposition that upon the receipt of the countermanding order from the defendant it was the duty of the plaintiffs to stop at once, and make the damage to the defendant as light as possible; but we have not found it necessary to consider how far the principle that a party to an executory contract, by a notice to the other party of his intention not to comply with its terms, can reduce his liability for damages, is applicable to this case, because we do not think that that question is fairly raised on this record. While the evidence as to the market value at the time and place of delivery was slight, still we cannot say as matter of law that it did not justify the finding made by the court.

Exceptions overruled.

(185 Mass. 156)

DANA v. DANA et al.

(Supreme Judicial Court of Massachusetts. Middlesex. Feb. 27, 1904.)

WILLS—CONSTRUCTION—INTENT OF TESTATOR—ESTATES DEVISED—LIFE ESTATES—POWER OF ABSOLUTE DISPOSITION—INTEREST OF REMAINDERMEN.

1. Whether the devisees under a will took only a life interest with a limited power of disposal, or one with full power both to use the income and expend the principal, is to be determined from the intention of the testator, ascertained from the provisions of the whole instrument.

2. A will devised all the residue of testator's estate to his wife, to hold and enjoy the same during her life. She was empowered to change the body of the estate into any form of investment, and to sell and dispose of any or all of it at her discretion, and as she thought necessary for her comfort and happiness, without accountability to any one. It further referred to "my wife's life estate as stated above," and then declared that the "reversion and residue of my said estate, if any," at her decease, was devised and bequeathed absolutely to certain of

¶ 2. See Sales, vol. 43, Cent. Dig. § 1099.

testator's relatives. *Held*, that the wife took, with her life interest, as ample a power to dispose of the estate as would be possessed by an owner in fee, and was not restricted in her disposition thereof to the use of only so much of the principal as might be necessary for her support, but could, if she saw fit, devote any part of the estate left to her to aid either charitable or philanthropic objects.

3. The fact that a wife has a private fortune amply sufficient for her support does not affect the legal force of testator's language, or cut down his clearly expressed intention in giving her an absolute power of disposition of property devised to her for life.

4. In construing a will, the language used by the testator, the extent of his estate, the mode of life in which his family have been reared, and the means provided by him in his lifetime for their culture and happiness, are all to be considered.

5. Where testator devised to his wife a life estate, with a power of disposal in fee, the devisees and legatees to whom the property was to go after the wife's death took a vested remainder, dependent, however, on the contingency of determination by the wife's exercise of the power conferred.

Case reserved from Supreme Judicial Court, Middlesex County; Henry K. Braley, Judge.

Bill by Richard H. Dana, trustee, against Richard H. Dana and others, executors, and others. Case reserved for the full court. Decree rendered.

J. Ralph Wellman, for plaintiff. Hollis R. Bailey, for defendants Lucia W. Longfellow and others. Edmund M. Parker, for defendants Richard H. Dana and others.

BRALEY, J. From the pleadings in this case, the question presented by the parties for our decision is whether, under the second clause of the will of James Greenleaf, his wife, Mary Longfellow Greenleaf, took only a life interest in the residue of his estate, with a limited power of disposal of the principal, or a life interest therein, with full power, not only to use the income, but also to expend the principal, either in whole or in part, as she might deem advisable for her own personal welfare and enjoyment. And the answer is to be sought for and found in the intention of the testator, which is to be ascertained from the provisions of the whole instrument.

At the date of the execution of the will it had been settled that a testator might make a testamentary disposition of his property in which he could devise and give a life estate with power to sell in the first taker, and a remainder over in any residue that might be left on the death of the life tenant. Harris v. Knapp, 21 Pick. 412; Lynde v. Estabrook, 7 Allen, 68. This will may well rest upon the law of these decisions. His principal purpose was to make, in the first place, ample provision for his wife, of whom he speaks in language of affection, and then, in clear and sweeping words, declares that after the payment of his debts she is to take all the residue of his estate, not only to have and to hold, but to enjoy, during her life. She also, at her pleasure, might change the body of the estate, so devised to her, into any form of investment that she deemed beneficial, and "sell and dispose of any, or all of it, at her pleasure and discretion," as she thought necessary "for her own comfort and happiness, without accountability to any person whatsoever." If the testator had stopped here, the language used would have been sufficient to pass a fee. Gen. St. 1860, c. 92, § 5; Chase v. Chase, 132 Mass. 473. But he went further, and in the last clause of his will he speaks of the estate created in his wife by the second clause as "my beloved wife's life interest therein as stated above," and then declares that the "reversion and residue of my said estate, if any," at her decease, is devised and bequeathed absolutely, and in fee simple, to certain of his relatives, who are specifically named. It would be difficult to employ language to more clearly and concisely express the purpose and intention of the testator than the words used by him. He gave to his wife, during her lifetime, as absolute and ample a power to dispose of the estate devised as would be possessed by an owner in fee. And it has been decided that such a power may be an incident of a life estate, and legally given to a life tenant. Johnson v. Battelle, 125 Mass. 453; Welsh v. Woodbury, 144 Mass. 542-545, 11 N. E. 762; Sawin v. Cormier, 179 Mass. 420, 60 N. E. 936.

If it be assumed, from the uncertain and indefinite allegations in the bill, that of the residue and principal of the estate devised to her, a small part of which it is conceded she has spent in her lifetime, an insignificant portion, when compared with the whole, was used by her for charitable purposes, the claim of the petitioner, as trustee under his will, that the executors of her will must make good such deficit, if it can be found, cannot be sustained. Her power to spend and use the principal was unlimited. She was to enjoy it, during her life, at her pleasure and discretion, and she was not required to render to any person an account of her use of the property. That she had a private fortune of her own, amply sufficient for her support, does not change the legal force of the language employed by the testator, or cut down his clearly expressed intention, by making his purpose depend in any degree upon the fact that she possessed a separate estate. No such limitation is imposed by him.

Neither was it his design to restrict her to the use of only so much of the principal as might be necessary for her comfortable physical support and existence. The power of disposal given to her was not for this object alone, though undoubtedly it was in the mind of the testator, and is included in the language used by him. But, in addition, she was to spend and enjoy it in the largest manner for her happiness, and nothing appears in the record to raise the suggestion that, in her use of the property, Mrs. Greenleaf wished to deplete the estate of her husband, in order to preserve or increase her own. If, through reasons of religion or of benevolence, and for her mental satisfaction, she chose to devote any part of the estate left to her in aid of either charitable or philanthropic objects, there is nothing in the terms of his will that restricts her from making such use of the principal. If the testator did not care to confine her discretionary powers, there is no duty incumbent on us to seek for reasons to limit their exercise. No general rule can be laid down that will be equally applicable to all cases, as what will be sufficient in one case to render the object of a testator's bounty free from anxiety, in providing means of support, by which contentment and enjoyment are secured and conferred, may, under other conditions, be wholly inadequate. The language used by the testator, the extent of his estate, the mode of life in which his family have been reared, and the means provided by him in his lifetime for their culture and happiness, are all to be considered. Lovett v. Farnham, 169 Mass. 1, 47 N. E. 246; Stocker v. Foster, 178 Mass. 591-599, 60 N. E. 407.

It must therefore be held that she took a life estate with a power of disposal in fee, while the devisees and legatees took a vested remainder, though their interest was dependent on the contingency that the exercise by her of the power conferred might determine their estate. Blanchard v. Blanchard, 1 Allen, 223; Kent v. Morrison, 153 Mass. 137-139, 26 N. E. 427, 10 L. R. A. 756, 25 Am. St. Rep. 616; Barnard v. Stone, 159 Mass. 224-225, 34 N. E. 272.

Decree accordingly.

(185 Mass. 253)

STANFORD v. HYDE PARK.

(Supreme Judicial Court of Massachusetts. Norfolk. Feb. 29, 1904.)

TOWNS—DEFECTIVE HIGHWAYS—INJURIES—ACTION—EVIDENCE—QUESTIONS FOR JURY.

1. Plaintiff alighted from a street car, carrying in her arms a sleeping child, and tripped over a stake in the street and sustained injuries. The stake projected about 14 inches above the ground, and there was evidence that it had been in the street for about six months, and it was shown that a large number of passengers alighted from the car where plaintiff did. *Held*, that the questions whether plaintiff was exercising due care, whether the stake caused the injury, whether, in view of the amount of travel, the way was reasonably safe, whether the defect might have been remedied by reasonable care, and whether the town had, or ought to have had by the exercise of reasonable care, notice of the defect, were questions for the jury.

Exceptions from Superior Court, Norfolk County; Edgar J. Sherman, Judge.

Action by Catherine E. Stanford against the inhabitants of Hyde Park. Verdict for plaintiff, and defendants bring exceptions. Exceptions overruled.

Plaintiff in this action alighted from a street car in one of the streets of defendant town, and a few feet from the track tripped on a stake, which projected about 14 inches above the ground in the street, and sustained injuries. It appeared that a great number of passengers alighted where plaintiff did, and that at the time of the accident she was carrying in her arms a sleeping child. There was evidence tending to show that the stake had been put in by engineers laying out a sewer system about six months before the accident.

Choate & Hall, for plaintiff. James E. Cotter, for defendants.

HAMMOND, J. This is a very plain case. There was but little conflict in the evidence, and it is unnecessary to recite it in detail, or to cite authorities to show that the questions whether the plaintiff was in the exercise of due care; whether the stake was the cause of the injury; whether, in view of the amount and character of public travel in that vicinity, the way was reasonably safe and convenient, or by reason of the existence of the stake was defective; whether the defect might have been remedied by reasonable care and diligence on the part of the town; and whether the town had, or by the exercise of proper care and diligence on its part might have had, notice of the defect—are questions, not of law for the court, but of fact for the jury. The first, second, and seventh requests were therefore properly refused. The other rulings requested, so far as material, were, in substance, given.

Exceptions overruled.

(185 Mass. 245)

MEHLINGER v. HARRIMAN.

(Supreme Judicial Court of Massachusetts. Suffolk. Feb. 27, 1904.)

Exceptions from Superior Court, Suffolk County; Wm. Schofield, Judge.

Action by Albert Mehlinger against one Harriman. Findings were for plaintiff, and defendant brings exceptions. Exceptions overruled.

Albert Mehlinger, pro se. Wm. B. Orcutt, for defendant.

HAMMOND, J. At the time the defendant delivered the note to Simeon Marcus, there was an oral agreement between them by which Marcus was not permitted to negotiate it to Riley. Although apparently Marcus attempted to violate that agreement, still he did not succeed; for the court finds that Smith purchased the note of Marcus, and thereafter held it until he sold it to the plaintiff. It is not shown, therefore, that the note was fraudulently put into circulation. The court further finds that before its maturity the plaintiff became a bona fide purchaser, giving as a consideration therefor his own note to Smith, who still holds it. These findings are warranted by the evidence. The plaintiff, upon the facts found by the court, took the note in due course of business (Rev. Laws, c. 73, § 69), and, there being no fraud, is entitled to recover its full value.

Exceptions overruled.

(185 Mass. 212)

McLAUGHLIN et al. v. RICE.

(Supreme Judicial Court of Massachusetts. Suffolk. Feb. 27, 1904.)

DEEDS TO HUSBAND AND WIFE—ESTATE BY ENTIRETIES—PAROL EVIDENCE.

1. Where a deed was made to two persons jointly without disclosing whether they were husband and wife, parol evidence was admissible to show such fact.

2. Under Gen. St. 1860, c. 89, §§ 13, 14, providing that conveyances made to two or more persons, except conveyances to husband and wife, should create a tenancy in common, a deed to husband and wife, executed while such statute was in force, created an estate by the entireties, under which the wife, on surviving her husband, became the sole owner of the land.

Exceptions from Superior Court, Suffolk County; Albert Mason, Judge.

Writ of entry between one McLaughlin and others and one Rice. From a judgment in favor of the tenants, the demandant brings exceptions. Overruled.

Henry J. Dubois and George A. King, for plaintiffs. Harrison M. Davis, for defendant.

LATHROP, J. 1. The first exception in this case and the first request for instructions raise the question whether, when land is conveyed by deed to A. and B., evidence is admissible to show that the grantees are husband and wife. We have no doubt that such evidence is admissible. If it were not, then a deed from a husband directly to his wife, which did not describe her as such, would be a valid deed, which could not for a moment be contended. In Morris v. McCarty, 158 Mass. 11, 32 N. E. 938, a deed was made to A. and B., the latter being described as the wife of A. It was held that, as B. was not in fact the wife of A., the grantees did not take an estate by entireties. It is the fact, and not the description or want of description, which determines the question. The first exception must therefore be overruled, and the first request for instructions was properly refused.

2. The third request for instructions was also properly refused. The deed being to a man and his wife, they took an estate by entireties, and not as tenants in common. The deed was executed in 1878, and, as the law then stood, the rights of the grantees, they being husband and wife, were the same as at common law. Gen. St. 1860, c. 89, §§ 13, 14. See, also, Pub. St. 1882, c. 126, §§ 5, 6. It was not until St. 1885, p. 679, c. 237, § 1, that the law was changed. In construing all conveyances prior to that statute, it has been held that a conveyance to a husband and wife conveyed an estate by entireties. Pray v. Stebbins, 141 Mass. 219, 4 N. E. 824, 55 Am. Rep. 462; Donahue v. Hubbard, 154 Mass. 537, 28 N. E. 909, 14 L. R. A. 123, 26 Am. St. Rep. 271; Morris v. McCarty, 158 Mass. 11, 32 N. E. 938; Phelps v. Simons, 159 Mass. 415, 34 N. E. 657, 38 Am. St. Rep. 430. The ruling of the court below that, as the wife survived her husband, she was the sole owner of the granted premises, and the finding for the tenant, were therefore right.

Exceptions overruled.

¶ 2. See Husband and Wife, vol. 26, Cent. Dig. § 73.

(185 Mass. 210)

ALBERT v. BOSTON ELEVATED RY. CO.

(Supreme Judicial Court of Massachusetts. Suffolk. Feb. 26, 1904.)

STREET RAILROADS—OPERATION—INJURY TO NEWSBOY—JUMPING ON MOVING CAR—DUTY AND LIABILITY OF COMPANY.

1. Plaintiff, a newsboy, 12 years of age, jumped on the running board of one of defendant's moving street cars for the purpose of selling papers. He testified that he was in the habit of jumping on and off moving cars, and it appeared that the car in question was going through a busy part of the city at about the usual speed, which the evidence, however, did not show was either increased or diminished before he was hurt. According to testimony in the case he became frightened at a motion from the conductor on the rear platform, and what he understood as an order from him to get off, and thereupon jumped off and was injured. His only right on the cars at any time to sell papers was under a contract which gave the right to enter and leave by the rear platform when not in motion, and not otherwise. *Held*, that he was a trespasser, to whom defendant owed no duty except to refrain from willfully or recklessly and wantonly exposing him to injury.

Exceptions from Superior Court, Suffolk County; J. B. Richardson, Judge.

Action by one Albert, by his next friend, against the Boston Elevated Railway Company, for personal injuries. There was a judgment for defendant, and plaintiff brings exceptions. Exceptions overruled.

Charles W. Bartlett, Elbridge R. Anderson, and Robert Levi, for plaintiff. P. H. Cooney and L. F. Hyde, for defendant.

KNOWLTON, C. J. The plaintiff, a newsboy 12 years of age, jumped upon the running board of an ordinary open street car as it was passing through Congress street, near State street, in Boston, for the purpose of selling his papers. He testified that he was in the habit of jumping on and off such cars when they were in motion. The testimony showed that the car was going at about its usual rate of speed, which we suppose was not great in that busy part of the city. There was no evidence that the speed was increased or diminished after he attempted to get on until after the accident. As he was changing hands, and trying to get out a paper to deliver to a man who sat near the middle of the car, he fell off, or intentionally jumped off, and was injured. There was testimony that the conductor, who was standing on the rear platform, made a motion and said something which the plaintiff did not understand, but thought was, "Get out of here!" or "Get off!" and that the plaintiff, being frightened, jumped off. He was on the running board but a very short time. To use his expression, "It all happened in a jiffy."

The plaintiff was a trespasser. His only right on the defendant's cars to sell newspapers at any time was under a contract between the defendant and his employer, in which it was stipulated that "newsboys shall enter and leave the cars by the rear platform, and while said cars are not in motion, and not otherwise." To him, as a trespasser, the defendant owed no duty except to refrain from willfully or recklessly and wantonly exposing him to injury. Metcalfe v. Cunard Steamship Company, 147 Mass. 66, 16 N. E. 701; Heinlein v. Boston & Providence Railroad Company, 147 Mass. 136, 16 N. E. 698, 9 Am. St. Rep. 676; Reardon v. Thompson, 149 Mass. 267, 21 N. E. 369. In speaking to the plaintiff, the conductor was only trying to enforce the rule which the plaintiff was violating. He was not near the plaintiff, who was in the middle of the car. He had no reason to expect that his command would cause the plaintiff serious injury. There was no evidence that he acted wantonly or recklessly in telling the plaintiff to get off. The case is fully covered by Mugford v. Boston & Maine Railroad, 173 Mass. 10, 52 N. E. 1078, and by Bjornquist v. Boston & Albany Railroad Company, 70 N. E. 53. See, also, Leonard v. Boston & Albany Railroad Company, 170 Mass. 318, 49 N. E. 621; Planz v. Boston & Albany Railroad Company, 157 Mass. 377, 32 N. E. 356, 17 L. R. A. 835.

Exceptions overruled.

(185 Mass. 226)

J. REGESTER'S SONS CO. v. REED et al.

KOLLER v. MOFFATT et al.

(Supreme Judicial Court of Massachusetts. Suffolk. Feb. 27, 1904.)

APPEAL—FINDINGS OF EQUITY COURT—CONCLUSIVENESS—BILLS AND NOTES—BONA FIDE PURCHASERS—BURDEN OF PROOF.

1. The finding of facts of the trial court, sitting in equity, with a full report of the evidence before it, will not be reversed on appeal unless it clearly appears to be erroneous.

2. Where it appears that notes were fraudulently put into circulation, the burden is on the indorsees thereof to show that they gave a valuable consideration for the same, and took them without knowledge of the makers' rights.

Appeal from Superior Court, Suffolk County.

Bills in equity by J. Regester's Sons Company against William J. Reed and others, and by one Koller against one Moffatt and others. From decrees for plaintiffs, defendants appeal. Affirmed.

Gaston, Snow & Saltonstall and H. S. Macpherson, for J. Regester's Sons Co. Walter A. Buie and Clarence F. Eldredge, for Wm. A. Clark, Jr., and George Warner. L. R. Clark, for Koller.

LATHROP, J. Each of these cases comes before us on an appeal from a decree of a single justice of the superior court sitting in equity, with a full report of the evidence taken before him by a commissioner appointed under a rule of court. The judge, at the request of the defendants, in each case made a finding of facts, and this finding is a part of the record. The familiar rule applies that in such an appeal this court will not reverse the finding of the court below unless it clearly appears to be erroneous. Dickinson v. Todd, 172 Mass. 183, 51 N. E. 976, and cases cited. We have examined the voluminous report of the evidence, and are of opinion that the findings of the judge were fully warranted. It would serve no useful purpose to review the evidence. The defendants contend that the findings must be supported by the evidence, including the inferences to be drawn from the written and spoken words, and the conduct of the parties and their witnesses, and that mere suspicion is not enough. So far we agree. But it appears from the evidence that the notes were fraudulently put into circulation, and the burden of proof was upon the defendants to show that they gave a valuable consideration for the same and took the notes without knowledge of the plaintiffs' rights. Merchants' National Bank v. Haverhill Iron Works, 159 Mass. 158, 34 N. E. 93; Savage v. Goldsmith, 181 Mass. 420, 63 N. E. 918. The defendants failed to satisfy the judge who heard the cases that they had sustained this burden, and they have failed to satisfy us.

The order therefore in each case must be: Decree affirmed.

(185 Mass. 130)

BJORNQUIST v. BOSTON & A. R. CO.

(Supreme Judicial Court of Massachusetts. Suffolk. Feb. 25, 1904.)

RAILROADS—INJURIES TO TRESPASSER—CHILDREN—WANTON NEGLIGENCE—USE OF LANGUAGE—BURDEN OF PROOF.

1. On evidence that a railroad servant was managing cars, there being nothing to show that any other person was in control of them at the time, the jury could find that it was within the scope of such servant's employment to keep trespassers away from cars.

2. To a trespasser on its cars a railroad owes no duty, except to refrain from willfully or wantonly and recklessly exposing him to danger.

3. Recklessness and wantonness on the part of a railroad servant in dealing with a trespasser on its train is not to be inferred from the mere use of language intended to influence the trespasser's voluntary action, though the language used is not necessary or proper, but

¶ 2. See Bills and Notes, vol. 7, Cent. Dig. § 1684.

only where it is so unreasonable or improper in reference to its probable effect on the safety of the trespasser as to indicate a wanton and reckless disregard of probable dangerous consequences.

4. Plaintiff, a boy of from eight to nine years of age, who lived near a railroad, and was familiar with trains, was injured in jumping off a slowly moving freight car, on which he was stealing a ride. The immediate cause of his jumping was an order of the brakeman to get off, "or I'll break your neck." *Held*, that there was no such apparent probability of the injury caused as to indicate in the language of the brakeman a wanton and reckless disregard for harmful consequences.

5. In an action for injuries to a boy trespassing on a freight car, the burden was on plaintiff to show reckless and wanton misconduct on the part of defendant's servant.

Exceptions from Superior Court, Suffolk County; Robt. J. Harris, Judge.

Tort for personal injuries by Charles Bjornquist, by next friend, against the Boston & Albany Railroad Company. There was verdict for plaintiff, and defendant excepted. Exceptions sustained.

S. A. Fuller and W. E. Bowden, for plaintiff. Samuel Hoar and Geo. P. Furber, for defendant.

KNOWLTON, C. J. The defendant was moving two or three oil tank cars on a short side track used for loading and unloading freight, close by its freightyard in Cambridge. The switching engine was behind the cars without being coupled to them, and the cars were pushed or "kicked" a short distance on the tracks, and left to stop from their own inertia. These were platform cars, constructed with a large tank extending longitudinally between points about two feet from the ends of the car, and with stakes set at intervals along the sides of the car at the edge of the floor, with an iron rod passing through the top of the stakes, leaving room to pass between the tank and the rod on each side. The plaintiff, a boy of ordinary intelligence, about 8½ years of age at the time of the accident, was a trespasser on the forward one of these cars; lying on his stomach, with his feet and legs hanging over the side of the car. At that point there was an iron step on the side of the car, and he had climbed up, taking hold of the stake, and was riding as the car was pushed by the engine. The floor of the car was about as high from the ground as his shoulders when he was standing, or, as he testified, about as high as the crutch which he used at the time of the trial. One Perry, a companion, three years older than he, had got up on the opposite side of the car with his feet on the step, which was an iron strap or loop attached underneath to the side of the car, and was riding, holding onto the upright stake which was near the end of the car. One of the defendant's servants, who is described as a brakeman, had uncoupled the engine from the car next it, and was riding on the car, when he saw one or both of these boys near the forward end of the forward car, and called out in a loud tone, "Get off there, or I'll break your neck." The boys immediately started to jump off, and the plaintiff fell so that his feet came upon the track, and he was seriously injured. His language in testifying was: "When I was going to jump off, I slipped. * * * There was a step there. I put my foot in that, and I was going to jump, and I slipped and went under the wheels." The defendant's servant was acting in the management of the cars just before the accident, and it does not appear that any other person was employed at that time in the control of them. On this evidence the jury might well find that it was within the scope of his employment to try to keep trespassers away from them. To the plaintiff, as a trespasser, the defendant owed no duty, except to refrain from willfully or wantonly and recklessly exposing him to danger. This is the uniformly recognized rule in regard to the management of a proprietor's business, and the performance of his ordinary duties. A question may be raised whether the rule is the same if the proprietor does anything which is directed to the trespasser, and is intended to affect immediately his conduct or condition. We are of opinion that in ordinary cases this makes no difference, if the action is in the exercise of the legal rights of the proprietor, and in other respects is in the proper performance of his duties. When this action takes the form of the intentional use of force upon the person of a trespasser, the force must be limited to that which is reasonable under the circumstances, in the exercise of his legal rights. Any excess may be punished as an assault and battery. This is because force upon the person of another is ordinarily harmful and injurious. One who uses it must guard his conduct so as not to go beyond his legal rights. So, if an action is brought for reckless and wanton negligence in dealing with a trespasser, and if the conduct relied on is the intentional use of force upon the person in an attempt to exercise one's legal rights, it may well be that, because of the injurious nature of the agency employed, wantonness and recklessness would ordinarily be inferred from any excess of intentional force beyond that which was reasonably necessary. But this principle is not applicable to a use of language which is intended to have no further effect than to influence the voluntary action of another. In the latter case the question is not whether the use of the language is entirely reasonable and proper, but whether it is so unreasonable or improper, in reference to its probable effect upon the safety of the person to whom it is addressed, as to indicate a wanton and reckless disregard of probable dangerous consequences.

In the present case, all that the brakeman did which is relied on as reckless and wanton negligence was to call out as above stated, and to walk forward in an ordinary way. According to the testimony of two of the plaintiff's witnesses, he was not on the car on which the plaintiff was, but on the one behind it. According to the testimony of the plaintiff, he was at the rear end of the car on which the plaintiff was, and from there was walking forward. If we assume that he was in charge of the cars, it was his duty to do all that he reasonably could to keep trespassers away from them. It was his duty, not only in reference to the interests of his employer, but in reference to the interests of the trespassers themselves. The dangers to trespassers about moving cars, especially in freightyards, are great and constant. The persons with whom the employé has to deal, whether vagrants trying to steal rides upon freight trains or boys seeking amusement upon moving cars in freightyards, are almost always of a bold and lawless kind. Sober reasoning, friendly advice, and gentle admonition, after they have accomplished their purpose, would in most cases be entirely ineffectual to prevent or diminish trespassing by such persons. From the necessity of the case, appeal must be made in some form and to some degree to fear, as a motive to induce obedience to proper rules. It is necessary and proper, in a reasonable way, to interfere with the enjoyment of boys taking rides in such places, rather than to permit them to complete their rides pleasantly. The evidence is that the plaintiff lived only 300 or 400 yards from the place of the accident, and that between his home and the railroad were open fields, where the boys were accustomed to play ball and other games. He testified that just before the accident he was returning from fishing, and had stopped with two other boys to play tag on the platform of one of the buildings of the oilworks at which cars were unloaded, and that as he saw the two tank cars and the engine, he called to Perry, his companion, "Come on, let's take a ride," and that they then ran and got upon the car furthest from the engine. It is hardly to be supposed that boys living so near and accustomed to play close by moving cars were ignorant of orders of their parents or others which forbade them to get upon the freight cars which were being switched back and forth in or near the yard. It is reasonable to infer that in dealing with such boys, quite as much for their own safety as for the interests of the railroad company, some show of severity would be needed on the part of the defendant's employés. These conditions are important in considering the conduct of the defendant's servant. He gave a single command, accompanied with a threat which no intelligent boy would interpret literally, but which implied a severe reproof, and a possibility of punishment if disobedience was repeated and persisted in. Except the use of this expression, which apparently was instantaneous, and perhaps almost involuntary, there was nothing said or done by him to which exception could be taken. Is this evidence of a wanton and reckless disregard for the personal safety of the boys? The conduct which creates a liability to a trespasser in cases of this kind has been referred to in the books in a variety of ways. Sometimes it has been called "gross negligence," and sometimes "willful negligence." Plainly it is something more than is necessary to constitute the gross negligence referred to in our statutes and in decisions of this court. The term "willful negligence" is not a strictly accurate description of the wrong. But wanton and reckless negligence in this class of cases includes something more than ordinary inadvertence. In its essence, it is like a willful, intentional wrong. It is illustrated by an act which otherwise might be unobjectionable, but which is liable or likely to do great harm, and which is done in a wanton and reckless disregard of the probable injurious consequences. This is a wrong of a much more heinous character than common inadvertence. See Aiken v. Holyoke Street Railway Company (Mass.) 68 N. E. 238, and cases there cited. In the present case there is no evidence to show when the brakeman first saw either of the boys, nor whether he had seen more than one of them before he spoke. His language seems to refer to but one person. It is at least as probable that he was speaking to the larger boy, Perry, who was standing on the step on the right-hand side of the car, as to the plaintiff. Perry's position was far more prominent than that of the plaintiff, who was lying on the floor of the car. The fact that the brakeman subsequently walked forward on the side where the plaintiff was is not significant, for, upon all the testimony, there was then nothing threatening in his attitude or manner. When he spoke the cars must have been going very slowly, for the testimony of both of the boys is that they started to jump off as soon as he spoke, and the cars moved only about 50 feet after the plaintiff fell. There was no evidence that the brakes were set at any time. Moreover, Perry testified that when he jumped off he passed around in front of the car and went away. If the cars, stopping of their own inertia, moved only 50 feet after the accident, they had then come almost to a state of rest. The question relates to the state of mind of the brakeman, which can be inferred only from the circumstances. If his language was addressed to the plaintiff, was there, from his point of view, such a probability that he would jump off before the car stopped as to involve any danger of falling? If the plaintiff should start to jump off before the car stopped, was there such a probability that he would get under the wheels as to indicate wantonness and recklessness on the part of the brakeman? There was a stake and a strap or loop step attached to the side of the car, just where the plaintiff was. Besides, the side of the car projected out beyond the track, and, if the plaintiff fell perpendicularly, he would not be likely to fall upon the track. The brakeman had no reason to think that a boy riding upon a car in that way would fail to use such care as he was capable of in getting off, whether he started before the car stopped or afterwards. The undisputed evidence shows that the plaintiff was not acting involuntarily, but was trying to jump from the step, when his foot slipped.

The right of a brakeman upon a train to perform his prescribed duties, even though performance involves something of peril to a trespasser, is stated in Leonard v. Boston & Albany Railroad Company, 170 Mass. 318, 49 N. E. 621. In Planz v. Boston & Albany Railroad Company, 157 Mass. 377, 32 N. E. 356, 17 L. R. A. 835, where the trespasser was injured in jumping from a moving freight train at the command of a brakeman, it was held that there could be no recovery. Mugford v. Boston & Maine Railroad, 173 Mass. 10, 52 N. E. 1078, is very similar to the present case, and it was held that there was no evidence of negligence on the part of the defendant's servant. In that case the plaintiff was a boy a little older than the present plaintiff, but the cars seem to have been running considerably faster than these. See, also, Bolin v. Chicago, St. P., M. & O. Railway Company, 108 Wis. 333, 84 N. W. 446, 81 Am. St. Rep. 911. In view of the duties which the defendant's servant had to perform, and the circumstances attending the accident, we discover no evidence that when he gave his command there was such an apparent probability that it would cause serious injury to the plaintiff as to indicate a wanton and reckless disregard for harmful consequences. If he had owed the plaintiff a duty to make provision for his safety, or to refrain from action which might in any degree expose him to danger, the case would be very different. If the question were whether he exercised such care for the plaintiff's safety as would be deemed reasonable for one charged with a positive duty to look out for him and protect him, it might well be submitted to the jury. If the brakeman's command was given to the plaintiff, as distinguished from the larger boy, in a different situation, it might well be found that he did not exercise a high degree of care for the plaintiff's safety. But such an omission falls short of recklessness which is equivalent to a willful wrong for which he would have been subject to criminal punishment if the accident had caused the plaintiff's death. The burden of proof was upon the plaintiff to show this grave misconduct of the defendant's servant. While we feel that the case is not free from difficulty, we are of opinion that there was no evidence which tends to show that he was guilty of a wanton and reckless disregard for human life and personal safety.

Exceptions sustained.

(185 Mass. 279)

CROWLEY v. FITCHBURG & L. ST. RY. CO.

(Supreme Judicial Court of Massachusetts. Worcester. March 2, 1904.)

CARRIERS—STREET RAILWAY—FALSE IMPRISONMENT—EJECTION FROM CAR—TRANSFERS—HARMLESS ERROR.

1. A regulation of a street railway company requiring a passenger changing from one line to another to produce a transfer or pay his fare is reasonable.

2. The rules of a street railway company required that a passenger, on transferring from one line to another, should produce a transfer, or pay his fare on the second line. Plaintiff, on leaving a car in order to transfer to another line, was not given a transfer by the conductor of the car he was leaving, but such conductor shouted to the other conductor that plaintiff had paid his fare, and that he should be passed. Plaintiff refused to pay a fare on the car to which he transferred, and was ejected by the conductor. *Held*, that the conductor had no right to disregard the rule, and had a right to eject plaintiff.

3. Plaintiff was guilty of an evasion of fare, within the meaning of Rev. Laws, c. 111, § 251, imposing a penalty on any one evading payment of fare on street cars.

4. The rules of a street railway required that a passenger, on transferring from one line to another, should produce a transfer, or pay his fare on the second line. Plaintiff, on leaving a car in order to transfer to another line, was not given a transfer by the conductor of the car he was leaving, but such conductor shouted to the other conductor that plaintiff had paid his fare, and that he should be passed. Plaintiff refused to pay a fare on the car to which he transferred, and he was arrested at the instance of the conductor, who afterwards made a complaint. Rev. Laws, c. 111, § 251, provides a penalty for evading payment of fare on a street car. In an action by plaintiff for false imprisonment, plaintiff offered to show that he had a conversation with the superintendent relative to the prosecution, and that an officer of the company asked for a continuance of the hearing on the complaint. *Held* that, while there was nothing to show that it was within the scope of the conductor's duty to cause plaintiff's arrest, yet, if it had been, the arrest was justified, because of plaintiff's violation of the statute, and hence the exclusion of the offered evidence was harmless.

Exceptions from Superior Court, Worcester County; Elisha B. Maynard, Judge.

Action by Jeremiah Crowley against the Fitchburg & Leominster Street Railway Company. Judgment for defendant, and plaintiff brings exceptions. Exceptions overruled.

J. E. McConnell, for plaintiff. Chas. F. Baker and W. P. Hall, for defendant.

MORTON, J. This is an action of tort to recover damages for an assault, and for a false and malicious arrest and imprisonment. The defendant operates two connecting lines of street railway on Main and Water streets in Fitchburg. A passenger paying his fare on one is entitled to a transfer taking him to his place of destination on the other. But if he changes from one line to the other, the rules of the company require him either to produce a transfer, or in default thereof to pay fare. The plaintiff lived on Water street, and got onto a Main street car to go to his home; changing cars at a place called "Depot Square." He offered a $20 bill in payment of his fare. The conductor was unable to change it, but told him that he would change it when he got to Depot Square, and did, taking out the fare. The Water street car was waiting, and the conductor of that car shouted to the plaintiff to "hurry up." The plaintiff turned to the conductor of the Main street car, and asked for a transfer, but the conductor said, "Never mind your transfer," and shouted to the conductor of the Water street car, who was about 20 feet away, to pass the plaintiff; that he was all right, and had paid his fare, and he (the conductor) had not time to give him a transfer. The plaintiff got upon the Water street car, and an altercation took place between him and the conductor in regard to the payment of his fare. The conductor demanded payment of fare, and the defendant refused, saying that he had paid it. The conductor took hold of him by the arm to eject him, but desisted on a threat of resistance by the plaintiff. The plaintiff did not pay his fare or produce a transfer, and the conductor called upon a policeman to arrest the plaintiff, which he did, and took him to the police station, where he was admitted to bail. The next morning the conductor made a complaint against the plaintiff, but when the case was called the plaintiff was discharged, no evidence being offered. The plaintiff offered to show that he had a conversation with one Sargent, the superintendent of the defendant company, relative to the prosecution of the complaint by the railroad company. There was no statement, if that is material, as to what the conversation was, or what the plaintiff expected to prove by it; and there was no evidence as to the authority of the superintendent, except such as might be inferred from the fact that he was superintendent. This offer, as well as an offer to show that an officer and employé of the company asked for a continuance of the hearing upon the complaint, were excluded, and the plaintiff duly excepted. At the close of the evidence the court directed a verdict for the defendant, and the case is here on exceptions by the plaintiff to this ruling, and the rulings in regard to the evidence offered by the plaintiff and excluded.

We think that the rulings were right. The rule that a passenger changing from one line to the other should produce a transfer, or pay his fare on the line to which he changed, was a reasonable rule, and was known to the plaintiff. Bradshaw v. So. Boston R. Co., 135 Mass. 407, 46 Am. Rep. 481. The conductor had no right to waive it or disregard it, and the plaintiff not having paid his fare on the Water street line, or produced a transfer from the Main street line, the conductor was acting within his rights, and in the performance of his duty, in attempting to eject the plaintiff from the car, and was not guilty of an assault in taking hold of the plaintiff's arm for that purpose. It is immaterial whether the conductor of the Water street car heard what was said to him by the conductor of the Main street car or not. If he did hear it, it was said to him by a conductor whose right to disregard the rules was, so far as appears, no greater than his own; and it gave the conductor of the Water street car no right to carry the plaintiff without the production of a transfer, or the payment, in default thereof, of a fare.

There is nothing to show that it came within the scope of the duty of the conductor of the Water street car to make a complaint against the plaintiff, or to cause his arrest and detention. But if it had been within the scope of his duty, the arrest and detention were clearly justified, and therefore the plaintiff was not harmed by the exclusion of the testimony that was offered. Rev. Laws, c. 111, § 251; Com. v. Jones, 174 Mass. 401, 54 N. E. 869; Dixon v. N. E. R. R., 179 Mass. 242, 247, 60 N. E. 581. The plaintiff knew that the rules of the road required the production of a transfer or the payment of a fare, and it was an evasion of fare, within the meaning of the statute, to ride without producing a transfer, or paying the fare required in default thereof. Com. v. Jones, supra; Dixon v. N. E. R. R., supra.

Exceptions overruled.

(185 Mass. 229)

SMITH v. WENZ.

(Supreme Judicial Court of Massachusetts. Suffolk. Feb. 27, 1904.)

LANDLORD AND TENANT—LEASE—PROVISIONS —CONSTRUCTION—FURNISHING STEAM —ACTION BY LANDLORD.

1. A provision in a lease to the effect that the lessee should have the privilege to connect a pipe to the steam supply pipe to draw steam for use in his confectionery business, provided the same could be done without extra expense to the lessor, did not mean that the steam should cost the lessor mathematically nothing, but that the lessee should be entitled to have furnished him steam which, having relation to the entire plant and the lessee's business, should be of no considerable cost to the landlord.

2. A lease provided that the tenant should have the privilege of connecting a pipe to the steam supply pipe to draw steam for use in his confectionery business, provided it could be done without extra expense to the lessor. The tenant requested such connection, and the landlord's engineer, who had charge of all matters connected with the steam, made the connection with the pipe which carried live steam from the boiler to the engine, and the tenant supposed he was not using any steam save that furnished under the lease. Rent bills were presented monthly and paid, and no demand made for compensation for the steam for more than four years after the commencement of the tenancy, when the landlord examined into the matter, and then claimed that the steam should have been taken after it left the engine. *Held*, that the landlord could not recover for steam furnished, before giving the tenant any notice that such use of the steam was not within the terms of the lease.

Report from Superior Court, Suffolk County; Albert Mason, Judge.

Action by one Smith against one Wenz. Judgment for plaintiff, and the case was reported to the Supreme Judicial Court. Judgment for plaintiff.

G. W. Anderson, for plaintiff. Samuel C. Bennett and Hugh D. McLellan, for defendant.

HAMMOND, J. This is an action of contract to recover for steam power, cooking steam, and water alleged by the plaintiff to have been supplied by her to the defendant. By the terms of the lease the defendant, a manufacturer of confectionery, was to hold as tenant certain portions of a building owned by the plaintiff, "including steam necessary to heat the existing heating apparatus during business hours in cold weather, * * * together with three horse power to be furnished by the lessor to a pulley on the premises during ordinary business hours." The lessee was "to put up his own shafting, belting and machinery"; and it was further provided that "if the lessor shall furnish and the lessee shall use power in addition to said three horse power, then the lessee" agrees to pay for such additional power "so used at the rate of $95 per year per horse power, in monthly proportions, on the days and as hereinafter provided, for rent." It was still further provided that the lessee was to have the "privilege to connect a pipe to the steam supply pipe to draw steam for use in the confectionery or in his business, when steam is in the supply pipe, provided same can be done without extra expense to lessor, or those representing her, either for making changes or for supplying steam." The lessee was to pay rent at the rate of $2,800 a year, in equal monthly payments of $236.67, on the 15th day of every month, and also an additional sum, as above stated, for extra horse power. The lease contained certain other provisions, but they do not seem to have any bearing on the question before us.

It therefore appears that ordinarily steam was used in this building both for heating and for power, and that, to the extent named in the lease, the lessee was entitled to use it for both purposes. It further appears that, in the business of manufacturing confectionery, steam could be used for "cooking," and consequently there was given to the defendant the right, under certain conditions, to draw steam from the supply pipe for that purpose. For this no extra compensation was to be paid. It was one of the rights the payment for which formed a part of the sum named as rent. The lease was dated May 15, 1898, and on that day the defendant began his occupation of the tenement. Shortly after this, at the request of the defendant, "the system of pipes running to his various heating kettles was connected with the pipe carrying the live steam from the boiler to the engine." The only question before us is whether the plaintiff is entitled to recover anything for this cooking steam.

The connection was made at the request of the defendant, and, as he supposed, in order that he might enjoy the privilege given him by the lease to use cooking steam. Neither in making the request, nor in using the steam, did he suppose, or have any reason to suppose, that he was using any cooking steam except that furnished under the terms of the lease. Nor does it appear that the plaintiff's engineer who made the connection supposed that he was doing anything not provided for by the lease. Whether the term "steam supply pipe" means, on the one hand, the pipe carrying the waste steam, after the same had been used by the engine, through the building, where it was used for heating purposes, as contended by the plaintiff, or, on the other, the pipe carrying "live steam" from the boiler to the engine, as contended by the defendant, it is certain that the connection was such as the defendant thought he was entitled to have, and that it was made by the engineer, who, as to all matters connected with the steam and mechanical appliances, had general charge as the agent of the plaintiff. It further appears that the rent bills were presented monthly and were promptly paid, that no demand was ever made upon the defendant for payment for cooking steam until the fall of 1902, when, owing to the extraordinary price of coal, the plaintiff made close examination into the matter of steam, and discovered the facts. The plaintiff's husband was her general agent in the management of the building, was frequently in and about it, including the leased premises, and he generally presented the monthly bills and received payment therefor. The court found that he, in the exercise of reasonable and proper care, should have known the facts about the connection and the use. The right to the use was conditional, it is true, but we agree with the trial court that the condition was not that the steam which the defendant was to have from the plaintiff's pipes should cost absolutely or mathematically nothing, but that the defendant should be entitled to have furnished by the plaintiff steam which, having relation to the entire plant and the defendant's business, should be of no considerable cost to the plaintiff. Whether at any time the steam used by the defendant was of any considerable cost to the plaintiff, or, in other words, whether at any time the defendant was using steam in violation of this condition, was a matter within the peculiar knowledge of the plaintiff, and not of the defendant.

Here, then, is a case where a defendant, intending to act under the terms of his lease and not otherwise, asks for the connection in order that he may use the steam; the connection is made by the engineer of the plaintiff for that purpose; and the defendant, acting all the time in good faith, proceeds to use the steam. There is no fraud or secrecy on his part. He believes, and has reason to believe from the conduct of the plaintiff and her husband, that all this is known to her, and that she acquiesces. Under these circumstances, justice to the defendant requires that he should be notified that, in the opinion of the plaintiff, at least, the use of the steam is no longer within the terms granted in the lease, so that the defendant may choose whether to discontinue the use or try to make some new arrangement. And the ignorance of the plaintiff, due to her own want of proper care in the management of her business, and not in any way to the conduct of the defendant, does not excuse her from giving such notice. The ruling that the plaintiff cannot recover for steam furnished before such a notice was right. See Boston Ice Co. v. Potter, 123 Mass. 28, 25 Am. Rep. 9.

In accordance with the terms of the report, there must be judgment on the finding for $1,322.69 and interest.

(185 Mass. 236)

AMERICAN TUBEWORKS v. TUCKER.

(Supreme Judicial Court of Massachusetts. Suffolk. Feb. 27, 1904.)

WILL—CONDITIONS—AGENCY—EVIDENCE—ESTOPPEL—INSTRUCTIONS.

1. Instructions as to a case as shown by an auditor's report, where there was other evidence introduced, being a ruling on the effect of a part of the evidence considered separately from the rest, were properly refused.

2. Where a will bequeathed the testator's business to his son, title not to vest till the son should give a guaranty that he would pay the debts owing on account of the business, this condition, being for the benefit of the beneficiaries under the will, does not give any right of action by one who transacted business with the son after the testator's death against the executrix for permitting the son to take charge of the business before giving the guaranty.

3. Evidence *held* sufficient to sustain a finding that a testator's business was being carried on by his son on his own account, and not as agent of the executrix.

4. Evidence in an action against an executrix on an indebtedness incurred by her son in carrying on the testator's business *held* to present a question for the jury whether plaintiff was misled by the actions of the executrix into believing that the son carried on the business as her agent, so as to estop her to deny that he was her agent.

Exceptions from Superior Court, Suffolk County; John A. Aiken, Judge.

Action by the American Tubeworks against Mary A. Tucker. Judgment for defendant, and plaintiff excepts. Exceptions overruled.

M. J. Creed, J. Porter Crosby, and Walter A. Buie, for plaintiff. Anson M. Lyman, for defendant.

HAMMOND, J. The plaintiff seeks to hold the defendant, first, upon the ground that she, as executrix of the will of her late husband, Isaac N. Tucker, was carrying on the business through her son, Charles, as her agent; and, second, on the ground that she, by her acts and omission to act when she should have acted, and by her conduct in general, permitted Charles to hold himself out as conducting the business for the estate, and the plaintiff, in reliance upon that representation, parted with its goods, and that therefore she is estopped to deny that she is individually responsible to the plaintiff. Shortly stated, the contention of the plaintiff is that the defendant is responsible either because she was the contracting party or because she is estopped to deny that she was.

The second, third, and fourth requests relate simply to the case as shown in the auditor's report, and, inasmuch as there was other evidence introduced at the trial, they are open to the objection that they were requests for a ruling upon the effect of only a part of the evidence considered separately from the rest, and it is well settled that that is a sufficient reason for the refusal of the court to give them. We pass, therefore, to the consideration of the first request, which was, in substance, that on the evidence a verdict should be ordered for the plaintiff. At the death of the husband in October, 1899, the situation was peculiar. He had been carrying on the plumbing business for years, but for the last few months of his life he had not been able to attend to it, and the son, Charles, "had been in entire charge thereof, consulting often with his father." The will contained a bequest to Charles of "the business now carried on by me, together with all stock in trade, apparatus, tools and utensils, books and book accounts, contracts, and all things pertaining to said business." Several conditions were annexed to the bequest, one of which was that, in addition to other sums, Charles should pay the "debts owing * * * on account of the business." The plain intent of the testator was that Charles, upon complying with the conditions, or giving a guaranty of compliance, should take the business as it was, with the right to all the assets, including book accounts and unfinished contracts, and should be liable to pay all the business liabilities then existing. In a word, the testator intended that both as to assets and liabilities his son should stand with reference to the business as he (the testator) stood at the time of his death. After the death of his father, Charles assumed charge and control of the business, and the defendant, neither as executrix nor as an individual, assumed any control or drew any money from the business; and the evidence tended to show that both the defendant and Charles believed that upon the death of the father the business passed under the will to Charles as his own, and that he took possession and carried it on not as the agent of his mother, but as legatee under the will. It is true that he collected the bills which were unpaid at the time of his father's death, and that he paid many of the business debts left by his father, but in doing all this the jury might have found that, as between him and the estate, he was acting under the rights granted to and the responsibilities imposed upon him as legatee by the will. To a certain extent, so far as respected the business, he had, upon this view, assumed as legatee to do what ordinarily is done by an executor. If he was thus acting, the fact is important, and it furnishes a reasonable explanation of his conduct in doing in the business many things the duty to do which primarily rested upon the executrix. So far as respects the inventory sworn to a few weeks after the testator's death and filed in the probate court in June, 1900, it may be said that, since the property in the business was a part of the assets of the testator's estate, it was the duty of the executrix to charge herself with it in the inventory; and that was so even if she had delivered the property to the legatee. Nor do we think that the method of keeping the bank account, as it is explained by the witnesses, is conclusive in favor of the view that the defendant was carrying on the business.

It is urged, however, by the plaintiff that the son had not complied with the conditions of the bequest, and that therefore the defendant had no right to turn the business over to him; and the twelfth request embodies that proposition in substance. Upon that point the jury were instructed to the effect that this requirement of a guaranty was for the protection of the beneficiaries under the will, and that, if the executrix saw fit to turn over the business to Charles without a guaranty, or before a performance of the conditions named in the will, she might be liable to any parties aggrieved by that action, but that the plaintiff was not such a party, so far as material to this case; and that while the fact that Charles had not complied with the conditions could be taken into consideration upon the question whether the business had been turned over to him, still it would not prevent Charles from carrying on the business on his own account. This seems to us to be correct. The question was whether Charles was actually carrying on the business on his own account with the consent of the executrix, and not whether she ought to have consented. Without a further recital of the evidence, it is sufficient to say that the question whether the business was being carried on by the son on his own account or as agent for the defendant was a question of fact, and that in the evidence before the jury there is no fact conclusive against the validity of the finding that the son carried on the business on his own account. So far, therefore, as respects the first ground upon which the plaintiff relies, it was not entitled, as matter of law, to a verdict in its favor.

We now pass to the question of liability by estoppel. Assuming that the defendant did not carry on the business, has her conduct been such as to estop her from setting up that defense? The auditor finds that "the plaintiff and its agents never knew, saw, or had any communication with the defendant," that she had nothing to do with the business, and that "there was no evidence that the plaintiff was misled by any verbal statements to it either by Charles B. Tucker or by the defendant." He also reports that, while the defendant never gave any notice to the plaintiff that she was not carrying on the business, or that the estate was not carrying it on, or that any change had been made in it, or that Charles B. Tucker was not her agent, still she testified before him that she never gave any authority to Charles to "purchase goods of the plaintiff, or of any one, in the name of the estate of I. N. Tucker, and that she never gave him authority to sign promissory notes for her, or for the estate of I. N. Tucker." The auditor further finds that "the goods in the account of the plaintiff were never * * * delivered to her." He further finds that "it did not appear when the plaintiff had actual notice of the death of Isaac N. Tucker," but that "the plaintiff's account was carried along on its books as charged to I. N. Tucker until May 4, 1900, after which all charges in the account were made to 'Estate of I. N. Tucker' "; that the defendant "never knew or heard of the plaintiff until this action was brought," but that "she knew that the business was being conducted in part under the name of I. N. Tucker and Estate of I. N. Tucker"; and that "the defendant supposed, and was acting under the belief, that Charles B. Tucker had a right under the will to take the property as his own." While there was considerable other evidence, still the jury may have thought that the auditor's conclusions upon these various points were right.

Upon the question of estoppel the plaintiff chiefly relies, however, on the conduct of the defendant with reference to the bank account kept in the name of "Estate of I. N. Tucker." The auditor finds that Charles used this, and no other, bank account in his business, drawing checks under the style of "Estate of I. N. Tucker, by Charles B. Tucker, Attorney." The defendant never drew any checks on this account. It appears that in December, 1899, the defendant signed a power of attorney authorizing Charles to draw, as her attorney, any check upon this account, and to indorse for deposit and collection any check payable to the estate, whether in the name of I. N. Tucker or Estate of I. N. Tucker, or herself as executrix. Charles testified before the auditor that he wanted this power because "checks kept coming in in name of the estate of I. N. Tucker." The jury may have found from all the evidence, including the testimony of Charles and the defendant, that, inasmuch as the old bills due the estate on account of the business as well as those due from the estate on the same account were to be settled in the name of the estate by Charles, in accordance with the conditions of the bequest to him, the purpose in giving this power of attorney was to enable him to do this part of the business, primarily a part of the defendant's duty as executrix; and that with one or two exceptions she never knew or supposed that he was using the power for any other purpose. Moreover, it is to be observed that the check of July 27, 1900—the only one set out or described in full, although signed by Charles as attorney for the estate—is payable, not to the plaintiff, but to the order of Charles B. Tucker, and is indorsed by him. It does not distinctly appear that any check signed in this way was ever made payable upon its face to the plaintiff, and each one may have been in the same form as the one just named. It is true that the notes were made payable to the order of the plaintiff, but that is not material on the question of the estoppel by the power of attorney. The evidence tends to show that the defendant never knew of the notes before the suit was begun. It is true that the auditor has found that the defendant knew the business was being conducted in part under the name of I. N. Tucker and Estate of I. N. Tucker, but that knowledge would not of itself make her liable.

But we do not further discuss the matter of her conduct with reference to the alleged estoppel, because it was a question for the jury whether the plaintiff was in any way misled by her actions as to the checks or in any other respect. The plaintiff never knew anything of this power of attorney. It does not appear that any single check signed thereunder was made directly to the plaintiff, or that the plaintiff relied in any respect upon the form of the check or signature in parting with its goods. While a strong argument might be made to show that the plaintiff was misled, still no witness called by the plaintiff testified to that effect. It is plain that on the evidence the questions arising out of the alleged liability on the ground of estoppel were questions for the jury. The court therefore properly declined to give the first ruling requested.

As already stated, the twelfth request was properly refused. The instruction to the jury as to the matter contained in the seventeenth request were accurate, and sufficiently full.

Exceptions overruled.

(185 Mass. 303)

MUSKEGET ISLAND CLUB v. TOWN OF NANTUCKET.

(Supreme Judicial Court of Massachusetts. Bristol. March 9, 1904.)

WITNESSES—EXPERTS—QUALIFICATION—QUESTION FOR COURT—LAND VALUES—EXCLUSION OF WITNESSES—SUFFICIENCY OF RECORD.

1. Whether a witness offered as an expert is qualified to testify as such is to be decided by the presiding justice as a question of fact, and his decision is conclusive unless upon the evidence it appears erroneous in law.

2. One who had been a resident of a town for 60 years, for 26 of which he was a farmer, and who had traded to a considerable extent for himself and others in land situated in the town; who had seen the land in question, and knew its situation and general character; had held important town offices for years—among others, that of assessor, in the discharge of which he had appraised the land for six different years about the time when it was taken—was qualified to testify as an expert to its value.

3. On an issue of the value of land taken for a park, while one of the uses to which the land was put was that of shooting, yet its market value was to be determined in view of all the purposes for which it was adapted or might be used.

4. Where the only question before the court was not whether the witness' testimony would be material, but whether he was qualified to testify as an expert, and he was excluded solely on the latter ground, an exception to the exclusion may be reviewed without incorporating in the record what the testimony of the witness would have been, or what was expected to be proved by him.

Exceptions from Superior Court, Bristol County; Fred K. Lawton, Judge.

Action for damages for land taken for a public park on the Island of Muskeget under St. 1895, p. 489, c. 442, by the Muskeget Island Club against the town of Nantucket. Respondent excepted to a refusal to admit the evidence of a certain witness to the land taken. Exceptions sustained.

Harvey N. Shepard, for plaintiff. Elder & Whitman, for defendant.

HAMMOND, J. The question whether a witness offered as an expert is qualified to testify as such is to be decided by the presiding justice as a question of fact, and his decision is conclusive unless upon the evidence it appears erroneous in law. Perkins v. Stickney, 132 Mass. 217. We cannot say that in coming to the conclusion that the several witnesses called by the petitioner were qualified the judge erred in law. In each case the evidence justified the finding. But we think that the evidence as to Folger did not warrant his exclusion. He testified that he had lived in Nantucket over 60 years, and for the last 17 years had held town offices, prior to which time he had been a farmer for 26 years; that he had known a great deal of all kinds of land in Nantucket, and had bought and sold for himself and other people; that he knew only by hearsay whether land had been sold for shooting places on the sandy beaches, but had heard of some sales on Eel Point for that purpose. He further testified that he had been an assessor of the town of Nantucket for six years, being the years 1888 to 1891, both inclusive, 1896 and 1897, and in that capacity had assessed the island of Muskeget; that he never had visited Muskeget, but had visited the Island of Tuckernuck and Eel Point and Smith Point, the western points of Nantucket, where his father had lived. He also testified that, while he never had been on Muskeget he had sailed within half a mile of it; that he knew it was a sand heap; that he knew nothing of the shooting

¶ 3. See Eminent Domain, vol. 18, Cent. Dig. § 356.

there except from his friends "who go shooting there"; and that he had seen a great deal of shooting on Smith and Eel Points, and had been there a great many times. We do not understand that any of these statements are taken to be untrue, or that the witness was excluded upon the ground of mental infirmity from age or any other cause. Here, then, is a man who has been a resident of the town for 60 years, for 26 years of which time he was a farmer; who has traded to a considerable extent for himself and others in land situated in the town; who has seen the land in question, and knows its situation and general character; who is somewhat acquainted with shooting in that vicinity; who has held important town offices for years; and who, above all, has been called upon, in the discharge of his official duty and under his official oath as an assessor for six different years close around the time when the land was taken, some before and some after the taking, to appraise this very land, and declare its market value. It seems clear that upon this testimony he is qualified as an expert. He was a typical islander, apparently of the most reliable character, had passed his life in that vicinity, and in many ways, especially in his capacity as an assessor, had had his attention called to this land, and in the latter capacity had valued it under an official oath. The knowledge, in part, at least, was acquired as an officer whose duty it was to ascertain the value of this land for purposes of taxation. See Swan v. Middlesex, 101 Mass. 173, 177. If it be said that the petitioner's claim was based upon the value of the land for shooting purposes, the answer is that, while that may have been one of the purposes to which it might be devoted, yet it could not have been certain that the jury would take that view, and the real question was its fair market value in view of all the purposes for which it was adapted or might be used. The fact also that Folger had not been upon the land was of but little, if any, importance under the circumstances, so far as respected its character. It was what it appeared to him to be—a sand heap.

It is argued by the petitioner that, inasmuch as the record fails to show what the testimony of Folger would have been, or what the respondents expected to prove by him, the exception to his exclusion should not be sustained; and in support of that proposition it relies upon those cases where an exception to the exclusion of a question has been overruled upon the ground that the record does not show what the witness was expected to say, or, if permitted to answer, would have said. In such a case it does not appear that the exclusion of the question resulted in the exclusion of any evidence material to the issue. But here it is plain that the only question then before the court was not whether the testimony of the witness, if he were allowed to give it, would be material, but whether he was qualified to testify as an expert; and he was excluded not because his testimony would be immaterial, but on the ground that he was not qualified to testify at all. We think that the rule upon which the petitioner relies should not be extended to such a case.

Exceptions sustained.

(185 Mass. 160)

In re DIRECTORS OF OLD COLONY R. CO.

(Supreme Judicial Court of Massachusetts. Suffolk. Feb. 26, 1904.)

RAILROADS—ABOLITION OF GRADE CROSSINGS—REIMBURSEMENT FOR EXPENSES.

1. Under St. 1890, pp. 463–465, c. 428, §§ 3–7, providing for the abolition of certain grade crossings by the Old Colony Railroad Company, commissioners were to decide what alterations were necessary, and prescribe how they should be made, etc., and the expense of abolishing the grade crossings, for a percentage of which the company was entitled to claim reimbursement from the commonwealth, was restricted to "the actual cost of the alterations, including in such cost the cost of the hearing and the compensation of the commissioners and auditors for their services and all damages" for the taking of the necessary land. St. 1892, p. 536, c. 433, under which the work was done, was enacted subject to the provisions of the former act, and the items of costs were the same in both, though the percentage to be borne by the company was reduced. *Held*, that the interest paid on money borrowed by the company to make alterations was not a part of the "actual cost" for which it was entitled to claim reimbursement.

Report from Superior Court, Suffolk County; Franklin G. Fessenden, Judge.

Petition by the directors of the Old Colony Railroad Company for reimbursement for the expense of abolishing certain grade crossings. The decree disallowed a certain item of expenditure, and the case is reported to the Supreme Judicial Court. Decree affirmed.

Andrew J. Bailey, for city of Boston. J. H. Benton, Jr., for Old Colony R. Co. Robt. G. Dodge, Asst. Atty. Gen., and Fred T. Field, for the Commonwealth.

BRALEY, J. Under St. 1892, p. 536, c. 433, the Old Colony Railroad Company has made the alterations and improvements called for by the act, and rendered necessary by the abolition of certain grade crossings of the tracks of the Boston & Providence Railroad Company according to the plan prescribed by commissioners duly appointed for that purpose under the provisions of St. 1890, p. 463, c. 428. The expenses of this work were to be paid in the first instance by the railroad company, and for that purpose it was authorized to issue and sell its stock from time to time in order to raise the money, but not to exceed an amount named. A certain percentage of these expenses was to be repaid to the company by the commonwealth, which in turn was to be reimbursed in part by the city of Boston. At reasonable periods of time as the work proceeded the company presented to the auditor for examination and allowance a statement of its disbursements and expenses connected therewith, and made a claim in each statement for interest at the rate of 4 per cent. actually paid for money hired by it, to carry out and complete the alterations, and improvements directed by the commissioners. In his twenty-first report the auditor states this claim as follows: "Item 5. Interest paid on money expended in payments for lands taken, damages caused, and construction, all as required to be paid under said acts, the same being interest at four per cent. on the several items of expenditures from their respective date of payment to the dates when the same were repaid under decrees of court providing for the payment thereof." No question is raised that interest has not been paid on the sums named and at the rate specified. Neither is it claimed that the postponement of the presentation of the final detailed statement in its entirety of this demand has caused any additional burden to the commonwealth, if it properly can be allowed, as interest is charged as an expenditure only from the date of payment to the date when a claim could be made for repayment to the extent of the reclamation permitted against the state. St. 1892, p. 536, c. 433, was a special act, and it was enacted subject to the provisions of St. 1890, pp. 463-466, c. 428, §§ 1-8, inclusive, in so far as these sections do not conflict with its terms. It does not appear that the Legislature intended to lay down any different rule under one, from that provided by the other, and the items of cost for which the company is to be reimbursed are the same in both acts, though the percentage of the whole outlay to be borne by it is reduced. The commissioners decide what alterations are necessary for the safety and convenience of the public, and "shall prescribe the manner and limits within which such alterations shall be made, and shall determine which party shall do the work," and "the railroad company shall pay sixty-five per cent. of the actual cost of the alterations, including in such cost the cost of the hearing and the compensation of the commissioners and auditors for their services, and all damages" for the taking of land necessary to carry out the alterations that have been ordered. St. 1890, pp. 463-465, c. 428, §§ 3-7. The cost incurred by the company, and for which it is to be finally repaid, are the necessary disbursements required to make the alterations ordered by the commissioners; and to meet this expense it may pay from funds in its treasury, or issue and sell its stock, or it might go into the market and hire what was necessary on its negotiable paper. The special act evidently contemplated paying for the work from time to time as it proceeded, and upon the report and allowance of the amount due by the auditor.

The ground upon which the petitioners put their claim is that money paid by way of interest on money used to pay for the alterations is a part of the "actual cost." In a broad sense this is true of a railroad company which is obliged to hire money to meet the obligation imposed by the statute. Interruption of the regular running of trains, caused by extensive changes in its tracks, loss of traffic that is thereby caused, and any consequential and incidental damages arising from the interruption necessarily incident to the adjustment of a railroad system, in whole or in part to the changes that may be required under these statutes may not improperly be called an expense to the company so affected. No illustration can make a distinction stronger than the case itself, for, if such an item is to be included either under the term "expense" or that of "actual cost," then there is no logical limit to sweeping into such a classification everything that directly or collaterally calls for expenditure, or cost, or loss by a railroad company that is compelled under the statute to carry out the order of commissioners, when approved by the court, for the abolition of one or more of the grade crossings of its road. That such a construction would open the door to let in claims that would be not only large in amount, but uncertain and contingent in their character, is reasonably clear. If the Legislature had intended to include such claims as a part of such cost and expenses caused by and arising from the alterations ordered under St. 1890, p. 463, c. 428, now Rev. Laws, c. 111, §§ 149-160, the act would have contained language making this intention clear.

The only attempt to enumerate the items of expense are those named in the statute, and the phrase "actual cost" means the cost of what is described; though, where damages are incurred in taking land to carry out the report of the commissioners, counsel fees and extra work done by selectmen, paid by a town in defending or settling a claim for such damages for land taken for the purpose of abolishing grade crossings, have been held to be included. Boston & Albany Railroad Co. v. Inhabitants of Charleston, 161 Mass. 32, 36 N. E. 688. With this exception, unless "actual cost" and "expense" are to be taken as equivalent in meaning to the term, full compensation for any and all expenses in whatever form they may be sustained, which is a construction that, in view of the language used, and the general purpose of the act for the abolition of grade crossings, cannot be adopted, it must be held that these words have the limited definition given to them by the statute, and cannot be extended to include the claim of the petitioners. Newton, Pet'r, 172 Mass. 5-10, 51 N. E. 183; Providence & Worcester Railroad Company, Pet'r, 172 Mass. 117-121, 51 N. E. 459; Selectmen o Norwood, Pet'rs, 183 Mass. 147, 66 N. E. 637; Selectmen of Westborough, Pet'rs, 184 Mass. 107-111, 68 N. E. 30.

Decree affirmed.

(185 Mass. 264)

MOORE v. RAWSON et al.

(Supreme Judicial Court of Massachusetts. Suffolk. March 2, 1904.)

PARTNERSHIP—ACCOUNTING—RIGHTS OF RETIRING AND CONTINUING MEMBERS—APPEAL AND ERROR.

1. In the absence of an exception to a ruling of a master, it will be presumed that the ruling has been accepted by the parties.

2. Where an individual, who had been engaged as a manufacturer under a trade-name, entered a partnership under an agreement that the place of business as well as the name and style of the firm should be the same as under the individual's ownership, the property right to the trade-name passed to the firm without being distinctly enumerated.

3. Where a partner, who is notified by his copartners of a dissolution of the firm under the terms of the contract of partnership, demands his share in the assets of the firm, and is met with a denial by the continuing members of the firm that he has any rights in the partnership property, it is not necessary for him to specify the various items that make up the property of the partnership in which he claims his rights as a partner in order to save himself from the possible defense of having waived any claim that there was a good will to the business.

4. Where a partnership is dissolved pursuant to its terms, the interest of the partners in the assets of the firm becomes several, subject only to the payment of the debts of the partnership and the proper settlement of the accounts between them.

5. Where a partnership is dissolved pursuant to its terms, the continuing members of the firm are estopped to deny that the good will of the partnership had no salable value, where they forcibly and wrongfully appropriate to their own use the property of which the good will was a part.

6. Where a partnership has been in existence for a time long enough to establish a business sufficiently permanent in character to include not only its customers but the incidents of locality and distinctive name, a good will exists which forms an asset of commercial value in a winding up between the partners.

7. The fact that the good will of a partnership may be difficult of appraisement, is no legal reason for denying to a retiring partner an appraisal where there is proof that he is entitled to it.

8. Where a partnership is dissolved pursuant to its terms, but the continuing members refuse to pay over to the retiring partner his share of the assets, the continuing members are placed in a fiduciary relation to him in the care and management of his share until they finally wind up and settle the affairs of the partnership.

9. Where a partnership is dissolved pursuant to its terms, but the continuing members refuse to pay over to the retiring partner his share of the assets, they are bound at his election to pay to him the share of the profits which his portion of the assets earned for the time the continuing members use his capital, or to allow interest for its use.

10. Where a partnership is dissolved pursuant to its terms, but the continuing members wrongfully refuse to pay over to the retiring partner his share in the assets, whether the continuing members shall be allowed anything for their skill and services for the time the retiring partner's assets are used is within the discretion and control of the court, and does not rest in contract made by partners.

11. Where a partnership was dissolved pursuant to its terms, but the continuing members refuse to pay over to the retiring partner his share of the assets, an allowance to them of so much of the net profits as are found to be due to their skill and ability is proper on accounting with the retiring partner, in which he elects to take his share of the profits arising from the continuation of the business.

Case Reserved from Supreme Judicial Court, Suffolk County; Jas. M. Barker, Judge.

Bill for accounting by one Moore against Daniel G. Rawson and another. Case reserved for Supreme Court on report of master. Decree ordered for complainant.

George R. Swasey and Michael J. Dwyer, for plaintiff. Warner, Warner & Stackpole, for defendants.

BRALEY, J. Between March 14, 1872, the time when the bill was filed, and the coming in of the master's report, this case has been pending before the court for more than 30 years. Those originally connected with it, either as counsel or appointed as masters to hear the parties on the issues to be tried, have been removed by death. A part of the pleadings have been either lost or destroyed, and the books of account of the partnership, kept at the office in Boston, and showing all its business transactions, were damaged almost to the point of destruction by the great fire of November, 1872. The defendant Daniel G. Rawson, the only member of the partnership who was familiar with the business of the firm and the contents of the books, became insane, and died without ever having given his evidence in the case; and the bookkeeper, who knew of its business transactions as shown by the books of account kept by him, also died before his testimony was taken. The masters to whom from time to time the case had been referred did not live to make any report, though in one instance all the evidence had been submitted and arguments made. In the beginning the plaintiff asked for the usual accounting arising upon the dissolution of the partnership, but as the case proceeded it broadened into an additional demand for actual profits received by the defendants from the use of his capital after dissolution. But no supplemental bill was filed, the defendants conceding that the plaintiff might have, under the original bill, equitable relief commensurate with his claims, subject, however, to any defense that they might interpose. On January 25, 1897, the case was again referred to a master, and his report, as amended and confirmed by an interlocutory decree of February 20, 1903, together with all questions of law raised and stated either in the report or open under the decree have been reserved for our decision.

It is plain from this brief recital of the history of the course of litigation that in any attempt now made to determine the questions raised many obstacles would be found, and embarrassments arise, not only by the death of witnesses, but from the absence of important evidence which had perished without any fault of the parties. But out of such testimony as could be found and presented the master has succeeded in making certain findings of fact, and in stating the rights of the parties, in a full and clear report. Though the plaintiff took a very large number of exceptions, it does not become necessary to take them up in detail, as they may be grouped and considered under the classification presented in the report and at the argument.

Before considering them, it becomes necessary to ascertain the plaintiff's legal standing, and his right to demand and receive an accounting from the defendants. The contract of partnership signed by the parties dated January 1, 1870, was formed "for the purpose of the manufacture and sale of boots and shoes," and among other stipulations provided that "this firm shall be dissolved at the expiration of any year hereafter (within the term of three years aforesaid) by the written consent and wish of any three members of said firm giving notice of such consent or wish in writing at such termination of any such years to each of the members thereof." Dissatisfaction over the conduct of the business by the plaintiff appears to have arisen between him and Daniel G. Rawson, and after a dispute over the affairs of the firm, on December 20, 1871, notice was given to the plaintiff by his partners, Daniel G. Rawson, W. B. Fay, and C. S. Goddard, of their intention to terminate the partnership at the expiration of the year 1871, as provided in the agreement. The master finds and reports that under ordinary conditions the dissolution took place, and the account should be stated, as at the close of business December 31, 1871, "but the destruction of the principal books of account by fire, the death of parties and witnesses, * * * make it impossible to state an accurate account as of December 31, 1871." "The master has endeavored to state the account of December 20, 1871, which was the date of the firm's annual taking of stock." No exception is taken to this ruling, and it must be treated as having been accepted by the parties. Upon all the evidence before him he finds and reports that at that time the amount due the plaintiff, exclusive of good will, upon a winding up and settlement of the affairs of the firm, was $13,529.58. As the defendants took no exceptions to the report, this finding must be considered acceptable to them, and of this sum they paid into court, for the use of the plaintiff, December 27, 1873, the amount of $12,483.63. It is the contention of the plaintiff that this sum should be increased by the value of his interest in the good will of the business, and also by the addition of profits which accrued subsequently on his share of the assets in their use by the defendants. Before the formation of the partnership the defendant Daniel G. Rawson was a manufacturer of boots and shoes, and carried on business under the name of "D. G. Rawson & Co.," with a factory at Worcester and an office in Boston. In the articles of partnership it was stipulated that the place of business, as well as the name and style of the firm, should be the same; and by force of the agreement, if there was any property in the trade-name, it passed to the firm, without being distinctly enumerated. Sohier v. Johnson, 111 Mass. 238-242; Whitcomb v. Converse, 119 Mass. 38-43, 20 Am. Rep. 311; Boon v. Moss, 70 N. Y. 470-473. After the dissolution by the enforced withdrawal of Moore, no change was made, but the defendants continued the business as before until December 31, 1872, when a new partnership was formed, consisting of four persons, three of whom were the retiring partners of the old firm, and the defendants in this case. No change, however, was then made either in the firm name, which continued to be that of "D. G. Rawson & Co.," or in the place where the business was located, and the defendants took over the assets of the old firm, not for the purpose of liquidation, but for use in their business. And the customers who had patronized the first continued to trade with them and the second partnership. The plaintiff retired not only from the firm, but also from the business that it carried on, while the defendants retained the old place of business, and conducted it, under the old firm name. In other words, no change, apparent or real, was made in an enterprise which was transferred bodily from the old partnership to the new, except that one partner was obliged to retire under the terms of the old contract, and after a short period, by a new agreement, another was taken in his place. The attitude of the defendants up to the time of the payment of the money into court was evidently that of a general denial of any right of the plaintiff to an accounting. Their conduct and motives in dissolving the firm are stated in their second answer in the words, "And they did so by reason of the incapacity, inattention, and inefficiency of the plaintiff in the affairs of the firm, and these defendants found it necessary to the safety and interests of the firm to close the partnership." No evidence was introduced to support this allegation, and the master reports that "up to the time of dissolution the plaintiff had devoted himself faithfully to the business of the firm," and during its existence he had sold substantially "eighty-five per cent." of all goods made by it, and "had a very substantial influence in building up the established list of customers." A trading partnership that had apparently achieved this large measure of success in its business, an appreciable part of which was due to the skill and ability of the plaintiff, might have a good will that upon dissolution would form a valuable part of its assets; and the plaintiff now contends that such good will existed, and that his interest therein is to be valued and added to his share of the assets already found.

When he demanded that his share in the assets of the firm should be paid over, it was not necessary for him to specify the various items that made up the property of the partnership in which he claimed his rights as a partner, in order to save himself from the possible defense of having waived any claim that there was a good will to the business. At the dissolution the interest of the partners in the assets of the firm became several, and subject only to the payment of the debts of the partnership and a proper settlement of the accounts between them. Yale v. Eames, 1 Metc. 486, 487; Sanborn v. Royce, 132 Mass. 594, 595; Pratt v. McGuinness, 173 Mass. 170, 53 N. E. 380; Bank v. N. O. & Carrolton R. R. Co., 11 Wall. 624, 20 L. Ed. 82. The general demand made by him was sufficient and broad enough to include its entire property. He was not asked to give a particular enumeration of the various items comprising it, but the attitude of the defendants towards him is well stated in the words of Daniel G. Rawson, who, at the interview in which the demand was made, "denied that there was anything of value to which the plaintiff had any right." Hoxie v. Chaney, 143 Mass. 592-594, 10 N. E. 713, 58 Am. Rep. 149. If the defendants had wound up and adjusted the affairs of the partnership by a sale of all of the property, and for the accomplishment of this result they had sold the business as a whole, and as designated by the firm name, the good will would have passed, and they must have accounted to the plaintiff for its value. Musselman's Appeal, 62 Pa. 81, 1 Am. Rep. 382; Boon v. Moss, ubi supra.

It is strongly argued by the defendants that the good will cannot be found to have any salable value, and it was not an asset, since the purchaser could not have used the firm name without the consent in writing of Daniel G. Rawson. Gen. St. 1860, c. 56, § 3; Lodge v. Weld, 138 Mass. 499. But no such question arises in this case, for by their conduct in forcibly and wrongfully appropriating to their own use the property of which the good will was a part they have put themselves in a situation similar to that which would have arisen on a sale of it either to themselves or by them to a stranger. Jones v. Dexter, 130 Mass. 380, 39 Am. Rep. 459; Mellersh v. Keen, 27 Beav. 236; Id., 28 Beav. 453. See Burchell v. Wild [1900] 1 Ch. 551. It is not possible, on the facts of this case, to direct the master to put up and sell by auction the good will, and it does not become necessary to consider whether the plaintiff at any time could have had its value determined in this way. Hutchinson v. Nay, 183 Mass. 355, 67 N. E. 601. While no rule can be laid down by which the good will of a trading partnership in all cases can be ascertained and its value fixed with mathematical precision and accuracy, yet, if it be assumed that a firm has been in existence for a time long enough to establish a business sufficiently permanent in character to include not only its customers, but the incidents of locality, and a distinctive name, these advantages constitute a going business enterprise; and it may then be said that the name and what is done under it go together, and a good will exists which forms an asset of commercial value in a winding up between partners. The fact that such an asset may be difficult of appraisement is no legal reason for denying to the retiring partner an appraisal, if it be proved that he is entitled to it. McMurtrie v. Guiler, 183 Mass. 451-454, 67 N. E. 358, and cases cited. And there seems in this case to have been at least sufficient evidence before the master from which he could find and determine not only the fact of its existence, but also the amount to be allowed to the plaintiff for his share in the good will of the firm of "D. G. Rawson & Co." at the date of dissolution. The length of time the firm had been in existence, the nature and character of its business, the fact whether it had been successful or unsuccessful, the average amount of net profits, the probability of the continuance of the business under the same name without competition in any form from a retiring partner, are some of the elements that may enter into such an inquiry.

As the trial proceeded before the different masters at some stage of the proceedings it appeared that the defendants had used the share of the plaintiff, including not only the first amount found by the master, but that amount increased by the value of his interest in the good will, in their business; and under the stipulation which was treated by the parties as a substitute for a supplemental bill he now claims that this share is to be increased by actual profits, and added to the sums already ascertained in finding the total amount that is due to him. From the date of dissolution, January 1, 1872, to December 27, 1873, the share of the plaintiff in the assets of the firm which had been dissolved was used by the defendants in their business; and it makes no difference in this case, in the measure of their accountability to him, whether this period of time is divided into the part in which they continued the business between themselves, or into that after the new partnership was formed, for during the entire time they used his share as forming a portion of their working capital. The conduct of the defendants, and the use by them of the plaintiff's property, placed them in a fiduciary relation to him, in the care and management of his share, until they had fully wound up and settled its affairs. Jones v. Dexter, 130 Mass. 380, 39 Am. Rep. 459; Knox v. Gye, L. R. 5 H. L. 656. They were called upon to act fairly and in good faith, and to use reasonable diligence in seeing that his interests were fully protected, and if they chose to use his property without his consent they must strictly account for any and all actual profits received by them from such use. Dunlap v. Watson, 124 Mass. 305–307; Freeman v. Freeman, 136 Mass. 260–262.

The rule has sometimes been stated that, owing to the great difficulty which may arise in determining the amount of subsequent profits and stating the account between those who are entitled to share them, liquidating or surviving partners who continue to use the capital of a retiring or deceased partner ought not to be held liable for profits on capital used, except in cases of gross fraud, or breach of trust. See Phillips v. Reeder, 18 N. J. Eq. 95. But it was said by this court in Robinson v. Simmons, 146 Mass. 167–175, 15 N. E. 558, 4 Am. St. Rep. 299, that, "as a general rule, where a surviving partner continues to use the capital of a deceased partner in the business, the representatives of the latter, in the absence of any agreement to control, have the election to demand either interest on the capital used or the profits earned by its use, and also all accretions to the fund owned by them. There is, however, no inflexible rule governing all cases, but each case depends upon its own circumstances and equities." Though this language was used with reference to the right of the representatives of a deceased partner to such an accounting, no sufficient reason appears why it does not apply equally to a case where the dissolution is not caused by death, but takes place under the terms of the articles of partnership. When the plaintiff demanded an accounting, and that his share of the assets should be ascertained and paid to him, the demand was met with a denial of such a right, and a refusal to grant his request. He was obliged to resort to a bill in equity to compel the defendants to do what by implication under their contract, which contained no provisions for a settlement of the partnership on its termination, they had agreed to perform upon a dissolution of the firm at their option; and after which, with the plaintiff's assent, they became bound within a reasonable time to wind up and settle the affairs of the partnership and pay him his proportionate part. No pretense was made by them that in good faith they had taken the partnership property at a fair valuation, and were ready to state the account on that basis, but they refused to pay anything, absolutely ignored him, and treated the property as their own. For this reason the case does not fall within the decision made in Denholm et al. v. McKay et al., 148 Mass. 434, 19 N. E. 551, 12 Am. St. Rep. 574, relied on by the defendants.

From the facts found by the master, the defendants must have known that the profits of the business had been large, and that the plaintiff was entitled to one-third of them under the partnership articles upon dissolution, or at the latest after a reasonable time had elapsed in which to reduce the assets to cash, if they assumed to act as partners in liquidation. Apparently, they could have paid the plaintiff as early as August 31, 1872, but they made no offer of any specific sum until the payment into court, and then the amount offered was less than that actually found to be due to him. Upon the dissolution of a partnership, in the absence of any agreement permitting him to charge for his services, the partner who winds up the business and disposes of the assets ordinarily is not allowed compensation. What he does is as much for his own benefit as for that of the retiring or the estate of a deceased partner; and it may be said that this is one of the burdens which may arise and is deemed incidental to the contract. If, however, the continuation of the business is consented to by those entitled to an account, then he is to be compensated for any extra services. Schenkl v. Dana, 118 Mass. 236. While it must be held, under the facts disclosed in this case, that there was no such assent by the plaintiff to the use of his money as will bring it within the line of decisions where, upon dissolution, the liquidating or surviving partner continues the business, and by consent uses the share of the retiring or deceased partner, and the situation of the defendants thus becomes analogous to that of trustees in their own wrong; yet the plaintiff cannot have compensation both by way of profits actually earned by his money, and at the same time interest on his capital. Robinson v. Simmons, ubi supra; Levi v. Karrick, 13 Iowa, 344. When the contract of partnership terminated, he was then to have his share as it stood at dissolution; but if, without his consent, the defendants used his capital, they must, at his election, give to him what, if anything, it had earned, or allow interest for its use. If any depreciation in the value of the assets taken over by them is found during the short period covered by the accounting, such decrease may be allowed, so far as it can properly be considered, in finding the amount of net profits. It is obvious that what would be just in one case might not be in another. He must now take one of two positions—either that the defendants, in their relation to him, had been guilty of bad faith and a breach of their trust, and must account, not only for the principal, but for all profits received by them by the wrongful use of his money, which is the measure of their liability; or he must be content with accepting interest in full satisfaction for the use of his principal. Robinson v. Simmons, ubi supra. The use by the defendants of the property of the plaintiff after August 31, 1872, which is the date found by the master when the share of the partners in the assets of the partnership could have been liquidated and paid, was unauthorized. But whether, under such conditions, they should be allowed anything for their skill and services is within the discretion and control of the court, and does not rest on any contract made by the parties. Robinson v. Simmons, ubi supra; Turnbull v. Pomeroy, 140 Mass. 117, 3 N. E. 15; Thayer v. Badger, 171 Mass. 279, 280, 50 N. E. 541.

It does not appear that the nature of the business presented any extraordinary difficulties, or called for more than ordinary business skill or ability, though, as a result of its continuance, large profits appear to have been realized. The defendants apparently kept in successful operation the business enterprise of which they had taken possession at the dissolution of the firm, and to this extent it may be found that the subsequent profits can be said to be due to their efforts.

In finding the net profits the master has allowed 8 per cent. by way of interest on capital and profits invested as capital by the defendants, but he does not state whether he finds that the sums which each of them would thus receive should be treated as equivalent to that part of the net profits due to their skill and services, and, if so, then the balance remaining would not be subject to any further reduction, but should be considered as the actual earnings of the whole capital invested, including the amount due to the plaintiff. It may be assumed that he regarded the contract of partnership as still controlling the rights of the parties; but if interest at the date of dissolution should be allowed on the original capital invested, after dissolution interest ought not to be charged until the balance has been found on a settlement between the parties, and a reasonable time has passed in which to wind up the affairs of the firm. Crabtree v. Randall, 133 Mass. 552; Bradley v. Brigham et al., 137 Mass. 545, 546. If, however, the defendants were entitled to be further allowed such part of the net profits as the master, upon the evidence before him, might find to be just and equitable, then, in order to give the plaintiff equality of participation, interest at the same rate for like periods of time after August 31, 1872, would have to be reckoned, not only upon his principal, but also upon that principal as augmented for each period by his share of the actual profits when found.

In order to avoid what might become a long and complex, if not impossible, statement of the accounts, the same result is substantially reached, and the plaintiff may have the net profits stand, without diminution by any credit of interest on the total capital and profits which have been invested in the business. From the net profits so stated such a sum is to be deducted as the master finds is solely attributable to the skill and services of the defendants, and the balance is to be treated as actual profits, in which the whole capital invested is entitled to share equally. This method of determining the share of each of the parties interested allows to the defendants the amount actually earned by their capital; and if it be said they lose interest the reply is not only that the original contract is not to control, which provided for interest at the rate of 8 per cent. on the capital invested during the life of the partnership, but the plaintiff also gets no interest upon his share, which they have used against his will, and in their own wrong. Dunlap v. Watson, ubi supra. An allowance to them of so much of the net profits as may be found due to their skill and ability is all that they are equitably entitled to receive. The plaintiff, therefore, after August 31, 1872, is to be allowed such portion of the actual profits as his amount of capital bears to the whole capital invested. Freeman v. Freeman, 142 Mass. 98-106, 7 N. E. 710; Dunlap v. Watson, ubi supra; Hartman v. Woehr et al., 18 N. J. Eq. 383-386; Featherstonhaugh v. Fenwick, 17 Ves. 298.

The result to which we have come may be stated as follows: The sum of $13,529.58 is to be treated as a constant factor in the problem of ascertaining the final amount due to the plaintiff. There is to be added to it the value of his interest in the good will of the firm at the date of dissolution, and the total amount represents his share in the assets of the partnership. This amount is to be further increased by the plaintiff's part of the actual profits accruing to him from the use of his money or share after August 31, 1872, and up to December 27, 1873. From the principal so found the partial payment of $12,843.63 is to be deducted, and on the new principal interest is to be computed at the rate of 6 per cent. from December 27, 1873, to the date of the entry of the final decree. The case must be recommitted to the master to make the necessary computations and findings and state the result in a final report.

Decree for the plaintiff accordingly.

(178 N. Y. 1)

DOLFINI v. ERIE R. CO.

(Court of Appeals of New York. March 4, 1904.)

RAILROADS—ACCIDENT AT CROSSING—CONTRIBUTORY NEGLIGENCE.

1. In an action to recover for injuries at a crossing, plaintiff testified that on a clear day, when 20 feet distant from the track, he saw nothing on the tracks. It appeared that from a point 75 feet distant there was an unobstructed view in the direction from which a train was coming for several hundred feet, and that, if he had looked as stated in his testimony, the train must have been in plain sight. *Held*, that his testimony was incredible, as a matter of law.

Appeal from Supreme Court, Appellate Division, Second Department.

Action by Peter D. Dolfini against the Erie Railroad Company. From a judgment of the Appellate Division (81 N. Y. Supp. 1124) affirming a judgment for plaintiff, defendant appeals. Reversed.

Henry Bacon and Joseph Merritt, for appellant. Edwin S. Merrill, for respondent.

CULLEN, J. On the record before us, we think that the plaintiff was clearly guilty of contributory negligence, precluding a recovery for his injuries, and that the motion of the defendant made on the trial to dismiss the complaint should have been granted. On a clear summer's afternoon, between 4 and 5 o'clock, the plaintiff was driving along a public highway in Orange county towards the intersection of such highway with the Erie Railroad, known as "Ryan's Crossing." The plaintiff was approaching the railroad from the south. When he had arrived in the vicinity of the crossing, there was a freight train going east on the track nearest to him. He testified that he waited until this train disappeared from his view towards the east, and thereupon started to cross the railroad; that when 20 feet distant from the near track he looked to the right or east and saw that nothing was on the tracks; that he continued across the railroad, and that, as he was passing over the northerly or west-bound track, his vehicle was struck by a passenger train coming from the east, and he received the injuries for which he brought the action. The horse was going "on a good, fair walk." At the scene of the accident the highway intersects the railroad at an acute angle. There was a much greater space than usual between the two tracks, in consequence of there having formerly been another track between them. The distance between the first or nearest rail of the east-bound track and the nearest rail of the west-bound track was 33 feet, and 11 feet further would carry any object clear of a train moving on the last-named track. The railroad crossed the highway on a straight course, which continued to the east for a distance of 1,050 feet, where it curved to the right. While the view of a traveler approaching from the south of this portion of the railroad was somewhat obstructed by a wall and trees until he reached a point 75 feet from the west-bound track, from that point the view was entirely clear. He could there see the railroad to the east for a distance of 800 feet. At 50 feet from the crossing he could see the road for 900 feet, and at 25 feet from the crossing for 1,000 feet. The grade of the railroad from the east to the crossing was slightly rising, and the grade of the highway towards the crossing was also rising. The speed of the train which struck the plaintiff's vehicle was from 30 to 35 miles an hour. If the plaintiff looked at the point stated in his testimony, the train at the time must have been two or three hundred feet west of the curve, and in plain sight. It is not sufficient that the plaintiff testifies that he looked, but did not see. Such a statement is incredible, as a matter of law. Matter of Harriot, 145 N. Y. 540, 40 N. E. 246.

The case before us is not like those often occurring at railroad crossings, where, as the traveler approaches the railroad at some points, he obtains a clear view of the track, and at other points his vision is obstructed by intervening obstacles. In such cases it may be that the traveler, though exercising due care, may fail to see the approaching train. Here, for at least 75 feet from the crossing, the view was clear and unobstructed. It is true that in the present case the crossing was unusually long, and therefore more than usual time would be required to pass over it. But the plaintiff had ample opportunity as he crossed the near or east-bound track, and also in the space between the two tracks, to discover whether any train was approaching on the far track. It is apparent that the accident was caused by the plaintiff's neglect to exercise ordinary caution to see whether there was any train coming from the east. At the time of the accident there were travelers on the other side of the railroad, including two who were driving vehicles, waiting until they could cross in safety. They had no difficulty in discovering the approach of the passenger train, and made no attempt to cross.

The judgment appealed from should be reversed, and a new trial granted; costs to abide the event.

PARKER, C. J., and GRAY, HAIGHT, MARTIN, and WERNER, JJ., concur. VANN, J., not sitting.

Judgment reversed, etc.

(178 N. Y. 9)

LORD et al. v. HULL.

(Court of Appeals of New York. March 4, 1904.)

PARTNERSHIP—ACCOUNTING—WHEN GRANTED.

1. An action for an accounting in equity will not lie where it is a mere incident to the settlement of a solitary matter in dispute between partners, not vital to either party, and where no dissolution is sought.

2. Two partners cannot maintain an action for an accounting against a third partner because of a dispute between them as to whether a certain contract with a third party was binding on the firm, or only the two copartners, where no dissolution of the partnership is asked, and there is no claim that the third partner was insolvent or had been guilty of any misconduct, or the books had not been properly kept, or that plaintiffs did not have access to them, and there was nothing involved in the accounting except the matter of the disputed contract.

Appeal from Supreme Court, Appellate Division, First Department.

Action by Austin W. Lord and others against Washington Hull and Kenneth M. Murchison, Jr. From a judgment of the Appellate Division (74 N. Y. Supp. 711) affirming a judgment for plaintiffs and Murchison, defendant Hull appeals. Reversed.

It is alleged in the complaint that in September, 1894, the plaintiffs and the defendant Hull formed a copartnership to carry on business as architects in the city of New York, at first for a definite period, but finally until certain work was finished, and that the time for the termination thereof was uncertain, owing to the large number of unfinished contracts on hand. The powers, rights, and obligations of the copartners were in all respects equal. On the 18th of February, 1896, a written agreement was made in the name of the firm with Kenneth M. Murchison, Jr., containing a promise "to pay him ten per cent. of the gross commissions for the work on the residence of William A. Clark," not yet completed. The rest of the complaint (Murchison not having been a party. when it was drawn) is as follows: "That a disagreement has arisen between the plaintiffs and defendant as to the payments which have been and are still to be made to the said Kenneth M. Murchison, Jr., and as to the obligations of the copartnership to the said Murchison, Jr., under the contract entered into by said copartners and said Murchison, being the agreement of February 18, 1896 (Schedule B, hereto annexed), hereinbefore set forth; that the defendant has withdrawn from the funds of the copartnership and has appropriated to his own use the sum of $945, which was a sum largely in excess of any and all sums to which he was entitled at the time of such withdrawal, and threatens to withdraw from the funds of the said copartnership from time to time hereafter such sum or sums as he may deem himself entitled to, irrespective of the rights of the plaintiffs; that the plaintiffs do not desire to dissolve the copartnership existing between them and the defendant, for the reason that the plaintiffs believe that the contracts entered into between such copartnership and William A. Clark, the owner of one of the works set forth in Schedule C, hereto annexed, and yet incomplete, require the exercise of the professional skill and ability of all the members of the said firm, which could not be secured upon a dissolution of the said copartnership, and that loss and damage would be sustained by the plaintiffs if such contracts were broken by the dissolution of said copartnership; that the plaintiffs are without an adequate remedy at law." There was no allegation that Hull was insolvent, or that there was any occasion for an accounting, except with reference to the Murchison contract. The relief demanded was an accounting as to all copartnership affairs to date, and an adjudication of the rights and obligations of the parties under their copartnership agreement and under the contract with Murchison. There was also a prayer for general relief, but none for an injunction, either temporary or permanent. The defendant Hull alleged in his answer that the agreement with Murchison was made without authority, and was not binding on the firm; that the plaintiffs had unlawfully paid him thereon large sums of money out of the funds of the firm; and that they threaten to continue such payments. A few days before the action was tried, Murchison moved at Special Term, on notice to the parties, to be made a party defendant, with leave to serve an answer upon both the plaintiffs and the defendant. The motion, although opposed, was granted, and no one appealed from the order. The answer of Murchison, served on all the parties, after certain denials, set forth, "by way of an equitable counterclaim," the agreement between himself and the firm, and alleged that the firm owed him the sum of $2,100 and upwards thereon. He asked for an accounting to ascertain the amount received by the firm as commissions from said Clark, and for judgment against the plaintiffs and the defendant Hull for the amount found due him, with other relief. The last set of copartnership articles provided "that upon completion of the works above mentioned a true and final accounting shall be made by the parties to this agreement each to the others, and all the property of the firm * * * shall be equally divided between them." Upon the trial it appeared from the testimony of the plaintiffs that there was "nothing to have an accounting about, except Mr. Murchison's share of those commissions." The trial judge found the facts as alleged by the plaintiffs and the defendant Murchison, and the decree entered held the Murchison agreement valid and binding upon the firm, interpreted its meaning in accordance with their contention, and awarded judgment in favor of the plaintiffs and against the defendant Hull for $1,415.27, with costs, and in favor of the defendant Murchison against the plaintiffs and the defendant Hull for the sum of $3,000, besides costs. Upon appeal by Hull to the Appellate Division, the judgment was in all things affirmed—two of the justices dissenting—and he now comes to this court.

John Henry Hull, for appellant. J. Albert Lane, for respondents Lord and others. Henry B. Culver, for respondent Murchison.

VANN, J. (after stating the facts). This action was brought by two copartners against the third for an accounting, without a dissolution, and it is not surprising that a challenge is interposed to the jurisdiction of the court. The contract of copartnership has existed as long as the common law, and a vast amount of business has been transacted by persons working together under this relation. The law upon the subject is founded on the custom of merchants, who have thus, in effect, made their own law, yet we find no well-considered case which approves of such an action as the one now before us. While the novelty of an action is by no means conclusive against it, still it is suggestive, when the history of the law relating to the subject shows many occasions and few efforts.

The general rule is that a court of equity, in a suit by one partner against another, will not interfere in matters of internal regulation, or except with a view to dissolve the partnership, and by a final decree to adjust all its affairs. Story on Partnership, § 229; Lindley, 567; Gow, 114; Parsons, § 206; Bates, § 910; Collier, § 236. It is not its office "to enter into a consideration of mere partnership squabbles" (Wray v. Hutchinson, 2 Mylne & Keen, 235, 238), or "on every occasion to take the management of every playhouse and brewhouse" (Carlin v. Drury, Vesey & B. 153, 158). If the members of a firm cannot agree as to the method of conducting their business, the courts will not attempt to conduct it for them. Aside from the inconvenience of constant interference, as litigation is apt to breed hard feelings, easy appeals to the courts to settle the differences of a going concern would tend to do away with mutual forbearance, foment discord, and lead to dissolution. It is to the interest of the law of partnership that frequent resort to the courts by copartners should not be encouraged, and they should realize that, as a rule, they must settle their own differences, or go out of business. As a learned writer has said: "A partner who is driven to a court of equity, as the only means by which he can get an accounting from his copartners, may be supposed to be in a position which will be benefited by a dissolution; in other words, such a partnership as that ought to be dissolved." Parsons on Partnership (4th Ed.) § 206. "If a continuance of the partnership is contemplated," as another commentator has said, "or if an accounting of only part of the partnership concerns is allowed, no complete justice can be done between the partners, and the fluctuations of a continuing business will render the accounting which is correct to-day incorrect to-morrow; and to entertain such bills on behalf of a partner would involve the court in incessant litigation, foment disputes, and needlessly drag partners not in fault before the public tribunals." 2 Bates on Partnership, § 910. Judge Story declared that "a mere fugitive, temporary breach, involving no serious evils or mischief, and not endangering the future success and operations of the partnership, will therefore not constitute any case for equitable relief. * * * It is very certain that, pending the partnership, courts of equity will not interfere to settle accounts and set right the balance between the partners, but await the regular winding up of the concern." Story on Partnership, §§ 225, 229.

While a forced accounting without a dissolution is not impossible, it is by no means a matter of course, for facts must be alleged and proved showing that it is essential to the continuance of the business, or that some special and unusual reason exists to make it necessary. Thus, Mr. Lindley, upon whom reliance was placed by the courts below, mentions three classes of cases as exceptions to the general rule: "(1) Where one partner has sought to withhold from his copartner the profits arising from some secret transaction; (2) where the partnership is for a term of years still unexpired, and one partner has sought to exclude or expel his copartner, or drive him to a dissolution; (3) where the partnership has proved a failure, and the partners are too numerous to be made parties to the action, and a limited account will result in justice to them all." The plaintiffs claim that this case belongs to the second class, and the courts below have so held; but, as we think, it does not come under any head of Mr. Lindley's classification, which is correct as far as it goes, and it goes as far in the direction of the plaintiffs' theory as any just classification that can be made.

There is neither allegation nor evidence that Hull tried to exclude or expel the plaintiffs, or to drive them to a dissolution, or that he did anything in bad faith or with an ulterior purpose. The controversy was confined to one point of difference—the Murchison contract—which was a matter of internal regulation. There was no dispute about anything else. The plaintiffs claimed that the contract bound the firm, and that it included all work done or to be done for Mr. Clark, while Hull claimed that it did not bind the firm, and that, if it did, it embraced only a part of that work. There was no difference in the computation of balances, or claim that the articles had been violated by either side, except with reference to that contract. The plaintiffs insisted that Hull had drawn out more than his share of the profits, because he drew one-third of the income without leaving one-third of the part going to Murchison, and that thus there was a balance against him. Hull claimed that the plaintiffs, in paying anything to Murchison, wasted the assets of the firm, and thus there was a balance against them. When the interlocutory judgment was made, the parties at once stipulated the respective balances on the basis of that decree, and thus obviated a reference, so that final judgment was entered without delay. Neither party desired an accounting, except as an excuse to sustain or defeat the Murchison contract. Exclusion from a small portion of the profits, paid or withheld in good faith on account of that contract, was not exclusion from the affairs of the firm, yet an accounting was sought only as a means of settling the dispute over that particular subject, which related simply to a detail in the management of the business. No discovery was asked for. There was no claim that Hull was insolvent, or that he had suppressed any fact, or had made secret profits, or had been guilty of bad conduct, or that the books had not been properly kept, or that the plaintiffs had been denied access to the books. There was no evidence that any partner had refused to give an account of all moneys received by him, or that there was error or omission of any kind in the accounts of the firm, except as limited to the Murchison agreement. It was easy to test the validity of that contract by simply withholding payment, forcing Murchison to sue, and raising the question by answer. That was not an equitable, but a legal, question. Murchison's claim did not differ from that of any firm creditor, except that the partners were at odds over its validity. "No action can be maintained by one partner against the other in respect to particular items of account pertaining to the partnership business." Thompson v. Lowe, 111 Ind. 274, 12 N. E. 477.

An accounting without a dissolution has never been allowed, under the circumstances of this case, by any court in this country or in England, so far as we can learn from the authorities cited by counsel or discovered by ourselves. A brief review of the leading cases will show that the principle upon which they rest has no application to the facts of the case before us. In Fairthorne v. Weston, 3 Hare's Ch. R. 387, the plaintiff bought into the business of an attorney, paying £700 down, and agreeing to pay 700 more at the end of five years, when the defendant was to retire, and the business was to belong to the plaintiff. During the five years the parties were to be copartners, sharing the profits and expenses equally. After a while the defendant, for the fraudulent purpose of getting rid of his contract, received money, and refused to account for it, excluded the plaintiff from all knowledge and control over the business, used insulting language toward him, and violated the copartnership agreement in other ways, and all in order to bring about a dissolution. A bill filed for an accounting, without a dissolution, was sustained upon the ground that the defendant was violating the contract in order to compel the plaintiff to submit to a dissolution upon very injurious terms, and that the court had power to support as well as dissolve a partnership. In Richards v. Davis, 2 Russell & M. 347, a copartnership for a long term had not expired, and the acting partner excluded the others "from the means of ascertaining the state of the partnership affairs." A bill for an accounting, and to permit the plaintiffs "to have access to all the books of the partnership," was sustained; but the court refused to make an order "for carrying on the partnership concerns, unless with a view to dissolution." It is claimed that this case was overruled by Knebell v. White, 2 Younge & C. Exch. 15, where it was held that a bill for an account of partnership transactions must pray for a dissolution, or the court could not take jurisdiction. From the fragmentary report of Harrison v. Armitage, 4 Mad. 143, it appears that the defendant denied that there was any partnership; and the court so held, but remarked orally that one partner might file a bill against another for an account without asking for a dissolution, although not in a case of interim management. The remark was obiter, and so limited as not to include the case we are considering, yet it is one of the few authorities relied upon by those who claim that courts of equity should open their doors to admit quarreling copartners. In Knowles v. Houghton, 11 Vesey, Jr., Ch. R. 168, the existence of the partnership was denied by the defendant, who claimed that the plaintiff "was merely employed as a clerk." An accounting was granted without a dissolution, the object being to establish the partnership. In Lascomb v. Russell, 4 Simons, 8, there was a partnership for seven years, "and so from seven years to seven years, till determined by notice." After the first period had expired, and one year of the second, a bill was filed for an account of the profits, upon the allegation that no settlement had been made for the last three years. In dismissing the bill, the court said: "With respect to the law of this court upon this subject, there is no instance of an account being decreed of the profits of a partnership on a bill which does not pray a dissolution, but contemplates the subsistence of the partnership. * * * With respect to occasional breaches of agreement between partners, when they are not of so grievous a nature as to make it impossible that the partnership should continue, the court stands neuter; but when it finds that the acts complained of are of such a character as to show that the partners cannot continue partners, and that relief cannot be given but by a dissolution, the court will decree it, although it is not specifically asked. Here a dissolution is not prayed for, and, if the court were to do what is asked, it would not be final." Under similar circumstances, Lord Eldon dismissed the bill in Forman v. Humfray, 2 Ves. & B. 328; observing "that, if a partner can come here merely for an account pending the partnership, there seems nothing to prevent his coming annually." In Taylor v. Davis, 4 Law J. (N. S.) 18, an injunction was granted, restraining the defendant from retaining in his sole possession, and excluding the plaintiff from access to, a book kept by the firm, and indispensable to the business. The book had been abstracted by the defendant, and he had threatened to burn it. In Marshall v. Colman, 2 Jacob & W. 266, the court declined to restrain the defendant from violating the articles of partnership, in refusing to use the name of the plaintiff as a part of the firm name in the transaction of firm business. The lord chancellor said: "It would be quite a new head of equity for the court to interfere where one party violates a particular covenant, and the other party does not choose to put an end to the partnership. In that way there may be a separate suit and a perpetual injunction in respect of each covenant, and that is a jurisdiction that we have never decidedly entertained." In Knebell v. White, 2 Younge & C. 15, previous conflicting decisions were considered, and the court said: "It may now, therefore, be considered as settled that, in the case of ordinary trading partnerships, an account of partnership transactions must be consequent upon a dissolution of the partnership." These cases illustrate, if they do not exhaust, the instances where the courts of England have interfered, or refused to interfere, when a dissolution of the firm was not asked. In this country the question does not appear to have been directly decided, at least not in this state. It was not involved in Sanger v. French, 157 N. Y. 213, 51 N. E. 979, nor in Traphagen v. Burt, 67 N. Y. 30, as will appear from an examination of the facts. The primary object of those actions was to establish a partnership with reference to a particular adventure, and they turned mainly on the existence and effect of an oral agreement between the parties. Our courts, and especially those having jurisdiction under the laws of Congress, have sometimes interfered by injunction in a flagrant case of danger and injustice, although no dissolution of the firm was contemplated. Marble Co. v. Ripley, 10 Wall. 339, 19 L. Ed. 955; Leavitt v. Windsor Land Co., 54 Fed. 439, 4 C. C. A. 425. This is quite different from an action for an accounting without a dissolution, where no especial reason is alleged or proved to show that one is necessary, or to authorize a departure from the general rule.

A court of equity will not take cognizance of an action for an accounting as a mere incident to the settlement of a solitary matter in dispute between partners, when it is not vital to either party or to the business, and dissolution is not sought. Actions to establish a partnership, the existence of which was denied by the partner in control to give a partner access to the books after persistent refusal, or to permit him to take part in the business from which he had been excluded, are founded on intentional and continuous wrongdoing, which, unless arrested, might subvert the partnership. When one party seizes or absorbs the entire business, or usurps rights of his copartner which are essential to his safety or the safety of the firm, or persists in misconduct so gross as to threaten destruction to the interests of all, the court may intervene to restore the rights of the innocent party, or to rescue a paying business from ruin. Extreme necessity only, however, will justify interference without a dissolution. There was no sufficient reason for an appeal to a court of equity in the case under consideration. There was no equity in the bill as filed by the plaintiffs, and none in the case made for them by the evidence. The defendant Murchison had an adequate remedy at law, and he can take nothing from his intrusion into the litigation, under the circumstances, for the questionable order admitting him as a defendant did not create a cause of action, nor add to the jurisdiction of the court. All the parties should be put back where they were before the action was commenced, and hence it is our duty to reverse the judgments below and dismiss the complaint, with costs to the defendant Hull against the plaintiffs and the defendant Murchison.

GRAY, O'BRIEN, HAIGHT, MARTIN, and CULLEN, JJ., concur. PARKER, C. J., absent.

Judgments reversed.

(178 N. Y. 5)

HARVEY v. BREWER et al.

(Court of Appeals of New York. March 4, 1904.)

MECHANICS' LIENS—PAYMENT OF ORDERS—FILING—NECESSITY.

1. Laws 1897, p. 521, c. 418, § 15, requires orders drawn by a contractor or subcontractor for moneys payable on the contract to be filed. *Held* not to affect payments made by the owner for labor or material furnished outside the contract.

2. The acceptance by the owner of a building of an order drawn on him by the contractor for money due under the contract, which order was payable to a subcontractor who had filed a lien for the amount, and the owner's promise in writing to pay it, accepted in satisfaction of his lien by the subcontractor, who thereupon discharged it, constitutes a payment, and the filing of the order is not requisite under Laws 1897, p. 521, c. 418, § 15, to make it valid against subsequent lienors.

Appeal from Supreme Court, Appellate Division, Second Department.

Action by William E. Harvey against George E. Brewer and others. From a judgment of the Appellate Division (81 N. Y. Supp. 840) affirming a judgment on report of the referee in an action to foreclose a mechanic's lien, defendants Garret L. Hardy and others appeal. Affirmed.

William B. Hurd, Jr., for appellants. William B. Anderson and William Williams, for respondent.

PARKER, C. J. In the year 1900 Dr. Brewer made a contract with one Conklin to build for him a house for $8,025. Conklin made a contract with the Van Brunt Plumbing Company to do a certain portion of the work, for which it filed a mechanic's lien on March 23d for $673. Two days later Conklin wrote a letter to Brewer, requesting him to pay to the Van Brunt Plumbing Company the sum due it, and for which its lien had been filed, and requesting him to deduct the sum from the last payment to Conklin on the contract price. This order Dr. Brewer accepted on April 3d, and promised, in writing, to pay the Van Brunt Plumbing Company such sum. Upon the receipt of this promise the agent of the company indorsed upon the back of it the following: "Accepted April 3, 1901, Van Brunt Plumbing Co., per Ryder." Nine days thereafter the Van Brunt Plumbing Company, in consideration thereof, satisfied the mechanic's lien and discharged it of record. A month and eight days later defendants Hardy, Voorhees, and others duly filed mechanics' liens. But in the meantime six other parties filed mechanics' liens for various sums, and in an action of foreclosure of the first lien filed it appeared that the balance due on the contract and for extras was insufficient to satisfy appellants' lien, and they insist that, notwithstanding the acceptance of Conklin's order of March 25th, and its subsequent payment on June 19th by Dr. Brewer, the latter was not entitled to be credited with such sum of $673 as a payment on account of the contract price and for extras. They insist that the transaction which we have described between Conkling, the Van Brunt Plumbing Company, and Dr. Brewer was within section 15 of the lien law (Laws 1897, p. 521, c. 418), which provides that "no assignment of a contract for the performance of labor or the furnishing of materials for the improvement of real property or of the money or any part thereof due or to become due therefor, nor an order drawn by a contractor or subcontractor upon the owner of such real property for the payment of such money shall be valid, until the contract or a statement containing the substance thereof and such assignment or a copy of each or a copy of such order, be filed in the office of the county clerk. * * *" This section is supposed to be due to a decision of this court in Bates v. Salt Springs Nat. Bank, 157 N. Y. 322, 51 N. E. 1033, holding that, in the absence of anything to the contrary in the contract, and before any notice of mechanic's lien is filed, the contractor may assign to his creditor, in payment of his debt, the whole or any portion of the moneys due or to become due under the contract, and the assignee acquires a preference over a subsequent lienor. That statute was recently before this court in Brace v. City of Gloversville, 167 N. Y. 452, 60 N. E. 779, where it is held to apply to public contracts as well as to those with private persons, and in that particular case it said that the order which was given for materials furnished to the contractor constituted an equitable assignment of the fund. That is the view taken by this court of such an order in McCorkle v. Herrman, 117 N. Y. 297, 22 N. E. 948, and in Bates v. Salt Springs Nat. Bank, supra. So, if what was done here was, in effect, either an absolute or equitable assignment of so much of the fund as the order named, it would come within the condemnation of section 15 of the lien law, supra. That section indicates that the Legislature was of the opinion that the protection of the laborers and materialmen made it necessary that notice of an assignment of the contract or the moneys due thereunder, or some part thereof, or an order drawn by a contractor upon the owner, ought to be given to those interested, and so it provided that such an assignment or order should not be valid "until the contract or a statement containing the substance thereof and such assignment or a copy of each or a copy of such order be filed" in the proper county clerk's office. It will be observed, however, that the section only applies to an assignment of the contract, or of the whole or some part of the moneys due or to become due thereunder, or an order drawn by the contractor or subcontractor upon the owner; so that it in no wise affects payments made by the owner on account of labor performed or materials furnished under the contract. The statute does not hinder or embarrass an owner who in good faith makes such a payment before the filing of liens. Now, the referee before whom this case was tried, and the Appellate Division as well, reached the conclusion that the transaction between Conklin, Dr. Brewer, and the Van Brunt Plumbing Company amounted to a payment of the $673 due the Van Brunt Plumbing Company, and for which it had filed a valid lien nearly two months before appellants' lien was filed. We concur in that view. A valid lien having been acquired by the Van Brunt Plumbing Company for $673 due to it, Conklin, the contractor, in order to secure an immediate satisfaction and discharge of the lien, gave to the company an order upon Dr. Brewer, the owner, for the amount due, which he at once accepted, and promised in writing to pay. That promise the Van Brunt Plumbing Company accepted in satisfaction of their lien, which was thereupon discharged of record. All this transpired before the filing of appellants' lien, and constituted a payment by the owner on account of the sum due under the contract with Conklin, for when the Van Brunt Plumbing Company accepted Dr. Brewer's written promise to pay the order drawn on him by Conklin, and discharged the lien of record, the legal effect of the transaction was, as against the contractor and subsequent lienors, precisely as if Dr. Brewer had immediately paid to the Van Brunt Plumbing Company the amount due to it and specified in the order of Conklin.

It follows that the judgment should be affirmed, with costs.

GRAY, O'BRIEN, BARTLETT, MARTIN, VANN, and WERNER, JJ., concur.

Judgment affirmed.

(69 Oh. St. 294)

MANHATTAN LIFE INS. CO. v. BURKE.

(Supreme Court of Ohio. Dec. 8, 1903.)

CONTRACT OF LIFE INSURANCE—LIABILITY—AMOUNT—ACTION ON POLICY—TENDER OF AMOUNT RECEIVED—SETTLEMENT—PLEADING.

1. Where, at the time of a compromise of a claim founded on a contract of life insurance, a dispute exists between the parties as to the liability of the company in any sum whatever, it denying that anything is owing, and an amount less than the claim is paid to the claimant in settlement of the controversy, and he executes a full acquittance and release, and surrenders the policy, an action at law on the policy cannot be maintained without a return

or a tender of the amount received, even though the party's assent to the settlement was obtained by the fraudulent representations of the other party, and the amount received as the settlement is in the petition credited as a payment on the policy.

2. Where in such case the contract of settlement is pleaded as a defense, a reply which simply alleges that the settlement was induced by fraud, but does not allege a payment or tender of the amount received, is not responsive to the answer, and is insufficient in law. Insurance Co. v. Hull, 37 N. E. 1116, 51 Ohio St. 270, 46 Am. St. Rep. 571, distinguished.

(Syllabus by the Court.)

On rehearing. Reversed.

For former opinion, see 69 N. E. 1135.

The action below was upon a policy of life insurance issued October 25, 1897, by the Manhattan Life Insurance Company, plaintiff in error, upon the life of one George Messmore, for $5,000, which policy was assigned November 24, 1897, by said Messmore to the defendant in error, plaintiff below, Joseph Burke. It was alleged in the petition that Messmore had deceased; that $2,000 had been paid plaintiff by the company on the policy May 31, 1899; and that $3,000, with interest, remained due, for which judgment was prayed.

Two defenses were interposed by the company. One that the procuring of the policy and its assignment to plaintiff were a mere scheme, devised to cover a gambling transaction, the plaintiff having no insurable interest in the life of Messmore, and that, a controversy having arisen, the same was compromised for the amount credited. The second defense set up that, after the death of Messmore, plaintiff, claiming to be the owner of the policy, demanded of the defendant that it pay to him the sum of $5,000, which payment the defendant, having been advised by its counsel that it was not liable therefor, refused to make, upon the ground, as then stated by it to the plaintiff, that the policy, having been taken out by him for his own sole use and benefit on the life of Messmore, in which he had no insurable interest, was a gambling policy, and that the plaintiff was not entitled to be paid or recover from the defendant any sum whatever under said policy. Thereupon the plaintiff and the defendant, the latter having been advised by counsel learned in the law that it was not liable to the plaintiff in any sum whatever on account of said policy, agreed to compromise and settle said disputed claim for the sum of $2,000, which sum the defendant, in pursuance of said agreement of compromise and settlement, paid to the plaintiff, which the plaintiff ever since has and still retains. In consideration of said payment and of the compromise and settlement of said disputed claim the plaintiff then and there delivered the policy to the defendant to be canceled, and also duly executed and delivered to the defendant the release, a copy of which is as follows:

"In consideration of two thousand dollars, this day paid and for good and valuable consideration thereto moving, the receipt whereof is hereby acknowledged, the annexed policy No. 108,540 on the life of George Messmore of or near Commercial Point, Ohio, heretofore issued by the Manhattan Life Insurance Co., of New York, is hereby surrendered, canceled and annulled, and all right, title and interest therein of any nature whatsoever is hereby absolutely and forever relinquished; and the undersigned for themselves and their personal representatives hereby guarantee the validity and sufficiency of this instrument, and that no claim will ever be made against said company, under or by reason of said policy. Witness my hand and seal this twenty-third day of May, 1899.

"Joseph Burke, Assignee. [Seal.]"

For reply to the first defense plaintiff pleaded a general denial, and as reply to the second defense he averred that the writing of the release was obtained from him by the fraud of the defendant, its officers and agents; also by their false and fraudulent representations made to the plaintiff that the said policy had never in fact been issued and was not a legal and binding contract; that the same had not in fact been assigned to plaintiff; that the company had not in fact ever assented to such assignment and transfer; that a mistake had been made by the agents of the company in the writing of the policy and in the assignment thereof which rendered the same worthless and void, which were made to the plaintiff by the agents of defendant and others in its employ who were neighbors of plaintiff and professed to be his friends, which employment was then unknown to plaintiff, and were aiding defendant to cheat and defraud plaintiff out of the policy and the money due him thereon. They also urged and advised plaintiff that he should not consult lawyers respecting the policy and the assignment and other matters connected therewith, and they thus overcame and overreached plaintiff, and prevented him from consulting counsel, he being unskilled in business affairs wholly unfamiliar and unacquainted with such matters and the law. And plaintiff, relying on such false and fraudulent representations, and believing them to be true, was overreached, and an unfair and unlawful advantage gained over him, and his signature obtained to a paper professing to surrender and cancel said policy.

The cause coming on for trial, the defendant, before the impaneling of a jury, moved the court for judgment upon the pleadings, both upon the ground of departure in the reply and that they disclosed the fact that the matter in controversy had been settled. This motion was overruled.

Testimony was then given to the jury by the plaintiff, over the objection of the defendant, tending to maintain the allegations of his petition. Testimony was then given by defendant tending to maintain its claim of settlement. Rebutting testimony was then given by plaintiff tending to establish the allegations of fraud in the reply.

At the conclusion of the testimony the defendant moved the court to arrest the case from the jury, which was overruled. Counsel for defendant then made this statement: "I want the record to show that the defense has refrained from offering testimony upon any issue except as to the fact of a settlement, for the reason that the plaintiff is not entitled to recover or maintain the present litigation, in the event of a settlement having been effected, without a tender back of the amount paid."

Counsel for defendant then requested the court to charge the jury that: "If you find that there was a settlement of the Messmore policy by the payment and acceptance of two thousand dollars in full of all claims under it, your verdict must be for the defendant, whether it was a settlement procured by fraud or not, for the reason that Burke makes no offer to restore the money so received." This was refused, and the substance of it was not given in the charge. Exceptions were noted to that refusal and to the charge. A verdict was then rendered for the plaintiff for the amount claimed, and, motion for a new trial being overruled, judgment was rendered on the verdict. That judgment was affirmed by the circuit court, and the company brings error.

Maxwell & Ramsey and Robert Ramsey, for plaintiff in error. M. A. Dougherty, for defendant in error.

SPEAR, J. (after stating the facts). The judgment of affirmance announced after the first hearing of this case (68 Ohio St. 681, 69 N. E. 1135) was not the unanimous decision of the court, three judges only concurring therein. The case having been more fully argued on the rehearing, and further considered by the court, is now for disposition as upon the original submission.

Counsel for the company at the trial rested its case upon two propositions, and they rest it upon the same propositions here. If their position is correct, then the judgments below are erroneous, and should be reversed; if not, then the judgments should be affirmed.

The propositions are that the reply is a departure not permissible under our rules of practice, and that under the facts as disclosed by the pleadings there could be no recovery, inasmuch as the plaintiff had failed to allege, as he had failed to prove, any return or tender back of the money received in the settlement. The two may be treated together, and, put in legal phrase, the proposition is: A compromise, although procured by fraud, is a bar to an action upon the original claim until rescinded by a tender back of the consideration paid. On the other hand, as an answer to this, it is claimed that where fraud has induced the agreement, the settlement is not binding, since fraud vitiates all contracts, and no tender back or payment is necessary to authorize a suit on the original contract where the judgment asked for will attain that result, which is this case.

In determining the vital legal question, however, it is important to keep in mind certain features of the controversy shown by the pleadings and the testimony. The plaintiff's suit was upon the original contract; it was not a suit to rescind a contract, or to reform it, nor an action for damages on account of fraud. No mistake is shown in the paper itself, nor is it alleged in the pleadings that the plaintiff signed any paper which he did not understand and did not intend to sign. The claim is that he was induced to agree to sign and to sign the contract—a contract of settlement otherwise lawful and valid—by the fraud and misrepresentation of the agents and employés of the company. The presence of a controversy between the parties as to whether any liability at all existed on the part of the company in favor of the plaintiff is shown by the allegations of the answer and as clearly shown by the testimony introduced by the plaintiff himself. It is also clear that, to settle this disputed demand, the execution of the release and surrender of the policy by the plaintiff was had, and the payment of the $2,000 by the company made.

The real question, then, is this: Where, at the time of the compromise of a claim founded on contract, a dispute exists between the parties as to the liability of the alleged debtor in any sum whatever, he denying that anything is owing, and an amount less than the claim is paid to the claimant in settlement of the controversy, can the party claimant maintain an action at law on the original contract without tendering back the sum received, even though his assent to the settlement was obtained by the fraudulent and false representation of the other party?

No dispute exists between counsel and we presume no doubt exists of the soundness of the general proposition that where a party to a compromise desires to set aside or avoid the same, and be remitted to his original rights, he must place the other party in statu quo by returning or tendering the return of whatever has been received by him under such compromise, if of any value, and so far as possible any right lost by the other party in consequence thereof. In an action to rescind the petition should allege the fact of such return or tender prior to, or at least contemporaneous with, the commencement of the suit. Further, as a general proposition, the rule obtains even though the contract of settlement was induced by the fraud or false representations of the other party; the ground being that, by electing to retain the property, the party must be conclusively held to be bound by the settlement. 8 Cyc.

of Law & Pro. 531. No further authorities seem necessary in support of these propositions.

Numerous exceptions have, however, been ingrafted on this general rule. One is that restoration is not necessary where the money received by the party was due him in any event, and if returned could be recovered back. Bebout v. Bodle, 38 Ohio St. 500, may be referred to as illustrative. An action was brought by Phœbe S. Bodle on a note signed by William Bebout as principal and Solomon Bebout as surety. Solomon pleaded his suretyship and an extension of time for payment by agreement to pay interest between the plaintiff and the principal maker without his consent. Plaintiff, by reply, admitted the agreement and receipt of the interest money, but alleged that the agreement to extend was procured by fraud. Solomon demurred to the reply, contending that as no offer to pay back the interest money had been pleaded the reply was insufficient. But the district court held, and this court held, that such payment back was not necessary, as, in any event, the principal maker owed the debt and all of it. Of course, the payment back would have been the doing of a vain thing, inasmuch as the plaintiff was admittedly entitled to the interest paid, whether by virtue of the settlement or by the principal maker's original liability, which liability was in no way impaired. The law does not require an idle ceremony. A less obvious distinction, at least one more likely to be misconstrued, is sought to be ingrafted to the effect that an offer to return is unnecessary if the judgment asked for will accomplish that result. If this be conceded as a naked proposition, yet its application to the case before us is not clear, and the decisions cited as illustrating it do not seem to closely resemble our case. The principal one is that of Allerton et al. v. Allerton, 50 N. Y. 670. The plaintiffs, the defendant, and one McPherson were partners. The defendant (who had managed the business), by fraudulent representations to plaintiffs as to the unprofitable character of the business, and that he (defendant), in conjunction with them, would sell out to McPherson, induced plaintiffs to unite with him in such sale upon being refunded the amount invested by them, and thereafter defendant represented that he had sold out, and paid to plaintiffs the money advanced by them, while in fact defendant did not sell, but retained his interest, and subsequently acquired McPherson's interest. The business was profitable, and defendant had received large gains and profits. They asked that the sale be declared void, that defendant account for all moneys received by him, and that they have judgment for their portion of the profits less the amount received. It is to be noted that this was a suit brought directly to set aside the alleged agreement. It was in chancery, tried by the court, and, as appears by the record, the plaintiffs were entitled to an accounting and to judgment, if the claim of fraud should be maintained. The court was appealed to as a court of equity by the injured parties, by a proper pleading, to rescind a contract induced by fraud and then for an accounting. They did not, as in the present case, attempt themselves to rescind and ignore the contract. The case gives little, if any, aid in determining our question. And that it does not apply to a case like ours is distinctly held by the same court in Gould v. C. C. N. Bank, 86 N. Y. 75, where the Allerton Case is referred to as an action in equity to rescind, in which the rights of the parties could be fully regarded and protected. The Gould Case, as is the case at bar, was an action on the original claim, and it was there held that one who seeks to rescind a compromise of a disputed claim on the ground of fraud must restore or offer to restore whatever of value he has received; that in an action at law upon the original claim the plaintiff must show that he thus rescinded the fraudulent compromise prior to the commencement of the suit; if no rescission is shown, a final determination of the court that plaintiff was entitled to more than the sum paid is no answer to the objection. A case involving a similar question is that of O'Brien v. C., M. & St. P. Ry. Co., 89 Iowa, 644, 57 N. W. 425. It is there held that where a settlement with an employé on account of damages sustained from a personal injury was procured by false representations that other witnesses to the accident were against him, and the promise that he would be given work as long as he behaved himself, which promise was broken, and that the employé was in such condition mentally as not to understand the effect of the release which he signed, such settlement is not a bar to an action for damages for the injury, and that a tender of the amount received is not necessary before an action on the original liability.

The record does not clearly show that the company disputed its liability at the time of the settlement, and a fair inference is that it did not; for it does appear that the court rested its judgment on the proposition that "one who attempts to rescind a transaction on the ground of fraud is not required to restore that which in any event he would be entitled to retain either by virtue of the contract sought to be set aside or of the original liability." This proposition is taken from the opinion and syllabus in Kley v. Healy, 127 N. Y. 555, 28 N. E. 593, and that case is relied upon as authority for the Iowa decision. That action was one brought to procure the cancellation of a satisfaction of a judgment upon the ground that it was obtained by fraud, and that the judgment be restored as a valid lien. The court held that the defendant would be entitled to what she had received, whatever might be the result of her action for a rescission. If the action failed, she was entitled to what had been paid; if she succeeded, the sum was less than she was concededly entitled to by the original judgment. Hence an offer to return was not necessary. Here, too, was an appeal to a court of equity to procure a rescission. It, like the Allerton Case, would seem to fall short of affording a solution of our case. The holding in the Kley Case is consistent with earlier New York cases, notably Cobb v. Hatfield, 46 N. Y. 533, and McMichael v. Kilmer, 76 N. Y. 36, and with a host of other cases in that state and elsewhere in which the general rule hereinbefore given is maintained.

After very full consideration of the controversy in all its bearings, and an extensive examination of authorities, we are satisfied that the case at bar comes within the general rule, and not within any of the exceptions sought to be ingrafted upon it. The rule may be briefly stated: If at the time of the agreement there was, without dispute, an amount due equal to the amount paid, as in Bebout v. Bodle, supra, and in Kley v. Healy, supra, then no tender is necessary; but if, at the time of the settlement, it is denied by the alleged debtor that anything is owing, and a dispute as to that liability exists, and that is settled by payment and release, then a return or tender is necessary. There being in this case a controversy between the parties, a disputed claim which the parties, being sui juris at the time, deliberately settled, the one executing a full and sufficient release, intending to do just what he did do, and the other paying a money consideration therefor, the release, whether obtained by fraudulent representations or not, is binding until set aside either by a tender or return of the money received, or by a direct proceeding in a court of equity for that purpose, upon equitable terms, and the claim for rescission in such case on the ground of fraud cannot be made by a reply.

It is to be borne in mind that the parties were settling a controversy. It was the settlement of this dispute that afforded the consideration for the compromise of the original claim. True it is that the amount received was discounted from the recovery. But that is no answer. We say as the New York court said in the Gould Case. Suppose the verdict had been the other way, what would have been the position of the defendant in respect to the money paid under the release? Clearly there would be no recourse to recovery back from the plaintiff. The compromise agreement is binding upon the plaintiff in error, and could not be rescinded or set aside at its instance. If binding on one side, it must be on the other so long as it exists. It did exist at the time this action was brought; it had not been rescinded; and consequently while it bound one party it must equally bind the other. Lyons v. Allen, 11 App. D. C. 543; E. T., V. & G. Ry. Co. v. Hayes, 83 Ga. 558, 10 S. E. 350.

It is urged with much confidence that the face of this policy was a liquidated demand, and that the payment of a less sum could not satisfy it, even though accepted as such, because there was no consideration for giving up the rest. The rule of law stated is good. But it is not correct to say that a policy of insurance is a liquidated demand. It is not identical with an instrument for the payment of money only nor the judgment of a court. The every day business of the courts shows to the contrary. The original consideration may be sufficient, and there may be a legal delivery of the instrument, and yet, when the event insured against occurs, there may be, and in a great many instances there are, good and sufficient defenses to a recovery. There was such defense pleaded in this case. To characterize such a contract as a liquidated demand is a consideration in terms. It is safe to say that a claim concerning which a defense may be made is not a liquidated claim, and if a defense is made it is a proper subject of compromise. One may buy his peace. The law favors the amicable settlement of disputes.

In argument it is urged that the plaintiff below signed the contract of release without knowing its contents; that in accepting the check for $2,000 he supposed he was receiving payment on the policy; and hence the release is not binding upon him, and there was no settlement. The plaintiff does testify that he did not read the paper; that he could not read writing, although he could write his own name, and that the signatures on the release and on the check are his; that he signed them. He undertakes to say, further, that he received this money as a payment on the claim. It is true, also, that the jury, in addition to the general verdict, returned answers to divers interrogatories in which it is found that the parties did not agree to settle; that the $2,000 was not paid plaintiff in full settlement of the policy; that the release and check did not express the intention of the plaintiff, etc. But the testimony of Burke himself leaves no sort of question but that he perfectly understood that the agents of the company were there to settle the entire claim; that they had no other purpose; and that, by signing and delivering the release and surrendering the policy, he was assenting to a settlement for the amount paid. He was sui juris, and in law able to look out for his own interests. The testimony respecting the alleged fraud would be potent in a suit properly brought, and the finding of the jury with respect to it might be conclusive of the facts in a suit involving them properly pending before a jury. But, over and against it all, there is the release and the surrender of the policy, and the retention of the money received, which are, while the contract of compromise remains unrescinded, controlling. In the words of another, restitution before absolution is as sound in law as in theology.

But it is insisted, finally, that the case is ruled by Insurance Co. v. Hull, 51 Ohio St. 270, 37 N. E. 1116, 46 Am. St. Rep. 571, and that to reverse the judgment below will be to overrule that case. We do not think so. The holding in that case involved the effect of a suppression of a criminal prosecution, and the decision is based on that fact. A contract attempted to be founded upon such consideration has no legal efficacy, it is against public policy, is void absolutely, and incapable of ratification. It is otherwise with a contract induced by fraud. Such contract is voidable only. We may not agree with all of the argument and all of the conclusions stated in the opinion by the learned judge who reported that case, but our case does not require any criticism upon the decision, much less an overruling of it. Indeed, the opinion itself, in the concluding paragraph, emphasizes the distinction between that case and one where the contract sought to be rescinded has been induced by fraud. The distinction was also made by the learned trial judge in his charge wherein he said to the jury, among other things, that if there was a settlement as claimed, and a promise that the plaintiff should not be prosecuted on the charge of burning the property formed no part of the consideration for such settlement, she could not recover; but, if such promise was a part of the consideration, the contract was void, and constituted no defense to the action.

We do not overlook the claim made in argument that the testimony of the plaintiff was that at the time of the settlement there were threats of imprisonment. He does so testify. But there is no claim made in the pleadings of the suppression of a criminal prosecution, nor was there any offer to amend the pleadings; and whether, if they had been amended and that charge made, the testimony would have supported it, we need not inquire. Besides, all the evidence was subject to the objection made at the outset of the trial.

As conclusion, we are of opinion that no right of recovery was shown on the part of plaintiff below, and that the judgments in his favor are erroneous. The former entry of affirmance will be set aside, and judgment for plaintiff in error will be rendered in accordance with this opinion. Reversed.

BURKET, C. J., and DAVIS, SHAUCK, PRICE, and CREW, JJ., concur.

(162 Ind. 204)

SCOTT v. CITY OF GOSHEN et al.

(Supreme Court of Indiana. Feb. 19, 1904.)

SCHOOL CITY—AUTHORITY TO BUILD SCHOOLHOUSE—PERMISSION BY CIVIL CITY—PROVISION FOR INDEBTEDNESS—CONSTITUTIONAL LIMITATION—CONSTRUCTION OF STATUTES.

1. Burns' Rev. St. 1901, § 5914, makes each incorporated city a distinct municipal corporation for school purposes, and authorizes it to contract and be contracted with, etc.; section 5920 makes it the duty of school trustees to establish a sufficient number of schools, and build or otherwise provide suitable houses, etc.; section 5975, enacted in 1873, authorizes any city or incorporated town, on the filing by the school trustees of a report to the common council showing the cost of school buildings undertaken, or the amount required to build them, to issue bonds therefor; section 5976 requires the proceeds of the bonds to be paid to the school trustees, to erect or complete such building, etc.; section 5977 (being section 3 of the act of 1873, as amended in 1875) provides for the collection annually of a special tax to pay the interest and principal of the bonds; section 5978, enacted in 1879, in an act supplemental to that of 1873, provides that, before the school trustees shall contract for a school building, they shall file a statement with the common council showing the necessity therefor, with an estimate of the cost, to be approved by the council. *Held*, that the civil city could not consent to the erection of a schoolhouse by the school trustees unless it provided for the indebtedness so incurred, or unless the school city had funds available therefor, and hence, where a civil city was already indebted beyond the constitutional limit of 2 per cent. on its assessed valuation, and the school city would not have funds sufficient to pay for a schoolhouse for 10 or 15 years, the erection of such building could not be authorized by the civil city, or legally undertaken by the school city.

Appeal from Circuit Court, Elkhart County; J. D. Ferrall, Judge.

Suit by John F. Scott against the city of Goshen and others. From a judgment for defendants, entered on sustaining demurrers to the complaint, plaintiff appeals. Reversed.

Vail & Wehmeyer, for appellant. Miller, Drake & Hubbell, for appellees.

MONKS, J. Appellant, a resident taxpayer of the city of Goshen, Ind., brought this action on August 8, 1902, to enjoin said city from permitting the school trustees of said city to contract for the construction of a high-school building which was to cost about $42,000, and to enjoin the school city and the school trustees from letting the contract for said school building, and issuing evidences of indebtedness for the cost thereof. Each appellee filed a separate demurrer for want of facts to the complaint, which was sustained, and, appellant refusing to plead further, judgment was rendered against him. The assignment of error calls in question the action of the court in sustaining each of said demurrers to the complaint.

It was alleged in the complaint and admitted by the demurrers that, at the commencement of the action, appellant was a resident taxpayer of said city; that the taxable property within the corporate limits of said city at the last assessment was $3,194,755, 2 per cent. of which was $63,895; that the indebtedness of the city was more than $119,000, $8,000 of which was evidenced by bonds issued by said city in 1896 for the building of a schoolhouse within said city; that the school city in February, 1902, obtained consent of said city of Goshen permitting it to build a new school building, to cost not more than $42,000, and that said city is threatening to let said permit continue; that the school city and its trustees are threatening to let a contract to a certain contractor named in the complaint for the construction of a school building in said city to cost $42,000, and that neither the city nor the school city has any money with which to pay for said building; that the school city and its trustees are threatening to issue to the contractor evidences of indebtedness of said school city for the construction of said school building amounting to $42,000, payable annually for 10 or 15 years out of the special school tax to be levied and collected for that purpose, and to levy each year a special school tax upon the property within said city largely in excess of the amount necessary for the current expenses of said school city, and to use said excess each year in payment of the evidences of indebtedness which they threaten to issue as aforesaid, the same to continue for a long period, to wit, 10 to 15 years.

Each incorporated city in this state is by statute made a "distinct municipal corporation for school purposes, by the name and style of * * * the city corporation, and by such name may contract and be contracted with, sue and be sued in any court having competent jurisdiction." Section 5914, Burns' Rev. St. 1901 (section 4438, Rev. St. 1881; section 4438, Horner's Rev. St. 1901). By section 5920, Burns' Rev. St. 1901, it is the duty of the school trustees of their respective townships, towns, and cities "to employ teachers, establish and locate conveniently a sufficient number of schools for the education of the children and build or otherwise provide suitable houses, furniture, apparatus or other articles and educational appliances necessary for the thorough organization and efficient management of said schools." Broad and comprehensive as their powers are, there are other provisions of the statute which clearly restrict the same. Sections 5917, 5918, 5929, 5930, 5975, 5978, Burns' Rev. St. 1901 (sections 4441, 4442, 4450, 4451, 4488, 4491, Rev. St. 1881; sections 4441, 4442, 4450, 4451, 4488, 4491, Horner's Rev. St. 1901); Wallis v. Johnson School Tp., 75 Ind. 368; Union School Tp. v. First Nat. Bank, etc., 102 Ind. 464, 474, 476, 2 N. E. 194. In 1873 the General Assembly passed an act entitled "An act to authorize cities and towns to negotiate and sell bonds to procure means with which to erect and complete unfinished school buildings, and to purchase any ground and building for school purposes, and to pay debts contracted for such erection and completion, and purchase of buildings and grounds, and authorizing the levy and collection of an additional special school tax for the payment of such bonds." Acts 1873, p. 60. The first section of said act, being section 5975, Burns' Rev. St. 1901 (section 4488, Rev. St. 1881; section 4488, Horner's Rev. St. 1901), provides "that any city or incorporated town in this state which shall by the action of its school trustee or trustees have purchased any ground and building or buildings, or may hereafter purchase any ground or building or buildings, or have commenced or may hereafter commence the erection of any building or buildings for school purposes, or which shall have by its school trustee or trustees contracted any debts for the erection of such building or buildings, or the purchase of such ground and building or buildings, and such trustee or trustees shall not have the necessary means with which to complete such building or buildings, or to pay for the purchase of such ground and building or buildings, or pay such debt, may, on the filing by the school trustee or trustees of said city or incorporated town, of a report under oath with the common council of such city, or the board of trustees of such incorporated town, showing the estimated or actual cost of any such ground and building or buildings, or the amount required to complete such building or buildings, or purchase such ground and building or buildings, or the amount of such debt,—on the passage of an ordinance authorizing the same by the common council of said city, or the board of trustees of such incorporated town, issue the bonds of such city or town." Section 2 of said act, being section 5976, Burns' Rev. St. 1901 (section 4489, Rev. St. 1881; section 4489, Horner's Rev. St. 1901), requires that the proceeds of the sale of said bonds shall be paid to the school trustees of the town or city "to enable them to erect, or complete such building or buildings and pay such debt." Section 3 of said act was amended in 1875 (Acts 1875, p. 29). The section as amended, being section 5977, Burns' Rev. St. 1901 (section 4490, Rev. St. 1881; section 4490, Horner's Rev. St. 1901), provides for the levying and collection annually of a special tax, sufficient to pay the interest and principal of said bonds as they fall due.

It has been held by this court that the bonds issued under section 1 of said act, being section 5975 (4488), supra, were not the obligations of the school city, but were the bonds of the civil city, and must be counted to ascertain whether the aggregate indebtedness of such civil city was in excess of the constitutional limit of 2 per cent. Wilcoxon v. City of Bluffton, 153 Ind. 267, 54 N. E. 110. It is evident that, whatever may have been the power, if any, of school cities and towns to borrow money before said act of 1873 took effect (Wallis v. Johnson School Tp., 75 Ind. 368), after it took effect they had no such authority.

In 1879 the General Assembly passed an act supplemental to said act of 1873. The title of the last-named act was the same as the title of said act of 1873, heretofore set out in this opinion, except that the same followed immediately after the words "An act, supplemental to an act entitled." The first section of said act of 1879, being section 5978, Burns' Rev. St. 1901 (section 4491, Rev. St.

1881; section 4491, Horner's Rev. St. 1901), provides "that before the school trustee or trustees of any incorporated town or city in this state shall purchase any ground for school purposes, or enter into any contract for the building of any school building or buildings, such school trustee or trustees shall file a statement with the trustees of such incorporated town or common council of such city, showing the necessity for such purchase of ground, or the erection of such building or buildings, together with an estimate of the cost of such ground or building, or buildings, and the amount of means necessary to be provided, to pay for such ground or building, or buildings; and such school trustee or trustees shall not purchase any ground, or enter into any contract for the building of any school building, or buildings, until such action be approved by the trustees of such incorporated town, or by the common council of such city: provided, however, that there shall be nothing in this act so construed as to affect any purchase of ground, or contract made for the erection of any building, or buildings, for school purposes, prior to the taking effect of this act." It will be observed that the statement required by said act of 1879 must contain substantially the same information as is required to be set forth in the report required by section 1 of the act of 1873 providing for the issuance of the bonds of the civil city. The act of 1879 was passed as supplemental to said bond act of 1873, and must therefore be read and construed in connection therewith, and as a part of section 1 thereof, being section 5975 (4488), supra. So construed, it is evident that the General Assembly, by passing said act of 1879, and making it supplemental to the act of 1873, intended that the board of trustees of the town, or the common council of the city, if consent was granted to purchase the ground or erect said buildings for school purposes, at the same time, and as a part thereof, should provide whatever means were necessary for that purpose by the issue and sale of bonds as provided by section 1 of the act of 1873, being section 5975 (4488), supra. If the school town or city would not have on hand money available for that purpose sufficient to pay cash for said ground, or for the erection of such buildings when completed, the board of trustees of such town, or the common council of said city, would have no power to consent to the purchase of the ground or the erection of the building, unless it provided the means necessary for that purpose by an issuance and sale of bonds under section 1 of the act of 1873, being section 5975 (4488), supra, and any consent given without making such provision would be void. If the board of trustees of the town, or the common council of the city, were unable to provide the means necessary for such purpose, on account of being indebted to or beyond the constitutional limit, or for any other reason, it would have no power to give consent to the purchase of the ground or erection of the buildings, and any consent given would confer no power on the school corporation.

It follows that in 1902, when this suit was brought, the school city of Goshen had no power to erect a building for school purposes, even if the common council consented thereto, unless the means necessary for that purpose had been provided by the common council under section 5975 (4488), supra, or the school city had or would have on hand money sufficient to pay for said building when completed, and which it had the right, under the law, to use for that purpose. The allegations of the complaint show that the city of Goshen had not made any provision under section 5975 (4488), supra, to pay for said school buildings, and could not make any, because it was indebted beyond the constitutional limit, and that the school city did not have any money on hand which it had the right to use for that purpose, and would not have a sufficient sum to pay for the same until the expiration of 10 or 15 years. It is evident that the court erred in sustaining each of said demurrers.

Constitutional questions are argued by appellant, but the conclusion we have reached renders the decision thereof unnecessary.

Judgment reversed, with instructions to overrule the demurrer of each appellee, and for further proceedings not inconsistent with this opinion.

(32 Ind. App. 442)

CHAMBERLAIN et al. v. WAYMIRE.

(Appellate Court of Indiana, Division No. 1. Feb. 18, 1904.)

On petition for rehearing. Petition overruled and opinion modified.

For former opinion, see 68 N. E. 306.

PER CURIAM. After re-examining the entire record in this cause, we have concluded that justice would be best subserved by directing a new trial. The petition for rehearing is overruled, and the mandate heretofore made is modified as follows: The judgment is reversed, and the trial court is directed to grant a new trial.

CHICAGO & E. R. CO. v. FOX.*

(Appellate Court of Indiana, Division No. 1. Feb. 18, 1904.)

NEGLIGENCE—DANGEROUS PREMISES—RAILROADS—TURNTABLE—PLACES ATTRACTIVE TO CHILDREN—INJURIES TO CHILD NON SUI JURIS—TRESPASSER—IMPLIED INVITATION.

1. Where a railroad company maintained an unguarded and unlocked turntable on its premises at a point where the same was traversed by various paths, used by the public without objection, and the railroad employés had knowledge that, notwithstanding its dangerous character, the turntable was used by children as a plaything without objection, and it could have been guarded or fastened without seriously interfering with the railroad's business, the railroad was

*Rehearing denied. Transfer to Supreme Court denied.

liable to a child non sui juris for an injury sustained while he was playing thereon, though he was a trespasser in so doing.

Appeal from Circuit Court, Porter County; W. C. McMahan, Judge.

Action by Edward L. Fox, a minor, against the Chicago & Erie Railroad Company. From a judgment in favor of plaintiff, defendant appeals. Affirmed.

W. O. Johnson and Johnston, Bartholomew & Bartholomew, for appellant. L. L. Bomberger, D. E. Kelly, and W. J. Whinery, for appellee.

BLACK, J. The appellee, an infant, suing by his next friend, recovered a judgment against the appellant for a personal injury. At the time of the injury, and for many years before, the appellant owned and maintained at the city of Hammond railroad yards, side tracks, switches, a roundhouse, and a turntable, in the southern part of the city. The tracks of the appellant's railroad ran nearly north and south, and the tracks of the Monon Railroad Company, west of the appellant's grounds, and running nearly parallel with the appellant's tracks, were graded up between 2 and 3 feet. Douglass street crossed these tracks about 2,000 feet north of the turntable, and bounded appellant's yards on the north. About 3,600 feet south of the turntable another street, crossing the tracks, bounded the appellant's yards on the south. The east side of Harrison Park, a public park of the city, was west of the Monon tracks, and about 300 feet from the turntable, which was situated in the western part of appellant's yards, in front of the roundhouse. Webb street, running east and west, ran along the north side of Harrison Park, and terminated at the west side of the Monon tracks, nearly opposite the roundhouse and turntable, while from that terminal point Park avenue extended northward along the west side of the Monon tracks. The southern portion of the appellant's grounds was inclosed by a wire fence, which ran east and west, passing about 3 feet south of the roundhouse. A beaten path ran from the Monon Railroad, at a point about 60 feet south of Webb street, eastward between the wire fence and the roundhouse, and thence northeastward to the turntable, in front of the roundhouse, and about 180 feet east of it. The grounds in which the roundhouse and the turntable were situated were uninclosed. A short distance north of the turntable was a large excavation on the appellant's grounds, filled with water, and used as a swimming pool. The roundhouse was in a dilapidated condition, and was not used by the appellant; but the turntable was occasionally used for turning locomotives, which were brought upon it by a track which approached from the north, and connected with the track upon the turntable. Harrison Park, containing 25 or 30 acres, was resorted to for picnicking and general outing in summer, and for skating and coasting in winter. Carrol street, one square north of Webb street, and parallel with it, extended westward to the Monon Railroad. There was a path extending from Webb street across the Monon Railroad to the west wall of the roundhouse, and thence around its north side to the north side of the turntable. Opposite the east end of an alley which ran east and west between Carrol and Webb streets, another path extended southeastward, passing the north side of the roundhouse, to the turntable. There was also a path from Williams street, one square north of Carrol street, which ran southeastward to the Monon tracks, and thence around the north side of the swimming hole. All these paths united with a path running along the tracks of the appellant. The turntable had an iron frame 58 feet in diameter, and turned on a pivot, above an excavation 18 inches in depth, and was supported at the circumference by wheels which ran on a track extending around the excavation. The frame was floored over, and had a track of two rails, and two handles at opposite sides for turning the table. It was used for turning freight engines, mostly, sometimes three or four times a day, and sometimes once or twice a week. The rails of the track upon the turntable and those of the side track connected with the table came close together when opposite to each other. The roundhouse and the turntable could be seen from the park, and were within 600 feet from the nearest dwelling house. The turntable was permitted by the appellant to remain unfastened. The roundhouse and the turntable were frequently resorted to as playing places by the children of the city, and they had been so used for a number of years before the appellee's injury. The railroad grounds and tracks in the vicinity of the turntable were traversed daily by large numbers of people going to and from their work, and were frequented by children who played in Harrison Park, especially when they were attending picnics. Appellant's employés and its man in charge of the roundhouse and turntable frequently had seen children playing on the turntable, and such employés had more than once turned the table for the children to ride on it, and had given children permission to turn the table, provided they would restore it to its former position. Appellant's agent in charge of its yards and tracks at Hammond knew that children frequented the turntable; but the employés of the appellant had never driven children away from the turntable, or forbidden them to use it or to ride upon it, or take any active measures to prevent them from using it. On two occasions before the injury of appellee, children 6 or 7 years old had been injured while playing on the turntable, and one of appellant's employés had carried away from the turntable a child injured there. The appellee, who was a boy not quite 6½ years old, resided with his parents on Douglass street. With the knowledge and consent of his father, he left his home after noon on Sunday, December 1, 1901, to go about five blocks, to visit some boy friends residing at the corner of Webb street and Homan street, which ran north and south along the west side of Harrison Park. He had often before been at the home of these friends; having lived in their neighborhood, and having been in the habit of playing with them. He afterward went across the street into Harrison Park, and across the park to the Monon tracks, at a point south of the turntable, seeking his brother and another boy. There he met two boys about 13 years old, going north along the Monon Railroad, and, at their suggestion, walked with them northward toward his home along that railroad. When they came to a point on the railroad opposite the turntable, and not on the appellant's grounds, the appellee noticed the turntable, and asked the other boys to go with him to it and give him a ride on it, which they did; going eastward along the path which ran between the wire fence and the roundhouse. The appellee had ridden on the turntable before. The appellee sat down on the went side of the turntable, and the other two boys moved it around by pushing upon its handles. The turntable was not fastened, but was open; the track thereon extending east and west. When the appellee, thus situated, had ridden about one-fourth of the way around, and had arrived at one of the rails of the track for the passage of locomotives on and off of the turntable, the rails of which projected over the brink of the excavation so as to meet the rails of the track upon the turntable, the appellee was caught by the projecting rail, and his left leg was torn and crushed, the bones thereof being broken, and his right leg was severely lacerated. He was carried home by the other two boys, and thence he was removed to a hospital, where, after some weeks of nursing, his left leg was amputated.

As the case is presented by counsel, no matter for decision is before us, except the question as to the duty of the appellant toward the appellee with respect to the turntable, taking into consideration all the facts of the case.

Assuming that a railroad company is under no obligations to lock or otherwise fasten or render immovable or to guard its turntable so situated, when not in use for the purpose for which it was constructed and maintained, so as to prevent a like injury under like circumstances to a person capable of appreciating the danger, it does not necessarily follow that no such obligation exists with reference to a child, who, because of its immaturity, and consequent want of reason and judgment, is not chargeable with negligence, or is capable of only a small degree of care for his own safety. In Lynch v. Nurdin, 1 Q. B. 29, the defendant's cart, in charge of his servant, having been left standing unattended in a street, where there were a number of children playing, while the cartman went into a house, the plaintiff, under 7 years of age, climbed upon the cart. Another boy led the horse a few steps, and the plaintiff fell off, and, the wheel running over him, his leg was thereby broken. The defendant was found liable, and, although it was considered that the plaintiff was a trespasser, and contributed to his injury by his own action, it was held that the trial judge properly left to the jury whether the defendant's conduct was negligent, and whether the negligence caused the injury. In the course of his opinion, Lord Denman, C. J., observed that, "If it were probable that large parties of young children might be reasonably expected to resort to the spot, it would be hard to say that a case of gross negligence was not fully established. But the question remains, can the plaintiff then, consistently with the authorities, maintain his action, having been at least equally in fault? The answer is that, supposing that fact ascertained by the jury, but to this extent—that he merely indulged the natural instinct of a child in amusing himself with the empty cart and deserted horse, then we think that the defendant cannot be permitted to avail himself of that fact. The most blameable carelessness of his servant having tempted the child, he ought not to reproach the child with yielding to that temptation. He has been the real cause of the mischief. He has been deficient in ordinary care; and the child, being without prudence or thought, has, however, shown those qualities in as great a degee as he could be expected to possess them." In Binford v. Johnston, 82 Ind. 426, 42 Am. Rep. 508, the defendant had sold pistol cartridges to two brothers, aged 10 and 12 years, respectively, and a toy pistol loaded with one of the cartridges was left by these boys lying on the floor of their home; and the pistol having been taken up by another brother, aged 6, and discharged, the ball struck and fatally wounded one of the two boys who purchased the cartridges. In the discussion of the case, the Supreme Court cited Lynch v. Nurdin, supra, with approval. In Indianapolis, etc., R. Co. v. Pitzer, 109 Ind. 179, 6 N. E. 310, 10 N. E. 70, 58 Am. Rep. 387, the court, after saying that intruders, whether infants or adults, cannot, as a general rule, impose any duties upon the person on whose property they intrude, and citing thereto a number of cases, said further: "These cases are to be discriminated from those in which one places dangerous agencies where trespassing children are likely to be injured by them, for here the company did what it was perfectly lawful for it to do, and that was to run a passenger train in the manner in which such trains are usually managed. The class of cases to which we refer, although numerous, have no application here." Citing a number of cases—

among them, Lynch v. Nurdin, supra, and Binford v. Johnston, supra. And the court went on to say: "The cases last cited all recognize the rule that children of tender years are not to be treated as persons of mature years. This is a reasonable and humane rule, and any other would be a cruel reproach to the law." See Beach, Contr. Neg. §§ 137, 140; Birge v. Gardner, 19 Conn. 507, 50 Am. Dec. 261, cited in Indianapolis, etc., R. Co. v. Pitzer, supra. Railroad Co. v. Stout, 17 Wall. 657, 21 L. Ed. 745, also cited in Indianapolis, etc., R. Co. v. Pitzer, supra, was like the case at bar, and there, as here, the defendant rested its defense on the ground that the company was not negligent. The court approved an instruction which submitted that question to the jury. See Stout v. Sioux City, etc., R. Co., 2 Dill. 294, Fed. Cas. No. 13,504; Pacific R. Co. v. McDonald, 152 U. S. 262, 270, 14 Sup. Ct. 619, 38 L. Ed. 434, et seq.; Beach, Contr. Neg. § 207.

The duty of the defendant in such cases may be based upon what we, perhaps, may call one species of implied invitation, not involving the actual intention or wish of the defendant that the plaintiff should come upon the defendant's premises or do the act which results in his injury, but consisting in leaving a thing exposed and unguarded which is of such nature as to tempt and allure young children or others not sui juris to play with it or otherwise use it, at a place where, within the knowledge of the defendant, such incompetent persons assemble, or are likely to do so; the injurious thing being such that the defendant may enjoy the use of such property for the purpose to which it is adapted, and for which it is intended, without leaving it in a condition thus dangerous to such persons, but at slight expense may so secure it, when not in such use, that it will not be thus dangerous. The so-called invitation or tortious allurement which would be a violation of duty will not be involved where the defendant cannot carry on his lawful business or pursuit in the necessary and ordinary manner, and at the same time take precautions to prevent injury to such incompetent persons through the indulgence of their natural instinct to seek enjoyment or diversion, in which case, the injury being attributable, not to the fault of the injured person, but, rather, to the indulgence of an innocent instinct, no blame is attached to the defendant. Thus, for instance, would be the case of the intrusion of a child upon a railway train during its temporary stoppage at a station for the discharge and the reception of passengers, where the child enters the car along with other persons. In such case the railway company does nothing not incident to the usual and necessary way of conducting its lawful business. So might be the case of a child jumping upon the steps of a moving railway train. But a turntable, not constantly, but only occasionally, used to change the direction of locomotive engines, may, without undue interference with the company's full enjoyment thereof, be securely fastened, without great expense or inconvenience, when not in use; and such precaution may even tend to the preservation of the property itself, which, however, would be a matter within its own discretion. To take such precaution that others shall not use the appliance is not injurious to the company, or a hindrance to the prosecution of its lawful business. It is not an undue application of the maxim of the law commanding one to so use his own as not to injure another, to hold that the unnecessary exposure of one's property, attractive and alluring to children, but dangerous, at a place, though on his own premises, where the owner so exposing his property knows or has good reason to believe that children do or will come for the indulgence of the natural inclination or instinct of young persons to ride upon moving objects, or otherwise to divert themselves in a manner to which such dangerous object is adapted, involves such disregard for the safety of such incompetent persons as to amount to what may be called unlawful allurement, and as to be attributable as an implied invitation, in a case where, but for such incompetency of the injured person, he would be regarded as a trespasser or a mere licensee.

The following from Cooley on Torts is quoted in Union Pacific R. Co. v. McDonald, supra: "In the case of young children, and other persons not fully sui juris, an implied license might sometimes arise when it would not on behalf of others. Thus, leaving a tempting thing for children to play with exposed where they would be likely to gather for that purpose may be equivalent to an invitation to them to make use of it." In Thompson, Com. on Neg. (2d Ed.) § 1827, referring to the subject of injuries to children from unguarded and unfastened railway turntables, it is said: "In view of its great danger to children—so shown by the numerous cases in the lawbooks founded upon injuries of this kind—the just and humane conclusion must be that if the railway company can, at slight expense or inconvenience to itself, keep it guarded from trespassing children, or locked so that they cannot use it, it should be held bound to do so, and should stand liable in damages if, in consequence of the failure of this duty, a child of tender years, to whom contributory negligence cannot be imputed, is injured while playing with it. This, on the one hand, allows the railway company the reasonable use of its property, while at the same time it refuses to release it from those obligations of social duty which rest upon all men in a state of civilized society." See, also, section 1036 et seq. of the same work. The care which it is the duty of the railway company to exercise in such a case is that degree of care which an ordinarily prudent person would, under similar circumstances, use to prevent injury to children. O'Malley v. St. Paul, etc., R. Co., 43 Minn. 289, 45 N. W. 440. In Barrett v. Southern Pacific Co., 91 Cal. 296, 27 Pac. 666, 25 Am. St. Rep. 186—an action to recover damages for personal injury to the plaintiff, a boy of 8 years of age, sustained while riding on a railway turntable—it was said: "If defendant ought reasonably to have anticipated that, leaving this turntable unguarded and exposed, an injury such as plaintiff suffered was likely to occur, then it must be held to have anticipated it, and was guilty of negligence in thus maintaining it in its exposed position. It is no answer to this to say that the child was a trespasser, and, if it had not intermeddled with defendant's property, it would not have been hurt, and that the law imposes no duty upon the defendant to make its premises a safe playing-ground for children." And the question as to the defendant's negligence was held to be the one to be decided by the jury. In Alabama, etc., R. Co. v. Crocker, 131 Ala. 584, 31 South. 561, it was said: "It is the apparent probability of danger, rather than the rights of property, that determines the duty and measure of care required of the author of such a contrivance, for ordinarily the duty of avoiding known danger to others may under some circumstances operate to require care for persons who may be at the place of danger without right." In such case, where an object on one's premises has caused injury to another, the question as to the usefulness of the object to the owner, by way of contributing to the full enjoyment of his right of proprietorship, may enter into the consideration of the question of negligence in the maintenance of the object in the condition which occasioned the injury; but also it should be considered, in such connection, whether such enjoyment may be had, consistently with safety to others, at such slight expense and inconvenience as the due consideration of the known or probable danger to others, under all the circumstances, would suggest to a reasonably prudent person in the use of his own property of the particular kind in question in like situation and condition. See Koons v. St. Louis, etc., R. Co., 65 Mo. 592; Ferguson v. Columbus & Rome R. Co., 75 Ga. 637; Id., 77 Ga. 102; Ilwaco, etc., Nav. Co. v. Hedrick, 1 Wash. St. 446, 25 Pac. 335, 22 Am. St. Rep. 169; U. P. R. Co. v. Dunden, 37 Kan. 1, 14 Pac. 501; Gulf, etc., R. Co. v. Styron, 66 Tex. 421, 1 S. W. 161; Gulf, etc., R. Co. v. McWhirter, 77 Tex. 356, 14 S. W. 26, 19 Am. St. Rep. 755; Callahan v. Eel River R. Co., 92 Cal. 89, 28 Pac. 104; Keffe v. Milwaukee, etc., R. Co., 21 Minn. 207, 18 Am. Rep. 393; Kansas Central R. Co. v. Fitzsimmons, 22 Kan. 686, 31 Am. Rep. 203; Nagel v. Missouri Pac. R. Co., 75 Mo. 653, 42 Am. Rep. 418; Evansich v. G., C. & S. F. R. Co., 57 Tex. 126, 44 Am. Rep. 586. The four cases last above cited are also cited in Indianapolis, etc., R. Co. v. Pitzer, supra. See, also, Ft. Worth, etc., R. Co. v. Robertson (Tex. Sup.) 16 S. W. 1093, 14 L. R. A. 781; Edgington v. Burlington etc., R. Co. (Iowa) 90 N. W. 95, 57 L. R. A. 561; Chicago, etc., R. Co. v. Krayenbuhl (Neb.) 91 N. W. 880, 59 L. R. A. 920; San Antonio, etc., R. Co. v. Skidmore (Tex. Civ. App.) 65 S. W. 215; City of Pekin v. McMahon (Ill.) 39 N. E. 484, 27 L. R. A. 206, 45 Am. St. Rep. 114; Young v. Harvey, 16 Ind. 314; Graves v. Thomas, 95 Ind. 361, 48 Am. Rep. 727; City of Indianapolis v. Emmelman, 108 Ind. 530, 9 N. E. 155, 58 Am. Rep. 65; Penso v. McCormick, 125 Ind. 116, 25 N. E. 156, 9 L. R. A. 313, 21 Am. St. Rep. 211; Cincinnati, etc., Co. v. Brown (Ind. App.) 69 N. E. 197.

Judgment affirmed.

(32 Ind. A. 456)

JOHNSON et al. v. BLAIR.

(Appellate Court of Indiana, Division No. 1. Feb. 18, 1904.)

APPEAL—JOINT ASSIGNMENT OF ERROR—RULING ON PLEADINGS OF ONE APPELLANT.

1. A joint assignment of error by three defendants to adverse rulings on the pleadings of only one of them presents nothing for review.

Appeal from Circuit Court, Grant County; H. J. Paulus, Judge.

Suit by James H. Blair against James Johnson and others. Judgment for plaintiff, and defendants appeal. Affirmed.

Davis & Davis, for appellants. A. R. Long, for appellee.

HENLEY, C. J. Appellant has assigned error: First, the trial court erred in overruling the demurrer to the complaint; second, the trial court erred in overruling the motion for a new trial. The appellants are James Johnson, David O. Ice, and John F. Jones, and they have jointly assigned error. It appears from the record that the demurrer, to the overruling of which appellants complained, was a separate demurrer of James Johnson, and that the motion for a new trial, to the overruling of which appellants have excepted, was the separate motion of appellant James Johnson. The assignment of error, for this reason, does not present any question. Appellants David O. Ice and John F. Jones could not be affected by any ruling of the trial court on a demurrer or motion for a new trial submitted separately by James Johnson. Goss v. Wallace, 140 Ind. 541, 39 N. E. 920; Armstrong v. Dunn, 143 Ind. 433, 41 N. E. 540; McFarland v. Pierce, 151 Ind. 546, 45 N. E. 706, 47 N. E. 1; Hatfield v. Cummings, 152 Ind. 280, 50 N. E. 817, 53 N. E. 231; Green v. Heaston, 154 Ind. 127, 56 N. E. 87; Sheeks v. State, 156 Ind. 508, 60 N. E. 142; Killian v. State, 15 Ind. App. 261, 43 N. E. 955; Board, etc., v. Fraser, 19 Ind. App. 520, 49 N. E. 42, 831; Stephens v. Smith, 27 Ind. App. 507, 61 N. E. 745.

Judgment affirmed.

¶ 1. See Appeal and Error, vol. 3, Cent. Dig. § 2985.

(32 Ind. A. 466)

T. J. MOSS TIE CO. v. HUFF.

(Appellate Court of Indiana, Division No. 2. Feb. 19, 1904.)

APPEAL—RECORD—INSTRUCTIONS—SALES—ACTION FOR PURCHASE PRICE OF RAILROAD TIES—ADMISSIBILITY OF EVIDENCE—REVIEW—NECESSITY OF OFFERED PROOF.

1. Under Burns' Rev. St. 1901, §§ 543, 544, relating to instructions, and enacting that a party excepting thereto shall not be required to file a formal bill of exceptions, but may write on the margin of each instruction, "Refused, and excepted to," or "Given, and excepted to," which memorandum shall be signed by the judge, etc., instructions cannot be made a part of the record on appeal unless they are filed.

2. In an action for the price of railroad ties defendant's witness testified that he bought ties from other people, and inspected them before he bought, as he did with plaintiff. He was then asked, "That was the custom, was it not?" *Held*, that his answer thereto was properly stricken out, his custom in the matter not being material.

3. Defendant asked its witness what the prices plaintiff received would indicate as to the place of delivery, and asked another witness, who had testified to his knowledge of the manner in which plaintiff had got out the ties in question, whether that treatment of the ties was a careful way of handling them. *Held*, that objections to these questions were properly sustained.

4. The defendant asked its witness, a practical tie man, to state whether it would have been possible, from the time he (the witness) took charge of the work until the expiration of the contract, to get off the ties. The question was urged as proper because plaintiff asked a commission, because he claimed he would have got the ties off, whereas defendant claimed that plaintiff had delayed until it found it necessary to send the witness to take charge of the work. *Held*, that an objection to the question was properly sustained.

5. Where, on appeal, the record shows that no offer to prove was made before an objection to a question had been sustained, no question is raised for review.¶

Appeal from Circuit Court, Vanderburgh County; H. A. Mattison, Judge.

Action by Henry A. Huff against the T. J. Moss Tie Company. Judgment for plaintiff, and defendant appeals. Affirmed.

James T. Walker, for appellant. Henning & Henning, for appellee.

COMSTOCK, J. Appellee (plaintiff below) brought this action against appellant to recover an amount claimed to be due him from appellant on account of the purchase for and delivery to the appellant of crossties at prices and on terms set out in the complaint. The complaint was in five paragraphs. Appellant answered the complaint by general denial and plea of payment. Appellant also filed a cross-complaint in four paragraphs, upon which issue was formed by general denial. No question is raised upon the pleadings, and further statement of them is not necessary. The jury returned a verdict in favor of appellee for $1,402.57. He remitted $648.23, and thereupon judgment was rendered in the sum of $754.24. Overruling appellant's motion for a new trial is assigned as error.

In support of the motion it is urged that the evidence is not sufficient to sustain the verdict. In passing upon this reason for a new trial it is enough to say that there is evidence fairly tending to sustain the verdict, and to refer to the rule that appellate courts will not weigh the evidence upon appeal.

Appellant insists that the court erred in giving to the jury instructions 4 and 6, and each of them. Appellee contends that the questions attempted to be raised upon these instructions cannot be considered, because the instructions are not properly in the record. Instructions may be made a part of the record in three ways: (1) By order of court; (2) by bill of exceptions; (3) under sections 543, 544, Burns' Rev. St. 1901, sections 534, 535 (Horner's Rev. St. 1901). In the case at bar they are not made a part of the record by order of court nor by bill of exceptions. An attempt is made to make them a part of the record under said sections of the statute. It does not appear that the instructions were filed. They are not, therefore, a part of the record. Ayres v. Blevins, 28 Ind. App. 102, 62 N. E. 305; Krom v. Vermillion, 143 Ind. 77, 41 N. E. 539.

W. S. James, a witness for appellant, upon direct examination testified that he bought ties from other people than the appellee, and that he inspected them before he bought them, the same as he did with Mr. Huff. The question was then put, "That was the custom, was it not?" Upon motion of plaintiff his answer was stricken out. The dealings of parties hereto was matter of contract. The custom of the witness was immaterial.

Appellant asked its own witness the following question (witness had testified that he was a representative of the Cincinnati Cooperage Company): "Now, supposing the price which Mr. Huff received was 30 and 35 cents for firsts, and 15 and 17 cents for seconds, what would that indicate as to the place of delivery?" Appellant asked its own witness, who had previously testified as to his knowledge of the manner in which appellee had gotten out the ties in question, and his condition in relation thereto, the following question, "You may tell the jury whether that treatment of the ties was a careful, proper, and prudent way of handling them?" Appellant also proposed to Mr. Burten, one of the witnesses, a practical tie man, who was familiar with the work of getting the ties off the land upon which the appellee was working, the following question: "From the time you took charge of the work until the expiration of the contract, tell the court and jury whether it would have been possible to get off those ties?" Appellant claims the question was proper, because Huff claimed he would have gotten the ties off, and asks commission for that reason; that he had delayed until the company found it necessary to send

¶ 5. See Appeal and Error, vol. 3, Cent. Dig. § 1283.

Burten to take charge of the work. In these various rulings there was no error. But, if the court had erred, no question is raised, because the record shows that no offer to prove was made before the objection to the question had been sustained. Pittsburgh, etc., R. Co. v. Martin, 157 Ind. 224, 61 N. E. 229.

Judgment affirmed.

(185 Mass. 202)

HUSSEY v. ARNOLD et al.

(Supreme Judicial Court of Massachusetts. Suffolk. Feb. 26, 1904.)

TRUSTS — LIABILITY OF TRUSTEES — ACTION AGAINST TRUSTEES—ATTACHMENT—LIEN—LIABILITY OF ESTATE.

1. In the absence of special limitation, a contract by one who is a trustee relative to the trust property binds him personally.

2. Several persons formed an association for investment in real estate and the management thereof, the property being vested in trustees, and the trust agreement provided that contracts entered into by the trustees should be in their names as such, and should provide against any personal liability on their part, and provided that those having a beneficial interest in the property should not be liable to any third person. One who had sold goods to the trustees brought an action at law against them, and attached certain property held by them as trustees. *Held*, that plaintiff acquired no lien, either legal or equitable, since under the agreement those beneficially interested could not be charged, and, if the trustees contracted, without limiting their liability, their personal liability so created could not be enforced against the trust property, and, if the trustees had a beneficial interest in the property, such interest could be attached at law.

Report from Superior Court, Suffolk County; Jas. B. Richardson, Judge.

Suit by George F. Hussey against Edward L. Arnold and others. Order dismissing the petition of W. B. Emery and others for a dissolution of an injunction granted complainants. Case reported. Affirmed.

G. W. Anderson, for W. B. Emery and others. Geo. Royal Pulsifer, for receivers.

KNOWLTON, C. J. Some of the defendants entered into an agreement establishing an association called "The Boston Associates," and appointing three trustees to conduct the business of the association, which was to be the investment, management, and use of property in real estate, in shares, in trusts and corporations, in bonds secured by mortgage upon real estate, and in other similar securities, with a view to obtain income and profit for the owners. These trustees were to hold the title to all the property that was paid in or acquired, and to manage it, subject to the provisions of the agreement, as they should see fit. Either of the trustees could be removed and a successor could be appointed by three-fourths in value of the shareholders, and, if not removed, they could fill vacancies in their board caused by death or resignation or otherwise. The trust could be terminated by a writing signed by three-fourths in value of the shareholders; but, if not so terminated, it was to continue for the term of 20 years after the death of the last subscriber to the agreement. Shares of $100 each, taken by the subscribers, and represented by certificates, could be transferred, and the transferee would thereby acquire the rights and be subject to all the obligations of the original owner. Each shareholder was to be liable for the amount subscribed by him, but he was not to be liable to any third person, nor for any amount in excess of his subscription. This association became insolvent, and a suit in equity was brought, and receivers were appointed to wind up its affairs. William B. Emery and Heber E. Emery, copartners under the name of W. H. & S. L. Emery, furnished coal to the trustees for the use of the association, for which they were not paid, and more than four months before the commencement of the suit in equity they brought an action at law against the trustees in their individual names, describing them as "Trustees of the Boston Associates," and attached on the writ all their right, title, and interest in and to any real estate in the county of Suffolk. At that time these trustees held in their names as trustees the title to certain real estate in Boston, which was acquired and held for the associates under this agreement. The plaintiffs in the action at law were enjoined in the suit in equity from proceeding to enforce the collection of their claim against the real estate under their attachment. They subsequently brought a petition in the suit in equity for a dissolution of the injunction, or for a decree establishing a lien in their favor upon the real estate. From an order of the superior court denying and dismissing their petition they appealed to this court.

The agreement creating the trust has peculiar provisions. The object of it, apparently, was to obtain for the associates most of the advantages belonging to corporations, without the authority of any legislative act, and with freedom from the restrictions and regulations imposed by law upon corporations. Article 12 of the agreement is as follows: "All contracts and engagements entered into by the trustees shall be in their names as trustees, and shall provide against any personal liability on the part of the trustees, and stipulate that no other party shall be answerable than the property in the hands of the trustees." We have already said that the subscribers were not to be liable to third persons, and it would seem, therefore, that the business of the trust was intended to be done in a way that would give no one dealing with it a right to bring an action at law against anybody to enforce any contract or liability of the association. The trustees held the legal title to all the property, and they alone could make contracts. Ordinarily, in the absence of special limita-

¶ 2. See Attachment, vol. 5, Cent. Dig. §§ 131, 171.

tions, trustees bind themselves personally by their contracts with third persons. Actions at law upon such contracts must be brought against them, and judgments run against them personally. This is because the relations of the cestuis que trustent to their contracts are only equitable, and do not subject them to proceedings in a court of common law, and the property held in trust is charged with equities which hold it aloof from the jurisdiction of a court of law to take it and apply it in payment of debts created by the trustees. Such debts, if proper charges upon the trust estate, can be paid from it under the authority of a court of equity.

Whether the trustees in this case, in dealing with the petitioners, provided against personal liability in accordance with the direction of the agreement, as they might do (see Shoe & Leather National Bank v. Dix, 123 Mass. 148, 25 Am. Rep. 49), does not appear. If they did, these petitioners cannot maintain an action at law against anybody. As agents and trustees under the agreement, they were not authorized to contract any debt which should charge the certificate holders. Of course, if an action at law cannot be maintained, there can be no effectual attachment in such a suit as the petitioners originally brought. If the trustees contracted in the usual way, without referring to anything which would limit the liability resulting from an ordinary contract, they are personally liable to these petitioners, and judgment can be obtained and enforced against them individually; but the trust property cannot be held under an attachment nor sold upon an execution for their personal debts. If, as we presume to be the fact, the trustees were also certificate holders having equitable interests in the property, these are not attachable in an action at law. They can be reached only through proceedings in equity. Rev. Laws, c. 159, § 3, cl. 7; Geer v. Horton, 159 Mass. 259, 34 N. E. 269; Wemyss v. White, 159 Mass. 484, 34 N. E. 718. On no ground, therefore, can it be held that the petitioners acquired a lien upon the real estate by their attempted attachment in the action at law. In the pending suit in equity they stand like other creditors. They have already proved their claim against the estate in the hands of the receivers, and they will obtain their share of the assets.

Our decision goes no further than to hold that, upon the facts shown, the petitioners have acquired no lien, legal or equitable, which gives them precedence over other creditors in the settlement of this trust. We do not attempt to determine whether all the provisions of this agreement are enforceable in the courts, or whether there are such considerations of public policy involved in an attempt of this kind to do business without a legal liability of anybody for debts incurred by the trustees as merit consideration by the Legislature.

Order affirmed.

(185 Mass. 219)

LANCY v. CITY OF BOSTON.

(Supreme Judical Court of Massachusetts. Suffolk. Feb. 27, 1904.)

EMINENT DOMAIN—COMPENSATION—EQUITABLE RELIEF—PRACTICE—LIMITATIONS.

1. Under St. 1897, p. 550, c. 519, authorizing the appointment of commissioners to consider the abolition of a certain grade crossing, and providing that damages caused by proceedings under the act might be recovered as provided by St. 1890, p. 464, c. 428, § 5, which declares that a petition for the assessment of damages shall be brought within one year after the decree confirming the decision of the commission, the court has no jurisdiction to entertain a petition after one year from such decree.

2. St. 1900, p. 57, c. 84, authorizing a recovery by persons whose property was injured by a change of grade of streets in connection with the abolition of a certain grade crossing, does not authorize a recovery by one whose property was taken for a highway by the commissioners appointed under St. 1897, p. 550, c. 519, to consider the abolition of the grade crossing.

3. Under St. 1897, p. 550, c. 519, relative to the abolition of a certain grade crossing, and providing that all persons damaged in their property may recover as provided by St. 1890, p. 464, c. 428, § 5, by petition to the superior court, etc., a property owner has no right to have the original petition to abolish the grade crossing amended, the proper course being to intervene.

4. Under St. 1897, p. 550, c. 519, relative to the abolition of a grade crossing, and providing that all persons damaged in their property may recover as provided by St. 1890, p. 464, c. 428, § 5, by petition to the superior court, etc., an owner of property taken for the improvement has a plain and adequate remedy at law, and is not entitled to equitable relief.

5. That the owner had no actual notice or knowledge that his land was taken was immaterial.

Report from Superior Court, Suffolk County; Jas. B. Richardson, Judge.

Petition by one Lancy against the city of Boston. There was judgment for defendant, and the case was reported to the Supreme Judicial Court. Affirmed.

W. O. Childs, for plaintiff. Samuel M. Child, for defendant.

LATHROP, J. This is a petition to the superior court, filed June 25, 1900, for a jury to assess damages for the taking of a parcel of the petitioner's land for a highway by the commissioners appointed under St. 1897, p. 550, c. 519, to consider the abolition of the grade crossing of Dorchester avenue and the railroad of the Old Colony Railroad Company. The decision of the commissioners was confirmed by the court on June 23, 1898. The taking by the commissioners was authorized by section 3 of the act, and by section 4 all damages suffered by any persons in their property by reason of anything done under the act might be recovered as provided in St. 1890, p. 463, c. 428. Section 5 of this act provides that a petition to the superior court for the assessment of damages shall be "brought within one year after the day of the date of the decree of the court confirming the decision of said commission." The respondent filed a general denial, and subsequently moved to have the petition dismissed for the reason that it was not filed in time; and the petitioner moved to amend the petition into a bill in equity, incorporating it as a paragraph in the original petition for the abolition of the grade crossing, by striking out the prayer for a jury, and substituting therefor a prayer that the damages be assessed by the court sitting in equity, and an allegation that the taking was without the knowledge of the petitioner, or notice to him; that he first learned of the taking about June 20, 1900; that the land was erroneously taken as the land of the Old Colony Railroad Company, and not as the land of the plaintiff; and that, if it had been taken as his, he would have had an award in his favor, and would have been notified of the taking. The judge ruled that the petition could not be maintained, granted the motion to dismiss, and ordered judgment for the respondent. The judge further ruled that, if the petition could be turned into a bill in equity, it could not be maintained for the assessment of damages, and reported the case for the determination of this court. If either of the rulings was wrong, judgment was to be entered for the petitioner for $200 and costs.

The first contention of the petitioner is that the petition can be maintained on the ground that the street was laid out, not as a part of the abolition of Dorchester avenue grade crossing, but as a separate municipal improvement; and to this point he cites Farwell v. Boston, 180 Mass. 433, 438, 62 N. E. 751. While there is broad and general language in the opinion, the only points decided were that section 4 of the Statutes of 1897, p. 552, c. 519, was intended "to insure compensation for all damages, but not to change the rule of damages," and that a petitioner whose access to a railroad was taken away by the removal of the railroad, and whose land was not taken in this connection, could not recover damages for the injury to his business. There is nothing in that case which bears upon the contention of the petitioner here as to the time in which the petition must be filed. Where a statute limits the time in which a petition for damages must be brought, the court has no jurisdiction to entertain a petition brought after that time has expired. Custy v. Lowell, 117 Mass. 78; Cambridge v. County Commissioners, Id. 79; Gately v. Old Colony Railroad, 171 Mass. 494, 51 N. E. 5—a decision under St. 1890, p. 464, c. 428, § 5. See, also, McGrath v. Watertown, 181 Mass. 380, 63 N. E. 889. The petition, therefore, was rightly dismissed.

It is not contended that the case falls within the provisions of St. 1900, p. 57, c. 84, and it is clear that it does not, for that statute is limited to persons injured by a change of grade of streets in connection with the abolition of the grade crossing of Dorchester avenue and the Old Colony Railroad.

The remaining question is as to the right of the petitioner to change the petition into a bill in equity by inserting it, with some changes, into the petition in the original proceedings to abolish the grade crossing. It is clear that, if the petitioner has any right to equitable relief, he has no right to have the petition in the original proceedings amended, and his proper course would be to file a petition in that case as an intervener. Middleborough v. New York, New Haven & Hartford Railroad, 179 Mass. 520, 524, 61 N. E. 107. But we are of opinion that he is not entitled to relief in equity. It is true that such relief was granted in the case last cited, but that was on the ground that the town which sought to recover damages for land taken within its borders could not avail itself of the relief afforded by section 5 of the Statutes of 1890, p. 464, c. 428, because it could not sue itself. The general rule of law is that where the Legislature authorizes the taking of land for a public use, and the taking is in accordance with the statute, and a plain and adequate remedy is provided for compensation, the remedy provided by statute is exclusive. Perry v. Worcester, 6 Gray, 544, 546, 66 Am. Dec. 431; Hull v. Westfield, 133 Mass. 433, 434; Boston Belting Co. v. Boston, 140 Mass. 44, 20 N. E. 320; Titus v. Boston, 149 Mass. 164, 166, 21 N. E. 310; Brainard v. Newton, 154 Mass. 255, 27 N. E. 995, where relief in equity was denied. In Gately v. Old Colony Railroad, 171 Mass. 494, 51 N. E. 5, it was contended that St. 1890, p. 464, c. 428, § 5, was unconstitutional, because it did not provide for notice to the owner whose land was taken; but it was pointed out in the opinion that the entire proceeding of taking the land was by a suit in court, and it was held that no further notice was required than that provided for in the statute. See, also, Appleton v. Newton, 178 Mass. 276, 59 N. E. 648, where this subject is discussed at length. The fact, therefore, that the petitioner had not, in fact, any notice or knowledge that his land was taken, is immaterial, if the provisions of the statute were complied with, and there is nothing to show that they were not complied with.

Judgment for the respondent affirmed.

(186 Mass. 288)

KELLEY v. SNOW et al.

(Supreme Judicial Court of Massachusetts. Bristol. March 9, 1904.)

TRUSTS—VALIDITY—POWER OF REVOCATION—DELIVERY OF PROPERTY—REVOCATION OF TRUST—WILLS—MARRIED WOMEN — CONSENT OF HUSBAND—CODICILS—CONSTRUCTION.

1. Where a trust deed recited a valuable consideration, contained apt words of conveyance, was under seal, and was delivered to the trustee, who received the same and agreed to carry out all the trusts therein stipulated, the legal title to the property, as between the parties, passes to the trustee even without delivery.

2. A trust of personalty is not invalidated by provisions that the donor during her life should have the use of the property and power to change the dispositions at any time on written notice to the trustee.

3. A deed conveying personalty to a trustee, to be distributed at the death of the donor, but providing that she should retain possession during her life, and should have power to change the dispositions on written notice to the trustee, was, in view of the donor's obvious purpose to make changes in the disposition of her property without her husband's consent, not a testamentary instrument, but a present conveyance of the property to take effect during the donor's lifetime.

4. Under the statutes, the power of a married woman over her personal estate during her lifetime is absolute so far as respects her husband, and she may give it away or convey it on such terms as she pleases, provided that the conveyance be real and not colorable, and is made to take effect in her lifetime.

5. The simple return of a trust agreement by the trustee to the donor will not of itself change the legal title of the trustee or the rights of the beneficiaries.

6. Where a trust deed reserved in the donor the right to change the disposition of the property to be made at the donor's decease, at any time, on written notice to the trustee, a revocation made by will, no notice having been given to the trustee during the life of the donor, was void.

7. Whether the facts showed a special trust in a bankbook held by another was a question of fact, and not of law.

8. Facts as found by a master *held* to warrant his conclusion that testatrix did not at any time intend to create a trust in favor of a certain claimant in a deposit in bank.

9. Under Pub. St. 1882, c. 147, § 6, providing that a married woman may make a will as if sole, except that no such will shall, without the written consent of her husband, operate to deprive him of her real estate, not exceeding $5,000 in value, where no issue survive her, or, in any event, of more than one-half of her personal estate, the consent of the husband is not necessary to the validity of his wife's will, so far as it does not interfere with his rights in her estate should he survive her.

10. Pub. St. 1882, c. 147, § 6, providing that a married woman may make a will as if sole, except that no such will shall, without the written consent of her husband, operate to deprive him of her real estate, not exceeding $5,000 in value, where no issue survive her, or, in any event, of more than one-half of her personal estate, does not change the common-law rule that consent by a husband to one will is not applicable to a subsequent will which changes substantially the disposition of the property as to which the consent is requisite.

11. Where a married woman's will was invalid for want of consent of her husband, he could not claim both his statutory rights in her property and also a specific legacy.

12. A codicil whereby testatrix ratified and confirmed her will "except as herein changed," and which did not mention an item of her original will, left the legacy contained in such item in force.

13. Clauses in a will providing for the disposition of a trust fund, and intended to be paid only from it, are inoperative where the attempted revocation of the trust by the will is void.

14. A clause in a will, providing that the trustee should hold in trust all the "rest, residue, and remainder" of the property, and pay the income thereof to a designated person for life, and so much of the principal as he deemed best, was sufficiently broad to cover everything in the estate not otherwise disposed of.

Case Reserved from Supreme Judicial Court, Bristol County; Marcus P. Knowlton, Judge.

Petition for instructions by Bernard F. Kelley, executor and trustee, against Benjamin F. Snow and others. Case reserved for the full court. Decree rendered.

The following are the will and codicils to the will of Mary Ann Snow:

"Know all men by these presents that I, Mary Ann Snow, of New Bedford, Bristol County, Massachusetts, being of sound and disposing mind and memory, do make, publish and declare this my last will and testament.

"First. I order my executor hereinafter named as soon as convenient after my decease to sell all my property, real, personal or mixed, and I hereby authorize and appoint my said executor to sell said property, both real and personal, either at private sale or public auction, and to make, execute and deliver all deeds, bills of sale or other instruments necessary to carry such sales into effect.

"Second. After the payment of all my debts, funeral expenses and the charges of administration, and the amount to which my husband, Benjamin F. Snow, would by law be entitled from the proceeds of said sale, I give and bequeath to Mary Ann Hammond, my niece, the sum of one thousand dollars.

"Third. All the rest, residue and remainder of my estate, real, personal or mixed, I give, devise and bequeath to Thomas R. Hillman in trust, nevertheless, for the following trust purposes only, viz: to keep the same safely invested and to pay over the income therefrom to Gracie Kirwin for and during the term of her natural life. At her death I direct my said trustee to pay over said trust fund, together with all accumulations of interest to the issue of said Gracie Kirwin if she die leaving issue surviving her. If the said Gracie should die leaving no issue surviving her I direct my said trustee to pay over said trust property in equal shares to Mary Ann Hammond, Thomas Meade, son of my brother, John Meade, and Bernard Kelly.

"Fourth. I nominate and appoint Thomas R. Hillman as executor of this will and request that he be not required, either as executor or trustee under this will, to furnish surety or sureties on his official bond.

"In witness whereof I have hereunto set my hand this twenty-third day of June A. D. 1892.

her
"Mary X Ann Snow.
mark.

"Signed, published and declared by the said Mary Ann Snow as and for her last will and testament in presence of us, who, at her request, in her presence and in the presence of each other have hereunto set our names as witnesses.

Henry B. Worth.
"Garry de N. Hough.
"Philip E. Macy."

"I, Mary Ann Snow make this codicil to my will above executed. I revoke and cancel in the second clause of my will the words, 'And the amount to which my husband, Benjamin F. Snow, would by law be entitled,' and I hereby give and bequeath to my said husband the sum of two thousand dollars, except as herein changed by this codicil I hereby ratify and confirm my said will.

"In witness whereof I hereto set my hand this twenty-third day of June A. D. 1892.

her
"Mary X Ann Snow.
mark.

"Signed, published and declared by the said Mary Ann Snow as and for a codicil to her last will, in presence of us, who at her request, in her presence and in presence of each other hereto set our names as witnesses both to the signature of Mary Ann Snow and Benjamin F. Snow her husband.

"Henry B. Worth.
"Garry de N. Hough.
"Philip E. Macy.

"I hereby consent to this codicil and the foregoing will as changed by this codicil.

"Benj. F. Snow."

"I, Mary Ann Snow, make this second codicil to my will dated June 23d 1892.

"I revoke section four of my said will and substitute therefor the following section.

"I nominate and appoint Bernard Kelley of Rochester, New York, executor of the foregoing will and codicil.

"In witness whereof I hereto set my hand this first day of November, A. D. 1893.

her
"Mary X Ann Snow.
mark.

"Witnessed by us and subscribed in the presence of the said Mary Ann Snow.

"Henry B. Worth.
"John L. G. Mason.
"Tillinghast Kirby."

"I, Mary Ann Snow, wife of Benjamin Snow of New Bedford, Bristol County, Massachusetts, make this codicil to my last will in manner following. My will and the codicil thereto are dated June twenty-third 1892, and my husband, Benjamin F. Snow, assented thereto and I hereby ratify and confirm said will and codicil except as herein changed.

"1. My friend Thomas R. Hillman has deceased and I appoint as executor of this will my nephew Bernard Kelly and I request that he be excused from furnishing sureties or a surety on his official bond. He shall have all the power given in said will to Hillman.

"2. The third clause in said will, wherein the rest, residue and remainder of my estate was given in trust to Thomas R. Hillman for the benefit of Gracie Kirwin I hereby cancel and revoke, also the bequests therein given at the end of said third clause to Mary Ann Hammond, Thomas Meade and Bernard Kelly and issue of Gracie Kirwin.

"3. Whereas the said Bernard Kelly entered into a trust agreement dated September eleventh, 1893, wherein he agreed upon receipt of eleven savings bank deposits to make certain disposition of the same as in said agreement contained. I do now cancel said disposition and revoke the same and in place thereof substitute the following bequests:

"4. I direct my executor to deposit with the Treasurer of the City of New Bedford the sum of two hundred dollars the income from which shall be used in the care and preservation of my burial lot in Oak Grove Cemetery in New Bedford.

"5. I give and bequeath to Bernard Kelly, my nephew, three thousand dollars.

"6. I give and bequeath to my sister, Elizabeth Kelly, two thousand dollars.

"7. I give and bequeath to my niece, Mary Ann Hammond, the sum of two thousand dollars, one half of my silver, one feather bed, three mats and one set gold band china crockery.

"8. To the following named persons I give and bequeath the sum of one thousand dollars each; Thomas Meade, son of my brother John Meade; John Meade, son of the aforesaid Thomas Meade; Mary Meade, daughter of Thomas and grand-daughter of my brother John Meade; Mary C. Hammond, daughter of said Mary Ann Hammond; Elizabeth E. Hammond, daughter of said Mary Ann Hammond; Herbert Hammond, son of said Mary Ann Hammond; Edward Kelly, son of my sister Elizabeth; William Meade, son of my brother John Meade; William Meade, son of Thomas and grandson of my brother John.

"9. All the rest, residue and remainder of my estate, real, personal or mixed I give, devise and bequeath to the said Mary Ann Hammond.

"In witness whereof I hereto set my hand this twenty-eighth day of June, 1901.

her
"Mary X Ann Snow.
mark.

"Signed, published and declared by the said Mary Ann Snow as and for a codicil to her last will and testament in presence of us, who at her request, in her presence and in presence of each other have hereto put our names as witnesses.

"Henry B. Worth.
"F. H. Freeman, Nurse.
"E. C. Coombs, Nurse."

The trust deed reads as follows:

"Know all men by these presents that I, Mary Ann Snow, of New Bedford, Bristol County, Massachusetts, for a valuable consideration, do hereby assign and transfer unto Bernard F. Kelley, of Rochester, New York State, all my personal property, consisting of my household furniture and furnishings and silver and clothing; and the following deposits in savings banks, viz: Money on account No. 72,088, New Bedford Institute for Savings; money on account No. 80,718, New Bedford Institute for Savings; money on account No. 52,083, New Bedford Institute for Savings; money on account No.

37,335, New Bedford Institute for Savings; money on account No. 44,665, New Bedford Institute for Savings; money on account No. 47,319, New Bedford Institute for Savings; money on account No. 56,762, New Bedford Institute for Savings; money on account No. 79,772, New Bedford Institute for Savings; money on account No. 26,431, New Bedford Five Cents Savings Bank; money on account No. 39,962, New Bedford Five Cents Savings Bank; money on account No. 14,261 Plymouth Savings Bank, Plymouth, Mass.—in trust, nevertheless, for the following trust purposes only and not otherwise, viz:

"First. Said Mary Ann Snow is to retain possession of the property hereby assigned, together with the bank pass books represent-in said savings bank deposits to collect the income during her life.

"Second. Said Mary Ann Snow shall have the power to change the following dispositions at any time upon written notice to said Kelley.

"Third. At the decease of said Mary Ann Snow, said Kelley shall then take possession of said property and bank books and shall distribute the same as follows, providing the following dispositions have not been changed.

"Fourth. To Mary Ann Hammond, wife of Herbert Hammond, one-half of my silver and one feather bed, three mats and one set gold band china crockery.

"Fifth. To Grace Kirwin, my son's natural child, the remainder of my silver and household furniture and clothing.

"Sixth. I direct my said trustee to deposit with the Treasurer of the City of New Bedford the sum of one hundred dollars, the income from which shall be used in the care and improvement of my burial lot in Oak Grove Cemetery, New Bedford, Mass.

"Seventh. To Norah Meade three hundred dollars.

"Eighth. To Bernard F. Kelley three thousand dollars.

"Ninth. My said trustee shall hold in trust the sum of two thousand dollars, and shall pay the income thereof to said Mary Ann Hammond during her natural life. If her husband shall die during her life said trustee shall thereupon pay to her the whole of said trust fund. At her decease if said fund shall not have been paid to her as aforesaid it shall then be paid to her issue surviving her.

"Tenth. My said trustee shall hold in trust the sum of five hundred dollars, and shall pay the income thereof to my brother James Mead during his life. At his decease said fund shall be paid over to George Mead, son of said James Mead.

"Eleventh. My said trustee shall pay to my sister Elizabeth Kelley the sum of one thousand dollars.

"Twelfth. My trustee shall hold in trust the sum of one thousand dollars, the income thereof to be paid to Thomas Mead, son of my brother John Mead, during his life. At his death said fund shall be paid to John Mead, son of said Thomas. If said John Mead die before his father, leaving issue surviving him, said fund shall be paid to such issue. If he leave no issue surviving him it shall be paid to his brothers and sisters who may be living at his father's death.

"Thirteenth. All the rest, residue and remainder of said property, my said trustee shall hold in trust and shall pay the income therefrom to said Grace Kirwin during her life; if it shall be considered expedient by my trustee he may pay to said Grace Kirwin such sums from the principal as he deems best. At her decease said fund or so much as remains shall be paid to the issue of said Grace if she die leaving issue surviving her. If no issue survive her said fund shall be paid to the issue of Elizabeth Kelley by right of representation as such issue may be determined at the death of said Grace Kirwin.

"Fourteenth. If said Mary Ann Hammond mentioned in section fourth, or George Mead, son of James Mead, or either of them die leaving no surviving issue, said trustee shall dispose of the fund herein given for the benefit of such person in accordance with the provisions of section thirteenth hereof.

"Fifteenth. The said Bernard F. Kelley hereby assents to the terms of the foregoing instrument and agrees to carry out all the trusts therein stipulated.

"In witness whereof we hereto set our hands and seals this eleventh day of September, 1893.

her
"Mary X Ann Snow. [L. S.]
mark.
"Bernard F. Kelly. [L. S.]

"Witnessed by Henry B. Worth.

"New Bedford, Sept. 11, 1893.

"Then personally appeared the said Mary Ann Snow and Bernard F. Kelley and acknowledged the foregoing instrument by them signed to be their free act and deed.

"Before me, Henry B. Worth,
"[Notarial Seal.] Notary Public."

"To the Treasurer of the Plymouth Savings Bank, Plymouth, Mass.

"New Bedford, Mass., Sept. 8th, 1893.

"For value received, I hereby assign and transfer to Bernard F. Kelley and his legal representatives, all the moneys that have been deposited, together with interest that has become due on account of Book No. 14,-261 in the Plymouth Savings Bank.

her
"Mary X Ann Snow.
mark.

"Witness to signature:
"Henry B. Worth."

The master's findings referred to in the opinion are as follows:

"(11) One of the savings-bank deposits included in the property which the trust instrument purports to assign and transfer to the petitioner is a deposit amounting to sixteen hundred dollars, represented by book No. 56,-762 in the New Beford Institution for Savings, standing in the name of the testatrix in trust for the respondent, Elizabeth Kelley, a sister of the testatrix. Elizabeth Kelley claims the deposit. The facts in the matter are these: The account was opened by the testatrix in trust, as above stated, in 1874. In does not appear that Elizabeth Kelley knew of its existence until 1885, when, at the request of the testatrix, she executed and delivered a written transfer of it to the testatrix. In 1889 the balance of the deposit, namely, $1,600, was carried to a new book, but under the same number and the same account, and, at the time when this was done, the testatrix signed and delivered to the bank the following declaration: 'Having deposited money in the New Bedford Institution for Savings as trustee, as represented by book No. 56,762, I hereby declare that no written trust exists, and that by the terms of said trust said deposit with its dividends is payable to me or my order during my life, and after my death to my estate.' No additional deposits were made on the account subsequent to this time, and the dividends, as they accrued, were drawn by the testatrix. In 1889, and prior thereto, the testatrix had a number of deposits of more than one thousand dollars each in the bank stated, standing, one in her own name, and the others in her name ostensibly in trust for various persons, but in reality for her own use. On several occasions subsequent to 1889 the testatrix told Elizabeth Kelley that she had put money in the bank for her, but she did not state how much or the name of the bank. On one of these occasions she said to Mrs. Kelley: 'If you will sell your house and come to live with me, I will help you more.' Mrs. Kelley, however, did not sell her house, and did not go to live with the testatrix. At different times subsequent to 1889 the testatrix told the daughter and son-in-law of Mrs. Kelley that she had put money in the bank for the latter, but she did not state how much, or designate the bank. The book was never delivered by the testatrix to Elizabeth Kelley, or to any one for her, but was always kept by the former in her possession until the day before she died, when she handed it, with the transfer to the petitioner signed by her when she executed the trust instrument, to Mary Ann Hammond to deliver to the petitioner upon her death. The trust instrument provides for the payment of one thousand dollars to Mrs. Kelley, and the third codicil contains a bequest of two thousand dollars to her. It does not appear that there was any deposit in the name of the testatrix, in trust for Elizabeth Kelley, other than this deposit. On the foregoing facts I find that it was not the intention of the testatrix at any time that Elizabeth Kelley should be the owner of the deposit in question, and I find that there was no completed transfer or gift of it to her by the testatrix.

"(12) In 1897, about four years after the execution of the trust instrument, the testatrix made a deposit of sixty-four dollars, on book No. 69,645, in the New Bedford Five Cents Savings Bank, in her name, in trust for Mary Hammond, meaning thereby her niece, the respondent Mrs. Mary Ann Hammond. At this time the testatrix had two other accounts in the same bank, each in excess of one thousand dollars, one in her own name, the other in her name ostensibly in trust for one Whitney, but in reality for her sole benefit. She continued to make deposits on the account in question until her death, the deposit then amounting to $1,050.52. Mary Ann Hammond claims this deposit. The facts in the matter, other than those above stated, are there: The testatrix, about a year before her death, said to Mrs. Hammond's husband, 'I am putting money in the bank in your wife's name for her.' On one occasion, after the account had been opened, the testatrix and Mrs. Hammond's husband being together in front of said bank, the former handed to the latter the book representing the deposit in question, together with a sum of money, and said to him, 'You take that in and deposit it; I am taking out a book for your wife.' The testatrix, about two weeks before her death, exhibited to Mrs. Hammond the book representing the deposit in question, and said to her, 'There is a book; I put money in for you.' The testatrix always kept the book representing the deposit in question in her possession until the day before she died, when she handed to Mrs. Hammond a bag containing said book and other bankbooks, and instructed her to deliver the bag with its contents to the petitioner, in the event of her death. A few days after the death of the testatrix, Mrs. Hammond delivered to the petitioner the bag with all the books in it, including the book representing the deposit in question. It does not appear that there was any deposit in the name of the testatrix, in trust for Mrs. Hammond, other than the deposit in question. The will provides for the payment of one thousand dollars to Mrs. Hammond; the trust instrument provides for the payment of the income of two thousand dollars to her during her life, and in a certain contingency for the payment of the principal sum to her; and the third codicil gives her two thousand dollars, and the rest and residue of the estate of the testatrix after the payment of debts and legacies. On the foregoing facts, I find that it was not the intention of the testatrix at any time that Mrs. Hammond should own the deposit in question, and I find that there was not a completed transfer or gift of it to her by the testatrix."

Grosvenor Calkins, for Bernard F. Kelley. F. A. Milliken and Oliver Prescott, Jr., for Elizabeth Kelley and others. Leml. T. Willcox and Wm. C. Parker, for respondent Benj. F. Snow. J. M. Browne and Merrill H. Browne, for Grace Kirwin and Norah Mead. F. A. Milliken, for Mary Ann Hammond.

HAMMOND, J. 1. The trust deed recites that it is executed "for a valuable consideration," contains words apt to convey the property, is under seal, which imports a consideration, and was delivered to Kelley, the transferee, who received the same and agreed "to carry out all the trusts therein stipulated." As between the parties, therefore, the legal title to the property passed to Kelley, even without delivery; and, so far as respected the form of the transaction, the trust was completely created. Upon its face the trust was valid, notwithstanding the provisions that the donor during her life should have the use of the property and collect the income of the bank deposits, and the further provision that she should have the power to change the "dispositions at any time upon written notice to" Kelley. Stone v. Hackett, 12 Gray, 233.

It is urged, however, by the husband of the donor, that the trust was invalid because it was in the nature of a testamentary instrument, and, moreover, was in fraud of his rights. It appears from the report of the master that the wife had determined to change the disposition of her property provided for by her will and codicil of June 23, 1892, but her husband refused to consent to the changes she desired to make. Whereupon, "by advice of counsel, and with the view to make the desired changes in a manner which would be effective without her husband's consent, she executed" this trust deed in duplicate, giving one copy to Kelley and retaining the other. There can be no doubt of her intention. She intended to put this property beyond the control of her husband, even if in doing that it was necessary to limit her own control or change her relation towards it. She was determined that he should have no power to say where it should go, either during her lifetime or after her death, and, in the light of the facts disclosed in the report, it is not difficult to see the grim determination with which she went to work. She transferred the legal title to Kelley, reserving to herself certain beneficial rights. The legal title passed at once, and all beneficial interest ceased at her death. It was a present conveyance, which took effect in her lifetime. She fixed, then, the terms of the trust. It is true that she had the power to change its terms, but the power was conditioned upon giving written notice to Kelley. This condition, especially when taken in connection with the entire absence of any express power by will, shows that the power was to be exercised and the changes were to take effect in her lifetime, and not by way of a will. In view of the purpose of the donor, the circumstances surrounding the transaction, the language of the instrument, the nature of the power given to her, it is clear that the instrument was not testamentary in its nature, but was a present conveyance of property, taking effect during the liftime of the donor, and that it was made in good faith for that purpose. Nor is the trust invalid as against the husband. Under our statutes the right of a married woman over her personal estate during her lifetime is absolute, so far as respects her husband. She may convey it or give it away upon such terms as she pleases, provided always the conveyance be real and not colorable, and is made to take effect in her lifetime. Leonard v. Leonard, 181 Mass. 458, 63 N. E. 1068, 92 Am. St. Rep. 426. The case is distinguishable from Brownell v. Briggs, 173 Mass. 529, 54 N. E. 251. The trust, therefore, was a valid trust at the time of its creation. It existed at the time of the donor's death. While it is true that Kelley, after keeping his copy for two years, returned it to the donor at her request, the master finds that her purpose in requesting its return does not appear, and it is evident that as late as June 28, 1901, several years after the return, she regarded the trust as still existing, for in her will executed by her on that day she attempts to cancel and discharge the trust agreement. But the return of the agreement, without more, would not change the legal title, which was in Kelley, nor the rights of the beneficiaries. The attempted revocation of the trust was void, because made by will, and no notice was given to Kelley during the life of the donor. The trust, therefore, at the time of the death of the donor, existed as it was originally created. By her death her beneficial life estate was determined, and the beneficiaries in remainder became entitled to their respective shares in accordance with the terms of the trust deed. It follows that the property covered by the trust must be so administered by the petitioner.

2. It is contended, however, by Elizabeth Kelley, one of the respondents, that one of the bankbooks named in the trust deed, namely, book No. 56,762 of the New Bedford Institution for Savings, was held by the donor in trust for her, and that she is therefore entitled to it. The facts bearing upon this matter are stated at length in the eleventh paragraph of the master's report. Whether they show a special trust in favor of Mrs. Kelley is a question of fact, and not of law. The facts fully warrant the conclusion, reached by the master, that the testatrix did not at any time intend to create a trust in favor of Mrs. Kelley in this deposit, and that there was no completed transfer or gift to her. This deposit must stand as a part of the trust.

3. A similar claim is made by the respondent Mary Ann Hammond to the bankbook No. 69,645 in the New Bedford Five Cents Savings Bank. This deposit was not included in the trust deed, but was a part of the estate owned by the testator at the time of her death. The facts with reference to this claim are set out in the twelfth paragraph of the report of the master, and they fully justify his finding that it was not at any

time the intention of the testatrix that Mrs. Hammond should own the deposit. No trust, therefore, is shown in it, and it is a part of the assets of the estate of the deceased.

4. At the decease of the testatrix her estate consisted of this last deposit, and of real estate of the value of $5,000; and the question on this branch of the case is, what disposition shall be made of this property, real and personal? The testatrix appears to have made a will and three codicils. At the time each was made she was the wife of Snow, the respondent, who was her third husband. She was childless, her only child, a son by a former marriage, having died unmarried, leaving, however, a natural daughter, Grace Kirwin, who lived with the testatrix until a short time before her death. The first will and codicil, executed simultaneously in June, 1892, provided in substance that all the property, real and personal, should be reduced to cash by the executor, that $2,000 should be paid to the husband, $1,000 to Mary Ann Hammond, and the balance should be placed in trust for Grace Kirwin for life, with remainder to her children surviving her, or, in default of such children, to the said Mary A. Hammond, Thomas Meade, and Bernard Kelley. To this will and codicil the husband duly consented. At this time the estate consisted of the real estate above named and of the personal property afterwards conveyed by the trust deed, and it is evident that, had the testatrix retained this property until her death, her husband, if then surviving, would, in the absence of the consent to her will, have received much more than $2,000. The second codicil simply changed the trustee and executor nominated in the will. The third was executed the day before the testatrix died, and by it the provisions of the will and first codicil, with the exception of the bequests of $2,000 to the husband and of $1,000 to Mary Ann Hammond, are radically changed. The trust created in the will as above stated is revoked, there is no bequest to Grace, and the estate remaining after the said bequests to the husband and to Hammond is divided among various legatees, the most of whom are not named at all in the first will. In a word, the will as changed by the third codicil is, with the exceptions above named, an entirely different will from that to which the husband consented, and this radical difference extends to the portion which, if the testatrix had died intestate, would have gone to him. What is the result as to the rights of the husband? Shall his consent to the will and first codicil be held to be a consent to the will as changed by the third codicil? At common law a married woman could not make a valid will of her real estate. Nor could she make a will of her personal estate (except, perhaps, as to that held by her to her own separate use) without her husband's license. 2 Bl. Comm. 498. Osgood v. Breed, 12 Mass. 525. In order thus to establish a will, however, a general consent that the wife may make a will was not sufficient. It was necessary that the husband should consent to the particular will made by the wife. 2 Bl. Comm. 498; Rex v. Bettesworth, 2 Strange, 891; Cutter v. Butler, 25 N. H. 357, 57 Am. Dec. 330. While under our statutes the real and personal estate of a married woman are her separate property, yet until very recently her power to dispose of it by will always has been subject to the condition that no will should operate to deprive the husband, without his consent, of certain rights therein at her decease. The testatrix died June 29, 1901. At that time Pub. St. 1882, c. 147, § 6, with its amendments, had not been repealed. It is true that in St. 1899, p. 544, c. 479, § 13, there was a provision for its repeal, but this last statute, having itself been repealed before it went into effect (see St. 1900, p. 119, c. 174, and p. 432, c. 450), never became operative, and it was not until St. 1900, p. 432, c. 450, which took effect January 1, 1902 (see St. 1901, p. 393, c. 461), that Pub. St. 1882, c. 147, § 6, as amended, ceased to be the law. This statute, as amended and in force at the time of the death of the testatrix, provided, so far as material to this case, that a married woman might make a will in the same manner and with the same effect as if she were sole, except that no such will should, without the written consent of her husband, operate to deprive him of her real estate, not exceeding $5,000 in value, where no issue survived her, or, in any event, of more than one-half of her personal estate. Pub. St. 1882, c. 147, § 6; St. 1885, p. 694, c. 255, § 1; St. 1887, p. 920, c. 290, § 2. The consent of the husband is not necessary to the validity of the will, so far as it does not interfere with his rights in the estate of the testatrix should he survive her. This consent is not in the nature of a transfer or conveyance of property in which the husband has any present right or interest, but it is only a waiver of any statutory right he might otherwise have to his wife's property after her decease. Silsby v. Bullock, 10 Allen, 94-96. It is manifest that the reason which leads a husband to consent to a particular will may be found, not only in the specific provisions therein made for him, but also in those which respect the other parts of the wife's property, especially that part which but for the will would upon her decease come to him. He might be willing to stand aside in the interest of his own child, and unwilling to do it in the interest of a person deemed by him undeserving, or for an object which did not commend itself to him. In the light of the principle prevailing, as before stated, at common law, namely, that the general consent of the husband that the wife might make a will was not sufficient, but that the consent must be to the particular will made, and of the principles applicable generally to a waiver, and of the

weighty and obvious objections to a contrary interpretation, we are of opinion that the consent required by the statute is like that theretofore required at common law, and that a consent to one will is not applicable, at least, to a subsequent will which changes substantially the disposition of the property as to which the consent is requisite. It follows that the husband in this case never consented to the will of his wife as finally allowed. He is entitled to her real estate to the value of $5,000, and to one-half of her personal estate, as if she had died sole. But of course he cannot have also the specific legacy of $2,000.

Under this rule the husband in this case will apparently take substantially all the real estate, and there will be only a little, if any, real estate, and but a small amount of personal property, remaining. It remains to be considered how this residue shall be distributed. It is plain that the testatrix did not intend by the third codicil to revoke the legacies contained in the second item of the original will. The bequest, therefore, of $1,000 to Mary Ann Hammond, must stand as originally drawn. It is also plain that the bequests contained in the fourth to the eighth clauses, both inclusive, of the third codicil, were intended to relate only to the distribution of the trust fund, and were to be paid only from it. This part of the will becomes inoperative. The language of the residuary clause in favor of Mary Ann Hammond, however, is broad enough to cover whatever may be left of the estate outside of the trust fund.

The result is that the petitioner holds the property named in the trust deed, including the deposit represented in book No. 56,762 in the New Bedford Institution for Savings, as trustee under the deed, and not as executor, and he is to distribute it in accordance with its terms. He holds the deposit represented by book No. 69,645, in the New Bedford Five Cents Savings Bank, as executor, as a part of the assets of the estate of the testatrix, free from any trust. The rights of the husband in the estate are as hereinbefore stated, and the residue of the estate goes to Mary Ann Hammond.

Decree accordingly.

(185 Mass. 137)

HUNT v. HOLSTON.

(Supreme Judicial Court of Massachusetts. Franklin. Feb. 26, 1904.)

TAXES—ARREST FOR NONPAYMENT—DEMAND FOR PAYMENT—SERVICE.

1. Under St. 1889, pp. 1020, 1021, c. 334, §§ 1, 4, requiring, as the foundation for an arrest for nonpayment of taxes, a demand for their payment "to be given to the person assessed," or sent to him by mail addressed to the town where he resided on the 1st day of May, a notice addressed and mailed to a town to which one had moved since the 1st day of May was insufficient, though it was actually received.

Report from Supreme Judicial Court, Franklin County; Robt. R. Bishop, Judge.

Action by William W. Hunt against John C. Holston. Report on plaintiff's exception to an order setting aside a verdict in his favor. Judgment for plaintiff.

Fredk. L. Greene and Wm. A. Davenport, for plaintiff. Dana Malone, for defendant.

MORTON, J. This is an action for assault and false imprisonment growing out of the arrest of the plaintiff for the nonpayment of his taxes by the defendant as tax collector of the town of Wendell. The question is whether the notice sent to the plaintiff constituted a proper demand. The court ruled that it did not, and the defendant excepted. There was a verdict for the plaintiff. The defendant filed exceptions, and also a motion to set aside the verdict, and for a new trial, which was allowed on the ground that the ruling in regard to the notice was erroneous. Thereupon the court reported the case to this court: If the ruling was right, and the setting aside of the verdict was wrong, judgment is to be entered on the verdict; if the ruling was wrong, and the setting aside of the verdict was right, then judgment is to be entered for the defendant.

The plaintiff was an inhabitant of the town of Wendell on May 1, 1897, and was duly assessed for a poll tax and a tax on real and personal estate. On September 5th of the same year he moved to Baldwinsville, in the town of Templeton, in Worcester county, leaving his taxes unpaid. On March 28, 1898, the defendant sent to him by mail, at Baldwinsville, a notice demanding payment of the taxes, which was duly received by the plaintiff. There was also testimony tending to show that the defendant had sent to the plaintiff a notice by mail directed to him in the town of Wendell, but a question whether such notice was sent was submitted to the jury, and they found that it was not. The plaintiff contends that the notice was defective in form, and that it should have been served on him personally, or, if sent by mail, should have been directed to him in the town where he resided on the 1st day of May in the year in which the tax was assessed. We assume, without deciding, that the notice was sufficient in form and substance, but we think that it was not served as required by the statute in force at the time the demand was made. The levying and collecting of taxes is a purely statutory matter, and persons arrested for the nonpayment of taxes have a right to require that the provisions of the statute shall be strictly followed. The law requires as the foundation for an arrest for nonpayment of taxes, or for the distraint of personal property, or the sale of real estate, a demand for their payment. Formerly this demand had to be made on the taxpayer in person. St. 1785, pp. 568, 569, c. 70, §§ 2, 5. The Revised Statutes added a provision that it could be made at the place of usual abode (Rev. St. c. 8, §§ 3, 11), and the General Statutes added the qualification, "if to be found within their precincts." The statute as it thus stood was re-enacted in Pub. St. 1882, c. 12, §§ 4, 14, and again in the codification of the statutes relating to the collection of taxes in St. 1888, pp. 362, 363, c. 390, §§ 8, 18. Then came St. 1889, pp. 1020, 1021, c. 334, §§ 1, 4, which provided that demand should be made by causing a statement of the amount of the tax with a demand for its payment to be given to the person assessed, or to be sent to him postpaid through the mail directed to the city or town where he resided on the 1st day of May in the year in which the tax was assessed. The question is, what was meant by the words "by causing to be given * * * to the person assessed"? it being plain that the notice that was sent by mail was not directed as required by the statute. The provision is used as the alternative of that relating to sending notices by mail, which would seem to exclude the sending of notices by mail except in the particular manner therein specified, and to require that the language should be construed as meaning the delivery of a notice to the taxpayer in person. It is possible, of course, to construe the alternative intended by the statute as that between causing notice to be actually given to the taxpayer and that sent by mail; in other words, between actual notice and notice by mail, which may be actual or not. The object of the Legislature was to secure notice to the taxpayer, and it was for the Legislature to say how notice should be given, and what should be regarded as sufficient notice. But for many years through successive re-enactments the notice required had been a personal notice, or a notice left at the last and usual place of abode, and it seems to us that the statute will have the meaning intended by the Legislature if it is construed as authorizing in addition a notice by mail in the manner therein prescribed. As the statutes now are (Rev. Laws, c. 13, §§ 1, 3), the service would have been sufficient, but, as we have already said, the question is to be decided according to the statutes in force at the time when the demand was made.

Although the report speaks of setting aside the verdict, we infer that the status quo has been so far preserved that judgment can be entered on the verdict. If not, judgment will have to be entered as by agreement of the parties for the amount of the verdict.

Ordered accordingly.

(178 N. Y. 91)

PEOPLE v. MOONEY.

(Court of Appeals of New York. March 15, 1904.)

MURDER—EVIDENCE.

1. Evidence *held* sufficient to sustain conviction of murder in the first degree.

Appeal from Supreme Court, Trial Term, Franklin County.

Allen Mooney was convicted of murder in the first degree, and appeals. Affirmed.

Robert M. Moore, for appellant. Gordon H. Main, for the People.

O'BRIEN, J. The defendant was convicted upon an indictment charging him with murder in the first degree. It is not necessary to say much about the case, and, except for the practice which has so long prevailed of giving in some form the reasons of this court for its conclusions in capital cases, we might very well affirm this judgment without any opinion at all. There is no dispute about the fact that the defendant, on the night of November 4, 1902, between 8 and 9 o'clock in the evening, entered a dwelling house at Saranac Lake through an unfastened rear door, and, having provided himself with a revolver, he proceeded to fire, and did fire, several shots, resulting in the death of two women, and the wounding of the man who was the proprietor of the place. The indictment charges him with the murder of one of the women named Thomas, who was one of the inmates of the house. It appears that the inmates did not bear a very high moral character, and there can be no doubt, from the evidence, that the defendant had for some time been intimate with the woman he is charged with killing. The proof tends to show that his motive was jealousy of another man, who was in the house on the same evening, but escaped injury by crawling under a bed. The other woman whom the defendant killed was an associate of Mrs. Thomas, and the defendant doubtless knew both of the women.

Before going to the house on the evening mentioned, the defendant had prepared himself for the tragedy by purchasing a revolver, and had strengthened his nerves by absorbing considerable strong liquor, but it does not appear that he was intoxicated to the extent of affecting his mind, or depriving him of the capacity to know and understand the character and quality of his acts and that they were wrong. The evidence produced in behalf of the prosecution tended quite clearly to show that the defendant fully prepared himself for the work which was consummated on that evening, and that the killing of the woman by the defendant was with a deliberate and premeditated design on his part to effect her death. There was proof of preparation on his part, of premeditation, and of motive, that was amply sufficient to warrant the jury in finding that he was guilty of the offense as charged. His conduct before the homicide, and his declarations after it was consummated, left no doubt that he was entirely conscious of the nature and quality of his act and knew that it was wrong.

The only defense attempted or suggested in behalf of the defendant was insanity, or such weakness or derangement of mind as to render him irresponsible in law for the act committed. It is scarcely worth while to go at much length into the details of this defense. It is quite sufficient to say that it rested largely, if not entirely, upon some vague proof that the defendant was subject to fits of epilepsy, and that his mother was afflicted in like manner. From these circumstances the jury was asked to find that the defendant at the time of the homicide was irresponsible for his acts. It is enough to say that, whatever there was of that defense, no one can reasonably claim that it was not properly submitted to the jury, and the jury, by the verdict, have found that the defense was untenable. It is difficult to see how, under all the facts and circumstances of the case, the jury could have reached a different conclusion. The learned trial judge explained to the jury with admirable clearness the law applicable to the question, and it is not, I think, within the recognized powers and functions of this court to disturb the judgment.

We have here a case that does not present a single question of law worthy of any consideration. There was really no controversy with respect to the fact that the defendant was the author of the death of the two women who fell victims on that evening either to his jealousy, his rage, or some other evil propensity. Indeed, that fact stands admitted. As to the defense of irresponsibility, at best it presented a question of fact for the jury, and it having been determined, as we think, according to the evidence, the duty of this court is performed by an affirmance of the judgment, since the record does not disclose even a single mitigating fact or circumstance. The defendant certainly had a fair trial, and nothing appears from the record that can raise a doubt in any reasonable mind as to the defendant's guilt.

The judgment of conviction must therefore be affirmed.

PARKER, C. J., and GRAY, BARTLETT, MARTIN, VANN, and WERNER, JJ., concur.

Judgment of conviction affirmed.

(178 N. Y. 50)

WALTERS v. SYRACUSE RAPID TRANSIT RY. CO.

(Court of Appeals of New York. March 15, 1904.)

NEGLIGENCE—NONSUIT.

1. In an action to recover for injuries alleged to have been sustained by the falling of a live wire on plaintiff, who was at the time riding on a bicycle, it was error to grant a nonsuit on the ground that the facts testified to by plaintiff and his witnesses were incredible and scientifically impossible—the case involving electrical phenomena—where it was not shown by science and common knowledge that such testimony was absolutely false.

Appeal from Supreme Court, Appellate Division, Fourth Department.

Action by Charles Walters against the Syracuse Rapid Transit Railway Company. From a judgment of the Appellate Division (82 N. Y. Supp. 82) affirming a judgment for defendant entered on a dismissal of complaint, plaintiff appeals. Reversed.

John H. McCrahon, for appellant. Charles E. Spencer, for respondent.

O'BRIEN, J. The plaintiff sought to recover damages for a personal injury that he claimed to have sustained in consequence of the falling upon him of a guy or stay wire, being a part of the defendant's overhead trolley system for operating its railroad. One end of the wire, which was about 120 feet long, was attached to the top of a pole, and the other end was attached to the main trolley wire. There is no dispute about the fact that this wire broke near the point where it was connected with the trolley, and at least 100 feet of it fell into the street below, a distance of about 22 feet. The plaintiff testified that he was at that moment riding on a bicycle through the street, underneath the wire, and that it fell upon him, coiled around his body, and communicated what he called a shock of electricity to him, which affected his heart and nervous system. The plaintiff's testimony was in many respects corroborated by other witnesses. The proof tended to show that the plaintiff was subjected to considerable physical suffering in consequence of the accident, but whether the injuries claimed to have been sustained were temporary or permanent does not appear from the proofs.

At the close of all of the testimony the learned trial judge granted a motion made by the defendant's counsel for a nonsuit, and to this ruling the plaintiff's counsel excepted. He also asked that the whole case made out by the evidence be submitted to the jury, which request was refused and an exception was taken. The case therefore presents the familiar question whether the plaintiff produced at the trial any evidence which he was entitled to have weighed and considered by the jury. There can, I think, be no doubt that the plaintiff's testimony, if believed, or, rather, if at all credible, tended to establish the cause of action stated in the complaint. The plaintiff has been nonsuited, and the judgment of nonsuit has been affirmed at the Appellate Division, on the sole ground that the facts to which he and his witnesses testified at the trial were utterly incredible, and in fact scientifically and physically impossible. It is upon that ground that the learned counsel for the defendant attempts to sustain the judgment in this court. The fact that the overhead wire attached to the defendant's trolley system fell at the time and place claimed, and came in contact, at least to some extent, with the plaintiff's person, was clearly established; but it was said that a stay or guy wire, one end of which was detached from the trolley, and the other end attached to a pole, could not possibly have communicated a current of electricity to the plaintiff's body. We are not able to understand how such an occurrence could have happened, but this court is not the judge of the credibility of testimony. We have frequently had occasion, in cases of accidents upon electric railways, to try and fathom some of the unaccountable freaks of electricity. We know that there are many things concerning its action that are imperfectly understood. What it does or may do under a given state of circumstances is perhaps not yet accurately known. It may be that the plaintiff's claim that he felt a shock of electricity when the wire coiled around his body was purely imaginary; but, if he tells the truth as to what followed, and the effect which the accident had upon him, there can be no doubt that in some way and from some cause he sustained bodily injuries. What the extent of these injuries was, and whether they were real, or in some degree feigned, was a question for the jury. If the plaintiff's testimony as to the circumstances attending the injury is incredible and impossible, it is as easy to expose the falsity and to demonstrate the truth before the jury as it is before the court.

All we mean to say is that the credibility and the weight to be given to the plaintiff's testimony should have been determined by the jury. It is not a very unusual thing for this court to feel constrained to affirm judgments in such cases where large recoveries have been had upon testimony quite as incredible as that of the plaintiff in this case. Moreover, it frequently happens that cases appear and reappear in this court, after three or four trials, where the plaintiff on every trial has changed his testimony in order to meet the varying fortunes of the case upon appeal. It often happens that his testimony upon the second trial is directly contrary to his testimony on the first trial, and, when it is apparent that it was done to meet the decision on appeal, the temptation to hold that the second story was false is almost irresistible. Yet in just such cases this court has held that the changes and contradictions in the plaintiff's testimony, the motives for the same, and the truth of the last version, is a matter for the consideration of the jury. Williams v. Del., L. & W. R. Co., 155 N. Y. 158, 49 N. E. 672. If this court is to be consistent with the position taken in that case, and in many other cases of like character, we cannot hold, as matter of law, that there was no proof in this case to sustain the plaintiff's cause of action. It often happens that science and common knowledge may be invoked for the purposes of demonstrating that a particular statement in regard to some particular accident must be absolutely false. In such cases the question is for the court. But in cases of doubt we think it is wiser and better to remit such controversies to the proper tribunal for settling facts and ascertaining where the truth lies, rather that assume the power to determine the facts ourselves. This is an old rule, and, while like all other rules, it may work hardship or injustice in a particular case, it is wiser to adhere to it. McDonald v. Metr. St. Ry. Co., 167 N. Y. 66, 60 N. E. 282; Place v. N. Y. C. & H. R. R. Co., 167 N. Y. 345, 60 N. E. 632; Hoffman House v. Foote, 172 N. Y. 350, 65 N. E. 169.

The judgment should be reversed, and a new trial granted; costs to abide the event.

BARTLETT, HAIGHT, VANN, CULLEN, and WERNER, JJ., concur. PARKER, C. J., absent.

Judgment reversed, etc.

(178 N. Y. 45)

JONES v. CITY OF BUFFALO.

(Court of Appeals of New York. March 15, 1904.)

MUNICIPAL CORPORATIONS—ILLEGAL REMOVAL OF EMPLOYÉ—REINSTATEMENT—SALARY.

1. On certiorari, the removal of a municipal employé appointed under the civil service law, and the appointment of another in his place, was declared illegal and vacated by an order of the Appellate Division, and the city appealed to the Court of Appeals, which affirmed the decision, whereupon the clerk was reinstated. *Held*, that he could recover against the city his salary from the time the city authorities were notified of the order of the Appellate Division vacating his discharge until the time he was reinstated.

Appeal from Supreme Court, Appellate Division, Fourth Department.

Action by George T. Jones against the city of Buffalo. From a judgment of the Appellate Division (79 N. Y. Supp. 754) reversing a judgment for defendant and granting a new trial, defendant appeals. Affirmed.

Charles L. Feldman, Corp. Counsel (Edward L. Jung, of counsel), for appellant. Frank Gibbons, for respondent.

O'BRIEN, J. The plaintiff was a clerk having charge of a bureau in the police department of the city of Buffalo, and he brought this action to recover his salary. The complaint was dismissed at the trial, but the judgment entered against the plaintiff has been reversed by the court below, and a new trial granted. From this order and the judgment entered thereon the city has appealed to this court, stipulating for judgment absolute in case the judgment appealed from is affirmed.

The facts are practically undisputed. It appears that on the 22d day of July, 1896, the plaintiff was appointed to the position referred to, and his right to the salary of the place accrued on that day. The appointment was made pursuant to the provisions of the civil service law (Laws 1899, p. 795, c. 370), and the position was held by him protected by all the restrictions of that statute upon the power of removal. The plaintiff could not have been removed except upon notice, and for cause judicially established. From the date of his appointment until the 7th day of June, 1899, the plaintiff continued to occupy and discharge the duties of the position and receive from the defendant the monthly salary or compensation therefor. Upon that day he was removed by the board of police commissioners, and, of course, prevented from discharging any of the duties pertaining to the position, although he offered to perform the same, and was at all times ready and willing to do so, and so informed the board. Immediately upon the plaintiff's removal he procured a writ of certiorari against the police board, with the result that the plaintiff's discharge was declared to be illegal and void, and was vacated and set aside by the Appellate Division of the Supreme Court on the 24th day of July, 1900. People ex rel. Jones v. Diehl, 53 App. Div. 645, 65 N. Y. Supp. 801. An appeal was taken from that decision to this court, and the order was in all things affirmed. 165 N. Y. 643, 59 N. E. 1128. The decision of this court was served upon the city authorities on the 30th day of January, 1901, and thereupon the board reinstated the plaintiff, who has ever since that time occupied the position, discharging the duties of the same, and receiving the salary therefor. When the police board removed the plaintiff, it immediately appointed another person in the place, who continued to occupy the position and perform the duties thereof until the time when the plaintiff was reinstated, and during this period the defendant paid to this incumbent the full salary. The comptroller and mayor of the city had knowledge of the fact of the plaintiff's removal by the police board and the reversal of that determination by the Appellate Division of the Supreme Court.

The question in this case is whether, when an officer or employé of a city protected by the civil service or by law against removal without cause has been illegally removed, and the illegality of the removal has been adjudicated by the courts, and notice thereof communicated to the city authorities, the municipality is protected from that time by payment of the salary made to a person who, by the adjudication, was a usurper, and not entitled to hold the place. The defense of the city in this case is that it has paid the salary which the plaintiff was entitled to receive to another person, whom the courts have held was not legally in the position. The point involved in this case was decided in this court in the case of McVeany v. Mayor, etc., of N. Y., 80 N. Y. 185, 36 Am. Rep. 600. The principle there laid down was stated by the court in these words: "So, also, where, after an adjudication against the one in the office and after notice thereof to the disbursing officer of the municipality, the intruder still continues to perform the duties of the office, the rendition of the services is in behalf of the one entitled to the office. The compensation accruing therefor belongs to him, and he may maintain an action against the municipality to recover the same, although the disbursing officer has paid it to the intruder." That would seem to be a reasonable rule. When it is once determined by the courts that the officer or employé was illegally removed, and that he should be reinstated, and notice of such determination is given to the municipal officer whose duty it is to pay, then the city ought to obey, and not defy, the decision of the court. In this case, when the mayor and comptroller had notice of the decision of the court that the removal was illegal and the appointment of the other person unauthorized, it made payment to the intruder at the peril of being subsequently compelled to pay the person who had the legal right to the salary. There is no hardship in this rule, since the city can always protect itself in case of a dispute between two parties as to the right to the salary by refusing to pay either, or, if sued by either, by then compelling them to interplead as in other cases where a party is subjected to conflicting claims by different persons for the same thing or the same debt or obligation.

Numerous cases have been cited by the learned counsel for the defendant, which he claims are inconsistent with the rule above stated. Martin v. City of New York, 176 N. Y. 371, 68 N. E. 640; Higgins v. Mayor, etc., of N. Y., 131 N. Y. 128, 30 N. E. 44; Demarest v. Mayor, etc., of N. Y., 147 N. Y. 203, 41 N. E. 405; Terhune v. Mayor, etc., of N. Y., 88 N. Y. 247; O'Hara v. City of New York, 46 App. Div. 518, 62 N. Y. Supp. 146; affirmed, 167 N. Y. 567, 60 N. E. 1117; Van Valkenburgh v. Mayor, etc., of N. Y., 49 App. Div. 208, 63 N. Y. Supp. 6. These cases have all been examined and explained in the learned opinion below. Jones v. City of Buffalo, 79 App. Div. 328, 79 N. Y. Supp. 754. It will be seen that the point presented in the case at bar did not arise in any of these cases. It was not held in any of them that the city would be protected by payment to a usurper after notice of an adjudication that he was such, and that the displacement of the rightful incumbent was illegal; and in some of them the principle asserted by the plaintiff's counsel in this case was impliedly recognized. In this case the learned court below reversed the judgment dismissing the complaint upon questions of law only, certifying that the facts had been examined, and no error found therein. This court is therefore justified in disposing of the case upon the principle that the facts hereinbefore stated have been conclusively established. We think that the case was correctly decided below, and that the order appealed from should be affirmed, and judgment absolute ordered for the plaintiff on the stipulation, with costs.

PARKER, C. J., and BARTLETT, MARTIN, VANN, and WERNER, JJ., concur. GRAY, J., absent.

Order affirmed, etc.

(178 N. Y. 26)

IDE v. BROWN et al.

(Court of Appeals of New York. March 15, 1904.)

COURT OF APPEALS—REVIEW—QUESTIONS FOR DETERMINATION—SPECIFIC PERFORMANCE—CONTRACT OF GUARDIAN.

1\. Code Civ. Proc. § 1022, relating to decisions on reports of referees on trial of issues of fact prior to Laws 1903, p. 237, c. 85, provided for a long and short form of decision, whereby the questions of fact were specially found under the long form, and the question of law which arose was to be determined by the judgment that was to be entered thereon. *Held*, that a judgment entered on a decision of the long form, when unanimously affirmed by the Appellate Division, establishes the facts as found, and the only question for the Court of Appeals is whether such facts authorized the judgment.

2\. A statutory guardian agreed that his ward should continue to live as a member of the family with a person with whom she had always lived in the position of daughter. *Held* to furnish no consideration for a promise by such person to bequeath her at his death a specified sum, and devise to her the house and lot in which he lived, so that on the death of such person, and failure to fulfill his promise, equity will not decree specific performance.

Martin, J., dissenting.

Appeal from Supreme Court, Appellate Division, Third Department.

Action by Kate L. Ide, by William T. Cowles, her guardian ad litem, against Louis M. Brown and others, executors of George W. Lee. From a judgment of the Appellate Division (83 N. Y. Supp. 1108) affirming a judgment for plaintiff, defendants appeal. Reversed.

Edgar T. Brackett and Stephen Brown, for appellants. J. A. Kellogg, for respondent.

HAIGHT, J. Section 1022 of the Code of Civil Procedure, prior to its amendment by chapter 85, p. 237, Laws 1903, provided that "the decision of the court or the report of a referee, upon the trial of the whole issues of fact, may state separately the facts found and the conclusions of law, and direct the judgment to be entered thereon, or the court or referee may file a decision stating concisely the grounds upon which the issues have been decided, and direct the judgment to be entered thereupon." Here were two forms of decision provided for, which were known by the profession, respectively, as the long and short form. The two forms thus provided for differed in this respect: Under the long form the material facts were specifically found, and then the question of law arose as to the judgment that should be entered thereon, while under the short form it was not necessary to find the facts, the trial court being required to state the grounds or reasons upon which judgment was directed, and upon review we were required to assume that the necessary facts to support the judgment were found; treating the decision similar to that of a verdict of a jury. In the case under consideration all of the material facts have been specifically found and separately numbered. The decision conforms in every particular to the provisions of the Code formerly known as the long form, and, in view of the fact that the judgment entered upon the decision has been unanimously affirmed in the Appellate Division, the facts, as found, are established, and the question with reference thereto for the determination of this court is whether such facts authorize the judgment that has been entered.

It appears from the facts found that on or about the 20th day of August, in the year 1900, one Colvin, acting as guardian of the plaintiff, who was then 16 years of age, entered into an agreement with George W. Lee, whereby it was mutually agreed that the plaintiff should continue to live with him as a member of his family, and in the position of a daughter, during his lifetime, and at his death he would bequeath to her the sum of $20,000, and, in addition, would devise to her the house and lot in which they resided, in the village of Glens Falls; that in pursuance of the agreement she continued to live with him as his daughter for the period of about eight months, when he died, leaving a will in which he bequeathed her only the sum of $5,000. The judgment entered directs specific performance of this contract.

My attention has been called to no case in which the question here presented has been the subject of adjudication in this court. There are numerous cases in which persons have entered into agreements to live with or take care of an aged person during the remainder of his or her life for a consideration promised to be made by bequest or devise, but the contracts in those cases have been made by adults, and not by minors who were incapable of entering into a valid contract. There is another class of cases in which infant children have been taken under agreement with their parents to be supported and maintained as the children of the foster parent during their minority, with a covenant to provide for them by will; but in these cases the custody and control of the infants terminated upon their arriving at their majority, and the contract was made by parents who were entitled to the society and services of their children.

In the case under consideration the plaintiff was 16 years of age, and had always lived in the family of the decedent. The contract was oral, and made by her guardian. The agreement bound her to continue to live with George W. Lee during the remainder of his life, whatever that period should be. She was to assume the character of a daughter, thus undertaking a daughter's duty to serve and care for an aged and decrepit parent. Had he continued to live until she became 25 or 30 years of age, she would have been still obligated to continue to live with and care for him. It was in consideration of this agreement that Lee promised to bequeath to her the sum of $20,000, and to devise to her the real estate mentioned. Had the agreement been that she should continue to live with him during her minority, or for the period of 5 years, it is quite possible that Lee would have fixed a different amount as measuring the consideration for her time and services during that period. But, as we have seen, such was not the contract, and the question therefore arises as to whether the guardian had any power to make the contract in question. As guardian, we assume that he had the power to provide for her support and maintenance during her minority; but upon her arriving at the age of 21 years his power as guardian terminated, and he had no power, by contract or otherwise, either after or before her arriving at her majority, to bind her thereafter in the disposition of her time, services, or property. It is true that Lee died a few months after the contract was made, but the happening of that event could not affect the validity of the contract, which speaks as of the time that it was made, and at that time it was not possible to know but that his life would continue until long after she should become 21 years of age. A guardian is not entitled to the services or society of his ward, and ordinarily he has no power to make a contract binding upon the person or property of the ward, unless authorized by a statute. Wuesthoff v. Germania L. Ins. Co., 107 N. Y. 580, 588, 14 N. E. 811. Woerner on Guardianship (section 49) says: "Neither can a guardian bind his ward either as to the person or the estate by any contract, but contracts entered into by the guardian in performance of his duty to educate and maintain his ward bind him personally and alone, save that the ward's estate is liable to reimburse him for reasonable expenditures made for his benefit." In 15 American & English Encyclopædia of Law (2d Ed.) p. 70, it is said: "The prevailing doctrine is that a guardian has no power to make a contract binding upon the ward or upon his estate, however proper and beneficial the contract may be, but the contract made by him imposes a personal liability upon himself, and his protection from loss lies in his right to charge the expenditures to the ward's estate in his account." See Andrus v. Blazzard (Utah) 63 Pac. 888, 54 L. R. A. 354; Copley v. O'Niel, 57 Barb. 299; Warren v. Union Bank of Rochester, 157 N. Y. 259, 51 N. E. 1036, 43 L. R. A. 256, 68 Am. St. Rep. 777.

These is no statute in this state authorizing a guardian to enter into a contract of this character. The only statute upon the subject appears in our domestic relations law (chapter 272, p. 232, of the Laws of 1896, § 72), under which a minor may bind himself or herself as a servant in any profession, trade, or employment for a term "not longer than the minority of such minor"; but contracts of this character are by the statute required to be in writing, and signed by the minor as well as by his guardian, and they are, as we have seen, expressly limited to a period within the minority of the minor. There is but one exception provided for in the statute, and that is in case of a minor coming from a foreign country, who may, for the purpose of paying his passage, make an indenture for a term of one year, although such term extend beyond the time when he will become of age. It appears to me that the contract, being for the life of Lee, was one that the guardian had no power to make for his ward, or in her behalf, and that it was therefore void.

The judgment should be reversed, and a new trial granted, with costs to abide event.

GRAY, J. I concur with Judge HAIGHT in his opinion in this case, upon the ground that the statutory guardian does not possess the power to bind the person of his ward by contract extending beyond the period of minority. I have been unable to find any precise authority covering the case, but I think the proposition true upon principle. We might assume that a parent, as such, and as a guardian by nature, might surrender the person of a child, under such a contract, and still find it difficult to infer a like authority in the general guardian, who is appointed under a statute designed to provide for the care of an infant's person and property only during the period of minority.

O'BRIEN, J. This is a controversy concerning the ownership of the estate of one George W. Lee, who died on the 6th day of May, 1901, leaving a will which was admitted to probate, and adjudged to be a valid will of real and personal estate. The will appears in the record in full, and covers nearly 10 printed pages. It bears date and was executed on the 7th day of August, 1900. The will made full and complete disposition of all his real estate, besides personal property, which, it is found, amounted to $300,000. The purpose of this action was to defeat the testamentary disposition thus made, and to procure a decree transferring all the real estate and $20,000 of the personal property to the plaintiff, and the judgment appealed from sustains and sanctions all the purposes of the action.

It is found that the plaintiff is an infant, born on the 24th of August, 1884; that her father and mother died prior to the year 1899, and that a guardian of her person and estate was duly appointed by the surrogate of the county, who qualified and entered upon the discharge of the duties of his trust; that at the time of the testator's death he was seised of certain real estate, which is described in two parcels, constituting the house and lot in which the testator lived prior to and at the time of his death. It has not been decided, and no one claims, that this will was in any respect invalid, but it is claimed and found that it was revoked or modified materially by certain events which took place before his death, and which will be set forth in full hereafter.

The class of cases presented by this record has now become quite common, and this will be a proper place to set forth the views of this court upon the questions involved, as stated in a case so recent that it may be said metaphorically that the ink is not yet dry on the opinion. Every member of the court concurred in what was then said. I did not myself take part in that decision, but I heartily agree to everything contained in the opinion; and, if my Brethren are now of like mind, there is only one possible view to be taken of this case. What was said in the opinion was in regard to a transaction just like the one in question, and the note of warning then sounded was in these words: "Such contracts are dangerous. They threaten the security of estates, and throw doubt upon the power of a man to do what he wills with his own. The savings of a lifetime may be taken away from his heirs by the testimony of witnesses who speak under the strongest bias and the greatest temptation, with all the dangers which, as experience shows, surround such evidence. The truth may be in them, but it is against sound policy to accept their statements as true, under the circumstances and with the results pointed out. Such contracts should be in writing, and the writing should be produced, or, if ever based upon parol evidence, it should be given or corroborated in all substantial particulars by disinterested witnesses. Unless they are established clearly by satisfactory proofs and are equitable, specific performance should not be decreed. We wish to be emphatic upon the subject, for we are impressed with the danger, and aim to protect the community from the spoliation of dead men's estates by proof of such contracts through parol evidence given by interested witnesses." Hamlin v. Stevens, 177 N. Y. 39, 69 N. E. 118. The opinion in that case expressly approved of Mahaney v. Carr, 175 N. Y. 454, 67 N. E. 903, quoting the very language of the opinion in the case where just such a transaction as the one in question was condemned as invalid. It also approved of another recent decision, which is Brantingham v. Huff, 174 N. Y. 53, 66 N. E. 620. If we follow these three recent decisions, I think the present judgment cannot stand.

It may be that some case, or, rather, some dicta, may be found to warrant the judgment as rendered, although I have not been able to find any. However that may be, I am inclined to follow the views of Chancellor Kent, who, when commenting upon the rule of stare decisis, said that many thousand cases could then be pointed out in the English and American Reports which had been overruled, doubted, or limited in their application. He added that "it is probable that the records of many of the courts of this country are replete with hasty and crude decisions; and such cases ought to be examined without fear, and revised without reluctance, rather than to have the character of our law impaired and the beauty and harmony of the system destroyed by the perpetuity of error." 1 Kent's Com. (13th Ed.) 477. And this court has recently given its approval to this doctrine in a case which reversed a rule of law which prevailed in this state for nearly half a century. Rumsey v. N. Y. & N. E. R. Co., 133 N. Y. 79, 30 N. E. 654, 15 L. R. A. 618, 28 Am. St. Rep. 600. But it is not necessary to invoke that doctrine in this case, since, whatever else may have been decided, it is safe to say that it has never yet been decided that a verbal arrangement such as appears in this record has been given such effect as to subvert the provisions of a will; and that is what has happened in this case, and that is the feature with which I propose to deal. We must therefore look at the record of the case, in order to see what it is about, and what the judgment under review has accomplished. Fortunately we have every single fact upon which this judgment rests plainly and explicitly stated in the decision, and these facts, so far as they are material, are as follows: "That during said year 1900, and on or about the 20th day of August of said year, said Addison B. Colvin, acting as guardian of the person and estate of said plaintiff, and having the custody and control of her person, entered into an agreement with said George W. Lee, wherein and whereby it was stipulated and mutually agreed that the said plaintiff should continue to live in the family of said George W. Lee until the death of said Lee, and that said Colvin should during said time permit the said George W. Lee to have the custody and control of said plaintiff as a member of his family, and in the position of a daughter, and that the said George W. Lee would treat said plaintiff in all respects as his daughter during his lifetime, and at his death would bequeath to her the sum of $20,000, and, in addition thereto, would at his death devise and transfer to her the house in which said George W. Lee then resided, on the southwesterly corner of Warren and Church streets, in the village of Glens Falls, Warren county, New York, together with the lot on which said house was situated, which said lot consisted of the parcels of real estate hereinbefore specifically described. That thereupon and thereafter, pursuant to said agreement, the said plaintiff continuously lived in the family of said George W. Lee, and in all respects conducted herself as his daughter, and to the time of his death remained in his family and conducted herself towards him in all respects as a member of his family, and during said time was subjected to the restraint, custody, control, and management of the said George W. Lee, who acted towards this said plaintiff in the relation of a parent; and said plaintiff fully performed all the duties and conditions of said contract and agreement on her part to be performed, and said Addison B. Colvin, her general guardian as aforesaid, performed all the duties and conditions of said contract on his part to be performed. That in violation of the said contract and agreement hereinbefore set forth, made between said Addison B. Colvin, as plaintiff's guardian, for and on behalf of said plaintiff, and said George W. Lee, the said George W. Lee failed at his death to bequeath to this plaintiff the sum of $20,000, and failed to devise to her the house and lot above described, and in all respects failed on his part to perform the agreement hereinbefore set forth, except that said George W. Lee in and by said last will and testament bequeathed to said executors, in trust, the sum of $5,000, and the accumulated income thereof; to be paid to said plaintiff in case, and in case only, that she should arrive at twenty-one years of age; and, aside from said contingent bequest, the said George W. Lee made no provision whatever for said plaintiff, either by his last will and testament or otherwise."

We are not concerned in the least with the circumstance that the decision below was unanimous. The sole question is whether these facts warrant the judgment given. The agreement set forth in this finding was a verbal one, and, although it is claimed it disposed of some $40,000 worth of property, not a single scrap of writing touching the transaction was ever made. It will be seen that the facts upon which the transaction rests in Mahaney v. Carr, supra, were found by the trial court, and the finding appears in the report of the case. If there is any difference, in substance or in principle, between the finding in that case and those in the case at bar, I have not been able to comprehend it. It may not be amiss to repeat here that the opinion in that case was to the effect that the finding of fact did not sustain the judgment; and the language in which that idea was expressed was quoted verbatim in Hamlin v. Stevens, supra, and seems to have met with the unanimous approval of the court. We must now meet a question which is identical, and that is whether the facts as found in this case can sustain the judgment for specific performance which the court awarded to the plaintiff.

The plaintiff is an orphan girl, not related in any way to the testator, and in her early childhood her mother, or some one interested in her, secured a home for her with the deceased. Assuming that the relations between her and the deceased were those that ordinarily exist between parent and child, these relations were not changed by what is claimed to have taken place a few months before the death of Mr. Lee. The plaintiff assumed no new duties or obligations in consequence of the conversation between her guardian and the deceased. If it be said that her guardian stipulated that she should live with the deceased during his life, no one can believe that, had he lived for 10 years more, and the plaintiff concluded to marry or to go elsewhere before his death, she was not at perfect liberty to do so. We are not in the least concerned with the relations of the parties, except for the few months preceding the testator's death, since there is no claim that the deceased owed the plaintiff anything when the verbal transaction took place. I have no doubt that the plaintiff is a very worthy young lady, but her personality has nothing to do with this case. In this court every case stands, or ought to stand, not on sentiment, but on laws. The single witness called to testify to the 15-minutes conversation that he had with the deceased, upon which this case rests, did not profess to remember the words of the conversation, but said that his narrative embraced the "spirit and sentiment" of the interview. The learned counsel for the plaintiff describes the things that underlie the judgment in these words: "The plaintiff occupied towards Mr. Lee practically the position of his child, as she naturally would, having been born and reared in his family. She called him by a pet name, 'Bompt.' She got his slippers for him, took off his shoes, ran on little errands for him, helped him to go to the table, got his cards for him, and generally waited upon him. Mr. Lee was in a feeble condition from the time of his last marriage. He had paralysis of the limbs and throat, his speech was difficult to understand, and he could not walk a step without taking hold of some one's arm." These must be regarded as weighty words, since they express in concise form the reason for the extensive relief that the judgment awards to the plaintiff. Let us assume that the plaintiff, instead of being a stranger to the testator's blood, was, as Judge Cullen once expressed it, "the child of his own loins"; that she was accustomed to address the deceased by the same pet name, and to do all the other things described above. Would her case then be any stronger than it is now? Manifestly not, but, on the contrary, it would be much weaker, and why that is so I have never been able to understand. Could the plaintiff, as one of the testator's children, maintain an action in equity for specific performance of the testator's verbal promise to make a new will or to change an old one? If not, then it is difficult to see how she is in any better position now. The conversation proved in this case is styled a "contract," and I will continue to use that term simply because it is convenient and expressive. That word imports mutual and binding promises between competent parties, upon a good consideration, to do or not to do some particular thing. At all events, that definition is quite sufficient for all the purposes of this case. The plaintiff made no promise whatever, nor was any valid promise made for her. The promise that the deceased made, as found, was that he would make a new will, or change one then existing, and it is said that such promise binds his estate. Now, that promise was either good and valid, or it was invalid, and in law no promise at all. If a court of equity cannot decree specific performance of such a promise, then that ends the case.

I do not think that there is any controlling authority in this state, that, when properly understood, holds that such a promise can be made the basis of a decree of specific performance. On the contrary, it is elementary law that it cannot. "A contract, to be specifically enforced by the court, must be mutual; that is to say, such that it might, at the time it was entered into, have been enforced by either of the parties against the other of them. Whenever, therefore, whether from personal incapacity to contract, or the nature of the contract, or any other cause, the contract is incapable of being enforced against one party, that party is equally incapable of enforcing it against the other, though its execution in the latter way might in itself be free from the difficulty attending its execution in the former." And "a party not bound by the agreement itself has no right to call upon a court of equity to enforce specific performance against the other contracting party, by expressing his willingness, in his plea, to perform his part of the agreement. His right to the aid of the court does not depend upon his subsequent offer to perform the contract upon his part, but upon its original obligatory character." Fry on Specific Performance (3d Ed.) § 440. Judge Gray said in Palmer v. Gould, 144 N. Y. 671, 39 N. E. 378: "It is a rule well settled by the cases that the specific performance of a contract for the sale of lands will not be decreed if the remedy be not mutual, or where one party only is bound by the agreement." These principles are too familiar to call for any extended discussion. They were applied by this court in the case of Mahaney v. Carr, supra, where the finding was the same as in this case. If the recent cases bearing upon this question are not satisfactory, it ought to be observed that the right of the plaintiff to maintain this action was decided adversely to her claim by this court more than 30 years ago (Shakespeare v. Markham, 72 N. Y. 400), and in more recent cases (Gall v. Gall, 64 Hun, 600, 19 N. Y. Supp. 332, affirmed in 138 N. Y. 675, 35 N. E. 515).

I understand that we all agree that the question is open in this court whether the findings of fact sustain the judgment. At all events, it is entirely safe to say that every member of the court has so stated in various cases, which I will not now take the trouble to cite, since I assume there is no question about it. No one claims in this case that the findings of fact are not to be taken as conclusive. The facts, indeed, were found upon evidence, some portions of which are far from satisfactory. But the appellants in this court must take the facts as they are found, and to say that a written decision of the trial court, in which every material fact stated in the complaint is expressly found and separately numbered, does not enable this court to know what the facts of the case are, in order to review the law, any more than it can know the facts the jury passed upon in a general verdict, would seem to be quite absurd.

But it is said that the agreement found in this case is equitable, and, of course, before we can tell whether it is equitable or otherwise, we must look at all the facts and circumstances of the case. There are some things in the record that seem to be considered important, and one of them is the fact that the plaintiff was born in the house which it is said was the gift of the testator to her before his death. I do not for a moment imagine that the place where this young lady was born is of the slightest consequence. Her case would be just exactly as strong as it now is if she had been born in some other house. It must be that these things are emphasized in order to show that the alleged contract under which the plaintiff claims is a wiser and more equitable disposition of the property of the deceased than that which he made by his will, but that would seem to be a departure from the sound views of the court in the case of Hamlin v. Stevens, wherein it is said that every man had a right to do what he would with his own.

This court is required to review judgments entered upon decisions. So far we have referred to the decision alone. We must now see what the judgment accomplishes in this case. The executors and trustees under the testator's will are ordered and directed to deliver to the plaintiff's attorneys a deed of the real estate described in the complaint and in the judgment, and so it has been held that this girl is entitled, under the facts found, to a specific performance of a verbal promise by the testator to devise to her by will a valuable piece of real estate. There is no claim or pretense that she ever had possession of this real estate, or that any other element or fact exists which is required in order to warrant a court of equity to decree the specific performance of a contract to convey land. When it is said that the contract in this case was equitable, I suppose it is intended to express the idea that it contains all the elements which courts of equity require in order to decree a conveyance. The testator, before this alleged contract was made, had executed his will by which he devised this land to others, and so the judgment decides that the testator's will by this verbal arrangement was pro tanto revoked or modified, but that is not all. The judgment commands the testator's executors and trustees to hand over to this girl, out of the testator's personal property, $20,000, and so it has been decided that a verbal promise by an old man to bequeath to a young girl by will $20,000 has enabled the plaintiff to have that promise specifically performed. I confess that I am not aware of any principle of law upon which such judgments can be rendered, and, indeed, no one claims that there is any principle at the basis of this decision. All we are told is that some case has so decided, but, when we come to examine these cases, it will be seen that the facts are very different from the case at bar; but, whatever the facts may be, the three recent decisions to which I have referred, have, I think, settled adversely the claim that such verbal promises can be used to subvert a will. If there is any legal principle that enables this young girl, by means of a verbal conversation between her guardian and the deceased, to acquire $40,000 of this old man's property—one-half of it being real estate—and thus work a revocation of his will, then I think this court owes a duty to itself, to the profession, and to the public to state the principle, to the end that the validity of such a transaction may be known and understood. I think that upon principle and the most recent authorities the judgment in this case is clearly wrong. To say nothing about the absence of any writing for the transfer of such a large amount of property to the plaintiff, what consideration was there which the law recognizes to warrant a court of equity in upholding this verbal agreement? What mutuality was there in this arrangement, as between this old man and the plaintiff, sufficient to warrant a court of equity to decree the things required in this judgment? Suppose she had left the testator's house the next day, and thus broken the agreement, as it is called; what remedy did he or could he have against either her or her guardian? The plaintiff was 16 years old when the alleged agreement was made. It is not claimed that she ever personally assented to the arrangement or was a party to it, and one of the things decided in this case is that a guardian can transfer the sole custody of his ward of that age without her consent, and bind her out to service without writing, to a third party, indefinitely, during the life of that party. Such an arrangement can furnish no consideration to support this transaction. The plaintiff had neither father or mother, brother or sister, or other relative. She was an orphan, and this old man gave her a good home, and educated her, and left her $5,000, and the accumulated income thereof, in his will. It was only eight months from the time that this alleged contract was made that the testator died, and so that was the period covered by his verbal arrangement called a contract. She had her home with him, and she has the $5,000 for her presence in his family for these few months. That gift is one of the few things in the will that the verbal arrangement does not seem to have disturbed. It strikes me that, as the world goes, the plaintiff was a very fortunate orphan to secure so good a home and to receive so substantial a legacy; but it would seem from the judgment in this case that equity will never be satisfied until it has added to the legacy all the testator's real estate, besides $20,000 of his personal property, on the ground that there was a verbal promise on his part to make another and a better will for the plaintiff, which promise must be specifically performed. Of course, the person who made the promise having died, it is impossible to produce the new will, but then equity always treats as done what ought to have been done, and hence the present judgment.

The deceased died, leaving a son, one brother, and two sisters, besides some nephews and nieces. After the gift to the plaintiff, which was in trust until after she arrived at the age of 21 years, he disposed of his estate for the benefit of the son and brother and sister and their descendants, giving a small legacy to another person. I am not quite able to see why this son and the brother and sisters and their children did not have as strong a claim upon the testator's bounty as the plaintiff, but this judgment gives to the plaintiff a large part of what the will gives to the son and the brother and sisters, and it is said that that is equitable. The only basis for all this is the verbal promise of the deceased to change his will, and, having neglected to make the change during his lifetime, a court of equity will make it for him after his death.

When the testator made the will disposing of his estate, he supposed that the law of the land was that he had the right to do what he would with his own, but in this, it seems, he was mistaken. He did not suppose that his will could be destroyed by calling a single witness to testify to a verbal interview with the testator, wherein it is said he promised to make another and better will. It seems from this case that the witness was not able to state the words of the interview, but only what he calls the "spirit and sentiment," and, that having been made to appear in the way suggested, a court of equity is asked to proceed and tear up the will as made, and substitute the verbal arrangement in its place, in whole or in part. If this can be permitted, it is pertinent to ask what becomes of the sacred right to make a will and have it respected, which this court asserted with so much vigor in Doble v. Armstrong, 160 N. Y. 584, 55 N. E. 302? Of course, no man, old, rich, and childless, can safely make a will, if it is always to be open to attack after his death, not, as heretofore, on the ground of incompetency or illegality of its provisions, but upon some kind of vague proof of a verbal arrangement to change it, or to make another will more favorable to strangers in blood, who may think they are equitably entitled to share in the estate.

It has been found as a fact, and is apparently considered very material, since the same thing is emphasized in the argument, that at the time of making the alleged contract, up to the time of his death, the testator "was a paralytic in speech and limbs; it being difficult for him to speak or walk." The prominence given to this fact in favor of the plaintiff illustrates the strange confusion of thought that pervades this case at every point and in all its features. It seems to be supposed that the verbal promise of a helpless paralytic and physical wreck, made a short time before his death, to change his will and make a new will, has peculiar claims on a court of equity for specific performance, whereas I suppose the truth to be that no court of equity, or any other court, ever thought of enforcing such a promise. It might, and doubtless would, produce one of those familiar lawsuits, if the promise was kept, in order to determine whether it was the old will or the new one that should prevail. I think it may be safely asserted that equity will never compel a paralytic, on the eve of death, to make a will. But the startling thing about the whole business is that it is earnestly contended in support of the judgment that this old man, paralytic and physical wreck as he was, having muttered a few incoherent words to the plaintiff's guardian that are to be dignified with the title of a "contract," bound himself and his estate to change his written will in favor of the plaintiff; and this, it is said, presents a transaction so attractive to a court of equity that its specific performance will be decreed.

The learned trial judge did find that the verbal arrangement expressed in the findings is in harmony with public policy, or at least not contrary to it. I always supposed that a verbal agreement to change a written will, already executed, disposing of the testator's estate, or a verbal arrangement of any kind, such as the one in question, for the disposition of property in view of death, and to take effect only upon the happening of that event, was distinctly contrary to public policy; and so, I think, this court has held. Matter of Kennedy, 167 N. Y. 171, 60 N. E. 442. Every one not only admits, but asserts, that these so-called contracts are dangerous, and, if so, it is difficult for me to see why public policy favors them.

I am in favor of reversing the judgment.

PARKER, C. J., and VANN, J. (and GRAY, J., in memorandum), concur with HAIGHT, J. VANN, J., concurs with O'BRIEN, J. MARTIN, J., dissents. CULLEN, J., not voting.

Judgment reversed, etc.

(178 N. Y. 20)

RIGAS v. LIVINGSTON, Commissioner of Public Works, et al.

(Court of Appeals of New York. March 4, 1904.)

CONTEMPT—VIOLATION OF INJUNCTION.

1. Plaintiff obtained an injunction in a suit against city officials to restrain the removal of a sidewalk fruit stand under Code Civ. Proc. § 604, subd. 1, which order forbade defendants and all other persons having knowledge of the order to remove the same. *Held* to restrain only defendants and those acting as their servants or agents, or in collusion with them, and not to affect the rights of the landlord of the property, who removed the stand in execution of the process of another court because of the default in rent of the owner of the stand, who was his tenant; so that he was not guilty of contempt in so doing.

Vann, J., dissenting.

Appeal from Supreme Court, Appellate Division, First Department.

Action by Peter Rigas against George Livingston, commissioner of public works of the borough of Manhattan, and others. From an order of the Appellate Division (83 N. Y. Supp. 1110) affirming an order adjudging Morris Levy guilty of contempt, he appeals. Reversed.

Gustavus A. Rogers, for appellant. Meyer Greenberg, for respondents.

CULLEN, J. The plaintiff was the occupant of a fruit stand on the sidewalk in front of No. 89 Park Row, in the city of New York. The appellant, Levy, was the tenant and occupant of the store in front of which the plaintiff's stand was located. Levy was anxious that the stand should be removed, and applied to the city authorities to have such removal effected. Thereupon the plaintiff brought an action in the Supreme Court against the commissioner of public works of the borough of Manhattan and the superintendent of the bureau of incumbrances to enjoin them from interfering with his stand. A temporary injunction was granted, which, after a hearing, was continued during the pendency of the action. This order purported in terms not only to restrain the defendants, but also "all persons having knowledge of this injunction order." Thereafter one Rosenblum, the son-in-law of Levy, landlord of the building, brought proceedings in the Municipal Court to dispossess Levy from his store. In these proceedings Levy made default, and a warrant for his removal was issued. Acting under this warrant, Loewenthal, a city marshal, and Dickman, the at-

¶ 1. See Injunction, vol. 27, Cent. Dig. §§ 435, 485, 486, 495.

torney for the landlord, removed and destroyed the plaintiff's stand. Thereafter application was made to punish Levy, Dickman, and Loewenthal for contempt. The proof tended to show that all of them were notified of the existence of the injunction. The Special Term adjudged the parties guilty of a civil contempt in impairing and prejudicing the plaintiff's rights, and fined them the sum of $150. Levy appealed to the Appellate Division (83 N. Y. Supp. 1116; 84 N. Y. Supp. 1143), where the order was affirmed. The court afterward allowed an appeal to this court, certifying the question, "Do the papers submitted by the respondent state sufficient facts upon which the order adjudging the appellant in contempt could properly be made?" It is a matter of regret that, since the learned Appellate Division deemed the case presented a question of law which ought to be determined by this court, it did not write any opinion, and we are thus deprived of the benefit of the views which that court entertained on the subject. The Special Term found that the appellant "did, by trick and scheme, violate said injunction order, and caused said stand to be removed." It is doubtful whether the proof was sufficient to justify this finding. Levy was not present at the removal of the stand, nor does it appear that he gave any instructions to the persons who actually removed the stand. It does appear that he was anxious to have the plaintiff ousted, and had some time previous to this occurrence threatened he would get the stand removed. It also appears that other summary proceedings had been taken by Rosenblum against Levy and the plaintiff to remove them. Those proceedings were dismissed. These facts, and the relationship between Levy and Rosenblum, create a very strong suspicion that Levy was a prime mover in all the transactions; but it is doubtful whether, in the face of Levy's sworn denial, they were sufficient in these proceedings, which are quasi criminal, to establish his guilt. However this may be, we are of opinion that the removal of the stand, though illegal, was not a violation of the injunction. The parties might have been sued for their trespass civilly, and, it is possible, criminally; but, however great their fault, it was not a contempt of court. The court had jurisdiction of the subject-matter of the action and of the defendants to the action, and the injunction was in all respects valid and binding on the parties. But the question is, what persons did it restrain? The power of the court to grant injunctions pendente lite is to be found in the Code of Civil Procedure (People ex rel. Cauffman v. Van Buren, 136 N. Y. 252, 32 N. E. 775, 20 L. R. A. 446), and this case falls within the first subdivision of section 604: "Where it appears, by affidavit, that the defendant, during the pendency of the action, is doing, or procuring, or suffering to be done, or threatens, or is about to do, or to procure, or suffer to be done, an act, in violation of the plaintiff's rights, respecting the subject of the action, and tending to render the judgment ineffectual, an injunction order may be granted to restrain him therefrom." In terms the Code authorizes an injunction against the defendants only, not the whole world. There are some exceptions to this rule—as in the case of proceedings for the dissolution of corporations which are in the nature of proceedings in rem, where the statute expressly authorizes an injunction against all creditors. Therefore, so far as the order purported to restrain all other persons having knowledge of the injunction, this provision was inoperative to enlarge its effect.

It is true that persons not parties to the action may be bound by an injunction if they have knowledge of it, provided they are servants or agents of the defendants, or act in collusion or combination with them. Such was the case of Daly v. Amberg, 126 N. Y. 490, 27 N. E. 1038, where the agents and employés of the manager of a theater disobeyed an injunction granted against their employer to restrain the representation of a play at his theater. So, in People ex rel. Davis v. Sturtevant, 9 N. Y. 263, 59 Am. Dec. 536, an injunction granted against the city of New York was held binding on the members of the common council of that city. Authorities illustrating the rule might be cited to an indefinite extent, but the underlying principle in all cases of this class, on which is founded the power of the court to punish for the violation of its mandate persons not parties to the action, is that the parties so punished were acting either as the agents or servants of the defendants, or in combination or collusion with them, or in assertion of their rights or claims. Persons, however, who are not connected in any way with the parties to the action, are not restrained by the order of the court. In High on Injunctions, vol. 2, p. 1112, it is said: "One who was not a party to the proceeding, and who has acquired no rights from any of the parties defendant pendente lite, is not guilty of a breach of injunction by exercising a right which belonged to him before the suit." In Spelling on Injunctions, vol. 2, p. 956, it is said: "One not a party to a suit in which an injunction has issued, nor an agent of such party, and to whom such injunction is not directed, cannot be held in contempt, or be punished for the violation of the writ, although the act prohibited be illegal in itself." In Batterman v. Finn, 32 How. Prac. 501, it was held that, to make a person not a party to the action liable for disobeying an injunction, the person should bear such a relation to the defendant as enables the latter to control his action. So it was held that lessees of the defendant, who had been enjoined from interfering with a water power, could not be punished for violating that injunction, it not appearing that they were acting in conspiracy or collusion with the defendant. In

Walton v. Grand Belt Copper Company, 56 Hun, 211, 9 N. Y. Supp. 375, it was held that an injunction could only issue against a party to the action. The same doctrine was held in Marty v. Marty, 66 App. Div. 527, 73 N. Y. Supp. 369. In People ex rel. Morris v. Randall, 73 N. Y. 416, Batterman v. Finn, supra, was quoted with approval, and it was held that a stranger to the restraining orders of the court was in no way affected by or bound to obey them. In the present case the injunction order determined that prima facie the plaintiff was authorized to maintain his stand as against the city of New York and its authorities. This was the only right passed upon on the application for the injunction, and the only right which could have been passed upon. The injunction order therefore properly restrained the city authorities from interfering with the plaintiff's stand. Had any of the city officials, or their employés or agents, or any third parties acting in aid of or in connivance with them, interfered with the stand, they would have committed a contempt of court. But it is not pretended that the city officials against whom the action was brought, or either of them, in any way, directly or indirectly, by act or solicitation, took part in the subsequent trespass on the plaintiff's property. The parties who removed the stand neither acted nor assumed to act under any right or authority of the city officials, but in execution of the process of another court, issued on a judgment not based on any claim of the city that the stand was a nuisance, but on a right asserted by a landlord to dispossess a defaulting tenant. It is true that this process offered no justification for the trespass on the plaintiff's property. That fact did not make them guilty of contempt, but liable as trespassers. A thief might have come along in the night and stolen the plaintiff's stand. He would have been guilty of larceny, but not of contempt of court.

The orders of the Special Term and of the Appellate Division should be reversed, and the application denied, but, under the circumstances, without costs.

PARKER, C. J., and GRAY, O'BRIEN, HAIGHT, and MARTIN, JJ., concur. VANN, J., dissents.

Orders reversed.

(178 N. Y. 84)

BATEMAN v. NEW YORK CENT. & H. R. R. CO.

(Court of Appeals of New York. March 15, 1904.)

INJURY TO EMPLOYÉ—DANGEROUS PREMISES—QUESTION FOR JURY.

1. Where plaintiff sustained injuries by falling through a trapdoor on defendant's premises, where she was employed, which was improperly replaced by her coservants, and such trapdoor had no hinges, and was a very tight fit, so that her coservants, who were working below the trapdoor, could not close it from below, it is a question for the jury whether the accident was not likely to occur because of the want of the hinges, so as to render defendant liable, under the circumstances, by failure to furnish a safe place for plaintiff to work.

Appeal from Supreme Court, Appellate Division, Fourth Department.

Action by Margaret Bateman against the New York Central & Hudson River Railroad Company. From a judgment of the Appellate Division (73 N. Y. Supp. 390) reversing a judgment for plaintiff, she appeals. Reversed.

Theodore E. Hancock, for appellant. A. H. Cowie and Frank Hiscock, for respondent.

BARTLETT, J. This is an action to recover damages for alleged personal injuries. The jury found a verdict in favor of the plaintiff for $1,000, and judgment was duly entered thereon.

The Appellate Division states in its order on reversing this judgment that it was upon questions of law only, and that the facts had been examined, and no error found therein. It is therefore incumbent on the plaintiff (appellant) to show that there was no error of law justifying the reversal of the judgment.

The plaintiff resides in the city of Syracuse, and at the time of her injury, the 17th of November, 1898, was employed by the defendant company as a cleaner in its freight office. She had filled this position since the May previous. In the floor of this office, outside of the desks, and in the space for the public, was a trapdoor, located near the wall of the building. It was proved that beneath the floor of this office was the heating plant, consisting of steam pipes and other appliances. The trapdoor in question was to enable plumbers to reach this plant when necessary to replace or repair the same. The space between the trapdoor and the ground was about three feet, the grade falling off toward the center of the building. The manner of the construction and operation of the trapdoor has a controlling bearing on this case. The plaintiff swore a carpenter as an expert, who had examined the premises, and he testified in part as follows: "This trap door that was in the floor was 25½ inches long and 22½ inches wide. It is on the east side of the freight office. * * * The edge of the hole is one foot from the mopboard on that side of the office. It extends out from that 22½ inches. The cover of this hole is made of the same material of which the floor is made. The boards are hard pine, an inch and an eighth thick. There are nine boards making this cover—nine pieces. There is a batten nine inches wide on the underside. The boards are screwed or fastened to this batten. * * * Now, the * * * floor is so made that it gives a bearing to each end of this little door of an inch and a half; and, when the door is laid down in its place, it is flush with the floor—smooth, so you walk over it. There are no hinges on it. * * * When down in its place properly, * * * it is virtually a portion of the floor, and is a good, tight fit. It fits flush with the floor. * * * If the door was in its proper position in the floor, one would possibly pass it without noticing that there was a trapdoor there. * * * I saw them take it out. The man that took it out had to take a little screw-driver and put it under this corner here to pry it up. Then, when I was done with my measurements, laid it down, gave it a kick with my toe to knock it back into its place, and it went down. * * * It fits in there very tight." At the time of the accident, plumbers were at work beneath the floor on the steam-heating apparatus, and had opened the trapdoor in order to reach the place. The plaintiff, at about half-past 8 o'clock in the afternoon, while engaged in her work, approached the south side of the office, near the location of the trapdoor. She thus testifies in this connection: "I hadn't worked on that side of the office before. I worked on the other side. * * * I had never seen this trapdoor. Didn't know of its existence. At the time I stepped on this door, we were just finishing up to get through; and the other woman came to me, and she asked me if I was through, and I said, 'Yes.' I was just wiping the desk, and went to reach up to wipe off the light; and, just as I stepped around the end of the desk, I stepped on this loose piece of floor, and it flew right up and struck me on the left knee, and, when I saw the floor opening, I felt my feet going from under me, and I made a twist to swing around, not to fall in, and then I went with harder force against the edge of the floor, and went right down through, and the loose piece of floor was between me and the tight floor that was in the hole. This piece of flooring tipped up in the hole. Both of my legs didn't go into this hole. The right foot went down to my body, and the other one—my knee—right in there. There was a radiator there. I struck against it when I was falling. * * * I remained in bed over three months steady. The doctor came sometimes twice a day, and he came every day for over three months. I had three broken ribs. Then, after I got up, the knee that I bruised in the fall— When I got up, my knee was sore. Inflammation set in. I was so weak I coudn't do any work." The witness also testified that at the time of the trial her knee was still troubling her, and that she had never regained her normal condition of health.

The trial judge submitted this case to the jury in an exceedingly fair charge. He stated to them, in substance, that in an action based on negligence the plaintiff must show that the injury happened by reason of some negligence on the part of the defendant, without any negligence on the part of the plaintiff that has contributed in any degree to the result; that the duty was upon the defendant to furnish a reasonably safe place for its servants, of whom the plaintiff was one, for the discharge of the duties that they were employed to perform. He then told the jury, with considerable elaboration, that he proposed to submit to them the question whether the defendant had, in view of the circumstances, discharged its full duty of furnishing a safe place for the plaintiff to work, the trapdoor having been constructed without hinges. He said: "According to the evidence of Mr. Hunt, this door, when it was fully in place, was apparently solid and tight. If so, the inference naturally would follow that, at the time the plaintiff stepped upon it and it had tipped, it had been removed to some extent from its original place, so that the tipping occurred; and the inference, perhaps, may be drawn (it is your duty to draw it, if anybody does) that the plumbers, who were at work below upon this day, when they went down, instead of placing this trapdoor squarely over the hole, left it raised a little upon one side, so that there was occasion for the tipping. If those employés, those plumbers below, were negligent in the manner in which they left it, if they were careless, I say to you, for the purpose of this case, the defendant is not liable for their negligence; and, if their negligence was the sole and only cause of the accident, then the plaintiff could not recover. If, however, the defendant was also careless; if it failed to furnish there a reasonably safe place; if, by reason of this door being constructed, as it was, without any hinges (which, as it is claimed, was an important circumstance, and that, of course, is for you), but constructed as it was, and being there just as it was, for the purpose for which it was there placed, and with such a liability as may be shown here of its being used; if the defendant failed to perform its duty, and therefore was careless, and such carelessness also contributed to the result—then the defendant would not be relieved because the employés were also negligent." The plumbers in question were in the permanent employ of the defendant company.

The Appellate Division approved the charge of the trial judge, save in one particular, where it submitted to the jury the question whether the defendant had performed the duty resting upon it of furnishing a reasonably safe place for plaintiff to work when discharging the duties of her employment. The learned court were of the opinion that this case falls within the rule laid down in Perry v. Rogers, 157 N. Y. 251, 255, 51 N. E. 1021, citing in that connection Hussey v. Coger, 112 N. Y. 614, 20 N. E. 556, 8 L. R. A. 559, 8 Am. St. Rep. 787; Filbert v. D. & H. C. Co., 121 N. Y. 207, 23 N. E. 1104; Hogan v. Smith, 125 N. Y. 774, 26 N. E. 742; Geoghegan v. Atlas S. S. Co., 146 N. Y. 369, 40 N. E. 507. The rule laid down in these cases is the correct one, and has been strictly adhered to by this court. We are constrained to differ with the court below as to the application of this rule in the present case. In Perry v. Rogers, supra, a very different situation was presented. The headnote of that case states the facts as follows: "When the employer of competent workmen engaged in blasting down a ledge of rock, on the face of which they necessarily work, has provided them with the necessary and proper appliances, and with a skillful foreman, the removal from a spot where a blast has been exploded of a threatening overhanging rock, made dangerous by the work, before undertaking to remove the blasted rock beneath, is an ordinary incidental detail, as to which the employer is not bound to direct a workman, but which may be properly left to the foreman; and if the foreman, on sending a workman to clear a blasted spot, omits to remove or to notify the workman to remove a threatening piece of rock before working directly under it, he is in that respect a fellow servant; and, if the piece falls and injures the workman, the negligence, if there is any, except on the part of the workman himself, is that of the foreman, as a fellow servant, and does not constitute a breach of the employer's duty." The Appellate Division quotes, in part, the following from the opinion of Parker, C. J., in that case: "But it has not been understood to be the rule in this state that in the performance of work of this character the master, after making his place in the first instance reasonably safe for the prosecution of the work, has any duty to perform, other than in the furnishing of safe appliances and the employment of competent and skillful employés." The Appellate Division then says: "Tested by the rule as thus declared, we fail to see how it can be said that the place in which the plaintiff was required to perform her work was unsafe in any sense for which the defendant was responsible. The cover for the trap was, beyond all question, so constructed as to withstand the greatest weight which under any conceivable circumstances would ever rest upon it; and, when adjusted in the manner designed by the defendant, it was not only flush with the floor, but it was a part of the floor, and just as firm and safe as any other part. Indeed, it appears that in such circumstances it was so firmly and closely fitted to the aperture for which it was constructed that it required some effort to remove it; and, this being so, the conclusion is irresistible that, but for the failure of the plumbers to replace the cover in the exact condition in which they found it, the plaintiff would have escaped the injury which subsequently resulted. It is possible that, if the cover had been adjusted by means of hinges, this particular accident would not have occurred; but, even assuming this to be so, it does not follow that the defendant's liability was established, for the fact still remains that with the means of adjustment which it had furnished, and which, so far as appears, had always theretofore proved sufficient, the place was both safe and suitable, within the rule cited, and, if so, the verdict of the jury had nothing upon which to rest." The learned Appellate Division, in thus summing up the evidence, has omitted, as it seems to us, the one controlling fact, which was a proper inference from the evidence, if the jury saw fit to draw it, that the plumbers, from beneath, could not close the trapdoor and bring it down to a level with the surrounding floor, for the reason that it was a very tight fit, and required considerable force from above to drive it back into position. It was for the jury to say whether what did happen was not likely to occur, in the absence of hinges on the trapdoor, which would have held it firmly in place, so that it would have been either wide open, and the aperture perfectly obvious, or practically closed, substantially covering the opening, and immovable if stepped upon. While there was no direct evidence as to the precise position of this trapdoor just prior to the accident, yet the plaintiff's testimony as to the manner in which she fell into the opening justified the jury in finding that the trapdoor was not placed squarely over the aperture, but was in a position which caused it to tip when she stepped upon it. We are of opinion that it was an open question for the jury to answer, under all the circumstances, whether the defendant had furnished a safe place, in which the plaintiff was required to work. It follows that there was no question of law presented justifying the reversal of the judgment in plaintiff's favor.

The order and judgment of the Appellate Division should be reversed, and the judgment of the trial court affirmed, with costs to plaintiff in all the courts.

O'BRIEN, HAIGHT, VANN, CULLEN, and WERNER, JJ., concur. PARKER, C. J., absent.

Order and judgment reversed, etc.

(178 N. Y. 63)

MEYER v. SUPREME LODGE K. P.

(Court of Appeals of New York. March 15, 1904.)

BENEFICIAL SOCIETIES—CERTIFICATE—CONSTRUCTION—WITNESS—PRIVILEGED COMMUNICATION.

1. A fraternal benefit corporation, organized under the acts of Congress, issued a certificate of membership, through its officers in Chicago, to a resident of New York, on which was printed an acceptance of the certificate, subject to all the conditions therein contained, which was signed by the applicant in New York. The conditions provided that the certificate was to take effect when the acceptance was executed. *Held* a New York contract, to be enforced according to the laws of that state.

2. Code Civ. Proc. §§ 834, 836, prohibiting the disclosure by a physician of professional information, unless the privilege has been expressly waived by the personal representatives

of the deceased, apply to a fraternal mutual benefit certificate, though it contains a waiver by the applicant.

3. Where a physician is called to treat a patient against his will, he becomes a patient by operation of law, and any information which is acquired by such physician in order to enable him to act is acquired in attending a patient in a professional capacity, within Code Civ. Proc. § 834, and is privileged.

Parker, C. J., and Gray, J., dissenting.

Appeal from Supreme Court, Appellate Division, Second Department.

Action by Henrietta Meyer against the Supreme Lodge Knights of Pythias. From a judgment of the Appellate Division affirming a judgment for plaintiff (81 N. Y. Supp. 813), defendant appeals. Affirmed.

Laurence G. Goodhart and Carlos H. Hardy, for appellant. Otto H. Droege and J. Lawrence Friedmann, for respondent.

VANN, J. The deceased was in extremis, incapable of acting or deciding for himself, and, from the necessity of the case, any one was authorized to call a physician to treat him. Without the knowledge or consent of the dying man, Dr. Bruso was called for that purpose, and for that purpose alone he attended. He found Mr. Meyer, the deceased, in bed in an upper room of a hotel, "suffering intense pain and vomiting." Meyer told him to get out of the room—that he did not want him there—but he did not leave. He remained to treat him as a physician, and, in order to treat him intelligently, tried to find out what the matter was. He learned from Meyer, partly in answer to questions, and partly through voluntary disclosures, that he had taken a preparation of arsenic, known as "Rough on Rats," "because he wanted to die." From this information, and from observation of the physical symptoms, he decided that Meyer was suffering from arsenical poisoning. Thus informed as to the nature of the disease, he at once administered a remedy, and soon followed it by another. The helpless man, without friends to aid or advise, hopeless of life and courting death, objected, and tried to curse him away from his bedside. The doctor, loyal to the instincts of his profession, refused to listen to the ravings of the would-be suicide, and continued to prescribe in order to relieve suffering and prolong life. Upon the trial he was not allowed to disclose the information acquired under these circumstances, and we are now to determine whether there was enough evidence to warrant the trial judge in deciding, as a preliminary question of fact, that such information was acquired "in attending a patient, in a professional capacity," and that it "was necessary to enable him to act in that capacity." Code Civ. Proc. § 834; Griffiths v. Met. St. Ry. Co., 171 N. Y. 106, 111, 63 N. E. 808.

The learned doctor was called as a physician, he attended as a physician, he made a diagnosis as a physician, and he administered remedies as a physician. In all that he did, he acted in a professional capacity. While it is true that in all he did he acted against the will and in spite of the remonstrance of a man whose condition imperatively called for professional treatment, still the meeting was professional in nature, and all that he said or did was strictly in the line of his profession. Was the subject any the less a patient, within the meaning and object of the statute, because he was forced to submit to ministrations designed to save his life? Was the doctor guilty of assault when he gave the hypodermic injection? Was he bound to leave him there to die, without an effort to help him? Was the statute designed to protect those only who are treated by consent, but not those treated through necessity? Does it not mean by a "patient" at least one who is consciously treated by a physician, even without his consent, when the facts tend to show that through bodily suffering his mind had partially lost its hold? Do our humane laws make it the duty of a physician to leave the bedside of a dying man, because he demands it, and, if he remains and relieves him by physical touch, hold him guilty of assault? Either Dr. Bruso was the physician of Mr. Meyer, or he committed an assault upon him, and was guilty of a crime. If the wife of the deceased had called the doctor, she would have acted as an agent by implied authority. The bell boy who in fact called him also acted upon implied authority, and, when the doctor came, the act of the agent in calling him, if subject to revocation in the actual case, would have been in the supposed case. While the doctor in either case could have retired, if he remained in either he remained as a physician, the sick man became his patient, and he was acting in a professional capacity when, as a duly licensed physician, he actually treated Mr. Meyer as a patient. When one who is sick unto death is in fact treated by a physician as a patient, even against his will, he becomes the patient of that physician, by operation of law. The same is true of one who is unconscious and unable to speak for himself. If the deceased had been in a comatose state when the physician arrived, the existence of the professional relation could not be questioned. The relation of physician and patient, so far as the statute under consideration is concerned, springs from the fact of professional treatment, independent of the causes which led to such treatment. An examination made in order to prescribe establishes the same relation. I am of opinion that Dr. Bruso, who treated the deceased at the hotel, occupied the same confidential relation to him as did the physicians at the hospital. The fact that the patient told the doctor several times to let him alone, as he wished to die, expressing himself in a brutal and profane manner, does not, in my judgment, negative the existence of the relation of physician and patient. As was said by Judge Earl in Renihan v. Dennin, 103 N.

Y. 573, 578, 9 N. E. 320, 321, 57 Am. Rep. 770: "Dr. Bontecou was a person duly authorized to practice physic. Whatever information he had about the condition of the testator he acquired while attending him as a patient. It is true that the testator did not call him or procure his attendance, but he did not thrust himself into his presence or intrude there. He was called by the attending physician, and went in his professional capacity to see the patient, and that was enough to bring the case within the statute. It is quite common for physicians to be summoned by the friends of the patient, or even by strangers about him; and the statute would be robbed of much of its virtue if a physician thus called were to be excluded from its provisions because * * * he was not employed by the patient, nor a contract relation created between him and the patient. To bring the case within the statute, it is sufficient that the person attended as a physician upon the patient, and obtained his information in that capacity." So, in People v. Murphy, 101 N. Y. 126, 4 N. E. 326, 54 Am. Rep. 661, it was held that the fact that the physician was selected and sent by the district attorney to attend the patient after the commission of a crime against her person did not affect the question.

When a physician is sent by a prosecuting officer to make a report upon the sanity of a prisoner, if he does not treat or prescribe for the subject, the statements of the latter are not protected. People v. Sliney, 137 N. Y. 570, 33 N. E. 150. But even though a physician is sent for the sole purpose of examining as to sanity, if he prescribes for the prisoner during the visit, the relation of physician and patient is thereby created, and the disclosures made are within the statute. People v. Stout, 3 Parker, Cr. R. 670; Weitz v. Mound City Ry. Co., 53 Mo. App. 39; Freel v. Market St. Ry. Co., 97 Cal. 40, 31 Pac. 730; Colorado Fuel & Iron Co. v. Cummings, 8 Colo. App. 541, 46 Pac. 875. See, also, Grossman v. Supreme Lodge (Sup.) 6 N. Y. Supp. 821; Grattan v. Metro. Life Ins. Co., 24 Hun, 43; Edington v. Mutual Life Ins. Co., 67 N. Y. 185. The fact of treatment is the decisive test in this case. Meyer was treated by the witness as a physician, and answered his questions, knowing that he was a physician, and that he was about to prescribe for him against his will. As was well said by the learned judges of the Appellate Division: "The language [of the statute] is broad enough to cover cases of medical attendance, whether such attendance results from the voluntary call of the patient upon the physician, or from the exigencies of the patient's situation. If the relation is that of a physician attending a patient in a professional capacity, no matter how the relation was brought about, the sections apply."

In Griffiths v. Met. St. Ry. Co., 171 N. Y. 106, 63 N. E. 808, relied upon by the appellant, there was no evidence that the physician acted in a professional capacity, or even that the supposed patient knew he was a physician. The doctor in that case testified that at the time he acquired the information he did not "treat him, in any sense, as a physician"; that his conversation with him did not relate to his physical condition, but was confined "to the method of the accident, and that whatever he said was entirely distinct from any treatment or visit of a physician, or anything of that sort"; that, while he had rendered "first aid" to the plaintiff in a drug store immediately after the accident, when no statement was made, "he did not think the plaintiff knew that he was the physician who treated him at the drug store; and that he did not advise him of the fact until after the plaintiff had given him a statement." Judge Werner, writing for this court, said: "Here there are no facts shown which would warrant the presumption that the relation of physician and patient existed, or that would justify the conclusion that the conversation the doctor was about to give had any relation to professional treatment."

I think that the statute impresses absolute secrecy upon all knowledge acquired by a physician in a sickroom that is necessary to enable him to properly treat the sick person, whether the treatment be with or without his consent. While I agree with Judge GRAY in his conclusion as to the first question considered by him, I differ as to the last, and, for the reasons stated, vote in favor of affirmance, with costs.

GRAY, J. (dissenting). The action was brought to recover against the defendant, a fraternal, mutual benefit corporation, organized under the acts of the Congress of the United States, upon a certificate of membership issued to Emanuel Meyer, by which it promised to pay upon his death to his wife, this plaintiff, the sum of $2,000. The defendant alleged in defense of the action that the death of Meyer was the result of suicide, which, within the terms of the agreement of the parties, avoided the certificate. Upon the trial of the issues, the defendant, claiming the affirmative, and not questioning plaintiff's preliminary proofs to establish a case under the allegations of her complaint, was allowed to begin with its defense, and its evidence was directed towards proving that the beneficiary committed suicide by taking poison. The trial judge submitted to the jury the one question "whether the deceased committed suicide," and, upon their answering "No" to the question, he directed judgment to be entered for the plaintiff. That judgment has been affirmed by the Appellate Division, and upon this appeal, in substance, the general argument of the appellant is that the waiver of the deceased, contained in his application for the insurance certificate, of all provisions of law then or thereafter in force prohibiting any physician from testifying to any information acquired by attendance upon him, was a part of a contract, which had been validly made in the state of Illinois, and that sections 834 and 836 of the Code of Civil Procedure of this state, under which such testimony is rendered inadmissible unless the statutory prohibition is waived upon the trial by the personal representatives of the deceased, are inoperative, as being in violation of the provisions of the federal Constitution which prohibit legislation in impairment of contracts. The argument, further, is that, as to one of the physicians called upon to testify for the defense, his testimony, certainly, did not come within the statutory prohibition, inasmuch as the necessary relationship of physician and patient did not exist.

With respect to the first of these questions raised by the appellant, whatever other answers might be made to the applicability of the provision of the federal Constitution relied upon, it is sufficient to say now that this contract was consummated in the state of New York, and is to be governed, in its enforcement, by the laws of that state. The beneficiary was a resident of this state, and there made his application for the insurance. The certificate issuing upon the application appears, from its language only, to have been signed by the officers of the defendant at Chicago, in the state of Illinois, on September 20, 1894; but upon it was printed the following clause: "I hereby accept this certificate of membership subject to all the conditions therein contained." And that had the signature of the applicant, followed by the words, "Dated at New York, this 28th day of September 1894, attest: Louis Riegel, Secretary Section 2179, Endowment Rank, K. of P." By the terms of the certificate, the agreement of the defendant was subject not only to the conditions subscribed to by the member in his application, but "to the further conditions and agreements hereinafter named"; and the clause containing his acceptance, above quoted, was one of those "further agreements." From these terms of the agreements of the parties, the only natural conclusion is that the place of the contract was where it was intended and understood to be consummated. Its completion depended upon the execution by the member of the further agreement indorsed upon the certificate, namely, to accept it "subject to all the conditions therein contained." The contract was not completed, in the sense that it was binding upon either party to it, until it was delivered in New York after the execution by the member of the further agreement expressing his unqualified acceptance of its conditions. As matter of fact, the promise of the defendant was to pay the insurance moneys to the plaintiff, who resided in New York—a feature giving additional local coloring to the contract. But the sufficient and controlling fact is that by its terms it was first to take effect as a binding obligation when the required agreement on the part of the member was executed by him.

The difficulty in this case, which, in my judgment, entitles the defendant to a new trial in the action, is the exclusion of the evidence of Dr. Bruso, called as a witness for the defendant, and asked to state a conversation had with Meyer, the deceased. This witness was a physician, having his office in the city of Buffalo, in this state, near to the Iroquois Hotel. He testified that, in the early morning, one of the bell boys of the hotel came for him, and, upon entering one of the rooms, he found a man in the bed, suffering from pain and vomiting. Objection being made to his evidence, which was in the form of a deposition, the court put the question: "Did this doctor treat him?" The defendant's counsel replied: "He inserted something hypodermically into the man against his wish." The objection to the testimony was sustained, the defendant excepted, and the whole deposition of the witness was excluded, under the previous ruling of the court that sections 834 and 836 of the Code of Civil Procedure applied. From the deposition thus offered and excluded, it appeared that the witness had a conversation with Meyer, which was narrated, so far as material, as follows: "I asked him what he had been doing, and he told me it was none of my damned business; that he didn't want me in there, and he wanted me to get out of there. * * * I looked around the room. * * * I found * * * a box of Rough on Rats * * * empty. * * * He told me he had taken it * * * because he wanted to die; * * * he didn't want to get well; * * * he didn't want me to do anything. * * * I prepared a hypodermic injection, * * * and stimulated him, so he would not die in the Hotel Iroquois. * * * When I was going to give him the hypodermic, he said: 'You [cursing him in foul language] keep away from here. Didn't I tell you before to keep away?' I paid no attention to him, and gave him the hypodermic." The witness was then asked if he knew what was the cause of the condition of the man, and he answered that it was arsenical poisoning, and that the symptoms evidenced it. The deceased was immediately conveyed from the hotel to the hospital, where he died soon afterwards. The evidence of Dr. Bruso was deemed inadmissible, under the provisions of section 834 of the Code of Civil Procedure, which prohibits a physician from disclosing "any information which he acquired in attending a patient, in a professional capacity, and which was necessary to enable him to act in that capacity." The agreement of the insured, contained in his application, which waived, for himself, his representatives and beneficiaries, "any and all provisions of law, now or hereafter in force, prohibiting * * * any physician * * * attending me * * * from disclosing, or testifying to, any information acquired thereby," and which expressly consented to such testimony being given in any suit, was held below to be insufficient to meet the requirement of section 836 of the Code of Civil Procedure, that the provisions of section 834 must be expressly waived upon the trial by the personal representatives of the deceased patient. Such a waiver was refused at this trial. Our recent decision in Holden v. Metropolitan Life Ins. Co., 165 N. Y. 13, 58 N. E. 771, justified the ruling below upon the question of the force of the waiver in the insurance contract. Theretofore it had been the rule to regard such a waiver as a binding part of the contract of insurance, and, as such, available to the insurer in any action upon the policy. Foley v. Royal Arcanum, 151 N. Y. 196, 45 N. E. 456, 56 Am. St. Rep. 621.

But was there disclosed that relationship of physician and patient between the deceased and Dr. Bruso which made operative the prohibitory provisions of section 834? As the inadmissibility of such testimony is only because of the statute, it is quite important that the case should come very clearly within its terms, however liberal the construction which we should give to an enactment intended to promote the ends of justice. The object of this legislation was to render privileged what communications are made between a physician and his patient, but, obviously it is essential that it shall appear that the person attended is his patient, in the sense in which such a term is ordinarily understood. In Griffiths v. Metropolitan Street Railway Company, 171 N. Y. 106, 63 N. E. 808, we quite lately had occasion to consider such a question under a state of facts not essentially dissimilar to that now before us. In that case the plaintiff brought his action to recover damages for injuries sustained through the negligence of the defendant's servant, a gripman upon one of its cars. The defendant called a physician as a witness who was at the scene of the accident when an ambulance arrived, and who rendered "first aid" to the plaintiff. The witness was also an attending physician at the hospital, to which the plaintiff was assisted by him in the ambulance, but he rendered no further services to him while in the hospital. The witness was asked to relate a conversation which he had with the plaintiff in the hospital subsequently, but the court sustained an objection to its admissibility, under section 834 of the Code, and the witness was not allowed to testify to what was said by plaintiff with reference to his sufferings or to the accident. When the case reached this court, it was held that the exclusion of the physician's evidence was an error, for which the judgment should be reversed, and a new trial had. The decision by this court rested upon the ground that the burden upon the plaintiff of showing that the evidence was within the statutory prohibition had not been met, and that the facts did not warrant the presumption that the relation of physician and patient existed. The opinion quite fully reviewed the cases illustrating the application of the statutory provision in question, and the rule was distinctly adhered to, that, to warrant the application, it must appear that the relation of physician and patient at the time existed, and that the information sought to be excluded was necessary to enable the physician to act as such. Previous to the Griffiths Case, that rule had been expressed in People v. Koerner, 154 N. Y. 355, 48 N. E. 730. Can we say that the rule applies to such a situation as that disclosed in this case, any more than it did in Griffiths' Case? I think not. It seems to me to be difficult to assert, with any gravity of countenance, at least, with Meyer rejecting the witness' presence and services, and cursing him for his interference, and with the witness' determined efforts to prevent Meyer from dying in the hotel, whose servants had summoned him, that the relation of physician and patient arose, and that the confidential relation existed which the statute has in view, and which, with a tender solicitude for a patient's interests, it is designed to safeguard.

The inadmissibility of the testimony of the hospital physicians rests upon a different basis. Both may reasonably be said to have been in attendance upon him as a hospital patient, but, in my opinion, the deposition of Dr. Bruso was erroneously excluded, and therefore I advise the reversal of the judgment.

O'BRIEN, BARTLETT, and MARTIN, JJ., concur with VANN, J. PARKER, C. J., concurs with GRAY, J. WERNER, J., absent.

Judgment affirmed.

(178 N. Y. 94)

WEINSTEIN v. WEBER.

(Court of Appeals of New York. March 15, 1904.)

WILL—CONSTRUCTION—VESTED REMAINDER—POWER OF SALE.

1. Testator devised to a person, who, after the execution of the will, became his wife, one-third of his estate during life, after her death two-thirds thereof to go to her children and one-third to his children, with full power in the wife to sell and dispose of any part of the estate, and also gave the remaining two-thirds of his estate to his children, share and share alike. *Held* not to create a general power of sale, but one accompanied with a trust, so that her children and those of the testator took vested remainders.

2. Where testator gave to his wife one-third of his estate for life, and at her death provided that two-thirds thereof should go to her children, and one-third to his, giving her power to sell, and a deed was executed by testator's executors of an undivided interest in lands owned by him, on which the widow indorsed an instrument purporting to convey all her right

and interest therein, such indorsement was not an exercise of the power of sale under the will, but only a conveyance of her dower in the two-thirds devised to testator's children, and her life estate in the one-third devised to her.

Appeal from Supreme Court, Appellate Division, First Department.

Action by Rachel Weinstein against Joseph Weber. From a judgment of the Appellate Division (81 N. Y. Supp. 62) affirming a judgment for plaintiff, defendant appeals. Affirmed.

The plaintiff sued to compel the defendant specifically to perform his agreement to convey a clear title to certain real estate, as demanded by the terms of a contract between them, or for the recovery back of the moneys paid by plaintiff upon the contract. The objection had been made to the title of the defendant that it was defective and unmarketable. The source of the title was in Adolphus Brown, to whom and to Felix Brown, his brother, simpliciter conveyances covering the premises in question had been made, as tenants in common. Adolphus Brown died in 1875, leaving a widow, Walli Brown, formerly Walli Goetz, and three minor children, between whom his will disposed of his residuary estate by the following clauses, viz.:

"First. I give, devise and bequeath unto my friend, Walli Goetz, all my furniture and household articles, and also one-third of the rest, residue and remainder of my estate, real as well as personal, to have and to hold the same unto her during her lifetime, and after her death to be divided in such a manner that two-thirds thereof shall go to her children, and one-third thereof to my children. I expressly provide however, that my said friend shall have possession of the property so given, devised and bequeathed to her, and be entirely free in administration of the same, with full power to sell and dispose of the same, or any part thereof, and shall not be required to give any security whatever.

"Secondly. I give, devise and bequeath the remaining two-thirds of all the rest, residue and remainder of my property, real as well as personal, to my children, to be divided between them, share and share alike; and I hereby provide that the property hereby devised or bequeathed to my children shall be converted into money, and the share of each child be safely invested in good security during his or her minority, and the interest or income derived therefrom to be applied to the education and maintenance of my said children until they have become of age respectively."

The will was proved as a will of personal property, only, and in 1876 the executors undertook to convey to Felix Brown the undivided interest in the premises owned by their testator, and it is out of the deed, which was delivered, that the difficulty in the defendant's title has arisen. Walli Goetz, named as a residuary legatee, in the will, subsequently to its execution married the testator, and, with her two children by a former marriage, survived him. She had no children by marriage with Brown. One of her children, a daughter, is still living, as Mrs. Bain, and Max Goetz, the other, died before his mother, leaving a daughter named Julia, a minor. Mrs. Brown died in 1897. Upon the deed of the executors to Felix Brown were indorsed the following instruments:

"Know all men by these presents, that I, Walli Brown, widow of Adolphus Brown, deceased, in consideration of fifteen hundred dollars to me paid by the within named Felix Brown, do grant, remise, release and quitclaim unto the said Felix Brown all my right, title, interest and dower in and to the within described premises. In witness whereof I have hereunto set my hand and seal this —— day of June, in the year one thousand eight hundred and seventy-six. Walli Brown. [L. S.] Signed, sealed and delivered in the presence of Louis A. Wagner.

"State of New York, City and County of New York, ss. On this 16th day of June, 1876, before me personally came Walli Brown, widow, to me known and known to me to be the person described in and who executed the foregoing release of dower, and to me acknowledged that she executed the same. Louis A. Wagner, Notary Public, Kings Co., N. Y."

At a date subsequent to the execution and delivery of this deed, the three children of the testator, Adolphus Brown, executed to the grantee, Felix Brown, conveyances of their interests in the premises, and he thereafter conveyed to this defendant. After this last conveyance, and at the time of the trial of this action, the defendant received from Mrs. Bain, the daughter mentioned of Walli Goetz, a release of her interest in the premises affected. That still left outstanding what interest may be in Julia, the daughter of Max, the son of Walli Goetz, mentioned as having predeceased her. It was held by the trial court that Max Goetz became vested upon the death of Adolphus Brown with one undivided half part of the remainder in two-ninths of the premises, after the expiration of the widow's life estate, and, as the defendant had never obtained a release of that interest from Max's daughter and heir at law, Julia, that his title is, to that extent, defective and unmarketable. Judgment was therefore directed for the plaintiff as prayed for, and, that judgment having been affirmed by the Appellate Division, the defendant appeals to this court.

Edward W. S. Johnston and Lewis S. Goebel, for appellant. Benjamin N. Cardozo and Moses Esberg, for respondent.

GRAY, J. (after stating the facts). The courts below have held, under the provisions of the testator's will, that the power of sale given to Mrs. Walli Goetz was not general and beneficial, that it was accompanied by a trust, and that her children and those of the testator took vested remainders in the life estate devised to her. It was held that the power of sale given to her by the will had not been exercised, through the instrument indorsed upon the deed of Brown's executors, and that it effected nothing more than a conveyance of her dower in the two-thirds devised to testator's children, and of her life estate in the one-third devised to her. We agree with the decision, and we do not see how different conclusions could be reached. It is clear that the children of Walli Goetz at the moment of the testator's death became vested with estates in remainder. Although he used the words "to be divided," in disposing of Mrs. Goetz's life estate after her death, no especial significance is to be given to them. Nothing in the will shows any intention on his part to prevent an immediate vesting. To the contrary, it is manifest that they were intended as words of gift, merely, just as, when giving to his own children upon his death, in the second clause, he uses the same words.

That being the situation upon the testator's death, his will conferred the power on Mrs. Goetz, then his widow, to sell the property composing the one-third of the residuary estate devised to her; but, had she validly executed the power, the proceeds would simply have taken the place of the property sold, and would have been held by her as life tenant. Matter of Blauvelt, 131 N. Y. 249, 30 N. E. 194. Her life estate had not been converted into a fee by the absolute power to sell, inasmuch as her children and those of her husband, as remaindermen, were interested in the exercise of the power. The will gave her no greater interest in the proceeds of a sale than in the land sold. She took the general power, not for her own benefit, but accompanied by a trust, and that brought it within the limitation in section 81 of the article on "Powers" of the Revised Statutes (9th Ed.) p. 3557. Having then a general power to sell the property, her release, indorsed upon the executors' deed of the premises, was not in execution of it, within section 155 of the real property law (Laws 1896, p. 583, c. 547), because she was not conveying some interest which she had only the right to convey by virtue of the power. Apparently, from the language of the release and of the notarial acknowledgment, she was conveying her right of dower in the premises sold, and, if any other right or interest belonging to her was the subject of her release, it was her life estate. Within the rule of the decision in Mutual Life Insurance Company v. Shipman, 119 N. Y. 324, 24 N. E. 177, as the testator's widow had independent interests in the property, her conveyance must be construed as relating to them, and the statutory provision validating a conveyance by the grantee of a power, as in execution thereof, although the power be not referred to therein, has no application. The learned Appellate Division, in reversing a judgment for the defendant rendered upon a previous trial, in an opinion by Justice Hatch, has so well and carefully discussed the question as to render needless further discussion by us. Weinstein v. Weber, 58 App. Div. 112, 68 N. Y. Supp. 570.

The appellant raises the additional question of the correctness of rulings rejecting evidence offered to prove that the property was owned and held by the copartnership of Felix Brown and Adolphus Brown. The effect of such proof, it is argued, would be to make the interest of Adolphus Brown personalty, which the conveyances in question by his executors and by his widow were competent to transfer. Whatever might be made of such proof to fortify the defendant's title, it is quite sufficient in such a case to say that a party will not be required to take a title which depends for its completeness upon parol evidence. As to that, I need only cite Moore v. Williams, 115 N. Y. 586, 22 N. E. 233, 5 L. R. A. 654, 12 Am. St. Rep. 844, as a case in point. An exception might be found, perhaps, where the title was vested upon such a notorious and generally known fact as that of adverse possession, which usually is capable of establishment beyond any reasonable doubt. But, to use the language in Moore v. Williams, such instances have "little analogy to one like this, where the lapse of time operates in a different way, and may speedily wipe out the only evidence competent to cure or remove the defect in the title tendered." Whether the premises were partnership property, and whether the conveyances of the executors and widow were in settlement of partnership matters, were questions of fact, and depended for their solution upon extrinsic evidence, to be gathered from partnership records or books, and from a restricted class of witnesses. A purchaser should not be compelled to take a title which he might have to defend by resort to such perishable evidence.

I think that the judgment appealed from was correct, and that it should be affirmed, with costs.

PARKER, C. J., and O'BRIEN, HAIGHT, MARTIN, VANN, and CULLEN, JJ., concur.

Judgment affirmed.

(178 N. Y. 75)

NEW YORK CENT. & H. R. R. CO. v. AUBURN INTERURBAN ELECTRIC R. CO.

(Court of Appeals of New York. March 15, 1904.)

APPEAL—REVIEW—ERRORS OF LAW—STREET RAILROADS—EXTENSION—PROCEDURE.

1. Where the findings of the trial court are supported by the evidence, and sustain a judgment rendered thereon which has been affirmed by the Appellate Division, failure to find other

facts claimed to have been established by the evidence is not error of law reviewable in the Court of Appeals.

2. Railroad Law, § 90 (Laws 1895, p. 791, c. 933), prior to the enactment of Laws 1902, p. 610, c. 226, in relation to the extension of street-surface railroads, provided that any such road extending its roads or constructing branches thereof might file in the offices in which its certificate of incorporation was filed a description of the roads and property upon which it was proposed to construct the extension, and on filing such statement and obtaining the consent of adjoining property owners might have the right to operate and maintain such extensions. *Held*, that a street-surface railroad corporation incorporated in 1895, which filed in 1901 a statement in conformity with sections 90 (Laws 1895, p. 791, c. 933) and 91 (Laws 1901, p. 1529, c. 638), has the right to construct an extension without the certificate of the Board of Railroad Commissioners as to public convenience and necessity thereof, as required by Laws 1902, p. 610, c. 266, which added to section 59a a provision for such certificate, so that an action brought by a steam railroad company to restrain a street railroad company from constructing an extension cannot be maintained on the ground that the certificate required has not been obtained.

Appeal from Supreme Court, Appellate Division, Fourth Department.

Action by the New York Central & Hudson River Railroad Company against the Auburn Interurban Electric Railroad Company. From a judgment of the Appellate Division (80 N. Y. Supp. 1144) affirming a judgment for defendant, plaintiff appeals. Affirmed.

Frank Hiscock, Thomas Emery, and Ira A. Place, for appellant. George Barron, for Skaneateles Railroad Company. William Nottingham, for respondent.

WERNER, J. This action was brought to restrain the defendant from constructing and operating an alleged proposed extension of its street-surface railroad between the village of Skaneateles and the city of Syracuse, in the county of Onondaga. The complaint was framed upon the theories: (1) That the alleged extension was invalid, because the defendant had failed to obtain from the Board of Railroad Commissioners a certificate that public convenience and necessity required it; and (2) that the so-called extension was such only in name, and was in reality a new road, the construction and operation of which was illegal without such certificate. These allegations of the complaint were met by the denials of the answer, and upon the issue thus joined and the proofs made the defendant was given a judgment, which has been affirmed by the Appellate Division.

The appellant now contends that the findings of fact and conclusions of law of the learned trial court do not support the judgment, because the allegations of the complaint and the evidence given in support thereof tend to prove the construction and operation of a proposed extension between Skaneateles and Syracuse, while the only findings and conclusions upon the subject are to the effect that a bona fide extension was projected and made between Skaneateles and Marcellus. Of this contention it is enough to say that there is evidence to support the findings and conclusions made, and these are sufficient to sustain the judgment rendered, unless the main contention of the plaintiff as to the construction of sections 59 and 90 of the railroad law (Laws 1895, pp. 317, 791, cc. 545, 933) is upheld, in which event the judgment must, of course, be reversed, without regard to the evidence or the findings of fact based upon it.

The failure of the trial court to find certain facts which the appellant claims to have established by evidence is not, in the present state of this record, an error of law reviewable by this court (National Harrow Co. v. Bement & Sons, 163 N. Y. 505, 57 N. E. 764); and, if there is any evidence to support the findings of fact actually made, the result in that regard is binding upon this court, even though a different conclusion should or might have been reached in the courts below (Ostrom v. Greene, 161 N. Y. 353, 55 N. E. 919). In the last analysis, therefore, the only question that we can review is whether the extension of defendant's road, projected and constructed as found by the trial court, was valid under the statute, without the certificate of the Board of Railroad Commissioners as to the public convenience and necessity thereof. The defendant was organized in 1895 for the purpose of constructing an electric street-surface railroad over certain routes described in its charter. One of these routes extended from a given point in the city of Auburn, in the county of Cayuga, over and along stated courses to the intersection of Genesee street with the easterly boundary of the village of Skaneateles, in the county of Onondaga. The defendant had complied with the then existing requirements of section 59 of the railroad law (Laws 1895, p. 317, c. 545), which, among other things, provided that "no railroad corporation hereafter formed shall exercise the powers conferred by law upon such corporations or begin the construction of its road * * * until the Board of Railroad Commissioners shall certify that * * * public convenience and a necessity require the construction of said railroad as proposed in said articles of association." The route above referred to was one of the routes specified in the defendant's articles of association. At the time of the commencement of this action the defendant had constructed and was operating about 6½ miles of its road over that route, from the point of its beginning in the city of Auburn to a point in Genesee street at or near its intersection with Jordan street in the village of Skaneateles, and was about to begin the construction of the remainder of its road along Genesee street from its intersection with Jordan street to the easterly boundary of the village of Skaneateles. After the completion of its road along this route, and on the 2d day of October, 1901, the defendant made and filed a statement and certificate of a proposed extension of its road from its easterly terminus in the village of Skaneateles, easterly along specified courses for a distance of about six miles to the village of Marcellus, in the county of Onondaga. This statement and certificate complied in all essential particulars with section 90 of the railroad law (Laws 1895, p. 791, c. 933), which provides that: "Any street surface railroad corporation, at any time proposing to extend the road or to construct branches thereof, may, from time to time, make and file in each of the offices in which its certificate of incorporation is filed, a statement of the names and descriptions of the streets, roads, avenues, highways, and private property in or upon which it is proposed to construct, maintain or operate such extensions or branches." Upon filing any such statement and upon complying with the conditions set forth in section 91 of the railroad law (Laws 1901, p. 1529, c. 638, which relates to the consents of the local authorities and adjoining property owners in cities and villages), "every such corporation shall have the power and privilege to construct, extend, operate and maintain such road, extensions or branches, upon and along the streets, avenues, roads, highways and private property named and described in its certificate of incorporation or in such statement."

The courts below have held that section 59 of the railroad law, as it stood in 1901, had no application to proposed extensions of then existing street-surface railroads, and that it was not necessary for the defendant to apply to the Board of Railroad Commissioners for a certificate of public convenience and necessity for the extension of its road above referred to. We concur in that construction of the statute. The history and the language of section 59 very clearly indicate the legislative purpose behind its enactment. When it first became a part of the railroad law in 1892, street-surface railroads were expressly exempted from its provisions. Thus it stood until 1895, when that exemption was removed. In plain and unequivocal language it referred only to new railroads to be constructed by railroad corporations thereafter to be formed. In 1902 it was amended (section 59a, Laws 1902, p. 610, c. 226) by providing that "any street surface railroad company which proposes to extend its road beyond the limits of any city or incorporated village by a route which will be practically parallel with a street surface railroad already constructed and in operation shall first obtain the certificate of the Board of Railroad Commissioners that public convenience and a necessity require the construction of such extension as provided in the case of a railroad corporation newly formed." During the whole of the period from 1890, when the present railroad law was originally enacted, down to 1902, when section 59 was so amended as to bring proposed extensions of street-surface railroads within the rule requiring the certificate of the board of railroad commissioners as to public convenience and necessity, section 90 has also been a part of the same law, and, although amended in 1893, and again in 1895, its substance has remained unchanged, and it has always dealt exclusively with extensions and branches of street-surface railroads. Thus we see that in 1890, when newly projected street-surface railroads were concededly exempted from the changed policy of the state towards its steam railroads, as manifested in section 59 of the railroad law, the statutory provision (section 90) for extensions of street-surface railroads was, in effect, the same as in 1895, when new street-surface railroads were placed upon the same footing as new steam railroads, and this was the condition of the statute down to 1902 when section 59 was amended as above stated.

The reasons for this difference in the earlier legislative treatment of the two kinds of railroads are obvious. Under the law as it stood prior to 1890 the requisite number of persons with sufficient capital could organize a railroad corporation and construct a railroad at any time and over any route they might choose. In the formative period of our state this was doubtless a most beneficent policy, and contributed very materially to the development of our commerce and resources. Experience, however, demonstrated that railroad enterprises are not exceptions to the ordinary trade laws of supply and demand. Ill-advised and speculative railroad enterprises soon emphasized the necessity of protecting not only existing railroad corporations against destructive competition, but the investing public against the disastrous consequences of indiscriminate and unrestricted railroad schemes backed by alluring but impracticable promise of gain. These were the conditions which brought about the enactment of section 59 as part of the railroad law. The reasons for then exempting street-surface railroads from its operations are equally apparent. At that time street-surface railroads were operated by horse power, chiefly in the larger cities, and they were comparatively few in number. With the advent of electricity as a motive power new conditions were created. Not only was urban traffic greatly augmented, but interurban street-surface railroads were projected on every hand, until the history of steam railroads found its counterpart in this new outlet for corporate enterprise and capital. In 1895 the Legislature again interposed—this time in favor of existing street-surface railroads and the investing public—by striking out of section 59 the exemption in favor of street-surface railroads, thus placing all railroads of every kind thereafter to be projected upon precisely the same footing. That this amendment of section 59 was not quite far-reaching enough has been made evident by later developments and legislation. After the legislation of 1895, section 90 of the railroad law still gave practically unlimited power to extend existing street-surface railroads. Under this power long interurban lines could be constructed by means of successive extensions, and existing lines could be paralleled by the same methods. To remedy this new phase of an old evil, section 59a was enacted in 1902, and, as the law now stands, no street-surface railroad corporation can extend its road beyond the limits of any incorporated city or village, 'if the effect of such extension will be to practically parallel any existing street-surface railroad, without first obtaining from the Board of Railroad Commissioners a certificate that public convenience and a necessity require such extension.

The construction of sections 59 and 90 of the railroad law, supported by their language and history, is re-enforced by several incidental considerations. While it is true that these sections must be read together, it is equally true that such a reading is useful only so far as the two sections relate to precisely the same subject. Originally, section 59 had reference only to steam railroads, and section 90 has always dealt exclusively with street-surface railroads. The railroad law has never permitted the extensions of steam railroads, while it has always provided for extensions of street surface railroads. The same legislative policy which in 1890 applied the provisions of original section 59 to steam railroads, excluded street-surface railroads from its operation, and, as that section related only to newly projected railroads, it is clear that the mere excision in 1895 of the exemption in favor of street-surface railroads had no other effect than to place the latter upon exactly the same footing with the former. Sections 59 and 90 were therefore entirely independent of each other until 1902, when the Legislature again announced a change of policy, not as to railroads generally, but only as to extensions of street-surface railroads as expressed in section 59a, which for the first time brought sections 59 and 90 into relations with each other. All this is supplemented by the practical construction that has been given to these sections by the Board of Railroad Commissioners and by the Legislature. The former, in its annual reports of 1897, 1898, and 1899, very pointedly called attention to the need of amendatory legislation in respect of street-surface railroad extensions; and the latter, in 1902, adopted the recommendations therein made by the enactment of section 59a. Much might be said as to the far-reaching effect of this practical construction, and the legal weight which should be given to it, but, since it is in perfect accord with our own view of the statute, we deem it unnecessary to further extend the discussion.

The judgment should be affirmed, with costs.

PARKER, C. J., and O'BRIEN, MARTIN, and VANN, JJ., concur. GRAY, J., not sitting. BARTLETT, J., taking no part.

Judgment affirmed.

(178 N. Y. 54)

SVENSON v. SVENSON.

(Court of Appeals of New York. March 15, 1904.)

MARRIAGE—ANNULMENT—FRAUD—CONCEALED DISEASE—APPEAL—AFFIRMANCE.

1. Where one of the parties at the time of the celebration of a marriage is affected with a chronic venereal disease, which fact is concealed, it is a ground for annulment of the marriage, under 2 Rev. St. pt. 2, c. 8, tit. 1, § 4, for fraud, even assuming that, at the time of the application for annulment, he had practically recovered.

2. The Appellate Division cannot affirm an unwarranted judgment dismissing a complaint in an action to annul a marriage on the ground of some supposed collusion between the parties, where no such issue was raised on the trial or determined by the trial judge.

Appeal from Supreme Court, Appellate Division, Second Department.

Action by Marguerite Svenson against Oscar H. Svenson. From a judgment of the Appellate Division (79 N. Y. Supp. 657) affirming a judgment for defendant, plaintiff appeals. Reversed.

The action was brought to procure an annulment of the marriage between the plaintiff and defendant upon the ground of fraud, in that the defendant, at the time of the marriage, was suffering from a chronic and contagious venereal disease, which he concealed from the plaintiff. The parties were married in the city of New York, March 29, 1900. The plaintiff was induced to consent to such marriage through representations made by the defendant that he was at the time in good health and physically able to consummate and discharge the marital functions, and she believed such representations and relied thereon. At the time of the marriage, and long prior thereto, the defendant was suffering from a chronic and contagious venereal disease, and knew such fact. He concealed from the plaintiff his real character and physical condition prior to such marriage, and she had no knowledge thereof. After the marriage he stated to her that it would be impossible for him to cohabit with her as man and wife by reason of such disease. At the time of the trial he had practically recovered. The plaintiff and defendant never cohabited as man and wife, and such marriage has never been consummated. As soon as she ascertained the falsity of such representations, and the defendant's true character and physical condition, she immediately left him, and did not afterwards cohabit with him. The foregoing are the facts as found by the trial court. As conclusions of law, it held that the marriage was not obtained by such fraud as called for an annulment or as would justify such relief, the defendant having since recovered, and it thereupon dismissed the complaint upon the merits. Upon appeal to the Appellate Division (79 N. Y. Supp. 657), that court in effect held that the trial court erred in deciding that the plaintiff could not recover upon the ground stated, but affirmed the judgment upon the theory that there was collusion between the parties upon the trial of the action, and for that reason alone the judgment was affirmed.

J. Stewart Ross, for appellant.

MARTIN, J. (after stating the facts). We share in the unwillingness of the learned Appellate Division to indorse the decision of the Special Term or the ground upon which is was based, or to assert the doctrine that an innocent and unsuspecting girl who marries a man afflicted with a chronic, contagious, and hereditary venereal disease, and who therefore refuses to consummate the marriage, may not procure a decree annulling the same because of the fraud involved in the existence of such a condition and its concealment from her.

The statute of this state relating to marriages and the annulment thereof, among other things, provides: "When either of the parties to a marriage shall be incapable, for want of age or understanding, of consenting to a marriage, or shall be incapable from physical causes, of entering into the marriage state, or when the consent of either party shall have been obtained by force or fraud, the marriage shall be void, from the time its nullity shall be declared by a court of competent authority." 2 Rev. St. pt. 2, c. 8, tit. 1, § 4. The findings of fact in this case were in the plaintiff's favor, and substantially included all the allegations of the complaint. But the relief sought was denied upon the ground that the defendant, two years after the marriage, had practically recovered. What a practical recovery from such a disease may import, where it has existed for more than two years, with the danger of its return and ultimate transmission, it is difficult, if not impossible, to determine. But it is certain, at least, that at the time of the marriage the defendant was incapable of meeting the obligations and performing the functions of the marital relation, and was morally and physically unfit to become or continue to be the husband of a pure and innocent girl. When he concealed that condition from her, and still induced her to marry him in ignorance thereof, he was guilty of a base and unmitigated fraud as to a matter essential to the relation into which they contracted to enter. Obviously, the principle that refuses relief in cases of ordinary ill health after the marriage contract has been actually consummated has no application to a case like this, where there has been no consummation, and the disease is one involving disgrace in its contraction and presence, contagion in marital association, and includes danger of transmission and heredity that even science cannot fathom or certainly define. The suppression of the presence of a disease including such dire and disastrous possibilities, directly affecting the marital relation, constitutes a fraud which clearly entitles the innocent party to a decree annulling the marriage contract, particularly when it has not been consummated. "Marriage begins by contract, and results in a status. If, before children are begotten, before debts are created, real estate involved, and the community have long recognized the relation, the injured party seeks relief from fraud, error, or duress, it seems clear that no consideration of public policy will prevent a court from annulling a marriage where the relation has not fully ripened into the complications of a public status. In such case the marriage is but little more than a contract, and, in view of the serious consequences to follow, the degree of fraud which vitiates a contract should be sufficient." Nelson on Marriage & Divorce, § 600. "Where there has been no consummation, any fraud which would be sufficient to annul a contract should in reason be sufficient to annul a marriage ceremony. No satisfactory reason of the law will justify the courts in declaring valid such a contract marriage, when tainted with fraud or duress, where the only effect will be the punishment of the innocent and the confiscation of his or her property by the deception. If the marriage is declared valid, it will exist in name only, preventing both parties from marrying again, and bringing the marriage relation into disrepute. Every reason for relief from fraud is applicable here, where a denial of relief is fraught with evil consequences much greater than those flowing from ordinary conduct." Id. 602. "Whatever of fraud, of error, or duress will vitiate any other contract, should ordinarily be received as sufficient to vitiate the mere marriage contract, whether executory or executed, viewed as a thing separate from the consummation which follows." 1 Bishop on Marriage & Divorce, § 166 et seq. This principle was very clearly and concisely stated by Woodward, J., in Di Lorenzo v. Di Lorenzo, 71 App. Div. 509, 519, 75 N. Y. Supp. 878, 886, as follows: "When, however, the fraud is discovered before the marriage is consummated, and the innocent party refuses to cohabit, the marriage is so inchoate and incomplete that the status of the parties is similar to that of parties to an executory contract, and may be annulled without violating any considerations of public policy." This court, in Kujek v. Goldman, 150 N. Y. 176, 179, 44 N. E. 773, 774, 34 L. R. A. 156, 55 Am. St. Rep. 670, in discussing the question of the marital relation, made this remark: "It is difficult to see why a fraud, which, if practiced with reference to a contract relating to property merely, would support an action, should not be given the same effect when it involves a contract affecting not only property rights, but also the most sacred relation of life." This principle seems quite applicable where the marriage rests in contract alone, and has not ripened into "the complications of a public status." Again, in Di Lorenzo v. Di Lorenzo, 174 N. Y. 467, 472, 67 N. E. 63, 64, which was an action to annul a marriage contract upon the ground of fraud, it was said: "The free and full consent, which is of the essence of all ordinary contracts, is expressly made by the statute necessary to the validity of the marriage contract. The minds of the parties must meet in one intention. It is a general rule that every misrepresentation of a material fact, made with the intention to induce another to enter into an agreement, and without which he would not have done so, justifies the court in vacating the agreement. It is obvious that no one would obligate himself by a contract if he knew that a material representation, entering into the reason for his consent, was untrue. There is no valid reason for excepting the marriage contract from the general rule. In this case the representation of the defendant was as to a fact, except for the truth of which the necessary consent of the plaintiff would not have been obtained to the marriage. * * * The minds of the parties did not meet upon a common basis of operation. The artifice was such as to deceive a reasonably prudent person, and to appeal to his sense of honor and of duty. The plaintiff had a right to rely upon the defendant's statement of a fact, the truth of which was known to her and unknown to him, and he was under no obligation to verify a statement to the truth of which she had pledged herself. It was a gross fraud, and upon reason, as upon authority, I think it afforded a sufficient ground for a decree annulling the marriage." In that case the representation was that the defendant had been delivered of a child of which the plaintiff was the father. While it may well be said that the cases to which we have previously referred are not precisely analogous to the case at bar, yet the principles laid down by the text-writers and in those cases establish a general doctrine more or less applicable to the case under consideration.

There is, however, another line of cases more closely resembling the case at bar, which will now be considered. Smith v. Smith, 171 Mass. 404, 408, 50 N. E. 933, 935, 41 L. R. A. 800, 68 Am. St. Rep. 440, was an action to procure a sentence of nullity of marriage. In that case it was held that it was within the power of the superior court to enter a decree declaring a marriage void, where it appeared that the libelant, after the ceremony and before the consummation of the marriage, on learning that the respondent was afflicted with a venereal disease, refused to live with him. The court, in discussing that case, said: "The case at bar rests solely upon fraud in regard to the bodily condition of the libelee. As we have already seen, the previous unchastity of the libelee is not enough to entitle the libelant to relief. Indeed, we are not quite certain from the report that the libelee might not have been constitutionally affected with the disease from his birth. But, on the findings of the judge, his concealed disease was such as would leave with him no foundation on which the marriage relation could properly rest. It had advanced to such a stage as probably to be incurable. The libelant could not live with him as his wife without making herself a victim for life, and giving to her offspring, if she had any, an inheritance of disease and suffering. While this case lacks the element of introducing a bastard child into the husband's family, which existed in Reynolds v. Reynolds, 3 Allen, 605, it has the element of a loathsome, incurable contagious disease to be communicated to the wife, which the other had not. Few, if any, would be bold enough to say that it was the duty of the libelant, on discovery of the fraud before the consummation of the marriage, to give herself up as a sacrifice, and to become a party to the transmission of such a disease to her posterity." This case was followed by the case of Vondal v. Vondal, 175 Mass. 383, 56 N. E. 586, 78 Am. St. Rep. 502, where it was held that the concealed existence of a venereal disease in one of the parties to a marriage which has been consummated is not a sufficient ground for the annulment of the marriage, but that case turned upon the fact of a presumed consummation of the marriage by cohabitation within four months after its celebration. In an anonymous case, 21 Misc. Rep. 765, 49 N. Y. Supp. 331, the facts were in all essential respects identical with the facts in this case, and it was held by the referee before whom it was tried that the marriage should be annulled upon the ground that the presence of such a disease was a fraud upon the plaintiff; that, the contract having been made in reliance upon the representation of the defendant that he was in good health, an annulment of the marriage was recommended. In that action the learned referee refers to an unreported case, decided in July, 1897, by Mr. Justice Truax, wherein a marriage was dissolved for fraud in the suppression by the defendant of the fact that he was affected at the time of the marriage with syphilis, which he gave to his wife, and which was transmitted to a child born of the marriage, who afterwards died. In Meyer v. Meyer, 49 How. Prac. 311, a similar doctrine was held. Ryder v. Ryder, 66 Vt. 158, 28 Atl. 1029, 44 Am. St. Rep. 833, is to the effect that if the wife, at the time of contracting the marriage relation, conceals from her husband the fact that she has chronic and incurable syphilis, it would amount to a fraud for which the marriage may be annulled, under the statute which provides, "The marriage contract may be annulled when, at the time of the marriage, either party * * * was * * * 'physically incapable of entering into the marriage state, or when the consent of either party was obtained by force or fraud."

Without further discussion of this question, we are clearly of the opinion that the plaintiff was entitled to the relief sought in this action, and this conclusion is justified by the principle of these authorities. It is evident that, the marriage not having been consummated, the usual considerations of public policy which apply to a case where the relation has by consummation of the marriage ripened into a public status do not exist here. There was between these parties little more than a contract to marry, and we are aware of no principle of public policy which would be subverted by annulling this marriage, or which requires us to compel the plaintiff to consummate the marriage and give herself up as a sacrifice to the possibilities involved in such a course.

As we have already seen, the learned Appellate Division entertained the same opinion as that reached by this court upon the merits of this action, but affirmed the judgment on the ground of some supposed collusion between the parties. No such issue was raised on the trial or decided by the trial court. Presumably that conclusion was reached principally from the fact that the defendant appeared by an attorney, who, on the trial, waived the provisions of section 834 of the Code of Civil Procedure in the manner required by section 836 of that act, thus enabling the plaintiff to prove by a physician the physical condition of the defendant when the marriage contract was entered into, which she could not have done in that manner except by such waiver. If there remained in the defendant a single spark of manhood, how could he have done otherwise? Moreover, the record tends to disclose that this course was pursued by the defendant to avoid being called as a witness and compelled to testify to his own ignominy and disgrace. It may be that upon the record the learned Appellate Division, by virtue of its right to examine into the facts, possessed authority to award a new trial upon the ground that the plaintiff was entitled to a decree annulling her marriage, but it had not the power to affirm an incorrect and unwarranted judgment upon some other supposed ground not tried or established at the trial, and thus defeat the plaintiff and conclusively deprive her of a judgment upon the merits, to which she was entitled. In Matter of Fitzsimons, 174 N. Y. 15, 25, 66 N. E. 554, 557, when the case reached the Appellate Division, the question upon which the motion was decided by the court below was ignored, and the court held, as a matter of law, that the agreement was unconscionable, and in that case, on appeal to this court, it was said: "Under the circumstances it seems impossible that the learned Appellate Division had any jurisdiction to review that question, when there was no issue raising it or trial presenting the facts relating thereto. Surely the appellant could not properly be thrown out of court, and have his petition dismissed and all relief denied, without an opportunity to be heard upon the question. * * * When that question has been passed upon by the trial court it may be properly presented to the learned Appellate Division for review, but until it is so presented that court has no right to determine the question. 'It is one of the fundamental principles of our law that questions of fact are to be tried and determined in a court of original jurisdiction, and it is not the appropriate function of an appellate court to determine controverted questions of fact and render final judgment upon such determination.'" Benedict v. Arnoux, 154 N. Y. 715, 724, 49 N. E. 326. Applying the principle of these authorities to the question under consideration, it becomes obvious that the Appellate Division exceeded its authority, as a court of review, by raising and deciding a new issue, and thereupon affirming a judgment which was otherwise invalid and should have been reversed.

The judgments of the Special Term and the Appellate Division should be reversed, and a new trial ordered, costs to await the final award herein.

PARKER, C. J., and O'BRIEN, BARTLETT, VANN, and WERNER, JJ., concur. GRAY, J., absent.

Judgments reversed, etc.

(185 Mass. 214)

LORD v. INHABITANTS OF WAKEFIELD.

(Supreme Judicial Court of Massachusetts. Middlesex. Feb. 27, 1904.)

MASTER AND SERVANT—PERSONAL INJURIES—ASSUMPTION OF RISK—DIRECTION OF SUPERINTENDENT.

1. An employé of a city owning an electric lighting system was directed by his superintendent to climb a pole and cut the wires, and, after cutting part of them, felt the pole tremble, and saw the remaining wires sag. He asked the foreman if he had not better guy the pole, and was told that the pole was all right, and to cut the wires. On cutting the other wires, the pole, which was rotten inside, fell, injuring the employé. *Held* that, as the risk was not obvious, and the superintendent was present, the employé did not assume the risk.

Exceptions from Superior Court, Middlesex County; Robert R. Bishop, Judge.

Action by Frederick N. Lord against the inhabitants of Wakefield. Judgment for defendant, and plaintiff brings exceptions. Exceptions sustained.

Hamilton & Eaton, for plaintiff. John Lowell and James A. Lowell, for defendant.

LATHROP, J. This is an action of tort, with a count at common law and several counts under St. 1887, p. 899, c. 270, and the amendments thereof, for personal injury sustained by the plaintiff while in the employ of the defendant. At the trial in the superior court at the close of the plaintiff's evidence a verdict was ordered for the defendant, and the case comes before us on the plaintiff's exceptions, with a full report of the evidence. The evidence is set forth at unnecessary length, and the facts in the case may be briefly stated. The defendant was a municipal corporation, engaged in the manufacture and distribution of electricity for lighting purposes, under St. 1891, p. 949, c. 370. Under section 16 of this act it was liable for any injury or damage to persons or property "happening or arising by reason of the maintenance or operation of the same, in the same manner and to the same extent as though the same were owned and operated by an individual or private corporation." See Rev. Laws, c. 34, § 28. The plaintiff had been in the defendant's employ at two different periods for four years and nine months. During that time he had worked as a trimmer, by which we understand a trimmer of arc lights, and had also been a general helper about the electrical works. He had set poles, helped string wires, and had put transformers on poles. On the day of the accident, June 18, 1901, some wires were to be cut to allow a church, which was to be moved, to pass between two poles. One Weare, the superintendent in charge of the wires and all outside work, was sent by the manager of the plant, with the plaintiff and a fellow servant, to attend to the cutting of the wires. Weare went up the pole to look after some fire-alarm wires which had fallen across the pole. Soon after, Weare ordered the plaintiff to go up the pole and cut the wires. This pole was about 25 feet high, and was set in 1890. In obedience to the order of Weare, the plaintiff went up the pole, and with one leg over the cross-arm and the other leg on a step of the pole cut two of the wires. The plaintiff then felt the pole tremble, and saw the other wires sag. He then said to Weare, who was standing at the foot of the pole, "Don't you think you had better guy this pole?" Weare replied, "The pole is all right; cut them down." The plaintiff then cut the wires, the pole fell, and the plaintiff was injured. The pole had entirely rotted away below the ground, and, though the outside was apparently sound, the pole was rotten for some distance above the ground.

The defendant does not contend that the plaintiff was not in the exercise of due care, nor that there was not evidence of negligence on the part of the defendant; and no question is made of Weare being a superintendent. The contention is that the fall of the pole was one of the risks which the plaintiff assumed, and that the defendant owed him no duty to inspect the pole. But the answer to this contention is that the plaintiff was acting under the direct and immediate control of the superintendent. The risk was not an obvious one, and the plaintiff might treat the language of the superintendent as an assurance from one who knew better than he did that he could work there in safety. Mahoney v. Bay State Pink Granite Co., 184 Mass. 287, 68 N. E. 234, and cases cited. The defendant relies principally upon the cases of McIsaac v. Northampton Electric Lighting Co., 172 Mass. 89, 51 N. E. 524, 70 Am. St. Rep. 244, and Tanner v. New York, New Haven & Hartford Railroad, 180 Mass. 572, 62 N. E. 993. We are, however, of opinion that the case before us is distinguishable from each of these cases. In McIsaac v. Northampton Electric Lighting Co. the plaintiff was an experienced lineman, and was sent off alone to remove two wires from one pole to another. He attempted to do the work in his own way, and was injured by the fall of the pole, owing to its rottenness below the ground. The plaintiff in that case knew that the life of a pole was limited, and that any pole after a time would become unsafe. In the case before us the plaintiff was not an experienced lineman. He was not sent off alone, but under the care and guidance of a superintendent, who was to give the orders, and whose orders he obeyed. There is nothing in the evidence to show that the plaintiff knew that the life of a pole was limited, or that the pole was an old one. It may be impracticable for an electric lighting company to have a long line of poles constantly inspected, so that an experienced workman, sent by himself to remove wires from a particular pole, has no right to assume that the pole is sound, and should, as a matter of precaution, inspect the pole for himself, there being no difficulty in ascertaining whether any particular pole is rotten or not. But in a case like the present we are of opinion that it was the duty of the superintendent to inspect the pole, as he must have known that when the wires were cut the pole would fall unless the pole was sound, and its condition was readily ascertainable. In Tanner v. New York, New Haven & Hartford Railroad, 180 Mass. 572, 62 N. E. 993, the plaintiff was an experienced lineman, and was set to work with others, under a superintendent, to remove wires from a number of old poles to new ones. The plaintiff knew that the pole was an old one, and knew the tendency of poles which had been set for a long time to rot beneath the surface of the ground. After he had thrown off the wires, they fell across a wire guy which connected the pole with a fence. The plaintiff told the superintendent that the wires were crossed on the guy, and asked him what he should do about it. The superintendent told him to cut it, and the pole fell. The court, in its opinion, says: "His question to the overseer was not whether it would be safe for him to cut the guy, and it could not be found fairly that the order was intended to be an expression that it was safe to cut it, or that the plaintiff had a right to interpret the order as such an expression." The court further says: "It was not a case in which the act of setting the workman to do a particular thing in a particular place might be understood fairly by the workman to be an assertion that the place was safe." In the present case, as we have already said, the plaintiff was not an experienced lineman, and he was set to work to do a particular thing in a particular place, under the supervision of a superior, who knew the fact that he was not an experienced lineman. While the conversation shows that the plaintiff was apprehensive of danger if the pole was not guyed, yet we are of opinion that it was a case where the jury could find that he might well yield his judgment to that of his superior, and obey the command. McKee v. Tourtellotte, 167 Mass. 69, 71, 44 N. E. 1071, 48 L. R. A. 542.

In this view of the case, it becomes unnecessary to consider the construction to be given to the provision of St. 1899, p. 295, c. 337, § 1, which provides: "Every person or corporation, private or municipal, owning or operating a line of wires over or under streets or buildings in a town, shall use only strong and proper wires safely attached to strong and sufficient supports, and insulated at all points of attachment." The portion of the section quoted is, in substance, the same as St. 1890, p. 358, c. 404, § 1, except that the earlier statute applied only to wires over streets in a city, while the later applies to wires over or under streets in a town. In Illingsworth v. Boston Electric Light Co., 161 Mass. 583, 37 N. E. 778, 25 L. R. A. 552, Chief Justice Field, in delivering the opinion of the court, left it undecided whether it was the intention of St. 1890, p. 358, c. 404, to give a private person a cause of action for any violation of the first section of the statute, if, in consequence of such violation, he suffers damage in his person or property. No such question arises here, for the right of action is given by St. 1891, p. 956, c. 370, § 16.

Exceptions sustained.

(185 Mass. 281)

COMMONWEALTH v. BOSTON TERMINAL CO.

(Supreme Judicial Court of Massachusetts. Suffolk. March 3, 1904.)

EMINENT DOMAIN—STATE LANDS—CONDEMNATION BY UNION DEPOT COMPANY—COMPENSATION—IMPLIED GRANT—CONSTRUCTION OF STATUTE.

1. Acts 1896, p. 520, c. 516, created the Boston Terminal Company, to build a union station and to provide terminal facilities for certain railroads. The power of eminent domain was conferred on the company, to be exercised under the laws of the commonwealth, which contemplated the assessment of damages. The railroad companies named were required to pay in, in cash, all the company's capital stock, before any land was taken. The company was required to convey to the city of Boston, without compensation, a certain portion of the land taken, constituting extensions of certain streets. *Held*, that the company could not avoid payment for lands of the state below low tide water mark, condemned by it and embraced within such street extensions, on the theory that the statute amounted to an implied grant; the sacrifice of the public rights of navigation and fishery being compensated by the new easement of way created by the extension of the streets.

Report from Supreme Judicial Court, Suffolk County; John H. Hardy, Judge.

Petition by the commonwealth against the Boston Terminal Company to secure compensation for land taken by the respondent below low tide water mark. Case reported and reserved to the Supreme Judicial Court upon petition, agreed facts, and demurrer. Overruling of demurrer affirmed.

Robert G. Dodge and Fredk. H. Nash, Asst. Atty. Gen., for petitioner. Samuel Hoar and Woodward Hudson, for respondent.

BRALEY, J. It must now be taken as settled that the territorial limits of the commonwealth extend one marine league from its seashore at the line of extreme low water, and the title to the land within these boundaries, except as it may have been granted to others or acquired by them previously to St. 1867, p. 676, c. 275, by prescription, is vested in the state. St. 1859, p. 640, c. 289; Gen. St. 1860, c. 1, § 1; Pub. St. 1882, c. 1, § 1; Dunham v. Lamphere, 3 Gray, 268-270; Wonson v. Wonson, 14 Allen, 71-82; Nichols v. Boston, 98 Mass. 39, 93 Am. Dec. 132; Com. v. Manchester, 152 Mass. 230-240, 25 N. E. 113, 9 L. R. A. 236, 23 Am. St. Rep. 820; Attorney General v. Revere Copper Co., 152 Mass. 444-450, 25 N. E. 605, 9 L. R. A. 510; Manchester v. Massachusetts, 139 U. S. 240, 11 Sup. Ct. 559, 35 L. Ed. 159.

In its sovereignty it represents not only the proprietary right formerly held by the King, and which at the Revolution was in the colony, and then passed by succession to the state, but it also became vested by the same event with jurisdiction and dominion over the common rights of the people at large to the free use of such tidal waters for fishing and navigation. Barker v. Bates, 13 Pick. 255-259, 23 Am. Dec. 678; Dill v. Wareham, 7 Metc. 438; Drake v. Curtis, 1 Cush. 413; Com. v. Alger, 7 Cush. 53-58; Com. v. Hilton, 174 Mass. 29, 30, 54 N. E. 362, 45 L. R. A. 475; McCready v. Virginia, 94 U. S. 391, 24 L. Ed. 248.

Whatever may have been the rights of the crown under the early common law, the King could not in recent times sell his proprietary interest in lands covered by such waters, so as to deprive his subjects of these rights. Weston v. Sampson, 8 Cush. 349, 351, 54 Am. Dec. 764; Attorney General v. Parmenter, 10 Price, 378, 412; Gann v. Whitstable Free Fishers, 11 H. L. Cas. 192, 217.

In this country the decisions of the courts of the several states as to the right of the state to devest itself of its trusteeship have not been uniform. The cases are collected and exhaustively reviewed and the principle discussed by Gray, J., in Shively v. Bowlby, 152 U. S. 1, 26, 14 Sup. Ct. 548, 38 L. Ed. 331. But the common law of this state, whatever the rule may have been in other jurisdictions, has not recognized this limitation as binding on the Legislature, to whom is given the control of all public rights.

Originally, and before the ordinance of 1647, the title of the colony to which the state succeeded included flats between high and low water mark. By that ordinance these flats not previously granted to individuals or appropriated to public uses became the property of the owner of the adjoining upland, "where the sea doth not ebb above a hundred rods, and not more wheresoever it ebbs further." Wonson v. Wonson, ubi supra. But the ordinance left unaffected the remainder of the public domain below the line established, and within the limit subsequently defined as a marine league therefrom.

The title or proprietary right is to the soil itself, not to the water that may cover it, either for a part or all of the time. That is, the state, having the absolute power to terminate the trust which is appurtenant to its ownership, can refuse to act longer as trustee, and convey its property, so that the grantee will hold it free from the trust. Boston v. Richardson, 105 Mass. 351, 356, 362, 363; Henry v. Newburyport, 149 Mass. 582, 585, 22 N. E. 75, 5 L. R. A. 179; Martin v. Waddell, 16 Pet. 367, 410, 10 L. Ed. 997; McCready v. Virginia, ubi supra.

The state, being vested with both rights, can by way of grant pass its interest by an act of the Legislature in lands that are below extreme low-water mark, and which, when filled by the grantee, will extinguish the right of user by the public (Res. 1856, p. 284, c. 76; St. 1860, p. 154, c. 200; Boston & Hingham Steamboat Co. v. Munson, 117 Mass. 34; Atty. Gen. v. Gardiner, 117 Mass. 492–499; Drury v. Midland Railroad, 127 Mass. 571–583, and note; Hastings v. Grimshaw, 153 Mass. 497, 27 N. E. 521, 12 L. R. A. 617), though, for the purposes of protection of the seashore, and securing to all of its citizens the right and benefit of unobstructed navigation of tidal waters, notwithstanding such grant, it may require the grantee to obtain its license or permission to wharf or fill before such waters can be displaced by any structure or filling. St. 1866, p. 107, c. 149; Pub. St. 1882, c. 19, § 8; Atty. Gen. v. Boston & Lowell Railroad Company, 118 Mass. 345–348; Atty. Gen. v. City of Cambridge, 119 Mass. 519. See, also, in this connection, Lake Shore & Michigan Southern Railway Company v. Ohio, 165 U. S. 365, 17 Sup. Ct. 357, 41 L. Ed. 747; Cummings v. Chicago, 188 U. S. 410, 23 Sup. Ct. 472, 47 L. Ed. 525; Montgomery v. Portland, 190 U. S. 89, 23 Sup. Ct. 735, 47 L. Ed. 965.

The commonwealth, then, must be held to have had a right of property in, and title to, the several parcels of land described in the petition, and all situated below the line of extreme low water. By the demurrer the respondent admits that it has taken this land by force of, and in accordance with, the provisions of St. 1896, p. 520, c. 516.

The Boston Terminal Company was organized under this act to build and maintain a union passenger station in the southerly part of the city of Boston, and to provide and operate adequate terminal facilities for the various railroad companies named therein, which, upon completion of the station, are required to occupy and use it. Its capital stock, amounting to $500,000, in the proportion of one-fifth to each, could be subscribed for and held by these various corporations, and "all said capital stock shall be paid in in cash by said railroad companies before the said corporation takes any land under this act," so that in this way the money estimated to be necessary to pay for the land to be taken for the site of the proposed station and its approaches would be paid in before the work was begun. The immediate government, direction, and control of its affairs was vested in a board of five trustees, one of whom was to be appointed by each of the five railroad companies. Instead of the railroad companies themselves uniting to build the station, the history of the statute indicates that it was apparently deemed best that the several persons named as incorporators should organize a corporation for this purpose. It was a plan undertaken in this form by those connected with or interested in the railroads to be benefited, and it is too plain for discussion that, standing by itself, it would be financially unprofitable, and must fail of success, and, though possessing a distinct and independent corporate existence, the respondent must be treated as a company created and organized as an auxiliary to them. Frazier v. New York, New Haven & Hartford Railroad Co., 180 Mass. 427, 62 N. E. 731. There is nothing in the act by which it was compelled to begin, go forward, and complete this work; but it may fairly be inferred and conceded that, if once commenced, then the plan was to be carried out according to the specified details, and to this extent it may be said to be mandatory. Bradford v. Old Colony R. Co., 181 Mass. 33, 35, 63 N. E. 6. But not rigidly so, for the language used as to the taking of land to change the streets is permissive. A certain amount of flexibility, at least, was left, so that, if the whole territory named was not necessary, or if the combination of the parts, to make up the whole, could be better adjusted by changes, such changes were permissible. If it be granted that the taking of the land for Dorchester avenue and Summer street, and for the station itself, must have necessarily included the lands described in the petition, yet it was open to the respondent, if it did not want to pay for what it must take, either to abandon its project, or petition for a change in the act. Under these conditions, it was within the power of the Legislature to determine in the first instance if the enterprise for whose benefit private property was to be appropriated was of such a character that the purpose of the respondent constituted a public use of the land, and the state might permit a part of its domain to be taken for such a use in fee, or a less interest therein without compensation, but such a grant must be made by a legislative act. Talbot v. Hudson, 16 Gray, 417. This brings us to the main contention of the respondent—that here such a grant should be inferred, because the land, after it was taken, still remained subject to a public easement; nearly one-half in area being used for public ways known as Dorchester avenue and Summer street, and the remainder for the station itself. Prince v. Crocker, 166 Mass. 347–361, 44 N. E. 446, 32 L. R. A. 610. And though the nature of the user by the public had changed from that of rights in navigable waters to those of reasonable facilities of access to and transportation as passengers on railroads that were common carriers, and into legally created highways for public travel, yet the easement in each instance was for the benefit of the public; and it must therefore have been intended that the latter easement should be taken and deemed to be a fair equivalent or set-off for the other, and it ought not to be held to pay for the land so taken. In taking the land authorized by the statute, a title in fee was to be acquired, either by purchase from the owners, or by the exercise of the right of eminent domain. This right could not, under the Constitution, have been legally given to the respondent, if it were not for the principle that land held by railroads, whether within the location necessary for the placing of tracks, or to afford access to them, is considered subjected to a public use. Talbot v. Hudson, ubi supra; Prince v. Crocker, ubi supra. But if a fee is taken, the title is not wholly within the control of the state, for, when the public use ceases, then land so held is the private property of the taker, discharged from the easement. Mt. Hope Cemetery v. Boston, 158 Mass. 509–512, 33 N. E. 695, 35 Am. St. Rep. 515, and authorities cited. There is no doubt that the title of the respondent in this case must be measured by the extent of the taking, which was in fee, and not of a mere easement; and the strength of the argument is weakened by this fact: that instead of relying on the construction now put forward, that a fee was granted by implication, and, if so, then the title passed absolutely by force of the act, and nothing further was necessary, it preferred to acquire and hold the land through the delegated right of eminent domain. "And if there is such a thing as a new title known to the law, one founded upon a taking by the right of eminent domain is as clear an example as can be found." Holmes, C. J., in Emery v. Boston Terminal Co., 178 Mass. 172–184, 59 N. E. 763, 86 Am. St. Rep. 473.

If it be said that under section 14 the respondent was subsequently required to convey, without compensation, to the city of Boston, so much of the real estate described in the petition that is now within the layout and location of Dorchester avenue and Summer street, and that it could not be compelled to part title to its property without compensation, even if the use was in part for the benefit of the public; the principal question involved is not affected, for the reason that the respondent was not obliged to accept the act, but, if it did, then it must be held to have assented to this condition. Hampshire v. Franklin, 16 Mass. 76–87.

While it is true that the people who use the facilities for travel from place to place furnished by the railroads occupying the terminal station, which, in a broad sense, can be held to include not only the building, but all the appurtenances that make it accessible and usable are benefited, yet so are the railroads themselves; and the nature of the undertaking itself, from whatever point of view, remains unchanged. It must accept the burdens while receiving the benefits. And the statute is to be construed as a legislative act by which the respondent was enabled to complete its scheme of a terminal station for pecuniary profit, though it was required to contribute a part of its property to another public use, made necessary solely to enable it to carry out its purpose.

It cannot be held that the state, any more than an individual, parts title in fee to real estate by implication alone, and if its land is to be granted in aid of a private corporation, even if the public may thereby be more largely accommodated. This intention must clearly appear by the express words of the act under which the grant is claimed. Com. v. Roxbury, 9 Gray, 451; Commissioners on Inland Fisheries v. Holyoke Water Power Company, 104 Mass. 446, 447, 6 Am. Rep. 247; Attorney General v. Jamaica Pond Aqueduct Corporation, 133 Mass. 361–365; The Charles River Bridge v. The Warren Bridge, 11 Pet. 420, 9 L. Ed. 773, 938.

There is no doubt that where the precise wording of a statute is such that, if exactly carried out, the result would not be what the Legislature intended, the literal language used may be rejected; but here the real design or object to be effected is precisely and clearly expressed, and the words used must therefore be given their ordinary meaning and construction, and which will carry that design into effect.

Though, in taking the lands prescribed by the terms of the act, it would be obliged to acquire those of the commonwealth included in such description, no intention appears to give this property of the state to the respondent, or to grant the right to gain title upon conditions other than those by which it was authorized to purchase or take land belonging to others. The authority to take, and the requirement of compensation to be paid for what is taken, go together, and are expressed in the same language as to both classes of owners. Com. v. Boston & Maine R. Co., 3 Cush. 25; Old Colony & Fall River Railroad Co. v. County of Plymouth, 14 Gray, 155, 161, ad finem; Grand Junction Railroad & Depot Company v. County Commissioners of Middlesex, 14 Gray, 553-565; Boston & Albany Railroad v. Cambridge, 159 Mass. 283, 284, 34 N. E. 382, and cases cited.

The ruling of the superior court was right, and the order overruling the demurrer is affirmed. So ordered.

(185 Mass. 233)

LAING v. MITTEN.

(Supreme Judicial Court of Massachusetts. Middlesex. Feb. 27, 1904.)

MALICIOUS PROSECUTION—WARRANT—SERVICE—ACTS OF OFFICER—AUTHORITY—LIABILITY OF PROSECUTOR—SLANDER—STATEMENTS TO MAGISTRATE — PRIVILEGE — INSTRUCTIONS—EVIDENCE.

1. In an action for malicious prosecution, an instruction that the burden was on plaintiff to prove that defendant, in instituting the criminal proceedings, acted maliciously and without probable cause, and that, in determining the question of probable cause, the jury should not consider the fact of acquittal, but should deal with the case as though it was new before them, was proper.

2. In an action for malicious prosecution, an instruction that defendant was liable for all the results of the prosecution, "no matter what happened," was cured by a subsequent instruction that defendant was liable only for that which would naturally arise, or be expected to happen, as the natural consequence of the service of the process.

3. Acts of an officer, in serving a warrant, in taking plaintiff out of bed at 1 o'clock at night, carrying him to a lockup in a patrol wagon with intoxicated people, and placing him in a cell not sufficiently warmed, etc., were within his authority under the process, and hence no recovery could be had therefor against the prosecutor in an action for malicious prosecution.

4. Words spoken by prosecutor to a magistrate at the time of the issuance of a warrant, importing that plaintiff had committed an assault on prosecutor, for which the warrant was issued, and evidence to the same effect at the trial under the warrant, were absolutely privileged, as spoken in judicial proceedings, though uttered maliciously.

5. Where, in an action for false imprisonment and malicious prosecution against defendant, arising out of a controversy between the parties in an armory, defendant contended that plaintiff had written a letter derogatory to defendant as an officer of the National Guard, and that plaintiff had written to defendant, apologizing for his conduct as a member of the Guard, such letters were properly excluded as too remote to the issues in controversy.

Exceptions from Superior Court, Middlesex County; John H. Hardy, Judge.

Action by John C. Laing against Anthony D. Mitten. From a judgment in favor of plaintiff, defendant brings exceptions. Exceptions sustained in part.

¶ 1. See Malicious Prosecution, vol. 33, Cent. Dig. §§ 50, 114.

The amended declaration contained three counts—the first, for false imprisonment; second, for slander; and the third, for malicious prosecution. Defendant was the captain of a company in the volunteer militia of Massachusetts, of which plaintiff was quartermaster sergeant, and, as such, had charge of the equipment room. Plaintiff's evidence tended to show that while plaintiff, at defendant's direction, was distributing arms and ammunition to the men in the armory, defendant came into the equipment room, and, after some conversation with reference to certain shells, spoke to plaintiff about a letter which he alleged plaintiff had written to the Adjutant General, complaining of defendant's conduct as an officer. Defendant then closed the doors of the equipment room and assaulted plaintiff, and, during the altercation, plaintiff seized the knob of a door, which came off in his hands, and struck defendant on the hand and head. After the knob had been pulled from the door, it could not be opened, and both plaintiff and defendant were imprisoned in the room. Defendant called for the janitor to unlock the door, and, as he came out, stated to the bystanders that plaintiff had assaulted him with a door knob. Defendant denied the assault on plaintiff, and claimed that he went into the room to relieve plaintiff of the keys, by reason of his misconduct as an officer in permitting intoxicated persons to have access to the room, etc. Subsequently defendant made complaint to a justice of the peace of plaintiff's assault with the door knob, on which a warrant was issued, and plaintiff was arrested. The arrest was not made in the usual manner, but plaintiff was taken from his bed about 1 o'clock in the morning by a force of three men, and was carried to the lockup in a patrol wagon with intoxicated people; and, at the time of the arrest, plaintiff's wife was ill, and needed his attention. At the lockup, plaintiff was put into a cell not sufficiently warmed, and suffered therefrom the aggravation of a disease contracted by him in the army, and the next morning was acquitted of the assault. Defendant offered in evidence a letter signed by a third person, and written to the State Adjutant General, complaining of defendant's conduct as an officer, and another written by plaintiff, apologizing for his condition in the armory, and for allowing men under the influence of liquor in the uniform room—offering to show that both letters were written by plaintiff—which the court excluded over defendant's exception. The court charged the jury, in substance, that the burden was on the plaintiff to show that, in instituting the criminal proceeding, defendant acted maliciously and without probable cause, and that on the question of probable cause the jury were not to consider the fact of acquittal, but were to deal with the case as though it were new before them, and say whether there was probable cause for it, under the circumstances. On the question of damages, the jury was also instructed that defendant would be liable for all the results of the prosecution, "no matter what happened," but such statement was followed "by a charge that defendant was liable only for what would naturally arise from the service of the process, or which naturally might be expected to happen as the natural consequence of such service."

John J. & Wm. A. Hogan, for plaintiff. William H. Bent, for defendant.

HAMMOND, J. The amended declaration contained three counts—the first, for false imprisonment; the second, for slander; and the third, for malicious prosecution. The questions before us arise upon the rejection of two letters offered by the defendant, and upon the instructions to the jury upon the second and third counts.

1. As to the count for malicious prosecution: The defendant stoutly contends that the charge to the jury upon this point was contradictory and confusing, and that it must have misled them. While some of the sentences, considered apart from their setting, might seem to give color to this criticism, still, upon a careful reading of the charge, we are of opinion that, in substance, the jury were told that the burden was upon the plaintiff to prove that in instituting criminal proceedings the defendant acted maliciously and without probable cause, and that upon the question of probable cause the jury were not to take into consideration the fact of the acquittal, but were "to deal with the case as though it was new before" them, "and say whether there was a probable cause for it, under all the circumstances." While upon the question of damages the jury were at first told that the defendant was to be held liable for all the results of the prosecution, "no matter what happened," this statement was subsequently corrected so as to hold the defendant liable only for that "which would naturally arise from the service of the process, or which naturally might be expected" to happen "as the natural consequence of the service of the process." As thus construed, the charge, both as to liability and damages, was sufficiently favorable to the defendant. The defendant was not liable for any acts of the officer done in excess of the authority conferred by the warrant, but, having started the prosecution, he was liable for everything done within such authority, and that was so even if the officer might have been a little more considerate than he actually was. Adams v. Freeman, 9 Johns. 117; Welsh v. Cochran, 63 N. Y. 181, 20 Am. Rep. 519. It may be said, in passing, that while the bill of exceptions recites that "the arrest was made in an unusual manner, and with acts of unnecessary and unwarrantable cruelty and indignity," the acts which are set forth in the bill, with the possible exception of the confinement in a cell not sufficiently warmed (and even this might have occurred with no fault upon the part of any person), are all plainly within the authority of the precept under which the officer acted. Unless there were acts besides those shown in the record to which the words "unnecessary" and "unwarrantable" are applicable, the words would not seem to imply an act beyond the authority of the process. The exceptions applicable to this count must therefore be overruled.

2. As to the count for slander: It appeared that the alleged slander consisted of the words spoken by the defendant to the magistrate, importing that the plaintiff had assaulted the defendant and struck him with a door knob, and also of the testimony to the same effect given by the defendant as a witness upon the trial of the complaint. The complaint was made to a magistrate having jurisdiction to receive it, and the trial took place in a court of competent jurisdiction. These words were therefore spoken in the course of judicial proceedings, and, being pertinent to the matter in hearing, were absolutely privileged, even if uttered maliciously. Hoar v. Wood, 3 Metc. 193; Kidder v. Parkhurst, 3 Allen, 393, 396, and cases cited; Watson v. Moore, 2 Cush. 133, 138; Morrow v. Wheeler & Wilson Mfg. Co., 165 Mass. 349, 43 N. E. 105. The instructions to the jury, allowing them to find for the plaintiff upon this count if they found that these statements thus made in the course of judicial proceedings were not made in good faith, were erroneous. It is suggested by the plaintiff that the jury might have founded their verdict upon the evidence which tended to show that the same words were spoken also at the armory, but we cannot know that such is the case. The exceptions to the instructions, so far as applicable to this count, must be sustained.

3. There was no error in the exclusion of the letters. Whether the letter of February 25th showed bias, and to what extent, depended somewhat upon whether the statements therein contained were true or false, and the court may well have thought that its admission would lead to an extended inquiry upon matters remote from the true issues. The letter of February 25th was so far remote from the true issues as to throw no light upon them. Both letters were properly excluded at the discretion of the court.

Exceptions as to the second count sustained. Other exceptions overruled.

(162 Ind. 213)

POTTER v. STATE.

(Supreme Court of Indiana. Feb. 23, 1904.)

INVOLUNTARY MANSLAUGHTER—CARRYING CONCEALED WEAPON.

1. That the pistol, by the accidental discharge of which deceased was killed while defendant was playing with him, was carried concealed by defendant, in violation of law, does not make

him guilty of involuntary manslaughter, under Burns' Rev. St. 1901, § 1981 (Horner's Rev. St. § 1908), declaring guilty of manslaughter one who kills another without malice, involuntarily, but in commission of some unlawful act.

Appeal from Criminal Court, Marion County; Fremont Alford, Judge.

William Potter was convicted of manslaughter, and appeals. Reversed.

W. E. Henderson, for appellant. C. W. Miller, Atty. Gen., L. G. Rothschild, C. C. Hadley, and W. C. Geake, for the State.

JORDAN, J. Appellant was tried before a jury in the lower court, and a verdict was returned finding him "guilty of manslaughter, as charged in the indictment." Over his motion for a new trial, the court rendered judgment on the verdict, assessing his punishment at imprisonment in the Indiana Reformatory for not less than 2 nor more than 21 years, and that he be fined and disfranchised. From this judgment he appeals, and assigns, among others, that the court erred in overruling his motion for a new trial.

The indictment upon which he was tried and convicted charged that William Potter on the 10th day of April, 1903, at the county of Marion, state of Indiana, "did then and there unlawfully, feloniously, and involuntarily, without malice, express or implied, kill one Hurva Garnett, by then and there, in a rude, insolent, and angry manner, unlawfully and feloniously shooting at and against and into the body of the said Hurva Garnett with a certain revolver, a dangerous weapon, which he, the said William Potter, then and there unlawfully had, loaded with gunpowder and leaden balls, concealed upon his person, he, the said William Potter, not then and there being a traveler, thereby mortally wounding the said Hurva Garnett, from which mortal wound he, the said Hurva Garnett, then and there died, contrary to the form of the statute," etc. The undisputed facts established by the evidence are substantially as follows: Appellant, a young colored man, about 24 years old, residing in the city of Indianapolis, was on the day of the homicide, which is shown to have been on some Sunday in the month of April, 1903, going to his home, in said city. As he was passing along the street near the corner of Rhode Island and Locke streets, the deceased, a boy about 18 years old, together with some two other boys, was standing at the corner of said streets. Appellant and the deceased, as it appears, were friends, and well acquainted with each other, and at times past had been in the habit of engaging in "friendly scuffles." As appellant approched the corner of the streets in question, he was engaged in tossing up a small ball; and, when he came up to the point where the deceased was standing, some friendly conversation or bantering occurred between them, in regard as to whether appellant could hit him with the ball which he had been tossing. The talk or bantering between the parties in question appears to have led up to a friendly play or "scuffle," during which a loaded revolver that appellant at the time was carrying concealed in his pocket, or somewhere about his person, was accidentally discharged; the ball therefrom passing through the clothing of appellant into the body of the deceased, from the effects of which the latter died.

Counsel for appellant contend that the verdict of the jury is contrary both to law and the evidence, and that the conviction of the accused cannot, thereunder, be sustained. Counsel for the state say in their brief: "This record presents a case which is somewhat novel in the annals of criminal jurisprudence in this state, if not in this country. The manner in which the deceased met his death, as shown by the record, was peculiar, to say the least; and whether appellant must suffer for the crime of involuntary manslaughter for circumstances created unintentionally, nevertheless unlawful, on his part, is the question presented for this court's consideration and solution."

Neither the facts as alleged in the indictment, nor as established by the evidence, constitute the crime of voluntary manslaughter. The pleader, in drafting the indictment, however, appears to have at least attempted to charge appellant with the offense of involuntary manslaughter. As the indictment is not assailed in this court, we need not determine its sufficiency as to the charge of involuntary manslaughter, but simply treat it, for the purpose of this appeal, as presenting such a charge. The crime of voluntary and involuntary manslaughter, as defined by the statutes of this state, is as follows: "Whoever unlawfully kills any human being without malice, express or implied, either voluntarily, upon a sudden heat, or involuntarily, but in the commission of some unlawful act, is guilty of manslaughter, and upon conviction thereof shall be imprisoned in the State Prison," etc. Section 1981, Burns' Rev. St. 1901 (section 1908, Horner's Rev. St.). The statute prohibiting the carrying of concealed weapons is as follows: "Every person, not being a traveler, who shall wear or carry any dirk, pistol, bowieknife, dagger, sword in cane, or any other dangerous or deadly weapon, concealed * * * upon conviction thereof, shall be fined in any sum not exceeding $500." Section 2069, Burns' Rev. St. 1901 (section 1985, Horner's Rev. St.). It is conceded, and properly so, that, at the time of the homicide, appellant was carrying the pistol in question in violation of the above statute. The question arises, then, did carrying the weapon unlawfully at the time of the homicide, in view of the other facts in the case, render the accused guilty of the crime of involuntary manslaughter, as charged in the indictment? The question, under the circumstances, as counsel for the state assert, is certainly a novel one, within the "annals of criminal jurisprudence," and we believe that a search for authorities to sustain the judgment below, under the facts, will be futile. The theory of the state in the lower court, as the case appears to have been placed before the jury under the evidence and instructions of the court, was that the carrying of the revolver concealed by appellant, in violation of the statute, was the commission of an unlawful act, from which the homicide resulted. It is undoubtedly true, as a general rule of law, that a person engaged in the commission of an unlawful act is legally responsible for all of the consequences which may naturally or necessarily flow or result from such unlawful act. But before this principle of law can have any application under the facts in the case at bar, it must appear that the homicide was the natural or necessary result of the act of appellant in carrying the revolver in violation of the statute. Section 2215, Burns' Rev. St. 1901, prohibits, under penalty, any person from hunting birds or other species of game with firearms on Sunday. If appellant, instead of carrying the pistol in question concealed, had been hunting with the weapon on Sunday in violation of the above statute, and when so hunting he had accidentally discharged it and killed Garnett, who happened to be standing near by, could it, in reason, be asserted that his death was due to appellant's unlawful act of hunting on Sunday? Certainly not. If, while engaged in hunting in violation of the statute, the pistol, through or by reason of the culpable negligence of appellant, had been discharged, and killed the deceased, the law, under such circumstances, would not have attributed his death to the unlawful act of hunting, but would have imputed it to such negligence. In fact, under such circumstances, the unlawful act of hunting would not be a factor in, or add anything to, the case. It would constitute nothing more than a separate and distinct offense. An eminent author on Criminal Law says: "It is malum prohibitum, and not malum in se, for an unauthorized person to kill game in England contrary to the statutes; and if, in unlawfully shooting at game, he accidentally kills a man, it is no more criminal in him than if he were authorized." 1 Bishop's New Criminal Law, § 332. See, also, 1 East's P. C. p. 260; 2 Roscoe's Criminal Ev. p. 800. With equal reason and force it may be asserted that the mere fact that the accused was unlawfully carrying the weapon in question at the time it was accidentally discharged is not, under the circumstances, a material element in the case, for it is manifest that such unlawful act did not, during the scuffle between the parties, render the pistol any more liable to be discharged than though the carrying thereof had been lawful. Of course, the law exacts of all persons the duty of being exceedingly cautious and careful in the use of or the handling the firearms or other dangerous agencies. Surber v. State, 99 Ind. 71. In fact, as a general rule, the law has such a high regard for human life that it considers as unlawful all acts which are dangerous to the person against whom they are directed, no matter how innocently they may be performed. A person will not be permitted to do an act which jeopardizes the life and safety of another, and then, upon plea of accident, escape liability for a homicide involuntarily resulting from his reckless or careless act or conduct. State v. Dorsey, 118 Ind. 167, 20 N. E. 777, 10 Am. St. Rep. 111; Gillett's Criminal Law (2d Ed.) § 502; 21 Am. & Eng. Ency. of Law (2d Ed.) 191, and cases cited. It is not charged in the indictment in this case that the homicide resulted from the reckless, careless, or negligent manner in which appellant was using or handling the pistol at the time it was discharged. Consequently, under the pleading, even though the facts could be said to justify or sustain such a charge, the case is not brought within the rule of culpable negligence, as affirmed and enforced in State v. Dorsey, supra, wherein the defendant was charged in the indictment with having carelessly and negligently run a locomotive engine into a passenger car, thereby killing a person who was a passenger thereon. It will be readily seen that, under the charge made by the indictment, the case at bar does not fall within that class of cases where the homicide is the result of culpable carelessness or negligence of the accused party in using or handling a dangerous weapon. 21 Am. & Eng. Ency. of Law (2d Ed.) pp. 191, to 195, inclusive, and cases cited in footnotes.

Without further comment upon the question involved, we conclude that the conviction of appellant was wrong. The judgment of the lower court is therefore reversed, and the cause remanded, with directions to the court to grant appellant a new trial. The clerk will issue the proper order for the return of the prisoner.

(162 Ind. 218)

McCARTY et al. v. STATE ex rel. BOONE et al.

(Supreme Court of Indiana. Feb. 24, 1904.)

INTOXICATING LIQUORS—DEATH FROM ILLEGAL SALE—SUFFICIENCY OF EVIDENCE.

1. The question of the sufficiency of evidence to support a verdict cannot become one of law, so as to be reviewable on appeal, unless there is an entire absence of evidence on a material point.

2. Plaintiff's decedent was taken into defendant's saloon in the afternoon so drunk that he fell on the floor. He there drank intoxicating liquors a number of times during the afternoon and evening, then sold to him by defendant's employés. When the saloon was closed, he went out, and others who had been in the saloon left him sitting on the porch, in a temperature below freezing. Twelve days later he was found dead in the vault of an outhouse immediately back of the saloon, into which he might have fallen, the water covering his body. A post mortem exhibited no external marks of violence. The physicians testified that his or-

gans disclosed no cause of death; that, in their opinion, he was not drowned; that there was no liquor in his stomach, and no odor of alcohol present; and that they could not state the cause of death. *Held*, that the jury were authorized to find his death was caused by defendant's unlawful sale of intoxicating liquor to him.

Appeal from Superior Court, Grant County; R. T. St. John, Special Judge.

Action by the state, on the relation of Rosella Boone and others, against James M. McCarty and others. From the judgment defendants appealed to the Appellate Court, whence it is transferred under Burns' Rev. St. 1901, § 1337u. Affirmed.

Henry & Elliott, for appellants. Elias Bundy, for appellees.

GILLETT, C. J. Action on a saloon keeper's bond to recover under the statute for loss of support by the death of one John R. Boone, caused by the unlawful sale of intoxicating liquor to him. The suit was brought on the relation of the widow and children of said decedent. The issue was formed by a general denial addressed to the complaint. A trial resulted in a verdict and judgment in favor of appellee. Appellants unsuccessfully moved for a new trial, and the refusal to grant such motion has been made the basis of this appeal. It is urged that there was no evidence showing an unlawful sale of intoxicating liquor to said John R. Boone, and that the jury was not justified in inferring that his death was caused thereby. There was evidence to the following effect: Boone, who was a periodical drinker, left his home on the morning of November 27, 1900, and did not return thereto. About 3 o'clock of the afternoon of the next day he was found lying in the yard back of the saloon of appellant McCarty. He was brought into said saloon in such a condition of intoxication that he fell to the floor. He drank intoxicating liquor in said saloon a number of times that afternoon and evening. The latter part of said evening he spent in sleep in the back room of said saloon. When the time came to close, he went out, and the other persons who had been in said saloon left him sitting on the porch thereof. He was not thereafter seen in life, so far as the evidence shows. The temperature that night was below freezing. Twelve days later the body of said Boone was found in the vault of an outhouse immediately back of said saloon. There was water in said vault, which entirely covered the body. The seat of said outhouse was so constructed that it might be possible to fall in the vault, as there was an open space 16 inches wide between the rear wall and said seat, extending the whole length of said outhouse, or about 4½ feet. A post mortem was held. There was no external mark of violence upon the body. The physicians who conducted the post mortem testified that an examination of the vital organs disclosed no cause of death. The brain and its membranes were apparently normal. There was no water or foreign substance in the lungs or in the trachea. The stomach bore some evidence of inflammation. It contained a small amount of mucous. It had no liquor in it, and there was no odor of alcohol present. The body was but little decomposed, and the only change in the external appearance thereof was due, according to the testimony, to the soaking of the skin. The physicians further testified that, in their opinion, the deceased was not drowned, that they perceived no evidence that he died from exposure, and that they could not state the cause of death.

It is not denied by counsel for appellants that the testimony of one of the witnesses (Graham) tends to show unlawful sales of intoxicating liquors to Boone by the servants of appellant McCarty during the afternoon and evening preceding Boone's disappearance. The mere fact that Graham was contradicted by a number of other witnesses, and that the physicians testified that there was no liquor in the stomach, and no odor of alcohol present at the time of the post mortem does not present an issue of law for our determination. Our function, in the consideration of cases of this character, is limited to the decision of law questions, and the question as to the sufficiency of evidence to support a verdict cannot become one of law unless there is an entire absence of evidence on some material point. Carver v. Forry, 158 Ind. 76, 62 N. E. 697, and cases there cited.

In our opinion, the jury was authorized to infer that Boone came to his death as a result of intoxication produced by such unlawful sales. The physicians may have been unable to venture a definite opinion as to the cause of death, but the jury was authorized to draw such inference. In reasoning from cause to effect, that body followed the evidence, instead of indulging in a vague and speculative doubt as to whether some third person might have caused Boone's death. One of two theories must be adopted: that he fell into the vault, or that, living or dead, his body was put in there by some one else. It was not material to the cause of action whether Boone died in the outhouse or not, for the question was as to whether his death was caused by the unlawful sale of intoxicants as charged. The theory of relators is based on known facts, and is reasonably adequate; while the suggested theory is not only wholly without evidence to support it, as before stated, but involves the improbability that any one would kill a practically helpless man, and the serious difficulty of determining how his life could be thus taken without an evidence of the fact which the physicians could detect. The evidence shows that in some way the body of Boone, dead or alive, fell into the vault. There was therefore this known fact upon which the antecedent evidence had a strong bearing.

and it was perfectly competent for the jury to infer from the whole evidence that his death was caused as charged. A fact being established, other facts may be, and often are, ascertained by inferences. While rein must be sometimes put on the imagination of juries, the process of reasoning in respect to inference is largely a matter of free logic. In R. v. Burdett, 4 B. & Ald. 95, 161, Abbott, C. J., said: "A presumption of any fact is properly an inference of that fact from other facts that are known. It is an act of reasoning, and much of human knowledge on all subjects is derived from this source. A fact must not be inferred without premises that will warrant the inference; but, if no fact could thus be ascertained by inference in a court of law, very few offenders could be brought to punishment." We perceive nothing in the fact that the evidence shows that Boone was not drowned which renders the conclusion reached by the jury inadmissible. If he did not, with his expiring breath, fall into the vault, it may be inferred that, having fallen in there, the water was not deep enough to submerge his head while standing upright. In that unspeakable place, death would soon relieve his suffering, whether he were drowned or not. The statute was intended to afford a remedy for an injury to the means of support, whether directly or remotely caused by the intoxication. Homire v. Halfman, 156 Ind. 470, 60 N. E. 154. The trial court did not err in overruling the motion for a new trial.

Judgment affirmed.

(162 Ind. 234)

PITTSBURGH, C., C. & ST. L. RY. CO. v. SEIVERS.

(Supreme Court of Indiana. Feb. 26, 1904.)

APPEAL—BRIEFS—RECITAL OF EVIDENCE—STATEMENT OF FACTS.

1. Under Sup. Ct. Rule 22, subd. 5 (55 N. E. vi), providing that, if the insufficiency of the evidence to sustain the verdict is assigned, the brief shall contain a condensed recital of the evidence, in narrative form, an appellant who has complied with this rule is entitled to have the question of its negligence and that of plaintiff's decedent, as shown by the evidence, considered, though the brief may have failed to comply with the rule in some other respects.

2. Under Sup. Ct. Rule 23 (55 N. E. vi), providing that the brief of appellee shall point out any omissions or inaccuracies in appellant's statement of the record, the court is justified, without referring to the record, in regarding an undisputed statement of facts in appellant's brief as correct.

On petition for rehearing. Overruled.

For former opinion, see 67 N. E. 680.

JORDAN, J. The grounds assigned by appellee for a rehearing herein may virtually be said to be but two, the first of which is that the court failed to decide an important question presented by appellee in regard to the construction of rule 22 of this court (55 N. E. v); second, that the evidence in respect to the contributory negligence of the deceased is conflicting, and hence the court erred in deciding that question adversely to appellee.

It is contended that appellant's counsel, in his brief, neglected to comply with the rule mentioned, and therefore the questions presented for our consideration ought not to have been considered. Appellant's brief disclosed, under proper captions, the nature of the action, what the issues were, as to how they were decided, as to what was the judgment of the court, and the errors relied on for a reversal. Appellant's brief also gave a concise statement of the record in relation to the issues and the determination thereof, a concise statement of the facts which, as appellant claimed, the evidence established, and which were relied on for a reversal upon the ground, among others, that such facts established that appellee's decedent was guilty of contributory negligence at the time of the accident. It is true that, under the caption of "Errors Relied on for a Reversal," the brief merely stated such errors generally, in like manner as they were specified in the assignment of errors. It is not essential, under the circumstances, that we decide whether appellant complied in all respects with the requirements of rule 22, for the only question determined was that the facts established by the evidence disclosed that the deceased was guilty of contributory negligence. Appellant had complied with the rule, so far as the evidence was concerned, by making a statement in its brief wherein a condensed recital of the evidence, in narrative form, was given. If it were conceded that it had disregarded the rule in part, nevertheless it had the right to invoke the consideration of the court upon the questions presented upon the evidence relative to its own negligence and that of appellee's decedent. Perry, etc., Co. v. Wilson (Ind. Sup.) 67 N. E. 183, and cases cited.

Counsel for appellee, in their brief, did not dispute the statement of facts contained in appellant's brief disclosing contributory negligence on the part of the deceased, but were content to rest upon the argument that the rule which exacts of a traveler at a railroad crossing the duty to listen and look in both directions for approaching trains before attempting to cross had no application under the facts in the case at bar. By reason of appellee's silence in her brief in regard to the facts stated by appellant in its brief, we were authorized, under rule 23 (55 N. E. vi), to treat and consider appellant's statement as accurate and true, without referring to the record. McElwaine-Richards Co. v. Wall, 159 Ind. 557, 65 N. E. 753. But we did not take advantage of this right, but examined the evidence contained in the record, in order to determine the question raised in respect to contributory negligence on the part of the deceased, and the adverse holding against appellee on that point was based upon the undisputed facts established by appellee's own witnesses, as shown by the record. If appellee's contention that the evidence upon the deceased's contributory negligence was conflicting could be sustained by the record, we would not hesitate to grant a rehearing. In addition to the fact that he neglected to look before entering upon the track, two other undisputed facts are established by the evidence: (1) If he had looked towards the east before going onto the track, he could have seen the approaching cars; (2) if he had not stopped on the track, he would have passed over in safety. The case, under the facts and circumstances, is not one which can be said to warrant the drawing of different inferences or conclusions, thereby falling within the rule affirmed in Malott v. Hawkins, 159 Ind. 127, 63 N. E. 308, "so that an impartial sensible man may draw the inference and conclusion that the injured person was guilty of contributory negligence, while another man, equally sensible and impartial, might draw a different conclusion." Under the evidence, the question was, did the deceased exercise such care as a person of ordinary prudence would have exercised under the same circumstances? From his conduct or acts in the matter under the particular circumstances of the case, but one inference or conclusion can be drawn, and that is that he did not exercise ordinary care. In such cases on appeal to this court the error committed by the trial court in rendering the judgment complained of is one of law, which this court is required to correct. Cleveland, etc., R. Co. v. Stewart (Ind. Sup.) 68 N. E. 170.

Counsel for appellee, in support of their petition for a rehearing, among other things, say that if the deceased "had stopped at the place suggested, namely, 3½ or 4 feet north of the north rail of side track No. 1, he would have been struck by the cars, as there was not room between the timbers which supported the stone crusher and the side track for a person to stand without being struck by a passing car." They assert that, when he stepped out into the space between these timbers and the north rail, had he looked east, he would have seen the cut of cars approaching within less than 20 feet of him at the rate of 12 miles per hour. They further assert that the deceased, being "in a place of danger, would have to retreat or advance, and, if he hesitated an instant, or made a mistake of judgment, such hesitation or mistake of judgment would not constitute contributory negligence." The infirmity of counsel's argument is that it attempts to construct a case outside of the evidence. The deceased, was not between the timbers and the track, and it appears that he had sufficient space in which to stand without being subjected to any danger. If counsel's assertion is true, then he went upon the track without looking, virtually in front of the approaching cars, and before he succeeded in clearing the track he was struck and killed. The case, under the facts, is not one in which it appears that appellee's decedent was placed in a position of danger through the negligence of appellant, and thereby became confused by his surroundings, and made a mistake in the choice as to the way or manner of escaping from such danger, and in so doing was killed by the cars. Before entering upon the track, it fully appears that he was in a place of safety, and went therefrom into one of danger, without exercising in the least the ordinary precautions imperatively exacted of all persons who place themselves in a similar position of danger. Wabash R. Co. v. Keister (Ind. Sup.) 67 N. E. 521, and cases cited; Rich v. Evansville, etc., R. Co. (Ind. App.) 66 N. E. 1028; Elliott v. Chicago, etc., R. Co., 150 U. S. 245, 14 Sup. Ct. 85, 37 L. Ed. 1068.

We have again given this case a careful consideration, and are constrained to hold that appellee's decedent is shown to have been guilty of negligence which proximately contributed to his death.

The petition for a rehearing is overruled.

(162 Ind. 193)

SCHOOL CITY OF RUSHVILLE et al. v. HAYES et al.

(Supreme Court of Indiana. Feb. 18, 1904.)

SCHOOLS — BONDS — VALIDITY — STATUTE — CONSTITUTIONAL LAW — SPECIAL LEGISLATION.

1. Successful bidders who have deposited the amount required by a board of school trustees for the purpose of bidding on an issue of school bonds, and which the board refused to return on refusal of such bidders to take the bonds on the ground of their invalidity, have such an interest in the subject of the statute under which the bonds were to be issued as to authorize them to contest the validity of the statute.

2. Acts 1903, p. 347, c. 198, § 1, providing that the board of school trustees of any school corporation in any city or town of the state having a population of not more than 4,545 nor less than 4,540, according to the last preceding United States census, may issue bonds and provide means to erect school buildings, or to pay debts incurred in erecting school buildings, is violative of Const. art. 4, § 22, forbidding the passage of any local or special laws providing for support of the common schools.

Appeal from Circuit Court, Rush County; Douglas Morris, Judge.

Action by William J. Hayes and others against the School City of Rushville and others. From a judgment for plaintiffs, defendants appeal. Affirmed.

Smith, Cambern & Smith and Gates Sexton, for appellants. Miller, Elam & Fesler and S. D. Miller, for appellees.

DOWLING, J. For the purpose of supporting its common schools by the purchase of grounds and the erection of buildings thereon, the school city of Rushville, with the approval of the common council of the civil city, determined to issue its bonds to the amount of $35,000, and to sell them to the highest bidder. Due notice of the intended sale was given by publication. The advertisement required that all bids should be accompanied by a certified check for 5 per cent. of their amount. The appellees sent in a sealed proposal for the whole of the bonds, together with their certified check for $1,750, being the amount required as a deposit. Their bid was the highest, and the board of school trustees awarded the bonds to them at the price offered. Afterward the appellees were advised that the act of the Legislature under which the bonds were issued was void, that it had been repealed before the commencement of the proceedings for the issue of the bonds, and that the bonds were invalid. They refused to complete the purchase, and demanded the return of the $1,750 deposited by them with their bid. The school city declined to surrender the $1,750, and insisted that the sale was valid, and the bonds legal. It offered to credit the amount of the deposit on the bid, and to deliver the bonds on payment of the balance of the bid, but, in the event of the failure of the appellees to complete the purchase of the bonds, it declared its intention to retain the $1,750 as a forfeiture, and to sell the bonds to other persons. Thereupon this suit was brought by the appellees to recover the amount of their deposit, or, in case the bonds should be held valid, to restrain the appellants from disposing of them to any other bidder, and to compel their delivery to the appellees. The complaint stated the foregoing facts, among others, and, a demurrer to it having been overruled, the school city and its board of trustees refused to plead further, and judgment was rendered in favor of the appellees. The decision on the demurrer is the error assigned.

Section 1 of the act of March 9, 1903 (Acts 1903, p. 347, c. 198), under which the school city proceeded in issuing its bonds, is as follows: "Be it enacted by the General Assembly of the State of Indiana: That the board of school trustees of any school corporation in any city or town in this state, having a population of not more than 4,545, nor less than 4,540, according to the last preceding United States census, which shall have purchased any ground or building * * * or may desire to purchase any ground, building or buildings, * * * may on the filing of a report, under oath, with the board of trustees of the incorporated town, or with the common council of the city in which such school corporation is located, showing the actual or estimated amount required to purchase such ground, erect building or buildings, or the amount of such debt, on the passage of a resolution approving the same by the board of trustees of such town, or common council of such city, may issue the bonds of such school town to an amount not exceeding in the aggregate thirty-five thousand dollars ($35,000), in denominations of not less than one hundred ($100), nor more than one thousand ($1,000) dollars, said bonds to bear not to exceed five per cent interest, and payable at any place that may be designated in said bonds, the principal in not less than one year nor more than fifteen years from the date of such bonds, and the interest annually, or semi-annually, as may be therein provided, to provide means to erect such building, or to pay such debt. Such board of school trustees may from time to time negotiate and sell as many of such bonds as may be necessary for such purposes, in any place, and for the best price that can be obtained therefor in cash: provided, that such bonds shall not be sold for less than their par value." Section 2 requires the school trustees to file with the county auditor a bond payable to the state of Indiana in a sum not less than the face value of the bonds, with security to be approved by the auditor, conditioned for the faithful and honest application of the proceeds of the sale of the bonds. Section 3 authorizes the levy of a special tax additional to that now provided for the payment of the interest and principal of such bonds. Section 4 directs the application of any surplus special school revenue to the payment of the interest and principal of any debt incurred under the act. Section 5 repeals all laws in conflict with the act. Section 6 declares an emergency requiring the immediate taking effect of the law. The main objection taken to this statute by the appellees is that it is local and special, and therefore void under the provisions of section 22, art. 4, of the state Constitution. The appellants answer that the act is general, and that the classification of cities named in it is a proper one. They also deny that the appellees have such an interest in the subject of the statute as to authorize them to contest its validity.

The latter position is clearly untenable. The appellees are directly interested in the question of the constitutionality of the act. The appellants assert a right under the statute to compel the appellees to pay to them the amount of their bid for the bonds, or, upon failure of the appellees to do so, to retain as a forfeiture the deposit of $1,750 which accompanied appellees' bid. If the statute is valid, these claims may be well founded and enforceable. If it is void, because in conflict with the Constitution, the appellees cannot be required to take and pay for the bonds, nor can the appellants lawfully retain the sum deposited by the appellees. The agreement between the parties contemplated the delivery to the appellees of valid obligations of the appellant school city to the amount of $35,000. Unless such obligations can be delivered, the appellees, as such purchasers, cannot be required to accept and pay for them.

It is not true, as asserted by appellants, that the school city and all its property owners and taxpayers are estopped to deny the validity of the bonds, and therefore that the rights of the appellees could not be prejudiced by the fact that the statute under which they were issued was void. The contrary has often been decided in this state and in other jurisdictions. Town of Winamac v. Huddleston, 132 Ind. 217, 31 N. E. 561; Alexander v. Johnson, 144 Ind. 82, 41 N. E. 811; Louisiana v. Wood, 102 U. S. 294, 26 L. Ed. 153; High on Injunctions, §§ 783, 784; Read v. Plattsmouth, 107 U. S. 868, 2 Sup. Ct. 208, 27 L. Ed. 414. If appellants' view of the law were correct, the restrictions of the Constitution in many cases would be vain and ineffectual. Any city or town could incur debts and issue notes or bonds in violation of the express prohibitions of that instrument, all of which would be enforceable, and against whose validity and payment neither the corporation itself nor its property owners and taxpayers could be heard to object. The payment of the bonds, if issued without authority, could be enjoined at the suit of any taxpayer, or, if sued upon, the corporation could resist their collection, on the ground that they were illegally issued. This being the case, the bonds would have no legal value in the hands of a purchaser, and an agreement to buy and to pay for them would be without consideration. Unless the appellees are permitted to reject the bonds if they were issued without authority of law, they will be compelled to pay more than $35,000 for securities for which the school city is not liable, and the collection of which cannot be enforced by legal process. It is very evident that the appellees have an interest in the question of the validity of the bonds, which entitles them to challenge the constitutionality of the statute under which they were issued.

The deposit of the check for $1,750 by the appellees at the time they made their bid did not constitute such a voluntary payment as deprived them of the right to demand its return and to recover it upon discovery of the fact that the proposed issue of the bond would be void. Gist v. Smith, 78 Ky. 367; Gwin v. Smurr, 101 Mo. 550, 14 S. W. 731; Louisiana v. Wood, 102 U. S. 294, 26 L. Ed. 153; Reed v. Plattsmouth, 107 U. S. 568, 2 Sup. Ct. 208, 27 L. Ed. 414. As the offer to purchase the bonds made by the appellees was conditional, they had the right to refuse to take the bonds on that ground also.

The act of March 9, 1903, purports to be a general law. It attempts to make a classification of cities and towns, and its operation is confined to the class so created. That class embraces cities and towns having a population of not more than 4,545 nor less than 4,540 according to the last preceding census. At the time of the enactment of the statute only one city in the state came within the prescribed description. The point to be determined on this appeal is whether this act is, in fact, general, or whether it is local and special, within the meaning of the Constitution. The views of counsel for appellants are thus stated in their brief: "The act itself is general in form, as it provides 'that the board of school trustees for any school corporation in any city or town in this state.'" No city or town is excluded. The only limitation is that such city or town should have a certain population under the last preceding United States census. This creates a class of cities. It is true that under the United States census of 1900 the city of Rushville is the only city that meets the requirements of the statute and can avail itself of the provisions of the act. But will this court say that under any future census there may not be 10 or 20 cities that will have all the qualifications required by this act? The organic law of the state, the aid of which is invoked by the appellees, to have this law destroyed, divides our government into general heads, to wit, the administrative, judicial, and legislative, and defines their general powers. The legislative is the only power in the state that can enact laws. The wisdom or frailty of their declared laws can only be measured or tested by limits imposed and prescribed by the Constitution. The intention of the legislators at the session of 1903 to create general classes for the support of common schools upon the basis of population is fully and conclusively shown by the several laws enacted at that session. They are as follows:

"First. An act relating to cities having a population of more than 100,000 to issue bonds, approved January 29, 1903 (Acts 1903, p. 5, c. 3). Second. An act authorizing school corporations of cities with a population not less than 2,820 nor more than 2,830 to create a debt to erect school buildings, approved February 4, 1903 (Acts 1903, p. 13, c. 6). Third. Authorizing school corporations of cities with a population of not more than 7,820 nor less than 7,800 to issue bonds for erection of school buildings, approved March 5, 1903 (Acts 1903, p. 175, c. 89). Fourth. Authorizing school trustees of cities with a population of not less than 7,095 nor more than 7,105 to issue bonds to erect school buildings, approved March 9, 1903 (Acts 1903, p. 239, c. 137). Fifth. Authorizing boards of school trustees in school cities with a population not less than 6,100 nor more than 6,130 to issue and sell bonds to construct school houses, approved March 9, 1903 (Acts 1903, p. 335, c. 191). Sixth. Act under which bonds are issued in case at bar, approved March 9, 1903 (Acts 1903, p. 347, c. 198). Seventh. General act applying to all cities in relation to creating school debts, approved March 9, 1903 (Acts 1903, p. 350, c. 200). Eighth. Authorizing boards to levy a tax to build schoolhouses in cities with a population of not less than 7,200 nor more than 7,700, approved March 10, 1903 (Acts 1903, p. 415, c. 224). Ninth. Authorizing boards of school trustees of cities or towns with a population not less than 3,410 nor more than 3,420 to issue bonds for school building purposes, approved March 11, 1903 (Acts 1903, p. 533, c. 245). Tenth. Authorizes boards of school trustees of cities or towns with a population not less than 4,025 nor more than 4,050 to issue and sell bonds for school building purposes. The Legislature thus created nine different classes authorizing boards of trustees in school cities or towns to provide means to erect school buildings. The purpose and intent of the Legislature cannot be doubted."

Under the Constitution of this state, cities and towns may be classified upon the basis of differences in population, and laws applicable to a single class may be regarded as general in their character, and not local or special. But the classification must be natural and reasonable, and not arbitrary. It must be founded upon real and substantial differences in the local situation and necessities of the class of cities and towns to which it applies. Where such a classification excludes from its operation cities and towns differing in no material particular from those included in a class, the statute cannot be upheld. It is obvious that cities having a population of 100,000 or more may require larger and more varied powers than such as contain a population of 10,000 or less. The political needs of the larger community may be of a different nature, and the forms and methods by which its affairs must be administered may be more extensive, complicated, and elaborate than those required in a municipality of smaller population. But can it be said that cities and towns having substantially the same population should be placed in different classes, and each class governed by a different set of laws? What reason requires that such distinctions should be made? Why should cities having a population not exceeding 4,545 nor less than 4,540 be placed in a separate class from cities having a population of not more than 5,000 nor less than 4,000? It is not possible that the political necessities of one of these classes founded on population alone could be different from those of the other. Why should the school corporation of a city of not more than 4,545 inhabitants nor less than 4,540 be authorized to issue bonds for the support of its public schools without submitting the question of the expediency of incurring the debt to the electors of the city, while the school corporation of every other city in the state incorporated under the general law is required to decide such question by a popular vote? In what respect does the one corporation differ from all others? The mode of classification furnishes a conclusive answer to the question. It consists solely in a trifling difference in population. The requirements of the statute serve no other purpose than to identify the particular city to which the statute shall apply. The fact that the act is declared to apply to all cities and towns having a population of not more than 4,545 nor less than 4,540, as shown by the last preceding census, does not relieve it from the vice of being a local and special law. The possibility that other cities and towns may hereafter meet the narrow conditions of the statute is not sufficient to take it out of the prohibition of the Constitution. Its legal foundation is not more secure than if it it had been declared to apply to all cities and towns bearing the name of "Rushville," as shown by the last preceding census. The classification is entirely arbitrary and artificial, and the plain command of the Constitution cannot be evaded by so weak and transparent a device.

Let it be supposed that the act of March 9, 1903, supra, is valid, what provision of the Constitution cannot be rendered nugatory by similar evasions? If cities and towns may be classified according to trifling differences in population, so may counties and townships. By means of statutes general in form, but local and special in purpose, resting entirely upon slight differences in population, every provision of section 22 of article 4 of the Constitution may be successfully evaded. Inferior in dignity and force of obligation only to the Constitution of the United States and the acts of Congress and treaties made under it, the state Constitution is the supreme law of the commonwealth. It is to be interpreted and applied in a reasonable manner. It is to be observed and obeyed, and not evaded and frittered away by distinctions and classifications which rest upon no rational or natural basis, and which deceive no one. When it declares that the General Assembly shall not pass local or special laws providing for supporting common schools and for the preservation of school funds, its mandate cannot be defeated by creating a class of cities differing in no material respect from scores of others in the state. The mere convenience of local communities, the financial necessities of particular cities, the conflicting views of citizens on the subject of the necessity for the erection of school buildings, are not sufficient to authorize legislation which the Constitution prohibits. Attempted evasions of the Constitution, the object of which is to meet and overcome such local and special conditions, cannot be tolerated. A due regard for the highest interests of the citizens of the state requires that all constitutional limitations and restrictions shall be firmly and constantly enforced. In Gulf, etc., Ry. Co. v. Ellis, 165 U. S. 150, 159, 17 Sup. Ct. 255, 41 L. Ed. 666, the court say: "But arbitrary selections can never be justified by calling them classifications. The equal protection demanded by the fourteenth amendment forbids this." In State v. Loomis, 115 Mo. 307, 314, 22 S. W. 350, 21 L. R. A. 789, quoted with approbation in Gulf, etc., Ry. Co. v. Ellis, supra, it was said by Black, J., that: "Classification for legislative purposes must have some reasonable basis upon which to stand. It must be evident that differences which would serve for a classification for some purposes furnish no reason whatever for a classification for legislative purposes. The differences which will support class legislation must be such as, in the nature of things, furnish a reasonable basis for separate laws and regulations. Thus the Legislature may fix the age at which persons shall be deemed competent to contract for themselves, but no one will claim that competency to contract can be made to depend upon stature, or color of the hair. Such a classification for such a purpose would be arbitrary, and a piece of legislative despotism, and therefore not the law of the land." Again, in State ex rel. Richards v. Hammer, 42 N. J. Law, 435, it was well said by the chief justice that: "Plainly, a law may be general in its provisions, and may apply to the whole of a group of objects having characteristics sufficiently marked and important to make them a class by themselves, and yet such law may be in contravention of this constitutional prohibition. Thus a law enacting that in every city in the state in which there are ten churches, there should be three commissioners of the water department, with certain prescribed duties, would present a specimen of such a law, for it would sufficiently designate a class of cities and would embrace the whole of such class, and yet it does not seem to me that it could be sustained by the courts. If it could be so sanctioned, then the constitutional restrictions would be of no avail, as there are few objects that cannot be arbitrarily associated, if all that is requisite for the purpose of legislation is to designate them by some quality, no matter what they may be, which will so distinguish them as to mark them as a distinct class. But the true principle requires something more than a mere designation by such characteristics as will serve to classify, for the characteristics which thus serve as the basis of classification must be of such a nature as to mark the object so designated as peculiarly requiring exclusive legislation. There must be substantial distinction, having a reference to the subject-matter of the proposed legislation, between the objects or places embraced in such legislation and the objects or places excluded. The marks of distinction on which the classification is founded must be such, in the nature of things, as will in some reasonable degree, at least, account for or justify the restriction of the legislation." See, also, Board v. Spangler, 159 Ind. 575, 65 N. E. 743; State ex rel. v. Parsons, 40 N. J. Law, 1; Dixon v. Poe, 159 Ind. 492, 65 N. E. 518, 60 L. R. A. 308; Commonwealth v. Patton, 88 Pa. 258; State v. Jones (Ohio) 64 N. E. 424; City of Cincinnati v. Trustees (Ohio) 64 N. E. 420; State v. Bargus (Ohio) 41 N. E. 245, 53 Am. St. Rep. 628; Rauer v. Williams (Cal.) 50 Pac. 691; Sutton v. State (Tenn.) 36 S. W. 697, 33 L. R. A. 589; Angel v. Cass County (N. D.) 91 N. W. 72; Indianapolis St. Ry. Co. v. Robinson, 157 Ind. 232, 236, 61 N. E. 197; Reed v. State, 12 Ind. 641, 648. The constitutional question presented in this case was not involved in any of the following: City of Indianapolis v. Navin, 151 Ind. 139, 47 N. E. 525, 51 N. E. 80, 41 L. R. A. 337, 344; City of Indianapolis v. Wann, Receiver, 144 Ind. 175, 42 N. E. 901, 31 L. R. A. 743; Consumers' Gas Trust Co. v. Harless, 131 Ind. 446, 29 N. E. 1062, 15 L. R. A. 505; Young v. Board, 137 Ind. 323, 36 N. E. 1118; Gilson v. Board, 128 Ind. 65, 27 N. E. 235, 11 L. R. A. 835.

For the reasons stated, we are constrained to hold the act of March 9, 1903, supra, unconstitutional, because special and local. The complaint therefore was sufficient, and the demurrer to it was properly overruled.

We find no error. Judgment affirmed.

(162 Ind. 183)

STATE ex rel. SHANKS et al. v. BOARD OF COM'RS OF CARROLL COUNTY.

(Supreme Court of Indiana. Feb. 18, 1904.)

ROADS—REPAIR—DUTY OF COUNTY COMMISSIONERS—STATUTES—CONSTRUCTION.

1. Under Acts 1895, p. 174, c. 82, granting the board of county commissioners power to purchase toll roads, and declaring that, when conveyed, the roads shall thenceforth be free, and shall be kept in repair as provided by law for the repair of other roads, the phrase "other roads" means other free roads of the class to which those purchased under the act would belong when conveyed to the county, in the absence of anything to indicate that the Legislature intended the contrary.

2. Under Acts 1901, p. 439, c. 202, § 1, declaring that by virtue of their office the commissioners of each county are thereby constituted a board of directors for all free gravel, macadam, and turnpike roads in their county, and vesting the management and control of such roads exclusively in the board, it is the duty of the board to take charge of and repair toll roads purchased pursuant to Acts 1895, p. 174, c. 82, granting the board of county commissioners power to purchase toll roads.

Appeal from Circuit Court, Carroll County; Truman F. Palmer, Judge.

Mandamus by the state, on the relation of Leonidas P. Shanks and others, against the board of commissioners of Carroll county. From a judgment for defendants, plaintiff appeals. Reversed.

Reeder & Sullivan, for appellant. John H. Cartwright and James P. Wason, for appellees.

JORDAN, J. This action was instituted by the relators, as citizens and taxpayers of Carroll county, Ind., to mandate the board of commissioners of that county, ex officio a board of directors of all free gravel, macadam, and turnpike roads, to assume the control and management of a certain toll road purchased by said board on the 7th day of May, 1901, from the Logansport & Burlington Turnpike Company. The board appeared to the action, and successfully demurred to the petition for want of facts; and, on the relators refusing to further plead, the court rendered judgment against them for costs.

The only error assigned is upon the ruling of the court in sustaining the demurrer to the petition. The material facts set up in the petition, in addition to those above stated, are substantially as follows: On the 8th day of January, 1901, a petition signed by 100 and more freeholders of Carroll county, Ind., was filed before the said board of commissioners, praying for the purchase of the Logansport & Burlington Gravel Road, which road at said time, and for many years prior thereto, was and had been owned and operated in said county as a toll road by said Logansport & Burlington Turnpike Company. The board, after considering said petition, appointed appraisers to appraise said toll road; and these appraisers on the 7th day of May, 1901, reported favorably in respect to the purchase of the road. On the same day the board of commissioners found that said report was in all things true, and thereupon entered an order for the purchase of the road; and on the same day the aforesaid turnpike company, by and through its proper officers, conveyed to said board of commissioners all of its right, title, interest, and franchise in and to said toll road, which conveyance was accepted by the board of commissioners, and thereupon the company surrendered and relinquished all management and control over the road, and have not since exercised any jurisdiction or management of control over the same. It is further alleged that more than 18 months have elapsed since the road was purchased and conveyed as aforesaid, but the board of commissioners have done nothing in respect to managing, maintaining, or repairing the road. It appears that, owing to the constant and great travel thereover, this road has become and is in bad condition and out of repair. Since the purchase and conveyance of the road to the county, the relators have frequently notified the board of its bad condition, and have often requested and demanded that the board of commissioners take charge of, manage, and repair said road, as provided by law for the maintenance and repair of other free gravel, macadam, and turnpike roads within said county, but said board has always refused to do so, and so continues to refuse. Copies of the petition, deed of conveyance, and other papers in the proceedings before the board in the matter of the purchase of the toll road in question were filed with the petition for mandate as exhibits. The prayer is that the court, by a writ of mandamus, compel said board of commissioners, as ex officio a board of directors of all free gravel, macadam, and turnpike roads in said county, to take charge of, and assume the management and control of, said road, and assign the same to one of its members, as provided by law for the maintenance and repair thereof, etc.

The material question at issue between the parties is as to whether, under the facts, the road in dispute, after its purchase and conveyance to the county, was one which said board, under the law, was required to assume the management and control thereof. The contention of counsel for appellant is that, after its purchase and conveyance, it became the duty of the board of commissioners, under the law, as ex officio directors of all free gravel, macadam, and turnpike roads of the county, to manage and control said road, and provide for the repair thereof, as required by an act of the Legislature approved and in force March 11, 1901 (Acts 1901, p. 439, c. 202). It is asserted that, upon the refusal of the board of commissioners to discharge this duty enjoined upon it by law, the performance thereof can be compelled by mandamus. Counsel for appellees, however, insist that by the provisions of an act of the Legislature approved March 9, 1895 (Acts 1895, p. 174, c. 82), under the authority of which it is conceded that the road in controversy was purchased, the Legislature did not intend that it should pass under the control and jurisdiction of the commissioners, but should be maintained and be repaired under the authority of the statutes pertaining to ordinary highways. It is therefore asserted, in opposition to the contention of appellant's counsel, that the act of the Legislature approved March 11, 1901, supra, can have no application to the control and repair of the road in controversy.

The opposite views entertained by the counsel of the respective parties in regard to the proper interpretation of the provisions of the act of 1895, supra, require an examination of the statutes—repealed and unrepealed—of this state enacted in relation to the construction and maintenance of free gravel, macadam, and turnpike roads, and also the laws pertaining to the purchase by boards of commissioners of toll roads for the purpose of converting them into highways to be open to the travel of the public thereover without the payment of toll. Reviewing these laws from the year 1877, it will be found that, by an act approved March 3d of that year, the construction by boards of commissioners of gravel, macadam, or paved roads, to be opened to the public free of toll, was authorized. Acts 1877, p. 82, c. 47. This law made no provision, however, for the repair of these roads. Consequently the necessity for some legislation in regard to their management and repair after their construction was recognized; and the Legislature, by an act approved March 24, 1879 (Acts 1879, p. 226, c. 115), provided that the board of commissioners of any county, by virtue of their office, should constitute a board of turnpike directors, under whose control and management all free gravel roads of the county were exclusively vested; and provisions were made therein for the maintenance and repair of these roads under the authority of the board of commissioners as such turnpike directors. This act of 1879, as originally passed, was apparently limited and made to apply only to free roads constructed by boards of commissioners, for section 3 expressly provided that "wherever the word turnpike occurs in this act it shall be taken and held to include all roads constructed or improved under the act entitled 'An act to authorize the county commissioners to construct roads, on petition of a majority of resident land owners along and adjacent to the line of said road,' approved March 3rd, 1877." In 1881 (Acts 1881, p. 531, c. 61) a law was passed authorizing the board of commissioners of any county, when petitioned by a certain number of freeholders and citizens thereof, to submit to the voters of the county, at an election as therein provided, the question of the purchase of any turnpike or toll road. If the majority of those voting at such election were in favor of purchasing the road in question, the board of commissioners were empowered to make the purchases, and thereupon the road was to be conveyed by a proper deed by the owners thereof to such board; and when so conveyed it became a free road. By section 5 it was provided that such toll roads, after becoming free turnpike roads, should be kept in repair the same as other free turnpike roads, under the act approved March 24, 1879. Vide section 6969c, Burns' Rev. St. 1901. In 1883 (Acts 1883, p. 121, c. 99), sections 1 and 3 of the act of March 24, 1879, supra, were amended. The latter section was changed to read as follows: "Sec. 3. Wherever the word turnpike occurs in this act, it shall be held and taken to mean and include all turnpike and gravel roads, either purchased or constructed by counties, and which are used as free turnpike or gravel roads." This is section 6874, Burns' Rev. St. 1901. On March 8, 1883, an act was approved which provided for the purchase by the board of commissioners of toll roads, and their conversion into free roads. Acts 1883, p. 183, c. 128. This act authorized the board to purchase such roads upon a petition signed by any number of stockholders of the toll road company owning over one-half of the stock thereof, and was also signed by a majority of the landowners whose lands would be benefited or assessed for the purchase of the road. Section 11 provided that all gravel or macadamized toll roads purchased and converted into free roads thereunder should be kept in repair the same as other free turnpike roads were authorized to be kept in repair by the act of 1879, supra. In 1885 (Acts 1885, p. 209, c. 85) sections 1, 2, 3, 4, 5, and 6 of this act were amended. By this amendatory act the board of commissioners was not only authorized to order the purchase of a toll road, but was required under the same proceedings to order the repair of the road at the time of its purchase; and the expense incurred in putting it in good repair, together with the expense incurred in the purchase thereof, was to be assessed upon all of the lands benefited within one mile and a half of either side of the road, and also upon all lands located within the same distance of the beginning and terminus of the road. The purpose of the provisions in regard to the initial repair of the road, and authorizing the expense of such repair to be assessed against the lands benefited within the prescribed taxing district, was manifestly to exempt the taxpayers of the county in general from being required to pay the expense of this particular repair, for it will be observed that the act of 1879, supra, provided that the money for keeping free roads in good repair should be raised by an assessment against all of the taxable property in the county. Section 11 of the act of March 8, 1883, supra, which, as shown, provided that toll roads purchased by the county should, after such purchase, be maintained and kept in repair as provided by the statute of 1879, supra, was left untouched by the amendatory act of 1885. Under an act approved March 8, 1889 (Acts 1889, p. 276, c. 137), boards of commissioners were empowered to purchase toll roads when petitioned to do so by 50 freeholders and citizens of the township or townships in which such roads were situated. In the event the proposition to purchase was authorized at an election by a majority of the voters of such township or townships, section 6 of this latter act provided that all roads purchased thereunder were to be free of toll, and should be kept in repair, "the same as roads constructed under the free gravel road law of the state." By an act approved March 3, 1899 (Acts 1899, p. 403, c. 170), the Legislature appears to have again declared that the board of commissioners of every county in this state should constitute a board of turnpike directors, and that the management, control, and repair of all the free turnpikes of the county should be vested in such board. The act of 1895, of which mention has already been made as the law under which the road in controversy was purchased, provides that the board of commissioners, when petitioned to do so by 100 freeholders of the county, shall be authorized to purchase any or all toll roads therein, and pay for the same as provided. It is provided by this act that the purchase money for such road or roads shall be paid out of any funds in the county treasury not otherwise appropriated or required for other purposes; and, in case there are not funds sufficient in the treasury, the board is authorized to issue the bonds of the county in order to raise the necessary money to pay for the road or roads so purchased. The latter part of section 5, p. 175, of the act of 1895, as originally enacted, and as the same section stands since its amendment in 1901 (Acts 1901, p. 51, c. 30), provides "that no money shall be paid or bond delivered to such vendor until a conveyance has been made of such toll road, including its franchise to such county. *And when so conveyed, said road shall thenceforth be free, and shall be kept in repair, as provided by law for the repair of other roads.*" (Our italics.) The act approved and in force March 11, 1901, supra, appears to have superseded the act of 1899, supra, regulating the repair of free gravel and turnpike roads. Section 1, p. 439, of this act of 1901, provides "That by virtue of their office the commissioners of each county in this state are hereby constituted a board of directors for all free gravel, macadam and free turnpike roads in such county under whose management and control all such roads are hereby exclusively vested. It shall be the duty of such board of directors at its first meeting after this act takes effect, to divide the free gravel, macadam and turnpike roads of such county into three districts, each district to contain as nearly as possible the same number of miles of such road. Said directors shall by agreement assign one of their number to each of said districts, and such director shall have entire charge of the district so assigned to him. Such director shall employ all labor and purchase all material necessary to keep the district under his control in repair. He shall oversee and superintend the labor employed, and see that faithful work is done." Section 2 authorizes the appointment by the board of directors of superintendents, who are required to execute an official bond to the board of commissioners, and are to have charge of the repair of all free gravel, macadam, and turnpike roads within their respective divisions or districts. Other sections of the act cover details in relation to the repair of this system of improved roads within the county.

It is contended by counsel for appellees that the part of section 5, p. 175, of the act of 1895 which we have embraced in italics, fully reveals that it was the intent and purpose of the Legislature that all toll roads purchased and conveyed to the county under the authority of that statute should not become a part of the class or system of free and improved roads of the county, to be controlled and repaired under the jurisdiction of the board of commissioners, acting as the board of directors, but, upon the contrary, the Legislature intended to charge the repair of such toll roads, after their purchase by the county, to the trustees and supervisors of the township or townships through which the road passed. It is contended that this particular purpose of the Legislature is fully disclosed in the closing part of section 5 of the act in question, which declares that, after the purchase and conveyance of the road to the county, it "shall be kept in repair as provided by law for the repair of other roads." Construing this particular provision in the light of the provisions enacted prior to the statute of 1895 relating to the same subject-matter, and, in reason, no such interpretation as that contended for by counsel for appellees can be adopted. The various acts to which we have referred, enacted as far back as 1879, fully reveal that it was the positive will and purpose of the Legislature to have all free gravel, macadam, and turnpike roads of the county constitute a particular system or class of roads, and to vest the exclusive management, control, and repair thereof in the board of commissioners, the members of which body were declared to be ex officio a board of turnpike directors. It fully appears from these statutes that the Legislature did not intend to confine this system of free and improved highways alone to roads which had been constructed as such under proceedings had before boards of commissioners, but intended, also, to include therein all toll roads which had been purchased and converted into free highways. It would be unreasonable to suppose that the Legislature, in the enactment of the act of 1895, intended to change its former policy or purpose, and depart from a method which in 1881 it had declared should apply to the management and repair of toll roads after their purchase and conversion into free roads. It will be observed that, under section 19 of the law of 1899 (Acts 1899, p. 348, c. 154) concerning county business, it is provided that "every estimate required by said section 16 to be prepared by the board of commissioners shall embrace, in items separate from each other, each of the following matters: * * * (8) Amount of repair of free gravel roads * * * naming each road, the length thereof, and the amount required therefor." It is provided in the same act that the amount required for such purpose shall be levied by the county council. This provision of the act of 1899 is certainly of force, as it serves to show that some four years after the passage of the act of 1895 the Legislature still considered the repair of all free gravel roads as a matter of county business, under the control of the board of commissioners. Again, considering the phrase "other roads," as used in the act in question, from another standpoint, and there can be no doubt in regard to the particular roads to which it refers. It will be noted that the Legislature, in enacting the act of 1895, supra, was dealing with the purchase of toll roads, and their conversion into free roads. The roads mentioned in the act are of a particular description or kind. Under such circumstances, the rule applicable to its construction, as asserted by the authorities, is "that where words of a particular description in a statute are followed by general words that are not so specific and limited, unless there be a clear manifestation of a contrary purpose, the general words are to be construed as applicable to persons or things, or cases, of like kind to those designated by the particular words." Nichols v. State, 127 Ind. 406, 26 N. E. 839, and authorities cited. In compliance with this canon of construction, as there is nothing to indicate that the Legislature intended the contrary, the phrase "other roads" must be construed as meaning other free roads of the class or kind to which those purchased under the act would belong when conveyed to the county.

We conclude, and so hold, that it devolved upon appellees, under the act of March 11, 1901, supra, to assume the management and control of the road in suit, and perform the duties in regard thereto as enjoined by that statute. The court therefore erred in sustaining the demurrer to the petition of the relators, for which error the judgment is reversed, and the cause remanded.

(162 Ind. 154)

EMMONS v. HARDING et al.

(Supreme Court of Indiana. Feb. 17, 1904.)

DEEDS—DELIVERY — ACCEPTANCE — PRESUMPTIONS—TIME—RELATION — IMPEACHMENT BY STRANGER—GRANTEE WITH NOTICE—QUESTIONS OF FACT.

1. Where appellant, presumably by oral direction, caused an appeal in an action to quiet title to be docketed in the Appellate Court, though the name of the court to which the appeal was taken was not shown in the assignment of error, as that court alone had original appellate jurisdiction over cases of the class to which this case belonged, though the procedure was irregular, the Appellate Court acquired jurisdiction, and the Supreme Court will take jurisdiction on its transfer, under Burns' Rev. St. 1901, § 1337u, because of the disparity in numbers of causes pending in the Appellate and Supreme Courts.

2. A subsequent acceptance by the grantee of a deed delivered by the grantor to a third person for delivery upon the grantor's death, or a ratification of the transaction, may, by the fiction of relation, validate the deed.

3. The delivery of a deed by the grantor to a third person, to be delivered to the grantee at the grantor's death, must be of such a character as to terminate the dominion of the grantor over the deed.

4. Although there is a presumption of acceptance by the grantee of a deed delivered by the grantor to a third person for delivery at the grantor's death, there is no actual acceptance until the grantee elects to claim under the deed.

5. The fiction of relation which carries back the acceptance of a deed, delivered by the grantor to a third person for delivery at the former's death, to the date of delivery by the grantor, cannot operate to the prejudice of strangers who have a standing to go behind the fiction and show the true time of acceptance.

6. A purchaser with notice of a prior deed delivered by the grantor to a third person to be delivered to the grantee therein at the grantor's death is in privity with the grantor, and has no standing, as a stranger, to attack the fiction of relation which carries back the date of the acceptance by the grantee in the former deed to the date of delivery by the grantor.

7. A daughter-in-law, with whom her father-in-law had resided for some years in his old age, and to whose husband he owed money, was not a grantee without equity in a deed by her father-in-law to her, executed and delivered to a third person in his lifetime, but not delivered to her till the father-in-law's death, and is not required to give way to a subsequent purchaser from the father-in-law, who had notice of the deed to her.

8. A deed delivered by a grantor to a third person to be delivered to the grantee at the grantor's death must take effect presently, and cannot take effect subsequently as a testamentary disposition of the property, although it may be delivered with the intention that the estate is not to be enjoyed in possession until after the grantor's death.

9. A delivery of a deed by a grantor to his agent leaves it subject to reclamation by him.

10. To constitute a delivery of a deed, there must be indicia, either by acts or words, of the intent of the maker to deliver the instrument as his deed; and where such acts or words unequivocally evince the purpose of the maker, the question of delivery is one of law, but ordinarily it is largely one of fact.

11. Statements of a grantor at the time of the delivery of a deed to a third person to be delivered to the grantee at the grantor's death *held* sufficient to authorize an inference of an intent to deliver the instrument in question as his deed.

¶ 2. See Deeds, vol. 16, Cent. Dig. § 134.

Appeal from Circuit Court, Kosciusko County; J. D. Ferrall, Judge.

Action by Ellen Emmons against Oscar A. Harding and others. From a judgment for defendants, plaintiff appeals. Transferred from Appellate Court under Burns' Rev. St. 1901, § 1337u. Reversed.

Summy & Lehman and Wood & Bowser, for appellant. John D. Widaman and Royse & Shane, for appellees.

GILLETT, C. J. This action was brought by appellant against appellees to quiet title to certain real estate. There was a trial by jury, and on the conclusion of the evidence the court directed a verdict in favor of appellees. Over a motion for a new trial, judgment was rendered on the verdict.

It is objected by counsel for appellees that the assignment of errors is defective, in that the name of the court to which the appeal was taken is not shown. Appellant, presumably by oral direction, caused the appeal to be docketed in the Appellate Court, and an order of submission was afterwards duly entered. That court alone has original appellate jurisdiction over cases of the class to which this belongs. If the case had been filed in this court, it would have been our duty to transfer it. Section 1362, Burns' Rev. St. 1901. The procedure of appellant in the particular stated was irregular, but the Appellate Court acquired jurisdiction by the steps taken, and, as the irregularity is not serious, we regard it as our duty to consider the appeal on its merits.

It remains to determine whether there was sufficient evidence to entitle appellant to go to the jury. The question was as to the delivery and acceptance of a deed. The real estate in question belonged to one Erastus H. Emmons, and was part of an 80-acre tract of land. In the spring of 1900 Emmons signed and acknowledged 11 deeds, describing in the aggregate said tract of land. The deeds were in favor of his 11 children, respectively, except that as to the portion intended for the benefit of his son Henry the deed was made in favor of the latter's wife, the appellant here. The land covered by said deed is the property in suit.

It consists of about 10 acres, on which is a house and a barn. In August, 1900, Emmons sent for a friend and neighbor, one Blue, and handed him said deeds, and also a writing, which contained directions concerning the disposition of said instruments. Emmons was at the time an old man, in failing health. He had resided with appellant and her husband upon said 80 acres of land for many years. We have only secondary, and somewhat fragmentary, evidence as to the writing which accompanied the deeds. It is in evidence that it contained a direction to Blue to hold the deeds until Emmons' death, and at "his death to deliver them to each one of the heirs." Said writing contained some further provisions to the effect that the crops were to be sold, and, if necessary, timber was to be sold (whether the timber was upon the tract embraced in the deed in favor of appellant does not appear), to meet the expense of Emmons' support and to pay the cost of his burial. A number of oral statements were made to Blue by Emmons at the time of the delivery of said papers. Thus, when the deed to appellant was turned over to Blue, Emmons said, "This is Henry's," and, upon Blue stating that it was made to Ellen (appellant), Emmons answered, "Yes, I made it to her." He then explained that he had done so because Henry was in debt, and he added that he thought it best to deed the land to her, so that she and Henry could have a home. In the course of said conversation Emmons further said that he did not owe any man a dollar; that he "did owe Henry some, but made that all right with him in deeding the land to pay him." He further said, with reference to his having lived with Henry and his wife, that "he had been sick, and a good deal of bother to them," and that "he thought it was right to give Henry that much." The bill of exceptions also shows the following in connection with the testimony of the witness Blue: "Q. What did he [Emmons, Sr.] say about making this deed to Ellen Emmons? A. He told me that Henry Emmons was in debt some, and for them to have a home he made it to — (The defendant objects.) The Court. What did he say about executing this deed to Mrs. Emmons—whether he did or not? A. Yes, sir; he did." At the time said papers were turned over to Blue, Emmons had and retained in his possession a box, which had a lock and key, wherein it was his habit to keep his personal papers. A few days after the above-mentioned conversation, one Smith, who was acting for appellant and her husband, stated to the elder Emmons that Henry and his wife requested that he "let the deed stand as it was, and they would give no further trouble at all from any book account or anything of that kind." Emmons answered that he would allow the deed to remain if there would be no further account, and if said Smith would be a witness to that fact; an assurance which the latter thereupon gave. A little later Emmons called on Blue, and stated that he had "changed things," or "changed his mind," and he demanded and received said deeds and the paper which had been delivered with them. On August 30, 1900, Emmons, Sr., and appellee Oscar concluded an oral negotiation for the sale to the latter of said 80 acres. He paid $1 down, and on the next day he received a deed, and made an additional payment. Said appellee admitted upon the stand that he had heard of the making of said former deeds, and that said Blue held them, and said witness further admitted that he destroyed said deeds, at the request of said Emmons, at the time he concluded his negotiations for the purchase of said land. Emmons died in April, 1901, before this suit was commenced. So far as described in the evidence, the deed in favor of appellant was unconditional. Appellant at least had nothing to surrender to avail herself of the deed, if it was delivered for her use and benefit. If it can be said that it was delivered with an express agreement between the father and Henry that the latter's account was to be canceled, there is room for the inference, from the statement of the elder Emmons, that Henry had agreed to it, so that nothing remained to surrender. The evidence also tends to show a subsequent acceptance by appellant, and a waiver of all claim to an account upon the part of Henry.

It is insisted by counsel for appellees that as the grantor took the deed from the hands of the person to whom it was intrusted, and executed a deed of the land subsequently, the courts should not treat the first deed as a conveyance of the land. A delivery of a deed to a third person, to be by the latter delivered upon the grantor's death, would appear at first thought to be open to the objection that there was lacking that meeting of minds which is essential to the validity of contracts. Nevertheless it is hornbook law that a subsequent acceptance of the instrument or a ratification of the transaction may, by the operation of the fiction of relation, validate the deed. It is to be observed that the instrument on its face purports to run in favor of the grantee, thus bringing him, in a sense, into privity with the grantor. Gibson v. Chouteau, 13 Wall. 92, 20 L. E. 534. It is required that the delivery to the third person be of such a character that all dominion over the deed upon the part of the grantor should terminate. The transaction is to be distinguished from an escrow. The instrument has been lodged with the third person to await the lapse of time, and not the performance of any condition, and there is nothing to prevent it from becoming the grantor's deed presently. Foster v. Mansfield, 3 Metc. (Mass.) 412, 37 Am. Dec. 154. In fact, the authorities proceed on the theory that a deed so delivered is for some purposes a present conveyance. Osborne v. Eslinger, 155 Ind. 351, 58 N. E. 439, 80 Am. St. Rep. 240, and cases there cited. This has been put on two grounds: (1) That the act of the third person in receiving the deed on behalf of the grantee is not void; and (2) that it is presumed that a person will accept a deed which imposes no burden on him. As to the first ground, reference may be made to the note to the case of Armory v. Delamire, in Smith's Leading Cases. In that note the annotators say: "A subsequent ratification of an act done in the name of the party who ratifies is tantamount to a prior command; nay, it has relation back to the time of the act done, and is in point of law, and may be described in pleading as, a command. So that where a person, if present at the time, could lawfully command any act to be done, any other person, though either wholly without authority, or exceeding the limits of his authority, would be justified in doing that act, provided he did it in the name, or as one acting by the authority, of the person entitled (whether to his advantage or not), and obtained his subsequent ratification." 1 Smith's Lead. Cases (11th Eng. Ed.) 361. This, if we may omit a few exceptions not necessary to note here, is a correct statement of the law. See 2 Bouvier's Inst. § 1816 et seq.

As to the second ground above stated—that of a presumed acceptance—it was once held that a disclaimer by matter of record was necessary to avoid the transaction, but it was afterwards adjudged otherwise. Townson v. Ticknell, 3 Barn. & Ald. 31. As stated by Justice Ventris in Thomson v. Leach, 2 Ventris, 98, a man "cannot have an estate put into him in spite of his teeth." But the presumption that a person will accept a pure, unqualified gift is so strong that the courts have quite generally manifested a disposition to act upon such presumption in the interim as a working rule for the operation of conveyances. See Lessee of Mitchell v. Ryan, 3 Ohio St. 377; 4 Kent, Com. p. *455, note.

There seems to be but one further question remaining in this connection, and that grows out of the fact that a subsequent acceptance is required. "Where the commencement, progression, and consummation of a thing are necessary to go together, there all of them are to be respected." 18 Viner's Abr. p. 288, tit. "Relation." It has been justly observed that, notwithstanding the presumption of acceptance, there is no actual acceptance of the title until the grantee has elected to claim under the deed. Knox v. Clark, 15 Colo. App. 356, 62 Pac. 334; Tuttle v. Turner, 28 Tex. 759, 773; Devlin on Deeds, § 285. See Hulick v. Scovil, 4 Gilm. 159; 4 Kent, Com. 454; 3 Wash. Real Prop. 292. As before stated, the failure of the minds to meet is supplied by the doctrine of relation. Of the application of the fiction mentioned it has been said: "Where there are divers acts concurrent to be done to make a conveyance, estate, or other thing, the original act shall be preferred, and to this the other acts shall have relation." 18 Viner's Abr. 290, tit. "Relation"; Landes v. Brant, 10 How. 348, 372, 13 L. Ed. 449; Bellows v. McGinnis, 17 Ind. 64; Ridgeway v. Bank, 78 Ind. 119; Hollenback v. Blackmore, 70 Ind. 234. One of the older writers on real property says: "There is no rule better founded in law, reason, and convenience than this: that all the several parts and ceremonies necessary to complete a conveyance shall be taken together as one act, and operate from the substantial part by relation." 5 Cruise on Real Property, 510. The reason of the doctrine is found in the desire of the courts to uphold the agreements of parties—"Ut res magis valeat quam pereat"—that the thing may prevail, rather than be destroyed. "Without necessity—'ut res magis valeat'—the law will never feign any nullity." Butler and Baker's Case, 3 Rep. *25. The leading limitation of the doctrine is found in the maxim, "In fictione juris semper æquitas existit"—a legal fiction is always consistent with equity. Broom's Leg. Max. p. *127. In the discussion of this maxim Mr. Broom says: "The law does not love that rights should be destroyed, but, on the contrary, for the supporting of them invents maxims and fictions. And the maxim, 'In fictione juris subsistit æquitas,' is applied by our courts for the attainment of substantial justice, and to prevent the failure of right. 'Fictions of law,' as observed by Lord Mansfield, 'hold only in respect to the ends and purposes for which they were invented. When they are urged to an intent and purpose not within the reason and policy of the fiction, the other party may show the truth.'" Leg. Max. *129. A number of limitations have been put upon the doctrine of relation that are now unnecessary to consider. Perhaps as good a general statement of the subject as can be found in the books is in Jackson v. Davenport, 20 Johns. side pp. 537, 551, where it was said that the doctrine "is upheld to advance a right, not to advance a wrong, or to defeat collateral acts which are lawful, and especially if they concern strangers. This limitation of the fiction, so as to prevent it from doing injury to strangers or defeating mesne lawful acts, is the common language of the books." See, also, Butler and Baker's Case, 3 Rep. 25; 18 Viner's Abr. p. 285, tit. "Relation"; Heath v. Ross, 12 Johns. 140; Hawley v. Cramer, 4 Cow. 717; Jackson v. Douglass, 5 Cow. 458; Baker v. Wheeler, 8 Wend. 505, 24 Am. Dec. 66; Pratt v. Potter, 21 Barb. 580. The view that strangers who have a standing to go behind the legal fiction of relation and show the true time of acceptance, are not to be prejudiced by such doctrine, has often been recognized in this state. Fite v. Doe, 1 Blackf. 127; Goodsell v. Stinson, 7 Blackf. 437; Woodbury v. Fisher, 20 Ind. 387, 83 Am. Dec. 325; German, etc., Co. v. Grim, 32 Ind. 249, 2 Am. Rep. 341; Ridgeway v. Bank, 78

Ind. 119; Brenner v. Quick, 88 Ind. 546; Jones v. Loveless, 99 Ind. 317. The exception stated has been carried so far, as shown by some of the above authorities, as to refuse to permit deeds to operate by relation as against intervening attaching creditors and others in analogous situations. We think, however, that appellee Oscar was not a stranger in the ordinary sense. If we assume that there had been a constructive delivery to appellant by the elder Emmons—a matter concerning which said appellee was put on inquiry—it may be said that he is in privity with his grantor, and as applied to such a case we think that, as a subsequent grantee with notice, said appellee stands on no better footing than that occupied by his grantor. The theory that a constructive acceptance is possible is now thoroughly established, and, as all the cases travel upon the postulate that, to make a sufficient delivery, the deed must pass out of the dominion of the grantor, it ought scarcely be held that one claiming under him, but with notice of all the facts, could take title if the first grantee afterwards accepted the benefit of the prior delivery. In Stone v. Duvall, 77 Ill. 475, where a bill had been filed by a grantor to set aside a deed of which there had been only a constructive delivery, the Illinois Supreme Court said: "To cancel the deed would be to permit Duvall to change his mind, and to defeat his act, deliberately done after consultation and advice taken, and done in accordance with his previously expressed purpose to convey to Mrs. Stone." If the grantor could not defeat the deed by action, it would seem that he ought not to be able to do so by a deed executed to a party who received the same with knowledge of the facts. Although the authorities generally announce that the doctrine of relation is not to be applied to strangers, yet those who are in privity with the grantor are treated as bound, according to the general statements found in the cases. Heath v. Ross, 12 Johns. 140; Hawley v. Cramer, 4 Cow. 717; Jackson v. Douglass, 5 Cow. 458. See Fite v. Doe, 1 Blackf. 127; German, etc., Co. v. Grim, 32 Ind. 249, 2 Am. Rep. 341. In Butler and Baker's Case, 3 Rep. 25, 29, Lord Coke states "that, as relations shall extend only to the same thing, and to one and the same intent, so they shall extend only between the same parties, and never shall be strained to the prejudice of a third person who is not party or privy to the said act." The question as to whether appellee Oscar acquired a right superior to that of appellant, assuming that there had been a prior constructive delivery to her, is virtually determined against him by the case of Smiley v. Smiley, 114 Ind. 258, 16 N. E. 585.

We are not authorized to regard appellant as a grantee without equity. "Family agreements and settlements are treated with especial favor by the courts of equity, and equities are administered in regard to them which are not applied to agreements generally, and this on the ground that the honor and peace of families make it just and proper to do so." 12 Am. & Eng. Ency. of Law (2d Ed.) 875. In Souverbye v. Arden, 1 Johns. Ch. 240, 255, it was said by Chancellor Kent: "A voluntary settlement, fairly made, is always binding in equity upon the grantor, unless there be clear and decisive proof that he never parted, nor intended to part, with the possession of the deed." Assuming a valid delivery of the instrument in which appellant was named as grantee, the case seems one in which the fiction of relation should be resorted to in order to work out equity. We cannot uphold both instruments, and it seems clear under the circumstances that, if the first instrument was ever the deed of the elder Emmons, the subsequent acceptance of it should have relation back.

The important question in the case is as to the intent of said Emmons at the time he delivered said instrument to Blue. He could not have it take effect subsequently as a testamentary disposition of a portion of his property, and, if he intrusted said instrument to Blue as his (said Emmons') agent, it is obvious that it did not pass beyond his control, and was therefore subject to be reclaimed. Under our statute it is possible to create a freehold estate to commence in futuro (section 3379, Burns' Rev. St. 1901); but, if it was not designed by Emmons that there should be any grant until after his death, the instrument could not with propriety be termed his deed. It is enough, however, if such an instrument is delivered with the intent that an estate in land shall thereby pass, although it may be contemplated that the estate is not to be enjoyed in possession until after the grantor's death. Wilson v. Carrico, 140 Ind. 533, 40 N. E. 50, 49 Am. St. Rep. 213; Cates v. Cates, 135 Ind. 272, 34 N. E. 957.

It is said that a deed may be delivered by words without acts, or by acts without words. One or the other is necessary that there may be some indicia of the intent of the maker to deliver the instrument as his deed. The act or the word may unequivocally evince the purpose of the maker, particularly when the instrument is lodged with the grantee; and the question of delivery may thus become one of law, but ordinarily the question of delivery is largely one of fact. Dearmond v. Dearmond, 10 Ind. 191; Somers v. Pumphrey, 24 Ind. 231; Nye v. Lowry, 82 Ind. 316; Lindsay v. Lindsay, 11 Vt. 621; Jones v. Swayze, 42 N. J. Law, 279; Babbitt v. Bennett, 68 Minn. 260, 71 N. W. 22; Hibberd v. Smith, 67 Cal. 547, 4 Pac. 473, 8 Pac. 46, 56 Am. Rep. 726; Bury v. Young, 98 Cal. 446, 33 Pac. 338, 35 Am. St. Rep. 186; Murray v. Earl of Stair, 2 Barn. & C. 82. Some of the above cases are much in point. Thus, in Murray v. Earl of Stair, supra, it was said: "Upon further consideration we are all of opinion that there ought to be a new trial in this case, and that it should be presented as a question of fact for the jury upon the whole evidence whether the bond was delivered as a deed to take effect from the moment of such delivery, or whether it was delivered to Saunders upon the express condition that it was not to operate as a deed until the death of the then Lord Stair, and then only upon the delivery up of the two promissory notes." It is argued by counsel for appellees that the evidence fails to disclose a purpose to dispose of an estate which is to pass immediately, and it was further argued by them that the evidence shows that the deeds were turned over to Blue as the agent of the maker. We think, on the contrary, that there were several statements made by said Emmons at the time he turned over the papers which were sufficient to authorize an inference of an intent to deliver the instrument in question as his deed, and that, therefore, the question of intent should have been left to the jury.

Judgment reversed, and a new trial ordered.

(162 Ind. 165)

MEYER et al. v. TOWN OF BOONVILLE et al.

(Supreme Court of Indiana. Feb. 17, 1904.)

MUNICIPAL CORPORATIONS—FRANCHISE FOR PUBLIC UTILITIES—POWER OF BOARD OF TRUSTEES—STATUTES—CONSTRUCTION—INJUNCTION—PARTIES PLAINTIFF—ADEQUATE REMEDY AT LAW.

1. Under Acts 1899, p. 216, c. 131, § 1 (Burns' Rev. St. 1901, § 4443r), providing that no ordinance for the purpose of granting a franchise for the establishment of any lighting plant for a town shall go into effect until 30 days after its passage, nor until voted for at the polls, if within 30 days after its passage a referendum is demanded by 40 per cent. of the legal voters of the town. a franchise for such purpose can only be granted by ordinance.

2. Acts 1899, p. 216, c. 131, § 1 (Burns' Rev. St. 1901, § 4443r), provides that no ordinance for the purpose of granting a franchise for the establishment of a lighting plant for a town shall go into effect until 30 days after its passage, nor until voted for at the polls, if within 30 days after its passage a referendum is demanded by 40 per cent. of the legal voters of the town. Acts 1879, p. 201, c. 98, subd. 16 (Burns' Rev. St. 1901, § 4357), provides that the boards of trustees of towns shall have power to make such ordinances as may be necessary to carry into effect the provisions of the act, but that every ordinance, unless in case of emergency, shall be published or posted at least 10 days before the same shall take effect. *Held*, that the acts are pari materia, and must be construed together.

3. The emergency provision of Act 1879, p. 201, c. 98, subd. 16 (Burns' Rev. St. 1901, § 4357), providing that the board of trustees of towns shall have power to make such ordinances as may be necessary to carry into effect the provisions of the act, but that every ordinance, unless in case of emergency, shall be published, etc., has no application to an ordinance granting a franchise for the establishment of a lighting plant.

4. Acts 1899, p. 216, c. 131, § 1 (Burns' Rev. St. 1901, § 4443r), provides that no ordinance for the purpose of granting a franchise for the establishment of a lighting plant for a town shall go into effect until 30 days after its passage nor until voted for at the polls, if within 30 days after its passage a referendum is demanded by 40 per cent. of the legal voters of the town. Acts 1879, p. 201, c. 98, subd. 16 (Burns' Rev. St. 1901, § 4357), provides that the boards of trustees of towns shall have power to make such ordinances as may be necessary to carry into effect the provisions of the act, but that every ordinance, unless in case of emergency, shall be published or posted at least 10 days before the same shall take effect. *Held*, that an ordinance granting a franchise for the establishment of a lighting plant is void where no publication or posting was made.

5. Where the trustees of a town passed an ordinance granting a franchise to establish a lighting plant for a town, the invalidity of the ordinance carries with it a provision requiring the town to take and pay for a certain number of street lights.

6. The publication required by Acts 1879, p. 201, c. 98, subd. 16 (Burns' Rev. St. 1901, § 4357), providing that the board of trustees of towns shall have power to establish such ordinances as may be necessary to carry into effect the provisions of the act, but that every ordinance, unless in case of emergency, shall be published, etc., is not dispensed with by an ordinance granting a franchise for the establishment of a lighting plant, declaring an emergency, and providing that it should be enforced only when a written acceptance of it is filed with the clerk of the town.

7. A minority of resident taxpayers may maintain injunction for relief against a consummated illegal act of the board of trustees of a town on allegation that they are such taxpayers, when it is apparent that their interest and the injury complained of are not different in kind from that of the public in general within the corporate limits of the town.

8. The remedy at law to defeat an injunction must be as plain, complete, and adequate, or as practical and efficient to the ends of justice and its prompt administration, as the remedy in equity.

Appeal from Circuit Court, Warrick County; E. M. Swan, Judge.

Action by Louis J. Meyer and others against the town of Boonville and others. From a judgment for defendants, plaintiffs appeal. Reversed.

Gilchrist, De Bruler & Weiman, for appellants. Edward Gough and L. A. Folsom, for appellees.

MONKS, J. Appellants, who are resident taxpayers of the town of Boonville, brought this action against said town, the members of the board of trustees of said town, and the Boonville Electric Light & Power Company to set aside two ordinances and the contract for lighting the streets of said town contained in one of said ordinances, and to restrain the carrying out of said ordinances or the exercise of any rights thereunder. The separate demurrer for want of facts of each defendant was sustained to the complaint, and, appellants refusing to plead further, judgment was rendered in favor of appellees. Each of said rulings is assigned for error.

The following facts, among others, are alleged in the complaint and admitted by the demurrers: In January, 1901, the board of trustees of the town of Boonville adopted two ordinances, by one of which a franchise for 50 years was granted to the Boonville Electric Light & Power Company, a domestic corporation, to use the streets, alleys, and public grounds of said town for the purpose of laying and maintaining and operating mains, pipes, and conduits therein, and supplying "heat, power, light, refrigeration, and allied purposes" to said town and the inhabitants thereof; "said heat to consist of steam, gas, water, or any other mode of heating said company may see fit to use." The other ordinance granted the same corporation a franchise for 10 years for using the streets, alleys, and public grounds of said town for the purpose of erecting thereon poles, posts, wires, or other necessary appliances "for the purpose of furnishing electric or other kinds of light, and necessary for the purpose of furnishing said town and its inhabitants with such light." By section 5 of the last-named ordinance the town of Boonville agreed to take a certain number of street lights for five years at a fixed price per annum, to be paid quarterly, with the right to take the same or an increased number of lights at the same price for an additional period of five years. Each ordinance declared that: "Whereas an emergency exists for the immediate taking effect of this ordinance, the same shall be in force whenever a written acceptance shall be filed with the clerk of said town by said company." The officers of the Boonville Electric Light & Power Company were present when said ordinances were passed, and immediately thereafter, in the presence of the board of trustees of said town, made and filed a written acceptance of the provisions of each of said ordinances. No publication or posting of either of said ordinances was ever made.

The granting by the board of trustees of a town or the common council of a city of a franchise to use the streets, alleys, and public places therein to erect poles and posts and to suspend wires thereon to furnish electric light to such town or city and its inhabitants, or to lay "pipes, mains, and conduits" to furnish gas, water, light, or heat to such town or city and the inhabitants thereof, is the exercise of a legislative power. Eichels v. Evansville, etc., R. Co., 78 Ind. 261, 263, 41 Am. Rep. 561; Wood v. Mears, 12 Ind. 515, 521, 74 Am. Dec. 222; Indianapolis, etc., Co. v. State ex rel., 37 Ind. 489, 496, 497; Citizens', etc., Co. v. Town of Elwood, 114 Ind. 332, 16 N. E. 624; Grand Rapids, etc., Co. v. Grand Rapids, etc., Co. (C. C.) 33 Fed. 659, 669; Des Moines, etc., Co. v. City of Des Moines, 44 Iowa, 505, 24 Am. Rep. 756; Elliott's Roads and Streets (2d Ed.) §§ 450, 455; 2 Smith on Mod. Law Mun. Corp. § 1309; Dillon on Mun. Corp. (4th Ed.) §§ 683, 691, 697, 698. But when the town or city enters into a contract with a second party, having such franchise, to light its streets and public grounds and buildings, or to heat its public buildings and offices by steam, hot water, or otherwise, or to furnish gas for that purpose, it exercises a business, and not a legislative power. Town of Gosport v. Pritchard, 156 Ind. 400, 406, 59 N. E. 1058, and cases cited. In 1899 the General Assembly passed an act entitled "An act vesting a right in the voters of any incorporated town in the state of Indiana, by a petition to refer any ordinance, agreement, contract, or measure enacted or proposed by the board of trustees of any incorporated town of this state, to a vote of the voters of such town and to reject the same by ballot," etc. Acts 1899, p. 216, c. 131. The first section of said act, being section 4443r, Burns' Rev. St. 1901, provides: "That no ordinance for the purchase or establishment of any waterworks or lighting plant, or the granting of any franchise for the establishment or operation of any waterworks, lighting plant, street railroad, telephone or telegraph company in any incorporated town in this state, shall go into effect until thirty days after its passage, nor until voted for at the polls, if within the said thirty days a referendum is demanded by forty per cent. of the legal voters of such incorporated town as shown by the last preceding election." The other sections of the act make provision for the filing of said petition, its form, and the holding of an election. It is also provided that such ordinances shall not go into effect unless approved by a majority of the votes cast for and against the same. Appellants insist that the ordinances in question come within the provisions of said act of 1899, and could not take effect until after the publication thereof, as required by the sixteenth subdivision of section 4357, Burns' Rev. St. 1901 (Acts 1879, p. 201, c. 98); that by the express terms of said act of 1899 all agreements, contracts, and measures for any of the purposes mentioned in said act of 1899 must be by an ordinance, which cannot take effect until 30 days after its passage, and that, therefore, the emergency clause of said sixteenth subdivision could have no application thereto. The part of section 4357 Burns' Rev. St. 1901 (Acts 1879, p. 201, c. 98), mentioned, reads as follows: "The board of trustees shall have the following powers: * * * Sixteenth. To make and establish such by-laws, ordinances, and regulations, not repugnant to the laws of this state, as may be necessary to carry into effect the provisions of this act, and to repeal, alter, or amend the same as they shall seem to require, but every by-law, ordinance or regulation, unless in a case of emergency, shall be published in a newspaper in such town, if one be printed therein, or posted in five public places, at least ten days before the same shall take effect." Whatever may have been the manner in which incorporated towns were required to contract for the purchase or establishment of waterworks or lighting plants, or to grant a franchise for the establishment or operation of any waterworks, lighting plant, street railroad, telephone or telegraph line, before the taking effect of said act of 1899, being sections 4443r–4443bl, Burns' Rev. St. 1901, it is evident that since it took effect the same can only be done by an ordinance. It is clear, therefore, that the Legislature intended that all the rules, regulations, and requirements in regard to the enactment and taking effect of ordinances should apply to such an ordinance, unless otherwise provided in said act of 1899. Said sixteenth subdivision of section 4357, supra, and section 1 of said act of 1899, being section 4443r, supra, are in pari materia, and must be construed together. State v. Gerhardt, 145 Ind. 439, 460, 461, 44 N. E. 469, 33 L. R. A. 313, and authorities cited; Shea v. City of Muncie, 148 Ind. 14, 21, 46 N. E. 138, and cases cited; Black on Interpretation of Laws, p. 206. As section 1 of said act of 1899, being section 4443r, supra, provides in express terms that such ordinance shall not "go into effect until thirty days after its passage, it is evident that the provision of the sixteenth subdivision of section 4357, supra, in regard to ordinances taking effect "in case of emergency" without publication, can have no application to ordinances coming within said act of 1899, section 4443r, supra. There is no provision, however, of said act of 1899 which in any way dispenses with or prevents the publication of the ordinances covered thereby, as required by said sixteenth subdivision of section 4357, supra. To hold that said provision for publication in section 4357, supra, was dispensed with would in many cases defeat the very purpose for which said act of 1899, sections 4443r–4443bl, supra, was enacted—that of referendum. Publication would advise the voters of the town of such ordinances, and give them an opportunity to obtain the benefit of said act; but, if no publication were made, they would in many, if not all, cases have no knowledge of such ordinances until the 30 days within which a petition for referendum could be presented had expired. Construing said section 4443r, supra, and said sixteenth subdivision of section 4357, supra, together, as we are required to do (Shea v. City of Muncie, 148 Ind. 21, 46 N. E. 138), it is clear that an ordinance coming within said act of 1899, sections 4443r–4443bl, supra, can only go into effect 30 days after its passage, when publication thereof has been made, as required by said sixteenth subdivision of section 4357, supra, not less than 10 days before the expiration of said 30 days. It is therefore the duty of the board of trustees at once upon the passage of any ordinances coming within the provisions of said section 4443r, supra, to make publication thereof as required by said sixteenth subdivision of section 4357, supra. What was said in Town of Gosport v. Pritchard, 156 Ind. 400, 406, 59 N. E. 1058, cited by appellees, in regard to "an emergency clause" and "publication" being unnecessary, had reference only to contracts made by a town in the exercise of its purely business powers, and not to the exercise of its legislative powers. The contract to light the streets of the town sued upon in that case was made in 1897, long before said act of 1899 took effect. It will be observed that said act of 1899, sections 4443r–4443bl, supra, involved in this case, requires that contracts for the purchase or establishment of waterworks or a lighting plant shall be by ordinance, which we have held in this opinion cannot take effect unless publication thereof is made as required by section 4357, supra. To this extent the law declared in Town of Gosport v. Pritchard, supra, as to the contracts of a town in the exercise of its purely business power, was changed by said act of 1899.

Appellees insist that, even of the ordinance granting the franchise for 10 years to use the streets, alleys, and public places in the town to erect poles, posts, etc., to furnish electric light to the town and its inhabitants, is void, that the section thereof containing the contract of the town to take and pay for a certain number of street lights is not within the provisions of the act of 1899, sections 4443r–4443bl, and is therefore valid without a declaration of emergency or publication, being the exercise of a purely business power. The rule is that, if a part of a statute or ordinance is void, other essential and connected parts are also void, but when that part which is void is clearly independent, and not essentially connected with the remainder, the latter will stand. Griffith v. State, 119 Ind. 520, 522, 22 N. E. 7 et seq.; 1 Dillon on Munic. Corp. (4th Ed.) § 421; 1 Smith's Mod. Law of Munic. Corp. § 542; 1 Beach on Pub. Corp. § 518. And when an agreement is invalid in part only, the part which is good may be enforced if it can be separated from the part which is bad, but, if not capable of separation, the whole agreement is invalid, and cannot be enforced. Clark on Cont. pp. 470–475; Hynds v. Hays, 25 Ind. 36; Consumers' Oil Co. v. Nunnemaker, 142 Ind. 560, 568, 41 N. E. 1048, 51 Am. St. Rep. 193; Gas Light, etc., Co. v. City of New Albany, 156 Ind. 406, 413, 414, 59 N. E. 176. The part of the ordinance containing the contract for lighting the streets of said town is not independent of, but is dependent on, the other parts thereof, and is inseparably connected therewith. Said contract depends entirely upon the provisions of the ordinance granting the franchise, and the fall of the latter carries with it the former.

Appellees contend that, even if the ordinance for 50 years, so far as it grants a franchise for the operation of a lighting plant, is void, because the same is within the provisions of the act of 1899, sections 4443r–4443bl, yet, as the part of said ordinance which grants a franchise for supplying "heat, power, refrigeration, and allied purposes" is not covered by said act of 1899, it took effect on the emergency declared, without publication. The power given the board of trustees by said sixteenth subdivision of section 4357, supra, "in case of emergency," was to provide that the ordinance should take effect on its passage, or at some time fixed and certain, before publication could be had, and not that it should take effect on a contingency or event that might or might not occur. The declaration of emergency for the immediate taking effect of said ordinances is inconsistent with the provision that the same take effect on the happening of an uncertain event, for such an ordinance may never go into force. It is clear, therefore, that the declaration of an emergency for the immediate taking effect of each of said ordinances contained therein, followed by a provision that it shall be in force only when a written acceptance of the same is filed with the clerk of the town, an act which may never be performed, is not sufficient to dispense with the publication required by said sixteenth subdivision of section 4357, supra. As no publication was made of said ordinances as required by law, it follows that they are not in force.

It is next insisted that appellants cannot maintain injunction, because the alleged grievances do not affect them "peculiarly and in some manner different from the general public," citing Dwenger v. Chicago, etc., Co., 98 Ind. 153; Cummins v. City of Seymour, 79 Ind. 491, 41 Am. Rep. 618; McCowan v. Whitesides, 31 Ind. 235. It is true that in an action by a private person to enjoin a public nuisance the complaint must allege facts showing that he has sustained a special injury different in kind from that sustained by the general public. Martin v. Marks, 154 Ind. 549, 553-557, 57 N. E. 249, and cases cited. This principle, however, which obtained as to public nuisance, does not apply in this state to actions brought by a resident taxpayer of a municipal corporation to enjoin an illegal or wrongful act, or, if consummated, to have relief against it. In such cases it has been uniformly held that one or more resident taxpayers may maintain such actions upon a mere allegation that they were resident taxpayers of such municipal corporation, when it was apparent that their interest and the injury complained of were not different in kind from that of the public in general within such corporate limits, but were the same. City of Valparaiso v. Gardner, 97 Ind. 1, 8, 49 Am. Rep. 416; Harney v. Indianapolis, etc., R. Co., 32 Ind. 244, 247, 248, and cases cited; Sackett v. City of New Albany, 88 Ind. 473, 480, and cases cited, 45 Am. Rep. 467; City of Madison v. Smith, 83 Ind. 502, 515; Noble v. City of Vincennes, 42 Ind. 125; Myers v. City of Jeffersonville, 145 Ind. 431, 44 N. E. 452; Board, etc., v. Templeton, 51 Ind. 266; Rothrock v. Carr, 55 Ind. 334; Warren County, etc., Co. v. Barr, 55 Ind. 30; Board, etc., v. Gillies, 138 Ind. 667, 672, 673, 38 N. E. 40, and cases cited; Adams v. City of Shelbyville, 154 Ind. 467, 495, 57 N. E. 114, 49 L. R. A. 797, 77 Am. St. Rep. 484; Brashear v. City of Madison, 142 Ind. 685, 36 N. E. 252, 42 N. E. 349, 33 L. R. A. 474; Wilcoxen v. City of Bluffton, 153 Ind. 267, 54 N. E. 110; Campbell v. City of Indianapolis, 155 Ind. 186, 57 N. E. 920; Hurd v. Walters, 48 Ind. 148, 150, and authorities cited; Zuelly v. Casper, 160 Ind. 490, 67 N. E. 185; Id., 160 Ind. 455, 67 N. E. 103, 63 L. R. A. 133; Scott v. City of La Porte (Ind. Sup.) 68 N. E. 278; Kimble v. Board, etc. (Ind. App.) 66 N. E. 1023, 1026-1028. See, also, Dillon's Munic. Corp. §§ 908, 909, 914-919, 921, 922; 2 High on Injunctions (3d Ed.) § 1236; New London v. Brainard, 22 Conn. 552; Scofield v. Eighth School Dist., 27 Conn. 499, 504. It is not enough to defeat injunction that there is a remedy at law. It must be as plain, complete, and adequate—or, in other words, as practical and efficient to the ends of justice and its prompt administration—as the remedy in equity. Xenia, etc., Co. v. Macy, 147 Ind. 568, 572, 573, 47 N. E. 147; Sackett v. City of New Albany, 88 Ind. 473, 480, 45 Am. Rep. 467, and cases cited.

Other questions are argued in the briefs, but the view we have taken of the case renders their determination unnecessary.

Judgment reversed, with instructions to overrule each of the demurrers to the complaint, and for further proceedings not inconsistent with this opinion.

(162 Ind. 146)

HANCOCK et al. v. DIAMOND PLATE GLASS CO. et al.

(Supreme Court of Indiana. Feb. 16, 1904.)

CONTRACT FOR EXPLORATION FOR GAS—TERMINATION — FAILURE TO PAY RENT — COMPLAINT—SUFFICIENCY—TENANCY AT WILL.

1. A contract between a landowner and a corporation granted the latter the exclusive right of putting down a gas well on a tract of land, in consideration for which the corporation agreed to deliver the landowner natural gas free of charge, and to pay $20 each year until it should put down a gas well. It was provided that the contract should run from the date, and be terminated whenever natural gas ceased to be used generally for manufacturing purposes, or when the corporation should fail to pay the annual rent for 60 days after it became due. A complaint by the owner in an action to recover a stipulated annual sum for a number of years, and damages for failure to furnish free gas, set out the contract, and alleged that no well had been put down, nor possession of the premises taken; that gas was furnished free until a certain date, prior to the commencement of the action, and the annual sum of $20 paid each year until five years before the action was commenced; and that natural gas was and had been used for manufacturing purposes. *Held* to state a cause of action.

2. Where a contract between a landowner and a corporation gave the latter the exclusive right of putting down a gas well on certain property, and provided that, until this was done, it should pay $20 per year for the exclusive privilege, and that the contract should be deemed terminated whenever it should fail to pay the rental price within 60 days after it became

¶ 2. See Mines and Minerals, vol. 34, Cent. Dig. § 208.

due, failure to pay did not terminate the contract, but merely gave the landowner the right to do so.

3. A contract between a landowner and a corporation, giving the latter the exclusive right to bore for gas, and providing that the corporation should pay a certain sum annually until it had put down a gas well, but that the contract should be terminated whenever natural gas ceased to be used generally for manufacturing purposes, or whenever the corporation should fail to pay the annual rental within 60 days after it became due, did not create a tenancy at will, within Burns' Rev. St. 1901, § 7089, providing that all general tenancies in which the premises are occupied by the consent, either express or constructive, of the landlord, shall be deemed tenancies at will.

Appeal from Superior Court, Howard County; Hiram Brownlee, Judge.

Action by Anna E. Hancock and others against the Diamond Plate Glass Company and others. From a judgment for defendants, plaintiffs appealed to the Appellate Court, from whence the cause was transferred to this court, under Burns' Rev. St. 1901, § 1337u. Reversed.

B. C. Moon, for appellants. Bell & Perdum and Blacklidge, Shirley & Wolf, for appellees.

HADLEY, J. Contract for exploring for natural gas. Suit to recover stipulated sum for delay in putting down a well. On June 18, 1891, appellants and appellee Diamond Plate Glass Company entered into a written contract whereby appellants "granted and contracted" to said appellee and its assigns 20 feet square of a certain described tract of 40 acres, to be located by mutual agreement, for the purpose and with the exclusive right of putting down a gas well thereon, with the right of ingress and egress, and to lay pipe and conduct gas therefrom. As a consideration for the grant, the gas company agreed to deliver to appellants, in the highway nearest their dwelling house on said 40 acres, free of charge, during the continuance of the contract, whatever amount of natural gas was necessary for domestic use in said dwelling, and, in addition thereto, to pay appellants on September 1st of each year $100 for each producing gas well drilled on the premises, and, until the company should put down a gas well on said premises, the company agreed to pay appellants on September 1st of each year $20 at the office of the company, in Kokomo. Appellants, on their part, further "covenanted and agreed," for themselves, their heirs, executors, and assigns, "not to drill, or suffer or permit others to drill, or put down, any other gas well, or wells, on any part of said entire forty-acre tract of land during the continuance of this contract." It was further covenanted that "this contract shall be deemed to commence at, and run from the date of signing hereof, and shall be deemed to have terminated whenever natural gas ceases to be used generally for manufacturing purposes, or whenever the second party [the gas company], or their assigns, shall fail to pay or tender the rental price, herein agreed upon, within sixty days of the date of its becoming due. And in the event of the termination hereof, for any cause, all rights and liabilities hereunder shall cease and terminate." It will be observed that there was no limit to the duration of the contract, except "when natural gas ceases to be used generally for manufacturing purposes," and that no time was fixed for the commencement or completion of a gas well. The Diamond Plate Glass Company assigned said contract to the Pittsburg Plate Glass Company, which assigned the same to appellee the Logansport & Wabash Valley Gas Company; each assignee, in turn, agreeing to perform all the covenants of the assignor. No gas well was ever put down or commenced on said premises, and none has been demanded or requested by appellants, though they were always ready and willing for the same to be done. No possession of the premises was ever taken. Natural gas was furnished appellants, free of charge, under the contract, from November 1, 1891, to December 25, 1900, when the supply was cut off by appellee Logansport & Wabash Valley Gas Company. The annual sum of $20 to be paid during the delay in sinking a well was paid, according to the contract, on each September 1st, from 1891 to 1895, inclusive, and sued for and recovered by appellants for the year 1896. Natural gas has been all the time since the execution of said contract, and still is, used generally for manufacturing purposes. There has been no forfeiture or surrender, or termination of the contract, further than may be implied by the failure of appellees to pay the annual sum of $30 since September 1, 1896, and the cutting off of appellants' free gas on December 25, 1900. The complaint founded on the written contract was filed September 19, 1902, and seeks to recover the stipulated annual sum of $20 for the several years from September 1, 1897, to September 1, 1902, inclusive, and damages in the sum of $75 for failure to furnish free gas from December 25, 1900, to the commencement of the suit. The contract and all the foregoing facts are fully and specifically set forth in the complaint. Appellees' demurrer to the complaint for insufficiency of facts was sustained, and, appellants refusing to amend, judgment was rendered against them for costs.

The only question presented by the appeal is the sufficiency of the complaint. Is it sufficient to constitute a cause of action? It seems to us, from the nature of the action—it being a suit for damages for breach of a covenant to pay—and facts averred in the complaint, that the name of the contract sued on, or the class to which it belongs, and whether it creates a lease, a license, or an easement, or either, is wholly immaterial, and will not warrant discussion, though argued at length by the parties. The subject-matter is one concerning which the parties might lawfully contract, and, having contracted, our simple duty, within the limits of settled principles, is to see that it is kept in accordance with the mutual understanding and agreement of the parties at the time it was made.

What, then, are the terms of the agreement? It will be observed that the contract clearly provides that it shall continue in force as long as gas is generally used for manufacturing purposes, be that 1 or 40 years. No time is agreed upon for the commencement or the completion of a well, and no express provision that one shall ever be constructed; but it is made very plain that no one but the glass company shall have the right to put down a well anywhere on the 40 acres "during the continuance of the contract," or so long as natural gas shall be used generally for manufacturing purposes. In other words, under the contract, the company, in unmistakable terms, has the exclusive right to take and control the output of gas from appellants' 40 acres during the period of supply. It may enter the premises tomorrow, sink a well, and extract through it the gas from under appellants' land, or, if it prefers, with appellants' acquiescence, it may postpone an entry, exclude others from the premises, save the expense of making a well, and draw the gas from under the land through its well, on other premises, on the other side of the road. So far as appellants are concerned, by the contract they surrendered to the glass company, for an agreed consideration, all the right and dominion they were able to bestow to all the gas underlying their 40 acres of land; the company to take its chance on the quantity, and pursue its own method in mining it, within the limits of the contract. On the part of the company, it agreed, in equally certain terms, to give appellants, for the valuable concession, a supply of free gas for domestic use, and pay them $20 in cash, not for one year, but for every year that might elapse before it made a well on the premises, and thereafter $100 per annum for each well. As we have seen, the company has not bound itself to construct a gas well on appellants' land within any specified time; but, so long as natural gas continues in general use for manufacturing purposes, it has bound itself to pay the annual sum of $20 until it does make such a well. The parties themselves have agreed upon the thing to be done, and the exact amount to be paid when done, and for the delay in the doing of it, and we cannot look beyond the agreement. It is not to be supposed for a moment that either party understood when the contract was entered into that the company was to have these valuable and continuing rights without rendering to appellants what was deemed to be a coequal, valuable, continuing consideration. Nor is it to be doubted that it was the mutual understanding that, as long as the company excluded others from mining the gas on appellants' land, it should be liable for the sum it agreed to pay for the right to do so. We must so view the agreement, because in accord with the plain, simple meaning of its terms, and in harmony with a proper sense of fairness and natural justice.

Is the contract still running? This question must be answered in the affirmative, unless it appears that it has expired by limitation, or been surrendered, forfeited, or otherwise terminated. It has not expired by limitation, for we are informed by the complaint that natural gas has been, all the time since the making of the contract, and still is, generally used for manufacturing purposes. It has not been surrendered. The complaint avers that no surrender has been made, and affirmatively shows that appellants, on their part, demanded, sued for, and recovered the first annual payment defaulted (1896), and are now in court, suing for all other due and unpaid installments, and that appellee, on its part, continued to make voluntary payments to 1896, and to supply appellants with the stipulated free gas from the beginning of the contract to December 25, 1900. There is no pretense on the part of appellee that anything transpired on December 25, 1900, to terminate the contract, beyond the shutting off of appellants' gas on that day; and this continued part performance, in the absence of any explanation thereof, is of itself sufficient acknowledgment that the contract was in force to that time. The complaint shows no forfeiture of the contract. It is averred that appellants have performed all the conditions on their part to be performed. But appellee claims that it terminated the contract in 1896, by failing for more than 60 days to pay the stipulated annual $20, called "rent," and relies upon that part of the contract which is expressed in these words: "This contract shall be deemed to commence at, and run from the date of signing hereof, and shall be deemed to have terminated whenever natural gas ceases to be used generally for manufacturing purposes, or whenever the second party [the glass company], its heirs, or assigns, shall fail to pay, or tender, the rental price herein agreed upon, within sixty days of the date of its becoming due. And in the event of the termination hereof, for any cause, all rights and liabilities hereunder shall cease and terminate." The promise to pay for what it received from the appellants was the covenant of the appellee, made for the sole benefit of appellants, and the manifest absurdity of the latter part of the provision makes it plain that the contract cannot be enforced according to its letter. A promise to pay cannot be fulfilled by a failure to pay. Performance cannot be effected by nonperformance, nor a covenant satisfied by 60 days' default. A similar provision found in many such instruments has led courts to look critically after the real intent of the parties; and in cases like this, and where it is not expressly provided that "either party" or that the covenantor shall have the right, it has been uniformly held, so far as we have observed, that the right of forfeiture may be exercised by the covenantee, and not by the covenantor. Such a provision is made for the security of the one who is to be benefited by a fulfillment of the promise, and not for the benefit of the one whose interest lies in nonfulfillment. Such contracts are construed to mean that upon failure of the operator to pay the well rental, or the promised sum for delay in beginning operations, the landowner may elect to put an end to the contract, and recover what is due him, or he may waive his right of forfeiture, and allow the contract to run, and enforce payments as provided in that instrument. An operator will not be allowed to set up his own default or wrong in discharge of his obligation to a landowner to pay for what he has bought. There is no doubt but an operator may be relieved of his obligation to put down a well, or to pay the sum promised for his failure, upon such terms as may be agreed upon in the contract, either of benefit to the landowner, or of inconvenience to himself; but a naked default or nonperformance, such as is set up in this case, cannot be held to discharge his obligation. Leatherman v. Oliver, 151 Pa. 646, 25 Atl. 309; Cochran v. Pew, 159 Pa. 184, 28 Atl. 219; Oil Company v. Crawford, 55 Ohio St. 161, 176, 44 N. E. 1093, 34 L. R. A. 62; Smith v. Miller, 49 N. J. Law, 521, 13 Atl. 39; Jackson v. O'Hara, 183 Pa. 233, 38 Atl. 624; Ahrns v. Gas Co., 188 Pa. 249, 41 Atl. 739; Edmonds v. Mounsey, 15 Ind. App. 399, 44 N. E. 196; Simpson v. Glass Co., 28 Ind. App. 343, 62 N. E. 753; Thornton's Law Relating to Oil & Gas, §§ 149, 151, and authorities collated; Barringer & Adams' Law of Mines, p. 148. We are unable to see how the principles pertaining to the relation of landlord and tenant are applicable to such a contract as the one before us, either where possession has or has not been taken under the contract. It seems to have been held in Diamond Plate Glass Co. v. Curless, 22 Ind. App. 346, 52 N. E. 782, and Same v. Echelbarger, 24 Ind. App. 124, 55 N. E. 233, that similar instruments, granting the right to explore for and remove gas or oil for an indefinite period, are, in effect, leases creating tenancies from year to year, under section 7089, Burns' Rev. St. 1901, which may be terminated by the tenant at the end of any year, without notice. But we cannot accept this view as correct. While a contract providing for an entry and removal of gas or oil from the premises is, perhaps, more than a license, we are unable to believe that it constitutes such a tenancy as is contemplated by sections 7089 and 7090 of the statute. It must be agreed that such a contract is equally binding on the parties to it. Suppose, for instance, that, under such a contract as this one, the operator shall enter and drill in a well which yields a much greater volume of gas, and is therefore much more valuable, than was anticipated by the landowner when he made the bargain; will any one contend that the latter may avoid his contract and eject the operator by a three-months notice to quit before the end of the first year, under section 7090? And yet this is precisely what the doctrine leads to. There appears from the complaint no good reason why the contract should not be enforced against appellees.

Judgment reversed, with instructions to overrule the demurrer to the complaint.

(162 Ind. 136)

WHISLER v. WHISLER et al.

(Supreme Court of Indiana. Feb. 16, 1904.)

APPEAL—ASSIGNMENTS OF ERROR—SUFFICIENCY—TRANSCRIPT.

1. On appeal the certified transcript of the record imports absolute verity, and statements of parties in a verified petition are not available to either dispute the record or to supply anything not therein disclosed.

2. Inasmuch as it is not the practice to demur to an assignment of errors, or to move to make them more specific, an assignment must be treated as though challenged for a deficiency.

3. Burns' Rev. St. 1901, § 2766 (Horner's Rev. St. 1901, § 2596), provides that the executors of a will under contest, and all others beneficially interested, shall be made defendants to the action. A complaint seeking to set aside a will, made the executor, L., a defendant in his representative capacity, but he was subsequently defaulted, and judgment rendered affirming the validity of the will, and on appeal by plaintiff the assignment of errors merely described one of the appellees as "L., executor." *Held*, that a contention on appeal that the executor, in his representative capacity, was not a necessary appellee, and that hence the assignment of errors was not insufficient for failing to describe the defendant executor in his representative capacity, was without merit, and the Supreme Court had no jurisdiction.

Petition to reinstate appeal. Denied.

For former opinion, see 67 N. E. 984.

JORDAN, J. Appellant has filed a petition praying that his appeal be reinstated on the docket of this court. The grounds assigned are substantially the following: (1) That the court erred in holding that Cornelius Lumaree, executor of the will of John Whisler, deceased, and Lewis Signs, trustee thereunder, were necessary parties to the appeal, or that either of them had any interest in the judgment from which the appeal is prosecuted. (2) That the names of all parties having an interest in the judgment below were named in full compliance with rule 6 of this court (45 N. E. v). (3) That it appears by the record that Lumaree, the executor of the will in question, was defaulted before the trial, and thereby passed out of the case, and that no judgment was rendered either in his favor or against him. (4) That Signs, the trustee, never accepted his trust, and therefore could not be a party defendant; that he was not brought into court either individually or in his trust capacity.

The petitioner's counsel, in their argument, insist that the names of all the parties interested in the judgment below, or who in any manner are affected thereby, are fully and correctly set out in the assignment of errors. The argument is further advanced that, inasmuch as Lumaree, the executor of the will, was defaulted before final judgment of the court was rendered whereby the validity of the will was affirmed, he in no sense can be said to be a party to such judgment, and hence has no interest in the appeal. It is said that it is disclosed by the verified petition herein that he was not the executor of the will at the time of the trial in this cause for the reason that he had been finally discharged prior thereto. In regard to Signs, the trustee, it is claimed that he was not served with process, and did not appear in the action. It may be said in passing that it must be remembered that in appeals to this court the certified transcript of the record imports upon its face absolute verity, and statements of parties or their counsel, whether verified or unverified, are not available to dispute the record, or to supply any matter not therein disclosed. Consequently appellant's statement in his petition that Lumaree, the executor of the will, had been discharged as such executor before the final judgment was rendered, is not available in the determination of that question.

We may properly note some of the things shown by the record in this cause. It appears that the purpose of the action was to contest and set aside, for several reasons, the last will of John Whisler, deceased. In this will the testator nominated and appointed Cornelius Lumaree the executor thereof, and, among other things, he, as such executor, was directed by the will to sell and convey certain property, and to pay the proceeds thereof over to Lewis Signs, as trustee, to be held by him in trust as therein provided. By section 2766, Burns' Rev. St. 1901 (section 2596, Horner's Rev. St. 1901), the executor of a will under contest, and all other persons beneficially interested therein, are required to be made defendants to the action. It is shown that the appellant herein, plaintiff below, filed an amended complaint in three paragraphs, whereby he challenged the validity of the will of John Whisler, deceased. To this complaint he made "Cornelius Lumaree, executor of the estate of John Whisler, deceased, with the will annexed," one of the defendants. As such defendant he appeared and successfully demurred for want of facts to each paragraph of the amended complaint, and thereupon leave by the court was granted to the plaintiff to amend the third paragraph of the complaint, and to file additional paragraphs thereto. The third paragraph appears to have been amended, and four additional paragraphs were filed, and made a part of the complaint. Under these paragraphs "Cornelius Lumaree, executor of the estate of John Whisler, deceased, with the will annexed," was continued as one of the defendants. Lewis Signs, trustee, and Lewis Signs in his individual capacity, together with others, were also made defendants. Some time subsequent to the filing of these additional paragraphs the record discloses that Lumaree, the executor of the will or estate of John Whisler, deceased, together with three other defendants, viz., David, John, and William Whisler, were called, and defaulted, and thereupon the cause was submitted to the court for a trial, and after hearing the evidence the court rendered a final judgment to the effect that the will in suit was valid, and ought not to be set aside on the grounds alleged in the plaintiff's complaint. Counsel's contention that, because Lumaree, the executor, was defaulted after he had successfully demurred to the paragraphs of the complaint as shown, but before the rendition of the final judgment, he was not affected by such judgment, and is not a necessary party appellee in this appeal, is certainly untenable. It will be observed by an examination of the assignment of errors as they appear in the principal opinion that two of the specifications of errors are based on the rulings of the trial court in sustaining "the demurrer of Lumaree, executor, to the first and second paragraphs of the amended complaint." Appellant's very act in making Lumaree, "executor," and also David, John, and William Whisler, parties appellee to the appeal, is certainly inconsistent with his present contention that these parties, by reason of their being defaulted, were not affected by the judgment, or interested in this appeal. Lumaree, the executor of the will in question, under the requirements of the statute cited, was not only a proper, but a necessary, defendant to the action; and the mere fact that he had been defaulted before the beginning of the trial did not excuse appellant from making him a party appellee in his fiduciary capacity in this appeal. Michigan, etc., Ins. Co. v. Frankel, 151 Ind. 534, 538, 50 N. E. 304. This rule applies as well in the case of an appellee as it does in regard to a co-appellant. Abshire v. Williamson, 149 Ind. 248, 48 N. E. 1027. The true test, as a general rule, for determining who should be made an appellee in an appeal to this court, is, has the party an interest in maintaining the judgment from which the appeal is prosecuted? Ewbank's Manual, § 149; Elliott's App. Proc. § 160. Appellant in the lower court was interested in overthrowing the will, and in this court he is interested in securing a reversal of the judgment by which the validity thereof was affirmed. The executor of the will, as a party below, was interested in a legal sense in defeating the overthrow of the will, and in this court he is certainly interested in sustaining the judgment by which its validity was affirmed by the trial court. His position below, under the circumstances, was certainly hostile or adverse to that of appellant, and as the appeal, in effect, may be said to be a continuation of the litigation, his attitude or interest is not thereby changed, but continues to be adverse to that of appellant. Elliott's App. Proc. § 159. Under the circumstances it was certainly necessary for appellant to make him, in his representative capacity, one of the appellees in the appeal, for it is an elementary rule of appellate procedure that, before the court will proceed to adjudicate upon the subject-matter of a cause, it must first acquire jurisdiction over all the parties whose rights or interests will be affected by the judgment rendered. Michigan, etc., Ins. Co. v. Frankel, supra; Abshire v. Williamson, supra; Lowe v. Turpie, 147 Ind. 652, 44 N. E. 25, 47 N. E. 150, 37 L. R. A. 233. As it was essential, in order to maintain the appeal in this cause, that all parties adverse to appellant should be named as appellees, the failure of appellant to comply with this requirement would necessarily have resulted in the dismissal of his appeal. O'Mara v. Wabash, etc., R. R. Co., 150 Ind. 648, 50 N. E. 821; Cole v. Franks, 147 Ind. 281, 46 N. E. 532; National Home, etc., Ass'n v. Huntsinger, 150 Ind. 702, 50 N. E. 381, and authorities there cited. It being necessary, for the reasons stated, for appellant to name Cornelius Lumaree, executor of the will of John Whisler, deceased, as an appellee, his failure to name and describe him as such in his assignment of errors would, in effect, be the equivalent of entirely omitting his name in his fiduciary capacity as appellee in the assignment, and under such circumstances the appeal would be dismissed.

It is not the practice in this court for parties to formally demur to an assignment of errors, or to move to make such pleading more certain or specific; hence the assignment made must be treated and considered by the court as though it had been challenged by an appellant's adversary for a deficiency therein. In considering the sufficiency of an assignment of errors, all ambiguities or uncertainties therein will be construed against the pleading. The court cannot indulge any presumptions, and thereby supply what the appellant, by his pleading, may have possibly or probably intended. Merely placing the word "executor" after "Cornelius Lumaree," without a further designation or description to show that he was the executor of some particular will, would be but the equivalent of naming him as appellee in his individual capacity. The term "executor," under such circumstances, would not serve to indicate that he was named as appellee in some particular fiduciary capacity or character. In Brown, Ex'r of Phillips, v. Hicks, Adm'r of Phillips, 1 Ark. 232, the court said: "There is a striking and wide difference between the averment in a declaration, 'executor, or being executor as aforesaid,' and the direct allegation 'as executor aforesaid.' In one instance 'executor, or being executor as aforesaid,' are mere words of description, having exclusive reference to personal identity. In the other the term 'as executor aforesaid,' has but one meaning, which is fixed by law, and that is the party against whom the charge is made is sued in his representative character. This being the case, the defendant in the action is not charged as the executor of Thomas Phillips, deceased, for the declaration nowhere alleges that he was sued as such, and the words used, 'executor as aforesaid,' are mere matters of description and surplusage, and the antecedent, as aforesaid, refers only to the personal description of the defendant." Certainly, unless we indulge in presumptions, it cannot be said that Lumaree was the executor of the will of John Whisler, deceased, and had been named as an appellee to the appeal in his representative capacity.

It is unnecessary that we consider further the question presented in respect to Signs, trustee, under the will, because the failure of appellant to properly name Lumaree the executor of the will must operate to dismiss the appeal, regardless of the question as to Signs.

After again giving the question in respect to the dismissal of the appeal herein a careful consideration, we are still satisfied that it was properly dismissed, and therefore the petition to reinstate is overruled.

(162 Ind. 210)

MARSH v. MARSH.

(Supreme Court of Indiana. Feb. 19, 1904.)

DIVORCE — ALIMONY — JUDGMENT — INSTALLMENTS—ENFORCEMENT—EXECUTION—CONTEMPT.

1. An order in a suit for divorce directing defendant to pay to the clerk for the support of plaintiff the sum of $4 a week until further order of the court, was in violation of Burns' Rev. St. 1901, § 1059, providing for a sum in gross.

2. A judgment for alimony under Burns' Rev. St. 1901, § 1059, is enforceable by execution, and not by proceedings for contempt.

Appeal from Circuit Court, Wells County; E. C. Vaughn, Judge.

Proceeding by Bessie Marsh against Fred Marsh to punish defendant for contempt for failing to comply with an order directing the payment of alimony. From a judgment dismissing the application, plaintiff appeals. Transferred from Appellate Court under section 1337u, Burns' Rev. St. 1901. Affirmed.

Mock & Sons, for appellant. Dailey, Simmons & Dailey, for appellee.

GILLETT, C. J. In connection with a decree of divorce rendered in favor of appellant against appellee it was ordered that appellee pay into the office of the clerk of said county, for the support of appellant, the sum of $4 each week from March 1, 1902, until

¶ 2. See Divorce, vol. 17, Cent. Dig. § 754.

the further order of court. September 9, 1902, on the application of appellant, appellee was cited for contempt for a failure to obey said order. On his motion the court struck out said application. Section 1059, Burns' Rev. St. 1901, provides: "The decree for alimony to the wife shall be for a sum in gross, and not for annual payments, but the court in its discretion may give a reasonable time for the payment thereof, by installments, on sufficient surety being given." In Miller v. Clark, 23 Ind. 370, there is pointed out the fact of the reversal of the legislative policy in substituting for divorce a mensa et thoro, with its incidental provision for the maintenance of the wife during the separation, a provision for an absolute divorce a vinculo matrimonii, and the payment of a fixed sum to the wife, in bar of any future claim for her support. "The allowance so authorized," said the court in the above case, "is named 'alimony' in the statute; but it is not the alimony of the common law, the right to which ceased to exist or reverted to the husband on the death of the wife, resulting from the fact that the marriage relation continued to exist until her death. But it is alimony under, and the creature of, the statute, given upon an equitable settlement between the parties upon the dissolution of the marriage and of all the relations of husband and wife theretofore existing between them." In providing that that portion of the decree in divorce cases relative to the provision for the wife shall not be for annual payments, it was evidently the purpose of the Legislature to prohibit all indefinite allowances for her support, and to require the court to confine its allowance to her to a fixed sum, on the theory that thenceforth the parties were to be strangers to each other. It is clear that the order in question does not conform to the statute, but we are not called upon to determine whether the order is void or only voidable. It is sufficient to dispose of this case to hold, as we are required to, that the order cannot be enforced by means of a proceeding for contempt. The allowance which the statute contemplates may be made to the wife on the rendition of a decree of divorce is to all intents and purposes a judgment, which may be collected on execution. Musselman v. Musselman, 44 Ind. 106. It has been held that suit may be maintained on such an allowance (Hansford v. Van Auken, 79 Ind. 302), and that it is a proper claim to file in an attachment proceeding. Farr v. Buckner, 32 Ind. 382. If the order in question is only voidable, we deem it clear, nevertheless, that the departure from the statute did not invest the trial court with any power to enforce its order by a method not authorized for the enforcement of what may be termed "statutory alimony." The fact that the alimony contemplated by statute is in the nature of an ordinary judgment, which may be enforced by execution, creates a strong implication against the existence of the prior and more drastic remedy of contempt, and this implication is strengthened by the express provision concerning the enforcement of certain interlocutory orders in such cases by attachment, and by the granting of a like remedy to enforce the allowance for the reasonable expenses of the wife in prosecuting or defending the action, when the divorce is granted the wife or refused on the application of the husband. The action of the Wells circuit court in dismissing the contempt proceeding against appellee was proper.

Judgment affirmed.

(163 Ind. 112)

TOMLINSON v. BAINAKA et al.*

(Supreme Court of Indiana. Feb. 23, 1904.)

PARTITION FENCES — ERECTION — STATUTES — PROCEEDINGS—CONSTITUTIONALITY —PLEADINGS.

1. Acts 1897, p. 184, c. 122 (Burns' Rev. St. 1901, § 6568), relative to partition fences, and providing for proceedings for the erection of the same, contains a proviso that persons owning land not inclosed by a fence to retain stock shall not be required to make or maintain a partition fence. *Held* that, inasmuch as such proviso is not contained in the enacting clause of the statute, a complaint in an action to enforce a lien for building a fence was not insufficient because it did not allege that the lands therein described were inclosed by a fence to retain stock.

2. Burns' Rev. St. 1901, § 6565, relative to partition fences and the proceedings for the erection of the same, describes seven kinds of fences, either of which is declared to be a lawful fence, but requires the township trustee to adopt "the plans and materials for such fence as is most commonly used by farmers in the township." *Held*, that in proceedings for the erection of a fence it was proper for the township trustee to limit the kinds of fence which might be erected to those varieties most commonly used in the township.

3. Where, in an action to foreclose a statutory lien for building a partition fence, defendant's answer was a general denial, it was necessary for plaintiff to prove all the facts necessary to give the township trustee authority to contract for the building of the fence, etc., as provided for by the statute (Burns' Rev. St. 1901, § 6566).

4. Where a demurrer was sustained to certain paragraphs of an answer other than the general denial, but all the evidence admitted was admissible under the general denial, any error in sustaining the demurrer was harmless.

5. Inasmuch as a suit to foreclose a statutory lien for building a partition fence under Acts 1897, p. 184, c. 122 (Burns' Rev. St. 1901, §§ 6564-6569), was one calling for the equity powers of the court, it was not error to deny a trial by jury.

6. Burns' Rev. St. 1901, § 6566, relative to the erection of partition fences and proceedings therefor, requires that the statement which the township trustee gives to the contractor on the completion of the fence shall be recorded in the mechanic's lien record of the county. *Held*, that such provision is not ineffective for the reason that there is no such record as the mechanic's lien record, but there is a compliance with the statute where the statement is filed in the record in which mechanics' liens are required to be recorded.

7. Acts 1897, p. 184, c. 122 (Burns' Rev. St. 1901, §§ 6564-6569), provides proceedings for

*Rehearing denied June 3, 1904.

the erection of partition fences, and it is made the duty of the township trustee to determine whether any fence shall be built, or an old one repaired, and what proportion of the cost shall be borne by a defaulting landowner. The trustee is required to estimate the cost of building, and to deliver to the defaulting owner an itemized statement of the cost of building, in performing which duties the trustee determines the sufficiency of the existing fence. If the defaulting landowner, within 20 days after notice from the township trustee, builds the fence, the township trustee must determine its sufficiency, and, if it is not built as required, the trustee is required to let the contract after due notice. *Held*, that the statute is not open to the objection that it is in violation of the fourteenth amendment of the federal Constitution on the ground that it provides no tribunal to determine the sufficiency of the existing fence, and no means of testing the sufficiency of the fence built by the landowner after notice.

8. Acts 1897, p. 184, c. 122 (Burns' Rev. St. 1901, §§ 6564-6569), providing for the erection of partition fences and foreclosure of lien therefor where they are erected by the township trustee pursuant to the statute, is not violative of Const. art. 1, § 20, as denying the right of trial by jury, merely because the statute does not provide how the action to foreclose the lien shall be tried; that matter being governed by section 412, providing generally how causes shall be tried.

9. Const. art. 1, § 20, prohibiting the denial of right of trial by jury, applies only to such cases as were treated as civil cases when the Constitution was adopted, and is not applicable to Acts 1897, p. 184, c. 122 (Burns' Rev. St. 1901, §§ 6564-6569), providing for the erection of partition fences and proceedings for the foreclosure of the lien therefor.

10. Acts 1897, p. 184, c. 122 (Burns' Rev. St. 1901, §§ 6564-6569), providing for the erection of partition fences and proceedings for the foreclosure of a lien where a partition fence has been erected by the township authorities after default of a landowner, is not violative of Const. art. 1, § 21, providing that no man's property shall be taken by law without just compensation.

11. A party will not be heard to question the constitutionality of a statute unless he shows that some right of his is impaired or prejudiced thereby.

Appeal from Superior Court, Marion County; James M. Leathers, Judge.

Action by George W. Bainaka and others against Frank M. Tomlinson to foreclose a statutory lien for building a partition fence. From a judgment in favor of plaintiffs, defendant appeals. Affirmed.

John S. Berryhill, for appellant. Wm. T. Brown, for appellees.

MONKS, J. Appellee brought this action against appellant to foreclose a statutory lien for building a partition fence between the land of appellant and another under the act of 1897 (Acts 1897, p. 184, c. 122, being sections 6564-6569, Burns' Rev. St. 1901). A trial of said cause resulted in a finding, and, over a motion for a new trial, a judgment in favor of appellee. The errors assigned and not waived call in question the action of the court in overruling appellant's demurrer to the amended complaint, in sustaining appellee's demurrer to the second and fourth paragraphs of answer, and in overruling appellant's motion for a new trial.

It is insisted by appellant that said amended complaint was insufficient, because it was not alleged that "the lands therein described were inclosed by fence to retain stock"; citing section 6568, Burns' Rev. St. 1901, being section 5 of said act of 1897. Said section provides that "persons owning land not inclosed by fence to retain stock shall not be required to make or maintain a partition fence." The rule is that, when the exception is in the enacting clause, it must be negatived in the pleading, but when it is in a subsequent section, or in a separate proviso in the same section, it need not be. Black on Interpretation of Laws, p. 272; Sedgwick on Const. of Statutes (2d Ed.) 50; Bliss on Code Pleading (3d Ed.) § 202; Heard's Stephen on Pleading, *443; Crawford v. State, 155 Ind. 692, 695, 696, 57 N. E. 931, and authorities cited; State v. Maddox, 74 Ind. 105; U. S. v. Cook, 17 Wall. 168, 21 L. Ed. 538; First Baptist Church v. Utica, etc., R. Co., 6 Barb. (N. Y.) 313, 319, and cases cited; Foster v. Hazen, 12 Barb. 547, 550; Faribault v. Hulett, 10 Minn. 30, 38 (Gil. 15); Toledo, etc., R. Co. v. Pence, 68 Ill. 524, 527, 528; Vanvasour v. Ormond, 6 Barn. & Cress. 430, 432; Steele v. Smith, 1 Barn. & Ald. 99. As the provision referred to by appellant is in a subsequent section of the act, under said rule it was not necessary to the sufficiency of the complaint that it be negatived therein.

Appellant next insists that the "statute provides for seven kinds of lawful partition fence, and as the township trustee, in violation of the statute, limited the kind to be built in this case to a less number, the complaint is insufficient for that reason." It is true that section 6565, supra, describes seven kinds of fences, either one of which is declared to be a lawful partition fence; but said section requires the township trustee to adopt "the plans and materials for such fence as is most commonly used by the farmers of such township." Under this provision it was the duty of the township trustee to limit the kinds of fence as therein provided.

Appellant says "the second paragraph of answer was a special denial that the acts done by Harding and the trustee were duly and properly executed to give jurisdiction of the matter of building the fence and of the person of appellant, and was for the purpose of requiring the plaintiff below to prove on the trial of the cause the facts conferring jurisdiction on the township trustee." The first paragraph of answer was a general denial, and, to entitle appellee to recover under the issues so joined, he was required to prove, among other things, all the facts necessary to give the township trustee authority to contract for the building of said partition fence and issue the certificate to appellee provided by section 6566, supra. If the fourth paragraph of answer was sufficient to withstand a demurrer for want of facts—a question we need not and do not decide—it was because it was good as an argumentative denial. All the evidence admissible under said second and fourth paragraphs of answer was admissible under said general denial. It follows that the error, if any, in sustaining the demurrer for want of facts to said second and fourth paragraphs of answer was harmless. Harding v. Cowgar, 127 Ind. 245, 249, 26 N. E. 799; Craig v. Frazier, 127 Ind. 286, 287, 26 N. E. 842; Wood v. State, 130 Ind. 364, 366, 30 N. E. 309; Board, etc., v. Chipps, 131 Ind. 56, 59, 29 N. E. 1066, 16 L. R. A. 228, and cases cited; Hoosier Stone Co. v. McCain, 133 Ind. 231, 233, 31 N. E. 956; Board, etc., v. Nichols, 139 Ind. 611, 618, 38 N. E. 526; Berkey v. City of Elkhart, 141 Ind. 408-410, 40 N. E. 1081; Saint v. Welsch, 141 Ind. 382, 389, 390, 40 N. E. 903; Harness v. State, 143 Ind. 420, 423, 424, 42 N. E. 813; Smith v. Pinnell, 143 Ind. 485-487, 40 N. E. 798, and cases cited; State v. Osborn, 143 Ind. 671, 680, 42 N. E. 921; Jeffersonville, etc., Co. v. Riter, 146 Ind. 521, 525, 526, 45 N. E. 697; Board, etc., v. State, 148 Ind. 675, 680, 48 N. E. 226; Pittsburgh, etc., R. Co. v. Hawks, 154 Ind. 547, 548, 55 N. E. 258, and cases cited; Troxel v. Thomas, 155 Ind. 519, 523, 524, 58 N. E. 725; Harris v. Randolph County Bank, 157 Ind. 120, 129, 60 N. E. 1025.

Appellant assigned as a cause for a new trial that the court erred in refusing to grant him a trial of said cause by jury. As this was a suit to foreclose a statutory lien against real property, the same called for the exercise of the equity powers of the court, and the court did not err in denying a jury trial. Albrecht v. C. C. Foster Lumber Co., 126 Ind. 318, 320, 26 N. E. 157; Brighton v. White, 128 Ind. 320, 323, 27 N. E. 620, and cases cited.

The other causes assigned for a new trial depend for their determination on the evidence, which, under the rule declared in Drew v. Town of Geneva, 159 Ind. 364, 366, 65 N. E. 9, is not in the record, and cannot be considered.

Section 6566, supra, requires that the statement which the township trustee gives to the contractor on the completion of the fence shall be recorded in the "mechanic's lien record of such county," and appellant insists that, as there is no such record, the same is ineffective. The section requires that said statement be recorded in the record in which mechanics' liens are required by law to be recorded. So construed, said provision is effective.

It is insisted by appellant that said partition fence law of 1897 (Acts 1897, p. 184, c. 122; sections 6564-6569, Burns' Rev. St. 1901) is in violation of the fourteenth amendment of the Constitution of the United States, because (1) said "act provides no tribunal to determine the sufficiency of the existing partition fence or the necessity of repairing the same or building a new fence"; (2) said act provides no means of testing the sufficiency of the fence built by the defaulting landowner after notice has been served upon him. It is one of the duties of the township trustee, after receiving the notice under section 6565, supra, to determine whether or not a new fence should be built or the old one repaired, and what proportion thereof should be done by the defaulting landowner. He is required to "estimate the cost of building such fence or the cost of repairing the same, as the case may be," and to deliver to the defaulting landowner "an itemized statement of the due proportion of such defaulting landowner, * * * the cost of building a new fence or of making repairs, as the case may be." In performing these duties the township trustee determines the sufficiency of the existing fence, and, if insufficient, whether or not the same should be repaired or a new fence built. If the defaulting landowner, within 20 days after he receives such notice from the township trustee, builds or repairs said fence, as the case may be, the township trustee must determine the sufficiency thereof, because, if not done substantially as provided in said notice, the trustee is required by section 6565, supra, to let the contract for such work to the lowest bidder after giving due notice thereof. If the defaulting landowner, within 20 days after receiving notice from an adjoining landowner, under section 6565, supra, repairs or builds his proportion of the partition fence, and notwithstanding this fact the township trustee is notified, his duties are the same. He determines whether or not the fence built or repaired by said defaulting landowner is a lawful fence, and whether the same is his proportion of said partition fence. It is evident that said act of 1897 (sections 6564-6569, supra) is not open to said objections.

It is next insisted that said act is in violation of section 20, art. 1, of the state Constitution, because it denies the right of trial by jury. Said act makes no provision in regard to how the action to foreclose said lien shall be tried, but that question is governed by section 412, Burns' Rev. St. 1901 (section 409, Rev. St. 1881, and Horner's Rev. St. 1901). Moreover, said section 20 of article 1 applies only to such cases as were treated as civil cases when the Constitution now in force was adopted, and not to cases of equitable jurisdiction, like the one before us. Allen v. Anderson, 57 Ind. 388; McMahan v. Works, 72 Ind. 19, 21; Wright v. Fultz, 138 Ind. 594, 38 N. E. 175; Laverty v. State, 109 Ind. 217, 224, 9 N. E. 774; Brighton v. White, 128 Ind. 320, 323, 324, 27 N. E. 620; Carmichael v. Adams, 91 Ind. 526; Rogers v. Union, etc., Co., 111 Ind. 343, 346, 12 N. E. 495, 60 Am. Rep. 701, and cases cited; Moore v. Glover, 115 Ind. 367, 373, 16 N. E. 163; Albrecht v. C. C. Foster Lumber Co., 126 Ind. 318-320, 26 N. E. 157; Van Sickle v. Belknap, 129 Ind. 558, 559, 28 N. E. 305.

It is next claimed that said act is in violation of section 21, art. 1, of the state Constitution, which provides that "no man's property shall be taken by law without just compensation." We have had statutes on this subject since 1807. Acts 1807, pp. 168–174; Acts 1818, p. 347; Rev. St. 1824, pp. 179–181, c. 38; Rev. St. 1831, pp. 224, 228, c. 84; Rev. St. 1838, pp. 262–266, c. 37; Rev. St. 1843, pp. 375–381, c. 22; 1 Rev. St. 1852, pp. 292–294, c. 38; Rev. St. 1881, §§ 4834–4858; Acts 1897, p. 184, c. 122 (sections 6564–6569, Burns' Rev. St. 1901). Laws compelling the building, maintaining, and keeping in repair of partition fences are enacted in the exercise of the police power, and are an ancient branch of legislation which has been uniformly sustained. Coster v. Tide-Water Co., 18 N. J. Eq. 54, 68, 69; McKeever v. Jenks, 59 Iowa, 300, 306, 13 N. W. 295; Talbot v. Blacklege, 22 Iowa, 572, 578; Wills v. Walters, 68 Ky. (5 Bush) 351; Gilson v. Munson, 114 Mich. 671, 72 N. W. 994; Tyler on Law of Boundaries and Fences, pp. 343–504; note to Myers v. Dodd, 68 Am. Dec. 629–635; 22 Cent. Law Journal, 197–203; 12 Am. & Eng. Enc. of Law (2d Ed.) 1047, 1048, 1050–1057; Myers v. Dodd, 9 Ind. 290, 68 Am. Dec. 624; Brady v. Ball, 14 Ind. 317, 319; Cook v. Morea, 33 Ind. 497; Bartlett v. Adams, 43 Ind. 447; Rhodes v. Mummery, 48 Ind. 216; Bruner v. Palmer, 108 Ind. 397, 9 N. E. 354; Haines v. Kent, 11 Ind. 126; State ex rel. v. Kemp, 141 Ind. 125, 40 N. E. 661; Enders v. McDonald, 5 Ind. App. 297, 31 N. E. 1056. In Tyler on Law of Boundaries and Fences, p. 343, it is said: "It may be affirmed here, however, that it is perfectly competent for the Legislatures of the several states to pass laws regulating the subject of boundary and division fences, whatever may be said of the constitutional right to require the maintaining of fences along the public highways. Wills v. Walters, 5 Bush (Ky.) 351." This court, in Myers v. Dodd, 9 Ind. 290, 292, 68 Am. Dec. 624, in considering the act of 1852 (Rev. St. 1852, pp. 292–294, c. 38), said: "Both parties were equally bound to maintain the partition fence. Either might have repaired it, and enforced contribution from the other, but, neither having done so, they stood upon their common-law obligations." In a note to this case in 68 Am. Dec. 629, it is said that such laws are "unquestionably a valid exercise of legislative power. Coster v. Tide-Water Co., 18 N. J. Eq. 54; McKeever v. Jenks, 59 Iowa, 300 [13 N. W. 295]."

It is not pointed out or shown by appellant how or in what manner his property has been or can be taken in violation of said section of the state Constitution. It is settled in this state that a party will not be heard to question the constitutionality of a law, or any part thereof, unless he shows that some right of his is impaired or prejudiced thereby. State v. Gebhardt, 145 Ind. 439, 450, 44 N. E. 469, 33 L. R. A. 313; Currier v. Elliott, 141 Ind. 394, 407, 39 N. E. 554.

Having considered all the questions properly presented by appellant, we find no available error. Judgment affirmed.

(162 Ind. 222)

ALBANY LAND CO. v. RICKEL.

(Supreme Court of Indiana. Feb. 25, 1904.)

AGENCY—CONTRACT—MUTUALITY—CONSIDERATION—ASSIGNMENT—RATIFICATION—SPECIAL INTERROGATORIES—SPECIAL JURY.

1. A contract between a land company and real estate agents whereby the latter agreed to sell the town lots of the company at a certain town at such prices as might be deemed advantageous, and the company agreed to pay the agents 10 per cent. on all sales, and to set apart certain lots for advertising purposes, etc., was not invalid for lack of consideration, absence of mutuality, or want of definite term of existence.

2. Where a firm of two members contracted to manage and sell lots of a corporation at a town other than that at which the partners resided, the fact that the business was carried on at the town where the lots were located by only one of the partners was not a breach of the contract.

3. Knowing assent by the principal to the assignment of a contract of agency is equivalent to an agreement to substitute the assignee as agent.

4. After a general verdict for plaintiff, it will be assumed on appeal that a material allegation of the complaint was proven.

5. A special interrogatory to which the answer, "Evidence not conclusive," is returned, must be treated as unanswered.

6. The contract of a firm to act as real estate agents for a corporation was assigned to one member of the firm, who proceeded with the business, selling lots and rendering monthly reports in his own name. The corporation accepted the reports and proceeds of the sales, and executed checks and other papers to the assignee in his own name. *Held* a ratification of the assignment.

7. Const. § 65, declares that the right to trial by jury shall remain inviolate. Burns' Rev. St. 1901, § 1859, provides that, where a party to a civil action demands a jury trial, the sheriff shall call a jury from the regular panel; section 531 provides that the court shall have power, when the business thereof requires it, to order the impaneling of a special jury; and section 1461 enacts that, where no lawful traverse jury shall be present at any term of court, it is the duty of the court, if the business thereof requires it, to cause a jury to be summoned from the bystanders. A jury case was set for trial two days before the regular panel for that term was summoned to appear, and a jury impaneled from the bystanders. *Held*, that on appeal, where there was no showing as to why the regular panel was not summoned to appear sooner, it would be presumed that there was justifiable cause for ordering the special jury.

Appeal from Circuit Court, Delaware County; W. A. Barnard, Special Judge.

Action by Wyllis D. Rickel against the Albany Land Company. From a judgment for plaintiff, defendant appeals. Transferred from the Appellate Court under section 1337u, Burns' Rev. St. 1901. Affirmed.

Thompson & Thompson, for appellant. Gregory, Silverburg & Lotz, for appellee.

HADLEY, J. Contract of agency for sale of real estate. Damages for breach. Appellee, Rickel, sued appellant, Albany Land

Company, for damages for the breach of a written contract which was in these words:

"This agreement made and entered into this eleventh day of January, 1895, by and between the Albany Land Company of Delaware County, Indiana, and Wyllis D. Rickel and Thomas H. Sprott of Auburn, Indiana, doing business under the firm name and style of Rickel & Sprott.

"Witnesseth, that the said Rickel and Sprott are to have charge of the real estate and personal property belonging to the Albany Land Company at the town of Albany, Delaware County, Indiana, and to sell and dispose of the same at such prices as the said Rickel and Sprott may deem to be to the best advantage of the said land company, and to locate factories upon the land of the said Land Company, upon such terms as may hereafter be agreed to by and between the parties locating the factories and the said Land Company:

"Said Land Company is to pay said Rickel & Sprott for their services in locating said factories, for taking charge and managing the affairs of said company, a commission of (10 per cent.) ten per cent. upon the sales of all lots and other real estate made by said Rickel & Sprott.

"The Land Company agrees to set aside 150 of their said lots which said Rickel & Sprott are to sell to persons residing in said town of Albany with an agreement with the purchasers of said lots that the money paid by them for said lots shall be used as bonuses to parties locating factories upon the lands of said company in said town of Albany, said Land Company agrees to set aside one hundred (100) lots to be sold to persons residing in various towns in the State of Indiana, at such prices as the said Rickel & Sprott may deem expedient for the purpose of advertising said town and inducing other persons to purchase lots of said company. It is further agreed and understood that the said Rickel & Sprott shall have the exclusive sale of said real estate herein mentioned.

"In Witness Whereof, we have hereunto set our hands and seals this 9th day of May, 1895. Albany Land Company, by N. T. Dalton, Sec'y. Rickel & Sprott."

The complaint, which was founded on the contract, in substance, alleged: That prior to the making of the contract the plaintiff and one Sprott were partners as real estate agents and brokers, residing and doing a large and profitable business in the town of Auburn, Ind., in the firm name of Rickel & Sprott. Appellant, Albany Land Company, was a corporation owning about 1,000 lots in the town of Albany, Ind., which latter town had about 1,000 inhabitants, was located in the gas field, and an eligible and favorable place for the location of manufacturing concerns. That the company, desiring to locate factories at Albany, and thereby to create a demand and market for its lots, solicited the plaintiff's firm, which had much experience and skill in the location of manufacturing plants, to enter into said contract. That, after entering into the contract, the plaintiff, for his firm of Rickel & Sprott, gave up his and their business at Auburn, and went to Albany, a distance of 90 miles, and at once entered upon a performance of said contract on the part of Rickel & Sprott, and did, at his firm's expense, in many newspapers, and by printed circulars distributed through the mails, advertise the advantages of Albany as a good and economical place for factories and for investments in town lots, and did visit many places in this and in other states, and personally solicited the location of factories and the purchase of lots, and did succeed in locating factories on the company's said lots, and in selling a large number of the lots. That on March 13, 1896, with the full knowledge and acquiescence of the company, Sprott, for a valuable consideration, assigned to the plaintiff all his interest in the business under said contract. That after said assignment the plaintiff continued to perform the conditions of the contract, with the full knowledge and acquiescence of the company, and did thereafter sell a large number more of said lots, and could and would, if permitted by the company, have sold all of them within the term of five years from the making of the contract; which was a reasonable time in which to make a sale of all. That the plaintiff faithfully, diligently, and successfully continued to perform all the conditions of the contract on his part to November, 1896, at which time the company, without the consent of the plaintiff, wrongfully and arbitrarily revoked said contract and agency. That the plaintiff was willing and able to continue the contract, and willing and able to perform all the conditions thereof, and make sale of all of the lots, and by the revocation of the contract and agency he was deprived of his profits, and not remunerated for his expenses, etc., whereby he was damaged. The appellant's demurrer to the complaint was overruled. The case was put at issue and submitted to a jury. Verdict and judgment for appellee, over a motion for a new trial, for $1,500.

Three alleged errors are assigned: First, the overruling of the demurrer to the complaint; second, the overruling of appellant's motion for judgment on the answers to interrogatories notwithstanding the general verdict; third, the overruling of the motion for a new trial.

1. It is merely suggested, not argued, that the complaint is bad, because the foundation contract is invalid for want of consideration, for want of mutuality, and for want of a definite term of existence. The complaint is clearly good against either and all of these alleged infirmities.

2. The jury returned with their general verdict answers to 535 interrogatories, which interrogatories and answers occupy 115 type-

written pages of the record. Four hundred and forty-six of these interrogatories were requested by counsel for appellant, but no attempt has been made in their brief to summarize or state in narrative form the facts disclosed by the answers. They have contented themselves by copying into their brief certain selected numbers, and announcing that they rely upon the particular answers thus indicated, in support of their motion for judgment notwithstanding the general verdict. Appellee has in like manner done nothing more than copy into his brief certain other numbers, as tending to overcome the force of those presented by appellant. We have, therefore, under clause 5 of rule 22 of this court (55 N. E. vi), considered only such of the interrogatories and answers as have been thus pointed out. They exhibit the following facts: On January 11, 1895, appellee, Rickel, and one Sprott were engaged as partners, under the name of Rickel & Sprott, in the real estate business at Auburn, Ind., and at said date entered into a contract with appellant, Albany Land Company (hereinbefore set out in the statement of the complaint), for the sale of a large number of lots which the company then owned at Albany, Ind. The contract was spread upon the minutes of the company on said day, but was not reduced to writing and signed by the parties until the following May 9th. Immediately upon entering into the contract, in January, 1895, Rickel went to Albany, and entered upon the performance of the contract for his firm, and moved his family from Auburn to Albany in the fall of 1895. Sprott continued to reside at Auburn, and to conduct the firm's business at Auburn, Kendalville, and other places, and occasionally visited Albany for a day or two at a time, and advised with Rickel concerning the sale of the company's lots. The partnership, at their own expense, advertised the company's lots for sale in various newspapers, and by printed circulars sent through the mails, and personally visited many places, and solicited the location and establishing of factories at Albany, no part of which expense was ever repaid to them. On March 13, 1896, Sprott assigned all his interest in the business under the contract with appellant to Rickel. Many lots had been sold by Rickel prior to said assignment, and 10 or more were sold by him afterwards, under the contract; but business was depressed and money scarce in the community, and there was but little demand or sale for lots at Albany during the year 1896, and no sales were made in May, June, July, August, September, or October of that year, and on October 21, 1896, the company, in writing, by Charles Smith, its president, peremptorily, and without assigning any reason therefor, revoked said contract and agency. After the assignment by Sprott to Rickel, the latter continued to make to the company monthly reports of sales, and of receipts and expenditures in the management of the company's real estate, and made such reports, and stated all accounts in his individual name, and the company executed to him checks and other papers in his individual name. It has been uniformly held by this court that special facts found by the jury in answer to interrogatories propounded to them will not prevail against the general verdict, unless such special facts, when considered of themselves, and after indulging all reasonable presumptions against them, are found inherently so repugnant and inconsistent with the general verdict, supported by all reasonable intendments, that they cannot be reconciled therewith, and one or the other is necessarily erroneous. The reason for the rule, as stated in City of South Bend v. Turner, 156 Ind. 423, 60 N. E. 273, 54 L. R. A. 396, 83 Am. St. Rep. 200, is "that the jury, in reaching a general verdict, is required to consider, as a whole, all the issuable facts proved in the case, while the court, in testing the force of isolated facts disclosed by answers to interrogatories, does not know and cannot know what other facts touching the same matters were proved before the jury to justify their verdict." Therefore any fact that might have been properly proved under the issues must be considered as proved, in determining the legal force of the special findings as against the general verdict. It is first contended that the contract sued on shows that the employment of Rickel & Sprott counted on the joint service of the partners in the sale of the company's lots, and on a special confidence in their combined judgment and influence in locating factories and in otherwise promoting sales, and as the special findings show that Sprott continued the firm's business at Auburn, and did not actively engage in the business of the company, and did, while the contract was running, assign to Rickel all his interest therein, it does thereby conclusively appear that the partners broke and abandoned the contract, and cannot, therefore, recover damages for a breach precipitated by themselves. Counsel for appellant overlook the fact that the contract between the parties contains no stipulation that the partners should both give up their established business at Auburn, and actively and conjointly engage in selling the land company's lots at Albany. It is not stated in the contract whether the business of the agency should be conducted immediately and personally by both or either of the partners, or whether they should, or not, give up their established business in Auburn and other places, or whether they should, or not, confine their operations in real estate to the business of the company at Albany. These things, being unexpressed in the contract, will be governed by what is reasonable and usual in such engagements and enterprises. The terms of the employment being general, it will be implied therefrom that the firm assumed only the obligation to devote to the business such a degree of diligence, energy, and skill, and such methods as are customary and usual with reasonably prudent and successful land agents in employments of like character and importance. But it cannot be implied from general terms that the partnership undertook to give up all other business of like character, or that both should devote all their time to this particular employment, or that both should for any of the time actively and personally engage in the particular employment. The rule is that, when a firm is employed, it is the partnership that is engaged as agent, and not the individual members; and, in the absence of anything to show a contrary intent, either partner may execute the power, and his act is the act of the partnership, and in strict pursuance of the power. Mechem on Agency, § 65; Deakin v. Underwood, 37 Minn. 98, 33 N. W. 318, 5 Am. St. Rep. 827; Eggleston v. Boardman, 37 Mich. 14. The finding that Sprott assigned his interest in the contract to Rickel is not in conflict with the general verdict. If it be assumed that the assignment effected a dissolution of the partnership, and that a dissolution operated ipso facto as a revocation of the agency, which may be said to be the general rule, still it was alleged in the complaint, and provable under the issues, that the assignment was made with the knowledge and consent of the company, and we must assume that it was so proved. And a knowing assent to the assignment was equivalent to an agreement to substitute the assignee for the assignor. But it is insisted by appellant that the findings show that the company gave no consent to the assignment, and the following interrogatory and answer are relied on: "Did the Albany Land Company ever consent to the assignment by Sprott of his interest in the contract between the firm of Rickel & Sprott and said Albany Land Company to said Rickel? Ans. Evidence not conclusive." This answer amounts to nothing, because it does not pretend to state what the fact was, as shown by a preponderance of the evidence. The answer that the evidence was not conclusive implies that there was evidence upon that point, but which did not reach that degree of cogency and force that may be termed conclusive. What the weight of the evidence showed is not stated, and the incident must therefore be treated as if the interrogatory had been left wholly unanswered. But conceding appellant's contention that the language is equivalent to a negative answer, still the general verdict must stand. Other findings show that after the assignment Rickel proceeded with the business of the agency in his individual name under the contract; sold lots for the company, seven of which brought $3,600, which sales the company knowingly approved and accepted; also received from Rickel monthly reports of the business rendered in his individual name, executed to him, individually, checks, receipts, and other papers; and for a period of seven months went on dealing with him in relation to the business of the agency in conformity to the terms of the contract. If the assignment was unauthorized, and the company afterwards knowingly accepted the fruits and benefits of Rickel's individual acts, such an acceptance was a ratification which clothed the transactions with all the validity and obligation that would have been imparted by a previous authority to do them. Hauss v. Niblack, 80 Ind. 407, 412; Mechem's Agency, § 148, and cases collated.

3. Over appellant's objection, the cause was submitted to a jury impaneled from the bystanders. This action of the court is claimed to be erroneous. The record shows that the cause was put at issue at the September term, 1900, and during that term set for trial before a jury, requested by appellee, on the 28th day of January, 1901; the same being a day in the next succeeding term. The members of the regular panel drawn for the January term had been summoned to appear on January 30th, and were not in attendance upon the court when said cause was called for trial on the 28th. Appellant demanded the regular panel, and objected to a special jury. The court entered an order reciting the absence of the regular panel, and that the business of the court required the calling of a special jury from the bystanders, whereupon a special jury was called; and appellant having exhausted its peremptory challenges, and challenged all persons for cause who were legally disqualified, over its objection the trial proceeded. "In all civil cases the right of trial by jury shall remain inviolate." So says the Constitution (section 65). But it does not say that the right to trial by the regular panel shall remain inviolate. And when a litigant in a civil case is accorded a trial by a jury possessed of all the statutory qualifications, he has received all that is guarantied by the fundamental law. The qualification of jurors and the method of their selection is left wholly to the Legislature. That body has provided (section 1859, Burns' Rev. St. 1901) that in civil actions, where the parties are entitled to a trial by jury, and either party shall demand such trial, the sheriff shall call a jury from the regular panel. Section 531, provides further, "The court shall have the power when the business thereof requires it, to order the empaneling of a special jury for the trial of any cause." These statutes apply to both criminal and civil cases. Section 528. It is clearly implied from these enactments that the provision for the impaneling of the jury from the regular panel is directory, only, to be obeyed as far as a proper dispatch of business before the court will allow, but if, for any cause, the regular panel is not available, and, in the sound dis-

cretion of the presiding judge, the business of the court requires the impaneling of a special jury for a particular case, it may be properly done. So it has been held that when a case is called, and the regular panel is out, considering their verdict in another case, the court may order a special jury from the bystanders. Evarts v. State, 48 Ind. 422; Myers v. Moore, 3 Ind. App. 226, 229, 28 N. E. 724. And when the regular panel has failed to agree, and become thereby disqualified in the case, a special jury may be ordered and a retrial had at the same term, over the objection of the defendant. Pierce v. State, 67 Ind. 354. Where the proper officers have failed or refused to draw and impanel a jury, "or where, for any other cause whatever, no traverse jury shall be present at any term of the court, it shall be lawful, and is hereby made the duty of the court, if the business thereof require it," to cause a jury to be summoned from the bystanders. Section 1461, Burns' Rev. St. 1901; Heyl v. State, 109 Ind. 589, 10 N. E. 916. It was manifestly the legislative intent to give the court, in controlling and expediting its business, a large discretion in determining when the calling of a special jury is required, and it is only when it clearly appears that a party has been unnecessarily deprived of a trial before the regular panel that the action of the court will be reviewed. Gillett's Cr. Law, § 827. The record here shows that the case was at a previous term set for trial on January 28th before a jury, requested by appellee, and that the regular panel was summoned to appear on January 30th. Why the jury was not summoned to appear until two days after the beginning of jury trials does not appear—whether by the fault or inadvertence of the court or the officers, or whether by agreement of the litigants. However it was brought about, it may well be assumed that the trial calendar was full of other cases, that the witnesses were in attendance, and that a postponement would delay and disarrange the other business of the court. We must therefore presume that the court had justifiable cause for ordering the special jury. Appellant cites Wilson v. State, 42 Ind. 224, in support of its position; but it is apparent that since the decision of that case this court has broken away from the narrow limits there laid down, and that case can no longer be regarded as an authority.

We find no error in the record. Judgment affirmed.

(33 Ind. App. 80)

MORAN v. LESLIE.*

(Appellate Court of Indiana, Division No. 2. Feb. 16, 1904.)

STREET RAILROADS—COLLISION—VEHICLES—DUTY OF MOTORMAN—CONTRIBUTORY NEGLIGENCE.

1 It is the duty of a motorman of a street railway car, when running the same through a crowded street, to have it under such control that he may stop or sufficiently check its speed to avoid collision, and to keep a vigilant lookout to the same end.

2. Where plaintiff, who was injured by a collision with a street car, before attempting to cross the track knew the car was approaching, and, after hesitating, struck his horse, and attempted to cross in front of the car at the suggestion of his companion, he was guilty of such contributory negligence as precluded a recovery for his injuries.

Appeal from Circuit Court, Gibson County; O. M. Welborn, Judge.

Action by Frank Leslie against Harold D. Moran, as receiver, etc. From a judgment in favor of plaintiff, defendant appeals. Reversed.

Gilchrist, De Bruler & Welman and L. C. Embree, for appellant. C. M. Seiler, Funkhouser & Funkhouser, G. K. Denton, and W. E. Stilwell, for appellee.

ROBY, J. This is an action brought by the appellee against the appellant to recover damages for personal injuries alleged to have been sustained by the appellee by reason of a collision of a street car operated by servants of the appellant with a wagon which the appellee was driving, and from which he was thrown by the collision while attempting to cross the track of the street railroad. The single assignment of error is that the court erred in overruling appellant's motion for a new trial. Under this assignment appellant argues that the verdict of the jury is not sustained by sufficient evidence; that the court erred in instructions given at its own instance and at appellee's request, and in refusing those requested by appellant. Appellee had a verdict for $3,000, remitted $600, judgment rendered for $2,400.

The Union Depot at Evansville is situated at the southeast corner of Main and Eighth streets. At its north end there was, when appellee received his injuries, a paved driveway 47 feet wide and 50 feet deep, ending at the railroad platforms, where mail and baggage are unloaded. Double street railway tracks are located on Main street west of said building and driveway. The sidewalk between the building and the car tracks was 11 feet wide. The space between the car track and the sidewalk was about 12 feet, and at the time of the accident was occupied by cabs and wagons. Appellee was the driver of a mail wagon covered and with a wire netting back of the seat. A train due at 9:35 p. m. was 35 minutes late, so that he had, after receiving mail from it, only 17 minutes in which to drive to the post office, and thence to the L. & N. Depot. A mail clerk assisted him in loading, and got into the seat with him. They drove out of the passageway and upon Main street, when they saw a street car 30 feet south, and coming north. The head of the horse was over the first rail of the east car track upon which track the said car was approaching, and appellee either

*Rehearing denied April 20, 1904.

¶ 1. See Street Railroads, vol. 44, Cent. Dig. § 214.

stopped or checked the horse to allow the car to pass. The mail agent said, "You have time to make it across," and appellee then hit the horse with the lines, and drove across the track. "When I got across, except the left hind wheel of the wagon, the car struck the left hind wheel," etc.

The verdict, in so far as it finds the motorman on the street car to have been guilty of negligence, is not without support in the evidence. It was his duty, when running the car along the street at such a place, to have it under such control as that he might be able to stop or check it to void collision, and also to keep a vigilant outlook to the same end. Had he done so, the collision would not have taken place, as is established by the general verdict. The quality of appellee's conduct does not depend upon the acts or omissions of the motorman. He saw the car approaching, knew that it was likely to strike him if he attempted to cross, hesitated, and then concluded, influenced by the expression of his companion, to race with it. This he did, and lost. He was guilty of contributory negligence in so doing, and the jury should have been so instructed.

Judgment reversed, with instructions to sustain motion for a new trial and for further proceedings.

(32 Ind. A. 457)

BRUNSON v. STARBUCK, Treasurer.

(Appellate Court of Indiana, Division No. 1. Feb. 19, 1904.)

TAXATION—OMITTED PROPERTY—ASSESSMENT—ACTS OF OFFICER—VALIDITY—PRESUMPTIONS—DESCRIPTION OF PROPERTY—ACTIONS—PETITION—BURDEN OF PROOF.

1. Under Burns' Rev. St. 1901, § 8587, requiring every administrator to pay taxes on the property of his decedent, and declaring that, on his failure so to do, the county treasurer shall present to the circuit or other court a brief statement in writing setting forth the fact and the amount of the delinquency, whereupon the court shall issue an order commanding the administrator to show cause why the taxes should not be paid, etc., a petition clearly showing the fact and the amount of the delinquency was sufficient, without alleging how the assessments came on the tax duplicate.

2. Where, in a proceeding against an administrator to recover unpaid taxes, the petition did not wholly omit the averment of any fact required by the statute, a special finding in favor of plaintiff was sufficient to cure error, if any, in overruling a demurrer to such petition.

3. Burns' Rev. St. 1901, § 8560, provides for the assessing of omitted property by the county auditor, and section 8531 makes it also the duty of the county assessor to assess such property. Section 8454 declares that, in entering personal property on the taxbooks, it shall be sufficient to describe the same as "personal property," which phrase shall comprehend all species of personal property belonging to the person charged. *Held*, that an assessment of omitted property placed on the tax duplicate by the auditor, described as "omitted personal property for the year 1889, $20,000," was not objectionable for failure to further describe the property.

4. Under Burns' Rev. St. 1901, § 8642, providing that no general tax assessed by an officer authorized to make assessments shall be held illegal for want of any matter of form not affecting the merits, and that all taxes assessed shall be presumed to be legally assessed until the contrary is affirmatively shown, an assessment of omitted personal property by a county auditor authorized to make such assessment by section 8560 is valid, unless overthrown by a preponderance of evidence.

5. Where an administrator, on an order to show cause why he should not pay taxes on omitted personal property assessed, answered that such assessment was invalid, on the ground that the findings of the board of review making such assessment were made without notice, and such findings did not show that notice was not given, the burden was on the administrator to establish such fact.

6. Where, in an action against an administrator to recover taxes on omitted personal property, the court found that decedent was the owner of personal property, consisting of cash, money loaned, mortgages, and oil-storage receipts, largely in excess of the amount returned by him for taxation, which amount was omitted from the schedule and escaped taxation, and that the amount of omitted personal property for each of the years named was a certain sum, and the amount of the tax owing thereon, the findings sufficiently described the omitted property.

Appeal from Circuit Court, Jay County; Clark J. Lutz, Special Judge.

Action by Eugene Starbuck, treasurer of Jay county, against Albert Brunson, administrator of the estate of Aaron W. Letts, Sr., deceased. From a judgment in favor of plaintiff, defendant appeals. Affirmed.

Dailey, Simmons & Dailey and Adair & La Follette, for appellant. C. W. Miller, Atty. Gen., W. C. Geake, C. C. Hadley, L. G. Rothschild, Merrill Moores, and F. B. Jaqua, for appellee.

ROBINSON, J. The predecessor of appellee as treasurer of Jay county filed in the circuit court his petition under section 8587, Burns' Rev. St. 1901, which provides that it shall be the duty of every administrator having the property of any decedent in charge to pay the taxes due upon the property of such decedent, and, upon his failure to do so, when there is money enough on hand to pay the same, the county treasurer shall present to the circuit court, or other proper court of the county, a brief statement, in writing, "setting forth the fact and amount of such delinquency," and the court shall at once issue an order, directed to such delinquent, commanding him to show cause within five days thereafter why such taxes and penalty and costs should not be paid. The petition recites that the petitioner is county treasurer; that the tax duplicates in his hands show delinquent taxes, penalty, and costs assessed against the property of appellant's decedent aggregating $4,416.91, which amount was due and unpaid; that appellant, administrator of the decedent, had in his hands as such administrator $4,527.00; and that appellee had demanded payment of such taxes, penalty, and costs of the administrator, which payment had been refused.

We do not agree with counsel for appellant

that the petition should state the facts showing how the assessments came on the duplicate. The petition clearly shows "the fact and amount of the delinquency," and this is all the statute, by its terms, requires. The language used in the statute manifestly means the fact of the delinquency and the amount of the delinquency. With this construction of the language used, the petition follows the statute, and was good against a demurrer. Moreover, as the complaint does not wholly omit the averment of any fact required by the statute, the special finding, it has often been held, would correct the error, if any, in the overruling of the demurrer.

The court found substantially the following facts: Aaron W. Letts, Sr., died intestate in August, 1902, having been a resident taxpayer of Jackson township, Jay county, for about 30 years. Before the commencement of this action the treasurer of Jay county demanded of appellant, as administrator of the estate of Letts, the payment of delinquent taxes in the sum of $4,416.91, which the administrator refused to pay. At the time of the filing of the petition herein, and since that time, the administrator has on deposit in bank, subject to his order, funds belonging to the estate in the sum of $4,500. During the years 1889 to 1898, inclusive, Letts was the owner of and in possession of personal property, consisting of cash on hand, money loaned, mortgages, and oil-storage receipts, largely in excess of the amounts returned by him for taxation, which amount in each of the above years he withheld from the assessing officer, and failed to return the same for taxation, but omitted the same from his schedule, whereby such property so owned by him in excess of the amount so returned by him escaped taxation during each of these years; that on the 10th day of January, 1899, and again on the 19th day of January, 1899, the county assessor, having discovered and received credible information and having reason to believe that the personal property of Letts had not been assessed for the years 1889 to 1898, inclusive, and that there had been an omission from the assessment books and tax duplicates for each of these years of personal property owned by him, gave Letts notice in writing for him to appear within 10 days and show cause why he should not be assessed, and why omitted property should not be added to the duplicate; that, on each of the dates specified, Letts appeared before the county assessor, but in each instance refused to give any information whatever concerning omitted property mentioned in these notices, and from information otherwise obtained the county assessor then made out and filed with the county auditor his written finding and order, in which he directed the auditor to place upon the proper tax duplicate of Jay county the sum of $20,000 for each of the years 1889 to 1898, inclusive, all as omitted property (the property omitted for these years being crude oil; oil-well supplies and fixtures; pipes, tools, and machinery of different kinds used in and about the drilling and operation of oil wells; bonds; notes; notes secured by mortgage; accounts, building and loan stock, and other accounts due Letts; money on hand and on deposit; money loaned; interest due; judgments and allowances in his favor; tax certificates; certificates of sheriff's sales; shares of stock in corporations; and goods and merchandise on hand). In this finding and order to the auditor, the county assessor stated the fact that Letts had been summoned before him on two occasions, at which times Letts refused to disclose any omitted property, or to give any information concerning the same; also stating certain efforts he had made to secure information, and that, from reliable information communicated to him, the assessor believed that the amount of omitted property was at least $20,000 more than had been returned for taxation for the years mentioned. This written instruction to the auditor was filed in the auditor's office, and constituted all the evidence and instruction upon which the auditor placed $20,000 for each of the years 1889 to 1898, inclusive, on the tax duplicate. That the instructions were not recorded in any book in the auditor's office, and no record was made of the same in the auditor's office, except that the tax duplicates were corrected by the auditor, who entered the same upon the duplicate in the hands of the treasurer. The court further found "that as to said sums, and each of them, the court finds that the same was so owned by said Aaron W. Letts, Sr., on the 1st day of April of each year therein named, and that the same had been omitted from taxation by reason of said Aaron W. Letts, Sr., failing to make correct and true assessment lists during each of said years, and upon the filing of the notice and report with the auditor, as such auditor, without any other evidence being heard or offered before him, he assessed said amounts during said several years, respectively, as omitted property which had unjustly escaped taxation, and thereupon the auditor corrected the proper tax duplicate, and entered the same upon such duplicate in his office, and also upon the duplicate then in the hands of the county treasurer, being the duplicate of 1898, and added said omitted property to such duplicate, and said auditor did thereupon file said report and order of the county assessor in his office, which was all the evidence upon which such correction was made by said auditor"; that the taxes due and owing by Letts upon the omitted property held by him during the years 1889 to 1898, inclusive, so charged upon the tax duplicate by the auditor, amounted to $8,486, but, without interest and penalty, the several amounts for the several years are, and each of them have been, due and owing from the time when the taxes for each of these years were due and payable; that the taxes have been carried forward by the auditor on each successive duplicate from 1899, and no part of the same has ever been paid; that each and all of the tax duplicates upon which was placed such tax assessments were put into the hands of the county treasurer for the purpose of collection. On the 13th day of July, 1899, the county board of review raised the assessment of Letts' personal property for the year 1899 from $7,850 to $35,000, and in obedience to this order the auditor placed $27,150 on the tax duplicate for the year 1900 as a raise of the assessment for the year 1899. That the taxes on this amounted to $371.95, which sum is included in the amount demanded of the administrator by the treasurer. This order of the board was entered of record in the proper record used by it for the making of such entries. In making the assessments of the omitted property, and in ascertaining the amount thereof, and in correcting the tax duplicate, and in placing the omitted property and taxes thereon, the county treasurer, auditor, the petitioner herein, and the board of review each and all acted in good faith; and the findings, orders, and proceedings of the assessor, auditor, and board of review were made and had in good faith, and without any fraud. The court stated as conclusions of law that the administrator should be ordered to pay out of assets in his hands $3,486, taxes assessed on omitted property; $371.95, tax assessed by the board of review, and $558.96, penalty and interest; in all, $4,416.91.

It is first argued by appellant's counsel that an assessment made by the county assessor, and placed upon the tax duplicate by the county auditor, attempting to make an assessment against property as omitted property, is invalid, where the property sought to be assessed is not described. Section 8560, Burns' Rev. St. 1901, provides for the assessing of omitted property by the county auditor; and section 8531, Burns' Rev. St. 1901, makes it also the duty of the county assessor to assess omitted property. Section 8454, Burns' Rev. St. 1901, provides that, "in entering personal property upon the proper tax books for the purpose of taxation, it shall be a sufficient description of the same to use the words 'personal property,' and such phrase shall comprehend and embrace all species of personal property belonging to the party charged therewith, on the tax books, and no more specific description or designation thereof shall be necessary." The finding shows that during the years in question the decedent was the owner of personal property largely in excess of the amount returned by him for taxation, and which he had failed to return for taxation, and states the kind of property, amounting to $20,000, which was placed upon the tax duplicate as omitted property, and that the sums placed on the duplicate were owned by the decedent at the times named, and had been omitted from taxation by reason of the decedent having failed to make true and correct assessment lists, and that the assessment made by the auditor for each of the years 1889 to 1898, inclusive, was on omitted personal property. The findings also show that the assessment was entered upon the duplicate for the year 1889, "Letts, Aaron W. Sr., omitted personal property, for the year 1889, $20,000," etc., and that the entry for each subsequent year up to and including 1898 was the same. See Reynolds v. Bowen, 138 Ind. 434, 36 N. E. 756, 37 N. E. 962. Section 8411, Burns' Rev. St. 1901, designates what the term "personal property," for the purpose of taxation, shall include; and section 8454, supra, expressly provides that, in entering personal property upon the taxbooks for taxation, it shall be sufficient to use the words "personal property." The statute (section 8560) giving the auditor power to assess omitted property also provides, "To enable him to do which, he is invested with all the powers of assessors under this act." In this proceeding by the treasurer, he acts from the duplicate placed in his hands by the auditor who made the assessment. Section 8642, Burns' Rev. St. 1901, provides that no general tax assessed by an officer authorized to make assessments, "or which, if made by another person, or may be adopted by such officer as his act, shall be held to be illegal or invalid for want of any matter of form in any proceeding not affecting the merits of the case, and which shall not prejudice the rights of the party assessed. And all taxes assessed upon any property in this state shall be presumed to be legally assessed until the contrary is affirmatively shown. * * *" Under this provision, the assessment made by the auditor must stand, if not overthrown by a preponderance of evidence. See Gallup v. Schmidt, 154 Ind. 196, 56 N. E. 443; Id., 183 U. S. 300, 22 Sup. Ct. 162, 46 L. Ed. 207; Saint v. Welsh, 141 Ind. 382, 40 N. E. 903.

It is further argued that the assessment placed on the duplicate by the auditor by order of the board of review is illegal, because the findings do not show any notice was given. Under section 8532, Burns' Rev. St. 1901, the board of review has power to add omitted property to an assessment. International, etc., Ass'n v. Board (Ind. App.) 65 N. E. 297; Graham v. Russell, 152 Ind. 186, 52 N. E. 806. This assessment made by the board was for the year 1899. What is said in argument about the action of the board in assessing omitted property for the years 1894, 1895, 1896, 1897, and 1898 need not be further noticed, as these taxes were not placed on the duplicate by the auditor. It is the rule that, where a court of general jurisdiction has jurisdiction of the subject-matter, it will be presumed, in the absence of an affirmative showing to the contrary, that jurisdiction of the person was acquired, where the person sought to be concluded was a party to the adjudication. Davis v. Taylor, 140 Ind. 439, 39 N. E. 551, and cases cited. And when the jurisdiction of an inferior court is once established, then all presumptions in favor of its proceedings apply as well as to courts of general jurisdiction. But "the proposition," said the court in Board v. Markle, 46 Ind. 96, that "the rule for jurisdiction is that nothing shall be intended to be out of the jurisdiction of a superior court but that which especially appears to be so, and, on the contrary, nothing shall be intended to be within the jurisdiction of an inferior court but that which is so expressly alleged (Peacock v. Bell, 1 Saund. 73), is recognized by all the authorities as correct." In Saint v. Welsh, Exr's, 141 Ind. 382, 40 N. E. 903, suit was brought by an executor to enjoin the collection of taxes assessed on omitted property added to the duplicate by the county assessor. In that case the court, by Jordan, J., said: "Where one assails the action or proceedings of a county assessor had in pursuance of the law of 1891, as was done in the case at bar, by an action seeking injunctive relief, in order to succeed he must establish that either the act or proceedings of such officer were void for a failure to comply with some material provision of the statute, which operated to the prejudice of the taxpayer complaining, or that the property, money, or means in question, subject to taxation, had been duly listed and returned therefor." See Adams v. Davis, 109 Ind. 10, 9 N. E. 162; Smith v. Rude Bros. Mfg. Co., 131 Ind. 150, 30 N. E. 947; Reynolds v. Bowen, supra; Gallup v. Schmidt, supra; Buck v. Miller, 147 Ind. 586, 45 N. E. 647, 47 N. E. 8, 37 L. R. A. 384, 62 Am. St. Rep. 436; Midland Ry. Co. v. State, 11 Ind. App. 433, 38 N. E. 57; Burns' Rev. St. 1901, § 8642.

When the appellant was called upon by petition to show cause why the taxes should not be paid, he filed an answer in three paragraphs. He was required to overcome the presumption that the taxes assessed were legally assessed. The burden upon him to aver and prove facts showing the tax to be invalid, in a suit by him to enjoin the collection of these taxes, would not have been different from the burden resting upon him in this proceeding. If he claimed that the assessment by the board of review was invalid because no notice was given, it was incumbent upon him to allege and prove the fact. This was not done. To sustain the petitioner, it was not necessary that the finding should show that notice was given; but, to sustain appellant, it was necessary that the finding should show that notice was not given. Gallup v. Schmidt, supra; Buck v. Miller, supra. The findings state that, in placing the omitted property on the tax duplicate, the officers acted in good faith and without any fraud. As the burden was upon appellant to show that the claim asserted by the officers was groundless, we cannot say that the findings are not sustained by the evidence. Saint v. Welsh, supra; Gallup v. Schmidt, supra.

It is further argued that the finding of facts does not sufficiently describe the omitted property sought to be taxed. It is found that during the years in question the decedent "was the owner of and in possession of personal property, consisting of cash on hand, money loaned, mortgages, oil-storage receipts, largely in excess of the amounts so returned by him for taxation," which amount was withheld from the officers, omitted from the schedule, and escaped taxation. The court also found the amount of "omitted personal property" for each of the years named, and the amount of taxes due and owing thereon. Under the rulings in the cases above cited, and under the statute, we think the omitted property was sufficiently described. Reynolds v. Bowen, supra; Gallup v. Schmidt, supra; Burns' Rev. St. 1901, §§ 8411, 8434.

Judgment affirmed.

(32 Ind. App. 554)

HATFIELD et al. v. CHENOWETH.*

(Appellate Court of Indiana, Division No. 1. Feb. 19, 1904.)

APPEAL—FINDINGS—REVIEW—RECORD — BILL OF EXCEPTIONS—CONTENTS—EVIDENCE.

1. An assignment that the finding of the court was not sustained by sufficient evidence, and that the amount of the recovery was too large, cannot be considered on appeal in the absence of the evidence.

2. Where a bill of exceptions purported to contain all the evidence, but it affirmatively appeared therefrom that such was not the fact, it could not be considered on appeal in determining questions not reviewable without all the evidence.

Appeal from Circuit Court, Huntington County; R. K. Erwin, Special Judge.

Action between James M. Hatfield and others and Lizzie C. Chenoweth. From a judgment in favor of the latter, the former appeal. Affirmed.

J. T. Alexander and J. M. Hatfield, for appellants. Spencer & Branyan, for appellee.

BLACK, J. The action of the court in overruling the motion of the appellants for a new trial is assigned as error, and under this assignment it is urged that the finding of the court was not sustained by sufficient evidence, and that the amount of recovery was too large. We cannot consider these matters without the evidence. There is a typewritten bill of exceptions, which formally purports to contain all the evidence; but it appears in the bill that certain papers said to be tax receipts were introduced in evidence, and that they are not set out in the bill. At the place where they should have been copied into the bill there is an unsigned statement in manuscript as follows: "By agreement of parties, the following sy-

*Rehearing denied March 10, 1904.

nopsis of Highland's tax receipts is substituted for the receipts." Then follows a typewritten page, the first item being as follows: "1891. Tax sale 1891 for $91.46." Next follow a number of columns of figures under the headings, "Year," "Tax," "Delinquency," "Total;" "Pd.," the amount of the column under the heading "Total" being set out in figures. Next is a heading as follows: "Gravel Road Tax, Special Assessment," under which are a number of columns of figures under the headings, "Year," "Amt.," "Del.," "Total," "Pd.," the amount of the column headed "Total" being set out there under the figures. It does not appear by whom or to whom taxes were paid. Some of the evidence before the trial court is not before this court. In making up or in copying the bill some of the evidence shown to have been introduced was purposely omitted. The bill contains something which was not introduced in evidence, substituted for evidence which was before the trial court in making its findings. The receipts should have been set out in full as introduced in evidence. It has very often been held that, where it affirmatively appears that any evidence introduced is not contained in the bill of exceptions, no question depending upon the consideration of all the evidence can be decided.

Judgment affirmed.

(33 Ind. A. 448)

FIDELITY & CASUALTY CO. OF NEW YORK v. SANDERS.

(Appellate Court of Indiana, Division No. 1. Feb. 18, 1904.)

BURGLARY INSURANCE—POLICY—CONSTRUCTION—CONDITIONS—LEGALITY—EFFECT—COMPLIANCE—PROOF OF LOSS—TIME—PLEADING—DEMURRER—APPEAL.

1. Where a policy of burglary insurance provided that the assured, on the occurrence of a burglary, should give immediate notice to the company's agent, or to the home office, and police authorities, and that a claim for loss should be forthwith made in writing, etc., such provisions were conditions precedent, and a compliance therewith was essential to insured's right to recover on the policy, unless waived.

2. Where a foreign insurance company inserted a provision in a burglary insurance policy requiring notice of loss to be given forthwith, in violation of Burns' Rev. St. 1901, § 4923, the insured was required to give notice and furnish proofs of loss within a reasonable time after the burglary.

3. Where, in an action on a burglary insurance policy, the complaint alleged that the burglary was committed on May 24, 1901, and "that afterwards" plaintiff notified defendant of the loss, but the suit was not begun until February 27, 1902, and the complaint did not aver plaintiff's compliance with all the conditions of the policy, the complaint did not sufficiently allege compliance with a provision requiring plaintiff to give notice within a reasonable time.

4. Where, in an action on a burglary insurance policy, the complaint did not allege a compliance with a provision requiring notice of proof of loss within a reasonable time, an averment that defendant, after notice of loss, sent an adjuster to adjust the same, but refused to pay the loss, without alleging the reason for such refusal, did not sufficiently allege a waiver of plaintiff's performance of such condition.

5. A waiver of compliance with a condition in a policy requiring service of proof of loss, in order to be effectual, must be made before the policy is forfeited because of insured's failure to perform the conditions thereof.

6. Where it was averred that burglars broke into plaintiff's building and broke a safe by working the combination and lock on the outer door of the safe, and did then, by the use of tools and explosives; break into the money drawer on the inside of the safe, breaking the lock therefrom, and extracting the drawer from the safe, taking therefrom money, etc., the complaint stated a loss within the policy insuring against loss by the felonious abstraction of money by burglars from a safe described, after entry into the same, effected by the use of tools or explosives directly thereon.

7. Where a complaint is tested by demurrer it cannot be aided by reference to other parts of the record on appeal.

Appeal from Circuit Court, Vermillion County; A. F. White, Judge.

Action by Flora Sanders against the Fidelity & Casualty Company of New York. From a judgment in favor of plaintiff, defendant appeals. Reversed.

Rhoads & Aikman, for appellant. Conley & Conley, for appellee.

ROBINSON, J. Suit by appellee upon a policy insuring against loss by burglary. Trial by court, and finding and judgment for appellee. Errors are assigned on overruling a demurrer to each of the two paragraphs of complaint, sustaining a demurrer to the second and third paragraphs of answer, and the refusal of a new trial. Against the sufficiency of each paragraph of the complaint it is argued that it is not averred that appellee had performed all the conditions on her part to be performed, nor are facts pleaded sufficient to constitute an excuse for their nonperformance. The averment in each paragraph is "that afterward the plaintiff duly notified the said defendant of said loss, and the defendant sent an adjuster to adjust the same, but said adjuster refused to pay and indemnify the plaintiff for such loss, although she has frequently demanded the same." The policy provides that the assured, upon the occurrence of a burglary, shall give immediate notice thereof to the company's agent, or to the home office, and to the police authorities; that, in the event of a claim for loss under the policy, the claim shall be made forthwith in writing, setting forth a particular account of the manner in which the burglary was committed, the date, the damage done to the property insured, the assured's interest in the property, other concurrent or similar insurance, and that the company, upon application therefor, will provide the assured with a blank for such statement of loss; that the company shall not be held to have waived any provision or condition of the policy, or any forfeiture thereof, by furnishing such blank, or by any act taken

¶ 5. See Insurance, vol. 28, Cent. Dig. § 1269.

in connection with the investigation of any claim; that no suit shall be brought under the policy until three months after the particulars of the loss, as before required, have been furnished, nor at all unless commenced within twelve months after date of the burglary.

The provisions above set out are conditions precedent to appellee's right to recover on the policy. It is essential to the sufficiency of the complaint that it should affirmatively show a performance of these conditions, or that a performance had been waived. Home Ins. Co. v. Duke, 43 Ind. 418; Commercial, etc., Co. v. State ex rel. 113 Ind. 331, 15 N. E. 518; Indiana Ins. Co. v. Capehart, 108 Ind. 270, 8 N. E. 285; Prudential Ins. Co. v. Meyers, 15 Ind. App. 339, 44 N. E. 55; Phenix Ins. Co. v. Rogers, 11 Ind. App. 72, 38 N. E. 865. Section 4923, Burns' Rev. St. 1901, relating to foreign insurance companies doing business in this state, and in force when the policy was issued, prohibits such company from inserting certain conditions in its policy; among others, that the insured shall give notice of the loss forthwith, or within the period of time less than five days. The statute provides that any condition inserted in a policy contrary to its provisions shall be void. Under this statute the provisions in the policy in suit that the insured shall give immediate notice of the burglary, and shall forthwith furnish proof of loss, are invalid; but, having been inserted in the policy, the most that can be required by the insurer of the insured is that the insured shall use reasonable diligence in giving the notice and furnishing proof of loss. Phenix Ins. Co. v. Rogers, 11 Ind. App. 72, 38 N. E. 865; Germania Fire Ins. Co. v. Columbia, etc., Co., 11 Ind. App. 385, 39 N. E. 304; Insurance Co. v. Brim, 111 Ind. 281, 12 N. E. 315; Pickel v. Phenix Ins. Co., 119 Ind. 292, 21 N. E. 898. Appellee then was required to give the notice and furnish proofs of loss within a reasonable time after the burglary, and the complaint should show that this was done, or an excuse for not so doing. Ordinarily, what is a reasonable time is a question of fact, but in determining the sufficiency of the facts pleaded as against the demurrer it may be a question of law. The complaint, after stating the facts of the burglary, which it is averred was on May 24, 1901, states "that afterwards" appellee duly notified appellant of the loss. Keeping in view the general rule that a pleading must be construed most strongly against the pleader, and the fact that this suit was begun February 27, 1902, there is nothing in the pleading to indicate at what time between the occurrence of the burglary and the filing of the suit the notice was given. There is no more authority for concluding that the notice was given a few days after the burglary than that it was given a few days before the suit was filed, nine months after the occurrence. So far as disclosed by the pleading, the notice may have been given at any time between these two dates. If the notice was given eight or nine months after the burglary—and we cannot presume, in aid of the pleading, that it was not so given—the notice was not within a reasonable time. It has been held that an unexplained delay of 50 days in giving notice of a loss under a fire policy requiring notice to be given within a reasonable time was an unreasonable delay. Pickel v. Phenix Ins. Co., 119 Ind. 291, 21 N. E. 898. See, also, Railway, etc., Assur. Co. v. Burwell, 44 Ind. 460; Whitehurst v. North Carolina Ins. Co., 52 N. C. 433, 78 Am. Dec. 246; Inman v. Western Fire Ins. Co., 12 Wend. 452; Trask v. State Fire, etc., Ins. Co., 29 Pa. 198, 72 Am. Dec. 622.

The complaint does not contain the general averment that appellee has performed all the conditions on her part to be performed, nor does it contain anything equivalent to this. The policy not only requires that notice of the burglary shall be given, but that, in the event of a claim, proof of loss shall be made. The only averment in this particular is "that afterward the plaintiff duly notified the said defendant of said loss." Even if this could be said to include both the notice of the burglary and the proof of loss required by the policy, it is no more than the conclusion of the pleader that the notice given and the proof of loss made, if any, were such as the policy required. The policy provides that, in the event of a claim for loss, the same shall be made in writing, duly subscribed by the assured, and shall set forth a particular account of the manner in which the burglary was committed, the date, a statement in detail of the damage done, a statement defining the assured's interest in the article or property, and of other concurrent or similar insurance, if any. It cannot be said that the above averment is equivalent to an averment in general terms that appellee had performed all the conditions precedent. In Home Ins. Co. v. Duke, 43 Ind. 418, where the complaint averred that, "And though proof of said loss has been duly made and notice given," the court said: "The allegation in the complaint of performance of the conditions precedent are not sufficient, either under the rules of the common law or under the Code." Does the complaint show a waiver of the performance of these conditions? The only averment that can be said to show a waiver is that appellee notified the company of the loss, "and the defendant sent an adjuster to adjust the same, but said defendant refused to pay and indemnify the plaintiff for such loss." There is a waiver of proof of loss where the company denies the validity of the contract, or asserts that the policy has been canceled (Commercial Ins. Co. v. State ex rel., 113 Ind. 331, 15 N. E. 518); or where it repudiates the contract, and denies all liability (Bowlus v. Phenix Ins. Co., 133 Ind. 106, 32 N. E. 319, 20 L. R. A. 400); or where the company's agent told the insured that the company was not liable, and would never pay any part of the policy (National, etc., Ins. Co. v. Strebe, 16 Ind. App. 110, 44 N. E. 768); or where there is a refusal to pay because the house was not occupied when burned (Home Ins. Co. v. Boyd, 19 Ind. App. 173, 49 N. E. 285); or where the company refuses to pay because the insured property was mortgaged (Western Assur. Co. v. McCarty, 18 Ind. App. 449, 48 N. E. 265). But it certainly could not be held that a refusal to pay because the notice and proof of loss had not been given as the policy requires would be a waiver of the performance of these conditions. And, so far as the pleading discloses, this may have been the reason for refusing payment. No reason whatever is given for the company's refusal to pay, and the pleading cannot be aided by the presumption that it refused to pay for some reason other than that the insured had failed to comply with these conditions. Moreover, the pleading should show the waiver to have become effective before the policy was forfeited through failure to perform the conditions. These conditions could be waived only within the time when appellee would have performed them; that is, a reasonable time. So that, if the company's refusal to pay, as pleaded, could be held to constitute a waiver, it does not appear that this refusal to pay was not after the contract, by its terms, was forfeited because of appellee's failure to perform the conditions. Railway, etc., Ass'n v. Armstrong, 22 Ind. App. 408, 53 N. E. 1037; Phenix Ins. Co. v. Pickel, 3 Ind. App. 332, 29 N. E. 432; American Fire Ins. Co. v. Sisk, 9 Ind. App. 305, 36 N. E. 659; Standard, etc., Ins. Co. v. Strong, 13 Ind. App. 315, 41 N. E. 604. Counsel for appellee cite the case of Indiana Ins. Co. v. Pringle, 21 Ind. App. 559, 52 N. E. 821. In that case the complaint, which was not tested by demurrer, averred that the insured had, on his part, fully performed every act which, by the terms of the policy, he was required to do, and that after the fire the company's adjuster and the insured agreed in writing upon the amount of the loss as covered by the policy, which writing was signed by the insured and the adjuster, on behalf of the company, and filed with the complaint as an exhibit. The only question discussed in that case was the refusal of a new trial. The court correctly held that it was unnecessary to decide whether the averments in the complaint set out a waiver, as upon the trial, without objection by the company, facts were testified to constituting a waiver of proof of loss.

It was further argued that the second paragraph does not aver such a loss as that insured against. In the policy appellant agrees to indemnify appellee for loss of money, etc., "in consequence of the felonious abstraction of the same by burglars from the safe or safes described in said schedule, * * * after entry into such safe or safes by such burglars, effected by the use of tools or explosives directly thereupon." It is averred that burglars broke into the building, "and did then and there break into said safe by working the combination and lock on the outer door of said safe, and did then and there, by the use of tools and force, break into the money drawer on the inside of said safe, breaking the lock therefrom, and extracting said drawer from said safe," taking therefrom money, etc. This averment shows a loss within the provisions of the policy. The policy makes no distinction between outer and inner doors. The pleading shows that the money and property were taken from a part of the safe that was entered by the use of tools and force. Aside from the rule that insurance policies should be liberally construed in favor of the assured, we think this policy means that, if the money or property in the safe is reached through the use of tools or explosives upon any part of the safe, the loss is covered by the policy. In this respect we think the second paragraph sufficient. But for the reasons above given the demurrer to each paragraph of the complaint should have been sustained. As the complaint was tested by demurrer, it cannot be aided by reference to other parts of the record, but must stand or fall by its own averments. Pittsburgh, etc., R. Co. v. Moore, 152 Ind. 345, 53 N. E. 290, 44 L. R. A. 638, and cases there cited.

Judgment reversed.

(32 Ind. A. 432)

TRENT et al. v. EDMONDS.

(Appellate Court of Indiana, Division No. 1. Feb. 18, 1904.)

FRAUDULENT CONVEYANCE — ATTACHMENT — DEBT NOT DUE—SUBSTITUTION OF PARTY—MODIFICATION OF JUDGMENT—PLEADING—APPEAL.

1. In an action for attachment and to set aside a fraudulent conveyance, where, after the death of a defendant, his administrator was substituted on petition and order of the court, and filed an answer, and does not appeal from the judgment rendered, his codefendant cannot complain on appeal that no amended or substituted complaint was filed, naming the administrator as a defendant.

2. Where land was conveyed without consideration in fraud of creditors, the conveyance may be set aside as against the grantee, who had knowledge of the fraudulent intent.

3. In an action of attachment, and to set aside a fraudulent conveyance, an allegation in the complaint that the grantor "was the owner in fee simple of the unincumbered title" was a sufficient allegation of ownership.

4. Under the express provisions of Burns' Rev. St. 1901, § 925, a creditor may attach land fraudulently conveyed, whether the debt is due or not.

5. Where plaintiff extended credit to the defendant's son, relying on a representation, made with defendant's consent, that the son owned a certain tract of land, the validity of a subsequent conveyance of the land without consideration to the defendant cannot, as against plaintiff, be sustained on the ground that a previous conveyance of it by defendant to his son was without consideration, to defraud creditors.

6. Under Burns' Rev. St. 1901, § 273, providing that, when a complete determination of the controversy cannot be had without the presence of other parties, the court must cause them to be joined, on the death of a party defendant the plaintiff is entitled to have an administrator appointed and substituted as a party, whether issues have been joined or not.

7. In an action of attachment and to set aside a fraudulent conveyance, the attachment properly issued against the grantee with notice of the fraud.

8. A motion to dismiss attachment proceedings against an alleged fraudulent grantee of land, made after final judgment, was too late.

9. In an action on notes and to set aside a fraudulent conveyance, in which the grantee was joined as a party defendant, he cannot complain of a personal judgment rendered against the administrator of the grantor on the notes.

10. In an action on notes, for attachment, and to set aside a fraudulent conveyance, the grantee with knowledge of the fraud cannot complain of the refusal of the court to modify the judgment so that the real estate should be sold only when the last note sued on should become due, and that only a lien be declared for the payment of the notes when the last one falls due.

11. Under the express provisions of Burns' Rev. St. 1901, §§ 401, 670, error which is not prejudicial to the complaining party is not sufficient to reverse a judgment; and, where the merits of a cause have been fairly tried and determined, and substantial justice has been done between the parties, a judgment should not be reversed.

Appeal from Circuit Court, Owen County; M. H. Parks, Judge.

Action by Andrew J. Edmonds against Edward B. Trent and another. From a judgment in favor of plaintiff, defendant Josiah Trent appeals. Affirmed.

Fowler & Spangler, for appellant. Willis Hickam, for appellee.

WILEY, P. J. Action by appellee against Edward B. Trent upon two promissory notes. Upon the filing of an affidavit and bond, a writ of attachment was issued. In his amended complaint, appellee alleged that, since the execution of the notes sued on, the payor had fraudulently and without consideration conveyed certain real estate to appellant, Josiah Trent, who was made a party defendant, for the purpose of defrauding his creditors. During the trial, Edward Trent died, and appellee filed a petition asking that an administrator for his estate be appointed, and such administrator substituted for him, and thereupon the petition was granted. John Foster was appointed administrator, gave bond, qualified, and was "substituted as party defendant in lieu of Edward B. Trent, deceased." There was a finding and judgment for appellee. Appellant Josiah Trent alone moved for a new trial, which motion was overruled. John V. Foster, administrator, is made a party appellant, but has filed a paper in this court in which he declines to join in appeal, and avers that the use of his name in the assignment of errors is without his knowledge or consent, and that he is content with the judgment as rendered.

Josiah Trent is therefore the sole appellant. He has assigned 31 errors. The 7th, 8th, 9th, 13th, 14th, 15th, and 16th specifications thereof are not proper assignments of error, and do not present any question for decision. The first four go to the sufficiency of the complaint, and may be considered together.

Appellant's first objection to the amended complaint is that it does not allege any cause of action against John V. Foster, administrator of the estate of Edward B. Trent. It did allege a cause of action against Edward B. Trent. His administrator has not attacked its sufficiency here by an assignment of error. A party seeking the reversal of a judgment has the burden of showing that his substantial rights were prejudiced by the errors of which he complains. Ewbanks' Manual of Practice, § 254; Poundstone v. Baldwin, 145 Ind. 139, 44 N. E. 191; Keller v. Reynolds, 12 Ind. App. 383, 40 N. E. 76, 280; Levi v. Drudge, 139 Ind. 458, 39 N. E. 45. If it be conceded that the complaint does not state a cause of action against Foster, it does not follow that appellant can take advantage of that fact. In this connection, it is fair to say that the special objection urged to the complaint is that, after Foster was substituted as the administrator of Edward B. Trent, no amended or substituted complaint was filed in which he was named as a defendant. This objection is highly technical, and, in view of the facts that he was substituted upon petition and order of the court and filed an answer, and is not now objecting to the sufficiency of the complaint as against him, the appellant cannot object for him. The complaint does state a good cause of action against appellant, for the only allegation made against him is that he became the fraudulent grantee of Edward B. Trent, and took the conveyance from him of the real estate in controversy with a full knowledge of the fraudulent intent, and that it was without consideration.

It is also urged that there is no averment in the complaint that Edward B. Trent was ever the owner of the real estate alleged to be fraudulently conveyed. The allegation is that he "was the owner in fee simple of the unincumbered title," etc. This is a sufficient allegation of ownership, but, if it was not, appellant could not take advantage of it, as shown above.

The remaining objection is that it affirmatively appears that the notes sued on were not due. Appellant was not a party to that issue. This was an action in attachment, and to set aside a conveyance of real estate as fraudulent. Under section 925, Burns' Rev. St. 1901, an attaching plaintiff may prosecute his action, whether his debt is due or not, and such statute settles the question adversely to appellant.

In making up the issues, appellant filed an affirmative answer, to which appellee replied. Appellant's demurrer to the reply was over-

¶ 7. See Attachment, vol. 5, Cent. Dig. § 835.

ruled, and such ruling is assigned as error. The sum and substance of the answer is that appellant, who was the father of Edward B. Trent, deeded the real estate to his son, without consideration, for the purpose of avoiding liability to one Harrington in a suit for slander, and placed the deed on record for the purpose of giving out the information and creating the impression that the land belonged to Edward B. Trent, and not to himself, for the purpose of defeating Harrington's suit. The reply alleges that the land was originally conveyed by Josiah Trent to his son Edward B. Trent, who resided thereon with his father, to defraud his creditors, and the deed placed upon record by him for that purpose; that, while the deed was thus upon record, Edward B., who was, aside from this land, insolvent, with full knowledge and consent of Josiah Trent, represented to appellee that he was the owner thereof, and that appellee, relying upon such representations, and believing them to be true, sold said Edward B. a restaurant and stock of goods, and took the notes in suit as payment therefor. It also avers that appellant and Edward B. colluded to cheat and defraud appellee by representing to him that the real estate was the property of Edward B.; that said collusion was for the fraudulent purpose of enabling Edward B. to purchase the goods of appellee; that they both shared in the goods thus purchased; that, after the death of Edward B., appellant claimed to be their owner as his heir; that appellee sold said goods upon the fact that Edward B. owned said real estate, and upon the representations made to him by both of said parties. If the answer was good, of which we have doubts, but do not decide, the reply stated facts to avoid the issue thus tendered, and hence was sufficient. As between appellant and Edward B., the conveyance by the former to the latter, although in fraud of creditors, was valid. Kitts v. Wilson, 140 Ind. 604, 39 N. E. 313; Edwards et al. v. Haverstick, 53 Ind. 348; Findley v. Cooley, 1 Blackf. 262; Springer v. Drosch, 32 Ind. 486, 2 Am. Rep. 356; Fouty v. Fouty, 34 Ind. 433. Justice Story says: "A conveyance of this sort [for fraud as against creditors] is void only as against creditors, and then only to the extent in which it may be necessary to deal with the conveyed real estate for their satisfaction. To this extent, and this only, it is treated as if it had not been made. To every other purpose it is good." Story, 1 Eq. Jurisp. § 371. Courts will not permit a person to take advantage of his own wrong or fraud. Thus, where one conveys his real estate to another without consideration, to avoid liability for debt, and in fraud of creditors, he will not be permitted to say that he was not guilty of fraudulent intent. The law makes such conduct fraudulent, and this is emphasized when an innocent vendor subsequently sells property to the original fraudulent vendee upon the faith and credit of the property thus conveyed to him. Personette v. Cronkhite et al., 140 Ind. 586, 40 N. E. 59; Shedd et al. v. Webb et al., 157 Ind. 585, 61 N. E. 233. Our conclusion is that the reply was not open to a successful attack of a demurrer.

The 10th, 11th, 12th, 19th, and 20th errors assigned may be considered together, as they relate to the same question, and arise under appellee's petition and motion to have an administrator appointed for the estate of Edward B. Trent, and have him substituted as a party defendant. Appellant moved to reject and strike out the petition and motion, which was overruled, and his motion and the ruling thereon are brought into the record by a bill of exceptions. As stated, Edward B. died before the final disposition of the case, and the action could only be prosecuted against his personal representative.

Four reasons are given why the motion to substitute should be stricken out: (1) Because the issues were joined, trial had, argument of counsel heard, and the cause finally submitted to the court; (2) that admitting the administrator as a party would require the making of new parties after the issues had been joined; (3) that by his substitution new parties were made, and new issues would have to be joined, and thus annul the trial that had already been had; (4) that a good defense cannot be set aside after issues are joined, trial had, and the cause submitted to the court for decision. The reasons stated in the motion are not altogether in harmony with the facts disclosed by the record. The record does not show that the issues were joined when the petition for substitution was filed. In any event, we have no doubt of the right, pending an action, where one of the parties dies, to have an administrator of such deceased party substituted. The action could not proceed otherwise. It does not necessarily follow that new issues must be made. The administrator in such case represents the deceased. After Foster was substituted, he appeared to the amended complaint, and made himself a party to the action by filing an answer admitting the allegations of the complaint, and consenting to a judgment allowing the claim against the estate and sustaining the attachment. We are not advised as to how appellant was injured by the substitution of Foster. He became the representative of the estate of the deceased, with which appellant had no connection, and with which he had no right to meddle. The motion to strike out was properly overruled.

Appellant, in his assignment, predicates error on the overruling of his motion to dismiss the attachment as against him, as affecting his interests in the real estate attached. Counsel say that the attachment proceedings should have been dismissed, so far as they affected the appellant, "for the reason that said appellant * * * was not in any manner a party to the attachment proceedings, neither did he in any manner appear to the attachment proceedings." If he did not appear to the attachment proceedings, we do not know what right he had to move to dismiss them. In any event, this action is prosecuted upon the theory that the conveyance by Edward B. to appellant was fraudulent, and hence void as to creditors. If it was fraudulent, then the property was the property of appellant, and subject to attachment. As between appellee and Edward B., that was the issue of fact for determination. If the conveyance was not fraudulent, then the title vested in appellant, in which event his ultimate rights could not have been prejudiced. The issue which he tendered, and which was the issue between him and appellee, was that the property was his, and not Edward B.'s. If, for no other reason, the motion was properly overruled because it was not made until after final judgment, it came too late.

The sixteenth specification of the assignment of errors is that "the court erred in rendering personal judgment on the notes in suit against the estate of Edward B. Trent, deceased." If this was a proper assignment of error, appellant could not take advantage of it, for the judgment rendered against the estate of Edward B. could in no way affect his rights. He can only complain of errors prejudicial to him.

Appellant moved in arrest of judgment, which motion was overruled, and such ruling is one of the errors relied upon for reversal. It is urged that the motion in arrest should have been sustained for four reasons (1) that the complaint did not state a cause of action against Foster, administrator; (2) that the notes were not due; (3) that the complaint does not aver that Edward B. Trent was at any time the owner of the real estate in controversy; and (4) that the real estate described in the complaint is not the real estate conveyed by Edward B. to appellant. Appellant cannot take advantage of the first reason urged in arrest of judgment, because he is not affected by it. If any one could complain, it was the administrator, and he waived the point by appearing and filing an answer consenting to judgment. There is no merit in the second reason assigned, because an attachment proceeding may be successfully prosecuted upon a note not due, under the express provisions of the statute. Section 925, Burns' Rev. St. 1901. An action in attachment and to set aside a fraudulent conveyance may be jointly prosecuted. Quarl v. Abbett, 102 Ind. 233, 1 N. E. 476, 52 Am. Rep. 662. The third reason urged in arrest of judgment was disposed of in passing upon the sufficiency of the complaint. There is no merit in the fourth reason urged. The real estate is sufficiently described and identified.

Appellant's motion to modify the judgment was also overruled. He asked in his motion that the judgment be modified so that the real estate attached be sold only when the last note sued on should become due, and that only a lien "be declared on said lands for the payment of said notes when said last note falls due." Also to modify the "judgment and decree in attachment, that any sum or sums of money in the hands of said Foster as administrator * * * shall be applied first to the satisfaction of plaintiff's judgment," etc. The judgment makes ample provision for the application of any funds in the hands of the administrator to the payment of the judgment, and therefore the last reason assigned for the modification of the judgment is unavailing. As to the first, we do not see how appellant is in a position to take advantage of it, even if the judgment is not technically correct. The court found that the conveyance from Edward B. to appellant was fraudulent, and that the latter took the conveyance with full knowledge of the fraud. The court also found that Edward B. after said conveyance was insolvent. There was ample evidence to support the attachment. The modification of the judgment, for which he asked, could in no sense affect his rights, and hence he cannot complain.

Under the statute (section 273, Burns' Rev. St. 1901) and the practice in this state, the trial court has wide latitude and discretion in admitting new parties. Where full and complete justice cannot be done without the bringing in of new parties, they should be brought in. Scobey v. Finton, 39 Ind. 275; Pickrell v. Jerauld, 1 Ind. App. 10, 27 N. E. 433, 50 Am. St. Rep. 192; Parker v. State ex rel., 132 Ind. 419, 31 N. E. 1114; Barner v. Bayless, 134 Ind. 600, 33 N. E. 907, 34 N. E. 502; Kirshbaum v. Hanover Ins. Co., 16 Ind. App. 606, 45 N. E. 1113.

This disposes of every question but the overruling of appellant's motion for a new trial. In that motion he assigned 30 reasons why it should be sustained. We cannot take up these several reasons seriatim, for it would extend this opinion to an unreasonable length, and not serve any useful purpose. The first and second reasons question the sufficiency of the evidence to support the finding and judgment. There is an abundance of evidence to support every material averment of the complaint, and, while there is some conflict, we cannot disturb the judgment on the evidence. The third reason is not discussed. The fourth to the nineteenth reasons, inclusive, allege error in admitting evidence over appellant's objections. A careful examination of the evidence thus admitted, in connection with all the other evidence, leads us to the conclusion that there is no reversible error in the admission of the evidence of which appellant complains. Under repeated decisions and the express provision of the statute, error which is not prejudicial to the complaining party is not sufficient to reverse a judgment; and where the merits of a cause have been fairly tried and determined, and substantial justice has been done between the parties, a judgment should not be reversed. Sections 401, 670, Burns' Rev. St. 1901; Ewbank's Manual, § 254; Elliott's App. Prac. §§ 631, 652; Poundstone v. Baldwin, 145 Ind. 139, 44 N. E. 191; Engrer v. Ohio, etc., Ry. Co., 142 Ind. 618, 42 N. E. 217; Schmidt v. Draper, 137 Ind. 249, 36 N. E. 709. The twentieth, twenty-first, and twenty-second reasons for a new trial charge errors in overruling appellant's motion to strike out certain evidence, and in refusing to permit appellant to answer certain questions propounded to him. There was no error in these rulings. All other questions attempted to be raised by the motion for a new trial have been disposed of adversely to appellant in this opinion.

The trial court reached the right conclusion, and the judgment is affirmed.

(32 Ind. A. 425)

EVANSVILLE & I. R. CO. v. HUFFMAN.

(Appellate Court of Indiana, Division No. 2. Feb. 17, 1904.)

RAILROADS—FENCING RIGHT OF WAY—STATUTE—ACTION—COMPLAINT—EXHIBIT.

1. The notice required to be given a railroad company under Burns' Rev. St. 1901, § 5324, providing that the owner of any lands abutting on the right of way of any railroad shall have the right, after giving 30 days' notice in writing, to enter on the right of way and build a fence on the failure of the railroad to comply with the law regarding the fencing of the right of way, is not a proper exhibit to a complaint in an action against the railroad to recover the expense of erecting such fence.

2. In an action against a railroad to recover the expense of erecting a fence pursuant to Burns' Rev. St. 1901, § 5324, providing that the owner of any lands abutting on the right of way of any railroad shall have the right, after giving a certain notice, to enter on the right of way to build a fence on failure of the railroad to comply with the law regarding the fencing of the right of way, a complaint which does not allege that the fence was built on the side of the defendant's railroad or right of way, nor give any excuse for not so doing, is insufficient.

3. In an action against a railroad to recover the expense of erecting a fence pursuant to Burns' Rev. St. § 5324, providing that the owner of any lands abutting on the right of way of any railroad shall have the right, after giving a certain notice, to enter on the right of way and build a fence on failure of the railroad to comply with the law regarding the fencing of the right of way, and that, "when he has completed the same," he may present for payment an itemized statement of the expenses thereof, a complaint which omits to allege the date the plaintiff entered on the defendant's right of way and built the fence, and the day on which it was completed, is insufficient.

Appeal from Circuit Court, Clay County; P. O. Colliver, Judge.

Action by Faustimus Huffman against the Evansville & Indianapolis Railroad Company. From a judgment for plaintiff, defendant appeals. Reversed.

D. P. Williams, John G. Williams, and George A. Knight, for appellant. G. S. Payne, for appellee.

ROBY, J. Suit by appellee to recover for fencing part of appellant's right of way. A demurrer to the complaint was overruled, and the correctness of such ruling is duly presented. By the statute upon which appellee's right rests, it is made the duty of railroad companies to build fences "on both sides of such railroad throughout the entire length," etc. Burns' Rev. St. 1901, § 5323. The following section authorizes the abutting landowner, under certain specified conditions, to enter upon the railroad right of way and build such fences, so far as his own land abuts upon the right of way of the railroad, and, "when he has completed the same, he may present for payment to the agent of such corporation, * * * an itemized statement verified by the affidavit of such person or his agent, of the expenses thereof. * * *" Burns' Rev. St. 1901, § 5324. The Illinois courts hold, under a statute similar in this regard to ours, that the duty of the company is not discharged by the erection of a fence 10 feet inside the right of way line. Railroad v. People, 121 Ill. 483-488, 13 N. E. 236. And it was held in that state that the company may not encroach upon the lands of the abutter; that it must build its fence upon its own right of way. W., St. L. & P. Ry. v. Zeigler, 108 Ill. 304. The Illinois statute considered in these cases was penal, and therefore strictly construed. The Indiana statute is remedial, and therefore liberally construed in favor of the accomplishment of the object sought. Midland Ry. v. Gascho, 7 Ind. App. 407, 34 N. E. 643; Chicago, etc., Ry. v. Woodard, 13 Ind. App. 296, 41 N. E. 544; Chicago, etc., Ry. v. Vert, 24 Ind. App. 78, 56 N. E. 139.

The complaint contains no averment that the fence was built upon the side of appellant's railroad or right of way, nor is any excuse given for not so doing. It is averred that notice was given by appellee to appellant on February 8, 1897, of his intention to enter upon its right of way "where the same passes over and through the lands aforedescribed of plaintiff." The notice is attempted to be made a part of the complaint by exhibit, but, not being the foundation of the action, such attempt was ineffective. Midland Ry. v. Gascho, 7 Ind. App. 407, 410, 34 N. E. 643; Chicago Ry. v. Vert, 24 Ind. App. 78, 56 N. E. 139. The language of the statute must be taken as it is—"on both sides of such railway track." The side of the railroad means to the abutting landowner exactly what it does to the railroad company. Where it is bound to build the fence, he may, other conditions justifying, build it. If, on account of the condition of the ground, it is impossible to put the fence at the extreme limit of the right of way, the company would not thereby be released from the duty to fence, nor would it be required to do that which is impossible. The landowner building for it might therefore find a condition justifying him in building otherwise than on the last inch of right of way, but no facts showing any such situation are set up in this complaint, and the demurrer to it should have been sustained. It is not a good complaint for a different reason. The statute authorizes the presentation for payment of an itemized statement of expenses "when he has completed the same." The averment made as to the completion of the fence is as follows: "That plaintiff on the —— day of 1898 entered on defendant's right of way and built a good and lawful fence, * * * and completed the same on the —— day of —— month of 18—." The omitted dates are essential to the appellee's cause of action. First Nat. Bank v. Deitch, 83 Ind. 131.

Other questions argued will not likely arise again, and are therefore not decided.

Judgment reversed and cause remanded, with instructions to sustain demurrer to complaint and for further proceedings.

(34 Ind. App. 248)

PACIFIC MUT. LIFE INS. CO. v. BRANHAM.*

(Appellate Court of Indiana, Division No. 2. Feb. 17, 1904.)

ACCIDENT INSURANCE—IMMEDIATE NOTICE—WAIVER—CONTINUOUS DISABILITY—INSTRUCTIONS.

1. A complaint on an accident policy, which stated that plaintiff, after the injury, was immediately and continuously disabled, and incapacitated from business, and so remained wholly incapacitated and prevented from performing any work for 15 months, was not objectionable on the ground that it failed to aver that the disability resulted immediately from the injury.

2. An accident policy insured against injuries resulting in immediate, continuous, and total loss of business time. Insured was injured, and some days thereafter underwent an operation which confined him to bed for four weeks, at the end of which time he was able to go to his office and perform a portion of his labor, which he did for nearly a month, when he again discontinued labor, and was treated for his injuries for over two months. He was then able to move about on crutches, with his injured limb in a plaster cast, but at the end of the month was compelled to remove this and take treatment for two months and a half, and after another period, during which he was able to use crutches and a cane, he took treatment steadily for several months, and was again operated upon. *Held*, that his disability was continuous, within the meaning of the policy.

3. Where an accident policy required immediate notice of injury, and the insurer, on receiving notice some time after the injury, sent insured blanks on which to furnish proof of injury and loss of time, giving particular instructions, and stating that, when the proofs had been made and insured was ready to resume his duties, the claim would be adjusted without unnecessary delay, the provision as to immediate notice was waived.

4. Where insured in an accident policy made proof of disability and loss of time to a certain date, under the advice of his physician that he would soon be well, he was not thereby precluded, in an action on the policy, from claiming the amount due for disability continuing after that date.

5. In an accident policy, agreeing to pay a certain indemnity for the immediate, continuous, and total loss of time necessarily resulting from injuries, the word "immediate" will be construed as applying to causation.

6. In an action on an accident policy, the court charged that, while there must be an immediate, continuing, and total loss of business time, there need not be a total loss of time beginning at the time the bodily injuries were first sustained, and continuing total for the period for which the indemnity is sought; and thereafter charged that the loss of time must be immediately consequent upon the injuries, and thereafter continuous during any period for which the plaintiff might recover, so that if the plaintiff suffered loss of time and afterwards his injuries improved, so that he suffered no loss of time, he could not recover for any period thereafter, although he might subsequently suffer total loss of time, but that the loss of time must be continuous. *Held*, that the two instructions were not contradictory or misleading.

Appeal from Superior Court, Vanderburgh County; John H. Foster, Judge.

Action by Hal H. Branham against the Pacific Mutual Life Insurance Company. From a judgment for plaintiff, defendant appeals. Affirmed.

J. E. Williamson, for appellant. C. L. Wedding, for appellee.

COMSTOCK, J. Appellee, who was plaintiff below, recovered judgment against appellant upon an accident policy issued to him by appellant. The policy is made a part of the complaint. The defendant answered in three paragraphs: First, a general denial. Second, that the plaintiff's disability was not immediately consequent upon the happening of the accident, which was March 8th, and the disability did not occur until March 24th, and that between those dates appellee was not continuously and totally disabled, in consequence of the injury, to perform the character of labor mentioned in the policy. The third alleged the plaintiff failed to give notice of the accident according to the terms of the policy. The case was tried by a jury, and a verdict returned for appellee in the sum of $922. $75 of this sum was remitted. Appellant's motion for a new trial overruled, and judgment rendered.

The errors assigned are, first, that the court erred in overruling appellant's demurrer for want of facts to the amended complaint; second, in overruling appellant's motion for a new trial.

It is urged that the complaint is bad because it fails to aver that the disability resulted immediately from the injury. The complaint, after alleging the receipt of the injury, avers that appellee "was so immediately and continuously disabled and crippled and wholly incapacitated for all business, labor, or calling, and so remained wholly incapacitated, disabled, and prevented from

*Rehearing denied. Transfer to Supreme Court denied.

¶ 5. See Insurance, vol. 28, Cent. Dig. § 1181.

performing any work or labor, or pursuing any calling, for the space of fifteen months," etc. The objection is not well taken.

Appellant next argues, in the order stated, that appellee's disability was not continuous; second, that his loss of time was not total. The provisions of the policy involved are (omitting the formal parts): "Against the effects of bodily injuries sustained within the terms of this policy, caused solely by external, violent and accidental means, the company will pay an indemnity of twenty-five and $^{00}/_{100}$ dollars per week, not exceeding fifty-two consecutive weeks, for the immediate, continuous and total loss of such business time as may necessarily result from such injuries alone."

The evidence shows that in March, 1900, appellee was 29 years old, and in good health, and was paymaster and chief clerk to the treasurer and purchasing agent of Peoria, Decatur & Evansville Railroad. At that time he held an accident policy in the appellant company promising the payment to him of $25 per week for the immediate, continuous, and total loss of such business time as might necessarily result from such injury alone. On the night of March 8th, while bowling in a tenpin alley, he slipped, fell, and wrenched his knee, which he thought unimportant at the time. Next morning his knee was swollen, was bathed and bandaged, and this treatment was kept up for five or six days, with no improvement. At the end of five or six days, or on the 13th or 14th of March, he consulted Dr. G. M. Young, the examiner for the appellant company, who continued the same general treatment, but without benefit, and at the end of a week, or about the 20th or 21st of March, he had to go to bed and be operated on. He remained in bed, under treatment, for four weeks; then, under the advice of the physician, he went to his office, exercising proper care, and performing such portion of his labor as he could, until the 20th of May, when he went to Indianapolis to consult a specialist, returned to Indianapolis on the 26th, where he remained until the 6th of August, when he was obliged to return home to Evansville because of the sale of his railroad. He returned home on crutches and in plaster of paris, and remained in that condition for a month. Under the direction of his surgeon he removed the plaster, and took a massage treatment until November, when he again returned to Indianapolis and was operated on. He remained in the hospital until December 15th, when he returned to Evansville, and was able to get around with crutches and cane until the middle of February, when he was obliged to again return for treatment to Indianapolis, where he was again operated on, and again spent three or four weeks in the hospital, returning to Evansville about the middle of March in plaster of paris, and remained in that condition until the 20th of April. About that time he took treatment from Dr. Young, who operated on him April 21st, and continued treating him until May 20, 1901, and this was his condition from about the middle of March, 1900, extending over a period of 15 months continuously.

From the evidence the jury was justified in concluding that appellee's disability was continuous, and, applying the rule laid down by the court in Commercial Travelers', etc., Ass'n v. Springsteen, 23 Ind. App. 671, 55 N. E. 978, that his disability was total. In that case the court approved the following instruction given by the court below: "This paragraph sets out as an exhibit a copy of the policy, and in said policy it is provided that no claim shall ever accrue unless it arises from physical bodily injury through external, violent, and accidental means, and then only when the injury shall, independent of all other causes, immediately and wholly disable the insured from performing any and every kind of business pertaining to his occupation as manager of the When Clothing Company. I instruct you that, as a matter of law, the meaning of this provision of the policy is not that the plaintiff must have been disabled so as to prevent him from doing anything whatsoever pertaining to his said occupation, but that he must have been disabled only to the extent that he could not do any and every kind of business pertaining to his occupation. He might be able to do a part and not be able to do all, and because he was not able to do all be deemed to be wholly disabled from doing any and every kind, provided, of course, that he was so disabled as to be prevented from doing subsequently all the necessary and material things in said occupation requiring his own exertions, and substantially his customary and usual manner of so doing. He might be able to do personally minor and trivial things not requiring much time or physical labor, and through others, acting under his direction, to do the heavier things, requiring physical exertion, which in the ordinary and proper performance of his duties he had heretofore done personally, and yet, because of inability to do these heavier things and more material things personally, be said to be wholly disabled within the terms of his policy; provided, further, that the things he was able to do personally do constitute substantially all of his said occupation." In the opinion many cases are collected. We do not deem it necessary to recite them.

We quote from Joyce on Insurance, in speaking of indemnity clauses of accident insurance contracts (section 3031), as follows: "The general purpose of such clauses is to furnish an indemnity to assured for the loss of time by reason of accident or injury which prevents him from prosecuting his business, and it would seem that this ought to refer to his inability to perform substantially the duties which are necessary to be done in the business to which the contract refers—an absolute physical inability to perform substantially the duties which are necessary to be done in the business to which the contract refers. An absolute physical inability ought not to be meant in all cases, for the injury might be of such a character as that common care and prudence would preclude the prosecution of said business."

From Kerr on the same subject (page 386): "Total disability does not mean absolute physical disability on the part of the insured to transact any kind of business pertaining to his occupation. Total disability exists although the insured is able to perform a few occasional acts, if he is unable to do any substantial portion of the work connected with his occupation. It is sufficient to prove that the injury wholly disabled him from the doing of all substantial and material acts necessary to be done in the prosecution of his business, or that his injuries were of such a character and degree that common care and prudence required him to desist from his labors so long as was reasonably necessary to effect a speedy cure." And from May (4th Ed. § 522): "Total disability from the prosecution of one's usual employment means inability to follow his usual occupation, business, or pursuits in the usual way. Though he may do certain parts of his accustomed work, and engage in some of his usual employments, he may yet recover, so long as he cannot to some extent do all parts, and engage in all such employments."

The policy contains the following provision: "Unless the claimant gives the company at San Francisco, California, immediate notice of any accident with full particulars, and name and address of insured, and furnish affirmative proof," etc., "all claims based thereon and hereon shall be forfeited." It is insisted that it was necessary for appellee to prove that notice was given as required by the policy. Appellee was injured March 8, 1901, and notice was given March 30, 1901. Appellant contends that the notice was insufficient because not immediate. It has been held in this state that "immediate" means within a reasonable time under the circumstances. Insurance Co. v. Brim, 111 Ind. 281, 12 N. E. 315. In Martin v. Pifer, 96 Ind. 245, at page 248, the court say: "The construction as given generally by the courts to the words 'immediately' and 'forthwith,' when they occur in contracts or in statutes, is that the act referred to should be performed within such convenient time as is reasonably requisite. In Phybus v. Mitford, 2 Lev. 75, decided more than two centuries ago, it was said: 'The word "immediately," although in strictness it excludes all meantimes, yet, to make good the deeds and intents of parties, it shall be construed such convenient time as is reasonably requisite for doing the thing.' This construction has prevailed since in most cases which have come to our attention. In re Blue, 5 El. 290; Snowball v. Dixon, 4 Y. & C. 611; Richardson v. End, 43 Wis. 316; Ins. Co. v. Ins. Co., 20 Barb. 468; Rokes v. Ins. Co., 51 Md. 512, 34 Am. Rep. 323; Railway, etc., Co. v. Burwell, 44 Ind. 460." See, also, Peele v. Fund Soc., 147 Ind. 543, 44 N. E. 661, 46 N. E. 990; Ins. Co. v. Baum, 29 Ind. 236; 1 A. & E. Ency. of Law (2d Ed.) 323; Employers', etc., Co. v. Light, etc., Co., 28 Ind. App. 437, 63 N. E. 54. In Pickel v. Phenix Ins. Co., 119 Ind. 291, 21 N. E. 898, a suit upon a fire insurance policy in which the policy contained the provision that in case of loss the insured should forthwith give notice thereof to the company, after citing Passenger Assurance Co. v. Burwell, supra, and other cases, held that a delay of 50 days, unexplained, was an unreasonable delay.

Appellee delayed giving notice because he did not deem the injury serious. The evidence, however, shows that upon receipt of notice of appellee's injury appellant sent blanks to him upon which to furnish proofs of accidental injury and loss of time from work, giving particular instructions to the appellee as to the proof, concluding, "When this is done and you are ready to resume your duties send all papers to this office and claim will be adjusted without unnecessary delay." This was a waiver of time in giving notice. The proof was warranted under the averment of the complaint that appellant denied all liability to plaintiff upon said policy. Towle v. Ins. Co., 91 Mich. 227, 51 N. W. 987; Kerr on Ins. § 191; Hohn v. Interstate Cas. Co. (Mich.) 72 N. W. 1105.

Another reason for a new trial is that the amount of recovery—$847—is too large. It is insisted that under no view of the case is appellee entitled to more than $378.55, being $25 per week for the time intervening between the 24th of March and August 6th, 19 weeks, at $25 per week, being the time which he claims he lost as set out in the original proofs which appellee testified he sent in but subsequently withdrew. Under the advice of his physician that he would likely be well soon, appellee made proofs for payment to August 6th. This would not preclude his making further claim for an amount justly due him for continuing disability. Hohn v. Interstate Cas. Co., supra.

In instructions Nos. 2, 3, 4, and 5, requested by appellant and refused, is presented its construction of the policy, viz., that "immediate," as used with relation to other words and terms of the policy, applied to time, and not to causation. Shera v. Oseon, etc., 32 Ont. 411, holds against appellant's claim. At most, it can only be said, for the claim of appellant, that the language employed is equally susceptible of two interpretations, in which event the one giving greater indemnity and sustaining the claim will be adopted. May on Ins. §§ 174, 175; Ins. Co. v. Woods, 11 Ind. App. 335, 37 N. E. 180, 39 N. E. 205; Ins. Co. v. Jones, 17 Ind. App. 592, 47 N. E. 342.

Instructions 2 and 2½ given were excepted to. It is claimed that they are misleading and contradictory; that instruction 2 does not require the jury to find a continuous total loss of business time, while 2½ does. Instruction 2 concludes as follows: "But while there must be an immediate loss of business time, and a continuing loss of business time, and a total loss of business time, there need not be a total loss of business time which must begin at the time the bodily injuries were first sustained, and continue total for the period of time for which the indemnity is sought." Two and one-half is as follows: "The loss of business must be immediately consequent upon the injuries sustained, and must be thereafter continuous during any period of time for which the plaintiff may recover. If the plaintiff suffered a loss of business time, and afterwards his injuries, if any, improved so that he suffered no loss of business time, he cannot recover for any period thereafter, although he may subsequently suffer a total loss of time by reason of his injuries. The loss of business time must be continuous. If, for example, on the 17th day of April his injuries, if any, became so much improved that he suffered no loss of business time therefrom, he could not recover for any period thereafter." Two and one-half differs from two in making clear the fact that after the loss of business time once ceases there can be no recovery after that time, although there may be a recurrence of the loss of time. We cannot concede that these instructions are contradictory or misleading.

The instructions given, considered as a whole, are not inconsistent, and are in harmony with the instruction approved in Association v. Springsteen, supra. In his able brief counsel for appellant cites authorities in support of the instructions refused, and of the proposition that the word "immediate" applies to time and not causation. We concede that the decisions are not in harmony upon the meaning of either "total disability" or the word "immediate."

The judgment is clearly right upon the evidence, and the judgment is affirmed.

(32 Ind. A. 488)

RUTHERFORD v. PRUDENTIAL INS. CO.

(Appellate Court of Indiana, Division No. 1. Feb. 16, 1904.)

APPEAL—RECORD—TRANSCRIPT—PRÆCIPE—STATUTES—REPEAL.

1. Burns' Rev. St. 1901, § 661, providing that, when an appealing party desires only a partial record, he is required to designate in writing the particular parts of the record to be certified, and such written direction shall be appended to the transcript, is mandatory.

2. Such section was not repealed by Acts 1903, p. 340, c. 193, § 7, providing that a person desiring a transcript of the record may file with the clerk a præcipe therefor, and, if he desires a transcript of the entire record, it shall be sufficient to so state in the præcipe; otherwise he shall indicate therein the parts of the record desired, etc.

3. Acts 1903, p. 340, c. 193, § 7, providing that any person desiring a transcript of the record, or any part thereof, for appeal, may file with the clerk a written præcipe therefor, etc., is directory only.

4. Where it affirmatively appeared from the record on appeal and from the clerk's certificate that the record contained a transcript of all the pleadings, rulings thereon, judgment, etc., it was immaterial that it did not contain any written præcipe or directions to the clerk to make and certify such transcript.

Appeal from Circuit Court, Perry County; C. W. Cook, Judge.

Action by Harry Rutherford against the Prudential Insurance Company. From a judgment in favor of defendant, plaintiff appeals. On motion to dismiss. Overruled.

W. A. Land and W. M. Waldschmidt, for appellant. George J. Lindeman and Patrick & Minor, for appellee.

WILEY, P. J. Appellee has interposed a motion to dismiss the appeal upon the ground that "no præcipe is incorporated in the transcript." This motion is predicated upon the act of March 9, 1903, "concerning proceedings in civil procedure" (Acts 1903, p. 338, c. 193). Section 7, p. 340, of that act, among other things, provides that "any party or person desiring a transcript of the record of any cause or proceeding, or of any part thereof, for appeal, may file with the clerk a written præcipe therefor. If such party or person desires a transcript of the entire record, it shall be sufficient to so state in the præcipe; if a complete transcript be not desired, then such party or person shall indicate in the præcipe the parts of the record desired. And in the event that any other party to the judgment shall desire a complete transcript of the record upon such appeal, or that any part or parts not required by the præcipe so filed shall be included in the transcript, he may file with the clerk his præcipe in like form. Such præcipe shall constitute a part of the record. * * * The præcipe shall be copied in the transcript immediately before the certificate of the clerk." Counsel for appellee assume that this statute is mandatory, and that the appealing party, whether he requires a partial or complete record, must so indicate by a præcipe, and such præcipe must be filed as a part of the record. Under section 661, Burns' Rev. St. 1901, where an appealing party desires only a partial record, he is required to designate in writing the particular parts of the record to be certified, and such written directions shall be appended to the transcript. This provision of the statute is mandatory. In such case the clerk, in his certificate, should specify what parts of the record he has copied. Reid v. Houston, 49 Ind. 181. If it does not appear that any præcipe was filed, it is the duty of the clerk to make out and certify a complete transcript of the cause. Barnes v. Pelham et al., 18 Ind. App. 166, 47 N. E. 648. The act of March 9th, supra, did not repeal section 661, supra. It will be observed from the quotation above from section 7 of the act of 1903 that the language is, "may file with the clerk a written præcipe therefor." This cannot be construed as being mandatory, as applied to a complete transcript of the proceedings to be used on appeal. Under this statute, if a præcipe is filed, whether for a complete or partial transcript of the proceedings below, such præcipe would become a part of the record, and should be copied in the transcript as directed. In this appeal there was no written direction to the clerk to make and certify a transcript of the proceedings below, and none was required. The transcript was evidently prepared according to the provisions of section 661, supra. It affirmatively appears, both from the record itself and the certificate of the clerk, that it contains a transcript of all the pleadings, the rulings thereon, the judgment, etc. This is sufficient.

Motion to dismiss overruled.

(32 Ind. A. 507)

HELVIE et al. v. McKAIN.

(Appellate Court of Indiana, Division No. 1. Feb. 26, 1904.)

NOTES—CONSIDERATION—ESTOPPEL TO DENY—EXPLANATION BY PAROL—APPEAL—WAIVER OF ERRORS.

1. Where the consideration of a note given by defendants to plaintiff was the furnishing of money to a corporation in which defendants were interested, and defendants received the consideration, they could not, having voluntarily and without fraud entered into the agreement, be heard to complain in a suit on the note on the ground of inadequacy or want of consideration.

2. The mere form of a note does not necessarily determine the relations to the note of the parties whose names appear thereon, but such relation may be shown by parol.

3. Questions presented by the assignment of errors, but not discussed in the briefs, are waived.

Appeal from Circuit Court, Delaware County; Ralph S. Gregory, Special Judge.

Action by Arthur A. McKain against Charles E. Helvie and others. From a judgment for plaintiff, defendants appeal. Affirmed.

Templer, Ball & Templer, for appellants. Harold Taylor, for appellee.

ROBINSON, J. Suit by appellee upon a note and to foreclose a mortgage. On December 13, 1899, appellant Helvie and others executed and delivered to appellee a note for $3,000; and, as part of the same transaction, appellant and wife executed to appellee a mortgage on certain land, promising in the mortgage to pay the sum so secured. Appellant Charles E. Helvie was a stockholder in, and president of, the Eureka Poterie Company, a corporation, which owed a balance of $3,000 purchase money. This sum was required to be paid within a few days to save the company from loss of its property by forfeiture, and appellant Helvie had attempted to secure from various sources that sum upon the note of the company, but failed. On the above date, appellant Helvie arranged with appellee for a loan of $3,000 upon appellant's agreeing to secure the payment of the same by mortgage, and in pursuance of this agreement the note, signed by appellant Helvie and other officers and stockholders in the company, and the mortgage, were executed. Appellee accepted the note, and discounted the same at a bank, and the proceeds, $3,000, passed to the credit of the company, and were expended by appellant Helvie and other officers of the company in paying the above indebtedness. Appellee is still the owner of the note and mortgage, both of which were delivered by appellant Helvie to appellee. The furnishing of the $3,000, to be used by appellant for the benefit of the company, by the payment of the indebtedness above mentioned, was the consideration agreed upon for the execution of the note, which consideration appellants received. The court's conclusions of law upon the foregoing facts were that appellee was entitled to a judgment upon the note, and to a decree of foreclosure.

The only questions argued by appellants' counsel are that there was no consideration passed from appellee to appellants, and that the evidence shows that appellee became and was a member of the company, and was a maker of the note, the same as those who signed it, and that when he paid the amount of the note to the bank he was only entitled to contribution from the other makers. It is found as a fact that the furnishing of the $3,000 to be used by appellants for the benefit of the company, by the payment of a purchase-money indebtedness, was the consideration agreed upon for the execution of the note by appellants to appellee, and that appellants received the consideration agreed upon. Appellants, having voluntarily and without fraud or deception entered into the agreement, and having received all they contracted for, could not be heard to complain on the ground of inadequacy or want of consideration. "The consideration agreed upon," said the court in Hardesty v. Smith, 3 Ind. 39, "may indefinitely exceed the value of the thing for which it is promised, and still the bargain stand. The doing of an act by one at the request of another, which may be a detriment or inconvenience, however slight, to the party doing it, or may be a benefit, however slight, to the party at whose request it is performed, is a legal consideration for a promise by such requesting party." See Wolford v. Powers, 85 Ind. 294, 44 Am. Rep. 16; Mullen v. Hawkins, 141 Ind. 363, 40 N. E. 797; Ditmar v. West, 7 Ind. App. 637, 35 N. E. 47. It is true that the mere form of a note does not necessarily determine the relations to the note of the parties whose names appear on the note, and that the actual relation may be shown by parol

¶ 2. See Bills and Notes, vol. 7, Cent. Dig. § 1723.

evidence. Lacy v. Lofton, 26 Ind. 324; Tombler v. Reitz, 134 Ind. 9, 33 N. E. 789. But whether appellee was the bona fide payee of the note, or was in effect one of the makers of the note, was determined by the court from all the evidence, and there is evidence to support the conclusion reached by the trial court.

There is evidence to support the findings. We find nothing in the record authorizing us to disturb the court's conclusion in this respect. The conclusions of law are clearly right upon the facts as found by the court, and the judgment follows the conclusions of law. Such questions presented by the assignment of errors as are not discussed by counsel in their brief are deemed waived.

Judgment affirmed.

(32 Ind. A. 477)

COMER v. BOARD OF COM'RS OF MORGAN COUNTY.

(Appellate Court of Indiana, Division No. 2. Feb. 23, 1904.)

OFFICER — COUNTY CLERK — CONVERSION — RIGHT TO SPECIAL COMPENSATION — APPEAL — DISCUSSION OF ASSIGNMENT OF ERROR.

1. A county may recover from an officer amounts unlawfully allowed him out of the county treasury, which he accepted and converted to his own use.

2. In an action by a county against an officer for conversion, the county's liability for breach of a special contract cannot be used as a set-off or counterclaim; the suit being in tort.

3. A county clerk is entitled to his per diem for attending the sessions of the circuit court, in addition to his salary.

4. Where a county clerk receives a salary, he is not entitled to special compensation for any official services, unless there is a statutory provision therefor.

5. A county clerk's claim for compensation, in addition to his salary, for making certificates of allowance to special judges of the circuit court, being official services, will be disallowed by the Appellate Court where he fails to point out any statute authorizing such compensation.

6. Errors assigned on appeal, and not discussed, are thereby waived.

Appeal from Circuit Court, Johnson County; James E. McCullough, Special Judge.

Action by the board of commissioners of Morgan county against William A. Comer. From a judgment in favor of plaintiff, defendant appeals. Reversed.

Miller & Barnett, A. M. Bain, and O. Matthews, for appellant. George W. Grubbs and Elliott, Elliott & Littleton, for appellee.

ROBY, J. Action by the board of commissioners of Morgan county against appellant to recover money alleged to have been received by him while serving as clerk of said county, and wrongfully kept and converted by him to his own use. That the county may recover from the officer amounts unlawfully allowed him out of the county treasury, which he accepted and converted to his own use, is established. Board v. Heaston, 144 Ind. 583, 41 N. E. 457, 43 N. E. 651, 55 Am. St. Rep. 192; State ex rel. v. Flynn (Ind. Sup.) 69 N. E. 159.

Appellant's third paragraph of answer admitted the retention of the amounts as charged in the complaint, but averred that while still in office he entered into a contract with appellee by which he was to make certain indexes for the use of the office and the public, and that thereunder he did make and deliver indexes to the value of $1,500; that the indexes called for by said contract were worth to him $4,500; and that while he was fulfilling his contract the board of county commissioners rescinded the same, and refused to allow him to proceed further with his work, whereby he was damaged, etc. A demurrer to this pleading was sustained, and such action is assigned as error. The suit being in tort "for the unlawful conversion of money," the contract liability, if any, relied upon, could not be used as a set-off or counterclaim thereto. Lake Shore, etc., R. Co. v. Van Auken, 1 Ind. App. 492, 27 N. E. 119; Brower et al. v. Nellis et al., 6 Ind. App. 323, 33 N. E. 672; Crowe v. Kell, 7 Ind. App. 683, 35 N. E. 186; Block v. Swango et al., 10 Ind. App. 600, 38 N. E. 55.

A special finding of facts was made, and conclusions of law were stated thereon. A part of said finding was to the effect that appellant was clerk of said county from November 17, 1894, to November 17, 1898, and received the money referred to in the finding during such term. The total amount received by him was $20,566.99, of which he accounted for and turned over $17,303.08, leaving a balance of $3,263.87, made up of items and amounts allowed to him for purposes which are stated in the finding. Of this sum, $1,106 was allowed to him for his per diem on account of attending the circuit court during its sessions. Sixty-six dollars of said sum was allowed to him for making certificates of allowances to special judges during the term time of said court.

One of the conclusions of law was that appellee was entitled to recover $1,106 allowed as per diem for attending court. This conclusion was incorrect, as declared by the Supreme Court since the case at bar was appealed. Seiler v. State, 65 N. E. 922; s. c. 67 N. E. 448; State v. Flynn, supra.

A further conclusion of law was that appellee was entitled to said sum of $66, received by him for making certificates of allowances for special judges as aforesaid. The general proposition is that a person who holds the office of clerk, receiving a salary for his services in that capacity, is not thereby precluded from recovering upon contracts made by him unofficially, and with regard to matters which are not included in his duties as such official, but official services are covered by the salary attached to the office, when some other statutory provision does not

¶ 2. See Set-Off and Counterclaim, vol. 43, Cent. Dig. § 29.

exist. State v. Flynn, supra. If there is any statute authorizing appellant's claim for special compensation on account of the service indicated, he should point it out. Ellis v. Board, 133 Ind. 91, 54 N. E. 382. This he has not done.

The court further found for appellee as to a large number of items, apparently of an official nature, the details of which are set out in the findings. To examine all the statutes which have or might have a bearing upon these items would involve a large amount of labor, and, in the absence of assistance from counsel, be in the end of uncertain value. The well-settled rule that errors assigned and not discussed are thereby waived is therefore invoked, and dispenses with the necessity for further statement of facts found.

The first conclusion of law, relating to the per diem allowance as aforesaid, was incorrect. The other conclusions, in so far as they were in appellant's favor, are not challenged, and, in so far as they are adverse to him, no error is made to appear.

The judgment is reversed, with instructions to restate the first conclusion of law in accordance herewith, and for further consistent proceedings.

(32 Ind. A. 480)

MILLER et al. v. WAYNE INTERNATIONAL BUILDING & LOAN ASS'N.

(Appellate Court of Indiana, Division No. 1. Feb. 23, 1904.)

BUILDING AND LOAN ASSOCIATIONS—BY-LAWS — MORTGAGES — CONSTRUCTION — FORECLOSURE—MORTGAGED PROPERTY — SALE — ASSUMPTION OF MORTGAGE—PURCHASERS' LIABILITY—COMPLAINT — FINDINGS — WRITTEN INSTRUMENTS—REFERENCE—ALLEGATION OF DEFAULT.

1. Under Burns' Rev. St. 1901, § 365, providing that when a pleading is founded on a written instrument the original or a copy must be filed with the pleading, where the instrument sued on is contained in the body of the complaint it need not be appended or otherwise further exhibited.

2. Where a written instrument sued on is copied in the complaint, it is not necessary that the complaint should set out the substance of such instrument in addition.

3. A complaint, in an action commenced October 29, 1901, to recover a building association loan, alleged that defendants failed and had refused to pay monthly dues on the stock, together with interest and premium as provided by the bond and mortgage, and that all the payments on the stock and loan that accrued since June 25, 1901, and for a long time before, and also the principal and interest on the loan, remained due and wholly unpaid. It further alleged that the total value of the shares securing the loan was only $36.44⅙, which included all defendants' payments on the stock and loan of $600, together with the earnings and profits. The association's by-laws, which constituted a part of the contract, were attached to the complaint, and contained a provision that all installments on stock should be due on the 1st, and delinquent after the 25th, of each month, and that, if interest, premium, or monthly installments remained delinquent for a period of three months, the entire principal sum mentioned in the bond and mortgage should be immediately due and payable. *Held*, that the complaint sufficiently alleged when payments were to be made, that the stock had not matured, and that defendants were in default.

4. Where by-laws of a building and loan association provided that the stock should be paid for in monthly installments of 80 cents, and that the stockholder's liability for such installments should be limited to 72, but that the stock would not mature until the loan fund portion of the monthly installments, with accumulated profits, should equal $100 a share, a complaint, in an action to recover a loan for which the borrower's shares had been pledged, which alleged that, though 72 installments had been paid, the shares were worth only $36.44⅙ each, sufficiently charged that the stock had not matured.

5. In an action on a building and loan association bond and mortgage, a finding referring to the bond and mortgage as "the same mentioned and set out in the complaint" was not objectionable for failure to set out the same in full.

6. An exception to the court's conclusions of law constitutes an admission, for the purposes of the exception, that the facts were correctly found.

7. In an action on a building association loan, a special finding that the borrowers sold the mortgaged real estate to defendant and executed their deed to him, conveying the real estate, which deed contained an agreement by which the grantee assumed and agreed to pay the mortgage securing such loan, and that defendant accepted the deed and placed it of record, was not objectionable for failure to find the ultimate facts on which defendant's liability rested.

8. A building association mortgage purported to secure the performance of the stipulations and agreements of the bond, the terms of which it recited, showing the various payments of premium, interest, stock installments, etc., which the mortgagor was required to pay, and declared that the mortgage should be binding on the mortgagor's assigns. On a sale of the real estate to defendant he assumed the mortgage, and thereafter made monthly payments, as had been made by the mortgagor. *Held*, that defendant was liable for all sums secured by the bond and mortgage, and was not entitled to claim that by reason of the fact that he was not a member of the association he was liable only for principal of the loan and interest.

9. Where the by-laws of a building association required payment of a monthly premium of not less than 50 cents a month on all loans, for each $100 borrowed, and a loan for $600 was made to the owner of six shares of stock, each of which was of the face value of $100, and each share was represented in the loan by that sum, a provision of the bond securing such loan, requiring payment of a premium of 50 cents a month for each share of stock, was a payment of premium, and could not be treated as dues on the stock.

Appeal from Circuit Court, Henry County; W. A. Barnard, Judge.

Action by the Wayne International Building & Loan Association against Jack Miller and others. From a judgment in favor of plaintiff, defendants appeal. Affirmed.

Forkner & Forkner, for appellants. Daniel Wait Howe and A. R. Feemster, for appellee.

BLACK, J. This was a suit brought by the appellee against the appellants, Jack Miller, James L. Watkins, and Maud R. Watkins, his wife, upon a bond executed by James L. Watkins, a member of the association, holding six shares of its stock of the face value of $100 each, for a loan of $600, and to foreclose a mortgage on real estate, executed by the borrowing member and his wife, the real estate afterward having been conveyed by the mortgagors to the appellant Miller, by a deed containing a provision by the terms of which the grantee assumed and agreed to pay the mortgage.

Among the objections urged against the complaint, the sufficiency of which was assailed by demurrer of Miller, counsel claim that there are no averments of the legal effect of the instruments sued on, or tendering any issue in respect thereto; that the instruments are simply copied into the complaint, with averments that they were executed. The statute provides that when a pleading is founded on a written instrument, the original or a copy thereof must be filed with the pleading. Section 365, Burns' Rev. St. 1901. If the copy of the instrument be contained in the body of the pleading, this is sufficient, and it need not be appended to the complaint, or otherwise further exhibited. Jones v. Parks, 78 Ind. 537; Adams v. Dale, 29 Ind. 273; Adamson v. Shaner, 3 Ind. App. 448, 29 N. E. 944; Reynolds v. Baldwin, 93 Ind. 57. In Mercer v. Herbert, 41 Ind. 459, it was held that when a pleading is founded upon a written instrument, and a copy is referred to in and filed with such pleading, it becomes a part thereof, and, in determining the sufficiency of the pleading, such written instrument is regarded and treated as composing a part thereof, and speaks for itself, and it is not incumbent upon the pleader to state the substance thereof. See, also, Cotton v. The State ex rel., etc., 64 Ind. 573; Jaqua v. Woodbury, 3 Ind. App. 289, 29 N. E. 573.

The complaint is next criticised on the ground that the instruments sued on "contain no definite promise to pay at any given or stated time, but only to pay generally," and that they "are to be discharged by the maturity of the stock, by means of monthly payments, until such maturity, 'as provided by the by-laws of said association,'" and that the by-laws are not made part of the contract, and therefore the alleged copy thereof filed with the complaint is no part thereof, and that the complaint is insufficient, therefore, in not showing that the instruments sued on were due and payable. The bond provides for the payment of monthly dues in a certain sum per month on each share of stock, as provided by the by-laws of the association, together with a premium of a certain sum per month on each share of stock, and interest on the loan at the rate of 6 per cent. per annum, "all to be due and payable on the first, and delinquent after the twenty-fifth day of each month, until such shares mature, as provided by the by-laws of said association." The mortgage, besides purporting to be executed as a security for the performance of the stipulations and agreements of the bond, sets out the provisions of the bond above stated. A copy of the by-laws was attached, and was referred to in the complaint as being attached thereto and made part thereof. The complaint alleged that the defendants "have failed and refused, and still fail and refuse, to pay the payments of monthly dues upon said stock, and of interest and premium, as provided for in said bond and mortgage, and that all the payments upon said stock and loan that have accrued and become payable since June 25, 1901, and for a long time before, and also the principal and interest of said loan, still remain due and wholly unpaid." It is further alleged that the total loan fund portion of the monthly installments paid upon the stock, together with the accumulated earnings and profits thereof, do not equal $100 per share, but that the shares are worth only $36.44⅓ each, and no more, and that the six shares at the commencement of this action were worth only $218.66, and no more, which sum included the entire amount paid by the defendants to the association upon the stock and loan, together with the accumulated earnings and profits thereof, and included all credits to which they were entitled upon the shares or upon the loan. The statute provides that in case of nonpayment of installments upon stock, or interest or premium, by borrowing stockholders, for three months, payment of principal, premium, and interest (without deducting the premium or interest paid) may be enforced by proceedings on their securities according to law. Section 4446, Burns' Rev. St. 1901. See, also, section 4449, Id. The suit was commenced October 29, 1901. The by-laws constituted part of the contract, and properly were made an exhibit. Hatfield v. Huntington, etc., Ass'n, 132 Ind. 149, 31 N. E. 532; Wohlford v. Citizens', etc., Ass'n, 140 Ind. 662, 40 N. E. 694, 29 L. R. A. 177. They contained a provision that all installments on stock should be due on the 1st, and delinquent after the 25th, of each month, beginning with the month in which the stock was dated; also a provision that, if interest, premium, or monthly installments on stock remained delinquent for a period of three months, the whole principal sum mentioned in the note or bond and mortgage should immediately become due and payable. We think the complaint indicated when payments were to be made, and that the stock had not matured, and that the defendants were in default, and that the loan was due and unpaid; and the complaint was sufficient in these respects to put them to their answer.

It is further urged against the complaint that, assuming the by-laws to be a part of the complaint, payments of stock dues were limited thereunder to 72 payments, and the pleading shows that number of payments to have been made, and therefore it would follow that the stock was matured. The by-laws provided that the stock, of the class taken by the borrower in this case, should be paid for in monthly installments of 80 cents, and that the stockholder's liability for such installments should be limited to 72 installments; but it was also provided in the by-laws that stock of such class should mature as soon as the total loan fund portion of the monthly installments, with accumulated profits, should equal $100 per share. It was sufficiently shown in the complaint that the stock had not thus matured.

The conclusions of law stated by the court upon its special finding of the facts are assailed. It is contended that the finding is insufficient because in the portion thereof relating to the execution of the bond and mortgage they are each referred to as being "the same mentioned and set out in the complaint," and in the portion of the finding relating to the by-laws they are said to be "the same mentioned in plaintiff's complaint, and attached thereto, and marked 'Exhibit A.'" The practice of referring, in a bill of exceptions containing the evidence, to an item of written evidence, elsewhere properly in the record, without setting it forth in the bill, has long obtained under judicial sanction. See Smith v. Lisher, 23 Ind. 500, 504; Kesler v. Myers, 41 Ind. 543, 552; Douglass v. The State, 72 Ind. 385, 389; Henry v. Thomas, 118 Ind. 23, 26, 20 N. E. 519. In the case last cited the practice is approved on the ground that to hold otherwise would be to require a needless incumbrance of the record. The taking of the exception to the conclusions of law was an admission, for the purposes of the exception, that the facts were correctly found. The bond, mortgage, and by-laws were already parts of the record. It was a common practice in the framing of special verdicts to thus refer to instruments constituting parts of the pleadings in the record, and the same practice has obtained in our courts in the statement of the facts in a special finding. It relieves the record of unnecessary repetitions, and we are not disposed to condemn the practice. See Cook v. McNaughton, 128 Ind. 410, 24 N. E. 361, 28 N. E. 74; Evans v. Queen Ins. Co., 5 Ind. App. 198, 31 N. E. 843.

It is further suggested, in relation to the special finding of the facts, that it is found therein that the Watkinses sold the mortgaged real estate to Miller, and executed to him their deed conveying the real estate to him, which deed is the same mentioned and set out in the complaint in this cause, which deed contained the following agreement: "The grantee herein assumes and agrees to pay the mortgage on the above described real estate to the Wayne International Building & Loan Association for six hundred dollars;" it being further found in the same connection that said deed was accepted by the defendant Miller, and placed of record in the office of the recorder of Henry county, Ind., at a date mentioned in a specified deed record, on a designated page thereof. It is claimed that this portion of the finding does not find the ultimate fact whether Miller agreed to anything, or what his agreement was. It is sufficiently found that a contract was made by the parties, and what the terms of the contract were. The legal conclusion from such facts would be that Miller became the principal debtor, and his grantor became his surety. The facts stated were evidentiary, but they were also the ultimate facts on which the legal liability of Miller was to be predicated. The deed furnished the foundation of the claim against Miller. See King v. Downey, 24 Ind. App. 262, 56 N. E. 680, and cases cited. Other objections to the finding seem to be based upon the assumption that the by-laws were not found by the court, an assumption which we have already said to be incorrect.

In discussing the motion for a new trial, it is contended that the amount of recovery was too large. In support of this objection it is said that Miller was not a member of the association, the stock never having been assigned to him; and it is contended, therefore, that he was not under any obligation to pay dues and premiums, and that all payments made by him should have been credited to the principal, and that therefore the finding is excessive in amount. The mortgage purported to be executed as a security for the performance of the stipulations and agreements of the bond, and recited the terms of the bond, showing the various payments to be made, and contained a stipulation that all the payments mentioned in the mortgage should be paid without relief from valuation and appraisement laws, and a provision that the mortgage should be binding upon the assigns of the mortgagors. All the obligations of the borrowing member were secured by the mortgage, as well as by the pledge of the stock. When the real estate was conveyed to Miller, no obligations of the borrowing stockholder to the appellee were thereby discharged, but Miller, by his assumption of the mortgage, became bound to pay what was thereby secured. Some monthly payments were made by the borrowing member before the conveyance, and many were afterward made by Miller. In the foreclosure proceeding, the accrued value of the stock was applied to lessen the amount of recovery, and the stock was canceled. The appellee was entitled to claim the benefit of the promise of assumption of the mortgage. The claim of Miller that he only became liable for the principal and interest thereon cannot be upheld.

One of the by-laws provided for the payment on all loans of a monthly premium of not less than 50 cents per month for each $100 borrowed. The bond, by its terms, provided for a premium of 50 cents per month on each share of stock. It is contended that an agreement to pay a premium on the stock was unauthorized by statute or the by-laws, and that such payments should be applied to the discharge of the debt. The bond containing such language was for a loan of $600 to the owner of 6 shares of stock, each of the shares being of the face value of $100, and each share being represented in the loan by that sum. It is manifest that the sums so to be paid by the terms of the bond were intended, as expressed, to be paid as premium by a borrowing member as such, and were not meant to be dues upon the stock, and they were treated as installments of premium upon the loan.

We do not find any available error. Judgment affirmed.

(33 Ind. A. 229)

NICHOLS v. BALTIMORE & O. S. W. R. CO.[1]

(Appellate Court of Indiana, Division No. 2. Feb. 24, 1904.)

RAILROADS—INJURIES AT CROSSINGS—DEATH—OPERATION OF TRAINS—SIGNALS—FRIGHTENING TEAMS — DUTY OF ENGINEER — CONTRIBUTORY NEGLIGENCE—BURDEN OF PROOF—PLEADING — INSTRUCTIONS—APPEAL—RECORD—BILL OF EXCEPTIONS—SEAL—ERROR—FAILURE TO ARGUE—WAIVER.

1. Under Burns' Rev. St. 1901, § 359a, providing that the burden of proof of contributory negligence shall be on defendant, a complaint in an action for wrongful death caused by defendant's alleged negligence is not objectionable for failure to allege that decedent was without fault.

2. In an action for wrongful death, an instruction that defendant had answered by general denial, which put the burden on plaintiff of proving by a preponderance of the evidence all material allegations of at least one paragraph of the complaint, was misleading in that it was calculated to impress the jury that the burden of the issue of contributory negligence was on plaintiff.

3. Where, in an action for wrongful death at a railway crossing, both paragraphs of the complaint charged defendant's failure to give the statutory signals on approaching the crossing, it was not error for the court to charge that if, on the approach of the train to the crossing, the engineer observed a team near the crossing, frightened and becoming unmanageable, it was his duty to refrain from giving signals or doing any act tending to increase the fright of the team; and if, by reasonable exertion, he could avoid the accident by stopping the train, it was his duty to do so, but that, if the train had reached a point where the law required signals to be given, and it was uncertain whether the train could be stopped before reaching the crossing, he must give the signals.

¶ 4. Whether a traveler approaching a railroad crossing must stop, in addition to looking and listening, before he attempts to cross, depends on the facts of each particular case.

5. The right of a railroad company to run its engines over crossings is limited by restrictions imposed by law and reasonable prudence with regard to signals, etc.

6. Under Burns' Rev. St. 1901, § 359a, providing that the burden of proof of contributory negligence in an action for injuries is on the defendant, an instruction that the law presumes that the injuries to plaintiff's decedent, of which he died, if he died from injuries received by a collision with defendant's engine at a railway crossing, were brought about by his own negligence, was error.

7. Where a mule team which deceased was driving became frightened and unmanageable as they approached a railway crossing, whether the engineer was justified in sounding an alarm signal, tending to increase the fright of the team, after the engineer had discovered them, was for the jury.

8. Where the appeal record is duly attested by the certificate of the clerk with the seal affixed, the fact that no seal was attached to the special bill of exceptions in which the instructions were set out did not preclude a review of the instructions.

9. A statement in a bill of exceptions that it contains all the instructions given was not falsified by a showing that a requested instruction of a particular number which the court modified was not in the record, since the modified instruction might have been given under another number.

10. Error in an instruction excepted to, but not argued, is waived.

11. Where objections were only made to the instructions given, it was immaterial that the bill did not include all the instructions requested.

Wiley, P. J., dissenting in part.

Appeal from Circuit Court, Lawrence County; W. H. Martin, Judge.

Action by Bettie F. Nichols, as administratrix of the estate of Charles L. Nichols, deceased, against the Baltimore & Ohio Southwestern Railroad Company. From a judgment in favor of defendant, plaintiff appeals. Reversed.

Edwards & Edwards and S. B. Lowe, for appellant. Gardiner, Gardiner & Slimp, R. N. Palmer, and Edward Barton, for appellee.

COMSTOCK, J. Appellant, the widow of Charles L. Nichols, deceased, as administratrix, brought this action against appellee to recover damages for the death of the decedent, caused by the alleged negligence of the defendant. The complaint is in two paragraphs. The accident occurred at a public highway crossing. The deceased and his son were riding in a road wagon drawn by two mules. The negligence attributed to the appellee in the first paragraph is (1) failure to give the statuory signals, (2) failure to check the speed of the train, and (3) unnecessarily giving the danger signals and ringing the bell of the locomotive with knowledge that the team was unmanageable. The negligence charged in the second paragraph is (1) failure to give the statutory signals, and (2) giving the danger signals and ringing the bell needlessly with knowledge that the team was unmanageable. Appellee answered by general denial, and the trial resulted in a verdict and judgment for appellee. The only error assigned is the overruling of appellant's motion for a new trial. Appellant relies for reversal upon the giving by the court, of its own motion, of certain instructions, and of other instructions given at the request of appellee. We will consider these instructions, following the order in which they are discussed in appellant's brief.

Instructions 1 and 2 given by the court of its own motion may be considered together. Instruction 1 purports to state the averments of the complaint as to the character of the

¶ 4. See Railroads, vol. 41, Cent. Dig. §§ 1043, 1050.

[1] Rehearing denied, 71 N. E. 170.

action, the corporate existence of the defendant, date of the accident, the negligence of the defendant, and that the deceased was without fault. The second instruction states the nature of the answer, that it is a general denial, that before plaintiff can recover she must prove by a fair preponderance of the evidence all the material allegations in one or more of the paragraphs of the complaint. The complaint contains no averment that the plaintiff was without fault; neither was such averment necessary. Burns' Rev. St. 1901, § 359a. The second instruction, stating that the defendant had answered by general denial, and that this answer put the burden upon the plaintiff of proving by a preponderance of evidence all the material allegations of at least one paragraph of the complaint, was well calculated to give the jury the impression that the burden of the issue of contributory negligence was upon the plaintiff.

Instruction 2½ stated it to be the law that if, on the approach of a railroad train to a highway crossing, the engineer in charge of the engine observed a team near the crossing, evidently frightened, and becoming unmanageable, it was the duty of the engineer to refrain from giving signals or doing any act that tended to increase the fright of the team; and if, by reasonable exertion, he could avoid the accident by stopping the train, it was his duty to do so. If, however, the train had reached a point where the law required signals to be given, and it is uncertain whether or not the train can be stopped before reaching the crossing, he must give the signals. It is claimed that this instruction treats the signals given by the engineer immediately before the accident and after the team and crossing came into view of the engineer, which was less than 500 feet from the crossing, and not 80 to 100 rods from the crossing, as signals required by law, while the law requires no signals to be given less than 80 rods from the crossing; that in the case at bar the place for giving the statutory signals was passed before the deceased and the crossing and the team came into the engineer's view. Both paragraphs of the complaint charge a failure to give the statutory signals. With the statement of the duty of the engineer when approaching a frightened team the appellant has no reason to complain. There was no error in giving it.

Against instruction 5 given at the request of appellee the point is made that it is not applicable where the deceased was involuntarily drawn upon the crossing by a frightened team, and was not attempting to cross the railroad; and that it assumes that the deceased went voluntarily upon the track. The instruction states generally the duty of a traveler in approaching a point upon a highway where a railroad track is crossed upon the same level to proceed with caution, to look and listen. The instruction does not, as we understand it, make the assumption charged. As an abstract statement of the law it is correct, with the exception of the statement that he must stop. Whether the traveler must stop before he attempts to cross must depend upon the facts of each particular case. This instruction could not have prejudiced the rights of the appellant in the light of the undisputed evidence that the deceased stopped, looked, and listened.

Instruction No. 10, complained of, is as follows: "The defendant had the right to run its locomotive engine over its railroad at the time it did when it collided with the wagon of the plaintiff's decedent, and at any time, day or night, that it pleased; and this the plaintiff is held to know, and the plaintiff's decedent to have known at the time of the collision." Upon the giving of general signals appellee had the right to operate its trains. The right of appellee to operate its trains was subject to the restrictions imposed by law and reasonable prudence.

Instructions 14 and 15 assume that decedent voluntarily drove upon the track, and are open to this objection which is made to them.

In instruction No. 16 the jury are told that "the law presumes that the injuries to plaintiff's decedent, of which he died, if you find he did die from injuries received by collision with defendant's engine at a highway and railway crossing, were brought about by his own negligence." We have set out the opening sentence of the instruction. It is not modified by anything that follows. This was error. The instruction, we think, is contrary to the spirit of recent legislation and decisions. Burns' Rev. St. 1901, section 359a (Horner's Rev. St. 1901, § 284a); Malott v. Hawkins, 159 Ind. 127, 63 N. E. 308; Southern Ind. Ry. v. Peyton, 157 Ind. 690, 61 N. E. 722; Texas, etc., Ry. v. Gentry, 163 U. S. 353, 366, 16 Sup. Ct. 1104, 41 L. Ed. 186; Baltimore, etc., v. Est. of Landrigan, 24 Sup. Ct. 137, 140, 48 L. Ed. —; Chesapeake, etc., Ry. v. Steele, 84 Fed. 93, 98, 29 C. C. A. 81; Norton v. Railroad Co., 122 N. C. 910, 928, 29 S. E. 886. The presumption is that the decedent was without fault, his negligence being a matter of defense.

Instructions 21, 22, and 23 are correct as abstract statements of the law. We are of the opinion that they were harmless, even if it be conceded that they are inapplicable, as claimed by appellant.

Instruction 24 is as follows: "If the engineer in charge of defendant's locomotive engine, as he approached the crossing, going at a high rate of speed usual to his train, and when two or three hundred feet from the crossing he saw Charles L. Nichols and his son, in a wagon drawn by two mules, approaching the crossing, and saw that his team did not stop when at a safe distance from the crossing, but continued going toward the crossing, the said engineer was justified in sounding the alarm signals of the locomotive, and it was his duty to do so, in order, if possible, to prevent the team from going onto the crossing in front of the locomotive." Without qualifications, this instruction is too broad. It will not be contended that, if the engineer discovered that the alarm signals were frightening or adding to the fright of the team, and making them unmanageable, it would still be his duty, as a matter of law, to continue giving the signals. Whether the engineer is justified in sounding an alarm signal after discovering the team is to be determined by the jury upon proper instructions under all the facts and circumstances proven.

It is contended by appellee that the instructions cannot be considered (1) because no seal is affixed to the special bill of exceptions in which they are set out. A seal is not necessary. The record is duly attested by the general certificate of the clerk with the seal affixed. (2) That the bill of exceptions shows that all of the instructions given to the jury were not copied into the special bill of exceptions. It is pointed out in this connection that appellant states that the court modified instruction 6 requested by appellee among those given by the court, but appellee states that said instruction does not appear in the record. As the modified instruction might have been given under another number, this is not conclusive that it is not in the record, in the face of the statement in the bill of exceptions that it contains all the instructions given. (3) That an attempted exception to instruction No. 8 is not properly reserved. Said instruction is not discussed, and any error which might have been based thereon is waived. (4) That all the instructions requested are not in the bill. Objections are only made to the instructions given. We conclude that the exceptions to the instructions are properly saved.

The judgment is reversed, with instructions to sustain appellant's motion for a new trial.

WILEY, P. J. I concur in the conclusion, but it is my judgment that instruction 24 is a correct statement of the law as applied to the facts. It was the duty of the engineer to give the signals of danger where he did, so as to give warning to the approaching travelers.

(32 Ind. A. 610)

ROBERTS v. KOSS et al.

(Appellate Court of Indiana. Feb. 26, 1904.)

BUILDING CONTRACTS—CONSTRUCTION — SUBCONTRACTOR — MECHANIC'S LIEN — NOTICE—APPEAL—RECORD—RIGHT TO OBJECT.

1. Under the express provisions of Burns' Rev. St. 1894, § 7262, on the service of notice by a subcontractor on the owner of a building, setting forth the amount of his claim and the service rendered for which the contractor is indebted, the owner is personally liable to such subcontractor for the amount of such indebtedness, not exceeding the amount due the contractor at the time the notice was served.

2. A building contract binding the contractor to furnish all material and labor done of whatsoever kind, and to do and finish complete the cleaning of the premises, excavations, grading, and filling in for the building in conformity with the drawings and specifications, which were made a part of the contract, included the removal of the soil on the lot above the level of the lower edge of the first-floor joists, and hence work done in removing such soil could not be charged as extras.

3. A finding by the trial court on a question of fact, which there is evidence to support, will not be set aside on appeal.

4. Where a building contract required the contractor to make certain excavations, and a subcontract for such excavations bound the subcontractor to do the excavating, grading, etc., for the building complete, in accordance with the drawings and specifications of the architect, and according to the contract between the owner and the contractor, a construction of the contractor's contract as to such excavations was binding on the subcontractor.

5. Where, in an action by a subcontractor for alleged extra work, the contractor filed a cross-complaint against the owners, and the subcontractor introduced such cross-complaint in evidence as a part of his case, whereupon it was copied in the record, and referred to in the court's findings and conclusions of law, the subcontractor could not object on appeal that the cross-complaint was not in the record.

Appeal from Superior Court, Marion County; Vinson Carter, Judge.

Action by J. Harry Roberts against William F. Koss and others. From a judgment in favor of defendants, plaintiff appeals. Affirmed.

Wm. V. Rooker, for appellant. Baker & Daniels and F. Winter, for appellees.

COMSTOCK, J. Suit by appellant, as a subcontractor, against the appellee Koss as principal contractor, and against appellees Lewis and the Realty Investment Company as owners of the premises on which certain buildings were erected, for the excavations of which the appellant did the work. The complaint was in two paragraphs, the first declaring on a special contract; the second being on a quantum meruit for work and labor done. There was exhibited with each paragraph a notice to the property owners to withhold from the principal contractor moneys which the subcontractor claimed were owing him for his services in the premises.

In his first paragraph of complaint the appellant averred: That on the 11th day of February, 1901, the appellee Lewis owned certain real estate, which was described. That on said date the appellee Lewis employed his co-appellee Koss to furnish all materials and labor and to do and finish the cleaning of said premises, excavations, grading, and filling in, concrete and rubble work, window sills and door sills, and coping for and in flat building "then and thereafter to be erected on Capitol avenue north of Eleventh street," the whole of said work to be done and finished in conformity with the drawings and specifications prepared by Adolph Sherrer, architect, which drawings and specifications were made a part of the contract, but which were not exhibited with the complaint because they were in the possession of the defendants. The written contract between Lewis and Koss, omitting the plans and specifications, marked "Exhibit A," was filed with complaint. That pursuant of his employment of principal contractor, and in partial performance thereof, the said Koss engaged the plaintiff to do the work and labor and furnish the materials for excavating said cellars according to said plans and specifications. That said employment of the plaintiff was evidenced by a memorandum in writing, but no copy of which was exhibited with the complaint, because the memorandum was in the custody and possession of the defendants. That plaintiff had performed all the conditions of said contract on his part to be performed. That in the course of the construction of the building the defendant the Realty Investment Company acquired an interest in the premises. That there was due and owing plaintiff on account of said work and labor done $1,136.80, on which sum interest was demanded because of unreasonable delay in payment. That plaintiff served on the defendant property owners notice in writing particularly setting forth the amount of plaintiff's said claim for which his employer was indebted to him, and stating that plaintiff held the owners responsible therefor. That when notice was given the owners were indebted to the principal contractor in a sum largely in excess of plaintiff's claim. That a copy of said notice in writing was exhibited with the complaint. That plaintiff had been obliged to employ an attorney to prosecute this action for the collection of the indebtedness, and his services were reasonably worth $200. Judgment was demanded for $1,500 and all proper relief.

In the second paragraph of complaint it was averred that the defendants were indebted to plaintiff for work and labor done and material furnished in and about the erection and construction of a building known as the "Lewis Flats," on certain described real estate, which said work and labor done, etc., were done and furnished by the plaintiff to the defendants at their special instance and request on and between February 11th and June 8th, both in 1901; that said work and labor done, etc., were reasonably worth $1,-200; that a bill of particulars of said work and labor done, etc., marked "Exhibit B," was filed, etc.; that there had been unreasonable delay in the payment, etc., by reason whereof plaintiff was entitled to have and recover interest, etc. Judgment was demanded for $1,500.

The Lewis-Koss contract, marked "Exhibit A," appears in the record. It recites an agreement February 11, 1901, between Lewis, as first party, and Koss, as second party, whereby and in consideration of the payments and covenants subsequently recited to be made and performed by first party the second party obliged himself "to furnish all materials and labor done of whatsoever kind, and to do and finish complete the cleaning of the premises, excavations, grading, and filling in, concrete and rubble work, and one coping for a new flat to be erected on Capitol avenue north of Eleventh street, in the city of Indianapolis, state of Indiana." It further recited that the work was to be done and finished in conformity with drawings and specifications prepared by Adolph Sherrer, which were made a part of the contract; that work was to be commenced immediately, and completed before March 30, 1901, and one-half of the work was to be finished before March 15, 1901; that the contractor was to execute a bond for the faithful performance of his contract and for the payment of all claims, liens, or demands whatsoever, etc., "that if any alterations, additions, or omissions are made in the work during its progress the value of the same shall be decided by the architects," etc.; that second party was to receive for the performance of the contract $5,975; that payments were to be made semimonthly, on architect's estimates, deducting 20 per cent. of the amount of each until the final estimate; that upon the completion of the work a final estimate was to be made, and upon a stipulated showing of the payment of claims against the property the balance was to be paid to second party; that liquidated damages in the sum of $25 a day were to be paid by second party to the first party for each and every day work remained unfinished beyond the term of the contract. The defendants Charles S. Lewis and the Realty Investment Company each answered the complaint with a general denial. The defendant William F. Koss answered, first, with a general denial; second, with a plea of payment; and, third, that the cause of action mentioned in the two paragraphs of complaint were one and the same; that all the work done was done pursuant of a special contract in writing between the plaintiff and the defendant Koss, a copy of which contract, marked "Exhibit A," was filed with the answer; that by the terms of that contract plaintiff agreed to do and furnish at and for the sum of $2,150 all the work, labor, and material required by the provisions of the memorandum; that before the bringing of this action the defendant Koss paid the plaintiff the full sum of $2,150. Exhibit A filed with the answer was the contract between Koss and the plaintiff, which the latter had not been able to exhibit with his complaint because the memorandum was in the defendants' possession. This contract, in so far as the two have concurrent terms, is upon the same form used in the agreement made between Lewis and Koss, which was exhibited with the complaint, and is summarized supra. The defendants' Exhibit A recites that the plaintiff, as second party, agrees to do and finish complete the cleaning of the premises, excavations, grading, and filling in for a new flat to be erected for Charles S. Lewis on Capitol avenue, north of Eleventh street, in the city of Indianapolis, etc., "the whole of said work to be done and finished in conformity with the drawings and specifications prepared by Adolph Sherrer, architect, and according to the contract made between Charles S. Lewis and William F. Koss, and dated February 9, 1901, which drawings, specifications, and contract are understood to be incorporated in and made a part of this agreement." The bond executed by the plaintiff to the defendant Koss to secure the performance of the contract is attached to Exhibit A. The plaintiff replied to the special answer of the defendant Koss with a general denial. The court made a special finding of facts including 17 items, and stated thereon 4 conclusions of law. The following are the conclusions of law: "(1) That the removal of the soil above the level of the lower edge of the first-floor joists is included in both the contract of the defendant Koss with the defendant Lewis and the contract of the plaintiff with the defendant Koss, and is not entitled to be charged for as an extra. (2) That the plaintiff is entitled to recover of the defendants Koss and Realty Investment Company the sum of $550 for attorney's fees, making in all the sum of $605, together with his costs. (3) That the defendant Koss is entitled to recover of the defendants Lewis and Realty Investment Company the sum of $1,375 and the further sum of $100 as attorneys' fees, making in all the sum of $1,475, together with his costs, and also to a foreclosure of the mechanic's lien on the real estate mentioned in his cross-complaint, and an order for the sale. (4) That whatever amount the Realty Investment Company shall pay upon the judgment in favor of the plaintiff shall operate as a credit upon the judgment in favor of the defendant Koss." To which conclusions of law, and to each of them, appellant excepts.

The appellant relies upon the following alleged error in the record for a reversal of the judgment, viz.: "The trial court erred in limiting the right of the plaintiff to recover as against Koss, the principal contractor, to the plaintiff's right to recover as against Lewis and the Realty Investment Company, the owners of the property. It is claimed that this limitation is shown by the absence of material facts from the finding, and it is impliedly the twelfth finding of fact and by the first conclusion of law. The twelfth finding is as follows: '(12) That if the excavation above the lower level of the first-floor joists is to be considered an extra, then there would be due to the defendant Koss the further sum of $714.30 from the defendant Lewis, and there would be due the plaintiff from the defendant Koss, the further sum of $564.30.' "

Appellant served notice on appellees in compliance with section 7262, Burns' Rev. St. 1894. Under the statute and the notice given thereunder, appellees were liable to appellant personally for whatever amount the original contractor, their co-appellee, was indebted to appellant; it being admitted that at the time the notices were given that they were indebted to their co-appellee in a larger sum than was claimed by appellant. The amount could only be determined by reference to the contract and the law governing the same which existed between appellant and appellee Koss, the statute making them liable for Koss' debt to appellant. So it is argued that the court erred in giving the same construction to the contract between appellant and Koss that it did to the contract between Koss and his co-appellees. We understand appellant to concede that the contract in question was correctly construed by the court as between these appellees and their co-appellee Koss, and this court so holds. But appellant insists that the court erred in its construction of the contract between appellant and appellee Koss. Appellee Koss claims that the question tried by the court below was one of fact whether the contracts of Koss and his subcontractor, Roberts, were entered into without knowledge on their part as to the locality of the lot upon which work was to be done, or of the nature and elevation of its surface above the sidewalk grade, and in reliance upon statements made to them by architect Scherrer that the grade line shown in the plan by referring to the point "r" in the court between the buildings correctly indicated the natural elevation of the lot above the grade of the sidewalk, and therefore that no earth or other materials would have to be excavated or removed above the grade line indicated at point "r." In addition to other evidence, the architect, Adolph Scherrer, testified that the contract did not show anything in reference to the natural surface of the ground upon which the proposed building was to be erected, and that the grade lines referred to were those of the finished work, or the work when completed; that the plan indicated that the top of the finished grade in the court was 18 inches higher than the sidewalk grade. The specifications provided that the premises are to be taken in their present condition, and that the contractor "is to remove above and below the grade line all contents necessary to be removed for the erection of the new structure." In addition, the architect, Scherrer, testified that he did not state to either Koss or Roberts or Koss' clerk, Fritz, that the grade line at point "r" indicated the natural elevation of the lot, and there was also evidence tending to show that the locality of the lot was known to Mr. Roberts before he entered into the subcontract with Koss, and also to Mr. Fritz, Mr. Koss' clerk. The contract between appellant and appellee Koss recites: "That for and in consideration of the payments and covenants hereinafter mentioned to be made and performed by the said party of the first part the said party of the second part does hereby covenant and agree to furnish all the material and labor of whatsoever kind, and to do and finish complete the cleaning of the premises, excavation, grading, and filling in for a new flat to be erected for Charles S. Lewis on Capitol avenue, north of Eleventh street, in the city of Indianapolis, state of Indiana. The whole of the said work to be done and finished in conformity with the drawings and specifications prepared by Adolph Scherrer, architect, and according to the contract made between Charles S. Lewis and William F. Koss, and dated February 9, 1901, which drawings, specifications, and contract are understood to be incorporated in and made a part of this agreement." The questions of fact upon which the rights of appellant and appellee Koss depend were determined by the court below against appellant. There was evidence to support the determination of the court, and we cannot, therefore, disturb the judgment.

Appellant admits that the statement of the issue made by appellee Koss and the evidence stated is correct, but is only applicable to the issue raised by his cross-complaint, and that such cross-complaint is not a part of the record in this appeal. The first special finding states the amount to be paid appellee Koss according to the contract between appellees Lewis and Koss, "a copy of which contract between said plaintiff and the said William F. Koss is filed with the cross-complaint of the defendant William F. Koss, marked 'Exhibit A.'" The cross-complaint is also referred to in the third conclusion of law. In the transcript of appellant's evidence it appears that counsel for appellant introduced in evidence "the cross-complaint of Wm. F. Koss, filed in this case on March 7, 1902, which was admitted in evidence, and read to the court, and copied into the record in full as 'Exhibit No. 11.'" It also appears that the court rendered judgment on the cross-complaint, from which no appeal is taken. Upon the foregoing showing appellant cannot be heard to say that the cross-complaint is not in the record. Appellee contends that the contract was ambiguous, and that the interpretation put upon it by the parties should control. We do not concede that it was. It was, however, construed by the court, and, upon all the evidence, correctly, as we think, and that construction was sustained by evidence. The contracts were, as to the question here involved, identical, and there should be one interpretation for all the parties interested.

Judgment affirmed.

HENLEY, C. J., and BLACK, ROBINSON, and ROBY, JJ., concur. WILEY, P. J., absent.

(33 Ind. App. 399)

BALPH et al. v. MAGAW.*

(Appellate Court of Indiana, Division No. 1. Feb. 23, 1904.)

FRAUDULENT CONVEYANCE — LIMITATIONS — PLEADING—NEW TRIAL—FORM OF MOTION—APPEAL.

1. Where a complaint alleged that a judgment debtor paid to the purchaser at an execution sale of his land the amount of his bid, and took an assignment of the certificate of sale to a third party, who held the title as a volunteer for the benefit of the debtor to prevent a resale of the land in satisfaction of an unpaid balance of the judgment, it was sufficiently alleged that the debtor paid for the certificate with his own money.

2. Under Burns' Rev. St. 1901, § 298, providing that limitations do not run while the defendant is a nonresident, where a personal judgment has been procured, the statute does not bar a subsequent action to subject to the payment of the judgment property which has been fraudulently conveyed by the judgment debtor to nonresidents, though more than six years have passed.

3. Burns' Rev. St. 1901, § 568, provides that a new trial may be granted on the ground "that the verdict or decision is not sustained by sufficient evidence, or is contrary to law." *Held* that, though a motion for a new trial because "the finding and judgment of the court is not sustained by the evidence" and "is contrary to law" might have been overruled because of its form, yet where it was granted the defect in form is not available on appeal.

Appeal from Circuit Court, Tipton County; James V. Kent, Special Judge.

Action by Theophilus Magaw, guardian, against James Balph and others. From a judgment in favor of plaintiff, defendants Balph and another appeal. Affirmed.

Blackidge, Shirley & Wolf and Oglebay & Oglebay, for appellants. W. A. Johnson and Gifford & Gifford, for appellee.

ROBINSON, J. The judgment in this case rests upon the amended third paragraph of complaint, which avers substantially the following facts: Appellee is guardian of certain minor heirs of Thomas and Mary Cox, deceased. In the lifetime of Thomas Cox, one McCloy executed to him a mortgage on certain described land to secure $6,000 unpaid purchase money. Cox assigned the notes as collateral security to the Union Bank to secure a loan from the bank to him for $3,000. Afterwards the bank obtained a personal judgment against McCloy for $6,-546, the decree providing that out of the judgment there should be paid the bank $3,-677.66, with interest; the remainder to be paid to Cox. After McCloy executed the mortgage, he sold part of the land to other parties, which portions so sold were ordered in the above decree to be not sold until the remainder of the mortgaged property had been exhausted. Afterwards the sheriff sold all the land except the parts which had been conveyed away by McCloy, and the bank purchased the same for $3,856.32, the same being full amount of its claim. That there remained due on the judgment in fa-

*Rehearing denied. Transfer to Supreme Court denied.

vor of Cox the sum of $4,000. That afterwards McCloy paid the bank the sum of their bid, and took an assignment of their certificate of purchase to one James Balph, and, the land not having been redeemed of record from the sale, at the end of the year McCloy procured a sheriff's deed to be made to Balph on such certificate. That Balph, under this deed, is claiming title to the land, but it is averred that he has no interest in or to the land, but holds the apparent title as a volunteer from and through such sale, for the use and benefit of McCloy. That the equitable title to the land sold on the decree is in McCloy, the title being so held for the fraudulent purpose of preventing a resale of the land in satisfaction of the unpaid balance of the judgment. That McCloy, aside from this real estate, is insolvent. That Balph and Balph are, and have been since 1890, nonresidents of the state.

The case went to trial upon the second, third, and fourth paragraphs of complaint. As the court found in appellants' favor on the second and fourth paragraphs, they could not have been injured by the court's ruling in the demurrer to these paragraphs. The record contains a general finding and judgment. Although the facts are set out as found, it amounts to no more than a general finding. The finding does not purport to be a special finding, and cannot be so considered.

It is first objected to the third paragraph of complaint that it is not averred that McCloy paid his own money for the certificate, and the case of Lipperd v. Edwards, 39 Ind. 165, is cited. It is said in that case that the fraud, if any, consisted in the purchase of the land by Lipperd with his own means, and vesting the title in his wife, with intent to cheat his creditors. While pleadings are to be construed most strongly against the pleader, yet we think that it may be said that the pleading sufficiently shows that McCloy paid his own money for the certificate. The averment is that he paid the bank the sum of their bid, and took an assignment of the certificate to Balph; that he afterwards procured a deed to be made to Balph; that Balph has no interest, but holds the title as a volunteer from and through such sale for the use and benefit of McCloy, the title being so held for the fraudulent purpose of preventing a resale of the land in satisfaction of the unpaid balance of the judgment. This action was not brought to obtain any judgment against McCloy. That judgment had already been obtained. It is now sought to subject certain land held by Balph to the payment of that judgment. The personal judgment against McCloy is in no way affected by the decree against Balph subjecting the land held by him to the payment of the judgment. The complaint avers that Balph and Balph are nonresidents of the state, and the proof shows that they have never been residents of the state. The statute of limitations does not bar the action. Burns' Rev. St. 1901, § 298. See, also, Bottles v. Miller, 112 Ind. 584, 14 N. E. 728; Mozingo v. Ross, 150 Ind. 688, 50 N. E. 867, 41 L. R. A. 612, 65 Am. St. Rep. 387.

Upon a former trial the court found in appellants' favor, but afterwards sustained a motion for a new trial. This ruling is now assigned as error. The only objection to this ruling is that the motion is not in the form required by statute, and for that reason should have been overruled. The sixth subdivision of section 568, Burns' Rev. St. 1901, is "that the verdict or decision is not sustained by sufficient evidence or is contrary to law." In the motion under consideration the causes stated are that "the finding and judgment of the court is contrary to the evidence," "the judgment and finding of the court is not sustained by the evidence," "the finding and judgment of the court is contrary to law." The trial court would have been authorized in overruling the motion because of its form. Hubbs v. State ex rel., 20 Ind. App. 181, 50 N. E. 402; Allen v. Indianapolis Oil Co., 27 Ind. App. 158, 60 N. E. 1003; Famous Mfg. Co. v. Harmon, 28 Ind. App. 117, 62 N. E. 306; Baltimore, etc., R. Co. v. Daegling, 30 Ind. App. 180, 65 N. E. 761; Lynch v. Milwaukee Harvester Co., 159 Ind. 675, 65 N. E. 1025. But we do not think this defect in form of the motion is available where the motion has been sustained. The court's ruling is not questioned on the merits. The trial was by the court, and we cannot question the conclusions of the court that the motion was sufficient to direct its attention to an error that it had committed. If there had been a mistrial, it was the court's duty to grant a new trial, and the court's conclusion that the showing made in the motion was sufficient should not be overthrown where it can properly be said some showing was made. The court could have concluded, the trial having been by the court, that the word "finding" used in the motion was equivalent to the word "decision" (Rodefer v. Fletcher, 89 Ind. 563; Rosenzweig v. Frazer, 82 Ind. 342; Christy v. Smith, 80 Ind. 573; Wilson v. Vance, 55 Ind. 394; Gates v. Baltimore, etc., R. Co., 154 Ind. 338, 56 N. E. 722), and, having done so, the court may have treated the word "judgment" in the motion as surplusage. "To authorize us to reverse a judgment," said the court in Barner v. Bayless, 134 Ind. 600, 33 N. E. 907, 34 N. E. 502, "on account of the abuse of the discretion of the lower court in granting a new trial, it should be made to appear, first, that there was a plain abuse of judicial discretion; second, that flagrant injustice had been done the complaining party; third, a very strong case for relief should be made." Carthage Turnpike Co. v. Overman, 19 Ind. App. 309, 48 N. E. 874. Appellant Balph's motion for a new trial was properly overruled. The affidavits filed in support of the motion do not show a sufficient excuse for his nonattendance at the trial. They proceeded to trial without objection. No motion was presented asking a continuance. Appellant has discussed, to some extent, the evidence. There is evidence to sustain the court's conclusion. It is not shown that any error harmful to appellant was committed in the admission of any testimony. We find no error in the record.

Judgment affirmed.

(33 Ind. App. 544)

TERRE HAUTE BREWING CO. et al. v. NEWLAND.*

(Appellate Court of Indiana. Feb. 24, 1904.)

INTOXICATING LIQUORS—ILLEGAL SALE—CIVIL LIABILITY — BREWING COMPANY — CONNECTION WITH SALE—ADMISSIBILITY OF EVIDENCE UNDER PLEADING.

1. A complaint by a mother dependent on her son for support for his death, occasioned by acute alcoholism resulting from purchases of intoxicating liquors from defendants, alleged that the defendant brewing company "colluded and connived and became a party in interest with" the saloon keeper in carrying on a saloon without a license, "and became interested in the profits and proceeds of said business, and received a part of said profits for its aid and participation in said business." *Held*, that under the charge of collusion proof of the connection of the brewing company with the saloon business was admissible.

2. A saloon began business without a license, having made a note to a brewing company in payment for license, which the company was to get for him. The note was not paid, and the company made no attempt to secure a license, though its agent telephoned the saloon keeper that a license had been granted. The saloon keeper leased a building for his business, the brewing company paying the rent and furnishing the liquor. The saloon was run without a license, and kept open on Sundays. *Held*, that the brewing company was liable to a widow, whose son, on whom she was dependent, died from acute alcoholism, after spending the greater part of Sunday in the saloon where he purchased intoxicants.

Wiley, P. J., dissenting.

Appeal from Circuit Court, Hancock County; E. W. Felt, Judge.

Action by Mary Newland against the Terre Haute Brewing Company and another. Judgment for plaintiff, and the brewing company appeals. Affirmed.

Marsh & Cook and Woolen & Woolen, for appellant. E. F. Ritter, W. O. Doan, and Mason & Jackson, for appellee.

ROBY, J. Action by appellee for damages on account of death of her son, 22 years of age, upon whom she avers that she was dependent. Verdict against Jacob Van Blaricum and the Terre Haute Brewing Company for $500. Motion for a new trial overruled, and judgment on the verdict.

The sole question presented on this appeal is the sufficiency of the evidence to sustain the verdict as against the brewing company, the alleged deficiency being lack of connection with the occurrence on its part. The complaint contains an averment as follows: "The defendant the Terre Haute Brewing Company colluded and connived and became a party in interest with the said defendant Van Blaricum in the conduct of said unlawful business at the beginning of the same as aforesaid, and became interested in the profits and proceeds of said business, and received a part of said profits for its aid and participation in said business." It is established without conflict of evidence, and mainly by the testimony of the defendant Van Blaricum, whose presence at the trial of the cause in Hancock county was procured on the second day of such trial through the service of a subpœna in Marion county and the payment of witness fees to him by appellee, that from December 24, 1901, until the time of the trial, June 13, 1902, he kept a saloon in the city of Indianapolis without any license to do so. The testimony also tends to show that he made a note to the appellant brewing company for $350 in payment for a license, which it agreed to get for him. The note had not been paid, and it is not shown that any attempt had been made by the brewing company, or any one else, to procure any kind of a license. Van Blaricum testified that the agent of the brewing company notified him over the telephone that a license had been granted. The agent denied having done so, but the finding of the jury was against him. The building in which Van Blaricum carried on his trade was leased to him by the owner on December 7, 1901. On that day the first installment of rent was paid by the brewing company. It paid the rent thereafter on the 1st days of January, February, March, April, May, and June, 1902, and on February 3d Van Blaricum assigned all his interest in the lease to it. Van Blaricum and the brewing company had an agreement by which he "would handle nothing else than our beer." It delivered to him before January 19, 1902, merchandise on various dates, amounting to $99, and up to the time of the trial to $838.80. The saloon was not only run without a license this entire time, but it was kept open every Sunday from morning until night. It is not denied that appellee's son on Sunday, January 19, 1902, died of acute alcoholism, after spending the greater part of the day in this saloon. He was taken to his mother's house, put on the doorstep. in the evening, and either was dead when she discovered him, or died shortly thereafter.

When two or more persons engage in the prosecution of an illegal enterprise, and in the violation of the law, it is elemental that each one of them becomes responsible for all the consequences resulting therefrom. The gravamen of this action is a tort; i. e., the unlawful sale of intoxicating liquor. If the evidence tends to show that the brewing company was a party to such sale, then the verdict against it under the allegations of the complaint as to collusion cannot be set

*Rehearing denied. Transfer to Supreme Court denied.

aside. Severinghaus v. Beckman, 9 Ind. App. 388, 36 N. E. 930; Mendenhall v. Stewart, 18 Ind. App. 262, 47 N. E. 943. The law regards substance, not form. If in fact defendant was a party to the illegal sales of liquor by reason of which appellee's son met his death, it is quite immaterial how its relation to the business was cloaked. The charge of collusion permits proof of its true attitude and connection therewith, if any. There is no room for division of responsibility. Van Blaricum cannot be allowed to defend himself by casting responsibility upon appellant because of its failure to get the license after having taken his note for the price and informing him that it had been granted. Neither can appellant evade its responsibility by its manner of keeping books. The question was, did these parties participate in the illegal business which caused the young man's death? The evidence shows that appellant identified itself with the business from the time the room was rented. It furnished every element that was necessary except the man to sell. That was Van Blaricum. It undertook to get a license. It is not shown to have made or caused any application to be made. It paid for the room and furnished the liquor knowing that it was being sold contrary to law, as is inferable from the fact, in connection with others, that its bills were furnished at different times, and in relatively small amounts. The sales of liquor made by it to Van Blaricum were illegal. Terre Haute, etc., Co. v. Hartman, 19 Ind. App. 603, 49 N. E. 864.

The verdict is not without support in the evidence, and it is not material what relations the parties, as between themselves, intended to create.

Judgment affirmed.

HENLEY, C. J., and BLACK, J., concur in result. ROBINSON and COMSTOCK, JJ., concur in opinion.

WILEY, P. J. (dissenting). I would be glad to concur in the majority opinion if I could see any way clear to do so upon any legal hypothesis based upon the theory of the complaint. Under the facts pleaded and the evidence in support thereof, I cannot believe there is any legal liability resting upon appellant. Trying to avoid the influence of any sentiment naturally aroused by the fact of the total disregard of the law on the part of Van Blaricum in selling liquor, as disclosed by the evidence, I deem it my duty to express my views of the law as applicable to the proven facts, and give the reasons which lead me to the conclusion that appellant is not liable. To do this I must be permitted to give a more detailed statement of the facts than appears in the prevailing opinion. The cause was commenced in the Marion superior court, and venued to the court below, where it was tried and determined. Appellee based her cause of action upon the death of her son, which she alleged in her complaint was caused by acute alcoholism, superinduced by the unlawful sale of intoxicating liquors to him by appellant and Van Blaricum. Appellant's demurrer to the complaint was overruled, answer in denial, trial by jury, and verdict against each of the defendants. Appellant's motion for a new trial overruled, and judgment on verdict. Each of these rulings are assigned as errors.

Appellee bottoms her right of action upon that provision of section 7288, Burns' Rev. St. 1901, fixing liability upon persons who illegally sell intoxicating liquors, as a result of which another is deprived of his or her means of support. She was a widow, and her son, Guy Newland, resided with her. He was of age, and in her complaint she avers that he was her only means of support. She also avers that Jacob Van Blaricum owned and kept a saloon in the city of Indianapolis; that he did not have a license to retail intoxicating liquors, but that in violation of law he sold liquors on Sundays and divers other times; that her said son was an industrious and hardworking young man, in good health, and out of his earnings contributed to her support; that said Van Blaricum, on Sunday, January 19, 1901, at his saloon, unlawfully sold to her said son intoxicating liquors, which he drank, and thereby became intoxicated, and while in a state of intoxication he continued to sell intoxicating liquors to him, and that he became so intoxicated that he was unconscious and helpless, and finally died as a result thereof. Appellee seeks to fix responsibility upon appellant by the following averments: "The defendant the Terre Haute Brewing Company colluded and connived and became a party in interest with the said Van Blaricum in the conduct of said unlawful business at the beginning of the same, as aforesaid, and became interested in the profits and proceeds of said business, and received a part of said profits for its aid and participation in said business. * * * And plaintiff further says that on account of the said unlawful sales * * * and the unlawful conduct of said saloon the collusion, connivance, and participation in said business by said defendant the Terre Haute Brewing Company, the intoxication and death of said son was produced as aforesaid," etc. It is somewhat difficult to determine the theory of the complaint as against appellant. It is charged that Van Blaricum conducted the saloon as proprietor, and that appellant colluded and connived and became a party in interest with Van Blaricum in the conduct of said unlawful business, and became interested in the profits of the business, and received a part of the profits. A pleading must proceed upon some definite theory, and the only theory upon which it can be said that any cause of action is stated against appellant is that it was a partner of and interested with Van Blaricum in conducting and running an unlicensed saloon, and that it shared in the profits. Appellee must recover, if at all, upon the theory of the complaint, and hence it must appear from the evidence that appellant colluded and connived with Van Blaricum in the sale to appellee's son, and became a party in interest, and shared in the profits of the business.

Appellant relies for a reversal solely upon the insufficiency of the evidence to support the judgment. The evidence, so far as it relates to the liability of appellant, is brief, and may be summarized as follows: Appellant is a brewer of beer, and sells its products to retailers. December 7, 1901, the owner of the building in which Van Blaricum conducted his saloon leased it in writing to him. The lessee assigned his interest in the lease to appellant February 3, 1902, which was after appellee's cause of action had accrued. The rent for the building was paid by appellant to the owner's agent from December 7, 1901, to June 30, 1902, and entered upon appellant's books as charges against Van Blaricum. The latter reimbursed appellant by paying the rent to its collector. Appellant was to receive from Van Blaricum the money advanced by it for rent, whether he got it out of his business or from some other source. So far as appellant's agent knew, Van Blaricum was not engaged in any other business. The complaint avers that Van Blaricum was the "proprietor" of the saloon, and the evidence shows that as such proprietor he opened his saloon and commenced business December 24, 1901. On that day he took possession of the premises under the lease to him. On the day of the alleged sales to appellee's son he did not have any license to sell intoxicating liquors. He gave a note, with surety, to appellant's agent, for $350, for which a license was to be procured for him. This note he did not pay. Prior to January 19, 1902, appellant's agent had not taken out a license in Van Blaricum's name. Van Blaricum testified that he believed that one Donnelly, appellant's agent, had told him by telephone, between Christmas and New Year, that his license had been granted. Appellant supplied Van Blaricum with beer from its brewery for him to sell in his saloon under a contract at $7.20 per barrel. That was appellant's regular price for beer by the barrel to retailers. From December 28, 1901, to June 7, 1902, appellant sold him beer at different times, amounting in the aggregate to $838.80, for which he paid in cash at different times $789.20, leaving a balance due June 7, 1902, of $49.60. Appellant paid the rent for the saloon building as an advancement from December 31, 1901, to June 4, 1902, which amounted to $270.18, and charged the several payments to Van Blaricum on its books. Of this amount he paid back to appellant, between January 14 and May 13, 1902, the sum of $120. It is in evidence that there was an agreement entered into between appellant's agent and Van Blaricum that, if appellant would advance the money for the license on the secured note, he would handle its beer exclusively, provided it would sell it to him at the market price of $7.20 per barrel. The evidence is uncontradicted that appellant received from Van Blaricum $7.20 per barrel, no more nor less, for all the beer sold him. There was no agreement between Van Blaricum and appellant that the latter should participate in the profits of the former's saloon business, and there is no evidence that it did participate therein. The evidence further shows that before the day on which the sales of liquor were made to appellee's son, as alleged, Van Blaricum had repaid to appellant a part of the first money advanced on the rent. On January 18, 1902, that being the day before the death of appellee's son, Van Blaricum had paid appellant for all beer previously sold him, and paid $7.20 per barrel therefor. The evidence as to the various facts stated is without conflict.

If any cause of action against appellant is stated, it is upon the theory that it colluded and connived with Van Blaricum in the unlawful sales, and participated with him in the profits. This theory cannot be sustained upon any hypothesis except upon the fact that appellant knew that Van Blaricum was selling liquor on Sunday. The fact that the sale was made to appellee's son on Sunday can have no weight, for the reason that the sale so made would have been unlawful even if he had had a license. There is no evidence to show that appellant knew he was selling liquors on forbidden days or hours, or that sanctioned, counseled, or abetted the same.

Counsel for appellee say in their brief that "the appellant not only furnished the liquors, room, and fixtures, but paid the rent where the business was conducted." I have read every word of the evidence, and there is not a scintilla of evidence that appellant furnished the fixtures, nor any facts from which such inference can be drawn. True, appellant did pay the rent by advancing the money, and also furnished the beer at the usual price to retailers. The money thus advanced and the beer thus sold were charged to him, and he paid all of it but a small balance. This is a statutory action, and it is well to look to the statute to determine the character of it, for what and against whom it may be maintained, and for what cause. The statute is as follows: "Every person who shall sell, barter or give away any intoxicating liquors, in violation of any of the provisions of this act, shall be personally liable * * * to any person who shall sustain any injury or damage to his person or property or means of support on account of the use of such intoxicating liquors, so sold as aforesaid," etc. Section 7288, supra. The facts do not disclose any element of a partnership between appellant and Van Blaricum. Neither do they show that the latter was the agent of the former in conducting the business. "Partnership is the relation subsisting between two or more persons who have contracted together to share, as common owners, the profits of a business carried on by all or any of them on behalf of all of them." Vol. 22 Am. & Eng. Encyc. of Law (2d Ed.) 13. In view of the undisputed facts, this effectually disposes of the question of partnership.

Persons claiming the benefit of a right of action conferred by statute must bring themselves within the provisions of the statute to secure such benefit. In this instance the right of action is given to a person who has been injured or damaged in his person or property or means of support, occasioned by the sale of intoxicating liquors, in violation of the provisions of the act which gives the right. It is a violation of the provisions of that act to sell without a license, to sell between 11 o'clock p. m. and 5 o'clock a. m., to sell on Sundays or holidays, and to sell to a person in a state of intoxication. As disclosed by the evidence, Van Blaricum violated three provisions of that statute, viz., he sold without a license, he sold on Sunday, and he sold to a person in a state of intoxication. Who sold appellee's son liquor in violation of the provisions of the statute? Was it appellant or Van Blaricum? Evidently the latter. Unless Van Blaricum was appellant's agent in making the sale, or they were partners in the business, there can be no liability against appellant, for it did not sell to appellee's son, for the statute limits the liability to the person who makes unlawful sales. It does not require any argument to support the proposition that the sale of beer by appellant to appellee, who was an unlicensed saloon keeper, was not a violation of any provision of that act. Legally it had a right to sell its beer to unlicensed saloon keepers, if it had no right to do so morally. I am not dealing with the legal question as to the rights of the parties, where a wholesale liquor dealer sells liquors to a retailer, where the former knows such liquors are to be unlawfully vended. The legal status of the parties to such a transaction has been adjudicated in this state, and correctly so, and that is that a seller is without remedy to enforce his contract. The relation existing between Van Blaricum and appellant may be simplified by an illustration: Suppose the former had had a license to retail intoxicating liquors when the latter sold him beer at wholesale. Unquestionably, the beer, when thus sold, would have become the property of the vendee. In such case he could have sold to whomsoever and whenever he pleased, and appellant would have been blameless. Suppose he had sold a part of it to appellee's son on a forbidden day, and when he was in a state of intoxication, in violation of law, from the results of which he had died, and appellee thereby deprived of her means of support, appellant, under such circumstances, would not have been liable, and no one could reasonably contend that it would be. It would have been just as much a violation of the law, under these circumstances, to have made the sales, as it was to have made them as he did without a license. The beer he had purchased of appellant prior to the time the sale to appellee's son is charged had been paid for, and was as much his as if he had had a license to sell before he purchased it. The question then resolves itself into the single proposition: Whose beer was it that was sold to appellee's son, and who sold it to him? This inquiry must be answered by declaring that it was Van Blaricum's beer, and was sold by him.

Neither is there a particle of evidence to support the allegation that appellant colluded and connived with Van Blaricum in the sale of its beer, or received any profits from the sale thereof. All it contracted to receive was the wholesale price of its beer at $7.20 per barrel, and it received this, except a small balance remaining unpaid.

There can be no doubt as to the theory of the complaint, as above stated; and the complaint, if good at all against appellant, was good upon the theory that it "colluded and connived with Van Blaricum, and became interested in the profits and proceeds of said business, and received a part of said profits for its aid and participation in said business." This implies a partnership. The record shows that it was upon this theory the case was tried. The trial court recognized that this was the theory as indicated by one of its instructions in which it told the jury that appellant was not liable unless it "had a pecuniary interest in the profits of such illegal sales and business, or was entitled, under the arrangement between the parties, to share therein." In their brief counsel for appellees have adopted a new theory, which is foreign to the one upon which the complaint proceeds and upon which the cause was tried. They say: "The relation between Van Blaricum and the appellant was mere associates in the conduct of an unlawful business, and as the appellant furnished the stuff and the room, and paid the rent, and owned the liquors which were placed in the saloon for the purpose and with the intent to be sold in violation of the law, it was the principal and Van Blaricum was a mere helper." It is the settled rule of law that the theory upon which a cause proceeded in the trial court should be the theory upon which the action of that court is tested on appeal. Louisville, etc., Ry. Co. v. Hughes, 2 Ind. App. 68, 28 N. E. 158; Cleveland, etc., Ry. Co. v. De Bolt, 10 Ind. App. 174, 37 N. E. 737.

Regardless of the fact that counsel apparently attempted to shift the theory of their complaint (in which case, it may well be remarked, it does not state any cause of action against appellant), we will review some of the authorities relied upon to support the judgment. The first case cited is that of

Phillips v. State, 20 S. E. 270, where the Supreme Court of Georgia announced as a legal proposition that: "Where one, by the use of his capital or credits, aids in procuring and furnishing whisky to another for the purpose of being unlawfully sold, and the former, by the agreement for conducting the business, is to receive, and does actually receive, a given per cent. of the costs of all the whisky so furnished and so sold, they are both guilty of selling the liquor unlawfully, whether, under the terms of such agreement, a technical partnership existed between them or not." That case is not in point upon any question here involved, because not pertinent to the facts disclosed by the record. In that case there was an agreement between the parties that they should participate in the profits, and the undisputed facts showed that they did participate. The facts showed there a partnership in the legal sense of the term. The following cases are cited and relied upon: White v. Buss, 3 Cush. 448; Mosher v. Griffin, 51 Ill. 184, 99 Am. Dec. 541; Tatum et al. v. Kelley, 25 Ark. 210, 94 Am. Dec. 717; Hill v. Spear, 50 N. H. 265, 9 Am. Rep. 205; Metcalf on Contracts, pp. 260, 261; Gaylord v. Soragen, 32 Vt. 110, 76 Am. Dec. 154; Aiken v. Blaisdell, 41 Vt. 655. As we review these last-cited cases, they are not decisive of any question here involved. They simply declare, or rather restate, a familiar and well-grounded rule that, where a party sells goods, wares, etc., which he knows is to be used for unlawful or illegal purposes, courts will not lend their aid to enforce such contracts of sale, but will leave the parties in the position they placed themselves. Under such circumstances they cannot invoke the intervention of courts for redress. Thus, where a party who was employed to train a horse for a race upon which money was bet, it was held he could not recover for his services, because it was in aid of an offense prohibited by law. Mosher v. Griffin, supra. So, where a dealer living in New York sold liquors to a person living in Vermont, to be sold in the latter state contrary to the law of that state, the seller knowing they were to be so sold in Vermont, it was held that the vendee could not recover their value. Gaylord v. Soragen, supra. Where guns were sold to be used in the War of the Rebellion, and a note given in payment, it was held that the seller could not recover, he knowing the purpose to which they were to be put, because he thus "concurred with and actively promoted the unlawful and treasonable purpose of the defendants." Tatum et al. v. Kelley, supra. The other cases are of similar purport, and need not be further noticed.

As above suggested, the evidence does not disclose any element of partnership, for it affirmatively appears that appellant sold Van Blaricum its beer under contract, for which he agreed to pay the regular wholesale price, and which in fact he did pay, all but a small balance. Neither does the evidence show any collusion or connivance between appellant and Van Blaricum in the sales made by the latter. If there was any, it must be inferred from the naked fact that appellant sold Van Blaricum beer at wholesale to be sold at retail, knowing that he did not have a license to so sell. No such inference can be indulged in view of the theory of the complaint and the undisputed facts. The complaint avers that Van Blaricum was the "proprietor" of the saloon, and that Van Blaricum unlawfully sold liquor to appellee's son, which caused his death. Assuming that Van Blaricum did sell liquor to appellee's son on Sunday, and when he was in a state of intoxication, he was guilty of violating three provisions of the statute: (1) He sold without a license; (2) he sold on a prohibited day; and (3) he sold to a person in a state of intoxication. The last two would have been unlawful if he had had a license. He could have been prosecuted under either one or all of the provisions of the statute thus violated. If he had had a license, and had been prosecuted for selling on Sunday, and to a person in a state of intoxication, it could not, upon any legal hypothesis or well-grounded reason, be contended that appellant could have been successfully prosecuted with him for such violation of the law. In such case its civil responsibility could be no greater than its criminal liability. And the violation of these two provisions of the liquor law, under the facts shown, was the direct cause of appellee's injury, and the result would have been the same if Van Blaricum had had a license. Again, suppose Van Blaricum had been indicted and prosecuted for making the sales he did to appellee's son without having first obtained a license. Could appellant have been indicted and successfully prosecuted with him? Evidently not, because Van Blaricum, and not appellant, sold the beer. It follows that the facts that Van Blaricum had no license, and appellant knew it, can in no wise fix liability against appellant, as it is not shown it made the sale, or profited by its results. This being a special statutory action, and such right of action is given alone against the person "who shall sell," etc., I do not see how the action can be maintained against one who did not sell, and was in no legitimate way connected with it. If I understand the proposition upon which my associates hold that appellant is liable, it is that expressed in the opinion that "where two or more persons engage in the prosecution of an illegal enterprise, and in violation of law, it is elemental that each one of them becomes responsible for all the consequences resulting therefrom." Concede that proposition to be true, it is not applicable to the facts here, for the reason that it is not shown that appellant engaged with Van Blaricum in the "prosecution of an illegal enterprise." The complaint makes no such charge, except by innuendo, and the evidence, in my judgment, does not support any such charge. The complaint avers that Van Blaricum was the "proprietor" of the saloon, and that Van Blaricum sold the liquor to appellee's son. Appellant and Van Blaricum are so disconnected by the facts from the sale to appellee's son as not to make them joint tort feasors. I understand the rule to be that, if there is no concert of action or unity of purpose between two or more persons in the commission of a tort, there is no joint liability, but in such event liability attaches to the one committing the tort.

These considerations lead to the conclusion that appellant is not liable, and the judgment should be reversed.

(185 Mass. 329)

SMITH et al. v. TOWN OF STOUGHTON.

(Supreme Judicial Court of Massachusetts. Middlesex. April 1, 1904.)

MUNICIPAL CORPORATIONS — CONTRACT — IMPOSSIBILITY OF PERFORMANCE—ACTION FOR BREACH—STATUTE.

1. A town had succeeded by purchase to the rights of a water company organized under St. 1886, p. 186, c. 240, for the purpose of supplying the inhabitants of the town with water. The statute authorized the company to take water, by purchase or otherwise, from certain specified sources, one of which was a certain brook, that being the only source specified in the law which it was possible to utilize. *Held*, that the town was limited to the same sources for its water supply as the corporation whose rights it purchased.

2. Where it appears, in an action against a town for damages for a refusal of the officers to permit plaintiffs to perform a contract in writing to put in certain wells and construct a system of waterworks for the town, that the town had no lawful authority to use the supply of water that it was proposed by the contract to furnish, the performance of the contract was impossible within the limits legally permissible to the parties.

3. There can be no recovery of damages for breach of contract, the performance of which is rendered impossible within the limits legally permissible to the parties.

4. A town succeeding to the rights of a water company contracted with plaintiffs to put in certain wells. In a suit to set aside a conveyance of a farm to the town, this contract was introduced incidentally, as dependent for its validity upon the ownership of the farm, which was purchased with reference to the use of the waters of a brook running through it. The only question determined was whether the commissioners had authority to buy the land, and no reference was made to the contract in regard to the wells. *Held*, that a dismissal of the bill was not res adjudicata as to the validity of the contracts for the sinking of the wells.

Exceptions from Superior Court, Middlesex County; John A. Aiken, Judge.

Action by one Smith and others against the town of Stoughton. From a judgment for plaintiffs, defendant brings exceptions. Exceptions sustained.

Samuel L. Powers, Oscar A. Marden, and Henry W. Dunn, for plaintiffs. T. E. Grover and E. F. Leonard, for defendant.

KNOWLTON, C. J. This is an action to recover damages for a refusal of the defendant to permit the plaintiffs to perform a contract in writing to put in certain wells and construct a system of waterworks for the defendant. The primary question is whether the contract relied on, in its application to the facts and to the contemplated mode, and the only possible mode, of performing it, was one that the defendant had a legal right to make; or, to put it in another form, whether the contract was possible of performance by the plaintiff, if the mode of performance was restricted to that which was within the legal rights of the defendant.

The only source for the supply of water from which the town was authorized to draw, at the place mentioned in the contract, was Knowles' brook. The method prescribed by the contract was by driving wells, each consisting of a 2½-inch iron pipe, and connecting them together by pipes to which a pump was to be attached. These wells were 25 or 30 or more feet deep, and in boring them it appeared that several feet below the surface there was a stratum of fine sand, several feet in thickness, which was nearly, but not entirely, impervious. Below this stratum there was a body of loose, coarse gravel, which, according to the contention of the plaintiffs, contained a large supply of water. The plaintiffs' witnesses testified that the water in this gravel came from a considerable distance, and, being confined by this stratum, could not find its way, except in a very small degree, into the brook; and that the water gathered from the apparent watershed of Knowles' brook was not a measure of the quantity that could be obtained from that locality. The water from all these wells flowed over their tops, and from one of them, when a covering was put on, leaving a small orifice, the water spouted up five or more feet. The general contention of the plaintiffs was that there was an actual watershed of from three to six square miles, exclusive of the apparent watershed of Knowles' brook, from which the water in this gravel was gathered, a large part of which could be reached by wells driven at the place prescribed in the contract. On the question whether it would have been possible for the plaintiffs to perform their contract, which called for a guarantied supply of 1,000,000 gallons of water per day throughout the entire year, the defendant objected to any evidence "that did not tend to show that the quantity of water called for * * * could be obtained from Knowles' brook, or other sources from which the town was authorized to take water, or which would naturally find its way into said brook or such other sources. But the court overruled the defendant's objection, and the defendant excepted." The plaintiffs' recovery was had upon the theory that this contract authorized the taking of water which had no connection with

¶ 3. See Contracts, vol. 11, Cent. Dig. §§ 1417, 1444.

Knowles' brook, but which came underground in large quantities from long distances, and which, by reason of the subterranean geological formation, could be drawn to the surface there by these wells. Knowles' brook flowed through a part of the farm owned by the defendant, on which the wells were to be put, and it had its origin there; but the apparent watershed pertaining to it was only about three-quarters or seven-eighths of a square mile. The defendant's farm contained 133 acres, some portions of which were a long distance from Knowles' brook. The jury were instructed that, under the contract, the plaintiffs might procure water anywhere within the boundaries of the farm.

The Stoughton Water Company was organized under St. 1886, p. 186, c. 240, for the purpose of supplying the inhabitants of the town of Stoughton with water. It was authorized to take water, by purchase or otherwise, from certain specified sources, one of which was Knowles' brook. It was important to private owners, as well as to the public, that its rights in reference to the sources from which it might draw water should be defined and limited. Accordingly, its franchise gave it the rights mentioned, and no others. As a corporation it had no powers but those given by its charter, and it could not take water and sell it to the inhabitants, either by purchasing lands and sinking wells, or otherwise, except from the authorized sources. See Bailey v. Woburn, 126 Mass. 418; Forbell v. City of New York, 164 N. Y. 522, 58 N. E. 644, 51 L. R. A. 695, 79 Am. St. Rep. 666; Bassett v. Salisbury Manufacturing Company, 43 N. H. 569. If it had attempted to do so, its act would have been ultra vires, and might have been prohibited in the interests of the commonwealth, or by a private person who was injuriously affected by it. The defendant town was authorized by the statute to purchase the franchise and rights of this corporation, and it exercised this authority. It succeeded to the corporation rights, and no others. It is limited to the same sources for its water supply as the corporation was. The only source of supply to which this contract relates, that can be used by the town, is Knowles' brook.

As against ordinary corporations, there are equitable limitations upon the defense of ultra vires to actions upon contracts partly or wholly executed. See Nims v. Mount Hermon Boys' School, 160 Mass. 177, 35 N. E. 776, 22 L. R. A. 364, 39 Am. St. Rep. 467, and cases there cited. Whether this defense could be availed of effectually in the present case, if the town had not purchased the franchise, and the original corporation were in the place of the present defendant, it is unnecessary to decide. There are additional considerations affecting suits against towns. A contract not authorized by law is not binding upon a town or its taxpayers, and the courts will not enforce it. Parsons v. Goshen, 11 Pick. 396; Minot v. West Roxbury, 112 Mass. 1, 17 Am. Rep. 52; Lowell Savings Bank v. Winchester, 8 Allen, 109; Allen v. Taunton, 19 Pick. 485–487; Anthony v. Adams, 1 Metc. 286; Claflin v. Hopkinton, 4 Gray, 502–504; Hood v. Lyson, 1 Allen, 103–105; Agawam Bank v. South Hadley, 128 Mass. 503–505; Lemon v. Newton, 134 Mass. 476–479. Neither the water commissioners as agents for the town, nor the town itself by a vote, could subject the taxpayers to a liability under a contract to take water from an unauthorized source. The plaintiffs do not deny this proposition, but they rest their principal contention upon the decision in Stoughton v. Paul, 173 Mass. 148, 53 N. E. 272, which they treat as an adjudication conclusive in their favor in this case. We do not so consider it. That was a suit in equity to set aside the conveyance of the farm to the town, and this contract was introduced incidentally, as dependent for its validity upon the ownership of the farm. It was decided that the votes of the town did not limit the authority of the water commissioners. It was assumed, upon the record then before the court, that the purchase of the farm was with reference to taking and using the waters of Knowles' brook. The single sentence in the report of the finding in reference to intercepting other subterranean waters as well as those flowing into Knowles' brook, and the evidence on that subject, were not introduced as showing the principal object of the purchase. The purchase of the large tract was justified on the ground that it was thought necessary for the preservation and purity of the sources of water supply, and taking the waters of Knowles' brook by interception and percolation was held to be permissible. In the opinion it is said that "the only question is whether the commissioners had authority to buy the land," and from the beginning to the end of the opinion it contains no reference to the contract now before the court. The validity of the present contract, in reference to the questions now raised, was not in issue, and a refusal of an injunction by a dismissal of the bill involved nothing as to the defenses to the contract which might be set up in an action at law afterwards. There was no jurisdiction in equity to enjoin proceedings under the contract on the grounds now relied on by the defendant. In reference to these matters, the remedy at law was complete and adequate. Neither as a part of the substance of the suit then tried between the parties, nor collaterally, was there any adjudication of the questions now before the court. An adjudication as to the purchase of the land was not an adjudication as to this contract, subsequently made.

Because the contract was for the construction of waterworks in connection with a supply which the town had no legal authority to use, and because performance of the contract was impossible within limits legally permissible to the parties, the plaintiffs were not entitled to damages for the defendant's refusal to perform it.

Exceptions sustained.

(185 Mass. 325)

CORCORAN v. CITY OF BOSTON.

(Supreme Judicial Court of Massachusetts. Suffolk. March 31, 1904.)

TAXATION—EXEMPTION—STATUTE.

1. Under Rev. Laws, c. 12, § 5, subd. 2, providing that the property of the commonwealth, except real estate of which the commonwealth is in possession under a mortgage for condition broken, shall be exempt from taxation, land held under a bond for a deed from the commonwealth, on which a private individual has erected buildings and engaged in the manufacturing business thereon, is exempt.

Exceptions from Superior Court, Suffolk County; Wm. Scofield, Judge.

Petition by one Corcoran against the city of Boston for the abatement of a tax assessed to the petitioner. Judgment for petitioner. Defendant excepts. Affirmed.

Chas. E. Hellier, for petitioner. Samuel M. Child, for respondent.

MORTON, J. This is a petition, under Rev. Laws, c. 12, § 78, for the abatement of a tax assessed to the petitioner as of May 1, 1902, by the assessors of Boston, for a parcel of land in South Boston, for which the petitioner had a bond for a deed from the commonwealth, and on which prior to May 1, 1902, he had erected buildings, and was carrying on business as a box manufacturer. The petitioner paid the tax under protest. The case was heard by the court upon agreed facts, with power to draw inferences; it being agreed that, if the petitioner was not liable to be taxed for the land, judgment should be entered for him for the amount of the tax, with interest. The court found and ordered judgment for the petitioner, and the case is here on exceptions by the respondent to the refusal of the court to give certain rulings that were requested, and to the rulings and findings that were made.

We think that the rulings and the refusals to rule were right. The statute expressly provides that "the property of the commonwealth, except real estate of which the commonwealth is in possession under a mortgage for condition broken," shall be exempt from taxation. Rev. Laws, c. 12, § 5, subd. 2. The language could not be plainer. The words "the property of the commonwealth" mean the same as "all the property of the commonwealth." And the fact that only one exception is made shows that no other exception could have been intended, and that a construction such as contended for by the respondent, namely, that the exception extends only to property held by the commonwealth for governmental purposes, would be unwarranted. The property that was taxed is the property of the commonwealth, notwithstanding the commonwealth has contracted to sell it to the petitioner, and the petitioner is in possession, and the exemption attaches to it so long as it continues to be the property of the commonwealth. The question now presented does not appear to have been passed upon in this state, but the plain implication of the language of the court in Inhabitants of Essex Co. v. Salem, 153 Mass. 141, 26 N. E. 431, is that if there had been an exemption from taxation in the case of counties, like that in the case of the property of the commonwealth, it would have been held that the property of the county was exempt from taxation, whether actually devoted to public uses or not. The court has found that the tax assessed to the petitioner was for the land described in the bond, and, for the reasons given, we are of opinion that the tax could not be legally assessed to him.

Judgment affirmed.

(185 Mass. 327)

MEADE v. BOSTON ELEVATED RY. CO.

(Supreme Judicial Court of Massachusetts. Suffolk. March 31, 1904.)

STREET RAILWAYS—INJURY TO PASSENGER WHILE ALIGHTING—NEGLIGENCE—EVIDENCE.

1. The question of negligence and contributory negligence is for the jury, there being testimony that when plaintiff, a passenger on a street car, attempted to alight, it was not in motion, and no signal had been given to start; that she looked at the starter all the time while she was getting out; that he could have seen her if he had looked; that he gave the signal before she had alighted; and that the car was started when she had got as far as the running board, throwing her down.

Exceptions from Superior Court, Suffolk County; Daniel W. Bond, Judge.

Action by one Meade against the Boston Elevated Railway Company. Verdict for plaintiff. Defendant excepts. Exceptions overruled.

Francis P. Garland, for plaintiff. M. F. Dickinson and Walter B. Farr, for defendant.

MORTON, J. This is an action of tort to recover damages for personal injuries sustained by the plaintiff while alighting from an open car of the defendant company at the Park Street Station, in the Subway, Boston. At the close of the evidence the defendant asked the court to rule that, upon all the evidence, the plaintiff was not entitled to recover. The court refused so to rule, and submitted the case to the jury, who returned a verdict for the plaintiff. The case is here on the defendant's exceptions to the refusal of the court to give the ruling thus asked for.

We think that the ruling was right. There was evidence tending to show that the plaintiff, with two ladies and three children, took a car of the defendant company at Arling-

¶ 1. See Carriers, vol. 9, Cent. Dig. §§ 1228, 1229, 1235.

ton to go to Charlestown. On arriving at the Park Street Station of the Subway, they alighted from the Arlington car, and crossed the platform to take the Charlestown car. When that car came along, the plaintiff got on to it about the middle. Her daughter went to get into the seat in front, but, finding it full, turned back to go into the seat where the plaintiff was, and the starter pulled her back. Thereupon the plaintiff attempted to get off the car, and got as far as the running board when the car started, and threw her down, causing the injuries complained of. There was testimony tending to show that the car was not in motion, and that no signal had been given to start it when the plaintiff attempted to get off. It could not be said, therefore, as matter of law, that she was not in the exercise of due care in attempting to get off as she did. It was the duty of the starter to see that passengers attempting to alight had safely done so, before he gave the signal to start the car. There was testimony tending to show that he gave the signal before she had alighted, and that he could have seen her if he had looked. The plaintiff testified that she looked at him all the time while she was getting out. We do not see, therefore, how it could have been ruled, as matter of law, that there was no evidence of negligence on the part of the defendant. The question whether the accident happened as the plaintiff and her witnesses testified that it did, or as the defendant and its witnesses testified that it did, was plainly a question for the jury.

Exceptions overruled.

(185 Mass. 345)

ROBINSON et al. v. NUTT.

(Supreme Judicial Court of Massachusetts. Middlesex. April 1, 1904.)

GIFT TO PARISH—SUBSCRIPTION—CONSIDERATION.

1. A subscription made to a parish in the form of a formal offer for the purpose of raising a fund to pay off the debt of the parish, on condition that the full amount of the debt should be raised by similar subscriptions, and that the current expenses of the parish would not be materially increased during the period of five years, in which the subscription was payable in installments, is supported by a sufficient consideration, where the acceptance of the offer and the performance of the conditions are shown by the parish in an action to recover the amount due on the subscription.

Appeal from Superior Court, Middlesex County.

Action by one Robinson and others against William Nutt, executor of the will of Maria Hayes, deceased, to recover installments due under a subscription paper, by the terms of which the testator agreed to give to the First Parish of Natick $5 a month for five years from and after April 1, 1900. The gift was conditional upon the raising of the entire indebtedness of the parish, and upon other conditions, the nature of which are stated in the opinion. In the superior court there was judgment for defendant, and plaintiffs appealed. Reversed.

William Reed Bigelow, for appellants. William Nutt, pro se.

BRALEY, J. The written agreement signed by the testatrix was an undertaking on her part by which she agreed to pay the sum of $60 a year for the term of five years, if certain requirements were fulfilled by the plaintiffs, who were the standing committee of the First Parish of Natick. From the agreed facts on which the case is submitted, the defendant concedes that these terms have been met and fulfilled, upon a full performance of which her subscription was made contingent and payable; and in his written argument the executor now denies any liability of the estate, except on the ground that the undertaking must be considered as wholly gratuitous, and therefore without any legal consideration to support it. If the offer is considered as a promise made by her, in common with others, to aid a religious society in which she was apparently interested, although not a member, it cannot be supported, for it falls within the class of what are called mere gratuitous or benevolent proposals, prompted by charitable or religious motives, of which the law will not require a performance. Cottage Street Methodist Episcopal Church v. Kendall, 121 Mass. 528, 23 Am. Rep. 286. The principal purpose was to raise a fund to pay the debt of the parish, to which she, in common with others, promised to contribute to the extent of the various subscriptions; and it becomes incumbent on the plaintiffs to go further, and they must, as persons to whom the promise was made, show an acceptance by them of her proposal, and the use by them of the fund contributed by her and others for the object stated in the subscription. Her subscription was really made in the form of a formal offer, which, being accepted by the plaintiffs, became an agreement under which they entered upon the performance of the contemplated plan, by obtaining additional subscriptions from others, and, as a result, the combined pledges made up the full amount required; and, when they applied the money received from time to time in reduction of the debt of the parish, the object upon which her promise depended had been accomplished. Williams College v. Danforth, 12 Pick. 541. But under the proposal the burden also rested on the plaintiffs, as one of the conditions, that the current expenses of the parish would not be materially increased, except in case of unavoidable necessity, and no unusual current expense should be incurred, unless a sum amply sufficient to meet it had been first obtained or provided; and, in order to receive the amount which she pledged, the plaintiffs were obliged to carry

¶ 1. See Subscriptions, vol. 45, Cent. Dig. § 6.

out this requirement for the period of five years, and the agreed facts contain enough to show that this was done by them in reliance on, and in order to obtain, the contribution made by her, as the several payments became due. A sufficient consideration to support the contract is found in the offer made and its acceptance, followed by a performance on the part of the plaintiffs as promisees, who, in reliance on her promise, assumed and performed the imposed duties on which her subscription depended, including the obligation of keeping the current expenses of the parish within certain required limits. Ladies' Collegiate Institute v. French, 16 Gray, 196, 201; Cottage Street Methodist Episcopal Church v. Kendall, supra; Sherwin v. Fletcher, 168 Mass. 415, 47 N. E. 197; Martin v. Meles, 179 Mass. 114, 60 N. E. 397; French v. Boston National Bank, 179 Mass. 404, 408, 60 N. E. 793.

Judgment for the plaintiffs.

(185 Mass. 361)

LIND v. LIND.

(Supreme Judicial Court of Massachusetts. Middlesex. March 31, 1904.)

CONTEMPT—MOTION TO DISMISS—TIME FOR FILING.

1. A motion to dismiss a petition for nullity of marriage on the ground that the petitioner is in contempt for not complying with an order of court is the proper way of bringing the contempt to the attention of the court, and need not be filed within the time allowed for pleas in abatement.

Exceptions from Superior Court, Middlesex County; Elisha B. Maynard, Judge.

Petition by James A. Lind against Annie F. Lind. Judgment dismissing the petition. Petitioner excepts. Affirmed.

This was an appeal by James A. Lind from an order dismissing a petition for nullity of marriage. Two motions were made by the respondent, Annie F. Lind. In the first it was alleged that the petitioner had failed to pay certain costs as ordered by the court in divorce proceedings, and in the second it was alleged that the respondent had procured a divorce from the petitioner in a libel brought before the petition for nullity, and that she had obtained a decree nisi in her proceeding, and that a motion for a rehearing filed by the husband had been denied by the superior court. It was alleged that the husband was in contempt of court, and in the motion the respondent prayed that the petitioner be adjudged in contempt, and his petition be dismissed. The docket of the superior court showed that the respondent's motion to dismiss the petition and the motion for contempt were filed on February 18, 1903, and the docket entry was further as follows: "February 19, petition dismissed. February 28, petitioner appeals."

Lougee & Robinson, for plaintiff. Geo. W. Poland, for defendant.

LORING, J. A motion to dismiss a petition for nullity of marriage on the ground that the petitioner is in contempt for not complying with an order of the court directing him to pay $30 into court for the expenses of the respondent does not stand on the same footing as a motion to dismiss a common-law writ for irregularities not going to the jurisdiction of the court, as the petitioner contends. Such a motion is the proper way of bringing the fact of the contempt to the attention of the court, and need not be filed within the time allowed for pleas in abatement. The petitioner was entitled to be heard on this motion, and on the record before us we assume that he was heard.

Judgment affirmed.

(185 Mass. 315)

GLASSEY v. WORCESTER CONSOLIDATED ST. RY. CO. (two cases).

(Supreme Judicial Court of Massachusetts. Worcester. March 31, 1904.)

NEGLIGENCE—PROXIMATE CAUSE.

1. Where a street railway company left a reel which had held feed wire lying on its side in the untraveled portion of a highway, and some boys rolled it down the street, striking plaintiff's carriage and injuring her, the negligence, if any, of the company in leaving the reel in the highway, was too remote to entitle plaintiff to recover.

Exceptions from Superior Court, Worcester County; Maynard, Judge.

Separate actions by Rachel Glassey and Andrew J. Glassey against the Worcester Consolidated Street Railway Company. Judgments for defendant in both cases, and plaintiffs except. Exceptions overruled.

A. P. Rugg and Charles W. Saunders, for plaintiffs. Charles C. Milton and Chandler Bullock, for defendant.

MORTON, J. These two cases were tried and have been argued together. At the close of the plaintiffs' evidence in the superior court, the presiding justice ruled, at the defendant's request, that the plaintiffs could not recover, and directed verdicts for the defendant. The cases are here on exceptions by the plaintiffs to these rulings. The case of the plaintiff Rachel, who is a married woman, is for injuries alleged to have been received by her in consequence of the negligence of the defendant in leaving a large reel by the side of or in Cameron street, in Clinton, which some boys rolled down the street, and which struck the carriage in which the plaintiff was driving, and threw her out, and caused the injuries complained of. The other action is by the husband for the loss of consortium and the expenses incurred by him by reason of the injuries to his wife.

The evidence would have warranted a finding, and, for the purposes of these cases, we assume that such was the fact, that the reel belonged to the defendant, and had had feed wire upon it, which had been strung upon its poles by persons in its employ. But it is not clear whether the reel was left on a vacant piece of land just outside the limits of the highway, or whether it was left within the limits of the highway. We assume, as most favorable to the plaintiffs, that it was left within the limits of the highway. The uncontradicted testimony shows, however, that it was left outside the traveled portion of the highway, lying on its side in the grass in a secure position. The plaintiffs introduced in evidence a by-law of the town forbidding persons to leave obstructions of any kind in the highway without a written license from the road commissioners or other board having charge of the streets, and they contend that, if the reel was left within the location of the highway, when forbidden by the by-law, that of itself constituted such negligence as renders the defendant liable. But the most, we think, that can be said of this contention, is that the leaving of the reel within the limits of the highway was evidence of negligence, not that in and of itself it rendered the defendant liable, or should be held, as matter of law, to have contributed directly to the accident. Hanlon v. South Boston R. Co., 129 Mass. 310. The question is whether, in leaving the reel lying on its side in the grass, near the road, the defendant ought reasonably to have anticipated that children passing along the street on their way to school, or for other purposes, would take it from the place where it had been left, and engage in rolling it up and down the street, and that travelers on the highway would thereby be injured. The question is not whether a high degree of caution ought to have led the defendant to anticipate that such a thing might possibly occur, but whether it ought reasonably to have been expected to happen in the ordinary course of events. In the former case the defendant would not be liable, and in the latter it might be held liable, notwithstanding an active human agency had intervened between the original wrongful act and the injury. The case of Stone v. B. & A. R. Co., 171 Mass. 543, 51 N. E. 1, 41 L. R. A. 794, furnishes an illustration of the former class of cases, and the case of Lane v. Atlantic Works, 111 Mass. 136, of the latter. It is clear that the plaintiff Rachel was in the exercise of due care. But assuming that the reel was left in the highway, and that that was some evidence of negligence, we think that such negligence was the remote, and not the direct and proximate, cause of the plaintiff Rachel's injury. The material facts, with the inferences to be drawn from them, are not in dispute, and in such a case the question of remote or proximate cause is one of law for the court. Stone v. B. & A. R. Co., 171 Mass. 543, 51 N. E. 1, 41 L. R. A. 794; McDonald v. Snelling, 14 Allen, 290, 299, 92 Am. Dec. 768; Hobbs v. London Southwestern R. Co., L. R. (1875) 10 Q. B. 111-122. The defendant's servants left the reel in a secure position, lying on its side in the grass, outside the traveled part of the street, and not in immediate proximity of it. As the reel was left, it was entirely safe. It was not possible for a slight or accidental movement to set it in motion so as to injure others, as in the case of Lane v. Atlantic Works, supra. The reel was large and cumbersome, and required active effort on the part of a number of children to move it from the place where it had been left onto the traveled part of the highway, and set it in motion. And in order to injure the plaintiff or any other traveler on the highway, it was necessary that it should be set in motion at a time when the plaintiff or other travelers were passing along the highway. In other words, in order to render the defendant liable, it must appear not only that it should have anticipated that, in the ordinary course of events, school children would take the reel from the position where it had been securely left, outside the traveled part of the road, but that they would set it in motion on the highway under such circumstances that it was liable to injure a traveler thereon. It seems to us that, conceding that there was evidence of negligence on the part of the defendant in leaving the reel where its servants did, they could not be required to anticipate that this would happen in the ordinary course of events, and therefore that the negligence was too remote. See Speaks v. Hughes (1904) 1 K. B. 138.

Exceptions overruled.

(185 Mass. 318)

EMERSON v. METROPOLITAN LIFE INS. CO.

(Supreme Judicial Court of Massachusetts. Essex. March 31, 1904.)

LIFE INSURANCE—BENEFICIARY'S RIGHT OF ACTION—SURVIVAL IN ADMINISTRATOR—INSTRUCTIONS—FINDINGS.

1. Under Rev. Laws, c. 118, § 73, providing that the person to whom a policy of life insurance is made payable may sue thereon in his own name, the right of action survives to the administrator of the beneficiary.

2. In an action on a life policy, the refusal of a requested instruction that if, on the date of the policy, insured was liable to have fits or bad spells or loss of consciousness, he was not in sound health, was harmless, in view of a finding that insured had no such difficulties.

Exceptions from Superior Court, Essex County; Chas. U. Bell, Judge.

Action by Ellius A. Emerson, as administrator of the estate of Mary A. Varney, deceased, against the Metropolitan Life Insurance Company. Judgment for plaintiff. Defendant excepts. Exceptions overruled.

Wm. H. Moody and Jos. H. Pearl, for plaintiff. Wm. M. Butler and Guy W. Cox, for defendant.

MORTON, J. This is an action upon a policy of insurance issued by the defendant company upon the life of one John C. Varney. The policy is dated June 13, 1898, and is for

$2,000. It is made payable "to Mary A. Varney, wife of the insured, * * * if living, otherwise to the legal representatives of the insured, upon receipt by the company at its home office and its approval of the proofs of death of the insured, made in the manner, to the extent, and upon the blanks required by condition sixth, and upon the surrender of this policy." John C. Varney died September 30, 1899. Proofs of death furnished by the defendant were filed with it by Mary A. Varney on or before October 12, 1899. Mary A. Varney died October 14, 1899, and the plaintiff is administrator of her estate. The proofs of death furnished by her were not acted on by the defendant, but an additional blank was furnished by it to be filled out by the physician who had attended Varney in 1871-1883 and 1885. The administrator completed this additional blank November 7, and filed it with the defendant November 8, 1899. The date of the writ was January 21, 1901. There was a verdict for the plaintiff, and the case is here on exceptions by the defendant to the refusal of the court to give certain rulings that were requested.

The first question is whether the action can be maintained by the plaintiff, as administrator of the estate of the wife. We think that it can. The applications are not before us, and it may be doubtful whether the contract contained in the policy is not a contract between the defendant and the wife. See Millard v. Brayton, 177 Mass. 533, 59 N. E. 436, 52 L. R. A. 117, 83 Am. St. Rep. 294. But, however that may be, it is expressly provided by Rev. Laws, c. 118, § 73, that "the person to whom a policy of life insurance, issued subsequent to the eleventh day of April in the year eighteen hundred and ninety four, is made payable may maintain an action thereon in his own name." The policy in this case was issued after April 11, 1894, and comes, therefore, within the statute. No good reason can be assigned why the right of action thus given should not survive and pass to the administrator when it has once vested, or why the right should be regarded as a purely personal privilege bestowed on the person to whom the policy is made payable. As we construe the policy, the defendant agreed to pay the wife, if living at the death of the husband, $2,000 at its office in New York, upon receipt and approval by the company of proofs of the death of the husband, made in the manner and to the extent and upon the blanks required, and upon surrender of the policy. The beneficiary could not, of course, be required to surrender the policy except upon payment, and, so far as appears, the defendant has refused to pay at New York or anywhere. The wife survived the husband, and proofs of death, on blanks furnished by the defendant, were filed with the defendant by the wife before her death. It is true that these blanks were not acted upon by the company, and an additional blank was sent, which was not completed and returned, till after her death, by her administrator. But the right of the wife, or of her estate, to the proceeds of the policy, depended primarily on her surviving her husband. It might be defeated by failure on her part or on the part of her administrator to comply with the conditions of the policy, but, subject to that contingency, the right to the proceeds of the policy vested in her. There is nothing to show that the proofs were not satisfactory as proofs of death, and we think, as already observed, that the action can be maintained by her administrator.

The application was made a part of the policy, and the answers and statements were declared to be warranties. One of the conditions on which the policy was issued was that the insured was at the time in sound health. The defendant contended that the insured was an epileptic at the time of the application, and that the answers to certain material questions were false, and on all the evidence requested the court to direct a verdict for the defendant, and to instruct the jury that if on the 13th of June, 1898, the date of the policy, the health of the insured was such that he was liable to have fits, or bad spells, or loss of consciousness, he was not in sound health at that time. The court declined to rule as thus requested, except so far as covered by the charge, and submitted the case to the jury with the question, "Did John C. Varney, the person insured, have epileptic fits prior to the date of his application for insurance—June 9, 1898?" which the jury answered "No."

There was much evidence tending to show that the insured was subject to epileptic fits at the time when the policy was issued, and that he died of epilepsy. But there was also evidence of a contrary character. It would serve no useful purpose to attempt to review the testimony in detail. The question was eminently one of fact for the jury, and was submitted to them with full instructions. They were specially instructed, amongst other things, that the policy did not attach unless at the date of delivery the insured was in sound health, and that the plaintiff could not recover unless he satisfied them, by a fair preponderance of the evidence, that the insured was in sound health on that day. This was, in substance, repeated. We doubt whether it could have been ruled as matter of law that the insured was not in sound health, if liable to have fits, or bad spells, or loss of consciousness. But, if it should have been so ruled, the defendant was not harmed by the refusal to instruct as requested, because the jury found that the insured was not subject to epileptic fits prior to the date of the application, and, consequently, that he was not liable to have fits, or bad spells, or loss of consciousness.

The result is that we think that the exceptions should be overruled. So ordered.

(185 Mass. 306)

MASSACHUSETTS MUT. LIFE INS. CO. v. GREEN.

(Supreme Judicial Court of Massachusetts. Hampden. March 30, 1904.)

ASSUMPSIT—MONEY PAID—PLEADING—ALLEGATION OF REQUEST—SUBSEQUENT PROMISE—CONSIDERATION—ACCOUNT ANNEXED—NECESSARY AVERMENTS.

1. A count alleging that by reason of certain facts defendant became bound to repay money to plaintiff, because paid out by plaintiff for defendant's benefit, but failing to state that the money was paid at defendant's request, is bad.

2. A subsequent express promise by defendant to pay a sum paid by plaintiff for defendant's benefit is not the equivalent of a previous request, so as to support a count in assumpsit for money paid.

3. Giving defendant an opportunity to examine her own accounts is no consideration for a promise on her part to repay a sum paid by plaintiff for defendant's benefit.

4. Under Practice Act (Rev. Laws, c. 173, § 6) cl. 7, providing that the common counts shall not be used unitedly, and clause 8, providing that a count on an account annexed may be used if one or more items are claimed, any of which would be correctly described by any of the common counts, a count on an account annexed, includes by intendment, with respect to the item stated in the account, all the allegations contained in the common counts, so that an allegation of a request by defendant to pay money expended by plaintiff for defendant's use is unnecessary.

5. A declaration to recover money paid by plaintiff for taxes on defendant's land, containing a count on an account annexed, a count alleging payment for defendant's benefit, a count alleging an agreement by defendant to repay, and one counting on a promise to repay if plaintiff would give defendant an opportunity to examine her accounts, was not bad because it also contained an allegation that all counts were for the same cause of action.

Appeal from Superior Court, Hampden County.

Contract by the Massachusetts Mutual Life Insurance Company against one Green to recover from defendant money paid by plaintiff for taxes assessed on real estate owned by defendant. A demurrer was sustained to the declaration, judgment was ordered for defendant, and plaintiff appealed. Affirmed in part and reversed in part.

J. B. Carroll and W. H. McClintock, for appellant. Wm. M. McClench, for appellee.

LORING, J. In this case both the plaintiff and the defendant owned land in the northeast one-fourth of section 13, township 37 north, range 13, in Cook county, Ill. The plaintiff received from the proper authorities a bill for taxes on a lot in said northeast one-fourth, which it paid, supposing it was for a tax on its land. It turned out subsequently that it was for a tax on the defendant's land, and thereupon this action was brought to recover the amount of the tax from the defendant. The declaration contained four counts. The first was a count on an account annexed; the second stated the facts, and concluded with a statement that by reason thereof the defendant became bound to repay the money to the plaintiff, because it was paid for the defendant's benefit; the third count added that, upon the mistake being discovered, the defendant agreed to repay the amount to the plaintiff; and in the fourth the plaintiff counted on a promise to repay the amount if the plaintiff would give the defendant an opportunity to examine her own accounts. It is alleged that all the counts are for the same cause of action.

The second count is bad because it is not alleged that the money was paid at the defendant's request. Roxbury v. Worcester Turnpike Corp., 2 Pick. 41; Winsor v. Savage, 9 Metc. 346; Middleborough v. Taunton, 2 Cush. 406; South Scituate v. Hanover, 9 Gray, 420; Bicknell v. Bicknell, 111 Mass. 265; Mansfield v. Edwards, 136 Mass. 15, 49 Am. Rep. 1. This defect in the second count is (so the plaintiff contends) cured by the allegation in the third and fourth counts of a subsequent express promise on the part of the defendant to pay this sum to the plaintiff. Its contention is that a subsequent promise is equivalent to a previous request, and that Gleason v. Dyke, 22 Pick. 390, is an authority for that proposition; that Gleason v. Dyke was cited with approval in Smith v. Bartholomew, 1 Metc. 276, 25 Am. Dec. 365, and never has been overruled. But, although it is not referred to by name, Gleason v. Dyke was overruled by Dearborn v. Bowman, 3 Metc. 155, so far as this ground for the decision in Gleason v. Dyke goes. The original case of Gleason v. Dyke was well decided on the ground that the plaintiff was forced to pay the money to protect the estate which the defendant had a right to redeem and did redeem. In the subsequent case of Winsor v. Savage, 9 Metc. 346, 348, it is again stated that a subsequent ratification is equivalent to an original request. But this statement was obiter, and Dearborn v. Bowman has since been affirmed on this point in Shepherd v. Young, 8 Gray, 152, 69 Am. Dec. 242, Chamberlin v. Whitford, 102 Mass. 448, and Moore v. Elmer, 180 Mass. 17, 61 N. E. 259, and must be taken to be the law of the commonwealth. It is not necessary to discuss the cases cited by the plaintiff from other jurisdictions.

The plaintiff has not argued that the fourth count is helped by the allegation of a consideration which it contains. The defendant's right to examine her own books was not within the plaintiff's control, and his giving her an opportunity to do what she had a right to do is not a valid consideration for a promise on her part.

But we are of opinion that the demurrer to the count on the account annexed should have been overruled. The defendant's contention here is that it is not alleged in the account annexed that the money was paid at the request of the defendant. It seems to

¶ 1. See Money Paid, vol. 35, Cent. Dig. § 25.

be assumed in Rider v. Robbins, 13 Mass. 284, that such an allegation was necessary at common law, while in Newmarket Iron Foundry v. Harvey, 23 N. H. 395, it seems to have been assumed that, when the account annexed was used for money paid, the law imported the allegation that it was paid at the request of the defendant. However it may have been at common law, we are of opinion that under the practice act such an allegation is, by legal intendment, included in the count. It is provided by the practice act (Rev. Laws, c. 173, § 6) cl. 7, that the common counts shall not be used unitedly, and by clause 8 that a count on an account annexed may be used if one or more items are claimed, any of which would be correctly described by any one of the common counts. The commissioners, in a note to these two sections as they were drafted by them (Hall's Mass. Practice Act, 160, 161), explain that their purpose in these two sections was to avoid the confusion resulting from the use of all the common counts unitedly. What was meant by that was that the practice of inserting a number of the common counts to be sure to cover the case proved at the trial led to confusion, and to avoid that confusion the use of more than one of the common counts for one cause of action or item was forbidden; and it was provided that, if the plaintiff was uncertain what common count would meet the case when the evidence was in, he could use a count on the account annexed, and that should be sufficient if the case proved would be correctly described by any one of the common counts. By the original practice act (St. 1851, p. 699, c. 233, § 2, cl. 7) the count on an account annexed could be used only when two or more items were claimed. This left a plaintiff who brought an action to recover for only one item in the predicament of not being able to insert more than one common count in his declaration, and of being forbidden to use the count on an account annexed under the statute, which allowed him to do so to meet his requirements in case he was not entirely certain what case would be shown in evidence when two items were claimed. This was corrected by the practice act of the following year, which allowed a plaintiff to use a count on an account annexed when only one item was claimed as well as when two or more were in issue. St. 1852, p. 224, c. 312, § 2, cl. 7. The result is that by force of the statute a plaintiff who counts on a count on an account annexed has, in legal intendment, made with respect to the item stated in the account annexed all the allegations contained in all the common counts, and the first count in the declaration standing by itself was good. We do not think that it is bad because it is alleged in the declaration that all counts are for the same cause of action. We cannot say that the plaintiff did not insert the count on an account annexed for the very purpose of having that count in the declaration in case he succeeded in showing at the trial that the money was paid at the defendant's request, and that he inserted the other three counts to meet his case if he did not succeed in proving the defendant requested it to pay the tax. The result is that the plaintiff has a right to go to trial for the purpose of proving that the money was paid at the defendant's request, but for that purpose only.

Judgment sustaining demurrer to first count reversed. Judgment sustaining demurrer to other counts affirmed.

(185 Mass. 324)

COMMONWEALTH v. BARKER.

(Supreme Judicial Court of Massachusetts. Suffolk. March 31, 1904.)

WITNESSES—COMPETENCY—HUSBAND AND WIFE—CRIMINAL PROSECUTION.

1. Under Rev. Laws, c. 175, § 20, subd. 2, providing that neither husband nor wife "shall be compelled to testify" in a criminal proceeding against each other, a husband or wife may testify in a criminal proceeding against the other, if willing to do so, irrespective of the want of consent of the one on trial.

Exceptions from Superior Court, Suffolk County; Danl. W. Bond, Judge.

One Barker was convicted of polygamy, and excepts. Exceptions overruled.

John D. McLaughlin, Asst. Dist. Atty., for the Commonwealth. P. H. Kelley, for defendant.

MORTON, J. This is an indictment against the defendant for polygamy. There was a verdict for the commonwealth, and the case is here on the defendant's exceptions. The person alleged to be the lawful wife of the defendant was called as a witness against him, and without the consent and against the objection of the defendant was allowed to testify to material facts tending to prove his guilt. The only question is whether she should have been allowed to so testify without his consent. At common law a married woman could not testify in such a case against her husband. Kelly v. Drew, 12 Allen, 107, 90 Am. Dec. 138. But by various statutes, which were consolidated in Gen. St. 1860, c. 131, §§ 13-16, the common law was greatly changed. It was changed still more by St. 1870, p. 301, c. 393, which was substantially re-enacted in Pub. St. 1882, c. 169, § 18 et seq., and in Rev. Laws, c. 175, § 20 et seq. It is now provided that "any person of sufficient understanding, although a party, may testify in any proceeding, civil or criminal, in court, or before a person who has authority to receive evidence, except as follows: First, neither husband nor wife shall testify as to private conversations with each other. Second, neither husband nor wife shall be compelled to testify in the trial of an indictment, complaint or other criminal proceeding against each other." Rev. Laws, c. 175, § 20. The effect of these provisions is to render every person competent to testify, except that husband and wife cannot testify to private conversations, or be compelled to testify in criminal proceedings against each other. There is nothing which prevents a husband or wife from testifying against the other in criminal proceedings if the one testifying is willing to do so. The competency of the one testifying in such a case does not depend on the consent of the other. The only limitation is that the husband or the wife cannot be compelled to testify. The case of Kelly v. Drew, supra, relied on by the defendant, arose under the General Statutes, and consequently is not applicable to the case before us. The statutes cited from other states differ materially from our own, and do not affect its construction.

Exceptions overruled.

(185 Mass. 310)

FIRST UNIVERSALIST SOC. IN SALEM v. BRADFORD, Treasurer.

(Supreme Judicial Court of Massachusetts. Essex. March 30, 1904.)

RELIGIOUS SOCIETIES—PROPERTY—TAXATION—EXEMPTIONS—DEVISES—SUCCESSION TAX.

1. St. 1889, p. 1211, c. 465, providing that the personal property of literary, benevolent, charitable, scientific, and temperance societies, and the real estate belonging to them and occupied by them or their officers for the purpose for which they were incorporated, shall be exempt from taxation, but that none of the real or personal estate of such corporation shall be exempt when any portion of the income or profits therefrom is divided among their members or stockholders, or used for other than literary, educational, benevolent, charitable, scientific, or religious purposes, etc., does not apply to religious societies, the houses, etc., of which are exempted from taxation by Pub. St. c. 11, § 5, cl. 7.

2. Whether a devise to a corporation is exempt from succession taxation imposed by St. 1891, p. 1028, c. 425, § 1, depends on whether the corporation is one whose property is generally exempt from taxation, and not whether the property which passes by the devise is exempt from yearly taxation under general laws.

3. The property of a religious corporation being generally exempted from taxation by Pub. St. c. 11, § 5, cl. 7, such a society was not subject to a succession tax imposed by St. 1891, p. 1028, c. 425, § 1, on the devise of a dwelling house and certain of the furniture contained therein, to be used by the church as a parsonage.

Case reserved from Supreme Judicial Court, Essex County; Jas. M. Morton, Judge.

Bill for instructions by the First Universalist Society in Salem to determine a claim of Edward S. Bradford, as State Treasurer and Receiver General, for a succession tax assessed on a devise and bequest to complainant. A probate decree was rendered holding that the property was not subject to the tax, and on appeal to the Supreme Court the case was reserved for the full court. Affirmed.

Frederic B. Greenhalge, Asst. Atty. Gen., for Treasurer. Wm. H. Rollins, for First Universalist Soc. in Salem.

LORING, J. Walter S. Dickson, by his last will and testament, which was duly admitted to probate in June, 1900, devised to the First Universalist Society in Salem a parcel of land, "with the dwelling house and outbuildings thereon (the same being used and occupied by me as a homestead) to be used and occupied only as a parsonage for said Church, and for the same purpose I give said Church all the carpets in my said homestead and all the furniture therein not otherwise disposed of by me." The Treasurer of the Commonwealth claims that a succession tax is due on this devise and bequest under St. 1891, p. 1028, c. 425, § 1, now Rev. Laws, c. 15, § 1. The devisee claims that the devise and bequest come within the clause excepting from the operation of the act property which shall pass "to or for the use of charitable, educational or religious societies or institutions the property of which is by law exempt from taxation."

This clause of exemption does not find in our statutes the counterpart which its language would lead one to expect. There is no clause in the general laws exempting the property of charitable, educational, and religious societies or institutions from taxation. More than that, there is no clause which in terms exempts the property of charitable and educational institutions from taxation. The only act in June, 1900, which applied to charitable and educational institutions, was St. 1889, p. 1211, c. 465, now Rev. Laws, c. 12, § 5, cl. 3. That act applies to "literary, benevolent, charitable and scientific institutions and temperance societies," and provides that the personal property of such institutions and societies incorporated within the commonwealth, and the real estate belonging to them and occupied by them or their officers for the purpose for which they were incorporated, shall be exempt, with a proviso that none of the real or personal estate of such corporations shall be exempt "when any portion of the income or profits of the business of such corporations is divided among their members or stockholders or used or appropriated for other than literary, educational, benevolent, charitable, scientific or religious purposes." Where the income of property is used to support the institution, the property of such institutions is exempt under the act when invested in personal securities, but is taxable when invested in real estate. The property of religious societies did not come within this act, but was dealt with by Pub. St. c. 11, § 5, cl. 7, now Rev. Laws, c. 12, § 5, cl. 7. That clause provides that "houses of religious worship owned by a religious society or held in trust for the use of religious organizations, and the pews and furniture except for parochial purposes," shall be exempt. Both the personal and real property of a religious society is taxable, even although the income is used to support religious worship (see Pub. St. c. 11, § 22, now Rev. Laws, c. 12, § 25; Trustees of Greene Foundation v. Boston, 12 Cush. 54; Boston Society of Redemptorist Fathers v. Boston, 129 Mass. 178); and this applies to real estate used as a parsonage (Third Congregational Society of Springfield v. Springfield, 147 Mass. 396, 18 N. E. 68).

The contention of the Treasurer is that the exemption clause in question is to be construed to provide that property which shall pass to or for the use of charitable, educational, or religious societies or institutions is to be exempt to the extent to which the property of such societies and institutions is exempt by general laws of taxation. We are of opinion that the exemption depends upon this question: Is the society or institution one whose property is generally exempt from taxation? and that the question was not: Is the property which passes to the society or institution one which will be exempt from yearly taxation under general laws?

In stating what the test is, we have stated that it is whether the property of the society or institution is generally exempt from taxation, because no charitable, educational, or religious society or institution is wholly exempt from taxation, as has already appeared. There are or may be charitable or educational institutions none of whose property is exempt, namely, institutions where "any portion of the income or profits of the business of such corporations is divided among their members or stockholders or used or appropriated for other than literary, educational, benevolent, charitable, scientific or religious purposes," and it evidently was intended to exclude these from this clause of exemption. The objection to the construction which the Treasurer is contending for is, in the first place, that it is not what the language used means. The act provides that property which passes to charitable, educational, or religious societies or institutions, "the property of which is by law exempt from taxation," shall be exempt from a succession tax; it does not provide that property which passes to such societies or institutions shall be exempt to the extent to which the property passing to them will be exempt from taxation when held by them. To adopt the construction here contended for is to read into the act a clause which is not there. In the second place, the thing dealt with by the two exemptions is altogether different. Exemption from the succession tax deals with the passing of property to a legatee or devisee; the exemption from yearly taxation deals with the holding of property—with the purpose for which property is held. As a rule, a legacy or devise is not given for a purpose. For that reason it would be difficult to apply the exemption from yearly taxation to the passing of property, and we do not think that the Legislature intended to adopt that as the test of exemption in case of the succession tax.

It happens in the case at bar that the property is devised and bequeathed for a parsonage; that is to say, it happens in the case we have before us that the way in which and the purpose for which the property devised and bequeathed is to be held is stated and established. But this is an accident, and an accident which is not only the exception rather than the rule, but is a rare exception. In most cases real estate is devised or personal property bequeathed to charitable, educational, or religious societies or institutions with a full right in the society or institution to use or transfer and convey it as it may please. There is no reason for supposing that the Legislature thought the form in which the property passes to it to be significant. There is no reason for supposing that, in case of a devise or a legacy to an educational institution, which can be changed by it the next day, the liability to a succession tax is to be determined by the fact that it is personal property, in which case it would not be taxable under the rule contended for by the Treasurer, in place of its being real estate, in which case it would be taxable under that rule.

And, again, there is no reason to suppose that the Legislature intended that a succession tax should be imposed on a legacy to a religious society, but not on a legacy to an educational institution. Yet if the contention of the Treasurer is right, this result would follow, for the personal property of an educational institution is exempt, while the personal property of a religious society is subject to yearly taxation.

For these reasons, we are of opinion that the test is this: Is the society or institution one whose property is generally exempt from taxation? Their houses of religious worship are the principal property held by religious societies, and we are of opinion that a bequest and a devise to a religious society is not subject to a succession tax.

Decree affirmed.

(185 Mass. 321)

SNOW v. NEW YORK, N. H. & H. R. CO. (two cases).

(Supreme Judicial Court of Massachusetts. Suffolk. March 31, 1904.)

CARRIER—INJURY TO PASSENGER—SPELLS OF DIZZINESS—SUBSEQUENT FALL—LIABILITY—LETTERS MAKING CLAIM—ADMISSIBILITY.

1. A passenger injured in a railroad collision, and suffering thereafter from attacks of dizziness, cannot recover for a broken wrist resulting from a fall occasioned by such an attack while she was standing in a sink to examine a leak in a water pipe.

2. Letters by a claimant for damages from a railroad company for personal injuries, stating the claim and the amount demanded, are admissible in a subsequent action for the injuries, as bearing on the genuineness and extent thereof.

Exceptions from Superior Court, Suffolk County.

Actions by Eva F. Snow and by Theodore Snow against the New York, New Haven & Hartford Railroad Company. Verdicts for plaintiffs insufficient in amount, and they except. Exceptions overruled.

James E. Cotter and James F. McAnarney, for plaintiffs. Choate & Hall, for defendant.

MORTON, J. These are two actions of tort, which were tried together. The first is for injuries received by the female plaintiff in a collision on the defendant's railroad on December 16, 1899, while a passenger; and the second is by the husband for expenses and loss of consortium. The liability was admitted, and the only question in each case was the amount of the damages. The verdicts were unsatisfactory to the plaintiffs, and the cases are here on their exceptions to certain rulings and instructions and to the admission of certain testimony.

There was testimony tending to show that, as the result of the injuries received, the female plaintiff became subject to attacks of dizziness, which continued at intervals from the time of her injury down to the time of the trial, which occurred in May, 1903, and there was testimony tending to show that on one occasion, when alone in her home several months before the trial, she got into a pantry sink by means of a chair, to see about a leak in the water pipe above the sink, and while standing in the sink had an attack of dizziness, and fell to the floor, and broke her wrist. She offered to show the pain and other inconveniences which she suffered from the broken wrist, but the court excluded the evidence, and instructed the jury not to consider the consequences of the broken wrist, as they were too remote, and the defendant was not responsible. The plaintiff excepted to these rulings and instructions, and this constitutes the first exception.

The case of Raymond v. Haverhill, 168 Mass. 382, 47 N. E. 101, would be decisive on this point except for the fact that it was a highway case. It was held in that case that the plaintiff, whose right ankle had been injured by a defect in a sidewalk in the defendant city, so that it became weak, and was liable at times to turn and fail to support her, could not recover for injuries received by her in consequence of a fall due to the failure of the ankle to support her as she was stepping from a chair to a settee while assisting in preparing for an entertainment in a public hall. It was held that the injuries so received were not the direct and immediate results of the injury received in consequence of the defect in the public way, but were due to a new and independent cause. It is true that cities and towns are not liable for consequential injuries resulting from defects in the public ways. Nestor v. Fall River, 183 Mass. 265, 67 N. E. 248. But there was a strong intimation in Raymond v. Haverhill, supra, that, if the action had been for negligence at common law, the later injuries could not have been considered as the natural and proximate result of the injury received in consequence of the defect in the sidewalk. And if in that case what took place was regarded as constituting a new and intervening cause—as it was—we do not see how what took place in the present case can be otherwise regarded. The breaking of the wrist certainly was not the direct result of the collision that caused, or may have caused, conditions which contributed to it, and but for whose existence it would not perhaps have happened. But it cannot be justly said, it seems to us, that the collision was the proximate cause of the broken wrist. That was due to her getting up into the pantry sink to look at the leak in the water pipe, and was the result of voluntary and independent action on her part. The plaintiff relies, amongst other cases, on Brown v. Chicago, etc., R. R., 54 Wis. 342, 11 N. W. 356, 911, 41 Am. Rep. 41. But this court expressly declined to follow that case in Raymond v. Haverhill, supra. We think that this exception must be overruled.

The remaining exception relates to the admission of two communications sent by the plaintiff to the defendant. The plaintiff objected to their admission on the ground that they related to a compromise of the plaintiff's claim. The letters cannot be regarded as offers of compromise. They were a statement of the plaintiff's claim and of the amount which she demanded, and were admissible as bearing upon the genuineness and extent of her injuries. See Snow v. Batchelder, 8 Cush. 513; Harrington v. Lincoln, 4 Gray, 563, 64 Am. Dec. 95.

Exceptions overruled.

(185 Mass. 380)

GERDING v. EAST TENNESSEE LAND CO. MOWRY v. SAME. MYRICK v. SAME. BEAL v. SAME.

(Supreme Judicial Court of Massachusetts. Suffolk. April 1, 1904.)

CREDITORS' BILLS — EFFECT — DECREES—EXTRATERRITORIAL FORCE—CREDITORS' ELECTION—WAIVER OF OTHER REMEDIES—NON-CONTRIBUTING CREDITORS.

1. A decree of the United States Circuit Court sustaining a bill as a general creditors' bill, and appointing receivers to take possession of the property of a corporation for the purpose of reducing it into money and distributing it pro rata among the creditors, has no effect, of its own force, beyond the territorial limits of the state in which the decree is entered, and, as a matter of comity, will not be allowed by courts of another state to prevail against any remedy which its laws afford to its own citizens against property of the corporation within its jurisdiction.

2. Where a nonresident creditor voluntarily becomes a party to insolvency proceedings, he thereby elects to take advantage of and become bound by those proceedings, and cannot thereafter resort to remedies against the property of the insolvent in other states, to which otherwise he would have a right to have recourse.

3. One who holds a judgment for his claim in insolvency proceedings in another state, which he has not sought to have avoided, cannot maintain a bill to enforce his demand by attachment of the insolvent's property in this state, irrespective of whether the person who reduced his claim to judgment had any authority so to do or not.

4. Creditors who elect to prove the interest due on bonds in insolvency proceedings thereby make election as to the bonds, and, by proving on such bonds as collateral, they elect to prove on the note secured by them, and cannot thereafter bring attachment proceedings to reach the principal of the debt in another state.

5. A creditor who elected not to contribute to the prosecution of suits under an order in insolvency proceedings that they should be conducted for the benefit of the contributors, but who lay by for nearly four years and a half after such election, and for nearly three years after the suits had been brought to a successful issue by the efforts of those who had contributed, had no standing in equity to maintain a bill to attach the funds made available by such suits.

Report from Supreme Judicial Court, Suffolk County; Jas. B. Richardson, Judge.

Separate bills of equitable attachment by Gerding, Mowry, Myrick, and Beal against the East Tennessee Land Company. In the Superior Court the case was reported to the Supreme Judicial Court. Bills dismissed.

Jerome Templeton, for plaintiffs. Wm. Hepburn Russell, Wm. Beverly Winslow, Lewis G. Farmer, and Geo. W. Easley, for defendant.

LORING, J. On November 18, 1893, a general creditors' bill was filed in the Circuit Court of the United States for the Southern Division of the Eastern District of Tennessee against the East Tennessee Land Company, a corporation created by the state of Tennessee, and having its principal place of business in that state. On November 20, 1893, a decree was made in said suit declaring that the land company was insolvent, directing all creditors to come in and prove their claims on or before April 1, 1894, and appointing receivers to take possession of its property and collect all sums due to it. Acting in pursuance of this decree, and of subsequent orders recited in the opinion in Hayward v. Leeson, 176 Mass. 310, 324, 57 N. E. 656, 49 L. R. A. 725, and hereinafter stated, suits were begun in the superior court of this commonwealth to recover from one Leeson and one Hopewell secret profits realized by them as promoters of the company. These suits were held by this court, in Hayward v. Leeson, to be well brought. It appeared, however, that there had been no assignment of these claims to the receiver, and for that reason it was held that the suits should have been begun in the name of the company. In pursuance of that opinion, the receiver was allowed to amend by making the company the nominal plaintiff. East Tennessee Land Co. v. Leeson, 178 Mass. 206, 59 N. E. 639. These suits have been before the court twice since then. East Tennessee Land Co. v. Leeson, 183 Mass. 37, 66 N. E. 427; East Tennessee Land Co. v. Leeson, 185 Mass. —, 69 N. E. 351. The suits now before us are four bills of equitable attachment, brought by persons claiming to be creditors of the East Tennessee Land Company for the purpose of having the funds which this court held were due to that company from Leeson and Hopewell applied in payment of the debts due these plaintiffs, respectively. Three of them were originally filed in October, 1900, and one (that by Beal) in December, 1902. They have been defended by the receiver in the name of the company.

The principal defense set up is that these plaintiffs have voluntarily become parties to the general creditors' suit in the United States Circuit Court in Tennessee, and for that reason cannot maintain these bills of equitable attachment in this state.

The decree of the Circuit Court of the United States sustaining the bill as a general creditors' bill, and appointing receivers to take possession of the property of the company for the purpose of reducing it into money and distributing it pro rata among the creditors of the company, has the same effect as an involuntary assignment in insolvency proceedings. It is settled in this country that such a sequestration has no effect, proprio vigore, beyond the territorial limits of the state in question, and that, as matter of comity, it will not be allowed by the courts of another state to prevail against any remedy which the laws of the latter afford to its own citizens against property of the company within its jurisdiction. Taylor v. Columbian Ins. Co. 14 Allen, 353; Witters v. Globe Savings Bank, 171 Mass. 425, 426, 50 N. E. 932. And we assume, for the purposes of this case, that citizens of other states, not citizens of the state in which the attachment is made, are entitled to the same rights against property in this state. See, in this connection, Blake v. McClung, 172 U. S. 239, 19 Sup. Ct. 165, 43 L. Ed. 432, and Id., 176 U. S. 59, 20 Sup. Ct. 307, 44 L. Ed. 371. See, also, Blake v. Williams, 6 Pick. 286, 308, 17 Am. Dec. 372; Sturtevant v. Armsby Co., 66 N. H. 557, 23 Atl. 368, 49 Am. St. Rep. 627; Paine v. Lester, 44 Conn. 196, 26 Am. Rep. 442; Milne v. Moreton, 6 Bin. 353, 6 Am. Dec. 466. Indeed, the courts of New York go so far as to extend this right to citizens of the same state as the insolvent. Barth v. Backus, 140 N. Y. 230, 35 N. E. 425, 23 L. R. A. 47, 37 Am. St. Rep. 545. Myrick is a citizen of Massachusetts. The other three plaintiffs are citizens of states other than the state of Tennessee; being Gerding and Beal, citizens of New York, and Mowry, a citizen of the state of Rhode Island.

We are of opinion that, where a nonresident creditor voluntarily becomes a party to the insolvency proceedings, he thereby elects to take advantage of, and become bound by, those proceedings, and cannot thereafter resort to remedies against the property of the insolvent in other states, to which otherwise he would have a right to have recourse. See Wilson v. Keels, 54 S. C. 545, 32 S. E. 702, 71 Am. St. Rep. 816. This depends upon a principle similar to that on which it is held that a creditor of another state, who voluntarily submits to such involuntary proceedings, is bound by a discharge granted in the course thereof, as to which see Cole v. Cunningham, 133 U. S. 107, 114, 10 Sup. Ct. 269, 33 L. Ed. 538.

It remains to state in detail the claims of each of the four plaintiffs, and in what way they have become parties, if they have become parties, to the insolvency proceedings in the Circuit Court of the United States for the Southern Division of the Eastern District of Tennessee:

The first bill now before us is brought by one Gerding as assignee of one Meissner. By deed dated February 1, 1893, Meissner conveyed to the East Tennessee Land Company a tract of land for $28,000. Of this purchase money, $500 was paid down, and three notes were given by the land company for the balance—one for $7,500, and the other two for $10,000 each—and these three notes were secured by 10 first mortgage bonds of the company, for $1,000 each. The first two notes have been paid. The note in question was dated February 1, 1893, and was due February 1, 1894. Meissner proved his note and the 10 bonds in the insolvency proceedings, and they are allowed in the decree establishing the debts of the East Tennessee Land Company. Before stating the terms of this decree, and how it dealt with the Meissner claim, it will be necessary to state more in detail the proceedings in the Circuit Court of the United States. On March 23, 1894 (that is to say, in the March next after the November in which the creditors' bill was filed), suit was brought by the Central Trust Company of New York, trustee under a mortgage of the property of the land company, to foreclose said mortgage; and, by an order dated the same day, the two suits were consolidated. On February 27, 1897, a decree was entered in the consolidated causes, in which, after it is declared that the mortgage was duly executed, that bonds secured by it are outstanding, and that the lien thereby created is a valid lien on the property thereby conveyed, it is decreed that the amount of the said mortgage debt which has been proved is $1,110,686.58, "and that bonds of said issue to the par value of $54,150 are outstanding, in addition to those proven in these causes, as enumerated above, for which no claims have been filed in these causes, and the names of the holders of which are unknown to the court, and that there is now due and payable to the holders of said $54,150 of bonds the principal of said bonds, together with interest thereon, as shall hereafter be proved to be unpaid thereon upon presentation of said bonds for payment out of the proceeds of sale as hereinafter provided:" It is then declared that the first bill "has been sustained as a general creditors' bill, and the assets of said corporation shall be sold and applied to the payment of its debts, under the several bills in these consolidated causes"; and it is decreed (1) by paragraph 11, that the receivers' indebtedness amounts to $9,631.10; (2) by paragraph 21, that the indebtedness of the company secured by vendor's liens on land of the company, which are prior in point of time to the time of the mortgage, is $141,794.15; (3) by paragraph 22, that the indebtedness of the company secured by vendor's liens which are subsequent in point of time to the time of the mortgage amount to $23,439.66; (4) by paragraph 23, that the indebtedness secured by pledge of personal property amounts to $202,407.09; and (5) by paragraph 24, that the amount of the unsecured debt of the company is $226,818.04. As part of each of the paragraphs aforesaid is a statement in detail giving the names of the several creditors, and the amounts found to be due to them, respectively, covered by the paragraph in question. The decree makes provision for the sale of the property of the company, and, after doing so, "it is further ordered, adjudged, and decreed that the several persons mentioned in paragraphs 11, 21, 22, and 23 of this decree are creditors of the East Tennessee Land Company to the amounts shown to be severally due them by the recitals in said paragraphs, and it is therefore adjudged and decreed that they have and recover from the East Tennessee Land Company the amounts severally due to them as aforesaid, and that, as to any balance due them after the proceeds of any and all properties upon which there are specific liens in their favor have been applied, they shall be general creditors of the East Tennessee Land Company, and, as such, entitled to their pro rata share of its general estate, and the proceeds of its property not otherwise appropriated under the terms of this decree; that the several persons mentioned in paragraph 24 of this decree are creditors of the East Tennessee Land Company to the amounts shown to be severally due them by the recitals in said paragraph, and it is therefore adjudged and decreed that they have and recover of the East Tennessee Land Company the amounts severally due them as aforesaid." Meissner's 10 bonds are included in the $1,110,686.58 mentioned in paragraph 11, and his note is included in the $141,794.15 mentioned in paragraph 21. By paragraph 32 of said decree it is provided that "no part of the distributive share herein directed to be paid to Frederick Meissner or Charles H. Younger upon their vendor's lien, or upon the bonds held by them as collateral security, shall be paid to them until the further order of this court." This proviso was inserted in said decree because it was claimed by the receiver that there is nothing due to Meissner, because, by the written agreement of purchase, a proportionate part of the price should be abated in case there was a failure of title in acreage warranted by the deed, and that there is in fact such a failure of title. Meissner assigned his claim to the plaintiff Gerding after the rendition of said decree. After the assignment Gerding brought a petition of intervention, which is still pending. The lands conveyed by Meissner "are in the possession of John K. Hayward as receiver of the East Tennessee Land Company, pending the determination of the rights of the parties under said petitions of intervention and the answers thereto in said consolidated causes." It is plain that the owner of the Meissner note, or of the bonds given as collateral security for the payment of it, has voluntarily become a party to the insolvent proceedings in the Circuit Court of the United States; that Gerding succeeded to his rights, and is now pursuing them in these proceedings. Under these circumstances, he cannot maintain a bill of equitable attachment against the property of the company in this commonwealth. As against this plaintiff, the title of the receiver is good, as matter of comity.

The second suit was originally brought by one Daniel A. Mowry. He died August 11, 1901, and Classen Mowry, the administrator of his estate, has been admitted to prosecute the bill. Mowry owned eight bonds, which he intrusted to one Schumacher, and which were proved by Schumacher, and are included in the $1,110,686.58 covered by paragraph 11 of the decree. It appears that there is a contest between Mowry and the Harriman Land Company as to whether Mowry's judgment has become its property, and Mowry is a stockholder in the land company. That is immaterial here. It appears further that Mowry also claims that Schumacher, to whom he intrusted his bonds, had no authority to have them reduced to judgment. Whether he had or not, judgment on them has been recovered in the consolidated causes, which Mowry has not sought to have avoided, although those causes are still pending. The owner of this claim now holds judgment for it in the insolvency proceedings, and cannot maintain this bill to enforce his demand by attachment of property in this commonwealth.

The third bill is brought by one Nathaniel W. Myrick, claiming by assignment from the executor and executrix of Nathaniel Myrick. Nathaniel was the holder of a note for $3,120 secured by mortgage bonds of the East Tennessee Land Company of the par value of $3,100. In addition, he held mortgage bonds of the face value of $11,000. The executor and executrix of Nathaniel Myrick "filed the interest coupons for a time prior to April 1, 1894, amounting to the sum of $717.85," in the insolvency proceedings in the Circuit Court of the United States, and they are included in the $1,110,686.58 covered by paragraph 11 of the decree. After the entry of this decree, covering, inter alia, these coupons, the executor and executrix assigned to the plaintiff the note for $3,120, the bonds, and claim for $717.85, under the decree of February 27, 1897. On the insolvency of the company and the bringing of the general creditors' bill, creditors were put to their election as to the course to be pursued by them, and among the creditors who had to make their election were the executor and executrix of Nathaniel Myrick. They elected to prove under the insolvency proceedings the interest due on said bonds which remained unpaid for a time prior to April 1, 1894. We are of opinion that they could not separate the debt in making an election, and that by proving on the coupons they made an election as to the bonds, and by proving on the collateral they made an election as to the note for $3,120, for which $3,100 of the bonds were held as security. The present plaintiff has succeeded to the rights of the executor and executrix, and to nothing more, and is precluded from maintaining this bill by the voluntary action of his assignor in becoming a party to the insolvency proceedings in the Circuit Court of the United States in Tennessee.

The fourth bill is brought by one Beal, who owns five bonds, of the face value of $5,000, being $5,000 of the $54,150 of bonds outstanding in the hands of persons unknown, covered by the concluding subsection of paragraph 11 of the decree of February 27, 1897. After the entry of this decree, to wit, on March 26, 1897, Beal filed his intervening petition in the insolvency proceedings. This was allowed, and referred to a master, who reported on July 12, 1897, that Beal owned the five bonds, and that there was due thereon, on July 1, 1896, the sum of $5,881.25. Subsequently, to wit, on July 2, 1898, Beal procured an order to be entered allowing him to dismiss his intervening petition and withdraw his bonds. It appears that on February 5, 1898, the Central Trust Company filed a motion in the consolidated causes "to discharge Receiver Hayward because the services of a receiver in these causes are no longer required; or (b) failing in this, that said Central Trust Company be absolved from the costs of the receivership hereafter." This came on to be heard, and on April 11, 1898, in the order entered on this motion, it is declared that there are still matters which require the services of a receiver; that from and after the entry of the order in question the costs and expenses of the receivership shall in no event be taxed to the trust company or to its sureties, nor to the funds produced or realized from the mortgaged property foreclosed therein. The order then recites that the chief purpose in retaining said receiver is for the enforcement of certain claims, the proceeds of which will go to the general creditors, and as to which the trust company is charged with no duty. Thereupon "it is ordered that the receiver continue the prosecution of said suits only in the event that creditors of the East Tennessee

Land Company who are parties to these causes shall provide securities for the costs of such suits, including the expenses of the receiver and his counsel, for such sums and in such form and amount as the clerk of the court may deem adequate and satisfactory, and to be sufficient to protect the Central Trust Company from being charged or liable for any such expense from the date of the entry of this order. It is further ordered that the creditors so indemnifying the receiver as aforesaid, and who shall elect to further continue the prosecution of said suits or actions, shall be entitled to the proceeds or benefits thereof to the extent of their respective claims, and to the proceeds of all property and assets hereafter coming into the hands of said receiver, to the exclusion of other creditors and persons who do not, within thirty days after notice to the solicitors for the respective parties of the entry of this order, join in providing security for the payment of further costs and expenses as hereinbefore required." On May 23, 1898, the Harriman Land Company, claiming to be entitled by assignment to claims covered by the decree of February 27, 1897; amounting to $1,224,397.80, filed its bond under said order. On June 24, 1898, it having been made to appear to the court that sufficient time had not been allowed to creditors residing at a distance, the time within which bonds could be filed was extended for 20 days; and, if creditors filed their bonds within said 20 days, it was ordered that they should have the same rights as those complying with the original order. Within said 20 days another creditor filed a bond. The suits in this commonwealth against Leeson and Hopewell have been prosecuted by the receiver since then under these orders. By the terms of the original order of April 11, 1898, any creditor who wished to participate in the prosecution of these suits had "thirty days after notice to the solicitors of the respective parties of the entry of this order" in which to make his election. Beal was then a party to the consolidated causes; appearing there by his solicitors, Washburn, Pickle & Turner. Moreover, when Beal withdrew, on July 2, 1898, the further time allowed for electing to share or not to share in these suits had not expired. Full opportunity was given to Beal to join in the prosecution of them at a time when the outcome of them had not become assured. When the bills against Leeson and Hopewell were filed in the superior court in this commonwealth, does not appear; neither does it appear when they were heard in that court. They first came on for hearing in this court in December, 1899, and the decision reported in 176 Mass. 310, was rendered January 15, 1900. That opinion may be taken to have brought those suits to a successful termination. When Beal filed the bill in equity now before us, does not appear. But it was not sworn to until December, 1902; that is to say, nearly three years after the suits against Leeson and Hopewell had become a success. The plaintiff Beal elected not to contribute to the prosecution of these suits. He allowed other creditors to contribute to the expense of conducting them under an order that they should be conducted for the benefit of the contributors. He lay by for nearly four years and a half after he elected not to contribute to the prosecution of these suits, and for nearly three years after these suits had been brought to a successful issue by the efforts of those who did contribute. He then undertook to step in and appropriate to himself the fruits of the expenditures of those who did contribute. He has no standing in equity to maintain such a bill. He does not stand in the situation he would have stood in, had these suits against Leeson and Hopewell been conducted at the expense of the company. They were in fact conducted by creditors, and at the expense of creditors. Under these circumstances, Beal, who elected not to contribute to these suits, must, in equity, yield to the prior rights of the creditors who contributed to them and prosecuted them to a successful termination.

It has been argued at length by the plaintiffs that the creditors' bill in Tennessee was a fraud on the court. In addition, we have been urged not "to permit the fund to be taken from its jurisdiction without assurance that the interest of creditors nonresident in Tennessee, and especially Massachusetts citizens, will be fully protected, and it is submitted that, upon the facts disclosed upon the record, no such assurance can be given, but, on the contrary, it appears that the administration in Tennessee will deny all of these plaintiffs any share or participation in the fund"; and they rely on what was said by this court in Buswell v. Order of the Iron Hall, 161 Mass. 224, 234–236, 36 N. E. 1065, 23 L. R. A. 846, in support of that request. The question in Buswell v. Order of the Iron Hall was whether this court should allow the Massachusetts assets collected by a Massachusetts receiver of an insolvent association, which had its origin and principal place of business in Indiana, to be administered in Massachusetts for the benefit of Massachusetts creditors, or whether we should direct those Massachusetts assets to be transmitted to the receiver in Indiana, to be administered there for the benefit of all creditors, including those who were citizens of Massachusetts. The investigation to be entered upon was an investigation as to the amount of the fund in the Indiana court, and the order of distribution adopted there. Without deciding that such an inquiry as was directed in that case could be made in such suits as those now before us, and that what was said there is applicable here, it is enough to dispose of the contention made here to say that there is nothing in the conduct of the case in the Circuit Court of the United States which raises a question as to these plaintiffs having justice done to them. It appears that the consolidated causes are still pending in the Circuit Court of the United States for the District of Tennessee, and for that reason that court can deal more fully with the rights of all parties. Indeed, no other court can deal so fully with the conflicting rights of all interested as that court, which has before it all the parties interested, who choose to intervene. So far as the contention that that suit is a fraud on that court, and has been used as an instrument of fraud in depriving these plaintiffs of their rights as creditors, it is enough to say that these bills are not, either with respect to the parties defendant or the allegations made, bills on which such a ground of suit can be pursued.

It appears that on February 2, 1903, an order was entered in these suits appointing a receiver to collect any sums paid by Leeson and Hopewell in the two suits brought against them in the name of the East Tennessee Land Company, to be held by him until the report in these suits had been heard by this court.

The entry in each of these suits must be: Plaintiff not entitled to maintain his bill. As against the plaintiff Hayward, receiver is entitled to the fund in the hands of the receiver in this suit. When the fund in the hands of the last-named receiver has been disposed of, this bill is to be dismissed, with costs.

(178 N. Y. 127)

TAFT v. LITTLE.

(Court of Appeals of New York. March 22, 1904.)

EVIDENCE AT FORMER TRIAL—ADMISSIBILITY—MEMORANDA—DECEASED WITNESS—BEST AND SECONDARY EVIDENCE.

1. Where plaintiff reads portions of the evidence taken on a former trial, on the ground that they contained admissions against defendant's interest, the latter may read any other portions of the same evidence which explained such admissions.

2. In order to refresh his memory, a witness may use memoranda as to certain items of work and materials, made by another and proved to be correct.

3. Where a witness in proceedings before a referee dies, and before the evidence is finally submitted the referee also dies, on a subsequent hearing before another referee such testimony is not inadmissible on the ground that the former hearing was not a trial within Code Civ. Proc. § 830, allowing evidence of a deceased witness taken at a former trial to be introduced where the parties against whom the testimony was offered had the opportunity to cross-examine such witnesses.

4. In an action to recover for work and material furnished under an oral agreement supplementary to a written contract, it was error to allow plaintiff's witness to testify what was extra work, without producing the contract and specifications, or accounting for their absence.

5. In an action to recover for extra work, the exclusion of a complaint in a previous action brought by plaintiff, a subcontractor, against his principal, covering the same claim, is error, where the issue is as to whether defendant had dealt directly with plaintiff as an independent contractor or as a subcontractor.

¶ 1. See Evidence, vol. 20, Cent. Dig. §§ 1083, 2418.

Appeal from Supreme Court, Appellate Division, First Department.

Action by Enos N. Taft, assignee of George Riker, against William McCarty Little, individually and as executor of Augusta McCarty Little. From a judgment of the Appellate Division (79 N. Y. Supp. 507) affirming a judgment in favor of plaintiff, defendant appeals. Reversed.

Alexander Thain and Burton Thompson Beach, for appellant. Robert Thorne, for respondent.

WERNER, J. The plaintiff, as assignee in bankruptcy of one George Riker, recovered a judgment against the defendant, individually and as executor of his mother's estate, for labor and materials furnished by Riker for the alteration of a building then owned by the defendant and his mother, and situate at the corner of Fourth avenue and Seventeenth street, in the city of New York.

The principal question litigated upon the trial was whether the labor and materials referred to were furnished by Riker upon the direct and independent request of the defendant, or whether the former was purely the subcontractor of the principal contractors, D. C. Weeks & Son, and was to look to them for payment of his claim.

Upon this issue the referee herein found that labor and materials of the value of $2,832.29 had been furnished by Riker directly to the defendant, at the latter's request, acting for himself and his mother, and judgment was directed accordingly. This judgment was unanimously affirmed at the Appellate Division, so that the only questions open to review in this court are those arising upon exceptions taken to rulings during the course of the trial.

1. The referee excluded certain evidence given by the defendant upon a former trial, which his counsel offered to read upon the last trial. The defendant was not present at the last trial, owing to his absence from the state. The action had been previously tried, almost to completion, before another referee, who died before the case was submitted to him for decision. Upon the last trial the plaintiff was permitted to read from the record of the former trial parts of the testimony then given by the defendant, because they were claimed to be admissions against his interest. Defendant's counsel offered to read from the same record other parts of defendant's testimony, insisting that they were explanatory of the parts introduced by the plaintiff, but, upon the objections of plaintiff's counsel, they were excluded. If the testimony offered by the defendant was in fact explanatory of that introduced by the plaintiff, it was clearly competent (Matter of Chamberlain, 140 N. Y. 390, 393, 35 N. E. 602, 37 Am. St. Rep. 568), but the learned Appellate Division held, and we think correctly, that there is nothing in the record

to show that the rejected evidence was explanatory of other evidence received at the instance of the plaintiff. Counsel for the appellant did, it is true, finally offer to read other parts of the record "explanatory of the questions and answers read by the other side," but this was followed by the reading of quite a number of questions, the answers to which are not printed in the record, and it is therefore impossible to determine whether the evidence which appellant's counsel thus sought to introduce was really explanatory or not. The ruling that appellant's counsel would be permitted to read "any part that gives the remainder of an answer to a question" indicated that the learned referee took too narrow a view of the subject, but, taking into account the vagueness of the record in this respect, as well as the fact that the judgment must be reversed in any event, we simply suggest, for the guidance of the court and counsel upon another trial, that, when plaintiff's counsel had read portions of defendant's evidence on the theory that they were admissions against his interest, it was competent for the defendant to have read in his own behalf any other portion of the same evidence tending to explain such admissions.

2. Defendant insists that it was error to permit the plaintiff's witness, Riker, to testify from a paper, made many years before the trial, as to certain items of work and materials, and their value. The record discloses that the paper was a memorandum made by Riker's bookkeeper from items appearing upon his books. These items were entered from original data furnished by Riker's foreman, under the supervision of Riker, and the latter testified, not only that he had personal knowledge of their correctness, but that, after glancing at the paper, he could speak from memory. This practice was well within the settled rule permitting the use of memoranda to refresh the recollection of a witness. Wise v. Phœnix Fire Ins. Co., 101 N. Y. 637, 4 N. E. 634; Bigelow v. Hall, 91 N. Y. 145, 147; Howard v. McDonough, 77 N. Y. 592.

3. Another group of exceptions taken by the defendant relates to the reading in evidence, on behalf of the plaintiff, of certain portions of the testimony of the deceased witness, D. C. Weeks, one of the firm who had the principal contract with the defendant for the alteration of the building in question. The trial on which this witness had testified was never formally terminated, because the former referee had died before the evidence was finally submitted to him. For this reason it is claimed that the former hearing was not a trial within the meaning of section 830 of the Code of Civil Procedure, which provides: "Where a * * * witness has died * * * since the trial of an action, * * * the testimony of the decedent * * * taken or read in evidence at the former trial or hearing, may be given or read in evidence at a new trial or hearing * * * by either party. * * *" It was admitted that on the hearing before the first referee the witness Weeks had been examined and cross-examined in the plaintiff's case, and that subsequently the defendant put in his case and rested. "The fundamental ground upon which evidence given by a witness, who afterwards dies, may be read in evidence upon a subsequent trial, is that it was taken in an action or proceeding where the parties against whom it is offered, or their privies, have had both the right and the opportunity to cross-examine the witness as to the statement offered." Young v. Valentine, 177 N. Y. 347, 69 N. E. 643. Here the defendant had full opportunity to cross-examine the witness, and availed himself of it. We think that the former hearing was a trial within the meaning and spirit of the section quoted. The appellant urges, however, that under the case of Beals v. Guernsey, 8 Johns. 446, 5 Am. Dec. 348, the record was not admissible without the production of the postea of the former trial. The postea is simply evidence that a trial was pending, and not that it was legally concluded. Pitton v. Walter, 1 Strange, 162; White v. Kibling, 11 Johns. 128. Here there was no question of the pendency of the former trial. The exceptions under this head, therefore, present no error.

4. A more serious question is presented, however, by the exceptions of the defendant to the evidence of the plaintiff's witness, Riker, and the evidence of the deceased witness, Weeks, read in behalf of the plaintiff, which was relied upon to show that the items involved in plaintiff's claim were extra work, and not included in the contract of the defendant with Weeks & Son. Early in the trial of the case it appeared that the work upon the defendant's building had been performed under a written contract between the latter and D. C. Weeks & Son, and pursuant to plans and specifications therein referred to. It was also shown that Weeks & Son had entered into a written subcontract with Riker, the plaintiff's assignee, for a portion of the work. It is true that the complaint herein was framed on the theory of a quantum meruit for work performed and materials furnished, and that defendant's answer was in effect simply a general denial; but, when it became evident that there were written contracts, plans, and specifications covering the bulk of the work and materials, these written instruments should have been produced to show whether the work and materials for which plaintiff now seeks to recover were within the original contracts or not. If, as claimed by the plaintiff, the written instruments could not be found, then the foundation should have been laid for the introduction of secondary evidence. But this was not done. Although there is some evidence tending to show that the contracts, plans, and specifications could not be found, the trial did not proceed upon the theory that the plaintiff was giving secondary evi-

dence of their contents. On the contrary, the plaintiff gave direct evidence tending to show the performance of work and the furnishing of materials, and their value. This was supplemented by the bald statements of witnesses that this work and these materials were extra, and were not within the original contracts, plans, and specifications. This summary method of establishing the plaintiff's case utterly ignored the rule that a claim for extra work or materials, based upon an alleged oral agreement, supplementary to a written contract which may or may not cover all the work and materials furnished, necessarily involves proof of the original contract, for without such proof it cannot be determined whether the claim for extra compensation is well founded or not. This rule is very simply and clearly stated by Lord Abinger, C. B., in Buxton v. Cornish, 12 M. & W. 426-429, as follows: "When an action is brought for work done, and a witness proves that the plaintiff did the work, but that it was done under a written contract, then you put in the contract for the purpose of showing what is included within it, and, when it is read, you find that the contract does not include the particular work for which the action is brought." See, also, Vincent v. Cale, Moody & M.; s. c., 3 Carr. & P. 481; and Collyer v. Collins, 17 Abb. Prac. 467, op. Leonard, P. J., 476. We think it was error for the learned referee to permit plaintiff's witnesses to state what was extra work, without producing the plans, specifications, and contracts, or at least properly accounting for their nonproduction.

5. The appellant also challenges the correctness of the referee's ruling excluding the complaint in an action by Riker, the plaintiff's assignor, against Weeks & Son, the principal contractors above referred to, and offered in evidence herein by the defendant. It is practically conceded that the allegations of that complaint covered the same work and materials for which the plaintiff now seeks to recover in this action, and it is obvious that the pleading was offered in evidence to contravene plaintiff's present claim. That it was competent for that purpose cannot be doubted, and the learned Appellate Division so decided; but it was thought that the erroneous ruling was harmless, because there was other evidence establishing the same fact, and because the referee had certified that he had allowed the plaintiff to recover only upon those items which were directly ordered by the defendant. These suggestions are well enough so far as they go, but the fact remains that the real question in the case was whether the defendant had dealt with Riker directly and as an independent contractor, or as the subcontractor of Weeks & Son. The complaint offered in evidence was not only a direct admission of the latter relation, but it contained an allegation that, under the terms of the contract between Riker and Weeks & Son, the defendant was at liberty during the progress of the work to request any alterations, additions, deviations, or omissions from the work provided for in the contract between Weeks & Son and the defendant, and that the value of the same should be added to or deducted from the contract price between Riker and Weeks & Son, as the case might be. Attached to that complaint was a copy of the contract between Riker and Weeks & Son, containing the covenant referred to. That contract was made in 1877, while the oral testimony of Riker was given in 1901, when the witness was 83 years of age, and when some of the details of the transactions between him and the defendant may well have passed from memory. Under these conditions the rejected evidence may have been of vital importance, and, for aught we know, might have changed the result.

There are other alleged errors of minor importance, which we shall not discuss. It is to be regretted that an action characterized by so many delays and vicissitudes as the one at bar should have to be sent back for a new trial, but the two principal errors above set forth are such that it is impossible to uphold the judgment herein, and it should therefore be reversed, and a new trial ordered, with costs to abide the event.

PARKER, C. J., and GRAY, O'BRIEN, BARTLETT, MARTIN, and VANN, JJ., concur.

Judgment reversed, etc.

(178 N. Y. 102)

PAIGE v. SCHENECTADY RY. CO. LANSING v. SAME. VAN EPPS v. SAME. BEATTIE v. SAME. THOMPSON v. SAME. WHITMYRE v. SAME.

(Court of Appeals of New York. March 15, 1904.)

HIGHWAYS—OWNERSHIP OF FEE—DEED—PRESUMPTIONS — STREET RAILWAYS — CONSENT TO CONSTRUCTION—ABANDONMENT OF USE—REVOCATION OF CONSENT.

1. Where the court, on the evidence, finds that a street was not a public highway, prior to 1664, at the time of the capitulation by the Dutch to the English, it is a finding that the Dutch law, which placed the title of the street in the public and not in the abutting owner, does not apply to such street.

2. Where a city conveyed land, describing it as abutting on a public street, the deed is presumed to carry title to the center of the street, subject to the right of way over it, where there was no reservation of title to the center of the street.

3. Where owners of the fee of the street on which their lots abut, have consented to the construction and operation of a street railway over the highway, they cannot withdraw such consent where there is no contract with the company giving them such right, without the consent of the state and the general public and the stockholders of the company; and an act by the receiver of the company, appointed in foreclosure, under an order limiting his authority to the management and protection of the property, in abandoning the use of such high-

way, does not destroy the rights acquired by the company under such consents, so as to entitle the consenting owners to an injunction restraining the subsequent operation of the road on the ground that the rights acquired by the street railway have been abandoned by the receiver.

4. Where a street railway company had obtained the consent of abutting owners to construction of its road in a highway, and thereafter a receiver appointed in foreclosure to manage the road abandoned that portion of the highway to which the consents attached, the fact that the company succeeding to its rights by purchase attempted to obtain the consent of the abutting owners to the reconstruction of that part of the railway abandoned by the receiver in no way impaired its rights under the original consent, and a proceeding to obtain the approval of its road, though unnecessary, was not destructive of such rights.

5. Where abutting owners consented to the building of a street railway on a highway, and thereafter a strip of land outside of the original street was acquired by the city under condemnation proceedings, an abutting owner who owned the fee to the center still held the fee to the land lying between the center of the street and the former boundary, and, where he did not consent to the construction of the railway over the premises, he is entitled to restrain the use by the railway of such strip.

Appeal from Supreme Court, Appellate Division, Third Department.

Action by Janet Franchot Paige, Caroline Paige Lansing, Belle Van Epps, Isabella Beattie, Louise A. Thompson, and Charles L. Whitmyre against the Schenectady Railway Company. From judgments of the Appellate Division (82 N. Y. Supp. 192) affirming judgments enjoining defendant from operating its railway on any part of Washington avenue in front of the premises of each of such plaintiffs, defendant appeals. Reversed in actions of Paige, Thompson, and Whitmyre, and affirmed as to the others.

The trial judge made a short decision in each action, and also made findings of fact, and directed the same to be attached to the decision therein. The Schenectady Street Railway Company, the predecessor of the defendant, obtained the consent of the local authorities of the city of Schenectady and the consent of the necessary number of abutting owners to the construction of a street railway in Washington avenue, in that city. The plaintiffs Paige, Whitmyre, and the predecessor in title of the plaintiff Thompson were among the property owners who consented to its construction. In September, 1891, after the railway on Washington avenue had been completed and was in operation, the company executed a mortgage upon its property and franchises, including the Washington avenue portion of its road, to the Central Trust Company of the city of New York. In August, 1893, Corra N. Williams, a stockholder and bondholder of the street railway company, brought an action in the United States Circuit Court on behalf of himself and all other creditors of said company, alleging its insolvency, and asked, among other things, that a receiver of the property of the railway company be appointed. Subsequently John Muir was, in that action, appointed receiver of all the property of the company, and duly qualified as such. In the following December, while the property was in the possession of such receiver, the Central Trust Company brought an action in the same court to foreclose the mortgage upon the property and franchises of said railway company. In that action George W. Jones was appointed receiver of its property on June 19, 1894, by an order which also provided that Muir, the receiver in the Williams suit, should turn over the property to Jones, and it directed him "to manage and operate the said railway and property, and to exercise the franchises of the said company, and to discharge the public duties, and to preserve and protect the said property in proper condition and repair so that it may be safely and advantageously used, and to protect the title and possession, and to secure and protect the business of the same." On or about October 2, 1894, D. Cady Smith and 19 others, owners of property on Washington avenue, presented a petition to the common council of the city of Schenectady, asking the consent of that body to the abandonment of the street railway on a portion of Washington avenue. A similar petition was presented on behalf of Jones, as receiver of the railway company in the foreclosure suit. The common council thereupon adopted a resolution authorizing Jones, as such receiver, to dispense permanently with the operation of its road between Church street and the Mohawk Bridge. After the adoption of such resolution, and with the consent of 20 abutting owners, Jones took up the rails on a portion of Washington avenue, and restored the pavement. There seems to be no evidence in the case that he obtained authority to abandon the road from the court which appointed him, from the railroad commissioners, or from the state. Nor does the proof disclose that he obtained the consent of the Schenectady Street Railway Company, or its stockholders or bondholders, or of the trustee under the mortgage. On September 1, 1894, a decree of foreclosure and sale was entered, and pursuant to that decree the property mentioned therein, which included the Washington avenue railway and franchise, was sold to one Kobbe and two others. This sale was confirmed by a decree of the court February 8, 1895, and a deed thereof was executed and delivered to them by the special master appointed to make such sale on or about February 9, 1895. Kobbe and the other purchasers also received deeds of such property, rights, and franchises from the Schenectady Street Railway Company and from George W. Jones. On February 14, 1895, Kobbe and the other purchasers conveyed the mortgaged property to the present defendant, which was incorporated on that day. The complaint in the foreclosure action, the decree of foreclosure and sale, and each of the foregoing deeds specifically described the franchise to maintain a railroad on Washington avenue. In 1901 the present defendant, claiming that the alleged abandonment of the railway by the receiver was ineffective, and also claiming a right under original proceedings instituted by it, independent of any right acquired from the Schenectady Street Railway Company, attempted to relay the tracks on Washington avenue, whereupon the present actions were brought. In each of the conveyances for the six lots owned by the plaintiffs the description of the lots bounded them upon the street. The defendant's railway is "in part on the half of the street towards the plaintiffs in all cases." On the trial it was stipulated that the plaintiffs had been in possession under their respective conveyances of the premises abutting on Washington avenue for 29 years. Upon the evidence and stipulation it is claimed by each of the plaintiffs that he or she owns the portion of Washington avenue in front of his or her premises to the center of the street. The defendant, however, sought to show that Washington avenue was in existence prior to August 27, 1664, and hence that it was originally a Dutch street, to which the Dutch law was applicable.

Marcus T. Hun and James A. Van Voast, for appellant. Douglas Campbell, for respondents.

MARTIN, J. (after stating the facts). Although our decision in the case of Peck v. Schenectady Ry. Co., 170 N. Y. 298, 63 N. E. 357, where we held that the use of a city street for the purposes of a street surface railroad operated by electric power imposes an added burden upon the property rights of the owners of the fee of the street, is in conflict with the rule adopted in most other jurisdictions, yet, as that case was most carefully and thoroughly examined and considered, and the conclusion reached that we should adhere to the former decision of this court upon the subject, that decision must now be regarded as final and conclusive—not to be overruled or avoided, even by indirection. Hence it follows that the owners of the fee in Washington avenue are entitled to defend against any improper invasion of or interference with their rights therein, unless they have been surrendered or impaired by some effective act of the plaintiffs or their grantors.

The defendant seeks to attack or impeach the validity of the title of the plaintiffs to the fee of the street on the ground that their premises extend only to the line of the street, and not to the center thereof. The claims upon which this contention rests are twofold: First, that Washington avenue existed anterior to 1664, and was consequently a Dutch street, to which the Dutch law applied, and placed the title of the street in the public, and not in the abutting owner; and, second, upon the authority of the case of Graham v. Stern, 168 N. Y. 517, 61 N. E. 891, 85 Am. St. Rep. 694, in which this court held that, where there was a conveyance of property in the city of New York bounded upon one of its streets, the presumption that the conveyance carried the fee to the center is offset, where the conveyance is by the municipal authorities, by the presumption that the municipality would not part with the ownership and control of a public street once vested in it to be forever held for the benefit of the public.

The first of these grounds is disposed of by the finding of the trial court, which, upon evidence sufficient to justify it, has found that Washington avenue was not in existence as a public highway prior to August 27, 1664, the date of the capitulation by the Dutch to the English. Consequently, under that finding, and with our view of the case, it becomes unnecessary to consider much of the historical evidence in these cases, which was so thoroughly and exhaustively discussed upon the argument and in the briefs of counsel, as, when, in 1664, the English took possession under the charter to the Duke of York, the common law of England followed. Mayor, etc., of N. Y. v. Hart, 95 N. Y. 443, 450; Canal Appraisers v. People, 17 Wend. 571, 583.

The contention of the defendant upon the second ground is that the title to the property claimed by the plaintiffs passed from the colony of New York, or from the local authorities of Schenectady, to the predecessors in title of the present owners, after Washington avenue had been opened, and while it was used as a public highway, and hence that, under the principle of the Graham Case, the presumption is that the public authorities, in making the several conveyances under which the plaintiffs claim, intended to retain the fee of the street, and that it should not pass to the grantees under such conveyances. Thus the question at once arises whether the principle of the decision in the Graham Case has any application to the facts and conditions existing in the cases at bar. Obviously, when Washington avenue became a public highway, the colony of New York was governed by the English law, under which the sovereign did not own the fee to the streets or highways, but only an easement upon the land over which they extended. Under the common law of England, the title to the land in a street or highway was not in the King, but in the lord of the manor, subject only to the easement of the public to a way over it. Goodtitle v. Alker, 1 Burr. 133, 135. In this state, as between a grantor and grantee, the conveyance of a lot bounded upon a street carries the land to the center, and there is no distinction in this respect between the streets of a city and country highways. The rights of the public in a street or highway are no higher or other than those of a mere easement, and the proprietors on each side presumptively own the soil in fee to the center thereof. Bissell v. N. Y. Central R. Co., 23 N. Y. 61; Wager v. Troy Union R. Co., 25 N. Y. 526, 529; White's Bank of Buffalo v. Nichols, 64 N. Y. 65, 71; Potter v. Boyce, 73 App. Div. 383, 77 N. Y. Supp. 24; Wallace v. Fee, 50 N. Y. 694; Holloway v. Southmayd, 139 N. Y. 390, 400, 34 N. E. 1047, 1052. The same rule applies where the conveyance is from the state or commonwealth, and the land is described as abutting upon a street, without any reservation or declaration of intention not to convey to the center. Such a conveyance, like a conveyance between individuals, is presumed to carry the title to the center of the street, subject to the public right of way over it. This was expressly held in Cheney v. Syracuse, O. & N. Y. R. Co., in which the opinion at Special Term was written by Judge Vann. That case was affirmed by the Appellate Division (8 App. Div. 620, 40 N. Y. Supp. 1108) upon the opinion of the Special Term, and also affirmed by this court (158 N. Y. 739, 53 N. E. 1128). Gere v. McChesney, 84 App. Div. 39, 82 N. Y. Supp. 191; Syracuse Solar Salt Co. v. Rome, W. & O. R. Co., 43 App. Div. 203, 60 N. Y. Supp. 40, affirmed in 168 N. Y. 650, 61 N. E. 1135; Ex parte Jennings, 6 Cow. 518, 16 Am. Dec. 447; Chenango Bridge Co. v. Paige, 83 N. Y. 178, 38 Am. Rep. 407; Smith v. City of Rochester, 92 N. Y. 463, 44 Am. Rep. 393.

The doctrine of these authorities renders it obvious that the plaintiffs and their grantors, under their deeds describing the property as bounded by the street or way, presumptively took title in fee to the center of the street, and must be regarded as the owners thereof. Therefore, under the principle of the Peck Case, they are entitled to restrain the defendant from operating its road over their premises, unless they consented thereto. The cases at bar are clearly distinguishable from the Graham Case, as in that case the city of New York was the owner in fee and in possession of the streets, and held the title thereto in trust for street purposes.

This brings us to the question of consent, which relates only to the cases of the plaintiffs Paige, Whitmyre, and Thompson, and involves the effect of their consents, or the consent of their predecessors in title, to the construction of the Schenectady Street Railway. That they originally consented to the construction of that road is abundantly proved, and not denied. But the contention of the plaintiffs named is that the railway was subsequently abandoned, and therefore their consents were nullified, and have no present effect or operation. The findings of the court upon this question are somewhat conflicting. By its first decision, which is in the short form, it stated as a ground therefor that the defendant was operating its railway upon Washington avenue in front of the premises of the plaintiffs without their consent. In its specific finding it found that the Schenectady Street Railway Company obtained the consent of the plaintiffs Paige, Whitmyre, and Charles Thompson, the predecessor in title of the plaintiff Thompson, and that they also consented to the change of motive power from horse power to electricity. In considering this question, the findings most favorable to the defendant must be accepted as true. Parsons v. Parker, 159 N. Y. 16, 53 N. E. 710; Israel v. Manhattan Ry. Co., 158 N. Y. 624, 53 N. E. 517.

The consents in this case were in writing, under seal, acknowledged by the parties, and were valid grants of the right to build and operate such railway over the street, including the premises of the above-named plaintiffs. Having been once given, and the railway having been constructed, they cannot be withdrawn, and are a bar to these actions, so far as the plaintiffs signing such consents are concerned, unless the rights under them which were acquired by the Schenectady Street Railway Company and transferred to the defendant have become invalid. Adee v. Nassau Electric R. Co., 65 App. Div. 529, 72 N. Y. Supp. 992, affirmed in 173 N. Y. 580, 65 N. E. 1113; Geneva & W. Ry. Co. v. N. Y. C. & H. R. R. Co., 163 N. Y. 228, 57 N. E. 498; Heimburg v. Manhattan Ry. Co., 162 N. Y. 352, 56 N. E. 899.

The claims of these plaintiffs are that the rights acquired under their consents were abandoned by the act of Jones, as receiver, in the mortgage foreclosure suit, and by the action of the common council of the city of Schenectady in consenting to the abandonment of the railway upon a portion of Washington avenue, including that in front of their premises. Jones was appointed receiver to manage and operate the railway and property belonging to the Schenectady Street Railway Company, to preserve and protect it in proper condition and repair, and to protect the title and possession thereof, and the business of the same. Under this limited authority, we can discover no principle upon which the receiver had a right to abandon any of the property belonging to such railway company without the consent of the company, of its stockholders, and the consent of the Legislature of the state. Nor was the common council clothed with any authority to compel or to authorize an abandonment of any portion of such street railway. While its consent might possibly waive any right the city possessed to enforce, or compel the enforcement of, a continued operation of the road, still it certainly could not, by any action upon its part, deprive the railway company of its rights, or affect the rights of the stockholders or the rights of the state and general public to require the company to continue the maintenance and operation of its road as originally constructed. These consents vested in the original railway company the right to maintain its road on Washington avenue in front of the plaintiffs' premises, and, having been once given, and the road constructed, they could not be withdrawn at the will of the owner, where, as in this case, there was no contract with the company to that effect, no consent by the state or general public, or by the stockholders of the company, and no consideration therefor. Adee v. Nassau Electric R. Co., 65 App. Div. 529, 72 N. Y. Supp. 992, affirmed in 173 N. Y. 580, 65 N. E. 1113; White v. Manhattan Ry. Co., 139 N. Y. 19, 34 N. E. 887; Heimburg v. Manhattan Ry. Co., 162 N. Y. 352, 356, 56 N. E. 899; Bellew v. N. Y., W. & C. Traction Co., 47 App. Div. 447, 62 N. Y. Supp. 242.

The right to maintain this railway upon Washington avenue in front of these plaintiffs' premises passed under the sale in the action of foreclosure, and ultimately vested in the defendant. Under the original consents, the railway company obtained a property right to construct and operate its road, which could not be destroyed by the action of the receiver or of the common council, or by the consent of a portion of the owners of the land abutting on the street, or by all. Moreover, in this case the receiver had no authority from the court to thus abandon a portion of the road. He was required to operate and conduct the business of the road in accordance with the laws of the state, which gave him no authority to abandon any portion of the mortgaged property. Erb v. Morasch, 177 U. S. 584, 20 Sup. Ct. 819, 44 L. Ed. 897. His functions were confined to the care and preservation of the property, and his appointment gave him temporary management of the railroad under the direction of the court, and nothing more. He did not represent the corporation, or supersede it in the exercise of its powers, except in relation to the possession and management of the property committed to his charge. Notwithstanding his appointment, the corporation was clothed with its franchise, which still existed. Such an appointment vested in the court no absolute control over the property. The possession taken by the receiver was only that of the court, and added nothing to the previously existing title of the mortgagees. Kneeland v. American Loan & Trust Co., 136 U. S. 89, 10 Sup. Ct. 950, 34 L. Ed. 379; Fosdick v. Schall, 99 U. S. 235, 251, 25 L. Ed. 339. Nor did the removal of the tracks by the receiver determine or forfeit the franchise of the original company over Washington avenue, so as to prevent the defendant, who had succeeded to its rights, from relaying its tracks thereon. Such abandonment only operated as a cause of forfeiture, of which the public alone could take advantage. Trelford v. Coney Island & Brooklyn R. Co., 6 App. Div. 204, 40 N. Y. Supp. 1150; Thompson v. N. Y. & H. R. Co., 3 Sandf. Ch. 625. A railroad corporation owes a duty to the public to exercise the franchise granted to it, and it cannot abandon a portion of its road and incur a forfeiture at its mere pleasure. A charter must be accepted or rejected in toto. If accepted, it must be taken as offered, and the company has no right to accept in part and reject in part. People v. Albany & Vermont R. Co., 24 N. Y. 261, 269, 82 Am. Dec. 295; Matter of Metropolitan Transit Co., 111 N. Y. 588, 19 N. E. 645; Collins v. Amsterdam St. R. R. Co., 76 App. Div. 249, 78 N. Y. Supp. 470; Goelet v. Metropolitan Transit Co., 48 Hun, 520, 1 N. Y. Supp. 74.

The right to construct and operate a street railway is a franchise which must have its source in the sovereign power, and the legislative power over the subject has this limitation: that the franchise must be granted for public, and not for private, purposes, or, at least, the grant must be based upon public considerations. It is well settled, on the soundest principles of public policy, that a contract by which a railroad company seeks to render itself incapable of performing its duties to the public, or attempts to absolve itself from its obligations without the consent of the state, is void, and cannot be rendered enforceable by the doctrine of estoppel; and any contract which disables the corporation from performing its functions without the consent of the state, and to relieve the grantees of the burden it imposes, is in violation of the contract with the state, and is void as against public policy. Fanning v. Osborne, 102 N. Y. 441, 7 N. E. 307; Union Pacific R. R. Co. v. Chicago, etc., Ry. Co., 163 U. S. 564, 581, 16 Sup. Ct. 1173, 41 L. Ed. 265; State v. Hartford & N. Haven R. R. Co., 29 Conn. 538; State v. S. C. & P. R. R. Co., 7 Neb. 357; City of Potwin Place v. Topeka Ry. Co. (Kan.) 36 Pac. 309, 37 Am. St. Rep. 312; State v. Spokane St. R. R. Co. (Wash.) 53 Pac. 719, 41 L. R. A. 515, 67 Am. St. Rep. 739; Rex v. Severn & Wye R. R. Co., 2 B. & Ald. 646.

Within the principle of the cases cited, it is obvious that the public had an interest in that portion of the Schenectady Street Railway which was constructed in Washington avenue, which could not be destroyed or abandoned without the consent of the state, and that the consents given by the plaintiffs survived the attempted abandonment of the railway upon Washington avenue. That such was the policy of the state is manifest, and, independent of the statute, neither the corporation, the common council, nor the receiver possessed any right to abandon the property or any part thereof. Nor could they destroy the effect of the consents of the plaintiffs through which the company acquired the right to construct its railway over the street. That such was the law anterior to the statute we have no doubt, and the statute, which is little, if any, more than a codification of the law as it previously existed, expressly provides that in case of the dissolution of the charter of a street surface railroad corporation, or upon its repeal, the consents of the owners and of the local authorities having control of the highway upon which the railroad shall have been constructed shall not be deemed to be in any way impaired, revoked, or terminated by such dissolution or repeal, but shall continue in full force, efficacy, and being. Railroad Law, § 105 (Heydecker's Gen. Laws, p. 3320, c. 39). The defendant was a reorganized corporation which, by virtue of such foreclosure and sale, acquired all the rights and franchises of the original company, and is bound to exercise the franchises of its predecessor. Stock Corporation Law, § 8 (Laws 1892, p. 1825, c. 688).

These plaintiffs also seek to have their consents held ineffective upon the ground that the defendant subsequently attempted to obtain the consent of the property owners to a reconstruction of its road on Washington avenue, and, having failed, has secured the approval of that route by the Appellate Division. The fact that the defendant, from abundant caution, acquired the approval of the court to run its road over that portion of Washington avenue, in no way forfeited or impaired its rights acquired under the original consents of these plaintiffs. That proceeding was, perhaps, unnecessary, but it was at most by way of further assurance, and not destructive of the rights already acquired. These consents being in the nature of conveyances of easements in the street, the right thereby acquired was not destroyed by reason of the proceeding which was taken to obtain the approval of the Appellate Division. Adee v. Nassau Electric R. R. Co., 65 App. Div. 529, 72 N. Y. Supp. 992, affirmed 173 N. Y. 580, 65 N. E. 1118. Without further discussion of this question, we are of the opinion that the consents of the three plaintiffs mentioned gave the Schenectady Street Railway Company the right to build and operate its railroad over Washington avenue in front of their premises; that no action of the receiver, the common council, or abutting owners has in any way invalidated or affected such consents, and that the same are in full operation and effect, and constitute a bar to their recovery in this action. Therefore the judgments in their favor should be reversed.

We are now brought to the consideration of a question which need be discussed only in its application to the Van Epps Case. Under this decision, by which we have held that the property of all the plaintiffs originally extended to the center of Washington avenue, and in view of our decision in the Peck Case, 170 N. Y. 298, 63 N. E. 357, it follows that, as to a part of the Van Epps lot at least, he originally owned the fee to the center of the street, and the defendant had no right to relay its tracks over his premises. It is, however, claimed that, inasmuch as the street was subsequently widened and a strip of land outside of the original street was taken, he cannot recover for that portion lying between the center of the street and the line of the lands thus taken. Without specially discussing the grounds upon which this claim is made, and thus unduly prolonging this already too lengthy opinion, we think it must be held that the fee to some portion of the land owned by Van Epps, and lying between the center of Washington avenue and the former boundary thereof, still rests in him, and that he is entitled to restrain the defendant from building its road across that piece of land, although its value can be little more than nominal. So far as this question applies to the land of the plaintiff Whitmyre, it need not be considered, as we have already held that, by virtue of the consent he executed, he has no right to maintain the action.

We have examined the various exceptions to the admission and rejection of evidence, but have found none that would justify a reversal, or that require special consideration. It follows that, as to the actions in which Paige, Whitmyre, and Thompson are plaintiffs, the judgments should be reversed and the complaints dismissed, and that, as to the actions in which Lansing, Van Epps, and Beattie are plaintiffs, the judgments should be affirmed.

Judgments in the Paige, Whitmyre, and Thompson actions reversed, and the complaints dismissed, with costs. As to the actions in which Lansing, Van Epps, and Beattie are plaintiffs, the judgments are affirmed, with costs.

PARKER, C. J., and O'BRIEN, HAIGHT, VANN, CULLEN, and WERNER, JJ., concur.

Judgments accordingly.

(178 N. Y. 136)

PEOPLE ex rel. RYAN v. WELLS et al.

(Court of Appeals of New York. March 22, 1904.)

MUNICIPAL CORPORATIONS—DEPUTY TAX COMMISSIONERS—REMOVAL.

1. Under amended Greater New York Charter (Laws 1901, c. 466, omitting section 887), which authorizes the deputy tax commissioners to hold office during the pleasure of the board of taxes and assessments, such officers became subject to removal as provided by section 1543, p. 636; and as a deputy tax commissioner is an officer, and so denominated in the charter, and as the duration of his term is not declared by law, the office is, under Const. art. 10, § 3, held subject to the pleasure of the appointing power.

On motion for rehearing. Denied.

For former opinion, see 68 N. E. 883.

Robert H. Elder, for the motion. John J. Delany, Corp. Counsel (James B. Bell, of counsel), opposed.

PER CURIAM. The motion for reargument in this case is based on the ground that the court overlooked the change effected in section 887 of the Greater New York Charter by the amended act of 1901, c. 466, p. 377. As originally enacted, this section provided in terms that the deputy tax commissioners should hold their office during the pleasure of the board of taxes and assessments, and be subject to removal by said board as deputies in the other city departments—a provision omitted in the amended act. We did not consider the effect of this amendment because the respondent based the claim that his removal was illegal upon the provisions of the civil service law. If his present contention that the elimination by the act of 1901 of the previous provision for removal is equivalent to an affirmative prohibition of removal, it would follow that the term of the relator as deputy tax commissioner was for life, and we are somewhat at a loss to discover what relevancy the civil service act, which is the only subject discussed before us, bore to the question. But for two reasons the contention cannot be sustained: First. The provisions of section 1543, p. 636, are comprehensive, and in terms apply to all officers and subordinates in the respective city departments, except where otherwise especially provided. When the special provision was eliminated from section 887, the case of the relator fell under the later section, and it may well be that the provision of the earlier section was omitted in the revision as unnecessary. Second. The position of the relator was an office, and is so denominated in the charter. By section 3 of article 10 of the Constitution, its duration not being declared by law, the office was held during the pleasure of the authority making the appointment.

The motion for reargument should be denied, with $10 costs.

PARKER, C. J., and O'BRIEN, BARTLETT, HAIGHT, VANN, CULLEN, and WERNER, JJ., concur.

Motion for reargument denied.

(178 N. Y. 118)

LEEDS v. NEW YORK TELEPHONE CO.

(Court of Appeals of New York. March 22, 1904.)

NEGLIGENCE—REMOTE AND PROXIMATE CAUSE.

1. Where defendant telephone company maintained a wire for over two years across a public street from an old brick chimney on a low building to another building at a considerable elevation, 200 feet away, and during the construction of a building the wire was struck by the boom of a derrick, operated by workmen engaged on the building, causing the chimney to be pulled over into the street, a part of which struck plaintiff, causing the injuries complained of, though the telephone company was negligent in maintaining its wire on the chimney, which inspection would have shown to have become unsound, its failure to inspect was not the proximate cause of the fall of the chimney, but it was the intervention of the derrick boom carelessly allowed to swing out into the street which caused the accident to occur, and plaintiff injured by the fall of the chimney cannot maintain an action therefor against the telephone company.

Vann, Cullen, and Werner, JJ., dissenting.

Appeal from Supreme Court, Appellate Division; Second Department.

Action by Florence S. Leeds against the New York Telephone Company. From a judgment of the Appellate Division (80 N. Y. Supp. 114) affirming a judgment in favor of plaintiff, defendant appeals. Reversed.

Eugene Lamb Richards, Jr., for appellant. Louis Hicks, for respondent.

GRAY, J. The plaintiff, while walking upon a street of the city of New York, was struck by bricks falling from a chimney, and she has sued the defendant for damages, upon allegations that its negligence was the cause of her injuries. The material facts may be briefly stated. One of the telephone wires of the defendant was attached to the chimney of a house at a height of some 39 feet above the ground, and thence was extended over the street and beyond to the roof of a building at a height of about 100 feet from the ground. The wire had been in that position for two years, with the permission of the municipal authorities, when the construction of a steel-frame building was commenced by the Jackson Architectural Ironworks on the side of the street opposite to the house from whose chimney the wire extended. On the third floor of the building in course of construction a derrick was placed for the purpose of lifting up materials for the framework. The mast of the derrick was 65 feet high, and the boom of the derrick was 55 feet in length, and was in such a position as to project beyond the sidewalk and 15 feet over the roadway of the street. A steel girder was being lifted by means of attachments from the end of the boom, and through some careless handling was allowed to swing against the wire with sufficient force to pull the chimney over. Some of the bricks fell upon the plaintiff, and produced the injuries complained of. There was evidence that the chimney had been weakened by age and decay, and the negligence of the defendant in maintaining its wire upon it, under the circumstances, is alleged, and is relied upon, as constituting an efficient and the approximate cause of the injury sustained.

I am not able to agree in this view, and, in my opinion, the negligence of the ironworks was an intervening, and the responsible, cause of the accident. The theory of defendant's negligence must rest upon the proposition that in the condition of the chimney, which inspection would have disclosed, the defendant should have foreseen possible interference with its wire in the course of the building operations on the other side of the street, and the possible consequence to the chimney. An apparent vice in this proposition is the assumption that, had the chimney been different, or newer, or sounder in its construction, it would have been able successfully to resist the strain caused by the blow of the great derrick boom against the wire. I doubt that we can indulge in such an assumption in order to find a concurring act or omission of duty. It seems to me that guilty or responsible concurrence in causing an injury involves the idea of two or more active agencies co-operating to produce it, either of which must be an efficient cause, without the operation of which the accident would not have happened. These few cases will suffice for the discussion of the doctrine: Hofnagle v. N. Y. C. & H. R. R. R. Co., 55 N. Y. 608; Ring v. City of Cohoes, 77 N. Y. 83, 33 Am. Rep. 574; Lowery v. Manhattan Ry. Co., 99 N. Y. 158, 1 N. E. 608, 52 Am. Rep. 12; and Laidlaw v. Sage, 158 N. Y. 73, 52 N. E. 679, 44 L. R. A. 216. A very good illustration is to be found in Sheridan v. Brooklyn City & N. R. R. Co., 36 N. Y. 39, 93 Am. Dec. 490, where the conductor of the car, in compelling the child to stand upon the platform, and the passenger's carelessness in trying to get off the car when in motion, were efficient and active agencies co-operating to cause the accident. The Barrett Case, 45 N. Y. 628, also furnishes a good illustration, where two cars of street railway companies collided at a crossing of tracks. In every such case the question is, what was the proximate cause of the occurrence, and, if concurrence in negligence is claimed, were the acts or omissions of the parties so closely related and co-operative as to make either a probable and an efficient cause? Could it be said of each cause that without its operation the accident would not have happened?

Was the specific act of negligence charged against the defendant in this case the natural and efficient, and hence a proximate, cause of the accident, or was it the result of the intervention of an independent cause, which defendant was not bound to anticipate, and without which the injury would not have happened? I think that the latter was the case. The negligent conduct of the persons in using the derrick upon the building was an unusual occurrence, and not such as should have been foreseen by the defendant. In Laidlaw v. Sage, 158 N. Y. 73, 52 N. E. 679, 44 L. R. A. 216, the definition of that which is the proximate cause of an event was expressed by Judge Martin as "that which, in a natural and continual sequence, unbroken by any new cause, produces that event, and without which that event would not have occurred; and the act of one person cannot be said to be the proximate cause of an injury when the act of another person has intervened and directly inflicted it." Shearman & Redfield on Negligence, § 26; Wharton on Negligence, § 134.

This is a case where the negligence of the ironworks intervened between the defendant's negligence in making use of an unsound chimney and the receipt by the plaintiff of her injuries, and the former's negligence, as a cause, was remote. The chimney was strong enough to sustain the wire, and the wire was far enough above the street to be out of the way of interference from usual street uses. We may assume that the defendant was negligent for continuing to maintain its wire upon a chimney which inspection would have shown to have become unsound, and still I do not think we could reasonably say that such conduct in the omission on its part of the duty of inspection was the proximate cause of the injury to the plaintiff. Remotely, it may have been a cause; but proximately it was simply the intervention of the derrick boom, carelessly allowed to swing out in the street, which enabled the accident to occur. In the sequence of events, the blow to the wire from the derrick boom was the causa causans, and that was the intervening act of another party. That was an independent force, which came in upon the existing situation and produced the plaintiff's injuries.

I think, on the state of facts disclosed by this record, that there was nothing to warrant a recovery against the defendant, and I advise that the judgment be reserved, and that a new trial be ordered, with costs to abide the event.

VANN, J. (dissenting). The jury found upon sufficient evidence that the plaintiff, while walking on a sidewalk in a public street of the city of New York, was seriously injured by bricks from a falling chimney, and that she would not have been injured but for the negligence of the defendant; yet judgment is about to go against her because another party was guilty of concurring negligence, which, blending with the negligence of the defendant, caused the chimney to fall. The defendant was negligent in attaching one of its telephone wires to a wornout and dangerous chimney standing on the inner line of the sidewalk, and leaving it there without inspection for more than two years, although it knew that the wire passed over a vacant lot in a part of the city well built up, and should have known that a large building had been in process of erection on said lot for three months prior to the accident, whereby the security of the wire was put in danger. The negligence of the third party, a contracting company engaged in erecting said building, consisted in such careless management of its operations as to cause the boom of a derrick to swing against the wire and topple the defective chimney down upon the plaintiff. As the wrong could not have been done without the concurring negligence of the two parties named, the negligence of each was an efficient and proximate cause, which rendered both liable, jointly and severally, for the natural result.

Concurring negligence is not an intervening cause within the meaning of the law, provided the result was a reasonable probability. If the defendant, acting with the average prudence of mankind, should have foreseen that interference with its wire was likely to occur through the building operations, of which it should have known, its negligence is not excused by the negligence of those engaged in erecting the building, because it was bound to the exercise of due care to prevent injury through the union of its own action with that of another. The law does not permit a public street in a crowded city to be turned from a place of safety into a place of danger by the joint action of two persons without holding both liable for such consequences as a reasonable man should have anticipated and provided against. The defendant could not create the dangerous situation, and leave it, making no effort to guard or watch it, and, when harm came therefrom to the plaintiff, as a result reasonably to be apprehended, plead in defense the intervening negligence of a third party, although the accident could not have happened but for its own negligence. The negligent act of a stranger did not excuse the negligence of the defendant, provided some such act—not necessarily the one which did occur, but any similar act that might have occurred—was liable to happen in the judgment of a man of ordinary prudence. The evidence made this a question for the jury, and their verdict, after affirmance by the Appellate Division, is conclusive upon us.

These views are supported by the following cases, which I regard as establishing the law of the state upon the subject: Congreve v. Morgan, 18 N. Y. 84; Colegrove v. N. Y. & N. H. R. R. Co., 20 N. Y. 492, 75 Am. Dec. 418; Sheridan v. Brooklyn City & N. R. R. Co., 36 N. Y. 39, 93 Am. Dec. 490; Webster v. Hudson River R. R. Co., 38 N. Y. 260; Barrett v. Third Avenue R. R. Co., 45 N. Y. 628; Ring v. City of Cohoes, 77 N. Y. 83, 33 Am. Rep. 574; Kunz v. City of Troy, 104 N. Y. 344, 10 N. E. 442, 58 Am. Rep. 508; Cohen v. Mayor, etc., of N. Y., 113 N. Y. 532, 21 N. E. 700, 4 L. R. A. 406, 10 Am. St. Rep. 506; Phillips v. N. Y. C. & H. R. R. R. Co., 127 N. Y. 657, 27 N. E. 978; Murphy v. Leggett, 164 N. Y. 121, 126, 58 N. E. 42; Rider v. Syracuse R. T. Ry. Co., 171 N. Y. 139, 155, 63 N. E. 836, 58 L. R. A. 125. In the Sheridan Case a child was compelled by the conductor of a crowded railway car to leave his seat and stand upon the platform, and while there he was thrown off and killed through the carelessness of another passenger in trying to get off while the car was in motion. The defendant was held liable, notwithstanding the fact that the carelessness of the passenger intervened between the carelessness of the defendant and the injury to the plaintiff's intestate. The court said: "It does not alter this liability that the wrong of a third party concurred with their own in producing the injury. * * * If they had not removed the deceased from his seat, and compelled him to stand upon the platform, he would have been unaffected by this illegal act of the young man. It was his violence, concurring with the defendant's illegal conduct in overcrowding their car and in placing the deceased upon the platform, that produced the disastrous result. It is no justification for the defendant that another party, a stranger, was also in the wrong." In the Barrett Case the plaintiff was injured by a collision between the cars of two horse railroad companies, the tracks of which crossed each other at an acute angle. The court, in sustaining a verdict for the plaintiff against the defendant upon whose car she was riding as a passenger, said: "If the acts of the defendant's servants contributed to the injury, the defendant must respond in damages to the plaintiff, although the negligent acts of the persons in charge of the other car also contributed to the same result; and the comparative degree in the culpability of the two will not affect the liability of either. If both were negligent in a manner and to a degree contributing to the result, they are liable jointly and severally." In the Ring Case it was said that: "When several proximate causes contribute to an accident, and each is an efficient cause, without the operation of which the accident would not have happened, it may be attributed to all or to any of the causes; but it cannot be attributed to a cause unless without its operation the accident would not have happened." In the Kunz Case the court said that "a defendant whose negligence was a constitutent element of the transaction, and without which the injury would not have happened, is legally responsible." In the Cohen Case we said: "In a case like this, where no obstruction would have existed but for the wrongful conduct of the defendant, it must be held responsible for the damage which it has caused by reason of the obstruction, even though it might have happened if the licensee had been careful in regard to the manner in which he exercised the assumed right granted him by the license. The defendant, under these circumstances, must take the risk of such care, and not an innocent passer-by." In the Phillips Case it was held that where, in an action to recover damages for injuries alleged to have been caused by the defendant's negligence, it appeared that there were two proximate causes of the injury, one the negligence of the defendant and the other an intervening occurrence happening without fault on the part of the plaintiff, she was entitled to recover. The same rule prevails elsewhere. Lane v. Atlantic Works, 111 Mass. 136; Koplan v. Boston Gas Light Co., 177 Mass. 15, 58 N. E. 183; Koelsch v. Philadelphia Co., 152 Pa. 355, 25 Atl. 522, 18 L. R. A. 759, 34 Am. St. Rep. 653; Pastene v. Adams, 49 Cal. 87; Kennedy v. Grace (C. C.) 92 Fed. 116; The Magdaline (D. C.) 91 Fed. 798; Felton v. Harbeson, 104 Fed. 737, 44 C. C. A. 188; Waller v. M., K. & T. Ry. Co., 59 Mo. App. 410; Lake Shore & M. S.

Ry. Co. v. McIntosh (Ind. Sup.) 38 N. E. 476; Burrows v. Gas Co., L. R. [5 Exch.] 67; 7 Id. 96. The evidence authorized the jury to find, and hence they are presumed to have found, that the negligence of the defendant concurring with that of the contracting company caused the accident, that the plaintiff would not have been injured without the negligence of the defendant, and that the result was such as should have been foreseen as a reasonable probability. These facts, as I think, render the defendant liable, and the judgment against it should therefore be affirmed.

PARKER, C. J., and HAIGHT and MARTIN, JJ., concur with GRAY, J. CULLEN and WERNER, JJ., concur with VANN, J.

Judgment reversed, etc.

(208 Ill. 198)

CHICAGO CITY RY. CO. v. LEACH.*

(Supreme Court of Illinois. Feb. 17, 1904.)

SERVANT'S INJURIES—FELOW SERVANTS—DEPARTMENT RULE—DIRECT CO-OPERATION—BUSINESS IN HAND—PERSONAL ACQUAINTANCE—NECESSITY—STREET RAILROAD EMPLOYÉS—QUESTIONS OF LAW—QUESTIONS OF FACT—BURDEN OF PROOF.

1. In an action for a servant's injuries, the plaintiff has the burden of proving the nonexistence of the relation of fellow servants.

2. A refusal to charge that the burden was on plaintiff to prove that he and the servant by whose negligence he was injured were not fellow servants was not error, where the question was covered by another instruction, stating that the burden of proof was upon plaintiff on several different propositions, and that he could not recover unless the fact that he and the other servant were not fellow servants was established by the preponderance of the evidence.

3. What facts will create the relation of fellow servants is a question of law, but whether such facts exist is a question of fact, unless there is no evidence fairly tending to prove that they are not fellow servants, and the undisputed facts showed that the relation existed, in which case the question again becomes one of law.

4. The relationship of fellow servants depends on the existence between servants of an association which enables them, better than the employer, to guard against risk or accident resulting from the negligence of each other. It does not rest in any degree upon personal acquaintance or actual previous association between the servants, but upon the relation of their duties to each other, and the respective positions they hold.

5. The conductor on one car of a cable company is not engaged in the "particular business" in which the gripman on a following car is engaged, so as to make the two fellow servants.

6. Where there is a direct co-operation between servants of a common master, there is nothing further necessary to make them fellow servants; but, where they are not directly cooperating in some particular work, their usual duties must require co-operation or actual association, to bring them within that relation.

7. The conductors and gripmen on the different cars of a street railway, who were in duty bound to run their cars in such a manner as not to injure the employés on other cars, and who had the same headquarters, were under the same superintendent, and governed by the same rules, were engaged in the same character of service, and were brought into such relation with each other as to depend on each other for their safety, with power to observe the manner in which each discharged his duties, and to influence each other by caution and example, and were thus, as a matter of law, fellow servants.

Ricks, Wilkin, and Magruder, JJ., dissenting.

Appeal from Appellate Court, First District.

Action by Thomas Leach against the Chicago City Railway Company. From a judgment of the Appellate Court (104 Ill. App. 30) affirming a judgment for plaintiff, defendant appeals. Reversed.

W. J. Hynes, S. S. Page, and H. H. Martin, for appellant. Wing & Wing and James C. McShane, for appellee.

CARTWRIGHT, J. This case was before us on a former appeal, when the judgments of the Appellate Court for the First District and the superior court of Cook county were reversed for error of the superior court in sustaining a demurrer to a plea of the statute of limitations. An additional count of the declaration, stating a new cause of action, had been filed after the statute had run, and issues of fact under that count had been submitted to the jury, and found in favor of appellee. Chicago City Railway Co. v. Leach, 182 Ill. 359, 55 N. E. 334. The case has since been tried upon proper issues, resulting in a verdict for appellee for $15,000, upon which judgment was entered. On appeal to the Appellate Court for the First District, the judgment was affirmed.

Plaintiff was a conductor on defendant's street railway, and, in his declaration, alleged that he was injured through the negligence of other servants of the defendant. On the trial he offered evidence tending to prove that his injury was caused by the negligence of Golden, a gripman; and the first alleged error consists in the refusal by the trial court of an instruction offered by defendant that the burden of proof was upon the plaintiff to prove, by a preponderance of all the evidence in the case, that he and Golden were not fellow servants. The instruction correctly stated the law as declared in Joliet Steel Co. v. Shields, 134 Ill. 209, 25 N. E. 569, where that subject was given full consideration, and where it was the determining question in the case. The charge in the declaration was that the plaintiff, a track repairer, had been injured by the negligence of other servants of the defendant in placing an iron mold in an insecure and dangerous position near the track; and the declaration neither alleged in express terms that they were not fellow servants of the plaintiff, nor such facts as would lead to that conclusion. It was held that in all actions for negligence the burden is upon the plaintiff to allege and prove such negligent acts of the defendant as will entitle the plaintiff to recover; that it is not

*Rehearing denied April 6, 1904.

¶ 1. See Master and Servant, vol. 34, Cent. Dig. § 806.

sufficient for one servant to prove that he has been injured by another servant of the common master, but that it is also necessary to prove that the relation of the servants is such as to render the master liable to one for the negligence of the other. In the subsequent case of Louisville, Evansville & St. Louis Consolidated Railroad Co. v. Hawthorn, 147 Ill. 226, 35 N. E. 534, where the declaration alleged that the plaintiff was a fence builder, and was injured by the negligence of a locomotive engineer, the court calling attention to the fact that in the Shields Case there was nothing in the declaration to show that the other servants were not track repairers with the plaintiff, held that it was not necessary to aver in the declaration, in so many words, that the negligent servant was not the fellow servant of the plaintiff, where the facts stated showed that the relation of fellow servant did not exist. In Chicago & Alton Railroad Co. v. Swan, 176 Ill. 424, 52 N. E. 916, the facts showing the relation of the two servants were stated, and showed that they were not fellow servants, and the same rule was declared. Of course, the rule as to pleading does not apply where the charge of negligence is against the master himself. Libby, McNeill & Libby v. Scherman, 146 Ill. 540, 34 N. E. 801, 37 Am. St. Rep. 191. Previous to the Swan Case, an opinion of an Appellate Court had been adopted in Chicago & Alton Railroad Co. v. House, 172 Ill. 601, 50 N. E. 151, in which it was said that, upon the question whether the servants in that case were fellow servants, appellant was the affirmant, though the declaration contained the negative allegation. No question as to the burden of proof was in any way involved, and it cannot be presumed that the Appellate Court attempted to overrule the decisions of this court on that question. Whatever may have been meant by the statement, if it was intended to establish a new rule as to the burden of proof, it was incorrect. There was no intention in adopting the opinion, or in the case of Hartley v. Chicago & Alton Railroad Co., 197 Ill. 440, 64 N. E. 382, which referred to it, to overrule the previous cases on that question. It appears to us, however, that the question where the burden of proof rested was properly and sufficiently covered by another instruction given at the instance of the defendant. That instruction stated that the burden of proof was upon the plaintiff upon several different propositions, and that he could not recover unless the fact that he and the gripman, Golden, were not fellow servants was established by a preponderance of all the evidence in the case. That instruction being correct and covering the ground, it was not error to refuse the instruction concerning which complaint is made.

At the close of the evidence the defendant requested the court to give an instruction of not guilty, which the court refused to do, and this ruling is the principal subject of discussion by the respective counsel. Plaintiff was injured by another train, on which Golden was the gripman, running against the rear of the train on which plaintiff was conductor while plaintiff was on the ground between the cars; and it is contended that his injury resulted from an ordinary hazard of his employment, and from his own negligence in going between the cars and not providing any lookout for approaching trains, and that the plaintiff and Golden were fellow servants of the defendant. The main question is whether plaintiff and Golden were fellow servants; the other questions being controverted questions of fact, which, in our opinion, were properly submitted to the jury.

What facts will create the relation of fellow servants between two employés of a common master is a question of law, and whether such facts exist is ordinarily a question of fact to be submitted to the jury; but where there is no evidence fairly tending to prove that they are not fellow servants, and the undisputed facts show that the relation exists, the question is one of law. If there is any evidence fairly tending to prove the required averment that they are not fellow servants, the court should submit the issue to the jury; but, if there is no controversy about the facts, and they bring the parties within the relation of fellow servants, so that a verdict to the contrary would not be supported by any evidence, the court should not submit the question to the jury. Abend v. Terre Haute & Indianapolis Railroad Co., 111 Ill. 202, 53 Am. Rep. 616; Chicago & Eastern Illinois Railroad Co. v. Driscoll, 176 Ill. 330, 52 N. E. 921. In this case there was no controversy as to the material facts concerning the relation between plaintiff and Golden as servants of the defendant, which were all either proved by the plaintiff, or admitted of record by his counsel upon the trial. If the evidence would justify different conclusions in any respect, it would be with regard to social relations and acquaintance which were wholly immaterial.

The undisputed facts were, in substance, as follows: The accident occurred on September 27, 1893, during the World's Fair. The defendant was operating a double-track cable street railway from Randolph street, on Wabash avenue, to Twenty-Second street, and thence on Cottage Grove avenue to Seventy-First street, in the city of Chicago. There was a loop at the north end, around which the cars ran. At the intersection of Madison street with Wabash avenue, one of the tracks ran east on Madison street one block to Michigan avenue, thence north two blocks to Randolph street, thence west on Randolph street one block to Wabash avenue, and thence south on Wabash avenue. Plaintiff's train consisted of a grip car and two passenger cars. McCarthy was the gripman, plaintiff was the conductor on the car next the grip car, and Baker was the conductor on the rear car. The train was made up at appellant's barn, between Thirty-Eighth and Thirty-Ninth streets, on Cottage Grove avenue, to make its regular trip north around the loop and back to the south. When the train was leaving the barn, plaintiff boarded it; and, after it had gone a few blocks, he discovered that there was too much slack between the grip car and his car, causing them to bump back and forth. It was his duty to correct this, but he waited to do so until he should reach the north end of the loop, when there would be few, if any, passengers, and he would have more time, and the cable ran at but half as high a rate of speed. The train ran north, and turned from Wabash avenue around the loop. When it reached the east side of Wabash avenue, and was about to turn into that avenue, it was stopped on Randolph street to shorten up the drawbars. The trains ran about two minutes apart, and there was about 300 feet of clear track between the rear of the train and the corner of Michigan avenue, around which the next train would come. The sun was shining, and it was a bright, dry, clear morning. Plaintiff got down from his car, and the gripman, McCarthy, fastened his brake, and went to the rear end of the grip car, and took hold of the next car to hold them together while plaintiff took up the slack. Plaintiff looked eastward, and there was no train in sight, and he then got down between the cars to make the necessary change. Neither McCarthy, the gripman, nor Baker, the other conductor, kept any lookout to see whether any other train was approaching. At the usual time the next train, in charge of Golden, came around the corner of Michigan avenue into Randolph street, and ran, without stopping or warning, against plaintiff's train, driving it around the curve into Wabash avenue, and knocking down the plaintiff, who was dragged along under the train, and seriously and permanently injured. The evidence tended to prove that Golden was looking to the northeast, and not looking out for plaintiff's train.

Defendant had over 500 gripmen and conductors running its trains, who all had the same headquarters and the same superintendent, and were governed by the same rules. The trains followed each other over the tracks, regulating their movements by the trains ahead. There were frequent stops and delays by obstructions and accidents, or something getting into the slot; and, if a train stopped, the one behind was required and accustomed to stop. If a train lost the cable, it would wait for the one behind to push it to a point where the cable could be taken up. Each train consisted of a grip car and one or more passenger cars, each of which had a conductor. The defendant had two lists—one of conductors, and the other of gripmen—and the men at the head of the gripmen's list ran with the men at the head of the conductor's list, and so on down the line. Whenever a conductor or gripman missed his run, quit the service, or was discharged, all those below him were moved up one point, so that a conductor generally ran with the same gripman; but, on account of the changes, plaintiff ran with many different gripmen. There is no evidence that he ever ran with Golden, and he did not remember that he had ever seen him, but they had run on the same line for several months.

The rule in this state as to what will constitute fellow servants has been very frequently defined and explained. This court has held the master to a stricter accountability for injuries to one servant by the act of another servant than courts in general. The generally prevailing rule that all servants of a common master are fellow servants was rejected, and it was held that, where a servant was employed in a department separate and distinct from that of a servant whose negligence caused an injury, the master would be liable. Ryan v. Chicago & Northwestern Railway Co., 60 Ill. 171, 14 Am. Rep. 32; Pittsburg, Ft. Wayne & Chicago Railway Co. v. Powers, 74 Ill. 341. The rule as to consociation was also adopted, and was first expounded at length in the case of Chicago & Northwestern Railway Co. v. Moranda, 93 Ill. 302, 34 Am. Rep. 168. In that case, servants of a common master were classified on the basis of their relation to each other at the time of an injury, or their usual duties. The rule established was that those are fellow servants who are co-operating at the time of an injury in the particular business in hand, or whose usual duties are of a nature to bring them into habitual association, or into such relations that they can exercise an influence upon each other promotive of proper caution. If they are not co-operating in some particular work, or if their usual duties are not such as to bring them into habitual association so that they may have the opportunity and power to influence each other to the exercise of caution, they are not fellow servants. It was said in that case that the rule of respondeat superior rests upon considerations of public policy, and is founded on the expediency of throwing the risk upon those who can best guard against it, and that the liability of the master must turn upon the same consideration. This is the principle underlying the application of the doctrine, whether it was adopted on grounds of public policy, or because the risk is assumed by the servant in entering the service; and the relation is made to depend upon the existence of association between servants, which enables them, better than the employer, to guard against risks or accidents resulting from the negligence of each other. The rule, however, does not rest in any degree upon personal acquaintance or actual previous association between the servants, but upon the relation of their duties to each other, and the respective positions which they hold. The rule, stated as a mere abstract proposition, might suggest previous personal acquaintance between individuals, and it is apparent from the opinion of the Appellate Court in this case that that court so regarded it, but this is clearly incorrect.

Counsel for the appellee concede that a personal acquaintance between the plaintiff and Golden was not essential to make them fellow servants; that it was the position which Golden held, and the position which the plaintiff held, which should determine the question; and that, if plaintiff had taken the position of some conductor who had been running the same train with Golden, they would be fellow servants while on the same train, even though plaintiff should be injured within a few minutes after his employment; and their claim is that the employés on different trains are not fellow servants. The classification is of servants as such, and not of individuals; and, if two servants are brought within the classification, they instantly become fellow servants, although they may never have seen each other before. That was the case in Abend v. Terre Haute & Indianapolis Railroad Co., supra, where it was held that a blacksmith and other employés in a wrecking crew, made for the occasion, became fellow servants. The nature of the employment determines the relation, and the rule must be uniform and capable of a reasonable application. To hold the master exempt from liability for an injury to one who had been long in his service, and had associated with the other employés, and to hold him liable for a like injury under the same circumstances to a new servant, would be wholly unwarranted.

One branch of the doctrine is that those are fellow servants who are directly co-operating with each other in some particular work, and it is contended that the particular work in hand at the time of the accident to plaintiff was the running of defendant's trains at the place of the accident, and therefore the employés on the two trains were fellow servants. The rule must have a reasonable and practical interpretation, and, if co-operation in particular work should be construed to mean identical work, the rule would not apply in any case, since no two servants would ever be doing the same identical thing at the same time. A conductor and gripman have separate duties, and yet they are directly co-operating with each other in the particular work of running a train. On the other hand, the particular work in hand does not include the general business of the master. The general business of the defendant was the running of trains on its road, and we do not see how the particular business in which plaintiff was engaged could be extended to include other trains which were following him. The question whether the qualifying words with respect to the exercise of influence modify both branches of the rule is of no importance. Where two servants are directly co-operating in the particular work in hand, they are brought into such relations that they may exercise such influence. Pagels v. Meyer, 193 Ill. 172, 61 N. E. 1111. The addition of qualifying words is wholly unnecessary, and, if there is direct co-operation, nothing further is required to bring them within the relation. Where the servants are not so directly co-operating in some particular work, their usual duties must require co-operation or habitual association.

The remaining question is whether the plaintiff and Golden were fellow servants, under the second branch of the rule, or, in other words, whether the usual duties of the employés of the defendant upon one train were of a nature to bring them into habitual association with the employés on the next train preceding or following them, so that they might exercise an influence upon each other promotive of proper caution. There is no similarity between the relation of servants on different trains on a steam railroad, which are run under orders and directed by a train dispatcher for the purpose of preventing interference and collisions, and the relation of servants on these trains, which followed each other over the tracks, and managed their trains with reference to each other. This case is very much like the case of Chicago & Eastern Illinois Railroad Co. v. Driscoll, supra, where it was held that yard crews employed to perform the same character of service at the same time, using the same tracks and working near each other, were fellow servants, though under different foremen. It was there held that an instruction to find for the defendant should have been given on that ground. In Leeper v. Terre Haute & Indianapolis Railroad Co., 162 Ill. 215, 44 N. E. 492, it was held that a finding by the Appellate Court that an injury to a fireman on one section of a train which was running in three sections was caused by the negligence of an engineer running another section, and that said servants were in the same general grade of service and the same line of employment, whose duty it was to be on constant guard not to injure each other, and whose relation was such as to promote caution for the safety of each other, was a finding that the servants were fellow servants. In this case the undisputed evidence was that plaintiff and Golden were in the same general service and the same general line of employment, and that it was the duty of the employés on one train to run it in such a manner as not to injure those on the train next preceding, and that the duties of employés on such trains were such as to bring them into habitual association, with power and opportunity to influence each other by advice and caution. They were, in the strictest sense, engaged in the same character of service, in which they were brought into such relations to each other as to depend upon each other for their safety, and with power to observe the manner in which each discharged his duty, and to influence each other by caution, advice, and example. There was no disputed fact to be submitted to the jury, and the facts proved by plaintiff or admitted brought him and Golden within the legal definition of fellow servants. It was therefore error to refuse the instruction asked for by the defendant.

The judgments of the Appellate Court and the superior court are reversed, and the cause is remanded to the superior court. Reversed and remanded.

RICKS, WILKIN, and MAGRUDER, JJ., dissenting.

(208 Ill. 282)

SCHUMANN PIANO CO. v. MARK et al.*

(Supreme Court of Illinois. Feb. 17, 1904.)

LANDLORD AND TENANT—LANDLORD'S POSSESSORY ACTION—JUSTICES—CONSOLIDATION OF ACTIONS—ACTION FOR RENT—INCONSISTENT REMEDIES.

1. Hurd's Rev. St. 1901, c. 79, § 53, provides that in all actions before a justice each party shall bring forward all demands which may be consolidated, and which, after consolidation, do not exceed $200. *Held* that, inasmuch as in suits under the forcible entry and detainer act the jurisdiction of the justice is not affected by the amount involved, a landlord may maintain at the same time two different actions to recover different premises held by his tenant under different leases.

2. The fact that a landlord had sued in assumpsit for past-due rents for a certain month, the rent being payable in advance, was no bar to proceedings for possession after nonpayment of the rent within the time fixed by the notice which the landlord is authorized to give by Hurd's Rev. St. 1901, c. 80, § 8.

Appeal from Appellate Court, First District.

Action of forcible detainer by Cyrus Mark and others, known as the Mark Manufacturing Company, against the Schumann Piano Company. From a judgment of the Appellate Court (105 Ill. App. 490) reversing a judgment of a justice, defendant appeals. Affirmed.

This was an action of forcible detainer, commenced on July 30, 1901, by appellees, partners, known as Mark Manufacturing Company, against appellant, the Schumann Piano Company, a corporation, before a justice of the peace in Cook county, to recover possession of the first, fourth, and fifth floors of a building known as Nos. 123 and 125 La Salle avenue, in the city of Chicago. Judgment was there entered in favor of the Mark Company, and the Schumann Company appealed to the circuit court of Cook county, where, upon a trial before the court without a jury, judgment was entered in favor of the latter company. From that judgment of the circuit court the Mark Company appealed to the Appellate Court for the First District, where the judgment of the circuit court was reversed, and judgment was entered in the Appellate Court finding the Schumann Company guilty as charged in the complaint, and adjudging that the appellants (appellees here) recover from the Schumann Piano Company the premises above described, together with costs, etc. This is an appeal prosecuted by appellant to reverse the judgment of the Appellate Court.

On June 14, 1900, the parties to this suit entered into a written lease, by which the premises here involved were demised to appellant by appellees for a term commencing July 1, 1900, and ending April 30, 1902, at a monthly rental of $250, payable in advance on the 1st day of each month. The lease provided, among other things, that the appellees leased the premises, "together with motive power, not to exceed twenty horse power, and sufficient heat in varnishing and finishing room during cold weather to prevent checking the varnish," and that the appellant would "pay (in addition to the rents above specified) for all power used in excess of the amount above specified the sum of five dollars ($5) per month for each horse power, the amount used to be determined by lessor by any of the ordinary methods, the maximum amount of power used at any one time to be the basis of calculation."

The first indication of trouble between the parties to the lease in reference thereto shown by the evidence appears from a letter written by appellant to appellees, dated March 19, 1901, in which there seems to have arisen some difficulty in reference to the power furnished, and it appears that appellees had rendered to appellant a bill for motive power in excess of 20 horse power, which appellant claimed was incorrect, and refused to pay. In the same letter complaint is made by appellant because of lack of heat in the varnish room, causing loss to appellant. It is therein stated that appellant had repeatedly taken this matter up with appellees, and that it had delayed making out a bill for damages until cold weather had passed, but that it would have the bill ready to present to appellees in a few days. On June 20, 1901, an itemized statement of account in the sum of $1,107 for refinishing pianos, claimed to have been made necessary from the checking of varnish caused from lack of heat in the varnish room during cold weather, $11.25 for delay in labor from damage from roof, and $90.90 for telephone, was sent to appellees, with a request to remit the amount of $1,209.15. On July 18, 1901, the attorney for the appellant sent a communication to appellees, together with a statement, showing $340 due for rent under the lease above referred to and under a lease for other parts of the same building for the month of July, leaving a balance of $873.05 due appellant, after adding interest for delay. On July 20, 1901, appellees commenced a suit in assumpsit against appellant in the circuit court of Cook county, returnable to

*Rehearing denied April 6, 1904.

the August term, 1901, thereof, to recover the rent for the month ending July 31, 1901. Among the pleas filed to this declaration was one of set-off, in which $2,000 is claimed by appellant as damages to its pianos by reason of the failure of appellees to furnish sufficient heat in the varnishing and finishing room to prevent checking the varnish, as required by the lease. On July 24, 1901, the appellees, through a constable, served a five-days notice on appellant, notifying it of the default in the payment of rent in the sum of $250, and demanding payment of the same on or before July 29, 1901, and informing appellant that in default of such payment the lease for the premises involved in this suit would be terminated. On the same day another notice from appellees was served on appellant demanding the sum of $25 as rent for the basement of the same building, which was held under another lease, and containing like provisions in case of default in the payment thereof. Suit was commenced under this notice on the same day the case at bar was commenced, and before the same justice of the peace, and judgment was rendered against appellant for possession of the basement.

Anson Mark, one of the plaintiffs, testified that the last month for which appellant paid rent under the lease here in question was June, 1901; that it did not pay the rent for July; that it was in possession of the premises at the time this suit was brought and at the time of testifying. The treasurer of appellant testified that the itemized statement as sent to appellees was correct, and that appellant had been damaged by reason of the checking of varnish, caused by a lack of heat in the varnishing room, in the sum of $1,107.

The Appellate Court incorporated in its judgment the following finding of facts: "The court finds that appellants, by written lease dated June 14, 1900, demised to the appellee the premises described in the complaint in this cause from July 1, 1900, till April 30, 1902, the appellee to pay as rent therefor the sum of $250 per month, payable monthly in advance, on the 1st day of each month; that the rent due July 1, 1901, was not, nor was any part thereof, paid by the appellees, or any of them; that July 24, 1901, appellants caused a five-days notice, in accordance with the statute in such case made and provided, to be served on said appellee, notifying appellee that, unless payment should be made of the said July rent, to wit, $250, on or before July 29, 1901, the said lease from appellants to appellee would be terminated, and that appellee did not pay said rent, or any part thereof, but therein made default, and did not surrender to appellants said demised premises or any part thereof." Propositions of law properly presenting the law questions arising in the case were passed upon by the circuit court, and that court held that the institution of the suit in assumpsit for the rent for the month of July barred a forfeiture of the lease prior to the expiration of that month. The Appellate Court reached the opposite conclusion on this legal proposition, and in accordance with that conclusion and its findings of facts entered the judgment now presented to this court for review.

A. D. Gash, for appellant. Daniel F. Flannery, for appellees.

SCOTT, J. (after stating the facts). Appellant refused to pay the rent due July 1, 1901, which was the rent for the ensuing month, for the reason that it claimed a larger amount due from the landlord on account of the failure of the landlord to furnish heat as provided by the lease. It is conceded by appellant that in this suit for forcible detainer it cannot successfully defend by showing that such damages exceeded the amount of rent due, but it is contended that appellees could not maintain this suit for the premises involved herein, for the reason that on the same day that this suit was begun another suit in forcible detainer was begun by appellees against appellant before the same justice of the peace for other premises demised to appellant by a separate lease, the contention being that one suit should have been brought for the possession of all the real estate described in both complaints, and that, as the real estate involved in this suit was not included in the complaint in the other suit, this suit cannot be maintained.

The statute relied upon by appellant in this regard is section 53 of chapter 79 of Hurd's Revised Statutes of 1901 (page 1116), which is as follows: "In all actions which shall be commenced before a justice of the peace, each party shall bring forward all his demands against the other, existing at the time of the commencement of the action, which are of such a nature as to be consolidated, and which do not exceed $200 when consolidated into one action or defense; and on refusing or neglecting to do so, shall forever be debarred from suing therefor;" and it is argued that under this statute appellees' causes of action in forcible detainer should have been consolidated. This section of the statute does not apply to proceedings under the act in reference to forcible entry and detainer. This construction is shown to be correct by the fact that the plaintiff is required to consolidate only such demands "as do not exceed $200 when consolidated into one action or defense." In suits under the forcible entry and detainer act the jurisdiction of the justice is not affected by the amount involved, and it is therefore apparent that a statute requiring the consolidation of demands which, when consolidated, do not exceed a certain amount, could not apply to rights of action accruing under a statute on which suits may be brought before a justice of the peace without reference to the amount involved. If it had been intended to require the consolidation of actions of this character, that intention would have been evinced by a statute on the subject containing no monetary limitation.

It is then urged that, as the appellees had brought a suit in assumpsit for the July rent, they could not forfeit the lease and maintain a suit for the possession of the real estate prior to August 1, 1901, for the reason that the beginning of a suit for the July rent is inconsistent with the act of appellees in terminating the tenancy prior to the expiration of the month of July. It is said that the suit in assumpsit and the proceeding under the forcible entry and detainer statute are inconsistent remedies for the enforcement of the same right, and that, having elected to first sue in assumpsit, the plaintiff cannot afterwards, during the period covered by the rents sued for, terminate the lease and sue for possession. This is a misapprehension of the situation. The landlord has two rights. One is to have the rent that is due paid; the other is, where the rent has not been paid, to proceed under the statute and obtain possession, if the rent be not paid within the time fixed by the notice which the landlord is authorized to give by section 8 of chapter 80 of Hurd's Revised Statutes of 1901, p. 1135. If, before the expiration of that notice, the rent is paid, any further proceedings for the possession are barred; but no attempt to collect the rent by a suit in assumpsit will bar the suit for possession unless the rent be actually paid within the time limited by the notice. A pending action for use and occupation will not invalidate a notice of the termination of the lease, for the landlord may only recover in his action for rent due at the time of the expiration of the notice, although he may claim rent to a later period. Taylor on Landlord & Tenant, § 485. The language quoted from Lord Coke in the case of Jackson v. Sheldon, 5 Cow. 457, also leads to the same conclusion.

The judgment of the Appellate Court will be affirmed. Judgment affirmed.

(208 Ill. 252)

CITY OF CHICAGO v. GOODWILLIE et al.*

(Supreme Court of Illinois. Feb. 17, 1904.)

MUNICIPAL CORPORATIONS—PUBLIC IMPROVEMENTS—ABANDONMENT—SECOND ORDINANCE.

1. A city, after the return of a verdict in proceedings to condemn land for a street, may in good faith dismiss the proceedings without notice to the adverse parties, and abandon the improvement.

2. A city council passed an ordinance authorizing the opening of a street. Proceedings to condemn the land were instituted, and the jury rendered a verdict awarding compensation. Afterwards the city dismissed the proceedings without notice to the adverse parties. After more than seven years from the passage of the ordinance, and more than five years from the dismissal of the proceedings, a second ordinance providing for the same improvement, and expressly repealing the first ordinance, was adopted by the council. *Held*, that the proceedings under the first ordinance were not a bar to similar proceedings under the second ordinance.

Scott, J., dissenting.

Appeal from Superior Court, Cook County; R. P. Goodwin, Judge.

Proceedings by the city of Chicago for the condemnation of land for a street. From a judgment sustaining the objection of Jennie D. Goodwillie and another to the report of the commissioners, the city appeals. Reversed.

This is a proceeding commenced by the appellant in the superior court of Cook county under an ordinance passed by the city council of the city of Chicago on April 2, 1902, for the opening of Lake View avenue from St. James place to Roslyn place, in the city of Chicago. The petition prayed that compensation and damages to the property affected by opening said avenue be ascertained, and that each piece of property benefited by said improvement be assessed its proportionate share of the cost of said improvement. The appellees, whose property was affected, appeared and filed objections. The only objection relied upon here to sustain the judgment of the court below is that on January 3, 1895, the city council of the city of Chicago passed an ordinance providing for the identical improvement specified in the ordinance which forms the basis of this proceeding; that in pursuance of the provisions of that ordinance a petition was filed in the circuit court of Cook county on March 12, 1895; that on December 23, 1896, a verdict was rendered in said proceeding fixing the compensation and damages to the property of the appellees at $23,250; and that on February 6, 1897, an order was entered on the application of appellant dismissing said proceeding without notice to appellees. The court sustained said objection, and dismissed the proceeding, and the city has appealed.

Edgar Bronson Tolman and Robert Redfield (Charles M. Walker, Corp. Counsel, of counsel), for appellant. Robert S. Cook (R. S. Thompson, of counsel), for appellees.

HAND, C. J. (after stating the facts). The contention of the appellees is that the proceeding had under the ordinance bearing date January 3, 1895, is a bar to this proceeding. We do not agree with such contention, but are of the opinion that the dismissal of said proceeding on February 6, 1897, put an end to the proceeding under the first ordinance. Bass v. City of Chicago, 195 Ill. 109, 62 N. E. 913.

The city, after the verdict was returned and before judgment thereon, had the right,

*Rehearing denied April 6, 1904.

if it acted in good faith, to abandon the improvement and dismiss the proceeding. 7 Ency. of Pl. & Pr. p. 674; McChesney v. City of Chicago, 188 Ill. 423, 58 N. E. 982. In each of the cases of Chicago, Rock Island & Pacific Railway Co. v. City of Chicago, 143 Ill. 641, 32 N. E. 178, Chicago, Rock Island & Pacific Railway Co. v. City of Chicago, 148 Ill. 479, 36 N. E. 72, and Illinois Central Railroad Co. v. City of Champaign, 163 Ill. 524, 45 N. E. 120, relied upon by appellees, judgment had been rendered upon the verdict, and an attempt was made to get rid of the judgment after the term had expired at which it was rendered, and the court held that the judgment was an adjudication between the parties which fixed the amount of compensation and damages; that, while a party seeking to condemn is not bound to take the property at the price fixed by the judgment, if the property is taken the question of compensation and damages is res judicata, and that the question of compensation and damages cannot be opened up and retried by filing a new petition—that is, the effect of the judgment cannot be gotten rid of by commencing a new proceeding. In this case the proceeding was dismissed before judgment, and the rule is that it is the judgment which concludes the parties, and not the verdict of the jury. Sayler v. Hicks, 36 Pa. 392. Mr. Greenleaf, in his work on Evidence (volume 1, § 510), says: "The rule is that, where the verdict was returned to a court having power to set it aside, the verdict is not admissible without producing a copy of the judgment rendered upon it, for it may be that the judgment was arrested or that a new trial was granted." "A verdict cannot ordinarily operate as an estoppel, or even be given in evidence, until it has received the sanction of the court and passed into judgment" (2 Smith, Lead. Cas. 687), "because it may happen that judgment was arrested or a new trial granted." Buller's Nisi Prius, 234.

It is urged, however, that the first ordinance remained in force, and that the city could not pass a new ordinance for the improvement covered by the first ordinance while that ordinance remained in force. We think that argument is fully answered by the fact that the first ordinance was repealed in express terms by the last ordinance, and that more than seven years had elapsed between the dates of the passage of the two ordinances, and more than five years elapsed from the date of the dismissal of the first proceeding and the date of the passage of the second ordinance. In McChesney v. City of Chicago, supra, it was apparent the improvement was not abandoned, but that it was the intention of the city to immediately re-enact the ordinance, and proceed to construct the identical improvement covered by the first ordinance. If it appeared here that the first proceeding was dismissed, and the ordinance which formed the basis of that proceeding was repealed solely with the view of immediately passing a new ordinance for the identical improvement, with the intention of instituting a new proceeding, the purpose of which was to enable the city to escape the effect of the verdict of the jury rendered in the first proceeding, and to enable it to again submit the question of compensation and damages to another jury, under the authority of the McChesney Case, supra, it would be clear that the improvement provided for by the first ordinance had not been abandoned by the city in good faith; but where a period of more than five years has elapsed since the first proceeding was dismissed and the second proceeding commenced we are not disposed to hold that the proceeding under the first ordinance can be interposed as a bar to the second proceeding under a new ordinance, although the improvement provided for under the new ordinance is identical with that provided for by the old ordinance.

The judgment of the superior court will be reversed, and the cause will be remanded to that court for further proceedings in accordance with the views herein expressed.

Reversed and remanded.

SCOTT, J., dissents

(208 Ill. 247)

WETHERELL v. JOHNSON et al.*

(Supreme Court of Illinois. Feb. 17, 1904.)

TRUSTS—PLEDGEE—PURCHASE OF PLEDGED PROPERTY—SUIT TO SET ASIDE BILL OF SALE—ALLEGATIONS—SUFFICIENCY.

1. Though a pledgee is a trustee, and cannot purchase the pledge at his own sale except on an agreement with the pledgor, a payee of a note, holding shares of stock as collateral, with power to sell at public or private sale without notice, may lawfully agree with the debtor to take the stock, as well as stock similarly pledged as security for another note, payable to another person in satisfaction of the notes.

2. An allegation, in a bill to set aside a bill of sale of stock made by complainant to a creditor in satisfaction of debts, that complainant's attorney in the matter was disqualified from purchasing the stock, is defective for failing to allege that he purchased the same, or that any stock was purchased through him, or that he had any interest in the purchase by the creditor.

3. An allegation, in a bill to set aside a bill of sale of stock made by complainant to a creditor in satisfaction of debts for which the stock was held as collateral, that the stock was worth a specified sum above the liens on it, is not an allegation of market value, and is defective for failing to aver that he could have sold the stock for more than he got for it, or that he was kept in ignorance of its value, or that he did not know its worth.

Appeal from Circuit Court, Cook County; E. F. Dunne, Judge.

Suit by Oscar D. Wetherell against Albert Johnson and others. From a decree dismissing the bill, plaintiff appeals. Affirmed.

*Rehearing denied April 6, 1904.

¶ 1. See Pledges, vol. 40, Cent. Dig. §§ 8, 130.

Eugene E. Prussing, pro se. Frank A. Bingham (H. W. Dikeman, of counsel), for appellant. John M. Curran and H. S. Mecartney, for appellees.

CARTWRIGHT, J. The circuit court of Cook county sustained demurrers of the appellees, Albert M. Johnson, Edward A. Shedd, Charles B. Shedd, Eugene E. Prussing, Louis G. Phelps, the National Life Insurance Company of the United States of America, the National Life Building Company, and R. E. Sackett, to the amended and supplemental bill filed on August 28, 1903, against them by the appellant, Oscar D. Wetherell. The alleged wrong against which complainant sought relief was the procuring from him on June 3, 1902, of a bill of sale for 9,010 shares of stock of said National Life Insurance Company pledged as collateral to his notes, in consideration of the release and cancellation of the notes. The prayer of the bill was that the court should cancel the bill of sale and all entries of the transfer in the records of the insurance company, and set aside a deed executed by the insurance company to the National Life Building Company of certain lots in Chicago, and order a reconveyance of the same, and restore complainant to his ownership of said shares. Complainant elected to stand by the bill, and the court dismissed it for want of equity.

The bill abounds in charges of wrongful intent and wicked design on the part of some of the defendants to take advantage of complainant and obtain his shares of stock without consideration, in violation of duty and of confidential and trust relations, but those charges are mere matters of vituperation, except so far as they are justified by facts alleged in the bill. There are charges that defendants (except the corporations) wrongfully confederated together to wrongfully take advantage of the confidential relations existing between the complainant and the defendant Prussing, and to wrongfully take advantage of the relation of trustees and cestui que trust existing between the complainant and the defendants Edward A. Shedd and Albert M. Johnson, and to wrongfully take advantage of the distressed financial condition of complainant, and his weak physical condition, and his wrought-up, feeble, and distracted mental condition, and that in pursuance of said confederacy and design the bill of sale was obtained. These charges also constitute the burden of the argument; but the question whether the court erred in sustaining the demurrers must depend upon the facts stated in the bill, and unless facts constituting fraud are therein specifically set out the decree must be affirmed.

The material facts stated in the bill as a ground for relief are as follows: That complainant was the owner of 9,468 shares of the capital stock of the National Life Insurance Company, a corporation with a capital stock of 10,000 shares, of the par value of $100 each; that he controlled other shares, and controlled the corporation through directors elected to promote his interest and to perform prescribed perfunctory duties as such directors; that the corporation was the owner of the real estate in the City of Chicago described in the bill, otherwise known as the "National Life Building"; that complainant was indebted for an unpaid balance of $120,000 on a note, with which he had pledged as collateral security 4,000 shares of said capital stock; that he owed another note for the principal sum of $100,000, with which was pledged as collateral 5,010 shares of said capital stock; that each note contained a power under which the holder could sell and deliver said shares of stock at public or private sale, without notice, for the payment of the note; that the notes were due; that the defendant Prussing was attorney for complainant in matters pertaining to said interests, and especially as to matters relating to the notes and stock, and, without complainant's knowledge, Prussing was also attorney and legal adviser of the defendants Edward A. Shedd and Albert M. Johnson, the holders of the notes, about the same matters; that complainant was financially distressed, 67 years of age, physically sick and feeble in body, mentally wrought up by the anxieties of business troubles, and on the verge of mental collapse; that the shares of stock were worth $500,000 above the liens thereon; that Prussing held before complainant the danger of a sale of the stock by the legal holders of the notes, and gave him to understand that said holders had it in their power to sell the stock and threatened to do so; that complainant, being greatly wrought up mentally, and distressed, executed the bill of sale of the stock on June 3, 1902, to defendant Johnson, for the stated consideration of one dollar, and the cancellation and release of said two promissory notes; that the complainant relied upon the advice of Prussing, and was influenced thereby to sign the instrument, without reading it or having it read to him; that neither the stock certificates nor the notes were present when he signed the bill of sale, and the recital that he received one dollar was untrue; that the notes were not surrendered until after the filing of the original bill, when they were left, on August 12, 1902, at the office of his attorney; that the individual defendants took control of the insurance company and caused the certificates of stock to be surrendered and new ones to be issued, and voted the stock and were elected directors; that afterward they formed the corporation the National Life Building Company, and caused a deed to be executed by the insurance company conveying the National Life Building to the new corporation; that the conveyance was in consideration of a conveyance of capital stock of the building company to the insurance company; and that in December, 1902, complainant caused a demand to be made upon defendants for the funds, money, stock, bill of sale, and other property belonging to him, which demand was refused.

There are no facts stated in the bill which would constitute a fraud. It is averred, as matter of law, that the relation of the defendants Albert M. Johnson and Edward A. Shedd to the complainant was that of trustees, that the power to sell the stock pledged as collateral was in the nature of a trust, and that they were therefore disqualified from dealing with the subject of the trust to their own advantage. A pledge is trust property, and the character of a pledgee is that of a trustee. Union Trust Co. v. Rigdon, 93 Ill. 458. The law does not permit a pledgee to purchase the pledge at his own sale except upon an agreement with the pledgor, because he has a duty to perform in relation to the property inconsistent with the character of a purchaser, and such a sale is voidable at the option of the pledgor. 22 Am. & Eng. Ency. of Law (2d Ed.) 891; Cook on Stock and Stockholders, § 479. The facts alleged in this case do not bring it within the rule, since there was no attempt by either Johnson or Shedd to purchase at his own sale, or to take advantage of the trust relation for his own benefit. Johnson could lawfully purchase the shares of stock from the complainant without any violation of duty, or they might agree that Johnson should take the stock in satisfaction of the notes, and that was what was done.

It is alleged that Prussing was disqualified from purchasing the stock because he was the attorney and confidential adviser of complainant; but it is not alleged that he did purchase the stock, or that any purchase was made through him, or that he had any interest in the purchase by Johnson. There is no showing whatever that the advice given by Prussing was not good and given in good faith. Complainant knew that the holders of the notes had power to sell the stock pledged as collateral, that the notes were past due, and that there was danger of the loss of the stock to him through the exercise of that power, and therefore the fact that Prussing advised him of such danger does not tend to show fraud. There is no averment in the bill that anything Prussing told the complainant was untrue, but, on the contrary, every statement made is shown by the bill to have been true. There is no fact stated which shows either mental or physical incapacity of complainant to enter into the contract or sell his stock, and, although complainant says he did not read the bill of sale or have it read to him, the bill shows he fully understood it, and was not deceived in any manner as to its contents. There is no complaint that he did not understand the nature of the transaction and the legal effect of the bill of sale.

It is alleged that the stock was worth $500,000 more than the liens upon it; but that is not an allegation of market value, and there is no averment that complainant could have sold the stock for more than he got for it, that he was kept in ignorance of its value, or that he did not know exactly what it was worth. No explanation is offered why complainant did not sell the stock for the great amount of money which it is alleged to have been worth, or that he was deceived or prevented in any manner from realizing its full value.

When the charges of wrongful motives, unsupported by facts, are eliminated, the bill is clearly insufficient to require an answer, and there was no error in sustaining the demurrers. The decree of the circuit court is affirmed.

Decree affirmed.

(208 Ill. 209)

WEBER v. BAIRD, Town Collector, et al.

(Supreme Court of Illinois. Feb. 17, 1904.)

TAXATION—ASSESSMENT—BOARD OF REVIEW—CHANGE IN ASSESSMENT—ENTRY IN BOOKS—PRESUMPTION—EQUITABLE RELIEF—PRODUCTION OF RECORD.

1. In a suit to restrain the collection of taxes, it will be presumed that the board of review performed the duty imposed on it by section 37 of the revenue act (4 Starr & C. Ann. St. 1902, p. 1119, c. 120, par. 111), and caused the changes which they made in the valuation of property to be made and entered upon the assessment books.

2. The courts cannot review the decision of the board of review as to the real value of property assessed, merely on the ground that the value fixed by the board is too great.

3. Since the manner in which the board of review conducts its investigation is such that the taxpayer is not advised of the proofs heard or information obtained by the board relative to the ownership by him of alleged omitted property, and he has no opportunity to contest the truth of such proof before the board, and cannot appeal from any decision of the board other than from a decision that certain property is not exempt, equity will afford a remedy and hear and determine whether the board correctly decided that the taxpayer was the owner of the property assessed against him as having been omitted by him from his schedule.

4. A taxpayer seeking the aid of a court of equity to review the action of the board of review in assessing property against him, omitted from his schedule, must produce in court the assessment books in which the board is required, by section 37 of the revenue act (4 Starr & C. Ann. St. 1902, p. 1119, c. 120, par. 111), to cause the changes in assessments made by them to be entered.

Appeal from Superior Court, Cook County; Jesse Holdom, Judge.

Bill to restrain the collection of taxes by William H. Weber against James Baird, town collector, and others. From a decree of dismissal, plaintiff appeals. Affirmed.

Thornton & Chancellor and Armand F. Teefy (James De Witt Andrews, of counsel), for appellant. James H. Wilkerson and Edwin W. Sims, Co. Attys., William F. Struckmann, Asst. Co. Atty., and Frank L. Shepard, for appellees.

¶ 2. See Taxation, vol. 45, Cent. Dig. §§ 879, 885.

BOGGS, J. The assessment of the personal property of the appellant for taxation in the year 1901 was increased by the board of review of Cook county from a total full value of $1,430, as assessed by the board of assessors, to the sum of $50,000, and taxes were extended against the appellant accordingly. He filed this his bill in chancery to enjoin the collection of the taxes extended upon the excess of an assessment above $1,430.

In the bill appellant alleged that on April 23, 1901, he filed with the board of assessors of Cook county a sworn schedule of all personal property owned and controlled by him on April 1, 1901; that said schedule was sworn to by him before a deputy assessor and accepted by the board of assessors, who assessed said personal property at the sum set forth in said schedule—$1,430; that he was afterwards notified to appear before the board of review and show cause why said assessment of $1,430 should not be increased; that he did so appear, and verified the correctness of said schedule, and informed the board of review that he did not own, nor did he have in his possession or control, any other personal property subject to taxation than that specified; that he was given to understand by said board of review that the amount of said schedule would not be disturbed and would be accepted by said board of review, and that he retired from said board of review believing that said assessment would not in any manner be increased; that he afterward noticed in the public press that his assessment had been fixed at the sum of $50,000; that he thereupon filed a protest with the board of review, and demanded a full public hearing; that he was not the owner of $50,000 worth of property, and that the amount of said assessment was ridiculous, absurd, outrageous, inequitable, and unjust; that, upon demanding to be heard of and concerning said assessment, he was informed by a member of the board of review, before whom the complainant appeared in connection with the assessment, that he would not accord the complainant any hearing upon the subject, and that he did not care what statements the complainant made in reference to the personal property owned by the complainant; that he (the member of the board of review) was not bound to and would not believe said statements, and then and there refused to hear the complainant any further, or to fix any time at which the complainant could be heard; that said assessment is unjust in every particular; that the complainant is not the owner of any property other than that scheduled by him, and that said sum of $50,000 is fraudulently excessive, and should be reduced to the sum of $1,430.

Answer was filed admitting that the board of assessors found the full value of complainant's property subject to assessment for said year to be the sum of $1,430, and assessed the same at one-fifth of said amount, and delivered the assessment so made to the board of review; that complainant was notified to appear and show cause why his assessment should not be increased, and that he did appear, and was heard fully; denying that complainant was informed by the said board of review, or by any one, that no increase would be made; alleging that thereafter the board, from information derived from the complainant at such hearing, and from information derived from other sources, and its own knowledge of the subject, increased the valuation to the sum of $50,000, and assessed the same at the sum of $10,000, and that the same was extended upon the collector's warrant, together with the taxes based thereon, for the sum of $554.30, and the same delivered to the town collector for collection; denying that the assessment made by the board of review is unauthorized, illegal, excessive, inequitable, or fraudulent; denying that the full value of complainant's personal property for the year 1901 did not exceed $1,430, but alleging it far exceeds that sum in value.

The cause was submitted to the court on the sworn testimony of appellant, together with a certified copy of the schedule or list made by appellant of his personal property subject to taxation for the year 1901, which he filed with the board of assessors, and which schedule the board of assessors returned to the board of review. The schedule was verified by the oath of the appellant in due form as required by the statute. The statement of appellant's property liable to assessment was given in said schedule as follows:

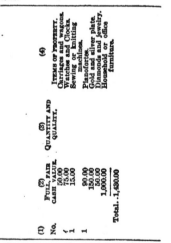

(1) No.	(2) Full, fair cash value.	(3) Quantity and quality.	(4) Items of property.
	50.00		Carriages and wagons.
	75.00		Watches and Clocks.
1	15.00		Sewing or knitting machines.
1	90.00		Pianofortes.
	150.00		Gold and silver plate.
	50.00		Diamonds and jewelry.
	1,000.00		Household or office furniture.
	Total..1,430.00		

The testimony of appellant was, in substance, as follows: "My business is that of a manufacturer of wagons. I signed and swore to said schedule and filed the same, and it contained a true list of all of my personal property of every kind, and the valuations of the same as therein set forth are the full, fair cash values of said property on that date. The full, fair cash value of all personal property owned or controlled by me on the 1st day of April, 1901, did not exceed $1,430. I got notice to appear before the board of review. I went there. Mr. West [a member of the board of review] questioned me about my return, and said it was reported I was rich. I told him, 'That is all I have got, and I should like to see anybody saying to the contrary, and would be able to explain that he was mistaken.' Mr. West questioned as to what I had. He put different questions to me. I forget now just what they were. I told him the schedule showed all the property that I had which was taxable."

It will be observed there is nothing in his testimony in support of the allegations of his bill that his schedule would be accepted by the board, and that he understood that the board was satisfied the schedule contained all property owned by him and subject to assessment. It does not appear with certainty whether the increase in the assessment complained of resulted from the conclusion of the board of review that the property mentioned in the schedule had been undervalued and that it was in fact of the value of $50,000, or whether the board of review ascertained and determined that appellant owned personal property subject to be assessed other than that contained in the schedule, and valued and assessed such other property. We would infer from the testimony of appellant the increase was not caused by a revaluation of the items of property appearing in his schedule.

The board of review possessed power, under the first subdivision of section 35 of the revenue act (4 Starr & C. Ann. St. 1902, c. 120, par. 109, p. 1117), to assess all property of the appellant subject to assessment which had not been assessed by the board of assessors, if any, and under the other provisions of the section the board had power to increase the valuation placed by the board of assessors on the property described in the schedule made by the appellant. Section 37 of the act (4 Starr & C. Ann. St. 1902, par. 111, p. 1119) provides: "Whenever the board of review shall decide to reverse or modify the action of the supervisor of assessments or board of assessors, or county assessor, or the assessment in any case, or to change the list as completed, or the assessment or description of any property in any manner, they shall cause the changes to be made at once and entered upon the assessment books." Under this section it became the duty of the board to have such changes made on the assessors' books as would show the action taken by them. If the board of review determined that the valuation placed by the board of assessors on any one or more of the articles or classes of property listed by appellant in the schedule was too low, it became the duty of the board, under said section 37, to fix and determine the true cash value of such property, and to change the valuation of such article or class of property in the appropriate column in the assessors' books to an amount which, in the judgment of the board of review, represented the true value of such article of property or class of property owned by the appellant. If the board determined that the appellant was the owner of property not included in the description of any of the classes of property specified in the schedule made by him, but falling within other classes of taxable property, it had power to ascertain and determine the value of such omitted property, to class it in compliance with the provisions of section 35 of the revenue act, and order the assessment to be so changed on the assessors' books as that such omitted property would appear for taxation on the assessment books in the appropriate column in such assessors' books prepared for property of that nature or class.

The record of the decision of the board of review upon the hearing of a charge that a taxpayer has property liable to assessment other than such as is contained in the schedule, or that the property listed in the schedule is of greater value than that fixed by the board of assessors, is made by entering the same on the assessment books, and in the proper column prepared in that book for the assessment of property of the nature and kind as that which, in the opinion of the board, had been omitted. The board cannot decide that a taxpayer shall pay taxes on an amount arbitrarily fixed by the board. The board has power to assess property, and has no power to order that an assessment be entered against the person of a taxpayer. It is to be presumed the board of review performed its duty, and that there is, therefore, a record on the assessment book for the year 1901 showing the action of the board and specifying the property which was assessed to the appellant. But the assessment book was not produced in evidence, nor do we find in the record any reference whatever to it. We, therefore, can know no more from this record than that the total personal property assessment of the appellant was increased, either by an increase made by the board in the value of the articles listed by him as liable to taxation, or by the assessment to him by the board of other property not mentioned in the schedule, but which the board decided was owned by him on the 1st day of April, 1901, and was subject to assessment for taxation. If the increase was the result of the investigation made by the board of review as to the true value of the property included in the schedule as made by the appellant, the decision of the board as to the real value of such property cannot be reviewed by the court on the ground, merely, that the value fixed by the board is too great. "The assessor and boards for review are invested with the only power to fix valuations, and their decisions can only be questioned for fraud or want of jurisdiction. * * * But while it is not the duty of courts, nor within the power of equity, to supervise the honest judgments of statutory officers as to valuations, equity will interfere if the valuations are fixed from improper motives and in disregard of duty. * * * It is the rule that an excessive valuation merely does not establish fraud, but the attending circumstances may be such as to lead to the conclusion that it was fraudulently and dishonestly made." New Haven Clock Co. v. Kochersperger, 175 Ill. 383, 51 N. E. 629. There is no evidence in this record to show that the property listed by the appellant was revalued at all by the board of review. It is fairly to be deduced from the testimony of the appellant that the increase arose from the decision of the board that the appellant was the owner of other property than that listed by him for assessment, and which other property the board decided should be assessed to him. As said before, we are to assume, primarily, that the board performed the duties devolving upon it by the statute, and that it caused such other property, which in the opinion of the board the appellant owned and on which he should pay taxes, to be "entered upon the assessment books," in pursuance of the requirements of said section 37 of the revenue act.

It would constitute a good ground of complaint that the board of review caused entries to be made on the assessment books assessing to appellant property which he did not possess or own, or so control as that it became his duty to report the same for taxation. But he did not produce the assessment books, nor state in his bill what appeared thereon. What the board did appears of record; or, at least, we must so assume in the absence of proof to the contrary. We think a court of equity may revise the decision of the board of review assessing property to a taxpayer as having been owned by him and subject to taxation and omitted from the schedule prepared by him. The manner in which the board of review conducts its investigation is such that the taxpayer is not advised of the proofs heard or information obtained by the board relative to the ownership by him of property said to have been omitted from the schedule, nor has he an opportunity to contest the truth of such proof or such information before the board. He cannot appeal from any decision of the board, other than from a decision that certain property is not exempt from assessment for taxation. Dutton v. Board of Review, 188 Ill. 386, 58 N. E. 953. Equity will therefore afford a remedy, and hear and determine whether the board correctly decided that the taxpayer was the owner of the property which the board assessed against him as having been omitted by him from his schedule. The inquiry in such an equitable proceeding is, what property did the board decide the taxpayer owned and had omitted from his schedule, and did he own that property? What the board decided is to be determined by the record made by the board of its decision. A taxpayer seeking the aid of equity must therefore show the record made by the board, and then he will be heard to show that he did not own the property there specified in the record. If, in fact, the board did not enter its decision on the assessment books, or if its decision did not show on such books the kind and class of property said to have been omitted, such failure would vitiate the assessment, unless in some way cured. But a taxpayer cannot ignore the record made by the board of review, which, if lawfully rendered, would show specifically the property or class of property which the board decided the taxpayer owned and had not listed for assessment, and be allowed to overturn the decision by seeking, in a general way, to deny that he had any other property than that he had listed.

The decree must be and is affirmed. Decree affirmed.

(208 Ill. 187)

CHICAGO UNION TRACTION CO. v. CITY OF CHICAGO.*

(Supreme Court of Illinois. Feb. 17, 1904.)

MUNICIPAL CORPORATIONS—STREETS—PAVING ORDINANCE—VALIDITY.

1. An ordinance provided for the paving of a street for a certain distance, which included intersections of three other streets, and declared that all ordinances and parts of ordinances inconsistent with its provisions were repealed. Prior to the passage of this ordinance, ordinances had been passed providing for the paving of the three intersecting streets, including the points of intersection, and the paving of the street intersections had been completed under the ordinances authorizing the paving of the three intersecting streets before application for confirmation of an assessment against property abutting on the first-mentioned street for the paving thereof. *Held*, that the ordinance repealed the prior ordinances relative to the paving of the intersecting streets, so that the court was without power to exclude from the assessment roll the cost of paving the three street intersections, and confirm the assessment less such reduction.

2. An ordinance authorized the paving of a portion of a street which included three street intersections, and prior ordinances authorizing the paving of the intersecting streets had also authorized the paving of such intersections. Before application for confirmation of an assessment under the first-mentioned ordinance, these intersections had been paved under the prior ordinances; and, before the passage of the first-mentioned ordinance, the contract for the paving of one of the intersecting streets had been let, and a judgment confirming an assessment against property benefited had been entered. Hurd's Rev. St. 1899, p. 374, c. 24, § 562, prohibits the city council from in any way staying or delaying the collection of the assessments levied under a prior ordinance

*Rehearing denied April 6, 1904.

for the purpose of collecting a fund to discharge the obligation of a paving contract, without the consent of the contractor and bondholder. *Held*, that the first-mentioned ordinance was void, as unreasonable and oppressive.

Appeal from Cook County Court; Frank Harry, Judge.

Application by the city of Chicago against the Chicago Union Traction Company for confirmation of an assessment for street improvement. From a judgment confirming the assessment, defendant appeals. Reversed.

Williston Fish and Louis Boisot (John A. Rose, of counsel), for appellant. William M. Pindell (Edgar Bronson Tolman, Corp. Counsel, and Robert Redfield, of counsel), for appellee.

BOGGS, J. This appeal brings before us the judgment of the county court of Cook county confirming a special assessment against the property of the appellant company, levied under an ordinance of the city of Chicago, for the purpose of paving with asphaltum the roadway of Belden avenue from the westerly line of North Clark street to the east curb line of Perry street, "except the intersection of Cleveland avenue with Belden avenue, and also except steam and street railway rights of way thereon between said points." Lincoln avenue, Larrabee street, and Halsted street also intersect Belden avenue between the termini of the improvement of that avenue as fixed by the ordinance. The ordinance was adopted December 17, 1902, and declared that all ordinances and parts of ordinances inconsistent with its provisions should be, and were, repealed.

It appeared from the stipulation entered into by the parties that a prior ordinance had been adopted by the city council of said city, providing for the paving of Larrabee street, July 1, 1901, and an ordinance providing for the paving of Halsted street had been adopted November 18, 1901, and an ordinance providing for the paving of Lincoln avenue had been adopted April 21, 1902, and that each of said ordinances included the paving of the street intersections of each of said streets with Belden avenue. It also appeared that, at the time of the adoption of the ordinance here under consideration, proceedings were pending in the county court for the construction of the improvement of each of said streets—Lincoln avenue, Larrabee street, and Halsted street—and that in said proceedings judgments had been entered confirming an assessment against property benefited by the improvements. It also appeared that, notwithstanding the adoption of the ordinance under consideration, for the paving of the entire roadway of Belden avenue between the points named, the city, under the prior ordinances, proceeded with the work of constructing pavements in the street intersections of Belden avenue with the before-mentioned three streets, and that at the time of the hearing of this cause the pavement of said street intersections had been completed under the prior ordinances. It was proven that, before the adoption of the ordinance here under consideration, the contract for the paving of the intersection of Halsted street and said Belden avenue had been entered into under the prior ordinance authorizing the improvement of Halsted street.

The estimate made by the engineer of the board of local improvements fixed the cost of the improvement in Belden avenue at $75,500. The assessment roll, as returned, asked assessments in the sum of $72,213.50. The court ascertained from the evidence that the estimated cost of paving the said three street intersections had been deducted from the estimated cost of the whole improvement, as described in the ordinance, and held that the court had power, under the statute, to order the roll recast, eliminating the cost of these three street intersections, and that, if such power should be exercised, the assessment roll would be returned into court for the same amount asked by the roll as returned, and adjudged that the assessment should be confirmed for the amount of the estimate of the engineer, less the estimated cost of the three street intersections.

The ordinance under consideration purported to repeal all ordinances and parts of ordinances inconsistent therewith. The ordinances providing for the improvement of Halsted street, Larrabee street, and Lincoln avenue, in so far as said ordinances, respectively, authorized and directed the paving of that part of Belden avenue which intersected each of said streets, were inconsistent with it. But at the time of its adoption the contract for the improvement of so much of Belden avenue as constituted the intersection of that avenue and Halsted street had been entered into under the prior ordinance, and the proviso to section 56 of the act of June 14, 1897 (Hurd's Rev. St. 1899, p. 374, c. 24, § 562), inhibited the city council from in any way staying or delaying the collection of the assessments levied under the prior ordinance for the purpose of collecting a fund to discharge the obligation of the contract without the consent of the contractor and bondholder. But so far as we are advised, no reason existed why the city council, in adopting the ordinance under consideration, could not have repealed the prior ordinances providing for the improvement of the intersections of Larrabee street and Lincoln avenue with Belden avenue. The action of the court in excluding from the estimate the cost of paving these street intersections was a holding, in effect, that the prior ordinances were in full force notwithstanding the declaration of their repeal in the latter ordinance, and that the latter ordinance was effective only in such parts of Belden avenue as were not covered by the prior ordinances, and that it was effective and was to be enforced on all other parts of the avenue according to its terms. In this the court fell into error. The ruling involved an assumption and an exercise by the court of authority legislative in character, which could be lawfully exercised only by the city council. The ruling was an attempt by the court to amend the ordinance last adopted by the city council. In American Hide & Leather Co. v. City of Chicago, 203 Ill. 451, 67 N. E. 979, we said: "An ordinance can be amended only by the body which had power to pass it." We think the court should have held the later ordinance to be unreasonable and oppressive upon the property holders and for that reason invalid. If enforced as adopted, it would subject the property benefited by the paving of the intersection of Halsted street and Belden avenue to a double burden of taxation for such paving, for the reason a judgment confirming an assessment against such property for the cost of paving the intersection had been entered under a former ordinance, and a contract had been entered into for the construction of the work under that ordinance, which it was beyond the power of the city council to interfere with, and it would render nugatory all proceedings had under the former ordinances looking toward the paving of the intersections of Lincoln avenue and Larrabee street with Belden avenue. In such status of affairs, the court should not have attempted to correct the defects in the exercise of legislative power by the council, but should have declared the ordinance to be unreasonable and oppressive, and for that reason refused to have enforced it, and thus left the city council free to take such action as should seem to that body to be just and proper in view of the actual situation of the improvements in the street.

The case of Noonan v. People, 183 Ill. 52, 55 N. E. 679, in no wise supports the action of the county court. In that case we held the later ordinance repealed the prior one, and that its provisions as to the paving of street intersections, to which both ordinances related, should prevail. Here the holding of the county court was that the prior ordinances are superior, and should be given effect. In the Noonan Case there had been no judgment of confirmation under the prior ordinance when the later ordinance was adopted, and we held that as the effect of the later ordinance was to repeal so much of the former ordinance as provided for the paving of the street intersections, in the proceeding for the confirmation of assessments under the prior ordinance the commissioners and the court might proceed upon the theory that that part of the ordinance which provided for the paving of the intersection of the streets, having been repealed by the later ordinance, was ineffective and no longer in force, and that the cost of the intersection should therefore be excluded from the estimate, and the judgment confirmed. Nothing there said can by any possibility be regarded as authority for the view that the county court in the case at bar might regard the later and repealing ordinance as ineffective, and exclude from the estimate and judgment of confirmation a part of the improvement ordered by such later ordinance to be made because the provisions of such later ordinance were inconsistent with the provisions of prior ordinances which the later ordinance declared should be repealed.

The county court should have denied judgment confirming the assessment, and thus the whole matter would have been remitted to the city council for such action as to that body should seem proper to be taken. If the city council should deem it proper to adopt an ordinance providing for the improvement of Belden avenue by paving the roadway of that street with asphaltum, except at the intersections of Lincoln avenue, Larrabee street, and Halsted street, they could lawfully do so, but the county court was without power to so enforce the ordinance under consideration as to effectuate that end.

The judgment must be, and is, reversed, and the cause will be remanded to the county court of Cook county with directions to that court to dismiss the petition.

Reversed and remanded with directions.

(208 Ill. 236)

STEGER v. TRAVELING MEN'S BUILDING & LOAN ASS'N et al.*

(Supreme Court of Illinois. Feb. 17, 1904.)

MORTGAGES — PRIORITIES — DEFECTIVE ACKNOWLEDGMENT—CURATIVE ACT—VALIDITY —EFFECT—REPORT OF MASTER.

1. A trust deed executed before 1903, conveying a homestead to a building association to secure a loan, the acknowledgment of which deed was taken by the secretary of the association, who was also a stockholder, as notary public, is void, and a subsequent deed of trust, duly executed and acknowledged before 1903, conveying the same homestead, creates a prior lien, unless the act of 1903 (Laws 1903, p. 120), curing defective acknowledgments, has a retroactive effect, so as to validate the lien of the building association from the time of the original transaction.

2. Laws 1903, p. 120, providing that deeds, mortgages, etc., wherein a corporation was a grantor or grantee, or mortgagor or mortgagee, in instruments which have been duly acknowledged before a notary public shall be adjudged by the courts as legally acknowledged notwithstanding the acknowledgments thereof were taken before a notary public who was at the time a stockholder or officer of the corporation, merely ratifies and confirms what the Legislature might have lawfully authorized in the first instance, and is not invalid as an exercise of judicial power.

3. The act merely binding the grantor or mortgagor by a contract attempted to be made, but which was void for defective execution, is not in violation of the Constitution, prohibiting the impairment of the obligation of a contract.

*Rehearing denied April 6, 1904.

4. The act cannot deprive a mortgagee in a mortgage executed prior to the passage of the act, or a judgment creditor in a judgment obtained prior to the passage thereof, of his vested right to priority over a prior mortgage executed to a building association, and acknowledged by the secretary and stockholder of the association.

5. A purchaser of such subsequent mortgage and judgment pending a litigation as to the priority of the mortgages and judgment, though taking the mortgage and judgment subject to the equities existing against them in the hands of the assignor, acquires rights which are prior to the rights of the building association, it having no equities which could overcome the legal and equitable rights of the assignor.

6. Where a building association, in loaning money to an individual, advanced part of the loan for a purpose other than for the improvement of the debtor's homestead, and held the balance until a building erected by the debtor was practically completed, when, for its own protection, it required releases of mechanics' liens, and distributed the money to the contractor and subcontractor, the debt so created was not one incurred for an improvement of the homestead within the meaning of the law making such debts first liens on the property.

7. A master in his report should clearly and concisely state the conclusions of fact and law, but should not make arguments on the law, with citation of cases and quotations from reports.

Appeal from Superior Court, Cook County; Jesse Holdom, Judge.

Suit by Chris G. Steger against the Traveling Men's Building & Loan Association and others. From a decree for defendants, plaintiff appeals. Reversed.

Frederick Mains, for appellant. Ives, Mason & Wyman, for appellee Traveling Men's Building & Loan Ass'n. C. Arch Williams, J. Erb, and Cyrus J. Wood, for appellees Joseph and Marcianna Strozewski.

CARTWRIGHT, J. The only question to be decided on this appeal is one of priority between liens held by the appellant and by the Traveling Men's Building & Loan Association, one of the appellees, upon a homestead estate in a lot in Chicago. The property, at the time the liens were created, was the homestead of Joseph Strozewski. The lien of the building association on the lot is by virtue of a trust deed executed June 18, 1894, by Joseph Strozewski and Marcianna, his wife, to the American Trust & Savings Bank, trustee, to secure an indebtedness in the sum of $3,300 for money loaned, with interest and penalties. The acknowledgment of this trust deed was taken by George J. Kuebler, a notary public, who was secretary of the building association, and a stockholder therein, and for that reason the estate of homestead was not released, and the trust deed created no lien upon it. Ogden Building & Loan Ass'n v. Mensch, 196 Ill. 554, 63 N. E. 1049, 89 Am. St. Rep. 330. The liens of the appellant were created by a trust deed executed by said Joseph Strozewski and wife on August 2, 1894, to L. L. Gilman, trustee, to secure the payment of four promissory notes to different persons, aggregating $443.70, and by a judgment recovered in the circuit court of Cook county on October 28, 1895, for improvements on the homestead premises, and an execution levied thereon. In the trust deed securing the notes held by the appellant the homestead estate was released, and the trust deed was acknowledged in accordance with the statute, so that it became a lien upon the homestead estate. The controversy is over the question whether the act in force May 15, 1903 (Laws 1903, p. 120), legalizing acknowledgments taken before stockholders or officers of corporations, had the effect to make the trust deed securing the building association a lien upon the homestead prior to the liens held by appellant.

The building association and the trust and savings bank, as trustee, filed their bill in the superior court of Cook county November 20, 1901, for the foreclosure of the trust deed securing the building association. Among the defendants were the holders of the four notes now owned by appellant and L. L. Gilman, the trustee, and Joseph Strozewski and his wife. Gilman, the trustee, and the holders of the notes, as well as Joseph Strozewski and his wife, in their answers set up the homestead estate, and alleged that the trust deed of the building association was null and void so far as that estate was concerned. Gilman and the holders of the notes claimed that their trust deed was a first lien on the homestead, and afterward filed their cross-bill to foreclose said trust deed, making the same averments. The owner of the judgment recovered for the improvement of the homestead premises answered the cross-bill, claiming a second lien on the estate of homestead, subject only to that of the trust deed to Gilman. Replications having been filed to all the answers, the issues under the original bill and cross-bill were referred to a master in chancery, who filed his report September 19, 1902, finding that there was a homestead estate in the premises; that the trust deed securing the building association was null and void as to such estate; that the trust deed securing the cross-complainants was a first lien on the homestead; that by the levy of an execution the judgment became a second lien on the estate of homestead; that the building association had a first lien on the excess over and above the homestead; that the Gilman trust deed was a second lien on such excess, and the judgment a third lien thereon. Other liens not involved in this appeal were also disposed of by the report. On December 15, 1902, the issues were again referred to the master on the question whether the trust deed securing the building association was a lien on the homestead as a debt incurred for the improvement thereof. The master filed his supplemental report on April 28, 1903, finding that said trust deed secured a debt in part for the improvement of the premises; that as to such part it was a first lien on the home-

¶ 7. See Equity, vol. 19, Cent. Dig. § 888.

stead estate, and that the Gilman trust deed and judgment were second and third liens. The case stood on exceptions to this report, when appellant, who had become the owner of the notes secured by the Gilman trust deed and of the judgment, by leave of court, together with Gilman, the trustee, filed a supplemental cross-bill on June 2, 1903, alleging the purchase of said securities as first and second liens in reliance upon the law as it existed at the time of the purchase, and claiming priority for his liens. The answer of the complainants in the original bill admitted the purchase of the securities by appellant on July 21, 1902, after examination of the records, and in the belief that they were first and second liens on the homestead; but averred that the indebtedness to the building association was incurred for the improvement of the homestead, with the exception of $750. The answer of Joseph Strozewski and wife set up the act of 1903, legalizing acknowledgments. Replications having been filed to the answers, it was stipulated that the issues should be submitted to the court on the evidence taken and reported by the master.

The material facts shown by the evidence are as follows: Joseph Strozewski, the owner of the premises occupied as a homestead, entered into a contract with John Skotnicki to erect a building thereon, and on May 22, 1894, Strozewski made application to the building association for a loan of $3,300, offering said premises and 33 shares of capital stock of the association as security, and stating that the property was incumbered by a mortgage for $750, and that he had agreed to pay the contractor $3,200 to complete the building. The application was accepted, and the trust deed was executed and acknowledged before the secretary of the association, who was also a stockholder. The association advanced money to pay the existing incumbrance and commissions, attorney's fees, insurance and other expenses, together with $200 to a subcontractor, amounting to $1,315.70. The balance of the loan was retained until August 2, 1894, when the building was completed, and it was insufficient to pay the entire amount due on the building. By agreement the contractor and subcontractors entitled to liens met at the office of the association on that day, and the balance of the loan was distributed among them upon their executing releases of their claims for liens. At the same time Joseph Strozewski and wife executed the four promissory notes to contractors, and secured them by the trust deed to Gilman, which was acknowledged so as to convey the homestead. They also executed two other notes for work on the building, on which the judgment was afterward entered. On July 21, 1902, appellant purchased the judgment and the notes secured by the trust deed to Gilman.

Upon the hearing the superior court entered a decree finding that the lien of the building association was a first lien on the premises, including the homestead estate; that the liens of appellant were subject thereto; that there was due the building association $3,856, including $300 for solicitor's fees; that on July 21, 1902, appellant, in consideration of $428.09, became the owner of the notes secured by the trust deed to Gilman; that the amount due thereon was $620; that on August 11, 1902, appellant, for the consideration of $202.62, purchased the judgment; that the act of 1903, legalizing acknowledgments, had the effect to make the trust deed securing the building association a valid and legal conveyance of the estate of homestead as against appellant, the same as though it had been originally acknowledged in accordance with the law; and that appellant purchased his notes and judgment before the passage of said act, but with knowledge that the building association claimed a lien on the homestead estate. The master was ordered to sell the property, and pay the amount due the building association, and bring the surplus into court.

The trust deed securing the building association, when executed, was null and void as to the estate of homestead (Ogden Building & Loan Ass'n v. Mensch, supra), and so remained until the curative act of 1903 took effect. The Gilman trust deed and the judgment are prior liens on the homestead estate, unless that act had a retroactive effect to validate the lien of the building association from the time of the original transaction. The validity of that act is attacked by appellant on several grounds. It is first contended that it is not a law, but a mere legislative direction to the courts to decide and adjudge in a particular manner, and is therefore an invasion of the province of the judicial department. The act provides as follows: "That all deeds, mortgages, or other instruments in writing relating to or affecting any real estate situated in this state, wherein a corporation was or may be the grantor, mortgagor, grantee or mortgagee, which have been acknowledged or proven before any notary public, justice of the peace or other officer authorized by the statutes of this state to take acknowledgments of such instruments in writing, when so acknowledged or proven, in conformity with the statutes of this state, shall be adjudged and treated by all courts of this state as legally executed and acknowledged or proven, notwithstanding such acknowledgments or proof of the execution thereof were taken before a notary public, justice of the peace, or such other officer who was, or may have been at the time of such acknowledgment, a stockholder or officer of such corporation; and all such acknowledgments or proof of such deeds, mortgages or other instruments in writing heretofore taken before any such notaries public or other officers, who were at the time of such execution, acknowledgment or proof, a stockholder or officer of such corporation, are hereby legalized." Laws 1903, p. 120.

There is language in the act which, standing alone, might be interpreted as a mandate of the Legislature to decide cases arising prior to the enactment according to the legislative will. The Legislature cannot exercise judicial power, either directly or through a legislative command; but the substance of this act is that acknowledgments taken before an officer or stockholder of a corporation shall be legal and valid, and that acknowledgments so taken before the passage of the act are legalized. That is not an exercise of judicial power, since it does not purport to settle suits or controversies, but only gives effect to acknowledgments in a matter under the legislative control. The Legislature might doubtless have provided by a prior law that an acknowledgment could lawfully be taken before an officer or stockholder of a corporation, and the act goes no further than to bind the mortgagor where the acknowledgment is void by reason of personal disability of the officer to take it. The Legislature may ratify and confirm any act which it might lawfully have authorized in the first instance, where the defect arises out of the neglect of some legal formality and the curative act interferes with no vested rights. United States Mortgage Co. v. Gross, 93 Ill. 483.

The next proposition is that the act is in violation of the Constitution, as impairing the obligation of a contract. It seems clear that it does not violate the obligation of the contract between the building association and Strozewski, but rather validates it, and makes it enforceable. It goes no further than to bind the mortgagor by a contract which he attempted to enter into, but which was void for defective execution. The intention of the parties failed merely through the disability of the officer. Neither does the act impair the contract between Strozewski and the parties secured by the Gilman trust deed. Their contract remains in force, to be executed according to its terms.

The third proposition we consider sound, and it is that the act cannot have the effect to deprive appellant of his vested rights, and transfer them to the building association, which would constitute a taking of property without due process of law. Under the law of the land the building association had no lien on the homestead prior to the passage of the curative act of 1903. After the execution of the trust deed securing the building association, Strozewski was still vested with a perfect, unincumbered title to the estate of homestead; and on August 2, 1894, that estate was conveyed to Gilman, in trust to secure the holders of the four notes. The judgment was recovered on two notes given for improving the homestead, and a levy was made on the homestead estate under an execution issued on that judgment. Under the law the judgment was a second lien on the homestead. A mortgage lien and a judgment which is a lien are each vested rights of property, and in this case both had become vested before the passage of this act. It is not within the power of the Legislature to transfer such vested rights from one to another. Lane v. Soulard, 15 Ill. 123; Russell v. Rumsey, 35 Ill. 362; Conway v. Cable, 37 Ill. 82, 87 Am. Dec. 240; Rose v. Sanderson, 38 Ill. 247. To make vested prior liens inferior and subsequent to a trust deed which was not a lien when such rights vested would be to transfer property from one to another by legislative enactment. Appellant was purchaser of the securities, pendente lite, and took them subject to all equities existing against them in the hands of his assignors, and subject to any decree which might have been entered against such assignors. Perhaps this would have been the case whether he purchased during the pendency of the suit or before. At any rate, it cannot be denied that he took the liens subject to any equities existing against the original holders. The building association, however, had no equities which could overcome the legal and equitable rights of appellant's assignors. Much of the argument on behalf of appellees relates to such supposed equities treated as synonymous with natural justice, but it must be remembered that, while equity is based upon moral right and natural justice, it is not coextensive with them. Equities are rights which are established and enforced in accordance with the principles of equity jurisprudence under some general principle or acknowledged rule governing courts of equity. 1 Pom. Eq. Jur. 46, 47. The building association did not, by virtue of its loan or its trust deed, acquire any equitable estate in the homestead. No court of equity would think of decreeing an equitable estate in a homestead under a mortgage which in the law did not create any lien. All deeds or instruments of writing for the alienation of a homestead are invalid unless the homestead is released in the manner prescribed by the statute, and, if a mortgage contains no release or waiver of the homestead, a court of equity cannot make the mortgage effectual against such estate. Stodalka v. Novotny, 144 Ill. 125, 33 N. E. 534. The lien of the building association was subject to the homestead estate of Strozewski, but in the trust deed to Gilman the homestead was released and waived, and in such a case the second mortgage is entitled to priority over the first to the extent of $1,000. Shaver v. Williams, 87 Ill. 469; Eldridge v. Pierce, 90 Ill. 474. The act can have no effect as against subsequent bona fide purchasers, who cannot be deprived of their property by legislative enactment. The right of a person having a vested interest is secure against any act of the Legislature. Cooley's Const. Lim. 378; Fisher v. Green, 142 Ill. 80, 31 N. E. 172. It would not be contended that, if Strozewski had conveyed the premises to a third person, the Legislature could deprive him of his title by validating the acknowledgment, so that the homestead estate could be appropriated to the payment of the debt to the building association. In the case of United States Mortgage Co. v. Gross, supra, it was held competent for the Legislature to validate a mortgage by a curative act, on the ground that the purchaser had no vested right to keep property released from a debt which he was paid for assuming. It would have been inequitable and unjust to permit a purchaser to hold valuable property discharged of a debt which was a large portion of the purchase price, and which he had agreed to pay. There are no such equities in this case.

It is urged, however, that the trust deed of the building association is a first lien, because it is for a debt incurred for the improvement of the homestead. The loan was made by the building association to Strozewski, who intended to apply the proceeds in payment for the new building. Part of the loan was advanced for other purposes, and the building association held the balance until the building was practically completed, when, for its own protection, it required releases of mechanics' liens, and at a meeting of all the parties interested distributed the money to the contractor and subcontractors. The debt was not a debt for making any improvement. As between the contractor and Strozewski the debt was for the improvement of the homestead, but as between Strozewski and the building association he was a borrower and it was a lender. The improvement was considered by the association in making the loan with reference to the sufficiency of the security, and the money was held and paid to the contractors for the protection of the lender. Money so borrowed and used in the improvement of real estate does not constitute a debt incurred for an improvement of the homestead, within the meaning of the law. Parrott v. Kumpf, 102 Ill. 423. In the cases of Austin v. Underwood, 37 Ill. 438, 87 Am. Dec. 254, and Magee v. Magee, 51 Ill. 500, 99 Am. Dec. 571, money was paid as purchase money directly to the vendor for the purpose of having land conveyed, and was not borrowed to pay for the land. Those cases were different from this, in which the debt was the debt of Strozewski to Skotnicki under the building contract, and money was borrowed to discharge the debt.

A question is raised as to the reasonableness of the allowance made to the master for reporting his conclusions, but counsel says that he submits it without argument. The reports, and especially the first one, consist of lengthy arguments, and quotations from decisions of courts, which are not proper to be contained in a report. Such a practice imposes unnecessary burdens upon litigants, and perhaps affords an apparent basis for exorbitant charges. The conclusions of fact and law should be clearly and concisely stated, and it is not a proper practice for the master to present a treatise on the law, with citations of cases and quotations from reports. That is the proper function of counsel, and the record should not be filled with such material. In view of the fact that the objection does not appear to be insisted upon, we are inclined to permit the allowance in this case to stand as made.

The decree of the superior court is reversed, and the cause is remanded to that court, with directions to enter a decree in accordance with the views herein expressed. Reversed and remanded.

(162 Ind. 250)

COUCHMAN v. PRATHER et al.

(Supreme Court of Indiana. Feb. 26, 1904.)

INTOXICATING LIQUORS — DEATH FROM INTOXICATION—ACTION AGAINST SELLER OF LIQUOR—STATUTES.

1. Burns' Rev. St. 1901, § 285, provides that, when the death of one is caused by wrongful act, the personal representative of deceased may have an action, if deceased might have maintained an action, had he lived. *Held*, that an action could not be maintained under section 285 for the death of a person, owing to his intoxication by reason of liquor sold him by defendant in violation of law, even though deceased would have had a cause of action, had he lived, but the remedy is limited to that given by section 7288, providing that every one who shall sell intoxicating liquors in violation of law shall be liable to any person who shall sustain an injury to his person or property, or in means of support, on account of the use of such liquor.

Appeal from Appellate Court, First Division.

Action by Harry S. Couchman against Cyrus A. Prather and others. From a judgment of the Appellate Court affirming a judgment in favor of defendants (68 N. E. 599) plaintiff appeals, under Burns' Rev. St. 1901, § 1337j. Affirmed.

S. R. Artman and J. C. Farber, for appellant. S. M. Ralston, Ayres, Jones & Hollett, Dupree & Slack, and Morrison & Morrison, for appellees.

GILLETT, C. J. This action was brought by appellant, under section 285, Burns' Rev. St. 1901. A demurrer was sustained to the amended complaint, and from the final judgment which followed this appeal is prosecuted.

It is charged in said amended complaint that from November 19, 1900, until June —, 1901, appellees were engaged in the business of selling intoxicating liquors at retail in the town of Thorntown, Boone county, Ind., without a license authorizing them so to do; that on May 23, 1901, and for a long time immediately prior thereto, said John S. Couchman possessed an uncontrollable appetite for intoxicating liquors, as appellees then well knew; that on said day they sold him intoxicating liquors in their said place of business, in quantities of less than a quart at a time, until he became drunk; that, while he was in a semiconscious condition as a result thereof, they then and there continued to sell and deliver to him additional intoxicating liquors, in quantities of less than a quart at a time, well knowing his condition, to be drunk by him as a beverage in said place, which liquor he then and there drank, and as a result he became so extremely intoxicated as to be unconscious of his condition and surroundings; that while intoxicated as aforesaid he attempted to drive in a buggy to his home; that while so doing he fell out of said buggy, breaking his neck and causing his death, as a result of appellees' wrongful acts as aforesaid, to the damage of certain persons, his next of kin, etc.

The threshold question in this case is as to the right of appellant to maintain this action under section 285, supra. That section is as follows: "When the death of one is caused by the wrongful act or omission of another, the personal representatives of the former may maintain an action therefor against the latter, if the former might have maintained an action, had he or she (as the case may be) lived, against the latter for an injury for the same act or omission. The action shall be commenced within two years. The damages cannot exceed ten thousand dollars; and must inure to the exclusive benefit of the widow, or widower (as the case may be), and children, if any, or next of kin, to be distributed in the same manner as personal property of the deceased." The pleading falls short of charging an assault and battery, as appellant's counsel admit, since it is not shown by averment that said Couchman did not voluntarily drink such liquors. It is therefore plain that at common law no cause of action would have existed in said Couchman for his injury, had he lived. This essential element in an action surviving to the personal representatives under the above statute, it is claimed, exists by virtue of section 7288, Burns' Rev. St. 1901. That section is in the words following: "Every person who shall sell, barter, or give away any intoxicating liquors, in violation of any of the provisions of this act, shall be personally liable, and also liable on his bond filed in the auditor's office, as required by section 4 of this act [§ 5315], to any person who shall sustain any injury or damage to his person or property or means of support on account of the use of such intoxicating liquors, so sold as aforesaid, to be enforced by appropriate action in any court of competent jurisdiction." Counsel for appellees contend that said section is to be construed in the light of the settled principles of the common law, and that, when so construed, the words "any person" are to be restrained so as not to give a person an action for his own participating wrong. This proposition need not be decided, if the administrator cannot sue, since the voluntary acts of Couchman in drinking such liquors would not be a defense in the suit of a third person.

Under the provisions of section 7288, supra, any person who has sustained "any injury or damage to his * * * means of support" on account of the use of intoxicating liquors sold in violation of the act of which the section is a part is given a complete cause of action. If an element of the right must be borrowed from said section 7288, we are at a loss to understand why the remedy should not be sought thereunder. A statute giving a remedy which did not exist at common law not only speaks affirmatively, but it also speaks negatively. In such circumstances the maxim, "Expressio unius est exclusio alterius," has a particular application. Sutherland, Stat. Const. § 325. So far as a remedy by way of damages is concerned, the rule is that when a new right is conferred by statute, and an adequate provision for its enforcement is therein made, the statutory remedy is exclusive. Storms v. Stevens, 104 Ind. 46, 3 N. E. 401; Sedgwick, Stat. & Const. Law, p. 94; Endlich, Interp. Stat. § 465; Sutherland, Stat. Const. § 399. In another section of the last-named work its author says: "Where a statute enumerates the persons or things to be affected by its provisions, there is an implied exclusion of others. There is then a natural inference that its application is not intended to be general." Section 327. "The rule is certain," said Lord Mansfield in Rex v. Robinson, 2 Burr. 799, 803, "that where a statute creates a new offense, by prohibiting and making unlawful anything which was lawful before, and appoints a specific remedy against such new offense, not antecedently unlawful, by a particular sanction and particular method of proceeding, that particular method must be pursued, and no other." In Storms v. Stevens, supra, it was said by Zollars, J., speaking for the court: "Where a statute creates a new right, and prescribes a mode of enforcing it, that mode must be pursued, to the exclusion of all other remedies. Such has been the settled law in this state for more than sixty years, and such is the law elsewhere. Lang v. Scott, 1 Blackf. 405, 12 Am. Dec. 257; Butler v. State, 6 Ind. 165; Martin v. West, 7 Ind. 657; McCormack v. Terre Haute, etc., R. Co., 9 Ind. 283; Toney v. Johnson, 26 Ind. 382; 1 Wait's Actions & Defenses, p. 42." It has often been asserted by this court that a person seeking a statutory remedy must show himself within the statute he invokes. Ezra v. Manlove, 7 Blackf. 389; Montgomery v. State ex rel. Southard, 53 Ind. 108; Weir v. State ex rel. Worl (Ind. Sup.) 68 N. E. 1023; American, etc., Co. v. Hullinger (on rehearing, at this term) 69 N. E. 460; Indianapolis, etc., Co. v. Foreman (at this term) 69 N. E. 669; Bartlett v. Crozier, 17 Johns. 439, 8 Am. Dec. 428, and cases there cited; Austin v. Goodrich, 49 N. Y. 266; Speirs v. Parker, 1 Durn. & East, 141.

It is our opinion, if the interpretation of appellant's counsel, that Couchman would have had a cause of action for the wrong done him, had he lived, be correct, that nevertheless such special statutory cause of action died with his person. Complications would arise from a holding that, in the circumstances of a case like this, suit could be maintained under section 285, supra. It would result in the action being instituted and controlled by a statutory trustee, instead of by the person injured in his means of support, in his individual capacity, as contemplated by said section 7288; and it is further to be observed that the basis of distribution is not the same under the two statutes. An examination of the authorities relative to the construction of statutes giving special rights of action for death shows that this court has always endeavored to construe such statutes in such a way as to prevent their overlapping. Ohio, etc., R. Co. v. Tindall, 13 Ind. 366, 74 Am. Dec. 259; Berry v. Louisville, etc., R. Co., 128 Ind. 484, 28 N. E. 182; Thornburg v. American Strawboard Co., 141 Ind. 443, 40 N. E. 1062, 50 Am. St. Rep. 334; Maule Coal Co. v. Partenheimer, 155 Ind. 100, 55 N. E. 751, 57 N. E. 710. We deem it clear that appellant had no standing to maintain this action.

The judgments of the Clinton circuit court and of the Appellate Court are affirmed.

(162 Ind. 316)

O'BRIEN v. HIGLEY et al.

(Supreme Court of Indiana. March 11, 1904.)

SALES—DELIVERY OF MATERIAL—TIME—CONTRACT—CONSTRUCTION—SALE BY SAMPLE—EVIDENCE—HARMLESS ERROR.

1. Where a buyer of paving bricks received them from the cars, and accepted them without objection, he could not thereafter object, in a suit for the price, that he was compelled to turn and reset a number of the bricks because of slight defects, which was the result of his own negligence and unskillful methods in laying them.

2. Refusal of the court to strike out evidence merely cumulative, if error, was harmless.

3. In an action for the price of bricks sold, the bills of lading for the cars on which the bricks were delivered were admissible in evidence.

4. Where a written contract for the sale of bricks contained a stipulation that the buyer should give a good and sufficient bond, or other security, for the payment of all sums due on account of the sale, and the buyer consented to such condition, evidence that the seller, before entering into the contract, had agreed to accept the buyer's contract with the city for the paving of a street, and his bond executed therefor, as sufficient security, was immaterial.

5. Where a street paving contractor purchased paving bricks according to samples, the buyer's paving contract with the city, and the bond accompanying it, were inadmissible in an action for the price of the brick.

6. Where loss sustained by a paving contractor in hauling and unloading defective bricks from the cars was solely due to his failure to inspect the bricks before taking them from the cars, he was not entitled to set off such loss in a suit for the price of the bricks.

7. Where a contract for the sale of paving bricks required shipments to begin "about October 20, 1900," time was not of the essence of the agreement.

8. Where a manufacturer of paving bricks agreed to begin deliveries under a sale about October 20, 1900, and the delay in failing to make the first shipment until November 1st resulted from the buyer's delay in furnishing the security called for by his contract, and by the seller's inability to procure cars, but such shipment was received without objection, and afterwards the buyer's only complaint was that the shipments were too frequent, the buyer could not object that the bricks were not delivered in time.

¶ 7. See Sales, vol. 43, Cent. Dig. § 217.

Appeal from Superior Court, Madison County; H. C. Ryan, Judge.

Action by Joseph L. Higley and others against Patrick T. O'Brien. From a judgment in favor of plaintiffs, defendant appeals. Transferred from Appellate Court under Acts 1901, p. 590, c. 259. Affirmed.

Greenlee & Call, for appellant. Ballard & Campbell, for appellees.

DOWLING, J. Action by the appellees against the appellant upon a contract in writing for the sale and delivery by the appellees of 512,000 bricks for street paving in the city of Alexandria, Ind. Answer, denial and payment. A counterclaim was filed, alleging damage to the appellant because of the failure of appellees to ship the bricks at the time fixed by the contract, because of the defective character of the bricks, and because of expense incurred by appellant in resetting and in hauling defective or worthless bricks. Reply in denial. The cause was tried by a jury, and a verdict was returned for appellees, with answers to special questions of fact. Motion for a new trial, stating some 15 separate reasons therefor. Motion overruled. Judgment for appellees. The error assigned is the overruling of the motion for a new trial.

The contract which was the foundation of the appellees' action provided (1) that the appellees should ship about 512,000 bricks, beginning about October 20, 1900; (2) that the appellees guarantied that 42 bricks would lay one square yard of pavement; (3) that the bricks delivered should correspond with the samples furnished. By the agreement the appellant promised (1) that he would receive all bricks shipped to him, and pay the freight on them; (2) that all bricks should be carefully handled; (3) that he would report promptly all car numbers that did not arrive in proper order, or that did not correspond with invoices and bills of lading; (4) that he would pay $17.50 per thousand on the 15th of each month for all bricks shipped the previous month, and that he would return all freight receipts; (5) that he would give good and sufficient bond or other security for the payment of the amount coming to the appellees on the contract. The writing itself declared that it contained the entire agreement of the parties.

1. The first, second, and third causes for a new trial go to the sufficiency of the evidence

to sustain the general verdict and the answers to certain interrogatories. There was evidence which supported the verdict and these findings of facts. In regard to the latter, while the appellant may have turned and reset a number of bricks because of slight defects, the proof showed that the appellant had received and accepted these bricks without objection, and that his trouble with them was the result of his own carelessness and his unskillful methods in laying them.

2. The fourth cause for a new trial was the refusal of the court to strike out the testimony of Mr. Barbour, who at first stated the number of bricks shipped to the appellant, but afterwards acknowledged that he derived his information chiefly from entries on the books of the appellees, and from other sources than his own personal knowledge. The error, if any, was a harmless one. There was no real controversy over the number of bricks shipped to and received by the appellant. The testimony of the appellant himself, as well as other evidence before the jury, fully proved the fact; and, if the testimony of Mr. Barbour had been stricken out, the result would have been the same. The bills of lading were closely connected with the transaction, and were properly admitted in evidence. The fact that a member of appellees' firm, previous to the making of the contract, read the agreement before that entered into by the appellant and the city of Alexandria for the improvement of one of its streets, together with the bond executed by the appellant for the fulfillment of that agreement, and stated that his firm would accept such contract and bond as sufficient security, upon appellant's contract with them, was immaterial, and the proof was properly excluded. When the latter agreement was made, a stipulation was inserted that the appellant would give good and sufficient bond or other security for the payment of all sums becoming due to the appellees on account of the sale and delivery of the bricks. The appellant consented to this condition, and signed the agreement so written. All previous negotiations and propositions were merged in and superseded by the written contract. For the same reason, the court did not err in excluding the contract with the city, and the bond accompanying it, when offered by appellant. The agreement between the appellant and the appellees required the latter to deliver bricks corresponding to certain samples furnished by them. This they were bound to do, but nothing more. The agreement contained the entire undertaking of the parties. The expense of hauling and unloading defective bricks on the street was attributable solely to the failure of the appellant to inspect them before he took them from the cars to the place where they were to be used. The ruling of the court excluding evidence of the cost of such hauling was correct.

The ninth, tenth, and eleventh causes for a new trial call in question the action of the court in permitting the appellees to prove that their failure to begin the shipment of the bricks to the appellant "about October 20, 1900," was due to his neglect to complete the execution of the contract by furnishing the required security under his contract with them until October 27, 1900, and their inability to get cars after the security was so furnished. It is objected that appellees alleged in their complaint that they had fully performed the contract, and that no pleading was filed by them which authorized proof of an excuse for nonperformance. The sufficiency of the excuse itself is also denied. To these propositions there are several good answers. Nothing in the agreement indicates that time was of the essence of the contract. No precise date for the first shipment of bricks was named, but the same was to be made "about October 20, 1900." The first shipment was received by the appellant November —, 1900, without objection; and afterwards his only complaint was that the shipments were too frequent, and the quantity of bricks sent too great for him to take care of. The delay of the appellant in furnishing the security called for by his contract with the appellees was the cause of their delay in making the first shipment. When the security was given, October 27, 1900, they were unable to procure cars, but succeeded in doing so November 1, 1900.

The twelfth, thirteenth, and fourteenth causes for a new trial were the alleged errors of the court in refusing to give instructions numbered 1, 3, and 4 tendered by appellant, and in giving instruction numbered 2 at the request of appellees. The appellees were bound to deliver bricks of the same kind and quality as the samples furnished by them. If the bricks delivered did not correspond with the samples, the appellant had the right to reject them. Before using them, it was his duty to inspect them; and he had no right to lay them in the street without inspection, and charge the appellees with the expense of removing, resetting, or hauling them away.

The jury made a considerable deduction from appellees' claim on account of bad or defective bricks and bricks not delivered, and, upon the whole record, the result reached was reasonable and just. We find no error. Judgment affirmed.

(162 Ind. 297)

SPAULDING v. STATE.

(Supreme Court of Indiana. March 10, 1904.)

HOMICIDE — EVIDENCE — SELF-DEFENSE — INSTRUCTIONS—NEW TRIAL—NEWLY DISCOVERED EVIDENCE—IMPEACHMENT—DILIGENCE —APPLICATION—AFFIDAVITS — FILING — EXCUSE.

1. Where, in a prosecution for homicide, defendant had knowledge before the trial that the question of his identity was being investigated, and that a certain witness had examined defendant and other prisoners for the purpose of selecting the person who killed deceased, a mo-

tion for a new trial for alleged newly discovered evidence that such witness designated another than defendant as the person who had struck deceased on two different occasions was properly denied.

2. Newly discovered evidence concerning the previous history, habits, and moral character of a witness who testified that defendant was the person who struck the blow which killed deceased was not ground for a new trial, where the only fact tending to excuse defendant's failure to procure such evidence at the trial was that the witness had been known at different times by different Christian names.

3. A motion for a new trial on the ground of newly discovered evidence should be accompanied by the affidavits of the witnesses by whom the new matter is expected to be proved, or an excuse for failure to file them.

4. A new trial will not be granted on the ground of newly discovered evidence which merely tends to contradict or impeach the state's witnesses.

5. In a prosecution for homicide, evidence *held* to sustain a conviction of murder in the first degree.

6. Where, in a prosecution for murder, it appeared that deceased had retreated to a wall, and was calling on defendant's sister to desist from stoning him, when defendant, who had not been present at the previous difficulty, rushed at deceased, and stabbed him once, inflicting a mortal wound, a requested instruction relating exclusively to the right of self-defense, and defendant's right to defend a relative or member of his family from unlawful attack, was properly refused.

Appeal from Criminal Court, Marion County; Fremont Alford, Judge.

Joseph Spaulding was convicted of murder, and he appeals. Affirmed.

Franklin McCray and Charles McGrorty, for appellant. John C. Ruckelshaus, C. W. Miller, Atty. Gen., W. C. Geake, C. C. Hadley, and L. G. Rothschild, for the State.

DOWLING, J. Upon a trial on an indictment for murder in the first degree, the defendant, Spaulding, was found guilty, and his punishment was assessed at imprisonment for life. A motion for a new trial was overruled, and judgment was rendered upon the verdict. The defendant appeals, and assigns for error the ruling on the motion for a new trial.

The reasons stated in the motion, and not waived by failure to discuss them, were: (1) That since the trial the defendant has discovered new evidence, material to him, which he could not with reasonable diligence have discovered and produced at the trial; (2) that the verdict is contrary to the evidence; (3) that the court erred in refusing to give an instruction tendered by defendant and numbered 1; (4) that the court erred in giving instructions numbered 8, 9, and 10.

This case is a very plain one. The sister of the defendant, in company with one Bud Wilson, met the deceased, Compotello, and a companion named Magdalena, who were Italians, on a narrow sidewalk of a street in Indianapolis, at about half past 9 o'clock at night. The parties unintentionally ran against each other. A quarrel followed, and some blows were exchanged by the men. Wilson ran off, and the Spaulding woman, who was with him, threw several stones at the Italians, one or more of which struck them. Some one shouted "Fight! fight! Lizzie Spaulding is in a fight." The defendant, who was near by in a saloon or gambling room, heard the noise, and ran toward the scene of the trouble. A crowd had gathered, composed principally of colored men, and Compotello had retreated to a brick wall, where he stood still, making no demonstration of any kind toward any one, but appealing to the woman who was throwing stones at them, saying, "Don't, lady, don't." Just at this time his companion, Magdalena, was attacked and knocked down in the street by one of the men who came out of the saloon with the defendant. Without inquiry as to the cause of the trouble, the defendant rushed at Compotello, who was close to the wall and who made no resistance, and stabbed him in the groin with a knife. The wounded man walked a short distance, bleeding profusely, and then fell upon his face in the street. He died in a few moments from the wound and consequent hemorrhage. Only one wound was found upon his body.

1. The newly discovered evidence for which a new trial was demanded was to the effect that Joseph James, one of the witnesses for the state, who testified that he was present when the homicide occurred, and that the defendant was the person who stabbed Compotello, had visited the county jail after the defendant had been placed there to await his trial, and that the witness had then designated another colored prisoner as the man who struck the deceased; that the witness came to the jail a second time, and that, at his request, four colored prisoners, including the defendant, were "lined up" before the witness, and that he again indicated that one of them, McGinness, struck the fatal blow. The affidavit alleged that these facts could be proved by Kurtz, the jailer, and by Pitts, his assistant, both of whom refused to make affidavits. It was further stated in the motion and affidavit that the witness Joseph James was a man of bad moral character; that the defendant could not discover the facts because the witness had been previously known by the name of Jesse James, and not Joseph James; and that the defendant could now impeach the moral character of the witness. No witnesses were named by whom this proof was expected to be made. The motion and the affidavit in support of it also charged that Samuel Shaffer, another witness for the prosecution, who swore on the trial that he saw the defendant strike the deceased, was a man of bad moral character and reputation.

This motion and the affidavit of the defendant in support of it were not sufficient to entitle the defendant to a new trial. The inspection of the colored prisoners by the

¶ 3. See Criminal Law, vol. 15, Cent. Dig. § 2401.

witness at the jail was enough to apprise the defendant that the subject of the identity of the person who stabbed Compotello was being investigated. It would naturally and reasonably have suggested the question upon cross-examination whether the witness had recognized the defendant at the jail as the guilty man. Again, no sufficient excuse is shown for the failure of the defendant to ascertain the facts concerning the previous history, habits, places of residence, and moral character of the witness Joseph James. Reasonable diligence always requires that such inquiries be made and pursued until some information, at least, is obtained. The fact that the witness was at one time known as Joseph James, and at another as Jesse James, did not prevent such inquiry, or constitute a serious obstacle to its prosecution. There is yet another objection to the motion and affidavit. They refer to the affidavits of Zula Barnhill and Mrs. James, the wife of the state's witness, neither of which was filed or appears in the record. As these were the only witnesses by whom the matters relied upon in this connection were expected to be proved, their affidavits should have accompanied the motion, or a legal excuse should have been shown for not filing them. Barnett v. State, 141 Ind. 149, 40 N. E. 666; Vandyne v. State, 130 Ind. 26, 29 N. E. 392; Quinn v. State, 123 Ind. 59, 23 N. E. 977; Shipman v. State, 38 Ind. 549; Gibson v. State, 9 Ind. 264. But, further, the object of the evidence said to have been discovered was to impeach and contradict the witness James by showing that he had on two occasions designated another man as the person who stabbed the deceased, and that his moral character was bad. It is well settled that a new trial will not be granted to enable the defendant to procure evidence to contradict or impeach a witness. Hire v. State, 144 Ind. 359, 43 N. E. 312; Meurer v. State, 129 Ind. 587, 29 N. E. 392; Pennsylvania Co. v. Nations, 111 Ind. 203, 12 N. E. 309; Sutherlin v. State, 108 Ind. 389, 9 N. E. 298; Hamm v. Romine, 98 Ind. 77; Morel v. State, 89 Ind. 275. Finally, the question arising upon the motion for a new trial because of newly discovered evidence was submitted to the court upon the affidavit of the defendant, and the oral testimony of Kurtz and Pitts, the jailer and his assistant, who had declined to make affidavits at the request of the defendant. The court found against the defendant. Its decision was not only not an abuse of its discretion in the matter, but was fully sustained by the evidence presented. The newly discovered evidence in regard to the witness Shaffer related wholly to the impeachment of the witness, and for that reason, as already stated, the refusal of the court to grant the new trial for this cause was not error.

2. The verdict was in strict accordance with the facts proved. Two witnesses, James and Shaffer, testified that the defendant was the man who struck or stabbed Compotello, and another, Mary Burgess, swore that after the homicide the defendant said to a sister, Hattie Spaulding, "I have cut a man over on Washington street about Lizzie. Have you got any money? I want to leave town." The situation and conduct of the Italians at the time the defendant made his attack on Compotello furnished the defendant no pretext for his savage assault. Compotello had literally "retreated to the wall." He was attempting to escape. He was being stoned by defendant's sister Lizzie Spaulding, and was begging her not to throw rocks at him. He was surrounded by colored men and women, who, if they did not actively assist or sympathize with his assailants, certainly did nothing to rescue or protect him. The defendant did not stop to ask the origin or nature of the trouble. He had his knife open, and with one terrible blow in the groin killed the Italian. There was nothing in his relationship to the woman who was throwing stones at Compotello, nor in her situation when he came upon the scene, which in any degree excused his unprovoked and unnecessary attack upon Compotello. There was simply an opportunity for violence, and he eagerly embraced it. So far as he knew or could judge, the man he assaulted was entirely innocent of any wrongdoing, and was himself the victim of an assault. There was here no provocation, real or apparent. The defendant rushed upon the Italian with an open knife in his hand, and, with a reckless disregard of the merits of the controversy in which his sister was engaged, he stabbed the man to death. The blow with the knife was not a mere chance cut, but was directed to one of the most vulnerable, exposed, and vital parts of the body. The evidence sustained the charge contained in the indictment in every particular, and authorized the jury to find, as they did, that the killing was felonious and with premeditated malice.

3. Instruction No. 1, asked for by the defendant and refused by the court, related exclusively to the right of self-defense, and the right to defend a relative, or member of one's family, from an unlawful attack. It was not applicable to any evidence in the case, and was calculated to mislead the jury. Instructions numbered 13 and 15 fully and fairly stated the law of self-defense, and the rule in regard to the right of a brother or other near relative to defend a sister or other member of his family from an unlawful injury at the hands of an assailant. The court did right in refusing to give the instructions requested. Hinshaw v. State, 147 Ind. 334, 47 N. E. 157.

We find nothing objectionable in instructions numbered 8, 9, and 10 given by the court.

The judgment was clearly right upon the evidence, and we find no error in the record. Judgment affirmed.

(182 Ind. 310)

KERR, County Auditor, v. PERRY SCHOOL TP.

(Supreme Court of Indiana. March 11, 1904.)

SCHOOLS AND SCHOOL DISTRICTS—PUPILS—TRANSFER — TUITION — STATUTES — CONSTRUCTION—PUBLIC POLICY—CONSTITUTIONAL LAW—TAXATION.

1. An objection that a statute is inequitable and unjust cannot be considered by a court, but is a matter within the exclusive jurisdiction of the Legislature.

2. Const. art. 10, § 1, requiring uniformity and equality in the rate of assessment and taxation of property within the taxing district or locality in which a particular tax is levied, applies only to assessments and taxation, and does not control the expenditure of money arising out of any assessment or taxation of property.

3. Acts 1901, p. 448, c. 204, provides for the transfer of school children from one district to another, and section 2 declares that, if such transfer is granted, the officers of the school corporation in which the child resides shall pay out of the special school fund to the corporation to which the child is transferred, as tuition, an amount equal to the annual per capita cost of education in the corporation to which such child is transferred, or such part of it as the term of enrollment of said child in the schools of the creditor corporation may require. *Held* that, where a child transferred from one district to another was enrolled for a longer period than he would have been entitled to in the district of which he was a resident, the tuition payable to the creditor district was not limited to the term of school held in the residence district, but was to be determined by the length of the term of the child's enrollment in the creditor district.

Appeal from Circuit Court, Monroe County; Jas. B. Wilson, Judge.

Action by Perry school township against Samuel M. Kerr, as auditor, etc., Monroe county. From a judgment in favor of plaintiff, defendant appeals. Reversed.

Henry A. Lee and Duncan & Batman, for appellant. Jos. E. Henley, for appellee.

JORDAN, J. Action in the lower court by Perry school township, Monroe county, Ind., to enjoin appellant, the auditor of said county, from drawing a warrant on the treasurer thereof in favor of the school city of Bloomington, to be paid out of the special school fund apportioned to said township. The money for which appellant was about to draw the warrant was for tuition due to the school city of Bloomington on account of the transfer of certain children of school age of appellee township, transferred for school purposes to the school city of Bloomington, under and in pursuance of an act of the Legislature approved March 11, 1901 (Acts 1901, p. 448, c. 204). Appellant unsuccessfully demurred to the complaint, and, on his refusal to further plead, judgment was rendered enjoining him from drawing the warrant in question, as prayed for in the complaint of appellee. The error assigned in this appeal is that the court erred in overruling the demurrer to the complaint.

¶ 2. See Taxation, vol. 45, Cent. Dig. § 88.

The first section of the above-mentioned act provides: "That if any child resident in one school corporation of the state may be better accommodated in the schools of another school corporation the parent, guardian or custodian of such child may at any time ask of the school trustee, board of school trustees or commissioners of the school corporation in which such child resides an order of transfer, which, if granted, shall entitle such child to attend the schools of the corporation to which such transfer is made, under the conditions hereinafter prescribed: provided," etc.

Section 2 of the act provides as follows: "If such transfer is granted, the school trustees, or board of school trustees, or commissioners of the school corporation in which such child resides, shall pay out of the special school fund to the school trustee, board of school trustees or commissioners of the school corporation to which such child is transferred, as tuition for such child, an amount equal to the annual per capita cost of education in the corporation to which said child is transferred; or such a part of it as the term of enrollment of said child in the schools of the creditor corporation may require; provided, that the per capita cost in high schools shall be calculated upon the basis of expenditures for high school purposes, and the per capita cost in grade schools shall be calculated upon the basis of expenditures for the schools below the high school: provided, that the rate of tuition per month shall not exceed two dollars in the high school, or one dollar and fifty cents in the grades. In calculating the per capita cost, only expenditures for the current year, not including permanent improvements and additions, shall be counted."

Section 4 (page 449) provides that the indebtedness for tuition between school corporations under the provisions of the act shall be due and payable February 1st and July 30th in each year. It is further provided in said section that: "If any school trustee or board of school trustees or commissioners refuse to pay any sums claimed by another corporation as due, the creditor corporation shall make a written statement of the case to the county auditor, who shall have power to hear and determine the matter. If he hold that a given sum is due the complaining corporation, he shall, in the next semi-annual distribution of school revenues, withhold such sum from the amount otherwise due the debtor corporation. Provided," etc.

The complaint, among other things, alleges that certain children therein named, prior to the school year 1901–02, were within school age, and residents of Perry township, and were by the proper authority transferred to the school city of Bloomington; "that on the 17th of October, 1902, there was filed, in the office of the auditor of Monroe county, a statement of the president and secretary of the board of trustees of the school city of

Bloomington of the annual per capita cost of education in the school city of Bloomington for school year 1901–1902 for the high school in said city, and also for the grades in the schools of said city, and also a statement of the money due to the school corporation July 1, 1902, on transferred children for school purposes from the corporation of Perry school township, which statement claimed a balance due from plaintiff of $235-25;" and asking that the auditor hear and determine the facts, and to withhold said amount from Perry school township in the next semiannual distribution of school revenues, and to issue a proper warrant therefor; that subsequently the matter was submitted to the auditor, who determined that amount was due, and that it would be withheld. The complaint then alleges that there were but five months of school in Perry township, and nine months in the city of Bloomington; that the transferred children in both high school and grades had the advantage of the nine months, while the untransferred had but five months; that a large majority of the children could not be better accommodated by being transferred to the city of Bloomington; that plaintiff tendered the city school trustees "the full amount claimed by said school city for a school term of five months, according to the estimate made by said school city for the cost of education per capita in said school city for said year." The complaint further alleges that the statute under which the transfer of the children was made is invalid, (1) because it is inequitable and unjust, and (2) that it is unconstitutional. Counsel for appellant insist that the pleading is manifestly insufficient, and that the demurrer thereto should have been sustained. Opposing counsel, in support of the complaint, argue that the threatened act of the county auditor to withhold $235.25 out of appellee's special school fund for the purpose of applying the same in payment of the tuition due to the creditor corporation, the school city of Bloomington, as the cost of the education of the children transferred from Perry township to the city schools, is illegal, for the reason that section 2 of the statute in question does not contemplate that the debtor school corporation shall be liable for or pay to the creditor corporation for a term of school which is in excess of the term in the debtor corporation. It is asserted that, inasmuch as it is shown by the facts alleged that the annual terms of the schools in appellee township continue only five months, while in the school city of Bloomington the terms are nine months in length, therefore the contention is that, under such circumstances, appellee is only liable to said school city for five-ninths of the per capita cost of each child transferred. As an illustration, counsel say that if the per capita cost for the annual term of the schools of said city is $18, then appellee, under a proper construction of section 2, would only be liable to pay $10—five-ninths of the total per capita cost in the city's schools. It is contended that, if the law is not open to this construction, then it must be held to be violative of section 1, art. 10, of the state's Constitution, which declares that "the General Assembly shall provide by law for a uniform and equal rate of assessment and taxation; and shall prescribe such regulations as shall secure a just valuation for taxation of all property, both real and personal," etc.

The claim made that the act in controversy, in its character or nature, is inequitable or unjust, if true, is not one which concerns the court. As to whether an act is expedient, wise, or just, is a matter to be determined by the legislative department, and its decision in that respect is not open to judicial review. State v. Gerhardt, 145 Ind. 450, 44 N. E. 469, 33 L. R. A. 313; Hedderich v. State, 101 Ind. 564, 1 N. E. 47, 51 Am. Rep. 768.

We cannot yield our sanction to the construction of section 2 for which counsel for appellee contends. In fact, it may be said that this section speaks clearly for itself, and requires no interpreting to reveal what it means. Under its provisions it certainly cannot be said that the Legislature intended that the debtor corporation should be liable for or pay any amount less than that prescribed by the plain letter of the law. The evident meaning of the clause in section 2 which reads, "or such a part of it as the term of enrollment of said child in the schools of the creditor corporation may require," is that, if the child transferred is enrolled for only six months in the schools of the creditor corporation, and the term of such schools is nine months, then the debtor corporation is required to pay the per capita cost for six months only. Or, in other words, it would be required to pay for what it received, and no more. Under such circumstances it cannot be said that in this respect the law is inequitable or unjust. The contention that if the statute means what it declares, then it is violative of section 1, art. 10, of the Constitution, is wholly untenable. This provision of our fundamental law clearly applies to assessments and taxation, and does not profess to control the expenditure of money arising out of any assessment or taxation of property. It deals with the uniformity and equal rate of assessment and taxation of property within the taxing district or locality in which the particular tax is levied. Bright v. McCullough, 27 Ind. 223; Loftin v. Citizens' Nat. Bk., 85 Ind. 341; Board, etc., v. State, 147 Ind. 476, 492, 46 N. E. 908, and cases cited; Kent v. Town of Kentland, 62 Ind. 291, 30 Am. Rep. 182; Robinson v. Schenck, 102 Ind. 307, 1 N. E. 698.

Appellee insists that taxes are not equal and uniform when all persons within the district or locality do not share equally in the benefits derived therefrom. But benefits derived from taxes levied, and the uniformity of assessment and taxation within the particular district or locality, are entirely different questions. As the act in question is neither invalid on the grounds assigned by appellee, nor open to the construction or interpretation for which its counsel contend, therefore it certainly has no foundation whatever upon which to base a right for an injunction against appellee to prevent him from drawing the warrant or withholding the money in dispute.

The court erred in overruling the demurrer to the complaint, for which error the judgment is reversed, and the cause remanded with instructions to sustain the demurrer.

(162 Ind. 258)

LENGELSON et al. v. McGREGOR et al.

(Supreme Court of Indiana. March 8, 1904.)

BILL OF EXCEPTIONS—SIGNING—TIME—ABSENCE OF JUDGE—NUNC PRO TUNC ORDER—DILIGENCE.

1. Where a bill of exceptions was not signed until after the term, nor within the time fixed by the court, it could not be considered on appeal, though appellant's failure to procure the signing thereof within the time resulted from the trial judge's absence from the state.

2. Where, during the time fixed by the trial judge for the preparation and service of a bill of exceptions, he left the state, thereby preventing appellant from procuring a settlement of his bill within the time limited, and appellant was diligent in the preparation of his bill, he was entitled to have the same signed nunc pro tunc.

3. After the trial of a case the court granted 60 days within which to prepare bills of exceptions, and on the fifty-ninth day appellant had prepared for signing two bills, one occupying 2 written pages of the record, and another embracing 60 typewritten pages. The judge being absent from the state at such time, appellant was unable to procure his signature to the bills within the time fixed, though there were 36 days after the end of the trial in which to prepare the bills before the judge left home. *Held*, that a finding that appellant had not exercised due diligence in presenting his bill, and was, therefore, not entitled to an order signing the same nunc pro tunc after the judge's return after the expiration of the time limited, was proper.

On rehearing. Petition overruled.

For former opinion, see 67 N. E. 524.

HADLEY, J. Appellant, in support of hi petition for a rehearing, very earnestly con tends that we erred in holding that his bil of exceptions containing the evidence was not properly in the record. He relies upon the maxim, "Actus curiæ neminem gravabit," to protect him against the loss of his bill of exceptions by reason of the absence of the trial judge from the state, when he, within the time allowed, did all he could to present the bill for settlement. The pith of his argument is that a court will not be permitted to throw a litigant off his guard by granting him a time beyond the term to prepare a bill of exceptions, and then defeat the privilege by absenting himself from the state until the time has expired. We have no disposition to deny the justness and reasonableness of the maxim invoked, to wit, "An act of the court shall prejudice no one," and will unhesitatingly give the principle force and effect in a case where it applies and we have authority to do so. It is doubtless the law that a litigant who has been awarded time for a bill of exceptions, and who has successfully completed his bill within the time, and who has been diligent in its preparation and presentation, should be afforded an opportunity to present it, and should not be deprived of the bill by the absence of the trial judge from the state. State v. Dyer, 99 Ind. 426; Fechheimer v. Trounstiene, 12 Colo. 282, 20 Pac. 704; Stonesifer v. Kilburn, 94 Cal. 33, 29 Pac. 332. But what we decided in the original opinion, and what we reaffirm here, is that the signing of exceptions under and at a date subsequent to the time allowed for the signing and filing of the same imparts no validity to the instrument as a bill of exceptions. The statute, though remedial in character, is mandatory, and prescribes the precise terms upon which exceptions may, after the term, be authenticated and incorporated into the record. And it is plain that we have no authority to treat any document or instrument of writing as a bill of exceptions unless upon its own face it shows affirmatively that the terms of the statute have been complied with, and, among other things, that it was presented to, or was settled and signed by, the trial judge within the time granted by the court. The doctrine rests upon the principle that, the statute being the only authority for a bill of exceptions after adjournment of the court, it can only be had upon the terms of the statute, and a bill signed by the presiding judge after the expiration of the time lawfully fixed is without authority or jurisdiction, and amounts to nothing more than if signed by the clerk. Rigler v. Rigler, 120 Ind. 431, 22 N. E. 776; Rubber Co. v. Midland, 63 Ohio St. 66, 57 N. E. 958; Neuman v. Becker, 54 Ohio St. 323, 46 N. E. 706; Walker v. Mortgage Company, 100 Ga. 84, 26 S. E. 75; 3 Cyc. p. 38; Daugherty v. Western Union Tel. Co. (C. C.) 61 Fed. 138. After expiration of the time allowed, the judge loses jurisdiction over the subject-matter, and cannot be reclothed with it by agreement of the parties. Long v. Newhouse, 57 Ohio St. 348, 366, 49 N. E. 79; Morris v. Watson, 61 Ill. App. 536. A failure of the stenographer to prepare the longhand manuscript of the evidence, though the party excepting has been diligent, is ineffectual as an excuse for signing or filing of a bill after time. Horbach v. Omaha, 49 Neb. 851, 69 N. W. 121. Pressure of official business upon the trial judge furnishes no reason or authority for him to sign a bill after the time has expired. Walker v. Mortgage Company, 100 Ga. 84, 26 S. E. 75. To take cog-

---

¶ 1. See Exceptions, Bill of, vol. 21, Cent. Dig. §§ 721, 73.

nizance of a bill of exceptions that shows upon its face to have been created in disobedience of the statute would be to hold that we have discretionary power to dispense with the law whenever we deem it proper to do so. In such cases, therefore, the only way for an aggrieved party to get his exceptions into the record is to procure the insertion of the proper date of presentation nunc pro tunc, and thus send up on appeal a bill fair upon its face. Rigler v. Rigler, supra; Kirby v. Bowland, 69 Ind. 290; Walton v. U. S., 9 Wheat. 651, 6 L. Ed. 182; Ferris v. Nat. Bank, 158 Ill. 237, 239, 41 N. E. 1118; Railroad Co. v. Morrison, Adams & Allen Co., 160 Ill. 288, 43 N. E. 393; Ewbank's Man. § 31. And if a party is able to show that he has been diligent in the preparation and presentation of his bill, and in good faith and in due season had his prepared bill at the court, office, residence, or other place within the judicial circuit where the judge might reasonably be expected to be, and was prevented from presenting the same by the absence of the judge from the state or judicial circuit, the act is such a presentation of the bill, if promptly presented to the court upon his return, as will authorize the latter, upon notice and motion, to insert nunc pro tunc the date when the presentation was defeated by his absence. Davis v. Patrick, 122 U. S. 143, 7 Sup. Ct. 1102, 30 L. Ed. 1090. The right, however, rests upon diligence, and upon the fact that the exceptor has done all he reasonably could do to secure the prompt approval of his exceptions. And whether he has been diligent or not must be determined by the sound judgment of the presiding judge upon the facts of the particular case. Here appellant was allowed 60 days from March 15th in which to prepare and file his bills of exceptions. He had them ready for presentation to the judge on the 59th day. In Daugherty v. Western Union, etc., Co. (C. C.) 61 Fed. 138, the answer in an application for removal was due February 13th. On that day the defendant's attorney, residing in an adjoining county, left home for the place where the court was held, by a passenger train which was due to arrive at 10 o'clock a. m., and which was only prevented by a very unusual snowstorm, with respect to which, Baker, J., said: "The failure to start for the place where the court was sitting until the day when the answer was due was such an act of negligence as to defeat the right of removal, without regard to the delay occasioned by the storm."

Bill of exception No. 1, based on a motion to modify the judgment, occupies 2 written pages of the record, and No. 2, containing the longhand manuscript of the evidence, embraces 60 typewritten pages. Because 60 days were granted did not excuse appellant from promptly and diligently proceeding with the preparation and presentation of his bills with as much dispatch as circumstances would reasonably allow. He could not be held blameless if he negligently postponed their preparation or presentation to the very end of the period. It is not shown that it would require anything like 60 days for appellant's attorney to prepare bill No. 1, or for the stenographer to write out the evidence. There were 36 days in which to accomplish the work before the judge left home. The judge was a special judge, resided in another county, and had no official or other known reason to keep him at home or in the circuit. There was no correspondence with the judge to ascertain whether he would remain at home to the end of the 60 days. Appellant might have had timely notice of the judge's intended absence from the state, and might have had ample time and opportunity to prepare and present his bills before the judge went away. These and other matters involving the question of diligence were properly cognizable by the court in determining whether appellant presented a case warranting the signing of his bills now for then. The court, from the known facts and the evidence before it, decided that appellant was not entitled to have his bills signed nunc pro tunc, and refused to so sign them. The conclusion thus reached in the nunc pro tunc proceeding was a judicial judgment upon the evidence before the court, and is impeachable on appeal only as ordinary judgments of the court.

The record shows that what purports to be bills of exceptions were signed by the judge 20 days after the expiration of the time granted therefor, to wit, June 4th, and when he had no jurisdiction of the subject-matter, and no power to impart validity to the documents as bills of exceptions. They must, therefore, be regarded as nullities, and as serving no purpose in the record.

The petition for a rehearing is overruled.

(162 Ind. 599)

VORIES v. PITTSBURG PLATE GLASS CO.[1]

(Supreme Court of Indiana. March 10, 1904.)

MUNICIPAL CORPORATIONS—STREET IMPROVEMENTS — SPECIAL ASSESSMENTS — NOTICE—HEARING—IRREGULARITIES — WAIVER — VALIDITY — ABUTTING OWNERS — BACK-LYING LANDS—STATUTES—CONSTRUCTION.

1. Burns' Rev. St. 1894, § 4290, provides that the owners of lots bordering on a street shall be liable for cost of improvement according to frontage, and in making the assessment such lots and unplatted lands shall be assessed on the ground fronting on such improvement back to the distance of 150 feet from such front line, and the city and the contractor shall have a lien thereon for the value of such improvement, provided that, where such land is subdivided or platted, the land lying immediately on the line of the improvement and extending back 50 feet shall be primarily liable, and, should that prove insufficient, then the second parcel, and other parcels in their order to the rear parcel of said 150 feet, shall be liable in their order, and such assessment shall be a lien on the property so assessed. Section 4293 requires the city engineer to make a final report of cost, giving the names of owners on the part of the street improved, and the number of front feet

[1] Rehearing denied.

owned. Section 4294 requires two weeks' publication of notice for hearing on the report, when any person aggrieved shall have the right to appear. *Held*, that an assessment on the abutting lots, founded on a report not giving the names of owners of back-lying lands within 150 feet, created a valid lien on such back-lying land, which was enforceable after sale of the abutting lots for a sum insufficient to pay the costs of improvement.

2. The owner of such back-lying land is entitled to appear and be heard on the question of special benefits, and the law is not unconstitutional as failing to provide for a hearing.

3. In Burns' Rev. St. 1894, § 4290, providing for assessments for improvements and that in making the assessments "against such owners for the improvement of such lots and parts of lots" shall be assessed, the word "of," between the words "improvement" and "such," being incapable of any sensible meaning, and the paragraph being complete without it, is to be rejected.

4. Section 4294 further provides that, if an assessment exceeds $50, the owner against whom it is made may secure a right to pay in installments by signing a waiver of illegalities. *Held*, that the signing of such waivers by abutting owners did not release the back-lying owners from the lien of the assessment.

Hadley, J., dissenting.

Appeal from Superior Court, Howard County; W. W. Mount, Special Judge.

Proceedings by William H. Voris against the Pittsburg Plate Glass Company to enforce the lien of an assessment for street improvements. From a judgment sustaining a demurrer to the complaint, plaintiff appeals. Reversed.

C. B. Masslich, C. M. Clay Buntain, and Willits & Voorhis, for appellant. Bell & Purdum, Blacklidge, Shirley & Wolf, B. C. Moon, and Charlton Bull, for appellee.

MONKS, J. Appellant brought this suit against the Pittsburg Plate Glass Company, the owner of back-lying real estate within 150 feet of a street in the city of Kokomo, improved in 1893, under the Barrett law, to enforce the lien of an assessment for said street improvement, on the ground that the subdivision primarily liable therefor had, at a judicial sale on a decree foreclosing said lien, proved insufficient to pay said assessment. A demurrer for want of facts was sustained to said complaint, and, appellant refusing to plead further, judgment was rendered against him. It appears from the complaint, among other things, that Joseph S. Amos was the owner of lots 20 and 21, lying immediately upon and adjacent to the line of said street improvement, neither of which extended back 150 feet from the front line thereof; that appellee plate glass company owned all the real estate lying back of each of said lots within said 150 feet. The city engineer, as required by section 4293, Burns' Rev. St. 1894, being section 6, Acts 1889, pp. 242, 243, described in his report said lots 20 and 21, and gave the name of Jacob S. Amos as the owner thereof. In said report the amount of the cost of the improvement due upon said lot 20 was $200.60, and upon said lot 21 was $212.50, which amounts were ascertained by the frontage of said lots, as provided in the fifth clause of said section 4293 (6), supra, but said back-lying real estate of appellee, Pittsburg Plate Glass Company, was not described in said report. After giving the notice required by section 4294, Burns' Rev. St. 1894, being section 7 of the act of 1889, as amended by the act of 1891 (Acts 1891, pp. 324–326), "no objection being made to said engineer's report, the common council of said city adopted the same and the assessments without alteration or amendment." The owners of the lots described in said report of the engineer signed and filed a written promise to pay said assessments as provided in said section 4294 (7), supra, and the city issued and sold street improvement bonds to pay for the improvement of said street, under section 4296, Burns' Rev. St. 1894, being section 8, Acts 1889, p. 244. Appellant is the owner of all the bonds, and the interest coupons attached thereto, so issued by said city of Kokomo, and the same, to the amount of several thousand dollars, are due and unpaid. In a suit in the court below, brought by appellant for that purpose, he recovered a personal judgment against said Amos on said written promise, and a decree foreclosing said assessment lien against said lots 20 and 21. Said lots were duly sold upon said decree, and the proceeds of said sale were not sufficient to pay the same. Said Amos was insolvent, and since the rendition of said judgment has been adjudged a bankrupt in the District Court of the United States for the District of Indiana. Under section 4296, Burns' Rev. St. 1894 (section 8, Acts 1889, p. 244), appellant, as the owner of bonds, has all the rights and interest of said city of Kokomo in and to the assessments and liens for the improvement of said street, with full power to enforce the collection thereof by foreclosure.

It is provided in section 4290, Burns' Rev. St. 1894, being section 3, Acts 1889, pp. 240, 241, that "the owners of lots or parts of lots bordering on such street or alley, or the part thereof to be improved, * * * shall be liable to the city for their proportion of the costs in the ratio of the front line of the lots owned by them to the whole improved line for street and alley improvements, * * * and the city or incorporated town shall have a lien upon such lots or parts of lots respectively from the time such improvement is ordered for such costs of improvement, * * *; and in making the assessment against such owners for the improvement of such lots or parts of lots and unplatted lands shall be assessed upon the ground fronting or immediately abutting on such improvement back to the distance of one hundred and fifty feet from such front line, and the city or incorporated town and the contractor shall have a lien thereon for the value of such improvement, provided however, that where such land is subdivided or platted, the land lying immediately upon and adjacent to the line of the improvement and extending back fifty feet, shall be primarily liable to and for the whole costs of the improvement, and should that prove insufficient to pay such costs, then the second parcel and other parcels in their order to the rear parcel of said one hundred and fifty feet shall be liable in their order." The word "of," between the words "improvement" and "such," in the part of said section 4290 (3) above set out, is incapable of any sensible meaning, and the clause in which it appears is complete and sensible without it. It is evident that said word was inserted through inadvertence or mistake, and should be rejected. Black on Interpretation of Laws, pp. 83, 84; Southerland on Construction of Statutes, § 260, p. 342; Endlich on Interpretation of Statutes, §§ 301, 302, pp. 409-412.

Construing the above-quoted provisions of said section 4290 (3), supra, in connection with sections 4293, 4294, Burns' Rev. St. 1894, it is evident that the common council of the city, or the board of trustees of the town, assess the special benefits of the improvement to each lot or parcel of ground abutting thereon to such lot or parcel of ground, regardless of whether the same extends back 150 feet or less from the front line thereof. Adams v. City of Shelbyville, 154 Ind. 467, 490, 491, 57 N. E. 114, 49 L. R. A. 797, 77 Am. St. Rep. 484. The city or town engineer in his report under section 6 of said act of 1889, being section 4293, Burns' Rev. St. 1894, only gives the description of the lots and parcels of ground bordering on the street or alley improved, and the names of the owners thereof, and the amount of the cost for the improvement due from such lots or parcels of ground determined by the frontage, regardless of whether the same extend back 150 feet or less from the front line thereof. City of Terre Haute v. Mack, 139 Ind. 99, 105-110, 38 N. E. 468. When, therefore, the common council of the city or board of trustees of the town have made the assessments to each of said abutting lots or parcels of ground so as to conform to the special benefits accruing to each of said abutting lots or parcels of ground, as provided in section 4294, Burns' Rev. St. 1894, whether by adopting said report of the engineer as made, or after altering or amending the same, such assessments, by the express provision of section 4290 (3), supra, are a lien, not only on the lots or parcels of ground bordering on said street or alley, but on the back-lying lots or parcels of ground, if any, within 150 feet of the front line thereof. While the subdivision or parcel of ground "lying immediately upon and adjacent to the line of improvement" must be first exhausted before the second parcel, and the others in their order, can be sold to pay the assessment, the same is a lien, not only on said first subdivision or parcel, but on all the subdivisions or parcels lying back thereof within said 150 feet from the front line, to the extent provided in section 4290 (3), supra, although owned by different persons, and who were not named in the report of the engineer or in the assessment made by the common council of the city or board of trustees of the town. Town of Woodruff Place v. Raschig, 147 Ind. 517, 523, 524, 46 N. E. 990.

The notice by publication required by section 4294 (7), supra, when made, gives the common council of the city or board of trustees of the town full and complete jurisdiction over the person of each person owning land within the taxing district of said improvement, whether the same abuts on the improvement or not. Said notice having been given, said owners of back-lying real estate, like the owners of real estate abutting on said improvement, are bound to know the law, and that their real estate is in the taxing district of said improvement, and will be subject to the lien of special benefits assessed in the manner and to the extent above stated. Hyland v. The Brazil, etc., Co., 128 Ind. 335, 340, 341, 26 N. E. 672. All of said owners of real estate within said taxing district, whether back-lying or abutting, have the right to appear before the committee or common council of the city or board of trustees of the town and be heard on the engineer's report, and object thereto, and have a hearing on the question of special benefits, which the law requires said common council or board of trustees to adjust so as to conform to the special benefits accruing to said abutting real estate. Adams v. City of Shelbyville, 154 Ind. 467, 484-491, 57 N. E. 114, 49 L. R. A. 797, 77 Am. St. Rep. 484; Leeds v. Defrees, 157 Ind. 392, 397, 61 N. E. 930; Hibben v. Smith, 158 Ind. 206, 208-211, 62 N. E. 447. It is true that only the special benefits to the abutting lots or parcels of ground are assessed by the common council of the city or board of trustees of the town; but, if any such lot or parcel of ground does not extend back 150 feet from the front line thereof, the owner of the real estate lying back thereof, and within said 150 feet, has such an interest in the assessment to such abutting lot or parcel of ground as entitles him to a hearing on the question of actual special benefits thereto, because his real estate is subject to the lien of said assessment, when made, to the extent provided in section 4290 (3), supra, and is liable to be sold to pay the same in the order prescribed in said section. It follows that, when the common council assessed the special benefits of said improvement to lot 20 at $200.50 and to lot 21 at $212.60, the same was not only an assessment against said lots, but, ex proprio vigore, was a valid assessment and lien against all the real estate lying back of each of said lots respectively, and within 150 feet of the front line thereof, to the extent provided in the proviso of section 4290 (3), supra, and was binding alike on the owner of said lots 20 and 21 and said Pittsburg Plate Glass Company, appellee, the owner of the back-lying real estate.

It is insisted that this construction of the Barrett law renders the same unconstitutional as to the back-lying real estate, on the ground that each owner of real estate, whether the same is abutting or back-lying, is entitled to a hearing on the question of the special benefits to his parcel of land; citing Adams v. City of Shelbyville, 154 Ind. 467, 57 N. E. 114, 49 L. R. A. 797, 77 Am. St. Rep. 484; Martin v. Wills, 157 Ind. 153, 60 N. E. 1021; Leeds v. Defrees, 157 Ind. 392, 61 N. E. 930; Wray v. Fry, 158 Ind. 92, 62 N. E. 1004. The only question before the court in the cases cited was the proper construction of the Barrett law, and this court held in those cases that said law provided that the real estate within the taxing district, prima facie, received special benefits from the improvement according to frontage, but that the common council of the city or board of trustees of the town had the power to alter or change the same so as to conform to the special benefits received, and that all persons aggrieved had the right to a hearing before such questions were determined. It was held that the law so construed was not obnoxious to any provision of the state or federal Constitution. It was not necessary, therefore, in said cases, to determine as to the constitutionality of a law which declared that the total cost of an improvement should be assessed equally against the frontage according to what is known as the "front-foot rule," without allowing or providing for a hearing as to special benefits to the real estate charged therewith, for no such law was before the court. None of said cases cited by appellee gives any support to its contention. What was said in Adams v. City of Shelbyville, 154 Ind. 467, 57 N. E. 114, 49 L. R. A. 797, 77 Am. St. Rep. 484, concerning a law which makes no provision for a hearing on the question of special benefits, and that such a law would be in violation of the fourteenth amendment to the Constitution of the United States, under the case of Norwood v. Baker, 172 U. S. 269, 19 Sup. Ct. 187, 43 L. Ed. 443, was clearly obiter dicta, for the reason, as we have shown, that no such question was before the court for decision. Adams v. City of Shelbyville, supra, did not overrule any of the following cases decided by this court: Ray v. City of Jeffersonville, 90 Ind. 567; City of Indianapolis v. Imberry, 17 Ind. 175; Flournoy v. City of Jeffersonville, 17 Ind. 169, 79 Am. Dec. 468; Palmer v. Stumph, 29 Ind. 329; City of New Albany v. Cook, 29 Ind. 220; Snyder v. Town of Rockport, 6 Ind. 237; Ross v. Stackhouse, 114 Ind. 200, 16 N. E. 501; Garvin v. Daussman, 114 Ind. 429, 16 N. E. 826, 5 Am. St. Rep. 637; Johnson v. Lewis, 115 Ind. 490, 18 N. E. 7; Weaver v. Templin, 113 Ind. 298, 14 N. E. 600; Goodrich v. Winchester, etc., Co., 26 Ind. 119; Law v. The Madison, etc., Co., 30 Ind. 77; Gilson v. Board, etc., 128 Ind. 65, 27 N. E. 235, 11 L. R. A. 835; Board, etc., v. Harrell, 147 Ind. 500, 504–507, 46 N. E. 124.

In Webster v. City of Fargo, 181 U. S. 394, 21 Sup. Ct. 623, 645, 45 L. Ed. 912; French v. Barber, etc., Co., 181 U. S. 324, 21 Sup. Ct. 625, 45 L. Ed. 879; City of Detroit v. Parker, 181 U. S. 399, 21 Sup. Ct. 624, 645, 45 L. Ed. 917; Cass Farm Co. v. City of Detroit, 181 U. S. 396, 21 Sup. Ct. 644, 645, 45 L. Ed. 914; Shumate v. Heman, 181 U. S. 402, 21 Sup. Ct. 645, 45 L. Ed. 922; Farrell v. West Chicago Park Com'rs, 181 U. S. 404, 21 Sup. Ct. 609, 645, 45 L. Ed. 916, 924; Town of Tonawanda v. Lyon, 181 U. S. 389, 21 Sup. Ct. 609, 45 L. Ed. 908 (cited in Martin v. Wills, 157 Ind. 153, 155, 60 N. E. 1021)—the Supreme Court of the United States held "that it is within the power of the Legislature of the state to create special taxing districts and to charge the cost of local improvements, in whole or in part, upon the property in said district, either according to valuation, superficial area, or frontage, and that it was not the intention of said court to hold otherwise in Norwood v. Baker, 172 U. S. 269 [19 Sup. Ct. 187, 43 L. Ed. 443]," and that a state law apportioning the entire cost of a street or alley improvement upon the abutting lots according to their frontage, without any hearing as to the benefits, was not in violation of the fourteenth amendment to the Constitution of the United States; that the Legislature, in enacting such laws, exercises, not the right of eminent domain, but that of taxation (2 Cooley on Taxation, [3d Ed.] pp. 1181–1183), and may, in the exercise of its discretion, direct the cost of the improvement to be charged to the land within the taxing district "in proportion to the position, the frontage, the area, or the market value of the lands, or in proportion to the benefits as estimated by" some body or person designated. See, also, Elliott on Roads and Streets (2d Ed.) §§ 558, 559, 560, 564, and cases cited; 2 Dillon on Munic. Corp. (4th Ed.) § 752; 2 Cooley on Taxation (3d Ed.) pp. 1180–1183, 1202–1206, 1217, 1222, 1226, 1227; Cass Farm Co. v. City of Detroit, 124 Mich. 433, 83 N. W. 108, and cases cited; Farrell v. The West, etc., Com'rs, 182 Ill. 250, 55 N. E. 325; Farrar v. St. Louis, 80 Mo. 379; Barber, etc., Co. v. French, 158 Mo. 534, 58 S. W. 934, 54 L. R. A. 492, and cases cited; Webster v. City of Fargo, 9 N. D. 208, 82 N. W. 732, 56 L. R. A. 156, and cases cited; Williams v. Eggleston, 170 U. S. 304, 311, 18 Sup. Ct. 617, 42 L. Ed. 1047; Parsons v. District of Columbia, 170 U. S. 45, 18 Sup. Ct. 521, 42 L. Ed. 943; Bauman v. Ross, 167 U. S. 548, 17 Sup. Ct. 966, 42 L. Ed. 270; Davidson v. City of New Orleans, 96 U. S. 97, 104, 24 L. Ed. 616; County of Mobile v. Kimball, 102 U. S. 691, 26 L. Ed. 238; Hagar v. Reclamation District, 111 U. S. 701, 4 Sup. Ct. 663, 28 L. Ed. 569; Wurts v. Hoagland, 114 U. S. 606, 5 Sup. Ct. 1086, 29 L. Ed. 229; Walston v. Nevin, 128 U. S. 578, 9 Sup. Ct. 192, 32 L. Ed. 544; Spencer v.

Merchant, 125 U. S. 345, 8 Sup. Ct. 921, 31 L. Ed. 763.

It is insisted by appellee that the bondholder succeeds only to the lien against the property owned by those who signed the waiver and promise to pay the assessment, and that, as the plate glass company did not sign such writing, appellant, the bondholder, has no lien on the back-lying real estate owned by it. Even if no bonds should have been issued by the common council of said city to procure the money to pay part of the costs of said improvement charged against said lots 20 and 21, and the real estate owned by the plate glass company, unless said company signed said waiver and promise—a question we need not and do not decide—still the execution of said writing by the owner of said lots 20 and 21 did not release the back-lying real estate of the plate glass company from the lien of said assessment. The bonds having been issued, and the money paid therefor by the bondholder used to pay the contractor, the bondholder is subrogated to the rights of the city and contractor to enforce the lien of said assessment against said lots 20 and 21, and the real estate lying back thereof, to reimburse him for the money so used. Appellant was not a mere volunteer, but, upon principles of equity and justice, is entitled to enforce the lien of said assessments. Davis v. Schlemmer, 150 Ind. 472, 478, 50 N. E. 373, and cases cited; Fowler v. Maus, 141 Ind. 47, 52, 54, 40 N. E. 56, and cases cited; Reed v. Kalfsbeck, 147 Ind. 148, 154, 155, 45 N. E. 476, 46 N. E. 466, and cases cited; Milburn v. Phillips, 143 Ind. 93, 42 N. E. 461, 52 Am. St. Rep. 403; Baker v. Edwards, 156 Ind. 53, 58, 59 N. E. 174, and cases cited; Watkins v. Winings, 102 Ind. 330, 331, 1 N. E. 638, Bodkin v. Merit, 102 Ind. 293, 296, 1 N. E. 625.

It follows that the court erred in sustaining the demurrer to the complaint. Judgment reversed, with instructions to overrule the demurrer to the complaint, and for further proceedings not inconsistent with this opinion.

HADLEY, J., dissents.

(162 Ind. 270)

SMITH v. SPARKS et al.

(Supreme Court of Indiana. March 8, 1904.)

PARTITION—MORTGAGES—FORECLOSURE—DECREES—PARTIES—COLLATERAL ATTACK—ORDER OF SALE—NONCOMPLIANCE—EFFECT.

1. Where a decree partitioning certain lands, and foreclosing a mortgage on the entire tract, directed the sheriff to first sell the two-thirds of the tract set off to S., and that, if such tract should be insufficient to satisfy the mortgage indebtedness, costs, and charges, then to sell the tract partitioned to the wife of the mortgagee, a sale of the entire tract in solido, after he had offered the rents and profits of the tracts, and then the tracts separately, and received no bids therefor, was unauthorized and void.

2. Where the one-third interest of the mortgagor's wife in mortgaged land had been severed and vested in her, as authorized by Act March 11, 1875 (Acts 1875, p. 178, c. 123), on a sale of the land in satisfaction of a judgment against the husband, it was proper for the court, in a suit for partition and to foreclose the mortgage on the entire tract, to decree that the two-thirds interest vested in the husband's creditor should be first exhausted, before resort should be had to the part set off to the wife.

3. Where a husband's interest in mortgaged land which had been vested in his creditor under an execution sale was ordered to be first sold, before resort should be had to the interest of his wife, set off to her under a partition decree, the sheriff's act in selling the entire property in solido was prejudicial to her, since she was thereby precluded from redeeming her interest alone, as authorized by Burns' Rev. St. 1901, § 780.

4. Where the interest of the wife of a mortgagor of certain lands had been severed as authorized by Act March 11, 1875 (Acts 1875, p. 178, c. 123), under a sale of the tract in satisfaction of a judgment against her husband, and a mortgagee of the entire tract was made a party to a suit by her for partition, wherein a decree was rendered partitioning the property and foreclosing the mortgage, such decree was not subject to collateral attack by the mortgagee or the purchaser at the sale in so far as it provided the order in which the property should be sold.

Appeal from Circuit Court, Wells County; Jno. M. Smith, Special Judge.

Action by Lovina Sparks and husband against William S. Smith. From a judgment in favor of complainants, defendant appeals. Transferred from Appellate Court, under Burns' Rev. St. 1901, § 1337u. Affirmed.

C. E. Sturgis and J. M. Berryhill, for appellant. J. K. Rinehart, for appellees.

JORDAN, J. Appellee, together with her husband, instituted this action to set aside a sheriff's sale to appellant of 80 acres of land situated in Wells county, Ind. Under the issues joined, a trial by the court resulted in a finding in her favor, and, over appellant's motion for a new trial, assigning the statutory grounds therefor, judgment was rendered setting aside and annulling the sale in question. The errors relied on for a reversal are (1) overruling a demurrer to the complaint; (2) denying a motion for a new trial. The complaint alleges and the evidence established the following facts: Appellees, Lovina and Phineas M. Sparks, were husband and wife at the commencement of this action, and such relation existed at and prior to the 13th day of February, 1897. Phineas M. Sparks, her husband, was the owner in fee simple of the land in controversy, and on that date he became indebted to the Connecticut Mutual Life Insurance Company to the amount of $600 for money borrowed by him of that company. To secure the payment thereof, he and his said wife executed a mortgage to the company on the said 80 acres of land. After executing this mortgage, but prior to the 2d day of May, 1899, a judgment was rendered in the Wells circuit court in favor of Elisha J. Felts against the said Phineas M. Sparks and another on a promissory note executed by them for the sum of $352.32,

After the rendition of this judgment, it appears that the judgment creditor, Elisha J. Felts, died testate, and William S. Smith, under his will, became the executor thereof. On May 2, 1899, as such executor, by virtue of a purchase at sheriff's sale, and a conveyance thereunder in satisfaction of said judgment, he became the owner in fee simple of an undivided two-thirds of said tract of land, and Lovina Sparks, as the wife of Phineas M. Sparks, became the owner in fee simple of the remainder by virtue of the statute of March 11, 1875 (Acts 1875, p. 178, c. 123; section 2669, Burns' Rev. St. 1901). She and said Smith, as the executor aforesaid, on said date held said land undivided as tenants in common, subject to the mortgage lien of the insurance company. On said 2d day of May, 1899, she filed a petition in the Wells circuit court praying for partition of the land in question. Smith, as the executor of Felts' will, and as the owner of the undivided two-thirds of said realty, and the mortgagee, the Connecticut Mutual Life Insurance Company, were made parties defendants to said action in partition, and each was duly notified of the pendency thereof. The insurance company appeared and filed its separate answer, and also filed a cross-complaint by which it sought to foreclose its mortgage upon the premises in question. To its cross-complaint it made the plaintiff and her said husband, together with William S. Smith in his individual and also in his trust capacity, and the widow and other devisees and heirs of the said Elisha J. Felts, defendants thereto, all of whom were duly summoned to answer the said cross-complaint. The proceedings for partition and to foreclose the mortgage under the cross-complaint were treated as one action and tried together; and the court, upon the trial of the isuses, found that the plaintiff Lovina Sparks was the owner in fee simple of the undivided one-third of said real estate, and Smith, as the executor aforesaid, was the owner of the remainder, and partition thereof was accordingly awarded, and commissioners were appointed and directed to make partition. The court further found in favor of the insurance company on its cross-complaint, to the effect that its mortgage was the first and best lien on the land, and that there was due and unpaid to it upon the mortgage indebtedness the sum of $674.08. A personal judgment was rendered against said Phineas M. Sparks upon the mortgage note for that amount, together with costs. The court ordered and decreed that the mortgage be foreclosed, and expressly decreed that the two-thirds of the mortgaged premises, as partitioned and set off to William S. Smith, executor of Felts' will, should be first sold by the sheriff of Wells county in payment and satisfaction of the mortgage indebtedness, interest, charges, and costs. It was further ordered and decreed that if the said two-thirds of the realty partitioned to Smith as executor should sell for a sum sufficient to pay and satisfy in full the mortgage indebtedness, together with all costs and charges thereon, then and in that event the one-third of the mortgaged premises partitioned and set off to Mrs. Sparks should be held by her free and discharged of the mortgage lien; but, in the event that said two-thirds did not sell for a sum sufficient to pay and satisfy in full said mortgage indebtedness, interest, costs, and charges, then it was ordered and decreed that the sheriff should proceed to sell under the decree the one-third partitioned and set off to her, for the purpose of satisfying the remainder due and unpaid upon the mortgage. It was also ordered that said sale should be made without relief from valuation and appraisement laws, and that a certified copy of the decree, under the hand of the clerk and the seal of the court, should be a sufficient warrant or authority to the sheriff to execute the same. At the same term of court, and as a part of the proceedings, the commissioners appointed by the court made their report, setting off to Lovina Sparks in severalty 20 acres of the said real estate; describing the tract so partitioned to her by metes and bounds. Sixty acres were set off by said commissioners to William S. Smith, executor aforesaid, as his interest in the entire tract of 80 acres. The report of the commissioners was approved, and the partition as made was confirmed by the court, subject to the lien of the mortgage of the Connecticut Mutual Life Insurance Company, and it was ordered and adjudged that the said Lovina Sparks should hold and occupy the tract of land partitioned to her. A certified copy of the aforesaid decree, including therein the order and judgment of the court in partition of the land, was duly issued by the clerk, under his hand and the seal of the court, to the sheriff of said county, and that officer duly advertised the premises for sale according to law on December 9, 1899. Upon said date it appears that the sheriff, in making the sale, did not obey or follow the commands of the decree whereby he was required to sell separately the part of the real estate set off to Mrs. Sparks on the happening of the event as mentioned. It is shown that he first offered the rents and profits of the 60 acres partitioned to Smith as executor, and, upon receiving no bid for the rents and profits, he then offered the fee simple of the said tract, but received no bid for the same. The sheriff then proceeded to offer the rents and profits of the 20 acres set off to Lovina Sparks, but, upon receiving no bid therefor, he then offered the rents and profits of the entire tract of 80 acres, but received no bid. Thereupon he offered the entire tract of 80 acres in fee simple, and appellant, William S. Smith, bid for the same $746.42. This bid being the highest and best bid, the sheriff, as it appears, struck off and sold the entire 80 acres to appellant for that price in full satisfaction of the mortgage indebtedness, interest, costs, and charges. On payment of the amount bid, a certificate of sale was issued to appellant by the sheriff. This is the sale complained of by appellees. The 60 acres set off to Smith as executor, under the facts alleged and established by the evidence, are shown to be of the value of $1,-333.33, and the 20 acres partitioned to Mrs. Sparks are shown to be of the value of $666.-67, making the total value of the 80 acres $2,000.

Reduced to a simple proposition, under the facts alleged and proven, the question presented is, was the sale by the sheriff of the 80 acres in solido unauthorized? That this question must be answered in the affirmative is well settled by the authorities. The sheriff, as shown, sold the 80 acres as an entirety, and not in separate tracts, as he was ordered to do by the decree, and thereby clearly violated the terms and provisions thereof. The legitimate question arising under the facts is not what the decree of the court should have been, for that was a matter which was settled in the action in the proceeding for partition and foreclosure. If the insurance company or any other party in that action was not satisfied with the decree and judgment of the court as rendered, then was the proper time to have interposed objections. The court, as it appears, had jurisdiction over the subject-matter and the parties in said proceedings, and its decree therein to the effect that the parts of the mortgaged premises as partitioned should be separately sold by the sheriff, and that the part or tract set off to Smith as executor should be first sold and exhausted before a sale should be made of the part partitioned to Mrs. Sparks was conclusive and binding upon all the parties in the action until set aside by a direct proceeding for that purpose. Grave v. Bunch, 83 Ind. 4. Under the positive mandate of the decree, there could be no sale of the one-third that was partitioned to Mrs. Sparks until the two-thirds held separately by Smith, as executor, under the partition, had been first sold. It was only in the event that his part failed to sell for a sum sufficient to satisfy the mortgage, interest, costs, and charges that resort could be had to the portion set off to Mrs. Sparks. It is certainly evident that any sale made under the decree, not authorized by the terms thereof, cannot be upheld, but must be set aside. Langsdale v. Mills, 32 Ind. 380. The question as to the manner in which the tracts should be sold was not left open to the judgment of the sheriff. This had been settled in advance by the court, and therefore was not a matter within the sheriff's discretion. It was the imperative duty of this officer to obey the commands of the decree, and he had no right or authority to depart therefrom. Meriwether v. Craig, 118 Ind. 301, 20 N. E. 769.

We may assume that the court was justified in molding its decree as it did. In Medsker v. Parker, 70 Ind. 509, it is held that in a case where the one-third interest of the wife in the mortgaged premises had been severed and vested in her under the provisions of the act of March 11, 1875, supra, it was right for the court to order that the two-thirds interest of the husband should be first sold and exhausted, before resort could be had to the part set off to the wife. The same holding is followed and affirmed in Leary v. Shaffer, 79 Ind. 567; Grave v. Bunch, supra; Crawford v. Hazelrigg, 117 Ind. 63, 18 N. E. 603, 2 L. R. A. 139; Hardy v. Miller, 89 Ind. 440; Main v. Ginthert, 92 Ind. 180; De Armond v. Preachers, etc., Society, 94 Ind. 59; Purviance v. Emley, 126 Ind. 419, 26 N. E. 167; Kelley v. Canary, 129 Ind. 460, 29 N. E. 11. This rule is asserted and upheld upon the theory that the wife, under the circumstances, occupies a position in relation to the mortgage somewhat analogous to that of a surety for her husband. That a sheriff's sale of property may be avoided and set aside, in an action instituted for that purpose, on account of the misconduct of the officer, or irregularity in making the sale, where such misconduct or irregularity is prejudicial to the interest or rights of the party complaining, is a well-settled proposition. Davis v. Campbell, 12 Ind. 192; Weaver v. Guyer, 59 Ind. 195; Jones v. Kokomo, etc., Ass'n, 77 Ind. 340; Brake v. Brownlee, 91 Ind. 359; 17 Am. & Eng. Ency. of Law (2d Ed.) 999; Rorer on Judicial Sales, § 1101. As shown, the sheriff was not empowered, under the decree, to sell as he did the mortgaged premises in solido, but was expressly ordered to first sell the tract set off to Smith as executor; and it was only in the event that this part failed to sell for a sum sufficient to satisfy the mortgage indebtedness, interest, costs, and charges, that he was empowered to resort to and sell the real estate partitiond to Mrs. Sparks. In this respect, at least, the officer seems to have wholly disregarded the terms of the decree. The decree of the court as certified to the sheriff in the manner therein provided was his sole warrant or authority for subjecting the land to sale, and his failure to obey its terms and provisions certainly operated to impair the substantial rights of Mrs. Sparks. Selling the land in a body at least resulted in placing impediments in the way of her statutory right of redemption. Had her tract been sold separately, as ordered, she would have been enabled to redeem as owner, under section 780, Burns' Rev. St. 1901, without redeeming the entire 80 acres. Holding, as she did, under the partition, a divided interest, she would not come within the express provisions of section 781, Burns' Rev. St. 1901, which permits a person having an individual interest in the property sold in one body to redeem as therein provided. This section vests in the owner of an undivided interest the right to redeem, provided he redeems the land sold as an entirety. Eiceman v. Finch, 79 Ind. 511.

But counsel for appellant assert that the partition proceedings in no manner affected the mortgagee, the insurance company, and therefore Mrs. Sparks' interest in the land at the time of the sale continued to be an undivided interest, and that she could have redeemed the entire real estate sold, and then had recourse against the two-thirds held by Smith as executor. But it must be remembered that the mortgagee, the insurance company, was a party to the proceedings in partition, and was therefore bound by the judgment of the court therein. As previously said, the question in this appeal is not what the judgment or decree of the court in the partition and foreclosure proceedings ought to have been, but the question is, what was the particular judgment as rendered? The familiar rule that a party cannot collaterally impeach a judgment precludes all parties to the proceedings in question from asserting that the court should have rendered a judgment therein different from the one in controversy.

It is evident, under the facts, that the judgment of the lower court is correct, and it is therefore affirmed.

(162 Ind. 303)

CINCINNATI, R. & M. R. CO. v. WABASH R. CO.

(Supreme Court of Indiana. March 10, 1904.)

INTERSECTING RAILROADS—CROSSINGS—APPROPRIATION—INJUNCTION—APPEAL.

1. One railroad company filed an instrument of appropriation to secure a right of way across another railroad, on which commissioners were appointed and an award made, which the defendant company sought to review by filing exceptions in the circuit court. *Held*, that the propriety of the rulings to be reviewed could not be raised on a bill by the defendant company to enjoin the construction of the crossing pending the review.

2. A ruling by the Supreme Court settles the law on the point in all subsequent stages of the case, no matter how the question may arise.

3. Burns' Rev. St. 1901, § 5160, provides that on the filing of papers by one railroad company seeking to appropriate a right of way across the line of another company the circuit court shall appoint appraisers, and on payment of the award by the company seeking the right "it shall be lawful for such corporations to hold the interests in such lands for the uses aforesaid," but the award may be reviewed, and that pending such appeal such company may take possession of the property, and the subsequent proceedings on appeal shall only affect the amount of compensation. A complaint by a railroad company against another demanded a crossing at grade, and the court ordered the defendant to make its road straight for 100 feet on each side of the crossing, which involved the elimination of a curve and the lowering of the outside rails 2½ inches. *Held* that, if the complaint did not imply a demand for such an order, it was at most voidable only, and the complainant was entitled to possession pending a review, and could not be enjoined from constructing the crossing.

Appeal from Circuit Court, Fulton County; A. C. Capron, Judge.

Bill by the Wabash Railroad Company against the Cincinnati, Richmond & Muncie Railroad Company to enjoin defendant from constructing a crossing on plaintiff's railway at intersection of the roads. From a decree granting a temporary restraining order, defendant appeals. Reversed.

R. A. Jackson, A. C. Starr, Harry Bernetha, H. P. Loveland, and R. J. Loveland, for appellant. Stuart, Hammond & Sims and Holman & Stephenson, for appellee.

HADLEY, J. Appellant, engaged in the construction of a railroad from Cincinnati to Chicago, the line of which intersects appellee's railroad at a point two miles west of Peru, Ind., having failed to agree with appellee with respect to said crossing, on October 29, 1901, filed in the office of the clerk of the Miami circuit court an instrument of appropriation of so much of appellee's railroad as would enable appellant to construct its railroad thereover. Proceedings were thereafter had under the statute, whereby, on November 28, 1901, an award was made fixing the point and manner of crossing, and the amount of the consideration to be paid by appellant at $4,000. The amount awarded was paid by appellant to the clerk of the Miami circuit court, for the use of appellee, on December 4, 1901, pursuant to the award. Exceptions to the award were timely filed by appellee, and afterwards, and while its exceptions remained undisposed of, appellee appealed the cause to the Appellate Court, which appeal was dismissed on the ground that the same was prematurely taken. Wabash Railroad Company v. Cincinnati, R. & M. Railroad Co., 29 Ind. App. 546, 63 N. E. 325. Before the appeal the venue of the cause was changed from the Miami to the Fulton circuit court, and was pending in the latter court when the appeal to the Appellate Court was dismissed. Said appeal was dismissed March 13, 1902, and on March 21, 1902, appellee filed in said cause its cross-complaint to enjoin appellant from taking possession of the condemned premises, and from constructing thereon a crossing, interlocking tower, etc., until the appropriation proceeding should be fully heard and determined by the Fulton circuit court; and on the following day, and without notice, and on said cross-complaint, procured the issuance, by the judge of the Fulton circuit court, of a temporary restraining order against appellant, and, appellant having appeared to said cross-complaint, the judge of said court, on March 28th, in vacation, granted appellee a temporary injunction restraining appellant from proceeding with the construction of said crossing until the next term, or further order of the court; from which action of the court in granting said temporary injunction this appeal is prosecuted.

An earnest effort has been made by counsel for appellee to bring into this action for injunction and into this appeal questions which belong exclusively to the appropriation proceeding, and which remain undisposed of and pending in the Fulton circuit court. A cross-assignment of error has been made calling in question the action of the Miami circuit court in overruling appellee's demurrer to appellant's instrument of appropriation in its orders and decrees establishing and relating to said crossing, and in overruling and sustaining divers subsidiary motions involving the sufficiency of the pleadings in the appropriation proceeding, and the regularity and legality of the order and decree made thereon. Appellee's exceptions to the award filed in the Miami circuit court, and which are still pending in the Fulton circuit court, embody the same facts that formed the basis of appellee's objections to the instrument of appropriation and order of decree of the court, and which are brought forward and presented in the cross-complaint as grounds for an injunction. It was held by the Appellate Court in the former appeal (29 Ind. App. 546, 63 N. E. 325), which ruling was subsequently, on October 8, 1902, upon appellee's application to transfer, reviewed and affirmed by this court, that all questions of law and fact which arose upon the instrument of appropriation, the interlocutory order and decree of the court, and award of the commissioners thereon, were by appellee's exceptions filed thereto and the appeal carried forward to the circuit court for final determination. This ruling settles the law on that point so far as this case is concerned, and rules in all subsequent stages of the case without reference to how the question may afterwards arise. Board v. Bonebrake, 146 Ind. 311, 45 N. E. 470, and cases cited.

The questions thus referred to the Fulton circuit court have not been considered and finally determined, and there they must remain until the body of the case is fully disposed of. Appellee cannot be allowed to execute a flank movement, and in a collateral way secure the adjudication of questions by this court until they have been first decided at nisi. It may be that when such questions are decided below it will have no ground of complaint. There is not a question argued or arises either upon the direct or cross assignment that does not arise and properly belong to the main case, and within the rule above mentioned, save only as to the right of appellant, upon its payment of the award, to take possession of the condemned premises and proceed with the construction of its crossing. The complaint shows that appellant was proceeding to do this, and, if it did not have the right, injunction will lie. If it did, it will not lie. And to this question we must confine ourselves.

We have many sections of the statute relating to the rights and obligations of railroad corporations in the construction of their railroads, in crossing other railroads, and in appropriating the property of others for their tracks; but so far as concerns the question before us it is only important to call attention to section 5160, Burns' Rev. St. 1901. It is therein provided that the corporation, having failed to agree with the owner, "shall deposit with the clerk of the circuit court of the county where the land lies a description of the rights and interests intended to be appropriated; and such land, rights and interests shall belong to such company, to use for the purpose specified by making, or tendering payment as hereinafter specified. * * * Upon filing such act of appropriation * * * the circuit court * * * of the county where the land lies, or judge thereof in vacation, upon the application of either party shall appoint three disinterested freeholders of such county to appraise the damages which the owner of the land may sustain by such appropriation. * * * They shall consider the injury which such owner may sustain by reason of such railroad, and shall forthwith return their assessment of damages to the clerk of such court setting forth the value of the property taken, or injury done to the property which they assess to the owner. * * * And, thereupon, such corporation shall pay to said clerk the amount thus assessed. * * * and upon making payment * * * in the manner herein required, it shall be lawful for such corporation to hold the interests in such lands * * * for the uses aforesaid. * * * The award of said arbitrators may be reviewed by the circuit court in which such proceedings are had, on written exceptions filed by either party in the clerk's office within ten days after the filing of such award; and the court shall make such order therein as right and justice may require, by ordering a new appraisement, on good cause shown. Provided that notwithstanding such appeal, such company may take possession of the property therein described, as aforesaid. and the subsequent proceedings on appeal shall only affect the amount of compensation to be allowed." The company's authority to take the property of another for the construction of its railroad proceeded from an exercise of the state's right of eminent domain. In conferring this right the Legislature might and did prescribe the exact terms of its enjoyment, within the limits of the Constitution. It is manifest from the statute that the Legislature intended that the right to appropriate should be summary and indefeasible by prepayment or tender of just compensation. and the exercise of the right in the mode prescribed. If the appropriating company is within the statute, and if its procedure is regular, it is entitled, upon the payment of the award into the clerk's office, to take possession of the property. All the right or power the landowner has in the transaction is to see that the proceeding is regular, and that the compensation awarded him is paid. If he feels aggrieved, either by the irregularity of the proceeding, or by the inadequacy of the compensation allowed, he may file exceptions to the award, and appeal the case to the circuit court; but such appeal shall not prevent the company from taking possession, and the proceedings on appeal shall affect only the amount of compensation. That is to say, no matter what may be established on appeal, it shall not defeat the right of the condemning company to the appropriation, but only the amount it may be required to pay for it. Doubtless the reason for making the right to such an appropriation unquestionable is that it contravenes public policy to permit an individual or corporation to impede, by litigation and incidental delays, the progress of a great enterprise, which involves important public interests, as well as the outlay of large sums of money. At any rate, it is settled by the decisions of this court that the proviso of section 5160, with respect to the right of the appropriating company to take immediate possession, means what it says. We quote from what is said in Railway Company v. Kinsey, 87 Ind. 517, the following: "The payment of the amount awarded by the appraisers gives the corporation a right to the immediate possession and a prima facie claim to the land, subject to an appeal in ten days after the award is filed. If no appeal is taken, at the end of the ten days the title vests and relates back to date of payment. If an appeal is taken, no title vests, and the corporation has no greater right than that of a license under the statute to hold possession and proceed with the construction of its road pending litigation. When the compensation has been finally fixed on appeal, then the corporation must pay or tender the compensation so fixed, and on failure to do so it acquires no title to the land, and its license to hold possession and prosecute its work ceases." See, also, Boyd v. Traction Co. (Ind. Sup. Jan. 5, 1904) 69 N. E. 398; Railway Co. v. Swinney, 97 Ind. 586, 593; Railroad Company v. Crawford, 100 Ind. 550, 557; Gas Trust Co. v. Harless, 131 Ind. 446, 452, 29 N. E. 1062, 15 L. R. A. 505, and cases there collated.

Appellee chiefly bases its claim for injunctive relief upon the following facts shown by the record: The place of the crossing in controversy is on a curve in appellee's railroad, by reason whereof the outer rail of its track at that point is 2½ inches higher than the inner rail. Appellant's instrument of appropriation claimed and demanded the right to intersect and cross appellee's railroad at grade, and the Miami circuit court, in determining the mode of crossing, prior to the assessment of damages as required by section 5158a, Burns' Rev. St. 1901, to make a practicable crossing at grade, on the level, among other things ordered that appellee's railroad be made straight for a distance of 100 feet on each side of the center line of the crossing, and that appellee so straighten it within 20 days, and in default appellant should thereafter have the right to enter and straighten it at appellee's cost. The insistence of appellee is that so much of the court's order as directed a change in the construction of its road, and the mandate that appellee accomplish the change within 20 days, or suffer appellant to enter and make it, is void, because it is a right not demanded in the instrument of appropriation, and consequently not appropriated; and notwithstanding the assessment of damages therefor, and payment of the same into the clerk's office for the use of appellee, it did not warrant the taking of possession, because the proviso of the statute only operates as to property that has been legally appropriated. There can be no doubt that it was within the jurisdiction of the court to make the order complained of upon a proper complaint; and whether a complaint, and demand for a railroad crossing at grade, is sufficient, as implying also a demand for whatever change in existing conditions may prove essential to effectuate the crossing, a judgment or decree rendered upon such complaint would not be void. At most it would be only voidable. It could not, therefore, be attacked in any other way than by appeal. In any view we take of the case, it is clear that injunction will not lie.

The order for a temporary injunction is reversed.

(163 Ind. 51)

AMERICAN MUT. LIFE INS. CO. v. BERTRAM.*

(Supreme Court of Indiana. March 9, 1904.)

LIFE INSURANCE — INSURABLE INTEREST — WAGERING POLICY — ASSIGNMENTS — PREMIUMS—RECOVERY—PARI DELICTO—LIMITATIONS—DEMAND—INTEREST.

1. A policy of life insurance issued on a life in which the beneficiary had no insurable interest, without insured's knowledge, was void, as being against public policy, and in violation of Act March 9, 1883, § 6 (Acts 1883, p. 204, c. 130), providing that when payments of assessments on a policy are made by a person other than the insured, and without his written consent, the beneficiary must have an insurable interest in the insured's life.

2. Defendant issued a policy to S., insuring the life of E., without her knowledge or consent, which was void for want of an insurable interest. S. thereafter assigned the policy to plaintiff, who was induced to accept the assignment by the false representations of defendant's agent, who had knowledge of its invalidity, that the same was valid and a good investment, and that plaintiff, who also had no insurable interest in insured's life, was entitled to take an assignment thereof. Thereafter, defendant's vice president and treasurer visited plaintiff, and, on being informed by her of the facts attending the assignment, ratified the same, and informed her that they were true; advising her to keep up her dues. Plaintiff thereafter continued to pay assessments on the policy until further tenders were refused, after which she ascertained that the policy was void, and sued to recover premiums paid. Act March 9, 1883, § 6 (Acts 1883, p. 204, c. 130), requires that when assessments on a policy, made by any person other than assured, are paid without his written consent, the beneficiary must have an insurable interest in insured's life; and section 9 makes it a felony for any person to knowingly issue a policy on the life of another without his knowledge or consent. *Held*, that the plaintiff was not in pari delicto with defendant, and was therefore entitled to recover the assessments paid by her on such policy.

3. Where an assignee of a void policy paid premiums thereon, believing it to be valid, and

*Rehearing denied May 31, 1904.

consented that such premiums should be converted by the insurance company to its own use, the statute of limitations did not begin to run against an action to recover such premiums until after demand made.

4. Where an assignee of a void insurance policy paid premiums sought to be recovered, believing the policy to be valid, she was not entitled to interest prior to demand made by her for their repayment, under Burns' Rev. St. 1901, § 7045, declaring that interest shall be allowed on money had and received for the use of another, and retained without his consent.

Appeal from Circuit Court, Elkhart County; J. D. Ferrall, Judge.

Action by Mary Bertram against the American Mutual Life Insurance Company. From a judgment in favor of plaintiff, defendant appeals, and plaintiff files cross-assignments of error. Case transferred from Appellate Court, as authorized by Act March 13, 1901 (Acts 1901, p. 590, c. 259). Affirmed on defendant's appeal, and reversed on plaintiff's cross-error assignments

Van Fleet & Van Fleet, for appellant. Crumpacker & Moran and Miller, Drake & Hubbell, for appellee.

DOWLING, J. This action was brought by the appellee to recover from the appellant premiums paid for insurance upon a policy alleged to have been void from the time of its execution. At the request of the parties, the court made a special finding of facts, and stated its conclusions of law thereon. Exceptions were saved by both parties, and judgment was rendered for the appellee for so much of the premiums as was paid by her within six years before the commencement of the action. Errors are assigned by the appellant upon each conclusion of law. The appellee assigns a cross-error upon the second conclusion.

Briefly stated, the facts were as follows: The appellant was a mutual life insurance company organized under the laws of this state, doing business on the assessment plan. On February 24, 1887, at the city of Elkhart, with full knowledge of the facts, it issued its policy of insurance to one Leander Stiles upon the life of one Mary Ellsworth, a resident of New York, without her knowledge. Stiles was not a creditor of Mrs. Ellsworth, nor was she under any kind of obligation, legal or moral, to him. She was related to him only as an aunt by marriage, and he was in no way dependent upon her. The consideration of the policy was the payment by Stiles of a membership fee of $25, and his agreement to make monthly payments of $6.80. The sum to be paid to Stiles, his heirs, administrators, or assigns, within 30 days after the death of Mrs. Ellsworth, and proof thereof, was his pro rata share of 80 per cent. of an assessment on all members of the insurance company—not exceeding, however, $4,000. Stiles paid the membership fee and the assessments for February and March, 1887. On March 2, 1887, in consideration of the agreement of the appellee to pay all subsequent premiums and assessments on the policy, he assigned to her a two-thirds interest in it. After such assignment the assessments were increased by appellant to $12 per month. The appellee paid all such premiums and assessments until October, 1890, when the appellant refused to receive any further payments, for the reason, as it alleged, that the policy had lapsed in consequence of the failure of the appellee to pay the October, 1890, assessment on the day it became due. Mrs. Ellsworth died in May, 1900, and, when payment of the amount named in the policy was demanded by the appellee, the appellant at first refused to pay it because the policy had lapsed on the nonpayment of the October, 1890, assessment: but afterwards, on June 13, 1900, it denied its liability on the ground that neither Stiles, who took out the policy, nor the appellee, to whom it was assigned, had an insurable interest in the life of Mrs. Ellsworth. The application for the policy was made by Stiles through one Gusten, an agent of the appellant. Gusten knew that the application was made without the knowledge or consent of Mrs. Ellsworth; that Stiles was not a creditor of Mrs. Ellsworth; that she was not obligated to him in any manner; that Stiles was not dependent upon her in any way; that she was an aunt of the said Stiles by marriage, only, and not otherwise related to him. The application was written by Gusten himself, and Stiles signed Mrs. Ellsworth's name to it in the presence of Gusten. The latter forwarded the application to the appellant, at Elkhart, Ind., and on February 24, 1887, the appellant, on this application, issued to Stiles the policy on the life of Mrs. Ellsworth. At the time of the assignment of the policy to the appellee, and prior thereto, Gusten, who was acting as the agent for the appellant, and who knew all the facts before stated, for the purpose of inducing the appellee to take an assignment of the policy, falsely and fraudulently represented to her that the policy was valid and all right; that she had a right to take an assignment thereof; that she would be entitled to receive payment thereunder in case of loss; that it was a good investment for her, and one by which she might save her money. The appellee was ignorant of all the facts of the case, and of the law in respect to them. She believed and relied on the representations of Gusten, the agent of the company, and was induced by them to take an assignment of the policy, and to pay to Stiles therefor all he had paid out thereon, including the membership fee and the said monthly assessments. She continued to pay the assessments thereafter, under the belief that the policy was valid. Some two months after the policy was assigned to her, Barney, the vice president and treasurer of the appellant, visited the appellee at her home, in Valparaiso, and she repeated to him all that Gusten had said to her in regard to the assignment of the policy. Barney thereupon, with full knowledge of all that had taken place, represented to her that everything was perfectly right, and advised her to keep her dues paid. The appellee thereafter, relying on these false representations and statements of Barney and Gusten, as agents of the appellant, continued to pay the monthly assessments on the policy until October, 1897. A few days after it became due, she tendered the October assessment, and from month to month thereafter she offered to pay each subsequent assessment, but her tenders and offers were refused. The total amount paid by the appellee on account of premiums and assessments was $1,574, which, with the interest thereon, amounted to $2,586.35. Before the commencement of the suit, the appellee demanded repayment to her of the amount so paid on account of the policy, but the appellant refused to repay the same, or any part of it. The action was commenced November 10, 1900.

The court's conclusions of law were "(1) that the said policy was void from the beginning; (2) that plaintiff is entitled to recover all moneys paid by her, with interest, within six years before the commencement of this action, being the sum of $1,007.35."

A reversal of the judgment is insisted upon by the appellant on the grounds (1) that the finding fails to show that the policy was issued without the knowledge or consent of Mary Ellsworth; (2) that it does not appear that the policy was invalid under section 6 of the act of March 9, 1883 (Acts 1883, p. 204, c. 136), either in the hands of Stiles or the appellee; (3) that public policy forbids a recovery by the appellee; (4) that the appellee can found no right upon a misrepresentation of the law; and (5) that the appellee has no superior equity against the other members of the appellant, as a mutual life insurance company.

Section 6 of the act of March 9, 1883 (Acts 1883, p. 204, c. 136), under which the appellant company was organized, declared that when payments of assessments on a policy were made by any person other than the insured, and without his written consent, the beneficiary must have an insurable interest in the life assured. Section 9 of the act made it a felony for any person to knowingly secure a policy on the life of another without his knowledge or consent. Stiles had no insurable interest in the life of Mrs. Ellsworth. All assessments were to be paid by him, and the policy was issued to him without her knowledge or consent. The contract of insurance, therefore, was void, both as against public policy, and by force of the statute. Continental Life Ins. Co. v. Volger, 89 Ind. 572, 575, 46 Am. Rep. 185; Prudential Ins. Co. v. Hunn, 21 Ind. App. 525, 52 N. E. 772, 69 Am. St. Rep. 380; Ruse v. Mutual Ins. Co., 23 N. Y. 516; May on Insurance (4th Ed.) § 74; Beach, Law of Insurance, § 850.

The question, then, is, had the appellee as the assignee of the policy, under the circumstances hereinbefore stated, the right to recover the premiums and assessments paid by her on account of the supposed insurance? The general rule is that an action will not lie to recover premiums paid upon an insurance which is illegal by reason of the policy being illegal by statute, or by reason of the illegality of the adventure insured. 14 English Ruling Cas. 533; Lowry v. Bourdieu, 2 Dougl. 468; Van Dyck v. Hewitt, 1 East, 96; Russell v. De Grand, 15 Mass. 35; Welsh v. Cutler, 44 N. H. 561; Feise v. Parkinson, 4 Taunt. 640; Anderson v. Thornton, 8 Ex. 425; Waller v. Northern Assur. Co., 64 Iowa, 101, 19 N. W. 865; Richards v. Marine Ins. Co., 3 Johns. 307; New York Life Ins. Co. v. Fletcher, 117 U. S. 519, 6 Sup. Ct. 837, 29 L. Ed. 934. But it is held that this rule does not apply where there has been no fraud on the part of the plaintiff, where the policy is void because of innocent misrepresentations, where the plaintiff has been induced to take out the policy by the fraud of the insurer, and is himself innocent, or where it is clear that the policy was not a wagering contract, but was taken out under a mistake in regard to the rights of the party insured. In this case it is to be borne in mind that the appellee herself did not take out the policy, but that, with the knowledge and consent of the appellant, and at its solicitation, she took an assignment of it. Upon the authority of Continental Co. v. Munns, 120 Ind. 30, 22 N. E. 78, 5 L. R. A. 430, the assignment is to be treated as a new contract, to which the assignee and the insurer are the parties. In Lowry v. Bourdieu, supra, the right to recover the premium paid upon a gaming policy issued in violation of an act of Parliament was denied; but Lord Mansfield said "he desired it might not be understood that the court held that, in all cases where money has been paid on an illegal consideration, it cannot be recovered back; that in cases of oppression—when paid, for instance, to a creditor to induce him to sign a bankrupt's certificate, or upon a usurious contract—it may be recovered, for in such cases the parties are not in pari delicto." In Fulton v. Metropolitan Life Ins. Co. (Com. Pl.) 19 N. Y. Supp. 660, the plaintiff, being solicited for life insurance by defendant's agent, took out policies on the life of her sister and brother, payable to herself; having signed their names to the application with the knowledge of the agent. After several years, she ascertained that the policies were void on that account, and brought an action to recover the premiums paid. It was held that the company was chargeable with the agent's knowledge of the invalidity of the policies, and that the plaintiff was entitled to recover, though the facts were never communicated to the company. In Waller v. Northern Assurance Co., 64 Iowa, 101, 19 N. W. 865, two policies of fire insurance were issued to the plaintiff as the absolute owner of the property insured, when he really held but a mortgage interest in it. No actual fraud was found in the representations concerning the title. The policies contained the condition that "if the interest of the assured in the property be any other than the entire, unconditional and sole ownership of the property, for the use and benefit of the assured, * * * it must be so represented to these companies, and so expressed in the written part of the policy, otherwise, the policy shall be void." The court said: "Under this condition, each of the policies was absolutely void, and incapable of binding or being enforced against defendants. * * * Each presents the case of a payment of money by plaintiff, and a failure to receive any consideration therefor, without any fraud or deception practiced by him. It is the simple case of money paid in good faith, and nothing in return received. No element of fraud exists which defeats plaintiff's rights. Nor is it a case of voluntary payment, for it was made with the expectation of receiving a consideration in return which has wholly failed, for the reason that the policy did not bind the defendants. Under familiar rules of the law, plaintiff is entitled to recover the amount of premiums paid, as money had and received to his use. This doctrine has been often recognized by the authorities as applicable in actions for the recovery of money paid as premiums upon policies where the risk did not attach, or the contract was void ab initio." The facts in Fisher v. Metropolitan Life Ins. Co., 160 Mass. 386, 35 N. E. 849, 39 Am. St. Rep. 495, were these: An agent of the defendant solicited the plaintiff's husband to effect an insurance on his life for the wife's benefit, which the husband refused to do. Afterwards the agent, without the knowledge of the husband, urged the wife to effect such insurance, and procured a physician to visit and converse with the husband, and thereafter to sign the requisite examination. The husband was not aware of the purpose of the physician in visiting him, nor did he know that any application had been made for insurance on his life. The wife signed her name and that of her husband to the application for insurance, and also to the examination form on the back of the application. The agent afterwards delivered to the wife a policy of insurance upon the life of her husband, payable to her in the event of his death, and the wife paid the premiums then and thereafter falling due for such insurance. The agent also delivered to the wife a book upon which receipts of money paid by her were, from time to time, acknowledged, and the book contained extracts from the rules and regulations of the company to which the policy was subject. Among others was a rule stating that under no circumstances could an application be written upon the life of a husband for the benefit of his wife without his consent, nor without an examination by the physician of the company, nor unless the applicant personally signed the examination form on the back of the application after the answers to the application had been made, and that any policy issued in violation of these rules should be void. In July, 1892, the wife claimed that she was first advised of the invalidity of the policy for want of the consent of her husband. She informed the president of the company by letter of that date that she had discovered that the policy had been issued against the rules of the company, and was not enforceable, and that the agent had told her at the time it was issued it was all right. She therefore stated that she wished her money back. The company did not make any direct reply to the letter, but afterwards one of its agents urged the wife to continue her payments, which she refused to do, and again demanded repayment of the money paid by her as premiums, which demand being refused, she brought her action. In ruling upon an exception to an instruction given to the jury, the court said: "If the plaintiff, in collusion with Bannigan, the defendant's agent, intended to cheat the company or practice a fraud upon it, then the money she has paid the company was paid in pursuance of this fraudulent intention, and she cannot recover it back; but, if she was innocent of any fraudulent intent, and was deceived by Bannigan, and induced by his fraudulent representations to make the application, then she could rescind the contract of insurance when she discovered the fraud, and recover back the amount of the premiums which she had paid. Hedden v. Griffin, 136 Mass. 229, 49 Am. Rep. 25." In Bales v. Hunt, 77 Ind. 355, this court held that while, ordinarily, relief against mistakes of law will not be afforded, yet, where the mistake was induced or encouraged by the misrepresentations of the other party to the transaction, and the plaintiff, through misapprehension or mistake of law, assumes obligations or gives up a private right of property upon grounds upon which he would not have acted but for such misapprehension, a court of equity may grant relief, if, under the general circumstances of the case, it is satisfied that the party benefited by the mistake cannot, in conscience, retain the benefit or advantage so acquired. See, also, Kerr on Fraud & Mistake, pp. 398, 400; Hollingsworth v. Stone, 90 Ind. 244; Kinney v. Dodge, 101 Ind. 573; Parish v. Camplin, 139 Ind. 14, 37 N. E. 607; Metropolitan Life Ins. Co. v. Bowser, 20 Ind. App. 557, 50 N. E. 86; Supreme Lodge, etc., v. Metcalf, 15 Ind. App. 135, 43 N. E. 893.

If the contract of insurance be illegal in its inception, the insured cannot recover the premiums paid, if the parties are in pari delicto. The controlling inquiry, then, in the present case, is, were the parties to the transaction equally in fault? It was said by Lord Mansfield in Browning v. Morris, Cowper, 790, 793, that "the rule is, 'In pari delicto potior est conditio defendentis,' and there are several other maxims of the same kind. Where the contract is executed and the money paid in pari delicto, this rule, as Mr. Dunning contended, certainly holds, and the party who has paid it cannot recover it back. For instance, in bribery, if a man pays a sum of money by way of a bribe, he can never recover it in an action, because both plaintiff and defendant are equally criminal. But where contracts or transactions are prohibited by positive statute, for the sake of protecting one set of men from another set of men—the one, from their situation and condition, being liable to be oppressed or imposed upon by the other—then the parties are not in pari delicto; and, in furtherance of these statutes, the person injured, after the transaction is finished and completed, may bring his action and defeat the contract." The rule is thus stated in 20 Am. & Eng. Ency. Law, 816: "It is one of the fundamental maxims of the common law that ignorance of law excuses no one. It is a maxim founded not only on expediency and policy, but on necessity. * * * It is therefore applied most rigidly at law, and is only relaxed in equity where the mistake is mixed with misrepresentation or fraud, or where the ignorance of the complainant has conferred upon the defendant a benefit which he cannot in good conscience retain." The language used by the court in Jestons v. Brooke, Cowper, 793, 795, is directly applicable to the case under consideration: "This is an action for money had and received, and therefore it is analogous to a bill in equity. The ground of the action is to recover half of the neat profits arising by the resale of certain goods purchased by the defendant, as stated in the report. The general question is whether the plaintiff ought to recover in an action for money had and received; that is, whether it is against conscience that the defendant should retain the whole profits of the goods in question to himself."

The present suit is not brought to enforce the illegal contract of insurance, or any right arising out of it. The appellee seeks only to recover from the appellant moneys paid by her to it without any consideration whatever. For, as the policy on the life of Mrs. Ellsworth was void from its inception, the appellant never incurred any risk, and the appellee never could have derived any benefit from it. At the time of the assignment of the policy, and immediately previous thereto, Gusten, acting as the agent of the appellant, and knowing all the facts which rendered the policy void, for the purpose of inducing the appellee to take an assignment of the policy, falsely and fraudulently represented to her that the policy was valid, that she would be entitled to recover payment thereunder in case of loss, and that the assignment would be a good investment for her. The appellee, who was a woman, believed these representations, and was induced by them to take an assignment of the policy from Stiles, and to reimburse him for his entire outlay up to that time. She also agreed to pay all future premiums and assessments. Within two months after the assignment was made, and when she had paid a comparatively small amount on the policy, Barney, the vice president and treasurer of the appellant, acting for it, visited the appellee at her home, and, when told by her what Gusten had said to her, with a full knowledge of the facts, also falsely represented to the appellee that the policy was perfectly right, and advised her to go on and keep her dues paid up. Relying on these false statements, the appellee paid to the appellant premiums and assessments on the void policy to the amount of $1,574. It cannot be said that the parties to this transaction were in pari delicto, or that the appellant ought, in good conscience, to retain the moneys paid to it by the appellee. The representations made to the appellee by the officers and agents of the company—one of them being its vice president and treasurer—were calculated to impose upon and mislead any one contemplating the purchase of a policy previously issued by the company. The parties did not stand upon an equal footing, and the officers and agents making the false representations to the appellee had every advantage over her which their special knowledge of the facts of the case, and of the law of insurance applicable to their company, could give. We think, too, that these representations that the policy was valid and would be paid were equivalent to a statement that it had been issued with the knowledge and consent of Mrs. Ellsworth, and that Stiles had such an interest in her life, as creditor or otherwise, as authorized him to take it out, so that the mistake of the appellee, occasioned by the fraudulent representations of the appellant's officers and agents, may be fairly regarded a mistake of fact as well as of law. The direct result of this mistake was that the appellee assumed obligations to pay the premiums and assessments on the policy, and that she parted with her money in discharging them.

In this connection, the fact is not to be overlooked that section 9 of the act of 1883 makes it a criminal offense for any person to secure a policy on the life of another without his knowledge or consent only when such act is done knowingly. The court expressly found that, in taking the assignment of the policy, the appellee was ignorant of the facts which rendered it void.

Our conclusion upon this branch of the case is that the appellant cannot, in good conscience, be permitted to retain the premiums and assessments paid to it by the appellee, and that she has the right to recover the same in this action.

A distinction between a mistake of law, affecting mere private rights, and such a mistake when the transaction is illegal by statute or is against public policy, may exist, as contended for by counsel for appellant;

but, giving to this distinction its fullest effect, it could not, under the circumstances of this case, as shown by the special finding, defeat the appellee's right to recover the premiums and assessments paid by her. She did not take out the policy. She violated no statute. She knowingly did no act prohibited by law or by public policy. She has not attempted to enforce the illegal contract, or make any claim under it. She admits that she has no claim against the appellant upon the policy. While she must give up the insurance upon the life of Mrs. Ellsworth, because the contract was void, it is equally necessary that the appellant should surrender the money it has received from her without right, without consideration, and solely through the fraudulent misrepresentations of its officers.

The point that the appellee has no equity which is superior to that of the members of the appellant association is without merit, and requires no consideration. The corporation received the money, and should repay it.

The trial court found that $1,574 had been paid by the appellee on account of premiums and assessments, and that the interest thereon amounted to $1,012.35, making a total of $2,586.35, but that the appellee was entitled to recover only the moneys paid by her within six years before the commencement of the action, with interest thereon. The cross-error assigned by the appellee calls in question the correctness of the conclusion limiting the appellee's right of recovery to the sums paid by her within six years before the commencement of the action, and we are asked to grant her affirmative relief, by requiring a restatement of this conclusion of law. It is well settled that this court has the right to grant such relief to the appellee, even where the judgment is not reversed. In discussing the subject of the assignment of cross-errors by the appellee, this court said in Feder v. Field, 117 Ind. 386, 388, 20 N. E. 129: "The rule [allowing the assignment of cross-errors] which has so long prevailed, and which we here sanction and carry to its just and logical result, does no injustice to any party. It prevents a multiplicity of appeals, and yet presents for adjudication the rights of all the parties properly brought before the court. It enables the court to finally adjudicate upon the whole controversy. It prevents one party from taking an advantage of the other by appealing, and, after the assignment of cross-errors, dismissing the appeal and carrying the entire case out of court. It brings the practice on appeal into harmony with the practice in the trial courts, and gives uniformity and consistency to our system of procedure. It simplifies the practice, and yet preserves all rights. In deciding that cross-errors may be assigned, we do not by any means decide that it is necessary to consider them in every instance. Nor do we decide that they are always, or even generally, of controlling effect. If, for instance, all that the appellee asks is an affirmance of the judgment, then all that it is necessary to do, in cases where an affirmance can be reached by disposing of the errors assigned by the appellant, is simply to consider and decide the questions presented by the appellant's assignment. It is not every case where cross-errors will entitle the appellee to affirmative relief, for in many cases they can do no more than prevent a reversal or settle a question of costs. Where, however, the entire record and all the parties are properly before the court on appeal, and it is manifest from the record before the court that the appellee has not received the relief to which he was entitled, this court may direct that it be awarded him. * * * With such a record before us, all questions should be decided, for otherwise the assignment of cross-errors would be an idle ceremony." Patoka Tp. v. Hopkins, 131 Ind. 142, 30 N. E. 896, 31 Am. St. Rep. 417; Johnson v. Culver, 116 Ind. 278, 19 N. E. 129; Thomas v. Simmons, 103 Ind. 538, 547, 2 N. E. 203, 3 N. E. 381; 2 Ency. Pl. & Pr. 970. The money received by the appellant from the appellee on account of premiums and assessments on the policy was so received, with the knowledge and consent of the appellee, to be applied in discharge of supposed obligations arising out of the transaction between the parties. Until the discovery by the appellee that the policy was void, and her rescission of it, the moneys so paid were held by the appellant, with her apparent consent, as its own. Under the particular circumstances of this case, we think a demand was necessary before bringing the action. The statute of limitations did not begin to run until such demand was made, or until the disavowal of the contract by the appellant. Then, too, the contract on the part of the appellant was wholly executory, and on the part of the appellee it was a continuous one. Taggart v. Tevanny, 1 Ind. App. 339, 357, 27 N. E. 511; Littler v. Smiley, 9 Ind. 116; Purviance v. Purviance, 14 Ind. App. 269, 272, 42 N. E. 364. Until June 13, 1900, both the appellant and the appellee treated the contract of insurance as a valid one, and acted under it. We think it clear that the statute did not begin to run against the claim of the appellee until June 13, 1900.

The trial court allowed interest upon the claim of the appellee from the date of the payment of the several premiums. We find no authority for this action of the court, and we have been referred to none. The provision of the statute on this subject is that interest shall be allowed on money had and received for the use of another, and retained without his consent. Burns' Rev. St. 1901, § 7045. According to our view of the case, interest should be calculated on the sum of the premiums and assessments paid by the appellee to the appellant only from the date of the demand made by her for their repayment. Stanley's Estate v. Pence, 66 N. E. 51, 160 Ind. —.

Judgment reversed on cross-error, and the Elkhart circuit court is directed to restate its second conclusion of law in conformity to this opinion, and to render judgment in favor of the appellee and against the appellant for the amount due.

(162 Ind. 278)

KRAUSE et al. v. BOARD OF TRUSTEES OF SCHOOL TOWN OF CROTHERSVILLE.

(Supreme Court of Indiana. March 9, 1904.)

CONTRACTS — DISCHARGE — IMPOSSIBILITY OF PERFORMANCE—DESTRUCTION OF SUBJECT-MATTER—RIGHTS OF PARTIES—BREACH OF CONTRACT—APPEAL—WAIVER — COLLATERAL CONTRACT—EFFECT.

1. The fact that a contractor unnecessarily delayed the completion of an annex to a building, although he had ample opportunity to complete it before performance was rendered impossible by the destruction of the old building and the annex by fire caused by lightning, as such fact had nothing to do with the destruction, did not render the contractor liable for failure to perform his contract.

2. A complaint against a contractor for failure to perform a contract to build an annex to a building, such performance having been rendered impossible by fire, which alleged a breach in the contractor's failure to proceed after the fire, constituted a waiver of a prior breach, consisting in the contractor's unnecessary delay in completing the building.

3. Where a contractor agreed to build an annex to a building, and after the work was nearly completed the building was destroyed by fire, the owner could not impose on the contractor an obligation to complete the work by offering to restore the old building.

4. Where a building to which a contractor had agreed to build an annex was destroyed by fire, the owner's remedy, if any, was in equitable assumpsit to recover for advancements in excess of expenditures; but, where the contractor had expended more than he had received under the contract, the payments made which had gone into the property would be treated as an execution of the contract pro tanto, leaving the loss, as it had fallen, on the respective parties.

5. The provision of a contract, for the construction of an annex to a building, that the owner should not be "in any manner answerable, accountable or responsible for any loss or damage" that might happen to the work, could not be extended so as to make the contractor answerable for a destruction of the original building by fire, caused by lightning, before the completion of the work.

6. The fact that, had an annex to a building been completed by the contractor without delay, the owner might have insured against the fire which destroyed the building and annex before completion, has no bearing on the question of the contractor's obligation to perform his contract after the fire.

7. Where a contract for the construction of an annex to a building provided that 80 per cent. of the value of the material and labor furnished should be paid, on the presentation of estimates, while the work progressed, and the balance on the completion of the work, and the building was destroyed by fire after the annex was almost completed, and the 80 per cent. had been paid, the contractor was not entitled to recover anything further, either on the contract or on a quantum meruit.

Appeal from Circuit Court, Bartholomew County; F. T. Hord, Judge.

Action by the board of school trustees of the school town of Crothersville against John Krause and others. From a judgment for plaintiff, defendants appeal. Transferred from the Appellate Court under Burns' Rev. St. 1901, § 1337j, subd. 2. Reversed.

Oscar Montgomery, Marshall Hacker, and W. T. Brannaman, for appellants. Stansifer & Baker and S. A. Barnes, for appellee.

GILLETT, C. J. This suit was instituted by appellee to recover on a bond executed by appellants for the faithful performance of a building contract. Certain of the appellants, constituting the firm of John Krause & Co., filed a cross-complaint to recover for a balance unpaid under the contract, and to this they added a paragraph on a quantum meruit. Issues were joined on the pleadings mentioned, and a trial resulted in a judgment in favor of appellee upon its complaint, and against said cross-complainants, on the issues tendered by them. Pursuant to request, the court found the facts specially. The findings are very long, and in the statement of the facts so found we shall not only summarize many of the findings, but shall omit matters which, for the purposes of this opinion, are irrelevant.

In October, 1898, appellee entered into a contract in writing with said John Krause & Co., whereby the latter agreed to furnish the materials for, and to erect and finish, an annex to a school building belonging to appellee, and to make certain improvements upon the latter building, for the sum of $3,853.35, "to be paid upon the completion of the work." Appellee agreed in said contract, in consideration of the agreements of said firm being strictly kept, that it would pay said sum to said firm, but provision was made in said instrument that, as the work progressed, estimates were to be furnished by the architect of materials, provided and labor performed, on which 80 per cent. of the value of said material and labor would be paid on the presentation of said estimates, the amount so paid to be deducted from the final estimate which the contract provided for. The fifth subdivision of said contract was as follows: "The party of the first part [the school town] shall not be in any manner answerable, accountable or responsible for any loss or damage that shall or may happen to said work or any part thereof, or for any of the materials or anything used or employed in finishing the same." Appellee reserved the right in said contract to place in position the heating apparatus and furniture at such times as it saw fit. The specifications attached to the contract provided that all the work, when finished, was to be turned over perfect, complete, and undamaged in every particular; that the whole work was to be inspected as it went on, and was to be accepted by the owner and architect before a final settlement was made. The character of the bond is indicated above. The building to which said annex was to be attached was a two-story brick structure, and the annex was of the same height. For a distance of 42 feet the west wall of the old building was to be the east wall of the new structure. The annex was to be so compactly and substantially joined to the old building as to constitute one building. One end of the lower sill or cord of the roof trusses was required to rest on said old wall, and the roof plates of the new building were to be fastened to the roof plates of the other building. The halls of the two buildings were to be arranged so that they would be continuous. Krause & Co. were also required under their contract to do considerable work on the old building, such as excavating, putting in underpinning, building a concrete floor, raising the tower, and doing the mason work in connection with the installing of the heating apparatus. On July 24, 1899, said firm had progressed with its work until it would have cost but $35 to complete the same, there being but one coat of paint and of varnish necessary to finish such undertaking; the value of the work done and materials furnished at that time, the court found to be but $35 less than the contract price. On the day aforesaid the old building was struck by lightning and thereby set fire to, and everything inflammable in both buildings was destroyed by such fire. As a result of the fire said common wall partially fell, and was so weakened that it had to be taken down. The remaining walls of the old building were also seriously injured. The court found that all that could have been done upon the old building after the fire, under said contract, was to build up the retaining walls in the furnace rooms to the floor line. It was further found that it would have been impossible for said contractors to build the roof of the annex, as provided for in the contract, without said common wall, and that without it the remainder of said structure, if built, would have been weak. With the exception of a few days' work done by two men during the week before the fire, no work had been done by said firm on said contract, according to the findings, after May 26, 1899. The court found that said firm could have completed its contract by June 15, 1899, and that it unreasonably and without excuse delayed the completion of said work. It is shown that appellee had advanced to said firm, prior to said fire, approximately 80 per cent. of the contract price. No estimates had been made or demanded. The concluding findings of the court show that after the fire appellee requested said firm to complete its contract; that the firm refused to do so, for the assigned reason that the old building was not in such condition as to make such work possible; that appellee then offered to restore the old building, so that the firm might complete its contract, but that the firm refused to agree to do so; that appellee then demanded that said firm pay back the money advanced on the work, which demand was refused.

The questions involved in this case are in many respects quite novel, at least so far as this court is concerned. The ancient case of Paradine v. Jane, Aleyn 26, is often referred to in the discussion of the question as to whether a covenant will be discharged by a subsequent event, happening without the default of the covenantor, which renders performance impossible. That case was an action of debt to recover rent. The defendant answered that he had been dispossessed by an alien army, which had occupied the premises until after the lease expired. There was no answer as to one quarter. The court said: "Where the law creates a duty or charge, and the party is disabled to perform it without any default in him, there the law will excuse him; * * * but where the party by his own contract creates a duty or charge upon himself, he is bound to make it good, notwithstanding any accident by inevitable necessity, because he might have provided against it by his contract." It will be seen that that case did not involve a question as to a covenant which it had become impossible to perform, since the defendant could pay rent, modo et forma as he had covenanted, notwithstanding the eviction. We regard it as thoroughly settled that the words of a mere general covenant will not be construed as an undertaking to answer for a subsequent event, happening without the fault of the covenantor, which renders performance of the covenant itself not merely difficult or relatively impossible, but absolutely impossible, owing to the act of God, the act of the law, or the loss or destruction of the subject-matter of the contract. Where performance is thus rendered impossible, the inquiry naturally arises as to whether there was a purpose to covenant against such an extraordinary and therefore presumably unapprehended event, the happening of which it was not within the power of the covenantor to prevent. The tempest, for instance, may destroy that which must exist if performance of the covenant is to remain possible, and it would seem evident in such a case that it was not within the contemplation of the parties that the maker of the covenant should answer in damages for what he could in no wise control. But, on the other hand, a person entering into a charter party might be answerable for delay caused by adverse winds, since it would be presumed that the parties contracted with such a possibility in mind. Shubrick v. Salmond, 3 Burr. 1637. A well-known English writer on the law of contracts says: "By the modern understanding of the law, we are not bound to seek for a general definition of 'the act of God' or vis major, but only to ascertain what kind of events were within the contemplation of the parties;" and he further says upon the same point: "We cannot arrive, then, at any more distinct conception than this: An event which, as between the parties and for the purpose of the matter in hand, cannot be definitely foreseen or controlled. In other words, we are thrown back upon the nature and construction of the particular contract." Pollock, Prin. of Contracts, 262. In Hayes v. Bickerstaff, Vaugh. 118, 122, it was declared "that a man's covenant shall not be strained so as to be unreasonable, or that it was improbable to be so intended, without necessary words to make it such, for it is unreasonable to suppose a man should covenant against the tortious acts of strangers, impossible for him to prevent, or, probably, to attempt preventing."

The leading case upon the subject of subsequent events rendering performance of covenants impossible is Baily v. Crespigny, 4 Q. B. L. R. 180. In that case a lessor had covenanted that neither he nor his heirs or assigns would allow any building on a piece of land of the lessor's fronting the demised premises. A railway company purchased this land under the compulsory powers of a subsequent act of Parliament, and erected a station upon it. It was held that the railway company, coming in under compulsory powers, whom the covenantor could not bind by any stipulation, was "a new kind of assign, such as was not in the contemplation of the parties when the contract was entered into," and that therefore the covenantor was discharged In the course of the opinion the court said· "There can be no doubt that a man may, by an absolute contract, bind himself to perform things which subsequently become impossible, or to pay damages for nonperformance; and this construction is to be put upon an unqualified undertaking, where the event which causes the impossibility was or might have been anticipated and guarded against in the contract, or where the impossibility arises from the act or default of the promisor. But where the event is of such a character that it cannot reasonably be supposed to have been in the contemplation of the contracting parties when the contract was made, they will not be held bound by general words which, though large enough to include, were not used with reference to the possibility of the particular contingency which afterwards happens. It is on this principle that the act of God is in some cases said to excuse the breach of a contract. This is, in fact, an inaccurate expression, because, where it is an answer to a complaint of an alleged breach of contract that the thing done or left undone was so by the act of God, what is meant is that it was not within the contract; for, as it is observed by Maule, J., in Canham v. Berry, 15 C. B. 619 (E. C. L. R. vol. 80), 24 L. J. C. P. 106, a man might by apt words bind himself that it shall rain tomorrow or that he will pay damages. This is the explanation of the case put by Lord Coke in Shelley's Case, 1 Rep. 98a: 'If a lessee covenants to leave a wood in as good a plight as the wood was at the time of the lease, and afterwards the trees are blown down by tempests, he is discharged of his covenant because it was thought that the covenant was intended to relate only to the tenant's own acts, and not to an event beyond his control, producing effects not in his power to remedy.' See Shep. Touch. 173. It is on this principle that it has been held that an impossibility, arising from an act of the Legislature subsequent to the contract, discharges the contractor from liability."

In Singleton v. Carroll, 6 J. J. Marsh. 527, 22 Am. Dec. 95, it was held that the defendant was not liable upon his covenant to return a slave who, without the fault of the defendant, had run away. It was there said: "The true ground, however, generally, upon which in such cases to rest the defense of the covenantor, is that the loss is not to be considered as provided against by a general covenant." See, also, Pollard v. Schaaffer, 1 Dall. 210, 1 L. Ed. 104, 1 Am. Dec. 239.

It has been questioned whether a fire caused by lightning is "an act of God," since fire can be prevented and also extinguished, but we need not consider this point. As to a general covenant, it is the law that the destruction of the subject-matter of the contract, thereby creating a physical or natural impossibility inherent in the nature of the thing to be performed, whether occasioned by vis major or otherwise, will discharge the covenant, provided the event occurred without the fault of the covenantor.

The destruction before completion of a house which a contractor had covenanted to furnish materials for, and to erect and complete, will not relieve him, for performance is not thereby rendered impossible, since he may build a new house; but if the contract is to bestow labor and materials upon a particular building, it is obvious that its destruction prevents a compliance with the undertaking. Pollock states that it is the admitted rule of English law that, if a chattel perish without the vendor's fault, performance is excused, although the promise is in words positive. Prin. of Cont. 263. Chitty says: "But in contracts from the nature of which it is apparent that the parties contracted on the basis of the continued existence of a given person or thing, a condition is implied that if the performance become impossible from the perishing of the person or thing, that shall excuse such performance." 2 Contracts (11th Am. Ed.) 1076.

In Taylor v. Caldwell, 3 Best & Smith, 826, where a music hall, engaged for concerts, had been accidentally destroyed by fire, it was held that both parties were thereby excused from the contract, because the general rule requiring absolute performance "is only applicable when the contract is positive and absolute, and not subject to any condition, expressed or implied." It was there also held that "where, from the nature of the contract, it appears that the parties must from the beginning have known that it could not be fulfilled unless, when the time for the fulfillment of the contract arrived, some particular specified thing continued to exist, so that, when entering into the contract, they must have contemplated such continuing existence as the foundation of what was to be done, there, in the absence of any express or implied warranty that the thing shall exist, the contract is not to be construed as a positive contract, but as subject to an implied condition that the parties shall be excused in case, before breach, performance becomes impossible from the perishing of the thing without the default of the contractor." See, also, Womack v. McQuarry, 28 Ind. 103, 92 Am. Dec. 306; Jamieson v. Ind., etc., Co., 128 Ind. 555, 28 N. E. 76, 12 L. R. A. 652; Lord v. Wheeler, 1 Gray, 282; Schwartz v. Saunders, 46 Ill. 18; Walker v. Tucker, 70 Ill. 527; Lorillard v. Clyde, 142 N. Y. 456, 37 N. E. 489, 24 L. R. A. 113; Niblo v. Binnse, *40 N. Y. 476; Brumby v. Smith, 3 Ala. 123; Cook v. McCabe, 53 Wis. 250, 10 N. W. 507, 40 Am. Rep. 765; Haynes v. Second Baptist Church, 88 Mo. 285, 57 Am. Rep. 413; Hall v. School Dist., 24 Mo. App. 213; Anglo-Egyptian Nav. Co. v. Rennie, L. R. 10 C. P. 271; Platt on Covenants, 582; 9 Cyc. 631, and cases cited.

The case of Butterfield v. Byron, 153 Mass. 517, 27 N. E. 667, 12 L. R. A. 571, 25 Am. St. Rep. 654, is quite in point. The court in that case, by Knowlton, J., said: "The fundamental question in the present case is, what is the true interpretation of the contract? Was the house, while in the process of erection, to be in the control and at the sole risk of the defendant, or was the plaintiff to have a like interest as the builder of a part of it? Was the defendant's undertaking to go on and build and deliver such a house as the contract called for, even if he should be obliged again and again to begin anew on account of the repeated destruction again and again of a partly completed building by inevitable accident, or did his contract relate to one building only, so that it would be at an end if the building, when nearly completed, should perish without his fault? It is to be noticed that his agreement was not to build a house, furnishing all the labor and materials therefor. His contract was of a very different kind. The specifications are incorporated in it, and it appears that it was an agreement to contribute certain labor and materials towards the erection of a house, on land of the plaintiff, towards the erection of which the plaintiff himself was to contribute other labor and materials, which contributions would together make a completed house. The grading, excavating, stonework, brickwork, painting, and plumbing were to be done by the plaintiff. Immediately before the fire, when the house was nearly completed, the defendant's contract, so far as it remained unperformed, was to finish a house on the plaintiff's land, which had been constructed from materials and by labor furnished in part by the plaintiff and in part by himself. He was no more responsible that the house should continue in existence than the plaintiff was. Looking at the situation of the parties at that time, it was like a contract to make repairs on the house of another. His undertaking and duty to go on and finish the work was upon an implied condition that the house, the product of their joint contributions, should remain in existence. The destruction of it by fire discharged him from his contract."

Counsel for appellee attach much importance to the fact that under the findings of the trial court the firm of John Krause & Co. had full opportunity to perform its contract before the fire occurred. It is insisted that this case does not fall within the general rule, because some of the authorities proceed on the supposition that the reason for nonliability upon the part of the covenantor rests on the fact that the other party impliedly covenants that the premises shall remain in condition for a sufficient length of time to permit the promisor to perform his contract. It may well be said, as we have seen that Mr. Chitty states, that a condition is implied that, if the performance becomes impossible from the perishing of the person or thing, that shall excuse performance. Such a construction would be a fair example of the doctrine, laid down by one of the old writers, that "constructions are to be with equity and moderation, to moderate the rigor of the law." Grounds of Law and Equity, 38 Ca. 49. We think the case is one for the application of the rule declared by Lord Bacon, that "general words are restrained according to the nature of the thing or person." Max. Reg. 10; Whart. Max. 207. We fail to perceive why the covenantor should be charged with a breach that had nothing to do with the impossibility, and we cannot understand how the covenantor can be relieved upon performance becoming impossible before breach, on the theory that the covenantee had violated his implied undertaking that the premises should continue in a fit condition, where it was impossible for him to prevent the happening of the event. The view that what is made an excuse for the covenantor is to be treated as a breach by the covenantee has been exploded by Appleby v. Myers, L. R. 2 C. P. 651.

The breach of contract on the part of the firm, set out in the trial court's findings, had nothing to do with the burning of the building. As observed in Pollard v. Schaaffer, 1 Dall. 210, 1 L. Ed. 104, 1 Am. Dec. 239, the property would have alike perished in the hands of the other party. The firm had proceeded to a point where the undertaking lacked but little of completion, and after the fire, when a demand to restore the work was made, the answer that performance was impossible was as sufficient, since the firm was not to blame for the destruction of the building, as it would have been had the fire occurred before the breach relied on. Appellee's complaint does not proceed upon the theory that the prior delay was a breach. The theory of that pleading is that the breach lay in the failure to proceed with the execution of the contract after the fire. The pursuit of said firm on the latter ground was a waiver of the prior breach, since the two theories are diametrically opposed to each other. If the position were taken that the delay was a breach which appellee had taken advantage of to terminate the right of performance and to seek damages on the contract, the very assuming of that position involves the view that appellee had devolved upon it the ownership of the building in its then state, together with the responsibility of ownership under the rule res perit domino, thus limiting the damages to the cost of completion, or $35. But this breach had to be passed over, in order that it might be asserted that said firm should have proceeded with the work after the fire, and with the assumption of the latter position the prior breach ceased to be a factor in the case.

We do not think that the rights of the parties were changed by the offer of appellee to restore the old building. The offer was made for the purpose of changing legal rights. There is no equity in a case of this kind, where the contractors have expended more money than they received in the execution of the contract. There must be a loss to some one. As observed by Lord Ellenborough, in Barker v. Hodgson, 3 Mau. & Selw. 267, "The question is, on which side the burden is to fall." When said firm entered into the original contract, the old building was standing, and it had a right to proceed presently with its contract. Appellee has no equity to demand that said firm carry out its contract after waiting until the old building can be restored, or that said firm accommodate itself to a new undertaking which would be different from the particular work which it obligated itself to do.

There have been decisions to the effect that substantial performance of covenants will be required where exact performance has become impossible. This proposition is no doubt true, as a general rule, especially in equity. Eaton v. Lyon, 3 Ves. Jr. 690. If the essence of an undertaking can be performed, that will be required. Thus, if a man covenants to build and complete a house by a certain day, the existence of the plague will excuse him, but he will be required to perform his undertaking afterwards. Bacon's Abr. Conditions (2). But the particular class of cases to which our inquiries relate seems to be distinguishable in that such cases proceed on the theory that the covenantor did not, presumptively, by his general words, contract against that which afterwards rendered performance impossible, if caused by the vis major or the loss or destruction of the subject-matter. If he did not covenant against such possibilities, there is no basis for requiring him to perform as near as may be. Lord Coke states, in his note to Shelley's Case (1 Rep. 98a), that if a lessee covenants to leave a wood in as good a plight as it was at the time of the lease, and the trees are blown down by tempests, "he is *discharged* [our italics] of his covenant, quia impotentia excusat legem"; and this was said, as pointed out in Pollard v. Schaaffer, supra, although it was obvious that the lessee might have planted new trees, or rendered damages in lieu of those which had fallen. It seems to us that if the covenantee has any remedy, where a particular building is accidentally destroyed, it must be in assumpsit, to recover, ex æquo et bono, for advancements in excess of expenditures, if any; but where, as here, the contractor had paid out more than he has received, we think that the payments made, which have gone into the property, must be treated as an execution of the contract pro tanto, leaving the rule to prevail, "Res perit domino." See Anglo-Egyptian Nav. Co. v. Rennie, L. R. 10 C. P. 271.

Another consideration must be borne in mind with reference to the asserted obligation of the firm to rebuild if appellee restored the old building, and that is that appellee was not under a corresponding obligation to rebuild for the accommodation of said firm. Suppose that the fire had occurred before the work on the annex had progressed to any considerable extent; would the school town have been required to restore its building, that the firm might avail itself of its contract? Obviously not. The occurrence of a fire which practically destroyed the original building put such a different aspect on the face of things that it could not be said that it was within the contemplation of the parties, when they entered into the contract, that, if a fire occurred, the old building should be restored. The observations of the court in Butterfield v. Byron, supra, are quite to the point upon the matter now under consideration. "It seems very clear," said the court in that case, "that after the building was burned, and just before the day fixed for the completion of the contract, the defendant could not have compelled the plaintiff to do the grading, excavating, stonework, brickwork, painting, and plumbing for another house of the same kind. The plaintiff might have answered, 'I do not desire to build another house, which cannot be completed until long after the date at which I desired to use my house. My contract related to one house. Since that has been destroyed without my fault, I am under no further obligation.' If the plaintiff could successfully have made this answer to a demand by the defendant that he should do his part towards the erection of a second building, then, certainly, the defendant can prevail on a similar answer in the present suit. In other words, looking at the contract from the plaintiff's position, it seems manifest that he did not agree to furnish the work and materials, required of him by the specifications, for more than one house, and, if that was destroyed by an inevitable accident just before its completion, he was not bound to build another, or to do anything further under his contract. If the plaintiff was not obliged to make his contribution of work and materials towards the building of a second house, neither was the defendant. The agreement of each to complete the performance of the contract after a building, the product of their joint contributions, had been partly erected, was on an implied condition that the building should continue in existence. Neither can recover anything of the other under the contract, for he has not performed the contract so that its stipulations can be availed of." See, also, Board of Com'rs, Crawford Co., v. Louisville, etc., R. Co., 39 Ind. 192, 200.

It is contended by counsel for appellee that the provision of the contract that the school town "shall not be in any manner answerable, accountable, or responsible for any loss or damage that shall or may happen to said work or any part thereof," amounted to a special provision which guarded against any implication that would leave appellee to bear any part of the loss or damage. We fail to apprehend how this provision, designed as a shield, can be converted into a sword. So far as the principal action is concerned, no one is endeavoring to hold appellee "answerable, accountable, or responsible for any loss or damage." In any event, it cannot fairly be contended that this provision made said firm responsible for the integrity of the old building. As it was the destruction of the building which belonged to appellee that made performance impossible, the special provision under consideration did not extend to such a case. As against such a contingency, the contract wholly failed to provide.

There is even less of merit in the contention that, if said firm had completed its contract without delay, appellee might have insured against fire. The latter had an increasing measure of risk during the progress of the work, and it was entirely optional with it whether it would insure against such risk. We cannot, however, admit that the mere right or privilege of entering into a collateral contract of indemnity can have anything to do with the construction of the original covenant to build.

We now address ourselves to a consideration of appellants' cross-complaint. The contract provided for the performance of a specific and entire work, for a consideration, as to the portion thereof now in dispute, which was to be paid upon the completion of the building. The firm had reached a point where it was not entitled to any further money until it had completed its contract. To this extent, at least, the contract was unapportionable, and the performance of the whole work was a condition precedent to a recovery upon the special contract. 1 Addison on Contracts, 400. There could be no recovery upon this contract, because it was unperformed, and the question as to the right to recover on a common count must depend upon where the loss must fall. In respect to a substantially like agreement relative to chattels, Judge Story says: "Suppose there is a contract to do work on a thing by the job (as, for example, repairs on a ship), for a stipulated price for the whole work, and the thing should accidentally perish, or be destroyed, without any fault on either side, before the job is completed, the question would then arise, whether the workman would be entitled to compensation pro tanto for his work and labor done, and materials applied, up to the time of the loss or destruction. It would seem that by the common law (independent of any usage of trade) the workman would not be entitled to any compensation, and that the rule would apply that the thing should perish to the employer and the work to the mechanic." Story on Bailments, § 426b.

The subject under consideration received an exhaustive consideration in Appleby v. Myers, L. R. 2 C. P. 651. That was a case stated, by consent, without pleadings. The contract was to install a steam boiler, engine, etc., in a building belonging to defendant, for a consideration to be paid on the completion of the work. The building was burned. The court said: "Where, as in the present case, the premises are destroyed without fault on either side, it is a misfortune equally affecting both parties, excusing both from further performance of the contract, but giving a cause of action to neither." It was also pointed out by the court that there was nothing illogical in holding that the plaintiffs were not entitled to pay, since, if the accidental fire had left the defendant's premises untouched, and had only injured a part of the work of plaintiffs, they would have been required to do that part over again to fulfill their contract to complete the whole.

Pollard v. Schaaffer, 1 Dall. 210, 1 L. Ed. 104, 1 Am. Dec. 239, was a suit on a covenant to deliver up demised premises at the end of the term in good order and repair. Plea, that the British army had forcibly taken possession of the premises and held the same until the term had expired, and that during said time said army had committed the waste complained of. McKean, C. J., in concluding an opinion well worth the perusal in connection with this case, said: "I am of the opinion that the defendant is excused from his covenant to deliver up the premises in good repair on the 1st of March, 1778: (1) Because a covenant to do this, against an act of God or an enemy, ought to be special and express, and so clear that no other meaning could be put upon it. (2) Because the defendant had no consideration nor premium for this risk, and it was not in the contemplation of either party. And, lastly, because equality is equity, and the loss should be divided; he who had the term will lose the temporary profits of the premises, and he who hath the reversion will bear the loss done to the permanent buildings."

The rule res perlit domino is very influential in all cases of this general character, and the only question is as to the application of the rule. See Story on Bailments, §§ 426, 426a. The following authorities support the view that the members of said firm cannot recover on their cross-complaint: Brumby v. Smith, 3 Ala. 123; Siegel v. Eaton & Prince Co., 165 Ill. 550, 46 N. E. 449; Lumber Co. v. Purdum, 41 Ohio St. 373; Fildew v. Besley, 42 Mich. 100, 3 N. W. 278, 36 Am. Rep. 433; Bishop on Contracts, § 588. As applied to this case, we may well adopt the following, which we take from 15 Am. & Eng. Ency. of Law, 1090: "In a case of this nature, the defendant (owner) receives no benefit, and, if he is equally blameless and irresponsible for the accident by which the property is destroyed, why should not the law leave the parties as it finds them, and let each suffer his own loss?" We think that neither said firm nor the appellee was entitled to recover in this case.

Judgment reversed, with directions to the trial court to restate its conclusions of law and to render judgment in accordance with this opinion.

(32 Ind. A. 519)

CHICAGO, I. & E. RY. CO. v. INDIANA NATURAL GAS & OIL CO.

(Appellate Court of Indiana, Division No. 1. March 8, 1904.)

APPEAL—RECORD—AMENDED PLEADINGS—CLERK'S CERTIFICATE.

1. Under Burns' Rev. St. 1901, § 662, providing that the clerk shall certify the amended pleadings only, but the original pleadings may be made a part of the record, on appeal, by exceptions or order of the court, the clerk can only certify the amended pleadings, and cannot, by indicating what portion of the pleadings was original and what amendment, inform the court, on appeal, with reference thereto.

2. Where, after the court has sustained demurrers to paragraphs of the answer, the complaint is amended, the answers should be refiled, so that, if the demurrers are again sustained, the record on appeal may be made up so as to present the answer and complaint as seen and considered by the trial court in ruling on the demurrers.

3. Where demurrers were addressed to the paragraphs of a pleading severally, and the court considered the paragraphs separately, and sustained the demurrers as to some of the paragraphs and overruled them as to others, the court on appeal cannot review the decision, unless the record shows the paragraphs held sufficient on demurrer, though such paragraphs were subsequently dismissed by the voluntary act of the pleader.

Appeal from Circuit Court, Grant County; H. J. Paulus, Judge.

Action by the Indiana Natural Gas & Oil Company against the Chicago, Indiana & Eastern Railway Company. From a judgment for plaintiff, defendant appeals. Affirmed.

Knight & Brown and Hawkins & Smith, for appellant. Miller, Elam & Fesler, S. D. Miller, W. O. Johnson, and C. C. Shirley, for appellee.

BLACK, J. The appellee filed its complaint against the appellant September 9, 1901. The appellant, September 27, 1901, filed its answer in eight paragraphs, the eighth being a general denial, and its cross-complaint in five paragraphs. October 7, 1901, the appellee filed its demurrer to each of the paragraphs of the answer, except the eighth, and also its demurrer, for want of sufficient facts, to each paragraph of the cross-complaint. October 29, 1901, the court sustained the demurrer to each of the first six paragraphs of the answer, and overruled the demurrer to the seventh paragraph of answer. At the same time the court overruled the demurrer to the first, fourth, and fifth paragraphs of cross-complaint, and sustained the demurrer to the second and third paragraphs of cross-complaint. November 18, 1901, the appellant dismissed its seventh paragraph of answer and its fifth paragraph of cross-complaint. December 2, 1901, the appellee amended its complaint. On the same day the trial was commenced, "the answer of general denial being treated as refiled after the filing of" the amended complaint. The appellee having introduced its evidence, the appellant dismissed its first and fourth paragraphs of cross-complaint, and the court, after hearing further evidence and argument, found for the appellee on its amended complaint. The appellant, by its assignment of errors, questions the action of the court in sustaining the appellee's demurrer to the first six paragraphs of answer, severally, and in sustaining the appellee's demurrer to the second and third paragraphs, severally, of the cross-complaint.

The transcript of the record before us contains the first six paragraphs of answer, but it does not contain the seventh paragraph. It contains the second and third paragraphs of cross-complaint, but it does not contain the first, fourth, or fifth paragraphs of cross-complaint. The complaint, it thus appears, was amended after the ruling upon the demurrers, and the appellant did not plead to the amended complaint, but upon the trial the answer of general denial was considered as if refiled. When the complaint was amended, the original complaint, to which the answers were directed, ceased to be a part of the record on appeal, unless brought in by bill of exceptions or order of court. Section 662, Burns' Rev. St. 1901. It was not within the province of the clerk to indicate what portion of the complaint certified up to this court was original and what portion was matter introduced by amendment, but it was his duty, under the statute above cited, to certify the amended pleading only. Thus, if sustaining a demurrer to an answer to an original complaint, afterward amended, can be made a material matter, it cannot be said that we are properly informed as to the averments of the pleading to which the answers were addressed. We ought in all cases to be certainly informed in a legitimate way of the precise question for decision as it was presented to the court whose ruling we are asked to review. The answers as to whose sufficiency our opinion is desired should have been refiled after the filing of the amended complaint, and if, then, demurrers directed to the answers thus refiled were sustained, the record could easily have been so made up as to present the answers and the complaint as seen and considered by the court in ruling upon the demurrers.

When the court sustained the demurrer to each of the first six paragraphs of answer to the original complaint, and sustained the demurrer to the second and third paragraphs severally of the cross-complaint, the seventh paragraph of answer, the demurrer to which was overruled, and the first, fourth, and fifth paragraphs of cross-complaint, the demurrer to each of which was overruled, were before the court below in the record; but we know nothing as to the averments of the pleadings thus held sufficient on demurrer, for they are not in the record on appeal. The demurrers were addressed to the paragraphs severally of the answer and to each paragraph of the cross-complaint, and the court below, therefore, considered the paragraphs of answer and the paragraphs of cross-complaint separately, and considered none of them jointly with other paragraphs of answer or cross-complaint, in ruling upon the demurrers; and we, in like manner, considering the paragraphs separately, cannot, as to any of the first six paragraphs of answer, determine whether or not there was any substantial difference between it and the seventh paragraph, or whether or not all the material averments of the second or the third paragraph of cross-complaint might have been made as available under one of the paragraphs of cross-complaint, the demurrer to which was overruled, as they would have been if the demurrer had not been sustained. Each paragraph of answer and each paragraph of cross-complaint before us in the record may have been regarded properly by the court as presenting no question that was not as effectually presented by another paragraph of pleading held sufficient on demurrer. If the rulings of the court were correct when made, they could not be rendered erroneous by the subsequent voluntary action of the appellant in dismissing his pleadings, the demurrers to which were overruled, and leaving them out of the record.

We are unable to say that there was any available error in the rulings questioned on appeal. Judgment affirmed.

(33 Ind. App. 484)

BOLDT v. EARLY.*

(Appellate Court of Indiana, Division No. 1. Feb. 26, 1904.)

VENDOR AND PURCHASER — SPECIFIC PERFORMANCE — EQUITIES — DISCRETION OF COURT—VENDEE'S FAILURE TO MAKE PAYMENTS.

1. The awarding of specific performances is a matter not of absolute right, but of sound discretion.

2. In a suit for a specific performance the burden is on plaintiff to show a full and complete performance, or offer to perform.

3. Though time be not of the essence of a contract for the sale of land as originally made, it may be rendered so by the conduct of the vendor and vendee subsequent to the making of the contract.

4. The fact that, after the vendee in a contract for the sale of land has failed to pay an installment of the purchase money, there has been a considerable increase in the value of the land, may be a sufficient reason for denying him specific performance.

5. At the time of a contract for the sale of land the vendor told the purchaser that the land was being sold that the vendor might pay his debts, and the value of the land was rising at that time. The purchaser failed to pay the second installment at the time it was due, and about seven months thereafter the vendor gave the purchaser notice that, if the moneys due were not paid by a certain date, about four months later, the land would be sold to some one else. During that time no payment was made, and the land continued to increase in value. Subsequently the purchaser tendered the money due. *Held*, that the purchaser was not entitled to specific performance.

Appeal from Circuit Court, St. Joseph County; W. A. Funk, Judge.

Action by Hilary Early against August Boldt. From a judgment in favor of complainant, defendant appeals. Reversed.

Frank E. Osborne and Wm. A. McVey, for appellant. F. R. Liddell and T. E. Howard, for appellee.

BLACK, J. The appellee sued the appellant for specific performance of a contract for the sale of land. The facts, as stated in the court's special finding, were substantially as follows: July 20, 1899, the appellant

*Rehearing denied May 17, 1904.

¶ 4. See Specific Performance, vol. 44, Cent. Dig. §§ 205, 207.

was the owner in fee simple and in possession of a certain tract of land in La Porte county, Ind., and the legal title thereof was still in him at the date of the court's finding. At the date first above mentioned the appellant entered into a written contract with the appellee for the sale of this land. By the terms of the contract, which was signed by both parties, and dated July 20, 1899, the appellant agreed to sell to the appellee the land in question, described, for the sum of $2,300, "of which I have received this day ten dollars, and agree to take $490.00 in thirty days, $500.00 in six months, at which time I will give a warranty deed conveying a perfect title free of any incumbrance, and take a mortgage on said land, payable in payments of $500.00 per year, with interest at six per cent., except one, the last note or payment to be $300.00. It is agreed that said notes shall be drawn payable on or before the date of ultimate maturity, and it is also agreed that payments can be made on the two specified payments first named herein, at any time previously, and the deed shall be made when the first $1,000.00 named is made. And the said Early hereby agrees to make the named payments as specified." August 25, 1899, the appellee paid the appellant under the contract $490, the latter accepting the same, and receipting to the former therefor. July 24, 1900, the appellee paid the appellant upon the contract $15.77, which the appellant accepted, receipting to the appellee therefor. July 24, 1900, the appellant caused a letter to be written to the appellee, which the latter received about the same date, advising the appellee that the time was past due for making the second payment of $500, which, by the terms of the contract, was to be made in six months from the date of the contract, and which, therefore, was due January 20, 1900, and informing the appellee that the appellant wanted to know what he was going to do about it soon; to which letter the appellee replied July 31, 1900, saying he would see the appellant before long, and would settle matters with him for the land. At the time of the making of the contract the appellee was a man of business experience, and was engaged in the real estate business, which he had been following for more than 30 years; and the appellant was a German, unable to read or write in either the German or the English language, and could talk the English language only brokenly, and understood it with difficulty. He had lived in the neighborhood of the land in question for 31 years. At the time of the making of the contract the appellee went to the home of the appellant, and prepared the contract himself, and it was there signed by the appellee, and was signed in the name of the appellant, in his presence, and with his consent, by the appellant's son; and at the same time the appellant informed the appellee that the former was selling the land because he was in debt, and wanted to use the money he would derive from the sale for the purpose of paying his debts; and in fact the appellant was in debt to the amount of about $1,300, and he used the $500 paid him as aforesaid by the appellee to pay a part of said indebtedness immediately upon the payment of the same to him. On or about August 30, 1900, the appellant, with one Henry Jahns, a neighbor, who acted as an interpreter for the appellant, called upon the appellee in the city of La Porte, and demanded of the appellee that he pay the $500 then past due; and the appellee then informed the appellant that the former had no money, and could not get any then, and could not make the payment. The appellant informed the appellee that the former needed the money to pay his debts, and the appellee then stated to the appellant that the former expected to sell a piece of land in a short time, from which he would get money to make the payment, and that he would make the payment soon; and the appellant then informed the appellee that unless he made the payment by Christmas he could not have the land, and that the appellant would sell it to some one else. On or about October 1, 1900, Herman Boldt, a son of the appellant, at the latter's request, again called upon the appellee in the city of La Porte, and inquired of him if he had as yet arranged to make the payment, to which the appellee replied that he could not pay then; that he had not yet been able to raise the money, but he would do so soon; in response to which Herman Boldt informed the appellee that unless he made the payment by Christmas he could not have the land, but the appellant would sell it to some one else. The appellee did not make any further payment before Christmas, 1900, and did not go to the appellant and give him any further information, or make any other arrangement with him whatever; but February 9, 1901, he left the state of Indiana and did not return until July 4, 1901. July 5, 1901, the appellant entered into a written contract with one Charles H. Tuesburg, by which the appellant promised and agreed to sell and convey the land in question for the price of $4,000, of which Tuesburg at the time paid the appellant $200, which the appellant used and applied to the payment of his debts; but the appellant at the date of the court's finding had not executed to Tuesburg any deed of conveyance for the land.

At the time of the making of the contract of the appellant and the appellee the land in question was marsh land, uncultivated, and unimproved, and there was a growing demand for such lands in that neighborhood, and such lands were increasing in value, of which fact the appellee had knowledge; and the appellant also knew that the land in controversy was increasing in value, and he fully understood the value of the land, and understood the contract between him and the appellee and all its provisions; and when the appellant and Jahns called on the appellee August 30, 1900, the appellant had learned and knew that the lands in the neighborhood in question were increasing in value. From the early spring of 1899 to August 30, 1901, the land in question had gradually increased in value about 25 to 40 per cent. July 11, 1901, the appellee learned that the appellant had entered into a contract for the sale of the land to Tuesburg, and the appellant on that day informed the appellee that the former had sold the land to Tuesburg. Thereafter, on August 30, 1901, the appellee called upon the appellant at his home, and offered him first $660, and presented three notes dated August 30, 1901, signed by the appellee, and payable to the appellant, two of them for $500 each and one for $300, due on or before one, two, and three years from date, respectively, with interest at the rate of 6 per cent. from date until paid, and a mortgage on the land in question securing the notes, signed and acknowledged by the appellee, and demanded of the appellant that he execute to the appellee a deed for the land. Immediately thereafter, on the same occasion, the appellee offered the appellant $1,160 and two notes, signed by the appellee, and payable to the order of the appellant, dated August 30, 1901—one for $500, due on or before one year after date, and the other for $300, due on or before two years after date—and also offered a mortgage on the land to secure the notes executed and acknowledged by the appellee; in response to which the appellant stated to the appellee that he had sold the land. At the time for the payment of $500 and the delivery of the deed, January 20, 1900, neither party did anything toward the performance of the contract. August 31, 1901, the appellee brought this suit in the La Porte circuit court, and filed in the office of the clerk of that court a lis pendens notice of the bringing of the suit. The appellee did not at any time after the making of the contract in suit until August 30, 1901, offer to pay the $500 which came due January 20, 1900, nor did he during that period execute or offer to execute notes and mortgage for the deferred payments. At all times from the date of the contract up to Christmas of the year 1900 the appellant was ready and willing and able to accept and receive the payments and notes and mortgage and execute and deliver to the appellee a warranty deed conveying title to the land in accordance with the contract. He never executed or tendered to the appellee a deed of conveyance for the land. August 11, 1900, the appellant authorized the appellee to cut the grass on the land, which he had done. April 12, 1901, the appellee paid to the treasurer of La Porte county $11.52 for the taxes assessed against the land for the year 1900. The court found that about the end of August, 1900, the appellant agreed with the appellee to an extension of the time for making payment upon the contract until Christmas, 1900. August 30, 1901, the appellee went to the appellant prepared to pay the money then due from the former to the latter upon the contract, and prepared to execute the notes and mortgage for the balance of the purchase money for the land, and prepared to tender said money and said notes and mortgage, but was informed by the appellant that he could not have the land, and that the appellant refused to carry out the terms of the contract with the appellee.

Upon these facts the court stated conclusions of law as follows: "(1) That the plaintiff is entitled to a specific performance of said contract by the defendant. (2) That the defendant shall execute and deliver to the plaintiff a good and sufficient warranty deed for said real estate, and should receive therefor from the plaintiff the amount of money, notes, and mortgage tendered to him August 30, 1901, or the full amount of the balance of the purchase price, which was due August 30, 1901, in cash, at the option of the plaintiff, as provided in said contract; and that if the defendant fails within a reasonable time to execute and deliver said deed and receive said consideration therefor, a commissioner should be appointed by the court to execute such deed, on the payment of such consideration into the hands of the clerk of this court for the use of the defendant."

By the terms of the contract the appellant, after receiving, at its date, the payment of $10, and after receiving in 30 days thereafter $490, was to receive in 6 months after the date of the contract—that is, on January 20, 1900—another payment of $500. He was then to execute the deed of conveyance, and to take a mortgage on the land to secure payment of the remainder of the purchase money, payable in three installments, represented by three notes bearing interest at 6 per cent.—two for $500 each, to mature ultimately one in one year and the other in two years from January 20, 1900, and one for $300, to mature ultimately in three years from that date; but these notes were to be drawn payable on or before such dates of ultimate maturity. The appellee agreed to make the payments as thus specified. There was also a provision that payments might be made on the installment of $490 due in 30 days and the installment of $500 due in 6 months at any time before their maturity, and in this connection it was provided that the deed should be made when the first $1,000 of the purchase money was paid. When the appellee offered to make payments and to give notes and mortgages on August 30, 1901, the installment of $500 payable January 20, 1900, had been due 1 year and 7⅓ months, and the time of this offer was more than 7 months after the date designated for the ultimate maturity of the first note contemplated by the contract for $500. The court rendered its special finding and its judgment

September 8, 1902. At that date, if the contract had been carried out according to its terms, all the installments of the purchase money would have been due except the final installment of $300, which would have ultimately matured in less than five months thereafter. In any view of the case, the appellant could not have been regarded as having been placed in a position where he could be required to make the deed before August 30, 1901. The court concluded September 8, 1902, that he should execute the deed, and should receive therefor the amount of money, notes, and mortgage tendered to him August 30, 1901, or the full amount of the balance of the purchase price due at that date in cash, at the option of the appellee.

It will have been observed that the court found that two offers of money, notes, and mortgages were made by the appellee on that day; but we notice that the judgment provided that the appellant should execute the deed and receive from the appellee $1,160, "being payments and interest due on August 30, 1901, together with his promissory notes for $800, secured by mortgage on the said land for the balance of the purchase money, or that he receive from the plaintiff; at the option of the plaintiff, $1,960 in cash, being the total amount due from plaintiff to defendant for said real estate on August 30, 1901." In stating in the finding of facts the offer of August 30, 1901, which included the proposition to pay $1,160, it is stated that the appellee offered the appellant two notes dated August 30, 1901—one for $500, due on or before one year after date, and one for $300, due on or before two years after date. The maturity of each of these notes would be seven months later than the ultimate maturity provided for in the contract. The notes, by the terms of the contract, were to draw interest at 6 per cent. It does not appear from the finding of facts that the notes offered along with the $1,160 in cash provided for any interest, and in the conclusions of law and the judgment it was not required that the notes to be given by the appellee should provide for any interest. It is well settled that the enforcement of specific performance of contracts rests in the sound discretion of the court, and the court will do what seems just and equitable under the peculiar circumstances of the particular case before it for decision. The awarding of specific performance by a court of equity is a matter not of absolute right, but of sound discretion; and a bill may be resisted on much weaker grounds than are necessary for its maintenance. Vawter v. Bacon, 89 Ind. 565. In a suit for specific performance the plaintiff must show that he has been ready, willing, and eager to perform, and the burden is upon him to show a full and complete performance or offer to perform on his part. Forthman v. Deters (Ill.) 69 N. E. 97. Though time be not of the essence of the contract originally, it may be so rendered by the conduct of the vendor or vendee subsequent to the making of the contract. Jackson v. Ligon, 3 Leigh, 161, 188. If, succeeding the fault of the vendee by failure to pay an installment of the purchase money at the time stipulated in the contract, there has been a considerable increase in the value of the property, this may be a sufficient reason for denying him specific relief; for the contract would thereby become an unequal one, and its specific enforcement would encourage delays by enabling the vendee to take advantage of changes in his favor, though he might have delayed intentionally, having purchased for speculation, and not meaning to perform unless favorable changes occur. Smith v. Lawrence, 15 Mich. 499. See, also, Mahon v. Leech (N. D.) 90 N. W. 807. In Brashier v. Gratz, 6 Wheat. 528, 5 L. Ed. 322, it was said by Mr. Chief Justice Marshall: "Another circumstance which ought to have great weight is the change in the value of the land. It was purchased at $22.50 per acre. Mr. Brashier [the plaintiff] failed to comply, and was unable to comply, with his engagements. More than five years after the last payment had become due the land suddenly rises to the price of $80 per acre. Then he tenders the purchase money, and demands a specific performance. Had the land fallen in value, he could not have paid the purchase money," he being insolvent. "This total want of reciprocity gives increased influence to the objections to a specific performance, which are furnished by this great alteration in the value of the article." Lapse of time, after maturity, before payment of purchase money, may generally be compensated by interest; and time will not be regarded as of the essence of such a contract as the one in suit merely because definite dates of performance are designated therein. Jackson v. Ligon, 3 Leigh, 161, 187; Fry, Spec. Perf. (3d Eng. Ed.) § 1077. Neither can inability to pay the purchase money when due, not attributable to the fault of the vendor, be regarded by the court as any excuse for failure to pay at maturity, or upon demand thereafter. In Ewing v. Crouse, 6 Ind. 312, where the provisions of the contract seemed to show that the parties at the time of the sale contemplated a literal performance within the period named, it was said that, if this view were incorrect, yet the subsequent conduct of the parties afforded sufficient proof that they regarded and expressly treated the time agreed on for the payment of an installment of purchase money as an essential element in the contract. The appellant was in debt when the contract was made, and he then informed the appellee that he was selling the land to pay his debts, and he applied upon his debts the moneys he received, which were not enough to discharge his indebtedness. The value of the land was rising gradually when the contract was made, as they both knew, and it had risen greatly afterwards. When payment, overdue, was demanded, the appellee was told that the money was needed to pay debts, which was the purpose of the sale, as he was apprised from the beginning. He was an experienced business man and dealer in real estate, and, while the land was rising greatly in value, he gave no reason for failure to pay except his alleged inability to do so. He had himself gone to the appellant for the making of the contract, the appellant being a man who imperfectly understood the English language, and who was desirous of freeing himself from debt. Having wholly neglected to comply with the demand for payment during the time limited by the notice, he continued thereafter to be in default, and made no offer until after he learned that the appellee had contracted to sell to another person.

While we need not treat the extraneous matters which we thus far have recounted as being sufficient to themselves alone to make time of the essence of the contract, they are not unworthy of the observation of a court of equity in considering the notice limiting the time of payment to Christmas, 1900, and the conduct of the parties thereafter. In Pomeroy on Contracts (2d Ed.) § 395, 3, it is said: "As the doctrine that time is not essential in the performance of a contract may sometimes work injustice, and be used as an excuse for unwarrantable laches, the following rule was introduced at a comparatively late period, and is now firmly settled, which prevents the doctrine from being abused by the neglect or willfulness of either party: If either the vendor or the vendee has improperly or unreasonably delayed in complying with the terms of the agreement on his side, the other party may, by notice, fix upon and assign a reasonable time for completing the contract, and may call upon the defaulting party to do the acts to be done by him, or any particular act, within this period. The time thus allotted then becomes essential, and, if the party in default fails to perform before it has elapsed, the court will not aid him in enforcing the contract, but will leave him to his legal remedy." It is further said in section 396: "The notice cannot be an arbitrary and sudden termination of the transaction. It cannot put an immediate end to a pending dispute or negotiation as to the title. It must allow a reasonable length of time for the other party to perform. And if it fails in any of these respects, it may be disregarded, and will produce no effect upon the equitable remedial rights of the party to whom it is given. The nature and object of the contract, the circumstances of the case, and the previous conduct of the parties are important, and, indeed, controlling, elements in determining the reasonableness of the notice. The notice, also, to be effectual in making the time allotted an essential element of the performance, must be express, clear, distinct, and unequivocal." See, also, to the same effect, Fry, Spec. Perf. (3d Eng. Ed.) § 1092 et seq. This rule appears, as stated by these text-writers, to be well and firmly established in England and America. In Taylor v. Brown, 2 Beav. 180, it was held that, while it was established by repeated decisions that, where the contract and the circumstance were such that time was not considered as of the essence of the contract, if any unnecessary delay was created by one party, the other had the right to limit a reasonable time within which the contract should be perfected by the other, and that in cases where the time was fairly limited by notice, stating that within such a period what was required must be done, or the contract would be treated as at an end, bills for specific performance afterward filed had been dismissed by the court, with costs; yet this rule was not applicable to a case of a notice given during the pendency of negotiations, stating that from the time and on the day of the giving of the notice the party giving it would consider the contract at an end. In Benson v. Lamb, 9 Beav. 502, where there was a delay of two months after the date designated for the completion of the contract, a notice of ten days, then given, was held sufficient to put an end to the contract, and specific performance was denied. In Wiswall v. McGowan, Hoff. Ch. 125, 138, it was said that either party to a contract for the sale of land, where no time has been fixed, or performance at the appointed time has been waived, may limit a day at which it must be fulfilled; but this must be a reasonable period according to the nature of the contract, affording the party a reasonable time to make his preparation, and of this period due notice must be given. See, also, Thompson v. Dulles, 5 Rich. Eq. 370; Mudgett v. Clay, 5 Wash. 103, 111, 31 Pac. 424; Chabot v. Winter Park Co. (Fla.) 15 South. 756, 43 Am. St. Rep. 192. And see Rummington v. Kelley, 7 Ohio, 97, pt. 2, where there was a long delay after the vendor informed the vendee of the immediate end of the contract and tendered him his notes. Specific performance was denied. We need not go so far in the case before us. In Hatch v. Cobb, 4 Johns. Ch. 559—a suit of the vendee for specific performance—it appeared that the plaintiff had made default in the payments, which, by the contract, were made a condition precedent to the conveyance, and the defendant had accepted one small payment subsequent to such default, but about six months thereafter the defendant repeatedly called for payment, and gave notice that, if the plaintiff did not pay him, he should be obliged to part with his interest in the land. No payment being made, the defendant assigned over his right to a third person, and the plaintiff, with knowledge of that fact, made a tender of the balance due on the contract, and filed his bill for specific performance, etc. The court, in holding that specific performance could not be decreed, said that the defendant was not bound to wait any longer upon the plaintiff, but had a clear right to exact immediate payment, or else to part with his interest in the land to another, in order to meet his own convenience or necessities. It was further said that, if the defendant had not parted with his interest before the filing of the bill, it might even have been a point deserving consideration whether the plaintiff was entitled to assistance when no accident, mistake, or fraud had intervened to prevent the performance of the contract on his part, and when, after indulgence and after considerable subsequent delay, he had twice been required to make payment and had omitted to do it. Where the time of performance specified in the notice to the defaulting party is expressly assented to by the latter, the reasonableness of the notice cannot be questioned by him. Miller v. Rice, 133 Ill. 315, 330, 24 N. E. 543. In Chabot v. Winter Park Co. (Fla.) 15 South. 756, 43 Am. St. Rep. 192, it was said: "Although the complainant was in default, he made no reply whatever to the notice. If he had desired still further extension of time, he should have let his wishes be known. If he considered that he had further rights in the matter, and that the Winter Park Company could not put a limitation of time upon him, he should have been prompt in the assertion of such rights. Failing to ask any further extension, or to assert any right, he must be held as acquiescing in the demand contained in the notice; and as abandoning all rights he might have had to enforce the performance of the contract." In that case the time fixed in the notice for the performance of the contract was nearly 40 days, and the act to be done was the payment of a sum of money. This was held to be a reasonable limitation, though one party lived in Massachusetts and the other was in Florida.

At all times from the making of the contract up to the date specified in his notice as the limit of time for payment the appellant was ready, willing, and able to receive and accept payment and notes and mortgage, and to execute to the appellee a deed of conveyance as stipulated in the contract. Being always met with the statement of inability of the appellee to pay, no occasion arose for express tender or offer of a deed of conveyance. Upon all the facts, we think the appellee is not entitled to the interposition of a court of equity, but should be remitted to his remedy at law.

The appellee has filed a cross-assignment of error in the overruling of his demurrer to certain paragraphs of answer, but, if the conclusion to which we have thus arrived be correct, there was no error in the ruling.

The judgment is reversed, and the cause is remanded, with instruction to state a conclusion of law in accord with the foregoing opinion.

(33 Ind. A. 532)

THIEME et al. v. UNION TRUST CO. et al.

(Appellate Court of Indiana, Division No. 1. March 8, 1904.)

WILLS—RIGHT OF SURVIVORSHIP—CONSTRUCTION.

1. Testatrix, by item 4 of her will, gave one-fifth of her estate, which included stock owned by her in a certain brewing company, to two of her grandsons. By item 6 it was provided that the survivor of the two grandchildren should take the whole of the fifth interest in the estate on the death of either during the life of the testatrix. In item 11 it was provided that, while testatrix desired those grandsons to have their full share of the stock in the brewing company, yet she did not desire that they should have anything whatever to do with the business of the company, and by the same item she appointed one of her sons a trustee for the grandsons, and empowered him to take charge of their part of the stock in the brewing company, and control it in the interest of the company, and provided that he should pay to them respectively, or to the survivor thereof, annually, the proportionate share of the dividend declared on the stock. *Held*, that under Burns' Rev. St. 1901, § 8136, providing that the survivor of persons holding personal property in joint tenancy shall have the same rights only as survivors of tenants in common, unless otherwise expressed in the instrument; the will did not create the right of survivorship between the grandsons in the ownership of the stock on the death of one of them after the death of the testatrix.

Appeal from Circuit Court, Clinton County; J. V. Kent, Judge.

Action by the Union Trust Company and another, administrators of the estate of John Thieme, deceased, against John H. Thieme, trustee, and others. From a judgment for plaintiffs, defendants appeal. Affirmed.

Kumler & Gaylord and A. Orth Behm, for appellants. J. E. McCullough and A. N. Wilson, for appellees.

HENLEY, C. J. This action was commenced by appellees, the administrators of the estate of John Thieme, deceased, against appellants John Henry Thieme, trustee under the will of Elizabeth Thieme, deceased, Edward Thieme, and the Thieme & Wagner Brewing Company. The action was to recover 148 shares of the capital stock of the Thieme & Wagner Brewing Company, which was held by the appellant John Henry Thieme in trust for the appellant Edward Thieme and John Thieme, appellees' intestate decedent. The appellant Edward Thieme was made a party defendant to this action in order that his interest, if any, in said capital stock might be determined; and the Thieme & Wagner Brewing Company was made a party defendant in order that the court might compel, by its judgment, such company to issue to appellees the stock claimed by them in case the judgment of the court was in appellees' favor. The appellant Edward Thieme filed a cross-complaint against appellees and his co-appellants, in which he claimed to be the owner of the 148 shares in the brewing company claimed by appellees. In this cross-complaint the will of Elizabeth Thieme, deceased, was set forth in full; the said Edward Thieme claiming that by the terms of said will he was the owner of the capital stock of said brewing company which is here in controversy. Upon motion of the appellees the venue of this cause was changed to the Clinton circuit court. The issue tried was made by answers of general denial filed by the defendants to both the complaint and the cross-complaint. The cause was tried by the court. The facts were found specially, and conclusions of law stated thereon. The only error assigned in this court is that the trial court erred in its conclusions of law on the special finding of facts. The facts found which are necessary to a proper determination of this case were the following: Elizabeth M. Thieme, a widow, died on the 29th day of April, 1895, and left surviving her as her sole and only heirs at law her sons, John Henry Thieme, Charles C. Thieme, and Frederick Thieme, and a daughter, Sophia Zumpe, and two grandchildren, Edward Thieme and John Thieme, sons of her predeceased son, William Thieme. That at the time of the death of the said Elizabeth neither of her grandchildren, Edward and John Thieme, were or ever had been married. That on the 25th day of December, 1891, the said Elizabeth executed her last will and testament, and after her death, to wit, on the 15th day of May, 1895, the said will was duly probated and recorded in the proper records of Tippecanoe county, and said will ever since has been and still remains in full force.

Item 4 of said will was as follows:

"Item 4.—I give, devise and bequeath to my children Charles C. Thieme, Sophia Zumpe, John Henry Thieme, Frederick Thieme, and my grandchildren, Edward Thieme and John Thieme, children of my son William Thieme, deceased, all of the remainder of the real and personal property of which I may die seized or possessed; the said grandchildren both together receiving the undivided ⅕ part thereof. And in case my said son Charles C. Thieme should die without issue, then, at his death ⅓ of the amount bequeathed to him hereby shall go to his wife, Frances, and the other ⅔ shall be divided among my other children and grandchildren, sons of my son William, as in this Item heretofore provided. And the share bequeathed by this clause to my said daughter Sophia Zumpe is made subject to the provisions contained in Item 10 of this will."

"Item 6.—And in case either of said grandchildren should die before my death, then his share shall go to the survivor; and in case both of said grandchildren shall die before I do, then the share, which under this will, would go to said grandchildren, or surviving grandchild, shall be divided among my surviving children, if living, or their children, should they be dead.

"Item 7.—I direct that in the distribution of the personal property each of my children and said grandchildren, Edward and John Thieme, shall have its proportionate share of the stock owned by me in the Thieme & Wagner Brewing Company, the shares of stock in said Brewing Company, which by this clause shall go to my daughter, Sophia Zumpe, shall be subject, however, to the conditions and stipulations contained in Item 10 of this will, and the shares of stock in said Brewing Company which by this clause shall go to my grandchildren Edward and John Thieme shall, however, be subject to the conditions and stipulations contained in Item 11 of this will."

"Item 11.—While I desire that my grandsons, Edward Thieme and John Thieme, shall have their full share of the stock in the Thieme & Wagner Brewing Company, viz.: together an undivided ⅕ thereof, yet I do not desire that they shall have anything whatever to do with the control or management of the business of said Company. I therefore appoint my son John Henry Thieme a trustee for said Edward and John Thieme, and hereby fully authorize and empower him to take charge of their part of the stock in said Brewing Company, and vote and control the same in the interest of said Company, and that he pay to them respectively, or to the survivor thereof, annually, their proportionate share of the dividends declared on said stock."

That John Henry Thieme, who was named by the testator as the executor of her will, duly qualified, and took upon himself the administration of said trust, and was by the circuit court of Tippecanoe county appointed trustees under said will for John and Edward Thieme, and has since such appointment, to wit, since the 7th day of October, 1895, continued to act as said trustee. That at the time of the death of the said Elizabeth she was the owner of 1,480 shares of the capital stock of the Thieme & Wagner Brewing Company, a corporation organized under the laws of the state of Indiana; and that 296 shares of said stock is the amount that came into the possession of said trustee under items 7 and 11 of said Elizabeth's will as the property here in trust for her grandchildren, Edward and John Thieme. That after the death of the said Elizabeth, and after said John Henry Thieme had qualified as trustee under item 11 of said will, the said Thieme & Wagner Brewing Company issued to said trustee two certificates of stock in said company, each of said certificates being for 148 shares of its capital stock, one of said certificates being numbered 25, and certifying that John Henry Thieme, as trustee of Edward Thieme, is the owner of 148 shares of the capital stock of the said brewing company; and one certificate, numbered 26, certifying that said John Henry Thieme, as trustee of John Thieme, is the owner of 148 shares of the capital stock of said brewing company. That the said Edward Thieme had no knowledge, prior to the commencement of this action, that the stock held by John Henry Thieme as trustee was represented by separate certificates. That neither the said John Thieme nor Edward Thieme, grandchildren of the said Elizabeth, deceased, made any disposition, during the lifetime of John Thieme, of the stock, or any part of it, owned by them in said brewing company, and willed to them as aforesaid by the said Elizabeth Thieme, deceased. That the said John Thieme, grandson of said Elizabeth, was married on the 17th day of October, 1900, to Lillian May, now Lillian May-Thieme, one of the appellees herein; and that the said John died in Marion county, Ind., on the 15th day of August, 1901, intestate, and leaving surviving him as his only heir at law his widow, Lillian May-Thieme. That on the 30th day of August, 1901, the said Lillian May-Thieme and the Union Trust Company of Indianapolis were, by the Marion circuit court, appointed administrators of the estate of the said John Thieme, deceased, and qualified and gave bond, and have ever since been acting as administrators of the estate of said decedent. That after the appointment and qualification of said administrators, and before the commencement of this action, said administrators made demand upon each of the defendants to this action that they claimed on behalf of said decedent's estate one-half of the 296 shares of stock held by John Henry Thieme, as trustee, in trust for Edward and John Thieme, and demanded that such steps be taken as would cause to be issued to them a proper certificate from said brewing company showing the ownership of 148 shares of said stock in the estate of John Thieme, deceased, represented by appellees herein.

The court's conclusions of law upon the facts found were that appellees, as the administrators of the estate of John Thieme, deceased, were entitled to have the title to 148 shares of the stock in the Thieme & Wagner Brewing Company held by John Henry Thieme as trustee quieted in them as the legal representatives of said John Thieme's estate, for the use and benefit of said estate, and that the said John Henry Thieme, as trustee, should transfer to appellees for the use and benefit of said John Thieme's estate 148 shares of said capital stock in said brewing company, and that he should execute all necessary papers and do all things necessary on his part to transfer and vest the title of said stock in the appellees. Judgment was accordingly so rendered.

Briefly stated, the question involved in this appeal is as follows: By the will of Elizabeth M. Thieme she disposes of 1,480 shares of stock in the Thieme & Wagner Brewing Company, owned by her at the time of her death. 296 shares of this stock were given to her grandchildren, John and Edward Thieme. The interests of said grandsons in this stock were equal. It is the claim of appellees that at the death of Elizabeth M. Thieme their decedent, John Thieme, became the absolute owner of one-half of the 296 shares of stock, and that by his death the trust created by item 11 of the will of Elizabeth M. Thieme was dissolved as to the said John's estate, and that they, as his administrators and legal representatives, are entitled to a judgment that the 148 shares in said brewing company are the property of the estate of their decedent. The appellant Edward Thieme claims that as the survivor of said grandsons he is the owner of the whole of said 296 shares. This is the whole question in the case.

It is statutory law in this state (section 8136, Burns' Rev. St. 1901) that "the survivors of persons holding personal property in joint tenancy shall have the same rights only as the survivors of tenants in common, unless otherwise expressed in the instrument." In the case of Johnson, Trustee, v. Johnson, 128 Ind. 93, 27 N. E. 340, the court, in reference to the effect to be given to the above-quoted statute, said: "Under this statute property held by two or more persons as joint tenants does not go to the survivors, unless it is so expressly stipulated in the instrument creating the estate." Under the statute and the construction given it by the Supreme Court as above cited, the decision of the question presented by this appeal must be based wholly upon a construction of the will; this will being the instrument by which the estate was created. Appellants, in order to sustain their position, must show that the will created a joint tenancy, and, in addition, that the will, by its express provisions, stipulated that the property so held should go to the survivor. The right of survivorship in personal property held by joint tenants cannot be conferred by implication or inference; it must be clearly expressed by the instrument creating the estate. By item 4 of the will in question the grandsons of the testatrix are given in clear and decisive terms one-fifth of her estate, which included the stock in the brewing company. In item 4 no restriction, condition, or limitation is placed upon the rights of the grandsons in the property so willed to them, nor is any reference made to any subsequent part of the will by which any conditions or limitations are attempted to be imposed. By item 6 of the will it is made plain that the only event in which the survivor of the two grandchildren should take the whole estate would be the death of one of them during the lifetime of the testatrix. Up to the seventh item of the will the property in controversy is given absolutely, in clear and decisive terms, to the grandchildren, without any expression of an intent to create the right of survivorship after the death of the testatrix. It is said in Langman v. Marbe, 156 Ind. 330, 58 N. E. 191: "It is the settled law that, when an estate in fee simple is clearly given a person, the estate so given cannot be cut down or modified by subsequent clauses in the will, unless the intention to do so is manifest from words as clear and certain as those which gave the fee-simple estate." See, also, Rusk v. Zuck, 147 Ind. 388, 45 N. E. 691, 46 N. E. 674; Mulvane v. Rude, 146 Ind. 476, 45 N. E. 659, and cases cited. The rule so announced is applicable to personalty and real estate. Mulvane v. Rude, supra; Ross v. Ross, 135 Ind. 367, 35 N. E. 9. It is from item 11 of the testatrix's will that the controversy has arisen as to the title to one-fifth of the stock in the brewing company. As we view this item of the will, its whole scope and purpose is to appoint a trustee and define his duties and powers. The first part of this item, viz., "While I desire that my grandsons, Edward Thieme and John Thieme, shall have their full share of the stock in the Thieme & Wagner Brewing Company, viz., together an undivided one-fifth thereof, yet I do not desire that they shall have anything whatever to do with the control or management of the business of said company," does not in any way attempt to take away from the grandsons, or either of them, their interest in the stock in the brewing company, but rather confirms in them the interest they had been given under a prior item of the will; the interest so given being the interest which, under the laws of descent, would have gone to their deceased father had he been living at the time of the testatrix's death. The second and last part of this item of the will, viz., "I therefore appoint my son John Henry Thieme a trustee for said Edward and John Thieme, and hereby fully authorize and empower him to take charge of their part of the stock of said Brewing Company and vote and control the same in the interest of said company, and that he pay to them respectively, or to the survivor thereof, annually their proportionate share of the dividends declared on said stock," appoints the trustee and defines his duty in relation to the one-fifth of the stock in the brewing company. The reference in regard to the duty of the trustee as to the stock and the income therefrom is invariably to the "one-fifth thereof" and their "share of the stock." And it is made the duty of the trustee to pay to each of said grandchildren "respectively" his share of the dividends declared on the one-fifth of the stock in the brewing company specifically devised to said grandchildren. But the testatrix goes further, and provides for a contingency which might have arisen under item 6 of her will had one of her grandchildren died prior to her death, and extends the provisions of item 11 to the survivor under item 6. We believe that the only construction which the intention of the testator and the words employed in this will will justify is that the title to the one-fifth of the stock in the brewing company at the death of the testatrix vested in the grandsons, Edward and John Thieme, they both surviving her; that the word "survivor," used in item 11 of the will, refers to a condition that might have arisen under item 6 of the will; that the right of survivorship to the title to the one-fifth of the stock of the brewing company which vested in Edward and John Thieme at the death of the testatrix was not in any way created or expressed by her will, and, this being true, it is immaterial, under the statute of this state heretofore cited, whether said grandchildren held the stock as tenants in common or as joint tenants; that upon the death of John Thieme, occurring after the death of the testatrix, one-half of the stock in the brewing company devised to Edward and John Thieme by the will of Elizabeth M. Thieme became a part of the estate of John Thieme, deceased, and within the control and management of his legally appointed administrator. The trial court so held.

Judgment affirmed.

(33 Ind. A. 532)

GROVES v. HOBBS.

(Appellate Court of Indiana, Division No. 1. March 8, 1904.)

APPEAL—STATEMENT—EVIDENCE.

1. There being no attempt to comply with Appellate Court rule 22, subd. 5 (55 N. E. vi), providing, if the insufficiency of the evidence to sustain a finding is assigned, the statement shall contain a condensed recital of the evidence, appellant is not entitled to a decision as to the sufficiency of the evidence.

Appeal from Circuit Court, Clinton County; Jas. V. Kent, Judge.

Action between Elizabeth Groves and Zachariah T. Hobbs. From the judgment, Groves appeals. Affirmed.

Fippen & Purvis and Gifford & Gifford, for appellant. Gavin, Davis & Gavin, for appellee.

ROBINSON, J. As there was no special finding of facts with conclusions of law in the case, the second, third, and fourth errors assigned, relating to these matters, present no question.

The first error assigned is overruling the motion for a new trial on the ground that the decision of the court is not sustained by sufficient evidence, and is contrary to law. It is insisted by counsel for appellee that the appeal should be dismissed, or the judgment affirmed, because of appellant's failure to comply with the rules of the court in the preparation of the transcript and brief. The fifth subdivision of rule 22 (55 N. E. vi) provides: "If the insufficiency of the evidence to sustain the verdict or finding, in fact or law, is assigned, the statement shall contain a condensed recital of the evidence in narrative form, so as to present the substance clearly and concisely." As no attempt whatever has been made to comply with this provision, appellant is not in a position to ask a decision upon the sufficiency of the evidence to sustain the finding. Boseker v. Chamberlain (Ind. Sup.) 66 N. E. 448; Security, etc., Co. v. Lee (Ind. Sup.) 66 N. E. 745; Indiana, etc., R. Co. v. Ditto, 158 Ind. 669, 64 N. E. 222. Moreover, a reading of the evidence shows that there is evidence to support the conclusion reached by the trial court.

Judgment affirmed.

(32 Ind. App. 550)

LUDWICK v. PETRIE et al. [1]

(Appellate Court of Indiana. Division No. 1. March 10, 1904.)

VENDOR AND PURCHASER—BREACH OF WARRANTY—ACTIONS—INSTRUCTIONS — IGNORING ISSUES—FRAUD—ABATEMENT OF PRICE.

1. Where, in an action for breach of warranty, complainant avers the execution of the deed, and failure of title to a portion of the land, and in a second paragraph asserts fraud of the vendor in misrepresenting the number of acres in the tract conveyed, an instruction is erroneous which directs a finding for defendant on facts provable under the first paragraph, without reference to the issue based on the fraudulent representation as to the number of acres conveyed.

2. Where a vendee is induced, by fraudulent representations of the vendor as to the number of acres, to pay more than he otherwise would for the land, he is entitled to an abatement of the purchase price.

3. A vendee need not rescind the contract in order to recover damages sustained by fraudulent representations as to the number of acres conveyed.

Appeal from Circuit Court, Huntington County; James C. Branyan, Judge.

Action by John Ludwick against Margaret Petrie and another. From a judgment in favor of defendants, plaintiff appeals. Reversed.

Lesh & Lesh, for appellant. Branyan & Feightner and G. W. Stults, for appellees.

HENLEY, C. J. Action by appellant for damages growing out of a breach of warranty in the deed of conveyance of certain real estate purchased by him of appellee. The complaint was in two paragraphs. The first paragraph of complaint contains averments covering the execution and delivery of the deed, the payment of the purchase price, the warranty covering 35.70 acres of land, the failure of the title to 6.70 acres of the land so conveyed and warranted, and the eviction of appellant therefrom by one holding the paramount title. The second paragraph of complaint, in addition to the averments which appear in the first paragraph, contains the following: That at the time of the purchase of the real estate appellee orally represented that a certain rail fence running south from the Maple Grove Gravel Road, near the buildings on the land conveyed, was the line fence, and formed the western boundary of said land; that such representations were false and fraudulent, and were falsely and fraudulently made, and that appellant relied upon and believe them to be true; that thereafter, and after appellant had purchased the real estate so pointed out to him, a survey was had of said land, and said line fence was removed a sufficient distance east to dispossess appellant of six acres of land. The material part of the deed, which was made a part of each paragraph of complaint, is as follows: "This indenture witnesseth that Margaret Petrie and Jacob Petrie, her husband, of Huntington County, Indiana, convey and warrant to John Ludwig of Huntington County, Indiana, for the sum of $3,500, the following real estate in Huntington County, Indiana, to wit: The following tract of land except 41 acres off the west side thereof, viz: that part of the reserve of ten sections at the banks of the Wabash river, granted by the United States to John B. Richardville, which is described as follows: Being north of the Wabash and Erie Canal and between tracts number 10 and 11, in the division of said reserve, and known as Carnot tract containing 80 acres, except 3.30 acres in the north part of said tract conveyed by Snap Richardson to John Roche by a deed dated December 21, 1852, and recorded in book H page 488 of the records of Huntington County, Indiana. Said 41 acres to be laid off by a line running from the Maple Grove Road south along the center of the lane to a point 4 rods south of the barn on said farm, thence east to a point from which a line runs to the south line of the tract will leave 41 acres on the west of the line so run, being in Town 28, range 9 east." An answer of general denial filed by appellee made the issue upon which the case was tried. The trial resulted in a judgment against appellant.

The questions presented to this court all arise under the assignment of error that the trial court erred in overruling appellant's motion for a new trial. The action of the trial court in regard to the giving of certain instructions, and in the refusal to give certain other instructions to the jury, and in the refusal to permit the introduction of certain evidence is assigned as cause for a new trial. The instructions given by the court to the jury were many in number, and seem to have been carefully prepared. The giving of instruction numbered 11, however, we think, constituted reversible error. The instruction referred to was as follows: "(11) I instruct you that by the express terms of the deed of conveyance set out in this complaint the defendant conveyed to the plaintiff the tract of land referred to as 'Carnot Tract,' except two specified parts thereof. The Carnot tract is referred to in this deed as containing 80 acres. Now, if the plaintiff was put in possession of and still holds all the Carnot tract left after cutting off the two tracts excepted in his deed, he cannot recover in this action, unless you find that the Carnot tract contained less than 80 acres. So, if the evidence fails to show that the Carnot tract contained less than 80 acres, your verdict should be for the defendants." If we concede that the law, as stated in this instruction, is cor-

[1] See 83 N. E. 770.

rect, it would only be correct as applied to the first paragraph of complaint; and, while the second paragraph of the complaint was not based upon the contract as evidenced by the deed, but was based upon the fraud of the vendor in misrepresenting the number of acres in the tract conveyed, the reference in the instruction to the deed of conveyance would not, we think, have the effect of directing the attention of the jury to the fact that the law as stated in the instruction was applicable alone to the case made by the first paragraph of complaint. The instruction took from the jury the evidence introduced upon the question of fraudulent representation of the amount of land conveyed, and, in effect, told the jury that, if certain facts were proven, which were only provable under the allegation of the first paragraph of complaint, their verdict must be for the defendants. It is the settled law in this state that if, by the fraudulent representations of the vendor as to the extent of, or the number of acres in, the tract of land about to be conveyed to him, the vendee is induced to enter into a contract that he would not otherwise have entered into, and to pay therefor more than he otherwise would have done, the vendee will be entitled to an abatement in the purchase price. King v. Brown, 54 Ind. 368; Tyler v. Anderson, 106 Ind. 185, 6 N. E. 600. Nor is the vendee compelled to rescind the contract in order to recover the damage suffered through the fraudulent representations. English v. Arbuckle, 125 Ind. 77, 25 N. E. 142; Nyswander v. Lowman, 124 Ind. 584, 24 N. E. 355. The second paragraph of complaint squarely presented an issue based upon fraudulent representation of the number of acres of land conveyed. Appellant produced evidence in support of this issue, and the court ought to have confined the effect of the instructions above set out to the case made by the first paragraph of complaint.

Other alleged errors are discussed by counsel, which we do not deem it necessary to consider. For the error in giving instruction No. 11 the judgment is reversed, and the trial court is directed to grant appellant's motion for a new trial.

(32 Ind. App. 540)

CLAYPOOL v. GERMAN FIRE INS. CO.[1]

(Appellate Court of Indiana, Division No. 2. March 9, 1904.)

MORTGAGES—PRIORITY—WAIVER—CONDITIONAL CHARACTER—SCOPE.

1. To enable a vendee to secure a loan to build a house, the vendor, who held a purchase-money mortgage, executed an instrument reciting: "I hereby waive the lien of my said mortgage and make it second and junior to the lien" of the mortgage to secure the subsequent loan. "The above waiver named in the agreement is made with the express understanding and as a consideration for my so doing" that a dwelling house of a certain cost should be built, free from liens, and insured, and interest on the second loan paid. *Held*, that the waiver was an absolute one; the matters recited as a consideration therefor, and to be performed by the vendee, being independent of the waiver itself.

2. Where the holder of a purchase-money mortgage waives priority, in favor of a mortgage given for a loan to build a house, the waiver will not include a commission on, and expenses incident to, the second loan, or insurance on the building paid out of the loan.

[1] Rehearing denied.

Appeal from Superior Court, Marion County; Jno. L. McMaster, Judge.

Suit by the German Fire Insurance Company against John P. Leyendecker and Edward F. Claypool. From a decree for plaintiff, defendant Claypool appeals. Reversed.

Jno. W. Claypool, Daniel Wait Howe, and Russell T. Byers, for appellant. Flores & Seidensticker and Wilson & Townley, for appellee.

ROBY, J. Action by appellee to foreclose a mortgage on a lot in Indianapolis, executed to it by John P. Leyendecker. Appellant, Claypool, was made a defendant, and filed a cross-complaint to foreclose a mortgage upon the same lot executed to him by said Leyendecker. He set up that his mortgage was given to secure unpaid purchase money, and that its lien was prior to the lien of appellee's mortgage, but that such priority had been waived by him, but only upon condition; that the conditions of such waiver had been broken, and it had thereby become null and void, wherefore he prayed foreclosure, and a decree of priority in his favor. A special finding of fact was requested and made, and conclusions of law stated thereon. The controversy relates solely to priority between the two mortgages. The facts found, so far as necessary to a determination of the issue stated, are as follows:

Prior to July 12, 1897, appellant, Claypool, was the owner of lot 200 in Morton Place, in Indianapolis; it being the lot described by said mortgages. On that day he conveyed it to Leyendecker, by warranty deed, in consideration of $1,600, $450 of which was paid in cash, and promissory notes secured by the mortgage referred to in the complaint were given for the residue. This mortgage was recorded within 45 days after its execution, and said notes were, when the suit was begun, all due and unpaid. There was an understanding at the time of the transaction, between the parties thereto, that, if the mortgagor should desire to build on the lot, the mortgagee would waive the priority of his mortgage in favor of a second mortgage executed by Leyendecker to one who would lend him money with which to build. Pursuant to this agreement, Claypool did on October 27, 1897, execute a written waiver to appellee, which instrument was of the following tenor:

"This indenture witnesseth, that whereas I hold a mortgage for $1,150 secured on lot number two hundred (200), in Morton Place, an addition to the city of Indianapolis, Indiana, dated August 16, 1897, recorded in Record Book 333, on page 272, of the records of Marion county, executed by John P. Leyendecker, and whereas said John P. Leyendecker desires to build a dwelling on said lot, I hereby waive the lien of my said mortgage and make it second and junior to the lien of a mortgage executed by said John P. Leyendecker to German Fire Insurance Company of Indiana, dated October 27, 1897, for $3,000, maturing in five years from date, and bearing interest at the rate of six per cent. per annum.

"The above waiver named in the agreement is made with the express understanding and as a consideration for my so doing, so that said parties shall build a dwelling house upon said lot on or before four (4) months from date hereof, to cost and be worth not less than $4,000 and to be free from any and all liens, and that they shall keep said building when completed insured in some good, reliable fire insurance company for not less than three thousand dollars, during the term of said loan of $3,000, for the benefit of said German Fire Insurance Company of Indiana, and in case of loss or damage by fire to said building the amount derived from said insurance company shall be paid on said loan or in repairing said building. And they will pay the interest on said loan when the same shall become due, and in case of default to make any such payments in thirty days after the same shall become due the said German Fire Insurance Company of Indiana shall proceed to foreclose said mortgage and notify me accordingly, or sell the same to me at its face value and accrued interest, as I may elect.

"Dated this 27th day of October, 1897.

"[Signed] Edward F. Claypool."

This instrument was duly acknowledged, and was duly recorded two days after its execution.

Leyendecker had previously made an agreement with appellee by which it was to loan him $3,000, to be secured by a mortgage on said lot; the loan not to be made until Claypool should execute a waiver of his prior mortgage. After the execution of such waiver as aforesaid, appellee did loan him $3,000. A house was in process of construction on the lot at the time. Its actual cost was $4,374.81. It is worth not less than $4,000. Mechanics' liens for $626.74 were filed against it. Taxes became delinquent to the amount of $315.07. After the commencement of this action, appellee paid $339.08 of said liens, taking assignments thereof; such payment being authorized by its mortgage. From the date of its loan to the completion of the house, appellee advanced $2,811.07, which was all expended in the erection of said house. One hundred and eighty-eight dollars and ninety-three cents was retained for the following purposes:

Commission on loan..................	$150 00
Insurance on building................	24 00
Expense incident to loan............	14 93

The commission on loan retained by appellee was distributed among the members of its finance committee. The $24 was paid as a premium for a policy of insurance. The $14.93 was paid for an abstract, an examination of it, etc. These sums were deducted with the consent of Leyendecker, but without notice to Claypool.

On April 27, 1898, the coupon interest note payable to appellee became due, and was not paid, and by reason of such default the entire debt to it became due. It served notice upon Claypool, and was notified by him to foreclose its mortgage; he, however, denying its priority. There is due appellee the principal sum, interest, and attorney's fees, $5,078.15, including delinquent taxes and assessments paid, and the amounts due for labor and material, and secured by lien, as aforesaid. Exclusive of the two latter amounts, there is due to it $4,367. The amount due on the mortgage to Claypool is $1,628.76.

The conclusions of law subordinated Claypool's mortgage to the lien of appellee's mortgage, and the amounts paid by it for the protection of its security. The correctness of the conclusions depends upon the terms and construction of the instrument above set out. Appellant's position is that the waiver was made upon condition that one of those conditions was that the house should be free from any and all liens; that such condition was broken, and the waiver therefore is inoperative. The instrument contains an express and immediate waiver of the priority of the purchase-money mortgage, made in the present tense. The language is, "I hereby waive the lien of my mortgage and make it second and junior," etc. This language is not consistent with an intention of making the waiver contingent. Its further terms are that the waiver is made with the express understanding and "as a consideration for my so doing that said parties shall build a dwelling house upon said lot on or before four months from date hereof, to cost and be worth not less than $4,000, and to be free from any and all liens, and that they shall keep said building when completed insured," etc. "* * * And they will pay the interest on said loan * * * also all taxes," etc. The consideration for a contract is a different thing from a condition upon which the contract is made to depend. A partial failure of consideration is entirely different in its consequences from the breach of a strict condition. The omission of any language to the effect that the waiver is made conditional or contingent tends to the conclusion that a condition was not meant. "The word 'condition' is not necessary to the creation of a condition. Any words that convey the proper meaning will create a condition." Stilwell v. Knapper, 69 Ind. 558, 570, 35 Am. Rep. 240; Am. & Eng. Ency. of Law, vol. 8, p. 60; 2 Parsons, Contracts, 526. The terms used must be construed in the light of established rules of construction. No language will be held to import a condition which does not expressly and clearly indicate that such was the intention of the parties. Forfeitures are odious, and conditions are not favored in law. Phenix Ins. Co. v. Lorenz, 7 Ind. App. 272, 33 N. E. 444, 34 N. E. 495; Halstead v. Jessup, 150 Ind. 85-87, 49 N. E. 821; Ellis v. Elkhart Co., 97 Ind. 247, 252. In doubtful cases the words of an instrument will be taken most strongly against the party using them. Wilson v. Corrico, 140 Ind. 533-536, 40 N. E. 50, 49 Am. St. Rep. 213; Davenport v. Gwilliams, 133 Ind. 142-145, 31 N. E. 790, 22 L. R. A. 244; Hunt v. Francis, 5 Ind. 302. Where an instrument creates a right, interest, or estate in unequivocal language, such right, interest, or estate cannot be cut down or destroyed by a subsequent provision in the same instrument, unless it is equally clear and explicit as that creating the same. Orth v. Orth, 145 Ind. 184-194, 42 N. E. 277, 44 N. E. 17, 32 L. R. A. 298, 57 Am. St. Rep. 185; Ross v. Ross, 135 Ind. 367-371, 35 N. E. 9; Mitchell v. Mitchell, 143 Ind. 116, 42 N. E. 465.

Counsel for appellant argue that, inasmuch as the instrument recites that the waiver is made in consideration of the performance of certain acts, it is therefore ineffective unless such acts are performed. This contention implies that the undertakings of the parties are dependent. Where a contract consists of dependent promises, the failure to perform by one party excuses the failure to perform by the other; but, where the promises are independent, the failure of one party to perform does not excuse a failure to perform upon the part of the other, but confers upon him a right of action for damages. McAlister v. Howell, 42 Ind. 15, 22, 23; Keller v. Reynolds, 12 Ind. App. 383, 40 N. E. 76, 280; Knights v. New England Co., 2 Cush. 271-286. Where the mutual promises which constitute a contract are not to be performed simultaneously, but where the acts to be performed by one party must or may precede those to be performed by the other, the promises are independent, and not dependent. Mountjoy v. Millikin, 16 Ind. 226; Watson v. Deeds, 3 Ind. App. 75, 29 N. E. 151; Wile v. Rochester Improvement Co., 24 Ind. App. 422-425, 56 N. E. 928. The intention of the mortgagor and appellant, Claypool, was to induce some one to loan the former money with which to build a house upon land owned by him, and in the improvement of which the latter was interested. It can hardly be said that the insurance of the house, not yet built, or the payment of interest upon a loan not yet made, were conditions precedent, not to an agreement to waive priority, but to an executed waiver thereof necessary to the negotiation of any loan. The waiver was executed in consideration of a number of distinct acts, part of which have been performed. It would be somewhat severe to hold it dependent for any validity upon the performance of each one of them. Appellee loaned its money, and the money so loaned went into the house, thereby increasing the value of appellant's security. It is entitled to priority only to the extent that its money was so applied. Loan Ass'n v. James, 13 Ind. App. 522, 41 N. E. 978; Loan Ass'n v. Moats, 149 Ind. 123, 48 N. E. 793.

An opinion was filed in this case on February 2d, and the judgment on that day was affirmed. Whether or not the sum of $188.93 retained by appellee, as heretofore set out, was included in the finding of the amount due, was at that time left to inference by appellants, and not referred to by appellee. In the argument on petition for rehearing, appellant showed by reference to the record that such sum was so included. Desiring that the result be as devoid of severity to either party as the circumstances permit, a rehearing was granted, and the point is treated as presented in the original brief. The appellant's right to priority exists only to the extent that its money was used in the construction of the house. The sum of $188.93, as aforesaid, was not so used. Such sum, therefore, ought not to have been included.

Judgment reversed and cause remanded, with instructions to state the twenty-first conclusion of law in accordance herewith, and for further proceedings.

(33 Ind. App. 404)

CLEVELAND, C., C. & ST. L. RY. CO. v. LINDSAY.[1]

(Appellate Court of Indiana, Division No. 2. March 11, 1904.)

MASTER AND SERVANT—INJURY TO BRAKEMAN—PLEADING—SUFFICIENCY—KNOWLEDGE OF DEFECTS.

1. In an action for wrongful death of a brakeman, a complaint averring negligence in bringing into the train a car with a defectively constructed coupling apparatus, without alleging that intestate did not know of the defect, or knowledge of defendant, is insufficient.

2. A complaint, in an action for wrongful death of a brakeman, averring that the engineer negligently disregarded signals, and ran the train at a negligent speed, by reason of which decedent, in making a coupling, was injured, and that because of defects in the brake pin it was necessary for the switchman to go between the cars while being moved at a dangerous speed, and decedent, by reason of such defect, was caught between the cars, is insufficient for lack of direct averments that the signals were disregarded, that the engineer was bound to obey the signals, that decedent did go between the cars, that he was caught between the cars, or that defendant had knowledge of the specified defects.

3. In an action for the wrongful death of a brakeman, occasioned by his being crushed between the cars because the insecure footing impeded his movements, an allegation that the yard had been carelessly left, so as to be rotted by time, is sufficient to show that defendant had knowledge of the defective condition, or that it had existed for sufficient time to charge it with knowledge.

4. Where the record does not show on which paragraph of the complaint the verdict was rendered, and allegations in certain paragraphs

¶ 1. See Master and Servant, vol. 34, Cent. Dig. §§ 832, 853.

[1] Rehearing denied, 70 N. E. 998. Transfer to Supreme Court denied.

were not referred to in an instruction, it cannot be urged that, the submission of the issues tendered by such paragraphs having been withdrawn by the instruction, the defendant was not injured by the submission in the first instance.

5. In an action for the wrongful death of a brakeman, the complaint charging a violation of duty, in that the engineer was to move the train in obedience to signals, and that, without notice or signals, after decedent had placed himself in a dangerous position, he carelessly moved the train rapidly, whereby deceased was injured, is sufficient as against a demurrer.

Appeal from Circuit Court, Hendricks County; Thomas J. Cofer, Judge.

Action by Leonia Lindsay, administratrix of Howard Lindsay, deceased, against the Cleveland, Cincinnati, Chicago & St. Louis Railway Company. From a judgment for plaintiff, defendant appeals. Reversed.

Elliott, Elliott & Littleton, for appellant. Wm. V. Rooker, for appellee.

COMSTOCK, J. Appellee brought this action, as administratrix of the estate of Howard Lindsay, deceased, against appellant, to recover damages for the death of appellee's decedent, occasioned by the alleged negligence of appellant. The cause was tried upon an amended complaint in five paragraphs, to each of which a general denial was filed. The trial resulted in a verdict and judgment for appellee in the sum of $2,500. The errors relied upon are the overruling of appellant's separate demurrers to each paragraph of the amended complaint, and the overruling of appellant's motion for a new trial.

Briefly summarized, the negligence attempted to be charged in the respective paragraphs of amended complaint is as follows: In the first: Bringing into the train upon which the plaintiff's intestate was to work a car with a wrong and defectively constructed coupling apparatus. In the second: That the engineer in charge of the engine attached to the train upon which the plaintiff's intestate was to work negligently disregarded signals, and ran the train at a negligent, careless, and wrongful rate of speed. In the third: That the coupling apparatus upon a car upon which the plaintiff's intestate was required to work was so out of repair as to require the plaintiff's decedent to go between cars, to uncouple them, when running at a great rate of speed, thereby causing his death. In the fourth: That the yards of the defendant, where the plaintiff's intestate was required to work, had been left broken and rotted and uneven, so as to render the place where he was required to work dangerous and unsafe. In the fifth: That the engineer moved the train, on which the plaintiff's intestate was at work, in disobedience of signals.

The first paragraph of the amended complaint, omitting the formal parts, is as follows:

"That on the 21st day of January, 1898, plaintiff's decedent was in the employ of defendant as switchman, in the yards of the defendant, east of and adjacent to the city of Indianapolis, and as such switchman was engaged in the discharge of the duties appertaining to his position, and in the performance of duties imposed upon him by those in charge and having authority over him, acting for and in behalf of said defendant. That on said date he was directed by those in authority, acting for and in behalf of said defendant, to throw the switches along the tracks of said defendant, and cut off and switch cars in a train of said defendant, at the time being operated along the tracks and switch of said defendant. That the train consisted of an engine and numerous freight cars, brought to the point of work by employés of defendant having charge thereof, and acting for and in behalf of defendant. That, among the cars of said train being so handled, there was one so defectively constructed and negligently brought into said train as to endanger the limbs and lives of those called upon to handle it in this, to wit: That the brake extended over and beyond the end of the car, and the lever upon the outside end of said car for operating the coupler had been placed in its construction or repair upon the wrong side of the car, and no lever or other thing for use as such had been placed on the side that should have had a lever; that the chain for upholding the link of said coupler was broken, and the lug of said pin was worn out and would not support said pin, of which fact plaintiff's decedent had no knowledge. That in the performance of his duties, and while said train was moving at a rapid rate of speed, plaintiff's decedent was required to separate the defective car, as aforesaid, from the car attached to it, and by reason of said careless and negligent construction, and said careless and negligent placing of said car entrain, plaintiff's decedent was compelled to go between said cars, and was crushed and mangled, so that he died from the effects thereof."

Various objections are made to this paragraph; among others, that it does not allege that the decedent did not know that the lever was on the wrong side; that it appears that the location of the lever caused him to go between the cars. The allegation so to the lever may be taken as showing the circumstances under which the decedent attempted to uncouple the cars. It does allege that he had no knowledge that the chain and pin were broken, but in this paragraph negligence is not attributed to that of which the decedent was ignorant. It is further pointed out that said paragraph does not allege the knowledge on the part of the employer. For these reasons the paragraph is bad. Ohio Valley, etc., Ry. Co. v. Goble, 28 Ind. App. 362, 62 N. E. 1025; Cleveland, etc., Ry. Co. v. Scott, 29 Ind. App. 519, 64 N. E. 896; Creamery v. Hotsenpiller, 24 Ind. App. 122,

56 N. E. 250; Atchison, etc., Co. v. Tindall (Kan. Sup.) 48 Pac. 12; Evansville, etc., R. Co. v. Duel, 134 Ind. 156, 33 N. E. 355.

The part of the second paragraph questioned by the demurrer is as follows: "That the engine, while manipulating such train, was in charge of an engineer of the defendant, acting for and in behalf of said defendant, and representing it in that capacity; and that said engineer, negligently and carelessly disregarding the signals given by him, ran such train at a negligent, careless, and wrongful speed along the tracks and the switches of said defendant, so as to endanger the lives and limbs of those called upon to perform their duties in connection with the running of such train. That plaintiff's decedent was directed by those in charge, acting for and in behalf of said company, to uncouple the cars of said train, and, while so attempting to do, the said engineer in charge of said train negligently and carelessly ran the same at such speed as to render the duty of plaintiff's decedent extrahazardous; and, while plaintiff was in the act of making such uncoupling, he was, by reason of such high speed, and the negligent and careless acts of said engineer, caught, crushed, and mangled in such manner that he died from the effects thereof." It contains no direct averment that the allegations that signals were disregarded, or that any signals were given, or that the engineer was bound to obey signals. The only allegations in this connection are by recital. Facts must be directly averred, and not pleaded by way of recital. Indiana, etc., R. Co. v. Adamson, 114 Ind. 282, 15 N. E. 5; Jackson School Tp. v. Farlow, 75 Ind. 118; Bliss on Code Pl. (3d Ed.) § 318.

The third paragraph contains the following: "That among the cars of said train being so handled there was one so out of repair, carelessly and negligently brought into said train, as to endanger the lives of those called upon to handle it, in this, to wit: That the chain connecting the lever with the line of the coupling connections had been broken, of which fact plaintiff's decedent had no knowledge, and was useless; and, in order to move the brake pin and uncouple the cars, it was rendered necessary by reason of such defects, so carelessly and negligently permitted by defendant, for the switchman to go between the cars while being moved at a dangerous and unreasonable speed, and make such coupling; and, by reason of such defect, this plaintiff's decedent was caught between said cars, and so crushed and mangled that he died from the effects thereof." It is not alleged that the decedent did go between the cars, nor that he was caught between said cars; nor is it alleged that appellant had knowledge of the defects specified.

It is alleged in the fourth paragraph that: "The yards of said defendant, at the place of the occurrence of the accident hereinafter spoken of, had been so carelessly and negligently left as to be broken and rotted by time and the actions of the elements between and on the tracks of said defendant as to render work to employés at all times hazardous, and especially at night; and that the flanges along the rails of defendant's tracks had become loose, uneven, and broken in such manner as to impede the movement of the employés required to work about the trains, and to render dangerous all coupling work about the point where the accident hereinafter complained of occurred, of which fact plaintiff's decedent had no notice or knowledge. That the plaintiff's decedent, in the performance of his duties, and while the train of the defendant was in action, was required to go between the cars of the defendant upon such uneven and broken ground, and across the tracks of the defendant, where the flanges were loose and unsafe to step upon or about, and that while there between such cars, in performance of his duties, he was caught; and the insecure and rotten footing and loose flanges so impeded and obstructed his movements as to prevent his escape, and threw him under said cars, whereby he was crushed and mangled, so that he died from the effects thereof."

It is urged against this paragraph that it does not allege that the defective condition of the yards was known to the defendant, or had existed for a sufficient length of time to charge it with knowledge thereof. The allegation that the yard had been so carelessly and negligently left as to be broken and rotted by time is sufficient to meet this objection. City of Huntington v. Burke, 21 Ind. App. 655, 52 N. E. 415.

Appellee calls attention to instruction 5½, given at the request of appellant, and claims that by this instruction the court took from the jury the issue, tendered by the first and third paragraphs of the complaint, respecting a defect in the coupling; that, the submission of the issues tendered by these paragraphs having been withdrawn from the jury, the appellant was not injured by the submission in the first instance. The instruction referred to is as follows: "There is no evidence that the B. and O. car, as the witnesses have designated it, was not in good repair when the plaintiff's intestate, Howard Lindsay, was injured. The uncontradicted evidence is that it was in good repair and proper condition, but that the coupling lever was on a different side of the car from which levers were generally placed on cars. Such evidence is not sufficient to show that the defendant was guilty of negligence in receiving such car, or in placing the same in one of its trains or cuts of cars." Said instruction only informed the jury that the coupling lever on said car was on a different side of the car from which levers were generally placed on cars, and that such evidence was not sufficient to show negligence on the part of the defendant in receiving such car or placing the same in one of its trains.

Other allegations in said paragraphs are not referred to in the instructions. Besides, in an instruction given at the request of appellee, reference is made to a defective coupling on a car which the defendant received from a connecting line. The record does not show upon which paragraph of the complaint the verdict was rendered.

The fifth paragraph contains the following: "That on the 21st day of January, 1898, plaintiff's decedent was in the employ of defendant as switchman in the yards of the defendant, east of and adjacent to the city of Indianapolis, and as such switchman was engaged in the discharge of the duties appertaining to his position, and in the performance of the duties imposed upon him by those in charge and having authority over him, acting for and in the behalf of said defendant. That on said date he was directed by those in authority, acting for and in behalf of defendant, to throw the switches along the tracks of said defendant, and cut off and switch cars in a train of said defendant at the time being operated along the tracks and switch of defendant. That such train consisted of an engine and numerous freight cars, brought to the point of work by employés of defendant having charge thereof, and acting for and in behalf of defendant. That the engine hauling such train was in charge of and under control of an engineer who was at the time acting for and in the behalf of such defendant, and that it was the duty of said engineer to move such train obedient to the signals of the switchman, whose duty it was to uncouple cars in such train. That on the night in question, it being exceedingly dark, such signals were given by a lantern, and plaintiff's decedent was doing the switching, and giving such signals according to the direction of the rules of the defendant. That, while it was exceedingly dark, plaintiff's decedent, by signal, notified the engineer to close up the slack in said train, so that he could uncouple cars, and, having so notified him, passed in between the cars to draw the coupling pin, and said engineer negligently and carelessly, without further notice or signal, caused said train to pass rapidly along such track and around the curve thereon, whereby plaintiff's decedent was caught between said cars and crushed and mangled in such a manner that he died from the effects thereof."

The objection made to this paragraph is that it does not allege what the rules were, nor in any manner attempt to describe any of the signals, or allege what signal was or was not necessary for any particular movement of the train; that no negligence is shown or charged except such as appears from the use of the words "negligently and carelessly"; that it does not allege the signal given was disregarded, or that any signal was necessary or required. In short, it shows no breach of duty to the injured party. The paragraph charges a violation of duty in this: that the engineer was to move the train in obedience to signals, and that without notice or signal, after the appellee's decedent had placed himself in a dangerous position, he carelessly caused the train to be moved rapidly, whereby the decedent received his injury. It is sufficient to withstand a demurrer.

It does not appear from the record upon which paragraph of the complaint the verdict was rendered. Therefore, without passing upon the motion for a new trial, the judgment is reversed, with instructions to sustain the demurrers to the first, second, and third paragraphs of the amended complaint.

(33 Ind. A. 547)

CLEVELAND, C., C. & ST. L. RY. CO. v. DRUMM.

(Appellate Court of Indiana, Division No. 1. March 10, 1904.)

ACTION FOR DEATH—DAMAGES—NEXT OF KIN—INSTRUCTIONS.

1. The presumption that a wife and children sustain a pecuniary loss in some amount by the death of the husband and father does not obtain in the case of next of kin who are in no wise pecuniarily dependent upon the decedent.

2. While, in an action for negligently occasioning death, brought for the benefit of the next of kin, the jury must determine the amount of recovery from the evidence by giving it such weight as their knowledge leads them to determine it should have, an instruction that the jury may estimate such damages "from the facts proved, in connection with their own knowledge and experience which they are supposed to possess in common with the generality of mankind," is erroneous, as in effect permitting the jury to consider matters not in evidence.

3. An instruction that, in estimating the pecuniary value of a decedent to her next of kin, the jury may consider the probable "or even possible" benefits which might result to them from her life, is erroneous, as permitting the jury to enter the domain of speculation.

Appeal from Circuit Court, Delaware County; Jos. G. Leffler, Judge.

Action by Enoch Drumm, as administrator, against the Cleveland, Cincinnati, Chicago & St. Louis Railway Company. Judgment for plaintiff, and defendant appeals. Reversed.

Thompson & Thompson, for appellant. Geo. H. Koons, for appellee.

ROBINSON, J. Appellee's decedent and her husband were killed in the same accident at a highway crossing. Appellee brings the statutory action, the damages to be recovered to inure to the benefit of the next of kin. Decedent left, as her next of kin, brothers and sister and a niece and nephews. The brothers and sisters, the youngest of whom is 55 years old, are married, settled in life, have homes of their own, and are the

¶ 1. See Death, vol. 15, Cent. Dig. § 77.

heads of families. The niece and nephews, children of a deceased sister of the decedent, lived with their father as a family, and had so lived since their mother's death. None of these next of kin depended upon decedent for pecuniary support or assistance.

The court gave, among other instructions, the following: "(11) The court instructs the jury that it is not necessary, in order to recover in this case, that the next of kin of the decedent, Rachel Driscoll, should have a legal claim on her, the said decedent, but that the administrator is entitled to recover for them for the pecuniary loss to them, if any. The jury may estimate such pecuniary damages from the facts proved, in connection with their own knowledge and experience, which they are supposed to possess in common with the generality of mankind, but in no case could such damages exceed ten thousand dollars. (12) The court instructs the jury that no precise rule for estimating the loss recoverable under this statute can be laid down. When the relation of the party whose death has been caused to those for whose benefit the suit is being prosecuted has been shown, and her obligation, if any, disposition and ability to earn wages or conduct business, and to care for, support, counsel, advise, and protect her next of kin named in the complaint, the matter then is submitted to the judgment and sense of justice of the jury. In estimating the pecuniary value of Rachel Driscoll to her next of kin, the jury may take into consideration the probable or even possible benefits which might result to them from her life, modified, as in their estimation they should be, by all the chances of failure or misfortune." It is not claimed that the decedent was under any legal obligation to support the next of kin for whose benefit this action was brought. The presumption that the wife and children sustain a pecuniary loss in some amount by the death of the husband and father does not obtain in a case like that at bar. For determining the pecuniary loss in such cases as this, any general rule is not possible, but such loss must of necessity depend upon the particular facts and circumstances of each case. From these particular facts and circumstances, as disclosed by the evidence, the jury must determine the amount of recovery. And such facts and circumstances so proven will necessarily be given such value and weight as the knowledge and experience of the individual jurors determine they should have. The first of the above instructions tells the jury, in effect, that, in estimating the pecuniary damages, they may consider something in addition to the facts proven. The pecuniary injury resulting from the death to the next of kin is uncertain and indefinite, but it must be determined wholly from the facts and circumstances proven. The assessment of damages in such a case "must proceed, not merely upon the pecuniary ability of the deceased, but rather upon the anticipations of pecuniary benefit which the surviving next of kin are shown to have had reasonable ground to indulge." Diebold v. Sharp, 19 Ind. App. 474, 49 N. E. 837; Commercial Club v. Hilliker, 20 Ind. App. 239, 50 N. E. 578; Wabash R. Co. v. Cregan, 23 Ind. App. 1, 54 N. E. 767; Louisville, etc., R. Co. v. Wright, 134 Ind. 509, 34 N. E. 314.

A part of the twelfth instruction is evidently based upon the following language of the court in Louisville, etc., R. Co. v. Buck, 116 Ind. 566, 19 N. E. 453, 2 L. R. A. 520, 9 Am. St. Rep. 883: "When the relation of the party, whose death has been caused, to those for whose benefit the suit is being prosecuted, has been shown, and his obligation, disposition and ability to earn wages or conduct business, and to care for, support, advise, and protect those dependent upon him, the matter is then to be submitted to the judgment and sense of justice of the jury." Admitting, without deciding, that this language might be held to apply where the next of kin were not dependent upon the decedent, yet the concluding part of the instruction is erroneous in informing the jury that, in estimating the pecuniary loss, they might take into consideration the probable or even possible benefits which might result to the next of kin from her life. The possible benefits which might result to the next of kin from the decedent's life would be altogether speculative. It has been held that a jury is not justified in basing its verdict upon "estimates of probabilities or chances," but in the instruction in question the jury is told it may consider possibilities. We have carefully considered the evidence upon this branch of the case, and from the relations that had existed between these next of kin and decedent for years prior to her death and at the time of her death, as disclosed by the evidence, we are not prepared to say that a correct conclusion was reached notwithstanding these erroneous instructions. Commercial Club v. Hilliker, supra.

The motion for a new trial should have been sustained. Judgment reversed.

(32 Ind. A. 556)

ELSBURY et al. v. SHULL.

(Appellate Court of Indiana, Division No. 2. March 10, 1904.)

SPECIFIC PERFORMANCE—PAROL CONTRACT FOR THE SALE OF LAND—COMPLAINT—ALLEGATIONS—NECESSARY PARTIES—POSSESSION OF LAND—NOTICE TO SUBSEQUENT PURCHASER—EFFECT.

1. A complaint in a suit for specific performance of a contract to convey land which alleges, as against defendant grantee of the defendant who had contracted to make such conveyance, that she knew at the time of the conveyance that plaintiff was in possession of said real estate, claiming it as his own, and that she took it subject to plaintiff's rights, is sufficient, though it does not aver that such defendant knew that plaintiff had entered into an agreement to purchase such land.

2. The complaint in a suit for specific performance of a contract to convey land need not allege a demand for a deed from the purchaser purchasing after the making of the contract, with knowledge thereof.

3. Where the complaint in an action for specific performance of a contract to convey land alleged that the vendor, for the purpose of avoiding his contract, pretended to convey the land to a grantee, the vendor was a necessary party, though the complaint did not claim damages against him, or aver that he claimed any interest in the land adverse to plaintiff.

4. A complaint in an action for specific performance of a contract to convey land which states the facts showing the performance of the conditions imposed on plaintiff is sufficient, without specifically averring that plaintiff has performed his part of the agreement.

5. A purchaser of land under a parol contract providing for the execution of a deed to the land on demand and payment of the purchase price, who entered into and continued in the possession of the land and made lasting improvements, is, on complying with the terms of the contract, entitled to a deed.

6. Defendant purchased a tract of land containing 2½ acres. The original grantor and his grantee supposed that the land included a strip adjacent to it, but the description in the deed did not include it. Subsequent to defendant's acquisition of the land by deed containing the same description as that contained in the deed to the first grantee, plaintiff agreed to purchase the strip from the heirs of the original grantor, and entered into possession thereof under the agreement. Thereafter defendant, with knowledge of plaintiff's possession, purchased the strip. *Held*, that defendant's title, as against plaintiff's claim, was ineffective.

Appeal from Circuit Court, Hancock County; Ed. W. Felt, Judge.

Action by Lucian N. Shull against George Elsbury and others. From a judgment for plaintiff, defendants appeal. Affirmed.

Marsh & Cook, for appellants. Jackson & Mason, for appellee.

COMSTOCK, J. The complaint in this action is in one paragraph, and avers, substantially, that on April 23, 1901, the appellants, other than Maggie Kemerly, together with Noah Elsbury, Joseph Elsbury, and Walter Elsbury, were the owners in fee simple, as tenants in common, of a certain strip of real estate in said county, 16 feet wide and 26⅝ rods long; that on said day the appellee purchased said strip of land of said owners, and thereupon went into immediate possession of the same under the provisions of said contract, and has remained in possession of the same under said contract of purchase since said date, and has made lasting improvements, by erecting a fence along the east side of said strip; that a deed of conveyance for said strip was to be executed to appellee on demand, and payment of the purchase money, in the sum of $40; that on April 29, 1901, the appellee tendered to the appellants, George Elsbury and Clara Sewell the sum of $8 each, and demanded a deed pursuant to said agreement, which was refused, and upon the filing of the complaint herein said sum was paid to the clerk of said Hancock circuit court for their use and benefit; that on April 30, 1901, said George Elsbury and wife and Clara Sewell and husband, Joseph, for the purpose of evading their said agreement, pretended to convey the same to said Maggie Kemerly, and that said Maggie Kemerly knew at the time that appellee was in possession of said real estate, claiming it as his own; and that said Kemerly took her conveyance subject to appellee's rights. Prayer that appellants George Elsbury, Clara Sewell, and Joseph Sewell, her husband, be compelled to execute to appellee a deed free from any claim or lien of Maggie Kemerly, or a commissioner be appointed to execute the same. To this complaint the appellants jointly and severally demurred, because the same failed to state facts sufficient to constitute a cause of action, which demurrer was overruled and excepted to. The cause was then put at issue by a general denial to the complaint. Upon request of appellants, the court filed a special finding of facts, with its conclusions of law drawn therefrom, to which appellants jointly and severally excepted. The court concluded, from the facts found, that the law was with the appellee, and that a commissioner ought to be appointed to execute to the appellee a conveyance for said real estate, and judgment was rendered accordingly.

Appellant Maggie Kemerly separately assigned errors, and, in her first and second specifications, challenges the sufficiency of the complaint, and, in her third, states that the court erred in its conclusions of law stated upon the special findings of fact, and each of them, separately and severally. The appellants jointly and severally assigned the same specifications of error.

It is claimed that the complaint is insufficient as against the appellant Kemerly because it does not aver that she took her conveyance with knowledge of the fact that appellee Shull had entered into an agreement to purchase. The complaint does aver that she knew at the time of the conveyance that appellee was in possession of said real estate, claiming it as his own, and that she took it subject to appellee's rights. Knowing of the possession, she cannot be permitted to deny that she had notice of the title under which the possession was enjoyed. Waterman on Spec. Per. § 64; Holmes v. Powell, 8 De G., M. & G. 572.

It is further claimed that the complaint is bad, as to the appellant last named, because it does not aver that a demand was made upon her prior to the institution of the suit. No demand of her was necessary, although it is the general rule that, where vendors contract to convey real estate upon demand, a demand is necessary before the commencement of the suit. In Kirkham v. Moore, 30 Ind. App. 549, 65 N. E. 1042—a suit for specific performance of a contract to convey real estate, in which a purchaser of the land aft-

¶ 5. See Frauds, Statute of, vol. 23, Cent. Dig. § 322.

er the commencement of the suit was made a party—this court held that the complaint need not allege a demand upon such purchaser for a deed. This holding was upon the ground that the purchase was with notice. Its reason is applicable to the question before us. The knowledge alleged, of appellee's possession, was notice of his equities. She took the real estate subject to appellee's claim, and she is in no better position than her grantors.

It is pointed out that there is no averment in the complaint of damages, or that George Elsbury or Clara Sewell claimed any right, title, or interest in the real estate adverse to the appellee, or any interest that was a cloud upon his title; that they were not, therefore, necessary parties, and, if proper parties, would only be liable for damages, having conveyed their supposed interest away; that a complaint in a suit for specific performance which is not in the alternative (that is, for specific performance or for damages) is not insufficient for that reason, although we may concede that damages should be alleged, to warrant judgment therefor. The claim is made the premise of the proposition that, as said George Elsbury and Clara Sewell conveyed prior to the institution of the suit, specific performance cannot be decreed against them. The complaint alleges that said defendants, for the purpose of avoiding their said agreement, pretended to convey the said land in question. As no claim was made and no judgment for damages asked against either of the appellants, they cannot be heard to complain of the absence of such averment from the complaint; and the complaint, instead of averring a conveyance, characterizes the act of said appellants as a pretense—in effect, as fraudulent. It is further claimed that the complaint is defective in failing to aver that the appellee performed on his part all the conditions of the agreement. The complaint, stating facts showing the performance of the conditions, renders the specific statement unnecessary. In Johnson v. Pontius, 118 Ind. 270, 20 N. E. 792, it is said that "a parol contract for the sale of real estate, the specific performance of which a court of equity will enforce, must be one that is complete and definite, and must be just and fair in all its provisions." The complaint before us sets up such a contract, and is sufficient to withstand a demurrer.

The special findings show, among others, the following facts: John Elsbury and his children inherited from Francisca Elsbury a tract of land supposed to contain 13½ acres, but which really exceeded that amount, the excess constituting the strip in controversy. Partition was had, and 2½ acres set off to John Elsbury, who sold and conveyed it to one Olvy, supposing at the time that the conveyance included the strip in dispute. Olvy conveyed by the same description to Mathew Kemerly, who thereafter conveyed to Maggie Kemerly, the appellant here. John Elsbury died in 1896. In 1901 his children and heirs made the contract referred to in the complaint, by which appellee, upon the payment of $8 to each of them, was to have a conveyance of said strip; the same being necessary to him as a way to and from his lands to a public highway from which he had no outlet. That, after said contract had been made, Maggie Kemerly paid said heirs $10 apiece, and a conveyance of said strip was made by them to her. Appellee had, however, previous to said conveyance, taken possession of the said land under the provisions of said contract, and built and erected a post and wire fence along the east line of the same, with the knowledge and consent of all said heirs; and, at the time of said conveyance, Maggie Kemerly had knowledge of the use, possession, and improvement of said strip by said appellee as aforesaid. She now claims that it was the intention of John Elsbury to convey said strip, notwithstanding the same was not included in the description; that she is entitled to hold it as against his heirs and those claiming under them, as appellee does. She purchased 2½ acres of land, and got it. She afterward purchased an adjacent strip from the heirs of John Elsbury by outbidding appellee, whose proposition had been accepted and become binding upon the parties and the land. As against him, the title so procured was ineffective. The allegations of the complaint are specially found, and exceptions to the conclusions of law concede that the facts upon which the conclusions are based are correctly found. In its conclusions of law, the court did not err. Nat. St. Bk. v. Sandford, etc., Co., 157 Ind. 10, 60 N. E. 699.

We have passed upon the controlling questions discussed. Appellee has done all in his power to fulfill the contract on his part. The specific execution of a contract is, in equity, a matter of sound discretion in the court. In the case before us, it seems to have been properly exercised. Judgment affirmed.

(208 Ill. 304)

SPENCE v. HUCKINS et al.*

(Supreme Court of Illinois. Feb. 17, 1904.)

WILLS—OTHER INSTRUMENTS — SIMULTANEOUS EXECUTION—EFFECT — EQUITABLE MORTGAGE —TESTAMENTARY CAPACITY—UNDUE INFLUENCE—EVIDENCE.

1. Testatrix, being in feeble health, was taken to defendant's house, and after complainant, her brother, had been solicited to provide for her during the remainder of her life in consideration of receiving her property, and had declined so to do, complainant and defendant met at the office of an attorney, where a contract was drawn providing that defendant should care for testatrix; that she should will defendant all her property, etc.; that he should pay certain sums to others; and that, in case testatrix should desire during her life to be released, defendant would release her on payment of sums expended and reasonable compensation for her care. Complainant joined in signing this con-

*Rehearing denied April 7, 1904.

tract, and at the same time a power of attorney was executed giving defendant power to manage testatrix's property, together with a will by which testatrix willed to defendant all of such property. *Held*, that such instruments should be construed according to their purport, and that the fact that they were all executed at the same time did not require that they should be construed as a single instrument, and, in effect, an equitable mortgage.

2. In a will contest, evidence reviewed, and *held* insufficient to establish want of testamentary capacity.

3. Where, prior to the making of a will by testatrix devising all her property to defendant in consideration of support, contestant, who was testatrix's brother, was offered her property on the same terms and refused, and he was present and participated in the execution of the will, and had full knowledge and gave his consent to the same, a finding that the will was not the result of undue influence was proper.

Appeal from Circuit Court, Cook County; J. L. Healy, Judge.

Bill by William H. Spence against George W. Huckins and others to set aside the will of Margaret Jane Spence, deceased. From a decree dismissing the bill, complainant appeals. Affirmed.

Appellant filed his bill in the circuit court of Cook county to contest the will of Margaret Jane Spence. Said testatrix and the appellant were brother and sister, and jointly owned 591 acres of land in Iroquois county, which they had farmed in partnership for many years. They had both resided upon this farm until about 15 years prior to testatrix's death, when the appellant married, and brought his wife to live with them. Trouble occurred between the wife and sister, and appellant moved to an adjoining farm, where he resided until 1900, when he moved to the city of Kankakee. Testatrix had never been married, and was 62 years of age. Her health had become very poor, and in August, 1900, she went to Colorado, hoping to be benefited by the change of climate. In November, 1900, she accidentally received an injury to her arm and shoulder. On January 7, 1901, she returned to Chicago, and was met at the train by the appellee George W. Huckins, who resided in Chicago with his wife and family, and was engaged in business there. He had been blind for many years, and had been intimately acquainted with testatrix and appellant from childhood, their mothers being sisters. Testatrix was taken to his house, and appellant notified of her arrival. In a day or two he came to Chicago to make arrangements for her future home, and the question arose whether she should live with Huckins in the city, with appellant in Kankakee, or whether appellant should rent her a house there, and secure some one to live with and keep house for her. They arrived at no definite conclusion, and on January 15, 1901, testatrix became suddenly and seriously ill. During her illness she was unconscious a part of the time, and it was much doubted whether she would live through the attack. During that sickness the question was discussed between Huckins and appellant as to the disposition of her property in case of her death. She gradually recovered, however, and regained the use of all her faculties, but was still unable to leave her bed, except to sit up for short periods in a chair. As soon as she grew better, the question was again raised with reference to her permanent home and with reference to the disposition of her property. She was anxious to remain in Chicago, where she could be treated by her chosen physician, and where she could be attended by a skilled nurse, and the proposition was made that appellant and his wife should move to Chicago into the house of Huckins, and take care of her. Huckins insisted that his wife was not able to perform the labor necessary to the proper care of her, and that some such arrangement should be made. These negotiations continued until March 5th, when Huckins sent for appellant, and informed him that something definite must be done. Appellant replied that testatrix had plenty of money to pay for her care, and that, if Huckins would assume the responsibility, he should be well paid for his trouble. Huckins replied that, as far as money matters were concerned, appellant could not give him more than testatrix had already offered, for the reason that she had made the proposition that if he would care for her during the remainder of her life she would give him, at her death, all her property. Huckins asked appellant what he thought of this arrangement, and told him to think it over for a day or two, and then decide what to do. Appellant returned to his home in Kankakee, talked the matter over with his wife, and returned to Chicago on March 7th, when he met Huckins, and together they went to the office of an attorney, and there stated to him that they wanted a contract drawn providing for the care of testatrix. They each furnished to said attorney the data from which the instruments involved in this case were prepared, and he at their request drew three instruments, one of which is in the nature of a contract between testatrix, the appellant, and Huckins, and provides, in substance, that testatrix shall will to Huckins all of her property, which will should be absolute and irrevocable, unless he should consent to discharge the agreement upon conditions therein contained. It also provided that she should convey, by deed or will, to Huckins, before her death, all her property, and that in consideration of said conveyance he should support and maintain her, and provide her with medical attention and nursing during the term of her natural life. He was also, by the agreement, to pay a Mrs. Dolly Finley the sum of $5,000 out of the property conveyed to him, and was to aid and assist, in a reasonable manner, George W. Yates, an uncle of testatrix, during his illness, provided the said Yates had not sufficient means of his own to support himself comfortably. He was also to erect a stone or cement fence around the family cemetery on the Spence farm, and pay to Elizabeth Jones an ample sum to remunerate her for her care of testatrix during her injury in Colorado; also to pay one-half of the price of a monument to be erected at the grave of testatrix's father and mother, and erect a monument over her own grave. The contract finally provides that, in case she should desire, at any time during her life, to be released from the terms of the agreement, Huckins should release her upon her payment to him of all the expense of every kind and nature, including support and maintenance, medicines, doctor bills, and nursing, and all money he should have paid out under the contract, and such further sum as should be deemed reasonable compensation for the trouble he had been put to in caring for her. The same contract provides that appellant, who joined in it, should not contest the conveyance so made by will or deed, and that he should be released of all liability of every kind or nature concerning said contract or the care of testatrix. Said attorney at the same time drew another instrument, purporting to be a power of attorney, which authorized Huckins to collect all of the rents and profits arising from the property of testatrix, and to apply the same towards her support and maintenance, giving him full power to manage and control her property. A third instrument was also drawn, purporting to be the last will and testament of said testatrix, Margaret Jane Spence, which willed to Huckins her property of every kind and character, but contained the same provisions with reference to Mrs. Dolly Finley, George W. Yates, and Mrs. Elizabeth Jones, and the erection of a cemetery fence and monuments stipulated for in the contract. After the three instruments had been drawn, copies were furnished to appellant, and were each read to him by the said attorney. The will, as first read, provided that Huckins should be executor of the same; but appellant objected to that clause, and at his request he was added as one of the executors, and provision with reference to his release from all liability was placed therein at his request. He then signed the contract, and it was signed by Huckins. Appellant then returned to his home in Kankakee, and Huckins took the three instruments to his home, where they were each properly executed by the testatrix on the next day. Thirty-one days after that she again became suddenly ill, and died April 10, 1901. After her death the will was filed for probate in the probate court of Cook county by appellant and Huckins, and duly admitted to probate, whereupon they were both appointed executors thereof. An inventory of the estate was filed, and they continued as executors until July, 1902, when appellant resigned, and filed this bill to contest said will.

The bill was filed upon the theory that the three papers above described, being executed at one and the same time, constituted, in law, but a single instrument, and were, in legal effect, but an equitable mortgage. That proposition or theory was submitted to the court below, and decided adversely to appellant, the holding there being that the first instrument was a simple contract, the second a mere power of attorney, and the third the last will and testament of the deceased. An issue of fact was then made on the allegation by the complainant that at the time of the execution of said papers the testatrix was of unsound mind, and unduly influenced by said Huckins and his wife, and under duress, which issue was submitted to and tried by a jury, and a verdict rendered in favor of the validity of the will. A decree was entered by the trial court in accordance with the verdict, to reverse which this appeal is prosecuted.

Appellant raises substantially the same question here as was urged in the trial court as to the construction of said three instruments in writing; also that the court erred in the refusal of certain instructions asked by the complainant, and in refusing to set aside the verdict as contrary to the evidence.

D. H. Stapp and H. L. Richardson, for appellant. Wing & Wing, for appellees.

WILKIN, J. (after stating the facts). The first question for our determination is the construction to be placed upon the three instruments mentioned in the foregoing statement. The evidence in the case is very clear on this point, and shows that said instruments were executed for the purpose of providing for the care and maintenance of said testatrix during her life. Offers had been made to appellant that, if he would arrange to care for her as she desired, he should have her property. This he declined to do, and the instruments in question were drawn for the purpose of inducing and enabling appellee George W. Huckins to do that which he (the appellant) could not or would not do. The contract, power of attorney, and will admit of no construction. They are neither indefinite, ambiguous, nor uncertain. The first states the terms under which said Huckins is to care for the testatrix; the second gives him power and authority to manage the property of the testatrix during her lifetime; and the third is, to all intents and purposes, a legally executed last will and testament by Margaret Jane Spence. The chancellor could do no more than to so construe and give them legal effect. Argument can make this no clearer.

It is next insisted that the trial court erred in refusing to give three instructions asked on behalf of complainant, but no specific reasons are set forth why they, or either of them, should have been given. We have examined them so far as we have been able to identify them from the argument of counsel, and are convinced that, in so far as they state correct principles of law, they were inapplicable to the facts of the case, and also that the jury was sufficiently instructed as to the law of the case, and therefore no substantial error was committed by their refusal, even if they had been otherwise correct.

Another ground of reversal here urged is that the verdict of the jury sustaining the validity of the will is contrary to the evidence, the contention being that the weight of the testimony sustains the averments of the bill that the testatrix was, at the time of the execution of that instrument, of unsound mind and memory, and that she was under the undue influence of appellee Huckins and his wife. This is a voluminous record of over 1,000 pages of evidence, the trial having lasted about a week. We have made a painstaking examination of the evidence as presented, both in the abstract filed by appellant and the additional abstract filed on behalf of appellees, and are clearly of the opinion that the verdict of the jury and decree of the court below are abundantly supported by the testimony. In the number of witnesses the preponderance of the evidence is with the appellees, and those who testified to the soundness of mind and memory of the testatrix had better opportunities for knowing and observing her mental condition than those who testified to the contrary. As an instance of this, Esther M. Gillett, the nurse who waited upon her in her last illness, was called as a witness on behalf of appellant, who appears to have been entirely disinterested and impartial, though she was appellant's own witness, and testified that in her opinion Miss Spence was of sound mind, and under no undue influence or restraint, at the time she signed her will. John Barlin, also a witness introduced on behalf of appellant, testified that in his opinion she was of sound mind; and the evidence of the two physicians who attended her in her last illness—Dr. White and Dr. Egert—both testified to the fact that she was fully competent to make a will, and in no way unduly influenced. Of those expressing a different opinion, some, at least, gave but indefinite and unsatisfactory statements, such as that "she was not a very sound-minded person," etc.

Much stress is placed by counsel for appellant on the fact that appellee Huckins, by the will in question, obtains many thousand dollars in money and property for wholly inadequate services rendered, and this is attempted to be construed into evidence of undue influence and want of mental capacity in the testatrix at the time the will and the contract were entered into. In the first place, at that time it was not and could not be known how long she would survive and he be required to provide for and take care of her. All of the money and property might be consumed during her lifetime, and therefore, it cannot be said that the transaction is evidence of her unsoundness of mind, or that she was improperly influenced in entering into the arrangement. Moreover, appellant was offered the opportunity of having the property if he would assume the burden of her care, maintenance, and support, and declined to accept it. He considered the matter fully with his sister, his own wife, and appellee Huckins. He was present at the time the papers were drawn up, and at his own request was made one of the executors of the will which he now seeks to impeach. A clause was also inserted in the contract at his request relieving him from all liability after her death, and he afterwards wrote a letter to Colorado, in which he stated that the property had been disposed of according to the wishes of his sister. After her death he made an effort to effect a settlement with Huckins for a division of the property. When the evidence is impartially considered, it leaves little doubt in the mind that, if his sister had continued to live through many years, and had been cared for by Huckins according to the terms and conditions of the contract and will, there would have been no attempt on appellant's part to regain the property. It was her sudden and unexpected death, which, it seems to us, prompted the bringing of the present suit.

In the preparation of the abstract filed by counsel for appellant his cross-examination was almost entirely omitted, to supply which omission, as well as other evidence left out of appellant's abstract, an additional abstract was filed by counsel for appellee. The cross-examination of appellant himself, as shown by the additional abstract, clearly shows that all the transactions called in question by his bill were entered into between his sister and Huckins with his full knowledge and consent, and that he must at that time have considered her as possessing testamentary capacity, and the ability to rationally enter into the contract which she signed. We are clearly of the opinion that the case made by his bill and the testimony offered in support of it fall far short of entitling him to the relief prayed.

The decree of the circuit court, being in conformity with this view, will be affirmed. Decree affirmed.

(208 Ill. 181)

BRUEGGEMANN v. YOUNG.*

(Supreme Court of Illinois. Feb. 17, 1904.)

ELECTION CONTEST—JURISDICTION OF CITY COURT.

1. An election contest, jurisdiction of which is given circuit courts by 2 Starr & C. Ann. St. 1896 (2d Ed.) p. 1661, c. 46 (entitled "Elections") § 97, is not a civil case, within City Court Act (Laws 1901, p. 136) § 1, giving city courts concurrent jurisdiction with circuit courts in all civil cases.

Appeal from City Court of Alton; J. B. Vaughn, Judge.

Election contest by Henry Brueggemann against Anthony W. Young. From an adverse judgment, contestee appeals. Reversed.

*Rehearing denied April 7, 1904.

An election was held on April 21, 1903, and the appellant, upon the canvass of the vote by the city council, was held to have been duly elected mayor of the city of Alton, and qualified as such. The appellee, who had been mayor for the preceding term, was a candidate for re-election, and, upon the appellant being sworn into office, filed his petition in the city court of the city of Alton to contest the election of the appellant. The appellant made a motion to dismiss the petition, on the ground that the city court was without jurisdiction to entertain said petition and to hear and determine said election contest. The court overruled the motion, whereupon the appellant filed an answer. A trial was had, which resulted in a finding and judgment against the appellant, and he has brought the record to this court for review by appeal, and has assigned as error the action of the court in overruling his motion to dismiss the petition filed by appellee for want of jurisdiction, and in holding the court had jurisdiction to hear and determine said election contest. Other assignments of error have been made upon the record, but, from the view entertained by the court upon the question of jurisdiction, that question alone will be considered.

Burton & Wheeler, Dunnegan & Leverett, David E. Keefe, and Levi Davis, for appellant. B. H. Canby and J. V. E. Marsh (John J. Brenholt, B. J. O'Neil, and E. C. Haagen, of counsel), for appellee.

HAND, C. J. (after stating the facts). The circuit courts of this state, by the act of 1895, amending section 97 of chapter 46, entitled "Elections" (2 Starr & C. Ann. St. 1896 [2d Ed.] p. 1661, § 97), are given jurisdiction to hear and determine contests of the election of mayors of cities. The section of the statute, as amended, conferring such jurisdiction, reads as follows: "The circuit courts in the respective counties, and in Cook county the superior court also, may hear and determine contests of the election of judges of the county courts, mayors of cities, presidents of county boards, presidents of villages, in reference to the removal of county seats and in reference to any other subject which may be submitted to the vote of the people of the county, and concurrent jurisdiction with the county court in all cases mentioned in section ninety-eight (98)." In King v. Jordan, 198 Ill. 457, 64 N. E. 1072, it was held that county courts were without jurisdiction to try contests of the election of the officers named in said section, and that the trial of such contests, by said section, outside of Cook county, had been committed exclusively to the jurisdiction of the circuit courts.

By section 1 of the act of 1901 (Laws 1901, p. 136), entitled "An act in relation to courts of record in cities," it is provided that the city courts organized under said act shall have concurrent jurisdiction with the circuit courts within the city in which the same may be located "in all civil cases and in all criminal cases arising in said city, and in appeals from justices of the peace in said city," and it is contended that, city courts having been invested with concurrent jurisdiction with the circuit courts, and jurisdiction having been conferred upon circuit courts to try contested elections of mayors of cities, the city courts have jurisdiction over such contests. The correctness of that contention depends upon whether an election contest is a "civil case." If the contest instituted by the appellee against the appellant is, within the meaning of the law, a civil case, as the circuit courts have jurisdiction of such a contest, and the city courts have concurrent jurisdiction with the circuit courts in all civil cases, it necessarily follows that the city court of the city of Alton had jurisdiction of said proceeding to contest said election, and was authorized to hear and determine said contest.

It has, however, been repeatedly held by this court that an election contest is not a case. The class of cases mentioned as civil cases in the first section of the city court act clearly was intended to include only law cases and equity cases as they were known to the common law, and such other actions since provided for by statute as belong to the same class or are of the same nature as previously existing actions at law or in equity in which personal or property rights are involved, and where a remedy for the recovery of property or for damages occasioned by the infringement of a right is given. The contest of an election is not an action at law or in equity, and does not belong to the same class and is not of the same nature as previously existing actions at law or in equity, and does not fall within the designation "all civil cases," over which concurrent jurisdiction is conferred upon the circuit and city courts. In Douglas v. Hutchinson, 183 Ill. 323, 55 N. E. 628, it was held that the circuit court of Cook county did not have jurisdiction to try a contest of an election for judge of the superior court of said county by virtue of the original jurisdiction conferred upon circuit courts by the Constitution, which provides circuit courts shall have jurisdiction of "all cases in law and equity" where there was no statute in force conferring jurisdiction upon said courts in that class of cases, as it was held an election contest was not a case in law or in equity. And in Moore v. Mayfield, 47 Ill. 167, which was a contest of the election of sheriff, it was held the proceeding was purely statutory, and was not a "case" within the meaning of the Constitution. And in People v. Smith, 51 Ill. 177, it was held the contest of an election was purely statutory, and without the aid of a statute it could not be brought before the circuit court. The cases of Jennings v. Joyce, 116 Ill. 179, 5 N. E. 534, Kreitz v. Behrensmeyer, 125 Ill. 141, 17 N. E. 232, 8 Am. St. Rep. 349, and Allerton v. Hopkins, 160 Ill. 448, 43 N. E. 753, are to the same effect.

As there was no statute in force conferring jurisdiction upon the city court of Alton to hear and determine a contest of the election of mayor, and such contest is not a civil case within the meaning of the statute which confers upon city courts jurisdiction concurrent with that of circuit courts, we are of the opinion that the city court of Alton was without jurisdiction to entertain the petition of the appellee, and to hear and determine the contest of the election of mayor of said city.

Appellee relies upon the case of Hercules Iron Works v. Elgin, Joliet & Eastern Railway Co., 141 Ill. 491, 30 N. E. 1050, as an authority sustaining the position that the city court had jurisdiction to hear and determine said contest. In that case it was held that the city court of Aurora had jurisdiction in proceedings, under the eminent domain act, arising within the territory limits of said city.

In the Douglas Case, supra, in considering the original jurisdiction conferred upon circuit courts by the Constitution, it was said, page 328, 183 Ill., and page 629, 55 N. E.: "The provision of the Constitution conferring original jurisdiction upon circuit courts includes the prosecution of every claim or demand in a court of justice which was known, at the adoption of the Constitution, as an action at law or a suit in chancery. It also includes all actions since provided for, in which personal or property rights are involved, which belong to the same class or are of the same nature as previously existing actions at law or in equity. Such are cases where the Legislature creates a new statutory remedy for the recovery of property, or for damages occasioned by the infringement of a right. There are many special statutory proceedings which involve rights, but which are not within the terms of the Constitution because they are not causes at law or in equity. This proceeding has never been regarded, under common-law or equity practice, as a cause at law or in equity, and is not of the same nature as such a cause."

The Constitution expressly provides that private property shall not be taken or damaged for public use without just compensation, and that such compensation, when not made by the state, shall be ascertained by a jury, as shall be provided by law. The statute providing the method to be pursued in fixing the compensation and damages to be paid the owner before private property shall be taken for public use is clearly a remedy for the recovery of damages occasioned by reason of the infringement of a right, and falls within that class of cases, covered by the Constitution, which is pointed out in the opinion in that case as that class of cases where the Legislature creates a remedy for the recovery for damages occasioned by the infringement of a right, and is a part of the original jurisdiction conferred upon circuit courts by the Constitution. The fact, therefore, that city courts are held to have jurisdiction in proceedings under the eminent domain act, does not establish that said courts have jurisdiction in cases of contested elections, as such contests are not actions at law or suits in equity, and do not involve personal or property rights such as have heretofore been enforced by an action at law or in equity, and are not for the recovery of damages occasioned by the infringement of a right. The distinction between a condemnation suit and a proceeding to contest an election is plain. The one is to recover a judgment for the amount of compensation and damages which the owner of private property has sustained by reason of the taking of his property for a public use, and may be said to be a "case," and falling within the language of the statute, "all civil cases," conferring concurrent jurisdiction upon city and circuit courts; while the contest of an election is a proceeding instituted for the purpose of determining which of the contestants has received the greater number of votes for a particular office. In Moore v. Mayfield, supra, it was said the proceeding to contest an election "is merely a statutory proceeding for recanvassing the votes cast at an election, in which the illegal votes may be rejected, and those which are legal may be counted, and the result ascertained; and the finding of that result is not a 'judgment,' in the sense in which that term is used in the law giving the right to prosecute a writ of error, nor is the proceeding by means of which that result is reached a 'case,' within the meaning of the Constitution. That term would refer more properly to an action at law or a suit in chancery, but this proceeding is neither one nor the other."

The judgment of the city court of Alton will be reversed, and the cause remanded to that court with directions to dismiss the petition. Reversed and remanded, with directions.

(208 Ill. 267)

CHICAGO CITY RY. CO. v. O'DONNELL.

(Supreme Court of Illinois. Feb. 17, 1904.)

STREET RAILWAYS — NEGLIGENCE—CONTRIBUTORY NEGLIGENCE—QUESTION FOR JURY —INSTRUCTIONS.

1. In an action against a street railway company for death resulting from a collision it appeared that deceased was driving behind a large covered wagon, and that when he reached a street intersection he pulled out from behind the wagon, and drove upon defendant's track, and his vehicle was struck by a car coming from the opposite direction. At the time he drove upon the track the car was between 100 and 200 feet distant, and there was no evidence tending to show that the bell was rung, or that he was conscious of any warning. *Held*, that the question whether deceased was guilty of contributory negligence was one for the jury.

2. In an action for negligent injuries it is not error for the court to define the meaning of the phrase "ordinary care" as applied to the conduct of either party.

¶ 1. See Street Railroads, vol. 44, Cent. Dig. §§ 214, 257.

3. In an action against a street railway company for death resulting from collision it appeared that deceased was driving behind a large covered wagon, and that when he reached a street intersection he pulled out from behind the wagon and drove upon defendant's track, and his vehicle was struck by a car coming from the opposite direction. At the time he drove upon the track the car was between 100 and 200 feet distant, and there was no evidence tending to show that the bell was rung, or that he was conscious of any warning. The court instructed that "ordinary care" was the degree of care which an ordinarily prudent person, situated as the deceased was "before and at the time of injury," would exercise for his own safety. *Held*, that the instruction was not erroneous on the theory that it might be construed as meaning that plaintiff might recover if deceased exercised ordinary care after driving upon the track, irrespective of any care before that.

4. The court refused to instruct that, if the jury believed that ordinary care on the part of deceased for his own safety required him, before driving upon the track, to look and ascertain whether a car was approaching, and if they believed that, if he had looked, he could have ascertained whether a car was approaching, and if they believed he did not look, and was injured in consequence, and because of his failure, there could be no recovery. *Held*, that it was error to refuse the instruction, and it was not erroneous on the theory that it assumed that if deceased saw the car he should, in no event, have driven upon the track.

5. The court refused an instruction requested by defendant to the effect that the issues to be tried were whether the car was carelessly managed, and whether it was traveling at a dangerous rate of speed, whether a bell was sounded, whether the car could have been stopped in time to have avoided a collision, and whether deceased was using ordinary care, and that, if the weight of evidence did not show deceased using such care, the jury need not concern themselves with the other issues. *Held*, that the instruction was erroneously refused, and it was not subject to the objection that it ignored the question as to whether defendant's servants kept a proper lookout.

6. The instruction was erroneously refused inasmuch as the jury had been instructed at plaintiff's request that if deceased, in the exercise of ordinary care, was killed in consequence of the negligence of defendant, as charged in the declaration, they should find defendant guilty; thus leaving the jury to determine what negligence was charged.

7. In an action against a street railway for death resulting from a collision it appeared that deceased was driving behind a large covered wagon, and that when he reached a street intersection he turned out upon defendant's track, and his vehicle was struck by a car approaching from the opposite direction; that at the time he turned out the car was between 100 and 200 feet distant, running about 12 miles an hour; and that its speed did not slacken perceptibly until the accident occurred. There was evidence tending to show that the bell was not rung, but there was some evidence that the motorman called out, and sought to warn deceased. *Held*, that the evidence did not show gross negligence on the part of defendant.

8. It was proper to refuse an instruction that deceased had no right to drive upon the track so as to obstruct or interfere with the passage of defendant's cars, there being no evidence tending to show that he sought to obstruct the track.

9. The trial court has no authority to arbitrarily fix the number of instructions that shall be presented or passed on.

10. The unauthorized conduct of the trial court in limiting the number of instructions that might be presented was not reversible error where only one of appellant's instructions was not passed on, and it would have been proper to have refused it if considered.

Appeal from Appellate Court, First District.

Action by Patrick H. O'Donnell, as administrator of the estate of John White, deceased, against the Chicago City Railway Company. From a judgment of the Appellate Court (108 Ill. App. 385) affirming a judgment in favor of plaintiff, defendant appeals. Reversed.

This is an appeal from a judgment of the Appellate Court affirming a judgment for $2,500 entered upon a verdict rendered by a jury in the superior court of Cook county against appellant in an action on the case prosecuted to recover damages on account of the death of John White. The declaration consisted of one count, and alleged that the defendant, through its certain servant then and there in charge of one of its street cars then and there being operated upon and along said railway upon Halsted street in a northerly direction towards and past Forty-Second street, so recklessly, carelessly, and negligently ran and drove the said street car at such a high and dangerous rate of speed, and without maintaining a proper lookout, and without giving suitable warning of the approach of said car, that as a result and consequence thereof said car then and there ran against and struck said wagon, etc. A plea of not guilty was filed.

The evidence discloses that at the time of the accident deceased was 74 years of age, and in the employ of a lumber company as a sort of errand man, and on the day of the accident was driving a one-horse carpenter wagon belonging to his employer. He had delivered some lumber, and was driving back towards the lumber company's office, south on Halsted street, and immediately before the accident was following a covered beer wagon. Halsted street runs north and south. Appellant had two street car tracks along Halsted street, the west line being called the "south-bound track" and the east line the "north-bound track." The beer wagon which deceased was following was going down the south-bound track very slowly, and about the time Forty-Second street was reached the deceased pulled his horse out onto the north-bound track, and either started to go around the wagon he was following or to turn east on Forty-Second street, there being a conflict in the evidence as to what he was trying to do, but the evidence shows that about the time he had pulled over onto the north-bound track he pulled back towards the south-bound track, and his wagon was struck by an electric car coming towards him on the north-bound track. White fell from his wagon, and died a short time afterwards. Forty-Second street intersects Halsted street on the east side, but does not extend west beyond Halsted street, the stockyards being to the west.

The errors urged are the failure of the court to direct a verdict for the appellant, the giving and refusing of instructions, limiting the number of instructions to be given and passed upon by the court, and alleged misconduct of the attorney for appellee in his argument to the jury.

William J. Hynes, James W. Duncan (Mason B. Starring, of counsel), for appellant. James C. McShane, for appellee.

RICKS, J. (after stating the facts). 1. It is urged that the court should have directed a verdict for appellant because White, plaintiff's intestate, was guilty of contributory negligence as a matter of law. It is contended that there is no evidence that the deceased used ordinary care for his own safety, and that the evidence, taken in the most favorable light to appellee, does not tend to show that the deceased did use ordinary care, but, on the contrary, shows that the deceased's injury resulted from his own negligence. Appellant concedes that it is generally a question of fact whether or not a given line of conduct amounts to the exercise of ordinary care, but takes the position that it is equally well settled that, where there is no conflict in the evidence, and where it can be fairly seen the injury was the result of the negligence of the party injured, the question becomes one of law, and in such case the court should instruct the jury to find for the defendant. In this position appellant insists it is supported by Beidler v. Branshaw, 200 Ill. 425, 65 N. E. 1086, North Chicago Street Railroad Co. v. Cossar, 203 Ill. 608, 68 N. E. 88, and in other cases cited in its brief.

The accident occurred in the morning. The sun was shining, but there was some mist. Appellee's contention is that when the deceased reached the north boundary of Forty-Second street he turned his horse in an easterly course, as if to cross Halsted street and go east along Forty-Second street, but that there was on the east line of Halsted street another beer wagon loaded with barrel beer that obstructed his way, and, seeing the approaching car of appellant coming from the south, and north bound, the deceased, in order to avoid a collision, turned his horse back towards the west to pass the car on the west side, but that the west track, which was only about five feet from the east track, was occupied, and the speed of the car was so great that before he could reach a place of safety the collision took place. Appellant's contention is that the deceased undertook to pass the wagon loaded with bottled beer, which he had followed on the south-bound track, that was immediately in front of him, and pulled out of Forty-Second street for that purpose; that the street, except as to the wagon going south along the west track, was free from obstructions; and that the deceased, in the exercise of ordinary care, should have seen the approaching car, and have refrained from turning out on to or near to the east track until the car had passed.

There is some conflict in the evidence as to where the deceased did leave the west track—whether at the north boundary or north curb of Forty-Second street or about the middle of Forty-Second street. Witnesses for appellee testified that the deceased left the track at the north boundary, or at the curb of Forty-Second street, and that the collision took place about the middle of the street, while other witnesses testified that the deceased left the west track about the middle of the street, and that the collision took place near the south curb. There is no conflict in the evidence but that the car, when the deceased did pull into the street, was between 100 and 200 feet south of him. There is a conflict in the evidence as to the speed of the car, but there is testimony tending to show that the speed of the car was about 12 miles an hour when the collision took place. In considering this question we are bound to take the testimony most favorable to appellee. The evidence most favorable to him tends to show that the deceased turned out of the west track at the north boundary of Forty-Second street, and that at that time the car was 200 feet away, and was traveling at the rate of 12 miles an hour, and that its speed was not perceptibly slackened until almost the moment of the collision. There is also evidence tending to show that the bell was not rung or gong sounded, and while there is evidence that shows that the motorman, and perhaps others, by calling to and by gesticulation sought to warn the deceased, there is no evidence that he was conscious of such warning. The evidence as to what course the deceased intended to pursue at the time he did pull out of the west track is only inferential, there being no evidence showing where he was going, or what for. His place of work was at 4824 Halsted street, or a little more than six blocks directly south of where he received his injuries, and at that time he was going south towards his headquarters, with his wagon empty.

We have for several years denied the contention that the failure to look and listen when approaching a railroad crossing was, as a matter of law, negligence, and have in recent years uniformly held that whether such failure was negligence was a question of fact, to be determined from all the facts and circumstances in the case. If, then, it was not negligence, as a matter of law, for the deceased to have changed his course at the street crossing and have turned out toward or upon the east track without looking and listening for a north-bound car, we are unable to say that, as a matter of law, the deceased was guilty of negligence in doing so when it appears that the car was 200 feet away from him, approaching a street crossing, and in the absence of evidence that he had any knowledge that such car was approaching. Appellant puts the question thus: "The sole question then arises, was his conduct in turning to the left upon the track, where he might come face to face with an approaching car, contributory negligence?" and we answer, "As a matter of law, no; as a matter of fact, it may have been." But to say that in a city, at the crossings of streets, every person in a conveyance who may veer from his course is guilty of negligence or want of ordinary care because he may come face to face with an approaching car and may incur an injury, is to say that, as a matter of law, every person driving along a street must take one course, and not deviate from it, at the risk of receiving injury for which he shall have no compensation under any circumstances. The beer wagon that was in front of the deceased when driving down the west track continued in its course, and when the injury occurred the two wagons were practically side by side, and whether it was the duty of the deceased, in the exercise of ordinary care, to have seen the approaching car 200 feet away at or before the time he pulled out of the west track, and have apprehended the danger of a collision, and have remained on the west track, or to have endeavored to have gone on east, down Forty-Second street, or turned back into the west track behind the wagon he had been following, or whether he might not, in the exercise of ordinary care, rely upon appellant so keeping its car in control in approaching the street crossing, and in the 200 feet it had to travel, that the same might be easily and safely stopped and collision avoided, were questions of fact, which we think were properly referable to the jury. Appellant concedes that the evidence tends to show negligence on its part. It was not error to refuse to direct a verdict of not guilty.

2. Complaint is made of appellee's instruction No. 20. The instruction reads: "The court instructs the jury that 'ordinary care,' as mentioned in these instructions, is the degree of care which an ordinarily prudent person situated as the deceased was, as shown by the evidence, before and at the time of the injury, would usually exercise for his own safety." It is said of this instruction that it confines the definition of ordinary care to the plaintiff's intestate, and, as other instructions referred to the care of appellant as well, the definition should have been broad enough to include both. It was not improper for the court to define to the jury the meaning of the term "ordinary care" as applied to the conduct of either of the parties. Appellant was urging contributory negligence as a substantive defense, and appellee was entitled to an instruction as to the line of conduct required of the deceased to show care on his part. The greater insistence of appellant is that the instruction is too narrow, and does not, in terms, submit the proposition that plaintiff's intestate must have exercised ordinary care in leaving the west track, and assumes that an ordinarily prudent person would be situated as the deceased was situated before and at the time of the accident; that the central inquiry was, not what the deceased did after getting into the situation, but was he in the exercise of ordinary care in getting himself into that situation; that, although the words "before and at the time of" are in the instruction, the jury were warranted in construing it to mean that the appellee might recover if, after leaving the west track, his intestate exercised the care an ordinarily prudent person would usually exercise. In support of this contention appellant cites North Chicago Street Railroad Co. v. Cossar, 203 Ill. 608, 68 N. E. 88, Illinois Central Railroad Co. v. Weldon, 52 Ill. 290, and Illinois Central Railroad Co. v. Creighton, 63 Ill. App. 45. In the Cossar Case time was not an element of the instruction complained of, but "the circumstance and in the situation" were to be the criteria, and we expressed the view that under it no time or circumstance, except that directly attendant upon the immediate accident was included in its terms, and that it was too narrow, as it excluded the requirement that the plaintiff should not negligently place herself in a position of danger. In the Weldon Case, supra, the instruction is not set out. The court say the instructions were confined to the conduct of the deceased whilst unloading the coal cars, during which he received his injuries, but that the central question was, did he exercise proper care and caution in entering the car under the circumstances, and that the latter question should have been submitted. In the Creighton Case, supra, the instruction was, "At the time of such alleged injuries exercising due care." The injury was caused in an effort of the plaintiff, an engineer, to reverse the lever on a locomotive and avert a wreck. The evidence tended to show that the difficulty in reversing the lever arose from the plaintiff having two days previously plugged certain holes in the cylinder in such manner that the lever could only be moved by great effort. The defense was contributory negligence. It was held that the instruction confining the due care to the time of the injury was too narrow, as it authorized the jury to find for the plaintiff if using due care at the time, although the injury may have been due to his gross negligence two days before. All that occurred in the case at bar from the time the deceased reached Forty-Second street to the time of the accident could not have exceeded two or three minutes, and the instruction required due care before and at the time of the injury, and we think was broad enough, and did not assume, as is contended, that the deceased was in the exercise of due care at any time.

The appellant's fourth instruction told the jury that White, the deceased, and appellant, were required to use the same degree of care to avoid the injury, and by appellant's eighth instruction the jury were told that if White was negligent and careless in driving his wagon at the time and place in question, and that such negligence caused his injury, appellee could not recover.

Appellant's instruction No. 12 was refused. It was as follows: "If the jury believe, from the evidence, that ordinary care on the part of White for his own safety required him, before driving to or upon the track parallel with the track upon which he had been driving, at the time and place in question and under all the circumstances in evidence, to look and ascertain whether or not a car was approaching along the north-bound track, and not to drive upon said track without so looking; and if the jury believe, from the evidence, that White, if he had looked, could, by the exercise of ordinary care, have ascertained whether or not a car was approaching along the said north-bound track; and if the jury further believe from the evidence that White did not so look and ascertain whether or not the car was so approaching, and that he was injured in consequence and because of his failure, if he did so fail to look and ascertain—then the court instructs the jury to find the defendant not guilty." Appellee says this instruction was properly refused, because it assumes that, if plaintiff's intestate saw the car approaching, he should, in no event, have driven upon the track; that it emphasized the question of his looking or failing to look; and that it was covered by other general instructions requiring him to exercise ordinary care to avoid the injury. We do not think any of the suggestions made justify its refusal. It assumes no fact, but submits the question as one of fact, to be determined from the evidence, whether plaintiff's intestate, in the exercise of ordinary care, should have looked for the car before turning out, and whether he did look; and then states that if he should have looked, and did not look, and was injured in consequence of his failure to do so, the jury should find the appellant not guilty. There was no other instruction that contained the proposition here presented, except instructions of a general character. The matter there presented was the chief ground of defense, and should have been submitted by the instruction offered. Mallen v. Waldowski, 203 Ill. 87, 67 N. E. 409; Chicago, Burlington & Quincy Railroad Co. v. Camper, 199 Ill. 569, 65 N. E. 448; Chicago & Eastern Illinois Railroad Co. v. Storment, 190 Ill. 42, 60 N. E. 104.

The court refused appellant's instruction No. 13, which was as follows: "The issues you are sworn to try in this case are as follows: Was the electric car which collided with the wagon in question carelessly and improperly driven or managed by the servant or servants of the defendant? Was the said electric car traveling at an unnecessarily high or dangerous rate of speed? Did the servant or servants of defendant negligently fail to ring a gong or bell at the time and place in question? Did the servant or servants of defendant in charge of said car know that White was in a position of peril in time to have stopped the car in time to have avoided the collision by the use of reasonable care on their part? Could the servant or servants of defendant in charge of the electric car, by the use of reasonable care, have seen that White was in a position of peril in time to have stopped the said car before the collision? Was White at and just before the time of the collision using ordinary care and caution for his own safety? If you conclude that the greater weight of the evidence does not show that White was using such care and caution for his own safety, you need not concern yourselves with the other issues, because in no event can the plaintiff be entitled to recover a verdict unless it has been shown by the greater weight of the evidence that such care and caution was used by White. If you do find from the greater weight of the evidence that such care and caution was used by White, you will examine the evidence bearing upon the other issues, and if you do not find the greater weight of the evidence, taken as a whole, will warrant you in answering one or more of them in the affirmative, you should find the defendant not guilty." And the court gave appellant's instruction No. 18, as follows: "The jury are instructed that the plaintiff cannot recover at all in this case against the defendant company unless the jury believe that the plaintiff has proved, by a preponderance of the evidence, the following propositions: First, that the plaintiff's intestate was exercising ordinary care for his own safety at and just prior to the time of the accident in question; second, that the defendant company was guilty of negligence in the manner charged in the declaration; and, third, that such negligence was the proximate, direct cause of the death of the plaintiff's intestate. And if you find from the evidence that the plaintiff has failed so to prove these propositions as stated, or that he has failed so to prove any one of them, he cannot recover against said defendant company, and you should find the defendant company not guilty." Appellee claims that by giving appellant's instruction No. 18, and other general instructions, the errors, if any, in refusing No. 13, were cured. Appellee further contends that instruction No. 13 ignores the charge in the declaration that appellant did not maintain a proper lookout; that the direction by the next to the last clause of the instruction refused, that the jury need not consider the other matters if they found the appellee's intestate was not in the exercise of due care and caution, ignored the question of the appellant's gross negligence, which the narr. was broad enough to cover, and there was evidence tending to support. As to the latter claim, we will not enter into a discussion, but will only say we think there was no evidence tending to support the charge of gross negligence on the part of appellant, and no instruction was asked by appellee upon the theory that there was. Under the fourth and fifth clauses the question of a proper lookout was included. The instruction was not subject to objection as to form or substance, and fairly stated the issues under the declaration, and, unless covered by other instructions, should have been given.

Instruction No. 13 was presented among the fifteen to which the court had limited each side, and after it was refused appellant offered three more instructions, numbered 16, 17, and 18, together with written suggestions why the court should consider the same, and 16 and 18 were given and 17 refused. Appellee only offered six instructions, and they were 19 to 24, inclusive, and were all given. By appellee's instruction No. 19 the jury were told that if White, in the exercise of ordinary care, was killed by or in consequence of the negligence of the defendant, as charged in the declaration, they should find the defendant guilty. The jury were thus to learn, as best they could, and determine for themselves, so far as the plaintiff was concerned, what actionable negligence was charged in the declaration; and the appellant, with such instruction given for appellee, was entitled to have the jury fairly and fully informed what negligence was charged in the declaration, and what acts or omissions of the defendant must be found to authorize the verdict of guilty. North Chicago Street Railroad Co. v. Polkey, 203 Ill. 225, 67 N. E. 793; Illinois Central Railroad Co. v. King, 179 Ill. 91, 53 N. E. 552, 70 Am. St. Rep. 93; West Chicago Street Railroad Co. v. Kautz, 89 Ill. App. 309. In the latter case the judgment of the trial court was reversed for failure to give an instruction almost identical with appellant's No. 13. We do not think the instructions given covered the issues in the case.

Appellant's ninth instruction began with the statement, "The court instructs the jury that White had no right to drive upon the railway track in question so as to obstruct or unnecessarily interfere with the passage of the defendant's cars." There was no evidence in the record tending to show White sought to obstruct or unnecessarily interfere with the passage of appellant's cars. The instruction assumed either the fact, or that there was evidence tending to support the statement. What followed in the instruction did not relieve it from such vice, and the court properly refused it.

Appellant's seventeenth instruction was refused. The court declined to examine or pass upon it, as it was in excess of the limit as to number which the court had fixed. The material parts of it were covered by appellant's instructions Nos. 2, 4, and 5, and its refusal was not error.

Complaint is made of the modification of some of appellant's instructions, but we do not find the modifications such as should be held to be error.

3. It is claimed by appellant that it was prejudiced by the manner and language of the court while fixing and enforcing the rule limiting the number of instructions. At the close of the plaintiff's case the court openly announced the rule limiting the total number of instructions to 30, allowing 15 to each side, and stated no more would be received and considered. When appellant offered its instructions there were eighteen, and the court insisted that counsel should select 15 of them to be passed upon; and it is claimed that in the colloquy between the court and counsel the court was gruff and arbitrary, and so spoke that the jury might infer that appellant was seeking both an unfair and illegal advantage. The language of the court is included in the bill and briefs, and is followed by the statement that it is doubtful if the jury heard what transpired. The manner of the court, more than the language, is complained of. The court was not authorized to arbitrarily fix the number of instructions that should be presented or passed upon. Chicago City Railway Co. v. Sandusky, 198 Ill. 400, 64 N. E. 990. By fixing the rule appellant was not injured, as all its instructions presented (and there were 18) were considered and passed upon but one—No. 17. It would have been proper to have refused it when considered. We cannot say whether the jury observed or heard what transpired as to the instructions, or what effect it had, if any, on the jury. It cannot be maintained that it was the proper thing for the court to establish an illegal rule, and become angry and show his displeasure because it was not acquiesced in.

4. The argument of counsel for appellee, in some of its features, was strenuously objected to by appellant, and the remarks were mostly withdrawn, and the objection sustained. To say the least, some of the remarks should not have been made, and we may hope will not be repeated upon the further trial for which this cause will be remanded to the superior court.

The judgments of the superior court and the Appellate Court will be reversed. Reversed and remanded.

(208 Ill. 312)

GRAFF v. PEOPLE.*

(Supreme Court of Illinois. Feb. 17, 1904.)

CRIMINAL LAW—APPEAL—CHALLENGE TO JURORS—WITNESS—WIFE OF CO-INDICTEE—CONSPIRACY — EVIDENCE — LEGAL EXISTENCE OF CORPORATION—MERGER OF MISDEMEANOR IN FELONY—CODEFENDANT PLEADING GUILTY—SURPRISE—HARMLESS ERROR—NEW TRIAL.

1. An appeal unauthorized in a criminal case will, in the absence of a motion to dismiss, be considered as a writ of error; everything essential to a hearing on writ of error being present.

2. Any error in disallowing challenge for cause to jurors is harmless; they having been challenged peremptorily, and defendant not having been compelled to take an incompetent juror.

*Rehearing denied April 7, 1904.

3. Allowing the wife of one jointly indicted with defendant, but who pleaded guilty before the trial, to testify, is not error.

4. On a trial for conspiracy, a conversation in furtherance of the common design, but not in defendant's presence, by one engaged in the conspiracy, though not named in the indictment, is admissible.

5. Cr. Code, § 613 (Starr & C. Ann. St. 1896, p. 1402, c. 38, par. 613), providing that user shall be prima facie evidence of the legal existence of a corporation, makes other evidence unnecessary, in the absence of countervailing proof, as well in the case of a foreign as a domestic corporation.

6. Where a conspiracy to obtain insurance money by false pretenses (a misdemeanor) is formed, and, in the course of carrying it out, arson (a felony) is committed, the misdemeanor does not merge with the felony, so as to prevent a conviction of the conspiracy.

7. Defendant cannot complain because a codefendant withdrew his plea of not guilty, and entered one of guilty, in the presence of the jury, after the state had rested, where it does not appear that the court or prosecution had notice that this was to be done, especially where the jury were instructed that his pleading guilty should not influence them.

8. The question of surprise in admission of evidence is not open to review where defendant merely objected to the evidence on the ground that the state had closed its case.

9. On a trial for conspiracy to obtain insurance money by false pretenses, a written statement made by a codefendant, at defendant's instigation, at the time of adjustment of the loss, relating to the value of articles claimed to have been burned, is admissible.

10. The specific pointing out, in an instruction, of an accomplice's testimony, though error, is not ground for reversal, where it cannot be seen that it resulted in harm.

11. Newly discovered evidence, being cumulative, does not require the granting of a new trial.

Appeal from Appellate Court, First District.

Barney Graff was convicted of conspiracy, and from a judgment of the Appellate Court (108 Ill. App. 168) affirming the conviction, he appeals. Affirmed.

Appellant, Barney Graff, in July, 1901, was jointly indicted with Ben Ettelson, Dave Ettelson, Fred Alexander, and George Samels, charged with a conspiracy to obtain money from the Buffalo German Insurance Company and the Rochester German Insurance Company of Rochester, N. Y., by false pretenses, with intent to cheat and defraud said companies. The defendants Fred Alexander and George Samels entered pleas of guilty before the trial of said cause, and testified in the case on behalf of the people. During the trial, and after the state had announced that it had closed its case, Ben Ettelson, another of the defendants, arose to his feet, and stated to the court that he desired to enter a plea of guilty, and to take the stand and testify as to the facts in the case; appellant and Dave Ettelson being the only remaining defendants standing trial.

The evidence discloses that for some time previous to January 1, 1901, appellant and Ben Ettelson, one of the codefendants, had been friends; and in the month of November, 1900, appellant, during an interview with Ben Ettelson, suggested that he get some one who would be willing to make some "easy money." Shortly afterwards Ettelson approached a man by the name of Clark Snyder with the proposition suggested to him by Graff, but Snyder refused to join in the scheme; and shortly afterwards Ettelson made the same proposition to Alexander, and he consented to become a party to the scheme. Thereupon Ettelson unfolded the scheme to Alexander; stating that he wanted him to start a cigar store, and to first select the store, and he (Ettelson) would arrange to have it stocked with cigars, and, after it was so stocked, they could make some "easy money." Alexander and Ettelson immediately began to look for a vacant store to rent, and during the latter part of December located one on the south side of the city of Chicago, in the building known as Nos. 469-471 Forty-Seventh street, which Ettelson stated to Alexander was "made to order" for their purpose. Ettelson then instructed Alexander to see one M. A. Pierce, who was the agent having the store for rent, and arrange for the renting of the same, which Alexander did, and informed Mr. Pierce that he intended to conduct a retail cigar store, and, being informed that the room rented for $30 per month, rented the same, and paid $30 in advance; the money being furnished by Ettelson. In a few days Ettelson, with Alexander, went to see George Samels, who was engaged in the cigar business; Ettelson introducing Alexander to Samels, and recommending him; saying anything sold to Alexander would surely be paid for. It appears, also, from the evidence, that Graff had in the meantime visited Samels, and informed him of Ettelson and Alexander's intention of going into the cigar business, and that he (Graff) would vouch for their responsibility, and that Samels could safely sell them a stock of cigars. After having the arrangements made with Samels for the cigars, Ettelson and Samels purchased secondhand fixtures. The fixtures and stock being placed in the store, Ettelson instructed Alexander to take out $3,000 insurance on the fixtures and stock. The fixtures cost $59, and the stock of cigars about $700. Alexander immediately went to see about the insurance, and, after some trouble, he succeeded in getting the two insurance companies named in the indictment to carry the insurance; $500 being placed on the fixtures, and $2,500 on the stock. Ettelson states that during all this time he was in daily communication with appellant, and that appellant advised him with reference to everything done. After the store was opened, ready for business, Alexander apparently took charge, which was some time after the middle of January, 1901. On January 31st (being nine days after the policies were received), Ben Ettelson, accompanied by his brother Dave, came to the store, bringing with them a five-gallon gasoline can, and in-

¶ 4. See Criminal Law, vol. 14, Cent. Dig. §§ 990, 991.

structed Alexander to place the can in the rear room; warning him not to place it near the fire. The same afternoon Ben Ettelson packed up a large amount of the stock of cigars, and removed them to his house. Between 12 and 1 o'clock in the morning, Ettelson and Graff came to the store and saturated everything with gasoline; and Ettelson states that some combustible material was used, which had been given him by appellant, and, a light being applied to the combustible material, an explosion resulted therefrom, and the place was consumed by fire. Ettelson and Graff ran from the premises. Ettelson, being badly burned, was compelled to call a physician, and was taken to the hospital, where he stayed for several weeks. Appellant sent for Alexander the next morning, and he came to appellant's place of residence, and had a talk with appellant, who informed Alexander that Ettelson had been badly burned at a fire at his place of business the night before, and that he would assist Alexander in getting the insurance money, and to call at 7 o'clock that evening, and he would tell him what to do, which he did, and was instructed to take the policies to Joseph Fish, an adjuster, which Alexander did. Fish stated it would be necessary to obtain statements showing the purchase price of the stock and fixtures. Alexander informed appellant of this fact, and appellant said to Alexander that he would attend to that, and at this time had Alexander make a false statement as to the amount of fixtures. Samels shortly afterwards called on appellant, and informed him that the stock of cigars had not been paid for. Appellant said to him that he would get his money as soon as the insurance money was collected, but informed Samels that, in order for him to get the money, it would be necessary for Samels to make out false statements showing that $3,000 worth of cigars had been purchased, instead of $700, which Samels did; sending the statement to Fish, the adjuster. Fish then began negotiations for a settlement on the insurance policies, and, after some delay, made a settlement with the companies for $1,500; the money all being turned over to appellant; Alexander receiving $150, and Ettelson receiving $300.

The case was tried before a jury, who found the appellant guilty of conspiracy to obtain money by false pretenses, as charged in the indictment, and fixed his punishment at a fine of $2,000, and imprisonment in the penitentiary, on which the court rendered judgment. The defendant Dave Ettelson was found not guilty. A writ of error was prosecuted to the Appellate Court by appellant, where the judgment of the circuit court was affirmed, and appeal was prayed and allowed to this court.

Appellant assigns as error (1) the action of the court in overruling a challenge, for cause, of jurors; (2) the admission of improper evidence: (3) insufficient proof of the existence of the corporations alleged to have been defrauded; (4) that the indictment charged a misdemeanor, while the evidence showed the offense to have been a felony, and that the misdemeanor merged in the felony, and that appellant should have been tried for the felony, being the burning of the building; (5) in the court permitting Ben Ettelson to withdraw his plea of not guilty, and enter a plea of guilty, in the presence of the jury, and then testifying for the state; (6) in permitting certain exhibits to be offered in evidence; (7) the giving and refusing of instructions; (8) the refusal of the court to grant a new trial by reason of newly discovered evidence.

Stedman & Soelke, for appellant. Charles S. Deneen, State's Atty., and Harry Olson, Asst. State's Atty. (Haynie R. Pearson and Samuel W. Jackson, of counsel), for the People.

RICKS, J. (after stating the facts). The law does not authorize an appeal in a criminal case, and, whenever a motion to dismiss such an appeal has been made, it has been allowed. In this case no motion of that kind was made, but the appearance of the people was entered, and there was a joinder in error. The cause was submitted for decision upon the errors assigned on the record, and, inasmuch as everything essential to a hearing upon a writ of error is before us, we will treat the case as being here on writ of error. That was done in Berkenfield v. People, 191 Ill. 273, 61 N. E. 96, where the record was in the same condition.

As to the first objection, it need only be said that the record fails to show that appellant was prejudiced in any way by reason of the court disallowing the challenge, for cause, of jurors, inasmuch as the jurors were challenged peremptorily, and appellant was not forced or compelled to keep any juror that was incompetent. Spies v. People, 122 Ill. 1, 12 N. E. 865, 17 N. E. 898, 3 Am. St. Rep. 320.

As to the second error assigned, the evidence objected to, first, was that of the witness Mrs. Alexander, who was the wife of one of the defendants named in the indictment, and was permitted to testify in rebuttal in corroboration of the testimony of her husband. Alexander had pleaded guilty before the beginning of the trial, and was not, so far as this record shows, a defendant; and we are unable to see why her testimony was not competent, the same as any other witness. In criminal cases, as a general proposition, a husband or wife cannot testify for or against one another, but here the wife was not testifying either for or against her husband. It is claimed, secondly, the court erred in permitting O. C. Kemp, the insurance adjuster, to testify to alleged conversations with Joe Fish, at which neither appellant nor any of the persons named in the indictment were present. Fish was the representative of appellant and Alexander, and went to Kemp with the proofs of loss; and in the conversations there does not appear to have been anything said, except in relation to the making and delivery of the necessary proofs of loss, which Kemp declined to accept, and said he regarded the claim as fraudulent. Conversations, to be admissible in evidence in a case where the defendant is charged with conspiracy, need not be in his presence, or in the presence of some one of the parties jointly indicted, so long as the conversation was in furtherance of the common design, and by one engaged in the conspiracy, whether named in the indictment or not. Lasher v. Littell (Ill.) 67 N. E. 373; Spies v. People, supra; Van Eyck v. People, 178 Ill. 199, 52 N. E. 852.

As to the third contention, the indictment charged, "the personal goods, funds, money, and property of the Buffalo German Insurance Company, a corporation organized and existing under and by virtue of the laws of the state of New York, * * * and property of the Rochester German Insurance Company of Rochester, N. Y., a corporation organized and existing under and by the laws of the state of New York," etc. Appellant contends that it became necessary for the prosecution to prove that the corporation had been organized and incorporated as alleged in the indictment. Proof of the actual exercise and enjoyment of the corporate powers and functions was made by the witness Kemp, who was the agent of the companies. Section 613 of the Criminal Code provides "that in all criminal prosecutions involving proof of the legal existence of a corporation, user shall be prima facie evidence of such existence" (Starr & C. Ann. St. 1896, p. 1402, c. 38, par. 613), and, where there is no countervailing proof, the proof of user sufficiently supports the allegations; and, as was said in the case of Kincaid v. People, 139 Ill. 213, 28 N. E. 1060: "The language is broad and comprehensive, including all criminal prosecutions involving proof of the legal existence of a corporation, and it is not, as is supposed, nor can it be, by any fair construction, confined to proof of the existence of an Illinois corporation only." Both corporations made and issued policies of insurance, and, after loss, still acting in their corporate capacity, compromised and adjusted the same, through their adjuster, with Fish, who was acting for and under the directions of appellant, and he received the money from the corporations as such. We think the evidence was ample upon this point.

Appellant's fourth contention is that the indictment in this case should have been under section 14 of division 1 of the Criminal Code (Starr & C. Ann. St. 1896, par. 48, c. 38, p. 1237), which section makes it a felony to burn or set fire to, or cause to be burned, any building or chattels, etc., insured against loss by fire, with intent to injure the insurer, instead of under section 46 of the same statute, for conspiracy, which is a misdemeanor. The argument proceeds upon the theory of the merger of the lesser offense (the conspiracy) charged in the indictment with the felony (arson), which was not charged in the indictment, but which was one of the overt acts pursuant to the conspiracy. At the common law, because of the marked difference between felonies and misdemeanors, arising not only from the dissimilarity and extent of the punishment and the consequences to the accused, but also the method of procedure, the theory of merger was evolved and generally obtained. Under an indictment for misdemeanor a person was entitled to the full privilege of counsel, to a copy of the indictment, and to a special jury, which, upon an indictment for a felony, he was denied. With these circumstances in view, it was considered that a person could not be found guilty of a misdemeanor upon an indictment for felony, although the misdemeanor formed a constituent of the felony and was complete, as he would lose substantial advantages of the method of trial provided for the misdemeanor; and where the indictment was for a misdemeanor, and the evidence necessary to establish it showed the commission of a felony, an acquittal would be directed in order that the prisoner might be indicted and tried for the felony. In such case the technically less crime of misdemeanor merged in the technically higher crime of felony, and it became a doctrine that, where the same criminal act satisfied the definitions of misdemeanor and felony, the misdemeanor was merged and gone, and the felony could alone be punished. It was also the rule at the common law that one charged with a felony could not be convicted of a misdemeanor, although the latter might be legally involved in the former, for, by the law as then administered, felonies and misdemeanors were classed as different things, and, where there was an indictment for a felony, if the proof failed to show a felony, but did show a misdemeanor, the person was detained in custody, to be indicted and prosecuted for the misdemeanor. So it has been held in both England and America that where an indictment was for a conspiracy to commit a felony, though the conspiracy would be a misdemeanor, if the object of the conspiracy was completed and a felony was committed, then the misdemeanor would merge in the felony. Commonwealth v. Kingsbury, 5 Mass. 106; People v. Mather, 4 Wend. 230, 21 Am. Dec. 122; State v. Hattabough, 66 Ind. 223.

In the modern criminal law, by reason of legislation and decisions of the courts, the distinctions in the trials of felonies and misdemeanors have been abolished; and in this state it has long been the law that a person charged with an atrocious offense may be convicted of any constituent offense of a lower degree, provided such minor offense is substantially included in the description in the indictment or accusation, and even without regard to the technical line of demarcation between felonies and misdemeanors. Herman v. People, 131 Ill. 594, 22 N. E. 471, 9 L. R. A. 182; Beckwith v. People, 26 Ill. 500; George v. People, 167 Ill. 447, 47 N. E. 741; Howard v. People, 185 Ill. 552, 57 N. E. 441. Where, however, the conspiracy alleged in the indictment is a misdemeanor, and the offense for the commission of which the conspiracy was formed is also a misdemeanor, and is completed, it has been uniformly held in this country that there is no merger. And so the rule applies if the conspiracy charged is a felony, and, when the completed crime is a felony, there is no merger, or, in other words, the rule of merger does not apply where both the conspiracy for which the person is indicted and the completed offense are both felonies or both misdemeanors. Orr v. People, 63 Ill. App. 305; Hamilton v. State, 36 Ind. 280, 10 Am. Rep. 22; Commonwealth v. McPike, 3 Cush. (Mass.) 181, 50 Am. Dec. 727; State v. Dowd, 19 Conn. 388; State v. Salter, 48 La. Ann. 197, 19 South. 265; Keefe v. People, 40 N. Y. 348. And it would seem that in conspiracies the rule of merger is confined to those cases where the conspiracy charged in the indictment would be a misdemeanor, and the crime, when completed, as charged in the indictment, is a felony, and the proof shows the completed crime. United States v. Gardner (C. C.) 42 Fed. 829; United States v. McDonald, 3 Dill. 545, Fed. Cas. No. 15,670; State v. Murphy, 6 Ala. 765, 41 Am. Dec. 79; State v. Lewis, 48 Iowa, 579, 30 Am. Rep. 407. And it is believed that, by the greater weight of authority, the rule of merger, as formerly existing at common law, has been to a great extent abrogated, and confined to very narrow limits. Bishop on New Crim. Law, §§ 791, 814, 815, 815a; Wharton on Crim. Law (8th Ed.) 1343, 1344. If the indictment be for a conspiracy, which is a misdemeanor, and the conspiracy comprises the doing of many things, and the proof shows that among the overt acts done pursuant to the conspiracy is a felony, it would seem the greater weight of authority is that a conviction may nevertheless be had for the conspiracy. Johnson v. State, 26 N. J. Law, 313; Commonwealth v. Blackburn, 1 Duv. 4; People v. Peterson, 60 App. Div. 118, 69 N. Y. Supp. 941; United States v. Rindskoff, 6 Biss. 265, Fed. Cas. No. 16,165; State v. Grant, 86 Iowa, 217, 53 N. W. 120; 20 Am. & Eng. Ency. of Law (2d Ed.) 605; 3 Greenleaf on Evidence, § 90; State v. Murray, 15 Me. 100.

The crime, under paragraph 48, could be committed without any conspiracy, and the crime charged in the indictment could have been devised and committed without arson. It so happens that arson was one of the means selected for the commission of the crime charged, but it was only one of them. The proof shows that the conspiracy charged in the indictment was primarily to obtain from the insurer insurance greatly in excess of the amount of the loss. It involved an outlay of about $750, and the pressing of a claim for $3,000. The fraud consisted in buying a small amount of goods, carrying a great portion of them away from the store, burning a small portion, and presenting false invoices of goods purchased. The defendant Samels, so far as the evidence discloses, was not a party to the conspiracy until after the arson, nor is it shown that he had any knowledge of the arson until after the fact. He could not have been indicted for arson, but only as an accessory after the fact, while he and all the others included in the indictment were, if the evidence is to be accredited, guilty of the crime charged in the indictment; and we cannot yield our assent to the contention that where a conspiracy is formed, including or requiring several acts for its consummation, and, because one of the acts may be of the nature that it is classed as a felony, therefore the conspirator must be indicted for the felony, and the conspiracy be disregarded. If the conspiracy charged were only to commit the crime of arson for the purpose of defrauding the insurance companies named in the indictment, then the contention made here would have much force. It is not shown that the details of the conspiracy were all developed or evolved at the inception of the conspiracy, which is the crime charged here, but that the plan grew with time, and after the arson the plan of increasing the demand against the insurance companies by having Samels who had sold to Ettelson and Alexander cigars to the amount of about $700, prepare and present, for use in the adjustment of the loss, invoices of sales to the amount of $3,000, seems to have been conceived. Samels had not been paid for his goods, and he was told that, in order to get his pay, it was necessary that he present the false invoices, which he did, and which made him a party to the conspiracy.

A careful examination of the American authorities cited by appellant upon this proposition will disclose that the only one that may be fairly said to be directly in point and tending to sustain his contention is Commonwealth v. Kingsbury, supra. From a careful reading of that case, it will appear that the conspiracy charged was to commit a felony, and that it was carried into effect, and the real matter before the court was not the question presented to this court, as would seem to be contended. In that case the Massachusetts court remarks that the rule of merger applies both in respect to misdemeanors and to felonies. This announcement is so contrary to authority that the case cannot carry with it the weight it otherwise might. It appears that the rule announced in that case was subsequently departed from in the case of Graves v. Graves, 108 Mass. 314. Hoyt v. People, 140 Ill. 588, 30 N. E. 315, 16 L. R. A. 239, does not seem to us to be authority upon the point here presented. The question there was whether the indictment was double. It charged a conspiracy to burn, and it also charged the burning of a certain building by the defendants. The indictment was held not double, but to be a good indictment for arson, and it was merely said in the discussion that "the conspiracy in such case is merged in the consummated act of burning."

It is very earnestly contended that, if this conviction be allowed to stand, appellant may be indicted and convicted of the crime of arson, under said paragraph 48, as it is urged that the present conviction cannot be pleaded in bar to an indictment for arson. We do not feel called upon to pass upon the question as to whether this conviction can be pleaded in bar to a prosecution under said paragraph 48. Whether it can or not does not furnish a sufficient reason for relieving appellant from the consequences of his own deliberate actions. If he has in fact committed two crimes, that are so distinct that the conviction of one may not be urged in bar of the other, the misfortune must be his own.

Complaint is made that the trial court permitted Ben Ettelson, a codefendant with appellant, after the people rested, to withdraw his plea of not guilty, and enter his plea of guilty, in the presence of the jury, and during the progress of the trial. We are unable to see how error can be predicated upon this matter. The court had no more control over Ben Ettelson than did appellant. He had the unquestioned right to plead guilty if he saw fit to do so, and the only proper place for him to do so was in open court. It is not shown or claimed that the court had any notice of Ettelson's intention to withdraw one plea and enter the other until it was done. Nor was it shown that the state had any notice of the intended action of Ettelson. It seems to have been upon the spur of the moment, and to have been somewhat dramatic. It may be that it had some influence with the jury, but neither the people nor the court was responsible for it. He was a codefendant with the appellant, and was being tried jointly with him, and there is no reason to assume that the court or the prosecution knew any more about his intended action than appellant. Be that as it may, and though it may have been an unfortunate circumstance for appellant, it was not one for which a blame can be attached to the court or to those representing the people. Appellant's counsel now state that both the appellant and his counsel were so surprised that they were dumbfounded, and it may be that they were greatly surprised; but they doubtless felt, as the court must have felt, that, however great the surprise, Ettelson was exercising a right that he unquestionably had, and, unless there was overindulgence by the court, which there does not seem to have been, or collusion by those representing the state, which is not shown, the incident must be regarded as one of those unfortunate things that sometimes happen in the course of a trial, for which no one in particular is to blame.

After Ettelson had pleaded guilty, the court reopened the case for the state and permitted the state to use Ettelson as a witness. The only objection interposed by appellant was upon the ground that the state had closed its case. It is admitted that it rested in the discretion of the court to reopen the case and permit the state to offer further evidence, but appellant now urges that he was surprised by the course Ettelson had taken, and by the offered testimony. Whether he was surprised, in a legal sense, is not shown by the record, as he did not object to the evidence upon the ground of surprise, or make any motion addressed to the court upon that theory. As far as the court could do so by instructions, the injurious effect, if any, of Ettelson's conduct, was repaired by appellant's fifty-second and fifty-third instructions. The jury were told that the fact that Ettelson had pleaded guilty in their presence should not influence them in arriving at their verdict, or be considered by them as any evidence of guilt of the other defendants.

At the time of the adjustment, Alexander, one of the codefendants, had a certain written statement, made by himself, and relating to the value of the fixtures that were claimed to have been lost by the fire. This exhibit was admitted in evidence, and is complained of by appellant. It was one of the efforts in the direction of the conspiracy by one of the conspirators for the accomplishment of the given purpose. The evidence was that it was made at the instigation of, and under the direction of, appellant, and we are unable to see any ground upon which it was not admissible.

Complaint is made as to the giving and refusing of instructions. Those given were 67 in number, and, from a careful review of them, and taken as a series, we think they fully and fairly presented the law to the jury, and that those that were refused were covered by other instructions given.

Instruction 47, given for the people, singled out and directed special attention to the evidence of Ben Ettelson. It told the jury that the testimony of an accomplice should be received with caution, and yet that a conviction might be had upon the uncorroborated testimony of an accomplice, and that if they believed, from the evidence, that the testimony given by Ettelson was true, they had the right to act upon it as true; that it should be weighed by the jury like the testimony of any other of the witnesses, or that the testimony of an accomplice, like all other evidence in the case, was for the jury to pass upon. By instructions 44 and 45, given for appellant, the jury were further and particularly cautioned to act with great caution and care, and subject to critical examination and scrutinization, in the light of all the other evidence in the case, the testimony of accomplices, and that they should not convict upon such testimony alone, unless, after a careful examination of it, they were satisfied, beyond a reasonable doubt, of its truth, and that they could safely rely upon it. It was error to have specifically pointed out the evidence of the witness Ettelson, and such action has been many times condemned by this court; but there was evidence of other accomplices to the same effect as Ettelson's, though not so full, and there was ample evidence in the record to warrant the verdict found, and we would not feel justified in reversing this case for the error committed, as we are unable to see that it resulted in harm to appellant.

Motion for new trial was made, and partially based upon newly discovered evidence. The evidence claimed to have been newly discovered was but cumulative, and was not sufficient to require the granting of a new trial.

We find no reversible error in the record, and the judgment of the Appellate Court will be affirmed. Judgment affirmed.

(208 Ill. 256)

CHICAGO TRUST & SAVINGS BANK et al. v. BALL.*

(Supreme Court of Illinois. Feb. 17, 1904.)

FRAUDULENT SALE—AFFIRMANCE—RESCISSION.

1. A bill showing fraud in the sale of stock to complainant, and alleging facts from which it followed that the stock had and could have no value (it being alleged that the corporation never did any business which, by its charter, it was authorized to transact, and that it had never done anything other than to pretend to guaranty commercial paper to enable defendants to exact usurious interest, and it not being pretended that the corporation owned any property), but praying, among other things, that defendants be required to surrender the stock to complainant, and be enjoined from disposing of it, shows an election, with knowledge of the facts, to affirm the sale, from which position complainant cannot be relieved by an amended bill to rescind the contract of purchase, which, besides enlarging on the charges of fraud, merely makes the additional statement that the stock was valueless when it was sold to him.

Appeal from Appellate Court, First District.

Suit by Joseph Charboneau, for whom David M. Ball, his executor, was substituted, against the Chicago Trust & Savings Bank and others. From a judgment of the Appellate Court (108 Ill. App. 321) affirming a decree for complainant, the bank and others appeal. Reversed.

On February 26, 1892, Joseph Charboneau exhibited his bill in the circuit court of Cook county against the appellant the Chicago Trust & Savings Bank, Daniel H. Tolman, and the Midland Company for injunction and relief. By a supplemental bill the appellants Cornelia T. Williams and Delmon W. Norton were made defendants. Pending the litigation, and after the bill and the amended bills had been filed and the evidence taken before the master, but before the hearing, Charboneau, the complainant, died, and upon the suggestion of his death David M. Ball, the appellee, who was the executor of Charboneau's will, was substituted as complainant.

The original bill was verified, and alleges that on the 16th of September, 1889, the complainant received a letter from the Midland Company, requesting him, if he was in need of money, to call, and that about the latter date he called on the Chicago Trust & Savings Bank for a loan of $750; that appellant Tolman was the president of the bank; that Tolman informed complainant that he would not loan money to complainant unless he would take stock in the Midland Company; that Tolman then exhibited to complainant a book, which purported to show the profits to be made by investing in the latter company; that the stock was worth $160, the par value being $100 per share, and that Tolman told complainant that if he would purchase stock in said company, and did not want it when paid for, Tolman would purchase it back; that the Midland Company was organized for the purpose of guarantying commercial paper of its stockholders, and was a sort of mutual benefit society, organized upon the plan of building and loan associations; that complainant was unacquainted with Tolman, the bank, and the Midland Company, and knew nothing about either of them, and, believing the statements of Tolman to be true, and relying thereon, purchased five shares of said stock in said company at the price of $800, and gave to the bank his judgment note for $750 and nine judgment notes for $80 each, due and payable in one, two, three, four, five, six, seven, eight, and nine months, with interest at 8 per cent., and received from the bank, or Tolman, or the company, the sum of $595 as the proceeds of his loan; that complainant did not know from which of said parties he received the loan, but the notes were made payable to complainant's order, and by him indorsed; that $155 was deducted from the face of the loan to make up $80 of the purchase price of the stock, $30 by reason of the pretended guaranty of the Midland Company upon the $750 note, and $45 discount to the bank; that the rate of interest he was to pay was 2½ per cent. a month in advance, besides purchasing the stock in said company; that when said $750 note became due he renewed the same for 90 days, paying at the rate of 2½ per cent. per month interest, in advance, on account of said renewal, and when the renewal note became due he paid the same in full; that by means of the premises the bank, Tolman, and the Midland Company obtained from complainant $106 above the legal rate of 6 per cent. interest, which they held for his use and benefit; that upon the payment of said $750 renewal note his certificate of stock was not delivered to him, but was retained until the last $80 note given on account of the purchase price of said stock

*Rehearing denied April 7, 1904.

in said company was paid; that he paid all of said notes, with 8 per cent. interest per annum; that on the 27th of March, 1891, he applied to Tolman for a loan of $500, and offered his stock in said company as collateral security; that said loan was made, and a judgment note for $500, payable four months after date, to the order of the complainant, was drawn and indorsed and delivered to Tolman, for the bank, and that complainant received $450, $50 of the said loan being deducted for interest for four months at the rate of 2½ per cent. per month, and $20, as pretended by Tolman, for the guaranty of said company, and the balance for interest to the bank; that the latter note was renewed from time to time until about the 27th of January, 1892, at which time complainant applied to the bank for a further renewal, but advised Tolman that he could not pay $50 for such renewal; that after offers and counter offers were made, the renewal was obtained by complainant paying $35 advance for a period of four months; that complainant had paid a large amount of illegal and usurious interest, which should be applied upon the said $500 note, which was still outstanding, and in possession of the defendants, or some of them. Complainant offered to pay the defendants, or such of them as might be the holder of said note, the amount justly and equitably due on accounting.

The bill then contains the allegation, upon the information and belief of complainant, that the Midland Company was planned, organized, and incorporated under the laws of Illinois by Tolman for the purpose and with the intent on the part of Tolman and the bank of using the same unlawfully and fraudulently as a means of acquiring large sums of money illegally and fraudulently and without consideration, by the sale, forfeiture, and resale of the stock of said company, and by compelling borrowers in the bank to become stockholders in the company, and to pay the rate of 1 per cent. a month on moneys borrowed by them from the bank in addition to the illegal interest charged by the bank; that said company had been so illegally and fraudulently used by said Tolman and the bank, and that said company had never transacted any business which, by its charter, it was authorized to transact, nor was it intended at the time of its organization by Tolman that it should transact such business; that it had never pretended to transact any business other than guarantying commercial paper of its stockholders; that the company, the bank, and Tolman were branches of one concern conducted and controlled by Tolman; that all moneys paid by complainant as compensation or illegal interest for the purpose of obtaining and renewing loans from the bank, which Tolman pretended were for the benefit of said company for guarantying paper, were in fact paid it at the request and under the requirements of Tolman and the bank, and that Tolman and the bank were in equity liable to account to complainant therefor, as well for other illegal interest paid the bank; that the bank and Tolman were principals, and said company was their agent; that the bank, Tolman, or said company had possession of complainant's note for $500 of date January 27, 1892, a large part of which had been paid, and that the defendants, or some of them, had also his certificate for five shares of the Midland Company stock, which he was entitled to possession of; and that said bank, Tolman, and the Midland Company should be enjoined and restrained from disposing of his said note or said certificate of stock of the Midland Company, and from entering judgment or taking other action upon said note. The prayer of the bill was that Tolman and the bank be held liable to complainant for the moneys paid for alleged guaranties of said company; that an accounting be had; that complainant's note be canceled and surrendered; that his certificate of stock in the Midland Company be surrendered and delivered to him; that injunction issue restraining defendants, etc., from selling, etc., the judgment note of $500 or causing judgment to be entered thereon, and from selling, assigning, forfeiting, or otherwise disposing of his certificate of the capital stock in the Midland Company.

Answers were filed to the bill and supplemental bill, and nothing further seems to have been done until December 15, 1894, when complainant filed what is termed his "engrossed bill," which states substantially all that is in the original bill or suit, and, in addition thereto, alleges that Tolman for years past has been president and general executive officer managing the business of the bank, and also president, treasurer, and executive officer, managing the business of the Midland Company; that prior to May, 1888, Tolman conceived the scheme of organizing a corporation to defraud the public, and for that purpose organized the Midland Company; that he first applied to the Secretary of State for a charter for a company to guaranty commercial paper, and was refused; that he caused three of his employés to make application to the Secretary of State, stating in the application the object of the company was to "secure information and furnish statements concerning the responsibility of persons and corporations, to conduct a merchandise commission business, and to contract in respect thereto"; that Tolman at the time did not intend that the company should conduct such business, but intended it to do a business of guarantying commercial paper as his agent, for the purpose of cheating and defrauding persons out of their money by selling them stock and pay money to said corporation for the pretended guaranties thereof; that said Tolman knew that said company was not authorized to guaranty anything; that the company was intended to be and was used by Tolman and the bank as a cover for usury and a device to assist them in getting usurious interest; that when complainant applied to the bank, through Tolman, its president, for a loan, he was informed he could not obtain the same without the guaranty of the Midland Company, and that he would be obliged to become a stockholder to obtain such guaranty; that said Tolman would sell five shares of stock; that the Midland Company was organized for the purpose of guarantying commercial paper, and was authorized by its charter to guaranty such paper, and had been in the past doing a prosperous business, and its stock was worth $100 per share; that since its organization it had been earning money rapidly, and inside of a year would be worth $250; that it charged 1 per cent. per month for guarantying paper of its stockholders, but the earnings of the company were so large that the stockholders would get back in dividends enough to make the interest very light; that it was organized on the plan of building and loan associations, for the mutual benefit of its stockholders; that he believed the statements and representations made by Tolman regarding the organization, objects, business, and profits of the Midland Company to be true, and relied thereon; that he knew nothing about the Midland Company or its charter powers, except as he was informed by Tolman; that Tolman did not show him the charter or books of the company; that the statements and representations made by Tolman to induce him to purchase such stock were false and fraudulent, and were known by said Tolman to be false and fraudulent at the time he made them; that said company did not do a profitable or prosperous business, and was not authorized to guaranty commercial paper of its stockholders or any one else, but was organized as a fraudulent device, and as the agent of Tolman and the bank, and that, instead of said stock being worth $160 per share, it was absolutely worthless; that proceedings were had in the superior court of Cook county, on the relation of the people, against said company, by which, on the 10th of February, 1894, a decree was entered arresting the charter of said company, and prohibiting it from doing business. The prayer of the bill is that the bank, Tolman, and said company be held parcels of one institution, and that Tolman and the bank be held liable for moneys paid by complainant for guaranties to said company; prays for an accounting, and that in the accounting he be given credit for $800 paid by him to Tolman for the certificate of stock in said company, and interest thereon; that said purchase be declared fraudulent and void, and that said certificate be decreed to belong to said Tolman, and offers to permit him to retain possession of the same; and for other and general relief.

The cause was referred to the master, who reported, finding that the evidence supported the allegations of the amended bill. Upon the coming in of the report the complainant further amended his bill on September 15, 1900, by alleging that he was ignorant of all the facts and circumstances respecting the Midland Company, its organization, charter powers, fraudulent character, stock and the value thereof, and relied entirely upon the misrepresentations and promises of Tolman, and believed them to be true, and never learned of their falsity, etc., until a long time after, to wit, immediately and within five years next preceding the filing of the original bill as to such matters as are therein stated, and immediately and within five years next preceding the filing of the amended and supplemental bill of complaint as to such matters as are therein stated.

Objections were filed to the report of the master and overruled, and exceptions before the chancellor and by him overruled, and a decree was entered finding that there was due complainant on account of the purchase price of the said stock and the interest thereon, and for usurious interest and pretended charges of the guaranty company, $1,777.50, and that there was due from complainant, upon his note, $753.20; awarded complainant execution against all the defendants, except Norton, for the amount decreed to him; and ordered that upon the payment of said amount there be paid to Norton therefrom the amount of the note and interest owing from complainant. An appeal was prayed and prosecuted to the Appellate Court, which rendered judgment affirming the decree of the circuit court, and this appeal was prosecuted.

C. E. Cleveland, for appellants. Bulkley, Gray & More, for appellee.

RICKS, J. (after stating the facts). This case and the case of Anderson v. Chicago Trust & Savings Bank, 195 Ill. 341, 63 N. E. 203, are, as far as we are able to determine from a careful review of the record, alike in all substantial features, and grow out of the same fraudulent conduct and combinations between Tolman and the appellant bank and the Midland Company that are shown in the cases of Murray v. Tolman, 162 Ill. 417, 44 N. E. 748, and Tolman v. Coleman, 104 Ill. App. 70. That the organization of the Midland Company was an unmitigated fraud for the purpose of enabling Tolman and the appellant bank to profit by usury under the pretense of guarantying commercial paper is too well settled by the former opinions of this court above referred to to require further comment, and that appellee's testate was one of the victims of that fraudulent combination cannot be doubted from the evidence contained in this record; but we cannot overlook the fact that at the time of the filing of the original bill in this case, which was verified, appellee's testate knew and declared that said Midland Company was organized and being used for fraudulent purposes, and at the same time insisted that he was the owner of stock in said company, of which appellants, or some of them, had possession, and which he called his stock, and prayed that appellants should be required to surrender the same up to him, and be restrained and enjoined "from selling, assigning, forfeiting, canceling, or otherwise disposing of his certificate of the capital stock in the Midland Company." It is true that in 1894, by what is termed his "engrossed bill," the complainant enlarged upon the charges of fraud made in the original bill, and then, in effect, for the first time asked that the transaction be rescinded because thereof, and offered to leave appellants in possession of said stock. But at that time it did not occur to the complainant to allege that he did not know, at the time of filing his original bill, that said Midland Company was a fraudulent organization; and in fact he could not have well so alleged, as in his original bill he had alleged that said Midland Company was a fraudulent organization, and was but an adjunct to and a part of the bank, and under the control and management of Tolman for the benefit of Tolman and the bank. In fact, the only new thing that he did allege by his amended bill that can be said to have been material was the fact that the stock of the Midland Company was valueless at the time it was sold to him, and that the representations as to its value were false and fraudulent. Although this same allegation was not contained in the original bill, that bill did contain the allegations that the company had never transacted any business which, by its charter, it was authorized to transact, and that it was not intended by Tolman that it ever should transact such business; that it had never transacted any business other than guarantying commercial paper, and that such guaranties were only a pretense and a cloak used by Tolman and the bank for exacting illegal and usurious interest; that the moneys paid to Tolman by complainant as compensation or illegal interest for the purpose of obtaining and renewing loans from said bank, which Tolman pretended were for the benefit of said company for guarantying paper, were in fact paid at the request of the bank.

If, then, the company had never done any business which it was authorized to do, and if all the business it had ever done was to aid the bank in collecting illegal interest, and these facts were known to the complainant when he filed his original bill, or he was so informed and believed, he must have known then that the stock of a corporation so conducting business was worthless. He must have known that the stock of any corporation not owning property—as it was not pretended that this corporation did own any—but depending upon the conduct of business for its value, and doing no business it was authorized to do, but being engaged only in a fraudulent scheme to aid a bank in collecting illegal interest, had no value, and could have none; and with such knowledge or information he insisted that he was the owner of the stock of said company, and that such stock was in the possession of appellants, or some of them, and that he was entitled to have the certificate for such stock restored to him, and desired to have appellants enjoined from canceling or assigning the same. It would seem that the mere statement, afterwards added, that the stock was worthless, would not be sufficient to relieve appellee's testate from the position of one who, with knowledge of the fraud, had elected to assert ownership to the property thus imposed on him.

The last amendment of the bill of September 15, 1900, was upon the suggestion of the master, contained in his report, that the bill lacked an allegation upon the point of the time of knowledge of the fraud; and when the allegation is looked to we find that it is in such general language—the language being, "immediately and within five years next preceding" the filing of the amended and supplemental bill—that little weight can be attached to it, and, so far as we have been able to determine from the record, there is no evidence whatever to support such amendment. The case seems to us to be upon all fours with the Anderson Case, and to be controlled by it. In the latter case we held that the attempt to rescind the purchase of the stock must be treated as first made at the time of the amendment of the bill, in 1894, which was the same time the bill in question was amended; and the view was there expressed that the amendment could not be carried back to the time of the filing of the original bill. That view seems applicable to the case at bar.

We find that appellee's testate paid $222.63 to Tolman under the pretense of the latter that such sum was a guaranty fee of the Midland Company, and we think a decree should be rendered allowing appellee to offset that sum against the note and interest which he owes and is held by appellants, and that that is the limit of the relief that can be granted him under the facts as shown by this record.

Appellants urge that the costs of the court below should be apportioned, but we do not think sufficient appears in the record to justify us in entering such order.

The judgment of the Appellate Court and the decree of the circuit court of Cook county are, and each is, reversed, and the cause is remanded to the circuit court of Cook county, with directions to enter a decree in conformity with the views herein expressed.

Reversed and remanded, with directions.

(208 Ill. 231)

BUTLER v. MILLER et al.*

(Supreme Court of Illinois. Feb. 17, 1904.)

BILL TO ANNUL SHERIFF'S DEED—GROUNDS FOR RELIEF—APPEAL.

1. In an action to set aside a sheriff's deed, the bill alleged the filing of a transcript of judgment for execution to sell the land, and attached a copy of the transcript to the bill. It was further alleged that by the transcript of judgment it appeared that a summons was issued by a justice against complainant and another, that service was had on the other defendant and judgment rendered against him, and summons in the nature of a scire facias subsequently issued against complainant and her codefendant, both of whom were served and appeared, and against both of whom judgment was rendered, execution thereon being returned unsatisfied, with a statement that neither of the defendants had personal property within the county. The bill then alleged that neither complainant nor her codefendant in the suit before the justice was ever served or appeared in that suit; that the scire facias was never served on complainant; that the return on the execution that complainant and her codefendant had no personal property was untrue and falsely and fraudulently made; and that complainant had no notice or knowledge of the suit before the justice, or the scire facias, or either of the judgments or of the transcript or sale, until long after such proceedings, and relief was sought on these grounds. The answer admitted the filing of the transcript, and that the document attached to the bill was a substantially correct copy thereof. *Held*, that on appeal plaintiff could not base her right to recover on the fact that the copy of the transcript attached to the bill showed that the summons was not signed by the justice, that the copy of the transcript contained no copy of the scire facias, and showed a continuance of the cause before the justice from the date on which judgment was rendered until several days later, even though the copy of the transcript was admitted to be substantially correct.

Error to Circuit Court, Cook County; O. H. Horton, Judge.

Action by Mary E. Butler against Martha A. Miller and others. From a judgment for defendants, plaintiff brings error. Affirmed.

John C. Wilson and William Slack, for plaintiff in error. Eldridge & Rose and Edward P. Vail, for defendant in error Martha A. Miller. Charles L. Bartlett, for defendants in error Marcus Langerman, Fannie Langerman, Charles Seth Burton, and Charles Seth Burton, as trustee.

SCOTT, J. This is a writ of error sued out of this court to review a decree of the circuit court of Cook county, entered on February 28, 1902, dismissing, for want of equity, a bill in chancery filed in that court on April 15, 1901, by Mary E. Butler, plaintiff in error, against Martha A. Miller, one of the defendants in error.

The bill, as amended, represents that on the 7th day of November, 1899, there was filed in the office of the circuit clerk of said county a "transcript of judgment for execution to sell land, a copy of which transcript of judgment" is attached to the bill; that by said transcript of judgment it appears that on the 14th day of August, 1899, before a justice of the peace in Cook county, at the suit of Julia C. Higbee against Mary E. Butler and Redmond F. Sheridan, joint defendants, a summons was ordered and issued, returnable August 22, 1899; that said summons was returned showing service on Sheridan, and that Mary E. Butler was not found; that on August 22, 1899, the cause was continued until August 29, 1899; that judgment was then taken against Sheridan for $70.55; that on September 25, 1899, summons in the nature of a scire facias was issued against Mary E. Butler, as defendant in said cause, returnable October 5, 1899; that said scire facias was duly returned by the constable, showing personal and timely service, by reading, to Mary E. Butler, and that on October 5, 1899, the case was called, plaintiff and defendant being present, evidence was heard, and judgment rendered against Mary E. Butler, together with Sheridan, for the sum of $60.55 and costs of suit; that on October 26, 1899, execution issued against both defendants, and was returned on October 28, 1899, in no part satisfied, and with a statement in the return thereon to the effect that the defendants in the execution had no personal property in the county whereof the constable could cause to be made the said judgment and costs, or any part thereof; that on November 9, 1899, execution issued out of the circuit court of Cook county, directed to the sheriff of that county for the collection of the amount of the said judgment and costs, against Mary E. Butler and Redmond F. Sheridan; that by virtue thereof, on the 11th day of November, 1899, the sheriff levied on certain real estate in said county of which complainant was the owner in fee simple, and sold the same on the 12th day of December, 1899, to Julia C. Higbee, to whom a certificate of purchase was duly executed, which was by her, on December 3, 1899, assigned to Martha A. Miller, and on March 13, 1901, the sheriff of said county executed to said Miller a sheriff's deed for the real estate in question.

The bill then charges, in substance, that said deed does not convey any title, for the reasons following: (1) The summons issued by the justice was never served on Sheridan, he never appeared in the suit before the justice, and judgment was rendered against him by the justice without jurisdiction. (2) The scire facias was never served on the complainant, Mary E. Butler, and she never appeared in the suit before the justice, and the judgment rendered against her and said Sheridan was rendered without the justice having jurisdiction of either. (3) The return on the execution, to the effect that complainant and Sheridan had no personal property out of which the judgment could be made, is untrue; that each had ample personal property out of which the execution could have been satisfied, and that the indorse-

*Rehearing denied April 7, 1904.

ment and return on said execution are false, and were fraudulently made. (4) Complainant never had any notice or knowledge of the pendency of the cause before the justice of the peace, or of the summons or scire facias, or of either of the judgments rendered in the cause, or of either of the executions, or of the transcript of the judgment, or of the sale, or of the execution of the certificate of purchase, or of the sheriff's deed, until about the 20th day of March, 1901, and that no demand was made upon her for the amount called for by the execution issued by the justice.

The bill further avers that the defendant took the assignment of the certificate of purchase with knowledge of the facts set out in the bill, and that the defendant is not the lawful owner of said real estate; that the title held by her in the same is held without legal or equitable right; that complainant is in possession of said real estate, and avers that the said sheriff's deed is a cloud upon her title; that she was not indebted to Julia C. Higbee in any sum at the time said judgment was rendered against her, unless by virtue of the assignment of some claim against her to said Higbee; that she was never informed of any such assignment, and offers to pay to Martha A. Miller, as assignee of Higbee, such amount, if any, as may be due her upon an accounting; prays that the deed may be set aside, and decreed null and void.

The defendant answered, admitting the filing of the transcript, and that the document attached to the bill "is substantially a correct copy of said transcript"; admitted the suit and the various steps in the proceedings as stated in the bill; but denied the existence of each and every of the causes upon which the bill places the right to the relief sought.

The cause was referred to a master to take the proofs. Upon the hearing before the master, complainant offered no evidence whatever. Defendant took the testimony of several witnesses, from which it conclusively appears that the summons was personally served, by reading, upon Sheridan; that the scire facias was personally served, by reading, on the complainant, as stated in the returns on those writs respectively; that the defendant was present before the justice of the peace on October 5, 1899, during the trial of the cause against her, and was then represented by counsel; that she had notice on November 25, 1899, that the said real estate would be sold by the sheriff at the time and place where it was thereafter sold. The master made his report accordingly, it was approved, and a decree was entered dismissing the bill for want of equity, and awarding costs against complainant.

Plaintiff in error seeks to have this decree reviewed for the reasons following: (1) The summons, as shown by the copy of the transcript attached to the bill, does not bear the signature of the justice of the peace. (2) Such copy of the transcript does not contain a copy of the scire facias. (3) Such copy of the transcript shows a continuance of the cause from August 29th to October 7th.

It is conceded that these objections were not specifically pointed out in the bill, but it is said that the bill made the copy of the transcript attached a part of the bill, and the answer admitted that the copy was substantially correct, and that, as these objections appear from an inspection of that copy, they must be considered as a part of the cause made by the bill. With this view we cannot concur. The bill recites the contents of the transcript—not the contents of the copy attached. From such recitals none of these objections appear. In fact, the statements of the bill would lead to the conclusion that they did not exist. For example, the bill recites that the transcript of the judgment on file in the office of the clerk shows that a "summons" was issued by the justice of the peace, from which the legal inference is that it was a lawful summons, bearing the signature of the justice. Had the bill based the right to relief on the objections now urged, defendant would have had an opportunity to introduce the transcript filed in the office of the clerk and attempt to meet the case now presented. The bill specifically states the grounds upon which the relief is sought, and they do not include either of the objections now made in this court. It is apparent that plaintiff in error made one case by her bill, and seeks to make another in this court upon this writ. That she cannot do this has been too frequently decided to now require the citation of authorities.

Plaintiff in error made several persons other than Martha A. Miller defendants in error. Such other persons moved in this court that the writ of error be dismissed as to them. The motion was taken to be determined with the case. The decision at which we have arrived makes unnecessary any disposition of the motion.

The decree of the circuit court will be affirmed. Decree affirmed.

(208 Ill. 369)

Appeal of BORDEN.*

(Supreme Court of Illinois. Feb. 17, 1904.)

TAXATION—PERSONALTY—SITUS—BOARD OF REVIEW—DETERMINATION — CERTIFICATION OF QUESTIONS—SUPREME COURT—REVIEW.

1. Hurd's Rev. St. 1899, p. 1453, c. 120, § 35, provides that if the board of review shall decide that property claimed to be exempt is taxable, and the party aggrieved prays an appeal, a brief statement of the case shall be made by the clerk under the direction of the board, and transmitted to the Auditor of Public Accounts, who shall present the case to the Supreme Court. *Held* that, where a case is presented under such section, the decision of the court must be based on the "brief statement" so certified.

*Rehearing denied April 7, 1904.

2. Stocks, bonds, and credits are taxable at the place of the owner's residence, though they are held by his agents in a foreign state, if such holding is for convenience only, and not for the purpose of enabling the agent to transact any business of which the property is the subject-matter or stock in trade.

Certified by Auditor of Public Accounts.

Proceedings by the board of review of Marion county for assessment of certain personal property against Theresa Borden, as executrix of the estate of Henry Lee Borden, deceased. From an order of the board of review assessing the property, the executrix prayed an appeal to the Auditor of Public Accounts, which was allowed, and the record certified to the Supreme Court. Affirmed.

L. M. Kagy, for appellant. H. J. Hamlin, Atty. Gen., for the People.

WILKIN, J. This is an appeal from the action of the board of review of Marion county in assessing against Theresa Borden, executrix of the last will and testament of Henry Lee Borden, deceased, certain stocks, bonds, and credits owned by the estate of her deceased husband, Henry Lee Borden, at the time of his death, and which, under his will, became vested in her. For several years prior to his death, Henry Lee Borden owned a farm and dwelling house in Tonti township, in Marion county, and lived there with his family a portion of each year up to the time of his death. He died on November 21, 1902, in California and was buried in New York. By his last will and testament he appointed his widow, Theresa Borden, the appellant herein, his executrix, and made her his sole legatee. The will was duly admitted to probate by the county court of Marion county, and letters of administration issued to said widow. L. L. Borden, a son of appellant, acting as her agent, gave in to the local assessor of Tonti township, for assessment for the year 1903, $50,350, in the name of appellant, individually. The board of review notified her to appear before it on September 10, 1903, and show cause why certain stocks, bonds, and credits owned by her should not be assessed; and on that date she appeared with her attorneys, and made a written answer to said notice, alleging that all the personal property belonging to the estate of Henry Lee Borden subject to taxation in said county had been duly listed and assessed by the assessor of Tonti township, and that certain shares of stock of the Home National Bank of Elgin, Ill., were not subject to taxation in said county, but were taxable in Kane county, and that the United States bonds held by said estate were exempt from taxation. She then listed numerous stocks, bonds, and credits which she alleged were not subject to taxation in the state of Illinois on April 1, 1903, for the reason that such stocks and bonds, on the 1st day of April, 1903, and at all times prior thereto, had no actual or constructive situs in the state of Illinois, but were held, owned, and controlled in the state of New York, and there had their legal situs, and therefore were not assessable in said Tonti township. She also filed with the board her affidavit, and that of her son L. L. Borden, in support of the allegations of her written answer, with the further statements that all stocks and bonds last above mentioned were held, owned, and controlled in the state of New York by agents of appellant for the purpose of enabling said agents to transact all business relating thereto in the state of New York, where said bonds, stocks, and credits had their legal situs on April 1, 1903, and had had their legal situs long prior to the death of Henry Lee Borden; that the appellant and Henry Lee Borden never had permanently resided in Tonti township or in Marion county, but had only used said farm, residence, and buildings in said county as a temporary abode for the purpose of spending the pleasant spring months of the year, and of occasionally stopping for the purpose of rest and recreation when not living elsewhere in the United States, the greater portion of the time, to wit, about 10 months in the year, having been spent out of the state of Illinois; that said stocks, bonds, and credits had no connection whatever with the business of appellant as executrix, or personally, in said county, but were separate and distinct therefrom, and all business transactions in relation thereto were conducted and carried on in the state of New York.

The board of review, after hearing these affidavits, certified that the foregoing was all the evidence heard or considered on the hearing of said matter, and made a written finding to the effect that the said Henry Lee Borden, for several years prior to his death, lived on said farm with his family a portion of each year, and during his lifetime, while living in said township, exercised the right of citizenship by voting at township elections in the township; that after his death said Theresa Borden, his widow, filed her petition, under oath, in the county court of Marion county, asking for probate of his will and testament, and in said petition she stated, under oath, that the said Henry Lee Borden was at the time of his death a resident of said county, and that she at that time was a resident of said county; that on the 1st day of April, 1903, said widow resided in said township, and had no other home or permanent residence elsewhere, and that on May 15, 1903, she reported all of these stocks, bonds, and credits to the county treasurer of Marion county, upon which to base the inheritance tax of the state of Illinois, which tax she paid to said county treasurer; that all of these stocks, bonds, and credits were listed to the local assessor of Tonti township for the year 1903 by L. L. Borden, her son and agent, and afterwards, at the request of said son, said local assessor received a new schedule, and erased from said assessment books all of the stocks, bonds, and credits in controversy herein, except the sum of $50,350, and that all of said assessments were made in the name of Theresa Borden individually, and not in her name as executrix, and that the same should be made in her name as executrix; that all of said stocks, bonds, and credits in controversy were kept by the said Henry Lee Borden, in his lifetime, in the hands of his agents in the state of New York, and have remained there in the hands of the said agents since his death; that the said stocks, bonds, and credits were not used by the said Henry Lee Borden in his lifetime, nor by his agents, either before or since his death, in any permanent business of the said Henry Lee Borden or the said agents in the state of New York, nor were they kept there, nor are they now kept there, for use in any particular business, and they were not in the hands of any agent of said executrix on the 1st day of April, 1903, in the carrying on of any business in which they were used or needed; and that the taxable situs of said stocks, bonds, and credits on April 1, 1903, was in said township and county, and an assessment was therefore ordered to be extended against said bonds by the said board of review, but not against the bank stock or United States bonds.

From this order of the board of review an appeal was prayed and allowed to the Auditor of Public Accounts, and the record has been certified to this court for our consideration, under section 35 of the revenue law of 1898 (Hurd's Rev. St. 1899, p. 1453, c. 120), which, among other things, provides: "If the board of review shall decide that property so claimed to be exempt is liable to be taxed, and the party aggrieved at the time shall pray an appeal, a brief statement in the case shall be made by the clerk, under the direction of the board, and transmitted to the Auditor, who shall present the case to the Supreme Court in like manner as hereinbefore provided." Our decision must be based upon such brief statement. The board of review found, according to that statement, that the deceased, Henry Lee Borden, was a resident of Tonti township, in Marion county, this state, at the time of his death, and that the appellant, in whom the property in question became vested under his will, resided in that township on the 1st day of April, 1903. As to her, there is nothing whatever in the affidavits set out in the statement to the contrary. No one pretends to dispute that fact. The recited facts also sustain the conclusion of the board that her deceased husband was a resident of that township, notwithstanding the fact that he did not permanently reside there. If his residence was not there, where was it? Presumably he had a residence at some place, but the affidavits of appellant and her son are both silent upon that subject. It is true, the stocks, bonds, and credits assessed as found were not in this state on the 1st of April, 1903, but were held in the state of New York. That fact alone would not, however, exempt them from taxation in Tonti township, where the owner resided; the rule being that where the owner of stocks, bonds, credits, or choses in action resides in this state, there is jurisdiction over his person and credits, which in law accompany him, and have their situs here for the purpose of taxation. Scripps v. Board of Review, 183 Ill. 278, 55 N. E. 700, and cases cited on page 284, 183 Ill., page 702, 55 N. E.; Ellis v. People, 199 Ill. 548, 65 N. E. 428.

In Metzenbaugh v. People, 194 Ill. 108, 62 N. E. 546, we said (page 116, 194 Ill., page 550, 62 N. E.): "The general rule is, the taxable situs of credits is the domicile of the owner. But an exception to the rule arises when the instruments which evidence the right of the owner to receive the indebtedness which constitutes the credits are in the hands of an agent of the owner for the purpose of enabling such agent to transact the business of the owner, in which business the credits constitute, as it were, the subject-matter or stock in trade of such business." Citing Hayward v. Board of Review, 189 Ill. 234, 59 N. E. 601, and Goldgart v. People, 106 Ill. 25. Appellant seems to have attempted, by the affidavits of herself and son, to bring the property in question within this exception to the general rule, but we are of the opinion that she has failed to successfully do so. It will be noticed that her affidavit, as well as that of her son, simply states that the property is held, owned, and controlled in the state of New York by agents of appellant for the purpose of enabling said agents to transact all business relating thereto in the state of New York, where said stocks, bonds, and credits had their legal situs on April 1, 1903, etc. In what particular business they were actually held and controlled there, does not appear from these affidavits—whether for the purpose of carrying on some business of which they are "the subject-matter or stock in trade of such business," or merely for convenience in receiving dividends thereon, is left altogether indefinite and uncertain—whereas the board of review finds and recites in its statement that said stocks, bonds, and credits were not used by the said Henry Lee Borden in his lifetime, nor by his agents, either before or since his death, in any permanent business of the said Henry Lee Borden or the said agents in the state of New York, nor were they kept there, nor are they now kept there, for use in any particular business, and they were not in the hands of any agent of said executrix on the 1st day of April, 1903, in the carrying on of any business in which they were used or needed, etc.

We entertain no doubt that, upon the showing in this record, the board of review correctly held that said stocks, bonds, and credits were taxable in the township of Tonti, in

Marion county, Ill., and its decision to that effect will accordingly be affirmed. Decision affirmed.

(208 Ill. 289)

VILLAGE OF LONDON MILLS et al. v. WHITE et al.

(Supreme Court of Illinois. Feb. 17, 1904.)

TELEPHONE COMPANIES—USE OF STREETS—CONSENT OF VILLAGE—MODE—ESTOPPEL—EQUITY PLEADING—MISJOINDER OF PARTIES—MULTIFARIOUSNESS—AMENDMENTS.

1. Hurd's Rev. St. 1901, c. 134, § 4, which provides for the erection of telegraph and telephone poles, posts, wires, etc., with the consent of the corporate authorities of a city, town, or village, except as it confers the power of eminent domain, applies both to corporations and natural persons.

2. Where a village board has, by resolution, granted to the owner of a telephone line the use of its streets and alleys in which to set poles and string wires for telephone use, and where the licensee, with the knowledge and tacit consent of the village authorities, has accepted and acted upon such resolution by erecting poles and stringing wires in the streets and alleys, the license so granted thereby becomes a contract, which is valid and binding on the parties thereto, and which cannot be revoked by the village, which is equitably estopped to assert that the consent required to be given by Hurd's Rev. St. 1901, c. 134, § 4, should, in the first instance, have been given by ordinance.

3. A bill charging that defendant telephone company and defendant village were conspiring together to drive complainants out of the telephone business in said village for the purpose of securing to defendant company exclusive control of the telephone business therein, and that, in furtherance of said conspiracy, defendant village was threatening to remove complainant's wires and poles, was not bad for misjoinder of parties defendant, in view of the further fact that it appeared from the averments of the bill that the village trustees and defendant company had joined in a corrupt combination for the purpose of securing to defendant company a telephone monopoly in the village.

4. Nor was the bill multifarious.

5. Amendments to a sworn bill were properly allowed without an affidavit showing valid excuse for failure to incorporate in the original bill the matters introduced by the amendments, where the amendments were entirely proper in their character, would not in any way change the cause of action, and would not contradict the averments of the original bill, and were not materially inconsistent therewith, but merely enlarged and amplified the statements of the bill so far as the charges therein contained were concerned, altered the prayers, and omitted certain words descriptive of the parties.

Appeal from Appellate Court, Third District.

Bill for injunction by Edward White and others, as co-partners under the name of Fairview-London Telephone Circuit, against the village of London Mills and others. From a judgment of the Appellate Court (105 Ill. App. 146) affirming a decree for complainants, defendants appeal. Affirmed.

On November 30, 1901, a bill for an injunction was filed by Edward White and others, appellees, against appellants, in the circuit court of Fulton county. The court permitted the complainants to amend their bill, and, as amended, a demurrer was interposed by appellants, which was overruled. A decree pro confesso was entered, and an injunction was awarded in accordance with the prayer of the bill. The cause was appealed to the Appellate Court for the Third District, where the decree of the circuit court was affirmed, and an appeal was thereupon taken to this court.

The bill alleges that the complainants are residents of this state, and, as copartners under the name of Fairview-London Telephone Circuit, have since April 2, 1900, operated a telephone system; that the system is used by members of the company, the public generally, and other connecting telephone companies; that the system connects the village of London Mills with Fairview, and furnishes telephonic communications for a large number of farmers, members of the circuit; that it has always been open to use by the public upon payment of customary charges, and is in competition with other lines; that it has expended the sum of $1,500 in constructing its plant, and has 31 miles of wire and 38 telephones; that on April 2, 1900, the circuit presented the following petition to the president and board of trustees of the village of London Mills: "The Fairview-London Telephone Circuit would respectfully ask that they be granted the privilege of using the streets and alleys of the village for the erection and maintenance of the necessary poles and wires for the proper communication of said circuit in the corporate limits of your village;" that said president and trustees, at a meeting on the same day, granted such privilege, and the following record was made and entered: "London Mills, April 2, 1900. A petition presented by the Fairview-London Telephone Circuit, asking privilege of using the streets and alleys of the village for the erection of a telephone circuit; petition granted;" that complainants immediately accepted said privileges, and spent $350 in erecting poles, wires, and other fixtures in said village; that they were erected so as not to interfere with the use of such streets and alleys; that complainants united with four other telephone companies (naming them) in establishing an exchange office, and have entered into a contract with those companies to jointly maintain the same, and are liable on that contract.

The bill further avers that the London Power & Electric Company was on March 13, 1901, incorporated for $2,500, under the laws of this state, "to conduct and maintain a suitable plant and necessary conducting apparatus in said village, to furnish said village and surrounding vicinity with electricity, light and power, and a system of water-works, and a telephone exchange," and sets out the names of the subscribers to the capital stock, and the number of shares subscribed for by each person. It then sets out the names of the persons at that time constituting the village board. The bill then avers that the London Power & Electric Company, by its stockholders, and the village officers, conspired and confederated together to secure to the London Power & Electric Company the exclusive control of the telephone business centering at said village; that in furtherance of such conspiracy the village board passed an ordinance, which is then set out in hæc verba, the substance of which, so far as the telephone system is concerned, provides that the right and permission are granted to the London Power & Electric Company to construct, erect, operate, and maintain poles, etc., upon the streets, alleys, and highways of the said village, for furnishing to the public communication by telephone, and a telephone exchange, and that these rights and privileges shall exist and continue to be exclusive and to be in force and irrevocable for 25 years, reserving the right to pass reasonable regulations pertaining thereto; that no telephone line or company entering and using the central or exchange office of said corporation shall be charged in excess of $1 per phone per year, nor in excess of $20 per year for any one line. This ordinance proceeds to repeal all ordinances, grants, or permissions in conflict therewith, with the proviso that lines and centrals already established in the village shall remain immune, and no change shall be made in them, except by mutual agreement, for a period of six months from the date of the ordinance.

The bill alleges that a majority of the village board that passed said ordinance were interested, as stockholders, in the London Power & Electric Company; that said ordinance was passed for the purpose of requiring all telephone companies to use the exchange office of said corporation at terms fixed by it, thereby increasing its profits; that appellees and the four other telephone companies using the joint exchange at the time this ordinance was passed permitted members of any one of them to use the lines and telephones of all five companies without charge; that after March 25, 1901, the London Power & Electric Company established its exchange, and by threats attempted to compel all other companies in said village to connect their lines with such exchange; that about May 1, 1901, two companies were permitted to enter said village without any license or permit from the village authorities, on condition that they would connect with the exchange of said corporation, and that they have not been molested since; that the village board passed another ordinance imposing a fine for making discrimination between persons, and providing that no telephone company should charge any individual or member of any line any fee which is not charged to each member of every line connected therewith, and should give to all individuals the same service accorded to others; that under this ordinance said board and the stockholders of said corporation threatened the companies having the joint exchange, and the operator in charge of such exchange, with prosecution under such ordinance unless free telephone service was accorded to the public, and free transfer fees to other telephone companies were allowed, all of which was done to compel the five companies to enter the exchange of said corporation.

The bill further alleges that another ordinance was passed by said board specifically naming the Fairview-London Telephone Circuit and two other companies, and providing that the rights and privileges granted to these and all other individuals and companies, except the London Power & Electric Company, were thereby revoked and repealed, but providing that the plants might be used and maintained until September 25, 1901, but that no change or extension should be made in such systems without the consent of said board, the London Power & Electric Company, and all other parties and companies interested; that a bill for an injunction was filed by the London Power & Electric Company against the companies operating the joint exchange, to restrain them from violating said ordinances; that one of these five companies withdrew from the joint exchange and entered the exchange of said corporation, and said suit was thereupon dismissed as to such company, and is still pending as to the other companies; that on November 7, 1901, a notice was served on the Fairview-London Telephone Circuit by the village authorities, notifying and requiring said circuit to remove from the streets and alleys of said village all poles, wires, and other fixtures used, owned, controlled, and operated by it upon and across any such streets and alleys within 30 days, and that, in case of failure to comply with such demand, the said village would take the necessary steps to remove such poles, wires, etc., according to law; that the London Power & Electric Company is counseling and advising with the village authorities to carry out said threats for the purpose of compelling all companies to enter their exchange or leave the village; that no such notice has been served on any company entering the exchange of said corporation.

The bill alleges that the foregoing ordinances are against public policy and void; that complainants believe said village is about to carry out the threat to remove the telephone appliances of complainants, which will result in irreparable loss.

The village of London Mills, the president and board of trustees of the village, and the London Power & Electric Company are made defendants. The bill asks that the ordinances be declared null and void, and that defendants be enjoined from carrying out their threats and from interfering with the telephone business of the complainants.

Chiperfield & Chiperfield and Thomas & Robison, for appellants. A. M. Barnett, Lucien Gray, and M. P. Rice, for appellees.

SCOTT, J. (after stating the facts). In this case the record of the president and board of trustees of the village of London Mills recites the presentation of the petition of the appellees, "asking the privilege of using the streets and alleys of the village for the erection of a telephone circuit," and shows that the permission was granted by resolution or motion. Acting thereon, appellees expended a considerable sum of money in establishing their lines along the streets and alleys of the village of London Mills. It is a necessary conclusion from the averments of the bill that these lines were so established with the knowledge of the village authorities, without objection from them, and with their tacit approval. Thereafter the village board passed an ordinance by which it was ordained that "all the rights, grants, privileges, franchises and permits in and to the streets, alleys and public places" which had been granted to appellees, were thereby revoked, repealed, and annulled. As a result of all which, appellees contend that the license granted to them has become a contract between appellees and the village which is irrevocable, while the position of appellant is that the right to use the streets and alleys for the purposes of appellees could be lawfully granted only by ordinance.

Sections 9, 10, and 17 of paragraph 62 of chapter 24 of Hurd's Revised Statutes of 1901 give to the president and board of trustees power to regulate the use of the streets in reference to the matters of this character. Section 4 of chapter 134 of Hurd's Revised Statutes of 1901, in terms, applies only to telegraph companies; but the act of which it is a part, we think, should be construed as applying also to telephone companies, and this section is as follows: "No such company shall have the right to erect any poles, posts, piers, abutments, wires or other fixtures of their lines along or upon any road, highway, or public ground, outside the corporate limits of a city, town or village, without the consent of the county board of the county in which such road, highway, or public ground is situated, nor upon any street, alley, or other highway or public ground, within any incorporated city, town or village, without the consent of the corporate authorities of such city, town or village. The consent herein required must be in writing, and shall be recorded in the recorder's office of the county. And such county board, or the city council, or board of trustees of such city, town or village, as the case may be, shall have power to direct any alteration in the location or erection of any such poles, posts, piers or abutments, and also in the height of the wires, having first given the company or its agent opportunity to be heard in regard to such alteration."

In City of Quincy v. Chicago, Burlington & Quincy Railroad Co., 92 Ill. 21, the city charter provided that "the city council shall have power to make all ordinances which shall be necessary and proper for carrying into execution the powers specified in this act." The city there, by resolution, granted to the railroad company the use of certain streets and alleys in which to lay its tracks, and, in accordance with that resolution, executed a deed to the company. It was contended by the city that the grant was void, because the city was only authorized to legislate in reference to its streets and alleys by ordinance. In reference thereto, this court said: "The action of the city council, though in the form of a resolution, we regard, with the conveyance made by the city, as a sufficient grant of possession by the city to the defendant for the purpose of constructing, maintaining, and operating its railroad tracks." While it is true that this court treated the deed as aiding the resolution, still the deed could only have been authorized by the resolution, so that, in the end, the legality of the grant depended upon the resolution itself, and upon acts done and permitted by the city which were in pursuance of the resolution.

It is argued in the case at bar that this court should not hold that such a grant can be evidenced by resolution, and made binding by acts done and permitted thereunder, because then the veto power cannot be exercised. The same objection existed to the action of the city council in the Quincy Case. There was nothing upon which a veto could operate in that instance. There the corporate authorities had recognized the validity of the permission obtained by the railroad company by the execution of a deed, and by permitting the railroad company to use the streets for many years. Here the president and board of trustees recognized the existence of the written consent held by the appellees by permitting them to erect their poles and string their wires in the streets in accordance with the terms of that written consent, and thereafter treated that consent so granted as having validity by the passage of an ordinance repealing or revoking it; and while but little credit, perhaps, is given to this resolution by an ordinance which mentions it but to repeal it, still it is evident that the village board regarded it as having force, or the course which that body would have pursued would have been to order the removal of the poles and wires, without attempting by ordinance to revoke the permission which had theretofore been granted to appellees.

It has been said that acts of the city which have for their object the carrying into effect of the charter powers granted to the city are legislative in their character, and it is well settled that acts of municipal corporations which are legislative in their character must be put in the form of an ordinance, and not of a mere resolution. Chicago & Northern

Pacific Railroad Co. v. City of Chicago, 174 Ill. 439, 51 N. E. 596; Village of Altamont v. Baltimore & Ohio Southwestern Railway Co., 184 Ill. 47, 56 N. E. 340.

There is, however, another line of cases, which we regard as controlling here, which hold that where, with the consent and without the objection of the city or village authorities, a structure is erected or an improvement made in a street under a permit granted by the authorities of the municipality, and where the structure or improvement is one for the erection or construction of which the city or village might lawfully grant permission, the doctrine of equitable estoppel applies and may be enforced against the municipal corporation, and it will not be permitted to show that the permission under which the work in question has been carried forward to completion was not granted with proper formalities in the first instance. City of Chicago v. Carpenter, 201 Ill. 402, 66 N. E. 362; People v. Blocki, 203 Ill. 363, 67 N. E. 809; Village of Winnetka v. Chicago & Milwaukee Electric Railway Co., 204 Ill. 297, 68 N. E. 407.

Appellants contend that the act of which section 4, supra, is a part, applies only to corporations. In so far as that act confers the power of eminent domain, this is true; but, in so far as it prescribes the method for obtaining the consent of corporate authorities to the erection of poles and the stringing of wires, it must be held applicable both to corporations and natural persons. Following the reasoning of this court in Chicago Dock Co. v. Garrity, 115 Ill. 155, 3 N. E. 448, "the clause should be read as including both incorporations and individuals."

We therefore hold that where a village board has, by resolution, granted to the owner of a telephone line the use of its streets and alleys, in which to set poles and to string wires for telephone uses, and where the licensee, with the knowledge and tacit consent of the village authorities, has accepted and acted upon such resolution by erecting poles and stringing wires in the streets and alleys, the license so granted thereby becomes a contract which is valid and binding upon the parties thereto, and which cannot be revoked by the village. Equity and good conscience require that the village of London Mills be not now heard to say that this written consent must in the first instance have been given by ordinance. It is now equitably estopped so to do.

There is said to be a misjoinder of defendants, for the reason that the relief which is sought is an injunction to prevent the removal of appellees' poles and wires, and that such removal is threatened only by the village authorities, wherefore the London Power & Electric Company is improperly joined, as the relief sought is not against it; and it is also urged that the bill is multifarious, in that the substance of the charge against the London Power & Electric Company is that it is seeking to avail itself of certain ordinances passed by the village of London Mills, and is conspiring with the village authorities to destroy the business of appellees, with the purpose of driving appellees out of the telephone business in the village of London Mills; and it is argued that, if these averments state a cause of action, it is one entirely separate and distinct from that stated against the village. The village, by its ordinance of August 22, 1901, attempts to divide its corporate powers, and to confer a part thereof upon the London Power & Electric Company, and also attempts to exempt the rights and privileges theretofore granted to that company from the operation of that ordinance, as appears from an inspection of sections 2 and 3 of that ordinance, which are in words and figures following:

"Sec. 2. All telephones, telephone poles, telephone lines, telephone centrals, and the fixtures belonging to the same, that were established, located and used in said village on the 25th day of March, 1901, and the companies, persons or corporations owning, using and controlling the same on the date last aforesaid, shall be permitted to remain in the same places and as they were located on the said 25th day of March, 1901, and the persons, companies or corporations owning or controlling the same on said date shall have the right to continue to so use and maintain the same until the 25th day of September, 1901: provided, however, that no change in location, no alterations in use and no extensions or additions to any of said telephones, telephone poles, telephone lines, telephone centrals, and the fixtures belonging to the same, shall be made during the time aforesaid, except by the mutual consent by the said village board, said London Power and Electric Company and all other parties and companies interested.

"Sec. 3. This ordinance shall be known as Special Ordinance No. 54, and shall be in effect from and after its passage and approval, and nothing herein contained shall be construed as affecting any of the rights and privileges heretofore granted to the London Power and Electric Company."

The bill charges that the London Power & Electric Company and the village are conspiring together to drive appellees out of the telephone business in the said village, for the purpose of securing to that company exclusive control of the telephone business in said village, and that, in furtherance of said conspiracy, the village authorities are threatening to remove the wires and poles of appellees. In view of these charges, and of the fact that it plainly appears from the averments of the bill that the board of trustees and the London Power & Electric Company joined in a combination, corrupt in its character, for the purpose of securing a monopoly of the telephone business in London Mills for that company, these objections based upon the grounds of misjoinder and multifariousness are not well taken.

The action of the court in permitting an amendment to the sworn bill in the absence of an affidavit showing a valid excuse for the failure to incorporate in the original bill the matters introduced by the amendment is assigned as error. The truth of the matters stated by the amendments was shown by an affidavit in support thereof, and is admitted by the demurrer. The amendments were entirely proper in their character. They do not in any wise change the cause of action. They do not contradict in any way the averments of the original bill, and they are not materially inconsistent therewith. If the amendments were obnoxious to either of these three objections last suggested, it would undoubtedly have been the proper practice to require a sworn showing that the statements made in the original bill, which the amendments contradict or alter, were made by excusable mistake, before permitting the amendment. The amendments merely enlarged and amplified the statements of the bill, so far as the charges therein contained were concerned. In addition, the prayer was altered, and words designating certain of the complainants as copartners composing a firm within the complainant copartnership, and words describing one of the complainants as an administrator, were omitted. Under these circumstances, the cases of Gregg v. Brower, 67 Ill. 525, Bauer Grocer Co. v. Zelle, 172 Ill. 407, 50 N. E. 238, and Fowler v. Fowler, 204 Ill. 82, 68 N. E. 414, warrant the conclusion that the court did not err in permitting the amendment to be made.

The judgment of the Appellate Court will be affirmed. Judgment affirmed.

MAGRUDER, J. (specially concurring). I concur in the conclusion reached by this opinion, and in the opinion itself, so far as it holds that, where a village board has by resolution granted to the owner of a telephone line the use of its streets and alleys in which to set poles and to string wires for telephone uses, and has, by ordinance subsequently passed, recognized the existence of the right so granted, such grant, where it has been set apart and acted upon by erecting poles and stringing wires, is valid. That is to say, such resolution, when followed by an ordinance recognizing the existence of the right granted by the resolution, will be upheld; but the resolution itself, if there were no subsequent ordinance recognizing the existence of the right granted by it, would not be a sufficient authority to confer such right.

I think that the granting of the use of the streets for the purposes named in the opinion must be deemed a legislative act, and that any action of a city council or village board, the effect of which is to grant to a corporation the use of the public streets, must be regarded as legislation of the highest character. Such a grant cannot be accomplished by a mere resolution.

In Chicago & Northern Pacific Railroad Co. v. City of Chicago, 174 Ill. 439, 51 N. E. 596, it was held by this court that the act of the city council in establishing the grade of a street is legislative in character, and must be put in the form of an ordinance, and not a mere resolution or order. The views upon this subject, expressed in Chicago & Northern Pacific Railroad Co. v. City of Chicago, supra, including the interpretation therein given to the case of City of Quincy v. Chicago, Burlington & Quincy Railroad Co., 92 Ill. 21, have been approved and adopted in the following cases, to wit: Village of Altamont v. Baltimore & Ohio Southwestern Railway Co., 184 Ill. 47, 56 N. E. 340; Claflin v. City of Chicago, 178 Ill. 551, 53 N. E. 339; Brewster v. City of Peru, 180 Ill. 126, 54 N. E. 233; Shannon v. Village of Hinsdale, 180 Ill. 206, 54 N. E. 181; People v. Mount, 186 Ill. 575, 58 N. E. 360; Craig v. People, 193 Ill. 201, 61 N. E. 1072. If the establishment of a street grade cannot be accomplished by a resolution, but must be effected by an ordinance, surely the granting of the use of a public street to a corporation should be by the high legislative act of an ordinance, and not by a mere resolution. In the case of City of Quincy v. Chicago, Burlington & Quincy Railroad Co., 92 Ill. 21, such a grant by a resolution was upheld simply because of the recognition of the rights of the corporation under the resolution referred to in that case for a period of over 20 years; and the resolution was there held to be binding because of the deed made under it, and the long possession held under such deed. The case is not authority for the position that such grant can be made by a resolution alone.

One of the reasons why it is an unfortunate doctrine to hold that the use of the streets can be granted to a corporation by a mere resolution is the fact that resolutions do not need to be submitted to the mayor for his approval. As was said in People v. Mount, supra (referring to authorities): "The wise and salutary provision of the statute which clothes the mayor with the veto power may be defeated by a city council by the simple election on its part to change the form of its legislative acts into resolutions, instead of embodying them in ordinances, if it be true that municipal legislation can be accomplished by mere resolutions." The mayor cannot exercise his supervisory power over the action of the council if important municipal legislation takes the form of a resolution. The responsibility to the people can be less easily evaded in the case of an individual than in the case of a body of men. Where so important an act is done by the common council as the granting of the use of the public streets to a corporation, the mayor should have the power to veto such an act, if, in his judgment, the granting of the privilege or franchise is unwise and against the interests of the people. This supervisory power of the mayor is apt to be defeated where the result is to be accomplished by a mere resolution, instead of an ordinance.

On Rehearing.

(April 7, 1904.)

Upon consideration of the petition for rehearing by the court, SCOTT, J., speaking for the court, delivered the following additional opinion:

It is now insisted the majority opinion heretofore filed in this cause, in so far as it holds that a natural person may acquire the right to maintain poles and wires for telephone purposes in the streets of a city or village, is in conflict with the case of Goddard v. C. & N. W. Ry. Co., 202 Ill. 362, 66 N. E. 1066. In that case it is held that the right to operate a street railway in this state is one that can be acquired and exercised under existing laws only by a corporation. Sections 11, 12, c. 134, Hurd's Rev. St. 1901, expressly recognize the right of natural persons to engage in the telephone business outside the incorporated limits of cities and villages, and we think that business one in which such persons may engage within cities and villages, subject, of course, to the limitation that they cannot exercise the power of eminent domain. The case at bar is thus distinguished from Goddard v. C. & N. W. Ry. Co., supra.

The petition for rehearing will be denied. Rehearing denied.

(208 Ill. 229)

THOMSON et al. v. BLACK.*

(Supreme Court of Illinois. Feb. 17, 1904.)

DEED OF TRUST—FORECLOSURE—APPORTIONMENT OF COSTS—APPEAL AND ERROR.

1. Where the court, in decreeing foreclosure of a deed of trust, finds the amount due on the notes secured by the trust deed, orders sale of the premises to satisfy the decree, and that the master, after sale, report the deficiency, if any, to the court, and provides that when the deficiency is ascertained it shall be allowed as a seventh-class claim against the estates of the makers of the notes and trust deed, which were in process of settlement in the probate court, an appeal, prior to the sale, attacking the decree in this respect, is premature.

2. Where, in an action to foreclose, the mortgagee recovered, and because of a premature appeal before the sale the question of the liability of the makers of the note and the trust deed could not be reviewed, any alleged error in refusing to apportion the costs cannot be reviewed.

Appeal from Appellate Court, First District.

Action by William P. Black, administrator, against George Thomson, administrator, and others. From a judgment of the Appellate Court affirming a judgment for plaintiff, defendants appeal. Affirmed.

*Rehearing denied April 7, 1904.

Fred H. Atwood, Frank B. Pease, William S. Corbin, and Chas. O. Loucks, for appellants. William R. Plum, for appellee.

HAND, J. This is an appeal from a judgment of the Appellate Court for the First District affirming a decree of the superior court of Cook county for the foreclosure of a trust deed, given upon certain real estate situated in said county, to secure the payment of 12 promissory notes for the sum of $500 each and interest. The decree found there was due the sum of $7,150 upon the notes secured by the trust deed, and ordered the sale of the premises described in said trust deed to satisfy said decree, and that the master, after sale, report the deficiency, if any, to the court, and provided that when the deficiency was ascertained the same should be allowed as a seventh-class claim against the estates of the makers of the notes and trust deed, which were in process of settlement in the probate court of Cook county.

The appellant has suggested no reason for reversing the decree of foreclosure and sale, but the principal question argued in his brief is the invalidity of that part of the decree which provides for the allowance of the deficiency after sale, if any, as a seventh-class claim against the estates of the makers, of the notes and trust deed. That question, however, is not before us for determination, as it is clear the appeal as to that part of the decree is premature. It cannot be determined what the deficiency will be until after a sale, and no sale had been made at the time of the appeal. There may be no deficiency after sale, and, if any, it may be less than $1,000, in which case an appeal will not lie to this court from the judgment of the Appellate Court without a certificate of importance. In Eggleston v. Morrison, 185 Ill. 577, 57 N. E. 775, which was a bill to foreclose a mortgage, where it was sought, before sale, to review the action of the trial court in entering a conditional deficiency decree, on page 579, 185 Ill., and page 776, 57 N. E., it was said: "An appeal will not lie from a finding or conclusion, either of law or fact, not accompanied by any final judgment or decree, and there can be no personal decree until there is a judicial determination of the amount due. That amount can only be ascertained after the sale, and such a decree as this is not final in that respect."

It is also contended that there was error committed by the trial court in refusing to apportion the costs, and in support of such contention it is said the costs were mainly incurred in establishing the liability of the makers of the notes and trust deed for the deficiency should the premises not sell for enough to satisfy the debt, and that the costs thus incurred should have been adjudged against the appellee. The appellee recovered on that issue upon the hearing, and in the state of this record, the question of the liability of the makers of the notes and trust deed not being before us for review, we are unable to say there was error committed in the refusal to apportion costs.

The judgment of the Appellate Court will be affirmed. Judgment affirmed.

(208 Ill. 218)

TELLURIDE POWER TRANSMISSION CO. et al. v. CRANE CO.*

(Supreme Court of Illinois. Feb. 17, 1904.)

SALES—ACTION FOR PURCHASE PRICE—DEFENSE—WARRANTY—RECORD—ESTOPPEL.

1. Where, in an action to recover a balance due on chattels sold, it is stipulated and made a part of the record that defendants purchased the chattels at an agreed price, defendants cannot assert that no joint contract by them is shown by the record.

2. In an action to recover a balance due on chattels sold, the questions as to what writings should be considered, and whether those considered constituted a written contract, or whether the written contract fully expressed the agreement between the parties, were for the court.

3. Where writings show a complete legal obligation, without any uncertainty or ambiguity as to the object and extent of the engagement, it is conclusively presumed that the whole agreement was included in the writings; and the fact that a point has been omitted which might have been embodied therein will not open the door to the admission of parol evidence.

4. Where defendants in an action to recover a balance due for chattels sold did not, in their written proposal to purchase, require a warranty, they are precluded from insisting on a warranty expressed in previous negotiations.

5. In the sale of an existing chattel, there is not, in the absence of fraud, any implied warranty of good quality or condition of the chattel.

6. Where the buyer of personal property saw the property before taking possession, and had opportunity to inspect it, and no concealment was used on the part of the sellers, or representations made by them respecting the quality, to induce the buyer not to examine it, buying without examination was at the risk of the buyer.

Appeal from Appellate Court, First District.

Action by the Crane Company against the Telluride Power Transmission Company and another. From a judgment of the Appellate Court (103 Ill. App. 647) affirming a judgment for plaintiff, defendants appeal. Affirmed.

This is an appeal from an affirmance by the Appellate Court of the judgment of the circuit court of Cook county in a suit by appellee to recover the balance due on a contract of sale of a quantity of iron pipe by appellee to appellants. August 13, 1896, the Telluride Power Transmission Company contracted with one T. B. Rhodes for the erection of a flume and pipe line. In furtherance of his contract, Rhodes gave appellee an order for pipe, specifying the kind of pipe required. The pipe was shipped to Ophir, Colo., as ordered, and there remained on the cars, owing to the fact that Rhodes became financially embarrassed, and unable to pay the freight and take the pipe from the cars. Being advised that Rhodes was unable to take up the Crane Company's draft and complete his contract with the Telluride Company, Mr. L. L. Nunn, the general manager of the Telluride Company, and one of the appellants here, went to Chicago and there had a conference with the representatives of the Crane Company relative to the completion of Rhodes' contract by appellants themselves, and concerning the quality of the pipe then on the cars at Ophir, which had been shipped to Rhodes by appellee. Afterward Nunn, being then in New York, wrote the Crane Company the following letter:

"The Telluride Power Transmission Co., Holland House, N. Y., Dec. 18, 1896. Crane Co., 10 North Jefferson St., Chicago, Ill.—Gentlemen: I am advised from Telluride, Colorado, that Mr. T. B. Rhodes is unable to take up your draft against bill of lading for about $2,000 on account of material ordered by him to complete a contract with the Telluride Power Transmission Company. We have advanced Mr. Rhodes a good deal beyond the payments provided for by our contract with him, and it is not entirely convenient for me to pay your draft while absent from Telluride. I shall return next month. If you will order the material delivered to us by the railway company and it passes the inspection of our engineer, we will receive it at once and pay your draft on February 1, and also greatly appreciate your courtesy in the matter. On account of the well-known strength of our company I have no hesitation in asking the credit. Mr. James Campbell, of St. Louis, is the president, and Mr. H. R. Newcomb, treasurer of the Savings and Trust Company of Cleveland, Ohio, is the treasurer of our company. Please telegraph me, care Holland House, New York, your decision. Yours truly, Lucien L. Nunn."

To this letter the Crane Company replied by wire under date of December 22d:

"Letter received; on receipt of your company's note due February 1 for nineteen hundred seventy-six dollars nine cents will order material delivered; write to-day. Crane Co."

It also wrote the following letter; stating, among other things:

"This amount does not correspond with the amount of our draft, which was $1,945.06. We had, however, deducted $31.03 for cash discount, on the understanding that draft was to be paid promptly. Of course, under the proposed arrangement this allowance will not be made. Your proposition is to pay us on February 1, provided the material, when delivered, passes the inspection of your engineer. We cannot consent to any condition of this character, because it is too general in its terms. We do not know what your arrangement was with Mr. Rhodes nor what kind of inspection would be required. We simply know the material we have furnished

*Rehearing denied April 7, 1904.

¶ 5. See Sales, vol. 43, Cent. Dig. § 754.

is strictly in accordance with Mr. Rhodes' order to us, and we shall not be willing to deliver it except on absolute payment or promise of payment. You will no doubt appreciate the correctness of our position on this point. Yours truly, Crane Co., O. P. Dickinson."

As this letter refused inspection, the telegram and letter were given no immediate attention by Mr. Nunn. On December 30, 1896, the Crane Company again wired, as follows:

"12/30/'96. L. L. Nunn—Please reply to our letter of twenty-second. Crane Co."

To this telegram Mr. Nunn replied by the following letter:

"Holland House, New York, Dec. 30, 1896. Crane Co., 10 North Jefferson St., Chicago, Ill.—Gentlemen: I greatly regret the delay in adjusting the matter of the pipe shipped to Mr. T. B. Rhodes at Telluride, Colo. I have but just returned from my Christmas vacation.

"My letter to you must have been very ambiguous, for you have entirely misunderstood my proposition. It was not to receive the pipe and then pay for it if satisfactory, but to ascertain by inspection whether it was such as we required, and if it was, to receive it immediately and pay for it on the first of February next. I am confident Mr. Rhodes is financially unable to comply with his contract with either you or us. Of course, as we did not order the pipe you do not expect us to take it and pay for it unless it is such as we can use, but if it is such as we require we are anxious to have it immediately, and, of course, will pay your price. I do not like to give a promissory note. Our company has never executed a note in its entire history. A note would add nothing to your security. If we take the material we are bound to pay for it.

"Please do me the courtesy of delivering this shipment to us without further delay, and I will telegraph my engineer to inspect it at once and receive it on the cars if he thinks the strength sufficient. Being away from home, I should like very much to have this favor. Kindly wire me on receipt of this.

"Very truly yours, L. L. Nunn."

To this letter the Crane Company telegraphed:

"Secretary Murphy will call and see you Wednesday night or Thursday morning."

Mr. Murphy called, but nothing was done in New York, and on January 22, 1897, appellee wired the Telluride Company as follows:

"Railroad wires pipes still uncalled for and must be disposed of without delay. Nunn, when here, agreed to accept pipe, and we supposed it taken before this. Why delay? Answer. Crane Co."

This was replied to on January 23d as follows:

"To Crane Co., Chicago, Ill.: Delay account complications with contractor, but practically settled. Propose accepting soon. Telluride Power Transmission Co."

On February 5, 1897, Nunn wrote the Crane Company this letter:

"Denver, Colo., Feb. 5, 1897. Crane Co., 10 North Jefferson St., Chicago, Ill.—Gentlemen: I was delayed in my return West by the very serious illness of my brother, and but just arrived here this morning. My engineer from Telluride met me, and explained the situation respecting the shipment of pipe to Mr. Rhodes at Ophir. The whole matter is certainly very badly mixed. Mr. Rhodes cannot be found. He has abandoned the matter, and the demurrage on the four cars since November 16, 17 and 18 amounts to something over $400. My firm has represented the railroad, as attorneys, ever since its construction. I called to-day and used all the influence I could to have the demurrage charge deducted, and succeeded to the extent of having it reduced to $100, which I believe is less than the actual expense incurred by the railroad company in pulling the cars backwards and forwards over the single switch at that place. My engineer informs me that we can use about one-half the pipe at the present time and the other half in the construction of a duplicate line which we purpose to put in during May and June. In the meantime we must order new pipe from you to complete both lines. The freight charges on these four cars amount to $1,174. If we pay this amount and the demurrage charges, making nearly $1,300, and place with you another order for pipe to complete two lines, we do not feel that we should pay for the half of the pipe which will not be used for some months, until we use it—or, to fix the date definitely, until June first—and, of course, we cannot afford to pay without charging to your account the demurrage.

"We regret very much that you have suffered any inconvenience and we are anxious to render you any assistance in our power, but, of course, we are not responsible for Mr. Rhodes' contracts, and it would seem from the condition he is in that he is entirely unable to make any use whatever of the pipe, and that you would therefore have it on your hands, with freight charges one way amounting to more than half the price of the pipe, and including return charges amounting to more than the entire price of the pipe. If you will instruct us by wire Monday morning to do so, we will settle with the railroad and stop further expense and will take the pipe at the original bill, paying one-half within a few days and the other half about June 1, charging you the amount paid for demurrage.

"I shall only be in Telluride a few hours on Monday, leaving there in the afternoon for our works in Utah and Montana. Kindly attend to this matter without delay, and wire me so that I can close it up while in Telluride. I might add, that owing to the long delay it is now immaterial to us whether we make use of the pipe at all before summer.

"Very sincerely yours, L. L. Nunn."

To this appellee immediately replied by wire:

"L. L. Nunn, Agent T. P. T. Co., Telluride, Colo.: We accept proposition contained in your letter fifth. Crane Co."

Appellee wrote the same day this letter:

"Chicago, Feb. 8, 1897. L. L. Nunn, Manager Telluride Power Trans. Co., Telluride, Colo.—Dear Sir: We received this morning your favor of the 5th, and as requested immediately wired you in reply, 'We accept proposition contained in your letter 5th.' This proposition is that you will take the pipe which we sold to T. B. Rhodes & Co., paying the freight and demurrage charges, and that you will then pay us the amount of our original bill less $100 demurrage, making payments one-half within a few days and the other half about June 1. The amount of the original bill referred to was $2,048.77. From this is to be deducted a freight allowance of $72.68, leaving the net amount $1,976.09, as stated in our letter of December 22, addressed to you in New York.

"We had rather expected to receive payment of the full amount now, but are willing to make the concession of time in view of all the circumstances, and especially because you promise to give us orders for additional pipe. We shall bo glad to receive such orders, and think that by dealing directly with you we shall avoid any misunderstandings.

"Yours truly, Crane Co., O. P. Dickinson."

Appellants then received and used the pipe in controversy.

Upon the trial the following stipulation was filed: "A question has arisen as to whether plaintiff or the defendants are entitled to open and close the argument in the above-entitled cause, and, for the purpose of disposing of the question, it is agreed between the parties hereto that theretofore the defendants purchased from the plaintiff a lot of pipe then on the cars at the town of Ophir, Colo., at the agreed price of $1,876.09; that $1,000 was paid on account of said purchase on June 29, 1897; and that no other payments have been made; and it is further agreed that defendants received said pipe, and that this agreement shall be read in evidence when the jury is sworn to try the issues in this case, or to the court if the jury should be waived, and that thereupon the defendants shall be permitted to offer their evidence, and that counsel for defendants shall have the opening and closing arguments." After receiving the pipe, appellants made a payment of $1,000, and appellee brought suit to recover the unpaid balance of $876.09.

Appellants filed separate pleas of the general issue and set-off, alleging that they were engaged in the business of generating electricity by water power, obtained by means of water conveyed by pipe lines, and that appellee sold them pipe to be used for that purpose, which pipe appellee guarantied was of a certain strength, quality, and thickness, of the very best material in the market, suitable for the purpose for which it was to be employed, of sufficient strength and quality to carry water as aforesaid, and to withstand the pressure consequent upon the transmission of such water; that the pipe was delivered and partly paid for, and appellants placed it in position for the transmission of such water, but that the pipe was not made in accordance with the specifications and requirements in the order for the same, nor was the pipe of the strength, thickness, and quality guarantied by appellee, nor was it of sufficient strength to carry such water; and that by reason of the poor quality of the pipe, and the poor, unskilled, and insufficient character of the workmanship on it, it burst repeatedly, and caused valuable lands and property of appellants to be overflowed, and, after being repaired, burst repeatedly, so that it could not be used for the transmission of such water, whereby the appellants were damaged to the extent of $50,000.

On the trial, appellants offered evidence to show that Rhodes, before giving his order, showed to Mr. Lee, the agent of appellee, his contract with the Telluride Company, and the profile showing the requirements and water pressure of the contemplated line; that Lee understood that the pipe was to have a safety factor of 5, and a tensile strength of 60,000 pounds to the square inch, and that said material of that quality would be furnished. They further offered to show that after the failure of Rhodes to complete his contract, when Mr. Nunn called upon the Crane Company in reference to the delivery to appellants of the pipe on the cars at Ophir, Colo., and mentioned the requirements of the pipe, he was assured by the representatives of appellee that the quality of the pipe was the very best. Appellants also offered to show that the pipe was installed and burst repeatedly under the water pressure, causing great damage; that the pipe was apparently burnt in welding, and had not the requisite tensile strength, nor a safety factor of 5. This evidence was admitted over the objection of appellee, and afterward stricken out by the court, and the jury were instructed to return a verdict in favor of appellee for $876.09; the court holding that the contract was in writing, and embraced in the letters and telegrams hereinbefore set forth. On appeal the Appellate Court sustained the trial court; holding that the letter of appellants of February 5, 1897, together with appellee's reply thereto by telegram and letter of February 8, 1897, constitute a written contract between appellants and appellee, in which all previous negotiations were merged. To reverse that judgment, appellants now prosecute this further appeal, contending that no contract is shown to have been entered into by both appellants; that the letters of February 5th and 8th, and the telegram of the 8th, do not constitute the agreement between the parties, but that it is to be found in all the negotiations, oral and written, which passed between the parties, and that, even if the letters of the 5th and 8th, and the telegram of the 8th do constitute the entire contract, the circumstances shown in evidence sustain the contention of an implied warranty of the fitness of the pipe sold for the purpose to which it was to be put.

Kraus, Alschuler & Holden, for appellants. James H. Barnard (E. M. Ashcraft and E. M. Ashcraft, Jr., of counsel), for appellee.

WILKIN, J. (after stating the facts). The action in this case is not brought upon the contract between the Crane Company and Rhodes to furnish pipe to the latter for the pipe line he had contracted to erect for the Telluride Company, but the suit is against the latter company and L. L. Nunn, the general manager of that company (appellants here), jointly, upon a contract for the sale of certain pipe at the time on cars at Ophir, Colo., which had been shipped by appellee to Rhodes on his contract, which he, by reason of his insolvency, was unable to perform; the pipe being thereby left upon the hands of appellee. Appellants contend that no joint contract by them is shown by the record. We do not think the position can be maintained. No plea in abatement or in bar was filed, and no proof offered on the point, but, by the stipulation of parties which was filed on the trial, the joint liability is admitted; and further discussion on the question is thereby rendered unnecessary.

It is again urged that the Appellate Court erred in holding that the letters of February 5th and 8th, and the telegram of February 8th, set forth in the foregoing statement, constitute the entire contract between the parties; it being insisted that the entire agreement is to be found in all the negotiations, oral and written, had between the parties, and that appellants had the right to show an express warranty of the pipe to them. The questions as to what writings should be considered, and whether or not those considered constituted a written contract, and whether or not the written contract fully expressed the agreement between the parties, were for the court. The rule is that when the writings show, upon inspection, a complete legal obligation, without any uncertainty or ambiguity as to the object and extent of the engagement, it is conclusively presumed that the whole agreement of the parties was included in the writings. The fact that a point has been omitted which might have been embodied therein will not open the door to the admission of parol evidence in that regard. Seitz v. Brewers' Refrigerating Co., 141 U. S. 510, 12 Sup. Ct. 46, 35 L. Ed. 837. In the case at bar the pipe in question was on the cars at Ophir, where it had been consigned to Rhodes. Rhodes was unable to take and pay for it, and appellants began negotiating for its purchase with a view of completing the pipe line themselves, which Rhodes had abandoned. Mr. Nunn had interviews with the representatives of the appellee, and exchanged letters and telegrams in relation to the proposed purchase by appellants, which finally culminated in Nunn's written offer, contained in his letter to appellee dated February 5, 1897. Appellee's telegram and letter of the 8th of February, accepting the offer, closed the deal. The rule is too well recognized to require citation of authorities that all preliminary negotiations, whether oral or written, are merged in the written contract. The offer by appellants to buy the pipe, which appears in Nunn's letter of February 5th, and the stipulation of terms therein upon which the purchase would be made, considered together with appellee's letter and telegram of the 8th accepting appellants' offer, constitute a contract in writing which is clear and unambiguous, both as to its object and extent. Considering these documents alone, without any reference to previous negotiations, they leave nothing to be explained. They contain all the elements of a complete written contract. If appellants had desired any further conditions, it was their duty to have so stipulated. The fact that, in their written proposal to purchase, they require no warranty of the pipe, precluded them from insisting upon it on the trial.

It is further urged that, conceding that the letters and telegram of February 5th and 8th constitute the entire contract between the parties, yet there is an implied warranty that the pipe was fit and suitable for the purpose for which it was intended to be used. The rule is that, if an article is to be made or supplied to the order of a purchaser, there is an implied warranty of the fitness of the article for the special purpose designed by the buyer, if that purpose be known to the vendor; but in the bargain and sale of an existing chattel there is not, in the absence of fraud, an implied warranty of good quality or condition of the thing sold. Benjamin on Sales, § 647; Mechem on Sales, §§ 1312-1316; Kohl v. Lindley, 39 Ill. 195, 89 Am. Dec. 294; Misner v. Granger, 4 Gilman, 69; Carondelet Ironworks v. Moore, 78 Ill. 65. In the case at bar the chattels in controversy were in existence, on the cars near appellants' works, where appellants passed them frequently during the several months they lay there. That the appellants knew and recognized that they could determine by inspection whether or not the pipe would suit them is evidenced by the fact that, in the preliminary negotiations for the purchase, Mr. Nunn stated that, if the pipe should suit their purpose, they would take it and pay for it. Where the purchaser of personal property sees the property before taking possession, and has every opportunity to inspect the same, and no concealment is used on the part of the seller, or representations made by him respecting the quality to induce the purchaser not to examine the same, the purchaser cannot recover on the ground of fraud and deceit. Carondelet Ironworks v. Moore, supra. In the case at bar, we do not think the evidence as to representations by appellee of the quality of the pipe, even if admitted, would make such a case of deceit or false statements, knowingly made, as would warrant a finding in favor of appellants, where it is shown that they had as good opportunity of testing and inspection as had appellee. There is no evidence whatever tending to prove that statements were made to appellants for the purpose of inducing them to waive the inspection which they first insisted on. The Crane Company simply wrote that it would not consent to make the sale dependent upon inspection by appellants' engineer. Here was an existing chattel, which, in the absence of an express warranty, appellants must be held to have purchased upon their own inspection, or, if they failed to do so, at their own risk.

The judgment of the Appellate Court is right, and will be affirmed. Judgment affirmed.

(208 Ill. 401)

LURIE et al. v SABATH et al.*

(Supreme Court of Illinois. Feb. 17, 1904.)

TRUSTS—ESTABLISHMENT—EVIDENCE—SUFFICIENCY—EQUITY—APPEAL.

1. On a bill by an insolvent to establish a trust for his benefit as against purchasers of his stock of goods and of judgments against him, evidence examined, and *held* insufficient to establish the trust.

2. In order to establish a trust, the evidence must be clear and satisfactory, not only as to its existence, but as to its terms and conditions.

3. Where the testimony was taken in open court by the chancellor, his findings will not be disturbed, unless against the clear weight of the evidence.

Appeal from Appellate Court, First District.

Bill by Josef Lurie and another against Adolph J. Sabath and others. A decree for defendants was affirmed by the Appellate Court (108 Ill. App. 397), and plaintiffs appeal. Affirmed.

Kraus, Alschuler & Holden, for appellants. John F. Holland, for appellees.

WILKIN, J. Appellants filed their bill in the circuit court of Cook county against appellees to establish a trust and for an accounting. Upon a hearing in open court before the chancellor, the bill was dismissed for want of equity. An appeal was prayed to the Appellate Court for the First District, where that order was affirmed, and this further appeal is now prosecuted.

*Rehearing denied April 7, 1904.

There is but one question raised for our determination, and that is whether the allegations of the bill alleging the trust were sustained by the evidence.

In 1892 the appellant Josef Lurie was appointed by the probate court of Cook county executor of the estate of Adolph Lurie, and at the same time was appointed guardian of Bertha, Albert, and Gottlieb, the three minor children of the latter. Prior to his death, Adolph and Josef Lurie had been engaged in the mercantile business in Chicago, conducting three stores. After the death of Adolph, and after the appointment of Josef as executor and guardian, as above stated, the business was continued by the latter until he sold an interest in the same to his son Max Lurie, and thereafter the stores were conducted by the father and son as partners; the latter, however, having but a small amount of money invested therein. The firm met with financial reverses, and finally failed, becoming insolvent. On November 23, 1898, the appellant Josef Lurie filed in the probate court of Cook county his report as guardian of the above-named minors, showing an indebtedness by him to them of $24,107.36, and at the same time asked that he be relieved as such guardian, and his successor appointed. His petition also set forth that he had no property except his interest in the three stocks of goods, two promissory notes amounting to $6,500, and two city lots, the value of which does not appear, incumbered for $600. The prayer of his petition was that he be permitted to turn said property over to his successor, and that he be credited by the court with the value thereof. The probate court accepted his resignation, and appointed Joseph Sabath, one of the appellees, as his successor, and ordered the property turned over to the latter, which he was ordered to hold until the further order of the court. The same order recited that the value of said property should be left for future determination by the court. Josef Lurie turned over all of said property except the three stocks of goods, which he was unable to deliver to his successor for the following reasons: Among the creditors of appellants and Adolph Lurie was the firm of John V. Farwell & Co., and on November 21, 1898, they sued out a writ of attachment, and the same had been levied upon said stocks of goods by the sheriff of Cook county on a claim of $22,000 due said firm. Immediately after that attachment had been levied upon the goods, and possession taken by the sheriff, negotiations were entered into, in which it was attempted to arrive at an agreement whereby the business could be continued, but, on account of fear of involuntary bankruptcy proceedings, no definite conclusion was reached; but on December 10, 1898, it was stipulated by all parties concerned that the stores should be opened by the sheriff for the retail Christmas trade, and, as a result of that agreement, $8,000 was realized from said stocks of merchandise. In order that the minors should be allowed to receive their pro rata share of whatever was realized from such sale, with the other creditors, the said Josef Lurie made and delivered to Joseph Sabath, as guardian, his promissory note for the sum of $24,107.36, dated back to November 23, 1898, due one day after date; being the amount which he owed the minors, as shown by his report of the date of said note. On December 1, 1898, suit was begun by Sabath on that note, and at the same time five other suits were commenced against the appellants. Judgments were rendered against them in the six suits for $48,531.79. On November 9, 1898, one A. J. Sabath, who was one of the bondsmen of Josef Lurie as guardian, and a man by the name of Alexander, bought the judgment of Farwell & Co., amounting to $22,000, paying therefor $10,500, and subsequently also purchased the judgments of certain other creditors. On December 28, 1898, the sheriff of Cook county sold at public auction the remainder of said stocks of goods, and the same were purchased by the same parties (that is, A. J. Sabath and Alexander) for $14,000, and the goods were turned over to them by said sheriff, and they thereafter retailed them in their own right, as owners. On December 29, 1898, after the merchandise had been sold and delivered to said parties by the sheriff, the superior court of Cook county entered an order distributing the net proceeds of the sale among the judgment creditors of appellants, upon which distribution A. J. Sabath, as assignee of Farwell & Co. and other creditors, received the sum of $4,537.22. It was then contended by appellants that the purchase of the judgments by A. J. Sabath and Alexander, and the purchase of the merchandise by them, were in trust for the benefit of appellants and said minors; and accordingly this bill was filed in the circuit court of Cook county, alleging that an oral agreement was entered into on November 23, 1898, by Josef Lurie and Max Lurie, of the one part, and Joseph Sabath, as guardian of the three minors, and A. J. Sabath and Alexander, of the other part, by which the appellants transferred their interest in the goods to the said A. J. Sabath and Alexander, who, in consideration thereof, agreed to buy up all the outstanding claims with their own money, and sell the goods, and, after reimbursing themselves, to turn over the balance to pay the indebtedness of Josef Lurie, and to account to the said appellants for any sum remaining. The allegations of the bill were specifically denied by appellees, thus forming the issue presented to us for decision.

The law is that, in order to establish the trust, the evidence offered by complainants below must have been clear and satisfactory, not only as to the existence of the trust, but also as to its terms and conditions. Furber v. Page, 143 Ill. 622, 32 N. E. 444; Francis v. Roades, 146 Ill. 635, 35 N. E. 232; Towle v. Wadsworth, 147 Ill. 80, 30 N. E. 602, 35 N. E. 73. The bill alleges that the trust was created on November 23, 1898, and an instrument in writing is set up in the bill, purporting to contain all of its terms and conditions; but, under the undisputed facts of the case, it is clear that no trust was or could have been created at that time, and, if it was created at all, it must have been not earlier than December 8th of that year; and the condition of the property on the latter date was such that we are unable to understand how the parties could have anticipated the subsequent events which occurred, and entered into the alleged agreement. On that date (December 8th) the property was in the hands of the sheriff under attachment, and negotiations were then pending between the parties and Farwell & Co. for a settlement. At that time the judgment against Lurie had not been purchased by A. J. Sabath and Alexander, nor had any of the goods been sold by the sheriff. The negotiations between the parties resulted in no agreement whatever, and the property was subsequently sold, as above stated. It is clear from the evidence that the writing set up in the bill was not prepared on December 8th, but was drawn up some 30 or 40 days after that date from a memorandum kept by one of the attorneys, and was never signed by A. J. Sabath and Alexander, or either of them, and, if presented to them for their signatures, they refused to sign it; nor was it signed by Joseph Sabath, the guardian. Manifestly, he could only have executed such an agreement under the authority of the probate court, and no such authority was given him. The contention that the order of that court on November 23, 1898, directing him, as guardian for the minor children, successor to Josef Lurie, to take possession of the property, which exceeded in value the liability of Lurie to the minors, authorized and made it his duty to enter into the alleged agreement, is wholly untenable. That order authorized the successor of Josef Lurie to take charge of all the property then in the possession of Josef Lurie, but this property was not then in his possession, and was subsequently sold without its having been returned to him. If the contention of appellants is true, the probate court by its order attempted to authorize the guardian to accept, in full payment of all claims due his wards, goods which were then in the possession of the sheriff of Cook county under writs of attachment aggregating in amount much more than was realized from their sale.

Appellants also insist that the sheriff's sale is evidence of the existence of the alleged trust, for the reason that the goods were sold for a sum far less than their actual value; and they say that, by reason of the trust agreement, competition was stifled, and they (the appellants) did not attempt to protect said goods from being sacrificed. The evidence, however, shows that the goods were variously estimated in value at from $30,000 to $40,000, and that at the sheriff's sale they brought $22,834. The sale was made in the usual manner of conducting sheriff's sales of that kind—that is, the goods were sold at auction to the highest bidder, different persons bidding on them; and it is not true, as we understand the evidence, that they were sold at a sacrifice or for an inadequate price at such forced sale, nor does it satisfactorily appear that the appellants had the ability or could have made them sell for a higher price. The action of A. J. Sabath and Alexander in buying them was consistent with their interests. They sustained no legal, substantial, or trust relations to the minors. A. J. Sabath was one of the bondsmen of Josef Lurie as guardian, who had become insolvent, and his bondsmen liable for his misappropriation of the minors' money. The action of A. J. Sabath in buying the goods was doubtless with a purpose to save himself from as much loss as he could upon that bond. All that he did was perfectly consistent with that purpose, and affords no evidence whatever of an existing trust, as alleged in the bill.

The evidence also strongly tends to show that this alleged trust was an afterthought on the part of Josef Lurie, who had improperly used the money of his wards in his own business, and thereby lost it. He was hopelessly insolvent, and his bondsmen were liable for the balance due his wards. On April 26, 1900, and on June 15th of that year, notwithstanding his former report of November 23, 1898, he filed petitions in the probate court in which he claimed that the deficiency in his account as guardian was caused by the natural loss and decline of the mercantile business, and not through any wrongful act or fraud on his part; and in those petitions he also claimed that the property turned over to his successor largely exceeded in value the amount of his liabilities to his wards, and asked the court to determine the amount of credit he was entitled to, and to discharge him and cancel his bond. In neither of these petitions did he say anything about a trust having been created between the parties to this suit, although, according to his bill, the trust agreement had been entered into on November 23, 1898.

We think the testimony in this record clearly preponderates in favor of the appellees. But even if it could be held otherwise, the witnesses appeared and gave their testimony in open court, in the hearing and presence of the chancellor; and the rule in such case, as often announced by this court, is that his finding will not be disturbed unless it can be said that it is against the clear weight of the evidence.

We are satisfied that the decree of the circuit court was in conformity with the law and the facts of the case, and that it was properly affirmed by the Appellate Court. Judgment affirmed.

(208 Ill. 192)

VOCKE v. CITY OF CHICAGO.*

(Supreme Court of Illinois. Feb. 17, 1904.)

HIGHWAYS — INJURY — TRIAL — STATEMENT OF LAW OF COUNSEL—INSTRUCTIONS.

1. While counsel may state to the jury what they believe the law to be, and base arguments thereon, it is the jury's duty to decide the case according to the law as given by the court.

2. Where the record does not show the statements of counsel to the jury as to the law, it will be presumed that they warranted an instruction that the jury should consider only the law as given by the court, and not as stated by the counsel.

3. An instruction that a person who uses a public street, and is familiar with it, must use reasonable care in proportion to any danger known to him, and that, therefore, if one injured saw, or by reasonable care could have seen, the danger, then he was bound to exercise ordinary care in view of all the circumstances, was erroneous, being confusing and misleading.

4. Where undisputed evidence showed that one driving along a street was thrown from his buggy and dragged some distance, and a wheel passed over him, and evidence conflicted as to whether ruptures which he had were caused by the accident, an instruction that, if the injuries were not caused by the accident, there could be no recovery, was erroneous, as barring a recovery for the injuries which were undisputed.

Magruder, J., dissenting.

Error to Appellate Court, First District.

Action by Herman Vocke against the city of Chicago. From a judgment of the Appellate Court affirming a judgment of the superior court in favor of defendant, plaintiff brings error. Reversed.

James C. McShane, for plaintiff in error.
John F. Smulski, City Atty. (Wm. J. Stapleton, of counsel), for defendant in error.

CARTWRIGHT, J. Herman Vocke, plaintiff in error, brought suit in the superior court of Cook county against the city of Chicago, defendant in error, for personal injuries received by him while driving along Ashland avenue in said city. The declaration charged the defendant with negligence in permitting a large hole to be and remain in said avenue, and alleged that in consequence thereof plaintiff was thrown from his vehicle to the ground, and dragged a considerable distance, and that one of the wheels passed over his body, causing serious and permanent external and internal injuries. There was a plea of the general issue, and on a trial the jury returned a verdict of not guilty. The court entered judgment on the verdict, and a writ of error was sued out from the Appellate Court for the First District, where, upon a review of the record, the judgment was affirmed, and a certificate of importance was granted.

The facts proved at the trial were as follows: Plaintiff was engaged in delivering newspapers twice a day with a horse and newspaper cart. He had finished delivering

*Rehearing denied April 7, 1904.

his evening papers on April 12, 1900, and was driving north, at about 7:30 p. m., on Ashland avenue, to Forty-Eighth street. In front of No. 5025 Ashland avenue there was a hole in the pavement about six feet wide east and west and two feet north and south. The street was paved with wooden blocks, and the place had been in bad condition for several months at least. The edges of the blocks around the hole would be worn until new blocks came out and others in turn became worn and loosened. There were street car tracks in the street, and the hole was about four feet east of them. It was dark, and plaintiff was driving on a trot, with the west wheel of his cart on the east car track, when the east wheel dropped into the hole, and he was thrown out. He held to the reins, and was dragged a considerable distance, and one of the wheels passed over him. The next day he was about his business, but had a boy to deliver the papers while he drove the horse. He had an old rupture, which had existed for seven or eight years, but there were two new ruptures, caused, as he claimed, by the accident. The testimony of the two doctors produced at the trial differed as to the cause of such new ruptures; the doctor for plaintiff testifying that they might have been caused by the accident and external injury, while the doctor for the defendant testified that they could not have been caused from pressure without, but resulted from pressure within. The evidence as to the hole in question varied but little, most of the witnesses saying it was about six inches deep—the depth of the blocks which had come out. Plaintiff testified that it was a foot deep.

The errors assigned consist in the giving of instructions at the request of defendant. One of the instructions so given was as follows: "The court instructs the jury that in considering this case it is not only your duty to decide the case according to the weight of the evidence, but it is also your duty to decide it according to the law as given you by the court, applied to the evidence. While it is true, as a matter of law, that the attorneys for the respective parties may state to you what they believe the law to be, and base arguments thereon, still, under your oaths and under the law, you have no right to consider anything as law except it be given you by the court; and you have no right to take the statement of any attorney as to what the law is, except the court gives you an instruction to the same effect; or, in other words, you should consider only that as law as given you by the court, and decide the case accordingly." It is the exclusive province of the court to decide all questions of law arising upon a trial, and to instruct the jury as to the law. It is not the function of counsel to instruct the jury, in argument or otherwise, and, if they desire to have the jury informed as to the law applicable to a given state of facts, they must present an instruction to the court for that purpose. This instruction was correct in telling the jury that it was their duty to decide the case according to the law as given by the court, and it also recognized the privilege of counsel to state what they believed the law to be, and to base arguments thereon. It may be that in making such statements the counsel may agree as to the law, and it may be correctly stated, so that it might be error to give an instruction of this character. The course of counsel in argument, however, may be such as to require such an instruction, and in this case we have no means of knowing what the statements of counsel as to the law were. Error is not presumed, and, as the record does not show the statements of counsel as to the law, we must assume that the instruction was necessary and proper. Assertions and argument to the jury by counsel as to the law cannot be made to take the place of instructions by the court.

Another instruction given at the request of defendant is as follows: "A person who uses a public street, and is familiar with the condition of the same, must exercise reasonable care in proportion to the danger, if any, known to him; and therefore, if you believe from the evidence that at the place of the alleged injury to the plaintiff there was a dangerous condition, and that the plaintiff saw, or by the use of reasonable care could have seen, the place complained of, then he was bound to exercise ordinary care on his part in view of all the circumstances; and if you believe from the evidence that he was injured through failure to exercise ordinary care, then, no matter how much the authorities of the city in charge of its streets have neglected their duty, no recovery can be had by the plaintiff in this suit, and in such case you should find the defendant, the city of Chicago, not guilty." It is a primary rule that instructions must be clear, concise, and plain, so as to be readily understood by the jury. This instruction is a vague, obscure, disjointed statement, rather calculated to mislead the jury than to enlighten them. Its first statement is that a person using a public street, who is familiar with its condition, must exercise reasonable care in proportion to the danger, if any, known to him. This is a correct statement of the law. If one knows of the dangerous condition of a street, he must exercise reasonable care in proportion to the known danger. That fact would call for the exercise of a higher degree of care than would be required in the absence of such knowledge, or where the person using the street would have a right to presume that it was reasonably safe. By the language of the instruction the next proposition is based on that rule, and the statement is that therefore (i. e., for that reason, or in consequence of that rule), if the jury believed from the evidence that the plaintiff saw, or by the use of reasonable care could have seen, the place complained of, he was bound to exercise ordinary care on his part, in view of all the circumstances. We do not understand what connection the rule as to actual familiarity with the condition of the street had with the ability of plaintiff to see the place complained of, with the use of reasonable care, if he did not in fact see it. The two propositions are not connected, and one does not follow from the other. The presumption of law is that a city will perform its duty, and the law imposes no duty on a traveler using a public street to anticipate negligence on the part of the city. He must use reasonable care for his own safety, but has a right to assume that the city has exercised ordinary care to keep the street in an ordinarily safe condition for persons using such degree of care. There was no instruction given in the case informing the jury either as to the presumption of law or what would constitute reasonable care on the part of one using a street. Plaintiff was bound to exercise ordinary care for his own safety in view of all the circumstances, but to tell the jury that he must exercise reasonable care in proportion to the danger if he was familiar with the street, and that if, by the exercise of reasonable care, he could have seen the place, then he must exercise reasonable care in view of all the circumstances, was both confusing and misleading.

Another instruction given was as follows: "The court instructs the jury that the plaintiff in this case is not entitled to recover for any injuries, infirmity, or sickness, if such there were, occurring at any time other than the time of the accident alleged in this case. The jury are further instructed that if you believe from the evidence that the plaintiff has failed to establish the fact that his alleged injuries or infirmities are the result of and were caused by the accident alleged in this case by a preponderance or greater weight of the evidence, then you should find the defendant not guilty." There was a controversy over the question whether the two later ruptures were caused by the accident, but there was no conflict in the testimony on the question that he suffered some injury from being thrown out of the cart and dragged. A jury would naturally understand this instruction as applying to the ruptures; but, if the jury concluded that they were not caused by the accident, that fact would not be a warrant for a verdict for the defendant, freeing it from all liability. The injuries, which were not disputed, may have been very slight, but, if there was a liability, plaintiff was entitled to some damages. Under the evidence the instruction should not have been given in that form.

The judgments of the superior court and Appellate Court are reversed, and the cause is remanded to the superior court. Reversed and remanded.

MAGRUDER, J., dissenting.

(208 Ill. 328)

BURKE v. SNIVELY et al.*

(Supreme Court of Illinois. Feb. 17, 1904.)

CONSTITUTIONAL LAW — CANALS — APPROPRIATIONS—ACTIONS—PARTIES.

1. A bill seeking to restrain the commissioners of the Illinois & Michigan Canal and certain public officials from applying certain sums of money appropriated to the maintenance of the canal by an act of the General Assembly (Laws 1903, p. 45), on the ground that the act was illegal and that the appropriation was not warranted by law, was not a suit against the state within the prohibition of Const. 1870, art. 4, § 26, declaring that the state shall not be made a party to any action at law or suit in chancery.

2. Const. 1870, § 3 (Starr & C. Ann. St. 1896, p. 206), provides that the Illinois & Michigan Canal shall never be sold or leased until the specific proposition for the sale or lease thereof shall first have been submitted to a vote of the people of the state at a general election, and have been approved by a majority of all the votes polled at such election; that the General Assembly shall never loan the credit of the state, or make appropriations from the treasury thereof, in aid of railroads or canals; provided that any surplus earnings of any canal may be appropriated for its enlargement or extension. *Held*, that the Legislature had power to operate the canal only to the extent that the income therefrom would defray the expenses, and that no moneys should be appropriated from the treasury of the state in aid of its operation, maintenance, or preservation, and hence that Laws 1903, p. 45, appropriating money for that purpose, was illegal.

3. On a bill by a taxpayer to restrain state officials from appropriating money to the maintenance of the Illinois & Michigan Canal contrary to Const. 1870, § 3 (Starr & C. Ann. St. 1896, p. 206), defendants could not make the objection that the provision of the state Constitution forbidding appropriation was void as impairing the obligation of a contract, contrary to the federal Constitution, because the grant of lands by the federal government in aid of the canal was conditioned on it being maintained by the state, as the defendants had no interest in the enforcement of the obligation of the contract.

Hand, C. J., and Wilkin, J., dissenting.

Appeal from Circuit Court, Sangamon County; J. A. Creighton, Judge.

Bill by Richard E. Burke against Clarence E. Snively and others. From a decree for defendants, plaintiff appeals. Reversed.

Darrow & Masters, for appellant. H. J. Hamlin, Atty. Gen. (Joseph N. Carter, of counsel), for appellees.

BOGGS, J. This was a bill in chancery filed in the circuit court of Sangamon county by the appellant against the appellees Snively, Newton, and Sackett, in their official capacity as commissioners of the Illinois & Michigan Canal, and the appellee James S. McCullough, as Auditor of Public Accounts of the State, and the appellee Fred A. Busse, as Treasurer of the State, to restrain the said Auditor of Public Accounts from drawing his warrant in favor of the said canal commissioners for certain sums of money

*Rehearing denied April 7, 1904.

¶ 3. See Constitutional Law, vol. 10, Cent. Dig. § 40.

appropriated by an act of the General Assembly approved May 15, 1903 (Laws 1903, p. 45), for the maintenance and protection of the Illinois & Michigan Canal, and for the necessary and extraordinary expenses thereof, and enjoining the said State Treasurer from paying any moneys out of the public funds of the state on any such warrant, should one be or have been drawn. A temporary injunction was issued as prayed. The defendants to the bill filed a joint answer thereto. The answer was accompanied by the affidavits of several persons, containing statements pertinent to matters alleged in the answer. A general replication was filed to the answer. The cause was submitted to the chancellor upon the bill, answer, and affidavits filed therewith, the replication to the answer, and a stipulation of the parties, in substance, as follows: That the bill of complaint, as verified under oath of said complainant, shall be considered as the evidence on his part; that the answer of said defendants, verified, together with the affidavits thereof, shall be considered as the evidence of one witness, if competent and received by the court, as to substance, on the part of the defendants; and that the court shall consider the averments of said bill and answer, and the statements in said affidavits, as evidence offered by the respective parties, and give to the same the same force and effect as though the testimony of said parties was taken in open court. The court overruled a motion entered by the appellant to strike the affidavits from the files, to which ruling exception was entered, and the appellant thereupon gave in evidence his bill, duly verified, and the appellees read in evidence their answer thereto and the affidavits filed in support of the answer. The decree of the court was that the bill should be dismissed and the injunction dissolved, from which decree the appellant has prosecuted this appeal.

The General Assembly of the state, at its session in 1903, adopted statutes authorizing the appropriation of $152,950 from the public moneys of the state for the purpose of providing means for maintaining the Illinois & Michigan Canal in a navigable condition, and maintaining and operating the Bridgeport pumping station and dredging the steamboat channel and basin at La Salle. The act authorized the Auditor of Public Accounts, on receipt of the certificate of the canal commissioners showing that the moneys are needed for the purposes for which the same were appropriated, to draw his warrant on the State Treasurer in favor of the canal commissioners for such sums so appropriated. The bill alleges that the complainant is a citizen of the state of Illinois, and the owner of real and personal property which is subject to taxation in said state and is taxed therein, and further alleges that such appropriations of the public moneys are prohibited by the provisions of the Constitution of 1870 with reference to canals, and that the acts of the Legislature authorizing such appropriations of the public moneys are therefore void, and the prayer of the bill is that such alleged misappropriation of the moneys of the state be restrained and enjoined. Appellees contend the bill is a suit against the state of Illinois, and should be dismissed for the reason that section 26 of article 4 of the Constitution of 1870 declares the state shall not be made a party to any action at law or suit in chancery.

The bill is not a suit against the state. It does not implead or ask any relief against the state. The relief asked is that officials of the state charged by law with the performance of official duties be restrained from a misuse of moneys intrusted to them, or from applying such moneys to purposes not warranted by law. The question to be determined is whether the state has, by law, authorized the payment from the public funds of sums of money to the commissioners of the canal, to be used in keeping in repair, improving, maintaining, and operating the Illinois & Michigan Canal. In equity the money in the state treasury is the money of the people of the state, and suits by a taxpayer to restrain the misappropriation by public officers of such money to an unauthorized purpose are not suits against the state. We have frequently maintained the jurisdiction of courts of equity to entertain bills in behalf of taxpayers to restrain misappropriation of funds by public authorities. Littler v. Jayne, 124 Ill. 123, 16 N. E. 374; Adams v. Brenan, 177 Ill. 194, 52 N. E. 314, 42 L. R. A. 718, 69 Am. St. Rep. 222. In Burritt v. Commissioners of State Contracts, 120 Ill. 322, 11 N. E. 180, this court entertained an original petition for a writ of mandamus to compel the commissioners to provide the petitioner, who was a justice of the peace, with a certain legal publication, to be paid for out of public moneys, and considered the contention on its merits. In German Alliance Ins. Co. v. Van Cleave, 191 Ill. 410, 61 N. E. 94, we upheld the jurisdiction of a court of chancery to restrain the insurance commissioner from paying to the Treasurer of the State moneys collected as taxes from certain insurance companies, and to enjoin the State Treasurer from receiving such taxes.

Public officials of the state who are charged by law with the duty of granting certificates or warrants purporting to authorize the payment of moneys from the treasury of the state may be restrained from issuing certificates or warrants for the payment of the public money for any other than purposes for which such moneys may be lawfully used, and the Treasurer of the State may be enjoined from paying public funds for purposes or objects not authorized by law. An unconstitutional statute is not law, and an appropriation of public funds in pursuance of an unconstitutional statute is a misuse of funds, which may be restrained by injunction. Suits of that character, such as bills to enjoin the Governor, Secretary of State, and Treasurer of State from selling lands of the state under an unconstitutional statute (Pennoyer v. McConnaughy, 140 U. S. 1, 11 Sup. Ct. 699, 35 L. Ed. 363), a suit against the Governor and other state officers to restrain the issuing of a bond in violation of a statute (Louisiana Board v. McComb, 92 U. S. 531, 23 L. Ed. 623), and a suit against the Auditor of a state to restrain the execution of an unconstitutional statute (Osborn v. Bank of the United States, 9 Wheat. 738, 6 L. Ed. 204), have been held not suits against the state, and not violative of constitutional provisions against impleading the state in any action at law or suit in chancery. We may therefore consider the contention of the appellant that the General Assembly was wanting in power to authorize the public moneys to be taken out of the treasury of the state and applied to maintenance and operation of the Illinois & Michigan Canal. The General Assembly possesses full, plenary power of legislation, in the absence of some inhibitory constitutional provision. It is composed of representatives of the people of the state, and may therefore exercise every legislative function not denied it by the Constitution, and not delegated to some other department of the state government.

The contention of the appellant is that the provision of the Constitution of 1870 which relates to the Illinois & Michigan Canal prohibits the Legislature from making any appropriations from the Treasury of the State for the maintenance and operation of the Illinois & Michigan Canal, or for the ordinary and necessary or extraordinary expenses of the canal. The constitutional provision referred to reads as follows: "The Illinois and Michigan Canal shall never be sold or leased until the specific proposition for the sale or lease thereof shall first have been submitted to a vote of the people of the state at a general election, and have been approved by a majority of all the votes polled at such election. The General Assembly shall never loan the credit of the state, or make appropriations from the treasury thereof, in aid of railroads or canals: provided, that any surplus earnings of any canal may be appropriated for its enlargement or extension." Const. 1870, separate section 3; Starr & C. Ann. St. 1896, p. 206. It will be observed the section consists of but two sentences. The first sentence inhibits the sale or lease of the Illinois & Michigan Canal, except by the authority of the people of the state, expressed at the polls at an election to be held throughout the state on a specific proposition for the sale or lease thereof. This sentence leaves unaffected the power of the Legislature to operate the canal and to make appropriations of the public moneys to defray the expenses of the operation, maintenance, or preservation thereof. Prior to the formation of the Constitution the canal had been operated under the direction and by the authority of the General Assembly, and an income had been derived in excess of all the expense of operation, and it was being so controlled, managed and operated at and during the time the constitutional convention was in session. Notwithstanding the fact that at the time of the formation of the Constitution of 1870, and also during all prior years after the completion of the canal, all the expenses of operation and maintenance of the canal had been met and discharged out of the tolls and earnings, and the income had each year exceeded the expenses of the operation and maintenance thereof, still we are advised, by the discussion that arose in the constitutional convention upon the question of the adoption of this sentence, and more particularly as to the adoption of the second sentence of the constitutional provision under consideration—the provision having been divided, and a separate vote had on each sentence—that it was to be apprehended that the more rapid means of transportation afforded by railroads, and the great increase in the number of railway lines in the territory contiguous to the canal, would divert traffic from the canal, and that in the future the tolls and income from the canal would most likely decrease and shrink away, and possibly fall below the amount necessary to defray the expenses of maintaining and operating it, and that in the not remote future the operation and maintenance thereof might, and probably would, become a burden and expense to the people, if the public moneys were not protected by the Constitution against legislative enactments making appropriations in aid of the canal, and to meet such deficiencies as might occur in the course of the operation and maintenance thereof. We hereinafter refer to this discussion, and quote the remarks of members of the convention. The second sentence of the constitutional provision here being considered, it is urged, was framed for the express purpose of protecting the treasury of the state in the event the canal should cease to be self-supporting. The second sentence may be here repeated for more convenient reference: "The General Assembly shall never loan the credit of the state, or make appropriations from the treasury thereof, in aid of railroads or canals: provided, that any surplus earnings of any canal may be appropriated for its enlargement or extension."

The Constitution of a state derives its force and authority from the vote of the people adopting it. For that reason it is a general rule that in construing the provisions of a Constitution the words employed therein shall be given the meaning which they bear in ordinary use among the people. The natural and ordinary meaning of the words is to be accepted, except where a word is used the meaning whereof is established by statute or by judicial construction. The word "aid," employed in the body of the sentence, has no such established meaning, or any technical meaning different from that given it by the lexicographers as the meaning thereof as understood generally among men. In ordinary acceptation it means to help; to support; to assist; to sustain; to succor or to relieve; and so it is defined by Mr. Webster. The inhibition against making appropriations from the treasury of the state in "aid" of canals, if the word "aid" be given its natural and ordinary meaning, would deny to the Legislature the power to appropriate money from the treasury for any of the purposes of the Illinois & Michigan Canal here asked to be enjoined, if the word "canals," used in the body of the sentence, includes the Illinois & Michigan Canal. If the proviso had not been appended to the body of the sentence, some weight and force would attach to the argument that the general word "canals," found in the body of the sentence, had no reference to the canal owned by the state; that it was absurd to speak of the state loaning its credit to itself, as the owner of the Illinois & Michigan Canal, and that a prohibition against the application of the public moneys in aid of canals should not, in reason, be understood to forbid the application by the state of moneys from the treasury to defray the necessary expenses of operating, repairing, maintaining, and preserving a canal which belonged to the state; that under the correct interpretation and construction the prohibition was against lending the credit of the state or appropriating the moneys of the state in aid of railroads or canals which individuals or private corporations owned, or were preparing to construct as the business enterprises of private proprietors. The true constitutional intent can, however, only be ascertained by the careful consideration of the entire sentence—the body thereof and the proviso—for one of the offices of a proviso is to qualify the generality of the body of the sentence of which it is a part, though it can have no potency to enlarge the scope or force of the enactment. Sarah v. Borders, 4 Scam. 341; Huddleston v. Francis, 124 Ill. 196, 16 N. E. 243; In re Day, 181 Ill. 73, 54 N. E. 646, 50 L. R. A. 519. The office intended to be served by the proviso here in review is clear. Manifestly the proviso, though the words "any canals" are employed therein, had and has reference only to the canal that was owned by the state—the Illinois & Michigan Canal. The state had the right to control and direct the application of the earnings of that canal, and of no other. Under the statutes then in force the "surplus earnings" of the Illinois & Michigan Canal were required to be paid into the treasury of the state, and the state had power to permit such surplus earnings to be drawn out of its treasury and applied to the extension or enlargement of the canal owned by the state. The state had no power to control the manner in which the surplus earnings of any canal other than the Illinois & Michigan Canal should be expended. The state owned but one canal—the Illinois & Michigan Canal—had power to control the surplus earnings of but that one canal, and the proviso had reference only to that canal. The words "any canal" were no doubt used in the proviso in an excess of caution, in order that the proviso might apply as well to any other canal of which the state might possibly afterward become the owner, in order that the restriction might be general and uniform, but it could in no contingency apply to a canal not owned by the state. The body of the sentence (the proviso being excluded) prohibits the appropriation of any of the public moneys "in aid" of canals generally. The proviso appended thereto authorizes the appropriation of the "surplus earnings" of the Illinois & Michigan Canal to the enlargement and extension of that waterway. The body of the sentence is general in its terms and its objects, and prohibits the appropriation of any of the public moneys in aid of any and all canals. The proviso qualifies the generality of this prohibition by excepting therefrom any moneys which have come into the treasury of the state from the "surplus earnings" of the Illinois & Michigan Canal, and by providing that any such surplus earnings may be devoted by the General Assembly to the purposes of enlarging or extending that canal. The rule of construction in such instances is that the proviso is to be strictly construed, and that it takes no case out of the prohibition declared in the body of the sentence, other than the precise case that is included in the terms of the proviso.

The Supreme Court of the United States, speaking through Mr. Justice Story, in the case of United States v. Dickson, 15 Pet. 165, 10 L. Ed. 689, said: "Passing from these considerations to another, which necessarily brings under review the second point of objection, we are led to the general rule of law which has always prevailed, and become consecrated almost as a maxim in the interpretation of statutes, that where the enacting clause is general in its language and objects, and a proviso is afterwards introduced, that the proviso is to be strictly construed, and takes no case out of the enacting clause which does not fairly fall within the terms of the proviso. In short, the proviso carves special exceptions, only, out of the enacting clause."

The proviso to the sentence of the Constitution here under consideration carves a special exception, only, out of the general inhibition found in the body of the sentence, and leaves the general inhibition in full force and vigor, save only to the extent it is qualified by the exception of the proviso. The proviso, therefore, takes out of the general inhibition that which, but for the proviso, would have remained within such general inhibition, and leaves within the general inhibition found in the body of the sentence all that is not specifically taken out by the terms of the proviso, strictly construed. The inhibition against the application of the public moneys that had or should be gathered into the treasury of the state, by taxation of the property of taxpayers of the state, to the purpose of "aiding" the canal, was not qualified by the proviso, or in any manner affected thereby. On the contrary, the presence of the proviso demonstrates that it was the understanding of the framers of the Constitution that the body of the sentence prohibited the appropriation of the public money in aid of the Illinois & Michigan Canal, and that the proviso was added for the purpose of so qualifying that prohibition that it might be lawful to use the "surplus earning" of that canal which should come into the treasury in enlarging or extending it, if the General Assembly should ever deem that course to be desirable. Therefore it seems to us to be so clear as to be beyond doubt or debate that the proviso was annexed to the sentence for the reason it was the understanding of the convention that the word "canals," employed in the body of the sentence, was intended to include the Illinois & Michigan Canal, and that the body of the sentence, in the absence of a proviso thereto, would absolutely inhibit the appropriation of any of the public moneys in aid of that canal, and that as to the Illinois & Michigan Canal an exception to the general inhibition was intended, namely, that appropriations of the surplus earnings of the Illinois & Michigan Canal might be made for the purpose of extending or enlarging it. Such being the object intended to be secured by the addition of the proviso, it is unmistakable that it was the understanding of the framers of the Constitution that the body of the sentence absolutely inhibited the appropriations of the public moneys in aid of or for any of the purposes of the Illinois & Michigan Canal, and that the proviso was added to qualify, in a degree, the generality of the language of the body of the sentence, and to limit the inhibition against the appropriation of any money from the treasury of the state to the purposes of, or in aid of, the canal, to such an extent as would leave it within the power of the Legislature to appropriate the moneys which had come into the treasury from the surplus earnings of the canal to the extension or enlargement of that waterway.

The constitutional intent, then, to be gathered from the entire provision, is that the power to sell or lease the canal shall remain with the people; that the control and management thereof, and the operation of the same, if that shall seem wise and best, should be possessed by the Legislature; to which power of management, control, and operation there was attached an inhibition against the application of the public moneys which should be derived from taxation of the property of the citizens of the state to any of the purposes of the canal, but that any moneys which should be paid into the treasury of the state as surplus earnings of the canal might be drawn therefrom and applied to the extension or enlargement of the canal. The constitutional intent was and is that the canal shall be self-supporting and that the people of the state shall not be taxed to aid it in any way.

In construing constitutional provisions the true inquiry is, what was the understanding of the meaning of the words used by the voters who adopted it? Still, the practice of consulting the debates of the members of the convention which framed the Constitution, as aiding to a correct determination of the intent of the framers of the instrument, has long been indulged in by courts as aiding to a true understanding of the meaning of provisions that are thought to be doubtful. The discussion in the constitutional convention of questions connected with the constitutional provisions here under consideration supports the construction we have given to it.

Mr. Archer, a member of the convention, said, among other things: "I am willing to vote for the proposition in these reports that this canal shall not be leased or sold, and that it shall forever remain the property of the state. Then, if it appears, in the course of a few years, that the canal is a burden; that it is unprofitable; that to lease or sell it would promote and secure the prosperity of the people better than to keep it, let the Legislature submit an amendment to the Constitution to that effect, revoke what has been done, and act upon the policy subsequently discovered to be correct and proper. But, Mr. Chairman, I will not by my vote inaugurate, however remotely, a system of appropriations for this canal beyond what its revenues may enable it to have appropriated to it." Debates, Const. Con. vol. 1, p. 374.

Mr. McCoy, another delegate, remarked: "We all know that this canal has been a fruitless enterprise. We all know that it has yielded nothing to the state of Illinois. We all know that there has been a large sum of money spent in its construction, and it cannot now be well claimed by the friends of the enterprise that the people of the state of Illinois are to be further taxed. * * * But I have no objection to this canal. It is an elephant on our hands. The gentlemen concede that we ought not to retain the animal on our hands much longer without special favor. I am decidedly in favor of its feeding itself for a while." Debates, Const. Con. vol. 1, p. 386, col. 2.

Mr. Washburn, also a delegate, gave expression to his views as follows: "If gentlemen would be satisfied with a simple provision that the Legislature should not sell or lease or dispose of this canal without the consent of the people, they could get it. We have no objection to that; we are willing to accede to that much, but that will not be accepted. That is not what is wanted. I believe members have gone so far as to say that would be no boon if they are prohibited from making appropriations for the canal. The appropriations are what they want, what they expect, and what we do not want you to have. We are willing for you to have your canal. We are willing you should keep all you have; we are willing you should run your canal and make all you can out of it—have all the benefits and proceeds of it—giving you the advantage of $7,000,000 over the people of the state; but do not ask us to tie the incubus of that canal on the people of the state for all time to come, so that you may have lever power wherewith to obtain future appropriations out of the Legislature." Debates, Const. Con. vol. 1, p. 431, col. 3.

Mr. Pillsbury, a member of the convention, manifestly understood that the inhibition prevented the appropriation of the public moneys to keep the canal in repair. He desired that the propositions contained in the second sentence of the constitutional provision should be so divided that the members might vote separately upon the question of inhibiting appropriations to "railroads" and the question of making appropriations in aid of "canals," and moved for a division of the proposition accordingly, and in support of his motion said: "Voting to aid railroads is a very different thing from voting appropriations to the canal which we already have. I do not wish to prevent the Legislature from protecting the property they already own, in case the interest of the people demands an appropriation to keep the canal in repair. I desire to vote upon the question freed from the connection with railroads." Debates, Const. Con. vol. 1, p. 468, col. 2.

Mr. Hayes also desired a similar division of the question, and in support thereof said: "Mr. President, I desire to divide the second branch so as to have a separate vote upon the proposition that the state shall make no appropriations to protect her property in the canal. I desire to have a separate vote upon that proposition." Debates, Const. Con. vol. 1, p. 485, col. 1.

Mr. Benjamin voted against the adoption of the constitutional provision we are considering, and in explanation of his vote said: "Mr. President, I desire to explain my vote. I am in favor of the proposition that the General Assembly shall not make appropriations from the treasury in aid of railroads, but I am opposed to any prohibition by which the General Assembly would be precluded from making appropriations from the treasury for the repair and preservation of the property of the state—the Illinois & Michigan Canal. I therefore vote no." Debates, Const. Con. vol. 1, p. 486, col. 3.

Mr. Merriam, another member of the convention, in explanation of the vote cast by him against the adoption of the provision, among other things said: "While I will very cheerfully vote in favor of the proposition to prevent the state from appropriating money for railroad purposes in any shape, I am opposed to the other part of the proposition, and therefore vote no." Debates, Const. Con. vol. 1, p. 486, col. 3.

Mr. Wagner, also a delegate, voted against the proposition, and when doing so said: "I vote no, for the reason that I believe that the proposition robs the state of its ability to take care of itself and protect the canal." Debates, Const. Con. vol. 1, p. 486, col. 3.

A contrary view of the meaning and effect of the constitutional provision was expressed but by one member of the convention, so far as we are advised, viz., Mr. Browning. That gentleman, in response to the statement of Mr. Benjamin that he was opposed to prohibiting the General Assembly from making appropriations of public moneys for the repair and preservation of the Illinois & Michigan Canal, and for that reason voted against the provision, expressed the opinion that the provision did "not touch the power of the General Assembly to keep the canal in repair." Debates, Const. Con. vol. 1, p. 486, col. 3.

It is therefore seen that the meaning we have given to the constitutional provision is the same as that given it by all but one of the members of the constitutional convention who, so far as we are advised, gave expression to their views in the debate.

Though it does not aid to the determination of the question of the power of the Legislature to make the appropriation in question, it is not inappropriate to remark that the fears entertained by members of the constitutional convention that more modern and more speedy means of transporting passengers and commodities would soon supplant the canal and divert traffic from it, and the canal would become practically of no use as a waterway or highway of traffic and commerce, and would cease to produce an income sufficient to pay the expenses connected with its management, and would, unless restrained by the Constitution, become a regular applicant at the door of the state treasury for appropriations of money of the taxpayers of the state, have been verified. In 1876 the tolls received for the use of the canal aggregated $113,293, but since that year there has been a marked and substantially gradual decrease in such receipts. In 1900 so little demand was there for the canal as a highway or waterway for transportation of persons or property that but $13,867 were paid as tolls. In 1901 the use of the canal for the purpose of trade or commerce was so little availed of that but $8,120 were collected from tolls. The gross receipts were much larger in all the years than the sums stated, but the excess arose from sales of ice privileges and sales of water power. But in addition to all receipts, of every character, during these years, heavy appropriations from the treasury of the state, amounting to something more than one-half a million dollars, have been asked and obtained from the public treasury to meet the deficiencies arising from the management and operation of the canal. The canal has practically fallen into disuse for any of the purposes of transportation of either persons or property, and has been perverted to mere commercial purposes of supplying water power to those along its banks and selling privileges to cut ice from its pools. It is no longer a highway of commerce.

It is argued by counsel for appellees, in support of the contention that the constitutional provision, under the proper construction thereof, does not deny to the General Assembly power to appropriate public moneys to defray the expenses of operating and maintaining the canal, that the first sentence of the constitutional provision is particular and specific, and relates to but one canal—the Illinois & Michigan Canal; that it deprived the Legislature of power to sell or lease the canal until authorized by a vote of the electors of the state; that this limitation on the power of the Legislature to sell or lease the canal demonstrated that the members of the constitutional convention were impressed with the importance of the canal to the people as a means of transportation of their commodities, and as having a tendency to check unjust and excessive charges by railroads; and that it is manifest that it was the constitutional intent that the Legislature should keep the canal in usable condition and operate it, even if it should become necessary to appropriate moneys gathered into the treasury by taxation of the property of citizens of the state generally, and that the inhibition contained in the second sentence is general, only, and does not specially inhibit appropriations of the public moneys to repair or maintain the Illinois & Michigan Canal, and hence that that which is specific and particular in the first sentence should control over that which is general in the second sentence. This argument is faulty in its premise, and hence erroneous in its conclusion. The restriction in the first sentence against the sale or lease of the canal by the General Assembly does not in express words or by fair implication impose it upon the Legislature, as a constitutional duty, to operate the canal, either while it could be made to pay or in the event it failed to earn enough to pay expenses. The restriction imposed no duty on the Legislature, but left the lawmaking body free to deal with the canal as its wisdom and judgment should dictate, save that the canal could not be sold or leased. This restriction alone considered, the Legislature had power to operate the canal even at the expense of the general taxpayers, or to abandon the operation thereof and let the canal remain idle and unused. No constitutional duty to operate the canal being declared by the first sentence, the general inhibition found in the second sentence against appropriations in aid of the canal is not in conflict with the first sentence.

The suggestion is made that this supposed conflict between the first sentence and the body of the second sentence may be reconciled by regarding the inhibition against lending the credit of the state, or making appropriations of the public moneys in aid of railroads or canals, as intended only to inhibit loaning the credit of the state or appropriating the public money to aid in building and constructing railways or canals, and as not intended to include and prohibit appropriations of the public moneys to meet and discharge indebtedness occasioned in the course of the operation of the Illinois & Michigan Canal; that it was only constructive work, building railroads or digging canals—not the expenses of operation—that was inhibited by the general language of the second sentence. In support of the suggestion it is pointed out that the proviso relates only to construction work—that is, the enlargement or extension of the canal—and only qualifies that which was inhibited by the body of the sentence, namely, aiding in constructive work. If such a construction could be given the sentence, the inhibition would be so restricted that there would be no prohibition against loaning the credit of the state or appropriating money from its treasury to aid any of the purposes of any railroad or canal, other than the work of building or constructing such railroad or canal. If that view is correct, the General Assembly may open the treasury of the state and draw therefrom the public money and apply it to the indebtedness of any railroad or canal, other than indebtedness incurred for what is called "constructive work." This would be, in substance, to embark again on the policy of fostering and supporting internal improvements by applying the moneys of the taxpayers to the discharge of the indebtedness of railroads and canals, a conclusion which is so inconsistent with the manifest intent of the framers of the Constitution as to be entirely beyond serious consideration.

The appellees further insist, to quote from their brief, that, "in construing a constitutional provision, an important rule to be observed—one often of a controlling character—is that a contemporaneous exposition by the legislative as well as of the executive branch of the state government is entitled to great weight in ascertaining the meaning of such provision, concerning the construction of which different minds might not agree." It appears from the record that the tolls received for the use of the canal during the years after the adoption of the Constitution of 1870 until the year 1877 exceeded the gross expenses connected with its management. In the year 1877 there was a deficiency of about $14,000, but no application was made to the Legislature for an appropriation by reason thereof. In 1878 the tolls exceeded the gross expenses in the sum of about $2,000, but in 1879 the gross expenses exceeded the tolls in the sum of something more than $8,000. Since 1879 the income of the canal as a highway or waterway of trade and commerce has dwindled away, until in 1901 the total tolls received amounted to but $8,120, the expenses for said year 1901 being $111,002. In 1879 the Legislature adopted an act appropriating the sum of $30,000 to be applied to the purpose of making necessary repairs and put and keep the canal in a navigable condition, to be used only after all the surplus earnings of the canal had been applied to such purposes. In 1883, in 1891, in 1897, in 1899, and in 1901, like enactments were adopted making appropriations in aid of the canal, and also in 1903, when the act here involved was adopted. The sum total of these appropriations exceeds one-half million of dollars, in addition to the sums specifically appropriated to construct the dams at Copperas Creek and Henry. The answer of appellees avers that the sums appropriated in 1879 and 1883, together amounting to $70,000, were not used on the canal, and that only a portion of the later appropriations were so used. To what purpose these moneys not used on the canal were applied is not disclosed, save that it is to be inferred such moneys were expended in and about the dams at Copperas Creek and at Henry, and therefore for the benefit of the canal. The additional sum of $76,452 was appropriated out of the public moneys to aid in building those locks and dams, and the earnings of the canal to an amount not disclosed were also devoted to the same purpose, under enactments of the General Assembly. These various enactments were approved by the chief executive of the state at the time of their adoption respectively. The earlier of these acts was not passed until nine years after the adoption of the Constitution, in 1870. Contemporaneous and continuous action of the General Assembly, sanctioned by the approval of the Governor, would be entitled to much weight. Bunn v. People, 45 Ill. 397. The literal meaning of "contemporaneous" is "living or existing at the time." 8 Cyc. 1145. While the principle of construction could not be fairly held to require perfect or literal coincidence in point of time, the lapse of time—of years—weakens the force of the influence of the enactment as a practical and contemporaneous construction of the provision. Out of that deference which is always due from the judicial to the executive and legislative departments of the state, these various enactments making appropriations in aid of the Illinois & Michigan Canal present themselves as worthy of our consideration as practical expositions of the meaning accorded to this provision of the Constitution by the different executives and Legislatures by whom the acts were respectively adopted.

We are referred, however, to an act of the General Assembly which was adopted on the 27th day of March, 1874, and approved by the then chief executive of the state. This enactment was passed five years earlier than the act of 1879, which was the first of the acts relied on by the appellees as a practical contemporaneous construction of the constitutional provision. The act of 1874 was passed within four years after the adoption of the Constitution, while nine years elapsed before the passage and approval of the act of 1879. Laws 1879, p. 6. The enactment of 1874 constitutes chapter 19 of our Revised Statutes of 1874. It provides that the canal commissioners shall continue to consist, as before, of three discreet and skillful persons to be appointed by the Governor, by and with the consent of the Senate. Section 9 of the act prescribes the duties of the commissioners. The second subdivision of the section is as follows: "Second—To cause the said canal, locks and dams and appurtenances to be kept in good and sufficient repair and condition for use, and whenever it shall be necessary for that purpose, they may, by themselves or their agents, enter upon and use, overflow or damage any contiguous lands, and procure and appropriate all such material as in their judgment may be necessary or proper to be used in making such repair, build or construct any dam, lock, or other improvement, and may take proceedings in their official name to ascertain the compensation therefor, in the manner at the time provided by law for the exercise of the right of eminent domain: provided, that the damages, cost of materials and improvements shall in all cases be paid out of the net proceeds derived from tolls." It will be noted that it was deemed important to append a proviso to the body of this subdivision of the section, specifically declaring that the cost of material used and of improvements authorized to be made, and the damages which might be incurred, if necessary, to keep the canal in good and sufficient repair and condition for use, should "in all cases" be paid out of the net proceeds derived from the tolls. This proviso indicates that the Legislature of 1874 understood the inhibition of the constitutional provision against making appropriations of the public moneys in aid of the canal as we have construed it, and that they attached the proviso as a limitation upon the power of the commissioners to make the repairs and improvements and exercise the power of eminent domain, and do the things specified in the body of the subdivision of the section, by restricting them in the exercise of such powers to the extent that the obligations thereby incurred could be paid out of the net proceeds of the tolls. This legislative interpretation of the constitutional provision was more nearly contemporaneous with the Constitution in point of time than the earliest of the enactments relied upon by the appellees as legislative construction of the constitutional provision.

A still earlier enactment, approved April 22, 1871, at the first session of the General Assembly after the adoption of the Constitution of 1870, indicates that it was the legislative understanding that the public moneys of the state were not to be appropriated in aid of the canal. The act is found on page 215 of the Session Laws of 1871-72. The preamble recites: "Whereas, the Illinois and Michigan Canal, and all remaining canal property, have reverted or are about to revert to the state, and it devolves upon the General Assembly to take the necessary steps to insure judicious and economical management of the same; therefore," etc. The first section provides that it shall be the duty of the canal commissioners of the state to examine and audit the accounts of their predecessors, the retiring board of trustees of the canal. The second section empowers the commissioners to take charge of and exercise full control over the Illinois & Michigan Canal, and to receive all moneys in the hands of the board of trustees belonging to the canal fund and to pay the same into the state treasury, and to receive all books, office buildings, and other property in the possession of the trustees, and directs the board of trustees to comply with the provisions of the act and account for and pay over to the commissioners all such moneys and deliver all such property promptly on the passage of the act. To the body of the second section were appended two provisos, as follows: "Provided, that any claim for which the state trustee is now liable may be prosecuted against the said commissioners, and shall be paid by them out of the resources of the canal: provided, that all moneys received for rents and tolls, not necessary for the expenses of the canal and for keeping the same in repair, shall be paid quarterly into the state treasury, and that the rate of tolls shall not be increased without the consent of the General Assembly." The first of the provisos disclaims any liability on the part of the state to pay any claim for which the board of canal trustees may be liable to answer, and directs that all such claims shall be paid out of the resources of the canal. The second proviso is in accord with the view that the expenses of the canal and of keeping the same in repair were to be paid out of moneys received from rents and tolls for the use of the canal.

In view of the earlier legislation with reference to the canal since the adoption of the Constitution, the enactments of 1879 and succeeding years, making appropriations out of the public moneys in aid of the Illinois & Michigan Canal, are shorn of much of the influence which otherwise might be accorded to them as aids to the true interpretation of the constitutional provision under consideration. It is a primary rule that the meaning of a constitutional provision is to be ascertained from the language employed therein, and that it is only when ambiguity is found, and the meaning is doubtful, that the extrinsic aid of practical construction given by other departments of the state is to be resorted to. 6 Am. & Eng. Ency. of Law (2d Ed.) p. 932, and authorities cited in note 5. In the case of Phœbe v. Jay, Breese, 268, speaking with reference to repeated enactments of the Legislature as aids to the construction of constitutional provisions, it was said: "If they have no power to pass an act, any number of repetitions of unconstitutional acts, or acts beyond the pale of their authority, can never make the original act valid." We are of the opinion that the true meaning of the constitutional provision with reference to the canal is that the Legislature should have power to operate it to the extent, and to the extent only, that the income of the canal would defray the expenses of operation, maintenance, and preservation, and that no moneys shall be appropriated from the treasury of the state in aid of the operation, maintenance, or preservation thereof, and that, if the earnings of the canal produced a surplus, appropriations of such surplus might be made to aid in the enlargement or extension of the canal should the Legislature deem it wise to so appropriate such surplus.

It is further urged that the state of Illinois procured the funds wherewith to construct the Illinois & Michigan Canal from the sales of lands granted to the state by the United States for the sole and only purpose of providing a fund to be applied by the state to the construction of a canal, and that the act of Congress granting said lands to the state for the purpose aforesaid contained the following proviso: "Provided, that said canal, when completed, shall be and forever remain a public highway for the use of the government of the United States, free from any toll or other charge for any property of the United States, or persons in their service, passing through the same: provided, that such canal shall be commenced within five years and completed within twenty years, or the state shall be bound to pay to the United States the amount of land previously sold, and that the title to the purchasers under the state shall be valid." It is further insisted that the said act of Congress was adopted by Congress and accepted by the state of Illinois long prior to the adoption of the Constitution of 1870, and that it then constituted a contract between the state of Illinois and the United States, obligating the state to forever keep and maintain the canal as a public highway or waterway for the use of the government of the United States, free from any tolls or other charges, for any person in the service of the United States or for any property of the United States passing through the same. Upon this insistence it is urged that if the provision of the Constitution of the state here under consideration is construed to mean that no appropriation of the public moneys belonging to the state shall be made and applied to the purpose of keeping the canal in proper condition for use as a public highway or waterway, free to be used by the federal government without charge or toll, the provisions of the state Constitution, so construed, would impair the obligation of the contract between the state and the general government, and would be void, as in contravention of section 10 of article 1 of the Constitution of the United States, which declares that no state shall enact a law impairing the obligation of a contract.

The question whether the cession of Congress, and the acceptance thereof by the state, constitute a contract on the part of the state to forever keep and maintain the canal in such condition that the general government may use it as a public highway, does not arise for determination. If such a contract arose out of the grant of the land and the acceptance thereof, the complaint that the provision of the state Constitution here under consideration, if construed to deny to the Legislature power to appropriate any sums whatever from the public treasury for the purpose of repairing or maintaining the canal in usable condition as a public highway, would impair the obligation of that contract, cannot be urged by the appellees, who appear in the suit only in their capacity as officers, which positions they hold under and by the authority of the Constitution of the state of Illinois and the statutes made in pursuance thereof. The rights of these appellees are not affected by any alleged impairment of the alleged or supposed contract between the federal government and the state of Illinois. The only person who may complain that a law impairs the obligation of a contract is one who has an interest in the enforcement of the obligation of the contract said to be impaired. Templeton v. Horne, 82 Ill. 491; 15 Am. & Eng. Ency. of Law (2d Ed.) 1059. If it shall be found that the grant of the lands and the acceptance thereof constitute a contract, and a question of the enforcement of the contract shall arise, the United States and the state of Illinois, in the exercise of the sovereign power which they respectively possess, it may be confidently asserted, will adjust their respective rights and obligations amicably, honorably, and justly. No obligation will be impaired or repudiated. The appellees are but servants of the state, charged, temporarily, with the performance of duties in and about certain public affairs of the state which the state has intrusted to them to be performed, and in that capacity they appear in this proceeding. They do not represent the United States, and have no power to submit for decision the question whether contract obligations accrued by reason of the cession and acceptance of the lands, much less to insist that, notwithstanding the changed conditions which have, it seems, rendered the canal wholly unnecessary, if not entirely useless, as a highway to the United States, the alleged contract can only be discharged by the specific performance thereof.

The circuit court fell into error in dismissing the bill. The relief prayed for should have been granted. The decree of the circuit court is therefore reversed, and the cause will be remanded to that court with directions to enter a decree perpetually enjoining the appellees according to the prayer of the bill.

Reversed and remanded, with directions.

HAND, C. J., and WILKIN, J. (dissenting). The question presented here for determination is one of legislative power, and the argument that the operation of the Illinois & Michigan Canal has ceased to be profitable, and therefore it should be abandoned, is beside the case. Such argument, if presented to the consideration of the Legislature, if founded on fact, might be worthy of its consideration, but when urged here as a reason for holding the statute unconstitutional is without force. If, however, it is to be given force, the facts should not be lost sight of that the canal thus far has not been a burden to the state, and the evidence in this record does not show it ever will be burdensome to the state. The original cost of the canal, which was approximately $5,000,000, was paid for from the sale of lands donated to the state by the general government for canal purposes, with the express understanding that the canal should be forever maintained by the state. From the time of its construction to the time of the filing of this bill the canal had earned more than $6,500,000, and there now remains in the state treasury, after paying all its expenses, and after refunding to the state all moneys appropriated for its use, the sum of $338,695.76.

At the time the Constitution of 1870 was adopted, the canal was the most valuable piece of property then owned by the state, and the framers of the Constitution, to guard against its sacrifice, inserted a provision in the Constitution, which was subsequently ratified by the people, that it should never be sold or leased unless the specific proposition for the sale or lease thereof should first have been submitted to a vote of the people of the state at a general election and approved by a majority of all the votes polled at such election. The adoption of that provision showed that it was the fixed intention of the people that they should not be deprived of said canal without their consent, and to effectuate such intention they took from the Legislature the power to transfer the canal to any person or corporation, even for a temporary period. The Constitution, it must be remembered, is a limitation upon and not a grant of power, and, the people having provided that the canal shall not be sold or leased, but shall remain the property of the state until they have consented that it might be disposed of by sale or lease, it would seem clear the Legislature, as their representative, has the right to provide for the preservation of the canal by the appropriation of funds from the state treasury so long as it belongs to the state, the same as it has for other property of the state, such as the State House, insane asylums, penitentiaries, etc., unless such power has been taken away by the Constitution, either in express terms or by necessary implication. It having been provided the canal cannot be sold or leased except upon the vote of the people, the implication would be that it should be maintained and operated until it was sold or leased, and not that it should be allowed to fill up and fall into decay; and the power to appropriate funds from the state treasury for such purpose would necessarily follow. The implications arising, therefore, are all in favor of the power to appropriate money for the operation and maintenance of the canal, rather than against it. This being true, we must therefore search the Constitution and be able to point out the clause therein which prevents the Legislature from appropriating funds from the state treasury with which to operate and maintain said canal, and, if such prohibition cannot be pointed out, the power exists, as the power is vested in the Legislature unless it has been taken away.

It is contended such limitation or inhibition is found in the following paragraph of the Constitution: "The General Assembly shall never loan the credit of the state, or make appropriations from the treasury thereof, in aid of railroads or canals: provided, that any surplus earnings of any canal may be appropriated for its enlargement or extension." We do not think the contention correct. It is a well-known fact that prior to the year 1870 municipal aid had been voted to assist in railroad construction in many municipalities throughout the state in a most wild and extravagant manner; that the members who sat in the constitutional convention held that year had not forgotton the schemes for a system of internal improvements which in the early history of the state had threatened to bankrupt the state, and that new schemes for the construction of canals to furnish drainage to the city of Chicago, for the reclaiming of the swamp and overflowed lands of the state, and to furnish a waterway connecting the Great Lakes and the Gulf, through the Illinois and Mississippi rivers, were again rife; and any one who will take the time to read what was said at the time the provision under consideration was before the constitutional convention will conclude at once that the words "the General Assembly shall never loan the credit of the state, or make appropriations from the treasury thereof, in aid of railroads or canals," were incorporated into the Constitution to prevent the Legislature from lending the credit of the state to or making appropriations from the state treasury in aid of railroads and canals which were not then built, and which, when constructed, were to be owned and controlled by private persons or corporations—at least, by parties other than the state—and that said provision does not apply to the Illinois & Michigan Canal.

This much seems to be conceded, but it is said the proviso following those general words, viz., "that any surplus earnings of any canal may be appropriated for its enlargement or extension," clearly refer to the Illinois & Michigan Canal, and prohibit an appropriation of funds from the state treasury for the maintenance and operation of said canal. We think the position untenable. It is conceded the usual office of a proviso is to limit the general provision which precedes it, and not to enlarge it. If this proviso is construed as a limitation, its effect would be to take from the general provision some subject which, by the general words used in the provision which precedes the proviso, would be included in the general provision, but in no event could it be held to import into the general provision a subject which was not there before. As the Illinois & Michigan Canal was not included in the general provision preventing the pledging of the credit of the state, or the appropriation of funds from the state treasury, in aid of railroads or canals, the same was not imported therein by the proviso, and therefore the appropriation covered by the act of the Legislature now in question is not prohibited by said constitutional provision, when considered separately or in connection with the proviso. It also appears from the debates in the constitutional convention, when the provision now claimed to inhibit the passage of the act making the appropriation in question was under consideration, that certain members of the convention were strongly in favor of the extension and enlargement of the Illinois & Michigan Canal westward to the Mississippi river, and it would seem, from the debate which then ensued, that the office of the proviso above set out was, in case the canal should be extended to the Mississippi river—which also involved its enlargement to a ship canal—to prevent the credit of the state and the moneys in the state treasury being used to pay for, or the state becoming liable in any manner for, the cost of such extension or enlargement, except in so far as the surplus earnings of the canal would pay for such extension and enlargement.

As no other express provision of the Constitution has been pointed out which it is claimed prevents the appropriation of moneys from the state treasury for the operation and maintenance of the Illinois & Michigan Canal, and as the provision pointed out does not in express terms or by implication even remotely refer to the expenses of operating or maintaining the canal, we take it there is no provision of the Constitution which prohibits such appropriation, and such was the view of the gentlemen who drafted the constitutional provision which has been relied upon to defeat said appropriation. While his view is not controlling, he was admittedly a profound lawyer. At the time the provision was being voted upon, he said "that this [the constitutional provision above quoted in full] does not touch the power of the General Assembly to keep the canal in repair," and in case of doubt we think the view as there expressed entitled to great weight, and that, after that view has been accepted and acted upon for more than 30 years by the executive and legislative departments of the state, it should not be set aside. In considering the constitutionality of a statute, it is the duty of the court to hold it constitutional unless the court can say it is clearly in conflict with the Constitution, and if the court is in doubt and two views are presented, one of which would sustain and the other overthrow the law, the court should adopt the one favorable to the law, and hold it constitutional.

(208 Ill. 415)

CITY OF ALEDO v. HONEYMAN.*

(Supreme Court of Illinois. Feb. 17, 1904.)

MUNICIPAL CORPORATIONS — DEFECTIVE SIDEWALKS—INJURIES—EXPERTS—HYPOTHETICAL QUESTIONS—OBJECTIONS—SUFFICIENCY—INSTRUCTIONS—REQUESTS TO CHARGE—APPEAL—INTERMEDIATE COURTS—QUESTIONS OF FACT—REVIEW—HARMLESS ERROR.

1. Where a judgment in favor of plaintiff in an action for injuries on a defective city sidewalk was affirmed by the Appellate Court, such affirmance conclusively settled a contention that the evidence did not show an injury to plaintiff's spine.

2. An objection to a hypothetical question on the ground that the facts assumed were not in evidence, but which failed to point out the facts claimed not to have been proved, was insufficient.

3. A party seeking the opinion of an expert, within reasonable limits, may put his hypothetical case as he claims it has been proven; leaving the opposite party, on cross-examination, to so change the question as to cover the facts as contended by him.

4. Where, in an action for injuries on a defective sidewalk, defendant asked instructions which required it to maintain a "sound and sufficient walk," it was not prejudiced by another instruction requiring the maintenance of sidewalks in a "good" and reasonably safe condition.

5. An instruction that the burden of proof was on the plaintiff, and that it was for her to prove her case by a preponderance of the evidence, "yet the degree of preponderance is not material," was not prejudicial by reason of the use of the words quoted.

6. Where, in an action for injuries on a city sidewalk, plaintiff had never been over the walk before, and did not know its condition, a requested instruction that the law requires a person who knows that a sidewalk is unsafe and dangerous to exercise care and diligence in going over the same was properly refused.

7. Requests to charge covered by the instructions given are properly refused.

Appeal from Appellate Court, Second District.

Action by Elizabeth A. Honeyman against the city of Aledo. From a judgment in favor of plaintiff, affirmed by the Appellate Court (108 Ill. App. 536), defendant appeals. Affirmed.

*Rehearing denied April 7, 1904.

¶ 3. See Evidence, vol. 20, Cent. Dig. § 2371.

McArthur & Cooke and Geo. W. Werts, Jr., City Atty., for appellant. Wood & Elmer and Bassett & Bassett, for appellee.

WILKIN, J. This is an action on the case brought by appellee to recover for personal injuries alleged to have been sustained by her upon a defective sidewalk of defendant. On August 3, 1901, she and her husband were passing along a wooden sidewalk on Walnut street, in said city. The husband stepped upon one end of a loose board in the walk, and the other end flew up, and tripped her, throwing her to the ground, and injuring her spine and one of her fingers. Upon a trial in the circuit court, judgment was rendered against the defendant for the sum of $1,200, which has been affirmed by the Appellate Court for the Second District.

It is insisted by appellant that the evidence does not show that the spine of appellant was injured, and considerable space in the brief and argument has been taken up in arguing that question. The judgment of the Appellate Court conclusively settled that and all other controverted questions of fact in favor of the plaintiff below and against the defendant.

Appellant claims that the trial court erred in refusing to sustain an objection made by its counsel to a hypothetical question put to one of appellee's witnesses. The objection made to the question was and is that the facts assumed by it were not in evidence, but such facts, claimed not to be in evidence, are nowhere specifically pointed out. In order to take advantage of the exception upon appeal to the court's ruling on the objection, counsel should have called the attention of the trial court to the particular evidence assumed in the question which was wanting. The rule applicable to hypothetical questions is that the party seeking the opinion of an expert may, within reasonable limits, put his hypothetical case as he claims it has been proven, and take the opinion of the witness thereon; leaving the jury to determine whether the case, as put, is the one proven. Grand Lodge I. O. M. A. v. Wieting, 168 Ill. 408, 48 N. E. 59, 61 Am. St. Rep. 123. In this case appellee had a right to ask the question, assuming only the elements as she claimed they appeared in the evidence; and, if the question so put did not fully and fairly cover all the points, then, upon cross-examination, counsel for appellant had a right to change the question so as to cover the facts which they contended were applicable to the case, and which reasonably appeared from the evidence; and, having failed to pursue that practice, they cannot now complain.

Objection is made to the first instruction given by the court on behalf of appellee. This instruction is directed to the duty of the defendant to keep its sidewalks in a reasonably safe condition, and says, in substance, that the defendant is bound to use reasonable care and caution to keep and maintain its sidewalks in good and reasonably safe condition. The objection is made to the use of the word "good." The duty of a city in maintaining its sidewalks has been frequently considered by this court, and the rule of law in that regard is well settled. This instruction would have been more accurate if the word "good" had been left out, but we do not think appellant was injured by its being inserted, especially as, in the seventh of its own instructions asked and given, the words "sound and sufficient" are used, which, in their connection, have the same import as the word "good" in the plaintiff's first instruction. Several instructions were given on behalf of each party which correctly defined the duty of the city in the care and maintenance of its sidewalks. The most that could be claimed would be that the instruction objected to was misleading, but, if it was subject to that objection, the defect was removed by those which correctly stated the law upon the same subject.

Appellant also objects to the fourth instruction given on behalf of appellee. This instruction lays down the rule that the burden of proof is upon plaintiff, and it is for her to prove her case by a preponderance of the evidence, yet the degree of preponderance is not material. The objection is made to the last sentence, "the degree of preponderance is not material." This instruction would also have been more correct without the words objected to, as the preceding words sufficiently state the rule sought to be announced, but we are unable to discover wherein the defendant was prejudiced by the inaccuracy.

The trial court refused to give the thirteenth and nineteenth instructions offered by appellant. These instructions are, in substance, that the law requires a person who knows that a sidewalk is in an unsafe or dangerous condition to exercise care and diligence in going over or upon such sidewalk, and that the law will not permit a person who knowingly and negligently goes upon such unsafe or dangerous sidewalk to recover damages sustained thereby. It may be conceded that these instructions lay down substantially correct propositions of law, but they were not applicable to the facts of the case, and were properly refused for that reason. The evidence shows that the appellee resided in New Boston, Mercer county, and that her injury occurred in the city of Aledo, in that same county, and that the appellee had never been upon or over the sidewalk in question before, did not know of its condition, and therefore was not charged with the care and diligence imposed by those instructions.

Complaint is also made of the refusal of the trial court to give the fourteenth and fifteenth instructions offered by appellant. These instructions state the law with reference to the notice necessary to appellant, and also the rule in case the jury should find said injury was the result of a mere accident. Both instructions are reasonably correct as statements of propositions of law, but the fifth, eighth, and eleventh given on behalf of appellant fully cover the same ground, and there was therefore no reversible error in the refusal of the fourteenth and fifteenth.

Our examination and consideration of all the instructions given lead to the conclusion that the jury was fully and fairly instructed, and that there was no substantial error in the refusal of those rejected.

We find no reversible error in the case, and the judgments of the circuit and appellate courts will therefore be affirmed. Judgment affirmed.

SCOTT, J., took no part in the decision of this case.

(208 Ill. 391)

DAUM v. COOPER.*

(Supreme Court of Illinois. Feb. 17, 1904.)

WATER COURSES — ALTERATION — DRAINAGE DITCHES—CONSTRUCTION—INJUNCTION—DAMAGE.

1. A landowner is entitled to change the course of a natural stream within the limits of his own land, provided that in so doing he does not cast on the land of an adjoining proprietor water which would not in the course of nature flow thereon, and he restores the stream to its original channel before such adjoining proprietor's land is reached.

2. After the institution of proceedings by drainage commissioners for the establishment of a drainage ditch to drain lands belonging to plaintiff and defendant, among others, plaintiff, in consideration of the abandonment of a proposed ditch, agreed that a ditch should be constructed eastwardly to the south end of a ditch then existing along the boundary of plaintiff's land, which he agreed to clean out and keep in good condition to conduct the water which came into it. Thereafter defendant, an adjoining landowner, in proceedings against the highway commissioners, authorized them to close a ditch which drained certain water courses over his land from a highway, whereupon defendant determined to cut a ditch on his own land, to lead from such water courses to, and connect with, the ditch which plaintiff had agreed to maintain. There was no proof that the construction of such ditch would turn more water into plaintiff's ditch than had previously been carried thereby, or that plaintiff would in any manner be injured. *Held*, that plaintiff was not entitled to enjoin the construction of the proposed ditch.

Appeal from Circuit Court, Lee County; O. E. Heard, Judge.

Bill by John Daum against Ira Cooper. From a decree dismissing the bill, plaintiff appeals. Affirmed.

Geo. D. O'Brien and Henry S. Dixon, for appellant. D. W. Baxter, for appellee.

BOGGS, J. This was a bill in chancery filed by the appellant, praying that appellee be enjoined from cutting a ditch in his (appellee's) farm, and causing water to flow out of its natural course to and upon the lands

*Rehearing denied April 12, 1904.

of appellant. The cause was heard upon bill, answer, replication, and proofs produced in open court, and a decree was entered dismissing the bill for want of equity, from which decree this appeal has been perfected.

A motion submitted by the appellee to dismiss the appeal for want of jurisdiction was reserved to the hearing, and will be overruled for reasons that will be made apparent in the course of the opinion.

The appellant and the appellee are the owners of adjoining farm lands in the town of Alto, in Lee county. The lands are all situated in section 29, town 39 north, range 2 east. The appellant is the owner of the west half of the southeast and the east half of the southwest quarter of said section, and the appellee's lands are described as the east half of the northwest and the northeast quarter of the said section. Appellee's dwelling is located on the northeast corner of the west half of the northeast quarter, which tract, together with the 80-acre tract immediately west of it, will be designated hereafter as the appellee's home place. A public highway runs east of this home tract of appellee's land, dividing it from the east half of the northeast quarter, which latter tract will be, for convenience, hereafter called the "Rody Place." This highway runs south along the east side of the lands of the appellant. There is a highway along the north side of appellee's lands. The following plat will aid to a clearer understanding of the location of these lands, and of what will hereafter be said in this opinion as to ditches and water courses:

Two small water courses ran from the Rody place across the highway westwardly into appellee's home tract, and another water course entered his home tract near the center thereof, on the north side. The natural flow of the water from all of these water courses was to the west and southwest. It seems from the testimony that the water did not flow in any well-defined channels in the westerly or southwesterly portion of appellee's home place, but that the land there was low and flat, and the water found its way in slight depressions to the west and southwest. The appellee contended, and the testimony in his behalf tended to show, that a portion of this water flowed from his land onto a portion of the northwestern corner of the lands of the appellant; but the testimony in behalf of the appellant tended to show that the water would, in a state of nature, flow across appellee's west line of his home place at points from 20 to 60 rods north of the northwest corner of the lands now owned by the appellant. The northwest portion of appellant's land and the southwest portion of appellee's land were flat and low and wet, and the truth of either contention could not be well declared from the proof.

The lands belonging to the appellant formerly belonged to one Jeptha Mitten. In the year 1871 the appellee and the said Jeptha Mitten, by mutual consent and agreement, constructed a line of ditches beginning on the west line of appellee's home place, about 100 rods north of his southwest corner, and extending thence south along the west line

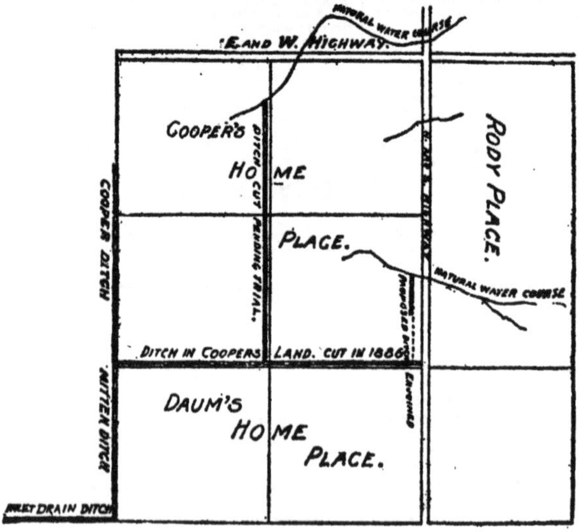

of the appellee's home place to the northwest corner of Mitten's land (now appellant's tract); thence south along the west line of Mitten's land a distance of 80 rods. Appellant became the owner of the Mitten land in 1875.

In 1886 the appellee claimed that the highway commissioners, in grading and improving the highways near the northeast corner of his home place, had obstructed the natural flow of the water coming from the east and north, and caused the same to flood his dooryard and premises about his house in the northeast corner of the home tract. This complaint on the part of the appellee resulted in an agreement with the commissioners of highways, made in 1886, under which the appellee was permitted to construct, and did then construct, at his own expense, a ditch in the west "bench" of the highway, which ran north and south, beginning in the west bench of the said highway, at the northeast corner of his home place, and extending from thence south to within about four feet of the south line of his land. This ditch intercepted the waters which would otherwise flow on the northeasterly portions of his home place because of the construction of the grade of the highway, and also the waters which would otherwise flow on the easterly part of his home place from the two water courses coming from the Rody place, and would conduct all such water down the ditch to the south end thereof, near the southeast corner of his home place. The appellee at the same time caused a ditch to be dug on his own land in the south part of his home place, from the south end of this ditch on the west side of the highway, west to his own ditch near the southwest corner of his home place. These ditches were constructed in 1886, and conducted the water which otherwise would have come upon the home place upon the northeast corner thereof, and from the Rody place, south in the ditch in the highway to the ditch leading west on his own land; thence in the latter ditch west to the appellee's ditch on the west line of his home place, and within a few feet of the north end of the Mitten ditch, into which latter ditch the water would then be conveyed by the ditch on the west line of appellee's land.

In 1888 the Inlet Swamp drainage district was organized, and a number of ditches were dug for the purpose of draining the lands west and south of that of these litigants. The plans of the drainage district contemplated the construction of a ditch from the north main ditch of the drainage district almost due northwest to the southwest corner of appellee's home farm, which was also the northwest corner of Daum's farm, and also the junction of the Cooper and Mitten ditches, and a few feet south of the western outlet of the ditch constructed by the appellee from the north and south highway in the south part of his home place to the southwest corner thereof, as before described. The appellant interceded with the commissioners of the drainage district, and induced them to abandon the proposed ditch to the southwest corner of appellee's land, and arranged with them to cut the ditch eastwardly to the south end of the Mitten ditch; and, to secure this action on the part of the commissioners, the appellant agreed with them that he would clean out the Mitten ditch, and keep it in good condition to conduct the water which came into it. After the construction of the Inlet drainage district ditch in the year 1888 until the year 1903 all of the water from appellee's farm came, by means of the ditch on the west side of his home place and the ditch from the highway on the south side of his place, into the Mitten ditch, and from thence to the ditch of the drainage district. The position of appellee is that he has the perpetual right to discharge the water from his ditch into the Mitten ditch on appellant's land, and to have the same flow therein, and it is for this reason we hold a freehold is involved.

In the year 1903, as the result of litigation between the commissioners of highways (the appellant being a member of the board) and the appellee, the commissioners, on payment of $250 to appellee, were authorized to close appellee's ditch in the west bench of the north and south highway, and to enter upon his lands where the two water courses which came through the Rody place entered his home lands, and open a way from the culverts for the water courses to enter on his land, and also to carry the water which had been diverted onto appellee's home place at his yard, in ditches along the north side of the east and west highway to a culvert, and thence through the culvert into and upon the appellee's land about 60 rods west of his house, and to there open a way in appellee's land a distance of 12 feet from the highway, in which to receive the water coming from the waterway under the culvert in the north and south highway, in order the same might flow onto appellee's land. The commissioners of highways constructed a culvert in the east and west highway at the proper point, made a ditch along the north side of that road, and opened a way in appellee's land for the water to be conveyed to and upon it from the highway. The commissioners also made two culverts where water courses which came from the Rody place crossed the highway running north and south, and in appellee's field, west of the more southerly of the culverts, the commissioners opened a way for the passage of the water into appellee's field, where it had previously gone in a state of nature. The appellee then determined to cut a ditch in his own land, to lead from the natural water course which came from the Rody place through the more southerly culvert in the north and south highway, south, to the ditch before mentioned, in the south part of his own land, which led to the west, and connected with the Mitten ditch at the southwest corner of appellee's land, and near the northwest corner of the land of the appellant, and to construct a dam or obstruction on his own land in the bed of the natural water course from the Rody place through the culvert in the north and south highway for the purpose of turning the water coming in such watercourse south into the proposed new ditch, whence it would reach the ditch in his land near the south line thereof, and from thence be conducted to the west into the Mitten ditch. The appellee, in pursuance of such plan, began to cut the ditch on his own land. The appellant thereupon filed this bill in chancery, praying for a writ of injunction restraining the appellee from completing the ditch, and from building any dam or barrier that would obstruct the natural flow of the water on his (appellee's) land, or divert the flow thereof from its natural course, and from in any manner interfering with the natural water courses extending across the lands of the appellee west of the north and south highway so as to cause any water to flow on the lands of the appellant.

We think the chancellor correctly ordered the bill to be dismissed. A proprietor of land may change the course of a natural water course within the limits of his own land, if he restores it to the original channel before the lands of another are reached, provided, in changing the course of the stream, he does not cast upon the lands of an adjoining proprietor water which would not in a course of nature flow upon such adjoining premises. 28 Am. & Eng. Ency. of Law (1st Ed.) p. 982.

It appeared from the testimony of a number of witnesses who testified in behalf of the appellee that the manner in which the appellee proposed to dig the ditch, and control the flow of the water coming upon his own land, was necessary to the proper tillage of his lands, and we find nothing in the evidence to controvert this position. There is no proof in the record that appellant has ever suffered any appreciable damage from water coming from appellee's ditches, though the only ditch from which waters could come to the injury of the appellant, viz., that running east and west in appellee's land from the southeast corner at the highway to the Mitten ditch, at or near the southwest corner, had been there more than 17 years before the bill was filed. The ditch which it was sought to enjoin appellee from constructing would not, it is clear, bring as great a quantity of water into this east and west ditch as had been conducted to it by the ditch along the west side of the highway during that period of 17 years, for during that time the ditch along the highway extended at least 100 rods further north than did the ditch which appellee was engaged in digging when enjoined, and consequently gathered and conveyed more water than would the proposed new ditch in appellee's field.

It was proven that since the issuance of the injunction the appellee had cut a ditch from the opening made by the commissioners of highways from the culvert in the highway at the north side of the home farm of the appellee to the ditch running east and west in the south part of his farm, from the highway to the Mitten ditch. It may be that this latter constructed ditch would bring some more water into the east and west ditch than had previously flowed therein, but the additional quantity, if any, would only be such as would fall upon his lands, for the ditch which existed along the highway along the east side of appellee's home place intercepted and conveyed the water from all the water courses that flowed onto the home place. It was also shown that the appellee had constructed a strong embankment on his land on the south bank of the east and west ditch, where this new north and south ditch emptied therein, and no reasonable grounds for fear of an overflow or the breaking of the bank of the ditch were disclosed by the proof.

There is no proof in the record that the appellant has ever suffered any appreciable damages from the efforts of the appellee to drain his lands. It was proven that at the northwest corner of the appellant's land, near the point where the appellee's east and west ditch intersects the ditch running north and south on the west side of his home place, the water had washed the banks of the ditch to such an extent as to loosen and cause to fall some of the posts of appellant's fence, and that appellant's cattle at one time escaped through the opening thus made; but we think it is well established by the proof that the appellant failed to comply with his contract to keep the Mitten ditch cleaned out and open, and that the injury to the bank at the northwest corner of his place was attributable to the fact that obstructions in the Mitten ditch caused the water to collect and stand in the ditch at appellant's northwest corner, and to soak and loosen the soil, and caused it to fall into the ditch, or "cave in," and that this neglect of the appellant caused the injury to his fence.

The appellant produced testimony to the effect that the water had begun to cut or wash away the bank of appellee's ditch on his land near the highway at the southeast corner of his home place, and also at another point still further west in the same ditch. The wash or break in the bank at the east end of this ditch near the highway was described as a hole in the bank 18 inches or 2 feet in width, but it was not clear that the wash or break had reached appellant's land. There was testimony tending to show this hole was within the limits of the highway, and, if so, it would be east of the terminus of the ditch that the appellant sought to have the appellee enjoined from cutting, and hence no further injury could occur from it. The appellee testified that the only hole he knew of was outside of his fence, and that it had not been caused by the action of the water, but had been cut by the appellant. The testimony as to the washing of the bank at the point further west on the ditch was that the dirt had been soaked or washed away sufficiently to expose the roots of the hedge fence. There was no proof that any water had passed from the ditch at either of the points into or upon the lands of the appellant. The opinion was expressed by witnesses for the appellant that, if the water continued to flow in the ditch, the banks, if not protected, would eventually be washed away, and that the water might then reach and damage the lands and crops of the appellant; but on cross-examination these witnesses conceded that if reasonable and proper care was taken to keep the ditches clean, and the banks and embankments repaired, the danger of injury to the appellant could be averted. The fact that the water had passed through this ditch for the period of more than 17 years without appreciable injury to the walls of the ditch or the lands of the appellant, no doubt, had great weight to convince the court there was little reason to apprehend injurious results in the future. The appellee testified that he intended to give careful attention to the banks and embankments of his ditches, and, if necessary, to support and repair any breaks that might be developed, with plank or stone, and to keep the ditches clean and open to the full extent thereof. The chancellor, it seems, was fully justified in concluding there was no reasonable ground for the apprehensions of the appellant that he would suffer any immediate injury. The apprehensions of injury and damage to lands in the future were merely conjectural, and not at all probable. The chancellor was fully justified in concluding there was no well-grounded apprehension of immediate injury or damage. Actual experience of many years had demonstrated that there was no reasonable ground to fear that the appellant would be irreparably damaged, either immediately or in the future. Under circumstances similar in all respects, we have uniformly held that the extraordinary restraining power of a court of equity should not be exercised. Thornton v. Roll, 118 Ill. 350, 8 N. E. 145; Wilson v. Dondurant, 142 Ill. 645, 32 N. E. 498.

The decree will be affirmed. Decree affirmed.

(208 Ill. 426)

BARNETT & RECORD CO. v. SCHLAPKA.*

(Supreme Court of Illinois. Feb. 17, 1904.)

INJURY TO EMPLOYÉ—SAFE PLACE TO WORK—DAMAGES—EVIDENCE—INSTRUCTIONS.

1. Evidence in an action by an employé for personal injuries arising from failure to provide a safe place to work examined, and *held* sufficient to justify the court in refusing a peremptory instruction for defendant.

2. The exception to the general rule as to the duty of the master to use ordinary care to provide a reasonably safe place to work, made where the character of the work is such that the relative safety of employés necessarily varies from time to time as the work progresses, and the work being done at times renders the place dangerous, applies only where the work being done necessarily renders the place dangerous, and not to a case where the danger could have been entirely obviated at a slight expense.

3. Where an employé, by command of his foreman, placed himself in a position of danger, and was injured, his knowledge of the danger would not defeat his right to recover, if, in obeying, he acted with ordinary care, under the circumstances.

4. A few minutes after an employé had finished digging in a tunnel, where he was sent to work by his foreman, he returned with a fellow employé who had requested him to assist in carrying a board; and, while doing so, the foreman crawled under the board as it was being carried, to get out of the way, and neither said anything to advise him of changed conditions, or of an order to keep out, to avoid danger. *Held*, that this amounted to an affirmance or repetition of the order to go into the tunnel previously given by the foreman, and, in an action for the resulting injury, justified an instruction leading the jury to conclude that they might find that he was in the tunnel in consequence of such order.

5. In an action for injury to an employé, an instruction as to the measure of damages, authorizing consideration of the future effect of the injury on plaintiff's ability "to work in his ordinary and former line of labor," correctly stated the law, and did not exclude consideration of what he might be able to earn in other lines of employment.

6. An instruction, in an action for injury to an employé, advising the jury as to the duty owing plaintiff as to his safety, was properly directed to the duty to him in particular, without regard to the safety of defendant's servants in general.

7. A servant has the right to presume that the master has used ordinary care to provide him a place reasonably safe in which to work, and need not make an examination to determine whether the place is safe; the danger not being apparent on ordinary observation.

8. In an action for injury to an employé, an instruction which sought to inform the jury that plaintiff could not recover if it were the result of an accident, without fault of either party, was properly modified by inserting a definition of the word "accident."

Appeal from Appellate Court, Second District.

Action by Casper Schlapka against the Barnett & Record Company. A judgment for plaintiff was affirmed by the Appellate Court (110 Ill. App. 672), and defendant appeals. Affirmed.

This suit was an action on the case brought by appellee against appellant in the circuit court of Peoria county, where, at the September term, 1902, a trial was had before a jury, and a verdict rendered in favor of appellee for $3,760. Motions for a new trial and in arrest of judgment having been made and overruled, judgment was entered on the verdict, and appellant appealed to the Appellate Court for the Second District. That

*Rehearing denied April 12, 1904.

¶ 7. See Master and Servant, vol. 34, Cent. Dig. §§ 714, 717.

court affirmed the judgment of the circuit court, and the case is now brought to this court by appeal.

The declaration consisted of two counts; the first charging that the appellant carelessly and negligently shored, propped, and braced the sides, walls, and banks of a certain ditch or tunnel which it was constructing, in a manner which was insecure, unsafe, and dangerous, and that plaintiff, not having knowledge of these defects, and being assured by defendant that said ditch or tunnel was a safe place in which to work, by the order of defendant's foreman commenced work therein, and while so engaged in his work the side walls and banks of the ditch or tunnel broke, caved in, and fell upon him, whereby he was injured. The second count differed from the first, in that it charged that defendant carelessly and negligently partially excavated and constructed the ditch or tunnel before plaintiff was employed by defendant, and that plaintiff had no knowledge that the excavating had been carelessly and negligently done theretofore, etc. To the declaration, defendant pleaded the general issue.

Appellant is a construction company, and during the summer of 1901 was engaged in erecting an annex to the Iowa Elevator, near the city of Peoria, and in constructing a ditch (referred to as a tunnel) connecting these two buildings, through which grain could be taken from one building to the other. This tunnel was 35 feet long, an average of 8 feet deep, and 12 feet wide at the bottom. Along both sides of the bottom of the tunnel, trenches about 3 feet wide and 18 inches deep were being dug, boards placed on each side of the trenches, and boxes constructed therein, into which concrete was placed to form the foundation or base for the walls of the tunnel. The sides of the tunnel did not rise perpendicularly, but sloped, so that the tunnnel was about 3 feet wider at the top than at the bottom. The tunnel was not covered. It was nothing more than a wide, open ditch. There was nothing whatever over it, except two railroad tracks which crossed it, and a shed, which the company's carpenter, on behalf of appellant, testified covered part of it; but at what part of the tunnel this shed was located, the evidence does not disclose. No other witness in the case testified in regard to the shed. The rails for the railroad tracks were fastened to ties which rested on I beams, and these beams were temporarily supported by upright timbers resting in mudsills at the bottom of the tunnel.

On August 6, 1901, appellee was employed by appellant to work for it. He commenced work in the afternoon of that day, helping dig a small outside ditch. The remainder of the afternoon he was engaged in removing stone from a box car. On the following morning he was ordered by appellant's foreman to work in one of the trenches in the bottom of the tunnel. He looked at the wall of the tunnel, and inquired of the foreman if it was solid, in response to which the foreman said that it was, and ordered plaintiff to proceed with work in the trench. Plaintiff worked at digging a short time, when, as he says, his services were no longer required there, and he went outside, and was at work on the surface of the ground. About five minutes after leaving this trench, and while he was standing at the mouth of the tunnel, a man carrying a board came up, and asked appellee to take one end of it and help carry it into the ditch. Appellee testified that this man was a stranger to him. Brown, a carpenter in the employ of appellant, testified that he was the man referred to by appellee. They carried the board in, appellee walking in the trench at the side of the tunnel on which the board was to be placed. Brown testified that the board was being taken in to shore the side of the tunnel, which he had observed a few minutes before was cracked and appeared unsafe, while appellee testified that the board was to be used in the trench in making the box for concrete. When appellee reached the place in this trench where he had been at work digging, the side of the tunnel caved in from the top, and a large amount of earth and bricks fell upon him, causing the injuries complained of in this suit.

About three days previous to the injury the side of another tunnel or ditch which appellant was constructing about 25' feet away from this one had caved in. The ground in both of these tunnels was of the same character. At the surface was filled or made ground, which was cohesive. Proceeding downward the soil became looser, and 7 or 8 feet below the surface there was a sandy soil. For a distance of about 16 feet on the side of the tunnel where appellee was injured, appellant had placed boards or timber against the side of the tunnel; but this support stopped about 12 feet from the place where appellee was injured, and at that place there was nothing whatever to keep the side from caving in. At or very near the place where the injury occurred, one of the railroad tracks crossed the tunnel, and for two or three nights previous thereto engines and cars had crossed on this track—a fact known to the master, but not to the servant. The passage of these engines and cars was apt to loosen the soil. A few minutes before the injury, machinery in the Iowa Elevator was started, and appellant's foreman noticed that it caused the earth on one side of the tunnel to vibrate, and noticed a crack in that side extending from the top to the bottom, and ordered the workmen out of the trench on that side of the tunnel.

Appellee swears he received no warning from any one until, carrying the end of the board, he reached the place in the ditch where he was injured, when the foreman, who was standing near by in the tunnel, called to him to go away or get out, but the side immediately caved in, and he had no time to get out of the trench before the earth fell on him. He testified that he had had no previous experience in making such excavations, or working about them.

At the close of plaintiff's evidence, and again at the close of all the evidence in the case, appellant submitted and requested the court to give to the jury an instruction in writing telling them to find the defendant not guilty, which the court refused to do. The alleged errors relied upon by appellant for a reversal of the cause by this court are the action of the court in refusing the peremptory instruction, the giving of appellee's first and fourth instructions, and modifying the fourth, eighth, ninth, and eleventh instructions offered by appellant.

Stevens, Horton & Abbott, for appellant. Harry S. Miller (Elmer J. Slough, of counsel), for appellee.

SCOTT, J. (after stating the facts). The evidence in this case, the substance of which is recited in the foregoing statement of facts, tends to prove that the master did not exercise ordinary care to provide a reasonably safe place for the servant to work in; that the master had knowledge of the danger; that the servant did not know of the danger, and had not equal means of knowing with the master. The peremptory instruction was therefore properly refused. Lake Erie & Western Railroad Co. v. Wilson, 189 Ill. 89, 59 N. E. 573; Momence Stone Co. v. Turrell, 205 Ill. 515, 68 N. E. 1078; Western Stone Co. v. Muscial, 196 Ill. 382, 63 N. E. 664, 89 Am. St. Rep. 325.

The danger was latent in its character, and arose, in great measure, from the formation of the soil through which the tunnel was excavated. Appellant had notice of this danger from the fact that, a few days before, a similar accident had occurred in another tunnel, through the same sort of soil, a short distance from this one. Appellee inquired, before going into the excavation, whether there was danger of the character which actually existed, and the reply of appellant's superintendent was substantially an assurance that there was none. He then went into the ditch and worked in one of the trenches along the side a short time, when, as he says, there were more men there than were needed, and he went outside to shovel away the earth that was thrown out on the side of the tunnel. Shortly after this it was discovered by the superintendent that the bank on one side was breaking away, and apt to fall in immediately. The men then remaining in the trench on that side were ordered out of the trench, but not out of the tunnel, on this account. Appellee swears that he heard no such order, and it is earnestly insisted that when he went back after this, helping a carpenter to carry a board in, he assumed the risk of injury from the accident which thereafter occurred. The answer to this is that the evidence on his part tends to show that he had not been advised of the impending danger. It does not appear that he had, or ought to have had, knowledge of any change in conditions which existed at the time he had been assured by the master's representative that there was no danger of the kind which in fact actually existed. He went into the tunnel carrying one end of the board in consequence of a request made by Brown, the carpenter. The evidence justifies the conclusion that the superintendent was present, heard this request, and saw appellee complying therewith. When they got into the tunnel with the board, plaintiff walked in the trench on the side where the bank caved in. As he and the carpenter carried the board along the tunnel, appellant's foreman crawled under it to get out of their way. Neither the superintendent nor the foreman said anything to him at that time in regard to the existence of the danger, and he swears that the board was to be used in making the box in the trench, while those who testify for appellant swear that it was to be used in shoring the bank where the break was anticipated.

Appellant cites Simmons v. Chicago & Tomah Railroad Co., 110 Ill. 340, and other similar cases, in support of the doctrine that the general rule that it is the duty of the master to use ordinary care to provide a reasonably safe place in which the servant may do his work is not applicable where the character of the work is such that the relative safety of persons there employed necessarily varies from time to time as the work progresses, and the work being done at times renders the place dangerous. It will be found, on examination, that these cases apply only where the work being done necessarily renders the place dangerous, as in mining coal, blasting stone, wrecking buildings, and other matters of a like nature. In this case the banks of the tunnel could have been given greater slope at a slight increase of the expense, and this would have entirely obviated the danger, or the sides could have been shored throughout the entire length, as they were throughout a portion of their length. This last expedient was said by witnesses for defendant below to be impracticable—a statement which the jury may possibly have discredited, as defendant also sought to show that it attempted to shore the side of the tunnel where this break occurred as soon as it was discovered that the earth had begun to give way.

Objection is made because the first instruction given on the part of appellee advised the jury that, if plaintiff had some knowledge of the attendant danger, still that if, in obedience to the command of the foreman, who had knowledge of the danger of obeying the command, the plaintiff placed himself in a position of danger, such knowledge as the plaintiff had would not defeat his right of recovery, if, in obeying the command, he acted with a degree of care and prudence and diligence that an ordinarily prudent man would have used under the circumstances. We think this instruction in accordance with the view expressed in Western Stone Co. v. Muscial, supra, where it is said (page 386, 196 Ill., page 66, 63 N. E., 89 Am. St. Rep. 325): "Even had appellee had some knowledge of the defect in the bank, yet the order of the master to proceed with the dangerous work would relieve him of the assumption of the risk, unless the danger was so manifest that a person of ordinary prudence would not have incurred it." It is said, however, that, if the instruction states a correct proposition of law, it was improperly given in this case, because it would lead the jury to conclude that they might find that appellee was in the tunnel at the time of the accident in consequence of the order given him by the foreman to go there in the morning, while appellant's position is that he was there, when he received the injury, as a mere volunteer, or at the request of the carpenter, who seems to have been a fellow servant. In view of the fact that the evidence tends to show that the superintendent was present and heard the carpenter request appellee to return to the ditch, and saw appellee complying with the request, and that the foreman crawled under the board as it was being carried into the trench, to get out of the way, and neither said anything to advise appellee of the changed conditions, or of the order that had been given to keep out of the trench in which plaintiff walked with the board, we think the conclusion not unwarranted that the conduct of the superintendent and the foreman at that time amounted to an affirmance or repetition of the order given by the foreman earlier in the day. The objection to the instruction is not well taken.

The fourth instruction given on behalf of the plaintiff was in reference to the measure of damages, and authorized the jury to take into consideration the effect, if any, of the injury in the future upon the plaintiff's ability "to work in his ordinary and former line of labor." This is said to exclude from the jury the consideration of what plaintiff might be able to earn in other lines of employment. The instruction had no such effect. It merely authorized the jury to consider the plaintiff's decreased ability, if any, to engage in his former occupations. It left them free to consider his earning capacity in other lines of employment. An instruction identical with this one in this respect was approved in Illinois Central Railroad Co. v. Read, 37 Ill. 484, 87 Am. Dec. 260, and has been ever since treated by this court as a correct statement of the law.

The court modified the defendant's fourth and eighth instructions, so that, as given, they advised the jury that if the defendant's "conduct and orders (having due regard to the safety of plaintiff) were such as a reasonably prudent person, having a like duty to perform as the defendant, would have done or given under similar circumstances, then the defendant was not negligent." The modification consisted in the insertion by the court of the words in parentheses, and the argument is that the instructions, as given, called special attention to the duty which the defendant owed to the plaintiff, which is said to have been no greater than its duty to its other servants; and the trend of the argument seems to be that, if the instruction had advised the jury that the defendant must have due regard to the safety of its servants, it would have been unobjectionable. We think in that form it would have been the subject of much more serious objection. The only duty in that respect for the consideration of the jury in this case was the duty owing to the plaintiff. The jury were being advised that the defendant was free from liability for an injury resulting from such conduct and orders as might be expected of a reasonably prudent person, and in that connection it was not improper to call their attention to the obligation resting upon the defendant in regard to considering the safety of the plaintiff. That is one of the things which a reasonably prudent person would consider under similar circumstances.

By the ninth instruction defendant asked to have the jury instructed that if plaintiff "had equal means and capacity" with the foreman of knowing the condition of the side of the tunnel, and the danger therefrom, and the foreman, before the plaintiff commenced work, expressed an opinion that the side of the tunnel was safe, the plaintiff would have no right to rely upon such opinion. The court's modification consisted in the insertion of the words "and capacity." The instruction, both as requested and as modified, is misleading. It should not have been given in either form, because the jury were apt to conclude therefrom that the servant should have made an examination to determine whether the place was safe. He was not required by the law to make an investigation for the purpose of learning the nature of the soil, and the danger, if any, resulting therefrom. He could not close his eyes to open and obvious dangers, but he had a right to presume that the master had performed his duty by using ordinary care to provide him a place reasonably safe in which to work, and it was not his duty to make an examination for the purpose of discovering whether there were latent or hidden dangers. Ross v. Shanley, 185 Ill. 390, 56 N. E. 1105; Western Stone Co. v. Muscial, supra. What the rights of the respective parties would be if the danger was one that was apparent upon ordinary observation, or where the danger was actually discovered by the servant, this instruction does not attempt to advise the jury. The error in giving this instruction was one that favored appellant. It cannot complain.

By defendant's eleventh instruction, it is sought to have the jury informed that the plaintiff could not recover if the injury was the result of an accident, without the fault of either plaintiff or defendant. The court modified the instruction by inserting a definition of the word "accident," which was not improper.

The judgment of the Appellate Court will be affirmed. Judgment affirmed.

(208 Ill. 364)

STORRS et al. v. CITY OF CHICAGO.*

(Supreme Court of Illinois. Feb. 17, 1904.)

MUNICIPAL CORPORATION — LOCAL IMPROVEMENTS—SPECIAL ASSESSMENT—SUPERINTENDENT OF SPECIAL ASSESSMENTS—DOUBLE IMPROVEMENTS—DESCRIPTION—EXEMPTIONS.

1. Though one who made an assessment for a local improvement was appointed for the purpose by the court in accordance with Hurd's Rev. St. 1899, p. 370, c. 24, § 38, yet where he signed the assessment roll as superintendent of special assessments, he acted in his official capacity, in compliance with the act of 1901 (Hurd's Rev. St. 1901, p. 385, § 38), providing that on the filing of a petition for local improvements the superintendent of special assessments shall make an assessment of the cost thereof.

2. While in proceedings under Hurd's Rev. St. 1899, p. 362, c. 24, concerning local improvements, an ordinance providing for sidewalks, under a single special assessment, on streets so separate that the sidewalks on one cannot benefit the property on another, is void, yet where there is no evidence of the relative location of the streets, it will be presumed the city council has not abused its discretion in this respect.

3. An ordinance providing that the owner of a lot may construct a sidewalk "in accordance with said ordinance" complies sufficiently with Hurd's Rev. St. 1899, p. 369, c. 24, § 34, giving the owner the right to construct a sidewalk, provided the work shall "in all respects conform to the requirements of such ordinance."

4. That a recommendation and estimate describe only a "cement sidewalk," does not render invalid an ordinance based thereon, providing for a cinder, cement, concrete, torpedo sand, and limestone walk.

5. To support the validity of an assessment, the burden is not on a city to show the cause of exemption from assessment of lots on the line of an improvement.

Appeal from Cook County Court; Frank Harry, Judge.

Proceedings by the city of Chicago against D. W. Storrs and others for confirmation of a special assessment. From a judgment confirming the assessment, defendants appeal. Affirmed.

F. W. Becker, for appellants. Robert Redfield and William M. Pindell (Edgar Bronson Tolman, Corp. Counsel, of counsel), for appellee.

WILKIN, J. Appellants prosecute this appeal to reverse a judgment confirming a special assessment rendered by the county court of Cook county for the construction of a cement sidewalk.

Numerous objections were filed in the court below, all of which were overruled. Those relied upon on this appeal for a reversal are: First, the assessment roll made by John A. May, not in the capacity of superintendent of special assessments, but as appointee of the court, was contrary to section 38 of the act of 1901 (Hurd's Rev. St. 1901, p. 385); second, the improvement is double; third, the ordinance is uncertain as to the depth and quantity of the filling; fourth, the provisions of the ordinance permitting owners to construct said sidewalk in accordance with said ordinance does not conform to section 34 of the improvement act (Hurd's Rev. St. 1899, c. 24, p. 369); fifth, the provisions of the ordinance that the whole cost thereof be paid by special assessment conflicts with section 94 of the improvement act (Hurd's Rev. St. 1899, c. 24, p. 382); sixth, the recommendation and estimate do not describe the improvement mentioned in the ordinance; and, seventh, that certain lots on the line of the improvement were improperly exempt from assessment by the ordinance, the burden being on the city to show the cause of exemption.

Section 38 of the act of 1901 (Hurd's Rev. St. 1901, p. 385), mentioned in the first objection, is as follows: "Upon the filing of such petition, the superintendent of special assessments, in cities where such officer is provided for by this act, otherwise some competent person appointed by the president of the board of local improvements, shall make a true and impartial assessment of the cost of the said improvement upon the petitioning municipality and the property benefited by such improvement." The assessment roll, as shown by the record, was returned by John A. May, and signed by him as "superintendent of special assessments," which is in conformity with the foregoing section. It appears, however, that the court below followed section 38 of the act of 1897 (Hurd's Rev. St. 1899, c. 24, p. 370), which provided that upon the filing of the petition the court should enter an order directing the superintendent of special assessments to make a true and impartial estimate, etc., and appointed John A. May superintendent of special assessments to perform that duty. It is contended that he made the roll as the appointee of the court, and not in his official capacity as superintendent of special assessments, because in his report, certificate, and affidavit he mentions his appointment by the county court of Cook county, etc., and it is said the words "superintendent of special assessments," following his signature, should be treated as merely descriptio personæ. This is too technical a view upon which to ground a reversal of the judgment below. The report, certificate, and affidavit all show that John A. May acted as "superintendent of special assessments of the city of Chicago," and the fact

---

*Rehearing denied April 7, 1904.

¶ 5. See Municipal Corporations, vol. 36, Cent. Dig. § 1174.

that he was appointed by the court did not invalidate his acts. The proper official acted in his official capacity.

The objection that the improvement is double demands more serious consideration. This proceeding is not under the sidewalk act of 1875 (1 Starr. & C. Ann. St. 1896, c. 24, p. 857), but under the statute concerning local improvements, approved June 14, 1897 (Hurd's Rev. St. 1899, c. 24, p. 362), and therefore the recent case of People v. Latham, 203 Ill. 9, 67 N. E. 403, is not authority on this question. The ordinance in the present case provided "that a cement sidewalk six feet in width be and is hereby ordered constructed on a system of streets as follows, to wit: On both sides of Sherman avenue from Railroad avenue to Seventy-Ninth street; both sides of Saginaw avenue from Seventy-Seventh street to Seventy-Eighth street; both sides of Seventy-Seventh street from Colfax avenue to Coles avenue," etc. Counsel for appellants attaches to his argument a diagram, which he claims shows the relative location of the streets upon which the sidewalks were to be built, and argues that the improvements are thereby shown to be distinct and separate. An insuperable obstacle in the way of the argument is that there is no proof whatever in the record upon which to base the assumption of fact upon which it is based. The only testimony introduced upon the hearing, as appears from the bill of exceptions, was that of E. C. Hathaway, a sidewalk inspector in the employ of the city, to the effect that he was acquainted with the location of the proposed improvement, and that the lots mentioned in the ordinance as excepted from its provisions had a cement or stone walk, and that in front of objectors' property was in bad condition, etc.; saying nothing whatever as to the relative location of the streets mentioned in the ordinance. The rule of law is well settled in this state on the question of double improvements. "The limits of the district [formed for a special assessment] rest in the discretion of the legislative power, and the courts will interfere only to correct a clear abuse of the discretion. In theory (and the practice should in all cases of imposing special taxes conform to the theory) the limits of the improvement should be so fixed as that the property to be taxed shall receive some benefit from the proposed improvement. Absolute equality, as already said, is not attainable; but if, in the combination of streets, and the like, they should be so separate and distinct that the making of one could not reasonably be said to benefit property situated upon the other, their combination would be clearly violative of the rule governing in such case." Davis v. City of Litchfield, 145 Ill. 313, 33 N. E. 888, 21 L. R. A. 563; Church v. People, 179 Ill. 205, 53 N. E. 554. "The extent of the improvement, and what shall be included within it, and its nature and character, are within the legislative discretion of the city council. Sidewalks on each side of the street may be included as a single improvement, as in Watson v. City of Chicago, 115 Ill. 78, 3 N. E. 430, and the improvement of different streets may be included in a single scheme of improvement, as in City of Springfield v. Green, 120 Ill. 269, 11 N. E. 261, and Wilbur v. City of Springfield, 123 Ill. 395, 14 N. E. 871. Burroughs on Taxation, § 146; Cooley on Taxation, 450, 451." Davis v. City of Litchfield, supra. The same doctrine is announced in the later decisions of this court. Drexel v. Town of Lake, 127 Ill. 54, 20 N. E. 38; Haley v. City of Alton, 152 Ill. 113, 38 N. E. 750; Palmer v. City of Danville, 154 Ill. 156, 38 N. E. 1067; Payne v. Village of South Springfield, 161 Ill. 285, 44 N. E. 105; Walker v. People, 170 Ill. 410, 48 N. E. 1010; Village of Hinsdale v. Shannon, 182 Ill. 312, 55 N. E. 327. Here the ordinance provided for a system of improvements, the sidewalks on the streets named to be in all respects the same, and, as already stated, there is no evidence in the record from which we can say that the city council abused its discretion in designating the district or system of streets designated, nor is there anything upon which to base a conclusion that the streets sought to be improved are so separate and distinct that the sidewalks upon one cannot reasonably be said to benefit property upon the others. So far as appears from the record, the improvement is single; as much so as was the scheme for the improvement of several streets in City of Springfield v. Green, or Wilbur v. City of Springfield, supra, and subsequent cases following them.

The third objection is substantially the same as one of those urged to a similar ordinance in the case of Gage v. City of Chicago, 203 Ill. 26, 67 N. E. 477, and there held to be without merit. See, also, Gage v. City of Chicago, 196 Ill. 512, 63 N. E. 1031.

The ordinance provides that the owner of any lot shall be allowed 40 days in which to construct said sidewalk, "in accordance with said ordinance," and it is contended, under the fourth objection, that this is not a compliance with section 34 of the statute (Hurd's Rev. St. 1899, c. 24, p. 369), which gives the owner the right to construct a sidewalk, "provided the work so to be done shall in all respects conform to the requirements of such ordinance." The argument is too refined and technical to deserve serious consideration.

We regard the fifth objection also without merit. The ordinance does not, as claimed by counsel, authorize the levy of an assessment to pay the costs and expenses of making and levying the assessment, which section 94 of the act of 1897 (Hurd's Rev. St. 1899, c. 24, p. 382) provides shall be paid by the municipality from its general funds.

The sixth objection is that the improvement set out in the ordinance provides for a cinder, cement, concrete, torpedo sand, and limestone walk, whereas the recommendation and estimate described only a "cement sidewalk." This objection was also held to have been properly overruled in Gage v. City of Chicago, 196 Ill. 512, 63 N. E. 1031.

The seventh and last objection is likewise disposed of adversely to the contention of objectors by the last-named case and what we said in Hyman v. City of Chicago, 188 Ill. 462, 59 N. E. 10.

The county court properly overruled each of the foregoing objections, and its judgment will accordingly be affirmed. Judgment affirmed.

(208 Ill. 387)

CITY OF CHICAGO v. W. D. KERFOOT & CO.*

(Supreme Court of Illinois. Feb. 17, 1904.)

MUNICIPAL CORPORATION—STREET IMPROVEMENT—PUBLIC HEARING—ESTIMATED COST —NECESSITY FOR FURTHER HEARING.

1. Under Hurd's Rev. St. 1901, c. 24, § 514, as amended by Laws 1901, p. 104, § 8, providing that at a public hearing on a proposed scheme of improving a street the board of local improvements shall adopt a resolution abandoning the scheme, or adhering thereto, or altering it in character and estimated cost, provided the change shall not increase the estimated cost more than 20 per cent., without a further public hearing, where a resolution is adopted at such a hearing changing the scheme, but not stating the estimated cost, a further public hearing is not necessary on a report of the civil engineer showing the estimated cost of the changed scheme to be less than that of the original scheme.

Appeal from Cook County Court; O. N. Carter, Judge.

Petition by the city of Chicago for confirmation of a special assessment against W. D. Kerfoot & Co. From a judgment refusing such confirmation, the city appeals. Reversed.

Robert Redfield (Edgar Bronson Tolman, Corp. Counsel, of counsel), for appellant. Mason Bros. (Louis M. Greeley, of counsel), for appellees.

RICKS, J. This is an appeal from a judgment of the county court of Cook county refusing confirmation of a special assessment, on the petition of appellant, levied to defray the cost of paving, curbing, and grading Twentieth street from Halsted street to South Center avenue, in the city of Chicago. The petition contained a copy of the ordinance, to which no objection is made. Accompanying the ordinance was the recommendation of the board of local improvements and the engineer's estimate of the cost of the proposed improvement.

It appears from the record that on November 26, 1902, the board of local improvements passed a resolution to improve the street named above by "plastering curb walls, resetting curbstones and curbing with limestone curbstones on limestone blocks, grading, and paving with re-pressed vitrified paving brick on two inches of sand and six inches of Portland cement concrete, joints filled with asphaltic cement, surface dressed with one-half inch of sand." The engineer's estimate of costs was $33,000, and was properly included in the resolution, and the public hearing was fixed for the 11th day of December, 1902. At the latter date, proper notice having been given, the public hearing was had, when it was determined to alter and change the improvement, and a resolution was accordingly passed amending the former resolution "so as to provide for the plastering of the curb walls, constructing granite concrete gutters and a granite concrete combined curb and gutter on cinders, grading, and paving with asphalt on six inches of Portland cement concrete, swept with natural hydraulic cement," and the engineer was directed and authorized to prepare an estimate of the cost of the improvement as amended, and the improvement was ordered to be proceeded with in accordance with the original resolution and the amendment thereof. The engineer made and presented his estimate, which showed the cost of the improvement as modified, and estimated to be $32,500. No other or further public hearing was had than that of December 11, 1902. On February 24, 1903, the secretary of the board of public improvements presented the estimate of the engineer and the draft of the ordinance for the improvement to the board, at a meeting held at that time, that the board might, if it approved the same, sign a certificate recommending the passage of the ordinance and the making of the improvement; and the board, having examined the same, attached their signatures to the certificate, and the certificate or estimate of the engineer and the ordinance were presented to the city council for action, which resulted in the ordinance passing, and the petition for the improvement being filed in the county court. The objection urged against this proceeding is that the estimate of the engineer was not considered by the board at the time of the public hearing, and that the board had no right to adopt a resolution for an improvement, or change or alter a former resolution, until the estimate of the cost of the proposed change is made and presented to the board and submitted at a public hearing; and it is urged that, unless this construction be placed upon the statute, the benefit of the public hearing to the taxpayer is lost, as it is said that at such hearing the property owner has a right to discuss before the board not only the necessity of the proposed improvement, and the nature thereof, but also the cost as estimated; and in support of this contention Clarke v. City of Chicago, 185 Ill. 354, 57 N. E. 15, is cited.

The above case is not in point. The facts there were entirely dissimilar to those in the case at bar. The improvement in that case was not abandoned at the meeting fixed for the public hearing, but at another and differ-

*Rehearing denied April 7, 1904.

ent meeting, after an ordinance had been passed under the first plan and proceedings for the special assessment instituted, while in the case at bar the change of plan was determined upon at the meeting for the public hearing, as provided by section 8. At that public meeting an estimate of the engineer was presented for the improvement, as intended by the first or original resolution, and was, no doubt, considered, and, so far as the court can know, it was developed upon that hearing, taking into consideration the necessity of the improvement or nature thereof and the cost as estimated, that it was better and more in keeping with the interest and wishes of the property holders to change the improvement to the one provided for by the ordinance. Whether a new estimate should have been made and presented and considered at that public hearing, or whether an adjournment should have been taken for the purpose of allowing an estimate to be made and a hearing upon that estimate, according to the proposed change of the improvement, must be determined by the provisions of the statute. The proceeding is statutory, and the board of local improvements is only required to pursue the statute, and the property holder is entitled to no more hearings nor to have any other matters considered at any hearing, than the statute requires. Upon that subject section 8 of the local improvement act (Hurd's Rev. St. 1901, c. 24, § 514), as amended by the amendatory act of 1901 (Laws 1901, p. 104), simply provides that the "board shall adopt a new resolution abandoning the said proposed scheme or adhering thereto, or changing, altering or modifying the extent, nature, kind, character and estimated cost, provided such change shall not increase the estimated cost of the improvement to exceed twenty (20) per centum of the same without a further public hearing thereon, as it shall consider most desirable; and thereupon, if the said proposed improvement be not abandoned, the said board shall cause an ordinance to be prepared therefor, to be submitted to the council or board of trustees." Thus it will be seen that by the statute it is not required that a further estimate be submitted to the property holders, or that a further or other public hearing be had, but the direction is that the "board shall cause an ordinance to be prepared therefor," the only limitation or restriction being that the change shall not increase the estimated cost of the improvement to exceed 20 per centum. McChesney v. City of Chicago, 205 Ill. 611, 69 N. E. 82; Washburn v. City of Chicago, 198 Ill. 506, 64 N. E. 1064. In the case at bar the cost of the improvement was decreased $500.

It is urged, however, that it was necessary that the board should consider the estimate of the civil engineer at some public meeting, and should formally approve the same. Such is not the requirement of the statute. It is nowhere required that the board shall approve the estimate of the civil engineer, but the requirement is that such board shall cause an estimate of the cost of such improvement to be made in writing by the engineer, over his signature, which shall be itemized to the satisfaction of the board. We think it sufficiently appears by this record that an estimate of the cost of the improvement as proposed to be made by the ordinance in question was made by the civil engineer, was presented to the board, and was itemized to its satisfaction, as the board certified the same, with the ordinance, to the council, with its recommendation for the passage of such ordinance. It is not questioned, nor, indeed, do we think it can well be, that the Legislature has authority to prescribe the steps and course necessary to be taken for such improvement, and that when it has done so the courts are not authorized to require more.

The objection urged and sustained by the county court should have been overruled.

The judgment of the county court is reversed, and the cause remanded for further proceedings in conformity with the views here expressed. Reversed and remanded.

(208 Ill. 437)

PEOPLE v. McCORMICK et al.*

(Supreme Court of Illinois. Feb. 17, 1904.)

INHERITANCE TAX—PROPERTY SUBJECT TO—TIME OF IMPOSITION.

1. Testator devised the residue of his estate to his son as trustee to be invested and managed for 20 years, with directions that from the net income an annuity of a specified sum should be paid during that period to testator's three children, and provided for the disposition of the income in case any of the children died during the period, and for the distribution of the residue at the end of the period, and for the contingency of each of the children dying prior to the expiration of the period without issue surviving the period. *Held*, that under Hurd's Rev. St. 1901, c. 120, § 366, imposing a tax on the transfer of property by will where one becomes "beneficially entitled in possession or expectation to any property or income thereof," the residuary estate could not be taxed until the expiration of the 20-year period, for until that time it could not be known who would be beneficially interested therein.

2. Testator bequeathed to his daughter $75,000, to procure for herself a home, the title to be vested in her for life, and, after her death, in her issue then living, and provided that, if she should not desire a home, the income should be paid to her until she should desire a home, or until the expiration of 20 years after his death, and, if a home was not procured within 20 years, the fund should become the property of the daughter if she survived the 20 years, while, if she died without issue before the expiration of 20 years, then the fund should go in part to the person appointed by her will and the other part to the residue of the testator's estate. *Held*, that under Hurd's Rev. St. 1901, c. 120, § 366, the fund could not be taxed until the expiration of the 20-year period, for until that time it could not be known who would eventually succeed thereto.

3. A testator devised the residue of his estate to a trustee, to be managed for 20 years, with

*Rehearing denied April 12, 1904.

directions to pay $20,000 a year to each of his three children out of the income thereof, and with a provision that, if all the children should agree in writing thereto, a larger sum should be paid to each. *Held*, that each of his children could not be deemed to be the owner of one-third of the income, so as to subject them to the transfer tax imposed by Hurd's Rev. St. 1901, c. 120, § 366, on the whole of the income, in the absence of an agreement disposing of the income to them.

Appeal from Cook County Court; O. N. Carter, Judge.

Proceedings by the people to determine the amount of the inheritance tax on the estate of Leander J. McCormick, deceased. From a judgment of the county court fixing the tax, the people appeal. Affirmed.

H. J. Hamlin, Atty. Gen. (E. M. Ashcraft, of counsel), for the People. Pence & Carpenter, for appellees.

SCOTT, J. This was a proceeding in the county court of Cook county to fix the inheritance tax in the matter of the estate of Leander J. McCormick, who died testate on February 20, 1900, leaving an estate, the market value of which was fixed in this proceeding in the county court, after making all proper deductions on account of indebtedness and expenses of administration, at $3,548,680.67. Leander J. McCormick left no widow, and his only heirs at law are his three children, Nettie L. Goodhart, R. Hall McCormick, and Leander H. McCormick. The will is quite lengthy, and provides for many contingencies that may arise in the 20 years next succeeding the death of the testator. A proper understanding of the questions involved requires that the substance of several of its paragraphs be stated at some length.

The third clause of the will gives to the daughter the sum of $75,000 to procure for herself a home, the title to be vested in her for life, and after her death in her issue then living, per stirpes. If she should not desire to own a residence, then the testator's trustee is directed to invest the fund and pay the income to her until she should desire a home, or until the expiration of 20 years after his decease. In case the home should not be purchased within the 20 years, then this fund is to become the property of the daughter provided she survive the 20 years, and, if the home is not procured and the daughter does not survive the 20 years, then the income for the remainder of the 20 years is to be paid to her surviving issue for the balance of the 20 years, when the principal of the fund is to be distributed to her surviving issue per stirpes. In case she dies without issue prior to the lapse of 20 years after the death of the testator, or leaving issue who die prior to the lapse of the said last-mentioned period of 20 years, then the proceeds arising from the sale of the residence, if one shall have been procured, or the principal of the fund if a residence shall not have been procured, is to be distributed, one-fourth as the daughter may by her last will appoint, and the remaining three-fourths to fall into the residue of McCormick's estate, and, if the daughter does not appoint any person to take the one-fourth, then it also falls into the residue of his estate.

The fifth clause devised to the son R. Hall McCormick, as trustee, and to his successors in trust, the residue of the estate of the testator, the same to be invested, managed, and controlled for a term of 20 years after the testator's death, and directs that from the net income of the estate an annuity of $20,000 shall be paid throughout said period of 20 years to each of the three children, with a provision that if all the children shall agree, in writing, thereto, a larger sum than $20,000 per annum shall be paid to each of them from the net income of his estate, provided such larger sum can be advanced without prejudice to the general interest of the estate. In case of the death of either of the children prior to the expiration of 20 years, then three-fourths of the annuity shall be paid to the issue of such child in such manner as such child shall by will appoint, and the other one-fourth of the annuity shall be paid to any person whom such child by last will may appoint, and failing such appointment as to either portion, respectively, the same to pass to the issue of the deceased child per stirpes, any increase in the amount of the annuity made in the manner aforesaid to take the same course, in the event of the decease of either child, as is provided for the annuity of $20,000 fixed by the will.

By the sixth clause it is provided: "It is my intention that up to the date of the full expiration of the twenty years after my decease * * * that none of the beneficiaries hereinafter mentioned are to take any interest in any of said property [referring to the residue of the estate] except the annuity and bequests hereinbefore mentioned, prior to the expiration of said twenty years." It is then provided that the trust shall terminate at the end of the 20-year period, and upon such termination the residue of the estate, with accumulations, is devised, share and share alike, to the three children. In case R. Hall McCormick is deceased at the termination of the 20-year period, with issue who survive that period, his portion of the residue is to be distributed among such persons as he may by his last will appoint, and, if no such appointment is made, then it is to be distributed equally among his children then surviving and the issue of any deceased child, such issue taking the share that the parent would take if living. In case Leander H. McCormick shall die prior to the expiration of the 20-year period, his portion of the residue, except the sum of $100,000, shall be paid to and vested in his children then surviving and the issue of any deceased child of his as he may by his last will appoint, and the said sum of $100,000 shall be paid to and vested in any person appointed by the last will of said Leander H. McCormick, and failing any such appointment as to either portion, respectively, of such share of Leander H. McCormick, that portion shall be paid to and vested in the child or children of Leander H. McCormick then surviving, share and share alike, and to the issue of any deceased child, such issue taking the share that the parent would if living. The same disposition is made of the portion of the residue devised to Nettie L. Goodhart, in case she dies prior to the expiration of the 20-year period, as is made of the portion devised to Leander H. McCormick in the event of his death prior to the expiration of that period.

The seventh clause provides for the contingency of each of the children dying prior to the expiration of the 20-year period without issue, or leaving issue none of whom survive the 20-year period. If R. Hall McCormick shall die under such circumstances, he is given a power of appointment by his will, whereby he may designate the person or persons who shall become entitled to and in whom shall vest in fee one-fourth of his portion of the residue, the remaining three-fourths of his portion of the residue to pass to the surviving children of the testator, and the issue of such as are deceased. If he does not exercise the power of appointment as to the one-fourth, then that is to pass with the three-fourths. The same provision is made in reference to Leander H. McCormick and Nettie L. Goodhart, except that each has the power of appointment as to $100,000, only, of his or her portion of the residue.

The county court treated the interest of Nettie L. Goodhart in the $75,000 fund as a life estate, ascertained the present worth of such life estate, and fixed the tax upon such present worth, and ascertained also the present worth of the interest of each of the three children in the annuity of $20,000 per annum, and fixed the tax on the sum so ascertained. That portion of the estate which is to pass into the possession of the three children of the testator at the expiration of the 20-year period was appraised at $2,903,506.67. The court below did not fix any tax against this remainder, for the reason, as stated in the order of the court, that the amount of the tax thereon is not now ascertainable, because it is impossible to determine who may be the beneficiaries of this portion of the estate, and what, if any, relation they may bear to the testator, or the amounts which they will take, respectively, at the termination of the trust provided for in the will; and the order recites that the determination of the amount of the tax on that portion of the estate is deferred until such time as the uncertainties are removed. It was shown by stipulation that the net annual income from the portion of the estate devised to the trustee is at least $100,000.

An appeal has been prosecuted to this court by the people of the state of Illinois, and upon the errors assigned it is contended: First, that a tax should have been fixed upon that portion of the estate which is to be distributed at the end of the 20-year period, on the theory that each of the three children took such an interest therein as was presently ascertainable and taxable under the statute; second, that a tax should have been fixed on the full amount of the $75,000 fund bequeathed for the use of Nettie L. Goodhart, instead of upon the present value of a life estate for her therein; third, that a tax should have been assessed upon the present value of the full amount of the net income of the estate of Leander J. McCormick for the period of 20 years from his death, on the basis that one-third thereof passed to each of his children.

It will be seen by an inspection of section 366 of chapter 120, Hurd's Rev. St. 1901, that the tax is to be imposed where the beneficial interest in property has passed to the person taxed, and such tax may be imposed against any person who "shall become beneficially entitled in possession or expectation to any property or income thereof." It has been said that the terms "beneficially entitled" and "beneficially interested," as used in statutes providing for a tax of this character, when considered with regard to the time when the beneficiary becomes so entitled or interested, are construed to refer to the time when the beneficiary has the title to the property or is entitled to the possession thereof, or when a contingent interest vests or when a defeasible interest becomes indefeasible (2 Woerner on American Law of Administration [2d Ed.] p. 691a); while a "beneficial interest," when considered as a designation of the character of an estate, is such an interest as a devisee takes solely for his own use or benefit, and not as the mere holder of the title for the use of another (In re Seaman's Estate, 147 N. Y. 69, 41 N. E. 401).

It will be observed from this section of the statute that where the property passes to certain persons related to the testator by consanguinity or affinity an exemption is permitted; that the exemption is greater and the rate of taxation lower in case of those most nearly akin, while the exemption is less and the rate higher in case of those farther removed; that in case of the stranger who is a beneficiary the rate of taxation is graduated according to the amount of property received, up to the sum of $50,000; in all cases where the succession exceeds that amount and passes to a stranger the rate is the same. It is therefore obvious that the amount of tax cannot be fixed until it is certainly known who the beneficiaries are, and what portion of the property each will take.

It is contended on the part of appellant that each of the three children of the testator takes a vested interest in the property that is to pass from the trustee at the termination of the 20-year period, while the view of counsel for appellees is that the interests devised in that property, which are to vest in possession at the end of that period, are contingent remainders. We will not indulge in any nice distinctions for the purpose of determining whether or not the interest in this residuary estate, into the possession of which each of the children of the testator is to enter at the end of the 20-year period, is, in the technical meaning of the term, a "vested estate." If it can be said to be vested, it is subject to a condition of defeasance, because, if either of the children of the testator dies prior to the expiration of the period, his or her title to this property will thereby be defeated. Nothing is left but a power of appointment, which may or may not be exercised, and it is therefore wholly uncertain at this time who will, when the 20 years shall have elapsed, possess the beneficial interest in this property, or in what proportion this property will be divided among the persons who succeed to the beneficial ownership thereof.

The condition contemplated by our statute as that which should authorize the imposition of the tax is one of practical and actual ownership—the possession of a title to something that can be conveyed. If either of the children of the testator, in this case, should convey, by deed, his or her interest in the remainder, and die before the expiration of the 20 years, the purchaser would take nothing, and under such circumstances to impose a tax upon either of the children of the testator on account of the right to succeed to the interest in the residuary estate would be to tax the shadow, and not the substance. It would result in taxing appellees upon their right to succeed to property, when, so far as any beneficial ownership is concerned, there never was a right of succession. The right to succeed, under such circumstances, is, for all practical purposes, a myth. Taxation to the taxpayer is intensely real. It should not be levied upon that which is unreal. If the estates now under consideration are contingent, they cannot be taxed until they are vested. If they are now vested, they are subject to an estate for years and subject to defeasance, and cannot be taxed until they become indefeasible. If they be executory devises, they cannot be taxed until the persons who will some time be beneficially entitled thereto are ascertained. Who can tell now whether R. Hall McCormick will die prior to the expiration of the 20 years? If so, will his issue survive that period? If he does not survive that period, will he or will he not exercise the power of appointment? It is impossible now to tell who will succeed to this portion of the residue of this estate. The situation is equally uncertain so far as each of the other children of the testator are concerned.

The right to tax is based upon the right to succeed. The amount of the tax is fixed by the amount of the property which, as a result of the right to succeed, passes to the beneficiary. The tax is levied on the succession, and not on the property as such. The rate must be determined by the amount of the succession where the beneficiary is a stranger, and the exemption, if any, must be determined by the identity of the person who succeeds. When the basis of the tax, the rate, and the exemption, if any, cannot be fixed, the tax itself cannot be fixed. No other course is left open, in the practical administration of the statute, than to postpone the assessing and collecting of the tax upon such remote and contingent interests as are incapable of valuation, and as to which the rate and the exemptions cannot be determined. Billings v. People, 189 Ill. 472, 59 N. E. 798, 59 L. R. A. 807; In re Hoffman's Estate, 143 N. Y. 327, 38 N. E. 311; In re Roosevelt's Estate, 143 N. Y. 120, 38 N. E. 281, 25 L. R. A. 695; In re Stewart's Estate, 131 N. Y. 274, 30 N. E. 184, 14 L. R. A. 836; In re Curtis' Estate, 142 N. Y. 219, 36 N. E. 887; In re Seaman's Estate, 147 N. Y. 69, 41 N. E. 401; In re Dow's Estate, 167 N. Y. 233, 60 N. E. 439; In re Sloane's Estate, 154 N. Y. 109, 47 N. E. 978. As is suggested by Mr. Justice Finch in the Hoffman Case, supra, "the state will get its tax when the legatees get their property."

An ordinary vested remainder, not subject to any condition or contingency, as where the property is given to A. for life with remainder to B., is, under the statute, immediately taxable as the property of B. upon the death of the testator, because there the estate is immediately vested in interest in the remainderman, his heirs and assigns. Nothing can defeat it. B.'s right is absolute; his deed will transfer the property; an execution against him and sale thereunder will convey it; his death cannot affect it; he is beneficially entitled to it "in expectation." This term "expectation," as used in our statute, has reference only to possession. The language is, "by reason whereof any person * * * shall become beneficially entitled, in possession or expectation, to any property or income thereof." The term "expectation" is used, not to denote an expectation of becoming vested both with the title and the possession where neither is now vested, but to denote a condition where the title is vested and the possession is deferred. The term "in expectation" is used in contradistinction to "in possession." Both contemplate a title vested and indefeasible, but in one instance the right of enjoyment is immediate, "in possession"; in the other it is postponed, "in expectation." As used in this statute, these words last quoted refer to the future possession of an estate now vested, and which is subject to the immediate enjoyment of another. It is true that in the case of Ayers v. Chicago Title & Trust Co., 187 Ill. 42, 58 N. E. 318, this court said that whether or not the remainders under consideration there were vested or contingent was not material, for the reason that they were "expectancies," within the meaning of the statute, and presently taxable as such. That language was unnecessary to the decision of that case so far as it referred to contingent remainders, because, as appears from a discussion of the subject found on page 60, 187 Ill., page 325, 58 N. E., the remainders in that case were vested remainders.

A brief consideration of a very common contingent remainder will show the fallacy of the doctrine that such a remainder is taxable immediately upon the death of the testator. Suppose A. devises $100,000 to his son B. for life, with the remainder to his son C. in case C. survives B.; if not, then to a stranger; and that the appraised value of the remainder exceeds $50,000. If the remainder goes to the son, $20,000 of it is exempt, and the rate of tax is $1 on every $100, while if the remainder passes to the stranger there is no exemption, and the rate is $6 on the $100. It is apparent that in such an instance the tax should not be fixed until the remainder vests.

As we have heretofore said, however, the right to impose the tax presently depends, not upon the character of the estate devised, with reference to its being a contingent or vested remainder, but upon the question whether the person who is now, or will ultimately be, entitled to a beneficial interest in the remainder, can be now identified, and whether the proportion thereof to which he will succeed can be now determined. What we have said in reference to the residuary estate disposes of the question presented in regard to the $75,000 fund. It cannot now be known who will be entitled to succeed to this fund, under the will, at the end of the 20-year period. The interest which the daughter takes therein will be defeated by her death, should it occur before the lapse of that time. It would not have been proper to have treated her as the absolute owner of this fund in fixing the tax.

So far as the tax on the income is concerned, it is apparent that the income of each of the children can be increased, provided all consent, in writing, to the increase, and such increase will not embarrass the administration of the fund, and the position of appellant is that as the children have the power to increase this fund until the aggregate amount of the annuity will equal the net income from the estate, subject to the condition just suggested, each must be held to be the owner of one-third of such net income. No authority is cited on this proposition. It has seemed to us, on reflection, that the theory of the counsel for the people is wrong in this respect, for the reason that the three devisees under consideration are not taxed jointly. If either one of them had the power to have his or her annuity increased to one-third of the net income of the estate, then we think each should be taxed upon the basis that he or she is the owner of one-third of the net income; but, before either is entitled to any portion of the income above the sum of $20,000 per annum, the written consent of the other two must be obtained, and one or both of the others may never consent, in which event each of the children would be taxed upon an increase which they do not receive. If such written document should at any time be executed, the sum added to the income of each would become taxable, and, as suggested by the written opinion of the learned jurist who determined this matter in the county court, it would be entirely proper at any time, upon the motion of those representing the people of the state of Illinois, to cite the trustee and the children to appear in that court for the purpose of ascertaining whether such an instrument has been executed and the income of each increased accordingly.

At the expiration of the 20-year period it will be certainly known who is beneficially entitled to the residuary estate and the remainder in the $75,000 fund. All doubts now existing will then be resolved. The exemptions and the rate can then be fixed without uncertainty. Then the legatee will get his property and "the state will get its tax." The imposition of the tax is properly deferred until that time.

The order of the county court will be affirmed. Order affirmed.

(208 Ill. 408)

STARRETT v. BROSSEAU.*

(Supreme Court of Illinois. Feb. 17, 1904.)

APPEAL—QUESTIONS OF FACT—REVIEW—ACTION AT LAW.

1. Hurd's Rev. St. 1899, c. 110, § 89, providing that no assignment of error in the Supreme Court which shall call into question the determination of the Appellate Courts on controverted questions of fact shall be allowed, applies only to actions at law, and not to suits in equity.

2. An action by a principal against the executor of her deceased agent on a claim which did not involve any breach of trust nor require an accounting, but was for a simple money demand based on an alleged error in a single transaction, is an action at law, though instituted in the county court in probate.

Appeal from Appellate Court, Second District.

Action by Henrietta H. Starrett against Noel Brosseau, executor of the estate of Truman Huling, deceased. From a judgment of the Appellate Court (110 Ill. App. 605), affirming a judgment for defendant, plaintiff appeals. Affirmed.

J. Starrett, for appellant. H. K. & H. H. Wheeler, for appellee.

BOGGS, J. Truman Huling, appellee's testator, and Milo Huling, were the executors of the last will of George V. Huling, deceased.

*Rehearing denied April 13, 1904.

The will bequeathed the residuum of the estate in equal parts to ten legatees, of whom appellant was one. On the 10th day of April, 1895, the executors made a partial distribution in cash and notes to each of the ten legatees, by which each legatee received in cash and notes $50,205.57. In order to accomplish this distribution, Truman Huling, deceased, advanced a considerable sum of money, and took therefor certain of the notes which belonged to the deceased, George Huling, the money so advanced being distributed to the legatees. Among the notes for which he so advanced the money were, so said Truman Huling claimed, certain notes which may be conveniently known as the "Fritz, Erzinger, and Fortin" notes. Subsequently the appellant placed the notes falling to her share in the distribution in the hands of Truman Huling, appellee's testator, for collection. Said Truman made a list in a small book, which he gave to the appellant, of the notes so held by him for collection for her, and in the list appeared the Fritz, Erzinger, and Fortin notes heretofore mentioned. On the 9th day of September, 1897, said Truman and Milo Huling, as executors, made final settlement of the estate of George Huling, deceased, and were discharged by the probate court from further duty in respect of said estate. After the settlement of the estate said Truman Huling continued to act as agent for the appellant in the matter of the collection of the principal and interest of her notes. In March, 1899, correspondence between the appellant and said Truman disclosed to the latter that the Fritz, Erzinger, and Fortin notes were listed, on the book he had given appellant, as belonging to her. He then insisted that an error had been made, by which these notes and the money which he had advanced for them were both distributed to the legatees, whereby each legatee received something more than $600 more than he was entitled to have. He advised all of the legatees, and after much correspondence his insistence was accepted as being correct, and it was further agreed that he should retain the Fritz, Erzinger, and Fortin notes, and that each legatee should pay the amount necessary from each, respectively, to correct the error and repay the appellant for the loss of the Fritz, Erzinger, and Fortin notes. This was done, and each of the legatees, other than the appellant, paid him $618.98, which he paid to the appellant to correct the error aforesaid. The appellant refunded the same sum by deducting the same from the proceeds of the collection of a note known as the "Maltman note," which said Truman held for collection for her. The adjustment of the alleged error was concluded on the 19th day of September, 1899. Truman Huling died in February, 1902. He left a will, which was probated, and the appellee qualified as executor. On the 8th day of April, 1902, the appellant filed a claim against the estate in the total sum of $1,391.35. In the claim she charged the deceased with the Fritz, Erzinger, and Fortin notes, and with the amount deducted from the Maltman note as her contribution to the refunding fund, and credited him with the amount paid to her which the other legatees had paid him as their contributions to the refunding fund. She also claimed interest from the date of the adjustment of the alleged error. The cause was heard before the county court, and judgment was entered against the claimant (the appellant). She perfected an appeal to the circuit court of Kankakee county. When the cause came on to be heard in the circuit court, the parties, by agreement, waived a trial by jury, and submitted the cause to the court for decision. A hearing resulted in the rejection of the claim, and the claimant perfected an appeal to the Appellate Court for the Second District. The Appellate Court affirmed the judgment of the circuit court, and the claimant has brought the case into this court by her further appeal.

The parties presented to the trial judge in the circuit court a number of propositions to be held as announcing correct legal principles applicable to the contentions, but it is not assigned as for error, or contended, that the court erred in ruling on said propositions or any of them. The contention for solution, as counsel for appellant urges, is whether, in making the distribution among the legatees of the estate of George Huling, deceased, said Truman Huling advanced money for the Fritz, Erzinger, and Fortin notes, and the money so advanced and the notes were both divided among the legatees. If such an error was not made, counsel for appellant contends said Truman Huling, as her agent, having her notes for collection, should have accounted to her for the principal and interest of the Fritz, Erzinger, and Fortin notes, and should return to her the $618.98 retained out of the proceeds of the Maltman note, admitting, however, that the amount paid by the other legatees through him to her should be deducted from the total of her claim. This, it is clearly seen, presents but a question of fact for decision. It is therefore pertinent to inquire whether, in view of the provisions of section 89 of the practice act (Hurd's Rev. St. 1899, c. 110), the appellant is entitled to have another hearing on a mere question of fact, or whether the determination of the circuit court and the Appellate Court as to the controverted question of fact in the case is final and conclusive. If the proceeding is to be regarded as a cause in chancery, the provisions of said section 89 of the practice act have no application, and appellant is entitled to have the testimony again considered in this court, and the weight thereof determined according to the judgment of this court. Henry v. Caruthers, 196 Ill. 136, 63 N. E. 629. In the case cited we investigated and determined the facts in a claim filed by the appellee, Caruthers, but his claim was against the deceased to recover a debt due from a copartnership of which the deceased was a member, other members of the firm being alive but insolvent. We held that an action at law might be maintained against the surviving partners, and that equity afforded a remedy against the legal representative of the deceased partner, and held that the proceeding was therefore to be regarded as a cause in equity, and might be reviewed by this court on the facts.

County courts sitting in probate have jurisdiction of both legal and equitable claims against a decedent, but a right of action at law against a person while living remains an action of the same nature against his legal representatives. It may be prosecuted in the circuit court as an action at law against the administrator or executor (Darling v. McDonald, 101 Ill. 370), or may be filed in the county court as a claim against the estate, and in the latter forum the proceeding is to be regarded as an action at law, so far as the provisions of the practice act under consideration are concerned. Whether instituted in the circuit court or in the county court in probate, if the action is one at law the Appellate Court is the final court of appeal as to controverted questions of fact.

It can hardly be questioned, it seems to us, that an action at law would have afforded an adequate remedy for the recovery of any amount due the appellant from the deceased. She did not seek a full accounting of the many transactions of the decedent as her agent. She did not claim that he had made a profit, out of the subject-matter of the agency, to which she was entitled under equitable principles. Her claim was specific, and touched but one of the transactions of the agency. The claim was not against him to recover because of any act or omission as the executor of George V. Huling. The two executors of the will of George V. Huling had fully settled the estate and had been discharged, and it is not proposed to disturb or question the correctness of that settlement. The decedent was the agent of the appellant, and as such had possession of her notes and securities, and possessed power to collect and receive payment of the same. The bare relation of principal and agent does not give jurisdiction to a court of equity to entertain a bill for the collection of amounts claimed to be due from the agent, or for an accounting. 16 Ency. of Pl. & Pr. 920. Equity does not exercise jurisdiction merely because a confidence is reposed or another is trusted with the performance of the acts for the benefit of another. Steele v. Clark, 77 Ill. 471. Courts of equity have entertained bills to enforce an accounting by an agent, but only when some special feature or features were present requiring the aid of chancery, as, for instance, that an agent has employed the subject-matter of the agency in an enterprise of his own and enjoyed a profit therefrom; or where there has been a failure to account amounting to a breach of trust; or if an accounting involves the examination of so many complicated transactions between the principal and the agent, or the latter, as agent, and other persons, that it would be impracticable to adjust them in an action at law; or where the principal is entitled not only to recover money, but also property which was or has become the subject-matter of the agency. In such cases equity will entertain a bill on the ground courts of law cannot afford an adequate remedy. 16 Ency. of Pl. & Pr. 920. The nature of the agency, the duties of the agent, may create a trust in the subject-matter of the agency, in which case equity will entertain a bill for an accounting and relief. In Weaver v. Fisher, 110 Ill. 146, a case of the latter character was presented, and we upheld the jurisdiction of a court of equity to grant relief. Bills in chancery were entertained in Smith v. Wright, 49 Ill. 403, for the reason an agent, who had been employed to obtain a land warrant for the principal, fraudulently procured the warrant to be located on land in his own name; and in Clapp v. Emery, 98 Ill. 523, the ground of equitable jurisdiction of an accounting was that the peculiar circumstances of the case constituted the agent a trustee and the transaction a trust; and in Davis v. Hamlin, 108 Ill. 39, 48 Am. Rep. 541, the agent was held a trustee, in equity, of a lease which, in violation of the trust reposed in him, he had procured to be executed to himself for his personal gain. The same equitable doctrine, that an agent who has dealt in the property of the agency for his own benefit will be deemed a trustee in equity, controlled in Reese v. Wallace, 113 Ill. 589; Vallette v. Tedens, 122 Ill. 607, 14 N. E. 52, 3 Am. St. Rep. 502; Roby v. Colehour, 135 Ill. 300, 25 N. E. 777; and Conant v. Riseborough, 139 Ill. 383, 28 N. E. 789.

It cannot, it seems to us, be questioned but that an action at law would have afforded adequate relief in the case at bar. There was no claim the agent had, in violation of his duty, dealt in the matter of the agency on his own account or for his own benefit, and that she was entitled to have him declared to hold the benefit of the transaction as in trust for her. It was not desired to open up the affairs of the agency generally. The account of the agent and his acts and doings were unquestioned save as to the one matter. The claim did not involve any alleged breach of a trust. It was for a simple money demand based upon an alleged error in a single transaction. Had the decedent not died, an action in assumpsit would have afforded an adequate remedy, or that action might have been instituted against the executor. In Eddie v. Eddie, 61 Ill. 134, which was an action at law, we said: "No one will contend that, if an error was committed in settling accounts by parties, the mistake or error might not be shown; and if it may be, and is, shown, then the party against whom the error was committed is not bound by that settlement as then made. This instruction only announces this rule, and is correct."

We think an action at law provided an adequate remedy, and that no ground for equitable interference existed. The proceeding is not, therefore, a proceeding in equity, but at law. The parties clearly regarded the proceeding as an action at law. They waived trial by jury, and submitted propositions of law to be held or refused by the court. This was the proper view, and, that being true, the statute has denied to the appellant another hearing in this court on mere controverted questions of fact.

No error of law appearing, the judgment of the Appellate Court is affirmed. Judgment affirmed.

(208 Ill. 419)

ILLINOIS STATE TRUST CO. v. ST. LOUIS, I. M. & S. RY. CO.*

(Supreme Court of Illinois. Feb. 17, 1904.)

EMINENT DOMAIN—FOREIGN CORPORATIONS—RAILROADS—PURCHASE—PARALLEL LINES—COMPLIANCE WITH STATUTES.

1. It is competent for the Legislature to delegate the exercise of the power of eminent domain to a foreign corporation, but the power cannot be exercised unless granted.

2. Laws 1899, p. 116, authorizing a foreign corporation in possession or control of a railroad situated within the state and belonging to a corporation of the state to purchase such railroad, and declaring that it thereby acquires the powers, privileges, and franchises of the corporation, and may exercise the power of eminent domain, provided that the act shall not permit any railroad company to purchase any parallel or competing line of railroad in this state, did not authorize the purchase of a line extending along the Mississippi river, within the state, by a foreign corporation owning a parallel road extending along the opposite side of said river in another state.

3. The purchase being contrary to the statute, the corporation could not exercise the right of eminent domain, and the owner of the land could raise the question in condemnation proceedings brought by the foreign corporation, and need not resort to quo warranto.

Appeal from St. Clair County Court; J. B. Hay, Judge.

Condemnation proceedings by the St. Louis, Iron Mountain & Southern Railway Company against the Illinois State Trust Company. From a judgment fixing the compensation to be paid, defendant appeals. Reversed.

Wise & McNulty, for appellant. W. S. Forman (L. D. Turner, of counsel), for appellee.

CARTWRIGHT, J. This is an appeal from the judgment of the county court of St. Clair county in a condemnation proceeding fixing the compensation to be paid by appellee, a foreign corporation, to appellant, for a strip of land 100 feet wide lying along and adjoining the original right of way of the St. Louis Valley Railway Company, in said county. The petition for condemnation was filed by appellee on May 29, 1903, and alleged that petitioner was a foreign corporation, formed by the consolidation of corporations organized and existing under the laws of the states of Missouri and Arkansas, and qualified under the laws of this state to do business in this state; that it was the owner of a railroad in this state running through the counties of St. Clair, Monroe, Randolph, Jackson, Union, Alexander, and Williamson, which was in operation, and that it was necessary in the operation of the said line of railway to have railroad yards located on the lands described in the petition. Appellant, the owner of the lands sought to be taken and appropriated to the use of the petitioner, moved the court to dismiss the proceeding, for the reason that the petitioner was a foreign corporation organized and existing under the laws of the states of Missouri and Arkansas, and not organized or chartered under the laws of this state, and that it had no right to institute the suit or exercise the power of eminent domain by condemning land in this state. Upon the hearing of the motion the petitioner offered evidence for the purpose of proving the incorporation of the Cairo & Fulton Railroad Company in the state of Arkansas and the St. Louis & Iron Mountain Railroad Company in the state of Missouri, and the consolidation of the two under the name of the St. Louis, Iron Mountain & Southern Railway Company, the petitioner, by virtue of the statutes of said states; which evidence, for the purpose of this decision, will be assumed, without passing on the question, to have been competent and sufficient for the purpose. Petitioner also offered in evidence articles of incorporation of the St. Louis Valley Railway Company for the construction and operation of a railway from East St. Louis through the counties of St. Clair, Monroe, Randolph, Jackson, Union, and Alexander to Cairo, and a deed of conveyance of said railway executed by the St. Louis Valley Railway Company to the petitioner. Defendant objected to the introduction of this deed on the ground that the St. Louis Valley Railway was a competing and parallel railway with the Iron Mountain & Southern Railway, and that by the statute a conveyance to the petitioner was prohibited. The objection was overruled. The petitioner also introduced testimony that the St. Louis Valley Railway was finished from the city of East St. Louis a distance of 122 miles, to a small place called "Gales," about 2 miles north of Thebes, and was in the possession of the petitioner. The witnesses testified that the general course of said railway was a little west of south, along the east side of the Mississippi river; that the St. Louis, Iron Mountain & Southern Railway of the

*Rehearing denied April 12, 1904.

¶ 1. See Eminent Domain, vol. 18, Cent. Dig. § 36.

petitioner was on the west side of the Mississippi river, in Missouri, and ran in the same general direction; that the two roads were practically parallel to Thebes, and when the St. Louis Valley Railway should be completed to Cairo they would run in the same direction, and be substantially parallel lines; that the St. Louis, Iron Mountain & Southern Railway started at St. Louis and ran to a point opposite Cairo; and that railroads so situated and running in the same direction are competitors for business. The court overruled the motion of defendant to dismiss the proceeding, and impaneled a jury to ascertain the compensation to be paid to the defendant. A verdict was returned, and a judgment entered upon it.

The power of eminent domain is an incident to sovereignty and inherent in the state, and can be exercised only on the occasion, in the mode, and by the agency prescribed by the Legislature. No other state can authorize the exercise of that power within this state, and the laws under which petitioner has its existence could not and do not purport to do so. The petitioner can have no legal existence in this state outside of the boundaries of the states where it was incorporated, and can exercise none of the powers conferred by its charter except by consent of the Legislature of this state. It is competent for the Legislature to delegate the exercise of the power of eminent domain to a foreign corporation (18 Am. & Eng. Ency. of Law [2d Ed.] 858), but the power can only be exercised when so granted. The power to take the property of the individual without his consent is against common right, and all acts authorizing such a taking are to be strictly construed. Chicago & Eastern Illinois Railroad Co. v. Wiltse, 116 Ill. 449, 6 N. E. 49; Chicago & Northwestern Railway Co. v. Galt, 133 Ill. 657, 23 N. E. 425, 24 N. E. 674. Unless both the letter and the spirit of the statute relied upon clearly confer the power, it cannot be exercised. Ligare v. City of Chicago, 139 Ill. 46, 28 N. E. 934, 32 Am. St. Rep. 179. The question under what conditions the power shall be exercised is purely legislative, but it is the duty of the court, when called upon, to decide whether the statutory conditions exist, and whether the taking of the property is within the statutory power conferred. Harvey v. Aurora & Geneva Railway Co., 174 Ill. 295, 51 N. E. 163.

The general statute providing for the exercise of the right of eminent domain does not embrace foreign corporations, and the only authority granted to them is contained in the act entitled "An act concerning the rights, powers and duties of certain corporations therein mentioned, authorizing the sale and transfer of any railroad, or railroad and toll bridge, and other property, franchises, immunities, rights, powers and privileges connected therewith or in respect thereto, of any corporation of this state to a corporation of another state, and prescribing the rights, powers, duties and obligations of the purchasing company," approved April 21, 1899. Laws 1899, p. 116. That act consists of a single section, and provides, in substance, that whenever a corporation organized under the laws of another state shall be in possession of a railroad situated in this state belonging to a corporation of this state, or shall own or control all of the capital stock of such corporation of this state, then the corporation of this state may sell and convey and the corporation of the other state may purchase, in fee simple or otherwise, such railroad, and hold in fee simple or otherwise the property so purchased, and may exercise the powers, privileges, and franchises of the corporation whose property is so purchased, and may, when necessary or proper, exercise, in the same manner as railroad corporations in this state are authorized to, the power of eminent domain in acquiring lands or property necessary or convenient for the betterment, maintenance, extension, or operation of such railroad, and for the construction, use, and maintenance of spurs, switches, side tracks, depots, stations, terminals, and other franchises to be used in connection with such railroad, with the following proviso: "That this act shall not be construed so as to permit any railroad company to purchase any parallel or competing line of railroad in this state." The evidence showed that the railroad of the petitioner and the one purchased within this state are parallel and competing roads, starting from St. Louis and East St. Louis, on the opposite sides of the Mississippi river, with connections through a terminal association at that point, and running to points on the opposite banks of the same river. The fact that they are separated by the river, constituting another public highway, is, of course, of no consequence; and, inasmuch as the act prohibits the purchase by a foreign corporation of a parallel or competing line of railroad in this state, the fact that they are in different states makes no difference. The purchase is one that is prohibited by the statute.

But it is contended that, if the purchase was illegal, the petitioner could still condemn the defendant's lands, and the legality of the purchase could only be inquired into by quo warranto. Counsel say that we so decided in the case of Thomas v. St. Louis, Belleville & Southern Railway Co., 164 Ill. 634, 46 N. E. 8. In that case a corporation of this state, authorized to construct and maintain a railroad and to take private property for its use by the exercise of the power of eminent domain, filed its petition to condemn a right of way. There was no claim that the franchise of the petitioner had been forfeited, or that the power to condemn had not been granted to it, but the defendants offered to prove that the railway of petitioner was a parallel line with that of another railway company, not a party to the proceeding, and that both lines were operated by the Illinois Central Railroad Company, which was not a party. The claim was that petitioner had entered into an illegal combination with another company, by which it might have exposed itself to penalties or to a forfeiture, but it was still in the possession and use of its franchise. A private individual cannot question the legal existence of a de facto corporation, and it was held that the court would not try the question whether the petitioner had in some way violated the law. In this case the motion to dismiss for want of power to condemn land in this state did not involve the question of the legal existence of the corporation where it was organized. The question was whether it had acquired the power to condemn the defendant's lands under the provisions of the act of 1899. That is not the same question decided in the case relied upon. The petitioner, as a corporation of another state, was required to bring itself within the terms of the act, and could only do so by proving the purchase of the St. Louis Valley Railway. It could only exercise the power to take the defendant's lands against its will by proving such purchase, and it could not make the purchase except under the conditions prescribed by the act. Instead of proving a purchase authorized by the statute, which would give it a right to condemn land for the improvement, maintenance, and use of the railroad so purchased, it proved a purchase prohibited by the act itself. In attempting to prove the power to condemn, it proved the illegality of the purchase and transaction. Petitioner was asking the aid of the court to exercise a right which it claimed had been delegated to it by the Legislature of this state, and the evidence showed that it had not complied with the condition upon which the power was delegated, but, on the contrary, had violated it. This court has uniformly held that a foreign corporation which has not complied with the conditions prescribed for transacting business in this state cannot maintain an action in the courts of the state. Cincinnati Mutual Health Assurance Co. v. Rosenthal, 55 Ill. 85, 8 Am. Rep. 626; Supreme Order of Iron Hall v. Grigsby, 178 Ill. 57, 52 N. E. 956; Thompson Co. v. Whitehed, 185 Ill. 454, 56 N. E. 1106, 76 Am. St. Rep. 51. The Legislature have power to impose such conditions upon foreign corporations for the exercise of powers or privileges in this state as they may choose, and such conditions must be complied with. The purchase of a railway prohibited by the act is illegal and void, and while in such a case the state might oust the foreign corporation from the exercise of the franchise within this state, we do not think that the courts ought to entertain a petition for condemnation where the petitioner does not bring itself within the statute delegating the power to condemn.

The judgment of the county court of St. Clair county is reversed and the cause remanded. Reversed and remanded.

(208 Ill. 375)

DAVIS et al. v. FIDELITY FIRE INS. CO. OF BALTIMORE et al.*

(Supreme Court of Illinois. Feb. 17, 1904.)

CONTRACTS—CONSTRUCTION — PRIOR NEGOTIATIONS—PAROL EVIDENCE—UNCERTAINTY.

1. After verbal and written negotiations between the parties looking towards the appointment of one as agent of the other, a letter of appointment was submitted by the principal, with the request that the agent make suggestions for its modification and alteration, and, after making proposed alterations, the letter was again sent to the agent. *Held*, that this letter constituted the contract, and was not to be modified by evidence of the prior negotiations.

2. A contract appointing an agent for an insurance company contained a paragraph headed "Duration of Appointment," and reciting that the object was "to establish a permanent insurance business in the territory assigned to you, on a solid basis and under conservative management, such as has been mutually discussed and agreed upon, and this contract is entered into between this company and yourselves with this understanding only," and the conclusion of the letter expressed a hope for a relation of long duration. *Held* that, if this provided for a permanent appointment, it might nevertheless be terminated at the will of either party.

3. That a contract appointing an agent was complete in terms, except that it did not state the duration, did not render it uncertain so as to admit parol evidence.

Appeal from Appellate Court, First District.

This is a bill of interpleader filed in the superior court of Cook county by the Illinois Trust & Savings Bank against Lewis H. Davis, John Shepherd, and John E. Shepherd, partners under the firm name of Davis & Shepherd, doing business in Chicago, and the Fidelity Fire Insurance Company of Baltimore, offering to bring into court the amount of a deposit in said bank of $12,016.79 in the name of said insurance company, subject to the check of said insurance company, signed by Davis & Shepherd, managers, which moneys, it is alleged, were claimed both by the insurance company and Davis & Shepherd. Answers and replications were filed, and the case was referred to a master to take the evidence of the respective parties and report his conclusions. On the coming in of the master's report, and after objections and exceptions had been overruled thereto, a decree was entered dismissing the bank from the suit, reimbursing it for costs and solicitors' fees, and releasing it from all claims of the defendants; also directing the bank to pay to Davis & Shepherd out of the fund $10,610 and their costs, and the balance to the insurance company. The insurance company prosecuted an appeal to the Appellate Court for the First District, where the decree was reversed, and the cause was remanded to the superior court with directions to enter a decree that the Illinois Trust & Savings Bank, after deducting its costs in the appellate and superior courts and its solicitors' fees in the Appellate Court, pay the balance of the de-

*Rehearing denied April 12, 1904.

posit in its hands to the Fidelity Fire Insurance Company, and that Davis & Shepherd pay all other costs in the appellate and superior courts; and a further appeal has been prosecuted to this court by Davis & Shepherd. Affirmed.

The appellants, Davis & Shepherd, in the spring of 1900 became the western agents of the Fidelity Fire Insurance Company, with offices in Chicago. They acted as such agents from May 1 to December 8, 1900, when the Western agency was discontinued, and the appointment of Davis & Shepherd was terminated. The deposit held by the Illinois Trust & Savings Bank was the earnings of the Western agency during that period, and the claim of Davis & Shepherd was that they had an equitable lien thereon for damages growing out of the wrongful termination of their agency in December, 1900, when they had been appointed the Western agents of said insurance company until May 1, 1905—that is, for the period of five years.

The negotiations leading up to the appointment of Davis & Shepherd as Western agents of said insurance company were begun in March, 1900, and were carried on by J. J. Courtney, representing the insurance company, who later became its president, and the members of the firm of Davis & Shepherd, and continued until the following June 16th, when they were completed, though the commencement of the agency was to be dated back as of May 1, 1900, about which time it appears that Davis & Shepherd began work for the insurance company. The first negotiations between Courtney and the members of said firm were in Chicago on March 22, 1900, which were followed by a letter from Davis & Shepherd, on March 24th, to J. J. Courtney, as president of the insurance company, written at Courtney's suggestion, embodying the substance of their conversation upon the 22d of March in the form of a proposition to be submitted to the board of directors of the insurance company, to represent the said company as its Western agents, with offices at Chicago. The letter is lengthy, and relates to certain matters concerning the Western branch of the company's business, and, in so far as it is material to the matters in controversy between the parties, is as follows:

"Chicago, Mch. 24, 1900.

"Mr. J. J. Courtney, Pres't, Brooklyn, N. Y.—Dear Sir: Referring to our conversation of yesterday. * * *

"Tenth—It must be the understanding that the contemplated arrangement is a permanent one, extending over a period of years,—not less than five nor more than ten is asked in such a contract,—for which employment the said named gentlemen will give their very best endeavor and their time in the development of said department.

"Eleventh—A percentage of five per cent. will be expected on the balance betwixt income and outgo in said department, to be paid Messrs. Davis & Shepherd.

"Thirteenth—Only upon the condition of establishing a permanent insurance business on a solid basis and under conservative management are these gentlemen willing to engage to open up and develop such department, and a contract will be entered into by them with this understanding only.

"Fourteenth—* * *

"At a very conservative estimate, and on $2500 lines, such as you suggest, an income in this territory of $150,000 for the first year may be expected, $200,000 second year, $250,000 third year, and $300,000 within five years. This means that the most conservative methods are to be used in the selecting of business and in the management of the department, and only the best business, through good agencies, selected."

April 15, 1900, Davis & Shepherd sent a telegram to Courtney at the company's office in Baltimore, in which it is stated that Mr. John Shepherd of their firm would be with him (Courtney) Friday (evidently referring to a later date), and saying, "He has our authority to close contemplated arrangements." The evidence shows that Mr. John Shepherd did go to Baltimore, where the matter of the agency was discussed with Mr. Courtney, and the testimony shows that, among other things, the duration of the agency was discussed, and Shepherd stated that he "would not enter into any arrangement that did not contemplate some length of time." During the month of May following, letters were written by Courtney to Davis & Shepherd which refer, in a general way, to the agency and their letter of appointment which was to be sent to them, and on May 7th Courtney sent a letter of that date to Davis & Shepherd in Chicago, in which was inclosed a draft of a letter of appointment of Davis & Shepherd as Western branch managers of the company. The first of these letters states, in substance, that the appointment had been wired to Davis & Shepherd; that this letter was in confirmation of the telegram; that the letter of appointment had been prepared "with the utmost care," though it was not signed; and that Davis & Shepherd, after having carefully read it, should make "whatever suggestions may occur to you for its modification or alteration in any particular," and return it to the office of the company for submission to its executive committee on the 16th of the month (May). This draft of letter of appointment is lengthy, and after the address, so far as material, is as follows:

"Western Department.

"Gentlemen: Referring to my visit to your city in March last, and to your favor of the 24th of March, as well as to the visit of your Mr. John Shepherd in April to this city for the purpose of perfecting arrangements for the establishment of a branch of this company, to be hereinafter styled as its 'Western Department,' with headquarters in your city, at Nos. 195-197 LaSalle street, we now take pleasure in advising you of your appointment as manager thereof, said appointment to date as and from the first of May, 1900. * * *

"In a general way we desire our line kept down to a conservative basis, for the reason that a company of the limited size and comparative youth of the Fidelity may prove of more benefit to its agents by writing conservatively for the first two or three years of its existence and later on increasing its lines, than by writing excessive lines at the start and be compelled to reduce them later. The Fidelity is in business to stay, and under your able representations should soon take a leading place in the agency field of the west. * * *

"Duration of Your Appointment.

"It is mutually recognized that this appointment has for its object not only the efficient supervision and proper conduct of all the company's business in the territory placed under your jurisdiction, but the active cultivation and material increase in the volume of its business in that area, particularly in the preferred classes, which will not involve the undue writing of term business, as alluded to heretofore. Our aim, which we understand to be shared by your good selves, is to establish a permanent insurance business in the territory assigned to you, on a solid basis and under conservative management, such as has been mutually discussed and agreed upon, and this contract is entered into between this company and your good selves with this understanding only."

The omitted parts of this letter refer to the territory covered by the agency, various details as to the conduct of the business, their office, its furnishings, books of account, bank account, and an estimate of the probable income of the business for its first, second, and fifth years, and other matters which cover 19 pages of typewritten matter in the record, and concludes as follows:

"In conclusion we desire to express the hope that our relations will prove mutually beneficial and of long duration and of the most harmonious nature.

"Awaiting the favor of your acknowledgment, touching upon all the features dealt with in this letter, I am, dear sirs,

"Yours very truly, ———, President."

Under date of May 12th, Davis & Shepherd reply to Courtney's letter of May 7th, and state, among other things, that "we are enclosing you a copy of the draft of letter of appointment, with some few modifications," and then proceed to refer to nine different headings of the draft of the letter of appointment, but make no reference whatever to the duration of the agency. Their letter closes with the following language: "Trusting that the several matters may meet with your approval, we beg to remain," etc. Inclosed with this letter Davis & Shepherd returned the draft of letter of appointment, with various marks and interlineations thereon, but leave that part thereof headed "Duration of Your Appointment," which has been above quoted, without any mark or modification.

Under date of June 14, 1900, Courtney wrote to Davis & Shepherd as follows: "Referring to our respects of the 7th of May, wherein we forwarded you a draft letter of appointment for your approval, and to your reply thereto of the 12th idem, containing your comments thereon, we now beg to advise you that we have re-written the said letter of appointment under the same date, viz., May 7, 1900, and incorporated therein such modifications as have proven necessary to accord with your suggestions. This we now enclose herein, and in order that the modifications referred to, and other matters needing comment, may be clearly understood, we recapitulate them under their several captions, as follows."

This letter then makes reference to all the suggestions of Davis & Shepherd contained in their letter of the 12th, and what had been done with reference thereto in the final letter of appointment, and closes with a request that Davis & Shepherd reply thereto in the "fullest detail without loss of time, and thus dispose, once and for all, of your appointment and its attendant conditions." The final letter of appointment was inclosed in this letter, and is the same as the original draft under the heading "Duration of Your Appointment," but in other respects is modified as above stated. To this letter Davis & Shepherd replied, acknowledging the receipt of the "letter of appointment," and also his letter setting forth certain subjects concerning it on which Courtney desired information. The letter then proceeds to give the information referred to, and concludes as follows: "Trusting that all the matters dealt with by you have been properly disposed of to your entire satisfaction, we are yours most truly, Davis & Shepherd, Managers." This letter contains no reference whatever to the duration of appointment, and, so far as the record shows, nothing further occurred between the parties thereafter with reference to that subject, and nothing appears from the record but this correspondence and the previous conversations between the parties relating to the term of the agency.

D. J. Schuyler and Thomas Bates, for appellants. James C. Hutchins and Max Baird, for appellee Illinois Trust & Savings Bank. Thomas Taylor, Jr. (George Whitelock and J. W. Taylor, of counsel), for appellee Fidelity Fire Ins. Co. of Baltimore.

HAND, C. J. (after stating the facts). From the view we take of this case it will be necessary to consider but one question, that is, was the firm of Davis & Shepherd appointed Western agents for the Fidelity Fire Insurance Company for the period of five years, or was their appointment for an indefinite period of time, and subject to termination by the insurance company upon its discontinuing its Western agency? From a consideration of all the evidence in the record, we think it clear that the agreement between the insurance company and Davis & Shepherd must be found in the letter of appointment bearing date May 7, 1900, and that all the conversations and correspondence between the parties leading up to that letter, and the acceptance of its terms by Davis & Shepherd, were in the nature of negotiations, and became merged in said letter of appointment when accepted.

The law is well settled that, when parties reduce to writing their agreement as finally agreed upon by them, all prior negotiations leading up to the execution of the writing are merged in the writing, and that parol evidence is not admissible to explain, contradict, enlarge, or modify the writing as it exists when executed. The writing, when executed becomes the repository of the agreement between the parties. In Memory v. Niepert, 131 Ill. 623, 23 N. E. 431, on page 630, 131 Ill., and page 432, 23 N. E., it is said: "Where parties have deliberately put their contract into writing, the rule doubtless is that the writing is the exclusive evidence of what the contract is." And in Clark v. Mallory, 185 Ill. 227, 56 N. E. 1099 (page 232, 185 Ill., and page 1100, 56 N. E.): "While courts will uniformly endeavor to ascertain the intentions of the parties in construing a contract between them, and for that purpose will look into the surrounding circumstances at the time the contract was executed if the language of the instrument is ambiguous or its meaning uncertain, still, when the language employed is unequivocal, although the parties may have failed to express their real intention, there being no room for construction, the legal effect of the instrument will be enforced as written. Intention of the parties is not to be determined from previous understandings or agreements, but must be ascertained from the instrument itself which they execute as their final agreement, otherwise written evidence of an agreement would amount to nothing."

In the conversation in Chicago on March 22d between Courtney and the members of the firm, in the letter of March 24th written by the firm to Courtney, and in the conversation in April between John Shepherd and Courtney in Baltimore, it is doubtless true that Davis & Shepherd were seeking to obtain an appointment for five years. This part of their proposition, however, does not appear to have been acceded to by the insurance company, and in the draft of the letter of appointment of May 7th, as first sent to Davis & Shepherd, the duration of the time of their appointment was left indefinite. They were asked to examine the letter, and to note such changes therein as they desired to have made. After an examination of the letter, which must have included an examination of the paragraph designated "Duration of Your Appointment," as it occupies a prominent position in the letter, Davis & Shepherd suggested a number of changes in the letter, none of which affected in any manner that part of the letter which fixed the duration of the time of their appointment, and the letter of appointment, upon the receipt of their suggestions, was rewritten by the company in accordance with their suggestions, but no change was made in the duration of the time of their appointment. The letter, as rewritten, was returned to them, and they accepted its terms, and their appointment thereunder, in writing. The proposition of Davis & Shepherd that they be given an appointment for five years, contained in the conversation had on the 22d of March, repeated in their letter of March 24th, and referred to by John Shepherd when in Baltimore, was not accepted by the insurance company, but what, in effect, was a counter proposition upon that subject, was submitted by the company in the draft of the letter of May 7th, which was sent to Davis & Shepherd for their examination, and which they afterwards accepted in writing. In Maclay v. Harvey, 90 Ill. 525, 32 Am. Rep. 35, it was held a letter written in reply to an offer, which restates the terms of the offer, but with some variations, though slight, cannot be regarded as the consummation of a contract, and requires an acceptance upon the terms thus stated, and, until unequivocally accepted, is only a mere proposition or offer. And in Anglo-American Provision Co. v. Prentiss, 157 Ill. 506, 42 N. E. 157 (page 513, 157 Ill., and page 159, 42 N. E.), it is said: "It is undoubtedly the rule that, where one party makes a proposition to another, an assent, to be valid so as to conclude an agreement or contract between the parties, must in every respect meet and correspond with the offer, neither falling short of nor going beyond the terms proposed, but exactly meeting them at all points, and closing with them just as they stand."

We have no doubt the parties fully expected that the Western agency of the insurance company and the business relation established between them would continue for some time, perhaps for a period of years. Still, the time the Western agency and the business relation between the parties were to continue was left indefinite by the agreement, and the insurance company was not bound to continue its Western agency, and neither party, by the terms of the agreement, could require the other to continue the relation thereby established between them longer than such relation was agreeable to both.

In Orr v. Ward, 73 Ill. 318, the contract sued on was an employment contract, in writing, for a salary and commission, which provided for the payment to the employé of $2,100 for the year 1873 and $2,400 for the year 1874, in semimonthly or monthly installments, and a commission on all sales in excess of $35,000. The appellee commenced work thereunder in January, 1873, and continued until June 11th of the same year, when the firm which had engaged him became insolvent, and he was discharged. Suit was brought to recover damages for not continuing appellee in the service of the firm. The court, on page 819, said: "We are to judge of the contract by what it contains. Having reduced it to writing, we must presume the parties have embodied in it their entire agreement. It contains no stipulation the firm will retain appellee for two years or any other fixed period. Their undertaking is to pay him at a certain rate of compensation if he shall discharge the duties assumed by him to be performed. No doubt it is true each party contracted on the supposition the business would continue through the space of two years, but appellant's firm did not obligate themselves to continue it for that length of time. As a matter of fact, it terminated much sooner. We have no authority to add to the contract as the parties have made it, enlarging the liability of either one of them, and have no disposition to do so."

If the duration paragraph be abbreviated by eliminating adjective and dependent phrases, it would then read as follows: "Our aim is to establish a permanent insurance business on a solid basis and under conservative management, such as has been mutually discussed and agreed upon;" and if it be admitted that this amounted to an agreement that the Western agency should be permanently continued and for a permanent appointment, we think it still might be terminated at the will of either party. In Lord v. Goldberg, 81 Cal. 596, 22 Pac. 1126, 15 Am. St. Rep. 82, the plaintiff testified that he said, "While it is a very good increase in salary, will it be permanent?" to which the defendant answered, "It will; it will last; it will be permanent." It was held the hiring was for an indefinite period. And in Gray v. Wulff, 68 Ill. App. 376, in a suit for a wrongful discharge, it was shown that the plaintiff, a musician, had written the defendant previous to the employment, saying, "I would prefer your house if you can guarantee a long engagement," and that the defendant had replied, "Be here Thursday evening." It was held that the term "long engagement" has no certain meaning, and that there was no employment for a definite time, and that the defendant had the right to discharge the plaintiff on giving him the customary notice. In Beck v. Walkers, 24 Pa. Cir. Ct. R. 403, it was said: "Though, by the contract, the employment is made expressly a permanent employment, the law still holds that the term is indefinite." And in Milner & Co. v. Hill, 19 Ohio Cir. Ct. R. 663, an employment contract was made by the appellee writing to appellants, after some previous correspondence: "Would you be kind enough to inform me what salary you will pay if only for the season, and what you will pay if for an annual or permanent position? And also please state whether the position soon to be vacant in your ingrain department is for the season, or permanent." Appellants answered: "In reply would say that the position in our ingrain department will be a permanent one. * * * Come at once." After a breach alleged, the court say: "Either party might terminate the contract at any time. * * * It is simply a statement that he has entered into a business that is permanent, rather than a temporary business, and it refers to the position itself, rather than to his employment for the position."

It is urged by appellants that the letter of appointment does not fully set forth the agreement between the parties, and therefore the case of Orr v. Ward, supra, and the other cases to the same effect cited by the appellee in its brief, do not apply to this case for that reason. We are of the opinion the letter of appointment does set forth the agreement between the parties, and that its terms are plain and unambiguous. While the agreement does not state the duration of the time of the appointment of Davis & Shepherd, but leaves the time of their appointment indefinite, that does not, in a legal sense, make the agreement uncertain or ambiguous. To admit parol evidence that the appointment was for a period of five years by reason of the fact that the time of their appointment is indefinite, would be to import into the agreement a provision which the parties deliberately omitted therefrom. In other words, to admit such testimony would be to make a new contract for the parties. This the court is powerless to do. Vail v. Northwestern Mutual Life Ins. Co., 192 Ill. 567, 61 N. E. 651.

Finding no reversible error in this record, the judgment of the Appellate Court will be affirmed. Judgment affirmed.

(162 Ind. 320)

CONSUMERS' GAS TRUST CO. v. LITTLER.

(Supreme Court of Indiana. March 15, 1904.)

GAS LEASE—CONSTRUCTION—IMPLIED CONDITION—WAIVER—FORFEITURE—NOTICE—JUDICIAL NOTICE.

1. By a written contract the first party agreed to sell all the oil and gas underlying his land to the second party, with the right to mine and transport it, no time being fixed for the beginning of operations nor for the completion of a well, and no express provision being made that a well should ever be drilled; but it was agreed that a sum should be paid annually by the second party till oil or gas was found, or till, in the judgment of the second party, they could not be found. If they were found, the first party was to receive a share. *Held*, that there was an

implied engagement by the second party to explore for oil and gas, which, if not performed in a reasonable time, entitled the first party to a forfeiture.

2. In construing a contract giving a license to drill wells in land for oil and gas, the court has judicial knowledge, as a matter of common knowledge, that gas or oil does not exist in paying quantities under all the lands within a recognized district, and that there is no other generally acknowledged way to determine whether it does exist than putting down a well.

3. Where under a contract the owner of land had the option to require, by claiming a forfeiture, that the other party should drill for gas and oil within a reasonable time, or to accept a certain sum annually for delay, his acceptance of an annual payment in advance was a waiver of performance for one year.

4. Where, by the acceptance of an agreed annual payment, the owner of land had waived his right to have the other party drill there for oil and gas up to a certain time, and at the expiration of that time he refused to accept another payment, he could not claim a forfeiture of the contract 15 days later, since that did not afford notice for a reasonable time of his intention to do so.

Appeal from Circuit Court, Grant County; H. J. Paulus, Judge.

Action by Joseph W. Littler against the Consumers' Gas Trust Company. From a judgment in favor of plaintiff, defendant appeals. Transferred from the Appellate Court under Burns' Rev. St. 1901, § 1337u. Reversed.

Miller, Elam & Fesler and S. D. Miller, for appellant. Charles & Brown and Hiram Brownlee, for appellee.

HADLEY, J. Appellee sues appellant to secure the cancellation and the quieting of his title against a gas and oil contract, the substance of which follows: It was entered into on October 15, 1896, by appellee and his wife, as first parties, and one Walley, assignor of appellant, as second party, hereinafter referred to as "Gas Company," and witnessed that the first parties, their heirs and assigns, in consideration of $1 in hand paid, sold to the second party, his heirs and assigns, all the oil and gas under certain described lands in Grant county, "together with the right to enter upon said lands at all times for the purpose of drilling and operating for oil, gas, or water, with the right to erect and maintain all necessary telephone lines, buildings, and structures for that purpose; and together with the right to lay, maintain, and remove all lines of pipe over and across said lands for the conveyance and transportation of oil and gas." "In consideration of the premises, the second party agrees to pay the first party the sum of forty dollars annually, beginning on the 15th day of October, 1896 [date of the contract], and until oil or gas is found in paying quantities, or this grant is terminated as hereinafter provided." The second party is not to drill any well within 300 feet of any building on the premises, and is not to use more than one acre of the ground with each well drilled. The first party is to have the use of the lands for agricultural or other purposes, except what is actually occupied in operating for gas or oil. The second party is to pay the first party all damages done to crops by reason of its operations in drilling wells or in laying, repairing, or removing pipe lines. If oil is found in paying quantities, the second party is to deliver to the credit of the first party in the pipe line with which it may be connected one-sixth part of the oil which may be saved. The first party is to have free gas for domestic purposes from the wells or pipe line on the premises, and, should gas be found in greater quantity than is required for use by the first party, the second party is to pay the first party "one hundred dollars each year for each and every well from which gas is used off the premises." If either gas or oil is found on the premises in paying quantities, "the part of oil to be delivered as aforesaid, or the sum per well for gas, shall be in lieu of the annual payment above provided," and such annual payment shall cease immediately. "It is agreed by the parties that whenever, in the judgment of the second party, his heirs or assigns, oil or gas, or either, cannot be found on the premises, or, having been found, have ceased to exist in paying quantities, and said party of the second part shall reconvey to the first party, their heirs or assigns, all the oil and gas in and under said premises, then all payments of every kind to be made to the first party by the terms hereof shall from and after said date cease and determine," and in case of a reconveyance the second party is to have the right to lay and maintain pipe lines for the transportation of oil and gas over the premises for ten years from "said date," and the right at any time to remove all machinery, fixtures, and property placed on the land. All payments under the contract to be made on October 15th of each year at a bank in Muncie. "In default of complete compliance on part of second party, or his assigns, renders this lease null and void." Signed by all contracting parties, and execution acknowledged before a notary public on said October 15, 1896. The deal embraces a quarter section of land. There was a separate contract for each 80 in same terms. The complaint is in three paragraphs. The first, being a general statutory count to quiet title, covers the whole farm. The second and third were addressed to the respective 80's, and each set out the contract in full. In addition to formal matters, the second and third paragraphs of complaint each allege the recording of the contract, the assignment thereof by Walley to the defendant, and recording of such assignment, the payment by defendant on or about October 15, 1900, of $40 as a consideration for the defendant's option and right to drill on the premises for one year from the last-named date to October 15, 1901, which payment was the exact amount due the plaintiff under the contract at the time it was paid, and nothing has since been paid thereon to continue the contract after that date; that on October 15, 1901, plaintiff refused, and still refuses, to longer continue the contract in force, or receive any further payments therefor, but declared the contract then terminated and forfeited; that neither defendant nor its assignor has ever drilled a well on said premises, nor has gas or oil ever been found thereon, nor has any one under the contract laid a pipe line thereon for oil or gas; that plaintiff is, and at all times has been, in possession, and neither Walley nor defendant has ever been in possession; that defendant claims rights under the contract. Prayer for cancellation and quieting title, etc. The defendant's demurrer to each the second and third paragraphs was overruled. In its answer to the second and third paragraphs it alleged, in substance, that the second party in the contract, Walley, was the agent of the defendant, took the contract for it, and afterwards made a formal assignment of the same to the defendant. It alleges the payment of the annual sum stipulated, $40, on or before the 15th day of October in each year, down to the 15th day of October, 1901, and an offer to pay for the year commencing on that date, and the refusal of the same by the first party upon the ground that first party had a right to terminate the contract, and intended to do so at that time; and that second party had been at all times ready to pay the same. It denied that the contract had ever been terminated as provided therein, and denied that the $40 annually was paid as a consideration for the option or right to drill for any one year, but avers that it was a part of the consideration for all the rights and property granted under the contract. It denied that it had ever been ascertained that in the judgment of said Walley or defendant oil or gas, or either, could not be found on the premises, or that, having been found, the same has ceased to exist and denied any reconveyance. Plaintiff's demurrer to each paragraph of the answer was sustained. Thereupon, defendant declining to answer further, judgment was rendered on demurrer against it annulling the lease and quieting plaintiff's title as against the same.

The only matter for decision is the sufficiency of the complaint and answers. They present the same questions, and will be considered together. It will be observed that the contract before us, like many others of its class, embraces indefinite and peculiar provisions. By it appellee purports to "sell" to appellant's assignor, for the consideration of $1, all the gas and oil underlying his land, and the right to enter at any time to mine and transport it. No time is fixed for the beginning of operations, nor for the completion of a well, nor any express provision that appellant shall ever drill a well. It is, however, stipulated that, as a further consideration, the company shall pay to appellee $40 each year on each 80, in advance on each October 15th, beginning on the day the contract was executed, until oil or gas is found in paying quantities, or until, in the judgment of the gas company or its assigns, oil or gas cannot be found on the premises, or, having been found, shall cease to exist in paying quantities. And whenever a well is drilled, if oil is found, the landowner shall have one-sixth part, and, if gas, he shall have $100 each year for each well, and that the one-sixth of the oil, or $100 per well, shall be in lieu of the annual acreage rental, which shall no longer be paid. There is nothing in the subject-matter of the contract to limit the power of the parties to enter into such mutual obligations as they liked. No fraud or overreaching is claimed, and it becomes our plain duty to give the instrument the effect intended by the parties at the time it was executed. "If there is one thing more than another public policy requires," said an eminent English jurist, "it is that men of full age and competent understanding shall have the utmost liberty of contracting, and that their contracts, when entered into freely and voluntarily, shall be held sacred, and shall be enforced by courts of justice." Printing, etc., Co. v. Sampson, 19 Law R. Eq. Cases, 462. What, then, was the contract? It is clear that the fundamental purpose of both parties was the exploration for gas and oil on the premises. The whole tenor of the contract shows that the prospective benefits and profits from gas or oil were the real considerations moving the contracting parties. To the landowner the manifest inducement was the rents and royalties he expected to enjoy if the gas company should find gas or oil in paying quantities; to the gas company, the right to exclude others from the premises, and the anticipated profits in vending the products of the wells it should drill. It will not do to believe that the landowner would for the pittance of 50 cents per acre per annum have knowingly incumbered his land situate in the gas district, and thereby reduced its selling value, by transferring, for an indefinite period, and for speculative purposes, the right to enter at the pleasure of the grantee or his assignee and mine the underlying gas or oil; or that he would have bargained away his prospects for large gains from the gas and oil under his land, with the knowledge that the same would be extracted through wells on other premises, and that his profits would be limited to the annual acreage rent during the process of extraction. It is as obvious as if expressed that the real intention of the parties was that the gas company or its assigns should, with diligence, and within a reasonable time, enter upon the premises and drill a well, and thereby test the existence or nonexistence and continuance of the fluids in paying quantity. We judicially know, as a matter of common knowledge, that gas or oil does not exist in paying quantities under all the lands within the recognized district, and that there is no other generally acknowledged way than putting down a well to determine whether or not it does exist. The company's undertaking to pay the landowner until, in the judgment of the company, "oil or gas cannot be found on the premises, or, having been found, has ceased to exist," clearly implies an engagement to explore and develop the premises. The stipulation does not contemplate an arbitrary judgment, but an honest one; a judgment that is justifiable by the results of a bona fide investigation; such as could only be arrived at by sending down the drill to where the oil or gas is or should be. The Louisville, etc., R. Co. v. Donnegan, 111 Ind. 179, 188, 12 N. E. 153; Elevator Co. v. Clark, 80 Fed. 705, 26 C. C. A. 100. The obligation to explore is such an essential part of the contract, though implied, as must be treated as a condition, which, if not performed within a reasonable time, entitled appellee to claim a forfeiture under the agreement that, "in default of complete compliance on the part of the second party, or his assigns, renders this lease null and void." Gadbury v. Gas Co. (Ind. Sup. May 14, 1903), 67 N. E. 259, and cases cited. But while appellant's default under the contract might be of a character to bestow upon appellee the right to demand a forfeiture, yet that right might be defeated by conduct amounting to a waiver. Equity looks with disfavor upon forfeitures, and when such is claimed it will closely scrutinize the demand, and will interpose to prevent it when its enforcement will operate inequitably or unconscionably. Thompson v. Christie, 138 Pa. 249, 20 Atl. 934, 11 L. R. A. 236; McCarty v. Mellen, 5 Pa. Dist. R. 425. "If there has been a breach of an agreement," says a distinguished author, "sufficient to cause a forfeiture, and the party entitled thereto either expressly or by his conduct waives it, or acquiesces in it, he will be precluded from enforcing the forfeiture." Pomeroy's Eq. Jr. § 451; Lynch v. Gas Co., 165 Pa. 518, 30 Atl. 984; Hukill v. Myers, 36 W. Va. 639, 15 S. E. 151. In this, as in other mutual agreements, the engagements are equally binding on the contracting parties. They must be equally fair and just in performance, and one will not be permitted to cause the other to suffer from an act which he himself induced. The contract imports a sale to appellant's assignor of all the gas and oil underlying appellee's farm, to be paid for in kind and by well rental after wells are put down. No time is indicated when a well shall be constructed or when exploring operations shall begin, but it is expressly stipulated that, until such well is put down, the company shall pay appellee on each 80 $40 per annum, in advance, beginning on the day the contract was made. When the contract was entered into it was problematical whether either gas or oil was to be found under appellee's land. He then, under the contract, had his election whether he would require, by claiming a forfeiture, the existence or nonexistence of gas or oil under his premises, to be determined within a reasonable time by drilling a well, or whether he would prefer delay, and the $80 per annum, rather than take his chance on the finding of gas or oil, and the possible total loss of any further revenue from the prospect. If he chose the former, under the vague and uncertain terms of the contract, equity required him to give appellant reasonable notice of his intention, or, what would be equivalent to such notice, refuse to assent to or accept a consideration for a postponement beyond a reasonable time. Hukill v. Myers, 36 W. Va. 639, 15 S. E. 151; Thropp v. Field, 26 N. J. Eq. 82; Double v. Heat & Light Co., 172 Pa. 388, 33 Atl. 694. If he chose the latter—as he did—the acceptance of the $40 at the time of the contract was a waiver upon a valid consideration of performance for one year. The acceptance of a like sum at the beginning of the second year was a like waiver for the second year, and likewise to the end of the five years for which such payments were made. So at the end of the latter period, to wit, October 15, 1901, the relations of the parties stood, with respect to appellee's right of forfeiture, precisely as they were at the moment the contract was executed. Up to October 15, 1901, appellee had no ground of complaint. He had consented to the delay, and had received a satisfactory consideration for it. Therefore this suit, commenced 15 days later, cannot be sustained. He could not go on, as the pleadings show, through a term of years, without complaint, or appearance of dissatisfaction, and by his conduct lull appellant into a sense of security and state of unpreparedness, and successfully claim a forfeiture, without such reasonable notice as would afford appellant a fair chance to discharge his obligation. The refusal of appellee on October 15, 1901, to accept the annual payment for another year, was notice that further delay in commencing operations was not approved, but we cannot say as a matter of law that it was sufficient notice under the circumstances. Appellant might not have possessed any drilling machinery, and there might have been none obtainable within the brief period of 15 days. Besides, we know as a matter of common knowledge that it is often impossible to complete a well in 15 days.

Judgment reversed, with instructions to sustain the demurrer to each the second and third paragraphs of the complaint.

(163 Ind. 190)

CONSUMERS' GAS TRUST CO. v. CRYSTAL WINDOW GLASS CO. et al.[1]

(Supreme Court of Indiana. March 17, 1904.)

GAS LEASE—FORFEITURE—NOTICE.

1. Where one by a written contract granted the exclusive right to drill in his land for gas

[1] Rehearing denied.

and petroleum for a certain rental and a share of the proceeds, where the drilling was delayed, he cannot, by refusal to accept the rental, immediately terminate the contract, and lease the rights to another party, but must give reasonable notice of his intention before doing so.

Appeal from Circuit Court, Madison County; Jno. F. McClure, Judge.

Action by the Consumers' Gas Trust Company against the Crystal Window Glass Company and others. From a judgment in favor of defendants, plaintiff appeals. Transferred from Appellate Court under act of March 13, 1901 (Acts 1901, p. 590, c. 259). Reversed.

Miller, Elam & Fesler, S. D. Miller, and Jno. W. Lovett, for appellant. Bagot & Bagot, for appellees.

DOWLING, J. This is a suit by the appellant against the appellees, the Crystal Window Glass Company and Jones and wife, for an injunction to prevent the Crystal Window Glass Company from entering upon the lands described in the complaint and sinking gas wells and conveying the gas therefrom. Issues were formed, and there was a finding and judgment for the appellees. The error assigned is the refusal of the court to grant a new trial upon the motion of the appellant.

The complaint was in two paragraphs, which were substantially alike, the first referring to the southwest quarter of the northeast quarter of section 21, township 22, range 8 east, containing 40 acres; and the second to another 40-acre tract adjoining that first described. The material facts alleged in the complaint were: That on April 27, 1899, the appellant was a corporation organized under the laws of this state for the purpose of leasing lands, acquiring the right to drill for natural gas, transporting such gas to Indianapolis, and selling the same at that city. That Jones was the owner of the lands mentioned in the complaint, and that on said day he and his wife entered into a contract in writing with the appellant, whereby they conveyed to appellant the exclusive right to drill for gas and petroleum upon said southwest quarter of the northeast quarter of said section 21, and to transport the same therefrom, together with certain other rights and privileges necessary to the full enjoyment of the said agreement. That at the time the said contract was made, and as a part of the same transaction, Jones and wife executed another lease upon the other 40 acres of the farm owned by him, on which he had a dwelling house and residence, which was occupied by him and his wife. That while appellant has not completed any well upon said 40-acre tract first described, yet it was a part of the consideration of the said contracts that the appellant should pay to the said Jones and wife the rents reserved in the said leases, and that it should also furnish to them gas for domestic purposes at their said residence free of cost, and upon their demand. That the appellant, with the consent of Jones and wife, had put down a line of pipe on their land on the highway on the east side of said tract. That appellant tapped its said pipe line, and connected a service pipe therewith for the use of said Jones and wife, and on December 21, 1901, began to furnish gas to Jones and wife for use in their said residence, and ever since has been and still is furnishing the same, and that Jones and wife are still accepting and using said gas under said contract. That appellant paid and that Jones and his wife received the rents under the contract for each year prior to and including the year ending April 27, 1902, and that it duly tendered in advance the rent for said land for the year ending April 27, 1903, and still offers to pay the same. That Jones and his wife refused to receive the money tendered as rent for the year 1903, and have wrongfully sought to repudiate their said contract, and are combining and conspiring with the appellee the Crystal Window Glass Company to deprive appellant of its rights under said lease and agreement. That on April 30, 1902, the appellees Jones and wife made a pretended contract with the said Crystal Window Glass Company whereby they attempted to grant, and said company to obtain, the exclusive right to drill wells for gas and oil, and lay pipe lines for the transportation of the same, upon the lands described in the complaint. That the appellant has performed all the duties and obligations imposed upon it by said lease, and that the same is in full force. That the appellees have entered into an agreement, the particulars of which are unknown to appellant, and that the Crystal Window Glass Company has entered upon said real estate and erected a derrick there preparatory to drilling a well and operating for petroleum and gas, and that they threaten to and have commenced drilling such well, and that they threaten to lay pipes upon said lands for the transportation of gas and oil if any is found, and to completely oust the appellant from said real estate, and to deprive it of all its rights under said lease and agreement. That an emergency exists requiring the issue of a temporary injunction without notice. Prayer for a temporary order, and on the final hearing for a permanent injunction.

The contract executed by Jones and wife and the appellant, referred to in the complaint, is substantially the same as the lease and agreement in Consumers' Gas Trust Company v. Littler (No. 20,246, decided by this court at its present term) 70 N. E. 363, and the evidence in this case is very much the same as in that. On the authority of that case, and for the reasons there stated, we hold that the appellees Jones and Jones could not terminate the contract abruptly without notice to the appellant by a refusal to accept the rent or compensation provided for by the contract. Such refusal to accept the rent can be construed only as an indication that the owners of the land objected to further delay on the part of the appellant in beginning operations under the contract, and that it must proceed to drill for gas or oil within a reasonable time after such refusal.

Judgment reversed, with instructions to sustain the motion for a new trial, and for further proceedings not inconsistent herewith.

(162 Ind. 353)

HAMMOND v. CROXTON et al.

(Supreme Court of Indiana. March 18, 1904.)

WILLS—POWERS—VALIDITY—ABSENCE OF BENEFICIAL INTEREST.

1. A naked power of disposition under a will may exist exclusive of any beneficial interest in the donee.

On petition for rehearing. Overruled.

For former opinion, see 69 N. E. 250.

DOWLING, J. We are asked to grant a rehearing in this cause, chiefly on grounds fully discussed in the original briefs, and which were carefully considered when the case was decided. In addition to the reasons formerly presented by counsel for a reversal of the judgment, it is now contended that the decision is in conflict with the rule announced in Mulvane v. Rude, 146 Ind. 476, 45 N. E. 659.

This case is readily distinguishable from that one. In Mulvane v. Rude the first item of the will was as follows:

"I give and bequeath to my beloved wife, Sophia P. Folsom in lieu of her interest in my lands, all my real estate in said town of Worthington, known and designated * * * as lots 21, 22, and the south half of lot 23, with all the appurtenances thereto belonging, and all the household and kitchen furniture, pictures, ornaments, and all other personal property of every description whatever belonging to me at the time of my decease, except money on hand or on deposit, notes, bills, bonds, and judgments of which I may be possessed at said time.

* * * * * * * * *

"Fifth. * * * And now, having full confidence in the judgment of, and integrity of my wife, and there being a strong probability that she may survive me for some years, and fearing that some of my heirs may be unworthy of any special bequest before the decease of my said wife, I have therefore made the terms of this will as hereinbefore written, and will add the following suggestions to my said wife: that whatever part of the legacies hereinbefore made to her, and shall not have been expended or otherwise disposed of by her, may at her decease be given by her to such of my legal heirs as in her judgment shall need and would make good use of the same. But in case my wife should die intestate, whatever part or amount of the real and personal property hereinbefore willed to her which shall remain unexpended or otherwise undisposed of by her at her decease, I do will and bequeath to my daughter, Emily J. Mulvane, and her heirs."

In giving a construction to the above will, this court said: "Under these rules counsel for appellant admit that the first item, considered alone, without regarding the fifth item, gave to the widow the real estate in fee simple, and the absolute title to the personal property." It was held, therefore, that the widow, Sophia P. Folsom, took an absolute title to the property in controversy, and that the devise over to the appellant, Emily J. Mulvane, was void because repugnant to the grant of the absolute estate first given to the widow.

In the case before us the real estate was not given absolutely to the widow of Edward T. Hammond, nor was it devised to her generally, or indefinitely with a power of disposition. The Hammond will in terms gave no estate or property whatever to his widow. It conferred on her a naked power of disposition, and nothing more. Such a power may exist exclusive of a beneficial interest in the donee. Whatever interest Frances Hammond took under the will arose from implication only.

The rules announced in Mulvane v. Rude are expressly recognized and approved in the original opinion. But the language of the two wills differs in every essential particular. The devise to the widow in Mulvane v. Rude is express, absolute, and in fee; while here no estate or interest whatever is described, and a naked power of disposition only is given. The same item of the will which confers on the widow a power to sell, plainly indicates the intention of the testator to create two estates, inconsistent with his supposed purpose to give to the widow an estate in fee simple.

We can discover no reason for any change of the original opinion herein, and the petition for a rehearing is overruled.

(162 Ind. 331)

INDIANA RY. CO. v. MORGAN.

(Supreme Court of Indiana. March 17, 1904.)

WILLS—POWERS TO EXECUTORS—DEVOLUTION OF TITLE—VENDEES OF HEIR—RIGHTS—ESTOPPEL—ACQUIESCENCE IN RAILROAD CONSTRUCTION.

1. Where a will gave a life estate to testator's widow, and provided that at her death the executor should sell the real estate, and after payment of certain legacies divide the proceeds among testator's children, the title during the life of the widow was not in the executor, but in the beneficiary children, who could convey the estate, and whose vendee was entitled to defend the same against all persons but the life tenant, and the right of the executor to sell when the contingency arose, and whatever injury he could prevent the life tenant from doing he could also prevent a stranger.

2. Where the owner of land, with full knowledge of his rights, stood by while an electric

¶ 2. See Estoppel, vol. 19, Cent. Dig. § 268.

railroad made a considerable excavation and embankment, and constructed its road on his farm, and made no protest except to the excavation of gravel, the railroad was justified in assuming that he assented to the construction of the road, and the owner was estopped to recover possession of the land, after the road had been completed, large sums of money expended, and the interest of the public in the road as a line of common carriage had become fixed.

3. The fact that the road had not the power of eminent domain was immaterial.

Appeal from Circuit Court, St. Joseph County; W. A. Funk, Judge.

Action by Henry C. Morgan against the Indiana Railway Company. From a judgment for plaintiff, defendant appeals. Transferred from the Appellate Court under Burns' Rev. St. 1901, § 1337u. Reversed.

Brick & Bates, for appellant. Anderson, Du Shane & Crabill, for appellee.

HADLEY, J. Appellee brought this suit on March 8, 1901. The first paragraph of the complaint is a common count to quiet his title to, and the second to recover mesne profits for the alleged wrongful occupancy with its railroad track and right of way, and without his authority, of, a strip of ground from 8 to 25 feet wide running east and west across his certain farm of 100 acres, and between the Vistula road and the bank of the St. Joseph river.

There is no controversy over the pleadings. The controlling question arises upon appellant's exception to the conclusion of law upon the special finding of facts. The facts found established, so far as material to the question involved, are in substance as follows: John M. Miller died testate in 1880, the owner of the farm of which the strip in dispute was a part, and by his will devised the land to his widow for and during the remainder of her life, and directed his executor, upon her death, to sell the land, and, after the payment of some small legacies, to divide the balance of the proceeds of the same equally among his three children, Henry C., Martha E., and Sarah A. Miller. The widow accepted the will, took possession of the land, and enjoyed the rents and profits thereof until her death, in 1899, when the land was conveyed by the executor as directed by the will. In 1893 Sarah A. executed to appellee, Morgan, for value, a warranty deed for an undivided one-third of said lands. A public highway known as the "Vistula Road," and running east and west across the land, has been opened and used for public travel to a width of 40 feet for more than 50 years, though its legal width was never defined. In 1894 the board of commissioners granted to the General Power & Quick Transit Company, a corporation organized as a street railroad company, a franchise to construct a street railroad upon and along the Vistula road, and providing that the track shall be laid north of said road wherever practicable to do so, and at no point should the south rail of said track be laid nearer than 20 feet to the center of said road. In 1895 said corporation constructed through the premises a railroad, connecting the town of Mishawaka with the city of South Bend, along the north side of the Vistula road, occupying a strip outside the limits of the highway, varying in width from 8 to 25 feet from the north line of the highway to the north line of the railroad track. After the company had cut and removed the timber and bushes that grew upon the line, and was engaged in constructing the grade, appellee, Morgan, first learned that said company proposed to and was engaged in constructing a street railroad on the land, and immediately, through his attorney, notified the company that he was informed that it had taken a large amount of gravel off the farm to be used in the construction of said road, and that he was the owner of an undivided one-third of the land, subject only to the life estate of the widow of John M. Miller, deceased, that the widow had no right to sell the gravel, and he should hold the company liable to him for one-third in value of the same. Henry C. and Martha E. Miller, the other two beneficiaries of the will, and the widow of John M. Miller, had knowledge of the location and construction of said railroad from beginning to end, and neither the said Henry, Martha, the widow of John M. Miller, nor appellee, at any time during the construction and operation of said railroad, prior to February 23, 1900, made any protest or objection to the location, construction, or operation of said railroad upon the land in controversy. The railroad was completed in 1895, and from January 1, 1896, to the commencement of this action the cars have been continuously run over the same at intervals of 15 minutes, and have carried from 1,500 to 4,000 passengers daily, including a large number of laborers who lived in one, and worked in the other, of said cities. On March 15, 1899, appellant, the Indiana Railway Company, by consolidation succeeded to the rights and obligations of the said General Power & Quick Transit Company, and after said last-mentioned date, in addition to the cars run between South Bend and Mishawaka, passenger and express cars from Goshen and Elkhart were run over said road to Mishawaka and South Bend, carrying passengers and light freight. The cost of construction of said railroad was $8,000 per mile. The widow of John M. Miller died in August, 1897, and in June, 1899, Henry C. and Martha E. Miller, the other tenants in common, and James S. Ellis, as executor of the will of John M. Miller, pursuant to the will, for value, executed to appellee a deed conveying to him the whole of said farm. On February 23, 1900, appellee, then being the owner of all of said farm, demanded of appellant payment for the value of the land occupied by said railroad.

The conclusion of law was that appellee is the owner in fee of the land described in the complaint, and entitled to the immediate possession thereof, and to have a judgment quieting his title thereto, and for $1 damages and costs, and judgment was rendered accordingly.

The real question is, does it appear from the findings that appellee is entitled to have his title to the land occupied by appellant for its track and right of way quieted as against such use and occupancy? Or—what means the same thing—is he entitled to oust the appellant from the premises? Appellee's right to pecuniary compensation for the land so occupied is not questioned by appellant, but it is vigorously maintained that appellee, having knowingly stood by and observed appellant's grantor, at great expense, construct upon the land a permanent railroad, make excavations and embankments thereon, without protest or objection, and having observed the operation of cars over it at regular and frequent intervals, carrying passengers and light freight, for more than five years, and a large number of inhabitants establish their homes and business along the line, induced so to do by the apparent easy, cheap, and comfortable means of transportation from their homes to and from their work and places of business, will not now, after such prolonged acquiescence, be permitted to oust appellant, and thus, by wresting from it possession of a part of said line, destroy said means of transportation, to the injury of the public. Whether appellant's contention shall be sustained depends largely upon whether appellee, as the grantee of Sarah A. Miller, held such an interest in the farm as would enable him to protect the estate against the encroachment of appellant's grantor. It is well to note that the will of John M. Miller gave a life estate to his widow, and then proceeds, "and after the death of my wife, I direct that the remaining real estate shall be sold by my executor, and out of the proceeds thereof shall be paid [certain small legacies] and the balance of the proceeds of said real estate shall be equally divided between my son, Henry G. Miller, and my two daughters, Martha E. and Sarah A. Miller." It has been uniformly held in this state since Doe v. Lanius (1852) 3 Ind. 441, 56 Am. Dec. 518, that a naked power given by will to an executor to sell land, for the purpose of paying legacies or making distribution, does not vest the title in the executor, but in the heir, who becomes entitled to the rents and profits until the power to sell is exercised. In no case can the heir be cut off by will, except by a devise of the estate, either expressly or by implication, to some one else. Bowen v. Swander, 121 Ind., and authorities collected on page 170, 22 N. E. 725. Under this rule, during the life estate of the widow, the title to the land in controversy was not in abeyance, nor in the widow, nor in the executor, but in the beneficiary children of the testator, and subject also to conveyance by them. Brumfield v. Drook, 101 Ind. 190. Therefore, as a remainderman, by purchase from Sarah A. Miller, appellee was entitled to defend the estate against all persons but the life tenant, and the right of the executor to sell it when the contingency arose; and, as such, whatever injury to the inheritance he might prevent the life tenant from doing, he might also prevent a stranger. Appellee was bound to know what his legal rights were in the premises, and it is evident that he did know, as it is shown by the special findings that, upon learning that appellant's grantor had taken possession of the land, and had cut away the trees and bushes, and was engaged in grading a railroad upon it, he immediately notified the company in writing that he was the owner of an undivided one-third of the farm, subject only to the widow's life estate, that the widow had no right to sell certain gravel that had been taken from the farm and used in the construction of the road, and he should hold the company liable to him for one-third in value of the same. Thus, with full knowledge of his rights, appellee stood by while the company made an excavation from 2 to 7 feet deep for a distance of 400 feet, and threw up an embankment from 1 to 3 feet high on the entire balance of the distance through his farm, without the slightest complaint or manifestation of displeasure at the proceeding. He must have known, when he proclaimed to the company his ownership, and demanded an accounting to him for the gravel, that whatever he might demand pay for he might decline to sell, except upon his own terms; and, furthermore, that whatever right he could assert to the gravel he could also assert to every other part or parcel of his estate. Having, therefore, gone to the pains of giving written notice of his purpose and intention with respect to the gravel, without expressing any complaint or dissent to the digging up and removal of the earth from one part of his farm to another, which he knew was being done in the construction of a railroad thereupon, the company had the right to assume from appellee's conduct that he assented thereto. His conduct was sufficient to justify the belief that he acquiesced in the construction of the road upon his land, and would be content to receive, at some subsequent time, pecuniary compensation therefor. He was at least silent when he ought to have spoken. Having thus permitted the construction and operation of the road to go forward until after a large sum of money has been expended, and the public has placed itself in such relation to the road as a line of common carriage as to be injuriously affected by a destruction of a part of it, appellee will not now be permitted to recover that which equity says he should not have. "Compensation he may recover, possession he cannot." Railroad Co. v. Allen, 113 Ind. 581, 583, 15 N. E. 446; Railroad Co. v. Berkey, 136 Ind. 591, 593, 36 N. E. 642.

Appellee argues that the rule above stated only applies to railroad corporations vested with the right of eminent domain, and that, since street railroad companies had no such power prior to 1901 (Acts 1901, p. 461, c. 207), it is not applicable to this case. No attempt is made to point out any principle of the law of eminent domain that will afford a reason for greater protection against being misled by false appearances, to railroad corporations having such right, than to those not having it. We assume that no such reason can be shown, for it seems to us very clear that the doctrine rests upon principles of public policy, and not upon the right of eminent domain. See Railroad Co. v. Passenger Ry., 167 Pa. 62, 31 Atl. 468, 46 Am. St. Rep. 659, 664.

Our conclusion is that appellee is not now entitled to the possession of the ground occupied by appellant's railroad, nor entitled to have his title thereto quieted. The judgment is therefore reversed, with instructions to restate the conclusion of law in accordance with this opinion.

(162 Ind. 608)

MATTHEWS GLASS CO. v. BURK.*

(Supreme Court of Indiana. March 16, 1904.)

SALE — CONTRACT—LEGALITY—CONSTRUCTION—PRICE—EVIDENCE.

1. Plaintiff's contract to sell window glass to defendant at prices a certain per cent. lower than those of the A. Glass Co., rebates included, not being to prevent competition, but to enable defendant to compete with the customers of the A. Co., and it not appearing that the nature and methods of the A. Co. were not known by plaintiff when it made the contract, it is no valid objection to defendant's demand for a reduction of price, on account of rebates made the A. Co., that such rebates were not in the ordinary course of trade, but to prevent competition, the price fixed by the A. Co. being less than cost of manufacture, and that such company was an unlawful combination to create a monopoly in the window glass business.

2. Plaintiff contracted to sell defendant the output of its glass factory during a certain season, at a discount of a certain per cent. lower than the lowest price made by the A. Glass Co., plaintiff to have the right to end the agreement if the price of glass fell 90 per cent. below an existing price list, and either party being authorized to cancel it on a week's notice; "payment for glass is to be made * * * promptly on receipt of same." *Held*, that the price of each shipment of glass was to be determined by the prices of the A. Co. existing at the time of its receipt, and was not affected by a subsequent reduction during the season.

3. Plaintiff having contracted to sell glass to defendant during a season, at prices depending on those to be fixed by the A. Glass Co., circular letters purporting to be addressed by such company to its customers, shown to be the means by which it informed its customers of its prices, received in the regular course of business, and recognized and acted on by such company, are admissible in an action for the price of glass sold by plaintiff to defendant.

Appeal from Circuit Court, Grant County; H. J. Paulus, Judge.

Action by the Matthews Glass Company against Benjamin F. Burk. From the judgment plaintiff appealed to the Appellate Court, whence the case is transferred under Act March 13, 1901. Reversed.

Manley & Strickler and C. L. Medsker, for appellant. Henry & Elliott, for appellee.

DOWLING, J. The appellant sued the appellee for a balance of $3,500, claimed to be due on account of eight car loads of window glass sold and delivered by the appellant to the appellee under a contract in these words:

"Marion, Indiana, October 26, 1899.

"It is hereby understood and agreed by and between Matthews Glass Company of Matthews, Grant County, Indiana, and Benjamin F. Burk of Marion, Indiana, that the former is to sell the latter virtually all the glass they make during the blast of 1899 and 1900 at a discount which will be 5 per cent. lower than the lowest price made by the American Window Glass Company, all rebates included, on all sizes single strength and on all sizes double strength to sixty united inches.

"On all sizes double strength sixty united inches and over, the price is to be 7½ per cent. lower as herein mentioned. On all shipments made to Marion, freight is to be allowed. If shipments are to be made other than to Marion, and as directed by said Burk, then no freight is to be allowed.

"The quality of all glass is to be fully up to standard brands. Should the price be lower than what would be equal to 90 per cent. from present list, then said Glass Company is to have the privilege of not furnishing in case they decide not to sell and if for any reason of dissatisfaction on the part of either party, this agreement may be annulled on one week's notice.

"Payment for glass is to be made by said Burk promptly on receipt of same less 2 per cent. Matthews Glass Company,

"Per A. Wuchner, Sec'y.

"Joseph Mayer, Prest.

"Benj. F. Burk."

The appellee filed an answer in denial, a plea of payment, and a counterclaim. The only material part of the counterclaim on this appeal is a demand for a reduction of the price of the glass on account of rebates made by the American Window Glass Company December 7, 1899, to which he alleged he was entitled by the terms of the foregoing contract. The first paragraph of answer to the counterclaim was a denial; the second, an argumentative denial; and the third averred that the rebates made by the American Window Glass Company to its customers were illegal, because not made in the ordinary course of trade, but for the purpose of preventing competition; that the price fixed by the American Window Glass Company was less than the cost of manufacture, and that the said company was an unlawful combination for the purpose of creating a monopoly in the window glass business. No reply was

*Rehearing denied May 11, 1904.

filed. A demurrer to appellee's counterclaim was overruled, and a demurrer to the third paragraph of appellant's answer to appellee's counterclaim was sustained. The cause was tried by the court, and there was a finding for the appellee. A motion for a new trial was overruled, and judgment was rendered on the finding. The rulings on the demurrer and on the motion for a new trial are assigned for error.

We find no error in the action of the court in sustaining the demurrer to the third paragraph of appellant's answer to the counterclaim. The purpose of the contract between the appellant and the appellee was not to prevent competition, but to enable the appellee to compete successfully with the customers of the American Window Glass Company. For all that appears in the pleadings, the nature of that corporation and its methods of doing business were as well known to the appellant when it entered into the contract with the appellee, as at any time afterward. The parties having seen fit to adopt the prices which might be fixed by the American Window Glass Company for the sale of its glass to its customers as the basis of the prices to be paid by the appellee to the appellant, neither of them can be heard to say that the American Window Glass Company was an illegal combination, and that its methods of dealing were unfair. They fixed the terms of the agreement with each other voluntarily and deliberately, and we can discover no reason why one of them should be released because prices went down instead of being advanced. If the prices of glass had been kept up by the American Window Glass Company, we cannot think that the appellant would have objected to the contract on the ground that the American Window Glass Company was an unlawful combination for the purpose of creating a monopoly in the business of manufacturing and selling window glass.

2. The principal controversy is over the proper construction of the contract. The appellant claims that the price to be paid for glass was 5 per cent. lower than the lowest price made by the American Window Glass Company, all rebates included, on all sizes single strength, and on all sizes double strength to 60 united inches; and 7½ per cent. lower than the lowest price made by the American Window Glass Company, all rebates included, on all sizes double strength, 60 united inches and over, less 2 per cent., up to the time of the delivery of each shipment to the appellee. The latter contends that price of the glass was to be computed upon the basis of the whole quantity sold and delivered after the transaction was completed, and that the total sum to be paid by the appellee to the appellant was to be 5 per cent. and 7½ per cent. less than the lowest prices at which the American Window Glass Company sold the same kind of glass, during the same period, all rebates included, less 2 per cent. The contract was an executory one, and contemplated the sale of the entire output of the appellant for the season of 1899-1900. The time and the quantity of the shipments were not fixed. It may be assumed that the glass was to be delivered as fast as manufactured in sufficient quantities to justify shipment. Payment was to be made by the appellee on receipt of each shipment. At what price? The contract answers the question. At a discount of 5 per cent. lower than the lowest price made by the American Window Glass Company, all rebates included, on all sizes single strength, and on all sizes double strength to 60 united inches; and on all sizes double strength, 60 united inches and over, at a discount of 7½ per cent. on prices fixed by the American Window Glass Company, less 2 per cent. The contract does not provide for the payment of any rebate by the appellant to the appellee. The purpose of the parties was to enable the appellant to undersell the American Window Glass Company. If the prices of glass fell 90 per cent. below an existing price list, the appellant had the right to end the agreement. Either party was authorized to cancel it upon one week's notice. All these provisions indicate that each shipment was to be treated as a separate sale and transaction, and that the price to be paid for the glass shipped was to be computed on the basis of the prices before that established by the American Window Glass Company existing at the date of the receipt of the glass. The agreement is the same in legal effect as if it had provided that payment for each shipment should be made at the market price, say at Chicago, on receipt of the glass. Any other construction would leave the price undetermined until the whole of the output of the factory should be received by the appellee, and neither party would know what the price would be until the end of the season. The provisions of the contract that the appellant might terminate it at any time when the price fell below 90 per cent. of the existing price list, and that either party might annul it on one week's notice, are inconsistent with the idea that the price to be paid for each shipment and delivery, depended upon the result of the action of the American Window Glass Company in fixing prices for the whole season. The language used in the contract concerning the payments by appellee is not without significance. The words of this provision are, "Payment for glass is to be made by said Burk promptly on receipt of same, less 2 per cent." It will be noticed that not even the definite article "the" is used before the word "glass." The intent of the parties appears to have been that all glass delivered should be paid for on delivery, and that such payment should close the transaction to that extent. It is clear that the parties had the right to adopt the method agreed upon for fixing the price to be paid for glass delivered and accepted under the

contract. There was nothing illegal in it, and both were bound by its terms. Having adopted this means, neither can be permitted to say that the method was not a fair and proper one. Mason v. Beard, 2 Ind. 505; Luthy v. Waterbury, 140 Ill. 664, 30 N. E. 351; Beymer, Bauman Lead Co. v. Haynes, 81 Me. 27, 16 Atl. 326; Champion Machine Co. v. Gorder, 30 Neb. 89, 46 N. W. 253; Talmadge v. White, 35 N. Y. Super. Ct. 219. Where goods are deliverable in periodical installments, and are to be paid for on the receipt of each installment, the price becomes due upon each delivery, and to that extent, when payment is made, the contract is to be treated as executed on both sides. In Veerkamp v. Hurlburd Canning, etc., Co., 58 Cal. 229, 41 Am. Rep. 265, the defendant agreed to take and pay for all the fruit raised by the plaintiff at a uniform rate per pound for all fruit so raised and delivered, at the works of the defendant. The plaintiff delivered and the defendant received the fruit under the contract, but the latter refused to pay for the fruit until all was delivered, and the plaintiff declined to deliver any more, and sued for the value of that delivered. It was held that as each lot was delivered and accepted the price agreed upon became due. So, too, in a recent case in this state—Neal v. Shewalter, 5 Ind. App. 147, 31 N. E. 848—plaintiffs agreed to sell and defendants to buy 4,000 barrels, to be delivered at defendants' mill by a fixed date. It was further agreed that defendants should buy from plaintiffs all the barrels they should use for one year from the date of the contract, at a price of 33 cents cash per barrel. The court construed this as an executory contract to sell, and not an absolute sale, and decided that, when any number of barrels was delivered and accepted, plaintiffs were entitled to payment at the contract price for the number delivered. See, also, State v. Davis, 53 N. J. Law, 144, 20 Atl. 1080; Matthews v. Hobby, 48 Barb. 167; Pineville Lumber Co. v. Thompson, 46 Minn. 502, 49 N. W. 204. Suppose that, in the present case, the price to be paid for glass delivered had been 5 per cent. less than the lowest market price at Chicago, payable on receipt of glass. Certainly no one could have claimed that this meant the lowest price at Chicago at any time during the whole period of delivery. Its obvious intent would be to fix the price upon the basis of the prices at Chicago at the date of the delivery of each installment of the goods delivered and accepted. As all the glass, except the last two shipments, was delivered to and accepted by the appellee before December 7, 1899, the date at which the American Window Glass Company made a rebate of 90 per cent. on single strength and 10 per cent. on all sizes of double strength glass, the appellee was bound to pay the price named by the contract, calculated upon the basis of the prices established and maintained by the American Window Glass Company at the date of each delivery and acceptance of glass, and he was entitled to no reduction of price on the rebate proposed and made by the American Window Glass Company to its customers December 7, 1899, except upon glass delivered and accepted after that date. The counterclaim rested upon a different construction of the contract, and the evidence was introduced upon the same theory. In our opinion, the evidence was not sufficient to sustain the finding.

No error was committed in admitting in evidence the circular letters purporting to be addressed by the American Window Glass Company to its customers. By fixing the price to be paid for glass by the appellee on the basis of prices thereafter to be established by the American Window Glass Company, the parties brought into their agreement the course of dealing of that corporation with its customers from time to time during the period of the delivery of glass under their contract. The letters were shown to be the means by which that corporation informed its customers of its prices for glass, and they were received by the appellee, or the Marion Window Glass Works, of which he was an officer, in the regular course of business, and were recognized and acted upon by the American Window Glass Company. They stood very much upon the footing of an ordinary price current, concerning which no very formal proof is ever required. Sloan v. Baird, 162 N. Y. 330, 56 N. E. 752; Gilbert v. Manning, 54 Hun, 99, 7 N. Y. Supp. 220; Parmeuter v. Fitzpatrick, 135 N. Y. 196, 31 N. E. 1032.

For the error of the court in overruling the motion for a new trial when asked for on the ground that the decision of the court was not sustained by sufficient evidence, the judgment is reversed, with directions to sustain said motion, and for further proceedings in accordance with this opinion.

(162 Ind. 580)

STATE ex rel. MOORE v. BOARD OF COM'RS OF CLINTON COUNTY et al.

(Supreme Court of Indiana. March 15, 1904.)

RAILROAD AID TAX—MANDAMUS FOR COLLECTION—CONFLICT WITH PRIOR INJUNCTION—JURISDICTION—PARTIES—PRIOR JUDGMENT FAVORABLE TO TAX.

1. Proceedings before a board of county commissioners, on petition of a taxpayer, to cancel a railroad aid tax, in which appeals were prosecuted to the circuit court and the Court of Appeals, will not be held coram non judice, on collateral attack, though prior to their commencement the board had made two adjudications against the right to have the tax collected, the board in the subsequent proceedings acting judicially and not ministerially.

2. Even if the statutory proceedings by taxpayer's petition to a board of county commissioners for canceling a railroad aid tax on the ground of nonperformance by the railroad company be exclusive, it does not preclude a resort to injunction to prevent the collection of the

tax, not only on account of nonperformance, but because of other matters rendering it void.

3. Even if an injunction restraining a board of county commissioners from entertaining proceedings for the enforcement of a railroad aid tax, and the county auditor and treasurer from collecting the same, be void so far as the board is concerned, yet, being valid as to the auditor and treasurer, it furnishes a sufficient defense to mandamus against the board to compel it to order the collection of the tax.

4. The fact that when a default injunction decree was made restraining a board of county commissioners from entertaining proceedings for the enforcement of a railroad aid tax, and the county auditor and treasurer from collecting it, the circuit court of another county, on change of venue, had decided an appeal from such board in such proceedings favorably to the tax, would not render the injunction decree void, the complaint not disclosing the existence of the appellate judgment.

5. The fact that the township is not a party defendant to a suit to enjoin a board of county commissioners, and county officers, from enforcing a township railroad aid tax, does not render the injunction decree void as to those who were made defendants and duly served.

6. A decree against a public officer operates upon the office and binds his successor.

7. Mandamus will not lie to compel a board of county commissioners to order the collection of a railroad aid tax which it has been enjoined from enforcing, especially where the personnel of the board has changed since the injunction decree was rendered on default.

On petition for rehearing. Overruled.
For prior opinion, see 68 N. E. 295.

Wm. R. Moore, A. W. Hatch, F. Winter, Clarence Winter, C. W. Miller, Atty. Gen., L. G. Rothschild, C. C. Hadley, and W. C. Geake, for appellant. Martin A. Morrison, Crane & Anderson, and Gavin A. Davis, for appellees.

GILLETT, C. J. A petition for a rehearing has been filed by appellee in the above cause. It is urged that we erred in holding that the judgment of the White circuit court was not void, although, before the institution of that proceeding, the board had ordered the tax canceled. The subsequent cause was not like a claim against the county, where the board merely audits and allows or rejects the claim. When the second proceeding arose, the board was acting in a judicial capacity. For such purpose it had been created as an independent tribunal to pass upon the rights of the taxpayers of the township. Its grant of power from the General Assembly to pass on that class of controversies constituted jurisdiction over the subject-matter. That jurisdiction was invoked by the petition which was filed to cancel the tax. Notice was given, pursuant to statute, of the pendency of the proceeding, with the result that another taxpayer, Bayless, appeared, and joined issue upon said petition, and also filed a cross-petition that the tax be ordered collected. No pleading setting up a former adjudication was filed by those seeking to have the tax canceled. The jurisdiction of the White circuit court and of this court, as well as of said board of commissioners, was each regularly invoked to pass upon the controversy, and judgment was pronounced in each instance. The proposition that in these circumstances the judgments so rendered were mere nullities seems to us to be most extraordinary. The jurisdiction of each of the courts above mentioned was regularly challenged to consider of its power to hear and determine. The exercise of this power was jurisdictional, and, if it were granted that a wrong result was reached in passing upon the power to proceed, the judgments relied on by relator were nevertheless impervious to collateral attack. None of the cases cited by appellee's counsel upon this point afford them any real support. They are either cases in which the board of commissioners was acting in a ministerial capacity, or where, in a judicial proceeding, an attempt was directly made to annul a prior judgment—a proceeding unauthorized by law.

One of the grounds on which counsel for appellee base their petition for a rehearing is that we failed to pass upon the sufficiency of the twelfth and fourteenth paragraphs of answer. The printed briefs in the cause were very voluminous, aggregating 600 pages. This fact, and the further one that appellee's counsel did not set out the substance of said paragraphs, in their brief on the cross-assignments of error, according to the numerical sequence, led us to overlook said paragraphs. We proceeded on the theory that all of the 23 paragraphs of special answer related to matters that pertained to or antedated the principal action. On a re-examination of this cause, we find that we were in error in this assumption. We shall therefore pass upon these answers now. Said paragraphs charge, in substance, that an action was instituted in the year 1893, in the Clinton circuit court, by certain resident freeholders of the township which voted said tax, suing on behalf of themselves and all other owners of real and personal property in said township liable to be assessed for said special tax, against the auditor and the treasurer of said county, and said board, to enjoin said auditor from putting said tax on the duplicate, and said treasurer from collecting said tax, and to enjoin said board from exercising any jurisdiction over any application which theretofore had been, or which thereafter might be, filed for the collection of said tax, and from paying any money or making any subscription of stock on account of said appropriation; that a summons against said officers and board was duly issued and served, and at the proper time they were defaulted; that thereafter such proceedings were duly had by said court in said action that said tax was adjudged null and void; and that a final decree of injunction was rendered against said officers and board as prayed. The answers further show that said complaint not only charged nonperformance by said railway company, but that other matters were set out which it was charged made the tax void. It is averred in the twelfth paragraph that Bayless and the relator, Moore, were at the time resident taxpayers of said township; and it was further charged in the fourteenth paragraph that said Moore had knowledge of the proceedings before the decree was rendered, and did not intervene therein.

The first objection urged by appellant's counsel to these answers is that the statutory remedy to cancel a railroad aid tax on the ground of nonperformance is exclusive, and that therefore the circuit court could not entertain jurisdiction in such a case. This objection, if well taken, does not go far enough. As pointed out above, other matters were pleaded as reasons for declaring the entire proceeding void. Injunction may be a proper remedy against an illegal and void tax. Smith v. Smith, 159 Ind. 388, 65 N. E. 183, and cases cited. This court has recognized the right in certain circumstances to enjoin a railway aid tax. Jager v. Doherty, 61 Ind. 528; Peed v. Millikan, 79 Ind. 86. If it were granted that a decree enjoining a board of commissioners from proceeding in a matter which was wholly within its jurisdiction would be invalid even on collateral attack, yet this is not such a case. As above pointed out, the complaint made a case where it was for the Clinton circuit court to determine whether, as a matter of law, the proceedings to aid in the construction of the railroad were not wholly void. English v. Smock, 34 Ind. 115, 7 Am. Rep. 215; Smith v. Smith, supra; Van Fleet, Collateral Attack, § 150. And see Board of Com'rs Owen Co. v. Spangler, 159 Ind. 575, 65 N. E. 743. It is also to be recollected that the decree in question went further than to enjoin said board, since it enjoined the auditor and treasurer from performing their respective duties. If the decree as to said latter officers is not void, it affords an answer to the mandate proceeding, since the peremptory writ will not issue where it appears that it would be nugatory in its results. Board of Com'rs Hamilton Co. v. State ex rel. Cottingham, 115 Ind. 64, 4 N. E. 589, 17 N. E. 855; State ex rel. Repp v. Cox, 155 Ind. 593, 58 N. E. 849.

It is next claimed by appellant's counsel that the Clinton circuit court could not enjoin the enforcement of the judgment of the White circuit court. If this proposition were granted, the answer to it is that the complaint did not disclose that the latter court had rendered any judgment. Such matter was therefore, at the most, but a defense. The effort of the plaintiffs in said action was to tear up the proceeding by the roots. The ulterior fact of the existence of such judgment did not render the adjudication relied upon by appellee void.

It is urged on behalf of appellant that the parties defendant to said action did not occupy such a relation to the matter in controversy as to invoke the jurisdiction of said court to determine the validity of said tax. The constitutionality of the act of May 12, 1869 (Acts 1869, p. 92), providing that counties and townships might aid in the construction of railroads, was upheld, in its provisions relative to counties taking stock in railroad companies, by holding, as the language of the act made it possible to do, that the county was not liable to the railroad company notwithstanding the favorable vote, and that the only means of enforcing the payment of aid voted was by mandate, brought after the collection of the tax, by one of the petitioners initiating the proceeding, or by some taxpayer of the county in which the aid had been voted. Lafayette, etc., R. Co. v. Geiger, 34 Ind. 185; Board of Com'rs Crawford Co. v. Louisville, etc., R. Co., 39 Ind. 192. This construction of the act has been followed as to townships voting such aid. Petty v. Myers, 49 Ind. 1; Jager v. Doherty, 61 Ind. 528; Bittinger v. Bell, 65 Ind. 445; Board Com'rs Hamilton Co. v. State ex rel. Cottingham, 115 Ind. 64, 4 N. E. 589, 17 N. E. 855. It has been held that the railroad company is not a necessary or proper party defendant in an action to have such a proceeding declared void. Jager v. Doherty, supra; Bittinger v. Bell, supra. In the latter case, where the action was to enjoin the county treasurer from collecting or attempting to collect a tax voted in aid of a railroad company, it was held that it was not necessary to make the board of commissioners a party defendant; but it was further held that the treasurer, by reason of his office, was both a proper and a necessary party defendant. It would seem, considering the posture of said Clinton county case, that the last-cited precedent would require us to hold that the board was at least a proper party defendant. All of the taxpayers of the township were represented as plaintiffs; the township in its corporate capacity was not empowered by statute to take any steps in the granting of such aid, while the board and the auditor and the treasurer had duties to perform, under the law, if the proceeds of tax should be paid over. We incline to the opinion that the board, as the agent of the township, was a proper party defendant under our Code. But even if we were to admit that there was no proper party defendant before the court, it would not follow that its injunction was void. It was, at least, binding as to the defendants to the action, they having been duly served with process. Keyes v. Ellensohn (Sup.) 30 N. Y. Supp. 1035; In re Ruppaner's Will (Sup.) 41 N. Y. Supp. 212.

An injunction is essentially a preventive remedy; mandamus operates much, in the relief it affords, like a decree for specific performance. Ordinarily, injunction restrains action; mandamus commands it. The question is whether one court should require a defendant to do a thing which another court of equal jurisdiction has forbidden.

Mandamus was originally a prerogative writ, and it does not issue now ex debito justitiæ. It issues at discretion, although this discretion is to be exercised in accordance with the rules that have been established concerning such practice. The writ is not granted where it will work injustice or introduce confusion and disorder. For these reasons a court will not ordinarily command the doing of an act which another court of competent jurisdiction has forbidden, where the doing of the act would subject the defendant to punishment for contempt. Ex parte Fleming, 4 Hill, 581; People ex rel. Humphrey v. Board, 30 Hun, 146; People v. Blackhurst (Sup.) 11 N. Y. Supp. 669; Ohio, etc., R. Co. v. Commissioners, 7 Ohio St. 278; People ex rel. Ives v. Circuit Judge, 40 Mich. 63; State ex rel. Mills v. Kispert, 21 Wis. 392; High, Extra. Leg. Rem. § 23; 2 Spelling, Inj. & Extra. Rem. § 1378. The Ohio case above cited was one where a mandate was sought to compel a board of commissioners to make a subscription for railroad stock in accordance with a vote that had been taken. There had been a prior injunction suit instituted against the commissioners to cancel the tax, and they had answered the bill. Such suit resulted in a final decree absolutely and perpetually enjoining the commissioners from subscribing to the stock. In disposing of the mandamus case, the Ohio Supreme Court said: "It is true that the Ohio & Indiana Railroad Company was not a party to the proceeding in chancery in which the decree of injunction was rendered, and that decree does not therefore bind or conclude the company by any of its findings; but it does nevertheless have the effect, while it exists in full force, to preclude the company from having the peculiar remedy which it now here seeks. If we were to award the peremptory writ of mandamus, we should command the commissioners of Wyandot county to do the very act which, by our decree of injunction in full force, they are forbidden to do. The idea of such inconsistency is wholly inadmissible. If the peremptory writ of mandamus were to issue, and the defendants failed to obey it, they would be liable to process for contempt; while, on the other hand, if they obey it, they would be equally in contempt for disobedience to the decree of injunction. Even where the order or decree of injunction is made by a court of competent jurisdiction other than that in which the mandamus is sought, the latter will not thus place a party between two fires by subjecting him to contradictory orders. Ex parte Fleming, 4 Hill, 581. Whether there be any way in which the Ohio & Indiana Railroad Company can get rid of the decree of injunction is a question not before us. As to that, it is at liberty to proceed as it may be advised, but we are clear that it cannot be done in this collateral proceeding." State ex rel. Mills v. Kispert, supra, has an especial application to this case. In that case the defendant's predecessor in office had been enjoined from doing the act which the alternative writ commanded. The court said: "Was the treasurer justified by the injunction in not paying over the money? It is maintained by the counsel for the relator that the injunction suit is collusive, and all proceedings in it void. We do not see any certain evidence of collusion on the part of Reinal, the treasurer. It would be a dangerous doctrine to establish that a defendant, enjoined from doing any particular act, may himself determine that the injunction is void, and disregard it. We think he did right in obeying the injunction, and that it is a protection to him so long as it is in force; and it cannot be annulled in this action. The remedy of the relator is not by mandamus, but by petition to be made a party to the injunction suit, or by some other proceeding."

Equity acts in personam, and in a very real sense it may be asserted that a court so acts in punishing for contempt for the violation of a decretal order of injunction. As was in effect pointed out in the principal opinion herein, although in another connection, a judgment estoppel, in a case where an officer is a party, operates upon the office. The successor is in privity with his predecessor. It is to be borne in mind in this case, therefore, since the personnel of the board has changed since the injunction suit, that while the board is bound by the result of such suit, yet its members are not personally responsible for any dereliction of duty upon the part of the former board in not appearing. There is therefore an especial reason in this case why the members of the board as now constituted should not be compelled to do an act which at their peril they would be required to justify if cited for contempt in violating the decree pleaded. We hold that paragraphs 12 and 14 of appellee's answer were sufficient, and that the court below erred in sustaining a demurrer to them.

As to the further grounds on which a rehearing is sought, we dispose of them with the statement that we remain content with the views expressed in the principal opinion.

In addition to the mandate heretofore entered by us, it is now ordered that the judgment sustaining a demurrer to said two paragraphs of answer be reversed. As no reason remains for the granting of a rehearing, the petition is overruled.

(162 Ind. 338)

CONNER v. ANDREWS LAND, HOME & IMPROVEMENT CO., Limited.

(Supreme Court of Indiana. March 18, 1904.)

CONTRACTS—MUNICIPAL IMPROVEMENT ASSOCIATIONS — BREACH — DAMAGES—BILLS AND NOTES—FAILURE OF CONSIDERATION—APPEAL —HARMLESS ERROR—ADMISSION OF EVIDENCE —STRIKING OUT PLEADINGS—WAIVER OF OBJECTIONS — FINDINGS OF FACT — BRIEFS — RULES OF COURT.

1. Where the facts found support, and the judgment of the court rests, on the second paragraph of the complaint, any error in overruling a demurrer to the first paragraph is harmless to defendant.

2. Overruling a motion to strike out parts of a pleading is not available error on appeal.

3. The modification of special findings and conclusions of law based thereon is not authorized.

4. Where plaintiff, a city improvement association, executed to defendant certain notes in consideration of an agreement on defendant's part to build a factory and equip it with at least 30 machines, which would employ in the neighborhood of 100 men, and defendant, after the building of the factory, only placed in it 10 machines, and never employed more than 11 men, the court was justified in concluding that the conditions on which the notes were given had not been complied with.

5. A finding that plaintiff, by reason of the nonperformance of the contract by defendant, was damaged in the sum of $6,000, was a finding of fact.

6. By excepting to the conclusions of law an appellant admits that the facts have been fully and correctly found.

7. A defendant is not harmed by a conclusion of law that on the payment of damages he should hold certain real estate free from all claims.

8. An assignment that damages are excessive presents no question for consideration in an action arising on contract.

9. A recital that the evidence of certain witnesses "was similar" to the evidence of other witnesses, is but a conclusion, and not a compliance with Sup. Ct. Rule 22 (55 N. E. v), requiring the particular evidence to be recited in narrative form.

10. Plaintiff, a city improvement association, conveyed to defendant certain lots, and paid him $6,000 in cash in consideration of the construction by defendant of factory buildings to be equipped with 30 machines, which would be sufficient to employ 100 men. Defendant, after the factory was completed, operated only 10 machines, and employed but from 2 to 11 men. Plaintiff brought suit for breach of contract, and the court awarded it $6,000 damages. *Held* that, as the breach of the contract entitling plaintiff to the damages awarded it was fully proven, defendant was not harmed by the admission of parol evidence as to negotiations between defendant and plaintiff leading up to the contract, in which plaintiff insisted on the insertion of a provision for the employment of 100 men by defendant, and defendant convinced plaintiff that the proposed number of machines would require that many men, whereupon plaintiff executed the contract without insisting on the incorporation of the provision in the written instrument.

Appeal from Superior Court, Allen County; John H. Aiken, Judge.

Action by the Andrews Land, Home & Improvement Company, Limited, against Ovid W. Conner. From a judgment for plaintiff, defendant appeals. Transferred from the Appellate Court under Burns' Rev. St. 1901, § 1337u. Affirmed.

J. D. Conner and Barrett & Morris, for appellant. Lesh & Lesh, Branyan & Freightner, J. B. Kenner, and Henry Colerick, for appellee.

JORDAN, J. Appellee upon a special finding of facts in the lower court recovered a judgment whereby it was awarded, among other things, $6,000, as damages. From this judgment appellant appeals, and relies on the following alleged errors for a reversal: (1) Overruling his motion to strike out parts of the second paragraph of the complaint; (2) overruling a demurrer to the first paragraph of the complaint; (3) error in the conclusions of law; (4) overruling motions to modify certain conclusions of law and finding of facts; (5) denying a motion for a new trial. The complaint is in two paragraphs and a demurrer to each was overruled. The answer was a general denial.

The following appear to be substantially the facts as alleged in the first paragraph of the complaint: On July 10, 1899, appellant and appellee entered into a contract in writing, by the terms of which it was agreed that appellee should convey to appellant certain real estate situated in the town of Andrews, state of Indiana, embracing lots Nos. 57 to 68, inclusive, in Cubberly & Bell's Addition, and also pay him $10,000, $6,000 of which was to be in cash, labor, or material, and $4,000 in two promissory notes of equal amount, containing certain specified conditions; in consideration of which appellant was to construct on said real estate factory buildings of given dimensions, and to equip said buildings by placing therein at the start not less than 30 new, or equivalent to new, machines, and an engine of sufficient power to operate the same, and to add thereto from time to time as the business might require. By the terms of said contract it was further stipulated that said notes were to be deposited in the First National Bank of Wabash, Ind., one to be paid within 60 and the other 90 days after the said buildings had been completed and the machinery placed therein and in operation; that on the failure on the part of appellant to equip said buildings with said machines, or to operate the same, or should he abandon said business or cause said machines to be removed at any time within five years, then the title to said lots should revert to appellee. The lots were duly conveyed to appellant, and $6,000 were paid to him in cash, labor and material, and said notes were duly executed. Appellant caused said buildings to be constructed, but failed to place therein 30 new and good machines as required of him. He also failed to operate said factory in substantial compliance with the terms of said contract, but, on the contrary, abandoned the business for which the factory was constructed. It is further averred that the aforesaid notes were transferred by appellant to Taylor, Dick & Dick; that by failure on appellant's part to comply with the terms of the contract said notes have become inoperative and void, and title to said property has reverted. A reconveyance was duly demanded, but refused. The prayer is for the cancellation of said notes and the deeds of conveyance, and that appellee be declared the owner of said lands. Copies of the contract and notes were filed with the complaint.

The second paragraph of the complaint differs from the first in that it alleges, in addition to the averments in the first: That the purpose of appellee company was to promote the general good and prosperity of the town of Andrews by aiding in the location of factories, which would furnish employment to a large number of citizens at remunerative wages. That with this end in view it obtained a large number of donation contracts and leases, from the proceeds of which it proposed to reimburse itself for any bonus paid out as an inducement for the location of a factory. A large amount of these subscription contracts and leases contained a specific stipulation that the money or rentals should be payable only upon the location of a factory and the operation thereof with not less than 100 employés. "That at the time said contract was entered into between plaintiff and said Conner, and before the signing thereof, the plaintiff informed the defendant of the manner in which it proposed to raise the money to reimburse and repay itself for the time and money by it to be expended, and of the stipulation in such contracts of subscriptions and leases as to the employment of 100 men in such factory, and insisted that such stipulation be also inserted in the contract with him. Conner thereupon stated that it would require from three to four men to operate each of the thirty machines specified in the contract, and, as the contract required the placing in said factory of at least thirty machines, and the operation thereof, that this would require at least one hundred men to operate said factory; and that the provisions in the contract were substantially equivalent to the proposed clause. He represented to the plaintiff that he did not desire to have a direct stipulation in said contract requiring him to operate such factory by the employment of one hundred men, because said contract had to be recorded in a public record, and that his employés would thereby learn of such stipulations, and take advantage thereof in demanding higher wages, else go on a strike, and thereby reduce the number of employés below the requirement of said contract. To convince plaintiff that it would require at least one hundred men to operate said machines, he requested plaintiff to send a committee to the factory at Wabash, Ind., known as the 'Underwood Factory,' where he represented they would find machines in operation identical with those with which he proposed to equip said factory, to ascertain how many men it would require to operate said machines. Plaintiff thereupon did send such committee to said factory at Wabash for said information, and was informed by the foreman thereof that said representations were true, and that it would in fact require one hundred men to operate such machines. Plaintiff believed these representations, and relied thereon in signing and delivering such contract, and with this understanding and belief the plaintiff signed and delivered said contract. It is alleged that such representations were made fraudulently by said Conner, and at the time he made the same he did not intend to employ one hundred men in such factory, and falsely represented such purpose only to induce plaintiff to execute said contract, and thereby get the said property and moneys from the plaintiff." The breach of said contract is then fully charged, whereby appellee became "unable to collect said donations and subscriptions and rentals from leases in a large sum, to wit, about twelve thousand dollars," and that the appellee sustained damages thereby in the sum of $10,000, for which judgment was prayed in addition to the relief sought by way of forfeiture of title to said lands and the cancellation of said notes.

The written contract referred to in each paragraph of the complaint, and entered into between appellant and appellee, omitting the signatures of the parties and the formal parts, is as follows:

"In consideration of the sum of ten thousand dollars ($10,000) to be paid me by the Andrews Land, Home and Improvement Company, as hereinafter stated, and the conveyance to me by good and sufficient warranty deed or deeds (a perfect title to be shown by an abstract to be furnished to me by you) of the following described real estate, situate in the town of Andrews, in the county of Huntington, in the State of Indiana, to wit: Lot Nos. 57, 58, 59, 60, 61, 62, 63, 64, 65, 66, 67, and 68, in the Cubberly & Bell's Addition to Andrews, I agree to construct a building or buildings for the purpose of manufacturing fine cabinet wares and other specialties upon the above described real estate, one building forty-eight by one hundred feet (48x100) with basement for shafting and machinery, constructed with brick with stone foundation. One building forty by one hundred (40x100) two stories of wood and corrugated iron or of equal floor area on stone foundation. In addition to this I will build an engine and boiler room of sufficient size for an engine of sufficient power to operate said factory with which I agree to equip said room. At the start I will place in the building or buildings not less than thirty new machines or those in proper condition, and add thereto as in my judgment the business will justify, additional machines, and such other buildings as additional machines and the increasing business will require. The foregoing ten thousand ($10,000) shall be paid to me as follows: Six thousand dollars ($6,000) in cash to be paid me in labor, material and cash during the construction of said building or buildings. I agree to accept such work and labor and material as I may need in the construction of said building or buildings as you may be able to furnish, which must be of the kind and quality which I demand and must be furnished at the market price. And whatever work and labor and material are furnished as stated and accepted by me shall be credited upon said six thousand dollars ($6,000) aforesaid, and the balance paid in cash as demanded aforesaid. Four thousand dollars ($4,000) which are to be represented by two notes of two thousand dollars ($2,000) each, to be deposited in the First National Bank of Wabash, $2,000 to be paid within sixty days and $2,000 to be paid within ninety days after said building or buildings are completed and the machinery aforesaid is placed therein and in operation. Said ten thousand dollars are to be acceptably secured and paid by you to me under the terms of this contract and proposition aforesaid. If within any time within five years I abandon the business or cause the machinery to be removed from said buildings, the lots and the buildings therepn shall revert to you if you so elect. You are to furnish the right of way for railroad switch. You are to guarantee that I can contract for and have delivered promptly native lumber at ten dollars ($10.00) per thousand feet to be used in building (only such as you furnish on subscription), good building brick delivered on the ground at five dollars ($5) per thousand. That lime stone laid in good lime mortar at one dollar and fifty cents ($1.50) per perch. I will have the building insured and in case of loss within five years will pay same to you unless I shall reconstruct within six months. In letting the contract for the foregoing named building, I will give you the preference on a contract for the same at the same price others will do it for.

"Andrews, Indiana, July 10, 1899."

The two promissory notes mentioned in the complaint and sought to be canceled are identical, except as to the date of maturity, the first of which reads as follows:

"$2,000. Andrews, Indiana, April 7, 1900.

"The Andrews Land, Home and Improvement Co., promise to pay Ovid W. Conner, or order, the sum of Two Thousand and 00/000 Dollars, payable within sixty days after the buildings are completed and the machinery is placed in said buildings and in operation as provided in a certain written contract, executed on the 10th day of July, 1899, by and between said company and said Conner. For value received and without relief from valuation or appraisement laws and with attorney's fees."

The signatures of the parties are omitted.

Taylor, Dick & Dick filed a cross-complaint, thereby seeking to recover judgment on the notes, to which appellee filed an answer pleading, in substance, the same facts alleged in the complaint. The court, at the request of the parties, made a special finding of facts and stated its conclusion of law thereon.

The facts found by the court follow and support in the main those alleged in the second paragraph of the complaint. In fact, it is apparent that the judgment of the court rests on this paragraph; therefore we need not consider the sufficiency of the first, for, if the trial court erred in overruling the demurrer thereto, such error, under the circumstances, would be harmless to appellant. Illinois, etc., R. R. Co. v. Cheek, 152 Ind. 663, 53 N. E. 641, and cases cited. By the first paragraph of the special finding the court finds that the plaintiff (appellee herein) is a corporation organized under the laws of the state of Indiana, and that its purpose was to promote the general good and prosperity of the town of Andrews, Ind., and the citizens thereof, by aiding in the location and construction of factories at or in said town, which would furnish employment to a number of its citizens and laboring men; that with this end in view, on the 10th day of July, 1899, it entered into the contract with the defendant as set out in the complaint. A copy of the contract is set out and embodied in the special finding. The second paragraph of the finding recites that under the averments of this contract there were conveyed to appellant the several lots described in the complaint, situated in the town of Andrews, Huntington county, Ind. The other paragraphs of the finding may, in a general way, be summarized as follows: Upon the conveyance to appellant of these lots he constructed the buildings as required, in which he placed at the beginning 30 machines, and thereafter added some others, but "only ten, in all, of them, were adequate for the business contemplated by the contract." The further facts in respect to the execution of the subscription contracts and leases containing conditions requiring the employment of at least 100 men, and the demand by appellee of appellant that a clause be inserted in the contract requiring him to employ 100 men, his explanation as to why he did not desire to insert such a clause, and his representations and statements made to appellant that the agreement therein to use 30 machines was, in effect, the equivalent of agreeing to employ 100 men, as the use of that number of machines would require 100 men to operate them, his suggestion and direction to appellee that it send a committee to the factory at Wabash, Ind., to ascertain if it would not in fact require 100 men to operate the 30 machines, the action of this committee and its report to appellee in regard to what it had ascertained at the Wabash factory, that appellee executed the contract in suit relying on said statements, and that both parties intended and agreed thereby that the factory should be operated with not less than 100 men, are fully found by the court. The court also finds the payment of the $6,000 by appellee, except a small balance of $9, and the execution by it of the two notes for $2,000 each, as set out in the complaint. It is further found that the construction of the building was completed in November, 1899, except as to an extra floor, which was placed therein in April, 1900, at which time all buildings were completed, and by April of the next year appellant had the aforesaid machinery placed therein and in operation. The court finds in respect to the solicitation, upon the part of appellant, of orders, and the filling thereof, and the delivery of all products by him for which orders had been obtained. It is further found that appellant operated the factory continuously from the 8th day of April, 1901, to the commencement of this action, but that from said date he only employed therein from 2 to 11 men, as the business required, but at no time did he employ more than 11 men in operating said factory. It is also found that none of the machines placed in said factory had been removed, nor has appellant abandoned the business for which said factory and buildings were constructed under the contract in question. The amount of money expended by appellant in operating the factory, the sum paid to him by appellee, and the amount paid by him for the machines, and their value, are facts also found. The court further finds that at no time since the execution of the contract in suit up to the time of the commencement of this action has appellant complied with said contract, either as to the number of men employed or as to the number of machines to be operated in said factory; that by the averments of the contract in question the court found that appellant bound himself to operate the factory with not less than 30 adequate machines, which would require the services of 100 men in their operation. At no time between the making of the contract in suit and the commencement of the action did appellant have or place in his factory more than 10 adequate machines. The fact that appellant assigned the two notes executed by appellee to Taylor, Dick & Dick as collaterals for a loan of money obtained by him from these parties, who accepted the assignment of said notes with notice that appellee had a defense thereto, are all found by the court. It is further found that on June 25, 1901, appellee made a written demand on appellant for a reconveyance of the lots, with which he refused to comply, but no demand was made that he comply with the contract as to the number of men to be employed or the number of machines to be used. It is further found that from the date of the contract to the beginning of this suit more than a reasonable time had elapsed for the entering upon and performance by appellant, upon his part, of the contract. The court also finds that the damages suffered by the plaintiff by reason of the nonperformance of the contract by the defendant is $6,000.

Upon the facts found by the court it stated the following conclusions of law: (1) That the title to the real estate in controversy, and described in said contract in finding No. 2, which title was vested in the defendant, does not revert to plaintiff by reason of the breach of the contract; (2) that the conditions upon which said two notes of $2,000 were given have not been completed within a reasonable time, and they are without consideration, and are void, and should be canceled; (3) that by reason of the defendant's failure to comply with his said contract plaintiff has been damaged in the sum of $6,000, which amount plaintiff is entitled to recover; (4) that upon the payment of said amount as herein adjudged the title to said real estate shall vest in said Ovid W. Conner, free of all claims of plaintiff by virtue of said contract.

Appellee excepted to the first and fourth conclusions of law, and appellant reserved exceptions to the second, third, and fourth, and over his motion for a new trial the court rendered judgment to the effect that the plaintiff recover of the defendant $6,000, together with costs, and further adjudged and decreed that on the payment of this judgment the defendant's title to said real estate conveyed to him by plaintiff be quieted. It was also decreed that the two promissory notes of $2,000 each, held by the cross-complainants, Taylor, Dick & Dick, should be canceled, and that plaintiff recover costs from these cross-complainants. The latter parties apparently abide by the judgment rendered against them, and decline to join in this appeal.

The first contention of appellant is that the court erred in denying his motion to strike out certain parts of the second paragraph of the complaint. It has been universally held by this court that overruling a motion to strike out parts of a pleading does not constitute available error. Appellant's motion to modify some of the special findings and conclusions of law thereon was properly denied for the reason that such procedure is not authorized. Chicago, etc., Ry. Co. v. State ex rel., 159 Ind. 237, 64 N. E. 860; Smith v. Barber, 153 Ind. 322, 53 N. E. 1014.

It is next insisted that the court erred in its second conclusion of law, whereby it stated that the conditions upon which the two notes in suit of $2,000 each were given had not been complied with within a reasonable time, and that these notes were without consideration, void, and should be canceled. Enos T. Taylor, Julius Dick, and Jacob Dick were the holders of these notes under an assignment for value by appellant. Appellee made these holders of the notes parties defendants to this action. They appeared and filed a cross-complaint seeking to recover upon the notes, alleging therein that they were the holders thereof for a valuable consideration. Issues were joined between appellee and them. The second conclusion of law was at least adverse to these defendants. This conclusion is justified by the facts found, and appellant's exception thereto was properly overruled.

He further complains of the third conclusion, wherein it is stated that the plaintiff, by reason of the defendant's failure to comply with the contract in suit, had been damaged in the sum of $6,000. It is claimed that there is no finding to sustain this conclusion. By the twenty-third paragraph of the special finding the court expressly finds that the plaintiff, by reason of the nonperformance of the contract by the defendant, is damaged in the sum of $6,000. This was a finding of a fact. Blair v. Blair, 131 Ind.

194, 30 N. E. 1076. By excepting to the conclusions of law appellant admitted that the facts had been fully and correctly found by the court. Louisville, etc., R. R. Co. v. Miller, 141 Ind. 533, 37 N. E. 343, and cases cited; Blair v. Curry, 150 Ind. 99, 46 N. E. 672, 49 N. E. 908.

Appellant complains of the fourth conclusion of law, by which the court adjudged that, on the payment of the damages awarded to appellee, appellant should hold the real estate free from all claims by virtue of the contract. Conceding, without deciding, as appellant contends, that this conclusion was not justified by the facts, nevertheless it is apparent that he was not injured or harmed thereby. Hence he has no grounds for complaint.

The reasons assigned in appellant's motion for a new trial and discussed by his counsel in this appeal are (1) that the damages are excessive; (2) that the evidence is not sufficient to support the finding of the court; (3) error of the court in admitting certain evidence. In regard to the assignment in the motion for a new trial that the damages are excessive, it may be said that such an assignment in an action as is this, arising out of a contract, presents no question for consideration. White v. McGrew, 129 Ind. 83, 28 N. E. 322; Smith v. Barber, 153 Ind. 322, 53 N. E. 1014. Appellant, in stating the evidence in his brief, has not complied with the requirements of rule 22 of this court (55 N. E. v). In several instances, after reciting the evidence of certain witnesses, it is asserted that the evidence of another witness mentioned "was similar." This was but a conclusion, and not a recital "in narrative form" of the particular evidence as required by the above rule. Under the circumstances, therefore, appellant is not in a position to demand as a matter of right a review of the evidence by this court in order that it may determine its sufficiency to sustain the special finding. But, notwithstanding appellant's failure to comply with the rule in question, we have examined and considered the evidence, and find that it supports the special finding and judgment.

It appears that at the trial the court, over the objections of appellant, permitted appellee to introduce evidence to show, in effect, that before the execution by the parties of the contract in question appellee demanded that a provision be inserted therein whereby appellant would expressly agree to employ in his factory 100 men, and insisted that it would not execute the contract in the absence of such a clause. Appellant, it appears, refused to comply with this request, stating that he would not stipulate in the contract to employ that number of men for the reason that the contract, when executed, would be recorded in the public records, and his employés would thereby be apprised that he had expressly bound himself to employ 100 men, and would be induced to strike for higher wages knowing that he was bound under the contract to employ that number of men. He stated to appellee that, inasmuch as he would agree in the contract to place or operate 30 machines, this would necessitate the service of 100 men to run that number. Appellee's representatives stated to him that they were not familiar with the machines proposed to be operated, and did not know how many men that number would require. He then suggested that they send a committee to a factory at Wabash, Ind., where machines similar to those proposed to be placed in his factory were in use, and that they would there ascertain that 30 machines would require 100 men to operate them. This committee was sent to the factory at Wabash, as suggested by him, and ascertained there that the statement which he made was correct, and that 30 machines of the kind proposed to be placed in the factory would require the services of 100 men in their operation. This appears to have satisfied appellee, and it stated to appellant that it would execute the contract without the express stipulation being inserted therein in regard to the employment of 100 men as it had previously demanded.

Counsel for appellant contend that this evidence was improperly admitted, for the reason that the contract in suit was complete on its face, and that parol evidence could not be received to vary, contradict, or add to its terms or provisions. There can be no controversy as to the correctness of this general rule of evidence, to which, however, the law recognizes exceptions. But as to whether the court erred or not in admitting this evidence is, in our judgment, under the facts, entirely immaterial, for, to say the least, appellant was not prejudiced thereby in any of his substantial rights. This evidence may be stricken out and rejected altogether and still the judgment of the court on the question of damages can be upheld. In fact, there is evidence given on the trial which proves that the operation of 30 machines by appellant would have required the employment of 75 to 100 men. The findings of the court, which are amply supported by the evidence, disclose a clear breach of the contract. Appellee is shown to have paid to appellant $6,000 as a part of the bonus, in labor, material, and money in the construction of the factory, and this is the amount of damages awarded to it. It is disclosed that, instead of operating 30 machines, as he agreed, he operated only 10, and employed in the factory from 2 to 11 men only. If he, under the circumstances, were suing appellee to recover the $6,000 which it had agreed to pay, certainly, in order to prevail, he would be required to establish that he had performed the conditions imposed upon him under the contract. Why, then, under the facts, should he be permitted to defeat appellee in recovering back the $6,000 which it paid to him in the faith that he would perform the conditions of the contract as he had agreed?

We have fully examined and considered all the points discussed by counsel for appellant, and are satisfied that the latter has no just grounds for a reversal of the judgment.

Finding no available error, the judgment is therefore affirmed.

RUSCHE v. PITTMAN.*

(Appellate Court of Indiana. Division No. 2. March 18, 1904.)

MECHANIC'S LIEN—STATUTE—CONSTRUCTION—REPAIRS.

1. Under Burns' Rev. St. 1901, §§ 7255, 7256, providing that a mechanic may acquire a lien on a building repaired, and on the interest of the owner of the lot on which it stands, a mechanic who makes repairs to a house on land in possession of one under contract of sale, holding bond for the deed, a portion of the price of which had been paid, is entitled to enforce his lien, as against the holder of the legal title, on surrender of the premises after cancellation of the contract of sale.

Appeal from Superior Court, Vanderburgh County; Jno. H. Foster, Judge.

Action by Henry Rusche against Annie Pittman. From a judgment for defendant, plaintiff appeals. Reversed.

Logsdon, Chappell & Veneman, for appellant. J. E. Williamson, for appellee.

WILEY, P. J. A demurrer to appellant's complaint was sustained by the trial court, and that ruling is the only question presented by the appeal.

The complaint avers that appellee sold to one Loigorte Arnold certain real estate by a written contract, and executed to her a bond for a deed, by the terms of which she bound herself, upon the full payment of the purchase money, which was to be paid in monthly installments, to convey to her. That under said contract the vendee took possession of the real estate, and occupied the same until her death. That during said time she paid appellee a part of the consideration, and that at the time of her death she was hopelessly insolvent, and left no property or assets whatever with which to pay debts. That after she took possession of said property she employed appellant to make certain repairs on the dwelling house situated thereon. That appellant, under said employment, performed labor of the value of $29. That, within 60 days of the time of completing said repairs, he filed notice of his intention to hold a lien on said real estate and dwelling house for the amount of his said claim, which notice of lien was duly and timely recorded in the recorder's office, etc. That, after the death of the said Loigorte Arnold, appellee declared forfeited and canceled said contract and bond, and took possession of said real estate, and still holds the same from the heirs of said Loigorte Arnold under the terms of the said bond. The complaint avers that of the purchase money the vendee paid $650, but is silent as to whether or not the contract of sale contained a forfeiture clause by which the vendor could declare a forfeiture in default of the payment of any installment of the purchase money. The prayer of the complaint is that said lien be enforced, and the real estate be sold to satisfy appellant's claim of $29.

Under the averment of the complaint, the vendee became the equitable owner of the property, and went into possession. It is important to inquire if she had any interest in the property, under her contract, to which appellant's lien could attach. As above suggested, she had an equitable interest therein. She paid $650 on the purchase price. She caused the repairs to be made while she was in possession under color of her equitable title. The lien was filed while she was in possession, and before appellee declared a forfeiture. The purchaser had such an interest in the property under the contract that she could have enforced specific performance upon payment of the entire purchase price. The statute provides that a mechanic may acquire a lien upon a building erected or repaired, "and on the interest of the owner of the lot or parcel of land on which it stands." Sections 7255, 7256, Burns' Rev. St. 1901. As such equitable owner of the property, the purchaser or vendee, while in possession, had a right to exercise control and dominion over it, and hence had a right to contract for repairs. As the vendee had an equitable interest in the property, it would seem that it would necessarily follow that the lien would attach to the extent of such interest, and the statutes cited substantiate this view. In McAnally et al. v. Glidden et al., 30 Ind. App. 22, 65 N. E. 291, it was held that, where labor liens attached under a leasehold, a voluntary surrender of the lease before its expiration, and the acceptance thereof by the lessor, would not operate to defeat such liens. In Montpelier, etc., Co. v. Stephenson et al., 22 Ind. App. 175, 53 N. E. 444, it was held that a lien for work and labor in the construction of a derrick for a lessee, to be used in the operation of an oil and gas well on leased premises, was not impaired by the forfeiture of the lease, where the lien attached prior to the forfeiture. In the recent case of Lengelsen v. McGregor et al. (Ind. Sup.) 67 N. E. 524, it was held that where a party purchased real estate with the intention of leasing it to his brother, and permitted him, with his knowledge and consent, to erect a building thereon, knowing him to be insolvent, the land was subject to a mechanic's lien in favor of the builder. In the case we are considering, Mrs. Arnold paid to appellant on the purchase price $650. She not only acquired an equitable interest in the property by virtue of

¶ 1. See Mechanics' Liens, vol. 34, Cent. Dig. § 335.
*Reversed on rehearing, 73 N. E. 473.

her contract, but, in addition thereto, she acquired a substantial interest therein by reason of the amount paid. Under the statute and in equity, appellant's lien should attach to the property to the extent of her interest therein. Appellant's claim amounts to only $29, which is insignificant in comparison to the amount paid appellee. While the complaint falls far short of being a model pleading, under the authorities cited, and upon equitable principles, it states a cause of action.

Judgment reversed, and the court is directed to overrule the demurrer to the complaint.

(34 Ind. App. 198)

UNDERWOOD et al. v. DECKARD.[1]

(Appellate Court of Indiana. Division No. 2. March 18, 1904.)

ESTOPPEL—IN PAIS—EQUITABLE—SUIT TO SET ASIDE JUDGMENT—LIMITATIONS—PARTITION OF LAND OF INFANT OWNER—JURISDICTION.

1. A person who does not induce another to change his position injuriously, and who is not guilty of any fraudulent conduct toward the latter, is not estopped from asserting his rights against the latter, who had knowledge of the facts.

2. An owner conveyed a part of his land to a married woman and her children, and another part to her husband and his children. The husband and wife, believing that the conveyance to them gave them the title in fee, sold the land to a third person. Subsequently the husband and wife and the third person discovered that the children had rights. The husband and the third person then instituted in the name of the children, who were minors, and the third person, an ex parte proceeding for partition. The children had no knowledge of the proceedings, and no one had authority to act for them. The husband was appointed commissioner, and the land was sold to the third person for the consideration given in the conveyance by the husband and wife. The children received no part of this consideration. *Held*, that the children, on attaining full age, were not equitably estopped, as against the third person, from asserting their rights.

3. A suit to set aside a judgment in ex parte proceedings for partition instituted in the name of plaintiffs, who were then minors, and a third person, because the court did not have jurisdiction of the persons of plaintiffs, as no one had authority to represent them, is not barred by the six-year statute of limitations, though fraud is an incidental cause of action.

4. Though an infant owner of real estate may maintain partition and procure the appointment of a commissioner to sell if the land is not divisible, the use, without authority, of the name of an infant owner, in partition proceedings, does not confer jurisdiction over the infant, so as to bind him by the decree rendered.

Appeal from Circuit Court, Monroe County; Newton Crooke, Special Judge.

Action by Hugh V. Underwood and others against James M. Deckard. From a judgment for defendant, plaintiffs appeal. Reversed.

George L. Reinhard, Seymour Riddle, and Gavin & Davis, for appellants. R. A. Fulk, Edwin Corr, and Duncan & Batman, for appellee.

COMSTOCK, J. Appellants brought this action against the appellee to have a certain judgment rendered against them and in favor of said Deckard in the Monroe circuit court set aside and declared null and void. The complaint is in two paragraphs, and alleges, in substance, that on the 20th day of January, 1893, the appellants and the appellee were the owners in fee simple, as tenants in common, of certain real estate therein described, situated in Monroe county, Ind., each being the owner of the undivided one-fifth interest thereof; that on the said 20th day of January, 1893, the appellee, without the knowledge or consent of either of the appellants, filed his petition in said court, joining the appellants with himself therein, in the form of an ex parte proceeding, wherein it was alleged that appellee and appellants were the owners of the real estate above referred to as tenants in common, each owning an undivided one-fifth interest thereof, and averring that said lands could not be divided without injury to the whole, and asking that a commissioner be appointed by the court to sell said lands and distribute the proceeds among the owners. Each paragraph further alleges that a commissioner was appointed by the court, who pretended to sell the whole of said lands to the appellee; that said pretended sale was by the commissioners reported to and approved by the court, deed made and approved, and a judgment of the court entered quieting the title to said lands in the appellee. It is further alleged that the appellants at the time were all infants, and that no process of the court was ever issued or served on them in said proceedings; that they had no knowledge of the proceedings until long time thereafter; that they had no next friend, statutory guardian, or guardian ad litem; that two of said appellants became 21 years old within two years prior to the beginning of the action; that the said court acted wholly without jurisdiction over the persons of said appellants, or either of them; that in fact there was no sale of said real estate by the said pretended commissioner to the said Deckard, and that no money or anything of value was ever given or promised to be given by the said Deckard or received by the commissioner for said lands; and that the appellants never directly or indirectly received anything whatever for or in consideration of the pretended sale of said lands; and that neither of the appellants ever consented to such proceedings or order of the court for the sale or transfer of said property; and that appellee at all times had full knowledge of all the facts. Demurrers were overruled to the complaint, and appellee answered in several paragraphs. Demurrers were sustained to each paragraph of the answer except the third and sixth, which are in the words and figures following, to wit:

"Par. 3. The defendant, further answering herein, says that after the purchase of the real estate mentioned in the complaint at

[1] Rehearing denied. Transfer to Supreme Court denied.

said commissioner's sale he immediately went into possession thereof and began to make, and from that time has made, valuable and lasting improvements thereon; that he has occupied the same as owner, and has exercised full acts of ownership thereover; that the plaintiffs have all lived in the immediate vicinity of said real estate during all of said time, have known his occupancy of said real estate and of the circumstances under which it was held during all of said time; that the eldest of said plaintiffs is now twenty-eight years of age; that the next one is twenty-six years, the next one twenty-four, and the youngest twenty-two years of age; and that neither of said plaintiffs at any time prior to the commencement of this suit made any claim or demand whatsoever against the defendant for said real estate, or any part thereof, or at any time made any complaint to this defendant of the irregularity of the said partition proceedings, but, upon the contrary, have recognized the validity of the same by making no complaint thereof, by renting the said real estate, paying the rent thereon, and by recognizing this defendant's ownership of the said real estate."

"Par. 6. The defendant, further answering each of the first and second paragraphs of the complaint separately and severally herein, says that the cause of action herein did not accrue within six years prior to the commencement of this suit."

The appellants replied to the third and sixth paragraphs of answer by general denial.

The issues were submitted to the court for trial, and the court made a special finding of facts. The special finding shows: That one Hugh Hill owned the land in question; that he conveyed a part to Susan M. Underwood and her children, and another part to Lafayette Underwood and his children. That said Susan and Lafayette are the mother and father, respectively, of the appellants. The deeds conveying said real estate were duly recorded in the proper deed record of said Monroe county, and possession immediately taken of said real estate by said Lafayette Underwood. In December, 1892, said Lafayette and Susan, being mistaken as to the legal effect of the deed made to them and believing in good faith that said deeds conveyed to them the entire amount of said real estate, undertook to sell and convey by deed of general warranty, in which they both joined, the entire amount of said real estate to one James M. Deckard, defendant, of Monroe county, Ind., who was likewise ignorant of any right, title, or interest which the children of said Lafayette A. Underwood and Susan M. Underwood had in said real estate, or any part thereof, and who likewise believed in good faith that said Lafayette A. Underwood and said Susan M. Underwood, at the time of said conveyance to him, the said Deckard, were the owners of all the said real estate. After the sale of the above-described real estate by Lafayette A. Underwood and Susan M., his wife, to said James M. Deckard, and immediately after the execution of the deed of conveyance therefor, the said deed was duly delivered to said James M. Deckard by the said Lafayette A. Underwood and Susan M. Underwood, and the said Deckard immediately went into possession and occupancy of all said real estate, and continued to occupy and cultivate the same until the present time, claiming it as his own land, and making lasting and valuable improvements thereon, repairing fences, making ditches, and cleaning up ground. Said Lafayette A. Underwood and Susan M. Underwood, at the time of the conveyance to them and their children of the said real estate by the said Hugh H. Hill, were the father and mother of the following named children, then living, and who are the plaintiffs in this cause: (1) Frank E. Underwood, about 2 years old at the time of said conveyances by said Hill to the said Underwoods; (2) William C. Underwood, between 4 and 5 years old at the time of said conveyances; (3) Thomas H. Underwood, between 6 and 7 years old at the time of said conveyances from said Hill to the said Underwoods; (4) Hugh V. Underwood, between 8 and 9 years old at the time of said conveyances. Neither said Lafayette A. Underwood nor the said Susan M. Underwood had any child or children living other than those above named. The consideration paid for said sale and conveyance of the real estate from Lafayette A. Underwood and Susan M. Underwood to said James M. Deckard was $1,650. The said children did not join in the conveyance from said Lafayette A. Underwood and Susan M. Underwood to said James M. Deckard, and had no knowledge of or connection with such sale, and had no knowledge or information that they, or either of them, had any interest in or title or right to said real estate. On the 20th day of January, 1893, the defendant, James M. Deckard, and the said Lafayette A. Underwood, having been informed of the interests of plaintiffs in said real estate, and for the purpose of placing the title of the plaintiffs in and to said severally described tracts of land of which said Deckard and said plaintiffs were then the owners by reason of said conveyance to them by their said uncle, Hugh H. Hill, and by reason of the deed of conveyance by Lafayette A. Underwood and wife to said Deckard, and in order to deprive the said plaintiffs of their said title to said land, instituted in the Monroe circuit court of Monroe county, Ind., then in session, a certain ex parte proceeding in the name of the said James M. Deckard and the plaintiffs in this action by petition to said court, in which petition the plaintiffs herein and the defendant, James M. Deckard, purported to join, stating that they (the plaintiffs and defendant herein) were the owners in fee simple and tenants in common of the real estate described therein, being the same real estate described in the complaint; and further stating that the said Deckard and these plaintiffs were each the owner of one undivided one-fifth of said real estate, and that the same was not divisible without injury to said parties, and asking that a commissioner be appointed by the court to make sale of said real estate, and distribute the proceeds thereof among the said parties according to their respective shares or interest.

The court, on said petition of the parties, solely on the statements contained in said partition, made a finding, decree, and judgment of the tenor and to the effect that the facts stated in said petition were true; that the petitioners were together the owners in fee simple and tenants in common of the real estate described in said petition; that the said defendant, Deckard, was the owner of one-fifth part in value of the said real estate, and that said Hugh V. Underwood, Thomas H. Underwood, William C. Underwood, and Frank E. Underwood were the owners of the other four-fifths in value of said real estate, and that partition thereof could not be made without injury to said parties; and the court further adjudged, ordered, and decreed that said Lafayette A. Underwood be appointed a commissioner to sell said real estate at private sale, at its appraised value, to be ascertained by appraisement as provided by law in such cases; but the court made no finding and gave no judgment on the subject that these plaintiffs were then all infants under the age of 21 years, which was true. The said Lafayette A. Underwood thereupon undertook to serve as such commissioner, and procured the appraisement of said real estate, which was appraised at the sum of $1,600, and filed bond, as required, to the approval of the court, and on the same day reported to the court that he had sold the said real estate, as such commissioner, to said James M. Deckard, for the sum of $1,650, cash in hand, and that said sum had been paid by said Deckard, and that said Underwood asked to be ordered to make said Deckard a deed of conveyance of said real estate as such commissioner, and to distribute the proceeds thereof among the petitioners according to their respective interests, which was accordingly done by the court in its order and judgment duly entered of record, and said deed was accordingly executed and delivered, and said Lafayette A. Underwood then and there reported the execution and delivery of the deed to said Deckard, which was indorsed by the court "Approved," and the distribution of the proceeds, and was then by the further order of the court discharged from further service as such commissioner. At the time said proceedings were had and said commissioner's deed was made it was understood and agreed between said defendant, Deckard, and said Lafayette A. Underwood that the money previously paid by said Deckard to said Underwood, together with the notes executed for the deferred payments, should be and constitute the consideration for the said commissioner's sale and deed of conveyance to said Deckard, and that the said Underwood would consider and treat said original consideration as the payment for said real estate received by him from said Deckard, and that he would charge himself with plaintiffs' portion of the proceeds, and pay the same over to the plaintiffs according to their respective shares of interest as they respectively became of the lawful age of 21 years, and there was no other consideration paid to or received by said Underwood as commissioner for the sale of said real estate or said deed of conveyance. The said Lafayette A. Underwood, then and there assuming without authority to act as the agent of these plaintiffs, then and there executed and filed of record receipts for the distributive shares of these plaintiffs, as their agent, purporting that each of said plaintiffs had received from him, the said Underwood, as commissioner, his respective share of the proceeds of said commissioner's sale, which was and is wholly untrue. At the time of the said ex parte proceedings before the said Monroe circuit court the plaintiffs herein were all minors and persons under the age of 21 years, and had no statutory guardian, and were not represented by next friend or statutory guardian or guardian ad litem, or in fact by any person who had authority to act for them or either of them; nor did they, or either of them, have any knowledge thereof; nor did they directly or indirectly consent to said proceeding or sale of said land by said Lafayette Underwood as commissioner, either by guardian, or in person, or in any manner. The said Lafayette A. Underwood had no authority whatever from the plaintiffs herein, or either of them, to represent them, or either of them, in said proceedings, or in any other proceedings for the partition or sale of said real estate; and said plaintiffs never authorized said proceeding to be instituted or carried on, or authorized or employed any attorney or other person to do so for them, or either of them. The plaintiffs herein have never received any portion of the purchase money paid by said defendant, Deckard, to said Lafayette A. Underwood, nor has either of said plaintiffs received any portion thereof, nor has the said Lafayette A. Underwood ever paid them, or either of them, nor any one of them, any portion of the purchase money of said real estate. No consideration was paid or passed between said Deckard and said Lafayette A. Underwood at the time of the said ex parte proceedings, or at any other time, on account of such sale as commissioner by said Underwood, except the agreement between them that the original purchase money paid by said Deckard for said land should be accepted by said Underwood, as commissioner, as the consideration for said sale by him to said Deckard and said commissioner's deed, and that said Underwood should charge himself with said amount in his report as such commissioner, and there was no other consideration whatever for such commissioner's sale and deed to said Deckard. There was in fact no sale of said real estate by said Lafayette Underwood, as such commissioner, to said James M. Deckard, except for the purpose of placing the title of the plaintiffs in said Deckard, and to perfect the title of said Deckard in said real estate on account of the defect of his title by reason of the attempted conveyance from said Lafayette A. Underwood and wife to said Deckard. The said defendant, James M. Deckard, at the time of said ex parte partition proceedings, and at the time he received and accepted the said commissioner's deed from said Underwood, had full knowledge of and was fully acquainted with the fact that these plaintiffs had each one undivided interest in said real estate, and that neither of said plaintiffs was actually present in court at said partition proceedings, and that neither of them was represented by any attorney or agent who was authorized to act for them, or either of them, except so far as their said father had authority to act or employ counsel for them. That said plaintiffs, when they learned of having interest in said real estate, took legal advice from practicing attorneys at Bloomington, the county seat of Monroe county, Ind., concerning their interest in said land and the bringing of an action to assert the same, and were advised by said counsel and believed that they could not maintain a suit for their right, interest, or title in and to said real estate until after the youngest of the brothers, to wit, the plaintiff Frank E., should arrive at the age of 21 years, and accordingly waited until that time and the 7th of January, 1901, instituted this suit to set aside the judgment in said ex parte partition proceedings in this court. That the said defendant immediately went into the possession of said real estate under said purchase and deed from Lafayette A. and Susan M. Underwood, and has continuously remained in open, notorious, exclusive, and adverse possession thereof until this time, made valuable and lasting improvements thereon, including repairing fences, making ditches, cleaning and clearing the ground, and still retains possession thereof. That at the time of the institution and the prosecution of the said proceedings in partition the plaintiffs were living with their father, the said Lafayette Underwood, as a part of his family, who was acting for or on behalf of the said children, who, for them, employed counsel, who, in connection with counsel employed by the defendant, instituted and conducted said proceedings in partition. The plaintiffs have continuously since the 20th day of January, 1893, lived in the immediate neighborhood of the said real estate, and knew of defendant's possession thereof. That in the year 1899, the plaintiffs Frank E. and Thomas Underwood rented, occupied and used a part of said real estate, renting the same from the defendant. The plaintiffs, except Frank E., heard they had an interest in said real estate and of the said partition proceedings and sale therein within six months from the 20th day of January, 1893, and during the years 1895 and 1896 were all fully informed of said partition proceedings and sale by Thomas J. Sare, an attorney at this bar, with whom they consulted for the purpose of asserting their right therein by suit or otherwise.

On the facts the court stated the conclusions of law, omitting the formal part thereof, as follows: (1) For the defendant, and that the plaintiffs take nothing by this suit therein; (2) that the plaintiffs' cause of action is barred by the statute of limitations. Appellants severally excepted to each of the conclusions of law. Judgment was rendered in favor of appellee.

Appellants assign as error the action of the court in overruling their demurrer to the third and sixth paragraphs, respectively, of appellee's answer, and in its first and second conclusions of law upon the facts specially found.

The third paragraph of answer attempts to plead an estoppel. There were no facts pleaded showing that appellee was induced by the conduct of appellants to change his position injuriously to himself. He had full knowledge of the facts. No fraud is charged against the appellants, nor that they deceived him to his injury. An estoppel in pais is not shown. The principle of equitable estoppel does not apply to the facts stated. Bonner's Law Dic. tit. "Estoppel"; Dezell v. Odell, 3 Hill (N. Y.) 219, 38 Am. Dec. 628; 11 Am. & Eng. Ency. of Law (2d Ed.) 421; Fletcher v. Holmes, 25 Ind. 458; Ross v. Banta, 140 Ind. 120, 34 N. E. 865, 39 N. E. 732; Tinsley v. Fruits, 20 Ind. App. 534, 51 N. E. 111.

The six-year statute of limitations pleaded in the sixth paragraph of answer is not applicable. Relief is sought against a judgment obtained without jurisdiction of the person of appellant. Fraud is an incidental, but not the primary, cause of the action.

In Wilson v. Brookshire, 126 Ind. 497, 25 N. E. 131, 9 L. R. A. 792—an action brought to set aside a sheriff's sale and to annul the deed made by the sheriff in pursuance of the sale, not because of any actual or constructive fraud, but because, owing to the relation which the purchaser sustained to the transaction, the judgment was actually paid and satisfied before the sale was made—in the course of the opinion, the court, by Mitchell, J., say: "The statute which provides that actions for relief against fraud shall be brought within six years applies to actions the immediate and primary object of which is to obtain relief from fraud, and not to actions which fall within some other class, even though questions of fraud may arise incidentally;" citing Eve v. Louis, 91 Ind. 457; Caress v. Foster, 62 Ind. 145. In Vanduyn v. Hepner, 45 Ind. 589, the foregoing quotation is copied from Eve v. Louis et al. Evidently the trial court held fraud to be the gist of the action. Both paragraphs of the complaint show an utter want of jurisdiction. That they also incidentally show fraud does not bring the action within the six-year statute of limitations. The court not having jurisdiction of the persons of the appellants in the ex parte proceedings, the statute cannot apply.

In the propositions of law laid down in the able brief of appellee's counsel, in the main, we concur. They are, however, based upon the erroneous theory that the complainants primarily seek relief from fraud. The demurrer to each of said paragraphs should have been sustained.

Appellee has assigned as cross-error the action of the court in overruling his demurrer to each paragraph of the complaint. In the argument in support of this specification of error it is insisted, as in the answer brief of appellee, that the complaint is based upon the fraud and collusion of the appellee, Deckard, and Lafayette Underwood. In this connection it is not necessary to repeat what we have already said as to actions in which the ground for the complaint is want of jurisdiction and fraud is only incidentally involved. The complaint avers, and the court has found, that the appellants were infants, and that without their presence, knowledge, or consent a decree was prepared which the court was led to adopt, and which, if it stands, will deprive them of property and any compensation therefor. Granted, as claimed by counsel, that an infant owner of real estate may maintain partition, and have the appointment of a commissioner to sell if the land is not divisible; it does not follow that the name of an infant may be used in proceedings in court without any authority, and that then such infant can be bound by a decree to which he never assented. The special findings show that in law appellants, as between the parties to this action, were not parties to the proceedings, and that the decree is a nullity, because there was no jurisdiction of the persons, as essential as jurisdiction of the subject-matter, and that, after appellee had purchased the real estate of the parents of the appellants for the purpose of divesting the title of appellants, and without any new consideration moving from the appellee, and without any consideration moving to appellants, and without their knowledge or consent, secured the decree which is sought to be set aside. Upon the facts found the conclusions of law should have been found in favor of appellants.

The judgment is reversed, with instruction to the trial court to sustain the demurrers to the third and sixth paragraphs of answer, and to restate the conclusions of law in favor of appellants.

STATE ex rel. STUART et al. v. HOLT et al.*

(Appellate Court of Indiana, Division No. 2. March 8, 1904.)

COUNTY TREASURER—ACTION ON BOND—TAXPAYER AS RELATOR—RIGHT TO SUE—INDIVIDUAL CAPACITY—JOINDER OF PLAINTIFFS.

1. Burns' Rev. St. 1901, § 251, requires that every case be prosecuted in the name of the real party in interest, and section 253 provides that actions on official bonds shall be brought in the name of the state of Indiana, upon the relation of the party interested. *Held*, that where a board of county commissioners and the county auditor, though conversant with the facts, refused to sue on a county treasurer's bond to recover for misappropriation and conversion of county funds, a private taxpayer, though not peculiarly interested, could sue as relator in behalf of the other taxpayers, whose number made the joinder of all impracticable.

2. Burns' Rev. St. 1901, § 251, requires that every case be prosecuted in the name of the real party in interest, and section 253 provides that actions on official bonds shall be brought in the name of the state on the relation of the party interested. A private taxpayer sued as relator in the name of the state, and also in his individual capacity, on the bond of a county treasurer, alleging the refusal of the county officers to do so. He alleged that "plaintiffs herein have been put to great labor and expense in the preparation and prosecution of this cause and in the employment of legal counsel herein," and prayed, as a reasonable compensation therefor, a per cent. of the recovery. *Held*, that there was a misjoinder of parties plaintiff, since the taxpayer as an individual had no cause of action on the bond, and his claim for reimbursement was antagonistic to his capacity as relator, in which he represented the public.

Appeal from Circuit Court, Marion County; H. C. Allen, Judge.

Action by the state of Indiana on the relation of Romus F. Stuart, and Romus F. Stuart, against Sterling R. Holt and others. Judgment for defendants, and plaintiffs appeal. Affirmed.

P. W. Bartholomew, for appellants. Wilson & Townley and Hawkins & Smith, for appellees.

WILEY, P. J. Suit by appellants against appellee Sterling R. Holt upon his official bond as treasurer of Marion county. The sureties on the bond, the board of county commissioners, and Harry B. Smith, auditor, were made party defendants, and they are all joined as appellees. The amended complaint is in a single paragraph, to which a demurrer was sustained. Appellants declined to plead further, and judgment was pronounced against them for costs. Sustaining the demurrer to the amended complaint is assigned as error. The assignment of error is joint.

In the amended complaint and the assignment of error, appellants are designated as follows: "State of Indiana ex rel. Romus F. Stuart, and Romus F. Stuart." It thus appears that Romus F. Stuart is suing as relator and in his individual capacity. There are several grounds of demurrer stated, but

*Rehearing denied. Appealed to Supreme Court. 71 N. E. 653.

those which challenge the capacity of appellants, jointly and severally, to sue, and the sufficiency of the amended complaint, are all that need be considered.

The amended complaint is voluminous, but, for the purposes of this opinion, its material averments may be briefly stated: It is averred that Romus F. Stuart is a resident taxpayer and freeholder, and that he had paid into the county treasury all taxes assessed against him which were due at the commencement of this action; that as such taxpayer he has an interest in all moneys paid into, paid out, and belonging to Marion county, in common and jointly with all taxpayers; that the number of taxpayers in Marion county exceeds 50,000, which renders it impracticable for them to all join as plaintiffs; "therefore the plaintiffs bring this action for their own, on behalf of, and for the benefit of all the taxpayers of Marion county, Indiana, and in trust for the county of Marion." The amended complaint then avers that appellee Holt was duly elected treasurer of the county, gave bond, which was approved, qualified, and served as such for two years. That, as such treasurer, large sums of money came into his hands. That he did not honestly and faithfully perform the duties of his office according to law, in this, to wit: (Here follows a detailed statement of the various alleged derelictions of his official duties, as breaches of his official bond, wherein it is charged that he misappropriated large sums of money belonging to the county, to his own use, and failed and refused to account for the same.)

From the view we have taken of the law, which requires an affirmance of the judgment, it becomes unnecessary to set out the several alleged breaches of the bond, but it is proper to refer to two of the charges against him, as follows: That he collected $9,746.36 interest on $70,000 of time warrants, and that he loaned to the county, through the board of commissioners, large sums of the county's money, upon which he collected interest in the sum of $23,882.41, and unlawfully appropriated the same to his own use. These items show the character of the charges of malfeasance.

As the action cannot be maintained in its present form, it is unnecessary to discuss or decide the many charges of the alleged culpability of appellee Holt. The complaint charges that, notwithstanding Holt violated the law as specifically stated, the board of commissioners unlawfully and illegally ordered that he be paid his salary for the two years of his term of office, in violation of law, and that the auditor unlawfully issued warrants therefor in the sum of $24,000, which were paid, and that he wrongfully and unlawfully refused to return the same to the treasury. The complaint avers that the members of the board of commissioners are made parties because they refused to become relators or plaintiffs, and that their consent to become relators or plaintiffs could not be obtained; that the auditor is made a party because he refused to bring this action as plaintiff or relator. It is then charged that the appellees, constituting the board of commissioners, and Harry B. Smith, auditor, had full knowledge of the facts set forth in the complaint, constituting the unlawful and illegal acts charged; that the said various sums of money were due and owing to the county; that it was their duty to the taxpayers to recover the same; that, notwithstanding said knowledge, they refused and still refuse to bring this action, and have unlawfully entered into a pretended settlement with said Holt upon his returning a small sum of money to the treasury, which said sum is not embraced in the sums due the county as set forth in the complaint, and which settlement was fraudulent and void as against the taxpayers of Marion county. The complaint alleges a demand upon and a refusal by appellee to pay into the treasury the various sums alleged to have been misappropriated by him. The last averment in the complaint, preceding the prayer, and one which we think is significant, is as follows: "And the plaintiffs herein have been put to great labor and expense in the preparation and prosecution of this cause, and in the employment of legal counsel herein; that a reasonable compensation to remunerate them in the premises is a sum of money equal to twenty-five (25) per cent. of whatever moneys may be recovered on the final settlement and adjudication of this cause."

If Romus F. Stuart as relator, and Romus F. Stuart in his individual capacity, may jointly prosecute this action as plaintiffs, then the merits of the controversy here presented may be determined, for the breaches of Holt's official bond are well pleaded, and the demurrer admits their truth. To enable them to succeed as joint plaintiffs, it must affirmatively appear from the complaint that they have a community of interest. If their interest is not joint, they cannot be joined as plaintiffs. The statute requires that "every case must be prosecuted in the name of the real party in interest." Section 251, Burns' Rev. St. 1901. To this there are exceptions, as provided by section 252, supra, viz.: "That an executor, administrator, trustee of an express trust authorized by statute may sue without joining with him, the person for whose benefit the action is prosecuted. A trustee of an express trust, within the meaning of this section, shall be construed to include a person with whom, or in whose name, a contract is made for the benefit of another." Under this latter section appellant Stuart, as relator or in his individual capacity, cannot be regarded as a trustee of an express trust, and hence we must resort to the first statute quoted, to determine whether or not the action is prosecuted by the real party in interest. If, under the allegations of the complaint, Romus F. Stuart, as relator, may be considered the real party in interest, it does not necessarily follow that Stuart, in his individual capacity, is also a real party in interest. This can only be regarded as an action on the official bond of a public officer, for alleged official breaches thereof. The statute provides that: "Actions upon official bonds, and bonds payable to the state shall be brought in the name of the state of Indiana, and upon the relation of the party interested." Section 253, Burns' Rev. St. 1901. Generally speaking, the party in interest in such action is the public, and, primarily, an individual citizen is not clothed with power to prosecute an action upon an official bond, for, within the meaning of the statute, he is not the party "interested." He is but one of the body politic, and does not in any capacity represent the public, or the party interested.

But conditions may arise by which a private citizen, or a number of private citizens collectively, may prosecute an action to right wrongs against the public and to protect the public interest. If this were not true, there would be no remedy for any wrongs that might be perpetrated. While it is not technically true, yet it is substantially so, that for every wrong there is at law or in equity an adequate remedy. Each county in the state is an involuntary subdivision of the state, and a corporation for governmental purposes. It is a part of the machinery of local government. By statute, the board of commissioners becomes the legal representative of the county, and is charged with the management of its affairs. It is the duty of such board to conserve and protect the best interests of the county, and this includes the duty of compelling payment of all just dues in its favor, and the additional duty of seeing that unjust demands are not made upon or paid out of its treasury. In doing this they do not act for themselves, but for the county, whose servants they are. Hence, if money has been improperly drawn from the treasury, or fraud practiced by which the rights of the public have been infringed, primarily, it is the duty of the board of commissioners, or in some instances the auditor, to proceed by law to redress the wrong, and recover and return to the treasury the misappropriated funds. It would be a travesty upon the law, and a rebuke to equity, to say that if a public officer or officers, charged with the duty to act in such case, would not act, the public would be without remedy. If this were true, public officers could conspire and collude with each other to loot the public treasury, practice all manner of dishonesty, and enrich themselves at the public's expense, and be beyond the reach of the law. Fortunately, the principle here involved has many times been before the courts and decided in the interest of the public, and according to equitable rules that appeal strongly to good conscience.

The right of a private citizen to prosecute an action directly against a public officer for a misappropriation of public funds, where the proper officers refused, upon demand, to do so, was affirmed by the Supreme Court in the recent case of Zuelly et al. v. Casper et al., 67 N. E. 103. True, in that case it was not an action on an official bond, but directly against the officer charged with the malfeasance, in which the board of commissioners was made a party because it refused to prosecute. The suit was brought by three taxpayers for the use and benefit of the citizens of the county, and it was held that under the averments of the complaint they could maintain the action. By analogy, the rule there declared leads to the conclusion that such action may be maintained upon the official bond of a public officer by the state, upon the relation of a citizen and taxpayer, for the use and benefit of the county. In the Zuelly-Casper Case, supra, a great many authorities are cited in support of the rule declared. The following cases are also illustrative of the principle involved: Kimble v. Board of Commissioners, etc. (Ind. App.) 66 N. E. 1023; Shepard v. Easterling, 61 Neb. 882, 86 N. W. 941; In re Coles' Estate (Wis.) 78 N. W. 402, 72 Am. St. Rep. 854; Quaw v. Paff, 98 Wis. 586, 74 N. W. 369; Land, etc., Co. v. McIntyre, 100 Wis. 245, 75 N. W. 964, 69 Am. St. Rep. 915; Mock v. City, etc., 126 Cal. 330, 58 Pac. 826; Webster v. Douglas County, 102 Wis. 181, 77 N. W. 885, 78 N. W. 451, 72 Am. St. Rep. 870.

It has been held that a taxpayer may protect from lawless waste a public fund by injunction. Board v. Markle, 46 Ind. 96; Deweese v. Hutton, 144 Ind. 114, 43 N. E. 13; Alexander v. Johnson, 144 Ind. 84, 41 N. E. 811; Dillon Municipal Corporations (1st Ed.) §§ 732, 736. It has also been held that a taxpayer has such an interest in the subject as entitled him to examine the records and files of the county auditor's office, under reasonable regulations, and that such right may be enforced by mandamus. State ex rel., etc., v. Kind, Auditor, 154 Ind. 621, 57 N. E. 535. In Zuelly v. Casper, supra, the court said: "The reasons given by the court in support of the right of a taxpayer to maintain an action to enjoin an unlawful disposition of public funds apply with equal force where the wrong had been accomplished, the fund dissipated, and the public officers whose duty it is to sue for and recover the money obstinately or corruptly refuse to act."

The allegations of the complaint show a flagrant misappropriation of public funds; that neither the board of commissioners nor the county auditor would bring the action; that there are over 50,000 taxpayers in the county, and it would be impracticable to join all of them as plaintiffs; and that the action is prosecuted for the use and benefit of all of the inhabitants of the county. These allegations, under the authorities, are sufficient to show a right of action in the individual citizen and taxpayer as a relator.

. If we were not confronted with the fact that there is joined in this case as plaintiffs, and as appellants, the state on the relation of Romus F. Stuart, and Romus F. Stuart individually, we would not have to proceed further. But unfortunately, and we use the term advisedly, in view of the facts alleged, and admitted by the demurrer to be true, such is the case. If it were not clear from the complaint why Romus F. Stuart, individually, was joined as a coplaintiff, it was made manifest in the oral argument, when, upon inquiry by the court, counsel for appellants admitted he was made a party, to the end that the interests of the relator might be fully protected as to costs and attorney's fees in the event of a successful termination of the action. The complaint seeks a recovery in favor of each of the appellants. To grant relief to two or more joint plaintiffs, without showing a common cause of action in all of them, a community of interest would be violative of a well-established and wholesome principle of law. We are unable to see any cause of action stated in the complaint that is common to both of them. They must each be a party in interest. One is a relator, who is suing for the use and benefit of all the county corporate; the other is suing to secure his costs and attorney's fees. From this viewpoint, it appears to us that, instead of their having a common interest, their interests are diametrically opposed. We thus have this anomalous condition: A citizen suing upon an official bond as a relator, and the same citizen suing upon the same official bond in his individual capacity. This is not in harmony with the rules of harmony. An individual, as such, cannot sue upon an official bond, and, if he can sue at all, it must be as a relator. Jackson v. Rounds, 59 Ind. 116, 119, 120. A proper and improper relator in an action upon an official bond can no more be joined as plaintiffs, than proper and improper plaintiffs could be joined in an action upon contract. In either case the complaint, to be good against a demurrer, must show a common cause of action in both plaintiffs, and that they are the real parties in interest. Their interest must be joint. Harris v. Harris, 61 Ind. 117; Martin v. Davis, 82 Ind. 38; McIntosh v. Zaring, 150 Ind. 313, 49 N. E. 164; Elliott v. Pontius, 136 Ind. 652, 35 N. E. 562, 36 N. E. 421; Whitney v. Fairbanks (C. C.) 54 Fed. 985.

The complaint having proceeded upon the theory that the relator is seeking to recover moneys for the use and benefit of the inhabitants of the county, which have been, as alleged, wrongfully misappropriated and withheld from the county, and Stuart, as an individual, is seeking to have a part of such moneys appropriated to his own use and benefit, it is upon that theory that it must be tested and judged on appeal. Upon this theory the complaint is not good, for it does not state a common or joint cause of action in favor of both of appellants. Where two or more plaintiffs join in an action, the complaint must show a cause of action in all, or it will fall before the attack of a demurrer for want of facts. Louisville, etc., Ry. Co. v. Lohges, 6 Ind. App. 288, 33 N. E. 449; Steinke v. Bentley, 6 Ind. App. 663, 34 N. E. 97; Brown et al. v. Critchell; 110 Ind. 31, 7 N. E. 888, 11 N. E. 486. The fallacy of the position assumed by appellants, that Stuart as relator and Stuart individually are properly joined as plaintiffs, is made manifest by an expression we find in the brief of their counsel. He says: "We believe it was entirely right and necessary to do so [to join Stuart individually], as covering and comprising both his personal interest and his interest as relator." There are two horns to this legal dilemma: (1) Stuart individually, under the averments of the complaint, has no interest whatever in the subject of the controversy; and, (2) if he had, it affirmatively appears from the complaint that such interest is antagonistic to that of the relator, who avers that he represents the public. In either event, even conceding that the complaint states a cause of action in favor of Stuart individually, it is evident that it does not state the same cause of action that it does in favor of the relator, and hence, under the well-settled rules of pleading, is subject to the successful assault of a demurrer.

These considerations necessarily leave the merits of the controversy unsettled, for the demurrer to the amended complaint was correctly sustained, and the judgment is affirmed.

(33 Ind. A. 563)

SCHEPMAN et al. v. BUHNER et al.

(Appellate Court of Indiana, Division No. 2. March 10, 1904.)

HIGHWAYS — ESTABLISHMENT — VIEWERS — APPOINTMENT — TIME OF MEETING — BOARD OF COMMISSIONERS—JURISDICTION—WRONGFUL EXERCISE—REMEDY.

1. Burns' Rev. St. 1901, § 6742, relating to the establishment of highways, provides for the filing of a petition and giving of notice, and requires the board of commissioners to "appoint three persons to view such highway." Section 6745 makes it the duty of the auditor to issue a precept to the sheriff commanding him to notify the viewers of the time of their meeting, and "such viewers at such time" shall proceed to view the highway. The report of viewers duly appointed showed that they did not meet until several days subsequent to that specified in the commissioners' order. *Held*, that their report was not void, as the commissioners had no authority to name the day on which they were to meet, and section 6743 directing the auditor to issue the precept as to time was directory, and not mandatory.

2. The remedy of any person aggrieved by the report of viewers that the highway petitioned for was not of public utility was not by motion to set aside the report, but was under Burns' Rev. St. 1901, § 6753, permitting action on a second petition on a bond for costs being filed by the petitioners.

Appeal from Circuit Court, Jackson County; T. B. Buskirk, Judge.

Proceedings by H. William Schepman and others against J. Henry Buhner and others for the establishment of a highway. From a judgment setting aside the report of viewers, the petitioners appeal. Affirmed.

O. H. Montgomery, for appellants. Jas. F. Applewhite, for appellees.

WILEY, P. J. Appellants filed their petition before the board of commissioners of Jackson county for the location of a public highway, and gave notice of the pendency thereof according to the provisions of the statute. At the next ensuing session of the board the petition was regularly presented, and the board, after having determined that due notice was given, appointed viewers to view the proposed highway and report at the next session of the board. In pursuance of section 6743, Burns' Rev. St. 1901, the auditor issued a precept to the sheriff commanding him to notify such viewers of the time, place, and object of their meeting, which was duly served. By the precept the viewers were directed to meet on the 18th day of April, 1901. At the next ensuing session of the board the viewers filed their report to the effect that the proposed highway would not be of public utility. Upon the filing of such report the petitioners appeared by counsel, and upon their unverified motion the board set aside the report as being void for the reason that the viewers did not meet until the 22d day of April, 1901, when the precept served upon them directed them to meet upon the 18th day of April. Thereupon the board appointed other viewers, who reported favorably, and such subsequent proceedings were had as that the road was ordered established, etc. After the second set of viewers had filed their report, appellees entered their special appearance, and moved that the appointment of the last viewers be set aside, and their report rejected, and that the board approve the report of the first set of viewers. This motion was based upon the proposition that the board of commissioners were without authority to appoint the second viewers after the first viewers had reported against the utility of the proposed highway, and that it was the duty of the board to approve the report of the first viewers and dismiss the petition. After final judgment was entered by the board of commissioners establishing the highway, appellees appealed to the court below, where they moved that the cause be dismissed on the ground that all subsequent proceedings after the report of the first viewers were void for want of jurisdiction. This motion the court sustained, and such ruling is the only error assigned.

The single question for decision is this: Was the action of the first viewers void because they did not meet and qualify on the day named in the precept? If it was, then the action of the board in setting aside their report was justified, for then it would be as if no report had been made. It is well to look to the statute relating to the proceedings in locating public highways. Section 6742, Burns' Rev. St. 1901, provides for the filing of a petition and the giving of notice, and makes it the duty of the board of commissioners, upon proof of notice, to "appoint three persons to view such highway." Section 6743, Burns' Rev. St. 1901, makes it the duty of the auditor to issue a precept to the sheriff commanding him to notify "such viewers of the time, place and object of their meeting. Such viewers at such time, after having taken an oath, * * * shall proceed to view the highway to be located," etc. Section 6744, Burns' Rev. St. 1901, provides that such viewers, or a majority of them, "shall make a report of their proceedings at the ensuing session of the board," etc. Section 6753, Burns' Rev. St. 1901, provides that, if the viewers report that the proposed highway would not be of public utility, then no second or subsequent petition shall be acted upon by the commissioners, unless the petitioners shall first file a bond with approved surety conditioned for the payment of costs should the viewers report that they deem the proposed highway to be of no public utility. If that part of section 6743, supra, to which we have referred, is mandatory, then there is some basis for appellants' contention that the action of the viewers was void because they did not meet and qualify on the day named in the precept. The objection made to the report of the viewers, as indicated by appellants' motion, is that they did not meet on the day and at the place fixed by the board. The viewers were appointed by the board upon the authority of section 6742, Burns' Rev. St. 1901, and that statute gives it no authority to name the day and place of their meeting. The board has exhausted its authority when it has appointed the viewers. It has been ruled that the commissioners' court is one of special and limited jurisdiction, and that it has no power but that conferred upon it by statute, and that it must employ such power in the mode prescribed. Helms et al. v. Bell et al., 155 Ind. 502, 58 N. E. 707. It has power to establish highways, but the conditions and manner of its exercise are clearly defined by statutes, and must be substantially observed, or the proceeding becomes a nullity. Helms et al. v. Bell et al., supra. As the board of commissioners had no power to fix a day and place for the meeting of the viewers, that part of its order was a nullity. Under section 6743, supra, it seems to be the duty of the auditor to fix a time and place for, and acquaint them with the object of, their meeting. In the discharge of their duties as viewers the petitioners, and no one else, have any concern. While there is nothing in the statute preventing the petitioners from being present while they are making their view, it is not contemplated that they should be present. They certainly have no right to attempt to influence their action in any manner, for they are appointed as disinterested parties, and assume an obligation to discharge their duties honestly and faithfully. The statute directing the auditor to issue his precept notifying them of the time, place, and object of their meeting must be regarded as directory, and not mandatory. If they do meet, take an oath, discharge their duties, and report within the time prescribed by statute, they have discharged the full measure of their duties within the meaning of the statute. Appellants, in their motion to set aside the report, wholly failed to make any showing that their rights were prejudiced by the failure to meet on the 18th of April. The report shows that they did qualify as viewers, and fully discharged their duties. It is not even contended that the report would have been different if they had met on the 18th instead of the 22d. It must be presumed that they exercised their best judgment, and acted honestly.

The viewers having reported that the proposed highway would not be of public utility, the jurisdiction of the commissioners' court to proceed farther, was at an end, with two exceptions: (1) To dismiss the petition, and render final judgment on the adverse report. (2) The petitioners might have filed a bond for costs, and presented a new petition, and thereupon other viewers might have been appointed. Section 6753, supra; McKee v. Gould, 108 Ind. 107, 8 N. E. 724; Jones v. Duffy, 119 Ind. 440, 21 N. E. 348. It thus appears that appellants had a complete remedy, of which they failed to avail themselves. Upon the filing of a report of viewers declaring that a proposed highway would not be of public utility, it is the duty of the commissioners' court to pronounce judgment upon it, and dismiss the petition, unless the petitioners avail themselves of their rights under section 6753, supra. Such report stands in the same relation to such board as the verdict of a jury to the court, and it is the duty of the board to pronounce judgment upon it, except in cases where the statute provides differently. There are two instances in which authority is given the board of commissioners to set aside the report of viewers and appoint viewers, and these are especially provided for by section 6746 and section 6750, supra. Where the report of the viewers is adverse to the petitioners, the board of commissioners have no right to set aside the report and appoint other viewers. This question is settled by the case of Doctor et al. v. Hartman et al., 74 Ind. 221.

Counsel for appellants rely upon the case of Hobbs et al. v. Board, etc., 103 Ind. 575, 3 N. E. 263, to support their contention that the report of the viewers was void because they did not meet at the time designated. That case arose under act of March 3, 1877 (Act 1877, p. 82, c. 47), providing for the construction of free gravel roads, and the provisions of the statute are very different from those relating to the location of public highways. By section 1 of the act power was conferred upon the board of commissioners to construct free gravel roads, and authorized the viewers appointed by the board to assess damages to landowners, etc. By section 2 it was made the duty of the board, upon the presentation of a petition and filing of a bond, to appoint three disinterested freeholders as viewers and a competent surveyor or engineer, to proceed "upon a day named by the commissioners, to examine, view, lay out or straighten said road, as in their opinion public convenience and utility require." The same section also provides that the auditor shall notify such viewers and surveyor of the time and place of their meetings, and also to give notice, which said notice shall state the time and place of said meeting, the kind of improvements asked for, the place of beginning, intermediate points, if any, and the place of termination. Section 3 prescribes the duties of the viewers and the manner of the assessment of damages in favor of parties affected by the improvement. The necessity of the meeting of the viewers at the time and place fixed under the provisions of the statute is made clear by what the court said in the case cited. The following language is used: "Of the time appointed for the meeting the statute imperatively requires that notice shall be given, and notice is always a fundamental requisite to the validity of such proceedings as those described in the complaint." The statute also provides that "it shall be the duty of such viewers and surveyor or engineer to meet at the time and place specified by the Commissioners." Rev. St. 1881, §§ 5092, 5093. See sections 6855–6857, Burns' Rev. St. 1901. Continuing, the court say: "We regard the publication of notice as essential to the validity of the proceedings, for unquestionably it is a jurisdictional matter. If the notice is essential, then a proceeding that frustrates its purpose and renders it fruitless cannot be valid. The purpose of a notice is to afford a party his day in court, and to give him a hearing upon the matter upon which an action of a judicial character is to be taken. If the viewers and surveyor do not meet at the time designated, the notice serves no useful purpose. Quite as well have no notice at all as to permit the viewers to disregard it, and hold their meetings at a time different from that designated in the notice. The landowners were not bound to appear at a time fixed by the viewers, and of which they had no notice. The viewers could have no jurisdiction except such as the order of the commissioners conferred, and, if they did not meet at the time designated in the order appointing them, and in the notice given pursuant to that order, they could exercise no jurisdiction at all." The holding in that case that it was necessary for the viewers to meet at the time and place designated by the commissioners and the notice rests upon the proposition that notice of the time and place is indispensably necessary to their jurisdiction. In a proceeding under that statute a landholder affected by the improvement had a right to appear before the viewers and present his grievances, for the statute provides that such viewers shall not be required to assess damages in consequence of the appropriation of any private property, etc., unless the owner or owners "shall have filed written application with said viewers giving a description of the premises," etc. The notice provided for in section 6856, supra, being section 2 of the act of March 3, 1877, is the notice that confers jurisdiction, and that is what the court had reference to when it said, in the case cited, that "the purpose of the notice is to afford a party his day in court, and to give him a hearing upon the matter upon which an action of a judicial character is to be taken." Not so here, for jurisdiction of all parties affected was acquired by the notice of the pendency of the petition and when it would be presented for hearing and action. In proceedings to establish a highway all parties affected have their day in court under the original notice, and those who claim damages on account of the location of a highway cannot be heard by remonstrance until after the original viewers have filed their report, and then such report must be favorable. As above suggested, they have nothing to do with the viewers, and their rights cannot possibly be prejudiced if the viewers do not meet and qualify at the time named in the precept. The proceedings under the highway statute and the free gravel road statute are so different that they are easily distinguished.

These considerations lead to the conclusion that the commissioners' court was without jurisdiction to set aside the report of the original viewers, it being against the public utility of the proposed highway, and to appoint other viewers. This being true, all subsequent proceedings were void.

Judgment affirmed.

(33 Ind. A. 607)

HENRY SCHOOL TP. OF HENRY COUNTY, IND., v. MEREDITH.

(Appellate Court of Indiana. Division No. 1. March 18, 1904.)

TEACHER'S CONTRACT — STIPULATIONS — CONSTRUCTION—TRUSTEE'S RIGHT TO TERMINATE CONTRACT—PLEADINGS—COMPLAINT — ALLEGATIONS—PAROL EVIDENCE — APPEAL—BRIEF AND ARGUMENT OF APPELLANT.

1. The rights of the parties to a written contract are not affected by parol statements, made at the time of its execution, materially varying its terms.

2. A complaint, in an action by a teacher to recover on the contract of employment the compensation earned for teaching the term, which alleged that without any cause the school trustee violated the contract, that on a specified day he notified the teacher that the school would be discontinued, and locked the doors of the schoolhouse, and refused to deliver the keys to the teacher so that she might enter the schoolhouse and continue to teach, averred that the trustee without cause prevented the teacher from continuing to teach.

3. Where a teacher's contract for a term of school commencing at a specified date does not specify the length of the term, parol evidence showing the length of the term is admissible.

4. The stipulation, in a contract purporting to employ a teacher for a term beginning on a specified date, that it "is to be good as long * * * as the trustee sees fit," does not authorize the trustee to terminate the contract arbitrarily and without cause.

5. The statement of points in appellant's brief made no reference to a motion for a new trial or the causes therein assigned, but the points related solely to the complaint. The argument was devoted to a discussion of the complaint with reference to alleged errors occurring on the trial, without identifying them with particular assignments of error in the motion or in the record. *Held* not a compliance with the rules of the court relating to the briefs and arguments of appellant.

Appeal from Circuit Court, Henry County; Jno. M. Morris, Judge.

Action by Nora Meredith against the Henry school township of Henry county. From a judgment for plaintiff, defendant appeals. Affirmed.

Fred C. Gause and William A. Brown, for appellant. E. H. Bundy and Nation & Beard, for appellee.

BLACK, J. The demurrer of the appellant, Henry school township, of Henry county, Ind., for want of sufficient facts, to the complaint of the appellee, Nora Meredith, was overruled. In the complaint it was alleged that during the year 1901 Sanford W. Compton was, and he still is, the duly elected, qualified, and acting trustee of the school corporation, and August 28, 1901, he, by written contract, duly entered of record, and signed by the appellee and Compton, as such school trustee, employed the appellee to teach the common school at District No. 9, in Henry township, Henry county, Ind., during the school term commencing September 9, 1901, at the sum of $2 per day. A copy of the contract was exhibited with the complaint. By its terms the appellee agreed to teach that school for the term commencing September 9, 1901, for the consideration of $2 per day, "to be paid thirty dollars per month and balance end of term," and faithfully to perform all the duties of teacher of the school. A number of duties to be performed by her were specified. The contract then proceeded as follows: "This contract is to hold good as long as there is twelve pupils or more, or as said trustee sees fit. The said trustee agrees to keep the school building in good repair; and to furnish the necessary fuel, furniture, apparatus, books and blanks, and such other appliances as may be necessary for the systematic and proper conduct of said school. And the said trustee, for and in behalf of

¶ 3. See Evidence, vol. 20, Cent. Dig. § 1884.

said township, further agrees to pay the said Nora Meredith for services, as teacher of said school," a sum equal to the whole number of days taught, at the rate of the above-named sum per day, "when the said teacher shall have filled all the stipulations of this contract." The contract contained a proviso as follows: "Provided, that in case the said Nora Meredith shall be dismissed from said school by said trustee, or his successor in office, for incompetency, cruelty, gross immorality, neglect of business, or a violation of any of the stipulations of this contract, or in case her license should be annulled by the county superintendent or state superintendent, she shall not be entitled to any compensation after notice of dismissal or notice of annulment of license." It was further alleged in the complaint that at the date of the contract the appellee was a regular licensed teacher of said county, and held the necessary license and certificate from the county superintendent of schools of said county, which license was in force on and after September 9, 1901, and never was revoked or annulled; that at the time of making the contract the trustee represented to the appellee that there were 19 children of school age in the district, 17 of whom would attend the school there, and that the term of school in that district would be of seven months' duration, and that, should nearly all of the school children of the district become affected with any contagious disease, it would be necessary to discontinue the school, and for the purpose of closing the school in that event it would be necessary to insert, and he did insert, in the contract, the words: "This contract is to hold good as long as there is 12 pupils or more, or as said trustee sees fit." It was alleged that on September 9, 1901, the appellee entered upon the work of teaching the school under the contract, and continued teaching until the —— day of October, 1901; that, soon after she commenced to teach the school, the trustee solicited, requested, and persuaded the parents of a number of the school children in the district to send their children to a school outside of that school district, in order to keep these children from attending the school taught by the appellee, and in order to keep the number of children attending the school taught by her at a less number than 12; that on the —— day of October, 1901, the trustee informed the appellee that the school would be discontinued from that date, and as teacher of the school she had no further duties to perform; that he then caused the doors of the schoolhouse to be locked, and the keys to be turned over to him, and refused to deliver the same to her, so that she might enter the schoolhouse and continue teaching the school; that she was not dismissed from the school by the trustee for incompetency, cruelty, gross immorality, neglect of business, or a violation of any of the stipulations of the contract; that he brought against her no charge or accusation of inability, incompetency, or other charge, but, without any cause whatever, he violated the contract "as aforesaid"; that the school was not closed or discontinued by the trustee on account of any contagious or other disease among the children of the school district; that she demanded possession of the keys to the schoolhouse, and demanded that she be allowed to enter the same and to continue teaching the school for the remainder of the term, to wit, 110 days, but said demands were refused by the trustee; that she was ready, able, and willing to teach the school the remainder of the term, but the trustee denied her that privilege, and prevented her from teaching the school the remainder of the school term; that during the time she was prevented from teaching the school she endeavored to secure other employment, but could not and did not earn anything; that on the —— day of October, 1901, the appellant paid on the contract the sum of $30; that there was due and unpaid on the contract the sum of $300; "wherefore the plaintiff demands judgment for three hundred dollars, and for all other proper relief."

The complaint proceeds upon the contract of employment, to recover the whole compensation that would have been earned for teaching during the entire term, upon the ground that, so far as the service agreed upon was not actually rendered, performance was prevented by the appellant, without right to do so, the appellee having been at all times ready and willing to teach, and having been unable to obtain other remunerative employment. The pleading contains many averments of inconclusive matter. It is not shown that the representation of the trustee concerning the number of children of school age in the district was false. So far as any statements alleged to have been made at the time of the execution of the written contract materially varied any of the provisions of the writing, they cannot be regarded as affecting the rights of the parties.

There is an averment that the trustee solicited, requested, and persuaded parents to send their children to another school, but it is not shown that he did so fraudulently, or by means of any false accusations or representations concerning the appellee or the school which she was teaching, and it does not appear that the trustee thus influenced or caused any children to go to the other school, or diminished the attendance at appellee's school. It is not shown how many pupils attended her school at any time, or that it was, by anything done by the trustee, reduced in number below 12 pupils, or to any extent. It does not appear from the pleading that any representation or statement of matter of fact to the appellee, or any conduct of his with reference to other persons, was injurious, or constituted or produced a cessation of her actual service. It is not shown that the sum of $30 paid her was the only sum paid her on the contract.

A number of matters are mentioned which it is alleged were not grounds or reasons for dismissal or discontinuance. It is alleged that "without any cause whatever said trustee violated said contract as aforesaid." This may be regarded as referring to the action of the trustee in informing the appellee that the school would be discontinued from the time of his giving the information, and that the appellee had no further duties to perform as a teacher of the school, and his action in causing the doors of the schoolhouse to be locked and the keys to be turned over to him, and his refusal to deliver the keys to her so that she might enter the schoolhouse and continue to teach. The complaint may be treated as averring that the trustee did thus without any cause whatever.

The length of the period of employment was not specified in the contract, but it purported to be a contract of employment of the teacher for a term of school commencing at a specified date, and we think the written contract in this regard might be aided and explained by parol evidence showing the actual length of the term. The appellee's performance of the contract could not rightfully be thus interrupted and terminated by her employer without any cause whatever, unless it can properly be held that such right was derivable from the reservation in the contract in the words, "This contract is to hold good as long * * * as the trustee sees fit." To constitute a contract, there must be a subsisting agreement between at least two parties. The agreement must be binding upon both parties. An agreement which is not to hold except as one of the parties sees fit would not be a contract. It cannot be supposed that the parties executed a written agreement, containing formal stipulations on the part of each contracting party, with the intention of accomplishing such a futile result. It cannot be concluded that by the insertion of such words it was contemplated by both the trustee and the teacher that, on any day after the latter had entered upon the service for the term, the former, arbitrarily and through caprice or prejudice, or without any reason or cause whatever, could terminate the service under the contract at once, and thereby cut off the contemplated compensation. To regard him as having a right to end performance under the contract, there must be some fitness in his act—at least, such an occasion for such action as to render his conduct referable to the exercise of a sound official discretion, though without the consent of the teacher. Therefore the complaint seems to be sufficient to put the appellant to its answer.

Issues were formed, upon a trial of which by jury a verdict in favor of the appellee was returned. The overruling of the appellant's motion for a new trial is assigned as error. So far as the appellant has sought to present to this court alleged errors occurring upon the trial, there has not been adequate compliance with the rules of this court relating to the appellant's brief and argument. Under the statement of points in the brief, the appellant makes no reference to the motion for a new trial or the causes therein assigned, but the points stated relate solely to the complaint. The argument is devoted in part to a discussion of the complaint, with references to alleged errors occurring on the trial, without any attempt to identify them with particular assignments in the motion, or any reference to such assignments in the record. In this way reference is made to two of a large number of instructions given, the only assignment in the motion ascribing error in the giving of instructions being directed to all the instructions jointly. There is intermingled in the argument a recital of some of the evidence, and mention of exceptions to the admission of certain evidence, without reference to the motion for a new trial, or to any of the assignments of causes therein, in the record. The same is true of instructions offered by the appellant, and rejected, stating that the evidence was not sufficient to entitle the appellee to recover, and directing a verdict for the appellant. The appellee was entitled, at least, to recover for the time of her actual service at the stipulated rate of compensation. To ascertain with necessary certainty that there were any available errors upon the trial would require this court to perform the work of the attorneys for the appellant, and would involve an ignoring of the requirements of the rules of this court relating to the appellant's brief and argument.

Judgment affirmed.

(33 Ind. App. 559)

INDIANA NATURAL GAS & OIL CO. v. GRANGER.[1]

(Appellate Court of Indiana. Division No. 1. March 17, 1904.)

MINES AND MINERALS—LEASES—CONSTRUCTION—CONSIDERATION—TERMINATION.

1. In construing a contract, the court will, if possible, give effect to all its parts, and its true meaning will be determined from a consideration of its provisions taken together as a whole.

2. An oil and gas lease for 12 years, and so long thereafter as petroleum "can be produced in paying quantities, or the payments hereinafter provided for are made in accordance with conditions attaching hereto," by which the lessee agreed to commence operations for drilling within one year, or, in lieu thereof, to pay to the lessor $20 a year, and to give the lessor one-eighth of all petroleum or mineral substances produced, or $100 a year for the gas from each well, contemplated, as the actual consideration, the development of the property, and not the mere payment of the small annual rental, and the lessee could not, merely by making the annual payments, hold the premises longer than 12 years without drilling or commencing to drill a well, but could only hold the premises after 12 years if oil and gas could be produced in paying quantities, and on payment of royalties and rentals.

¶ 2. See Mines and Minerals, vol. 34, Cent. Dig. § 200.

[1] Rehearing denied. Transfer to Supreme Court denied.

Appeal from Circuit Court, Grant County; H. J. Paulus, Judge.

Action by Charles F. Granger, trustee, against the Indiana Natural Gas & Oil Company. From a judgment for plaintiff, defendant appeals. Affirmed.

W. O. Johnson, Blacklidge, Shirley & Wolf, and Foster Davis, for appellant. St. John & Charles, for appellee.

ROBINSON, J. Suit by appellee to cancel a gas and oil lease. In the second paragraph of complaint, appellee avers that he is now, and since 1892 has been, the owner and in possession of certain described land; that on April 14, 1888, Elizabeth Morgan, the then owner, with her husband, executed and delivered to the assignor of appellant a certain instrument or lease. The lease recited that the lessors, their heirs and assigns, for and in consideration of the sum of $10 to them paid, the receipt of which is acknowledged, and for the further consideration thereinafter mentioned, and on account of covenants thereinafter contained, lease to the lessee, his heirs and assigns, two acres of a certain tract of land, which tract and the two-acre tract are described, "for the purpose and with the exclusive right of drilling and mining and operating for petroleum, gas or any mineral substances on said land and appropriating the said products so obtained to his [the lessee] own use and benefit, except as hereinafter provided, and removing the same from said land, for the term of twelve years and so long thereafter as petroleum or mineral substances can be produced in paying quantities, or the payments hereinafter provided for are made according to the terms and conditions attaching thereto." The lessee is given the privilege of using from the premises sufficient wood and water to conduct drilling and mining operations, to erect upon and move from the premises buildings, machinery, tanks, pipe lines, and other property necessary for such business, and a right of way to the places of drilling, lessee to pay all damages to growing crops. The lessee agrees to give the lessor one-eighth of all petroleum or mineral substances produced, or, if gas alone should be found in sufficient quantities and under circumstances making it profitable to pipe the same to other localities, the lessee shall pay to the lessor $100 per annum for the gas from each well when so utilized, and sufficient gas to heat and light the dwelling on the premises, such payment to be accepted by the lessor as a full consideration and in lieu of any other royalty. The lessors further covenant and agree with the lessee, his heirs and assigns, "neither by themselves nor by any other person or persons, company or corporation, in any way or manner, to cause or suffer the rights herein granted on said two acres to be executed on the balance of the land described herein, so long as this agreement as to said two acres remains in force"; the lessor to have the use of the land for tillage. The lessee agrees "to commence operations for said drilling or mining purposes within one year from the execution of this lease, or in lieu thereof for delay in commencing such operations, and as a consideration for the agreements, contained herein, thereafter to pay to the said party of the first part [the lessor] twenty dollars per annum, payable in advance on the 14th day of April in each year, until such operations are commenced and a well completed"; a deposit to the credit of the lessor in a bank named to be considered a payment under the terms of the lease. Should the lessee fail to make such payments, or either of them, within 30 days from the time the same is due, then the lease to be null and void. The lease was duly acknowledged and recorded. It is further averred that appellant became the owner of the lease by assignment in 1890, and claims to have some interest in the land on account of the lease; that at no time since the execution of the lease has the lessee, nor those claiming under him, including appellant, taken any possession of the land, and no well has been drilled thereon; that appellant caused to be paid the sum of $20 per year for the period of 12 years, and that the same was received by appellee, and those under whom he claims, for the 12 years; that the $20 per year was received by appellee from appellant as payment for the privilege of entering thereon by appellant to prospect for oil or gas during the period of one year, for which the payments were made, and for no other purpose; that at the end of the 12 years, no possession having been taken and no well drilled, appellee refused to receive any further payments, and so notified appellant and the bank that he would not receive any further rental on the lease, but that he had elected to terminate the same; that the last $20 accepted was on the 14th day of April, 1899, which continued the lease in force until April 14, 1900; that the lease is null and void, because the term for which it was given has expired, and no well for oil or gas has been drilled; and that the same should be canceled of record. Prayer that the lease be declared void, and a commissioner appointed to cancel the same of record. A demurrer to this paragraph of complaint was overruled. Appellant's second paragraph of answer admits the execution of the lease, and alleges that by the terms of the lease it should continue in force as long as appellant should continue to make the payments agreed upon; that a deposit in the bank named should be considered a payment under the terms of the lease; that appellant has at all times made the payments required by the lease on or before the 14th day of April each year; and that all payments were made that were due prior to the beginning of this action, according to the terms of the lease, by depositing the payments in the bank named in the lease at the times mentioned in the lease, and that nothing is due appellee. To this answer a demurrer was sustained. The complaint in this case was filed April 16, 1902.

It is a well-settled rule that in construing a contract the court will, if possible, give effect to all its parts, and that its true meaning will be determined from a consideration of all its provisions taken together as a whole. While the lease contains a stated consideration of $10, yet it is manifest that the substantial consideration that moved the grantor to execute the lease was the hope of profits or royalties if gas or oil should be found. Gadbury v. Ohio, etc., Gas Co. (Ind. Sup.) 67 N. E. 259. It is quite true that it is not the duty of the court to make a contract for parties, nor can the court, in the absence of fraud or bad faith, relieve a party from an improvident contract that he had voluntarily entered into. But a consideration of the whole lease shows very clearly that it was the intention of both parties to develop the land for gas and oil. The lessor leases the land to the lessee for the purpose and with the exclusive right of drilling, mining, and operating for oil and gas, and this extends to the whole 40-acre tract, "for the term of twelve years, and so long thereafter as petroleum or mineral substances can be produced in paying quantities, or the payments hereinafter provided for are made according to the terms and conditions attaching thereto." The lessee agreed to commence operations for drilling and mining purposes within one year from the execution of the lease, or, "in lieu thereof, for delay in commencing such operations, and as a consideration for the agreements contained herein, thereafter pay" to the lessor twenty dollars per year in advance, until such operations are commenced and a well completed. Why did the parties insert the 12-year clause? Appellant's argument is that during the 12 years it was bound to pay the rental, and after the 12 years it could pay it or not, at its option. But does the lease give the appellant an option for an indefinite time to either put down a well or pay the $20 per annum? Is the instrument an option merely, and the $20 a year the price of it? If so, why was anything said in the lease about when operations should commence, and why was the stipulated payment to be made "until" such operations are commenced and a "well completed"? It is not necessary to inquire whether the lessor was bound to let the lessee hold the land for 12 years without attempting to develop it, because it was held by the lessee for 12 years, and the payments for delay were accepted by the lessor. But, giving effect to all the provisions contained in the lease, we think a reasonable and equitable interpretation is that the lessee, by making the annual payments, could not hold the premises longer than 12 years without drilling or commencing to drill a well, and that the lessee could hold the premises as long beyond the 12 years as oil and gas could be produced in paying quantities, upon payment of the royalties and well rentals. It was manifestly intended that the property should be developed, and that it should be developed within a certain time. We think this construction gives effect to what was manifestly the controlling intention of the parties. In Western, etc., Gas Co. v. George, 161 Pa. 47, 28 Atl. 1004, with a lease almost identical with that at bar, and where the term was 2 instead of 12 years, the court said: "The continuance of the lease beyond the definite term was contingent upon the finding of oil or gas in paying quantities, and on the payment to the lessor in such case of his share of the oil produced, or the stipulated sum for each well from which gas was obtained and sold. The primary and essential condition to any extension of the lease after the lapse of two years from its date was the finding of oil or gas in paying quantities within that time, and the secondary condition was that the rent reserved for the oil or gas found should be paid in conformity with the covenants in relation thereto." See Federal Oil Co. v. Western Oil Co. (C. C.) 112 Fed. 373; Consumers' Gas Trust Co. v. Littler (Ind. Sup. No. 20,246, decided March 15, 1904) 70 N. E. 363.

Judgment affirmed.

(33 Ind. A. 605)

STATE, to Use of CRAM, Drainage Com'r, v. ELLIOTT et al.

(Appellate Court of Indiana. Division No. 1. March 17, 1904.)

DRAINAGE—BENEFITS—ASSESSING LAND IN ANOTHER COUNTY.

1. Though a drainage ditch is all in one county, in which proceedings to establish it originated, the circuit court of that county has jurisdiction to assess benefits to lands in an adjoining county benefited thereby.

Appeal from Circuit Court, Marshall County; A. C. Capron, Judge.

Action by the state, to the use of Quincy Cram, drainage commissioner, against David A. Elliott and others. Judgment for defendants. Plaintiff appeals. Reversed.

Geo. W. Beeman, Jas. C. Fletcher, H. A. Logan, C. W. Miller, Atty. Gen., L. G. Rothschild, C. C. Hadley, and W. C. Geake, for appellant. W. B. Hess, for appellees.

HENLEY, C. J. This action was commenced by appellant to enforce the payment of a ditch assessment. The question presented for determination by this appeal is, had the circuit court of Stark county, Ind., jurisdiction to assess benefits to lands situated in Marshall county, Ind.? The question was presented by an answer which was held sufficient as against appellant's demurrer addressed thereto.

The facts, as we gather them from the record in this appeal, are that the ditch, for the construction of which the land in Marshall county was assessed, was wholly located in the adjoining county of Stark; that the source of the ditch was so near to the county line dividing the counties of Stark and Marshall that its effect was to drain and benefit lands in Marshall county, and the lands so benefited were assessed for the construction of the ditch.

We think the Supreme Court has settled the question presented by this appeal in favor of appellant. In Crist v. The State ex rel. Whitmore, etc., 97 Ind. 389, the court held that the commissioner of drainage of Huntington county had authority to assess lands in Grant county affected by a ditch constructed in Huntington county, the court saying: "The further point is made that the commissioner of drainage of Huntington county had no authority to assess land affected by such ditch in Grant county. We think otherwise. The statute clearly authorizes the construction of a ditch, affecting lands in different counties, by a single commissioner of drainage." To the same effect, see, also, Denton et al. v. Thompson, 136 Ind. 446, 35 N. E. 264; sections 5623, 5625, 5627, 5629, Burns' Rev. St. 1901. The case of Denton v. Thompson, supra, holds that, whether the construction of a public drain be under the authority of the circuit court or of boards of commissioners, if the drain extends into two or more counties, it must be considered as a unit throughout its whole extent, and the proceeding must be under one authority. This must necessarily be the mode of procedure, because, if more than one board of commissioners or court could take jurisdiction of different parts of a drain, one court or board of commissioners might order its construction, while another might determine that the part of the drain over which it had jurisdiction should not be established, and thus defeat the whole purpose of the law. The same reasoning must prevail where the source of the drain, all of which is constructed in one county, is so close to an adjoining county as to beneficially affect lands lying in the adjoining county. If this were not true, the lands benefited in the adjoining county would escape their just share of the expense of constructing the drain. It has never been doubted, in actions for partition, that the court in the county where the action was commenced, and in which a part of the real estate sought to be affected by the proceedings was situated, had jurisdiction to try and determine the action, even though lands in many other counties in the state were included. The court in which the proceeding is commenced has and retains jurisdiction over all lands affected by the action, and this was what the Legislature intended should be the effect of the statutes authorizing the construction of public drains. The action to collect a ditch assessment must be brought in the county where the land affected is situated. Dowden v. The State ex rel., 106 Ind. 157, 6 N. E. 136. This the appellant has done. But the jurisdiction to assess benefits upon all lands affected by the construction of a drain, like the one in the case at bar, whether the lands be in one or more counties, must be in the drainage commissioner of the court or board of commissioners of the county in which the proceeding to establish the drain originated. The demurrer to the second paragraph of appellee's answer should have been sustained.

Judgment reversed, with instructions to the trial court to sustain the demurrer to the second paragraph of answer, and for further proceeding in accordance with this opinion.

(33 Ind. App. 284)

RARIDEN v. RARIDEN.*

(Appellate Court of Indiana, Division No. 1. March 15, 1904.)

DIVORCE—ALIMONY—REMARRIAGE—APPEAL.

1. It being within the power of the Appellate Court, on appeal from a judgment for alimony, to reverse the decree of divorce as well as the judgment for alimony, where the appellant has placed it beyond the court's power to do this by remarriage his appeal from that portion of the judgment awarding alimony will be dismissed.

Appeal from Circuit Court, Newton County; C. W. Hanley, Judge.

Action by Esther B. Rariden against Elliott Rariden for a divorce. Divorce granted to defendant on his cross-complaint, and judgment against him for alimony and attorney's fees. From the judgment for alimony and attorney's fees alone, he appeals. Dismissed.

Davidson & Boulds, for appellant. Hanly & Woods, for appellee.

ROBINSON, J. Appellee sued for divorce. Appellant answered in denial, and filed a cross-complaint asking a divorce. Appellee answered the cross-complaint in denial. Upon a trial the court denied appellee's petition, and granted appellant a divorce upon his cross-complaint, and gave judgment against him in appellee's favor for alimony, and an allowance for attorney's fees. Appellant's motion to modify the judgment by reducing the amount of alimony and allowance was overruled, and exception taken. His motion for a new trial upon the question of alimony and allowance only was overruled. He has assigned as error the court's refusal to modify the judgment as to alimony and allowance, and the refusal of a new trial. Appellee moves to dismiss the appeal upon a showing that, since the submission of the cause, appellant remarried, and that he and the woman he married are now living together as husband and wife.

"Alimony," as here used, is purely incidental to a divorce proceeding, and is an allowance out of the divorced husband's estate made to the divorced wife for her support and maintenance. In this state it has no existence as a separate and independent right. It must be adjudged, if at all, in the

*Rehearing denied June 1 1904.

divorce proceedings, and cannot be the subject-matter of an independent suit. The court is required to make such decree for alimony as the circumstances of the case shall render just and proper. Burns' Rev. St. 1901, § 1057. The court bases its decree for alimony upon all the facts and circumstances disclosed in the divorce proceedings, including all matters of property which have transpired between the parties. Muckenburg v. Holler, 29 Ind. 139, 92 Am. Dec. 345. "In adjudging alimony," said the court in Hedrick v. Hedrick, 28 Ind. 291, "all the evidence in the case ought to be considered and acted upon, and then the subject is often a difficult one. It is not yet controlled by definite rules, and the determination of each case must therefore depend upon its own circumstances and an enlightened sense of justice and public policy." And it has been held that the appellate tribunal cannot say that alimony in a case is excessive, in the absence of the testimony on which the divorce was granted. Ifert v. Ifert, 29 Ind. 473. In Hedrick v. Hedrick, 128 Ind. 522, 26 N. E. 768, it was held that, in determining the amount of alimony, the court may "inquire into the circumstances of the parties, ascertain the amount of property owned by the husband at the time, the source from whence it came, the ability of the husband to pay, by reason of his financial circumstances, his income, and his ability to earn money, as well as his inability to earn money on account of ill health; and, upon a full investigation, it is the duty of the court to make such an allowance for alimony as is just and proper." In fixing the amount of the alimony, the court may consider the conduct of the husband, and the wrongs perpetrated by him upon the wife. Gussman v. Gussman, 140 Ind. 433, 39 N. E. 918. In all the authorities the fact is emphasized that alimony is an incident of the divorce. While it is, in a sense, a separate judgment, and may be in a particular case modified or disallowed by the appellate tribunal without in any way affecting the decree of divorce, yet, in another sense, it is in no manner a judgment separate and apart from the decree of divorce, as a reversal of the decree of divorce, in and of itself, sets aside the judgment for alimony. And while the appellate tribunal, upon an appeal for that purpose only, may make such modifications of the allowance of alimony as right and justice require, it may, also, upon an appeal by the party who secured the divorce, and who questions only the allowance of the alimony, reverse the decree of divorce, and remand the case for the trial court to hear and consider the entire case de novo. In Yost v. Yost, 141 Ind. 584, 41 N. E. 11, appellant was granted a divorce, and was awarded $100 alimony, and appealed, and questioned only the amount of alimony, and the court's refusal to allow any sum as attorney's fees in the prosecution of her petition. It was held that the trial court, as to these matters, did not exercise a proper judicial discretion; and the case was reversed both as to the decree of divorce and as to the alimony, and a new trial ordered upon all issues. The court, by Jordon, J., said: "As this court, in the exercise of appellate jurisdiction, has the power to so mold its judgment and mandates as to secure the proper relief or justice to the party or parties entitled thereto, we should much prefer to exercise that power in order to provide a way by which this result might be obtained without disturbing that part of the decree divorcing the parties. But as the value of the property owned by appellee may have changed since the judgment was originally rendered, and likewise the circumstances and conditions of both parties, it will be proper and right, and better, perhaps, we think, subserve the ends of justice, for the lower court to hear and consider the entire case de novo." That is to say, when, in the case at bar, appellant appealed from the judgment for alimony and allowance for attorney's fees, he placed it within the power of the appellate tribunal, if a consideration of the case showed that justice required it, to reverse the case not only as to the alimony and allowance, but also as to the decree of divorce, and direct a new trial upon all the issues. Whether, upon the whole record in this particular case, justice would or would not require that the trial court should consider the entire case de novo, is not material, as it is necessary that a general rule should be declared. Under the above authority it might be necessary in any case to reverse that part of the judgment and decree granting the divorce. But by his marriage, by which he has accepted the benefits of that part of the decree, he has made it impossible for the court to do what the justice of the case might require that it should do. He has accepted the benefits of a particular part of a judgment, which might or might not be permitted to stand, upon an adjudication of the question he is urging by his appeal, and by so doing has waived his right to prosecute his appeal. See Garner v. Garner, 38 Ind. 139; Stephens v. Stephens, 51 Ind. 542; Sterne v. Vert, 108 Ind. 232, 9 N. E. 127; McGrew v. Grayston, 144 Ind. 165, 41 N. E. 1027; Manlove v. State, 153 Ind. 80, 53 N. E. 385; Martin v. Bott, 17 Ind. App. 447, 46 N. E. 151; Keller v. Keller, 139 Ind. 38, 38 N. E. 337.

The appeal is dismissed.

(33 Ind. App. 171)

RABORN v. WOODS et al.*

(Appellate Court of Indiana, Division No. 1. March 16, 1904.)

APPEAL—WAIVER—ACCEPTANCE OF BENEFITS OF JUDGMENT.

1. A plaintiff in ejectment, who enters into possession of that portion of the land awarded to him, thereby waives his right to appeal from the judgment.

*Rehearing denied May 17, 1904.

¶ 1. See Appeal and Error, vol. 3, Cent. Dig. § 979.

Appeal from Superior Court, Madison County; H. C. Ryan, Judge.

Action by William Raborn against Jesse Woods and another. From a judgment granting insufficient relief, plaintiff appeals. Dismissed.

W. F. Edwards and Bagot & Bagot, for appellant. Kittinger & Diven and Shirts & Fertig, for appellees.

HENLEY, C. J. This was an action in ejectment. The complaint, omitting the caption, was in one paragraph, in the following words:

"The plaintiff, William R. Raborn, complains of the defendants, Jesse Woods and Eliza Woods, and says that he is the owner in fee, and that he is entitled to the possession, of the following described real estate, situated in Hamilton county, state of Indiana, to wit: The south half of the northwest quarter of section 35, township 19, range 5 east; that said defendants unlawfully detain the same, and unlawfully keep him out of the possession thereof, to his damage in the sum of $300. Wherefore the plaintiff prays the court that he have judgment against the defendants for the possession of said real estate," etc.

To this complaint defendants answered the general denial, and filed a cross-complaint in four paragraphs. The cause was submitted for trial upon the issues, and a verdict and judgment rendered to the effect that the appellant was entitled to the possession of the east half of the 80-acre tract of land described in his complaint, and that the defendants were entitled to the possession of the west half of said tract, and that their title to said land be quieted.

Appellant's motion for a new trial, as a matter of right, was overruled, and this action of the trial court is the only error assigned. Appellees have filed a verified special answer in bar to the errors assigned, and ask that this appeal be dismissed. It appears from this answer that, after the rendition of the judgment in this cause in the trial court, the appellant took possession of that part of the tract of land recovered by him under said judgment, and has ever since held the same, and has appropriated to his own use the rents and profits arising therefrom, and has exercised and is exercising all acts of ownership over the same. The Supreme Court, in McGrew v. Grayston, 144 Ind. 165, 41 N. E. 1027, said: "The right of appeal, though conferred by statute, may be forfeited and waived in many ways. It is an established principle of law that a party cannot prosecute an appeal, and thereby seek to reverse a judgment, the benefits of which he has accepted voluntarily and knowing the facts. After such acceptance he is estopped to reverse the judgment on error, and the same may be treated as a release of errors. * * * This rule is founded on the principle that a party in a court of justice will not be allowed to acquire advantages by assuming inconsistent positions." The case of Sonntag v. Klee, 148 Ind. 536, 47 N. E. 962, is not unlike the case at bar. That case was an action by appellees against appellants for the possession of certain real estate and machinery located thereon. The judgment of the court gave to appellants a part of the machinery. They appealed, and pending the appeal took possession of that part of the property awarded to them by the judgment of the trial court. In dismissing the appeal the court said: "We are of the opinion that this question has been settled against the contention of appellants both by the statute and by the rulings of this court. In section 644, Burns' Rev. St. 1894, it is said, 'The party obtaining judgment shall not take an appeal after receiving any money paid or collected thereon;' and in Sterne v. Vert, 108 Ind. 232, 9 N. E. 127, it was accordingly held that a party cannot accept the benefit of an adjudication, and yet allege it to be erroneous." It appears in this case that appellant has elected to receive the benefit of what he is alleging is an erroneous judgment and decree of the court. He has taken possession of the land awarded to him by the judgment, and is receiving the rents and profits therefrom, and is here seeking a reversal of the decree as to the other part of the land, which by the judgment of the court was given to appellees. This he cannot do. A reversal of the judgment under the assignment of error could only result in a new trial of the whole case. The parties to the action could not be placed in the same position that they occupied at the time the action was commenced, because it is alleged, and is not denied, that appellant accepted the benefit of the judgment and decree, and is in possession of a part of the real estate. Appellees at the time the action was commenced were in possession of all the property described in the complaint. We think the case falls fully within the rule that a party cannot accept any benefit of an adjudication, and afterward allege it to be erroneous. Glassburn v. Deer, 143 Ind. 174, 41 N. E. 376; McCracken v. Cabel, 120 Ind. 266, 22 N. E. 136; Patterson v. Rowley, 65 Ind. 108; Rarlden v. Rarlden (Ind. App., decided at the present term) 70 N. E. 398. The appellant has waived any errors committed in the proceedings leading up to the judgment from which he has appealed.

The appeal is dismissed.

(32 Ind. A. 583)

BASS et al. v. CITIZENS' TRUST CO.

(Appellate Court of Indiana, Division No. 2. March 15, 1904.)

FRAUDULENT CONVEYANCE—HUSBAND AND WIFE—COMPLAINT—APPEAL AND ERROR—MOTION FOR NEW TRIAL—STATUTE.

1. Where the record shows no request for special findings of fact and conclusions of law

thereon, as required by Burns' Rev. St. 1901, § 560, findings so designated in the record will be treated on appeal as general findings.

2. Where it is not alleged, in a complaint to set aside a fraudulent conveyance of real estate, that the grantor was a resident householder, a contention that the complaint is bad, because affirmatively showing that the grantor had no property except the $500 he borrowed from plaintiff's decedent, which was the subject-matter of the litigation (a less amount than allowed as an exemption to a resident householder), and that his investment of it in real estate, which he conveyed to his wife, could not be in fraud of creditors, is without merit.

3. A contention that a complaint to set aside a fraudulent conveyance from husband to wife is bad, as against the wife, because it does not show that she had any knowledge of the fraudulent intent of her husband, is without merit, where the complaint charges her with knowledge of the facts, and avers that she did not pay any part of the consideration.

4. The reason for granting a new trial, "that the decision is contrary to the evidence," is not designated by the statute as a ground for a new trial, and is unknown to the law.

5. Failure to state a reason for a new trial as one of the points relied on by appellant, and to make an argument in support of it, is a waiver of the question, though it is assigned as a reason for granting a new trial in the motion therefor.

6. In an action to set aside a fraudulent conveyance from a husband to wife, the question of the right of the husband to an exemption as a resident householder cannot be raised by motion to modify, but should be presented by answer and tendering issue thereon before trial.

7. In an action to set aside a fraudulent conveyance from a husband to wife, the question of the right of the husband to an exemption as a resident householder is not presented on the evidence, where it is not assigned as a reason in the motion for a new trial that the decision is not sustained by sufficient evidence.

Appeal from Circuit Court, Lawrence County; W. H. Martin, Judge.

Action by the Citizens' Trust Company, administrator of the estate of Jacob Y. Bates, deceased, against Hugh Bass and others. From a judgment for plaintiff, defendants appeal. Affirmed.

S. B. Lowe, for appellants. E. K. Dye, Edwards & Edwards, and Brooks & Brooks, for appellee.

WILEY, P. J. Action by appellee against appellants to set aside a conveyance of real estate, as fraudulent, and subject it to the payment of a judgment against Hugh Bass in favor of the estate represented by appellee. The complaint was in one paragraph, to which a demurrer was overruled. Answer in denial. Finding and judgment for appellee. Appellants' motion for a venire de novo, a new trial, and to modify the judgment, were each overruled. All rulings adverse to appellants are assigned as errors.

There is in the record what purports to be a special finding of facts, and conclusions of law stated thereon. In all cases triable by the court, a general finding is authorized by the statute, except where one or both of the parties properly request the court to make a special finding of facts, and state its conclusions of law thereon. Section 560, Burns' Rev. St. 1901. In the absence of such request being made, and where it does not affirmatively appear from the record that it was made, and the court makes a special finding of facts, it will be treated as a general finding. Such request will not be implied. Elliott's App. Prac. § 732, and authorities there cited. Under the authorities, we can only treat the special finding as a general finding. All questions attempted to be raised by the record which depend upon the special finding of facts for their determination cannot be considered. Appellants' motion for a venire de novo was upon the ground that the special finding was so defective, uncertain, and ambiguous that no judgment could be rendered thereon, and that the special finding "set out conclusions of law," and "did not find the facts." Appellants also excepted to the conclusions of law, and have assigned error predicated thereon. Under the rule stated, these questions will not be considered. This leaves for consideration the sufficiency of the complaint, the motion for a new trial, and the motion to modify the judgment.

The substance of the complaint is that Hugh Bass purchased real estate, and had the conveyance made to his wife and co-appellant for the purpose of defrauding his creditors; that at the time of said conveyance said Hugh Bass had no property left subject to execution, nor has he since had; that said Rebecca Bass paid no part of the consideration for said real estate; that said Hugh Bass borrowed of Jacob Y. Bates, now deceased, the sum of $500, which was applied to the payment of the purchase price of the real estate so purchased; and that appellant Rebecca had full knowledge of such facts. The complaint further shows that when Hugh Bass borrowed the $500 he gave a note therefor; that said note had been reduced to a judgment, execution issued thereon, and returned nulla bona. The objections urged to the complaint are: (1) That it affirmatively appears that Hugh Bass had no property except the $500 he borrowed of Bates, and hence that was a less amount than was allowed as an exemption to a resident householder, and his investment of it in real estate, which he had conveyed to his wife, could not be in fraud of creditors. If there is any merit whatever in this contention, it is not available here, for the evident reason that it does not appear from the complaint that he was a resident householder. We can indulge no presumption in favor of a pleading. The allegation is not that he had no property, but that he had no property subject to execution. If a person can create an honest debt by borrowing money and investing it in real estate in the name of his wife, and thus avoid liability, the law is lame and morals are lax. (2) That the complaint is bad as against appellant Rebecca because it does not show that she had any knowledge of the fraudulent intent of her husband. It charges her with knowledge of the facts, and that she did not pay any part of the consideration. This is sufficient. Eiler v. Crull, 112 Ind. 318, 14 N. E. 79; Eve v. Louis, 91 Ind. 457; Hanna v. Aebker, 84 Ind. 411.

Appellant's motion for a new trial assigns the following errors: (1) The special finding is contrary to law; (2) the decision is contrary to law; (3) the special finding is contrary to the evidence; (4) the decision is contrary to the evidence. From the fact that the special findings cannot be considered, the first and third reasons are eliminated. The fourth is not designated by the statute as a reason for a new trial, and is unknown to the law. There is but one statutory reason stated for a new trial, and that is the second—that the decision is contrary to law. Appellant has not even stated this reason as one of its points relied upon, and no argument is made in support of it. This is a waiver of the question.

Although the evidence is brought up by a bill of exceptions, its sufficiency to sustain the decision is not presented by the motion for a new trial. Hence the assignment that the court erred in overruling the motion for a new trial can only present such questions as are properly embraced in it. Counsel for appellants have discussed the question of the right of appellant Hugh Bass to an exemption as a resident householder. The question is attempted to be raised by a motion to modify and upon the evidence. If he desired to avail himself of such statutory right, he should have presented such question by answer, and tendered an issue thereon before trial. Having waited until a finding and judgment against him, he has slept on his rights. McNally v. White, 154 Ind. 163, 54 N. E. 794, 56 N. E. 214. Neither is the question presented on the evidence, for it is not assigned as a reason in the motion for a new trial that the decision is not sustained by sufficient evidence.

We find no error. Judgment affirmed.

(33 Ind. App. 476)

CITY OF HUNTINGTON v. LUSCH.*

(Appellate Court of Indiana. Division No. 1. March 11, 1904.)

DEFECTIVE HIGHWAY—PLEADING NOTICE—QUESTION FOR JURY—LEADING QUESTION—RULINGS ON EVIDENCE—PHOTOGRAPHS AS EVIDENCE.

1. Allegations in the complaint for injury from a horse being frightened at a stump in a city street, and running over the unprotected precipitous side of the street, that the stump was there and the side of the street left unprotected for two weeks, so that the city knew thereof and failed to remedy it, is a sufficient allegation of notice to the city of the defects.

2. Whether a stump remained in a city street so long that the city authorities should have taken notice of its presence, and whether it was a thing adapted by its appearance to frighten a horse, are questions for the jury.

3. The question to one's own witness, "This is the only instance, that you know of, isn't it?" is objectionable as leading.

4. Defendant, having procured a ruling excluding plaintiff's evidence of the happening of an event, may not complain that he was not thereafter allowed to prove it had not happened.

5. Photographs of the part of the street where the accident occurred, showing the stump which frightened the horse, are admissible, with evidence that there had been no material change in the appearance of the place, and that the photographs correctly represented it at the time of the accident.

Appeal from Circuit Court, Huntington County; J. C. Branyan, Judge.

Action by John Lusch against the city of Huntington. Judgment for plaintiff. Defendant appeals. Affirmed.

Lesh & Lesh, for appellant. Watkins & Morgan, for appellee.

BLACK, J. The amended complaint of the appellee contained two paragraphs, and the appellant's demurrer to each of them, for want of sufficient facts, was overruled. In each paragraph the appellee sought the recovery of damages for injury to himself and the death of his horse and injury to his vehicle. In the first paragraph it is alleged that by reason of the negligence of the appellant in leaving, or permitting to be left, a large stump on the street of the city, named Front street, along which appellee was driving on or about March 31, 1902, about 120 feet east of its intersection with Briant street, of that city, his horse became scared, and shied at the stump, running off into the river on the north side of the street; that the appellant negligently left the stump in the street; that the stump "was there for some time, to wit, ten days; and that by reason of its being there for a long period the city was bound to take notice of said stump being in said street, and that said defendant was negligent in permitting said obstruction to remain for a long period, and that said city had reasonable time to remove said obstruction, which defendant refused and negligently failed to remove," etc. In the second paragraph it was alleged that the street in question, for 200 feet or more, was along and on the south bank of Little Wabash river, the bank of which was perpendicular and 10 feet high above the water, which was 8 feet deep; that "there are no barricades or fence" along the top of the bank, or anything to prevent horses hitched to buggies and wagons, and becoming frightened, restless, or unmanageable, from falling into the river from the north side of the street; that on March 31, 1902, the appellee was driving along the street, and by reason of the negligence of the appellant leaving, and permitting to be left, a large stump, that had been torn up by the roots, on the street, the appellee's horse became frightened, and shied to the right, and by reason of the negligence of the city in not erecting barricades

*Rehearing denied. Transfer to Supreme Court denied. 71 N. E. 647.

¶ 1. See Municipal Corporations, vol. 36, Cent. Dig. § 1714.

on the north side of the street, where the street was unsafe and dangerous, the horse ran to the right, and fell over the bank into the river; that the horse was drowned in the river, etc.; "that said stump was left in said street and said bank on said river left unprotected by barricades for a long time, to wit, two weeks, and so long that defendant knew of such obstruction, and failed to erect barricades, or might have known by the use of ordinary and reasonable diligence," etc.

The only objection urged against the complaint, fully illustrated by the portions thereof we have set out, is that neither paragraph sufficiently shows notice to the municipal corporation of the alleged defects. It is not alleged in either of the paragraphs of complaint before us that any of the defective conditions stated were caused by the direct act or order of the city or by any person acting under its authority. It is not charged in either paragraph that the city thus placed, or caused to be placed, the stump in the street, but it is alleged in the first paragraph that the appellant negligently left the stump in the street, and that by reason of the negligence of the city in leaving the stump, or permitting it to be left, in the street, the horse shied at the stump, running off into the river. In the second paragraph the absence of barricades, etc., was alleged in the present tense, without any charge of negligence in that allegation. It was further alleged that on a date mentioned the appellee was driving along the street, and that by reason of the negligence of the city in leaving the stump, and permitting it to be left on the street, the horse became frightened and shied, and by reason of the negligence of the city in not erecting barricades the "horse ran to the right, and fell over the bank into the river."

It is not directly shown that, the city having caused the street to be so made that barricades were necessary to render it safe, it had negligently failed to so render it safe by never having provided reasonably sufficient barricades. It is not certainly shown that the street was rendered unsafe, either by reason of the presence of the stump, or because of the absence of barricades, by the direct act, order, or authority of the municipal corporation.

A city must not only make and keep in a reasonably safe condition the traveled portion of its streets, but also it is required to take such measures as are dictated by ordinary prudence to protect persons lawfully using a street, and exercising therein ordinary care from falling into dangerous places along the side of the street. City of Delphi v. Lowery, 74 Ind. 520, 39 Am. Rep. 98. But when it is sought to hold a city responsible for an injury to one in making such use of its streets, caused by a defect therein, the fault ascribed to the city being its neglect or omission to keep the street in repair, or caused by a defect therein created by wrongful act of another person, it is a rule of pleading in this state that it is not sufficient merely to charge the municipal corporation with negligence, but the complaint must also contain an averment that the city had notice of the defect which caused the injury, or such facts must be alleged that the court may determine as a legal conclusion therefrom that the city had notice, or under the circumstances ought to have known, of the defect in time to have remedied it before the occurrence of the injury. The city, in such case, is responsible for failure to exercise reasonable diligence to repair or to prevent injury, after knowledge of the dangerous defect, or after it ought to have known of it in the exercise of reasonable care and diligence. It should appear that the city had time to remedy the defect and make the way safe after it became known to the city, or after the city ought to have discovered it.

The question whether or not the stump had remained in the street so long a time that the municipal authorities should have taken notice of its presence there, as well as the question whether or not it was a thing adapted to frighten a horse, was a question of fact for the jury. Barr v. Village of Bainbridge (Sup.) 59 N. Y. Supp. 132.

In Scoville v. Salt Lake City, 11 Utah, 60, 39 Pac. 481, it was said: "The question of notice is not alone determined from the length of time a defect has existed, but also from the nature and character of the defect, the extent of the travel, and whether it is in a populous or sparsely settled part of the city."

In City of Indianapolis v. Murphy, 91 Ind. 382, in discussing the evidence, it was said that there was testimony that the defect in the alley had existed for the period of six weeks preceding the injury, and that "from the length of time the defect had existed, and the other facts and circumstances of the case, the jury was warranted in inferring knowledge on the part of the city."

In Turner v. City of Indianapolis, 96 Ind. 51, it was decided that, before the city could be held liable for not removing the obstruction there in question, a large rock, from the street, it must be shown by averments in the complaint that it had notice of the existence of the obstruction in the street, and that a reasonable time had elapsed before the accident for the removal of the same, or that it had remained there so long as to justify the presumption of such notice.

In City of Logansport v. Justice, 74 Ind. 378, 39 Am. Rep. 79, there was an instruction to the jury that, if the defective condition of the bridge in question "had continued for several days or weeks, then the city will be presumed to have notice such as will bind her in that regard." It was said by the court that the jury specially found that the bridge had been in the condition it was in at the time of the injury for "about two weeks," and that there had been negligence on the part of the city, or of her street commissioner, at and before the accident, to keep the bridge in repair when it was discovered to be out of repair. The court said: "Under any ordinary circumstances—and the evidence discloses nothing extraordinary—the fact of a bridge having been out of repair and in a dangerous condition so long would warrant an inference of knowledge on the part of the officers of the city, or some of them having duties in reference thereto, of the fact." See, also, City of Indianapolis v. Scott, 72 Ind. 196.

In Town of Spiceland v. Alier, 98 Ind. 467, it was said: "It may be that if the complaint alleged that the defect in the sidewalk existed for six or even three months before the injury the appellant's notice of such defect would be presumed."

In City of Evansville v. Wilter, 86 Ind. 414, where the injury was caused by a large stone lying on the sidewalk, it was alleged in the complaint that the city had negligently, wrongfully, and unlawfully allowed and permitted the stone to so lie upon the sidewalk, both day and night, for several months. This was held sufficient to show that the city, if diligent in the discharge of its duty, must have had notice of the obstruction.

In Town of Elkhart v. Ritter, 66 Ind. 136, the complaint alleged that the excavation in the sidewalk was upon one of the streets of the town most used by the public for ordinary business purposes, "and was by the defendant so negligently and carelessly allowed to remain several days prior to said accident, without any proper or sufficient guards, light, notices, or railings to warn people and prevent them from falling therein." It was held that the complaint stated facts from which the clear inference was that the town had knowledge of the excavation and its condition.

In City of Aurora v. Bitner, 100 Ind. 396, a paragraph of complaint was held sufficient wherein it was alleged "that for more than —— days before the time of the injury hereinafter complained of the defendant allowed the boards of said crossing to become loose and insecure, and that the defendant had notice that said crossing was in an insecure and dangerous condition for more than two days prior to the time of said injury, but that she wholly failed, neglected, and refused to repair the same."

The complaint is poorly composed, but we have concluded that such meaning may be gathered from its somewhat rambling averments as to require us to hold the pleading to be not insufficient in the matter to which the appellant's objection relates.

The appellant's motion for a new trial was overruled. One of the causes stated in the motion was alleged error in sustaining the appellee's objection to a question propounded on redirect examination of one of appellant's witnesses, who had resided near the place of the injury for a number of years. In the motion the question was stated thus: "Is this the only instance that any horse went over the bank, that you know of?" In the bill of exceptions the question is shown to have been as follows: "This is the only instance that any horse ever went over the bank, that you know of, isn't it?" The question propounded by appellant to his own witness was objectionable as being leading and plainly suggestive of the answer desired. If evidence that the witness had not knowledge of any other instance of a horse going over the bank might be regarded as tending to prove that no other horse had done so when the circumstances were the same as those of the case on trial, and might be received for such purpose, yet it appears in the record that upon the motion of the appellant the court had previously excluded evidence introduced by the appellee that another horse scared at the stump in question, and shied away from it. Having procured a ruling of the court, whether correct or erroneous, excluding such affirmative evidence, the appellant could not consistently complain of the court's exclusion of his proposed negative evidence.

Another ground assigned in the motion for a new trial was the introduction in evidence of each of two photographic views of the place where the injury occurred, one of them showing the stump in question, the ground of objection being that the photographs were not taken at or about the time of the injury, or when the things shown were situated as at that time, but things were changed and shifted by interested parties and the photographs taken. The appellee had testified that a day or two after the injury he passed along the road, and that then the stump was not in the street, but had been rolled into a vacant lot; but he further testified that when the photographs were taken the stump had been brought back, and was in the same place; that it was placed by Mr. Morgan or some one in the same identical place, as near as it could be placed there. The court permitted the photographs to be exhibited to the jury, in connection with all the other evidence in the case, but stated that the jury were not to be bound by the photographs; that they might apply the evidence with them. There being evidence to the effect that there was no material change in the appearance of the place of the injury, and that the photographs correctly represented the place at the time of the injury, the court did not err in admitting the photographs in connection with the other evidence in the case. Keyes v. The State, 122 Ind. 527, 23 N. E. 1097; Miller v. The Louisville, etc., R. Co., 128 Ind. 97, 27 N. E. 339, 25 Am. St. Rep. 416; Douglass v. The State, 18 Ind. App. 289, 48 N. E. 9.

It is claimed that the court erred in some of its instructions to the jury, and in rejecting a number of instructions proposed by the appellant. Upon comparing the instructions given with each other, and considering these instructions as a whole, we find that the court fairly represented the case to the jury, and in its instructions sufficiently covered the pertinent and correct instructions which were rejected.

The evidence cannot be regarded by us as insufficient. It was within the province of the jury, as before stated, to determine upon the evidence whether or not the stump was an object adapted by its appearance to frighten horses passing along the street. The question as to the appellee's contributory negligence was properly left to the jury, under the instructions of the court. There was evidence not merely as to the value of the property, but also as to personal injury of a serious nature suffered by the appellee, and we are unable to determine that the amount of recovery in the sum of $400 was too large.

Judgment affirmed.

(32 Ind. A. 593)

HOFFERBERT v. WILLIAMS et al.

(Appellate Court of Indiana. Division No. 1. March 16, 1904.)

NEW TRIAL AS OF RIGHT—ACTION INVOLVING TITLE—COMPLAINT—ESTOPPEL—SETTING ASIDE ORDER FOR NEW TRIAL.

1. A complaint alleged that plaintiff was in possession of lands that he owned in fee, and that defendants continuously trespassed thereon by driving over the same, claiming some right adverse to plaintiff, which constituted a cloud, and that the trespasses were an injury; and the prayer was for damages, for the trespass, for an injunction, and the quieting of plaintiff's title. *Held*, that plaintiff was not entitled to a new trial as a matter of right, under the statute providing for the granting of a new trial as of right in actions for the recovery of the possession of real estate, and for determining and quieting title, brought against one who claims title to or interest in the real estate adverse to the plaintiff, although the defendant is not in possession.

2. Where a new trial was granted as a matter of right, under the statute, in favor of plaintiff, though defendants failed to except to the order, and subsequently filed an answer to an amended complaint, and asked a continuance, defendants were not estopped to move for the striking out of the order granting the new trial.

3. A new trial as a matter of right having been erroneously granted, the court had a right, before entry on such trial, to set aside the order awarding it.

Appeal from Circuit Court, Huntington County; J. T. Cox, Special Judge.

Suit by William P. Hofferbert against John W. Williams and others. From an order setting aside an order granting plaintiff a new trial as a matter of right, he appeals. Affirmed.

Spencer & Branyan, for appellant. Watkins & Morgan, for appellees.

BLACK, J. The appellant was the plaintiff, and in his complaint it was stated that he was the owner in fee simple and in possession of a tract of land in Huntington county, particularly described, containing about 5½ acres; that the appellees "continuously and repeatedly trespass thereon by driving over the same with teams and vehicles without plaintiff's consent, and over his objection, and that they claim some title or interest therein adverse to plaintiff's title, and the right to enter thereon, and deny plaintiff's title thereto, which claim and denial of title is repeated and circulated, to plaintiff's damage in the sum of $100, and which prevents the sale of plaintiff's said real estate, and constitutes a cloud thereon, and such trespasses are a continuing injury to plaintiff's possession, to his damage in the sum of $100. Therefore plaintiff asks judgment for $200 damages, and for a decree perpetually enjoining said defendants, and each of them, from trespassing on plaintiff's said real estate, or interfering with plaintiff's possession, or slandering plaintiff's title, and that he also have a decree quieting his title to said real estate, and for all other proper relief." The issue formed on this complaint was tried by jury, the verdict being for the appellees, whereupon, on a subsequent day of the same term, judgment was rendered that the appellant take nothing by his suit herein, and that the appellees recover of him their costs. On the next following day, upon his motion made orally, and bond filed by the appellant, the court ordered a new trial as of right. At a subsequent day of the same term the appellant filed an amended complaint, in which he alleged "that he is the owner in fee simple and in the possession of a tract of land situate in said county [describing it]; that the defendants claim that said land was, prior to plaintiff's purchase thereof, dedicated by his grantors to the public for use by the public as a highway, and said defendants persist in such use and such claim, which use is wrongful, and such claim is false, and injurious to the plaintiff, and a cloud upon his title, which prevents the sale thereof, to the damage of the plaintiff in the sum of $100. Wherefore plaintiff asks judgment and a decree of the court quieting his title to said real estate, and for $100 damages for interfering with his possession and title, and for all other proper relief." The appellees answered this amended complaint by general denial, and at a subsequent term the court, upon the motion of the appellees, struck out the order granting a new trial as of right. This action of the court is questioned on appeal. The statute provides for the granting of a new trial as of right in actions for the recovery of the possession of real estate, and also in actions for determining and quieting the question of title to real estate, brought by any person either in or out of possession, or by one having an interest in remainder or reversion, against another who claims title to or interest in the real estate adverse to the plaintiff, although the defendant be not in possession.

The question whether the appellant was entitled to a new trial as of right may be determined by deciding upon the character of his original complaint. Whatever may be said of the amended complaint filed after the granting of the new trial, he cannot complain of the action of the court in depriving him of a new trial, without cause shown therefor, if the issue was not such as to entitle him to such additional trial. The tendency of the decisions is not to extend the terms of the statute allowing new trials as of right to cases other than those clearly falling within its provisions. Butler University v. Conrad, 94 Ind. 353. In that case it was held that where a cause of action to quiet title to real estate, or to recover possession thereof, is improperly joined with a cause of action in which a new trial as of right is not allowable, the law as to new trials relating to causes of action of the latter class should govern, and a new trial as of right should not be granted. In Bradford v. School Town of Marion, 107 Ind. 280, 7 N. E. 256, it was said: "If the judgment was for the defendant generally, and was an adjudication of all the issues presented, then, since the parties saw fit to litigate causes of action which were improperly joined, in some of which either party would have been entitled to a new trial as of right, with an action for damages, in which a new trial as of right was not allowable, the order granting a new trial was improperly made, and that which set it aside was correct." A new trial as of right will not be granted where title to real estate is but incidentally involved. Davis v. Cleveland, etc., R. Co., 140 Ind. 468, 39 N. E. 495; Thompson v. Kreisher, 148 Ind. 575, 47 N. E. 1059. In Wilson v. Brookshire, 126 Ind. 497, 25 N. E. 131, 9 L. R. A. 792, the rule is said to be that when a cause proceeds to judgment, which embraces a substantive cause of action, in which a new trial as a matter of right is not allowable, then, even though it embraces other causes in which a new trial as of right is allowable, the policy of the law is to regard that cause of action as controlling in which a second trial as of right is not permitted. Where the action was originally one for injunction and damages, and so continued to the end, and there was a supplemental complaint seeking damages and possession, and also a cross-complaint to quiet title, it was held that a new trial as of right could not properly be demanded. Richwine v. Presbyterian Church, 135 Ind. 80, 34 N. E. 737. See, also, Taylor v. Calvert, 138 Ind. 67, 37 N. E. 531. In Bennett v. Closson, 138 Ind. 542, 38 N. E. 46, it was held that if two or more substantive causes of action proceed to judgment in the same case, whether properly or improperly joined, if one of them would entitle the losing party to a new trial as of right, and the other would not, a new trial as of right will not be granted. See, also, Jones v. Peters, 28 Ind. App. 383, 62 N. E. 1019. In Nutter v. Hendricks, 150 Ind. 605, 50 N. E. 748, where a paragraph of complaint seeking damages for trespass and an injunction was joined with another paragraph for the recovery of the possession of real estate, and the cause went to finding and judgment on both paragraphs, it was held that a new trial as of right was not demandable. The court said that "if the whole case made by the complaint is not one to recover possession of, or to quiet title to, real estate, or both, then a new trial without cause shown is not provided for or allowable by law." See, also, Seisler v. Smith, 150 Ind. 88, 46 N. E. 993. In Atkinson v. Williams, 151 Ind. 431, 51 N. E. 721, it was held that where the complaint, judging from its general scope and tenor, sought only the recovery of damages for an alleged trespass to real estate, and an injunction to prevent the threatened continuation of the same, on the ground that the plaintiff had no other adequate remedy, neither party was entitled to a new trial as of right.

The amended complaint filed after the granting of the new trial as of right showed that the appellees were merely claiming that the real estate in question was a public highway, and were using it as such, and did not show that they were claiming or exercising any private title or interest in the real estate. An apparent purpose of the amended complaint was to prevent the future use by the appellees of the real estate as a highway, and their claiming the right to such use, and to recover damages for such past "interfering" with the appellant's "possession and title." In Miller v. City of Indianapolis, 123 Ind. 196, 24 N. E. 228, the complaint against the city and others alleged that the plaintiff was the owner of real estate described; that the defendants had unlawfully, wrongfully, illegally, and forcibly taken possession of the same, and, without having condemned the same, were threatening to do great and irreparable damage to the same, in that they were threatening to cut down the trees and vines thereon, and to plow the land and grade it, and to make a street over and upon it, without leave or license from the plaintiff, and with full notice that the plaintiff was the owner thereof, and under a claim that the real estate was a public street of the city; the prayer being that, as against the defendants, the plaintiff's title be quieted, and that the defendants be enjoined. It was held that there was no error in overruling the plaintiff's application for a new trial as of right. It would seem that if a plaintiff, after his application for a new trial as of right has been sustained, so amends his complaint as to present a cause of action as to which the statutory provision for the granting of a new trial as of right would not be applicable, there could be no error in setting aside the order so granting him a new trial. However this may be, in the original complaint it was not sought to recover compensation or damages for use and occupation, or for deprivation of possession. It was alleged that the appellant was in possession. There was a substantive charge of trespass

—an injury to the possession—and the plaintiff demanded a judgment for damages for trespass, and a decree enjoining the appellees from trespassing on the real estate, or interfering with the appellant's possession. Though there were intermixed in the pleading general and formal allegations proper for a complaint in a statutory action to quiet title, there were included, not merely as incidental to such an action, but distinctly, averments peculiarly applicable to a common-law action for trespass on land. We need not determine whether or not another common-law cause of action was stated. It is true that in an action for ejectment the plaintiff may, as a statutory incident, recover in the same action for use and occupation for six years next before the commencement of the action, but a distinct cause of action as at common law for trespass on land is not an incident to an action for possession or to quiet title. If the cause of action for trespass had been set forth in one paragraph, and the averments peculiar to the statutory action to quiet title had been set forth alone in another paragraph, it could not be doubted that the appellant would not be entitled to a new trial as of right, provided by the statute only for actions of ejectment and actions to quiet title; and we think no such advantage should accrue to a plaintiff merely because he has intermingled in one paragraph a cause of action for which such a new trial is provided with another distinct cause of action, as to which he can obtain a new trial only upon a showing of sufficient cause, as provided by another statute.

Counsel for the appellant seems to be of the opinion that by failing to except to the order granting a new trial as of right when the order was made, or afterward during the term, the appellees waived objection to the order, and that by filing an answer to the amended complaint, and by agreeing in open court to a day for trial, and by asking a continuance, without objecting to the granting of a new trial, the appellees were estopped to claim that the order was erroneous. The appellees have not appealed, assigning as error the action of the court in granting the new trial; but the appellant has taken upon himself the onus of establishing that the court erred to his prejudice in setting aside an order for a new trial, not yet entered upon, to which he had no right, but by which the right of the appellees under a judgment duly rendered in their favor was put in jeopardy without any sufficient cause. Unless we could say that the appellant was entitled to a new trial without the assignment of any cause therefor, because of the character of the issues involved, we cannot hold that the court might not properly set aside its erroneous order when the appellees thus, for the first time, assail it for the protection and reinstatement of their judgment. Judgment affirmed.

(33 Ind. App. 600)

HARRIS v. PITTSBURG, C., C. & ST. L. RY. CO.[1]

(Appellate Court of Indiana. Division No. 2. March 17, 1904.)

CARRIERS — INJURY TO PASSENGER — DANGEROUS STATION GROUNDS—PLEADING — ISSUES — PROXIMATE CAUSE — BURDEN OF PROOF — QUESTION FOR JURY.

1. It is the duty of a railroad company to provide a safe place for passengers to alight.

2. It is not negligence per se for a passenger to alight from a moving train.

3. In an action against a railroad for injuries sustained by a passenger by slipping on an icy platform when he alighted from a train, *held* that under the evidence the question whether plaintiff was guilty of contributory negligence was for the jury.

4. In an action against a railroad for injuries sustained by a passenger, the complaint alleged that the injury was owing to the fact that when the passenger stepped on a platform on alighting from a train he slipped upon an accumulation of ice, and there was evidence that at the time plaintiff alighted the train was in motion. *Held*, that the question as to the proximate cause of the injury was in issue.

5. The issue was one of fact for the jury.

6. Under the express provisions of Burns' Rev. St. 1901, § 359a, in an action for injuries contributory negligence is a matter of defense.

7. The burden on defendant of showing contributory negligence does not shift throughout the trial.

Appeal from Circuit Court, Clark County; Jas. K. Marsh, Judge.

Action by Lloyd Harris against the Pittsburg, Cincinnati, Chicago & St. Louis Railway Company. From a judgment in favor of defendant, plaintiff appeals. Reversed.

H. W. Phipps and L. A. Douglas, for appellant. M. Z. Stannard, for appellee.

ROBY, J. In this action appellant sought to recover damages alleged to have been caused by the negligence of appellee, a railroad corporation. He is averred to have been a passenger upon one of appellee's passenger trains running from Louisville, Ky., to Jeffersonville, Ind. Pearl street, in said last-named city, was a regular stopping place, and was announced by those in charge of the train, which stopped to discharge and receive passengers. Appellant avers that he then stepped from the lower step of the rear end of the coach in which he was riding upon the platform provided by appellee for such use. It is further averred that said platform was heavily covered with ice and sleet, which appellee had negligently permitted to remain thereon for a period of 10 days prior thereto, failing to remove the same, and thereby negligently failing to make said platform reasonably safe for passengers to alight upon; that when stepping from said train he stepped upon such ice and sleet, which caused his feet to slip from under him, inflicting the injuries complained of; which are averred to have been the direct result of appellee's said negligence. He further says that he did not

¶ 2. See Carriers, vol. 9, Cent. Dig. § 1281.

[1] See 77 N. E. 1061.

know that said ice and sleet were on the platform, and that appellee's servants failed to inform him of the same, wherefore, etc. The issue was formed by a general denial, the cause submitted to a jury, and upon the conclusion of the evidence the court, upon appellee's motion, instructed the jury to return a verdict in its favor.

Appellant's motion for a new trial was overruled, and such action is assigned as error. The only question which need be considered relates to the giving of the peremptory instruction, and that involves a consideration of the evidence. The specific negligence counted upon is that the appellee allowed its platform to be unsafe, by reason of which appellant slipped and fell at the time he alighted from said train. The action of the court in giving the peremptory instruction was based upon the hypothesis that the evidence established contributory negligence, and it is not, therefore, necessary to consider the evidence except as it relates to that subject. The testimony of appellant was as follows: "I was sitting about middle ways of the car, and when they stopped I got up and started out to the platform, and as I got to the platform the train kind a moved off, but I started on down the steps, and when I got to the bottom I put my right foot down to the ground, and when I went to put the other foot down my feet both went from under me, and my shoulder went this way. I think the forward end of the second coach struck my shoulder and threw me forward." His further testimony was, in effect, as follows: The platform was dark. It was dark around the place where the cars stopped. He could see the ground. The ice made him slip. He did not see the ice when he stepped off the coach. "When I came down, the train started to move, and I had my hands on both the handles; and when I got down I put my right foot down, and I stepped with my left, and when I let go my feet went from under me. Q. You say the train was moving some when you got off? A. Yes, sir. Q. How fast? A. The engine had just started up. Q. About what rate of speed would you say the train was going when you alighted from the train? A. About half a mile an hour. The engine kind a set onto the curve." There were lights in the train and in the depot, and an electric light in the rear of the train as it stopped, which would ordinarily illuminate the platform, but, owing to the train standing between it and the platform, did not do so at this time; the place where the appellant alighted being in the shadow so made, which extended four feet from the train. He knew that the streets and unprotected places in Jeffersonville were covered with ice and sleet. He was familiar with the locality and with appellee's train service. There was no roof over the platform. He could have alighted at the Wall Street Station, 600 feet further on. The point where appellant fell was about 15 or 20 feet east of the station building. It was in evidence that on three occasions during that "icy spell" one of appellee's employés spread ashes on the platform. It was the duty of appellee to provide a safe place for its passengers to alight. Ill., etc., R. v. Cheek, 152 Ind. 669, 53 N. E. 641, and cases; Louisville, etc., R. Co. v. Lucas, 119 Ind. 590, 21 N. E. 968, 6 L. R. A. 193; Penn. R. v. Marion, 123 Ind. 418, 23 N. E. 973, 7 L. R. A. 687, 18 Am. St. Rep. 330; Lucas v. Penn. Ry., 120 Ind. 205, 21 N. E. 972, 16 Am. St. Rep. 823.

The appellee's first contention is "that a passenger who voluntarily alights from a moving train is guilty of contributory negligence." The contention cannot be proved. It is not negligence per se for a passenger to alight from a moving train. Louisville & N. R. Co. v. Crunk, 119 Ind. 542, 21 N. E. 31, 12 Am. St. Rep. 443; Penn. Ry. v. Marion, 123 Ind. 415, 23 N. E. 973, 7 L. R. A. 687, 18 Am. St. Rep. 330; Louisville, E. & St. L. C. R. Co. v. Bean, 9 Ind. App. 240, 36 N. E. 443. The circumstances and conditions under which he acts must all be considered in determining the fact, and whether he exercised reasonable and ordinary care is a question for the jury; the exception being found only when the act is of such a character as to admit of but one inference. The speed at which the train is moving is an essential and important circumstance. If a passenger were to deliberately leap from a train running 60 miles an hour between stations it would be impossible to justify such an act as that of a reasonably prudent man, but such conclusion would be deduced, not from the mere act of alighting from a moving train, but from the act of alighting from a train so moving and under such conditions. Each case must be determined upon its own facts, which of necessity vary greatly. Louisville & N. R. Co. v. Crunk, supra; Louisville, E. & St. L. C. R. Co. v. Bean, supra; Penn. Ry. v. Marion, supra; Cin. Ry. v. Revalee, 17 Ind. App. 665, 46 N. E. 352. In the case of Toledo, St. L. & K. C. R. Co. v. Wingate, 143 Ind. 125, 37 N. E. 274, 42 N. E. 477, the conditions surrounding plaintiff's attempt to alight from the train were such, aside from the movement thereof, as to show contributory negligence on her part, when considered in connection therewith. The train in Reibel v. Cin. Ry., 114 Ind. 476, 17 N. E. 107, was running at a high rate of speed. The decedent was found to have jumped from the train moving six miles an hour in order to avoid being carried by the station. The rule announced by the court was that a passenger must not attempt to get on or off a moving train while in motion, if it be obviously dangerous to make the attempt. Considering the slow movement of the train, that it had been stopped at a platform for the purpose of discharging passengers, who were thereby invited to alight, appellant's lack of information as to the dangerous condition of the platform, the duty of appellee to keep the same in a reasonably safe condition, the situation of the lights, appellant's right to assume that appellee had discharged its duty in keeping the platform in a reasonably safe condition, and the other circumstances in the case heretofore set out, the question was clearly one for the jury. Penn. Ry. v. Marion, supra; Louisville Ry. v. Lucas, supra; Thompson, Comm. on Law of Neg. 3015.

It is contended on the one hand that the sole cause of appellant's fall was the icy platform; that he had left the train, and that its motion had nothing to do with his fall. On the other hand, that the allegations of the complaint limit recovery to an injury received while alighting from the train, and that the proximate cause of the fall was the negligent act of alighting from a moving train. The negligence counted upon related to the unsafe condition of the platform. If the injury was caused by leaping from a moving train in the dark, the allegation would be unproven, and there could be no recovery, irrespective of the contributory negligence. The question of proximate cause was therefore in issue. If the judge was authorized to decide that issue in appellee's favor, the binding instruction was justified, but the issue was not one of law. It was an issue of fact, an issue to be determined as other issues of like character. Ry. Co. v. Martin (Ind. App.) 65 N. E. 591. The burden of establishing contributory negligence was on appellee. Burns' Rev. St. 1901, § 359a. This burden did not shift. The evidence was sufficient to take the cause to the jury. Reversed, and cause remanded, with instructions to sustain motion for a new trial, and for further proceedings not inconsistent herewith.

(32 Ind. A. 587)

WEAVER et al. v. MEYER.

(Appellate Court of Indiana, Division No. 2. March 15, 1904.)

ADMINISTRATION—CONVERSION OF PROPERTY OF ESTATE—ACTION—BY WHOM BROUGHT—PLEADING—EVIDENCE.

1. A complaint alleging that an executor had managed a decedent's estate as such executor till his own death, and had never separated the income from the body of the estate, but handled it as a part of the estate, sufficiently shows that he had never so far executed his trust that the fund ceased to belong to the estate, or that an administrator de bonis non appointed after the executor's death could not maintain an action against persons who had wrongfully secured possession of the fund.

2. The title to personal property passing, under Wisconsin law, to the executor or administrator of a decedent, where a testator in that state bequeathed money and securities to his widow for life, and then to his son, who was made executor, and the son never intended to part with title to the property, the proper party to maintain an action for a conversion of the property after the son's death was the administrator de bonis non, though the widow had been placed in possession of the property.

3. In proceedings by an heir for the appointment of an administrator de bonis non, the widow of the decedent appeared and objected to the appointment; denying that the applicant was an heir, and alleging that the estate had been fully administered. On trial the findings were for the applicant, and an administrator was appointed. *Held* that, in an action by him for property of the estate, which the widow had conveyed to the defendants to conceal it, the record of these proceedings was conclusive on defendants; they being in privity with the widow.

4. In an action by an administrator de bonis non for property of the estate which the testator's widow was alleged to have wrongfully conveyed to the defendants, the record of a suit in which her son (since deceased) had secured a divorce, and in which the legitimacy of his daughter had been adjudicated, was admissible, as tending to explain the widow's action as an attempt to prevent the granddaughter from inheriting from the testator.

Appeal from Circuit Court, Clay County; P. O. Colliver, Judge.

Action by Richard Meyer, Jr., administrator, against George W. Weaver and others. From a judgment in favor of plaintiff, defendants appeal. Affirmed.

Coffey & McGregor, for appellants. A. R. Bushnell, Geo. H. Knight, and A. W. Knight, for appellee.

ROBY, J. Action by appellee to recover money averred to belong to the estate of James Moore. The appellants, and the appellant Weaver separately, demurred to the complaint, and the action of the court in overruling said demurrers is presented by proper assignment.

The facts set up in the complaint are, in effect, as follows: James Moore died intestate in Grant county, Wis., on April 30, 1885, where he had lived for many years. He left surviving his widow, Sarah Moore, and his son, John S., the only child, and by his will bequeathed the use of his estate to his widow during her life, and at her death to his said son, who was appointed executor. The will was duly probated, and said John S. qualified as executor, entered upon his duties as such, took possession of the estate, and made a partial inventory thereof. The family had lived together before the father's death, and afterward the mother and son continued to do so until June 6, 1891, when John S. departed life, leaving his widow, Addie Moore, and one child, Alma (now Alma Fox), his sole heirs. All the property in the family was that owned originally by James Moore, amounting to about $10,000, mostly in money and securities; possession thereof being held by John S., until his death, as executor. Under the Wisconsin statute, the title to all this property passed to the executor; legatees and heirs acquiring title only through the judgment of distribution made by the county court having jurisdiction. At the death of John S. Moore, his mother took possession of all said estate, and secretly carried $5,000 to Brazil, Clay county, Ind., where the defendant Weaver, her brother-in-law, Dilley, her brother, and Carpenter, a relative by marriage of Dilley, resided, and with them conspired and confederated to conceal said sum from the persons entitled thereto, and from the person who should be appointed administrator de bonis non of the estate of James Moore, and, to convert the same to their own use, fraudulently invested the same in building association stock in the name of said Sarah. Afterwards Sarah Moore, a constant citizen of Wisconsin, remarried in Grant county, Wis., with one Garthwaite, and lived with him until March, 1894, when she died, leaving, under the law of Wisconsin, as her sole heir, her said granddaughter, Alma. Defendants and said Sarah fraudulently concealed the facts connected with the Indiana transaction, and upon her death her second husband, conspiring with appellants to conceal the same, and to wrongfully convert the money to their own use, contrived that Dilley should take out letters of administration in Clay county on the estate of said Sarah, which he did in pursuance of the same purpose. "Defendant Weaver wrongfully trumped up a false and fraudulent account against said Sarah Garthwaite for $1,250," which Dilley fraudulently admitted. Dilley trumped up a fraudulent claim for $202 for his services, and $150 as attorney's fees. In order to further carry out said fraud upon the court, Dilley filed his report in final settlement, showing that Sarah Garthwaite left no child, or descendant of any child of hers, surviving her; that she left her husband, Garthwaite, her sole heir at law, from whom Dilley had procured an assignment of his interest in said estate, both of them knowing that Garthwaite had no interest therein, and intending to deprive the persons rightfully entitled thereto, and impose upon the court. Afterward Dilley filed his final settlement report, showing distribution to himself, and receipting to himself for the same. The appointment in Wisconsin of an administrator de bonis non of the estate is set out. Search for assets is shown, resulting in the discovery of the fraud alleged, in July, 1900; and it is averred "that at the said city of Brazil, in the said Clay county, Indiana, and at the time and in the way and manner aforesaid, the defendants, and each of them, unlawfully intermeddled with said moneys and property of the estate of the said James Moore, deceased, which so came into and was in the said state of Indiana as aforesaid, and with the income and proceeds thereof, and unlawfully converted the same to their own use, as this plaintiff is informed and believes, whereby the estate of the said James Moore, deceased, and this plaintiff, has been and is deprived of the use, interest, and income which it and he might and could otherwise have derived and had thereof and therefrom, to the plaintiff's injury and damage $10,000." Wherefore, etc.

The proposition insisted on by appellant is that if John S. Moore, as executor of the estate of James Moore, so far executed his trust as to reduce the assets of the estate to money, pay the debts, and pay over to Sarah Moore (Garthwaite) the fund in controversy, then such fund ceased to belong to said estate, and cannot be recovered by this administrator. The complaint contains an averment as follows: "That from the time of the death of the said James Moore, deceased, up to the time of the death of the said John S. Moore, the said John S. Moore, as such executor, had and retained the possession of all the estate of said James Moore, deceased, and by and with the consent and with the assistance of his mother, the said Sarah Moore, handled and managed the same as such executor, and they both had their living therefrom, and no part of the income was ever by them, or either of them, in any way segregated or set or kept apart from the body of the said estate, but the whole of the income thereof was by both of them always handled as part and parcel of the body of said estate, as this plaintiff is informed and believes." It follows that, even under appellant's statement of the law, the demurrer for want of facts was correctly overruled. The proposition above stated is asserted, in argument, to apply to the evidence, under the grounds for a new trial that the verdict is not supported by it, and is contrary to law. The fourteenth instruction requested by appellants, and refused, contains a statement of the law based upon the hypothesis claimed by appellants. It is unnecessary to consider the instruction refused, for the reason that, so far as it was a correct expression of the law, the fifteenth instruction given is equivalent to it. Under the Wisconsin law, "personalty, except heirlooms, or limbs of the inheritance which descend with it to the heir, is never inherited. Upon the owner's death the legal title goes to the executor or administrator. * * * In any case when the title to personalty comes to legatee or distributee, it comes from the executor or administrator, not from the testator or ancestor. The title of the executor or administrator intervenes between testator and legatee, between ancestor and next of kin." Murphy v. Hanrahan, 50 Wis. 485, 490, 7 N. W. 436. The will gave to Sarah Moore the use of all the testator's property during her life. She thereby became entitled to the income therefrom; such property consisting, as it did, of money and securities. Eddy v. Cross, 26 Ind. App. 643, 60 N. E. 470; Golder v. Littlejohn, 30 Wis. 344; Meyer v. Garthwaite, 92 Wis. 571, 575, 66 N. W. 704.

The verdict of the jury includes a finding that John S. Moore did not intend to part with title to said money and securities. In the absence of a completed gift by him to her, it would have been his duty at her death to have resumed possession of such property, had it been delivered to her in specie, and to have then transferred it to the person entitled thereto. Golder v. Littlejohn, supra.

The mere possession of the property did not authorize her to dissipate or give it away. She could not thus defeat the will of her husband, by which only its use during life was given her. It follows that after the death of the mother the representative of the estate was the only person entitled to possession of said property, and was therefore the proper party to bring this suit, based upon its wrongful conversion. The verdict, in so far as it relates to the connection of the appellants with the transaction, is supported by evidence.

John S. Moore was thrice married. From the mother of Alma he was divorced. After his death the guardian of Alma applied to the county court of Grant county, Wis., for the appointment of an administrator de bonis non of the estate of James Moore. Sarah Moore (Garthwaite) appeared in this proceeding and objected to such appointment; denying, in her objections, that Alma was the child of John S. Moore, or his heir, and asserting that said estate had been fully administered. Trial was had, evidence heard, finding made for the applicant, and an administrator appointed as prayed. The record of this proceeding was introduced in evidence on the trial of the case at bar. There was no error in admitting such evidence. Appellants are in privity with—claiming under—Sarah Garthwaite. The judgment therefore concludes them upon the facts in issue.

The record of the divorce suit between John S. Moore and the mother of Alma Moore was also introduced in evidence. The legitimacy of the daughter was then adjudicated and declared. The facts disclosed by these records illustrate and explain the action of said Sarah in seeking, with the aid of her second husband and appellants, to prevent a full administration in Wisconsin upon the estate of James Moore; resulting, as it evidently would have done, in the payment to the daughter of whatever surplus might ultimately remain for distribution. There was no error in the admission of the evidence.

A brief of 294 pages has been filed by appellants. Thirty-four grounds for a new trial were enumerated in the motion therefor, as high as 11 causes being named in a single specification. The alleged errors are referred to in the brief, although the reference comes short in many instances of such an argument as is necessary on appeal. We are not able to say that error was committed, requiring a reversal of the judgment. Sarah Garthwaite evidently determined that the granddaughter whom she refused to acknowledge should not inherit. The appellants undertook to assist her in preventing it. After her death they proceeded to consummate the fraud. There is no room for division of responsibility between them. The judgment appealed from was for $5,000. It accords with the merits of the controversy, and is therefore affirmed.

(178 N. Y. 147)

GMAEHLE v. ROSENBERG et al.

(Court of Appeals of New York. March 29, 1904.)

INJURY TO EMPLOYÉ—NOTICE TO MASTER—COMMON-LAW LIABILITY.

1. Laws 1902, p. 1748, c. 600, provides that a master shall be liable for the negligence of the superintendent, and section 2 (page 1749) requires notice to be given to the employer as a condition precedent to the maintenance of an action to recover damages for personal injuries under the act. *Held*, that a complaint in an action to recover for the death of an employé because of the alleged negligence of the master in the erecting of a scaffolding states a good cause of action based on a common-law liability of the master, and it is unnecessary to allege that a notice was given the employer in accordance with the provisions of such act.

Gray, J., dissenting.

Appeal from Supreme Court, Appellate Division, First Department.

Action by Charles Gmaehle, administrator of Charles Gmaehle, against Morris Rosenberg and others. From an order of the Appellate Division (84 N. Y. Supp. 1127) reversing a judgment of the Special Term overruling a demurrer to the complaint and sustaining the demurrer, plaintiff appeals. Reversed.

Morris Hillquit, for appellant. David Steckler, for respondents.

CULLEN, J. The action is brought, administrator of servant against master, to recover damages for the death of the servant, charged to have been caused by the negligence of the master. The allegations of the complaint as to the fault on the defendants' part are that they erected and caused to be erected a scaffold in such a negligent, improper, and unsafe manner that the same gave way and fell while the plaintiff's intestate was working thereon, by which said intestate received injuries causing his death. The defendants demurred to the complaint as not stating facts sufficient to constitute a cause of action, in that it failed to allege that notice of the time, place, and cause of the injury to the deceased was given to the employers as prescribed by section 2, p. 1749, of chapter 600 of the Laws of 1902. The demurrer was overruled by the Special Term, but this decision was reversed by the Appellate Division, which has certified to us the following question: "Is the service of a notice of the time, place, and cause of the injury by the servant upon the master within 120 days after the occurrence of the accident, as provided for by chapter 600 of the Laws of 1902, entitled 'An act to extend and regulate the liability of employers to make compensation for personal injuries suffered by employees,' a condition precedent to the maintenance of an action against the employer to recover damages for personal injuries sustained by the employé after the passage of said act?"

The complaint does not charge any liability based on the provisions of the statute of 1902. It was the settled law of this state prior to the enactment of the statute that the master was bound to exercise reasonable care to provide the servant a safe place to work and safe and suitable machinery and appliances with which to work, and that for a failure to exercise such a degree of care he was liable to the servant for any injury caused thereby. This was what our courts and the courts generally throughout the country have held to be the common-law liability of the master. Under this rule the complaint stated an entirely good cause of action, and it was unnecessary to rely on any statute enacted in favor of the employé. By the first section of the act of 1902 it is provided that an employé, or, in case of death, his personal representatives, shall have the right of compensation for such injury or death where the injury was caused (1) by reason of any defect in the condition of the ways, works, or machinery connected with or used by the employer, due to the negligence of the employer or the person intrusted by him with the care of such ways, works, and machinery; (2) by reason of the negligence of any superintendent of the employer, or any person acting as such, or whose principal duty is that of superintendence. The second section prescribes: "No action for recovery of compensation for injury or death under this act shall be maintained unless notice of the time, place and cause of the injury is given to the employer within one hundred and twenty days and the action is commenced within one year after the occurrence of the accident causing the injury or death." It will be seen that by the terms of the statute the requirement of notice to the employer is limited to "actions for the recovery of compensation for injury or death under this act." The learned court below was of opinion, however, that the statute dealt with the whole subject of the master's liability for defective ways, works, or machinery, and that, therefore, from the time of its enactment all causes of action for those defects, whether they were such as previously existed or not, were subjected to the qualification that notice must be given to the master within 120 days after the occurrence of the accident. It is also insisted that the statute gives no new cause of action, and that hence it must be construed as regulating such causes of action as were given by the common law. Now, while we are not prepared to say whether the statute has in any respect increased the liability of the master for defective ways, works, or machinery, it is clear that it has given an additional cause of action where it prescribes that the master shall be liable for the negligence of the superintendent, or any person acting as such. At common law, while the master was liable for the fault of his alter ego, to whom he intrusted the whole management of the work, with the power to employ and discharge servants, he was not liable for the negligence of foremen, merely, as such. Loughlin v. State of New York, 105 N. Y. 159, 11 N. E. 371. Moreover, unquestionably the statute does not cover the whole liability of the employer to the employé. The master is bound to exercise reasonable care in the selection and employment of competent co-servants, and, if the character of the business requires it, to promulgate and enforce proper rules for the conduct of the business. It cannot be denied that these, and probably other, liabilities remain unaffected by the statute. Reliance is placed by the learned Appellate Division upon the title of the statute, "An act to extend and regulate the liability of employers to make compensation for personal injuries suffered by employees." But if it were the legislative intent to deal generally with the subject of the liability of employers, it is difficult to see why the statute did not deal with their responsibility for incompetent fellow servants or insufficient rules, as well as for defective appliances, or why the statute did not prescribe broadly that in all actions of employés against employers the prescribed notice should be given. We think the legislative intent is reasonably clear. The Legislature, deeming that by the act it was about to extend the liabilities of masters to their servants (to what extent they effectuated this purpose it is unnecessary now to determine), thought it wise to safeguard the new liabilities by requiring that notice should be given the master of the accident for which it was sought to recover compensation. But it was only the new or extended liability that it was intended to subject to such safeguard. This intent is clearly expressed when the Legislature limited the requirement for notice to actions for injuries or death "under this act." Section 2 of the act is a substantial reproduction of certain provisions of the English and Massachusetts statutes on the subject. In Ryalls v. Mechanics' Mills, 150 Mass. 190, 22 N. E. 766, 5 L. R. A. 667, it was held that, where the plaintiff declared on the common-law liability of the master to his servant, it was unnecessary to give the statutory notice. The same doctrine was held by the Appellate Division in the Second Department in Rosin v. Lidgerwood Manufacturing Company, 89 App. Div. 245, 86 N. Y. Supp. 49. In the view of those courts we concur, except that we do not intimate any approval of the position of the learned court in the Lidgerwood Case that the statute, if given the broad construction accorded it by the court below, would be unconstitutional. With that question we do not deal.

The order of the Appellate Division should be reversed, and the interlocutory judgment entered on the decision of the Special Term affirmed, with costs in all the courts, and the question certified answered in the negative.

PARKER, C. J., and HAIGHT, MARTIN, and WERNER, JJ., concur. GRAY, J., dissents. O'BRIEN, J., not voting.

Order reversed, etc.

(178 N. Y. 137)

NEW YORK UNIVERSITY v. LOOMIS LABORATORY.

(Court of Appeals of New York. March 22, 1904.)

TRUST—EVIDENCE TO ESTABLISH—DECLARATIONS OF AGENT.

1. An agent was authorized to buy land, and equip a laboratory thereon for instruction in medical sciences, with moneys furnished by an unknown principal, and to convey the property when completed, and the corporation organized was to manage the laboratory. The agent declared that the laboratory was to be held for the exclusive use of the medical department of a certain university. *Held*, that where there was evidence that the statements of the agent were unknown to and unauthorized by the principal, and he denies that he assented to or ratified them when made known by the agent, and it was shown that he furnished the money to the agent, and that the agent had no title or interest except as agent, his statements are insufficient to create a trust on the property in favor of the university named by the agent.

Appeal from Supreme Court, Appellate Division, First Department.

Action by the New York University against the Loomis Laboratory. From a judgment of the Appellate Division (74 N. Y. Supp. 175) affirming a judgment for defendant, plaintiff appeals. Affirmed.

George A. Strong, for appellant. Charles E. Miller and Bronson Winthrop, for respondent.

VANN, J. The plaintiff was incorporated in 1831, by a special act of the Legislature, "for the purpose of promoting literature and science," and is an institution of learning well known by its popular and corporate name of "The New York University." Laws 1831, p. 207, c. 176. The defendant was incorporated in 1887, also by special act, "with all the privileges and immunities of a seminary of learning for the promotion of original research in chemistry, biology and pathology, and for elementary teaching in these branches." Laws 1887, p. 410, c. 329. The object of this action was to establish a trust in favor of the plaintiff with reference to all the property held by the defendant in its own name, and to enjoin the defendant from excluding the plaintiff from the benefit and enjoyment thereof. The theory of the plaintiff is that in December, 1887, Dr. Alfred L. Loomis held the real estate in question in trust for the plaintiff, and that without consideration he conveyed it to the defendant upon the same trust, but without expressing it in the deed; that the defendant now refuses to recognize the trust, and threatens to form a union with some "rival institution," and to place the property under its control. The theory of the defendant is that no trust ever existed with reference to said property, and that although it was authorized, by the act which brought it into existence, in its discretion to transfer all its real and personal property to the plaintiff, and thereupon cease to exist, it has never done so, and has no desire to do so. The trial justice, by a decision in the short form, dismissed the complaint upon the ground that no trust was ever created in favor of the plaintiff as to any property held by the defendant, and the judgment entered accordingly was unanimously affirmed by the Appellate Division.

While the facts are placed beyond our control by the united action of the courts below, it is necessary to examine the evidence to some extent, in order to properly consider the questions of law presented by the rulings made during the trial. The main evidence relied on by the plaintiff to establish the trust was as follows: In 1887 Dr. Loomis, although one of the faculty, was not a member of the council or governing board of the plaintiff, but was one of the eight directors of an institution incorporated in 1883, for "educational and scientific purposes," under the name of the "Medical College Laboratory of the City of New York." Laws 1883, p. 132, c. 125. On the 23d of March, 1887, Dr. Loomis made a report to the directors of the Medical College Laboratory, a stranger to the alleged trust, in which he made the following statement: "About one year ago a gentleman gave me a power of attorney to spend one hundred thousand dollars for him in the erection and equipment of a laboratory building for the exclusive use of the faculty and students of the Medical Department of the New York University. He designated that it should be known as the 'Loomis Laboratory of the Medical Department of the New York University'; that when completed it should be handed over to a board of trustees, who should hold it in trust for the use of the faculty and students, as already indicated; that in every way, and as might from time to time be indicated by the faculty, it should be used to increase the teaching facilities of the Medical Department of the University; that if at any time the council of the University was to assume the pecuniary obligations of the faculty and take the college building, the trustees of the laboratory may transfer the laboratory property to the council. In accordance with the wishes of the donor, I have had a bill introduced into the Legislature, incorporating the laboratory. * * * I have also had all the necessary steps taken * * * for the completion of the building by 10th September, 1887, according to the contracts presented. The donor will give the faculty any legal documents which they may wish, guaranteeing to them that the laboratory and its equipment shall always be for their use in laboratory teaching. It is understood that the trustees are to be simply the custodians of the property and of any endowment which the laboratory may receive." This report was accepted and ordered spread upon the minutes. On the 12th of December, 1887, Dr. Loomis presented to the defendant a deed dated that day, by which he and his wife, in consideration of $1, conveyed to the defendant the lot on which the laboratory building stands. In presenting the deed to the defendant's board of trustees, as their minutes show, he made the following statement: "In November, 1886, a friend gave me the authority to expend for him $100,000 in the purchase of grounds and the erection and equipment of a laboratory in connection with the Medical Department of the University of the City of New York. The only stipulations were that the name of the donor should remain a secret, and the laboratory should be called the 'Loomis Laboratory.' I was to expend the money in the manner which seemed best to me for the accomplishment of a perfect laboratory in every respect. In February, 1887, I purchased the ground, 35x100 feet, adjoining the University Medical College, for $17,700, and in March I accepted the plans and specifications * * * for the erection of a suitable building. In the following April the contracts for the erection of a building according to the specifications were signed by the builders, and the work of construction was immediately commenced, and completed in January, 1888, at the cost, with apparatus which was purchased during the construction, of $101,600. During this construction and at the time of its completion I received from the donor $101,600, and presented to him the vouchers for the moneys expended. I now deliver to this corporation the deed of the land and building." The trustees of the defendant accepted the deed, and passed a resolution thanking the donor for his gift. There was no evidence that Dr. Loomis ever stated to the plaintiff that the gift was for its benefit, or that he made any statement on the subject, except to the two other independent corporations. The plaintiff apparently never heard of the alleged trust until after all rights had become fixed, although evidence was given by one witness tending to show that Dr. Loomis, who was not living at the time of the trial, once stated to the chancellor of the university that a sum of money had been placed in his hands for its benefit, and that it was to be put into a laboratory building. Subsequently the present structure was erected, and on the front thereof the following inscription was placed: "Loomis Laboratory of the Medical Department of New York University." There was also evidence that some of the professors of the university had used the building, and had given instruction to its students therein.

While there was other testimony, this was the strength of the plaintiff's case, and it was met by evidence of the following character: It appeared, without contradiction, that Col. Oliver H. Payne furnished the money to buy the land, as well as to erect the building, and that he subsequently endowed the institution. Col. Payne testified that he furnished the money to Dr. Loomis during the years 1886 and 1887. He was asked, "What instructions did you give Dr. Loomis about the use of the money?" Subject to objection and exception, he answered as follows: "I told him to buy a lot and to build and equip a laboratory, to be transferred later to a corporation to be organized under the act of the Legislature, to be called the 'Loomis Laboratory.' I told him that it was my object to build a laboratory for original research and elementary teaching in scientific medicine, and that this laboratory was to be entirely independent; and I intended, as I did afterwards, to endow it with sufficient funds to run it. I desired and instructed him to have five trustees; two of those trustees I insisted should be himself and his son; the other three he should select; that the property, when completed, should be transferred to the Loomis Laboratory Association, to be governed entirely by these five trustees; that the articles incorporating the Loomis Laboratory should state exactly what the object of my gift was and intention." Col. Payne further testified that there was never a word said by him to any one that the money should be used in the interest or for the benefit of any institution other than the defendant. No mention was at any time made of the plaintiff, its medical department, faculty, or students in any conversation between himself and any person or persons. In December, 1886, he went to Europe for his health, and before leaving had a long interview with Dr. Loomis, during which he said he would give him a power of attorney "authorizing him to expend $100,000 for me in the erection and equipment and the buying of the lot for the laboratory, * * * and that this was to be transferred to the company to be organized under the act of the Legislature, to be called the 'Loomis Laboratory.'" Dr. Loomis had such a paper prepared, and it was duly executed by Col. Payne, who never knew or heard of any statement made by the doctor to the trustees of the defendant in relation to this property, and no such statement was made to them or to any one by his authority. He never knew of the inscription on the front of the building, and did not authorize it to be placed there. Upon his return from Europe in June, 1887, Dr. Loomis showed him the act of the Legislature which embodied what he was authorized to do, and also contained a clause that under certain circumstances the trustees should have power to transfer the property to the plaintiff, which he had not authorized. Dr. Loomis explained that this clause was inserted by advice of his attorney to provide for the contingency that the trustees might become tired of the trust and wish to wind up the institution. When this explanation was made, Col. Payne raised no objection. After the incorporation Col. Payne gave the further sum of $80,000 to the defendant to endow it and make it absolutely independent. He did not know that Dr. Loomis was connected with the New York University, or was a professor in that institution. No word ever passed between these men to indicate any intention other than that the institution thus founded was to be entirely independent. Col. Payne never said anything to Dr. Loomis, nor authorized him to say anything to others, about the erection and equipment of a laboratory building for the exclusive use of the faculty and students of the medical department of the plaintiff, or that the institution founded by him should be known as the "Loomis Laboratory for the Medical Department of the New York University," or that when completed the building should be handed over to the board of trustees to hold in trust for the use of its faculty and students. Col. Payne positively denied a statement made by a witness for the plaintiff that he had assented to the declaration of Dr. Loomis upon hearing it read early in 1887. Much of this evidence was received subject to the objection that it was incompetent and immaterial, and exceptions were duly taken to the rulings of the court.

Mr. Stetson, who drew the power of attorney referred to by Col. Payne, was asked to state its contents. This was objected to by the plaintiff, not as secondary evidence, but upon the ground that "other statements made at other times by the alleged trustee in a controversy of this character cannot be put in evidence; they do not tend to nullify the statement he may have made at any time establishing the trust." The objection was overruled, an exception was taken, and the witness answered: "The power of attorney was my own suggestion to Dr. Loomis. It contained authority to Alfred L. Loomis to go on and create liabilities, make contracts for the purchase of land and the erection of a building up to the amount of $100,000," but did not state what was to be done with the building. Subject to a similar objection, Mr. Stetson was permitted to testify that Dr. Loomis afterward informed him that the power of attorney had been signed by the donor of the money.

Dr. Lewis A. Stimson testified that he was one of the trustees of the defendant, and from 1878 to 1898 was a member of the medical faculty of the plaintiff; that instruction was given in the Loomis Laboratory to some of the students of the medical department of the university, but the fees for such instruction were paid by the students to the Loomis Laboratory, and were not received by the university or its medical department. During his cross-examination, the annual catalogues issued by the plaintiff in 1888 and 1889 were identified by him, and he testified that proofs were sent to the members of the faculty for examination, and that the catalogues themselves were distributed generally. Each catalogue contained the statement that through the liberal gift of an unknown friend of the university a laboratory building had been erected which by a condition attached to the gift was to be known as the "Loomis Laboratory of the Medical Department of the University of the City of New York." These statements were offered in evidence by the plaintiff, but were excluded upon the objection of the defendant.

This reference to the various exceptions and the condition of the evidence when they were taken shows that they raise no reversible error, because, if the evidence excluded had been received and that taken under objection had been excluded, the plaintiff could not have prevailed. Its evidence, even if the catalogues, which were excluded, had been received, was not sufficient to establish a trust. Independent of the question whether the defendant had power to hold property in trust for another corporation, no reasonable view of the testimony would authorize a decision in favor of the plaintiff.

It is conceded that Col. Payne created the property. He bought the land and erected the building, appointing Dr. Loomis as his agent for that purpose, instead of employing a broker or contractor. He furnished all the money, and Dr. Loomis accounted to him therefor by presenting vouchers showing how it was expended. No one else had put a dollar in the property when the deed was delivered to the defendant and the gift thereby completed. Until then the gift was inchoate, or merely in contemplation, and Col. Payne still owned the property as the beneficial owner. While Dr. Loomis held the title a short time, he never was the owner of the lot or the building, for he bought and built as the agent of Col. Payne. He did not use his own money, but the money furnished by another, and when the laboratory was completed it belonged to the one who had provided the money and under whose direction it had been expended. Dr. Loomis could neither use it for himself nor give it to another, except as authorized by his principal. It was his duty to convey to such person or corporation, and to such only, as Col. Payne designated. The defendant does not stand in his shoes, but in those of his principal, for whom he acted in all things, and without whose authority he could not lawfully act at all. He had no volition in the premises, and could take no independent action. His unauthorized declarations bound no one but himself, and when he said that the property was for the benefit of the plaintiff he created no obligation and conferred no right, because there is no evidence that the real owner authorized the statement. He could not impress a trust upon the property, for he had neither interest nor authority, but was simply the conduit for the passage of the gift from the donor, who brought the laboratory into existence, to the donee, who was specially organized to take and enjoy it. An agent or trustee cannot confer authority upon himself, but is bound to faithfully apply the property intrusted to him according to the confidence reposed in him. If Dr. Loomis, as a sworn witness, had testified to his authority to make the declaration upon which the plaintiff relies, a different question would be presented. No such evidence, however, was given by any one, and hence the doctor's naked declaration is without legal force. Col. Payne had the right to do as he wished with his own property, and there is no proof that he ever uttered a word or did an act showing that he intended to give anything to the plaintiff or for its benefit, at least until the title of the defendant was complete. While others may have said that he so intended, there is no evidence that he ever said so or authorized them to say so. Doubtless there was an honest misunderstanding as to the purpose of the unknown donor, but he was not responsible for it, although his modest method of doing good may have led to it. The property did not come from Dr. Loomis, but from Col. Payne, and evidence of what the former said about it is of no importance unless authorized, and proof of authority to make any declaration upon the subject was wholly wanting. He was authorized to convey to the defendant and to no one else, but he was not authorized to attach a condition to the conveyance for the benefit of the plaintiff. It was not his property nor his gift. Over and over again, and before the gift was complete, he stated that he was acting only as the agent of a friend who had furnished the money to erect a laboratory, but who wished that his name should be kept secret. He did not assume to do anything or say anything in his own name, but simply in behalf of another. What he did was authorized and bound all concerned, but what he said was unauthorized and bound no one but himself.

Moreover, aside from the fact that, if the rulings excepted to had been reversed, the result could not have been changed, the evidence received was competent, and that excluded was incompetent. We will notice only those especially relied upon by the plaintiff. The instructions of Col. Payne to Dr. Loomis, as well as the power of attorney, were competent, as part of the res gestæ, to show the capacity in which Dr. Loomis acted in purchasing the land and erecting the building. They did not contradict, but corroborated, his statement that he was acting as agent throughout the entire business. They confirmed his declaration that he was acting for an undisclosed principal, and showed that he did not assume to act for any one else. They measured the nature and extent of his authority, for they made him the attorney of Col. Payne to make the contracts for him which brought the laboratory into existence. They lay at the root of the subject, for they antedated substantially all that was done by the attorney in fact, and were the charter of his power. In connection with the act incorporating the defendant, which was passed to carry out the wishes of the donor, they show his method, object, and intention. They constitute the most material and important evidence contained in the record.

The catalogues were properly excluded, because a trust cannot be created by the declarations of a party in his own favor, when they are not brought to the knowledge of the creator of the trust. What the plaintiff said was of no importance unless Col. Payne knew of it, and there is no evidence that he ever saw either catalogue. The fact that Dr. Loomis and others had read the statement did not bind Col. Payne. If all the world had seen it and he had not, it would still be a self-serving declaration. If one proclaims in the most solemn manner that certain property belongs to him, he can take nothing from it unless the real owner directly or indirectly assents to it.

The question in relation to certain personal property which did not come from Col. Payne is not raised by any exception, and we cannot consider it. The decision of the Special Term was in the short form, the facts not being stated, and the exception thereto presents nothing which survives unanimous affirmance.

The judgment should be affirmed, with costs.

PARKER, C. J., and O'BRIEN, BARTLETT, MARTIN, and WERNER, JJ. (GRAY, J., in result), concur.

Judgment affirmed.

(185 Mass. 349)

GRAHAM v. MIDDLEBY et al.

(Supreme Judicial Court of Massachusetts. Norfolk. April 2, 1904.)

ALTERED INSTRUMENTS—ADMISSIBILITY OF EVIDENCE—CONTRACT—INTENTION OF PARTIES—SELF-SERVING DECLARATIONS—INSTRUCTIONS—ACTION ON BOND—ASSIGNMENT OF SECURED CONTRACT—CONSIDERATION—EFFECT OF SALE—NOTICE TO GRANTORS.

1. Where an action on a bond, the execution of which plaintiff proves, is defended on the ground of a subsequent alteration, the burden of proof does not shift to defendant, but it is for the plaintiff to prove the contract on which he has declared.

2. Plaintiff purchased a patent storage battery from defendant, taking two written contracts, by one of which defendant agreed to repay the purchase money if the sale was enjoined, and by the other agreed to assume the expense of any litigation brought against plaintiff for the use of the battery. These papers were accompanied by a bond, and plaintiff claimed that the three were fastened together when received

¶ 1. See Alteration of Instruments, vol. 2, Cent. Dig. § 240.

by him. There was evidence that defendant's officers, who were obligors in the bond, regarded the contracts as a unit. The defense to plaintiff's action on the bond was that it was intended to secure only one of the contracts, and that after its execution the letter "s" was added to the word "contract," in blue ink, with a pen; the remainder of the bond being typewritten. *Held*, that admitting the bond in evidence without requiring an explanation of the alteration was not error.

3. A company selling a patent storage battery executed two contracts—one for the repayment of the purchase money in case the sale was enjoined, and the other to indemnify the purchaser for the expense of any litigation brought against him on account of the use of the battery. These contracts were accompanied by a bond. *Held*, in an action on the bond, that evidence of a conversation between the obligees, before it was signed, to the effect that they understood that only one of the contracts was secured thereby, was inadmissible, whether treated as a declaration in their own favor not communicated to the purchaser, or on the ground that, as the purchaser had no knowledge of the private understanding, he had a right to rely on the bond and contracts in the form in which he received them.

4. Cross-examination of the company's treasurer, who testified to the execution and delivery of the bond and contracts, as to a statement in his own interest as to the scope of the obligation, made before the delivery, and when the purchaser was not present, was likewise inadmissible, even to contradict him, his interpretation of the contractual rights of the parties not having been offered; and this was true, though he might have been found to entertain hostile feelings towards one defendant.

5. Though parol evidence of the understanding of the signer of a blank contract is admissible to show that it was not filled out as he authorized, the rule does not extend to admitting evidence of conversations between the obligors in a bond, prior to its execution, on the issue of a material alteration of the instrument after execution.

6. In an action on an obligation averred by defendant to have been materially altered after execution, an instruction that the burden of proof is on plaintiff to show that the instrument was signed by defendant in the form in which it appeared is properly refused, where the court has instructed that, if the instrument has been materially altered, defendant is not liable.

7. An action on a bond to secure the performance of contracts was defended on the ground that it was given to secure only one contract, and that after delivery the word "contract" was changed by the obligee to the plural form. *Held*, that the fact that the bond and the accompanying contracts were detached and separate at the time of signing would not discharge the obligors, if it was found that they understood that all the instruments formed but one obligation, and were to be executed, and then fastened together and delivered by one of their number.

8. The fact that a contract to secure the performance of which a bond is given has been assigned to a third person is no defense to the obligee's action on the bond.

9. A sealed instrument imports consideration.

10. Failure to demand performance of a contract for repayment of the purchase money of a chattel, to secure performance of which a bond is given, is no defense to an action on the bond, where it is not shown that during the interval the conditions had changed so as to compel the obligors to assume a burden from which they would have been relieved if the obligee had acted earlier.

11. A company vending a patent storage battery contracted to repay the purchase money in case the sale was enjoined, and its officers gave a bond to secure performance of this contract. *Held*, that no formal notice to them of a breach of the contract was necessary before bringing suit on the bond.

Exceptions from Superior Court, Norfolk County; Edgar J. Sherman, Judge.

Action by one Graham against one Middleby, Jr., and others. Verdict for plaintiff, and defendants except. Exceptions overruled.

This was an action of contract to recover $6,000 from defendants, as signers of a bond guarantying the performance of certain contracts of the Hatch Storage Battery Company. At the trial the principal defense was that the bond was in fact given to guaranty, not the contract annexed to the plaintiff's declaration, but a certain written contract to furnish counsel and to defend any application for an injunction against the use of a battery purchased by said Graham of the Hatch Company, and that the word "contract," in the condition of the bond, had been changed after the bond was signed by the defendants, and without their consent, by the addition of the letter "s," in blue ink, with a pen; the remainder of the bond being typewritten.

Z. S. Arnold and W. G. A. Pattee, for plaintiff. Anson M. Lyman, for defendants.

BRALEY, J. By the terms of the bond, the defendants were held to the obligation that their principal should perform its agreements made with the plaintiff, contained in two separate contracts, of even date with its execution. As the bond was typewritten, any change or addition by letters in manuscript would be apparent on inspection; but it could not be said that the addition of a single letter to a word in a typewritten instrument is so unusual or extraordinary as to take it out of the common rule of practice that in such a case it is within the discretion of the trial court, after proof of execution, to permit it to be read in evidence. If the alteration was of an immaterial nature, the integrity of the obligation would not be impaired; but, if the change was such as to substantially vary the contract, this would constitute a defense. If the execution of the bond is proved, the burden does not change, but the defendant meets the evidence of the plaintiff by proof that the contract in evidence is not that put in suit, and in such a case the burden of proof remains on the plaintiff throughout the trial to prove the contract upon which he has declared. Wilde v. Armsby, 6 Cush. 314, 318; Ely v. Ely, 6 Gray, 439; Lincoln, Adm'r, v. Lincoln, 12 Gray, 45; Ives v. Farmers' Bank, 2 Allen, 236; Wilton v. Humphreys, 176 Mass. 253, 257, 57 N. E. 374. But in dealing with this exception the course pursued by the parties at the trial must be recognized. The ruling admitting the bond was not made alone on the view that where a party offers a written instrument to support a contract set forth in the declaration, and on inspection it is apparent that either before or after delivery there may have been an alteration, and the burden remains on the plaintiff to satisfy the jury that the contract offered was the one made by the defendant, and it may be put in evidence on proof of its execution without further explanation; nor that there may not be cases where an inspection of the writing apparently shows such a material alteration that it is then within the discretion of the judge presiding at the trial to require the plaintiff to offer some explanation of the alteration before permitting it to be read, even though the signatures of the parties to be bound may be admitted or proved. But here there were three papers—the bond and two agreements—one to repay the plaintiff any money that might be paid by him to the Hatch Storage Company if it was enjoined from vending the storage battery which it claimed the right to make and sell under certain patents held by it; the other referring to the assumption of the expense of any litigation connected with legal proceedings brought against the plaintiff for the use of the battery; but each bearing the same date, and simultaneously delivered. It was claimed by the plaintiff that these papers, in the form in which they appeared, were fastened together, and thus received by him; and the question presented, and on which the court ruled, ought not to be separated from this aspect of the case, it being apparently understood that, if the papers were delivered in this form, there had not been any subsequent alteration. Beyond the fact of an apparent change, there was nothing to prove any alteration by him, while there was evidence that it was the understanding of the officers of the company, including the defendants, that the bond and contracts, though separate, were really to be treated as one transaction. So that the substantial issue was this: Whether the several papers constituting the contract shown by the bond were left with the treasurer by the defendants, to be by him delivered to the plaintiff, in the condition disclosed by each paper when offered in evidence. Their offer of proof of a conversation between themselves before the bond was signed, when the conditions to be inserted were under discussion, and it was then understood that the only undertaking was an agreement to save the plaintiff harmless from the costs of impending litigation, whether treated as a declaration in their favor, and not communicated to the plaintiff, or put on the ground that, as he had no knowledge of such a private understanding, he had a right to rely on the bond and contracts in the form in which the treasurer delivered them to him, and whose general authority to act was apparently undisputed, was inadmissible. Taft v. Dickinson, 6 Allen, 553; White v. Duggan, 140 Mass. 18, 19, 2 N. E. 110, 54 Am. Rep. 437.

The question excluded in the cross-examination of the treasurer of the company falls within a similar limitation. He had testified to the execution and delivery of the bond and contracts, and any statement made by him before they were handed to the plaintiff, and when the latter was not present, cannot be treated as evidence, for the statement alleged to have been made was in his own interest; nor to contradict him as a witness, because his interpretation of the contractual rights of the parties had not been offered, and clearly was irrelevant (Carter v. Gregory, 8 Pick. 165; Whitney v. Houghton, 125 Mass. 451; Burns v. Stuart, 168 Mass. 19, 46 N. E. 399), even if it might also be found that he entertained feelings of hostility towards one of the defendants (Quigley v. Turner, 150 Mass. 108, 22 N. E. 586).

The defendants strongly urge that these conversations were competent evidence to show that they did not execute the bond, under the decision made in Smith v. Jagoe, 172 Mass. 538, 52 N. E. 1088. But the cases are different. In the case cited the plaintiff had executed a mortgage drafted on a printed form, with blank spaces which were not filled in, and had given authority to the mortgagee to have it filled out by inserting words to cover a single article of personal property. This was done, but other chattels were also named; and, having brought a writ of replevin for them, he was allowed to prove against the defendant, to whom the mortgage had been assigned, that the articles named in the writ were not covered, as no authority had been given to include them in the mortgage. Here the defendants executed an instrument which at the time of signing, under either view, was completed; and no argument is open that it was signed and delivered in blank, or fraudulently procured by the plaintiff.

The question now presented is not one of authority to write a contract above the signatures of the parties to be bound, and which must be strictly followed, but whether the contract itself, at the time of signing, was fully expressed as to all of its terms, or has since been materially altered.

One of the principal arguments of the defendants on this part of the case relates to the refusal to give the eighth request, in which the fact of annexation at the time of execution is again joined with the rule that the burden of proof was on the plaintiff to show that the bond was signed by the defendants in the form in which it appeared. As we have already said, this stated the law correctly. But no particular or set form of words are recognized, by which the principle is to be defined. Any language that conveys to a jury the substance of the rule and its application is sufficient, and it is enough to say that the judge was not required to instruct in the language requested. Norwood v. Somerville, 159 Mass. 105, 112, 33 N. E. 1108.

In the instructions given, which presented

the question in different ways, they were told that, if the contract had been materially altered, the defendants would not be liable; and they must have plainly understood that, in order for the plaintiff to prevail, he must satisfy them that the bond introduced in evidence was the same in all parts as when it was signed.

Whether the several papers were annexed at the time of signing, or were detached and separate, would not discharge the defendants as obligors, if it was found that they understood that the bond and contracts formed one obligation, and were to be executed, and then fastened together and delivered by the treasurer, who was one of their number. They could do this with their own hands, or by the hand of their agent, as the jury have specially found. Com. v. White, 123 Mass. 430, 434, 25 Am. Rep. 116; Greene v. Conant, 151 Mass. 223, 225, 24 N. E. 44.

There remain for consideration the other rulings requested, all of which were refused.

Whatever may be the duty of a party who rescinds an executed contract to return anything of value he may have received under it, the express agreement of the company, under which the plaintiff acted, provided for a termination of the contract and repayment of the money if an injunction prevented the use of the battery. That such an injunction issued, and was not dissolved within 60 days thereafter, is not disputed, and the condition upon which the obligation of indemnity arose was broken.

But the suit being brought in the name of the obligee, the fact that this contract had been assigned furnished no defense. The action is on the bond to recover the penalty, not on the agreement to secure the performance of which it was given, and the amount of damages which he may be entitled to recover is not before us. Rev. Laws, c. 177, §§ 9, 10; Austin v. Moore, 7 Metc. 116, 124.

Being a sealed instrument, a consideration was imported by the form of the undertaking. Hayes v. Kyle, 8 Allen, 300, 301. Neither is it shown that, because more than 60 days elapsed after the injunction issued, and before notice was given to the company, demanding repayment of the amount paid under the contract, conditions had changed, so that the defendants were compelled to assume a burden from which they would have been relieved if the plaintiff had acted earlier, or had made a demand on them for payment before bringing suit. Besides, they held the office of directors in the company, and must be presumed to have known of its financial condition, as well as its title to the patent under which it manufactured the battery and sold it to the plaintiff. The corporation of which they were officers undertook to sell to him a storage battery for which he paid a large sum of money. Evidently its right to make and sell the battery under certain patents held by it was open to legal attack, and the agreement recognized this by the recitals contained in it. Their obligation matured when their principal failed to perform its contract, and no formal notice to them by the plaintiff was required of its default. Watertown Fire Ins. Co. v. Simmons, 131 Mass. 85, 86, 41 Am. Rep. 196; Welch v. Walsh, 177 Mass. 555, 59 N. E. 440, 52 L. R. A. 782, 83 Am. St. Rep. 302.

This disposes of the various questions raised at the trial, and, as no error of law appears, the order must be: Exceptions overruled.

(185 Mass. 122)

HUDSON v. BAKER.

(Supreme Judicial Court of Massachusetts. Suffolk. Feb. 26, 1904.)

MUTUAL BENEFIT ASSOCIATION—RECEIVERSHIP—DELINQUENT TREASURER—ACCOUNTING—EFFECT OF TREASURER'S RECEIPT—CHARGING SAME ITEMS TWICE—EFFECT OF AUDITOR'S REPORT—JOINT LIABILITY OF TREASURER AND SECRETARY—SECRETARY'S PAYMENT TO PLAINTIFF—DEFENSE.

1. While a receipt is not an estoppel, but the giver thereof may show that he has not received the sum stated, yet where, in an action by the receiver of a mutual benefit association against a delinquent treasurer, the payment of certain items to him is evidenced by his receipts, and negatived only by entries in his books of account, the latter are to be treated as declarations in his favor, and he is properly charged with the items shown in the receipts.

2. In an action by the receiver of a mutual benefit association against its delinquent treasurer, the auditor was required to determine whether the amount of certain checks drawn to defendant's order should not be charged to him, in addition to amounts receipted for by him. Plaintiff's counsel admitted that only a portion of the amount of the checks should be added, the rest being covered by the receipts. On a motion to recommit, defendant requested that the auditor specifically find and report whether or not the amount of the checks was not accounted for in the debits in his books, and in a supplemental report the auditor found that the defendant was to account for all funds with which he charged himself, or was proved to have received, whether he charged himself with them or not, and reported that the amount of the checks was received in addition to the other sums stated. *Held* that, in view of the supplemental report, the contention that the admission of plaintiff's counsel was binding on the auditor was without force.

3. In an action by the receiver of a mutual benefit association against its delinquent treasurer, it appeared that defendant had charged himself with a certain sum, though the money had never been actually paid to him. Defendant claimed that this sum was included in a suspense fund, made up of money paid plaintiff by the secretary, and which represented property of the association wrongfully appropriated by the latter, and asked to be credited with the amount. The auditor found that, after the secretary informed the treasurer of the amount of collections on hand, it became the treasurer's duty to receive and account for such collections, and if he allowed the secretary to retain any portion without a sufficient warrant, and such portion was misappropriated, defendant would be liable, and the misconduct of the secretary would be no defense. *Held*, that this ruling was proper, as the plaintiff had a right to pursue both the secretary and the defendant to the extent of obtaining judgment against each, and a court of common law could not compel plain-

tiff to apply money conditionally received from one joint debtor, but not actually appropriated, in favor of another who was equally liable.

Report from Superior Court, Suffolk County; Robt. O. Harris, Judge.

Action on contract by Samuel H. Hudson, as receiver of the Northern Mutual Relief Association, against William H. Baker, as treasurer of such association, to recover money alleged to have been received by defendant, and not accounted for by him. On report from the superior court. Judgment for plaintiff affirmed.

G. W. Anderson, for plaintiff. Edward Lowe, for defendant.

BRALEY, J. In the usual course of business, the secretary of the association, which was a fraternal assessment insurance company, received from time to time all money due from "subordinate associations," and from assessments levied upon "members at large." It then became his duty to make payments to the treasurer, at the end of each week, of the sums thus received. Whenever these payments were made, the treasurer gave him a receipt for the amount paid, and, in stating the account, the defendant has been charged with the face value of the several vouchers; but he contended, as a matter of fact, that a less amount in some instances had been paid to him than was shown by the entries on his books of receipts and expenditures. The auditor, however, ruled, and it was affirmed by the court, that the defendant was bound by the receipts given, and must be charged with the amounts shown by them. Nothing is stated by way of explanation, showing why it was made, and its application to the evidence before him, but the ruling alone is given. If the defendant took the position that his books of account, wherein he debited himself with the payments received from the secretary, were to be taken as conclusive evidence in his favor, the ruling was right. By signing and delivering the receipts, he acknowledged what they recited, and, having signed them, in the absence of fraud or mistake, he was bound to this extent by his voluntary act; and the entries made by him must be treated as declarations in his favor, and can stand no better as evidence than declarations ordinarily made by a party in his own behalf. But if it was intended to hold that the receipts were equivalent to an estoppel, and it was not open to the defendant to show by way of explanation that he had not received the various sums stated, it was wrong. For it is familiar law that a receipt is always open to explanation or contradiction by oral testimony. Stackpole v. Arnold, 11 Mass. 27, *32, 6 Am. Dec. 150. With more or less of doubt, taking the entire report as a guide, the ruling must have been limited to the first ground, and did not preclude the defendant from explaining or contradicting the receipts, and it must have been so understood by the parties.

The next ruling reported relates to the effect of certain admissions made by counsel for the plaintiff at the trial. It became important to determine whether certain checks drawn by the secretary to the order of the defendant, and amounting to $2,014.86, should be charged to him, in addition to the amounts appearing in the receipts. When this question was raised, counsel for the plaintiff admitted that only the sum of $808.62 should be added, as the difference of $1,206.24 between the two was covered by the receipts; and the defendant claims that this admission was binding on the auditor, and it was error on his part to subsequently state the account, charging the defendant, in addition, with the face value of all of the checks. It should be observed, in reply to the position taken by him, that in his motion to recommit, which was granted, he asks, among other requests, that the auditor may specifically find and report "* * * whether or not said sum is not accounted for, in the debits on the defendant's books, prior to the first day of December, 1900." In his report the auditor finds "the defendant is to account for all funds of the association with which he charges himself, or which he is proved to have received, whether he charged himself with them or not," and reports that the amount of the checks was received in addition to the other sums stated. The admission was made on the express ground that the defendant should not be charged twice for the same debt, and it must have been so understood at the time by him; but, under the subsequent finding in the supplemental report that this has not been done, the objection ceases to have any force or effect.

During the trial it appeared that the secretary held the receipt of the treasurer for $900, with which the latter had charged himself through a mistake of fact that the money had been actually paid to him. By an arrangement between them, this amount was included, as the defendant claimed, in a suspense fund, made up of money paid to the plaintiff by the secretary, and which represented property of the association wrongfully appropriated by him; and it may be inferred, though not fully stated in the report, that it was understood, if the defendant was held liable for this sum, the secretary should not be called upon to make reimbursement. But the defendant asks to be credited with this portion of the fund. While it is clear, under the by-laws of the association, that the secretary is primarily responsible, the defendant is held liable also to account for it, under a finding made by the auditor, and which is supported by the evidence before him, that, after the secretary had made known to the treasurer the amount of collections on hand, it became his duty to pay them to the defendant, who became bound, under the duties of his office, to receive and account for them; and if he allowed the secretary to retain any portion of the money, without giving him a sufficient warrant, and, while so retained, it was misappropriated, the defendant would nevertheless be liable, and the misconduct of the secretary would not constitute a defense. As between the parties, the plaintiff has the right to pursue them both to the extent of obtaining judgment against each, but he can have but one satisfaction of his debt; and the ruling that the defendant could not avail himself of this defense was made rightly, for a court of common law could not compel the plaintiff to apply money conditionally received from one joint debtor, but not actually appropriated, in favor of the other, who was equally liable for the debt. Vanuxem v. Burr et al., 151 Mass. 386-389, 24 N. E. 773, 21 Am. St. Rep. 458; Burnham v. Windram, 164 Mass. 313, 41 N. E. 305. The fund, however, is held by the receiver as an officer of the court which appointed him, and is in its possession and control; and justice requires that, in some form of procedure, the equities arising from the situation of the parties interested should be adjusted. It will be open to the defendant, if it becomes necessary, to bring the matter to the attention of the court by a petition in the suit in equity in which the receiver was appointed.

Judgment affirmed.

(185 Mass. 391)

METROPOLITAN COAL CO. v. BOUTELL TRANSPORTATION & TOWING CO.

(Supreme Judicial Court of Massachusetts. Suffolk. April 2, 1904.)

CONTRACTS—OFFER—ACCEPTANCE — MATERIAL VARIATION—EFFECT—WAIVER.

1. An acceptance that varies from the offer in any substantial particular cannot be deemed an acceptance of the offer, but is an independent proposal.

2. The variance between an offer made by defendant to charter its vessels for a term "beginning before November 1st and continuing until May 1st," and plaintiff's acceptance, fixing the period of service "from Nov. 1 to May 1," is a material variance, and, in the absence of assent by defendant to the independent offer made in such acceptance, there is no valid contract.

3. A person making an offer to charter its vessels did not waive the variation in his offer and the other person's acceptance, and agree to the substitution proposed by the latter, when he did not know of the variation.

Exceptions from Superior Court, Suffolk County; Albert Mason, Judge.

Action to recover damages for breach of a contract for the charter of a tug and barges by the Metropolitan Coal Company against the Boutell Transportation & Towing Company. Verdict for plaintiff for $50,000, and defendant excepts. Sustained.

Robert M. Morse and Charles E. Hellier, for plaintiff. Eugene P. Carver and Addison C. Burnham, for defendant.

BRALEY, J. If it be assumed that the plaintiff succeeded in establishing the fact that William H. Mack was the general agent of the defendant, and, as such, had authority to make an agreement by which it would be bound, the more important and decisive question between the parties remains to be decided, and that is whether the evidence was sufficient, as a matter of law, to prove the contract set out in the declaration. The contract, if any, was made by an offer and reply in writing, and the only variance is the time referred to in each when the agreement was to take effect, and the defendant was to become entitled to the daily price to be paid by the charterer. No uncertainty appears in the language of the offer. The words "beginning before November 1st and continuing until May 1, 1900," were used in the proposal dated September 26, 1899, and may be construed as meaning that at any time after September 26th, and before November 1st, the defendant was ready to make an agreement to charter its tugboat and barges for continuous service, ending May 1st of the following year. Whatever business plans or projects may have been contemplated by the manager or agent of the defendant, it does not become important to consider, as he had a right to fix in his offer the date when the proposed service should commence. There were no negotiations directly between the parties, but whatever was done took place through a firm of shipbrokers to whom the original offer was addressed, and by them it was communicated to the plaintiff. On September 28, 1899, the plaintiff sent to the brokers an alleged acceptance, in which the conditions contained in the offer were stated, with the exception of the time in which the contract was to be performed. Instead of "beginning before November 1st, 1899," the letter of the plaintiff fixed the period of service "from Nov. 1, 1899, to May 1, 1900." This letter was not sent to the defendant, but the brokers were content to inform its agent on the same day by letter that the offer had been accepted, and giving the date of performance as being "from November 1st or earlier to May 1st." The transaction remained in paper, and stopped at this point, as there is no evidence of any further steps being taken by them.

While the intent of the parties to the proposed contract should not be defeated by any overrefined or too technical construction of the language used, an acceptance that varies from the offer, at least in any of its substantial particulars, cannot be deemed an assent to the proposition to which it is sent in reply, but it is to be classed as an independent proposal. Where a contract is in writing, the agreement is to be found from the language used. In a contract formed by a written offer followed by an acceptance in writing, it is the acceptance which furnishes the required element of agreement, and, indeed, binds the offerer to perform his undertaking according to its terms, because the offer has now become a contract, by the mutual under-

¶ 1. See Contracts, vol. 11, Cent. Dig. § 100.

standing and assent of the parties to what is to be performed. The contract is made and completed by an offer followed by a simple, unconditional acceptance. Stoddard v. Ham, 129 Mass. 383, 385, 37 Am. Rep. 369; Husse v. Horne-Payne, L. R. 8 Ch. Div. 670. When the defendant offered to charter its vessels for a definite time, clearly stated, it was not an assent to or acceptance of its offer for the plaintiff to name another period, even though the date of termination in the contract proposed and that stated in the reply was the same. Harlow v. Curtis, 121 Mass. 320; Lincoln v. Gray, 164 Mass. 537-540, 42 N. E. 95, 49 Am. St. Rep. 480; Horne v. Niver, 168 Mass. 4, 46 N. E. 393; Eliason v. Henshaw, 4 Wheat. 225, 4 L. Ed. 556; Minneapolis & St. Louis Railway Co. v. Columbus Rolling Mill Co., 119 U. S. 149, 7 Sup. Ct. 168, 30 L. Ed. 376; Hyde v. Wrench, 3 Beav. 334.

Assuming, without deciding, that the time named, "from November 1st or earlier to May 1st," may have been the same, in legal effect, as "beginning before November 1st and continuing until May 1, 1900," it is enough to say for the purpose of this case that it was not the proposition submitted to the brokers by the plaintiff, or transmitted by them to the defendant.

The law that an undisclosed principal may avail himself of a contract entered into for his benefit by his agent, when acting within the limits of his authority, or may ratify his unauthorized acts, is undisputed; but the plaintiff puts its case on the contract claimed to have been made by the offer, followed by its letter of acceptance, and not on the letter of the brokers, which in fact conveyed a different proposition from that which they were authorized by their principal to transmit. The brokers were not the general agents of the plaintiff, and their authority to act rested on the terms of the letter, which did not become an acceptance until either it had been sent or its contents communicated to the defendant by the plaintiff's authority. Coddington v. Goddard, 16 Gray, 436, 444, 445; Morris v. Brightman, 143 Mass. 149, 151, 9 N. E. 512. This was the ground on which recovery was sought, and the trial proceeded on the theory that there was no substantial variance between the offer and the reply. Whether the plaintiff, upon ratification of the action of the brokers in its behalf, could have maintained an action against the defendant, is a question that was not raised, and is not before us. On the face of the papers, the contracting parties never assented to the same period of time in which the agreement was to be performed, and no contract was established. When the new term as to time was introduced, the letter of the plaintiff cannot be treated as an acceptance, but must be considered as a new offer or counter proposal, and, in order to become a contract, would have to be accepted by the defendant. Gowing v. Knowles, 118 Mass. 232, 233. To meet this difficulty, the plaintiff is obliged to resort to a construction that treats this difference as one so immaterial in its nature that it is not within the principle discussed. The right to begin the term of service is put by the defendant at any time before November 1st, but the letter of the plaintiff fixes the date as from November 1st. If the most favorable construction is given to this interpretation, and the reply is considered as a formal acceptance, the period would begin, apparently, November 2d, as there is nothing to show that it was intended to include the day from which the time of service began to run. Walker v. John Hancock Mutual Life Ins. Co., 167 Mass. 188, 189, 45 N. E. 89, and cases cited. Or the same legal proposition may be put in another form. Under the offer, the latest day would have been October 31st; by the acceptance, the earliest November 2d, when the time of performance became of binding force and effect. A variation of two days seems to be unavoidable, and their value in money is substantial, and measures the pecuniary difference between the offer and the acceptance. Such a difference, if insisted upon, cannot be treated as of a trifling or immaterial character. It became incumbent upon the plaintiff to go still further, and it evidently contended at the trial that there had been a waiver on the part of the defendant of so much of the offer as related to the time when the term of service should begin, and the ruling given "that in this case, on the evidence, the court finds that the trivial variation in language, if amounting to a variation in substance, was waived," was wrong. A waiver must be found, if at all, either in the language, or conduct of William H. Mack, the general manager of the defendant. From the uncontradicted evidence, it is plain that he never saw or knew of the contents of the communication of the plaintiff to the brokers, and, after their letter to him, no further correspondence or interviews took place either with them or the plaintiff. The telegrams sent by him could not, therefore, be considered as a waiver of any part of the offer. Neither can the fact that certain forms of a proposed charter party were shown to him on September 27th, to which he made no objection, but only asked if the president of the plaintiff corporation would sign, aid the plaintiff in this contention, for the reason that the brokers, after obtaining the president's assent, never disclosed that fact to him. In order to hold that he waived the variation, and agreed to the substitution proposed by the acceptor, it must appear that he knew of it. Ft. Payne Coal & Iron Co. v. Webster, 163 Mass. 134, 137, 39 N. E. 786; Holdsworth v. Tucker, 143 Mass. 369, 376, 9 N. E. 764. For the doctrine of waiver rests on the ground that the party to be bound knows of the change, and intentionally, by express words, or impliedly by his conduct, assents to a modification or abandonment of his legal rights which are to be affected, and thereafter the parties proceed upon the substituted or new agreement thereby created. Kent v. Warner, 12 Allen, 561, 563; Rogers v. Rogers, 139 Mass. 440, 443, 1 N. E. 122.

The result is that the parties are finally left to the documentary evidence alone for a determination of their contractual relations, and, as there had been no acceptance, the defendant had not become bound by any contract with the plaintiff. It follows that the telegram of October 7th, directed to and received by the brokers, operated as a recall of its offer, and terminated their agency. Lincoln v. Gray, ubi supra. The first, second, and fourth rulings requested by the defendant should have been given.

Exceptions sustained.

(185 Mass. 436)

CRONAN v. ADAMS et al.

(Supreme Judicial Court of Massachusetts. Suffolk. April 2, 1904.)

WILLS—CONSTRUCTION—VESTED INTEREST.

1. Testator's will provided that a portion of the income of a fund should be paid to certain annuitants, and the remainder added to the principal, and that on the death of all the annuitants the fund should be conveyed to the youngest of the issue of A., whose descent should be wholly in the male line from A., and, in default, that it should be conveyed to others. *Held*, that the youngest of the issue of A., whose descent was wholly in the male line, and who was living at the time of testator's death, did not take a vested interest, but the same was to go to the person answering the description at the death of the last annuitant.

Case Reserved from Supreme Judicial Court, Suffolk County; James M. Morton, Judge.

Bill by one Cronan, as administrator of the estate of Julius Adams, deceased, to determine whether Isaac Murray Adams took a vested interest under the will. Cause reserved for the full court. The will of testator construed, and the question determined.

Charles H. Donahue, for petitioner. George R. Swasey, guardian ad litem for Marjorie Adams and others. Hiram P. Harriman, guardian ad litem for Isaac Murray Adams. Henry W. Hardy, guardian ad litem for contingent interests.

LATHROP, J. The will of Julius Adams, executed December 23, 1898, and admitted to probate on May 24, 1900, after certain specific legacies, gave the remainder of his estate to the Carney Hospital, in trust, to pay from the income of the estate to each of the children of Durward Adams $500 a year during the life of each child, and to the child of Alice, deceased daughter of said Durward, $500 a year during its life. Then follow several other annuities to be paid from the income, and this clause follows: "The remainder of the income of said estate I direct to be added to the principal of the estate during the lives of said annuitants, and on the death of all, I direct the Carney Hospital to take to its own use one quarter of all the estate, and to convey the residue to the youngest Adams of the issue of Durward Adams whose descent is wholly in the male line from said Durward, in default I direct the trustee to convey said residue to the youngest of the issue of Julius Adams Ulman, in default I direct the trustee to convey said residue to the youngest of the issue of Durward Adams, in default I direct the trustee to convey said residue to the youngest of the issue of Elizabeth A. Ulman, in default I direct the Carney Hospital to take to its own use the said residue."

The only question presented is whether Isaac Murray Adams, who, when Julius Adams died, was and now is the youngest Adams of the issue of Durward Adams whose descent is wholly in the male line, takes a vested interest in the residue, or whether the person who answers the description is to be determined when the last annuitant dies, and so the interest is contingent. We are of opinion that the latter construction is the true one. In the first place, what is to be distributed consists not only of the residue, but of the accumulated income, and this could not vest at the testator's death. This tends to show that "the vesting of the whole was postponed till the arrival of the event on which the distribution is made to depend." Hale v. Hobson, 167 Mass. 397, 45 N. E. 913, per Morton, J. In the next place, we are of opinion that the scheme of the will shows that a contingent interest was intended. If Isaac Murray Adams took a vested interest, there was no need of the elaborate scheme of the testator, by which, on the death of the last annuitant, the residue was to be disposed of. Isaac Murray Adams was living both when the will was made and at the death of the testator, but in the residuary clause he is not mentioned by name. The intention of the testator, evidently, was that some one person in the four classes he mentions should take, according to the circumstances existing at the death of the last annuitant, and so the person cannot be determined until that time arrives.

Decree accordingly.

(185 Mass. 445)

CARLISLE et al. v. LIBBY.

(Supreme Judicial Court of Massachusetts. Suffolk. April 2, 1904.)

ACTION FOR RECOVERY OF LAND—TENANT'S TITLE—EVIDENCE—ADMISSIBILITY.

1. The fact that a tenant in a writ of entry to recover real estate had a deed to the property executed subsequent to an attachment under which demandant claimed title did not affect his title under foreclosure of a mortgage executed

by the attachment debtor prior to the attachment.

2. Where the tenant in a writ of entry to recover real estate claimed title under a foreclosure of a mortgage executed by a mortgagor prior to the attachment of the mortgagor's property, under which demandant claimed title, evidence of an oral agreement between the mortgagor and a grantee under a deed subsequent to the attachment was inadmissible, not being binding on the tenant, though the mortgagor's grantee had executed a deed to the tenant.

3. Evidence of the oral agreement would not be admissible, even if the tenant claimed title under the deed to him from the mortgagor's grantee.

4. Evidence of the oral agreement was inadmissible, there being no proof tending to show that the tenant had any knowledge thereof.

Report from Superior Court, Suffolk County; John A. Aiken, Judge.

Writ of entry to recover real estate by Harry H. Carlisle and others against Elihu Libby. The trial court excluded certain evidence, and reported the case to the Supreme Judicial Court. Judgment on finding for tenant.

The excluded evidence was the testimony of two witnesses, as follows: "That Jerome Rumery was an officer and director of the Rumery-Libby Company, a corporation duly organized under the laws of the state of Maine, and having its usual place of business in Portland, Maine. This corporation was composed of Elihu Libby, the tenant in this action, who owned forty shares of the stock and was president of the company. The other stockholders were Charles C. Libby, son of the tenant, who owned ten shares, and Jerome Rumery, treasurer of the company, who owned twenty-four shares. The Rumery-Libby Company was a creditor of Mrs. Marshall to the amount of $1,300. The conveyance was made at the request of Rumery to secure that indebtedness, and upon his promise to pay the two mortgages when due, the taxes, the attachment of the demandants, and to reconvey to Mrs. Marshall at such time within three years that she should satisfy the claim of the Rumery-Libby Company, and reimburse him for his expenditures on account of the demanded premises. On or about October 25, 1894, Rumery made an appointment with counsel for the demandants to pay off their claim in the original action against Marshall. Demandants' counsel went to the office of counsel for the Rumery-Libby Company to receive payment, and to discharge the attachment and suit against Mrs. Marshall. He was then and there informed that the claim could not be paid, because Mrs. Marshall had just filed a petition in insolvency."

John J. Higgins, for demandants. Benj. B. Dewing, for tenant.

LATHROP, J. We are of opinion that the evidence offered was rightly excluded. The title of the demandants was by virtue of an attachment made on August 7, 1894, in an action of contract, which we assume, though this is not clearly stated in the report, was against Mrs. Marshall. This title was subsequently perfected by a sale on execution on July 3, 1896. The land, however, at the time of the attachment, was subject to two mortgages—one made by Mrs. Marshall to one Dartnell on June 8, 1894, for $700, payable in six months, and another made on the same day to one Trevelli for $3,000, payable in three years. The tenant does not claim title under the warranty deed from Mrs. Marshall to Rumery, of August 21, 1894, and the deed of September 17th of the same year, from Rumery to himself, but under a foreclosure of the mortgage given by Mrs. Marshall to Dartnell, which was assigned to Rumery on December 7, 1894, and foreclosed on June 15, 1895, by a sale to one Dewing under a power contained in the mortgage. Dewing on the same day conveyed the land to Mrs. Rumery, and on September 13, 1895, Mrs. Rumery conveyed it to the tenant.

There is nothing in the report to show that there was any contention that the Dartnell mortgage was not properly executed, or that all the legal requirements were not properly complied with in the foreclosure sale. This sale gave the tenant a title superior to that of the demandants, and the fact that the tenant had a prior deed did not affect his title under the foreclosure.

There is nothing in the offer of proof relating to the oral agreement between Rumery and Mrs. Marshall at the time when she made the conveyance to him which can in any way bind the tenant, as he does not claim under this conveyance. Even if he did so claim, the evidence would not be admissible in this action. Cranston v. Crane, 97 Mass. 459, 93 Am. Dec. 106; Wilson v. Black, 104 Mass. 406. Nor does the offer of proof tend to show that the tenant had any knowledge of the oral agreement between Marshall and Rumery.

Judgment on the finding.

(185 Mass. 434)

HILLIER et al. v. FARRELL et al.

(Supreme Judicial Court of Massachusetts. Middlesex. April 2, 1904.)

EQUITY — MASTER'S REPORT — PROCEEDINGS — DRAFT OF REPORT—OBJECTIONS—WAIVER—REVIEW.

1. Chancery rule 31 requires a master in chancery to prepare a draft of his report, and to notify counsel, who may suggest alterations, and if, thereafter, either party is not satisfied, he is allowed a specified time for bringing in written objections, and no exception is to be allowed without a special order, unless founded on an objection made before the master; and rule 32 provides that in every case the exceptions are to briefly specify the matter excepted to. *Held* that, where a master files his report without giving a party opportunity to file objections, the party's remedy is by motion to recommit the report, and the master's negligence does not entitle the party to a consideration of objections not filed.

2. Though a party objects to evidence offered before a master, if he files no written objections

or exceptions to the report the questions are not open to review.

3. Exceptions to a master's report are to be confined to objections disallowed or overruled by the master.

4. Where a party does not make any objection, as provided by the rule, to the report of a master, the report will not be revised.

Case Reserved from Superior Court, Middlesex County; James B. Richardson, Judge.

Bill by one Hillier and others against one Farrell and others. Reserved on pleadings, special master's report, and agreed facts. Complainants awarded an injunction restraining the erection of a building.

Henry R. Skinner, for plaintiffs. John E. Abbott, for defendants.

LATHROP, J. This is a bill in equity filed in the superior court to have the defendants restrained by injunction from proceeding with the erection of a building within 18 feet of Belmont street, contrary to certain restrictions contained in a deed. The case was referred to a master, who found that this lot and others were sold pursuant to a general scheme or plan. It appears from the master's report that the case was heard on agreed facts and oral evidence, and that the defendants objected to the admission of certain portions of the oral evidence. On the filing of the master's report, no objections or exceptions were taken. The justice of the superior court who heard the case reserved it for our consideration upon the pleadings, the master's report, and the agreed statement of facts.

No regard appears to have been paid to the thirty-first and thirty-second rules in chancery of this court, which, by force of law, apply to the superior court as well as to this court. The thirty-first rule requires the master to prepare a draft report, and to notify the counsel, who may suggest such alterations thereof as they may think proper. The master then settles the draft report, and again notifies the counsel. If either party is not satisfied, he is allowed five days for bringing in written objections, and these are to be appended to the report. No exception is to be allowed to the master's report, without a special order of the court, unless founded upon an objection made before the master, and shown by his report. The thirty-second rule relates to the filing of the exceptions and setting them down for argument, and further provides: "In every case, the exceptions shall briefly and clearly specify the matter excepted to, and the cause thereof; and the exceptions shall not be valid as to any matter not so specified." If the master filed his report without giving the defendants an opportunity to file objections to it, their remedy was to move to recommit it. Lamson v. Drake, 105 Mass. 564.

The defendants have argued questions of evidence before us founded upon objections taken when the evidence was admitted; but, as they filed no written objections or exceptions to the master's report, these questions are not open to them, under the rules above referred to. Exceptions to a master's report are to be confined to objections disallowed or overruled by the master. Copeland v. Crane, 9 Pick. 73. If no exception is taken, this court cannot revise the finding of a master. Popple v. Day, 123 Mass. 520; Roosa v. Davis, 175 Mass. 117, 55 N. E. 809. See, also, Gray v. Chase, 184 Mass. 448, 68 N. E. 676.

We are also of opinion that, for the reasons given above, we are not called upon to revise the report of the master in other respects. If parties desire to have a master's report revised, they should comply with the rules of the court.

The only dispute between the parties was whether the restrictions imposed in the deed to the defendants were for the benefit of their grantor, or were imposed in pursuance of a general scheme upon this lot and other lots owned by the plaintiffs. On the findings of the master, the plaintiffs were entitled to an injunction. So ordered.

(185 Mass. 439)

STEVENS v. BRADFORD.

(Supreme Judicial Court of Massachusetts. Plymouth. April 2, 1904.)

TAXATION—INHERITANCE TAX—TIME FOR PAYMENT—STATUTES—CONSTRUCTION.

1. The payment of the tax on a devise of property in trust, the income of which was to be paid to the beneficiary during his life, with remainder to the nieces and nephews of the testator surviving, under a will probated in 1899, is postponed until the persons entitled thereto come into possession of their property, under St. 1902, p. 881, c. 473, which went into effect in 1902, providing that in all cases where there has been or shall be a devise liable to collateral inheritance tax, to come into actual enjoyment after the expiration of one or more life estates, the tax on such property shall not be payable until the persons entitled thereto shall come into actual possession of such property, since the statute is retrospective as well as prospective.

Case Reserved from Supreme Judicial Court, Plymouth County; Jas. M. Morton, Judge.

Petition to the probate court by one Stevens to obtain instructions regarding payment of collateral inheritance tax on a devise under the will of Charles E. Stevens, deceased. From the decree the State Treasurer appealed, and the case was reserved by a single justice of the Supreme Judicial Court for the full determination of the full court. Decree modified and affirmed.

Samuel D. Elmore, for petitioner and life tenant. Frederic B. Greenhalge, Asst. Atty. Gen., for the treasurer.

LATHROP, J. This is a petition to the probate court by the executor and trustee under the will of Charles E. Stevens to obtain the instructions of that court upon the following facts alleged in the petition and admitted by the answer: Charles E. Stevens,

¶ 4. See Equity, vol. 19, Cent. Dig. § 905.

by his will, which was admitted to probate on November 2, 1890, bequeathed and devised certain property to the petitioner, in trust to pay the net income to Frederick T. Stevens during his life, and upon his decease to divide and pay over the remainder to the nephews and nieces of the testator living at the decease of Frederick T. Stevens. The question presented is whether the collateral inheritance tax of this commonwealth is now payable by the executor upon the property to be held in trust until the death of Frederick T. Stevens, or whether the payment of the tax is postponed by St. 1902, p. 381, c. 473, until the person or persons entitled thereto come into possession of their property. The probate court made a decree that the tax was not now payable, but was postponed by St. 1902, p. 381, c. 473, until the person or persons entitled thereto should come into possession of their property, and added the words: "In other words, that statute is prospective, and not retroactive, in relation to said tax." From this decree the State Treasurer appealed, and the case was reserved by a single justice of this court for our determination.

The question presented depends upon the construction to be given to St. 1902, p. 381, c. 473. This statute, which took effect upon its passage, June 12, 1902, reads as follows: "In all cases where there has been or shall be a devise, descent or bequest to collateral relatives or strangers to the blood, liable to collateral inheritance tax, to take effect in possession or come into actual enjoyment after the expiration of one or more life estates or a term of years, the tax on such property shall not be payable nor interest begin to run thereon until the person or persons entitled thereto shall come into actual possession of such property, and the tax thereon shall be assessed upon the value of the property at the time when the right of possession accrues to the person entitled thereto as aforesaid, and such person or persons shall pay the tax upon coming into possession of such property. The executor or administrator of the decedent's estate may settle his account in the probate court without being liable for said tax: provided, that such person or persons may pay the tax at any time prior to their coming into possession, and in such cases the tax shall be assessed on the value of the estate at the time of the payment of the tax, after deducting the value of the life estate or estates for years: and provided, further, that the tax on real estate shall remain a lien on the real estate on which the same is chargeable until it is paid." The decree of the judge of the probate court is inconsistent, and we are of opinion that he was right in the first part of his decree, and wrong in the words added, and that the latter words should be stricken out. The statute is clearly retrospective, and not merely prospective. It applies to "all cases where there has been or shall be a devise," etc. To construe it as relating merely to devises, descents, or bequests, subsequently to the passage of the act, would give no effect to the words "has been." The use of the words expresses a clear and unequivocal intent on the part of the Legislature that the statute should operate retrospectively as to all estates where the tax has not been paid. In Commonwealth v. McCaughey, 9 Gray, 296, it is said by Mr. Justice Metcalf: "For it is an anciently established rule in the interpretation of statutes that such a sense is to be made upon the whole statute that no clause, sentence, or word shall prove superfluous, void, or insignificant, if by any other construction they may all be made useful and pertinent. 1 Show. 108; Bac. Ab. Statute, 1, 2. See, also, Opinion of the Justices, 22 Pick. 571, 573." The statute in question was very likely passed to relieve a hardship which was imposed by the preceding laws, by which, in case of a legacy of $10,000 in trust to pay the income to A. during his life, with remainder to B., the tax was taken out of the capital, and A. received the income of only $8,000, although a legacy to him would not be taxable. In Minot v. Winthrop, 162 Mass. 113, 125, 38 N. E. 512, 26 L. R. A. 259, where this was held, it was said by Chief Justice Field: "Perhaps a simpler way than that prescribed by statute would have been to levy the tax at the end of the life estate upon the whole of the fund to be paid to the legatee in remainder." This suggestion of the chief justice has been followed in the statute before us.

The decree of the probate court, amended as we have already stated, is to be affirmed.

(185 Mass. 363)

CHICAGO TITLE & TRUST CO. v. SMITH.

(Supreme Judicial Court of Massachusetts. Hampshire. April 1, 1904.)

ACTION ON JUDGMENT—LEX FORI—DEFENDANTS.

1. An action on a foreign judgment is governed by the law of the state in which the suit is brought.

2. An action on a foreign judgment is defeated by pleading and proof that defendant was never served with process, and did not authorize an appearance in the action in which the judgment was rendered.

Exceptions from Superior Court, Hampshire County; L. Le B. Holmes, Judge.

Action by the Chicago Title & Trust Company against one Smith. Finding for defendant, and plaintiff brings exceptions. Exceptions overruled.

J. Arthur Wainwright, for plaintiff. J. C. Hammond and H. P. Field, for defendant.

BARKER, J. The plaintiff, as receiver of the Chicago Paper Manufacturing Company, an Illinois corporation, seeks to recover upon an alleged judgment rendered in the superior

¶ 2. See Judgment, vol. 30, Cent. Dig. § 1469.

court of Cook county, Ill., on July 3, 1901, in an action begun on October 3, 1890, in favor of the plaintiff, as such receiver, whereby that court adjudged and decreed that the plaintiff, as such receiver, recover of and from the defendant the sum of $17,922.19, and that execution issue therefor against the defendant. The present action was begun on November 11, 1901, and was heard by the court without a jury, with a finding for the defendant on July 29, 1903. A memorandum of the presiding judge filed on the same date shows that he found that the Illinois judgment was invalid because the defendant was not served with process in the Illinois suit, and that the appearance entered for him was not authorized or ratified by him, so that the Illinois court had no jurisdiction to enter judgment against him therein, although he then was a citizen of Illinois. Before the judgment was entered, the defendant had removed from Illinois, and when the judgment was entered he was a resident of New York. The case is here upon exceptions to the introduction of evidence by the defendant tending to show that he never was served with process in the Illinois suit, and never knew of or authorized any appearance for himself therein. There is also an exception to the striking out of a part of a reply of a witness to a question put to him in taking his deposition.

1. The principal contention of the plaintiff is that, because the defendant was a citizen of Illinois, he can contest the validity of the judgment only by proceedings for its review in the courts of the state where it was rendered. The record contains no evidence of the law of Illinois, and it well may be that by that law the defendant, if sued in Illinois upon the judgment, could defend by showing that he had not been served with process, and had not entered or authorized an appearance. But if we assume that by the law of Illinois a judgment debtor in a judgment obtained there has no remedy when sued there upon the judgment but by proceedings to review or annul the judgment, when the same judgment debtor is sued here upon the judgment his defenses here are not regulated by the law of Illinois, but by the law of Massachusetts. When brought into our courts, he has a right to have the same law administered which our courts give to our own citizens or to those of any other state. When a judgment debtor is sued here upon a judgment, the defenses open to him depend upon the fact as to where the judgment was entered. If in our own courts, the defense of want of service, and that he never appeared, is not open, and usually can be availed of only by proceedings to revise or annul the judgment. Hendrick v. Whittemore, 105 Mass. 23; McCormick v. Fiske, 138 Mass. 379. The only exception, made after the adoption of the fourteenth article of the amendments of the Constitution of the United States, is that a nonresident of Massachusetts against whom a judgment in personam has been rendered here, who neither was served personally with process nor appeared in the action in which the judgment was entered, is not obliged, when sued here upon the judgment, to resort to a writ of error to reverse it. Needham v. Thayer, 147 Mass. 536, 18 N. E. 429. See Eliot v. McCormick, 144 Mass. 10, 10 N. E. 705. But when the judgment sued on here is not a domestic judgment, and is one rendered in another state or jurisdiction, the defendant may plead and prove that he was not duly served with process, and did not authorize an appearance in the action in which the judgment was entered. Gilman v. Gilman, 126 Mass. 26, 30 Am. Rep. 646; Wright v. Andrews, 130 Mass. 149. In Finneran v. Leonard, 7 Allen, 54, 83 Am. Dec. 665, the judgment was a domestic one, and in Engstrom v. Sherburne, 137 Mass. 153, the defendant appeared in the Nevada court. The defendant in the present instance is within our rule, which governs whenever foreign judgments are sued on in our courts, and the evidence excepted to was admitted rightly.

2. The part of the answer of the witness excluded under the plaintiff's exception was not responsive to the question. For that reason it was excluded rightly.

Exceptions overruled.

(185 Mass. 366)

PENNSYLVANIA IRONWORKS CO. v. HYGEIAN ICE & COLD STORAGE CO.

(Supreme Judicial Court of Massachusetts. Bristol. April 1, 1904.)

SALES — CONTRACT — CONSTRUCTION—SUIT FOR PURCHASE PRICE—DEFENSES—DEFECT IN ARTICLE—NOTICE BY BUYER—WAIVER.

1. Plaintiff delivered to and erected on defendant's premises an ice-making plant. For the purpose of settling differences growing out of that transaction, plaintiff agreed to deliver on defendant's premises, for its plant, a 20-ton evaporating apparatus of a certain type, or other type of equal capacity. Defendant agreed to deliver to plaintiff the part of the plant previously installed which the new apparatus would supersede, and agreed to pay in a month from the delivery a specified sum, unless within that time it notified plaintiff that the apparatus failed to accomplish the results guarantied by a third person, and requested its removal. The agreement stated that the month between the delivery of the apparatus and payment was given to enable defendant to determine whether the capacity of the apparatus was 20 tons. *Held* that, under the agreement, defendant was required to pay for the apparatus in one month, unless it did not have the 20-ton capacity, or unless defendant notified plaintiff that it did not accomplish the results guarantied by the third person.

2. A buyer under a contract requiring him to pay the purchase price within a month after delivery, unless in the meantime it appeared that the article did not have a stated capacity, or unless he notified the seller that it did not accomplish the results guarantied, and requested its removal, who kept it for over a month without notifying the seller that it did not accomplish the results guarantied, could not show, when sued for the purchase price, that the arti-

cle produced unsatisfactory results, in the absence of evidence showing a waiver by the seller of the condition as to notice, or that the buyer was excused from complying with it.

3. Where a contract required a buyer to pay the purchase price in a month after delivery, unless he notified the seller that the apparatus did not come up to the guaranty and requested its removal, the fact that, on the buyer expressing dissatisfaction, efforts were made to improve the apparatus, so that it would produce better results, did not constitute the notice and request required by the contract, or establish a waiver on the seller's part, or furnish a valid excuse for failing to comply with the contract.

Exceptions from Superior Court, Bristol County; Frederick Lawton, Judge.

Action by the Pennsylvania Ironworks Company against the Hygeian Ice & Cold Storage Company. There was a verdict for plaintiff, and defendant brings exceptions. Exceptions overruled.

J. W. Cummings and C. R. Cummings, for plaintiff. Richard P. Borden, for defendant.

MORTON, J. This is an action to recover money alleged to be due under a written contract, and also upon an account annexed. At the trial it was agreed that the only matters in dispute were, first, the sum of $1,500, alleged to be due under the written contract; second, a balance of $68, also alleged to be due under the written contract; and, third, a claim made by the plaintiff on account of certain machinery which the defendant was to deliver to the plaintiff on the cars at Fall River. There was a verdict for the plaintiff, in part directed by the court, and in part upon matters submitted to the jury, and the case is here upon exceptions by the defendant to the exclusion of evidence that was offered and rejected, and to the refusal of the presiding justice to give certain instructions that were requested.

The case depends, it seems to us, upon the construction to be given to the written contract. There had been a previous contract between the plaintiff and defendant, under which the plaintiff had delivered to and erected on the defendant's premises, at Fall River, an ice-making plant; and, for the purpose of settling and adjusting matter growing out of that contract, the contract in question was entered into. The plaintiff agreed to deliver on the defendant's premises in Fall River, and in the location required by its ice-making plant, a 20-ton evaporating apparatus, of the "Lillie" type, or of some other type of equal capacity; and the defendant agreed to deliver to the plaintiff, on the cars at Fall River, that portion of the plant previously installed which the Lillie apparatus superseded. The defendant also agreed to pay to the plaintiff in one month from the delivery the sum of $1,500, unless within that time it notified the plaintiff that the apparatus had failed to accomplish the results guarantied by the company, with which the plaintiff contracted to furnish it, and requested its removal. This company was the Sugar Apparatus Manufacturing Company. The contract stated that the month between the delivery of the apparatus and the payment of the $1,500 was given in order that the defendant might have the opportunity to determine whether the capacity of the apparatus was 20 tons, as called for by the contract. A copy of the contract between the plaintiff and the Sugar Apparatus Company was attached to the duplicate original of the contract between the plaintiff and defendant furnished to the defendant, but was in no other way made a part of that contract; the only reference to it being that already mentioned. As we construe the contract between the plaintiff and defendant, the plaintiff was to deliver on the premises of the defendant, in Fall River, in the location required by the existing plant, a 20-ton evaporating apparatus, of the Lillie or of some other equal type, and within one month after the delivery the defendant was to pay the plaintiff $1,500, unless in the meantime it appeared that the apparatus had not a capacity of 20 tons, or unless the defendant notified the plaintiff that it did not accomplish the results guarantied by the Sugar Apparatus Company, and requested its removal. The plaintiff did not guaranty that the apparatus would furnish merchantable ice, free from impurities and odors, or that it would work satisfactorily in connection with the ice-making plant already installed. Indeed, it would seem from the correspondence that was put in without objection that the plaintiff did not believe that the Lillie apparatus would accomplish the results desired, and that the defendant was content to take the risk. All that the plaintiff was required to do was to deliver the apparatus upon the defendant's premises in the location required, and thereupon the defendant became bound to pay the plaintiff $1,500 in one month, unless it turned out that the apparatus was not of 20-ton capacity, or unless the defendant notified the plaintiff that the apparatus failed to accomplish the results guarantied by the Sugar Company, and requested its removal. It is conceded that the contract did not require the plaintiff to set up the apparatus. The uncontradicted evidence showed that the apparatus was delivered upon the premises of the defendant, and in the location required, and that the defendant kept and used it, and that it was included in the property conveyed by the defendant when the plant was sold. In view of the uncontradicted evidence that it was delivered as required, evidence that it was not accepted was immaterial. There was no contention that it was not of 20-ton capacity, or that the defendant had delivered to the plaintiff the apparatus superseded by it. The fact, if it was a fact, which the defendant offered to show, that the apparatus produced bad ice, was immaterial. If the defendant was dissatisfied with the apparatus, it was bound, under the contract, to notify the plaintiff within a month after the delivery, and request its removal. There was nothing to show that it did so, or that those provisions of the contract were waived by the plaintiff, or that anything occurred to excuse the defendant from complying with them. It is true that the defendant expressed dissatisfaction, and that efforts were made to improve the apparatus so that it would produce better ice; but this fell far short of the notice and request required by the contract, or of establishing a waiver on the part of the plaintiff, or of furnishing a valid excuse on the part of the defendant for not complying with the provisions of the contract. Without attempting to review and consider here the various rulings and refusals to rule to which exceptions were taken, we deem it enough to say that we discover no error in any of them, or in the way in which the case was submitted to the jury.

Exceptions overruled.

(185 Mass. 371)

McSWEENEY v. COMMONWEALTH.

(Supreme Judicial Court of Massachusetts. Middlesex. April 1, 1904.)

EMINENT DOMAIN—DAMAGES—SURFACE WATER—VENDOR AND PURCHASER—WARRANTY—EASEMENTS.

1. St. 1894, p. 283, c. 288, relative to the taking of land for park purposes, provides for the payment of all damages sustained by any person or corporation by the taking of land or any right therein, and that damages shall be assessed by a jury of the superior court in the same manner as is provided by law with respect to damages sustained by the laying out of ways. *Held*, that a landowner whose land was not taken was not entitled to damages because of an accumulation of surface water on his land on account of the grade of a parkway.

2. Easements by implied grant are those which are strictly necessary to the principal thing granted, and mere convenience is not enough.

3. A drain for a dwelling and for surface water would not be held to have passed as an easement by implied grant in the absence of evidence of its necessity.

4. One conveying with full covenants of warranty is estopped to claim any easement in the land conveyed.

Exceptions from Superior Court, Middlesex County; Frederick Lawton, Judge.

Petition by one McSweeney for an assessment of damages occasioned by a taking of land, under St. 1894, p. 283, c. 288. Judgment for the commonwealth, and petitioner brings exceptions. Exceptions overruled.

Moses Holbrook and M. Sumner Holbrook, for petitioners. Robert G. Dodge, Asst. Atty. Gen., for the Commonwealth.

LATHROP, J. This is a petition for the assessment of damages alleged to have been occasioned to the land of the petitioners in Everett by the acts of the metropolitan park commission in taking certain land and constructing a parkway thereon, under St. 1894, p. 283, c. 288, and St. 1895, p. 504, c. 450. At the close of the petitioners' evidence, the jury was directed to return a verdict for the respondent, and the case is before us on the petitioners' exceptions to this ruling.

No part of the petitioners' land was taken by the park commissioners, but a portion of the adjoining lot was taken up to within a few feet of the petitioners' boundary line. On the northerly side of the parkway the land slopes up gradually for some 300 feet to Chelsea street. During the work of construction of the parkway, an underground drain pipe running across the rear of the petitioners' land and the land taken was broken by the employés of the commission, within the limits of the land taken, and permanently obstructed. The petitioners' land is situated on Ferry Street Extension, which runs from Chelsea street down to the parkway, but is not connected therewith. The petitioners bought their land in October, 1892, from one Peters, who owned at the time, either alone or jointly with one Hadley, 5½ acres of land, of which the petitioners' land was a part. In 1890 Peters built a drain across his land, running from a point about 100 feet below Chelsea street down across the land afterwards sold to the petitioners, and land afterwards sold by Peters and Hadley to one Bench in 1895. This drain emptied into a creek in the marsh below. The drain, Peters testified, was designed for the drainage of the houses which might afterwards be built on the land, and also to take the underground water from the springy soil near the beginning of the drain, and it was so constructed that rain water could get into it. The drain was broken on May 31, 1901, and on the next day the petitioners' cellar was flooded to the depth of a foot and a half or more, and water remained in the cellar until July 15, 1901, when a connection was made with a sewer of the city of Everett that had just been put through Ferry Street Extension. The water which came into the cellar was house sewage from 18 families living between the petitioners' lot and Chelsea street. The effect of the water was to injure the house, and the petitioners were obliged to take a room in another house for six or seven weeks. Since that time, whenever there is a heavy rain, surface water has come through the cellar wall into the cellar. This water came down Ferry Street Extension, and was accumulated near the parkway. At the time of the trial a drain was being built to take care of this surface water. At the time the land was sold to the petitioners, there was no other house on the 5½-acre lot. The plumbing of the petitioners' house was connected with the drain by Peters after the petitioners bought the land. The deed to the petitioners was a warranty deed in the usual form, and it contained no grant of an easement in the drain, nor any reser-

¶ 2. See Easements, vol. 17, Cent. Dig. § 44.

vation of a right to Peters to drain the sewage or water from his remaining land through the petitioners' land.

St. 1894, c. 288, § 5, provides for the payment of "all damages sustained by any person or corporation by the taking of land or any right therein." The additional provision that damages shall be "assessed by a jury of the superior court in the same manner as is provided by law with respect to damages sustained by the laying out of ways" has reference only to the mode of procedure, and not to the elements of damage for which recovery may be had. Hay v. Commonwealth, 183 Mass. 294, 67 N. E. 334. As no part of the petitioners' land was taken, we are of opinion that they cannot recover for the temporary injury done to their land by the accumulation of surface water caused by the parkway being at a higher grade than the foot of Ferry Street Extension. See Lincoln v. Commonwealth, 164 Mass. 368, 374, 41 N. E. 489; Chelsea Dye House & Laundry Co. v. Commonwealth, 164 Mass. 350, 41 N. E. 64, and cases cited.

The remaining question is whether the petitioners had an easement in the land taken for the maintenance of the drain. There was no easement by grant in the land taken, nor was there any by prescription. If the petitioners' land had any easement, it was by implied grant; but easements by implied grant are those which are strictly necessary to the principal thing granted, and mere convenience is not enough. Nichols v. Luce, 24 Pick. 102, 35 Am. Dec. 302; Buss v. Dyer, 125 Mass. 287; Johnson v. Knapp, 150 Mass. 267, 23 N. E. 40; Cummings v. Perry, 169 Mass. 150, 47 N. E. 618, 38 L. R. A. 149. In the case at bar there was no evidence that the drain was necessary.

At the time the conveyance was made to the petitioners, the drain was used only for the purpose of carrying off underground water from land above them, some distance from their lot. The petitioners do not contend that they have been injured by having the drainage from their house cut off temporarily; but they contend that they have been injured by the sewage from the houses that had been built above them, after the conveyance to them had been made, being cut off and coming into the cellar of their house. It is difficult to see upon what ground the petitioners can claim an easement in the land taken for the purpose of having the sewage of the houses above them pass through their land and that taken. The petitioners were not compelled to receive the drainage from the houses above them, unless it can be said that when Peters conveyed to them he impliedly reserved a right of drainage for his remaining land. But this cannot be said, in view of of the covenants of warranty and freedom from incumbrances in the deed to the petitioners. Carbrey v. Willis, 7 Allen, 364, 83 Am. Dec. 688; Adams v. Marshall, 138 Mass. 228, 52 Am. Rep. 271.

While Peters owned the entire lot of 5½ acres he could acquire no easement in the drain, and, when he conveyed to the petitioners by a deed containing full covenants of warranty, both he and those claiming under him were estopped to claim any interest in the granted premises. Carbrey v. Willis, ubi supra. The petitioners, therefore, were not obliged to receive the sewage from the land above, and might have stopped up the drain where it entered on their land.

The order, therefore, must be: Exceptions overruled.

(185 Mass. 419)

TABBUT v. AMERICAN INS. CO.

(Supreme Judicial Court of Massachusetts. Suffolk. April 1, 1904.)

FIRE INSURANCE—PROPERTY HELD ON CONDITIONAL SALE—MEASURE OF RECOVERY.

1. Where one in possession of personal property, purchased on payments under conditional sale, insures her interest under a policy of fire insurance indemnifying the insured to the extent of her loss, she is entitled to recover from the insurer, on the destruction of the property by fire, only the amount represented by her payments on the purchase price and interest thereon.

Appeal from Superior Court, Suffolk County; Jas. B. Richardson, Judge.

Action by one Tabbut against the American Insurance Company. From a judgment for plaintiff for less than claimed, plaintiff appeals. Affirmed.

D. C. Linscott, for plaintiff. Bryant, Griswold & Howard, for defendant.

KNOWLTON, C. J. The plaintiff, having in her possession a piano which she held under a contract of conditional sale, obtained insurance on it in the sum of $300, by a policy in the Massachusetts standard form, in the defendant company. The piano having been destroyed by fire, she brings this action to recover under the policy. The contract under which she held the piano acknowledged her receipt of it "by way of conditional sale," and contained an agreement to pay $5 at that time, and $4.50 on the 1st day of each month thereafter, until the sum of $215, which was stated to be its value, should be paid in all, together with interest on all balances at the rate of 6 per cent. per annum. She agreed that the instrument was to remain the property of the person from whom she received it until all of the payments should be made, and that it should not be removed from the house without his written consent, and that, on her failure to perform the agreement according to its terms, he might take immediate possession of it and hold it free from all claims and demands. He signed an agreement that she might retain possession of it if she made the stipulated payments, and that he would give her a bill of sale of the instrument on her fulfillment of the agreement. At the time of the fire she had made four payments, amounting to $20. Although the title was not in her, it is conceded by the defendant that she had an insurable interest, and that the policy, which was in the common form, covered her interest, whatever it might be. Williams v. Roger Williams Insurance Company, 107 Mass. 377–379, 9 Am. Rep. 41; Fowle v. Springfield Fire & Marine Insurance Company, 122 Mass. 191–194, 23 Am. Rep. 308; Wainer v. Milford Mutual Fire Insurance Company, 153 Mass. 335–340, 26 N. E. 877, 11 L. R. A. 598; Doyle v. American Insurance Company, 181 Mass. 139, 63 N. E. 394. But her interest was not that of ownership of the instrument, and destruction of the piano by fire would not deprive her of the general property in it. It has often been held in such cases that the risk of loss by destruction without the fault of either party is upon the person who retains the title. After the property had been burned, the plaintiff was not bound by her agreement to pay. Thompson v. Gould, 20 Pick. 134; Weed v. Boston & Salem Ice Company, 12 Allen, 377–380; Wells v. Calnan, 107 Mass. 514, 9 Am. Rep. 65; Swallow v. Emery, 111 Mass. 355; Sloan v. McCarty, 134 Mass. 245. From the nature of the agreement, it is manifest that the parties contemplated, as a condition of performance by each, the continued existence of that to which the contract related. Butterfield v. Byron, 153 Mass. 517, 27 N. E. 667, 12 L. R. A. 571, 25 Am. St. Rep. 654.

The question in dispute is what sum the plaintiff is entitled to recover as damages. It is agreed that, if she is entitled to recover the full value of the piano, judgment is to be entered for $215, and interest and costs. If her right to recover is limited to the amount she had paid at the time of the loss, with interest thereon, judgment is to be entered for $20, and interest and costs. The case was presented on facts agreed, with a statement that the plaintiff had no insurable interest in the property, "except as shown by, or as may be inferred from, the facts" agreed. The plaintiff appealed from a judgment in her favor for the smaller sum.

It is unnecessary to determine whether the interest of the plaintiff had any value in particulars not stated, as the burden was upon her to prove her damages. She had a possessory right, founded on a conditional sale, with the privileges pertaining to it which are given by Rev. Laws, c. 198, p. 1708, §§ 11–13. She had made payments amounting to $20, of which she was entitled to the benefit under her contract. No facts are stated which warrant the recovery of more than $20 and interest, unless she was entitled to the full value of the property. A contract for insurance against fire, in the form prescribed by our statute, is a contract of indemnity, and the assured is only entitled to be put in the same condition pecuniarily that he would have been in if there had been no fire. His damages are not to be diminished because he has collateral contracts or relations with third persons which relieve him wholly or in part from the loss against which the insurance company agreed to indemnify him. King v. State Insurance Company, 7 Cush. 1, 54 Am. Dec. 683; Suffolk Insurance Company v. Boyden, 9 Allen, 123; Haley v. Manufacturers' Insurance Company, 120 Mass. 292–297. This principle, as applied to mortgages in some of the cases cited, has now become unimportant in this commonwealth, by reason of the provisions in the standard policy requiring a mortgagee to assign his mortgage to the insurance company, if requested. Rev. Laws, c. 118, p. 1146, § 60. As a general proposition, it is applied broadly, but it has no effect to enlarge an insurable interest, the value of which fixes a limit to the amount to be paid under a policy in common form. In Washington Mills Manufacturing Company v. Weymouth Insurance Company, 135 Mass. 503–507, it was said that "the insurer cannot complain if he pays no more than the value of the property he has insured, no more than the sum insured upon it, and no more than the interest of the insured at the time of the loss." But this was said in reference to the effect of collateral contracts and conditions, and not in reference to an enlargement of the interest of the assured, for the protection of which the insurance was obtained. It has application in the present case, in the fact that the defendant cannot diminish its liability in this suit for the interest owned by the plaintiff at the time of the fire, on account of any right which the plaintiff now has under her contract with the vendor. The plaintiff, in taking her insurance upon the property, became entitled to indemnity only to the extent of her interest. Doyle v. American Insurance Company, 181 Mass. 139, 63 N. E. 394. Her interest was that of a holder of an executory contract to purchase the property at a given price, of which she had paid a part. That interest was lost by the fire, and for that loss she is entitled to be paid. We are of opinion that the ruling was right.

Judgment affirmed.

(185 Mass. 337)

TOBIN v. CENTRAL VERMONT RY. CO.

(Supreme Judicial Court of Massachusetts. Suffolk. April 1, 1904.)

RAILROADS—RECEIVERS—INJURIES TO SERVANT—SALE OF ASSETS—DEED—CONSTRUCTION—LIABILITY OF GRANTEE—FOLLOWING ASSETS—STATE COURTS—JURISDICTION.

1. Where, at the time plaintiff was injured while acting as a fireman of a locomotive, he was in the employ of receivers of the railroad, appointed by the federal court, who were in complete control of its property and were operating the road, the receivers were not the agents either of the railroad company or of a subsequent corporation to which the property was sold under a decree of the federal court, so as to authorize plaintiff to maintain an action of tort for his injuries against such purchasing corporation.

2. The discharge of receivers of a railroad company appointed by the federal court relieved them from all personal liability for injuries to a fireman while the road was being operated by them.

3. Where the assets of a railroad company in the hands of receivers were conveyed under a decree of the court to defendant railway company, organized for that purpose, by a deed of the receivers, under which the grantee assumed and agreed to perform their obligations, a fireman, injured while in the receivers' employ, through their negligence, being a stranger to the conveyance, could not claim under it against the grantee.

4. Plaintiff's claim against the receivers, if any, not having been recognized by them either as to liability or by any sum as liquidated damages, was not within a provision of the deed requiring the grantee to pay "all debts, obligations, and liabilities of the receivers."

5. Where a decree for the sale of a railroad's property in the hands of receivers provided that on confirmation of the sale the purchaser should take title to all the railroad's property so purchased, subject to the lien of any and all debts, obligations, and liabilities of the receivers previously or thereafter lawfully incurred or arising out of the operation of the railroad by the receivers, and the deed provided that the grantee assumed all debts, obligations, and liabilities of the receivers, which were expressed in the deed, neither the purchase of the property, which had been increased by the receivers to an amount larger than plaintiff's claim, nor the terms of the decree, were sufficient to transform the liability of the receivers for negligently injuring plaintiff, while in their employ as a fireman, from a tort to a right sounding in contract, or raise an implied contract obligating the grantee to pay for such injuries.

6. Where the assets of a railroad company were sold to defendant by a decree in receivership proceedings in the federal court, the state court will not take jurisdiction of a suit by a fireman, injured by the negligence of such receivers while in their employ, to recover damages for the injuries, to be paid out of the assets.

Appeal from Superior Court, Suffolk County.

Action by one Tobin against the Central Vermont Railway Company. From a judgment sustaining a demurrer to the declaration, plaintiff appeals. Affirmed.

S. A. Fuller and W. E. Bowden, for appellant. J. L. Thorndike and E. R. Thayer, for appellee.

BRALEY, J. In a declaration that by amendment finally contained five counts the plaintiff seeks to hold the defendant liable "in an action of contract or tort, it being doubtful to which of these classes it belongs." The substantial allegations admitted by the demurrer state that the plaintiff, while in the employment of receivers duly appointed by the Circuit Court of the United States for the District of Vermont to take possession of and operate the line of railroad owned and controlled by the Central Vermont Railroad Company, sustained personal injuries when acting as a fireman on one of the locomotive engines then in use. Afterwards, under a decree of the court, the receivers sold the railroad, with its equipment and property, to the defendant, and the sale was subsequently affirmed. In the decree, among other directions, it was provided that "on confirmation of such sale the purchaser or purchasers shall take title to the railroad property so purchased, subject to the lien of any and all debts, obligations, and liabilities of the receivers heretofore or hereafter lawfully incurred by or under the authority of the court, or arising out of the operation of such railroad by the receivers, and subject also to the right of this court to compel payment of the purchase price in the manner hereinbefore provided." At the time the sale was made and the title passed the earnings from the operation of the road while in the hands of the receivers, and which had been expended by them in its equipment and improvement, amounted to a larger sum than the damages demanded in this action. No averment is made that permission to bring suit had been granted by the court having jurisdiction of the property, and by whose decree it had been sold, and it further appears that the receivers have been discharged, without having recognized or settled the plaintiff's claim. In order to maintain an action of tort the plaintiff must prove a wrongful act by the defendant, from which he has suffered damages to his person; but the negligence of which he complains, and that caused his injuries, was the alleged carelessness of the receivers, who at the time were acting for the court, and could not be considered as the agents or servants, even, of the Central Vermont Railroad Company: while it is too clear for discussion that no such relation arises between them and the defendant, a corporation, organized apparently to take the property under the sale ordered by the court, and retaining the old corporate name except that "railway" is substituted for "railroad," and neither the old nor the new company can be held to have taken by inheritance their liability to the plaintiff. Archambeau v. New York & New England Railroad Co., 170 Mass. 272, 273, 49 N. E. 435. Their discharge by the court of which they were officers, and under whose appointment they acted, relieves them from all personal liability of the nature described, and no action at law can now be maintained against them by the plaintiff. Archambeau v. Platt, 173 Mass. 249, 53 N. E. 816. He is therefore compelled to rely on an alleged contractual right, based on the conveyance made in conformity to the decree, in order to recover in an action of contract. But if the deed of the receivers is given the effect of a deed poll, by which the grantee assumes their obligations and agrees to perform them, the plaintiff was not a party to the transaction, and, being a stranger to the conveyance, cannot in law claim under it. Coffin v. Adams, 131 Mass. 133; New England Dredging Co. v. Rockport Granite Co., 149 Mass. 381, 21 N. E. 947; Creesy v. Willis, 159 Mass. 249-251, 34 N. E. 265; Clare v. Hatch, 180 Mass. 194, 62 N. E. 250. All that the defend-

¶ 2. See Railroads, vol. 41, Cent. Dig. § 846.

ant undertook and was called upon to carry out and perform appears to have been expressed in the deed, and no right of recovery can be founded on the fact that it bought a property which may have been increased in value under the management of the receivers. If it be assumed, without deciding, that the plaintiff's construction of the phrase "all debts, obligations, and liabilities of the receivers" is broad enough to include his cause of action, it does not appear that his claim has ever been recognized either as to liability or by any sum as liquidated damages. No relation arising out of any contract existed between the plaintiff and the receivers, and his right to recover, if at all, arose solely out of an alleged tort on their part. The purchase of the property by the defendant under these conditions, and the terms of the decree, and nothing more, are not sufficient to transform the tortious act into a right sounding in contract, or to raise an implied contract that in some manner the plaintiff is to be paid compensation for his injuries by the defendant. Massachusetts General Hospital v. Fairbanks, 129 Mass. 78, 37 Am. Rep. 303; Brooks v. Allen, 146 Mass. 201, 202, 15 N. E. 584; Borden v. Boardman, 157 Mass. 410, 32 N. E. 469. See Jesup v. Wabash, St. Louis & Pac. Ry. Co. (C. C.) 44 Fed. 663-665.

The plaintiff, however, urges in support of his contention that in some form of action he can reach and apply the assets passed by the receivers to the defendant in satisfaction of his damages; that the decree of sale and conveyance transferred the property subject to the receivers' liability to him, or created an equitable lien in his favor, and that he has a remedy in equity; and suggests that an amendment, changing his action at law into a suit in equity should be allowed in accordance with Rev. Laws, c. 159, § 6. But the extent and nature of the obligation with which the property was to be charged, and the time and manner of payment, as well as the procedure to be used to determine and enforce such a right, were all within the jurisdiction and control of the court that administered the property and marshaled the assets of the corporation, and by whose decree the sale was made and confirmed. No other tribunal can so well interpret these decrees or pass on the rights and adjust the equities of the parties arising under them. There is no imperative rule of law or of comity that requires us to take jurisdiction of this litigation, which may well be remitted to the determination of the court under whose authority the original proceedings were begun, and where, for this purpose, they may be treated as still pending. Howarth v. Lombard, 175 Mass. 570, 573, 575, 56 N. E. 888, 49 L. R. A. 301; Buck v. Colbath, 3 Wall. 334, 341, 345, 18 L. Ed. 257; Porter v. Sabin, 149 U. S. 473-479, 13 Sup. Ct. 1008, 37 L. Ed. 815; Byers v. McAuley, 149 U. S. 608-614, 13 Sup. Ct. 906, 37 L. Ed. 867.

Judgment affirmed.

(185 Mass. 409)

MARCUS et al. v. CLARK et al.

(Supreme Judicial Court of Massachusetts. Suffolk. April 1, 1904.)

VENDOR AND PURCHASER — AGREEMENT FOR CLEAR TITLE—PRIOR INCUMBRANCES—WAIVER—ACTION BY PURCHASER—EVIDENCE—COMPETENCY.

1. Where a contract for the sale of land called for a conveyance free from incumbrances, on payment of a specified sum, within a certain time, but the purchasers knew of certain restrictions during the time they were entitled to a conveyance, and were satisfied to take a conveyance subject thereto, the existence of the restrictions did not put the vendors in the wrong, and plaintiffs in an action for breach of the contract had to show a wrongful refusal to convey subject to the restrictions.

2. A contract for the sale of land called for a conveyance free from incumbrances, and the purchaser sued for damages on the ground that the vendors had, prior to the contract, placed certain restrictions on the property. The vendor introduced evidence that one representing plaintiffs had, the day after the time limited in the agreement expired, sought to procure an extension on the ground that there was difficulty in getting the purchase money. *Held*, that it was proper to exclude evidence in rebuttal that the real, but undisclosed, purpose was that plaintiffs desired further time to see if they could handle the property with the restrictions on it.

3. A contract for the sale of land called for a conveyance free from incumbrances, and the purchasers sued for damages on the ground that the vendors had, prior to the contract, put restrictions on the property. *Held* that, though the suit was for the benefit of one to whom the purchasers had assigned their contract during the time limit of their agreement, evidence of a request made by the purchasers for an extension of time during which they might secure the necessary purchase money was admissible where no notice of the assignment has been given to the vendor.

4. In a suit by the purchasers in a contract for the sale of land, the pleadings being on the basis of an affirmance of the contract and damages for its breach, plaintiffs, on failing to establish the breach, were not entitled to recover the value of a note given by them in part payment.

Exceptions from Superior Court, Suffolk County; Albert Mason, Judge.

Action by Marcus and others against Clark and others. Verdict for defendants, and plaintiffs bring exceptions. Exceptions overruled.

F. T. Hammond and Wm. B. Orcutt, for plaintiffs. John J. Higgins and Henry A. Wyman, for defendants.

LORING, J. This is an action on a written contract for the purchase and sale of land to recover damages suffered by the purchaser from the sellers' failure to fulfill their part of the agreement. The contract called for a conveyance by the defendants free from incumbrances upon payment of $25,000 within 60 days from the date thereof. Five thousand dollars of the purchase money was paid by the assignment of a note immediately after the contract was signed. The contract was dated August 28, 1902, and was assigned by the plaintiffs to one Jennings on the day it was executed. The plaintiffs proved that on July 18, 1902 (a little more than a month before the contract here sued on was executed), the defendants had entered into a covenant with the city of Boston by which they imposed restrictions on the land in question. The case was heard by a single judge without a jury, who found as a fact that the plaintiffs had full knowledge of the restrictions when the contract was made, but that the fact "that the plaintiffs and their assignee, Jennings, had full knowledge of the restrictions at the time of the making of the agreement, and upon which the action is based, is not material to the construction of said agreement." The 60 days expired on October 27, 1902. The plaintiffs have argued that, inasmuch as the defendants, by their prior covenant of July 18th, had put it out of their power to perform the obligation which they assumed in their contract of August 28th, it was not necessary for the plaintiffs to aver and prove that they were ready and willing to perform the agreement. But the judge has found as a fact that during the time when the plaintiffs were entitled to a conveyance on paying the balance of the purchase money the plaintiffs were satisfied to take a conveyance subject to these restrictions as a full performance of the defendants' obligation to make a conveyance under the contract, and never expected to receive anything else; and that the objection by reason of the restrictions was an afterthought, which was first put forward after the time for performance had expired. This is a finding that the objection based on these restrictions was waived, and that both parties to the contract were proceeding on the footing that it had been waived. The existence of the restrictions under this finding did not put the defendants in the wrong, and the plaintiffs, to maintain this action, had to prove that the defendants had wrongfully refused to convey subject to the restrictions. The sixth ruling requested was rightly refused.

The next exception argued by the plaintiffs is one to the exclusion of evidence. The defendants introduced evidence tending to show that on the day after the time limited in the agreement had expired, Jennings came to the defendants' attorney and stated that "he had difficulty in getting the money," and asked for an extension of time. The plaintiffs offered to show in rebuttal by Jennings that the real purpose for which he asked for an extension was that he "desired further time to see if he could handle the property with the restrictions on, which he had recently found to exist," which purpose was not disclosed to the defendants or their attorney. It is immaterial what undisclosed and secret purpose Jennings may have had, so long as he stated to the defendants' attorney that his reason for an extension was difficulty in raising money; and this was the only reason stated by him. This evidence was rightly excluded.

The next exception argued by the plaintiffs is to the ruling of the judge admitting evidence of "talks between the witness and the plaintiffs after the assignment was executed." It appeared from the writ that this action was brought in the names of Alfred A. and Simeon Marcus "for the use and benefit" of Jennings, the assignee. The talks admitted were between one Schon, who, as a real estate broker, originally brought the land to the attention of the assignors, the nominal plaintiffs, and who was sent by them to one Page, who acted as broker for the defendants in the sale covered by the contract sued on. Schon was allowed to testify that "about the end of September or the beginning of October" Marcus asked him to get Mr. Page to give an extension, because "I [Marcus] haven't got the money"; that witness saw Page, and the offer was refused; that thereupon Marcus instructed the witness to offer Mr. Page $1,000 for an extension of time, to be forfeited as liquidated damages if the purchaser failed to perform his agreement; that this was refused; and that subsequently Marcus said to him: "I guess I will drop it. Mr. Page won't give an extension, and they cannot give any title, and there are restrictions;" that witness replied, "I told you that there were park restrictions all the time, especially before you went down to see Mr. Page;" and that "this conversation took place probably the middle of October." If the plaintiffs' assignee did not notify the defendants of the assignment, he was bound by the action of his assignors, who were the original parties to the contract, and the only parties known to the defendants. Any request for an extension made by the original parties to the contract under such circumstances is admissible against the assignee. The presiding judge may have admitted the evidence on this ground. In addition to this, Jennings had previously testified that "he knew the Marcuses were having difficulty in raising the $20,000 required to complete the contract; that is why he went to Mr. Wyman [the defendants' attorney] to get an extension"; and it appeared later from Jennings' testimony in rebuttal that the plaintiffs were to raise the balance of the purchase money for him, and were to have all realized from a subsequent sale of the land over the purchase money paid and $8,000 owed to Jennings by the plaintiffs. It further appeared that Jennings left the whole matter of raising the money to the plaintiffs; that Jennings did not take any action in the matter until the last day within which the purchase money could be paid; and that all he did on that day was to make an appointment to meet the defendants' attorney on the next day. This request for an extension, made by a person interested in the contract when the request was made, is admissible, although the action is now brought for the exclusive use and benefit of the other party to the agreement. The plaintiffs were not injured by the admission of this evidence.

The plaintiffs have further argued that on the facts stated the defendants are not entitled to retain the note which was assigned to them as part payment of the purchase money, and that, in any event, the plaintiffs are entitled to recover the value of it, on the principle of Burk v. Schreiber, 183 Mass. 35, 66 N. E. 411. But the case at bar is not a case like Burk v. Schreiber, where an action was brought to recover back a part payment on rescission of the contract under which it was made. No such claim was made in the court below. The pleadings go on the basis of affirming the contract and claiming damages on the ground that it was broken, and the rulings asked for by the plaintiff went on the same basis.

Exceptions overruled.

(185 Mass. 375)

GUGLIELINO et al. v. CAHILL.

(Supreme Judicial Court of Massachusetts. Suffolk. April 1, 1904.)

ACTION ON ACCOUNT—EVIDENCE—ADMISSIBILITY.

1. In an action on account for labor performed to the amount of $364 defendant claimed that the plaintiffs had agreed to do the work for $350, and put in evidence a contract signed by the plaintiffs by their mark, showing that to have been the contract price. Plaintiffs did not fully complete the work, denied the contract price was $350, and one of them testified that it was $700. *Held* that, on the question of the probability of the execution of the contract in the manner and form as testified to in behalf of defendant, defendant was entitled to show by experts that $350 was a fair market price of the work called for by the written agreement.

Exceptions from Superior Court, Suffolk County; John A. Aiken, Judge.

Action by one Guglielino and others against one Cahill. Verdict for plaintiffs, and defendant brings exceptions. Exceptions sustained.

C. E. Washburn and O. E. Kaine, for plaintiffs. Daniel B. Ruggles, for defendant.

LATHROP, J. This is an action on an account annexed for labor performed to the amount of $364, less $112 paid, leaving a balance due of $252, for which amount, with interest, a verdict was returned. At the trial in the superior court there was evidence that the defendant was a contractor to build a schoolhouse, and that he sublet a portion of the work to a firm named Cullen Bros., by whom the plaintiff was employed to do some of the work. One issue in the case was whether the plaintiffs signed a written agreement with Cullen Bros. to do the work for $350, and an agreement was put in evidence, purporting to be signed by the plaintiffs by their mark. The plaintiffs denied signing this agreement, and one of them testified that the price for which they agreed to do the work was $750, and not $350; that, after he had been working some days, without receiving any pay from Cullen Bros., he went to the defendant, and said that, unless he got some money, the men would put on a lien, and that the defendant said that he did not want any liens on the work, and would see that the men were paid. The defendant testified that he did not make a new agreement with the plaintiffs; that one of them called on him for money, and that, after seeing one of the Cullens, he made certain payments to the plaintiffs, charging them to the account of Cullen Bros.; and that the plaintiff with whom he had the conversation told him that the price of the work in the contract with the Cullens was $350. There was evidence that the plaintiffs did not fully complete the work.

The only exception in the case is the following: "The defendant offered to show by experts, duly qualified, that $350 was a fair market price for the work called for by the written agreement." This evidence was offered on the question of the probability of the execution of the contract in manner and form as testified to in behalf of the defendant. This evidence was excluded.

We are of opinion that the evidence for the purpose for which it was offered should have been admitted. The question is fully covered by our previous decisions. Bradbury v. Dwight, 3 Metc. 31; Upton v. Winchester, 106 Mass. 330; Brewer v. Housatonic Railroad, 107 Mass. 277; Norris v. Spofford, 127 Mass. 85; Nickerson v. Spindell, 164 Mass. 25, 27, 41 N. E. 105; Copeland v. Brockton Street Railway, 177 Mass. 187, 58 N. E. 639, 83 Am. St. Rep. 274.

Exceptions sustained.

(185 Mass. 406)

HARVARD BREWING CO. v. PRATT.

(Supreme Judicial Court of Massachusetts. Middlesex. April 1, 1904.)

CORPORATIONS—OFFICERS—COMPENSATION.

1. Where one invests money with others in the organization of a corporation, and is made an officer thereof, on condition that he would ask no salary until he learned the business, and is later, pursuant to his request therefor, put on salary, he cannot recover compensation for the period prior to his being put on salary, though he rendered some services for the corporation during that time.

Appeal from Superior Court, Middlesex County; Edward P. Pierce, Judge.

Action by the Harvard Brewing Company against one Pratt, administrator of the estate of John H. Coffey, to recover money paid to Coffey, as treasurer of the plaintiff corporation, for shares of stock in the company, and which money had not been turned over to the company. There was also a claim for money received by Coffey for merchandise sold. Finding of $11,095.65 for the plaintiff, and defendant appealed. Affirmed.

Knox & Coulson, for appellant. Nathan D. Pratt and John J. Devine, for appellee.

KNOWLTON, C. J. The evidence in this case tends to show that the defendant's intestate, who was the treasurer of the plaintiff corporation, appropriated to his own use at different times various large sums of money which belonged to the plaintiff, and which this action is brought to recover. The question presented for our consideration relates to the first item in the defendant's declaration in set-off, which is as follows: "To services and expenses of defendant's intestate as treasurer and general manager prior to 1895, twenty-three months, at $300.00, $6,900.00." This item the auditor disallowed. and the parties have agreed that his report shall be taken as an agreed statement of facts, and that, if the agreed facts warrant the conclusion reached by the auditor, the judgment shall follow the auditor's finding; otherwise the finding for the plaintiff shall be reduced by the sum of $4,375. The facts in relation to this item stated in the auditor's report are as follows: "In the spring of 1893, before said brewery was built, and before the plaintiffs had started in business, said Coffey, who had theretofore been engaged in the meat and provision business, agreed with the plaintiffs to put a certain amount of capital into the corporation, and work as treasurer and general manager of the same long enough to learn the business, before he would ask any salary, provided he should be appointed to the position of treasurer and general manager. Said Coffey was appointed to such position, and rendered some services to the plaintiffs in the same up to January 1, 1895, when, in consequence of his request made in December, 1894, to be informed 'when he would go on salary,' he was granted a salary of $2,500 per annum, to begin with January 1, 1895. Such salary was, in December, 1897, raised to $3,600 per annum, and such sums were respectively drawn by said Coffey as his salary while treasurer. I find that said Coffey never made any claim upon the plaintiffs for salary or compensation for services rendered as treasurer and general manager previous to January 1, 1895, until June 16, 1898, when, trouble having arisen over the brewery affairs between the plaintiffs and said Coffey, a letter was received by said Coffey from the plaintiffs, as follows." Then follows a letter from the plaintiff, by the chairman of its executive committee, to the defendant's intestate, bearing date June 13, 1898, informing him that for reasons well known to him the committee would recommend to the board of directors, at a meeting to be held on June 16th, his dismissal from the office of treasurer, and suggesting that, if he should conclude to be present at the meeting, or tender his resignation in writing, he would relieve the committee from an unpleasant duty. A reply to this letter was sent, as follows:

"Lowell, June 16, '98.

"John Joyce, President Harvard Brewing Company—Sir: Before voting on treasurership, vote to pay my first year's salary and expenses, also thirty-five hundred dollars which I put in for a cash start, making a total of seventy-five hundred dollars, which is only a small part of what I have spent for the brewery.

Salary,	$2,500.00
Expenses,	1,500.00
Cash put in for start on books,	3,500.00
	$7,500.00

"Respectfully yours, John H. Coffey."

"No evidence was submitted of any other request to or demand on the plaintiff by said Coffey that he should be paid for services rendered the plaintiffs prior to January 1, 1895."

The burden of proof was on the defendant to establish his claim for the amount of this item. The agreement of the parties presents the question whether the auditor was bound, as matter of law, to find affirmatively that the plaintiff was indebted for these services. Ingalls v. Hobbs, 156 Mass. 348, 31 N. E. 286, 16 L. R. A. 51, 32 Am. St. Rep. 460; Dyer v. Swift, 154 Mass. 159, 28 N. E. 8. We think it very plain that he was not. All there is to sustain the defendant's contention is that in the spring of 1893 the defendant's intestate was appointed treasurer, under an agreement that he should work long enough to learn the business before he would ask for any salary, and that "he rendered some services to the plaintiffs" prior to his request. made in December, 1894, "to be informed when he would go on salary." The arrangement under which he was serving up to that time, the fixing of a salary of $2,500 per annum to begin January 1, 1895, in response to this request, his taking his salary at that rate and at a subsequently increased rate without ever asking for anything for services prior to January 1, 1895, until after he was informed that he was likely to be removed from his office, and other facts which appear in the report, well warranted the finding of the auditor that this item was not established as a valid claim against the plaintiff.

Judgment affirmed.

(185 Mass. 402)

COMMONWEALTH v. HUDSON.

(Supreme Judicial Court of Massachusetts. Plymouth. April 1, 1904.)

EVIDENCE — CONFESSION — ADMISSIBILITY — WHEN VOLUNTARY—QUESTION FOR COURT.

1. Where a confession is offered in evidence, the question whether it is voluntary is primarily for the presiding judge, and where the testimony is conflicting, the judge, if he decides that it is

¶ 1. See Criminal Law, vol. 14, Cent. Dig. §§ 1219, 1220, 1267.

admissible, should instruct the jury that they may consider all the evidence, and should exclude the confession, if, on the whole evidence, they are satisfied that it was not defendant's voluntary act.

2. Whether a confession is voluntary or not depends on whether the language of the arresting officer, to the effect that defendant "had better tell the truth," or "Don't you think it better to tell the truth?" or similar language, when taken in connection with the surrounding circumstances, and with other language spoken, such as a subsequent statement by the officer that he could "offer defendant no hope or favor whatever," shows that the confession was made under the influence of some threat or promise.

Exceptions from Superior Court, Plymouth County; Robt. O. Harris, Judge.

One Hudson was convicted of setting fire to a barn and excepted. Exceptions overruled.

C. A. McLellan, for plaintiff. Asa P. French, for the Commonwealth.

HAMMOND, J. 1. "When a confession is offered in evidence, the question whether it is voluntary is to be decided primarily by the presiding justice. If he is satisfied that it is voluntary, it is admissible; otherwise it should be excluded. When there is conflicting testimony, the humane practice in this commonwealth is for the judge, if he decides that it is admissible, to instruct the jury that they may consider all the evidence, and that they should exclude the confession, if, upon the whole evidence in the case, they are satisfied that it was not the voluntary act of the defendant." Morton, J., in Commonwealth v. Preece, 140 Mass. 276, 277, 5 N. E. 494, citing cases. That practice was followed in the present case, and the question is whether the evidence on the voir dire warranted the judge in coming to the conclusion that the confession was voluntary. While it may be true that when an arresting officer tells his prisoner that he "had better tell the truth," the general rule is that the confession is inadmissible; still, after all, the real question in any case is whether such or similar language, when taken in connection with the surrounding circumstances, and with other language spoken in the same or some prior interview, shows that the confession was made under the influence of some threat or promise, so that it was not voluntary. Commonwealth v. Nott, 135 Mass. 269, and cases cited; Commonwealth v. Kennedy, 135 Mass. 543. Even if it be assumed that the question, "Don't you think it better to tell the truth?" is in substance equivalent to saying in a direct form that "it is better to tell the truth," still the subsequent statement by the officer that he could "offer the prisoner no hope or favor whatever" must be considered in connection with it. After a careful perusal of the whole evidence, we think that the presiding justice was warranted in coming to the conclusion that the confession was not procured by threat or promise, but was the free and voluntary act of the defendant.

2. The question whether tramps were in the habit of going into the barn was properly excluded, as also was the evidence as to the cost of the building. Under the circumstances of this case the presiding justice may well have thought that those matters were too remote to be of any practical use to the jury in deciding upon the guilt of the defendant or the credibility of the witness Smith, who was the owner of the building.

Exceptions overruled.

(185 Mass. 442)

KENNEDY v. MERRIMACK PAV. CO.

(Supreme Judicial Court of Massachusetts. Middlesex. April 2, 1904.)

MASTER AND SERVANT—NEGLIGENCE—MACHINERY—CONTRIBUTORY NEGLIGENCE—APPARENT DANGERS.

1. A master employing as engineer a machinist by trade, and a licensed engineer, is not bound to change a set screw on a revolving shaft, or point it out to the employé, in order to relieve himself from liability for an injury sustained by the employé by his clothes being caught in the set screw.

2. A servant—a machinist by trade, and an engineer for 10 years—was injured by his clothes being caught in a set screw on a revolving shaft. At the time of the injury he was employed as engineer, and had been so employed for 9 days. He testified that he did not know of the existence of the set screw, but he had had ample opportunity to ascertain its existence. The danger from the shaft was apparent, and he knew that shafts have set screws. At the time of the accident he could have gone a safer way, or he could have stopped the engine, over the running of which he had full control. *Held* guilty of contributory negligence precluding a recovery.

Exceptions from Superior Court, Middlesex County; John H. Hardy, Judge.

Action by one Kennedy against the Merrimack Paving Company. Verdict for defendant, and plaintiff brings exceptions. Overruled.

John J. & Wm. A. Hogan, for plaintiff. F. E. Dunbar, for defendant.

LATHROP, J. This is an action of tort for personal injuries sustained by the plaintiff while in the employ of the defendant. The declaration contained three counts. At the trial in the superior court the plaintiff elected to proceed upon the second and third counts. The second count was at common law for being set to work in an unsafe place. The third count was under St. 1887, c. 270, § 1, cl. 1, and alleged a defect in the condition of the ways, works, or machinery. At the close of the evidence for the plaintiff the judge directed a verdict for the defendant, and the case is before us on the plaintiff's exceptions to this ruling.

The plaintiff was a man 39 years old. He was a machinist by trade, and had been an engineer for 10 years before the injury, and was duly licensed as such under the laws of the commonwealth. At the time of the accident, June 20, 1902, the plaintiff had been employed by the defendant 9 days as an engineer. The defendant was a manufacturer of asphalt. Its plant was divided into three parts—the first, where the asphalt was put into large kettles, underneath which fires were lighted and the asphalt liquefied. The other two parts were placed upon an ordinary flat car, about 45 feet long and 7 feet wide, located upon a spur track of a railroad. The boiler, air tank, and engine were at one end of the car, and at the other end were two steam jackets and a machine containing sand drums. These drums were about 3 feet in diameter and 20 feet in length. Between the engine and the steam jackets there was a rectangular space 3½ or 4 feet wide, 6 feet measuring across the width of the car, 6 feet in height, and partly open at the top. In this space was the main shaft, 2½ inches in diameter. It was about 10 feet long, and extended across and beyond the sides of the car. It rested upon bearings attached to the floor of the car, and was about 2½ feet from the floor. On each end of the shaft, on the outside of the bearings, was a collar, fixed and adjusted with set screws, and outside of these collars on each end of the shaft was a pulley about 4 feet in diameter; the one on the side of the car where the plaintiff was injured having a 12-inch face. On the main shaft, and just inside the bearing at this side of the car, was the hub of an old wheel or pulley, about 4 inches in length, measuring along the shaft, and of a diameter of about 4 inches, including the diameter of the shaft. There were five broken spokes sticking out of this hub from three-quarters of an inch to an inch and a quarter. The hub was attached to the shaft by a set screw extending out from the outward surface of the hub about 2 inches. The main shaft was 17 inches from the engine, and about 2 feet from the steam jackets. On the morning of the injury, one Gately, who appears by the evidence to have had charge of the works in the absence of the general superintendent, called to the plaintiff to help him put on a belt which had slipped off a pulley attached to the main shaft. The belt was put on, but slipped off two or three times. Then Gately decided to put a stick to keep the belt on, and said to the plaintiff: "I want you to go in there and block up that stick." The plaintiff went up a ladder to the platform of the car, and turned round from the ladder, with his right foot between the air tank and the main shaft, a space 17 inches wide, intending to step over the shaft, when his overalls were caught at the right knee, and his clothes were stripped off by being wound around the old collar. He caught hold of an upright plank, but finally fell to the platform of the car, and was injured. There was evidence from the plaintiff and Gately that there was another way to reach the place where the stick was, which would have been safe, and would not have necessitated stepping over the shaft. The plaintiff further testified that he had entire charge of the boiler and engine of the defendant's plant; that he knew the shaft was revolving and the machinery running; that he did not know that there was a set screw in the hub; that he did not know whether the hub was serving as a collar or not; that it might have been so serving; that he knew of the use of set screws in various places; that all machinery has them; that a pulley generally has a set screw; and that he did not know how near to the shaft he was when caught, as he was looking for the plank.

Upon this evidence, we are of opinion that the ruling at the trial was right. The plaintiff was a man of experience, and, while he testified that he did not know of the existence of the old collar on the shaft, he had ample opportunity to ascertain its existence. The defendant was not bound to change his machinery, or to point out to the plaintiff the fact of the existence of the set screw or the collar. The danger from the revolving shaft was apparent, and, as such shafts have collars fastened to them by set screws—a fact well known to the plaintiff—his getting so near the shaft as to be caught was an act of negligence. Moreover, he could have gone by a safer way; and, unless he chose to take the risk of stepping over a revolving shaft, he could have stopped the engine, over the running of which he had full control. Demers v. Marshall, 178 Mass. 9, 59 N. E. 454, and cases cited.

Exceptions overruled.

(185 Mass. 356)

SAWYER et al. v. COMMONWEALTH.

(Supreme Judicial Court of Massachusetts. Worcester. April 1, 1904.)

EMINENT DOMAIN—WATER SUPPLY—CONDEMNATION OF PROPERTY—DAMAGES—INJURY TO BUSINESS—ITEMS TO BE CONSIDERED—INTEREST—COMMISSIONERS—REPORT.

1. Under St. 1895, p. 573, c. 488, § 14, providing for petitions for the determination of damages caused to business by carrying out the act to provide for a metropolitan water supply, and for commissioners to determine the damages to real estate, machinery, and business, and to report their determinations to the court, it is the commissioners' primary duty to decide all questions of law and fact and reach a conclusion as to the amount of damages. It is not their duty to report the evidence, nor their findings as to the particulars on which their conclusion is founded, except so far as is reasonably necessary to present such questions of law as are raised before them.

2. Under a petition to determine damages to an established business, caused by the carrying out of the act to provide for a metropolitan water supply (St. 1895, p. 573, c. 488, § 14), the commissioners properly rejected evidence of an actuary as to the expectation of life of the individual members of the firm.

3. Under St. 1895, p. 573, c. 488, § 14, relative to a metropolitan water supply, which provides that persons owning an established business in a certain town on April 1, 1895, may have their damages, caused by a decrease in its value, determined, such damages should be as-

sessed in reference to conditions existing April 1, 1895.

4. The provision of St. 1895, p. 573, c. 488, § 14, relative to the determination of damages caused by the carrying out of the act for a metropolitan water supply, that interest may be included in such damages, and in such value and at such rate and for such time as the commissioners may deem just and equitable, which provision is applicable to the assessment of damages to a business as well as to other assessments, leaves the allowance of interest for damages to a business to considerations of equity, in reference to the time when the damage is actually suffered, and does not make it dependent on an arbitrary rule.

5. In determining damages to a business, caused by carrying out St. 1895, p. 573, c. 488, § 14, providing for a metropolitan water supply, sums allowed to partners as a reasonable compensation for services rendered in the business should be deducted in determining its value as a producer of income.

6. In determining damages to a business, caused by carrying out St. 1895, p. 573, c. 488, § 14, providing for a metropolitan water supply, the value of the good will of the business is not ascertainable, as a matter of law, at so many years' purchase of the average annual net profits of the business prior to the taking, although such net profits are important evidence as to the value of the good will.

7. In determining damages to a business, caused by carrying out St. 1895, p. 573, c. 488, § 14, providing for a metropolitan water supply, the income of the business after the passage of the act may be considered.

Case Reserved from Supreme Judicial Court, Worcester County; John W. Hammond, Judge.

Petition by Henry O. Sawyer and others, as copartners, under St. 1895, p. 573, c. 488, § 14, to recover damages for diminution in value of the petitioners' business by carrying out the act to provide for a metropolitan water supply. The commissioners filed their report, and the petitioners moved to recommit the same, and the commonwealth moved for its acceptance. Case reserved for the full court. Motion to recommit denied, and report accepted.

John R. Thayer, Arthur P. Rugg, and Henry H. Thayer, for petitioners. Ralph A. Stewart, Asst. Atty. Gen., for respondent.

KNOWLTON, C. J. The petitioners, as copartners, on the 1st day of April, 1895, owned and were carrying on in West Boylston an established business, namely, that of proprietors of a store and dealers in general merchandise. Their partnership agreement was to expire on January 21, 1899. They bring this petition under St. 1895, p. 573, c. 488, § 14, to recover damages for diminution in value of their business by the carrying out of the act to provide for a metropolitan water supply. The case was referred to commissioners under the above section, and it is reserved for this court upon the questions of law raised by a motion of the petitioner to recommit the report of the commissioners, and a motion of the respondent for its acceptance.

The first contention of the petitioner is that the report should be recommitted because it fails to state with sufficient fullness the principles of law and the findings of fact on which the decision was founded. Under the statute a petition in a case of this kind is "for the determination of such damages," and the commission is to "determine the damage and value of the real estate, machinery, and business, and from time to time report their determinations on the petitions of such owners to said court," and it is primarily the duty of the commissioners to decide all questions of law and fact, and reach a conclusion as to the amount of damages. Ordinarily, it is not their duty to report the evidence, nor their findings as to the particulars on which their conclusion is founded. In this respect there is ordinarily not so much occasion to go into detail as in the report of an auditor or a master in chancery, who is not expected to report the evidence unless by special order of the court. See Newell v. Chesley, 122 Mass. 522; Boston & Worcester Railroad Company v. Western Railroad Corporation, 14 Gray, 253-259; Bowers v. Cutler, 165 Mass. 441, 43 N. E. 188; In re Butterick et al., Petitioners (Mass.) 69 N. E. 1044; De Las Casas, Petitioner, 178 Mass. 218, 59 N. E. 664; Id., 180 Mass. 472, 62 N. E. 738. When a question of law is raised at a hearing before a commissioner, or an auditor, or a master, it is usually his duty to report the facts with sufficient fullness to enable the court properly to deal with the question; or, if he himself is in doubt about a question of law which enters into the result, he well may frame his report in a way to present it clearly to the court. Parker v. Nickerson, 137 Mass. 487-493. But under the present statute commissioners are not expected to report with more fullness than is reasonably necessary properly to present such questions of law as are raised before them.

The petitioners, at the hearing before the commissioners, made thirteen separate requests for rulings. Seven of these were given, and three were refused. Two were given with modifications. The remaining one was practically covered by a ruling given, and it became immaterial. We are of opinion that the commissioners in their report presented everything necessary to an understanding of the questions, and that the motion to recommit it should be overruled.

The evidence of an actuary as to the expectation of life of the three individual members of the firm does not appear to have been material. It is very seldom that facts are shown, in a case of this kind, which will make the testimony of an expert actuary important. Copson v. New York, New Haven & Hartford Railroad Company, 171 Mass. 233, 50 N. E. 613; Rooney v. N. Y., N. H. & H. R. R. Co., 173 Mass. 222, 53 N. E. 435. We have no doubt that the commissioners treated the business as one which was expected to continue, and which would have continued, but for the enactment of the statute, until the expiration of the partnership agreement. If the partnership should be dissolved by the death of one of the partners, and if the business was valuable, the good will then existing would be a part of the partnership assets. There was no error in rejecting this evidence.

The first request for rulings was "that damages should be assessed as of the time (a) of the passage of chapter 488 [page 565] of the Acts of 1895, or (b) of the filing of the taking of the water." The commissioners ruled "that damages should be based upon the business shown to exist on April 1, 1895," but declined to make the ruling requested. We are of opinion that their ruling was right. The statute makes the existence of an established business on April 1, 1895, more than two months before the passage of the act, a condition precedent to recovery. In this way it is made impossible for one, after the passage of the act, or within two months before it, to establish a business for the purpose of subsequently claiming damages for an injury to it. The same reason applies to changes in the condition of the business by an increase in its magnitude or otherwise. The statute requires that the damage shall be assessed in reference to conditions existing on April 1, 1895. Earle v. Com., 180 Mass. 579, 57 L. R. A. 292, 91 Am. St. Rep. 326. We interpret the request as referring to this subject, and not to the time when the right to petition for the assessment of damages accrued. If it were construed as referring to the latter subject, it would be of no consequence except as bearing upon the question how much interest should be allowed. On this point the statute expressly provides "that interest may be included in such damages, and in such value, and at such rate, and for such time as the commission may deem just and equitable." This provision is applicable to the assessment of damages for diminution in the value of a business as well as to other assessments under the same section. St. 1895, p. 573, c. 488, § 14. The purpose of this provision is to leave the allowance of interest to considerations of equity in reference to the time when the damage is actually suffered, rather than to make it dependent upon an arbitrary rule.

The commissioners rightly refused to rule "that, in determining the net income of a business under this act, any sum or sums paid by way of salary to partners, all of whom are giving all their time, attention, and activity to it, should not be deducted." Such sums as are allowed to partners as a reasonable compensation for services rendered in a business are rightly deducted in determining the value of the business as a producer of income, and in assessing damages for interference with it.

The proposition "that the value of the good will of a business is ascertainable as a matter of law at so many years' purchase of the average annual net profits of the business prior to the taking," stated in the tenth request for a ruling, was erroneous. The net profits of the business for several years prior to the taking were important evidence as to the value of the good will, but for many reasons they might be more or less than would be likely to be earned later.

The request "that upon the evidence the court must find a total destruction of the business initiated by the passage of the act" has not been considered in argument, except on the question whether the commissioners were bound to report the whole evidence. The twelfth ruling requested was given with a modification, namely, that the income of the business after the passage of the act might be considered in determining the injury to the business caused by the act. This modification was plainly right.

Motion to recommit denied. Report accepted.

(185 Mass. 335)

HEBB v. WELCH.

(Supreme Judicial Court of Massachusetts. Suffolk. April 1, 1904.)

CONTRACTS—AMBIGUOUS PHRASE—PAROL EXPLANATION—BREACH—DAMAGES.

1. Parol evidence, though not admissible to vary the terms of a written contract is admissible to explain language in such a contract ambiguous by reason of unexpressed terms.

2. A contract for all the plumbing work in a stable and house provided that it should be accepted by the plumbing inspectors of the city, and referred to a "drain for soil pipe to cesspool," and "lay a six-inch Akron drain pipe from soil pipe to cesspool," but contained no requirement that a soil pipe should be put in the stable. *Held*, on an issue whether the contract required a soil pipe in the stable, that the contract was ambiguous, and hence evidence showing what "all plumbing" meant, and that a soil pipe would be necessary to render the plumbing acceptable to the inspectors, was competent.

3. Where a contractor for plumbing in a building failed to put in required appliances, the measure of the owner's damages was the cost of labor and material necessary to put in the appliances.

Exceptions from Superior Court, Suffolk County; Daniel W. Bond, Judge.

Action by one Hebb against one Welch, trustee. Judgment for plaintiff, and defendant brings exceptions. Exceptions overruled.

David T. Montague and Wade Keyes, for plaintiff. John A. Sullivan and John M. Maloney, for defendant.

BRALEY, J. This is an action of contract brought by the plaintiff to recover damages by reason of the failure of the defendant to carry out and perform an agreement in writing by which he undertook "to do all the plumbing work on two houses and one stable * * * according to the plans and specifications * * * the work to be completed in a substantial and thorough manner accepted by the plumbing inspectors of the city of Boston and to the satisfaction of the said W. C. Hebb." The defendant

¶ 3. See Damages, vol. 15, Cent. Dig. §§ 222, 224.

failed and refused to put in a soil pipe in the stable and make the necessary connections, claiming that this work was not required under the contract and specifications. At the trial in the superior court, without a jury, this contention was not sustained, and he was found liable in damages by reason of his failure to perform the contract; and, under his exceptions, this raises the principal question in the case.

The rule invoked by the defendant, that parol evidence is not admissible to vary the terms of a written contract, is well settled. St. Louis Mutual Ins. Co. v. Homer, 9 Metc. 39, 40. But it does not apply when the language used is ambiguous by reason of unexpressed terms, and resort must be had to extrinsic evidence to determine the meaning and extent of the language employed by the contracting parties. Such evidence is admissible, not to vary what is written, but to complete the instrument. Sargent v. Adams, 3 Gray, 72, 63 Am. Dec. 718; Stoops v. Smith, 100 Mass. 63-66, 1 Am. Rep. 85, 97 Am. Dec. 76; Keller v. Webb, 125 Mass. 88, 28 Am. Rep. 209; New England Dressed Meat and Wool Co. v. Standard Worsted Co., 165 Mass. 328-332, 43 N. E. 112, 52 Am. St. Rep. 516. In the contract under consideration the specifications for the stable, among other things, referred to a "drain for soil pipe to cesspool," and "lay a six-inch Akron drain pipe from soil pipe to cesspool," but contained no requirement that a soil pipe should be put in the stable. At the trial the defendant claimed that under it he had not contracted to put in a soil pipe, and resort must be had to the meaning of the words "all plumbing work on * * * one stable * * * and work to be * * * accepted by the plumbing inspectors of the city of Boston," to ascertain if his contention can be supported. In order to determine what was the intention of the parties, the conversation of the plaintiff with the defendant at and before the signing of the contract, in which the various items of work were discussed, including the plumbing in the stable, in order to fix the contract price, was competent, as well as evidence of what was necessary to be done in order that the plumbing might be "accepted by the plumbing inspectors of the city of Boston." Keller v. Webb, ubi supra. This testimony did not contradict any of the terms of the writing, but only showed in detail what was included under the general expressions used of "all plumbing," and that a soil pipe would be required in the stable before such plumbing would be acceptable to the inspectors. New England Dressed Meat & Wool Co. v. Standard Worsted Co., ubi supra; Alvord v. Cook, 174 Mass. 120, 54 N. E. 499. When the defendant declined to carry out the contract as proved, the plaintiff had a legal right to recover compensation for all damages he had suffered. Such damages would be measured by the cost of labor and materials necessary to finish the designated work, and which the defendant had failed to perform. Olds v. Mapes-Reeve Construction Co., 177 Mass. 41-43, 58 N. E. 478; National Machine & Tool Co. v. Standard Machinery Co., 181 Mass. 275-278, 63 N. E. 900. All the evidence is not reported, but enough appears in the bill of exceptions to make it apparent that this was the rule of law followed by the superior court.

Exceptions overruled.

(185 Mass. 426)

In re SULLIVAN.

(Supreme Judicial Court of Massachusetts. Suffolk. April 1, 1904.)

ATTORNEYS—DISBARMENT — REINSTATEMENT — ORDER DENYING WITHOUT PREJUDICE TO ANOTHER PETITION.

1. The provision in an order denying a petition for reinstatement as an attorney that it is denied without prejudice to the filing of another petition of like tenor after a designated future date relieves the petitioner from the effect of the order on a petition filed after the designated date, and does not preclude him from a hearing on the merits on a petition filed before that date, founded on other facts, and is not objectionable.

Appeal from Superior Court, Suffolk County; Francis A. Gaskill, Judge.

Petition by Cornelius P. Sullivan for reinstatement as an attorney and counselor at law. From an order denying the petition without prejudice to the filing of another petition after a specified date, the petitioner appeals. Affirmed.

Cornelius P. Sullivan, pro se.

KNOWLTON, C. J. The petition recites that the petitioner was duly admitted to practice as an attorney and counselor at law in the courts of this commonwealth, and that he was subsequently disbarred by a decree of the superior court. He asks that the decree may be vacated, or so far modified as to permit his reinstatement and readmission as an attorney. The order of the superior court is as follows: "Petition of Cornelius P. Sullivan for reinstatement as attorney at law denied, without prejudice to his filing another petition of like tenor after July 1, 1906." The record shows no finding of fact, nor any statement of evidence. The only question of law before us is whether, as the petitioner contends, that part of the order which relates to the filing of another petition is illegal. This petition purports to be founded largely on matters involved in the proceedings at the time of his disbarment, and, more than anything else, is a petition for a review of those proceedings. If the order stopped with the word "denied," and if a petition founded on the same averments should be hereafter filed, the court might treat the matter as res judicata, and hold that the judgment on this petition was a bar. It was doubtless for the benefit of the petitioner, and to relieve him from this effect of the order on a petition filed after July 1, 1906, that the provision as to another petition was added. We do not understand the provision as intended to preclude the petitioner from a hearing on the merits upon a petition filed before July 1, 1906, founded on facts not included in the present petition. Doubtless the court could not make an order which would have that effect. We construe this part of the order as wholly favorable to the petitioner, and as free from legal objection.

Order affirmed.

(185 Mass. 414)

EMERSON, Tax Collector, v. TRUSTEES OF MILTON ACADEMY.

(Supreme Judicial Court of Massachusetts. Norfolk. April 1, 1904.)

TAXATION OF REAL ESTATE—PROPERTY OF LITERARY INSTITUTION—EXEMPTION.

1. The real estate of an academy, contiguous with the school site, and occupied by the residences of teachers and as playgrounds for the pupils, is exempt from taxation under Rev. Laws, c. 12, § 5, cl. 3, exempting the real estate of literary institutions, owned and occupied by them or their officers for the purposes for which they are incorporated.

Report from Superior Court, Norfolk County; Wm. Schofield, Judge.

Action by one Emerson, as tax collector, against the trustees of Milton Academy. On report from the superior court. Judgment for plaintiff affirmed.

Felix Rackemann and Ralph W. Dunbar, for plaintiff. Louis D. Brandeis and William H. Dunbar, for defendant.

KNOWLTON, C. J. This is an action to recover taxes assessed upon the real estate of the defendant corporation. The case is submitted upon an agreed statement of facts, with an agreement that the court may draw any proper inferences from the facts stated. From a judgment for the defendant, the plaintiff appealed to this court. The only question is whether the court was warranted in finding for the defendant upon the competent facts stated.

The judge found that Milton Academy is a literary institution, within the meaning of Rev. Laws, c. 12, § 5, cl. 3, and that all the property described in the agreed statement consists of real estate owned and occupied by the academy or its officers for the purposes for which the academy was incorporated. The land in question consists of three lots—the Hunt lot, the Ware lot, and the Vose lot—together containing about 33 acres. Besides these, the defendant owns the original academy lot, of small area, which is agreed to be exempt from taxation, and another lot, not connected with it, which is agreed to be taxable. The plaintiff contends, as matter of law, that the agreed facts do not warrant a finding that the three first mentioned lots are occupied for the purposes for which the defendant was incorporated.

The law applicable to cases of this kind was considered at some length in Mt. Hermon Boys' School v. Gill, 145 Mass. 139, 13 N. E. 354, and more fully in the recent case of Phillips Academy v. Andover, 175 Mass. 118, 55 N. E. 841, 48 L. R. A. 550. It has also been applied under varying conditions in many other cases. Massachusetts General Hospital v. Somerville, 101 Mass. 319; Williams College v. Williamstown, 167 Mass. 505, 46 N. E. 394; Amherst College v. Amherst, 173 Mass. 232, 53 N. E. 815; Harvard College v. Cambridge, 175 Mass. 145, 55 N. E. 844, 48 L. R. A. 547. The same principle runs through all these decisions. It is that the purposes mentioned in the statute refer to the direct and immediate result of the occupation of the property, and not to the consequential benefit to be derived from the use of it. An occupation and use of real estate to produce income to be expended for the purposes for which the institution was incorporated is not within the statute, while an occupation whose dominant purpose is directly to accomplish some one of the objects for which the corporation was established is within it. If incidentally there are results of the use which would not entitle the property to exemption, that is immaterial, so long as the dominant purpose of the occupation is within the statute. The dominant purpose of the managing officers of the corporation in the use of the property which they direct or permit is often, although not always, controlling. So long as they act in good faith, and not unreasonably, in determining how to occupy and use the real estate of the corporation, their determination cannot be interfered with by the courts. There may be honest differences of opinion among persons of good judgment as to whether it is wise to use real estate in a particular way for its direct effect in promoting the purposes for which an educational corporation was established. In such cases the managing officers have the responsibility and duty of deciding. A decision plainly unreasonable, which affects the rights of third parties, might be disregarded by the court in a case of this kind, but a decision within the limits of reasonable determination should be given effect.

Upon two of these lots there were dwelling houses, with their appurtenances, occupied by teachers in the academy with their families, under an arrangement with each teacher that he should be paid a stated sum per annum, and, in addition, should have the use of the dwelling house. It is agreed that the defendant deems it important to have several masters living on the academy premises, as an aid in preserving discipline, and in bringing about closer relations with the pupils, and that the arrangements with these teachers were made with this end in view. The corporation has adopted this use of these

¶ 1. See Taxation, vol. 45, Cent. Dig. §§ 396, 397.

houses as a settled policy. The three lots in question adjoin the original academy lot and one another, and the boundary fences formerly standing between them have been removed. On the Vose lot a baseball field has been prepared, about 2½ acres in area, with additional space for spectators and less frequent plays when the ball is batted to a long distance, making the whole area about 4 acres. On the Ware lot there is a football field, which, with additional space required for players and for spectators, occupies about 2 acres. The Vose lot, containing about 14 acres, was received by gift from Miss Sarah Forbes Hughes, and by unanimous vote of the trustees was accepted on the following terms in part, namely: "Said land shall not be built upon, but shall be kept open for a playground for all pupils of said Milton Academy, except that at any time the said trustees may, in their discretion, select about one and one-fourth acres of said land near the southerly boundary thereof, for the purpose of building a suitable house and other buildings thereon for the use of the head master of Milton Academy; except that at any time the said trustees may, in their discretion, select about one-half an acre of said land near the northerly boundary thereof, and may place or build and maintain thereon a building or buildings belonging to said academy; except that at any time the said trustees may, in their discretion, select a site near the easterly or southerly boundary thereof, and place or build and maintain thereon a gymnasium or other athletic building; and except that said trustees may, if they deem it advisable, convey to the town of Milton, for such consideration as they deem best, such strip or strips of land as may be necessary to widen the adjoining streets to the limit of one hundred feet or less, but no more. If at any future time said Milton Academy shall cease to be a nonsectarian school, or shall be removed to other premises than those now occupied by it, all of said land shall be conveyed by said Milton Academy to the town of Milton for a public playground; but nothing in this shall be so construed as to give to the town of Milton any rights of any kind whatsoever in regard to said land, until such forfeiture or abandonment shall have taken place." Of the Ware lot, comprising about 16⅙ acres, from one-third to one-half is low and swampy. This part could be used and improved for buildings or for any purpose requiring a firm, dry field, only at large expense. Of the remainder, a part is thinly wooded in places, with small trees, growing near together, and in other places with large trees, detached or in small groves, and a part is pasture, with a poor growth of grass and small shrubs. "The defendant deems it important for the health and enjoyment of the pupils of the academy, and essential for the maintenance of the academy and the successful accomplishment of its purposes, that the grounds of the academy should furnish ample opportunity for recreation in the open air, and that the pupils should have at least all the open space now furnished by the academy grounds for exercise and recreation, and the academy desires to keep at least the whole area of these fields for such use. The defendant also deems it important for the interests of the academy maintained by it, and the successful accomplishment of its purposes, that the school buildings and grounds should be protected against the close proximity of other buildings, and against the possible use of land near the academy for purposes detrimental to the academy. In the judgment of the defendant's officers, all of the land then and now owned by it, as shown on the plan, was and is required for these purposes. The pupils do in fact constantly use the unimproved parts of the fields above referred to as recreation grounds, walking and roaming over them, playing games that do not require the ground to be improved or laid out, and going into the swampy part for amusement, and in the winter for some rough skating. It has always been the purpose of the defendant, since their acquisition, that such use should be made of the fields."

We have no doubt, upon the facts agreed, that the officers of the defendant corporation, in good faith, are occupying and intending to occupy this real estate in a way which they deem directly promotive of the purposes for which the defendant was incorporated. In view of the location of this academy, the number of its students, and the kind of educational work which it was intended to do, we cannot say that the occupation of these three lots in the manner described, with a view to the direct effect, in a broad way, upon the education of the scholars, is so unreasonable as to be forbidden to the trustees under the law. The amount of land so held and used is considerable, and, if the corporation was limited by strict necessity, less would be sufficient; but it properly may avail itself of opportunities to provide liberally for the physical training, and the social, moral, and esthetic advancement of the pupils who are intrusted to its charge. The justice of the superior court was authorized by the parties to draw proper inferences of fact, and we are of opinion that he was well warranted in finding that the property was occupied for the purposes for which the defendant was incorporated, within the meaning of the statute relative to exemption from taxation. The incidental uses which have been made of the barn and shed and stables connected with the dwelling houses do not deprive the property of its exemption from taxation. These uses are like those which were held permissible, in connection with other uses for educational purposes, in Trustees of Wesleyan Academy v. Wilbraham, 99 Mass. 599, and in Mt. Hermon Boys' School v. Gill, 145 Mass. 139, 13 N. E. 354.

Judgment affirmed.

(185 Mass. 422)

CONVERSE v. UNITED SHOE MACHINERY CO. et al.

(Supreme Judicial Court of Massachusetts. Suffolk. April 1, 1904.)

CORPORATIONS—CONSPIRACY TO INJURE—RIGHT OF STOCKHOLDER TO SUE.

1. An action at law cannot be maintained by a stockholder of a corporation for conspiracy to injure and ruin the corporation.

Appeal from Superior Court, Suffolk County.

Action by one Converse against the United Shoe Machinery Company and others. From a judgment for defendants, plaintiff appeals. Affirmed.

Whipple, Sears & Ogden, for plaintiff. C. A. Hight, for defendants.

KNOWLTON, C. J. This is an action at law brought against the defendant corporation and the three other defendants, who were sued personally, for conspiring to injure and ruin another corporation, the Guddu Sons Metal Fastening Company, in which the plaintiff is a stockholder. The averments of the declaration are, in substance, that the three personal defendants "conceived a plan of acquiring, by purchase or otherwise, the control of said Guddu Sons Metal Fastening Company, and of absorbing its rights, patents, and other property into the said United Shoe Machinery Company, of which they were officers and directors," and that afterwards, combining and conspiring with the defendant corporation to injure the property of the other corporation, they acquired a majority of the stock of this other corporation, and elected themselves directors and officers thereof, and, as such officers and directors, were guilty of various misfeasances in the control and management of the corporation, greatly to the injury and damage thereof, and of the plaintiff's share and interest therein. Each of the defendants demurred to the declaration, and the case is before us on the plaintiff's appeal from a judgment for the defendant, founded on an order sustaining the demurrer. Numerous grounds of demurrer are stated, several of which we need not consider.

The defendants contend that the declaration is vague and indefinite, and that it does not set forth with sufficient certainty the cause of action relied on. We will not stop to consider this part of the demurrer, for, if it is overruled, there are other particulars in which the case stated fails to show a ground of recovery. All the wrongs done or intended, set out in the declaration, are wrongs against the corporation in which the plaintiff is a stockholder, and, except through the corporation, they have no relation to the plaintiff. She was not affected by the defendants' conduct, except as every other stockholder was affected. Against her as an individual there was no conspiracy, and against her as an individual no wrong was done directly. There is no direct legal privity between her, individually or as a stockholder, and these defendants. She has an interest in the corporation, and in the conduct of its officers affecting its property; but this interest in the transactions of the officers is not legal, but equitable, and it cannot be made the foundation of an action at law against the officers. That an action at law cannot be maintained in a case of this kind was clearly shown by Chief Justice Shaw in Smith v. Hurd, 12 Metc. 371, 46 Am. Dec. 690. The plaintiff must find her remedy for such a wrong through a suit by the corporation or through a bill in equity, if she is unable to induce action of the corporation or its officers for the benefit of stockholders. Peabody v. Flint, 6 Allen, 52; Brewer v. Boston Theatre Company, 104 Mass. 378; Dunphy v. Traveller Newspaper Association, 146 Mass. 495, 16 N. E. 426; Richardson v. Clinton Wall Trunk Company, 181 Mass. 580, 64 N. E. 400; Allen v. Curtis, 26 Conn. 456; Conway v. Halsey, 44 N. J. Law, 462; Ritchie v. McMullen, 79 Fed. 522, 25 C. C. A. 50. The averment of conspiracy adds nothing, in legal effect, to the other averments of the declaration. Parker v. Huntington, 2 Gray, 124–127; May v. Wood, 172 Mass. 11, 51 N. E. 191.

Judgment affirmed.

(185 Mass. 424)

NATIONAL BANK OF THE REPUBLIC v. DELANO et al.

(Supreme Judicial Court of Massachusetts. Suffolk. April 1, 1904.)

NOTES—JOINT MAKER—HUSBAND AND WIFE—NOTE TO HUSBAND—VALIDITY OF CONTRACT.

1. Pub. St. 1882, c. 77, § 15, providing that every person becoming a party to a note by signature in blank on the back thereof should be entitled to notice of nonpayment, the same as an indorser, did not render one who so signed a note before it was delivered and took effect as a binding contract liable other than as a joint maker.

2. A wife cannot become liable to her husband on a note, whether her relation to it is that of a maker or indorser.

3. Where one signs a note on the back in pursuance of a previous agreement, he is a joint maker, and not an indorser, even though the note had taken effect prior to his signature.

Exceptions from Superior Court, Suffolk County; Robt. R. Bishop, Judge.

Action by the National Bank of the Republic against Mrs. Lizzie Delano and another. Verdict for defendants, and plaintiff brings exceptions. Exceptions overruled.

Charles H. Sprague, for plaintiff. S. L. Whipple and J. B. Crawford, for defendants.

KNOWLTON, C. J. The exceptions in this case relate to 5 of the 16 promissory notes on which the suit was brought. These notes, bearing date November 13, 1897, were

¶ 2. See Bills and Notes, vol. 7, Cent. Dig. § 568.

signed by C. R. Delano, were payable to the order of George S. Delano, and on the back of each appeared the following indorsements: "Mrs. Lizzie Delano. Pay to the order of National Bank of the Republic, Boston, Mass. George S. Delano." The payee and the defendant were husband and wife, and the maker of the notes was their son. The notes were given by the son to the father in payment for a three-eighths interest in his business, in connection with the formation of a partnership between them. According to the testimony of the defendant, she signed them before they were signed by her son. According to the testimony of her husband, she brought them to him with his son's signature upon them, and gave them to him while he was eating his dinner, and he put them into his pocket and kept them until the meal was over, when he asked her to sign them, and she immediately affixed her signature.

The exception is to the direction of a verdict for the defendant on the ground that she was a joint maker of these notes running to her husband, and that her contract was void. If she signed before the notes were delivered and took effect as binding contracts, she was a joint maker, under the law of Massachusetts in force when the notes were made. Union Bank v. Willis, 8 Metc. 504, 41 Am. Dec. 541; Bryant v. Eastman, 7 Cush. 111; Pearson v. Stoddard, 9 Gray, 199; Richardson v. Boynton, 12 Allen, 138, 90 Am. Dec. 141. See Rev. Laws, c. 73, § 81. St. 1874, p. 463, c. 404 (Pub. St. 1882, c. 77, § 15), which required demand and notice to hold parties signing in that way, still left their promise that of joint makers. State Street Trust Company v. Owen, 162 Mass. 156-160, 38 N. E. 438; Mulcare v. Welch, 160 Mass. 58, 35 N. E. 97; Legg v. Vinal, 165 Mass. 555, 43 N. E. 518; Brooks v. Stackpole, 168 Mass. 537, 47 N. E. 419. A promissory note made by a husband to his wife, or by a wife to her husband, is absolutely void; and the same rule applies to a contract of indorsement, and to any other contract purporting to create a liability upon a note. Fowle v. Torrey, 135 Mass. 93; Roby v. Phelon, 118 Mass. 541; Browning v. Carson, 163 Mass. 255, 39 N. E. 1037; National Granite Company v. Whicher, 173 Mass. 517, 53 N. E. 1004, 73 Am. St. Rep. 317.

These principles are sufficient to sustain the ruling and dispose of the case, unless the evidence of the husband that he had the notes in his possession a short time before the defendant signed them makes a difference. If her signing was in pursuance of a previous agreement, she would be a joint maker, even though the notes had taken effect before she signed. Hawkes v. Phillips, 7 Gray, 284; Moles v. Bird, 11 Mass. 436, 6 Am. Dec. 179. If she signed after the notes had taken effect, her contract, whether of guaranty, or of whatever kind that purported to create a legal obligation, was still a contract with her husband, made upon notes held by him as owner, and it was void, as it would have been if she had signed as a maker or indorser. Chapman v. Kellogg, 102 Mass. 246; Abbott v. Winchester, 105 Mass. 115. In every possible aspect of the evidence, the contract of the defendant which appears upon the note was a contract with her husband, and was therefore void.

Exceptions overruled.

(186 Mass. 341)

ROTH v. ADAMS et al.

RAND et al. v. SAME.

(Supreme Judicial Court of Massachusetts. Suffolk. April 1, 1904.)

LANDLORD AND TENANT—DUTIES OF LANDLORD—REPAIRS—BREACH OF COVENANT—EVICTION—IMPLIED WARRANTIES—GUARANTY OF RENT—BREACH—APPEAL—WAIVER OF OBJECTIONS.

1. A guaranty of payment of rent, under seal, imports a consideration, sufficient to support it as a binding agreement, whether executed concurrently with or after the signing of the lease.

2. Where a guaranty of payment of rent contains no requirement that the lessor should obtain judgment against the lessee as a condition precedent to the guarantor's being called on to make payment, no such requirement is implied, and a failure of the guarantor to pay the rent when due is a breach of his covenant, and a cause of action in favor of the lessor at once accrues against him.

3. Where, under the terms of a guaranty of payment of rent, it was the duty of the guarantor to ascertain whether the lessee had kept his covenants with the lessor or her representatives, neither she nor they were required to give notice of the lessee's default before bringing suit against the guarantor.

4. The fact that a lessor permitted a portion of the premises which remained in her possession and control to fall into a state of decay, to the personal annoyance of the lessee, does not necessarily prove such an interference with the lessee's occupancy of the demised premises as to amount to either an eviction or breach of the covenant for quiet enjoyment.

5. In the absence of fraud or concealment by the lessor of the condition of the estate at the date of the lease, the rule of caveat emptor applies, for there is no implied warranty on the part of the landlord that the premises are tenantable, or even reasonably suitable for occupation.

6. Unless the landlord agrees in the lease to make repairs or remedy defects, decay and dilapidation of the buildings are no defense to an action for the accruing rent against either the tenant or a guarantor of the rent.

7. Exceptions abandoned by plaintiff in argument if one defendant should be held liable are treated as waived, such defendant being held liable.

Exceptions from Superior Court, Suffolk County; Henry N. Sheldon, Judge.

Separate actions of contract by Bridget Roth and by Arnold A. Rand and others, executors, against Roland M. Adams, lessee, and Charles S. Hall, his guarantor. In the superior court plaintiffs excepted to a ruling that a lessee and guarantor could not be pursued in the same action, and defendant Hall

¶ 5. See Landlord and Tenant, vol. 32, Cent. Dig. §§ 441, 443.

excepted to a verdict for plaintiffs against him. Exceptions overruled.

Henry F. Naphen, Walter A. Buie, and Charles H. Morris, for plaintiffs. J. W. Pickering, for defendant Chas. S. Hall.

BRALEY, J. The short form of guaranty written on the lease follows the language of a similar contract construed in Sartwell v. Humphrey, 136 Mass. 396, and the nature of the undertaking of the defendants is clearly and precisely expressed. Being an instrument under seal, a consideration is presumed, and is sufficient to support it as a binding agreement, whether executed concurrently with or at a time subsequent to the signing of the lease. Hayes v. Kyle, 8 Allen, 300, 301. By its stipulations the punctual performance on the part of the lessee of the covenants of the lease was guarantied. It is not contended that the executors, or their testatrix in her lifetime, designedly allowed the rent to become in arrears in order to favor the lessee, the principal debtor, to the injury of the guarantor; and a failure by him to pay the rent reserved at the time when it became due and payable would be a breach of his covenant, and a cause of action would at once accrue to the lessor against the defendant. No limitation of the nature now suggested by him is expressed in the contract, and, while he might have made his promise to pay contingent on the failure of his principal to pay any judgment the lessor might recover if he failed to keep this covenant, it is a sufficient answer to say that he did not do so, but was content to make his liability unconditional and absolute.

If there was no express requirement in the contract of guaranty that the lessor should first obtain judgment for the rent against the lessee as a condition precedent to his being called upon to make payment, none is to be read into it by implication, and it must be construed like any written agreement, where the parties have seen fit clearly to state the extent of an obligation by which they are severally to be bound. Under its terms it became the duty of the defendant to ascertain whether the lessee had kept his covenants with the plaintiff, or her representatives, and neither she nor they were required first to give notice of this default of the lessee before bringing suit against the defendant. Welch v. Walsh, 177 Mass. 555, 59 N. E. 440.

No discussion of the joinder of both as parties defendant in this case is called for, as the plaintiffs at the trial, under a ruling sufficiently favorable to the defendant, and made at his request, were compelled to elect between them, and made their election to pursue him alone.

In the next question presented by the defendant's exceptions he contends that the evidence offered by him that the board of health had condemned a portion of the premises as dangerous, and unfit for habitation, was wrongly excluded, because such condemnation amounted to an eviction by the lessor, which would either suspend payment of the rent or justify their abandonment by the lessee. Independently of the facts that the tenant took the leasehold estate whether it included the brick building alone or in addition the wooden building and ell, as he found it, that he agreed to keep the premises in repair, that no substantial change of condition had taken place during his tenancy, and that he left solely because his business had declined and trade had followed his former customers to other localities, it is not shown that the lessor or her representatives had interfered with the tenant's estate in such a manner as to exclude him from, or permanently deprive him of, its full use and enjoyment as it existed at the date of the demise. Skally v. Shute, 132 Mass. 367; Smith v. McEnany, 170 Mass. 76, 48 N. E. 781, 64 Am. St. Rep. 272. If, upon conflicting testimony, the jury could have found that the wooden building and ell remained in the possession of the lessor, although she permitted them to fall into a state of decay, to the personal annoyance of the lessee, this does not necessarily prove such an interference with his occupancy of the demised premises as to amount to either an eviction or a breach of the covenant for quiet enjoyment; at least where the tenant still continues in possession and use of them. International Trust Co. v. Schumann, 158 Mass. 291, 33 N. E. 509. Besides, his offer of proof contained no attempt to show any fraud or concealment by the lessor of the condition of the estate at the date of the lease, and the tenant took the premises as he found them, for there is no warranty implied in law on the part of the landlord that they are tenantable, or even reasonably suitable for occupation, and the rule of caveat emptor applies. Stevens v. Pierce, 151 Mass. 207, 23 N. E. 1006; Bertie v. Flagg, 161 Mass. 504, 37 N. E. 572. But by the provisions of the lease the landlord entered into no contract to make any repairs that might be needed, or to remedy defects that might arise during the tenancy of the lessee, and, unless such an agreement is found, the decay and dilapidation of the buildings would not be a defense to an action for the rent as it accrued. Foster v. Peyser, 9 Cush. 242, 248, 57 Am. Dec. 43; Welles v. Castles, 3 Gray, 232, 235; Szathmary v. Adams, 166 Mass. 145, 44 N. E. 124. Such a defense is equally ineffectual by a guarantor who, for the purpose of performing this covenant, by his contract, stands in place of the tenant, and the collateral undertaking is as broad as the terms of the contract guarantied. Clark v. Gordon, 121 Mass. 330; Warren v. Lyons, 152 Mass. 310, 25 N. E. 721, 9 L. R. A. 353.

This discussion of the principles of law involved in the case covers all that is necessary to be said, as the rulings requested and refused stated in different ways the legal propositions already considered. No error of law appears, and, as the plaintiff's exceptions were abandoned at the argument if the defendant was held liable for the rent, we treat them as waived, and the order must be:

Exceptions overruled.

(186 Mass. 448)

CITY OF CAMBRIDGE v. JOHN C. DOW CO.

(Supreme Judicial Court of Massachusetts. Middlesex. April 4, 1904.)

PUBLIC HEALTH—MELTING AND RENDERING ESTABLISHMENT—INJUNCTION—JURISDICTION OF SUPREME JUDICIAL COURT.

1. Rev. Laws, c. 159, § 1, provides that the Supreme Judicial Court and the superior court shall have original jurisdiction of all cases cognizable under the general principles of equity jurisprudence, and section 2 gives to the Supreme Judicial Court original jurisdiction in equity of all cases cognizable under the provisions of the state statutes, and which are not within the jurisdiction conferred by the preceding section, etc. Chapter 75, § 141, provides that the Supreme Judicial Court or the superior court shall have jurisdiction in equity, upon the application of the board of health of a city or town, to enforce such board's orders. Section 108 provides that whoever uses a building for a melting or rendering establishment, without first obtaining the written consent of the mayor and aldermen, etc., and a board of health, if any, shall forfeit a certain sum for each month, etc., the provision not to apply to premises so occupied on May 8, 1871. Section 110 gives the superior court jurisdiction in equity to restrain the occupancy, etc., of any building for such purposes. Section 111, as originally enacted in St. 1901, p. 86, c. 134, provided that any person, etc., engaged in "killing horses, or in the rendering of horses or other animals," should make application to the board of health for a license. In the Revised Laws this was changed to read, "killing horses or in the carrying on of a melting or rendering establishment," etc., but the rest of the section retains the language of the statute of 1901, and shows that the section was intended to apply to a melting and rendering establishment used in connection with dead horses or other large animals. The remedy for violating section 111 is a fine or imprisonment. *Held*, that the Supreme Judicial Court had no jurisdiction of a bill by a city, having a board of health, to enjoin a melting and rendering establishment carried on since 1860, without a license, in which horses were never killed, and neither horses nor other dead animals rendered, it not appearing that the board of health had passed a general or special order applicable to the case.

Case Reserved from Supreme Court, Middlesex County; Jas. M. Morton, Judge.

Suit by the City of Cambridge against the John C. Dow Company. Reserved on bill and answer. Bill dismissed.

Gilbert A. A. Pevey, City Sol., for plaintiff. Geo. L. Mayberry, for defendant.

LATHROP, J. This is a bill in equity in which the plaintiff seeks to have the defendant restrained by injunction from carrying on the business of melting and rendering on certain land in Cambridge. The case comes before us on the bill and answer. From these it appears that when the bill was filed the defendant was carrying on, and had carried on continuously since 1860, in Cambridge, without a license, the business of melting and rendering of grease and tallow, and making food for fowls from oyster and other sea shells; but that the defendant never killed horses, and never did any rendering of horses or other dead animals, and never had used or required in its business trucks or wagons for the removal of dead animals. There was a board of health in Cambridge.

The principal question is whether the court has original jurisdiction in the matter. The court undoubtedly has jurisdiction to restrain a nuisance, but there is nothing in this bill to show that the trade carried on by the defendant is a nuisance, or that the board of health, under the powers given it by law, has passed any general or special order applicable to the case, and Rev. Laws, c. 75, § 141, do not apply. The court also has power, aside from its general jurisdiction, when such power is given it by statute.

The plaintiff refers in his brief to Rev. Laws, c. 75, §§ 73, 110, but these sections confer jurisdiction upon the superior court, and have no reference to this court. Nor is there anything in Rev. Laws, c. 159, §§ 1, 2, which affects this case. Section 1 of this chapter gives to both courts "original and concurrent jurisdiction in equity in all cases and matters of equity which are cognizable under the general principles of equity jurisprudence." Section 2 gives to the Supreme Judicial Court "original and exclusive jurisdiction in equity of all cases and matters of equity which are cognizable under the provisions of any statute, and are not within the jurisdiction conferred by the provisions of the preceding section, unless a different provision is made; and the superior court shall have like original and exclusive, or like original and concurrent, jurisdiction only if the statute so provides." The case presented by the bill might come within Rev. Laws, c. 75, § 108, and the jurisdiction would be in the superior court, under section 110, but for the provision in section 108 that "the provisions of the section shall not apply to any building or premises which were occupied or used for such trades or occupations" on May 8, 1871.

The plaintiff further contends that the case comes within Rev. Laws, c. 75, § 111, and that section 108 relates to places, and section 111 to persons. But section 108 applies to persons as much as section 111. By its terms, "Whoever occupies or uses a building for carrying on therein the business of slaughtering cattle, sheep or other animals, or for a melting or rendering establishment," etc., without first obtaining permission of certain boards named, shall pay a certain penalty. Then follows the provision already cited as to buildings. Section 111 is taken from St. 1901, p. 86, c. 134, which began as follows: "Any person, firm or corporation engaged or desiring to engage in the business of killing horses, or in the rendering of horses or other animals, shall * * * make application to the board of health of the city or town where the business is to be conducted, for a license to carry it on." The language of the first part of this section was changed by the joint special committee, on the consolidating and arranging of the Public Statutes, so as to read: "A person, partnership or corporation engaged in or desiring to engage in the business of killing horses, or in the carrying on of a melting or rendering establishment," etc., and in this form the Legislature enacted the law. It may well be doubted, however, whether any change in the law was contemplated either by the committee or the Legislature, or whether any change was in fact made. The rest of the section, which retains the language of the Statutes of 1901, shows that the section has no application to an establishment such as the defendant was carrying on, but was intended to apply to a melting and rendering establishment used in connection with dead horses or other large animals. Thus, before granting a license, the board of health must be "satisfied that the applicants have a suitable building and plant in a situation approved by said board, and that they have suitable trucks or wagons for the removal of dead animals." The board of health is also required to notify the board of cattle commissioners of the granting of any such license. The licensees are required to report to the board of cattle commissioners every animal received by them which is found to be infected with a contagious disease. There is also this further provision: "No unlicensed person shall carry on the business of killing horses or of melting and rendering." It seems to us reasonably clear that "melting and rendering" refers to horses or other large animals whose bodies are received before they are dismembered, and that other kinds of melting and rendering were supposed to be covered by section 108. However this may be, the remedy provided for a violation of the section is a fine or imprisonment, and nothing is said as to any other judicial remedy.

As the plaintiff has not brought the case within the general equity jurisdiction of the court, or within any statute giving this court jurisdiction, the order must be:

Bill dismissed.

(185 Mass. 430)

WILSON v. MULLONEY.

(Supreme Judicial Court of Massachusetts. Suffolk. April 2, 1904.)

EVIDENCE—WRITTEN CONTRACTS—VARIANCE BY PAROL—MORTGAGES—REDEMPTION—CONDITIONS—STRICT PERFORMANCE.

1. The rule that parol evidence is not admissible to vary the terms of a written contract does not apply to third persons who are not parties to the contract.

2. On a bill in equity to redeem a mortgage, the fact that strict performance of the conditions agreed upon has not been had is no defense.

Appeal from Superior Court, Suffolk County; Chas. U. Bell, Judge.

Bill in equity by John C. Wilson against John D. Mulloney. From a decree for plaintiff, defendant appeals. Affirmed.

James P. Barlow and John D. Mulloney, for appellant. Joseph A. Harris, for appellee.

LATHROP, J. This is a bill in equity, filed in the superior court, against the assignee of the Smith & Gardiner Supply Company, to restrain the foreclosure of a mortgage given to the plaintiff by the Automatic Time Stamp & Register Company, and assigned by him as collateral security to the Smith & Gardiner Supply Company. The plaintiff also sought by the bill to redeem the mortgage so assigned, and on payment of the amount due to have the mortgage reassigned to him. The case was sent to a master, and it appears from his report that in March, 1896, the Automatic Time Stamp & Register Company, hereinafter called the "Stamp Company," a manufacturer of certain patented devices for stamping letters and other papers, contemplated a business connection with the Smith & Gardiner Supply Company, hereinafter called the "Supply Company," by which the latter was to become the selling agent of the former's goods within the United States for the period of three years. On March 21, 1896, the plaintiff, who was the president of the stamp company, met the president of the supply company, and the two presidents made the following contract:

"Boston, Mass., March 21, 189-. The Automatic Time Stamp and Register Co., Boston, Mass.—Gentlemen: We have this day loaned you fifteen hundred dollars ($1,500) and have taken your note for three (3) months for that amount, together with an assignment of a mortgage made by your company to John C. Wilson as collateral security for the said loan. We agree to take time stamping, or printing apparatuses at the discount price set forth in a contract entered into by and between your company and the Smith & Gardiner Supply Company, to the amount of fifteen hundred dollars ($1,500) within three (3) months from this date, in the manner above set forth, and upon the full amount of said note being paid without interest as aforesaid, we agree to reassign said mortgage to the said John C. Wilson and to cancel the said note. Smith & Gardiner Supply Co. By John F. McNamee, Treas. [Corporate Seal.]"

The note in question was as follows: "Boston, March 21st, 1896. $1,500.00. For Value received, we promise to pay to Smith & Gardiner Supply Co., or order, the sum of Fifteen hundred Dollars no/100 in Three months from this date. The Automatic Time Stamp

¶ 1. See Evidence, vol. 20, Cent. Dig. § 1967.

& Register Co. Per Lowell M. Palmer, Treas."

On the margin of the note was written: "Secured by assignment as collateral, mortgage of personal property in Boston."

The treasurer of the stamp company delivered the note to the treasurer of the supply company, and received from him in return the company's check for $1,500. On this check the stamp company received $1,500 in cash. On the same day the letter above set forth was written. The supply company afterwards gave orders for goods to the stamp company, which were filled, and further performance of the agreement was abandoned by both parties. On April 18, 1899, the stamp company, by its treasurer, in the presence of the plaintiff, tendered the defendant, as assignee of the supply company, $94.58 in cash, being the balance between the amount of goods furnished, as charged by the stamp company to the supply company, and the amount of the note, and demanded a return of the note. The plaintiff also demanded a reassignment to himself of the mortgage. The master found that the tender was insufficient because it was not made until after the note became due, and no tender was made of interest between the time the note became due and the date of the tender. The plaintiff offered evidence to show that it was understood and agreed between him and the supply company that goods furnished by the stamp company to the supply company should be received and accepted as payments on account of the note, until the same was fully paid. This evidence the master refused to admit, and ruled that there was no ambiguity in the letter of March 21st, or in the note, and that evidence tending to show an understanding or agreement prior to or contemporaneous with the making of these instruments was not admissible. The master thereupon found for the defendant. On the filing of the report in the superior court, it was recommitted to the master to hear the parties further upon the question whether any contract was made between the plaintiff and the supply company as to the application of credits of the stamp company to the release of the plaintiff's mortgage, and, if such contract was made, what were its terms. The master heard the parties, and reported that three witnesses testified that the understanding between the parties was that, when the supply company should have received goods which amounted to the face of the note, the supply company was to reassign to the plaintiff personally the mortgage, which had been assigned by him to the supply company as collateral security for the $1,500. The master reported the evidence on this subject, and it supports a finding in the plaintiff's favor. When the case came before the superior court again, a decree was ordered, on January 12, 1903, "that the mortgage assigned by said plaintiff to the Smith & Gardiner Supply Company be reassigned to the plaintiff upon his paying over to the defendant the sum of $89.58, with interest thereon to date of this decree, amounting in all to $154.69, and that the plaintiff recover costs, to be taxed by the clerk." The case is before us on the defendant's appeal from this decree, taken on January 14, 1903.

We are of opinion that the decree must be affirmed. There is no technical objection to the evidence introduced by the plaintiff to show that the contract alleged to have been made by the defendant was made. The plaintiff was not a party to the contract, and was not bound by its terms. The rule that parol evidence is not admissible to vary the terms of a written contract does not apply to third persons who are not parties to the contract. Badger v. Jones, 12 Pick. 371; Kellogg v. Tompson, 142 Mass. 76, 6 N. E. 860; Spooner v. Cummings, 151 Mass. 313, 23 N. E. 839; McMasters v. Ins. Co. of North America, 55 N. Y. 222, 14 Am. Rep. 239; New Berlin v. Norwich, 10 Johns. 229; Johnson v. Blackman, 11 Conn. 342, 351; Edgerly v. Emerson, 23 N. H. 555, 565, 55 Am. Dec. 207. But, apart from this consideration, the agreement contained in the letter of March 21st was made for the benefit of the plaintiff. He was the owner of the mortgage assigned to the defendant, and was interested to have that mortgage reassigned to him as soon as the $1,500 was paid in the manner stated in the letter. If the defendant chose to make an additional oral contract with him to reassign the mortgage to him upon the performance of the conditions contained in the letter, there is no reason why it should not be held to the performance of the agreement. It cannot seriously be contended that on a bill in equity to redeem a mortgage, the fact that the strict performance of the conditions agreed upon have not been performed is any defense.

Decree affirmed.

(178 N. Y. 208)

ZANDER v. NEW YORK SECURITY & TRUST CO.

(Court of Appeals of New York. April 8, 1904.)

NEGOTIABLE INSTRUMENT—CERTIFICATE OF DEPOSIT—LOSS—INDEMNITY.

1. A trust company issued a certificate of deposit payable to the depositor and her assigns on return of the certificate, which was assignable only on the books of the company. *Held* not a negotiable instrument, and the provision protected the company dealing with the holder thereof, as it appeared on its books, from any liability to persons to whom it might have been transferred without the knowledge of the company.

2. Where a trust company issues a certificate of deposit payable to the depositor and her assigns on the return of the certificate, the company is not estopped to deny its liability to any assignee on its failure to require a return of the certificate as a condition for the payment of the amount deposited, so that on an action by a depositor on a lost certificate he need not first indemnify the company from liability.

Appeal from Supreme Court, Appellate Division, First Department.

Action by Caroline Zander against the New York Security & Trust Company. From a judgment of the Appellate Division (81 N. Y. Supp. 1151) affirming an interlocutory judgment of the Special Term overruling a demurrer to the complaint (78 N. Y. Supp. 900), defendant appeals. Affirmed.

Charles A. Boston, for appellant. Philip L. Wilson, for respondent.

CULLEN, J. The action is brought on a certificate of deposit issued by the defendant to the plaintiff for the sum of $500, which it is alleged the plaintiff has inadvertently lost or destroyed. The complaint further alleged that payment of said certificate had been demanded, but that the defendant refused to pay the same unless the plaintiff would give it a sufficient bond of indemnity against loss by reason of the failure to produce the certificate, which bond the plaintiff has been unable and unwilling to give. To this complaint the defendant demurred as not stating facts sufficient to constitute a cause of action. The demurrer has been overruled, and judgment entered thereon awarding to the plaintiff unconditionally the amount due on the certificate.

The only point the appellant seeks to raise on this appeal is its right to indemnity from liability on the lost certificate. It contends that, as the plaintiff has refused to give such indemnity, the complaint should be held not to state a good cause of action, or at least that the judgment of the courts below should be so modified as to award the plaintiff a recovery only on the delivery of such indemnity. The certificate of deposit which is the subject of this suit is in the following form:

"$500. No. 3711.

"The New York Security and Trust Company.

"New York, July 11, 1901.

"Has received from Caroline Zander the sum of five hundred dollars of current funds, upon which the said company agrees to allow interest at the annual rate of three per cent from this date, and on five days notice will repay, in current funds, the like amount, with interest, to the said Caroline Zander or her assigns, on return of this certificate, which is assignable only on the books of the company. The right is reserved by this company, upon giving five days notice, to reduce the rate, or discontinue the payment of interest on this certificate, or pay the principal, such notice to be given personally or through the mail, directed to the address named in the books of the company."

The defendant's argument is twofold: First, it urges that the certificate is a negotiable instrument; second, that, if it should not be held to be a negotiable instrument, the defendant, on account of the provision therein contained that the amount due is payable on the return of the certificate, would, in analogy to the law relating to certificates of stock, be liable to third parties who might acquire, for value, the certificate. Doubtless a certificate of deposit may be issued in the form of a negotiable instrument. Frank v. Wessels, 64 N. Y. 155. But from our examination of the subject there seems to be no uniform usage in commercial circles or with monetary institutions as to their forms. Some are plainly negotiable, some equally plainly are not negotiable, while between the two extremes are many of the debatable class. The instrument before us is payable to the plaintiff or her assigns. While the usual terms employed to confer negotiability on an instrument for the payment of money are to make it payable to order or bearer, still instruments payable to assigns have been held to be negotiable in cases where it was apparent from the whole nature of the instrument and the language employed that such was intended to be their character. Brainerd v. N. Y. & Harlem R. R. Co., 25 N. Y. 496; Citizens' Savings Bank v. Town of Greenburgh, 173 N. Y. 215, 65 N. E. 978. See Negotiable Instruments Law (chapter 612, p. 724, § 29, Laws 1897). Therefore, had the first sentence of the certificate terminated with the words "on return of this certificate," it might be claimed, not without force, that the certificate was intended to be negotiable. But the words quoted are followed by the provision, "which is assignable only on the books of the company." We think the clear effect and intent of this provision was to render the instrument nonnegotiable, and to protect the company in dealing with the holder of the certificate as such holder might appear on the books of the company, without liability to third parties, to whom, unknown to the defendant, it might have been transferred. If such were not the object, we are at a loss to discover any purpose which it was intended to subserve. This construction is fortified by the subsequent provision for reduction of rate of interest or payment of principal upon notice to the address named in the books of the company. We conclude, therefore, that, from a consideration of the language of the certificate as a whole, it is not a negotiable instrument.

Nor do we think that the defendant can be rendered liable to any assignee by way of estoppel for its failure to require a return of the certificate as a condition for the payment of the amount deposited. The case of stock certificates is not analogous to that of certificates of deposit. The object of requiring a surrender and return of the certificate as a condition precedent to the transfer of stock is to give to such certificates a certain degree of negotiability, which, without this condition, could not be obtained. No consideration of that character is applicable to instruments for the payment of money. If one wishes to make a pecuniary obligation negotiable, the law permits him to do so, and it is readily accomplished by making the obligation payable to bearer or to order. There is therefore no reason in such a case for resorting to the indirect means used in the case of stock certificates—means which are effective only to a limited extent. Moreover, the two instruments differ entirely in character. A stock certificate is merely a muniment or representative of title. The stock which it represents exists apart from the certificate, and its existence is contemplated to endure so long as the corporation continues. The owner, as he appears on the books of the company, is entitled to the dividends or profits, and it is only when he seeks to transfer his title to another that a surrender of the outstanding certificate is required as a condition precedent to the issue of a new one. But an instrument for the payment of money contemplates payment at some time, either at a date fixed or on demand. The condition that the certificate be surrendered at the time of its payment is no more than the law would require without a provision to that effect. Bailey v. County of Buchanan, 115 N. Y. 297, 22 N. E. 155, 6 L. R. A. 562. This condition is qualified, however, by an implied exception in the case of loss or destruction. Frank v. Wessels, supra; Wilcox v. Equitable Life Assurance Society, 173 N. Y. 50, 65 N. E. 857, 93 Am. St. Rep. 579. Such a requirement expressed in a certificate, therefore, does not constitute an estoppel in favor of a purchaser for value, as it would in the case of a stock certificate. As the defendant can incur no liability from the failure to produce and surrender the certificate on its payment, it follows it is not entitled to indemnity.

The judgment appealed from should be affirmed, with costs.

GRAY, O'BRIEN, HAIGHT, MARTIN, and VANN, JJ., concur. PARKER, C. J., absent.

Judgment affirmed.

(178 N. Y. 167)

NEW YORK CEMENT CO. v. CONSOLIDATED ROSENDALE CEMENT CO. et al.

SAME v. CONSOLIDATED ROSENDALE CEMENT CO.

(Court of Appeals of New York. April 5, 1904.)

CANAL — SALE — PUBLIC HIGHWAY—OBSTRUCTION — TOLLS — RIGHTS OF PURCHASER—INJUNCTION—TRIAL—DECISION—LONG OR SHORT FORM.

1. Laws 1899, p. 958, c. 469, authorized the Delaware & Hudson Canal Company to lease, sell, or discontinue its canal. Acting under such statute, the canal company conveyed the entire canal and its appurtenances to a domestic steamboat company, with all the franchises of the grantor in connection with the ownership and operation of the canal. The steamboat company operated the canal for about three years, charging the tolls provided by the act under which the canal company was organized, when it conveyed the east 12 miles of the canal to plaintiff, a domestic manufacturing company, reserving to itself and its successor and a certain person named the right at all times, when the canal was operated, to use it for boats, whether light or loaded, without charges of any kind. The entire canal, except such 12 miles, was abandoned. *Held* that, the entire canal, except the 12 miles, having been abandoned, and the grantee having continued to use said 12 miles for itself and such persons as it saw fit to permit, the said 12 miles are a public highway, and must be regarded, for the purpose of transportation, a public highway, to be operated under the restrictions placed upon the original canal company by the act under which it was organized.

2. Where a cement company, long before the sale of the east 12 miles of the Delaware & Hudson Canal, erected cement works on that part of the canal on the assumption that its product should be conveyed to tide water at rates fixed by the charter of the canal company, it can maintain a bill against the purchaser of the 12 miles of canal from the grantee of the original canal company, restraining it from excluding plaintiff's boats from the canal, and imposing illegal tolls, plaintiff being thereby subjected to damages peculiar to itself, in which the public have no interest.

3. Whether the exercise by the grantee of a canal company of a franchise granted by the state to the canal company is ultra vires is a question between the state and such purchaser, which the purchaser is estopped from raising by assuming that the canal is its private property, kept open for its private use.

4. After introduction of certain evidence on a case brought to trial before a jury, an agreed statement of facts was spread upon the record, whereupon plaintiff rested. Defendant moved to dismiss on the ground that facts constituting a cause of action had not been proved. *Held*, that on the grant of such motion and judgment entered in accordance therewith there can be no decision in the short or long form, and consequently no presumption of facts found in favor of the successful party.

O'Brien, J., dissenting.

Appeals from Supreme Court, Appellate Division, Third Department.

Actions by the New York Cement Company against the Consolidated Rosendale Cement Company and others and the same plaintiff against the Consolidated Rosendale Cement Company. From judgments of the Appellate Division (81 N. Y. Supp. 1137) affirming judgment in favor of defendants, plaintiff appeals. Reversed.

John J. Linson, for appellant. A. T. Clearwater and Alfred C. Pettè, for respondents.

BARTLETT, J. Action No. 1 seeks to prevent the collection of illegal canal tolls, and action No. 2 to restrain defendant from excluding plaintiff's boats and freight from the canal in question. These actions were tried and argued together on one set of briefs, although there are two records. No opinions were written below after the trial of the actions, but two were handed down at Special Term and one in the Appellate Division on motions for injunctions pendente lite. 37 Misc. Rep. 746, 76 N. Y. Supp. 469; 38 Misc.

Rep. 518, 77 N. Y. Supp. 1093; 76 App. Div. 285, 78 N. Y. Supp. 531.

The question presented by these appeals is an exceedingly narrow one when the facts, as settled by agreement, are carefully considered. The Delaware & Hudson Canal Company, by grant of the Legislature of this state (Laws 1823, p. 305, c. 238), constructed a canal between the Delaware and Hudson rivers, a distance of 110 miles, and operated the same for over 70 years as a common carrier of coal and other freight, charging tolls fixed by the act of 1823. This court held, when a subsequent enlargement of the canal was in progress, that the Delaware & Hudson Canal Company possessed the power under its charter to exercise the right of eminent domain. It was also held that the canal, "though not strictly a public work, is yet of the nature of one, as much as a railroad, and is to be regarded as a public work in the same sense." Selden v. D. & H. C. Co., 29 N. Y. 634, 638, 641, 642. In 1899 the Legislature amended the act of 1823 (Laws 1899, p. 958, c. 469) in important particulars by inserting therein certain new sections. We are concerned with sections 3 and 4. Section 3 reads as follows: "Whenever it shall appear to the managers of said canal company that it is able to fulfill the aforesaid purpose of opening and of mining and bringing to market a supply of stone coal which is found in the interior of the state of Pennsylvania more economically by rail over its own or other lines than by its canal, it shall be lawful for said company, and it is hereby authorized and empowered by vote of said managers, to lease, sell or discontinue to use or maintain said canal, or any parts thereof, which in their judgment are no longer necessary for said purpose." The managers of the canal company were thus authorized to do one of three things at their election, viz., lease, sell, or discontinue to use or maintain said canal, or any parts thereof. On the 24th day of June, 1899, the Delaware & Hudson Canal Company conveyed to the Cornell Steamboat Company, a domestic corporation, the entire canal and its appurtenances, and "all the franchises owned, possessed, used, or enjoyed by the grantor in connection with the ownership, use, and operation of said canal." The Cornell Steamboat Company continued to operate said canal in the same manner as its predecessor, charging only the tolls provided by the act of 1823, until about the 20th of March, 1902, when it conveyed, by deed similar to the one it had received, the east 12 miles of said canal, beginning at the tide lock at Eddyville, in the town of Ulster, county of Ulster, and ending at the easterly line of the town of Marbletown, in said county. It is conceded that at the time of this conveyance to the defendant the remaining part of the canal, extending westerly about 98 miles to Honesdale, in Pennsylvania, had been entirely abandoned. The plaintiff and defendant are large manufacturers of hydraulic cement, their works being on the line of said 12 miles of canal. The defendant's is located near the westerly end thereof, and the plaintiff's is about five miles from the Hudson river. The plaintiff corporation transported its cement by this canal to tide water for many years, and until shortly after the conveyance to the defendant corporation by the Cornell Steamboat Company on or about March 26, 1902, paying only the tolls provided by the act of 1823, being a fraction less than four cents per barrel. The Cornell Steamboat Company, in conveying to the defendant corporation, reserved to itself, its successors and assigns, and to a certain person named, his heirs, legal representatives, or assigns, the right at all times, so long as said canal is operated, to pass canal boats through the canal, whether light or loaded with sand, stone, or cement slag, without paying toll or charges of any kind therefor.

It appears in the agreed statement of facts that after the defendant company had acquired the 12 miles of canal aforesaid it claimed to own that portion of the canal as a private waterway, and that it kept it open and in operation for its own private use only; that it was under no obligation to allow the plaintiff or any other person to use it and to transport their goods thereon, but it offered, for the accommodation of the plaintiff, to allow it such use and transportation if it would pay therefor at the rate of 16 cents per barrel for the cement so transported; and it claimed that, unless the plaintiff would pay the sum asked by the defendant company, it could be excluded from the canal. Thereupon the plaintiff, after making tender of the legal rates of toll, began the two actions to which reference has already been made, insisting that the tolls were prohibitory.

It is to be observed that in this agreed statement of the facts it is not admitted by the plaintiff that this canal is a private waterway, and that it is kept open and in operation only for the private use of the defendant company. The statement is that this situation is claimed by the defendant company, and the one important question presented by this appeal is whether this remaining 12 miles of canal has been in law abandoned and discontinued. There was no effort made to prove at the trial that this portion of the canal had been abandoned in conformity to the provisions of section 4 of the act of 1899. The provisions of this section are most significant, and disclose what the Legislature had in mind when it provided for the discontinuance of the canal, or any parts thereof. Section 4 reads as follows: "Whenever the said company shall exercise the power and authority granted in section three of this act to discontinue to use or maintain said canal, or any part thereof, it shall, within a reasonable time thereafter, restore the highway crossings of such part of said canal as is so discontinued to their former state, so far as the same can be done, either by the removal of the bridges thereover and the approaches thereto and filling in the bed of the canal at such crossings, or in such other way as may be found most practicable for that purpose. It shall also be the duty of said company, in the event of such discontinuance of said canal, or any part thereof, to make such provision for the private crossings over that part of said canal so discontinued as will furnish those entitled thereto a suitable crossing thereover, either by the removal of the bridges and approaches now existing at and for such private crossings and filling in the bed of the canal thereat, or in such other way as may be found most practicable for that purpose. It shall also be the duty of said company, in the event of such discontinuance of said canal or any part thereof, to make such provision for the streams now discharging into said canal on that part of it which may be so discontinued as will restore them to their original channels; but where to make such restoration has become, or is now, impossible, such provision shall be made for the discharge of the water of such streams from said canal as the existing situation now permits, and as will avoid injury to other property. It shall also be the duty of said company, its successors or assigns, to take such precautions and make such provision for the carrying away of water that may flow into the bed of such portion of said canal as may be discontinued as will prevent such stagnant pools of water therein as are liable to become injurious to public health." This section clearly contemplates that the water is to be removed from the canal; that the highways which had been carried over it by bridges of sufficient height to permit large boats to pass underneath would be lowered to their former position before the canal was constructed, either by the removal of the canal bridges and the filling in of the bed of the canal, or in some other practicable way. The same provision is made for private crossings. The provisions as to the treatment of streams discharging into the canal, and the stagnant pools of water therein, all show that the Legislature contemplated a complete discontinuance and abandonment of the prism for transportation purposes.

The situation disclosed by this record is: (1) We have the Cornell Steamboat Company, the grantor of the defendant, reserving the right of its boats to navigate the canal light or laden without the payment of tolls. (2) We have the defendant offering the plaintiff to transport its product if the latter consents to pay 16 cents per barrel instead of 4 cents. (3) In the absence of proof we are permitted to assume that this 12 miles of canal stands precisely as it has existed for years. There was no abandonment up to the time of the trial. The question is not involved in this case whether the defendant may, in the future, at its option, discontinue this canal by actually doing so and complying with the provisions of section 4 of the act of 1899. The real question is whether the defendant, the successor in interest of the Delaware & Hudson Canal Company in the ownership of this waterway, which has been held by this court to be a public highway, can, so long as it exists and is used for the purposes of the defendant and such third parties as it sees fit to permit, be successfully claimed to be private property. We are of the opinion that it must be held as matter of law, under the conditions disclosed by this record, that this 12 miles of canal is a public highway, and operated under the restrictions of the act of 1823; and that if the defendant transports the product of the plaintiff to tide water it must confine itself to the tolls provided for in the act of 1823. If the position which has been assumed by the defendant company can be maintained, it has the liberty to use this canal as private property, and charge the general public along its route desirous of sending freight to tide water such rates as it sees fit. There is but one way for defendant to rid itself of the public burden imposed by this use, and that is to abandon it under the provisions of the act of 1899. We are of opinion that so long as this canal is used for the purpose of transportation it must be regarded as a public highway, and the defendant rests under all the restrictions and liabilities imposed upon the Delaware & Hudson Canal Company originally.

The defendant comes within the principle decided by the Supreme Court of the United States in Munn v. Illinois, 94 U. S. 113, 125, 130, 24 L. Ed. 77. Mr. Justice Waite, referring to the police powers, says (page 125, 94 U. S., 24 L. Ed. 77): "Under these powers the government regulates its citizens, one toward the other, and the manner in which each shall use his own property when such regulation becomes necessary for the public good. In their exercise it has been customary in England from time immemorial, and in this country from its first colonization, to regulate ferries, common carriers, etc., and in so doing to fix a maximum charge to be made for services rendered, for accommodations furnished, and articles sold." The learned judge further states (page 130, 94 U. S., 24 L. Ed. 77): "Common carriers exercise a sort of public office, and have duties to perform in which the public is interested. New Jersey Navigation Co. v. Merchants' Bank, 6 How. 382 [12 L. Ed. 465]. Their business is therefore 'affected with the public interest' within the meaning of the doctrine which Lord Hale has so forcibly stated." We have already pointed out that this court held in regard to the canal that, while it is not strictly a public work, yet it is in the nature of one, as much as a railroad, and is to be regarded a public work in the same sense. Selden v. D. & H. C. Co., 29 N. Y. 634, 638, 641, 642. The precise point decided in the Munn Case, supra, was that, when the owner of property devotes it to a use in which the public has an interest, he in effect grants to the public an interest in such use, and must, to the extent of that interest, submit to be controlled by the public for the common good as long as he maintains the use. He may withdraw his grant by discontinuing the use. See, also, People v. O'Brien, 111 N. Y. 1, 18 N. E. 692, 2 L. R. A. 255, 7 Am. St. Rep. 684; Gue v. Tidewater Canal Co., 24 How. 257, 16 L. Ed. 635; McEntee v. Kingston Water Co., 165 N. Y. 27, 58 N. E. 785.

The defendant raises the point that a bill in equity praying for a perpetual injunction restraining the defendant from imposing illegal tolls and excluding the plaintiff's boats and freight from the canal is not the proper remedy. The remedy suggested is mandamus. But we are of opinion that under the facts it was competent for the plaintiff to seek the restraining power of a court of equity to prevent the exaction of illegal tolls and exclusion from a public highway. An action can be maintained, although the matter is one of common right, where damage peculiar and personal to plaintiff is shown.

In discussing the general question whether the restraining powers of a court of equity will be exercised in favor of the plaintiff corporation in the case at bar, we are to keep in mind the precise situation. This is not the case where the general rights of the public alone are involved, and the plaintiff received only such injury as is common to other citizens interested in the maintaining of this canal. We have here a state of facts that shows the plaintiff to have been specially damaged. This canal had been in operation for a period of nearly 70 years when sold to the Cornell Steamboat Company. Before that sale the plaintiff had erected expensive cement works on the banks of the canal five miles from tide water, where the canal locks its boats into the Hudson river at Rondout. This expenditure of money we are bound to infer from these facts was made in view of the existence of the canal, and the further fact that the rate of tolls was fixed by the charter of the canal company under the laws of Pennsylvania and New York. In other words, the plaintiff company proceeded upon the assumption that its product could be conveyed to tidewater at rates fixed by law that would enable it to compete with other cement companies contending for the market. Mr. Morawetz in his work on Corporations (2d Ed.) § 1042, says: "It is well settled that a court of chancery has jurisdiction to grant equitable relief against a corporation at the suit of an individual whenever a sufficient cause for the relief is shown upon the ordinary principles of equity jurisprudence; and the fact that the act of the corporation against which relief is sought involves an unauthorized exercise of corporate powers, or other breach of the law, is wholly immaterial under the circumstances." In the case of Delaware & Raritan Canal Co. v. Camden & Atlantic R. R. Co., 16 N. J. Eq. 321, it was held that where, by the act of the Legislature, the plaintiff companies were fully and effectually protected until a certain date from railroad competition between the cities of New York and Philadelphia, an injunction was the proper remedy to secure to the plaintiffs the enjoyment of a statutory privilege. In Rowe v. Granite Bridge Corporation, 21 Pick. 344, it was held that, although indictment is the proper remedy in the case of a public nuisance, where it is absolutely necessary that such a nuisance should be immediately suppressed a court of chancery may interfere by injunction until the slower process of indictment can be put in motion. This case discloses the dual remedy, and illustrates the legal principle that equity will lay hold of a corporation to enforce not only public but private rights. We have been cited in support of the proposition that equity will not interfere in such a situation as is now presented to the case of Knickerbocker Ice Co. v. Shultz, 116 N. Y. 382, 389, 22 N. E. 564. This case involves the construction of a dike on the Hudson river shore that rested upon land under water, the title to which was still in the state. The plaintiff had for many years before the construction of the dike been accustomed to cutting ice in the Hudson river and drawing it over the premises in question to the shore. The dike interfered with this mode of harvesting ice, and the plaintiff thereupon brought an action to restrain the defendant from erecting or maintaining it. The court held that this was a purpresture; that is, an invasion of the right of property in the soil while the title to the same remained in the people. A nuisance in such a case as this is an injury to the common right of the public in navigating the river, and these questions can only be tested in an action at the suit of the people. It will be observed that in this case the plaintiff had no absolute vested property right which it was seeking to protect, but invoked a remedy which, under the conditions disclosed, rested in the people, and could only be invoked by the Attorney General.

Two other cases have been cited to us in this connection, viz., Lansing v. Smith, 8 Cow. 146; same case on appeal, 4 Wend. 25, 21 Am. Dec. 89; also case of B. M. C. Co. v. L. C. & N. Co., 50 Pa. 91, 88 Am. Dec. 534. In 8 Cow. 146, it was held that in the case of erections working a common injury to the owner of docks, etc., and unauthorized by statute, no action would lie at the suit of an individual unless there was some injury from the erection peculiar and personal to him. In 50 Pa. 91, 88 Am. Dec. 534, it was held that a bill in equity to enforce the performance of public duties by corporations could not be maintained by a private party in the absence of special right or authority. In Milhau v. Sharp, 27 N. Y. 628, 84 Am. Dec. 314, this court said: "To entitle a party to relief by injunction, who is sustaining or about to sustain a peculiar injury from a public nuisance, it is also necessary that the injury should be such as cannot be well or adequately compensated in damages at law, or such as, from its continuance or permanent mischief, must occasion a constantly recurring grievance, which cannot be otherwise prevented but by injunction." The principle which we are now considering is applied not only in cases of public nuisance, but to those involving similar situations to the one at bar. See, also, Mudge v. Salisbury, 110 N. Y. 413, 18 N. E. 249; West Point Iron Co. v. Reymert, 45 N. Y. 703; Corning v. Troy, I. & N. Co., 40 N. Y. 191; Mills v. Hall, 9 Wend. 315, 24 Am. Dec. 160; Ogden v. Gibbons, 4 Johns. Ch. 150; Covington Stock-Yards Co. v. Keith, 139 U. S. 128, 11 Sup. Ct. 461, 35 L. Ed. 73; Butchers' & Drovers' Stock-Yards v. L. & N. R. Co., 67 Fed. 35, 14 C. C. A. 290. In Covington Stock-Yards Co. v. Keith, supra, a bill in equity was filed against a Kentucky railroad company to foreclose a mortgage and to appoint a receiver. After the appointment of the receiver a petition was filed in the foreclosure proceeding requiring the receiver to show cause why he should not deliver to the plaintiff live stock consigned to him at some suitable place outside of the yards of the company. The Supreme Court of the United States held that a railroad company holding itself out as a carrier of live stock is under a legal obligation, arising out of the nature of its employment, to provide suitable and necessary means and facilities for receiving live stock that may be offered for shipment over its road and connections, as well as for discharging said stock after it reaches the place to which it is consigned. A final decree issued compelling the company to provide such facilities.

The defendant raises the further point that the exercise by the Consolidated Rosendale Cement Company of the franchise granted by the state to the Delaware & Hudson Canal Company would be ultra vires. This is a question between the defendant and the state of New York, with which the former has no concern, as it is estopped from raising it by voluntarily assuming the position which it now occupies. So long as the state of New York raises no objection in the premises, the defendant will not be heard to complain.

A new point has been raised in this court which seems to have escaped the vigilance of counsel, as their briefs are silent concerning it. It is urged that we have, in each of the cases that have been argued together, a situation which is absolutely fatal to the plaintiff's appeal, as the decision of the learned trial court is in the short form, and the judgment in favor of the defendant was unanimously affirmed; that in such a situation the decision of the trial court has the same effect as the verdict of a jury, and all the facts must be deemed to have been found in favor of the successful party. In each of the cases, so far as the proceedings at the trial are concerned, a similar situation is disclosed by the record, which includes the clerk's minutes, as follows: The cases were duly called for trial in the city of Kingston, Ulster county, and it was agreed that they should be tried together. A jury was duly impaneled, and the counsel for the plaintiff, after opening his case, introduced in evidence an agreement between the Delaware & Hudson Canal Company and the Cornell Steamboat Company, also a deed of the Cornell Steamboat Company to the Consolidated Rosendale Cement Company. It was then agreed between counsel that certain undisputed facts were involved in the actions, which were spread upon the record in full, and duly appear in the cases now before us on this appeal. Thereupon the plaintiff rested, and counsel for defendant, without offering any evidence, moved in each case to dismiss the complaint on the ground that facts had not been proved sufficient to constitute a cause of action. The motion in each case was granted, and plaintiff duly excepted. There could be no decision in a jury case, with the facts stipulated, in the short or long form, and, consequently, no presumption of facts found in favor of the successful party.

The judgment appealed from should be reversed, and new trials granted in each case, with costs to abide the event.

O'BRIEN, J. (dissenting). The parties to this action, plaintiff and defendant, are manufacturing corporations organized and existing under the laws of this state providing for the creation of corporations of that character. Both are engaged in the same business; that is, the manufacture and sale of cement. The plaintiff's plant is located in the same county as that of the defendant, and both corporations are competitors in business. The purpose of this action was to compel the defendant to carry the products of the plaintiff, its competitor, to market through a canal or waterway which the defendant insists is its private property and an adjunct to its business. The contention that the defendant is bound by law to furnish facilities for the transportation of the plaintiff's products to market, and thus to aid its competitor in the transaction of its business, cannot fail to arrest attention, and to invite an inquiry with respect to the grounds upon which the plaintiff's claim rests.

By chapter 238, p. 305, of the Laws of 1823, the Delaware & Hudson Canal Company was incorporated for the purposes described in the preamble to the statute, the first clause of which is as follows: "Whereas, it is desired that a channel should be opened through which the city of New York and other cities of this state may receive a supply of stone coal which is found in the interior of the state of Pennsylvania." The statute, among other things, prescribed the maximum rate of toll which the corporation should be entitled to charge for merchandise transported in water craft over or through the canal at four cents per mile for every ton of such products as are produced by the parties to this action. It was also enacted that if the corporation should neglect or refuse to keep in repair and good order any dam, lock, or sluice of their own construction, or should neglect to remove any obstacle which might occur, so that boats, rafts, or other vessels might safely use the navigation of the canal in the manner provided by the act, the corporation shall for every such offense forfeit and pay the sum of $100, to be sued for and recovered in any court of competent jurisdiction, one-half to the use of the informer and the other half to the use of the poor of the township or county where the neglect may occur; and the service of process upon the toll gatherer in the proper county, and next to the place where the offense shall have been committed, shall be held as good and as available in law as if served on the president of the said corporation. The corporate body thus created constructed a canal or public waterway, in compliance with the provisions of the statute, from Honesdale, in the state of Pennsylvania, to tide water at Eddyville, on the Rondout creek, a tributary of the Hudson river. This waterway furnished transportation for all merchandise through that section until the year 1899. The length of the canal was about 110 miles. By chapter 469, p. 958, of the Laws of 1899, the original act of incorporation was amended, and the third section of the amendatory act reads as follows: "Whenever it shall appear to the managers of said canal company that it is able to fulfill the aforesaid purpose of opening and of mining and bringing to market a supply of stone coal which is found in the interior of the state of Pennsylvania more economically by rail over its own or other lines than by its canal, it shall be lawful for said company, and it is hereby authorized and empowered by vote of said managers, to lease, sell or discontinue to use or maintain said canal, or any parts thereof, which in their judgment are no longer necessary for said purpose." And it was further provided in the next section that, when the company should exercise the power granted in the preceding section, to discontinue to use or maintain the canal, or any part thereof, it should within a reasonable time thereafter restore the highway crossings of said canal as are so discontinued to their former state, so far as the same can be done; and in case that the canal, or any part thereof, shall be discontinued, it was bound to make provision for the private crossings over the same. It is found that the canal company, on the 24th of June, 1899, sold and conveyed the canal to the Cornell Steamboat Company, which continued to occupy the canal in the same manner and charging the same tolls as theretofore until the 26th of March, 1902, except that it did not carry the coal of the Delaware & Hudson Canal Company. The steamboat company, on the 26th day of March, 1902, sold and conveyed the east 12 miles thereof to the defendant in this case. The remaining part of the canal, extending westerly about 98 miles to Honesdale, in the state of Pennsylvania, has been entirely abandoned. It is no longer used as a canal, but is in different portions thereof diverted and devoted to different uses. The defendant is a large manufacturer of cement, having its works near the westerly end of the 12 miles of the canal purchased by it, and it uses the 12 miles to transport its products to market. The plaintiff is also a manufacturer of cement having its works about 5 miles from the river, where it was located during the time that the canal company and the steamboat company owned the canal; and during that time used it to transport its products to the river, and had paid for such transportation to both corporations the rates fixed by the act of 1823. After the defendant had acquired the 12 miles aforesaid, it claimed to own that portion of the canal as a private highway, and that it be kept open and in operation for its own private use only. It asserts that it was under no obligation to allow the plaintiff or any other person to use it or transport goods thereon, but it offered, for the accommodation of the plaintiff, to allow it such use and transportation if it were paid therefor at the rate of 16 cents per barrel for the cement so transported, and it claimed that, unless the plaintiff would pay the sum so demanded, it should be excluded from the canal.

The plaintiff's complaint was dismissed at the trial and the judgment has been unanimously affirmed below. There is no finding in the case as to whether the sum demanded by the defendant from the plaintiff for the use of its waterway was unreasonable or otherwise; and the contention of the plaintiff is that it is now entitled to use the 12 miles purchased by the defendant in the same way and subject only to the same tolls fixed by the original statute. I think the fair construction of the act of 1899 is that the Legislature thereby intended to permit the canal to be abandoned or discontinued entirely as a public waterway, and that, when so discontinued or abandoned, the powers, duties, and obligations of the company or its grantees as public carriers ceased. It seems to be conceded that after the passage of the act of 1899 the canal company could, at its election, have discontinued the canal and filled up the prism, thereby wholly depriving the public of its use as a waterway. If the company had found it to its advantage to divide the canal into parcels one mile in length over its entire distance, then, under the plaintiff's construction, every part or any part of the ditch so sold must continue to be a public highway, and every owner by himself or in connection with every other owner would become a common carrier. The statute permitted the sale or discontinuance of the canal in parts, and 98 miles of it has certainly been abandoned, and no longer used as a canal, but in the language of the findings is in different portions devoted and diverted to different uses. If the defendant's purchase had been of a single mile instead of 12 miles, the same question would arise that is now presented. could it be reasonably asserted that it was bound to keep this one mile open for the use of the public as a canal? The circumstance that the fragment which the defendant purchased is 12 miles instead of 1 mile does not change the question. No duties or obligations survived after the sale to the defendant different from the duties or obligations of the numerous other parties who became purchasers of some fragments, more or less, of this original waterway. What the defendant took by its purchase was the physical property without the franchises, and without assuming the duties and obligations to the public of a common carrier. It is of no consequence that the conveyance to the defendant or its grantor assumed to convey the original franchise of the canal. In the absence of special statutory authority, which does not exist in this case, neither an individual nor a corporation, such as the defendant is, can buy a franchise in the market like other property. A franchise to a corporation to exercise the powers and perform the duties of a common carrier proceeds from the state in the exercise of its sovereignty, and when the canal company that originally received the franchise abandoned it under the authority of the statute the defendant did not succeed to its powers any more than did the other numerous purchasers of the other fragments.

If the plaintiff is right in the contention that the obligations and duties imposed upon the original canal company have devolved upon the defendant, then the defendant must be subject to the same penalties and liabilities. What the plaintiff complains of is that the defendant has closed these 12 miles of the canal to the public, and as to the plaintiff has obstructed free navigation, and excluded it from the use of the same as a public highway. If that be so, then the plaintiff is entitled to recover from the defendant in an action at law, not only all damages accruing to it from the defendant's refusal to open the canal to the public, but also is entitled to recover a penalty of $100 for each refusal to comply with the plaintiff's demands. It would follow from this that the plaintiff has a perfect remedy at law, and that a court of equity has no jurisdiction. The controversy simply involves a dispute between the parties to this action as to the ownership of the easterly end of what was originally a canal 110 miles long. The defendant claims that it owns the land, the prism, and every other physical object connected with the same. The plaintiff denies that claim, and insists that it is still a public highway, over which it has a right to transport its goods. If the defendant is a common carrier, as the plaintiff claims, then it can be compelled to do its duty by mandamus or by an action for damages; but I doubt if any controlling authority can be found that justifies the interference of a court of equity by writ of injunction. On the contrary, I think the law is well settled the other way. The rule that governs in such cases was stated by Judge Andrews in Moore v. Brooklyn City R. R. Co., 108 N. Y. 98, 15 N. E. 191, as follows: "The threatened violation of a mere naked legal right, unaccompanied by special circumstances, is not a ground for injunction, when, as in this case, legal remedies are adequate to redress any resulting injury. If the defendant violates its charter, or fails to perform the conditions under which it exercises its franchises, or if in the management of its trains or business it unlawfully occupies or obstructs the public highway, the remedy in the one case is by a proceeding in behalf of the people by the Attorney General to annul or forfeit its franchise, and in the other by indictment or proceedings under the statute." And by Judge Ruger in Thomas v. Musical M. P. Union, 121 N. Y. 45, 24 N. E. 24, 8 L. R. A. 175: "It is therefore a cardinal rule of equity that it will not entertain jurisdiction of cases where there is an adequate remedy at law, or grant relief, unless for the purpose of preventing serious and irreparable injury. These principles are elementary, and lie at the foundation of all equitable jurisdiction. Equity, therefore, interferes in the transactions of men by preventive measures only when irreparable injury is threatened, and the law does not afford an adequate remedy for the contemplated wrong." The principle thus stated has never been departed from in this court. On the contrary, it seems to me that the rule has been observed, if not extended, in a very recent case. People ex rel. Corscadden v. Howe, 177 N. Y. 499, 69 N. E. 1114. The authorities are clear and numerous to the effect that a bill in equity will not lie in a case like this. And in some of the cases the facts are almost identical with the case at bar. B. M. C. Co. v. L. C. & N. Co., 50 Pa. 91, 88 Am. Dec. 534; Saylor v. Pa. Canal Co., 183 Pa. 167, 38 Atl. 598. The owners of a ferry, a stage coach, or a railroad are doubtless conducting a business that is affected with the public interests, but I am not aware of any authority for the proposition that, if they refuse to perform their proper functions, and exclude an individual, or even the whole public, from the accommodations with which the business is charged, they can be disciplined in that regard by an injunction from a court of equity. The remedy in such cases is by mandamus, or by action at law for damages, or to recover the statutory penalties for a refusal to grant the accommodations.

Moreover, I am unable to see how a manufacturing corporation can exercise the fran-

'chise of operating a public canal or railroad. A corporation has no right to exercise any franchises not conferred upon it by law, and I am not aware that there is any law that has conferred upon a manufacturing corporation the powers, duties, or obligations of a common carrier. It cannot acquire by grant the power to engage in a business not embraced within the scope of its charter. The Attorney General may bring an action to dissolve any corporation that is engaged in the exercise of any franchise not conferred upon it by law. Code Civ. Proc. § 1798. And it would seem to follow that such an action might be maintained against the defendant in behalf of the people, providing it could be shown that it has actually usurped such powers and is assuming to exercise such a franchise. A court of equity will not compel a manufacturing corporation to do things which, if done, would subject it to dissolution and death in an action in behalf of the people. I cannot believe that the Legislature intended, when authorizing the canal company to sell or discontinue the canal in fragments, to impose upon the various purchasers the duties and obligations of the original corporation. It is quite certain that the statute which authorizes the sale or discontinuance of the canal is silent with respect to the franchise, and it must have reverted to the state, unless it is distributed among the various owners who at present are in possession of the property. The defendant doubtless had the power, within the scope of its charter, to buy the land and the other physical objects which constitute these 12 miles of waterway, but it had no power to acquire by grant, or to exercise the powers and privileges originally granted to the canal company. If it acquired any of the powers so conferred, it acquired them all, and these powers included the right to exercise the power of eminent domain and various other things utterly foreign to the functions of a manufacturing corporation. It is of no consequence that the defendant in some instances has permitted others to use the waterway. That is a voluntary act on its part, and does not proceed from any legal obligation. The defendant may permit its neighbors to cross its land or use its real estate for their convenience, and it may charge what it deems a reasonable compensation for the privilege. But when it is contended that it is obliged to do it, that presents quite another and different question, and that is what the plaintiff claims and insists upon. It seems to me that the fallacy involved in the argument in behalf of the plaintiff consists in assuming that the original franchise granted to the canal company has followed all the fragments of the original property which composed it, when by statute the owners of the property were authorized to discontinue it or abandon it, which is the same thing, and neither the original franchise nor any obligation or duty attached to it survived or devolved upon the purchasers. By the original statute a corporation was created for the express purpose of constructing and operating a canal. It was a private enterprise, but certain privileges and franchises were conferred upon the corporation, and delegated to it by the sovereign, and thus it was authorized to exercise some of the powers of government, such as the right to condemn land, to recover from any one obstructing or in any way injuring the waterway or anything connected with it four times the damages actually sustained, and other powers quite unusual in the case of private corporations. If the duties and obligations of a common carrier have been cast upon the defendant, the rights and privileges conferred must have accompanied them, and are now possessed by it, and hence it would follow that the defendant, as a mere manufacturing corporation, has acquired powers and privileges not possessed by any other manufacturing corporation in the state.

The statute prohibits any corporation from exercising any corporate powers except such as are expressly conferred by its charter or by-law, or are necessary to the exercise of the powers expressly enumerated and given. Where did the defendant, a mere manufacturing corporation, get the power to operate and maintain a canal, or railroad for the transportation of passengers and goods? By what authority can it exercise the powers and privileges of a transportation company? The contention of the learned counsel for the plaintiff imposes upon him not only the burden of showing that the defendant possessed all these powers, but that a court of equity will command and compel their exercise upon the demand of the plaintiff. If the duties of a common carrier have been imposed upon the defendant, as the plaintiff claims, the result has been accomplished in no other way than by a conveyance of the physical property to the defendant by an intermediate owner under statutory authority to "discontinue to use or maintain the canal." Under the exercise of that authority the canal has ceased to exist as such, since it was sold in fragments, and, if the defendant purchased a larger fragment than the other purchasers, it took the fragment with only the same burdens and obligations as the others did. It had the power to become the owner of any land necessary for its own operations, and, if that land happened to be covered with water, as was the case, it could float its own products on the water like any other private owner, but it was not bound in law to permit others to do so. The defendant could not become a transportation company by any private grant, nor did the governmental powers delegated to the canal company, which we call a franchise, pass to it through a deed like covenants which run with the land. The Legislature, I think, conferred authority upon the owners of the canal to discontinue its use or maintenance as a public highway, and it has been discontinued and abandoned under that authority.

The Legislature declared in explicit terms that the managers and owners of the canal might discontinue and abandon it as a public highway when, in their judgment, it was no longer useful or necessary for the purpose of its original construction, namely, the transportation of coal. The use of the waterway for the accommodation of the plaintiff, or for any other purpose than a channel for carrying coal, was not contemplated. The abandonment of the canal as such was made to depend entirely upon the judgment of the managers that it was "no longer necessary for said purpose"; that is to say, for the purpose of carrying coal. They determined that it was no longer useful for that purpose, and hence it was abandoned and sold, and the plaintiff has no right to insist that a fragment of it shall be kept in life for its private use. If the plaintiff wanted it retained for its own manufacturing or transportation operations, it could have outbidden the defendant at the sale, and, if that happened, there can be little doubt that the plaintiff would have assumed the same position with respect to its use by the public that the defendant assumes now.

It is suggested that the defendant cannot set up the defense of ultra vires, and cases are cited to show that a corporation cannot avoid its contracts or defend its wrongful acts on the ground that it had no power to make the contract or to do the thing for which a party sues to enforce a liability. No one disputes that principle, or questions the authority of the cases cited, but they have no application whatever to this case, for the plain reason that the defendant is not sued upon any ultra vires contract or act. What it is sued for is for refusing to make contracts, or to do things or to engage in a business which, as a manufacturing corporation, it is forbidden to do. The question is not when or how a corporation may defend on the ground of ultra vires, but whether a court of equity will compel a manufacturing corporation against its will and protest to do things and to engage in a business not within its chartered powers or permitted by law. If any case or any authority can be found to sustain the proposition that a court of equity will make such a decree, and thus compel the corporation to incur the risk of corporate death, then such a case or authority is pertinent; but it is entirely safe to assert that no case or authority of this kind can be found. It does not meet the point at all to cite cases to show that a corporation will not be permitted to repudiate its contracts or affirmative acts by the plea of ultra vires. What is sought to be accomplished in this case is to compel a manufacturing corporation to make ultra vires contracts, and to enter into business relations, and to exercise powers not conferred upon it by law, and the exercise of which is prohibited. Some principle or some authority to sustain that claim is what is very much needed in this case.

The exclusion of the plaintiff from the use of the 12 miles purchased by the defendant is not a special wrong peculiar to the plaintiff, but to the whole public, of which the plaintiff is a part. The injury, if any, is in common with the whole public, and not special to itself. The principle is quite familiar that under such circumstances a private party cannot maintain an action for an injunction, either in his own behalf or in behalf of the public. If the defendant, as alleged, has obstructed or closed up a public highway, and wrongfully excluded the whole public from the use of the same, the remedy is by action in the name of the people by the Attorney General. Knickerbocker Ice Company v. Schultz, 116 N. Y. 382, 22 N. E. 564; Lansing v. Smith, 8 Cow. 146; B. M. C. Co. v. L. C. & N. Co., 50 Pa. 91, 88 Am. Dec. 534; Saylor v. Pa. Canal Co., 183 Pa. 167, 38 Atl. 598; Wakeman v. Wilbur, 147 N. Y. 657, 42 N. E. 341. There is no finding that takes the case out of this principle.

There is another view of this case, which is founded upon the condition of the record. The decision is in the short form, and the judgment in favor of the defendant was unanimously affirmed. In such a case the decision of the trial court has the same effect as the general verdict of a jury, and all the facts must be deemed to have been found in favor of the successful party. In the case at bar the plaintiff cannot succeed unless certain facts are found in its favor. (1) It must be found that the canal was never abandoned, but is still a public highway, and that is a question of fact, or at least a mixed question of law and fact. (2) It must be found that the defendant purchased the 12 miles, and assumed control of it, not as a private waterway, but as a public highway. (3) It must be found that the defendant prevented the plaintiff from using a public highway to transport its goods, and that plaintiff sustained specific damage different from the damage to the whole public. These facts, and all other facts in the case, instead of being found in favor of the plaintiff, have been found in favor of the defendant, under the doctrine of our own decisions, and if any question survives to this court after the unanimous decision it ought to be pointed out, so that we may know just what the rule is in such cases and what are the exceptions, if any. The plaintiff cannot succeed in this appeal, unless we hold not only that these propositions are still open in this court, but are to be assumed in favor of the plaintiff and against the judgment. If that is so, then I can only say that I am utterly unable to understand the meaning of the numerous decisions of this court on the question. One of the most recent is that of Hutton v. Smith, 175 N. Y. 375, 67 N. E. 633, where the following proposition was decided: "Where a judgment entered upon a decision of the trial court in the short form is unanimously affirmed by the Appellate Division, the Court of Appeals is concluded thereby, and, whatever the views of the court may be, it must assume that facts sufficient to sustain the decision were necessarily found by the trial court." In the case of City of Niagara Falls v. N. Y. C. & H. R. R. R. Co., 168 N. Y. 610, 61 N. E. 185, the question was whether the locus in quo was a highway or private property. That is the question in this case, but in that case it was held that no question survived the unanimous decision, although it appeared that the railroad had written title of record to the land. There are many other cases to the same effect, all so recent that their scope must be well understood. If I am wrong in supposing that the case at bar must share the same fate, it ought not to be difficult to point out wherein this case differs from others, where the decision is in the short form and unanimously affirmed.

I think there was no error in the disposition of this case by the courts below, and that the judgment should be affirmed, with costs.

HAIGHT, VANN, CULLEN, and WERNER, JJ., concur with BARTLETT, J. O'BRIEN, J., reads dissenting opinion. PARKER, C. J., absent.

Judgment reversed, etc.

(208 Ill. 456)

CHICAGO & A. RY. CO. v. PULLIAM.*

(Supreme Court of Illinois. Feb. 17, 1904.)

RAILROADS—CROSSINGS—INJURIES—CONTRIBUTORY NEGLIGENCE—SIGNALS—EVIDENCE—QUESTION FOR JURY—INSTRUCTIONS.

1. Where, in an action for injuries at a railroad crossing, plaintiff testified that when he arrived at a street near the track, and as he passed along the street toward the main track, he looked north and south for trains, and when he reached the track he slowed his team to a walk, and looked north and south, and back north again, when, for the first time, he saw a limited passenger train coming right upon him, and that the short alarm whistle then given attracted his attention, and there was also evidence that there were obstructions to sight and hearing as a person was crossing the track, it was proper for the court to submit the question of his contributory negligence to the jury, though other witnesses testified that they saw the train coming before plaintiff got on the track, and attempted to warn him by calling to him, waving their arms, etc.

2. In an action for injuries at a railroad crossing, evidence of several witnesses that they did not hear the bell rung, though they admitted that they did not know definitely whether it was rung or not, was sufficient to justify an instruction authorizing a recovery if there was a failure to ring the bell at least 80 rods from the crossing, though defendant's evidence was to the effect that the bell was rung automatically, and had been ringing for more than a mile before reaching the crossing.

Appeal from Appellate Court, Third District.

Action by Floyd J. Pulliam against the Chicago & Alton Railway Company. From a judgment in favor of plaintiff, defendant appeals. Affirmed.

Patton & Patton (William Brown, of counsel), for appellant. Robert H. Patton and T. J. Nuckolls, for appellee.

CARTWRIGHT, J. The appellate Court for the Third District affirmed a judgment of the circuit court of Sangamon county in this suit for $1,500 in favor of appellee for personal injuries caused by appellant's train at a street crossing in the village of Auburn. Plaintiff was 18 years old, and was engaged in hauling ice to an icehouse from a car on the side track of defendant in said village. At the time of the accident he drove from the icehouse in a northerly direction along a highway parallel with and adjoining the right of way on the southeasterly side until he reached Monroe street, and then turned west across the track of the Pawnee Railroad and several side tracks of defendant to the main track. The weather was cold, and he was standing up in the wagon. When he reached the main track, the limited train approaching from the north struck the wagon and threw him out, causing the injuries for which the suit was brought.

At the close of the evidence the defendant moved the court to instruct the jury to find it not guilty. The motion was overruled, and the instruction refused, and the ruling is assigned as error. The charges of the declaration were negligence, generally, in the management of the train, a failure to give statutory signals before reaching the crossing, and a violation of the ordinance of the village of Auburn regulating the speed of trains. The train was running at a much higher rate of speed than was permitted by the ordinance, and it is not claimed that there was no evidence tending to prove negligence in that respect on the part of the defendant. The ground on which it is contended the instruction should have been given is that there was no evidence that the plaintiff was in the exercise of reasonable care for his own safety, but that, on the contrary, the evidence conclusively showed that, if he had exercised such care, he would have avoided the injury. The evidence of the respective parties on that question is as follows: Plaintiff testified that when he arrived at Monroe street, and as he passed along that street toward the main track, he looked north and south for trains; that, when he reached the railroad tracks, he slowed his team to a walk; that when he was on the side tracks he looked north, and then looked south, and looked back north again, and the train was coming right there; that the team was then on the main track; that the short whistle given as an alarm was the first thing that attracted his attention to the train; and that he did not see it before. On the part of the defendant, a witness testi-

*Rehearing denied April 14, 1904.

fied that he was standing on the north side of the street, just west of the railroad, when he saw plaintiff coming toward the track; that plaintiff had a cap pulled down over his ears; that the witness "hollered" at him four times to keep off the track, or he would get run over; that plaintiff never looked up, but was standing in the wagon, not looking for trains or anything else; and that he did not think plaintiff heard him. Another witness testified that he was standing south of the street crossing; that he "hollered" to the plaintiff three times; that the first time was just after the plaintiff had crossed the Pawnee track, and witness called twice after that; and that plaintiff did not appear to hear him, and, if he did, he did not pay any attention. The man for whom plaintiff was hauling ice was on a load of ice east of the track, going south, and testified that as plaintiff's horses were on the turn into Monroe street, when the witness was about 100 feet from him, the witness threw up his hand as a warning, and motioned to him, but he could not say whether he saw the warning. There were some obstructions to sight and sound, but they were some distance from the crossing: the first one being the station building, more than a block north. Although the existence of such obstructions does not excuse the exercise of care on the part of one approaching the crossing, the fact is proper to be considered in connection with all the other facts of the case. Obstructions to the view or hearing may require greater care and attention to ascertain whether a train is approaching, but they may sometimes have a tendency to render such care and attention unavailing. The care required is such as a reasonably prudent person would ordinarily exercise under the same circumstances, and in this case the testimony of plaintiff was sufficient to entitle him to have the question submitted to the jury. It was not error to refuse the request to take the case from the jury, and the judgment of the Appellate Court upon the controverted question of fact is conclusive.

The only other error alleged is the giving of the second and fifth instructions at the request of the plaintiff, which authorized a recovery if the plaintiff was in the exercise of due care for his own safety, and there was a failure to ring the bell at least 80 rods from the crossing. The objection to these instructions is that there was no evidence on which to base them. It is contended that not only was there no evidence tending to prove that the bell was not ringing, but, on the other hand, the evidence showed conclusively, without any conflict, that the bell was ringing for more than a mile from the place of the accident. The evidence on the part of the defendant was that the bell was rung automatically, and was ringing for more than a mile before reaching the crossing. All the witnesses agreed that the whistle was blown when it became apparent that plaintiff was going upon the crossing and there was likely to be a collision. Several witnesses for the plaintiff testified that they did not hear the bell, but none of them knew definitely whether it was ringing or not. It is urged that this evidence was too unsubstantial as the basis of an instruction, because one witness said he was hard of hearing, and another had his cap pulled down over his ears, and none of them were paying any attention to the question whether the bell was ringing or not. The evidence was admissible on the question whether the bell was rung or not, and it is not error to give an instruction based on the hypothesis that a fact exists, although the court may be of the opinion that the evidence is very slight, or that the great weight of the evidence disproves the existence of the fact. The court cannot exercise its judgment as to the weight of the evidence in giving or refusing instructions. We do not think it was error to submit the issues to the jury, or to give the instructions complained of.

The judgment of the Appellate Court is affirmed. Judgment affirmed.

(185 Mass. 455)

COGSWELL v. HALL.

(Supreme Judicial Court of Massachusetts. Norfolk. April 7, 1904.)

MONEY HAD AND RECEIVED — ACTION — COMPLAINT—AMENDMENT—HUSBAND AND WIFE—ADVANCEMENTS BY WIFE—RESULTING TRUSTS—DESCENT—EVIDENCE—COMPETENCY.

1. The heir of a decedent contracted with decedent's widow, whereby she received the amount realized on the sale of certain real estate of the estate which was subject to her right of dower, and of which sum she was to have the income of one-third during her life, and at her death the principal was to be paid to the heir, and the remainder she was to retain as a loan from him. In an action for money had and received, brought by the heir against the executor of the widow to recover the moneys, the declaration did not contain a count declaring specifically for the money that represented the value of the estate in dower, and an amendment was allowed in which that part of plaintiff's claim was set out in a separate count. *Held*, that the amendment was not improper on the ground that it introduced a new cause of action, which would otherwise have been barred by limitations.

2. The question whether plaintiff had intended, when he brought his action, to include the substance of the amended count as a part of his demand, was within the discretion of the trial court.

3. It appearing that the first count in the declaration included the demand which was subsequently set up specifically in the new count by amendment, the discretion of the trial court in deciding as a matter of fact that plaintiff had intended to claim the matter set up in the new count was not abused.

4. Inasmuch as the principal held by the widow as a substitute for her dower was not received to plaintiff's use, so as to be recoverable under the first count, and under the agreement made with him he would become entitled to its possession as his separate property only at her death, it was proper to permit the amendment so as to enable plaintiff to maintain his action for the cause for which it was brought.

5. In an action by an heir of a decedent against the executor of the decedent's widow plaintiff claimed that the money received on the sale of certain real estate belonging to the decedent's estate had been turned over to the widow under a contract with him whereby two-thirds of it was to be a loan, and she was to have the interest on one-third as representing her dower interest, the entire sum to be repaid to plaintiff at her death. *Held*, that it was open to the defendant to show a resulting trust, in that when the property was originally purchased she had contributed an aliquot part of the purchase price.

6. As tending to support the defense, conversations between the widow and her husband in the presence of third parties, and her conduct, inconsistent with the alleged contract, was admissible, under Rev. Laws, c. 175, § 67, declaring that, if the cause of an action brought against an executor is supported by oral testimony of a promise made by the testator, evidence of statements made by testator, and evidence of his acts and habits, tending to show the improbability of the making of such promise, is admissible.

Exceptions from Superior Court, Norfolk County; Chas. A. De Courcy, Judge.

An action by Charles F. Cogswell against Newbert J. Hall for moneys had and received. Verdict for plaintiff, and defendant brings exceptions. Exceptions sustained.

Everett C. Bumpus, Frank E. H. Gary, and John B. Sullivan, Jr., for plaintiff. Marcellus Coggan and George L. Dillaway, for defendant.

BRALEY, J. On the death of his father, the plaintiff, who appears to have been his only heir at law, entered into an agreement with his mother, of whose will the defendant is executor, by which she received the sum of $6,000, being the price of certain real estate left by his father, who died intestate, and subject to her right of dower. The details of the transaction are not fully disclosed, but from the testimony of the plaintiff it may be inferred that of this sum she was to have the income of $2,000 during her life, in place of her life interest in the land, and at her death the principal was to be paid to him. The remainder of the money she retained as a loan from him, on which she was to pay interest; but neither the time when the debt became due and payable nor the rate of interest to be charged appears in the bill of exceptions, and the only witness to the alleged contract was the plaintiff. As the original declaration did not contain a count declaring specifically for the money that represented the value of her estate in dower held by her at her death, an amendment was offered and allowed, in which this part of the plaintiff's claim was set out in a separate count. The defendant apparently opposed the allowance of this amendment upon the ground that it "introduced a new cause of action that would otherwise be barred by the statute limiting actions against executors to two years after their appointment," though there is no statement in the bill of exceptions giving the date of the appointment of the executor, or that he had given the notice required by statute (Rev. Laws, c. 139, § 1; Id. c. 141, § 9). Instead of this being a conclusive reason in favor of its disallowance, it might well be considered a sufficient cause for its being granted, for otherwise the plaintiff might lose a meritorious claim.

The other objection—that the conditions stated at the beginning of the trial had not arisen under which the amendment should be allowed—was wholly within the discretion of the presiding justice, as well as the further question of fact, raised by the defendant, whether the plaintiff, when he brought his action, intended to include the substance of the amended count as a part of his demand. Such an objection becomes of slight importance when it appears that the first count of the declaration included all the items for the full amount as money had and received to the plaintiff's use. But the principal held by her as a substitute for her dower was not received to his use, and under the agreement made with him he would become entitled to its possession as his separate property only at her death. Driscoll v. Holt, 170 Mass. 262, 49 N. E. 309; Adams v. Weeks, 174 Mass. 45, 46, 54 N. E. 350; Golding v. Brennan, 183 Mass. 286-289, 67 N. E. 239. To meet this difficulty, and enable the plaintiff to maintain his action for the cause for which it was brought, the amendment was allowed properly.

The remaining exception relates to the exclusion of evidence offered by the defendant that his testatrix originally contributed $3,000 towards the purchase of the land, and had the right to appropriate to her own use upon receipt of the price for which it sold, so much as would repay her this amount. The plaintiff's case rested upon his testimony of an express agreement with his mother. He took the position that, as heir at law of his father, he became entitled at the time of sale to two-thirds of the money received by her, and at her death to the remainder. It was open to the defendant to prove that when the property was originally bought Mrs. Cogswell contributed an aliquot part of the purchase price. Skehill v. Abbott, 184 Mass. 145, 68 N. E. 37. If so, and the money advanced by her was not a gift to her husband, there was a resulting trust in her favor, which she could have established, if necessary, by a bill in equity against him in his lifetime. Livermore v. Aldrich, 5 Cush. 431-435; Hayward v. Cain, 110 Mass. 273-277; Lombard v. Morse, 155 Mass. 136, 29 N. E. 205, 14 L. R. A. 273; Frankel v. Frankel, 173 Mass. 214, 53 N. E. 398, 73 Am. St. Rep. 266. And the plaintiff, as his heir at law, who claims title to the estate left by him either as land or the proceeds of its sale, is in no different situation. Day v. Worcester, etc., R. R. Co., 151 Mass. 302, 307, 23 N. E. 824; Holland v. Cruft, 3 Gray, 162-180; Dana v. Dana, 154 Mass. 491, 28 N. E. 905; Rines v. Batchelder, 62 Me. 95. From the discussion appearing in the bill of exceptions, when this evidence was offered by the defendant it was excluded for the reasons that the inquiry was collateral to the general issue of indebtedness then on trial, and, as she settled her husband's estate upon his death, and never claimed a resulting trust, her conduct was legally inconsistent with the position taken by her executor. Such a view only affects the weight to be given to the evidence, but leaves the question of admissibility untouched. The jury were not obliged to believe the testimony of the plaintiff, and his evidence could not be treated as absolutely establishing the business relation between him and his mother, to which he had testified. His case rested upon an express promise made by her to pay to him the price of the land under the terms already stated. By way of reply to this claim, and to support his defense that at least one-half of the amount that came into her possession was due to her in repayment of money advanced at the time when the estate was bought, the defendant was clearly within the statute permitting proof not only of declarations made by her, which would include the conversation between herself and husband, in the presence of a third party, but also of her conduct, as being inconsistent with such a contract, and thus tending to contradict it. Rev. Laws, c. 175, § 67; Brooks v. Holden, 175 Mass. 137–140, 55 N. E. 802; National Granite Bank v. Tyndale, 179 Mass. 390–395, 60 N. E. 927.

Exceptions sustained.

(185 Mass. 451)

WHITE v. McPECK et al.

(Supreme Judicial Court of Massachusetts. Suffolk. April 4, 1904.)

PARTNERSHIP — DEBTS—INSURANCE—LAPSE OF POLICIES—WAIVER—NOTES—CONSIDERATION—INSTRUCTIONS—APPLICABILITY TO EVIDENCE.

1. Where it is provided in a partnership agreement that certain insurance policies on the lives of the partners should be taken out, the premiums on such policies, as between the partners, are partnership debts.

2. Where the insurer subsequently accepts money due as premiums, the lapse of the policy for failure to pay them is waived.

3. A promise, on the part of an insurance agent, to forward premiums out of his own funds for insured, is a valid consideration for a note given for the premiums.

4. Where there was evidence of an agreement between partners to keep up insurance policies on each other's lives, which there was no deliberate decision on the part of defendant partner to break, and also evidence of a subsequent ratification by defendant of a note given by the other partner to plaintiff for premiums, a charge, in an action on the note, to find for defendant if plaintiff received notice that defendant did not wish to keep up the insurance, "and subsequently, without the assent of defendant," plaintiff secured the note in question, was properly refused, as inapplicable to the evidence.

Exceptions from Superior Court, Suffolk County; John A. Aiken, Judge.

¶ 2. See Insurance, vol. 28, Cent. Dig. § 1056.

Action by James G. White against Neal E. McPeck and Hammond Braman. There was judgment for plaintiff, and defendant Braman excepts. Exceptions overruled.

The defendant Braman made the contentions embodied in the following rulings: First. That the note declared on, on the facts, was not given for partnership purposes. Secondly. That the note declared on, on the facts, was without consideration. Thirdly. That if the plaintiff or his agent received notice from the defendant Braman that he, the defendant Braman, did not wish to continue the expense incident to the policies of insurance in question, and subsequently, without the assent of said Braman, the plaintiff secured from the defendant McPeck the note in question, such action on the part of the plaintiff was in fraud of the defendant Braman, and the plaintiff cannot recover against the defendant Braman.

Robert W. Nason and Thomas W. Proctor, for plaintiff. Whipple, Sears & Ogden and W. M. Lindsay, for defendant.

LORING, J. This is an action on a promissory note dated July 15, 1902, signed McPeck & Co. The defendants, McPeck and Braman, at that time were partners. The plaintiff put in evidence showing that he was and is the agent of the Travelers' Insurance Company; that McPeck and Braman became partners on February 8, 1902; that before this partnership was formed McPeck had been doing business with one Alexander as a partner; that on February 8th McPeck held a policy on the life of Alexander in the Travelers' Insurance Company, represented by the plaintiff, payable to him, McPeck, and Alexander held a policy on McPeck's life, payable to him (Alexander). When Braman became a partner of McPeck, and Alexander ceased to be a partner, Braman asked to have the policy on McPeck's life transferred to him, and this was done "in consequence of his request," in the words of McPeck in his testimony. McPeck's testimony immediately after this is as follows: "Subsequently he took out this policy payable to me; this was one of the agreements between us." The third quarterly premium on the policy payable to Braman fell due April 24, 1902, and the second quarterly premium on the policy payable to McPeck fell due June 15th. On or about July 2d the plaintiff sent his bookkeeper to demand the premiums; he returned, and reported that Braman told him that he and McPeck had decided not to continue the insurance any longer. A day or two afterward the plaintiff saw McPeck, and said to him that he was surprised that Braman and he were not going to continue "this partnership agreement which you made," and, on being asked what he meant, replied, "Braman told my bookkeeper the other day that you had decided not to continue that insurance any longer." To which McPeck replied that, "if

Braman told you that, it is untrue; we have had no such conversation, and I fully intend to keep up this insurance, and Mr. Braman, if he carries out the agreement which we made originally, should carry out his part of the contract, and if you will accept a partnership note—it is not convenient for me to give you a check today for those premiums—but if you will accept a partnership note I will give it to you." In pursuance of this conversation the note sued on was given, and the plaintiff, on July 29th, paid the premiums to the company out of his own money. At the trial in the superior court the defendant McPeck was defaulted, and Braman introduced no evidence material on the matters now before us. Braman asked the court to rule that on the facts the note was not given for partnership purposes, was without consideration, and "that if the plaintiff or his agent received notice from the defendant Braman that he, the defendant Braman, did not wish to continue the expense incident to the policies of insurance in question, and subsequently, without the assent of said Braman, the plaintiff secured from the defendant McPeck the note in question, such action on the part of the plaintiff was in fraud of the defendant Braman, and the plaintiff cannot recover against the defendant Braman."

The defendant contends, in support of the first ruling asked for, that, the application for each policy having been made by the person insured, the premium was due from each, and was not a partnership debt, and that this conclusion is re-enforced by the provision contained in each policy that the person taking out the policy can revoke the designation of the beneficiary at pleasure. But there was evidence that one of the terms of the partnership agreement between McPeck and Braman was that these policies should be taken out and kept in force. That made the premiums, as between the partners, partnership debts.

In support of the second ruling asked for, the defendant Braman contends that by its terms the policy became void on the premiums not being paid at maturity, and that it appears on the face of the policy that no agent can extend the time for payment of premiums, nor can the contract be altered except by the written agreement of the company, signed by the president, vice president, secretary, or assistant secretary. But, if the company subsequently accepted the money due as premiums, the lapse of the policy for the failure to pay them would be waived. The conversation in which the plaintiff agreed to take a note warranted the judge in finding that he agreed to forward to the company the premiums out of his own funds; that promise was a valid consideration for the note.

We are of opinion that, on a fair construction of the third ruling asked for, the question presented by it is whether the giving of the notice prevented the plaintiff from recovering on this note if Braman originally agreed to keep these policies in force, and never in fact decided to break his agreement, and the plaintiff in good faith believed such to be the fact, or if the giving of the note was ratified by Braman after it was given. In addition to the evidence already stated, McPeck testified, and this testimony was uncontradicted: "I told Mr. Braman, before we signed the note, we would have to sign and pay it, and we would pay it. I did not say what we would do. I told him I signed it after it was done, and he made no objection to it." In this state of the evidence we think that the words "and subsequently, without the assent of said Braman, the plaintiff secured from the defendant McPeck the note in question," refers to an assent on Braman's part having been expressly given by Braman after the notice was given, and does not refer to there having been originally an agreement to keep up the policies, and no deliberate decision by Braman to break it, nor to the note having been ratified by him after it was given.

Exceptions overruled.

(185 Mass. 376)

CHILD et al. v. CHILD et al.

(Supreme Judicial Court of Massachusetts. Suffolk. April 1, 1904.)

WILLS — CONSTRUCTION—VESTED REMAINDER—MISTAKE—SUPPLYING WORDS.

1. Testator's will provided that, on the death of his widow, certain property should be conveyed "in equal shares to and among such of my brother and sisters, L., S., and F. and the children of my sister M., deceased," said children to take by representation, "and in case my said brother F., or either of my sisters, or any of the children of M. * * * die in my lifetime or before said trust shall terminate leaving children," they "shall take the parent's share by representation." A child of M., living at the decease of testator, died without issue before testator's widow, and after her death his executor sued, claiming that he died possessed of a vested interest; but the surviving children of M. claimed that the sentence in the will should be completed by supplying the words "as survive my wife," or their equivalent. *Held*, that plaintiff's testator had a vested interest, since, if the mistake consisted in the omission of a dependent clause, instead of the insertion of the words "such of," it was a matter of conjecture what the clause was.

Case reserved from Supreme Judicial Court, Suffolk County; Jas. M. Morton, Judge.

Bill by George F. Child and another, as executors of the will of Samuel G. Child, against George F. Child and others, to determine whether Samuel G. Child took a vested interest under the will of James Guild. Case reserved for the full court. The clause of the will mentioned in the opinion provided that certain property on the death of the widow should be conveyed "in equal shares to and among such of my brother and sisters, Louisa Guild, Sarah Ann Chandler and Frederic Guild and the children of my sister, Mary D. Child, deceased (said children of Mary D. to take the parent's share by right of representation), and in case my said brother Frederic, or either of my said sisters, or any of said children of Mary D. Child, deceased, above named, die in my lifetime or before said trust shall terminate leaving children, such children shall take the parent's share by right of representation."

Charles E. Hellier, for complainants. Arthur E. Denison and W. Stanley Campbell, for respondents.

LORING, J. It is plain that, if the words "such of" had not been inserted in the twelfth clause of the will, the plaintiffs' testator would have had a remainder vested, subject to be divested by his dying leaving issue him surviving at the date of his decease. It is also plain that a mistake has been made in drafting the will. The sentence and limitation which were begun by the words "such of" stand unfinished and incomplete. And finally it is plain that the mistake was either in the insertion of these words, or in the omission of the description and limitation begun by them. The surviving children of Mary D. Child, who are the defendants here, ask us to hold that the mistake consists in omitting the rest of the sentence, and to correct the mistake by reading into this article of the will the words "as survive my wife," or their equivalent. The leading case in this commonwealth on supplying words in a will is Metcalf v. Framingham, 128 Mass. 370, which has been often cited and followed. It is not the province of the court to conjecture what the intention of the testator would have been, had the omission been called to his attention. It is the more restricted duty of ascertaining his intention by construing the words which he has used, and of supplying the words which the court finds necessary to express that intention fully. It cannot supply words to give effect to an intention which he has not expressed by the words used by him. In construing the particular words in question, they are to be construed in the light of the will as a whole. See Bradlee v. Andrews, 137 Mass. 51, 53; Towle v. Delano, 144 Mass. 95, 99, 10 N. E. 769. See, also, Lord Halsbury in Inderweck v. Tatchell [1903] A. C. 120, 122. Or, as it was well put by Vice Chancellor Page Wood in Hope v. Potter, 3 Kay & J. 206, 209, 210, cited and relied on by the defendants, words can be supplied only where it is plain, by necessary implication, what the words to be supplied are. If we pass by the difficulty that it is no more than a conjecture whether the mistake in the case at bar consists in leaving in the words "such of," or in leaving out the dependent clause, and assume, in favor of the defendants, from the presence in the will of the words "such of," that the mistake consists in the omission of the dependent clause, it is a matter of conjecture what the omitted dependent clause is. It must be gathered from the gift over contained in the following sentence—the sentence with which the article ends—construed in the light of the rest of the will. This sentence makes provision for the brother or any of the sisters, or any of the children of the deceased sister, Mary, "leaving children," in case they die either during the lifetime of the testator, or during the continuance of the trust for the life tenant, and the provision made is that "such children shall take the parent's share by right of representation." Judged by this sentence, the omitted clause was to confine the provision made by it to the class consisting of the brother, the sisters, and the children of the deceased sister, Mary, who did not die leaving children; but there is nothing to indicate by necessary implication (to use the phrase used by Vice Chancellor Page Wood) that the prior gift to the class above named was to such of that class as survived the duration of the trust for the life tenant, and did not include all of the class who survived the testator, and who subsequently died, leaving no children them surviving at the date of their several deaths. It is at least a matter of conjecture which of these two was the provision contained in the omitted clause, and for that reason no missing words can be supplied. Indeed, if we were at liberty to indulge in conjectures of this kind, it is at least as probable that the omitted clause did include those surviving the testator, and dying not leaving children at the date of their several deaths. The gift over is a gift to take effect in case the brother or any sister or any child of the deceased sister, Mary, should die "in my lifetime or before said trust shall terminate," and the omitted clause (following the tenor of the following sentence containing the gift over) may well have been a clause which, together with the words of the will, gave the remainder to "such of my brother and sisters and children of my deceased sister as shall have survived me and shall not die leaving children before the termination of the trust." The case principally relied on by the defendants is Donnell v. Newburyport Hospital, 179 Mass. 187, 60 N. E. 482. That is a case where there was a gift over by way of substitution, and the gift over was not commensurate with the previous gift. It was held that the gift over was to be cut down to fit the previous gift.

A decree must be entered declaring that Samuel G. Child had a vested interest in the land described in the bill of complaint, and directing the $7,500, the proceeds of the sale of the interest of Samuel G. Child, to be transferred to the plaintiffs as executors. So ordered.

(178 N. Y. 213)

WALDEN v. CITY OF JAMESTOWN.

(Court of Appeals of New York. April 8, 1904.)

MUNICIPALITIES—NOTICE OF INJURY—DEFECTIVE STREETS—EVIDENCE—DAMAGES.

1. Where a charter of a city provides that, when an action is brought against it for personal injuries caused by defective sidewalks or streets, plaintiff must show notice in writing, given within 48 hours after the accident, to the city officers, service of such notice within 72 hours thereafter is sufficient, where, up to the time of the preparation and service of the notice, plaintiff was suffering such pain from her injuries that she was unable to transact business.

2. In an action to recover for personal injuries, plaintiff's physician testified that she was suffering from concussion of the spine. *Held*, that he could testify as an expert that the injury was permanent, and that the progressive result thereof might be paralysis.

Appeal from Supreme Court, Appellate Division, Fourth Department.

Action by Emma J. Walden against the city of Jamestown. From a judgment of the Appellate Division (80 N. Y. Supp. 65) affirming a judgment for plaintiff, defendant appeals. Affirmed.

James L. Weeks, for appellant. Benjamin S. Dean, for respondent.

BARTLETT, J. This action is brought against the defendant, the city of Jamestown, to recover damages for personal injuries alleged to have been received on the 8th day of April, 1900, within said city, on one of its traveled thoroughfares, known as "Warren Street."

On the day in question the plaintiff, in company with her daughter, was on the way from her residence to church, and, in attempting to pass over the sidewalk of said street, experienced a serious fall in consequence of the defects existing therein, being thrown forward, striking on her left knee and head, thereby sustaining painful injuries. The referee found, in substance, that in consequence of this fall the patella of plaintiff's left knee was dislocated, and that she also received a severe shock or fall, which occasioned pain and suffering and produced a condition of partial unconsciousness, disqualifying her for a certain time from transacting business; that directly after receiving such injuries the plaintiff was removed into an adjoining residence, and there cared for to some extent; she was then removed to her own home. The trial of this action took place some 18 months after the accident. The referee found, in substance, that the injury to the plaintiff occasioned her much suffering during the greater part of the time since the accident; that in consequence thereof she had been unable to attend to her household duties, or to perform any large amount of work or labor; that she is now afflicted with spinal irritation and its attendant results, which were occasioned by said injury and by the shock received by her at the time of said injury, and that plaintiff had sustained loss and damage to the amount and extent of $1,800; that the accident to the plaintiff and the injuries received by her were the result of the negligence of the defendant in failing to keep and maintain the sidewalk in a safe and proper condition at the place where the accident occurred. The referee further found that in and by the terms and provisions of the charter of the defendant (Laws 1898, p. 675, c. 231, § 2) it is, among other things, provided as follows: "Where any action is brought against said city to recover damages for a death or personal injuries caused by defective sidewalks or streets, the plaintiff must show that notice in writing of the place where said accident occurred out of which said claim arose, was given to the mayor, city clerk, or some alderman of said city within forty-eight hours after the happening thereof in order to maintain such action. Such notice shall be in addition to the written notice hereinbefore required." The referee found, in substance, that no notice in writing or otherwise was given by the plaintiff, in pursuance of the requirements of said section, within 48 hours after the occurrence of such injury, but that on the 11th day of April, 1900, a notice in writing was prepared and signed by the plaintiff, and served upon the city clerk of the defendant. It is further found that up to the time of the preparation and service of this notice the plaintiff was suffering much pain through and in consequence of such injuries, and was in a condition where she was unable to transact business. The question is thus presented whether the failure by the plaintiff, under these circumstances, to serve this preliminary notice within the period of 48 hours prescribed by the charter of the defendant, is a bar to the present action.

The counsel for the plaintiff argued in this court the point, among others, that this exceedingly brief time allowed for the service of the preliminary notice is not only unreasonable, shocking the sense of justice, but is unconstitutional as depriving the plaintiff of property without due process of law. This question was discussed by both counsel with ability, but, as we are of opinion that there was a substantial compliance with the statute, it is unnecessary to pass upon the constitutional question. We have the finding that the notice was served within 3 days, or 72 hours, after the accident, and that up to the time of its preparation and service the plaintiff was unable to transact business. It would, indeed, shock the sense of justice if this charter provision was construed so as to hold this service insufficient. It cannot be reasonably presumed that the intention of the Legislature in enacting this charter would lead to any such unjust con-

¶ 1. See Municipal Corporations, vol. 36, Cent. Dig. § 1706.

clusion. It is a fundamental canon of construction "that a thing which is in the letter of a statute is not within the statute itself, unless it is within the intention of the makers." Riggs v. Palmer, 115 N. Y. 506, 509, 22 N. E. 188, 5 L. R. A. 340, 12 Am. St. Rep. 819. This court has recently had occasion to examine the question as to substantial compliance with similar provisions, which are not to be regarded as statutes of limitation on a right of action, although a failure to observe them might be insisted upon as a bar. In Missano v. Mayor, etc., of N. Y., 160 N. Y. 123, 54 N. E. 744, it was held that a notice, which in other respects complied with the law requiring the filing with the corporation counsel of the city of New York of a notice of the intention to commence the action, as a condition to the maintenance of it against the municipality for damages for personal injuries, is not prevented from being a substantial compliance with the statute by the fact that it was directed to and filed with the comptroller, instead of the corporation counsel, as required, it being admitted by the defendant that the notice, after its receipt by the comptroller, was sent by him to the corporation counsel and filed by the latter in his office. In Sheehy v. City of New York, 160 N. Y. 139, 54 N. E. 749, the statute required the filing with the corporation counsel of a notice of an intention to commence an action, as a condition for the maintenance of it against certain cities, including the city of New York, for damages for personal injuries. Held, that the statute was substantially complied with by a notice which, while not stating in terms an intention to commence an action, fulfills the purpose of the statute by informing the corporation counsel of the nature of the claim, the place where and the circumstances under which it arose, and of a purpose to enforce it. This court said: "While, in an action like this, the statute must be substantially complied with, or the plaintiff cannot recover, still where an effort to comply with it has been made, and the notice served, when reasonably construed, is such as to accomplish the object of the statute, it should, we think, be regarded as sufficient." This charter provision requiring a notice of 48 hours is common in the municipal charters of this state, and has been dealt with in a satisfactory manner, by applying the rule of substantial compliance, in the Appellate Divisions. See particularly Green v. Village of Port Jervis, 55 App. Div. 58, 66 N. Y. Supp. 1042. It is an accepted maxim that the law does not seek to compel a man to do that which he cannot possibly perform. Broom's Legal Maxims (4th Ed.) 178. And this reasonable rule has been applied in many cases. Harmony v. Bingham, 12 N. Y. 99, 62 Am. Dec. 142; Matthews v. American Central Ins. Co., 154 N. Y. 449, 463, 48 N. E. 751, 39 L. R. A. 433, 61 Am. St. Rep. 627; Herter v. Mullen, 159 N. Y. 28, 39, 43, 53 N. E. 700, 44 L. R. A. 703, 70 Am. St. Rep. 517; Buffalo & L. Land Co. v. Bellevue L. & I. Co., 165 N. Y. 247, 254, 59 N. E. 5, 51 L. R. A. 951.

The counsel for the appellant raises the additional point that the judgment should be reversed for the reason that certain evidence given by the plaintiff's family physician over his objection and exception was error. This evidence related to the question of possible permanency of the injuries received in the spine, which had developed a well-marked case of spinal irritation and concussion; also as to the progressive character of this nerve injury. We are entirely satisfied with the manner in which the learned justice, writing for the Appellate Division, has disposed of this point, and adopt his reasoning and the conclusion reached—that no reversible error was committed in the admission of this evidence. The referee has not found, as he might have done, in view of the expert evidence, that the injury is permanent, nor that the progressive result of this spinal trouble may be paralysis. He found that at the time of the trial, about 18 months after the accident, the plaintiff was unable to attend to her household duties or perform any large amount of work or labor, and that she was afflicted with spinal irritation and its attendant results. The very reasonable amount of damages awarded of $1,800 would seem to indicate that the referee was alone influenced in fixing that amount by the situation at the time of the trial.

The judgment appealed from should be affirmed, with costs.

PARKER, C. J., and GRAY, O'BRIEN, HAIGHT, MARTIN, and CULLEN, JJ., concur.

Judgment affirmed.

(178 N. Y. 153)

MEDICAL COLLEGE LABORATORY OF CITY OF NEW YORK v. NEW YORK UNIVERSITY.

(Court of Appeals of New York. April 5, 1904.)

DEED — CONSIDERATION—PAROL EVIDENCE—RECONVEYANCE.

1. An incorporated medical college conveyed by deed certain property to a university with which it had a nominal connection for the consideration of $1 and an agreement by the grantee to pay the debts of the grantor. There were no debts, and the statute authorizing the conveyance provided that the rights of any creditors of the grantor should not be impaired by the conveyance. The resolutions authorizing the transfer and the acceptance thereof showed that the agreement to pay the debts was not part of the consideration. *Held*, that parol evidence was admissible to show the real consideration.

2. Where a deed from a medical college to a university expressed only a nominal consideration, evidence of negotiations prior to the deed,

¶ 1. See Evidence, vol. 20, Cent. Dig. § 1912.

showing that the inducement leading to the conveyance was a statement by the representative of the university having apparent authority that, if the college would turn over its property to the university, the medical committee of the latter should have entire control of the college, and that the professors should succeed to the powers theretofore exercised by the medical faculty, and that the medical committee should be constituted of people acceptable to the medical faculty, together with evidence that after the deed was executed the university had placed itself in such condition that it could not carry out the agreement, will support a decree ordering a reconveyance.

Appeal from Supreme Court, Appellate Division, First Department.

Action by the Medical College Laboratory of the City of New York against the New York University. From a judgment of the Appellate Division (78 N. Y. Supp. 673) affirming a judgment for plaintiff, defendant appeals. Affirmed.

David B. Hill, for appellant. Elihu Root, Bronson Winthrop, and Henry L. Stimson, for respondent.

PARKER, C. J. The judgment under review requires the reconveyance to plaintiff of property it conveyed to defendant by a deed dated February 8, 1897, which recites a consideration of $1, and contains an assumption of debts, if any, by the grantee. But the property, which was worth about $150,000, was unincumbered, and plaintiff was not indebted to any one. Defendant paid nothing for the property; and the ground upon which the decree of reconveyance is rested is that certain promises made to the officers and directors of plaintiff by representatives of defendant were not kept—indeed, that such promises were repudiated by defendant—and, as plaintiff would not have made the conveyance but for them, it is entitled to have the property restored to it.

About 10 years after the creation of defendant a number of physicians of prominence associated, and established a medical school in connection with the university, in pursuance of the following university statutes:

"(1) All expenses for building, apparatus, museum, etc., are to be provided for by the medical faculty and the council shall be in no ways responsible for expenses incurred by the medical faculty.

"(2) Each graduate shall pay to the treasury of the university $20, $10 of which shall be given to the chancellor for each diploma furnished by him, and this shall be the only tax required by the council from the students or faculty.

"(3) Nominations to fill vacancies and to establish new professorships shall come from the faculty to the council.

"(4) The faculty shall have power to make any by-laws for their own government and that of the students, which shall be compatible with the character and general statutes of the university to regulate the terms of instruction and the fees from students, and to recommend students for diplomas."

At the following meeting of the university council a change was made, providing that the medical faculty should make nominations to fill vacancies in their number, and that the council, with concurrence of the faculty, might prescribe the requisite qualifications of medical students. It will be seen that the faculty was to govern the medical school and to assume all financial responsibility; vacancies in the medical faculty were to be filled by the council, but only on the nomination of the faculty; and defendant was to issue diplomas, receiving a fee of $20. Practically, therefore, the medical faculty organized a college nominally connected with the university, but in effect a self-governing, independent, proprietary school. The school prospered, and in 1843 the faculty purchased a building, and put it in order at an expense of $60,000. Their museum and apparatus were valued at $30,000. Other property was bought and improvements made, and after 1882 a college building was erected on land purchased by the faculty, who held title as tenants in common. Some of the faculty had made presents of substantial value to the college. Others had advanced moneys, receiving certificates showing the amount advanced, which it was expected would be returned. Friends of the faculty had made substantial contributions. In 1883, page 132, c. 125, of the Laws of that year was enacted, incorporating the Medical College Laboratory of the City of New York, this plaintiff. The eight members of the faculty were made incorporators by the act, which directed that they should constitute the first board of directors, which should be self-perpetuating. To this corporation the faculty conveyed the real estate. Some years later an attempt was made to strengthen the college by bringing into the board of directors three laymen —D. Willis James, Charles E. Miller, and Francis L. Stetson—three incorporators resigning for that purpose. The corporation was still under the control of the medical faculty, however, as they composed a majority of the board. The school continued to prosper, and in 1891 Col. Oliver H. Payne —a friend of the doctors composing the faculty, and very much interested in their work —gave them a sum sufficient to discharge the mortgage debts upon the property, and to pay the certificates (supra) issued for moneys loaned prior to the incorporation. At the time, therefore, that the negotiations commenced about which we are to speak, plaintiff owned a large property, free from debt, and was conducting a medical school, which, so far as its management and government were concerned, was apparently an independent institution, but called a department of the New York University. Defendant was able to show that $1,000 was received by the medical school through university sources, but with that exception all the money seems to have been given or raised by the directors of plaintiff. There were negotiations looking to a transfer of the property to the university in 1876 and in 1886. But we need not give the details. They were of importance to the trial court and the Appellate Division as tending to show whether plaintiff and defendant stood in the position of bargainors prior to negotiations in issue here, and hence of value in passing upon the character of the later negotiations. But that evidence is not specially helpful to this court, which is confined to the inquiry whether there is evidence tending to establish the making of promises which led to the conveyance and its subsequent breach.

In the latter part of 1896, Dr. Stimson, of plaintiff's medical faculty, spoke to the chancellor of the university about the removal of one of the professors. The latter suggested that the better, if not the only, way, was for the medical college to surrender its property to the university, and place itself under the management of the university council. It seems that the medical committee of the council—the only part of the council, aside from the chancellor, that had had anything to do with the affairs of the medical college—had not once met during the administration of the then chancellor, a period of upwards of 10 years. This nonaction was accredited to the fact that the medical college had maintained practically an independent status. The desirability of interesting the medical committee was considered. The chancellor suggested the filling of two vacancies with friends of the medical college, so that in case of the transfer of the property the medical committee could control and direct the medical college, and that the faculty select two men to be elected to the council with that end in view. The faculty did suggest Henry F. Dimock and Charles E. Miller, then a director of plaintiff. The chancellor does not agree with Dr. Stimson that he said the medical committee should control and direct the medical college. It is not of moment whether he made so broad a statement, for plaintiff's claim does not rest on that promise. They agree, however, that they were trying to evolve a plan by which the medical committee should be so composed as to be satisfactory to plaintiff, thus bringing about closer relations between the university and the medical college. Whatever the details of the negotiations, they resulted in the election of Dimock and Miller to the medical committee, the former being made chairman. The other members were Col. Oliver H. Payne and Charles T. Barney, with the chancellor ex officio. A little more than a month after the election of Dimock and Miller, Dr. Pardee, the dean of the medical college, and a director and the secretary of the corporation, received from the chancellor a letter inclosing this resolution of the executive committee of the university: "Resolved, that the New York University by its executive committee invites the University Medical Laboratory Corporation and the Loomis Laboratory Corporation to confer with a subcommittee consisting of Mr. Henry F. Dimock and the chancellor of the University respecting the expediency of the transfers thus recommended." This resolution, it will be seen, advised plaintiff that Mr. Dimock and the chancellor had authority to represent defendant in such negotiations. Plaintiff contends that it was led to convey its property upon the faith of promises made by these representatives of defendant, that such promises were not kept, and that defendant has placed itself where it is impossible for it to keep them. Thus arises its claim—sustained by the courts below—that it is entitled in equity to a reconveyance of the property. After receiving the letter and resolution, Dr. Pardee sent to each member of plaintiff's board of directors copies of them, and called a meeting of the board for the 19th of December. A majority of the board assembled, and Mr. Dimock appeared, according to the terms of the resolution of the executive committee of the defendant, as its accredited representative. It was at this meeting, called under these circumstances, that the promises were made, if at all, which plaintiff's directors insist led it to convey the property. Plaintiff claims that it was promised that, if it would turn over all its property to the university, the medical committee of the council of the university should have entire management and control of the affairs of the medical college, which should succeed in the appointment of professors to the power theretofore exercised by the medical faculty, and that the medical committee should always remain constituted of people acceptable to the medical faculty, and that such result should be accomplished by the election of members to the university council who were agreeable to the medical faculty.

Now, our first inquiry is, is there evidence tending to support the claim of plaintiff that such promises were made by the representatives of defendant? Dimock's testimony as to what occurred at this meeting is: "I said to these gentlemen that I had come, together with the chancellor, as a committee from the university to lay before them some of the reasons why we thought it would be well for them to pass that property over to us, and to state some of the conditions on which we were willing to receive it. I explained to them— I told them I supposed they knew, of course, that this medical committee, called the medical committee of the university, had been reconstituted, as I understood, in accordance with their wishes, and that it consisted of Colonel Payne, Mr. Miller, Mr. Barney, myself—and I was the chairman—and the chancellor ex officio. I explained to them—what I supposed they knew—that that was a very friendly committee to them, and, as I understood, two of the members, Mr. Miller and myself, had been elected to the council at their suggestion, to be placed on the committee, and that, of course, Colonel Payne was the great benefactor of their institution. I said to them that, if they passed their property over to the university, the university would engage that that committee—the medical committee—should always remain constituted of people who were acceptable and satisfactory to the governing faculty; that, as vacancies occurred, members of the council who were agreeable or acceptable to them would be appointed to the place, and that that committee, so constituted, would have and should have the entire management and control of the property to be turned over, and of the affairs of the medical college; and that it should succeed, in the appointment of professors, to the power that had been exercised by the governing faculty theretofore. I explained to them that these things would be done if the property was turned over."

In this testimony of Dimock is to be found every element of the promise upon which plaintiff relies. There is the assurance that the reorganization of the medical committee was for the express purpose of so constituting the committee as that it should be absolutely satisfactory to the medical faculty, in that it should assure to that faculty that practical control of the institution which they and their predecessors had had for the something more than half a century of its existence, and which had built for it a substantial reputation as an educator in the field of medicine—a reputation in which the faculty, as well as their predecessors, took a just pride. This testimony of Dimock shows that the medical committee was not made satisfactory to the medical college for a temporary purpose merely, but that it was to continue to the end satisfactory to the medical faculty, and the assurance of its continuance was in the promise that the medical committee should always remain constituted of people acceptable and satisfactory to the medical faculty, and that such committee was to have the entire control and management of the property.

We need not further analyze Dimock's testimony, for we have seen that it was broad enough to cover the claim of plaintiff that defendant, through its representatives, promised, in substance, that the medical faculty should continue to be the leading factor in the conduct of the medical college.

Dimock's testimony is corroborated by several, if not all, of plaintiff's directors present on the day Dimock made the statement referred to to the board. It is contradicted by the chancellor in so far as the alleged promises of Dimock in behalf of defendant were concerned. The latter is quite confident no promises were made. But it is not for us to weigh the testimony. That duty devolved upon the Special Term and the Appellate Division, to which the Constitution gives the right to review evidence. This court is limited to the inquiry whether there is evidence to support the determination of the court. Now, as we have seen, such evidence is to be found in the testimony of Dimock, and hence we need not examine the evidence further on this subject.

But, says defendant, the committee had no authority to make any such promises, and defendant should not be held bound by representations made by agents in excess of the authority conferred. But the answer is that defendant conferred upon Dimock and the chancellor the apparent authority to make all the representations made when it formally invited the representatives of plaintiff to confer with these gentlemen touching the transfer. Representations and promises made by Dimock and the chancellor under such circumstances plaintiff had the right to rely upon as being made with the consent and approval of defendant. Plaintiff conveyed the property on the strength of the promises, and equity will compel a reconveyance if defendant either will not or cannot make good the promises.

The same principle controls this situation as was applied in Rackemann v. Riverbank Improvement Co., 167 Mass. 1, 44 N. E. 990, 57 Am. St. Rep. 427. In that case an agent of B., with authority to sell lots, promised A. that, if he would buy a lot at a certain price, B. would not sell any other lots on a certain plan at a less price. Relying upon that promise, A. purchased the lot. Within a year B. sold two lots at a less price. A. filed a bill in equity for a rescission of the purchase. Defendant repudiated, as unauthorized, the contract of its agent. Plaintiffs insisted that, having relied upon the promise, they were entitled to rescission. The court was of that opinion. It said: "The defendant would not have secured the advantage of the sale to the plaintiffs except for the offer and promise of its agent. The defendant employed him to offer its land ror sale. He made the offer of a lot to the plaintiffs, accompanied by the promise which has been mentioned. The plaintiffs agreed to take the land with the promise. It turns out that they got the land without the promise. The defendant cannot retain what is beneficial in the transaction, while disclaiming what is onerous. When it repudiates the means by which plaintiffs were brought to contract with it, this entitles the plaintiffs to give up the contract altogether, unless there is some other objection to their doing so. The rule in this respect is the same, whether the unauthorized act of the agent was fraudulent, or merely matter of warranty or promise." In that case, as in this, the promise was oral, made without authority, and was the inducing cause of the contract. We are agreed that Rackemann's Case is authority here. This judgment, therefore, is supported by the evidence, provided defendant has placed itself where it cannot possibly make good the promises made to plaintiff by its representatives.

It was found at Special Term that by reason of defendant's acts since the conveyance, and for other reasons, it is not possible that the property should be employed and used for and in accordance with the promise and agreement under which defendant acquired it.

Our next inquiry must be whether there is some evidence to support that finding. The deed, as we have noted, was executed February 8, 1897, and accepted by the council of defendant on the 1st of March following. Eighteen days later, negotiations were formally commenced by the executive committee of the council for the consolidation of plaintiff with the Bellevue Hospital Medical College. By the 12th of April the negotiations gave such assurance of success that the medical committee of defendant adopted a resolution calling for the resignations of eight members of the medical faculty as one step toward consolidation. The resignations were promptly tendered. May 3d the medical committee reported the university statutes regulating the performance of the duties of the faculty and appointing the officers and professors of the faculty. This report was adopted. On May 24th, however, the council received a protest from the former faculty of the Bellevue Hospital Medical College against the action taken by the medical committee. The council reconsidered the report of the medical committee. A substituted report was drafted, which stripped the medical committee of the power it supposed it possessed, and left the former medical faculty of plaintiff in the minority in the governing faculty of the new, or consolidated, college. The original report and the substitute were referred to the medical committee. That committee then presented a compromise report acceptable to the old faculty, but not satisfactory to the council of defendant, which so amended it as to render it unacceptable to the faculty. Efforts were made by the members of the former medical faculty to bring about an abandonment of the plan of consolidation. A hearing was had June 9, 1897, in which all of the professors of plaintiff and some from the Bellevue Hospital Medical College appeared, and favored abandonment of the plan of consolidation. Two days later the executive committee adopted resolutions approving the plan. Thereupon consolidation of the two colleges, so far as defendant could accomplish it, was effected.

The various steps in the total estrangement of those persons representing plaintiff and defendant—such as the refusal of the former members of the medical faculty to accept chairs offered to them, the tender of such chairs and their acceptance by others who were strangers to the college and its work, the annual election of members of the council, at which there was a refusal to elect Mr. Dimock a member of the medical committee, followed by an immediate tender of the resignations of Messrs. Payne, Barney, and Miller—followed each other in rapid succession. The mere recital of these events make their own comment, and, supplementing the action of the executive committee in consolidating the two colleges, demonstrate that there is evidence to support the determination of the learned trial judge that a situation has arisen which makes it impossible that the property should be employed and used in accordance with the promises made to plaintiff, and under which defendant acquired title. A decree, therefore, directing a reconveyance furnishes the method by which equity could more nearly than by any other work out justice between the parties.

Defendant insists that this oral testimony touching the negotiations prior to the deed should not have been received. It was seasonably and properly objected to, and if defendant is right in its contention the judgment cannot stand. The deed recites that it was given "in consideration of the sum of one dollar paid by the party of the second part, and of the agreement herein made by the party of the second part to assume and pay the debts and obligations of the party of the first part, if any there be." If the recital had stopped with the assertion that the deed was given in consideration of the sum of $1, there could be no question of the right of plaintiff to prove by parol the real consideration. It is always open to a party, where a nominal consideration is expressed, to show what the real consideration was, and to compel performance by the grantee in case he has refused to keep the promise or do the thing which constituted the actual consideration. In this case, however, the recital does not stop with the acknowledgment of the nominal consideration, but continues with the statement of an agreement made by the party of the second part to assume and pay the debts and obligations of the party of the first part, if any. Now that agreement on its face expresses a good consideration, and hence defendant insists that evidence may not be introduced to contradict it, and to show that, in addition to an agreement to pay the debts, defendant agreed to do something else. But plaintiff contends that this recital should not be given the weight which would ordinarily attend it between individuals, for the reason that the act of 1892, which authorized the conveyance, provided that "the rights of any creditor of the said the Medical College Laboratory of the City of New York shall not be thereby impaired," and hence it is said that if there were any debts they were as much of a charge upon the land as if such an amount was secured by mortgage, and therefore their payment by the grantee—if it would keep the property—was in effect required by the statute, independently of the agreement stated in the deed; that the recital of the agreement in the deed was therefore unnecessary and without force, for such would have been the obligation of defendant taking title pursuant to the statute, even though there had been no such recital.

Plaintiff also urges that it is alleged in the complaint and admitted in the answer that there were no debts, so that defendant assumed no burden whatever in taking the deed, and that such fact is of importance in that it tends strongly to establish the claim of plaintiff that the recital was inserted in accordance with that which was understood to be in effect the command of the statute, rather than as part of the agreement between the parties, both of which understood there were no debts. Several answers are attempted to be made to this argument, but the most serious one is that an attack upon the deed is necessary in order to reduce this recital to an expression without force or value, as the parties perhaps understood it to be. While this is so, the evidence which reduces its value to nothing was properly before the court. That there were no debts was established by the pleadings, while the statute, the resolution of plaintiff corporation directing the conveyance and the insertion therein of this provision, and the evidence of acceptance by defendant, were all read in evidence, without objection. That being so, the fact was established that the agreement to pay the debts did not form any part of the consideration, and the situation presented was one where the court was at liberty to treat the deed as if it did not contain such a recital, and, instead, stated merely a consideration of $1. In such case oral evidence is permissible to show the inducement for the deed—the promise which led to its making—and the failure of defendant to make good the promise appearing to be made upon its authority, and upon which plaintiff relied.

As we think the oral evidence was admissible under the peculiar circumstances to which we have referred, it follows that the judgment must be affirmed, with costs.

GRAY, MARTIN, VANN, CULLEN, and WERNER, JJ., concur. HAIGHT, J., absent.

Judgment affirmed.

(178 N. Y. 194)

PEOPLE ex rel. CONNECTING TERMINAL R. CO. v. MILLER, Comptroller.

(Court of Appeals of New York. April 8, 1904.)

FRANCHISE TAX—DOMESTIC CORPORATIONS—EARNINGS—INTERSTATE COMMERCE.

1. Where the entire business of a domestic corporation consists in the transportation of grain and other products from ports outside of the state to ports and places in the state, and of personal property from ports in the state to ports in other states, and its entire gross receipts from its business are derived from such transportation, and not otherwise, its earnings are "earnings derived from business which is of an interstate character" within Laws 1894, p. 1303, c. 562, § 11; Laws 1896, p. 857, c. 908, § 184, which forbid the imposition of any tax on the business of interstate commerce, and are not subject to the franchise tax imposed by Laws 1880, p. 706, c. 542, § 6; Laws 1881, p. 484, c. 361, § 6; Laws 1896, p. 857, c. 908, § 184.

¶ 1. See Commerce, vol. 10, Cent. Dig. §§ 114, 128.

Cullen, Martin, and Vann, JJ., dissenting.

Appeal from Supreme Court, Appellate Division, Third Department.

Certiorari by the state, on the relation of the Connecting Terminal Railroad Company, against Nathan L. Miller, State Comptroller. From an order of the Appellate Division (82 N. Y. Supp. 582) affirming a determination of the defendant assessing a franchise tax, relator appeals. Affirmed.

Henry Galbraith Ward and Sidney Ward, for appellant. John Cunneen, Atty. Gen. (William H. Wood, on the brief), for respondent.

O'BRIEN, J. On the 6th day of June, 1900, the comptroller of this state imposed a tax upon the gross earnings of the relator, amounting to $11,537.27, together with a penalty of $1,153.73, amounting in all to $12.691, for taxes claimed to have accrued to the state for 17 years previous to that date, under the amendatory act, section 184, c. 908, p. 857, Laws 1896. This was the first occasion when the state claimed the right to impose a franchise tax, as it is called, upon the relator. The relator filed a petition with the comptroller, asking him to revise and cancel the tax on the ground that it was in violation of the Constitution of the United States, which confers upon Congress the power to regulate commerce with foreign nations and among the several states, and that it was in violation of the provisions of the law of this state, and especially of section 11, c. 562, p. 1303, Laws 1894, and section 184, c. 908, p. 857, Laws 1896, which, in effect, forbid the imposing of any tax upon the business of interstate commerce.

The relator, in its petition, stated that it was a domestic corporation organized under the laws of this state authorizing the formation of railroad companies, passed April 2, 1850, and the several acts supplementary to or amendatory thereof, the object of said corporation being for the business of conducting and operating a railroad for the purposes provided by said statutes. It was also alleged that the entire business of said corporation consists in the transportation of personal property, consisting of grain and other products, from ports outside of the state of New York to ports and places in the state of New York and of personal property carried by the petitioner from ports in the state of New York to ports in other states, and that its entire gross receipts from its business are derived from such transportation, and not otherwise; and that no part of said business and no part of its gross receipts are for local business carried on in this state; and that, all of the business of the petitioner being of the character above mentioned, the levy of such assessment or tax by the comptroller is contrary to the provisions of the Constitution and laws of the United States, and is therefore not justified to any extent whatever. These allegations of fact are not denied in the return of the comptroller, and hence they stand admitted upon the record, and the only question presented by this appeal is as to the legal effect of these undisputed facts upon the tax or demand which the state has imposed upon the relator. It appears that the relator owns a piece of land of the width of about 1,650 feet, fronting on the Niagara river in the city of Buffalo, upon which it has a grain elevator and freight warehouse and several lines of railroad tracks. These tracks are used to afford facilities for access to its elevator and warehouse by cars owned by other companies and for loading and unloading such cars. It owns no engines, cars, or boats. The entire business is transacted in Buffalo, and consists in loading and unloading and storing grain and other freights, which, on the one hand, come from places outside of the state and are destined for points in the state or elsewhere, and, on the other, which come from points in the state and are destined to places in other states. It handles no local freight whatever. All its receipts are from such business, and come from the payment to it by the several companies or carriers who employ it of fixed charges per bushel on the grain handled and a fixed rate per ton on the package freight, which charges include elevator service and the use of the yards for car storage and car service over its tracks. These charges also cover a 10-days storage privilege, and for freights remaining longer than that an additional storage charge is made. The shortest storage privilege is about 10 days and the longest about 3 months. This work is done by the relator for various railroad and other transportation companies having terminals on Buffalo Harbor.

It is somewhat difficult at first view to consider the relator as a transportation company, but, inasmuch as it has incorporated and exists under the general railroad law, it must, I think, for all the purposes of this case, be considered as a corporation of that character. Its principal business operations consist in the transshipment of grain which it takes into its elevator from boats or water craft upon the river or lake and discharges into cars to be carried by railroads to New York or other ports on the Atlantic seaboard. In this way it moves the freight or property, whatever it may consist of, about 500 feet, and only that part of the route is covered by the relator's operations, whether the freight is destined for the East or the West. It may be assumed from the nature of the business that the property is carried under bills of lading from the point of shipment to the point of ultimate destination, and the relator is employed by the carriers to aid in the transshipment of the property at Buffalo. Looking at the transactions of the relator in a general way, the mind readily arrives at the conclusion that it is engaged in the business of interstate commerce within the fair meaning of the law, but when we come to an examination of the cases on this question the conclusion may not be so clear. There is great difficulty in determining from the authorities what operations are and what are not interstate commerce. A reference to a few of the cases will show the perplexities that beset the subject at almost every point. In Munn v. Illinois, 94 U. S. 113, 24 L. Ed. 77, it was held that a state law regulating the charges of elevators in Chicago engaged in the business of storing and delivering grain to carriers for transportation to ports and places in other states was not in conflict with the commerce clause of the federal Constitution. That decision was subsequently reaffirmed and followed when the validity of a similar statute of this state was before the court. Budd v. New York, 143 U. S. 517, 12 Sup. Ct. 468, 36 L. Ed. 247. It has been held that a state statute regulating the freight charges of railroads upon property delivered to the railroad in one state to be transported to another state under one contract and by one voyage was an unauthorized interference with interstate commerce. Wabash, St. L. & P. Ry. Co. v. Illinois, 118 U. S. 557, 7 Sup. Ct. 4, 30 L. Ed. 244. It was held that a state statute requiring railroad corporations operating railroads within the state to pay an annual franchise tax based upon its gross receipts was valid, although the railroad in that case was partly within and partly without the state, and was operated as a part of a line or system extending beyond the state and into other states. Maine v. Grand Trunk Ry. Co., 142 U. S. 217, 12 Sup. Ct. 163, 35 L. Ed. 994. So it was held that a state tax upon the gross receipts upon a steamship company incorporated under its laws derived from the transportation of persons and property by sea between different states and to and from foreign countries was a regulation of interstate and foreign commerce in conflict with the exclusive powers of Congress under the Constitution. Phila. & Southern M. S. S. Co. v. Penn., 122 U. S. 326, 7 Sup. Ct. 1118, 30 L. Ed. 1200. It has just been decided by the same court that a cab service maintained and operated in the city of New York by the Pennsylvania Railroad Company for the purpose of transporting to various points therein its passengers conveyed to that city by ferry from its railroad terminus in an adjoining state was taxable upon its gross receipts under a state law, the service beginning and ending in the city of New York, not being a part of the interstate commerce transacted by the railroad corporation; and that the capital employed by it in the maintenance of such cab service is not exempt from the taxation imposed by the statute of this state relating to franchise taxes upon corporations. The final conclusion of the court in the case was that the business was an independent local service, preliminary or subsequent to interstate transportation. That decision affirmed the judgment of this court in the case of People ex rel. Penn. R. R. Co. v. Knight, 171 N. Y. 354, 64 N. E. 152. It has been held that this same railroad company, whose lines extend into other states, but not into this state, operating in connection with its road a ferry across the Hudson river to the city of New York, where it has terminal facilities used in receiving and delivering freight and passengers, collecting in that city the money due for transportation of freight to and from it, and selling therein passenger tickets, employing a large number of clerks and laborers, was engaged in interstate commerce, and its operation in the city of New York was of that character, and that it was not taxable by this state upon such business. I am not aware that this decision has ever been questioned. People ex rel. Penn. R. R. Co. v. Wemple, 138 N. Y. 1, 33 N. E. 720, 19 L. R. A. 694. The difficulty of formulating from these decisions, apparently in conflict with each other, any rule or principle to govern this case, must be quite apparent. In this condition of the authorities the best that we can do is to state briefly what seems to us to be the reasonable view of the law on this subject when applied to the facts of the case.

There is one feature of the case as to which there is no conflict in the authorities, and that is that interstate commerce cannot be taxed or burdened or restricted in any way by state laws, and the only question that we have to deal with now is whether the relator's operations are such that they can be held to be the transaction of the business of interstate commerce. Fortunately, there is no dispute about the facts of the case so far as they describe the relator's business. They have already been stated, and they stand admitted in the record. It is quite true that all of its operations are conducted within the state of New York, but I apprehend that the circumstance does not show that the business is something other than interstate commerce. We have the other fact that it is engaged in no local business whatever, and that it is but a mere link in the chain of transportation of grain and other property from the Western states to the seaboard and from the East to the West. If, as the court of last resort with respect to such questions has often held, interstate commerce consists in intercourse and traffic between the states, either by navigation or otherwise, for the transportation of persons and property and the purchase, sale, and exchange of commodities, the relator's operations would seem to fall fairly within that definition. What the relator does with respect to the property in transit from one state to another is just as essential and substantial a part of the process of interstate transportation as anything else that it does, or can be done, in order to complete the carriage of goods by water and by land from one state to another state. Indeed, except for the important part that the relator takes in the process of transportation, the commercial intercourse described in the record could not take place at all. The first part of the route in the process of transportation is covered by water craft upon the Lakes and the last part by railroads, but, between these two links in the line of transportation the relator's operations, which are not independent or local, but a part, and most essential part, of the process of transporting property by the owner in one state to the purchaser or consignee in another state, intervene. Hence the relator's earnings upon which the tax in question was imposed would plainly appear to be derived from the business of interstate commerce. McCall v. California, 136 U. S. 104, 10 Sup. Ct. 881, 34 L. Ed. 392.

But, whatever the rule of the federal court may be with respect to such a case as this, we have another guide, and that is the words of our own statute under the authority of which the tax in question was imposed. That statute in terms defines the gross earnings that are subject to the tax, and declares that they "shall in no event include earnings derived from business which is of an interstate character," and in adjusting such taxes the state officers are commanded to exclude all the earnings "of an interstate character." The question, then, is whether the earnings of the relator upon which the tax in question was imposed were "derived from business which is of an interstate character," or were "earnings of an interstate character." The character of the earnings must be interstate unless they are purely local, and the record, as we have seen, admits that they are not local. Independent of this admission, however, it would seem to be a reasonably plain proposition that the relator's earnings derived from the transportation of property in transit from one state to another—that is to say, in conveying it by means of elevators and railroad tracks from the boats on the lake to the railroad cars on the land—are "earnings of an interstate character," and it can make no difference in principle whether the distance over which the property was so conveyed was 500 feet or a mile.

The order appealed from should be reversed, with costs, and the assessment canceled.

PARKER, C. J. I concur with Judge O'BRIEN as to that portion of the tax which was levied after the enactment of chapter 562, p. 1302, Laws 1894, for, while this is an excise tax imposed on the corporation as authority for it to do business, the statute expressly prohibits the inclusion in the estimate of gross earnings for the basis of taxation "earnings derived from business which is of an interstate character." The tax for the years subsequent to 1894 seems to me to be levied on that basis, and upon no other. As to so much of the tax, however, as was assessed upon relator for the years prior to 1894, and levied by virtue of section 6, c. 361, p. 484, Laws 1881, it seems to me the levy could stand under the authorities. That section authorizes a tax upon its corporate franchise and business in this state at the rate of five-tenths of 1 per centum upon the gross earnings within this state of said corporation or company or association. This court holds in People v. Equitable Trust Co., 96 N. Y. 388, that when such a tax is imposed on a domestic corporation it is a tax on its corporate franchise; when imposed on a foreign corporation it is a tax on its business—a distinction based on the fact that corporate franchises are only taxable within the jurisdiction which creates them, and where alone they can be said to have a situs. This holding is affirmed in terms in People ex rel. Penn. R. R. Co. v. Wemple, 138 N. Y. 1, 8, 33 N. E. 720, 19 L. R. A. 694. Very recently we had before this court People ex rel. U. S. Aluminium P. P. Co. v. Knight, 174 N. Y. 475, 67 N. E. 65, in which it is unanimously held that the capital of domestic corporations invested in letters patent, United States bonds, or copyrights may be appraised for the purpose of ascertaining the amount of the franchise tax, the same as other property. Judge Vann, in speaking of certain cases, says (174 N. Y. 482, 67 N. E. 68) that "they involve the principle that while a tax cannot be assessed upon property that is exempt by act of Congress, it may be imposed upon the franchise of a corporation to which such exempt property belongs, and may be measured by the value thereof." Why does not the principle of that case apply to so much of this one as involves the tax prior to 1894? The state has no right to tax United States bonds, patent rights, copyrights, or interstate commerce, but it may place an excise tax upon a domestic corporation for its right to do business as a corporation, and in measuring the amount of such tax there may be taken into consideration, as we hold in that case, the value of government bonds, patents, or copyrights, although nonassessable as such by the state. Why, therefore, may not be taken into consideration, in measuring the amount of an excise tax assessed as an authority for the corporation to do business in the state, the volume of interstate commerce business done by it? But one answer to the question could result, it seems to me, from a careful reading of the statute of 1881 in the light of the authorities cited, but those of my associates that agree that the earnings of this corporation are of an interstate character are of the opinion that, inasmuch as section 184 of the tax law, passed in 1894 (Laws 1896, p. 857, c. 908), provides that the comptroller shall settle the taxes levied under the act of 1881 for the two years immediately preceding 1894 by excluding the earnings of an interstate character, the Legislature intended to prevent the collection of past taxes based on such earnings. As intention must be gleaned from the language of the statute, it is difficult to reach that conclusion by the application of any of the rules of statutory construction; inasmuch as the provision referred to embraces only the two years immediately preceding 1894. But as the Legislature may have assumed that the taxes prior to that time had been collected, I shall, for the purpose of making a decision, concur in the result reached by Judge O'BRIEN.

GRAY, J. I shall concur with the opinion of Judge O'BRIEN. The acts of 1894 and of 1896, which conferred authority upon the comptroller to impose additional franchise taxes, by its terms directs that officer "in no event to include earnings derived from business which is of an interstate character." If that officer cannot impose the tax upon the relator's earnings since the enactment of that law, I think he is quite without authority in this proceeding to impose taxes for the years prior to the enactment upon earnings of the relator derived from business of an interstate character.

CULLEN, J. (dissenting). So far as the claim is made that the tax imposed on the relator is in conflict with the federal Constitution, I assume that the decisions of the Supreme Court of the United States are conclusive upon us. Such is certainly their effect so far as they declare state regulations of commerce to be invalid. It may be that, if a state court should hold a statute of the state repugnant to the federal Constitution in a case in which similar statutes have been held by the Supreme Court not to be repugnant, the decision would not be subject to review by the Supreme Court. But, granting this, the action of the state court would be wholly unreasonable. Now, if the appellant's contention is to be determined by the decisions of the Supreme Court of the United States, it may be summarily disposed of by a very short syllogism. In the case of interstate transportation the Legislature of a state cannot prescribe the charge to be made even for the part of the transportation within the state. Wabash, St. L. & P. Ry. Co. v. Illinois, 118 U. S. 557, 7 Sup. Ct. 4, 30 L. Ed. 244. But the state can prescribe the charges to be exacted for services by the Buffalo elevators engaged like that of the relator in the transfer of grain from lake vessels to warehouses or cars. Budd v. New York, 143 U. S. 517, 12 Sup. Ct. 468, 36 L. Ed. 247. Therefore, the services of such elevators do not constitute part of interstate transportation.

I am frank to say that oftentimes, especially in the development of new principles of law, or in their application to new states of fact, the greatest and wisest of courts may not be able to foresee to what extent the logic of its doctrine will carry it, nor to state the limits and qualifications of that doctrine. It might, therefore, lead to an erroneous result to select two propositions determined by a court, between which decisions there had intervened a long period of time, and each of which might be made without appreciating its bearing on the other, and from those propositions to deduce a third as a necessary conclusion. But the present case is free from any such source of error. The doctrine of the Wabash Case was reaffirmed by the Supreme Court in Covington, etc., Bridge Company v. Kentucky, 154 U. S. 204, 14 Sup. Ct. 1087, 38 L. Ed. 962, and the case is cited with approval to this day. The Budd Case was decided on the authority of Munn v. Illinois, 94 U. S. 113, 24 L. Ed. 77, which is the pioneer case on the subject, and was itself reaffirmed in Brass v. North Dakota, 153 U. S. 391, 14 Sup. Ct. 857, 38 L. Ed. 757. In the last case it was said by Justice Shiras, delivering the opinion of the court: "In the cases thus brought to this court from the states of Illinois and New York [Munn and Budd Cases] we were asked to declare void statutes regulating the affairs of grain warehouses and elevators within those states, and held valid by their highest courts, because it was claimed that such legislation was repugnant to that clause of the eighth section of article 1 of the Constitution of the United States which confers upon Congress power to regulate commerce with foreign nations and among the several states, and to the fourteenth amendment, which ordains that no state shall deprive any person of life, liberty, or property without due process of law, nor deny to any person within its jurisdiction the equal protection of the law." It is clear that the objection that a state statute prescribing the charges of elevators and warehouses could not be upheld if such services constitute a part of interstate commerce was present in the mind of the court when it decided the elevator cases, though the dominant question in those cases was the alleged invasion of private property rights. In the Munn Case it was said: "It was very properly said in the case of the State Tax on Railway Gross Receipts, 15 Wall. 232, 21 L. Ed. 146, that 'it is not everything that affects commerce that amounts to a regulation of it, within the meaning of the Constitution.' The warehouses of these plaintiffs in error are situated and their business carried on exclusively within the limits of the state of Illinois. They are used as instruments by those engaged in state as well as those engaged in interstate commerce, but they are no more necessarily a part of commerce itself than the dray or the cart by which, but for them, grain would be transferred from one railroad station to another. Incidentally they may become connected with interstate commerce, but not necessarily so. Their regulation is a thing of domestic concern, and certainly until Congress acts in reference to their interstate relations the state may exercise all the powers of government over them, even though in so doing it may indirectly operate upon commerce outside its immediate jurisdiction." In connection with the Budd Case there was argued and decided in the Supreme Court of the United States the case of New York ex rel. Annon v. Walsh, 143 U. S. 517, 12 Sup. Ct. 468, 36 L. Ed. 247. Annon was the owner of floating elevators which were moved from point to point in the harbor of New York, and it was in this respect only that his case differed from that of Budd. Of such floating elevators the court said: "So far as the statute in question is a regulation of commerce, it is a regulation of commerce only on the waters of the state of New York. It operates only within the limits of that state, and is no more obnoxious as a regulation of interstate commerce than was the statute of Illinois in respect to warehouses in Munn v. Illinois. It is of the same character with navigation laws in respect to navigation within the state, and laws regulating wharfage rights within the state, and other kindred laws." There was a vigorous dissent in the Budd Case, but the dissent proceeded solely on the ground that the state statute before the court was an invasion of private property. Of the nature of elevator services Judge Brewer said: "It will not do to say that the transferring of grain through an elevator is one step in the process of transportation, and that, therefore, they are quasi common carriers, discharging public duty, and subject to public control. They are not carriers in any proper sense of the term. They may facilitate carriage. So does the boxing and packing of goods for transportation."

There is nothing in the case of this relator that distinguishes it from those of Munn, Budd, Annon, and Brass. The fact that the grain elevated or stored was on its journey from points without the state to points within the state or to points beyond the state was present in those cases as in this. Indeed, the argument of the majority of the court in the Budd Case in support of the right of the state to prescribe the rate of elevator charges proceeded largely on the circumstance that 120 millions of bushels of grain were annually shipped to Buffalo from the West, and, after transportation through the state, either by canal or railroad, a large part of it was, by the use of the floating elevators, transferred to ships to be distributed in the markets of the world. It may be true that the grain is carried through bills of lading, though that fact does not appear in the record. But to those bills of lading, whatever their character, the relator is a stranger. The evidence is: "In 1901 we handled through the elevator about ten million bushels of grain, the records of which were entirely with the Lehigh Valley Railroad. We had no bills of lading. We knew nothing of the grain at all except as we received directions from the Lehigh Road. The Lehigh Valley would have all the information, of course." The services of the relator were rendered not under the terms of a through bill of lading, but under a contract with the railroad company or navigation company, were performed entirely within this state, and the price charged included an option of 10 days' storage in the warehouse, though the time of storage might be increased on payment of an additional charge. It thus appears that the business of this relator does not differ from that of other elevator owners and warehousemen in Buffalo, nor is it distinguishable in character from the work performed by stevedores in unloading vessels. It is true the grain is moved by the operations of the elevator a distance of about 500 feet horizontally. In this respect, however, it does not differ from every crane or derrick on a wharf by which a cargo is moved at least from the hatchway to the pier. To the foregoing authorities may be added the declaration of the general doctrine on the subject found in Covington, etc., Bridge Company v. Kentucky, 154 U. S. 204, 14 Sup. Ct. 1087, 38 L. Ed. 962: "As was said by Mr. Justice Miller in the Wabash Case: 'It is impossible to see any distinction in its effect upon commerce of either class between a statute which regulates the charges for transportation and a statute which levies a tax for the benefit of the state upon the same transportation;'" that is to say, the power of a state to tax and the power to regulate charges are coextensive.

If I have rightly interpreted the authorities cited, it may safely be said to be the settled law of the Supreme Court of the United States that the work done by the relator is not of an interstate character. While the question before us arises under our own statute, I think that that statute is to be interpreted in the light of the federal decisions, since the action of the Legislature in exempting a business of an interstate character in computing the liability of the relator to taxation was undoubtedly dictated by the consideration that interstate commerce was under the control of Congress, and it could not have been intended to except any transportation or commerce as of an interstate character except such as the federal courts might hold to be, under the Constitution of the United States, within the control of Congress. Moreover, I do not see how we can hold that the work of the relator is of an interstate character without overruling the decision of this court in the Budd Case (People v. Budd, 117 N. Y. 1, 22 N. E. 670, 682, 5 L. R. A. 559, 15 Am. St. Rep. 460), for, if the elevation and transfer of grain is a part of interstate commerce, the Legislature of the state cannot prescribe the charge to be made therefor. If these views are correct, it is unnecessary to further discuss the nature and character of elevator and warehouse services.

The order appealed from should be affirmed, with costs.

HAIGHT, J., concurs with O'BRIEN, J. PARKER, C. J., and GRAY, J., in memoranda, concur in result with O'BRIEN, J. MARTIN and VANN, JJ., concur with CULLEN, J.

Order reversed.

(208 Ill. 267)

CHICAGO CITY RY. CO. v. O'DONNELL.

(Supreme Court of Illinois. April 7, 1904.)

SUPREME COURT PRACTICE—PETITION FOR REHEARING—ARGUMENT.

1. Supreme Court Rule 30, providing that a petition for rehearing shall state concisely the points supposed to have been overlooked or misapprehended by the court, and that it shall contain no argument, will be strictly enforced, and any petition found on examination to contain any argument whatever will be immediately stricken from the files, without being considered on the merits.

On petition for rehearing. Petition stricken.

For former opinion, see 70 N. E. 294.

SCOTT, J. This is a petition for rehearing. The practice in reference to the presentation thereof is regulated by rule 30 of the rules of practice of this court, which provides that such a petition shall state "concisely the points supposed to have been overlooked or misapprehended by the court, with proper reference to the particular portion of the original abstract and brief relied upon. In no case will any argument be permitted in support of such petition. This rule will be strictly enforced, and any petition in violation thereof will be stricken from the files."

A rehearing may be had in this court when any material fact has been overlooked or misapprehended, or where the court has failed to determine some proposition of law that is of controlling importance in the cause, and the only legitimate office of the petition for rehearing is to show, by a terse and accurate statement, the court's inadvertence, with reference to such portions of the brief or abstract, as will sustain petitioner's position. The petition under consideration is a gross violation of this rule. It contains more than 30 pages of printed argument, and is practically a reargument of the cause. Help-

¶ 1. See Appeal and Error, vol. 3, Cent. Dig. § 3234.

ful arguments, both oral and printed, are welcomed by this court. It is our earnest desire that a litigant should avail himself to the fullest extent of his right to argue, orally and otherwise, his cause in this forum. The proper time to argue, however, is at the time of submission, and when a case has been fully argued, has received careful consideration, and been decided, a reargument in a petition for a rehearing can serve no useful purpose. All that is proper in that respect is a reference to that portion of the brief and argument which petitioner conceives will show the error of the court.

The practice of arguing cases in petitions for rehearing has been gradually increasing in this court. The rule has not been enforced, because the court, as a body, has been loth, and especially has the writer of the opinion assailed been loth, to have a petition of this character stricken, lest there might possibly be error in the judgment, which would remain unchallenged and uncorrected if that course was followed; but the abuse of the rule has become so prevalent in this respect that the consideration of the arguments contained in these petitions has become an intolerable, as well as a useless, burden. The great majority of such petitions now filed in this court are but rearguments. So far as the one now before us is concerned, in view of the fact that counsel filing it was no doubt aware that the rule in question had not been heretofore strictly applied, we have examined the petition far enough to ascertain the points relied upon, and deem them without merit.

Every petition for rehearing hereafter filed in this court, which, upon examination, is found to contain any argument whatever, will be immediately stricken, without being considered upon the merits at all. Rule 30 will be rigidly enforced. The petition for a rehearing in the case at bar will be stricken from the files.

Petition stricken.

(185 Mass. 398)

ABBOTT et al. v. FROST.

(Supreme Judicial Court of Massachusetts. Middlesex. April 2, 1904.)

TAXATION—ASSESSMENT OF MORTGAGED REAL ESTATE—TO WHOM ASSESSED—TAX SALES—RIGHT OF PURCHASER—RIGHT OF MORTGAGEE—TIME OF SALE—ALIENATION BEFORE NOTICE OF SALE.

1. Under St. 1882, p. 131, c. 175, requiring the assessors to assess the interest of the mortgagor and mortgagee of real estate to each respectively, and providing that, if the mortgagor or mortgagee fails to bring to the assessors a statement of the amount due to the mortgagee, no tax shall be invalid for the reason that the mortgagee's interest therein has not been assessed to him, real estate may lawfully be assessed to the mortgagor in possession in case either he or the mortgagee fails to make the required statement, and hence a tax is not invalid simply because the mortgagee was not recognized in the assessment.

2. Where real estate is lawfully assessed to the mortgagor alone, a sale for delinquent taxes is valid as against the mortgagee.

¶ 3. A sale of real estate for delinquent taxes, lawfully assessed to the mortgagor in possession, under St. 1888, p. 366, c. 390, § 30, as amended by St. 1889, p. 1023, c. 334, § 9, providing that taxes assessed on real estate shall constitute a lien thereon from the 1st day of May until the expiration of two years from the 1st day of October of the year in which the taxes are assessed, and, if such tax remains unpaid for 14 days after demand therefor, it may with all incidental charges be levied by sale of the real estate, passes the entire title in the land to the grantee by the collector's deed, freed from the mortgage.

4. Under St. 1888, p. 366, c. 390, § 30, as amended by St. 1889, p. 1023, c. 334, § 9, making taxes on real estate a lien thereon from the 1st day of May until the expiration of two years from the 1st day of October of the year in which the taxes are assessed, and providing that, if the tax remains unpaid for 14 days after demand, the land may be sold within the two years, "or after the expiration of said two years if the estate has not been alienated prior to the giving of the notice of such sale," a purchaser of real estate for delinquent taxes at a sale after the expiration of the two years obtains as good a title if there has been no change in the ownership of the estate as if the sale had been made within the two years.

5. The entry of a mortgagee for the purpose of foreclosure under Rev. Laws, c. 187, § 1, and the subsequent sale under the power in the mortgage, after notice of the tax sale for delinquent taxes lawfully assessed to the mortgagor in possession, is not an alienation of the property, within St. 1888, p. 366, c. 390, § 30, as amended by St. 1889, p. 1023, c. 334, § 9, authorizing a sale of real estate for delinquent taxes after the expiration of two years "if the estate has not been alienated prior to the giving of the notice of such sale."

Appeal from Superior Court, Middlesex County.

Bill in equity by one Abbott and another, the present owner and mortgagee of real estate, against one Frost, alleging that certain taxes on the real estate were illegal, and that a tax sale was invalid. From a decree dismissing the bill, plaintiffs appeal. Affirmed.

Curtis Abbott, for appellants. W. Adams, for appellee.

BRALEY, J. Unless the sale of the premises described in the bill was invalid because the tax assessed had ceased to be a lien at the time of sale, there is no cloud on the title of the plaintiffs, and the suit cannot be maintained. For all of the time covered by the several assessments the property was subject to a mortgage duly recorded, but neither the mortgagor nor mortgagee brought in to the assessors any statement under St. 1882, p. 131, c. 175, requiring them to ascertain and fix a value on the interest of each in the real estate, and in the absence of any compliance with this preliminary requirement it could be lawfully assessed to the mortgagor in possession. Such assessments are permitted by our laws relating to taxation, and have been held to be in strict accordance with

¶ 3. See Taxation, vol. 45, Cent. Dig. § 1466.

their provisions. Pub. St. c. 11; St. 1889, p. 837, c. 84; Worcester v. Boston, 179 Mass. 41, 49, 60 N. E. 410.

Before St. 1881, p. 646, c. 304 (subsequently Pub. St. 1882, c. 11, §§ 13-15), when land subject to a mortgage was assessed to the mortgagor in possession the entire estate was assessed, and there was no division or separation of the legal and equitable titles, and the lien for the tax was as broad as the assessment. No distinction between these titles before possession by the mortgagee under foreclosure proceedings is recognized, and the tax assessed and the sale for its payment covers and includes both estates. Parker v. Baxter, 2 Gray, 185. If the object of this enactment was to prevent double taxation, and to require that the interest of each should be respectively ascertained, and in all cases they should be separately assessed or taxed as joint owners, it was subsequently amended so that, from being mandatory in terms, provision was made that real estate subject to a mortgage could be legally assessed to the owner in possession unless either the mortgagor or mortgagee had given to the assessors, within the time for bringing in lists of taxable property, a sworn statement of the amount due under the mortgage. St. 1882, p. 131, c. 175.

It is agreed that the mortgagor was in possession for the whole period, and it does not appear that either he or the mortgagee made any effort to have the respective interest of each assessed. Unless either complied with the statutory provision made for their benefit, they need not be deemed joint owners, and a tax otherwise lawfully imposed did not become invalid because the mortgagee had not been recognized in the assessment. Worcester v. Boston, ubi supra; Cummins v. Christie, 179 Mass. 74, 60 N. E. 396, 88 Am. St. Rep. 357. If a sale follows, it is commensurate with the tax lien, for in theory the taxing power assesses with one hand, and at the same time demands payment with the other, and, if the assessment is valid, a sale for its collection properly made is also valid. Hill v. Bacon, 110 Mass. 387.

At the time these taxes were assessed, and when the sale took place, St. 1888, p. 366, c. 390, § 30, as amended by St. 1889, p. 1023, c. 334, § 9, provided that, "* * * if such tax remains unpaid for fourteen days after demand therefor, it may with all incidental charges and fees be levied by sale of the real estate within said two years, or after the expiration of said two years, if the estate has not been alienated prior to the giving of the notice of such sale." When a sale of real property under this and similar statutes is made for taxes lawfully assessed, the entire title or interest in the land passes to the grantee by the deed of the collector, and it does not become essential to inquire whether his title is to be considered as the result of all previous titles, and which are transmitted to him by operation of law, or a new title conferred under a taking by the sovereign power to enforce a public right to which property under our Constitution is generally made subject. See Harrison v. Dolan, 172 Mass. 395, 398, 52 N. E. 513; Emery v. Boston Terminal Co., 178 Mass. 172, 184, 59 N. E. 763, 86 Am. St. Rep. 473. Such a lien constitutes a charge or incumbrance on the land without which it could not be sold, and at any time within the limitation a sale or conveyance would vest in the purchaser an absolute title to the whole estate, freed from the mortgage which was in existence, and all outstanding incumbrances. Hunt v. Boston, 183 Mass. 303, 305, 67 N. E. 244, and cases cited.

The plaintiffs contend that at the time of sale the statutory lien had expired, at least as to a part of the taxes, and as the sale cannot be divided and held good in part, and invalid as to the remainder, it was not effectual to cut off the mortgage. They also take the further position that, after the express limitation of two years had run, the sale, though effectual to transfer the interest of the mortgagor, left the estate of the mortgagee unaffected, and that it did not pass title to the whole property. Sherwin v. Boston Five Cents Savings Bank, 137 Mass. 444. But if the tax for each year constituted a lien, the last tax having priority over preceding taxes, yet the collector might sell separately or make a single sale for all the taxes. Keen v. Sheehan, 154 Mass. 208, 28 N. E. 150; Pixley v. Pixley, 164 Mass. 335, 41 N. E. 648; Lancy v. Snow, 180 Mass. 411, 62 N. E. 735. In these cases, however, no question seems to have arisen like that now presented. Here the difficulty arises when an attempt is made to determine whether the lien expires in all cases with the limitation of two years. Notwithstanding the lapse of time, the nature and extent of the charge upon the estate does not change, but is coextensive with the condition of the title at the time of assessment, and when it first attaches, and continues to be the same throughout. The whole land is held, and not the mere interest of the individual to whom it is taxed, and the manner of assessment, if legally made, really defines the extent of what must be treated as a lien to which it is the legislative intention to make all other titles subordinate. Langley v. Chaplin, 134 Mass. 82, 87; Hunt v. Boston, ubi supra. The lien attached at the time the taxes were severally assessed, and for the statutory period of two years the estate could not be devested of this paramount claim by any subsequent incumbrance or change of ownership. But if the precedent condition of alienation which works a discharge of the lien does not arise, then no change has taken place in the title which operates to free the property made subject to it until the tax is paid or the estate sold. Kelso v. Boston, 120 Mass. 297, 299. Where there has been no change in ownership, the estate is still subject to the taxes assessed, and remains liable to be sold for their payment, and the purchaser, if all statutory requirements have been followed, gets as good a title as if the sale had been made within the period of two years. The entry of the mortgagee for the purpose of foreclosure under Rev. Laws, c. 187, § 1, and the subsequent sale under the power in the mortgage, were after notice of the tax sale had been given, and did not work a change in the title, as the alienation of the property contemplated by the statute, in order to destroy the right of the collector to sell, must occur in point of time before notice of such sale is given. If the mortgage had ceased to be a legitimate incumbrance at the time of entry or foreclosure by sale, those claiming under it acquired no estate in fee, and the plaintiffs have no title to be clouded. A sale, therefore, under the conditions disclosed by the record in this case, whether made before or after the qualified limitation of two years had run, as to each of the taxes, must be held to have passed to the purchaser a good title free from all incumbrances, subject only to the right of redemption given by law to the owner of those lawfully claiming under him. Rev. Laws, c. 13, § 35. If the sale was valid, the plaintiffs have not made out a case that entitles them to equitable relief.

Decree affirmed.

(185 Mass. 458)

REGIS et al. v. J. A. JAYNES & CO. et al.

(Supreme Judicial Court of Massachusetts. Suffolk. April 12, 1904.)

TRADE-MARKS AND TRADE-NAMES — PROPERTY RIGHTS—INFRINGEMENT—PROOF—NOTICE —INJUNCTION.

1. Where plaintiff compounded a dyspepsia cure, marking the boxes in which it was sold with the word "Rex," from which her family surname was derived, and filed such name as a trade-mark, as authorized by St. 1895, p. 519, c. 462, § 1, and subsequently continuously used it as a trade-mark on such medicine, she thereby acquired an exclusive property right in the name.

2. Any word or device that has for its principal object to identify the owner of specific goods prepared and sold by him, may constitute a valid trade-mark.

3. Where plaintiff had previously and continuously used a trade-mark, and defendant thereafter adopted a mark so similar that buyers were likely to be deceived, and purchase defendant's goods for those of plaintiff, it was no defense to a suit to restrain defendant's use of its mark that it was not originally intended as an imitation.

4. In a suit to restrain defendants' use of a trade-name alleged to be an imitation of a name previously used by plaintiff, a mere comparison of the words showing similarity is insufficient, without proof that from the form of manufacture of the goods, the names, labels, shape of the receptacles in which they are sold, etc., there exists a reasonable probability that purchasers using ordinary care will be deceived by the similarity of names.

5. Where defendants, after notice that their trade-mark was an infringement and imitation of plaintiff's mark, continued to permit their names to appear in the same form of advertisement, and continued to sell their preparation without any change of name, shape, or label, such conduct constituted a direct and intentional infringement.

6. Complainant manufactured and sold a dyspepsia cure under the trade-name of "Rex." The remedy was compounded in two kinds of tablets, to be taken in connection with each other. Defendants thereafter compounded a dyspepsia cure in the same form, which it sold under the name "Rexall." *Held* that, though the form of the receptacles and the labels attached were dissimilar, yet, since persons not familiar with the exact appearance of each might be deceived, plaintiff was entitled to an injunction, though there was no proof of actual damages sustained.

Case Reserved from Supreme Judicial Court, Suffolk County; Henry K. Braley, Judge.

Bill by Ellen M. Regis and another against J. A. Jaynes & Co. and others to enjoin an alleged infringement of said Regis' rights to the use of the word "Rex" as a trade-mark or trade-name. On reservation from the Supreme Judicial Court. Decree for plaintiffs.

Edward S. Beach and Arthur P. Hardy, for complainants. Robert F. Herrick, for defendants.

BRALEY, J. When the plaintiff, Ellen M. Regis, first compounded her preparation in the form of pills, she marked on the boxes in which they were sold the word "Rex," from which her family surname was derived. She not only adopted and attached it as the distinctive feature indicative of the origin, identity, and proprietorship of her cure for dyspepsia, but filed it as a trade-mark, under St. 1895, p. 519, c. 462, § 1. No evidence appears that at any time she has abandoned or ceased to use it, but the contrary is true. She has formed a partnership with her son, and from small sales in its original form and within a circumscribed territory, other and more attractive combinations have been made, and the business has slowly increased in value and extended into larger fields. This is enough in the present case to establish an exclusive right of property in the plaintiffs to the device or name used in their business. Burt v. Tucker, 178 Mass. 493, 59 N. E. 1111, 52 L. R. A. 112, 86 Am. St. Rep. 499; Lawrence Manufacturing Company v. Tennessee Manufacturing Company, 138 U. S. 537, 11 Sup. Ct. 396, 34 L. Ed. 997. It may be conceded that words which are merely descriptive of the style and quality of an article cannot be appropriated and used for this purpose by the manufacturer in the description of his wares to the exclusion of a similar use by others; but any words or devices that have for their principal object to make plain the identity of the owner with the specific goods prepared and sold by him are not so classed, but may constitute a valid trademark. Lawrence Manufacturing Co. v. Lowell Hosiery Co., 129 Mass. 325, 327, 37 Am. Rep. 362; Frank v. Sleeper, 150 Mass. 583, 23 N. E. 213; Samuels v. Spitzer, 177 Mass. 226, 58 N. E. 693; Lawrence Mfg. Co. v. Tennessee Mfg. Co., supra; Columbian Mill

Co. v. Alcorn, 150 U. S. 460, 14 Sup. Ct. 151, 37 L. Ed. 1144. Although the subsequent origin of the mark or name used by the defendants on their cure for dyspepsia is not stated, it is found that it was not originally intended as an imitation of that of the plaintiffs, but may be considered as a fanciful term invented by the United Drug Company, and which was used to denote a particular proprietary medical compound put up and sold by it or its licensees. But if no intention to wrongfully injure the plaintiffs is manifested in the origin of "Rexall," this does not constitute a defense where priority of ownership and continuous use is shown of the device or mark of which it is found to be an imitation, and buyers are likely from the resemblance to be misled and purchase the defendants' cure when they desire to buy and believe they are getting the remedy made by the plaintiffs. Gilman v. Hunnewell, 122 Mass. 139; Burt v. Tucker, supra; North Cheshire & Manchester Brewery Co. v. Manchester Brewery Co. [1899] A. C. 83. A mere comparison of the different words, devices, or designs which may be used for the purpose of a trade-mark is not enough to make out the main fact to be proved, but the plaintiffs must go further, and establish the essential proposition on which a case like this depends, that, taking all the circumstances, the form of manufacture, names, labels, shape of boxes, or receptacles in which they are sold, there exists a reasonable probability that purchasers using ordinary care will be deceived by the similarity of names, and led into mistaking one medicine for the other. McLean v. Fleming, 96 U. S. 245, 24 L. Ed. 828. Among the various findings and rulings made by the master the only one now material is that in which he decides this principal issue of fact, and to which the single exception argued by the defendants was taken.

An examination of the report shows that the remedies are compounded in the form of two kinds of tablets, to be taken in connection with each other, and in this respect there was a likeness between them, though the boxes used for each in form, and the labels attached, are so dissimilar that persons of ordinary intelligence, if no further resemblance was found, could easily distinguish them; yet upon the whole, in connection with the similarity of names, the similitude becomes such that purchasers not familiar with the exact appearance of each, and the boxes and labels with which they are sold, and exercising the care and observation of the average buyer, are likely to mistake the defendants' preparation for that of the plaintiffs. This finding is well supported by the evidence and subsidiary findings stated in the report, and under our rule, where all the evidence is not reported, therefore becomes final, and is not to be disturbed. East Tennessee Land Co. v. Leeson, 183 Mass. 37, 38, 66 N. E. 427. But he further determined that within a common territorial area the United Drug Company, with the knowledge and consent of the defendants, who are represented in the advertisements as sole agents for its sale, has advertised, while they to a very limited extent have sold, this medicine as a specific for the same disease; but it did not affirmatively appear that such competition in trade at the time the bill was filed had led to any actual injury to the business of the plaintiffs, and for this reason he declined to assess damages. Presumably their prompt action, which did not allow sufficient time to pass before suit to ascertain the effect on their trade, had to a very large degree forestalled results which they feared might follow from, and probably would have been caused by, the unauthorized acts of the defendants. If at common law an action for damages caused to a manufacturer whose goods were put upon the market under a trade-mark and had acquired a distinctive value and reputation could be maintained against another trader who fraudulently copies and places on the goods made by him a similar mark or label, in equity relief can be granted not only as to damages already suffered, but an injunction can be awarded restraining such unlawful use in the future. Thomson v. Winchester, 19 Pick. 214, 31 Am. Dec. 135; Marsh v. Billings, 7 Cush. 322, 332, 54 Am. Dec. 723; Lawrence Mfg. Co. v. Lowell Hosiery Co., supra; Holbrook v. Nesbitt, 163 Mass. 120, 39 N. E. 794. If the choice of the trade device used by the defendants was innocent, and not copied from the name used by the plaintiffs, yet it appears, and the master has found, that after notice given to them that their continued use of it was wrongful, because of the fact that it was an imitation of the plaintiffs' trade-mark, they still allowed their names to appear in the same form of advertisement, and continued to sell their preparation without any change of name, shape, or libel. Such conduct of itself affords strong presumptive evidence of fraud. Orr v. Johnson, 13 Ch. Div. 434. And their acts, from that time at least, must be considered as a direct and intentional infringement. New England Awl & Needle Co. v. Marlborough Awl & Needle Co., 168 Mass. 154, 46 N. E. 386, 60 Am. St. Rep. 377; American Waltham Watch Co. v. United States Watch Co., 173 Mass. 85, 53 N. E. 141, 43 L. R. A. 826, 73 Am. St. Rep. 263; Flagg Mfg. Co. v. Holway, 178 Mass. 83, 59 N. E. 667; Viano v. Baccigalupo, 183 Mass. 160, 67 N. E. 641; Upman v. Forrester, 24 Ch. D. 231; Manhattan Medicine Co. v. Wood, 108 U. S. 218, 2 Sup. Ct. 436, 27 L. Ed. 706. Although the master has decided that the plaintiffs have not yet suffered any monetary loss, equity interferes when title and successful imitation have been established, to prevent the impairment or destruction of the right itself, notwithstanding it may also be found that the reputation and use of the plaintiffs' remedy may be confined to a relatively small section of the state when compared with the field occupied by the defendants, and probably is less widely known and sold, and much inferior to their specific in popularity. Such a disparity in volume of trade or in reputation, if held to be decisive as a limitation of the extent to which relief should be granted, affords no opportunity ordinarily for the organization and development of a business, though founded on a valid trade-mark, where, from a small and feeble beginning, if not subjected to unlawful interference by rivals, it may become a large and profitable enterprise, which the owner has a right to foster and establish; for the injury suffered in such a case is the same in kind, though it may differ in degree. Shaver v. Shaver, 54 Iowa, 208, 210, 212, 6 N. W. 188, 37 Am. Rep. 194.

While the public are deceived, and buy the spurious production in the belief that the imitation is the original article, yet the jurisdiction to award an injunction may well rest on the ground that, where a substantial business has been built up, the output of which has become known to buyers under a designated device or name, such designation, when lawfully established, whether treated technically as a trade-mark or tradename, is property in the same sense as the instrumentalities which the owner uses in making the specific thing that he vends in the market in this form. So that the proprietor of such a trade product, if another, without authority, uses similar devices intending to represent by them that the goods are identical, is entitled to protection from this wrongful and fraudulent appropriation of his property. Weener v. Brayton, 152 Mass. 101, 25 N. E. 46, 8 L. R. A. 640; Bradley v. Norton, 33 Conn. 157, 87 Am. Dec. 200; McLean v. Fleming, ubi supra; Hall v. Barrows, 32 L. J. C. 548, 551; Millington v. Fox, 3 Mylne & C. 338.

As the plaintiffs have made out a case, they are entitled to an injunction to prevent and restrain further interference with the use and enjoyment of their property, and the defendants' exception to the master's report must be overruled, and the report confirmed.

Decree for the plaintiffs accordingly.

(185 Mass. 427)

EMERSON v. WARK.

(Supreme Judicial Court of Massachusetts. Middlesex. April 2, 1904.)

WITNESSES—IMPEACHMENT—WITNESS CALLED BY PARTY.

1. Under Rev. Laws, c. 175, § 24, which allows a party to contradict a witness produced by him, by evidence other than of bad character, and also allows him to prove previous inconsistent statements, and section 22, which allows a party to call and cross-examine the adverse party, a contestant of a will, who calls the one charged with having used undue influence in the procurement of the will, does not hold him out as entitled to credit or to be believed.

Exceptions from Supreme Judicial Court, Middlesex County; William Caleb Loring, Judge.

Probate proceedings by George W. D. Emerson, as executor of the last will of Harriet D. Emerson, against Wark, contestant. There was a verdict for petitioner, and contestant excepted. Exceptions sustained.

Hiram P. Harriman and John F. Neal, for contestant. Geo. L. Mayberry, for executor.

LATHROP, J. This is a petition for the admission to probate of an instrument purporting to be the last will of Harriet D. Emerson, which named the petitioner as executor. At the trial before a single justice of this court, sitting with a jury, the case was tried on three issues. The first related to the soundness of mind of the testatrix; the second, to whether the signature to the will was that of the testatrix; and the third was as follows: "Was Harriet D. Emerson unduly influenced in the execution of said instrument by the said George W. D. Emerson?" The jury answered these questions in favor of the petitioner, and the contestant alleged exceptions.

During the trial the contestant called the petitioner as a witness, and examined him. The only exception relied upon before us was to the charge of the judge in regard to this witness, which was as follows: "There is one rule of law that I ought to bring to your attention, and that is this: When a party in litigation in court puts a person upon the stand as a witness, they put him forward as a person who is entitled to credit—to be believed as a witness. In this case the contestant put George Emerson upon the stand as a witness. In doing that, they put him before you as a person who is entitled to be believed. It does not follow from that that they cannot dispute facts that he testifies to. If a party in litigation puts a person on the stand, and he testifies to something, the person that puts him on is at liberty to prove that what he says is not true; but, in putting him on, they put him before you as a person entitled to be believed. And that it is proper that you should consider in this case, in connection with what George Emerson testified to." We are of opinion that this ruling was wrong, and was prejudicial to the contestant. It is incongruous to claim that a party who calls an adverse witness, or the other party to the cause, and who is entitled to cross-examine him because he is adverse, thereby holds him out as entitled to credit, when the only object in calling him is to obtain such evidence as may be elicited favorable to his own side. In the case at bar the adverse party was the person charged with using undue influence. It cannot be said that by calling Emerson the contestant held him out as a person entitled to credit or to be believed. This would be equivalent to saying that a witness whom the party calling him may impeach in a particular manner is nevertheless held out as entitled to credit. To ascertain the meaning of St. 1869, p. 743, c. 425, § 1 (now Rev. Laws, c. 175, § 24), it is necessary to consider the law as it existed at the time the statute was passed. It was held in the case of Adams v. Wheeler, 97 Mass. 67, argued in 1867, that, while a party could introduce evidence of any competent and material fact, though that fact had been denied by one of his own witnesses, and although the evidence might have the effect of discrediting that witness, he could not introduce evidence for the mere purpose of impeaching the credit of a witness whom he had himself produced. To meet this rule of law, St. of 1869 was passed, which, while it provides that a party producing a witness cannot impeach his credit by evidence of bad character, allows him to contradict him by other evidence, and also allows him to prove that the witness had "made at other times statements inconsistent with his present testimony." St. 1870, p. 302, c. 393, § 4 (now Rev. Laws, c. 175, § 22), provides as follows: "A party to a cause, who shall call the adverse party as a witness, shall be allowed the same liberty in the examination of such witness as is now allowed upon cross-examination." In Ryerson v. Abington, 102 Mass. 526, 530, it is said by Mr. Justice Gray, in commenting on the statutes of 1869: "This statute abrogates the rule of the common law, by which a party who had called a witness was deemed to have held him out as worthy of credit, and was therefore not allowed to prove by other witnesses statements previously made by him, inconsistent with his present testimony, which would not be admissible as independent evidence, and which could have no effect but to impair his credit with the jury." So, too, in Brooks v. Weeks, 121 Mass. 433, 435, it is said by Mr. Justice Endicott: "The object of the statute is simply to allow the party to impeach the credibility of his witness by showing, in the manner pointed out, that he has made statements inconsistent with his testimony." The instruction given in the case before us tended to mislead and confuse the jury, and to impose a burden upon the contestant which may well have affected the result. Indeed, at common law, the rule prohibiting the impeachment of a witness by the party calling him has not been always strictly applied in the case of an adverse or a hostile witness. It is said in 1 Stark. Ev. 248: "In the case of an adverse witness, it may frequently happen that what he states in favor of the party who calls him may be regarded as truth unwillingly wrung from a reluctant witness, while his counter statements are open to great suspicion. In all such cases, former declarations by the witness are obviously of importance, with a view to ascertain what part of his statement ought to be discredited, whilst credit is given to the rest. The ordinary rules as to the examination of an adverse witness supply an analogy in favor of the affirmative of the present question in all cases, at least, where the witness is apparently an adverse one." See, also, Becker v. Koch, 104 N. Y. 394, 10 N. E. 701, 58 Am. Rep. 515; Webber v. Jackson, 79 Mich. 175, 44 N. W. 591, 19 Am. St. Rep. 165. In Garny v. Katz, 89 Wis. 230, 61 N. W. 762, the defendant asked the judge presiding at the trial to instruct the jury that the plaintiff, having called the defendant as a witness in his own behalf, held him out as worthy of credit. This request was refused, and on appeal it was held that the action of the judge was right.

We are therefore of opinion that the order must be: Exceptions sustained.

(162 Ind. 379)

NATIONAL MASONIC ACCIDENT ASS'N v. McBRIDE.

(Supreme Court of Indiana. March 31, 1904.)

ACCIDENT INSURANCE — CONDITIONS — PROOFS OF LOSS—WAIVER—EVIDENCE.

1. A condition in an accident policy requiring delivery of proofs of injury within 90 days after the accident, and declaring that a failure to comply therewith should result in a forfeiture of the amount payable under the policy, is for the benefit of the insurer, who can waive a strict compliance therewith.

2. In an action on an accident policy, evidence reviewed, and *held* sufficient to sustain a finding that the insurer had received the necessary proofs within the time required, and, if not, it had waived its right to insist on forfeiture for an alleged failure to furnish the same in time.

Appeal from Circuit Court, Miami County; J. T. Cox, Judge.

Action by Cicero R. McBride against the National Masonic Accident Association. From a judgment in favor of plaintiff, defendant appealed to the Appellate Court, which transferred the case to the Supreme Court under Acts 1901, p. 590, c. 259 (Burns' Rev. St. 1901, § 1337u). Affirmed.

Reasoner & O'Hara, for appellant. Loveland & Loveland, for appellee.

DOWLING, J. The appellee recovered a judgment against the appellant upon an accident policy issued by the latter, and the association appeals.

Error is assigned upon the ruling of the court denying a new trial. The causes stated in the motion were that the finding of the court was contrary to law, and that it was not sustained by sufficient evidence. The policy and by-laws required that in case of minor injuries, such as the one sustained by the appellee, a written notice, signed by the member, should be given to the secretary of the association, at Des Moines, Iowa, within

¶ 1. See Insurance, vol. 28, Cent. Dig. § 1368.

10 days from the date of the injury, with full particulars thereof, stating the nature of the injury, and the full name, address, and occupation of the assured. It was also provided in the policy and by-laws that written or printed proofs must be completed and delivered to the association within 90 days from the happening of the accident, and that such proofs should state whether the member was wholly or partially disabled, and the time when such disability would probably terminate. A by-law of the association declared that all proofs must be sworn to by the claimant, and accompanied by a sworn certificate of a physician. Failure to furnish such proofs and evidence within the time specified was to be conclusively deemed a waiver of any right or claim to benefits. All assessments and premiums were promptly paid by the appellee, and all the conditions of the policy were faithfully performed by him, up to the time of the accident. On June 26, 1900, the appellee met with a railroad accident, and sustained thereby a severe bodily injury, which was directly caused by external, violent, and accidental means not excepted in the by-laws of said association, involving a fracture of the left leg between the knee and ankle, and the dislocation of the left elbow, which totally disabled him for more than 1 year. Within 10 days after the accident, the appellee gave to the appellant the required notice, together with a statement of additional facts, but did not furnish sworn proofs or the certificate of the physician until after the expiration of 90 days from the date of his injury. The issues made upon the pleadings were whether the appellee had performed the conditions of the contract, and, if not, whether the association had or had not waived the delivery of the proofs within the 90 days.

The only breach of the contract relied upon by the appellant on the trial was the failure of the appellee to deliver the proofs mentioned in the policy and by-laws within the time prescribed, and on this ground alone a forfeiture of the claim of the appellee for the indemnity promised by the association was asserted. The condition that, in default of the delivery of the proofs required within 90 days after the accident, the right to claim the sum promised to be paid by the association should be forfeited, was entirely for the benefit of the insurer. But the appellant had the right to waive strict compliance with it, and in such cases very slight circumstances have been held sufficient evidence of the intention of the insurer not to take advantage of the breach or to insist upon the forfeiture. Hollis v. State Ins. Co., 65 Iowa, 459, 21 N. W. 774; Replogle v. The American Ins. Co., 132 Ind. 360, 366, 31 N. E. 947; Insurance Co. v. Norton, 96 U. S. 234, 24 L. Ed. 689; Hartford Life Ins. Co. v. Unsell, 144 U. S. 439, 449, 12 Sup. Ct. 671, 36 L. Ed. 496.

There was some evidence that the conduct of the appellant and its local agent, Augur, was such as to lead the appellee honestly to believe that he need not furnish the proofs within the time named in the policy, and that if he furnished them afterward it would be a sufficient compliance with the stipulation of the policy concerning them. He did afterwards deliver them, and they were unobjectionable in form. The question whether Augur was a general agent of the appellant, and the nature and scope of his authority, as recognized and acted upon by the appellant, together with the statements made by Augur to the appellee, were questions of fact proper to be submitted to the trial court.

It appeared, also, that the first statement sent by the appellee to the association, at Des Moines, Iowa, contained much more than mere notice of the occurrence of the accident and the particulars required by the policy and by-laws, and that it included substantially all the information required in the proofs of loss or injury. There was evidence, too, of a custom of the association, upon notice of an accident covered by a policy, to send to the assured blanks for the proofs it demanded, but that no such blanks were received by this appellee.

Upon this and similar evidence, the court found that the appellant received the necessary proofs within the 90 days, or that, failing to do so, it waived its right to insist upon a forfeiture in consequence of this breach of the contract. We cannot say that these conclusions were not authorized by the proof.

For these reasons, the court did not err in overruling the motion for a new trial. Judgment affirmed.

(162 Ind. 374)

LAKE SHORE & M. S. RY. CO. v. GRAHAM.

(Supreme Court of Indiana. March 31, 1904.)

RAILROADS — PERSONS ON TRACK — DEATH — SWITCHMAN — GENERAL VERDICT — SPECIAL FINDINGS—CONFLICT—PRESUMPTIONS.

1. Though all presumptions must be indulged in support of a general verdict as against the answers to special interrogatories, the party in whose favor the general verdict is rendered can invoke no fact in his favor under such presumption that he would not have been allowed to prove.

2. Where, in an action for death of a railroad switchman, the jury specially found that deceased, with knowledge that the engine by which he was struck was approaching him, and which he could have seen if he had looked, failed to look, and, though fully possessed of his senses of sight and hearing, made no effort to avoid the collision, which he could have done by merely stepping off the ends of the ties, on which he was walking in violation of a rule of the company, a verdict in favor of plaintiff was in irreconcilable conflict with such special finding, though deceased at the time was intently looking for a link, and believed that the engine would stop before it reached the place where he was working, or prior to that time would be switched onto another track.

Appeal from Circuit Court, La Porte County; Lucius Hubbard, Judge.

Action by William Graham, as administrator of the estate of James S. McGuire, deceased, against the Lake Shore & Michigan Southern Railway Company. From a judgment in favor of plaintiff, defendant appeals. Reversed.

Miller & Drake and S. C. Hubble, for appellant. A. C. Harris, N. F. Wolf, and F. C. Cutter, for appellee.

HADLEY, J. This action was brought by appellee against appellant to recover damages for the death of James S. McGuire, while in the employ of appellant as a switchman in its Park Manor yards, in Chicago. The action is under the statute of Illinois, for wrongfully causing death, and the damages sought to be recovered are for the benefit of the widow and children of the deceased. The negligence charged is (1) that a locomotive was run in said yards, where McGuire was engaged in the service of appellant, without ringing a bell or giving him any notice or warning of its approach, at an unlawful rate of speed, to wit, 10 miles an hour, contrary to an ordinance of the city of Chicago then in force; (2) appellant permitted the bell on its locomotive to get and remain out of repair, so that it could not be rung, and the locomotive was run up to and against McGuire, while he was engaged in service, without any notice or warning by ringing of the bell or otherwise, and by reason thereof he was struck and injured; (3) negligence of the engineer in charge of the locomotive in failing to look ahead, and in driving the locomotive against McGuire; (4) failure of appellant to make and publish rules and regulations for the guidance and control of its employés in the handling of locomotives and cars in its switchyards; (5) the engineer and fireman in charge of the locomotive were incompetent, which was known to appellant and not known to McGuire. The complaint was put at issue by the general denial. With a general verdict for appellee, the jury returned answers to divers interrogatories. Appellant's motion for judgment in its favor on the answers so returned was overruled, which action of the court presents the only question for decision.

We recognize as well established in this state that a general verdict must stand if it can be upheld under any supposable state of facts provable under the issues, and that all presumptions must be indulged in support of the general verdict and against the special answers. But such presumptions must be reasonable, and relate only to such facts as might have been proved under the issues as formed. Therefore in this case, in support of his general verdict, appellee can invoke no fact in his own favor, or against appellee, that he would not have been allowed to prove within the limits of his complaint.

The special findings of the jury are in substance as follows: McGuire was employed by appellant on July 7, 1894, as a switchman in its yards at Park Manor, Chicago, and was injured on August 5, and died therefrom August 19, 1894. The accident happened about noon. Two parallel tracks known as Nos. 2 and 3 ran in a northwesterly direction. No. 3 was on the north of No. 2. The space between them was smooth and level, and seven feet wide. McGuire was familiar with the yard. He and another switchman were standing between tracks 2 and 3, about 300 feet north of where track 3 connects with the lead track, when a locomotive came off of lead track onto track 3. There was nothing to prevent McGuire from seeing the locomotive as it entered upon track 3, and he did know that it had entered upon said track, and that it was proceeding on the same in a northwesterly direction. While the locomotive was thus approaching on track 3, McGuire started also in a northwesterly direction, walking between tracks 2 and 3 on the south ends of the ties of track 3, and had walked a distance of 70 feet before the locomotive overtook and struck him. He knew the engine was approaching him, and could have seen it at any time if he had looked, but he did not look. He could have seen where the locomotive was at any time after it entered upon track 3, before it struck him, if he had looked. At the time he fully possessed the senses of sight and hearing. There was nothing to prevent him from stepping off the ties, and thus avoiding a collision with the engine. If he had been giving attention to his surroundings at the time, he could have avoided the injury by avoiding a collision with the locomotive. He did nothing to avoid injury from the approaching engine. It was not necessary for him to be walking where he was on track 3 when he was injured. McGuire was at the time familiar with the following rule of the company: "All [employés] are especially cautioned not to walk upon, nor to stand upon the tracks, except when necessary to do so; and as much as may be, to prevent the public from going upon the tracks." There was no strike, or disturbance of any kind in appellant's yards at Park Manor at the time of the injury, and McGuire was not performing any services as deputy United States marshal, and was engaged only in performing the duties of switchman, and with which duties he was familiar. The bell on the locomotive was not ringing, but the locomotive was making a noise, and could have been heard by one with ordinary hearing at least 100 feet away. The engineer in charge was not careful and competent, and did not see McGuire as the engine approached him.

Assuming that appellant's negligence was proved, we are unable, by any proper range of fancy, to find that McGuire was himself without fault. The gravamen of the negligence complained of is the running down of McGuire with an engine which at the time was being unlawfully speeded, and which was driven upon him without ringing the bell, or giving him any other notice or warning of its approach. With respect to this alleged misconduct on the part of the appellant, the findings show that McGuire could have escaped injury therefrom by the exercise of reasonable care. It is exhibited by the findings that he was familiar with the yards and his duties as switchman, and with good sight and hearing, in the full light of day, he deliberately stepped onto track 3 in front of an oncoming engine, when it was not necessary for him to do so, and when he knew that it was in violation of the company's rules. He not only stepped onto the track, but proceeded on the end of the ties northwesterly, with the knowledge that the locomotive was approaching him from the rear on the same track, and, without looking or listening, or at least without heeding, walked thereon 70 feet before being struck by the engine. It was not alone the speed, or the failure to ring the bell or give other notice or warning of the approaching engine that caused McGuire's injury, for without any other warning he heard, or might have heard, the rumbling of the coming engine at least a hundred feet away, and, even if the locomotive was running at the rate of 10 miles an hour, as alleged, while it covered 100 feet he had plenty of time to take a single step off the end of the ties into a place of safety. He was on the track in violation of the company's rules, knew the engine was approaching but a short distance away, and we are informed by the jury that if he had been giving attention to his surroundings he might have avoided injury by avoiding a collision with the engine. And under the law he was bound to give attention to his surroundings. Railway Co. v. Hedges, 118 Ind. 5, 11, 20 N. E. 530.

No situation of probable danger would excuse him from looking out for his own safety. And the more threatening the danger, the greater the caution required. Railway Co. v. Stommel, 126 Ind. 35, 25 N. E. 863. A railroad track is of itself a suggestion of danger, and walking on the ties so near a rail as to be struck by a passing engine, with the knowledge that one was approaching but a short distance away, was a situation requiring great attention and care, and the failure to give such attention and care constituted negligence. Pennsylvania Co. v. Meyers, 136 Ind. 242, 36 N. E. 32; Railway Co. v. Hill, 117 Ind. 56, 18 N. E. 461. What if McGuire was intently looking for a link or a coupling pin, and had been told and believed that the engine would stop where he and the other switchman had been standing? What if he had signaled the engine to stop, and had seen the steam shut off, or had been informed by a superior that he would send the engine back to come in on track 2, and believed it would be done? None of these, or like things which might have been proved, would have dispensed with the duty to look and listen while occupying the track unnecessarily, or have justified such an abandonment of all care as to disregard the noise of the moving engine a hundred feet behind him. Pennsylvania Co. v. Meyers, 136 Ind., at page 260, 36 N. E. 32.

We are wholly unable to summons any state of facts provable under the issues that will make the decedent's conduct consistent with his freedom from fault, and we must therefore conclude that the special findings of the jury are in irreconcilable conflict with the general verdict, which implies due care, and that the general verdict must yield. It follows that the court erred in overruling appellant's motion for judgment upon the answers to interrogatories, notwithstanding the general verdict.

Judgment reversed, with instructions to sustain said motion, and render judgment thereon for the defendant.

GILLETTE, C. J., concurs in result.

(163 Ind. 417)

GUTHRIE v. CARPENTER et al.

(Supreme Court of Indiana. April 1, 1904.)

BUILDING CONTRACTS — PAROL ALTERATION — SURETIES — DISCHARGE — DELAY—ACTIONS—PLEADING—INSTRUCTIONS—VERDICT—APPEAL —HARMLESS ERROR.

1. In an action on a building contract, an order requiring plaintiff to file the plans of the building with his complaint was not reversible error, since, if such filing was not required, the addition of the plans would be regarded as mere surplusage.

2. In the absence of a motion to have the plans of a building detached from the complaint in an action on a building contract, and excluded from the pleadings to be delivered to the jury, plaintiff was not entitled to object, on appeal, that such plans were not properly a part of the complaint, and should not have been submitted to the jury.

3. Where a building contract provided that the owner should pay claims for labor and material, and should only pay to the contractor the difference between the amount so paid and contract price on completion of the building, but such provisions, together with other material requirements of the contract, were thereafter orally modified on a sufficient consideration, so that the owner paid the contract price directly to the contractor, etc., without the knowledge or consent of the contractor's surety, the surety was thereby discharged.

4. In an action for damages for delay in completing a building, a defense pleaded, that the contractor delayed the completion of the work at plaintiff's request, stated a sufficient excuse for not complying with such provision of the contract.

5. A change in the construction of a building by direction of the supervising architect employed by the owner, who at the time was acting as the owner's agent to direct such change, was binding on the owner.

6. Where in an action on a building contract the jury's answers to special interrogatories showed that no allowance had been made for ex-

¶ 3. See Principal and Surety, vol. 40, Cent. Dig. §§ 162, 284.

tra work pleaded as a set-off, error of the court, if any, in overruling a demurrer to the paragraph of the answer pleading such set-off, was harmless.

7. In an action against a building contractor and the surety on his bond, a verdict, "We, the jury, find for the defendant S., release from bond," was general, and not objectionable in containing the words "release from bond," such words being mere surplusage.

8. Where an instruction referred to and was applicable to a paragraph of the answer to which no demurrer had been sustained, the fact that by mistake the instruction referred to the number of a paragraph of the answer to which a demurrer had been sustained was not reversible error, in the absence of evidence in the record from which prejudice could be found.

Appeal from Circuit Court, Delaware County; Jos. G. Leffler, Judge.

Action by Thomas S. Guthrie against James Carpenter and others. From a judgment in favor of plaintiff for less than the relief demanded, he appealed to the Appellate Court, which transferred the case to the Supreme Court under Acts 1901, p. 590 (Burns' Rev. St. 1901, § 1337u). Affirmed.

Geo. H. Koons, for appellant. Gregory, Silverburg & Lotz, for appellees.

DOWLING, J. Action for damages by appellant against the appellees on a contract in writing by which the appellee Carpenter, as principal, and the appellee Simmons, as surety, in consideration of $4,000 to be paid to Carpenter by appellant, agreed to construct for appellant a dwelling house according to certain plans and specifications referred to in the contract, and made part of it to complete the work within the time named, and to keep the same free from liens for work and materials. The complaint avers performance by appellant of all the conditions of the contract on his part, and charged divers breaches on the part of the appellees, the principal of which were a failure to complete the work within the time fixed by the agreement, failure to do certain work specified in the contract, and failure to pay certain bills for material and labor furnished and performed on said house, for which liens were filed, and which appellant was compelled to pay and discharge. On motion of the appellees, the appellant was required to file with his complaint a copy of the plans referred to in the agreement. Carpenter filed an answer in six paragraphs, to one of which, the fifth, a demurrer was sustained. These answers were a denial, a plea of payment, and answers in avoidance of the allegations of delay and failure to build according to the plans and specifications. Simmons, the surety in the agreement, answered in four paragraphs, consisting of a general denial, a plea of payment, and other answers alleging alterations of the contract without his consent. The third paragraph of this answer went out on demurrer. Appellant moved to strike out the allegations of the supposed changes in the plans and specifications. This motion was overruled. He demurred to the fourth paragraph of the answer, and to each specification of change in the contract mentioned therein. These demurrers were overruled. Replies were filed to all paragraphs of the separate answers of the appellees remaining in the record. The cause was tried by a jury, who returned a general verdict for appellant against Carpenter, assessing appellant's damages at $223.90, together with answers to the questions of fact submitted to them. The verdict as to Simmons was in these words: "We find for the defendant, James L. Simmons, release from his bond. Thomas B. Snell, Foreman." Appellant moved for judgment for $424.15 on the special answers of the jury, which motion was overruled. Motions for a venire de novo and for a new trial were also overruled, and judgment was rendered on the verdict.

1. The decision of the court sustaining appellees' motion to require the appellant to file the plans of the building with his complaint did not constitute reversible error. While it was not necessary to make the plans a part of the complaint, it would not have been improper to do so in the first instance, and, if filed, they would at most have been surplusage, and surplusage does not vitiate a pleading. Even if erroneous, the decision was not prejudicial to the appellant. The plans were an indispensable part of his proof, and must have come before the jury in the evidence. The objection that, if made a part of the complaint as an exhibit, the jury were thereby enabled to take them to their room, thus giving them an undue influence as a part of the evidence, is not sustained by any rule of pleading or practice. But, if such a result was feared, the question should have been presented by a motion to detach the objectionable paper from the complaint, and to exclude it from the pleadings to be delivered to the jury. As no motion of this kind was made by the appellant, it must be presumed that he consented to the delivery of the plans to the jury.

2. The second, third, fourth, and sixth errors assigned relate to the sufficiency of the fourth paragraph of the answer of the appellee Simmons. The defense set up in this paragraph was that Simmons was released and discharged from liability as surety on the contract of his co-appellee Carpenter by reason of material alterations of the contract without his knowledge or consent. The specific deviations from the requirements of that agreement, and the changes in the nature and value of the portions of the work to be done under it, pointed out in the answer, were of a very material and important character, and many of them directly and injuriously affected the surety by increasing his apparent liability. For example, in the first specification it is stated that all bills for materials and labor were to be paid by the appellant to the persons holding such claims, and that the amounts so paid were to be deducted from the total consideration for the building of the house, and that only the residue was to be

paid to the appellee Carpenter. This condition was a most important one to Simmons, as surety for the contractor, Carpenter. If carried out, it afforded him complete protection against liability upon that condition of the contract which bound his co-appellee, Carpenter, to keep the property free from mechanics' and materialmen's liens. But the answer alleges that, instead of paying for the labor and materials in the manner provided for by the agreement, the appellant paid the whole of the contract price for building the house directly to the contractor, the appellee Carpenter. It is not essential that the terms or conditions of a written agreement should be altered by another writing, or by changes inserted therein by interlineation. Such alterations may be by parol, and the acts of the parties mutually assenting to departures from the conditions of the original contract may result in a complete change in the agreement between them. Not only were these deviations from the conditions and requirements of the contract material, but they were made upon a valuable consideration, as is clearly apparent from the averments of the answer. Referring again to the change in the mode of payment of the contract price for the construction of the building, the consideration for each payment made to the contractor was the work done and the materials furnished. The payment to the contractor was clearly a benefit to him. The consideration for each change in the plans and specifications was the agreement of the contractor to substitute other kinds of work, or different materials, at the request of the appellant. The paragraph expressly avers that each of these changes and alterations was made by the appellant and the contractor without the knowledge or consent of Simmons, the surety. Any material alteration of or deviation from the contract, made by the parties upon a sufficient consideration, and without the consent of the surety, was sufficient to discharge the latter. As the jury found that many of the changes and alterations alleged in the fourth answer of Simmons were in fact made, and as they were material and were made upon a valuable consideration, without the consent of the surety, it was a matter of no importance that other changes named in the answer were not sufficient to work the release of the surety.

3. The third paragraph of Carpenter's answer alleged that the said appellee delayed the completion of the house at the request of the appellant. This defense is pleaded to that part of the complaint only which charges that the appellee Carpenter failed to finish the house within the time fixed by the contract. The answer stated a sufficient excuse for not finishing the work within the contract limit.

4. If the change made in the construction of the north wall of the laundry room was by the direction of the supervising architect employed by the appellant, and who was at the time acting as appellant's agent to direct such change, it was binding on the appellant. The fourth partial answer of the appellee Carpenter was sufficient.

5. The sixth paragraph of the answer of Carpenter alleged that the appellee did certain extra work not included in the contract, and that the work and labor therefor were furnished by him at the cost named in the paragraph. This answer is assailed on the ground that it did not allege that the extra work was done at the request of the appellant, or that the amount claimed therefor was due and unpaid. It appears from the special answers of the jury that this extra work was paid for by the appellant. The jury, therefore, allowed nothing for it on the set-off, and the appellant was not harmed by the ruling on the demurrer.

6. None of the special findings is inconsistent with the general verdict, nor did the facts shown by them entitle the appellant to judgment.

7. The reasons stated for the award of a venire de novo were not such as entitled the appellant to that writ and remedy. The verdict was general both as to Carpenter and Simmons. As to the latter, it was in these words: "We find for the defendant, James L. Simmons, release from bond." The words "release from bond" were superfluous, but were entirely consistent with the general finding in favor of that defendant. One of the defenses set up by Simmons was that by changes in the contract, made without his consent, he was discharged from liability. The words "release from bond" merely indicated the ground on which the jury found in his favor. There was neither ambiguity nor uncertainty in the verdict, and hence no reason for a writ of venire de novo.

8. Various grounds were assigned for a new trial, and, among others, it was averred that the assessment of the amount of recovery was too small. The evidence was not brought up. The special answers covered only a part of the issues and facts in the case, and these answers, considered in connection with the averments of the complaint and the general verdict, afford no basis for the conclusion that the appellant was entitled to a larger sum than was given him. One of the answers stated that only $776 was paid to appellee Carpenter, and from this fact it must be inferred that the residue of the $4,000 remained in the hands of appellant, and was used by him not only for the purpose of paying the ordinary bills for labor performed and materials furnished, but also to discharge a portion, at least, of the amount of the claims for which liens were taken upon the property.

9. We have carefully examined the instructions given and refused, but have found no error in the proceedings of the court. We do not consider it necessary to set them out in detail. Although the third paragraph of the answer of the appellee Simmons, which went out on demurrer, was referred to by its

number in instruction numbered 13, it is evident that the fourth paragraph of Simmons' answer was intended, and the instruction was applicable to it. Moreover, as the evidence is not in the record, we cannot say that the error, if any occurred, was wrongful to the appellant. In our view of the case, the conclusion reached was just and correct, and no error in the record requires us to disturb it.

Judgment affirmed.

(162 Ind. 382)

NORTHWESTERN MUT. LIFE INS. CO. v. KIDDER.

(Supreme Court of Indiana. March 31, 1904.)

INTERPLEADER — REQUISITES—STATUTES—CONSTRUCTION—CLAIMANTS — COMMON SOURCE—PRIVITY — CORPORATIONS — RECEIVERS — INSOLVENCY—RIGHTS OF CREDITORS.

1. Burns' Rev. St. 1901, § 274, providing that a defendant against whom an action is pending on a contract, at any time before answer, on affidavit that a person not a party to the action, and without collusion with him, makes against him a demand for the same debt, on due notice to such person and the adverse party, may apply to the court for an order to substitute such person in his place, on depositing the money in court, etc., did not create a new cause of interpleader, but was a mere substitute for the equitable remedy by an independent suit, and is governed by the same rules.

2. After insurer had delivered a check to the beneficiary in payment of a liability on a life insurance policy, certain creditors of a corporation, which, it was alleged, insured controlled, claimed to be entitled to the fund on the ground that insured had paid premiums on the policy from the corporation's assets, and that it was insolvent, and demanded that insurer stop payment on the check, which it did. *Held*, that since such creditors and the beneficiary did not claim the proceeds of the check from a common source, and there was no privity between the insurer and the creditors, or between insurer and the corporation or its receiver, insurer was not entitled to compel the parties to interplead as to their rights to such proceeds.

3. Where a life insurance company delivered a check to the beneficiary, which was received in full payment and in satisfaction of the policy, which was surrendered, the company was thereby estopped from denying that the beneficiary was the real party in interest when the check was executed.

4. Where an insolvent corporation was in the hands of a receiver at the time a liability on a policy insuring its managing stockholder accrued, any claim of the corporation to share in the proceeds of such policy on the ground that the premiums had been paid from the corporation's assets was enforceable only by such receiver; and hence the insurance company was not entitled to interplead the beneficiary and creditors of the corporation, who had asserted a claim to the proceeds of such policy, and notified the insurer thereof.

Appeal from Circuit Court, Vigo County; Jas. E. Piety, Judge.

Action by Kate Kidder against the Northwestern Mutual Life Insurance Company. From a decree sustaining a demurrer to defendant's bill of interpleader, it appeals. Affirmed.

B. V. Marshall and Baker & Daniels, for appellant. McNutt & McNutt, for appellee.

MONKS, J. Appellee sued appellant on February 12, 1902, in the Vigo circuit court, upon a bank check dated January 25, 1902, for $10,000, drawn by appellant upon the Wisconsin National Bank of Milwaukee, payable to appellee. Appellant on February 25, 1902, filed an interpleader, and sought therein to have other alleged claimants substituted as defendants in its place, and to be discharged from liability to either party on its depositing in court the amount of said check, interest, and costs, as provided in section 274, Burns' Rev. St. 1901 (section 273, Rev. St. 1881; section 273, Horner's Rev. St. 1901). At the same time appellant filed proof of service of notice of said interpleader on the other alleged claimants. A motion by appellee to make the pleading more specific was sustained by the court. Afterwards, on July 11, 1902, appellant filed a verified amendment to its interpleader. Appellee on the same day filed a demurrer to appellant's amended interpleader, and at the same time appellant filed a motion to strike said demurrer from the files "for the reason that the statute on the subject of interpleaders does not contemplate demurrers thereto." On July 12, 1902, the court overruled said motion and sustained said demurrer to appellant's amended interpleader, and on the same day rendered final judgment in favor of appellee against appellant for the amount of said check, interest, and costs. The errors assigned and not waived are: "(1) The court erred in sustaining appellee's motion to make appellant's interpleader more specific; (2) the court erred in overruling appellant's motion to strike out appellee's demurrer to appellant's amended interpleader; (3) the court erred in sustaining appellee's demurrer to appellant's amended interpleader."

It appears from appellant's amended interpleader that appellant, a foreign corporation, on September 6, 1894, executed its policy of life insurance, by which it promised to pay to appellee, wife of Edson W. Kidder, of Terre Haute, Ind., upon proof of the death of said Edson W. Kidder, the sum of $10,000; that said Edson W. Kidder died on January 12, 1902, said policy being at that time in full force for the sum of $10,000, and thereafter, upon due proof being made by appellee, the beneficiary in said policy, of the death of said Edson W. Kidder, appellant, at Milwaukee, Wis., on January 25, 1902, signed the check sued upon, and on January 27, 1902, caused the same to be delivered to appellee, at Terre Haute, Ind., in payment of said life insurance policy, and the same was received by the appellee as a payment in full of said policy, and she at the same time surrendered said policy to appellant as fully paid. On January 28, 1902, after said check had been delivered to appellee and said life insurance policy surrendered as aforesaid, certain national banks and trust companies located in Connecticut, Massachusetts, Pennsylvania, and Rhode Island, claiming to be creditors of the W. L. Kidder & Son Milling Company, of Terre Haute, Ind., demanded of appellant the payment to them of the $10,000 payable under said policy, and notified appellant not to pay said insurance policy on the life of said E. W. Kidder to appellee, stating that said insurance was paid for by said milling company, and that said corporation was insolvent, and said fund belonged to its creditors; and, if checks had been delivered by appellant to any one on account of said insurance, a demand was made that appellant stop payment thereof. That appellant had no notice of the claim of said creditors until January 28, 1902. On January 30, 1902, the Wisconsin National Bank of Milwaukee, by direction of appellant, refused payment of the check sued upon. On February 11, 1902, said creditors notified appellant that said E. W. Kidder, the person "insured in said policy, was at the time of his death practically the only stockholder of W. L. Kidder & Son, and dominated its board of directors; that he had for a considerable time been largely indebted to said corporation, and that it had for a long time been insolvent; that portions of its moneys had by said E. W. Kidder been wrongfully diverted from the creditors of said corporation to the payment of the premiums on said policy of insurance issued by appellant, and that the creditors asserted ownership of the whole proceeds of said life insurance policy by reason of said alleged wrongful diversion of the funds under said circumstances"; that, although said insurance policy was issued long prior to the formation of the corporation of W. L. Kidder & Son, "the later premiums were paid after the organization of W. L. Kidder & Son, and from the funds of that corporation; and that the creditors could at least claim a proportion of that insurance, and should assert a claim to the whole of it." At the time the check sued upon was in the hands of appellant's agent at Terre Haute for delivery to appellee, a number of the creditors of the W. L. Kidder & Son Milling Company were informed of said fact, and they made no objection thereto; and neither they nor the receiver of said W. L. Kidder & Son Milling Company gave any notice to appellant's said agent before or at the time the settlement was made with appellee, and said check delivered to her. A receiver of the W. L. Kidder & Son Milling Company was appointed by the Vigo circuit court, and had entered upon the discharge of his duties before January 27, 1902.

Section 274, Burns' Rev. St. 1901 (section 273, Rev. St. 1881; section 273, Horner's Rev. St. 1901), under which said interpleader was filed, is as follows: "A defendant against ..n action is pending upon a contract, ..ecific real or personal property, may, at any time before answer, upon affidavit that a person not a party to the action, and without collusion with him, makes against him a demand for the same debt or property, upon due notice to such person and the adverse party, apply to the court for an order to substitute such person in his place, and discharge him from liability to either party, on his depositing in court the amount of the debt, or delivering the property, or its value, to such person as the court may direct; and the court may, in its discretion, make the order." Said section 274 (273), supra, is a copy of section 122 of the New York Code of 1851 (Voorhees' Code 1851, p. 82); and it has been uniformly held that the same created no new cases of interpleader, but that the statutory remedy as to all cases falling within its provisions is a mere substitute for the equitable remedy by independent suit, and is governed by the same rules. Sherman v. Patridge, 11 How. Prac. 154, 4 Duer, 646; Vosburgh v. Huntington, 15 Abb. Prac. 254, 257; Pustet v. Flannelly, 60 How. Prac. 67, 69; Delancy v. Murphy, 24 Hun, 503; Stevenson v. New York, etc., Co. (Sup.) 41 N. Y. Supp. 964, 965, 966, 10 App. Div. 233, 235; Venable v. New York, etc., Co., 49 N. Y. Super. Ct. 481; Wells v. National City Bank (Sup.) 58 N. Y. Supp. 125, 126-128; Standley v. Roberts, 59 Fed. 836, 841, 8 C. C. A. 305; Nelson v. Goree, 34 Ala. 565, 576, 577; Johnson v. Maxey, 43 Ala. 521, 541; 3 Pomeroy's Eq. Jurisprudence, § 1329. It is laid down in 3 Pomeroy's Eq. Jurisprudence (2d Ed.) § 1322, "that the equitable remedy of interpleader depends upon and requires the existence of the four following elements: * * * (1) The same thing, debt, or duty must be claimed by both or all the parties against whom the relief is demanded. (2) All their adverse titles or claims must be dependent, or derived from a common source. (3) The person asking the relief—the plaintiff—must not have or claim any interest in the subject-matter. (4) He must have incurred no independent liability to either of the claimants; that is, he must stand perfectly indifferent between them, in the position merely of a stakeholder." It must also appear from the facts alleged in the interpleader that the plaintiff cannot pay either claimant without hazard to himself; in other words, that the third party's claim has some reasonable foundation, or that there is some reasonable doubt as to whether the stakeholder would be reasonably safe in paying out the money. Nofsinger v. Reynolds, 52 Ind. 218, 225; Crane v. Burntrager, 1 Ind. 165, 169; Ketcham v. Brazil, etc., Co., 88 Ind. 515, 517; Bassett v. Leslie, 123 N. Y. 391, 399, 25 N. E. 386; Crane v. McDonald, 118 N. Y. 648, 654, 23 N. E. 991; Trigg v. Hitz, 17 Abb. Prac. 436, 439-441; Hinsdale v. Bankers', etc., Co. (Sup.) 76 N. Y. Supp. 448; Id., 72 App. Div. 180, 76 N. Y. Supp. 448; Lennon v. Metropolitan, etc., Co. (City Ct. N. Y.) 45 N. Y.

Supp. 1033, 1034; Roberts v. Vanhorne, 21 App. Div. 369, 370, 47 N. Y. Supp. 448; Stevenson v. New York, etc., Co. (Sup.) 41 N. Y. Supp. 964; Id., 10 App. Div. 233, 41 N. Y. Supp. 964; The Nassau Bank v. Yandes, 44 Hun, 55; Baltimore, etc., Co. v. Arthur, 90 N. Y. 234, 237, 238.

Where there is no privity between the claimants—where their titles are independent, not derived from a common source, but each asserted as wholly paramount to the other—the stakeholder is obliged, in the language of the authorities, to defend himself as well as he can against each separate demand. A court of equity will not grant him interpleader. Pearson v. Cardon, 2 Russ. & M. 606, 609–612; Crawshay v. Thornton, 2 Myine & C. 1, 19–21; Nikolson v. Knowles, 5 Madd. 47; Pfister v. Wade, 56 Cal. 43; Third Nat. Bank v. Lumber Co., 132 Mass. 410; 3 Pomeroy's Eq. Jur. (2d Ed.) 1324. The same rule is declared in Crane v. Burntrager, 1 Ind. 165, 168; The White Water, etc., Co., v. Comegys, 2 Ind. 469, 472, 473; Kyle v. Mary Lee Coal Company, 112 Ala. 606, 20 South. 851; Gibson v. Goldwaithe, 7 Ala. 281, 42 Am. Dec. 592; Stone v. Reed, 152 Mass. 179, 183, 184, 25 N. E. 49; Fairbanks v. Belknap, 135 Mass. 179; Morristown Nat. Bank v. Beninger, 26 N. J. Eq. 345; Bartlett v. Sultan (C. C.) 23 Fed. 257; United States Trust Co. v. Wiley, 41 Barb. 477, 479, 480; Snodgrass v. Butler, 54 Miss. 45; Scott v. Midland, etc., R. Co., 2 Ir. C. L. R. 83, 85. This rule in regard to privity was abrogated in England by the common-law procedure act of 1860, § 12, and in California in 1881 by section 386, of the Code of Civil Procedure. 3 Pomeroy's Eq. Jurisprudence (2d Ed.) § 1324, note 1; Atterborough v. St. Katharine's Dock Co., L. R. C. P. D. 3, 450, 455, 456, 457; Lazarus v. Harris, 9 N. S. Wales, 148; Bartlett v. Sultan (C. C.) 23 Fed. 257, 258. It is said in 3 Pomeroy's Eq. Jurisprudence (3d Ed.), in a note to section 1327, on page 204: "As a general rule, when A. and B. are bound by express contract, A. cannot maintain an interpleader suit against B., or a person holding or claiming under him, and a stranger who claims under an antagonistic and paramount title. A. is under an independent liability to B. For example, a vendee of real or personal property, with respect to his liability to pay the purchase price, cannot interplead his vendor and a third person claiming to own the property by an independent, antagonistic title. James v. Pritchard, 7 Mees. & W. 216; Trigg v. Hitz, 17 Abb. Prac. 436; Shehan's Heirs v. Barnett's Heirs, 6 T. B. Mon. 592."

There is no privity between appellant and said creditors of the milling company, or between appellant and said milling company or its receiver; and said creditors do not claim said check, or the debt represented thereby, through any privity with appellee, but by a title paramount and adverse to her. Appellant is not, as to appellee, a mere stakeholder, but is the debtor of appellee, standing in privity with her alone. It is shown by the interpleader that the check executed by appellant to appellee was delivered by appellant and received by appellee in payment of the life insurance policy. Thereafter no recovery could be had by appellee on the policy. Her only remedy, if payment of the check was refused, was to sue upon the check. The debt evidenced by the policy was extinguished. Sutton v. Baldwin, 146 Ind. 361, 364, 45 N. E. 518, and cases cited. As against appellee, the payee in said check, appellant was estopped from denying that she was the real party in interest when the check was executed. Johnson v. Conklin, 119 Ind. 109, 110, 21 N. E. 462; Blacker v. Dunbar, 108 Ind. 217, 220, 9 N. E. 104; Rogers v. Place, 29 Ind. 577; Offutt v. Rucker, 2 Ind. App. 350, 354, 27 N. E. 589. When appellee accepted said check as a payment of said policy, it became her check, just as if appellant had paid her so much money. Patroni v. Campbell, 12 Meeson & Welsby, 277, Parke, B., on page 278. By the execution of said check, appellant incurred a personal liability to appellee, different from that which could be claimed by said creditors. 3 Pomeroy's Eq. Jur. §§ 1323, 1324, 1326, 1327, and notes; United States Trust Co. v. Wiley, 41 Barb. 477; Sherman v. Partridge, 11 N. Y. Super. Ct. Rep. (4 Duer) 646–648; Basset v. Leslie, 10 N. Y. Supp. 483; Id., 123 N. Y. 396, 25 N. E. 386; Trigg v. Hitz, 17 Abb. Prac. 436; Bechtel v. Sheaffer, 117 Pa. 555, 560–564, 11 Atl. 889, and cases cited; Pfister v. Wade, 56 Cal. 43; Crawshay v. Thornton, 2 Myine & Cr. 1, 20–24; Lindsey v. Barron, 6 C. B. 291, 60 Eng. C. L. 289; Patroni v. Campbell, 12 M. & W. 277; James v. Pritchard, 7 M. & W. 213, 8 Dowl. 890; Stanley v. Sidney, 14 C. & W. 800; Baker v. Bank of Australia, 1 C. B. N. S. 87, Eng. C. L. 515; Lazarus v. Harris, 9 N. S. Wales, 148.

If the said creditors were substituted for appellant, as asked for in the interpleader, the litigation between them and appellee would not determine said question of estoppel between appellant and appellee, but would deprive her of her right to enforce the same against appellant. Under the authorities cited, interpleader will not lie in such a case unless the third party sought to be brought in claims by a derivative title. In this case it would be one who claims the check by a title derived from the payee, Kate Kidder. It must acknowledge, and not deny, her title to the check. 3 Pomeroy's Eq. Jur. pp. 2044, 2045, and notes; Bechtel v. Sheaffer, 117 Pa. 555, 562, 563, 11 Atl. 889. The authorities hold that, even if the check was secured by mistake or appellee's fraud, appellant could not set up such a mistake or fraud in a proceeding of this kind. 3 Pomeroy's Eq. Jur. p. 2041; Mitchell v. Northwestern, etc., Co., 26 Ill. App. 295, 296.

Moreover, interpleader cannot be maintained unless it is shown that the third party sought to be substituted under said section 274, supra, is in existence and capable of interpleading. Metcalf v. Hervey, 1 Ves. 246, 248, 249; Browning v. Watkins, 10 Smedes & M. 482; Briant v. Reed, 14 N. J. Eq. 271, 276.

It will be observed that at the time appellant was notified by said nonresident creditors of W. L. Kidder & Son Milling Company not to pay said insurance policy or the check to appellee, and at the time of filing said interpleader, said corporation was insolvent, and in the hands of a receiver appointed by the Vigo circuit court—the court in which this action was brought. It is well settled that when the property of an insolvent corporation is in the hands of an assignee under the state insolvency laws, or a receiver or a trustee in bankruptcy, he represents the creditors, and has the exclusive right to recover and protect the assets of the corporation, and that such actions cannot be maintained by the creditors in their own names. First National Bank v. Dovetail, etc., Co., 143 Ind. 534, 539, 42 N. E. 924, and cases cited; National State Bank v. Vigo County National Bank, 141 Ind. 352, 356, 40 N. E. 799, 50 Am. St. Rep. 330, and cases cited; Voorhees v. Indianapolis Car Co., 140 Ind. 220, 239, 240, 39 N. E. 738; Vorhees v. Carpenter, 127 Ind. 300, 301, 302–305, 26 N. E. 838, and cases cited; Conner v. Long, 104 U. S. 228, 26 L. Ed. 723; Moyer v. Dewey, 103 U. S. 301, 26 L. Ed. 394; Trimble v. Woodhead, 102 U. S. 647, 26 L. Ed. 290; Glenny v. Langdon, 98 U. S. 44, 25 L. Ed. 43, and cases cited; Barder v. Bank, 4 B. R. 163, 166; In re Rothschild, 5 B. R. 587; Bump on Bankruptcy (10th Ed.) 147; High on Rec. (3d Ed.) §§ 314, 315, 320.

Even if Edson W. Kidder did use the money of said milling company in the payment of the premiums on said insurance policy in such manner or under such circumstances as to entitle said corporation or its creditors to maintain an action against appellant therefor, or against appellee when she received the proceeds of said policy, to recover the same or any part thereof, after the appointment of the receiver by the Vigo circuit court, such action, under the authorities cited, could be maintained only by such receiver, and he could be compelled by order of court to bring and prosecute such suit. Whatever right, if any, said milling company or its creditors had to recover the proceeds of said policy, or any part thereof, or the premiums paid thereon, from appellant or appellee, was vested in the receiver of said company, for the benefit of all the creditors, and said receiver alone had the right to recover the same. It is evident that said creditors were not, on account of said receivership, capable of interpleading with appellee, if substituted in place of appellant under section 274, supra.

It follows from what we have said that the amended interpleader of appellant was insufficient.

Whether or not it was proper practice to entertain and sustain a motion to make the interpleader filed by appellant more specific, and to permit a demurrer to be filed to the amended interpleader, and sustain the same, is immaterial, for the reason that the appellant's interpleader was clearly insufficient, and the result reached in holding the amended interpleader bad was correct. Mansfield v. Shipp, 128 Ind. 55, 57, 27 N. E. 427.

The notice to said creditors under section 274 (273), supra, was served on their attorney, a resident of this state, who gave the notice and made the demand upon appellant for said creditors in regard to said insurance policy and check. It is insisted by appellee that said notice, under section 274 (273), supra, must be personally served on each of said creditors; and that the service on said attorney was not sufficient to give the court below jurisdiction over their persons. Sections 314, 421, Burns' Rev. St. 1901; Allen v. Cox, 11 Ind. 383; Harkness v. Hyde, 98 U. S. 476, 25 L. Ed. 237; Patroni v. Campbell, 12 M. & W. 277, on page 278. As the reasons already given are sufficient to sustain the action of the trial court in holding the amended interpleader insufficient, we need not determine this question.

Judgment affirmed.

(32 Ind. A. 700)

STOUT v. WILLIAM CAMPBELL CO.

(Appellate Court of Indiana, Division No. 2. March 31, 1904.)

APPEAL—VERDICT—WEIGHT OF EVIDENCE—REVIEW.

1. A judgment will not be reversed on appeal on the ground that the verdict is contrary to the evidence, where there is some evidence to support it.

Appeal from Superior Court, Marion County; James M. Leathers, Judge.

Action by the William Campbell Company against Hulda A. Stout. From a judgment in favor of plaintiff, defendant appeals. Affirmed.

H. J. Everett, for appellant. Florea & Seidensticker, for appellee.

COMSTOCK, J. Appellee brought this action upon account against appellant for goods and merchandise sold and delivered by appellee to appellant. The cause was put at issue by general denial. A trial by jury resulted in a verdict in favor of appellee for $428.40, for which amount, over appellant's motion for a new trial, judgment was rendered. The overruling of the motion for a new trial is the only error assigned.

The reasons set out in the motion for a new trial discussed are that the verdict is not sustained by sufficient evidence, and that it is contrary to law. A written brief thereon has been filed by appellee to dismiss the appeal for failure to comply with a rule of the court. We have not considered the question raised by the motion named, but have read the evidence, and find that the verdict is not without support. Under the uniform rule governing appellate courts the judgment will not be disturbed.

Judgment affirmed.

(32 Ind. A. 642)

PARK v. PARK.

(Appellate Court of Indiana, Division No. 2. March 31, 1904.)

NOTES — LIMITATIONS — ACKNOWLEDGMENT — SUFFICIENCY—FINDINGS OF FACT—CONCLUSIONS OF LAW—REVIEW.

1. Burns' Rev. St. 1901, § 302, provides that no acknowledgment or promise shall be evidence of a new contract to take a case out of the statute of limitations, unless it be contained in some writing signed by the party to be charged. *Held*, that an acknowledgment is not sufficient to take a case out of the statute, unless it is of such a character that a new promise, sufficient to revive the debt, can be fairly inferred therefrom.

2. Burns' Rev. St. 1901, § 302, provides that no acknowledgment or promise shall be evidence of a new contract, so as to take a case out of the statute of limitations, unless the promise be contained in a writing signed by the party to be charged. On proceedings to collect a note from the estate of a decedent, the administrator relied on section 294, under which the note was barred by expiration of time, and the court found as a fact that on a certain date the decedent acknowledged in writing on the back of the note that it was due and unpaid, and the court found as a conclusion of law that the note was not barred. *Held* that, the written acknowledgment not being set out in the finding, the finding was insufficient to sustain the conclusion of law.

Appeal from Circuit Court, Morgan County; H. C. Barnett, Special Judge.

Proceedings by Josie M. Park to collect a claim from the estate of Benjamin P. Park, deceased. From a judgment in favor of claimant, Jeff. T. Park, as administrator, appeals. Reversed.

Jas. V. Mitchell and D. E. Watson, for appellant. C. G. Renner and Jno. C. McNutt, for appellee.

ROBY, J. Appellee commenced this proceeding by filing a claim against the estate, upon which she recovered judgment for $551.50, in accordance with the conclusions of law stated by the court, upon facts specially found, at the request of the parties.

In view of the disposition to be made of this appeal, it is not necessary to consider questions arising upon the pleadings or evidence, they not being likely to arise upon a retrial. It is established by the finding of facts that the note which forms the basis of the claim was executed by the decedent on November 10, 1886, and was by its terms due one day thereafter. The statute of limitations, by which actions upon promissory notes are required to be commenced within 10 years, was pleaded by the administrator. Subdivision 5, § 294, Burns' Rev. St. 1901. Appellee, tacitly admitting that the section cited is applicable and prima facie conclusive, sought to take the case out of the statute by proof of a written acknowledgment. The seventh finding of fact is as follows: "That on the 19th day of April, 1899, said Benjamin P. Park, then in life, acknowledged in writing on the back of said note, duly signed by him, that the said note was due and unpaid." The second conclusion of law was: "That the note mentioned in the claim herein is not barred by the statute of limitations, but is a legally existing claim against the estate of the decedent, Benjamin P. Park, no part of the same ever having been paid."

"No acknowledgment of promise shall be evidence of a new or continuing contract whereby to take the case out of the provisions of this act, unless the same be contained in some writing signed by the party to be charged thereby." Section 302, Burns' Rev. St. 1901; Kisler v. Sanders, 40 Ind. 78. No acknowledgment is sufficient to take the case out of the operation of the statute, unless it is of such a character that a new promise, sufficient to revive the debt, can be fairly inferred therefrom. McNear v. Roberson, 12 Ind. App. 87, 93, 39 N. E. 896. The written acknowledgment relied upon is not set out in the finding. Whether it was of such a character as to require the court to construe it in accordance with the conclusion of law stated cannot, therefore, be determined. In the absence of the writing itself, it cannot be said as matter of law that the inference of a promise to pay arose therefrom. If the acknowledgment is coupled with expressions which repel the presumption of a promise or of intention to pay, it will not be sufficient to avoid the operation of the statute. McNear v. Roberson, supra. The inference is one of fact. Christian v. State, 7 Ind. App. 417, 423, 34 N. E. 825; Mozingo v. Ross, 150 Ind. 688, 50 N. E. 867, 41 L. R. A. 612, 65 Am. St. Rep. 387. The acknowledgment must be considered in connection with the accompanying circumstances. McNear v. Roberson, supra; Conwell v. Buchanan, 7 Blackf. 539; Goldsby v. Genth, 5 Blackf. 436; Ft. Scott v. Hickman, 112 U. S. 150, 5 Sup. Ct. 56, 28 L. Ed. 636. A special finding in which no inference is drawn, the ultimate fact not stated, the writing relied upon not set out, and the circumstances attendant upon its execution not shown, is not sufficient to sustain a conclusion of law to the effect that the claim is not barred by the statute, it appearing that otherwise the statute has run.

The interests of justice require that there be a retrial of this cause. The judgment is therefore reversed, and the cause is remanded with instructions to sustain appellant's motion for a new trial, to permit the parties to reform the issues if they shall so desire, and for further consistent proceedings.

¶ 1. See Limitation of Actions, vol. 33, Cent. Dig. §§ 597, 598.

INDIANAPOLIS ST. RY. CO. v. MARSCHKE.*

(Appellate Court of Indiana. April 1, 1904.)

STREET RAILWAYS—COLLISION WITH VEHICLE—CONTRIBUTORY NEGLIGENCE—DRIVER'S FAILURE TO LOOK.

1. The driver of a vehicle who, in order to pass a wagon in front of her, turns, without looking for cars, onto a street car track in front of a car approaching from the rear in plain view, is guilty of contributory negligence.

Roby and Black, JJ., dissenting.

Appeal from Superior Court, Marion County; Vinson Carter, Judge.

Action by Bertha A. Marschke against the Indianapolis Street Railway Company. Judgment for plaintiff, and defendant appeals. Reversed.

Winter & Winter, for appellant. P. W. Bartholomew and R. F. Stuart, for appellee.

WILEY, P. J. Appellee was injured by one of the appellant's cars colliding with a buggy in which she was riding, and prosecuted this action to a successful termination in the court below to recover damages for such injury. The question of appellant's negligence, as charged in the complaint, and appellee's freedom from negligence, were issues of fact, which the jury, by its general verdict, resolved in her favor. The court submitted interrogatories to the jury upon specific questions of fact, which were duly answered, and upon such answers appellant moved the court to render judgment in its favor, notwithstanding the general verdict, which motion was overruled. Appellant moved for a new trial, which was also overruled. The rulings on these two motions are the only errors assigned, and will be considered in their order.

The evidence shows that appellee was injured on Virginia avenue, in the city of Indianapolis, about 500 or 600 feet southeast from the top of the viaduct. She was driving on the avenue, going in a southeasterly direction. Appellant has a line of street railway tracks on said avenue. Outgoing cars run over the southeast track, and incoming cars over the northeast track. The grade from the top of the viaduct extends a distance of 500 or 600 feet to the intersection of Louisiana street, running east and west. As appellee was driving southeast on the avenue, one of appellant's cars was going in the same direction, and descending the grade. She was driving far enough from the track on which the car was approaching for it to pass without striking her buggy. There was another buggy or wagon in front of her which she desired to pass, as she was driving more rapidly, and to get by it turned to the left, toward the track, and came in such close proximity to it that the car could not pass without striking it.

The specific facts, as exhibited by the answers to interrogatories, reduced to narrative form, are as follows: Appellee was injured, at the intersection of Virginia avenue and Louisiana street, by one of appellant's cars striking her buggy. The distance from the top or crown of the viaduct to Louisiana street is about 600 feet. The view along the right-hand track, between where appellee was and the crown of the viaduct, was unobstructed, and a car on such track could have been seen, by one traveling by the side of the track, after it got to the top or crown of the viaduct, at any point between there and Louisiana street. Appellee was driving southeast on Virginia avenue, descending the grade from the viaduct, and such a distance from the track that a car could pass the buggy without striking it. The motorman on the car saw appellee driving beside the track, and could see that there was room for his car to pass without striking her buggy. At a point about 100 feet from where she was struck, appellee found a wagon in front of her, which was stopped or going slower than she was. She desired to pass such wagon by driving between it and the track on which appellant's car, by which she was struck, was approaching. The car was then between her and the top of the viaduct, and was in sight from any point on the avenue between the center of Louisiana street and the top of the viaduct. There was nothing to prevent appellee from seeing the car, if she had looked, from the time it came over the top of the viaduct until it struck her. Appellee was driving at a speed not exceeding five, and not less than four, miles per hour. The speed of the car, after it came over the top of the viaduct, was not to exceed 20 miles per hour. When appellee found the wagon in her way, she turned her buggy to the left to pass between it and the right-hand track, and in so doing approached so close to the track that the car could not pass without striking it. The wagon in front of appellee was an indication to the motorman that appellee intended to turn to pass the wagon, thus getting nearer the track. The motorman knew, or had reason to know, that appellee would turn toward the track before she actually began to make the turn. The motorman, or no one in charge of the car, could have stopped it in time to have prevented it from striking appellee after she began to turn toward the track. When the car was at the top of the viaduct, appellee was about halfway between that point and the center of Louisiana street at its intersection with Virginia avenue.

The particular negligence with which appellant is charged, in the language of the complaint, was "one of defendant's cars, negligently propelled by defendant's servants at a rapid and dangerous rate of speed, * * * without ringing the gong or sounding any alarm of its approach, * * * carelessly and negligently ran the running

¶ 1. See Street Railroads, vol. 44, Cent. Dig. §§ 212, 215.

*Rehearing denied. Transferred to Supreme Court, 77 N. E. 945.

board and other parts of said car upon and against plaintiff's buggy, * * * and threw plaintiff therefrom," etc. The rate of speed at which the car is alleged to have been running was 20 miles per hour. By its general verdict the jury found that appellant was guilty of negligence as charged, and that appellee was without fault on her part. The general verdict must therefore stand, unless it is overcome by the facts specially found. If the facts thus found show that appellant was not guilty of negligence as charged, or that appellee, by her own negligence, contributed to her injury, then such facts would be in irreconcilable conflict with the general verdict, and would be of controlling influence. Appellant's learned counsel argue that the answers to the interrogatories affirmatively show that the appellee was guilty of negligence in turning her buggy onto the track, for it is established that the car was between her and the top of the viaduct before she began to turn in toward the track, and was in plain view from any point on Virginia avenue between the top of the viaduct and the intersection of Virginia avenue and Louisiana street, and there was nothing to prevent her from seeing it if she had looked. The question of appellee's negligence must be determined in view of the rule, so firmly established in this state, that the law will presume that she actually saw what she could have seen, if she had looked, and heard what she could have heard, if she had listened. Young v. Citizens', etc., Ry. Co., 148 Ind. 54, 44 N. E. 927, 47 N. E. 142; Cones v. Cincinnati, etc., Ry. Co., 114 Ind.; at page 114, 16 N. E. 638; Lake Erie, etc., Ry. Co. v. Stick, 143 Ind. 449, 41 N. E. 365. If she could have seen the approaching car, by looking, in time to have escaped colliding with it, it will be presumed, in case of collision, either that she did not look, or, if she did, she did not heed what she saw. Such conduct is held to be negligence per se. Ohio, etc., Ry. Co. v. Hill, 117 Ind., at page 61, 18 N. E. 461; Cones v. Cincinnati, etc., Ry. Co., 114 Ind., at page 330, 16 N. E. 638; Lake Erie, etc., Ry. Co. v. Stick, supra; Young v. Citizens', etc., Ry. Co., supra. If it was negligence for her to drive on the track so an approaching car would strike her, without first looking, then she could not recover, for by her own act she contributed to her injury. In Young v. Citizens', etc., Ry. Co., 148 Ind. 54, 44 N. E. 927, 47 N. E. 142, such conduct was declared to be negligence. The case of Kessler v. Citizens' Street Railway Co., 20 Ind. App. 427, 50 N. E. 891, decides the identical question we are now considering, with this exception: In that case appellee was driving on a street where appellant operated a line of street cars, and was driving at a safe distance from the track so a car could pass. To get around a wagon in front, appellee turned on the track about 40 feet in front of a car going in the same direction. The motorman did not have any warning that appellee was going to turn onto the track, and could not have stopped the car in time to avoid a collision after he discovered the danger. Upon these facts it was held that appellant could not recover. Here the jury found that the wagon in front of appellee was an indication to the motorman that appellee intended to turn to pass it, and that he knew, or had reason to know, she would turn toward the track. We think this finding is largely speculative, and more the statement of a conclusion than a substantive fact. The finding casts upon the motorman the presumption that she would deliberately imperil her life and safety by driving on the track, when he had a right to presume that she would not do so.

If it was negligence for appellant to run its car at the rate of speed it did, it was likewise negligence for appellee to drive upon the track in front of it, when she had ample opportunity of seeing its approach, if she had looked, and could thus have avoided injury. The law is too well settled to be longer in doubt that a person must exercise his own faculties so as to avoid danger, if he can reasonably avoid it; and a failure to do so, if it contributes proximately to the injury, will prevent the one thus injured from recovering damages therefor. Salem-Bedford Stone Co. v. O'Brien, 12 Ind. App. 217, 40 N. E. 430. If appellee had looked, she could have seen the approaching car, and realized her impending danger, and thus avoided injury. This she did not do, but deliberately placed herself in a place of peril, without taking any precaution for her safety. The two essential elements of contributory negligence are want of ordinary care by the plaintiff, and a casual connection between such want of care and the injury. Salem-Bedford Stone Co. v. O'Brien, supra. Here these two elements combine, for appellee did not use ordinary care, and there was a direct and casual connection between such want of care and the injury.

It is unnecessary to discuss the relative rights of a street car company and a traveler to the use of the street occupied by street car tracks. The simple question here involved is this: Can a person, traveling upon a street, deliberately drive or walk in front of an approaching car, without looking or taking any precautions to avoid a collision, and recover for resulting injury? This question must be answered in the negative, for the authorities so hold. The cases cited are in point. In the recent case of Indianapolis Street Ry. Co. v. Tenner, 67 N. E. 1044, this court held that a party who had alighted from a street car and passed back of it, and upon the track on which cars traveled in the opposite direction, without looking or listening for the approach of cars, was guilty of contributory negligence, and could not recover. The facts in that case made a more favorable showing for appellee than they do here, for there the view of the approaching car was obstructed by the car from which she alighted, and she could not see the approaching car until she had passed behind the one upon which she had been riding. Here appellee could have seen the car that injured her, if she had looked, at any time after it came over the top of the viaduct, and when it was four or five hundred feet away, and continuously to the time it struck her. The facts specially found are in irreconcilable conflict with the general verdict, in that they show appellee was guilty of contributory negligence.

Judgment reversed, and the court is directed to sustain appellant's motion for judgment on the answers to interrogatories and render judgment accordingly.

COMSTOCK, J., and HENLEY, C. J., concur. ROBINSON, J., concurs in result. BLACK, J., dissents. ROBY, J., dissents, and files dissenting opinion.

ROBY, J. (dissenting). In order that applicable legal conclusions be correctly stated, it is essential that the facts to which they relate be expressed specifically and with certainty. The negligence charged against appellant was that it ran an electric car along one of the principal streets in the city of Indianapolis at a dangerous rate of speed, without signal of any kind, in the same direction that appellee was driving in a buggy, and ran the same against her vehicle, overthrowing it, and inflicting personal injuries upon her. The issue was formed by denial, and upon trial she had a verdict for $950, the appeal being taken from a judgment thereon.

The burden of establishing contributory negligence was upon appellant, and the general verdict, being against it, is conclusive, unless the answers to interrogatories by the jury are irreconcilable therewith. The occurrence complained of was not a collision at the crossing of a steam railroad over a public highway. The collision was not caused by an attempt by the appellee to cross the tracks of an electric railroad at the crossing of an intersecting street. It was not caused by an attempt to cross such track between intersecting streets or at any other place. It did not take place on a country road or crossing, but in one of the main streets in the largest city of the state. A superficial resemblance does not make legal propositions applicable to one set of facts applicable to another, and analogies, charming as they appear, need to be carefully scrutinized, else they confuse and mislead, instead of pointing the way. By the general verdict it is established that appellant negligently inflicted the injuries complained of as alleged. The answers to interrogatories show that appellee was injured at the intersection of Virginia avenue and Louisiana street; that she was driving southeast on the avenue, on the right-hand side of the car tracks, on a descending grade from the viaduct, and such a distance from the track that a car could pass without striking the buggy. About 100 feet from where she was struck she found a wagon stopped, or going slower than she in the same direction. Desiring to pass it she drove between it and appellant's track, approaching near enough to the track so that the car could not pass without striking the buggy. She was driving at a rate of four to five miles an hour. The distance to the crown of the viaduct was 600 feet. The view along the track to that point was unobstructed, there being nothing to prevent her seeing the approaching car if she had looked. The motorman could see appellee, and that there was room to pass without striking her buggy. The speed of the car after it came over the viaduct did not exceed 20 miles an hour. He knew, or had reason to know, that she would turn towards the track before she did so. The wagon ahead of her was an indication to that effect. When the car was at the top of the viaduct, appellee was about halfway between that point and Louisiana street.

If contributory negligence can be adjudged as a matter of law upon these answers, it must be on the ground that failing to see the approaching car was per se negligence, without regard to other facts or the existing circumstances. Such holding would be wholly contrary to precedent. Since the carefully considered decision and exhaustive opinion by Wiley, J., in Street Railway v. Damm, 25 Ind. App. 511, 58 N. E. 564, it is not open to question that the "rigid and stringent rule governing crossing steam railway tracks that intersect highways and streets * * * is not applicable here, for the reason that persons about to cross a street car track in a city, at the intersection of streets, are not held to that high degree of care required of passengers crossing steam railroad tracks." If such rules do not apply to persons crossing the tracks, they do not apply to those driving along the streets, as appellee was doing. So that, in consideration of the questions presented by this appeal, steam crossing cases may be eliminated.

Young v. Ry. Co., 148 Ind. 54, 44 N. E. 927, 47 N. E. 142, cited by appellant, was decided long before Railway v. Damm, supra, and at a time when the burden was on the plaintiff to show his freedom from fault, and came to the Supreme Court on a special verdict. No general verdict was returned. The attendant presumptions did not arise, and it is not authority for overthrowing a general verdict upon answers to interrogatories, which show that the party injured did not see the approaching car, unless such failure is shown by such answers to have been inexcusable in connection with conditions which then existed. There can be nothing better settled than that one who deliberately casts himself in front of an approaching vehicle, whether wagon or car, cannot recover resulting damages. Moran v. Leslie (Ind. App.) 70 N. E. 162; Ry. v. Helvie, 22 Ind. App. 515, 53 N. E. 191; Kessler v. Ry., 20 Ind. App. 427, 50 N. E. 891.

The above-cited cases are typical illustrations of the principle. The facts stated in the answers to the interrogatories in the case at bar, remembering always that "all reasonable presumptions are indulged against the special answers and in support of the general verdict, and if the general verdict, thus aided, is not in irreconcilable conflict with the answers, it must stand" (Ry. v. Peyton, 157 Ind. 690, 697, 61 N. E. 722), come very far from bringing appellee within this principle. It is not stated therein how far appellant's car was from appellee when she started to drive around the wagon. "It is found as a fact that they [she] saw or did not see the car, but that there was nothing to prevent one seeing it who looked in the direction from whence it was coming." Ry. Co. v. Damm, 25 Ind. App., at page 518, 58 N. E. 567; Union Trac. v. Vandercook (Ind. App.) 69 N. E. 486. It cannot be said, as a matter of law, that it is negligence to cross the track without looking when the car is 50 feet distant. An undisclosed distance will not warrant such conclusion against one who was attempting to cross the track, or as against one who had no purpose to do so. When she started to go around the wagon ahead, "He [she] did not know that a car was approaching at the rate of 40 [20] miles an hour. Had he [she] seen the car when that distance away, and there was nothing to lead him to believe that it was running any faster than the ordinary rate of speed, his attempt to cross the track in front of the car would not have been, as matter of law, negligence. An attempt to cross in front of a street car running at an ordinary rate of speed, 50 feet distant, is not, as matter of law, negligence." Union Trac. v. Vandercook (Ind. App.) 69 N. E. 488; Ry. Co. v. Damm, supra.

The general verdict finds that no signals were given. The answers do not show that any were given. Their absence is therefore established. "While the failure of those in charge of the car to give the required signals would not excuse appellee from the exercise of due care, yet the jury might consider that fact, in connection with all the circumstances attending the accident, in passing upon the conduct of appellee." Union Trac. v. Vandercook, supra; Louisville v. Williams, 20 Ind. App. 576, 51 N. E. 128.

The high rate of speed at which the car was running is another circumstance bearing upon the quality of her act, while if the motorman made any attempt to check or stop his car after she turned toward the track, or at any other time, it has not been found. The findings are wholly silent as to what the appellee was doing, and to where her attention was directed, when she started around the wagon. So far as shown, the street may have been crowded with vehicles and the crossings filled with footmen, toward whom she was bound to exercise due care to avoid running them down. If she was so engaged, and was for that reason unable to look behind her at the critical moment, such fact must be considered for what it is worth upon the question of contributory negligence. "He did not see nor hear the car. If he had, it would have been his duty to have attempted to get off the track. He was not required to constantly look behind him." Ry. Co. v. Darnell (Ind. App.) 68 N. E. 612; Ry. Co. v. Damm, supra; Louisville v. Williams, supra. That every person must exercise his faculties to avoid collision with street cars or other vehicles, so as to avoid danger therefrom, if he can reasonably do so, is not only declared by the authorities, but is dictated by common sense. Whether one has done this must depend upon the attendant circumstances, and where, as in this case, they are not fully shown by the answers to the interrogatories, there can be no judgment as against the general verdict, unless there be some controlling act or omission that under any circumstances would be negligent. Neither can it be implied that appellee ought to have turned out on the other side of the wagon she was passing. The answers do not show that there was sufficient room, or any room, for her to do so. It is not incumbent upon her to show why she did not turn away from the track instead of towards it. The general verdict does that. It thus appears, without going further, that the quality of appellee's acts were dependent upon much the statement of which is omitted from the answers to the interrogatories, and that the question was for the jury. Ind. Pipe Line, etc., v. Neusbum, 21 Ind. App. 361, 369, 52 N. E. 471; Peirce v. Ray, 24 Ind. App. 302, 313, 56 N. E. 776.

The application of the decisions as to collisions at the crossing of steam railroads to collisions between travelers upon the streets, in favor of the owner of the heaviest vehicle, is, in my opinion, an unwarranted innovation, and why, in making it, the established rules by which answers to interrogatories returned in connection with a general verdict have always been judged should be wiped out, as is done by the main opinion, I cannot understand. Not desiring to be a party to either departure, I dissent.

(178 N. Y. 223)

WETYEN v. FICK et al.

(Court of Appeals of New York. April 8, 1904.)

DOWER—ACTION—LIMITATIONS—NONRESIDENT DEFENDANTS—SERVICE BY PUBLICATION.

1. Under Code Civ. Proc. § 1596, a widow must begin an action for dower within 20 years from the death of her husband, unless she is at such time under disability, or unless the right of dower has been adjudged by a decree of court, or been recognized under seal, in which case the time after the husband's death previous to the

recognition or adjudication of dower, or the time under which the widow was under disability, must be excluded.

2. Where a widow begins an action for dower more than 20 years after her husband's death, the cause of action is not exempted from the limitations of Code Civ. Proc. § 1596, by section 401, providing that if, when a cause of action accrues, a person is without the state, the action may be commenced within the time limited after his return by the fact that the defendants have not been in the state since the husband's death, as by section 414, subd. 1, the general provisions of the Code as to limitations do not apply to a case where a different limitation is specifically prescribed by law.

3. Under Code, § 1597, providing that, if any property in which dower is claimed is actually occupied, the occupant thereof must be made defendant in the action, and when it is not so occupied the action may be brought against some person exercising acts of ownership thereupon or claiming title thereto, a widow can bring action for dower against tenants or occupants, so that the statute of limitations provided by Code, § 1596, is not prevented from running because the life tenant and owners in fee were nonresidents.

4. Under Code Civ. Proc. § 438, subd. 5, providing for service by publication where the complaint demands judgment that defendant be excluded from interest in or lien upon specific real or personal property within the state, or that such an interest in favor of either party be defined and enforced, an action for dower may be commenced where such parties are nonresidents, and there was no occupant of the premises, or any person exercising acts of ownership.

Appeal from Supreme Court, Appellate Division, First Department.

Action by Adeline Wetyen against Peter W. Fick and others. From a judgment of the Appellate Division (85 N. Y. Supp. 592) in favor of defendants upon a submission of controversy, plaintiff appeals. Affirmed.

David Ackerman, for appellant. Henry Hill Pierce and Harry E. Lee, for respondent Peter W. Fick. Herbert M. Johnston and George W. McAdams, for respondent Anna M. C. Breckwedel.

BARTLETT, J. The case embodied in this submission is for dower in certain real estate situated in the city of New York. The plaintiff is the widow of the late John H. Wetyen, who died March 29, 1863, seised in fee simple of the real estate in question. The plaintiff was married some time previous to the year 1850 in the city of New York. There were four children of the marriage—one daughter, Anna M. C., and three sons—all of whom survived their father. The deceased left a last will and testament, which is set forth in the submission herein, but its terms are not material, as no question respecting the same is raised by either counsel. Prior to 1880 the plaintiff's daughter, Anna M. C. Wetyen, married Peter W. Fick, and a daughter was born to them, Anna M. Fick. Anna M. Wetyen, the mother, took title to a portion of the real estate in question under the will of her father, and upon her death in 1880 her husband, Peter W. Fick, one of the defendants herein, became a tenant by the curtesy in the real estate of which she died seised. It is unnecessary to refer to the details in the chain of title vesting the fee of this entire real estate in which dower is now claimed in the defendant Anna M. Fick, the granddaughter of the plaintiff. The plaintiff and her children resided in the city of New York for eight years after the death of her husband on March 29, 1863. She then removed to New Jersey, taking her children with her. All the parties, both plaintiff and defendants, have since resided in the state of New Jersey, with the exception that for one year the defendants herein lived in the city of New York. It appears by the submission as follows: "Since the death of said Anna in 1880 the defendants have collected, received, and used for their own benefit all the rents and profits from the premises in question, and are now in possession of said premises, and claim title thereto." It further appears that no demand was made by the plaintiff for her dower until the 24th day of March, 1903, which was 40 years, lacking 5 days, after the death of her husband.

Several questions were submitted under this agreed case, but the principal one is whether the plaintiff's claim for dower is barred by the statute of limitations. The limitation of the action for dower is contained in the Code of Civil Procedure, § 1596, which reads as follows: "An action for dower must be commenced by a widow, within twenty years after the death of her husband; but if she is, at the time of his death, either: (1) Within the age of twenty-one years; or (2) insane; or (3) imprisoned on a criminal charge, or in execution upon conviction of a criminal offense, for a term less than for life; the time of such a disability is not a part of the time limited by this section. And if, at any time before such claim of dower has become barred by the above lapse of twenty years, the owner or owners of the land subject to such dower, being in possession, shall have recognized such claim of dower by any statement contained in a writing under seal, subscribed and acknowledged in the manner entitling a deed of real estate to be recorded, or if by any judgment or decree of a court of record within the same time and concerning the lands in question, wherein such owner or owners were parties, such right of dower shall have been distinctly recognized as a subsisting claim against said lands, the time after the death of her husband, and previous to such acknowledgment in writing or such recognition by judgment or decree, is not a part of the time limited by this section." This section thus provides that an action for dower must be commenced by the widow within 20 years after the death of her husband, subject to certain exceptions. It also points out the manner in which the 20-years limitation may be extended 20 years more. It is the claim of the plaintiff (appellant) that, although the 20 years, by this section, have apparently run against her, as there was no extension of the period of limitation by writing or judgment, yet, nevertheless, the running of the statute was prevented by the fact that at no time since her husband's death have the defendants resided in the state of New York for 20 years. This claim is based on the provisions of chapter 4 of the Code of Civil Procedure, entitled "Limitation of the Time of Enforcing a Civil Remedy." Two sections contained in title 3 of this chapter, which is entitled "General Provisions," are relied upon. Section 401 reads in part as follows: "If, when the cause of action accrues against a person, he is without the state, the action may be commenced within the time limited therefor, after his return into the state." Exceptions are contained in title 3 qualifying the time fixed for the running of the statute in various cases. Section 414 of this title is headed, "Cases to Which This Chapter Applies," and reads in part as follows: "The provisions of this chapter apply, and constitute the only rules of limitation applicable, to a civil action or special proceeding, except in one of the following cases: (1) A case, where a different limitation is specially prescribed by law, or a shorter limitation is prescribed by the written contract of the parties." The remaining provisions of this section are immaterial at this time.

It is the contention of the counsel for plaintiff that section 1596 is not within the exception of section 414, and consequently section 401 applies. The counsel for defendants argues that section 1596 was intended to be complete in itself, and falls within the exception of section 414, subd. 1, above quoted, as it contains a different limitation specially prescribed by law. In order to answer the question now submitted it is necessary briefly to consider the history of the statute of limitations applicable to the action for dower. At common law and under the revised laws of this state there was no statute of limitation applicable to an action for dower, and the widow had her entire lifetime in which to enforce that right. In the revision of the Statutes of 1827 the commissioners inserted a new section in the title treating of estates in dower, reading as follows: "Sec. 18. A widow shall demand her dower within twenty years after the death of her husband; but if, at the time of such death, she be under the age of twenty-one years, or insane, or imprisoned on a criminal charge or conviction, the time during which such disability continues shall not form any part of the said term of twenty years." 1 Rev. St. (1st Ed.) p. 742, pt. 2, c. 1, tit. 3.

In the report of the commissioners to revise the statute law for 1827 (page 75; 5 Edmunds' R. S. [Ed. 1863] p. 334) they submitted the following note, referring to section 18, above quoted: "1 Rev. Laws, p. 60, § 1, allows a widow her lifetime to prosecute for her dower. By the revised statute of limitations a woman must demand every other estate in lands to which she may be entitled within twenty years, subject to the exceptions contained in the preceding section. If it be an object in any case to quiet titles, to protect honest purchasers, and to excite to a vigilance equally beneficial to the claimant and to others, it is conceived that this case requires the necessary provisions to attain it as much, if not more, than any other." We have here set forth the reason of the revisers in creating this limitation as to actions for dower, which was to quiet titles, to protect honest purchasers, and to excite to a vigilance equally beneficial to the claimant and to others. When the Code of Civil Procedure was enacted, section 18, above quoted, was incorporated into the first part of section 1596, with slight verbal changes not affecting the general meaning. The section remained as so enacted until amended in an important particular in 1882 (chapter 277, p. 344), when was added the following: "And if at any time before such claim of dower has become barred by the above lapse of twenty years, the owner or owners of the lands subject to such dower being in possession, shall have recognized such claim of dower by any statement contained in a writing under seal, subscribed and acknowledged in the manner entitling a deed of real estate to be recorded, or if by any judgment or decree of a court of record within the same time and concerning the land in question, wherein such owner or owners were parties, such right of dower shall have been distinctly recognized as a subsisting claim against said lands, the time after the death of her husband, and previous to such acknowledgment in writing or such recognition by judgment or decree, is not a part of the time limited by this section." It was undoubtedly the intention of the Legislature of 1882, in adding this amendment, to embody in the section provisions calculated to more completely carry out the intention of the revisers as expressed in their report in 1827, to quiet titles, to protect honest purchasers, and to excite to a vigilance equally beneficial to the claimant and to others. A careful reading of this amendment discloses that the Legislature intended the statute of limitation in the action for dower should be contained in one section, wherein a different limitation was specially prescribed by law within the exception of section 414 of the Code, subd. 1. That is to say, the section, as thus amended, provided an original limitation of 20 years, but upon the last day of the 20 years it was rendered possible for the owner of the land subject to dower being in possession to recognize the claim of dower in a writing under seal, subscribed and acknowledged in the manner entitling a deed of real estate to be recorded, or the claim of dower could be recognized by any judgment or decree of a court of record within the same time, and concerning the land in question, and wherein the owner thereof was a party. In case of recognition in either form thus pointed out the 20 years intervening between the death of the husband of the widow and the date of the writing or judgment is not a part of the time limited by this section. In other words, it was possible for the parties in interest to double the time of limitation mentioned in the statute, making it 40 years instead of 20, and in legal contemplation a special limitation. The object of requiring the writing to be under seal and acknowledged in the manner prescribed for the execution of a deed, or by judgment or decree of a court of record, obviously was to make the extension of time a matter of record, so that any one taking title to real estate, encountering a dower right, could, by consulting the provisions of the Code and the records of the county, ascertain whether or not such claim of dower was valid and existing. If, as is claimed by plaintiff, the intention of the Legislature was to apply to this section the provisions of section 401, which stops the running of the statute when the defendant is without the state, it would necessitate investigation as to a claim for dower, the validity of which could not be ascertained by an examination of the records. It would require a search in a foreign jurisdiction to ascertain if the interested parties had lived there, and, if so, how long, whether living or dead, their present residence, and other details that could only be preserved in affidavit form, and at best very unsatisfactory when incorporated into an abstract of title. In many instances it is highly probable that it would be impossible, after the lapse of years, to follow out such inquiries with a fair measure of success. In construing this section limiting actions for dower, an important question of public policy is involved, which distinguishes it from any other provisions of the Code dealing with the subject of limitations. This question of public policy is set forth in the revisers' notes already quoted, and is further evidenced by the amendment of the section in 1882. If the argument of the counsel for plaintiff (appellant) is sound, it would practically defeat the object of the revisers.

We have considered the question thus far under the assumption that the tenant by the curtesy and the owner of the fee, although residing in the state of New Jersey for more than 20 years, are necessary parties to this action. An action for dower seeks to determine an estate in land, and according to the present provisions of the Code, which are substantially a re-enactment of the Revised Statutes upon the same subject, the occupant of the premises must be made defendant in the action. Section 1597 of the Code, entitled "Against Whom Action to be Brought," reads as follows: "Where the property, in which dower is claimed, is actually occupied, the occupant thereof must be made defendant in the action. Where it is not so occupied, the action must be brought against some person exercising acts of ownership thereupon, or claiming title thereto, or an interest therein, at the time of the commencement of the action." We have already pointed out that the submission contains the following clause: "Since the death of said Anna, in 1880, the defendants have collected, received, and used for their own benefit all the rents and profits from the premises in question, and are now in possession of said premises and claiming title thereto." We have here a clear period of 20 years after 1880 when these defendants were residents of the state of New Jersey, and during that time had collected all the rents and profits from the premises in question. The rents and profits could not have been so collected unless there had been a tenant in the premises. It therefore follows that the widow could at any time have instituted this action for dower by making the tenant a party. In Ellicott v. Mosier, 7 N. Y. 201, Chief Judge Ruggles, writing at a time when the widow could maintain ejectment for her dower, said: "Before the adoption of the Revised Statutes, the plaintiff's remedy at law would have been by an action of dower. The object of that action is to obtain or compel an assignment of dower by the heir or other owner of the land subject to the widow's right. It could therefore be brought only against the owner or the tenant of the freehold. No other person could assign the dower. Hurd v. Grant, 3 Wend. 340; Park on Dower, 265; Coke's Littleton, 35a; Beddingford's Case, 9 Coke, 17. The action of dower was abolished in 1830, and the action of ejectment substituted in its place. 2 Rev. St. 303, §§ 2, 4, 304, 310, 313. By section 4 the action must be brought against the actual occupant of the land if there be one, and in terms this section applies as well to actions of ejectment for dower as to other actions of ejectment. The consequence is that in a case where the premises in which dower is claimed are in the actual occupation of a tenant for years the action of ejectment for dower, if it can be sustained at all, must be brought against the actual occupant, and not against the tenant of the freehold." This practice has been perpetuated in the Code of Civil Procedure, as above quoted, and regulates the necessary parties in the widow's action for dower. Furthermore, if we assume that there was a period of time when there was no occupant of the premises, or any person exercising acts of ownership thereupon, and the plaintiff had been compelled to join as defendant the nonresident person claiming title thereto, the situation would present no obstacle to the widow immediately beginning her action, as service could be made by publication under section 438 of the Code, subdivision 5, which provides that the service by publication can be made "where the complaint demands judgment that the defendant be excluded from a vested or contingent interest in or lien upon specific real or personal property within the state; or that such an interest or lien in favor of either party be enforced, regulated, defined, or limited; or otherwise affecting the title to such property." It is therefore clear that the statute of limitations has run against the plaintiff, and her claim for dower is consequently barred.

The plaintiff's counsel raises the further point that the former decisions of this court are controlling, and hold that section 401 applies to section 1596. Three cases are cited as sustaining this claim, viz., Hayden v. Pierce, 144 N. Y. 512, 39 N. E. 638; Titus v. Poole, 145 N. Y. 414, 40 N. E. 228; Hamilton v. Royal Ins. Co., 156 N. Y. 327, 50 N. E. 863, 42 L. R. A. 485. In the Pierce and Poole Cases the question arose under section 1822 of the Code, which provides, in substance, that an action on a claim against the estate of a decedent which has been disputed or rejected must be brought within the period of six months. In the Pierce Case it was claimed that section 401 applied, which provides that if, when a cause of action accrues against a person, he is without the state, the action may be commenced within the time limited therefor after his return into the state. In the Poole Case it was argued that section 405 of the Code applied, which provides that: "If an action is commenced within the time limited therefor, and a judgment therein is reversed on appeal, without awarding a new trial, or the action is terminated in any other manner than by a voluntary discontinuance, a dismissal of the complaint for neglect to prosecute the action, or a final judgment upon the merits, the plaintiff, or, if he dies, and the cause of action survives, his representative may commence a new action for the same cause, after the expiration of the time so limited, and within one year after such a reversal or termination." Both of these cases involved the construction of section 414. It was conceded that, if section 1822 could be regarded as establishing a different limitation, specially prescribed by law, within the language of section 414, then the sections arresting the running of the statute of limitations could not affect the situation, and defendants' defense of the statute would have to be sustained. In the Poole Case Chief Judge Andrews said (145 N. Y. at page 423, 40 N. E. 230), referring to section 414: "That section, so far as it affects the question now under consideration, is as follows: 'Sec. 414. The provisions of this chapter apply and constitute the only rules of limitation applicable to a civil action or special proceeding except in one of the following cases: (1) A case where a different limitation is specially prescribed by law or a shorter limitation is prescribed by the written contract of the parties.' The general purpose of the exception in this section seems plain. It was to preserve limitations prescribed by special statute, or by the contract of parties, and to prevent any misapprehension that actions subject to special limitations by statute or contract were affected by the periods of limitation prescribed in chapter 4 in the several classes of action therein specified. The statutes prescribing special and unusual limitations are numerous." In the Hamilton Case the question arose under a short statute of limitation contained in the standard policy of fire insurance, and it was there claimed that, notwithstanding the provisions of section 414 of the Code, section 399 applied, and prevented the running of the contract period of limitation. The latter section provides, in substance, that an attempt to commence an action in a court of record is equivalent to the commencement of it within each provision of chapter 4 of the Code, which limits the time for commencing an action when the summons is delivered to the sheriff of the proper county with the intent that it shall be actually served.

In the above cases the question was considered whether a period of limitation, standing by itself in a section of the Code, or a contract of the parties, could be regarded as creating such a special and unusual limitation as to bring it within the exception contained in section 414, subd. 1. It was held that, to treat a period of limitation standing by itself as subject to no statutory exceptions whatever, would be to work gross injustice, and to ignore the plain intention of the Legislature. In the case at bar we have already given in detail the reasons that have led us to the conclusion that section 1596 of the Code stands by itself, and contains a different and unusual limitation specially prescribed by law, and consequently is not affected by the provisions of chapter 4 of the Code, which deals with the limitation of the time of enforcing a civil remedy, and that it clearly falls within the exception of section 414 of the Code, subd. 1.

The judgment appealed from should be affirmed, with costs to the defendants separately appearing.

PARKER, C. J., and GRAY, O'BRIEN, and HAIGHT, JJ., concur. MARTIN and CULLEN, JJ., concur in result.

Judgment affirmed.

(178 N. Y. 219)

LIBERTY WALL PAPER CO. v. STONER WALL PAPER MFG. CO.

(Court of Appeals of New York. April 8, 1904.)

COUNTERCLAIM—BURDEN OF PROOF—ASSIGNMENT—EVIDENCE.

1. Under Code Civ. Proc. § 974, where defendant interposes a counterclaim and demands an affirmative judgment, he has the affirmative of the issue and the burden of proof; and where he must, to support the counterclaim, show that he was the owner of a certain contract when the action was brought, it is error to admit an undated writing in evidence, purporting to be an assignment of the contract, where it is shown by cross-examination that it was actually signed after the action was brought; and such er-

ror is not cured by the submission to the jury of the specific question whether, at the time the action was begun, the contract had been signed.

Appeal from Supreme Court, Appellate Division, Third Department.

Action by the Liberty Wall Paper Company against the Stoner Wall Paper Manufacturing Company. From a judgment of the Appellate Division affirming a judgment for defendant (79 N. Y. Supp. 1137), plaintiff appeals. Reversed.

Edgar T. Brackett and William E. Bennett, for appellant. John L. Henning, for respondent.

O'BRIEN, J. The issues in this case arise upon the defendant's counterclaim and the reply thereto, the affirmative cause of action set out in the complaint having been disposed of in a former decision of this court. 170 N. Y. 582, 63 N. E. 1119. The counterclaim was for damages claimed to have been sustained by the defendant for breach of a written contract entered into between the plaintiff and one Stoner, bearing date the 28th day of April, 1899. By the terms of this contract, the plaintiff agreed to sell, make, and deliver to Stoner paper hangings to the amount of between $25,000 and $50,000, on terms and prices as thereinafter stated, during the seasons of 1899 and 1900, so that it was a contract to last practically for two years. Stoner agreed to purchase from the plaintiff not less than $25,000 net; nor more than $50,000 net, in paper hangings—an order for not less than $10,000 net as soon as the samples were ready to show to the trade. It was further stipulated that Stoner should, under the contract, be entitled to the exclusive sale of the plaintiff's goods in the states of Iowa and Nebraska, excepting points thereafter to be agreed upon by the parties to the contract. Stoner, some time after the execution of this contract, organized the defendant corporation, which is controlled substantially by himself and his wife, and it is claimed that the contract was subsequently assigned by Stoner to the defendant. At the trial the defendant had a verdict on the counterclaim, upon which judgment was entered, and it has been unanimously affirmed by the court below.

The record before us presents three principal questions: (1) Whether the contract was assignable; (2) whether it ever was in fact assigned; and (3) whether there was any ruling in favor of the defendant at the trial, to which exception was taken, that constitutes a legal error.

If this was a contract merely for the sale and delivery of a certain quantity of goods at a specified price, and the relations created by the contract were simply those of buyer and seller, then there can be no question but the contract is assignable; but it is claimed that, inasmuch as the contract gave to Stoner the exclusive sales of the plaintiff's goods in the two states named, excepting points thereafter to be agreed upon by the parties, it created personal relations between the parties, that rendered the contract nonassignable. And it is further claimed that as certain points in the two states were thereafter to be excepted by agreement, and since that agreement was never made, the contract is in itself still incomplete, in the sense that it could not have been transferred. This question may not be entirely free from difficulty, and authorities are cited by both parties in support of their respective contentions. We do not think that it is necessary now to pass upon that question, since there must be a new trial of the case for the reason which will be presently stated.

If the contract was in fact assigned to the defendant prior to the commencement of this action, it was in some way other than an assignment in writing. It is claimed that there was a parol assignment and delivery that vested the interest in the defendant for all the purposes of the action. It may have been, and probably was, upon the proof in the record, a question of fact whether such assignment actually took place. There can be no assignment of a written contract unless the parties intended that an assignment should take place, and this intent must be manifested by some act or transaction sufficient to transfer the title from one party to another. Whether the proof in this case justifies the conclusion that there was an assignment in fact, we need not now express any opinion. There is no doubt, however, upon the record, that one of the principal questions controverted at the trial was whether the defendant had acquired the title to this contract by an assignment of any kind from Stoner, and on that issue some evidence was given in behalf of the defendant, which was objected to, and which we think is fatal to the judgment.

The defendant gave in evidence what purported to be a written assignment of the contract by Stoner to itself. It appeared to be properly executed, but, upon cross-examination of Stoner, the fact was disclosed that this writing, which was without date, was actually signed subsequently to the commencement of this action, and about the time of the first trial. As to the time when this alleged written assignment was made, there is really no dispute between the respective counsel. When the defendant interposes a counterclaim, and thereupon demands an affirmative judgment against the plaintiff, the mode of trial of an issue of fact arising thereupon is the same as if it arose in an action brought by the defendant against the plaintiff for the cause of action stated in the counterclaim, and demanding the same judgment. Code Civ. Proc. § 974. The defendant therefore had the affirmative of the issue and the burden of proof. It was bound to establish the fact that it was the owner of this contract at the time of the commencement of this action, and it is very obvious that it had no right to give in evidence for the consideration of the jury what purported to be a written assignment, which, as was disclosed by the cross-examination, had been made after the commencement of the action. It was obliged to stand or fall upon such rights as it had at the time that the suit was commenced. The issue which the defendant presented by the litigation, that it had become the assignee of the contract, was a vital one, and the evidence referred to must be held to have prejudiced the plaintiff. The fact that the trial court submitted to the jury the specific question whether there had been an assignment at the time of the commencement of the action does not change the situation. A written assignment, without date, executed by Stoner to the defendant subsequent to the commencement of the action, must, in any view of the case, have been misleading with the jury. The finding of the jury upon the specific question thus submitted was that the assignment took place prior to the commencement of the action, but, if that verdict was procured by the admission of evidence that was incompetent and calculated to mislead, then the judgment ought not to be permitted to stand, and the parties must be remitted to a new trial.

The judgment should therefore be reversed, and a new trial granted; costs to abide the event.

PARKER, C. J., and HAIGHT, MARTIN, CULLEN, and WERNER, JJ., concur. GRAY, J., concurs in result.

Judgment reversed, etc.

(70 Oh. St. 16)

BOWMAN LUMBER CO. v. ANDERSON et al.

(Supreme Court of Ohio. March 8, 1904.)

SALE AND DELIVERY OF CHATTELS—ABSENCE OF EXPRESS WARRANTY—ACCEPTANCE BY BUYER.

1. By an executory contract for the sale and delivery of chattels of a described grade or quality the seller becomes bound to deliver goods of the character described, but, in the absence of express terms of warranty, no obligation is imposed upon him which survives the acceptance by the purchaser of an article delivered by the seller in good faith as in the performance of the contract if the acceptance is with full knowledge of all the conditions affecting the character and quality of the article.

(Syllabus by the Court.)

Error to Circuit Court, Shelby County.

Action by the Bowman Lumber Company against one Anderson and others, doing business as the Buckeye Churn Company. From a judgment of the circuit court reversing a judgment for plaintiff, it brings error. Reversed.

The lumber company brought suit in the court of common pleas against the churn company to recover the amount due on two car loads of poplar lumber sold and delivered by the plaintiff to the defendants, the petition being in the short form authorized by the Code. The churn company answered, denying the allegations of the petition, and alleging by way of counterclaim that the defendants had purchased from the plaintiff ten car loads of No. 1 select and common poplar lumber under a memorandum of sale made in writing; four cars had been delivered under said contract and paid for at the contract price of $20.25 per thousand feet; that the two items included in plaintiff's account sued upon represented two additional cars upon said contract, which were not of the quality and kind bought and stipulated for by said contract, but inferior thereto, and only of the value of $18.50 per thousand feet; that the defendants refused to receive the said two cars upon said contract, and at once notified the plaintiff that the same were not of the grade or quality purchased, and were worth only said sum of $18.50, which they then agreed to pay for the same; that at the time said two cars were shipped poplar lumber of the grade and quality contracted for had materially advanced in price in the market; that the defendants had requested the plaintiff to deliver lumber of the kind and quality contracted for, which it had refused to do, and at all times refused to deliver the remaining four cars. It asked judgment by way of counterclaim for $260.69 on account of the defects in the two cars, and for the further sum of $420.50 for failure to deliver the remaining four cars.

By reply plaintiff admits that four cars were delivered and paid for by the defendants; that they agreed to pay for each installment of lumber when delivered; that the two items of the account upon which it sued represented two additional cars delivered upon said original contract; but denied the other allegations of the answer. Plaintiff further replied that upon the delivery of said two cars of lumber under said contract the defendants objected to the grade thereof, and refused to pay the contract price therefor; that thereupon the plaintiff tendered the said defendants the freight advanced by them; that the plaintiff demanded the return of said lumber, and permission to remove it in order that it might substitute other lumber therefor; that the defendants refused to permit such removal, and actually used the lumber in their business.

Upon the trial it appeared without contradiction that the contract was for ten cars of No. 1 select and common poplar lumber at the price of $20.25 per thousand, delivered; that four cars were delivered and paid for, the controversy arising over the fifth and sixth cars shipped; that when these cars were received by the purchasers they unloaded them, placed the lumber in the yard of their factory, and inspected it; that they notified the seller that the lumber was not of the grade contracted for, but proposed to retain the same, and pay for it at $18.50 per thousand feet. This proposition the seller rejected, and insisted that the lumber should be paid for at the contract price or returned at its expense, it to furnish other lumber in its place. The parties retained this position during a considerable correspondence, and when a representative of the seller came to adjust the matter the purchasers refused to pay the contract price, and refused to permit him to remove the lumber. About three months after the receipt of the lumber the purchasers used it in their business, the seller not having consented thereto except as it might be received under the contract. Evidence was also introduced tending to show that the lumber was inferior to that described in the contract. The seller, regarding the refusal of the purchasers to pay for lumber received as terminating the contract, refused to deliver the remaining four cars. The defendants also introduced evidence to show that the market price of such lumber had advanced while the controversy was in progress. The court, in substance, instructed the jury that if they should find from the evidence that the purchasers had accepted the two cars as being a part of the contract, and after inspection and ascertainment of its real grade and quality, without any agreement between themselves and the seller, appropriated the lumber to their own use, as a matter of law they had accepted it, and the question whether it was or was not of the kind provided for in the contract was not a question for the consideration of the jury; that it was the duty of the plaintiff to furnish lumber of the kind described in the contract, but when lumber was delivered by the seller, as in performance of the contract, and, with knowledge of its character, accepted by the purchasers, they could no longer make objection upon the account of the grade, quality, or price; that this would be the rule of law, in the absence of any fraud or deceit practiced by the seller. The jury returned a verdict for the plaintiff for the full amount claimed in its petition, and this, a motion for a new trial having been overruled, was followed by judgment. On petition in error the circuit court reversed the judgment for error in the instruction.

Gilbert & Shipman, for plaintiff in error. Andrew J. Hess and John F. Wilson, for defendants in error.

SHAUCK, J. (after stating the facts). Unless the purchasers were justifiable in refusing to pay the contract price for the two cars of lumber which they received and did not pay for, the seller might lawfully regard the contract as terminated thereby, and refuse, as it did refuse, to deliver the remaining four cars which the contract contemplated. We therefore concur in the view taken by the circuit court upon this point that the only question to be determined is whether the trial judge correctly instructed the jury with respect to the obligation of the purchasers to pay for the two car loads the price stipulated in the contract. In the court of common pleas the words "select and common," indicating the grade of the lumber, were regarded as merely words of description which imposed upon the seller no obligation which would survive the receipt, inspection, and use by the purchasers of the cars which the seller had shipped in good faith as in performance of the contract. In the circuit court the words were regarded as being both a description and a warranty; the warranty imposing upon the seller an obligation which survived the acceptance and use of the lumber by the purchasers with full knowledge of all the defects therein, which, upon the trial, they sought to make available as a defense to an action for the contract price.

Undoubtedly, in sales of this character, the particular subject of the contract not being designated or identified, the seller becomes charged with an obligation to furnish an article of the description contained in the contract, and the purchaser does not become bound to accept any other. In some of the cases cited this obligation of the purchaser is called a "warranty." That in some cases he is liable to the same extent as he would be upon a warranty is clear. That he incurs such liability in all cases of this character cannot be sustained by either the reasons involved or by the discriminating cases. It is not doubted that if the particular subject of this contract had been identified, the rights and liabilities of the parties would be determined under the rule caveat emptor. What modification, or apparent modification, of that rule does justice require in view of the fact that the subject of the contract was not present or designated? Obviously, it is that the purchaser should have the same opportunity for effective inspection of the subject which would have been afforded by its actual identification at the time of the sale. The instruction was given in the present case in view of evidence tending to show, or, more accurately, conclusively showing, that upon the arrival of the two cars at the factory of the purchasers they removed the lumber from the cars, made the inspection, which, according to their testimony upon the trial, showed that it was not in accordance with the description in the contract, and refused, for that reason assigned, to make payment of the contract price, proposed to take it at the lower price as lumber of an inferior grade, and, the seller not assenting thereto, refused to permit it to remove it at its own expense, and to substitute other lumber, which should be acceptable to them and in compliance with the contract; and that after three months they used it in their business—the seller always insisting that it should be accepted under the contract, or that it should be permitted to substitute other lumber. The obligation of the seller was to furnish lumber of the amount and grade described. No terms were employed appropriate to an obligation that these particular cars should be of that grade, nor does any consideration of justice to the purchasers require that such obligation should be imposed upon the seller regardless of intention. Its offer was to perform its contract, and the purchasers should not be permitted to coerce it into the acceptance of a price arbitrarily fixed by themselves, or to the submission to a jury of a price which had been fixed by the agreement of the parties.

It is admitted that the instruction given is in accordance with the doctrine declared and the point decided in Pierson et al. v. Crooks et al., 115 N. Y. 539, 22 N. E. 349, 12 Am. St. Rep. 831. The case involved the rights of the parties to an executory contract for the sale of chattels not identified and the effect of acceptance by the purchasers. The court said: "The quality is a part of the description of the thing agreed to be sold, and the vendor is bound to furnish articles corresponding with the description. If he tenders articles of an inferior quality, the purchaser is not bound to accept them. But if he does accept them, he is, in the absence of fraud, deemed to have assented that they correspond with the description, and is concluded from subsequently questioning it. This imposes upon the vendee the duty of inspection before acceptance, if he desires to save his rights in case the goods are of inferior quality. There is in such case no warranty of quality which survives acceptance, and the vendee cannot reject the goods after acceptance, or recover damages for inferior quality. He can do nothing inconsistent with the right of rejection, or do what is only consistent with acceptance and ownership, without precluding himself." Of the numerous cases in which the same view has been taken, Chanter v. Hopkins, 4 M. & W. 399, attracts attention because of Lord Abinger's discriminating criticism of the unfortunate use of the word "warranty" in cases of this character. His criticism is commended by Mr. Benjamin in his work on Sales, § 600. While it is true that some of the decided cases cannot be reconciled with the view of the subject here taken, discrimination will show that they do not constitute the "weight of authority," even if that be taken to refer to mere numbers. Such discrimination will attend to what is decided, rather than to what is said. It will recognize that mere reception may not be acceptance; that the purchaser is not precluded from subsequently asserting that the article does not conform to the description by the fact that in the due course of trade he has disposed of it without opportunity to inspect, and that neither opportunity to inspect nor actual inspection will preclude him from subsequently complaining of defects which are of such a nature that they would not be disclosed by any practicable inspection.

Judgment of the circuit court reversed, and that of the common pleas affirmed.

SPEAR, C. J., and DAVIS, PRICE, and CREW, JJ., concur. SUMMERS, J., not participating.

(70 Oh. St. 1)

STATE v. SCHILLER.

(Supreme Court of Ohio. March 8, 1904.)

MURDER IN FIRST DEGREE—INSTRUCTIONS—RECOMMENDATION TO MERCY—RECOMMENDATION FOR PARDON.

1. On the trial of an indictment for murder in the first degree, where the court instructs the jury that, if they shall find the defendant guilty as charged, they may, if they think proper, recommend mercy, and further instructs them that the legal effect of such recommendation by them will be to change the punishment of the accused from death to imprisonment in the penitentiary for life, such instruction is a correct and sufficient charge or instruction on that subject.

2. On the trial of such indictment the court is not required to instruct the jury that no person so convicted and imprisoned "shall be recommended for pardon by the board of pardons, or for parole by the board of managers of the penitentiary, except upon proof of innocence established beyond a reasonable doubt," and the omission to so instruct the jury is not error.

(Syllabus by the Court.)

Error to Circuit Court, Mahoning County.

At the May term, 1903, of the court of common pleas of Mahoning county the defendant in error, Michael G. Schiller, was indicted, tried, and convicted of the crime of murder in the first degree for the killing of his wife, Mary Schiller. The defendant in error filed his motion for a new trial, alleging and specifying therein as reasons why a new trial should be granted him: First. That the court of common pleas erred in admitting, over the objection of the defendant, the testimony of one Mike Louch, who testified as to a conversation had with the defendant in the city prison of the city of Youngstown two days after the commission of the alleged crime, and while Mary Schiller was yet alive, in which conversation the accused told witness "that, if Mrs. Schiller recovered, he would soon be out of there, and then he would kill her if he had to follow her to the old country to do it." Second. That the court erred in giving instructions to the jury in this: "That he did not state to them the full legal effect of finding the accused guilty of murder in the first degree with a recommendation of mercy." Third. That "the verdict is not sustained by sufficient evidence, and is contrary to law." This motion for new trial was at the same term, to wit, on July 29, 1903, overruled by the court, and thereupon the defendant, Michael G. Schiller, was duly sentenced to be electrocuted on November 10, 1903. Error was prosecuted by said Michael G. Schiller to the circuit court of Mahoning county, where the judgment of the court of common pleas was reversed for

¶ 1. See Homicide, vol. 26, Cent. Dig. § 663.

alleged error in the charge to the jury of the trial court, and the cause was remanded to said court of common pleas for further proceedings. The plaintiff in error herein now seeks a reversal of this judgment of the circuit court, and asks an affirmance of the judgment of said court of common pleas. Judgment of circuit court reversed, and of common pleas affirmed.

J. M. Sheets, W. R. Graham, and Frank L. Baldwin, for the State. Frank L. Oesch and R. C. Huey, for defendant in error.

CREW, J. (after stating the facts as above). On the hearing of this case in the circuit court upon the petition in error of Michael G. Schiller that court set aside the verdict of conviction and reversed the judgment of the court of common pleas on the sole ground that said court of common pleas erred in its instruction to the jury touching the law which gives to a jury on the trial of an indictment for murder in the first degree the right, upon conviction of the accused, to recommend mercy. The finding and judgment of the circuit court, as shown by the entry upon its journal under date of November 6, 1903, was as follows: "The said parties appeared by their attorneys, and this cause was heard upon the petition in error, together with the original papers and pleadings, and a duly certified transcript of the orders and judgment of the court of common pleas of said county in the case of the State of Ohio v. Michael G. Schiller, and was argued by counsel; on consideration whereof the court find that in the record and proceedings aforesaid there is error manifest upon the face of the record to the prejudice of the plaintiff in error, in this, to wit: That there is error in the charge of the trial court to the jury in that the court failed to charge what would be necessary for the accused to show in order to obtain pardon, in case of the verdict of guilty of murder in the first degree, with a recommendation of mercy, if made by the jury, and that there are no other errors apparent on the record. It is therefore considered, ordered, and adjudged by this court that the judgment and proceedings of the said court of common pleas in said action be, and the same hereby are, set aside, reversed, and held for naught," etc.

That the circuit court was right in its finding that there was no error apparent upon the record in said proceedings, judgment, and trial in the court of common pleas, except it be found in the charge of the court, as stated in this entry, counsel for defendant in error seem now to concede, for no claim or contention is made by them in this court, either in oral argument or in their printed brief, that such finding of the circuit court was unwarranted or erroneous. Neither is it claimed, or even suggested, here that the trial court erred in the admission of testimony, or that the verdict of the jury was not supported by competent and sufficient evidence. Nor do we find in this record, after a careful examination of the same, anything which, in our opinion, would warrant or justify such claim or contention, if made. There is presented, then, by this record, for our consideration, the single question, did the court of common pleas err in its charge to the jury, or in its failure to charge and instruct the jury as to just what effect the conviction of defendant, with a recommendation of mercy, would have upon his right thereafter to receive a pardon or obtain a parole. Section 6808, Rev. St., provides as follows: "Whoever purposely, and either of deliberate and premeditated malice, or by means of poison, or in perpetrating, or attempting to perpetrate, any rape, arson, robbery, or burglary, kills another, is guilty of murder in the first degree and shall be punished by death, unless the jury trying the accused recommend mercy, in which case the punishment shall be imprisonment in the penitentiary during life. Provided, however, that murder in the first degree as herein defined shall continue to be a capital offense within the meaning of the Constitution. And provided, further, no person convicted of murder in the first degree shall be recommended for pardon by the board of pardons, or for parole by the board of managers of the penitentiary, except upon proof of innocence established beyond a reasonable doubt." In the charge and instruction submitted to the jury the trial court, after defining murder in the first degree, and after carefully and correctly describing and defining the several lesser crimes embraced and included in the charge as made in the indictment, and after instructing the jury that it was competent for them if, under the law, the evidence should justify and warrant it, to acquit the defendant of the principal charge—that of murder in the first degree—and to find him guilty of either of the lesser crimes embraced or included in said indictment, said to the jury as follows: "The forms of verdict covering the different aspects of the crime charged in this indictment will be given you on retiring, and you will use such form as conforms to your finding of fact. The first is that of a general verdict finding the defendant, Michael Schiller, guilty of murder in the first degree, as he stands charged in the indictment. The second form is exactly like the first with the addition of four words, which are, 'The jury recommend mercy.' The statute of this state, as changed some years ago, provides that the jury may, in a case where it finds the defendant guilty of murder in the first degree, if it thinks proper, recommend mercy; the legal effect of such recommendation being to change the penalty of death fixed for the simple finding of murder in the first degree to imprisonment for life."

It is admitted that the instruction thus given, touching the effect of a recommendation of mercy, is, so far as it goes, unobjectionable, and free from error; but it is insisted by counsel for defendant in error, and was so held by a majority of the circuit court, that the trial judge should have gone further, and should have advised and instructed the jury that no person convicted of murder in the first degree, with a recommendation of mercy, shall be recommended for pardon by the board of pardons, or for parole by the board of managers of the penitentiary, except upon proof of innocence established beyond a reasonable doubt; and it is argued here that it is not enough that the court should have said to the jury that, if they should find the defendant guilty of murder in the first degree, and should recommend mercy, the legal effect of such recommendation would be to make his punishment imprisonment in the penitentiary for life, but that it became and was the imperative duty of the court to go further, and call their attention to the last proviso of section 6808, Rev. St., and to instruct and advise them that one so convicted cannot be recommended for pardon by the board of pardons, or for parole by the board of managers of the penitentiary, except upon proof of innocence established beyond a reasonable doubt; and it is claimed that the failure of the court to so advise and instruct the jury was error, for which the judgment of conviction in this case was properly reversed by the circuit court. We do not concur in this view, and cannot assent to the correctness of this claim. In this case the trial judge fully, fairly, and correctly instructed the jury as to the rules of law that should govern and control them in their consideration of the evidence in determining the question of the guilt or innocence of the accused, and instructed them that, if they should find the defendant guilty of murder in the first degree, it would be their privilege and their right to recommend mercy, and further informed and instructed them as to the effect such recommendation would have upon the penalty or punishment to be imposed; the language of the charge in that behalf being as follows: "The legal effect of such recommendation being to change the penalty of death, fixed for the simple finding of murder in the first degree, to imprisonment for life." The jury was thus correctly advised not only as to their right to recommend mercy, but as to the effect of such recommendation as well. More than this the defendant was not entitled to. Yet, notwithstanding the fact that the jury was thus told by the court in express terms and in plain and positive language that if they found the defendant guilty, and recommended mercy, his punishment would be imprisonment in the penitentiary for life, we are asked in this case to indulge the presumption and to assume as a fact that the jury withheld such recommendation of mercy merely because they were not instructed by the court that after conviction and sentence of the defendant the board of pardons would not be at liberty and was without right, except upon proof of innocence, to recommend his pardon or release. We find nothing in this record to warrant such inference or conclusion, or to justify any such holding, especially in view of the fact that the jury was told without qualification that his punishment would and must be, in case they recommended mercy, imprisonment for life. No request was made by defendant or his counsel for any further or additional charge on this subject, and no objection was made or exception taken to this particular portion of the charge as given; the only exception taken or noted by counsel for defendant being a general exception to the charge as a whole. It is a familiar and very general rule of practice, applicable alike to criminal and civil causes, that mere partial nondirection or incomplete instruction as to a particular matter or issue does not of itself constitute reversible error in the absence of a request for more specific and comprehensive instructions upon the particular point or issue involved. In the majority opinion of the circuit court in this case the judge announcing the same, in commenting upon that portion of the charge of the trial court last above quoted says: "He [the trial judge] says, in case you recommend mercy 'the legal effect of such recommendation is to change the penalty of death, fixed for the simple finding of murder in the first degree, to imprisonment for life'; rather than death, the legal effect will be imprisonment in the penitentiary for life. No, no. It is not the legal effect of finding him guilty of murder in the first degree with the recommendation. That is not the legal effect of it. The legal effect of it was to shift the penalty to imprisonment in the penitentiary for life, with the provision that follows in the statute that under no circumstances shall he be released unless he makes his innocence appear beyond a reasonable doubt. That is the legal effect of it. We insist that when he told the jury that the legal effect, if they found the party guilty of murder in the first degree with the recommendation of mercy, would be imprisonment for life, he did not state the fact to the jury as defined by the law, but the legal effect as charged would be imprisonment in the penitentiary for life, with the addition to it that neither the governor, nor board of pardons, nor the warden of the penitentiary, nor any other person affected, could release him, except upon proof of his innocence beyond a reasonable doubt." With all due respect to the learned judge who delivered this opinion, we submit that he misconceived and misinterpreted the scope and effect of the last proviso of section 6808, Rev. St. Had the trial court charged the jury, as suggested in this opinion of the circuit court, that if they found the defendant guilty of murder in the first degree, and recommended mercy, the effect of such recommendation would be to shift or reduce his punishment to imprisonment in the penitentiary for life, but without the right or possibility of pardon except upon proof of his innocence beyond a reasonable doubt, such charge would have been both misleading and erroneous, and would have been a misstatement both of the law and the fact. By section 11, art. 3, of the state Constitution, the Governor is invested with full power to pardon for all crimes and offenses except for treason and in cases of impeachment; and the right so given is in no wise affected or abridged by the last proviso of section 6808, Rev. St. Neither is the right of the Governor to exercise this pardoning power dependent upon the action or recommendation of the board of pardons, for it is provided by section 409-49, Rev. St., that: "The Governor shall have full power, notwithstanding the action of said board, to grant or reject any application for the granting of a pardon, commutation of sentence, or reprieve, if, in his judgment, the public interests would thereby be promoted."

We have very carefully examined the record in this case, and find no error in the record and proceedings of the court of common pleas. After such examination we are entirely satisfied that the defendant in error, Michael G. Schiller, was fairly tried, was rightfully convicted, and that this judgment of conviction should be affirmed. It follows, therefore, that the judgment of the circuit court should be, and the same hereby is, reversed, and the judgment of the court of common pleas is affirmed.

Judgment of the circuit court reversed, and that of the court of common pleas affirmed.

SPEAR, C. J., and DAVIS, SHAUCK, PRICE, and SUMMERS, JJ., concur.

(70 Oh. St. 30)

GOYERT & VOGEL v. EICHER et al.

(Supreme Court of Ohio. March 8, 1904.)

APPEAL—AGREED STATEMENT OF FACTS—WHEN PART OF THE RECORD—BILL OF EXCEPTIONS—JOURNAL ENTRY.

1. An agreed statement of facts, although in writing, signed by counsel of all parties, and filed, does not become a part of the record unless brought upon the record by a bill of exceptions, or the facts as agreed upon are stated in the journal entry as the court's finding of facts.

(Syllabus by the Court.)

Error to Circuit Court, Hamilton County.

In the matter of the estate of Bridget Glenn, deceased. Goyert & Vogel, creditors, filed exceptions to the inventory filed in the court by Frank Eicher, administrator. From an order of the circuit court reversing a judgment of the common pleas and of the probate court, the creditors bring error. Reversed.

¶ 1. See Appeal and Error, vol. 3, Cent. Dig. § 2403.

Closs & Luebbert, for plaintiffs in error. Jacob Krummel and John J. Gasser, for defendant in error.

SPEAR, C. J. The controversy which forms the ground for contention here originated in the probate court of Hamilton by the filing of exceptions by Goyert & Vogel, creditors of the estate of Bridget Glenn, deceased, to the inventory of the personal property of said estate filed in that court by Frank Eicher, administrator. A preliminary point in the case turns upon the proper solution of the question whether or not a certain agreed statement of facts, signed by counsel and filed in that court, should be treated as a part of the record. If this be held in the affirmative, then, as to that question, the judgment of the circuit court reversing the judgments of the common pleas and of the probate court should, as to that branch of the case, be affirmed; if in the negative, then the circuit court's judgment should be reversed, and the judgments of the common pleas and probate court affirmed.

The journal entry in the probate court with respect to the agreed statement was this, and this only: "This cause came on to be heard on the exceptions of Goyert & Vogel, creditors of the estate of Bridget Glenn, deceased, to the inventory of the personal property of said estate heretofore filed herein by Frank Eicher, administrator, and on submission of the agreed statement of facts, with the exhibits thereto attached, and the court doth find," etc.

Three cases are cited by the circuit court in this opinion, which, it is insisted by counsel for defendant in error, establish the proposition that the agreed statement is to be regarded as a part of the record under review, and, the facts being thus established, the rule of law applied by the circuit court is correct. It is proper to here briefly consider these cases. In Ish v. Crane, 13 Ohio St. 574, it is said by Sutliff, J., in the opinion, that "it is insisted by counsel of defendants that by virtue of this paper, dated August 27, 1860, now in this court, placed among the papers, the agreed statement of facts upon which the case was submitted in the district court, and reserved to this court, is annulled, and that the case is to be regarded by this court as if the agreed statement of facts were withdrawn from the files, and that the case is to be decided barely upon the pleadings. The counsel of plaintiff, on the other hand, has argued the case, and seems to rely fully upon the agreed statement of facts. How, then, is this agreed statement of facts to be regarded—as revoked or still in operation upon the parties? It has long been the practice in this state, as well as in the courts of other states, for counsel to mutually agree upon a state of facts, and to reduce the agreement to writing and file it in the case, instead of being to the trouble and expense of taking proof by depositions or otherwise to show the facts. And when such agreement is reduced to writing and signed by the parties or their counsel, and filed in the case, I think the general understanding, both of the bar and court, has been that the same was to be regarded, until set aside by the court, as a special verdict of a jury, expressing the result of the proof made by both parties, and so belonging to both parties that neither party could withdraw the same." This is the opinion of a learned judge, and is entitled to great weight; but it is, after all, a general statement, and is to be restrained to the facts of the case. And it is to be specially noted that the question on which this branch of the case turned was whether or not a paper signed by counsel for defendant, and served by copy on counsel for plaintiff, found with the papers filed in and belonging to the case, though neither filed in the case nor proven, which purports to be a revocation of the agreed statement, could be treated as annulling that statement. The court held that it could not, the syllabus being: "Where a case has been submitted upon an agreed statement of facts, reduced to writing and signed by the counsel of the respective parties, such agreement cannot be withdrawn, or the agreement retracted by either party, except by leave of court, on cause shown." Thus it will be seen that the question which we have was not, so far as appears, matter of contention in the case cited. Nor is it distinctly shown by the opinion whether the statement originally filed in the common pleas had been incorporated into the record or not. It does appear, however, that the cause, being pending in the district court on error to the common pleas, was reserved for hearing in this court, and that it was heard in the district court on the agreed statement of facts. It is, we think, reasonable to assume that objection to the statement was not made in either court, and that the only point with respect thereto made in this court related to the effect of the attempted retraction by a paper dated after the cause reached this court. Another case cited is that of Brown v. Mott, 22 Ohio St. 149. That was a case brought under section 495 of the Code (now section 5207, Rev. St. 1892), providing for the bringing of an action by the filing of an agreed statement and submission, without process or pleading. The third case cited is McGonnigle v. Arthur, 27 Ohio St. 251. The record in this case shows that all the testimony offered before the trial court was in an agreed statement of facts, in writing, carried into the record, and found by the trial court to be all the testimony offered by the parties. It seems entirely clear that neither of these cases rules the case at bar.

Some confusion has arisen in practice with respect to the office of an agreed statement of facts, and how such statement is to be evidenced in order to authorize a review of the judgment. The rule in this state ought by this time not to be the subject of doubt. We understand it to be that in order to enable a party, in a case tried upon testimony, or upon an agreed statement of facts, to avail himself of a review on error, the facts—all of them—should be found by the court and incorporated in the record, or brought into the record by a bill of exceptions. Section 5300, Rev. St. 1892, provides that when the decision objected to is entered on the record, and the grounds of objection appear in the entry, the exceptions may be taken by the party causing it to be noted at the end of the entry that he excepts. But (section 5301) "when the decision is not entered on the record, or the grounds of the objection do not sufficiently appear in the entry * * * the party excepting must reduce his exceptions to writing," etc. In other words, in the latter case he must present a bill of exceptions. There is no provision of statute constituting a paper called an "agreed statement of facts" a part of the record, nor can such paper be regarded as part of the record for review on error simply because the same is filed in the case. The filing does not bring it into the record any more than the filing of a deposition or of the court's charge to the jury makes either a part of the record. It is only for errors appearing on the record that a judgment may be reversed. In the present case the grounds of objection do not appear in the entry, for there is no incorporation in the entry of any facts on which the decision is based. The decision is not, therefore, entered on the record, within the meaning of the sections cited, nor do the grounds of the objection sufficiently appear in the entry.

It has long been settled law in Ohio, and remained the law until the act of October 22, 1902 (Laws 1902, p. 16), that a paper purporting to be a bill of exceptions cannot be regarded by a reviewing court as part of the record, unless it is made so by an entry on the journal showing its allowance, and identifying it with reasonable certainty. Hill v. Bassett, 27 Ohio St. 597. Nor will a reviewing court, on error, regard any matter which is not proper matter of record. Goldsmith v. State, 30 Ohio St. 208. Nor can an exception to a charge of a court be considered where the charge and exception appear only as part of the journal entry. Lockhart v. Brown, 31 Ohio St. 431. The reason of these rules applies as well, we think, to an agreed statement of facts as to the other papers referred to.

Since, therefore, the agreed statement, although signed by the counsel and filed in the probate court, was not a part of the record presented to the common pleas, that court had only before it for consideration in the error case the petition in error, the original papers (that is, the inventory and exceptions thereto), and the transcript of the docket and journal entries of the probate court; and, since the common pleas had power to reverse only for errors apparent on the record, it could do no other than affirm the judgment of the probate court.

Other questions are argued, but it is unnecessary to consider them.

We are of opinion that there is no error in the judgment of the common pleas affirming that of the probate court, and that both judgments should be affirmed. This results in a reversal of the judgment of the circuit court. Reversed.

SHAUCK, PRICE, CREW, and SUMMERS, JJ., concur.

(70 Oh. St. 11)

STEVENSON v. STATE.

(Supreme Court of Ohio. March 1, 1904.)

CRIMINAL LAW—CHALLENGES—NUMBER ALLOWED.

1. A defendant on trial in a criminal case for other than a capital offense is entitled to challenge but two jurors peremptorily.

2. The last paragraph of section 5177, Rev. St., as amended April 29, 1902 (95 Ohio Laws, 308), giving to each party the right to challenge peremptorily four jurors, furnishes the rule and determines the right of peremptory challenge only in civil causes. It has no application in criminal cases.

(Syllabus by the Court.)

William Stevenson was convicted of arson, and applies for leave to file petition in error. Leave refused.

Scott & Peck, Boothman & Newcomer, and Harris & Cameron, for plaintiff in error. Edward Gaudern, Pros. Atty., for the State.

PER CURIAM. At the October term, 1903, of the court of common pleas of Williams county, the plaintiff in error, William Stevenson, was tried and convicted of the crime of arson. A motion for new trial was made and overruled, and thereupon he was by said court sentenced to imprisonment in the Ohio penitentiary for the term of four years. From this judgment of the court of common pleas error was prosecuted to the circuit court of Williams county, where, on January 16, 1904, said judgment was affirmed, and the cause was remanded to said court of common pleas for execution of sentence. The case is now here upon the application of plaintiff in error for leave to file in this court a petition in error to reverse the judgments of the courts below. It appears from the record in this case that on the impaneling of the jury to try this cause in the court of common pleas the accused, William Stevenson, demanded the right to challenge peremptorily four of the jurors summoned in said cause, and the bill of exceptions herein recites that: "Thereupon, the jurors being sworn upon their voir dire, counsel for the state peremptorily challenged two jurors and the counsel for the defense peremptorily challenged two jurors, and thereupon counsel for defendant asked leave to exercise a third peremptory challenge, and did challenge one C. T. Wyatt, a juror, peremptorily, which challenge the court did overrule, to which ruling of the court counsel for the defendant at the time excepted." This ruling and action of the court in overruling the defendant's peremptory challenge to the juror Wyatt, which was the third peremptory challenge exercised by defendant, is here assigned as error. The single question presented by this assignment is whether or not, under our statutes, since the amendment to section 5177, Rev. St., passed April 29, 1902 (95 Ohio Laws, 308), giving to each of the parties to a civil action the right to peremptorily challenge four jurors, the defendant in a criminal case is entitled to have and may rightfully exercise a like number of peremptory challenges in a criminal prosecution. The determination of this question necessarily involves a consideration of certain of the statutory provisions relating to and governing the right of challenge, respectively, in civil and criminal cases, and especially does it involve a consideration of the construction and effect proper to be given to paragraph or subdivision 9 of section 7278, Rev. St. 1892, hereinafter considered.

Section 5176, Rev. St., enumerates and defines what shall be good ground for principal challenge, or challenge for cause, in civil cases. These are nine in number, and with but a single exception none of them are ground for challenge in a criminal prosecution, except in so far as they are made so by adoption by force of the provision of paragraph 9 of section 7278, Rev. St. 1892. Section 5177, as amended April 29, 1902, provides for challenges to the favor and for peremptory challenges in civil cases, and gives to each of the parties to a civil action the right to challenge peremptorily four jurors. Section 7277 of the Criminal Code prescribes the number of peremptory challenges that shall be allowed the defendant in a criminal prosecution; and section 7278 of the Criminal Code enumerates and defines what shall be ground for challenge for cause in criminal cases, and after enumerating eight grounds or causes for principal challenge it is provided by the ninth paragraph of said section that "the same challenges shall be allowed in criminal prosecutions that are allowed to parties in civil cases." No other or further right of challenge for cause or of peremptory challenge is given by statute to the defendant in a criminal prosecution, except by section 7272, Rev. St. 1892, in capital cases.

It is the claim and contention of plaintiff in error that under favor of the provisions of paragraph 9 of section 7278, above quoted, since the amendment to section 5177 of the Civil Code there are permitted and allowed to defendant in a criminal case not only the same challenges for cause, but the same number of peremptory challenges as are by said amendment given and allowed to each of the parties in civil cases. Such was not, we think, the purpose and intention of the Legislature in amending section 5177, Rev. St., nor is any such effect to be given said amendment because of the provisions of paragraph 9 of section 7278, Rev. St. 1892. The Legislature in this state has enacted separate and distinct codes of procedure to govern the practice in civil and criminal cases, and in each has expressly provided what challenges, for cause and peremptory, shall be allowed the parties in each particular class of cases; yet nowhere in the Criminal Code is any provision to be found that in terms gives to a defendant more than two peremptory challenges in a criminal case, except in prosecutions for capital offenses. If, then, the Legislature had intended to make so important a change as to give to a defendant four peremptory challenges in a criminal case where theretofore but two such challenges had been permitted or allowed, it is hardly reasonable to assume that it would have undertaken to effect such purpose by amending a section of the statute which related and applied exclusively to practice in civil cases, rather than by amending and extending the provisions of the section of the Criminal Code defining and prescribing the number of peremptory challenges allowed a defendant in a criminal case, thereby leaving such result to be effected and accomplished, if at all, by mere inference or construction, instead of by positive enactment. That paragraph 9, as originally enacted, was not intended to apply to or to include peremptory challenges, but that its purpose and office was merely to so extend the right of challenge in criminal cases as to embrace and include therein the grounds of principal challenge, or challenge for cause, in civil cases, affirmatively appears from the language of such provision itself. As originally passed, May 6, 1869 (66 Ohio Laws, 307), this provision read as follows: "The same challenges for cause shall be allowed in criminal prosecutions that are allowed to parties in civil cases." By subsequent revisions of the section, of which this paragraph was a part, the phraseology of the section has been changed, and the words "for cause" have been omitted from this paragraph; yet the change so made is not such as to evidence any design or purpose on the part of the Legislature to thereby extend its provisions, or to make them apply to causes of challenge other and different from those specified in the paragraph as originally enacted, and the rule is well established by the repeated adjudications of this court that "in the revision of statutes neither an alteration in phraseology nor the omission or addition of words in the latter statute shall be held necessarily to alter the construction of the former act. And the court is only warranted in holding the construction of a statute, when revised, to be changed, when the intent of the Legislature to make such change is clear, or the language used in the new act plainly requires such change of construction." State ex rel. v. Commissioners of Shelby County, 36 Ohio St. 326; State v. Vanderbilt, 37 Ohio St. 640; State ex rel. v. Stockley, 45 Ohio St. 308, 13 N. E. 279.

The right of peremptory challenge is purely a statutory right, and can only be exercised in such cases and to the extent expressly authorized and allowed by statute. In Ohio, under our Code of Criminal Procedure, the only right of peremptory challenge expressly given a defendant in a criminal case, other than in capital cases, is that given by section 7277, Rev. St. 1892, which is as follows: "Except as otherwise provided the prosecuting attorney and every defendant may peremptorily challenge two of the panel, and any of the panel for cause." As to the right of peremptory challenge it is only "otherwise provided" by section 7272, Rev. St. 1892, in capital cases, wherein the defendant is entitled to challenge 16 of the jurors peremptorily. Goins v. The State, 46 Ohio St. 460, 21 N. E. 476. The court of common pleas was therefore right in this case in limiting the defendant, Stevenson, to two peremptory challenges.

As to the other assignments of error, we think it enough to say that we have carefully examined and considered all of them, and find no error in the record.

Leave refused.

SPEAR, C. J., and DAVIS, SHAUCK, PRICE, and CREW, JJ., concur.

(70 Oh. St. 25)

In re KLINE.

(Supreme Court of Ohio. March 8, 1904.)

CRIMINAL LAW—REPEAL OF STATUTE—EFFECT ON PENDING CASE—HABITUAL CRIMINAL ACT.

1. Where a statute defining a crime and prescribing the punishment therefor is repealed at any time before final judgment in a prosecution thereunder, such repeal forecloses all further proceedings in such prosecution unless a contrary intent appears in the repealing statute; but when such repeal occurs after final judgment it does not in any respect vacate or modify such judgment or render it invalid.

2. A conviction and sentence under section 3788-11, Rev. St. 1892, commonly known as the "Habitual Criminal Act," does not confer upon the prisoner a right to be paroled at the discretion of the board of managers, which remains to him after the repeal of said act.

(Syllabus by the Court.)

In the matter of the application of one Kline for writ of habeas corpus.[1] Writ refused.

M. B. Earnhart and Thomas H. Hennessey, for relator. J. M. Sheets, Wade H. Ellis, and Smith W. Bennett, for respondent.

¶ 1. See Criminal Law, vol. 14, Cent. Dig. §§ 17, 18.

DAVIS, J. The relator is imprisoned in the penitentiary of this state under a sentence imposed on the 1st day of July, 1889, by the court of common pleas of Montgomery county. He was tried, convicted, and sentenced under an indictment for burglary and larceny and for being an habitual criminal. The return and answer of the respondent shows that the relator was found guilty, as charged, of burglary and larceny, and that he was adjudged to be imprisoned and confined in the penitentiary of this state and kept at hard labor for three years; and that, having also been found guilty of being an habitual criminal, it was "adjudged by the court that on the expiration of the term for which he has heretofore been sentenced he shall not be discharged from imprisonment in the penitentiary, but shall be detained there during his natural life, as provided in section 2 of an act passed May 4, 1885, and found in volume 82, Ohio Laws, p. 237." The act here referred to was known as section 7388-11, Rev. St. 1892, and it was repealed May 6, 1902 (95 Ohio Laws, p. 410). The relator demurs to the answer, and insists that, the "habitual criminal act" having been repealed, there is no longer any warrant for detaining him under his sentence as an habitual criminal, his sentence for burglary and larceny having expired. The relator was legally tried, convicted, sentenced, and committed under a valid statute. Blackburn v. State, 50 Ohio St. 428, 36 N. E. 18. Not only is the case res adjudicata, and beyond the reach of the courts, but it is in process of execution as a final judgment. If the courts could resume jurisdiction, and interfere with the execution of sentence, after regular procedure, judgment, and commitment under sentence, there could be no final judgment, and no end to a legal controversy. The Legislature cannot intervene and vacate the judgment of the courts, either directly or indirectly, by repeal of a statute under which the judgment was rendered, because that would be an exercise of judicial, and not of legislative, power. 1 Black on Judgments, § 298. "Legislative action cannot be made to retroact upon past controversies, and to reverse decisions which the courts, in the exercise of their undoubted authority, have made; for this would not only be the exercise of judicial power, but it would be its exercise in the most objectionable and offensive form, since the Legislature would, in effect, sit as a court of review to which parties might appeal when dissatisfied with the rulings of the courts." Cooley on Constitutional Limitations (7th Ed.) 136. The only remedy left to the adjudged criminal, if the case calls for any remedy, is a resort to the pardoning power, which is vested in the executive. The repeal of a statute which authorizes a prosecution and conviction, if before final judgment, ends all proceedings under it, unless a contrary intent appears in the repealing statute; but a repeal after final judgment will neither vacate the judgment nor arrest the execution of the sentence. This view of the law is fully sustained by the authorities cited by the counsel for the respondent, and after diligent search we have not been able to find any to the contrary.

It is further argued in behalf of the relator that by virtue of the statute which is now repealed he acquired, along with the sentence, a substantial and irrepealable right—the right to a parole, at the discretion of the board of managers—which still adheres to the prisoner, notwithstanding that the statute has been repealed. The weakness of this argument is exposed when we consider the nature and purpose of this statutory provision. In State v. Peters, 43 Ohio St. 629, 4 N. E. 81, this court held that this statute (section 7388-11, Rev. St. 1892) was constitutional, and that it did not interfere with the executive or judicial departments of the state government, and the court so held for the reason that the statute did not undertake to confer upon a prisoner the right to a pardon, absolute or conditional, nor to commute the sentence, nor to modify the sentence by shortening the term or by discharging the prisoner. The court construed this statute as being merely a "disciplinary regulation," which was clearly within the power and discretion of the Legislature to make or not to make. As a disciplinary regulation it would no more confer a vested right upon the prisoner than would any other rule or regulation which may be promulgated from time to time for the regulation of prisons and prisoners. It is not an essential part of the prisoner's sentence, and in its very nature and object it is subject to modification or repeal. And for the reason that it is not a part of the sentence, but extraneous to it, and because it is only a tentative rule for prison government, a repeal of such legislation neither takes away any right of the prisoner nor in any manner affects his sentence theretofore made and put into execution. The prisoner still has the right to appeal to executive clemency for a pardon, and until a pardon shall be granted a sentence lawfully made and carried into effect under a valid statute must be enforced, although the statute has been repealed.

Demurrer overruled, and writ refused.

SPEAR, C. J., and SHAUCK, PRICE, and CREW, JJ., concur. SUMMERS, J., not participating.

(162 Ind. 433)

CITY OF ALEXANDRIA v. LIEBLER.

(Supreme Court of Indiana. April 5, 1904.)

MUNICIPAL CORPORATION — STREET — INJURY — NEGLIGENCE—PLEADING—APPEAL—BILL OF EXCEPTIONS.

1. Where a complaint for injuries from being thrown from a vehicle by reason of a row of blocks in a street, projecting above the surface,

alleged that the defendant city "negligently and carelessly" placed and maintained the blocks there, and that it allowed them to remain there a long time with full knowledge that they rendered the street dangerous, it was unnecessary to allege that the blocks were not useful and necessary for crossing the street.

2. Where the appellant filed a præcipe, as provided by Burns' Ann. St. 1901, § 661, directing the clerk to certify a transcript of certain papers, including the bill of exceptions containing the evidence in the cause, but he certified the original bill instead, it is no part of the record, and cannot be considered on appeal.

Appeal from Superior Court, Madison County; H. O. Ryan, Judge.

Action by Valentine Liebler against the city of Alexandria. From a judgment in favor of plaintiff, defendant appeals. Transferred from the Appellate Court under Burns' Ann. St. 1901, § 1337u. Affirmed.

James A. May, for appellant. Bagot & Bagot, for appellee.

JORDAN, J. Appellee successfully prosecuted this action in the lower court to recover damages for personal injuries sustained by reason of the negligence of appellant in maintaining an obstruction in one of its streets. The errors assigned and relied upon for reversal are: (1) Overruling the demurrer to the complaint; (2) overruling appellant's motion for a new trial.

The facts, as alleged in the complaint, may be summarized as follows: On July 2, 1901, and for many years prior thereto, the defendant was a municipal corporation, and during all of the time it was such corporation there was a public street within its corporate limits known as "Broadway," which was generally accepted and used by the public for travel thereover. There was another street therein known as "Sheridan Avenue." These two streets intersected each other. On the said 2d day of July, 1901, and for many years prior thereto, the defendant, it is alleged, negligently and carelessly kept, maintained, and allowed to remain on and across said Broadway street, at the point where said street intersected Sheridan avenue, an obstruction consisting of a row of wooden blocks. These blocks were about 10 inches in diameter and 2 feet in length, and were securely sunk into the ground beneath the surface of the street to a depth of 16 inches, and extended 8 inches above the surface of the street, and were so placed and fixed as to constitute a dangerous obstruction to the use of said street by the public, and greatly endangered the life and limbs of persons traveling thereover in vehicles, all of which facts were well known to the defendant for a long time prior to the alleged accident. On the said 2d day of July, plaintiff (appellee herein) was traveling over the street in a one-horse vehicle, and, when within 100 feet of said obstruction, the horse drawing said vehicle became frightened, and, by reason of said fright, ran along said street in the direction of said obstruction; the plaintiff all the time using his best efforts and endeavors to check and control the horse, and to so guide him that the vehicle would not come into contact with said row of blocks. Regardless of his best efforts and endeavors to control and stop the horse, and to avoid coming into contact with the obstruction, the horse, on account of his fright, ran the vehicle in which plaintiff was seated rapidly and with much force against said blocks, and the wheels thereof came into contact with said blocks, thereby stopping the vehicle and throwing it high into the air, by reason of which the plaintiff was thrown therefrom, with great force and violence, onto the hard surface of the street, and against said row of blocks, whereby he was greatly wounded, crippled, and maimed, his leg being broken, etc. A particular description of his injuries is given. It is charged that he received his injuries wholly and solely by reason of the negligence and carelessness of the defendant in placing, maintaining, and allowing said blocks to remain in said street as an obstruction thereof. It is further alleged that the horse which he was driving was ordinarily gentle and docile, and that he was frightened without any fault of the plaintiff, and that the latter exercised ordinary care for his own safety and welfare, and, to prevent injury to himself, he used and employed his best efforts and endeavors to manage and control said horse, and prevent his vehicle from coming into contact with said obstruction.

The only objection pointed out and urged against the sufficiency of the complaint by appellant's counsel is that it fails to disclose that the row of blocks in question were not useful and necessary to the street. Counsel for appellant contend that if the blocks were necessary and useful in muddy weather, to enable persons to cross the street, then appellant had the right to maintain them. But the complaint, as shown, charges that the defendant "negligently and carelessly" placed and maintained the blocks in the street, that they constituted a dangerous obstruction therein, and that the defendant allowed them to remain for a long time, with full knowledge that they rendered the street dangerous to persons traveling thereover in vehicles. The burden was upon appellee to establish the negligence of which he complained, but certainly he was not required to allege in his complaint, in addition to the facts averred, that the blocks were not necessary and useful for the purpose of crossing the street. As to whether the pleading is sufficient in other respects, we do not determine. It is certainly manifest, however, that it is not open to the objection pointed out and urged by counsel for appellant. In support of its sufficiency in general, counsel for appellee cite the following cases: Town of Fowler v. Linquist, 138 Ind. 566, 37 N. E. 133; Senhenn v. City of Evansville, 140 Ind. 675, 40 N. E. 69; Lake Erie, etc., R. Co. v. McHenry,

10 Ind. App. 525, 37 N. E. 186; City of Indianapolis v. Marold, 25 Ind. App. 428, 58 N. E. 512; Town of Odon v. Dobbs, 25 Ind. App. 522, 58 N. E. 562.

The other and remaining grounds advanced and discussed by appellant's counsel for reversal depend upon the evidence, which is not properly in the record, for the reason that the clerk of the lower court has, in violation of appellant's præcipe, certified the original bill of exceptions, embracing the evidence, together with the rulings of the court in respect to the admission and rejection of certain evidence, instead of a transcript thereof. It is disclosed that appellant filed a præcipe, as provided by section 661, Burns' Ann. St. 1901, whereby it directed the clerk to certify a true and complete transcript of certain designated papers and entries, including the bill of exceptions, containing the evidence in the cause. The præcipe is attached to, and made a part of, the record in this appeal. The clerk, instead of complying with appellant's express direction to make a transcript of the bill of exceptions embracing the evidence, upon the contrary, has certified up the original bill. That the latter, under the circumstances, is not a part of the record, and that neither the evidence embraced therein, nor the rulings of the court in admitting and rejecting certain evidence can be considered, is well settled. See Johnson v. Johnson, 156 Ind. 592, 60 N. E. 451; Chestnut v. Southern Ry. Co., 157 Ind. 509, 62 N. E. 32; Berry v. Chicago, etc., Ry. Co., 158 Ind. 668, 64 N. E. 82; Marcy Mfg. Co. v. Flint, etc., Co., 158 Ind. 173, 63 N. E. 207; Drew v. Town of Geneva, 159 Ind. 364, 65 N. E. 9; Mankin v. Penn Co., 160 Ind. 447, 67 N. E. 229.

There being no error presented, the judgment is therefore affirmed.

(163 Ind. 120)

SEYMOUR WATER CO. et al. v. CITY OF SEYMOUR.*

(Supreme Court of Indiana. March 30, 1904.)

MUNICIPAL CORPORATIONS — FRANCHISE—CANCELLATION — COMPLAINT—SUFFICIENCY — RESCISSION—ADEQUATE REMEDY AT LAW—MANDAMUS—QUIETING TITLE.

1. A complaint by a municipal corporation alleged the passage of an ordinance granting to defendant water company an exclusive right to establish a waterworks system in plaintiff city, and to supply the city and inhabitants with water at an exorbitant and unreasonable price for an unreasonable and illegal time. It was further alleged that the franchise was ultra vires, and that defendant had executed a deed of trust, and assigned to the trustees therein all hydrant rentals, because of which the trustees claimed to have some interest in the contract, which claim was adverse to the plaintiff. It was prayed that the contract be revoked and declared void. There were no allegations that a waterworks system was ever built, or that the water company was attempting or threatening to occupy the streets under the franchise, or asserted any claim or title adverse to the city, or that the franchise was a cloud on the city's title. *Held* not sufficient to state a cause of action against the water company for quieting title, under Burns' Ann. St. 1901, § 1082, providing that an action may be brought by any person having an interest against another who claims title to or interest in real property, adverse to him, for the purpose of quieting the question of title.

2. Neither was it sufficient to state a cause of action against the trustees, because not showing that they claimed any interest in real property.

3. The complaint, however, was for the cancellation of the contract, and not to quiet title.

4. A contract between a municipal corporation and a water company, granting to the latter the exclusive right to furnish water to the city and its inhabitants, at an unreasonable and exorbitant rate, and for an unreasonable and unlawful length of time, will not be canceled by a court of equity without a showing of some matter specially calculated to invoke the jurisdiction of equity.

5. Mandamus is an action at law.

6. The performance of quasi public duties growing out of the acceptance of municipal grants may be enforced by mandate.

7. Rescission of a franchise granted by a city to a water company, in acceptance of which the water company agreed to furnish a certain pressure for fire protection, and to furnish water fit for domestic purposes, will not be decreed by a court of equity on the ground that the company has not complied with its contract in these respects, inasmuch as the city has an adequate remedy at law by mandamus to compel the water company to fulfill the conditions of its contract.

Appeal from Circuit Court, Jennings County; A. G. Smith, Special Judge.

Action by the city of Seymour against the Seymour Water Company and others. From a judgment for plaintiff, defendants appeal. Reversed.

Merrill Moores and O. H. Montgomery, for appellants. Shea & Wood, Elliott, Elliott & Littleton, Lincoln Dixon, and Burt New, for appellee.

GILLETT, C. J. This suit was instituted by appellee against appellants. The complaint was in two paragraphs, each of which was challenged by demurrer by each of appellants. The demurrer was overruled, and by proper assignments of error the question as to the sufficiency of said paragraphs is presented for our consideration.

The first paragraph is as follows:

"That the plaintiff is a municipal corporation existing under and by virtue of the laws of the state of Indiana. The defendant the Seymour Water Company is a corporation organized under, and existing by virtue of, the laws of the state of Indiana. The defendant the Farmers' Loan & Trust Company of New York is a corporation organized under, and existing by virtue of, the laws of the state of New York. Merrill Moores, trustee herein, is a citizen of the city of Indianapolis, in the state of Indiana. That on the 7th day of March, 1889, the common council of the city of Seymour, plaintiff herein, passed an ordinance in the words and figures follow-

*Rehearing denied June 8, 1904.

¶ 6. See Mandamus, vol. 33, Cent. Dig. § 265.

ing: [At this point there is set out a copy of an ordinance purporting to grant to one Willett E. McMillan, his heirs and assigns, the right to establish a waterworks system to supply said city and its inhabitants with water, and an undertaking by the city to rent a certain number of hydrants. Without explanatory averment, there is next set out what purports to be a formal acceptance.] That said city council, by its said action and by its said ordinance, attempted to grant to one Willett E. McMillan an exclusive franchise and monopoly to supply the city of Seymour and its inhabitants with water for a period of from thirty to sixty years, as provided in said ordinance, at an exorbitant and unreasonable price, and for an unreasonable and illegal time; thereby imposing unreasonable burdens upon said city and the inhabitants thereof. That said ordinance attempts to grant an exclusive contract and franchise, and is ultra vires, contrary to public policy and the Constitution of Indiana, and is wholly void. That on the 23d day of July, 1889, the said Willett E. McMillan, mentioned in said ordinance, assigned and transferred all his rights and interest to and in said contract to the defendant herein, said Seymour Water Company, and that the defendant the said Seymour Water Company has no right, title, or interest to or in said contract, except as the assignee of said Willett E. McMillan, which assignment is in the words and figures following: 'Seymour, July 23, 1889.' For value received I hereby sell, assign, transfer and set over to the Seymour Water Company all rights of every description growing out of the within contract. Willett E. McMillan.' The plaintiff further avers that on the 1st day of August, 1889, the defendant the Seymour Water Company executed to the defendants the Farmers' Loan & Trust Company of the City of New York and Merrill Moores, trustee, a deed of trust and mortgage upon the said property of the said Seymour Water Company in and about the city of Seymour, plaintiff herein. The plaintiff further avers that the said Seymour Water Company assigned to the said defendants, trustees, all the hydrant rentals to be paid by said city to said Seymour Water Company, and directed said city to pay said water rentals to said trustees; that said trustees, because of the premises herein set out, claim to have some interest in said contract, which claim is adverse to the interest of this plaintiff, and on the same side as the defendant waterworks company. Wherefore the plaintiff prays the court that said contract be revoked and declared to be null and void and of no force and effect; that the said city and its inhabitants be relieved from its burdens; and that the defendants, and each of them, be forever enjoined from attempting to enforce and ever claiming any rights under said contract."

The second paragraph omits the ultra vires charges, but alleges, in addition to the other averments of said first paragraph, the following:

"That said defendant the said Seymour Water Company, defendant herein, had fully failed and refused to comply with the terms of said contract, in this, to wit: (1) That said defendant has wholly failed and refused to supply water suitable for domestic purposes, as provided for in section 1 of said ordinance, but that said water supply to the plaintiff city and its inhabitants has at all times been very impure and wholly unfit for domestic and drinking purposes. (2) That said defendant has wholly failed and refused to comply with section 14 of said ordinance, which requires said defendant to furnish fire pressure for fire service to the amount of one hundred pounds to the square inch. Plaintiff avers that such fire pressure has never been furnished to the amount of one hundred pounds to the square inch, but that said fire service furnished has been notoriously inadequate and insufficient, to the great loss and damage of the said city and its inhabitants."

In determining the sufficiency of the first paragraph of complaint, as against the Seymour Water Company, it will be profitable to note some matters which said paragraph omits to allege. It does not charge (1) that a waterworks system was ever built or maintained by said company or by any one else in pursuance of said contract and franchise, or that anything has been done by virtue thereof; (2) that said water company is attempting or threatening to use or occupy the streets or other public places of said city under said grant; (3) that said water company is asserting any claim or title by virtue of said grant, either adverse to the city or otherwise; (4) that said grant is a cloud upon the city's title.

Counsel for appellee contend that said paragraph is sufficient to quiet title. Section 1082, Burns' Ann. St. 1901, provides that "An action may be brought by any person, either in or out of possession, or by one having an interest in remainder or reversion, against another who claims title to or interest in real property adverse to him, although the defendant may not be in possession thereof, for the purpose of determining and quieting the question of title." The principles upon which the statutory action to quiet title are based are, in a large measure, of equitable origin; and, while such principles have been influential in the construction of the statute, yet the fact remains that the proceeding as it now exists is essentially the creature of legislative enactment. Ragsdale v. Mitchell, 97 Ind. 458; Trittipo v. Morgan, 99 Ind. 269; Johnson v. Taylor, 106 Ind. 89, 5 N. E. 732; Puterbaugh v. Puterbaugh, 131 Ind. 288, 30 N. E. 519, 15 L. R. A. 341. In Johnson v. Taylor, supra, it was said concerning such statutory action that "the plaintiff or cross-complainant must allege in his complaint or cross-complaint that he is the owner of certain real estate, or of a certain interest therein (describing the same), and that the claim of the defendant to his action or cross-action, in or to such real estate or interest therein, is adverse to the title asserted by the plaintiff, or is unfounded and a cloud upon plaintiff's title." It should be stated in this connection, however, that, in view of the Code, a complaint to quiet title is not to be condemned because of the lack of any merely formal statement as to the nature of the defendant's claim, or of its relation to or its effect upon the plaintiff's title, where the general facts alleged supply such formal allegations as a necessary influence. Caress v. Foster, 62 Ind. 145; Kitts v. Willson, 106 Ind. 147, 5 N. E. 400; Rausch v. Trustees, etc., 107 Ind. 1, 8 N. E. 25; Bisel v. Tucker, 121 Ind. 249, 23 N. E. 81; Wilson v. Wilson, 124 Ind. 472, 24 N. E. 974; Island Coal Co. v. Streitlemier, 139 Ind. 83, 37 N. E. 340.

The above sufficiently indicates the standard by which a complaint to quiet title must be measured, and, judged by this standard, the paragraph of complaint in question falls far short of stating a cause of action under the statute against said company.

As to the other appellants, the question as to the sufficiency of said first paragraph, viewed as a complaint to quiet title, is more doubtful, but we have concluded that it is not sufficient as to them. What the property is upon which said appellants have a deed of trust and mortgage, is altogether in doubt. We infer that "said property" is tangible in its character, since it is alleged to be "in and about the city of Seymour," but we have looked in vain for any corresponding antecedent. So far as the assignment of hydrant rentals is concerned, it is to be considered that it is not alleged that a water plant has been constructed. In other words, it does not appear that there is any corporeal tenement out of which a rent could issue. We are not permitted to infer, in support of a barren allegation that there has been an assignment of hydrant rentals, that the assignment was of such a character as would, if valid, permit the assignees to proceed upon their own initiative to do any act to the prejudice of appellee's real estate. As we have seen, the statute provides that the action to quiet title is to be brought against one "who claims title to or interest in real property adverse to" the plaintiff, "for the purpose of determining and quieting the question of title." Here the interest to which it is alleged that said appellants lay claim is not an interest in real property, but an "interest in said contract." Such an interest might exist, and it might be adverse or opposed to the interest of appellee; and yet it might be of such a limited character, owing to the terms of the assignment, as in no wise to cloud the title of appellee to its real property.

All of these matters of uncertainty may be passed, however, because it is evident, when said paragraph is viewed from the standpoint of its general scope and structure, that it was intended as a paragraph to cancel a contract, and not as one to quiet title. This sufficiently explains why there was no averment in said paragraph that the water plant had been built, as the second paragraph and the evidence disclose. It was said by this court in Platter v. City of Seymour, 86 Ind. 323, 326: "To permit an isolated statement to control the scope and meaning of a long and involved pleading would be destructive of all certainty in pleading, result in injury to litigants, and impose upon the trial court the burden of looking into out of the way places to discover if disconnected and irrelevant allegations existed which might change the drift of the general averments of the complaint. Such a system would make pleadings mere traps for the ensnaring of the adverse parties, and would give to pleadings a protean character, which all rules of practice condemn." Many authorities might be accumulated from our Reports in support of the doctrine of Platter v. City of Seymour, supra, but we quote the above observations, since they are, for the most part, singularly apposite to this case.

The paragraph in question is to procure the cancellation of a contract, and upon that theory it must be judged. Such a complaint must state facts sufficient to invoke the equity powers of the trial court. Assuming, as we may do, against the pleader, that the waterworks plant has not been built, has any showing been made which would warrant the exercise of the equitable jurisdiction to decree cancellation? Prof. Pomeroy states that where an estate, interest, or right is legal, the exercise of the jurisdiction of equity to decree cancellation "depends upon the adequacy of the legal remedies; a party being left to his affirmative or defensive remedy at law where full and complete justice can thereby be done." Eq. Jur. § 1377. See also Ins. Co. v. Bailey, 13 Wall. 616, 20 L. Ed. 501; Noah v. Webb, 1 Edw. Ch. 604; Globe Mut. Life Ins. Co. v. Reals, 79 N. Y. 202; Farmington Village Corp. v. Sandy Riv. Nat. Bank, 85 Me. 46, 26 Atl. 965; Wooden v. Wooden, 3 N. J. Eq. 429; Boardman v. Jackson, 119 Mass. 161; New York, etc., Co. v. Traders', etc., Co., 132 Mass. 377, 42 Am. Rep. 440; San Diego Flume Co. v. Souther, 90 Fed. 164, 32 C. C. A. 548; McMillen v. Mason, 71 Wis. 405, 37 N. W. 253; County of Ada v. Bullen Bridge Co., 5 Idaho, 79, 47 Pac. 818; Hardy v. Newton First Nat. Bank, 46 Kan. 88, 26 Pac. 423.

As the above authorities evince, some reason for equitable interference must always be shown in a bill or complaint for cancellation, where the remedy is not sought for the protection of an equitable estate, interest, or right. In Hamilton v. Cummings, 1 Johns. Ch. 517, Chancellor Kent upholds the power of equity to decree cancellation of instruments void at law, but he adds: "While I assert the authority of the court to sustain such bills, I am not to be understood as encouraging applications where the fitness of the exercise of the power of the court is not pretty strongly displayed." In Town of Venice v. Woodruff, 62 N. Y. 462, 20 Am. Rep. 495, it was said: "Whether, therefore, the question be regarded as one of jurisdiction or of practice, it is established by the later decisions that some special ground for equitable relief must be shown, and that the mere fact that the instrument ought not to be enforced is insufficient, standing alone, to justify a resort to an equitable action." As very appropriate here, although the language was used with reference to the remedy of injunction, we quite the following from the opinion of Dillon, J., in Home Ins. Co. v. Stanchfield, 2 Abb. U. S. 1, 6, Fed. Cas. No. 6,660: "No principle is more familiar than the one that where the law affords a full, complete, and adequate remedy, equity will not interfere. 'Chancery,' says Lord Bacon, 'is ordained to supply the law, not to subvert the law.' 4 Bac. Works, 488. In other words, the parties must litigate in the law courts, unless there are good and legal reasons for invoking the aid of equity."

If appellee is right in its theory that there are illegal provisions in the ordinance, which condemn it as a whole, then its invalidity may be said to be apparent upon a mere inspection. Our statute authorizes the quieting of title against adverse claim, although the instrument on which it is based is void on its face. Bishop v. Moorman, 98 Ind. 1, 49 Am. Rep. 731. And see Reynolds v. First Nat. Bank of Crawfordsville, 112 U. S. 405, 5 Sup. Ct. 213, 28 L. Ed. 733; Green v. Glynn, 71 Ind. 336. Prof. Pomeroy states that the refusal to treat such instruments as clouds operates in many instances as a denial of justice. Eq. Jur. § 1399. But however this may be, it is certain, in the absence of statute, that, if an instrument which is void on its face can be canceled at all, it can only be done upon the averment and proof of some matter specially calculated to invoke the jurisdiction of equity, since the instrument itself could not be put to a wrongful use. Story, Eq. Jur. § 700; Pomeroy, Eq. Jur. §§ 1377, 1399. Appellee's own theory as to the nature of the instrument, therefore, condemns the paragraph in question, when regarded in its proper light as a mere complaint to cancel a contract.

Whether a case could be said to have been made out, as a matter of evidence, had the facts pleaded in said paragraph been shown upon a trial, where there would have been a right to indulge inferences, is another question. See American, etc., Co. v. Hullinger (Ind. Sup.) 69 N. E. 460. We hold said paragraph does not state a cause of action against appellants.

As heretofore shown, the second paragraph of complaint disclosed inferentially that the Seymour Water Company built and was engaged in operating a water plant in said city of Seymour. Said paragraph proceeds on the theory that there is a right to a decree of rescission for nonperformance in respect to the character and pressure of water provided. The two remedies—rescission and cancellation—complement each other, and are referable to the same general head of equity jurisprudence. The lack of an adequate remedy at law is the ground on which the jurisdiction of rescission, as well as of cancellation, is asserted by courts of chancery. Story, Eq. Jur. § 688. Rescission is the converse of specific performance. In a suit to annul a partially executed contract, the power of the court is sought, not to carry out and accomplish what the parties have begun, but to undo what they have accomplished. "Equity may refuse to revoke where it would decline to execute." Delamater's Estate, 1 Whart. 362; Du Bois Borough v. Du Bois City Waterworks Co., 176 Pa. 430, 35 Atl. 248, 34 L. R. A. 92, 53 Am. St. Rep. 678. The Supreme Court of the United States has declared that "the cancellation of an executed contract is an exercise of the most extraordinary power of a court of equity." Atlantic Delaine Co. v. James, 94 U. S. 214, 24 L. Ed. 112. In view of these considerations, a complaint for the rescission or cancellation of a contract which has been wholly or partially executed by the opposite party should show a necessity for such remedy, and especially should such complaint show the lack of an adequate remedy at law.

The writ of mandamus is an extraordinary remedy, but the action is at law, and, since the writ has lost its prerogative character, the proceeding is treated as in the nature of a civil action. The performance of quasi public duties growing out of the acceptance of municipal grants may be enforced by mandate. Portland, etc., Co. v. State ex rel. Keen, 135 Ind. 54, 34 N. E. 818, 21 L. R. A. 639; Jackson v. Suburban R. Co., 178 Ill. 594, 53 N. E. 349, 49 L. R. A. 650: People ex rel. Bush v. New York Sub. Water Co. (Sup.) 56 N. Y. Supp. 364; Merrill, Mandamus, § 27; 19 Am. & Eng. Ency. of Law, 876. In City of Topeka v. Topeka Water Co., 58 Kan. 349, 49 Pac. 79, the city sought a rescission of a franchise to the water company for failure to extend its mains as required by contract. In holding that the action would not lie, the court said: "The state is not asking to reclaim the franchises bestowed by it upon the company, but the city seeks an annulment of the contract because of the nonperformance of a condition subsequent, and the failure to perform this condition is not made a ground of forfeiture. If, however, the company failed to carry out the purpose of its organization, and willfully violated the provisions of the ordinance other than those specified as grounds of forfeiture, an annulment might in some instances be had; but, as has been before observed, a forfeiture is always abhorred, and, according to repeated decisions of this court, it will ordinarily not be declared where there is another adequate remedy. State ex rel. v. Wilson, 30 Kan. 661, 2 Pac. 828; Tarbox v. Sughrue, 36 Kan. 225 [12 Pac. 935]; Weston v. Lane, 40 Kan. 479 [20 Pac.

260, 10 Am. St. Rep. 224]. See, also, 5 Thompson on Corporations, § 6608; High on Extraordinary Legal Remedies (3d Ed.) § 649; 4 Am. & Eng. Encyc. of Law, 293, and cases cited. As determined in the cited cases, the court is vested with some discretion in such a proceeding; and, since it is slow to adjudge the extreme penalty where the law has provided other sufficient remedies, the question arises, is mandamus a suitable and sufficient remedy? It has already been determined that a corporation organized to promote public works, and which has been granted a franchise by a city through an ordinance, may be compelled to perform its duties toward the public by a proceeding in mandamus. City of Potwin Place v. Topeka R. Co., 51 Kan. 609 [33 Pac. 309, 37 Am. St. Rep. 312]." See, also, State ex rel. v. Galena Water Co., 63 Kan. 317, 65 Pac. 257.

If the acceptance of the grant by the water company imposed upon it a duty to furnish a better quality of water than could be obtained from the stipulated source of supply at the place of intake, the averments of the paragraph of complaint should have shown that no remedy short of the drastic one sought would be sufficient. If, in view of the contract and the condition of the water supply, filtration were required, mandamus to compel the company to filter would not only be a remedy less harsh than that of forfeiture, but the suggested remedy would possess the merit of operating with directness upon the wrongful omission. The observation with reference to mandamus applies also to the matter of insufficient pressure. The circumstances would have to be quite exceptional to warrant a court, sitting as a court of equity, in indirectly enforcing a forfeiture for the nonperformance of a condition subsequent; and, as circumstances warranting such course are not shown in the paragraph under consideration, we adjudge said paragraph insufficient.

Judgment reversed, with an instruction to sustain the demurrer of appellants to both paragraphs of complaint.

(163 Ind. 321)

FARMERS' INS. ASS'N OF MADISON COUNTY v. REAVIS et al.[1]

(Supreme Court of Indiana. April 6, 1904.)

INSURANCE — BY-LAWS — WAIVER—INTERROGATORY TO JURY.

1. Burns' Ann. St. 1901, § 555, authorizing the submission to the jury of interrogatories on the issues of the cause, does not authorize the submission of the question whether the general verdict is based on the first or second paragraph of the complaint, and the answer to such an interrogatory must be treated as surplusage; that not being one of the issues in the cause.

2. Where a by-law of a mutual insurance association provides that all members using gas must have good regulators, and that the association is not responsible for any loss by fire if this requirement is not met, but the association issues a policy and accepts premiums thereunder, with full knowledge that the insured violates this condition, it will not be permitted to insist on a forfeiture therefor.

Appeal from Circuit Court, Delaware County; Joseph G. Lefler, Judge.

Action by Jesse F. Reavis and others against the Farmers' Insurance Association of Madison County. From a judgment in favor of plaintiffs, defendant appeals. Transferred from the Appellate Court under Burns' Ann. St. 1901, § 1337u. Affirmed.

Kittinger & Diven, for appellant. Ball & Needham and Carver & Ballard, for appellees.

HADLEY, J. Appellees sued appellant in two paragraphs. By the first they seek to recover on a fire insurance policy the value of the property destroyed, and by the second they seek recovery upon an account stated. Upon the issues joined there was a trial by jury, and with a general verdict in favor of appellees the jury returned answers to a large number of interrogatories. The overruling of appellant's motion for judgment in its favor on the answers to the interrogatories notwithstanding the general verdict, and the sustaining of appellees' motion for judgment on the general verdict, are the only questions presented for decision.

The material facts, as shown by the answers to interrogatories, are as follows: Appellant is a mutual insurance company. Its board of directors consisted of one member from each township of the county. It was the duty of each director to receive all applications for insurance in his respective township, make surveys and estimates of value of property to be insured, collect all fines and assessments, on account of losses, made upon members holding insurance in his township, and to keep a record of all transactions in regard to membership and insurance in his said territory. All resident owners of farm property are eligible to membership in said association upon paying a fee of $5 and agreeing to pay all assessments on account of losses. In case of a loss it was the duty of the secretary of the company without delay to examine the premises, "and after taking such steps as he may deem necessary for the purpose he shall determine the amount of the loss sustained." A by-law of the company, in force at the time of the insurance, provides: "Sec. 13. All members of this association using gas are required to have good regulators at their houses and the pipes that are in their houses clear of leaks. The association is not responsible for any loss that may occur by fire if these requirements are not complied with." On May 28, 1894, appellant wrote a policy of insurance upon the dwelling house and contents of appellees. John L. Thomas at the time was the secretary of appellant, and Perry Heritage a di-

¶ 2. See Insurance, vol. 28, Cent. Dig. §§ 1041, 1042.
[1] Rehearing denied, 71 N. E. 905.

rector for the township in which the property insured was situate. Heritage, as township director, solicited and prepared appellees' application for insurance, and was at the time informed that appellees were burning gas from a high-pressure line without a regulator. The property was destroyed by fire December 8, 1896. During all the period from the issuing of the policy to the destruction of the property Heritage knew that appellees were using gas without a regulator, and prior to December 23, 1896, reported the same to the company, and with such knowledge during all of said time continued to and did assess, collect, and receive from appellees all assessments and premiums accruing upon said policy. Three days after the fire, Heritage, as director, and John L. Thomas, as secretary, of the company, visited appellees' premises, and took down a list of the property claimed to be destroyed, and fixed the value thereto, after which appellee Jesse F. Reavis inquired of Thomas when they should get their money, and the latter answered that the company would take 30 days to investigate, and if it found nothing crooked or wrong, the company would pay the money at the end of that time. The value of the insured property destroyed was $517, and the value of the property insured was $1,200. Appellees, after April 6, 1896, at no time procured from the company a permit to use gas from a high pressure line. At the time and before the fire appellees supplied their lights and cooking stove with gas through a low-pressure regulator, and their sitting room grate with gas from a high-pressure line through a three-eighths pipe without a regulator.

Appellant grounds its defense on appellees' use of natural gas from a high-pressure line without a regulator, in violation of the company's by-laws. Appellees seek to avoid the answers by replying that the company solicited, accepted, and continued appellees' risk, and demanded, collected, and retained from them all premiums and assessments, with full knowledge that they were supplying their grate from a high-pressure line without a regulator other than double key valves.

Among its other findings, the jury answered in response to an interrogatory that its verdict was based on the second paragraph of complaint. Appellant's first contention is that this was equivalent to a finding for the defendant on the first paragraph, and, as the other findings show there was no account stated between the parties, as alleged in the second paragraph, there is, therefore, no basis for the general verdict to rest upon, and it must fail. The interrogatory in question should not have been submitted to the jury. The answer called for was not such a fact on the issues of the cause as is contemplated by section 555, Burns' Ann. St. 1901, and, being unauthorized by the statute, must be treated as surplusage. Stone Co. v. Dearmin, 100 Ind. 162, 66 N. E. 609; Stone Co. v. Morgan, 160 Ind. 241, 66 N. E. 696; Stone Co. v. Hilt, 26 Ind. App. 543, 59 N. E. 97. If such a finding is desirable, it should be sought through the medium of the general verdict. We must not lose sight of the fact that in testing all questions of conflict between the general verdict and special findings of the jury we must assume that every fact provable under the issues, which is essential to the support of the general verdict, was by the jury found established. This rule has been affirmed so often that we deem it unprofitable to cite cases.

It is insisted that the use of gas by appellees in their grate without a good regulator, in violation of section 13 of the company's by-laws, forfeited their right of recovery. While it is true that the answers to interrogatories show that the by-laws provided that members (or insured persons) were "required to have good regulators at their houses," and that in default of which the association would not be liable for any loss by fire, it is also shown by such answers that a director of appellant, whose duty it was to solicit, supervise, and accept all insurance from the township, and to collect the initiation fee and all fines and assessments that should be levied against the policy, and to keep a record of all the company's business in his township, and who did solicit appellees' insurance, and did prepare, approve, and accept appellees' application, and forward the same to the secretary of the company for an issuance of the policy, was at the time of taking such application fully informed by appellees that they were using gas without a regulator. It also appears that this information was by the director, prior to December 23, 1896—which we must presume was at the time of forwarding the application—reported to the company. It is still further shown that, after being thus informed, and continuing so informed from the date of the policy to the time of the loss, the company continued to demand, collect, and retain all regular premiums and assessments made against appellees' policy prior to the burning of his property. Having, with knowledge of the broken condition, demanded and collected the assessments, appellant, with the money in its possession, will not be heard to say that appellees had no insurance for the money that was paid. When the company received notice that appellees were using gas without a regulator, it might have refused to issue the policy, or, if such notice was received after the policy had been issued, it might have declined to make further assessments or received further payments and canceled the policy; but, having gone on making and collecting assessments, and holding out to the insured the reasonable belief that the policy was valid, the company will not now be permitted to insist upon a forfeiture. "It is abundantly settled," said Mitchell, J., in Havens v. Ins. Company, 111 Ind. 92, 12 N. E. 138, 60 Am. Rep. 689, "that, notwithstanding conditions in the policy, if at the time the insurance was effected, or afterwards there were conditions, uses, or incidents of the risk which were in conflict with the conditions in the policy, and which were known to the insurer or its agent, whose knowledge is imputed to the company, such conditions, uses, or incidents cannot be used to defeat a recovery after a loss has occurred. Issuing or continuing a policy of insurance with full knowledge by the company of existing facts, which, according to a condition of the contract, makes it voidable, is a waiver of the condition." See authorities collected on page 92, 111 Ind., and page 138, 12 N. E., 60 Am. Rep. 689. See, also, Ins. Company v. Neiwedde, 11 Ind. App. 624, 39 N. E. 534; Aid Association v. Bodurtha, 23 Ind. App. 121, 53 N. E. 787, 77 Am. St. Rep. 414. It follows that the special finding of the jury that appellees were using gas without a regulator was not in conflict with the general verdict, and appellant's motion for judgment was properly overruled.

Judgment affirmed.

(162 Ind. 448)

VAN BUSKIRK et al. v. STOVER.

(Supreme Court of Indiana. April 7, 1904.)

PARTITION—APPEAL—ASSIGNMENTS OF ERROR—MOTION FOR NEW TRIAL—MOTION TO VACATE COMMISSIONER'S REPORT.

1. On appeal in partition, assignments that the court erred in refusing a trial of the issues joined on the pleadings and in rendering a judgment over objection without hearing evidence on the issues cannot be considered, since, under Burns' Ann. St. 1901, § 1202 (Rev. St. 1881, § 1188; Horner's Ann. St. 1901, § 1188), providing that the practice in partition suits shall be the same as in civil suits, these questions must be presented by motion for a new trial, and, if the motion is overruled, by assigning the ruling as error.

2. Under Burns' Ann. St. 1901, § 570 (Rev. St. 1881, § 561; Horner's Ann. St. 1901, § 561), providing that an application for a new trial must be made at the term at which the decision is rendered or the first day of the next term, where a motion for a new trial in a partition suit was not made till the second term after it was decided, the court's action in overruling the motion will not be considered on appeal.

3. The burden of proving the grounds of a motion to set aside and vacate the report of commissioners in a partition suit is on the parties who make the motion.

Appeal from Circuit Court, Madison County; John F. McClure, Judge.

Action by Lydia Stover against Frank Van Buskirk and another. From a judgment in favor of plaintiff, defendants appeal. Transferred from the Appellate Court under Burns' Ann. St. 1901, § 1337u (Acts 1901, p. 590, c. 259). Affirmed.

John R. Thornburgh and D. L. Bishopp, for appellants. Chipman, Keltner & Hendee, for appellee.

MONKS, J. This action was brought by appellee against appellants for partition of real estate. Appellants Van Buskirk and Van Buskirk filed an answer in two paragraphs, the first being a general denial. It was alleged in the second paragraph that said real estate could not be "partitioned without great and permanent damage to said land and to the interest of the defendants therein, and that it will be to the best interest of all the parties that a commissioner be appointed, and said real estate be sold." The other appellants, being minors, answered in two paragraphs by a guardian ad litem, the first paragraph being a general denial. The second paragraph of the answer of said guardian ad litem was substantially the same as that part of the second paragraph of Van Buskirk's answer above set out.

The transcript of the record proper shows that at the October term, 1901, of the court below, said cause was submitted to the court for trial, and the court found for the appellee, and entered an interlocutory judgment for partition, and appointed commissioners to set off to appellee her interest in said land. At the January term, 1902, of said court, said commissioners filed their report showing that they had set off to appellee her share in said land, describing it. Appellants filed exceptions to said report, and moved to vacate and set the same aside. Afterwards, at the April term, 1902, of said court, said exceptions and motion to set aside and vacate said report were overruled by the court, and final judgment approving said partition rendered. At said term, on May 9, 1902, appellants Van Buskirk and Van Buskirk filed a motion for a new trial, and on the same day said guardian ad litem of said infant appellants filed a motion for a new trial. Each of these motions was overruled by the court. The errors assigned are: "(1) The court erred in refusing to give the appellants a trial of the issues joined on the pleadings filed therein. (2) The court erred in rendering a judgment against the appellants over their objections without hearing any evidence on the issues formed in said cause. (3) The court erred in overruling the appellants' motion to set aside and vacate the report of the commissioners in partition. (4) The court erred in overruling appellants' motion for a new trial."

In partition cases, when a party is dissatisfied with the finding of the court on the issues joined, or claims that the court erred in admitting or excluding evidence, or that the court erred in making its finding and rendering judgment without hearing any evidence on the issues formed, or has been aggrieved by any action of the court at the trial, his remedy is by motion for a new trial, as in ordinary cases. Clark v. Stephenson, 73 Ind. 489, 493, 494; section 1202, Burns' Ann. St. 1901 (section 1188, Rev. St. 1881, and section 1188, Horner's Ann. St. 1901). The first and second errors assigned refer to matters which must be presented to the court below by a motion for a new trial, and, if such motion is overruled, by assigning said ruling as error in the court to which the cause is appealable. Said assignments of error therefore present no question for review in this court. Zimmerman v. Gaumer, 152 Ind. 552, 554, 555, 53 N. E. 829; Singer v. Tormoehlen, 150 Ind. 287, 289, 49 N. E. 1055; Elliott's App. Prac. § 347. It will be observed that the issues in said cause were tried and the interlocutory judgment rendered at the October term, 1901, of the court below, while the motion for a new trial of said issues was not filed until the second term of said court thereafter. Section 570, Burns' Ann. St. 1901 (section 561, Rev. St. 1881, and section 561, Horner's Ann. St. 1901), reads as follows: "The application for a new trial may be made at any time during the term at which the verdict or decision is rendered; and if the verdict or decision be rendered on the last day of the session of any court, or on the last day of any term, then, of the first day of the next term of such court, whether general, special, or adjourned." It is clear that said motion was filed too late to present any question to the trial court, and the assignment that the court below erred in overruling said motion presents no question for review in this court. Allen v. Adams, 150 Ind. 409, 50 N. E. 387.

The grounds of the motion to set aside and vacate the report of the commissioners, which were proper objections to said report, required proof to sustain them. The burden of making this proof was upon appellants, and the bill of exceptions does not show that any evidence was given in support of said grounds of objection. Clark v. Stephenson, 73 Ind. 494. The record therefore does not sustain the third error assigned.

Judgment affirmed.

(162 Ind. 174)

DUNN v. STATE.*

(Supreme Court of Indiana. Feb. 18, 1904.)

CRIMINAL LAW—APPEAL—BILL OF EXCEPTIONS—TIME FOR FILING—PRESUMPTION AS TO SIGNING—ORIGINAL BILL—MOTION FOR NEW TRIAL—SPECIFICATION OF ERROR—SUFFICIENCY—OTHER OFFENSE—ADMISSIBILITY OF EVIDENCE.

1. Burns' Ann. St. 1901, § 1916, provides that all bills of exceptions in criminal prosecutions must be made out and presented to the judge at the trial, or within such time thereafter as he may allow, not exceeding 60 days from the time judgment is rendered. A verdict of guilty was returned November 7, 1901, and motion for new trial filed November 9th and overruled December 2d, when 120 days were given in which to file a bill of exceptions. On the same day a motion in arrest was made, which was not decided until February 3, 1902, when judgment was rendered on the verdict, and 60 days given defendant within which to prepare and file a bill of exceptions. The bill was presented March 6th and signed and filed March 26th. *Held*, that the signing and filing were within time.

2. Where the signing and filing of a bill of exceptions appeared to have been done on the same day, it will be presumed, in the absence of a contrary showing, that the bill was signed before it was filed.

3. Under the express provisions of Burns' Ann. St. 1901, § 638a, it is proper, on the appeal of a criminal case, to make the original bill of exceptions containing the evidence a part of the record.

4. A motion for the new trial of a criminal case, which assigns as a ground therefor "error of law occurring on said trial in this: that the court erred in permitting the state to ask its witness C., on rebuttal, and in permitting said witness to answer, the following question," setting out the question in full, which is susceptible of an answer yes or no, only one of which could have prejudiced defendant, specifies the error complained of with sufficient certainty, though the witness' answer is not given.

5. In a prosecution for murder, where accused on cross-examination has denied making a statement involving an admission of adultery eight years previous, and wholy disconnected with the present offense, it is error to admit in rebuttal evidence of such statement, whether such evidence be viewed as going to the substance of the issues or as impeaching the credibility or moral character of the accused.

Monks and Dowling, JJ., dissenting.

On rehearing. Reversed.

For former opinion, see 67 N. E. 940.

Henry Colerick and Barrett & Morris, for appellant. C. W. Miller, Atty. Gen., W. L. Taylor, E. V. Emerick, S. M. Hench, F. A. Emerick, W. C. Geake, C. C. Hadley, and L. G. Rothschild, for the State.

HADLEY, J. Appellant was found guilty of murder in the first degree, and his punishment assessed at imprisonment in the state prison for life. The only error assigned and not waived is the overruling of his motion for a new trial.

The questions presented arise upon the bill of exceptions, which counsel for the state insist is not in the record, because not presented to and signed by the judge and filed within the time allowed by statute. The verdict was returned November 7, 1901. Appellant's motion for a new trial was filed November 9, 1901, and overruled December 2, 1901. One hundred and twenty days were given in which to file a bill of exceptions. On the same day a motion in arrest of judgment was made, which was not decided until February 3, 1902, when it was overruled, and judgment was rendered on the verdict. The court on that day gave the appellant 60 days within which to prepare and file a bill of exceptions. The bill was presented to the judge March 6, 1902, and the same was duly signed and afterwards filed March 26, 1902. The signing and filing appear to have taken place on the same day. The points are made that the court was not authorized to grant the 120 days from December 2, 1901, for the filing of the bill, nor to allow 60 days from February 3, 1902, for such presentation and filing; that it does not appear that the bill was filed after it was signed by the judge; and that a copy, and not the original bill containing the evidence, should have been

*Rehearing granted January 15, 1904.

certified to this court. The statute regulating the filing of bills of exceptions in criminal cases is as follows: "All bills of exceptions in a criminal prosecution must be made out and presented to the judge at the time of the trial, or within such time thereafter as the judge may allow, not exceeding sixty days from the time judgment is rendered." Section 1916, Burns' Ann. St. 1901. At the time the motion for a new trial was overruled, an exception was properly reserved. The 120 days granted by the court for the filing of the bill of exceptions did not expire until April 1, 1902, nor extend more than 60 days beyond the date of the judgment. The bill was filed 51 days after the judgment was rendered, and was within the time allowed. Besides, it appears that at the time the judgment was rendered the court made a further order allowing the appellant 60 days from that date to prepare and file his bill, and the time so allowed did not expire until April 4, 1902. Under either order, the bill was filed in time. Barnaby v. State, 106 Ind. 539, 7 N. E. 231; Colee v. State, 75 Ind. 511; Hunter v. State, 102 Ind. 428, 1 N. E. 361; Bruce v. State, 141 Ind. 464, 40 N. E. 1069; Hunter v. State, 101 Ind. 406; Herron v. State, 17 Ind. App. 161, 46 N. E. 540. Where the signing and filing of the bill appear to have been done on the same day, it will be presumed, in the absence of anything to the contrary in the record, that the bill was signed before it was filed. Martin v. State, 148 Ind. 519, 47 N. E. 930; Bradley, etc., Co. v. Whicker, 23 Ind. App. 381, 55 N. E. 490. Under the act of 1897 (Acts 1897, p. 244, c. 162; Burns' Ann. St. 1901, § 638a), it was proper to make the original bill of exceptions containing the evidence a part of the record. The act expressly extended to criminal cases. Adams v. State, 156 Ind. 596, 59 N. E. 24.

There were many reasons presented by appellant as grounds for a new trial. In the course of his cross-examination the prosecuting attorney asked the defendant if he did not tell Edna Cothrell, as he took her to Churubusco, that he (witness) had taken Alpha Bennett and her sister to the World's Fair at Chicago, and that they had registered at the hotel as man and wife, occupied the same room, and had a good time. Appellant answered the question in the negative. Subsequently, in rebuttal, the court permitted Edna Cothrell, over appellant's objection, to testify concerning the statement denied by appellant. This ruling of the court is challenged, and urged as a reason for a new trial. It is insisted by appellee that the subject-matter complained of is not set forth in the motion for a new trial with sufficient certainty to present any question, because neither the answer nor the substance of the answer to the question is set out in the motion. The assignment in the motion for a new trial is as follows: "Error of law occurring on said trial in this: that the court erred in permitting the state to ask its witness, Edna Cothrell on rebuttal, and in permitting said witness to answer, the following question: 'Edna, I will ask you to state to the jury whether or not at that time, in that conversation you had with Dunn going to Churubusco or coming from Churubusco, he stated to you that during the World's Fair that he had taken Alpha Bennett and sister with him to Chicago, and that they had registered at the boarding house or hotel as man and wife, whether they occupied the same room and had a good time?'" The record shows that the witness answered the question, "Yes, sir." A litigant who desires to present to an appellate tribunal for review rulings of the trial court made in the course of the trial, and which he deems erroneous and prejudicial, is required to state such controverted matter in a motion for a new trial in such terms as will clearly indicate to the court the identity of the particular subjects and rulings complained of. The principal object of the rule is to give the trial court a further opportunity to consider and correct any error he has made while the case is still under his control. State v. Swarts, 9 Ind. 221, 222. If the challenged ruling relates to the admission of evidence, it is not necessary that the question and answer be set out in full, but the law and its purposes are satisfied if the name of the witness and the subject and substance of the point are stated in such language as will apprise the trial court with reasonable certainty of the character and scope of the particular ruling. Humphries v. Marshall's Adm'r, 12 Ind. 609; Shirk v. Cartwright, 29 Ind. 406; Evans v. State, 67 Ind. 68. As was declared in Ohio, etc., R. Co. v. Stein, 133 Ind. 243, 257, 32 N. E. 831, 832, 19 L. R. A. 733: "It is not the practice, and it is not incumbent on a party in a motion for a new trial, to set out in detail a verbatim copy of the evidence admitted over objection, or offered and refused, or a verbatim statement of the objections made to its introduction. It is sufficient if the evidence be referred to with such certainty as to call the attention of the court to it and to the ruling in relation thereto, so that the judge could not mistake the matter and the ruling alluded to and complained of by the party filing the motion." This statement was quoted approvingly in Springer v. Byram, 137 Ind. 16, 24, 36 N. E. 361, 23 L. R. A. 244, 45 Am. St. Rep. 159. The fullest discussion of the rule in question that is found in the reports of this court is in the case of McClain v. Jessup, 76 Ind. 120, 122, where Elliott, J., speaking for the court, said: "The motion must 'name the witness and the part of his testimony which was improperly received or disallowed.' We do not mean to hold that it is necessary to state in full the particular evidence received or excluded, but that it is necessary to point out with reasonable certainty the particular part of the evidence. This may be done by naming the point or subject upon which the evidence was offered and refused in cases where it is excluded, or by naming the subject or point upon which it was received in cases where error is alleged upon the admission of evidence. This, or other similar modes, will fairly and certainly direct attention to the character of the ruling complained of, and afford both the trial and appellate courts a clear and full view of the questions arising upon the ruling." The following language was used by this court in Crowder v. Reed, 80 Ind. 1, 6: "Where a motion for a new trial points out with reasonable certainty the particular testimony offered and excluded, it is sufficient. It is not necessary, nor, indeed, proper, that the motion should recite at length the questions propounded, or rehearse the testimony proffered. The object of the motion is to point out with reasonable certainty the ruling complained of, and thus enable the trial court to review its own rulings, and to present the question to the appellate court in such a manner as that it can be properly understood and decided. While the motion must designate the particular ruling complained of, it is not necessary that there should be any detailed statement of the questions asked or evidence offered. We think the motion in this case points out with reasonable certainty the particular ruling sought to be reviewed, and that it supplies such information as fully designates the question sought to be presented for consideration." In the still later case of Isler v. Bland, 117 Ind. 455, 459, 20 N. E. 303, 304, it was said: "There can be no deviation from the well-settled rule which requires that a motion for a new trial, in order to present any question, must point out with reasonable certainty the particular evidence objected to and excluded, and so designate it as to enable the court, without searching the whole record, to ascertain what evidence was offered and excluded to which the motion applies."

Without setting out everything in hæc verba, it is difficult to see how more certainty could be observed than is revealed by the assignment in the motion for a new trial. The court is informed that the testimony complained of was given in rebuttal, that it was given by Edna Cothrell, that it related to a statement made by the defendant in a conversation between witnesses and defendant in going to or from Churubusco on a particular occasion, and the question itself is set forth in the precise words submitted to the witness over the defendant's objection. The question was answerable by yes or no. A negative answer could have done no harm. That the answer was in the affirmative would be implied to any intelligent court from the fact that the party against whom it was directed was in court complaining about it. The way the subject was presented to the court left no room for conjecture, or even doubt, as to the particular item of evidence and ruling referred to, and this was abundantly sufficient.

Was the admission of the testimony erroneous? The record shows that it was a part of a conversation the defendant had with witness about six months before the trial, and related to an incident that occurred in another state, more than eight years before, and which merely implied voluntary adultery with a woman who is not claimed to have sustained any connection with or relation to the crime charged against the defendant. Nor is it pointed out how the crime of adultery at that remote period supported or proved the charge of murder in any other way than to strengthen the probability of its commission by showing the immoral or dissolute character of the defendant. The evidence being offered and admitted in rebuttal, perhaps we should assume that it was allowed upon the theory that it was proper for the state to contradict the defendant, who had denied on cross-examination that he had told the witness any such thing. But, in the absence of cautionary advice by the court to the jury, how are we to know in what way the jury received it, whether as substantive evidence in support of the corpus delicti or in contradiction and impeachment of the defendant as a witness. Upon either theory we know of no rule or principle of evidence by which the admission of the testimony can be sustained. It is a rule as old as the law itself, subject to numerous exceptions, all of which fall so far short of the facts of this case that we deem it unprofitable to notice them, that substantive evidence in both civil and criminal cases must be confined to the facts embraced within the issues joined, and that no such evidence is competent that does not form a link in the chain of proof which naturally and reasonably tends to establish some material fact in the case as made between the parties. One reason of the rule is to avoid a distraction of the court and jury by a multiplicity of issues. Another is to secure to the defendant a fair and impartial trial, which cannot be accomplished in a criminal case without affording him protection against surprise, and unpreparedness to defend his conduct and character, when unexpectedly assailed. The defendant is only expected to come prepared to answer the particular charge preferred against him in the indictment, and which must be set forth in such terms as will apprise him of just what he has to meet, and to sustain the credibility of his witnesses, if he desires, in the event they are assailed. And the law will not permit the state to depart from the issue, and introduce evidence of other extraneous offenses or misconduct that have no natural connection with the pending charge, and which are calculated to prejudice the accused in his defense. Bonsall v. State, 35 Ind. 460; McIntire v. State, 10 Ind. 26; People v. Sharp, 107 N. Y. 427, 456, 14 N. E. 319, 1 Am. St. Rep. 851; Costelo v. Crowell, 139 Mass. 588, 2 N. E. 698; Thompson v. Bowie, 4 Wall. 463, 470, 18 L. Ed. 423; People v. The Justices, 10 Hun,

158; Suttin v. Johnson, 62 Ill. 209; Cotton v. State, 17 South. (Miss.) 372; Gillett's Ind. & Col. Ev. § 57. It is equally well settled that the court may in its discretion permit a witness on cross-examination, including a defendant in a criminal case, to be interrogated as to specific extraneous offenses, and conduct, calculated to degrade him, and thus impair his credibility as a witness. But in every such case the party propounding the interrogatory is bound by the answer the witness gives, and will not be permitted to introduce substantive evidence to contradict it. Hinkle v. State, 157 Ind. 237, 61 N. E. 196; Stalcup v. State, 146 Ind. 270, 275, 45 N. E. 334; Ford v. State, 112 Ind. 373, 384, 14 N. E. 241; Gillett's Ind. & Col. Ev. § 91. In another sense the testimony was, in effect, an impeachment of the defendant's moral character by a specific act of immorality which is not allowed. Griffith v. State, 140 Ind. 163, 166, 39 N. E. 440, and cases cited. In any view we may take of the evidence, its admission was erroneous. There was other evidence tending to prove that the defendant was of a lecherous and dissolute disposition, and this particular statement claimed to have been addressed to a girl but 14 years of age, late in the evening, while being conveyed by him in his buggy, is of a character to greatly prejudice the defendant before the jury. Grave as the crime of which the defendant stands convicted may be, he was at least entitled to a legal trial. This we are convinced he has not had, and not knowing how far, if at all, the erroneous evidence contributed to his conviction, a new trial must be awarded.

Judgment reversed. The clerk will issue the proper order for a return of the prisoner.

MONKS, J., dissents. DOWLING, J., dissents, and will prepare an opinion.

(162 Ind. 464)

JORDAN v. GRAND RAPIDS & I. RY. CO.

(Supreme Court of Indiana. April 8, 1904.)

RAILROADS—INJURY TO TRESPASSERS—MEASURE OF CARE—EVIDENCE.

1. A boy eight years of ago, who climbed on a box car to look at a sale of stock in an adjacent stockyard, was a trespasser.

2. A railroad company is not required, before moving cars standing on a side track, to examine them, to prevent injury to possible trespassers thereon.

3. A railroad company is not liable for injuries to a trespasser unless the injuries are purposely or recklessly inflicted, or it has knowledge of the injured person's danger in time to have prevented the injury.

4. In an action for negligence causing almost instantaneous death, a particular description of the various injuries was properly excluded.

5. In an action against a railroad company, plaintiff alleged that defendant negligently moved certain cars which had been standing on a side track, and on which plaintiff's decedent and other persons were sitting and standing, watching a sale of horses in an adjoining stockyard. *Held*, that evidence that a sale of horses at the same place on a former occasion attracted boys and men to that vicinity was not admissible to show that the railway company had notice that any one was on the cars.

6. In an action for negligence causing death of plaintiff's infant son, in which the evidence did not show liability on the part of defendant, the exclusion of evidence of plaintiff's occupation and the amount of his property was harmless.

¶ 3. See Railroads, vol. 41, Cent. Dig. §§ 1238, 1261.

Appeal from Circuit Court, Jay County; John M. Smith, Judge.

Action by John Jordan against the Grand Rapids & Indiana Railway Company. From a judgment for defendant, plaintiff appealed to the Appellate Court, from whence the cause was transferred to this court, under Acts 1901, p. 590, c. 259 (Burns' Ann. St. 1901, § 1337u). Affirmed.

McGriff & Bergman, for appellant. Zollars & Zollars, for appellee.

DOWLING, J. The complaint in this case was in two paragraphs—the first averring that the appellee willfully, purposely, and intentionally inflicted fatal injuries upon the infant son of the appellant, by suddenly attaching a locomotive to two cars standing on a siding, on one of which appellant's son, a child eight years of age, with the knowledge of the appellee, its agents and employés, was sitting or standing, and, without warning, putting the same in motion, thereby causing the child to leap or fall in an attempt to escape therefrom; and the second alleging that the child was killed by the negligence of the appellee, its agents and employés, in so attaching the locomotive and suddenly starting the cars without warning the child, or giving him an opportunity to escape from the car. The cause was tried by a jury, and, at the conclusion of the evidence for the plaintiff, the court gave a peremptory instruction for a verdict for the defendant, which was thereupon returned. Over a motion for a new trial, judgment was rendered for the defendant. The error assigned is the ruling upon the motion for a new trial. The alleged insufficiency of the evidence to sustain the verdict, the exclusion of certain evidence offered by the appellant, and the giving of the peremptory instruction, were the reasons for which a new trial was demanded.

The facts material to a decision of the questions before us were these: On the day of the accident, the appellee owned, and for some time before that had operated, on its own land, a main railroad track, two side tracks, one of which was on the east side of the main track, and the other on the west side, all lying near together, and also a spur track running from the southwest end of the east side track, in a southwesterly direction, to the property of the Haynes Milling Company. Appellee also owned certain lots inclosed by high board fences, adjacent to its main track and side tracks, and about five feet from the east track, used as stockyards, in which horses and other domestic animals were temporarily kept for shipment, delivery, or sale. On September 2, 1901, the day of the accident, after advertisement by posting, a public sale of wild horses from the West took place at these stockyards, and the lassoing, capture, and management of the animals attracted some 75 or more persons, who stood or sat on cars on appellee's tracks, watching the men and horses. Among these spectators were several young boys. These persons could have been seen by the employés of the appellee while they were switching cars. Appellant's son, a boy eight years old, small in size, but of ordinary intelligence, strength, and activity, was among them. With some 15 or 20 other men and boys, to obtain a better view of the yards, he climbed to the top of an empty box car standing on the side track near the sheds in the stockyards, and overlooking them, and sat down on the roof of the car. The car was not attached to a locomotive, but, with two or three other cars, had been in the same place for several days. While these cars were so standing on the side track, persons in charge of a locomotive engaged in switching cars at this point, and probably in the employment of appellee, caused the said engine to be run along and over the said main track, and near the place where the said sale was in progress, in full view of said place and of the persons on and about the cars who were watching the men and animals in the stockyards. Shortly afterwards, during the same morning, the persons in charge of the said locomotive ran it upon the said east side track, and coupled it to the empty box cars on which the said men and boys, including appellant's son, were standing or sitting, without any previous notice of their intention to do so. When the engine approached the cars, some one shouted to the persons on the cars that the locomotive was coming, and that they had better get off. The engine was in full view of the men and boys on the cars, and was making considerable noise, puffing steam and running over switches. When the coupling took place, the men and boys ran northward on the cars, and tried to get off. Some of them jumped on the stock sheds, a few children were taken off by their parents, and others climbed down. Appellant's son, who was on the third car from the engine, and another boy on the second car, were unable to get off, because of the number of persons who were jumping and climbing off. The former arose and stood on the top of the car some four or five feet from its north end, and acted as if he intended to climb down, but fell off between the cars, and was run over and killed. The train was moving slowly, and he fell at the moment when the engine was stopped, and the cars "jarred back." He was shaken off. The other lad descended the car ladder and reached the ground in safety. While the switching was going on, the conductor of the switching train was on the ground, and stood for several minutes near the corner of the stock sheds, watching the men and horses in the yards. He uncoupled one of the cars while the engine and its crew were switching on those tracks.

Counsel for appellant insist upon two main propositions: (1) That it appears from the evidence that the acts of the employés of the appellee which caused the death of appellant's son were done under such circumstances as evinced a reckless disregard for the safety of the child, and a willingness to inflict the injury, and therefore that the injury was a willful and an intentional one, for which the appellant was entitled to recover, even if the child was a trespasser on appellee's cars, and was guilty of contributory negligence; and (2) that the injury to and killing of the child were caused by the negligence of the appellee's employés in failing to warn the child of his danger when the engine was coupled to the standing cars, and to give him time to escape, the boy being of tender years and incapable of contributory fault.

It is manifest that the boy, although an infant in years, was a trespasser. Udell v. Citizens' Street R. Co., 152 Ind. 507, 513, 52 N. E. 799, 71 Am. St. Rep. 336. It cannot be said that he was upon the top of the empty box car by the invitation or permission of the railroad company. There was no proof that the appellee gave any invitation or license, express or implied, to any one to get upon its cars for the purpose of looking over the fences and watching the men and animals in the stockyards. The sales took place inside the yards, and the persons attending them for the purpose of examining the horses or purchasing them were not outside the yards, nor on the tops of the cars. The men and boys on the cars were merely idle spectators, gathered by chance, and sustaining no relation to the railroad company except that of trespassers upon its property. It was not proved that the employés of the appellee knew or had reason to believe that any person remained on the cars after the coupling to the locomotive took place. The law did not require them to search the cars for trespassers before moving them. Udell v. Citizens' Street R. Co., supra. The appellee, by its switching crew, was engaged in its proper and necessary business, which required that cars should be moved from point to point on its tracks with greater or less celerity. The lives of scores of travelers might be jeoparded by delay in getting cars off of sidings, and in failing to clear the main track of freight or other trains or cars, and rapidity in the performance of such work did not constitute negligence. The circumstances were not such as to authorize the inference that the trainmen must have seen and known that the child was in a situation of peril. All the cases hold that, in order to render a defendant liable for an injury to a mere trespasser, he must have had knowledge of the situation of the trespasser in time to have prevented the injury, or that the injury was purposely or recklessly inflicted. Louisville, N. A. & Erie Ry. Co. v. Bryan, 107 Ind. 51, 7 N. E. 807; Indianapolis, P. & C. R. Co. v. Pitzer, 109 Ind. 179, 6 N. E. 310, 10 N. E. 70, 58 Am. Rep. 387; Krenzer v. Pittsburg Ry. Co., 151 Ind. 587, 43 N. E. 649, 52 N. E. 220, 68 Am. St. Rep. 252; Palmer v. The Chicago, etc., R. Co., 112 Ind. 250, 14 N. E. 70, and cases cited. The engine was in plain view of all the persons on the cars as it approached, and it was making a noise by puffing steam and by running over switches. Before it reached the cars near the stockyards, the men and boys on the cars were warned by a volunteer that it was coming, and were admonished to get off the cars. All did so except David Ray Jordan and Glen Kinsey, two small boys. After the coupling was made, the train moved off slowly, and one of the boys climbed down the car ladder in safety. Appellant's son was about to do the same thing, when the sudden stopping of the train caused him to fall off. The evidence does not show that the engineer and the other persons in charge of the train evidenced any disregard for the safety of the child, either in making the coupling, or in moving or in stopping the train. The child was sitting on the top of the third car back from the engine. The duty of the engineer and fireman required them to look forward along the track. Pittsburgh, etc., Ry. Co. v. Fraze, 150 Ind. 576, 50 N. E. 576, 65 Am. St. Rep. 377. It does not appear that they could have seen the boy if they had looked back over the train. The evidence fell far short of proving an intentional injury, or of establishing the fact of such a reckless disregard of the safety of the child as amounted to a willingness to injure him. Palmer v. The Chicago, etc., Ry. Co., 112 Ind. 250, 14 N. E. 70; Louisville, etc., Ry. Co. v. Bryan, 107 Ind. 51, 7 N. E. 807; Cooley on Torts, 674; Terre Haute, etc., R. Co. v. Graham, 95 Ind. 286, 48 Am. Rep. 719. It is equally clear, for the reasons already given, that the appellee was not guilty of actionable negligence in failing to warn the child that the locomotive was about to be attached and the cars moved. The evidence was insufficient to charge the appellee with knowledge, express or implied, of the presence of the child on the car and in a place of danger. If the boy had been seen by the engineer or train crew on the top of the car before the train started, or while it was running, a different question would have been presented. But in the absence of proof that they did see him, or that they ought to have looked, and could have discovered him if they had done so, the appellee could not be held responsible for the accident.

2. The death of the child was almost instantaneous, and was caused by his fall from the top of the box car under the wheels of the moving train. A particular description of the various injuries he received was not material, and the evidence of these injuries was properly excluded.

3. The court did not err in refusing to admit evidence of a sale of horses at the appellee's stockyards on a former occasion which had the effect of attracting boys and men to that vicinity. Such evidence did not prove that the appellee invited or expected trespassers on its property, nor did a single occurrence of this character require the appellee to anticipate that its cars would be occupied by sightseers, and that its ordinary business of moving its cars and trains on its tracks in that vicinity could not be carried on without special warnings to persons who might congregate outside of the stock yards.

4. As the facts proved did not make the appellee liable for the death of appellant's son, the refusal of the court to admit evidence of the occupation of the appellant and the value of his property, even if erroneous, was harmless.

Giving to the evidence for the appellant its full legal effect, and allowing every reasonable inference from the facts proved, we are of the opinion that it failed to establish the allegations of either paragraph of the complaint, and that it would not have supported a verdict in his favor. Had such a verdict been returned, it would have been the duty of the court to have sustained a motion by the appellee for a new trial on the ground of the insufficiency of the evidence. In view of the failure of the proof to support the complaint, the direction of the court to the jury to return a verdict for the defendant was necessary and proper.

Judgment affirmed.

(162 Ind. 442)

QUINN v. CHICAGO & E. R. CO.

(Supreme Court of Indiana. April 6, 1904.)

RAILROADS—CROSSING—INJURIES—CONTRIBUTORY NEGLIGENCE—LOOK AND LISTEN.

1. Railroad crossings are places of extraordinary danger, in passing over which all persons competent to exercise care for their protection and safety are required by law to use their faculties of sight and hearing, when such use is possible, and to act upon the presumption that engines or trains may be expected to pass at any moment.

2. The rule is without exception that, where an injury is not willfully inflicted, the injured person must himself be without fault contributing to the accident, in order to hold the one inflicting the injury liable.

3. A pedestrian who stood on or near a railroad track at a crossing at which there were two or more tracks, and, while awaiting the passing of a train on one of the other tracks, was struck by another train moving toward the crossing on the track upon or near which he was standing, and which, while in plain view, he failed to observe, although he had ample time to do so, because of watching the movements of

the other train, and of the fact that the air was full of dust, was guilty of such contributory negligence as to preclude a recovery for his injuries.

Appeal from Circuit Court, Jay County; John M. Smith, Judge.

Action by Barton W. Quinn, administrator of the estate of Robert A. Boblett, deceased, against the Chicago & Erie Railroad Company. From a judgment for defendant, plaintiff appeals. Transferred from the Appellate Court under Burns' Ann. St. 1901, § 1337o. Affirmed.

D. B. Ninde, D. B. Erwin, and Headington & Whiteman, for appellant. W. O. Johnson, Adair & La Follette, A. P. Beatty, and L. J. Hackney, for appellee.

DOWLING, J. This action was brought by the administrator of the estate of Robert A. Boblett, deceased, against the Chicago & Erie Railroad Company, to recover damages on account of injuries resulting in the death of Boblett, alleged to have been caused by the negligence of the railroad company. The complaint was in a single paragraph, and the answer a general denial. The cause was tried by a jury, who returned a general verdict for the plaintiff, with answers to numerous questions of fact. The court sustained defendant's motion for judgment in its favor on the answers of the jury to the questions submitted to them. The plaintiff appeals, and the ruling on the motion for judgment is the error assigned.

Omitting its formal parts, the complaint stated the following facts: On August 5, 1899, and for more than one year previous to that date, the appellee owned and operated a line of railroad extending from Chicago, Ill., to and through Decatur, Ind. Said railroad passed through the city of Decatur from east to west, intersecting a public street of said city running from north to south, and known as "Third Street." In addition to its main track so intersecting said street, the appellee maintained a side track on the south side of the main track, and parallel with it, running across said street eastward to appellee's freighthouse in said city. On said day, while appellant's decedent was passing northward along the sidewalk on the west side of said Third street, and south of said side track, a train of freight cars, with an engine attached to the east or far end of said train, was standing on said side track east of said Third street, and 10 feet distant therefrom. Said train was standing still, without sign or signal that it would be moved, except upon due notice to passers-by. As the decedent approached the said crossing, he carefully watched for dangers which might arise from moving trains upon said railroad, and took notice of said train so standing on said side track. When he was about to step upon said track, appellant's east-bound freight train approached said crossing from the west, and the decedent then and there stopped to await the passing of said through freight train on said main track. While he was waiting for the passing of said train, appellee's servants negligently, and without notice or warning to the decedent by bell or whistle or otherwise, moved the said freight train before that standing on said side track. By reason of the passing of said freight train on the main track, and the noise and dust occasioned thereby, the decedent was unable, by the exercise of the utmost care and diligence, to hear or become aware of the approach of said freight train on said side track, and he had no knowledge of its approach. In consequence of the negligence of the appellee in failing to warn him of the approach of said train on said side track, the decedent was struck by the west end of said train, and sustained injuries from which he died on the same day. Said injuries were occasioned entirely by the negligence of the appellee, and without fault on the part of the decedent.

The answers of the jury to the questions submitted to them established these facts: Third street was one of the public streets of the city of Decatur, and was 60 feet wide. Two tracks of the appellee's railroad, described as the main track and the side track, crossed Third street at right angles. On August 5, 1899, between 10 and 11 o'clock in the forenoon, the day being clear, the decedent came along Third street, carrying a basket of clothes on his right shoulder, and approached the tracks. He was acquainted with the railroad crossing at Third street, and possessed ordinary intelligence. His eyesight and hearing were good. When he arrived at the crossing, a through freight train on the main track was moving toward Third street. When he was from 60 to 80 feet south of the side track, appellee's freight engine, with two loaded cars, went east on the side track, and, when he reached the crossing at Third street, this engine and these cars were standing still near Winchester street, which was about 315 feet east of Third street. The engine and two cars were then from 250 to 260 feet east of the crossing. The east end of that portion of the train on the side track which had been cut off from the two cars was about 600 feet westward from the crossing. The decedent stopped near the south rail of the side track, and remained on or near the track about two minutes, watching the through freight train on the main track, which passed in front of him, and only a few feet away, at a speed of from eight to ten miles per hour. No obstruction prevented him from seeing the engine and two cars on the side track, and, if he had looked eastward, he could have seen them when they were standing still, or after they started westward, when they were approaching him. While decedent's attention was directed to the train on the main track, the local freight engine and the two cars were run back westward at a speed of about four miles per hour, and struck the decedent while he was standing on or near the side track.

Counsel for appellant say in their brief: "These findings, taken in connection with the allegations of the complaint and the evidence which could have been introduced under the issues as joined, raise the flat and simple question whether there can be a recovery when a foot traveler on a public street, approaching a railroad crossing where there are two tracks, sees a train standing motionless on the track nearest him, and goes upon or near that track, and stands there, awaiting the passing of a train upon the further track, to which his attention is directed, and while so standing, with his attention directed to the passing train, is struck by the train upon the first track backing noiselessly down upon him, without signal or warning of any kind being given him of its approach."

The effect of the general verdict is that the railroad company was negligent in moving its train westward on the side track, and that no signal of the starting or approach of said train was given by the ringing of the bell, the sounding of the whistle, or otherwise. The only question is whether negligence on the part of the decedent contributed to produce the injury complained of. In other words, do the answers of the jury show that, as a matter of law, the decedent himself was negligent, and that his want of care for his own safety was one of the causes of the accident and injury?

Railroad crossings on streets and highways have always been recognized as places of extraordinary danger, and, when passing over the intersecting tracks, all persons competent to exercise care for their own protection and safety are required by the law to use their faculties of sight and hearing, when such use is possible, and to act upon the presumption that engines or trains may be expected to pass in either direction at any moment. It is also a matter of common knowledge that trains are often moved backward along the track, and that when running slowly they make but little noise. The place of danger at a street crossing is upon the track, and within a short distance outside the rails. If a traveler voluntarily or without reasonable cause stops on the track, or so near it as to expose himself to injury by passing trains, and, while in such a position of danger, fails to look in both directions and to listen for the noises which ordinarily indicate the approach of a train, and is struck by a locomotive or car negligently run upon the track, his own want of care must be held to be one of the causes of the accident, and there can be no recovery for the injury. In this state the rule is without exception, where the injury is not willfully inflicted, that the injured person must himself be without fault contributing to the production of the accident, if the defendant is to be held liable. The Bellefontaine Ry. Co. v. Hunter, Adm'r, 33 Ind. 335, 356-306, 5 Am. Rep. 201; The Ohio, etc., Ry. Co. v. Hill, Adm'r, 117 Ind. 56, 18 N. E. 461; Chicago, etc., Ry. Co. v. Hedges, Adm'r, 118 Ind. 5, 20 N. E. 530; The Pennsylvania Co. v. Meyers, Adm'x, 136 Ind. 242, 36 N. E. 32; Morford v. Chicago, etc., Ry. Co., 158 Ind. 494, 498, 499, 63 N. E. 857; Baltimore, etc. R. Co., v. Talmage, 15 Ind. App. 203, 43 N. E. 1019; Smith v. Wabash R. Co., 141 Ind. 92, 40 N. E. 270; Pittsburgh R. Co. v. Fraze, 150 Ind. 576, 50 N. E. 576, 65 Am. St. Rep. 377.

In the present case the tracks of the appellee were straight, and the view from the point where the decedent stood was unobstructed for more than 300 feet eastward, and upwards of 600 feet westward. While standing still, the western end of the train which afterwards struck the decedent was about 250 feet eastward from him, and was in plain view all the time. When it started toward him, at a speed of four or five miles per hour, if the decedent had looked in its direction, he must have seen it before it reached Third street, and ample time would have been afforded him to get off the track. The circumstance that his attention was directed to a train passing on the north track constituted no excuse for his failure to observe the train approaching him on the south track, nor for his negligence in standing upon the south track, or very near to it. If the movement of the train on the north track filled the air with dust, thereby obscuring the view up and down the south track, this was but an additional reason for the exercise of greater vigilance on the part of the decedent. Oleson v. Lake Shore, etc., R. Co., 143 Ind. 405, 42 N. E. 736, 32 L. R. A. 149; Cincinnati R. Co. v. Duncan, 143 Ind. 524, 42 N. E. 37. If this condition existed, common prudence required that the decedent should get off of and away from the track. The decedent had a basket of clothing on his right shoulder, and this probably prevented him from seeing the train as it came toward him. Had he turned his face eastward, or if he had put the basket down when he went upon the track, he must have discovered the coming train, and could instantly have stepped aside into a place of safety. He failed to take this natural and reasonable precaution, and his want of care for his own safety certainly contributed in some degree, and, as we think, in a very considerable degree, to occasion the accident and injury.

The answers of the jury established the fact of contributory negligence on the part of the decedent. This being sò, there could be no recovery by the plaintiff, and the court did not err in rendering judgment for the defendant. Judgment affirmed.

(162 Ind. 460)

LAFAYETTE & I. RAPID RY. CO. v. BUTNER et al.

(Supreme Court of Indiana. April 8, 1904.)

RAILROADS—CONDEMNATION PROCEEDINGS—RIGHT OF APPEAL.

1. No appeal lies from an order of the circuit court denying an application for the appointment of appraisers in a proceeding to condemn lands for the purpose of a right of way, instituted under Burns' Ann. St. 1901, § 5160, providing for the condemnation of land for railroad purposes.

Appeal from Circuit Court, Boone County; James L. Clark, Special Judge.

Proceeding by the Lafayette & Indianapolis Rapid Railway Company against Charles F. Butner and others to condemn lands for railroad right of way. From an order denying the application of the railway company for the appointment of appraisers, it appeals. Transferred from Appellate Court under section 1337u, Burns' Ann. St. 1901. Appeal dismissed.

O. B. Jameson, Chas. M. Zion, and Geo. P. Haywood, for appellant. Pierre Gray and S. M. Ralston, for appellees.

GILLETT, C. J. This was a proceeding instituted under section 5160, Burns' Ann. St. 1901, by the above-named company, to condemn certain lands for the purposes of a right of way. The Boone circuit court permitted issues of fact to be framed upon the instrument of appropriation, and, after hearing evidence as to such issues, entered an order refusing to appoint appraisers. From such order said company has attempted to appeal to the Appellate Court. The threshold question in this case is whether we have any jurisdiction over this proceeding, or, in other words, whether such an appeal will lie. The statute under which the proceeding was had makes no provision for an appeal from such an order. The only provision made for an appeal is to a trial court, and such appeal cannot be taken until after the award has been made. In so far as final judgments under the Civil Code are concerned, appeals can only be taken from the judgments of "circuit courts and superior courts." Section 644, Burns' Ann. St. 1901. A subsequent section of the Civil Code provides for appeals from certain interlocutory orders made by a court or judge (section 658, Burns' Ann. St. 1901), but appeals in instances like the present are not thereby authorized. Other express provisions for appeals may be found in the statutes, but such provisions do not affect the pending question. Sections 1337a–1337l, Burns' Ann. St. 1901, and Acts 1903, p. 280, c. 156, relative to the jurisdiction of this court and of the Appellate Court, are but supplemental to the express provisions for appeal which the statutes contain. It will be seen, upon this state of legislation, that, if the proceeding in question can be said to be a civil action at the stage it had reached below, the right of appeal would depend upon the accidental circumstance as to whether the application for the appointment of appraisers was denied in term time or in vacation. We do not believe that this was the purpose of the General Assembly, and we are therefore at once led to doubt whether an appeal is authorized from an order denying an application for the appointment of appraisers.

But an even more substantial reason urges us to the conclusion that such an appeal will not lie. The statute which authorizes the condemnation of land for railroad purposes does not relate to actions according to the course of the common law, but relates to special proceedings more nearly comparable to inquests than to civil actions. The very provision of the statute as to the taking of an appeal by exceptions to the award impliedly forbids a resort to any other statute for authority to appeal during the preliminary stages of the proceeding. The power of eminent domain inheres in sovereignty, and, in the division of powers, falls within the domain of the legislative authority. The mode of exercising the right is for the Legislature, in the absence of constitutional restraints. Secombe v. Milwaukee, etc., R. Co., 23 Wall. 108, 23 L. Ed. 67; Anderson v. Caldwell, 91 Ind. 451, 455, 46 Am. Rep. 613. The tribunal which the state provides to assess the damages must be impartial, but there is no requirement that the tribunal should be a court. It is proper, however, to provide for a judicial examination into the question as to whether the conditions which are required to exist to warrant the appropriation have been observed. Boom Co. v. Patterson, 98 U. S. 403, 25 L. Ed. 206; Searl v. School Dist., 124 U. S. 197, 8 Sup. Ct. 460, 31 L. Ed. 415.

Whether the statute we are considering contemplates that the court or judge shall permit issues to be made and tried before the appointment of appraisers, we need not and do not determine. Our present purpose is to evince the proposition that the proceedings are special at the stage indicated, and that therefore a right of appeal is not to be implied from the general language of the Code relative to such right.

Proceedings of this character may, upon appeal from the award, become so far analogous to civil actions as to be governed by the provisions of the Code in regard to the procedure; but they are not civil actions in their earlier stages, but are statutory proceedings of a special nature. Lake Shore, etc., R. Co. v. Cincinnati, etc., R. Co., 116 Ind. 578, 19 N. E. 440. In 2 Cyc. 540, it is stated: "It is a well-settled rule in most jurisdictions that where a tribunal exercises a special, limited jurisdiction, conferred by statute, and in which the proceeding is not according to the course of the common law, no appeal lies from its action therein, unless expressly provided by statute." In holding that an appeal would not lie to the circuit court from an order of a board of county commissioners in a proceeding to relocate a county seat, this court, in a comparatively early case, said: "The ground upon which our ruling is based is that this is a special proceeding, for a special purpose, based upon a special statute, which gives no right of appeal, and, being a special proceeding, it cannot be governed by the general statute, and that consequently no right of appeal exists." Bosley v. Ackiemire, 39 Ind. 536. See, also, Board Com'rs Scott Co. v. Smith, 40 Ind. 61; Cole v. Howard, 56 Ind. 330; Board Com'rs Jackson Co. v. State ex rel., 147 Ind. 476, 46 N. E. 908; French v. Lighty, 9 Ind. 475. There are a number of authorities involving condemnation proceedings which support the view that an appeal is unauthorized in an instance of this kind. In Wilmington, etc., R. Co. v. Condon, 8 Gill & J. 443, it was said: "There is no appeal expressly given to the Court of Appeals under the act of Assembly investing the county court with the power of reviewing and confirming or setting aside inquisitions like the present. From the nature and course of their proceedings, this power of review is a fit subject for litigation in a county court, but is wholly inappropriate to the jurisdiction of this court. It is a special, limited jurisdiction given to the county court, from the decision of which no appeal lies to any other tribunal." In New York, etc., R. Co. v. Marvin, 11 N. Y. 276, the question was presented as to the right to appeal to the Court of Appeals from an order of the Supreme Court confirming the report of commissioners in a condemnation case. The Code of New York allowed an appeal from "a final order affecting a substantial right made in a special proceeding," but it was held in the case mentioned that an appeal would not lie under said statute, as the railroad act of the state had created an entire system for ascertaining the value of lands so taken. In dismissing the appeal, the court said: "The whole proceeding is a special creation of the statute, and seems designed to form a complete system of itself, entirely independent of the general provision of the statute authorizing appeals to this court." See, also, Valentine v. City of Boston, 20 Pick. 201; Norfolk, etc., R. Co. v. Ely, 95 N. C. 77; Brown v. Phila., etc., R. Co., 58 Md. 539; Kundinger v. City of Saginaw, 59 Mich. 355, 26 N. W. 634; McNamara v. Minn. Cent. R. Co., 12 Minn. 388 (Gil. 269); Conter v. St. Paul, etc., R. Co., 24 Minn. 313; State v. Rapp, 39 Minn. 65, 38 N. W. 926; Hartley v. Keokuk, etc., R. Co., 85 Iowa, 455, 52 N. W. 352; Raleigh, etc., R. Co. v. Jones, 23 N. C. 24.

There is no right of appeal except as it is granted by statute. Lake Erie, etc., R. Co. v. Watkins, 157 Ind. 600, 62 N. E. 443. Our conclusion is that provision has not been made for an appeal as has been here attempted.

Appeal dismissed.

(162 Ind. 428)

CHICAGO, I. & L. RY. CO. v. TOWN OF SALEM.

(Supreme Court of Indiana. April 5, 1904.)

JURISDICTION—VIOLATION OF TOWN ORDINANCE—APPEAL.

1. Under Burns' Ann. St. 1901, §§ 4346–4346d, constituting the town clerk a court, and giving that court exclusive jurisdiction of all prosecutions for the violation of town ordinances, the circuit court has no jurisdiction of an action for the violation of a town ordinance.

2. Where the lower court had no jurisdiction of an action to recover a penalty under a town ordinance, the court on appeal had no power to determine the validity of the ordinance.

Appeal from Circuit Court, Orange County; Thos. B. Buskirk, Judge.

Action by the town of Salem against the Chicago, Indianapolis & Louisville Railway Company. From a judgment for plaintiff, defendant appeals. Reversed.

E. C. Field and H. R. Kurrie, for appellant. Mitchell & Mitchell and George H. Hester, for appellee.

MONKS, J. Appellee, in 1902, brought this action against appellant in the Washington circuit court to recover the penalty for an alleged violation of an ordinance of said town. The venue of said cause was changed to the court below, where appellant filed a motion to dismiss said cause for the reason that the circuit court had no jurisdiction thereof. The court below overruled said motion, to which ruling appellant excepted. A trial of said cause resulted in a finding and judgment against appellant. The assignment of errors calls in question the action of the court in overruling said motion to dismiss the action and the validity of said ordinance. The Legislature passed an act (Acts 1901, pp. 57, 58, being sections 4346–4346d, Burns' Ann. St. 1901) creating the court of town clerk, and gave said court exclusive jurisdiction of all prosecutions for the violation of the ordinances of the town. Baltimore, etc., R. Co. v. Town of Whiting (Ind. Sup.) 68 N. E. 266. It is evident that after said act took effect the circuit court had no jurisdiction of prosecutions for the violation of town ordinances except when appealed from the judgment of the town clerk to that court. State v. Board, etc., 101 Ind. 69; Board, etc., v. Maxwell, Id. 268. As this is a prosecution for the violation of a town ordinance, the court below erred in overruling said motion to dismiss the same. The court below having no jurisdiction over this cause, it follows that this court has no power on this appeal to determine the validity of said ordinance.

Judgment reversed, with instructions to sustain appellant's motion to dismiss said action for want of jurisdiction over the subject-matter.

(163 Ind. 202)

BOYCE v. TUHEY.[1]

(Supreme Court of Indiana. April 7, 1904.)

MUNICIPAL CORPORATIONS — LOCAL IMPROVEMENTS—SEWERS—MANNER OF CONSTRUCTION —DISCRETION OF COUNCIL—PROCEEDINGS OF COUNCIL — COLLATERAL ATTACK — JURISDICTION.

1. Acts 1889, p. 237, c. 118 (Burns' Ann. St. 1901, § 4288 et seq.), expressly empowers the common councils of cities to order the construction of sewers, and to assess the cost thereof against the lots or parts of real estate benefited thereby.

2. Where a city council adopted, and confirmed an assessment for a sewer, its judgment in the matter, so long as it acted within its jurisdiction, was conclusive on property owners until set aside in some direct proceeding, and was not open to collateral attack unless the defects in the council's proceedings affected its jurisdiction, irrespective of whether the property owner appeared and was accorded the hearing before a committee and the council to which he was entitled by Burns' Ann. St. 1901, § 4204, or not.

3. Under Acts 1889, p. 237, c. 118 (Burns' Ann. St. 1901, § 4288 et seq.), empowering city councils to order the construction of sewers, and to assess the cost thereof against property benefited, a city council is invested with authority in its discretion to cause sewers to be constructed with all useful appurtenances, such as manholes, subsoil drains, flushing tanks, outlets, connections with the premises of property owners, service pipes, etc., and the fact that connections with private premises are provided for as appurtenant to the sewer does not invalidate the council's action or render the improvement a private one.

4. Questions as to the method to be adopted for connecting sewers with the premises of property owners are matters largely within the discretion of the city council, which discretion will not be judicially reviewed when properly exercised.

Appeal from Circuit Court, Delaware County; J. G. Lefler, Judge.

Action by Edward Tuhey against James Boyce. From a judgment for plaintiff, defendant appeals. Affirmed.

C. L. Medsker, for appellant. Warner & Brady, for appellee.

JORDAN, J. Appellee sued appellant to foreclose a lien on certain described real estate, arising out of the assessment of benefits by reason of the construction of a sewer in the city of Muncie, Delaware county, Ind.

The complaint contains but one paragraph, and alleges facts, in substance, as follow: At a regular meeting of the common council of the city of Muncie, held July 27, 1891, said council adopted, by a vote of three-fourths of all its members, a resolution declaring it necessary to construct a sewer in said city on Main street, from Madison street east to Beacon street. The sewer was to be constructed of vitrified sewer pipe, of the diameter of 12 inches, with a subsoil drain pipe 4 inches in diameter, and with the necessary house connections and other appurtenances. The resolution declared that the entire cost thereof should be assessed against and collected from the lands and lots benefited thereby. The 24th day of August, 1891, was fixed as the day upon which objections might be made to the construction of said improvement. The clerk was directed to give the required notice of the time and place when such objections would be heard. This notice appears to have been duly given by publication in the Muncie Daily Times. It appears that at the time fixed the council heard the objections, and thereafter an ordinance was introduced ordering the construction of said sewer. On the 31st day of August, 1891, at a regular meeting of the common council, this ordinance was passed and adopted by a vote of five-sixths of all the members composing the council. By this ordinance, among other things, it was ordered and directed that the sewer should be denominated "Main Street Sewer No. 1," and should be constructed according to the plans and specifications therefor on file in the office of the civil engineer of said city, including the necessary subsoil drains, manholes, lampholes, flushing tanks, specials, catch-basins, and house connections, and that the cost arising out of the construction of the sewer should be assessed against and collected from the owners of the lands and lots benefited thereby.

The proper notice for receiving bids and letting the contract for the construction of the improvement was ordered to be given. This notice is shown to have been given. On the 28th day of September, 1891, the day fixed for letting said contract, the firm of Kinsey & Tuhey, composed of Thomas W. Kinsey and the appellee herein, submitted a bid to the council for the construction of the sewer. By this bid they offered and proposed to construct the sewer for certain specified prices, for furnishing and laying pipes, etc., among which it was specified for furnishing and laying 4-inch pipe for house service or connections, including detachable covers and cement joint, per lineal foot, 15 cents. Other prices in regard to excavations, manholes, lampholes, flushing tanks, etc., were specified and set forth in this bid, which is shown to have been the lowest and best bid received for the construction of said sewer. This bid was accepted by the council, and thereafter, on the 9th day of October, 1891, it entered into a written contract with the said Kinsey & Tuhey for the construction of the sewer, in conformity with the resolution, ordinance, plans, and specifications.

It is disclosed that on the 6th day of September, 1892, the sewer was completed in accordance with said contract, and was so reported to the common council, and the improvement was by it accepted as completed. It is further shown that the city engineer filed his final report and estimate of the total

[1] Rehearing denied.

cost of the sewer, the entire length of which was 1,928 feet, and the total cost for the construction thereof was $3,795.20. In this report a description of each lot, part of lot, parcel of ground, or real estate benefited by the construction of the sewer was given, together with the special benefits derived, and which should be assessed against each lot, part of lot, or part of ground described. The amount of said special benefits as estimated against the real estate of appellant in said report was $439.29. After the filing of this report the matter was referred by the council to its committee of sewers and drains, which committee was ordered to meet on the 23d day of September, 1892, at 10 o'clock a. m., at which time it was ordered a hearing should be had upon said report and estimate of benefits. Due notice as required by the statute was given in respect to the time and place of the meeting of said committee, before which all persons aggrieved were to be accorded a hearing. On September 26, 1892, the committee made its report to the common council, to the effect that the estimates made in the engineer's report were full and correct, and that the said sewer had been constructed according to contract, and recommended therein that the report and estimate of benefits made by the engineer be adopted and confirmed by the common council. Thereupon the said council accepted and adopted said report, and assessed the benefits therein set forth upon the real estate therein described. All of which appears to have been done by a resolution adopted by the council, setting forth and describing the real estate assessed, etc. Appellant was the owner of the real estate described and assessed as benefited by the said improvement to the amount of $439.20, and this amount is the assessment involved in this case.

In 1893 said Thomas W. Kinsey assigned and transferred to appellee all of his interest and right in and to the assessment in suit, and appellee is the sole owner thereof. On the 14th day of February, 1900, appellee notified appellant and others, against whose property assessments had been made, that the same were due and payable to him, and, if not paid on or before the 22d day of that month, suit would be commenced to collect them. In fact, it may be said that the complaint discloses that all of the necessary steps prescribed by the statute for the construction of the improvement in question were properly taken by the common council. The prayer of the complaint is that the lien arising out of said assessment be declared and established, and that the same be foreclosed, with interest and attorney's fees, etc. The action was commenced on the 10th day of March, 1900.

Appellant unsuccessfully moved the court to require the plaintiff to make his complaint more specific by separating the total amount of assessments made against appellant's property into two parts, so as to show (1) the amount assessed for the cost of the construction of the sewer; (2) the amount assessed for the cost of house connections. Appellant filed an answer consisting of 20 paragraphs, the first of which was a general denial. This was subsequently withdrawn. By the second paragraph he set up as a defense that the action had not accrued within six years. The substance of the third paragraph is that the plaintiff's cause of action was for work and labor done in the construction of the sewer named in the complaint, and for house connections; that the cost of constructing these connections is included in and constitutes a part of the assessment in suit. It is alleged that the defendant is unable to state, and does not know, the amount of the cost of the house connections, and that said connections were no part of the sewer; that they were simply private connections, and for the private use of persons who were supposed to desire the use thereof; that the connections were not used by appellant, and were made over his objection and remonstrance, and, so far as plaintiff's cause of action is based thereon, the same did not accrue within six years before the commencement of this action. The fourth paragraph alleges that the common council of the city of Muncie declared by resolution that it was necessary to construct the sewer mentioned in the complaint, with house connections; that these connections were ordered to be constructed of 4-inch sewer pipe, this pipe was to be placed in the street, and was to extend from the sewer to a point 12 inches beyond the curb line in front of each piece of property or division thereof. It is further alleged that these house connections were solely for the private use of the property owners along the line of the sewer for house sewage, and were no part of the sewer. The defendant, it is alleged, remonstrated in writing against the construction of the sewer as ordered; that the assessment sued on is for work done in the construction of the sewer and said house connections. It is averred that the council had no power, right, or authority to construct said connections as a part of the sewer, and that therefore the resolution, ordinance, assessment, and contract as set out in the complaint are all illegal and void. Each of the other paragraphs of the answer under the facts therein alleged proceeds upon the theory that the common council had no power or authority to provide for constructing the sewer with house connections.

Appellee successfully demurred to each of the paragraphs of the answer. Upon the court's sustaining the demurrer to these paragraphs, appellant refused to further plead, but elected to abide by the rulings of the court on the demurrer. Thereupon the court rendered judgment in favor of the appellee, foreclosing the lien, etc. From this judgment appellant appeals. The validity of the ordinance being in question, the jurisdiction is lodged in this court.

The insufficiency of the complaint is assailed for the first time under the assignment of errors. The other alleged errors are predicated on the rulings of the court in denying the motion to make the complaint more specific, and in sustaining the demurrer to each of the paragraphs of the answer.

It is insisted by counsel for appellant that the court erred in overruling the motion to make the complaint more specific, for the reason that the pleading disclosed an assessment for two kinds of improvement: First, for the construction of a sewer; second, for the construction of house connections. It is asserted that the first is a public improvement, and the second is but a private improvement. Therefore it is contended that appellant was entitled to be advised by the complaint as to what was the cost alone of the house connections. It is insisted also that the complaint must be held bad under the assignment of error assailing its insufficiency of facts, for the reason that it shows that the resolution, ordinance, and contract therein mentioned were to construct a sewer and house connections. The propositions discussed by appellant's counsel and relied on for reversal are each advanced upon the theory that the common council of the city of Muncie had no power or authority under the law to order the construction of the sewer in controversy with the connections in question. In fact, it may be said that counsel's contentions are entirely upon the theory or assumption that the connections to the sewer are separate and independent of the principal improvement, and are not appurtenant thereto; that they constitute a private improvement, over which, it is insisted, the council, under the law, had no jurisdiction, and therefore the resolution, ordinance, contract, and assessment made in pursuance thereof are all illegal and void, and open to the collateral attack interposed by the answer.

We do not regard appellant's contentions as well taken, or, in other words, we are satisfied that, under the facts and the law applicable thereto, they are wholly untenable. It is evident, from the steps shown to have been taken by the common council in the construction of the improvement in controversy, that it proceeded under what is known as the "Barrett Law," enacted in 1889. Acts 1889, p. 237, c. 118; section 4288 et seq., Burns' Ann. St. 1901. Under the provisions of this law the common council was expressly empowered to order and cause the construction of sewers, and to assess the cost thereof against the lots or parts of real estate benefited thereby. Sections 4288-4290, 4292-4294, Burns' Ann. St. 1901. It has been settled by the decisions of this court that in actions like the case at bar, to enforce a collection of assessments for public improvements, the property owner will not be permitted to contest or assail such assessments, unless it appears that the proceedings under which the improvement was made were void for want of jurisdiction. In the case of City of Indianapolis v. Holt, 155 Ind. 222, 57 N. E. 966, 988, 1100, the right to contest the assessment was expressly authorized by the statute under which the city was controlled; hence, under the circumstances, that case is not applicable to the question arising in the case at bar. The general rule denying the right of a property owner in an action like this to attack the assessment or contest the enforcement thereof, is based on the fact that such a contest is collateral. The fact that the proceedings may have been erroneous or irregular will not render them open to a collateral assault, unless the defects or irregularities are of such a character as to affect the jurisdiction of the council or other body in ordering the particular improvement. Studabaker v. Studabaker, 152 Ind. 89, 51 N. E. 933, and cases there cited; City of Elkhart v. Wickwire, 121 Ind. 331, 22 N. E. 342; McEneney v. Town of Sullivan, 125 Ind. 407, 25 N. E. 540; De Puy v. City of Wabash, 133 Ind. 336, 32 N. E. 1016; Hibben v. Smith, 158 Ind. 206, 62 N. E. 447. Appellant, by the provisions of section 4294, supra, if aggrieved by his assessment, was entitled to a hearing before the committee and the common council, and the latter was authorized to alter or modify the assessment made against his property. Adams v. City of Shelbyville, 154 Ind. 467, 57 N. E. 114, 49 L. R. A. 797, 77 Am. St. Rep. 484. Whether he appeared before the common council and was accorded a hearing, or not, is, however, immaterial, for it is shown that the council adopted, approved, and confirmed the assessment in controversy, and, so long as it kept within the limits of its jurisdiction under the law, its decision or judgment in the matter, either right or wrong, in the absence of fraud, is conclusive and binding upon him and all other persons concerned, until set aside or annulled in some direct proceeding upon grounds recognized by the law as sufficient for that purpose. Hibben v. Smith, supra.

But counsel for appellant contends that the doctrine of collateral attack cannot be regarded in this case, for the reason that the council has undertaken to construct two improvements, one public and the other private. It is asserted that, so far as house connections were concerned, the common council had no jurisdiction, and therefore its proceedings leading up to the construction of the sewer and the making and confirmation of the assessments are absolutely void. But counsel, in his assertion that two distinct and separate improvements were ordered and constructed by the council, is manifestly mistaken, and is not sustained by the facts in the case. The resolution adopted by the common council declared a necessity for the construction of a 12-inch sewer, "with subsoil drain pipes 4 inches in diameter, and with the necessary house connections and other appurtenances." The ordinance whereby the construction of the sewer was ordered provided that it should be made according to the plans and specifications on file in the office of the city civil engineer, including the proper and necessary subsoil drains, manholes, lampholes, flushing tanks, special, catch-basins, and house connections, and that the cost of the improvement should be assessed against and collected from the lands and lots benefited thereby. The statute, it will be observed, expressly empowers the common council to construct or cause sewers to be constructed. It is true that the statute does not in express language declare that the sewers authorized thereby shall be constructed in any particular manner or with any particular connections. The rule, however, is elementary that the grant of a principal power carries with it by implication all other powers necessary to carry out the principal power conferred, and thereby make effectual and complete whatever is authorized to be done by the principal or general authority granted. Conn v. Board, 151 Ind. 517, 51 N. E. 1062; Studabaker v. Studabaker, supra; 25 Am. & Eng. Ency. of Law (2d Ed.) p. 238. Tested by this rule, the common council, under the general power conferred by the statute to make the improvement in question, was invested with authority within its discretion to cause it to be constructed with any and all appurtenances essential to its usefulness or completion as a whole, or, in other words, all which necessarily conduced to and rendered it serviceable, beneficial, and lasting for the purpose for which it was constructed. Kirkland v. Board, 142 Ind. 123, 41 N. E. 374; Murphy v. City of Peoria, 119 Ill. 509, 9 N. E. 895; Palmer v. City of Danville, 154 Ill. 156, 38 N. E. 1067; Elliott on Roads & Streets (2d Ed.) §§ 461, 505, 563, and 580; Coburn v. Bossert, 13 Ind. App. 359, 40 N. E. 281. Whatever was necessary to make the sewer complete and useful for the purpose for which it was intended was a matter to be determined by the council.

The sewer in question as ordered to be constructed must be considered as a unit or as an entirety, and while it may embrace as parts thereof necessary appurtenances, such as manholes, subsoil drains, flushing tanks, outlets, connections, and service pipes, etc., in order to make it beneficial and useful to the public in general, and also beneficial and useful to the property owners who were assessed for the cost of its construction, nevertheless all such parts or appurtenances thereof united to constitute but a single public improvement. The property owners along the line of the sewer and the vicinity thereof whose property was benefited were, as we may assume, assessed, for its construction, the special benefits inuring to the property by reason of the improvement. Certainly, under the circumstances, they acquired the right to use the sewer for all legitimate or proper purposes, under such reasonable restrictions as might be imposed by the municipal authorities. Elliott on Roads & Streets (2d Ed.) § 471; City of Ft. Wayne v. Coombs, 107 Ind. 75, 7 N. E. 743, 57 Am. Rep. 82. The sewer, as it appears, was not only intended for the use of the city or public in general, but also for the use of property owners along its line or vicinity whose property was specially benefited thereby. The ordinance, in fact, provided that the cost of its construction should be assessed against the lots and lands benefited thereby. The very right to assess property for a public improvement like this is based upon the theory that special benefits will, incidentally, at least, inure to the owners thereof. Zigler v. Menges, 121 Ind. 99, 22 N. E. 782, 16 Am. St. Rep. 357; Barber Asphalt Co. v. Edgerton, 125 Ind. 455, 25 N. E. 436; Elliott on Roads & Streets (2d Ed.) § 22; 10 Am. & Eng. Ency. of Law (2d Ed.) 225. Evidently, under the circumstances, in planning the sewer, it became necessary to make provisions for tapping it, so as to enable property owners assessed to use it as was intended. The common council was therefore necessarily confronted with the question as to the best method to be adopted for such purpose. Possibly the council may have had under consideration the plan of constructing such taps by means of pipes in the shape of a "Y," to be placed and fitted into the sewer at certain intervals, which appears to be the method commonly adopted. It is manifest that to provide for tapping the sewer after its completion by this method would, as argued by appellee, necessarily result from time to time in disturbing the street by digging trenches therein, etc.

The question as to the method to be adopted for connecting the sewer with the premises of property owners was a matter largely within the discretion of the common council, and when such discretion is properly exercised it is not open to judicial review. Coburn v. Bossert, supra; Elliott on Roads & Streets (2d Ed.) § 580; Palmer v. City of Danville, supra; 25 Am. & Eng. Ency. of Law (2d Ed.) 240. The council, it seems, decided that the necessary connections of the sewer for the use of property owners should be provided by means of the pipes as specified. These pipes, as shown, were to be laid wholly within the limits of the street, and were to extend from the sewer to a point 12 inches beyond the curb line. Under the rule heretofore stated, the particular method which should be adopted for the construction of the connections was a matter within the sound discretion of the council, and its decision in the premises is not open to judicial review. The connections in question, as disclosed, were a necessary part of the sewer, and conduced to make it useful and available. Being constructed with the connections, as a part thereof or appurtenant thereto did not in any manner serve to render the sewer a private, instead of a public, improvement, as designed by the law.

We conclude that there is nothing disclosing that the common council was not authorized under the law to order and construct the sewer, with the connections in question as parts thereof. Therefore appellant's contention that the proceedings of the council were illegal and void is not sustained. The six-years statute of limitations set up in the answer did not constitute a bar to this action. It follows that the rulings of the court of which appellant complains present no available error, for the reasons herein stated.

Judgment affirmed.

(162 Ind. 430)

HAMILTON et al. v. HAMILTON.

(Supreme Court of Indiana. April 5, 1904.)

CONTRACTS—SPECIFIC PERFORMANCE—MORTGAGES TO PAY DEBTS—HUSBAND AND WIFE—DEBTS OF HUSBAND—ASSUMPTION BY WIFE—SURETYSHIP—INTEREST.

1. Mere inadequacy of consideration is not of itself sufficient reason for refusing specific performance.

2. A contract by which a wife received certain mill property, was to be saved harmless from a mortgage on property held by her, and was to have a portion of a certain mortgage debt of her husband paid, and in return was to deed certain property to the other party in the contract, and was also to allow a trustee to collect the profits of the mill property to pay certain debts of her husband, and, when she received a deed thereto, was to mortgage such property to the trustee, constituted an entire contract, and the consideration moving to her therein was sufficient to support the undertaking to mortgage the property to pay her husband's debt.

3. The promise of a wife, in a contract in which certain benefits moved to her, to mortgage property, which the contract provided was to be deeded to her, to pay her husband's debts, could be availed of and made the foundation of suit by a surety on one of her husband's debts who had paid the same.

4. A mere option, if founded on a valuable consideration, may be enforced.

5. Where a husband deeded certain property in trust to sell the same, and to pay 12 designated items of indebtedness, and to turn the balance of proceeds of sale over to his wife, the wife, not being a party to the deed, and having no interest in the proceeds until all debts were paid, could not complain of the action of the trustee in paying the debts in an order other than that designated.

6. A wife, who, on a consideration moving to her estate, agrees to execute with her husband a mortgage on her property to pay her husband's debts, is not a surety, but a principal.

7. Where a wife, on a consideration moving to her estate, agreed to execute a mortgage on property to be deeded to her to a trustee to pay her husband's overdue debts, the mortgage would be deemed payable presently.

8. One who was surety on a note of a husband, and who subsequently paid the same, was as to the wife, who, on a consideration moving to her estate, assumed her husband's indebtedness, also a surety, and the note which he paid thus fixed the rate of interest between himself and the wife, under Burns' Ann. St. 1901, § 1233, providing that a surety on a written instrument who pays the same may recover the rate of interest fixed by the instrument.

9. One who refused to execute a mortgage to pay a debt long overdue, in pursuance of a contract so to do, could not complain of a decree charging the indebtedness on the land and ordering a sale thereof.

Appeal from Circuit Court, Whitley County; J. W. Adair, Judge.

Action by Samuel Hamilton against David Hamilton and another. From a judgment for plaintiff, defendants appeal. Affirmed.

Marshall, McNaguy & Clugston, for appellants. A. A. Adams, N. G. Hunter, and Alvah Taylor, for appellee.

GILLETT, C. J. This suit was instituted to establish and enforce a lien against certain real estate belonging to appellant Abigail Hamilton. No further statement concerning the issues need be made, in view of the posture of the case on appeal. Pursuant to request, the trial court filed special findings of fact, together with conclusions of law. There was a judgment in favor of appellee in the sum of $1,103.50 against appellant David, and a decree adjudging that said real estate was subject to a lien on such account, and ordering said real estate sold to pay said amount. The errors assigned question each of the conclusions of law, and also the action of the court in overruling the motion for a new trial.

Stated in form, to some extent condensed, the facts found specially are as follows: November 13, 1888, said David Hamilton, being in failing financial circumstances, executed two deeds. The first deed was to his wife, Abigail Hamilton, and described a number of pieces of property, one of which, characterized in the findings as the "business property," was worth $7,000, and was incumbered by a mortgage for $2,750 and interest. It is found that she paid no consideration for the latter property. The second of said deeds was to appellee and to Levi J. Noftzger, and conveyed 420 acres of land, in trust, to pay out of the proceeds of sales thereof 12 items of indebtedness of the grantor, aggregating $15,650, and the expenses of the trust, and to pay the balance to said Abigail. The grantees mentioned in said deed of trust effected a sale of all of said land, except a tract of 120 acres, and with the proceeds of said sale paid all of said debts, except an amount owing to one James O. Cole, and $3,000 due to one Freiburg, which latter sum was secured by mortgage on said unsold tract of land. The amount due Cole stood seventh in the order of priority fixed in the deed, but the trustees, believing that they would be able to realize enough to pay all of the debts, at the request of said David, applied the money received by them from such sale on other debts mentioned in said deed, with the result that on October 18, 1889, said indebtedness to Cole remained unpaid. On said day said David and appellee, the latter describing himself as "trustee," executed a note in settle-

¶ 1. See Specific Performance, vol. 44, Cent. Dig. § 151.

ment of the amount due Cole, which was then $1,373.42. The note was payable one year after its date. On June 9, 1891, when the affairs of the trust were in the condition above indicated, appellants and one Tyler entered into a contract, by which appellant Abigail was to deed said business property to Tyler, and the latter was to turn over to her his interest in a flour mill, subject to a $750 mortgage. An option of purchase was outstanding on the latter property in favor of certain tenants. By his contract Tyler assigned the contract and lease of his tenants to said Abigail, and covenanted to make her a deed if said tenants did not purchase. Tyler, in addition, was to assume, and agree to save appellants harmless from, the mortgage on said business property, which then amounted to $2,733.55, and he was to pay $1,014.45 in cash, $1,000 of which was to be applied on said Freiburg mortgage. It was further provided in said contract, for the recited purpose of "relieving all of said property from any liabilities which are claimed against said real estate," that one Noftzger be appointed a trustee to receive the proceeds of said option contract and to collect the rents, and he was directed to apply the moneys received by him to pay: (1) The $750 mortgage, (2) the Cole note, (3) taxes which had accrued against said business property, (4) any incumbrance or charge on said business property by reason of any debt of said David which Tyler might be compelled to pay, (5) the expenses of the trust created by said contract and the expenses of said prior trust, and the balance, if any, said trustee was directed to pay to said David. It was further provided that, if said Abigail should receive a deed for said property, she and her husband would execute a mortgage to said trustee to pay the liabilities imposed by the first four of said numbered items. As a part of said transaction, and upon the considerations stated in the contract, the trustees of said former trust deeded said 120 acre tract of land to said Abigail. She accepted said deed and caused it to be recorded, and she accepted also the lease mentioned in said contract. She joined her husband in the execution of a deed to Tyler for said business property. Tyler paid the $1,000 to Freiburg, as had been agreed, and also paid the mortgage on said business property. On October 22, 1893, said tenants having refused to take said mill property, Tyler executed a deed to said Abigail for said property, in which deed it was recited that it was made subject to all of the conditions of said contract between said parties. It is expressly found that she accepted this deed and caused it to be recorded. It was further found that the trustees of said first-mentioned trust duly executed and discharged the same. Appellee was compelled to pay, as surety, $1,103.50 on said Cole note, which payment fully satisfied said note. Noftzger refused to act as trustee under the Tyler contract, and failed, neglected, and refused to make demand of said Abigail that she execute a mortgage as provided in said contract. On or about December, 1893, subsequent to the acceptance of said deed to the mill property, appellee "made and tendered a mortgage to the defendant, and made demand for the execution thereof, to secure the payment and discharge of said Cole debt, so paid by said Samuel, in pursuance of said contract sued upon, which demand was refused."

The eleventh and seventeenth findings of the court are as follows: "(11) That in the execution of said contract sued on, and the undertaking by her to pay the debt of James O. Cole, as therein stipulated and expressed, she did not become surety for the payment of said debt, but the same was an original undertaking and promise on her part for the purchase money for said mill property, and is part of the consideration for said contract." "(17) That the contract of June 9, 1891, was fully read over, and its contents and provisions explained, to the defendants and each of them, at and before the same was signed, and that no fraud or misrepresentation was practiced or made to induce defendants, or either of them, to sign the same."

The conclusions of law were stated as follows: "The court therefore concludes, as a matter of law from the foregoing facts, that said defendant David Hamilton is indebted to said plaintiff, Samuel Hamilton, in the sum of $1,103.50; that the same is and ought to be declared a lien on said mill property, as described in said contract of June 9, 1891; and that, in default of the payment of said sum, said lien ought to be foreclosed, and the said property ordered sold to pay the same."

In briefing this cause, appellants' counsel have omitted to so classify their points that it can be determined in each instance whether the point is urged with reference to the validity of a conclusion of law, or whether it is presented as a ground for a new trial. In view of this we shall, in the main, consider the argument for a reversal in the order of its presentation upon the brief.

It is strongly urged upon our consideration by counsel for appellants that the evidence shows that the contract of June 9, 1891, was procured from said Abigail by sharp and unscrupulous practices, if not by actual fraud; that the parties did not meet on an equality; and that the contract obtained was of such a harsh and unconscionable character that a court of equity should refuse to order it specifically performed. We have carefully read the evidence in the case, and have reached the conclusion that there was not such an uncontradicted showing as would warrant us in overthrowing the finding. If we were to look only to the testimony of appellants, a pretty strong case would be presented, but both are disputed upon many vital points by other witnesses. It is not questioned that said David fully understood the character of the business transacted on said day. If he was not honestly representing his wife's interests at that time, but was seeking rather to get his debt paid by imposing upon her, the evidence strongly tends to show that appellee was not aware of such unfaithfulness. The contract was read over to her, and she had the opportunity of fully acquainting herself with the facts. The trial court did not find in favor of said Abigail on her averments as to the circumstances in which she was induced to execute the contract, and in view of the testimony we are bound by this result.

It is argued that she had an equity in said business property of about $4,200, and that the transaction she entered into involved a clear sacrifice of her interests. In determining what was best for her to do in the circumstances which the evidence shows to exist, the problem was not altogether clear. Cole was demanding that some arrangement be made to better secure his debt, the mortgages on the business property and on the 120-acre tract of land were due, and the mortgagees were seeking payment. Assuming the values of the properties exchanged to be as disclosed by the special finding, it appears that by the exchange she incurred a loss to the extent of the debt due Cole, and assumed a mortgage debt upon the mill property of $750; but, on the other hand, she was relieved from the payment of a much larger mortgage on the business property, and procured $1,000 to be applied upon the mortgage upon the farm. In addition, the arrangement involved the closing up of the first trust, and the investing her with title to the remaining farm land, subject to a $2,000 mortgage. Moreover, the debt to Cole which she was assuming was one that was already hanging over her husband, so that if she paid it she would be at least relieving him to that extent, a fact calculated to appeal to a wife who was not altogether self-centered. There was oral evidence to the effect that the provision in said contract that the balance of the proceeds received by the trustee should be paid to said David was inserted so that he could draw the money for her. The court below did not find upon this point, but it is immaterial, for, as the lessees did not elect to purchase the mill property, and as said Abigail consequently took a deed for the same, said provision never became operative.

It was not essential, however, to the enforcing of said contract, that it should have appeared that said Abigail received in benefit to her estate the full value of what she surrendered. Mere inadequacy of consideration is not in and of itself a sufficient reason for refusing specific performance. Fry, Spec. Per. §§ 418-426; Pomeroy on Contracts, § 194; Note to Seymour v. Delancey, 15 Am. Dec. 299; 26 Am. & Eng. Ency. of Law, 26, 27.

It cannot be said that there was no consideration for the promise to pay the indebtedness to Cole. The contract was entire in its character, and the considerations which moved to said Abigail went to the support of the undertaking on which this action is based. Jordon v. Indianapolis Water Co., 159 Ind. 337, 64 N. E. 680.

The promise to pay said indebtedness was one of which appellee had a right to avail himself. Claypool v. Board, etc., 132 Ind. 261, 31 N. E. 665. No one could doubt, as it seems to us, that, as a contract made for his benefit, appellee had a right to take advantage of it. The consideration moving from Tyler was sufficient to support the contract. Even a mere option, if founded on a valuable consideration, may be enforced. 26 Am. & Eng. Ency. of Law, 30; South, etc., R. Co. v. Highland Ave., etc., R. Co., 98 Ala. 400, 13 South. 682, 39 Am. St. Rep. 74.

Said Abigail has no cause of complaint because the indebtedness to Cole was not paid in the order of its priority. She was not a party to the deed to said trustees, and had no interest in the proceeds of sales made by them until after all 12 of the items of indebtedness mentioned in said instrument were paid, so that the order of their payment could not concern her.

The fact that appellants engaged to execute a mortgage conditioned to pay the debt to Cole did not make said Abigail a surety. Upon a consideration which moved to her estate, she undertook, as principal, to pay such debt. Looking at the contract as an entirety, it is evident that it was the purpose of the parties, in so far as they were authorized to bind all concerned, to cast upon the property of said Abigail the burden of paying the whole debt. The undertaking was original and primary in its character, and she was the principal therein. The eleventh finding, when taken in connection with the findings as a whole, shows that she was not a surety.

A question is raised by appellants' counsel as to the sufficiency of the demand made by appellee for the execution of the mortgage, but the point made, as we understand it, goes only to the question as to the power of said Abigail to make the debt of her husband a primary obligation as to her. We perceive no element of uncertainty in the contract relative to the execution of the mortgage. Taking the whole contract together, it must be said that the mortgage was payable presently, and as appellee became, as between him and said Abigail, a surety, we think that the note to Cole fixed the rate of interest. Section 1233, Burns' Ann. St. 1901. There having been a refusal to execute a mortgage to pay a debt long overdue, appellants cannot complain of a decree charging the indebtedness upon the land and ordering a sale thereof. It having become necessary for the trial court to exercise its equitable jurisdiction in appellee's behalf, it was proper, in the circumstances, for the court to continue its active jurisdiction until full justice was done between the parties. Brace v. Doble, 3 S. D.

110, 52 N. W. 586; Peake v. Young, 40 S. C. 41, 18 S. E. 237; 20 Ency. Pl. & Pr. 479.

A question has been raised as to the propriety of finding that said Abigail was not a purchaser for value of the land conveyed to her in 1888. In the view we take of this case, it was immaterial whether she was a purchaser for value or not.

We observe that, in addition to the decree fixing a lien upon the real estate, and ordering it sold in case of nonpayment, there was also a personal judgment against David. No question is made upon this point, and we do not, therefore, determine whether he was liable.

Judgment affirmed.

(32 Ind. App. 633)

WILKINSON v. VORDERMARK et al.

(Appellate Court of Indiana, Division No. 1. March 31, 1904.)

ACTIONS—ABATEMENT—DEATH — SUBSTITUTION OF REPRESENTATIVES—APPEAL—DEFECT OF PARTIES.

1. Under Burns' Ann. St. 1901, § 272, providing that actions shall not abate by death, but may be continued by or against the successor in interest of the deceased party, in supplementary proceedings to subject personal property fraudulently transferred to the payment of alimony, where one of the defendants died, her personal representatives, and not her heirs at law, should have been substituted.

2. Under Burns' Rev. St. 1901, §§ 272, 648, 649, 675, providing that actions do not abate by the death of a party, and providing for the substitution of the proper representatives where the death of a party is suggested on the record before trial or judgment, the substitution of the proper representatives should be made in the trial court, and not in the Supreme Court.

3. In case of the death of a party defendant it devolves on the plaintiff, and not on the other defendants, to cause a substitution of the proper representative.

4. It is against the policy of the law which forbids several appeals in one cause to inquire on appeal whether there was error in finding in favor of certain defendants, where the interest of a deceased defendant had not been adjudicated as against her personal representatives, and the substitution of such representative would still have to be had in the lower court, but the appeal will be dismissed for want of parties.

Appeal from Circuit Court, Whitley County; Jos. W. Adair, Judge.

Supplementary proceedings by Millie A. Wilkinson against Henry P. Vordermark and others. From a judgment for certain defendants, plaintiff appeals. Dismissed.

T. E. Ellison and Ninde Bros., for appellant. W. G. Colerick, for appellees.

BLACK, J. This was a proceeding supplementary to execution, brought by the appellant, Millie A. Wilkinson, who had been the wife of Henry P. Vordermark, from whom she had obtained a divorce with a judgment for alimony. She sought to subject to execution on this judgment certain personal property alleged to have been disposed of fraudulently by her late husband. She made defendants in this proceeding the execution defendant, John W. Vordermark, the Ft. Wayne & New Haven Turnpike Company, the Tri-State Building & Loan Association of Ft. Wayne, and three of the execution defendant's children, namely, Harry Vordermark, Mary Maud Vordermark, and Lillian Ada Vordermark. The appellant recovered judgment against all these defendants. From this judgment an appeal was taken to the Supreme Court, and it appears from the judgment on appeal as shown in the record before us and in Vordermark v. Wilkinson, 147 Ind. 56, 46 N. E. 336, that the judgment of the trial court was reversed as to Harry Vordermark and Mary Maud Vordermark because of an error in overruling their demurrer for want of sufficient facts to the complaint, and, as a benefit derivable from the appeal from the necessity of the case, the judgment, so far as it incidentally affected the building and loan association by requiring the turning out for sale by the sheriff of certain stock of that association claimed by Harry Vordermark, was vacated; and as to all the other defendants the appeal was dismissed because not brought in proper time. This left the judgment as to such other defendants in full force and effect and unappealable. It was held by the Supreme Court that an interest in a certain sum of money claimed by Mary Maud Vordermark, and certain shares of stock of the building and loan association and a certain sum of money claimed by Harry Vordermark, constituted the only property in question upon that appeal.

The cause having been redocketed in the trial court, and the opinion of the Supreme Court, above mentioned, having been filed in the year 1898, further proceedings were had in that court. As appears by an entry of September 23, 1901, the parties then appeared, "and the death of Mary Maud Vordermark is suggested to the court"; but it does not appear from the record that any person or persons were formally substituted as her representatives. Afterward the venue was changed from the Allen circuit court to the court below, and the cause was there again tried by the court in November, 1901, and the court found, amongst other things, "in favor of the defendant Harry E. Vordermark, the heirs at law of Mary Maud Vordermark, who died during the pendency of this action, intestate, and leaving her father, Henry P. Vordermark, her brother, Harry E. Vordermark, and her sister, Lillian Ada Vordermark, surviving her as only heirs at law, and the Tri-State Building & Loan Association. And the court doth further find in favor of the plaintiff as against the defendants Henry P. Vordermark, John W. Vordermark, and Lillian Ada Vordermark and Ft. Wayne & New Haven Turnpike Company, and that the judgments heretofore rendered against them in this action by the Allen circuit court, of Allen county, Indiana, at its April term, 1893, and each of them, should be preserved and maintained, as said judgments were by the Supreme Court of Indiana on appeal therefrom affirmed." It was thereupon adjudged that "Harry E. Vordermark, the heirs at law of Mary Maud Vordermark, and the Tri-State Building & Loan Association, and each of them, do have and recover of the plaintiff their and each of their costs in this action expended; and it is further decreed and adjudged by the court that the plaintiff do have and recover of the defendants Henry P. Vordermark, John W. Vordermark, Lillian Ada Vordermark, and the Ft. Wayne & New Haven Turnpike Company the relief granted her in and by the judgments so rendered in her favor or against them in the said Allen circuit court, which appears elsewhere in the record of this action, and which judgments were affirmed by the Supreme Court of Indiana, and her costs in this action by her expended, so far as the same relate to said defendants."

The appellant's motion for a new trial, stating as grounds therefor that the finding against her was not sustained by the evidence, and that it was contrary to law, was overruled; and this ruling is alone assigned as error. In the assignment the plaintiff Millie A. Wilkinson is named as the appellant, and all the defendants, as named in the introductory part of this opinion, were named as the appellees, all, including Mary Maud Vordermark, in their individual characters, and no person in any representative capacity. The appellant, by her appeal, seeks the reversal of the judgment against her in favor of Harry Vordermark, the heirs at law of Mary Maud Vordermark, and the Tri-State Building & Loan Association. It appears from the record that Mary Maud Vordermark died while the cause was pending in the Allen circuit court. No representative was substituted for her formally, but the court below in its finding and judgment, treating the cause of action as surviving against her heirs at law, found and adjudged in their favor against the appellant. She could not be a party to the appeal. Having died before finding and judgment, the action did not thereby abate, but the action might have been allowed by the Allen circuit court or by the court below on motion or supplemental complaint, to be continued against her proper representative. Section 272, Burns' Ann. St. 1901. As the proceeding related solely to personal property, her personal representative, and not her heirs at law, should have been substituted for her before judgment. Since the cause has been in this court the appellant filed her motion here that Henry P. Vordermark, Harry Vordermark, and Lillian Ada Vordermark be substituted as appellees to answer as to the interest of Mary Maud Vordermark, deceased, supporting the motion by an affidavit of an attorney for the appellant, stating that Mary Maud Vordermark "one of the appellees in said cause, died prior to this appeal, leaving surviving her as her sole heirs at law her father, Henry P. Vordermark, her brother, Harry Vordermark, and her sister, Lillian Ada Vordermark, all of whom were parties defendant in said suit, and are appellees in this appeal." This motion was overruled at the time of its presentation, very properly; for the record shows that her decease was suggested before trial or judgment, and the statutes contemplated substitution of the proper representative in the trial court, and not in this court, in such case. Sections 272, 648, 649, 675, Burns' Ann. St. 1901. And, furthermore, if it were a proper case for substitution of a representative, the personal representative, and not the heirs at law, of the deceased party, would be the proper representative. It devolved upon the appellant, the plaintiff, to cause the substitution of a proper representative for the deceased defendant, and not upon any of the other defendants. There was no cause of action against the heirs at law of the deceased party defendant on trial, and the appellant could not have been entitled to a finding against them in such capacity. Without herself causing the substitution of a proper representative, she suffered judgment to be taken against her in favor of the heirs at law of the deceased defendant, making no objection to the substitution, and then named the deceased defendant as an appellee; and the heirs at law as such, in whose favor the court found, are not parties here.

If it may be said that there has been no adjudication upon the interest of the deceased defendant as against her personal representative, and that the substitution of such representative may still be made in the court below, it would be against the policy of the law forbidding several appeals in one cause to proceed to inquire whether or not there was error in finding in favor of the other defendants who recovered against the appellant.

The interest of the deceased defendant is not represented in this court. She cannot be made a party, being deceased, and no representative of the decedent is a party. A portion of the persons in whose favor the judgment appealed from was rendered are not before us. The want of proper parties is attributable to the appellant alone. We cannot either reverse or affirm the judgment rendered by the trial court as a whole or in part in the condition of the cause as presented to us. See Vordermark v. Wilkinson, 142 Ind. 142, 39 N. E. 441; Lawson v. Newcomb, 12 Ind. 439; Clodfelter v. Halett, 92 Ind. 426; Holland v. Holland, 131 Ind. 196, 30 N. E. 1075; Ewbank's Man. §§ 149, 150.

Appeal dismissed.

(34 Ind. App. 239)

WALKER v. SAWYER'S ESTATE.*

(Appellate Court of Indiana, Division No. 2. March 30, 1904.)

CONTRACTS — RECOVERY ON — CONDITIONS PRECEDENT—PROPORTIONATE PAYMENT—DEMAND—NECESSITY—PLEADING.

1. To entitle one to recover on a contract, his complaint must show compliance on his part with the terms thereof.

2. Where an agreement recited the payment by A. of $1,183.64 in the purchase of a lot, and also the fact that further expenditures would be necessary to perfect title, and that B. had rendered certain services, and should be compensated by a conveyance of title to an undivided one-half of the premises, on payment by him within a year of one-half the expenses incurred by A. in perfecting title, the payment by B., within the year, of one-half of $1,183.64, was a condition precedent to his receiving the stipulated compensation; and his duty to pay the same was not conditional on any demand by A. for payment, irrespective of whether such demand or a statement of indebtedness was necessary to obligate B. to tender and pay his proportion of the subsequent expenses, the amount of which was unliquidated.

Appeal from Circuit Court, Marion County; H. C. Allen, Judge.

Proceedings on a claim by Ivan M. Walker against the estate of J. Warren Sawyer, deceased, and against Sara R. Sawyer, administratrix. From a judgment for defendant, claimant appeals. Affirmed.

Chambers, Pickens & Moores, for appellant.

COMSTOCK, J. Appellant filed his claim against the estate of J. Warren Sawyer, deceased, and against Sara R. Sawyer, administratrix of said estate, in the circuit court, based upon the following contract:

"This memorandum witnesseth: That J. Warren Sawyer has this day purchased the interest of James Murphy of Philadelphia, Pa., in and to lot number twenty (20) in square number two (2) in North Park Addition to Indianapolis, together with certain tax liens held by others, the total amount paid therefore by said Sawyer to this date being Eleven Hundred and Eighty-three and $^{64}/_{100}$ dollars ($1,183^{64}/_{100}$) and that the said Sawyer is now proceeding to take other steps for the perfecting of the title to said lot in him which will involve the payment by him of additional sums, costs and expenses.

"That Ivan N. Walker, negotiated said purchase for the said Sawyer and is to be compensated therefor upon the following terms and conditions, and not otherwise, to wit:

"The said Walker shall within one year from this date pay the said Sawyer, one-half the sums, costs and expense which may hereafter be paid by said Sawyer in perfecting the title to said lot, with ten per cent. interest on one-half of all sums so paid by said Sawyer from the date of such payments by Sawyer, to date of payment to him by Walker, and upon such payment by said Walker within said period, said Sawyer shall convey, assign and transfer to said Walker an undivided one-half of his title and interest in and to said lot and thereupon said parties shall be the tenants in common of all the title and interest acquired in said lot.

"If said Walker shall not make the payments within the period named, time being of the essence of this contract, he shall receive no compensation for his said services, and shall have no right to acquire any title or interest in or title to said lot.

"In consideration of the agreements herein contained upon the part of said Sawyer, the said Walker agrees that if the said Sawyer when he sells said lot or his interest therein shall fail to realize a sum sufficient to reimburse him for all sums invested in said lot, with interest, then said Walker shall pay to said Sawyer one-half of the loss sustained by said Sawyer, i. e., one-half of the sum necessary to be added to proceeds of the sale to equal the investment in said lot and interest.

"Witness our hands this 13th day of May 1891, in duplicate. J. Warren Sawyer. Ivan N. Walker."

The complaint sets out the contract as above, and avers that said contract related to the purchase and sale of lot 20 in square 2 in North Park Addition to the city of Indianapolis, for which Sawyer had paid the price of $1,183.64; that, by the terms of this contract, Sawyer was to make further payments in perfecting the title to said lot; that, of the exact amount of this payment which appellant was to repay, the said Sawyer never advised claimant; that the claimant incurred certain expenses in connection with the improvement of the said property, amounting to about $40; that, because the property was advancing rapidly in value, it was deemed best, between the appellant and the said decedent, that no sale should be made during the year provided for in the contract; that said property was held by the said Sawyer until May 15, 1897, when Sawyer sold it for $5,833. The claim goes on to allege the full performance by the claimant of all the conditions of the contract required of him, and his willingness and readiness at all times to pay the said Sawyer, on demand, the amount of moneys due under said contract, which amount claimant has never paid, because not advised by the said Sawyer. Under the contract and allegations of the complaint, it is alleged that the appellant is entitled to one-half of the profit derived from the sale of the lot, after deducting the purchase price and expenses advanced by the decedent, to which should be added the amount paid by the claimant for improvements. Appellee demurred to the claim upon the ground that the same

¶ 2. See Contracts, vol. 11, Cent. Dig. § 1664.

*Rehearing denied. Transfer to Supreme Court denied.

did not state facts sufficient to constitute a cause of action. The demurrer was sustained. Appellant excepted, and refused to amend, and the court rendered judgment against appellant in favor of appellee.

The only question presented by the appeal is the sufficiency of the complaint. To entitle appellant to recover, the compliance with the terms of the contract by him should appear from the averments of the complaint. The averments show that he "was ready and willing at all times to pay to said Sawyer, on demand, the amount of money due from him for the original price and any sum for costs, expenses or taxes that may have been paid by said Sawyer, but the said Sawyer never advised him of the amount so due." It is claimed by appellant that the contract imposed no obligation upon him to tender Sawyer reimbursement for money expended until Sawyer should submit an account of the same, and make demand for such reimbursement—in other words, that a party is not liable to make a tender until the person to whom the tender is due shall advise him of the amount he must tender. If this proposition is true as to an unliquidated debt, where a question of forfeiture arises, it is not applicable to the facts before us. The contract recites that Sawyer had at the date of the contract (May 13, 1891) expended on the purchase $1,183.64. The amount was definite and certain. It was not exclusively in the knowledge of the decedent. As to it, no demand or statement was necessary for its payment within the year appellant obligated himself. This payment, whatever view may be taken of his failure to pay the obligations which may have arisen under the contract, was the condition precedent to his receiving compensation for his services in negotiating the purchase of the lot, and of his right to acquire any title or interest therein. The payment of the sum was not dependent on the performance of a condition by the decedent which by its terms might not be performed until after the date at which the money was to be paid. Front St., etc., Co. v. Butler, 50 Cal. 574, cited by appellant, is not applicable. Appellant cites cases to the effect that the law will not require a party to perform an impossibility, nor declare a forfeiture for a breach of a condition precedent, at the behest of another, who by his act has rendered the performance of the condition precedent impossible. The deceased is charged with no act hindering the payment of the agreed purchase price, or in any manner causing delay in its payment. By a contract which the parties were competent to make, appellant's right to acquire any title or interest to said lot was limited to a certain time within which he was to do certain things, failing in which, he forfeited all that he contracted for.

It is alleged in the complaint that appellant expended $40 on the improvement of said lot. Upon proper showing, such item might be made the basis of a claim against the estate. Such claim is not made in the complaint under consideration.

Judgment affirmed.

(32 Ind. A. 623)

JOHNSON v. STALEY et al.

(Appellate Court of Indiana, Division No. 2. March 30, 1904.)

CONTRACTS—CONSIDERATION—ACCEPTANCE BY MINOR — PRESUMPTIONS — IMPLICATIONS OF REASONABLENESS — PLEAS IN ABATEMENT — WAIVER—APPEAL—BILLS OF EXCEPTIONS.

1. A plea in abatement setting up nonresidence and service outside of the state was properly overruled when filed after a demurrer for want of facts, and a second demurrer for lack of jurisdiction and misjoinder of causes of action.

2. It is not the office of a bill of exceptions to supply that which is essential to the validity of a judgment.

3. When other order-book entries made by the clerk are in conflict with the bill of exceptions, the latter will control.

4. A promise to refrain from instituting suit to have the promisor's grandmother declared of unsound mind is sufficient consideration for a contract by which a recent purchaser of property from the grandmother agrees to pay the promisor a sum of money.

5. Acceptance of a contract made by a third person for the benefit of a minor is presumed from its beneficial character.

6. Where an agreement for the sale of land to pay a debt fixes no time within which the sale should be made, or the price at which the property should be sold, the law implies that it will be sold within a reasonable time, and that the price and terms will also be reasonable.

Appeal from Circuit Court, Hancock County; E. W. Felt, Judge.

Action by Gertie O. Staley and others against Thomas V. Johnson. From a judgment for plaintiffs, defendant appeals. Affirmed.

H. L. Hutson, for appellant. Marsh & Cook, for appellees.

ROBY, J. This action was begun June 5, 1897. The third paragraph of the complaint, upon which the judgment rests, was filed June 14, 1901. Appellant thereupon secured a continuance until the following term, and had judgment for the costs thereof. He subsequently demurred for want of facts, and later filed a second demurrer for want of facts, lack of jurisdiction both of person and subject-matter, and misjoinder of causes. Thereafter he filed a plea in abatement, setting up that the only service of process had upon him was made outside of the state, and that he is a resident of Ohio. On motion the plea was stricken out. There was no error therein. Eel River R. Co. v. State, 155 Ind. 439, 57 N. E. 388.

The court, at the request of the parties, made a special finding of facts, and stated conclusions of law, following which the order-book entry is: "Thereupon the defendant objects and excepts separately to each finding of fact and to the conclusions of law as stated by the court." A bill of exceptions subsequently filed contains the following statement: "The court thereupon stated and filed its conclusions of law upon the facts found, to which conclusions of law the defendant then and there at the time excepted." Appellees insist that the statement of the bill cannot be considered. It is not the office of a bill of exceptions to supply that which is essential to the validity of the judgment. Bowen v. State, 108 Ind. 411, 9 N. E. 378; Gray v. Singer, 137 Ind. 257, 36 N. E. 209, 1109. These authorities are not in point, for the reason that the exception, or its form, is not essential to a valid judgment. When other order-book entries made by the clerk are in conflict with the bill of exceptions, the latter will control. Alley v. State, 76 Ind. 94, 95; Ry. Co. v. Adams, 112 Ind. 302, 303, 14 N. E. 80; Ewbank's Man'l, § 34, p. 47.

The finding is to the effect that on December 4, 1896, Hannah Johnson was the owner of 80 acres of land in Hancock county, worth $45 per acre. Gertie and Bessie Staley are the minor children of Robert L. Staley. Their mother, whose only children they were, died intestate in 1894, and was the daughter of Hannah Johnson. The Staleys lived on the land, Hannah living with them for 12 years, and until August, 1896, when she went to Ohio to visit her son, the appellant, intending at the time to return in a few weeks. On December 4, 1896, she conveyed said land, which constituted her entire estate, to appellant, in consideration of $100, and his agreement to maintain her for life; said deed being recorded four days after its execution. Later, in December, a neighbor of Robert L. Staley went to Ohio to see Mrs. Johnson, and to learn the circumstances under which the conveyance was made, her mental condition, and intention with regard to appellees. Appellant refused to permit her to talk with the neighbor, except in his own presence; and, under his influence, said Hannah declined to return to Hancock county, but declared her intention that the granddaughters, who, with appellant, are her only heirs, should have their inheritance out of her estate, which was in fact her intention. Said Hannah, when she visited appellant, was past 73 years old, could not write her name, and was susceptible to his influence and control. In January, 1897, a suit was commenced in the Hancock circuit court, at the instance of Robert L. Staley, to declare said Hannah of unsound mind. It was subsequently dismissed on account of the claim that she was then a citizen of Ohio. A few days prior to March 15, 1897, said Robert L. sent an attorney to Ohio to obtain evidence upon which to institute an action against defendant, or to make a compromise, if possible, that would enable his children to receive a part of their grandmother's estate. Said attorney informed appellant that unless he paid to appellees $1,000, as their share in said estate, they would at once commence suit to set aside said deed on the ground of undue influence of appellant over said Hannah, and of her unsoundness of mind. Said attorney told appellant that he could sell said land for $60 per acre. In order to prevent such suit, and in order to compromise plaintiffs' claim, and in consideration that said legal proceedings should not be instituted, and that said conveyance might not be set aside or declared invalid for said reasons or for any other reasons, appellant executed a written instrument by which he promised to pay appellees $1,000, and directed said attorney to sell said real estate; the instrument, as executed, being in terms as follows: "Deerfield, Ohio, March 15th, 1897. This is to certify that I, Thomas V. Johnson, of Deerfield, Ohio, have this day placed in the hands of Albert W. Hammer, the following real estate, to wit: [describing it.] The conditions of the agreement are such that the said Albert W. Hammer is to sell the above-described real estate at such price and on such terms as I may direct, and I further agree to pay or direct the said A. W. Hammer to pay, out of the money received for the above real estate, the sum of one thousand ($1,000.00) to the guardian of Gertie O. and Bessie J. Staley, of Warrington, Ind. Thomas V. Johnson." Said Robert L. acted upon such settlement, said proceedings were not instituted as otherwise intended, and said contract remains in full force and effect. Said minors never had possession of said instrument, or did any affirmative act to indicate an acceptance thereof. The settlement was accepted and approved by the father, and was beneficial to his daughters. No sale of said real estate was made. An offer of $45 per acre was refused by appellant. In December, 1897, appellant notified Hammer that he did not recognize the right of the latter to procure a purchaser under such contract. Appellant is still the owner of the real estate, has refused to pay said $1,000, and denies liability therefor. The conclusion of law was that the plaintiff was entitled to recover $1,000, with interest.

The granddaughters had no property right in the possessions of their grandmother. So far as they were concerned, she could sell or give her land away at her pleasure. They could not maintain an action against her or against appellant on account of such disposition. A suit to have a guardian appointed, in order that her estate might be preserved for her own use and benefit, might have been instituted. An agreement not to sue is a good consideration, generally speaking. Doan v. Dow, 8 Ind. App. 324, 327, 35 N. E. 709; Ditmar v. West, 7 Ind. App. 637, 35 N. E. 47; Purviance v. Purviance, 14 Ind. App. 278, 42 N. E. 364. By refraining from causing the institution of an action to declare the grandmother of unsound mind, appellees suffered no direct pecuniary loss, but appellant manifestly received a direct and immediate pecuniary benefit; he holding a deed for land recently conveyed by her to him. It was competent for him to buy his peace, and, having received all the consideration for which he had contracted, there is no reason why he should be relieved from payment of the price. Acceptance of a contract made by a third person for the benefit of a minor is presumed from its beneficial character. Goelz v. People's Savings Bank (Nov. term, 1903) 67 N. E. 232; Copeland v. Summers, 138 Ind. 219, 223, 35 N. E. 514, 37 N. E. 971.

The agreement fixed no time within which the sale of said real estate should be made by Hammer. The law implies, therefore, a reasonable time. It is not claimed that the undertaking on appellant's part was repudiated because of a failure to sell within a reasonable time. The contract fixes no price at which the land should be sold. The price and terms to be fixed by appellant would therefore also be required to be reasonable. It appears that an offer of what the land was worth was made and refused. No question of the contract having been procured by fraud is presented by the findings.

The court did not err in its conclusions of law. Other questions argued are not presented by the record, and are not, therefore, considered.

Judgment affirmed.

(33 Ind. App. 356)

STAUFFER et al. v. CINCINNATI, R. & M. R. CO.*

(Appellate Court of Indiana, Division No. 1. March 29, 1904.)

EMINENT DOMAIN — CONDEMNATION PROCEEDINGS — DAMAGES—APPRAISEMENT—WHAT INCLUDED—BUILDINGS—ADJUDICATION OF APPRAISERS — CONCLUSIVENESS—ESTOPPEL—ACCEPTANCE OF AWARD—INJUNCTION—GROUNDS —PLEADING—WRITTEN INSTRUMENTS.

1. Burns' Ann. St. 1901, § 365, providing that where a plea is founded on a written instrument the original or a copy must be filed with the pleading, does not require a railroad, when suing to enjoin the removal of buildings from a strip of land acquired for a right of way by condemnation proceedings, to set out in, or file with, the complaint the instrument of appropriation, as the action is not based on it.

2. To authorize an injunction, the violation of plaintiff's rights must be of such a nature as is, or will be, attended with substantial or serious damage.

3. That a complete remedy at law exists does not prevent the granting of an injunction, but to accomplish such result the remedy must be plain and adequate, and as practical to the ends of justice as the remedy in equity.

4. Under Burns' Ann. St. 1901, § 5160 et seq., providing that railroads appropriating land shall deposit with the clerk of court a description of the rights and interests to be appropriated, and that such land, rights, and interest shall belong to the company on making payment, and further providing that appraisers shall consider the injuries sustained by the owner, and return their assessment of damages to the clerk, setting forth the value of, or injury to, the property, the appraisers should value the land taken with the buildings on it, and it will be presumed that the buildings are included in the award.

5. The award by appraisers in condemnation proceedings is an adjudication of damages by a competent tribunal, and at the expiration of the time allowed for appeal it is, to an extent at least, in the nature of a judgment.

6. Where a property owner accepts and retains the damages assessed in condemnation proceedings, he cannot claim greater damages, either in a direct appeal or in a collateral action.

7. Where a railroad is entitled to the possession of land through condemnation proceedings, the facts, if true, that it only acquired an easement therein, and that the dwelling house of a property owner did not pass to the railroad in the condemnation proceedings, but remained the property of the former owner, and that the appraisers made their award, without reference to the value of the building, on the theory that it did not pass to the railroad, do not give the former property owner a right to go on the land and remove the building.

Appeal from Circuit Court, Pulaski County; J. C. Nye, Judge.

Action by the Cincinnati, Richmond & Muncie Railroad Company against John Stauffer and others. From a judgment for plaintiff, defendants appeal. Transferred from the Supreme Court under Act March 12, 1901 (Acts 1901, p. 567, c. 247, § 10). Affirmed.

Geo. Burson and William Spangler, for appellants. F. L. Dukes, S. Bybee, and Robbins & Starr, for appellee.

ROBINSON, J. Appellee sued to enjoin appellants from removing certain buildings from a strip of land it had acquired for a right of way by condemnation proceedings. The complaint shows that the appraisers awarded appellants $2,980, which sum was paid into the clerk's office and was paid to and accepted by appellants on the same day. It is also averred that on the premises are located, at the present time, certain buildings, which appellants are attempting to remove, and thereby irreparably damaging appellee.

As the action is not based upon the instrument of appropriation, it was not necessary to set it out in the complaint or to file it as an exhibit. It is only where the action is founded on a written instrument that the original, or a copy, must be filed with the pleading. Burns' Ann. St. 1901, § 365.

It is a general rule that, to authorize a court of equity to interfere by injunction, there must be something more than a mere violation of a plaintiff's rights; it must appear that this violation is of such a nature as is, or will be, attended with substantial or serious damages. But it is not enough that there is a complete remedy at law. "If the remedy at law," said the court in Watson v. Sutherland, 5 Wall. 74, 18 L. Ed. 580, "is sufficient, equity cannot give relief, but it is not enough that there is a remedy at law; it must be plain and adequate, or, in other words, as practical and efficient to the ends of justice, and its proper administration, as the remedy in equity." Boyce v. Grundy, 3 Pet. 210, 7 L. Ed. 655; English v. Smock, 34 Ind. 115, 7 Am. Rep. 215; Clark v. Jeffersonville R.

¶ 2. See Injunction, vol. 27, Cent. Dig. § ...

*Rehearing denied. Transfer to Supreme Court

Co., 44 Ind. 248; Thatcher v. Humble, 67 Ind. 444; Fitzmaurice v. Mosier, 116 Ind. 363, 16 N. E. 175, 19 N. E. 180, 9 Am. St. Rep. 854; McAfee v. Reynolds, 130 Ind. 33, 28 N. E. 423, 18 L. R. A. 211, 30 Am. St. Rep. 194; Town of Winamac v. Huddleston, 132 Ind. 217, 31 N. E. 561; Alexander v. Johnson, 144 Ind. 82, 41 N. E. 811; Bishop v. Moorman, 98 Ind. 1, 49 Am. Rep. 731; Denny v. Denny, 113 Ind. 22, 14 N. E. 593.

The first paragraph of answer admits the condemnation proceedings and the payment of the award to the clerk, does not deny its acceptance by appellants, and alleges that on the land taken, and in which appellee acquired only an easement, was the dwelling house of appellants, which did not become the property of the appellee by reason of the condemnation proceedings, but is and has been at all times the property of the appellants, which they have the right to remove from the right of way, and that appellee has no title or interest therein. The second paragraph further alleges that the building is not needed and cannot be used by appellee in the construction and operation of its roads, that the appraisers believed and acted upon the theory that the house did not pass by reason of the condemnation proceedings, and that the award was made without taking into consideration the value of the building. The third paragraph alleges, in addition, the acceptance of the award by the appellants, that the appraisers acted on the theory that appellants could remove the building, and did not take into consideration the value of the house, but, on the contrary, did award, as part of the damages, and allow them, $150 as and for expense and cost of removing the building from the right of way.

The statute conferring power on railroads to appropriate land (section 5160 et seq., Burns' Ann. St. 1901) provides that the corporation shall deposit with the clerk of the court "a description of the rights and interests intended to be appropriated; and such land, rights and interests shall belong to such company, to use for the purpose specified, by making or tendering payment" as provided. It is further provided that the appraisers "shall consider the injury which such owner may sustain by reason of such railroad, and shall forthwith return their assessment of damages to the clerk of such court, setting forth the value of the property taken, or injury done to the property which they assess to the owner." Provision is also made for the review of the award by the court upon application of either party, upon which a new appraisement may be ordered.

When the appraisers were appointed in the condemnation proceedings, it was their duty to appraise the land taken. The house on the land taken was a part of the realty, and could not be considered by the appraisers except in connection with the land. "The term 'land,'" says the author in Lewis' Eminent Domain (2d Ed.) § 285, "in statutes conferring power to condemn, is to be taken in the legal sense, and includes both the soil and buildings and other structures on it, and any and all interests therein." Brocket v. Ohio, etc., Ry. Co., 14 Pa. 241, 53 Am. Dec. 534; State v. Reed, 38 N. H. 59; Mills, Eminent Domain, §§ 49, 228. The building in question being a part of the real estate, it must be presumed that it was included in the award of the appraisers. If this award was not satisfactory to appellants, they could have appealed and had the award reviewed by the circuit court. The award by the appraisers was an adjudication upon the question of damages by a competent tribunal, and at the expiration of the time allowed for an appeal it was, to an extent at least, in the nature of a judgment. Not only was there no appeal, but appellants accepted and retain the award as made. Had appellants appealed from the award, and, pending the appeal, had accepted the damages assessed by the appraisers, such acceptance would have precluded them from taking further proceedings for the recovery of greater damages. Baltimore, etc., R. Co. v. Johnson, 84 Ind. 420. The effect of appellant's answers is, indirectly, to impeach the award by attempting to show that the value of the building was not included in the damages. The same reason that would preclude them, having accepted and retained the damages assessed, from claiming greater damages in a direct appeal, precludes them from questioning the award in the manner attempted in the answers. Where land upon which buildings are situated is condemned, the parties might agree concerning the buildings, but a rule should not be declared that would permit the company to appropriate the land and leave the building to the owner. See City of Kansas v. Morse (Mo.) 16 S. W. 893; Dodge v. Burns, 6 Wis. 514; Mississippi, etc., Co. v. Ring, 58 Mo. 491; Mills, Eminent Domain, § 329. Moreover as the complaint shows the appellee is entitled to the possession of the land through the condemnation proceedings, the facts alleged in the answers are insufficient to show any right on the part of appellants to go upon the land condemned and remove the building.

Judgment affirmed.

(32 Ind. A. 638)

LOGANSPORT & WABASH VALLEY GAS CO. v. ROSS.

(Appellate Court of Indiana, Division No. 1. March 31, 1904.)

GAS—LEASE—SUIT BY LESSOR—CANCELLATION—QUIETING TITLE—SUFFICIENCY OF COMPLAINT.

1. In a suit by the lessor in an oil lease to cancel the same and quiet title, the complaint alleged provisions of the lease whereby the lessee was to drill a well within three months, or thereafter pay the lessor a specified yearly rental

¶ 1. See Mines and Minerals, vol. 34, Cent. Dig. §§ 204, 206.

until the well should be drilled. It was also alleged that a well had been drilled, but no oil found; that the well had been abandoned; that complainant had re-entered the premises; and that after the abandonment of the well the lessees had assigned their contract to defendant. *Held*, that the complaint was insufficient as against a demurrer; there being no showing of a failure on the part of the lessees to perform any covenant, and the fact that the unproductive well was abandoned not entitling the lessor to a forfeiture.

Appeal from Circuit Court, Grant County; H. J. Paulus, Judge.

Suit by Marietta E. Ross against the Logansport & Wabash Valley Gas Company. From a decree for complainant, defendant appeals. Reversed.

W. O. Johnson, Foster Davis, and Blacklidge, Shirley & Wolf, for appellant. Manley & Strickler, for appellee.

ROBINSON, J. Suit by appellee to quiet title, and to cancel a gas contract executed to a firm and assigned to appellant. The first paragraph of complaint is the statutory form of action to quiet title. The second paragraph avers the execution on November 11, 1898, of a written agreement between appellee and a firm named, and avers that the firm afterward (March 19, 1900) "sold and assigned its interests in the said contract to" appellant, "who is now the owner thereof." This written agreement, set out in full in this paragraph, recited that appellee, in consideration of $1 and the covenants and agreements thereinafter contained, "hereby grants and conveys unto" the firm "all the oil and gas in and under the following" 92 acres of land described, "together with the exclusive right to enter thereon at all times for the purpose of drilling and operating" for gas or oil; "to erect, maintain and remove all buildings, structures, pipes, pipe lines and machinery necessary for the production, storage and transportation" of oil and gas; appellee to have the right to use the premises for farming purposes. The firm agreed to drill a well upon the premises within three months from date, or "thereafter pay the first party for further delay a yearly rental of forty-six dollars until said well is drilled"; such rental, when due, to be deposited in a bank at Marion; should the firm refuse to make such deposits or pay the rental when due, such refusal to be construed by both parties as the act of the firm for the purpose of surrendering the rights granted, and the instruments, in default of such rental payments, to be void without further notice. Should oil be found, the firm agreed to deliver to appellee one-eighth part thereof, and to pay $100 for each gas well; appellee to have gas for domestic purposes free of expense. The firm "may at any time reconvey this grant and thereupon this instrument shall be null and void." It is further averred that by the terms of the contract the firm and its assigns were given the right to enter upon the real estate described for the purpose of drilling and operating thereon for oil and gas; that the contract further provided that the firm should drill a well upon the premises within three months from the date of the contract, and that it did, in pursuance of the agreement, on February 9, 1899, enter upon the land, and drilled a well thereon for oil and gas, but that the well proved to be dry and unproductive of either oil or gas, and was by the firm about the last of February, 1899, abandoned and plugged, and the derrick used in drilling the same was torn down and removed from the premises, and all the other property and material used in and about the drilling of the well was taken away from the premises by the firm, and the well and premises wholly abandoned; that upon such abandonment appellee took full and complete possession of the real estate, and ever since that time has been and now is the owner thereof; that appellant never had possession of the real estate, or any part thereof, for any purpose whatever; that appellant is claiming the written contract is yet in full force and effect, and by reason thereof, and of the assignment of the same to it by the firm, to have some right, title, and interest in and to the land, which claim is adverse to appellee's rights, and which claim is without right and unfounded, and a cloud upon appellee's title. Prayer that the contract be canceled and released of record, and that appellee's title to the real estate be quieted. A demurrer to the second paragraph of complaint was overruled. The complaint was filed September 9, 1901.

The demurrer to the second paragraph of complaint should have been sustained. It sets out a contract under which appellant, through its assignor, was given certain rights, and contains provisions by which such rights might be continued by the payment of certain annual payments. It avers that appellant is claiming some interest in the land by virtue of the contract. So far as shown by the pleading, both parties may have treated the contract as in force up to the time this suit was brought. The fact that an unproductive well was drilled and abandoned does not necessarily show an abandonment of the contract itself, or of the rights of the grantees themselves. Moreover, the complaint shows that the firm considered the contract in force, as it assigned it to appellant nearly a year after the unproductive well was abandoned. The pleading does not rely upon any failure of appellant or its predecessors to keep any of the covenants of the contract, but relies entirely upon the fact that an unproductive well was abandoned and no other put down before the beginning of this suit. Appellee has not shown herself entitled to the forfeiture of the lease, within the rule declared in Consumers' Gas Trust Co. v. Littler (Sup. Ct., No. 20,246, decided March —, 1904) 70 N. E.

363. The contract is set out in full, and contains provisions under which it may have been continued in force with appellee's consent. The fact that appellee took possession after the well was abandoned would not necessarily be inconsistent with continuing the contract in force. The agreement contains no provision that the abandonment of an unproductive well will work a forfeiture of the lease. Sufficient facts are not averred to show that appellee claimed a forfeiture of the lease at any time before the suit was brought.

Judgment reversed.

(32 Ind. A. 619)

MAKEEVER v. BLANKENBAKER et al.

(Appellate Court of Indiana, Division No. 1. March 29, 1904.)

APPEAL — RECORD—PRÆCIPE—BILL OF EXCEPTIONS.

1. Where on appeal the præcipe did not direct the clerk to certify the original bill of exceptions, that document, though certified by the clerk, cannot be considered.

Appeal from Circuit Court, Jasper County; Jno. C. Nye, Special Judge.

Action between John Makeever and William B. Blankenbaker and others. From a judgment for the latter, the former appeals. Affirmed.

Ferguson & Wilson and W. H. Parkison, for appellant. Foltz, Spitler & Kurrie, for appellees.

HENLEY, C. J. This is an appeal from the judgment of the Jasper circuit court establishing a highway. The questions presented by the assignment of error and not waived by failure to discuss them all arise under the motion for a new trial, and require the presence of the evidence for their proper determination. Counsel for appellee contend that the evidence cannot be considered by this court because the bill of exceptions containing the evidence is not properly a part of the record. The præcipe filed by appellant with the clerk of the circuit court did not direct or request such clerk to certify to this court the original bill of exceptions containing the evidence. It has been repeatedly held that only such papers and entries as are designated in the præcipe are properly a part of the record on appeal, and the præcipe in the case at bar did not in any way direct or request the clerk to certify to this court the original bill of exceptions containing the evidence. Chestnut v. Southern Ind. R. Co., 157 Ind. 509, 62 N. E. 32; Johnson v. Johnson, 156 Ind. 592, 60 N. E. 451; Brown v. Armfield, 155 Ind. 150, 57 N. E. 722; McCaslin v. Advance Mfg. Co., 155 Ind. 298, 58 N. E. 67.

The transcript in the case at bar was filed in this court on February 21, 1903, and the act of March 9, 1903 (Acts 1903, p. 338, c. 193), was not then in force. The certificate of the clerk shows that the record contains the original bill of exceptions embracing the evidence. The evidence cannot be considered for any purpose, and the record does not present any available error.

Judgment affirmed.

(32 Ind. A. 614)

BOWEN v. GERHOLD et al.

(Appellate Court of Indiana, Division No. 1. March 29, 1904.)

TENDER—PAYING MONEY INTO COURT—MORTGAGES—SUIT FOR REDEMPTION—COMPLAINT—SUFFICIENCY—APPEAL.

1. The maker of a note secured by mortgage sued to have the instruments decreed satisfied; alleging that a portion of the amount of the note was for usurious interest, and that such payments had been made that, computing interest at the legal rate, a certain amount was due, which had been tendered in lawful money and refused, and that, to keep this tender good, plaintiff had deposited the said money with the clerk. It was prayed that, if the tender was insufficient, the court should find and decree the amount due, which plaintiff offered to pay. The record showed that, at the time of filing the complaint, plaintiff paid into court the amount named in the complaint, "in gold, good and lawful money of the United States." *Held*, that it was immaterial whether the manner of payment alleged amounted to a payment of money into court, or whether the complaint showed a paying in of money of such kind as is necessary for keeping a tender good, inasmuch as the record showed that the money paid in was legal tender, paid in the presence and under the supervision of the court.

2. Even if the complaint could not be construed as alleging that the money paid into court was the same that had been tendered, it nevertheless stated a cause of action for redemption; an equitable tender of the amount the court might find to be due being sufficient, though a strict legal tender was not shown.

3. In a suit by the maker of a note secured by mortgage to have the instruments decreed satisfied on the ground that the debt had been partially paid, and the balance tendered, defendant filed a cross-complaint seeking to foreclose, and plaintiff pleaded payment, averring the same facts stated in the complaint. The court found for plaintiff, and decreed satisfaction of the note and mortgage. *Held* that, on appeal, alleged error in overruling a demurrer to the answer to the cross-complaint would not be considered.

Appeal from Circuit Court, Carroll County; F. F. Palmer, Judge.

Action by Adam Gerhold against John A. Cartwright and others. From a judgment for plaintiff, defendant Abner T. Bowen appeals. Affirmed.

L. D. Boyd, for appellant. Jno. L. Sims and Jno. H. Gould, for appellees.

BLACK, J. The appellee Adam Gerhold brought suit against the appellant and the appellees John A. Cartwright and Edward Bowen. The appellant's separate demurrer to the complaint for want of sufficient facts was overruled. It was alleged, in substance, in the complaint, that the plaintiff, August 14, 1896, executed to the defendants his promissory note to pay in 60 days thereafter $538.62 to the defendants, who then and ever since that time were partners doing a banking business under a firm name stated; that the defendants had and retained possession of the note, so that the plaintiff was unable to file a copy thereof; that, concurrently with the execution thereof, to secure the payment thereof, the plaintiff executed to the defendants his mortgage, a copy of which was exhibited, whereby, it was alleged, the plaintiff and his wife mortgaged and warranted to the defendants certain described real estate in Carroll county, and August 18, 1896, the defendants caused the mortgage to be duly recorded, etc. The complaint contained allegations, about which no question is made, to show that a portion of the amount of the note was for usurious interest, and that the plaintiff had paid the note in part. It was then alleged that at the beginning of this suit, computing interest at 8 per cent. per annum, and deducting the payments, there was due the defendants the sum of $226.90, and no more; that October 1, 1902, before the commencement of this suit, the plaintiff tendered to the defendants, in payment of the note and mortgage, "the sum of two hundred and seventy-five dollars, in lawful money, which was even more than the amount due them, which said defendants refused to accept, and, to make and keep said tender good, the plaintiff has deposited with the clerk of this court the said money, subject to the order of said defendants. Wherefore plaintiff prays that the court decree satisfaction of said note and mortgage; that they surrender possession of said note to the plaintiff, and enter satisfaction of said mortgage upon the record thereof in the office of the recorder, or that the court direct the clerk of this court to enter such satisfaction; if the court shall find that said tender is sufficient, that the court find and decree the amount due to the defendants, which plaintiff offers to pay; and for all other proper relief."

The appellant objects to the complaint on the ground of insufficiency of the allegations relating to the tender. It appears from the record that the complaint was filed in open court October 25, 1902 (the note and mortgage being payable in 60 days after August 14, 1896), and that at the time of filing the complaint "the plaintiff also pays into court the sum of two hundred and seventy-five dollars in gold, good and lawful money of the United States." We think that, in such a condition of the record, the question suggested by counsel, as to whether payment of the money to the clerk of the court—the manner of payment alleged in the complaint—amounts to a payment of the money into court, and also the question as to whether the complaint shows a paying in of money of such kind as is necessary for keeping a tender good, are immaterial questions, inasmuch as it affirmatively appears that the money paid in was not merely lawful money, but was legal-tender money, and that it was paid in the presence and under the supervision of the court. If it cannot be said that it is shown that the "lawful money" alleged to have been tendered was the same money paid into court, and therefore legal-tender money, it does not necessarily follow that the complaint did not show any cause of action. It was averred that the note secured by the mortgage included, as a part of the amount for which it was given, usurious interest, and part payment was alleged, and it was claimed that only a portion of the sum represented by the note was due; and an offer of payment, and a refusal thereof, were stated. While it was claimed that the amount paid into court, so shown by the record to be legal-tender money, was all that was due, and more, the plaintiff, in the complaint, proceeding upon the theory that the court should ascertain the amount really due, proposed that, if the court should find that the tender was insufficient, it should find and decree the amount due the defendants, which amount the plaintiff offered to pay, and he prayed for all proper relief. We think the complaint may be regarded as sufficiently showing a cause of action for redemption by the mortgagor, the suit being "really one to free the mortgagor's land from the incumbrance, to compel the mortgagee to accept the amount actually due, if any, and to discharge the mortgage of record." Pom. Eq. Jur. § 219. It was not necessary that the complaint should show a strict legal tender, kept good by bringing the money into court. An equitable tender, such as was made in the conclusion of the complaint, was sufficient. See Kemp v. Mitchell, 36 Ind. 249, 254; Spath v. Hawkins, 55 Ind. 155; Coombs v. Carr, 55 Ind. 303; Nesbit v. Hanway, 87 Ind. 400; Horn v. Indianapolis Nat. Bank, 125 Ind. 381, 25 N. E. 558, 9 L. R. A. 676, 21 Am. St. Rep. 231; Dawson v. Overmyer, 141 Ind. 438, 40 N. E. 1065.

The appellant filed an answer in several paragraphs—one of them a general denial. He also filed a cross-complaint against the plaintiff and others alleged to have some interest in the land subordinate to the mortgage; the appellant alleging that the note was made to him under the firm name, and seeking to enforce payment thereof, and the foreclosure of the mortgage. The plaintiff answered the cross-complaint—the facts set forth in the third paragraph, pleaded as an answer of payment, being like those averred in the complaint. The only other question pressed in the appellant's brief relates to the action of the court in overruling his demurrer to this third paragraph of answer to his cross-complaint. The court adjudged the note and mortgage satisfied, and directed the clerk to enter satisfaction upon the record of the mortgage, and adjudged that the appellant take nothing upon his cross-complaint. It was also adjudged that the money paid into court by the plaintiff belonged to the appellant, and the clerk was directed to deliver the same to the appellant. It was further adjudged that the plaintiff pay and satisfy the costs herein, to and including the filing of his complaint, and that the appellant pay and satisfy all other costs. We have deemed it necessary to determine whether or not the third paragraph of answer to the cross-complaint stated facts sufficient for an answer to a complaint upon the note and mortgage. The only ground of attack upon the judgment against the appellant, upon the complaint of the plaintiff, Gerhold, is the alleged insufficiency of his complaint, which we regard as sufficient. There could be no foreclosure of the mortgage if the mortgagor, who took the initiative, established his right to have satisfaction thereof entered of record. No error being shown, requiring a reversal of the conclusion thus reached, it does not seem to be material whether or not the answer to the cross-complaint for the foreclosure of the mortgage was technically sufficient. To reach that conclusion, it was necessary for the court to find not merely all the material facts stated in that paragraph of answer, but also such additional facts as were shown in the complaint, but not shown in that answer. The court expressly found the complaint to be true.

The judgment for the plaintiff on his complaint, and against the appellant on his cross-complaint, does not proceed upon the ground of payment before suit brought; nor is the judgment, or any part of it, based upon the theory of a strict tender before suit, kept good by bringing the money tendered into court, in which regard the answer is attacked here. It sufficiently appears that the judgment is not affected by any supposed error in ruling upon this demurrer. Having upheld the suit of the plaintiff upon its own merits, it necessarily followed that there could be no foreclosure of the mortgage, and that there could be no recovery upon the cross-complaint; and we would not be justified in reversing the entire judgment because of an infirmity in the answer pleaded as a bar to the cross-complaint, seeking the foreclosure of the mortgage, such infirmity consisting of inadequacy of the averments of the answer to show a tender made before suit brought, and kept good thereafter.

Judgment affirmed.

(32 Ind. A. 656)

BICKELL v. STATE.

(Appellate Court of Indiana, Division No. 1. April 5, 1904.)

CRIMINAL LAW—COMMON GAMBLER—INDICTMENT.

1. Under Burns' Ann. St. 1901, § 2180, providing that whoever, for the purpose of gaming with cards or otherwise, travels from place to place, or frequents any place where gambling is permitted, or engages in gambling for a livelihood, is a common gambler, all the acts mentioned disjunctively in the statute may be charged conjunctively in a single count of an indictment as constituting a single offense.

2. Under Burns' Ann. St. 1901, § 2180, defining a common gambler as one who, "for the purpose of gaming with cards or otherwise," does certain acts, an indictment for being a common gambler should charge the kind of gaming indulged in.

Appeal from Circuit Court, Allen County; Edward O'Rourke, Judge.

Jacob Bickell was convicted of being a common gambler, and appeals. Reversed.

S. M. Hench, for appellant. E. V. Emerick, C. W. Miller, Atty. Gen., W. C. Geake, C. C. Hadley, and L. G. Rothschild, for the State.

ROBINSON, J. Appellant was indicted, tried, and convicted under the statute providing that "whoever, for the purpose of gaming with cards or otherwise, travels about from place to place, or frequents any place where gambling is permitted, or engages in gambling for a livelihood, is a common gambler, and upon conviction" shall be fined. Burns' Ann. St. 1901, § 2180. The indictment charges that the appellant was on a day named, "and on divers other days thereafter and previous, found unlawfully wandering about from place to place for the purpose of gambling, frequenting gambling rooms and houses, and in the practice and habit of gambling, and then and there and thereby gaining his livelihood," contrary to the statute. Overruling appellant's motion to quash is the only question presented.

The statute defines the offense, and such acts as the statute mentions are necessary elements of the offense, and must be established by proper evidence. A common gambler is a person who does the certain acts mentioned by the statute. The statute has made it an offense to do any one of three things, all of which are punishable alike. These several things are mentioned disjunctively, and in such cases it is a general rule that all the things mentioned in the statute may be charged conjunctively in a single count as constituting a single offense. State v. Stout, 112 Ind. 245, 13 N. E. 715; Fahnestock v. State, 102 Ind. 156, 1 N. E. 372; Marshall v. State, 123 Ind. 128, 23 N. E. 1141. If the indictment is insufficient, it is because it fails to charge that the offenses therein enumerated were committed "with cards or otherwise." This statute formerly read as it does now, except the words "or engages in gambling for a livelihood" were omitted, and, as it then read, it was construed in Howard v. State, 64 Ind. 516, where the charge was unlawfully frequenting, for the purpose of gaming with cards, a place where gambling was permitted. In answer to the objection that the affidavit should have specified the kind of gambling which was permitted in the room, and that appellant frequented the room for the purpose of gaming with cards, at the kind of game that was permitted therein, the court, holding this to be unnecessary,

¶ 1. See Gaming, vol. 24, Cent. Dig. § 235.

said: "If the defendant frequented the room for the purpose of gaming with cards, it was wholly immaterial what kind of a game at cards was permitted, or what kind the defendant frequented the room to play at." See State v. Allen, 69 Ind. 124; Webster v. State, 8 Blackf. 400; State v. Maxwell, 5 Blackf. 230; Courtney v. State, 5 Ind. App. 356, 32 N. E. 335; Gillett's Criminal Law, §§ 480, 481. Under the above decisions, we think the indictment should charge the kind of gaming committed or indulged in; that is, if the gaming was with cards, the indictment should so state, or the indictment should charge some one or more acts which are characterized by the statutes of the state as gaming.

Judgment reversed.

(33 Ind. A. 6)

BELL et al. v. BITNER.

(Appellate Court of Indiana, Division No. 1. April 7, 1904.)

CONTRACTS — PLEADING CONTRACT — PAROL OR WRITTEN — PRESUMPTION — LANDLORD AND TENANT — ACTION FOR RENT—DEFENSE — ANSWER—DEMURRER.

1. Where a contract counted on in a pleading is not alleged to have been in writing, it will be presumed to have been in parol.

2. In an action for rent due plaintiffs as owners of land, and which had accrued since they became owners, the answer alleged a contract between defendant and the former owner, defendant's lessor, whereby he agreed that, if defendant would make improvements, he would pay defendant for such labor and expenses at the termination of the tenancy; alleged the making of the improvements, that the tenancy had terminated, and that defendant had withheld the sum sued for to discharge his equitable lien. *Held*, that the answer was demurrable; it not alleging that defendant had any lien on the rents, or that there was any personal liability on the part of plaintiffs, and there being no effort in the pleadings to follow the real estate for the purpose of enforcing any lien.

Appeal from Circuit Court, Howard County; W. W. Mount, Judge.

Action by Jane Bell and others against William Bitner. From a judgment in favor of defendant, plaintiffs appeal. Reversed.

Gifford & Gifford and Joseph P. Gray, for appellants. Gifford & Nash and Blacklidge, Shirley & Wolf, for appellee.

ROBINSON, J. Suit by appellants for $625 rent. Appellee answered in four paragraphs: First, general denial; second, payment; third, that appellee rented the land from one James Bell, the owner, and entered as a tenant from year to year; that about the 1st day of October, 1884, Bell agreed with appellee that if appellee would make improvements, in the way of a house and barn, fencing, clearing the land of stumps, digging wells, etc., Bell would pay him for such work, labor, and expense incurred in making such improvements, when appellee should have to leave the farm, and his tenancy on the farm had terminated, and that appellee should have to pay for certain seed sown during the last year of the tenancy; that appellee did make improvements, as shown by a bill of particulars filed as an exhibit, and occupied the land from the date of such agreement until March 1, 1901; that Bell died in July, 1895, leaving the lands to appellants, and appellee continued to occupy the land, holding possession of the land to secure the payment of his equitable lien for such improvements, and for the purpose of being reimbursed out of the rents of the land for the improvements made under the contract when he should have to leave the farm; that in 1900 appellants sold the land to one Hinkle, and gave appellee three months' notice to give possession March 1, 1901, and, in pursuance of such notice, appellee gave possession to the owner, and withheld the sum of $625 of the rents, and applied the same to the discharge of his equitable lien. The fourth paragraph alleges, in addition, that appellants, having knowledge of appellee's contract with Bell, directed him to continue as tenant under that contract, and that appellants, in consideration of the peaceable possession on March 1, 1901, and the release of an equitable lien thereon for such improvements, assumed and agreed to pay for the improvements made prior to the death of Bell, alleged to amount to $1,155, when appellee should leave the farm; that, in pursuance to such agreement, appellee released his equitable lien and gave possession. Demurrers were overruled to the third and fourth paragraphs of answer, and a verdict rendered in appellee's favor as to the complaint, and in appellee's favor upon the fourth paragraph of answer for $375 in excess of the amount claimed by appellants. Appellee remitted $375, and judgment was rendered against appellants for costs.

The demurrer to the third paragraph of answer should have been sustained. As the pleading does not show the contract concerning the improvements to have been in writing, it is presumed it was in parol. It is not shown that the agreement was a part of the contract of leasing. This is not an action to recover possession of land which a tenant claims the right to hold until improvements provided for in the contract of leasing are paid for. Mullen v. Pugh, 16 Ind. App. 337, 45 N. E. 347. Nor is it an action of ejectment against a tenant in possession under a written lease, in which it was provided that certain improvements to be made by the tenant should be paid for by the lessor at the end of the term. Ecke v. Fetzer, 65 Wis. 55, 26 N. W. 266. The complaint is an action to recover rent due appellants as owners of the land—rent which has accrued since they became such owners. It is not claimed in this paragraph that appellee has any equitable or other lien on the rents due appellants, nor that there is any personal liability on the part of appellants for the amount claimed to

¶ 1. See Contracts, vol. 11, Cent. Dig. § 1642.

be due appellee, nor does the pleading seek to follow the real estate for the purpose of enforcing any lien. This answer shows no more than a claim against the estate of James Bell for the value of improvements made under a contract with him while appellee was his tenant, and pleads no facts showing a right to claim the value of such improvements as a set-off to the demand of appellants for rents which have accrued to them as owners of the land.

Judgment reversed.

(32 Ind. A. 665)

STATE v. PETERMAN.

(Appellate Court of Indiana, Division No. 1. April 6, 1904.)

COMPULSORY EDUCATION — STATUTES — CONSTRUCTION—WHAT CONSTITUTES SCHOOL.

1. A parent in good faith employed a teacher formerly employed in the public schools to teach his child. It was arranged that the child should be taught all the branches taught in the public schools, at the regular public school hours. The child attended the teacher's home regularly every school day, and received instruction equal to that which could have been received at the public schools. The teacher did not advertise herself as keeping a private school, and had no regular tuition fixed, nor any school equipments, and made no arrangement to take other pupils. *Held* a compliance with Burns' Ann. St. 1901, § 6033a, providing that every parent shall be required to send his child to a public, private, or parochial school each school year for a term not less than that of the public schools where the child resides.

Appeal from Circuit Court, Montgomery County; Jere West, Judge.

Clarence Peterman was prosecuted for a violation of the compulsory educational law. From a judgment of acquittal, the state appeals. Affirmed.

James B. Murphy, Clyde H. Jones, C. W. Miller, Atty. Gen., L. G. Rothschild, C. C. Hadley, and W. C. Geake, for the State. C. W. Burton and Whittington & Whittington, for appellee.

HENLEY, C. J. Appellee was prosecuted for an alleged violation of section 6033a, Burns' Ann. St. 1901, of the compulsory educational law. The statute referred to is in the following words:

"Sec. 6033a. That every parent, guardian or custodian, having control or charge of any child or children between the ages of seven and fourteen years, inclusive, shall be required to send such child or children to a public, private or parochial school, or to two or all of these schools, each school year, for a term or period not less than that of the public schools of the school corporation where the child or children reside: provided, that no child in good mental and physical condition shall for any cause, any rule or law to the contrary, be precluded from attending school when such school is in session.

"Sec. 6033b. * * * The truant officer shall see that the provisions of this act are complied with, and when from personal knowledge, or by report or complaint from any resident or teacher of the township under his supervision, he believes that any child subject to the provisions of this act is habitually absent or tardy from school, he shall immediately give written notice to the parent, guardian or custodian of such child that the attendance of such child is required at school, and if within five days such parent, guardian or custodian of such child does not comply with the provisions of this section, then such truant officer shall make complaint against such parent, guardian or custodian of such child in any court of record for violation of the provisions of this act. * * * Any such parent, guardian or custodian of any child who shall violate the provisions of this act shall be adjudged guilty of a misdemeanor and upon conviction thereof shall be fined in any sum not less than five dollars, nor more than twenty-five dollars, to which may be added, in the discretion of the court, imprisonment in the county jail not less than two or more than ninety days."

It was shown by the defendant (appellee) upon the trial, that, immediately after he was served with notice by the truant officer, he employed one Mrs. Hugelheim to teach his said child at the home of said Mrs. Hugelheim, she living at said time in the town of Mace, about one-fourth of a mile from the residence of the defendant; that the said Mrs. Hugelheim was a competent teacher, in every way qualified to teach in the public schools, and that she had for several years taught in the public schools of said Montgomery county, and was a very successful teacher, and was recognized by the superintendent of said county as a good, efficient, well-qualified, and successful teacher; that it had been two years since she had taught in the public schools, and one year since she had held a teacher's license, but that she had never been refused a teacher's license or failed on an examination, but had quit teaching school by reason of her getting married, and at the time said arrangement was made with her by said defendant she was a married woman, but had no children, and her husband was not at home from Monday until Saturday evening; that it was arranged with said Mrs. Hugelheim that she should teach said child all the branches and whatever was taught in the public schools, and that she should go to her home at the regular public school hours in the morning, and should remain during the whole day, and be under the training and discipline of the said Mrs. Hugelheim, and that she should have her at a desk studying or have her reciting during all the time from half past 8 in the morning until 4 in the afternoon, except that she should have 15 mines' intermission in the morning at the regular intermission time at the public school, and should have an hour's intermission at noon, and 15 minutes' intermission in the afternoon; that she was to teach said child during the public school or year from the time she took said child to the time said public school would close for the year 1903; that no definite amount was agreed upon to be paid by said defendant to said Hugelheim for her said services in said matter, but that it was agreed that he would pay her whatever was right; that said child commenced attending at the home of said Hugelheim, and she commenced teaching and training her according to said contract, on the 22d day of January, 1903, and that said child has attended at said home of said Hugelheim regularly every school day in the week, and has been taught by said Mrs. Hugelheim according to said arrangements, and has received instructions equal to that to which she would have received, had she attended the public schools, and has advanced as fast or faster than she did while attending public school, and that said teacher has regularly attended her at all times, and has given her proper instructions and has taught her all the branches that she would have been taught, had she attended the public school; that the said Mrs. Hugelheim did not advertise herself as keeping a private school, and had no regular tuition fixed, and had no school equipments, other than a study table and a desk owned by said child, and a blackboard upon said desk, and that she had said child sit most of the time at her desk in the sitting room, but sometimes, when she thought said child, on account of her age, should move around, she allowed her temporarily to be in the kitchen, and that said Mrs. Hugelheim had no arrangements to take any other pupils for instruction; that there was evidence from which said jury could find that said arrangement was entered into in good faith in an honest effort to carry out the provisions of said section of the statute providing for compulsory education, and that all children between certain ages should attend a public, private, or parochial school during the school year of the district in which they live, and that it was the intention of said defendant to keep his said child at school under said arrangements with said Mrs. Hugelheim, and that the said Mrs. Hugelheim intended to keep said child regularly at her studies during the same time that she would have been, had she attended the public school, and that the said Mrs. Hugelheim gave her and will continue to give her the same instruction that she would have received, had she attended the said public school, and that the said Mrs. Hugelheim was capable and able to give said child said instruction; that the said Mrs. Hugelheim did not advertise herself as keeping a private school, and was not known in the neighborhood as the keeper of a private school, and she did not desire to receive or attempt to get other pupils than the defendant's said child, and had not made up her mind at that time to receive other pupils, should they apply, and had no regular tuition fixed and no regularly prescribed terms of school, and that the said Mrs. Hugelheim had never attempted to run a private school before, or to receive pupils for instruction; that it was agreed between the said defendant and the said Mrs. Hugelheim that she should teach said child under said agreement as long as the public schools in that township were in session, and for a time or period not less than that of the public schools of the school corporation where said child resided, and give her a course equal, if not superior, to that of the public schools. It was also shown that appellee's child had been attending the public school of the district in which he resided until taken therefrom by him on account of some disagreement with the teacher and the school authorities. Upon trial, the jury returned a verdict of not guilty.

Appellant complains of the action of the court in refusing to give certain instructions, the discussion of which, we think, will cover every question raised by the appeal. The whole question in this case is, what is a private school, within the meaning of the statute? The contention of the appellant is clearly stated in the following instruction, which was refused by the court: "(3) A private school, within the meaning of the law under which this prosecution is conducted, means a reputable private school, organized and conducted as such in good faith by a reputable person or persons, who possess the necessary qualifications as teacher or teachers, or in which such teacher or teachers were provided, and who have the proper equipment for conducting such a school, and who hold themselves out as conducting such a school." We think the instruction was properly refused, because it is radically wrong. A school, in the ordinary acceptation of its meaning, is a place where instruction is imparted to the young. If a parent employs and brings into his residence a teacher for the purpose of instructing his child or children, and such instruction is given as the law contemplates, the meaning and spirit of the law have been fully complied with. This would be the school of the child or children so educated, and would be as much a private school as if advertised and conducted as such. We do not think that the number of persons, whether one or many, make a place where instruction is imparted any less or more a school. Under a law very similar to ours, the Supreme Court of Massachusetts has held that the object and purpose of a compulsory educational law are that all the children shall be educated, not that they shall be educated in any particular way. Commonwealth v. Roberts, 34 N. E. 402.

The other instructions tendered by appellant and refused, of which complaint is made, were perhaps not so radical as the one quoted, in their general definition of a private school, and the duty of the parent under the statute; but they were all wrong, and tainted with the general proposition which pervaded appellant's argument to the effect that the law has to do with the way or place where a child shall be educated. In State v. Bailey, 157 Ind. 329, 61 N. E. 731, 59 L. R. A. 435, the court said: "The natural rights of the parent to the custody and control of his infant child are subordinate to the power of the state, and may be restricted and regulated by municipal laws. One of the most important natural duties of the parent is his obligation to educate his child, and this duty he owes not to the child, only, but to the commonwealth. If he neglects to perform it, or willfully refuses to do so, he may be coerced by law to execute such civil obligations. The welfare of the child and the best interests of society require that the state shall exercise its sovereign authority to secure to the child the opportunity to acquire an education. Statutes making it compulsory upon the parent, guardian, or other person having the custody and control of children to send them to public or private schools for longer or shorter periods during certain years of the life of such children have not only been upheld as strictly within the constitutional power of the Legislature, but have generally been regarded as necessary to carry out the express purpose of the Constitution itself." But what is all this for? Why does the state take control of the child, under certain circumstances, at a certain period of its life? Its purpose is "to secure to the child the opportunity to acquire an education," which the welfare of the child and the best interests of society demand. The result to be obtained, and not the means or manner of attaining it, was the goal which the lawmakers were attempting to reach. The law was made for the parent, who does not educate his child, and not for the parent who employs a teacher and pays him out of his private purse, and so places within the reach of the child the opportunity and means of acquiring an education equal to that obtainable in the public schools of the state. The instructions given by the court to the jury were, to say the least, as favorable to appellant as our construction of the statute would warrant.

The appeal of the state is not sustained.

(33 Ind. A. 1)

CARR v. HUNTINGTON LIGHT & FUEL CO.

(Appellate Court of Indiana, Division No. 1. April 7, 1904.)

MINES AND MINERALS—OIL AND GAS LEASES—INTEREST OF LESSEE—FORFEITURE—QUIETING TITLE—COMPLAINT—SUFFICIENCY OF DESCRIPTION.

1. Where defendant entered on land and produced gas under an instrument by which plaintiff conveyed all the oil and gas on the premises, together with the exclusive right to enter thereon to drill and operate for oil and gas, maintain and remove buildings, pipes, machinery, etc., in consideration of certain payments to be made, defendant acquired a vested interest in the land for the purposes named in the instrument.

2. The breach of a covenant by defendant to develop plaintiff's land for oil in accordance with a contract giving defendant the right to enter on the land for the purpose of operating for gas and oil does not give plaintiff the right to declare a forfeiture or procure the cancellation of the contract.

3. A complaint praying that plaintiff's title be quieted to a certain tract of land, "except a one-half acre tract surrounding each of said three wells," is insufficient in definiteness in its description of the land.

Appeal from Superior Court, Grant County; Hiram Brownlee, Judge.

Action by Alonzo W. Carr against the Huntington Light & Fuel Company. From a judgment for defendant, plaintiff appeals. Affirmed.

John A. Kersey, for appellant. St. John & Charles, for appellee.

HENLEY, C. J. Appellant commenced this action against appellee to quiet his title to the northeast quarter of the southwest quarter and the northwest quarter of the southeast quarter of section 18, township 24 north, range 9 east, in Grant county, Ind. The controversy grows out of the claims of appellee under an agreement entered into by the parties to the action on the 3d day of October, 1898, and which, omitting the formal parts, was in the following words:

"In consideration of the sum of Forty ($40.00) Dollars, and the covenants and agreements hereinafter contained, A. W. Carr and wife, first party, hereby grant and convey unto the Huntington Light and Fuel Company, second party, heirs or assigns, all the oil and gas in and under the following described premises, together with the exclusive right to enter thereon at all times for the purpose of drilling, or operating for oil, gas or water, to erect, maintain and remove all buildings, structures, pipes, pipe lines and machinery necessary for the production, storage and transportation of oil, gas or water, providing that the first party shall have the right to use said premises for farming purposes (except such part as is actually occupied by second party), namely: A lot of land situate in the township of Monroe, county of Grant, in the state of Indiana, as is described as follows, to wit: The northeast (¼) of the southwest (¼), and also the northwest (¼) of the southeast (¼) all in Section eighteen (18) township twenty-four (24) north, range nine (9) east, containing in all eighty acres more or less.

"The above grant is made upon the following terms:

"Second party agrees to drill a well upon said premises within twelve months from this date, or thereafter pay in advance the first party for further delay a yearly rental of forty ($40.00) dollars, until said well is drilled.

"Such rentals, when due, shall be deposited in Marion Bank, at Marion, Grant county, State of Indiana.

"Should second party refuse to make such deposits, or pay to first party on these premises, or at present residence of first party, the said rental when due as aforesaid, such refusal shall be construed by both parties hereto as the act of second party for the purpose of surrendering the rights hereby granted, and this instrument, in default of the rental payments, shall be null and void without further notice from second party.

"Should oil be found in paying quantities upon these premises, second party agrees to deliver to first party in the pipe line with which he may connect the well or wells, one-eighth (⅛) part of all oil produced and saved from the premises.

"Should gas be found second party agrees to pay first party One Hundred ($100.00) Dollars yearly, payable annually in advance, for each and every well from which gas is transported, or used off the premises, so long as the same is so transported.

"First party shall have free of expense, gas by March 15, 1899, to use at his own risk, to light and heat the dwellings and for domestic use, on said premises, by making connection at the N. W. corner of the southwest (¼) of Sec. (18) Township (24) North, Range (9) East.

"Second party shall bury, when requested so to do by the first party, all oil and gas lines, and pay all damages to growing crops, timber and fencing, caused by the aforesaid operations.

"No well shall be drilled nearer than 800 feet of the buildings now on the premises, without the consent of the first party, and no well shall occupy more than one-half acre.

"All additional taxes arising from increased valuation on each (½) acre drilled, caused by said operations thereon, shall be paid by the parties of the second part.

"Second party may at any time reconvey this grant, and thereupon this instrument shall be null and void.

"Should gas be found and not utilized from said land, rental shall be paid the same as gas well rental after 30 days from completion of well, if oil is found in paying quantities, same to be marketed within six (6) months from completion, or pay One Hundred Dollars per year until pipe line is laid in said Territory."

It is averred in the complaint, which is in one paragraph, that appellant is the owner of the fee of the real estate heretofore described; that appellee claims an interest in said real estate by reason of the lease heretofore set out, which is made a part of the complaint; that said lease was made for the purpose of exploring and developing said land for gas and oil by means of wells to be drilled thereon by appellee, and not for the purpose of enabling the lessee to hold the land, or any part thereof, and prevent the same from being developed; that there are many gas and oil wells drilled and being drilled by appellee upon lands adjacent to appellant's said land, and that gas and oil is being taken in large quantities from said wells, thereby taking the gas and oil from under appellant's said land; that "four of said wells on said adjacent lands are at distances from plaintiff's land as follows: One at 115 feet, one at 282 feet, one at 280 feet, and one at 600 feet; and all are pumping and producing oil in paying quantities, and are taking the same from plaintiff's said land." The complaint further avers that appellee has not, during the three years during which it has held the land, diligently or in good faith developed the land so held for either gas or oil, but has drilled only three wells on the 80 acres of land so held; that said wells were drilled only for gas; that if they had been drilled deeper, in Trenton rock, they would have produced oil in paying quantities; that, but for appellee's claim under said lease, appellant could procure the development of all his land for gas and oil. The complaint then concludes as follows: "Said defendant's interest in said lands under and by virtue of said lease, and on account of said three wells, extends to and includes one-half acre for each well, they being, respectively, in the center of such one-half acre tract; and the defendant having a right of ingress thereto and egress therefrom over the other lands of the plaintiff for the purpose of obtaining and transporting gas from said three wells. All the residue of said eighty-acre tract of land belongs absolutely to the plaintiff, the defendant failing and refusing to develop the same as aforesaid, and its said claim is wrongful and a cloud upon his title. Wherefore the plaintiff prays the court that his title to all said eighty-acre tract of land, except a one-half acre tract surrounding each of said three wells, and on the center of which, respectively, each of said wells is, and the right of access thereto for the purpose of transporting gas therefrom, be quieted in him, and that said lease be canceled."

The trial court sustained appellee's demurrer to the complaint. The sufficiency of the complaint is the only question presented by this appeal. The complaint shows that appellee entered upon the land and caused to be drilled three gas wells, and that appellant received and is receiving therefrom, under the agreement, the sum of $300 per annum. Through the instrument and entry and the production of gas thereunder, appellee acquired a vested interest in the land for the purposes named in the lease. McKnight v. Mfrs. N. G. Co., 146 Pa. 185, 23 Atl. 164, 28 Am. St. Rep. 790; Harris v. Ohio Oil Co., 57 Ohio St. 118, 48 N. E. 502; Heller v. Dailey, 28 Ind. App. 555, 63 N. E. 490. Assuming that the appellee impliedly covenanted to reasonably develop and operate the land for oil, and that appellee had broken the implied covenant as to the development for oil, appellant's remedy is not by way of forfeiture or cancellation of the contract. Harris v. Ohio Oil Co., supra.

The complaint in the case at bar is insufficient for the further reason that the description of the real estate, the title to which is sought to be quieted, is insufficient. Jones v. Mount, 30 Ind. App. 59, 63 N. E. 798, and cases cited.

Judgment affirmed.

ROBINSON, J., concurs in result.

(33 Ind. A. 659)

EVANSVILLE & T. H. R. CO. v. CLEMENTS.

(Appellate Court of Indiana, Division No. 2. April 6, 1904.)

RAILROADS — CROSSING INJURIES—NEGLIGENCE —FAILURE TO WARN—CONTRIBUTORY NEGLIGENCE—CARE REQUIRED—LOOKING AND LISTENING — OBSTRUCTIONS TO VIEW — EFFECT— INSTRUCTIONS—CURE—TRIAL—INCONSISTENCY OF VERDICT WITH FINDINGS.

1. The action of a railroad in running a train at a speed of 60 miles an hour through a village without ringing a bell, or sounding a whistle, or giving any signal of its approach to a crossing, is negligence.

2. A general verdict prevails over special findings if there could have been, under the issues, proof of supposable facts not inconsistent with those specially found, sufficient to sustain the general verdict.

3. In an action against a railroad for crossing injuries, a charge that it was defendant's duty to give the statutory signals on approaching a crossing, and if it failed to do so, and injury resulted therefrom, the defendant would be guilty of negligence, and if the engineer failed to sound the whistle and ring the bell, and by reason of such failure the accident occurred, and plaintiff was injured without negligence on his part, the verdict should be for him, was not open to the objection of relieving plaintiff from the exercise of ordinary care.

4. A railroad track on the level with the highway is in itself a warning of danger, and, if a traveler's view is obstructed, he is admonished of that danger, and must exercise caution commensurate therewith.

5. Failure of an engineer to sound his whistle or ring his bell on approaching a crossing does not relieve a traveler on the highway from the use of care and ordinary prudence for his own safety.

6. It is not negligence with respect to a traveler on a crossing for a railroad to maintain buildings on its right of way reasonably necessary for the prosecution of its business.

7. There is no duty on a railroad to maintain a watchman at a crossing in a small village.

8. A pedestrian approaching a railroad crossing is not excused from looking and listening for an approaching train because of buildings placed by the railroad on its right of way obstructing the pedestrian's view.

9. A bad instruction is cured only by its withdrawal.

Appeal from Circuit Court, Knox County; O. H. Cobb, Judge.

Action by Lawrence Clements against the Evansville & Terre Haute Railroad Company. From a judgment for plaintiff, defendant appeals. Reversed.

¶ 4. See Railroads, vol. 41, Cent. Dig. § 1057.

Iglehart & Taylor and Emison & Moffett, for appellant. Cullop & Shaw, for appellee.

COMSTOCK, J. The appellee brought this action against the appellant to recover damages for injuries to his person received in a collision with one of the appellant's passenger trains at a street crossing in Oaktown, Knox county, Ind. Judgment was rendered in favor of the appellee upon the verdict of the jury for $1,000. With their general verdict the jury returned answers to interrogatories. Motions by the appellant for a judgment on the answers to the interrogatories and for a new trial were overruled. The errors assigned relate to the overruling of these two motions and in overruling a demurrer to the complaint.

The complaint avers, in substance, omitting the formal parts, that the railroad of the appellee runs through the business and residence portion of Oaktown, a place of 600 inhabitants; that it intersects therein a much-traveled public highway, which runs east and west, the railroad running north and south; that on the north side of the street, and up to and along its line, and along and up its tracks on the east side, the appellee maintained a depot building 25 feet high, 30 feet wide, and 60 feet long, and north of the depot on its right of way a hand car house 20 feet by 12 feet and 12 feet high; that these buildings obstructed the view of trains by travelers approaching the crossing from the east; that the plaintiff was driving a team along the highway from east to west, and approaching the crossing in a careful and prudent manner, stopping, looking, and listening, but neither seeing nor hearing a coming train; that while he was attempting to cross over the crossing in a careful and prudent manner the defendant negligently ran one of its trains from the north, and approaching the crossing at a speed of 60 miles an hour, and, without sounding any whistle or ringing any bell to warn travelers of its approach, collided with the plaintiff, throwing him a distance of 20 feet or more, and inflicting upon him permanent injuries; that, had it not been for the obstructions, or if the defendant had given the proper signals, the collision would not have occurred. Negligence is also alleged on account of the failure to maintain a watchman at the crossing, and the injury is charged to have resulted from the above acts of commission and omission.

The objection made to the complaint is that it shows no actionable negligence, and that no negligent act producing the alleged injury is charged. It alleges that the train was run at a speed of 60 miles an hour without ringing a bell, or sounding a whistle, or giving any signal of its approach to a dangerous crossing. It charges substantially that the train was negligently run against appellee. Acts are charged as follows: maintaining obstructions to the view, failing to keep a watchman at the crossing to give warning, running at a high rate of speed without giving signal or warning, and it is averred that because of any and all of the acts of commission and omission the plaintiff was injured.

The failure to give any warning is of itself an act of negligence, and the complaint is therefore sufficient to withstand a demurrer.

As to the motion for judgment on the answers to the interrogatories notwithstanding the general verdict, we need only allude to the rule that the general verdict prevails over the special findings, if there could have been, under the issues, proofs of supposable facts not inconsistent with those specially found, sufficient to sustain the general verdict; or, in other words, sufficient to reconcile the general verdict with special answers. Rhodius v. Johnson, 24 Ind. App. 406, 56 N. E. 942, and cases cited; Sponhaur v. Malloy, 21 Ind. App. 287, 52 N. E. 245, and cases cited at page 300, 21 Ind. App., 52 N. E. 245. The special verdict finds appellant negligent in failing to give the statutory warning signals. This is not contradicted by any facts specially found. It also finds appellee's freedom from fault. Even if we concede, for the purpose of the argument, that there are special findings in apparent conflict with the general verdict upon the question of appellee's negligence, we cannot say that under the issues proofs of supposable facts could not have been made sufficient, with the facts found, to reconcile the general verdict with the answers to interrogatories.

Certain instructions, to which we will refer, were given to the jury, and exceptions duly taken. Instruction 1 in effect informed the jury that it was the duty of the defendant to give the statutory signals when approaching the crossing of a public highway, and, if there was a failure to do so, and injury occasioned therefrom, defendant would be guilty of negligence, and that, if the jury believed from the evidence that the engineer or person in charge of the engine from which the accident occurred failed to sound the whistle or ring the bell, and that if, by reason of such failure, the accident occurred, and the plaintiff was injured without negligence on his part, the verdict should be in his favor. The objection is made to this instruction that it relieved appellee from the exercise of reasonable and ordinary care under the existing conditions. We do not so understand the instruction. It only designates certain acts of appellant as negligent.

The conclusion of the second instruction is as follows: "So that in this case, if you find from the evidence that the plaintiff, on approaching the crossing on the highway, exercised due care, and employed his senses of seeing and hearing to ascertain if the train was approaching, and thereby avoid danger; and if you further find that he could not see the train because of obstructions, and that he did not hear it because there were no signals, and that he did not know a train was approaching—then the plaintiff would be justified in presuming that there was no train approaching, and that he could pass over the crossing in safety." The objection urged is that, if the plaintiff knew of obstructions to the view, he had no right to assume that he could cross in safety. The railroad track on the level with the highway is itself a warning of danger. Obstructions to the view admonish the traveler of the peril to which he is exposed. Caution must always be exercised commensurate with the known danger. The failure of the engineer to sound the whistle or ring the bell does not relieve the person approaching the highway from the use of care and ordinary prudence for his safety. What is ordinary care in one case would not be ordinary care in another under a different state of facts. "In proportion as the danger increases must the vigilance of the person attempting to cross increase." Oleson v. Lake Shore R. R. Co., 143 Ind. 405, 42 N. E. 736, 32 L. R. A. 149, and cases cited; Towers v. L. E. & W. R. R. Co., 18 Ind. App. 684, 48 N. E. 1046, and cases cited.

In instructions 6, 11, 12, and 13 the court instructed the jury upon the question of appellant's negligence, in substance, that they might consider, among other facts, whether or not the appellant kept a watchman at said crossing, and whether or not it permitted and maintained any obstructions on its right of way. It was not negligent for the appellant to maintain buildings upon its right of way reasonably necessary for the prosecution of its business. The law did not impose upon appellant the duty of maintaining a watchman, yet from the parts of the instruction referred to the jury might reasonably infer that the maintenance of the buildings and the failure to maintain a watchman were acts of negligence for which it was liable. "No weight can properly be given to the finding that the failure of defendants to have a light or flagman at the sidewalk crossing to warn plaintiff of the approach of the locomotive, is negligence." Winchell v. Abbot, 77 Wis. 376, 46 N. W. 665. Said instruction 12 concludes as follows: "If such obstruction, so placed there by the railroad company, would prevent a person traveling upon said highway from both seeing and hearing an approaching train, then it would be useless on his part to look and listen for an approaching train. The law would not require him to do that useless act, and therefore he would be excused for not doing so." The instruction excuses appellee, because of the obstruction named, from exercising reasonable care for his own safety. Within sight, if not within hearing, of danger (for the crossing was itself warning of danger), the jury were told that appellee had no duty to perform, since to look and listen would be useless. The jury might fairly be misled into the belief that appellee, failing, as he testified, to see or hear the approaching train at a distance of 60 feet from the crossing, under the circumstances related, might, without further regard for his safety, proceed upon his way. This was error. Upon the part of appellee it was claimed that the error of these instructions is cured by others given. This we cannot concede. A bad instruction is cured only by its withdrawal. Because of said instructions, and for the reason that we are not prepared to say, from the record, that a right result has been reached, the judgment is reversed, with instructions to sustain appellant's motion for a new trial.

ROBY, J. I concur upon the ground that it was the duty of the traveler to use reasonable care to avoid collision, notwithstanding any negligence of the railway company.

(33 Ind. A. 655)

HALLAGAN v. TANNER et al.

(Appellate Court of Indiana, Division No. 1. April 5, 1904.)

APPEAL—PARTIES TO JUDGMENT—QUESTIONS REVIEWABLE—DISMISSAL.

1. In an action against several defendants the only judgment rendered was one in favor of plaintiff against some of the defendants, and on appeal plaintiff complained of the overruling of his motion for a new trial as to a defendant against whom no judgment was rendered, and in overruling his motion for a new trial generally, but no complaint was made of anything at the trial save instructions claimed to have prejudiced plaintiff as against the defendant in question. *Held*, that the appeal will be dismissed, since, there having been no judgment either in favor of or against the defendant in question, no question as to him was presented.

Appeal from Circuit Court, White County; T. F. Palmer, Judge.

Action by Patrick Hallagan against George W. Tanner and others. Judgment was rendered in favor of plaintiff against some of the defendants, and the cause dismissed as to others, and plaintiff appealed to the Supreme Court. Cause transferred from the Supreme Court to the Appellate Court. Appeal dismissed.

Foltz, Spitler & Kurrie and Reynolds, Sills & Reynolds, for appellant. E. B. Sellers and J. B. Wilson, for appellees.

BLACK, J. This cause has been transferred from the Supreme Court to this court. The appellant, by his complaint, sought to recover the value of certain cattle alleged to have been converted by the defendants therein to their own use, and also to recover the amount of the proceeds of alleged sales of such cattle. Upon the trial by jury of issues formed a verdict was returned for the appellant against two of the defendants, the Sansom Commission Company and Simeon A. Dowell, and in favor of all the other defendants named as such in the complaint, being Stephen W. Thayer and six other persons. All these defendants, together with certain others, who were garnishees, and as to whom the appellant had dismissed during the trial, are named as appellees in the assignment of errors. The appellant addresses his attack against the action of the court in overruling his motion for a new trial as to the defendant Stephen W. Thayer alone. The judgment was rendered in favor of the appellant against the Sansom Commission Company and Simeon A. Dowell, and there does not appear to have been any judgment in favor of or against any other party. There being no final judgment, so far as appears from the record, to which the appellee Thayer was a party, we cannot take any action affecting his rights. The appellant does not claim here that judgment was not correctly awarded him as against the Sansom Commission Company and Simeon A. Dowell, and there was no other judgment; that is, the judgment actually rendered is not attacked. It is true there was also a motion of the appellant for a new trial of the cause generally, the overruling of which also is assigned as error, but there was not stated therein any cause referring to the amount of the recovery, and in his brief appellant has addressed his attention only to certain instructions by which it is claimed his cause was prejudiced as against the defendant Thayer. The case is not so presented that any question affecting Thayer can be decided, and the only apparent purpose of the appeal fails.

Appeal dismissed.

(33 Ind. A. 27)

BALTIMORE & O. S. W. R. CO. v. HUNSUCKER.

(Appellate Court of Indiana, Division No. 2. April 7, 1904.)

SERVANT'S INJURIES—SAFE PLACE TO WORK—APPLICATION OF DOCTRINE—CONTRIBUTORY NEGLIGENCE—FAILURE TO EXERCISE SENSES—PLEADINGS—SUFFICIENCY—FELLOW SERVANT'S ACT—JUDGMENT—REVERSAL—PLEADINGS BAD IN PART.

1. Any danger at a place where a wreck on a railroad has occurred is as open and obvious to an employé sent to remove such wreckage as it is to the railroad, and, the purpose of clearing away the wreckage being to make the place safe, the rule as to the master's duty to furnish a safe place to work does not apply.

2. In order that a complaint for a servant's injuries may be good against a demurrer for want of facts, it must show an absence of knowledge on the part of the servant of the defects or dangers of which he complains; and a general allegation of want of such knowledge is insufficient, in the face of allegations from which it is evident that the servant must have known of the defects or dangers, or that he had the same means or opportunities for such knowledge as the master.

3. The relations between master and servant are reciprocal, each being obligated to use care, diligence, and caution; and, where the servant fails to use his natural senses, he must suffer the consequences, although he did not discover the danger to which he was exposed.

4. Under Burns' Ann. St. 1901, § 7083, making railroads liable for injuries to employés where the injury results from the negligence of any person in its service, to whose order the injured employé was bound to conform and did conform, a complaint alleging that defendant's

superintendent of wreckage, to whom was delegated authority to control the work of clearing away wreckage, had full power to control defendant's servants, including plaintiff; that plaintiff conformed to such orders, and was at the time of his injuries performing his duties in obedience thereto; and that plaintiff's injuries were caused wholly by reason of the negligence of the superintendent in failing to use a derrick to hoist a car bolster which was too heavy to be loaded by hand, and in ordering plaintiff, with other employés, to take hold of such car bolster and load the same, and failing to warn plaintiff of the danger, of which plaintiff did not know—stated a cause of action.

5. Where a complaint for a servant's injuries is in two paragraphs, one good and the other bad, and it does not appear from the record on which paragraph the verdict and judgment for plaintiff rests, such judgment will be reversed, where the trial court overruled a demurrer to the bad paragraph of the complaint.

Appeal from Circuit Court, Jackson County; Thomas B. Buskirk, Judge.

Action by William Hunsucker against the Baltimore & Ohio Southwestern Railroad Company. From a judgment for plaintiff, defendant appeals. Reversed.

McMullen & McMullen and O. H. Montgomery, for appellant. Burton & Vance and McHenry Owen, for appellee.

WILEY, P. J. Action by appellee to recover damages for personal injuries inflicted by the alleged negligence of appellant. Complaint in two paragraphs, to which a demurrer was overruled. Answer in two paragraphs, to the second of which a demurrer was overruled. Reply in denial, trial by jury, general verdict for appellee, and answer to interrogatories. Appellant's motion for judgment on the answers to interrogatories and for a new trial overruled. Appellant also moved to reject and dismiss appellee's complaint on the ground that he refused to submit to an examination as a witness prior to the trial, which motion was also overruled. All rulings adverse to appellant are assigned as errors. Appellee has assigned as cross-error the overruling of his demurrer to the second paragraph of answer.

The first paragraph of complaint avers that appellee was in the employ of appellant as a sectionman; that he was 40 years of age, in good health, and was of great physical strength; that on the 19th of June, 1901, while so employed, there was a wreck of freight cars on appellant's road, by which some cars were derailed and broken into fragments; that it was necessary to clear away said wreckage, to place the derailed cars back on the track, and, in clearing away said wreckage, it became necessary to hoist and load and haul parts of the broken cars away; that it became necessary for the superintendent of wreckage to take charge of the work, and it was the duty of the sectionmen to obey his orders and directions, and said superintendent ordered and directed the sectionmen, including appellee, to assist in the work; that the superintendent of wreckage had the necessary appliances, derrick, tools, and implements to clear away the wreckage, and had the same in process of operation, and, in addition thereto, had cars, engines, and trains for the purpose of carrying the wreckage away; that it was a part of appellee's duty to assist in clearing away said wreckage; that, in performing said work, there was used for loading the heavy parts a derrick, until near its completion, when it became necessary to load heavy pieces, known as a "car bolster," which weighed about 1,500 pounds; that, in loading the same, the superintendent of wreckage ordered and directed the sectionmen, including appellee, to take hold of the same with their hands and load it into one of the "dump or side-dump" cars, which had a high siding; that, in attempting to load it, several of the employés, including appellee, took hold of it, which was irregular in shape, had bolts, bolt heads, or plates projecting on the sides or edges, which prevented it from slipping on the top of the car, and, when they had placed one end on the top of the end of said dump car, there was a bolt or bolt head or plate projecting from the underside, which made it necessary to lift the said car bolster so it would pass said point and slip over the end into the car, but, in attempting to do so, the bolster was too heavy for the number of men who could get hold of it to handle it, and, appellee being at the end of the bolster, with his hands and right shoulder under and attempting to support it, and standing on the ground, and being lower than the top of the dump car, and those engaged in trying to load it in the car being unable to hold it, by reason of its weight, it slipped back against appellee's shoulder, and, being unable to extricate himself and escape, he had to hold the same, whereby he was injured. (Here follow the particulars of the injuries appellee sustained.) This paragraph of complaint then charges appellant with these specific acts of negligence, to wit, that the said car bolster was too large and heavy and ill shaped to be loaded on a car by the personal and manual efforts of the sectionmen, and should have been hoisted and loaded by the derrick which was there and in use, and could have been supplied by the exercise of reasonable care; that to so attempt to load the same into a car, with the sides and ends thereof eight to ten feet high, was dangerous to life and limb, and was known to be so by appellant, and that appellant also knew that the proper and safe way to load the said car bolster was by the use of the derrick; that appellee had no knowledge of the great weight of the car bolster, nor of the danger or unsafety of attempting to hoist and load it in the manner attempted; that he had no knowledge or notice that there were upon the sides and edges of the car bolster any bolts, bolt heads, or plates projecting therefrom, and did not know it was dangerous to attempt to load it, until the same had been placed upon the top of the end of the car, at which time it became impossible for him to extricate himself from danger, without almost certain death to himself and great injury to his fellow laborers. It is then averred that "his said injuries were incurred wholly by reason of the carelessness, negligence, and failure to furnish him with a reasonably safe and suitable place to work."

In the second paragraph of complaint, appellee seeks to fix the liability upon the appellant, under subdivision 2 of section 7083, Burns' Ann. St. 1901, commonly known and designated as the "Employers' Liability Act." If is averred that one Hodnapp was appellant's superintendent of wreckage, to whom was delegated authority to manage and control the work of clearing away wreckage on the lines of its road; that said Hodnapp had full power and authority to manage and control the work of clearing away the wreckage of broken cars and débris, and had full power to control and manage the servants and laborers of appellant, including appellee; that said Hodnapp had authority to give orders and directions, which appellee and other employés were bound to obey and conform to; that appellee did so obey and conform to said orders and directions, and was at the time of his injuries performing his duties in conformity and obedience to said orders. It is further alleged that appellee's injuries were caused wholly by reason of the negligence and carelessness of said Hodnapp, that said superintendent should have used the derrick to hoist and load the car bolster, which appellant had provided; that it was too heavy to be loaded by hand, and to attempt to load the same by hand was dangerous and unsafe, but Hodnapp, disregarding his duty to appellee to provide him a reasonably safe and suitable place in which to work, ordered and directed appellee, with other employés, to take hold of said car bolster and load the same, well knowing it was too heavy to be handled with reasonable safety, and negligently failed to warn appellee of the danger; that said Hodnapp, by giving said order and direction, made the place of work dangerous and unsafe; and that appellee did not know of such danger. It is also further alleged that appellee, at the time of and prior to his said injury, had no knowledge of the great weight of said car bolster, nor of the danger and unsafety of so attempting to hoist and load the same into the car by hand, and that he was in the exercise of due care and diligence for his own safety, and was free from any fault or negligence on his part. It will be observed that in this paragraph of complaint no charge of negligence is made on the ground that bolts, bolt heads, and plates were projecting from the car bolster.

It is shown by the first paragraph of complaint that it was a part of appellee's duties as a sectionman to assist in clearing up wreckage within his territory. The first paragraph is a common-law count for injuries sustained while appellee was in the line of his duty, and that his injuries resulted from appellant's negligence. The acts of negligence charged are both acts of omission and commission, in that it was negligence to omit to use the derrick in loading the car bolster, and that it was also negligence to attempt to load it by manual strength, as detailed. The direct cause of appellee's injury, as shown by this paragraph, was a projecting bolt on the car bolster, which kept it from slipping over the end of the car into which it was being loaded, and, by reason of its great weight, caused it to slip back on appellee's shoulder. The first paragraph avers that appellee had no knowledge or notice that there were upon the edges or sides of the car bolster any bolts, bolt heads, or plates projecting therefrom, and did not know that it was dangerous or unsafe to assist in the attempt to load said car bolster until the same had been placed on the end of the car. There is wanting in the complaint any averment that appellee could not have known, by the exercise of reasonable care, that there were projecting bolts, bolt heads, or plates on the car bolster, before he began to move it, or that he could not have known, by the exercise of reasonable care, that it was dangerous to undertake to move it in the manner described. True, the first paragraph alleges that appellee's injuries were the result of the carelessness, negligence, and failure of duty of defendant, and its failure to furnish him a reasonably safe and suitable place to work, yet it seems clear from the general and specific allegations that the sufficiency of this paragraph cannot be upheld upon the theory that appellant did not furnish appellee a reasonably safe place to work. It is shown that a part of appellee's duties was to assist in clearing away wrecks. A place where a wreck on a railroad has occurred, with the wreckage present, may or may not be a place of danger. It is evident that such a place is as open and obvious to the employé as it is to the employer. If the place is dangerous, the danger is apparent to all who have an opportunity of observing it. The surroundings, conditions, and situation are subjects of observation to all alike. The purpose of clearing away and removing the wreckage is to make the place safe, and it would seem that under such conditions the doctrine that it is the duty of the master to use reasonable care in making the working place of his servant reasonably safe would not apply. The complaint shows further that appellant did furnish suitable machinery and appliances with which to do the particular work in which appellee was engaged, for it did furnish a derrick, and the complaint avers that it was the proper appliance with which to load the car bolster. It is shown by this paragraph that the direct cause of appellee's injuries was the great weight of the car bolster, and a bolt in it which kept it from slipping onto the car when placed on the top of the siding. The car bolster is not specifically described, but it is averred to be "a heavy piece of car," which weighed about 1,500 pounds. An object of that weight must be of considerable size. Appellee was a man of mature years, and had the same opportunity of observing the shape, size, and general character of the car bolster as appellant's superintendent of wreckage had. It is not averred that its dangers were latent. The bolts, bolt heads, and plates that projected from it were as open and obvious to his view as to the master's. When he, with other employés, first took hold of it to place it in the car, he must have discovered its great weight. He knew as well as the master did the height it had to be lifted, for the car into which it was to be placed was on the track, and was visible to all. He says in his complaint that the top of the car was from eight to ten feet high. Notwithstanding the averment of want of knowledge on his part of the danger incident to loading the car bolster, and the projecting bolts, etc., yet we are confronted with the physical fact, from which there is no escape, that these things were open and obvious to one using ordinary care. He knew also that the derrick was not being used in this particular work.

A complaint of this character, to be good against a demurrer for want of facts, the obligation rests upon the plaintiff to disclose an absence of knowledge on his part of the defects or dangers of which he complains. It is firmly established by the decisions that the general allegation of the absence of knowledge will be overcome by allegations from which it is evident that the servant must have known of the defects or dangers, or had the same means or opportunity for such knowledge as the master had. Louisville, etc., Ry. Co. v. Kemper, 147 Ind. 561, 47 N. E. 214; Peerless Stone Co. v. Wray, 143 Ind. 574, 42 N. E. 927; Sheets v. Chicago, etc., Ry. Co., 139 Ind. 682, 39 N. E. 154; Ames v. Lake Shore, etc., Ry. Co., 135 Ind. 363, 35 N. E. 117. In Louisville, etc., Co. v. Kemper, supra, it was said: "Where the alleged defects are of such a character as that their perils are open and obvious, it would seem but a contradiction of terms to say, in the absence of peculiar circumstances denying an opportunity for observation, that, while so open and obvious to the servant as the facts specially alleged disclose, the general allegation of want of knowledge is overcome by such special allegations." The case of Citizens', etc., Ry. Co. v. Brown, is in point. 29 Ind. App. 185, 64 N. E. 98. There appellee, who was in appellant's service as a servant, was called upon to assist in moving a heavy iron "frog," and averred that while so engaged he was pulled over and injured, that the work was dangerous, that appellant knew of such danger, and that appellee was ignorant thereof. There was no averment in the complaint that the danger was latent, and it was held that, if it was a dangerous undertaking, the danger was as obvious to appellee as it was to appellant. The complaint there failed to aver that the dangers to which appellee was exposed were not apparently such that they could have been avoided by the use of ordinary care, and the complaint was held bad. In Wortman v. Minnich et al., 28 Ind. App. 31, 62 N. E. 85, it was held that the servant assumed those risks which were open and obvious, or which he could have discovered by the exercise of ordinary care, and the fact that he did not know of the defects which caused his injury could avail him nothing, where he had equal opportunity with the master, and could, by ordinary observation, have seen them. See, also, Stuart v. New Albany, etc., Co., 15 Ind. App. 184, 43 N. E. 961. In Peerless Stone Co. v. Wray, supra, appellee was injured by the giving away of a bank of dirt, clay, and stone as he was passing near it. It was alleged in his complaint that he had no knowledge that said "dirt, clay, and stone had been loosened and left without any support"; that appellant knew there was danger of its falling; and that there was danger in passing near it. There was no allegation that appellee did not know of the danger. It was held by the Supreme Court that it was apparent from the allegations that appellee had at least an equal opportunity with appellant to have known that the embankment mentioned was unsupported, that it was open to his observation, and that, if he had exercised ordinary care, he would have known such fact. The court said: "The rule is that obvious defects or dangers, open to the ordinary, careful observation, or such as are or should be known by the exercise of ordinary care, are assumed by the employé. The paragraph may therefore be considered the same as if the averment that appellee had no knowledge that the embankment was unsupported were eliminated, but, whether so considered or not, it is clear that the averment of want of knowledge on the part of appellee was not sufficient." In Griffin v. Ohio, etc., Ry. Co., 124 Ind. 326, 24 N. E. 888, it was held that, where the danger is alike open to the observation of both the master and servant, they are upon an equality, and that the master is not liable for an injury incident to the business. The following cases are also in point: Day v. Cleveland, etc., Ry. Co., 137 Ind. 206, 36 N. E. 854; Vincennes Water Co. v. White, 124 Ind. 376, 24 N. E. 747; Indiana, etc., Ry. Co. v. Daily, 110 Ind. 75, 10 N. E. 631.

In the case we are considering, appellee was a man of mature years and judgment, and in such case the law does not cast upon the master the duty of becoming eyes and ears for his servant, where there is nothing to prevent the latter from using his own eyes and ears to avoid danger. The relations that necessarily exist between master and servant are largely reciprocal, and the law imposes upon each of them the duty of using care, diligence and caution. Men must use the senses with which they are endowed; and, where one fails to do so, he alone must suffer the consequences, and he is not excused where he fails to discover danger, if he made no attempt to employ the faculties that he possessed. Day v. Cleveland, etc., Co., supra; Brazil, etc., Co. v. Hoodlet, 129 Ind. 327, 27 N. E. 741; Lake Shore, etc., Ry. Co. v. Pinchin, 112 Ind. 592, 13 N. E. 677; Stewart, Adm'r, v. Pa. Co., 130 Ind. 242, 29 N. E. 916; Pa. Co. v. Meyers, Adm'r, 136 Ind. 242, 36 N. E. 32.

For the infirmities of the first paragraph of complaint to which we have referred, the demurrer should have been sustained.

As above stated, by the second paragraph appellee seeks to fasten liability upon appellant under the provisions of the employers' liability act of 1893 (Acts 1893, p. 294; section 7083, Burns' Ann. St. 1901). Section 1 of that act provides "that every railroad * * * shall be liable for damages for personal injury suffered by any employé while in its service, the employé so injured being in the exercise of due care and diligence, in the following cases: * * * Second. Where such injury resulted from the negligence of any person in the service of such corporation, to whose order or direction the injured employé, at the time of the injury, was bound to conform, and did conform." Under the averments of the second paragraph of the complaint, the general doctrine of fellow servants or of assumed risks is not controlling. The statute is clear and explicit, and is its own interpretation. It simply provides that where an injury results to any person in the service of a corporation embraced therein, from the negligence of any person in the service of such corporation, to whose order or direction the injured employé, at the time of the injury, was bound to conform, and did conform, the master shall respond in damages, provided the injured party was in the exercise of due care and diligence. This embraces the doctrine of vice principal, by which the person in authority, to whose orders the employé is bound to conform and does conform, represents and acts for the corporation. To contradistinguish the difference between the doctrine of the co-servants' rule and that applicable under this statute, the Supreme Court has applied this threefold test: (1) Was the offending servant clothed by the employer with authority to give orders to the injured servant that the latter was bound to obey? (2) Did the injury result to the latter from the negligence of the former while conforming to an order of the former, that the injured servant was at the time bound to obey? (3) Was the injured party at the time of the injury in the exercise of due care and diligence? Louisville, etc., R. Co. v. Wagner, 153 Ind. 420, 53 N. E. 927; Thacker v. Chicago, etc., R. Co., 159 Ind. 82, 64 N. E. 605, 59 L. R. A. 792; Indianapolis Gas Co. v. Shumack, 23 Ind. App. 87, 54 N. E. 414. Measured by the rule declared in these cases, the second paragraph of complaint states a cause of action under subdivision 2 of section 1 of the act of March 4, 1893 (section 7083, supra). The demurrer to it was properly overruled.

It does not, however, affirmatively appear from the record upon which paragraph of complaint the verdict and judgment rest. In such case a judgment for the plaintiff below will be reversed because of the action of the court in overruling a demurrer to a bad paragraph of complaint. Cincinnati, etc., R. Co. v. Voght, 26 Ind. App. 665, 60 N. E. 797.

Judgment reversed, and the court below is directed to sustain the demurrer to the first paragraph of complaint.

(33 Ind. A. 8)

ATKINSON v. STATE.

(Appellate Court of Indiana, Division No. 1. April 7, 1904.)

INTOXICATING LIQUORS — PERMITTING PERSONS TO ENTER SALOON ON PROHIBITED DAYS— INDICTMENT—EVIDENCE—SUFFICIENCY.

1. An objection that an indictment does not state facts sufficient to constitute an offense, made for the first time on appeal, is unavailing, if a public offense be charged against defendant, though the indictment be insufficient on a motion to quash.

2. An indictment charging a statutory offense in the language of the statute, or in terms substantially equivalent thereto, is sufficient.

3. An indictment alleging that defendant, being the holder of a retail liquor license, and being engaged, as owner and proprietor, in the sale of liquors, did permit certain persons, not members of his family, to enter, on Sunday, the room where liquors were sold, sufficiently charges the offense described in Burns' Ann. St. 1901, § 7283c, making it unlawful for a licensed liquor dealer to permit others than members of his family to go into the room where liquors are being sold on days when the sale of liquor is prohibited by law.

4. Burns' Ann. St. 1901, § 7278, provides that the applicant for a retail liquor license shall publish a notice stating the "precise location of the premises" in which he desires to sell. Section 7283 authorizes the county auditor to issue a license to the applicant, with the privilege of permitting liquor to be drunk on the premises, as stated in the notice, and which license shall state the place of sale. Section 7283a requires the applicant to specifically describe the room in which he desires to sell liquor, and the location thereof; and, if there is more than one room in the building in which liquors are intended to be sold, the applicant shall specifically describe and locate the room. Section 7283b requires a licensed liquor retailer to provide for the sale of liquor in a room separate from any other business, and no devices for amusement or partitions of any kind shall be permitted in such room. Section 7283d requires that any room where liquors are sold under a license must be on the ground floor, and in a room fronting the street. The application for a license, the published notice thereof, and the order granting the same, described the real estate by metes and bounds, or lot, and the premises were designated as the north room of a building; describing the room, giving the dimensions thereof, and the entrances thereto. The business under the license was conducted

on the entire ground floor of the building. The floor was divided by a partition extending to within about three feet of the ceiling. There were two doors in the partition. The bar was located on the north side of the partition, and on the other side there were pool tables. The doors in the partition were kept open through the week, but closed on Sunday. The dimensions of the room on the bar side of the partition were less than the dimensions given in the papers required for the issuance of the license. *Held*, that to permit persons not members of the licensee's family to enter on Sunday the part of the room occupied by the pool tables constituted a violation of Burns' Ann. St. 1901, § 7283c, making it unlawful for a licensed liquor dealer to permit others than members of his family to enter, on days when the sale of liquor is prohibited, the room where liquors are sold.

Appeal from Circuit Court, Jay County; John M. Smith, Judge.

John W. Atkinson was convicted of crime, and appeals. Affirmed.

James J. Moran and Charles Shockney, for appellant. C. W. Miller, Atty. Gen., L. G. Rothschild, C. C. Hadley, and W. C. Geake, for the State.

BLACK, J. In the indictment in this case it was charged that the appellant, John W. Atkinson, late of, etc., on, etc., at, etc., "being then and there the holder of a license issued under the laws of the state of Indiana to sell intoxicating liquors at retail in quantities of less than a quart, in said county, and being then and there engaged, as the owner and proprietor, in the sale of said intoxicating liquors, under and by virtue of the license and authority aforesaid, in a certain storeroom then and there being, did then and there unlawfully permit" eight persons named, "who were not then and there members of his family, to go and enter into said room where intoxicating liquors were then and there sold as aforesaid, the said day being the first of the week, commonly called Sunday; contrary," etc.

It is assigned as error that this indictment does not state facts sufficient to constitute a public offense. The objections urged against the indictment are, first, that the words "at a time" are not inserted after the words "being then and there the holder of a license issued under the laws of the state of Indiana to sell intoxicating liquors at retail in quantities of less than a quart"; second, that the indictment does not show that the liquors were sold in a room where a license could lawfully be granted, or that the license covered a room wherein intoxicating liquors could be sold by virtue of a license. An indictment may be thus attacked by the defendant for the first time on appeal, but such attack will not prevail except where there is an omission in the indictment of some criminal charge; and mere want of certainty in the statement of the facts constituting an offense cannot be ground for so questioning the indictment. Such an assignment will not prevail if a public offense be charged against the defendant, though there be such want of specific certainty in the charge that the indictment would be insufficient on motion to quash. State v. Noland, 29 Ind. 212; Stewart v. State, 113 Ind. 505, 16 N. E. 186; Elliott, App. Proc. § 488. To avoid prolixity, general pleading is allowed in all cases where the subject comprehends a multiplicity of matter and a great variety of facts (Shinn v. State, 68 Ind. 423); and it is a general rule, that in defining a criminal offense in an indictment, it is sufficient to charge the statutory offense in the language of the statute, or in terms substantially equivalent thereto. State v. Beach, 147 Ind. 74, 46 N. E. 145, 36 L. R. A. 179; Chandler v. State, 141 Ind. 106, 39 N. E. 444; Lay v. State, 12 Ind. App. 362, 39 N. E. 768; State v. Allen, 12 Ind. App. 528, 40 N. E. 705. It is expressly enacted that no indictment or information shall be deemed invalid, nor shall the same be set aside or quashed, nor shall the trial, judgment, or other proceedings be stayed, for any defect or imperfection which does not tend to the prejudice of the substantial rights of the defendant upon the merits. Section 1825, Burns' Ann. St. 1901. And if the offense charged is stated with such a degree of certainty that the court may pronounce judgment, upon a conviction, according to the right of the case, the indictment will be in this respect sufficient. Section 1824, Burns' Ann. St. 1901. The proceeding is based upon section 7283c, Burns' Ann. St. 1901, by which it is provided as follows: "Any room where spirituous, vinous, malt or other intoxicating liquors are sold by virtue of a license under the laws of the state of Indiana shall be so arranged that the same may be securely closed and locked, and admission thereto prevented, and the same shall be securely locked and all persons excluded therefrom on all days and hours upon which the sale of such liquors is prohibited by law. It is hereby made unlawful for the proprietor of such a place and the business herein contemplated of selling intoxicating liquors, to permit any person or persons other than himself and family to go into such room and place where intoxicating liquors are so sold upon such days and hours when the sale of such liquors is prohibited by law," etc. The punishment to be inflicted for a violation of this section is prescribed in the next following section. Sunday is one of the days upon which the sale of intoxicating liquors is prohibited by law. Section 2194, Burns' Ann. St. 1901. The indictment, we think, sufficiently charged the offense described in section 7283c, supra.

The cause was tried by the court, and the overruling of the appellant's motion for a new trial is assigned as error, and it is claimed in his behalf that the evidence was insufficient to uphold the conviction. The dispute relates to the evidence concerning the place into which the persons named in the indictment, other than the appellant and his family, were permitted to go on the day designated.

The saloon was on the ground floor of a two-story brick building fronting on High street, in the town of Redkey, the lot extending southward from that street something more than 150 feet. The business as actually conducted by the appellant was carried on in the entire space of the ground floor of the building, there being an entrance by a front door on High street, and there being also an entrance by a back door somewhere in the rear portion of the building. There was next to the street a compartment in which was located a bar; behind the bar and south of it, extending across the room, was a partition constructed of boards about four feet high, above which was open lattice work, the size of the openings or "meshes" being described as about five inches, which extended upward to within about three feet from the ceiling. There were two doors in this partition, affording entrance to and from the portion of the room in rear thereof, one of the doors being behind the bar, affording passage to a space behind a counter in the room in rear of the partition. Some of the witnesses testified that in these openings in the partition there were hanging curtains. It was in evidence, however, that there were in both openings doors of pine wood, provided with locks, and closed and locked. In the portion of the place in rear of this partition there were some pool tables, and it was spoken of in the testimony of some of the witnesses as a poolroom, and was used as such, and the business both in the front and rear portions of the room—that is, on both sides of the partition—was owned and controlled by the appellant.

The evidence showed that all the persons mentioned in the indictment as being present on the Sunday in question were on that day in the portion of the room behind the partition, one of them being the appellant's barkeeper, and that a part of the time another of his barkeepers also was there, when a number of the persons named in the indictment, other than the appellant or members of his family, were present. The ages of those present, other than the barkeepers, were, of one 15 years, of three 16 years, of one 23 years, and one was referred to in the testimony as a boy, and the age of another was not shown. So far as shown, they came in at the back door. It was not shown that any of these persons was in the portion of the room north of the partition. The doors in the partition were kept open through the week, but it was in evidence that the appellant locked the doors in the partition on the inside, or north side thereof, upon the night of the preceding day, Saturday; and it did not appear that these doors, or either of them, was opened or unlocked on the Sunday in question. The young men thus present were sitting around in the "poolroom," drinking beer and talking. There was testimony that the portion of the room in front of the partition was about 25 feet wide, and also that it went back 24 feet 10 inches. The appellant himself testified that he did not authorize anybody to enter the place of business or suffer anybody to enter it on the day in question, but there was evidence that one of the barkeepers, above mentioned, had a key to the back room.

The appellant's application for license, the published notice thereof, and the order of the county board granting the license were introduced in evidence. In all of them there was a description by metes and bounds of the real estate or lot on which the building in question was located, and in each of them the premises on which the intoxicating liquors were to be sold were designated as the north room on the ground floor of the two-story brick building situated on said real estate described, and said room was in each of said papers described by metes and bounds, indicating a depth of 28 feet 6 inches, and a width in part of 17 feet and in part of 19 feet 4 inches. The order for a license contained also the following language: "Said room fronts on High street in said town, and is entered therefrom by means of a door, and has two doors in south end leading to the south room; all doors are provided with locks and keys, and can be securely locked. Said room has a large glass front facing High street, which permits an unobstructed view of the entire room when blinds and screens are removed." The published notice also, though not the application, contained the same language last above quoted. In the application no permission was asked to carry on any other business than that of selling intoxicating, etc., liquors, with the privilege of allowing the same to be drunk on the premises, at and in the room located on the ground floor fronting upon High street, in the north room of the two-story brick building at No.——— High street, situated upon the premises described. In the license was the following: "And the board further order that no device for amusement, or music, or game of any kind or character, or sale of anything other than intoxicating liquors, be allowed in or on said premises, except that which is expressly provided by law."

We must make some reference to the statutes relating to the place where intoxicating liquors may be sold under license, so far as they seem to affect the question for decision. The person desiring to obtain the license must publish "a notice stating the precise location of the premises in which he desires to sell." Section 7278, Burns' Ann. St. 1901. The county auditor is to "issue a license to the applicant for the sale of such liquors as he applied for, with the privilege of permitting the same to be drunk on the premises as stated in the aforesaid notice, which license shall specify the name of the applicant, the place of sale and the period of time for which such license is granted." Section 7283, Burns' Ann. St. 1901. The person applying for license, in the application, must specifically describe the room in which he desires to sell such liquors, and the exact location of the same, and, if there is more than one room in the building in which such liquors are intended to be sold, said applicant shall specifically describe and locate the room in which he desires to sell such liquors in such building. Section 7283a, Burns' Ann. St. 1901. The licensed retailer is required to "provide for the sale of such liquors in a room separate from any other business of any kind, and no devices for amusement, or music of any kind or character, or partition of any kind, shall be permitted in such room; provided, that nothing in the provisions of this act shall be construed to forbid the sale of cigars and tobacco in such place of business; and provided further, that if such applicant for license desires to carry on any other or different business, he shall state the same in his application for license, and the same may be granted or refused by the board of commissioners hearing such application, and such permission shall be stated in the license, if granted." Section 7283b, Burns' Ann. St. 1901. The section upon which this prosecution is based (section 7283c) has been already set out herein.

Any room where intoxicating liquors are sold by virtue of a license must be situated on the ground floor or basement of the building and "in a room fronting the street or highway upon which such building is situated, and said room shall be so arranged, either with window or glass door, as that the whole of said room may be in view from the street or highway, and no blinds, screens or obstructions to the view shall be arranged, erected or placed so as to prevent the entire view of said room from the street or highway upon which the same is situated during such days and hours when the sales of such liquors are prohibited by law." Section 7283d, Burns' Ann. St. 1901.

It seems to be the intent of the statutes now in force that the place and premises contemplated therein for the selling of intoxicating liquors in less quantities than a quart at a time, with the privilege of permitting the drinking thereof on the premises under and by virtue of a license, must be one single room, which may be viewed throughout its entire extent or space by a person looking through the prescribed window or glass door from the street on which the room must front. A back or side room used in connection with the business of selling intoxicating liquors under a license, and in aid, promotion, or furtherance of such business, is not contemplated as permissible under the statute. No business of any kind other than selling liquors and permitting the drinking thereof is to be carried on in this room, and no devices for amusement or music of any kind or character, or partition of any kind, are to be permitted in this room, except that the sale of cigars and tobacco in such place of business—that is, in such room—is not forbidden, and except, also, that if the applicant desires to carry on any other or different business, and state such desire in his application for license, the county board may grant or refuse permission thereof. So far as the place of selling is concerned, it is not necessary in the notice (the statutory provision for which has not been changed since the year 1875) to state more than the precise location of the premises; and the license must be for the sale of liquors with the privilege of permitting them to be drunk on the premises, as stated in the notice, and must specify the place of sale; and in the application the particular room and its exact location must be specifically described. There are numerous requirements as to what the holder of a license must do with reference to the room and the business, as to which the statutes do not expressly require that reference be made in the application, notice, or license, if we except the matter of carrying on some other kind of business in the room. See Gates v. Haw, 150 Ind. 370, 50 N. E. 299. Here there seems to have been an attempt to evade the statutes by inserting in the application and notice a description of the room by metes and bounds, and procuring such description in the order of the board, with other unnecessary matter, and by providing a prohibited amusement in the room outside of such metes and bounds, and separated from the bar by a partition forbidden by law. The statute classes appliances for amusement in connection with the retailing of intoxicating liquors as constituting an unlawful accompaniment of a licensed saloon or drinking place, unless expressly permitted by the license, when the amusement must be furnished in the same room where the liquors are sold and drunk, and not elsewhere. The purpose of the statute under which the appellant was prosecuted is to prevent, so far as possible, the evasion of the law by licensed dealers through sales of liquor at times when it is, by the lawmaking power of the state, deemed to be detrimental to the welfare of society to make such sales. It is true that the appellant could not properly be convicted of one statutory offense for conduct which did not constitute such particular offense, though it may have furnished ground for prosecution under another statute; yet, if his conduct constitute an offense for which he is prosecuted, he can derive no benefit from its being also an offense for which he is not prosecuted; and we must seek to uphold and enforce the intention of the Legislature, and not permit evasion of the law by subterfuge. The appellant was carrying on the business of a saloon keeper under and by virtue of a license containing, unnecessarily and by his procurement, a description by metes and bounds of the room, being a false description of the premises in which the business was conducted. During the week the prohibited poolroom was a part of his saloon behind a prohibited partition. It did not cease to be a part of the room in which he was licensed to sell by the locking of the partition doors on Sunday. Though it be merely incidental to the offense, yet, having arrived at such conclusion, we may not improperly say that subjecting immature persons to temptation, and thereby inducing them to countenance such violation of law, whether for paltry gain or gratuitously, should be strongly reprobated by all who have occasion to remark upon the matter.

Judgment affirmed.

(209 Ill. 252)

MALLIN v. WENHAM et al.

(Supreme Court of Illinois. April 20, 1904.)

ASSIGNMENT OF WAGES—VALIDITY—PUBLIC POLICY—EXEMPTION LAWS—BANKRUPTCY.

1. Where one is in the actual employment of another, and is receiving wages thereunder, though not under a contract for a definite period, he may make a valid assignment of his future earnings.

2. An assignment of future earnings is not against public policy so as to render it void.

3. Statutes exempting wages from execution do not render invalid a contract assigning future earnings.

4. Under Bankr. Law July 1, 1898, c. 541, § 67d, 30 Stat. 564, 565 [U. S. Comp. St. 1901, p. 3449], providing that liens given in good faith and for a present consideration, which have been recorded if record thereof was necessary to impart notice, shall not be affected by the act, an assignment of future earnings under an existing contract of employment, where the consideration has been received, is not superseded by a discharge in bankruptcy of the assignor.

Appeal from Appellate Court, First District.

Bill by James H. Mallin against Charles F. Wenham and another. From a judgment of the Appellate Court (103 Ill. App. 609) reversing a decree in favor of complainant, he appeals. Affirmed.

In this case a bill is filed by appellant, Mallin, against appellee and Armour & Co. Mallin, for several years prior to the commencement of this suit, was employed continuously by Armour & Co. on a salary of $100 per month. He had no definite contract of employment, but was employed from month to month. Between October, 1897, and June, 1898, he from time to time borrowed money from appellee at usurious rates of interest. He obtained $342 more from Wenham than he ever paid back. On June 3, 1898, to secure his indebtedness to Wenham, he executed and delivered an assignment of wages, as follows:

"For a valuable consideration to me in hand paid by C. F. Wenham, the receipt whereof is hereby acknowledged, I do hereby transfer, assign and set over to said C. F. Wenham, his heirs, executors, administrators or assigns, all salary or wages, and claims for salary or wages, due or to become due me from Armour & Co., or from any other person or persons, firm, copartnership, company, corporation, organization or official by whom I am now or may hereafter become employed, at any time before the expiration of ten years from the date hereof.

"I do hereby constitute, irrevocably, the said C. F. Wenham, his heirs, executors, administrators or assigns, my attorney, in my name to take all legal measures which may be proper or necessary for the complete recovery and employment of the claim hereby assigned, and I hereby authorize, empower and direct the said Armour & Co., or any one by whom I may be employed as above, to pay the said demand and claim for wages or salary to the said C. F. Wenham, his executors, administrators or assigns, and hereby authorize and empower him or them to receipt for the same in my name.

"J. H. Mallin.

"Chicago, Ill., third day of June, 1898."

On May 3, 1899, Mallin filed his petition in bankruptcy, and his indebtedness to C. F. Wenham was scheduled in his bankruptcy proceedings, and Wenham had notice thereof. On October 23, 1899, he obtained his discharge in bankruptcy. Subsequently Wenham brought suit in the name of Mallin, for the use of Wenham, against Armour & Co., claiming the wages of Mallin by virtue of the above assignment. Mallin thereupon filed his bill without offering to repay the $342, or any part thereof, and prayed that said assignment be declared null and void, and that Wenham be restrained from prosecuting any suit against Armour & Co. or in any manner interfering with Mallin's salary. It was so decreed by the trial court, which decree, on appeal to the Appellate Court, was reversed, and judgment entered in behalf of appellee. The Appellate Court having granted a certificate of importance, the case is now before this court. The appellant urges as error the action of the Appellate Court in refusing to affirm the decree of the circuit court in reversing said decree and in directing the circuit court to dismiss the bill of complaint. The assignments of error and the argument of appellant raise the following questions: (1) Whether an assignment transferring wages to be earned in the future under an existing employment is valid; (2) is such an assignment against public policy? (3) the effect of a discharge in bankruptcy of a debtor, upon security or liens created by assignment.

H. H. Reed (A. R. Urion and A. F. Reichmann, of counsel), for appellant. Morse Ives and George I. Haight, for appellee.

RICKS, J. (after stating the facts). In respect to the first proposition mentioned,

¶ 1. See Assignments, vol. 4, Cent. Dig. § 20.

the authorities are ample and conclusive to the effect that an assignment of wages to be earned in the future, under an existing employment, is valid. This precise question has frequently been passed upon by the courts of the different states and of England, and, so far as we are advised, the courts of dernier ressort have, without exception, upheld such contracts, where they have been for a valuable consideration and untainted with fraud. The authorities are to the effect that it is not necessary that there be an express hiring for a definite time, but the existence of the employment at the time of the assignment is sufficient. In the case at bar appellant was, and had been for some time previous, in the actual employ of Armour & Co. at a fixed price per month. It is true, such employment was not of any definite duration, and appellant might abandon the same at any time, or his employer might discharge him. The subject-matter of the contract had but a potential existence, but it was such a property right as might legally be disposed of. The remarks of the court in Thayer v. Kelley, 28 Vt. 19, 65 Am. Dec. 220, are very pertinent to the subject in hand, and we here quote them: "When the debtor is in the actual employment of another, and is receiving wages under a subsisting engagement, an assignment by him of his future earnings may be made, not only for the security and payment of a present indebtedness, but for such advances as he may find it necessary to obtain. This principle is fully established by the cases to which we were referred. Weed v. Jewett, 2 Metc. 608, 37 Am. Dec. 115; Brackett v. Blake, 7 Metc. 335, 41 Am. Dec. 442; Field v. Mayor of New York, 6 N. Y. 187, 57 Am. Dec. 435; Emery v. Lawrence, 8 Cush. 151. The debtor in this case, at the time of his assignment to the claimants, was in the actual employment of the trustees under a subsisting contract, at a given price per day, and had in that manner labored for them for some two or three years previous; and though he had the right to leave their employment and they had the right to discharge him, yet so long as that relation existed between them we think the authorities are satisfactory in holding that the claimants were entitled to receive, under that assignment, his accruing wages in payment of the advances which they had made." In support of the above doctrine reference is made to the following cases: Kane v. Clough, 36 Mich. 436, 24 Am. Rep. 599; Manly v. Bitzer, 91 Ky. 596, 16 S. W. 464, 34 Am. St. Rep. 242; Metcalf v. Kincaid, 87 Iowa, 443, 54 N. W. 867, 43 Am. St. Rep. 391.

The second proposition urged by appellant is that the assignment in question is against public policy, and for that reason ought not to be upheld. This question was raised in the case of Edwards v. Peterson, 80 Me. 367, 14 Atl. 936, 6 Am. St. Rep. 207, and the court there held such an assignment did not contravene public policy, and quoted with approval from the case of Smith v. Atkins, 18 Vt. 461, in which case it was said: "It is argued that such contracts are so much against public policy that they ought not to be supported, but we think they are rather beneficial, and enable the poor man to obtain credit when he could not otherwise do it, and that without detriment to the creditors." And, further, in the Edwards Case, supra, the court say, speaking of an assignment of wages to be earned in the future: "It cannot be said to contravene public policy. Smith v. Atkins, 18 Vt. 461. The consideration was most meritorious, and the assignment was not given to delay creditors." And, further: "The true doctrine seems to be that, to make a grant or assignment valid at law, the thing which is the subject of it must have an existence, actual or potential, at the time of such grant or assignment. But courts of equity support assignments, not only of choses in action, but of contingent interests and expectations, and also of things which have no present actual or potential existence, but rest in mere possibility only"—citing numerous cases. Appellant, in this connection, calls attention to the statutes and exemption laws of this state, and insists that the liberal provisions made by the Legislature for the indigent and poorer classes indicate the adoption of a broad and liberal public policy toward the classes named, and that it is the duty of this court to so construe the law that the class and individuals so favored by the statute shall be compelled to accept of its beneficent provisions. Such is not the province of this court. The citizens of the state have a right to contract, and there is no law forbidding one from selling or assigning any property he may have. A person has the same right to assign his wages that he has to mortgage his homestead or to mortgage personal property that is exempt from execution. The statute provides liberal exemptions, of which a person has the right to avail himself if he so desires, but, if he does not, the courts are powerless to help him. The duty of the courts in instances of this kind is well laid down in the case of Carroll v. City of East St. Louis, 67 Ill. 568, 16 Am. Rep. 632 (on page 579, 67 Ill., 16 Am. Rep. 632): "It is the legislative, and not the judicial, power in the state that must control and give shape to its public policy. That power does not pertain to the courts. They can only observe that policy and apply it to cases as they arise, without changing or obstructing it." Also, in the case of Frorer v. People, 141 Ill. 171, 31 N. E. 395, 16 L. R. A. 492, it was said (page 185, 141 Ill., and page 399, 31 N. E., 16 L. R. A. 492): "Other instances of statutory regulations of private rights are in lien laws in favor of homesteaders, mechanics, etc., limitation laws, the statute of frauds, and other statutes relating to evidence, laws in regard to pleadings, exemption laws, and insolvent laws. But these all relate, not to the power to contract in regard to matters of general right, but to the remedy for the enforcing of contracts, as to which the Legislature may make such regulations as the public welfare seems to demand, so long as, under pretense of regulating the remedy, it does not impair the right itself." We also indorse the doctrine laid down in Greenhood on Public Policy, pp. 116, 117, as follows: "The power of the courts to declare a contract void for being in contravention of sound public policy is a very delicate and undefined power, and, like the power to declare a statute unconstitutional, should be exercised only in cases free from doubt. Before a court should determine a transaction which has been entered into in good faith, stipulating for nothing that is malum in se, to be void as contravening the policy of the state, it should be satisfied that the advantage to accrue to the public for so holding is certain and substantial, not theoretical or problematical. He is the safest magistrate who is more watchful over the rights of the individual than over the convenience of the public, as that is the best government which guards more vigilantly the freedom of the subject than the rights of the state."

The assignment of appellant's wages was simply a lien on the same so long as he remained in the employ of Armour & Co. and until the indebtedness secured thereby was satisfied. Should appellant quit his employment with Armour & Co., he would, by that act, destroy the assignment as security; or, should he pay his debt to Wenham, he could not be injured in any way by his assignment. Thus it will be seen that there is but little to support appellant's contention that the assignment was a harsh and unconscionable bargain. In the case of Kane v. Clough, supra, the assignor made an assignment "of all the wages that might thereafter become due to him from the defendants," and the transaction was upheld. In the case of Weed v. Jewett, supra, the assignment was "for all sums of money that may now be due to me from the Chicopee Manufacturing Company," etc., "for labor performed in their service," and the court, in concluding its opinion in that case, say: "This was a proper subject of contract or agreement, and when the labor was performed the company were bound to pay according to their undertaking."

The question of usurious interest is not an element in this case, but, if relief is desired to be had against such, appellant has his proper remedy. The record, however, discloses that appellant has obtained $342 in actual cash, which he has not repaid.

We cannot see that there is anything intrinsically vicious in an assignment of wages. The assignor in such case simply draws upon his future prospects to supply present needs, which may be of the most urgent and pressing character. There is no law in this state to prevent a poor person from mortgaging or pledging any or every article of property he possesses as security for his debts, and such a privilege may be of great value. On the whole, we see no reason or right for holding the assignment in question here void as against public policy.

It is next insisted by appellant that because of bankruptcy proceedings had by him the assignment is unenforceable. This position, we think, is wrong. The only effect of a discharge in bankruptcy is to suspend the right of action for a debt against the debtor personally. It does not annul the original debt or liability of the debtor. In Bush v. Stanley, 122 Ill. 406, 13 N. E. 249, the court said (page 416, 122 Ill., and page 253, 13 N. E.): "The discharge is analogous, in effect, to the statute of limitations, in so far as it does not annul the original debt, but merely suspends the right of action for its recovery." In Pease v. Ritchie, 132 Ill. 638, 24 N. E. 433, 8 L. R. A. 566, this court further said (page 646, 132 Ill., and page 434, 24 N. E., 8 L. R. A. 566): "It is no doubt true that appellant's discharge in bankruptcy operated as a bar to any action which might be brought to recover any debt or obligation existing at the time he was declared a bankrupt, and after-acquired property was exempted from being taken in satisfaction of any such debts. But if any creditor had a lien or an equitable claim, by mortgage or otherwise, upon any property of the bankrupt, such right or rights would remain unaffected by the proceedings in bankruptcy." In the case of Edwards v. Peterson, supra, an employé had given an assignment of his wages. Subsequently he filed a petition for discharge under the insolvent law of the state, and in its opinion the court there said: "The rule laid down by Judge Story in Mitchell v. Winslow, 2 Story, 630, seems to have been very generally held by all chancery courts in this country. He says: 'It seems to me a clear result of all the authorities that whenever the parties, by their contract, intend to create a positive lien or charge either upon real or personal property, whether then owned by the assignor or contractor or not, or, if personal property, whether it is in esse or not, it attaches in equity as a lien or charge upon the particular property as soon as the assignor or contractor acquires a title thereto, against the latter and all persons asserting a claim thereto under him, either voluntarily or with notice in bankruptcy.'" The language above quoted is also quoted with approval in the case of Gregg v. Sanford, 24 Ill. 17, 76 Am. Dec. 719. In the case of Champion v. Buckingham (Mass.) 42 N. E. 498, it was held that a creditor who has not proved his debt in bankruptcy is still, after discharge of the debtor, a subsisting creditor against him to the extent of his debt, which he is entitled to have paid out of the proceeds of a policy of insurance on the life of the debtor assigned to him by the debtor and beneficiary to secure subsisting demands in favor of the creditor, and it was said that the discharge did not extinguish the debt or demand, but that the effect of such discharge is analogous to that of the bar of the statute of limitations, which only goes to bar a creditor's remedy, and does not wipe out the debt. In discussing the right of a creditor to maintain an action on a collateral agreement as security after the debt so secured has become barred by the statute of limitations, it was said in Shaw v. Silloway (Mass.) 14 N. E. 783: "If there is an actual pledge, and the debt becomes barred, this does not give to the debtor a right to reclaim his pledged property. The debt is not extinguished; the statute only takes away the remedy. Hancock v. Insurance Co., 114 Mass. 156. In case of a mortgage of real or personal estate the security is not lost though the debt be barred. Thayer v. Mann, 19 Pick. 535. The rule is the same where there is a lien. Spears v. Hartly, 3 Esp. 81; Higgins v. Scott, 2 Barn. & Adol. 413; In re Bromhead, 16 L. J. Q. B. 355. And there appears to be no good reason why an independent collateral agreement given by way of guaranty or other security should not outlive the remedy upon the debt which it was given to secure, under proper circumstances." Section 67d, Bankr. Law July 1, 1898, c. 541, 30 Stat. 564, 565 [U. S. Comp. St. 1901, p. 3449], provides: "Liens given or accepted in good faith and not in contemplation of or in fraud upon this act, and for a present consideration, which have been recorded according to law, if record thereof was necessary in order to impart notice, shall not be affected by this act." In this case there is no question of notice of the assignment, nor was it such a one as required any notice to be given; consequently we think the assignment in question was one "not affected by this act." We think the decided weight of authority is to the effect that a discharge of a debtor in bankruptcy is but a personal release, and does not exonerate the effects of the debtor to which a valid lien has attached, and which is not expressly annulled by the provisions of the bankruptcy act.

The assignments of error, we think, are without merit, and the judgment of the Appellate Court should be and is affirmed.

Judgment affirmed.

(209 Ill. 277)

SUPREME LODGE KNIGHTS & LADIES OF HONOR v. MENKHAUSEN et al.

(Supreme Court of Illinois. April 20, 1904.)

MUTUAL BENEFIT SOCIETIES—MURDER OF INSURED BY BENEFICIARY—RIGHT OF HEIRS TO RECOVER ON CERTIFICATE.

1. Public policy does not prevent the recovery of the amount of a benefit certificate by the heirs of the insured, who has been murdered by the beneficiary.

¶ 1. See Insurance, vol. 28, Cent. Dig. § 1958.

2. Laws 1887, p. 205, § 1, authorizes the organization of mutual benefit societies for the purpose of furnishing benefits upon the death of a member to the widow, heirs, or relatives, legal representatives, or designated beneficiaries of such deceased members, and Laws 1893, p. 130, requires that payment of death benefits shall be made only to the families, heirs, blood relations, affianced husband or affianced wife of, or to persons dependent upon, the member. *Held* that, where the beneficiary in a mutual benefit certificate murders the insured, recovery on the certificate is not thereby defeated, the criminal act merely operating to place the beneficiary outside the class designated by the statute, so that the heirs of insured are entitled to recover on the certificate.

Appeal from Appellate Court, Fourth District.

Action by Olivie Menkhausen and others against the Supreme Lodge Knights and Ladies of Honor. From a judgment of the Appellate Court (106 Ill. App. 665) affirming a judgment for plaintiffs, defendant appeals. Affirmed.

This was an action of assumpsit in the circuit court of St. Clair county by appellees against the Supreme Lodge Knights & Ladies of Honor. The declaration was filed to the January term, 1902, of that court, and consisted of one special count for the amount of a certain benefit certificate. It sets out the facts that on March 22, 1893, the defendant issued its policy of insurance on the life of Elizabeth Menkhausen in the sum of $1-000, payable, at her death, to her husband, Gustav Menkhausen; that on November 9, 1893, Elizabeth Menkhausen departed this life, and that due proof was then and there furnished the defendant of her death, according to the rules, laws, and regulations of the defendant; that said Gustav Menkhausen, on August 6, 1895, instituted a suit upon said policy, and the defendant appeared and filed a plea. This plea is then set out in full, the substance of which was that Gustav Menkhausen willfully murdered his wife, and was sentenced to be hung, but that the sentence was commuted by the Governor to imprisonment for life, and that said Gustav was, at the time of filing the plea, in the penitentiary under such sentence. The declaration further avers that the only issue in said suit was whether the fact that Gustav Menkhausen murdered his wife was a bar to his suit; that upon a trial a verdict was returned for the defendant, judgment was entered on the verdict, and that judgment is still in force. It is averred by the declaration that the defendant is organized under the laws of Kentucky, Missouri, and Indiana for the purpose of promoting benevolence and charity by establishing a relief fund, from which, on satisfactory evidence of the death of a member, a sum not exceeding $5,000 shall be paid to such member of his or her family, or person dependent upon or related to him or her, as he or she may have directed; that the defendant is doing business in this state, and has complied with the laws thereof governing fraternal beneficiary societies; that the by-laws of the defendant provide that a benefit may be made payable to the wife or husband, children and grandchildren, parents, brothers and sisters, grandparents, nieces and nephews, cousins, aunts and uncles, or to the next of kin who would be distributees of the personal estate of the member upon his death intestate, in the order above named. It is then averred that by reason of the death of Elizabeth Menkhausen, and proof of that fact, and by reason of the fact that because of her death at the hands of Gustav Menkhausen it became impossible for him to recover upon said policy or benefit certificate or to receive the proceeds thereof, the said amount named in said certificate became due and payable to the plaintiffs herein, and that the defendant has not paid the said sum of $1,000 to the plaintiffs, or to any other person, but refuses so to do. The declaration then avers that Elizabeth Menkhausen died intestate, leaving plaintiffs as her only children and heirs at law; that plaintiffs were members of her family, were her heirs and blood relations, and were dependent upon her for their support. A demurrer interposed by the defendant to this declaration was overruled by the court, and, the defendant electing to stand by its demurrer, judgment was entered in favor of the plaintiffs for $1,000. An appeal was taken by the lodge to the Appellate Court for the Fourth District, where the judgment of the circuit court was affirmed. The Appellate Court granted a certificate of importance, and appellant appealed to this court.

Appellant urges as reasons why the demurrer should have been sustained, the following: First. Because appellees have no right, title, or interest in said benefit certificate, or any part thereof, and cannot maintain any action thereon. Second. The act of the Legislature of June 22, 1893 (Laws 1893, p. 130), for the organizing and management of fraternal beneficiary societies, has no application to this case, as it was passed after the benefit certificate was issued; and the act of the Legislature approved June 16, 1887 (Laws 1887, p. 204), under which this benefit certificate was issued, confers no authority on appellees to maintain this suit. Third. The murder of the assured by the beneficiary named in the benefit certificate was not one of the risks insured against and covered by the benefit certificate, and therefore no action can be maintained on said benefit certificate, or for the amount therein specified, by appellees against appellant.

J. M. Hamill (Ashcraft & Ashcraft, of counsel), for appellant. Turner & Holder, for appellees.

SCOTT, J. (after stating the facts). The beneficiary named in a benefit certificate who feloniously takes the life of the insured cannot recover from the fraternal beneficiary society, and it is now urged that public policy also requires us to hold that in such a case there can be no recovery by any person whomsoever against such a society, and that under such circumstances not only is the certificate void, but the obligation of the society to pay to any one whomsoever is canceled, and rendered absolutely inoperative. The cases relied upon by appellant are of two classes: First, where the insured was murdered by the beneficiary, and suit was brought by the criminal, or some one claiming through him; and, second, where the insured was executed in pursuance of the sentence of a court of competent jurisdiction for a crime committed by him or her. Neither class of cases is in point here. The only reason in favor of appellant's contention that seems to us of weight is found in the fact that the beneficiary might be incited to commit murder by the fact that, if unable to collect the benefit himself, it would be payable to some other person or persons in whose welfare he was interested. Human experience teaches that those willing to commit murder and assume the risk of punishment for the benefit of others are so few in number that consideration thereof becomes well-nigh inconsequential. But, even were it otherwise, if the rule suggested by appellant were established, it is perceived that the society would then profit by the murder, and an incentive be created for the destruction of the life of the insured that the interest of the insurer might be advanced. The contract between the society and the insured contained no provision absolving the society from liability in the event that she was murdered by the beneficiary, and public policy does not require us to read such a condition into the agreement. If it did, it would also require us to hold that the beneficiary could not recover on the policy if the insured was murdered by another, acting independently of and against the desire of the beneficiary, because it is within the realm of possibility that such other, without the connivance or knowledge of the beneficiary, might commit the crime solely for the purpose of enriching the latter. If societies of the character of appellant desire to be protected from such contingency, that object must be accomplished by a condition to that effect written into their contracts, failing which the law will not absolve them from liability. Cleaver v. Mutual Reserve Fund Life Ass'n, 1 Q. B. 147; Schmidt v. Northern Life Ass'n, 112 Iowa, 41, 83 N. W. 800, 51 L. R. A. 141, 84 Am. St. Rep. 323. In the absence of a contract to that effect, public policy will not permit the society to appropriate unto itself the fund which it has agreed to pay, merely because the life of the insured has been unlawfully taken.

It is suggested, however, that this certificate was payable alone to Gustav Menkhausen, and that no recovery can be had thereon except by him, or by those claiming through him, and that, as he cannot recover, no one can recover on the certificate. We do not regard this as a suit upon the certificate. A careful examination of the declaration leads us to conclude that it is a suit to recover the benefit, $1,000, which the appellant undertook, by its constitution and by-laws to pay to the person, within certain classes, who should be designated by Elizabeth Menkhausen; and that, the action is upon the obligation of appellant as evidenced by its constitution and by-laws, and not upon the certificate. These rules or laws of this organization recite its purpose to be the establishment of a relief fund, from which, upon the death of a member, a benefit shall be paid to the person designated by the member in the certificate, and that such benefit may be made payable by the member to the wife or husband, the children, grandchildren, parents, certain other persons of the whole or half blood, or the next of kin who would be distributees of the personal estate of the member, in the order above named. By the act of 1887, which was in force when the certificate in question was issued, it was provided, in substance, that societies of the class to which appellant belongs might be organized for the purpose of furnishing benefits, upon the death of a member, "to the widow, heirs, relatives, legal representatives or the designated beneficiaries of such deceased member." Laws 1887, p. 205, § 1. By the act of 1893 (Laws 1893, p. 130), which became effective a few months after the issuance of this certificate, it was provided, so far as material here, that payment of death benefits should be made only to the "families, heirs, blood relations, affianced husband or affianced wife of, or to persons dependent upon, the member." Hurd's St. 1895, c. 73, par. 258. It will be observed that by the spirit of each of these three enactments the children of the deceased would stand next in order after the husband or wife. "Upon the death of a member, where the person claiming to be his designated beneficiary is outside of the classes eligible as beneficiaries of his insurance, the member's heirs at law, who are within such classes, are entitled to the insurance. There being no selection of a beneficiary authorized to take, the fund goes to them. Palmer v. Welch, 132 Ill. 141 [23 N. E. 412]; Alexander v. Parker, 144 Ill. 355 [33 N. E. 183, 19 L. R. A. 187]." Baldwin v. Begley, 185 Ill. 180, 56 N. E. 1065. We think the correct view to take is that Gustav Menkhausen, by his act in taking the life of his wife, placed himself outside the classes from among whom she might designate a beneficiary, and he could not thereafter take the fund, or any part thereof, either as the beneficiary named in the certificate or as heir or heir at law of his wife. The situation, so far as his rights and those of appellees and appellant are concerned, we think is precisely the same as though, after the issuance of this certificate, he had been divorced from Elizabeth Menkhausen, and she had thereafter died without having any alteration made in the certificate. Under such circumstances he would have no interest in the certificate, but the proceeds thereof would be payable to the heirs of the insured, nothing to the contrary appearing in the certificate, the constitution and by-laws of the order, or the laws of the state under which it operates. Tyler v. Odd Fellows' Mutual Relief Ass'n, 145 Mass. 134, 13 N. E. 360; Schonfield v. Turner, 75 Tex. 324, 12 S. W. 626, 7 L. R. A. 189; Order of Railway Conductors v. Koster, 55 Mo. App. 186. In Schmidt v. Northern Life Ass'n, supra, and in Cleaver v. Mutual Reserve Fund Life Ass'n, supra, growing out of the Maybrick murder, the same question was presented as is now before us. In both cases it was held that the fact that the beneficiary had murdered the insured did not cancel the obligation of the insurer, and in both cases the administrator of the insured was allowed to recover on the theory that the insurer held the fund in trust for the estate of the deceased; and in the case at bar it is argued that, if there could be a recovery at all, it must, under the authority of these cases, be in the name of the administrator of the estate of Elizabeth Menkhausen. It is very evident that neither the constitution and by-laws of appellant nor the laws of this state contemplate the payment of a benefit of this character to the administrator of the member. The purpose is to pay it directly to the beneficiary, whoever that may be, without the intervention of administration; and where, as here, the law determines the persons who are entitled to the fund, the suit is properly brought in the names of such persons, and in this case there is no occasion for a resort to equity.

Rule 15 (47 N. E. vii) of this court indicates the manner in which a brief and argument should be prepared for presentation here. Counsel on both sides of this controversy have failed to observe that rule. A compliance therewith is materially helpful in the consideration of causes in this court. It should be followed in every instance.

The judgment of the Appellate Court will be affirmed. Judgment affirmed.

(209 Ill. 296)

CRERAR et al. v. DANIELS.

(Supreme Court of Illinois. April 20, 1904.)

LANDLORD AND TENANT—TERMINATION OF LEASE—PROPERTY OF TENANT—REMOVAL—TRADE FIXTURES—DEMURRER TO EVIDENCE—PEREMPTORY INSTRUCTIONS—TRIAL BY COURT—LEGAL PROPOSITIONS—REQUESTS—FINDINGS OF FACT.

1. A motion made at the close of the evidence "that the court find the issues for the defendants" is, in effect, a demurrer to the evidence.

2. A lease of a dock to plaintiff provided that any planking necessary should be done at plaintiff's expense. Thereafter, during negotiations for renewal, the lessor stated that it made no claim to the planking placed on the dock by

plaintiff, and preferred that plaintiff should remove the same. The dock having subsequently been leased to defendants, they notified plaintiff to "remove his coal and other property" therefrom, but, when plaintiff attempted to remove the planking, he was stopped by defendants' agents; but defendant subsequently credited plaintiff's claim for the value of the planking as a set-off to rent charged for the use of the dock. *Held*, in an action to recover the value of such planking, that whether there was in fact a surrender of the premises by plaintiff without removal of the planks, or whether they were trade fixtures, etc., were so much questions of fact that it was not error for the court to refuse to grant a peremptory instruction in favor of defendants.

3. Under Prac. Act, § 41 (Hurd's Rev. St. 1901, c. 110, § 42), providing that either party is authorized to submit to the court written propositions to be held as law in the decison of the case, propositions requested which were mere requests to the court to make certain specific findings of fact were properly refused.

Appeal from Appellate Court, First District.

Action by Edwin F. Daniels against John Crerar and another. From a judgment in favor of plaintiff, affirmed by the Appellate Court (109 Ill. App. 654), defendants appeal. Affirmed.

Goodrich, Vincent & Bradley (Warren Nichols, of counsel), for appellants. Tenney, Coffeen & Harding (J. H. Wilkerson, of counsel), for appellee.

RICKS, J. This is an appeal by the appellants, John Crerar and R. Floyd Clinch, from an affirmance by the Appellate Court for the First District of a judgment against them for $600 in favor of appellee, Edwin F. Daniels, plaintiff, in the circuit court of Cook county. The Appellate Court, in granting this appeal, granted a certificate of importance. In May, 1893, appellee leased from the Illinois Central Railroad Company a certain dock for one year. By various extensions, however, the lease was extended to May 1, 1897, about which time the representative of appellee had an interview with the manager of this part of the business of the lessor with reference to a continuance of the lease for another year. Appellee was considering moving to another dock, and requested and received further time for his consideration. About the 23d of May the appellee informed the lessor he would not renew the lease, and just about this time the said lessor made a lease of the dock to appellants, though said lease was dated May 1, 1897. When the appellee first leased the dock, it was not planked; and he immediately planked the entire dock by laying stringers along the ground, and nailing planks thereon, filling in earth when necessary. Appellee in July, 1897, attempted to remove the planking so placed by him, but was prevented by appellants, who had procured a lease of the dock from the owner. Appellee, after such attempted removal, demanded of appellants the value of the improvement, and, payment being refused, this suit was instituted.

The lease to appellants, and also that to appellee, contained this provision: "It is mutually understood and agreed that any planking required to be done on the pier hereby leased shall be done at the expense of the parties of the second part." Appellee's lease also contained a provision to the effect that the lessor, on giving 60 days' notice to the lessee, might terminate the lease. During the conversation between the representatives of appellee and the lessor as to the extension of the lease after May, 1897, the lessor's representative stated that the lessor made no claim to the planking placed by appellee on the dock, and preferred that appellee should remove it. Appellee, after the expiration of his lease, in May, 1897, continued to occupy the dock in question with two or three hundred tons of coal which he had thereon. Appellants did not move their office to this dock until in October, 1897. On July 9, 1897, appellee received a notice from appellants, in which it was stated that unless appellee removed his "coal and other property" from the dock by July 15, 1897, appellants would take steps to collect rent for the use of the dock, and to dispose of the property. Appellee then started to remove the planking, but was stopped by appellants' agents. After this appellee sent appellants a bill for $750 for the planking, and, in reply to the demand for an immediate removal, appellee insisted that under his lease he had 60 days in which to remove his property. No attention being paid to appellee's first bill sent appellants for the planking, subsequent bills were sent. Finally, in reply to one of date November 1, 1897, appellants sent appellee a statement, charging appellee with $866.66, and crediting him with $750, the amount of appellee's bill for planking. Appellants' bill was for rent of the dock, claimed by appellants from appellee.

A jury was waived by agreement of the parties, and both questions of law and fact were submitted to the court. Propositions were submitted by appellants to the trial judge to be held as law. One only (No. 12) of these propositions was held as requested.

At the close of the plaintiff's evidence, and also at the close of all the evidence, appellants made a motion to have given, and offered, the following instruction: "The court finds the issues for the defendants." The legal effect of offering this instruction was to demur to the evidence. First Nat. Bank v. Northwestern Nat. Bank, 152 Ill. 296, 38 N. E. 739, 26 L. R. A. 289, 43 Am. St. Rep. 247. There is evidence in the record showing that the owner of the premises recognized the right of appellee, as owner of the property in question, to remove the same. There is also evidence in the record showing that appellants sent two or three statements to the appellee, claiming rent for the premises during his occupancy of the same and after the expiration of the term of his lease, and that appellants finally sent a general statement to appellee, in which they charged him with $866.66 for rent, and credited him with $750, the amount claimed as the value of the property in question. There was also evidence that appellee had not surrendered up the dock upon which the planking in question had been laid by him, and that, when appellants gave him notice to remove his coal and other property from the dock, he began to remove the planks in question, and was stopped by the agents of appellants from doing so. These matters of evidence certainly fairly tended to support appellee's case, and whether there was in fact a surrender of the premises without the removal of the planks, or whether they were trade fixtures or other form of personal property, were so much questions of fact that we are not disposed to hold it was error in the court to refuse the peremptory instruction.

Complaint is made of the refusal of the court to mark "Held" 11 alleged propositions of law submitted to it. The first proposition was: "The court finds that the planks, planking, stringers, and surface improvements in question in this case were fixtures." The second is in the same language, and asks the court to hold that they are trade fixtures. By the third the court was asked to hold that the "plaintiff surrendered possession of the dock in question on the date of the expiration of his lease, and that the planks, planking, stringers, and surface improvements in question, at the time the premises were surrendered by the plaintiff, had not been removed or attempted to be removed by the plaintiff." The fourth asked the court to hold that the same materials designated in the previous instructions were annexed to the realty, were adapted for the use or purpose of the realty to which they were attached, and were intended by the plaintiff to be annexed to the realty. By the fifth the court was asked to hold that the property sued for had no such market value, in law, as entitled the plaintiff to recover against defendants. The sixth was that such property, located as it was, had no market value. The seventh was that the defendants leased the realty in question, and took possession thereof, with the property claimed upon the same; and that plaintiff had no right, against the defendants, to enter upon the realty and take possession of and remove said property.

We have set out enough of these propositions that their real character may be seen, and it is quite apparent that none of them are propositions of law, but are simply requests to the court to make certain specific findings of facts involved in the consideration of the case. By section 41 of the practice act (Hurd's Rev. St. 1901, c. 110, § 42), either party is authorized to "submit to the court written propositions to be held as law in the decision of the case." This provision of the statute authorizes the offering of propositions of law to be passed upon by the court, so that questions of law arising in the case as to the applicability, force, and effect of the evidence may be preserved and passed upon by courts of review. They are termed propositions of law to be held or refused by the court, in contradistinction to the instructions that are to be presented and given for the guidance of juries; but, so far as their substance and form is concerned, they must in all material respects be the same. Any form of stating a proposition of law that would not be proper in an instruction to a jury would likewise be improper when offered to the court trying a cause in the absence of a jury. Such propositions should state the law only, and not assume a state of facts existing or attempt to find a given fact or state of facts. They should be framed upon a hypothesis which there are facts in the record tending to establish, and should ask the court that, if those facts are found by the court, the law applicable to those facts is as stated in the propositions. As we said in First Nat. Bank v. Northwestern Nat. Bank, 152 Ill. 301, 38 N. E. 739, 26 L. R. A. 289, 43 Am. St. Rep. 247: "The statute does not contemplate that, under the cloak of written propositions of law, a party litigant shall have the right to call upon the court to find in his or its favor, seriatim, all the special or particular facts involved in the evidence; and, dehors the statute, it is not a common-law function of a judge, in a common-law action, to make special findings of fact." In County of La Salle v. Milligan, 143 Ill. 321, 32 N. E. 196, we said (page 345, 143 Ill., page 203, 32 N. E.): "Proposition 13 submitted by appellant was properly refused. By it the court was required to hold as a fact that the sheriff had 'collected from sources other than the county, during each year of his term as sheriff, fees in excess of the salary or compensation allowed him by the board.' The fact is not stated hypothetically, and the opinion of the court as to the law arising thereon asked, as may be done where the hypothesis assumed finds support in the evidence; but the court, if it held the proposition, was compelled to assume the fact as established. This is improper. The purpose of the statute is to enable the party to submit propositions with a view to obtaining the opinion of the court upon material and controlling principles of law only, and, when the proposition calls for the opinion of the court upon a question of fact, it may properly be refused. For aught we can know or are required to know the court found the fact directly at variance with the proposition." The last remark of the court in the above quotation is quite applicable to the case before us. It is evident from the judgment of the court that upon all the questions of fact proposed by the appellants the court entertained a different view to that requested to be held. The views herein above expressed are but the reiteration of the declarations of this court in Gilbert v. Sprague, 196 Ill. 444, 63 N. E. 993; O'Flaherty v. Mann, 196 Ill.

804, 63 N. E. 727; In re Tobin, 196 Ill. 484, 63 N. E. 1021; Field v. Crawford, 146 Ill. 136, 34 N. E. 481; Board of Supervisors v. Commissioners of Highways, 164 Ill. 574, 45 N. E. 983; Order of Foresters v. Schweitzer, 171 Ill. 325, 49 N. E. 506.

Whether the plank and stringers for which recovery is sought in this case were personal property, or whether they were trade fixtures which might be removed by the tenant, or whether they had become attached to and a part of the realty, and passed with the lease to appellants, were questions of fact, in determining which appellants were entitled, if they wished, to have the legal effect of any state of facts appearing in evidence passed upon by the court by propositions of law submitted for that purpose. The trial court found that the property sued for was personal property, for which recovery could be had, and gave judgment accordingly; and, as the Appellate Court affirmed the judgment of the trial court, we must presume that it found the facts the same way. There being, then, no further propositions or questions of law presented for our consideration, it becomes our duty to affirm the judgment of the Appellate Court, which is accordingly done. Judgment affirmed.

(209 Ill. 172)

CHICAGO TITLE & TRUST CO. v. CITY OF CHICAGO.

(Supreme Court of Illinois. April 20, 1904.)

INJUNCTION—WRONGFUL ISSUANCE—DAMAGES—ADEQUACY—INJURIES—PROXIMATE CAUSE.

1. Where, in a proceeding to assess damages for the wrongful issuance of an injunction restraining defendant from taking sand from the shore of Lake Michigan, opposite his property, as the same was washed up, it appeared that such washings were intermittent, and depended on the action of the wind and the waves, and, if not immediately removed, would be washed back into the lake, and defendant was unable to give an average of the amount of the accumulations, and was unable to say how much he lost from sand which he could have sold but for the injunction, which continued some 10 months, except that before the injunction he took from $15 to $70 worth a day, and after the injunction from $15 to $40 worth, a judgment awarding $500 for sand which he could have sold but for the injunction was as large as the evidence would warrant.

2. Where an injunction restraining the defendant from taking sand from the shore of Lake Michigan, opposite his property, and selling the same, did not prevent him from removing sand deposited outside his premises, or erecting a close fence to prevent it from drifting over his lawn, and the proximate cause of the deposit of sand on the lawn was the heavy winds which blew on the lake shore, and not the injunction, defendant could not recover damages for injuries to his lawn by such sand deposits on the injunction being held to have been wrongfully issued.

Appeal from Appellate Court, First District.

Action by the city of Chicago, substituted as complainant for the town of Lake View, against the Chicago Title & Trust Company, as executor of the estate of Parker R. Mason, deceased, substituted in his place after his death pendente lite. From a judgment in favor of defendant for less damages for the wrongful issuance of an injunction than the amount claimed, affirmed by the Appellate Court (110 Ill. App. 395), defendant appeals. Affirmed.

Edward Roby and Arthur Humphrey, for appellant. Granville W. Browning (Edgar Bronson Tolman, Corp. Counsel, of counsel), for appellee.

WILKIN, J. Blocks 5 to 16 of Pine Grove Subdivision, in Cook county, extend from Evanston avenue to Lake Michigan. Blocks 6, 7, and 12 are so laid out that each is bounded on the east by a line marked on the plat of the subdivision, and between this east line and the shore of Lake Michigan is a strip of land 2,172 feet long north and south, by about 160 feet wide east and west. Since 1871 one Parker R. Mason had been in possession and claimed to own the land in front of block 7, extending from the east lot line to the lake shore, together with considerable other land to the north and south of it, being in all about 1,858 feet long. The lake washed sand and gravel upon this strip from time to time, which had a merchantable value, and which Mason was in the habit of removing and selling. When holes were dug in the sand for the purpose of removing it, the wind and water, in the course of time, would refill them; and, if the sand was not removed immediately as it washed upon the shore, it was carried away and buried in the lake. On September 25, 1884, the town of Lake View filed its bill of complaint in the superior court of Cook county against Mason and other defendants, asking for an injunction restraining them from digging, carrying, and carting away or selling any of this sand or gravel, or from entering on the strip of ground for the purpose of dredging out or hauling away sand from the bottom of Lake Michigan. A temporary injunction was granted and served upon the defendants, and it continued in full force and effect until July 13, 1885, when it was dissolved. On August 15th following, Mason filed his suggestion of damages, asking, first, a solicitor's fee for procuring the dissolution of the temporary injunction; second, $10,000 damage for the value of sand and gravel which he was enjoined from removing during the continuance of the injunction; and, third, $1,000 damage to his lawn, lying west of the strip in controversy, by reason of the sand blowing and drifting thereon. On August 6, 1887, the town of Lake View became a part of the city of Chicago, and the city was substituted as complainant. Before the final hearing on the suggestion of damages, Mason died, and the Chicago Title & Trust Company, his executor, was substituted as defendant. The original case was heard in July, 1892, and a decree was entered sustaining the bill, and restoring and making perpetual the preliminary injunction as issued September 25, 1884, and as dissolved July 13, 1885. That decree was reversed by this court (163 Ill. 351), and upon a rehearing a decree was rendered confirming the title to the strip in Mason. On July 5, 1902, upon a hearing on the suggestion of damages, a decree was entered for $500 solicitor's fee, and $500 damage for the value of sand and gravel which Mason had been prevented from removing during the pendency of the injunction; and the third suggestion of damages, i. e., injury to the lawn, was rejected altogether. An appeal was prayed to the Appellate Court by the claimant, where the decree was affirmed, and a further appeal has been taken to this court.

No complaint is made as to the $500 solicitor's fee allowed by the decree of the superior court. In the Appellate Court the city assigned a cross-error upon the allowance of the second $500 upon the ground that there was no warrant for the same either in the law or the evidence; but in this court that assignment of error has been withdrawn, and appellee simply insists that the order of the Appellate Court should be affirmed. Appellant, however, very earnestly insists that said $500 is inadequate, and that the evidence shows that a very much larger amount of damages was sustained on that item; also that the third suggestion of damage should have been allowed; and these two last questions are alone presented for our decision.

The evidence as to the quantity of sand and gravel which might have been removed and sold during the life of the injunction, and the price which could have been obtained for it, is altogether too uncertain, indefinite, and unsatisfactory to furnish a definite basis for the estimation of damages. The quantity of sand and the intervals of its deposit are largely left to conjecture. The wind and waves deposited it on the beach, and, if it was immediately removed, it could be used, but, if not, it washed back in the lake and was lost. At times for days, and even weeks, no deposits whatever were made. In other words, the accumulations were governed by the condition of the weather. No attempt was made by appellant to average the amount of the accumulation; and, even if that had been done, the evidence shows that some of it was deposited in the streets, and some of it in front of block 12, which did not belong to Mason, a considerable distance north of his property. There is nothing, therefore, in the evidence to show how many days from September 25, 1884, to July 13, 1885, sand or gravel could have been obtained, or sold after being obtained. Mason himself testified he could not tell how much he sold; that he kept no books, except for a few months in 1888 and 1889, and did not even know what those books showed even for that period; that sometimes the money for the sand was paid to him, sometimes to the hired man, sometimes to his children, and sometimes it was not paid at all. The most that he could say was that before the injunction he took from $15 to $70 worth of sand per day, and after the injunction from $15 to $40 per day. Conceding that the testimony in this record tends to show that some loss was occasioned by the injunction on the second item in appellant's suggestion of damages, it is impossible to definitely fix the amount of such loss. Nor can it be fairly said that it exceeded the sum allowed by the superior court. In fact, we think that estimate, $500, is quite as large as the testimony would, in any view, sustain.

The third item is based upon an alleged filling up of the defendant's (Mason's) lawn with sand drifting upon it from accumulations outside of his inclosure while the injunction was in force, in consequence of which sand blew over the fence upon his lawn. The evidence shows that sand drifted all over that section of the country as snow drifts, and had been doing so for many years. One witness testified that, from the time Mason first made his lawn, he had to shovel sand from the fence to keep it out of his yard, and this he had kept up for 17 years; that the lawn would be covered with sand the next morning after it had been cleared off; and that there was a continual sand storm. Moreover, the injunction did not restrain Mason from removing the deposit outside of his fence to prevent its drifting upon his yard, or from building a close fence to protect his lawn. The city could not be held responsible for his negligence or failure to take such steps for his own protection, nor for unusual windstorms. The proximate cause of the injury was the heavy winds which blew upon the lake shore, and not the issuing of the injunction. Damages recoverable for the wrongful suing out of a writ of injunction must be such as naturally and approximately result therefrom, and remote or speculative damages cannot be taken into consideration. There is also an entire absence of evidence to show the amount of the injury claimed under this item, and, even if the proof was otherwise satisfactory, no recovery could be had.

There is no substantial merit in this appeal, and the judgment of the Appellate Court is affirmed. Judgment affirmed.

(209 Ill. 429)

CHICAGO UNION TRACTION CO. v. CHUGREN.

(Supreme Court of Illinois. April 20, 1904.)

PERSONAL INJURY — FUTURE DAMAGES — INSTRUCTION — CONTRIBUTORY NEGLIGENCE — STANDARD OF CARE—APPEAL FOR PURPOSES OF DELAY.

1. In a personal injury case the evidence showed that plaintiff's left shoulder had been dislocated, the bones of the nose fractured, and a cut made over the right eye, exposing the bone.

Evidence for plaintiff disclosed that at the time of the trial—more than a year and a half after the accident—his left arm could not be raised above a horizontal line; that the natural motion was limited, and an attempt to raise it higher caused pain; that the vision of the right eye was diminished one-fourth or one-third, and that the defective eyesight was permanent, and likely to increase. *Held*, that an instruction permitting a recovery for future pain or suffering, or future inability to labor and transact business, was proper, though there was evidence that at the time of the trial plaintiff was still employed as a teamster, and was earning the same wages as before the accident.

2. In an action for personal injuries it was not error, in instructing on contributory negligence, to define ordinary care as that care and foresight to avoid danger which a person of ordinary prudence, caution, and intelligence would "usually" exercise under the same or similar circumstances.

Appeal from Appellate Court, First District.

Action by Emil Chugren against the Chicago Union Traction Company. From a judgment of the Appellate Court, First District (110 Ill. App. 545), affirming a judgment for plaintiff, defendant appeals. Affirmed.

John A. Rose and Louis Boisot (W. W. Gurley, of counsel), for appellant. Castle, Williams & Smith (Ben M. Smith, of counsel), for appellee.

CARTWRIGHT, J. This is an appeal from a judgment of the Appellate Court for the First District affirming a judgment of the superior court of Cook county in favor of appellee against appellant for damages resulting from a collision of an electric car of appellant and a wagon loaded with timothy seed, on which appellee was riding and driving the team hauling the same across the tracks of appellant, by which he was thrown to the ground and injured. The errors assigned consist in giving two instructions to the jury at the request of the plaintiff.

The first instruction related to the assessment of damages in case the plaintiff should recover, and authorized the jury to take into consideration any future pain or suffering or future inability to labor or transact business, if any, that the jury might believe, from the evidence, the plaintiff would sustain by reason of the injuries received. The objection is that it permitted a recovery of damages for an element of injury which there was no evidence tending to prove was reasonably certain to occur. The allegations of the declaration were sufficient to admit proof of a permanent injury. The evidence showed that, as a result of the collision, the left shoulder of the plaintiff was dislocated, and there was a fracture of the bones of the nose and a cut over the right eye, extending across it and exposing the bone. The evidence for the plaintiff was that at the time of the trial—more than a year and a half after the accident—the left arm could not be raised above the horizontal line; that the natural motion was limited, and an attempt to raise the arm higher than a horizontal line caused pain; that the vision of the right eye was affected and diminished to the extent of one-fourth to one-third, and that the defective eyesight was permanent, and likely to grow worse. This testimony tended to show that there was some permanent injury which would affect the ability of the plaintiff to labor, and that the future damages mentioned in the instruction were reasonably certain to result. On the other hand, there was evidence that at the time of the trial plaintiff was still a teamster, and was earning the same wages as before the accident. This evidence was proper to be considered by the jury on the question of future damage, but it was not error to give the instruction based on the evidence for the plaintiff.

The second instruction was devoted to the subject of contributory negligence and the degree of care required of the plaintiff, and the objection to it is that in fixing the standard of ordinary care it was stated to be that care and foresight to avoid danger which a person of ordinary prudence, caution, and intelligence would usually exercise under the same or similar circumstances. Counsel say that the word "usually" had no proper place in the instruction; that plaintiff was required by law to exercise such care as a person of ordinary prudence would exercise under the same or like circumstances; that a person possessed of ordinary prudence, caution, and intelligence may exercise great care sometimes and at other times no care at all, and that when exercising no care he is not acting as a person of ordinary prudence. Counsel also object to the instruction as limiting the care required of the plaintiff to the time of the accident. The instruction includes the endeavor or attempt of the plaintiff to cross over the tracks of the defendant and also the time while on the tracks, which covers the whole period of the occurrence, and it is not limited to the time of the accident. It is true that men who are generally prudent and cautious are sometimes careless or inattentive to danger, and that the standard of ordinary care is to be determined from what prudent men generally or ordinarily do, and not on occasions where there may be a lapse from their usual habit of care. The jury are to determine what a reasonably prudent man would ordinarily do in a given state of circumstances. We think the instruction is not subject to the criticism offered, but that it conforms to the rule contended for by counsel.

Appellee moves the court to assess damages against the appellant on the ground that the appeal was prosecuted merely for delay. We cannot say that the appeal was taken for that purpose, and not in good faith, and the motion is denied.

The judgment of the Appellate Court is affirmed. Judgment affirmed.

(208 Ill. 492)

EWEN v. WILBOR.

(Supreme Court of Illinois. April 20, 1904.)

BILLS AND NOTES — SURETIES — PROTEST — INLAND BILLS — DEMAND — ACTIONS—PEREMPTORY INSTRUCTION—TIME FOR REQUEST—BURDEN OF PROOF—PREPONDERANCE OF EVIDENCE —APPEAL—OBJECTIONS—WAIVER—SET-OFF.

1. After the evidence was all in, defendant's motion for a verdict was denied, and argument thereon refused. After some other argument, defendant offered a series of instructions, the third of which was a peremptory one. *Held*, that it was too late.

2. An instruction that, in a suit on a note, if the defendant sets up a failure of consideration, he must establish such failure by a preponderance of the evidence, and that the burden of proving "any" defense is upon the defendant, followed by an instruction that by a "preponderance of the evidence" is meant the greater weight of the evidence, was not erroneous, as leading the jury to believe that the word "any" referred to every other defense than those spoken of in the instructions.

3. An instruction that "by a 'preponderance of the evidence' was meant the greater weight of the evidence" was correct.

4. A declaration contained two special counts, in effect declaring on a note, and also contained the consolidated common counts; but the special pleas all began by stating that the causes of action in the several counts were the same as contained in the special counts, and the evidence all related to the special counts. Defendant, the guarantor of the note, pleaded failure of consideration, and contended that as there was a contemporaneous written agreement with the note and referring to it, which was specially pleaded by plaintiff, the suit was not on the note. *Held*, that the suit was "an action on a note," within 2 Starr & C. Ann. St. 1896, p. 2802, c. 98, § 9, declaring that in such actions the defendant may plead failure of consideration; and therefore the burden of proof was on defendant.

5. Where defendant objected to the admission in evidence of the protest of a note, on the specific objection that it was not competent because the suit was against the guarantor, he could not, on appeal, raise the question that the protest could only be proved by a certified copy of the record kept by notaries.

6. The urging of a single specific objection to evidence is a waiver of all other objections.

7. The statute relating to the duties of notaries public has changed the common law, and made inland bills the subject of protest.

8. It was not error to refuse an instruction that there was no evidence of a demand on the note in suit, where there was a certificate of protest in evidence.

9. The Supreme Court cannot determine the sufficiency of the evidence after a verdict affirmed by the Appellate Court.

10. Plaintiff advanced money to a patentee, under a written agreement that, if the patentee should succeed in procuring certain contracts for the use or sale of the article patented, plaintiff should share in the profits and the note become nugatory; otherwise, the money advanced should be returned, if the plaintiff so chose. The agreement recited that, in order to better secure said sum in event repayment should be demanded, the patentee executed and delivered his note therefor, payable on demand after six months, to be guarantied by defendant. *Held*, in an action against defendant on the note so executed, in which he set up the written agreement, that the note was not subsidiary or collateral to the agreement, and demand on the note alone was sufficient.

11. The surety pleaded that plaintiff held money which he owed to the patentee, and which he ought to apply to the note, but that the patentee, who was insolvent, had, in conspiracy with plaintiff, released him from paying such debt. *Held*, that evidence that the patentee and plaintiff had entered into contracts relative to extending the patents subsequent to the contract and note sued on, and in no manner relating thereto, and that the patentee had released plaintiff from obligations incurred under such subsequent contracts, was not admissible in support of the plea.

12. In a suit against the surety of a note, he could not set off a claim on account due the principal by the plaintiff, assigned to the surety after the suit was brought.

13. Unliquidated damages arising out of contracts or covenants disconnected from the subject-matter of the plaintiff's claim are not such claims or demands as constitute the subject-matter of set-off.

Magruder, J., dissenting.

Appeal from Appellate Court, First District.

Action by Albert G. Wilbor, Jr., against John M. Ewen. From a judgment of the Appellate Court (99 Ill. App. 132), affirming a judgment for plaintiff, defendant appeals. Affirmed.

This appeal is from a judgment of the Appellate Court, affirming a judgment of the circuit court of Cook county in favor of appellee, against appellant, for $1,250. The declaration was filed on March 9, 1894, and consisted of two special counts and the consolidated common counts. The first special count alleged that on June 7, 1893, Warren Ewen, Jr., at Chicago, executed and delivered to the plaintiff his promissory note, in and by which he promised to pay, "on demand, after six months after the date of said note, to the order of said Albert G. Wilbor, Jr., $1,250, at the office of said Warren Ewen, Jr., in Chicago, for value received"; that the defendant, John M. Ewen, on June 7, 1893, at the same time and place of the execution of said note, and as part of the same transaction, guarantied the prompt payment of said note by the following writing on the back of said note, to wit:

"For value received, I hereby guarantee the payment of the within note at maturity, or at any time thereafter.

"John M. Ewen."

The count then alleges presentment of the note and demand for payment thereof after maturity, according to the tenor of the same, but that neither the said Warren Ewen, Jr., nor the said John M. Ewen, nor any one on their behalf, did or would pay the same, by means whereof defendant became liable, etc. The second special count alleged that on the same day and year Warren Ewen, Jr., was indebted to the plaintiff in the sum of $2,000; and in consideration that the plaintiff "would forbear and give time to the said Warren Ewen, Jr.," for the payment of said indebtedness "until he, the said plaintiff, should make payment thereof after six months thereafter, he, the said defendant, undertook and then and there in writing faithfully promised the said plaintiff to pay him the said last-named sum of $2,000, for value received"; that defendant, relying on said promise, did forbear and give time, etc., but Warren Ewen, Jr., did not and has not paid the same, of all of which the defendant had notice, whereby defendant became liable, etc. The promissory note declared on in the first count was a renewal of a note in the same words and figures, dated November 15, 1892, which was also guarantied by the defendant.

To the plaintiff's declaration the defendant, John M. Ewen, filed a plea of the general issue and seven special pleas, all based, in whole or in part, upon the following contemporaneous agreement entered into between the plaintiff and Warren Ewen, the maker of the note described in the declaration, as follows:

"This agreement, made this 15th day of November, A. D. 1892, by and between Warren Ewen, Jr., party of the first part, and Albert G. Wilbor, Jr., party of the second part, both of the city of Chicago, Illinois, witnesseth: That whereas the said party of the first part is the owner of the rights in certain territory of the United States for certain patents known as the 'multicolor dry process,' and has applied for certain other letters patent for improved process of making blue prints, and is about to apply for others, and is likely to improve upon the same, and to use, invent, and to own other patent processes for copying; and whereas, said party of the first part believes and represents unto the said party of the second part that by reason of the superiority of said processes over all others he can procure the same, some or all of them, to be adopted by the United States government for general use in the making of plats, prints, and drawings used by the government architects in and about all United States government architectural work: Now, therefore, in consideration of the premises and of the further sum of one ($1.00) dollar in hand paid by the said party of the second part to said party of the first part, and of other good and valuable considerations, the receipt of which is hereby acknowledged, the said parties of the first and second parts, respectively, do hereby mutually covenant, promise, and agree, each with the other, as follows:

"First. The said party of the first part hereby agrees to use his best endeavors to procure the adoption by the said government of said processes for use in all government architectural work, and in the event of being successful in procuring the same, or any of them, to be so adopted, all profits and other benefits arising therefrom are to be shared by the parties hereto in equal proportions. Whatever contract, agreement, or arrangement that shall or may be made with said United States government regarding said processes, or any of them, shall be made between said government on the one hand and Warren Ewen, Jr., and Albert G. Wilbor, Jr., on the other hand; the intention being that each of the parties hereto shall take in his own name and own an undivided one-half interest in any and all contracts, agreements, or arrangements that may or shall hereafter be made with the United States government respecting the use of said processes, or any of them.

"Second. The said party of the second part has, upon the ensealing and delivery of these presents, deposited with the said party of the first part, as a special deposit and earnest of good faith herein, the sum of twelve hundred and fifty ($1,250) dollars, the receipt of which is hereby acknowledged by said first party. Said sum of twelve hundred and fifty ($1,250) dollars shall be held by said party of the first part as a special deposit; but it shall, immediately upon the receipt of said second party of a duly executed agreement or contract between the United States government and the parties hereto, providing for the adoption for general use in government work of any of said processes, become the property of the said party of the first part, to compensate him in full for his services and the sale to the said party of the second part of said one-half interest in said contract or agreement, and in all other such contracts, agreements, and arrangements as shall hereafter be made with the United States government respecting the use of the said processes, or any of them, as above mentioned: Provided, however, that unless said contract or agreement with the said government is consummated on or before May 15, A. D. 1893, said sum of twelve hundred and fifty ($1,250) dollars shall, at the option of said party of the second part, be then returned by said first party to said second party, and then and in that case this agreement shall be ended and from thenceforth absolutely null and void. Should said second party, however, not elect to have said sum of twelve hundred and fifty ($1,250) dollars returned to him, as aforesaid, it shall continue to be held by said first party as such special deposit aforesaid until said government contract or agreement shall be made, or until demanded by said party of the second part, when it shall be at once due and payable to him. In order to better secure the repayment of said sum of twelve hundred and fifty ($1,250) dollars in the event that repayment thereof should be demanded, the said party of the first part has made, executed, and delivered his note of hand for said sum, of even date herewith, payable on demand after six months after date, to the order of said party of the second part, at the office of said first party, Chicago, Illinois, and has procured said obligation to be guarantied by John M. Ewin, of Chicago, Illinois.

"Warren Ewen, Jr. [Seal.]
"Albert G. Wilbor, Jr. [Seal.]"

The first and second special pleas alleged that the $1,250 mentioned in the above agreement was not deposited as alleged.

Replications to these two pleas were filed, which took issue that the deposit was not made, and the evidence showed that appellee drew in favor of the maker of the note two checks, one for $1,000 and one for $250. Five other special pleas were filed, setting up other transactions between the plaintiff and the maker of the note, in the third of which it was averred that the $1,250 mentioned in the contemporaneous agreement was afterwards, by and with the consent of the plaintiff, and without the knowledge of the defendant guarantor, applied to the payment of expenses of a joint venture and agreement entered into by the plaintiff and the maker of the note, by reason whereof the defendant, as guarantor, was discharged from all liability for the return of the special deposit mentioned in said contemporaneous agreement. The fourth additional plea averred that the plaintiff never demanded of the maker of the note the return of the special deposit. The fifth additional plea alleged that plaintiff had in his hands the sum of $3,000, which was the property of the maker of the note, and, with knowledge of the insolvency of the maker, fraudulently contriving and intending to injure the defendant and fix his liability as a surety for the return of the special deposit mentioned in the contemporaneous agreement, procured the maker of the note to execute and deliver to the plaintiff, without any good and valuable consideration, a release and discharge from all claims which the maker of the note had against the payee thereof, by reason of which the defendant, as guarantor, was discharged from all liability. The sixth additional plea averred certain contracts were entered into between the payee of the note and the maker thereof, by which the payee was desirous of raising the sum of $1,250, and the maker of the note made certain representations to the defendant guarantor to induce the latter to guaranty the note as accommodation paper, to enable the payee to raise the sum of $1,250, and that the note in suit was a renewal of said note for the same purpose, and was delivered and accepted solely as accommodation paper for the purpose aforesaid, and without any intention of creating any liability on the part of the guarantor to the plaintiff, whereby there was an entire want of consideration as between the guarantor and the plaintiff. The seventh special plea was a plea of set-off.

The note sued on was offered in evidence, and attached thereto was a notary's certificate of protest in words as follows:

"State of Illinois, County of Cook, City of Chicago—ss.: Be it known that on this ninth day of December, in the year of our Lord 1893, Isaac W. Brown, a notary public duly commissioned and sworn, and residing in the city of Chicago, in Cook county and state of Illinois, at the request of the Merchants' Loan and Trust Company, went with the original note which is above attached to the office of Warren Ewen, Jr., in the city of Chicago, during ordinary business hours, and demanded payment thereon, which was refused. Whereupon I, the said notary, at the request aforesaid did protest, and by these presents do solemnly protest, as well against the maker of said note, the indorsers thereof as all others whom it may or doth concern, for exchange, re-exchange, and all costs, charges, damages, and interest already incurred by reason of the nonpayment of the said note. And I, the said notary, do hereby certify that within forty-eight hours from the time of such protest, due notice thereof was put in the post office at Chicago, as follows: Notice for Warren Ewen, Jr., Chicago, Ill.; for John M. Ewen, Chicago, Ill.; for A. G. Wilbor, Jr., Brookline, Mass.—each of the above-named places being the reputed places of residence of the person to whom this notice was directed. In testimony whereof I have hereunto set my hand and affixed my official seal the day and year first above written.

"I. W. Brown, Notary Public."

Issue was taken on the several pleas, and on trial before a jury in the circuit court of Cook county a verdict and judgment were entered for the sum of $1,250 in favor of the plaintiff. A motion for a new trial was overruled, to which the defendant excepted, and an appeal was prosecuted to the Appellate Court for the First District, where that judgment was affirmed. From the judgment of the Appellate Court this appeal is prosecuted.

Numerous errors were assigned in the admission and exclusion of testimony and the giving and refusing of instructions.

Henry Schofield and Geo. M. Wilson, for appellant. Charles M. Walker and Charles M. Sherman (J. N. Swarts, of counsel), for appellee.

RICKS, J. (after stating the facts). We will first consider the contention of appellant that a peremptory instruction should have been given by the trial court, directing a verdict in his favor. The record shows that after the evidence was all in, and while counsel were discussing motions before the court, defendant's counsel stated that he desired to enter a motion for a verdict for the defendant, which motion the court denied. Counsel then insisted upon being heard upon the motion, but the court refused to hear arguments concerning it. Some other argument was indulged in, and then the defendant offered 12 instructions in a series, the third of which was: "Upon the evidence in this case, your verdict must be for the defendant." This is the first offer of an instruction to find for the defendant, so far as is shown by the record; and, as we have frequently held, it was not in apt time, and was therefore properly refused. Peirce v. Walters, 164 Ill. 560, 45 N. E. 1068; Chicago Great Western Railway Co. v. Mohan, 187 Ill. 281, 58 N. E. 395; West Chicago Street Railroad Co. v. Liderman, 187 Ill. 463, 58 N. E. 367, 52 L. R. A. 655, 79 Am. St. Rep. 226. Moreover, we have already passed upon that identical question in this case on a former appeal (Wilbor v. Ewen, 183 Ill. 626, 56 N. E. 342), in which we said (page 632, 183 Ill., page 344, 56 N. E.): "The Appellate Court, however, bases its judgment of reversal on the ground, as appears from the recitation found in its judgment, that the circuit court erred in refusing an instruction to find for the defendant. If the evidence introduced on the trial in the circuit court, with all proper inferences to be drawn therefrom, fairly tended to prove plaintiff's cause of action, the circuit court did not err in refusing to give the instructions to find for the defendant. Upon looking into the record, which is proper to be done in a question of this character, it will be found there is ample evidence tending to prove the plaintiff's cause of action." The cause being again considered in the Appellate Court, it rendered its judgment affirming the judgment of the circuit court, and this appeal is prosecuted from that judgment. It is clear, then, so far as the facts are concerned, or so far as the record was made up at the time the cause was considered by this court, it is now in the same condition as then, the record not having been returned at any time to the trial court, and there can be no reason for this court changing its views then expressed.

Complaint is made by appellant of instructions Nos. 1 and 2 given for appellee. Instruction No. 1 in substance told the jury that in a suit upon a note, if the defendant sets up a failure of consideration of the note, either in whole or in part, he must establish such failure by a preponderance of the evidence, and that the burden in proving any defense to the note is upon the defendant. The word "any" in this instruction appears to have been underscored. Instruction No. 2 told the jury that "by a preponderance of the evidence is meant the greater weight of the evidence." The complaint seems to be that there were other defenses than the failure of consideration, and that the word "any" must have been understood by the jury as synonymous with "every." It is not urged that the definition of the term "preponderance of the evidence" is wrong, and this court has held it correct. Schroeder v. Walsh, 120 Ill. 403, 11 N. E. 70. In fact, it is said that it states an abstract principle of law accurately, but that by the arrangement of the two instructions the court practically told the jury they must render the verdict they did. The action was upon a note, and pleas of failure of consideration were interposed. Instruction No. 1 spoke of no other pleas or defenses, and we do not think the jury were misled by the word "any" to believe that it referred to every other defense than those talked about in the instructions.

Appellant contends that the action was not upon the note, and that the burden was upon appellee. It is certain that the declaration contains two special counts in effect declaring upon the note. It also contained the consolidated common counts; but the special pleas all began by stating that the causes of action in the several counts are one and the same, to wit, that stated in the first count, and the evidence all related to the special counts. The position of appellant is that as there was a contemporaneous written contract between Warren Ewen, Jr., the maker of the note in question, and appellee, and which is set out in the statement in this case, and which referred to the note in question, and which was specially pleaded by appellee, it therefore follows the suit is upon both the written contract and the note. We do not think so. In our view, the suit was "an action on a note," within section 9, c. 98, p. 2802, 2 Starr & C. Ann. St. 1896, notwithstanding the contemporaneous agreement, and none the less so because of the fact that the suit is against the guarantor, and not against the maker, of the note. The note was a commercial instrument, governed by the rules of practice relating to such instruments. It was complete in itself, and there cannot be the slightest question but, had default been made, a judgment upon the note would have stood any test to which it could have been subjected. The special contract was a matter of special defense interposed by the appellant, and while it might be that, being a contemporaneous agreement, it should be considered together with the note when offered in evidence and the final consideration of the case being at hand, we think it cannot be said that the suit was upon anything except the note. The execution of the note was not put in issue in any way. When it was admitted in evidence, it made a prima facie case for the plaintiff. The fact that appellee had set up special defenses did not prevent its having that effect. Boudinot v. Winter, 190 Ill. 394, 60 N. E. 553; Stocks v. Scott, 188 Ill. 266, 58 N. E. 990; Miller v. Balthasser, 78 Ill. 302. The defenses set up by the special pleas were affirmative defenses, and they were the only defenses which any of the evidence tended to prove. The burden of those special defenses was upon appellant, and the court so properly told the jury.

The note had been protested, and when it was offered the plaintiff also offered the notary's certificate of protest. When this was offered appellant's counsel said: "I object to the protest. The suit is not against Warren Ewen, the maker of the note, but it is against the guarantor, and the protest is not competent evidence." The protest was attached to the note, and the note was offered in evidence without objection. It is now sought to raise the question that the protest could only be proved by a certified copy of the record required by the statute to be kept by notaries in such matters. That is not the question that was presented to the trial court. The distinction between the objection to evidence because of its competency and because of its sufficiency is well defined. Had the objection now insisted upon been urged at the trial, appellee could doubtless have had the notary make the certificate it is now said was necessary (Herrick v. Baldwin, 17 Minn. 209 [Gil. 183], 10 Am. Rep. 161); and to allow appellant to urge one objection upon the trial and another in this court would be to place appellee at an unfair advantage. The objection that the certificate of protest related to matter between other parties than those to the suit, and was therefore incompetent, which was the one urged, is not within the contention that the certificate was insufficient. Appellant, having urged the single and specific objection, thereby waived all other objections. Garrick v. Chamberlain, 97 Ill. 620; Walcott v. Gibbs, Id. 118; Newell v. Woolfolk, 91 Hun, 211, 36 N. Y. Supp. 327; Laliman v. Hovey, 92 Hun, 419, 36 N. Y. Supp. 662.

It is further insisted that the note in question, being an inland bill, was not the subject of protest; that by the law merchant only foreign bills could be protested. This court is committed to the view that the statute in relation to the duties of a notary public has changed the common law in this particular, and that inland bills are now the subject of protest. Montelius v. Charles, 76 Ill. 303.

Appellant offered instructions 4, 5, 6, and 7. By the fourth instruction the court was asked to hold that appellee could not maintain his suit, unless demand for payment had been made on Warren Ewen, Jr., the maker, and that there was no evidence of such demand. and appellee could not recover. By the fifth instruction the court was asked to hold that appellee could not recover, unless, prior to the suit, he had demanded of Warren Ewen, Jr., the special deposit of $1,250 mentioned in the contract of November 15, 1892, and that there was no evidence of such demand. The sixth instruction stated that the appellant was sued as guarantor, and his liability must be found in the strict letter and precise terms of the contract, and cannot be extended by construction or implication. The seventh instruction was predicated on the sixth, and stated that the note sued on is payable on demand after six months from its date, and that appellant is not liable unless such demand was made upon Warren Ewen, Jr., the maker, and that suit against appellee was no evidence of a demand against the maker. These instructions were refused, and the jury were instructed that "a demand on the note in evidence is a sufficient demand by the plaintiff for a return of the deposit under the contract." It was the duty of the court to refuse the fourth and fifth instructions offered, for the reason that the certificate of protest, which strongly tended to show a demand on Warren Ewen, Jr., the maker, and notice to appellant thereof, and his default, was in evidence. The sufficiency of that evidence was a question for the jury in the first instance, and as it found for appellee under a proper instruction on that point, and that judgment was affirmed by the Appellate Court, the question of the sufficiency of the evidence in that regard is not open for our consideration. The sixth and seventh instructions might properly have been given; but we do not think, under the whole record, the result could have been different had they been given, and their refusal was not reversible error.

Appellant urges that a demand on the note was not a sufficient demand, and urges that there was no personal demand made on Warren Ewen, Jr., on the note, and that a demand at the place and time of payment that would be sufficient under the law merchant, as applied to commercial paper, was not enough to fix the liability of appellant, which, he says, was controlled by the written agreement of November 15, 1892, between appellee and Warren Ewen, Jr. Whether personal demand for the payment of the note was made on Warren Ewen, Jr., was a question of fact, and we think there was evidence tending to show such demand, and the findings of the jury and the Appellate Court settled that question so far as this court is concerned. It is our opinion that a demand for the payment of the $1,250 note, made upon Warren Ewen, Jr., and his failure or refusal to pay, was a sufficient demand, as the parties by the written agreement expressly stipulated that the note for the payment of the $1,250 should be given, and that appellant should guaranty its payment, which was done. We cannot accept the view that appellant's liability is dependent entirely upon the provisions of the written agreement, or that his guaranty is simply a guaranty of his brother's obligations to appellee as the same are expressed in said agreement. To so hold would be to disregard the note entirely, and create a contract for the parties that they never entered into. Neither can we accept appellant's theory that the note is to be construed as a collateral security for the performance by his brother of the promises set forth in said agreement to return the special deposit in controversy when demanded. We hold that said note, instead of being intended to be subsidiary or collateral to the special agreement, was, in fact, a step in the direction of carrying out one of its provisions, and that the execution of said note operated to extinguish and render nugatory all that portion of the said written agreement providing for the return of said deposit upon demand by appellee. This view disposes of appellant's third and fourth special pleas.

Appellant by his fifth special plea set up

that appellee had $3,000 in his hands which he owed Warren Ewen, Jr., and which he should have applied on the debt secured by the note sued on, and, for the purpose of fraudulently collecting the amount of the note in question from appellant, appellee and said Warren Ewen, Jr., fraudulently entered into an agreement, without consideration and for the fraudulent purpose aforesaid, by which said Warren Ewen, Jr., who was insolvent, released appellee from the payment thereof, to the injury of appellant as surety. Issue was joined on this plea, and to support it appellant offered in evidence other written contracts, made prior to the contract of November 15, 1892, by which the parties undertook to work and extend the use of the process of Warren Ewen, Jr., in other fields and in a different manner from the provisions of the contract of November 15, 1892, and in no way relating to it, and then showed by Warren Ewen, Jr., who is appellant's brother, that he released appellee from certain liabilities under those contracts. The transactions to which that settlement related were in no part the contract of November 15, 1892, and the allegation that appellee had the right to apply or hold the moneys owing to Warren Ewen, Jr., by appellee, if any, on the payment of or as security for the special deposit or note sued on, was the mere conclusion of the pleader. The record shows that at the time the release was made the note in suit was not only not due, but by the express terms of the contract of November 15, 1892, it was dischargeable by means other than the payment of money, at the option of the defendant, Warren Ewen. In the light of these facts appellee not only had no right to apply the money he may have owed appellant's brother to the discharge of this note, but he would have violated a positive legal duty by doing so. To have given appellant the benefit of his plea, he must have shown, or offered to show, that the demand released was for money that, as between appellee and himself, appellee had a right to apply, and as to appellant it was his duty to apply, upon the note in question. This the evidence did not even tend to establish. In our opinion, appellee's alleged liability to Warren Ewen for material, etc., under the contracts of July and September, 1892, was not a "security," within the doctrine of subrogation, and that appellant's remedy on this branch of the case, if he has a remedy, is a proceeding in equity in the nature of a creditors' bill.

Appellant, by his seventh plea, pleaded a set-off of moneys due from appellee to Warren Ewen, Jr., alleged by appellant to have been assigned to him on September 1, 1893, by said Warren Ewen, Jr., and to support that plea relied in part on the same evidence offered under the fifth plea and other evidence offered, among which was a written assignment from Warren Ewen, Jr., dated September 1, 1893. Appellee's counsel asked leave to inquire about the paper offered, when the witness Warren Ewen, Jr., said the assignment was made on the day of the trial. This writing, upon objection, the court excluded from the evidence. Appellant offered no witness except Warren Ewen, Jr., who testified that the real consideration for the execution by him of the release of August 30, 1893, was a parol promise by appellee to bear one-half the expenses incurred and to be incurred by him in trying to get the government to adopt his patent process. This claim is the foundation of appellant's set-off. The written assignment, having been made after the suit was brought and on the day of the trial, was inadmissible as evidence proving a sale of the account, as the claim sought to be set off must have been held by appellant at the time the suit was brought. Pettis v. Westlake, 3 Scam. 535. That was the only evidence offered of the assignment of the debt, or tending to show that said plea of set-off had been filed by appellant with the knowledge and consent of Warren Ewen, the maker of the note sued on.

But, waiving this point, all the evidence touching this set-off might have been properly excluded, had the court been requested to do so. It is fundamental that unliquidated damages arising out of contracts or covenants disconnected from the subject-matter of the plaintiff's claim are not such claims or demands as constitute the subject matter of set-off, under the statute. Hawks v. Lands, 3 Gilman, 227; Sargeant v. Kellogg, 5 Gilman, 273. The set-off claimed in this case was for alleged moneys expended by Warren Ewen, Jr., under and upon an entirely distinct contract from that under which the note was given, and in no way related to it, upon a common project between appellee and said Warren Ewen, Jr., in which the latter claims appellee was to bear half the expense, and in which he testifies there was never any accounting or settlement or agreement as to the amount expended or the amount to be paid by the appellee. Had the suit been against Warren Ewen, Jr., directly, and not against the appellant, the plea of set-off should have failed.

Errors are assigned upon the action of the court below in excluding certain testimony of the witness Warren Ewen, offered in support of his plea of no consideration, being the first, second, and sixth special pleas. We have examined the record on this point, and are of the opinion that appellant was in no way prejudiced in the presentation of his defense of no consideration by the action of the court in this regard.

All that we said in our former opinion as to the irregular manner in which the case was argued by counsel for appellant was fully justified by the facts, and the petition for rehearing cannot be regarded in any other light than as a reargument of the case in violation of our rules. We have, however, re-examined the questions involved, and are satisfied with our former conclusion that the judgment of the Appellate Court should be affirmed.

Judgment affirmed.

MAGRUDER, J., dissents.

(208 Ill. 597)

AMERICAN HOIST & DERRICK CO. v. HALL.

(Supreme Court of Illinois. April 20, 1904.)

FRAUDULENT CONVEYANCES—BURDEN OF PROOF—ADVERSE WITNESS—CREDIBILITY—WEIGHT OF EVIDENCE.

1. That the grantor and grantee in an alleged fraudulent conveyance were relatives does not change the rule that the burden is on the creditor seeking to set aside such conveyance to prove the fraud, such fact being merely a circumstance tending to excite suspicion.

2. Where a creditor in an action to set aside an alleged fraudulent conveyance called the alleged fraudulent grantee as his own witness, and such grantee's testimony tended to show that the conveyance was not fraudulent, and plaintiff introduced no other evidence, plaintiff was not entitled to have such conveyance set aside on the ground that the grantee's evidence was suspicious and not entitled to credit.

Appeal from Appellate Court, First District.

Action by the American Hoist & Derrick Company against William E. Hall and another. From a judgment of the Appellate Court affirming a judgment in favor of defendants (110 Ill. App. 463), plaintiff appeals. Affirmed.

Hoyne, O'Connor & Hoyne, for appellant. John W. Smith, for appellee.

WILKIN, J. On January 9, 1899, the appellant filed a creditors' bill to set aside certain conveyances of real estate made by Charles E. Hall to his son William E. Hall, the appellee. The bill charges that the conveyances were made without any consideration, and for the purpose of hindering, delaying, and defrauding the creditors of Charles E. Hall, and that the appellee, William E. Hall, holds the property in secret trust for the benefit of Charles E. Hall. The bill made Charles E. Hall a party defendant, but he died during the pendency of the suit.

On October 20, 1898, the appellant recovered a judgment against Charles E. Hall in the circuit court of Cook county for $4,453.56 and costs of suit, upon three promissory notes dated September 15, 1897, signed by the Minnehaha Granite Company, and guarantied by Charles E. Hall and others. An execution was issued upon this judgment against Charles E. Hall, and on December 20, 1898, it was returned nulla bona. The property in controversy is situated in the city of Chicago, and is known as 3550 Vernon avenue, 7143 South Chicago avenue, 8457–8459 Ontario avenue, and 5235 Wabash avenue. The deed conveying the Vernon avenue property is dated July 21, 1897, and purports to have been acknowledged upon the same day, and filed for record September 28, 1897. It recites a consideration of $7,000, and warrants the premises to be free and clear of incumbrance. The deeds conveying the other pieces of property are all dated September 28, 1897, and purport to have been acknowledged upon the same day, and filed for record October 1, 1897. The deed conveying the South Chicago avenue lot recites a consideration of $2,000, subject to an incumbrance of $600. The deed conveying the Ontario avenue lot recites a consideration of $2,000, and the deed for the Wabash avenue lot recites a consideration of $1,000, and states that the property is subject to an incumbrance of $3,000.

The cause, being at issue, was referred to a master in chancery, who made his report, recommending that the bill be dismissed for want of equity. Exceptions were filed to this report, and were overruled by the chancellor, and the bill dismissed, at complainant's cost. An appeal was prayed to the Appellate Court, where the order of the circuit court was affirmed, and a further appeal has been prosecuted to this court.

There are two questions raised upon this appeal. It is first insisted by appellant that the evidence sustains the allegations of the bill, and that the chancellor erred in dismissing it. Upon the trial before the master the appellee, William E. Hall, was placed upon the stand by appellant, and he gave the principal testimony appearing in the record. He testified that all of the properties in controversy had been in the name of his father, Charles E. Hall, for a great many years before they were conveyed to him; that the father, though holding the title, had no interest whatever in the Vernon avenue property, but it belonged to him (the witness), and at the time of the conveyance was occupied by him as a homestead, and had been so occupied for several years. He also testified that he had for many years owned a half interest in all of the other pieces of property, and they were purchased by himself and his father on their joint account, each owning a half interest; that the title to all the properties was taken in his father's name, because, witness being a physician, he feared blackmailing suits might be brought against him for malpractice; that by the deeds of conveyance in controversy he acquired from his father only the other half interest in the properties, other than the Vernon place; and that his father's half interest in the properties was conveyed to him in part payment of a large indebtedness which his father owed him for money loaned from time to time, during many past years, and to help his father pay his share of the purchase price of the same, and for

¶ 1. See Fraudulent Conveyances, vol. 24, Cent. Dig. § 801.

improvements, repairs, and taxes on the property. He further testified that prior to January, 1895, he carried a small pocket memorandum book in which he entered the amounts advanced by him to his father, but had lost it, and at the time of the loss it showed the balance which his father owed him to be $7,280; that on the 3d day of January, 1895, his father called at his office, and he then informed his father of the balance due him; that thereupon his father took from his pocket a small memorandum book in which he kept account of the sums received by him from the witness, and, after looking it over, said the balance of $7,280 was correct, and that thereupon he (the witness) directed his bookkeeper to enter this balance in his office ledger, and he himself entered it in a small memorandum book in which he afterwards kept his account of all sums advanced by him to his father after that date. He also testified that he loaned his father a considerable amount of money to invest in the Minnehaha Granite Company, and, after the investment was made, lost confidence in the company, and in December, 1895, went to his father and demanded from him a deed to the Vernon avenue property, and a settlement of all accounts against his father, but they came to no definite understanding at that time, except that the father promised to convey the Vernon avenue property to him; that in the following March he called upon his father a second time, and demanded a settlement, and in July thereafter both he and his father went to the office of Elisha Whittlesey, Jr., his attorney, and there went over their accounts, and then and there agreed that the father was indebted to him in the sum of $9,862, and that the father should convey to him his one-half interest in all of the properties in part payment of that amount, and should execute a deed to him for the Vernon avenue property; and that in pursuance of that agreement the deeds in controversy were executed for such prima facie indebtedness existing between them. Outside of this testimony there was very little, if any, direct evidence offered by appellant tending to sustain the allegations of its bill.

It is claimed, however, that such testimony is uncertain, contradictory, and suspicious, and a great deal of the briefs and arguments of counsel for appellant is devoted to pointing out such uncertainties and contradictions. If this evidence should be treated as unworthy of belief and of no weight or credit whatever, it would be of no avail to the appellant, because in that event it would be left without proof to sustain the allegations of the bill. All transactions are presumed to be fair and honest until the contrary is proven. Appellant having alleged fraud, the burden was upon it to prove that allegation by a preponderance of the evidence. Schroeder v. Walsh, 120 Ill. 403, 11 N. E. 70; O'Neal v. Boone, 82 Ill. 589; Bear v. Bear, 145 Ill. 21, 33 N. E. 878; Merchants' Nat. Bank v. Lyon, 185 Ill. 343, 56 N. E. 1083. The fact that the alleged fraudulent transaction occurs between relatives will not change the rule as to the burden of proof; the relationship being merely a circumstance which may excite suspicion, but will not of itself amount to proof of fraud. Wightman v. Hart, 37 Ill. 123; Schroeder v. Walsh, supra; Merchants' Nat. Bank v. Lyon, supra. Appellant voluntarily put appellee upon the witness stand and made him its own witness, thereby vouching for his credibility; and while it is true it was not bound by his conclusions, and might contradict him by other witnesses, yet it could not impeach him. Mitchell v. Sawyer, 115 Ill. 650, 5 N. E. 109; Bowman v. Ash, 143 Ill. 649, 32 N. E. 486; 1 Greenleaf on Evidence, § 442. The fact that no note or receipts were passed between the parties at the time of the alleged settlement, and that the title was first placed by appellee in his father for an improper purpose, to avoid blackmail, and that tax receipts and entries in books may have been altered after the death of the father, and prior to the hearing of this cause, would only tend to cast suspicion upon the testimony of its own witness, and clearly would not amount to proof that the conveyance sought to be impeached was made without consideration, and for the purpose of hindering, delaying, and defrauding the creditors of Charles E. Hall. But in addition to this, we find, upon an examination of the record, that appellee was corroborated in his testimony as to the main facts by other witnesses. One witness testified that he was present at the time of the settlement between appellee and his father, and that he went over their accounts with them, and aided them in arriving at the balance due; another testified that she was present on many occasions, and saw various sums of money paid by appellee to his father; another testified to many acts of ownership exercised by the appellee over the different pieces of property here in controversy long before the conveyances were made, such as letting contracts for painting, papering, plumbing, and repairs, which were paid for by appellee; and still another witness testified that appellee placed one of these pieces of property in his hands for sale before the transfer by his father to him. The evidence also shows that the conveyances were made only about two weeks after the notes were given upon which complainant obtained its judgment, and more than a year prior to the entry of that judgment. From all the facts and circumstances in evidence in the case, we are unable to see upon what theory the allegations of the bill could have been sustained.

It is further insisted on behalf of appellant that the court below erred in refusing to admit the testimony of a witness named Waixel at the hearing on the master's report. The cause had been referred to the master, and he had taken the evidence and reported the same, together with his conclusions of law and fact. Exceptions had been filed to that report, and while they were under consideration by the chancellor the testimony of the witness was offered. We have held that, as a general rule, it is error for the court, under such circumstances, to hear evidence not considered by the master. Smith v. Billings, 170 Ill. 548, 49 N. E. 212; Brueggestradt v. Ludwig, 184 Ill. 24, 56 N. E. 419. There is nothing in this record to bring the case within any exception to the rule.

We are of the opinion that the decree of the circuit court dismissing the bill was clearly in conformity with the law and evidence produced upon the hearing, and that the Appellate Court properly affirmed the same. Decree affirmed.

(209 Ill. 389)

GOOD et al. v. BANK OF EDWARDSVILLE et al.

(Supreme Court of Illinois. April 20, 1904.)

APPEAL—ABSTRACT OF RECORD—FAILURE TO FILE.

1. A case will not be considered on its merits where abstract of the record has not been filed as required by Supreme Court rules.

Appeal from Circuit Court, Madison County; Charles F. Moore, Judge.

Bill in chancery by Ida May Good and others against the Bank of Evansville and others. From the decree, complainants appeal. Affirmed.

Charles E. Gueltig, B. G. Waggoner, and Mr. Bradshaw, for appellants.

HAND, C. J. This was a bill in chancery, filed in the circuit court of Madison county, for partition and to construe the will of Thomas W. Smith, deceased. No abstract of the record has been filed. The rules of this court require that the party bringing a case to this court shall in all cases, on or before the second day of the term, file in the clerk's office a complete abstract of the record. In case of a failure to file an abstract, the court will decline to consider the case upon its merits, and the judgment or decree of the lower court will be affirmed. For a failure to file an abstract, the decree is affirmed.

Decree affirmed.

(209 Ill. 84)

JACKSONVILLE & ST. L. RY. CO. v. WILHITE.

(Supreme Court of Illinois. April 20, 1904.)

EMINENT DOMAIN—CONDEMNATION OF PROPERTY — VALUATION — INSTRUCTIONS—APPEAL—ASSIGNMENTS OF ERROR — RIGHT TO COMPLAIN OF ERROR.

1. In proceedings by a railroad company to condemn real estate for a switch, requested instructions are properly refused as argumentative which tell the jury that they should not assess damages on the basis of what the owner would take for his property, or for what sum he or they would be willing to let the railroad go across the lands, but must keep in mind the actual fair cash market value as the only proper element of damage; and that it is the jury's duty to try the case fairly, and render a verdict on a fair consideration of the evidence, even though the manner in which the lands will be cut up might excite their sympathy.

2. An objection on appeal to instructions as erroneous and prejudicial, without pointing out any specific error therein, is insufficient, and will be deemed a waiver of such error.

3. A party cannot assign error in an instruction where the same fault appears in one given at his own request.

Appeal from Macoupin County Court; J. B. Vaughn, Judge.

Proceedings by the Jacksonville & St. Louis Railway Company to condemn the real estate of W. H. Wilhite. From the judgment, the petitioner appeals. Affirmed.

Mastin & Moss and Keefe & Peebles, for appellant. Knotts & Terry, for appellee.

WILKIN, J. On October 26, 1903, the appellant railway company filed its petition to condemn a strip of land belonging to W. H. Wilhite, the appellee, for the purpose of constructing a switch to connect its main line with a switch or spur leading to the plant of the Royal Colliery Company, near the city of Virden, in Macoupin county. Upon a hearing before a jury judgment was entered in favor of appellee for $730, and from this judgment an appeal has been prayed to this court.

Appellee's land, consisting of 28 acres, is in the extreme northeast corner of the section, and its length east and west is about four times its width north and south. It is immediately west of the corporate limits of the city of Virden. The main line of appellant's track crosses the 28 acres from its northwest corner in a southeasterly direction, and the portion in controversy is that part of the tract which lies south and west of the track, being triangular in shape, and containing 8.05 acres. The right of way for the switch sought to be condemned is about 520 feet long and 60 feet wide, and crosses this 8.05 acres, extending in a semicircle from the main track in a northwesterly, westerly, and southwesterly direction to the Royal Colliery Company switch. The part of the triangle actually taken by the proposed switch is .65 of an acre. The portion left north of the switch is 1.3 acres, and the portion south 6.1 acres. The question upon the trial was as to the value of the .65 of an acre actually taken and the damage to that part of the 8.05 not taken.

The evidence upon the trial was conflicting, but no point is made here as to the competency of any of it, nor as to the weight to be given to it. Neither is the right of the petitioner to condemn the land questioned. The only insistence is that the issue was a very narrow and simple one, and the testimony conflicting, rendering it especially important to appellant that the jury should have been fully and correctly instructed as to the law, which, it is claimed, was not done.

Complaint is first made of the refusal of two instructions offered by appellant. They are as follows:

(1) "You are instructed in this case that it is the law that you shall not assess the damages to Mr. Wilhite in this proceeding for land actually taken or damages to land not taken on the basis of what the owner would take for it, or for any part of it, or for what sum he would be willing to let the railroad go across his lands, or for what sum you would be willing to let the railroad go across your lands if you owned them; that these matters are improper to be taken into consideration by the jury either in fixing the value of the land actually taken or in assessing the damages to the land not taken. You must at all times keep in your minds that the actual fair cash market value of the land that is taken for the Y in this case, and the decrease (if any is shown by the evidence) in the fair cash market value of the land not taken, by reason of the construction of the switch or Y in question, are the only proper elements of damage in this case, and compensation that you are to consider."

(2) "You are further instructed that it is your duty in this case to try the case fairly and impartially, and to return your verdict after a fair and candid consideration of all the evidence, without regard to any sympathy that you may have for the defendant landowner in this case; and, even though the manner in which the Y in question may cut through the lands of Mr. Wilhite may excite your sympathy, you must see to it that your sympathy does not in any way enter into or control your verdict in this case as against the evidence introduced upon the trial."

These instructions are both open to the objection that they do not state propositions of law, but are in the nature of arguments. It is claimed by appellant that the first was approved by this court in the case of Kiernan v. Chicago, Santa Fé & California Railway Co., 123 Ill. 188, 14 N. E. 18. This is a misapprehension. The instruction there considered and approved is wholly unlike the one here refused. Nor is the contention that the second announces a correct rule of law tenable. However, on behalf of appellant, 10 instructions were given by the court, and they fully covered all the principles of law applicable to the case. Several of these told the jury what elements they should take into consideration in estimating the damages to and value of the land. While it is true that no instruction given contained some of the elements of those refused, yet they did direct the jury that they must be governed by the law and the evidence in the case. We have carefully examined the evidence, and also all of the instructions given by the court, and entertain no doubt that the jury were fully and correctly instructed on behalf of the petitioner, and that there was no error in the refusal of either of those refused. We have frequently held that it is sufficient if the jury has once been instructed upon any proposition involved in a case. Chicago City Railway Co. v. Fennimore, 199 Ill. 9, 64 N. E. 985; Henry v. People, 198 Ill. 162, 65 N. E. 120; North Chicago Street Railroad Co. v. Williams, 140 Ill. 275, 29 N. E. 672.

Complaint is also made of the first and last instructions given by the court on behalf of appellee. The only objection is that these instructions are erroneous, and were prejudicial to the rights of appellant, pointing out no specific objection to either of them. We have held in many cases that it is the duty of the party complaining of an instruction to point out wherein it is erroneous, and it is no part of our duty to search for errors on which to base a judgment of reversal. When the objection is in general terms, the appellant will be deemed to have waived the error. Razor v. Razor, 142 Ill. 375, 31 N. E. 678. It may, however, be suggested that appellant cannot be heard to complain of appellee's first instruction, for the reason that its last given instruction covers the same ground, and is to the same effect, and the rule is that a party cannot assign for error the giving of an instruction of the same character as one given at his request. Sibley Warehouse Co. v. Durand & Kasper Co., 200 Ill. 354, 65 N. E. 676, and cases cited on page 357, 200 Ill., and page 677, 65 N. E.

We find no reversible error in this record, and the judgment of the county court is affirmed. Judgment affirmed.

(209 Ill. 38)

ROBERSON v. TIPPIE et al.

(Supreme Court of Illinois. April 20, 1904.)

HOMESTEAD—NATURE OF ESTATE—DESCENT—CONVEYANCE—LIENS.

1. By the homestead act of July 1, 1873, the householder became vested with an estate in land, measured by its value, and where his interest, whether in fee for life or for years, does not exceed $1,000 in value, the homestead estate embraces his entire title and interest, leaving no separate interest in him to which liens can attach, or which he can alien distinct from the homestead estate.

2. On the death of the householder, the homestead estate, by operation of law, devolves on the surviving husband or wife for his or her life, and on the children of the household during the minority of the youngest, and the heirs at law take a reversionary interest, expectant upon the termination of the estate for life and for years.

3. 2 Starr & C. Ann. St. c. 52, § 4, providing that no release or conveyance of the homestead estate shall be valid unless the same is in writing, subscribed by the householder, and his or her husband or wife, applies to deeds made by husbands to their wives, and a conveyance of the homestead, not exceeding in value $1,000, by a householder to his wife, she not joining therein and acknowledging the same as required by the statute, is absolutely void, and passes no title.

¶ 3. See Homestead, vol. 25, Cent. Dig. § 183.

4. Since, at the date of her husband's death, the fee simple in the homestead estate vests in the husband's heirs, subject only to the homestead and widow's dower, the widow can have no claim or lien on the homestead for money which she had invested therein during her husband's lifetime.

Appeal from Circuit Court, Franklin County; P. A. Pearce, Judge.

Bill by Lydia L. Roberson against Julia Tippie and others. From a decree dismissing the bill, complainant appeals. Affirmed.

O. H. Layman, for appellant. W. H. Hart, for appellees.

WILKIN, J. On March 27, 1903, appellant filed her bill against appellees, who are the children and heirs at law of Levi Y. Roberson, deceased, to enforce the specific performance of a contract. The allegations of the bill are as follows: On September 29, 1889, the appellant, at the age of 29 years, was married to Levi Y. Roberson, who was then 61 years of age. Each had been previously married, and eight children had been born to the said Levi by his former wife, all of whom had reached their majority and left home before his marriage with appellant. Appellant had one child by her former marriage, and on August 3, 1894, there was born to her and the said Levi Y. Roberson a child, which is still living. At the date of the marriage of appellant and Roberson he was the owner of certain real estate described in the bill, which was at that time his homestead, and continued to be the homestead of appellant and the said Levi Y. Roberson to the date of his death, and since that time has continued to be the homestead of appellant. After the birth of their child the said Roberson on January 5, 1892, for a consideration of $500, paid by appellant, executed a warranty deed to her for said homestead, and put her in possession thereof, and she has continued in such possession since that date, paying all taxes thereon, and has made valuable improvements thereon. By the omission of appellant, who was then the wife of the said Levi Y. Roberson, to sign said deed, the same was inoperative to pass the legal title to the land, but the equitable title thereto by virtue of said deed was in appellant. The said Levi Y. Roberson died January 25, 1903, and left appellant, his widow, and the appellees, his children and grandchildren, surviving him, as his only heirs at law. The bill prays that appellant be vested with the title to said real estate, with a prayer for general relief. A demurrer was filed to the bill, and the same was sustained by the chancellor. The bill was then amended by adding the following allegations: That "the $500 paid by appellant for said land was used by the said Levi Roberson in repairs and planting an orchard on said land, and otherwise improving it, and in equity appellant was entitled to be reimbursed, and to have an equitable lien on said land for the same; that at the time said Levi Roberson made said deed he was not indebted to any person, and said sale was free from fraud or circumvention of all kinds; that, in case specific performance cannot be decreed, the court find the amount paid by appellant; and that a lien be decreed to exist in her favor against said lands for the same, and, if not paid, that the land be sold to pay the same." To this bill, as amended, a demurrer was sustained, and the amended bill dismissed for want of equity, at the cost of appellant, and from that order she appeals.

The one question presented for our decision is the correctness of the ruling of the chancellor sustaining the demurrer and dismissing the bill, which involves the construction to be placed upon section 4 of chapter 52, entitled "Exemptions," 2 Starr & C. Ann. St. p. 1874. That section provides, in substance, that no release, waiver, or conveyance of the homestead estate shall be valid unless the same is in writing, subscribed by the householder, and his or her husband or wife, etc. It went into force and effect July 1, 1873, and we have held that prior to this act the right of homestead was a mere exemption, and, when the householder in whom the exemption existed conveyed without the formal waiver of homestead, the effect was to transfer his title to the land, but so far as it affected the homestead right the operation of the deed was suspended until the exemption was extinguished. But by the act of 1873 the householder became vested with an estate in the land, measured and defined by the value, and not by the extent or quality, of his interest in the land or lot; and when the interest of the householder in the premises, whether in fee, for life or for years, does not exceed $1,000 in value, the homestead estate comprises and embraces his entire title and interest, leaving no separate interest in him to which liens can attach, or which he can alien distinct from the estate of homestead. The estate of homestead thus created is based upon the title of the householder, and can have no separate existence independently from the title, which constitutes one of its essential elements, and from which it is inseparable. Upon the death of the householder, in whom the estate of homestead is primarily vested, the estate, by operation of law, devolves upon the surviving husband or wife for his life or her life, and upon the children of the household during the minority of the youngest; and the heirs at law take a reversionary interest only, expectant upon the termination of the estate for life and for years created by the statute. The statute, which declares that no conveyance of the homestead shall be valid unless the same is in writing, subscribed by the householder and his wife, applies to deeds made by husbands to their wives, and therefore a conveyance of the homestead, not exceeding in value $1,000, by a householder to his wife, she not joining therein and acknowledging the same as required by the statute, is absolutely void, and passes no title whatever. Kitterlin v. Milwaukee Mechanics' Mutual Ins. Co., 134 Ill. 647, 25 N. E. 772, 10 L. R. A. 220; Anderson v. Smith, 159 Ill. 93, 42 N. E. 306; Dinsmoor v. Rowse, 200 Ill. 555, 65 N. E. 1079. By this bill it is shown that the homestead estate here involved did not exceed in value $1,000 when attempted to be conveyed. The deed to appellant was therefore a nullity, conveying no title or interest in the premises, and at the date of her husband's death the fee-simple title therein vested immediately in his heirs, subject only to her right of homestead and dower. This being so, she could have no claim or lien upon the property for the $500 invested therein, either in law or in equity. It cannot be seriously contended that the allegations of the bill are sufficient to entitle her to the specific performance of a contract, or to authorize a decree declaring her the equitable owner of the land. Her right to recover the amount paid for the homestead may be a subsisting valid claim against her husband's estate, but that question is not involved in this action.

We entertain no doubt that the demurrer to the amended bill was properly sustained, and the order dismissing the same for want of equity, at complainant's cost, must be affirmed.

Decree affirmed.

(209 Ill. 241)

WEST CHICAGO ST. RY. CO. v. DOUGHERTY.

(Supreme Court of Illinois. April 20, 1904.)

PERSONAL INJURIES—EXTENT OF INJURY—EVIDENCE—EXPERT TESTIMONY—EARNING CAPACITY—INSTRUCTIONS.

1. In an action for personal injuries, plaintiff on the first trial complained only of an injury to his hip and ankle, but on the second trial offered evidence tending to prove that an oblique inguinal hernia and a detachment of the retina of one eye resulted from the accident, and on a third trial proved that he was still suffering from the hernia, and that the eye had grown so much worse since the second trial that the eyeball had to be removed. There was evidence that before the accident plaintiff was able-bodied and healthy, suffering from none of the ailments complained of, and that shortly after the accident the hernia and injury to the eye became apparent, and continued to grow worse until the last trial. It was also in evidence that the injuries might have been caused by the accident, and were of such a nature as to develop slowly, so that they might not be discovered until after the first trial. *Held*, that evidence as to these injuries was properly admitted on the third trial.

2. In an action for personal injuries, the opinion of a physician as to the cause of an injury to plaintiff's eye was competent, though witness had not examined plaintiff until long after the accident.

3. In an action for personal injuries, evidence that for several years plaintiff had worked in a rolling mill, receiving $100 a month, was admissible on the issue of earning capacity, although he had quit his position about two months before the accident, and was at that time working as a laborer, receiving much less.

4. In an action for personal injuries, an instruction that "the court does not intimate to you an opinion as to whether one party was in the exercise of ordinary care, or the other party was guilty of negligence as alleged. These questions are for your determination alone from the evidence in the case," was not erroneous as impressing the jury that they were at liberty to decide regardless of the instructions, where other instructions expressly stated that the instructions must be accepted as the law of the case, that the jury should look to the evidence for the facts and to the instructions for the law, and that the evidence and instructions should alone control the verdict.

Appeal from Appellate Court, First District.

Action by Martin Dougherty against West Chicago Street Railway Company. From a judgment of the Appellate Court (110 Ill. App. 204) affirming a judgment for plaintiff, defendant appeals. Affirmed.

John A. Rose and Louis Boisot (W. W. Gurley, of counsel), for appellant. Waters & Johnson and Edward Maher, for appellee.

WILKIN, J. This is an action on the case, brought by appellee to recover for personal injuries caused by a collision between one of the appellant's cable cars and a one-horse wagon in which appellee was riding. The case has been tried three times. Upon the first trial appellee obtained a judgment for $3,000, which was reversed by this court (170 Ill. 379, 48 N. E. 1000) because of the refusal of an instruction asked by the defendant. Upon the second trial he obtained judgment for $5,500, which was reversed by the Appellate Court (89 Ill. App. 362) because of the modification of an instruction asked by the defendant. At a third trial he again recovered a judgment for $6,000, which has been affirmed by the Appellate Court for the First District, and this further appeal is prosecuted.

The accident occurred on October 6, 1892, about 7 o'clock in the morning, on Milwaukee avenue, at the intersection of Wabansia avenue. Milwaukee avenue runs northwest and southeast, Wabansia avenue runs east and west, intersecting it. There is a jog in the latter at Milwaukee avenue of about 175 feet to the northwest. Appellant has a double-track railroad on Milwaukee avenue, upon which it operates cable cars. The appellee, at the time of the accident, was riding in an open express wagon, together with three other fellow laborers, going to their work. The wagon was driven west on Wabansia avenue, and when it arrived at Milwaukee avenue the driver, one James O'Brien, turned northwest on the right side of the street, outside of the car tracks, and proceeded northwest on Milwaukee avenue until he arrived opposite the middle of that part of Wabansia avenue which extends west from Milwaukee avenue. There was a car coming from behind, which passed the wagon shortly before it reached the point at which those in the wagon wished to turn out of Milwaukee into Wabansia avenue. As soon as the car passed them, the driver turned the horse to the left, and drove behind it, directly upon another track, upon which a car was approaching from the northwest. The horse got across the track, but the wagon had not cleared it when the corner of the car struck the rear wheel, overturning the wagon, and throwing the occupants upon the pavement, causing the injury to appellee for which he sues.

It is first insisted that the trial court erred in admitting evidence of injuries to plaintiff which, it is claimed, were in no way connected with or caused by the accident. Upon the first trial the only injury complained of was to the left hip and ankle. Upon the second trial, in addition to those injuries, evidence was offered tending to prove that plaintiff had an oblique inguinal hernia and a detachment of the retina of the left eye, resulting from the accident. Upon the third trial he proved that he was still suffering from the hernia, and that his eye had grown so much worse since the second trial that the eyeball had to be removed. It is claimed by appellant that these last two injuries were not caused by the accident, but were afterthoughts on the part of the plaintiff, and that the testimony concerning them should have been excluded. The evidence is to the effect that before the accident plaintiff was a strong, able-bodied, and healthy man, suffering from none of the ailments complained of on the trial, and that shortly after the accident the hernia and injury to the eye became apparent, and continued to grow worse from that time until the last trial. There is evidence not only tending to show that these ailments have existed since the accident, but also that they might have been caused by the injury sustained at that time, and that they were each of such a nature as to develop slowly; also that they could have been caused by the accident, and not be discovered by the plaintiff until after the first trial. While these facts and theories are strenuously denied and disputed by witnesses for the defendant, producing an irreconcilable conflict in the testimony, the questions raised were for the consideration of the jury under proper instructions from the court. We think the evidence was competent, and that no error was committed in admitting it. The same may be said of the statements of Dr. Fellows, a witness introduced by the plaintiff, giving his opinion as to the cause of the injury to the eye, notwithstanding the fact that he had not examined the plaintiff until long after the accident occurred. The testimony was competent. Its weight and credibility were for the jury.

Appellee testified that he had worked for 16 years in a rolling mill, shoveling iron ore, and received $100 per month, but that about two months before the accident he had quit the mill, and at the time of receiving his injury was working as a laborer, shoveling dirt and laying sewer pipe, for which he received much less, and he was permitted, over appellant's objection, to state that he had earned $100 per month in the mill. It is claimed that this evidence was erroneous, and gave the jury a wrong basis upon which to estimate the plaintiff's damages. The position is untenable. In the case of West Chicago Street Railroad Co. v. Maday, 188 Ill. 308, 58 N. E. 933, plaintiff was permitted to state what wages he had earned at his trade, which he abandoned five years before the accident, and we there held that the admission of the testimony was not such prejudicial error as should reverse the judgment. The evidence admitted by the court below was of wages earned only two months before the alleged injury. We do not regard the evidence incompetent. It was proper to be considered by the jury, together with the other evidence of plaintiff's earning capacity, in fixing the amount of his damages.

Complaint is next made of the fifth instruction given on behalf of appellee, as follows: "You are instructed that the question whether or not the plaintiff, Dougherty, exercised ordinary care for his personal safety immediately before and at the time of the occurrence of the injury complained of is a question of fact, to be determined by you from the evidence before you; and you are further instructed, as a matter of law, that the question of whether or not the defendant, the West Chicago Street Railway Company, was guilty of negligence, as alleged in the declaration, is for your determination, also, from the evidence before you; and you are further instructed, as a matter of law, that if you find, from the evidence, that the defendant has been guilty of negligence, as charged in the declaration, and that such negligence caused the injury to the plaintiff complained of in the declaration, and that immediately before and at the time of such injury the plaintiff was in the exercise of ordinary care for his personal safety, then your verdict should be for the plaintiff; and you are further instructed that the court does not intimate to you an opinion as to whether one party was in the exercise of ordinary care or the other party was guilty of negligence, as alleged. These questions are for your determination alone, from the evidence in the case." It is insisted that this instruction is misleading and erroneous, because it tends to place the jury independent of the court, and to give them the impression that they were at liberty to decide the questions of negligence and of ordinary care, regardless of the instructions of the court. It is certainly not a model of perspicuity, and, standing alone, might be subject to the criticism made upon it. Even then the jury could hardly have been misled by it to the defendant's prejudice. It was, however, only one of many instructions offered by the parties, some of which expressly told the jury that the instructions must be accepted as the law of the case; that the jury should look solely to the evidence for the facts and to the instructions for the law, and that the evidence in the case and the instructions of the court as to the law should alone govern and control the verdict of the jury. By these instructions the jury were fully informed as to the consideration they were required to give to the instructions by the court as to the law of the case.

The instructions, considered as a series, were quite as favorable to defendant as it had a right to ask or expect.

All controverted questions of fact having been settled adversely to the appellant by the judgment below, and, no substantial errors of law being here pointed out, the judgment of the Appellate Court must be affirmed.

Judgment affirmed.

(209 Ill. 124)

CHICAGO & E. I. RY. CO. v. WHITE.

(Supreme Court of Illinois. April 20, 1904.)

MASTER AND SERVANT — FELLOW SERVANT — WHAT CONSTITUTES — JURY QUESTION—RAILROAD BRAKEMAN — INJURY BY COLLISION — ASSUMPTION OF RISK—INSTRUCTIONS—TECHNICAL EXPRESSIONS.

1. Servants of the same employer, directly co-operating in the particular business in hand, or whose usual duties bring them into habitual association, are fellow servants, though they are employed in different departments of the service.

2. The relation of fellow servants does not depend on personal acquaintance.

3. Whether a railroad brakeman and members of a switching crew were fellow servants, involving the issues of direct co-operation in the business in hand and of habitual association, *held* properly submitted to the jury.

4. A railroad brakeman, fatally injured while between the cars of a train in a yard, made up ready for its journey, caused by the yard switching crew sending a number of cars, without an attending brakeman, onto the track, in making a flying switch, did not assume the risk of the switching crew's negligence; it appearing that, while it was customary to kick the cars upon tracks without any brakeman to attend them, it was not customary to kick them on tracks where there was a standing train.

5. In an action for the death of a railroad brakeman, the objection that there was no proof to sustain an allegation in the declaration that he was directed to go between the cars where he was injured cannot be taken for the first time in the Supreme Court, where it was not made in the Appellate Court.

6. The fact that, in instructing in an action for the death of a servant, the court employs the term "respondeat superior" to express the master's liability, without explaining its meaning, is not ground for reversal on defendant's appeal, where the rule as to liability for negligence of a fellow servant—that being the defense relied on—was fully given in another instruction.

Appeal from Appellate Court, First District.

Action by Byron H. White against the Chicago & Eastern Illinois Railway Company. From a judgment of the Appellate Court affirming a judgment for plaintiff, defendant appeals. Affirmed.

Calhoun, Lyford & Sheean, for appellant. James C. McShane, for appellee.

CARTWRIGHT, J. This is an appeal from a judgment of the Appellate Court for the First District affirming a judgment of the superior court of Cook county in favor of appellee and against appellant in an action on the case prosecuted to recover damages for the death of Samuel C. Woodward, a brakeman in the employ of appellant, who was killed in its railroad yard in Chicago on December 22, 1900. At the conclusion of the evidence, the defendant asked the court to instruct the jury to return a verdict of not guilty. The court refused to give the instruction, and the refusal is assigned as error, and is the principal subject of argument by counsel on both sides.

It was proved, and is not denied, that the death of Woodward resulted from the negligence of other servants of the defendant, and it is contended that the negligent servants were fellow servants with Woodward. The declaration consisted of a single count, alleging that Woodward was employed by the defendant as a brakeman on a train of cars standing on the side track of defendant in its railroad yard in Chicago; that the train had been made up, and was headed south; that deceased went between cars to repair an air brake; and that while there the defendant carelessly and negligently backed another train against his train and killed him. There was little or no controversy as to the facts, and the material facts proved are as follows: Woodward was head brakeman on a freight train which made daily trips between Chicago and Brazil, Ind., leaving Chicago about 12 o'clock. The crew to which he belonged took the train out usually three times a week. The railroad yard in Chicago extended from Thirty-Third to Thirty-Seventh street, and consisted of two divisions, known as the "New Yard" and the "Old Yard." The old yard was on the west, and contained tracks numbered from 1 to 18. The new yard was on the east side, and contained tracks numbered from 1 to 26; and all the tracks formed a continuous system, connected by lead tracks and switches, and forming one yard. Defendant had two switching crews employed in this yard—one at the north end, which broke up and switched trains arriving in the yard from the road, setting the cars on various tracks to go to other roads or to freighthouses, and the other at the south end, which made up trains to go out on the road. When a freight train came in from the south, it stopped on any track which was unoccupied, and the engine was detached and went to the roundhouse at the north end of the yard, and it was the duty of the head brakeman to accompany the en-

¶ 1. See Master and Servant, vol. 34, Cent. Dig. § 479.

gine for the purpose of throwing switches. Trains were generally made up to go out on the road by the south-end crew, and, when ready to go out, the engine was taken from the roundhouse to the head of the train, which was made up for departure, and it was the duty of the head brakeman to accompany it. It would take any track that might be unoccupied to the head of the train. In going to and from the roundhouse the engine was liable to traverse the whole length of the tracks in the yards, passing over the same tracks and through the same switches as the switching crews. In making up trains the crew at the south end would switch from one track to another, and in breaking up trains the switch crew at the north end used the various switch tracks in the same way. There was no dividing line between the switch crews, and they worked all over the yard, wherever their duties called them. On the day of the accident the train on which Woodward was head brakeman was made up as usual, consisting of about 20 coal cars, with a way car at the north end. The train was standing at the south end of the yard, and the crew to which Woodward belonged took the engine to the south end of the train and coupled to it; and Woodward commenced to examine the air brakes, starting from the engine, to see if they were in working order. There was a defect or leak in the air hose two or three cars from the engine, and Woodward went between the cars to fix the leak. While he was between the cars, the switch crew at the north end kicked 13 cars from the north end of the yard upon the track, without a brakeman on them, and they ran rapidly down the track, striking the rear of Woodward's train with such force as to move it two or three car lengths before it could be stopped, and he was run over and killed. He had been employed as brakeman for five or six months on this train, and before that had been a clerk in the office at the yard, and during all the time of his employment the manner in which trains were broken up and switched and made up was the same as at the time of his death. The switch crew in the yard were under the direction and control of the yardmaster, and the road crews, while in the yard, were also under his direction, but from the time the train was ready to leave until it returned to the yard they were under the direction and control of the trainmaster.

Woodward was a servant of the defendant, and, his death having been caused by the negligence of other servants of the same master, the request of defendant for the instruction raised the question whether there was any evidence fairly tending to prove that the relations of the servants were such as to render the defendant liable, or, in other words, that they were not fellow servants. If the only conclusion to be drawn from the evidence was that they were fellow servants, the instruction should have been given; but, if different conclusions on that question might be reached from the evidentiary facts before the jury, it was not error to refuse the instruction. One of the things to be considered on that question is whether the servants were employed in the same or different departments of the service. The evidence was that the negligent switch crew and Woodward were not employed in the same department. The switch crews were under the control of the yardmaster, and performed all their work under his direction, while the road crew, in the general performance of their duties, were under the control of the trainmaster; and yet, when they were in the yard at Chicago, they were to some extent brought within the same department as the switch crews in handling their engine. Under the rule in this state relating to fellow servants, which is based so largely upon the doctrine of association in the performance of duties, the separation into different departments is not a conclusive test. In one sense, switching crews at different places remote from each other are in the same department; and yet, if they do not directly co-operate with each other, and their usual duties are not such as to bring them into habitual association, they are not fellow servants; and, on the other hand, where there is association between the servants in the performance of their duties, they are fellow servants, although in some sense employed in different departments. In Joliet Steel Co. v. Shields, 146 Ill. 603, 34 N. E. 1108, the rule is stated as follows (page 609, 146 Ill., and page 1110, 34 N. E.): "Persons may be fellow servants, although not strictly in the same line of employment. One person may be employed to transact one department of business, and another may be employed by the same master to transact a different and distinct branch of business; but if their usual duties bring them into habitual association, so that they may exercise a mutual influence upon each other, promotive of proper caution, such persons might be regarded as fellow servants. North Chicago Rolling Mill Co. v. Johnson, 114 Ill. 57 [29 N. E. 186]." If servants are directly co-operating in the particular business in hand, they are fellow servants, although their ordinary duties are in different departments. Abend v. Terre Haute & Indianapolis Railroad Co., 111 Ill. 202, 53 Am. Rep. 616. If, therefore, Woodward and the north-end switch crew were at the time of the accident directly co-operating in the particular business of the defendant then in hand, or if their usual duties were of such a nature as to bring them into habitual association, so that they might exercise an influence upon each other promotive of proper caution for their mutual safety, then they were fellow servants, notwithstanding their employment in different departments of the service.

Appellant claims that the particular business in hand when the accident happened was the whole business of the railroad yard, which consisted of receiving trains from the road, breaking them up, and distributing cars for freighthouses and other roads, making up freight trains and dispatching them on the road, and the moving of cars and trains for all these purposes. It is quite evident that direct co-operation in particular business does not mean the same thing as habitual association in the performance of duties, since, if that were so, there would be no occasion for stating two branches of the rule. Direct co-operation in a particular business is distinguished from indirect co-operation or co-operation in the general business of the master. Different persons employed in this extensive yard in some capacity, or who had occasion to be there in performance of different or separate duties, might be engaged in doing different parts of the same work, and promoting the general business of the master, and their duties be such as to bring them into habitual association, although not directly co-operating in a particular part of the work. The duties of the road crew respecting a train did not begin until the duties of the switch crew making it up ended, and the duties of the crew on the incoming train ceased before those of the switch crew began; and under the rule declared in Chicago & Alton Railroad Co. v. Hoyt, 122 Ill. 369, 12 N. E. 225, they could not be said, as a matter of law, to be directly co-operating in the particular business in hand. That question was properly submitted to the jury as one of fact.

On the question whether the duties of Woodward and the switch crew were such as to bring them into habitual association, so as to exercise an influence over each other, promotive of proper caution, the evidence was that the road crew, including the head brakeman, would take the engine, when uncoupled, and run over the track to the roundhouse, and would take it from the roundhouse and run over the tracks to couple on the outgoing train, and in doing so they ran through the yard over the tracks where the switch crews were working. It is contended by appellant that this fact established such habitual association between the two classes of servants as would make them fellow servants, in the law. Counsel for appellee says that they were not fellow servants, because Woodward was not even acquainted with the members of the north-end crew, and therefore the two could not have exercised an influence over each other promotive of proper caution. The fact of personal acquaintance does not determine the relation, but it depends upon the nature of the duties of the different servants, and the incidents of the employment. Whenever the requisite conditions are established, either by co-operation in a particular business then in hand, or duties which imply habitual association, that moment the relation commences, and under the law the servants are fellow servants. Whether they are fellow servants does not depend upon the accident of acquaintance or the length of time the men have worked together. World's Columbian Exposition v. Lehigh, 196 Ill. 612, 63 N. E. 1089. Any other rule would be vague, indefinite, and impracticable. It would be a question how long the servant must be employed before sufficient acquaintance would be established, and a sufficient opportunity given for advice, counsel, and caution, so that the servant would cease to have a right of action against the employer. The conclusion might depend upon friendship, which would induce friendly counsel and advice, or personal enmity, which would prevent or prohibit it. The fellow-servant rule rests both upon considerations of public policy, and upon the rule that when a servant enters the employment he assumes all the ordinary risks of such employment, including the negligence of fellow servants associated with him, and both reasons for the rule have been recognized by this court. He assumes the risks as to all those whose duties bring them into habitual association with him, or who may be directly co-operating with him in some particular business in hand at the time of an accident. There was evidence tending to prove that the duties of the road crew and switch crews while in the yard brought them into habitual association, but the evidence was not of such a nature that but one conclusion could have been drawn from it, and therefore the question was properly submitted to the jury. Whether the proper conclusion was drawn from the facts was finally settled by the Appellate Court, and is not subject to review here.

It is also contended that the instruction should have been given because, even if Woodward was killed by the negligence of a servant who was not his fellow servant, yet the risk of such a collision and injury as occurred was assumed by him. As already stated, one who enters the service of another contracts to assume the risk of the negligence of fellow servants, and he also assumes all the risks or hazards usually incident to the employment. He is chargeable with the ordinary conditions under which the employment is conducted, and is presumed to have notice of dangers and defects which are patent and obvious, either in the premises where the work is done, or the methods of doing the work. It is also true that the question whether an accident or injury is included in the risks of the employment is to be determined from the question whether it is an accident or injury liable to occur in the ordinary prosecution of the business, and it is not necessary to the assumption of such risks that the same accident should have happened before. A servant, however, does not assume the risk of a negligent manner of doing the work by other servants who are not his fellow servants, unless it is customary to do the work in that manner. The risk of such an act is not one of the usual or ordinary hazards of the employment. In this case the evidence was that, while it was customary to kick cars upon tracks without any brakeman to attend them, it was not the custom to kick them on tracks where there was a standing train, as was done in this case. The evidence tended to show that an out-going train was made up on a separate track, and not on one used for kicking cars upon. We conclude that the court was right in refusing the instruction.

The next proposition of counsel is that there was no proof to sustain an allegation of the declaration that Woodward was directed to go between the cars, and that he went in obedience to orders. This point was not made in the Appellate Court, and will therefore not be considered.

The last proposition of appellant's argument is that the court erred in giving the first instruction at the request of the plaintiff. The instruction used the term "respondeat superior" to express the liability of a master for a negligent act of his servant, without any explanation of what it meant, and also stated a principle of law to be within the rule, when it was in fact without the rule, or an exception to it. The jury may have had no idea of the meaning of the words "respondeat superior," and the instruction was apparently copied from a judicial opinion written for professional men. The general language often used in instructions conveys a very indefinite idea of the law of fellow servants, and the language of opinions as to co-operation, habitual association, and the like, has but little tendency to enlighten a jury upon that question. The giving of such instructions and the practice of making use of phrases unintelligible to the ordinary juror is disapproved. There was, however, nothing that could be said to be incorrect in the instruction, and the twelfth instruction given at the request of defendant seems to have been a much clearer statement of the rule, and doubtless gave the jury an understanding of the relations of fellow servants.

We find no reason for reversing the judgment. The judgment of the Appellate Court is affirmed. Judgment affirmed.

(209 Ill. 452)

CHICAGO & A. RY. CO. et al. v. PETTIT.

(Supreme Court of Illinois. April 20, 1904.)

RAILROADS—NEGLIGENCE—EVIDENCE—CONTRIBUTORY NEGLIGENCE.

1. Plaintiff, who had charge of a grain elevator, noticed that a car loaded with corn was leaking; and he told the conductor not to move the car any further than he had to, as he wanted to fix it, and he asked the conductor if he was through switching, to which the conductor replied in the affirmative. About half an hour later, plaintiff crawled in on the top of the south truck of the car, and, while lying on his back, mending the car, the locomotive threw a number of other cars against that one, whereby plaintiff was injured. Plaintiff was familiar with the method of switching at that point, and knew that the conductor might receive orders to do additional switching. *Held*, that plaintiff was guilty of contributory negligence, precluding recovery.

Magruder, J., dissenting.

Appeal from Appellate Court, Third District.

Action by Jacob A. Pettit against the Chicago & Alton Railway Company and another. From a judgment of the Appellate Court affirming a judgment in favor of plaintiff, defendants appeal. Reversed.

William Brown, A. E. De Mange, and E. M. Hoblit, for appellants. A. J. Barr and Welty, Sterling & Whitmore, for appellee.

HAND, C. J. This is an appeal from a judgment of the Appellate Court for the Third District affirming a judgment of the circuit court of McLean county in favor of the appellee for $7,500 against the appellants, as owner and lessee.

The plaintiff was in charge of a grain elevator owned by Claggett Bros., at Lexington, in said county. The defendants, at that place, which is on the main line of the Chicago & Alton Railway, have double tracks and a side track. On the morning of the accident two cars, one loaded with oats and one with shelled corn, stood upon the side track. The car loaded with corn was leaking, and the plaintiff went beneath the car to repair the same. While he was under the car, lying upon the axle and brake beam, the engine of a freight train which was engaged in switching in the Lexington yards threw a number of cars against the car plaintiff was repairing, and he was injured.

At the close of the plaintiff's evidence, and again at the close of all the evidence, the defendants asked the court to instruct the jury to return a verdict in their favor, which the court declined to do, and the action of the court in that regard is the principal error relied upon by the defendants for a reversal of the case.

The plaintiff testified that, as the freight train pulled into Lexington on the morning of the injury, he met the conductor near the station; that he inquired of him if he had any empty cars for his firm; that the conductor replied "No," but said he had a car of grain doors for them; that about that time the car of grain doors was pushed in on the side track; that it struck the loaded cars; and that he then noticed the car loaded with corn was leaking. He said: "They didn't strike very hard. I didn't notice very much about it." He also testified he then said to the conductor: "Don't move the car any further than you have to. I want to fix it;" that the conductor said, "All right;" that he then said to the conductor, "Are you through switching? I am going to fix that car," to which the conductor replied, "Yes." It appears that the freight train was then placed upon the west track to permit the north-bound passenger train to pass upon the east track; that the plaintiff was engaged in looking after his affairs for about 30 minutes, when he got a board, saw, hammer, and nails, and crawled in, feet first, upon the top of the south truck of the car, and while he was lying upon his back upon the axle and brake beam, engaged in mending the bottom of the car, the engine crossed over upon the side track for the purpose of placing a cattle car at the loading chute, which was upon the side track, north of the elevator, and moved the car upon which plaintiff was at work.

While contributory negligence is ordinarily a question of fact for the jury, if the undisputed evidence clearly shows the accident occurred by reason of the negligence of the plaintiff, and not by that of the defendants, there can be no recovery. The weight of the evidence is a question for the jury, but whether there is any evidence fairly tending to support a cause of action is a question for the court. The plaintiff seeks to excuse his recklessness in placing himself in the helpless position in which he found himself when he was injured on two grounds: First, that it was the custom for elevatormen in Lexington to repair leaky cars before shipment, and that, in accordance with such custom, he had gone beneath said car; and, secondly, that plaintiff notified the conductor he was about to repair the car, and the conductor informed him he was through switching. It would seem clear the defendants could not be held liable for the injury unless the persons in control of the engine knew, or by the exercise of reasonable care ought to have known, the plaintiff was beneath the car. The evidence does not show that the conductor was notified that it would be necessary for the plaintiff to go in on top of the truck to repair the leak, and the plaintiff admitted it was about 30 minutes from the time he talked with the conductor until he went in upon the top of the truck to repair the car. The plaintiff had been engaged in business at Lexington for about 11 years. He was familiar with the method in which the defendants did switching at that point, and, had he repaired the car immediately after the conversation with the conductor, he could have done so without risk. He, however, waited some 30 minutes before setting about to make the repairs. In the meantime the conductor had received orders to do other switching, which plaintiff admits he knew were likely to be given to the conductor. In view of that fact, it was negligence on the part of the plaintiff, 30 minutes after he had talked with the conductor, to go beneath said car without notifying the conductor or some other member of the train crew that he was beneath the car, engaged in repairing the bottom of the car. Had the plaintiff gone beneath the car immediately after talking with the conductor upon his arrival in Lexington, and been injured by reason of cars being thrown against the car which he was repairing, the defendants possibly would have been liable. This, however, he did not do, but waited some 30 minutes before commencing to make said repairs, and until the conductor had received orders to do additional switching, which orders the plaintiff knew were likely to be given to the conductor, by telegraph or otherwise, while he was waiting in Lexington; and then, without notice to the defendants or any of their agents, the plaintiff went under the car, and while there was injured. The law, under such circumstances, did not require the agents of the defendants to search beneath the cars standing upon the side track to ascertain whether the plaintiff was beneath them, or to search him out elsewhere to learn whether he was in a place of safety, before they might rightfully proceed with their work. It was the duty of the plaintiff, having waited the length of time he did after talking with the conductor, before placing himself in the perilous position in which he was found after his injury, to take all necessary steps to protect himself from injury by reason of moving cars. This was not done by his statements to the conductor made upon the arrival of the train, and the law will not shift that duty to the defendants without proof that the agents of the defendants in charge of the engine had notice that the plaintiff was beneath the car, making repairs, at the time the engine was driven on the side track after the passenger train had left Lexington; and the record is entirely devoid of any evidence showing or tending to show that the agents of the defendants knew or had any reason to suspect that the plaintiff was beneath the car at the time the engine was run in on the side track, and the car under which he was at work moved, while there is ample evidence in the record to show that the plaintiff recklessly went beneath the car by the moving of which he was injured, at a time when the agents of the defendants did not know he was going under the car to make repairs, and that he did not notify the conductor, or any other member of the train crew in charge of the engine, that he was going under the car, or take any precaution to protect himself from injury, or to give warning to the defendants that he was under the car and would be injured if the car was moved. We are of the opinion, by reason of the negligence of the plaintiff, a recovery cannot be had in this case.

The judgment of the appellate and circuit courts will be reversed, and the cause remanded. Reversed and remanded.

MAGRUDER, J., dissenting.

(209 Ill. 350)

DICKINSON v. GRIGGSVILLE NAT. BANK et al.

(Supreme Court of Illinois. April 20, 1904.)

WILLS — CONSTRUCTION—LIFE ESTATE—STOCKS —INCOME—CONVEYANCE OF STOCK—CONSIDERATION—EVIDENCE —ESTOPPEL.

1. An estate for life may be created in personalty of a durable nature, with remainder over.

2. Testator's will gave his wife one-third of his personal property for her own use during her natural life, and provided that at her death the one-third bequeathed to her should be divided between the children, and the executor delivered to the widow, as part of such third of the personalty, shares of bank stock. *Held* that, the subject-matter of the bequest being one-third of the personal estate, and not of specific consumable articles, the widow did not take an absolute estate in the stock, and was entitled only to the income thereof.

3. Where testator's will gave his widow one-third of the personalty for life, and the widow received from the executor in cash, in different payments, the full amount adjudged to her as the balance due on her widow's award, and thereafter received certain shares of stock, a contention that such shares were a part of the award was without merit.

4. Where testator's will gave his widow a life estate in one-third of his personalty, and the executor, as a part thereof, turned over to the widow certain shares of stock, and one of the children induced the widow to execute an assignment to him, she to retain all dividends during her lifetime, and he laid a dollar on the table before the widow in order that it might constitute consideration, but it was not shown whether the widow ever really received the dollar or not, such child was not a bona fide purchaser, and obtained neither a legal nor equitable title to the stock.

5. Testator's will gave his widow one-third of his personalty, with remainder over to his children, and as a part of such third certain shares of stock were turned over to her by the executors, and subsequently a son procured an assignment of such stock from the widow, and secured from a daughter an instrument reciting that she agreed to the transfer in consideration of one-third of five shares, and thereafter, in a suit to contest the validity of such assignment, it did not appear that the son taking the assignment transferred to the daughter any portion of his interest in any of the stock. *Held*, that the writing in question did not transfer the legal or equitable right to the daughter's interest.

6. Testator's will gave his widow one-third of his personalty, with remainder over to the children, and shares of bank stock were turned over to her by the executor. Subsequently she assigned some of the shares to one of the sons, the dividends to be paid to her during her life, and the bank executed a certificate to him, but retained the same in its possession, delivering to him a duplicate on which was a statement that the original would be delivered on the death of the widow. Dividends on the stock were paid to the widow, but the son voted at bank elections, as the owner of the stock. On the death of the widow other children demanded their interest under the will of their father, and the bank filed a bill of interpleader. *Held*, that the conduct of the bank had not been such as to estop it to require the son to whom the assignment had been made to litigate his claim of ownership.

Appeal from Appellate Court, Third District.

Bill of interpleader by the Griggsville National Bank against Ferdinand W. Dickinson and others. From a decree of the Appellate Court affirming a decree determining the rights of defendants, Ferdinand W. Dickinson appeals. Affirmed.

Edward Doocy, for appellant. A. C. Matthews and R. N. Anderson, for appellees.

BOGGS, J. This was a bill of interpleader, filed by the Griggsville National Bank, in which it was averred that the bank was the custodian of 11 shares of the capital stock of said bank; that the complainant had no interest in said shares of stock, but that the appellant, Rev. Ferdinand W. Dickinson, claimed to be the sole owner of 8 of said shares of stock, and the appellees, his brother, Samuel W. Dickinson, and his sister, Myra B. Cushing, each claimed to be the owner of an undivided one-third of said 11 shares of stock, and that said appellant was the owner of the other one-third of said shares of stock. The bill averred the claimants had demanded that the bank should surrender the stock to them, respectively, according to their claims of the ownership thereof, and the prayer of the bill was that the claimants should be required to interplead, and litigate between themselves their respective rights, interests, and title to said 11 shares of the said bank stock. The cause was heard on the bill, answers of the defendants, and replications thereto, and a decree was entered finding the parties claimant of the stock were each entitled to an undivided one-third of the 11 shares, and ordering the complainant bank to deliver the shares of stock in accordance with such finding, and decreeing that the costs should be paid by the appellant. The appellant brought the cause into the Appellate Court for the Third District by appeal, and from a judgment entered in that court affirming the decree of the circuit court has prosecuted his further appeal to this court.

The shares of bank stock here in controversy, and also 2 other shares of such stock not here involved, making 13 shares in all, were the property of one Justin Dickinson, deceased, at the time of his death. He died in Pike county, Ill., on the 20th day of June, 1885, and left, him surviving, Betsey E., his widow, and two sons, the appellant and Samuel W. Dickinson, one of the appellees, and one daughter, the appellee Myra B. Cushing. Said deceased left a last will, which was duly admitted to probate in Pike county, and letters testamentary were issued to Thomas Turnbull. The will, so far as necessary to be here considered, is as follows:

"First. I give, devise and bequeath to my beloved wife, Betsey E. Dickinson, the homestead in the city of Griggsville, in which we now live, for her own use during her natural life, and one-third of all personal property that I may die possessed of, for her own use during her natural life. * * *

"Third. * * * And at the death of my wife, the one-third bequeathed to her, and the homestead, to be equally divided between

¶ 1. See Life Estates, vol. 33, Cent. Dig. § 4.

Samuel Wales Dickinson and Ferdinand W. Dickinson, my sons, and Myra B. Cushing, my daughter."

On the 4th day of May, 1886, the executor, Turnbull, delivered and assigned to the widow, Betsey E., the said 13 shares of bank stock, on which the executor and the widow placed a value of $2,200, the shares of stock being worth a premium above their par value. The widow, Betsey E., departed this life on the 13th day of December, 1900.

The appellant contends that under the true construction of the will the widow was entitled to one-third of the personal property of the testator, with full and absolute power to sell and dispose of the same, and that she so received said shares of bank stock; and his further contention is that he bought from the widow, his mother, eight of such shares, being eight of the shares now in the possession of the appellee bank, and that he thereby became the sole and absolute owner of eight of the said shares. The appellees, brother and sister of the appellant, contend that under a true construction of the will the widow had only a life estate in one-third of the testator's personal property, and that the executor delivered these shares of stock to her as constituting one-third in value of the entire personal property of the testator, and that the widow thereby became entitled only to the benefit of the income from the stock, and had no power to sell the absolute title to the same. They further insist the proof shows the alleged purchase of the shares by the appellant from his mother was a mere pretense; that he had paid no legal consideration therefor; and that he entered into the transaction with the fraudulent intent to wrong them, and with full knowledge that the widow had no power to make a lawful transfer of the title to the shares of stock to him.

Appellant first contends that the gift to the widow of one-third of the personal property of the testator "for her own use during her natural life," found in the first clause of the will, invested the widow with unlimited power to sell such property if she saw fit to do so, and that the limitation over of the same property to the children of the testator, found in the third clause of the will, is repugnant to the bequest in the first clause, and for that reason void. The defect in that contention is that by the express terms of the first clause a life estate, only, is given the widow. This being true, the limitation over is not repugnant to the principal bequest, and, as we said in Welsch v. Belleville Savings Bank, 94 Ill. 191, the doctrine the limitation over is void has no application when the principal bequest is in express terms of an estate for life, only. An estate for life may be created in personal property of a durable nature, with remainder over, and in such case the property remaining is to be distributed to the remaindermen. Boyd v. Strahan, 36 Ill. 355; Trogdon v. Murphy, 85 Ill. 119; McCall v. Lee, 120 Ill. 261, 11 N. E. 522. A specific bequest, for life, of chattels of such nature the use whereof consists in their consumption or their destruction, may carry the absolute title (Burnett v. Lester, 53 Ill. 325; 24 Am. & Eng. Ency. of Law [2d Ed.] 437); but where the bequest is not of specific articles of property, but of the residue, which consists in part of chattels not of a durable nature, the gift is not of the absolute title of the consumable chattels and for life of the durable, but is of the income or use for life, and the property is reserved for the remaindermen; and in such case, if the property, or a portion of it, is of that character that it will be consumed, or will perish in its use, it may be ordered to be sold, and the income paid to the life tenant, and the principal secured for the remaindermen (Burnett v. Lester, supra; Welsch v. Belleville Savings Bank, supra; Buckingham v. Morrison, 136 Ill. 437, 27 N. E. 65). The bequest in the case at bar is to the widow "for her use during her natural life." The subject-matter of the bequest is the one-third of the residue of the personal estate of the testator, not of specific consumable articles. The gift to the widow was therefore of the one-third of the personal estate for her life, and she did not take an absolute, vendible estate therein.

We have investigated the contention of the appellant that his mother, the widow of the testator, received the said 13 shares of stock, or a portion of them, in payment of the amount adjudged to her as the balance due on her widow's award, and find the contention is not well grounded. The widow received from the executor, in cash, in different payments, the full amount adjudged to her as the balance due her on her widow's award. The shares of stock were in the hands of the executor after the payment of the widow's award and all other legal demands against the estate, and constituted a part of the residue of the estate of the testator. The widow was entitled to one-third of such residue, and the 13 shares of stock were delivered to her by the executor as being, in value, one-third of the residue of the personal estate of the testator. She did not take an absolute estate in the shares of stock, but only a right to enjoy the income arising therefrom during her natural life. The appellant had full knowledge of the provisions of the will, accepted a bequest provided for him therein, well knew that the shares of stock constituted a part of the residue of the personal property of which his father died seised, and of the manner and purpose of their transfer by the executor to his mother, and consequently could not obtain, by purchase from her, any greater interest than she herself had in the shares of stock.

Aside from this, the appellant cannot be regarded as a bona fide purchaser of the shares of stock. It does not appear that he paid any consideration for the assignment of the shares to him. The transaction was that he induced his mother to execute an assignment to him of the shares of stock without any consideration whatever, she to retain the right to receive all dividends during her lifetime. The assignment was merely voluntary. But it was suggested to the appellant that a consideration was necessary to make the transfer legal, and he thereupon, as he testified, laid a dollar on the table before his mother. It does not appear whether the mother ever received the dollar or not. There was only a very thinly veiled pretense of a sale. The appellant thereby obtained neither a legal nor equitable right or interest in or to the shares of stock.

The appellant procured the appellee, his sister, Mrs. Cushing, to sign the following instrument in writing:

"In consideration of one-third of five shares in the Griggsville National Bank, I agree to the transfer of eight shares by Betsey E. Dickinson to Ferdinand W. Dickinson. Mrs. Myra B. Cushing."

He insisted that thereby Mrs. Cushing ratified the transfer by the mother of the eight shares of stock to him. The chancellor declined to give this effect to the writing. Mrs. Cushing contended that her signature to the instrument was obtained by false representations on the part of the appellant, and that she received no consideration for its execution. The second of these contentions was well supported, and we therefore do not find it necessary to decide the first of them. The appellant did not assign or transfer to Mrs. Cushing any portion of his interest in the other five shares of the stock; does not admit in his pleadings that Mrs. Cushing is entitled to his interest in the other five shares; but his contention in his answer is that he is entitled to the eight shares absolutely and entirely, and to an undivided one-third of the remaining five shares. The writing did not invest appellant with the legal or equitable right to Mrs. Cushing's one-third interest in the eight shares.

The appellant contends the bill of interpleader ought not to have been entertained by the court. We think the appellee bank was entitled to a decree requiring the appellant and his brother and sister to interplead, and to procure the court to determine, as between themselves, their respective rights and interests in the shares of stock. The executor assigned the shares of stock held by the deceased to the widow. The bank issued a new certificate—No. 98—to the widow for 13 shares of stock. When the transaction occurred between the appellant and his mother, the widow, whereby he claims to have become the owner of the 8 shares of the stock, the widow indorsed on the certificate for the 13 shares an assignment of 8 shares to the appellant, and authorized the bank to make the "necessary transfer on the books of the bank." The bank executed a certificate—No. 100—for eight shares of the stock to the appellant, but retained the same in the possession of the bank and delivered to the appellant a duplicate thereof, on the face of which a statement was written in red ink, in substance to the effect that the same was a duplicate of the certificate No. 100, and that the original certificate was to be delivered to the appellant at the death of his mother, Betsey E. Dickinson. During the lifetime of the mother the dividends on the stock were paid to her, but the appellant was permitted to vote at bank elections as the owner of the stock. When the widow died the bank had in its possession the certificate No. 100 for the eight shares of stock. The appellant demanded the bank should deliver it to him. The appellees, Samuel W. Dickinson and Myra B. Cushing, advised the bank of the facts connected with the alleged transfers and assignments of the shares of stock, and that said appellees, respectively, claimed to be entitled to an undivided one-third of the eight shares mentioned in the certificate which was in the possession of the bank, and demanded that the bank should account to them accordingly. The position of counsel for the appellant seems to be that the bank, having recognized the appellant as the owner of the said eight shares of stock by permitting him to vote, as such owner, at the elections for directors, should be deemed estopped to question his ownership, or to require him, by way of a bill of interpleader, to litigate his claim of ownership in the courts. There is neither fraud nor misrepresentation charged against the bank, or that the appellant was induced by the action of the bank, or in reliance thereon, to take any steps or change his position or course to his injury. The appellant was not in any wise injured or prejudiced by the action of the bank in permitting him to vote as the owner of the shares, and therefore when that right was challenged the bank was not estopped to require him to interplead and defend his title to the stock and his right to be regarded as the owner thereof. The claim of appellant was unjust and inequitable, and was properly denied.

The judgment of the Appellate Court is affirmed. Judgment affirmed.

(209 Ill. 17)

WALKER v. FREEMAN.

(Supreme Court of Illinois. April 20, 1904.)

LIMITATIONS—NEW PROMISE—CONDITIONS—QUESTION OF LAW—APPEAL.

1. Whether certain letters admitted to have been written contained a new promise to pay a debt, sufficient to remove the bar of limitations, is a matter of law for the court.

2. An appellant cannot complain of the error in submitting to the jury the question whether certain letters contained a new promise to pay a debt, sufficient to remove the bar of limitations, where he asked instructions on the the-

¶ 1. See Limitation of Actions, vol. 33, Cent. Dig. § 729.

ory that it was a question for the jury, and asked that special findings on this point be submitted to the jury.

3. Letters wherein the maker of a note expressed his purpose to pay what he owed the payee, and offered to make a new note, contained such a new promise as removed the bar of limitations, though he claimed a deduction from the amount of the note for services he had rendered.

4. Statements in letters concerning a note given by the writer that he would pay when he was able, that he expected a raise of salary, and that he had other indebtedness to which he felt he must give preference, do not render a promise to pay conditional, so as to prevent it from removing the bar of limitations.

5. Letters written by the maker of a note to an agent of the payee in February, 1890, January, 1891, and March, 1892, may be considered together in determining whether there was a new promise to pay the note, sufficient to remove the bar of limitations.

Appeal from Appellate Court, First District.

Action by Reuben R. Freeman, executor of the estate of W. A. Koontz, deceased, against Amos W. Walker. From a judgment of the Appellate Court (110 Ill. App. 404) affirming a judgment in favor of plaintiff, defendant appeals. Affirmed.

John H. Bradley, for appellant. Alden, Latham & Young, for appellee.

RICKS, J. This was a suit upon a promissory note executed by appellant, dated March 15, 1883, payable one day after date. The declaration consisted of the common counts, with affidavit of merits attached. The plea of the statute of limitations and a plea of set-off were pleaded. To the plea of the statute of limitations appellee replied, alleging a new promise in writing.

The main question presented by this record is whether certain letters written by appellant contain sufficient admissions by the debtor of a new promise to pay to remove the bar of the statute. The material portions of the several letters are as follows: In a letter of date February 23, 1890, written to the agent of the holder and payee of the note in question, appellant says: "Please give me the principal of the note Mr. Koontz holds against me, date, per cent., and when it was due. Please state these particularly. I had hoped to begin paying interest on his note, at least, but now that I have yours to pay I will have to delay his. Let me hear soon." On January 31, 1891, appellant wrote as follows to the agent, John M. Stroup, at Sedalia, Ohio: "Dear Sir I have been expecting to write you for some time concerning my indebtedness to Mr. Koontz, and have only delayed because I have not seen my way clear to pay even the interest on the note and keep along with the expenses of my little family, living being very high in Chicago and suburbs. I did write you a long while ago wishing to renew my note, giving new note for principal and interest, less a fair remuneration for looking after rents and the farms generally. I now write you, friend Stroup, and ask you to arrange the matter with Mr. Koontz, as he is getting old, and such matters, I presume, annoy him. I will pay every cent I owe him, if I live, but I must have time. I now can see my way clear to pay at least the interest for next year, and possibly some on the principal, if I am not disappointed in my school prospects for next year. Since leaving Windsor I have relied on my own resources and have only been able to keep up current expenses, having to compete with old men teachers here, and my salary, in consequence, being small. But my prospects are brightening, and I want to arrange to meet my note just as fast as I can. Had I not been disappointed in my expectations with father I would have met this note before, but as it is I must pay it along now just as I can save from my salary. Father and I, however, are not estranged. Now, this is what I want to do and what I want to get Mr. Koontz to do: I want to give a new note for amount due first of February, having five years to pay it in, bearing seven per cent. interest, I agreeing to pay interest annually and as much on note as I can. I feel that by that time I can pay it off. Now, let the new note include principal of old note and interest up to February 1, 1891, less amount due me for looking after matters. Do you think $50 a year is unreasonable? I have an account of all moneys received and paid out, kept at the time, but cannot come upon it yet, but I am sure it is in my papers somewhere. But you will remember we settled up in the spring of 1883, some time. Do urge upon Mr. Koontz not to feel that I have through choice delayed making any provisions to meet my note. Nothing will please me better than to be able to meet my note against me, as I hope to, but I have had a pretty hard time, but I'll come out all right." On March 13, 1892, appellant wrote as follows to Mr. Koontz: "Yours of recent date forwarded to me, and I am sorry, and even mortified, not to be able now, and long before, to settle up matters with you. I have been teaching for the last few years, but live as economically as we can I don't get ahead any yet; but I do hope to get an increased salary in the course of a year or eighteen months, if not greatly disappointed. I had hoped all the time to get an advanced salary so as to begin paying on the note, but I have not been able to do so. * * * It is my purpose to begin paying you off as soon as I can, and as soon as I get this borrowed money paid back I will put my first savings toward paying you. I do trust you will not be greatly grieved by being kept out of payment so long, but it is all I can do now."

The note sued on was made at Shelbyville, Ill., March 15, 1883, and was for $1,199.25, due one day after date, with interest at the rate of 8 per cent. per annum. The evidence discloses that it was in a settlement between appellant and appellee's testate. It appears that Koontz, the payee, owned land in Shelby county, but lived in Ohio; that he made appellant his agent to lease and manage the lands, and that appellant acted as such agent from 1874 to 1883; that it was his duty to manage and rent the lands, pay the taxes, and collect the rents, and pay them over to Koontz. The evidence tends to show that appellant failed to pay the taxes, and failed to do other things that were incumbent upon him in the line of his agency, and that he also failed to remit the amounts that he collected, but appropriated them to his own use. In 1883 one John M. Stroup, the son-in-law and agent of Koontz, the owner of the land, came out to Illinois and made a settlement with appellant of the moneys that were due Koontz, and at which the balance of $1,199.25 mentioned in the note was found to be due Koontz, and the note given. The note was never paid, nor any part of it, and the suit at bar was brought. Pending the suit the payee died, and appellee, Freeman, as his executor, was substituted as plaintiff.

The case has been tried four times before a jury in the circuit court of Cook county, and three appeals have been prosecuted to the Appellate Court. 67 Ill. App. 309; 94 Ill. App. 357; and 110 Ill. App. 404. The principal controversy in all the trials has arisen over the proper construction and legal effect of the letters above set forth. The circuit court, in the trial from which this appeal is prosecuted, seems to have entertained the view that the effect of these letters and their construction were matters for the determination of the jury. Under this view, the court instructed the jury at length by instructions stating the law applicable to such case, and explained to them all the elements necessary to constitute a new promise within the meaning of our statute. Notwithstanding the death of the payee of the note, the appellant was allowed to testify as to his set-off. The note and interest at the time of the trial amounted to $3,008.52, and the jury found for appellee $1,321.11; thus allowing nearly $1,700 of set-off, which consisted of the services and expenses of appellant in and about the agency in looking after the farms for the period for which the rents accrued that the note in question was given for. On appeal to the Appellate Court the judgment of the circuit court was affirmed. Appellant prosecutes this appeal, and complains of the action of the trial court in the giving and refusing of instructions.

It is first complained that the court should have construed the letters in evidence, and have directed the jury as to their legal effect, and told them, as a matter of law, whether the letters were sufficient to raise the new promise required by the statute. The letters were the only evidence of the new promise. In this contention we think the position of appellant is sound. The letters were admitted to have been written to the payee of the note and his agent, and to have been in relation to the note sued on; and, so far as the liability upon the note was concerned, the only question was whether the matters contained in the three letters did constitute a new promise, and was undoubtedly a question of law. Ennis v. Pullman Palace Car Co., 165 Ill. 161, 46 N. E. 439; Kamphouse v. Gaffner, 73 Ill. 453; Belden v. Woodmansee, 81 Ill. 25; Illinois Central Railroad Co. v. Foulks, 191 Ill. 57, 60 N. E. 890; Kendall v. West, 196 Ill. 221, 63 N. E. 683, 89 Am. St. Rep. 317. But appellant is in no condition to complain of this error, as he asked and the court gave instructions upon the same theory, and asked the court to submit to the jury five special findings. By the first the jury were asked to give the date of the letter from which they found the written promise, if they found one. By the second the jury were asked, if they found a new promise, to give the language or that part of any letter from which they found the same. By the third the jury were asked, "Do you find that there was a written promise by the defendant to pay the note in the letter of date February 23, 1890?" The fourth and fifth requests for findings were in the same language, and related to the letters of date January 31, 1891, and March 18, 1892, respectively. All these findings, except the second, the court submitted as requested.

The appellant offered a number of instructions to the effect that neither of the above letters contained an unconditional or unqualified promise to pay the note, and that there was not sufficient in either of the letters from which such promise could be implied. These instructions were refused by the court, and we think properly. To take a case out of the statute, the new promise need not be an express promise to pay. If the debtor clearly admits the debt to be due and unpaid, and uses language of an intention to pay, it will be considered an implied promise sufficient to take the case out of the statute. Wooters v. King, 54 Ill. 343; Ayers v. Richards, 12 Ill. 146; Parsons v. Northern Illinois Coal & Iron Co., 38 Ill. 430; Mellick v. De Seelhorst, Breese, 221, 12 Am. Dec. 172. If the debt be identified with such certainty as will clearly determine its character, and show a present, unqualified willingness and intention to pay, that is sufficient to constitute the new promise, within the requirements of our statute. Keener v. Crull, 19 Ill. 189.

The contention that whatever promise may be found in these letters is a conditional one, we are unable to accede to. The most that can be said as to a condition is that appellant, in the letter of January 31, 1891, claims that there is an amount that is unliquidated, and that is due him for services as agent, which he is entitled to have set off or deducted from the note, and suggests that $50 a year for the time he was agent would be a reasonable amount. This supposed condition was not upon the theory that the note was not to be paid, or that appellant's promise to pay the note was upon the condition that such deduction would be acceded to by the payee of the note; but that expression is found in connection with an offer to give a new note for the debt, less the amount that should be agreed upon as a just allowance to appellant for his services. Preceding that expression is the express declaration, found in another part of the letter, that appellant would pay every cent he owed the payee of the note, and that he could see his way clear to pay at least the interest for the next year, and possibly some of the principal. Following the expression with reference to giving the new note in that letter, appellant requests Mr. Stroup, the agent, to urge upon the payee of the note the fact that the delay in the payment of the note has not been through the choice of appellant, and that nothing would please appellant better than to be able to meet the note, and that appellant would come out all right.

There is no force in the argument that the statements by appellant, in substance, in his letters, that he will pay when he is able, and that he expects soon to have an increase in his salary, and that he had other indebtedness to which he felt it his duty to give preference, and which he would first pay before paying the note in question, made the promise conditional. Such promises are to be performed in the future. If appellant had the money, and was ready and able to pay, instead of making promises to pay, he would have paid, and ended the matter; but he was confessing his inability and declaring his desire and intention to pay, and simply because he was unable, at the time of the promise, to carry out that intention, because of the smallness of his salary, or the extent of his other obligations, and so stated, his promise did not become conditional. Horner v. Starkey, 27 Ill. 13; Sennott v. Horner, 30 Ill. 429; Rolf v. Pilloud, 16 Neb. 21, 19 N. W. 615, 970; Devereaux v. Henry (Neb.) 19 N. W. 697; McNear v. Roberson (Ind. App.) 39 N. E. 896; Coffin v. Secor, 40 Ohio St. 637.

Appellant also contends that only the letter of January 31, 1891, can be looked to in determining whether a new promise was made. All these letters related to the same note, as appellant testifies, and were therefore upon the same subject-matter; and, although not so proximate in time as usually happens in such case, yet, in determining whether a new promise was made, and whether that promise was unconditional, we think all the letters should be taken into consideration. In the first, he asks for a particular description of the note that he owes, and states that he hoped to begin paying interest upon that note, but, because of a debt that he owes Stroup, he is compelled to delay; in the second, he seems to have received the information he wished, and there repeatedly makes the declaration of his intention to pay; and in the third, to the payee, we find a clear acknowledgment of the debt, the expression of contrition and mortification by appellant that the matter had so long remained unpaid, and his declaration, "It is my purpose to begin paying you up as soon as I can, and as soon as I can get this borrowed money paid back I will put my first savings toward paying you." We are unable to see why all these letters may not be looked to, and, if in any one of them or all of them there is present sufficient language from which a clear and unqualified promise to pay the debt may be found, such promise could be given effect, and appellant be bound thereby, as all of said letters were the writings of appellant.

As we have said, the court should have construed these letters, and, as we now hold, should have instructed the jury that they did contain an unqualified promise to pay the debt, thereby removing the bar of the statute. If appellant had not become a party to the error in failing to so instruct the jury, it would still be doubtful if there is reversible error in the case. The jury found just what the court should have instructed them to find, and, in the allowance of the set-off to appellant and the admission of testimony, was more favorable to him than he was entitled to have. There should be an end to this litigation. No complaint is made of instructions affecting the set-off, and appellant received all the benefit under that plea that he was entitled to.

The judgment of the Appellate Court is affirmed. Judgment affirmed.

(208 Ill. 621)

JONES et al. v. VILLAGE OF MILFORD.

(Supreme Court of Illinois. April 20, 1904.)

APPEAL—RECORD—BILL OF EXCEPTIONS—PRESERVATION OF OBJECTIONS.

1. An objection to the finding and judgment of a lower court which does not relate to the pleadings or appear on the face of the judgment itself is reviewable in the Supreme Court only by an exception taken in the court below and preserved by bill of exceptions, and a recital in the transcript prepared by the clerk that on the judgment being entered the appellant prayed an appeal, which was allowed, is insufficient.

Appeal from Iroquois County Court; Frank Harry, Judge.

Proceedings by the village of Milford for the confirmation of a special tax for a street improvement. From a judgment confirming the special tax, Alba M. Jones and others appeal. Affirmed.

Robert Doyle, for appellants. Morris & Hooper, McClellan Kay, and J. H. Dyer, for appellee.

HAND, C. J. This was an application in the county court of Iroquois county for the confirmation of a special tax, according to frontage, upon the property benefited, for the paving and curbing of a part of Axtell avenue, including street and alley intersections, in the village of Milford. The appellants appeared and filed objections as to their property. The legal objections were overruled, a jury was waived, and the questions of benefits and whether they had been properly apportioned were submitted to the court, which questions were decided adversely to the appellants, and the special tax was confirmed.

The only manner in which the correctness of the finding and judgment of the county court in confirming the special tax is attempted to be challenged in this court by the appellants is by a recital in the transcript prepared by the clerk of the county court, to the effect that, upon judgment of confirmation being entered, the appellants prayed an appeal to this court, which was allowed. This is not sufficient to bring before this court for review the errors assigned upon the record, which only question the finding and judgment of the county court. This court has repeatedly held that an objection to the finding and judgment of a lower court, which does not relate to the pleadings or appear upon the face of the judgment itself, can be preserved for review in this court only by an exception duly taken in the court below and preserved by bill of exceptions. Martin v. Foulke, 114 Ill. 206, 29 N. E. 683. In Bailey v. Smith, 168 Ill. 84, 48 N. E. 75, after setting out section 60 of the practice act, it was said (page 85, 114 Ill., and page 684, 29 N. E.): "It is only a decision so excepted to that can be assigned for error, and the exception can only be taken and preserved by means of a bill of exceptions. The errors here assigned question only the finding and judgment, and the record contains no exception to such finding or the judgment rendered, neither of which is so much as mentioned in the bill of exceptions." And in People v. Chicago & Northwestern Railway Co., 200 Ill. 289, 65 N. E. 675, on page 290, 200 Ill., and page 676, 65 N. E., the court said: "It does not appear from the bill of exceptions that an objection was preferred or any exception taken to the finding and judgment of the trial court. * * * The authority to certify that an objection was made and exception taken to the action of the court in entering judgment rested in the presiding judge of the court, not in the clerk. Such an objection can only be preserved and brought to our judicial notice by being incorporated into the bill of exceptions." And in Cincinnati, Indianapolis & Western Railway Co. v. People, 205 Ill. 538, 69 N. E. 40, on page 541, 205 Ill., and page 42, 69 N. E., it was said: "No proposition of law respecting those taxes was submitted, and the only complaint is that the final judgment of the court upon the law and the evidence was wrong. There was no exception to that judgment, and as to those taxes it must be affirmed." As the questions sought to be presented for our consideration on this appeal were not preserved in such manner that they can be reviewed by this court, the judgment of the county court must be affirmed.

Judgment affirmed.

(209 Ill. 109)

LIBBY, McNEILL & LIBBY v. BANKS.

(Supreme Court of Illinois. April 20, 1904.)

MASTER AND SERVANT—PERSONAL INJURIES—DUTIES OF MASTER—QUESTION FOR JURY—INSTRUCTIONS.

1. The question of whether or not plaintiff's evidence is sufficient to justify submission of the issues to the jury is one of law.

2. It is the duty of the master to use reasonable care to provide his servant with a safe place in which to work.

3. Whether or not a master provides his servant with a safe place in which to work is a question of fact for the jury.

4. Instructions having no foundation in the evidence should not be given.

Appeal from Appellate Court, First District.

Action by Mary E. Banks against Libby, McNeill & Libby. From a judgment of the Appellate Court (110 Ill. App. 330) affirming a judgment for plaintiff, defendant appeals. Affirmed.

F. J. Canty and R. J. Folonie, for appellant. Richolson & Levy (C. Stuart Beattie, of counsel), for appellee.

RICKS, J. This was an action on the case for damages, brought by appellee against appellant for personal injuries sustained by her. The only question arising on this record, except the refusal of one instruction, is whether the trial court erred, at the close of all the evidence, in refusing to give the peremptory instruction asked by appellant, who was the defendant below, directing the jury to find the issues for the defendant. A verdict was returned in favor of appellee. Judgment was entered on the verdict by the trial court, and this judgment, on appeal, was affirmed by the Appellate Court, and a further appeal is prosecuted to this court.

The question before this court to decide, in the court's refusal to grant the peremptory instruction, is one of law, and not one of fact, the motion being in the nature of a demurrer to the evidence; that is, admitting the evidence in favor of the plaintiff to be true, does it, together with all legitimate conclusions which may be drawn therefrom, fairly tend to sustain the plaintiff's cause of action as laid in her declaration? If it does, then, as a matter of law, the plaintiff is entitled to have her case passed upon by the jury. And whether this evidence is weak or strong is not a question for this court, as the judgment of the Appellate Court, in respect to the facts, where there is any evidence fairly tending to support the judgment, is final, and cannot be reviewed by this court. Metropolitan West Side Elevated Railway Co. v. Fortin, 203 Ill. 454, 67 N. E. 977. The evidence discloses that on or about

August 1, 1900, appellee, a woman 40 years of age, was in the employ of appellant, and was working at the time on the third floor of the packing plant of appellant, sweeping and cleaning the rooms underneath a loft or platform on which were stored goods belonging to appellant, and while so engaged the loft fell (there being on the loft, at the time it fell, four men, together with over 3,000 pounds of goods stored thereon), pinning appellee to the floor, and permanently injuring her. The loft is described by appellant, in substance, as follows: It consisted of a platform about 8 feet from the floor, 16 feet long, and approximately the same width. This was supported at the four corners, and braced by supports descending from the ceiling down to the sides of the platform. Attached to the south and also to the north supports were planks running parallel with the floor and 8 feet above it, which acted as joists at either end for the support of the same, and 4 by 4 beams running north and south supported the weight of the material on this loft. On these 4 by 4's boards were placed, forming a flooring, and iron braces, consisting of rods, were attached to the wall.

The first count of the declaration, in substance, charges that plaintiff was ordered to sweep below the loft used by defendant as a storeroom, and thereupon it became and was the duty of the defendant to keep and maintain said loft in a proper and safe condition and repair, so as to not endanger the life and limb of plaintiff; yet the defendant did not regard its duty or use due care in that behalf, but, on the contrary thereof, then and there carelessly, negligently, and wrongfully failed to keep said loft in proper and safe repair and condition, etc. The second count alleges that defendant maintained a certain loft used as a storeroom; that the plaintiff was hired to perform certain services, to wit, to sweep the floor below said loft, and in the course of her duty and employment did so; and then and there it became and was the duty of the defendant not to overload the said loft so as to endanger the life and limb of the plaintiff, yet the defendant did not regard its duty in that behalf, but negligently and wrongfully overloaded said loft, etc. The evidence is conflicting in reference to the manner in which the loft was constructed, appellee claiming, and the evidence tending to show, that the south end of the platform rested against the dressing room, and the other end of it rested on 2 by 4's, and a 2 by 4 to keep it from shaking was nailed up against the building at the northwest, and was only supported by two scantlings. Appellee also denied that there were iron braces or rods attached to the wall.

The evidence tends to show that the platform was built for the purpose of hanging beef to dry, and afterwards was also used to pile thereon such things as were necessary to be put out of the way, and at the time it fell there were piled upon it, besides the four men, 250,000 mincemeat cartons, tables, wrapping presses, barrels, water tank, etc., in all weighing to exceed 4,000 pounds. It was the appellant's duty to use reasonable care to provide the appellee with a safe place in which to work, and whether the structure was properly built and kept in a proper and safe condition, or whether the same was negligently and wrongfully overloaded, and therefore unsafe, were questions of fact for the jury, and not of law to be decided by this court, and after a careful review of the evidence we are of the opinion there is evidence tending to establish plaintiff's cause of action, and it was not error for the trial court to refuse the peremptory instruction.

It is also urged that the court's refusal to give a certain instruction along with a series of instructions was error, but it is sufficient to say of this refused instruction that it was upon the question of fellow servant, and there was no evidence upon which to base it, and it was therefore not error to refuse it.

The judgment of the Appellate Court will be affirmed. Judgment affirmed.

(209 Ill. 264)

LEHMANN et al. v. WARREN WEBSTER & CO.

(Supreme Court of Illinois. April 20, 1904.)

CONTRACT—GUARANTY — PERFORMANCE — TIME —PREVENTION BY OTHER PARTY.

1. Where a contract to install a heating plant contained a guaranty to make good any defects that might be apparent within a year from the completion of the apparatus, and within that time, while the contractor was endeavoring to make the plant effective, he was prevented from doing so by removal of the entire plant, he was entitled to recover the entire contract price for the plant.

Appeal from Appellate Court, First District.

Cross-actions between Augusta Lehmann and others and Warren Webster & Co., consolidated by stipulation. From a judgment of the Appellate Court (110 Ill. App. 298) affirming a judgment of the circuit court, Augusta Lehmann and others appeal. Affirmed.

Willis Smith and Henry L. Wallace (Jno. W. Smith, of counsel), for appellants. Randall W. Burns, for appellee.

RICKS, J. This is an appeal from a judgment of the Appellate Court for the First District affirming a judgment of the circuit court of Cook county.

Appellants were the representatives of the ownership—disregarding as immaterial in this discussion the substitution of parties—of a block of stores and flats, all of which were occupied by tenants. The appellee was the owner and engaged in the installation of what was known as the "Webster System of Steam Heating," which was represented as being more economical and furnishing a more perfect system of heating than was then installed in said stores and flats. As a result of the negotiations on the subject, appellee submitted to appellants a written proposition, which was subsequently accepted February 7, 1898, in and by which appellee agreed to furnish and erect the said system of steam heating, with all the necessary appliances and connections therewith, in said stores and flats, for the consideration of $3,983. By the terms of the contract, the appellants were to pay for the labor and materials 85 per cent. of the contract price as the work progressed, and the other 15 per cent. 30 days after its completion, the total of which should not exceed $2,900, and provided: "The balance of the above named price ($1,083) is to be paid at the end of the present heating season and the demonstration of the above guaranties." The contract contained certain guaranties by appellee as to completeness and efficiency of its system. It also contained the following provision: "We [appellee] will make good any defect in workmanship, materials or effectiveness that may be apparent within one year from the completion of the apparatus, without cost to you." Appellee, shortly after the execution of this contract, proceeded to change the heating system then in place in these buildings, and known as the "Gravity System" to the "Webster System." Appellee stopped work on the plant in May, 1898, as after that date there was no heat to test the work as it progressed, but again resumed work in October of the same year as the date of the contract, and while still working on the plant, about December 13th, was stopped by the Lehmann estate, now represented by appellants.

Appellants claim that the heating system was all installed before the work was discontinued in May, 1898, but was not in perfect working order, as contemplated by the contract, and that, when the heating season opened in the fall of 1898, appellee began a series of tests, and resorted to various expedients to make the system furnish the necessary heat, but with unsatisfactory results, and this was continued up until the 12th of December, when the demands of the tenants in the Lehmann buildings became so urgent that on December 13th appellants disconnected appellee's system. Appellee, however, contends that, when the work of completing the system was resumed in the fall of 1898, an insufficient and irregular quantity of steam was furnished by the Lehmann estate, because of the diverting of the steam to sinking an artesian well and other purposes, and by reason thereof appellee was not able to properly complete its work, and, besides, it was subjected to various other annoying impediments in the completion of its work, and finally the Lehmann estate, while appellee was still working on the system, and when it was almost completed, without justification or excuse, ripped out the whole plant and confiscated a portion of its property. On July 18, 1899, the suit of appellants against the appellee was instituted for the collection of the amounts theretofore paid on the above contract, and it was claimed appellee had not kept good its provisions. On August 3, 1899, the appellee brought suit in assumpsit against appellants on the aforesaid heating contract for the balance claimed to be due under the same. As the rights of each of the parties arose out of the same transaction, and being between the same parties, the two cases were, by stipulation, consolidated by the court, and tried as one case; the trial resulting in a verdict and judgment in favor of appellee for $1,604.18, the remaining portion of the contract price. From this judgment an appeal was prosecuted by appellants to the Appellate Court for the First District, which court affirmed the judgment of the trial court.

The errors of the Appellate Court in affirming the judgment of the trial court, as alleged and stated by appellants, are as follows: (1) The circuit and appellate courts erred in holding that appellee had one year for completing the contract and making the heating system installed under the contract comply with its terms; (2) the circuit and appellate courts erred in holding that the disconnecting of the heating system by appellants on December 13, 1898, more than six months after its erection and installation, was a violation of appellee's right to complete the contract, and prevented a compliance with the warranty, and therefore gave it a right of action to recover the unpaid portion of the contract price.

Appellants have assigned numerous specific errors, and discuss in their argument various objections; but, as we understand them, they relate either to questions of fact, with which we have nothing to do, or to the giving and modification of certain instructions. The objections as to the instructions are all upon the theory that the court misconstrued the contract, and shaped the instructions according to such erroneous construction. The misconstruction contended for, as above set forth, was that, under the terms of the contract between the parties, the court held the appellee had one year after the making of the contract to make the heating system contracted for complete, and comply with the terms of the contract, and that appellant's disconnection of said system while appellee was still working upon the same and endeavoring to bring it up to the required standard, and before the expiration of one year from the acceptance of the contract, was a violation of appellee's right to complete said contract.

The contract is devoid of any express statement when the system should be installed and completed. But whatever may be said as to the uncertainty in this particular, it does expressly provide that appellee "will make good any defect in workmanship, materials or effectiveness that may be apparent within one year from the completion of the apparatus." There is no question but what appellee was endeavoring to make good the effectiveness of the system of heating contracted for, when the Lehmann estate, in less than one year from the date of the acceptance of the contract, interfered and prevented further action on the part of appellee. As held in People ex rel. v. Holden, 82 Ill. 93, a party who prevents a thing being done within the time stipulated will not be allowed to avail of the nonperformance he has himself occasioned, and thus avoid his agreement.

Giving to the contract in question the interpretation that we feel compelled, from the language, to give it, we perceive no material error in the instructions complained of; and, indeed, it is only upon a different construction of the contract that appellants urge their objections. In the light of such circumstances, no good purpose can be served in setting out more fully the instructions complained of, or going more fully into this discussion.

The judgment of the Appellate Court will be affirmed. Judgment affirmed.

(209 Ill. 206)

DAVIS et al. v. UPSON et al.

(Supreme Court of Illinois. April 20, 1904.)

WILLS—SUIT IN CHANCERY TO CONTEST VALIDITY—JURISDICTION OF PROBATE COURT—VERDICT OF JURY—SETTING ASIDE—AUTHORITY OF CHANCELLOR—EXECUTION OF WILLS—WHAT LAW GOVERNS.

1. In a proceeding to contest the validity of a will by a bill in chancery under the statute of wills (3 Starr & C. Ann. St. 1896, p. 4035, c. 148, par. 7) authorizing a bill to contest the validity of a will admitted to probate, and providing that, if such a bill is filed, an issue at law shall be made up whether the writing produced be the will of the testator, the question of the jurisdiction of the probate court to admit the will to probate does not arise.

2. The property of a decedent at the time of her death consisted of cash on deposit in New York and bonds of an Illinois corporation and other choses in action which were simply debts due to the decedent. The bonds and a portion of the choses in action were in the hands of decedent's agent in Illinois, who held them as agent. The decedent, at the time of her death, and for a long time prior thereto, was a resident of New York. *Held*, that the validity of decedent's will, so far as it depended on the proper execution thereof, must be determined by the law of New York.

3. In a bill in chancery to contest the validity of a will on the ground that it was not executed according to the laws of New York, the state of the domicile of the decedent, and on the grounds of undue influence and testamentary incapacity, the jury returned a general verdict that the writing produced was not decedent's will, and special findings to the effect that the will was not executed according to the laws of New York, that there was no undue influence, and that decedent had testamentary capacity. *Held*, that what really occurred at the execution of the will was a question for the jury, and its verdict was obligatory on the court, and though, if it regarded the verdict palpably against the weight of the evidence, it could set the verdict aside, and grant a new trial, it could not vacate the verdict and enter a decree based on his conclusions that the will was duly executed.

4. Where the bill in a suit to contest the validity of a will on the ground that it was not executed according to the law of the domicile of the testator recited the statutes of the state of the testator's domicile relative to the execution of wills, and alleged with detail of facts that the will was not signed or acknowledged and attested by witnesses as required by such laws, the pleadings did not entitle the proponents of the will to a judgment notwithstanding the verdict of the jury finding that the will was not duly executed.

Appeal from Appellate Court, First District.

Bill by Lydia F. Upson against Lewis H. Davis, executor of the will of Cynthia M. Cameron, deceased, and others, to contest the validity of the will of the deceased. From a judgment of the Appellate Court (110 Ill. App. 375) reversing the decree of the Superior Court sustaining the will and directing that a decree be entered vacating the probate of the will, the executor appeals. Reversed.

D. J. & D. J. Schuyler, Jr. (D. J. Schuyler, of counsel), for appellant. Alden, Latham & Young and James C. Rogers, for appellees.

BOGGS, J. This was a bill in chancery filed by the appellees in the superior court of Cook county to contest the validity of the will of Cynthia M. Cameron, deceased, and of the codicil thereto. The bill alleged that said Cynthia M. Cameron, at the time of the execution of the alleged will and codicil, was a resident of the state of New York, and it recited the statutes of the state of New York in reference to the execution and attestation of wills, and averred that the alleged will and codicil were not executed and attested in compliance with such statutes of the state of New York. The bill further alleged the execution of the will had been induced by fraudulent arts and devices and undue influence exercised by the appellants, and also that the said Cynthia M. Cameron was not of sound mind and memory at the time of the making of the alleged will and codicil. The answer admitted the testatrix was a resident of the state of New York at the time of her death, and had been for a long time prior thereto; that prior to the execution of the will, to wit, on the 2d day of March, 1893, decedent caused to be placed in the hands of the appellant, Lewis H. Davis, a resident of the city of Chicago, in the state of Illinois, a large part of her estate, consisting of notes, notes secured by mortgage, and moneys, to be held and invested by said Davis for her use and benefit, and to pay the decedent as much of the income thereof as she might from time to time require; that said Davis was, by the direction of the testatrix, named as executor and trustee in the will; that the testatrix sent the will and the codicil to said Davis in Chicago, with directions to said Davis to retain possession of her property and invest and keep the same invested, and pay to the decedent the income thereof as might be from time to time requested by her; that said Davis retained possession of said will and codicil and personal property, securities, etc., and after the death of the decedent, on February 28, 1898, filed the will and codicil with the clerk of the probate court of Cook county for probate, in accordance with the provisions of the statutes of Illinois; that said will and codicil were admitted to probate on May 4, 1898; that no objections were made to the probate thereof, or appeal taken from the order of court admitting the same to probate, and that letters testamentary issued to said Davis, and he subsequently qualified, and thereafter filed an inventory, which was approved; that the property and estate of the decedent at the time the will was probated and at the date of the filing of the inventory were in the possession of said Davis; that decedent was not the owner of any real estate in the state of Illinois, but was the owner of personal property as inventoried by said Davis. The answer denied that the testatrix had been induced by any undue influence to execute the will or the codicil, or that she was lacking in mental power to execute the same, and averred that the will and the codicil had been executed and attested in the form and manner required by the statutes of the state of New York.

The case was heard before the court and a jury. The court submitted to the jury the following special interrogatories or findings to be answered by the jury: "First. Was the said Cynthia M. Cameron, at the time of the execution and attestation of the writing purporting to be the last will and testament, with the codicil thereto, of said Cynthia M. Cameron, dated February 13, 1895, unduly influenced to make said writing of February 13, 1895; and, if so, by whom? Second. Was the said Cynthia M. Cameron, at the time of the execution and attestation of the writing in evidence purporting to be the last will and testament, with the codicil thereto, of said Cynthia M. Cameron, on February 13, 1895, of sound mind and memory? Third. Was the document purporting to be the codicil to the last will and testament of Cynthia M. Cameron, deceased, dated February 13, 1895, executed in accordance with the laws of the state of New York? Fourth. Was the document purporting to be the last will and testament of Cynthia M. Cameron, deceased, executed in accordance with the laws of the state of New York?" The court also submitted the form for a general verdict that the writing in evidence purporting to be the last will of the said decedent was or was not her last will and testament, according as the jury might determine. The jury returned as their general verdict that the paper writing was not the last will and testament of the decedent, and in response to the special interrogatories replied that neither the will nor the codicil was executed in accordance with the laws of the state of New York, and that the testatrix was of sound mind and memory, and that the execution of the will was not induced by undue influence. The appellant executor filed his motion to set aside the general verdict of the jury and for a decree declaring the instrument of writing to be the last will and testament of the said Cynthia M. Cameron, notwithstanding the verdict of the jury. The chancellor granted this motion, and entered a decree accordingly, declaring the written instrument to be the valid last will and testament and codicil of said Cynthia M. Cameron, deceased, and dismissing the bill for want of equity at the cost of the contestants. The contestants prosecuted an appeal to the Appellate Court for the First District. The Appellate Court found from the pleading and the proof that said Cynthia M. Cameron was not a resident of the state of Illinois, and did not own any real estate in the state, and on these facts held that the probate court of Cook county, Ill., was wanting in jurisdiction to grant the probate of the will, and for that reason reversed the decree of the superior court, and remanded the cause, with directions to the superior court to enter a decree setting aside and vacating the probate of said will and codicil by the probate court of Cook county, and all its proceedings in that regard. From this judgment of the Appellate Court this appeal has been perfected to this court.

We think the Appellate Court erred in holding that the decree should be reversed because of any supposed or actual want of power or jurisdiction in the probate court of Cook county to admit the will to probate, and also erred in directing that a decree be entered in the superior court setting aside and vacating the probate of the will and codicil in said probate court and all of the proceedings of said probate court in respect of the said will and codicil. It is correct that the decree of a court may be attacked collaterally when it appears from the face of the record jurisdiction to entertain and decide the cause was wanting. But the question whether the probate of the will was valid and effectual did not arise in the cause. The proceeding was a bill in chancery, filed under section 7 of the statute of wills (3 Starr & C. Ann. St. 1896, p. 4035, c. 148, par. 7) to contest the validity of the will. This section authorizes a court of equity to entertain a bill to contest the validity of a will, and the statute provides that, if such a bill is filed, "an issue at law shall be made up whether the writing produced be the will of the testator or testatrix or not, which shall be tried by a jury in the circuit court of the county wherein such will, testament, or codicil shall have been proven and recorded as aforesaid, according to the practice of courts of chancery in similar cases." The proceeding is statutory, the object being to give the contestant of a will an opportunity to thoroughly investigate all the circumstances relating to the execution of the will, the capacity of the maker thereof to execute the instrument, and other facts affecting the validity of the will. The statute definitely and distinctly states the issue to be heard and determined in the proceeding is whether the writing produced be the will of the decedent. No issue relating to the validity of the order admitting the will to probate is provided for by the enactment.

It is not within the general jurisdiction of courts of equity (in the absence of enabling statutes) to entertain bills to set aside the probate of wills on the ground the probate court was lacking in jurisdiction. Luther v. Luther, 122 Ill. 558, 13 N. E. 166; 23 Am. & Eng. Ency. of Law (2d Ed.) 136–138. If the probate court was lacking in jurisdiction of the subject-matter, as found by the Appellate Court, the judgment admitting it to probate could be vacated by motion entered either at the term at which the judgment was made or at any subsequent term. If jurisdiction was lacking, the proceedings resulting in the admission of the will and codicil to probate is void, and may be set aside at any time by motion in that court. Wright v. Simpson, 200 Ill. 56, 65 N. E. 628. No contrary doctrine is announced in Chicago Title & Trust Co. v. Brown, 183 Ill. 42, 55 N. E. 632, 47 L. R. A. 798. That was a petition filed in the probate court to revoke the probate of a will on the ground the court had erroneously held one of the attesting witnesses to be a competent or credible witness. This alleged error did not touch the jurisdiction of the probate court, but only the correctness of the decision rendered by the court. In that case an expression is found from which the implication might arise that in a bill in chancery filed under the statute to contest the validity of the will the probate of the will might be contested and vacated. It was there said: "Appellees might have set aside the probate by an appeal to the circuit court, as provided by statute, or by bill in chancery brought within the time provided in the statute." In the case then before the court it was sought, by motion in the probate court, to vacate the order admitting the will to probate on the ground one of the attesting witnesses to the will was not a credible or competent witness. That objection affected the validity of the will, and the expression, if confined, as it should be, to the case in hand, is correct, and not inconsistent with what has been said herein. It may be in some instances the remedy provided by section 7 of the chapter on wills has been referred to in the opinions of this court as a proceeding to set aside the probate of a will, but such expressions are but inaccuracies. The effect of a decree under such a bill holding that a will is invalid operates practically to set aside, or rather to render nugatory, the probate of the will, for the reason the will being invalid, the probate thereof becomes inoperative. The issue in such cases is whether the will is valid, and whether the will was presented to the proper probate court for probate is not involved. The order of the court admitting the will to probate is not even competent to be produced in evidence. Craig v. Southard, 148 Ill. 37, 35 N. E. 361. No question could arise in respect of the jurisdiction of the probate court to enter an order admitting the will to probate.

The property of the decedent at the time of her death consisted of cash on deposit in New York and bonds of the Chicago City Railway Company, an Illinois corporation, and other choses in action, which, in law, were simply debts due to the decedent. The railroad bonds and a portion of the notes and choses in action were in the hands of the appellant, Davis, in Chicago, who held them as the agent of the decedent. The decedent, at the time of her death, had her domicile in the state of New York. The rule we think to be uniform that when personal or movable property only is the subject of the bequests in a will, the validity of a will, so far as it depends on the proper execution thereof, is to be determined by the law of the domicile of the decedent, without regard to the law of the place where such personal property may be found. The forms and solemnities necessary to a valid execution of the will and codicil of the decedent were such as were required by the law of the decedent's domicile, the state of New York. 22 Am. & Eng. Ency. of Law (2d Ed.) 1364. The laws of that state were proven, and much testimony was produced bearing on the question whether the requirements of that law had been complied with in the matter of the attestation of the will by the decedent and the witnesses thereto. The jury considered the testimony on these points, and in answer to special interrogatories decided that neither the will nor the codicil thereto had been executed in accordance with the laws of the state of New York. The general verdict that the writing produced was not the will of the decedent was consistent with these findings, and inconsistent with the other special findings of the jury to the effect that the decedent was of sound mind and memory, and under no constraint. The chancellor possessed rightful power to set aside the general verdict and grant a new trial, but was wanting in power to vacate the verdict and enter a decree based on his own conclusions as to the validity of the will. It was indispensable to the validity of the will that it should appear it had been executed and attested in compliance with the laws of the state of New York. The issue of compliance or noncompliance was submitted to the jury for decision. Whether the will, on its face, appeared to have been attested in compliance with the formalities required by the law of the state of New York was a question of law, but what really occurred at the time of the execution and attestation of the will was a matter of fact to be determined by the jury from the testimony produced before them, and whether what in fact occurred constituted a compliance with the laws of the state of New York was a question of fact for the jury, under proper instruction from the court as to the law. Masonic Orphans' Home v. Gracy, 190 Ill. 95, 60 N. E. 194. The verdict of the jury on that issue was not advisory, merely, to the chancellor, but was obligatory on the court, in like manner as is a verdict in an action at law. Rutherford v. Morris, 77 Ill. 397; Long v. Long, 107 Ill. 210; Biggerstaff v. Biggerstaff, 180 Ill. 407, 54 N. E. 333. If the chancellor regarded the verdict as palpably against the weight of the evidence, it was his province and his duty to set the verdict aside, but he should in that event have granted a new trial. It was error to decree that the bill should be dismissed for want of equity. The bill recited the statutes of the state of New York relative to the execution and attestation of wills and codicils, and averred, with detail of fact, that the will was not signed or acknowledged by the deceased as required by the law of that state, and that the witnesses did not attest or witness the will as required by such laws. The pleadings did not entitle the proponents of the will to a judgment non obstante veredicto, and the decree cannot be supported on the theory the court was authorized to render the same notwithstanding the verdict of the jury. Ambler v. Whipple, 139 Ill. 311, 28 N. E. 841, 32 Am. St. Rep. 202; 11 Ency. of Pl. & Pr. 914.

The judgment of the Appellate Court and the decree of the superior court are each reversed, and the cause is remanded to the superior court for such other and further proceedings as to law and justice shall appertain.

Reversed and remanded.

(209 Ill. 56)

STONE et al. v. SALISBURY et al.

(Supreme Court of Illinois. April 20, 1904.)

RES JUDICATA—ESTOPPEL—JURISDICTION OF COURT—SUBMISSION TO JURY.

1. A decree of partition of the property of a decedent, naming a certain person as his child and heir, is not conclusive on the heirs of his widow in a subsequent controversy, in which the property assigned to the person so named is not involved, as to the parentage of such person, where that question was not put in issue in the partition suit.

2. Deeds by a widow, of the property of her deceased husband, to one named as his child and heir, do not estop the widow or her heirs from denying that the grantee in the deeds was her child and heir, where the property granted in the deeds was not involved.

3. Under Hurd's Rev. St. 1901, c. 22, § 40, providing that in any cause in equity the court may direct an issue to be tried by a jury, it was proper, in a suit to set aside a will, to submit to the jury the question whether the complainant was the heir at law of the testatrix, to determine whether the court had jurisdiction; the verdict being advisory only.

Appeal from Circuit Court, Cook County; R. S. Tuthill, Judge.

Suit by Mary Snell Stone and another against Frank L. Salisbury, executor, and others. From a decree in favor of defendants, plaintiffs appeal. Affirmed.

Benjamin F. Richolson, Samuel Richolson, and Alexander M. Savage, for appellants. A. S. Trude, George A. Trude, and M. Marso (John Mayo Palmer, of counsel), for appellees.

RICKS, J. On April 16, 1900, the appellants, Mary Snell Stone and Albert J. Stone, her husband, filed a bill in the circuit court of Cook county to set aside the will of Henrietta Snell, deceased. The bill alleges that appellant Mary Snell Stone is a daughter and heir at law of Henrietta Snell, and, after designating the other heirs at law and setting out the will, and alleging that the same was duly exhibited in the probate court, and letters thereon issued to the executrix and trustees under the will, and the trust accepted by them, charges that the attesting witnesses did not sign the said will at the request of the testatrix, or in her presence, or in the presence of each other; that the testatrix did not sign said will in the presence of said attesting witnesses, and did not know the nature of the instrument she signed at the time of executing the same; and that at said time the testatrix was not of sound and disposing mind and memory. The bill further alleges that Albert J. Snell, a son of the testatrix, and one of the legatees and devisees under the will, and Frank L. Salisbury, his attorney, who is appointed executor of said will, and who drafted the same, used and exercised many undue arts and fraudulent practices, and resorted to falsehood and misrepresentation, to induce the testatrix to sign said instrument; that the testatrix never read said will or knew its contents, and at the time of the execution thereof was under the improper restraint and undue influence of said Albert J. Snell and Frank L. Salisbury, and was a victim of fraud and compulsion, and that said will is not the will of the testatrix; that, subsequently to the signing of said will, many erasures and interlineations were made therein; that, after said erasures and interlineations were made, the said will was not signed by anybody. The prayer of said bill is that said instrument in writing, and the probate thereof, may be set aside and declared null and void, and not the last will and testament of said Henrietta Snell; that the said estate of the said Henrietta Snell be distributed among her heirs at law (naming them, and naming appellant Mary Snell Stone as one of them). Appellees, Albert W. Adcock, Homer M. Thomas, and Frank L. Salisbury, executors and trustees under the will, filed their answer, in which they deny that Mary Snell Stone is the daughter of Henrietta Snell, and deny that she is interested in the estate of said Henrietta

Snell, or interested in the question of whether the writing produced and admitted to probate is or is not the last will and testament of said Henrietta Snell; deny that any undue influence had been exercised by Frank L. Salisbury and Albert Jerome Snell, and deny all other charges of fraud and misrepresentation alleged in the bill; deny that erasures were made after the will was executed, and that the testatrix was of unsound mind; and deny that the appellant Mary Snell Stone is an heir at law and a legal representative and daughter of the said Henrietta Snell. The other defendants answered, denying the charges of fraud and imposition, and denying that the will in question was not the true last will of the testatrix, but neither confessing nor denying the allegation of the bill that appellant Mary Snell Stone is a daughter and heir at law of the testatrix, but calling for strict proof in that regard. To these answers, replications were filed, and the cause was submitted to trial before a jury. The court, of his own motion, formulated and presented to the jury two issues to be passed upon by them. The first issue submitted was, "Is Mary Snell Stone the daughter of Henrietta Snell?" The second was, "Is the writing produced in evidence, purporting to be the last will and testament of Henrietta Snell, deceased, the true last will and testament of said Henrietta Snell, deceased?" When the case was submitted to the jury for consideration, and at the request of the appellant Mary Snell Stone, four special interrogatories were also submitted to the jury, which, with the answers thereto as found by the jury, were as follows: "(1) Is complainant Mary Snell Stone the daughter of Henrietta Snell, deceased? No. (2) Was there any undue influence exercised by Albert J. Snell over Henrietta Snell, connected with or operating upon and influencing her at the time of the alleged execution of the will in question? No. (3) Was there any undue influence exercised by Frank L. Salisbury over Henrietta Snell, connected with or operating upon and influencing her at the time of the alleged execution of the will in question? No. (4) Was the said Henrietta Snell, at the time of the execution and attestation of said writing read in evidence, purporting to be the last will and testament of said Henrietta Snell, capable of intelligently comprehending the extent of her property, the disposition she was making of her property thereby, the nature of the claims of others upon her, and the effect of the provisions of said alleged will? Yes." With these special findings the jury returned their general verdict, finding that Mary Snell Stone was not the daughter of Henrietta Snell, deceased, and that the writing produced in evidence, purporting to be the last will and testament of Henrietta Snell, was her last will and testament. Motion for a new trial was overruled, and a decree dismissing the bill was entered, and this appeal prosecuted.

The record is voluminous, containing about 2,000 typewritten pages, and it will be impossible, within the limits of this opinion, to go into an extended review of all the evidence upon all the questions presented. Nor do we think such course necessary to a proper disposition of the case. In the view we entertain of it, the controlling questions lie within comparatively narrow limits.

The testatrix was the widow of the late Amos J. Snell, who came to a violent death February 9, 1888, and from him the testatrix derived the large estate here in controversy. The testatrix and Amos J. Snell were married in 1846, and the undisputed evidence is that the only child that was born of both their bodies between the time of their marriage and 1857 was a male child, who was born within a year or so after the marriage, and who lived but about three weeks. In 1857 a son, Albert Jerome, was born. In 1863 a daughter, Grace Henrietta, and in 1867 another daughter, Alice Eva, were born. These were the only children born as the issue of the bodies of Amos J. Snell and Henrietta Snell, the testatrix. On the part of the proponents a large number of witnesses testified relative to the history and supposed parentage of the appellant Mary Snell Stone, and no witness was called to contradict or controvert what these witnesses testified to upon that subject. Their testimony shows that Amos J. Snell and the testatrix settled in Jefferson Park, near the city of Chicago, in the year 1851; that in the year 1853 Patrick Hughes and his wife, Anne Hughes, came from Rome, N. Y., to Jefferson Park, and built a little house upon the land of Amos Snell, where they resided. The party who met them at the train upon their arrival, and who was in the employ of Amos J. Snell, was a witness, and testified that at the time of their arrival they had with them two little girls, which they represented to be, and who were understood to be, and were accepted by all who knew them to be, their children. These girls were named Mary and Rosa. After Patrick and Anne Hughes, with these children, had resided at Jefferson Park two or three years, Anne Hughes, the wife of Patrick Hughes, and the supposed mother of these children, died. They were in poor circumstances and Patrick Hughes was advanced in years. A Mrs. Burns, a sister of Anne Hughes, also lived at Jefferson Park at the same time, and was a witness in this case upon this question. After the death of Anne Hughes, these two little girls were taken by Mrs. Burns, their aunt, and kept for a time, when, by some arrangement between the father, Patrick Hughes, and Amos J. Snell, they were both taken to his (Snell's) house. The time they were taken to the house of Amos J. Snell is not definitely fixed, and the witnesses (and there were a number of them) state that the child Mary was at that time from five to seven years old. After both these girls had remained at the house of Amos J. Snell for a time, the child Rosa was taken by Brockman Hopkins, who resided at or near Jefferson Park, and from that time the appellant Mary Snell Stone resided in and as a part of the family of Amos J. Snell, and took the name of Mary Snell, and by that name she was married from the home of Amos J. Snell; the marriage invitation designating her as the daughter of Amos J. Snell and Henrietta Snell. Mrs. Burns, the aunt of appellant Mrs. Stone, was not in New York at the time of the birth of the latter, but was here in Illinois, and no witness did or could testify to actual knowledge of the parentage of appellant Mrs. Stone; but the story of her being brought from Rome, N. Y., to Jefferson Park in 1852 or 1853 by Patrick and Anne Hughes, and being known as their child, and of her having lived with them until the death of Anne Hughes, and with Mrs. Burns after Anne Hughes' death, is not disputed or questioned by anybody. It is also shown that, after Mary Hughes was taken to the home of Amos J. Snell, the latter visited Judge Rucker, the then county judge, as we understand from the record, with a view of having papers drawn for the adoption of appellant Mrs. Stone; but, upon arriving at the office of the judge, he was found busy, and the matter was deferred to some subsequent time. There is no evidence showing that appellant Mary Snell Stone was ever legally adopted by Amos J. Snell, and such is not the claim of appellants.

A family Bible was also introduced, which bears date of publication of 1875. In this Bible was a family register, recording marriages, births, and deaths. The register was originally written in the hand of some professional penman, and not by Amos J. Snell or the testatrix or any member of the Snell family. As originally written, it contained the entry, "Mary Snell was born March 31, 1851, in the State of Illinois." The undisputed evidence shows that, after this entry was made, the testatrix erased the name "Snell" and the word "Illinois" from the register, and in her own hand and after the given name "Mary" wrote the name "Hughes," and instead of "Illinois" wrote "N. Y." There was also introduced in evidence as having belonged to the testatrix, a birthday Scripture text-book. Under each day of the month this book contained a passage of Scripture and a verse, and on the opposite page a blank for memoranda. The undisputed evidence discloses that opposite the date "March 31," in the handwriting of the testatrix, was the following entry: "Mary Snell, born March 31, 1851, in the State of Ill." When the entry was made does not appear from the evidence, and the book in which it was made has no date of its publication; but the evidence discloses that, after this original entry was made, the testatrix erased the name "Snell" and the word "Ill." from it, and substituted the name "Hughes," and, for the state, "N. Y."

The testatrix had a box in a safety deposit vault, and some time prior to her death—the date not being definitely known—she placed therein an envelope with this inscription:

"The pictures of the family; for them to look at and read the contents of the writing; give them to the three children. Mother."

The envelope contained two pictures of her son Albert, one of her daughter Grace, one of her daughter Alice, and one of herself. Inclosed with these pictures was the following writing, in the hand of the testatrix:

"Love each other for me. Grace, treat Albert as a brother. Alice, you treat Albert as a brother. Albert, treat Grace and Alice as your sisters, for me, for me.—Mother.

"This is sacred; don't pass this by as if it was not worth while to think of. Look over the past and forgive. Your Heavenly Father will forgive you."

These are the express declarations of the testatrix as to her children, and the manner in which they are named absolutely excludes the idea that there could have been any other. Appellant Mrs. Stone does not seek to overcome this testimony by counter testimony as to her origin, but urges that the appellees are estopped by certain conduct of the testatrix, and certain legal proceedings to which she was a party, to now deny the fact that she was a daughter of the testatrix. When Amos J. Snell died, the testatrix petitioned the probate court to grant letters of administration to herself and Albert J. Stone, one of the appellants. In that petition she stated that Amos J. Snell left him surviving Mary Snell, as one of his children and heirs at law, and in the settlement of his estate she was treated as his child, and the same distributive share of his estate given to her as was given to his children, Albert J., Grace, and Alice. Also, after the death of Amos J. Snell, the testatrix filed a bill for the assignment of her dower and the partition of his lands, in which appellant Mrs. Stone was designated as one of the heirs at law of Amos J. Snell, and, pursuant to this, a decree was entered upon the petition, and, pursuant to the decree, partition deeds were exchanged between the children of Amos J. Snell and appellant Mrs. Stone; and it is particularly urged that in the partition proceedings it was adjudicated that Mrs. Stone was the daughter of Amos J. Snell, and that, having been a party to that decree, the testatrix was bound by it, and could not by her will, nor could the appellees, as her privies in estate, cast doubt upon the parentage of Mrs. Stone.

It may be first remarked that the property involved in the litigation now at bar is not the property derived by appellant Mrs. Stone through that proceeding, or any part of it, and that by neither this proceeding nor the will in question is it sought to in any manner affect the title to any of the property that passed to appellant Mrs. Stone by virtue of the partition proceedings or the settlement of the estate of Amos J. Snell. The vital question here is, is appellant Mrs. Stone a daughter and heir at law of the testatrix? The partition suit was a friendly suit, and the matter of heirship was not made an issue or question, nor was there any contest whatever upon that subject, and should have little weight in the present controversy. Wadhams v. Gay, 73 Ill. 415; Farwell v. Great Western Tel. Co., 161 Ill. 522, 44 N. E. 891. The most that it can be said these proceedings, or any act done under them, tended to show, was that appellant Mrs. Stone was the daughter of Amos J. Snell; and the relation that she bore to Mrs. Snell was not in question, nor in any manner adjudicated or affected. It is true that if it had been definitely shown that appellant Mrs. Stone was born after the marriage of Amos J. Snell and the testatrix, and that she was the daughter of Amos J. Snell, the legal inference favoring legitimacy would be that she was also the daughter of testatrix. But this presumption is not a conclusive one, and may be overcome by proof, and must give way to the actual facts. Orthwein v. Thomas, 127 Ill. 554, 21 N. E. 430, 4 L. R. A. 434, 11 Am. St. Rep. 159.

As to the rule of res judicata here invoked, the property to be affected by this proceeding is different and other property than that involved in the suit and proceedings relied upon; and it seems to be well established that, before the rule has application in such a case, it must appear that the identical question was in fact adjudicated in the former proceeding. The distinction seems to be that, where the second suit is about the same matter or cause of action, then all matters that could have been, as well as all matters that actually were, put in issue and determined in the former suit, are presumed to have been so put in issue, and as to them the rule applies; but when the second action is as to a different cause of action, or in reference to a different matter, or relating to different property, then the rule has no application, except as to such matters as were actually in litigation and actually decided in the former proceedings relied upon as res judicata. Riverside Co. v. Townshend, 120 Ill. 9, 19 N. E. 65; Cromwell v. County of Sac, 94 U. S. 351, 24 L. Ed. 195.

As we have said, the question was not presented in the partition suit whether Mary Snell Stone was a daughter of Henrietta Snell. It is true that that question might have been presented by denying that appellant Mrs. Stone was the child of Amos J. Snell in the partition suit, and the proof as shown by this record, and which we presume would have been used if the question had been in controversy, would have shown that she was not the daughter of either Henrietta Snell or Amos J. Snell. But as is said in the case of Cromwell v. County of Sac, supra: "It is quite right that a defendant should be estopped from setting up in the same action a defense which he might have pleaded, but has chosen to let the proper time go by, but nobody ever heard of a defendant being precluded from setting up a defense in a second action because he did not avail himself of the opportunity of setting it up in the first action." And so in this case, in the same action the heirs of Henrietta Snell would have been estopped from bringing forward, as a ground of defense, the fact that Mary Snell Stone was not the daughter of Amos J. Snell, but they are not in a subsequent suit, upon a different cause of action, precluded from availing themselves of such ground in proving Mary Snell Stone is not the daughter of Henrietta Snell.

The will in question was made February 2, 1899, and the testatrix died on the 24th day of February, 1900. In 1895 the testatrix filed a petition, under the burnt records act, to establish title to certain real estate to which it appeared Amos J. Snell had at some time had title. In stating who were the children and heirs of Amos J. Snell, the testatrix alleged in her petition that the three children, Albert, Grace, and Alice, were his only children and heirs at law. She further stated, upon information and belief, that appellant Mary Stone would claim, as an heir at law, some interest in the property, and made her a party defendant to the petition, and she was regularly served and brought into court. The decree found that the said three children were the only heirs at law of Amos J. Snell, and it would be as reasonable to contend that this proceeding was conclusive upon appellant that she was not a child and heir at law of Amos J. Snell, as it is to make the contrary contention from the proceeding in partition.

A number of deeds were made to Mrs. Stone, to which the testatrix was a party, as grantor, affecting properties that belonged to the estate of Amos J. Snell, in which the consideration was love and affection, and in some of which Mrs. Stone was mentioned as a child and heir of Amos J. Snell; but in none of these deeds was Mrs. Stone named as the child of the testatrix, and, if she had been, we are unable to see why that should conclude the testatrix in other transactions relating to other property than that conveyed by the deeds. We know of no principle of estoppel that would be applicable, but it would be merely an evidentiary fact tending to show the relationship. The principle of estoppel, as we understand it, only applies to the property conveyed by the deed in which the recital is made, and may be invoked to quiet and establish such title. It is a special application of the rule of estoppel which precludes a grantor in a deed from making any declaration of fact, contrary to the recitals of his deed, which would affect the title conveyed. It is true that the evidence discloses many acts and declarations of both Amos J. Snell and the testatrix showing a very sincere affection for, and deep interest in, Mrs. Stone. It is but natural that it should be so. Nor are such facts inconsistent with the contention of appellees. Mrs. Stone was the child of neither Amos J. Snell nor of the testatrix. Living in the relation that she did to the family for the number of years shown by the evidence, and taken to the family when there was no child of their bodies in the family, it is neither unreasonable nor unnatural that one or both of them should become greatly attached to her, and permitting her to share in the distribution of the estate of Amos J. Snell was but a recognition of the attachment that he bore and showed toward her; but it does not seem sound to contend that, because she was so recognized as a beneficiary of the estate of Amos J. Snell, therefore she must, as a matter of law, be recognized as the child and heir of the testatrix, and be recognized as one interested in her estate and entitled to contest her will.

It is contended that it was improper to submit to the determination of the jury the question of the jurisdiction of the court, and that it was a matter for the court itself to decide. The court did decide it, but first took, as we think it had a right to do, the advisory verdict of the jury upon the question, which was one of fact. Section 40 of chapter 22 of Hurd's Revised Statutes of 1901 provides, among other things: "The court may, in its discretion, direct an issue or issues to be tried by a jury, whenever it shall be judged necessary in any cause in equity pending therein." This was unquestionably a case in equity. The fact that the statute specifically authorizes the contest of wills in a court of chancery, and directs that an issue at law shall be made up, whether the writing produced be the will of the testatrix or not, which shall be tried by a jury, does not in any other respect distinguish such a case from any other suit or proceeding in chancery in matters of procedure. The bill in this case alleged that Mary Snell Stone was a child and heir at law of, and interested in the estate of, the testatrix. It alleged all that the statute required, and whether those allegations were true became a question of fact. They were denied in the answer, and an issue of fact was thereby tendered. The case is unlike that of Jele v. Lemberger, 163 Ill. 338, 45 N. E. 279, where the contestant, Joseph Lemberger, stated on the face of the bill that he was of the empire of Germany. In that case an answer was filed denying the general allegations of the bill, but upon a hearing the relief prayed was granted, and the decree was reversed by this court upon the ground that it appeared upon the face of the bill that the complainant, being a resident and citizen of the empire of Germany, could not, under the alien law, inherit, and was not a party in interest, and that the bill should have been dismissed. In Russell v. Paine, 45 Ill. 350, it is said: "Where the evidence is contradictory, depends upon slight circumstances, the veracity of witnesses is involved, and where the manner, intelligence, and relation of witnesses to a case must have their proper weight, it is highly desirable that the issue should be tried by a jury." The chancellor was not required to submit this question to a jury, and, when he saw fit to do so, the verdict or finding was advisory, only. It was his duty to render such decree as the law required, under the evidence. He might have disregarded so much of the verdict entirely as related to the capacity of appellant to bring the suit, and entered such decree as in his judgment the case demanded, non obstante veredicto. Guild v. Hull, 127 Ill. 523, 20 N. E. 665.

It must have been apparent to the chancellor that, if the issue as to whether Mary Stone was the child of the testatrix should be settled adversely to the contestant, that would terminate the case; that it was one of fact, and might involve the testimony of many witnesses. No motion was made by appellant Mrs. Stone to try this issue separately, or to first try the issue as to her right to maintain her bill as a legal heir of the testatrix, or as one interested in her estate. So far as the record discloses, she voluntarily proceeded with both questions submitted to the jury; and, if costs were made upon the issue whether the writing was the will of the testatrix or not, and that evidence became immaterial because the jury and the court found that complainant bore no such relation to the estate of the testatrix, or to the testatrix, as entitled appellant Mrs. Stone to contest the will, she is not now in a position to complain.

In Way v. Way, 64 Ill. 406, which was a divorce proceeding, and in which it was necessary that the complainant make the statutory allegations as to residence, and the allegation was that the complainant was a resident of Chicago, Cook county, Ill., and answer was filed denying the allegations of the bill, including that of residence, the question of fact was submitted to the jury, and the practice was approved by this court. In that case it was said (page 408): "In this case the court had jurisdiction, if the bill was true. Its truth was denied, and, when the complainant failed to sustain his allegations by proof, the question of the jurisdiction of the court for the first time arose."

Complaint is made that, if this decree be allowed to stand, it will work great hardship upon appellant Mary Stone, as it will cast doubt upon her parentage. We are unable to concur in this view. We think this record fairly establishes her parentage. But if the contrary be true, appellant Mrs. Stone instituted the suit which raised the controversy, and the consequences must be with her, and not with the courts.

Holding, as we do, that appellant Mary Snell Stone was not a party in interest in the estate of Henrietta Snell, within the meaning of the law relative to contests, and therefore not entitled to prosecute this suit, we deem it unnecessary to examine or pass upon the questions relating to the execution of the will, the disposing mind of the testatrix, and the influences, if any, that operated upon her in making it.

Upon a mature consideration of the entire record, we think the decree entered was such as both law and equity demanded, and it is affirmed. Decree affirmed.

(209 Ill. 142)

COLES COUNTY v. GOEHRING.

(Supreme Court of Illinois. April 20, 1904.)

COUNTIES—LIMIT OF TAXATION—INCURRING INDEBTEDNESS—PROVISIONS FOR PAYMENT—COUNTY WARRANTS OR ORDERS—INTEREST—REPAIRS OF COURTHOUSE—LIABILITY OF COUNTY—COUNTY BOARD—MECHANICS' LIENS OF SUBCONTRACTORS.

1. Const. 1870, art. 9, § 8, providing that counties shall not assess taxes in excess of 75 cents per $100 valuation, unless authorized by vote of the people, is not a limitation on the power to contract a debt; the only restriction in the Constitution on this being in section 12, providing that no county shall become indebted in excess of 5 per cent. of the taxable property therein.

2. Before a county board made a contract for repairs of the courthouse, it, by resolution, appropriated 75 per cent. of the tax levy of the year for such repairs. *Held*, that the question of the power of the board to make the contract was not affected by such fund being thereafter applied to other purposes.

3. A contract of a county for repairs of its courthouse for a certain sum—the work to be paid for during the construction, monthly, on the basis of 85 per cent. of the value of the labor performed and material in place in the building, as estimated by the architect, in interest-bearing orders, bearing interest from date thereof, and the balance in interest-bearing county orders, bearing interest from date thereof, on the completion and acceptance of the building—does not create the character of indebtedness contemplated by Const. art. 9, § 12, to pay which that section requires a direct annual tax to be provided at the time of incurring the indebtedness; said section contemplating a bonded or an analogous indebtedness, drawing interest each year, and falling due all at one time, or from year to year.

4. County warrants or orders reciting merely that they are "to be paid out of any moneys in the county treasury not otherwise appropriated" are void under Rev. St. c. 146a, § 2, providing that, when there is no money in the county treasury, the proper authorities may provide for warrants against and in anticipation of the collection of any taxes already levied, provided that the warrants shall show on their face that they are payable solely from said taxes when collected, and not otherwise.

5. That in an action on a contract for repairing a county building, payable in county orders, certain of them, which were not included in the judgment, were not surrendered, is no reason for reversing the judgment for plaintiff; such orders not being under his control, they being void and unenforceable, and it being impossible to bring another action on the contract.

6. Where a contract for work on a county building does not provide for the payment of interest, but for the payment of the contract price in orders, to draw interest, interest cannot be recovered, the orders being void, so that there is no express agreement for interest, necessary to make a county liable therefor.

7. A county board having contracted for repairs of the county courthouse under the authority given by Rev. St. c. 34, §§ 24, 26, and the courthouse having been completed to the satisfaction of the county authorities, and accepted and appropriated to the use of the county, recovery may be had therefor, though the contract provided for payment in county orders, and the orders given were invalid.

8. Under Rev. St. c. 34, § 26, making it the duty of the county to provide a suitable courthouse, when necessary, and the finances of the county will justify it, the questions of necessity and of the finances justifying it are for the county board.

9. A judgment against a county for repairing a county jail should be no less because of mechanics' liens of subcontractors, under Rev. St. c. 82, § 24; their only claim being a lien on the money that is to be paid plaintiff.

Error to Circuit Court, Coles County; H. Van Seller, Judge.

Action by S. S. Goehring against Coles County. Judgment for plaintiff. Defendant brings error. Modified.

This is an action of assumpsit, begun on December 20, 1901, in the circuit court of Coles county by the defendant in error, Goehring, suing for the use of certain banks and other persons, against the plaintiff in error, the county of Coles, on a contract entered into between the plaintiff in error and the defendant in error on September 20, 1898, for the repair and reconstruction of the courthouse in said county. The declaration, as originally filed on December 20, 1901, consisted of three counts. The first count was a consolidated common count. This first count was amended on April 7, 1902, and, as amended, not only contained the usual common counts, including a count for money found to be due on an account then and there stated between the parties, but also included a claim for interest. The second and third counts were special counts upon the contract hereinafter mentioned. The special counts allege, by apt averments, that the work was done on the contract, and that the courthouse was accepted by the county. The plaintiff in error demurred to the special counts, and the demurrer was overruled. A plea of general issue was filed to the declaration, with the stipulation that all defenses to the merits that could be made under any plea well pleaded could be made under the plea of the general issue. The case was then tried by the court without a jury. After hearing the case, the court rendered a judgment in favor of the defendant in error and against the plaintiff in error for $95,204.31. Exceptions were taken by the plaintiff in error to the judgment. An appeal was prayed and allowed, but never perfected, and this writ of error is sued out from this court for the purpose of reversing said judgment.

The contract, made on September 20, 1898, between Samuel S. Goehring, as party of the first part, and the county of Coles, acting through a building committee appointed by the board of supervisors of said county, party of the second part, provides as follows:

"The party of the first part agrees with the party of the second part to furnish labor, and material to repair the courthouse on the public square in the city of Charleston, county of Coles, in conformity with the proposals, plans and specifications prepared by C. W. Rapp, architect, as mentioned in the printed proposals, which plans and specifications and proposals are hereby made a part of this contract, for the sum of $85,727.00, payable as hereinafter mentioned. The stone, used for the facing, to be Coles county buff sandstone, and the stone used for trimmings to be of the first quality of gray sandstone. The said work to be completed within one year from this date, provided that any delay, occasioned by the failure of the party of the second part to deliver possession of the ground and building to be repaired; and the time for completion shall be extended for a period equivalent to the time lost. Said work to be done under the direction of the architect, acting for the parties of the second part; but no change or alteration to be made from the plans and specifications, without the written consent of the parties hereto. Said work to be paid for during the construction to the parties of the first part, monthly on the basis of eighty-five per cent. of the value of the labor performed and material in place in the building, as estimated by the architect, in interest-bearing county orders, bearing seven per cent. interest per annum from date thereof, and the balance in interest-bearing county orders, bearing seven per cent. interest per annum from date thereof, upon the completion and acceptance of the building.

"Said party of the first part hereby agrees to give bond within three days from this date, according to the proposals aforesaid.

"The above and foregoing contract to be binding upon the party of the first part, his heirs, executors, administrators and assigns, and upon the party of the second part. Should the party of the first part fail or refuse to proceed with the contract for a period of ten days, according to the spirit thereof, the building committee shall have the right to take possession of all material and complete the work at the expense of the party of the second part.

"Witness our hands and seals this September 20, 1898. Samuel S. Goehring. [Seal.] County of Coles (By the Building Committee of the County Board). J. K. Bardin, Chairman. [Seal.] Ivory W. Merritt, Sec. [Seal.]"

Seven other members of the board signed under their hands and seals.

On July 11, 1898, at a regular meeting of the board of supervisors of the county, a communication from R. Alexander, the then county treasurer, to the board, was read. This communication stated that the office provided for the county treasurer was too small, badly lighted, and located between the ladies' water-closet and the main water-closet; that it had no ventilation; that it was contaminated with the poisonous gases from those closets, and that there were no vaults for the records or papers, and no place for necessary books and files; that it was unhealthy and unsanitary, and not convenient to accommodate the large number of people constantly called to the treasurer's office; that it was necessary to provide another and better office for the county treasurer; that the courthouse cannot be rearranged to provide more room for this office, as the other offices are overcrowded; that there were no offices or rooms for the county judge, state's attorney, coroner, county surveyor, and other officials, and no room to make them; that the building had been erected so long that it was doubtful whether it could be added to, with the present old walls, without endangering the structure; that it was necessary to have vaults and more room for the treasurer, and room for his books and papers; that it has been for years so unhealthy for the incumbent that each treasurer has been constantly alarmed for his health; that some provision should be made for a proper office for the county treasurer, so that he can transact his business according to law, and preserve his books and papers in a fireproof vault as provided by law; and that, in case of a fire in the present condition, the loss to the county would be beyond computation.

At the July term, 1898, the committee on grounds and buildings of the board of supervisors reported that they had examined the courthouse, and found that there was a general demand for additional room in the offices, and for more vault room; that, in view of the rotten brick, crumbling walls, and insecure foundations, it was a serious matter whether the walls could be repaired without constructing entirely new walls and new roof; that the building was cold in winter, and, for want of ventilation, hot in summer; that the courtroom is totally inappropriate for the uses for which it is designated; that there are in fact no jury rooms of any convenience; that the vaults for the records are crowded to the last degree, because the tremendous gain in population has made demands which were not anticipated when the courthouse was last reconstructed; that the board has wasted many times the cost of a new courthouse in idle repairs, which is now lost; that the reason therefor proceeded from the erroneous idea that to renew the whole structure would entail a heavier tax levy on the people; that the improvement has been delayed on that score, when the facts are that the levy can only be 75 cents on the $100, and that rate has been laid for many years; that, if the extra money is put in in constructing a permanent building, and the necessary saving is made in the accounts, the county may have a new courthouse without additional taxation. The report recommended that the board work on those lines, and that the walls and roof be rebuilt in whole or in part.

A resolution was then adopted by the board, appointing a special committee to obtain plans and specifications from some competent architect, and to advertise for bids for the repairing and reconstruction of the courthouse in accordance with such plans and specifications. The resolution, after reciting that it was made the duty of the county board of each county by statute to erect when necessary, and keep in repair, a suitable courthouse, and provide proper rooms and offices for the several courts of the county, and for the county board, county clerk, county judge, circuit clerk, sheriff, coroner, state's attorney, county superintendent, county surveyor, clerks of courts, and to provide suitable furniture therefor; and reciting that the present courthouse was not suitable, and had not the proper rooms, nor the necessary fireproof vaults, and was improperly lighted and ventilated and dangerous, and a menace to the life and health of all persons attending upon the court; and reciting that complaint had been made by the officers of the county, and by the building and grounds committee, of the lack of room, etc., and declaring that the courthouse was wholly inadequate and out of keeping with the standing of the county—it was thereupon resolved that the courthouse and offices be repaired by placing a modern system of heating therein; that the vaults be enlarged, so as to make room for the records, files, etc.; that the courtroom be remodeled so as to be convenient and suitable; that the roof be remodeled and repaired so as not to leak or be unsafe; and that suitable rooms for juries and for the county officers be constructed, enlarged, and remodeled, so as to be convenient, and of the proper capacity to transact business. A committee was then appointed, consisting of nine members of the board, to obtain plans and specifications; that public advertisements should be inserted asking for bids; that said committee be authorized to let the contract to the lowest responsible bidder; that the contract, if let, should specify the completion thereof at the earliest possible time.

This committee reported at the September meeting that they had employed C. W. Rapp, an architect, to prepare plans and specifications, which were open to public inspection, and their report was approved by the county board, and the county clerk was ordered to issue county orders, bearing 7 per cent. interest from date, to be used in payment of any and all accounts made for repairing and construction of the proposed building according to the plans and specifications adopted; and it was further resolved that the special committee be known, on the records and in its contracts, as the "Building Committee of the Coles County Board of Supervisors," and that 75 per cent. of the then present levy be, and it was, appropriated for the repair of the courthouse; and the county clerk was directed to issue county warrants in anticipation of the collection of the taxes for the ensuing year.

September 20, 1898, the building committee reported that they had advertised for bids, and that defendant in error, Goehring, bid the sum of $85,727, he being the lowest bidder; and thereupon the contract was awarded to him, and his bond was approved and accepted, and the contract hereinbefore set forth was made with him. On September 28, 1898, possession of the courthouse grounds was delivered to Goehring, and he was to receive 5 per cent. on the cost of the structure, of which the sum of $1,285.95, was paid to him in cash.

The work was commenced under the supervision of Rapp, the architect, who reported to the board the progress of the work, and made estimates of the value of the work performed, and of the material placed in the building. On these estimates, orders were from time to time issued by the county board on the basis of 85 per cent. of the amount due on the estimate in accordance with the contract. These orders provided for 7 per cent. interest, and were sold to the usees in this case.

In December, 1898, a resolution was adopted by the board that the claim of S. S. Goehring for $3,194.66, second monthly installment for repairing the courthouse, be audited and allowed, and the county clerk directed to draw and deliver to him an order in the following form: "State of Illinois, Coles County. This certifies that the county board of Coles county did on the 7th day of December, 1898, audit and allow S. S. Goehring the sum of $3,194.66, on the second monthly installment for repairing the courthouse to be paid to him or his order twelve months after date hereof, together with seven per cent. interest per annum, as provided in his contract for repairing the courthouse; this order to be paid out of any moneys in the county treasury not otherwise appropriated." Other orders were issued for various amounts from time to time; the last being dated September 14, 1900, and the face of the orders, without interest, amounting to $82,004.62. The difference between $82,004.62 and $95,204.31, the amount of the judgment, to wit, $13,199.69, was for interest upon the orders.

On September 7, 1900, the building committee made the following recommendation: "We, your committee, after having carefully examined the repairs made upon Coles county courthouse, would respectfully recommend that building be received, and that S. S. Goehring be paid in full for his contract." It was ordered that the recommendation and report be approved, and that the building be received, and that the keys of the courthouse be turned over to the chairman of the board of supervisors, and by him to the sheriff, and that the sheriff and chairman proceed to move the county officers into the courthouse at once, which was done. The circuit and county courts have held their sessions in the courthouse, as thus reconstructed, since that time, and all the county officers have occupied offices in the courthouse since September, 1900. The grand and petit juries have occupied rooms therein during the terms of court, and the records of all the county officers have been kept therein since September, 1900.

Upon the hearing of the case before the trial judge without a jury, twelve propositions of law were held for plaintiff, and four for the defendant. Three propositions of law submitted by the defendant below were modified by the court, and held as modified. Seventeen propositions of law submitted by the defendant below were refused by the court.

John. F. Voigt, Jr., State's Atty., J. F. Hughes, A. J. Fryer, and D. T. McIntyre, for plaintiff in error. James W. & Edward C. Craig, Craig & Kinzel, Charles C. Lee, and Andrews & Vause (Swift, Campbell & Jones, of counsel), for defendant in error.

MAGRUDER, J. (after stating the facts). The questions presented by the record arise out of the propositions of law as held and refused and modified by the trial court.

1. It is claimed on the part of plaintiff in error, the county of Coles, that the contract for the repair and reconstruction of the courthouse, as set out in the statement preceding this opinion, was void, as having been executed without authority of law. The contract is claimed to be void upon the alleged ground that when it was made the county of Coles had already assessed taxes to the amount of 75 cents per $100 valuation, and that, when the levy to that amount was reached and exhausted in the payment of current expenses, the county had no power to contract any further indebtedness, unless authorized by a vote of the people of the county. Section 8 of article 9 of the Constitution of 1870 is as follows: "County authorities shall never assess taxes, the aggregate of which shall exceed seventy-five cents per $100.00 valuation, except for the payment of indebtedness existing at the adoption of this Constitution, unless authorized by a vote of the people of the county." The equalized valuation of the property of Coles county for the year 1897 was $5,213,228, and the tax levy for that year, at 75 cents per $100 valuation, produced about $39,099.21. The equalized valuation of the property of the county for the year 1898 was $5,167,602, and the tax levy of 75 cents per $100 valuation produced about $38,757.01. It is contended by plaintiff in error that, whether the tax levy for 1897 or for 1898 is taken, it was inadequate to pay the ordinary running expenses of the county, and that, when the contract in question was made, there was a deficit which amounted to a sum somewhere between $35,000 and $50,000. It is therefore said that the county having levied the total amount which it was authorized to levy without a vote of the people, and such amount so levied having been required for the payment of current expenses and borrowed money, the county was without authority to go in debt to the amount of $85,727 for the construction of a courthouse without submitting to the vote of the people of the county the question, whether taxes should be assessed to an amount exceeding 75 cents per $100 valuation. In other words, the position taken is that the prohibition against an assessment of taxes, the aggregate of which shall exceed 75 cents per $100 valuation, is, by implication, a prohibition against the creation of a debt or the making of a contract, when the amount of the levy of 75 cents per $100 valuation is necessary to pay current expenses or existing indebtedness, without a vote of the people, as required by said section 8 of article 9. The objection thus made makes the prohibition against the assessment or levy of taxes equivalent to a prohibition against the incurring of an indebtedness. The theory upon which the objection is based is that the incurring of an additional indebtedness under such circumstances necessitates the making of a levy of taxes in excess of the amount named in section 8, as a means of paying such indebtedness. As counsel say in their brief: "The forbidding of the levy of the tax without a vote of the people is the forbidding of the creation of the debt rendering such increased tax necessary. The forbidding of the result is the forbidding of the means which create that result. If the effect is forbidden, then the cause which created that effect is also forbidden."

A limitation upon the power to levy taxes is not necessarily a limitation upon the power to contract a debt. Hitchcock v. Galveston, 96 U. S. 341, 24 L. Ed. 659; Jackson County v. Rendleman, 100 Ill. 379, 39 Am. Rep. 44; Andrews v. Knox County, 70 Ill. 65; Mills v. Gleason, 11 Wis. 470, 78 Am. Dec. 721; Rendleman v. Jackson County, 8 Ill. App. 287; Town of Kankakee v. McGrew, 178 Ill. 74, 52 N. E. 893; City of Danville v. Danville Water Co., 180 Ill. 235, 54 N. E. 224; Baltimore & Ohio Southwestern Railroad Co. v. People, 200 Ill. 541, 66 N. E. 148; Ketchum v. Buffalo, 14 N. Y. 361; Opinion of Justices, 126 Mass. 567; 1 Story on the Constitution, § 880; City of Galena v. Corwith, 48 Ill. 423, 95 Am. Dec. 557. Section 12 of article 9 of the Constitution provides that "no county, city, township, school district, or other municipal corporation, shall be allowed to become indebted in any manner or for any purpose, to an amount, including existing indebtedness, in the aggregate exceeding five per centum on the value of the taxable property therein, to be ascertained by the last assessment for state and county taxes, previous to the incurring of such indebtedness.

Any county, city, school district, or other municipal corporation, incurring any indebtedness as aforesaid, shall before, or at the time of doing so, provide for the collection of a direct annual tax, sufficient to pay the interest on such debt as it falls due, and also to pay and discharge the principal thereof within twenty years from the time of contracting the same." The equalized valuation of property in Coles county for the year 1897 being $5,213,228, 5 per cent. of the same is $260,661.40; and, the equalized valuation of the property in that county for the year 1898 being $5,167,602, 5 per cent. of the same is $258,380.10. It is not claimed or shown by the proofs in the record that the indebtedness of Coles county on September 20, 1898, when the contract here in question was made, was more than $50,000, outside of the amount specified in the contract for the construction of the courthouse made on that date. If the $50,000 be added to the $85,727, the amount for which the courthouse was contracted to be built, the sum would make $135,727. The latter amount is far less than either $258,380.10 or $260,661.40. Even if the indebtedness of the county should be put at $167,529, as it appears to be from some of the resolutions adopted by the county board in June, 1901, the total indebtedness of the county would still be less than either $258,380.10, or $260,661.40. Therefore, by incurring the indebtedness for the repairing and reconstruction of the courthouse, the county did not become indebted, if all prior indebtedness theretofore existing be included, to an amount exceeding, in the aggregate, 5 per centum on the value of the taxable property in the county, as ascertained by the last assessment for state and county taxes previous to the making of the contract. The only prohibition against incurring indebtedness which the Constitution imposes is that embraced in section 12 of article 9. No county is allowed to become indebted in any manner or for any purpose to an amount, including existing indebtedness, in the aggregate, exceeding 5 per centum on the value of the taxable property therein, to be ascertained by the last assessment for state and county taxes previous to the incurring of such indebtedness. In discussing the application of this section 12 to the incurring of indebtedness by towns in Town of Kankakee v. McGrew, 178 Ill. 74, 52 N. E. 893, we said (page 81, 178 Ill., page 894, 52 N. E.): "That the aggregate indebtedness of the town shall not exceed the constitutional limitation is the only restriction upon the power of a town to become indebted to discharge such duties devolved upon it by law." In Culbertson v. City of Fulton, 127 Ill. 30, 18 N. E. 781, we said (page 38, 127 Ill., page 783, 18 N. E.): "The indebtedness, however, can only be regarded as void to the extent of the amount of the excess over the constitutional limit. Up to and under that limit the indebtedness is valid. The inhibition operates upon the indebtedness, and not upon the form of the debt."

The proof is not altogether clear that the tax levy for the year 1898 of 75 cents per $100 valuation was entirely exhausted by the payment of the current expenses for that year. It is not entirely clear from the proof that, at the time the contract was made, Coles county was indebted in the sum of $50,000, or that its finances were not sufficient to pay the amount due upon the contract at the time therein specified, and also to pay what would be required for current expenses. Out of the money on hand at the time the contract was made, the county paid $1,144.97 thereon. The receipts of the county for taxes for the year 1898 amounted to $47,612; for 1899, to $43,850; and for 1900, to $48,129. Before the contract was made, to wit, on September 14, 1898, a motion was made and adopted by the county board "that seventy-five per cent. of the present levy be hereby appropriated for repairs of courthouse, and that the recommendations of the committee be concurred in and adopted as the act of the county board." At the same time a motion was made and adopted to the effect that "the county clerk be directed to issue such county orders as the building committee may request, and to issue county warrants in anticipation of the collection of taxes for the ensuing year, as may be directed by the building committee." Seventy-five per cent. or three-fourths of the tax levy for the year 1898, to wit, $47,612, was $35,709. By its action the county board appropriated $35,709 out of the tax levy of 1898 for repairs upon the courthouse. The proceedings show that, in the opinion of the county board, the necessary repairs and reconstruction of the courthouse could be effected out of the levy of 75 cents per $100 valuation without additional taxation. The fact that such fund of $35,709 may have been misappropriated, or applied to other purposes than the payment of the warrants or orders in question, does not affect the question of power of the board to make the contract in question. County of Pope v. Sloan, 92 Ill. 177.

2. It is said, however, by counsel for plaintiff in error, that, under the second sentence of section 12 of article 9 of the Constitution, the county, before or at the time of making the contract, should have provided for the collection of a direct annual tax sufficient to pay the interest on the debt incurred by the making of the contract, as it fell due, and also to pay and discharge the principal thereof within 20 years from the time of contracting the same. We have held that the second sentence of section 12 "has reference to indebtedness, the amount whereof has become fixed and absolute, and the payment thereof deferred to a stated period in the future." City of Danville v. Danville Water Co., 180 Ill. 235, 54 N. E. 224; Town of Kankakee v. McGrew, 178 Ill. 74, 52 N. E. 893. We also said in Baltimore & Ohio Southwestern Rail-

road Co. v. People, 200 Ill. 541, 66 N. E. 148 (page 553, 200 Ill., page 152, 66 N. E.): "In construing this part of section 12, we held that, within the five per cent. limit, it was lawful for a municipality to contract debts without providing for a direct annual tax, unless payment of such indebtedness is deferred to a fixed future period, and which bears interest." It is a serious question whether the debt contracted by the contract here entered into is a debt that falls due at a fixed future period, and bears interest. Here the work was "to be paid for during the construction to the parties of the first part, monthly on the basis of eighty-five per cent. of the value of the labor performed and material in place in the building, as estimated by the architect, in interest-bearing county orders, bearing seven per cent. interest per annum from date thereof, and the balance in interest-bearing county orders, bearing seven per cent. interest per annum from date thereof, upon the completion and acceptance of the building." It is questionable whether this provision created a debt that fell due at a fixed period in the future. It would seem that the Constitution contemplated a bonded indebtedness, or an analogous indebtedness, which draws interest each year, and falls due all at one time, or falls due from year to year. In Baltimore & Ohio Southwestern Railroad Co. v. People, supra, the city of Flora had contracted to purchase an electric light plant, and had provided for the payment of a debt that the light company had on its plant, in the sum of $13,000, payable in yearly installments of $1,000 each, and bearing 6 per cent. interest, and it was there claimed that this was a debt that came within this same constitutional inhibition; and we there held that "the case at bar does not fall within the provisions of the section, as construed by this court." In City of Danville v. Danville Water Co., supra, it was held (page 244, 180 Ill., page 226, 54 N. E.) that "the obligation of a city under an ordinance fixing the reasonable rate of annual rental to be paid for water hydrants does not create that character of indebtedness contemplated by section 12 of article 9 of the Constitution of 1870, to pay which that section requires a direct annual tax shall be provided at the time of incurring the indebtedness. Said section of the Constitution, in the respect under consideration, has reference to indebtedness, the amount whereof has become fixed and absolute, and the payment thereof deferred to a stated period in the future." See, also, Town of Kankakee v. McGrew, supra.

It is further insisted on the part of the plaintiff in error that these orders or warrants issued by the county board under the contract in question were void, as not being in compliance with section 2 of chapter 146a of the Revised Statutes. That section 2 provides as follows: "That, whenever there is no money in the treasury of any county, township, city, school district or other municipal corporation to meet and defray the ordinary and necessary expenses thereof, it shall be lawful for the proper authorities of any county, township, city, school district or other municipal corporation, to provide that warrants may be drawn and issued, against and in anticipation of the collection of any taxes, already levied by said authorities for the payment of the ordinary and necessary expenses of any such municipal corporation, to the extent of seventy-five percentum of the total amount of any said tax levy: provided, that warrants drawn and issued under the provisions of this section, shall show upon their face that they are payable solely from said taxes when collected, and not otherwise, and shall be received by any collector of taxes in payment of the taxes, against which they are issued, and which taxes, against which said warrants are drawn, shall be set apart and held for their payment." 3 Starr & C. Ann. St. (2d Ed.) pp. 3994, 3995, c. 146a. We are inclined to think that these warrants or orders are invalid, as not being in compliance with the statute above quoted. They recite upon their face that they are "to be paid out of any moneys in the county treasury not otherwise appropriated." They do not show upon their face that they are payable solely from taxes already levied, and from said taxes when collected, and not otherwise. They can only be drawn and issued against and in anticipation of the collection of the taxes already levied, and must so show upon their face. In addition to this, they are required by the statute to be countersigned by the county treasurer, and they are not so countersigned. Rev. St. 1885, c. 35, § 10, par. 3; 1 Starr & C. Ann. St. (2d Ed.) p. 1136, c. 35. The proof is not clear that, when these warrants were drawn, there was any money in the treasury for their payment. In Town of Kankakee v. McGrew, supra, we held that when there is no money in the treasury, and there is no tax in course of collection, such a warrant or order is void. See, also, Strodtman v. County of Menard, 56 Ill. App. 120; Amos v. Burrus, 11 Ill. App. 383; Locke v. Davison, 111 Ill. 19. We are of the opinion that the warrants or orders issued under the contract were void.

The contract price, as has already been stated, was $85,727. The judgment was rendered for $82,004.62, as principal, and $13,199.69, as interest. The sum of $82,004.62 is the amount of the certificates or warrants which were surrendered upon the trial to be canceled, and was the entire amount of the contract price, less $1,144.97 that was paid in cash to the defendant in error, and less $2,577.41, the amount of the two certificates or warrants that were not surrendered. It is claimed on the part of the plaintiff in error that the judgment should be reversed because two orders were not surrendered. It is not claimed or shown that these two orders were under the control of the plaintiff below, or the usees in this suit. The court below, in rendering the judgment, did not include the two orders which were not surrendered. Of this the plaintiff in error cannot complain. There can never be another suit on this contract. Inasmuch as the orders are held to be void, the objection that they were not surrendered for cancellation is without force. Inasmuch as they are void, they cannot be enforced against the county, and their possession, if surrendered, would be of no benefit to the county. Paul v. Kenosha, 22 Wis. 266, 94 Am. Dec. 598. Counsel for defendant in error, as we understand their brief, admit these orders to be void. They say in their brief: "In addition to this, if the orders are void, and every one agrees that that is true, adopting the language of the Supreme Court of Wisconsin in the case of Paul v. Kenosha, 22 Wis. 266, 94 Am. Dec. 598, where the contention was made that certain bonds, held to be void, were not surrendered for cancellation, 'we are really at a loss to imagine what earthly benefit the possession of the bonds would be to the city.' "

It follows that, the orders provided for in the contract being void, the judgment below was erroneous to the extent of $13,199.69, which was the amount of interest allowed. The judgment should have been for only $82,-004.62. The contract did not provide for the payment of interest, but provided for the payment of the amount therein named in orders which were to draw interest. The orders being void, interest cannot be recovered, as the contract does not provide that the amount, for which the courthouse was to be repaired and reconstructed, to wit, $85,727 should draw interest, but only that the county orders in which that amount was to be paid were to draw interest. We have held that "a municipal corporation, under the uniform ruling of this court, is not chargeable with interest on claims against it, in the absence of express agreement therefor; the only exception being where money is wrongfully obtained and illegally withheld by it." City of Danville v. Danville Water Co., 180 Ill. 235, 54 N. E. 224; City of Peoria v. Construction Co., 169 Ill. 36, 48 N. E. 435; Vider v. City of Chicago, 164 Ill. 354, 45 N. E. 720; City of Pekin v. Reynolds, 31 Ill. 529; City of Chicago v. People, 56 Ill. 327. There is nothing in the proofs to bring the present case within such exception. The orders being out of the way as being invalid, there is no express agreement for the payment of interest, and therefore it was error in the trial court to allow the same.

3. But in the case at bar the declaration contains the common counts, and declares for interest, and for an amount due upon an accounting. A suit will lie against a county under the common counts, for the building of a jail or a courthouse, where the work has been done and the house accepted. County of Jackson v. Hall, 53 Ill. 440; Maher v. City of Chicago, 38 Ill. 266; Clark County v. Lawrence, 63 Ill. 32. Although the warrants or orders were here offered and received in evidence, yet the defendant in error did not rely upon them wholly as legal evidence of indebtedness, but introduced the record kept by the county board, which showed that the amounts of these orders, as accounts and demands against the county, were presented to the board and found to be correct, and audited by the board as just demands against the county. As was said in Town of Kankakee v. McGrew, supra: "The record of these proceedings of the board was offered as evidence of an accounting, and was accepted by the court as sufficient to sustain a right of recovery under the count of the declaration averring liability by reason of an accounting between the parties * * * This record constitutes the best evidence as to the proceedings of the board, and it was produced before the court. It established prima facie an accounting between the parties. We find no evidence in the record tending to overcome the prima facie case thus made by" defendant in error.

In the present case the defendant in error completed the courthouse to the satisfaction of the county authorities, and the latter accepted it and appropriated it to the use of the county. Their records also show that, when they accepted the building, they acknowledged the price fixed by the contract for the construction of the building to be due to the defendant in error. Where a contract has thus been performed, and nothing remains to be done but the payment of the money, a suit may be maintained on the common counts. Where the law charges a municipality with the performance of certain duties, involving the creation of obligations and indebtedness, and authorizes it to exercise powers, which may result in the creation of legal demands against it, it may be necessary for it to perform these duties and exercise these powers, even if there is no money in its treasury, and no tax has been levied or is in process of collection. Town of Kankakee v. McGrew, 178 Ill. 74, 52 N. E. 893. Where a statute, in authorizing a municipal corporation to exercise a certain power, specifically regulates the mode in which that power is to be exercised, but the municipal authorities exercise it in a manner different from that prescribed by the statute, the municipality will be estopped from setting up the irregular exercise of the power when it is called upon to pay for what it has received, where the proof shows that it has received and accepted the benefit of the contract thus irregularly entered into. Westbrook v. Middlecoff, 99 Ill. App. 327.

Section 24 of chapter 34 of the Revised Statutes provides that "each county shall have power * * * to make all contracts and do all other acts in relation to the property and concerns of the county necessary to the exercise of its corporate powers." 1

Starr & C. Ann. St. (2d Ed.) p. 1085, c. 34. Where power is thus given to do a thing, there is given at the same time, by implication, authority to use the necessary means by which that thing can be done. Dutton v. City of Aurora, 114 Ill. 138, 28 N. E. 461.

Section 26 of the same chapter 34 provides as follows: "It shall be the duty of the county board of each county: First. To erect or otherwise provide when necessary, and the finances of the county will justify it, and keep in repair, a suitable court house, jail, and other necessary county buildings, and to provide proper rooms and offices for the accommodation of the several courts of record of the county, and for the county board, county clerk, county treasurer, recorder, sheriff and the clerks of said courts, and to provide suitable furniture therefor. But in counties not under township organization, no appropriations shall be made for the erection of public buildings, without first submitting the proposition to a vote of the people of the county, and said vote shall be submitted in the same manner and under the same restrictions, as provided for in like cases in section 27 of this act; and the votes therefor shall be 'For taxation,' specifying the object, and those against shall be 'Against taxation,' specifying the object." 1 Starr & C. Ann. St. (2d Ed.) pp. 1089, 1090, c. 34. The county of Coles is under township organization, and it is apparent from the reading of section 26 that it has authority to erect a courthouse without submitting the proposition as to such erection to a vote of the people. The county board is itself the judge of the necessity of building the courthouse. The duty imposed upon the board in reference to this matter is imperative, as shown by the use of the words "it shall be the duty." In Andrews v. Knox County, 70 Ill. 65, we said (page 69): "Among the duties imposed by law upon the board of supervisors, and in imperative language, is to build, as often as may be necessary, courthouses and jails, or cause the same to be repaired, in their respective counties, at the expense of such counties. About this they have no discretion. * * * The time when, the style, capacity, and cost of such erections, are wholly committed to them, with no responsibility to any power save the people." The word "necessary," as here used, is not to be interpreted as referring to such measures as are absolutely and indispensably necessary, but as including all appropriate means which are conducive or are adapted to the end to be accomplished, and which, in the judgment of the board, will most advantageously effect it. Juilliard v. Greenman, 110 U. S. 421, 4 Sup. Ct. 122, 28 L. Ed. 204. The word "when," as used in section 26, precedes not only the word "necessary," but also precedes the words "the finances of the county will justify it." The board is not only to determine when it is necessary to erect the building, but also when the finances of the county will justify it. The words "when the finances of the county will justify it" cannot be construed to mean that the county has no power to make a contract for the repair or reconstruction of a courthouse unless it has the cash in its treasury. The fifth paragraph of said section 26 shows that "finances" include all debts and liabilities of every description, and the assets, and other means of discharging the same. In passing upon the question, the county board takes into consideration everything in connection with the fiscal affairs of the county, and if, in good faith and without fraud, it determines that the finances justify the erection of the courthouse, the person with whom the contract is made to build the same is not bound to inquire into the correctness of their determination. The conclusion which the board comes to upon the subject is the one that must control. Here the board was confronted with such a condition of affairs that it seemed proper and right to provide for the repairing and reconstruction of the courthouse. The old courthouse was not merely unsuitable for the purposes for which it was erected, but is shown "to have been dangerous and a menace to the life and health of all persons required to be in attendance upon the court." The board found that the cost of the construction of the courthouse could be met by the tax of 75 cents on the $100, and, while the result may have proved that they were mistaken upon this subject, yet there is nothing to show that there was any want of good faith or any fraud on the part of the board. Inasmuch as it was the legal duty of the county board to repair and reconstruct the courthouse, it was proper that it should discharge that duty and exercise the power conferred upon it by the statute; it having clearly appeared that the performance of that duty would not necessitate an expenditure to an amount which, together with existing indebtedness of the county, would exceed the 5 per cent. limitation imposed by the Constitution. As was said in Town of Kankakee v. McGrew, supra: "The restrictions of said sections 1 and 2 of chapter 146a are upon the power of the town to draw warrants for the payment of money, not upon its power to incur obligations and indebtedness." The same rule would apply to a county, as to a town.

Statutes tending to effect objects of great public utility are to receive liberal and benign interpretation. Potter's Dwarris on Statutes, 203, note. Section 27 of said chapter 34 provides that "whenever the county board shall deem it necessary to assess taxes the aggregate of which shall exceed the rate of seventy-five cents per $100.00 valuation * * * the county board may * * * provide for the submission of the question * * * to a vote of the people," etc. The statute thus leaves it to the county board to determine when it shall be necessary to submit the question there indicated to the people. "Where the county court of a county is invested with jurisdiction and power to order the erection and repair of bridges, and is charged with the duty of taking care of and maintaining the poor, a limitation in the general revenue laws as to the rate or amount of taxes which may be annually levied for bridges and paupers does not measure the legal power of the county court to bind the county by contracts otherwise binding for those purposes." Beach on Public Corp. p. 792. See, also, County of Christian v. Merrigan, 191 Ill. 484, 61 N. E. 479.

In Fitzgerald v. Harms, 92 Ill. 372, Harms had a contract for work in reference to the foundation of the courthouse of Cook county, and there the court refers to the powers of the county, as contained in sections 24, 25, and 26 of chapter 34, above referred to, and says (page 375): "We shall not stop to inquire whether the claim of the contractor was meritorious or not. We have referred briefly to some of the leading facts, for the purpose of showing that the claim was one of a character that came within the jurisdiction and power of the county board to settle and adjust. Under the statute the board of commissioners had the power to erect a courthouse, it had the authority to make all contracts necessary to the exercise of its corporate powers, and it was likewise intrusted with power to examine and settle all accounts against the county, and all accounts concerning the receipts and expenditures of the county." And the lower court was there sustained in its refusal to enjoin the county board, which was shown not to have acted fraudulently or corruptly or by collusion, from settling and adjusting the claim against the county there under consideration. See, also, Jackson County v. Rendleman, 100 Ill. 379, 39 Am. Rep. 44; County of La Salle v. Milligan, 143 Ill. 321, 32 N. E. 196; Seagraves v. City of Alton, 13 Ill. 366; County of Vermilion v. Knight, 1 Scam. 97.

In County of Jackson v. Hall, 53 Ill. 440, it was held that the county of Jackson was estopped from denying liability, although there was no contract made for the building of a jail, inasmuch as the jail was accepted by the county authorities and used by them when completed; and it was there said (page 443): "The county judge and his associates are empowered by law to provide a sufficient county jail, whenever the means are such as to justify it. * * * Having such power, and having received the jail and issued bonds for its payment, the county thereby becomes liable, and cannot avoid the action of the court."

In Hitchcock v. Galveston, 96 U. S. 341, 24 L. Ed. 659, where a city agreed to pay for sidewalks in city bonds, and the bonds were held to be invalid, it was decided that the city was liable upon its contract, and that, although it had agreed to pay in a way in which it had no power to pay, yet, having received the property, it was estopped to deny its power to contract; and it was there said by the Supreme Court of the United States: "It is enough for them [the plaintiffs] that the city council have power to enter into a contract for the improvement of the sidewalks; that such a contract was made with them; that under it they have proceeded to furnish materials and do work, as well as to assume liabilities; that the city has received and now enjoys the benefit of what they have done and furnished; that for these things the city promised to pay; and that, after having received the benefit of the contract, the city has broken it."

It makes no difference that the contract in the case at bar provided for payment in county orders, and that these county orders are invalid. In Hitchcock v. Galveston, supra, it was said: "If payments cannot be made in bonds because their issue is ultra vires, it would be sanctioning rank injustice to hold that payment need not be made at all. Such is not the law. The contract between the parties is in force, so far as it is lawful."

As was said in Badger v. Inlet Drainage District, 141 Ill. 540, 31 N. E. 170: "The doing of the thing in a proper way is a legitimate charge upon the revenues of the municipality; and so, when it is done and is accepted and enjoyed by the municipality, the municipality gets what it had authority to get in a different way, and it should therefore pay for it what it would have had to pay, had it got it in the right way." See, also, Town of Bruce v. Dickey, 116 Ill. 527, 6 N. E. 435; Maher v. City of Chicago, 38 Ill. 266; City of Chicago v. Norton Milling Co., 196 Ill. 580, 63 N. E. 1043.

4. It is claimed by the plaintiff in error that this judgment cannot be sustained because the proof shows that there were liens to the amount of about $12,000 filed by certain subcontractors against the warrants and orders or money due the contractor upon the erection of the courthouse, as provided by section 24 of chapter 82 of the Revised Statutes, being the mechanics' lien act (2 Starr & C. Ann. St. [2d Ed.] p. 2572, c. 82), and which section 24 was recently passed upon by this court in West Chicago Park Com'rs v. Western Granite Co., 200 Ill. 527, 66 N. E. 37.

So far as the warrants or orders are concerned, the liens can be of no avail, inasmuch as such warrants or orders are here held to have been invalid. This suit is brought for the purpose of determining whether the county is liable to pay to the contractor for the benefit of the usees the money due by the terms of the contract. The filing of the claims for these liens cannot prevent defendant in error from obtaining judgment. A different question may arise when the time comes for the county to pay the money due upon the judgments. These claimants of liens, even if the defendant in error is indebted to them, would obtain nothing if the defendant in error should not be successful in this litigation. In other words, the success of the defendant in error in this litigation is for the benefit of the claimants of liens. The question here is whether the county owes money to the defendant in error, and not whether the county owes money to the lien claimants. The latter have no direct claim against the county. Their only claim is a lien upon the money that is to be paid to the defendant in error, and if the amount of the lien claims were deducted from the amount of the judgment, and the claimants should enforce their liens against the money that would be coming to the defendant in error on this judgment, defendant in error would be obliged to pay double the amount of the liens. Zimmerman v. Wead, 18 Ill. 304; Tedrick v. Wells, 152 Ill. 214, 38 N. E. 625.

Our conclusion is that the judgment of the court below was correct to the extent of $82,004.62, but that it was erroneous in allowing interest upon the orders or warrants in question to the amount already stated. Therefore the judgment of the circuit court of Coles county is affirmed as to the sum of $82,004.62, and reversed as to the balance thereof, consisting of such interest as aforesaid. It is not necessary, however, to remand the cause to the lower court, but judgment is here entered for $82,004.62, together with interest thereon at the legal rate from the date of the entry of the judgment in the court below, to wit, April 12, 1902. Partly affirmed, and judgment here.

(209 Ill. 9)

ILLINOIS CENT. R. CO. v. SCHEFFNER.

(Supreme Court of Illinois. April 20, 1904.)

RAILROADS—INJURIES TO TRAVELER AT CROSSING—EVIDENCE—SPECIAL INTERROGATORIES—DECLARATION—SUFFICIENCY.

1. Where the verdict is based on a count of the declaration which states a good cause of action, a motion in arrest of judgment for the insufficiency of the declaration is properly denied, and it is not necessary to determine whether the other counts are sufficient.

2. In an action against a railway company for injuries to a traveler at a railroad crossing, plaintiff testified that as he approached the crossing he observed a freight train passing east; that while he was from 300 to 400 feet from the track, and again as he started down the incline of the highway leading to the track, he saw the freight train still going east, and looked to see whether any train was approaching from the west, but saw none. Looking westerly from the highway at the beginning of the incline, a train, if approaching from the west about 400 feet away, would be partially visible only; that is, the smokestack of the engine and tops of the higher cars would be seen. Plaintiff was driving at a trot from five to six miles an hour, and he did not slacken his speed as he approached the track. On reaching the track a gasoline motor car passed on the track, frightening his horse, causing the injuries complained of. This motor car could not be seen by plaintiff as he approached the track. *Held*, that there was evidence tending to show that plaintiff exercised due care, making the question of his contributory negligence a question for the jury.

3. Where, in an action against a railway company for injuries to a traveler at a railroad crossing, the court submitted the question in the special verdict whether defendant was negligent in the manner in which a motor car approaching the crossing was managed, the refusal to submit the question as to what the negligence consisted of was proper.

4. A special interrogatory in case the jury are to return special findings is improper, unless a responsive answer would be inconsistent to some general verdict that might be returned.

5. Where the court has charged that no duty rested on a party to perform a particular act, the refusal to submit to the jury the special interrogatory whether the party was negligent for not doing the act is proper.

6. Where the court could not presume that any particular method was the ordinary method of operating a gasoline motor car, and there was no evidence showing the ordinary method, the court could not instruct the jury that defendant had the right to run the car in the ordinary method.

Appeal from Appellate Court, Second District.

Action by John Scheffner against the Illinois Central Railroad Company. From a judgment of the Appellate Court, affirming a judgment for plaintiff, defendant appeals. Affirmed.

This is an appeal from the Appellate Court for the Second District, which affirmed a judgment of the circuit court of Stephenson county for $2,000, in favor of appellee, against appellant. The suit was an action of trespass on the case, to recover for a personal injury alleged to have been received on account of negligence of appellant. Upon a trial in the circuit court the jury found for appellee, and assessed his damages at the amount above stated. Motions for a new trial and in arrest of judgment were respectively overruled, after which judgment was rendered upon the verdict in favor of appellee.

It was stipulated by the parties to the suit that the portion of the railroad in question was constructed in 1887 by the Chicago, Madison & Northern Railroad Company, and was leased to appellant in April, 1888.

The appellee received the injuries complained of at a crossing of this railroad and a public highway in Stephenson county on October 5, 1900. The railroad track, which is a single track, runs east and west, and the highway runs north and south. The highway was located on the same line for a number of years prior to the construction of the railroad. When the railroad was built, the company made a cut at this place for its roadbed, and excavated earth for a distance of several hundred feet west of the highway. The testimony shows that this cut varies in depth, being 9.7 feet in depth at the crossing with the highway, and 16.1 feet deep farther west. West of the latter point the cut grows shallower until it comes to grade, and 475 feet west of the crossing is a bridge. At about 550 feet west of the crossing another cut begins, which runs on west about a half mile. The railroad company also excavated the approaches of the highway to the crossing, both north and south of the track, making the track for travel in the highway 14 feet wide, and the distance between the tops of the banks of the cut in the highway 39 feet. Commencing at the crossing, this excavation extends south in the highway for a distance of 200 feet. The cut is about 10 feet deep next the track, and gradually slopes up to the natural level of the earth to the south. A person traveling in an ordinary buggy, emerging from the cut in the highway from the south, cannot see west past the bank until within about 30 feet of the track.

On October 5, 1900, appellee was driving a gentle horse in the highway towards this crossing, coming from the south. When within about 80 rods of the crossing he saw a freight train pass at the crossing, going east. Before entering the cut in the highway he looked east and west twice for smoke from an engine, or other indications of trains, but saw none except the freight train traveling east from the crossing. He entered the cut in the highway and proceeded north, his horse trotting, until his horse's head was within a few feet of the track, when a small car, propelled by a gasoline motor, and called a "motor car," upon which four officers or employés of appellant were riding, passed in front of him, going east. His horse jumped to the right, pulling the buggy into a small ditch, overturning it, and throwing appellee out on the railroad track, from which he suffered severe injuries.

The platform of the car in question stood 2 feet above the track. The seat extended 18 inches higher. On each corner of the car was a flag about 2 feet long and 20 inches wide—2 of them white and 2 green. When the car crossed the highway these flags were unfurled.

The 4 officers of appellant above referred to testified that when within 50 or 75 feet of the highway the car was stopped, and one of them got upon the seat of the car and looked up and down the highway to see if any one was coming; that this person reported that no one was in sight; that the car was then started, and was going at the rate of about 5 miles an hour when it crossed the highway. The person referred to as having looked for travelers in the highway testified that his height was 5 feet 8½ inches, that the seat of the car on which he stood was 3 feet 6 inches above the track, and that he could see the surface of the highway for a considerable distance south of the cut in the highway, and there was no person in sight thereon at the time he looked.

Appellee testified that he heard no sound, and received no warning of the approach of the car, before his horse jumped to the right, overturning the buggy, and that he did not see the motor car until just before it appeared in front of his horse, on account of the bank along the south side of the track.

At the close of plaintiff's case, and again at the conclusion of all the evidence, appellant moved the court to instruct the jury to find the issues for the defendant, at the same time offering an instruction to that effect. In each instance the court overruled the motion and refused the instruction.

J. H. Stearns (Wm. Barge, of counsel), for appellant. Burchard & Burrell, for appellee.

SCOTT, J. (after stating the facts). The appellant questions the sufficiency of the declaration by a motion in arrest of judgment. The first count in the declaration is, in substance, the same as that approved by this court in Chicago City Railway Co. v. Jennings, 157 Ill. 274, 41 N. E. 629, the only material difference being that in that case it is charged that the negligence resulted in a collision, while here the averment is that the negligence resulted in frightening the horse, as a consequence of which the carriage was overturned, and the plaintiff thrown out and injured. We are unable to perceive any distinction. The question is whether negligence is properly charged. Whether the statement of the negligence be then followed by appropriate language showing that it resulted in a collision or in frightening the horse, and consequent injury to the driver, can make no difference in the legal sufficiency of the pleading. The first special finding shows that the defendant was found guilty of the negligence charged by the first count, and, that stating a good cause of action, the motion in arrest was properly denied. It is unnecessary to determine whether the objections urged to other counts of the declaration are well taken. Baltimore & Ohio Southwestern Railway Co. v. Alsop, 176 Ill. 471, 52 N. E. 253, 732.

At the close of the evidence of the plaintiff, and again at the close of all the evidence, defendant moved that the jury be instructed to return a verdict in its favor. This motion was overruled in both instances, and it is now urged that there was no evidence which, with the reasonable inferences to be drawn therefrom, warranted a verdict in favor of the plaintiff. In presenting this question, counsel state that they are barred by the verdict of the jury and the finding of the Appellate Court from raising in this court the question whether appellant was guilty of negligence. This must be on the basis that there was some evidence tending to show negligence on the part of the railroad company, but it is urged that there is absolutely no proof tending to show appellee was in the exercise of ordinary care for his own safety. "Although it is true that the question of contributory negligence is ordinarily a question for the jury, yet when there is no conflict in the evidence, and the court can clearly see that the injury was the result of the negligence of the party injured, it should not hesitate to instruct the jury to return a verdict for the defendant." Beidler v. Branshaw, 200 Ill. 425, 65 N. E. 1086.

As the plaintiff approached the railway

crossing from the south, according to his testimony he observed a freight train passing east. After that, while he was three or four hundred feet from the railroad track, and again as he started down the incline of the highway which leads to the track, he observed this freight train still going east, and looked to see whether any train was approaching from the west, and saw none. Looking westerly from the highway at the south end of the incline, the train, if it were approaching from the west, after passing into the cut about 400 feet west of the crossing, would be only partially visible; that is, the top of the smokestack of the engine and the tops of the higher cars, only, would project above the bank, except at the deepest part of the cut, where the engine and highest cars would be entirely hidden. The motor car in that cut would be entirely invisible from this place of observation, and it appears that a train in the cut west of the bridge could not be seen from this point. Plaintiff was driving at the rate of five or six miles an hour. His horse was trotting. He did not slacken speed as he approached the track, and it is urged that this was contributory negligence. As the train going east had just passed, the jury might reasonably find that the exercise of ordinary care did not require plaintiff to guard against danger from that direction. He looked west as he started down the slope leading to the track, and satisfied himself that there was no train approaching within a distance of several hundred feet from that direction. Danger of injury by ordinary locomotives or cars would then be lessened by hastening across the track. Such a course, it is true, disregarded the possibility of a collision with a car of the character of that which was then approaching from the west, but the danger from such a car is much less than that from an ordinary train, and its passage, ordinarily at least, is much less frequent. The course which plaintiff pursued was promotive of safety, so far as danger from the ordinary train or engine was concerned. The quicker he crossed the track, the more speedily he would be entirely out of danger from any such train or engine approaching from a point beyond the range of his vision west of the bridge, but this course was not promotive of safety so far as danger from cars of the character of this motor car was concerned. Under such circumstances we think the evidence tended to show the exercise of due care, and the question was one for the jury.

Appellant requested the court to submit to the jury seven questions of fact, with directions to return special findings in response thereto. The third, fifth, and sixth were submitted as requested.

The first inquired whether the servants of the defendant were negligent in the manner in which they approached the crossing in question with the motor car, and, "if so, in what respect." The court struck out the quoted language, which was proper, and the jury answered the question, so modified, in the affirmative. The material question under the first count of the declaration was whether the servants of the defendant approached the crossing with the motor car in a negligent manner. If they did, and that negligence occasioned the injury while the plaintiff was in the exercise of due care for his safety, then the finding of the jury in response to the portion of the question stricken out would merely have been their statement of facts evidentiary of the ultimate fact—negligence.

The second and seventh questions, we think, related to immaterial facts; that is, the general verdict would not have been in any wise affected, no matter how those interrogatories had been answered had they been submitted to the jury. A special interrogatory of this character is not proper unless some answer responsive thereto would be inconsistent with some general verdict that might be returned, so that the court would be required to disregard such general verdict by virtue of section 58c of chapter 110 of Hurd's Revised Statutes of 1901, which provides: "When the special finding of fact is inconsistent with the general verdict, the former shall control the latter and the court may render judgment accordingly." These two special interrogatories were properly refused. Chicago & Northwestern Railway Co. v. Dunleavy, 129 Ill. 132, 22 N. E. 15; Chicago Exchange Building Co. v. Nelson, 197 Ill. 334, 64 N. E. 369.

The fourth was as follows: "Was the defendant negligent in not removing the bank of rock and earth on its right of way west of the highway in question?" One of the counts of the declaration charged the defendant with negligence in not removing this bank, and this interrogatory should have been submitted had the court not instructed the jury, on the part of the defendant, that no duty rested on the railroad company to remove this bank. When the jury had been so instructed, there was no necessity for submitting an interrogatory which would merely have been an invitation to the jury to find against the instruction of the court.

In instructions numbered 8 and 9, asked by the defendant, the court struck out phrases which advised the jury that the defendant had the right to run the car "in the ordinary and usual method for operating and running such cars and machines." This so-called "motor car" is one of a somewhat unusual kind. We do not think it in such common use that the court could, without any evidence on the subject, presume that any particular method was the ordinary and usual method of operating and running such cars, and, in the absence of proof showing the ordinary and usual method, the court should not have instructed the jury that the defendant had the right to follow such method.

We have carefully considered the instructions refused which were offered by appellant and to which our attention has been called by the brief and argument, and are of the opinion that in the refusal thereof no error was committed. The jury were fully and fairly instructed. The judgment of the Appellate Court will be affirmed.

Judgment affirmed.

(209 Ill. 330)

THE FAIR v. HOFFMANN.

(Supreme Court of Illinois. April 20, 1904.)

TRIAL—REMARKS OF COUNSEL—WITHDRAWAL—PREJUDICE — INSTRUCTIONS—REFUSAL—NUMBER — LIMITATION — APPEAL—OBJECTION TO EVIDENCE—REFERENCE TO RECORD—BRIEFS—PRINTING TESTIMONY—EXCEPTION—RIGHT TO ALLEGE ERROR.

1. It is a violation of the rules of the Supreme Court for appellant to insert in its brief and argument a large number of pages of testimony which appellant's counsel deems favorable to it.

2. Where evidence objected to is not pointed out, and no reference is made to the pages of the abstract where the same may be found, and the abstract, containing 128 pages, is not indexed, such objections will not be reviewed.

3. Where it did not appear from the record that injury was likely to result to defendant from remarks of plaintiff's counsel to the jury, which, on objection, he immediately withdrew, and told the jury not to consider, the making of such remarks is not reversible error.

4. The court may properly refuse requested instructions substantially covered by other instructions given.

5. Error of the court in limiting the number of instructions cannot be reviewed where no objection or exception was taken thereto at the trial.

6. Where defendant did not offer any instructions in excess of the limit imposed by the court. it could not object on appeal that it was prejudiced by the court's order limiting the number of instructions.

Appeal from Appellate Court, First District.

Action by Rudolph Hoffmann against The Fair. From a judgment in favor of plaintiff, affirmed by the Appellate Court (110 Ill. App. 500), defendant appeals. Affirmed.

Albert E. Dacy, for appellant. Brandt & Hoffmann (Oscar C. Miller and L. M. Ackley, of counsel), for appellee.

RICKS, J. This was an action on the case brought by appellee against appellant in the superior court of Cook county for alleged injuries received by appellee through the negligence of a driver of one of appellant's delivery wagons. It appears that on November 16, 1900, appellee, who was at the time engaged in the business of selling sewing machines, was, together with William Stein, driving northwest along Lincoln avenue, in the city of Chicago, in a one-horse wagon, in which they carried with them a sewing machine; that about the time they came to the intersection of Bernice avenue, an east and west highway, a two-horse wagon owned by appellant was being driven at a rapid trot westward along Bernice avenue, and, while appellee was crossing the intersection of the two streets, appellant's wagon turned northward along Lincoln avenue and passed appellee; and it is claimed by appellee that appellant's wagon, while passing, struck his wagon, breaking the shafts and harness, and one leg of the machine in the wagon, and also bending both axles of the wagon, and throwing appellee over the dashboard upon the ground, and he was thereby bruised and hurt in such a manner that he was unable to attend to any business for a considerable length of time. Upon the trial of the case, a verdict was rendered for appellee for the sum of $1,500, and on appeal to the Appellate Court the judgment was affirmed.

No peremptory instructions were asked by appellant, and no error argued or relied upon, except improper remarks made by appellee's counsel in the argument of the case before the jury, the refusal of the court to give the fifteenth instruction asked by appellant, the admission of certain evidence, and the limiting of the instructions by the court.

Appellant's brief and argument in this case contain 67 pages of testimony which counsel for appellant deems favorable to it. This is in violation of the rules of this court. The only evidence objected to is not pointed out, or reference made to the pages of the abstract where the same may be found, nor is the abstract, which contains 128 pages, indexed; and for these reasons the evidence complained of will not be considered by this court.

In reference to the improper remarks made by counsel for appellee, we cannot say that we approve of some of them, as they were improper, but the most objectionable ones were withdrawn by counsel, who told the jury that they were not to consider them; and, while this procedure does not always entirely cure the injury, if any is done, yet, unless it is apparent from the record that some injury was suffered or did likely result by reason of such remarks, they will not be considered as reversible error, and, after a review of the evidence, we do not consider the remarks of counsel sufficient error to reverse upon.

It is next urged that it was error to refuse instruction No. 15. While this instruction presented the law properly, it was not error to refuse it, for the reason the appellant's eighth, eleventh, and thirteenth instructions contained, in substance, all that the fifteenth did. Moreover, appellant's instructions were more liberal than it was entitled to.

The next error relied upon is the court's limiting the instructions. It is sufficient to say of this alleged error that no objection or exception was taken to the limiting of the instructions. The error cannot, therefore, be considered. If there had been an exception taken to the order limiting the number of instructions, we would not feel disposed to reverse for the mere error in making such order, unless it should further appear that appellant's rights were prejudiced thereby; and, as appellant offered no instructions in excess of the limit, we are unable to say that appellant's rights were in any manner prejudiced.

Finding no reversible error, the judgment of the Appellate Court will be affirmed. Judgment affirmed.

(209 Ill. 339)

CHICAGO & E. I. R. CO. v. ZAPP.

(Supreme Court of Illinois. April 20, 1904.)

RAILROADS—INJURIES AT CROSSING—METEOROLOGICAL DATA—LETTERPRESS BOOKS—ORIGINAL RECORD—INSTRUCTIONS—WITHDRAWAL—REMARKS BY COURT—MODIFICATION—ARGUMENT OF COUNSEL—HARMLESS ERROR.

1. Where a witness in charge of the United States weather bureau in a certain city recorded the meteorological conditions on blank forms, from which they were copied by a letterpress into a book kept in his office, and the sheets sent to Washington, the book in which such data was copied produced in court by such witness, and not the sheets, constituted the original record.

2. Where the judge, after having read a requested instruction to the jury which had been marked "Given," stated that he wished to modify it, and immediately concluded not to give the same, and orally so stated to the jury, whereupon he marked it "Refused," the instruction being plainly erroneous, and defendant's right to review the same having been preserved by the court's marking the same "Refused," defendant was not prejudiced by the court's oral statement that he wished to modify the instruction, which was objectionable under Prac. Act, § 53, providing that the court shall not modify instructions given otherwise than in writing.

3. In an action for injuries at a railroad crossing, a requested instruction that if plaintiff could have discovered the approaching train by ordinary care in time to have enabled her to avoid the accident by the exercise of ordinary care on her part, "and that she did not exercise such care," the jury should find the defendant not guilty, was properly modified by adding the clause quoted.

4. Where, on objection to remarks made by plaintiff's counsel in argument, the court sustained the objection, and directed the jury to disregard the remarks, and nothing which was said could have prejudiced defendant's case, the making of such remarks was not reversible error.

Appeal from Appellate Court, First District.

Action by Casendeign Zapp against the Chicago & Eastern Illinois Railroad Company. From a judgment in favor of plaintiff, affirmed by the Appellate Court (110 Ill. App. 553), defendant appeals. Affirmed.

Calhoun, Lyford & Sheean, for appellant. W. S. Johnson and John R. Philp, for appellee.

BOGGS, J. The action below was case, to recover damages for personal injuries sustained by the appellee through the alleged negligence of the appellant company. On the trial before the court and a jury judgment was awarded the appellee in the sum of $7,000, and the same was affirmed in the Appellate Court for the First District on appeal. By this its further appeal the appellant company asks reversal of the judgment on four grounds, namely: (1) That the court admitted improper testimony on behalf of the appellee; (2) that the court erred in orally instructing the jury as to the law of the case; (3) that the court erred in modifying instruction No. 22 asked by the appellant company; and (4) that counsel for the appellee was guilty of an abuse of the right of argument to the jury. We will consider these alleged errors in the order in which they are stated by counsel.

1. The appellee received her injury at the crossing of Archer avenue and appellant's railroad, in Chicago, and it became important that the jury should know the condition of the weather on the day and hour of the accident. The appellee called Prof. Henry J. Cox, who testified that he was in charge of the United States weather bureau at Chicago, and as such was the custodian of the record of the weather conditions of the local bureau at that station. The witness produced what he testified to be such record, and was permitted to read therefrom to the effect that it was "raining, with dense fog," on the day and hour in question. He further testified that the record of the meteorological conditions was made up for each month on blank forms provided by the department at Washington, and that a copy of the same was taken by a letterpress in the book which the witness produced, and that the original sheet was sent to Washington. Appellant insists the original sheets constituted the record, and that that which appeared in the letterpress book in Chicago was secondary evidence, and not admissible in the absence of testimony showing that neither the original nor a certified copy thereof could be obtained. We think the book which was produced in court was properly regarded as the record. The record of the Chicago office might have been made by writing the facts as to the meteorological conditions in a record book kept for that purpose, and making copies from the book to be sent to the department at Washington. That would have necessitated the additional labor of twice writing the data desired to be preserved. As a mere matter of convenience and saving of labor, the plan was adopted of writing such data first upon a loose sheet of paper or blank form, and transferring the same to the record book by means of a letterpress, which might be much more speedily done than by the slow process of writing. The mere fact the data were first placed upon the loose sheet or paper or blank form does not necessarily establish that it constituted the record. It was not prepared for the purpose of constituting the record, but for the purpose of serving as a copy of the record. The record consisted of what appeared in the book. Counsel for the appellant are in error in contending that the wit-

ness was permitted to testify as to the purport of the record. The book was produced by the witness in court, and, as we understand it, the witness read from the record.

2. The last instruction which the judge had marked "Given" was No. 25, given for the appellant. The court read the instruction to the jury, and after reading it said to the jury: "I wish to modify that instruction; I will not give that instruction, gentlemen of the jury." The court then marked the instruction "Refused," and it was not allowed to go to the jury with the other instructions. The appellant preserved objections and exceptions to the oral remarks of the court and to the action of the court in refusing to give the instruction. Counsel for the appellant do not now urge that the court erred in marking the instruction "Refused." It was clearly erroneous, and ought not to have been given. The contention of counsel is that the instruction having been marked "Given," and having been read to the jury, was given to the jury, within the meaning of the word "Given" as used in section 53 of the practice act (3 Starr & C. Ann. St. 1896, c. 110, par. 54, p. 3048), and that the oral remarks of the court were a direct violation of that clause of the said section of the practice act which provides that the judge "shall in no case, after instructions are given, qualify, modify, or in any manner explain the same to the jury otherwise than in writing." It seems from the remark of the court that the judge thereof entertained, in the first instance, the intention to modify the instruction, but that he immediately determined not to do so, but to refuse to give it. Any modification of the instruction should, of course, have been in writing, had the giving of the instruction to the jury been fully completed; but the instruction was not modified, but was withdrawn by the court. If the instruction had been delivered with the other instructions to the jury, whether the court could only have lawfully withdrawn it by giving his reasons therefor in writing or executing a written order for its withdrawal is not presented by the record for decision. It would be absurd to say that if the court, when reading a series of instructions to the jury, discovers, after reading one of them that had been marked "Given," that it is erroneous, and would mislead the jury, he cannot orally state to the jury that such instruction is withdrawn, but that he must allow the instruction, as written, to go to the jury, and withdraw it by delivering with it a written order for its withdrawal or a written instruction not to consider it. The court having read the instruction to the jury, the jurors might imply from the oral remark of the court that he wished to modify it—that it did not correctly state the principle of law to which it was directed; and in view of that possible implication the proper practice would have been to modify the instruction, in writing, so that it would correctly state the rule of law to which it applied, and to give it, so modified, with the other instructions to the jury. But as the instruction was plainly erroneous, and might have misled the jury to the injury of the appellee, and as it was marked, in writing, "Refused," thus preserving the right of the appellant to have its refusal reviewed, it is plain the appellant was not prejudiced by the irregularity.

3. The court modified instruction No. 22, asked by the appellant, and gave it as so modified. The refusal to give it as asked is assigned as for error. The instruction as given is as follows, the modification being in brackets: "The court instructs the jury that if you believe, from the evidence, that the plaintiff could have discovered the approaching train, by the exercise of ordinary care, in time to have enabled her to avoid the accident by the exercise of ordinary care on her part, [and that she did not exercise such care,] you will find the defendant not guilty." The instruction directed a verdict for the appellant company, and for that reason it was proper to so modify the instruction as to make it effective only in the event the jury should find the appellee did not exercise ordinary care for her own safety.

4. During the argument in behalf of the appellee counsel for the appellant interposed an objection to the remarks that were being made to the jury. The court sustained the objection, and directed the jury to disregard what counsel had said. The objectionable remarks were but the beginning of a discussion touching upon a phase of the labor question, and were immediately objected to and so promptly ordered to be disregarded by the court that nothing was said which could have in any manner prejudiced the cause of the appellant. The record contains further remarks of counsel during the argument, but no further objection was made thereto.

Finding the record free of error of reversible character, the judgment will be affirmed. Judgment affirmed.

(209 Ill. 321)

CHICAGO CITY RY. CO. v. BARKER.

(Supreme Court of Illinois. April 20, 1904.)

STREET RAILWAYS—NEGLIGENCE—PERSONAL INJURIES—RES IPSA LOQUITUR—RUNAWAY CAR—PLEADING.

1. Failure of a person about to cross a railroad track to stop and look is not negligence per se.

2. Where plaintiff in an action against a street railway company for personal injuries testified that he looked for an approaching car before going on the track, the alleged fact that, if plaintiff had looked, he must have seen the car which injured him, does not justify the Supreme Court, on appeal, in saying that there was no evidence that plaintiff was in the exercise of ordinary care; the credibility of plaintiff's testimony being a question of fact.

3. While plaintiff was driving along defendant railway company's track, his vehicle was struck from the rear by a sprinkling car hav-

¶ 1. See Railroads, vol. 41, Cent. Dig. §§ 1050, 1172.

ing no one in charge of it, and plaintiff was injured. The motorman who had been in charge of the car had fallen off some distance from the point of collision, from the effects, as he testified, of an electric shock. *Held* to raise a presumption of negligence on the part of defendant.

4. In an action for personal injuries from negligence, in which the occurrence of the accident raises a presumption of negligence, the question whether defendant's explanatory evidence sufficiently rebuts the presumption is one of fact for the jury.

5. Where the declaration in an action against a street railway company for personal injuries alleged that defendant carelessly, negligently, and wrongfully ran and managed its car, there was no charge of specific acts of negligence, precluding plaintiff from relying on the presumption of negligence arising from the happening of the accident.

Appeal from Appellate Court, First District.

Action by John Eick against the Chicago City Railway Company. From a judgment of the Appellate Court conditionally affirming a judgment for plaintiff, defendant appeals. Pending the appeal, plaintiff died, and Charles Barker, as administrator, was substituted as appellee. Affirmed.

This is an action on the case, brought on August 23, 1900, in the superior court of Cook county, to recover damages for personal injuries claimed to have been suffered by John Eick in consequence of a collision between one of appellant's electric sprinkling cars and a wagon in which Eick was driving. The declaration, as originally filed, consisted of two counts, to which the general issue was pleaded. Subsequently the plaintiff discontinued his action as to the first count, and the cause went to trial before the jury upon the issue tendered by the second count. The jury returned a verdict of guilty, and assessed the plaintiff's damages at $5,000, and judgment was entered on the verdict. From this judgment the appellant prosecuted its appeal to the Appellate Court, and there, upon the requirement of a remittitur of $1,500, which was entered, the Appellate Court entered judgment for the plaintiff in the sum of $3,500. The present appeal is prosecuted from the judgment so entered by the Appellate Court. The suit was originally begun in the name of John Eick, but, during the pendency of the appeal from the Appellate Court to this court, Eick died intestate, and the present appellee, having obtained letters of administration upon his estate, has been substituted as appellee.

The second count of the declaration alleges that on or about May 14, 1900, in Chicago, the defendant below (appellant here) was owning, controlling, and operating a street railway extending upon and along a certain public highway, to wit, West Forty-Seventh street, and on said street railway was owning, controlling, and operating a certain electric sprinkling car, and then and there said car was proceeding in a westerly direction towards and near the crossing of said West Forty-Seventh street with a certain other public highway, to wit, South Oakley avenue, and plaintiff was then and there riding, as he had a right to do, on a certain wagon on West Forty-Seventh street, and proceeding in a westerly direction some distance in front of said car, and was in the exercise of due care and diligence, and then and there the defendant so carelessly, negligently, and wrongfully ran and managed the said street railway and car that, by and through the carelessness, negligence, and mismanagement of the defendant, said car then and there ran from behind against and into the plaintiff's wagon, on which he was then and there riding as aforesaid, and with great force and violence then and there threw and knocked the plaintiff from and off the said wagon to and upon the ground there, by means whereof, etc.

The facts are substantially as follows: Forty-Seventh street runs east and west, and appellant has a double-track street railway thereon. The east-bound cars are run over the south track, and the west-bound cars over the north track. About a block east of Oakley avenue appellant's tracks on Forty-Seventh street are crossed from southeast to northwest by what are known as the "Panhandle Railroad Tracks," the distance across which at this point is about 100 feet. On May 14, 1900, Eick was riding west upon Forty-Seventh street in a covered wagon, drawn by one horse, upon the north or west-bound track of appellant's railway. There appears to have been upon this track at that time repair work going on at the railroad crossing, and there were piles of material upon the crossing, which made it necessary to use the south or east-bound side of the street to cross the railroad tracks going either way. Upon reaching the Panhandle crossing, Eick stopped, waited for a freight train to pass, then drove over the tracks of the steam railroad south of appellant's tracks because of the obstruction aforesaid, and, when he had passed the crossing, turned back into the north track. After Eick had proceeded 40 or 50 feet in the north or west-bound track, his wagon was suddenly struck in the rear by the sprinkling car. This sprinkling car was a tank about three feet high, and set on ordinary street car wheels, and was not as high as a man's head. The car was an electric motor sprinkler, carrying a water tank, and had been in charge of a single motorman. Before Eick went upon the north track, the sprinkler was east of the railroad tracks, and about 150 yards in his rear. The sprinkler, coming from the east towards the west, was running wildly, with no one in charge of it, and struck Eick's wagon from behind, so that the horse and wagon were forced to one side, and Eick was thrown out of the wagon. The car was stopped a short distance farther on at Oakley avenue by a man who jumped upon the same and disengaged the trolley. At a point about 150 yards east of the Panhandle crossing, the motorman who had been in charge of the sprinkling car fell or was knocked off from the same, and, as soon as he fell, jumped up and attempted to catch the trolley rope, so as to stop the car, but he failed in his attempt, and the car passed on until it struck Eick's wagon.

Mason B. Starring, for appellant. Richolson & Levy (C. Stuart Beattie, of counsel), for appellee.

MAGRUDER, J. (after stating the facts). At the close of all the evidence the appellant requested the court to give an instruction, directing the jury to find the defendant not guilty, and it is the contention of the appellant that the trial court erred in refusing this instruction. It is claimed by the appellant "that there was no evidence to sustain the verdict of the jury as to the issue, either of the appellant's negligence, or of ordinary care on the part of appellee." The question, which concerns this court is not whether there was any evidence to sustain the issues involved, but whether there was any evidence tending to establish the cause of action in the case.

1. It is said that Eick did not exercise ordinary care for his own safety. There is evidence tending to show that he did exercise such care. When he turned, after passing the steam railroad crossing, from appellant's south track into the north track, he swears that he looked back to the rear, or east, and did not see the sprinkling car. It is true that the wagon in which he was riding was a covered wagon, but he stated that he stretched himself out to one side and looked back. It is not evidence of negligence per se that a person does not stop and look back before crossing the track of a railroad, and it is a question for the jury to say whether the failure to so stop and look is, or is not, negligence. Chicago City Railway Co. v. Fennimore, 199 Ill. 9, 64 N. E. 985. In the case at bar the testimony of Eick shows that he did look, and that, as a result of his look, he saw nothing approaching in his rear. The argument of the appellant is that his evidence upon this subject was not true, because, under the circumstances, if he had looked, he must have seen the sprinkler approaching. This argument involves a discussion of the facts, which is inappropriate before this court, except so far as it is necessary to determine whether or not the evidence tends to sustain the cause of action. Chicago City Railway Co. v. Martensen, 198 Ill. 511, 64 N. E. 1017. It was a question for the jury to decide, from all the circumstances in the case, whether or not the testimony of Eick was true. The testimony is clear and positive on his part that he did look, but whether he looked in such a way as to show that he thereby exercised ordinary care for his own safety, or not, was a matter entirely within the province of the jury to determine. The only ground upon which appellant seeks to show that Eick was not exercising ordinary care is the alleged untruthfulness of his testimony that he looked to see what was behind him This being so, we are not prepared to say that there was no evidence tending to show that he exercised ordinary care.

2. This is a case for the application of the doctrine res ipsa loquitur. While Eick was riding west in his wagon upon the north side of the street, as he had a right to do, an electric motor car belonging to, and under the management of, appellant, and used for sprinkling purposes, with no motorman or any other person upon it or in control of it, ran up from the rear and struck Eick's wagon, and threw him out upon the ground, and inflicted the injuries for which this suit is brought. This collision gives rise to a presumption of negligence on the part of the appellant, and the burden of proof was upon the appellant to rebut that presumption. The meaning of the maxim res ipsa loquitur is that, while negligence is not, as a general rule, to be presumed, yet the injury itself may afford sufficient prima facie evidence of negligence, and the presumption of negligence may be created by the circumstances under which the injury occurred. "Where negligence is thus presumed from the occurrence of the injury, defendant is called upon to rebut the prima facie case by showing that he took reasonable care to prevent the happening of such injury." Hart v. Washington Park Club, 157 Ill. 9, 41 N. E. 620, 29 L. R. A. 492, 48 Am. St. Rep. 298. In Hart v. Washington Park Club, supra, quoting from Scott v. Docks Co., 3 Hurl. & C. 596, it was said: "There must be reasonable evidence of negligence. But when the thing is shown to be under the management of the defendant or his servants, and the accident is such as, in the ordinary course of things, does not happen if those who have the management use proper care, it affords reasonable evidence, in the absence of explanation by the defendant, that the accident arose from want of care." North Chicago Street Railway Co. v. Cotton, 140 Ill. 486, 29 N. E. 899. In the same case, quoting from Addison on Torts (volume 1, § 33), the rule was thus stated: "Where the accident is one which would not, in all probability, happen if the person causing it was using due care, and the actual machine causing the accident is solely under the management of the defendant, * * * the mere occurrence of the accident is sufficient prima facie proof of negligence to impose upon the defendant the onus of rebutting it."

There is no doubt here from the evidence that this electric sprinkling car which caused the accident was under the management and control of the appellant. When it was about 150 yards in the rear and east of the point where Eick's wagon turned to go upon the north track, the motorman in charge of the sprinkling car fell from it to the ground. He was the only person who at the time was upon the car, which had one platform in the rear and one platform in front. At the time when the motorman, whose name was Foley, fell from the sprinkling car, he had one hand on the brake handle of the car, and the other hand on the barrel tank, but without apparently holding onto anything. While in this position he turned to look back, and says that when he did so he received a shock which threw him from the car. His testimony is, in part: "I don't know whether I was looking back to see whether there were kids, or what was the matter. I put one hand on the brake handle, and I think I was looking back to see whether there was any water going out of the tank, * * * and the other back on the barrel, and I looked back over the tank; and at that instant, when I put back my hand, I got a shock and fell off involuntarily." It is evident that the motorman received no serious or long-continued injury from the shock, because his own testimony shows that, as soon as he struck the ground, he jumped up and ran after the sprinkler, and attempted to loosen the trolley wire. He says: "I jumped up the moment I fell. I got up as quick as I could, and made one jump to see if I could catch the trolley rope. I failed to get that."

It was for the jury to say, whether the motorman fell from the car on account of an electric shock, which, he says, he received, or whether he fell off as the result of his own conduct in looking back over the barrel without securing a sufficient hold upon some part of the car to prevent himself from falling off. Whether his statement was true—that an electric shock was the cause of his fall—was a matter to be determined by the jury. The testimony introduced by the appellant was to the effect that there was no way in which the electric apparatus could cause such a shock; that no person had ever heard of such an accident before; that the witness had run the car for three weeks, and during all the morning of that day, without any accident, the accident having occurred about 1 o'clock; that the car was of the best and highest standard of construction; that it was inspected by expert workmen every night; and that any repairs which were needed were promptly made.

The contention of the appellant is that, if it was necessary for it to rebut the prima facie presumption of negligence raised by the occurrence of the accident in the manner stated, it did so by showing that the motorman was thrown from the car by an electric shock which the appellant was unable to anticipate or prevent, and that therefore it should not be held responsible because the car was not in the control of any one when it struck Eick's wagon. It was a question for the jury to determine whether the explanation of the accident sufficiently rebutted the presumption in question. The credibility of such rebutting evidence is held by the authorities to be a question for the jury. Uggla v. West End Street Railway Co., 160 Mass. 351, 35 N. E. 1126, 39 Am. St. Rep. 481; O'Flaherty v. Nassau Electric Railway Co. (Sup.) 54 N. Y. Supp. 96. In actions brought for damages alleged to result from fire caused by the escape of sparks from locomotive engines, the fact of the communication of the fire to the property destroyed or injured is taken as prima facie evidence to charge with negligence the corporation or other person who at the time of the injury is in the use and occupation of the railroad, and in such cases "the question whether the defendant's evidence was sufficient, under all the circumstances, to rebut the prima facie proof of negligence, arising from the undisputed fact that the fire was communicated from the engine was clearly a question of fact for the jury, and as to which the judgment of the Appellate Court is conclusive." Louisville, Evansville & St. Louis Consolidated Railroad Co. v. Spencer, 149 Ill. 97, 36 N. E. 91; Cleveland, Cincinnati, Chicago & St. Louis Railway Co. v. Hornsby, 202 Ill. 138, 66 N. E. 1052. As is said by the Appellate Court in their opinion deciding this case: "In the case at bar, it was for the jury to consider whether the explanation offered by appellant relieved it from the presumption of negligence raised by the undisputed facts. If appellant ran its car in an unsafe condition, evidence tending to show such condition was admissible under the second count."

It is said, however, on the part of the appellant, that the declaration in this case charged specific acts of negligence, and that therefore Eick was not entitled to rely upon presumptive negligence. The cases of West Chicago Street Railroad Co. v. Martin, 154 Ill. 523, 39 N. E. 140, and Chicago & Eastern Illinois Railroad Co. v. Driscoll, 176 Ill. 330, 52 N. E. 921, are relied upon in support of this position. But the facts of the latter cases, when carefully examined, will show that they have no application to the case at bar. The declaration here charges that the appellant "carelessly, negligently, and wrongfully ran and managed its car." If the appellant placed the sprinkling car under the control of a motorman, who lost control of it by his own carelessness, then the sprinkling car was not properly run and managed by the appellant. We think that the declaration is sufficiently general in its terms to take the case at bar out of the rule announced in the cases last referred to. The second count of the declaration here does not charge that any servant of the appellant was guilty of specific acts of negligence, but charges that the appellant itself carelessly ran and managed its electric sprinkling car. The second count of the declaration does not state in or by what specific acts the carelessness in driving or managing the car was manifested—whether by running at a greater rate of speed than safety or prudence required, or by improper and insufficient exercise of control on the part of the motorman, or by some other means. "Carelessness and impropriety are not descriptive of specific acts, but of a class of acts only, which may include an indefinite number of specific acts, each differing in its character from the others." Chicago, Burlington & Quincy Railroad Co. v. Harwood, 90 Ill. 425.

We are of the opinion that there was sufficient evidence tending to show that the appellant was guilty of such negligence as caused the injury to justify a submission of the question of negligence to the jury.

Accordingly the judgment of the Appellate Court is affirmed. Judgment affirmed.

(208 Ill. 608)

ILLINOIS CENT. R. CO. v. SMITH.

(Supreme Court of Illinois. April 20, 1904.)

MASTER AND SERVANT—INJURIES TO SERVANT—DEFECTIVE APPLIANCES—EVIDENCE—OPINIONS—QUESTIONS IN ISSUE—INSTRUCTIONS—INTERMEDIATE APPEALS—REVIEW OF EVIDENCE—OPINIONS OF APPELLATE COURT—ASSIGNMENTS OF ERROR—REVIEW BY SUPREME COURT.

1. In an action for injuries to a railroad employé engaged in dumping ballast cars, he claimed that, in attempting to save himself from a fall caused by a jar of the train, he threw one foot back to the platform of the car behind, and that his foot went through a hole mashed through the planks and a part of the sill, down on the drawbar, and was injured. The defect in the platform was denied by defendant, and, in corroboration of plaintiff's testimony, he claimed that the injury showed it was caused by his foot being caught between two uneven surfaces, while defendant claimed that it was crushed between two even surfaces. *Held*, that evidence of physicians, who examined plaintiff immediately after the injury, that the foot must have been injured by coming in contact with two uneven surfaces, was not expert testimony, but was direct testimony as to how the injury occurred and what caused it, and was therefore inadmissible.

2. In an action for injuries to a servant by reason of an alleged defective car platform, an instruction that the burden was on the plaintiff to prove his case by a preponderance of the evidence, which was satisfied if the jury believed that the greater weight of evidence established that the platform was out of repair as alleged, and that such condition was the cause of plaintiff's injury, and the condition of the platform was the result of defendant's negligence, of which defendant had notice, and that at the time plaintiff stepped on the platform, if he did step on it, he was in the exercise of due care for his own safety, he was entitled to recover, was erroneous, as ignoring the question of assumption of risk, and declaring that defendant would be liable if it had notice of the defective condition of the platform, regardless of the time when it received such notice.

3. Where a case is appealed to the Appellate Court, and it is assigned as error that the verdict is contrary to the manifest weight of the evidence, it is the duty of the Appellate Court to weigh the evidence and determine such question.

4. Though the opinions or decisions of the Appellate Courts are required to be included in appellant's brief or otherwise on an appeal to the Supreme Court, error cannot be assigned on such opinions, so as to authorize the Supreme Court to review an assignment that the Appellate Court erred in refusing to weigh the evidence on an objection that the verdict was contrary to the manifest weight of evidence.

Appeal from Appellate Court, Third District.

Action by Charles Smith against the Illinois Central Railroad Company. From a judgment in favor of plaintiff, affirmed by the Appellate Court, defendant appeals. Reversed.

J. S. Wolfe and G. W. Gere (John G. Drennan, of counsel), for appellant. Ray & Dobbins, for appellee.

HAND, J. This is an action on the case, commenced in the circuit court of Champaign county by appellee against the appellant to recover damages for a personal injury sustained by appellee while in the employ of the appellant as a section hand and engaged in dumping "gondola" cars loaded with ballast. The declaration contained one count, and the general issue was pleaded, and the jury returned a verdict in favor of the appellee for $3,000, upon which, after overruling a motion for a new trial, judgment was rendered, which judgment has been affirmed by the Appellate Court for the Third District, and a further appeal has been prosecuted to this court.

The appellee, with one Garretson, was dumping cars. This was done by getting upon the platform at each end of the car and operating a lever. After they had dumped several cars, appellee got up to dump another car, and while he was on the platform the train was violently jarred by the shutting down of the locomotive, and his left foot, while he was attempting to save himself from falling, was in some manner caught between the coupling machinery of the cars and crushed. The appellee testified that when the jar occurred he was in the act of stepping from the car that had just been unloaded to the platform of an adjoining loaded car; that he was thrown backward, and, to prevent himself from falling, caught hold of the brake of the car he was facing and threw one foot back to the car he had just left; that in the platform of that car, over the drawbar and coupling machinery, and just back of where the "deadwood" should have been, there was a hole mashed through the planks and a part of the sill which supported them; and that his foot went through the hole, and down upon the drawbar beneath the platform, and was injured. Three witnesses on behalf of the appellant testified they reached appellee before he was released, and that his foot was caught between the lip of the drawbar and the deadwood, and that his foot was not in a hole. Five witnesses testified they examined the car on which appellee was injured, immediately after the injury, and that the deadwood was intact and there was no hole in the platform, and two witnesses testified they inspected the cars of the train, of which the car in question formed a part, upon the morning of the injury, and that they were in good repair and there were no holes in the platforms thereof.

Appellee sought to support his testimony, which was otherwise uncorroborated, by the testimony of the two physicians who treated him for the injury. Dr. J. A. Huffman, who saw appellee immediately after the injury, over the objections of the appellant, testified in part as follows: "Q. Describe, if you can, how the injury must have been made—whether with a flat surface or not, or a round surface, or an uneven surface. A. My impression is, it was done by some projection penetrating the bottom of the foot. Q. How, in your opinion, was the injury inflicted? A. By the foot being caught between two projections—something that would penetrate the bottom of the foot. It would be uneven. It could not have been flat. Q. I am asking your opinion as to what kind of surface would cause the twisting of the foot in that way—an even or an uneven surface? A. An uneven surface." Dr. Z. E. Matheny, who was called to see appellee the day of the injury, also testified, over the objection of the appellant, in part as follows: "Q. Describe what kind of a surface that injury could have been inflicted by—whether an even or an uneven surface. A. Well, judging from the appearance of the wound, I would judge it was an uneven surface that caused it. Q. You may state, after your examination of the foot and seeing its twisted condition, if you have any opinion as to how it was twisted into that shape. A. It could have been caught between two uneven surfaces and twisted around that way; could not have been inflicted by flat and even surfaces." Appellee testified that his foot was caught between two uneven surfaces, and all of the appellant's evidence tended to show that his foot was caught and crushed between two even surfaces. The evidence on that point was directly contradictory.

The first question, therefore, presented for consideration, is, was the testimony of the physicians above set forth competent evidence to be received in corroboration of that of appellee? Three objections are urged against the competency of said evidence: First, that the matter involved no particular science, skill, or knowledge in order to formulate the opinion given; second, that the matter could have been concisely and lucidly described to the jury; and, third, that the testimony, though in form an opinion, was in reality the statement of the very fact the jury was to determine. It seems to us clear, if the physicians who were called had confined their evidence to a description of the condition of the foot of appellee as they found it after the injury, the jury, from such evidence, would have been in as good condition as they to determine whether the injury had been caused by the foot being crushed between even or uneven surfaces, and that to permit the witnesses to testify the injury was caused from the foot being caught between two uneven, and not two even, surfaces, was to permit them to usurp the province of the jury, and to testify to the facts which were to be determined by the jury, which all the authorities agree is not permissible.

In Hellyer v. People, 186 Ill. 550, 58 N. E. 245, which was an indictment for murder, the trial court permitted a number of physicians to give their opinions upon the question as to whether or not the wounds found upon the body of the deceased were such as would likely have been inflicted upon a person, while living, by being struck by a railroad train running at the rate of 35 miles per hour. This court held the evidence incompetent, and on page 558, 186 Ill., and page 248, 58 N. E., said: "The subject of the proposed injury [inquiry] was a matter of common observation, upon which the lay or uneducated mind is capable of forming a correct judgment. In regard to such matters experts are not permitted to state their conclusions. In questions of science their opinions are received, for in such questions scientific men have superior knowledge and generally think alike. Not so in matters of common knowledge. Milwaukee & St. Paul Railway Co. v. Kellogg, 94 U. S. 469, 24 L. Ed. 256. 'Whenever the subject-matter of inquiry is of such a character that it may be presumed to lie within the common experience of all men of common education moving in the ordinary walks of life, the rule is that the opinions of experts are inadmissible, as the jury are supposed, in all such matters, to be entirely competent to draw the necessary inferences from the facts testified of by the witnesses.' Rogers on Expert Testimony, § 8; Ohio & Mississippi Railway Co. v. Webb, 142 Ill. 404, 32 N. E. 527. As a general rule, the opinions of witnesses are not to be received in evidence merely because such witnesses may have had some experience or greater opportunities of observation than others, unless such opinions relate to matters of skill and science. Robertson v. Stark, 15 N. H. 109; Marshall v. Columbian Ins. Co., 7 Fost. (N. H.) 157; Protection Ins. Co. v. Harmer, 2 Ohio St. 452, 59 Am. Dec. 684; People v. Bodine, 1 Denio, 281; Westlake v. St. Lawrence, etc., Ins. Co., 14 Barb. 206; Smith v. Gugerty, 4 Barb. 614; Folkes v. Chudd, 3 Doug. 157; 1 Smith's Lead. Cas. (5th Am. Ed.) 630; Daniels v. Mosher, 2 Mich. 183. An expert cannot be asked whether the time during which a railroad train stopped was sufficient to enable the passengers to get off (Keller v. Railroad Co., 2 Abb. Dec. 480), or whether it was prudent to blow a whistle at a particular time (Hill v. Railroad Co., 55 Me. 438, 92 Am. Dec. 601); nor can a person conversant with real estate be asked respecting the peculiar liability of unoccupied buildings to fire (Mulry v. Insurance Co., 5 Gray, 541, 66 Am. Dec. 380). The opinions of witnesses should not be asked in such a way as to cover the very question to be found by a court or jury. Chicago & Alton Railroad Co. v. Springfield & Northwestern Railroad Co., 67 Ill. 142. Where the matter inquired about requires no special knowledge, and may be determined by a jury upon a sufficient description of the facts in regard to it, it is not proper to receive the testimony of experts. Hopkins v. Indianapolis & St. Louis Railroad Co., 78 Ill. 32; City of Chicago v. McGiven, 78 Ill. 347; Pennsylvania Co. v. Conlan, 101 Ill. 93."

In Chicago & Alton Railroad Co. v. Lewandowski, 190 Ill. 301, 60 N. E. 497, which was a personal injury case, the appellant called a number of railroad men as expert witnesses, who testified that in their judgment a person could not be struck by a locomotive engine, pulling a train of freight cars and running at the rate of 25 or 30 miles an hour, and survive, while the appellee called a number of medical men, who testified that in their opinion a person could be struck by a train moving at said rate of speed, and thrown that distance, or even a greater distance, and live. On page 309, 190 Ill., and page 500, 60 N. E., the court said: "It is said it was error to allow the medical witnesses to give expert testimony upon such subject, as it called for their opinions upon subjects that were outside of their profession. We think the record shows that the witnesses for the appellee were as well qualified to speak upon the subject as those called by the appellant. We are of the opinion, however, that the subject inquired about was not a proper subject for expert testimony; but, as the error was invited by appellant, it cannot now complain. The subject of the proposed inquiry was upon a matter of common observation, upon which the jury were capable of forming a correct judgment, and upon which they would be more likely to be misled and confused, than enlightened, by the opinions of the so-called experts."

In Treat v. Merchants' Life Ass'n, 198 Ill. 431, 64 N. E. 992, where the defense interposed to the policy was suicide, on page 436, 198 Ill., and page 994, 64 N. E., the court said: "The court did not err in refusing to permit Dr. Mathews to express an opinion as to whether the wound was accidentally or purposely inflicted. That was a question for the jury to pass upon, after they had been put in possession of the facts surrounding the death of Helliwell."

In City of Chicago v. McGiven, 78 Ill. 347, which was an action on the case to recover damages claimed to have been sustained by the plaintiff falling upon a sidewalk, by reason of having stepped upon a piece of glass which was imbedded in the walk for the purpose of affording light to the area under the walk, the plaintiff, upon the trial, called a number of architects, and, against the objection of the defendant, proved by them that in their opinion a glass such as that which the evidence showed was inserted in the sidewalk, and upon which the plaintiff claimed to have slipped and fallen, was unfit to be used as a part of the walk, and was unsafe for such use. On appeal it was held the admission of the testimony was reversible error. In disposing of the question it was said (page 349): "The general rule is that the opinions of witnesses are inadmissible as evidence; that they are to testify to facts, and the jury are to draw the inferences and form the opinions which are to govern the case. The present case is supposed to come within the exception to the rule that on questions of science, skill, or trade, or others of the like kind, persons of skill, sometimes called 'experts,' are permitted to give their opinions in evidence. But this is on the ground of necessity, when the facts in issue are not themselves accessible by evidence, and it is a matter of necessity to call in the experienced or instructed opinions of such witnesses. The opinions of witnesses should not be received as evidence where all the facts on which such opinions are founded can be ascertained and made intelligible to the court or jury. Clark v. Fisher, 1 Paige, 174, 19 Am. Dec. 402; Mayor, etc., of New York v. Pentz, 24 Wend. 668; Linn v. Sigsbee, 67 Ill. 75. * * * The question whether the glass was unsafe by reason of the too great smoothness or slipperiness of its surface was not a question of science or skill. The decision of that question required no special knowledge, and it was easily determinable by the jury, upon a sufficient description of facts pertaining to the glass, and the use of it in a sidewalk, being given by witnesses. We do not perceive why mere proof of the naked facts could not enable the jury themselves to draw the inference whether the glass was safe or unsafe. The real question for the jury was, not whether the glass was safe, but whether it was reasonably safe. The not improbable effect of obtruding upon the jury the opinions of these architects that the glass was unsafe might be that the jury would regard them as deciding the whole question, and so accept them, and repose on them as such, without further inquiry and deciding for themselves whether the sidewalk might not have been reasonably safe."

In Chicago & Alton Railroad Co. v. Springfield & Northwestern Railroad Co., 67 Ill. 142, which was a condemnation suit, the contractor of appellee was called as a witness and asked, "If you put in the cut the work you propose to do and have described, what would be the damages to the defendant?" to which he replied, "There would be no damage." In sustaining an exception to the question, this court held the question called for an opinion covering the very question which was to be settled by the jury, and left to the jury no duty but that of recording the finding of the witness; that it permitted the witness to usurp the province of the jury; and that it was not competent to ask the opinion of an expert witness in such a way as to cover the very question to be found by the jury.

In State v. Rainsbarger, 74 Iowa, 196, 37 N. W. 153, counsel for defendant asked a witness, who was a physician, "how the wounds upon the defendant were probably made." The trial court excluded the evidence. The Supreme Court, in reviewing the ruling upon that question, said (page 204, 74 Iowa, and page 157, 37 N. W.): "The evidence was rightly excluded. It sought for an expression of opinion based upon matters which were to be weighed and considered by the jury, and determined upon the exercise of their own judgments, and not upon the opinion of another. The matters upon which the question was based were not peculiarly within the knowledge of the witness, or of the profession to which he belonged."

In People v. Hare, 57 Mich. 512, 24 N. W. 843, a physician who had examined the wound was asked: "From the appearance of the wound, what would you say it was caused by?" The court said (page 512, 57 Mich., and page 846, 24 N. W.): "We think the objection to this question was well taken. * * * The question calls for the fact which was to be found by the jury. What might have caused it would have been proper, but what did cause it was the real question for the jury."

In Cannon v. People, 141 Ill. 270, 30 N. E. 1027, Dr. Applington was called as a witness by the people. He testified that he assisted at the post mortem examination of the body of the deceased, described the nature, character, and extent of the wounds, and stated which wound, in his opinion, was the immediate cause of death. He was then shown a pair of shears, and asked, "Examine these shears, and tell the jury whether or not the wounds upon the body of Martin Ryan were likely to have been produced with that instrument." He answered: "They could have been produced with that instrument; yes, sir." The court, on page 277, 141 Ill., and page 1028, 30 N. E., said: "The question was clearly improper and invaded the province of the jury. The question whether the wounds were or were not inflicted in the manner alleged in the indictment, or with the instrument alleged, was one of fact, for the jury to determine from all the evidence, and in no sense was the proper subject of opinion by experts."

The appellee has referred to a number of decisions of this court, notably Illinois Central Railroad Co. v. Latimer, 128 Ill. 163, 21 N. E. 7, Village of Chatsworth v. Rowe, 166 Ill. 114, 46 N. E. 763, Illinois Central Railroad Co. v. Treat, 179 Ill. 576, 54 N. E. 290, and Shorb v. Webber, 188 Ill. 126, 58 N. E. 949, and of the courts of last resort in other states, which, it is insisted, sustain the position that the opinion evidence above referred to is competent. An examination of those cases discloses the fact that they, generally, are cases where physicians have been allowed to express an opinion as to what might have caused the injury, the cause of which was then being investigated; but none of them, so far as we have been able to discover, sustain a course of examination which calls for an opinion from the expert as to what caused the injury, and they all recognize the fact that the question of what did cause the injury is a question of fact for the jury, and not for the witness. In the Latimer Case a physician was permitted to express the opinion that fright would cause heart trouble; in the Rowe Case, to state the condition which he found in the plaintiff's knee could have been produced by a fall upon a sidewalk; and in Lacas v. Detroit City Railway Co., 92 Mich. 412, 52 N. W. 745, that a violent fall might produce displacement of the womb. The opinions of the physicians here were expressed upon a vital and closely contested point in the case. They were not asked how the injury, in their judgment, might have occurred or been produced, but the questions propounded to them were, "How the injury must have been made," "How, in your opinion, was the injury inflicted?" and it was ruled, "If he knows, or if he has any idea, how it was made, he can tell." "If he has any opinion, after examining the wound, as to how it occurred, he may state it." It is apparent, from the questions and answers and the rulings of the court, that the opinions of the physicians took the form, not of opinions as to how the injury might have been produced, but of direct testimony as to how it occurred and what caused it, which was the very question which the jury were called upon to decide. In view of the evidence, which was in irreconcilable conflict upon the question as to how the injury occurred, the testimony of the physicians necessarily had great weight with the jury in determining that question, and in all probability aided in producing a verdict in favor of appellee which otherwise might have been in favor of the appellant.

At the instance of appellee the court gave to the jury the following instruction: "The court instructs the jury that, while it devolves upon the plaintiff in this cause to establish his case by a preponderance of the evidence, yet by this it is not meant that he must necessarily produce the greater number of witnesses, but simply that he must prove his case by evidence shown on the trial which outweighs that produced on behalf of the defendant, where the whole evidence is considered together; and if the jury believes that the greater weight of evidence in this case establishes that the platform was out of repair, as alleged, and that such condition of the platform was the cause of his injury, and that the condition of such platform was the result of defendant's negligence, and that the defendant had notice thereof, and that at the time the plaintiff stepped upon such platform, if you believe, from the evidence, that he did step upon it, he was in the exercise of due care for his own safety, then the plaintiff will be entitled to recover."

The evidence was conflicting, and it was essential to a proper trial of the case that the jury be correctly instructed as to the principles of law which should govern them in a decision thereof. We think the instruction subject to two criticisms: First, it states, if the appellant had notice of the defective condition of the platform, it would be liable, regardless of the time when it received such notice; and, second, it ignores the question of assumed risk. In order that the appellant might be held liable for the defective condition of the platform, it was necessary that it have notice of such defective condition for a sufficient length of time to enable it to notify appellee thereof or to repair the same; and if appellee had notice of the defective condition of the platform, and continued to work upon it without objection, he assumed the risk of being injured by reason of such defective condition. Goldie v. Werner, 151 Ill. 551, 38 N. E. 95; Chicago & Eastern Illinois Railroad Co. v. Heerey, 203 Ill. 492, 68 N. E. 74. And the instruction was not cured by the instructions given on behalf of the appellant, as the jury were directed thereby, if they found the facts therein to be true, that plaintiff was entitled to recover. In Pardridge v. Cutler, 168 Ill. 504, 48 N. E. 125, on page 512, 168 Ill., and page 127, 48 N. E., it was said: "The law applicable to different questions may be stated in separate instructions, and the entire law applicable to all the questions involved in a case need not be stated in each. In such case the instructions supplement each other, and, if they present the law fairly when viewed as a series, it will be sufficient. But if an instruction directs a verdict for either party, or amounts to such a direction in case the jury shall find certain facts, it must necessarily contain all the facts which will authorize the verdict directed."

It is also assigned as error that the Appellate Court refused to consider all the evidence in the case, or to weigh the evidence upon controverted questions of fact presented to that court for decision. It was assigned as error in the Appellate Court that the verdict is contrary to the manifest weight of the evidence. This court has held it is the duty of the Appellate Court, upon such assignment of error, to weigh the evidence and determine whether the verdict is against the weight of the evidence, as that court, upon such an assignment, is the only appellate tribunal in this state that can determine that question, since this court, in actions at law, is permitted, under the statute, to review only questions of law. (Voigt v. Anglo-American Provision Co., 202 Ill. 462, 66 N. E. 1054; Chicago City Railway Co. v. Mead, 206 Ill. 174, 69 N. E. 19). The statute requires that the opinions or decisions of the Appellate Courts upon the final hearing of cases therein pending shall be reduced to writing and filed in the case in which rendered, and the rules of this court require that in all cases brought from the Appellate Courts to this court the party bringing the same to this court shall file, as an appendix to his brief or otherwise, a copy of the opinion of that court rendered in the case, including the statement of facts; and, although this court may rightfully look into such opinion for the purpose of advising itself as to the questions considered and how they were disposed of by the Appellate Court, error cannot be assigned upon the opinions of said courts, and this court is powerless to consider the assignment of error that said court refused to weigh or consider the evidence upon controverted questions of fact presented to that court for its determination and decision.

For the errors pointed out herein, the judgments of the Appellate and circuit courts will be reversed, and the cause remanded to the circuit court for a new trial.

Reversed and remanded.

(209 Ill. 53)

CITY OF PEORIA v. OHL et al.

(Supreme Court of Illinois. April 20, 1904.)

LOCAL IMPROVEMENTS—ENGINEER'S ESTIMATE—SUFFICIENCY.

1. The local improvement act (Laws 1897, p. 102, as amended by Laws 1901, p. 102) provides that the board of local improvements, in proceedings for the construction of sidewalks, may submit to the city council an ordinance providing for the proposed improvement, together with an estimate of the cost, to be made by the engineer, which shall be itemized to the satisfaction of the board. An estimate of an engineer presented to a city council with an ordinance for the construction of a sidewalk gave the cost of the proposed sidewalk in a gross sum. *Held* insufficient.

Appeal from Peoria County Court; W. J. Clemmons, Judge.

Proceedings by the city of Peoria for the confirmation of a special assessment, to which John Ohl and others filed objections. From a judgment sustaining the objections and dismissing the proceedings, the city appeals. Affirmed.

Walter H. Kirk (William M. Barnes and Henry C. Fuller, of counsel), for appellant. Geo. K. Beasley, for appellees.

HAND, C. J. This was a proceeding in the county court of Peoria county to confirm a special tax to pay for constructing a cement sidewalk upon one of the public streets of said city under the local improvement act of 1897 (Laws 1897, p. 102), as amended in 1901 (Laws 1901, p. 102). Objections to the confirmation of the special tax were filed by appellees, as to their property, on the grounds that the local improvement act, as amended, is unconstitutional, and that no sufficient itemized estimate of the cost of the improvement was made by the engineer of the board of local improvements prior to the passage of the ordinance providing for the construction of the sidewalk. The court sustained the last objection and dismissed the proceeding, and an appeal has been prosecuted to this court by the city.

The only question presented for our consideration upon this appeal is, was the estimate of the engineer presented to the city council with the ordinance providing for the construction of the sidewalk in compliance with the requirements of the local improvement act as amended in 1901?

The estimate of the engineer presented to the city council with the ordinance is in the following form:

"At the request of such board I submit below an estimate of the cost of constructing the sidewalk above described and as designated in and in accordance with the ordinance therefor hereto attached, including the labor, material and other expenses attending the same, as provided by law, viz.:

451 lineal feet of sidewalk six (6) ft. in width	$301 00
Court costs, collections, etc., 6%	18 06
Total	$319 06

"And I hereby certify that in my opinion the above estimate does not exceed the probable cost of the above proposed improvement.

"Peoria, Illinois, August 10, 1903.

"Respectfully submitted, H. E. Beasley, City Engineer and Eng. of such Board."

Section 7 of the local improvement act of 1897 provides all ordinances for local improvements to be paid for wholly or in part by special assessment or special taxation shall originate with the board of local improvements; that the board may originate such improvements upon petition or upon its own motion; that in either case the board shall adopt a resolution describing the proposed improvement, which shall be at once transcribed into the records of the board; that the board, by said resolution, shall fix a day and hour for the public consideration thereof, which shall not be less than 10 days after the adoption of the resolution, and shall cause an estimate of the cost of such improvement to be made in writing by the engineer of the board over his signature, which shall be itemized to the satisfaction of the board, and which shall be made a part of the record of such resolution; that at least a five-days notice of the public hearing shall be given to the person who paid the general tax for the last preceding year on each lot, block, tract, or parcel of land fronting upon the proposed improvement, which notice shall contain the substance of the resolution and the estimate of the cost of the improvement; and that the extent, nature, kind, character, and estimated cost of the improvement may be changed at the public hearing. The statute also provides that, if the board deem an improvement desirable, it shall adopt a resolution therefor, and shall prepare and submit an ordinance therefor to the city council. By the amendment of 1901 it was provided that in proceedings only for the laying, building, constructing, or repairing of sidewalks, water-service pipes, or house drains, no resolution, public hearing, or preliminary proceedings leading up to the same shall be necessary, but in such proceedings the board may submit to the city council an ordinance, together with its recommendation and the estimate of the cost of the improvement made by the engineer as herein provided for, and that such proceedings shall have the same force and effect as though a public hearing had been had thereon.

It is clear that under the original act the same steps were required to be taken to raise a fund by special assessment or special taxation with which to pay the cost of constructing a sidewalk under that act as are required in cases of other local improvements constructed thereunder; and it is equally clear that the provisions of the original act providing for the engineer's estimate of the cost of a sidewalk, and that it should be itemized, were not changed by the amendment. Under the amendment, the preliminary resolution, a public hearing, the giving of notice thereof, etc., in proceedings for the laying, building, constructing, and renewing of a sidewalk, are not necessary; but the provision that an itemized estimate of the cost of all local improvements, which would include a sidewalk, as provided for by the original act, was not affected by the amendment, and the itemized estimate which the amendment provides shall be submitted to the city council with a sidewalk ordinance is the engineer's itemized estimate of the cost thereof designated in the statute prior to the amendment thereof. That being true, it is clear an estimate by an engineer which gives the cost of a proposed sidewalk in a gross sum, as was the case here, is not a compliance with the provisions of the statute requiring that the cost thereof be itemized. Bickerdike v. City of Chicago, 203 Ill. 636, 68 N. E. 161. In the Bickerdike Case it was said by counsel on behalf of the city that all that the property owner is entitled to be informed of is the character of the improvement, the extent of the improvement, and the cost thereof; and it was urged it would be of no possible benefit for the property owner to know the cost of the different materials which enter into the construction of the improvement. In reply to that argument, the court held the statute in express terms required the estimate of the engineer to be itemized, and was mandatory, and said the requirements of the statute are not merely for the purpose of enabling the board to act, but are also for the benefit and protection of the owners of property to be assessed, and for their protection the requirements of the statute must be complied with.

It was also held in that case that the proceedings prior to the adoption of the ordinance required by the statute were jurisdictional, and, unless they were complied with, no valid ordinance could be passed. Our conclusion therefore is that the estimate presented with the ordinance to the city council was not in compliance with the statute, and that the county court did not err in refusing to confirm the special tax.

It is urged that the estimate in the case of Adcock v. City of Chicago, 172 Ill. 24, 49 N. E. 1108, is substantially like the estimate in the case at bar. That proceeding, however, was carried on under the act of 1872 (Laws 1871-72, p. 218), which did not require, as does the act under which this proceeding is being carried on, that the estimate of the engineer of the cost of the improvement be itemized.

It is also said the record in the case of Gage v. City of Chicago, 203 Ill. 26, 67 N. E. 477, shows that the estimate of the cost of the improvement in that case, which was for a cement sidewalk, is in form the same as the estimate in this case, and that the judgment of confirmation in that case was affirmed by this court. An examination of the opinion of this court filed in that case will disclose the fact that the question here presented was not there considered by the court.

The judgment of the county court will be affirmed. Judgment affirmed.

(209 Ill. 316)

BAUER et al. v. LUMAGHI COAL CO.

(Supreme Court of Illinois. April 20, 1904.)

CONTRACT—SPECIFIC PERFORMANCE — LACHES—MUTUALITY—DEFINITENESS OF DESCRIPTION.

1. Where no effort was made to enforce a contract of sale of a right of way till the death of the vendor, a year and half after the execution of the contract, and no suit was brought to enforce it till more than five years after its execution, this delay, unexplained, is such laches as will defeat specific performance.

2. Where, by a written contract, one agreed to convey a right of way whenever the other party should demand it and tender the agreed price, the contract was lacking in mutuality, so that specific performance cannot be enforced.

3. A contract for the conveyance of a right of way for a railway track—"said tract, after it intersects the west line of the land of said B. in section 3, T. 2, N. R. 8 W., to run in a southerly or southeasterly direction, following the ravine along and southeasterly over the west half of the S. W. ¼ to where it intersects the north line of section 10"—is too indefinite in its description of the land to be enforced by specific performance.

Appeal from Circuit Court, St. Clair County; B. R. Burroughs, Judge.

Bill by the Lumaghi Coal Company against John Bauer and others. From a decree in favor of complainant, defendant Bauer appeals. Reversed.

¶ 2. See Specific Performance, vol. 44, Cent. Dig. §§ 89, 90, 95.

Messick & Crow, for appellant. Winkelmann & Baer, for appellee.

WILKIN, J. Appellee filed its bill in the circuit court of St. Clair county, against appellant and others to enforce the specific performance of a written contract entered into by George Bauer and Conrad Rupprecht. The bill alleges that on October 15, 1897, Bauer and Rupprecht entered into the following contract, to wit:

"It is agreed between George Bauer, of St. Clair county and State of Illinois, party of the first part, and Conrad Rupprecht, of the county and State aforesaid, party of the second part, as follows: Said party of the second part is desirous of having a railroad switch or track lead from a point on the Vandalia railroad track near where said railroad intersects the Collinsville and Caseyville wagon road, in the northeast quarter of section 4, T. 2, N. R. 8 W., said track, after it intersects the west line of the land of said Bauer in section 3, T. 2, N. R. 8 W., to run in a southerly or southeasterly direction, following the ravine along and southeasterly over the west half of the S. W. ¼ said section 3, T. 2, N. R. 8 W., over the land of said George Bauer to where it intersects the north line of section 10, T. 2, N. R. 8 W., said N. W. ¼ belonging to the heirs of Leon Hoereth, in which lands said party of the second part and his wife have an interest, and the object and intention of said switch or track being to connect with a coal mine, which it is intended hereafter to open and operate on the lands of said heirs of Leon Hoereth. Now, in consideration that said party of the first part shall grant and give the right of way, with sufficient ground to build said switch or railroad track, fifty feet wide, if deemed necessary by the party of the second part, his heirs and assigns, when said Conrad Rupprecht shall demand the same in writing, or whatever any other person or persons or corporation to be named in writing by said Conrad Rupprecht or his heirs and assigns shall demand the same in writing from the said party of the first part or his assigns and heirs, and whatever said Conrad Rupprecht, his heirs and assigns, or any person or persons or corporation named by him or his heirs and assigns shall pay as cash for such privilege or right of way the sum of three hundred dollars ($300) in advance, then the said party of the first part hereby agrees and binds himself to give and convey, by sufficient deed, the said right of way over and through the premises above described and of the width aforesaid, if deemed necessary by the party of the second part or his heirs and assigns. But in no event shall any conveyance be made or signed by said Bauer, or his heirs and assigns, until the consideration money for said right of way be first paid, or his heirs and assigns. And it is further agreed that on all crossings along said right of way the same shall be protected by suitable cattle guards.

"Witness our hands and seals this 15th day of October, 1897. George Bauer. [Seal.] Conrad Rupprecht. [Seal.]

"Witness: Benjamin Boneau."

The bill further avers that the said George Bauer, without having executed said deed, died March 14, 1899, owning the lands described in said tract, and leaving as his only heirs at law the appellant herein, John Bauer, and Maggie Bertrand, and that a coal mine is about to be opened on the premises described in said contract, and that on March 1, 1903, the complainant demanded, in writing, that said defendants make conveyance of said right of way as provided in said contract, and tendered the money for the same, which was refused. The prayer is for a specific performance of said contract.

The defendants filed their answer, setting up several defenses against the contract—among others, alleging that appellee and its grantors have slept on their rights, if they ever had any, and that their claim has become stale, and not the proper subject for relief in a court of equity; also that the agreement is void as a contract, for want of mutuality in rights and remedies. Upon a hearing before the chancellor upon bill, answer, replication, and evidence, a decree was entered for complainant, enforcing the performance of the contract, and from that decree this appeal has been perfected.

There are several errors assigned by appellant, but a consideration of two of them will effectually dispose of the case.

The specific performance of a contract is not a matter of absolute right, even upon a case made by the proofs, but depends upon well-understood rules and principles applicable to the facts and circumstances of each case. The contract, in itself, must be reasonable, fair, just, mutual, certain, and unambiguous. Barrett v. Geisinger, 148 Ill. 98, 35 N. E. 354; Koch v. National Union Building Ass'n, 137 Ill. 497, 27 N. E. 530; Gould v. Elgin City Banking Co., 136 Ill. 60, 26 N. E. 497. And, after these requirements have been established, whether or not the performance of the contract shall be decreed rests in the sound discretion of the chancellor. Chicago, Burlington & Quincy Railroad Co. v. Reno, 113 Ill. 39; Beach v. Dyer, 93 Ill. 295. The discretion cannot be arbitrarily exercised, but must be governed by legal rules and principles. Phillips v. South Park Com'rs, 119 Ill. 626, 10 N. E. 230; Allen v. Woodruff, 96 Ill. 11. Nevertheless the court has the right, and it is its duty, to consider all the facts and circumstances of the case in hand, and do equity between the parties. It is always the duty of a party seeking to enforce a contract specifically to act with diligence in the performance of the same on his part, and it is the well-settled doctrine of courts of equity, both in England and this country, that great delay of either party, unexplained, in the performance of the terms of a contract, or in not prosecuting their rights under it by filing a bill, or in not prosecuting a suit for such performance with diligence when instituted, constitutes such laches as will forbid the interference of a court of equity, and so amount, for the purpose of a specific performance, to an abandonment of the contract. Hatch v. Kizer, 140 Ill. 583, 30 N. E. 605, 33 Am. St. Rep. 258; Fry on Specific Per. 218; Hough v. Coughlan, 41 Ill. 130. The evidence in this record shows that the contract was made October 15, 1897. George Bauer, one of the contracting parties, died March 14, 1899. The bill to enforce the contract was not filed until the September term, 1903, of the circuit court. There is nothing whatever in the record to explain the delay, but the evidence is wholly silent on that point. The parties to the contract did nothing towards its enforcement until after the death of George Bauer, a year and a half after it was executed. The contract was not assigned by Rupprecht to the appellee until 1902. In the absence of evidence to explain this long delay, we think, under the foregoing authorities, appellee and his assignor have been guilty of such laches as will, in law, defeat a specific performance.

The contract is also lacking in mutuality. It is said in Beach on Modern Law of Contracts (volume 2, § 885): "As a general rule, specific performance will not be decreed in any case where mutuality of obligation and remedy does not exist." And in a note to this text it is said: "The general principle is that, where the contract is incapable of being enforced against one party, that party is equally incapable of enforcing it against the other." In Beard v. Linthicum, 1 Md. Ch. 345, Chancellor Johnson held "that, if one of the parties is not bound or is not able to perform his part of the contract, he cannot call upon the court to compel specific performance by the opposite party." And in the subsequent case of Duvall v. Myers, 2 Md. Ch. 401, the same judge said, in substance, "that the right to the specific execution of a contract depends upon whether the agreement is obligatory upon both parties, so that, upon the application of either against the other, the court can compel a specific performance." We quoted the above authorities with approval in the case of Tryce v. Dittus, 199 Ill. 189, 65 N. E. 220. Also, see 22 Am. & Eng. Ency. of Law (1st Ed.) p. 1019. One cannot read the contract in this case without being impressed with the fact that it was so worded that if, in the future, the coal business should prove profitable, and Rupprecht or his assigns could gain an advantage by taking an easement, then they would have a right to demand it, and could compel Bauer to convey, but, if the coal business did not open up favorably, and it would be no advantage to Rupprecht, then Bauer would have no right to compel a specific performance, and would be powerless to force Rupprecht to do anything. It was therefore lacking in that element of mutuality required under the decisions above quoted, and therefore could not be specifically enforced in a court of equity. The contract, bill, and written demand made by appellee are also very indefinite as to the description of the land required by the right of way; and for this reason, also, the contract could not be enforced in a court of equity, even though appellee had been diligent in enforcing its rights.

For these reasons, the decree of the circuit court will be reversed, and the cause remanded, with directions to dismiss the bill. Reversed and remanded, with directions.

(209 Ill. 201)

SIEGEL, COOPER & CO. v. NORTON.

(Supreme Court of Illinois. April 20, 1904.)

NEGLIGENCE — PROXIMATE CAUSE—CONTRIBUTORY NEGLIGENCE—EVIDENCE—SUFFICIENCY—INSTRUCTIONS.

1. Where defendant's superintendent knew that plaintiff was going to work in an elevator shaft, plastering the same, and told the operatives of the elevator not to run it below a certain story, but they did so, whereby the car struck and injured plaintiff, defendant was guilty of negligence.

2. Such negligence was the proximate cause of the injury.

3. In an action for injuries sustained by plaintiff while plastering in an elevator shaft in defendant's building, because of the elevator having been negligently lowered to the point where he was at work, plaintiff's employer, the contractor for the plastering, testified that defendant's superintendent assured him it would be safe to work in the shaft. *Held*, that such testimony was not objectionable because of the fact that the superintendent's statement was not made in the presence of plaintiff.

4. Plaintiff, who was employed by one who had contracted to do plastering in an elevator shaft of defendant's building, while engaged in doing the plastering, was injured because the elevator was allowed to descend below a certain story, contrary, according to plaintiff's evidence, to directions which defendant's superintendent had given to the operatives of the elevator, and in an action for the injuries the operative of the elevator testified that the first two or three trips he stopped at the story below which the elevator should not have been allowed to pass. *Held*, that an objection to a question put by defendant to the operative as to why he stopped at that story was properly sustained, it being immaterial whether he stopped there in obedience to instructions or for some other reason.

5. In an action for injuries sustained by plaintiff while working in an elevator shaft in defendant's building, owing to the elevator having descended and struck him, the question of plaintiff's contributory negligence *held* one for the jury.

6. Where, on appeal, there is nothing appearing in either the record or abstract to indicate that it does not contain all the instructions, and those set out are numbered consecutively, an assignment of error as to an instruction will not be refused consideration merely because there is no statement that no instruction was omitted.

7. Where plaintiff, employed by a contractor for the plastering work in defendant's building, was injured while plastering in an elevator shaft, owing to the elevator operatives allowing it to descend contrary to the instructions of their superintendent, who knew of plaintiff's situation, any negligence on the part of plaintiff's employer in not blocking the elevator shaft would not inure to the benefit of defendant, so as to relieve it from liability.

Appeal from Appellate Court, First District.

Action by Dominick Norton against Siegel, Cooper & Co. From a judgment of the Appellate Court, affirming a judgment in favor of plaintiff, defendant appeals. Affirmed.

O. W. Dynes, for appellant. Edmund S. Cummings, for appellee.

CARTWRIGHT, J. The Appellate Court for the First District affirmed a judgment recovered by appellee in the superior court of Cook county against appellant for damages resulting from a personal injury alleged to have been due to the negligence of appellant. From the judgment of affirmance this appeal was prosecuted.

It is first contended that the trial court erred in ruling on the admission of evidence. The facts which the evidence on the part of the plaintiff tended to prove are substantially as follows: Plaintiff was in the employ of Peter Ray, a contractor, who took the job of patching the plastering on the walls and beams of two elevator shafts in the basement of defendant's department store. In doing the work Ray was an independent contractor, and not an employé of the defendant. The elevators were used for carrying freight, and about three feet above the main floor of the building there was a landing for the delivery of freight into an alley. The distance from the basement floor to the main floor was about 13 feet, and the platform was about 16 feet above the basement floor. Before beginning the work Ray and plaintiff had a talk with William Weber, defendant's superintendent. Weber showed them the places that were to be plastered and patched, and told them that they could stop the elevators from running below the alley landing or main floor while they were working beneath. Ray assented to do the work with that arrangement, and Weber called the boys operating the elevators and told them that the men were going into the elevator shafts to do some patching, and ordered them to run the elevators in accordance with the arrangement while the work was being done. The contractor, Peter Ray, then left, and plaintiff commenced the work, assisted by John Ray, the son of his employer, as helper. The work was completed in one of the elevator shafts, the elevator not running below the alley landing while the work was being done. When the work in that shaft was completed, and plaintiff was going into the second shaft, he and his helper, Ray, told the boy who was running the elevator that they were going in there, and the boy said, "All right." Plaintiff stood on a stepladder while doing the work, and the elevator made two or three trips, stopping at the alley landing above him. The next trip, without any warning or notice, the elevator descended below the alley landing to the main floor, or below, and struck the plaintiff, throwing him to the bottom of the shaft, breaking his hip bone, and otherwise injuring him.

The evidence proved the defendant guilty of negligence which was the proximate cause of the injury, and there was no evidence tending to prove the contrary. The alleged erroneous rulings on the admission of evidence were made on the examination of plaintiff's employer and the boy who ran the elevator. The employer, Ray, testified that Weber assured him it would be perfectly safe to work in the elevator shaft under the arrangement made, and this testimony was objected to because Weber's statement was not made in the presence of plaintiff. The purpose of the testimony was to show the arrangement for stopping the elevator under which Ray set the plaintiff to work, and to prove the negligence of the defendant in disregard of the agreement. It was not necessary that the arrangement should have been made in the presence of the plaintiff. On the examination of the boy who was running the elevator, he testified that he stopped at the alley landing on the first two or three trips, and was then asked by defendant's counsel why he stopped there. An objection to the question was sustained. Counsel for defendant contended that it was material to show whether he stopped there in obedience to instructions or for some other reason, and he now says that he wanted to prove that the boy had loads for the alley landing, and stopped there for that reason. Defendant was not prevented from proving that fact, if it was a fact, but the reasons which actuated the boy in stopping at the alley landing were immaterial. It was the duty of the defendant to operate its elevator in such manner as not to injure the plaintiff while properly working under it in the shaft, and any reasons that existed for stopping at the alley landing on the first two or three trips would afford no justification for the subsequent disregard of duty.

It is also urged that the court should have directed a verdict for the defendant on the ground that plaintiff was not in the exercise of ordinary care for his own safety. The helper, John Ray, testified that just before the accident he cautioned plaintiff that the elevator boy might forget himself; that he saw the elevator coming down, and commenced yelling; that plaintiff did not have a chance to make an answer, but looked up and commenced to yell just before the elevator struck him. The elevator boy testified that he heard the shouting in the shaft and heard the ladder fall. It could not be said, as a matter of law, that the plaintiff, who was working on the stepladder with tools in his hands, had time to get out of the way or could have avoided the injury by the exercise of ordinary care. That question was properly submitted to the jury.

Complaint is also made of the refusal of the court to give two instructions asked by the defendant, the first of which stated that the relation of master and servant did not exist between plaintiff and defendant, and that negligence on the part of plaintiff's employer was not negligence for which the defendant would be liable; and the second stated that if the jury should believe, from the evidence, that the sole cause of the accident was negligence on the part of the employer, the verdict should be not guilty. Counsel for appellee replies that this assignment of error cannot be considered, because the record and abstract do not show that the instructions contained therein are all the instructions given to the jury by the court. We have frequently held that where the abstract does not contain all the instructions given we will not consider an assignment of error on the refusal of an instruction, for the reason that there may have been another covering the point contained in the refused instruction. But that is not the case here. There is nothing appearing in either the record or abstract to indicate that they do not contain all the instructions. In practice, the instructions are usually separate and numbered, together constituting the charge of the court to the jury, and where the record and abstract purport to give the instructions it is not necessary to state that no part of the connected series has been omitted. In this case the instructions given at the instance of each party and the instructions refused are numbered consecutively, and there is nothing indicating that anything is omitted, so that there is no warrant for assuming that there has been any omission. We are of the opinion, however, that these instructions were not based on any evidence in the case, and could not have benefited the defendant if given. It is true that the relation of master and servant did not exist between plaintiff and defendant, and that defendant was not liable for any negligence of plaintiff's employer, but it was responsible for its own negligence, which was proved and not disputed. However negligent plaintiff's employer might have been, his negligence would not have relieved defendant of liability. The ground for insisting that the employer was negligent is that he did not put in a beam or timbers or block the elevator shaft to protect the plaintiff from possible negligence of the defendant. If there were any warrant for saying that the employer was negligent in that respect it would not inure to the benefit of the defendant. The jury could not have found that the sole cause of the accident was negligence on the part of the employer, which would have been in direct contradiction of every fact proved on the trial.

We find no error in the record. The judgment of the Appellate Court is affirmed. Judgment affirmed.

(209 Ill. 432)

JOEST v. ADEL et al.

(Supreme Court of Illinois. April 20, 1904.)

BILL OF REVIEW—PARTITION—FORMER DECREE—VACATION — DEMURRER — DETERMINATION — WAIVER—HOMESTEAD—DOWER — ASSIGNMENT —SALE—CONSENT OF TENANT—DOWER—WAIVER—SOLICITOR'S FEES—APPORTIONMENT.

1. Where defendant demurred to a bill in the nature of a bill of review and also for partition, it was error for the court to render a decree pro confesso against defendant on default, while the demurrer was pending and undisposed of.

2. Where defendant demurred to a bill, his failure to be present at each stage of the subsequent proceedings to see and insist that the issue presented by the demurrer was disposed of did not constitute a waiver thereof.

3. Where a bill was filed in part for the purpose of reviewing and setting aside a former assignment of dower and homestead to defendant, and also for partition, it was error for the court, without entering any order, to reopen the former decree and, without disposing of defendant's homestead and dower rights so previously assigned, to proceed to review the former proceedings and decree of partition.

4. Where a partition decree found that one of the parties was entitled to homestead and dower in the premises, but failed to require the commissioners appointed to make division to set off the homestead, and allot dower if the same could be done consistently with the interests of the parties, and, if not, then to appraise the value of each piece and report the same to the court, as required by Hurd's Rev. St. 1901, c. 106, § 22, the decree was erroneous.

5. Where dower and homestead had been assigned to defendant in certain real estate ordered to be sold under a partition decree, a sale of such property free and clear of defendant's homestead and dower interest, without defendant's written consent, required by Hurd's Rev. St. 1901, c. 106, § 22, was erroneous, though defendant had previously executed a mortgage on the property, in which he had waived his homestead and dower.

6. Where defendant in good faith set up a good defense to a petition in the nature of a bill of review and for partition, it was error for the court to require him to pay a part of the solicitor's fee under Hurd's Rev. St. 1901, c. 106, § 40, relating to partition, and providing that, when the rights of all the parties are properly set forth in the petition, the court shall apportion the costs, including a reasonable solicitor's fee, among the parties in interest, unless the defendants, or some of them, shall interpose a good and substantial defense.

Error to Circuit Court, Monroe County; W. P. Early, Judge.

Bill by Louis Adel and others against Valentine Joest. From a decree in favor of plaintiffs, defendant brings error. Reversed.

Jos. W. Rickert, for plaintiff in error. Winkelmann & Baer, for defendant in error Mehrmann.

WILKIN, J. Christine Joest was the owner in fee of the 80 acres of land involved in this litigation. She and her husband, Valentine Joest, plaintiff in error here, executed two mortgages on the land, one to Ellen Hall and the other to Louis Adelsberger, in each of which they released their homestead and dower rights. Christine died testate on January 15, 1900, leaving, surviving her, her husband, Valentine, and certain children by a former marriage. On August 14, 1900, Valentine, the husband, filed his petition in the circuit court of Monroe county for the assignment of his homestead and dower in said lands, and a decree was therein rendered assigning 50 acres thereof as and for his homestead and 10 acres as and for his dower. On February 10, 1902, the present bill was filed by the devisees of Christine Joest, which was twice amended. The second amended bill was filed on October 7, 1902, and is in the nature of a bill of review, seeking to set aside the decree assigning homestead and dower to plaintiff in error, and for partition, subject to his rights, etc. To that amended bill he filed a demurrer, which the court failed to dispose of, but entered a decree pro confesso against him, ordering partition of the lands, and appointing commissioners for that purpose, but they reported the premises not susceptible of division, and appraised the same at $1,000. Thereupon a decree of sale was entered, in which it was ordered that the land should be sold free of the homestead and dower of plaintiff in error, and out of the proceeds of such sale there should be paid, first, $867.68, being the amount due on the said mortgages, in which Christine and Valentine had released their homestead and dower. The premises were sold for $1,700, and to the master's report of sale plaintiff in error filed exceptions, which were overruled by the court, and a deed thereupon executed to the purchaser. Out of the proceeds of the sale the mortgages were paid off, and the balance remains in the hands of the master in chancery. Valentine Joest prosecutes this writ of error to reverse said decree of partition and sale.

It is first insisted that the court below erred in not ruling on the demurrer of plaintiff in error, and in entering a default against him before the same was disposed of. As already said, the second amended bill was in the nature of a bill of review, and also for partition. It alleged that the decree assigning homestead and dower to plaintiff in error was erroneous, and ought to be reviewed, revised, and set aside, for the reason that no proof was made that Christine Joest was the owner in fee of said real estate, and because of the discovery of new and material evidence in said cause, etc., which said new matter complainants did not know of, and could not by reasonable diligence have known, so as to make proof thereof previous to and at the time of the hearing and pronouncing of said decree. Plaintiff in error's demurrer was to this bill, in which he alleged, as special ground of demurrer, that there was no error in law apparent on the record assigning to him homestead and dower upon his bill of August 14, 1900, and that complainants did not allege in their bill any new matter, discovered since the entry of the former decree, authorizing its reversal or modification. On March 25, 1903, while the demurrer was still pending and undisposed of, the plaintiff in error was defaulted by the court, and a decree pro confesso entered against him, as above stated. This was clearly reversible error. No default could be entered against him while the demurrer was pending and undisposed of. McKinney v. May, 1 Scam. 534; Laflin v. Herrington, 17 Ill. 399; Kankakee & Seneca Railroad Co. v. Horan, 131 Ill. 288, 23 N. E. 621.

It is claimed by defendants in error that plaintiff in error by his silence waived his right to insist upon his demurrer. The position seems to be that it was his duty to see that the demurrer was disposed of, and, failing to do so, it is said he was silent. We do not understand that a party who has presented an issue to the court is required to be present at each stage of the subsequent proceedings to see and insist that that issue be disposed of. Here the defendant, having presented an issue of law, had a right to assume that the court would properly dispose of the same, as was its duty, without entering a default against him, and it was the duty of counsel for the complainants to see that that issue was so disposed of. There is nothing in the record which shows that plaintiff in error did anything to mislead the court or counsel, or that he has in any way estopped himself by acquiescence in the decree below. This error must therefore work a reversal of that decree.

There are, however, other serious defects in the proceedings, proper to be considered and obviated, if another hearing shall be had. The bill was filed, in part, for the purpose of reviewing and setting aside a former decree assigning dower and homestead to the plaintiff in error. Upon such a bill the court, upon opening the former decree, should have affirmed, revised, reversed, or modified the same according to the equities of the parties, but the chancellor, without entering any order to reopen the decree, proceeded to review the former proceedings, and decreed the partition, heard the cause, and disposed of the rights of the parties without making any order whatever disposing of plaintiff's homestead and dower rights previously assigned him. In other words, the division and partition of the premises were decreed in total disregard of such former assignment. Manifestly, this was error. The decree should have first granted leave to reopen and review the former decree, and then, by proper orders, indicated to what extent, if any, the rights and interests of the parties should be affected by such review. Adamski v. Wieczorek, 170 Ill. 373, 48 N. E. 951.

The decree of partition, as rendered, finds that Valentine Joest is entitled to homestead and dower in the premises, and, in appointing commissioners to make the division and partition among the parties, it fails to require them, before making such division and partition, to set off the homestead and allot dower in the premises, if the same can be done consistently with the interests of the parties, and, if not, then to appraise the value of each piece, and a true report make to the court. The failure to so order the commissioners was a violation of section 22 of the partition act (Hurd's Rev. St. 1901, c. 106, § 22), as construed in Hickenbotham v. Blackledge, 54 Ill. 318.

The decree of sale orders the premises sold free and clear of the homestead and dower of plaintiff in error, without his consent in writing having been given to such sale. This was also error, and in violation of section 32 of chapter 106, supra, and contrary to the decisions of this court in Cribben v. Cribben, 136 Ill. 609, 27 N. E. 70, Drake v. Merkle, 153 Ill. 318, 38 N. E. 654, and Merritt v. Merritt, 97 Ill. 243.

In answer to the last proposition, it is insisted that the dower and homestead of plaintiff in error was duly and properly released in the mortgages executed by him, and, consequently, the court committed no error in ordering the premises sold free and clear of such incumbrance. If the proceeding had been to foreclose either or both of said mortgages, there could be no doubt as to the propriety of the court granting an order of sale free and clear of the estate so released, but then plaintiff in error would be entitled to his equity of redemption. This, however, is not a foreclosure proceeding, but for partition, with allegations in the bill seeking a review of former proceedings under which homestead and dower had once been assigned, and it was clearly erroneous for the decree now before us to order a sale without the consent in writing of plaintiff in error.

It is further urged that the chancellor erred in allowing a solicitor's fee of $75 to the complainants' solicitor. Section 40 of chapter 106, entitled "Partition," provides that, "when the rights and interests of all the parties in interest are properly set forth in the petition or bill, the court shall apportion the costs, including the reasonable solicitor's fee, among the parties in interest in the suit, so that each party shall pay his or her equitable portion thereof, unless the defendants, or some one of them, shall interpose a good and substantial defense to said bill or petition. In such case the party or parties making such substantial defense shall recover their costs against the complainants according to equity." There is nothing in the record to show that plaintiff in error did not urge his defense to the bill of complainants in good faith, and we think it was error to require him to pay any part of said solicitor's fee.

The decree will be reversed, and the cause remanded to the circuit court for further proceedings in accordance with the views herein expressed. Reversed and remanded.

(209 Ill. 461)

PEOPLE ex rel. BIBB v. MAYOR, ETC., OF CITY OF ALTON.

(Supreme Court of Illinois. April 20, 1904.)

SCHOOLS—RACE DISCRIMINATION—EVIDENCE—SUFFICIENCY—VERDICT—MANDAMUS—REFUSAL OF WRIT—PRACTICE.

1. In mandamus proceedings by a colored parent to compel the admission of his children to a public school without discrimination on account of color, a verdict finding that there had been no discrimination *held* to be without evidence to support it.

2. Where a verdict is unsupported by the evidence, it is the duty of the court to set it aside and award a new trial.

3. In mandamus proceedings by a colored parent to compel the admission of his children to a public school, the fact that the relator's children had been kept out of school so long by illegal discrimination that the writ would do them no good is not sufficient ground for refusing to enforce the law.

4. Where no motion was made in the trial court to set aside a verdict for respondents in mandamus proceedings commenced in the Supreme Court, and referred to a circuit court for trial on issues of fact, the relator is not entitled to a peremptory writ, though the averments of the petition are clearly proved, requiring the Supreme Court to set aside the verdict.

Original petition filed in the Supreme Court, on the relation of Scott Bibb, for a writ of mandamus against the mayor and common council of the city of Alton, to compel them to admit relator's children to a public school, without discrimination on account of color. The issues of fact were sent to the circuit court of Madison county for trial, and a verdict in favor of defendants on the trial thereof was certified to the Supreme Court. Verdict set aside, and new trial ordered.

For former opinions, see 54 N. E. 421; 61 N. E. 1077, 56 L. R. A. 95.

John J. Brenholt, for relator. E. B. Glass and L. D. Yager, for respondents.

CARTWRIGHT, J. The relator, Scott Bibb, a colored citizen of the city of Alton, instituted this proceeding for a writ of mandamus requiring the respondents, the mayor and members of the common council of the city of Alton, to allow the children of the relator to be admitted to the Washington School, or the most convenient of the public schools of the city and school district of Alton to which they have the right of admission, without excluding either of them on account of their color or descent. The issues of fact in the case were certified to the circuit court of Madison county for trial, and a verdict in favor of respondents upon the first trial, certified to this court, was set aside on account of erroneous rulings of the circuit court in excluding competent and material evidence offered by the relator; and the circuit court was directed to submit the issues to another jury, and to proceed in accordance with the views then expressed. People v. Mayor of Alton, 179 Ill. 615, 54 N. E. 421. The issues were again tried, and a second verdict in favor of respondents was certified to this court, and was set aside for error of the circuit court in giving an instruction and submitting a special finding. The circuit court was directed to again submit the issues to another jury, and to proceed in accordance with the views expressed by this court. People v. Mayor of Alton, 193 Ill. 309, 61 N. E. 1077, 56 L. R. A. 95. A full statement of the case and the facts will be found in the opinions heretofore filed. The issues have been tried again, and a verdict in favor of the respondents has again been certified to this court.

The evidence upon the last trial was substantially the same as upon previous trials. It was proved by the relator, without dispute or contradiction, that his children had been attending the Washington School, and that when the school opened in September, 1897, they and all other colored children in the city of Alton were excluded from that school and all other schools except the Douglas and Lovejoy Schools; that policemen of the city of Alton, who were under the control and subject to the direction of the mayor and common council, were stationed at the doors of all the schoolhouses except the Douglas and Lovejoy Schools; that the police officers were in uniform, with their stars, and armed with policemen's clubs, and acting in their capacity as policemen; that the white and colored children received cards assigning them to certain schools; that only colored children received cards directing them to the Douglas and Lovejoy Schools, and only white children received cards assigning them to the other schools; that the policemen stationed at the said schools forcibly excluded the colored children and prevented their entering such schools; that the children formed in line outside of the school buildings, and, as they came to enter the schoolhouses, the policemen separated them, driving the colored children away and telling them to go to the schools they were assigned to, pushing them out of the line or off from the steps, and allowing the white children to go in; that this was continued for two or three weeks; and that the relator's children were assigned to the Lovejoy School, more than a mile farther from his residence than the Washington School, which they had attended. There was no attempt whatever to disprove such facts, but there was evidence in behalf of the relator of statements of teachers and officials of the city showing their intention to exclude colored children from schools attended by white children, which was contradicted. There was evidence for the relator that teachers said they were ordered not to allow colored children to attend their schools, and were not allowed to teach colored children; that policemen said that they were told by their superiors not to allow children to go in without a permit; that the mayor had told them to do as they did; and also evidence

¶ 2. See New Trial, vol. 37, Cent. Dig. § 135.

that the mayor said he would make the niggers go to the schools built for them, if it took the whole police force. Those persons, with one accord, denied that they ever made any of the remarks attributed to them, showing their intention; and a witness for the defendants, who had been city treasurer, postmaster, and alderman, and was a member of the city council when the ordinance abolishing the school districts and putting them all into one district was passed, testified that, at the time said ordinance was passed, "there was nothing said about a conspiracy by the mayor or council, in changing the ordinance, to exclude the colored children of Alton." The respondents confined themselves to evidence that they had not declared their intention to violate the statute of the state, or made a record of their illegal acts in disregard of the law, and such evidence had no tendency to prove that the intention clearly manifested by their acts did not exist. Whether the denials were true, or were due to failing memory, or to some other cause or motive, the fact, if it is a fact, that the intention was not declared, does not in any manner affect the rights of the parties. The acts proved manifested the intention of the parties, and afford a sure and reliable guide as to its character, regardless of the question whether they said they were going to violate the law or not. It would be incredible that the police would do what they did without the direction of their superiors to whom they were amenable, or that their acts, continued for the length of time they were, could have been without the direction and approval of the respondents, or that there could have been any other object than the exclusion of the colored children from the public schools, with the exception of the Douglas and Lovejoy Schools. Counsel for respondents can scarcely be serious in insisting that there is no evidence of any plan to discriminate, or of any discrimination, against any colored child. They cannot suppose that the court would be so simple and credulous as to adopt such a view. Evidence of the character contained in this record would be accepted by any impartial juror as conclusive evidence of an intention even in the gravest and most serious offense involving life or liberty, and the verdict can only be accounted for as a product of passion or prejudice. It is contrary to all the facts proved, and absolutely without support in the evidence. In such case, where the verdict clearly appears to be unsupported by the evidence, it is the duty of the court to set it aside and to award a new trial. People v. Town of Waynesville, 88 Ill. 469.

It is urged by respondents that relator's children are now nearly grown, and that they have been out of school so long that the writ will do them no good, and it should be denied for that reason. We do not regard the fact that there has been a denial of their legal rights for such a length of time as a sufficient ground for refusing to enforce the law.

Counsel for the relator urges that a peremptory writ of mandamus should be awarded on the ground that the evidence in the record shows the relator to be entitled to it. It is true that the averments of the petition were clearly proved, that there was no evidence tending to prove the contrary, and that the verdict was against the evidence. In that condition of the evidence, the relator might have moved the circuit court to direct a verdict in his favor, which doubtless the court would have done. The issues were sent to the circuit court for trial, in conformity with the practice governing the trial of issues of fact in actions at law before a jury, and such a direction would have been in accordance with such practice. In the present condition of the record, the verdict must be set aside and a new trial granted.

The verdict certified to this court is set aside, and the circuit court is directed to submit the issues to another jury, and to proceed in accordance with the views expressed in this opinion and the previous opinions filed in this case. Verdict set aside and new trial ordered.

(209 Ill. 261)

SPRINGER v. LIPSIS.

(Supreme Court of Illinois. April 20, 1904.)

CHATTEL MORTGAGES — NOTES — VALIDITY AS AGAINST SUBSEQUENT LIENORS—APPEAL.

1. The judgment of the Appellate Court is conclusive as to questions of fact.

2. If a mortgagee of chattels takes possession of the property before any other right or lien attaches, his title under the mortgage is good against everybody, although the mortgage was neither acknowledged nor recorded.

3. The fact that a note secured by a chattel mortgage does not state upon its face that it is so secured does not render it void as between the parties, if possession of the mortgaged property is taken before the lien of a third party attaches.

4. Where it is claimed on appeal that evidence was improperly admitted, but the evidence is not pointed out, or reference made to the abstract where such evidence may be found, the court will not examine the entire abstract to ascertain if any evidence was improperly admitted.

Appeal from Appellate Court, First District.

Action by Samuel R. Lipsis against Warren Springer and another. From a judgment of the Appellate Court (110 Ill. App. 109) affirming a judgment for plaintiff, defendant Springer appeals. Affirmed.

W. N. Gemmill, for appellant. David R. Levy and Douglas C. Gregg, for appellee.

RICKS, J. This is an action in trover brought by Samuel R. Lipsis, appellee, against Warren Springer, appellant, and Charles A. McDonald. The action grew out of a lease made by appellant to Louis Hammerslough for certain rooms at Nos. 214 and 216 South

¶ 2. See Chattel Mortgages, vol. 9, Cent. Dig. § 265.

Clinton street, Chicago. The lease was to continue from the 15th day of June, 1896, to the 30th day of November, 1897. On the 21st day of May, 1896, Hammerslough, with the consent of appellant, assigned the lease to the Midland Printing Ink Works, and on October 14, 1897, there was due appellant rent in the sum of $229.20 under the terms of the lease; and, being unable to collect the same, he levied a distress warrant, and, after obtaining judgment, advertised and sold all the personal property in said building, which appellant claimed was owned by said company, and at the sale, which was conducted by McDonald, appellant purchased the property for the sum of $200. It appears that on December 21, 1896, the Midland Printing Ink Works gave a chattel mortgage on all the personal property in said building to appellee to secure a promissory note for $2,000, which appellee held against the company; and it is claimed by appellee that on October 1, 1897, he took possession of the property through his agent, Mr. Rosenwald. It is insisted by appellant that the mortgage and note were both void, the mortgage being made in Kansas City, out of the state, and acknowledged by a notary public; and the note did not state upon its face that it was secured by a chattel mortgage. During the pendency of the suit, McDonald died, and an order was entered suggesting his death, and directing the cause to abate as to him. The cause was tried before a jury, resulting in a verdict for plaintiff for the sum of $1,-035. An appeal was prosecuted to the Appellate Court, where the judgment was affirmed, and a further appeal is prosecuted to this court.

No objection is raised to the giving or refusal of instructions, except the refusal of the court to give appellant's peremptory instruction at the close of all the evidence.

The first and main question argued by appellant is as to the sufficiency of the instrument purporting to be a chattel mortgage; but, under the view we take, it makes no difference whether the chattel mortgage was perfect in every respect or not, so it was good between the parties, as the main question in the case is, who had possession of the goods on October 14, 1896, at the time of the levy of the distress warrant. It is not denied by appellant that his claim would not become a lien until after the levy of the distress warrant, and it being a question of fact for the jury as to who was in possession at the time of the levy of the distress warrant, and the jury, under proper instructions, having found for appellee, and that finding having been sustained by the Appellate Court, the question cannot be considered by us. It makes no difference whether the mortgage was properly acknowledged or in proper form, if possession had been taken of the property by a person having a lien. If a mortgagee takes possession of mortgaged property before any other right or lien attaches, his title under the mortgage is good against everybody, although it is neither acknowledged nor recorded, or if the record be ineffectual by reason of any irregularity. First Nat. Bank v. Barse Live Stock Commission Co., 198 Ill. 232, 64 N. E. 1097. Appellant acknowledged that he knew of appellee being in possession, and wrote Mr. Rosenwald a letter notifying him that he would hold him responsible for the rent; the letter being as follows: "Chicago, October 11, 1897. Mr. M. H. Rosenwald, Att'y in fact for S. R. Lipsis, Kansas City—Dear Sir: You are hereby notified that I will hold you responsible for rent of the premises 214–216 S. Clinton St., under lease from me by Midland Printing Ink Company, during the time you are in possession. Yours truly, Warren Springer, Per Gallup."

It is next argued that the note is void for the reason it does not state upon its face that it is secured by a chattel mortgage; but, as between the parties, it was not necessary for the note to state this upon its face, if possession of the goods was in fact taken before the lien of a third party attached. Sellers v. Thomas, 185 Ill. 384, 57 N. E. 10.

It is next insisted that the damages awarded are excessive, but this is not a matter for investigation by us, as the judgment of the Appellate Court is final upon this question.

It is next contended that the court erred in admitting the mortgage in evidence for the reason that it never had the effect of establishing a lien in favor of the mortgagee; but we do not agree with appellant upon this proposition, as the mortgage was good between the parties, and it was proper evidence to prove the indebtedness and the contract between the parties to the mortgage.

It is also stated by the appellant in his brief that the court improperly admitted evidence concerning the value of the property in question, and that witnesses were permitted to testify as to the value of the property who knew nothing about it whatever; but no such evidence is pointed out, or reference made to the abstract where such evidence may be found. Under these circumstances, we will not examine the entire abstract in order to ascertain if any improper evidence was admitted.

After a careful examination of the record, we are satisfied that there is evidence tending to support the judgment, and the judgment of the Appellate Court will therefore be affirmed. Judgment affirmed.

(209 Ill. 42)

METROPOLITAN LIFE INS. CO. v. PEOPLE.

(Supreme Court of Illinois. April 20, 1904.)

LIFE INSURANCE—REBATE OF PREMIUM—STATUTORY PENALTY—COMPANY'S LIABILITY FOR ACT OF AGENT—AMENDMENT OF DECLARATION—LIMITATIONS—JUDGMENT AGAINST DEFENDANT SERVED.

1. A life insurance company is liable for the statutory penalty denounced by Laws 1891, p. 107, for permitting discrimination between insurants, though the rebate of premium is allowed by its agent without its knowledge, and in violation of its instructions.

2. A life insurance company and its assistant superintendent were sued for the statutory penalty denounced against life insurance companies and their agents, jointly and severally, by Laws 1891, p. 107, prohibiting discrimination between insurants, the suit being begun within two years of the rebate of premium relied on. The declaration alleged the name of the insured, the date of the policy, and the allowance of the rebate. On the trial, and more than two years after the rebate, the state amended by substituting the name of the local agent for that of the assistant superintendent. *Held* that, as the name of the agent was not a matter of essential description of the offense, the amendment did not change the cause of action so as to enable the company to plead limitations.

3. Laws 1891, p. 107, denounces a penalty against life insurance companies and their agents, jointly and severally, for permitting discrimination between insurants. Practice Act, § 9 (Hurd's Rev. St. 1899, c. 110, § 10), authorizes a plaintiff to take judgment on a defendant served, and have the cause continued as to a defendant not served. *Held*, that it was proper to render judgment against an insurance company in an action for the penalty, and continue the case against its agent, who, though a party, had not been served.

Error to Appellate Court, Fourth District.

Action by the people against the Metropolitan Life Insurance Company. Judgment of the Appellate Court, Fourth District (106 Ill. 516), affirming a judgment for plaintiff, and defendant brings error. Affirmed.

Whitnel & Gillespie, for plaintiff in error.
David J. Cowan, for the People.

CARTWRIGHT, J. The state's attorney of Jackson county brought an action of debt in the name of the people of the state of Illinois, in the circuit court of said county, against the Metropolitan Life Insurance Company and M. M. Maddox, to recover the statutory penalty for a violation of the act in force July 1, 1891 (Laws 1891, p. 107), prohibiting any life insurance company from making or permitting any discrimination between insurants of the same class and equal expectation of life. The declaration contained five counts, and charged that the defendant the Metropolitan Life Insurance Company was a life insurance company incorporated under the laws of the state of New York and doing business in this state; that the defendant M. M. Maddox was an agent of said company; and that the said defendants, in writing a life insurance policy on the life of Otis E. Harvick, made and permitted an unjust discrimination by paying and allowing to the insured a special rebate of a premium in the sum of $8.41. Defendants appeared, and filed a plea of nil debet. The cause was submitted to the court for trial without a jury, and it was proved at the trial that M. M. Maddox, of Mound City, Ill., was an assistant superintendent of the insurance company; that P. A. Johnson was an agent of the company, under Maddox, at Vienna, Ill.; that Maddox and Johnson negotiated with Otis E. Harvick, of Vienna, for insurance; that Harvick agreed to take two policies—one on his own life and another on the life of his mother; that the policy on the life of the mother was not issued, and Harvick thereupon refused to take the one issued on his own life; and that, after Maddox had left, Johnson arranged with Harvick to accept the policy and pay $10 premium, and the balance, $8.41, was rebated. The premium was $18.41, of which the agent was to receive $11.05 and the insurance company $7.36. Johnson accounted to the company for $7.36, to which it was entitled. Agents of the insurance company were not authorized to allow any rebate, and the ratebook issued by the company prohibited rebates. At the conclusion of the evidence leave was given the plaintiff to amend the declaration by striking out the name of M. M. Maddox and inserting the name of P. A. Johnson. The alleged rebate occurred more than two years prior to the amendment, and the insurance company again filed its plea of nil debet and a plea of the statute of limitations of two years. Plaintiff demurred to the plea of the statute of limitations, and the demurrer was sustained. The insurance company then submitted propositions of law to the effect that, if the rebate was allowed by an agent without the knowledge and consent of the company, and the company had not ratified the act, it would not be liable; that there could be no recovery for any rebate allowed by P. A. Johnson, and that there could be no recovery for any such rebate by P. A. Johnson more than two years prior to the amendment of the declaration. These propositions were refused by the court, and exception was taken to the ruling. There was no appearance by the defendant Johnson, and, the court not having acquired jurisdiction of him, the cause was continued as to him. The court found the insurance company guilty, and entered judgment against it for $500 and costs. From this judgment the insurance company appealed to the Appellate Court for the Fourth District, where the judgment was affirmed, and the writ of error in this case was sued out to review the judgment of the Appellate Court.

It is first contended that the court erred in not holding to be the law the proposition that if the rebate was allowed by an agent without the knowledge and consent of the plaintiff in error, and it had not ratified the act, it would not be liable. The contrary of this proposition was decided in the cases of

Franklin Life Ins. Co. v. People, 200 Ill. 594, 66 N. E. 378, and Id., 200 Ill. 619, 66 N. E. 379. The suit, although civil in form, was brought for a penalty for a violation of public law, and was, in effect, a criminal prosecution. The general rule is, as contended by counsel, that a principal is not liable criminally for an act of his agent committed without express or implied authority; but there have always been well-recognized exceptions to the rule, such as violations of the revenue laws, the creation or maintenance of nuisances, or the publication of libels. Well-recognized exceptions arise under police regulations prohibiting acts hurtful to the comfort, welfare, and safety of society, such as the adulteration of food and drink, the sale of intoxicating liquor in violation of law (Noecker v. People, 91 Ill. 494), or a failure to stop a train at a railroad crossing (Indianapolis & St. Louis Railroad Co. v. People, 91 Ill. 452). In such cases to give immunity to the principal would be to undermine and practically destroy the protection afforded to the people in general by the laws. The nature of the insurance business and the interest of the public in it are such as to subject it to regulation under the police power, and the statute which prohibits discrimination in favor of individuals between insurants of the same class and with equal expectation of life is a valid exercise of that power. 22 Am. & Eng. Ency. of Law (2d Ed.) 933. A corporation can only act through an agent, and the act of the agent within the scope of the business intrusted to him is the act of the principal. If there is a violation of the statute, the law wisely throws the responsibility for the act upon the corporation, which has the best opportunity to prevent it; and it is liable whether it has authorized the act or not.

It is next argued that the court erred in sustaining the demurrer to the plea of the statute of limitations and refusing the proposition of law that there could be no recovery, under the amended declaration, for an offense more than two years prior to the amendment. The question whether Johnson could have pleaded the statute of limitations is not now involved, but, if he could, the plea is a personal privilege and defense, which can be availed of only by the person for whose benefit the statute inures, or such other person as stands in his place or stead. Fish v. Farwell, 160 Ill. 236, 43 N. E. 367. A mere change in a party to a suit does not, of itself, change the cause of action or ground of recovery; and, unless the cause of action is a new one, the amended declaration is not subject to the statute of limitations. Thomas v. Fame Ins. Co., 108 Ill. 91. So far as plaintiff in error is concerned, the suit was begun within the time allowed by the statute, and, unless the amendment introduced a new cause of action, the demurrer was properly sustained. The question whether a new cause of action was introduced, or whether the identity of the original cause of action was preserved, is to be determined as a question of law by an inspection of the original and amended declaration. The statute declares that the insurance company and agent shall be jointly and severally subject to the penalty, and the charge in the original and amended declaration was that plaintiff in error and its agent, in writing a policy of insurance on the life of Otis E. Harvick on January 13, 1900, allowed to the said Harvick a rebate of $8.41. If the suit had merely been dismissed as to Maddox, or the averment as to him or his agency had been stricken out, the declaration would still have stated a good cause of action against plaintiff in error. The discontinuance as to Maddox and substitution of Johnson did not make the cause of action a new or different one, unless the name of the agent was a matter of essential description of the offense, and we do not think that was so. The name of the agent did not in any manner define, qualify, or limit the cause of action or the offense. The amended declaration did not present a different cause of action, and the demurrer was properly sustained, and the proposition of law refused.

After the amendment, the court, having no jurisdiction of Johnson, continued the cause as to him, and rendered judgment against the plaintiff in error, and it is insisted that the judgment was erroneous on that account. The action was civil in form, and was governed by the practice in civil cases. Section 9 of the practice act (Hurd's Rev. St. 1899, c. 110, § 10) authorizes a plaintiff to proceed to judgment against a defendant on whom process is served, and to have the cause continued as to a defendant not served.

The judgment of the Appellate Court is affirmed. Judgment affirmed.

(209 Ill. 176)

FUGMAN et al. v. JIRI WASHINGTON BUILDING & LOAN ASS'N.

(Supreme Court of Illinois. April 20, 1904.)

MORTGAGES—ACKNOWLEDGMENT—NOTARY PUBLIC—STATUTES—RETROACTIVE EFFECT—VESTED RIGHTS.

1. An acknowledgment of a trust deed containing a release of homestead before a notary who is a stockholder and director in the beneficiary corporation is void, and creates no lien on the homestead estate.

2. Act May 15, 1903 (Laws 1903, p. 120), providing that deeds, mortgages, etc., wherein a corporation was grantor or grantee or mortgagor or mortgagee in instruments which have been duly acknowledged before a notary public, shall be adjudged by the courts as legally acknowledged, notwithstanding the acknowledgments were taken before a notary who was at the time a stockholder or officer of the corporation, has no retrospective operation, as against the holder of a lien acquired before the act was passed; and hence the beneficiary in a trust deed validly acknowledged after the acknowledgment of a former trust deed before a stockholder and di-

¶ 1. See Acknowledgment, vol. 1, Cent. Cent. § 109.

rector in the beneficiary, but before the passage of the act, is entitled to priority over the first trust deed.

Error to Superior Court, Cook County; Jesse Holdom, Judge.

Action by the Jiri Washington Building & Loan Association against Jacob Fugman and others. From a judgment for plaintiff, defendant Fugman brings error. Reversed.

George F. Barrett, for plaintiff in error. Charles Vesely and Charles T. Farson, for defendant in error.

CARTWRIGHT, J. On July 20, 1896, Auguste Peters was the owner of a lot in Cook county of the value of less than $1,000, which she occupied, with her husband, Heinrich Peters, as a homestead; and on that day said Auguste Peters and Heinrich Peters, her husband, executed their trust deed to John Stropnicky, trustee, to secure the payment to the Jiri Washington Building & Loan Association of an indebtedness of $700 of said Heinrich Peters for money loaned. The trust deed contained a release of the homestead estate in the body and acknowledgment, but it was acknowledged before John Pecha, a notary public who was a stockholder and director in the corporation thereby secured. For that reason the trust deed did not become a lien on the homestead estate. Afterward, on August 1, 1896, said Auguste Peters and Heinrich Peters, her husband, executed a trust deed to Charles Loughridge, trustee, to secure the payment of their notes, amounting to $460, payable to Henry Schwartz. This trust deed contained a release of homestead, and was acknowledged so as to release the homestead estate and become a valid lien thereon. In the first week of November, 1896, Jacob Fugman purchased the notes secured by this trust deed for $460. Auguste Peters and Heinrich Peters occupied the lot as a homestead until July 24, 1901, when they left it. On February 27, 1902, the building and loan association filed its bill in the superior court of Cook county to foreclose the trust deed securing it, and made Jacob Fugman a party defendant, with others. Fugman answered the bill, alleging the existence of the homestead estate, and that the trust deed sought to be foreclosed created no lien thereon, by reason of the insufficient acknowledgment. Fugman then filed his cross-bill to foreclose the trust deed securing the notes held by him, claiming that said trust deed was a prior and superior lien to the one securing the building and loan association. The cross-bill was answered, and, replications having been filed, the cause was referred to a master in chancery. At the time of the hearing the lot was in possession of persons placed there by Schwartz. The master reported his conclusions that the trust deed securing the building and loan association was a first lien on the lot, and that the trust deed securing Fugman was a second lien, and found the amount due each, with solicitor's fees. The court overruled exceptions of Fugman to the report, and entered a decree of foreclosure in accordance with the report. The writ of error in this case was sued out to bring the record into this court, and in the assignment of errors the validity of the statute passed to legalize acknowledgments taken before officers and stockholders of corporations is questioned.

The principal question determining the priority of liens between the trust deeds was decided in Steger v. Traveling Men's Building & Loan Ass'n (Ill.) 70 N. E. 236. The acknowledgment of the trust deed securing the building and loan association before Pecha, a director and stockholder, and therefore pecuniarily interested in the debt secured, was not authorized by law, and the trust deed created no lien upon the homestead estate. Ogden Building & Loan Ass'n v. Mensch, 196 Ill. 554, 63 N. E. 1049, 89 Am. St. Rep. 330. The lot being of less value than $1,000, the trust deed was inoperative to create a lien upon any part of the property. The trust deed securing the notes held by Fugman contained a release and waiver of the right of homestead both in the body of the deed and in the acknowledgment, and it created a valid lien upon the lot. The act of May 15, 1903 (Laws 1903, p. 120), passed for the purpose of validating acknowledgments taken before officers and stockholders of corporations, could not operate retrospectively, so as to affect liens vested before its passage. Where an acknowledgment is necessary to transfer an estate, and there is no acknowledgment, the Legislature cannot supply the defect, which would be to transfer the estate of one person to another by a legislative act. Russell v. Rumsey, 35 Ill. 362. But where there is an acknowledgment conforming to the requirements of the law for the transfer of the estate, but the officer before whom the acknowledgment is taken has not been authorized by law to take it, the Legislature may cure the defect by a subsequent statute, provided they do not interfere with vested rights. Logan v. Williams, 76 Ill. 175. In this case the owners of the homestead estate attempted to convey it in conformity with the statute, but failed because the officer was disabled, by personal interest, to take the acknowledgment. In case the homestead estate should be extinguished by abandonment or surrender, the trust deed would become operative. There was in fact an acknowledgment, which was illegal only on account of the personal interest of the officer, and this disability the Legislature might remove as between the parties to the instrument. A curative statute of that kind, however, cannot operate to interfere with the rights of third persons vested at the time it takes effect. 1 Cyc. 610. So far as an act purporting to validate defective acknowledgments impairs vested rights, or affects the rights of strangers to the instrument, it is void. 1 Am. & Eng. Ency. of Law (2d Ed.) 568. The lien of Fugman was a vested right at the time the act of 1903 took effect, and the Legislature had no power to change its status or destroy it.

The premises were abandoned on July 24, 1901, and the homestead estate was thereby extinguished. The rights of Fugman had become vested, and the trust deed securing his notes is entitled to priority. Eldridge v. Pierce, 90 Ill. 474.

The decree of the superior court is reversed, and the cause is remanded to that court, with directions to enter a decree of foreclosure in accordance with the views herein expressed. Reversed and remanded.

(208 Ill. 633)

PEOPLE ex rel. CALDWELL et al. v. McDONALD et al.

(Supreme Court of Illinois. April 20, 1904.)

DRAINAGE DISTRICTS—ESTABLISHMENT—REVIEW—QUO WARRANTO—LANDS—DIFFERENT TOWNSHIPS—INFORMATION—DEMURRER—DIFFERENT COUNTS—CONSTRUCTION—PLEAS—WITHDRAWAL—DISCRETION—REVIEW.

1. The granting of leave to withdraw a plea and interpose a demurrer to a petition is within the discretion of the trial court, and will not be reversed unless abuse of such discretion is shown.

2. Where an information in the nature of quo warranto to review the acts of drainage commissioners in organizing a drainage district contained two separate and distinct counts—the first denying jurisdiction on the part of the commissioners, and the second consisting of a general charge of usurpation—such counts, on demurrer, must be considered independently of each other.

3. Where the record of an establishment of a drainage district does not contain sufficient facts to show that all the acts required to be performed by the commissioners have been done, the performance of such acts cannot be presumed.

4. Where an information in the nature of quo warranto to review the establishment of a drainage district by commissioners of a single township alleged that the commissioners at their first meeting found that lands embraced in the petition, including the lands of relators, were benefited by the maintenance of the open ditch then existing, and would be damaged if such ditch was closed, and that some of the lands so benefited were located in another township, by reason of which the commissioners had no jurisdiction to establish the district, under 4 Starr & C. Ann. St. 1902, c. 42, pp. 470, 471, requiring districts to include all lands to be benefited by maintaining the ditches, and all lands which would be damaged by filling the original ditch, and requiring districts to be organized by commissioners of highways of both townships, where the lands benefited lay in more than a single township, and the information further alleged that the district organized did not include all the lands benefited by maintaining the ditches, but that a large body of such lands and a large portion of the ditches properly belonging to the districts lay in another township, it was not demurrable on the ground that it alleged that the districts included all the lands which the commissioners found were benefited.

Appeal from Circuit Court, Moultrie County; W. G. Cochrane, Judge.

Information in the nature of quo warranto by the people, on relation of Chauncey Caldwell and others, against J. J. McDonald and others. From an order sustaining a demurrer to the information, relators appeal. Reversed.

W. K. Whitfield, State's Atty., for the People. Eden & Martin and Miller & Sentel, for relators. Harbaugh & Thompson, Ed C. Craig, and I. R. Mills, for appellees.

RICKS, J. On the 16th day of May, 1903, the state's attorney of Moultrie county, upon the relation of Chauncey Caldwell and others, filed an information in the nature of a quo warranto against the appellees to test the legality of the organization of a drainage district organized under section 76 of the farm drainage act (4 Starr & C. Ann. St. 1902, c. 42, pp. 470, 471), in Jonathan Creek township, in said county. The information consists of two counts. The first count purports to set out the proceedings for the organization of the district, and charges that the district was illegally organized, because the ditches that were found to be made by the voluntary action of the owners of the lands, and the lands involved in the system of combined drainage, lay in both Jonathan Creek and Lowe townships, in said county, and that therefore a union district, extending into both townships, should have been organized, instead of a district comprising lands in Jonathan Creek township alone. The second count in the information is the ordinary and general charge of usurpation. To the information appellees filed their plea of justification, and to this plea a number of replications were filed by appellants, and rejoinders to the replications, and the cause was set down for trial for the 22d day of October, 1903. Upon that date appellees made their motion to be allowed to withdraw their plea and all subsequent pleadings, and to file demurrer to the information. This motion the court allowed, imposing as terms the payment of all costs, including the fees of the witnesses summoned for that day. A general demurrer assigning special causes was filed, and, upon a hearing thereof by the court, it was sustained, and the information quashed. Exceptions were taken to the action of the court in permitting the withdrawal of the pleas and the order sustaining the demurrer. Appellants stood by their information, and prayed and prosecuted this appeal.

The granting of leave to the appellees to withdraw the plea and interpose the demurrer was so far within the discretion of the court that this court would not be warranted in reversing upon such ground unless it were shown that, in the exercise of its supposed discretion, the court had abused its powers. Leigh v. Hodges, 3 Scam. 15; New England Ins. Co. v. Wetmore, 32 Ill. 221; Miles v. Danforth, 37 Ill. 156; Leonard v. Patton, 106 Ill. 99; High on Ex. Legal Rem. (3d Ed.) par. 717, p. 673. The court in this case imposed upon appellees the payment of all costs as the terms upon which the order was made, and we cannot say there was an abuse of discretion, or such injury to appellants as calls for a reversal upon that ground.

We think, however, the judgment of the circuit court should be reversed. The information contained two counts, and, as has been said, the second count is a general charge of usurpation; charging that the appellees, "for the space of twenty days last past and more, in the county aforesaid, unlawfully have usurped and held jurisdiction over certain lands of relators [describing the lands], and then and there, on, to wit, the 27th day of April, A. D. 1903, at the county aforesaid, have pretended to organize a drainage district under the provisions of section 76 of the farm drainage act, * * * upon the petition of one John Fulton, and to include therein said lands of relators, and other lands, without having had any jurisdiction or authority of law to organize said proposed drainage district, and said commissioners then and there, under said pretended order, have proceeded to classify the lands of relators, and other lands, for the purpose of assessing benefits to said lands on account of the said proposed improvements to be made under the drainage district organized under said pretended order, and under said pretended assessment said commissioners are attempting to take or levy upon the property of relators, and to take the lands of relators upon which to improve or construct the ditches in said proposed drainage district, without due process of law; and said commissioners still do have and execute jurisdiction over said lands without any right, warrant, or title whatever, which jurisdiction over said lands said commissioners of highways, during all the time aforesaid, at the county aforesaid, upon the people of the state of Illinois aforesaid, have usurped, and still do usurp," etc.

Appellees say of this count of the information that it is but a continuation of the first count, and that if it be not, and be treated as an independent count, still, inasmuch as it alleges the same organization of a drainage district, of the same number, on the 27th day of April, 1903, the court is authorized to regard it as the same matter, and to look to the first count, and apply the allegations of that count to the second, and thus hold that, both relating to the same thing, and the first count showing, as appellees contend, that they rightfully are exercising the acts complained of, the demurrer should have been sustained to both counts alike.

We do not adopt the view that the counts are not distinct and separate, nor do we know of any rule of pleading by which the allegations in one count may be looked to in passing upon the sufficiency or insufficiency of another count. Appellees proceed in their argument upon the theory that the two counts shall be construed as one, or at least that they shall stand or fall together, and the greater part of the argument is devoted exclusively to matters contained in the first count of the information. With reference to that count, they say that there were presented to the trial court two propositions—one a proposition of law, and the other a proposition of fact. The proposition of fact is that the allegations of the information show a clear and legal right upon the part of appellees to hold the offices and exercise the franchise complained of in the information, and appellees invoke the rule announced in the case of People ex rel. v. Ottawa Hydraulic Co., 115 Ill. 281, 3 N. E. 413, where it is said (page 288, 115 Ill., page 416, 3 N. E.): "Where a number of individuals assume to act as a corporation, an information containing a general denial of their right to do so will be sufficient to put them to their plea of justification; but if the information attempts to set out their title, as was done here, and the facts disclosed for that purpose, when taken in connection with other facts appearing upon the face of a public statute, make the title good, the information will be necessarily bad." And appellees argue that the first count of the information does state facts which disclose, when taken in connection with the public law, namely, the farm drainage act, the clear legal right of appellees to exercise the acts complained of. Appellees then follow the various allegations of the information, which, in general terms, point out the various steps taken by appellees for the organization of the district in question; and it may be said that, in a general way, the information does show that appellees, in the organization of the district in question, did take all the steps required by the statute to legally perfect such an organization. Appellees further say that section 31 of article 4 of the Constitution, which was adopted in 1878, authorizing the General Assembly to permit the owners of land to construct drains, ditches, and levees for agricultural, sanitary, or mining purposes, across the lands of others, and "provide for the organization of drainage districts and vest the corporate authorities thereof with power to construct and maintain levees, drains and ditches," etc., gives the General Assembly plenary power to adopt such methods and confer the powers of organization upon such bodies as it sees fit, and that, having done so, those bodies so constituted are possessed of all the powers conferred upon them by the General Assembly, and all other powers necessary to make the powers thus conferred effective; that in the organization of drainage districts the Legislature has seen fit to confer upon the commissioners of highways, who organize drainage districts under section 76, in question, the power to determine what lands shall be included in the district; and that, when the commissioners have so determined, their finding is final. If this position be admitted to be sound, we are still unable to adopt the view that the information in this case shows sufficient to support the contention of appellees. By section 76 of the farm drainage act, which is found in chapter 42 of 4 Starr & C. Ann. St. 1902, pp. 470, 471, districts organized thereunder are to "include all the lands to be benefited by maintaining these ditches"; and further on in the section the General Assembly has sought to put a further interpretation upon that meaning by declaring, "It is the intent of this act to include all lands that would be damaged by filling the original ditch."

We are not called upon to determine what effect the interpretation placed upon the act by the Legislature shall have upon this court, but it is clear from the provisions of the act that the intention was that all the lands to be benefited by maintaining the ditches should be included in the district, and, to effectuate this end, three classes of ditches are provided for: The district where the lands lie in a single township, and which we may regard as a unit of drainage under this act, and which may be organized by the commissioners of highways of the township; districts where the lands lie in two townships, for which three commissioners of highways from the two townships are selected and make the organization, and which are denominated "union districts"; and districts where the lands involved lie in three or more townships, which are called "special districts," and which latter districts can only be organized in the county courts. These provisions for the various kinds of districts were for the purpose of providing a proper body that should have jurisdiction over the lands involved in the combined system of drainage, whether the same be confined to one or to a number of townships. Whether the application for the organization of the district be made to the commissioners of a single township, or to two townships, or to the county court, one of the things to be determined, and which we regard as jurisdictional, is the territorial extent of the proposed district. The county court has no authority to organize a district in a single township, nor have the commissioners of a single township authority to organize a district where the lands involved in the system of drainage extend into two or more townships. It is true that we have said that such bodies, in determining what lands shall be included in the districts, are called upon to exercise judgment, and that their acts in that respect are of a judicial character, and, unless fraud be charged, are not subject to review by quo warranto. Mason & Tazewell Drainage District v. Griffin, 134 Ill. 330, 25 N. E. 995; People ex rel. v. Cooper, 139 Ill. 461, 29 N. E. 872; Gauen v. Moredock Drainage District, 131 Ill. 446, 23 N. E. 633; People ex rel. v. Mineral Marsh Drainage District, 193 Ill. 428, 62 N. E. 225. But it must be borne in mind that the commissioners of highways, when acting in the organization of a drainage district, are exercising a special authority conferred upon them by the statute, and in favor of their acts there are no intendments or presumptions of law. Whatever they do must be found from their record, and, unless sufficient is found that it can be said that they have acted upon the particular matters required, the law does not, and the courts cannot, presume that they have done so. The information alleges that the commissioners, at their meeting at the time of the organization of the district, found that "lands embraced in said petition, including the lands of the relators, are benefited by the maintenance of the open ditch, and would be damaged if closed." The allegation in the information that raises the question of the jurisdiction of appellees to organize the district is that the district did not include all the lands benefited by maintaining the ditches, but that a large body of the lands and a large portion of the ditches that properly belonged in the district lay in Lowe township. There is no allegation in the information that the commissioners determined that the district, as organized or as petitioned for, or as proposed to be organized, included all the lands to be benefited by maintaining the ditches.

The point here discussed may be well illustrated by quoting from an averment of the plea of appellees that was withdrawn, in which plea the order and finding of the commissioners at their preliminary meeting, had after their examination of the lands for the purpose of determining the jurisdictional questions set forth, is as follows: "We further found that the lands specified in said petition are all the lands that will be benefited by maintaining said drainage ditches, and are all the lands that will be benefited by the proposed improvements." No such allegation as the above is found in the information, and, if it were, we would be disposed to hold that the demurrer to the first count of the information was properly sustained, as there are no allegations of fraud on the part of the commissioners, or that fraud operated in any way in the organization of the drainage district. But from the mere allegation in the information that the lands that were included in the district in fact are benefited by the maintenance of the open ditch, and would be damaged if it were closed, we are not authorized to indulge the presumption, or to hold that equivalent to the allegation, that the commissioners examined not only the lands included in the petition, but the lands involved in the same system of drainage, and that the lands included in the district were all the lands interested in maintaining the ditches.

The demurrer should have been overruled. The judgment is reversed, and the cause remanded for such further proceedings as to law and justice shall appertain. Reversed and remanded.

(209 Ill. 396)

BOYD et al. v. McCONNELL et al.

(Supreme Court of Illinois. April 20, 1904.)

WILLS—CREDIBLE WITNESSES—PERSONS INTERESTED—TESTAMENTARY TRUSTEES.

1. A "credible witness," within 3 Starr & C. Ann. St. p. 4026, c. 148, § 2, requiring wills to be attested in the presence of the testator by "two or more credible witnesses," is a witness who is not for any legal reason disqualified from giving testimony generally, or, by reason of interest or other disqualifying statutory cause, incompetent to testify in respect to the particular subject-matter under investigation.

2. Testatrix bequeathed pecuniary legacies to M. College and to M. Hospital, provided such hospital be in full working condition at her decease; otherwise the money was to be paid to B. in trust for such institution until such time as, in his judgment, the hospital should be fully equipped; but if, after three years, the hospital should not be so equipped, B. should pay such legacy to certain other institutions in equal shares. At testatrix's death the hospital was not in working condition. *Held*, that all of the legatees under such provision of the will being corporations organized for charitable and religious purposes, and not for profit, B., not being financially interested in such bequests, and another, who witnessed the will, though trustees of M. College, were not incompetent as witnesses thereto.

3. Since the judgment admitting the will to probate, though admissible in an action against B. for maladministration of the trust to show the fact of probate of the will, would have no tendency to show any violation of duty on his part, he was not rendered incompetent as a witness on the ground that the record might be used for or against him in such an action.

Appeal from Circuit Court, Warren County; Jno. A. Gray, Judge.

Petition by J. E. McConnell and others for the probate of the will of Mary A. Graham, deceased, to which Rebecca Boyd and others filed objections. From an order of the circuit court reversing an order of the county court refusing probate, and admitting the will to probate, contestants appeal. Affirmed.

George M. Boyd and Melvin A. Kidder, for appellants. Hanna & Clendenin and Safford & Graham, for appellees.

BOGGS, J. This record presents the question whether or not it was correctly ruled by the circuit court that W. T. Campbell and E. J. Blair were competent attesting witnesses to the will of Mary A. Graham, late of Warren county, deceased. The will contained, among others, the following bequests: "I devise, give and bequeath to the Monmouth College five hundred dollars ($500.) I give, devise and bequeath to the Monmouth Hospital five hundred dollars ($500) should the said hospital be in full working condition, receiving and caring for patients, at the time of my decease, if not, the money shall be paid to E. J. Blair, M. D. (without bond), to hold in trust for said institution until such time as in his judgment the said hospital is fully equipped for caring for patients and actively at work. If, after three years after the above-named money shall have come into the possession of Dr. E. J. Blair, the said Monmouth Hospital (the Monmouth Hospital is to be interpreted a general hospital under the care and control of the physicians and citizens of the city of Monmouth, in the county of Warren and State of Illinois) is not fully equipped as described above, then the said Dr. E. J. Blair shall pay the full amount of the five hundred dollars ($500) to the board of church extension and to the board of education of the United Presbyterian Church of North America, in equal shares." The evidence disclosed that at the time of the making of the will, and the attestation thereof, the attesting witnesses, W. T. Campbell and E. J. Blair, were members of the board of trustees of Monmouth College, to which institution the bequest of $500 was given, and that the E. J. Blair, M. D., to whom the bequest to the Monmouth Hospital was to be paid in the event the hospital should not be in "full working condition" at the time of the death of the testator, is the same E. J. Blair who signed the will as an attesting witness. The evidence further showed that the Monmouth Hospital was not in full working condition, receiving and caring for patients, at the time of the death of the said Mary A. Graham.

Section 2 of chapter 148, entitled "Wills" (3 Starr & C. Ann. St. p. 4026), requires that all wills shall be attested in the presence of the testator by "two or more credible witnesses." A "credible witness" means a witness who is not for any legal reason disqualified from giving testimony generally, or by reason of interest or other disqualifying cause, under our statute, incompetent to testify in respect of the particular subject-matter under investigation. Sloan v. Sloan, 184 Ill. 579, 56 N. E. 952. The presumption is that one offered as a witness is competent to testify, and the burden is therefore upon one who objects to state and prove the grounds of his objection. Campbell v. Campbell, 130 Ill. 466, 22 N. E. 620, 6 L. R. A. 167. The ground of objection here urged as to these witnesses is that they are both interested as members of the board of trustees of Monmouth College, and that the witness Blair is by the will constituted a trustee of the fund bequeathed primarily to the Monmouth Hospital, and, in the event of the hospital failing to become entitled thereto, bequeathed to the board of church extension and board of education of the United Presbyterian Church of North America, in equal shares. It is also urged that the witness Blair is charged with the discharge of active duties as a trustee under the will, and is bound to exercise ordinary prudence and diligence in the discharge of such duties, and is answerable for losses, deficiencies, or injuries arising from affirmative or negative violations of such duties.

We are unable to see that either of the witnesses will either profit or lose financially as the direct legal effect and operation of the admission of the will to probate, or the rejection thereof. Monmouth College is a corporation organized for educational purposes, and Monmouth Hospital is a corporation organized for charitable purposes. The board of church extension and the board of education of the United Presbyterian Church are organized and maintained for the furtherance of religious education, and other purposes religious in their nature. Neither of these organizations was created or is maintained for pecuniary profit. It appeared in the evidence that neither Campbell nor Blair, as trustee of the college, received any compensation. Campbell was secretary of the board of education of the United Presbyterian Church, and received compensation for such clerical services; but we find nothing in the testimony to indicate that his compensation would be increased or diminished, or at all affected, if, under the alternative of the will, the bequest of $500 should be received by and divided between the board of education and the board of church extension of the said church. Nor is there any proof in the record to show that the permanency of his position as secretary depended upon bequests or devises in wills, or on donations or gifts to the board of education. The will made no provision for the payment of compensation to Dr. Blair as trustee, and he was therefore not entitled to charge or receive payment for such services. Cook v. Gilmore, 133 Ill. 139, 24 N. E. 524; Buckingham v. Morrison, 136 Ill. 437, 27 N. E. 65. The act of June 17, 1891 (3 Starr & C. Ann. St. 1896, c. 148, par. 22, p. 4046), which provides that compensation may be allowed to trustees appointed by a will, though no provision is made in the will for compensation, by the express language of the enactment has no reference to trustees of trusts for charitable purposes. Neither Blair nor Campbell could, therefore, have compensation for his services as trustee under the will. They had, therefore, no pecuniary interest in the bequests. An interest in the furtherance of the educational and religious purposes that the bequests were intended to aid no doubt existed in the minds of the trustees, but the interest which will constitute a disqualifying cause of objection must be pecuniary in its nature. See 1 Greenleaf on Evidence, § 386. The true test of the interest of a witness is that the witness will either gain or lose financially as the direct result of the proceeding, or that the record will be legal evidence for or against him in some other action. 1 Greenleaf on Evidence, § 390.

In the supposititious event suggested by counsel for the appellants, that if Blair should, as trustee under the will, come into possession of the bequest to the hospital, and it should be alleged he had affirmatively violated some of the duties imposed on him as trustee, and suit should be instituted to recover for a loss alleged to have been thereby occasioned to the funds in his hands, counsel urge the will and the record of its probate would be admissible in evidence either for or against him on such action; hence it is argued he is incompetent for the reason the record in the case of the proceeding to probate will be legal evidence against him in another action. In some cases the record of judgments may be received in evidence against others than the parties, as, when a judgment is entered against a master for the negligence of his servant, the judgment is admissible in a suit by the master against the negligent servant. The record of a judgment entered against a master for the negligence of his servant or act of an agent is admissible in evidence in a subsequent proceeding by the master against the servant or agent to prove the fact that such a judgment had been rendered for such an amount, and on such and such allegations. 1 Greenleaf on Evidence, § 404. In Galena & Chicago Union Railroad Co. v. Welch, 24 Ill. 31, and Chicago & Rock Island Railroad Co. v. Hutchins, 34 Ill. 108, which were actions against employers to recover for the negligence of the employés, the employés were held to be incompetent to testify as witnesses, for the reason the record in the case would be admissible in any action that the employers might in the future bring against the employés, respectively, to recover the amount which the employers had been required to pay under the doctrine of respondeat superior. In Bruner v. Battell, 83 Ill. 317, a bill in chancery was filed to compel specific performance of a contract calling for the sale of land, and the question arose whether an agent of Battell, the vendor, was a competent witness to testify to an alleged payment by the vendee. It was held the agent was incompetent, because of the fact the vendee had died; but we there said that, if the cause depended on the question whether the agent had been guilty of some tortious act or negligence in respect of which he would be liable over to the principal, he would be incompetent, because the record of the suit would be evidence against him in any such future action. But the judgment admitting a will be probate, though admissible in an action against one who had acted as a trustee under the will for the purpose of showing the fact of the probate of the will, would have no tendency to show any improper deflection of the funds held in trust, or any other violation of duty or delinquency on the part of the trustee. Mr. Blair was not, therefore, incompetent on the ground the record might be used for or against him in such other action. The court did not err in holding said Campbell and Blair were competent attesting witnesses to the will.

The judgment will be affirmed. Judgment affirmed.

(209 Ill. 457)

ST. LOUIS & O. RY. CO. v. UNION TRUST & SAVINGS BANK.

(Supreme Court of Illinois. April 20, 1904.)

EMINENT DOMAIN—JURY—METHOD OF DRAWING—CHALLENGE TO THE ARRAY—TIME—OBJECTIONS—WAIVER — INSTRUCTIONS—APPEAL—REVIEW OF EVIDENCE—MOTIONS—BILL OF EXCEPTIONS.

1. A motion to dismiss a petition cannot be reviewed where the motion does not appear in the bill of exceptions.

2. Where an eminent domain proceeding was set for hearing in vacation, it was proper for the clerk to draw a jury in the manner prescribed by Hurd's Ann. St. c. 47, § 6, instead of in the mode prescribed by chapter 78, § 8, fixing the method of drawing jurors for the trial terms of the courts specified.

3. Where no objection to a juror was made until after the jury were accepted and sworn, a challenge thereafter to the array was too late.

4. An instruction that the weight of the testimony does not necessarily depend on the greater number of witnesses, but that the jury may consider all the facts and circumstances appearing from the evidence, and determine from that which of the witnesses are entitled to the greater weight, and that, if they believe that the evidence of the smaller number of witnesses on one side is more credible than the testimony of a greater number of witnesses on the other side, then the evidence preponderates on the side of the smaller number of witnesses, is proper.

5. Objections to evidence will not be reviewed where the evidence objected to is not pointed out and the court is not referred to the page in the abstract where the same may be found.

6. Where, in an eminent domain proceeding, the evidence on the question of damages was conflicting, a verdict of a jury who viewed the premises will not be disturbed as against the weight of evidence.

Appeal from St. Clair County Court; J. B. Hay, Judge.

Condemnation proceeding by the St. Louis & O'Fallon Railway Company against the Union Trust & Savings Bank. From a judgment in favor of petitioner, defendant appeals. Affirmed.

Walter S. Louden and Martin D. Baker, for appellant. Winkelmann & Baer (Dill & Wilderman, of counsel), for appellee.

RICKS, J. It is shown upon the docket in this court that this is a suit of the St. Louis & O'Fallon Railway Company against the Union Trust & Savings Bank, when, in fact, it should be the Union Trust & Savings Bank, appellant, against the St. Louis & O'Fallon Railway Company, appellee, and is upon a petition filed in the St. Clair county court on August 31, 1903, in vacation, by the said St. Louis & O'Fallon Railway Company against the Union Trust & Savings Bank and others, to condemn certain lands for yard purposes for the use of the said railway company. Before the beginning of the trial, and also after the introduction of evidence by the parties, motions were made by appellant to dismiss the petition, and the same were overruled. On September 15, 1903, a jury was impaneled and sworn, whereupon appellant challenged the array, and the challenge was overruled. The jury were then taken in charge by an officer and viewed the premises, and on September 18, 1903, returned into court, and, evidence being introduced by the parties, a verdict was rendered allowing appellant, as compensation for its land taken and damages to land adjoining and not taken, $13,672.75, from which an appeal is prosecuted by the Union Trust & Savings Bank.

It is first contended by appellant that the overruling of the motions to dismiss the petition of appellee was error. But the bill of exceptions does not show the motions or rulings of the court and exceptions thereto, the motion being copied in the record by the clerk, and we have repeatedly held that, in order for this court to pass upon motions made in a cause, they must appear in the bill of exceptions and be certified to by the trial court. Such being the condition of the record with reference to the motions, we are not authorized to pass upon this alleged error.

The next contention is that the court should have sustained the challenge to the array of jurors, for the reason that the said jurors were improperly drawn, and it is argued by appellant that the only proper method of drawing jurors is that provided under section 8 of chapter 78 of Hurd's Annotated Statutes of 1899, which is: "At least twenty days before the first day of any trial term of any of said courts, the clerk of such court shall repair to the office of the county clerk, and in the presence of the county judge and of such county clerk, after the box containing said names has been well shaken by the county clerk and being blindfolded shall without partiality, draw from said box the names of a sufficient number of said persons then residents of said county," etc. This contention would be correct if a trial was to be had in term time, but the record shows that in this case the trial was in vacation, and by a special provision of the statute the selection of jurors in cases tried under the eminent domain act, where the petition is filed in vacation, is provided for. Section 6 of chapter 47 of Hurd's Annotated Statutes of 1899 provides: "In cases fixed for hearing of petition in vacation, it shall be the duty of the clerk of the court in whose office the petition is filed, at the time of issuing summons or making publication, to write the names of each of sixty-four disinterested freeholders of the county on sixty-four slips of paper, and, in presence of two disinterested freeholders, cause to be selected from said sixty-four names twelve of said persons to serve as jurors,—such selection to be made by lot and without choice or discrimination; and the said clerk shall thereupon issue venire," etc. The record shows that the jurors were properly drawn, as provided for in the above section 6, in the first

¶ 3. See Jury, vol. 31, Cent. Dig. § 544.

place, the clerk having complied with the statute in every respect.

But it is insisted that only 11 of the jurors selected were properly served, and that one of the jury was on the panel irregularly. But nothing was said and no objection made, at the time, to any irregularity, nor until after the jurors were accepted and sworn. The challenge to the array was then too late. St. Louis & Southeastern Railway Co. v. Casner, 72 Ill. 384.

It is next insisted the court erred in giving instructions asked by the petitioner. Only one of the instructions, however, is pointed out, that being the first, and it is as follows: "You are instructed that the weight of the testimony does not necessarily depend on the greater number of witnesses sworn on either side of a question in dispute, but you are at liberty, as jurors, to consider all the facts and circumstances appearing from the evidence in the case, determining from that which of the witnesses are worthy of the greater credit; and if you believe, from the evidence, that the evidence of a small number of witnesses on one side is more credible and trustworthy than the evidence of the greater number on the other side, then the evidence preponderates on the side of the smaller number of witnesses." We are unable to find any error in this instruction, as we think it, as a whole, properly states the law.

It is next insisted the court admitted improper evidence. But there is no evidence pointed out or any citation made to the abstract to any improper evidence, and it is not the duty of the court to read the entire abstract through to determine whether there is any improper evidence admitted or not. It is the duty of the attorney to point out the evidence complained of, and refer the court to the page in the abstract where the same may be found. This not having been done, it is not our duty to consider the objection raised.

It is insisted that the verdict is against the weight of the evidence, and that the judgment is entirely inadequate for the property taken and damages to property not taken. But we have repeatedly held that the verdict of a jury in a condemnation proceeding will not be disturbed where the premises were viewed by the jury and there is any considerable conflict in the evidence as to the value. In this case there was a sharp conflict in the evidence upon the question of damages. A jury of freeholders were selected and went upon the premises and viewed the same, and under such circumstances were given many advantages, in the ascertainment of the proper damages, not possessed by a court of review, and a verdict rendered in such case will not be disturbed.

Finding no reversible error, the judgment of the county court of St. Clair county will be affirmed. Judgment affirmed.

(209 Ill. 269)

BARKMAN v. BARKMAN.

(Supreme Court of Illinois. April 20, 1904.)

RES JUDICATA—DECISION ON JURISDICTION—DIVORCE—WIFE'S RIGHT TO HOMESTEAD.

1. Where, on appeal from an order modifying a decree of divorce after the expiration of the term at which it was rendered, by terminating plaintiff's homestead right in the property, the Appellate Court holds that it was beyond the power of the court to modify the decree at that time, such an adjudication is not res judicata of plaintiff's right to the homestead.

2. Hurd's Rev. St. 1901, c. 52, § 5, provides that in divorce the court granting the decree may dispose of the homestead estate according to the equities of the case. A wife obtained a divorce on account of cruelty, securing $4,000 alimony out of the husband's $12,000 estate, as well as $250 solicitor's fee. She was also awarded a lease for two years of a flat previously occupied by her and her husband, and the latter was enjoined from interfering with or molesting her in the possession thereof. Otherwise the decree was silent as to the wife's homestead interest. *Held*, on a bill seeking to have a homestead in the premises set off to the wife, that her right thereto was terminated by the divorce, notwithstanding her allegations that her husband had deserted her several times before the decree.

Appeal from Circuit Court, Cook County; E. O. Brown, Judge.

Suit by Sophia Barkman against John G. Barkman. Decree for defendant, and plaintiff appeals. Affirmed.

This is an appeal from an order of the circuit court of Cook county sustaining a demurrer to appellant's bill of complaint, and dismissing the same, as amended, for want of equity. The amended bill sets up facts substantially as follows: The complainant and defendant were married in 1874, and had lived, for several years prior to the filing of said bill, in a three-flat building in Chicago, occupying the upper flat. This property was owned in fee by defendant. The bill alleges that on several occasions the defendant had deserted complainant, and finally she filed her bill for divorce, charging cruelty. On October 20, 1899, complainant was awarded a divorce on the ground of cruelty, and by an injunction defendant was ordered to desist from interfering with or molesting complainant in the enjoyment and possession of the flat which she occupied, pursuant to the provisions of the decree. The decree of divorce gave complainant $4,000 as and for alimony in full, $250 solicitor's fee, and decreed that the defendant execute and deliver to her a lease of the flat previously occupied by them, from the date of said decree to November 1, 1901, and also gave her the custody of two minor children. After the entry of this decree, and after the expiration of the term at which it was rendered, defendant (appellee) filed his petition in said cause, asking that the decree be so modified that it should specifically terminate the dower and homestead rights of complainant, and the prayer of the petition was by the circuit court granted. From that order an appeal was taken to the

Appellate Court, where it was held that the decree could not be modified after the term at which it was rendered, and the order of the circuit court was reversed. The lease to appellant was given her as provided by the decree, she signing and accepting the same. At the expiration of the period provided in the lease, appellee brought forcible detainer proceedings against appellant. Appellee was successful in this forcible detainer proceeding in the circuit and Appellate Courts, and now appellant seeks to enjoin appellee from suing on the forcible detainer bond, and also asks that a homestead be set off to her in the said premises.

Masterson & Haft, for appellant. Kitt Gould, for appellee.

RICKS, J. (after stating the facts). Appellant sets up in her bill the proceedings in Barkman v. Barkman, 94 Ill. App. 440, and insists that the judgment of the Appellate Court in that case is res judicata of the question of homestead here involved. In this contention we think appellant misapprehends the effect of that proceeding. It was supplemental to the original decree of divorce, and sought to change the same by adding to an order cutting off appellant's dower and homestead, and a holding was made in the circuit court that the granting of alimony in the sum of $4,000 in gross and the order for the lease to appellant of the homestead for two years were in lieu of and in full of all rights of alimony, homestead, and dower. The only question before the Appellate Court was the power of the circuit court to change the decree in these regards at a term subsequent to the term at which the original decree was entered. The Appellate Court held the circuit court had no such power, and for that purpose did not have jurisdiction of the cause. Having found that the circuit court did not have jurisdiction, and having reversed the decree of the circuit court upon that ground, that ended the duty and power of the Appellate Court, and anything said by the Appellate Court in its opinion as to the rights of the parties as to homestead and dower was aside from the question before it, and cannot be urged as res judicata when those questions are raised properly in a court having jurisdiction. The judgment of the Appellate Court left the original decree of the circuit court for divorce and alimony stand as a final decree. By the latter decree appellant. out of an estate of about $12,000 possessed by appellee, was awarded $4,000 alimony and $250 solicitor's fee, and given, free of rent, a lease on the premises here claimed as a homestead for two years. That decree was silent as to dower and homestead rights of appellant, except that the two years' lease was provided for.

In an action of divorce the court has full and complete jurisdiction of the parties and the subject-matter, and it may decree the payment of money in such amounts and in such manner as to it appears just and equitable. By the statute (Hurd's Rev. St. 1901, c. 52, § 5) it is provided: "In case of a divorce, the court granting the divorce may dispose of the homestead estate according to the equities of the case." The "equities of the case" may require that it be given for life, or, as in this case, for but a limited time; and, where the decree makes no specific disposition of the homestead, its disposition must be as directed by statute. Stahl v. Stahl, 114 Ill. 375, 2 N. E. 160. The case just cited is decisive of this case. In that case Catharine Stahl had obtained a divorce from Christian Stahl for extreme and repeated cruelty. The decree was silent as to homestead and dower rights. The circuit court having held that Catharine Stahl, the divorced wife of Christian Stahl, was entitled to a homestead of the value of $1,000 and to dower in the remainder, this court, on appeal to it, stated (page 379, 114 Ill., page 161, 2 N. E.): "The circuit court erred in its decree as to homestead. Section 5, c. 52, Rev. St. 1874, provides: 'In case of a divorce, the court granting the divorce may dispose of the homestead estate according to the equities of the case.' Here the court granting the divorce made no order with respect to the homestead. The disposition of it, therefore, must be as directed by statute. After the divorce the homestead estate remained and continued in Christian Stahl, the householder and owner in fee of the premises. Upon the granting of the divorce Catharine Stahl's relation of wife to Christian Stahl was severed. She then became entirely disconnected with the homestead estate, and had no right pertaining to any property of Christian Stahl by virtue of having been his wife, except dower saved by the statute, the divorce having been for the misconduct of the husband, and the alimony which was allowed. * * * Now, if, after the divorce and before his second marriage, Christian Stahl had been minded to release or convey the homestead, he could have done so by his own deed alone, as he would have had then no wife to join with him in the deed."

Appellant contends that the case just cited is not applicable to the case at bar. We do not admit the distinctions urged by her. It is contended in the present case that the defendant in the divorce proceedings (appellee here) had deserted the complainant, and by reason thereof the title to the homestead estate inured to complainant. The complainant, however, was given a divorce on the ground of defendant's cruelty, and an injunction was granted restraining defendant from interfering with or molesting complainant in her possession of the premises, which, under the decree, she was to have the right to occupy for two years. Under such conditions no estate of homestead, because of alleged desertion, can be held to have vested in complainant. Besides, when the decree of divorce was granted, the court had the right to adjust the property rights of the parties, including the homestead, "according to the equities of the case," and in doing so the question of desertion was proper to be considered by him.

Practically the same question presented here, and under a statute similar to ours, was decided, along the same line as the Stahl Case, in Rosholt v. Mehus (N. D.) 57 N. W. 783, 23 L. R. A. 239. Many of the cases urged by appellant in this case were similarly urged in that case, and the reasoning of the court there is so applicable we quote it here (page 786, 57 N. W., page 243, 23 L. R. A.): "The statute says (Comp. Laws, § 2585): 'The court, in rendering a decree of divorce, may assign the homestead to the innocent party, either absolutely or for a limited period, according to the facts in the case and in consonance with the law relating to homestead.' It would appear from this language that the Legislature, so far from intending that the homestead should pass to the innocent party by virtue of the statute alone, thought it necessary to give the court express power to so dispose of it by decree. We are entirely unable to see any good reason why, after the chancellor, in the exercise of the broad and liberal discretion in him vested, has given the innocent family every protection the circumstances admitted or their needs required, the law should then step in and transfer to them, at the expense of the husband, another and very material estate, to wit, the homestead owned and theretofore occupied by him. Particularly must this be true when, as in this case, the decree of divorce casts upon the husband the continuing duty of supporting that family, by compelling him to pay certain monthly payments. It is not to be believed that the law will then grasp the very property out of which the husband must realize the money to make those payments, and transfer it to the family, and yet hold him for the payments. We deem it better for the innocent party, better for the fee owner, better as a rule of property, that the interests of the respective parties in the homestead should be fixed by the decree in the divorce proceeding, and, when that decree is silent, the homestead, like all other realty, must remain in the possession of the party holding the record title, discharged of all homestead rights and claims of the other party; and this we deem the result of the better authorities"—citing Heaton v. Sawyer, 60 Vt. 495, 15 Atl. 166; Wiggin v. Buzzell, 58 N. H. 329; and Biffle v. Pullam, 114 Mo. 50, 21 S. W. 450.

The cases from this court cited by appellant on this point are not, in our judgment, in conflict with the rule announced in the Stahl Case, which we think is applicable to the case at bar. In the cases so cited the homestead right was specifically awarded in the decree of divorce, or the facts clearly showed a desertion, and such conditions as created, under the statute, a right to the homestead in the party held to be entitled to it. Under the facts disclosed in this case, we think the decree of the circuit court was correct, and the same will be affirmed.

Decree affirmed.

(209 Ill. 414)

CHICAGO & G. T. RY. CO. et al. v. HART.

(Supreme Court of Illinois. April 20, 1904.)

RAILROADS — LEASE—NEGLIGENCE OF LESSEE—INJURY TO SERVANT—LIABILITY OF LESSOR.

1. A railroad company owning a railroad track, which it leases to another corporation, is liable for injuries to an employé of the lessee arising from the negligence of the lessee alone; 3 Starr & C. Ann. St. 1896, p. 3247, c. 114, par. 53, which authorizes railroads to lease their roads or any part thereof, not relieving a railroad corporation of liabilities which would attach if it operated the road itself.

Scott, Cartwright, and Ricks, JJ., dissenting.

Appeal from Appellate Court, First District.

Action by Henry Hart against the Chicago & Grand Trunk Railway Company and another. From a judgment of the Appellate Court (104 Ill. App. 57) affirming a judgment in favor of plaintiff, defendants appeal. Affirmed.

Kenesaw M. Landis (Albert M. Cross, of counsel), for appellants. James C. McShane, for appellee.

BOGGS, J. The judgment entered in the superior court of Cook county in favor of the appellee and against the appellant companies, in the sum of $6,000, was affirmed in the Appellate Court for the First District on appeal, and it is now before us on a further appeal.

The action was in case to recover the damages for personal injuries sustained by the appellee by the negligence, as he alleged, of the appellant companies in permitting a switch engine to become and remain in an unsafe and defective condition; one of the journals of the said engine having become worn and weakened, and by reason thereof broke and gave way, and caused the said engine to be derailed, whereby the appellee was injured.

On the 22d day of December, 1880, the appellant the Chicago & Grand Trunk Railway Company, an Illinois corporation (hereinafter, for convenience, called the "lessee company") and the appellant the Grand Trunk Junction Railway Company, also an Illinois corporation (hereinafter called the "lessor company") entered into an agreement whereby the Junction Company agreed, among other things, to construct a line of railroad and to lease the same to the Grand Trunk Company for a stipulated annual rental, and did construct such line of railroad and leased the

¶ 1. See Railroads, vol. 41, Cent. Dig. §§ 802, 803, 813.

same to the Grand Trunk Company. It appeared from the agreement that the lessor company, by its charter, had power to construct and operate the contemplated and leased line of railroad. On the 19th day of June, 1899, the Grand Trunk Company, as such lessee, was operating trains of cars over said line of road. The appellee was in its employ as a switchman, and was injured while in the discharge of his duty in that capacity by reason of the breaking of a worn and defective axle or journal of a switch engine, and the judgment herein was rendered in an action against both the lessor and the lessee companies to recover damages for such injuries. Judgment was awarded him against both companies, and such judgment was affirmed as aforesaid in said Appellate Court.

Counsel for the appellant companies present but a single question for decision, and that is whether, as the cause of action is based solely upon the alleged negligence of the lessee company, any liability is established against the lessor company. It is conceded by appellants that under the law of this state the lessor and lessee of a railway track are jointly and severally liable to the general public for all damages resulting from the negligent acts of the lessee while operating engines and cars on that track, but it is contended that this rule does not apply to an employé of the lessee whose cause of action results solely from the negligence of his employer, and this presents the only question for our determination.

There is a conflict in adjudicated cases on the question whether a lessor railroad company is liable to a servant of the lessee company for injuries occasioned by the negligence of the lessee company in the operation of the leased road. Mr. Elliott, in his work on Railroads (volume 2, p. 610), says that he inclines to the opinion that the lessor company is not so liable where the injuries to the servant of the lessee company are caused solely by the negligence of the lessee company in operating the road, but this author says that the weight of authority is against the view that he is inclined to adopt. We think this court is committed to the view held by the current of authorities on the question, and, moreover, that, in sound reason, and as the better public policy, the doctrine should be maintained that the lessor company shall be required to answer for the consequences of the negligence of the lessee company in the operation of the road, not only to the public, but also to servants of the lessee company who have been injured by actionable negligence of the lessee company.

The charter of the lessor company empowered it to construct this line of railroad and operate trains thereon. It became its duty to exercise those chartered powers, otherwise they would become lost by nonuser. The statute authorized it to discharge that duty through a lessee, and it adopted that means of performing the duty which the state had created it to perform. The statute which authorized it to operate its road by means of a lessee did not, however, purport to relieve it of the obligation to serve the public by operating the road, nor of any of the consequences or liabilities which would attach to it if it operated the road itself. 3 Starr & C. Ann. St. 1896, p. 3247, c. 114, par. 53. Statutory permission to lease its road does not relieve a railroad company from the obligations cast upon it by its charter unless such statute expressly exempts the lessor company therefrom. Balsley v. St. Louis, Alton & Terre Haute Railroad Co., 119 Ill. 68, 8 N. E. 859, 59 Am. Rep. 784. While the duty which rests upon the lessor companies to operate their roads is an obligation which they owe to the public, the permission given by the Legislature, as the representative of the public, to perform that duty through lessees, has no effect to absolve such companies from the duty of seeing that the lessee company provides and maintains safe engines and cars, and that the employés of the lessee companies to whom is intrusted the operation of their roads are competent, and that they perform the duties devolving upon them with ordinary care and skill, for upon the character and condition of safety of such engines and cars and on the competency and care of such employés depend the lives and property of the general public. As a matter of public policy, such lessor companies are to be charged with the duty of seeing that the operation of the road is committed to competent and careful hands. The General Assembly of this state, though willing to permit railroad companies to operate their lines of road by lessees, refrained from relieving the lessor companies from any of their obligations, duties, or liabilities. Therefore it is that though a railroad company may, by lease or otherwise, intrust the execution of its chartered powers and duties to a lessee company, this court has expressed the view the lessee company, while engaged in exercising such chartered privileges or chartered powers of the railroad company, is to be regarded as the servant or agent of the lessor company.

In West v. St. Louis, Vandalia & Terre Haute Railroad Co., 63 Ill. 545, appellee railroad company had contracted with the firm of McKeen, Smith & Co. to construct its road and the appurtenances thereto. The superintendent of the firm employed the appellant, West, as a workman to assist in building a freighthouse for the railroad company. The timbers used in the construction of the freighthouse were treated with a liquid in which corrosive sublimate was an ingredient, to prevent decay. West was injured by breathing the fumes of this liquid, and by handling the timbers to which the liquid had been applied. He brought an action against the railroad company to recover damages for the injury, but was defeated in the trial court on the ground that the contractors alone were liable. The appellant contended that the work in which he was injured was being done for the benefit of the railroad company and by its authority, and "that the contractors must be considered its servants, for whose wrongful acts in the performance of their work the company must be held responsible." In support of that contention, counsel for appellant cited a number of cases decided in this court. We said as to such cited cases (page 546): "There is a radical distinction between each of these cases and that at bar. These were all cases in which redress was sought against a chartered company for wrongs done by persons while in the performance of acts which they would have had no right to perform except under the charter of the company. The court laid down the salutary rule that as to such acts the company could not escape corporate liability by having the acts performed or the work done by contractors or lessees. These persons must be regarded in such cases as the servants of the company, acting under its directions, and the company must see that the special privileges and powers given to it by its charter are not abused"—and, after making reference to the facts in such cases, deduced the following principles therefrom: "But between all these cases and the one at bar there is a radical difference. In these the wrong for which the action was brought was committed in the performance of acts which were performed by virtue of the authority of the company derived from its charter, and could have been performed in no other way. In such cases the public has the right to hold the company responsible, because it is really the company that is acting. The personal actors may, as between themselves and the company, be lessees or contractors, and the company may have its action against them for indemnity, according to the terms of its private contract; but they are, as to the public, the servants or agents of the company so long as they are doing what they could not do except by the chartered authority of the company. * * * The principle we consider to be substantially this: The company may be held liable when the person doing the wrongful act is the servant of the company and acting under its directions, and, though such person is not a servant as between himself and the company, but merely a contractor or lessee, still he must be regarded as a servant or agent when he is exercising some chartered privilege or power of the company, with its assent, which he could not have exercised independently of such charter. In other words, a company seeking and accepting a special charter must take the responsibility of seeing that no wrong is done through its chartered powers by persons to whom it has permitted their exercise."

While the liability enunciated by the declaration of the court is left to rest upon the ground that the injury was inflicted while in the performance of acts which could only be performed under the charter of the company, and therefore to be regarded as having been performed by servants or agents of the company, whether independent contractors or lessees, we had occasion in the later case of Balsley v. St. Louis, Alton & Terre Haute Railroad Co., supra., to consider what had been said in the former case of West v. St. Louis, Vandalia & Terre Haute Railroad Co., supra, and we then said (page 71, 119 Ill., page 860, 8 N. E., 59 Am. Rep. 784): "The reason for holding a railroad company responsible for the performance of all the duties and obligations imposed upon it by its charter or the general law of the state while it is being operated by a lessee does not, we conceive, rest upon the narrow ground alone of the latter being in the exercise of a franchise which belongs to the former, and in so acting is to be held as the servant or agent of the lessor corporation. In consideration of the grant of its charter, the corporation undertakes for the performance of duties and obligations towards the public; and there is a matter of public policy concerned, that it should not be relieved from the performance of its obligations without the consent of the Legislature."

A railroad company is granted a charter for the purpose of enabling it to perform duties for the benefit of the public. Such a company does not take, as one of its general powers, the right to substitute another to discharge those duties as its lessee. 23 Am. & Eng. Ency. of Law (2d Ed.) 776; 2 Elliott on Railroads, §§ 429, 430. In the absence of statutory authority to execute a lease, any attempt to do so is ultra vires; and the acts of the lessee in the operation of the road under such a void lease are, in legal contemplation, the acts of an agent of the railroad company. 23 Am. & Eng. Ency. of Law (2d Ed.) 777, 778. A lease, though authorized by an act of the Legislature, does not operate to relieve the lessor company of any duty or liability imposed by its charter unless the enabling statute contains an exemption therefrom. Balsley v. St. Louis, Alton & Terre Haute Railroad Co., supra; 23 Am. & Eng. Ency. of Law (2d Ed.) 784; 2 Elliott on Railroads, §§ 429, 430. Therefore it is that in the discharge of an act, the performance of which devolved upon the lessor company as a chartered power or duty, the lessee, under our statute authorizing a railroad company to perform its chartered powers through the medium of a lessee, is but the agent or servant of the lessor company, to the same extent as if the lease had been executed in the absence of statutory authority.

In the absence of a statutory exemption from liability for the negligence of the lessee company, the obligation to respond for such negligence is also to be maintained upon grounds of public policy. The fact the contract relation is between the employé and the lessee company, and was voluntarily entered into by the employé with the lessor company alone, cannot be allowed to control. The public are interested in the safe and efficient transportation of passengers and property over the line of road the lessor herein was given power to construct and operate. Competent and careful servants, well-constructed engines and cars, which are properly inspected and kept in good and safe condition of repair, are essential to the speedy and safe transportation of passengers and property. That such engines and cars to be used in the operation of the railroad shall be provided and kept in good repair is a chartered duty, compliance wherewith is of the greatest concern to the general public. No more effective means of compelling performance of that duty can well be conceived than to hold the lessor company responsible to all the world for the actionable negligence of the lessee company. The negligence of the lessee company here complained of is that it failed to keep its locomotive engine in safe and usable condition, and that negligence endangered not only those in the employ of the lessee company, but also the general public; and considerations of public policy are involved and must control in determining the liability of the lessor company. The obligation to provide cars and engines that are reasonably safe, and servants that are reasonably competent and skillful, which was cast upon the lessor company by the grant to it of its corporate powers, is not shifted to one with whom it has contracted to operate its road as lessee, but remains to be discharged by the lessor company to all the public; and to relieve it of that duty as to its employés would invite negligence from which injury to the public would likely occur. The lessee's employés are a part of the general public, and the lessor company is liable to them for the actionable negligence of the lessee company to the same extent as if such workmen were in the employ of the lessor company. The liability rests not only on the ground the lessee company, in discharging the corporate powers and duties of the lessor company, is but the agent or servant as to all others than the lessor company, but also on the ground that sound public policy demands that all corporations which the state has created, and given special provileges and powers, shall stand charged with the obligations and duty to see that such privileges and powers are properly exercised and discharged, unless relieved by express authority of the lawmaking department of the state.

The judgment must be, and is, affirmed. Judgment affirmed.

SCOTT, CARTWRIGHT, and RICKS, JJ. (dissenting). The question whether a railroad company owning a right of way, roadbed, and track lawfully leased to another company is liable for damages to a servant of the lessee, injured solely by the negligence of his employer, is one which has not been before presented to this court. The general statements quoted in the opinion of the majority from earlier decisions in this state dealing with the relations of the lessor company to the public and to persons other than servants of the lessee must be limited by the facts appearing in those cases, and should not, therefore, be deemed of controlling importance here. Authorities in other states are not entirely unanimous. The question was first presented to the Supreme Court of North Carolina in the case of Logan v. N. C. R. R. Co., 116 N. C. 940, 21 S. E. 959, where it was said: "A part of the original duty imposed by the charter was to compensate servants in damages for any injury they might sustain, except such as should be due to the negligence of their fellow servants. The employé is deemed, in law, to contract ordinarily to incur such risks as arise from the carelessness of the other servants of the company; but where the lessor company would be liable, if it had remained in charge of the road, to a person acting as its own servant, we see no reason why it should not be answerable to him when employed by the lessee." This rule has been steadily adhered to by the North Carolina court, and has been reaffirmed in Harden v. N. C. R. R. Co., 129 N. C. 354, 40 S. E. 184, 55 L. R. A. 784, 85 Am. St. Rep. 747; James v. Western N. C. R. R. Co., 121 N. C. 523, 28 S. E. 537, 46 L. R. A. 306; Smith v. Atlanta & C. R. R. Co., 42 S. E. 139; and Brown v. Atlanta & C. Air Line Ry. Co., 42 S. E. 911. The only other case to which we have been referred announcing the same doctrine is the case of Macon & Augusta Railroad Co. v. Mayes, 49 Ga. 355, 15 Am. Rep. 678. That case, however, has been criticised and weakened by the Supreme Court of that state in later cases, and finally, in the case of Banks v. Georgia R. R. & B. Co., 112 Ga. 655, 37 S. E. 992, the liability of the lessor company to the employé of the lessee for an injury caused by the negligence of the lessee is denied where the lease is made under legislative authority, although the statute authorizing the lease was without a provision exempting the lessor for the lessee's negligence; and in discussing the Mayes Case it was said: "In that case the company owning the road was held liable for a tort to an employé of the company using the franchise, occasioned by the negligence of his co-employé, but there was no legislative authority for the latter company to use the franchise. Indeed, there was no lease at all. And therein lies the marked distinction between that case and the one in hand." In the Banks Case the earlier decisions of the court are reviewed and discussed, and the conclusion reached denies the liability of the lessor. In the case at bar it is conceded that the lessor company had lawful right and authority to make the lease of its tracks to the lessee company, so that the case cited from 112 Ga., 37 S. E., seems to be fairly in point.

An able discussion of this question is found in E. L. & R. R. R. Co. v. Culberson, 72 Tex.

375, 10 S. W. 706, 3 L. R. A. 567, 13 Am. St. Rep. 805, where it is said, discussing the general rule of the liability of the lessor: "The reason for the rule is the protection of the public who need the protection. The passenger and the shipper of goods have no option, but must avail themselves of the services of the lessees, whether the lease is authorized or not. The law will not permit the owner of the road to shirk its duty to them by turning over its road to another company, nor will it permit it to deny its liability where it has allowed such other company, without authority of law, negligently to injure wayfarers over the track or property along the line. There is no privity between the persons injured, in such case, and the operating company. It is not so with an employé who voluntarily enters the service of the latter company with a knowledge of the facts, and participates knowingly in the wrong, if wrong it be. Where in similar cases a recovery has been permitted against a lessor, it has usually been allowed upon various considerations of public policy: First, because the franchises granted are in the nature of a personal trust, and sound policy demands, so far as the general public is concerned, that the corporation receiving the grant should be held responsible for the proper execution of the powers granted; and, second, for the reason that to deny the responsibility of the lessor would enable a railroad to shirk its responsibility and to injure the public by placing its property under the control of irresponsible parties; and, third, because a person who has received an injury at the hands of the operating company, and was ignorant of the relations between that company and the owner of the road, might be at a loss to determine against which to bring his action, and thereby placed at a disadvantage in seeking a redress of his wrongs. None of these reasons apply in the case of the servant of a lessee who is injured through the neglect of his employer. He needs no protection as one of the general public, because he can enter the service, or not, as he chooses. He is under no compulsion to take employment from an irresponsible company, and he certainly knows whom to sue for a wrong inflicted through his employer's neglect, for the latter is certainly liable to him in such a case. The reason of the rule which holds the lessor liable fails in case of an employé of the lessee, and we think that to follow it in a case like this would be to give it an arbitrary, and not a reasonable, application." The same view of the matter is taken in Indiana, Kentucky, Virginia, California, Georgia, and the federal courts. B. & O. & C. R. R. Co. v. Paul, 143 Ind. 23, 40 N. E. 519, 28 L. R. A. 216; Swice v. M. & B. S. R. Co. (Ky., decided June 20, 1903) 75 S. W. 278; V. M. Ry. Co. v. Washington, 86 Va. 629, 10 S. E. 927, 7 L. R. A. 344; Lee v. S. P. R. R. Co., 116 Cal. 97, 47 Pac. 932, 38 L. R. A. 71, 58 Am. St. Rep. 140; Banks v. G. R. & B. Co., 112 Ga. 655, 37 S. E. 992; Hukill v. M. & B. S. R. Co. (C. C.) 72 Fed. 745.

The editors of the American State Reports state their conclusion thus: As to employés of a lessee corporation, the weight of authority, whether the lease is authorized or not, is to the effect that they cannot recover from the lessor for injuries received through the negligence of such lessee or its servants or agents. 58 Am. St. Rep. 155. In the American & English Encyclopædia of Law, vol. 23 (2d Ed.) p. 785, after setting out the rule in reference to the liability of the lessor company to the public as it exists in this state, it is said: "The rule of liability which has just been stated does not apply to the lessees' servants who may be injured by the lessees' negligence."

As the view of the majority has been rejected by every one of the numerous courts in the Union to which it has been presented, except North Carolina, and, after having been once adopted by the Supreme Court of Georgia, has been there discredited, and the case announcing it overruled, we think the language quoted by Mr. Justice BOGGS from Elliott on Railroads, to the effect that the weight of authority supports that view, incorrect. The researches of court and counsel in the case at bar certainly do not warrant the conclusion of that author, but, on the contrary, show that every court, save one, has reached the opposite conclusion.

This court has frequently spoken of the lessee company as the agent or servant of the lessor in discussing the relations of the latter with persons other than the employés of the former, and, in a general sense, this is a correct view to take of the situation. The lessor, by accepting its charter, assumes the duties of a common carrier, and when, by the lease, it causes another to assume those duties, it becomes liable to the public for their performance in a lawful manner, and the lessee is its agent and servant for the purpose of meeting its obligations in this respect, so far as the public is concerned; but the lessee cannot be said to be the agent or servant of the lessor with respect to a contract with the employé of the former who enters his master's service moved solely by the inducements contained in the contract itself, and not because he finds that employer operating its trains over the lines of a road which he is by the necessities of business or travel impelled to use.

The lessee's position is different from that of one who, under a contract with the owning company, is engaged in work which can be carried on only under the charter of the latter. The contractor, in laying the track, is engaged in doing a work which he is specifically directed and required to do by the terms of his contract. The lessee of the track, in operating trains over the same, is enjoying a privilege accorded by the charter to the lessor; but it is not required by the contract, so far as the lessor is concerned, to operate any particular train or do any specific work. The contractor is much nearer to the owning corporation than is the lessee. The contractor is, under the immediate direction and control of the owner, bound to do specific work as required by the contract with the owner, while, so far as any specific work is concerned—the running of any particular train or the using of any particular engine—the lessee exercises its own option.

On the principal question—that of the liability of the lessor—the reasoning of the court of last resort of Texas seems unanswerable. As there suggested, the landowner whose real estate adjoins the right of way, the traveler who uses the highway crossing the railroad track, the shipper of freight who must have his goods carried over the leased line, the passenger who finds it necessary to travel over the same line of road, are all brought into such relations as they occupy with the company operating the trains, without their consent. So far as they are concerned, the lessor has obtained from the state a charter to operate the trains, and then, without the consent of these persons, has constituted another in its stead to perform the duties and meet the obligations which it assumed by accepting its charter. The public had no voice in making the contract of substitution. They are compelled to deal with the lessee whether they will or not, and an enlightened public policy has therefore made the lessor company liable for all the wrongs visited by the lessee upon the public, which has been compelled to deal with an agency selected by the lessor alone. The employé of the lessee is in a different category. The making of the lease has not compelled him to enter the employ of the lessee. His relations with the latter result from the contract which he has voluntarily made with it, and not from the fact that his relations with it have been forced upon him by the acts of the lessor company, as is the case with the general public. His rights as such employé result wholly from the contract of employment which he voluntarily made, and which he was not obliged by circumstances resulting from the act of the lessor company to enter into.

The reasoning of the majority opinion, based upon the consideration of public policy, seems to us entirely untenable. The argument is that, because the public interest requires that the safest appliances should be used by the lessee company, the lessor company should be held liable for injuries resulting to the servants of the lessee from the negligence of the latter, that the lessor may thereby be induced to require the lessee to provide such appliances. The same reasoning leads to the conclusion that the lessor company should be liable for the wages of the employé, that the most efficient and faithful may be hired; that it should be liable to the builder, that cars and locomotives of the highest grade may be secured. But it has not yet occurred to the creditor of an insolvent lessee, seeking a debtor who can pay, to assert any such claim against a lessor company. It is only for the proper exercise of powers conferred by charter, and which can be exercised only under and by virtue of the charter, that the lessor is responsible. Hiring a switchman or purchasing or repairing a locomotive requires the exercise of no such powers. Such things may be done by any one.

We therefore conclude that a railroad company owning a railroad track which, by a lawful contract, it leases to another, is not liable for damages resulting to the employé of the lessee from the negligence of the lessee alone.

On reason, we deem the judgment of the court below wrong, and the great current of authority, as shown by references hereinabove contained, certainly requires its reversal.

(209 Ill. 444)

CHICAGO UNION TRACTION CO. v. CITY OF CHICAGO.

(Supreme Court of Illinois. April 20, 1904.)

MUNICIPAL CORPORATIONS—PUBLIC IMPROVEMENTS—RESOLUTIONS—ENGINEER'S ESTIMATE—RECORD — STATUTES — CONSTRUCTION—ACTIONS—SUBJECT-MATTER—JURISDICTION—OBJECTIONS—GENERAL APPEARANCE—WAIVER—NEW TRIAL—GROUNDS—OBJECTIONS ON APPEAL.

1. Where no rule is entered or applied for to compel a party moving for a new trial to file a written motion stating the grounds relied on, and no objection is taken in the trial court that the reasons for the new trial were not stated in writing, such objection cannot be urged on appeal.

2. Where an objection to a judgment confirming a special assessment for street paving was one which challenged the jurisdiction of the court over the subject-matter, such objection was not waived by a general appearance.

3. A first resolution for a street improvement reciting that the improvement was thereby originated, the estimate of the cost being $17,000, "which estimate is hereby referred to and made a part of this resolution by reference," but which estimate was not transcribed on any record of the board whatsoever, did not comply with Local Improvement Act 1897, § 7 (Hurd's Rev. St. 1899, c. 24, § 513), requiring that the estimate of the cost of the proposed improvement "shall be made a part of the record of the first resolution."

4. The fact that the engineer's estimate, together with all similar estimates, were kept on file in the office of the board of local improvements, were properly indexed, open, and immediately accessible to any person, did not constitute a substantial compliance with such section.

5. Since Local Improvement Act 1897, § 7 (Hurd's Rev. St. 1899, c. 24, § 513), requiring the estimate of the cost of a proposed improvement to be made a part of the record of the first resolution authorizing the same, applies to the entire state, a construction of such statute by the board of local improvements of a city, different from the legal construction thereof, could not be adopted.

Appeal from Cook County Court; L. C. Ruth, Judge.

Action by the city of Chicago against the Chicago Union Traction Company. From a judgment confirming a special assessment for street paving, defendant appeals. Reversed.

Williston Fish and Louis Boisot (John A. Rose and Garnett & Garnett, of counsel), for appellant. Robert Redfield and Frank Johnston, Jr. (Edgar Bronson Tolman, Corp. Counsel, of counsel), for appellee.

SCOTT, J. This is an appeal from a judgment of the county court of Cook county confirming a special assessment for paving a part of Sheffield avenue, in the city of Chicago. Among other objections filed by appellant in that court was one to the effect that the estimate of the cost of the improvement made by the engineer was not made a part of the record of the first resolution of the board of local improvements, and the same question is presented here. All objections filed were overruled by the court below, and after trial by jury the assessment roll was confirmed.

The motion for a new trial was not in writing. It is preserved in the bill of exceptions. It does not disclose the reasons upon which it was based, and counsel for appellee therefore urge that, as the objection above suggested is not mentioned or particularly specified in that motion, it cannot now be considered. The better practice is to file a motion for a new trial in writing, and to state therein the grounds relied upon. If the party moving does not do this in the first instance he will be ruled to do so on application, or the court may enter such a rule of its own motion; but where such a rule is not entered or applied for, and no objection is taken in the court below on the ground that the reasons are not stated in writing, such objection to the motion for a new trial will be waived, and cannot be urged in an appellate tribunal. Ottawa, Oswego & Fox River Valley Railroad Co. v. McMath, 91 Ill. 104; Bromley v. People, 150 Ill. 297, 37 N. E. 209; West Chicago Street Railroad Co. v. Krueger, 168 Ill. 586, 48 N. E. 442.

Appellant entered a general appearance in the county court, and this is said to be a waiver of the jurisdictional objection that the estimate was not made part of the record of the resolution, for the reason that such an objection must be made under a special appearance, and that, where the appearance is general, an objection to the jurisdiction cannot afterwards be interposed. This is true where the summons or notice is defective, or has not been served in the manner required by statute, and the court's jurisdiction of the party defendant is questioned. In this case appellant was properly in court. This objection is one which challenges the power of the court to proceed, for the reason that certain preliminary proceedings were so defective that the court did not obtain jurisdiction of the subject-matter, and an objection of this character is not waived by a general appearance. 12 Ency. of Pl. & Pr. p. 186; Way v. Way, 64 Ill. 406.

Section 7 of the local improvement act of 1897 (Hurd's Rev. St. 1899, c. 24, § 513) provides that the estimate of the cost of the proposed improvement "shall be made a part of the record" of the first resolution. This resolution in the case at bar contains the following: "Be it resolved by the board of local improvements of the city of Chicago, that a local improvement be and the same is hereby originated, to be made within the city of Chicago, * * * the estimate of the cost of such improvement made by the engineer of the board being $17,000, which said estimate is hereby referred to and made a part of this resolution by reference." It will be observed that this resolution, except as to the amount of the estimated cost, is identical with the resolution which this court had under consideration in Kilgallen v. City of Chicago, 206 Ill. 557, 69 N. E. 586, where we held that such a reference to the estimate, when contained in the resolution, did not show compliance with the statute, for the reason that the estimate was not thereby made a part of the record of the resolution; and here, as there, the resolution was properly spread upon the record of the board, as required by section 7, supra, but the estimate was not transcribed upon any record whatever.

Appellee contends, however, that this case is distinguished from the Kilgallen Case by the fact that, in addition to such reference in the resolution to the estimate, it here appears that this estimate, together with all similar estimates, was kept on file in the office of the board of local improvements, open and accessible to all persons, and that said estimate has been so on file since the day the first resolution of the board was recorded in the book containing the record of such resolutions; that there is also kept in said office, open and accessible to all persons, an index book to such estimates, so kept and made that the estimate in any particular case and in the case at bar may readily be found by reference to that index, and that any person may, by application to the clerk in charge, or by personal search, easily secure access to such estimates. The purpose of the Legislature evidently was to require the preservation of the first resolution in a permanent memorial, and to have the estimate made a part of that memorial, so that the property owner, turning to the record of the resolution, would also have before him at the same time the information to be obtained from the estimate. It is apparent, considering this statute in the light of that purpose that no distinction between this case and the Kilgallen Case is shown. There is nothing more on the record which contains the resolution here than there was in that case. The estimate can only be found by a reference to a different record, which is termed an index. This case, therefore, is controlled by the Kilgallen Case.

The law does not require that the estimate shall be incorporated in or made a part of the resolution itself, but it should be made a part of the record thereof; that is, it should be spread upon the record of the board of local improvements with the record of the first resolution. If, from the portion of the resolution above quoted, the words, "and made a part of this resolution by reference," had been stricken out, and the words, "and which shall be transcribed upon the records of this board immediately following the record of this resolution," or other words of similar import, had been inserted in lieu thereof before its passage, and then, if the estimate had been spread upon the record immediately following the record of the resolution, the statute would have been satisfied.

It appears that the practice followed in this case has been followed in all cases by the board of local improvements in the city of Chicago, and it is urged, citing People v. Fidelity & Casualty Co., 153 Ill. 25, 38 N. E. 752, 26 L. R. A. 295, that, "where the execution of statutes is confided to a particular department of the government, the court will regard, and in doubtful cases adopt, the construction acted on by such department." This is wholly inapplicable here, for the reason that the execution of this statute is confided to the corporate authorities of all the cities, villages, and incorporated towns in this state, and not alone to the board of local improvements of the city of Chicago. Counsel's argument would lead to the statute receiving one construction in one city and a different construction in another.

It is unnecessary to discuss the other errors assigned.

The judgment will be reversed, and the cause remanded to the county court. Reversed and remanded.

(209 Ill. 70)

ALLEMAN v. HAMMOND et al.

(Supreme Court of Illinois. April 20, 1904.)

TAX DEEDS—DESCRIPTION—UNCERTAINTY—ESTOPPEL.

1. Where a tax deed described the land as "the east side (except the south-east corner) of the north-west quarter of section 31, Twp. 24, N., R. 4, E. 4th P. M.," etc., the deed was void for uncertainty of description, since the excepted portion could not be ascertained or located from the deed.

2. Where an owner of land procured the same to be assessed for taxes, but it was not shown that he had any knowledge of the description by which the clerk attempted to describe the land, or that he adopted such description, he was not estopped from claiming that a tax deed containing the same description as that by which the land was assessed was void for uncertainty of description.

Appeal from Circuit Court, Carroll County; Oscar E. Heard, Judge.

Action by Douglas Alleman against Robert Hammond and others. From a judgment in favor of defendants, plaintiff appeals. Affirmed.

George L. Hoffman and Henry Mackay, for appellant. Franklin J. Stransky and Ralph E. Eaton, for appellees.

BOGGS, J. The appellant claimed title in fee to a part of the northwest quarter of section 31, town 24 north, range 4 east of the fourth principal meridian, in Carroll county, in virtue of a deed made in pursuance of a judgment ordering the said land to be sold for delinquent taxes, and brought this, an action of ejectment, against the appellees to recover possession of the premises as owner in fee. The plea was not guilty, and a jury was impaneled to try the issue. The court refused to permit appellant's tax deed to go in evidence, and directed a peremptory verdict for the appellees, and appellant has appealed.

The description in the deed of the land purported to be conveyed thereby was as follows: "The east side (except the south-east corner) of the north-west quarter of section 31, Twp. 24, N., R. 4, E. 4th P. M., in county of Carroll and state of Illinois, containing 115.15 acres." The excepted portion in the southeast corner of the east side of the northwest quarter is in no manner described and cannot be ascertained or located from the description in the deed. The excepted tract not being ascertainable, it is, of course, uncertain what remained to be conveyed. When the land intended to be conveyed cannot be located from the description thereof in the deed, the deed is void for uncertainty. Shackleford v. Bailey, 35 Ill. 387; 4 Am. & Eng. Ency. of Law (2d Ed.) 802.

The contention of the appellant that Robert Hammond, one of the appellees, acting for himself and the other appellees, procured the lands to be assessed for taxation by the description found in the deed, and that the appellees became thereby estopped to deny that such description was sufficient, without being conceded to be good in point of law, may be disposed of by saying that the proof which was heard, against the objection of the appellees, did not show that the appellees, or either of them, procured the land to be described, for assessment and taxation, by such description. The only proof upon the subject was that Robert Hammond told the deputy county clerk of the county that he "wanted to put the balance of this quarter section that was not assessed on the tax books," and said to the deputy that he "wanted the unsurveyed portion of the 160 acres assessed." Hammond testified as follows: "The clerk took the assessment book, and found out what land was assessed in that quarter section. He made up the amount assessed—or, no; he set down 160 acres, and subtracted 44.85 from it. I don't know what writing the county clerk done in the assessor's book. I don't remember whether he read it off to me or not. I suppose it was placed on the tax books—knew, of course, that it was. I supposed the description by which it was placed on the tax books was the east part—the unsurveyed part, either way. By the unsurveyed part I mean the part that lays within the meandered line of this lake the surveyed land borders on. In that conversation nothing that I remember of was said about the southeast corner by any one. 'Except southeast corner' was placed in there because it was inclosed in a fence. We had it inclosed. The west portion of the northwest quarter at that time was surveyed, to my knowledge—not anything else to my knowledge. I don't know why the term 'southeast corner' was placed by the county clerk in this book. All the lands within the meandered line of Sunfish Lake, in the northwest quarter, I asked him to put on the tax books." It appeared from this testimony that the clerk formulated the description from what the witness told him about the land. There was no proof that Robert Hammond knew the description by which the clerk attempted to describe the land, or adopted such description, even if by adopting the same the judicial proceedings resulting in the execution of the tax deed should be regarded as containing a valid description of the land. The deed was properly excluded.

The judgment is affirmed. Judgment affirmed.

(209 Ill. 73)

TOWN OF VANDALIA et al. v. ST. LOUIS, V. & T. H. R. CO. et al.

(Supreme Court of Illinois. April 20, 1904.)

CORPORATIONS—RECEIVERS—APPOINTMENT—INTERLOCUTORY ORDERS—APPEAL—RECEIVER'S CERTIFICATES—ISSUANCE.

1. Where, in a suit by stockholders of a railroad company which had been leased to another railroad company in the hands of a receiver, a receiver was appointed and directed to bring suit to recover the rent, but was unable to do so for lack of funds, the court appointing such receiver had jurisdiction to authorize him to issue receiver's certificates to raise money for that purpose, though the claim for rent was the only property in the hands of such receiver.

2. In the absence of statute authorizing it, an order appointing a receiver cannot be reviewed either on appeal or by writ of error.

3. Since the only statute authorizing an appeal from an order appointing a receiver is Hurd's Rev. St. 1899, p. 226, c. 22, § 52, providing that, whenever an interlocutory order or decree is entered appointing a receiver, an appeal may be taken therefrom to the Appellate Court, but that no appeal shall lie or writ of error be prosecuted from the order entered by the Appellate Court in any such appeal, where an order appointing a receiver was affirmed by the Appellate Court as modified, whether such order was proper could not be reviewed by the Supreme Court on a subsequent appeal from a different interlocutory order prior to the rendition of final judgment.

4. Objections that defendant's answers in a suit in which a receiver of a corporation was appointed should have been held sufficient to overcome the evidence for the plaintiffs, and that the court was not justified in finding fraud and mismanagement charged in the bill, and that others alleged to be indebted to the corporation should have been made defendants, did not deprive the court of jurisdiction to appoint such receiver.

Error to Appellate Court, Fourth District.

Bill by the town of Vandalia and others against the St. Louis, Vandalia & Terre Haute Railroad Company. From an order of the Appellate Court (109 Ill. App. 498) reversing a circuit court order authorizing a receiver of the St. Louis, Vandalia & Terre Haute Railroad Company to issue receiver's certificates to raise funds with which to prosecute an action against the receiver of the Terre Haute & Indianapolis Railroad Company to recover rent due under a lease of the Vandalia Railroad Company's property, the town of Vandalia and other stockholders of the Vandalia Company bring error. Reversed.

Charles W. Thomas, for plaintiffs in error. John G. Williams and T. J. Golden, for defendants in error.

CARTWRIGHT, J. The plaintiffs in error, who are stockholders of the St. Louis, Vandalia & Terre Haute Railroad Company, filed their bill in the circuit court of Bond county against the said railroad company and its directors and executive officers, the defendants in error, charging said directors and officers with mismanagement of the affairs of the corporation and managing the same in the interest and for the purposes of other railroad companies in which they were interested as officers or otherwise, to the prejudice of the complainants and others as stockholders. The bill alleged that the said directors and officers had fraudulently issued preferred stock entitled to dividends at 7 per cent. before any dividend could be declared on other stock, for the purpose of diverting the funds of the corporation and absorbing its earnings so that holders of common stock should receive no dividend; that they had fraudulently appropriated funds of the company to pay for construction, betterment, and equipment furnished to it; that the railroad and equipment had been leased to the Terre Haute & Indianapolis Railroad Company, and was in the possession of a receiver of that company appointed by the Circuit Court of the United States for the District of Indiana; that the Pennsylvania Railroad Company, through the agency of the Pennsylvania Company, acquired a large interest in the Terre Haute & Indianapolis Railroad Company, and had obtained entire control, through its board of directors, of the St. Louis, Vandalia & Terre Haute Railroad Company, the defendant; that no steps were taken by said officers and directors to collect large amounts of rent which were due from the lessee, and that said directors and officers acted in the interest of the Pennsylvania Railroad Company and the Terre Haute & Indianapolis Railroad Company, in which they were interested, in disregard and violation of their duty as such directors and officers. The bill charged them with a purpose to continue such fraudulent conduct and disregard of their duty, and prayed for an injunction against further misappropriation of the funds of the St. Louis, Vandalia & Terre Haute Railroad Company, and for the appointment of a receiver to take charge of the property of said corporation, except the railroad property in the custody of said receiver, and to collect all moneys due or to become due said corporation, including moneys due for rentals, and to commence and prosecute suits and collect moneys wrongfully paid out, and also for general relief. The defendants answered, denying the material averments of the bill, and, replications having been filed, a hearing was had, and the court, on September 27, 1901, appointed a receiver of the property of the St. Louis, Vandalia & Terre Haute Railroad Company, except its railroad and the equipment thereof, and authorized said receiver to reduce said property to his possession, and to bring suits generally, in his discretion, without limit or restraint. From that decree the defendants prosecuted an appeal to the Appellate Court for the Fourth District. The Appellate Court affirmed the decree so far as the appointment of a receiver was concerned, but reversed it as to the provisions authorizing the receiver to bring suits against whomsoever he might choose, in his own discretion. 103 Ill. App. 363. The order was modified by the Appellate Court so that the receiver was authorized to bring suit for the collection of rent due the corporation at his own discretion, or to forfeit the lease in case of nonpayment; but he was not authorized to commence or prosecute any other suits without leave of the court. The circuit court was directed to enter the order as so modified, and, the cause having been reinstated in the circuit court, the order was entered.

After the reinstatement in the circuit court the receiver filed his application asking for leave and direction to bring certain specified suits and proceedings which were alleged to be necessary to protect the estate in his hands and to administer his trust as a receiver. The court granted the application, and on September 18, 1902, entered an order authorizing said receiver to demand from the receiver of the Terre Haute & Indianapolis Railroad Company the rent then due, or from time to time to become due, under the lease, and to declare a forfeiture of the lease in case of nonpayment; to bring suit against the Terre Haute & Indianapolis Railroad Company, or its receiver, or both, either by intervention in the United States court or otherwise; and to commence and prosecute a suit or suits against the Pennsylvania Railroad Company and the Pennsylvania Company for moneys received by them belonging to the corporation of which he was receiver. Afterward the receiver filed his petition, stating that he had demanded from the receiver of the Terre Haute & Indianapolis Railroad Company, the lessee, the rent due under the lease; that there was in the hands of said receiver over $600,000 of such rents due to the Vandalia Company; that the United States court had entered an order directing the receiver, in his discretion, to pay the rent due and to become due under the lease to the Vandalia Company, with certain deductions; that there was on deposit with the Pennsylvania Company the sum of $279,000 belonging to the Vandalia Company; and that said receiver of the lessee and other railroad companies refused to pay him anything, and that he was without means to employ counsel to carry out the order and decree of the court. He therefore asked for authority to issue receiver's certificates to such an amount as might be necessary for such purpose. On November 17, 1902, the court granted the petition, and entered an order authorizing the receiver to borrow $20,000, and to issue certificates bearing interest, which should be a lien upon the rents, issues, and profits of the corporation, subject to its bonded debt, and payable out of the first moneys coming into his hands, and to use the proceeds for the employment of counsel and for the necessary purposes of prosecuting the suits. From that order the defendants again appealed to the Appellate Court for the First District, which reversed the order (109 Ill. App. 498), and the writ of error in this case was sued out to review said judgment of reversal.

The reason given in the opinion of the Appellate Court for reversing the order was that there was no property in the possession of the receiver, and nothing upon which to base the certificates, except the uncertain results of the proposed litigation, and therefore it was an improper exercise of the powers of the court to authorize the certificates to be issued and placed on the market. Defendants in error make no attempt to defend the reasoning of the Appellate Court or to justify the judgment for the reasons given, but say that the real question involved is whether the receiver was lawfully appointed in the first instance. It is very clear that the reasons given afford no ground for reversing the order of the circuit court and requiring that court to abandon all attempts to enforce its own decrees. To appoint a receiver and authorize him to bring suit upon an apparently valid claim, and then deny him the means to do so, would be without precedent and without justification. There was no denial of the averments of the petition, and it is not denied by counsel for defendants in error that the Terre Haute & Indianapolis Railroad Company or its receiver owes the Vandalia Company a very large amount of money. The receiver refused to pay it, and it was necessary to the administration of the receivership that the suit should be brought. The reason for borrowing the money was that the receiver might execute the decree of the court and obtain possession of the property committed to his care, and the power of the court to authorize him to borrow money upon the faith of the large sum due cannot be doubted. The fact that the result of the litigation is not certain affords no reason for refusing the authority. If the certificates are negotiated, they must be sold to persons who will take the risk that the rentals will be recovered. The power to issue receiver's certificates is to be exercised very largely in the discretion of the court, and, if the discretion is not abused, the act of the court will not be reversed or set aside. In this case the circuit court was governed by the principles regulating the exercise of judicial discretion, and the Appellate Court erred in reversing the order.

The defendants in error make no claim that the order of the circuit court appealed from was not proper if there was a lawful receivership, but they insist that the circuit court erred in appointing the receiver, and the Appellate Court erred in affirming the appointment on the former appeal, and they have assigned cross-errors to the following effect: That on the appeal from the order now in question authorizing the receiver to borrow money the Appellate Court should have examined the entire record, and dismissed the bill for want of equity; that the decree of the circuit court appointing the receiver was void for want of power to make such appointment, and the Appellate Court should have so held; and that the Appellate Court should have reversed the original decree and all orders made in the case. On this writ of error neither party has raised any question of the right of defendants in error to appeal from the order of the circuit court to the Appellate Court, or the right of plaintiffs in error to sue out the writ of error from this court to review the judgment of the Appellate Court, and we regard the jurisdiction in each case as conceded. The history of the case, as given above, shows that there was an appeal from the order appointing the receiver to the Appellate Court, and that that court approved of the appointment, and affirmed the order, with a modification as to the directions to the receiver. That appeal was taken by virtue of a statute authorizing it, and in the absence of such a statute the order could not have been reviewed, either by appeal or writ of error. An order appointing a receiver which does not settle or adjudicate rights of property is interlocutory, and no writ of error lies to review it. The mere appointment of a receiver with authority to reduce the estate to his possession does not determine any right nor affect the title of either party. He is the officer of the court appointed on behalf of all parties to take the possession and hold it for the benefit of the party ultimately entitled. Coates v. Cunningham, 80 Ill. 467. A decree removing a receiver is not a final decree, but interlocutory merely, and a writ of error does not lie to review it. Farson v. Gorham, 117 Ill. 137, 7 N. E. 104. The right of appeal in any case is a statutory right, and it does not exist except where given by the statute which creates, limits, and controls the right. No appeal lies from an order appointing a receiver unless the statute authorizes an appeal. 2 Cyc. 611. The right of appeal from an order appointing a receiver must therefore be found in the statute, and can only be exercised as therein provided. The only statute authorizing the appeal from the order appointing the receiver is the act to provide for appeals from interlocutory orders granting injunctions or appointing receivers, in force July 1, 1887. Hurd's Rev. St. 1899, p. 226, c. 22, § 52. That act provides that whenever an interlocutory order or decree is entered in any suit pending in any court in this state appointing a receiver an appeal may be taken from such interlocutory order or decree to the Appellate Court of the district wherein is situated the court granting such interlocutory order or decree. No further appeal is allowed, but it is prohibited in the following language: "No appeal shall lie or writ of error be prosecuted from the order entered by said Appellate Court in any such appeal." Of course, a judgment of the Appellate Court affirming an interlocutory order does not change the character of the order affirmed, which remains interlocutory, and may be reviewed, as one of the steps in the case, in this court, upon a final disposition of the case; but there can be no further appeal or review until there is a final adjudication. In this case there has been no final order, judgment, or decree determining the rights of the parties. The controversy has not been determined. Questions of fact in issue are unsettled. No execution has been awarded, and nothing has been done except to appoint a receiver, and to authorize him to recover property, and for that purpose to issue certificates which will be a lien upon the property when recovered. To permit a review of the interlocutory order appointing the receiver, and the judgment of the Appellate Court affirming it, whenever any step is taken in the administration of the receivership, would be to nullify the provision of the statute limiting the appeal to the Appellate Court.

It is contended, however, that the circuit court was lacking in jurisdiction to appoint a receiver, and that the order of appointment is for that reason absolutely void, and may be attacked at any time. Wherever the court has jurisdiction of the subject-matter and of the necessary parties, its appointment of a receiver cannot be questioned in a collateral proceeding, whether erroneous or not. Richards v. People, 81 Ill. 551. However erroneous such an order may be, it is binding not only on the parties, but everywhere, until reversed by superior authority. If the court has no jurisdiction to appoint a receiver, as in a case where there is no law authorizing the appointment, the order of appointment is absolutely void, and it may be attacked collaterally. People v. Weigley, 155 Ill. 491, 40 N. E. 300. This is not a collateral attack in which the appointment or the receiver's title is involved, and the order of appointment is not void. The court had jurisdiction of the subject-matter and of the parties necessary to give the jurisdiction.

Defendants in error say that their answers ought to have been held sufficient to overcome the evidence, and the court was not justified in finding the fraud and mismanagement charged in the bill, and that other parties alleged to be indebted to the corporation ought to have been made defendants. Whether such claims are well founded or not, they do not affect in any way the jurisdiction of the court to appoint a receiver for the corporation, which was in court with its officers and directors against whom the charges were made. The defendants in error were parties to the suit, and bound by the order until it should be set aside by competent authority. The only appeal allowed by law was to the Appellate Court, and its decision was conclusive until there should be a final adjudication in the case.

The judgment of the Appellate Court is reversed, and the decree of the circuit court is affirmed. Judgment reversed.

(208 Ill. 577)

ORTMEIER v. IVORY.

(Supreme Court of Illinois. April 20, 1904.)

AGENCY—COLLECTION OF NOTE—EVIDENCE OF AGENCY—IMPLIED AUTHORITY.

1. Proof of authority to make a loan of money does not amount to evidence of authority to collect either the principal or interest.

2. Complainant requested a broker to find some one to whom complainant could loan a sum of money. The broker made a loan of such an amount to defendant, advancing his own money and taking a note and mortgage, which he turned over to complainant, and complainant paid over the amount to the broker. Defendant paid the broker for obtaining the loan. Subsequently defendant made payments of interest to the broker, who remitted to complainant, and on some occasions complainant requested the broker to notify defendant when the interest was due. *Held*, that the evidence did not show that the broker was the agent of complainant in receiving payments.

3. While an exception to a ruling of the court is not necessary in chancery cases, it is necessary, on appeal, to show by the record that any question presented for review was involved below and an adverse ruling made.

Appeal from Appellate Court, Second District.

Suit by Patrick Ivory against Henry Ortmeier and others. From a decree in favor of complainant, defendant Henry Ortmeier appealed to the Appellate Court, where the judgment was affirmed (109 Ill. App. 361), and from such judgment he appeals. Affirmed.

On September 26, 1901, Patrick Ivory, the appellee, filed a bill in the circuit court of Jo Daviess county to foreclose a mortgage upon certain lands in that county. Henry Ortmeier, Lotta Ortmeier, Martin M. Mitchell, Luther Geddings, August Gerke, and Herman Janssen were made parties defendant. The complainant afterwards dismissed his bill as to the defendants Martin Mitchell and Luther Geddings. The remaining defendants answered the bill, alleging that the mortgage indebtedness had been fully paid, to which answer the complainant filed a replication. August Gerke filed a cross-bill praying that Patrick Ivory be decreed to deliver up the mortgage and release the same on the records in the recorder's office. Complainant answered the cross-bill, and Gerke replied to the answer. Later Gerke died, and his executor was substituted. The evidence was heard by the chancellor in open court, and a decree was rendered in favor of the appellee, ordering a sale of the premises described in the bill, unless the mortgage indebtedness, interest, and costs should be paid within 30 days. Henry Ortmeier prosecuted an appeal from this decree to the Appellate Court for the Second District, where the decree was affirmed, and he now appeals to this court.

The facts in the case are substantially as follows: Appellant applied to Louis Rowley, a real estate agent, for a loan of $1,200. Appellee had previously told Rowley that he had $1,200 to loan, and had requested Rowley to find a borrower for that amount. Rowley loaned the money to appellant, taking as security therefor a note dated May 4, 1894, due three years after date, with interest at 6 per cent., payable to Patrick Ivory at the Galena National Bank, and secured by a real estate mortgage. A short time afterwards Rowley turned the note and mortgage over to appellee, receiving therefor from appellee $1,200, the principal of the note. Ortmeier paid Rowley $12 for obtaining this loan for him, but Rowley made no charge against Ivory for anything done in connection with the transaction. At the time Ortmeier delivered the note and mortgage to Rowley, the latter gave to Ortmeier his business card, and told him to send the interest and principal to him. For four years thereafter Ortmeier sent the interest to Rowley annually, and, when received, Rowley notified appellee of the fact, and appellee sent one of his sons to Rowley with the note. Rowley paid the money to the son, took a receipt therefor, and credited the amount on the back of the note, and the money and note were then taken by this son to appellee, and Rowley sent Ortmeier the receipt. On April 29, 1899, Ortmeier sent Rowley the interest due the following May, and also $700 of the principal, and the latter wrote him, stating that he might retain the balance of the money another year, and inclosing a receipt for the remittance, signed "Patrick Ivory, per R." Rowley only paid the interest to Ivory, and said nothing about receiving any part of the

¶ 1. See Principal and Agent, vol. 40, Cent. Dig. § 300.

principal. On February 20, 1900, Ortmeier went to Rowley's office and paid the balance of the principal, $500, together with interest in full. Ortmeier informed Rowley that he was about to sell his farm and move away. Rowley did not have the note and mortgage, those papers being in the possession of Ivory, but promised to get them, and suggested to Ortmeier that he had better leave them with Rowley until after Ortmeier had moved, to which he agreed. Rowley gave Ortmeier his personal receipt for this payment, specifying in the receipt for the $500 that it was in full of Ivory's note. Rowley prepared a deed from Ortmeier to Gerke, the purchaser of the land, and also prepared an abstract showing the Ivory mortgage satisfied. Ortmeier paid for drawing the deed, and Gerke paid for the abstract. On May 5, 1900, Rowley paid to Ivory $72 as the annual interest on the note, saying nothing to him about the principal, or any part thereof, being paid, and had it credited on the note. Between May 4, 1900, and May 4, 1901, Rowley died, without having paid to appellee the principal of the note, and without informing him that he had received it. In May, 1901, Ivory wrote to Ortmeier informing him that the interest was due, and referring to the death of Rowley. Ortmeier did not reply to this letter, and on June 12, 1900, appellee again wrote to appellant demanding the interest. Appellant answered this letter, replying that he did not owe Ivory anything. On March 2, 1900, Gerke, having secured the deed above referred to from Ortmeier, mortgaged the land to Herman Janssen to secure a note for $3,400. Rowley had negotiated five other loans for Ivory besides this one, and had collected and paid to Ivory the interest in practically the same manner as he did in the Ortmeier loan. There is, however, no evidence, other than the fact of receiving and paying money to Ivory, to show that he was acting as Ivory's agent in collecting those loans. One of the loans was made to King, who was a witness on the trial of this cause for appellant, and he testified that in obtaining his loan Rowley was acting as his agent, and that he paid him for his services.

The only reasons urged by appellant for reversing the judgment of the Appellate Court are that the evidence shows that Rowley was the agent of Ivory, and had authority to receive and collect the principal of the note; that the mortgage was satisfied by the payment of the $1.200 and interest to Rowley, and that the court erred in not dismissing the bill as to the wife of appellant and Gerke's executor, and in not adjudging costs occasioned in making them parties against appellee.

M. H. Cleary, for appellant. Sheean & Sheean, for appellee.

SCOTT, J. (after stating the facts). The evidence is not sufficient to show that Louis A. Rowley was the agent of Patrick Ivory to collect. It appears that Ivory told him he had $1,200 to loan, and requested him to find a place for it. Shortly afterward Ortmeier applied to Rowley for a loan, and Rowley took his note for $1,200, payable to Ivory, secured by a real estate mortgage. When Ortmeier delivered his note and mortgage to Rowley, the latter paid over the money, and Ivory did not part with his funds until Rowley delivered the note and mortgage to him at a later time. It would appear, therefore, that Rowley advanced his own money to Ortmeier in the first instance. Rowley directed Ortmeier to make remittances of interest and principal to him, and Ortmeier did so by mail, and the interest payments were in turn paid by Rowley to Ivory, but the principal, when paid, he embezzled. It is shown that, in other instances where Rowley had loaned the money of Ivory, the same course had been pursued in making payments, except that no other misappropriation appears. Ivory swears that Rowley never was his agent for any purpose, and the other evidence in the case is entirely consistent therewith, so far as the existence of any right to collect Ivory's money is concerned. There is no evidence that Ivory ever placed any money in Rowley's possession to be loaned, or that Rowley ever had possession of any of the evidences of indebtedness after the money loaned thereon by Ivory had passed out of the hands of the latter. The fact that Rowley received money from the borrowers and paid it to Ivory, and that Ivory requested Rowley to notify Ortmeier when the interest was due, and after the death of Rowley wrote Ortmeier of his decease, and requested the debtor, in view thereof, to remit to him, Ivory, consists as well with the theory that Rowley was the agent of the borrower as with appellant's contention that he was the agent of the lender. We think the conclusion warranted that such payments were made through Rowley by the borrowers at his solicitation, his purpose being thus to keep in touch with both borrower and lender for the purpose of promoting the loan brokerage carried on by him, and under such circumstances he would be acting as the agent of the borrower in receiving the payments. It does not appear that either party ever paid him anything for his services in collecting money and turning the same over to the mortgagee.

Viewing this evidence from the standpoint of appellant, the most that can be said is that it tends to prove that Rowley was Ivory's agent to make the loan in the first instance, but proof of authority to make the loan is not evidence of authority to collect either principal or interest. Cooley v. Willard, 34 Ill. 68, 85 Am. Dec. 296; Thompson v. Elliott, 73 Ill. 221; Fortune v. Stockton, 182 Ill. 454, 55 N. E. 367.

Lotta Ortmeier, the wife of appellant, and Dow, the executor of Gerke, appellant's grantee, were made defendants. It is now assigned as error that the court should have dismissed the bill as to them, and adjudged the costs occasioned by making them parties against appellee. As suggested by counsel, an exception to a ruling of the court is both unnecessary and improper in chancery, but it is necessary to show by the record that any question presented in a court of review was involved in the suit below and an adverse ruling made there. It does not so appear here.

The judgment of the Appellate Court will be affirmed. Judgment affirmed.

(209 Ill. 390)

REED v. FLEMING et al.

(Supreme Court of Illinois. April 20, 1904.)

NOTES—EXECUTION BY PRESIDENT OF CORPORATION—INDIVIDUAL LIABILITY—EFFECT OF SEAL—BURDEN OF PROOF.

1. Defendant signed certain notes, his signature being followed by the words, "Prest. Mt. Carmel Lgt. & Water Co.," and the imprint of a seal showing the words, "The Mt. Carmel Light & Water Company, Mt. Carmel, Illinois. [Seal.]" The notes recited that they were payable "as per agreement on reverse side," and by this agreement they were to be paid in first mortgage bonds, at par value, of the corporation, as soon as they could be issued in the regular and legal way, without reference to the date of the note. *Held*, that the notes were the obligations of the corporation, and not of defendant individually.

2. Where a defendant is sued on notes bearing his signature, followed by words indicating his presidency of a corporation, and having the corporate seal attached, the burden is on the plaintiffs to prove the obligations to be individual promises of the defendant.

3. Where a defendant is sued individually on notes which on their face appear to have been executed by him as president of a corporation and under its seal, it is immaterial to his taking advantage of the variance that the authenticity of the seal is not established.

Error to Appellate Court, Second District.

Action by Frank C. Fleming and Ashley R. Cadwallader, partners under the firm name of Fleming, Cadwallader & Co., against William S. Reed. Judgment of the Appellate Court, Second District (102 Ill. App. 668), affirming on writ of error a judgment for plaintiffs, and defendant brings error. Reversed.

Francis M. Lowes (George N. B. Lowes, of counsel), for plaintiff in error. Charles E. Woodward (Lincoln & Stead, of counsel), for defendants in error.

CARTWRIGHT, J. Frank C. Fleming and Ashley R. Cadwallader, partners under the firm name of Fleming, Cadwallader & Co., brought their suit in the circuit court of La Salle county against William S. Reed, plaintiff in error, and filed their declaration in the common counts in assumpsit. There was a plea of the general issue by the defendant, and, a jury having been waived, the cause was submitted to the court for trial. Plaintiffs, to maintain the issue on their part, offered in evidence two written instruments, viz.:

"$2,500.00. Chicago, May 6th, 1893. On or before July 15th, after date, we promise to pay to the order of Fleming, Cadwallader & Co., as per agreement on reverse side, twenty-five hundred and No/100 Dollars, at Central State Bank, West Lebanon, Inda. Value received, with interest at 6 per cent. per annum. William S. Reed, Prest. Mt. Carmel Lgt. & Water Co." Seal as follows: "The Mt. Carmel Light & Water Company, Mt. Carmel, Illinois, Seal."

Upon the back appears the following: "May 6th, 1893. It is agreed & understood between the parties to this contract that this note is to be paid in 1st Mortg. Bonds of the par value of the Mt. Carmel Light & Water Co., Mt. Carmel, Ill., as soon as the bonds can be issued in the regular & legal way without reference to the date of the note."

"$2,500.00. Chicago, May 6th, 1893. On or before July 15, 1893, after date —— promise to pay to the order of Fleming, Cadwallader & Co., as per agreement on reverse side, twenty-five hundred and No/100 Dollars, at Central State Bank, West Lebanon, Inda. Value received, with interest at 6 per cent. per annum. William S. Reed, Prest. Mt. Carmel Lgt. & Water Co." Seal as follows: "The Mt. Carmel Light & Water Company, Mt. Carmel, Illinois, Seal."

Upon the back appears the following: "May 6, 1893. It is agreed and understood between the parties to this contract that this note is to be paid in 1st Mortg. Bonds at par value of the Mt. Carmel Light & Water Co., Mt. Carmel, Ill., as soon as the bonds can be issued in the regular way and legally without reference to the date of the note."

To the introduction of these instruments defendant objected, but the objection was overruled, and he excepted. The defendant then offered the articles of incorporation of the Mt. Carmel Light & Water Company, and a certificate of increase of capital stock of said corporation under seal, showing that defendant acted as president thereof. The defendant submitted to the court propositions of law that the notes introduced in evidence were, as matter of law, the notes of the Mt. Carmel Light & Water Company, and not the individual notes of the defendant, and that when the seal of the corporation is attached to a note, and the name of the president of the corporation is signed to the note, with his official designation and the name of the corporation, the note is prima facie the note of the corporation. These propositions were refused, and the court found the issues for the plaintiffs, and entered judgment against the defendant for $7,312 and costs. The defendant excepted to the refusal of said propositions, the ruling of the court, and the judgment, and removed the record by writ of error to the Appellate Court for the Second District. The Appellate Court affirmed the judgment, and the writ of error in this case is prosecuted to review the judgment of the Appellate Court.

There was no extrinsic evidence as to the consideration for the notes, or by whom it was received, or of any facts or circumstances connected with their execution, and the objection to them, when offered in evidence, raised the question whether they appeared upon their face to be obligations of the defendant or of the Mt. Carmel Light & Water Company. That question was to be determined by looking into the terms and provisions of the instruments, and the manner of their execution, for the purpose of interpreting them according to the intention of the parties. When an officer of a corporation enters into a contract which he is authorized to make, and which purports to be the contract of the corporation, he assumes no liability. In such a case the contract is the contract of the corporation, and not of the officer; but he may pledge his own credit when in fact acting for the corporation, if by the language of the contract he binds himself to its performance. If, instead of attempting to bind the corporation, he uses words to charge himself he will be personally liable, although he adds to his name descriptive words identifying himself. In such a case his mere official designation will not exempt him from liability. So it has often been held that mere words of description of the maker of the note will not relieve him from liability unless it appears that he acted as agent for a disclosed principal, intending to bind that principal. Powers v. Briggs, 79 Ill. 493, 22 Am. Rep. 175; McNeil v. Shober & Carqueville Lithographing Co., 144 Ill. 238, 33 N. E. 31; Hately v. Pike, 162 Ill. 241, 44 N. E. 441, 53 Am. St. Rep. 304. The fact that the intention of the parties is generally discoverable upon examination of the instrument was stated in Scanlan v. Keith, 102 Ill. 634, 40 Am. Rep. 624, as follows (page 642, 102 Ill., 40 Am. Rep. 624): "Most generally there is that on the face of the instrument itself, and especially where the execution is witnessed by the seal of the corporation attached thereto, that indicates unmistakably it is the obligation of the corporation. It is seldom any one takes such paper under the belief it is the obligation of the officers executing it on behalf of the corporation." And again: "It is inconceivable a person familiar with the business transacted by a corporation, taking a note executed by its officers under its corporate seal, should believe he was obtaining the individual note of the officers whose names are attached to it. It needs no extrinsic evidence to show such a note is the obligation of the corporation. Such is the common understanding from what appears on the face of the instrument itself." In this case the instruments were signed by the defendant, William S. Reed, president of the corporation, and under its corporate seal. The words, "Prest. Mt. Carmel Lgt. & Water Co.," might be regarded as words of mere personal description if nothing more appeared, but the seal of the corporation could not possibly be regarded in that light. The seal of the corporation is in no way descriptive of the president or any other officer, but is used to evidence and authenticate papers and obligations of the corporation. It belongs to the corporation as such, and cannot properly be attached to the obligations of an individual. The seal of a corporation appearing upon an instrument is prima facie evidence of the assent of the corporation and of authority to execute the instrument. Springer v. Bigford, 160 Ill. 495, 43 N. E. 751.

But counsel say that the authenticity of the seal was not established, and that it did not prove itself, and therefore the obligation was personal. In Phillips v. Coffee, 17 Ill. 154, 63 Am. Dec. 357, it was held that the execution of an instrument by the president of a bank with the seal affixed afforded prima facie evidence that it was the seal of the bank, and that this rule does not dispense with the evidence that a seal is the seal of a corporation, but adopts a rule of prima facie evidence of the fact. Whatever the correct rule may be on that subject, the question before the court was whether the instruments appeared upon their face to be the individual obligations of the defendant. The burden was on the plaintiffs to allege and prove an individual promise of the defendant, and it was not for him to show that the obligation was not his. He might become personally liable for acting without authority when he assumed to act as though he was authorized, but that question was not presented by pleading or proof. The instruments, when offered without any proof, appeared upon their face to have been executed by the defendant as the president of a corporation, under the seal of that corporation. They therefore appeared upon their face to be the obligations of the corporation. It was afterward shown, without contradiction, that the Mt. Carmel Light & Water Company was a corporation and that defendant acted as its president.

There are other, and perhaps stronger, reasons for the conclusion that the instruments were obligations of the corporation. In considering whether the corporation or the defendant was expected to perform the agreement it is important to consider which would be able to perform it. The promise was to pay, according to the agreement on the reverse side, the sum of $2,500, with interest at 6 per cent. The agreement upon the back was thereby incorporated into the face of the instrument, and the obligation was to pay $2,500, with 6 per cent. interest, in the first mortgage bonds of the Mt. Carmel Light & Water Company, at their par or face value, as soon as the bonds could be issued in the regular way, and legally, without reference to the date of the notes. The instruments did not call for $2,500 in value of the bonds, but for bonds amounting to that sum on their face, regardless of value. There was no provision as to time of payment of the bonds or the rate of interest, and if they were issued on long time, without interest, they might be worth very much less than par, or with other conditions they might perhaps be worth a premium. The agreement, then, was to deliver mortgage bonds, with a certain face value, which had never been issued, and which the corporation alone could issue. They could not have been the property of the defendant when the instruments were executed, nor did he have it in his power to issue or deliver them. It was not in the power of the defendant to fix the maturity of the bonds, the rate of interest, or anything else affecting their value. That power rested in the corporation itself, which could fulfill the obligation. It would hardly be supposed that an individual would bind himself to pay $2,500, with 6 per cent. in cash, on a failure to deliver bonds which might be worth much less, where there was no provision as to maturity of the bonds or rate of interest, and where he would have no absolute right to control the terms, issue the bonds, or obtain them in the market. It seems, from the terms of the instruments, to have been intended that the corporation should perform the promise, and we think the court erred in admitting the instruments in evidence, and refusing the propositions of law.

The judgments of the Appellate Court and circuit court are reversed, and the cause is remanded to the circuit court. Reversed and remanded.

(208 Ill. 518)

ZELLERS v. WHITE.

(Supreme Court of Illinois. April 20, 1904.)

GAMING—RECOVERY OF SUMS LOST—STATUTES—AGENCY—PLAYING WITH CHIPS.

1. Hurd's Rev. St. 1901, c. 38, § 132, provides that any person who shall at any time or sitting, by playing at cards, lose to any person so playing any money amounting to $10, and shall pay the same, may sue and recover the money by action in assumpsit. *Held* that, in such action, the declaration should refer in apt language to the act of which section 132 is a part.

2. A variance between the averments of the declaration and the proof, which is the ground of a motion to instruct the jury to find for defendant at the close of plaintiff's evidence, must be particularly specified in the motion.

3. Hurd's Rev. St. 1901, c. 38, § 132, provides that any person who shall at any time or sitting, by playing at cards, lose to any person so playing any money amounting to $10, and shall pay the same, may sue and recover the money by action in assumpsit. *Held*, that one who employs others to play a game of cards in his interest is responsible to the loser for money lost to his servants.

4. Where those engaged in a game of poker purchased chips furnished by the proprietor of the place where the game took place, each chip representing a sum of money deposited with the proprietor, and which chip was redeemable when presented to the proprietor by the holder thereof, the fact that the game was played with chips, instead of with money, did not relieve the winner from liability under the statute.

5. All that transpires in playing a game of cards from the time certain players begin playing together on any one occasion until they cease playing together on that occasion, no matter how many hands are played, is to be regarded as one "sitting," within the statute.

6. Where plaintiff and others engaged in a game of cards with defendant, and at the close of the game defendant had won all the money which had been lost by plaintiff directly to him, and also that which had been lost by plaintiff to the others, defendant was liable to plaintiff for his entire loss.

7. In an action under the statute, the fact that there was a variance between the proof fixing the date when the gambling occurred and the bill of particulars filed with the declaration was not material; it not appearing that plaintiff had ever played at the place in question, except on the occasion in question.

8. In an action under the statute to recover money lost at cards which had been played with persons employed by defendant to play in his interest, the court instructed that no winning of the plaintiff could be set off against his demand for loss, unless obtained from the defendant at the same sitting. *Held*, that the instruction was not prejudicially erroneous because the word "defendant" was not followed by the words "or his agent or agents"; there being no question of any set-off on account of winnings in the case.

Error to Appellate Court, Second District.

Action by Lawrence White against Jacob Zellers. From a judgment of the Appellate Court (106 Ill. App. 183), affirming a judgment in favor of plaintiff, defendant brings error. Affirmed.

This is a suit in assumpsit, brought on December 3, 1901, by Lawrence White against Jacob Zellers in the circuit court of La Salle county. The declaration consisted of the common counts, with a copy of the account sued on. Before pleading to the declaration the defendant obtained a rule on the plaintiff to file a specific bill of particulars. This bill of particulars, when filed, showed the cause of action to be for "money lost gambling night Oct. 30–31, 1901, $100." Defendant in error then filed the general issue. The cause was tried before a jury, and a verdict was rendered in favor of the plaintiff for $70. After overruling a motion for a new trial made by the defendant, the court rendered judgment upon the verdict. The Appellate Court for the Second District has affirmed this judgment, and Zellers now brings the cause to this court.

During the trial of the cause leave was granted to the plaintiff, over defendant's objection, to amend the bill of particulars, by substituting the words and figures, "Oct. 31 and Nov. 1," for "Oct. 30–31." The evidence as to whether the poker game in question took place on the night of October 31st and morning of November 1st, or on the night of October 30th and morning of October 31st, is conflicting. On all three of these dates, however, plaintiff in error was conducting a saloon and bowling alley on the first floor of a building in the city of Ottawa and gaming rooms on the second floor of that building. He at that time had working for him

¶ 6. See Gaming, vol. 24, Cent. Dig. § 61.

in the gaming rooms two men, named, respectively, Kaiser and Downey. Downey was manager of the gaming rooms, and Kaiser was employed to operate a roulette wheel therein. On the night on which this game commenced, Zellers met White in the bowling alley, informed him that there would be a game of draw poker that night, and asked him if he was going to stay around, to which White replied that he was. The game started about 10 o'clock at night, with White, Downey, Kaiser, and four others in the game, and ended about 5:15 o'clock the next morning, with White, Kaiser, Downey, and one of the other four men in the game. These men did not play with money, but with chips furnished by Zellers' employés; each chip representing a certain sum of money deposited with the employé, and the house would redeem the chip when presented by the holder thereof. White paid for the chips furnished him, but the evidence tends to show that Kaiser and Downey did not pay for those furnished them, that they were playing for Zellers, and that any money or chips won by them belonged to Zellers. At the conclusion of the game White had paid $80 for chips, and had lost all of his chips in the game. Zellers and Downey had won a larger amount. They did not present these chips for redemption, but Zellers came to the room, took all the money from the till which had been paid in for chips, including the $80 paid by White, and took it away with him. A few days afterwards White demanded of Zellers the money lost by him in this game. Zellers refused to give it to him, and White thereupon commenced this suit.

Immediately after plaintiff had rested his case, the defendant moved the court to instruct the jury to find for the defendant. The motion was renewed, and an instruction advising the jury to find for the defendant offered at the close of all the evidence. The court overruled the motion and refused the instruction, which is assigned as error. Other grounds urged for reversing the judgment are that the court permitted the bill of particulars to be amended during the trial, that it refused to admit evidence offered by plaintiff in error to show that White swore before the grand jury that the game took place on October 26th and 27th, and that it permitted White to testify that Downey and Kaiser got the losings. The giving of instructions numbered 2, 3, 4, 5, and 6 for defendant in error, refusing instructions numbered 12, 13, 14, 15, 16, 17, 18, 19, and 20 offered by plaintiff in error, and modifying instructions numbered 8, 10, and 11, also offered by plaintiff in error, are pointed out as errors committed by the trial court necessitating a reversal of the cause.

Henry M. Kelly, for plaintiff in error. George H. Haight (M. T. Moloney, of counsel), for defendant in error.

SCOTT, J. (after stating the facts). Section 132 of chapter 38 of Hurd's Revised Statutes of 1901 reads as follows: "Any person who shall, at any time or sitting, by playing at cards, dice or any other game or games, or by betting on the side or hands of such as do game, or by any wager or bet upon any race, fight, pastime, sport, lot, chance, casualty, election or unknown or contingent event whatever, lose to any person, so playing or betting, any sum of money, or other valuable thing, amounting in the whole to the sum of $10, and shall pay or deliver the same or any part thereof, the person so losing and paying or delivering the same shall be at liberty to sue for and recover the money, goods or other valuable thing, so lost and paid or delivered, or any part thereof, or the full value of the same, by action of debt, replevin, assumpsit or trover, or proceeding in chancery, from the winner thereof, with costs, in any court of competent jurisdiction. In any such action at law it shall be sufficient for the plaintiff to declare generally as in actions of debt or assumpsit for money had and received by the defendant to the plaintiff's use, or as in actions of replevin or trover upon a supposed finding and the detaining or converting the property of the plaintiff to the use of the defendant, whereby an action hath accrued to the plaintiff according to the form of this act, without setting forth the special matter."

This suit is to recover money lost at draw poker. The declaration is an ordinary declaration in assumpsit, and does not refer in apt language, as it should do, to the act of which said section is a part, for the purpose of showing that it counts thereon. At the close of the evidence for White, the plaintiff, Zellers, the defendant, moved the court to instruct the jury to find a verdict for the defendant, and it is now stated that one of the grounds was a variance between the pleadings and the proof resulting from this omission in the declaration. The motion was not in writing. At the time of making it counsel tendered an instruction in the following words: "The court instructs the jury that the plaintiff has failed to show by any evidence that he played cards with defendant on the 31st day of October or 1st day of November, 1901, or that he lost money to defendant on those days in the playing of cards, and you will therefore return the following verdict: 'We, the jury, find for defendant; no cause of action.'" As the motion itself did not specify any ground upon which it was based, and as the instruction offered in connection therewith does show the ground upon which the defendant sought to have the jury instructed in his favor, the defendant cannot now be heard to urge that the motion was based upon the failure of allegata et probata to agree. A variance between the averments of the declaration and the proof, which is the ground of a motion to instruct the jury to find for defendant at the close of the plaintiff's evidence, must be particularly specified in the motion. Probst Construction Co. v. Foley, 166 Ill. 31, 46 N. E. 750; Illinois Central Railroad Co. v. Behrens, 208 Ill. 20, 69 N. E. 796. We will, therefore, not consider the error assigned in this regard. Had this matter been properly called to the attention of the court, the declaration could, and no doubt would, have been amended, and the objection obviated.

Again, at the close of all the evidence, the defendant moved the court to instruct the jury for the defendant, and it is now urged that there is in the record no evidence which tends to support the verdict. It appears from the evidence of plaintiff, which, for the purposes of this motion, must be taken as true, that he began playing draw poker at about 10 p. m., and continued until about 5 a. m. the next morning; that among those playing were Frank Downey and Chester Kaiser, who were in Zellers' employ and playing for him; that plaintiff lost during the time $80, and that Downey and Kaiser won a little over $100, which was made up of the $80 lost by plaintiff and small amounts lost by others. The money lost by plaintiff was not all lost on any one hand, nor, in the first instance, was it all won by either Downey or Kaiser. Some portions of his losses passed to other persons in the game temporarily, and finally from them to the agents of Zellers, so that in the end they were the only winners, and had won an amount in excess of the losses of the plaintiff. The game was not played by betting money directly. Chips were purchased from Zellers, or "the house," as the witnesses expressed it, and at the end of the game or sitting, if the purchaser by any chance had any of the chips left, or if they had been won by persons other than Zellers' agents, the house redeemed them, paying for each the price for which it had been sold.

It is first urged that as Zellers, in person, did not play in the game, there can be no recovery from him. We think this too narrow a construction of the statute. It appears from the evidence that in his gambling room roulette was also played. If the position of counsel be correct, and Zellers employed an insolvent individual to operate the wheel for him, as a result of which the wheel or the operator won the money of the player for Zellers as the proprietor, the player would be unable to recover from the winner. The proposition carries with it its own answer. What Zellers did by another in this instance he did by himself, and he is responsible for the money won for him by such other. Plaintiff could sue the agent or the principal, at his election. Plaintiff in error relies upon the case of Kruse v. Kennett, 181 Ill. 199, 54 N. E. 965, as authority for the statement that the doctrine of agency has no application so far as the question of the violation of this penal statute is concerned. In that case the suit was brought against brokers or commission agents to recover money lost in gambling in grain options, and in response to the contention that the plaintiff should have brought his suit against the person or persons with whom the brokers had transactions to counterbalance those of plaintiff, and who, in fact, profited by the losses of the plaintiff, it was held that the broker was a "winner," within the meaning of the statute, but there was no holding that the suit could not be maintained against such other person or persons who had profited by the transaction.

It is then said that because that which was actually staked on the game was the chips, and there is no evidence in this record that they had any intrinsic value, there is no evidence of the loss of "money or other valuable thing, amounting in the whole to the sum of $10." The correct view is that the chips were merely markers to indicate the amount of the money lost or won, the money itself being actually deposited with the gaming house keeper as a stakeholder, to be paid by him to the owner thereof as such owner was indicated by the possession of the chips which the keeper had given in exchange therefor, and that the loss of the chips was a loss of the money which they represented.

Attention is then called to the fact that many hands of draw poker were played—one every two minutes, according to the statement of the defendant—during the hours the plaintiff was engaged in play, and that each hand is a game, and that in each hand the plaintiff would win or lose; that when he lost, and that hand was played, the transaction was ended; and the person to whom that loss was paid, it is urged, is the only person from whom such loss could be recovered, and that the plaintiff could not recover money which he had so lost to some person other than the defendant's agents, because, in the end, such agents won the money from such other person, who had in the first instance won it from the plaintiff. Counsel urges that a strict construction of the statute leads to this conclusion, and authorities are cited in support of the doctrine that penal statutes should be strictly construed. This is the general rule, but it is only one of the rules to be applied in determining the meaning of an enactment of that character. In Hamer v. People, 205 Ill. 570, 68 N. E. 1061, the following language from Sedgwick on Construction of Statutes was cited with approval (page 573, 205 Ill., and page 1063, 68 N. E.): "The rule that statutes of this class are to be construed strictly is far from being a rigid and unbending one, or, rather, it has in modern times been so modified and explained away as to mean little more than that penal provisions, like all others, are to be fairly construed according to the legislative intent as expressed in the enactment." And in that case it was also said that the object of construing penal statutes, and all other statutes, is to discover and give effect to the true legislative intent, and the rule requiring strict construction of penal statutes is not to be applied with such unreasonable strictness as to defeat the true intent and meaning of the enactment.

The purpose of the Legislature in the enactment of this statute was to lessen, and, if possible, to prevent, gambling. The evils resulting therefrom are among the most pernicious that afflict modern society. The practice destroys in its devotees all desire to engage in legitimate employment or business. The loser becomes intent on recovering his losses at the gaming table, and is frequently driven to embezzlement and theft. The winner acquires a contempt for the small gains of honest pursuits. He spends the profits of unlawful hours in idleness and debauchery, among dissolute companions. Thrift is destroyed. Wholesome pleasures soon pall upon the taste. The ties of home and domestic life are disregarded, and eventually annihilated, by the craze for gaming, and by the feverish excitement with which it fires its followers. Being itself unlawful, it creates and encourages contempt for all law, and weakens every legal restraint and every honest impulse. Financial ruin and moral degradation alike inevitably overtake every man who cannot resist its allurements, no matter with what degree of skill he engages in the nefarious business. Section 132, supra, is calculated to make its gains unavailing to the winner, and to remove, to some extent, at least, the incentive to play. If the loser, after a long night at draw poker, must sue the man who won from him on each hand for the amount lost on that hand, and cannot have this remedy unless the sum so lost on that hand equal or exceed $10, the statute, for all practical purposes, would not be applicable to draw poker. This form of gambling became so common recently that it was denominated the "national game" of the American people. Its peculiar terms and phrases have found their way into common use in our language, where their aptness for the purposes for which they have been borrowed attracts the attention of many to this game, and no doubt leads them to a closer acquaintance with it, when, but for a familiarity with its expressions thus obtained, they would not have sought its beguilements. The interpretation placed upon this statute by appellant, so far as this seductive game is concerned, would enable the winner to substantially escape the salutary and chastening effect of this law, and deprive him of the refined pleasure which results from making restitution for wrongdoing. The Legislature certainly did not intend that this game, which is a very common vice, should escape the ban of this section of the Criminal Code.

Keeping in view the wrong at which the statute is aimed, and giving consideration to the use of the word "sitting," in this section, we think the proper construction is that all that transpires in playing the game of draw poker from the time certain players begin playing together on any one occasion until they cease playing together on that occasion, no matter how many hands are played, may be regarded as one transaction or "sitting," and that all those who have won more than they have lost during the sitting are "winners," and all those who have lost more than they have won during the sitting are persons "losing," within the meaning of the statute; that all money or other valuable thing staked upon the game at any time during the sitting is to be regarded as in play so long as the sitting continues; and that the liability of the winner to the person or persons losing is measured by the net amount of his own winnings. Resort may be had to equity, where necessary, for the purpose of making proper adjustments between the various winners and the various losers.

It is also claimed that there was a variance between the proof fixing the date when the gambling occurred and the bill of particulars filed with the declaration. We do not regard the statement of the date in this bill of particulars as material. It does not appear that plaintiff ever played in defendant's gaming room, except on this occasion. There are cases where the court below may, on motion, properly require the plaintiff to particularly identify, by date or otherwise, in his statement of account, the transaction or transactions on which he relies, and the plaintiff may be required to confine his proof to transactions so identified. Such a case was not here presented. We think the rulings upon the admissibility of evidence correct.

What we have said disposes of objections to the action of the court in passing on instructions, except as to instruction No. 4 given on the part of the plaintiff, which contains this language: "No winning of the plaintiff can be set off against his demand for loss in this suit, unless obtained from the defendant at the same sitting." The objection to this instruction is that the word "defendant" should have been followed by the words "or his agent or agents." There is no question of any set-off on account of winnings in the case. Plaintiff only sought to recover the net amount of his losses. Defendant did not offer evidence of any winnings that should have been deducted or set off. The error in the instruction, if any, was harmless.

The judgment of the Appellate Court will be affirmed.

Judgment affirmed.

(209 Ill. 291)

STEBBINS v. PETTY et al.

(Supreme Court of Illinois. April 20, 1904.)

EQUITY—CANCELLATION OF DEEDS—BREACH OF GRANTEE'S AGREEMENT TO SUPPORT GRANTOR—DEATH OF GRANTEE—FAILURE TO PERFORM BY MINOR HEIRS—EFFECT—CONVEYANCE TO MARRIED WOMAN—RIGHT OF SURVIVING HUSBAND.

1. The cancellation by courts of equity of deeds executed in consideration of the agreement of the grantee to support the grantor, on the grantee's failure to perform, is based on the theory that the grantee's refusal to comply with his contract raises a presumption that he did not intend to comply with it in the first instance, making the contract fraudulent in its inception.

2. Where a grantor conveying land reserves a life estate, the surviving husband of the grantee, dying in the grantor's lifetime, has no present interest in the land conveyed.

3. An owner conveyed his land to his adopted daughter, reserving a life estate. The consideration of the conveyance was the grantee's agreement to support and care for the grantor during life. The grantee complied with the agreement during her lifetime. The grantee left two children, three and six years of age, respectively. *Held*, that the failure of such children to properly support the grantor after their mother's death did not warrant the cancellation of the deed; their failure not raising the presumption that the agreement for support was fraudulent in its inception.

Appeal from Circuit Court, Pike County; Harry Higbee, Judge.

Suit by Luther Stebbins against Joseph Petty and others. From a decree dismissing the bill on sustaining a demurrer thereto, plaintiff appeals. Affirmed.

On May 27, 1903, appellant commenced this suit in equity in the circuit court of Pike county. The bill alleges that Luther Stebbins, the complainant, on October 21, 1868, became seised in fee of certain real estate situated in that county; that he occupied the land as a home until about July 10, 1902, when he conveyed the same (being all of his property) to his adopted daughter, Emily Petty, reserving a life estate to himself therein; that Emily Petty died on October 31, 1902, leaving, her surviving, Joseph Petty, her husband, and Estill Miller Petty and Marion Luther Petty, her minor children; and that she left no assets or personal property whatever. The bill then alleges that the deed of July 10, 1902, a copy of which is attached to the bill and made a part thereof, contains the following condition: "Reserving, however, a life estate in said land, and in further consideration of this deed the said grantee, Emily Petty, agrees and binds herself, her heirs and assigns, to properly maintain the said grantor, in sickness and in health, during his natural life, which undertaking of support and maintenance is hereby made a lien on the land hereby conveyed, situated in said Pittsfield township, county of Pike and State of Illinois." The bill then alleges that Emily Petty accepted the conditions of said deed; that since the death of Emily Petty her husband and said children have failed to support and maintain the complainant; that they have been often requested to do so, but have refused; that the complainant has made repeated requests of said Joseph Petty to pay for the complainant's board and support—and sets out that said Joseph Petty, in his own right and as the natural guardian of said minors, has refused, and still refuses, to carry out the agreement of Emily Petty contained in said deed. It is alleged that the consideration of the deed has utterly failed, and that said children are minors; and the court is asked to appoint a guardian ad litem for them. The prayer of the bill is that the deed be canceled and set aside, and complainant reinvested with the title in fee to the land, and for general relief. Joseph Petty and the two children above mentioned are made defendants. The consideration expressed in the deed from Luther Stebbins to Emily Petty is "$100 and love and affection, in hand paid." The circuit court appointed Jefferson Orr and W. E. Williams as guardians ad litem for the infant defendants. The defendants demurred to the bill. The demurrer was sustained, and a decree was entered dismissing the bill at complainant's costs. This is an appeal from that decree.

Matthews & Anderson, for appellant. Jefferson Orr, W. E. Williams, and Williams & Grote, for infant appellees.

SCOTT, J. (after stating the facts). It has been frequently held in this state that where a grantor conveys land, and the consideration is an agreement by the grantee to support, maintain, and care for the grantor during the remainder of his or her natural life, and the grantee neglects or refuses to comply with the contract, the grantor may, in equity, have a decree rescinding the contract and setting aside the deed, and reinvesting the grantor with the title to the real estate. Frazier v. Miller, 16 Ill. 48; Oard v. Oard, 59 Ill. 46; Jones v. Neely, 72 Ill. 449; Kusch v. Kusch, 143 Ill. 353, 32 N. E. 267; Cooper v. Gum, 152 Ill. 471, 39 N. E. 267; McClelland v. McClelland, 176 Ill. 83, 51 N. E. 559; Fabrice v. Von Der Brelie, 190 Ill. 460, 60 N. E. 835. A careful examination of these cases leads to the conclusion that the intervention of equity in such cases has been sanctioned in this state on the theory that the neglect or refusal of the grantee to comply with his contract raises a presumption that he did not intend to comply with it in the first instance, and that the contract was fraudulent in its inception, wherefore a court of equity will not permit him to enjoy the conveyance so obtained.

It appears from this bill that the grantee herein complied with her contract during her lifetime. Nothing that she did, therefore, raises any presumption that she was animated by any fraudulent purpose in accepting this conveyance. Joseph Petty, her husband, has no present interest in this real estate, as the grantor reserved to himself a life estate therein. Her heirs are the appellees Estill Miller Petty and Marion Luther Petty, aged, respectively, three and six years. Will the failure of these minor children to properly maintain the grantor after the death of the mother lead to the conclusion that the contract was fraudulent in the beginning? We are referred by appellant to the cases of Patterson v. Patterson, 81 Iowa, 626, 47 N. W. 768, Knutson v. Bostrak, 99 Wis. 469, 75 N. W. 156, Glocke v. Glocke, 113 Wis. 303, 89 N. W. 118, 57 L. R. A. 458, Wanner v. Wanner, 115 Wis. 196, 91 N. W. 671, and Lockwood v. Lockwood, 124 Mich. 627, 83 N. W. 613, as authorities for the proposition that appellant has the same remedy in equity against these minors that he would have had against their mother, had she survived and refused or neglected to perform her contract. None of these cases are cases where the rights of the grantee had passed to minors. In Cree v. Sherfy, 138 Ind. 354, 37 N. E. 787, however, the grantee, until his death, supported the grantor, and thereafter the grantor obtained relief of the character here sought against the minor heirs of the grantee. In Indiana, as well as in the other states, excepting Illinois, where the courts of last resort have considered contracts of this character, so far as we have been referred to their decisions by appellant, the relief is placed on the theory that the agreement to maintain will be read into the deed as a condition subsequent, and that the latter instrument will be construed as though the granting portion thereof were followed by words stating that it is made upon condition that the grantee support and maintain the grantor so long as the latter lives. Under such a construction, it is apparent that, whenever support and maintenance were not furnished to the grantor, no matter what occasioned the default, unless performance was excused by him, he could enforce the condition. We have never so construed these deeds. In the case of Gallaher v. Herbert, 117 Ill. 160, 7 N. E. 511, where the father conveyed a quarter section of land to his son in consideration of natural love and affection and $200 per year, to be paid to the father as long as he lived, this court expressly refused to hold that the conveyance was upon a condition subsequent, saying: "The words 'upon condition' do not occur, and there are no other words of equivalent meaning." No reason appears why a different construction should be given by us to a deed which requires support and maintenance to be thereafter furnished, instead of money to be thereafter paid.

These minor children, having no legal guardian, in the absence of some legal proceeding resulting in a decree or judgment providing for the enforcement of the contract of their mother against their property, which remains unsatisfied, cannot be held, in equity, either to have refused or neglected to comply with the contract of their mother. They are peculiarly the wards of a court of chancery. We must recognize the fact that, without the aid of a court of competent jurisdiction, their property cannot be applied to the satisfaction of this obligation, nor can they themselves elect to refuse to perform this contract; nor, in the absence of a decree or judgment against them, can it be said that they have negligently failed to comply with the terms of the agreement. It will scarcely be urged that the failure of two children of tender years to furnish support to the grantor, under the circumstances disclosed by this bill, raises a presumption that the contract had its inception in a fraudulent purpose on the part of their mother.

The grantor is entitled to support and maintenance as in the lifetime of Emily Petty. A lien securing the same is reserved by the deed, and he has the undoubted right to foreclose that lien if he so elects.

The decree of the circuit court will be affirmed. Decree affirmed.

(209 Ill. 50)

HERDER v. PEOPLE.

(Supreme Court of Illinois. April 20, 1904.)

CRIMINAL LAW—REVIEW OF EVIDENCE—NECESSITY OF MOTION FOR NEW TRIAL—PENITENTIARY SENTENCE—VERDICT FINDING DEFENDANT'S AGE—INDETERMINATE SENTENCE.

1. The sufficiency of the evidence to support a verdict of guilty in a criminal prosecution cannot be reviewed on error where no motion for a new trial was made.

2. It is not necessary, to support a sentence to the penitentiary for an indeterminate period, that the verdict should find the defendant's age.

3. Where a crime is punishable by imprisonment in the penitentiary for an indeterminate period, the jury are not required to fix the time of imprisonment by their verdict.

Error to Circuit Court, Peoria County; T. N. Green, Judge.

James Herder was convicted of robbery, and brings error. Affirmed.

J. W. Culbertson, for plaintiff in error. W. V. Tefft, State's Atty., and Edwin Hedrick, Asst. State's Atty. (Oliver R. Barrett, of counsel), for the People.

HAND, C. J. The plaintiff in error was indicted jointly with Ed. Colvin and James Shufeldt for the crime of robbery by the grand jury of Peoria county, and, upon a trial—his co-defendants not having been arrested—was found guilty, and sentenced to the penitentiary for an indeterminate period.

It is first assigned as error that the verdict was contrary to the evidence. The plaintiff in error made no motion for a new trial. The question of the sufficiency of the evidence to support the verdict is not, therefore, raised upon this record, and is not presented to this court for determination. In Call v. People, 201 Ill. 499, 66 N. E. 243, 94 Am. St. Rep. 160, on page 500, 201 Ill., and page 244, 66 N. E., 94 Am. St. Rep. 100, it was said: "The rule is well settled in this state that, where there has been a trial by jury, the errors relied on for a reversal in this court must have been first called to the attention of the trial court by motion for a new trial, and an opportunity given that court to correct the same (Illinois Central Railroad Co. v. Johnson, 191 Ill. 594, 61 N. E. 334); and, if the motion is overruled, the motion, ruling of the court thereon, and an exception thereto, must be preserved by bill of exceptions. In the case of Graham v. People, 115 Ill. 566, 4 N. E. 790, at page 569, 115 Ill., and page 791, 4 N. E., the court say: 'But even if the verdict was not supported by the evidence, we could not reverse the judgment for that reason, because the bill of exceptions does not show that any motion was made in the court below for a new trial on that account.'"

It is next assigned as error that the verdict is insufficient to support a judgment of conviction, as the jury did not find by the verdict the age of plaintiff in error. The record is silent as to the age of plaintiff in error, except in this: That he testified while upon the stand as a witness in his own behalf that he had resided in the city of Peoria 23 years. It was, however, not necessary that the jury, by their verdict, find the age of the plaintiff in error. Sullivan v. People, 156 Ill. 94, 40 N. E. 288; Porter v. People, 158 Ill. 370, 41 N. E. 886; Doss v. People, 158 Ill. 660, 41 N. E. 1093, 49 Am. St. Rep. 180.

It is also assigned as error that the jury failed to fix by their verdict the time of imprisonment of the plaintiff in error in the penitentiary. It was held, in Hagenow v. People, 188 Ill. 545, 59 N. E. 242, People v. Murphy, 202 Ill. 493, 67 N. E. 226, and Glover v. People, 204 Ill. 170, 68 N. E. 464, that the statute, where the crime is punishable by imprisonment in the penitentiary for an indeterminate period, does not require the jury to fix the time of the imprisonment of the defendant by their verdict.

Finding no reversible error in this record, the judgment of the circuit court of Peoria county will be affirmed. Judgment affirmed.

(209 Ill. 193)

HESS et al. v. KILLEBREW et al.

(Supreme Court of Illinois. April 20, 1904.)

WILLS—TESTAMENTARY CAPACITY—WHAT CONSTITUTES — EVIDENCE — SUFFICIENCY—JUDGMENT AGAINST EXECUTOR—APPEAL—FINDINGS OF TRIAL COURT—REVIEW.

1. Where witnesses of apparent equal respectability, candor, and fairness testified on both sides in a will contest based on testamentary incapacity, the court on appeal cannot hold that the witnesses of the proponents are the more credible, or had the better opportunity to form correct opinions.

2. The fact that a testator, at the time of the execution of his will, contested on the ground of testamentary incapacity, transacted some small matters of business, such as furnishing money to pay interest on a mortgage and taxes, and to buy food for stock, is not controlling in favor of testamentary capacity, especially in view of a showing that during the same period some of his acts were inconsistent with sanity.

3. Where a testator has capacity to transact ordinary business, the law presumes that he possesses testamentary capacity, but a person incapable of transacting ordinary business is not necessarily also incapable of making a will.

4. On a will contest on the ground of testamentary incapacity the witnesses of the contestant were asked whether testator was capable of transacting business, and the question was answered in the negative. Others testified that he was crazy, another that he was mentally deranged, and others that he was not in his right mind. Many of the witnesses detailed occurrences and transactions showing testamentary incapacity. *Held*, that the evidence of the contestant was not based on too high a test of testamentary capacity.

5. A jury in the trial of a suit in equity disagreed. The parties stipulated that the case should be tried by the judge presiding at the trial on the evidence heard by the jury. The stipulation provided that a transcript of the evidence should be made, and submitted to the judge for use by him in deciding the case. *Held*, that the findings of the judge were entitled to the same weight as if he had heard the evidence without the intervention of a jury.

6. The findings of a court on conflicting evidence orally delivered by the witnesses will not be disturbed on appeal unless clearly against the preponderance of the evidence.

7. A judgment of the Supreme Court in a will contest, in which the executor was the proponent, affirming the decision of the trial court finding against the validity of the will, will be against the executor in his capacity as executor, and the question whether his costs shall be a charge against the estate must be determined when he presents his account current to the county court.

Appeal from Circuit Court, Pike County; Harry Higbee, Judge.

Bill by Finis Killebrew and others against Jacob D. Hess, executor of the will of Levi Killebrew, deceased, and others, to set aside the probate of the will. From a decree for complainants, defendant Hess appeals. Affirmed.

This is an appeal from a decree of the circuit court of Pike county, rendered at the June term, 1903, setting aside an instrument dated January 18, 1902, which had been admitted to probate in that county as the will of Levi Killebrew, deceased, who departed this life on the 26th day of January, 1902, leaving as his heirs at law his children Finis Killebrew, William Killebrew, Zerilda Burbridge, and his grandchildren Albert Smith, Burton Smith, and Francis M. Smith, children of a deceased daughter, who were complainants in the bill to set aside the will, and his children Spencer Killebrew, Pearlina Hamner, and Robert Killebrew, who, with John Hamner, the husband of Pearlina, and Jacob D. Hess, executor and trustee under the will, were the defendants to the bill. The first clause of the will creates a trust in Jacob D. Hess, the executor, conveying to him the real estate of the deceased, consisting of about 320 acres of land; authorizes him to lease the same and collect the rents, issues, and profits therefrom, and pay the expenses of maintenance of the land, for the period of 15 years, and at the end of that period to divide the land, according to the best judgment of the trustee, among Spencer Killebrew, Pearlina Hamner, and Robert Killebrew, or their children. The second clause bequeaths to the trustee all the personal property of the deceased, and directs him to convert it into cash within five years after the death of Levi Killebrew. The third clause directs that the proceeds of the personal property, together with the net amount of money arising from the rents, shall be loaned or reinvested by the trustee, as his judgment dictates, until the end of the 15-year period, when it is to be distributed, according to the judgment of the trustee, among the same persons to whom the land is to pass at that time. The fourth clause recites that his heirs, other than the three named in the first clause of the will, have already received their shares of his estate.

The will, which was drawn by Jacob D. Hess, was admitted to probate on June 30, 1902, and the bill to set it aside was filed on October 8, 1902, the grounds of the contest being that at the time of the execution of the instrument in question Levi Killebrew was not of sound mind and memory, and that it was the result of undue influence exercised by Pearlina Hamner and members of her family. Spencer and Robert Killebrew answered, admitting the incapacity of Levi Killebrew to make the will in question. Pearlina Hamner and Jacob D. Hess answered, denying the mental incapacity, and denying the exercise of undue influence. At the April term, 1903, complainants amended their bill by averring that defendants were each estopped from claiming under said pretended will, for the reason that on January 29, 1902, all the heirs of the deceased, including all the devisees named in the will, excepting the trustee, joined in a contract providing that any will made by the deceased should be considered null and void, and that the property of the deceased should be divided among his heirs as in case of his intestacy. To this amendment a demurrer was sustained. At the same term the cause was tried, and the jury disagreed, and was discharged. Thereupon the parties entered into a stipulation providing that a jury be waived, and that the cause be submitted to the judge of the court upon the evidence which had been submitted to and heard by the jury, the same as if the said evidence had been addressed to the court on a trial by the court without the intervention of a jury, and provided that the stenographer should furnish to the court the transcript of the evidence which had been heard by the jury. At the June term, 1903, the court found that the writing in question was not the last will and testament of Levi Killebrew, for the reason that at the time of its execution he was of unsound mind, and mentally incapable of making a will, and a decree in accordance therewith passed, setting the same aside, and declaring the proceedings by which it was admitted to probate null and void. Jacob D. Hess, as executor, alone appeals.

W. H. Crow, Frank S. Dulaney, and William Mumford, for appellant. Jeferson Orr, A. Clay Williams, and Edward Yates, for appellees.

SCOTT, J. (after stating the facts). It is assigned as error that the court erred in holding that the burden of proof was on proponents to show by a preponderance of the evidence that the testator was of sound and disposing mind when he made the purported will. Appellant fails to indicate by a reference to the record where any such holding is evidenced. No propositions of law were submitted by either party to be passed upon by the court, and the question under consideration does not seem to arise upon this record.

The other assignments of error may be included in the general statement made by appellant that the finding of the court is contrary to the evidence. For the purpose of establishing the mental capacity of the testator, proponents took the testimony of 29 witnesses, and on this question 26 witnesses testified on behalf of contestants. As is usual in such cases, the testimony is contradictory and irreconcilable. Levi Killebrew, at the time he executed this instrument, was 76 years of age. He had been a farmer all his life, and for a considerable period had been a widower. He had been suffering from a cancer of the face for a number of years, and this finally caused his death. A few weeks prior to his decease, while on his way to Pittsfield, he stopped at the residence of his daughter, Pearlina Hamner, intending to pass the night with her, and then proceed on his way. The next few days, however, were so cold and disagreeable that he did not venture out, but became weaker, and thereafter was unable to leave. His condition from that time to the time of his death was pitiable. One of his eyes was eaten out entirely, and the flesh on that side of his face, from the eye to the corner of his mouth, was gone. The bone of the jaw on that side was also bare. He soon after became confined to his bed, and there remained until the time of his death. He was greatly distressed by an accumulation of phlegm in his throat, and on account of the condition of his face was unable to relieve himself. He was unable to drink in the ordinary way, and water was given him from a bottle, the mouth of which was passed into the back part of his mouth. He was a great sufferer, gradually growing weaker, and died eight days after the execution of the purported will.

Appellant urges that the witnesses who gave opinion evidence in favor of the testamentary capacity of the deceased were more credible and better informed than those testifying favorably for the contestants. So far as we are able to determine from the record there is no basis for this conclusion. Several of those testifying on behalf of the appellant were closely allied to Pearlina Hamner, and the testimony of several others is not of that positive character that carries conviction. The subscribing witnesses to the will, Thomas Harpole and Vinton E. Smith, when called by the proponents, merely identified their signatures to the attestation clause. Later they were called by contestants. Harpole then testified that he had known Levi Killebrew ten years; that he sat up with him three or four nights during his last illness; that at times he seemed rational, and at others he did not; that witness could not swear that he was of sound mind when he executed the will. Smith, called by contestants, testified that he also watched with Killebrew several nights about the time the will was executed, and that he was exceedingly feeble, and the witness stated that he was unable to testify that the deceased was of sound mind and memory when he executed the instrument in question. Two physicians, who appear to be entirely disinterested, and men of intelligence, testified that they saw him in his last illness, and, in substance, that he was not of sound mind. It also appears that the deceased intelligently transacted some matters of business down almost to the time of his death, and even after he came to his daughter's house on this last occasion; but that one of his sons for several years had generally attended to his business affairs. Evidence on the part of the contestants tended to show that his mind had been failing for several years. Witnesses of apparently equal respectability, candor, and fairness testified on both sides of this case on the principal question involved, and we have been unable to join with appellant in the conclusion that those for proponents are shown to be more credible, or to have had better opportunity for forming correct opinions.

It is then urged that the circumstances are all in favor of the testamentary capacity of the deceased, and the basis of this argument is found in the evidence to the effect that at and about the time of the execution of the will, and during his illness at his daughter's, Levi Killebrew transacted some small matters of business. These were of trifling character, such as furnishing money to pay interest on a mortgage and to pay taxes and to buy food for stock. We do not regard them as of controlling importance, especially in view of the fact that he said and did things during the same period inconsistent with sanity. In January, for example, when his son called his attention to a lack of food for the stock, he told him to sharpen the sickle and go out and mow some grass for them. His statement to Mr. Hess, at the time the will was drawn, that certain of his children had received their shares from his estate, seems to have been a delusion, as none of them had received from him any substantial amount.

It is then urged that the evidence for the contestants did not meet that offered for the proponents. Those who testified on behalf of the defendants generally gave it as their opinion that Levi Killebrew had mental capacity "to transact ordinary business" at the time of the execution of the will, which would include or be as great a capacity as was required to make this testamentary disposition of his property; and it is urged that the witnesses who testified for the complainants expressed the opinion that Killebrew did not have mental capacity "to transact ordinary business," and it is said that this was too high a test; that a man might not have mental capacity to transact ordinary business, and still have testamentary capacity; that the evidence for contestants therefore entirely fails to show a want of testamentary capacity; and in this connection we are referred to the case of Waugh v. Moan, 200 Ill. 298, 65 N. E. 713, where it is said (page 303, 200 Ill., page 714, 65 N. E.): "If a testator has capacity to transact ordinary business, the presumption arises that he is capable of doing any act requiring no greater capacity, which would include the act of making a will. But the converse of this proposition is not true, and it cannot be said, as a matter of law, that, because incapable of transacting ordinary business, a person is incapable of making a testamentary disposition of his estate." We have examined the questions propounded to the witnesses on behalf of the contestants, and find that they are not the same in every instance. In some cases the inquiry was whether Levi Killebrew was able to transact business, which would mean any business, and a response in the negative would deny testamentary capacity. Some of the witnesses testified that he was crazy; another that he was mentally deranged; others that he was not right in his mind. Many of them detailed occurrences and transactions from which the conclusion might very properly be drawn that the testator lacked testamentary capacity. While appellant's statement of the law in this regard is correct, the record is not in such condition as that the application of that legal proposition necessitates or authorizes a reversal.

When this case was tried before the jury, Hon. Harry Higbee, one of the judges of that circuit, presided, and under the stipulation the case was tried by the same judge upon the evidence which had been heard by the jury, and it is contended that the finding of facts is not entitled to the same weight, when reviewed in this court, as it would have been had the evidence been heard by the chancellor with a view of determining what the facts were in the first instance; and it is said that, as the stipulation provided for the making of a transcript of the testimony, which, in accordance with the provisions of the stipulation, was submitted to the chancellor to be used by him in determining the cause, his finding should be treated as though the evidence had all been taken by depositions, and he had not enjoyed the advantage of seeing and hearing the witnesses testify. The chancellor who presides at the trial of a question of fact before a jury must necessarily observe the appearance and demeanor of the witnesses upon the stand for the purpose of qualifying himself to pass upon a motion for a new trial, which may be based upon the ground that the verdict is against the preponderance of the evidence. He thereby necessarily obtains the same impressions in reference to the credibility of the various witnesses that he would obtain if he were hearing the testimony for the purpose of determining himself what the facts were. In the one instance he must determine what witnesses are worthy of credit, to enable him to determine whether the verdict should stand. In the other he must use precisely the same means to advise himself what weight should be given to the testimony of those who speak from the witness stand, to enable him to determine what the finding of fact should be. In this case the determination of the presiding judge in reference to the facts is entitled to the same weight as though he had heard the evidence without the intervention of a jury. Where the trial court, in a trial without a jury, has had an opportunity of seeing the witnesses and of hearing their testimony as it is delivered orally, the findings of such court upon mere questions of fact, when the testimony is conflicting, will not ordinarily be disturbed on appeal, unless such findings are clearly and manifestly against the preponderance of the evidence. Lane v. Lesser, 135 Ill. 567, 26 N. E. 522; Burgett v. Osborne, 172 Ill. 227, 50 N. E. 206; Delaney v. Delaney, 175 Ill. 187, 51 N. E. 961; Phelan v. Hyland, 197 Ill. 395, 64 N. E. 360. In our judgment, so far as we can determine from the record, the evidence in this case not only does not clearly and manifestly preponderate against the finding, but does not preponderate against it at all.

The appellees ask that a judgment be rendered here against the appealing executor, in his individual capacity, for the costs of this court. The judgment here will be against him in his capacity as executor. If, when he presents his account current to the county court, he asks credit for money paid in satisfaction of that judgment, the question whether he should be allowed to charge the estate with the money so paid will arise and will be an open one, if exception be taken to the report, in that respect, by any person interested in the administration of the estate.

The decree of the circuit court will be affirmed. Decree affirmed.

(208 Ill. 646)

MISERVEY et al. v. PEOPLE ex rel. HANBERG, County Treasurer.

(Supreme Court of Illinois. April 20, 1904.)

MUNICIPAL CORPORATIONS — SIDEWALKS—SPECIAL TAXATION—ITEMIZED BILL OF COSTS.

1. Under 1 Starr & C. Ann. St. 1896, p. 857, providing that the cost of construction of sidewalks in cities and towns shall be paid by special taxation, etc., and, on failure of property owners to construct a sidewalk as required, it may be constructed by the city, and the cost collected from the property owner, in which case a bill of the cost of the sidewalk, showing in separate items the cost of grading, materials, laying down, and supervision, shall be filed in the office of the clerk, etc., failure of a bill to show the cost of the separate items invalidates a special tax levied therefor.

Appeal from Cook County Court; L. C. Ruth, Judge.

Application by the people, on relation of John J. Hanberg, county treasurer, for the sale of certain land for delinquent special tax, to which S. T. Miservey and another file objections. From an order of sale, objectors appeal. Reversed.

George A. Mason (William J. Donlin, of counsel), for appellants. Frederick W. Pringle, for appellee.

BOGGS, J. The appellants appeared in the county court of Cook county and filed objections to the application of the county collector for judgment for a special sidewalk tax levied against certain lots and parcels of land belonging to the appellants under an ordinance adopted by the village of Oak Park. The ordinance provided for the construction of a plank walk, particularly described in a former general ordinance, which was made a part of the later ordinance, to be constructed and laid and materials furnished in accordance with the provisions of section 1 of an act entitled "An act to provide additional means for the construction of sidewalks in cities, towns and villages," approved April 15, 1875 (1 Starr & C. Ann. St. 1896, p. 857), the cost thereof to be paid by special taxation of the lots and parcels of land contiguous to the proposed sidewalk, in proportion to the respective frontage of the lots on the walk. The ordinance, in obedience to the first section of the act, provided that the owner of any lot should be allowed 30 days after the adoption and publication of the ordinance in which to construct the sidewalk in front of his property, and thereby relieve his property from the special tax. These objectors did not construct sidewalks in front of their respective properties. Prior to the adoption of the ordinance the village of Oak Park entered into a contract with the firm of Goetter & Hillmann, in which it was agreed that said firm should be employed by the village, for the period of one year, to furnish all materials and labor and lay all plank sidewalks ordered to be laid by the village, which should not be laid by the owners of the property, at and for the price of 34 cents for each lineal foot. The said firm, acting under said contract, after the expiration of the said 30 days which the appellants were given in which to lay the walk had expired, procured the materials, furnished the labor and completed the walks in front of appellants' properties, respectively, and the special tax sought to be here collected is for the cost of constructing said sidewalks under such contract.

Section 3 of the act relied upon to authorize the levy of this special tax provides that, if the owner of a lot fails to construct a sidewalk in front thereof as required by the ordinance, the same shall be constructed by the village, and that the cost thereof may be collected by levying a special tax on the lot in pursuance of the ordinance. Said section 3 further provides "that a bill of the cost of such sidewalk, showing in separate items the cost of grading, materials, laying down and supervision, shall be filed in the office of the clerk of such city, town or village, certified to by the officer or board designated by said ordinance to take charge of the construction of such sidewalk, together with a list of the lots or parcels of land touching upon the line of said sidewalk, the names of the owners thereof, and the frontage, superficial area, or assessed value as aforesaid, according as said ordinance may provide for the levy of said costs by frontage, superficial area or assessed value, whereupon said clerk shall proceed to prepare a special tax list against said lots or parcels, and the owners thereof, ascertaining by computation the amount of special tax to be charged against each of said lots or parcels and the owners thereof, on account of the construction of said sidewalk, according to the rule fixed for the levy of such special tax by said ordinance, which special tax list shall be filed in the office of said clerk." Section 4 of the same act makes it the duty of the clerk of the village to report in writing to such general officer of the county as may be authorized by law to apply for judgment against lands or lots delinquent for taxes or special assessments all lots or parts of lots upon which such special sidewalk tax shall be unpaid. Section 5 of the act requires such general officer to apply for a judgment and order of sale of all lots on which such special tax shall be returned delinquent.

A certified bill of the cost of the sidewalk, showing in separate items the cost of "grading, materials, laying down, and supervision" thereof, is the basis for a special tax list to be prepared by the clerk. It is intended for the protection of the owners of the property to be specially taxed, and is an indispensable step in the levy of a legal special sidewalk tax. Holland v. People, 189 Ill. 348, 59 N. E. 753; Craig v. People, 193 Ill. 199, 61 N. E. 1072; People v. Smith, 201 Ill. 454, 66 N. E. 298. The village in the case at bar caused the sidewalks to be constructed by the said firm of Goetter & Hillmann at a contract price of 34 cents per lineal foot, and filed the bill of costs with the clerk of the village accordingly. The bill did not, as the statute requires, show in separate items the cost of grading, materials, laying down, and supervision of the work, but only the amount paid by the village to the contractors per lineal foot. This contract price may have been more than the cost of grading, materials, laying down, and supervision; but it is immaterial whether it is more or less. It is not required of the property owner to show the contract price was excessive in order to defeat the tax, nor would proof that the contract price was less than the value of the material and cost of the work avail to maintain the legality of the proceeding for a judgment for a special tax. The right to levy a special tax is purely statutory, and the statute requires that an itemized bill of the cost of the walk shall be filed. This requirement is for the protection and benefit of the property holder, and cannot be dispensed with, and a certified bill of the amount contracted by the village per lineal foot substituted. The property of the citizen may be legally charged only with its proportionate part of the actual cost of the materials used in the walk and a like proportionate part of the cost of grading, laying down, and supervising of the work of putting down the walk, and the bill of costs must disclose these different items of the cost of the work in order to warrant the imposition of a special tax on the property of the citizen.

For the reason indicated herein, the judgment of the county court must be, and is, reversed, and the cause will be remanded for further proceedings consistent with this opinion.

Reversed and remanded.

(209 Ill. 120)

GAGE et al. v. CUMMINGS et al.

(Supreme Court of Illinois. April 20, 1904.)

VENDOR AND PURCHASER—MUTUALITY OF CONTRACT—SPECIFIC PERFORMANCE.

1. Where one of complainants contracted with defendant to exchange lands, and the contracting complainant did not have title to all the lands which he had agreed to exchange, title to the remainder being in the other complainant, but they executed deeds for such lands and tendered them to defendant, complainants could not maintain a suit for specific performance, because of the fact that at the time the contract was entered into it could not have been enforced by defendant.

Appeal from Superior Court, Cook County; Jesse Holdon, Judge.

Suit by Henry H. Gage and others against Norman P. Cummings and others. From a decree dismissing the bill, complainants appeal. Affirmed.

On July 30, 1902, Norman P. Cummings, one of the appellees, and Henry H. Gage, one of the appellants, entered into a written contract with each other for the exchange of certain land therein specifically described, Cummings to make conveyance to Mary B. Gage, and Gage to convey to either Cora C. Willett or said Cummings. Gage was also to pay the sum of $1,000 cash, and give a note for $5,000, to be secured by trust deed on the property to be conveyed to him by Cummings. Each was to furnish the other, within five days, a complete abstract of the property showing good and merchantable title in the respective parties, and ten days were to be allowed to examine the title, and sixty days to cure defects therein. All deeds were to be passed and negotiations closed at the office of the Chicago Title & Trust Company within five days after the titles should be found good, and the contract was to be held by that company for the parties thereto. The contract was signed by Norman P. Cummings and Henry H. Gage. The abstracts furnished showed title in Cummings to the property which he had agreed to convey, but showed title to part of the property agreed to be conveyed by Gage to be in Mary B. Gage. On August 8, 1902, before the title to the Gage property had been examined by Cummings, Gage deposited with the trust company two warranty deeds to Cora C. Willett, as grantee, conveying all the property which he had by the contract agreed to convey, one of the deeds being from Gage and his wife to the property the title of which was in his name, and the other from Mary B. Gage, his wife, and Henry H. Gage to the property the title of which was in Mary B. Gage, and at the same time deposited $1,000 in cash with the trust company. He also gave the trust company written instructions that the deeds and money were to be delivered to Norman P. Cummings when Cummings should deliver a deed from himself and wife to Mary B. Gage for the property which he had agreed to convey.

On October 24, 1902, the appellants filed a bill in the superior court of Cook county against Norman P. Cummings, Annie A. Cummings, and Cora C. Willett for specific performance of the contract. A demurrer interposed by Annie A. Cummings was sustained, and the bill was dismissed by the court as to her. The other two defendants, who are appellees here, filed separate answers, to each of which appellants filed a replication. The evidence was taken in open court, and a decree was rendered finding that by reason of the fact that Mary B. Gage was not a party to the contract, and did not sign the same, and therefore could not be held bound to convey the property the title to which was in her, there was such want of mutuality in the contract that the same ought not, in equity, be enforced against Norman P. Cummings, and dismissing the bill for want of equity. Complainants in the bill appeal to this court.

Simeon Straus, for appellants. Alfred E. Barr, for appellees.

SCOTT, J. (after stating the facts). This is a contract between Norman P. Cummings and Henry H. Gage, and provides for the conveyance of real estate by each. Mary B. Gage is not a party to the agreement, and it contains no recital to indicate any purpose that she should be a party thereto. It is not a unilateral or option contract, but provides absolutely for the conveyance of all the real estate therein described. The title to a part of the real estate which Gage agreed to convey was vested in Mary B. Gage. It is apparent that as the rights of the parties existed when that contract was concluded, Cummings would have had no right, at any time, to enforce specific performance thereof because Mary B. Gage was not bound thereby, while it is apparent from the contract that the purpose was that the owner of all the real estate therein described should, upon the execution of the contract, be bound to convey, and not that Mary B. Gage, the owner of a part of that which Gage had agreed to convey, should have an option whether or not she would accept the contract. As the rights of the parties were fixed by that contract, barring the question of a lack of mutuality, Gage, at its maturity, would have had a right to enforce specific performance thereof against Cummings, while Cummings could not enforce specific performance against Gage, for the reason that Gage was not the owner of all the real estate which he had agreed to convey.

"A contract to be specifically enforced by the court must be mutual; that is to say, such that it might, at the time it was entered into, have been enforced by either of the parties against the other of them. Whenever, therefore, whether from personal incapacity, the nature of the contract, or any other cause, the contract is incapable of being enforced against one party, that party is equally incapable of enforcing it against the other, though its execution in the latter way might in itself be free from the difficulty attending its execution in the former." Fry on Specific Performance, § 286; Waterman on Specific Performance, § 196; 2 Beach on Modern Law of Contracts, § 885; Pomeroy on Contracts (2d Ed.) § 166; Tryce v. Dittus, 199 Ill. 189, 65 N. E. 220; Beard v. Linthicum, 1 Md. Ch. 345; Duvall v. Myers, 2 Md. Ch. 401; Luse v. Deitz, 46 Iowa, 205.

Applying this test to the contract before us, it is apparent that the decree of the court below is correct, for the reason that under the contract as executed Cummings could not have specifically enforced the same against the owners of the real estate which Gage agreed to convey.

It is urged, however, that Mary B. Gage, within the time limited by the contract for the conveyance of the real estate by Henry H. Gage, executed her deed and placed it in the hands of a trustee, to be delivered to Cummings whenever he complied with the contract on his part, and that this was an acceptance of the contract on her part, and that thereafter it could have been specifically enforced by either party thereto. This contract was not one made subject to the acceptance or approval of Mary B. Gage, and therein it is distinguishable from a so-called option contract, which, in accordance with its terms, becomes binding as a contract for the purchase and sale of real estate between the parties only when the person entitled to exercise the option accepts, while the contract before us is one which, if binding upon the owners of the real estate as a contract of purchase and sale at all, must have been binding at the moment of its execution.

Appellants rely upon the case of Dresel v. Jordan, 104 Mass. 407. In so far as that case expresses views at variance with those hereinabove set forth, we deem it opposed to the great current of authority and to the better reason. Moreover, it is distinguishable in some respects from the case at bar, while Luse v. Deitz, supra, is exactly in point.

The decree of the circuit court will be affirmed. Decree affirmed.

(209 Ill. 284)

WALLER v. PEOPLE.

(Supreme Court of Illinois. April 20, 1904.)

HOMICIDE—EVIDENCE—SUFFICIENCY—REBUTTAL —WITNESSES — IMPEACHMENT — CAUSE OF DEATH — VENUE — PROOF — INSTRUCTIONS — SELF-DEFENSE—CONSIDERATION OF DEFENDANT'S TESTIMONY — TRIAL — MISCONDUCT OF JURY—SEPARATION OF JURORS—JUDGMENT—FORM—HARMLESS ERROR.

1. Evidence *held* sufficient to support a conviction of murder, the defense being self-defense.

2. Where defendant's witnesses testified that a witness for the state, in stating to them the circumstances of the affair, did not say that defendant kicked him (witness), whereas he testified on the trial that defendant did kick him, it was proper for the state, in rebuttal, to introduce testimony of witnesses that at the time of the occurrence said state's witness, in rehearsing the circumstances to them, said that defendant did kick him.

3. Upon the trial, testimony as to what a witness for the state had said in reciting the circumstances of the killing was properly excluded, where no foundation had been laid on the cross-examination of such witness for the testimony.

4. Where the evidence of the physician attending deceased described a wound which any one of average intelligence would know was mortal, it was not necessary, in proof of the cause of death, for the physician to have given his opinion that the wound was mortal.

5. Evidence showing that the killing took place at Mitchell's mill, at West End, in Saline county, Ill., is sufficient proof of venue.

6. Under Hurd's Rev. St. 1899, p. 689, which requires the clerk, after judgment in a criminal case, to deliver a certified copy of the judgment to the sheriff, who shall, "without delay," convey the convict to the penitentiary, while the judgment should not provide for removal "within a reasonable time," such a provision in a judgment will not be ground for a reversal where it is not shown that there was any delay or postponement in the execution of the sentence, so as to show that defendant suffered any harm on account thereof.

7. The jury should not be allowed to separate while deliberating on their verdict on a trial for murder, under circumstances where any harm could possibly come to the defendant from the separation.

8. An affidavit stating that while the jury were deliberating on their verdict, with the officers in charge, one of the jurors separated from the others, and went about 150 yards, and was absent from the balance of the jury for a considerable space of time, without showing the length of the time, where he went, or what the circumstances were, or that he was not in charge of an officer all the time, or that he had any opportunity to communicate with any other person, was insufficient to justify a new trial.

9. An instruction, in the language of Cr. Code, div. 1, § 149, that, to constitute self-defense, it must appear that the danger was so urgent that, in order to save defendant's own life or to prevent great bodily harm, the killing of the other was absolutely necessary, although, if standing alone, it would have been erroneous, as ignoring apparent danger, was not error, where all the sections of the Criminal Code relating to homicide were given to the jury, and with them section 148, declaring homicide justifiable where the circumstances are sufficient to excite the fears of a reasonable person as to the necessity of killing in self-defense, and the court also gave other instructions to the effect that the danger need not be real if the appearances and circumstances were such as to raise a belief of existing danger in the mind of a reasonable person.

10. An instruction that the credibility and weight of defendant's testimony were for the jury, and that they might consider his manner of testifying, the reasonableness of his account of the transaction, and his interest in the case, and should consider his testimony and determine whether it was true or not, was not open to the objection of telling the jury that they were not bound to treat defendant's testimony the same as that of other witnesses.

Error to Circuit Court, Saline County; A. K. Vickers, Judge.

Richard Waller was convicted of murder, and brings error. Affirmed.

M. S. Whitley, for plaintiff in error. H. J. Hamlin, Atty. Gen., and A. E. Somers, State's Atty., for the People.

CARTWRIGHT, J. On September 15, 1902, during an altercation with Joshua Pemberton at West End, in Saline county, the plaintiff in error, Richard Waller, when from 18 to 25 feet from Pemberton, fired his revolver at him, and killed Gus Mitchell, who was reclining on the porch of his mill at one side and from 8 to 12 feet from Pemberton. Plaintiff in error was indicted for the murder of Mitchell, and upon a trial was found guilty, and sentenced to the penitentiary for a term of 18 years.

It is first contended that the judgment is not justified by the facts proved, which are substantially as follows: Gus Mitchell was sitting on the porch of his mill, with his legs over the edge, and Joshua Pemberton was standing on the ground, leaning on the porch with his elbows, and talking with him. Defendant, who had been with a company that had a jug of whisky, and, according to his account, had taken two drinks, came to them, and asked Pemberton whom he voted for the previous spring for school director.

Defendant and John Dean had been opposing candidates, and Pemberton replied that he voted for Dean. Pemberton, testified that defendant called him a "damned old rascal," and kicked him on the knee. Defendant, in his testimony, denied this. Pemberton then picked up a block of water oak 2 inches wide, 3 inches in length, and 1¼ inches thick; and, as defendant backed away from him, Pemberton threw the block, striking him on the hand, or perhaps on the hand and nose, as he threw up his hand at the time. Defendant instantly drew his revolver and fired, killing Mitchell. The defense was that the shot was fired in self-defense, although defendant testified that he meant to shoot over Pemberton's head. The evidence justified the jury in finding that defendant provoked the difficulty, and that he did not fire the shot in self-defense. Pemberton was a small man, weighing 122 pounds, and was over 60 years of age. He was not attempting to assault defendant, and did not have any weapon or missile at the time the shot was fired. Defendant was about 39 years old, and weighed about 175 pounds. He was at a safe distance, and was in no danger whatever of any serious bodily harm. He testified that, after throwing the block, Pemberton stooped and picked up a club; but defendant also testified that he fired as quick as he could get his revolver out after he was struck by the small block, and it is quite clear from all the evidence that such was the case. The evidence justified the verdict.

The next proposition of counsel is that the court improperly permitted the people to introduce evidence in rebuttal. Various witnesses on the part of defendant testified that the witness Pemberton, in stating to them the circumstances of the affair, did not say that defendant kicked him before he threw the block. There was no evidence of any contradictory statement by Pemberton, and the testimony in question was for the purpose of raising an inference that his testimony that he was kicked was a recent fabrication. In rebuttal the people were allowed to introduce the testimony of witnesses that, at the time of the occurrence, Pemberton, in stating the circumstances, said that defendant kicked him before he threw the block. The evidence was limited to about the time of the occurrence. As a general rule, proof of statements made by a witness out of court harmonizing with his testimony is inadmissible, but where it is charged that his story is a recent fabrication, or that he has some motive for testifying falsely, proof that he gave a similar account of the transaction when the motive did not exist, or before the effect of the account could be foreseen, is admissible. Gates v. People, 14 Ill. 433; Stolp v. Blair, 68 Ill. 541. It was not claimed that Pemberton had ever made any different or contradictory statement, but the attempt was to show that he had recently fabricated the story, because he did not state on the prior occasions that defendant kicked him. The evidence was limited to its legitimate purpose, and was properly admitted.

It is next objected that the court refused proper evidence on behalf of defendant. Henry Stucker was one of those testifying that, in conversation with him, Pemberton did not say anything about defendant kicking him. He was then asked if Pemberton said anything as to whom defendant shot at, and if he did not say that defendant shot at him and hit Gus Mitchell. No foundation had been laid on the cross-examination of Pemberton for this testimony, and the court sustained an objection to the questions. We do not see in what respect the testimony would have contradicted Pemberton if it had been admitted, and we think the ruling was right.

It is next contended that there was no proof of the cause of the death of Gus Mitchell. The doctor attending Mitchell testified that he was with him two-thirds of the time until his death; that he was suffering from a gunshot wound; that the ball entered the left side, and ranged upward and to the right, passing through the peritoneum and along the intestines, and in several places passed through the coils of the intestines, and passed through the stomach, and upward into the back part of the right lung; and that Mitchell died. The objection is that the doctor should have given his opinion that the wound was mortal. The evidence described a mortal wound, and the proof of the cause of death would not have been more convincing if the doctor had added his opinion. Where the facts proved are such that every person of average intelligence would know, from his own knowledge or experience, that a wound was mortal, all the requirements of the law are met.

It is also insisted that the venue was not proved. The evidence was that the shooting took place at Mitchell's mill, in West End, in Saline county, Ill., and the venue was clearly proved.

The next point made is, that the judgment is void because it requires the sheriff to convey the defendant to the penitentiary within a reasonable time. The court is required to pronounce judgment, and section 18 of division 14 of the Criminal Code then requires that the clerk of the court shall forthwith deliver a certified copy of the judgment to the sheriff or other proper officer of the county, who shall without delay convey the convict to the penitentiary of the state, and deliver him to the warden thereof. Hurd's Rev. St. 1899, p. 639. The judgment should not provide for removal within a reasonable time, but the presumption is that the clerk and sheriff performed their respective duties under the statute; and there is nothing to show that there was any delay, or that the statute was not literally complied with. There was no postponement, in the judgment, of the execution of the sentence, and it was not inconsistent with the performance of their duties by the clerk and sheriff. Inasmuch as it does not appear that plaintiff in error suffered any harm on account of the form of the judgment, it is not ground for reversal.

The next point made is, that a motion for a new trial should have been sustained because the jury were allowed to separate while deliberating on their verdict. The motion was supported by an affidavit that, while the jury were deliberating on their verdict two officers were in charge of the jurors, and that one of such jurors separated from the others, and went about 150 yards, and was absent from the balance of the jury for a considerable space of time. In a case of this character the jury should not be allowed to separate, while deliberating upon their verdict, under circumstances where any harm could possibly come to the defendant from the separation. McKinney v. People, 2 Gilman, 540, 43 Am. Dec. 65; Jumpertz v. People, 21 Ill. 375. There may be circumstances, however, that would necessitate a juror being absent from the others for a time in charge of an officer, and there is nothing in the affidavit to show that the juror was not in charge of an officer all the time, or that he had any opportunity to communicate with any other person. The affidavit does not state the length of time that the juror was separated from the jury, where he went, or what the circumstances were, and we regard it as insufficient to justify a new trial.

Objections are made to some instructions given at the request of the people. The jury were very fully instructed, at the request of the defendant, upon every proposition of law favorable to him, including the law of self-defense, but it is insisted that the court erred in giving the ninth instruction on that subject at the request of the people. This instruction was a copy of section 149 of division 1 of the Criminal Code, and if it had been given alone, as the only instruction on the subject of self-defense, it would have been erroneous, as ignoring the doctrine of apparent danger. Gainey v. People, 97 Ill. 270, 37 Am. Rep. 109. It is not error, however, to give such an instruction as a part of a series of instructions fairly presenting the law of self-defense. McCoy v. People, 175 Ill. 224, 51 N. E. 777. In this case all the sections of the Criminal Code relating to homicide were given to the jury, including sections 148 and 149. The court also gave to the jury, at the request of the people, the 14th, 15th, and 18th instructions, recognizing fully the right of self-defense in cases where the danger is only apparent, and at the instance of defendant gave the 11th, 12th, 13th, 14th, 15th, 16th, 17th, and 18th instructions, informing the jury fully that the danger need not be real, if the appearances and circumstances are such as to raise a belief of existing danger in the mind of a reasonable person. The jury were fully instructed on the subject, and could not have misunderstood that the necessity for taking life need not be actual, but may be only apparent, if the apprehension of danger is reasonable and well grounded from the surrounding circumstances.

The thirteenth instruction given at the request of the People is objected to as placing the plaintiff in error in a different class from other witnesses, and not requiring the jury to treat his testimony the same as that of others; and the decision in Hellyer v. People, 186 Ill. 550, 58 N. E. 245, is relied upon. In that case the jury were told that they were not bound to treat the defendant's testimony the same as that of the other witnesses. But the instruction in this case is entirely different. In this case the jury were told that the credibility and weight of his testimony were for them; that, in testifying, they might take into consideration his manner of testifying, the reasonableness or unreasonableness of his account of the transaction, and his interest in the case, and they should consider his testimony and determine whether it was true or not.

We find no error in the record, and the judgment is affirmed. Judgment affirmed.

(209 Ill. 246)

KINKADE et al. v. GIBSON et al.

(Supreme Court of Illinois. April 20, 1904.)

EJECTMENT—EVIDENCE—JUDGMENTS—ADMISSIBILITY—EXECUTIONS—SCIRE FACIAS—DEATH OF JUDGMENT DEBTOR—LIEN OF JUDGMENT—EXECUTION AGAINST HEIRS—NOTICE TO ADMINISTRATOR—SERVICE.

1. An assignment of errors must be signed by plaintiff or his attorney, or the appeal will be dismissed on motion.

2. In ejectment a judgment was admissible in evidence, although it did not recite service of summons on defendant, where the summons was in evidence, and showed personal service on defendant more than 10 days before the first day of the term of court at which the judgment was rendered.

3. In ejectment, a judgment having been admitted in evidence, it was error to admit an execution which varied from the judgment in an essential particular.

4. In ejectment, a judgment on a scire facias was properly admitted, though it did not affirmatively show service of the writ on defendant, where the writ had been admitted, with a return thereon showing due service.

5. Since the statute requiring notice to be given to an administrator before issuing execution on a judgment against his decedent does not specify a different mode of service, the notice must be personally served.

6. Under the statute requiring notice to be given to an administrator before issuing an execution on a judgment against his decedent, while evidence that the notice was mailed is insufficient to show service, yet such evidence, together with testimony of the administrator that he received a notice, and took it to the attorney who sent it, who explained it to him, sufficiently shows the statute to have been complied with.

7. In ejectment, where defendants had no title under the limitation act, payment of taxes by them was immaterial, and receipts showing such payment were improperly admitted.

8. Hurd's Rev. St. 1899, pp. 1048 to 1053, provide that, when execution is not issued within a

year from the rendition of judgment, the lien of the judgment ceases, but execution may issue within 7 years, and will become a lien from the time of the delivery of execution to the sheriff. Where a person against whom a judgment is rendered dies, execution may be issued, without a revivor of the judgment against the heirs, after the expiration of 12 months from such death, on 3 months' notice to the legal representative or heirs of the existence of the judgment. *Held* that, on the death of a judgment debtor, execution can be issued, and will become a lien, while the title remains in the heirs, at any time within 7 years after the entry or revivor of the judgment, not including the 12-months delay on account of the death of the judgment debtor.

Appeal from Circuit Court, Richland County; P. A. Pearce, Judge.

Ejectment by J. M. Kinkade and others against Emily J. Gibson and others. From a judgment for defendants, plaintiffs appeal. Affirmed.

Levi Clodfelter, for appellants. Allen & Fritchey and H. G. Morris, for appellees.

CARTWRIGHT, J. This is a suit in ejectment brought by appellants, the heirs at law of James Kinkade, deceased, in the circuit court of Richland county, against the appellees. There was a plea of not guilty, and an affidavit that the parties claimed title from a common source. Upon a trial before the judge without a jury, the issue was found for the defendants, and judgment was rendered against the plaintiffs for costs.

Upon the back of the transcript a paper has been pasted, on which there appears what was evidently intended as an assignment of errors, but it is not in the form of such an assignment, and is not signed. The assignment of errors is the pleading of the appellant or plaintiff in error, and must be signed by him or his attorney. 2 Ency. of Pl. & Pr. 960; 2 Cyc. 1002. If a motion had been made to dismiss the appeal for want of a proper assignment of errors, the appeal would have been dismissed. There was no motion to dismiss the appeal, and, the cause having been submitted for decision, we have concluded to consider the case as presented by counsel.

James Kinkade, at the time of his death, on August 23, 1893, was the owner of certain premises in Richland county, and plaintiffs are his heirs at law. At the January term, 1884, of Richland county, James S. McCartney, for the use of James McWilliams, recovered a judgment in assumpsit by default against said James Kinkade for $410.90 and costs. At the January term, 1891, that judgment was revived by default on scire facias against said James Kinkade. No execution was issued after the revivor before the death of James Kinkade, on August 23, 1893. After his death, execution was issued on October 24, 1894, by virtue of which the sheriff levied upon and sold said lands to James McWilliams, and, the lands not being redeemed, a deed was executed to McWilliams, and he conveyed to Emily J. Gibson, one of the defendants.

There are several objections to rulings on the admission of evidence. Plaintiffs objected to the introduction of the original judgment for the reason that it did not recite service of summons on James Kinkade. The objection was overruled, and in this there was no error, for the reason that the summons was in evidence, and showed personal service on Kinkade more than 10 days before the first day of the term of court at which the judgment was rendered.

The defendants offered in evidence an execution dated June 30, 1884, running in the name of James S. McCartney, for the use of James McWilliams, against James Kinkade. The execution was objected to, and the objection overruled. In this the court erred. An execution must conform to the judgment. Hobson v. McCambridge, 130 Ill. 367, 22 N. E. 823. And this execution did not follow the judgment in an essential particular, but appeared to have been issued on a different judgment. The case must be treated as though the first execution issued on the judgment was on August 24, 1894, after the death of the judgment debtor. But in our opinion, neither the rights of the parties, nor the result of the suit, was affected by the erroneous ruling.

The judgment on the scire facias was objected to on the specific ground that it did not affirmatively show service of the writ upon the defendant. The writ had been admitted in evidence, with a return thereon showing it had been duly served, and the specific objection made was properly overruled. The judgment is exceedingly informal, and there is a variance between the writ and the judgment in the name of the nominal plaintiff; but the variance was not made a ground of the objection, and there was no ruling on that subject to be reviewed. The purpose of a revivor is to renew a dormant judgment, and to give it its original force as a lien on the judgment debtor's property, and the proper form of the judgment is to award execution for the amount of the original judgment, with interest from its rendition, and costs. We think that this judgment, although not in the best form, contains the essentials of a judgment of revivor.

It was objected that there was no sufficient evidence that notice was given to the administrator before issuing execution, as required by the statute. An attorney testified that he sent a notice to the administrator, and filed a copy with the clerk of the county court, but that the copy had been lost from the files. The statute does not specify a different mode of service of the notice, and therefore it must be personal. Chicago & Alton Railroad Co. v. Smith, 78 Ill. 96. The evidence that the notice was mailed was not sufficient, but the administrator testified that he received a notice, and took it to the attorney who sent it, and that the attorney explained it to him. The notice was actually received by the administrator, and we regard the statute as having been complied with.

The levy on the lands and subsequent proceedings were objected to on the ground that the description of the premises was uncertain. The declaration is not abstracted, and the abstract does not show, in any manner, what lands plaintiffs were seeking to recover. The levy and subsequent proceedings were sufficiently definite as to part of the lands, at least; and, as the abstract does not show what lands plaintiffs were suing for, we cannot say that the levy did not describe them.

Several receipts showing payments of taxes by the defendants were improperly admitted in evidence. There was no title in the defendants under the limitation act, and the question who paid the taxes was immaterial. The tax receipts, however, did not affect the result in any way, and the judgment cannot be reversed on account of their admission.

The principal question is whether the premises could be sold under an execution issued after the death of James Kinkade on a judgment which was not a lien upon the premises at the time of his death. No execution was issued within a year after the judgment of revivor, and the lien of the judgment therefore expired in the lifetime of the judgment debtor. By the statute a judgment of a court of record is a lien on the real estate of the person against whom it is obtained, from the time it is rendered or revived, for a period of seven years. When execution is not issued within one year from such rendition, the lien so created ceases, but execution may issue within seven years, and will become a lien from the time of the delivery of the execution to the sheriff. In case of the death of a person against whom a judgment is rendered, execution may issue and a sale be made without reviving the judgment against his heirs; but no execution can issue until after the expiration of 12 months from his death, nor until his legal representative or heirs shall have had 3 months' notice of the existence of the judgment. Hurd's Rev. St. 1899, pp. 1048-1053. After the expiration of one year from the judgment of revivor, James Kinkade could have sold the premises discharged of the lien of the judgment; but, if he had been living when execution was issued, it would have become a lien upon the premises when delivered to the sheriff. The claim here is that, the title having passed to the heirs after the lien had expired, they took the premises unaffected by the judgment, and that the execution afterward issued did not become a lien. We are of the opinion that execution could be issued and would become a lien while the title remained in the heirs, at any time within 7 years after the judgment was revived, not including the delay on account of the death of the judgment debtor. The cases relied upon by counsel are where an execution could not have been issued so as to become a lien if the judgment debtor had been living. The statute fixes no limitation to the issuance of execution against the lands of the deceased judgment debtor, other than the general provision and the provision that the delay on account of the death of the defendant shall not be considered as any part of the time for issuing execution. The provision is general that execution may issue against the real estate of the deceased judgment debtor, provided that no execution shall issue until after the expiration of 12 months, and after notice to the legal representative or heirs. There seems to be no sufficient reason why the lands of the deceased judgment debtor should not be subject to execution within the statutory period, so long as they are held by his heirs or devisees. The death of the judgment debtor does not change the legal status of the judgment, and the statute only affects its enforcement by staying execution for a fixed period.

There is no material error in the record, and the judgment is affirmed. Judgment affirmed.

(209 Ill. 358)

MILLIGAN v. MACKINLAY.

(Supreme Court of Illinois. April 20, 1904.)

PARTNERSHIP—UNINCORPORATED STOCK SYNDICATE—RELATION OF MEMBERS—ACTION AT LAW BY ONE PARTNER AGAINST ANOTHER PARTNER—WHEN MAINTAINED.

1. The members of an unincorporated stock syndicate, formed to buy, subdivide, and sell real estate for profit in a city, are partners, so that an action at law will not lie in favor of one member against another member on a demand growing out of the transactions of the syndicate until a settlement and a balance struck.

2. One partner cannot maintain an action at law against another partner for the amount found due in a suit for an accounting, unless the latter partner is guilty of fraud in withholding payment of the sum adjudged due.

Appeal from Appellate Court, Second District.

Action by James Milligan, Jr., against Thomas E. Mackinlay. From a judgment of the Appellate Court (108 Ill. App. 609), affirming a judgment of the circuit court sustaining a demurrer to the declaration and dismissing the suit, plaintiff appeals. Affirmed.

This is an appeal from a judgment of the Appellate Court for the Second District, affirming a judgment of the circuit court of La Salle county sustaining a demurrer to the declaration in an action on the case and dismissing the suit. The declaration, as amended, contained two counts, the first of which alleged that the plaintiff and defendant were members of a stock company or syndicate, not incorporated, called the "South Ottawa Improvement Association," and generally known and spoken of as the "Highland Syndicate," formed to buy, subdivide, and sell real estate for profit in the city of Ottawa; that defendant was chosen and acted as secretary of the same, and by virtue of his office as secretary received and collected, in trust for said syndicate, large sums of money belonging to it, and wrongfully, fraudulently, and maliciously, at the time of the collection of said sums, during the years 1887 to 1895, appropriated the same to his own use, with the intention of never accounting therefor, and embezzled the same, and that he has never accounted for or paid over the same; that plaintiff, being a member of said syndicate and entitled to a share of its assets, on October 1, 1896, filed a bill against the defendant and others, charging the receipt of large sums of money by the defendant, as such secretary, which were never completely accounted for, and praying that an accounting be made and the rights and interests of all the parties be determined by the court; that the defendant filed an answer denying the allegations of the bill; that thereafter the master made a report, and a decree was entered by the court finding defendant indebted to the syndicate in the sum of $5,147.78 and that the defendant had forfeited his interest in said syndicate; that it was decreed by the court that the defendant was indebted to the plaintiff, on account of his proportion of the money embezzled, in the sum of $1,008.15, and that plaintiff have judgment therefor; that said decree and findings are in full force, and not in any part or manner reversed, annulled, or satisfied, and so the defendant wrongfully and maliciously defrauded plaintiff out of said sum of $1,008.15. The second count, in addition to the general statement of facts contained in the first count, charged that the syndicate was not a partnership, and states that the defendant has no property subject to execution, and that said court of chancery cannot enforce the payment of the sum found due from the defendant to the plaintiff.

Lester H. Strawn, for appellant. D. B. Snow, for appellee.

HAND, C. J. (after stating the facts). We are of the opinion that the declaration did not state a cause of action, and that the demurrer thereto was properly sustained. Under the decisions of this court, the relation existing between the members of said syndicate was that of partners (Morse v. Richmond, 97 Ill. 303; Winstanley v. Gleyre, 146 Ill. 27, 34 N. E. 628); and the doctrine is well settled that an action at law will not lie in favor of one or more partners, or their representatives, against one or more copartners, or their representatives, upon a demand growing out of a partnership transaction, until there has been a settlement of accounts and a balance struck. 15 Ency. of Pl. & Pr. p. 1005. As it does not appear from the declaration that the defendant has been guilty of fraud in withholding payment of said sum since the decree was entered, an action in tort in favor of the plaintiff will not lie for the amount found to be due him by the decree. To hold that an action in tort would lie in favor of the plaintiff would be to hold, in case of the misappropriation of funds by a partner, that, so soon as the amount due each partner upon a bill for an accounting had been determined, the partner in arrears would become immediately liable in tort to his copartners, respectively, for the several amounts found to be due them, the effect of which would be to make the decree the basis of an action of tort, and not the wrong of the defendant, as prior to the entry of the decree no action at law could be maintained against the partner in default by his copartners, or either of them. Such is not the office of a decree in chancery.

The judgment of the Appellate Court is affirmed.

Judgment affirmed.

(209 Ill. 437)

HUTCHINSON et ux. v. COONLEY.

(Supreme Court of Illinois. April 20, 1904.)

VENDOR AND PURCHASER—WRITTEN CONTRACT—MERGER—PERFORMANCE OF CONDITIONS—OFFER IN COURT.

1. Where, after an oral agreement for the sale of a lot, and the giving of a receipt by the vendor for the first payment, showing the terms of the sale, and after the price was fully paid and the vendees went into possession, but the vendor refused a deed on account of certain unadjusted matters between them, a formal contract was executed for the adjustment of all financial matters between them, their rights under the former negotiations were merged in this contract, so that ejectment could not be maintained against the purchasers till they failed to perform its terms.

2. Where a contract for the adjustment of matters between parties, including the sale of a lot of which the vendees were already in possession, called first for the vendor to furnish an abstract showing title to the lot, this was a condition precedent; and, till it was performed, the vendees were under no obligation either to make or keep good a tender or otherwise.

3. A condition in a contract for the sale of land requiring the vendor to furnish an abstract showing the title subject only to an incumbrance of $1,000 was not satisfied by furnishing an abstract showing a trust deed securing three notes, of $1,000 each, and an offer to surrender two of the notes, and to have interest paid on the third to date, but unaccompanied by any satisfaction signed by the grantee of the trust deed.

4. In ejectment against purchasers in possession under a contract of purchase of the land in question, an offer by the plaintiff, in open court, to perform the terms of the contract, is unavailing, since the rights to be determined are those that existed at the commencement of the action.

Appeal from Circuit Court, Cook County; C. M. Walker, Judge.

Action by John S. Coonley against John Hutchinson and wife. From a judgment in favor of plaintiff on a directed verdict, defendants appeal. Reversed.

This was an action of ejectment, brought in the circuit court of Cook county by John S. Coonley, appellee, against John Hutchinson and his wife, Annie Hutchinson, appel-

¶ 4. See Ejectment, vol. 17, Cent. Dig. § 64.

lants, to recover two certain lots in the city of Chicago. Both parties claim title from Imogene L. Hanchett Cobb, formerly Imogene L. Hanchett. At the conclusion of all the evidence, the jury returned a verdict for the plaintiff, Coonley, in compliance with a peremptory instruction which was given upon his motion.

The evidence in chief on the part of the plaintiff consisted of three deeds—one dated October 1, 1892, from Imogene L. Hanchett Cobb to Frank J. Hanchett; one dated August 21, 1896, from Frank J. Hanchett to Buell M. Cobb; and one dated December 12, 1898, from Buell M. Cobb to John S. Coonley, the appellee.

The evidence of the defendants tended to show that on July 22, 1887, John Hutchinson and Annie Hutchinson purchased the lots in question from Imogene L. Hanchett for the sum of $400, agreeing to pay therefor $50 down, and the balance at the rate of $10 per month; that John Hutchinson was a carpenter, and it was agreed that the $10 per month could be paid either in cash or in carpenter work done for Imogene L. Hanchett; that no deed was delivered or writing signed when the sale was made, but that on the following day Imogene L. Hanchett called at the Hutchinson home, and John Hutchinson there paid her the $50 which it had been agreed should be paid down, and received the following writing signed by her: "South Englewood, July 23, 1887. Received of John Hutchinson fifty dollars ($50) to apply on lot, said lot to cost four hundred dollars ($400). Imogene L. Hanchett;" that, about a week after the sale of the lots, Imogene L. Hanchett stated to John Hutchinson that she was under contract with the person from whom she had purchased the lots to erect a house thereon during the fall of 1887, and offered to advance the money for materials to be used in constructing such house if Hutchinson would build it; that this offer was accepted, and the house was erected according to the agreement; that appellants moved into the house on October 6, 1887, completed it that fall, and have resided there ever since; that the agreement concerning the lots and that concerning the house were entirely separate transactions; that it was agreed that all payments, either in cash or work, were to be credited on the purchase price of the lots until the $400 was paid; that appellants paid to Imogene L. Hanchett more than $400, in cash and work, between July 22, 1887, and February, 1889, the last of such payments being made during the latter month; that after February, 1889, she was on several occasions requested to execute a deed to the lots, but that, although admitting that the lots were fully paid for, she refused to execute such deed until all other financial matters between them were adjusted.

On November 8, 1889, John Hutchinson and wife and Imogene L. Hanchett signed the following instrument: "This agreement witnesseth, that the matters of business between Imogene L. Hanchett, of South Englewood, Cook county, Illinois, and Anna Hutchinson and John Hutchinson, of the same place, have been all adjusted, and it is agreed by and between them that there is this day due to said Imogene L. Hanchett from said Anna Hutchinson and John Hutchinson, on account of the sale of lots three and four (3 and 4), in block fourteen (14), in W. O. Cole's subdivision of the north $90^{87}/_{100}$ acres of part of the northeast quarter of section 5, town 37, north, range 14, east, third principal meridian, in Cook county, Illinois, and all improvements thereon, and for all moneys advanced to them by her for purchase of horse and all other advances, the sum of $2,143.16. For this balance to be adjusted by the assumption of a mortgage of at least $1,000, with interest at seven per cent. payable half-yearly; a payment in cash of at least $500, to be paid in cash, and balance to be secured by second mortgage payable in five years after date, with interest at seven per cent. half-yearly, with privilege to pay sums of $50 or more at any payment of interest on the principal sum. It is understood that the mortgage of $1,000 shall be payable on or before maturity. This contract to be consummated so soon as the abstract and papers are furnished and examined within fifteen days, or as much sooner or as soon thereafter as the deed is ready and the title accepted."

Previous to signing the above instrument, Imogene L. Hanchett, without the knowledge of the appellants, had executed a trust deed on the lots in question to one Waughop to secure three promissory notes, each for $1,000. The evidence for appellants tends to show that, after signing the instrument of November 8th, Imogene L. Hanchett refused to carry out the terms thereof; that she submitted an abstract of title to Lowrey, the legal adviser of appellants, which showed the trust deed of $3,000 to Waughop to be a lien upon the lots; that Lowrey objected to the title because of the abstract, and told her that as soon as it was adjusted he would pay the $500, but that she refused to do anything about the mortgage, and stated that she would not carry out the agreement of November 8th; that afterwards Lowrey tendered to her $500 in gold, and requested that she execute a deed to the premises "and straighten up the deal with them," but that she refused to accept the money "or have anything further to do with the deal." The evidence does not show that any specific offer was made by appellants to assume a mortgage of $1,000, nor any tender of or offer to execute a second mortgage. According to Lowrey's testimony, the $500 in gold was placed in the bank, and was subsequently checked out by him in the payment of personal claims, and there were numerous occasions thereafter when he did not have that amount of money on deposit in the bank.

According to the testimony of one Arnold, during the first part of August, 1899, he (Arnold), acting on behalf of appellee, went to the Hutchinson home, and there tendered to John Hutchinson a warranty deed to the property, signed by Coonley and wife, as grantors, to John Hutchinson and Annie Hutchinson, grantees; also an abstract of title to the lots; and that he offered to have canceled two of the notes secured by the mortgage, leaving one note for $1,000 unpaid, but with interest thereon paid to date; that Hutchinson said he knew nothing about what Arnold was tendering, and would have nothing to do with it. John Hutchinson testified in reference to this transaction that Arnold called at his house with papers in his hand, and stated that he wanted to get a settlement between Hutchinson and Coonley; that he said he was ready with the abstract and deed; that he handed witness the agreement of November 8th, but that witness handed it back to Arnold and told him that Lowrey, his attorney, had instructed him to have no dealings with Arnold in the matter, but to send Arnold to him, Lowrey. Nothing further was done by any of the parties towards carrying out the agreement of November 8, 1889, up to October 19, 1899, the date when this suit was commenced.

The action of the court in directing a verdict for the plaintiff is urged as the cause for a reversal of the judgment below.

Frederick Arnd (Charles Arnd, of counsel), for appellants. Arthur W. Underwood, for appellee.

SCOTT, J. (after stating the facts). We regard the rights of the parties under the contract evidenced by the receipt as being merged in the written agreement of November 8, 1889. After the execution of that agreement, Hutchinson and wife were purchasers in possession under a contract of purchase, and a suit in ejectment could not be maintained against them until they had in some manner made default in the performance thereof. Stow v. Russell, 36 Ill. 18; Kilgour v. Gockley, 83 Ill. 109; Chicago & Eastern Illinois Railroad Co. v. Hay, 119 Ill. 493, 10 N. E. 29.

The first thing in point of time required by this contract was that Imogene L. Hanchett should furnish an abstract showing title in her, as contemplated by that contract, namely, a title subject only to a mortgage securing a note for $1,000, due one year after date, with interest at 7 per cent., payable half-yearly; principal and interest payable on or before maturity, at the option of the payor. This was a condition precedent, with which she had to comply before the Hutchinsons were under obligation to do anything at all. Howe v. Hutchison, 105 Ill. 501. Shortly after November 8, 1889, she did furnish an abstract; but it showed a trust deed on the property in favor of John W. Waughop for $3,000, and was objected to for that reason. She had placed this incumbrance on the property after its sale to the Hutchinsons, without their knowledge. The evidence tends to show that thereafter the Hutchinsons tendered her the $500 which they were to pay in cash, and requested that she close the matter up in accordance with the terms of her agreement, but that she refused to accept the same, and then stated that she would not carry out the contract. The evidence shows that this tender has not been kept good. That is a matter of no consequence, as there was no occasion to make it until an abstract was furnished in accordance with the terms of the contract. Such an abstract never has been furnished. In August, 1899, one Arnold, acting for appellee, offered to John Hutchinson a warranty deed for the property, signed by the then owners thereof, accompanied by an abstract of title to the lots certified to April 29, 1899, which still showed the Waughop trust deed for $3,000. The debt thereby secured was evidenced by three notes of $1,000 each. At the time of making the tender, Arnold offered to surrender two of these notes, and credit interest on the third to that time. The deed so offered recited that it was subject to an incumbrance of $1,000. This was not a compliance with the contract in reference to furnishing the abstract. Appellants were entitled to an abstract certified down to the date of its delivery, or as near thereto as it could be certified in the orderly transaction of business. Further, this abstract showed a trust deed on the property securing three notes for $1,000 each. It should have shown satisfaction of that instrument to the extent of two of the three notes by it secured, or should have been accompanied by an instrument, signed by Waughop, showing satisfaction to that extent. What authority Arnold had to deliver the notes does not appear, and it is not claimed that he made any offer or had any authority to have the mortgage satisfied pro tanto of record. At this time John Hutchinson, who, from his testimony, does not appear to have been a man of much business ability, referred Arnold to his attorney, but Arnold did not take the matter up with him. The evidence does not show that appellants have ever been in default. The condition of the title, as shown by the abstract, has never been such that the Hutchinsons could have accepted a deed from appellee or his grantors as a substantial compliance with the contract. At all times since the execution thereof the amount secured by the trust deed on the property has exceeded the amount of the unpaid purchase money mentioned in the agreement.

On the trial, counsel for appellee offered in open court to comply with the contract. This offer avails nothing, and was not properly made in the presence of the jury, as the rights to be determined in the case are those that existed at the time suit was commenced.

It was error to instruct the jury to find for plaintiff. The judgment of the circuit court will be reversed, and the cause remanded. Reversed and remanded.

(209 Ill. 180)

GANNON v. MOLES et al.

(Supreme Court of Illinois. April 20, 1904.)

DEED AS MORTGAGE—BURDEN OF PROOF—SUFFICIENCY OF EVIDENCE—CONVEYANCE BY GRANTEE—EFFECT.

1. The burden of proof is on a party claiming that an absolute deed is a mortgage to sustain his claim by clear and convincing evidence.

2. Evidence in a suit by the owner of realty, conveyed by a deed accompanied by a written defeasance, to have a deed from her grantee to a third person declared also a mortgage, examined, and *held* insufficient to show that such third person did not actually purchase the property.

3. Where a grantee in a deed accompanied by a written defeasance deeds to a third person, to whom the original owner afterwards assigns her equity, the intention of all the parties being to invest such third person with the absolute title, he takes such title, notwithstanding his grantor was merely a mortgagee.

Error to Appellate Court, Second District.

Action by Bridget Gannon against Fred R. Moles and others. Judgment of the Appellate Court affirming a decree for defendants, and plaintiff brings error. Affirmed.

This is a bill filed on January 4, 1902, in the circuit court of Kane county by the plaintiff in error against the defendants in error for the redemption of a farm of 220 acres in that county. The defendant in error Haish, one of the defendants below, filed no answer, and the bill was taken as confessed against him. The defendant in error Moles, the other defendant below, filed an answer, denying the material allegations of the bill, and to his answer a replication was filed. The cause was heard in open court before the chancellor, and all the witnesses who were examined upon the hearing testified orally. The court below found that the defendant in error Moles did not hold the title to the farm as security, but was an absolute purchaser, and had paid the full consideration, which was the fair cash value of the land, and dismissed the bill at complainant's costs. Plaintiff in error, the complainant below, took an appeal to the Appellate Court, where the decree entered below was affirmed. The case is brought here by writ of error for the purpose of reviewing the judgment of affirmance entered by the Appellate Court.

Jones & Rogers and J. E. Matteson, for plaintiff in error. D. B. Sherwood, for defendants in error.

MAGRUDER, J. (after stating the facts). The question presented by the record is largely a question of fact, and that question of fact is whether, under the circumstances shown by the evidence, the farm formerly owned by the plaintiff in error was purchased by the defendant in error Moles, or whether he held the title thereto as mortgagee, merely, subject to redemption by plaintiff in error.

The material facts are substantially as follows: On and before October 14, 1893, plaintiff in error was indebted in the sum of about $5,830.68 to the defendant in error Jacob Haish, of De Kalb county, and, in order to secure such indebtedness, conveyed to Haish her farm of 220 acres in Kane county by an absolute deed of conveyance. By the terms of the deed, the grantor, Bridget Gannon, a widow, of the town of Virgil, in Kane county, conveys, for the expressed consideration of $5,830.68, to Jacob Haish, of the city of De Kalb, in De Kalb county, the farm in question, which deed was recorded on November 7, 1893. At the same time, to wit, on October 14, 1893, articles of agreement were executed between Jacob Haish, of the first part, and Bridget Gannon, of the second part, wherein it was provided that, if the party of the second part should first make payment and perform the covenants thereinafter mentioned on her part to be made and performed, said party of the first part covenanted and agreed to convey to the party of the second part, in fee simple, subject to the same incumbrances as were then on the land, the said farm, by a good and sufficient warranty deed; and the party of the second part thereby covenanted and agreed to pay to the said party of the first part the sum of $5,339.77 two years after date, with interest at 7 per cent. This defeasance or article of agreement was signed by both Jacob Haish and Bridget Gannon under their seals.

The deed, so executed by plaintiff in error to the defendant in error Haish, though absolute on its face, was a mortgage, when considered in connection with the written defeasance executed simultaneously with it. "The doctrine is well settled that a deed absolute in terms, if intended to secure an indebtedness, is a mortgage, whether the intention is manifested by a written defeasance, by parol declarations, or by the acts of the parties." Cassem v. Heustis, 201 Ill. 208, 66 N. E. 283, 94 Am. St. Rep. 160, and cases cited on page 215, 201 Ill., page 286, 66 N. E., 94 Am. St. Rep. 160. Indeed, it is not denied by either of the parties to this litigation that the deed and defeasance above described constituted a mortgage, as between the plaintiff in error and defendant in error Haish.

The evidence shows that Haish held one or more mortgages, or other evidences of indebtedness, against the plaintiff in error, besides that represented by the deed and defeasance as above set forth. About January, 1895, Haish began to press the plaintiff in error for the payment of her indebtedness to him; and the plaintiff in error applied to the defendant in error Moles, who was her son-

¶ 1. See Mortgages, vol. 35, Cent. Dig. §§ 96, 109.

in-law, the husband of her daughter Katie, to assist her in her pecuniary troubles. On January 11 and 12, 1895, meetings were held at the bank of Haish, in De Kalb, for the purpose of ascertaining the amount of the indebtedness of plaintiff in error to Haish, and for the purpose of consummating the arrangement, which is claimed by Moles to have been a sale of the farm to him, and by plaintiff in error to have been merely a mortgage of the farm by her to Moles. At one or both of the meetings on January 11th and 12th, there were present Haish and Mrs. Gannon, the plaintiff in error, and her two sons, Edward L. Gannon and William P. Gannon, and Moles, the defendant in error, and R. N. Botsford, who appeared to act as attorney for both Moles and Mrs. Gannon. The whole matter was settled and arranged in the manner herein stated on the afternoon of January 12, 1895; the parties differing in their testimony as to the precise hour in the afternoon when the business was concluded. At that time Haish, holding the title to the farm, with the consent of Mrs. Gannon, executed a deed of the farm to Moles. This deed bears date January 12, 1895, and is signed by Jacob Haish and his wife, and conveys to Fred R. Moles, of Chicago, the farm in question, for an expressed consideration of $8,661.58. The sum of $8,661.58 was there ascertained to be the amount of the indebtedness due from plaintiff in error to Haish, and this amount was agreed upon as such indebtedness by all the parties. The whole amount of the consideration named in the deed was not then paid by Moles to Haish; but Moles paid to Haish $2,661.58 in cash, and executed to Haish a mortgage upon the farm of 220 acres so deeded to him by Haish to secure a note for $6,000, payable five years after date, with interest payable annually at the rate of 6 per cent. per annum. The payment of $2,661.58 and the execution of the mortgage for $6,000 settled the indebtedness of plaintiff in error to Haish.

On October 14, 1893, the day on which the defeasance was executed by Haish and Mrs. Gannon, she, by indorsement thereon, assigned and transferred, for the expressed consideration of $1,000, all her right, title, and interest in and to said defeasance or contract to her two sons, William P. Gannon and Edward L. Gannon. This written assignment was signed by Mrs. Gannon. It is not altogether clear from the evidence what the object of this assignment to her sons was. She had another son, named Tom Gannon, with whom she had had some litigation, and Tom Gannon held against her a judgment for $1,000, upon which he subsequently filed against her a creditors' bill. Whether at that time she actually owed her sons William and Edward a debt, for the security of which she transferred her contract with Haish to them, or whether the assignment to them was made for the purpose of preventing the enforcement of the judgment of her son Tom against the property, is not altogether clear.

On January 11, 1895, William and Edward Gannon, by a written instrument executed under their hands and seals, for an expressed consideration of $3,000, sold, assigned, and transferred unto Fred R. Moles all their right, title, and interest in and to said contract, therein designated "the within contract," with full power and authority to Moles to exercise all rights and privileges therein granted to them. On January 11 and 12, 1895, Moles paid to Edward and William Gannon, in cash, $338.42. At the same time he executed his three notes—one for $1,000, payable on or before October 14, 1895, to the order of Edward Gannon, with interest at 6 per cent.; one for $1,000, payable one year after date to the order of William M. and Edward Gannon, with interest at 6 per cent.; and another for $1,000, payable on or before October 14, 1895, to the order of William Gannon, with interest at 6 per cent. The sum of $8,661.58, paid by Moles to Haish in cash and by mortgage, as above stated, and the check for $338.42 paid to Edward and William Gannon, and the three notes, each for $1,000, payable, one to the order of Edward and William Gannon both, and one to the order of Edward Gannon alone, and the other to the order of William Gannon alone, made altogether the sum of $12,000.

Defendant in error Moles claims that he bought the farm from his mother-in-law, Mrs. Gannon, for $12,000, and paid for it by discharging her indebtedness to Haish, and by paying to her sons $3,338.42 in the check and notes above mentioned. The plaintiff in error claims that Moles paid off for her her indebtedness to Haish, and made an additional loan to her of the balance of the money advanced by him, and that the deed made to Moles by Haish was merely intended to be a security for the $12,000 so claimed by her to have been advanced by Moles for her.

On January 12, 1898, Moles paid the note and mortgage for $6,000 held by Haish, and a release of the mortgage was on that day executed to him by Haish. When the three notes, of $1,000 each, were executed by Moles, on January 11 and 12, 1895, they were not at once delivered either to Mrs. Gannon, or to her sons William and Edward, or either of them, but they were retained by Botsford until the judgment held by Tom Gannon against his mother should be paid or settled. The understanding among all parties was that these notes should be held by Botsford, and that, out of the money to be realized upon them, the judgment of Tom Gannon should be paid, and, when it was so paid, then the notes were to be delivered up either to Mrs. Gannon, or her sons Edward and William. About December 23, 1895, the attorney of Tom Gannon and Botsford and Moles held a meeting at Geneva, and there a settlement was made with Tom Gannon, and he accepted $500 in payment of his judgment. This sum of $500 was taken out of one of the notes which had been executed by Moles, and which was then due. At that time, or before that time, written instructions had been given to Botsford by Edward and William Gannon that upon the settlement of the judgment the notes should be given up by Botsford to Mrs. Gannon. On December 23, 1895, Moles paid the $3,000—$500 to discharge the Tom Gannon judgment, and $2,500 to Mrs. Gannon. Of the $2,500 thus obtained by Mrs. Gannon, she retained $500, and placed the remaining $2,000 in the hands of a lawyer to invest or lend out for her.

Upon the foregoing state of facts, the question arises whether the relation between Moles and plaintiff in error was that of mortgagee and mortgagor, or vendor and vendee. The Appellate Court, in its opinion, makes an elaborate review of all the evidence, and concludes that the transaction amounted to a sale of the farm to Moles, and not a mortgage of the same. There is great conflict in the evidence. As to the oral testimony, the evidence of Botsford and Moles sustains the view of the latter, that the transaction was a sale, while the testimony of Mrs. Gannon and her two sons, William and Edward, tends to sustain the opposite theory, that the transaction was merely a mortgage. We shall not attempt to analyze all the testimony upon this subject, nor to pass upon the credibility of the witnesses who contradict each other. The testimony was given orally in open court before the chancellor. He saw the witnesses, and could better judge of their credibility than we can from the record. "When the trial court has had an opportunity of seeing the witnesses, and of hearing their testimony as it is delivered orally, the findings of such court upon mere questions of fact, when the testimony is conflicting, will not ordinarily be disturbed on appeal, unless such findings are clearly and manifestly against the preponderance of the evidence." Burgett v. Osborne, 172 Ill. 227, 50 N. E. 206; Schoonmaker v. Plummer, 139 Ill. 612, 29 N. E. 1114; Van Vleet v. De Witt, 200 Ill. 153, 65 N. E. 677. After a careful examination of the testimony, we are of the opinion that the chancellor below and the Appellate Court have reached the correct conclusion. We will only refer to some of the written evidence which shows the transaction to have been a sale of the farm by Mrs. Gannon to her son-in-law.

The law presumes, in the absence of proof to the contrary, that a deed is what it purports to be—that is to say, an absolute conveyance; and the burden of proof is upon the party claiming such an absolute deed to be a mortgage to sustain his claim by evidence sufficient to overcome this presumption of the law. Heaton v. Gaines, 198 Ill. 479, 64 N. E. 1081. To show that a deed absolute on its face is a mortgage, the evidence must be clear and satisfactory and convincing. Helm v. Boyd, 124 Ill. 370, 16 N. E. 85; May v. May, 158 Ill. 209, 42 N. E. 56. We have said that, "without an ownership in lands, there can be no mortgage of them." Heaton v. Gaines, supra, and cases there cited. We have also said that, in order to establish the fact that a deed absolute on its face is a mortgage, it must appear that a debt existed from the mortgagor to the alleged mortgagee. Rue v. Dole, 107 Ill. 275; Freer v. Lake, 115 Ill. 662, 4 N. E. 512; Heaton v. Gaines, supra; Burgett v. Osborne, supra. In the case at bar there is no evidence that any indebtedness existed from Mrs. Gannon to Moles. It is claimed on the part of the plaintiff in error that when Haish, who held the title to the farm, executed a deed to Moles, Moles merely became thereby an assignee of the mortgage security held by Haish. De Clerq v. Jackson, 103 Ill. 658. It is true that under ordinary circumstances, and when there is nothing to show to the contrary, a grantee of one who holds under a deed on its face absolute, but in legal effect a mortgage, occupies the position of an assignee of a mortgage. But in the present case there is nothing to show that such was the position occupied by Moles when he received the deed from Haish. Immediately upon the execution of the deed to him, and as soon as the title was thereby vested in him, he executed a mortgage to Haish upon the property for $6,000, thereby treating himself as the owner of the property. No deed was executed to Moles by Mrs. Gannon. The execution of the mortgage for $6,000 by Moles to Haish was made with Mrs. Gannon's knowledge and consent. On January 4, 1895, Moles wrote a letter to Mrs. Gannon, inclosing to her the copy of a letter which he had written to Haish, and which he afterwards sent to Haish, and in that letter the borrowing of $6,000 upon the property by a proposed purchaser is referred to. Whether Mrs. Gannon was really indebted to her sons Edward and William in any amount or not, it is certainly true that all of the $12,000 paid by Moles over and above what was necessary to pay off the indebtedness to Haish went to Mrs. Gannon, except $338.42, which was paid to her two sons. Of the remaining $3,000, she received $2,500 in cash, and $500 was expended to pay the judgment against her held by her son Tom. There is nothing in the evidence, or in any of the circumstances developed by the proof, to show that what was paid by Moles over and above the indebtedness to Haish was a loan, and not purchase money. Indeed, all the circumstances point to the conclusion that it was purchase money, and not a loan.

On January 3, 1895, after Mrs. Gannon had called upon Moles, in Chicago, and asked him to buy the farm, she wrote a letter to her daughter Katie, the wife of Moles, in which she says: "Dear Katie: I received your letter. Fred [that is, Moles] can take it at $12,000.00, and our blessing, and I want him to take it at once, as I would be crazy before a month." Other letters and other testimony show that the reference in this letter is to a purchase of the farm by Moles at $12,000. When plaintiff in error said, "Fred can take it at $12,000.00 * * * and I want him to take it at once," she refers to his taking the farm at $12,000. In reply to this letter thus written by Mrs. Gannon on January 3d, Moles wrote to her on January 4th as follows: "Yours of last night at hand and contents noted. Find enclosed copy of the letter I have sent to Haish. You can show it to the boys, and tell them what arrangements you made with me, because, if they are not satisfied, I don't want to take the farm, and in fact it is only an accommodation to you that I go into it. I will go and see Ranstad and Botsfield when I am at Elgin Monday; then I will know how to talk to those at Elgin. * * *. You could have the boys tell Mr. Haish that you have a purchaser for the place, but don't say what the price is, or who it is. He might decide to pay you more than what I have offered you." In the copy of the letter written to Haish which Moles inclosed in his letter to Mrs. Gannon, he tells Haish that he can get a purchaser for the farm, who wants five years' time on $6,000 at 6 per cent., and asks him if he can make such a loan; and he then says: "If you would favor me with an itemized statement of your claims against the farm, so that I can explain them to Mrs. Gannon, I think we can close this deal immediately with a satisfactory settlement. I don't fully understand what condition her affairs are in with you, as I understand you have the deed of the farm, and she has a contract of return sale within two years at a certain sum; if such is right, the purchaser I have will settle with her, and you can convey the property to the purchaser on the terms as before stated." On January 7, 1895, Mrs. Gannon answered this letter of January 4th by a letter to her daughter, in which she says: "Dear Katie: I received your letter. * * * Katie, for God's sake, let ye not let your mother and father's grand home go to the stranger. * * * So don't think but you are making money by buying that farm, that has everything on it, nothing wanted on it, good fences, and the buildings are the best in the township," etc. These letters all show that the parties had in view a sale of the farm by Mrs. Gannon to Moles, and not a transfer from Haish to him as mortgagee. She was unable to pay her indebtedness to Haish, and he was threatening the foreclosure of a mortgage that he held upon the property. Her attorney, Mr. Botsford, had advised her to sell the farm, in order to get as much out of her equity of redemption as possible before any foreclosure proceedings should be commenced.

The two sons of Mrs. Gannon, William and Edward, were unable to be present at the meeting in December, 1895, where the Tom Gannon judgment was settled, and the notes against Moles were turned over to Mrs. Gannon, and paid to her. Edward L. Gannon on December 17, 1895, in view of the impossibility of his being present at that meeting, wrote the following letter to Mr. Botsford: "Being in a position where I am not certain of a leave of absence being granted me, I give my mother, Mrs. B. Gannon, full power to act for me in all matters pertaining to late sale of the farm, and also the disposition of all notes held by you." Edward Gannon, who was present on January 11th and 12th when the transaction took place by which the indebtedness to Haish was settled, and the title to the farm was transferred to Moles, speaks of it in this letter of December 17, 1895, as the "late sale of the farm." It is singular that he should thus speak of it as a sale, if it was understood at the time by his mother and his brother and himself that it was merely a transfer of the rights of Haish as mortgagee to Moles, and that Moles held the property as mortgagee, subject to redemption by Mrs. Gannon. When Mrs. Gannon said in her letter on January 7, 1895, to her daughter, "you are making money by buying that farm," she could have referred to nothing else than an offer by Moles to buy the farm. Indeed, she was urging her daughter and the husband of the latter to buy the farm. All this is inconsistent with the idea of a mortgage.

If the intention was that Moles should buy the indebtedness which Haish held against Mrs. Gannon, and hold it subject to her right of redemption, it is singular that he should have paid to Mrs. Gannon, or to her sons for her, $3,338.42 over and above the indebtedness due to Haish. We find nothing in the evidence to satisfy us that this latter amount constituted a loan.

One of the strongest circumstances to show that the transaction was a sale, and not a loan, was the fact that the defeasance agreement was on January 11, 1895, assigned by William and Edward Gannon to Moles, and taken up and held by him. By the terms of that defeasance, as originally executed, Haish was to make a conveyance to Mrs. Gannon upon her paying to him a certain amount of indebtedness. If the deed of Haish to Moles was merely an assignment of the mortgage to Moles, then it would appear that an agreement of defeasance should have been executed between Mrs. Gannon and Moles, or at least the old agreement of defeasance should have been held by Mrs. Gannon or her son. Instead of this, however, the defeasance agreement is assigned and surrendered to Moles, the grantee in the deed from Haish of the property in question. Having the title to the farm by a deed from Haish, Moles is also allowed to keep the only written evidence in existence that the transaction between Haish and Mrs. Gannon was a security. There is some evidence tending to show that some paper was executed on the afternoon of July 12th, after Mr. Botsford had left the room where the settlement was made, which paper was said to embody an agreement on the part of Moles to allow a repurchase of the property by Mrs. Gannon. In regard to this matter, however, she and her son Edward are contradicted by their letters, as well as by the testimony of Botsford and Moles. We are unable to say, therefore, that the testimony preponderates in favor of the theory contended for by the plaintiff in error and her counsel. If it was the intention that there should remain in her the right of redemption, it is singular that her counsel, who was there advising her, should not have compelled Moles to put in writing some evidence of the rights of Mrs. Gannon in this regard. So, also, there is nothing to show that any evidence was retained of the amount of the indebtedness which is alleged to have existed between Mrs. Gannon and Moles after the settlement on January 12, 1895. If he was making a loan to her, and not buying the farm, he would certainly, as a prudent man, have taken from her some evidence of her indebtedness to him. No such evidence, however, was then retained or is now produced.

We concur in the following views expressed by the Appellate Court in their opinion deciding this case: "It is also worthy of notice that, while the bill alleges it was agreed between complainant and defendant that the deed from Haish to defendant was for the purpose of vesting title in him to hold as security for the money he had advanced, it is nowhere stated that such agreement was in writing, nor is any such paper as the Gannons testified to mentioned or referred to in the bill. The decree finds, and we think not unwarrantedly, that the $12,000 paid by Moles was the fair value of the land at that time, and, in view of all the evidence, we are unable to say that the court erred in dismissing complainant's bill. It is insisted, as a matter of law, that, as Haish's title was that of a mortgagee, Moles necessarily took title as a mortgagee also. We do not think this correct. If all the parties interested agreed that Moles should become the absolute owner of the land, and if the deed from Haish and the assignment to him of the agreement from Haish to reconvey were intended to vest in him the legal and equitable title, we think what was done had that effect. Complainant and her sons, the only persons besides Haish having any interest in the land, requested and procured the deed to be made to Moles, he paying the full consideration thereof; and her two sons, also with her knowledge and consent, assigned and transferred to Moles the agreement from Haish to reconvey, thus vesting in him absolute title, and, having done this, she cannot now be heard to repudiate it."

The judgment of the Appellate Court is affirmed. Judgment affirmed.

(208 Ill. 460)

McKEVITT v. PEOPLE.

(Supreme Court of Illinois. April 20, 1904.)

ROBBERY — INDICTMENT — IDENTIFICATION OF PROPERTY—MOTION TO QUASH—PLEA—MOTION TO STRIKE OUT—MISTAKE—WITNESSES—CREDIBILITY—COMMISSION OF CRIME—EVIDENCE—RESISTANCE OF ARREST—VERDICT—SENTENCE.

1. A motion to quash the indictment cannot be considered after plea, unless the plea is withdrawn upon leave.

2. The objection that an indictment for robbery does not describe the property with sufficient certainty is not ground for quashing the indictment.

3. The testimony of defendant in a criminal case is insufficient of itself to show that a plea of not guilty was entered by mistake, and hence a motion to correct the records in this respect, based upon the offered testimony of defendant alone, is properly denied.

4. An oral motion, made after verdict of guilty, to amend the record in a criminal case by striking out a plea of not guilty, claimed to have been entered by mistake, but not showing when defendant first discovered the mistake, was properly denied.

5. In a prosecution for robbery, prosecuting witness testified that he recognized defendant at once when he saw him after his arrest, and that, though he had been taken to see several other men, he knew that none of them was the right man. No objection was made to the testimony as to having seen several other men until after it was given. *Held*, that defendant was not prejudiced by refusal to strike it out.

6. The fact that a witness in a criminal case has been convicted of an infamous crime can be shown to affect his credibility only by introducing the record of conviction, and not by cross-examination.

7. In a prosecution for robbery the prosecuting witness testified that a certain person looked like the man who was with defendant at the time of the robbery, and thereafter this man, as a witness for defendant, testified that he did not see defendant during the month in which the robbery took place, but did not testify that he was present when the robbery took place, and that defendant was not. *Held*, that this did not tend to show that defendant did not commit the crime, and hence error in allowing the state to prove by cross-examination that witness had been convicted of an infamous crime was harmless.

8. In a prosecution for crime it is proper to show that defendant resisted arrest.

9. Hurd's Rev. St. 1901, c. 38, § 426, declares that no person shall be disqualified as a witness by reason of having been convicted of any crime, but that such conviction may be shown for the purpose of affecting his credibility. Section 279 declares that every person convicted of certain crimes shall be deemed infamous, etc., provided that the section shall not apply to any person sentenced to the State Reformatory at Pontiac. *Held*, that the proviso does not exclude a person sentenced to the State Reformatory from the operation of section 426, but that the fact of conviction followed by sentence to the reformatory may be shown to affect the credibility of a witness.

10. An indictment charged robbery, and also that at the time defendant was armed with a revolver, with intent to kill if resisted, and had two confederates present, armed in the same manner, to aid and abet. On trial the jury found defendant guilty of robbery "in the manner and form as charged in the indictment." Defendant was sentenced for the crime of "robbery, etc." *Held*, that "etc." was meaningless, and the verdict and sentence were merely for robbery.

¶ 1. See Indictment and Information, vol. 27, Cent. Dig. § 473.

Error to Criminal Court, Cook County; Chas. G. Neeley, Judge.

Michael McKevitt was convicted of robbery, and brings error. Affirmed.

Plaintiff in error was indicted at the September term, 1902, of the criminal court of Cook county, for the crime of robbery. The indictment, consisting of one count, charges that Michael McKevitt, on February 14, 1902, in said county of Cook, made an assault upon one Patrick Cahill, and then and there put said Cahill in bodily fear and danger of his life, and against the will of said Cahill did feloniously and violently, by force and intimidation, from the person of said Cahill rob, steal, take, and carry away money, personal goods, and property of the said Cahill, the indictment enumerating numerous treasury notes of the denomination of $100 down to $2, bank bills of denominations unknown to the grand jury, greenbacks of denominations unknown to the jury, silver coin of the United States, enumerating 500 of each of the denominations of $1 down to one dime, 500 pieces of nickel coin of the United States, 100 pieces each of gold coin of the denominations of $20 down to $1, and two keys of the value of 10 cents each, and further charges that the said Michael McKevitt then and there was armed with a revolver, with the intent, if resisted, to kill and maim said Cahill, and that said McKevitt then and there had two confederates present, whose names are unknown to the jurors, said confederates being armed so as to aid and abet said McKevitt. No motion was made by the plaintiff in error to quash the indictment before pleading to the indictment. The record shows a plea of not guilty made by him on September 26, 1902. The verdict of the jury was as follows: "We, the jury, find the defendant, Michael McKevitt, guilty of robbery in manner and form as charged in the indictment." Plaintiff in error moved for a new trial and in arrest of judgment, which motions were respectively overruled and exceptions taken. He was then "sentenced to the penitentiary of this state at Joliet for the crime of robbery, etc., whereof he stands convicted."

In the bill of exceptions there appears a recital, under date of November 17, 1902, that on that date "defendant, by his counsel, moved the court to quash the indictment," with reasons therefor, and further reciting that this motion was overruled.

The evidence on the part of the people shows that Patrick Cahill kept a saloon at the northwest corner of Thirty-Sixth street and Parnell avenue, in the city of Chicago; that there were two doors leading from the street into the saloon building, the one on the east side opening on Parnell avenue and the one on the south side opening on Thirty-Sixth street; that on the night of February 14, 1902, two men came into the saloon by the south door, and at the same time the plaintiff in error came in at the east door; that one of the two men first mentioned asked Cahill for a glass of beer, and at the same time McKevitt made a sign to them; that as Cahill turned to get the beer one of the men struck Cahill on the head with a revolver. Cahill testified that he got the revolver away from the man, and struck him on the head with it, while Frank Cahill, a son of Patrick Cahill, testifying on the part of the people, said that the revolver used by his father was one that had been kept in the saloon for some time. Patrick Cahill further testified that he struck this man repeatedly on the head with the revolver, until his hand was covered with blood and the revolver slipped from his hand; that he held on to the man, and knocked him down three times; that while he was beating this man the man said, "Oh, Cahill! that is enough!" that McKevitt jumped over the bar and fired twice at the son, who ran upstairs, and McKevitt went to the cash drawer and took $2 in United States money, a lead half-dollar that had been there for some time, and two keys; that the man with whom Cahill was fighting called to McKevitt for help, and McKevitt came up, put his revolver against witness' stomach and fired, the bullet being subsequently taken out of Cahill's back; that Cahill's son returned, and the men ran out of the saloon.

A police officer, named McCarthy, on the part of the people testified, over the objection of plaintiff in error, that on June 10, 1902, he was walking on Wells street, and heard quarreling in a saloon on that street; that he went in, and saw McKevitt in the saloon with a revolver in his hand; that he went up to him, and McKevitt pointed the revolver at witness, and said, "I will clear you and the whole bunch out of this," and snapped the weapon; that witness took the revolver from plaintiff in error, and called two other officers to help arrest him; that while taking him to the station two more revolvers were taken from him while he was attempting to use them on the officers. The other two police officers testified to facts corroborating McCarthy concerning the arrest and finding of the revolvers on the person of plaintiff in error and his attempts to use those revolvers. McCarthy did not inform McKevitt that he was arresting him for the robbery of Cahill, nor did any one else. They had no warrant for him, and did not know that he was wanted for that robbery. The three revolvers, together with the cartridges they had contained, were admitted in evidence over the objection of plaintiff in error.

Both Patrick Cahill and his son testified that McKevitt on the night of the robbery wore a short coat and a soft fedora hat, and that this night was the first time they had seen him.

The defendant, on his part, testified that he never had been in the saloon in question, and that he did not take part in the assault upon Patrick Cahill nor in the robbery; that he never wore a short coat or soft fedora hat, but always wore a long coat and a hard derby hat. When Patrick Cahill was being cross-examined, counsel for McKevitt called one McKnight into court, and Cahill then said that this man McKnight looked like the man with whom he had fought at the time of the robbery. Later, McKnight, on the part of plaintiff in error, testified that he was the person whom Patrick Cahill had so identified, and that he did not see plaintiff in error at any time during the month of February. The people, on cross-examination of this witness, were permitted by the court (over defendant's objection that this was not the best evidence) to show that this witness had been convicted and sent to the penitentiary for a robbery, which, however, did not appear to be this robbery of Patrick Cahill. The record of a prior conviction of plaintiff in error for the crime of robbery, for which he was sentenced to the reformatory at Pontiac, was also admitted in evidence on the part of the people in rebuttal.

After the motion for a new trial had been overruled, plaintiff in error moved the court to strike the plea of "not guilty" from the record on the ground that plaintiff in error had not entered such plea, and that the same had been entered by mistake of the clerk of the court, and offered to testify to certain facts to show that such plea had not been made by plaintiff in error, whereupon the court said: "You ask me to strike something from the record which you say is not there. The motion is overruled;" and refused to hear the evidence offered by plaintiff in error in support of the motion.

Charles P. R. Macaulay, for plaintiff in error. H. J. Hamlin, Atty. Gen., Charles S. Deneen, State's Atty., and F. L. Barnett and John R. Newcomer, Asst. State's Attys., for the People.

SCOTT, J. (after stating the facts). The motion to quash the indictment seems to have been made after plea. Such a motion cannot be considered after a plea is entered, unless, upon leave obtained, the plea is first withdrawn. The basis of the motion was that the description of the money ($2) which the prosecuting witness, Cahill, claimed was taken from him, was included with the description of many pieces of money of other kinds, so that it was impossible for the defendant to tell what money he was charged with taking by force from Cahill. This is not ground for quashing the indictment. If the defendant is entitled to any relief, under such circumstances, for the purpose of enabling him to determine which of the money described in the indictment the prosecution seeks to show was stolen by him, it is by motion of another character.

After the motion for a new trial had been overruled, defendant below sought first to have the record amended by striking out the plea of not guilty which appeared upon the record, for the reason that the defendant never had pleaded, and for the reason that the plea of not guilty had been entered by a mistake of the clerk of the court, and, upon this motion being overruled, make a motion in arrest of judgment, based upon the same grounds, which motion was also overruled. Where a defendant charged with a felony has not pleaded, he may, in the event of conviction upon trial, have the judgment arrested (Johnson v. People, 22 Ill. 314; Yundt v. People, 65 Ill. 372; Hoskins v. People, 84 Ill. 87, 25 Am. Rep. 433); and where the record erroneously shows that a plea of not guilty has been entered, the defendant, upon establishing that fact, may, if he act with diligence, have the record corrected at any time prior to the adjournment of the court at the term at which final judgment in the cause is entered. Phillips v. People, 88 Ill. 160; May v. People, 92 Ill. 343; Knefel v. People, 187 Ill. 212, 58 N. E. 388, 79 Am. St. Rep. 217. In this case the defendant offered to show by his own evidence that the plea was erroneously entered. This is not enough. The testimony of the defendant alone is not sufficient to successfully impeach the record. Gillespie v. People, 176 Ill. 238, 52 N. E. 250. The action of the court in this instance was proper for another reason. The motion and offer were made orally. It does not appear therefrom when the defendant first knew the record showed the plea. It was his duty to make this motion at the earliest possible moment. Before such a motion should be entertained, it should be supported by the affidavit of the defendant or by his offer to testify to facts showing that it was interposed at the earliest opportunity after he had learned that the record did not speak the truth. For aught that appears here, he may have known the condition of the record in this respect before the jury was called into the box. If he did, he could not juggle with the court by waiting to ascertain what the verdict was before determining whether to seek a correction of the record. Upon a motion so shown to be made in apt time it would be the duty of the court to determine what the fact was, and make the record accordingly.

When Patrick Cahill was testifying, he stated that he recognized McKevitt at once when he saw him after his arrest; that he had been taken by the police to see several other men, but knew that none of them was the right man. Defendant moved to strike out the statement in reference to other men, which was overruled by the court. Whether he had been to look at other men was wholly immaterial, unless, indeed, it could be shown that he had identified some other man as being the man who did the things with which he charged McKevitt. The testimony might well have been stricken out, but it seems to have been given without any objection being made prior to the statement, and we do not think a failure to strike it out prejudiced the defendant.

During the cross-examination of Cahill counsel for defendant called Michael McKnight to come into court, and Cahill then testified (indicating McKnight), "That man is very like the McKnight with whom I said I was fighting." When McKnight testified on the part of the defendant, the assistant state's attorney was permitted to show on his cross-examination that he had been imprisoned in the penitentiary at Joliet for robbery. This was highly improper. In a criminal case it is proper to show that a witness has been convicted of an infamous crime for the purpose of affecting his credibility, but this can be done only by the introduction of the record of the conviction. Bartholomew v. People, 104 Ill. 601, 44 Am. Rep. 97; Kirby v. People, 123 Ill. 436, 15 N. E. 33; Simons v. People, 150 Ill. 66, 36 N. E. 1019. If this man's testimony, standing alone, showed that McKevitt was not in Cahill's saloon at the time of the robbery, this error would necessitate a reversal of this cause. The prosecuting attorney, who thus violated a fundamental rule of practice, should not be permitted to sustain a verdict if his conduct has contributed to the conviction of the defendant. Counsel for defendant in error argues that the facts in question were developed in ascertaining where McKnight resided, and states that it is always proper to ascertain the residence of a witness, but that the evidence in this case "discloses why this usual and ordinarily harmless question as to residence and occupation was exceedingly objectionable to the gentleman from Joliet." The matter is not to be disposed of in this flippant manner. The prosecuting officer did not cross-examine this man at all upon the testimony given by him in chief. He merely sought to show, and did show, his conviction. Besides, after the witness had testified that he was undergoing imprisonment at Joliet, the further fact was elicited, by an additional cross-question, that this was in consequence of a conviction for robbery, so that it was not solely an investigation of the place of residence. Improper conduct is not excused by a statement that the purpose is proper. The law does not permit the interrogation of a witness in regard to his residence, or any other subject, where the result will be to show by oral testimony that which can be legally shown only by testimony of a different character. The objection to this cross-examination came from the defendant. The record is in this situation: Cahill and his son, Frank, positively identified McKevitt as one of the robbers. McKnight was only shown to have been present and participating by Cahill's uncertain identification of him when he was called into court during Cahill's cross-examination in the manner above stated. McKevitt denied the charge, but did not account for his whereabouts at the time the crime was committed. This robbery took place in the month of February, 1902. The only thing McKnight testified to which it can be contended bears on the issues was that he (McKnight) did not see McKevitt at any time during February, 1902, and that in itself did not tend to show that McKevitt did not commit the crime. McKnight did not testify that he was in the saloon at the time of the robbery, or that McKevitt was not. McKnight's testimony is entirely consistent with his own absence from and McKevitt's presence at the saloon when the crime was perpetrated. The only reasonable conclusion that the jury could draw from the proof, if they believed McKnight, was that he was at some place other than the scene of the robbery at the time it occurred, and that Cahill's uncertain identification of him was a mistaken one. Had McKnight sworn that he was there at the time the crime was committed, and that McKevitt was not, a situation would be developed in which the argument of counsel for plaintiff in error would be unanswerable. This error was therefore harmless.

It is also urged that it was improper to show that McKevitt resisted the police officers at the time of his arrest. We think this was proper in the first instance. If the person arrested was under the impression that he was being arrested for some other offense than the one for which he is being tried, and resisted because he did not want to be apprehended for such other offense, or for any reason other than a desire to avoid a prosecution and trial for the offense for which he is being tried, the burden rests upon him to show that fact by cross-examination or otherwise.

The defendant testified in his own behalf, and for the purpose of affecting his credibility the people offered in evidence the record of the criminal court of Cook county, showing that he had theretofore been convicted of robbery, and sentenced to the Illinois State Reformatory at Pontiac. This is said to have been improper, for the reason that the Legislature has relieved persons who have undergone punishment in the reformatory from the consequences attendant upon a conviction of infamous crime where the punishment is by imprisonment in the penitentiary. This is a misapprehension. The statute of 1845, which is still in force, provides: "No person shall be disqualified as a witness in any criminal case or proceeding by reason of his interest in the event of the same, as a party or otherwise, or by reason of his having been convicted of any crime; but such interest or conviction may be shown for the purpose of affecting his credibility." Hurd's Rev. St. 1901, c. 38, § 426. By a statute passed in the same year it was provided as follows: "Every person convicted of the crime of murder, rape, kidnaping, willful and corrupt perjury or subornation of perjury, arson, burglary, robbery, sodomy or other crime against nature, incest, larceny, forgery, counterfeiting or bigamy, shall be deemed infamous, and shall forever thereafter be rendered incapable of holding any office of honor, trust or profit, or voting at any election, or serving as a juror, unless he is again restored to such rights by the terms of a pardon for the offense, or otherwise, according to the law." In 1899 the Legislature amended this section by adding thereto the words following: "Provided, however, that the foregoing shall not apply to any person who has been heretofore convicted and sentenced, or who may be hereafter convicted and sentenced to the Illinois State Reformatory at Pontiac." Hurd's Rev. St. 1901, c. 38, § 279. This amendment relieves the person who has been convicted and imprisoned in the reformatory for one of the crimes specified in the last-mentioned section from those civil disabilities visited by that section upon one who has been convicted of the same crime, and whose age is such that imprisonment in the penitentiary is the lawful punishment; but the amendment does not in any wise affect the operation of section 426, above quoted. The purpose of the Legislature evidently was to lessen the misfortunes consequent upon conviction of any of the specified offenses in the cases of persons who, on account of their youth, were imprisoned in the reformatory, instead of in the penitentiary, the object being to extend a leniency to the youthful offender which is denied to one of greater maturity. If the Legislature took the view, as urged by the plaintiff in error, that when a young culprit was discharged from the reformatory his reformation would be such that the fact that he had been convicted of one of the crimes denounced as infamous should no longer affect his credibility, and should not be offered in evidence for that purpose, that body failed to express that view in any legislative enactment. Section 426, supra, is not altered by the amendment to section 279, supra, made in 1899. It is the conviction for infamous crime, and not the nature or mode of punishment, that may affect credibility. Bartholomew v. People, supra.

The indictment charged McKevitt with robbery, and further charged that he was at the time armed with a revolver, with the intent, if resisted, to kill and maim Patrick Cahill, and that McKevitt had two confederates present, armed in the same manner, to aid and abet him in the robbery. The jury found him "guilty of robbery in manner and form as charged in the indictment." By the judgment of the court the defendant was sentenced for the crime of "robbery, etc.," and it is said that this is so indefinite that it is impossible to tell whether the sentence was for robbery in the ordinary acceptation of the term, in which event the maximum punishment is imprisonment for 14 years in the penitentiary, or whether it is for robbery in the more aggravated form, which may be punished by imprisonment in the penitentiary for the natural life of the offender. Following the reasoning of this court in Turley v. People, 188 Ill. 628, 59 N. E. 506, it cannot be said that the manner and form of the robbery include the intent with which it is charged the defendant was animated while armed with the revolver, or the purpose for which he had confederates present. He could not be punished for the more aggravated form of this crime unless it appeared from the verdict that the jury had found him guilty thereof. He might have been found guilty, if the evidence warranted, of robbery when armed with a dangerous weapon, with the intent specified in the statute, or of robbery with a confederate present for the purposes designated by the statute, in either of which instances he could be imprisoned for life. In the judgment before us, the letters "etc." are meaningless. The defendant, by the verdict, was found guilty of robbery, and the judgment of conviction is for robbery of that character for which the maximum punishment is imprisonment in the penitentiary for 14 years. The verdict cannot be held to be a finding that the defendant was guilty of the graver crime with which he is charged in the indictment, unless such graver crime is specifically designated or described in the verdict itself. Where the verdict of a jury finds the accused guilty of a certain part of an offense only, the effect is an acquittal of the residue. 22 Ency. of Pl. & Pr. p. 958.

A patient examination of this record reveals no reversible error.

The judgment of the criminal court will be affirmed. Judgment affirmed.

(209 Ill. 33)

SUPREME COUNCIL ROYAL ARCANUM v. PELS.

(Supreme Court of Illinois. April 20, 1904.)

MUTUAL BENEFIT CERTIFICATE—SUICIDE—MEANING OF TERM.

1. A provision in a mutual benefit certificate that no benefit shall be paid if assured commits suicide refers to intentional self-destruction, and does not prevent payment in case of suicide at a time when the assured is incapable, by reason of unsoundness of mind, to resist an insane impulse to take his own life, or to understand the moral character, consequences, and effect of the fatal act.

2. A provision in a mutual benefit certificate that no benefit shall be paid on the death of a member committing suicide, unless the person claiming under the certificate shall prove that prior to the suicide the member had been judicially declared insane, or was under treatment for insanity at the time the act was committed, or was then in the delirium of other illness, operates only to entitle the beneficiary to recover after a death by suicide by proving that assured had been judicially declared insane, or was under treatment for insanity, or was in the delirium of other illness, but does not make such proof indispensable to a recovery after suicide; proof that the member was insane at the time of the suicide entitling the beneficiary to a recovery, though the other facts be not proved.

¶ 1. See Insurance, vol. 28, Cent. Dig. § 1956.

Appeal from Appellate Court, First District.

Action by Eugenie Brudi Pels against the Supreme Council Royal Arcanum. From a judgment of the Appellate Court (110 Ill. App. 409) affirming a judgment for plaintiff, defendant appeals. Affirmed.

H. H. C. Miller and W. S. Oppenheim, for appellant. William Vocke, for appellee.

BOGGS, J. In this an action of assumpsit brought by the appellee against the appellant to recover upon a mortuary certificate issued by the appellant on the 6th day of April, 1899, providing for the payment of a benefit in the sum of $3,000 to the appellee in the event of the death of her husband, Emil Ernst Pels, judgment was entered in the sum of $3,000 in the superior court of Cook county in favor of the appellee, and the judgment was affirmed by the Branch Appellate Court for the First District. A further appeal perfected by the Royal Arcanum, appellant, has brought the record into this court.

To the declaration the appellant filed a plea of the general issue, and also a special plea in bar. The special plea averred: "Emil Ernst Pels, husband of plaintiff, in his application for membership in the defendant order, dated November 28, 1895, covenanted that he and his beneficiaries would and should conform to and abide by the constitution, laws, rules, and usage of the said council and order then in force or that might thereafter be adopted; that section 473 of the code of constitutions and laws of the defendant in force at the time of the death of the said Pels was as follows: 'No benefit shall be paid upon the death of a member who shall commit suicide within five years from and including the date of his initiation, * * * unless the person or persons claiming under such certificate or membership shall establish and prove affirmatively that prior to such suicide the member had been judicially declared insane, or was under treatment for insanity at the time the act was committed, or was then in the delirium of other illness;' and that, in violation of the said section, said Pels did, within five years from his initiation, commit suicide by taking poison, not being then judicially declared insane, nor under treatment for insanity, nor in the delirium of other illness." The assured came to his death by his own act on the 21st day of May, 1900; being within the period of five years after his initiation into the appellant order.

The trial court, in ruling on the admissibility of evidence, and in granting and refusing instructions, construed the word "suicide," used in the by-law, to mean "voluntary, intentional self-destruction," and that the by-law therefore did not present a bar to a right of recovery, if, when the deceased took his own life, he was so affected with insanity as to be unconscious of the act or of the physical effect thereof, or was driven to the commission of the fatal act by an insane impulse which he had not the power to resist. In Grand Lodge I. O. M. A. v. Wieting, 168 Ill. 408, 48 N. E. 59, 61 Am. St. Rep. 123, the phrase "commit suicide" was declared to be of like meaning as those other phrases, "take his own life," "die by his own hand," and "die by his own act," and that all of such phrases conveyed the idea of voluntary and intentional self-destruction. "Suicide is the act of designedly taking one's own life." 24 Am. & Eng. Ency. of Law (1st Ed.) p. 490. In the Wieting Case, supra, the application for the beneficiary certificate and the certificate provided that, should the assured commit suicide, the beneficiaries should only be entitled to receive the amount which had been paid in as premiums or assessments on the policy. We there held that, under such provisions of the certificate, only the return of the amount which had been paid into the benefit fund could be recovered if the assured, while in the possession of his ordinary reasoning faculties, intentionally took his own life; but that if his reasoning faculties were so far impaired that he was unable to appreciate the moral character, general nature, consequences, and effect of the act of self-destruction, or that he was impelled thereto by an insane impulse which he had not the power to resist, the entire amount of the mortuary benefit might be recovered. That is, we held that the words "commit suicide" were applicable only to a case of voluntary, intentional self-destruction—the act of a sane mind. The trial court therefore properly so construed those words in the by-law in question, and for that reason ruled that the by-law had no effect to exonerate appellant from liability if the death of the member was occasioned by his own act at a time when such assured was incapable, by reason of unsoundness of mind, to resist an insane impulse to take his own life, or to understand the moral character, general nature, consequences, and effect of the fatal act.

The rulings of the court on questions of the admission or rejection of testimony, and in giving and refusing instructions, were in harmony with the construction given by the court to the meaning of the words "commit suicide." One may have sufficient mental power to form the intention to do the physical act which will result in death, and also intend to bring about that result by such act, yet, if he is driven to the formation of that intention and the commission of the act by an insane impulse which he has not the power to resist, and which overwhelms his moral nature, his death is not regarded as a voluntary and intentional act of self-destruction, but as though it were the result of accident or of some irresistible external force. Such would have been the construction given to the by-law if it had gone no farther than to declare that the appellant should be exonerated from liability to pay a mortuary benefit if the assured should commit suicide within five years from the date of his initiation. But the effect of the further provisions of the by-law was to empower the beneficiaries to fix liability to pay the beneficiary fund by showing that the assured had been officially declared insane, or was under treatment for insanity, at the time he took his life, or was then in the delirium of other illness. Under the by-law, therefore, proof that the assured had been judicially declared insane, or was under treatment for insanity, or was in the delirium of other illness, at the time he took his life, would effectually fix the liability of the appellant to pay the mortuary benefit. That is, such proof was equivalent to that which the law would require to establish liability in the absence of the qualifying provisions of the by-law, namely, that the assured was affected with unsoundness of mind to such a degree that his moral nature had been overcome, and he had lost the power to resist an insane desire or impulse to take his own life. The effect, therefore, of the qualifying provisions of the by-law, was to relieve the beneficiaries from the duty of producing proof to establish the degree of insanity with which the assured was affected in all cases where the assured had been judicially declared to be insane, or where at the time of his death he was under treatment for insanity, or was then in the delirium of other illness; but it had no effect to exclude such beneficiaries from participation in the benefit fund in cases where the assured had not been judicially declared insane or was not under treatment for insanity, but whose mental faculties at the time he committed the fatal act were impaired by insanity to such an extent that he was unable to understand the moral effect of the act and its general nature and character from a moral point of view, or was so weakened and unsound that he was unable to resist an insane impulse to take his own life. The beneficiaries might avail themselves of the advantages offered by the bylaw, but there was no reason, if they could do so, why they might not take upon themselves the greater burden of proof which the law would cast upon them in the absence of the qualifying phrases of the by-law.

These observations answer all of appellant's contentions, save a refined, if not hypercritical, criticism of an instruction given by the court at the request of the appellee relative to the effect of the verdict of the coroner's jury as prima facie proof of the statements therein contained. The court gave, as requested, an instruction as to the verdict of the coroner's jury which supplemented that given on behalf of the appellee, and removed all just ground of complaint as to the accuracy and correctness of the charge, as a whole, on this branch of the case.

The judgment must be, and is, affirmed. Judgment affirmed.

(208 Ill. 582)

PITTENGER v. PITTENGER et al.

(Supreme Court of Illinois. April 20, 1904.)

DEEDS — CANCELLATION — AGREEMENT TO SUPPORT GRANTORS — BREACH — EVIDENCE — SUFFICIENCY — FRAUD — PRACTICE — JURY IN EQUITY — FINDINGS — FORCE AND EFFECT.

1. The fraud or undue influence which will avoid a deed must be directly connected with the execution of the instrument.

2. A deed made in consideration of the support of the grantors will only be set aside in equity where there has been an entire failure or refusal to perform the agreement, or at least such a substantial failure to perform as would render the performance of the rest a thing different from what was contracted.

3. In a suit by a widow to set aside a deed from herself and husband to their son, in consideration of his agreement to support the parents during their lives, evidence considered, and *held* insufficient to show a breach of this agreement.

4. It requires clear and conclusive evidence to show that a person's signature to a contract was obtained by fraud.

5. Where a chancellor submitted questions of fact to a jury, the verdict was merely advisory, and could be set aside or disregarded.

6. In a chancery case, in which questions of fact were submitted to a jury, error in instructions was unimportant.

7. In a chancery case, it will be presumed that the court disregarded the irrelevant evidence, and predicated the finding upon legal, admissible evidence.

Appeal from Circuit Court, Christian County; Truman E. Ames, Judge.

Suit by Julia A. Pittenger and others against John B. Pittenger. From a decree for complainants, respondent appeals. Reversed.

This is a bill filed on February 28, 1902, in Christian county, by the appellees against the appellant, praying that a certain deed executed by John Pittenger, Sr., during his lifetime, and the appellee Julia A. Pittenger, his wife, conveying 80 acres of land, described in the bill, to the appellant, John B. Pittenger, their son, be set aside, canceled, and declared null and void, and that the appellees (complainants below) and the appellant (defendant below) be vested with the title to said land as the widow and heirs at law of the said John Pittenger, Sr. An answer was filed to the bill by the appellant, denying the material allegations thereof. To this answer, replication was filed. A jury was called, to whom certain questions of fact were submitted upon motion of the complainants below. Under instructions given by the court on behalf of both parties, the jury returned a verdict embodying their answers to the questions so propounded to them. At the August term, 1903, the court rendered a decree substantially in accordance with the bill, setting aside the deed in question, and declaring the same to be null and void. The decree recites that the court "considered the evidence so offered on said trial, and the issues so found by said jury," and the court found "from the evidence and the issues so

¶ 1. See Deeds, vol. 16, Cent. Dig. § 165.

submitted to said jury" that the allegations of the bill were true, etc.

The material facts of the case, as shown by the pleadings and proofs, are substantially as follows: John Pittenger, Sr., being on September 14, 1898, an old man, about 80 years of age, and the appellee Julia A. Pittenger, his wife, an old lady, about 75 years of age, executed on that day a warranty deed conveying, for an expressed consideration of $4,000, to their son, the appellant, John B. Pittenger, the 80 acres in question. This deed was signed both by John Pittenger, Sr., and his wife, Julia A. Pittenger, in the presence of Charles Brooks and J. A. Burchfield, as witnesses, and acknowledged before one Lyman G. Grundy, a notary public, and also an attorney at law, and was recorded on September 15, 1898. The fee of the land was in John Pittenger, Sr., and not in his wife, and the premises were then occupied by John Pittenger, Sr., and his wife as a home. At the same time, on September 14, 1898, John B. Pittenger, appellant here, executed a contract in writing wherein, in consideration of the execution and delivery to him of the warranty deed so executed by his father and mother, the appellant agreed, "for himself, his heirs, executors, and assigns, to provide for the support and maintenance of the said John Pittenger and Julia A. Pittenger for and during their natural lives, and furnish and supply them with the reasonable comforts and necessaries of life, suitable to their condition, including such medicines and medical attendance as they may require"; and it was therein "further agreed and understood that the said John Pittenger and Julia A. Pittenger shall have the right to retain the possession of said premises where they now reside as their home, free of charge, to be so occupied by them until their death, unless, by further agreement hereafter, some other arrangements for their home shall be made." The original agreement, as executed on September 14, 1898, contained a provision that the appellant would pay to his father and mother, in addition to the performance of the matters mentioned above, the amount of $100 a year as long as they lived, or, in case of the death of either of them, he would pay the said amount to the survivor as long as he or she should live. The contract, so made on September 14, 1898, contemporaneously with the deed, and signed by the appellant, was subsequently modified and changed by leaving out the provision which required the appellant to pay the sum of $100 per year. The record contains a letter, dated October 28, 1899, signed by John Pittenger, Sr., and Julia A. Pittenger, his wife, addressed to L. G. Grundy, the attorney who drew the original deed and contract, which letter was as follows: "You may recollect of writing a memorandum of agreement for John B. Pittenger on the 14th day of September, 1898, and in that writing is mentioned the payment annually of $100.00 to us, or our survivor. We do not need that amount of money and you may mark that part off of that agreement, so that no one in the future can make him or his heirs or his executors any trouble, or cause him or them to pay that amount." This letter was received by Grundy, and, in pursuance thereof, a new contract, drawn by him, and dated October 30, 1899, was executed by John B. Pittenger, and was the same in all respects as the contract of September 14, 1898, except that it left out the provision in regard to the payment of $100 per year. Thereupon the old contract was destroyed, and two copies of the new contract of October 30, 1899, were executed, and one of them was retained by the appellant, and the other was delivered to his father and mother. The latter copy was produced upon the trial from the possession of the complainants below (appellees here). On February 1, 1900, John Pittenger, Sr., died intestate, leaving his widow, the appellee, Julia A. Pittenger, and two sons, the appellant, John B. Pittenger, and the appellee Charles Pittenger, and a number of grandchildren, who are minors suing here by their next friend, Charles Pittenger. The complainants in the bill below were the widow and the son Charles and the grandchildren, and the defendant was the present appellant. The bill charges that the deed was procured by the appellant through fraud and undue influence, and without any intention of in good faith caring for and supplying the comforts and necessaries of life to the said John Pittenger, Sr., and Julia A. Pittenger, his wife, while they lived, and that the sole object of the appellant was to get possession of the property. The bill furthermore charges that during the lifetime of John Pittenger, Sr., and since his death, the appellant has neglected and refused to furnish his father and mother with proper and suitable clothing and proper and suitable eatables and necessary fuel, and has neglected to pay the $100 already mentioned; that he has permitted the appellee Julia A. Pittenger to remain alone and neglected, and refused to get any one to care for her, or to furnish her and keep for her a supply of water and fuel; that the bread he furnished to her during a portion of the time was old and stale, etc. The answer of the appellant denied all the allegations in regard to the failure to support his father and mother, and claimed that he had faithfully performed the contract made for their support, and in consideration of which the deed was executed to him. The answer denied that the deed was obtained by any fraud or undue influence, but was entered into voluntarily, and in order that the grantors therein might be supported and cared for in their old age. The answer also sets up that in October, 1899, the provision in the contract in regard to the payment of the $100 was eliminated therefrom by the written direction of his father and mother, and upon their statement that they did not need the $100 specified in the contract, and that the letter of October 28, 1890, and the contract executed on October 30, 1899, were deposited in a certain bank named in the answer. The answer alleges that the attorney, Grundy, went to the house of John Pittenger, Sr., and Julia A. Pittenger at their request, and at the request of the appellant, and drew the papers above referred to, the terms of which were dictated by the said John Pittenger, Sr., in the presence of Julia A. Pittenger, and read over by them both and voluntarily signed by them both, and that the original contract was destroyed by him at the request of John Pittenger, Sr., and that Julia A. Pittenger was informed in regard to the same. The answer denies all the allegations as to failure to support or maintain his father and mother in accordance with the contract, and denies that the appellant refused to supply them with water, fuel, or bread, etc.

J. E. Hogan and L. G. Grundy, for appellant. J. C. & W. B. McBride, for appellees.

MAGRUDER, J. (after stating the facts). The issues presented by this record are principally issues of fact. On September 14, 1898, the father and mother of appellant executed to him a deed of their homestead farm, consisting of 80 acres, upon condition that he would support them during their natural lives, and furnish and supply them with the reasonable comforts and necessaries of life, suitable to their condition, including such medicines and medical attendance as they might require, giving them the right to retain the possession of the premises as their home free of charge, to be kept by them until their death, unless by further agreement thereafter some other arrangement for their home should be made, and also that he would pay them the sum of $100 in money per year. The main question of fact is whether or not the appellant has fulfilled the contract so made by him.

One of the charges in the bill is that the deed in question was procured by fraud and undue influence. We find no evidence whatever in the record to sustain this charge. The fraud or undue influence which will avoid a will or deed must be directly connected with the execution of the instrument. Guild v. Hull, 127 Ill. 523, 20 N. E. 665; Francis v. Wilkinson, 147 Ill. 370, 35 N. E. 150. The evidence shows that the deed was executed voluntarily by John Pittenger, Sr., and Julia A. Pittenger, his wife, on September 14, 1898. At that time the fee of the property was in John Pittenger, Sr., and Julia A. Pittenger had only the interests of homestead and inchoate dower. John Pittenger, Sr., lived, after the execution of the deed, until February 1, 1900, at which time he died, still owning the fee. There is no testimony whatever in the record that the appellant failed to properly support and maintain his father and mother during this period. The testimony introduced for the purpose of showing appellant's failure to carry out the contract is in relation to his alleged treatment of his mother after his father's death. The contract did not provide for the support of the heirs of John Pittenger, Sr., but only for the support of himself during his lifetime, and of his wife during her lifetime. When he died, therefore, the contract was ended, so far as he was concerned. The complainants below have only sought to prove that appellant failed to properly support his mother, and pay her $100 a year, after the death of the father, on February 1, 1900. The questions involved, therefore, which relate to the manner in which the contract was carried out after the death of the father, divide themselves into two parts: First, was the appellant at fault in not furnishing his mother proper support and maintenance after the death of his father? And, second, was he at fault in not paying her $100 a year in money, as it was provided that he should do in the original contract of September 14, 1898?

1. Appellant lived, with his wife and children—he having been married some 26 years, and being over 50 years of age—on his farm, about a quarter of a mile distant from the farm here in controversy, being the home of his mother. By the terms of the contract, she had a right to remain upon the home farm free of charge, and occupy it, until her death. But the contract contemplates that, by agreement with her, some other arrangement might be made for a home for her. The proof shows that the appellant offered her a home at his house, and tried to persuade her to come and live with him, instead of living alone upon the farm here in controversy. She did once or twice go to his house, and remain there a month or more, but left and went back to her own home, because of the noise made by appellant's children, or others concerned in the management of his farm. She also stated that her husband had requested that she should remain upon the home farm. Her determination to remain upon the farm, instead of living with the appellant, required him to furnish her with the necessary supplies for living at her own home, and also to furnish her with company, or somebody to stay with her and look after her in her old age. We think the proof shows, by an overwhelming preponderance, that the appellant fulfilled his obligations in this regard. The appellee Julia A. Pittenger remained at the home farm, with the exception of an occasional visit for a few weeks to the appellant's house or to the house of her brother, from the time of her husband's death up to the time of the beginning of this suit, in February, 1902, and subsequently thereto. Charles Pittenger, her son, had not lived with his father and mother for a number of years, and had not visited the old home for a number of years until the death of his father, when he came to

the latter's funeral. He had received, as the evidence shows, a considerable amount of money from his father during the latter's lifetime, but contributed nothing to his mother's support after his father's death. In the fall or winter of 1901 he came back and visited his mother, and the evidence tends strongly to show that the dissatisfaction which she then began to show was due to the influence of her son Charles. She asked of the appellant that he give or lend to her son Charles the sum of $400, which he refused to do. In the recent case of Huffman v. Sharer, 191 Ill. 79, 60 N. E. 866, which was similar in many respects in its facts to the case at bar, this court said (page 84, 191 Ill., page 868, 60 N. E.): "The testimony of the plaintiff in error demonstrated that his mind has been greatly impaired by age, and his memory and judgment much weakened; and his testimony, together with the other proofs in the case, fully warranted the finding of the master, which was approved by the court, that his present dissatisfaction with the terms of the conveyance was inspired by other interested parties, who have ulterior designs to forward, which it is not to the best interest of the plaintiff in error should be promoted." While all of this language may not be applicable to the facts of the present case, yet a portion of it is so applicable; that is to say, the dissatisfaction of the appellee Julia A. Pittenger with the contract made by her son for her support, and with the execution of the deed, is shown by the testimony to have been inspired by interested parties, who had ulterior designs to promote.

While the evidence in this case does not show that there was any fraud or undue influence exercised over the grantors in procuring the execution of the deed here sought to be set aside at the time of the execution of the same, yet the doctrine laid down in McClelland v. McClelland, 176 Ill. 83, 51 N. E. 559, and the cases therein referred to and commented upon, is invoked for the purpose of carrying back the testimony in regard to what occurred after the death of John Pittenger, Sr., and making it apply to the intention of the appellant at the time the deed was made. The doctrine thus sought to be invoked is that, where there is a failure to perform contracts of this kind, a court of equity will entertain jurisdiction to set aside a deed upon the ground that the circumstances justify the inference of an abandonment of the contract, and a presumption of a fraudulent intent in entering into the contract. In other words, it is claimed by the appellees that the appellant failed to properly maintain and support his mother after the death of his father, and that his conduct in this regard gives rise to the presumption that he entered into the contract originally, and obtained the deed, with a fraudulent intent. We have no fault to find with this doctrine, which has been laid down by this court in a number of cases, but we fail to see that the appellant was guilty of any such conduct in this case as to justify the presumption that his original intention in obtaining the deed was fraudulent. The testimony upon which the court below based its decree is principally that of the appellee Julia A. Pittenger and her son Charles, and a son or daughter of the latter. The interest and bias of this testimony are apparent upon its face, while the testimony as to the fulfillment of the contract by the appellant comes from disinterested parties, and is of a convincing character. In the first place, while the contract does not specify that the appellant was obliged to secure and provide families or persons to reside with his mother in her home, yet the evidence shows that he did so, and that he paid them with his own money for their services in this respect. The evidence is too voluminous to justify us in analyzing and commenting upon all of it, but a few salient features may be noticed. For instance, from February 1, 1900, the time of the death of the appellant's father, up to and after February, 1902, when this suit was begun, there were only a few weeks when the appellant's mother was without company upon the home farm. In February, 1900, Laura Burchfield, a niece of Mrs. Pittenger, stayed with her until appellant could procure some one to go there, and was paid for so doing by the appellant. Elias Burton and his wife went to live with her in March, 1900, and stayed with her until September of the same year. Mrs. Pittenger then went to the appellant's home, and remained there awhile. Then, in November, one Rhodes and his wife came to her home, and stayed with her until about March, 1901. Then one Christian and his wife stayed with her from March 1, 1901, until about September of the same year. Then other parties, to wit, Bertha Neff and Charles Mitchell and a son of appellant, stayed with her at different times. Then one Mrs. Amanda Kiger came and stayed with her until about New Year's day in 1902. During this time, also, one Hamilton Cole stayed there a month or so, and also Ida Pittenger, appellant's daughter, stayed there four weeks or over. After that a man named Pope, and his wife, came and stayed with her. All these persons were procured to attend upon Mrs. Pittenger by her son, the appellant, and nearly all of them were paid by him to do so. Without further comment upon this branch of the testimony, it is sufficient to say that the appellant procured 10 or 12 families or individual persons, not including his son and daughter, to stay with Mrs. Pittenger from February, 1900, until about October, 1902. After the beginning of this suit, in February, 1902, she left the farm for a considerable time, and lived with her brother or her nephews and nieces, and during all this time the appellant paid her board to the parties with whom she so lived.

The evidence also shows that, during the time when his mother remained on the farm, the appellant himself went there several times a week, and some member of his family was there almost every day, and he sent to his mother fresh milk and butter and provisions, and also sent her fuel and ice, and did all that he could to make her stay comfortable. The testimony that she was well provided for comes from neighbors and persons thus living with her, who can have no possible interest in this suit. Their testimony is overwhelmingly convincing to the effect that the appellant not only provided her with attendants or companionship, but provided her also with provisions and other necessaries of life. A few persons were put upon the stand, who stated that, at certain times when they took meals there, the bread would be stale or heavy, and at one time the well was broken, or there was some difficulty about getting water; but these were small matters, and of minor importance. A slight or partial neglect on the part of one of the contracting parties to observe some of the terms or conditions of the contract will not justify the other party in abandoning or rescinding the same. A deed or contract made in consideration of the support of the grantors will only be set aside, in equity, where there has been an entire failure or refusal to perform the agreement, or at least such a substantial failure to perform the contract in respect to material matters as would render the performance of the rest a thing different from what was contracted. As was said in Weintz v. Hafner, 78 Ill. 27: "Appellee had no right to rescind the contract, and recover the purchase money paid, unless appellant had failed, in a substantial manner, to observe his part of the contract. A slight or partial neglect on the part of one of the parties to a contract to observe some of the terms or conditions thereof will not justify the other party to at once abandon the agreement. As was said in Selby v. Hutchinson, 9 Ill. 319, in order to justify an abandonment of the contract, and of the proper remedy growing out of it, the failure of the opposite party must be a total one. The object of the contract must have been defeated or rendered unattainable by his misconduct or default. For partial derelictions and noncompliances in matters not necessarily of first importance to the accomplishment of the object of the contract, the party injured must still seek his remedy upon the stipulations of the contract itself." See, also, Leopold v. Salkey, 89 Ill. 412, 31 Am. Rep. 93; City of Elgin v. Joslyn, 136 Ill. 525, 26 N. E. 1090. We think that, under the evidence here, an effort was made by the appellant in good faith to effect a substantial compliance with the agreement, and that such effort was successful. The evidence tends to show that Mrs. Pittenger, who was an old lady, upwards of 80 years of age, at the time when most of these transactions occurred, would become dissatisfied with persons living with her, so that they were obliged to leave. Many of her complaints, which seemingly reflected upon the conduct of the appellant, were, as matter of fact, due to the whims and fancies of old age, and a feeling of loneliness natural to her after the death of her husband. She declined appellant's offer to take her to his home, and to give her the best room in his house, if she desired it. But when she remained in her own home, or went elsewhere, she was always supported by the appellant at his own expense, and, as we read the testimony, adequately and comfortably. In addition to this, there is abundance of testimony in the record proving declarations which were made by the appellee Julia A. Pittenger as to the appellant's kindness to her. Before she fell under the influence of her son Charles, she frequently stated to other people—who so testify—that the appellant had done all for her comfort which she could ask, and furnished her with all the necessaries which she required.

2. The second ground upon which the failure to keep his contract is charged against the appellant is that he neglected to pay the $100 per year which the original contract required him to pay. In explanation of this matter the appellant introduced the evidence set forth in the statement preceding this opinion, which shows that the original contract was subsequently changed and modified by leaving out the provision requiring the payment of the $100 per year. The letter, directing that the contract be changed in this regard, was signed by John Pittenger, Sr., and Julia A. Pittenger, his wife. There is not a particle of evidence to show that the letter was not signed voluntarily by John Pittenger, Sr. Mrs. Pittenger admits that she signed the letter, and that she did it at the request of her husband, who had already put his signature to the letter before he asked her to do so. The reason given in the letter for relieving appellant from the necessity of paying this $100 is that it was not needed by his father and mother. The proof shows that he gave his mother money from time to time, and the testimony of persons who lived with her shows that they were authorized by the appellant to make purchases for her, requiring money, and subsequently paid for by him. Mrs. Pittenger states in her testimony that, when she signed the letter consenting to the modification of the contract in the respect named, she did not know that the provision regarding the $100 was to be left out. There is, however, a considerable amount of testimony in the record by outside parties to the effect that she stated to them at different times that the appellant was relieved from the necessity of paying this $100, because she and her husband did not need it. Her testimony upon this subject is weakened by the evidence of witnesses who swear to her declarations to the contrary of what she testifies to. A duplicate of the contract of October, 1899, was within her control, or within the control of some of the appellees here act-

ing with her, for more than two years after the death of John Pittenger, Sr.; and, if any fraud had been practiced in modifying the original contract by leaving out the provision in regard to the $100, it is singular that the silence of the second contract upon this subject was not noticed. It would seem natural that the omission of the $100 from the modified contract would have been noticed during this long period, if there had been any fraud in procuring the modification of the contract. Mrs. Pittenger's name having been signed to the letter, consenting to the change in the contract, it requires clear and conclusive testimony to show that she was deceived or imposed upon in any way when she so signed the letter, in view of the fact that her husband signed it at the same time, and requested her to sign it.

3. Some stress is laid by the appellees upon the fact that certain issues in this case were submitted to the jury, and that the answers returned by the jury to the questions propounded to them were in favor of the appellees and against the appellant upon the points here involved. In reply to this it is sufficient to say that, where a chancellor submits controverted questions of fact to a jury, the verdict or finding of the jury is advisory merely. He may adopt the verdict, or set the same aside, and resubmit the question to the jury, or he may disregard it and enter such a decree as in his judgment equity demands. "He may enter his decree after setting the verdict aside, or without setting it aside." Guild v. Hull, 127 Ill. 523, 20 N. E. 665. We think that some of the instructions which were given to the jury by the court were misleading and erroneous, but inasmuch as the verdict was advisory, merely, and not binding upon the chancellor, the error in this regard is unimportant in determining the correctness of the decree which was finally rendered. It will be presumed that the court disregarded irrelevant evidence, and predicated the findings upon legal, admissible evidence. Notwithstanding the fact that there was here a submission of certain questions to be determined by the jury, we yet think that the only material question to be considered by us is whether the decree rendered by the court is sustained by the evidence; that is, by the legal testimony, such as is admissible under the established rules of evidence. Peabody v. Kendall, 145 Ill. 519, 32 N. E. 674. The final decree shows that it was based not only upon a consideration by the chancellor of the evidence, but also upon a consideration of the finding made by the jury; and it may be that the chancellor did not rely as completely upon his own interpretation of the evidence as he would have done if there had been no action on the part of the jury. But in view of the character of the testimony in this case, we cannot resist the conclusion that the jury were carried away by sympathy for this old lady, as they rendered a verdict which is contrary to the weight of the evidence. In our opinion, the decree of the court is not sustained by the proof.

Accordingly the decree of the circuit court is reversed, and the cause is remanded to that court, with directions to dismiss the bill. Reversed and remanded.

(208 Ill. 473)

BLINN et al. v. GILLETT et al.

(Supreme Court of Illinois. April 20, 1904.)

WILLS—CONSTRUCTION—INTENTION OF TESTATOR—LIFE ESTATES—STOCK DIVIDENDS.

1. Testator's will gave his wife the profits of certain bank stock for life, and provided that if, during her life, any bank should wind up its business and distribute its capital, she should be entitled to receive all sums payable on its certificates, and be empowered to reinvest the principal, which principal should, after the death of the wife, be distributed as thereinafter directed. A subsequent residuary clause provided that the proceeds of the sale of all personal property other than bank stock should be distributed among testator's children, and a subsequent clause provided that on the death of the wife all bank stock remaining unsold, and all money arising from the sale of bank stock, should be distributed among the children who should survive the wife, in certain specified amounts, and that in case any of the children should die before the wife, leaving a child or children, they should take in equal parts the share of the bank stock which their parents would have taken had they survived the wife, and that if any child should die, leaving no child, before the wife, then the share of such child should be divided among the survivors. *Held* that, in accordance with the evident intention of the testator, the will should be construed as meaning that any moneys arising from the voluntary liquidation of banks should pass to the children who survived the wife, and not under the residuary clause.

2. A stock dividend which evidences a conversion by the corporation into capital of earnings accumulated during the stockholder's lifetime goes to the remainderman under his will as a part of the corpus of the estate, and not to the life tenant, under a clause devising the income to the life tenant.

3. Where a will gave testator's widow the life estate in certain bank stocks, with remainder over to the children who might survive her, a stock dividend issued after the death of the testator was not intestate property passing under a residuary clause of the will, but went to the remaindermen under that clause of the will devising the stock.

Appeal from Appellate Court, Third District.

Suit by Jessie D. Gillett, as administrator de bonis non with the will annexed of the estate of John D. Gillett, deceased, to obtain a construction of the will. From the decree Edward D. Blinn, as successor to Inez M. Gillett, as administratrix of the estate of John P. Gillett, deceased, and others, appealed to the Appellate Court, where the decree was affirmed (110 Ill. App. 37), and from such decree they appeal. Affirmed.

This was a bill in chancery filed in the circuit court of Logan county by Jessie D. Gillett, administrator de bonis non with the will annexed of the estate of John D. Gillett, de-

¶ 2. See Life Estates, vol. 33, Cent. Dig. § 35.

ceased, for the purpose of obtaining a construction of the will of John D. Gillett so far as it affects the disposition of certain bank stock, and the proceeds thereof, owned by John D. Gillett at the time of his death.

John D. Gillett departed this life testate on the 24th day of August, 1883, leaving, him surviving, his widow, Lemira P. Gillett, and his children, Emma S. Oglesby, Grace A. Littler, Nina L. Gillett, Amaryllis T. Gillett, Mary C. Hill, John P. Gillett, Jessie D. Gillett, and Charlotte L. Barnes. At the time of the death of John D. Gillett he owned the following bank stock: First National Bank, Lincoln, Ill., 100 shares, par value $10,000; First National Bank, Farmer City, Ill., 30 shares, par value $3,000; Farmers' National Bank, Pekin, Ill., 15 shares, par value $1,500; Illinois National Bank, Springfield, Ill., 100 shares, par value $10,000; Farmers' National Bank, Springfield, Ill., 50 shares, par value $5,000; First National Bank, Mt. Pulaski, Ill., 10 shares, par value $1,000; National State Bank, Bloomington, Ill., 30 shares, par value $3,000—total amount of stock, par value, $33,500. The paragraphs of the will of John D. Gillett, deceased, which affect the disposition of said bank stock, are Nos. 9, 23, and 24, and read as follows:

"Ninth—I give and devise to my wife, in case she shall survive me, for and during the period of her natural life, all the use, interest, dividends and profits that may accrue during such period on or from any share of bank stock which I may own at the time of my death. She shall be entitled to the possession of all certificates representing such stock, and to vote them in person or by proxy during her life. If, during the life of my said wife and after my death, any of the banks in which I shall own said stock shall wind up its business and distribute its capital among its stockholders, my said wife shall be entitled to receive and receipt for all sums payable on the certificates so to be held by her for life. She is hereby empowered to re-invest the principal of said stock as safely as possible, and to collect and retain to her own use all interests and profits derived from such investment during her natural life. The principal so invested shall, after the death of my said wife, be applied and distributed as hereinafter directed. If my said wife shall become satisfied, at any time after my death, that it would be wise and judicious to sell any part of said bank stock, she is hereby fully empowered, by and with the advice and consent of my said executors, to sell any part or all of the stock so owned by me in the banks at Pekin, Mt. Pulaski, Farmer City and Bloomington. In the event of making such sale she shall invest the proceeds thereof as aforesaid, and shall be entitled to take to her own use, as her own property, all the interest and profits arising from such investment during her natural life. At her death the principal so invested shall be applied as hereinafter directed."

"Twenty-third—I hereby direct that the proceeds of the sale of all my personal property, other than bank stock, and not otherwise herein disposed of, together with the proceeds of all debts and demands due or to become due me, and of all real estate in this last will declared and directed to be disposed of as personalty, shall be applied and disposed of by my executors as follows: They shall first pay to my daughter Emma Susan Oglesby the sum of $10,000, and they shall divide the remainder of the proceeds of said personal property in equal parts amongst all of my said children"—naming them, and providing that if any of his children shall depart this life before him, leaving children, the children should take the parent's share; or if they died before him, leaving no children, then the proceeds of said debts, demands, and personal estate to be divided in equal parts among the survivors or their descendants.

"Twenty-fourth—In case my said wife shall not survive me, I give and bequeath all my bank stock as follows: To Emma Susan Oglesby $5000; to Grace Adeline Littler $5000; to Nina Lemira Gillett $5000; to Mary Catherine Hill $4000; to Jessie D. Gillett $4000; to Amarilla Tuttle Gillett $3000; to Charlotte Lancraft Gillett $3000; and the remainder, if any, to my son, John Park Gillett. I direct that said stock shall be distributed by my executors, not on the face or par value of said stock, but on its market or selling value, so that the share given to each of my said children shall amount in real value to the sum above specified as intended for her. If there shall not be sufficient stock to make up the sums indicated, then I direct that all of said bequests shall abate pro rata. If any of my said children shall depart this life before me leaving any child or children who shall survive me, then such child or children shall take in equal parts amongst them the share or shares which his, her or their deceased parent or parents would have taken if alive. If any of my said children shall depart this life before me leaving no child or children who shall survive me, then the share or shares of such deceased child or children shall be divided in equal parts amongst my surviving children named as aforesaid, the surviving children of any of my children so named as aforesaid to take in equal parts amongst them the share or shares which his, her or their deceased parent or parents would have taken if alive. If my said wife shall survive me, I give and bequeath all my bank stock that shall remain unsold at the time of her death, and all money arising from the sale of said bank stock by my wife, in manner following, to-wit: To each of my following named children who shall survive my said wife the following parcels or portions, to-wit: To Emma Susan Oglesby $5000; to

Grace Adeline Littler $5000; to Nina Lemira Gillett $5000; to Mary Catherine Hill $4000; to Jessie D. Gillett $4000; to Amarilla Tuttle Gillett $3000; to Charlotte Lancraft Gillett $3000; and the remainder, if any, to my son, John Park Gillett. I direct that my executor shall make distribution, not on the par value or face of said stock, but on the basis of the market or selling value thereof, so that the share given to each of said children shall amount in real value to the sum above specified as intended for her. If my bank stock, together with the money arising from the sale of any part thereof, shall not be sufficient to discharge said specific bequests, then each bequest shall abate pro rata. If any of my said children shall depart this life before my said wife leaving any child or children who shall survive my said wife, then such child or children shall take in equal parts amongst them the share or shares of said bank stock and money which his, her or their deceased parent or parents would have taken in the event of surviving my said wife. If any of my said children shall depart this life before my said wife leaving no child or children who shall survive my said wife, then the share or shares of said bank stock and money which would otherwise go to such deceased child or children shall be divided in equal parts among the survivors of my children named as aforesaid, the surviving children of any of my children so named to take in equal parts amongst them the share or shares which his, her or their deceased parent would have taken if alive at the death of my said wife. I distinctly direct and declare that in bequeathing said bank stock, and any money that shall arise from the sale of any part thereof by my said wife, it is my desire and intention that none of my children named as aforesaid, or their children or descendants, shall take any vested interest in said stock or money until the death of my said wife, in case she shall survive me, and that until the death of my said wife, and the consequent vesting of said titles and interests, my said children and their descendants shall not be entitled to sell, transfer or encumber any of said stock or money or any interest therein, and that the same shall be wholly free from all judgments, attachments, executions and legal processes against any of my said children or their descendants until or unless said title or interest shall become vested in them by the death of my said wife."

In 1895 the Farmers' National Bank of Pekin went into voluntary liquidation, and there was paid to the executors of John D. Gillett, deceased, the sum of $2,175, which amount represented the net value of the Gillett stock in that bank. During the same year the First National Bank of Farmer City went into voluntary liquidation, and there was paid to the executors of John D. Gillett, deceased, the sum of $3,420, which amount represented the net value of the Gillett stock in that bank; and in the year 1900 the National State Bank of Bloomington went into voluntary liquidation, and there was paid to the executors of John D. Gillett, deceased, the sum of $3,750, which amount represented the net value of the Gillett stock in that bank; and these sums, which aggregate the sum of $9,345, were paid by the executors to the widow, Lemira P. Gillett.

At the time of the death of John D. Gillett the capital stock of the First National Bank of Lincoln was $50,000, surplus $50,000, and its undivided profits $13,169.41. Shortly after the death of John D. Gillett the directors and stockholders of that bank, with the consent of the Comptroller of the Currency, increased the capital stock of said bank from $50,000 to $100,000, and 100 shares, of the par value of $100 per share, of the new stock, was issued to the widow, Lemira P. Gillett, the certificate which she received therefor being certificate No. 122, for the sum of $10,000. From that time to the time of her death Lemira P. Gillett held the original and the new stock in said First National Bank of Lincoln, and received the cash dividends thereon as they accrued and were paid, and at the time of her death the new stock was worth $20,000.

Grace A. Littler died without leaving her surviving a child, or children or the descendants thereof, in May, 1891, and leaving a last will, in which she bequeathed all personal property that she might own at the time of her death to her husband, David T. Littler. John P. Gillett died testate on September 8, 1901, without leaving, him surviving, a child or children or the descendant thereof, and leaving Inez M. Gillett as his widow. On the 21st day of September, 1901, Lemira P. Gillett, widow of John D. Gillett, deceased, died testate, and by her last will bequeathed all the bank stock owned by her in the First National Bank of Lincoln to Charlotte L. Barnes in trust for Joan Gillett Barnes and William Barnes, Jr., the children of Charlotte L. Barnes, who are made parties defendant to the bill.

Answers and replications were filed, and David T. Littler and Inez M. Gillett averred that the will of John D. Gillett did not make any specific devise of the proceeds of the stock of banks that had voluntarily gone into liquidation, but that the same passed under the residuary clause in the will of John D. Gillett, deceased, to all of his children, share and share alike; and Charlotte L. Barnes, as trustee, averred that she claimed certificate No. 122, for $10,000 of stock in the National Bank of Lincoln, under the will of Lemira P. Gillett, deceased, for the benefit of her said children.

The decree of the circuit court found certificate No. 122 passed, upon the death of Lemira P. Gillett, to the children of John D. Gillett who survived their mother, Lemira P. Gillett, and that the money in the hands of Lemira P. Gillett, received by her from the national banks which had voluntarily gone into liquidation, belonged to the children of John D. Gillett, deceased, who survived their mother, Lemira P. Gillett, and that, Grace A. Littler and John P. Gillett having died prior to the death of their mother, David T. Littler and Inez M. Gillett took no interest in said bank stock or said fund. David T. Littler and Inez M. Gillett excepted to that part of the decree that found that the fund received by Lemira P. Gillett from banks that had gone into voluntary liquidation passed to the children of John D. Gillett, deceased, who survived their mother, Lemira P. Gillett, and also to that part of the decree that found that David T. Littler and Inez M. Gillett took no interest either in the fund derived from the banks that had gone into voluntary liquidation or in certificate No. 122, and Charlotte L. Barnes, as trustee, and her children, who appeared by guardian ad litem, excepted to that part of the decree that found that certificate No. 122 did not pass under the will of Lemira P. Gillett to Charlotte L. Barnes, in trust for her children. Since the commencement of this suit David T. Littler has departed this life, testate, and Stephen L. Littler, his personal representative and sole heir, has been substituted in his stead. Inez M. Gillett and Stephen L. Littler, as the personal representatives of John P. Gillett, deceased, and David T. Littler, deceased, respectively, and Charlotte L. Barnes, as trustee, prosecuted an appeal to the Appellate Court for the Third District, where the decree of the circuit court was affirmed, and a further appeal has been prosecuted to this court. Edward D. Blinn has been substituted as administrator of the estate of John P. Gillett, deceased, in lieu of Inez M. Gillett.

Hugh Crea and Hugh W. Housum, for appellant Charlotte L. Barnes, as trustee. Beach, Hodnett & Trapp, for Nina L. Gillett and Emma S. Oglesby, appellees. Hamilton & Catron and R. C. Maxwell, for Jessie D. Gillett, administratrix.

HAND, C. J. (after stating the facts). The first question presented for consideration is, to whom did the $9,345 received from the banks that had gone into voluntary liquidation belong upon the death of Lemira P. Gillett? The rule is fundamental that in construing a will the intention of the testator, if legal, should control, and to ascertain such intention the entire will should be considered in the light of all the circumstances surrounding the testator at the time the will was made. In Decker v. Decker, 121 Ill. 341, 12 N. E. 750, on page 354, 121 Ill., and page 756, 12 N. E., the court said: "In every case calling for construction, the question of first importance is, what was the testator's intention?" And in Finlay v. King's Lessee, 3 Pet. 346, 7 L. Ed. 701: "The intent of the testator is the cardinal rule in the construction of wills, and if that intent can be clearly perceived, and is not contrary to some positive rule of law, it must prevail." And in Johnson v. Askey, 190 Ill. 58, 60 N. E. 76, on page 61, 190 Ill., and page 76, 60 N. E.: "The rule is well settled that in construing a will the intention of the testator must control, and to ascertain such intention the entire will should be considered in the light of all the circumstances surrounding the testator at the time the will was made."

If those paragraphs of the will of John D. Gillett which deal with the bank stock of the testator be read as a whole, it will appear clear, we think, that the testator intended his widow should have the absolute control of his bank stock, or the funds arising therefrom, during her lifetime, and that no interest therein should vest in his children or their descendants so long as the widow should live, and that the testator, upon the death of Lemira P. Gillett, intended that the principal of his bank stock, in whatever form it might be at that time—that is, whether in stock, cash received from the sale of stock, or cash received from banks that had gone into voluntary liquidation—should be divided among his then surviving children and the descendants of deceased children. By paragraph 9 it is provided, if his wife survive him, for and during her natural life she shall have "all the use, interest, dividends and profits that may accrue during such period on or from any share of bank stock which I may own at the time of my death," and, in case any of the banks in which the testator owned stock should wind up their business and distribute their capital, it is provided the widow shall be entitled to receive the funds received from such banks upon liquidation, and she is given the right to reinvest the principal and to retain to her own use all interest and profit derived from such reinvestment during her natural life. She is also given power, with the advice and consent of the executors, to sell any part or all of the stock in certain of said banks, and in case of such sale she is given authority to reinvest the proceeds arising therefrom, and is to have as her own property all the interest and profit arising from such investment, and at her death the principal arising from a voluntary liquidation shall "be applied and distributed as hereinafter directed," and in case of sale the principal shall "be applied as hereinafter directed." While the stock, or the funds arising from a sale of the stock or from a voluntary liquidation of any bank, remained in the widow's hands, no distinction is made with reference to the profit arising therefrom, whether in the form of dividends upon the stock, interest upon the money, or profit upon the investment. It is all treated as income, and is given to the widow for life.

As showing the intention of the testator with reference to the division of his bank stock upon the death of the widow, we think the first part of paragraph 24 of the will has an important bearing. The testator there provides in what proportions he desires his bank stock divided among his children in case he shall survive his wife, and provides that in case any of his children shall die before he dies, leaving a child or children them surviving, such child or children shall take the share of the parent, and that in case a child shall die before he dies, without leaving a child or children him surviving, the share or shares of such deceased child shall be divided in equal parts among his surviving children, and that the surviving children of any of his children shall take the share which their deceased parent would have taken if living, thereby clearly manifesting an intention that the principal of his bank stock should be divided among his children and the children of his deceased children. In the same paragraph, after devising the income of the bank stock to his wife for life if she should survive him, upon her death he divides the bank stock among his children in the same proportion he had provided it should be divided among them upon his death in case he should survive his wife, and then provides that it is his intention that, in case his wife survive him, none of his children or their children or descendants shall take any vested interest in said stock until after the death of his wife, and that they shall not have the ability to transfer it, and it shall not become liable for their debts by attachment, execution, or other legal process, and, in case of his widow's death subsequent to his death, limited the right of his children or their descendants to take said bank stock to those who should survive his widow.

It is conceded said limitation applies to the bank stock and to the principal in the hands of the widow at the time of her death, derived from the sale of bank stock, but it is said that no such limitation applies to the fund in the widow's hands received from the banks which had gone into voluntary liquidation. The clause of the will which disposes of the bank stock, and the proceeds thereof, after the death of Lemira P. Gillett, reads as follows: "If my said wife shall survive me, I give and bequeath all my bank stock that shall remain unsold at the time of her death, and all money arising from the sale of said bank stock by my wife, in manner following," etc.—which clause does not include the moneys received from the banks which have gone into voluntary liquidation, unless the following or similar words, "and moneys received by her from banks which have gone into voluntary liquidation," can be legitimately read into that clause of the will, and it is earnestly insisted by the appellants to read such words into that clause of the will would be to make a new will for the testator. If the effect of reading into that clause of the will the words above specified would be to change the clause and to make it include something which it did not include before, manifestly the words cannot be read into the clause. But we do not so view the matter. The words are read into the clause to make plain what is the manifest intention of the testator, considering the will as a whole, but which intention the testator has not accurately or completely expressed by the words he has used. And the authorities are clear this may be done. In Glover v. Condell, 163 Ill. 566, 45 N. E. 173, 35 L. R. A. 360, on page 584, 163 Ill., and page 179, 45 N. E., 35 L. R. A. 360, the language of Mr. Jarman in his work on Wills (2 Rand. & Tal. [5th Am. Ed.] p. 60) is quoted with approval. He there says: "It is established that where it is clear on the face of a will that the testator has not accurately or completely expressed his meaning by the words he has used, and it is also clear what are the words which he has omitted, those words may be supplied in order to effectuate the intention as collected from the context." And in that case the court read into the will the words "of the income," or "of the interest," or "of the dividends," the insertion of which words, it was said, "effectuates the clear intention of the testator, and is necessary to give expression to his meaning." To the same effect is 29 American and English Encyclopedia of Law (1st Ed.) p. 372, where it is said: "Where it is clear on the face of the will that the testator has not accurately or completely expressed his meaning by the words he has used, and it is also clear what are the words which he has omitted, those words may be supplied in order to effectuate the intention as collected from the context."

A glance at paragraph 23 of the will, wherein the testator directs that all of his personal property, other than bank stock, shall be divided in stated proportions among his children, shows that the testator considered the bank stock and the funds which might arise therefrom, and so treated it, as having been fully disposed of by other provisions of the will, and the clause in relation to the disposition of the fund arising from banks in liquidation, and the clause in relation to the disposition of the fund proceeding from sales of stock, are in substantially the same language, and both refer to future directions in the will for the distribution of both funds. It would seem to follow that the provision, "I give and bequeath all my bank stock that shall remain unsold at the time of her death [the widow's death], and all money arising from the sale of said bank stock by my wife, in manner following," should be held to cover and include all money from both sources. If this position be not correct, then it would appear the testator, when dealing with these two funds, intentionally disposed of one fund and left the other to pass under the residuary clause of the will, although both funds were the proceeds of bank stock received by the widow subsequent to his death. This is not probable. In paragraph 24 of the will it is provided that in case any of the children of the testator should die before his wife, leaving a child or children, then such child or children should take in equal parts the share or shares of said bank stock and money which his, her, or their deceased parent or parents would have taken in the event of surviving the wife of the testator; again, that if any child of the testator should die, leaving no child, before the death of his wife, then the share of such child in such bank stock and money should be divided among the surviving children of the testator or their descendants; and, further, that none of the children or descendants of children of the testator shall take any vested interest in said stock or money until the death of the wife. It seems apparent the money arising from stock in liquidated banks, as well as money derived from sales of stock by the widow, was alluded to in these clauses of the will when the testator spoke in general terms of bank stock and money; and this reference to money in this connection strengthens the position that the testator intended to dispose of all moneys derived from both the sale of stock and the liquidated banks to his children or their descendants who survived the widow, by the provisions of his will, other than the residuary clause.

Our conclusion is that the fund in the hands of Lemira P. Gillett, received from banks which had gone into voluntary liquidation, upon her death went, under the terms of the will of John D. Gillett, deceased, to his children who survived his widow.

The next question presented for determination is, did the 100 shares of stock of the First National Bank of Lincoln represented by certificate No. 122, issued to Lemira P. Gillett as a stock dividend, belong to her at the time of her death, and pass, by virtue of her will, to Charlotte L. Barnes as trustee, or did the same belong to the estate of John D. Gillett, deceased, and pass to his devisees, under the terms of his will, at the death of Lemira P. Gillett? It appears that the stock issued to Lemira P. Gillett was paid for with the earnings of said bank which had accumulated prior to the death of John D. Gillett. In the case of De Koven v. Alsop, 205 Ill. 309, 68 N. E. 930, it was held that a stock dividend which evidenced a conversion by the corporation into capital of earnings accumulated during the stockholder's lifetime goes to the remaindermen as a part of the corpus of the estate, and not to the life tenant under a will devising the income of the estate to the testator's widow for life and directing the residue to be divided among others at her death. That case considers all the questions urged upon the consideration of the court bearing upon the phase of this case now under consideration, and is conclusive against the right of Charlotte L. Barnes, as trustee, to hold the stock issued as a stock dividend to Lemira P. Gillett by the First National Bank of Lincoln.

The contention is made by appellants other than Charlotte L. Barnes that, if it is held certificate No. 122 does not pass to Charlotte L. Barnes as trustee, then the shares represented by said certificate are so far intestate property that they pass under the residuary clause of the will of John D. Gillett, deceased, to all his children, which would include the devisees of his deceased children. We do not agree with this contention. In Gibbons v. Mahon, 136 U. S. 549, 10 Sup. Ct. 1057, 34 L. Ed. 525, it is said: "A stock dividend really takes nothing from the property of the corporation, and adds nothing to the interests of the shareholders. Its property is not diminished, and their interests are not increased. After such a dividend, as before, the corporation has the title in all the corporate property. The aggregate interests therein of all the shareholders are represented by the whole number of shares, and the proportional interest of each shareholder remains the same. The only change is in the evidence which represents that interest, the new shares and the original shares together representing the same proportional interest that the original shares represented before the issue of the new ones." The new shares of stock represented the surplus earnings of the bank, and go to the remaindermen under the will of John D. Gillett, deceased, the same as the surplus or improvements made with the surplus would have gone had no stock dividend been made. In Minot v. Paine, 99 Mass. 101, 96 Am. Dec. 705, the court said (page 107, 99 Mass., 96 Am. Dec. 705): "It is obvious that if the directors had made no stock dividend, but had invested the income in permanent improvements, making no increase of the number of shares, the improvements would have been capital, belonging to the legatees in remainder."

We think it clear that certificate No. 122, upon the death of Lemira P. Gillett, became the property of the children of John D. Gillett, deceased, who survived Lemira P. Gillett, his widow.

Finding no reversible error in this record, the judgment of the Appellate Court will be affirmed. Judgment affirmed.

(208 Ill. 529)

BOOKER v. BOOKER et al.

(Supreme Court of Illinois. April 20, 1904.)

UNRECORDED CONVEYANCE — ACTUAL NOTICE — SUFFICIENCY OF EVIDENCE — CONSTRUCTIVE NOTICE — GRANTEE'S MORTGAGE — NOTICE TO AGENT — WITNESSES — HUSBAND AND WIFE — SETTING ASIDE CONVEYANCE — INADEQUACY OF CONSIDERATION.

1. In an action by claimants under an outstanding unrecorded deed to set aside a conveyance by the holder of the record title to a wife in her own right, the husband is a competent witness, under the exceptions in 2 Starr & C. Ann. St. 1896, p. 1837, c. 51, par. 5, forbidding a husband or wife to testify for or against each other as to any transaction or conversation occurring during marriage, except where the wife would, if unmarried, be a plaintiff or defendant, or where the litigation shall concern her separate property.

2. Mere inadequacy of consideration is not ground for relief to claimants under an outstanding unrecorded title, seeking to set aside a deed by their grantor of record to a subsequent purchaser.

3. Evidence, in an action by claimants under an outstanding unrecorded title to set aside a deed by their grantor of record to a subsequent purchaser, examined, and *held* insufficient to show actual notice to such purchaser of the outstanding title.

4. A recorded mortgage, made to a third person by the grantee in an outstanding unrecorded deed, does not put a subsequent purchaser from the holder of the record title on inquiry as to the outstanding title.

5. Notice to a mere messenger in a transaction, who is not acting as agent therein, is not notice to his employer.

6. Notice to an agent is not notice to his principal, where the presumption that the agent will communicate his knowledge to the principal is rebutted by the fact of his antagonistic interest.

7. In 1882 a wife procured an attorney to purchase certain realty for her, taking a conveyance in his own name, and then deeding to her by unrecorded deed. The wife died in 1887. Her husband's second wife obtained a deed from the attorney in 1894, which she recorded, and under which she took possession, remaining therein, and paying taxes on the property. Claimants under the first wife resided in the county during the entire time. In 1899 they filed a bill to set aside the second wife's deed. The only excuse for their delay was that the husband had falsely represented to them that the second wife had no conveyance. *Held*, that the suit was barred by the laches both of the first wife and of those claiming under her.

Appeal from Circuit Court, Shelby County; S. S. Dwight, Judge.

Suit by Jennie Booker and others against Lettie C. Booker. From a decree for plaintiffs, defendant appeals. Reversed.

This is an appeal from a decree of the circuit court of Shelby county, granting the relief prayed in a bill filed by appellees against appellant. The allegations of the bill were, in substance, that on February 25, 1882, a certain 40-acre tract of land was sold at an administrator's sale, under a decree of the county court of Shelby county, to pay the debts of one William Davis, deceased; that prior to the sale Nancy Booker, who was then the second wife of John W. Booker, employed T. F. Dove, a lawyer at Shelbyville, in said county, to purchase the land in his own name for her; that said attorney made the purchase for $1,020, taking a deed to himself, and two days later conveyed the land to said Nancy, which latter deed was never filed for record, but was left in the custody of the grantor, Dove; that Nancy Booker borrowed at the same time $800 from one Minerva Cooper with which to pay a part of the purchase money, giving her note therefor, due in five years, secured by a mortgage on said land, which was duly recorded, and that she afterwards paid all of that mortgage indebtedness, except the sum of $400; that after her death, which occurred on March 20, 1894, and after the marriage of John W. Booker with his present wife, Lettie C. Booker, the latter, by collusion with her husband, fraudulently procured and obtained the execution and delivery of another deed from said Dove to the land, who, through and by means of the fraudulent collusion and deceitful arts of the said Lettie C. and John W. Booker, executed to Lettie C. Booker a second deed, which she fraudulently filed for record in the recorder's office of the said county; that at the time of the execution of the said deed Lettie C. and her husband, John W. Booker, well knew that the land was purchased by Nancy Booker in her lifetime, and that she had paid to said Dove the full amount of the purchase price, and that he (Dove) had made a deed to her, and that she had executed the said mortgage to Minerva Cooper, and well knew that the deed executed by the said Dove to Lettie C. was procured and obtained in fraud of the rights of the children of the said Nancy Booker; that after the making of the last-mentioned deed Lettie C. borrowed $400 from one Smith, securing the same by a mortgage on the land, dated March 20, 1894, which mortgage was duly recorded, and that the said John W. Booker had fully paid said mortgage indebtedness, and that said Lettie C. has never paid any part of the same. It is then alleged that whatever title Lettie C. Booker holds to the land is fraudulent, and should be declared null and void, and that her title should be decreed to be held in favor of complainants, and the trust executed by decree and partition of the land made. The bill offers to reimburse Lettie C. for any sums due her.

John W. Booker, the husband, and one Lincoln Booker, a minor son of Lettie C. and John W. Booker, together with Lettie C. Booker, were made parties defendant. John W. made no answer to the bill, and it was taken as confessed against him. Lincoln Booker answered by his guardian ad litem, and Lettie C. filed her answer, denying all knowledge of the execution of the alleged deed from Dove to Nancy Booker, and averring that at the time she purchased the land and obtained her deed from Dove she inquired particularly of him, as well as of her codefendant (her husband) John W. Booker and others, as to the rights and ownership of Dove, and of his power to convey the same, and was assured by them that he (Dove) was the absolute owner of the land and had complete right to convey the same, and that she never heard that right questioned or disputed until the filing of the present bill; that she has not now, and never had, any knowledge or information whatever of any conveyance of the land by Dove to Nancy Booker, or of any lien executed by said Nancy to Minerva Cooper, or of any mortgage by the former to the latter, or the payment of such indebtedness by said Nancy; that she is an utter stranger to all such matters, and denies the same, but admits that, if any deed was ever made to said Nancy

¶ 6. See Principal and Agent, vol. 40, Cent. Dig. § 689.

Booker, it was never filed for record. She denies all fraud and collusion on her part in obtaining her deed from Dove, or that she fraudulently filed the same for record. She admits that on March 20, 1894, she borrowed $400 from one Smith, and gave a mortgage upon the land to secure the same, but denies that John W. Booker paid any part of said indebtedness, and avers that she paid the money so borrowed to Dove as part of the purchase price, and subsequently paid the entire amount so borrowed to said Smith. She admits that she holds title to the land, and denies that she holds the same in fraud of complainants' rights, or that there is any trust to be executed by her. She then avers that at the time of her marriage to John W. Booker she owned a small amount of property in her own right, which he, by certain devices and schemes, attempted to obtain, and represented to her, among other things, that said Dove was the absolute owner of the land in question, and that it could be bought to good advantage, and that she, yielding to his solicitations, bought the same in good faith, for a valuable consideration, without notice, etc; that she at the time procured an abstract of title to the land, which showed that T. F. Dove was the owner of the same, by which she was enabled to make said mortgage loan from Smith. She further sets up that prior to the death of the said Nancy Booker the land had been sold for taxes, and a tax title perfected in Dove on September 12, 1889, and the deed duly recorded; that immediately upon receiving her deed from Dove she entered into possession of the land, and has ever since been and still is in the open, exclusive, and actual possession of the same under the claim and belief that she was and is the absolute owner thereof, all of which has all the time been known to complainants; that she has paid all the taxes assessed thereon for each and every year since and including the year 1894, and is now the sole owner thereof. She charges that her codefendant John W. Booker is only nominally a defendant; he causing himself to be made a defendant, etc. She sets up and relies upon the laches of said Nancy Booker, and the complainants claiming through or under her, as a bar to all right of recovery in the present action.

To the answer of Lettie C. Booker a general replication was filed, and the cause heard upon oral testimony taken in open court. The decree finds the issues for the complainants, and orders the deed from T. F. Dove to Lettie C. Booker set aside and declared null and void, but that she have a first lien upon the land for $574.50, and that partition be made subject to said lien. It then finds the interests of the respective parties complainant, and of the defendants John W. Booker and the infant, Lincoln Booker; the said Lincoln Booker and John W. Booker deriving their interests through the death of one of the sons of Nancy Booker. Other facts necessary to a decision of the case appear from the opinion.

Walter C. Headen, for appellant. W. C. Kelley, for appellees.

WILKIN, J. (after stating the facts). The undisputed evidence in the case is that prior to February 25, 1882, John W. Booker procured T. F. Dove to purchase the land in question for Nancy Booker, and that the administrator's deed to Dove, his quitclaim deed to Nancy Booker and her mortgage to Minerva Cooper were executed as alleged in the bill. The deed to Nancy was withheld from record by the directions of John W. Booker for some ulterior purpose which he does not explain. There is no dispute as to the fact of its delivery, and that it was the same day returned to Dove, and remained in his possession until the hearing of the present cause. It is not claimed that Nancy Booker was at any time in possession of the land. On March 20, 1894, T. F. Dove and wife executed and delivered to the appellant, Lettie C. Booker, a quitclaim deed for the same land, which was recorded two days later. Prior to the execution of the latter deed the land had been sold for taxes, and a tax deed executed therefor, to one William W. Hess, dated June 8, 1888, and filed for record on the day of its date; and on September 12, 1889, Hess and wife by quitclaim deed conveyed the same to Dove in consideration of $75, and that deed was also duly filed for record March 22, 1894. There also appears to have been a tax deed to the same land executed to one Michael Montgomery, dated February 2, 1892, and filed for record the same day; but, so far as the evidence in this record shows, that title is outstanding. On March 20, 1894, the date of the deed from Dove and wife to the appellant, she borrowed of one D. C. Smith, through one John D. Millar, $400, for which she gave her promissory note and executed a mortgage upon the land to secure the same, due five years from date, with 10 coupon interest notes, for $14 each, due semiannually, and that mortgage was recorded March 22, 1894. In order to obtain said loan, she procured an abstract of title to the land, for which she paid $9.50, and she also paid Millar $10 commission. The proceeds of the Smith loan were paid to Dove in consideration of the deed by him to her. Immediately upon receiving her deed she entered into and has remained in possession of the land from that time to the present. She has also paid the taxes thereon for the years 1894 to 1902, inclusive. Nancy Booker, through whom complainants claim title, died March 8, 1887, leaving two children—Jennie Booker, one of the complainants, born in 1887, and John Wesley Booker, who died before reaching his majority, and unmarried, about the year 1898; and his alleged interest in the land in question descended to his father, the said John W. Booker, his sister, Jennie Booker, the complainants Finley and Elbridge Booker, his half-brothers by a former marriage of his father, and his infant half-brother, defendant Lincoln Booker. At the time the bill was filed the half-brothers Finley and Elbridge Booker were, respectively, about 32 and 34 years of age. The former has lived in the state of Kansas for the past 3 or 4 years, and the other complainants and the defendant John W. Booker have at all times resided in Shelby county, this state, in which the land is located.

Without reference to the tax title which he held at the time of his conveyance to the appellant, the title of record to said land was in T. F. Dove, and it is admitted by counsel for the complainants that, unless the evidence shows that the appellant took her deed with actual or constructive notice of her grantor's prior conveyance to Nancy Booker, her title must prevail; and such is unquestionably the law of this state. As was said in Grundies v. Reid, 107 Ill. 304: "Our law protects the purchasers of real estate in their purchases of the same as the title appears of record, unless there be notice of something to the contrary." Many later decisions of this court are to the same effect.

The only evidence in this record tending to prove actual notice to the appellant of the unrecorded deed to Nancy Booker is the testimony of John W. Booker, nominally her codefendant and her husband. It is insisted on behalf of appellant that he was incompetent to testify for or against his wife, Lettie C. Booker. The litigation is "concerning the separate property of the wife," and the action is one "in which she would, if unmarried, be defendant." Therefore, under the exceptions to paragraph 5, c. 51, p. 1837, 2 Starr & C. Ann. St. 1896, he was competent to testify for or against her. McNail v. Ziegler, 68 Ill. 224; Pain v. Farson, 179 Ill. 185, 53 N. E. 579, and cases cited; Cassem v. Heustis, 201 Ill. 208, 66 N. E. 283, 94 Am. St. Rep. 160.

The credibility of the testimony of the said John W. Booker presents a different question. Though joined with his wife as a defendant, he was not only hostile to her in interest, but so manifested his hatred and prejudice against her upon the witness stand that he was repeatedly rebuked by the court and admonished by his own counsel, and it is admitted now that no excuse can be offered for his misconduct as a witness. His testimony is to the effect that he told his wife all about the prior deed, and that she took her title with actual knowledge that Dove had previously conveyed the land; but in view of his unjustifiable conduct, and his manifestation of bias against the appellant and partiality in favor of the complainants, we cannot receive his testimony without at least some grains of allowance. He had not lived with his wife for several years, and she squarely contradicted him as to his having told her anything whatever about the condition of the title to the land or the deed to his former wife, Nancy; and she swears, without qualification, that she had no knowledge or information from him, or any one else, that the title was in any way defective. He also swore positively that he himself paid off the Smith mortgage. He said: "I furnished every dollar of the money myself to pay off the Smith loan." The appellant swore directly to the contrary—that she paid that entire indebtedness; and in that she was corroborated by the testimony of John D. Millar, to whom the money was paid. On this proposition the chancellor must have disbelieved John W. Booker and given credit to the appellant; otherwise, she would not have been given a first lien on the land for the amount of that loan and interest. She further testified that at the time she took her deed from Dove she inquired of him whether the title was good, and was told that it was, and she gives in detail a conversation with him on that subject, to the effect that she was getting a perfect title, in which she was corroborated by her sister, who was present and heard the conversation. It is true that Dove did not remember the conversation. He testified: "I don't remember seeing Lettie C. Booker about the time I made the deed to her. I don't remember the circumstance of Lettie C. Booker and her sister, Sylvia, coming to my office to inquire about the title to the land. I cannot say they didn't, because I have no recollection of it whatever. I don't remember any conversation with her until after suit was brought." When it is remembered that the conversation took place several years prior to his attention being called to it, and in all probability being one of many similar transactions which occur in an attorney's office, it cannot be fairly said that his evidence is at all contrary to or inconsistent with that of appellant and her sister. It is true, the consideration paid for the land by appellant was much less than—perhaps not to exceed—one-third its actual value; and while inadequacy of consideration is not, of itself, a ground for relief, as contended by counsel for appellees, it is nevertheless a circumstance to be considered in determining the good faith of the purchaser. It cannot, however, be fairly said in this case that, because the appellant purchased the land for a grossly inadequate price, she is chargeable with knowledge of the prior unrecorded deed, because, upon the same line of reasoning, it could be said she would not have paid $500 or more for a title which she knew to be absolutely worthless. She testified that she knew that she was purchasing the 40 acres for less than it was worth, and was induced to buy it for that very reason. To hold that, because she paid an inadequate consideration for the land, she ought therefore to be held chargeable with notice of the defect in her title, would be to authorize the setting aside of every title obtained for a grossly inadequate price, which the law will not permit. The fact that the land had been sold for taxes, and two tax deeds executed therefor, must also be considered as affecting the market value of the land. We have endeavored to carefully and impartially consider the testimony in this record, and have been forced to the conclusion that the complainants failed to prove by that preponderance of testimony which the law imposes upon them that the appellant had actual notice of the execution of the deed to Nancy Booker.

It is, however, earnestly insisted that the facts and circumstances surrounding the transaction and parties at the time of the execution of appellant's deed are sufficient, in law, to charge her with constructive notice of the deed to Nancy, and upon this ground, in all probability, the learned chancellor based his finding and decree. On this branch of the case it is first contended that the record of the mortgage executed by Nancy Booker to Minerva Cooper in January, 1882, was, in law, notice to the appellant of the unrecorded deed from T. F. Dove to said Nancy; and reliance in support of this position is placed upon the cases of Ogden v. Haven, 24 Ill. 57, and Morrison v. Morrison, 140 Ill. 560, 30 N. E. 768. We do not regard those cases in point. In the Ogden Case, the mortgage from Tooley to Haven, the former owner, was duly recorded, and it was said (page 60): "We think the presumption of fact, as well as of law, is that Ogden at that time saw the record of that mortgage. Finding the title in fee in Haven, and subsequently a mortgage to him from a third person, was well calculated to excite suspicion that Haven must have conveyed the land to Tooley by some conveyance not of record"—and it was held that that mortgage was sufficient to arouse the suspicion of the subsequent purchaser. But the case did not turn upon that fact alone. There was there abundant evidence of actual notice. In the later case of Morrison v. Morrison, supra, the mortgage, which was held to be constructive notice of the prior unrecorded deed, was given to the owner of the fee, as shown by the record, and we said (page 576, 140 Ill., and page 772, 30 N. E.): "If plaintiff in error made such examination [i. e. of the record], she found, or, if she had made examination, she would have found, a title in fee in her grantor, and a subsequent mortgage on part of the N. W. ¼ of section 9, made by her brother, while in possession, to Abend, as trustee, to secure a promissory note made by her brother and payable to the order of her grantor. It would seem that notice of the record of such a mortgage is sufficient to put a purchaser on inquiry as to any unrecorded conveyance"—citing Ogden v. Haven. The facts here are entirely different. The mortgage which, it is claimed, should in law charge the appellant with constructive notice of the unrecorded deed was not executed to her grantor, but to a third party. It cannot be seriously contended that in every case where the records show a conveyance from one party to another, third persons are chargeable with notice that the grantor had a title from some other person. To so hold would render nugatory the statute relating to the registration of deeds of conveyance.

In St. John v. Conger, 40 Ill. 535, the action was ejectment, in which the plaintiff claimed title through a deed from one McNemony to Peter H. Schenk, improperly recorded in Madison county; the land being situated in Knox county. There was a mortgage from McNemony to Schenk, properly recorded, and a deed from Schenk to Whittemore, and a chain of conveyance from Whittemore to the plaintiff. The original deed from McNemony to Schenk had never been recorded in Knox county. The defendant claimed under a deed from the heirs of McNemony to one Lancaster, duly recorded. A judgment in favor of the plaintiff and against the defendant was reversed by this court, and it was said (page 537): "It is also urged that the subsequent deed from Schenk to Whittemore should have put the defendant, and those under whom he claims, upon inquiry as to whatever title Schenk had. This proposition, in effect, is that, if a person has made a deed of a tract of land having no recorded title, he must nevertheless be supposed to have some title, and subsequent purchasers must take notice of whatever title he had. Much as registry laws have been frittered away by the doctrine of putting parties upon inquiry, we do not think any court has ever gone to the extent of adopting this rule. It would substantially defeat the object of registry laws. Their object is to provide a public record, which shall furnish to all persons interested authentic information as to titles to real estate, and enable them to act on the information thus acquired. This rule would require a person purchasing from one who has the title on record to take subject to the unrecorded deeds of persons claiming under a chain of title having no connection of record with the true source of title. If such purchaser is to be held to notice of such a chain of title at all, he has the right to presume, in the absence of any other information, that whatever title the persons claiming under such chain have is on record, as the law requires it to be, and that they have no title if the record shows none. Here the record shows that Schenk had a mortgage from the owner, and when the defendant purchased he had a right to presume the grantees under Schenk had acquired only his interest as mortgagee. That was all the record disclosed, and any other construction would make the record a snare." The Ogden Case is then referred to and distinguished.

In Kerfoot v. Cronin, 105 Ill. 609, where A., in whom the record showed no title, made a deed of trust to B. for certain real estate, which was recorded, and which recited that it was given to secure two notes of the grantor to C., in whom the record of deed showed the title for the purchase money of the property, and C. indorsed and sold the notes, and after the record of the trust deed sold and conveyed the premises to innocent parties for value, who had no knowledge of any prior conveyance by him to A., or of the deed from A. to B., or the recitals therein, it was insisted that the record of the deed from A. to B. was notice to such subsequent purchaser from C. of the existence of the deed or of its recitals; but we held the contrary, on the ground that both A. and B. were strangers to the chain of title acquired by the purchasers, and we said (page 617): "The principle contended for by appellant's counsel would, as we conceive, require every record that might possibly affect real estate to be thoroughly examined before a party could be protected in taking a title to or lien upon real estate, the expense and burden of which would practically put an end to all transactions of that kind. The law imposes no such burden. In the present instance the defendants were only required, in the absence of actual notice, to see whether the records showed any, and what, deeds by or judgments against Walker. They were not required to run through with the alphabet, and see if, by possibility, in some deed, no matter by or to whom, it is mentioned that the grantee is a trustee for Walker, and that the deed is made to secure the payment of the purchase money."

We are unable to perceive upon what principle the appellant was chargeable with notice that Dove had conveyed the title to Nancy Booker, because of her mortgage to Mrs. Cooper, and hold that the record of that mortgage was not, as a matter of law, sufficient to arouse her suspicion or put her upon inquiry.

Another position insisted upon by counsel for appellees is that John W. Booker, in the purchase of the land by Lettie C. from Dove, was her agent, and that she is chargeable with notice of the facts known to him. In the first place, we do not think the evidence shows that he was her agent in that transaction. He was, at most, nothing more than a mere messenger. Doyle v. Teas, 4 Scam. 202. Generally, in order to create an agency, there must be an appointment of the agent by the principal and an acceptance of such appointment. The agency may be implied, as well as expressed; but the proof in either case must be clear and satisfactory in order to bind the principal. It is also true, as a general proposition, that notice to the agent of facts learned by him while actually engaged in the business of his principal is notice to the principal. Notice to the agent, to be notice to the principal, must, as a general rule, be given to the former while acting in the course of his employment. An exception to the rule, however, is that the principal may be bound by knowledge of his agent obtained in a former transaction—that is, one not connected with his employment—provided the knowledge is so definite as that it is, or must be presumed to have been, present in the agent's mind and memory at the time of the performance of his duties for the principal. These rules are based upon the presumption that the agent has acquired knowledge which it is his duty to impart to his principal, and upon the presumption that he has performed or will perform that duty; and hence, even where the agency is clearly established and his knowledge sufficiently proven, whenever it appears that the agent has a motive or interest in concealing the fact from his principal, the latter will not be bound. No one can read the evidence in this record without reaching the conclusion that John W. Booker had a fraudulent and selfish purpose in keeping the deed to his wife, Nancy, off of the records of the county, and also in his dealings with his present wife. If he acted as her agent, it is clear that he was not seeking or desiring to protect her interests. In other words, the presumption that he would discharge his duty by disclosing to his wife the facts known to him is completely overcome by his conduct and personal interest in the matter. To say that she should be chargeable with the knowledge obtained by John W. Booker of the unrecorded deed in 1882, not communicated to her, is, it seems to us, unreasonable and grossly unjust.

We are further of the opinion that under the facts of this case the right of action in the complainants and the defendant John W. Booker is clearly barred both by the laches of Nancy Booker and those claiming under her. She obtained her deed in 1882. She died in 1887, some five years after she obtained the deed. The appellant obtained her deed in 1894, and immediately took possession of the premises, and has remained in such possession to the present time, paying all taxes assessed thereon. The complainants, except Elbridge Booker, have resided in the same county in which the land is situated during all this time, and he has only been absent three or four years. This bill was not filed until 1899, five years after the appellant placed her deed upon record and entered into possession of the land. Under the repeated decisions of this court, this delay, unexplained, is such laches as will defeat the right of recovery. In Howe v. South Park Com'rs, 119 Ill. 101, 7 N. E. 333, we said (page 117, 119 Ill., and page 346, 7 N. E.): "The doctrine of laches, as understood by the court, has been often declared by its previous decisions [citing cases]. The principle that lies at the foundation of all the cases in this court on this subject is, the party who challenges the title of his adversary to real property must be diligent in discovering that which will avoid the title or render it invalid, and diligent in his application for relief. Unreasonable delay, not explained by equitable circumstances, has always been declared evidence of acquiescence, and will bar relief." The only pretense of an excuse for the delay in this case is that the complainants were kept in ignorance of the facts by the false representations to them of John W. Booker, their father. He says: "I told this falsehood about this transaction to all my children. I have said to each of them—I will not say at one time—but I was asked this question, 'Is it true that Lettie has a deed to this land?' and I said, 'No.' I repeatedly said that. I intentionally and willfully made the statement. I deceived my children. I kept up that course until they found out better. I don't know whether they caught me in the lie or not, but it was a lie," etc. It can scarcely be seriously contended that such statements, if they were in fact made, would be a sufficient reason for the delay. The complainants themselves make no explanation whatever—in fact, did not testify. Appellant's deed to the land was a matter of public record, and she was in the open, exclusive possession of the same. Those seeking to challenge her title were bound to take notice of her claim and act with reasonable diligence. They had no right to rely on the false statement of their father that she had no deed.

On the whole record we are convinced that the court below was in error in granting the prayer of complainants' bill, and its decree will accordingly be reversed, and the cause remanded, with directions to dismiss the bill.

Reversed and remanded.

(208 Ill. 623)

TOLEDO, ST. L. & N. O. R. CO. et al. v. ST. LOUIS & O. R. R. CO. et al.

(Supreme Court of Illinois. April 20, 1904.)

EQUITY — JURISDICTION—RAILROADS—INJUNCTION—VIOLATION—EVIDENCE—SUFFICIENCY—DAMAGES.

1. A court of equity will not lend its aid to enforce a forfeiture because of a breach of condition subsequent in a deed.

2. A court of equity is without jurisdiction to hear and determine a bill to remove a cloud from the title to real property, where the lands in controversy are in the possession of the defendant to the bill, unless some other ground of equitable cognizance appears.

3. The determination of the question of ownership of real property is not within the jurisdiction of a court of equity, where no ground of equitable jurisdiction is alleged in the bill and proved at the hearing.

4. Mere statements in a bill on which chancery jurisdiction might be maintained, but which are not proved, will not authorize a decree on such parts of the bill as, if standing alone, would not give the court jurisdiction.

5. Though a court of equity will restrain by injunction the commission of trespasses to real property which would result in irreparable injury to the owner, yet, where defendant is in possession of real property, claiming under a deed, and where the only acts which complainants seek to enjoin are the construction of a roadbed, and laying a railroad track thereon, which is claimed to be an injury to another railroad company, one of the complainants, for the reason that the proposed roadbed is to be several feet lower than one which it desires to construct on practically the same line, equity has not jurisdiction; the purpose of the bill not being to preserve the real estate in its present condition and free from injury until this title can be determined at law, but to have determined the ownership and right of possession.

6. Where complainants in a bill in equity have an adequate remedy at law, the failure of the defendant to state in his answer that complainants have an adequate remedy at law does not confer jurisdiction to determine a question not otherwise cognizable in equity.

7. A nondefendant railroad succeeded to the rights of the defendant railroad, and was engaged, under the defendant's charter, in completing the construction of defendant's line, when a bill in equity was filed, and a temporary injunction issued against defendant. The nondefendant's solicitors appeared and secured a dissolution of the injunction, receiving their fees and expenses from the nondefendant road. *Held*, that a decree awarding defendant damages for the fees and expenses of the solicitors was proper.

8. Where damages are recoverable at law in a suit on an injunction bond, they may be allowed by the chancellor in the same suit in which the injunction was issued, on suggestion.

9. Evidence that a railroad company which had been enjoined from proceeding with the construction of its line on a certain strip of land proceeded with the work of construction outside the strip, but on one occasion, by mistake, in blasting, the workmen got over the line, and on the enjoined strip, and one shot was discharged there, and the workmen were then taken off that strip, is insufficient to show a violation of the injunction, in the absence of a finding or decree of the court below relating thereto.

¶ 2. See Quieting Title, vol. 41, Cent. Dig. § 2.

Appeal from Circuit Court, Pope County; W. W. Duncan, Judge.

Suit by the Toledo, St. Louis & New Orleans Railroad Company and another against the St. Louis & Ohio River Railroad Company and others. From a decree for defendants, complainants appeal. Affirmed.

This is an appeal from a decree of the circuit court of Pope county dismissing a bill for an injunction which had been filed by the appellant railroad company and Jacob W. Michell, and assessing damages against appellants for the wrongful suing out of the injunction writ. The bill was on January 5, 1903, presented to the master in chancery of Pope county, who on the same day ordered a temporary injunction to issue, which was served on appellees January 6, 1903. An answer was filed to this bill, but the transcript does not show the date of filing. On January 17, 1903, appellees applied to Hon. A. K. Vickers, one of the judges of the First Judicial Circuit, for a dissolution of the injunction. The cause was continued to the 23d day of the same month, at which time a hearing was had upon the pleadings and affidavits filed by the respective parties, and the motion for a dissolution of the injunction was taken under advisement until January 27th. On the latter date the judge ordered the temporary injunction dissolved. On April 18, 1903, appellants filed an amended bill. Appellees answered the amended bill, and appellants replied to the answer. Appellees also filed suggestions of damages.

The cause then proceeded to a hearing before the court, and resulted in the decree above mentioned.

The evidence shows that the St. Louis & Ohio River Railroad Company, one of the appellees, was incorporated on June 18, 1900, under the name of Chicago, St. Louis & Ohio River Railroad Company, for the purpose of constructing a railroad from a point on the Ohio river at or near Golconda, in Pope county, to a point on the Chicago & Eastern Illinois Railway in Johnson county. This latter terminal was afterwards changed to a point on the Illinois Central Railroad in Johnson county. The name was also changed to St. Louis & Ohio River Railroad Company. The appellant company was incorporated on March 18, 1902, for the purpose of constructing a railroad from a point in Shelby county to a point on the Ohio river in Massac county.

North of Golconda, in Pope county, a high bluff extends up the Ohio river for a distance of about two miles, and between this bluff and the river is a narrow pass. Appellant Jacob W. Michell was, prior to July 1, 1901, the owner of two adjoining tracts of land, the south tract containing 58¾ acres, and the north tract 16 acres, both tracts having the Ohio river as the eastern boundary line. This pass constituted the eastern portion of each of these two tracts, extending from the south line of section 18, town 13 south, range 7 east, to the north line of the 16-acre tract. About 800 feet south of the north line of the latter tract, and in the pass, was a large rock, designated in the pleadings and by the witnesses as the "Big Rock."

The plan of the appellee railroad company, in constructing its system, included the building of a branch line from Golconda and an incline track to the river, by means of which connection could be established with boats at some suitable point. With this object in view, it surveyed a line north from Golconda, and proceeded to obtain the right of way along the route surveyed. Adopting a point on the line which was denominated "Zero," as the survey proceeded stakes were placed at intervals of 100 feet and numbered with minus numbers; the first stake north of the zero point being designated "Minus 1," and each stake to the north being given the next higher minus number than the one immediately south of it.

Prior to July 1, 1901, the appellee railroad company had surveyed and set stakes through the pass referred to, up the Ohio river, to a point near the big rock on the Michell land, at which point a stake was set, marked "Minus 74." On the latter date the appellee company procured from Jacob W. Michell a warranty deed for a right of way over that portion of the two tracts of land above mentioned which constituted the pass, described as follows: "From the point where the center line of said railroad, as now located and staked out for a part of the distance across said land, crosses the south line of fractional section 18, town 13, south, range 7, east of the third principal meridian, to a point eleven hundred and thirty feet northwardly from the first said point, a strip of land one hundred feet in width on the westerly side of said center line, and on the easterly side of said center line a strip of varying width, extending from said center line to the Ohio river; and from the aforesaid point eleven hundred and thirty feet northwardly from the south line of said section 18 to a point in the north line of the south part of fractional northeast quarter section 18, a strip of land one hundred feet in width on the westerly side and seventy-five feet in width on the easterly side of the center line of said railroad as the same is now located and staked out for a part of the distance and as it may hereafter be staked out for the remainder of the distance across said land." The deed then proceeds: "Also the right to construct, operate and maintain a railroad upon the said strip of land, wherever the same may be surveyed and located upon the said tracts of land by the grantee herein, its successors and assigns, and to have, hold and use the land extending fifty feet on either side of the meridian line of the said railroad for all the uses and purposes of a railroad right of way." It also contains the following condition: "This deed is to be null and void unless the grantee, its successors or assigns, shall construct said railroad by the first day of January, A. D. 1903." The deed was acknowledged by Jacob W. Michell and wife on August 17, 1901, and was recorded on February 1, 1902. At the time it was executed the appellee railroad company had made no survey and had established no line north of the stake marked "Minus 74."

The appellant company, desiring to use the pass in question for its railroad, on July 26, 1902, obtained from Jacob W. Michell and wife a quitclaim deed for a right of way over the two tracts of land in question, described as follows: "A piece of land one hundred feet in width, and as many more feet in width as may be required for the excavations and embankments, and for material for embankments, for so much of said railway as may pass through the following described land, to wit: The south part fractional northeast quarter section 18, sixteen acres, and also the fractional southeast quarter section 18, fifty-eight and three-fourths acres. This last being granted over said land west of the right of way heretofore granted to the Chicago, St. Louis and Ohio River Railroad Company, across part or all of said land in said last description, all in the county of Pope and State of Illinois." This deed was acknowledged and filed for record on the same day it was executed. During the latter part of September or the first part of October, 1902, the appellant company surveyed a line through the pass, and set stakes along the proposed route from the north end to the south end of the Michell land.

On December 13, 1902, the appellee company surveyed and located its line from the stake marked "Minus 74" to the north line of the Michell land, but did not have its road constructed on the land in question by January 1, 1903. It did, however, have a line constructed and trains running over that part of its system between Reevesville, on the line of the Illinois Central, in Johnson county, and Golconda, by that date, and had 60 or 70 per cent. of its construction work done on the Michell land.

On January 3, 1903, Michell and his wife executed a warranty deed to the appellant company, conveying to it the following described real estate: "Beginning at a point where the center line of the Toledo, St. Louis and New Orleans railroad, as now staked out, crosses the south line of fractional section 18, town 13, south, range 7, east of the third principal meridian, said point being about one hundred and forty-five feet west of the northeast corner of Jacob D. Rauchfuss' land; thence west along said section line to a point thirty feet distant, measured at right angles to said center line of railroad; thence northwardly to a point in the north line of a sixteen-acre tract of land owned by said Michell in the south part of fractional northeast quarter section 18, said point being about one hundred and ten feet west of the crossing of the north line of above described sixteen-acre tract and the center line of Toledo, St. Louis and New Orleans railroad as now staked out; thence east along said north line of sixteen-acre tract to the Ohio river; thence in a southerly direction, following meanderings of the said river, to the south line of section 18; thence west along said section line to the place of beginning; all in the county of Pope and State of Illinois, as shown by the plat hereto attached." The description in this deed includes the right of way granted to the appellee railroad company by the deed of July 1, 1901, and this deed was filed for record on the same day it was executed.

The appellee railroad company had not constructed its railroad over the Michell land by January 5, 1903, but its servants, together with the servants of the McArthur Bros. Company, which latter company had the contract to clear off and grade the right of way for the appellee railroad company, were proceeding with the construction of the railroad on the land described in the deed of January 3, 1903, to the appellant company, and were pulling up the stakes set by the latter company, when the temporary injunction issued; and the following day it was served on both of the appellee companies and their servants, restraining them from interfering, meddling with, or possessing the real estate in question, and from interfering with the appellant company in its work upon said land. Appellants charge that appellees disregarded the injunction writ, and proceeded with the construction of the road after it had been served, and before it was dissolved, doing part of the work at night. Appellees deny any violation of the writ.

It appears from the evidence that the Illinois Central Railroad Company was constructing this road for and by authority of the appellee railroad company. The McArthur Bros. Company was paid by the former railroad company, as were also the men who made the survey and supervised the work of construction. The suggestion of damages filed by the McArthur Bros. Company was disallowed. Damages to the amount of $621.40 were allowed to the appellee railroad company on account of solicitors' fees and expenses. The evidence of these solicitors shows that they were employed and paid by the Illinois Central Railroad Company, and that they had made no charge against, and had received no money from, the St. Louis & Ohio River Railroad Company.

The grounds urged by appellants in this court for a reversal of the decree are, first, that the condition contained in the deed of July 1, 1901, to the effect that the deed should be void if the road was not constructed by January 1, 1903, was broken by the grantee, and that the conveyance by Michell to the appellant company on January 3, 1903, was a sufficient re-entry on the part of Michell to divest the appellee railroad company of all right and title it had obtained by virtue of the deed to it; second, that said deed of July 1, 1901, is void for uncertainty as far as it attempts to convey any land north of the stake marked "Minus 74;" third, that if the title to the land north of the stake marked "Minus 74" remained in Michell until lines were located to which the deeds could attach, the appellant company, having first surveyed a route, had the better right to the land embraced in its survey; fourth, that the court erred in assessing damages in favor of the appellee railroad company for solicitors' fees, because the solicitors were employed and paid by the Illinois Central Railroad Company, which was not a party to this suit.

E. B. Green, D. G. Thompson, Theo. G. Risley, and W. S. Phillips, for appellants. W. W. Barr and R. J. Stephens (J. M. Dickinson, of counsel), for appellees.

SCOTT, J. (after stating the facts). 1. It is sought by the amended bill herein to set aside and annul the deed dated July 1, 1901, from Jacob W. Michell and wife to the St. Louis & Ohio River Railroad Company, hereinafter referred to as the Ohio River Company, on account of fraud and misrepresentation in procuring the same. The proof is not sufficient to warrant relief on this ground, and counsel do not press this question in this court.

2. The amended bill prays that the deed

of July 1, 1901, be set aside for the reason that the condition subsequent therein contained, which is set out verbatim in the foregoing statement of facts, was not complied with by the grantee, and that, as a consequence, its right to the real estate in question has been forfeited. In this respect the complainants seek to enforce a forfeiture because of a breach of a condition subsequent in the deed. A court of equity will not lend its aid for that purpose. 2 Story's Eq. Jur. § 1319; Douglas v. Union Mutual Life Ins. Co., 127 Ill. 101, 20 N. E. 51.

3. The amended bill also seeks to set aside and annul the deed of July 1, 1901, on the ground that, prior to the filing of the bill herein, the condition subsequent had been broken, and the title had revested in Michell, and that he had on January 3, 1903, conveyed the real estate to appellant the Toledo, St. Louis & New Orleans Railroad Company, hereinafter referred to as the Toledo Company, and that the said deed of July 1, 1901, is a cloud upon the title of the last-named appellant, and should be set aside for that reason. It is unnecessary to determine whether the condition had been complied with, or whether the title of the grantee under the deed containing that condition had been divested. The condition was to be fulfilled by January 1, 1903. On that date, and for several days prior thereto, and from that time down to the time of the service of the temporary injunction herein, it conclusively appears from the testimony of all the witnesses in the case that appellees were in the possession of the strip of ground which the Ohio River Company claims to own, by virtue of the deed which is alleged to be a cloud upon the title of the Toledo Company, and had thereon a large force of men and teams, and were engaged in constructing thereon a railroad grade. A court of equity is without jurisdiction to hear and determine a bill to remove a cloud from the title to real estate where the lands in controversy are in the possession of the defendant to the bill, unless some other ground of equitable cognizance appears. Lundy v. Lundy, 131 Ill. 138, 23 N. E. 337; Glos v. Randolph, 133 Ill. 197, 24 N. E. 426.

4. The amended bill also prays for a permanent injunction restraining the defendants from interfering with the Toledo Company's possession of a portion of the real estate which the Ohio River Company claimed to hold under its deed from Michell, and from constructing thereon a roadbed, and laying thereon a railroad track, and that if, before a final hearing, the defendants shall enter upon such real estate and construct thereon a railroad track, they be restrained from removing the same therefrom, and that, if they be in possession on a final hearing of the bill, they be decreed to surrender the possession to the Toledo Company, and that, if it be found that the Ohio River Company has any right or title to the land claimed as a right of way by the Toledo Company, it be decreed to release and quitclaim the same to the Toledo Company on such terms as shall seem equitable. It is apparent that by this branch of the bill the only matter presented is the question, who is the owner of, and entitled to the possession of, the real estate which was in the possession of the Ohio River Company? This is clearly a question for a court of law. It is only on the theory that a freehold was involved that an appeal could have been taken directly to this court.

The grounds hereinabove spoken of under the first, second, and third divisions of this opinion are the only other grounds upon which the interference of a court of equity is invoked. Complainants' right to equitable relief on either of those three grounds fails for reasons hereinbefore stated.

While it is true that a court of equity, which has jurisdiction of a cause by reason of the existence of some ground of equitable jurisdiction, for the purpose of doing complete justice between the parties, may, in addition to the equitable relief, afford relief of a character which in the first instance is only obtainable in a suit at law, still, to authorize relief of the latter character, some special and substantial ground of equitable jurisdiction must be alleged in the bill and proved upon the hearing. Mere statements in a bill upon which the chancery jurisdiction might be maintained, but which are not proved, will not authorize a decree upon such parts of the bill as, if standing alone, would not give the court jurisdiction. 12 Ency. of Pl. & Pr. p. 165; Daniel v. Green, 42 Ill. 472; Logan v. Lucas, 59 Ill. 237; Gage v. Mayer, 117 Ill. 632, 7 N. E. 97; County of Cook v. Davis, 143 Ill. 151, 32 N. E. 176.

It is apparent that upon this branch of the case nothing is involved except the possession and title to real estate. The Ohio River Company was in possession claiming title in fee simple under its deed from Michell. The Toledo Company claims to be the owner and entitled to the possession under its conveyances from Michell. The following language from Daniel v. Green, supra, is applicable: "To permit this bill to be maintained would be to hold that purely legal titles may be tried by a suit in chancery, instead of by an action of ejectment, in every case to recover lands adversely held. * * * Without the equity powers of the court have been brought into action by the main purpose of the bill, the court will not try legal titles, and decree the surrender of adverse possession. When it does so, it is only incident to its legitimate equity jurisdiction."

We are reminded that a court of equity will restrain by injunction the commission of trespasses to real estate which would result in irreparable injury to the owner. Authorities stating that doctrine are not applicable where, as here, defendant is in possession of the real estate, claiming the same under a deed, and where the only acts which complainants seek to enjoin are the construction of a roadbed, and laying a railroad track thereon, which is claimed to be an injury to the Toledo Company, for the reason that the proposed roadbed is to be several feet lower than one which it desires to construct upon practically the same line. Such an injury, even if the Toledo Company be the owner of the land over which the road is to be constructed, is one readily adjusted in a suit at law. This is not a bill for the purpose of preserving the real estate in its present condition, and free from injury, until the title thereto can be determined at law, but its purpose is to have a court of equity determine the ownership and right of possession.

Counsel for appellants state the gist of this controversy in the following language: "In the reign of Cæsar Augustus all highways in the Roman Empire led to Rome, and in the case at bar all other questions lead up to the important and controlling question, who was the owner of, and had right to, the strip of right of way in controversy at the time the original bill was filed?" The thoroughfare which leads to the solution of this problem passes through a court of law.

It is said, however, that, as the answer to the amended bill does not state that complainants had an adequate remedy at law, appellees should not now be permitted to contend that a court of equity cannot in this case properly determine the title to this property, and in support of that proposition we are referred to Monson v. Bragdon, 159 Ill. 61, 42 N. E. 383; Village of Vermont v. Miller, 161 Ill. 210, 43 N. E. 975; and Kaufman v. Wiener, 169 Ill. 596, 48 N. E. 479. This doctrine must be accepted with the qualification found in the latter case, which is, "provided, of course, the subject-matter of the litigation and the character of the relief are not foreign to the power of a court of equity." We think the subject-matter of the litigation presented by this branch of the bill under consideration so foreign to the power of a court of equity as to bring this case within the quoted language. The bill, on its face, states a good cause of action, because it is alleged in apt words that the deed of the Ohio River Company was obtained by fraud and misrepresentation. The lack of jurisdiction did not appear on the hearing until that question was disposed of. We think this rather falls within the class of cases discussed in Richards v. Lake Shore & Michigan Southern Railway Co., 124 Ill. 516, 16 N. E. 909, of which it is there said: "It is a fundamental principle that parties to a suit cannot, by consent, confer jurisdiction with respect to the subject-matter of the suit, by stipulation or consent, for that is fixed by the law, and is consequently beyond the control of the parties." Unless this be the correct view, parties may by agreement confer upon a court of equity the power to try suits, not only in ejectment, but in replevin, trespass to the person, and other matters equally foreign to the jurisdiction of that court. An action of ejectment in a court of law must be resorted to where, as here, the parties desire to contest the validity of conflicting titles. "An action of ejectment cannot be tried in a court of equity by bill or cross-bill." Gage v. Mayer, supra; Parker v. Shannon, 114 Ill. 192, 28 N. E. 1099.

5. The damages awarded by the court below were for the fees and expenses of solicitors in securing a dissolution of the temporary injunction. Two objections are urged: The first is that it appears from the record that these solicitors were not employed by either of the appellees, but were employed by the Illinois Central Railroad Company. This question does not seem to have been specifically presented to the court below, and the position of appellants now virtually is that the decree is not sustained by the evidence in this respect. It appears from the testimony, however, that the Illinois Central Railroad Company, prior to the beginning of this suit, had succeeded to the rights of the Ohio River Company, and, under the charter of the latter, was engaged in doing the work on the Michell land; that the contractors and employés who constructed the roadbed and laid the track were contractors and employés in the service of and paid by the Illinois Central Railroad Company; and that the latter was in fact, under the law, the agent of the Ohio River Company in constructing the line north of Golconda and across the Michell land. A person or corporation exercising the power conferred by charter upon another corporation is the servant of the latter. Lesher v. Wabash Navigation Co., 14 Ill. 85, 56 Am. Dec. 494; Chicago, St. Paul & Fond du Lac Railroad Co. v. McCarthy, 20 Ill. 385, 71 Am. Dec. 285; Pennsylvania Co. v. Ellett, 132 Ill. 654, 24 N. E. 559. Under the circumstances, we think that the employment by the Illinois Central Railroad Company was employment by the Ohio River Company.

It was also objected that no damages should have been allowed for the reason that appellees violated the temporary injunction. In the case of Colcord v. Sylvester, 66 Ill. 540, we held that this did not constitute a defense to an action at law on the injunction bond for wrongfully suing out the temporary injunction, and that, while the parties enjoined who disobey the writ would be amenable to the action of the court as for a contempt, still their disobedience would not deprive them of their action on the bond to recover damages occasioned by the wrongful issuance of the injunction. Appellants insist that a different rule prevails where the defendant files his suggestion of damages and seeks to have an allowance in the same suit in which the injunction issued, for the reason that he who comes into equity must do so with clean hands. We are not impressed with this argument. The question is, are the damages recoverable by the defendant? It seems to be conceded that they would be recoverable in a suit at law on the injunction bond. We think, if they can be so recovered, they may be allowed by the chancellor upon suggestion.

Moreover, it does not certainly appear that the injunction was violated. The line of the Ohio River Company follows its survey across the Michell land. The Toledo Company had also surveyed a line across this land. Where the two lines of survey for the center lines of the tracks of the respective companies cross the south line of the Michell land, they are 70 feet apart. They approach each other gradually as they go north. About 1,500 feet north, on the center line of the Ohio River Company, a stake was driven, which is known in the litigation as "Station Minus 74." From there on north the lines, still approaching each other, soon become so close together that the tracks of the two companies would occupy practically the same ground to a point 800 feet north of Station Minus 74, where the line of the Ohio River Company terminates. The temporary injunction restrained the defendants from operating on a strip of land extending entirely across the Michell real estate, and which is spoken of in this litigation as the "enjoined strip." At the south line of the Michell land the east line of this strip is 35 feet east of the line of the Toledo Company, and continues north parallel with the line of the Toledo Company, intersecting the center line of the Ohio River Company at Station Minus 74. That portion of the roadbed of the Ohio River Company which is north of Station Minus 74 is in the enjoined strip, while that south thereof is outside the enjoined strip, practically speaking. The east line of the enjoined strip does not cross the tracks of the Ohio River Company at right angles, but crosses them diagonally, and, as appears from the testimony of the witnesses, would cross the center line of the tracks at Station Minus 74. When the temporary injunction was served, about 60 or 70 per cent. of the work of construction on the Michell land had been done. Thereafter, and while the injunction was in force, a large amount of construction work was done and rails were laid on the Michell land. The evidence of appellees is that this work was all done south of Station Minus 74, and not on the enjoined strip, except that on one occasion, by mistake, in blasting, the workmen got over the line and on the enjoined strip, and one shot was discharged there, and the workmen were then taken off that strip. On the other hand, witnesses for appellants testified that work was done north of Station Minus 74 on the roadbed of the Ohio River Company while the injunction was in force. In this state of the evidence, and in the absence of any finding or decree by the court below on the subject, we are not disposed to hold there was a violation of the injunction.

The decree of the circuit court will be affirmed. Decree affirmed.

(209 Ill. 361)

SENFT v. VANEK.

(Supreme Court of Illinois. April 20, 1904.)

MORTGAGES—EQUITY OF REDEMPTION—CONTRIBUTION — PURCHASER PENDENTE LITE — AMENDMENTS OF PLEADINGS—DISCRETION OF COURT.

1. Two persons purchasing, at a judicial sale, separate parcels of land subject to a common mortgage, must, as between themselves, pay the common mortgage in proportion to the value of their respective parcels.

2. Though, as a general rule, a complaint as to the character of a mortgage foreclosure sale should be made on the confirmation of the report of the sale, an owner of the equity of redemption who files a bill, three days after the order approving the sale, in the court in which the sale was made, attacking the character of the sale, is not barred by laches.

3. The allowance of amendments to pleadings in chancery suits is a matter resting in the discretion of the court, which will not be interfered with on appeal unless abused.

4. A grantee in a trust deed to secure a debt executed after the entry of a decree of a sale of the land under mortgage foreclosure, and before the sale, is in the position of a purchaser pendente lite, and whatever interest he acquires is subject to the lien of the foreclosure decree.

5. Plaintiff and defendant purchased at a judicial sale separate parcels of land. Plaintiff's parcel was worth $400, and defendant's parcel was worth nearly $6,000. The two parcels were subject to a common mortgage. At the sale under foreclosure of the common mortgage, plaintiff's parcel was alone sold to defendant for a sum over $6,000, the amount paid being sufficient to pay the debt, interest, and costs. *Held* that, as plaintiff and defendant were liable for the payment of the common mortgage in proportion to the value of their respective parcels, plaintiff was entitled to redeem on paying his proportion.

Appeal from Appellate Court, First District.

Suit by John Senft against Jakub Vanek. From a decree of the Appellate Court (110 Ill. App. 117) affirming a decree dismissing the bill, complainant appeals. Reversed.

This is a bill filed on October 4, 1900, in the superior court of Cook county, which, as finally amended, is substantially a bill to secure an equitable redemption from a foreclosure sale. Some of the defendants demurred to the bill, and some of the defendants answered the bill. A reference was taken during the progress of the proceedings to a master in chancery, who made a report, to which exceptions were taken, and said report was approved and confirmed. Upon the sustaining of a demurrer by one of the defendants to the amended bill, the court below dismissed the bill for want of equity. An appeal was taken to the Appellate Court, where said decree of dismissal has been affirmed. The present appeal is prosecuted from such judgment of affirmance.

The facts are substantially as follows: On

January 10, 1898, Anthony Kozel owned lot 2, and all of lot 1 (except the east 21 feet 5 inches thereof), in a certain subdivision in Cook county. On that day Kozel and his wife executed a deed of trust conveying all of said premises to Moses E. Greenebaum, as trustee, to secure their note of that date for the sum of $4,500. Subsequently, on April 5, 1898, Kozel and his wife, by quitclaim deed, conveyed said premises to Marie Kucaba, who, on April 6, 1898, to secure her three notes, aggregating the sum of $2,800, executed, with her husband, three separate trust deeds of that date, thereby conveying to said Kozel, as trustee, to secure said last-named notes, the said premises, together with another lot, described as lot 3 in block 4. Subsequently, in a cause in the circuit court of Cook county wherein Charles F. Woolley was complainant and Marie Kucaba and others were defendants, the three trust deeds executed by her and her husband were foreclosed, and a decree of sale was entered, in pursuance of which, on June 13, 1898, the master in chancery of the circuit court sold at public sale said lot 2 to the appellee, Jakub Vanek, and issued a certificate of sale to him, and at the same sale and at the same time sold to Charles Vesely said lot 1 (except the east 21 feet 5 inches thereof), and issued a certificate of sale to him, which latter certificate was subsequently assigned by said Vesely to the appellant, Senft. On September 14, 1899, the master executed a master's deed conveying said lot 1 (except the portion above named) to said Senft, and on September 20, 1899, the master executed to said Vanek a deed to said lot 2, both of which deeds were filed for record.

When Senft and Vanek, appellant and appellee, acquired their titles as aforesaid from the master to lot 1 (except the east 21 feet 5 inches thereof), owned by Senft, and lot 2, owned by Vanek, said premises were both subject to the deed of trust executed by Kozel and wife to Greenebaum to secure $4,500, as above stated. That is to say, the Greenebaum deed of trust for $4,500 was a common incumbrance upon the lots owned by Senft and Vanek.

On May 18, 1900, said Greenebaum and others, individually, and as trustees and successors in trust, filed a bill in the superior court of Cook county against said Kozel and wife, and said Vanek and Senft, and others, for the purpose of foreclosing said trust deed for $4,500. On July 19, 1900, a decree of foreclosure was entered by the superior court, finding that there was due to the complainants, the Greenebaums and others, the sum of $5,960.98, and directing that, in default of the payment thereof, the master should sell said lot 2 and all of lot 1 (except the east 21 feet 5 inches thereof), or so much thereof as might be necessary, to pay the amount due the complainant. On August 16, 1900, said premises were sold by the master at public vendue, whereupon the appellee, Jakub Vanek, offered and bid for said lot 1 (except the east 21 feet 5 inches thereof) the sum of $6,178.56, and the master thereupon struck off and sold to said Vanek said lot 1 (except the east 21 feet 5 inches thereof) for said last-named sum, which was the highest and best bid for the premises. The amount realized from said sale was sufficient to satisfy the amount due the complainants, including the costs, so that no other part or portion of said premises was offered for sale; and said lot 2, owned by the appellee, Vanek, was withdrawn, and not sold. The sale was reported to the superior court, and approved and confirmed by it on October 1, 1900. Thereupon, three days after said confirmation, to wit, on October 4, 1900, the present bill was filed in the superior court of Cook county. The present bill represents that the Greenebaum mortgage or trust deed for $4,500 was a common lien against that part of lot 1 owned by Senft, and lot 2, owned by Vanek, and that Senft and Vanek were responsible for the payment of said mortgage indebtedness according to the value of their respective lots, and states the respective amounts which each lot should have contributed towards the payment of the amount due upon the decree of foreclosure, to wit, $6,178.56 with interest.

On July 27, 1900, after the decree of foreclosure on July 19, 1900, in the Greenebaum suit, and before the sale on August 16, 1900, in that suit, Vanek and wife executed to Arthur W. Draper, trustee, and Adolph F. Kramer, successor in trust, a deed of trust, conveying all of lot 1 (except the east 21 feet 5 inches thereof), and all of lot 2, to secure the payment of the note of said Vanek for $2,000, dated July 27, 1900, due in five years, and also 10 interest coupon notes of $55 each. This latter trust deed was made before Vanek had title to said part of lot 1, and is alleged in the bill to have been without consideration, and made with intent to defraud Senft, and against his rights in lot 2 as aforesaid; and the bill charges that said last-named trust deed was null and void. The bill makes as parties thereto all of the persons above named, together with the holders of the notes secured by the trust deed from Vanek and wife to Draper, and prays that said last-named trust deed may be set aside, and declared null and void as against the rights of Senft; that an account may be taken, and for contribution and subrogation.

Samuel Strauss, claiming to be the owner of the note for $2,000 secured by the trust deed to Draper, and Draper, trustee, and Kramer, successor in trust, filed a demurrer to the bill on October 29, 1900. Jakub Vanek and Anna Vanek, his wife, filed a general demurrer thereto on November 5, 1900. On December 3, 1900, the superior court overruled the demurrers of all said defendants. Jakub Vanek and Anna Vanek, his wife, elected to stand by their demurrer, and on December 8, 1900, Strauss and Draper and

Kramer filed a joint and several answer. In this answer all the facts recited in the bill, down to the acquisition of their titles by Senft and Vanek, were admitted to be true; it was denied that the premises owned by Vanek were worth $12,000, or that the trust deed to Draper was fraudulent and void, or that the premises owned by Vanek and Senft were responsible for the payment of the common incumbrance resting upon them, according to their respective values; the answer alleges that the note secured by the deed of trust to Draper was given to secure a loan of $2,000, made to Vanek by Strauss "for the express purpose of enabling said Vanek to discharge the indebtedness then resting upon said lot 2, and secured by said trust deed from said Kozel as aforesaid"; that from and after July 27, 1900, and up to August 16, 1900, said Samuel Strauss held said sum of $2,000 for the benefit of said Jakub Vanek, subject to said Jakub Vanek's order to be used as aforesaid, and that on August 16, 1900, said Samuel Strauss paid said sum of $2,000 to said Jakub Vanek, and said sum of $2,000 was paid by said Vanek to said Wirt E. Humphrey, master in chancery, at the sale of said lot 1 (except the east 21 feet 5 inches thereof) as aforesaid, the same being a parcel of said sum so paid by said Jakub Vanek at said sale of said lot, and being $2,000 of the $6,178.56 so paid by said Jakub Vanek as aforesaid; that the entire amount, to wit, said sum of $2,000, remains unpaid, and that the trust deed to Draper, securing the same, was not made for the purpose of defrauding Senft. The answer admits that, when Vanek executed said trust deed to Draper, he had no title to said lot 1 (except the part above named), and that Vanek and wife did not intend thereby to convey said part of lot 1, but that the same was, by a mistake of the scrivener, inserted therein; that the intention of Vanek was to convey by said trust deed all of lot 2 only, which was at that time owned by him; "and that, said sum of $2,000 having been used by said Vanek in the payment and satisfaction of the indebtedness due upon said lot 2, secured by the trust deed from Anthony Kozel to Moses E. Greenebaum, as aforesaid, said defendant should be subrogated in equity, as against said Senft, to the rights of the mortgagees in said case of Henry E. Greenebaum et al. v. Anthony Kozel et al. in and to lot 2, said lot 2 having thus contributed $2,000 of the $6,178.56 necessary to satisfy the indebtedness due under said mortgage to said Greenebaum."

On October 28, 1901, a decree was entered by the court, sustaining the validity of the trust deed made by Vanek to Draper to secure $2,000, and finding that said sum of $2,000 was paid by Strauss to Vanek, and used by Vanek in making his bid of $6,178.56 for the purchase of the fractional portion of lot 1 at said master's sale, and that said lot 1 (except the east 21 feet 5 inches thereof) was included by a mistake of the scrivener who prepared the deed of trust, contrary to the intention of the parties, and that therefore said portion of lot 1 is not included in the trust deed, and said trust deed is not a lien upon said fractional portion of lot 1. The decree of October 28, 1901, finds that said fractional portion of lot 1 was a strip of land 8 feet 7 inches in width, and that, when the same was purchased by said Vesely, it was worth the sum of $400, and that said lot 2, when originally sold to Jakub Vanek, was worth the sum of $10,000, with the buildings thereon; that said fractional portion of lot 1 was subject to the payment of $237.64, being $^1/_{26}$ of the common incumbrance, and said lot 2 was subject to the payment of $5,940.92, being $^{25}/_{26}$ of the common incumbrance; that, by bidding $6,178.56 for said part of lot 1, Vanek removed the common incumbrance from lot 2, so as to make it rest entirely upon said portion of lot 1; that, by paying the amount of his bid, to wit, $6,178.56, Vanek received a master's certificate of sale; that into this certificate is merged the entire incumbrance formerly resting upon said lot 2 and said fractional portion of lot 1; "that, instead of Senft's portion of lot 1 being subject to the payment of $237.64, the sale and certificate of Vanek operated to subject said fractional portion of said lot 1 to the payment of $6,178.56, in order to redeem from said sale; that said Senft has not lost his land, nor has he paid any money, and therefore is not entitled to contribution; that said Senft should be permitted to redeem his said land from this particular certificate holder, the said Jakub Vanek, upon paying $237.64, the equitable share of the common incumbrance resting upon his said strip, together with lawful interest, and no more, had he elected so to do; that the equity of redemption remaining in said Senft is inconsistent with the theory of an absolute sale; that the bid of said defendant, Vanek, cannot be treated as if it were the bid of a third person not interested in the premises incumbered, and as if the said sum of $6,178.56 were paid simply for the value of the land owned by Senft." The decree then fixes the master's fees at a certain sum, and decrees that the trust deed from Vanek and wife to Draper be declared null and void, and of no effect, so far as it affects lot 1 (except the east 21 feet 5 inches thereof), but adjudges the trust deed to be a good and valid and subsisting lien upon said lot 2 only; and the decree thereupon dismisses the bill of complaint for want of equity, and concludes with this provision: "Nothing in this decree shall in anywise affect the rights of Vanek or Senft with reference to lot 1."

On November 1, 1901, an order theretofore entered, dismissing the bill as against Vanek and his wife, was set aside, and leave was given to Senft, the complainant below, to file an amendment to his bill, and a rule entered upon Vanek and his wife to plead, answer, or demur to the bill as amended; and this order recites that it was entered over the objection of counsel for defendant, Vanek. On November 27, 1901, pursuant to leave so granted by the court, an amendment was filed to the bill by Senft, substantially in pursuance of the findings so as above made in the decree of October 28, 1901, and alleging that said fractional part of lot 1, owned by Senft, was only worth $400, and that lot 2 owned by Vanek was worth $10,000, and that Vanek should have contributed towards the payment of said sum of $6,178.56 25/26 thereof, and Senft should have contributed only 1/26 of said sum, such being the relative values which their premises bore to the amount due under the decree with costs; that is to say, said part of lot 1 owned by Senft was subject to the payment of $237.64, and lot 2, owned by Vanek, was subject to the payment of $5,940.92; that in law said Senft is only entitled to redeem from said sale by tendering and paying to the master who made such sale the full amount realized from the sale for said portion of lot 1 to said Vanek as above stated, to wit, the sum of $6,178.56; that Senft has not the money with which to redeem said property, and is unable to pay said sum, with interest from the time of sale, and to require him so to do would result in the loss of all his right in and to said premises, and that thereby a great injustice would be entailed upon him; that Vanek, in bidding an amount representing 25 times the value of said fractional portion of lot 1 owned by Senft, was actuated in so doing by malicious and evil motives, and that said bid was a fraud upon said Senft, and made for the purpose of preventing and depriving him from exercising the right, secured to him by the law, of redeeming from said sale, and also for the purpose of unlawfully securing to Vanek the title to said portion of lot 1 owned by Senft. The bill as thus amended alleges that the trust deed to Draper is absolutely null and void as against the rights of Senft in said portion of lot 1. The prayer of the bill, as thus amended, is that Senft may be allowed to redeem said portion of lot 1 by paying Vanek or the master the sum for which the lot was in law and equity responsible as its proportion of said common incumbrance, to wit, the sum of $237.64, with interest from August 16, 1900, which sum orator avers he is ready and willing to pay and tenders to said Vanek; that, upon making said payment, Vanek, as the holder of said master's certificate, be ordered to execute to Senft a quitclaim deed of all his interest in said portion of lot 1, and, in the event of his failing to do so, that the master in chancery be directed to issue to Senft a certificate of redemption as to said part of lot 1, upon payment to the master of $237.64, with interest as aforesaid; and for such other and further relief as equity may require. On December 13, 1901, Vanek and his wife filed their general demurrer to the bill as so amended. On January 13, 1902, the defendants below moved to strike the amendment from the files, but this motion was overruled. The demurrer, however, was sustained, and leave given to the complainants to file an amended bill instanter, to which the defendants were ruled to plead, answer, or demur within 10 days.

Thereupon, on January 13, 1902, Senft filed an engrossed amended bill, alleging that the decree of sale entered on July 19, 1900, in said foreclosure proceeding of Greenebaum v. Kozel, was a lien on both lot 2 and said fractional portion of lot 1; that by said decree the indebtedness against said lots was not apportioned according to the relative shares for which each of said lots was properly chargeable in equity. The prayer of the engrossed amended bill was that the purchase by Vanek at the master's sale on August 16, 1900, should be decreed to be a payment by Vanek of the lien upon lot 2 and said portion of lot 1 of said decree of July 19, 1900, and that, so far as Vanek paid more than the proportion equitably resting upon lot 2, as between him and Senft, the excess should be decreed to be a lien upon said fractional part of lot 1, and Vanek subrogated to the lien of said decree to that extent only, so far as said part of lot 1 is concerned; that Senft be permitted to pay such portion, with lawful interest to Vanek, and that, upon such payment, the sale of August 16, 1900, may be set aside and vacated, and the decree of July 19, 1900, be satisfied, and the lien thereof discharged, so far as said part of lot 1 is concerned; that, upon making said payment, Vanek be ordered to surrender his master's certificate to Senft, or to execute to him a quitclaim deed of his interest in said part of lot 1, or that the master be ordered to issue to Senft a certificate of redemption as to said part of lot 1. On January 18, 1902, a general demurrer was filed by Vanek to the engrossed amended bill, and, on February 3, 1902, an order was entered sustaining said demurrer and dismissing the bill for want of equity. It is from said last-named decree so dismissing the bill that an appeal was taken to the Appellate Court, where the decree of the superior court was affirmed.

Charles Vesely, A. Morris Johnson, and Chas. T. Farson, for appellant. Mancha Bruggemeyer, for appellee.

MAGRUDER, J. (after stating the facts). Upon reading the statement of facts which precedes this opinion, no other conclusion can be reached than that the appellant, Senft, by trickery, if not by fraud, has been deprived of his statutory right of redemption. The Greenebaum mortgage or trust deed was an incumbrance which rested both upon lot 1 (except the east 21 feet 5 inches thereof) and lot 2, the former belonging to Senft and the latter to Vanek. In other words, the two properties of appellant and appellee were subject to the Greenebaum mortgage for $4,-500. Appellant and appellee acquired title to their respective lots at the same time; that is to say, each obtained a master's deed to his property in pursuance of a sale foreclosing trust deeds, which were second mortgages, subject to the Greenebaum mortgage. When they bought their respective lots, the Greenebaum mortgage rested upon them as an incumbrance, and they were both subject thereto.

In Carpenter v. Koons, 20 Pa. 227, it was said by the Supreme Court of Pennsylvania, speaking through Chief Justice Black: "Two purchasers at a sheriff's sale, subject to a mortgage which is a common incumbrance on the land of both, stand on a level. Neither of them has done or suffered anything which entitles him to preference over the other. Equality is equity. They must pay the mortgage in proportion to the value of their respective lots." In 19 Am. & Eng. Ency. of Law (2d Ed.) p. 1280, it is said: "Where lands subject to an incumbrance are sold in parcels to different purchasers at the same time, all the purchasers must contribute ratably toward the discharge of the common encumbrance"—citing Chase v. Woodbury, 6 Cush. 143; Brown v. Simons, 44 N. H. 475; Ex parte Merrian, 4 Denio, 254; Alley v. Rogers, 19 Grat. 366; Rodgers v. McCluer, 4 Grat. 81, 47 Am. Dec. 715. In Sawyer v. Lyon, 10 Johns. 32, it was held that, "where two persons purchase separate parcels of a lot of land previously mortgaged, and one of them afterwards pays more than his share of the mortgage money, in proportion to the part of the lot owned by him, he may call on the other for contribution of his aliquot share, or such part of it as has been so paid." The proofs show, in the case at bar, that the portion of lot 1 owned by Senft, which was a strip of land only 3 feet 7 inches in width, was worth $400, and that lot 2, owned by Vanek, with the buildings thereon, was worth $10,000. Upon the principle that equality is equity, appellant and appellee were under obligations to pay the Greenebaum mortgage, resting upon their respective lots, in proportion to the value of such lots. As between themselves, they were under obligation to contribute ratably towards the discharge of the Greenebaum trust deed, which was a common incumbrance. The record shows that the proportion of the incumbrance which was justly payable by the appellant was $237.64, and the proportion thereof which was justly payable by the appellee was $5,940.92. When the sale under the foreclosure of the Greenebaum trust deed was made on August 16, 1900, Vanek, one of the defendants with Senft in that foreclosure proceeding, and being under obligation to pay his proportion of the mortgage, bid for the part of lot 1 owned by Senft the whole amount of principal and interest due by the terms of the decree, to wit, $6,178.56. Inasmuch as, by this bid, the whole debt found due by the decree was paid off, it was unnecessary for the master to sell lot 2, belonging to Vanek, and that lot was freed from the lien of the decree, and was saved to Vanek without sale. As appellant's lot was only worth $400, there could be no object in his paying $6,178.56, together with statutory interest, for the purpose of redeeming the same. No man would consent to pay $6,178.56 in order to redeem a lot which was worth only $400. The whole matter was so ingeniously managed by Vanek that appellant's right of redemption was substantially cut off, because made worthless.

It is said that the appellant should have presented his objections to the sale when the master made his report of sale, and when such report of sale came up for confirmation. The report of sale was approved on October 1, 1900. It is true, as a general rule, that a complaint as to the character of a master's sale, or as to the mode of bidding thereat, should be made upon the coming in of the master's report of sale for confirmation. But the present bill was filed October 4, 1900, only three days after the order approving the sale, and it was filed in the superior court of Cook county, the same court in which the foreclosure proceeding, wherein the sale was made, was pending. Both the foreclosure proceeding begun by the Greenebaums, and the present bill to redeem from the sale, were pending in the same court, and the application embodied in the present proceeding was filed in the court only three days after the report of sale was confirmed. Under these circumstances we are of the opinion that appellant was not too late in calling the attention of the court to the character of the sale, as to the manner in which the property was struck off.

The appellee, Vanek, has assigned cross-errors, alleging that the court below erred in permitting the appellant to amend his original bill and to file an amended bill. It has always been held in this state that the question of amendments in chancery proceedings is one which is very largely in the discretion of the court. We are not prepared to say that the discretion was abused in this case.

The decree of sale under the Greenebaum foreclosure was entered on July 19, 1900. A little more than a week thereafter, to wit, on July 27, 1900, Vanek executed a trust deed to one Draper to secure $2,000 upon lot 1 (except the east 21 feet 5 inches thereof) and all of lot 2. This trust deed was executed some 20 days before August 16, 1900, when the foreclosure sale took place. It is admitted in the answers that the execution of the trust deed to Draper was for the purpose of borrowing $2,000 to be paid upon the bid to be made on August 16, 1900, by Vanek for said part of lot 1. Lot 2 was thus made to furnish at least $2,000 towards the coming bid of $6,718.56. Lot 2 was thus made to furnish a portion of the money necessary to pay the amount due by the decree, not by offering the same at the sale under the decree, as the decree of foreclosure provided, but by the execution of a mortgage by the defendant, Vanek, in advance of the sale. If, when the sale came off, and the part of lot 1 owned by appellant was first offered for sale, $4,718.56 only had been bid, it would have been necessary to offer lot 2 for sale, in order to raise the remaining $2,000, necessary to pay the whole amount due upon the decree. By mortgaging lot 2 in advance of the sale, it was made to pay the $2,000 in a different way and by a different process, but so as to seriously impair appellant's right of redemption, and seriously increase the burden resting upon his property. It is admitted in the answers that this $2,000 was retained by the owner of the money between July 27, when the trust deed securing it was executed, and August 16, 1900, when the sale was made, and was only handed over to be paid upon the bid upon the day of sale itself.

When Vanek executed the trust deed to secure the $2,000 to Draper, Draper or Strauss, owning the note for $2,000 secured by the trust deed, stood in the attitude of a purchaser pendente lite. Draper, the trustee, or Strauss, the holder of the note, took whatever interest they obtained in lot 2 subject to the lien of the decree of sale owned by the mortgagees, the Greenebaums; and if lot 2 had been sold to a third party at the master's sale, the purchaser of lot 2 would have taken the property freed from the lien of the trust deed to Draper. The decree of sale ordered that lot 2 be sold, not that lot 2, subject to a trust deed for $2,000, should be sold. Strauss and Draper were thus interested in having the whole amount due upon the trust deed bid upon the part of lot 1 owned by Senft, because thereby the lien of the trust deed for $2,000 was kept intact and prevented from being annihilated by the sale. The parties interested in the incumbrance for $2,000 were interested in preventing lot 2 from being offered for sale at all. Thus, in advance of the sale, the scheme concocted by these parties interfered with the proper conduct of the sale, and prevented competition at the sale. No third party would bid more than $6,178.56 for the part of lot 1 owned by Senft, because it was only worth $400. When, therefore, Vanek bid that amount, there was an end of the sale. Vanek, codefendant with Senft, was the only person who could be benefited by bidding for the fractional lot 1 so much more than it was worth. It is a singular fact that the incumbrance to Draper securing the $2,000 was executed not only upon lot 2, but also upon lot 1 (except the east 21 feet 5 inches thereof). After the sale was made and the answers were filed, it was alleged that the insertion of the description of said portion of lot 1 in the trust deed to Draper was a mistake, and that there was no intention of creating a lien upon said part of lot 1.

We pause not to discuss the question whether the doctrine of contribution, or the doctrine of subrogation, has any application to the present case. A court of equity will not permit a fraud or a trick to deprive a party of his right under the statute to redeem his property at a reasonable figure, and at a figure somewhere in the neighborhood of the real value of the property. It never could have been the intention of the statute that one defendant should pay so much for the property of his codefendant, when both of their properties were subject to the same incumbrance, that such codefendant would be virtually deprived of the power to redeem his property. We think that the decree entered by the court on October 28, 1901, fixing upon $237.64 as the proper amount of the incumbrance to be paid by appellant, was correct.

If, before the sale, Vanek, owning lot 2, worth $10,000, had gone into court and paid off the whole amount due upon the decree, to wit, $6,178.56, so as to prevent a sale, he would have had a right to demand of Senft that he should pay to him $237.64, being the proportion of the indebtedness which it would be the duty of the appellant to pay, according to the value of his lot, as compared with the value of the appellee's lot and with the amount due upon the decree. In view of the manner in which the sale was conducted, and in view of the bid made by Vanek, codefendant with Senft, the sale here was nothing more than a payment of the whole amount of the mortgage by Vanek, but a payment made in such a way as to take away from the appellant his property, and prevent the exercise of the right of redemption.

For the reasons above stated, we are of the opinion that the court below erred in dismissing the bill for want of equity. Accordingly, the decree of the superior court of Cook county, and the judgment of the Appellate Court affirming that decree, are reversed, and the cause is remanded to the superior court with directions to proceed in accordance with the views herein expressed.

Reversed and remanded.

(208 Ill. 544)

PARMELEE et al. v. PRICE et al.

(Supreme Court of Illinois. April 20, 1904.)

CORPORATIONS—LIABILITY OF STOCKHOLDERS—STATUTES—ACTION BY CONTRACT CREDITOR—LIMITATIONS—CREDITORS' BILL.

1. While the issuance of stock by a corporation in return for property which has been fraudulently overvalued is voidable as to creditors or other stockholders prejudiced thereby, it is binding on the corporation.

2. Hurd's Rev. St. 1901, c. 32, § 8, provides that every stockholder shall be liable for the debts of the corporation to the amount unpaid on the stock held by him, and that, when an ac-

tion is brought to recover a debt from the corporation, the stockholders may be proceeded against at the same time, whether the amount unpaid on their stock has been called in or not, as in cases of garnishment. *Held*, that it is not necessary that a creditor shall have obtained a judgment and had an execution returned "No property found," but he may commence his proceedings against the corporation and the stockholder simultaneously.

3. Limitations commence to run in favor of a stockholder against an action under the statute from the time when the debt against the corporation falls due.

4. Where a stockholder's stock has been issued to him as fully paid up, because of his having turned over property to the corporation at a fraudulent overvaluation, no cause of action under Hurd's Rev. St. 1901, c. 32, § 8, accrues against such stockholder in favor of a creditor of the corporation.

5. Hurd's Rev. St. 1901, c. 32, § 25, provides that if any corporation allow any execution or decree to be returned "No property found," or shall dissolve or cease doing business leaving debts unpaid, suits in equity may be brought against all stockholders liable in any way for the debts of the corporation, by joining the corporation in such suit, and each stockholder may be required to pay his pro rata share of the debts to the extent of the unpaid portion of his stock after exhausting the assets of the corporation. *Held* that, where a corporation has ceased doing business and has debts, a contract creditor may proceed under the statute, although he has not obtained judgment and had execution returned "No property found."

6. The fact that Hurd's Rev. St. 1901, c. 32, § 25, authorizes the contract creditor of a corporation which has ceased to do business and left debts to proceed in equity against the corporation and the stockholders without having obtained a judgment and had execution returned "No property found," does not render it unconstitutional, as violating the constitutional guaranty of the right of trial by jury, since the remedy given is one which did not exist at common law.

7. Hurd's Rev. St. 1901, c. 32, § 25, provides that, if any corporation shall cease to do business leaving debts unpaid, suits in equity may be brought against all persons who were stockholders at the time or liable in any way for the debts of the corporation, by joining the corporation in the suit, and each stockholder may be required to pay his pro rata share of such debts or liabilities to the extent of the unpaid portion of his stock. Chapter 83, § 15, relative to limitations, provides that actions not otherwise provided for shall be commenced within five years after the accrual of the cause of action. *Held*, that a suit under said section 25 by the creditor of a corporation against a stockholder whose stock has been paid for by property at a fraudulent overvaluation is subject to the limitations of chapter 83, § 15.

8. Hurd's Rev. St. 1901, c. 32, § 25, provides that, if any corporation cease business leaving debts unpaid, suits in equity may be brought against all persons who were stockholders at the time or liable in any way for the debts of the corporation, by joining the corporation in such suit, and each stockholder may be required to pay his pro rata share of such debts or liabilities to the extent of the unpaid portion of his stock. Chancery Act (Hurd's Rev. St. 1901, c. 22) § 49, provides that, whenever an execution shall have been issued against the property of a defendant and returned unsatisfied, the party suing it out may file a bill in chancery to compel the discovery of property, and that the court may decree satisfaction of the judgment out of any property belonging to the defendant or held in trust for him. *Held*, that where a corporation ceased business leaving debts, so that a cause of action under said section 25 then accrued to a contract creditor of the corporation against stockholders whose stock had been issued in return for property at a fraudulent overvaluation, limitations then commenced to run against proceedings by such creditor under section 49.

9. The relation between a stockholder and the corporation is not such that unpaid subscriptions in the subscriber's hands are a trust fund, so as to prevent limitations running against a suit by a creditor of the corporation against the stockholder.

10. Hurd's Rev. St. 1901, c. 83, § 22, provides that, if one liable to an action fraudulently conceals the cause of action from the one entitled thereto, it may be commenced at any time within five years after the person entitled to bring it discovers it. Held, that an allegation that a creditor had no knowledge of the existence of the cause of action does not amount to a statement that the debtor fraudulently concealed it.

¶ 3. See Corporations, vol. 12, Cent. Dig. §§ 1090, 1091.

Appeal from Appellate Court, First District.

Suit by H. L. Parmelee and others against Vincent C. Price and others. From a judgment of the Appellate Court (105 Ill. App. 271). affirming a decree dismissing the bill for want of equity as to the defendants Price and another, complainants appeal. Affirmed.

In May, 1890, the Interior Building Company was organized as a corporation under the laws of this state, with a capital stock of $125,000. The license to open books for subscription to the capital stock was issued to Vincent C. Price, Henry F. Vehmeyer, and C. August Ebert. Price subscribed for $48,000 of the capital stock, Vehmeyer for $32,000, and the remainder of the $125,000 was subscribed for by C. August Ebert, R. C. Price, and G. K. Williams. At or about the time of the formation of this company a plant for the manufacture of sash, doors, blinds, and woodwork pertaining to buildings was purchased from James B. Goodwin, as assignee of the estate of the C. J. L. Meyer & Sons Company, insolvent, for $25,000, that amount being furnished for the purchase of the plant by said stock subscribers according to the proportion and ratio of their subscriptions to said capital stock, and the plant was turned over to the Interior Building Company to apply on the stock subscriptions at the sum of $100,000. The subscribers to the capital stock also paid into the company $25,000 in cash in the proportion and ratio of their said subscriptions, and thereupon the entire capital stock of the company was issued to said subscribers in the amount subscribed for by them, respectively, as full-paid stock. No other money or thing of value was ever paid by said subscribers on account of their subscriptions. The plant was not, at the time of its purchase from Goodwin, nor has it been since that time, worth more than $25,000.

Between and including the 16th and 23d days of May, 1895, separate suits at law were commenced by the several appellants herein against the Interior Building Company; all of said suits being brought in the circuit court of Cook county except one, and that one being brought in the superior court of that county. Judgment was recovered in each of these cases, the dates of the judgments rendered ranging from March 9, 1896, to April 12, 1897, and in each instance an execution was issued, which was returned by the sheriff of Cook county with an indorsement that he had demanded of the Interior Building Company, by its president, Vincent C. Price, money or property to satisfy the writ, and it having failed to satisfy the same, or any part thereof, and the sheriff not being able to find any property of the defendant within his county on which to levy the writ, he therefore returns the same "No property found and no part satisfied."

On May 16, 1895, judgment by confession was entered in the circuit court of Cook county against the Interior Building Company in favor of the Lincoln National Bank of Chicago for $20,065.23 and costs. An execution was issued on this judgment, and a levy made on all the property of the company. On May 17, 1895, two bills were filed against said company by certain creditors in the circuit court of Cook county, to which all its stockholders and stock subscribers were made defendants. These suits were afterwards consolidated, and on May 20, 1895, a receiver was appointed for the company, who collected all its assets, and, after paying the expenses of the receivership, applied the remainder of the assets to the bank's judgment, in pursuance of the final decree entered in the consolidated causes, by consent of all the parties thereto, on October 31, 1899. No decree was entered in these cases dissolving the company and winding up its affairs, or finding any of the parties thereto liable on account of their subscriptions to the capital stock of the company. The bill was dismissed, by the consent decree, as to all allegations of such liability, and only questions arising with respect to the administration of the affairs of the company by the receiver were adjudicated in those cases. The appellants here were not parties to the consolidated causes.

The above facts are set out in a creditors' bill filed in the superior court of Cook county on May 25, 1901, by appellants against the Interior Building Company, Vincent C. Price, and Henry F. Vehmeyer, to compel the two defendants last named to pay the judgments obtained by appellants against said company, on the ground that the Goodwin property had been fraudulently overvalued, and charging that Price was indebted to said company in the sum of $28,800 on account of unpaid subscription to the capital stock, and Vehmeyer in the sum of $19,200 on the same account. Vehmeyer filed a general demurrer to the bill. Price also filed a demurrer, showing as causes therefor, first, that the cause of action was barred by the statute of limitations; second, that complainants are barred by the adjudication in the consolidated causes above referred to; third, that complainants have been guilty of laches; and, fourth, the bill is defective in not making C. August Ebert, R. C. Price, and G. K. Williams parties to the bill. The demurrers were sustained, and the bill was dismissed for want of equity as to the defendants Price and Vehmeyer. The Appellate Court for the First District has affirmed the decree of the superior court, and appellants now appeal to this court. The only question here presented is whether the cause of action above stated is barred by section 15 of chapter 83 of Hurd's Revised Statutes of 1901.

William S. Corbin, for appellants. Musgrave, Vroman & Lee, for appellee Price.

SCOTT, J., after stating the facts, delivered the opinion of the court.

This is an ordinary creditors' bill, brought under section 49 of the chancery act (Hurd's Rev. St. 1901, c. 22), by which it is sought to enforce the liability of Vincent C. Price and Henry F. Vehmeyer for unpaid subscriptions to stock in the Interior Building Company, a corporation, which is the principal defendant, and against whom appellants had obtained judgments.

Section 25 of chapter 32 of Hurd's Revised Statutes of 1901 provides: "If any corporation or its authorized agents shall do, or refrain from doing any act which shall subject it to a forfeiture of its charter or corporate powers, or shall allow any execution or decree of any court of record, for a payment of money, after demand made by the officer, to be returned 'No property found,' or to remain unsatisfied for not less than ten days after such demand, or shall dissolve or cease doing business, leaving debts unpaid, suits in equity may be brought against all persons who were stockholders at the time, or liable in any way, for the debts of the corporation, by joining the corporation in such suit; and each stockholder may be required to pay his pro rata share of such debts or liabilities to the extent of the unpaid portion of his stock, after exhausting the assets of such corporation. And if any stockholder shall not have property enough to satisfy his portion of such debts or liabilities, then the amount shall be divided equally among all the remaining solvent stockholders. And courts of equity shall have full power, on good cause shown, to dissolve or close up the business of any corporation, to appoint a receiver therefor who shall have authority, by the name of the receiver of such corporation (giving the name), to sue in all courts and do all things necessary to closing up its affairs, as commanded by the decree of such court. Said receiver shall be, in all cases, a resident of the state of Illinois, and shall be required to enter into bonds, payable to the people of the state of Illinois, for the use of the parties interested, in such penalty and with such securities as the court may, in the decree or order, appointing the same, require. In all cases of suits for or against such receiver, or the corporation of which he may be receiver, writs may issue in favor of such receiver or corporation, or against him or it, from the county where the cause of action accrued to the sheriff of any county in this state for service."

The Interior Building Company, on May 20, 1895, being then insolvent, passed into the hands of a receiver, who then took possession of all its property and effects, and afterwards administered them in the interests of its creditors. It never resumed business. The bill herein was filed May 25, 1901. We think its averments show that the corporation ceased doing business, leaving debts unpaid, more than five years prior to the time of the filing of this bill. At that time it was indebted to all of the appellants, and their debts were due and payable. After that, and within five years prior to the filing of this bill, the appellants recovered judgments at law against the corporation. Executions were issued thereon and returned "No property found," except in the case of one of the appellants, whose judgment was recovered more than five years prior to the filing of the bill herein. The execution on that judgment, however, was issued and returned after the filing of this bill, and that appellant thereafter became a party complainant upon petition for that purpose, not having been a party to the bill as originally filed. The demurrer was sustained in the superior court, and the decree of that court was affirmed in the Appellate Court, on the theory that the stockholder is entitled to the benefit of the five-year statute of limitations; that a suit by a creditor to enforce the liability of a stockholder, under section 25, for an unpaid stock subscription, must be brought within five years after the corporation shall "cease doing business, leaving debts unpaid," in the language of that section; and that immediately upon the corporation ceasing to do business, leaving debts unpaid, any creditor of the corporation whose debt is due has a right of action which then accrues against the stockholder, and can immediately begin a suit in equity to enforce payment of his debt, joining the corporation and the stockholders, under the provisions of that section, without first reducing the claim to a judgment at law against the corporation. Appellants argue that simple contract creditors cannot file a bill under section 25, supra, and that a right of action would not accrue to the creditor against the stockholder until a judgment had been obtained against the corporation and an execution returned nulla bona.

It appears from the bill that the stock of appellees was paid for partly in cash and partly in property, and that this property was fraudulently overvalued to such an extent that in fact only 40 per cent. of the subscription was paid. While this transaction was voidable as to creditors or other stockholders prejudiced thereby, it was binding upon the corporation. Bouton v. Dement, 123 Ill. 142, 14 N. E. 62.

Section 8 of chapter 32 of Hurd's Revised Statutes of 1901 provides: "Every assignment or transfer of stocks, on which there remains any portion unpaid, shall be recorded in the office of the recorder of deeds of the county within which the principal office is located, and each stockholder shall be liable for the debts of the corporation to the extent of the amount that may be unpaid upon the stock held by him, to be collected in the manner herein provided. No assignor of stock shall be released from any such indebtedness by reason of any assignment of his stock, but shall remain liable therefor jointly with the assignee until the said stock be fully paid. Whenever any action is brought to recover any indebtedness against the corporation, it shall be competent to proceed against any one or more stockholders at the same time to the extent of the balance unpaid by such stockholders upon the stock owned by them, respectively, whether called in or not, as in cases of garnishment. Every assignee or transferee of stock shall be liable to the company for the amount unpaid thereon, to the extent and in the same manner as if he had been the original subscriber."

Under this section of the statute it will be observed that the liability of the stockholder is primary, and not collateral or secondary. He is directly liable to the creditor, whether the assets of the corporation are sufficient to pay its debts or not. The creditor can collect either from the corporation or from the stockholder, as he sees fit, as we have held that the creditor may sue the corporation and garnish the stockholder at the same time, that it is not necessary to obtain a judgment and have an execution returned "No property found" before instituting the garnishment proceeding, but that both may be set on foot at the same time. World's Fair Excursion Co. v. Gasch, 162 Ill. 402, 44 N. E. 724. This, however, is where the stockholder is still liable to the corporation. It is for the unpaid portion of his subscription. In such case an action accrues to the creditor and against the stockholder as soon as the debt against the corporation falls due, and the statute of limitations runs in favor of the stockholder from that time. In the case at bar, however, no right of action accrued to the creditor under section 8, supra, for the reason that, as between the corporation and the stockholder, the stock subscription was fully paid. A garnishing creditor in a proceeding by garnishment can assert no greater rights against the garnishee than could his debtor. Webster v. Steele, 75 Ill. 544; Richardson v. Lester, 83 Ill. 55. Consequently appellants' right of action against the stockholders in the case at bar did not accrue until they had a right to proceed in equity to set aside the fraudulent arrangement by which the stock had been issued in exchange for property received by the corporation at a fraudulent overvaluation. In that respect this case differs from one where, as in World's Fair Excursion Co. v. Gasch, supra, the corporation has accepted from the subscriber, in full payment of the subscription, a sum of money less than the amount of the subscription. In such case there is no consideration for the satisfaction of the unpaid portion of the subscription, and the corporation can maintain a suit therefor.

The question whether a simple contract creditor can maintain an action under section 25, supra, was considered by this court in Butler Paper Co. v. Robbins, 151 Ill. 588, 38 N. E. 153. It was there objected, as here, that the complainant "had no standing in a court of equity to maintain a bill to wind up the corporation, as such a suit can only be brought after the recovery of judgment and the return of execution unsatisfied"; and this court, although holding that in that case any objection to the jurisdiction of the court had been waived, still said in reference to this point (page 620, 151 Ill., and page 161, 38 N. E.): "We think this objection is not well taken. The printing company was incorporated under the general act of April 18, 1872, and had ceased doing business, leaving debts unpaid, and the complainant was one of its creditors and stockholders, and, under section 25 of said act, had the right, we think, to file this bill. In Hunt v. Le Grand Roller Skating Rink Co., 143 Ill. 118, 32 N. E. 525, this court said: 'It is provided in said section that suits in equity may be brought against a corporation and its stockholders, and all persons liable in any way for the debts of said corporation; but it is not stated in express terms by whom such suits in equity may be prosecuted. It is manifest, however, that the statute provides a remedy in the nature of a creditors' bill, and is designed to aid creditors in the collection of their debts.' "

If the construction which appellants place on section 25, supra, which was first enacted in 1872, is correct, than the creditor has no greater right under that section than he has under section 49, supra, which was enacted in 1845, and its enactment, so far as it confers rights upon creditors, was useless. It will be observed that by one clause of that section the right to maintain a suit in equity is conferred if the corporation shall permit an execution issuing from a court of record to be returned " 'No property found,' or to remain unsatisfied for not less than ten days" after demand. This is said by appellants to be necessary before any suit can be maintained by any creditor under that section at all. If so, what, then, is the meaning of the words following almost immediately in the section; "or shall dissolve or cease doing business, leaving debts unpaid"? It seems apparent that the right to maintain a suit was thereby conferred upon a creditor, without any reference to whether an execution had issued for the collection of his debt. By section 8, obtaining a judgment and the issuance and return of an execution nulla bona as a condition precedent to garnishing the stockholder was dispensed with. The purpose of the Legislature in enacting that section was to facilitate a recourse to the unpaid subscription, and it seems reasonable to conclude that the same purpose was in view in enacting section 25, and that the latter section was intended to accomplish in suits in equity what section 8 accomplished at law, namely, to enable the creditor to proceed against the stockholder without the delay incident to the recovery of a judgment and the issuance of an execution against the corporation.

It is urged, however, that, if section 25 be construed as permitting the creditor to proceed thereunder before reducing his chose in action to judgment, a construction will be placed upon that section which will render it unconstitutional, for the reason that the parties would thereby be deprived of the right to a trial by jury. The constitution of 1870 guaranties the right to a trial by jury practically as that right existed at the common law. It does not give the right to a jury trial in any class of cases in which that right did not exist at common law. Where a new class of cases is directed by the Legislature to be tried in chancery, and it appears, when tested by the general principles of equity, that they are of an equitable nature, and can be more appropriately tried in a court of equity than a court of law, the chancellor will have the right, as in other cases in chancery, to determine all questions of fact without submitting them to a jury. Ward v. Farwell, 97 Ill. 593; Chicago Mutual Life Indemnity Ass'n v. Hunt, 127 Ill. 257, 20 N. E. 55, 2 L. R. A. 549. The constitutional provision in question "introduced no new rule of law, but merely preserved the right already existing. It does not apply to suits in equity, or to any statutory proceeding to be had in courts of equity." Keith v. Henkleman, 173 Ill. 137, 50 N. E. 692. The remedy given by this section is one which did not exist at common law. The relief sought may involve the taking of an account between the corporation and the stockholder and between the various stockholders, the appointment of a receiver, and a marshaling of the assets of the corporation. It is apparent that the machinery of the common law is inadequate for these purposes, and that the right of a trial by jury does not exist.

In this case we have been supplied with exhaustive briefs. The examination of the cases to which we have been referred from jurisdictions other than our own has been of little assistance, for the reason that the laws fixing the liability of stockholders and regulating the procedure to enforce that liability vary so radically in the different states that decisions announced outside our own commonwealth afford no guide in placing a construction upon section 25 of our act on corporations. We hold that a right of action accrues to a creditor against a stockholder whose stock, as between the shareholder and the corporation, has been paid for by property taken at a fraudulent overvaluation, whenever the corporation ceases doing business leaving debts unpaid, and that the creditor may proceed immediately to enforce this right of action in equity, under section 25, supra, without first reducing his claim against the corporation to judgment at law. The liability of the stockholder resides in the fact that he has subscribed for and taken stock, for which the law requires he should pay, in money or property, the full amount of his subscription. His liability to the creditor is not a liability upon his contract of subscription, and is not dependent upon any call being made upon him by the corporation, as in case where the corporation seeks to collect the same, but is a liability resulting from the statute, consequent upon the fact that he is a shareholder, and the action of the creditor against him is a "civil action not otherwise provided for," within the meaning of section 15 of chapter 83 of Hurd's Revised Statutes of 1901, and is therefore governed by the five-year statute of limitations.

It is suggested, however, that the creditor has the right to elect whether he will proceed under section 25, supra, or section 49, supra; that, if he proceeds under the latter, he cannot bring a suit against the stockholder until he has had an execution returned "No property found"; and that the statute, therefore, would not begin to run against him until the execution was so returned, so far as his remedy under the latter section is concerned. This would place the power in the hands of the creditor to extend the statute of limitations far beyond any period of time contemplated by the Legislature. If his debt against the corporation was evidenced by writing, he has 10 years in which to bring his suit at law against the debtor, and after the recovery of a judgment he may take out an execution at any time within 7 years; and, if he may institute a proceeding against the stockholder at any time within 5 years thereafter, it makes a period of 22 years after the maturity of the debt against the corporation within which the creditor may proceed against the stockholder. It is manifest that such a holding would be against that public policy which has led to the enactment of statutes of limitation. That act "was intended as a statute of repose, to prevent fraud, and to afford security against stale demands, which might be made after the true state of the transaction may have been forgotten or be incapable of explanation by reason of the death or removal of witnesses," and this purpose should be kept in view in construing that statute. Where two methods are provided by statute by which a creditor of a corporation may enforce the liability of a stockholder for his unpaid stock subscription, the statute of limitations begins to run whenever a right accrues to the creditor to proceed directly against the stockholder by either method, and when the statutory period, counting from that time, has elapsed, the right to proceed by either method is barred. Conklin v. Furman, 48 N. Y. 527; Cottell v. Manlove (Kan.) 49 Pac. 519; First Nat. Bank v. Greene, 64 Iowa, 445, 17 N. W. 86, 20 N. W. 754.

There is nothing whatever in the relation of a stockholder to the corporation or to a creditor on which to base the argument of counsel for appellants that the unpaid subscription is, in the subscriber's hands, a trust fund for the benefit of the creditors of the corporation, and that, consequently, the statute of limitations does not apply. The relation of the stockholder who has not paid for his stock to the corporation or the creditor is the ordinary one of debtor.

The Martin-Barriss Company is the complainant that was made a party, upon petition, after the filing of the original bill, in the manner herein above mentioned, and it is averred, as to that company, that it had no knowledge of the fraud by which it was wrongfully made to appear that appellees had fully paid for their stock until the month of May, 1901, and it is therefore said that as to that company the statute of limitations did not begin to run until that time. Section 22 of chapter 83 of Hurd's Revised Statutes of 1901 provides: "If a person liable to an action fraudulently conceals the cause of such action from the knowledge of the person entitled thereto, the action may be commenced at any time within five years after the person entitled to bring the same discovers that he has such cause of action, and not afterwards." It will be observed that, to prevent the running of the statute, it must be shown that the person liable to the action "fraudulently conceals the cause of such action." No such fraudulent concealment is averred. The mere statement that the creditor had no knowledge of the existence of the cause of action does not amount to a statement that the person liable has fraudulently concealed the cause of action, and is not sufficient to prevent the application of the statute of limitations. Conner v. Goodman, 104 Ill. 365.

The judgment of the Appellate Court will be affirmed. Judgment affirmed.

(209 Ill. 222)

ORR et al. v. YATES et al.

(Supreme Court of Illinois. April 20, 1904.)

EQUITY — JURISDICTION—TRUSTS—WILLS—CONSTRUCTION—DETERMINABLE REMAINDER—UNCERTAINTY—ACCOUNTING.

1. Equity has jurisdiction of a bill to determine whether on the face of a will a trust was created; the bill asserting that the trust was illegal, and that defendants deny such illegality.

2. A will, after giving the real estate to testator's wife, provided: "I devise to my daughter my personal property * * * and in fee simple all the real estate. * * * That is to say, that if at the death of my wife * * * my daughter, M., shall then be living, the fee to said real estate shall vest in her, and in the event * * * M. shall not be living but shall leave a living child * * * then the fee shall vest in said child. * * * But in the event that at the death of * * * my wife, said M. shall not be living, then * * * said fee, if not disposed of by M., shall vest in my brothers." *Held*, that M. was not given an absolute power of disposition, and therefore took only a vested remainder, determinable on her death before that of her mother.

3. A trust will not fail merely because of uncertainty in whom the fee will vest in case the first beneficiary dies leaving issue—a contingency which may not arise.

4. A trust is not void because the times and manner of accounting for rents and profits are not fixed.

5. The declared purpose of testator in creating a trust being to create a competency for his daughter, and the trustee being authorized to turn the property over to her for such period as he sees fit, he ceasing to be liable for the rents during such period, she is entitled to all the income of the property as it accrues.

6. The provision of a will creating a trust, that the trustee may turn the property over to the beneficiary for such period as he may see fit —he ceasing to be liable for the rents during such period—is not contrary to the idea of a trust, but simply vests in him a discretion not inconsistent with his duties as trustee.

7. Under a will devising land in trust to pay the income to testator's daughter, declaring the purpose to provide a competency for her, and to create a fund that shall not be liable for her debts, and providing that no part of the rents or profits or use of the land shall be applied to the payment of any debt contracted by her, such freedom from liability is only before the rents and profits are paid to her.

8. A trust is not rendered void by the provision of the will authorizing the trustee, in the event of his sickness, old age, or for any other good cause appearing to him, to appoint his successor. His action, if arbitrarily or unwisely exercised, will be controlled by the court.

Appeal from Circuit Court, Pike County; Harry Higbee, Judge.

Suit by Mary Maria Yates and another against Jefferson Orr and others. From a decree, defendants appeal. Reversed.

William Mumford and L. T. Graham, for appellants. Vandeventer & Woods, A. G. Crawford, and Matthews & Anderson, for appellees.

WILKIN, J. Mary Maria Yates and Lydia Yates, her mother, the daughter and widow of William H. Yates, who died testate on September 16, 1902, filed their bill in chancery in the circuit court of Pike county against Jefferson Orr, as trustee and executor, and certain devisees in the last will of William H. Yates, to construe his will and grant certain relief therein prayed. The bill alleges that said will, by its first clause, gave the lot and residence where the family resided at the date of testator's death to his wife, Lydia Yates; that by the second clause she was given one-half of the personal property, and by the third, all of the real estate for life, except the Putz farm. The fourth clause, the construction of which is involved in this litigation, is as follows:

"I devise to my daughter, Mary Maria Yates, one-half of all my personal property, including choses in action, and in fee simple all the real estate that I may die seized of, except the farm known as the Putz farm, which is herein otherwise disposed of. That is to say, that if, at the death of my wife, Lydia Yates, my daughter, Mary Maria Yates, shall then be living, the fee to said real estate shall vest in her, and in the event the said Mary Maria Yates shall not be living but shall leave a living child or children, then the said fee shall vest in said child or children. But in the event that at the death of Lydia Yates, my wife, said Mary Maria Yates shall not be living, and no child or children or descendants of child of said Mary Maria Yates shall be living, then, in such case, said fee, if not disposed of by Mary Maria Yates, shall vest in my brothers and sisters, Catherine Rush, Emma Fisher, Monroe Yates, Edward Yates, Ella M. Orr and Mattie McMahon, in equal parts, and their heirs and assigns, and in the event of the death of either of said brothers or sisters such share shall descend to the heirs of such deceased brother and sister.

"I being desirous of providing a competency for my daughter, Mary Maria Yates, and to create a fund that will not be liable for her debts in any manner whatever, and that will secure to her a living, I devise to Jefferson Orr, trustee [describing the land], said above described tract of land constituting what is commonly known and called the Putz farm, to have and to hold in trust for the sole use and benefit of Mary Maria Yates for and during her natural life; and in the event of the death of the said Mary Maria Yates without child or children or descendants of child, then to have and to hold for the sole use and benefit of Lydia Yates, my wife, if she shall be living, during her natural life, and at the death of Lydia Yates, my wife, and Mary Maria Yates, my daughter (if said Mary Maria Yates dies without child or descendants of child), the fee to the said last described tract of land known as the Putz place shall be equally divided between my brothers and sisters and their heirs and assigns, as herein provided for the division of my other real estate herein devised, that is to say, in equal parts.

"I hereby authorize said trustee to turn the management of said estate over to Mary Maria Yates, and Lydia Yates, for any period of time that he may deem best. It is a part and condition of this devise to said trustee that no part of the rents or profits or use of said lands shall be applied to the payment of any judgments against the said Mary Maria Yates or on any debt contracted by her, but the sole object and purpose of said devise is to create a fund that shall be kept free from the said Mary Maria Yates' contracts and judgments against her; that if said trustee shall turn the management of said Putz farm herein devised to the said Mary Maria Yates and Lydia Yates, then said trustee shall not be accountable for the rents and profits in any manner while the same shall be under the management of said Lydia Yates and Mary Maria Yates. I hereby authorize and empower Jefferson Orr, my said trustee, in the event of sickness, failing health, old age, or any other good cause appearing to him, he may appoint some suitable person to execute said trust."

It concludes by nominating Jefferson Orr sole executor of the will and guardian of the daughter, Mary Maria Yates; giving him, as such guardian, full power and authority to manage whatever property she shall be the owner of, or to which she is entitled.

The bill further alleges that said pretended last will is ambiguous and uncertain, and that the legal effect of said fourth clause is to vest the life estate in the widow, Lydia Yates, of the lands mentioned in said clause, except the Putz farm, and the remainder in fee absolute in the daughter, and that the limitation over to the brothers and sisters of testator is null and void, as tending to limit the estate in fee given to said daughter; that the remaining portion of the fourth clause, devising the Putz farm in trust, is ambiguous and uncertain, and does not provide what shall become of said trust fund in the event of the death of said appellees without leaving descendants; that the same is in violation of the rule against perpetuities; that no provision is made for the accounting by said trustee or cestui que trust; and that for these reasons that portion of said pretended will should be set aside and declared null and void. The prayer is that the will may be construed by the court, and that portion of it which creates a trust set aside upon the ground of uncertainty and remoteness; that Mary Maria Yates be declared to be the owner in fee simple of all of the lands mentioned in said pretended will; and that the management and control of said Putz farm may be turned over to her upon her reaching her majority.

To the bill the defendants filed a general and special demurrer, which was overruled, and they elected to stand by the same. The cause was submitted for hearing upon the issue so formed, and a final decree rendered adjudging that all of the real estate, except the home place and Putz farm, was vested by the will in fee simple absolute in the said Mary Maria Yates, subject to the life estate of said Lydia Yates; that the limitation over to the brothers and sisters of the testator is void, because it attempts to limit the fee already given to the daughter after giving her a general power of disposition in fee; and that the trust attempted to be created by the fourth clause in Jefferson Orr of the Putz farm is void for uncertainty, incompleteness, and ambiguity, and declaring the same null and void. The decree then adjudges that said Mary Maria Yates is seised of a life estate, by said will, in the Putz farm, and that upon her death the said Lydia Yates, if Mary Maria Yates shall die without child or children or descendants thereof, will be seised of a life estate therein, and in the event that said Mary Maria dies leaving child or children, or descendants thereof, the fee simple in the premises, after the death of both Mary Maria and Lydia Yates, will vest in said child or children or descendants thereof, but in the event of the death of said Mary Maria without child or children, or descendants thereof, then, upon her death and the death of said Lydia, the fee simple in said farm will vest in said brothers and sisters. From that decree the defendants prosecute this appeal.

The first assigned error relied upon is that the circuit court had no jurisdiction to entertain the bill, for the reason that it attempts to settle purely legal titles, and not to enforce the alleged trust, or to construe and determine the complainants' rights thereunder, but denies the existence of any trust; setting up the legal title of the complainants, and asking the court to adjudge the same in them. It is admitted by all parties that courts of equity are wanting in jurisdiction in such cases where purely legal titles are involved. Harrison v. Owsley, 172 Ill. 629, 50 N. E. 227, and cases cited. It is, however, equally well settled that, upon bills by executors or trustees, courts of chancery have power to construe wills creating trusts, in order to enable executors or trustees to perform the duties imposed upon them in the administration of the trust, and that, having acquired jurisdiction for that purpose, they will retain it for the purpose of construing other provisions of the same will. Nor do we understand this latter rule to be confined to cases in which the bill is filed by a party charged with the execution of the trust, but may be invoked by a cestui que trust or other party interested. Longwith v. Riggs, 123 Ill. 258, 14 N. E. 840, and authorities there cited; Minkler v. Simons, 172 Ill. 323, 50 N. E. 176. The bill in this case sets out the will of the testator, and alleges that it is ambiguous and uncertain, and that the trust attempted to be created contravenes well-established principles of law, and is therefore void, but it also avers that the defendants deny such illegality, and insist that it is legal and valid. This presented an issue to be determined by the court—whether, upon the face of the will, a trust was created—and we are unable to see why a trust was not directly involved in that issue. It is true, the chancellor held that there was no valid trust contained in the will, but his jurisdiction could not be made to depend upon that conclusion. If he had held there was a trust, and construed the same, there would seem to be no reasonable ground for the contention that his decree was invalid for want of jurisdiction. It is also insisted on this branch of the case that the bill seeks the judgment of the court on a mere future contingency which may never happen, but that is one of the questions to be determined upon a construction of the will. We think the ruling of the chancellor upon this question was correct.

On the merits of the case, two questions are presented for decision: First, did the court below err in construing the first paragraph of the fourth clause, above set out, as vesting the title in fee absolute in the real estate therein mentioned in Mary Maria Yates, subject only to a life estate in her mother? and second, in decreeing the trust provided for in the second paragraph of that clause of the will to be absolutely null and void?

As already shown, the court below held, and the argument of counsel for appellees is, that by the first paragraph Mary Maria Yates is given the fee-simple title, with an absolute power of disposition in all the real estate of which the testator died seised, except the Putz farm, and that therefore, the subsequent provisions of that paragraph are void; relying upon the rule that, where there is a devise of an unlimited power of disposition of an estate in such manner as the devisee may think fit, a limitation over is inoperative and void by reason of its repugnance to the principal devise. Hamlin v. United States Express Co., 107 Ill. 443, is a case recognizing and approving the rule, and citing prior decisions of this court to the same effect. Many later decisions follow the rule, and it is not questioned here. On the other hand, it is earnestly insisted by counsel for appellants that, properly construed, that paragraph of the will gives to the daughter, Mary Maria Yates, after the life estate given to Lydia Yates by the third clause, the remainder in fee determinable, liable to be defeated by her death in the lifetime of her mother by the executory devise over to any child or children of Mary Maria Yates who may survive her, and be living at the time of the death of her mother, and, if none should be living, then to the testator's brothers and sisters.

Counsel for appellants are not entirely agreed as to whether the remainder in fee to said Mary Maria Yates is a vested or contingent remainder, of which we will speak later. They do agree, however, that the fee, in either event, is a base or determinable one. There is perhaps no rule of construction, as applied to wills, more universal than that "the intention of the testator, to be gathered from the entire will, must govern. * * * So far is this principle carried, that the court say in 8 Wils. 141: 'Cases on wills may guide us to general rules of construction, but unless a case cited be in every respect directly in point, and agree in every circumstance, it will have little or no weight with the courts, who always look upon the intention of the testator as the polar star to direct them in the construction of wills.'" Boyd v. Strahan, 36 Ill. 355. It may be regarded as a judicial maxim that effect should be given to the several parts of a will, so as to render no component part inoperative. The intention of the testator must govern, and that must be ascertained, if possible, from the language of the instrument. The cases in this and other courts laying down and following this rule are almost without number, and need not be cited. It is never departed from, unless to give effect to the manifest intention of the testator would result in the violation of some established rule of law or public policy. It cannot be denied that the construction adopted by the court below and insisted upon by counsel for appellees in the present case results in a palpable violation of that rule. It is based solely upon the first sentence in that paragraph, and ignores entirely the expression, "That is to say, that if, at the death of my wife, Lydia Yates, my daughter, Mary Maria Yates, shall then be living, the fee to said real estate shall vest in her," etc. If we take into consideration the entire language of the paragraph, we are forced to the conclusion that the testator intended the absolute fee-simple title should vest in his daughter if she survived her mother, and, if the mother should survive her, the fee should vest in any child or children of the daughter who should be living at the death of the life tenant, Lydia Yates, but if no such child or children, or descendants of such, should then be living, and the said Mary Maria Yates should not have disposed of the property, the fee should vest in his brothers and sisters. In other words, the construction adopted by the learned chancellor, and contended for by counsel for complainants below, renders nugatory all the qualifying language of the will, and defeats the clearly expressed purpose of the testator, whereas the interpretation placed upon the entire paragraph by counsel for appellants will give effect to all the language there used, and carry out the intention of the testator. Therefore, if the latter construction can be adopted without violating established rules of law, the decision of the court below must be held erroneous and reversed. It is true, the language, "and in fee simple all the real estate that I may seized of," etc., standing alone, would vest the absolute fee-simple title in the daughter, and, if she had been given such a title, the unqualified power of disposition would necessarily follow; but, following our previous decisions, the subsequent words must be held to qualify or explain the expression "fee-simple title," so as to give the daughter but a base or conditional fee, determinable upon her death before that of her mother. The words "that is to say" clearly mean the same as if the testator had said, "by this I mean that if," etc., or "provided if, at the death of my wife," etc.

Perhaps the case most directly in point sustaining this interpretation is Friedman v. Steiner, 107 Ill. 125. The thirteenth item of the will then under consideration by the court was as follows: "I give and bequeath all the rest and residue of my said estate, real, personal and mixed, of which I shall die seized, possessed or entitled to, unto my beloved wife, Rebecca Steiner, and unto her heirs and assigns forever, to the total exclusion of any and all person or persons whatsoever: provided, however, upon the express condition hereby made by me, in case the said Rebecca Steiner, after my decease, shall die intestate and without leaving her surviving lawful issue, * * * that then and in such event all the rest and residue of my said estate so bequeathed and devised unto her * * * shall at once be converted into money by my executor, and the said money shall be paid over * * * as follows, namely:" (Then follows a disposition of the proceeds.) In the construction placed upon that item, Mr. Justice Dickey, speaking for the court, said (page 130): "We recognize the rule of law that 'conditions that are repugnant to the estate to which they are annexed are absolutely void,' yet, in the construction of a will, we must consider all the words of the will, including all provisos and conditions, for the purpose of ascertaining what estate the testator intended to confer by the granting words of the will; and, weighing the words of the proviso, we think they do qualify the granting words, and do show that the testator did not intend to confer upon his wife a fee simple absolute in this property. Kent says: 'Fee simple is a pure inheritance, clear of any qualification or condition, and it gives the right of succession to all the heirs generally. * * * It is an estate of perpetuity, and confers an unlimited power of alienation.' Such an estate, we think, was here granted to Mrs. Steiner, except in so far as the same is qualified by the words of the proviso, and we think the words of the proviso do qualify the estate granted, and reduce it below that of a fee-simple estate; but this reduction, below a fee simple absolute, extends no farther than the express words of the proviso declare or necessarily imply." And it was there further said: "The interest of Mrs. Steiner in the lands of the estate of her deceased husband is not an estate in fee simple, but is 'an estate in fee determinable.'" The same doctrine has been repeatedly reannounced in similar cases.

In Koeffler v. Koeffler, 185 Ill. 261, 56 N. E. 1094, the will construed gave an estate in fee simple to the natural son of the testator, with the condition that, if he should die before his twenty-fifth year, the testator's brother or his heirs should be the heirs of the son, etc. After quoting at length from the opinion in the Friedman Case, it was held that the interpretation in that case had been recognized in the several cases there cited, and it was said (page 269, 185 Ill., page 1096, 56 N. E.): "This rule of interpretation has, in effect, become a rule of property in this state, and in the will under consideration it must be held that the title of the son, Gustav Adolph Koeffler, is a fee determinable, which he can convey and make absolute in the purchaser; but, upon his death without issue him surviving, the title to all the estate not disposed of would pass to the heirs of his deceased uncle, Carl August Koeffler." See, also, Frail v. Carstairs, 187 Ill. 310, 58 N. E. 401, and Becker v. Becker, 206 Ill. 53, 69 N. E. 49, citing cases. Though not material in the decision of this case, the rule undoubtedly is, "If the owner of a determinable fee conveys in fee, the determinable quality of the fee follows the transfer." 4 Kent's Com. p. 10; Smith v. Kimbell, 153 Ill. 368, 38 N. E. 1029, cited in Koeffler v. Koeffler, supra; Becker v. Becker, supra. And in so far as a different doctrine is announced in the Friedman Case, it has not been approved. Otherwise it is the law of this state.

Cases have frequently arisen in which, under the same rules of construction, language of itself sufficient to convey an absolute fee-simple title has been held to vest but a life estate. In Healy v. Eastlake, 152 Ill. 424, 39 N. E. 260, we said (page 429, 152 Ill., page 261, 39 N. E.): "By the second clause of the will there was devised to the daughter, Alice, all the property, real and personal, 'subject, however, to the conditions hereinafter following.' That the language is sufficiently broad to vest the personal property absolutely and the real estate in fee is not questioned, and, unless a limitation is placed thereon by the subsequent clauses of the will, as we have seen may be done, the absolute title passed to the devisee." But we held the effect of the conditions named was to modify the general words of the first paragraph of the second clause of the will, to terminate the estate devised to the daughter, Alice, with her life.

In Siegwald v. Siegwald, 37 Ill. 430, the will contained this clause: "I give and bequeath unto my beloved wife, Antonia, all my real and personal estate, wheresoever situated, in fee simple and absolute, forever —that is to say, that my said wife shall have all of the benefits thereof until the expiration of her life, at which time my son, Anton, shall be the only heir of real and personal estate what may be left;" and it was held that the wife took only an estate for life in the real estate, and remainder in fee to the son. Chief Justice Walker, delivering the opinion of the court, said (page 436): "Had the devise contained no language designed to operate as a limitation, the will would have been free from all difficulty. The first clause, unaffected by the words of limitation, unquestionably vested a fee simple absolute; and plaintiff in error insists that they are repugnant to the devise, and are therefore inoperative, and leave an estate in fee in the devisee, and not a life estate. Wills, like all other instruments, must be so construed as to effectuate the intention of the testator, and that intention must be ascertained from the language employed in the instrument itself; and, in arriving at the intention, all of the language employed must be considered. It seems to be evident that the testator did not intend to devise to his widow a fee simple absolute; otherwise he would not have added the limiting clause. Had that been the intention, he had fully accomplished the purpose without employing the latter clause; but, when he did so, it must have been to limit or qualify the estate already devised." And so in the present case. If the testator, William H. Yates, had intended to give his daughter the fee simple absolute, he would have stopped with the first sentence of the paragraph under consideration; but, having added the limitation, we must conclude that he intended to give her a less estate.

In Bergan v. Cahill, 55 Ill. 160, the will provided as follows: "First, I give, devise and bequeath to my beloved wife, Johanna Morris, all my real estate and personal property; also one cow; all, without reserve, I give unto my beloved wife. N. B.—In case my wife is not supported by her children, so as it may be necessary for her bodily comfort, I give her power to sell and dispose of any or either of the two lots which I now possess and own in Underhill's addition to the city of Peoria; also I hereby declare it my wish that after my wife's decease, whatever property, real or personal, of which she may be possessed or which she may own at the time of her decease, shall be devised and bequeathed to my faithful son, Martin, providing that he pays over unto my daughter, Julia, $100, or an equivalent." And it was held that the intention of the testator was to give the wife but a life estate, and upon her death the fee to the son, subject to a legacy to the daughter. Justice Thornton, delivering the opinion of the court, there said: "The first clause in the will clearly indicates the intention of the testator to devise all his property to his wife. In the last clause the power to sell upon a contingency, and the declaration of a wish that his faithful son, Martin, should have whatever property the wife might die possessed of, cast some doubt upon the intention. There is some apparent contradiction. A will, however, should not be rendered void by mere repugnancy. We must gather the intention from the entire instrument. Sometimes a clause posterior in position will denote a subsequent intention. The gift of an estate of inheritance in lands may be restricted by subsequent words."

And so decisions might be cited almost without limit. Generally the words "fee simple" mean an absolute estate of inheritance, but not necessarily so. A title in fee simple determinable is, in a qualified sense, a fee-simple title; and where, as here, the language is followed by a clearly expressed qualification, it must be held that the testator used the first words in that sense.

Counsel for appellees seem to understand that Friedman v. Steiner, supra, and kindred cases, are not in harmony with the later decisions of this court in Wolfer v. Hemmer, 144 Ill. 554, 33 N. E. 751; Jones v. Port Huron Thresher Co., 171 Ill. 502, 49 N. E. 700; Burton v. Gagnon, 180 Ill. 345, 54 N. E. 279; and Lambe v. Drayton, 182 Ill. 110, 55 N. E. 189. The Jones Case is clearly distinguishable, and in the Burton Case the construction of the will under consideration was not concurred in by a majority of the court. When the language used in the wills construed in the other two cases is considered, they are not thought to be in conflict with the earlier cases. Manifestly they do not, nor were they intended to, overrule Friedman v. Steiner, and the long line of cases following it. We think the doctrine of those cases clearly applicable to this case, and, as stated in Koeffler v. Koeffler, supra, having become a rule of property in this state, it should not now be departed from. Moreover, we entertain no doubt that the doctrine is founded in reason and well supported by authority. It cannot be seriously contended, nor do we understand counsel to insist, that the language in the last sentence of the first paragraph, "if not disposed of by Mary Maria Yates," etc., can be construed to give her the unqualified power of disposition. In fact, those words confer no power whatever.

Our conclusion is that, by the terms of her father's will, Mary Maria Yates took the fee-simple title in remainder after the termination of her mother's life estate, determinable upon her death before that of her mother. The remainder in fee would seem, upon all the authorities, to be a vested remainder, and not merely contingent. Chapin v. Nott, 203 Ill. 341, 67 N. E. 833, and cases cited on page 358, 203 Ill., 67 N. E. 833.

Did the court err in holding the second paragraph of the fourth clause void? It seems to be conceded that the decree was based upon the allegations of the bill that the trust attempted to be provided for in that paragraph is "void for uncertainty, incompleteness, and ambiguity." The point is made, however, by counsel for appellees, that, at most, the trust there provided for is a mere passive or dry trust; the legal title to the Putz farm vesting absolutely in Mary Maria Yates by operation of the statute of uses. If the premise of this proposition is correct, the conclusion cannot be denied. We are at loss, however, to perceive how a valid trust could be held to exist, under the provisions of the will, without also holding that active duties are imposed upon the trustee; and the point need not, therefore, be considered separately. It may be conceded that the declaration of a trust must be reasonably certain in its material terms, and that this requisite of certainty includes, first, the subject-matter or property embraced within the trust; second, the beneficiaries or persons in whose behalf the trust is created; third, the nature and quantity of interests which they are to have; and, fourth, the manner in which the trust is to be performed. If the language is so vague, general, or equivocal that any one of these necessary elements of the trust is left in real uncertainty, the trust must fail, or, if any one of the three things necessary to constitute a trust is wanting (that is, first, sufficient words to raise it; second, a definite subject; and, third, a certain or ascertained object), the trust will fail. It is not practicable to adopt any specific definition of a trust which can be applied to all cases. Many attempted definitions are to be found in the text-books and decided cases, but it is unimportant here to accept one rather than another. All must agree that it is not necessary to the validity of a trust that every element necessary to constitute it must be so clearly expressed in detail in the instrument creating it that nothing can be left to inference or implication. No particular form or words are necessary, but, wherever an intention to create a trust can be fairly collected from the language of the instrument and the terms employed, such intention will be supported by the courts. Fisher v. Fields, 10 Johns. 495; 2 Story's Eq. Jur. § 980; Hagan v. Varney, 147 Ill. 281, 35 N. E. 219.

It is conceded by counsel for the appellees that the requisites of certainty as to the subject-matter of the trust and the beneficiaries are in this will sufficiently expressed, but their contention is that there is a failure to show the nature and quality of interest which the beneficiaries under the will are to receive, and that the manner in which the trust is to be executed by the trustee does not definitely appear from the language employed. The subject-matter or property embraced in the trust is the Putz farm. The beneficiary is Mary Maria Yates, or, in case of her death without child or children or descendants of child, Lydia Yates.

As will be seen from the foregoing statement, the ambiguity, uncertainty, and indefiniteness averred in the bill are, first, that the will does not provide what shall become of the said trust fund in the event of the death of Mary Maria Yates without leaving descendants; second, that it is void, as violating the rule against perpetuities—no point, however, being attempted to be made on this allegation; third, that no provision is made for the accounting by the trustee to his cestui que trust; and, fourth, that there is no provision as to when the trustee shall turn over the trust fund to the cestui que trust or to any one else.

The declared purpose of the testator in creating the trust is to provide a competency for his daughter—that is, not merely a bare living, but a sufficiency for her support, maintenance, and education according to her degree and position in life—and that such fund shall not be liable for her debts in any manner whatever. The duration of the trust as first provided is expressly made during the natural life of the daughter, but, if she dies without descendants, then during the life of her mother, Lydia Yates. Upon the death of the daughter leaving no descendants, and the death of her mother, the trust will terminate, and the fee, by the express language of the will, vest in the brothers and sisters. The only uncertainty is as to what shall be done with the trust property in case Mary Maria Yates dies leaving issue. Will it go to such issue in fee, or will it fall back into the estate as intestate property, and descend to the heirs of William H. Yates? Our opinion is that it will vest in the issue of Mary Maria Yates. That seems to be the fair inference from the language used. If she dies without issue, then the trust continues during the life of Lydia Yates, and the fee vests in the brothers and sisters. If Mary Maria Yates dies, leaving issue, that is clearly the end of the trust, and it seems to be the intention of the testator that the fee shall vest in her issue. This construction is in harmony with the rule of law that, where a party disposes of his estate, the presumption is that he intended to dispose of all of it, and courts will so construe the will as to leave no part of the estate as intestate property. But suppose this view cannot be sustained; must the entire trust fail? We think not. The duration of the trust is now definite, and may never become uncertain. Certainly a court will not defeat the clearly expressed intention of a testator because a contingency may arise in the future which will render the trust uncertain. But it may be possible that the question as to where the fee goes in case Mary Maria Yates dies leaving issue cannot finally be determined upon this record. In case William H. Yates left a son or other heirs who were not made parties to this bill, they would be entitled to be heard on the question as to whether the Putz farm shall vest in the issue of Mary Maria Yates, or descend to all of the heirs of William H. Yates.

The fact that the times and manner of accounting for the rents and profits of the trust estate are not fixed cannot render the trust void. The law will compel the trustee to render accounts in proper manner and at proper times. The absence of specific directions as to when and in what manner the trustee shall render his accounts simply leaves that matter to be determined by construction. If the trustee and cestui que trust disagree on that subject, the courts may be resorted to for a settlement of the differences. In such a case the parties, and, if necessary, the court, would be compelled to take into consideration the nature of the property, how and when the rents and profits will probably accrue, and all other facts and circumstances affecting the question. 2 Perry on Trusts, §§ 821-843; Lehman v. Rothbarth, 159 Ill. 270, 42 N. E. 777; Carpenter v. Davis, 72 Ill. 14; Hale v. Hale, 125 Ill. 399, 17 N. E. 470.

It is clearly the duty of the trustee to turn over all the rents and profits of the farm as they accrue. The trustee has nothing whatever to do with the question as to what is reasonably necessary for the support and maintenance of the cestui que trust. The trust is not merely to provide her a bare support. Her father provides this trust in order to secure her a competency; that is, a sufficiency for her support, etc. She is therefore entitled to all of the income arising from the farm set apart by her father for her. That he intended her to have it all is further manifested by the provision authorizing the trustee to turn the property over to her and her mother for such period as he may see fit, he ceasing to be liable for the rents during such period. We are unable to concur in the view that this provision is contrary to the idea of a trust. It simply vests in the trustee a discretion to rent the property to others, or let the daughter and her mother use and enjoy it for such period as he may choose. Such a discretion is not inconsistent with his duties as trustee. Rife v. Geyer, 59 Pa. 393, 98 Am. Dec. 315. Whom the rents and profits shall go to at the death of Mary Maria Yates is sufficiently disposed of by what has already been said. These rents and profits do not accumulate in the hands of the trustee, but are paid over to the cestui que trust, or her guardian during her minority, as they are received. How they shall be used during her minority would be for the guardian to determine, and after she becomes of age she can do as she pleases with her own. If rents and profits have accrued and have not been collected and paid over at the time of her death, they would go to her administrator or executor, like any other property of which she may die seised. The fund created, which is not to be liable for her debts, does not refer to the rents and profits after they are paid to her, but does refer to the farm from which they arise; to the rents and profits before they are paid into the hands of the trustee, and also while they are in his hands.

The point that the fact that the will authorizes the trustee, in the event of his sickness, old age, or for any other good cause appearing to him, to appoint his successor, renders the trust void, is clearly without force. His action in that regard, if arbitrarily or unwisely exercised, would be controlled by the courts upon application of the cestui que trust, even without this provision. There can be no doubt that the court would have the power to appoint some suitable person to execute the trust if for any reason Jefferson Orr became incapable of doing so.

Conceding that the trust provisions of this will are not altogether explicit and absolutely certain, yet these uncertainties are such as a court of equity will aid by construction, and not such as will defeat the intention of the testator to provide in his own way for his daughter.

We are of the opinion that it was error in the court below to hold the trust absolutely null and void. It follows that so much of the decree as finds a life estate in Mary Maria Yates is also erroneous. The decree of the circuit court will therefore be reversed, and the cause remanded for further proceedings in accordance with the views herein expressed. Reversed and remanded.

(209 Ill. 88)

HEPPE et al. v. SZCZEPANSKI et al.

(Supreme Court of Illinois. April 20, 1904.)

EXECUTOR'S FINAL REPORT—SERVICE ON MINOR HEIRS—ORDER SETTING ASIDE REPORT—SALE OF REALTY—FRAUDULENT CHARACTER—JURISDICTION OF MINORS—TRUST DEED—SUBSEQUENT PURCHASER—NOTICE—IMPROVEMENTS BY CO-TENANT—CONTRIBUTION.

1. Notwithstanding 1 Starr & C. Ann. St. 1896, pp. 336, 337, c. 3, par. 112, provides that no final settlement shall be made and approved unless decedent's heirs have been notified thereof in such manner as the court may direct, it is immaterial whether minor heirs were properly served with notice of an executor's final report and his discharge, where the order was favorable to the minors, in that a release of a portion of the widow's award was thereby approved.

2. A probate court has jurisdiction to set aside at a subsequent term an order discharging an executor.

3. 1 Starr & C. Ann. St. 1896, p. 329, c. 3, par. 103, provides that, where a petition is filed by a personal representative for the sale of realty, the heirs must be served by reading the summons to them, or leaving a copy thereof at their usual place of abode with some member of the family 10 years old or more, and informing such person of the contents thereof. After releasing a portion of her award, and the discharge of the executor, a widow, who occupied realty as co-tenant with her minor children under decedent's will, began negotiations for a loan on the property with an attorney, who had the widow's brother execute a deed of trust to him. The next day this deed was recorded, and the widow, by the attorney, petitioned for an order vacating the executor's discharge and withdrawing the widow's release of her award as executed by mistake, and for a sale of the realty to pay the award. This order being secured, the executor petitioned for permission to sell the property; the summons being served on the minor heirs by leaving a copy thereof with the widow. The property was sold as unincumbered to the widow's brother, who, on the same day that he received a deed, executed a conveyance to the widow, who afterwards conveyed to the executor. No consideration was paid for any of these deeds, and the brother was not present at the executor's sale, and knew nothing about it. It did not appear that any credit was made on the widow's award. *Held*, that the proceedings were collusive and fraudulent, being really in the interest of the widow as a party adverse to the minor heirs, so that the service had on

them by leaving process with the widow was insufficient to give jurisdiction of their persons.

4. After a release of the balance of her award and a discharge of the executor, a widow began negotiations for a loan with an attorney, who prepared a trust deed to himself, which was executed by the widow's brother, who at the time had no title to the property. The widow then petitioned for an order setting aside the executor's discharge, and her release, and for sale of the realty. The order was granted, and on the executor's sale the widow's brother became the purchaser, and immediately conveyed to the widow. *Held*, that purchasers of the trust deed were charged with notice that the proceedings were fraudulent as to minor heirs, whose interest in the property was not bound by the trust deed.

5. The purchaser of an incumbrance on real estate is charged with notice of the rights of parties in possession.

6. A tenant, against whom improvements made by a co-tenant without his knowledge are to be charged, will be charged, not with the price thereof, but only with his proportion of the amount which, at the time of partition, they add to the value of the premises.

Appeal from Circuit Court, Cook County; L. Honoré, Judge.

Suit by Rosalia Szczepanski and others against Mary Heppe, as executrix of the last will of George Heppe, deceased, and others. Decree for plaintiffs, and Mary Heppe and certain other defendants appeal. Affirmed.

This is a bill, filed in the circuit court of Cook county on June 19, 1899, by the appellees against the appellants, and other parties herein named, for partition, and for the removal of certain deeds and trust deeds as clouds upon the title of the appellees. Answers were filed to the bill, and a reference was taken to a master in chancery, who took testimony, and reported the same and his conclusions. A final decree was rendered substantially in accordance with the prayer of the bill and for partition, and appointing commissioners to make the same. The present appeal is prosecuted from such decree.

The facts are substantially as follows: On January 10, 1895, Frank Szczepanski died testate, owning lot 33 in block 8 in Sherman's addition to Holstein, in Cook county, being the property here sought to be partitioned, and left, him surviving, his widow, Katharina Szczepanski, and four children, to wit, Martha Szczepanski, Stanislava Szczepanski, Rosalia Szczepanski, and Marianna Szczepanski. Said testator by the terms of his will gave to his wife and four children said property in equal shares. His will was probated in the probate court of Cook county on February 8, 1895. Joseph Kucharski was executor of the will; letters testamentary having been issued to him on February 8, 1895. On March 5, 1895, an inventory was filed and approved, which showed the property in question, and on the same day an appraisement of personal property, amounting to $408.52, and a widow's award of $1,330, were approved in said probate court. Proof of heirship was made in the estate, and on March 5, 1897, the executor filed his final report, dated March 2, 1897, which was approved on March 30, 1897, and therein recites that the personal property, which was appraised at $408.52 on March 11, 1895, was turned over to the widow to be applied on her award. Katharina Szczepanski, widow of Frank Szczepanski, married one Witt Obecny after the death of her husband, Frank Szczepanski. The probate court on March 30, 1897, ordered that such final report should stand as a final account, and that the executor should be discharged. After the death of Frank Szczepanski, the widow and children lived on the premises as a homestead, and at the time of the final decree herein were occupying the same as a homestead. After the death of their father, Martha Szczepanski and Stanislava Szczepanski died, leaving their mother and the appellees herein their heirs at law. On June 10, 1897, Katharina Obecny applied to Theodore H. Schintz for a loan upon the premises in question for the purpose of improving the same. Schintz asked her if she could get a man in whom they could place confidence, and said that, if she could, he would fix matters and make the loan, whereupon she requested her brother, Kazmierz Kluczynski, to help her out, and took him down to Schintz's office. On that day (June 10, 1897) Schintz having previously prepared a note for $4,000 and a trust deed to himself as trustee to secure the same, Kluczynski signed said note and trust deed; the note being due five years after date, with interest at 6 per cent. per annum, secured by 10 semiannual interest notes, and the trust deed conveying the premises above described. This note for $4,000 and the trust deed to Schintz as trustee were without any consideration when executed; Kluczynski having received no money for the execution thereof. The trust deed was recorded on the next day, June 11, 1897.

On June 11, 1897, Katharina Obecny filed in said probate court her petition, by Schintz and his partner as attorneys, asking that the order of March 30, 1897, declaring the estate settled, be vacated, and that she have leave to withdraw her receipt for the balance of her widow's award, and that an order might be entered directing the executor to sell the real estate to pay such widow's award. Thereupon, on June 21, 1897, the probate court entered an order, reciting therein that Katharina Obecny, formerly Katharina Szczepanski, widow of the deceased, Frank Szczepanski, came, by Schintz and another, her solicitors, and presented her petition, asking for leave to withdraw her receipt for the balance of her widow's award due her as widow of said deceased, the said receipt having been signed by her by mistake, and also came Joseph Kucharski, the executor, by his solicitors, and also came Rosalia Szczepanski and Marianna Szczepanski, minor heirs of said deceased, by their guardian ad litem, and that it appeared to the court, from evidence introduced, that said

¶ 5. See Mortgages, vol. 35, Cent. Dig. § 684.

widow signed said receipt by mistake, and that she was not in fact paid to exceed the sum of $400; and the court, being fully advised in the premises, ordered that the said widow have leave to withdraw the receipt for the balance due her on said widow's award, the same having been signed by her by mistake, and that Joseph Kucharski, executor of the last will, etc., proceed to sell the real estate of said deceased to pay such balance, after presenting to the court a just and true account of the personal estate and debts of said deceased, as required by statute.

Subsequently, on September 7, 1897, the executor filed in the probate court a petition, setting up all the proceedings theretofore taken as hereinbefore detailed; that said Rosalia and Marianna are both unmarried, and are minors, having no guardian residing in Illinois; that the only persons interested in the estate, as legatees or devisees, are the widow and children above named; that the testator died, owning the property above mentioned, which at the time of his death was in the possession and occupation of his widow and her family; and that no persons other than those above named held liens against the estate, or any part thereof—and praying that Katharina Obecny and Witt Obecny and Rosalia and Marianna Szczepanski may be made defendants and summons issued as to them, and a guardian ad litem be appointed for them, and upon a final hearing that a decree may be entered for the sale of the property described in the petition. The summons issued upon the petition for the sale of the real estate to pay the balance of $921.48, due the widow upon her award, was not served personally upon the appellees, who are minors, but was served upon them by leaving a copy with their mother, Katharina Obecny, a member of the family of the age of 10 years and upwards, and informing her of the contents thereof, on the 9th day of September, 1897. Thereafter, on October 8, 1897, a decree was entered by the probate court ordering a sale of the property. The decree recites that the petition for sale was taken as confessed by the widow and her husband, and that the appellees were served with process. The decree appointed a guardian ad litem for the minors, and sets forth the entry of the order of March 30, 1897, and the filing of the petition on June 11, 1897, for the vacation of said order, and also finds that the personal estate was insufficient to pay the claims allowed, and that the deficiency amounts to $921.48, besides expenses of administration; and the decree thereupon ordered that said real estate should be sold for cash at the judicial salesroom of the Chicago Real Estate Board, No. 57 Dearborn street, in Chicago, "subject to the dower and homestead rights of the widow of said deceased," and that said petitioner make report of his proceedings. The notice of the sale, dated October 14, 1897, as published and posted, announced that all the right, title, and interest of Frank Szczepanski, deceased, in the property in question, would be sold for cash on November 12, 1897, and stated that the lot was improved by a one-story cottage, and subject to the dower and homestead rights of the widow of said deceased, and also that said premises were unincumbered, and that no deed would be delivered until the sale had been reported to and approved by the probate court. On November 12, 1897, the executor, Joseph Kucharski, reported that he had sold the premises for $1,100 to Kazmierz Kluczynski, and that the same were struck off to him, he being the highest and best bidder therefor, which report of sale and the sale were confirmed in open court on November 16, 1897.

Afterwards, on November 18, 1897, the executor executed a deed of the premises to said Kluczynski, which deed was recorded on November 18, 1897; and on the same day (November 18, 1897) Kluczynski and wife conveyed the premises, for an expressed consideration of $6,000, to Katharina Obecny, who was the sister of said Kluczynski. On November 20, 1897, Witt and Katharina Obecny executed a trust deed to Frederick H. Winston, trustee, to secure the sum of $2,000, with interest, of which note and trust deed the F. J. Dewes Brewery Company is the owner. The note for $4,000, dated June 10, 1897, and payable five years after date, and secured by the trust deed on these premises to Schintz, is owned by the appellant, Mary Heppe, executrix of the last will of George Heppe, deceased, and Elizabeth Heppe, Emma Heppe, William Heppe, and Mary Heppe. The trust deed given to Schintz was for the purpose of securing a loan for the building of improvements on said premises, the estimated cost of which was fixed by Schintz at $5,000; but, the trust deed being for only $4,000, Katharina Obecny, or her husband, or both of them, deposited $1,000 with Schintz. Schintz paid out $2,936.62 toward the construction of the new building on the premises, of which about $1,000 was the cash deposited by Katharina Obecny and her husband. The amount due on the note and trust deed to Schintz is the sum of $1,936.62. At the time Schintz made the loan the premises were improved by a small brick cottage, which had a store and two rooms, and since making the loan the premises have been improved by a three-story brick building, in which Katharina Obecny occupies one flat and three rooms and the store, and keeps and boards the children, and has a homestead therein, and collects the rents from the balance of the premises. On January 7, 1899, Katharina Obecny and Witt Obecny conveyed the premises to Joseph Kucharski, subject to an indebtedness of $5,100. No homestead right was ever set off in said proceeding.

The final decree of the court, entered on

December 16, 1903, finds the facts in regard to the death of the testator and the interests of his devisees as they have been above stated, and also finds the facts in regard to the filing of the petition on June 21, 1897, and the petition for the sale of the premises, and the decree of sale entered on October 8, 1897, and the report of the executor that he had made such sale and sold the premises to Kazmierz Kluczynski for $1,100, and the confirmation of the sale on November 10, 1897, and the delivery of an executor's deed to the purchaser. The decree further finds "that the purchaser at said sale never attended the same, and knew nothing about it, and that nothing was paid for the deed, and that no consideration passed therefor; that on November 18, 1897, the purchaser at such sale conveyed said premises to Katharina Obecny for the pretended consideration of $6,000, and that no money passed, and none was intended to pass"; that on November 20, 1897, Witt and Katharina Obecny executed the trust deed above named to Winston, as trustee, to secure $2,000; and that the notes for $2,000 are owned by the F. J. Dewes Brewery Company. The decree further recites the execution of the trust deed and note for $4,000 to Schintz, as trustee, and that said note is owned by Mary Heppe and the other appellants above named. The decree further finds "that the trust deed last aforesaid is no lien whatsoever upon the property in question; that the probate court of Cook county was without jurisdiction to vacate said final order, declaring said estate settled and discharging the executor, and order the sale of said real estate to pay said widow's award, after the lapse of two terms of said probate court from the day said final order was entered discharging the executor; that the proceedings in said probate court, and the pretended sale of said premises by the executor, are absolutely void, and of no force or effect whatsoever; that the complainants are each the owners in fee simple of an undivided six-twentieths of said premises, free and clear of the lien of each and all of said trust deeds, hereinbefore found to have been executed; that Katharina Obecny is the owner in fee simple of the remaining eight-twentieths part of the said premises, subject only to the trust deed to Frederick S. Winston as trustee, given to secure the note of $2,000 aforesaid." The court thereupon entered a decree in accordance with the findings aforesaid, and directed that partition be made, and appointed commissioners for that purpose. The defendants below Kazmierz Kluczynski, Katharina Obecny, Witt Obecny, Joseph Kucharski, Theodore H. Schintz, trustee, and Chicago Title & Trust Company, successor in trust, were defaulted, and order pro confesso was entered against them.

Albert H. Meads, for appellants. Arnold Tripp, for appellees.

MAGRUDER, J. (after stating the facts). By the death of the testator, Frank Szczepanski, on January 10, 1895, his widow and four daughters became, as devisees by the terms of his will, the owners each of an undivided one-fifth interest in the lot, described in the bill herein and sought to be partitioned. By the subsequent death of two of the children, who were minors, the appellees, the two surviving children, also minors, became the owners, each, of an undivided six-twentieths of the premises in question, and the widow, Katharina Obecny, then the wife of Witt Obecny (formerly Katharina Szczepanski), became the owner of an undivided eight-twentieths of said lot. Therefore the widow, Katharina Obecny, and the appellees, Rosalia Szczepanski and Marianna Szczepanski, minors, were tenants in common, owning the respective undivided interests above named at the time of the transactions hereinafter named.

No claims whatever appear to have been filed by creditors against the estate of the deceased testator, Frank Szczepanski. The widow's award was fixed by the appraisers at $1,330, and the whole amount of the personal property was appraised at $408.52. After the personal property, amounting to $408.52, was applied upon the widow's award, there remained a deficiency of $921.48. In March, 1897, the executor made his final report, and attached to the report was a receipt by the widow for the $408.52 to be applied on her award of $1,330, and also attached to such final report was a release by the widow of the balance of her award, to wit, $921.48. As a part of the receipt and release, so attached to the executor's final report, the widow assented that such report be accepted as a final report, and that the executor, Joseph Kucharski, be discharged from all further duties as the executor of the last will of her deceased husband. Accordingly, on March 30, 1897, an order was entered by the court, by the terms of which such final report was accepted, and the executor was discharged. It appears from such portions of the record of the probate court in the estate of the deceased testator as were introduced in evidence that on March 5, 1897, a written notice to the appellees, being then minors, was drawn by the attorneys of the executor, to the effect that he had filed his final report, and would, on March 19th, ask to have the executor discharged from further service and the report confirmed. This notice was served by leaving copies with Rosalia and Marianna Szczepanski, the appellees herein, on March 9, 1897. Section 112 of the act in regard to the administration of estates provides "that no final settlement shall be made and approved by the court, unless the heirs of the decedent have been notified thereof, in such manner as the court may direct." 1 Starr & C. Ann. St. 1896, pp. 336, 337, c. 3, par. 112. It does not appear here that this service of notice upon the minor devisees in person was a service "in such manner as the court may direct"; it not being shown that the court made any direction upon the subject. But it is immaterial whether the appellee minors were properly served with notice of the filing of the final report and the discharge of the executor, or not, because the final order of March 30, 1897, was favorable to the minors, in that thereby the unpaid portion of the widow's award, to wit, $921.48, which was a claim against the estate, was released at the same time when the executor was discharged. The estate of the minors was thereby relieved from liability for said portion of the widow's award so released.

Subsequently, however, on June 11, 1897, a petition was filed by the widow, who had then become the wife of Witt Obecny, and who was a tenant in common in the ownership of the premises with the minor appellees, to set aside the order discharging the executor and releasing the balance of the widow's award remaining after applying the amount of the personal property thereon. Afterwards, and in pursuance of this petition, an order was entered by the probate court on June 21, 1897, vacating the order of March 30, 1897, discharging the executor, and in such order of vacation it was recited that the widow should have leave to withdraw her receipt for the balance of the widow's award upon the ground that the same had been signed by her by mistake, and it was therein ordered that the executor proceed to sell the real estate of the deceased to pay such balance, after presenting to the court a just and true account of the personal estate and debts of the deceased, as required by statute.

First. It is contended on the part of appellees, and it was found by the court below in its decree, that the order of June 21, 1897, vacating the previous order of March 30, 1897, was void, as having been made at a term subsequent to that at which the vacated order was entered. After the order of March 30, 1897, was entered, two terms had passed before the order of June 21, 1897, was entered, which set aside the previous order discharging the executor. We are unable to agree with the court below in the view that the court was without jurisdiction to enter the order on June 21, 1879, for the reason that it was made at a subsequent term to the order of March 30, 1897. Undoubtedly the general rule is that, after a term has passed, a court has no authority or discretion at a subsequent term to set aside a judgment or to amend it, except in matters of form and for the purpose of correcting clerical errors. Ayer v. City of Chicago, 149 Ill. 262, 37 N. E. 57, and cases referred to on page 266, 149 Ill., page 58, 37 N. E. It has been held by this court in a number of cases that the county court or probate court, in the settlement of estates, is vested with equitable as well as legal powers, and that, in the adjustment of accounts of executors, administrators, and guardians, the county court has equitable jurisdiction and may adopt equitable forms of procedure. Millard v. Harris, 119 Ill. 185, 10 N. E. 387, and cases on page 198, 119 Ill., page 394, 10 N. E.; Spencer v. Boardman, 118 Ill. 553, 9 N. E. 330; Shepard v. Speer, 140 Ill. 238, 29 N. E. 718. In the latter case of Shepard v. Speer, it was said the probate court, when adjudicating upon matters pertaining to the settlement of estates, is clothed with authority to exercise equitable powers like a court of equity. A court of equity would certainly have power to set aside such an order as that of March 30, 1897, if the entry of the latter order had been procured by fraud, or was due in any way to accident or mistake. Fraud, accident, and mistake are well-established grounds of equity jurisdiction. The order of June 21, 1897, entered by the probate court, setting aside the previous order, recites that the receipt and release executed by the widow, giving up the balance that was due to her upon her award, were so executed by mistake. The order recites that it appeared to the court from evidence introduced that the widow signed such receipt by mistake. Therefore the probate court, in the exercise of its equitable powers, had a right to set aside and vacate the order discharging the executor, even though such action was taken by it at a subsequent term. In Schlink v. Maxton, 153 Ill. 447, 38 N. E. 1063, it was held that the probate court, in the exercise of its equitable jurisdiction, might, on motion at a subsequent term, set aside its own order allowing a claim against an estate, if mistake or fraud had intervened; and in that case it was said: "So, here, although the term of court at which an allowance was made, has passed, it may, for such cause as would move a court of equity upon a bill filed, entertain a motion to set aside the allowance." In Strauss v. Phillips, 189 Ill. 9, 59 N. E. 560, the cases of Millard v. Harris, supra, and Schlink v. Maxton, supra, were referred to and approved. See, also, Marshall v. Coleman, 187 Ill. 556, 58 N. E. 628; Tanton v. Keller, 167 Ill. 144, 47 N. E. 376; Wright v. Simpson, 200 Ill. 56, 65 N. E. 628.

It is a matter of doubt, however, although the probate court may have had jurisdiction to enter the order of vacation at a subsequent term, whether, when the order of vacation was entered, the court had jurisdiction over the persons of the minors. The order, vacating the previous order discharging the executor and reinstating the claim of the widow for the balance of $921.48 due upon her award, was against the interest of the minors. It restored a claim which had been released, and directed that their land should be sold for the payment of that claim. It was important, therefore, that they should have notice. It is true that the order of June 21, 1897, makes the following recital: "And also come Rosalia Szczepanski and

Marianna Szczepanski, minor heirs of said deceased, by their guardian ad litem." But it nowhere appears in the record that they received any actual notice that the order of June 21, 1897, vacating the order discharging the executor would be applied for. When a guardian ad litem is appointed to act for a minor, it must be for a minor who is a party to the suit. "A guardian ad litem has been defined to be a person appointed by a court of justice to prosecute or defend for an infant in any suit to which he may be a party." 10 Ency. of Pl. & Pr. p. 616. It is nowhere shown that these appellees, who are minors, and who own twelve-twentieths of the land ordered to be sold, were made parties by any service of any kind. Nor is there any order showing the appointment of a guardian ad litem to represent them. The order of June 21, 1897, not only vacated the previous order of March 30, 1897, but it contained also the following order, to wit: "That Joseph Kucharski, executor of the last will and testament of said deceased, proceed to sell the real estate of said deceased to pay such balance," etc. Section 99 of the act in regard to administration of estates provides that the widow, heirs, and devisees of the testator or intestate, and the guardians of any such as are minors, etc., shall be made parties. 1 Starr & C. Ann. St. 1896, p. 325, c. 3, par. 99. We are inclined to the opinion that the order of June 21, 1897, at least so far as it directed the executor to make a sale of these premises, was void, as against these appellees, for want of jurisdiction over them by proper service of notice or process. The order of June 21, 1897, does not recite or state that such minors had due notice, but merely recites that a guardian ad litem, whose appointment is not shown, came into court when the order was entered. The master found in his report "that the record does not establish the fact that said Rosalia and Marianna Szczepanski were served with notice of the presentation of said petition to withdraw said receipt and to sell said real estate." In the case at bar there is no recital of service in the order of June 21, 1897, which cures the failure of the record to show service. Law v. Grommes, 158 Ill. 492, 41 N. E. 1080; Burr v. Bloemer, 174 Ill. 638, 51 N. E. 821; Botsford v. O'Conner, 57 Ill. 72.

Second. Independently, however, of any question as to the void character of the order of June 21, 1897, the record discloses such facts as make it inequitable to sustain the sale and transfer made of the interest in the property in controversy, which belonged to the minor appellees. The vacation of the order which discharged the executor, and the reinstatement of the released claim of the widow for the balance due upon her award, were not made in good faith for the purpose of realizing by a sale an amount of money necessary to pay what was due her. A scheme was concocted by Theodore H. Schintz, acting with Katharina Obecny and her husband, Witt Obecny, and her brother, Kazmierz Kluczynski, which had for its object the acquisition of such a title to the interests of the appellees in this lot as would enable Schintz to make a loan thereon. When Mrs. Obecny and her husband went to consult Schintz on June 10, 1897, he suggested to them to find some one whom they could trust, and she thereupon named her brother, Kluczynski. On the very next day, to wit, June 11, 1897, Schintz, as attorney for Mrs. Obecny, filed a petition for her to set aside the order, by which the balance due on her widow's award had been released and the executor had been discharged. At the same time he drew a note for $4,000, and the trust deed to himself as trustee, securing the same upon the whole of the lot, including the interests, not only of the appellees, but of the widow. He thereupon induced Kluczynski, the widow's brother, to sign the note and trust deed; the former being payable to the latter's own order and indorsed by himself. Kluczynski says that he received no money when he signed the note and trust deed, and that he did not know what he was signing. He was merely requested to sign such papers as would enable his sister and brother-in-law to obtain some money to put up a new building upon the lot in question. The trust deed to Schintz to secure the note for $4,000 was dated June 10, 1897, and recorded on June 11, 1897, the very day on which the petition to set aside and vacate the order of March 30, 1897, was filed. At the time when this trust deed to Schintz was executed, Kluczynski had no title at all to this lot, or any portion of it. The record showed that the title was in Katharina Obecny and her two minor children, the present appellees. After the order of June 21, 1897, vacating the previous order had been entered, and after the trust deed securing the note for $4,000 had been executed and recorded, then a petition was filed in the probate court by the executor for the sale of the lot, in order to pay the $921.48 due to Mrs. Obecny upon her award. This petition was filed on September 8, 1897. On October 8, 1897, an order was entered directing a sale of the property at public vendue for cash, in order to realize the amount of money to pay the deficiency due upon the widow's award. After notices published and posted, a sale was made on November 12, 1897, of the whole of the lot to Kluczynski for the sum of $1,100. This sale was reported to the probate court and approved. But the probate court was evidently imposed upon. The evidence shows clearly that Kluczynski was not present at the sale and knew nothing about it. He did not pay for the purchase of the property, to the executor making the sale, the sum of $1,100, or any other sum; nor did his sister, Mrs. Obecny, pay any money. Both she and the purchaser, Kluczynski, swear that they paid nothing, and knew nothing about the approval of the sale. There is nothing to show that this $1,100 was paid into court, or that any portion of it was credited upon the widow's claim for the balance of her award. The notice of the sale announced that the property was unincumbered, and would be sold subject to the dower and homestead of the widow. At the time when this announcement was made that the property was unincumbered, the trust deed to secure $4,000 to Schintz was on record, but evidently was not regarded by Schintz, who conducted the proceedings, as constituting an incumbrance upon the property. After the sale was made, and on November 18, 1897, a deed was executed by Joseph Kucharski, the executor, alleged to be in pursuance of the sale at public vendue, to Kluczynski, the pretended purchaser, but no money was paid by him for the deed. On the same day, to wit, November 18, 1897, Kluczynski executed a deed and conveyed the premises to his sister, Katharina Obecny. No consideration was paid by Mrs. Obecny to her brother for this deed. Subsequently, on January 7, 1899, Mrs. Obecny and her husband conveyed the premises to the executor, Joseph Kucharski. No consideration was paid for this deed by Kucharski.

We regard all the proceedings in the probate court from June 11th down to the time of the execution of the deed by Kluczynski to Mrs. Obecny as having been fraudulent, and instituted for the purpose of depriving these appellees of their interest in this property. In fact, there was no executor's sale, but merely a sham sale. The forms of the law were made use of to put a title in Kluczynski, the brother of Mrs. Obecny, who had executed a mortgage or trust deed upon the property to Schintz on June 10, 1897, more than five months before the executor's sale was made to him as a pretended purchaser. The whole object of the proceeding was to get some sort of title in Kluczynski as purchaser at the executor's sale, so as to connect him with the trust deed previously executed to Schintz. The conclusion is warranted by the evidence that the real party in interest was Katharina Obecny, acting under the advice and direction of Schintz. Although the sale was nominally made to her brother, Kluczynski, yet it was really to her and for her benefit, as the property was deeded to her on the very day on which the executor made a deed to Kluczynski. She filed the original petition asking that the order, which had discharged the executor and released her claim against the estate, should be vacated. It is true that the petition for the sale of the property to pay the balance due upon the widow's award was filed in the name of the executor, Kucharski; but it was really filed by Mrs. Obecny and for her benefit, and the sale was made for her benefit. She was herself the owner of eight-twentieths of the property which was sold. In buying the property through her brother, she was buying eight-twentieths of what already belonged to her. Counsel for appellant, in answer to the charge that the record nowhere shows any payment by Kluczynski to the executor of $1,100 bid by him, says in his brief: "It may have been paid by the widow giving to such purchaser a receipt for the amount of her award, and allowing the purchaser to turn such receipt into court." If the purchase money was paid by crediting the same, or a part thereof, upon what was due the widow upon her award, then the widow was the real purchaser, although the name of her brother was used as such purchaser. Such credit is only made at a public sale where the purchaser at the sale owns the debt for which the sale is made. The property was not sold to pay any debt or claim which was due to the pretended purchaser, Kluczynski. If there was a real sale, therefore, it was the duty of Kluczynski to pay the money, and not to turn in a receipt from his sister for the amount due from her upon her award.

It being true, then, that this was a sale in fact to Mrs. Obecny, and that the petition to the court for the sale of the property to pay the balance due on the widow's award was really a petition by Mrs. Obecny, though filed in the name of the executor, it necessarily follows that there was no such service in this case upon the minors as gave the probate court jurisdiction to enter the decree of sale which was entered. Where a petition is filed by an administrator or executor for the sale of real estate to pay debts, the heirs must be made parties, and must be served with summons. Section 103 of the act in regard to administration (1 Starr & C. Ann. St. 1896, p. 329, c. 3, par. 103) provides that "the service of summons shall be made by reading thereof to the defendant, or leaving a copy thereof at the usual place of abode, with some member of the family of the age of ten years and upwards, and informing such person of the contents thereof, which service shall be at least ten days before the return of such summons." The minor appellees were made parties defendant to the petition for sale, and summons was issued against them. The return of the sheriff upon the back of the summons shows that he "served this writ on the within-named Rosalia Szczepanski and Marianna Szczepanski by leaving a copy thereof for each of them at their usual place of abode with Katharina Obecny, a member of their family of the age of 10 years and upwards, and informing her of the contents thereof this 9th day of December, 1897." In other words, the summons was served upon these two minor devisees and heirs by leaving a copy thereof with their mother, who was not only a tenant in common with them in the ownership of the premises, but was proceeding adversely against them for the purpose of subjecting their interest in the premises to the payment of her widow's award, or, rather, who was trying through the machinery of the law to put the title to their interest in her brother and in herself for purposes of her own. This court has held in a number of cases that, where a bill in chancery is filed against minors to subject their land to sale, the service of the summons by the delivery of a copy thereof to the complainant, informing him of its contents, will confer no jurisdiction on the court as to the persons of the defendants, and the decree of sale rendered on such service will be void as to them. Hemmer v. Wolfer, 124 Ill. 435, 16 N. E. 652; St. Louis & Sandoval Coal & Mining Co. v. Edwards, 103 Ill. 472; Lee v. Fox, 89 Ill. 226; Filkins v. O'Sullivan, 79 Ill. 524; Clark v. Thompson, 47 Ill. 25, 95 Am. Dec. 457. In the case at bar, Katharina Obecny, acting in the name of the executor, Kucharski, was the real complainant in this petition for the sale of this property. Indeed, in the petition which she filed for the vacation of the order of March 30, 1897, in her own name, she asked that the property might be sold. There was no service upon her minor children, except by leaving a copy of the summons with her, the real, though not nominal, complainant in the petition, and stating the contents of it to her. We do not regard this service, under the decisions referred to and upon principle, as sufficient. Her interest lay in the direction of keeping a knowledge of the filing of the petition from the very children for whom she accepted service. We are, therefore, of the opinion that the court acquired no jurisdiction over these appellees to enter the order of sale against their property.

The only persons who have taken the present appeal, and who assign errors here, are the appellants, who own the note and trust deed executed to Schintz as trustee. The owners of the second trust deed to Winston are not here complaining. None of the other defendants below are here complaining. The only defendants who answered were the holders of the incumbrances. The executor, Kucharski, the alleged purchaser, Kluczynski, and Mr. and Mrs. Obecny, and Schintz, the trustee, were all defaulted below. The only parties, therefore, whose rights can here be considered, are those of the appellants, who purchased from Schintz the note and trust deed executed to him. The appellants, or their deceased ancestor, George Heppe, claim that they paid $4,000 for this mortgage to Schintz. It is very certain that he only applied about $1,900 of it toward the erection of the new building upon the premises in question. The appellants cannot be regarded as purchasers in good faith without notice of the rights of the appellees, in view of what has already been stated. The salient facts, which have been set forth, were shown by the record in such a way that appellants were affected with notice of the scheme which was concocted to deprive these children of their property. Appellants must have known, and could not have helped knowing, that, when they purchased the trust deed from Schintz, Kluczynski, the maker of that trust deed, had no title whatever to the property. Exactly when they made the purchase of the $4,000 note is not shown by the evidence. Counsel say in their brief that they purchased the note a few weeks after it was executed, but we find no evidence in the record to show that fact; but, even if it was purchased after the sham sale to Kluczynski, there was enough upon the record to put them upon inquiry, so that, if they had made such inquiry, they could not have failed to ascertain the true character of the proceedings taken in the probate court, the effect of which was illegally and fraudulently to deprive these appellees of their property. In other words, the appellants purchased the trust deed to Schintz with notice of its real character.

The improvements, which were put upon this property, were put upon it by Mrs. Obecny, who owned an undivided interest as tenant in common with the appellees. This property was the homestead of the testator, the father of appellees, when he died, and was occupied as a homestead by the widow and these children when the transactions herein narrated occurred. Parties, purchasing the incumbrance, had full notice of the rights of the appellees from their possession of the property. Where compensation is allowed for improvements, made by one tenant in common without the knowledge of the others, the compensation will be estimated, so as to inflict no injury on the co-tenant against whom the improvements are charged. It is said here that the new building, which was erected by Mrs. Obecny upon these premises, benefited the property of these appellees, and that they should be charged with their proportionate share of the cost of the improvements. The co-tenant, against whom such improvements are charged, will be charged, not with the price of the improvements, but only with his proportion of the amount which, at the time of the partition, they add to the value of the premises. Cooter v. Dearborn, 115 Ill. 509, 4 N. E. 388; Rowan v. Reed, 19 Ill. 21. The master, whose report in this case was confirmed, found that the value of improvements on the lot in 1897 was $1,500, and that the value of the lot in 1897 was $2,500, making a total amount of $4,000 for lot and improvements. We are not prepared to say that the evidence does not sustain this finding of the master. Indeed, much of the testimony shows a greater value of the lot and improvements than the amount so found by him. But he also finds in his report that he is unable, from the evidence, to state the present value of said premises. Nor do we find any evidence in the record showing such present value. It is impossible to state, therefore, the amount which the improvements added to the value of the premises. This being so, it is impossible to charge the appellees with their proportion of the amount which, at the time of the partition, the improvements will have added to the value of the premises, if, under the facts of this case, they are justly chargeable with such proportion. As, however, this is a matter which concerns the appellees and their mother as between themselves, it is not necessary for us to pass upon it, as the mother has taken no appeal and assigned no errors, and is not complaining of the decree below.

After a careful consideration of the whole record, we are unable to say that the chancellor below erred in holding that the appellees are each the owner in fee of an undivided six-twentieths of the lot described in the bill, free and clear of the lien of the trust deed executed by Kluczynski to Schintz as trustee, and also of the lien of the other trust deed hereinbefore mentioned. Accordingly, the decree of the court below is affirmed.

Decree affirmed.

(209 Ill. 333)

SHACKLEFORD et al. v. ELLIOTT et al.

(Supreme Court of Illinois. April 20, 1904.)

RESULTING TRUSTS—PURCHASE OF LAND—SOURCE OF PURCHASE MONEY—EVIDENCE—SUFFICIENCY—DESCENT OF INTEREST OF BENEFICIARY.

1. On an issue as to whether lands purchased by a husband in his own name had been paid for with moneys belonging to the wife, evidence considered, and *held* to show such to have been the case.

2. On an issue as to whether lands purchased by a husband had been paid for with moneys furnished by the wife, the fact that the bond given on the sale of the lands recited that the husband gave his note was not conclusive on the question whether such note was given, or whether there was a cash payment, as claimed.

3. Where, on an issue as to whether lands purchased by a husband in his own name had been paid for with money belonging to the wife, the mother of the wife testified that she furnished the money, but also testified that she first gave it to her daughter as a gift, a contention that the evidence showed that the money was furnished by the mother, so that there could be no trust in favor of her daughter, was untenable.

4. Where, in a chancery suit, there is little or no conflict in the evidence, and the finding of the chancellor appears to be erroneous, it will be reversed.

5. The interest of a beneficiary in a resulting trust in lands descends to his heirs, who are entitled to a decree conveying the title to them.

Appeal from Circuit Court, Franklin County; P. A. Pearce, Judge.

Suit by Mary A. Elliott and others against Oscar Shackleford and others for an assignment of dower and partition. From a decree dismissing the cross-bill of defendants, and granting the relief prayed for by complainants, defendants appeal. Reversed.

E. E. Denison, for appellants. Pillow & Smith, for appellees.

RICKS, J. The appellee Mary A. Elliott, formerly the wife of Henry L. Shackleford, now deceased, at the November term, 1903, of the Franklin county circuit court filed her bill for assignment of dower and partition of certain lands (being 60 acres) in said county. She alleged that on September 14, 1899, said Henry L. Shackleford died seised of the lands in question, leaving complainant, formerly Mary A. Shackleford (then Mary A. Elliott), as his widow, and appellants, Oscar, William, Callie, and Orvie Shackleford, and Lawrence Henry Shackleford, his only children and heirs at law. Lawrence Henry Shackleford died in infancy, and was the child of complainant and said Henry L. Shackleford. The other mentioned children were the children of Henry L. Shackleford and a former wife, Ella Shackleford, and, being infants, by next friend filed their answer to said bill, denying the interest of complainant in said land as in her bill alleged, and averring that, of the 40 acres, part of the said 60 acres mentioned in the bill, Henry L. Shackleford was seised in trust for his former wife, Ella Shackleford, the mother of appellants, and after her death he held the same in trust for said appellants. Appellants also filed their cross-bill, averring that in 1894 Lucretia Guthrie, mother of the said Ella Shackleford and grandmother of appellants, being desirous of making her daughter a gift of some land, gave her certain money ($200) in two installments, of $100 each, which the said daughter, Ella Shackleford, gave to her husband, Henry L. Shackleford, and requested him to purchase for her the 40-acre tract in question; that, of the $100 so first given Henry L. Shackleford, he paid $50 as a cash payment on said purchase, the balance being used in improvements; that, instead of taking a bond for a deed to his wife, the said Henry L. Shackleford caused one to be made in his own name, and that the wife supposed said bond was taken in her name; that afterwards the said Lucretia Guthrie gave to her daughter, on April 30, 1895, the balance of the purchase price for said land, who in turn gave it to her husband, and requested him to finish paying for the same and obtain for her a deed; that the said Henry L. Shackleford did so apply the money, but took the deed in his own name, instead of his wife's, but without her knowledge or consent; and that by reason of such acts the said Henry L. Shackleford held said lands in trust, as above declared. The cross-bill further avers the death of Ella Shackleford, intestate, October 17, 1897, leaving the said Henry L. Shackleford, her husband, and appellants, her children, her only heirs at law; also stating that said Henry L. Shackleford afterwards married one Mary A. Pippy, who afterwards became Mary A. Elliott, the complainant in the original bill. The cross-bill further avers that the said 40 acres descended, by the death of their mother, to appellants, and said Henry L. Shackleford only held the same in trust for them, and denies that the said Mary A. Elliott had any interest in the same, and prays that the court may decree the title in said land to be in said appellants. The cause was heard by the chancellor without the intervention of a jury, and a decree was entered dismissing the cross-bill and granting the relief prayed for in the original bill. This action of the chancellor the appellants assign as error, and prosecute this appeal.

Appellants contend that the evidence offered in support of their cross-bill proves conclusively that the 40 acres of land in controversy was purchased by Henry L. Shackleford with the money belonging to his wife, Ella Shackleford; that he was sent to buy the land as her agent, and fraudulently took the title in his own name; that an implied or resulting trust arose in favor of Ella Shackleford; that Henry L. Shackleford held the land in trust for his wife until her death, and afterward in trust for her children, the appellants. In support of the cross-bill, appellants offered in evidence the deed to Henry L. Shackleford to the 40 acres of land here in question; the consideration mentioned in the said deed being $150. Appellants also introduced the testimony of seven witnesses. This evidence of appellants is uncontradicted; defendants in the cross-bill offering no evidence, except the bond for a deed to the land in question. This bond bears date November 21, 1894, and runs from the grantors of the land to Henry L. Shackleford, and mentions in the condition that the said Shackleford had that day given said grantors two promissory notes—one for $50, due June 1, 1895, and one for $100, due one year after date—and, upon the payment of said notes on or before maturity, a deed to the lands described would be made.

In our judgment, the evidence shows that in November, 1894, Lucretia Guthrie, the mother of Ella Shackleford, gave her said daughter $100, with which to buy land. It was intended as a gift, and was handed to her in the form of silver and paper money, in the home of Henry Shackleford, and in his presence. Said Ella Shackleford held the money for a while, and afterwards gave it to her husband, with the request that he purchase the land here in controversy for her. Henry Shackleford bought the 40 acres, taking a bond for a deed in his own name. It is not clear whether, at the time of receiving this bond, any cash payment was made or not. The bond shows that two notes were given—one for $50, due June 1, 1895, and one for $100, due one year after date—the notes being payable on or before maturity. There is evidence, however, that the $50 was paid in cash, and the balance of the first $100 was used in improvements. There is also evidence to the effect that, when Shackleford returned home, he told his wife he had "her bond" for a deed to the land. She was a sickly woman, and did not investigate the bond, but relied upon the statement that it was in her name. When the other payment became due, Mrs. Guthrie again gave her daughter $100, which the daughter turned over to her husband to finish paying for the land. He returned, and told her he had "her deed," putting it away in a trunk. The wife never investigated it herself, but relied upon the statements that it was hers, and knew no different until, later on, the husband requested her to join in a mortgage of this land; and, when she thus discovered that the title was not in her, she gave way to tears, and protested, in the husband's presence, that the title was hers. Several witnesses testified to statements made by Henry Shackleford to the effect that this land was purchased with money furnished his wife by her mother, and that it was his wife's land, and he intended her children to have it. There is also evidence to the effect that up to the time of the commencement of this suit the complainant in the original bill, Mary A. Elliott, also disclaimed any interest in said land; saying that her husband had told her it was bought with his first wife's money, and belonged to her children.

Inasmuch as appellee offered no testimony in conflict with the testimony offered by appellants, it is not necessary for us to set out more fully the evidence in support of the cross-bill. Enough has already been stated, when uncontradicted, to clearly indicate that appellants were entitled to the relief sought by their cross-bill.

Appellee, however, contends that the recitals of the bond showed that no cash payment was made for the land, and that Henry L. Shackleford gave his individual notes therefor. The notes were payable on or before maturity, and the $50 note, if executed at all, may have been paid the same day of its execution. But whether paid then or not, the testimony is to the effect that it was paid with the money given Shackleford by his wife for the purchase of this land. There is no evidence that Shackleford ever put a cent of his own money into this purchase. His own admissions refute the contention that he did. There is evidence, uncontradicted, to the effect that he had no visible means with which to make this purchase. It is not shown that he ever even claimed that he did make the purchase with his own money. It can by no means be logically contended that the mere recitals in the bond are at all conclusive that a $50 note was given instead of a cash payment. The facts and circumstances disclosed by the record are in entire harmony with appellants' theory of the case, and directly contrary to that of appellee's.

Appellee, however, urges that the evidence shows that the purchase money for the land was furnished by the mother of Ella Shackleford, and hence there could be no resulting trust in favor of the mother of appellants. The record does not bear out this contention. While Lucretia Guthrie, the mother of Ella Shackleford, did testify that she furnished the money in question, she also said that she first gave it to her daughter as a gift, and that afterwards the daughter turned it over to her husband, with a request that he purchase the land for her. The admissions of Henry L. Shackleford are also to the same effect.

It is next insisted by the appellee that the chancellor who entered the decree herein saw and heard the witnesses, and his findings should not be disturbed. Where the testimony is very conflicting, and requires to be weighed and balanced in order to determine its proper effect, under the well-established rule, such contention is of great force; but in a case like the one at bar, where there is little or no conflict, the rule does not apply. As we read the record in this case, the entire purchase money for the 40 acres here involved was furnished by Ella Shackleford, and with the distinct and declared intention that the purchase was to be for her benefit, and the title to be taken in her name; and, under such circumstances, the law is too well settled to require the extended citation of authorities to support the conclusion that a resulting trust was established in favor of Ella Shackleford, and on her death descended to her children. Fleming v. McHale, 47 Ill. 282.

The decree herein will be reversed, and the cause remanded to the circuit court of Frankin county, with directions to that court to grant the relief prayed in the cross-bill of appellants. Reversed and remanded.

(208 Ill. 603)

MICHAELS v. PEOPLE.

(Supreme Court of Illinois. April 20, 1904.)

CRIMINAL LAW—CONFESSIONS—OFFER TO SETTLE—EVIDENCE—PROCEEDINGS BEFORE FOREIGN JUSTICE OF THE PEACE.

1. In a criminal prosecution, papers purporting to be the files of an attachment suit brought against defendant before a justice in another state were not admissible, in the absence of any authentication or evidence that the alleged justice was such in fact, or as to his jurisdiction.

2. Offers by a person arrested for forging a check to settle the matter by paying the amount of the check, or a greater sum, were not confessions, so as to authorize an instruction on the subject of confessions in a prosecution for the crime.

Error to Circuit Court, Peoria County; T. N. Green, Judge.

Samuel B. Michaels was convicted of forgery, and brings error. Reversed.

Joseph A. Weil, for plaintiff in error. H. J. Hamlin, Atty. Gen., William V. Tefft, State's Atty., and Geo. B. Gillespie, Asst. Atty. Gen., for the People.

CARTWRIGHT, J. Plaintiff in error was convicted in the circuit court of Peoria county upon an indictment charging him with forging a check in the name of C. Schilling & Co., of San Francisco, Cal., on the Third National Bank of San Francisco, dated October 10, 1901, for $75, payable to the order of W. E. Hull. The evidence tended to prove that on the date of the check a person representing himself to be Mr. Schilling, of Schilling & Co., of San Francisco, Cal., gave to William E. Hull, manager of Clarke's Distillery, at Peoria, an order for 100 barrels of Clarke's rye whisky, to be shipped to San Francisco; that this person bought in Peoria three or four diamonds, amounting to $150, and afterward stated that the purchase made him short of money, and he must wire for funds to get to Denver; that Hull offered to let him have money, and he drew the check in question, for which Hull gave him $75. The defendant was arrested in Memphis, Tenn., on January 24, 1903, and was brought to Peoria, where the trial took place in November, 1903. The principal question of fact was the identity of the defendant with the person who drew the check, and upon that subject the evidence was contradictory. He was identified with more or less certainty by several persons who saw the man who drew the check in Peoria, while some others failed to identify him as such person. There was evidence, consisting of the book of the hotel where he boarded and the testimony of witnesses, that on the date of the check he was staying at said hotel in Chicago with his wife.

We are of the opinion that the defendant did not have a fair trial, and that the judgment must be reversed on account of prejudicial error in the admission of evidence and in giving an instruction at the request of the people. Joseph Farnbacher, of Memphis, Tenn., was called as a witness for the people, and testified that he was a clerk and deputy sheriff in the office of F. W. Davis, a justice of the peace in that city. He produced several papers purporting to be the files of an attachment suit for $75 brought by said W. E. Hull against the defendant before said F. W. Davis, as a justice of the peace, and testified to the signatures of the justice subscribed to the same. The papers consisted of an affidavit for a writ of attachment signed by W. E. Hull, and sworn to before the said F. W. Davis, a bond, a writ of attachment issued by Davis, a return by the sheriff showing service, and that he garnished the State National Bank, and a statement signed by the bank that there was $1,000 to the credit of the defendant in the bank. There was a memorandum on the process which the witness testified that he had written: "Settled by the defendant paying into court the amount of debt and costs this 26th day of January, 1903." He testified that he went over to the city prison, where the defendant was confined, and brought him into the justice court to his attorney, and after a consultation the attorney paid into court the amount for which the suit was begun, and costs. These papers were then offered in evidence, and were admitted over the objection of the defendant. The papers were not authenticated in any manner, and there was no attempt to authenticate them, under the act of Congress or otherwise. There was no evidence that F. W. Davis was a justice of the peace in Tennessee, and our courts do not even take judicial notice who are justices of the peace within this state, beyond the county where the court is held. There was no evidence as to the jurisdiction of justices of the peace in that state, and the alleged files of the suit were not admissible in evidence. Brackett v. People, 64 Ill. 170. The defendant testified that he was not out of the jail on that day; that he was never in the office of the justice of the peace; that, if the money was paid, it was by his intended bondsman as a deposit and security for the claim. The reply made on behalf of the people is that the papers were admissible because they were not intended to prove a judgment against the defendant, but merely to prove the settlement of the suit by payment of the amount for which the writ was issued and costs. We do not understand that the nature of the inference to be drawn from evidence affects the competency of the evidence, or dispenses with the necessity of legal proof of facts. The papers were offered to prove the commencement of the attachment suit before a supposed justice of the peace in another state, the garnishment of moneys of the defendant in the bank, and the settlement of the suit by paying the amount demanded and costs of the proceedings. They were not legal evidence of such facts.

The court gave to the jury the following instruction at the instance of the people: "The jury are instructed that if you believe, from the evidence, beyond a reasonable doubt, that the defendant has made any confession of the crime charged in this indictment, freely and voluntarily, that confession, if so proven, is of itself sufficient to warrant the conviction of defendant, if you otherwise believe, from the evidence, beyond all reasonable doubt, that the crime charged was committed by some one." There was no evidence that the defendant had made any confession of the crime charged in the indictment, but, on the contrary, the evidence for the people was that he constantly denied that he was guilty. There was, however, evidence which it was proper for the jury to consider on the question of guilt or innocence, to which the instruction would naturally be applied by the jury. When the defendant was arrested at a hotel in Memphis, he was taken to the room of J. P. Carter, a traveling salesman for the distillery firm, and he was there accused of the crime. William E. Hull testified: That, when taken to the room, the defendant said: "What is all this about?" That witness said: "Mr. Schilling, you know what it is about. You forged a check on me for $75." That defendant denied it, and said his name was not Schilling, but was Michaels, and said: "Why, Mr. Hull, I will give you back your $75." That he talked with the detectives, and said he would like to fix it up, and said: "Mr. Hull, I will give you ten times that amount to settle this up." Carter testified that the defendant asked why he was arrested, and Hull said, "You passed a bogus check on me at Peoria;" that defendant said, "Can this thing be fixed up?" and also asked what was the amount of the check, and was told that it was $75. Ike Wolf, a detective, testified that, when defendant was called "Schilling," he said, "My name is not Schilling;" that defendant then asked Hull what this was for, and Hull said, "You passed a bogus check for $75 on me at Peoria;" that defendant then said, "Can't this be fixed up?" that Hull said, "No," and defendant then said, "I will pay ten times $75." W. S. Lawless testified that defendant wanted to know what was the matter, and witness addressed him as Mr. Schilling; that defendant said his name was not Schilling but was Michaels; that defendant was told he was arrested for passing a bogus check, and he asked how much it was, and he said he could fix that up —that he would even give 10 times that amount. The defendant denied that he offered to settle or fix the matter up, and his version of the conversation was that he sent for the proprietor of the hotel, and asked him to go his security for $75; that some one said it would take more, and he said he would furnish security for 10 times that amount. The proprietor of the hotel testified that, when he was sent for, defendant asked him if he would go his security for $75; that one of the officers said that would not cover the amount of the claim; and that defendants said he could give 10 times that amount. This, with the evidence before referred to, of settling the claim before the justice, did not amount to a confession, which is a voluntary acknowledgment of a person charged with the commission of crime that he is guilty of the offense. It is a voluntary declaration by a person charged with a crime of his agency or participation in the crime. 8 Cyc. 562. It is not equivalent to statements, declarations, or admissions of facts criminating in their nature or tending to prove guilt. It is limited in its meaning to the criminal act, and is an acknowledgment or admission of participation in it. 6 Am. & Eng. Ency. of Law (2d Ed.) 520; 1 Greenleaf on Evidence, § 170; Johnson v. People, 197 Ill. 48, 64 N. E. 286. By the instruction the jury were advised that a confession by the defendant, if proved, was of itself sufficient to warrant a conviction, if the corpus delicti were otherwise proved. The jury would naturally assume that the testimony as to what defendant said when arrested was evidence of a confession of the crime with which he was charged, and, with the evidence that the check was forged, was sufficient to justify his conviction. There being no evidence tending to prove a confession, it was prejudicial error to give the instruction.

The judgment of the circuit court is reversed, and the cause is remanded. Reversed and remanded.

(209 Ill. 215)

McCRACKEN et al. v. PEOPLE.

(Supreme Court of Illinois. April 20, 1904.)

EMBEZZLEMENT—INDICTMENT—INSTRUCTIONS—TRIAL—ARGUMENT TO JURY—EVIDENCE—SUFFICIENCY—DISTURBANCE ON APPEAL—CRIMINAL LAW—PRINCIPALS AND ACCESSORIES.

1. An indictment charging that defendants fraudulently converted to their own use certain property, "which said property had been delivered to the said defendants as bailees," being substantially in the words of the statute, was sufficient, without alleging the facts which constituted the bailment.

2. In a prosecution for embezzlement, a charge specifically pointing out accused, and calling attention to his testimony, and stating that, if he had willfully and corruptly testified falsely to any fact material to the issue, the jury had the right to entirely disregard his testimony, was not error.

3. In a prosecution for embezzlement, where defendants introduced in evidence a contract whereby they were to care for the body of the person whose property they embezzled, at his death, and to furnish him certain clothing during his life, and, in arguing to the jury, defendants' counsel insisted that the money which defendants had embezzled was in consideration of the obligations they had assumed in signing the contract, it was proper for the state's attorney, in reply to this argument, and in discussing the evidence, to refer to the insolvency of defendants.

4. The Supreme Court will not set aside a conviction based on conflicting evidence unless a reasonable and well-founded doubt of the guilt of accused arises from all the evidence.

5. In a prosecution for embezzlement of property delivered to defendants as bailees, evidence *held* sufficient to support a conviction.

6. Under the statute providing that one who stands by, and aids, abets, or assists, or who, not being present, has advised, encouraged, or abetted, the perpetration of a crime, is a principal, and punishable accordingly, where defendants co-operated together in the conversion to their own use of money intrusted to them as bailees, they were equally guilty, irrespective of which one of them actually received the money from the bailor.

Error to Criminal Court, Cook County; Geo. Kersten, Judge.

Ole G. McCracken and Enos E. McEldowney were convicted of embezzlement, and bring error. Affirmed.

Heron, Long & Stanton, for plaintiffs in error. H. J. Hamlin, Atty. Gen. (Charles S. Deneen, State's Atty., and John R. Newcomer, Asst. State's Atty., of counsel), for the People.

WILKIN, J. The plaintiffs in error, Ole G. McCracken and Enos E. McEldowney, were indicted by the grand jury of Cook county, charged with larceny as bailees. The indictment alleged that the plaintiffs in error, on the 1st day of April, 1901, fraudulently and feloniously did embezzle and fraudulently convert to their own use a large amount of personal goods, funds, money, and property (describing current money of the United States in various denominations, bank bills and gold and silver coin of various denominations), all of the value of $200; also one draft, the same then and there being an instrument of writing, for $300, then and there of the value of $300, being the personal goods, funds, money, and property of one Henry M. Ramey, which said property had been delivered to the said plaintiffs in error as bailees. In subsequent counts the form of the charge included an allegation that the property was intrusted to the defendants as bailees, that they were agents in the employ of Henry M. Ramey, and that the property was received as such agents, etc. A motion was made to quash the indictment, which was overruled; and, upon a hearing before the court and a jury, plaintiffs in error were found guilty as charged in the indictment, and sentenced to the penitentiary.

The facts in the case are substantially as follows: Henry M. Ramey was an old man, about 75 years of age, who lived in Ohio, and had an incurable disease. He was desirous of going to Chicago and getting into the Home for Incurables, situated in the southern portion of the city, which is an institution for the care of elderly people who are afflicted with incurable diseases. If, at the time of the admission of patients, they are able to do so, they are expected to pay at least something to the home; the amount depending altogether on the particular case. Ramey had a niece in Chicago—a Mrs. Amelia Browder—who lived in the same building and on the same floor with the defendant McEldowney, and they were intimate friends. There was considerable talk between McEldowney and Mrs. Browder, and between the former and the defendant McCracken, with reference to getting the old gentleman into the home. In several of such conversations it was suggested that the old gentleman bring at least $300 with him when he came from Ohio for the purpose of securing his admission, and such a request was written to Ramey by his niece, Mrs. Browder. Some two or three weeks prior to Ramey's arrival in Chicago, Mrs. Browder informed plaintiffs in error that her uncle had finally obtained the $300 from friends in Ohio, and would bring it with him. When he arrived he was met at the train by McEldowney, and taken to the home of Mrs. Browder; and the next day McEldowney took McCracken up to the house to see him, and introduced him as a friend who would assist in getting him into the home. After this there were many conversations between the parties, and the plaintiffs in error visited the home and talked with Mr. Mitchell, the general manager, concerning Ramey's admission. Finally Ramey gave McEldowney the draft for $300, and McEldowney placed it in the bank in his own name; and afterwards, in conversations between both of the plaintiffs in error and the superintendent of the home, they stated to him on different occasions that they thought it possible that Ramey could raise at least $100 to secure his admission. Arrangements were finally completed whereby the old gentleman

¶ 1. See Embezzlement, vol. 18, Cent. Dig. §§ 50, 51.

was to be admitted upon the payment of that sum. Plaintiffs in error signed a contract to the home, at the time of Ramey's admission, whereby they agreed to provide him with proper clothing during his residence in the home, take care of his body in event of his death, and provide it with a suitable burial. The $100 was paid to the home, and $25 had been previously paid to McCracken by McEldowney, and the remainder of the $175 was drawn out of the bank; McEldowney retaining $100, and paying McCracken $75. About one year after this took place, the home learned the facts, and sent for plaintiffs in error, and demanded that the funds be turned over to the home. This they refused to do, and the result was their indictment and conviction, as above stated.

The first ground of reversal insisted upon is that the indictment is insufficient, in that it fails to allege the facts which constituted the bailment; and the case of Johnson v. People, 113 Ill. 99, is relied upon as sustaining the point. That case is clearly distinguishable from this. The indictment here is not for a common-law offense, but is for the crime of larceny as bailee, as defined by our statute. If it had been for larceny by the common law, it would have been necessary to set out the particular facts which constituted the crime, as held in the case cited; but we have held in many cases that, where the offense is statutory, it is sufficient to allege it in the words of the statute, provided it sufficiently defines the crime. Strohm v. People, 160 Ill. 582, 43 N. E. 622; Meadowcroft v. People, 163 Ill. 56, 45 N. E. 303, 35 L. R. A. 176, 54 Am. St. Rep. 447. This indictment charges plaintiffs in error with larceny as bailees in substantially the words of the statute, and was therefore good, under the foregoing decisions, and the trial court committed no error in overruling the motion to quash.

Objection is next made to the refusal of instructions numbered 1, 3, and 4½ asked by the defendants, and to the giving of the seventeenth at the instance of the people. Those refused were drawn upon the theory that Ramey was not the owner of the property at the time of the alleged embezzlement. They did not correctly state the law applicable to the facts in the case, and for that reason were properly refused. But in addition to this fatal objection to each of them, the fourth requested by the defendants, and given as modified, correctly stated all the elements constituting the crime charged, and necessary to be proved. The objection to the seventeenth instruction given on behalf of the people is that it specifically points out the accused, and calls attention to their testimony; stating that, if they have willfully and corruptly testified falsely to any fact material to the issue, the jury had the right to entirely disregard their testimony, etc. The contention is that it erroneously calls particular attention to the defendants, instead of relating to the witnesses generally. It is substantially in the language of instructions approved in Hirschman v. People, 101 Ill. 568; Leigh v. People, 113 Ill. 372; and Siebert v. People, 143 Ill. 571, 32 N. E. 431. There was no error in giving the instructions as asked.

Complaint is next made of certain statements made by the state's attorney, in his closing argument to the jury, with reference to the insolvency of plaintiffs in error. A contract was introduced in evidence by plaintiffs in error, signed by them, in which they agreed to furnish certain clothing and care for the body of Ramey at his death. This contract was delivered to the home at the time Ramey was admitted. It appears from the evidence that, for one year after his admission, plaintiffs in error had not paid anything for clothing or other necessaries under that contract; and, upon the argument before the jury, their counsel insisted that the $100 which they had each retained was in consideration of the obligation which they had assumed in signing said contract. In reply to this argument, and in discussing the evidence in the case, the state's attorney made the remark complained of. We think, from an examination of the argument of counsel on either side, the remarks objected to were not improper, but were in reply to those which had been made by counsel for the defendants.

It is also insisted that the verdict is not supported by the evidence, and for that reason the judgment of conviction should be reversed. It was admitted by both of the defendants that, out of the $300, they each received $100. Ramey testified that he gave the money or draft to McEldowney, with instructions to pay it to the home when he (Ramey) was admitted, and that McEldowney agreed to do so. He further testified that he had numerous conversations with both defendants upon the same subject, in each of which the money was mentioned—they agreeing to pay the $300 to the home—and also that on at least one occasion he stated to McEldowney that he hoped to be able to reward him for his trouble in assisting him in getting into the home, and McEldowney replied, "I am not working for money, and all I wish is to assist you to get into the home." The testimony clearly shows that the old man did not know until more than a year after he had been admitted that the home did not receive the $300, and Mrs. Amelia Browder testified that she heard McEldowney tell him that it would be necessary for him to pay $300 in order to get into the home, and that, during all the conversations between her uncle and the defendants, she never heard either of them say a single word about taking or receiving any portion of the $300 for their services. The evidence also shows that they frequently went to the home and had conversations with the general manager, and on several occasions told him they believed the old gentleman might possibly be able to raise $100 among his friends, and that they then well knew that he had provided $300, and had paid it over to McEldowney, which was in the bank in his (McEldowney's) name, and that they were at that time trying to induce the general manager to receive him for $100, and at the same time impressing Ramey with the belief that it would be necessary for him to pay $300. There is also evidence in the record to the effect that, on the day he was admitted, McEldowney had by some means obtained possession of certain papers and agreements which had been sent to Ramey by the home through the mail for his signature, and that McEldowney had signed the same himself, and had McCracken sign them, without allowing the papers to get into Ramey's hands, apparently for the purpose of concealing the fact that they were not paying the whole of the $300 to the home; the papers themselves containing the statement that Ramey was to be admitted upon the payment of but $100. McEldowney kept the papers in his own possession when he took Ramey to the home, and the latter did not know at any time where they came from, when they were signed, or what they contained. It is true that many of these facts were denied by the defendants, but their guilt or innocence was a question to be determined by the jury from all the facts and circumstances proven upon the trial. They saw the witnesses and heard them testify, as did the presiding judge; and it is well settled that this court will not, under such circumstances, set aside the verdict, unless we are able to say, after a consideration of all the evidence, that a reasonable and well-founded doubt of the guilt of the accused arises therefrom. There is an abundance of evidence in this record to the effect that the conduct of the defendants in their dealings with Ramey and the Home for Incurables was inconsistent with honesty and fair dealing, and we are convinced that the verdict below is fairly supported by the evidence.

It is insisted by counsel for McCracken that he was wrongfully convicted, for the reason that the $300 was received by McEldowney, and on the day Ramey was taken to the home he paid McCracken $100, and that no part of the $300 was in the latter's hands until that time, and that he is not, therefore, guilty as charged in the indictment. It is the law of this state that he who stands by, and aids, abets, or assists, or who, not being present, aiding, abetting, or assisting, hath advised, encouraged, aided, or abetted, the perpetration of a crime, shall be considered a principal, and punished accordingly. We think the evidence before the jury warranted the conclusion that the defendants acted and co-operated together in the conversion to their own use of the $200. It is therefore unimportant which one of them actually received the money from Ramey.

On the whole record, we find no substantial grounds of reversal, and the judgment of the criminal court of Cook county will accordingly be affirmed. Judgment affirmed.

(208 Ill. 508)

RUDDELL v. WREN et al.

(Supreme Court of Illinois. April 20, 1904.)

WILLS—CONSTRUCTION—DEVISEES—CLASS—PERSONS INCLUDED—CONTINGENT REMAINDERS—PARTITION.

1. A will devising real estate to testator's daughter for life and to her children surviving her, if any, otherwise to testator's brothers and sisters, and, in case any of them shall be dead at the time of the death of the daughter, then the share of such deceased brother or sister should go to and be equally divided among his or her children, constituted a devise in remainder only to such brothers and sisters of the testator as survived him, and hence the daughter of a brother who predeceased testator took no interest in the property.

2. Testator devised real estate to his daughter for life, remainder to her children, if any survived her, otherwise to testator's brothers and sisters, and, in case any one or more or all of them should be dead at the time of his death, then the share of such deceased brother or sister should go to and be equally divided among his or her children, share and share alike. At the time of suit brought for partition, testator's daughter, though married, was 50 years of age, and had never had any children. *Held*, that the remainder to testator's brothers and sisters was a contingent and not a vested remainder, and hence no partition could be had during the daughter's life.

Appeal from Circuit Court, Adams County; Albert Ahers, Judge.

Suit by James T. Ruddell against Benjamin Wren and others. From a judgment dismissing the bill, complainant appeals. Affirmed.

This is a bill, filed in the circuit court of Adams county by James T. Ruddell, in his own right, against the appellees, for the partition of some 250 acres of land in that county. A demurrer was filed to the bill, and sustained, and a decree was entered dismissing the bill for want of equity. The present appeal is prosecuted from such decree of dismissal. The allegations of the bill are substantially as follows:

One Nicholas Wren died testate on September 28, 1901, seised in fee of the land here in controversy, and leaving, as his only child and heir at law, his daughter, Elnora Alice Alkire. By the terms of the will the appellant, James T. Ruddell, was appointed executor. Nicholas Wren had no other child or children than the said Elnora Alice Alkire, nor descendants of any deceased child or children. The will was admitted to probate in the county court of Adams county on November 19, 1901, and appellant qualified as such executor, and has been since, and is still, acting as executor of said will.

After provision is made in the first clause for the payment of the funeral expenses and debts, the second and third clauses are as follows:

"Second—I give, devise and bequeath unto my beloved daughter, Elnora Alice Alkire, all the real and personal property that I may own wherever situated at the time of my death for and during her natural life, subject, however, to the condition and provision that she (my said daughter) shall never encumber said real estate or any part thereof by mortgage or any otherwise.

"Third—After the death of my said daughter, it is my will that, if she shall leave her surviving any child or children, that such child or children shall have, and I do hereby give, devise and bequeath to him, her or them in equal parts, if there be more than one child, all of my real estate and personal property; and in case my said daughter shall die without leaving any child or children, then and in that event I give, devise and bequeath in equal parts, share and share alike, all my real and personal estate to my brothers and sisters, and in case any one or more or all of them shall be dead at the time of the death of my said daughter, then the share of such deceased brother or sister shall go to and be equally divided among his or her children, share and share alike."

Elnora Alice Alkire, at the time of the filing of the bill, was past the age of 50 years. As is alleged in the bill, Nicholas Wren left him surviving three brothers and four sisters, namely, Benjamin Wren, Thomas Wren, Andrew J. Wren, Millie Lowe, Avarilla Wood, Jennie Burton, and Sarah Wible, and no others. There were two brothers and two sisters who died before the testator, Nicholas Wren, died, to wit, John Wren, Washington Wren, Lizzie Ballard, and Drusilla Smith. The two brothers and the two sisters, who predeceased the testator, Nicholas Wren, left children and grandchildren, all of whom are shown by an exhibit to the bill, and all of which children and grandchildren, as well as the brothers and sisters, are parties defendant to the bill. The interests alleged to be owned by them are set out in the bill. Elnora Alice Alkire, the life tenant mentioned in the will, has no child or children, never has had any, and probably never will have. All the shares set forth in the bill are alleged to be subject to the life estate of the appellee Elnora Alice Alkire. Among the children of John Wren, deceased, a brother of the testator, Nicholas Wren, who died before the testator, Nicholas Wren, is a daughter, named Euphemia E. Bramlet, alleged in the bill to be the owner of $^{6}/_{660}$ths of the premises in question. On April 1, 1902, said Euphemia E. Bramlet executed a quitclaim deed, as a widow, and as a daughter of John Wren, deceased—John Wren being a deceased brother of Nicholas Wren—conveying to Mrs. Robert S. Alkire (Elnora Alice Alkire) all her right, title, and interest in and to the lands described in the bill. On June 10, 1902, Elnora Alice Alkire and R. S. Alkire, her husband, executed a quitclaim deed conveying to the appellant, James T. Ruddell, all their interest in the land described in the bill, reserving, however, to the grantor Elnora Alice Alkire a life estate in and to the said real estate, thereby intending to convey the same interest theretofore received by deed from Euphemia E. Bramlet. By virtue of these deeds the appellant, complainant below, claims to be the owner of $^{6}/_{660}$ths of the premises in question, and alleges that he is a tenant in common with the brothers and sisters of the deceased testator, and with the children and grandchildren of those brothers and sisters of the deceased testator who died before the testator died, all subject, however, to the life estate of the said Elnora Alice Alkire.

Walter Bennett, for appellant. U. H. Keath and Vandeventer & Woods, for appellees.

MAGRUDER, J. (after stating the facts). All the interests of the parties to this proceeding claiming to be the owners as tenants in common of the premises sought to be partitioned, are admitted to be subject to the life estate of the testator's daughter, Elnora Alice Alkire. Undoubtedly, reversioners and remaindermen owning interests in fee in land subject to an unexpired life estate are entitled to partition. Scoville v. Hilliard, 48 Ill. 453; Drake v. Merkle, 153 Ill. 318, 38 N. E. 654. But we are of the opinion that the appellant here, complainant below, was not entitled to partition, and that his bill was properly dismissed by the chancellor, for the reasons hereinafter stated.

First. Section 1 of the partition act provides "that when land, tenements or hereditaments are held in * * * tenancy in common * * * any one or more of the persons interested therein may compel a partition thereof," etc. 3 Starr & C. Ann. St. 1896 (2d Ed.) p. 2912. The appellant was therefore required, in order to entitle himself to a partition of the premises, to show that he was the owner of an interest therein as tenant in common with the parties against whom the partition is sought. The appellant has no such interest in the land here in controversy. The daughter of the testator is given a life estate. After the expiration of the life estate her surviving children, if she leaves any, take the property; but, in case she dies without any children, then the property is given to the brothers and sisters of the testator, with the provision that, in case any one or more of such brothers and sisters shall be dead at the time of the death of his said daughter, then the share of such deceased brother or sister shall go to and be equally divided among his or her children, share and share alike. The exact language of the will is, "then and in that event I give, devise and bequeath in equal parts, share and share alike, all my real and personal estate to my brothers and sisters." The bill alleges that the testator, Nicholas Wren, left him surviving three brothers and four sisters, naming them, and the demurrer admits this allegation to be true. These three brothers and four sisters were all living at the death of the testator. It is these brothers and sisters, or their children, who are to take in case the life tenant shall die without issue. The will makes no provision for the children or grandchildren of the brothers and sisters of the testator who died before his death. "A will takes effect at the death of the testator." Scofield v. Olcott, 120 Ill. 362, 11 N. E. 351. The brothers and sisters referred to who were to take were the brothers and sisters who should be alive at the death of the testator. The only interest which the appellant, the complainant below, has in the land sought to be divided, is such interest as he obtained through the deed executed by Euphemia E. Bramlet, but Euphemia E. Bramlet was the daughter of John Wren, a brother of Nicholas Wren, the testator who died before the testator. Euphemia E. Bramlet, therefore, had no interest whatever to convey, nor can she, in any event or under any circumstances, take any interest in the property under the will of the testator. When a man makes a devise to his brothers and sisters surviving him at the time of his death, he does not include in such devise his nephews and nieces, or grandnephews and grandnieces, who are the children of brothers and sisters, who have died before the date of his own death.

Second. The remainder which was to go under the third clause of the will of Nicholas Wren to his brothers and sisters, or the children of any of them, after the death of his daughter without issue, cannot be regarded as otherwise than a contingent remainder. If it is a contingent remainder, and not a vested remainder, then there can be no partition made at this time of the premises in controversy.

The third clause of the will reads in part as follows: "After the death of my said daughter it is my will that, if she shall leave her surviving any child or children that such child or children shall have and I do hereby give, devise and bequeath to him, her or them in equal parts, if there be more than one child, all of my real estate and personal property; and in case my said daughter shall die without leaving any child or children, then and in that event I give, devise and bequeath in equal parts, share and share alike, all my real and personal estate to my brothers and sisters." If the portion thus quoted were all of the third clause, then the four sisters and three brothers of the testator, who were alive when he died, would have taken immediately upon his death a vested estate, subject to open up and let in the children of the life tenant, in case she should have children. In other words, the remainder to the brothers and sisters would have been a vested remainder. A vested remainder has been defined by this court as follows: "A vested remainder is an estate to take effect after another estate for years, life or in tail, which is so limited that, if that particular estate were to expire or end in any way at the present time, some certain person, who is in esse and answered the description of the remainderman during the continuance of the particular estate, would thereupon become entitled to the immediate possession, irrespective of the concurrence of any collateral contingency." Boatman v. Boatman, 198 Ill. 414, 65 N. E. 81. In the case of Boatman v. Boatman, supra, it was held that a devise of the residue of the testator's property to his eight children, share and share alike, except that the share of one son should be a life estate only, the remainder in fee to go to any child or children surviving him, or, if he left no child or children, then to his brothers and sisters, created a vested remainder in such brothers and sisters, regardless of the fact that children might thereafter be born to the life tenant, and the remainder be thereby divested. In case the third clause of the will of Nicholas Wren had contained nothing except the portion last above quoted, then the brothers and sisters of Nicholas Wren, living at the time of his death, would be the only persons in esse who could answer the description of remaindermen. The mere fact that children might afterwards be born to Elnora Alice Alkire, and might survive her, would not render the interest of the brothers and sisters of the testator living at the time of his death contingent. Such brothers and sisters at the death of the testator would have become seised of a vested remainder in the land in which the daughter had a life estate. The remainder would have been liable to be divested by the birth of a child to Elnora Alice Alkire, who should survive her. To the same effect, also, is the recent case of Chapin v. Nott, 203 Ill. 341, 67 N. E. 833. In the latter case it was held that a deed to the grantee and the heirs of her body, and, in the event of her death without issue, the land to revert to three named persons in being, passed a vested remainder to such persons, subject to defeasance by the birth of issue to the grantee, and, if any of such persons died before the grantee, her interest passed to her heirs.

But the third clause of the will here under consideration, in addition to the portion so last quoted and commented upon, ends as follows: "And in case any one or more or all of them shall be dead at the time of the death of my said daughter, then the share of such deceased brother or sister shall go to and be equally divided among his or her children, share and share alike." This language makes the remainder which was to go to the brothers and sisters, or, in case of the death of any of them, to the children of those dying, a contingent remainder. "A contingent remainder is one limited to take effect either to a dubious and uncertain person, or upon a dubious and uncertain event."

2 Blackstone's Com. 168; Haward v. Peavey, 128 Ill. 430, 21 N. E. 503, 15 Am. St. Rep. 120; Thompson v. Adams, 205 Ill. 552, 69 N. E. 1. The remainder which is devised to take effect upon the death of the life tenant, Elnora Alice Alkire, without leaving any child or children, is to dubious and uncertain persons. If the brothers and sisters of the testator who were alive when he died survive the life tenant, Elnora Alice Alkire, she leaving no child or children, they become entitled to the estate, but their title is conditional upon their being alive at the time of Elnora's decease. If either one of the brothers and sisters is dead at the time of the decease of the life tenant, his or her share is to go to his or her children. As it is uncertain whether either one or more of the brothers and sisters of the testator will die before the death of the life tenant, it is uncertain whether the shares of the brothers and sisters will belong to them or to such children of theirs as may be alive when the life tenant dies. So, also, the title of the child or children of any brother or sister who may be dead at the time of the death of the life tenant is conditional upon such child or children surviving the parent. The facts of this case thus bring it within the doctrine of the case of Thompson v. Adams, supra. In the latter case the will provided as follows: "Fourth—And upon the death of my said wife, Elizabeth Adams, while she remains my widow, then and in that event it is my will, and I hereby order and direct that my said estate, both real and personal, then remaining, be then equally divided between my said two daughters, Elizabeth Rebecca Adams and Emma Matilda Thompson, wife of said Charles Francis Thompson, or the survivor of them, their heirs and legal representatives, share and share alike. Fifth —In the event of the death of either one of my said daughters, leaving a child or children her surviving, during the lifetime of my said wife, Elizabeth Adams, then the entire distributive share so bequeathed to such deceased daughter hereunder shall at once, upon the death of my said wife, Elizabeth Adams, descend and pass to the surviving child or children of such deceased daughter forever, share and share alike;" and, in interpreting the fourth and fifth clauses of the will as thus quoted, it was there held that remainders which, in case of the death of the life tenant without remarrying, were to go to her daughters who survived her, and to grandchildren who survived their parents, but whose parents died before the grandparent, the widow, were contingent.

There is a manifest uncertainty as to the persons who will be ultimately entitled to the remainder of the estate of Nicholas Wren at the time of Mrs. Alkire's death, in case she die without child or children. The brothers and sisters of the testator are by the express terms of the will not to take the estate unless they survive Mrs. Alkire's death and she leaves no issue, and, if they do not survive her death, the children of such as are dead at that time take their parent's share as purchasers under the will, and not by descent from their parent. Bates v. Gillett, 132 Ill. 287, 24 N. E. 611. It follows that the remainder cannot be properly partitioned before the death of Mrs. Alkire, because any brother or sister of the testator who dies in her lifetime can take nothing in the remainder if she afterward die without issue, and the children of such brother or sister so dying will not take anything by descent, as the will expressly directs that the children of such deceased brother or sister shall in such case take the parent's share, not by descent from their father or mother, but from the testator directly, and as purchasers under the will. The uncertainty as to the individuals who shall thus take and enjoy the remainder at Mrs. Alkire's death, if she leave no child or children, distinguishes the case at bar from the case of Boatman v. Boatman, supra. The rights and interests of the parties interested cannot be declared in a decree for partition made before Mrs. Alkire's death. Suppose such decree should now be entered, and one of the brothers and sisters of the testator living at the time of his decease, should be dead at the time of Mrs. Alkire's death, the decree would not be binding upon the child or children of such deceased brother or sister. The third clause expressly provides that "then"—that is to say, at the death of Mrs. Alkire (Strain v. Sweeny, 163 Ill. 603, 45 N. E. 201)—the share of such deceased brother or sister shall go to and be equally divided among his or her children, "share and share alike;" and, this being so, such children, not being parties to this suit nor represented here, would not be bound by the decree for partition.

Even, therefore, if this partition proceeding were begun by one of the devisees under the will, who holds an interest as a tenant in common, it could not be maintained because the remainder to go to the brothers and sisters or their children is a contingent one, and the persons who are to take that remainder at the death without issue of Mrs. Alkire are uncertain, and cannot now be ascertained.

For these reasons, the decree of the circuit court dismissing the bill is affirmed. Decree affirmed.

(209 Ill. 25)

CHICAGO & A. RY. CO. v. BELL.

(Supreme Court of Illinois. April 20, 1904.)

INJURY TO EMPLOYÉ—NEGLIGENCE—PLEADING AND PROOF—DEMURRER—DUTY TO WARN —COST OF ABSTRACT.

1. Error in overruling a demurrer to the declaration is waived by subsequently pleading to the merits.

2. Under the charge of the declaration, in an action for injury to one engaged in a cinder pit in cleaning out cinders and ashes from engines, he being struck while coming out of the pit by

an engine coming onto the pit, that defendant did not provide proper notice or signals to warn plaintiff that an engine was about to be moved over the pit, there can be no recovery; the evidence showing that a method was adopted by defendant whereby the engine was to come to a stop, and then move over the pit, while some one stood at the side and showed where it should stop, and that on the occasion when plaintiff was injured this method was disregarded by his fellow servants.

3. There is no duty of an employer to inform an employé that engines will without notice be run onto a pit where ashes are taken out of the engines where the employer has provided a method for the approach of the engines to be made with proper signals and notice.

4. In case of an adult, capable of understanding and appreciating ordinary dangers, engaged in an ash pit in cleaning out ashes from engines which come onto it, there is no duty of the employer to warn him of the danger of coming out of the pit without looking to see if an engine is approaching.

5. The Supreme Court rules as to condensing the evidence in the abstract not being observed, costs of the abstract will not be taxed.

Appeal from Appellate Court, Third District.

Action by Thomas Bell against the Chicago & Alton Railway Company. From a judgment of the Appellate Court, affirming a judgment for plaintiff, defendant appeals. Reversed.

Henry C. Withers and Henry T. Rainey (Wm. Brown, of counsel), for appellant. D. J. Sullivan, for appellee.

CARTWRIGHT, J. The Appellate Court affirmed a judgment recovered by appellee in the circuit court of Greene county against appellant for damages on account of a personal injury sustained while in its employ. The defendant demurred to the declaration, and, its demurrer being overruled, it filed a plea of the general issue.

The first point made by counsel is that the demurrer should have been sustained, and that the court erred in overruling it. This alleged error is not contained in the assignment of errors upon the record, and could not be considered if it were an error; but, the defendant having pleaded to the merits after the demurrer was overruled, error cannot be assigned on the ruling. Barnes v. Brookman, 107 Ill. 317.

At the close of all the evidence produced at the trial, defendant moved the court to exclude the evidence and direct a verdict of not guilty. The motion raised the question whether there was any evidence which, with all proper inferences to be drawn therefrom, fairly and reasonably tended to support the cause of action alleged in the declaration. If there was, the court was right in overruling the motion; but, if there was not, the motion should have been sustained.

There were two counts in the declaration, in each of which it was alleged that the plaintiff was employed by the defendant in the capacity of a laborer to work in a certain cinder pit, and that he was wholly inexperienced in such work and unacquainted with the perils connected with it. In the first count it was further alleged that it became the duty of the defendant to inform the plaintiff of such dangers as were not obvious to the employment; that engines were run over the cinder pit without notice to the employés working therein; that the defendant failed to inform him of the dangers attending the employment, and that engines would be so driven over the pit without notice to him; and that he was struck by an engine driven over the pit without notice, and his left hand was run over, necessitating the amputation of three fingers. The second count alleged that it was the duty of the defendant to use reasonable diligence to see that the place where plaintiff was required to work was reasonably safe, and to use reasonable diligence to inform him of perils connected with his duties which were not known to him and not obvious to the employment. The negligence charged in that count was that the defendant caused one of its engines to be driven over the pit without providing proper notice or signals, or any means, by which plaintiff might know that the engine was about to be so driven over the pit.

The testimony of the plaintiff, and all the evidence in the case most favorable to him, tended to prove the following facts: Defendant had a roundhouse in the city of Roodhouse, where engines coming in from the road were cleaned and prepared to be sent out on another trip. Northeast of this roundhouse was a building equipped with machinery for coaling engines, and between the rails of the track over which the engines were driven to be coaled there was a cinder pit for cleaning out the cinders and ashes. The pit was variously estimated at from 80 to 100 feet in length, and it was of the full width between the rails and from 3½ to 4 feet deep. In the pit there were tubs, which ran upon tracks in the bottom of the pit, and into which the ashes and cinders from the engines were raked. When the tubs were full of cinders, they were dumped into a hole at one end of the pit, from which they were elevated by machinery into cars and removed. Plaintiff had been a farmer, and moved from the farm to Roodhouse, and went to work for the defendant. He worked for about 10 days oiling journals at the stockyards, and afterwards applied for work to the foreman at the roundhouse, who had charge of coaling and cleaning the engines, and he was employed to work in the cinder pit. He was inexperienced in that kind of work and knew nothing about it. He came to the cinder pit the next morning just before 7 o'clock, when the night force was still at work. A man was at work in the pit under an engine raking cinders into a tub, and plaintiff told him that he came to take his place, but that he knew nothing about the work. The man showed him how to rake out the cinders, and got out of the pit, and plaintiff took his place. The method of doing the work was to run an engine over the cinder pit, and to stop it at the right place over one of the tubs. One man would then get on the engine, and knock the fire and cinders out into the ash box of the engine, and he was called the "fire knocker." The other man would get under the engine in the pit, and rake the ashes into a tub. The men would then accompany the engine to the wood pile, and put on wood to start the fire, and the engine would then be coaled. John Shinnall was the fire knocker working with the plaintiff. When plaintiff first went to work, they finished cleaning the engine that was over the pit, and then went with it to the wood pile, and, after being coaled, it was taken back into the roundhouse. The engines came to the cinder pit from the north, and some time afterward two engines came on together. Shinnall opened the switch and let the engines upon the track, and then got on the front engine and rode down to the pit. The engine stopped, and Shinnall got out where he could see when the engine was directly over a tub, and signaled the engineer where to stop. This was called "spotting" an engine, and plaintiff was told to watch Shinnall spot the engine, as that would be part of his duties. When the first engine was properly placed over the pit, Shinnall got up in it and knocked the cinders and fire out, and plaintiff went into the pit and raked the ashes. That engine moved on, and the other engine was spotted in the same manner, and the fire and cinders were knocked out and raked as in the former case. The two engines then moved on to the wood pile, and Shinnall went with them, after directing plaintiff to dump the cinders into the hole and get the tubs ready for the next engine that might come in. Plaintiff pushed the tubs along on their track and dumped them. He then drew one of the tubs along in the pit toward the north, walking backward, or nearly so, with his hands on the tub, drawing it after him. Another engine was then approaching the cinder pit from the north, backing up, according to the usual custom, and moving very slowly, at about 3 miles an hour, or an ordinary walk. When plaintiff got to the place where he wished to leave the tub he was drawing he placed one hand upon the rail and the other on the tub, and commenced to raise himself out of the pit, when he was struck in the back by the tender of the engine. He did not look toward the north, and testified that there was no obstruction to his view, and that, when down in the pit, he could see an approaching engine for 800 feet if he looked. He testified that he did not give any attention to the question whether an engine might be approaching, because he supposed that they would look out for him, and not come on the pit until he was ready. His hand was caught between the wheel of the tender and the rail, and three fingers were cut off. He was not informed that engines would be run upon the pit without notice to him. One of the men was hanging on the steps of the engine, facing the gangway, and watching the track ahead of the engine. When plaintiff started to raise himself out of the pit, that man and Shinnall both saw him, and both cried out. The man operating the engine stopped it at once, and it did not move over 4 or 5 feet.

It is fundamental that a plaintiff must recover, if at all, upon the case stated in his declaration, and that he cannot allege specific negligence of one kind and recover upon proof of negligence of another character. Chicago, Burlington & Quincy Railroad Co. v. Bell, 112 Ill. 360; North Chicago Street Railway Co. v. Cotton, 140 Ill. 486, 29 N. E. 899; Chicago & Eastern Illinois Railroad Co. v. Driscoll, 176 Ill. 330, 52 N. E. 921. It is therefore necessary for the plaintiff to prove facts from which the law would raise a duty of the defendant to give him notice that its engines were run upon the cinder pit, for the purpose of cleaning them, without notice to him, as alleged in the first count, or that the defendant had failed to provide any proper notice or signals that engines were about to be driven over the pit, as alleged in the second count. There was absolutely no evidence tending to prove the charge in the second count that the defendant did not provide proper notice or signals to warn the plaintiff that an engine was about to be moved over the pit. On the contrary, the evidence on that question tended to prove that a perfectly safe and proper method had been adopted. Plaintiff testified that the engines which had come in that morning had stopped before they were moved over the pit, and that they then moved down slowly under the direction of Shinnall, who showed them where to stop, and that he expected, if another engine came in, it would do the same thing. Plaintiff's witness Shinnall testified that the custom was to give signals, and that the engine would just stop, and stand, and come over the pit in accordance with his signals. The method adopted by the defendant, which the evidence tended to prove, was for the engine to come up and stop, and then move over the tubs, while the fire knocker or cleaner stood at one side and spotted the engine, or showed precisely where it was to stop over the tub. There was no fault in the defendant in that respect, but the evidence tended to show that in this instance the method was disregarded. If so, it was disregarded by fellow servants of the plaintiff, for whose negligence the defendant was not liable. If the men in charge of the engine at the time of the accident were negligent, or failed to give proper and reasonable notice to the plaintiff, their negligence was that of servants in the same department with the plaintiff, engaged in the same line of employment, and directly co-operating with him in the work in hand. They were, therefore, fellow servants, and the relation did not depend upon the accident of acquaintance or the length of time they had worked together. World's Columbian Exposition v. Lehigh, 196 Ill. 612, 63 N. E. 1089. As to any such negligence, if any there was, the declaration did not state, nor the evidence tend to prove, any cause of action. It is true, if the injury resulted from the combined negligence of fellow servants and of the defendant, the plaintiff might still recover. Chicago & Northwestern Railway Co. v. Gillison, 173 Ill. 264, 50 N. E. 657, 64 Am. St. Rep. 117. But if it is a fact that the method of doing the work adopted by the defendant was a proper and safe one, and provided for proper signals and notice, the charge in the first count also failed, and there could be no duty of the defendant to inform the plaintiff that engines would be run over the pit without notice.

Ordinarily, one engaging in any employment assumes the ordinary risks and hazards of the business in the manenr in which it is conducted, and there is no duty of the master to warn and instruct him as to dangers which are patent to persons of ordinary intelligence. One who attempts to do work which exposes him to obvious and known dangers assumes the risk. Indianapolis, Bloomington & Western Railroad Co. v. Flanigan, 77 Ill. 365. When there are special risks, which are not obvious or patent, and of which the servant is not cognizant, it is the duty of the master to notify him of such risks. United States Rolling Stock Co. v. Wilder, 116 Ill. 100, 5 N. E. 92. If the servant is ignorant and inexperienced, it is a duty to warn him of dangers not obvious to one without experience; but there is no duty to notify or instruct him as to dangers which are open and apparent to every person. In this case the plaintiff was an adult, capable of understanding and appreciating ordinary dangers, so that the rule as to infants or those who are incompetent to fully understand and appreciate dangers cannot be invoked in his behalf. The work was performed in the daytime, there was no obstruction whatever to view, the track extended in a straight line as much as 300 feet from the cinder pit in the direction from which the engines came, and they were moved very slowly to and over the pit. Plaintiff could not have been ignorant of the fact that he would be injured by an engine running over the pit while trying to climb out as he did; and, as such a danger was perfectly open and obvious, it was not the duty of the defendant to instruct him that such a thing was dangerous. He was employed in the open cinder pit, and necessarily knew that engines would be run over it. If it could be said that there was any evidence tending to prove a habit or custom of running engines over the pit without notice, there can be no question that the danger arising therefrom was patent and obvious to any person of ordinary intelligence.

The evidence did not tend to prove the negligence charged in the declaration, and the motion to exclude it and direct a verdict should have been sustained.

In the abstract furnished by the appellant the rules of this court are violated by failure to condense the evidence in narrative form. Most of it is printed at length by questions and answers, where there was no objection or exception to any question or answer requiring it to be so printed. The clerk, in taxing the costs, will not include any cost of the abstract.

The judgments of the Appellate Court and the circuit court are reversed, and the cause is remanded to the circuit court.

Reversed and remanded.

(209 Ill. 112)

HARTFORD FIRE INS. CO. v. PETERSON.

(Supreme Court of Illinois. April 20, 1904.)

INSURANCE—POLICIES—CANCELLATION—LOSS—DIVISION—MORTGAGEE'S INTEREST—ACTIONS—PARTIES—INTERMEDIATE APPEAL—FINDINGS OF FACTS—JUDGMENTS—REVIEW.

1. Where a policy was issued to the owner of a building, who paid the premium, providing that the loss, if any, should be payable to a mortgagee for the owner's account, a suit on the policy was properly brought in the name of the owner for the use of the mortgagee.

2. Where an action on a policy was tried on a written stipulation as to the facts, which contained only the evidentiary facts, and the Appellate Court found the facts different from those found by the circuit court, it was the Appellate Court's duty to incorporate into its judgment the ultimate facts on which its judgment was based.

3. In an action on a policy, a finding by the Appellate Court that insured had not ratified the action of the agent of the mortgagee, to whom the policy was payable in case of loss, in surrendering the policy for cancellation, was a finding on a question of mixed law and fact which was conclusive on the Supreme Court.

4. After a policy sued on had been issued, providing that insurer should not be liable for a greater proportion of any loss than the amount insured by the policy should bear to the whole insurance, whether valid or not, or by solvent or insolvent insurers, and authorizing cancellation by the insurer on five days' notice, the insurer notified its agent to cancel the policy, and he obtained the same from the agent of a mortgagee to whom it was payable, in case of loss, for the mortgagor's account. Insurer's agent thereupon canceled the same without the mortgagor's knowledge, and issued another policy for the same amount in another company, which he delivered to the mortgagee. No premium was ever paid on the second policy, except the premium paid by the mortgagor to the agent for the first policy, no part of which was ever returned as required in case of cancellation, and after loss insured brought suit on both policies. *Held* that, though the attempted cancellation of the first policy was void, the insurer thereunder was only liable for one-half the loss, not exceeding the amount of the policy.

Appeal from Appellate Court, First District.

Action by Andrew Peterson, for the use of the Masonic Building, Loan & Savings Association, against the Hartford Fire Insurance Company. From a judgment in favor of defendant, reversed by the Appellate Court, defendant appeals. Reversed.

¶ 1. See Insurance, vol. 28, Cent. Dig. § 1564.

This was an action of assumpsit, commenced in the circuit court of Cook county by Andrew Peterson, for the use of the Masonic Building, Loan & Savings Association, against the Hartford Fire Insurance Company, to recover the amount of a policy for the sum of $1,700 issued by said insurance company to Peterson on March 24, 1893, upon a dwelling house belonging to Peterson, located upon premises situated in Hegewisch, Cook county, Ill., which was destroyed by fire on October 5, 1893, and upon which property said Masonic Building, Loan & Savings Association held a mortgage to secure the payment of Peterson's bond for the sum of $2,200, and which insurance, in case of loss, the policy provided should be payable for Peterson's account to the Masonic Building, Loan & Savings Association. The insurance was taken out by Peterson through William M. Martin, the agent of the appellant at Hegewisch, for which Peterson paid to Martin the premium thereon, which amounted to $18, and the policy was delivered by Martin, at the request of Peterson, to the building association. Martin failed to remit the premium to the insurance company, and on August 26, 1893, the insurance company instructed Martin to cancel the policy. He went to the office of the building association and informed its secretary, Colven B. Burt, that the insurance company had directed him to cancel the policy. Burt thereupon gave the policy to Martin, who returned it to the insurance company, and it was indorsed, "Canceled and charged back, August 26, 1893." Martin thereupon delivered to Burt the policy of the Firemen's Insurance Company of Chicago, of which he was also agent, for the sum of $1,700 upon said dwelling house, which was accepted by Burt in lieu of the policy of the Hartford Fire Insurance Company which he had surrendered to Martin. No premium other than the $18 which had been paid before that time by Peterson to Martin was ever paid upon either of said policies.

The policy of the Hartford Fire Insurance Company contained the following provision: "This policy shall be canceled at any time at the request of the insured, or by the company, by giving five days' notice of such cancellation. If this policy shall be canceled as hereinbefore provided, or become void or cease, the premium having been actually paid, the unearned portion shall be returned on surrender of this policy or last renewal, this company retaining the customary short rates, except that when this policy is canceled by this company by giving notice it shall retain only the pro rata premium."

Peterson had no notice that the policy of the Hartford Fire Insurance Company had been surrendered and canceled, or a new policy in the Firemen's Insurance Company issued in lieu thereof, until after the dwelling house had been destroyed by fire, and no part of the premium paid by Peterson to Martin was ever returned to him. On October 17, 1893, Peterson served upon W. H. Taylor, who was the manager of the loss department in Chicago of the Hartford Fire Insurance Company, the following notice:

"Please take notice that the dwelling situated on lot 68, block 22, of Calumet and Chicago Canal and Dock Company's addition to Hegewisch, was totally destroyed by fire October 5, 1893, at 11 P. M. Insured in your company as policy 958, issued by your agent, W. M. Martin, March 24, 1893. My notice would have been given you earlier, but that your agent, W. M. Martin, was notified and was present at the fire.

"Andrew Peterson."

At the time of the service of said notice, Taylor denied the Hartford Company was liable upon said policy, and, after some discussion with Peterson with reference to the matter, Taylor wrote the following statement upon the back of said notice, which was signed by Peterson:

"Chicago, October 17, 1893.

"Now comes Andrew Peterson and states that the within and foregoing statement is not correct, and was signed by him not knowing that he claimed insurance in the Hartford Insurance Company on his dwelling, and further states that he did not have any insurance on his dwelling in the Hartford but did have a policy on said dwelling in the Firemen's Insurance Company of Chicago.

"Andrew Peterson.

"Subscribed and sworn to before me this 17th day of October, A. D. 1893.

"[Seal.] W. H. Taylor, N. P."

Afterwards, Peterson made proof of loss to the Firemen's Insurance Company, and subsequently instituted this suit against the Hartford Fire Insurance Company, and also upon the same day brought suit against the Firemen's Insurance Company upon the policy issued by that company and delivered to the building association, which suit is still pending. The case against the Hartford Fire Insurance Company was tried before the court without a jury, upon a written stipulation of facts, and judgment was rendered in favor of the insurance company. Peterson prosecuted an appeal to the Appellate Court for the First District, where the judgment of the circuit court was reversed, and the cause was remanded to the circuit court with directions to render a judgment in favor of Peterson against the Hartford Fire Insurance Company for the sum of $1,700, with interest at 5 per cent. per annum from December 5, 1893. 87 Ill. App. 567. The case was brought to this court upon appeal by the insurance company, and the judgment of the Appellate Court, in so far as it directed the circuit court to enter a judgment against the insurance company for damages and interest, was reversed. 187 Ill. 395, 58 N. E. 1095. The case was redocketed in the circuit court, where, upon a retrial before the court without a jury, upon a stipulation in writing as to the facts, judgment was again rendered in favor of the insurance company, and Peterson prosecuted an appeal to the Appellate Court for the First District, where the judgment of the circuit court was reversed, and the Appellate Court rendered judgment in favor of Peterson, and against the insurance company, for $1,700, with interest thereon at the rate of 5 per cent. per annum from December 17, 1893, and an appeal has been prosecuted to this court by the insurance company.

The Appellate Court, when the case was there the last time, made the following finding of facts: "The court finds that the policy sued upon was a valid and binding contract at the time the loss by fire occurred upon the premises in said policy described, and that appellant has not released, surrendered, or canceled said policy, and did not authorize or ratify its surrender or cancellation."

Bates & Harding, for appellant. Daniel F. Flannery, for appellee.

HAND, C. J. (after stating the facts). It is first contended that the Masonic Building, Loan & Savings Association is the real party in interest herein, and that the suit should have been brought in its name, and not in the name of Peterson for its use. The policy was issued to Peterson, who was the owner of the property insured, and paid the premium. The policy provided in case of loss the insurance should be payable for his account, and he was interested in the collection of the policy, to the end that the amount thereof might be applied in satisfaction of his mortgage indebtedness to the building association, and we are of the opinion the suit was properly brought in his name for the use of the association. Illinois Fire Ins. Co. v. Stanton, 57 Ill. 354; St. Paul Fire & Marine Ins. Co. v. Johnson, 77 Ill. 598; Westchester Fire Ins. Co. v. Foster, 90 Ill. 121.

In the case of Queen Ins. Co. v. Dearborn Savings, Loan & Building Ass'n, 175 Ill. 115, 51 N. E. 717, relied upon by appellant, the right of the mortgagee to bring the suit in its name does not appear to have been challenged, and that case is therefore not an authority against the position that the suit was properly brought in the name of the insured for the benefit of the mortgagee. In Illinois Fire Ins. Co. v. Stanton, supra, it was said (page 356): "The interest only of the mortgagor was insured, but the policy contained a clause that in case of loss the money should be paid to McClellan, the mortgagee. The contract being with the mortgagor, the legal title vested in him, but it was for the benefit of the mortgagee. Hence the suit was properly brought in the name of Matthew Stanton, the assured, for the use of the beneficiary."

It is next contended that Peterson ratified the action of Burt in surrendering the policy of the Hartford Company for cancellation, and in accepting the policy of the Firemen's Company in lieu thereof, and that by reason of that fact no recovery can be had against the Hartford upon its policy. The case was tried upon a written stipulation as to the facts. The stipulation contained only the evidentiary facts, and, the Appellate Court having found the facts different from the circuit court, it was its duty to find and incorporate into its judgment the ultimate facts upon which it based its judgment (Purcell Co. v. Sage, 189 Ill. 79, 59 N. E. 541; National Linseed Oil Co. v. Heath & Milligan Co., 191 Ill. 75, 60 N. E. 834; Irwin v. Northwestern Life Ins. Co., 200 Ill. 577, 66 N. E. 386), and, that court having found that Peterson had not ratified the action of Burt in surrendering the Hartford policy for cancellation, and in accepting the Firemen's policy in lieu thereof, which finding, like that of waiver and other kindred questions, is a question of mixed law and fact, this court is bound by such finding. It is therefore conclusively established upon this record that Peterson did not ratify the action of Burt in surrendering the Hartford policy, and in accepting the Firemen's policy in lieu of that policy.

The policy of the Hartford Fire Insurance Company contained the following provision: "This company shall not be liable under this policy for a greater proportion of any loss on the described property * * * than the amount hereby insured shall bear to the whole insurance, whether valid or not, or by solvent or insolvent insurers, covering such property;" and it is contended that the Appellate Court erred in rendering judgment for the full amount of the policy issued by the Hartford Company against that company, and it is insisted that in no event should a judgment be rendered against said company for a greater sum than one-half the amount of the loss sustained by Peterson by reason of the destruction of said property by fire. We are of the opinion the contention is correct. At the time the property was destroyed there were two policies of insurance thereon—one issued by the Hartford Company for $1,700, and one by the Firemen's Company for $1,700—and the policy upon which this suit is brought provides in express terms that the Hartford Company shall not be liable for a greater proportion of any loss than the amount which its policy shall bear to the whole insurance on said property, whether valid or not, or by solvent or insolvent insurers. It appears that after the fire Peterson was notified of the issuance of the Firemen's policy, whereupon he made proof to that company of loss, and instituted a suit upon the policy. We think that, within the meaning of the clause in the Hartford policy providing for an apportionment of the loss in case of other insurance upon the property, the policy issued by the Firemen's Company should be treated as insurance upon the property, and that the loss should be apportioned in accordance with the terms of the Hartford policy.

It is, however, said by appellee that the question of the apportionment of the loss between the Hartford and Firemen's Companies was not raised in the Appellate Court, and that that question cannot be raised here for the first time. It is true, as a general proposition, that questions not raised in the Appellate Court will not be considered in this court, and it is conceded that question was not raised in that court. In the Appellate Court, however, the Hartford Company was appellee, and was attempting to sustain the judgment of the circuit court, which was in its favor, while in this court it is appellant, and is attacking the judgment of the Appellate Court, which was against it; and we are of the opinion, as the provision in the Hartford policy now relied upon to show that the insurance should be apportioned appeared upon the face of the record in that court, and should have been considered by that court in determining the amount of its judgment, the question may be raised in this court by appellant, although it is raised here for the first time.

The judgment of the Appellate Court will therefore be reversed, and the cause remanded to that court with directions to find the amount of the loss occasioned by the destruction by fire of the property insured, and to render a judgment against the Hartford Fire Insurance Company for an amount equal to one-half of said loss, with interest at 5 per cent. from the 17th day of December, 1893, but in no event should the said judgment exceed the sum of $1,700 and interest.

Reversed and remanded, with directions.

(209 Ill. 133)

DE WITT COUNTY et al. v. LEEPER et al.

(Supreme Court of Illinois. April 20, 1904.)

WILLS—SUIT TO CONTEST VALIDITY—NECESSARY PARTIES—DECREE—PARTIES BOUND.

1. A county having the legal title to land conveyed to it under 1 Starr & C. Ann. St. (2d Ed.) p. 550, c. 21, par. 1, for cemetery purposes, which cemetery is under the management of trustees authorized by Act July 1, 1887 (1 Starr & C. Ann. St. [2d Ed.] p. 554, c. 21, par. 22), has no financial interest in a will providing that a cash legacy shall be used to build a receiving vault in the cemetery, and for the improvement of the cemetery, but without designating by whom the money is to be expended, and hence is not a necessary party in a suit to contest the validity of the will.

2. A will provided that a legacy should be used for the erection of a vault in, and the improvement of, a cemetery, the legal title to which was in a county, but under the management of trustees. In a suit to contest the validity of the will, the cemetery trustees were made parties. *Held*, that the county, being, in effect, a party to the proceeding, through the cemetery trustees, was bound by the decree rendered therein.

Appeal from Circuit Court, Logan County; J. H. Moffett, Judge.

Suit by the county of De Witt and others against James M. Leeper and others. From a decree for defendants, complainants appeal. Affirmed.

Arthur F. Miller, State's Atty., for appellant county of De Witt. Baldwin & Stringer and Lemon & Lemon, for other appellants. Blinn & Harris, for appellees.

HAND, C. J. Martha E. Cornelius died in Logan county possessed of real and personal property of the value of $15,000 or more. A paper purporting to be her last will and testament was admitted to probate by the county court of that county, which, omitting the formal part, is as follows:

"First. I order and direct that my executor hereinafter named pay all my just debts and funeral expenses as soon after my decease as conveniently may be.

"Second. After the payment of such funeral expenses and debts I give, devise and bequeath all my real estate, consisting of 87½ acres to the east and near Atlanta, also my city residence, to be sold, and from the proceeds thereof I direct that a receiving vault made of marble and stone, and a vault for the remains of John L. Cornelius, my husband, and myself and Ed Leeper. Also that my bank stock in Farmers' National Bank, Pekin, Illinois, be sold, and the proceeds all be used for improvement of the Waynesville cemetery. From the sale of the farm $1,000 to go to James M. Leeper of Ottawa, Kansas, if living; if dead to be used in the improvement of Waynesville cemetery where all my relatives are buried, namely, my mother, sister and others.

"Lastly. I make, constitute and appoint J. P. Heironymus, without bond, of Atlanta, Illinois, to be the executor of this my last will and testament, hereby revoking all former wills by me made."

In March, 1900, James M. Leeper, her nephew, and a legatee named in the will, filed a bill in chancery in the circuit court of said county to contest the will on the ground of mental incapacity and undue influence. The other heirs of Mrs. Cornelius, the executor of her will, and the Waynesville Cemetery were made parties defendant. The heirs made default, but the executor and the trustees of the Waynesville Cemetery appeared by their respective solicitors and answered the bill. A replication was filed, issues were made up, and upon a trial the jury found against the will; and the court, after overruling the motion for a new trial made by the executor and the trustees of the Waynesville Cemetery, entered a decree upon the verdict setting the will and the probate thereof aside, which decree remains in full force, no appeal having been prosecuted or writ of error sued out to reverse the same. Subsequent to the disposition of the bill of Leeper to set aside the will by the entry of a final decree, the county of De Witt and William W. Dunham, William C. Whiteman, and I. J. Atchison, as trustees of the Waynesville Cemetery, filed an original bill in the circuit court of Logan county against the heirs of Martha E. Cornelius, deceased, and other persons who, it was alleged, had an interest in the subject-matter of the suit, for a construction of the said will, and to have the same carried into effect according to the terms thereof, notwithstanding the proceedings to contest the same commenced by Leeper, and the entry of the decree in that suit, on the ground that the title to the lands comprising the Waynesville Cemetery is vested in the county of De Witt, and the county of De Witt was not made a party defendant to said proceeding to contest the will; it being averred in the bill that, by reason of the failure to make the county of De Witt a party defendant to that proceeding, the decree entered therein as to it is wholly null and void, and the will, and the probate thereof, as to said county, remains and is in full force and effect. Defendants filed a plea setting up the proceedings in the chancery suit brought by Leeper to contest the will, in extenso, in bar of the present suit. The plea, upon argument, was held good; and the complainants having refused to reply thereto, and having elected to stand by their bill, the bill was dismissed for want of equity, and an appeal has been prosecuted to this court.

Is the decree entered in the suit to contest the will of Martha E. Cornelius, deceased, binding upon the county of De Witt? We think it is, for two reasons. If the will had been valid, the county of De Witt would have had no interest in the fund which the testatrix sought to set aside, with which to erect a public and private vault and to improve Waynesville Cemetery, and it was not, therefore, a necessary party to the suit to contest the validity of the will; and, if it be conceded that, had the will been valid, the county of De Witt would have had an interest in the fund set aside by the will to be used in constructing said vaults and to otherwise improve said cemetery, and it was therefore a necessary party to the proceeding to contest the will, it was, although not in name, in law and in fact a party to said proceeding, and bound by the decree entered in that case, and the question of the validity of said will is, as to it, res judicata, and cannot again be relitigated in this proceeding.

1. The act of 1851 (1 Starr & C. Ann. St. [2d Ed.] p. 550, c. 21, par. 1) entitled "An act to provide for the dedication of land for cemetery purposes" authorizes the conveyance in perpetuity of lands in limited quantities to the county in which the land is situated, for the use of any society, association, or neighborhood, as a burying ground or place for the interment of the dead; and the land now comprising the Waynesville Cemetery was conveyed to De Witt county by deed or devise under the provisions of said act, the effect of which was to place the legal title to said premises in the county of De Witt, to be held in trust for the use for which said land was dedicated by the donor; that is to say, for a burying ground or a place for the interment of the dead. By section 1 of an act of the Legislature entitled "An act to provide for the proper care and management of county cemetery grounds," in force July 1, 1887 (1 Starr & C. Ann. St. [2d Ed.] p. 554, c. 21, par. 22) it is provided that, where any grounds have heretofore been or may hereafter be conveyed to any county in this state for burial places, it shall be lawful for the board of supervisors, in counties under township organization, to appoint three trustees to take charge and control of such grounds. The trustees of the Waynesville Cemetery, who caused an answer to be filed in the chancery suit commenced by Leeper to contest the will, and the trustees of the Waynesville Cemetery, who appear in this suit, are the same persons, and were appointed by the board of supervisors of Logan county trustees of the Waynesville Cemetery, under the provisions of said section, in the year 1892, and have ever since their appointment been in possession and had control of said Waynesville Cemetery. Section 2 of said act provides that it shall be the duty of said trustees, so soon as may be after their appointment, to organize by appointing one of their number president, and another one of their number clerk; also to appoint a treasurer, who may or may not be one of their number, who, before entering upon the duties of his office, shall give bond, with security, in such sum as the judge of the county court may require, for the safe care and management of all the moneys which may come into his possession as such treasurer. Section 3 defines the duties of the treasurer. Section 4 provides said trustees may cause any such grounds to be surveyed into lots, streets, and alleys, of such size and shape as they think best for proper management thereof, and cause a plat of the survey to be made and recorded in the recorder's office of the proper county, and may also sell and make deeds of conveyance of any lots or parts of lots for family or individual use for burials, at such price and on such terms as they may think best, to create a fund to keep the grounds in good repair, and purchase, where necessary, additional grounds thereto, and any sale so made shall vest the purchaser or his legal representatives with the right to make any improvements on the part so purchased as he may desire, subject to any general rules or regulations of the trustees. Section 5 provides that, where any county board has heretofore appointed trustees to take charge of county cemetery grounds, the acts of such trustees shall be legalized, in so far as they are not inconsistent with the provisions of this act, and that the treasurer and trustees so appointed shall hereafter be subject to be governed by the provisions of said act. Section 6 provides the county board shall have power to remove from office any trustee appointed by it, and to fill all vacancies which may in any way occur. Section 7 provides the compensation of the trustees and treas-

urer shall be fixed by the county board. The effect of this act is to give the trustees appointed thereunder the management, supervision, and control of county cemetery grounds, except in so far as their conduct may be controlled by the right to remove them from office, which is vested in the county board.

It will be seen from an examination of the provisions of the will that Martha E. Cornelius did not intend to bequeath the fund arising from the sale of her farm, residence, and bank stock to the county of De Witt or the Waynesville Cemetery, but she provided her farm, residence, and bank stock should be converted into money, and after the payment of her debts, funeral expenses, and $1,000 to James M. Leeper, if living, the balance of the fund was to be used to build a receiving vault, a vault for the remains of her husband, herself, and Leeper, and for the improvement of the Waynesville Cemetery. Neither does the will specify by whom the money was to be expended. It being silent upon that subject, the presumption would be the testatrix intended the person named by her as executor should carry into execution the plans which she had evolved for improving and beautifying said cemetery, alone or in conjunction with the trustees, the legal custodians of the property upon which she sought to provide, by her will, her estate should be largely expended in making improvements. The county of De Witt has no beneficial interest in the cemetery. It holds only the naked legal title to the lands comprising the cemetery, and the management and control of the cemetery are vested in the trustees. The funds belonging to the cemetery are held by its treasurer, who is required to give bond for their safe-keeping. The purposes for which its funds shall be expended rest wholly within the discretion of the trustees, and if the fund derived from the sale of the farm, the residence, and the bank stock of Mrs. Cornelius had been paid by her executor to the treasurer of Waynesville Cemetery, the manner in which it should have been expended by the erection of a receiving and private vault and the improvement of the cemetery grounds would have rested solely with the trustees. The county took title to the real estate comprising the Waynesville Cemetery by virtue of the deed or will through which it derives title, but the property sought to be disposed of by this will was to be converted into cash and expended, either under the direction of the executor or the trustees of the cemetery, or both, in making the improvements specified in the will upon the cemetery grounds. There was therefore no attempt to bequeath the fund to the county, and it took no interest in the fund. The most that can be said is, the county holds the naked legal title to the land comprising the Waynesville Cemetery, upon which the testatrix sought to provide a receiving vault and private vault should be erected, and other improvements made, from a fund which was to be derived from a sale of her farm, residence, and bank stock. The expenditure of this fund in accordance with the terms of the will could in no way have benefited De Witt county. It held the legal title to the premises comprising the Waynesville Cemetery at the time the will was executed, and, were the will valid, it would continue to hold only the legal title after the improvements contemplated by the testatrix had been made. The value, however, of that legal title, would not be enhanced by the improvements. Its interest in the land would remain the same whether the will was held valid or invalid. The public were interested in having the improvements made. The interests of the public, however, were represented, not by the holder of the legal title, but by the trustees of the cemetery, who had ample power, in case they received the fund, to execute the will of the testatrix by making the improvements provided for in the will. This the county of De Witt would be powerless to do, except in so far as it was represented by the board of trustees of the Waynesville Cemetery. We conclude, therefore, that the county of De Witt had no financial interest in the probate of the will of Martha E. Cornelius, deceased, and was not a necessary party to the bill to contest the same for mental incapacity and undue influence.

Second. If, however, it be conceded that the county of De Witt had such an interest in having the will of Martha E. Cornelius, deceased, carried into effect, that it ought to have been made a party to the bill to contest her will, we think De Witt county, though not in name, was in law and in fact, a party to that proceeding, and should be held to be bound by the decree entered in that case. The county could act only through its agents, and for all purposes connected with the management and control of the Waynesville Cemetery the trustees of the cemetery were the representatives of the county. The Waynesville Cemetery was named as a party defendant in the bill to contest the will, the board of trustees appeared in that suit and filed an answer in its name, and, when defeated, could have caused the decree entered in that case to have been reviewed by appeal or writ of error (People v. McCormick, 201 Ill. 310, 66 N. E. 381), and, having failed to pursue that remedy, the right of De Witt county or the Waynesville Cemetery to have the estate of Martha E. Cornelius converted into cash and used in erecting vaults or otherwise improving said cemetery was foreclosed by that decree. In Hale v. Hale, 146 Ill. 227, 33 N. E. 858, 20 L. R. A. 247, on page 256, 146 Ill., page 867, 33 N. E., 20 L. R. A. 247, it is said: "It is unquestionably a general rule, subject, however, to certain well-recognized exceptions, that in proceedings in equity the interests of parties not before the court will not be bound by the decree. But among the exceptions is one growing out of convenience or necessity in the administration of justice, which has given rise to what is known as the 'doctrine of representation.' Thus, where it appears that a particular party, though not before the court in person, is so far represented by others that his interests receive actual and efficient protection, the decree may be held to be binding upon him." And in McCampbell v. Mason, 151 Ill. 500, 38 N. E. 672, on page 508, 151 Ill., page 674, 38 N. E., the court said: "It is doubtless the general rule that in proceedings in equity the interests of parties not before the court will not be affected by the decree. But this rule is subject to certain well-recognized exceptions. Thus, where a party is before the court by representation, and in such way that his interests must be deemed to have been as fully and effectually presented and protected as they would have been if he had been personally present, his rights will be concluded."

The interests of the inhabitants of the county of De Witt residing in the vicinity of the cemetery were fully represented in the case to contest the will by the trustees of the Waynesville Cemetery (Harmon v. Auditor of Public Accounts, 123 Ill. 122, 13 N. E. 161, 5 Am. St. Rep. 502), and we are of the opinion the county of De Witt is bound by the decree entered in that case, and that the chancellor ruled correctly in sustaining the plea and dismissing the bill.

The decree of the circuit court will therefore be affirmed. Decree affirmed.

(209 Ill. 302)

BEIDLER et al. v. KING.

(Supreme Court of Illinois. April 20, 1904.)

PARTY WALLS—CONTRACT FOR CONSTRUCTION—CONSTRUCTION OF CONTRACT—DESTRUCTION OF WALL—RELATIVE DUTIES OF PARTIES—NEGLIGENCE—FALLING OF WALL—DAMAGES—ACTIONS—INSTRUCTIONS.

1. A contract between adjoining owners for the construction of a party wall provided that defendant should build the wall, and that plaintiff should have the right to join to and use the wall along any part thereof on payment to defendant of half the full value of the part of the wall so used by plaintiff, and that, if it should become necessary to repair or rebuild any portion of the wall after plaintiff should have used or paid for a portion, then the cost of such repairing or rebuilding should be borne equally by the parties to the extent that they might be using the wall. *Held*, that the contract meant that each party should pay one-half of the cost of repairs to that portion of the wall which was being used by both, and defendant was burdened with the repairing of that portion of the wall which plaintiff had not used.

2. Defendant would not be deprived of his title to that portion of the wall which stood on the ground of plaintiff merely because the wall had become so weakened by a fire as to be no longer suitable for a party wall.

3. Where the owner of a burned building permits the walls thereof to remain standing, and they subsequently fall, he is liable to an adjoining owner for any damage occasioned by such fall.

4. In an action against the owner of a burned building for damages sustained by an adjoining owner because of the falling of a wall, the question whether defendant was negligent in not having the wall taken down sooner *held* one for the jury.

5. Where the owner of premises adjoining those on which stood a burned building called the attention of the owner of the building to the fact that the standing wall was liable to fall, she had a right to presume that the owner would perform his duty in respect thereto, and was not guilty of contributory negligence.

6. A contract between the owners of adjoining lands for the building of a party wall required defendant to build the wall, and provided that plaintiff might join to it at any time or any portion thereof by paying half the value of the portion of the wall used by her. The building of defendant which was joined to the wall was destroyed by fire, and the wall fell on plaintiff's building and demolished it; and in an action for damages the court instructed that, until plaintiff exercised her right to pay for and use some portion of the wall, defendant had exclusive control, and plaintiff had no interest in the wall. *Held* that, while the instruction might have been properly refused, it could not have misled the jury, and hence was no ground for reversal.

7. An instruction that if defendant's portion of the wall, as a result of his negligence, fell and pulled over a portion of the wall which plaintiff paid for and was using, which otherwise would not have fallen, she might recover, was not erroneous, on the theory that it ignored the fact that her part of the wall might have been weak, defective, and out of plumb; it appearing that the portion of her wall which came down was carried out of plumb prior to the fall by the progress of the wall above it, which had not been used by her.

8. A contract between adjoining owners for the building of a party wall required defendant to build the wall, and provided that plaintiff should be entitled to join to any portion of the wall on payment of one-half of the value of the portion used by her. Subsequently she joined to a portion of the wall, and thereafter a fire occurred in defendant's building, and the party wall fell on plaintiff's buildings and demolished them. *Held*, that plaintiff had no right to go on the portions of the wall not paid for by her for the purpose of preventing the wall from falling.

9. Where, in an action for damages because of the alleged negligence of defendant, the court instructed, on behalf of defendant, that there could be no recovery if plaintiff was guilty of contributory negligence, the fact that the instruction given by the court of its own motion, in which all the elements necessary to a recovery were stated, failed to state that plaintiff could not recover if she had been guilty of contributory negligence, was not reversible error.

Appeal from Appellate Court, First District.

Action by Emily A. King against David Beidler and others. From a judgment of the Appellate Court (108 Ill. App. 23), affirming a judgment in favor of plaintiff, defendants appeal. Affirmed.

On August 24, 1887, Emily A. King, being the owner of the east half of lot 8, in block 70, in the original town (now city) of Chicago, and Jacob Beidler, being the owner of the west half of said lot 8, entered into an agreement which, after reciting the desire of the parties that a party wall of sufficient thickness for a six-story brick building should be erected, the center line of which

¶ 3. See Adjoining Landowners, vol. 1, Cent. Dig. § 58.

should be located on the west line of the east 2½ feet of the west half of said lot, which 2½ feet the said Emily A. King agrees to purchase from the said Beidler for the sum of $1,000, proceeds as follows: "Now, therefore, this indenture witnesseth, and it is hereby mutually covenanted and agreed by and between the parties hereto, in consideration of the premises, that the said party of the first part [Jacob Beidler] may so build and erect a party wall, of such thickness and in accordance with plans already prepared by architect, and in accordance with the ordinances of the city of Chicago, to make and constitute the east wall of such building as he may decide to erect, so that the center line of such party wall shall and may be located on the west line of the east two and one-half (2½) feet of the west half of said lot eight (8). And this indenture witnesseth further, and the said party of the first part does hereby covenant and promise and agree, that the said party of the second part [Emily A. King], her heirs, administrators, and assigns, shall and may at all times hereafter have the full and free right and privilege of joining to and using the said party wall above mentioned, as well below and above the surface of the ground, and along the whole length or any part of the length thereof, any building which she or they, or any of them, may desire or have occasion to erect on the said lot so owned by the said party of the second part, and to sink the joists of such building or buildings into the said party wall to the depth not exceeding four (4) inches: provided always, nevertheless, and on the express condition, that the said party of the second part, her heirs, administrators, executors, or assigns, as aforesaid, before proceeding to join any building to the said party wall, or to any part thereof, and before making use thereof, or breaking or cutting into the same, shall pay unto the said party of the first part, his heirs or assigns, the full moiety or one-half part of the full value of the whole of said party wall if used, or of such portion thereof as shall be used as a party wall by said party of the second part, which value shall be the cost price at the time when such party wall is to be used by said party of the second part, as fixed, estimated, and determined by two competent, disinterested builders of said city of Chicago, one of whom shall be chosen by the party of the first part, or his heirs, executors, administrators, and assigns, and one of whom shall be chosen by the said party of the second part, or her heirs, executors, administrators, or assigns. * * * And the parties hereto further covenant and agree that, if it shall become necessary to repair or rebuild any portion of said party wall or walls before the said party of the second part shall use or pay for her portion of the same, the expense or cost of such repairing or rebuilding shall be borne by the said first party; and, further, if it shall become necessary to so repair or rebuild after the said party of the second part shall have used or paid for her portion of said wall, then and in that event the cost of such repairing or rebuilding shall be borne equally by the parties hereto; to the extent that they are each using said wall. It is further mutually covenanted and agreed by and between the parties hereto that this agreement shall be perpetual, and at all times be construed as a covenant running with the land."

On the same date Jacob Beidler deeded to Emily A. King the east 2½ feet of said lot 8, and thereafter erected a wall, in pursuance of said contract, 183 feet long and 94 feet high, which constituted the east wall of a double factory building, 90 feet wide by 180 feet long, and six stories high. Appellee erected a two-story and basement brick barn upon her lot, using a part of the party wall as the west wall of the barn. This barn was erected by first building a small portion, and then adding to it from time to time, up to 1895. As additions were made she acquired from Jacob Beidler such portions of the party wall as she needed, paying therefor in the manner provided by the contract. At the time of the fire hereinafter mentioned she had paid for and was using the party wall for a distance of 119 feet, measured south from the north end of the party wall, and 38 feet in height. After the erection of the Beidler building, Jacob Beidler died, leaving appellants as his only heirs. On October 17, 1899, at 12:40 a. m., the east half of the double building erected by Jacob Beidler was destroyed by fire. The east wall, or party wall, was left standing, but was badly damaged. On the same day that the fire occurred appellee sent a notice to appellants, informing them that the wall was in a dangerous condition and liable to fall on her property at any time, and notifying them to protect the same at once. On the following day the commissioner of buildings of the city of Chicago served a notice of like import upon appellants. On October 20, 1899, appellants contracted with one Benson to take down this wall, and about 4 o'clock in the afternoon of the latter date 3 men were started on this work. The force of men was subsequently increased on later days to 6 or 7, and then to 9 or 10, and finally to 12 or 15. On October 28, 1899, the wall fell to the east upon the building of appellee, entirely demolishing that building. The evidence tends to show that from the time of the fire this wall was bulged out, the greater projection being in the third story, from the bottom and about midway of the wall from north to south; that on the morning after the fire the top of the wall was but little, if any, out of alignment, and the bulge did not extend below the third story, but as time passed the wall inclined more and more to the east, until it fell; that there was a crack in the wall, commencing at the top of the north end of the wall and extending diagonally toward the south to the bottom of the wall at its south end. The evidence also tends to show that with a sufficient force of men the wall could have been taken down in four or five days, that the wall was not tied or braced in any manner after the fire, and that a larger number of men could have been worked at tearing it down than were employed at that work at any time. When it fell, only about a story and a half of the wall had been removed.

On January 24, 1901, appellee commenced an action on the case for the recovery of damages to her property occasioned by the falling of this wall, making the owners of the property defendants to the suit. A trial before a jury resulted in a verdict for $7,778.40 for appellee, upon which the court rendered judgment, after overruling a motion for a new trial. Appellants appealed to the Appellate Court for the First District, where the judgment of the circuit court was affirmed. This appeal is from the judgment of the Appellate Court. Appellants presented a peremptory instruction to the court, to be given to the jury, both at the close of the plaintiff's evidence, and again at the close of all the evidence. The court refused to give the instruction in each instance. Appellants complain of the action of the circuit court in giving instructions numbered 11, 12, 13, 14, 15, and 18 for the plaintiff, and in giving one instruction at its own instance. They also complain of the refusal to give the peremptory instructions requested by them, and of the refusal to give instructions numbered 6 and 7 offered by appellants.

William J. Lacey, for appellants. Arthur Humphrey (Thomas Bates, of counsel), for appellee.

SCOTT, J. (after stating the facts). The principal controversy in this case is determined by a construction of the party wall contract. Appellants' position is that, after appellee had paid for and used a portion of the party wall, she was then liable, under that contract, for a portion of the repairs to the entire wall, and that, it being her duty to assist in keeping the entire wall in repair, she cannot recover damages resulting from a failure to repair the party wall. The language of the contract in reference to repairs is as follows: "And the parties hereto further covenant and agree that, if it shall become necessary to repair or rebuild any portion of said party wall or walls before said party of the second part shall use or pay for her portion of the same, the expense or cost of such repairing or rebuilding shall be borne by the said first party; and, further, if it shall become necessary to so repair or rebuild after the said party of the second part shall have used or paid for her portion of said wall, then and in that event the cost of such repairing or rebuilding shall be borne equally by the parties hereto, to the extent that they are each using said wall." Under the above contract it is said that appellee was bound to pay her share of any repairs to any portion of said party wall in the proportion which the part of the wall that she had paid for bears to the entire wall; that is, if she was using the north one-half of the wall, or had paid one-half of the cost thereof, she would then have paid for and would have been the owner of the one-fourth part of the entire wall, and, if the south half of the wall needed repairs, she would be liable for one-fourth of the expense thereof, even though she owned no part of that half of the wall. The intention of the parties was that she should pay for this wall and use the same in such portions thereof as she might elect from time to time, and we think the contract simply means that she should be liable for repairs to that portion of the wall for the one-half of which she had paid. The language is, "the cost of which repairing or rebuilding shall be borne equally by the parties hereto, to the extent that they are each using said wall." This means that each shall pay one-half of the cost of the repairs to that portion of the wall which is being used by both; that throughout that extent of the wall which was used by each each should bear one-half of the expense of repairing or rebuilding. The preceding language plainly shows that Beidler was to pay all the necessary expenses of repairing or rebuilding that portion of the wall which appellee had not used, and to the cost of which she had contributed nothing.

In Mickel v. York, 175 Ill. 62, 51 N. E. 848, this court said (page 70, 175 Ill., and page 851, 51 N. E.): "The contract in this case expressly provides that plaintiff, before making any use of or joining any building to the wall, shall pay or secure to the defendant York the full moiety or one-half part of the value of the said party wall, or so much thereof as shall be joined thereto or used, which value shall be the cost price at the time when such wall is to be used. The contract expressly provides, further, that York shall build that wall. By the terms of that contract York retained the ownership of what he had placed upon the plaintiff's land until he should be paid for it, and he had a right to have it supported on the land of plaintiff under this contract. The wall having been built on the plaintiff's land under this agreement, which amounts to a license with an interest, is not thereby incorporated and lost in the land or lot, but remains a separate property, still belonging to the builder until he is paid therefor. York, therefore, was the owner of this wall, and was liable for any and all damage for failing to maintain it in a safe condition." In the case at bar appellants were the sole owners of the entire wall, except that part thereof which was being used by appellee, and the rights and liabilities of the parties were the same with respect to that portion of the wall of which appellants were the sole owners as they would have been with reference to the entire wall, had appellee neither purchased nor used any part thereof. The cases referred to by appellants, of the class of City of Peoria v. Simpson, 110 Ill. 294, 51 Am. Rep. 683, holding that, where the same duty rested upon two parties to make repairs, both may be said to be guilty of negligence if the repairs be not made, are not in point.

It is then urged that, as this contract does not expressly provide for rebuilding the "whole" of this wall, it cannot be rebuilt under this party wall contract, and that, upon its usefulness as a party wall being destroyed by the fire, it was as though the wall itself was absolutely and entirely destroyed, and appellee became the owner of that portion thereof which stood on her land, and that consequently the injury resulted from her failure to care for her own property. It is unnecessary here to determine whether the wall can be rebuilt under this contract as a party wall. The contract contains this language: "Provided always, nevertheless, and on the express condition, that the said party of the second part, her heirs, administrators, executors, or assigns, as aforesaid, before proceeding to join any building to the said party wall, or to any part thereof, and before making use thereof, or breaking or cutting into the same, shall pay unto the said party of the first part, his heirs or assigns, the full moiety or one-half part of the full value of the whole of said party wall, if used, or of such portion thereof as shall be used as a party wall by said party of the second part, which value shall be the cost price at the time when such party wall is to be used by said party of the second part." We think this language applicable to this wall so long as it stood, and that the owner of the wall would not be deprived of his title to that portion thereof which stood on the ground of appellee merely by the fact that the wall had become so weakened by the fire as to be no longer fit for the purpose for which it was originally built.

So construing this contract, we come now to a consideration of the error assigned upon the refusal of the court to instruct the jury to find for the defendants at the close of all the testimony. In support thereof it is said that there is no evidence of negligence on the part of the defendants, and that there is no testimony showing the exercise of due care by the plaintiff. The general rule is that where a fire has occurred in a building, destroying the inner portion of the building and leaving the walls, if the owner negligently permits the walls to remain standing, and they thereafter fall, the owner of the wall is liable to the adjacent owner for the resulting damage. 1 Wood on Law of Nuisances, § 225; Schwartz v. Gilmore, 45 Ill. 455, 92 Am. Dec. 227; Mickel v. York, supra. In this case the attention of appellants was called to the condition of this wall immediately after the fire, on the morning of October 17, 1899. They did not begin the work of taking down the wall until the evening of October 20, 1899, and then only with a force of 3 men, when a force greater in number than 15 could have been used in the work. The evidence is that the wall could have been taken down in from four to five days with a sufficient force of workmen; that is, with as many men as could have worked thereon. It also appears that, after the work of taking down the wall began, it was suspended one day under the direction of the fire department of the city of Chicago. It fell on the 28th. It is apparent that, if a force of men in proper numbers had been put to work on the wall at the earliest possible moment, it would have been entirely removed before the day on which it fell. The longer the wall stood, the greater was its inclination to the east. Had a stronger force been at work earlier, the upper portion of the wall would have been sooner removed, and the tendency of the wall to lean to the east would thereby have been lessened. Some evidence was offered tending to show the difficulty about securing men to work on this wall on account of the danger of its falling. This evidence does not show such an effort to secure the necessary men to take down this wall as the emergency required of men of ordinary prudence. A small force was kept continually at work, except on the day when they were interfered with by the fire department. We are not able to say from the evidence, as a matter of law, that, by the exercise of measures such as a reasonably prudent man would have used, men sufficient in number to take the wall down at the earliest possible moment could not have been obtained. The evidence tended to show negligence on the part of appellants.

It is then urged that, inasmuch as appellee took no steps herself to prevent the wall falling, beyond notifying appellants of its dangerous condition and demanding that they remove it, she was guilty of contributory negligence. Laying aside for the moment the question of her right to do anything with the wall, we think she was entitled to assume that the appellants, whose attention had been called to the condition of the wall, would perform their duty in respect thereto, and we cannot, therefore, hold as a matter of law that she was guilty of contributory negligence. The peremptory instruction was properly refused.

The eleventh instruction given on the part of appellee is an abstract proposition of law. By it the jury are informed that, until Emily A. King exercised her right to pay for and use some portion of the wall, Jacob Beidler and his heirs were the owners and had exclusive control thereof, and that she had no right, title, or interest in the said wall, or any part thereof. This instruction might better have been made to apply alone to that part of the wall to the cost of which she had not contributed and which she was not using. This instruction, however, is an accurate statement of the law, and, while it might properly have been refused, we do not think it could have misled the jury, and, unless it appears to the court that such instructions tend to mislead the jury, the judgment will not be reversed on account of the giving thereof. Healy v. People, 163 Ill. 372, 45 N. E. 230.

Appellee's eighteenth instruction was to the effect that if defendants' portion of the wall, as a result of their negligence, fell and pulled over a portion of the wall which plaintiff had paid for and was using, which portion last mentioned would not otherwise have fallen, she may recover the entire amount of damages sustained by her, resulting from the fall of the entire portion of the wall which fell upon her premises. It is said that this instruction ignores the fact that Mrs. King's part of the wall may have been weak, defective, and out of plumb, and may have contributed to the fall. We do not think it objectionable on this account, as it plainly appears from the evidence that the portion of her wall which came down in the catastrophe was carried to the east, prior to the fall, by the progress of the wall above it in that direction.

Instructions numbered 12, 13, and 14, and one given by the court of its own motion, are all criticised for the same reasons. No. 13 is in the following language: "The court instructs the jury that as a matter of law the plaintiff had no right to go on or touch the portion of said east wall of said building not paid for by her, for the purpose of preventing the same from falling, or for any other purpose." The first and second objections to these instructions are disposed of by what we have already said. The third is that appellee had the right to enter upon the premises, if necessary, and also upon any part of the wall, for the purpose of bracing the wall to prevent the same from falling upon her property. We are referred in this connection to the case of Field v. Leiter, 118 Ill. 17, 6 N. E. 877. That case deals with the right of entry for the purpose of reinforcing a party wall under the contract then before the court, and the contract there is held to give one party the right of entry upon the premises of the other for the purpose of strengthening the foundation of the wall. No such provision is found in the contract in the case at bar. The portion of the wall to which these four instructions applied was the sole property of appellants. The contract gave to appellee no right to use or deal with the wall, or any portion thereof, in any manner, until she should have paid one-half the cost thereof. These instructions were correct. Appellants rely upon the case of Insurance Co. v. Werlein, 42 La. Ann. 1046, 8 South. 435. That case, however, turns upon certain provisions contained in the Louisiana Code which are not found in our statute, and the case is, therefore, of no assistance in determining this question.

The objection urged to instruction No. 15 is that it advised the jury that Mrs. King was entitled to recover if the wall fell through the negligence of the defendants, and omitted the qualification that it must appear that she was in the exercise of due care. This question does not arise upon this instruction, which is to the effect that the fact that Emily A. King paid for and used a portion of the east wall does not bar a recovery for damages occasioned by the fall of another portion of that wall, resulting from negligence on the part of the defendants. This objection is also made to instruction No. 18, which we have heretofore considered in regard to a different complaint made to the action of the court in giving the same.

In the instruction given by the court of its own motion, in which all the elements which must be found by the jury to warrant a verdict in favor of the plaintiff are stated, they are told that, to warrant a recovery, they must "find that the plaintiff was without fault," and in an instruction given on the part of the defendants is this language: "And if the jury believe, from the evidence, that the plaintiff was guilty of negligence contributing to the injury, then the plaintiff cannot recover, and the jury should find for the defendants." It is a familiar rule that the instructions must be considered as a series. In considering the same objection which is now made, this court, in Wenona Coal Co. v. Holmquist, 152 Ill. 581, 38 N. E. 946, said (page 591, 152 Ill., page 949, 38 N. E.): "Third, error in the instructions given for the plaintiff is complained of. The first instruction is objected to upon the ground that it does not require the exercise of ordinary care by the plaintiff. This is true, if the instruction is considered by itself; but all the instructions, both those given for the plaintiff and those given for the defendant, must be considered together as one charge. Upon examining the instructions given for the defendant, we find that five of them distinctly and in express terms say to the jury that the plaintiff cannot recover unless he shows that at the time of the injury he was in the exercise of ordinary care. Plaintiff's first instruction, although unnecessarily announcing the now obsolete doctrine of comparative negligence, is not inconsistent with the five instructions of the defendant, which require the exercise of ordinary care as a condition to the right of recovery; and, when it is read in connection with such instruction, it could not have misled the jury. This view is sustained by the following decisions of this court: Willard v. Swansen, 126 Ill. 381, 18 N. E. 548; Chicago, Burlington & Quincy Railroad Co. v. Warner, 123 Ill. 38, 14 N. E. 206; Village of Mansfield v. Moore, 124 Ill. 133, 16 N. E. 246; Calumet Iron & Steel Co. v. Martin, 115 Ill. 358, 3 N. E. 456;

Chicago, Burlington & Quincy Railroad Co. v. Johnson, 103 Ill. 512; Chicago & Alton Railroad Co. v. Johnson, 116 Ill. 206, 4 N. E. 381." No instruction advised the jury that the plaintiff could recover if she was guilty of negligence herself. It is, therefore, not a case where the instructions are inconsistent with each other, so that the jury could not tell which instruction to follow; but it is a case where an element lacking in one instruction is supplied by another, and the exception is, therefore, not well taken.

Instructions numbered 6 and 7, asked by the defendant, were refused. Each would have advised the jury that, if the plaintiff had knowledge of the dangerous and unsafe condition of the wall, and could at a moderate expense have prevented its fall, it was her duty to have incurred this expense. What we have already said in discussing instruction No. 18 given on the part of the plaintiff disposes of the errors assigned upon the refusal of these instructions 6 and 7.

The judgment of the Appellate Court will be affirmed.

Judgment affirmed.

(208 Ill. 562)

SWEDISH-AMERICAN TELEPHONE CO. et al. v. FIDELITY & CASUALTY CO. OF NEW YORK.

(Supreme Court of Illinois. April 20, 1904.)

INDEMNITY INSURANCE—PREMIUMS—EXAMINATION OF BOOKS OF ASSURED—RIGHT TO ORDER FOR EXAMINATION — VALIDITY—CONTEMPT OF COURT—APPEAL.

1. An order authorizing a party to an action to examine certain books belonging to and in the possession of the adverse party, issued under Hurd's Rev. St. 1901, c. 51, § 9, giving the court power to compel the production of the books of the adverse party, does not authorize any unreasonable search or seizure of the adverse party's books in violation of Const. U. S. Amend. 4, and Const. Ill. art. 2, § 6, guarantying the right to be secure against unreasonable searches and seizures.

2. An assured, in an indemnity policy stipulating that the insurer shall have the right to examine the books of the assured so far as they relate to the compensation paid to its employés, is estopped from asserting that an order authorizing such examination, issued under Hurd's Rev. St. 1901, c. 51, § 9, authorizes unreasonable searches and seizures, in violation of Const. U. S. Amend. 4, and Const. Ill. art. 2, § 6.

3. An indemnity policy provided that the premium should be based on the compensation paid by assured to its employés during the policy, and stipulated that the insurer should have the right to examine the books of the assured so far as they relate to the compensation paid by the assured to its employés. In an action by the insurer to recover premiums, the insurer averred that the assured had not fully paid the premiums and had denied the insurer the privilege of examining assured's books relating to the compensation paid to its employés, and that it had reason to believe that the books would show a larger pay roll than alleged by the assured. The attorney of the insurer averred that the insurer could not prepare for the hearing of the case unless permission was granted to examine the books of assured, and that affiant knew of no other source from which the evidence contained in the books could be procured. *Held*, that the insurer was entitled to an order for the examination of the assured's books, under Hurd's Rev. St. 1901, c. 51, § 9, giving the court power to compel the production of books containing pertinent evidence.

4. Where the court has jurisdiction of the parties and the subject-matter of the suit, and legal authority to make an order, a party refusing to obey it, however erroneously made, is liable for contempt.

5. A proceeding to punish for contempt of court for a violation of an order issued under Hurd's Rev. St. 1901, c. 51, § 9, giving the court power to compel the production of books containing pertinent evidence, is a civil remedy intended to enforce a private right of a party litigant, and the party in contempt can only be relieved by compliance with the order.

6. Hurd's Rev. St. 1901, c. 51, § 9, giving the courts in any action before them power to compel the production of books containing evidence pertinent to the issue on "good and sufficient cause shown and reasonable notice thereof given," does not limit the time when books are to be produced to the trial of the action, but empowers the courts to require the production of books in the cases specified, whether before trial for the purpose of preparing for the same, or at the trial to be used as evidence.

7. Where an assured in an indemnity policy agreed that the insurer should have the right to examine the assured's books at all reasonable times, an order compelling the assured to permit an examination of its books is not improper, because made before trial of an action by insurer for premiums, for the purpose of preparing for trial.

8. Hurd's Rev. St. 1901, c. 51, § 9, giving courts in any action pending before them power to compel the production of books containing evidence pertinent to the issue, obviates the necessity of proceeding by bill of discovery in order to secure an examination of the books of a party litigant by the adverse party.

9. An order adjudging a party litigant in contempt of court for a violation of an order entered for the benefit of the adverse party is directly appealable to the Supreme Court.

Appeal from Circuit Court, Cook County; E. F. Dunne, Judge.

Action by the Fidelity & Casualty Company of New York against the Swedish-American Telephone Company and another. From a judgment adjudging the telephone company and its officers and attorney guilty of contempt, they appeal. Affirmed.

This is an appeal from an order, entered by the circuit court of Cook county on January 9, 1904, in a certain suit in assumpsit, brought by the appellee against the appellant the Swedish-American Telephone Company, imposing a fine upon said telephone company of $25, and imposing a fine upon the appellant Fayette S. Munro of $1,050, for contempt of court in refusing to comply with an order for the production of the ledger and journal of the telephone company, and all sheets and memoranda, which were a part thereof, showing the entries or memoranda contained therein, "which pertain to money expended as compensation to employés of the said defendant for services rendered during the time covered by the policy of insurance issued by the plaintiff to said defendant, to wit, from the 7th day of June, A. D. 1901, to the 7th day of June,

¶ 4. See Contempt, vol. 10, Cent. Dig. § 63.

A. D. 1902, inclusive, within 10 days from this date, upon plaintiff giving to the defendant 24 hours' notice, said examination to take place at the office of defendant's attorney, room 734, 159 La Salle street, Chicago, Illinois," which said order was entered on the 27th day of November, 1903.

The suit in assumpsit was begun on January 6, 1903, by the appellee, the Fidelity & Casualty Company of New York, against the said telephone company, and the declaration, as originally filed therein, consisted of the common counts, to which a plea of the general issue was filed. Subsequently, an additional count was filed, setting forth a certain contract between said telephone company and said casualty company, which was in the nature of an indemnity, by which the casualty company agreed to indemnify the telephone company against all loss which might be suffered by the latter company by reason of personal injury suits or claims arising out of accidents to the employés of the telephone company. The consideration, stated in the contract of insurance or indemnity, was twofold: First, the sum of $84 as a premium; and, second, a promise by the telephone company to pay an additional premium, to be computed upon a percentage of its pay roll, to wit, a sum of money equal to $^{42}/_{100}$ of 1 per cent. of the total amount that the telephone company should expend during the period covered by the insurance contract for labor and services of its employés employed on its premises in Chicago. The amended or additional count averred that the payroll at the end of the year June 7, 1902, exceeded the sum of $20,000, etc. A copy of the original contract, called a "liability policy," is set out in the additional count, and the clause upon which the additional premium is based is as follows: "The premium is based on the compensation to employés to be expended by the assured during the period of this policy. If the compensation actually paid exceeds the sum stated in the schedule hereinafter given, the assured shall pay the additional premium earned; if less than the sum stated, the company will return to the assured the unearned premium pro rata. But the company shall first retain not less than $25, it being understood and agreed that this sum shall be the minimum earned premium under this policy." The policy contained a further clause, the first sentence of which is as follows: "The company shall have the right and opportunity at all reasonable times to examine the books of the assured, so far as they relate to the compensation paid to his [its] employés, and the assured shall, whenever requested, furnish the company with a written statement of the amount of such compensation during any part of the policy period, under oath if required."

On December 16, 1903, after it was made to appear to the court that all parties and persons had been duly notified that a rule would be asked for upon the telephone company, and upon its president and secretary and attorney, to appear before the court and show cause why they and each of them should not be attached and punished for contempt in refusing and neglecting to obey the order entered on November 27, 1903, and after it had been made to appear to the court by affidavits heard and filed that the telephone company, its president, secretary, and attorney, had each refused and neglected to obey said order of November 27, 1903, it was thereupon, on December 16, 1903, ordered by the court that the telephone company, its president, secretary, and attorney, should each appear before the court within three days from that date to show cause why they and each of them should not be attached and be punished for contempt. In the order, entered on January 9, 1904, imposing the fines as above stated, it was recited that the telephone company and Fayette S. Munro, its attorney, were guilty of contempt, in that each of them willfully refused and neglected to comply with the order of the court, entered on November 27, 1903, and failed to show cause why they should not be attached and punished for contempt of court, as ordered by the court to do, and which order they and each of them were duly notified of, and which order they and each of them had ample opportunity to comply with. The telephone company filed no affidavits denying the allegations contained in the affidavits filed by the casualty company. But the counsel of the telephone company objected to the entry of the order on November 27, 1903, for the alleged reasons that said order was not authorized by any statute of Illinois nor by the common law, but was contrary to the common law and the statutes, and to public policy, and to the Constitutions of the United States and of the state of Illinois. These objections were overruled by the court, to which action of the court the telephone company took exception. It was agreed that the objections to the order, together with the ruling thereon and exceptions, should be considered as having the same effect as if filed, made, and taken in writing in the form of a motion to vacate the order.

The affidavits filed by the appellee, after stating the terms and conditions of the policy as above set forth, stated that the telephone company had not fully paid to the casualty company the premium agreed to be paid as consideration for said insurance, and had not allowed the casualty company, its agents or representatives, or any of them, to examine its books of account, in so far as they related to compensation paid to the telephone company's employés during the period of the insurance contract, but on the contrary, had denied the casualty company the right to make such examination, and refused to permit it, or its agents, or any of them, to make such examination, although repeatedly requested to do so; that at reasonable times the agent and auditor of the casualty company presented himself at the regular place of business of the telephone company, where its books of account were kept, and requested to be permitted to make an inspection of said books, in so far as the same related to compensation paid to its employés during the period covered by the insurance contract, and such requests were refused and denied; that, upon request, such agent had examined a portion of the books of the telephone company, but had been refused permission to examine the ledger, journal, or cash book, and that he had reason to believe that said books would show a larger pay roll than the pay roll presented to him by the books which he had examined; that from his examination there was due on the policy the sum of $54.-72, and he had no other methods of obtaining the information concerning the books of the telephone company. The affidavit of the attorney for the casualty company stated, in addition to the above allegations, that, unless permission was granted to see the books, the casualty company would be unable to properly prepare its case for hearing, and that the evidence contained in said books was pertinent to the issue and necessary to the proof of the plaintiff's case; that said books and memoranda of accounts were wholly in the custody and control of the telephone company, and liable to be lost and destroyed; and that affiant knew of no other source from which the evidence contained in the books and memoranda aforesaid could be obtained.

Fayette S. Munro, for appellants. O. W. Dynes, for appellee.

MAGRUDER, J. (after stating the facts). The order punishing the appellants herein for contempt of court was made under and in pursuance of section 9 of chapter 51 of the Revised Statutes (Hurd's Rev. St. 1901), in regard to evidence, etc. Section 9 is as follows: "The several courts shall have power in any action pending before them upon motion, and good and sufficient cause shown, and reasonable notice thereof given, to require the parties, or either of them, to produce books or writings in their possession or power, which contain evidence pertinent to the issue." 2 Starr & C. Ann. St. (2d Ed.) p. 1842, c. 51, par. 9.

First. The first contention made by the appellants is that section 9 above quoted is unconstitutional, as being in contravention of the Constitutions of the United States and of the state of Illinois. The constitutional provisions which are claimed to be violated are those which protect "the right of the people to be secure in their persons, houses, papers and effects against unreasonable searches and seizures." Const. U. S. Amend. 4; Const. Ill. § 6, art. 2; 1 Starr & C. Ann. St. (2d Ed.) pp. 36, 108. It is also claimed that section 2 of article 2 of the Illinois Constitution, which provides that "no person shall be deprived of life, liberty or property without due process of law," is violated (1 Starr & C. Ann. St. [2d Ed.] p. 100); and that there is also a violation of the similar provision contained in section 1 of article 14 of the amendments to the federal Constitution (1 Starr & C. Ann. St. [2d Ed.] p. 38). It cannot be said that the enforcement of the order requiring the appellant telephone company to produce its books for inspection authorizes any unreasonable search or seizure of appellant's papers or books. This is so for two reasons: First, the books were left in the possession of the telephone company, and the permission given to the appellee was simply to look at certain portions of the books while they remained in the possession and custody of the appellant company at its attorney's office in Chicago: second, the contract which the appellant company made with the appellee prior to the entry of the order stipulated as follows: "The company [the appellee] shall have the right and opportunity at all reasonable times to examine the books of the assured [appellant], so far as they relate to the compensation paid to the employés." The appellant company thus stipulated in writing that the appellee might do what the order of the court authorized it to do. The appellant company by this stipulation waived the right to insist upon the protection afforded to it by the constitutional provision against unreasonable searches and seizures, even if there would have been a violation of such constitutional provision without the stipulation in question. The appellant company is therefore estopped from evading the obligations of its contract by insisting upon the protection thus insured to it by the Constitution.

It is to be noted that the amount of the premium to be paid to appellee by the terms of the insurance policy, so far as it exceeded a certain fixed amount, depended upon a percentage of the total amount which the telephone company should expend during the period covered by the insurance contract for the labor and services of its employés. Forty-two one-hundredths of 1 per cent. of such amount was the premium agreed to be paid by the appellant company to the appellee. It is manifest, therefore, that the amount of the premium could not be determined without knowing what sum had been expended during the period in question for the labor and services of its employés by the appellant company; and this sum could not be ascertained without an inspection of appellant's books. It was for this reason that the appellee was to have the right and opportunity at reasonable times to examine the books of the assured, so far as they related to the compensation paid to the employés. In Fidelity & Casualty Co. v. Seagrist, Jr., Co., 79 App. Div. 614, 80 N. Y. Supp. 277, where it appeared that the premium, payable under a policy of insurance insuring an employer against liability for injuries suffered by his employés and others during the term of the policy, was based upon an estimate of the compensation to be paid to the employés during the period of the policy, and the policy provided that, if the compensation actually paid should exceed the amount stated in the schedule attached to the policy, the employer should pay the additional premium earned, and that, if it was less than the amount stated in such schedule, the insurance company would return to the employer the unearned premium, and where the policy further provided, as does the policy in the case at bar, that the insurance company should have the right at all reasonable times to examine the books of the employer, so far as they related to the wages paid to the employés, it was held that the court had power, upon a petition of the insurance company, alleging that the employer had falsely misrepresented to it the amount of wages paid to its employés, to compel the employer to produce his books for inspection, showing the payments made to his employés, in order to enable the insurance company to frame its complaint in an action to be brought by it to recover additional premiums. It was also held in that case that, although the order there entered was too broad in permitting the plaintiff to inspect books not necessary to determine the question involved, yet that the order should be so modified as to require the defendant to produce and deposit with the clerk of the court the books of original entry, which showed the payment to its employés during the period covered by the policies of insurance, and which were in use during that period. The precise question here involved seems to have been decided, in the New York case above referred to, under a policy similar to the one here sued upon, and under a statutory provision similar in its terms to section 9, as above quoted.

Counsel for appellants seems to entertain the idea that the case of Lester v. People, 150 Ill. 408, 23 N. E. 387, 37 N. E. 1004, 41 Am. St. Rep. 375, is an authority for the contention here made that said section 9 is unconstitutional. We do not so understand the Lester Case. In that case it was held that an order for the production of a party's books on the trial, to be used as evidence in a proper case and upon a proper showing, was not an unreasonable seizure of such books, but that an order of court, by which they were taken from his custody and committed to that of a third person for an indefinite period of time, and for an inspection generally into all his affairs by the opposite party and his counsel, with leave to take copies of the entries therein, was unwarranted by the law, and was a palpable violation of the constitutional right of a party to be secure against unreasonable seizure of his papers and effects. But no such order was entered in the case at bar as the order which was condemned in the Lester Case. The order here is for the production of the books of the appellant company to be used as evidence in a proper case and upon a proper showing. The order granted permission to the appellee, its agent or attorney, to examine the ledger and journal of the telephone company, and all sheets and memoranda, which were a part thereof, showing the entries or memoranda contained therein, which pertained to money expended as compensation to employés of the said defendant for services rendered during the time covered by the policy of insurance. The examination was by the terms of the order limited to such entries or memoranda as pertained to money expended as compensation to employés. It did not authorize an examination of the appellant company's books, so far as those books related to other transactions than merely the amount of compensation paid to the employés. The order cannot, therefore, be regarded as amounting to an unreasonable seizure of the books. On the contrary, the nature of the order brings the present case within the terms of the decision made by this court in Pynchon v. Day, 118 Ill. 9, 7 N. E. 65, where the action was assumpsit, and where section 9 of chapter 51 was quoted and commented upon. In Pynchon v. Day, supra, the action was for the recovery of moneys placed in the defendant's hands by plaintiff as margins in the purchase and sale of stocks by the defendant, as agent of plaintiff, and the plaintiff made a motion, supported by affidavit, for an order compelling the defendant to submit his books of account during the time of the dealing between the parties to the plaintiff's inspection, and it was there said in relation to section 9 (page 14, 118 Ill., and page 66, 7 N. E.): "There was here full liberty given for the examination and inspection of all accounts pertaining to transactions between plaintiff and the defendants, the refusal only being to allow the examination, and inspection of the accounts which appellees kept with their other customers." And it was there also held that, although "the court will not compel a party to submit for inspection his books of accounts with other persons not parties to the suit, when it is not made to appear that they contain evidence pertinent to the issues, yet that the statute authorizes the court, upon cause shown and proper notice, to require either party to a suit to produce books or writings in his possession or power which contain evidence pertinent to the issue." In the case at bar, the order was such an order as was approved of in Pynchon v. Day, supra. Where books are to be produced, the defendant will have leave to seal up and conceal all such parts of them as, according to his affidavit previously made and filed, do not relate to the matters in issue. 3 Greenleaf on Evidence, § 301; Pynchon v. Day, supra. If the order requiring the production of the books limits the examination to such matters as are pertinent to the issue, there will be no infringement upon the constitutional privilege of protection against unreasonable search and seizure. In Rigdon v. Conley, 31 Ill. App. 630, it was said by one of the Appellate Courts of this state, speaking of section 9: "The power given by this section is in furtherance of justice, and is to be exercised in aid of parties litigant, whenever proper application is made to the court and it is shown that the books or writings contain evidence pertinent to the issue between the parties." In the case at bar, the affidavits, whose substance is set forth in the statement preceding this opinion, made a clear case for the production of such books as were necessary in order to show the amount of money expended as compensation to its employés by the appellant company during the time covered by the policy of insurance.

While it is true that a party cannot be guilty of contempt of court for disobeying an order which the court had no authority to make, yet if the court has jurisdiction of the parties and the subject-matter, and legal authority to make the order, the party cannot refuse to obey it, however improvidently or erroneously made. Leopold v. People, 140 Ill. 552, 30 N. E. 348. In the case at bar there can be no question as to the power and jurisdiction of the court to entertain the action in assumpsit, in which the order in question was here entered. Prosecutions for contempt may be instituted for the purpose of punishing a person for misconduct in the presence of the court, or with respect to its authority or dignity, and in such case they are criminal in their nature; but, when such a prosecution is instituted in order to afford relief between parties to a cause in chancery, it is civil, and is sometimes called remedial. People v. Diedrich, 141 Ill. 665, 30 N. E. 1038. The proceeding here is purely a civil remedy, intended to enforce the private right of one of the parties litigant, and is intended to compel the doing of an act necessary to the administration of justice in enforcing such private right. In the class of cases where the purpose is to advance the civil remedy of the other party to the suit, and where the penalty inflicted is intended to be coercive, the party in contempt can only be relieved by compliance with the order. Lester v. People, supra. In this state the circuit court has the right and power in a suit at law to punish for contempt persons who refuse to comply with its proper orders. Clark v. People, Breese, 340, 12 Am. Dec. 177; Stuart v. People, 3 Scam. 395; People v. Wilson, 64 Ill. 195, 16 Am. Rep. 528; Clark v. Burke, 163 Ill. 334, 45 N. E. 235; Dahnke v. People, 168 Ill. 102, 48 N. E. 137, 39 L. R. A. 197. For the reasons above stated, we are of the opinion that the order on the appellant company to produce its books in this case was not a violation of either the federal or state Constitution.

Second. The contention of the appellant company is that section 9 of chapter 51, as above quoted, does not confer upon the circuit court power to compel the production of documents prior to the trial of the case, but should be construed to apply only to the production of documents at the trial of the case. It is also contended by the appellant company that the proper method for a party litigant to obtain evidence pertinent to the issue and in the control of his adversary is by a bill of discovery, or a subpœna duces tecum. The language of section 9 does not limit the time when books or writings are to be produced to the trial of the cause. On the contrary, the several courts are given power to require the production of such books or writings "upon motion and good and sufficient cause shown," whether before the trial, for the purpose of preparing for the same, or at the trial, to be used as evidence. The contract of the parties here provides that the appellee shall have the right and opportunity to examine the books of the assured "at all reasonable times." We see no reason why an examination of the books at a time before the trial, in order to prepare for trial, is not as much an examination at a reasonable time as an examination of the books upon the trial itself. At common law, in an action ex contractu, where the instrument sued upon was in the possession of the defendant, and where the plaintiff was either an actual party or a party in interest, and was refused inspection of the instrument upon request, the court was authorized to grant a rule on the defendant to produce the documents, or give the plaintiff a copy, when the production was necessary to enable him to declare against the defendant. 1 Greenleaf on Evidence (15th Ed.) § 559. In the case at bar, from the very nature of the contract between the parties, the only method by which the amount due to the plaintiff below could be ascertained was by an examination of the defendant's books, and the parties, in view of this situation, have expressly agreed that the plaintiff should be entitled to such examination. Without that examination the appellee would not be able to set up in its declaration the amount of premium due to it, because such amount is dependent upon the amount paid as compensation to the employés of the telephone company. There may be expressions in the case of Lester v. People, supra, which limit the production of the books of the opposite party to the trial of the cause; but a careful examination of the language in that case will show that it was not intended to make such limitation, provided a proper showing was made that the books contained entries tending to prove the issues.

Nor do we think that it was necessary to file a bill of discovery in order to secure an examination of the books. In Lester v. People, supra, it was said in reference to section 9 above quoted, as follows (page 418, 150 Ill., page 388, 23 N. E., 41 Am. St. Rep. 375): "The evident purpose and design of this statute was to furnish to a party litigant a speedy and summary mode by which, under the order of the court, to obtain written evidence, pertinent to the issue, which might be in the possession and control of his adversary, and thus obviate the necessity of a bill of discovery, seeking the same end." In 3 Chitty's Practice, 432, 434, it is said: "Anciently, if a plaintiff had neglected to secure in his possession a part of a deed or agreement wanted in order to frame his declaration, he was obliged to file a bill in a court of equity for a discovery; * * * but now, to save the expense and delay of that proceeding, * * * a judge at chambers will make an order, or the court a rule, for the defendant to produce the document and give a copy to the plaintiff, at his expense, in order that he may declare thereon." In Greenleaf on Evidence, vol. 1, § 477, it is said: "The motion for a rule to inspect and take copies of books and writings, when an action is pending, may be made at any stage of the cause, and is founded on an affidavit, stating the circumstances under which the inspection is claimed and that an application therefor has been made to the proper quarter and refused." If such motion may be made at any stage of the cause, it can as well be made before the trial as at the trial. In Greenleaf on Evidence, vol. 1, § 559, it is said: "The production of private writings in which another person has an interest may be had either by a bill of discovery in proper cases, or in trials at law by a writ of subpœna duces tecum, directed to the person who has them in his possession. The courts of common law may also make an order for the inspection of writings in the possession of one party to a suit in favor of the other." "The object of a court of equity in compelling discovery being to enable itself or some other court to decide on matters in dispute between the parties, the right of discovery is limited by the purpose with reference to which alone it is conferred, and will not for that reason extend beyond the exigencies of the question or questions about to be tried." Kerr on the Law of Discovery, pp. 14, 15, 17. If a bill of discovery were filed, instead of the entry of such an order as is here under consideration, the right of such discovery would be limited to the exigencies of the question about to be tried. Here, the order is limited to the exigencies of the question about to be tried; that is, to the entries or memoranda, contained in the books, which pertain to the money expended as compensation to the employés of the appellant. As the same limitation to such entries in the books as are pertinent to the issue involved exists at chancery as in orders entered under section 9, there can be no necessity of the delay required by a bill of discovery in equity. Section 9 was intended in actions at law to be a substitute for the bill of discovery. The order provided for in that section may be made "in any action pending before them" (the courts). The words, "in any action pending before them," exclude the idea that the evidence sought to be obtained can only be acquired by a bill of discovery. "Any action" includes a suit at law as well as a bill in chancery. Where the affidavits filed state facts entitling one of the parties to an inspection of the books, it is no answer that such party could get the books by subpœna. Rigdon v. Conley, supra.

No complaint is made on the part of the appellants of the amounts imposed by the court below as fines upon the appellant company and its attorney, nor is any question made as to the right of appeal directly to this court. As this is a civil proceeding, such right of appeal is recognized in the following cases: Lester v. People, supra; People v. Diedrich, supra; Leopold v. People, supra.

In any view which we are able to take we are unable to reach any other conclusion than that there was no error in the action of the circuit court in entering the order here sought to be reviewed. Accordingly, the judgment of the circuit court of Cook county is affirmed.

Judgment affirmed.

(209 Ill. 344)

BELT RY. CO. OF CHICAGO v. CONFREY.

(Supreme Court of Illinois. April 20, 1904.)

MASTER AND SERVANT—INJURIES TO SERVANT—RAILROADS—COUPLING CARS—DEFECTIVE APPLIANCES — INSPECTION—NEGLIGENCE—CONTRIBUTORY NEGLIGENCE—ISSUES AND PROOF—EVIDENCE—QUESTIONS FOR JURY—INSTRUCTIONS.

1. Where, in an action for injuries to a switchman while attempting to couple a car, the declaration alleged that defendant negligently permitted the drawbar and the appliances and devices necessary to the making of a coupling to a car to be in a dangerous, defective, and unsafe condition, the declaration was sufficiently broad to authorize the introduction of evidence that the car was not provided with a "grab-iron" at the end thereof, and that the lack of such "grab-iron" contributed to the injury.

2. Where, in an action for injuries to a switchman while attempting to couple certain cars, one of the cars was alleged to be defective, in that the drawbar had a lateral play of from four to six inches, plaintiff was entitled to show the ordinary or average play of drawbars on other cars having the same make of car couplers.

3. In an action for injuries to a switchman alleged to have been caused by the excessive lateral play of a drawbar of a car he was engaged in coupling, evidence that there were no ferules on certain bolts which, had they been present, would have reduced the play of the drawbar, and that there were no retaining bolts in the coupler which, if present, would have had a similar effect, was properly admitted.

4. Where a statement of a witness out of court was introduced for the purpose of impeachment to show that it was contradictory to his testimony, it was not objectionable as hearsay.

5. In an action for injuries to a switchman by reason of a defective coupling on a car, while he was attempting to couple such car to another, evidence held to require submission to the jury of the questions whether defendant was guilty of negligence in failing to properly inspect the car before directing it to be moved, and whether plaintiff was guilty of contributory negligence in attempting to couple the car with knowledge that it had not been inspected.

6. In an action for injuries to a switchman by reason of a defective coupler, it appeared that

defendant had ample time to inspect the car and discover the defects, and there was no evidence that such switchman had "equal means" or "a like favorable opportunity" to ascertain the condition of the coupling and appliances before attempting to use them. Defendant requested a charge that, though the defects existed at the time ot the injury, plaintiff was not entitled to recover if defendant used reasonable care to have the car inspected before the accident, and if plaintiff knew of such defects, or if "he had equal means with the defendant of knowing or learning of the same." *Held*, that it was not error for the court to modify such instruction by striking the words quoted, and inserting in lieu thereof a requirement that such defects must have been so obvious that any switchman in the exercise of ordinary care would have observed them.

Appeal from Appellate Court, First District.

Action by William F. Confrey against the Belt Railway Company of Chicago. From a judgment in favor of plaintiff, affirmed by the Appellate Court, defendant appeals. Affirmed.

Edgar A. Bancroft, for appellant. James W. Duncan and C. Leroy Brown, for appellee.

BOGGS, J. The action below was case by the appellee to recover damages for personal injuries sustained by him by reason of the alleged negligence of the appellant company. Judgment was entered in favor of the appellee in the superior court of Cook county, and the same was affirmed by the Appellate Court for the First District. This is an appeal from such judgment of affirmance.

The appellant company operates a connecting line of railway engaged exclusively in transferring freight cars belonging to other railroads or transportation companies to and from certain railroads which enter the city of Chicago, and to and from certain industries in that city. The appellee was in its employ as a switchman, and on the 27th day of August, 1899, while attempting to couple a coal car to a box car, received the injuries for which the action was brought. The coal car had a "Janney," "Master Car Builder's," or "Tower" coupler. The box car had an old style link-and-pin drawbar and coupler.

The appellee was permitted, over the objection of the appellant company, to introduce proof showing that the box car was not provided with a "grab-iron" at the end of the car when the coupling was being made, and that the lack of such grab-iron contributed, in part, to his injury. It is complained that the declaration did not charge that the appellee's injuries resulted from or were contributed to by the lack of such grab-iron. The first and second amended counts of the declaration alleged that the appellant company "negligently and carelessly handled said car, upon which the drawbar and appliances and devices necessary and used for and in aid of coupling were in a dangerous, defective, and unsafe condition, and the said defendant carelessly and negligently permitted the said car, and the said drawbar, and said devices and appliances necessary and used for and in aid of coupling, to be and remain in an unsafe, dangerous, incomplete, and defective condition." The evidence showed that one of the purposes to be served by a grab-iron was to aid switchmen in coupling and uncoupling the cars. The averments of the declaration were therefore sufficiently comprehensive to warrant the admission of the testimony.

Appellee claimed that when the cars came together to be coupled the drawbar of the box car moved too far to the west of the Janney coupler, thus permitting the two cars to come together and crush and injure him. Evidence was produced by the appellee tending to show that the drawbar had a lateral play of from four to six inches, and, over the objection of the appellant, the appellee was permitted to prove the ordinary or average play of drawbars in that make of car couplers. We think the proof so objected to was proper. It tended to show a defective condition of the coupler. Other testimony objected to by the appellant company, in substance, that there were no ferules on certain bolts, which, had they been present, would have reduced the play of the drawbar, and still other evidence that there were no "retaining bolts" in the coupler, which, had they been present, would have restrained the play of the drawbar (also objected to), was properly admitted. It was the duty of the appellant company to inspect the cars which it transferred with reasonable care, in order to ascertain whether they were reasonably safe to be handled and coupled by its employés. The evidence tended to show that a reasonable examination of the coupling appliances on the box car would have disclosed that the drawbar had too much lateral play.

The complaint that the court admitted hearsay testimony is groundless. The statement referred to as hearsay was for the purpose of impeachment of the witness, whose statement out of court was proved as being contradictory to his testimony as a witness.

We have considered the complaint that the conduct and remarks of the trial judge interfered with a fair and impartial hearing of the cause. In the main, this objection relates to a colloquy between court and counsel, arising out of the persistent insistence of counsel for the appellant that the averments of negligence in the declaration were not broad enough to admit proof that no grab-irons were on the box car. The court was clearly right in the ruling made, and though it may be that while announcing the ruling, and in stating the reasons therefor, during which there were interruptions by counsel, the court indulged in expressions that might well have been omitted, we find no reason justifying the declaration that a fair and impartial hearing was at all affected by what occurred.

Counsel for the appellant presses with

great vigor the complaint that the court erred in refusing to peremptorily direct the jury to return a verdict for the defendant. The first ground of this motion, which was that the plaintiff relied for recovery largely upon the alleged want of a grab-iron on the box car, and that the declaration did not authorize any such ground of recovery, has been considered in passing upon the admissibility of the evidence, and determined adversely to the appellant.

The second ground urged in support of this alleged error of the court is that the evidence wholly failed to show that the plaintiff's injuries were due to any breach of duty which the appellant company owed to the switchman. It was the duty of the appellant company, as its counsel concedes, to cause the cars which its employés were expected to transfer on its tracks to be inspected with reasonable care, in order that its employés might not be subjected to the danger of injuries from defective or insufficient appliances for coupling the cars together. The declaration alleged the failure to perform this duty of inspection with reasonable care, and the evidence tended to show that the box car in question was not inspected at all. The inspector employed by the appellant company, and who appeared as a witness in its behalf, testified as to the proper mode and manner of inspection. He stated that the inspector should go around each car, examine the drawbars, the drawtimbers, the sills, the ends of the car, the trucks, the sides of the car, the side doors, and the brakes. The evidence further tended to show that a reasonably careful examination of the coupling appliances would have disclosed to the inspector that the drawbar of the box car was not in order—was too loose and had too much lateral play—and also would have disclosed that there was no grab-iron on the car. There was therefore evidence so far tending to support the charge of negligence as to make the determination of that issue a question of fact for the jury.

The third ground upon which the court was asked to peremptorily instruct the jury is that the injury to the plaintiff resulted from his own want of care. The evidence tended to show the plaintiff performed the work of coupling the cars in the ordinary and usual way in which prudent switchmen do such work. The evidence so tending to show this consisted not only of proof of the acts of the appellee, but also of the testimony of expert and experienced switchmen. It was the custom of the car inspector of the appellant company to place marks on each car inspected by him, and on the car in question there were no such marks. The appellee observed that the car did not bear such marks before or just as he stepped between the cars to make the coupling, and it is urged that it was contributory negligence on his part to attempt to couple a car which he knew had not been inspected. The appellee was acting under the general instructions or orders of the appellant company to couple the cars together. He knew, of course, either that the box car had not been inspected, or that the inspector had failed to place his mark upon it. Finding no mark there did not necessarily mean that the coupling appliances of the car were defective or dangerous. It meant no more, at the most, than that the car had not been inspected. Nevertheless, the coupling and its appliances might be entirely safe. There was no defect in the coupling that was open to view. There was no grab-iron, but he did not observe that such was the case until he saw that the drawbar of the box car had slipped past the "knuckle" of the Janney coupler of the coal car, at which time he sought to take hold of the grab-iron to save himself from injury, and thus learned that there was none on the car. The case is not one where the employé voluntarily encounters the hazards of a known danger. The law has no rule declaring, as a matter of law, what a prudent and careful workman should do in the situation in which the appellee was placed. That was for the jury to determine, under proper instructions from the court.

The sole complaint of the rulings of the court in instructing the jury is that certain of the instructions asked by the appellant company were modified by the court. The only modifications of any importance were of instructions in which the appellant company sought to have the court advise the jury that if the appellee had "equal means" with the appellant company, or "as favorable opportunity" as had the company, to know and learn of the alleged defective condition of the coupling, the law would not permit a recovery in the case. These instructions, as modified, directed the jury, in substance, that if the appellee, before he attempted to make the coupling, could, by the exercise of ordinary care, have observed or become advised of the condition of the drawbar and grab-iron, he could not recover. The duty of inspecting the cars rested upon the company. It had ample time to make the inspection, and every opportunity to discover the defects, both such as were obvious and such as could only be ascertained by strict or close inspection. The appellee had to act under the pressure of great haste, with no opportunity to observe other than the most obvious defects. There was no evidence tending to show the appellee and the appellant company had "equal means" or like "favorable opportunities" to ascertain the condition of the coupling and the appliances in aid thereof. There being no proof tending to establish that test of appellee's right of recovery, the court correctly declined to give the instructions as asked. As modified, the duty and obligation of the appellee and of the appellant company were correctly declared; as asked, the duty of inspection was erroneously cast equally upon the appellant company and the appellee.

The judgment must be and is affirmed. Judgment affirmed.

(178 N. Y. 263)

SIMONS v. SUPREME COUNCIL A. L. H.

(Court of Appeals of New York. April 26, 1904.)

ACCORD AND SATISFACTION—EVIDENCE—PROTEST.

1. Beneficiaries in a certificate of life insurance issued by a fraternal benefit society disagreed with it as to the amount due under the certificate, the society insisting that the amount named in the policy was reduced to a certain sum by an amendment of the by-laws passed after the issuance of the certificate, and refused to pay that sum until the beneficiaries signed a certificate acknowledging payment of the policy and surrendered it for cancellation. *Held*, that the acceptance by the beneficiaries of a draft for the amount tendered by the society, and the signing and delivery of the certificate required, were evidence of a settlement by the beneficiaries with full knowledge of all the facts, and sufficient to establish an accord and satisfaction.

2. Where the beneficiaries under a benefit certificate and the benefit association disagreed as to the amount to be paid under the certificate, and the association tendered to the beneficiaries the amount which the association claimed to be due, and the beneficiaries accepted the same and executed a certificate of surrender of the policy, which was signed by both of the beneficiaries, the fact that one of them wrote above his indorsement, "Receipt below given for $1,900 only," while the beneficiaries had claimed a larger amount, was not a protest affecting the legal effect of the surrender certificate.

Appeal from Supreme Court, Appellate Division, Second Department.

Action by John H. Simons against the Supreme Council American Legion of Honor. From a judgment of the Appellate Division (81 N. Y. Supp. 1014), affirming a judgment for plaintiff, defendant appeals. Reversed.

Henry A. Powell, for appellant. John T. Booth and George P. Breckenridge, for respondent.

PARKER, C. J. Defendant insists that it should have had judgment against plaintiff, on the ground that plaintiff's claim grows out of a situation which was included in an accord and satisfaction; that there was a dispute between plaintiff's assignors and defendant as to the amount due the former from the latter—an honest dispute—which resulted in the proposition by defendant to pay a given sum, and no more, in settlement of the matter, for which sum a draft was accepted. Now it is the settled law of this state that, if a debt or claim be disputed or contingent at the time of payment, the payment, when accepted, of a part of the whole debt, is a good satisfaction, and it matters not that there was no solid foundation for the dispute. The test in such cases is, was the dispute honest or fraudulent? If honest, it affords the basis for an accord between the parties, which the law favors, the execution of which is the satisfaction.

The father of the assignors of plaintiff obtained a benefit certificate, or policy of insurance, issued by defendant, whereby the latter agreed to pay to the beneficiaries, plaintiff's assignors, $5,000 upon proof of the death of insured. Insured died October 2, 1900. Had he died two days earlier, this controversy could not have arisen, as then, according to the policy and defendant's by-laws, the beneficiaries would have been entitled to $5,000 beyond dispute, and a payment of a less sum would not have prevented the beneficiaries or their assignors from maintaining an action to recover the balance. But defendant had amended its by-laws months before, so as to reduce the amount payable on all policies maturing after October 1, 1900; $5,000 policies being reduced to $2,000. Defendant's by-laws—made a part of the policy—authorized amendment. So, when insured died, this policy represented but $2,000, according to the by-laws. This court recently held that such an amendment is without power, and therefore ineffective. Weber v. Supreme Tent of K. of M., 172 N. Y. 490, 65 N. E. 258, 92 Am. St. Rep. 753. But that was not the position of the courts of this state prior to the amendment. Indeed, nearly seven years before the amendment, the General Term of the Fifth Department, in Hutchinson v. Supreme Tent of K. of M., 68 Hun, 355, 22 N. Y. Supp. 801, held that defendant had power to make an amendment substituting for a disability benefit an annuity of 10 per cent. thereof. Therefore defendant's amendment—in addition to being sustained by the authorities in some other jurisdictions—was supported by the only decision of importance in this state at that time bearing upon the subject.

It is not pretended that defendant's representative fraudulently represented to plaintiff's assignors that the policy had been reduced to $2,000. It had been so reduced by the formal action of defendant, and according to a decision in this state its action was legal. When, therefore, its representative insisted that the policy had been reduced to $2,000, he stated the contract as defendant understood it and believed it to be. And hence, when he said that, after deducting 5 per cent., as to which there is no controversy, there would remain but $1,900 due the beneficiaries, he stated defendant's belief accurately. The beneficiaries asked for the $5,000. They were disappointed at the reduction. Here, then, was the dispute. The beneficiaries could have refused to accept the $1,900, and brought suit for the entire amount. But the only decision of moment in this state upon the subject held that defendant's action was authorized and legal. The only other course open was to settle. The law wisely favors settlement, and where the parties are in a position to deal with one another at arm's length, as these parties were, the law will support their settlement. How is the settlement in this case evidenced? By the acceptance of the draft for $1,900 by the beneficiaries after they had been told by defendant's representatives that such sum would be paid only on condition that the beneficiaries sign the blank surrender form and give up the policy. About this there is no controversy whatever. The beneficiaries had the policy, upon which they could bring action for $5,000, and they surrendered it to get a draft for $1,900, when they were told that that was all that was due and all they could have, and that they should not receive that unless and until the surrender certificate was signed and delivered up with the policy. The beneficiaries accepted the terms when they signed the surrender certificate, delivered the policy, and accepted and used defendant's draft for $1,900. It is not disputed that this transaction took place.

The beneficiaries would have it now that one of them protested. But there is no protest in the papers. The surrender, which was indorsed upon the certificate of insurance, was signed by both beneficiaries, and reads: "Undersigned beneficiary, named in the within benefit certificate, acknowledges having received the amount herein agreed to be paid, and this certificate is hereby surrendered to the Supreme Council American Legion of Honor for cancellation." Now, above that indorsement one of the beneficiaries, Howard L. Keyser, wrote the following: "Receipt below given for $1,900 only. 2—27—'01." That statement represents the simple fact that they received under the certificate $1,900. And it does not affect the character and legal effect of the instrument any more than as if the certificate of surrender had stated that "Undersigned beneficiary, named in the within benefit certificate, hereby acknowledges having received $1,900, the amount herein agreed to be paid." It simply adds to the surrender certificate, which says the beneficiaries have received the amount agreed to be paid, what that amount was. There is very little evidence of protest in the testimony of the beneficiary Keyser. But, if it were far stronger, it could have no legal effect as against the written evidence of this settlement, consisting of the signed surrender of the policy and the draft payable to the beneficiaries, and not received until after the signing of the surrender and the delivering up of the policy, as testified to by the beneficiary Keyser. He said defendant's representative told him, before he would give him the draft: "The policy must be surrendered and this receipt signed. * * * He told me I had to give up the policy, and had to sign that blank form there, and that, if I failed to do so, I would not get the $1,900. After doing that, he delivered the draft to me, and that is all I ever received." This the beneficiaries followed by surrendering the policy for cancellation, which act, under the decision of this court in Larkin v. Hardenbrook, 90 N. Y. 333, 43 Am. Rep. 176, would deprive the beneficiaries of the right to maintain an action, although no consideration was paid, as it operates in law as a release and discharge of the maker's liability, in the absence of fraud or mistake.

That decision, standing alone, would, perhaps, require a reversal of this judgment. But it is not invoked for that purpose, as in my view an accord and satisfaction in law was established by plaintiff's proofs. That case is cited in order, primarily, that attention may be called to a portion of the reasoning of the court. Judge Miller said (all of his associates concurring) that "there certainly could not be higher evidence of an intention to discharge and cancel a debt than by a destruction and surrender of the instrument which created it to a party who is liable by virtue of the same." The surrender of the policy in this case, with the statement in writing that it was surrendered for cancellation, was evidence of an intention to discharge and cancel the policy. It was not only evidence of it, but evidence of such a vigorous character that, according to the opinion quoted, there could be no higher evidence of such an intention. This case, however, is stronger in favor of defendant than that. There, there was no evidence that plaintiff received anything. Here, plaintiff's assignors received $1,900, which they admitted they were told they would not receive unless they did surrender the policy for cancellation. There is no evidence of any kind in contradiction of this evidence of intention, so that no opportunity is presented for a submission of such a question to the jury. There was no question for the jury. No fraud is claimed. The controversy was honest. Neither witness nor circumstance questions it. And there was a settlement with full knowledge on the part of the beneficiaries of the situation, as well as with knowledge that, unless they surrendered the policy, they could not receive a cent. There is no question for the jury on that subject, for one of the beneficiaries testifies to it. With that knowledge they accepted the draft and surrendered the policy, saying over their signatures that they surrendered it for cancellation. If that written evidence could be disputed, it is not, and so there is no question for the jury on that subject; and hence by competent and undisputed evidence is made out every element of an accord and satisfaction.

An attempt is made by counsel for plaintiff to persuade us that this case is so nearly analogous to Komp v. Raymond, 175 N. Y. 102, 67 N. E. 113, as to prevent our disposition of the case by the application of well-established legal principles. As I understand the facts of that case, the decision is not applicable to this one; but the general principles laid down in that case are in harmony with those asserted here. In Komp's Case the parties differed as to the amount due and as to the meaning of their contract. Plaintiff finally accepted the amount defendant conceded to be due, and receipted for the same; but he offered to prove that he did so with the distinct understanding that, if he could bring proof to defendant that he was wrong, defendant would pay the balance, and at the same time he said: "If you do not pay me that balance I will take the thing to court, and we will leave it to a court and jury to settle." This evidence was rejected, and this court holds he had a right to prove it. But in the case under consideration no such act was proved, nor was any attempt made to prove it, or to prove any other fact tending to cut down the legal force and effect of the surrender in writing of the policy in consideration of the draft.

The judgment should be reversed, and a new trial granted, with costs to abide the event.

GRAY, O'BRIEN and HAIGHT, JJ., concur. MARTIN and CULLEN, JJ., concur in result on the ground that the question whether there was an accord and satisfaction was under the evidence a question for the jury and should have been submitted to them. BARTLETT, J., not voting.

Judgment reversed, etc.

(178 N. Y. 247)

PEOPLE v. KOEPPING.

(Court of Appeals of New York. April 26, 1904.)

MURDER—EVIDENCE—APPEAL—NEW TRIAL—REVIEW.

1. Evidence *held* to sustain conviction of murder in the first degree.

2. The Court of Appeals will not interfere with the discretion of the trial court in denying a motion for new trial because of the alleged misconduct of a juror.

Appeal from Supreme Court, Trial Term, Orange County.

Albert Koepping was convicted of murder in the first degree, and appeals. Affirmed.

Wilton Bennett, for appellant. A. V. N. Powelson, Dist. Atty. (A. H. F. Seeger, of counsel), for respondent.

GRAY, J. The defendant was indicted for the crime of murder in the first degree, upon the charge of having willfully and deliberately killed John G. Martine by shooting him with a revolver. Being put upon his trial, he was found guilty, as charged in the indictment, by the verdict of a jury, and judgment of death was passed upon him on June 17, 1903.

I perceive no valid reason for our interference with this judgment, either in the commission of some serious error upon the trial, or upon a consideration of the course of that trial with respect to its fairness and to a due regard to the defendant's legal rights. That the defendant killed the deceased he did not deny. His defense was that he had committed the act in self-defense. The wife of the deceased was present, and testified, and the conflict between her testimony and that given by the defendant was left to the jurors to decide upon the credence they might give to either in the light of the facts and circumstances which the evidence disclosed prior to and at the time of the homicide. The defendant, a young man 22 years of age, and German by birth, became a boarder in the house of the deceased, whose family consisted of a wife of 38 years of age and of four children between the ages of 18 and 4. The deceased was 40 years of age, and worked as a glove cutter in an establishment in the village of Port Jervis, where was also his family residence. The evidence tended to establish that he was more or less addicted to intemperate drinking, and when under the influence of liquor was apt to be quarrelsome. After having boarded a few weeks with the deceased, the defendant left, in consequence of some friction between them; but he soon was permitted to return, and to remain for several months. On February 18, 1903, the day before the homicide, the deceased ordered him to leave the house, and a quarrel arose over the amount of his indebtedness. According to his testimony—which received corroboration from that of another witness—the deceased then threatened him with a pocketknife in the course of the altercation, and a bystander took the knife away. The defendant left, and went to the house of one Weiser, at a late hour in the evening, and asked to be allowed to remain that night. Weiser and his wife testified to his having said that he was chased by the deceased out of the house; that he spoke abusively of the deceased, and threatened to "fix" him. The next morning he went back to the house of the deceased, occupied himself in various ways for some time, and while there the latter returned home. According to the wife of the deceased, he told the defendant to hurry out of the house, and the latter said that he would. After the deceased had procured some articles for which he had returned, he entered the dining room, removed some of defendant's clothes from a chair, sat down in it, and commenced to clean his finger nails with his pocketknife. The defendant complained of his throwing his clothes around. Going into the adjoining parlor for some household purpose, while there she heard the noise of the shooting. The deceased came into the hallway between the rooms, exclaimed "I am shot," and fell across the threshold of the parlor, dead. She had heard no other noise of any struggle, and the dining room showed no evidences of any disturbance.

According to the defendant, he was preparing to take his departure, when the deceased returned, and, upon going for his clothes, which the latter had thrown around, was attacked by him with a knife. He then was handed a revolver by the wife of the deceased, and was told to defend himself. He shot four times at the deceased to protect himself—the first time to frighten him—and afterwards went out and gave himself up to the authorities. The autopsy revealed three bullet wounds, one in the breast and two in

¶ 2. See Criminal Law, vol. 15, Cent. Dig. § 3071.

the back. The situation of the parties in the room was shown to have been such as to evidence that the first two shots were fired directly at the deceased, one of them passing over his head and lodging in the wall, and that the last two shots were fired at him as he was leaving, or escaping from, the room. The defendant had three exits from the room readily available to him. The pistol used belonged to the deceased, and, according to his wife's evidence, had been kept for some time in the drawer of a piece of furniture standing in the hallway near the defendant's bedroom on an upper floor. It appeared that he went upstairs after the deceased had returned home. The knife with which the defendant said that the deceased had threatened him, and which the wife said he had been using in cleaning his nails, was found in his open hand as he lay upon the floor. Upon the argument counsel described it as a jackknife, and it was referred to in the charge as a pocketknife.

The case, as it was submitted to the jurors, was one clearly for their determination. What conflict of testimony there was in the narration of events between the defendant and the wife of the deceased was for the jury to consider and to decide. There was evidence tending to affect the credibility of the latter's statements, as there was to affect the former's. The charge of the trial judge was perfectly fair, and no objection was taken to it.

The defendant's counsel argues that the verdict was not warranted, because of the absence of any evidence to show a motive for the commission of the crime charged, or to show premeditation and deliberation on the part of the defendant. It would be quite immaterial if no motive had been shown, in view of the admission and the proof of the killing of the deceased; but the evidence did furnish ground for the inference of a motive in the defendant's desire to revenge himself for the treatment he had received. Premeditation was evidenced in the threats testified to have been made by the defendant against the deceased on the previous evening, and both premeditation and deliberation were inferable from the evidence relating to his conduct on the morning of the homicide. He then returned to the house of the deceased, between 9 and 10 o'clock, and remained until about 11 o'clock, when the deceased also returned. Although knowing, as he says, that the deceased was in a quarreling mood, he did not leave the house. When the deceased arrived, the defendant was in the kitchen, and angry words passed between them there. He states that he then went upstairs and came down again, and the homicide almost immediately followed. The significance of the fact of his going upstairs, it may be observed, is in the opportunity afforded him of getting the pistol; which, as the wife of the deceased testified, was kept in a stand near his bedroom door. The only reason he gives for going upstairs when his clothes were in the dining room, and when he was, at the moment, dressing in the kitchen, was "to tie his tie." In my opinion, that was a frivolous and incredible explanation of a significant fact in the chain of evidence to show premeditation. Then he shoots at the deceased four times, and, evidently enough, the first shot was directly at his object, for there was but one breast wound, which, according to the physicians, was fatal. The other two shots struck him in the back; indicating, in view of the situation described, that the deceased was going from the defendant, and trying to leave the room. Thus the jurors had abundant justification for believing that the defendant committed the crime with deliberate intention. They could hardly, in my opinion, have come to any other conclusion rationally. There was time for the defendant to reflect upon what he would do, and to decide to accomplish his purpose, even if the jury believed his story that the wife handed him the revolver at the moment. However short the interval of time, the mind works with sufficient celerity for him to have been able to meditate a purpose to kill this man, instead of avoiding a conflict, as he might have done. He was the younger man, coming into a room where the older man was sitting in his chair. Behind and to the right of him were exits, readily available to leave the room or the house, and his theory of defense that the shooting was to protect his life is without any foundation in the surrounding circumstances. To justify the taking of life in self-defense, the person accused must show, not merely that he believed he was in imminent peril, but that the act was necessary in order to effect his escape. It was the defendant's duty to avoid the attack, and there is not the slightest ground for an inference that he had done all in his power to avoid the necessity of killing. People v. Kennedy, 159 N. Y. 346, 54 N. E. 51, 70 Am. St. Rep. 557. The question of deliberation and premeditation was one for the jury upon sufficient evidence, and we should not be warranted in disturbing their verdict.

After the conviction the defendant moved for a new trial upon the ground of the misconduct of one of the jurors. Affidavits were read to the effect that the juror had publicly discussed the case upon evenings during the trial, and that he had expressed an opinion of the defendant's guilt. The juror named denied wholly the allegations in the moving papers. His sworn statements were corroborated by those of others within whose observation he had been, and there were furnished to the trial judge affidavits which evidenced the juror's good standing and reputation in the community. The denial of the motion, therefore, upon the facts as disclosed, was within the exercise of the court's discretion. With that exercise of discretion this court will not interfere, as a general rule, and nothing in these facts would justify a departure from that rule.

I advise the affirmance of the judgment of conviction.

PARKER, C. J., and O'BRIEN, BARTLETT, MARTIN, and CULLEN, JJ., concur. HAIGHT, J., not voting.

Judgment of conviction affirmed.

(178 N. Y. 254)

PEOPLE v. BORGSTROM.

(Court of Appeals of New York. April 26, 1904.)

CRIMINAL LAW — CHALLENGE OF INDIVIDUAL GRAND JUROR—TRIAL JURY—CHALLENGE TO PANEL—WAIVER.

1. Under Code Cr. Proc. § 238, providing that there should be no challenge allowed to the panel or the array of the grand jury, but the court may discharge the panel and order another for certain causes, and section 237, providing that the district attorney may challenge an individual grand juror, the person held to answer for a crime may challenge an individual grand juror; and the fact that he is confined in jail, awaiting the action of the grand jury, does not prevent him from exercising that right, and a motion therefor to dismiss an indictment on the ground that, by reason of imprisonment, accused had no opportunity to challenge individual grand jurors, is properly denied.

2. On a criminal trial, counsel for defendant challenged the panel of the trial jurors on the ground that they had not been selected as prescribed by law, but were chosen by a special jury law for the county, which was unconstitutional, as counsel offered to prove; and, on request so to do by the trial court, counsel had no evidence to produce, and examined each juror, and withdrew all challenges to each before being sworn. *Held*, that the challenge to the panel was properly overruled as waived.

Appeal from Supreme Court, Trial Term, Westchester County.

Oscar Borgstrom was convicted of murder in the first degree, and appeals. Affirmed.

David H. Hunt and David Verplanck, for appellant. J. Addison Young, Dist. Atty., for the People.

BARTLETT, J. The defendant took the life of his wife under circumstances of great atrocity, and his counsel seek by this appeal to reverse the judgment of conviction on questions of law only.

The record discloses that the defendant was unjustly jealous of his wife, frequently quarreled with her, and threatened on several occasions to kill her. His actions finally became so violent that the deceased swore out a warrant for his arrest, and placed it in the hands of an officer to serve. The evening of the murder, April 13th, was Monday, and the officer appeared the Saturday night previous to arrest the defendant on the warrant in his possession. When the arrest was about to be made, the deceased relented, for the reason, as stated by the officer, that "she said she didn't like to do it on account of its being Easter Eve, Saturday night, and tomorrow was Sunday, and she wanted to go to communion." No arrest was consequently made, and the following Monday evening, while his wife sat sewing at her work table, the defendant passed behind her, cutting her throat and nearly severing the head from the body.

Two legal questions are presented for consideration: (1) That the defendant was unlawfully deprived of his opportunity to challenge any one of the individual grand jurors who found the indictment against him, and that the grand jury was drawn under the special jury law for Westchester county, which is unconstitutional; and (2) that the trial jurors returned to serve at the term when the defendant was tried were not selected, drawn, and served in the manner and form prescribed by the Code of Civil Procedure, but were so selected under the special jury law for the county of Westchester, being chapter 401, p. 1016, of the Laws of 1892, as amended by chapter 269, p. 532, of the Laws of 1893.

We will first consider the claim that the defendant was deprived of his right to challenge the individual grand jurors, and that the grand jury was improperly drawn under the special jury law for Westchester county. The indictment herein was filed the 24th of June, 1903, and the defendant was duly arraigned thereon the following day. At that time the defendant submitted an affidavit that he was destitute of means wherewith to employ counsel, and asked the court to assign the counsel who appeared for him on this appeal. His request was granted. The counsel so appointed moved to dismiss the indictment on the ground, substantially, that the defendant had been confined in jail continually from his original arrest, and was under such restraint at the time of the impaneling of the grand jury, and consequently was not afforded an opportunity to challenge any individual grand juror, which right was a substantial one, conferred upon him by section 237 of the Code of Criminal Procedure. The court denied the motion, and the defendant duly excepted. The counsel for the defendant thereupon filed a challenge in writing to the panel of grand jurors, and moved to set aside or quash the indictment on the ground that the special jury law for Westchester county was unconstitutional, as contravening article 3, § 18, of the Constitution of this state. The court thereupon overruled the challenge, and the defendant duly excepted.

The defendant was brought to trial on the 30th day of October, 1903. At the opening of the trial the counsel for the defendant called the attention of the court to the fact that at the time of the arraignment the defendant had interposed an objection to the effect that on the occasion of the impanelling and swearing of the grand jury he was confined in jail, and had no opportunity to exercise his right of challenge to any individual grand juror. Nothing appears to have been said at that time as to the challenge to the panel of grand jurors drawn under the special jury law for Westchester county. The district attorney suggested that it was an objection interposed usually in capital cases, and said: "I do not suppose you propose to argue it." The court said: "No; I have no knowledge on the subject, and overrule the objection." The counsel for the defendant then filed a challenge to the panel of trial jurors, which will be presently considered.

The motion made by defendant to dismiss the indictment on the grounds already stated is sufficiently answered by the fact that there is no provision of law permitting it. An indictment may be set aside on motion when it is not found, indorsed, and presented as prescribed in the Code of Criminal Procedure; also when a person has been improperly permitted to be present during the session of the grand jury while the charge embraced in the indictment was under consideration. Code Cr. Proc. § 313. The court can, undoubtedly, in addition to the grounds above stated, set aside an indictment where the constitutional rights of the defendant are invaded. People v. Glen, 173 N. Y. 395, 66 N. E. 112. No constitutional rights of the defendant are here involved, but they are clearly subject to legislative control.

Section 238 of the Code of Criminal Procedure provides as follows: "There is no challenge allowed to the panel or to the array of the grand jury, but the court may, in its discretion, at any time discharge the panel and order another to be summoned, for one or more of the following causes." The causes that follow are immaterial at this time. Section 237 of the Code of Criminal Procedure reads: "The district attorney in behalf of the people, and also a person held to answer a charge for crime, may challenge an individual grand juror." It is the obvious right of a defendant, under a criminal charge before indictment, to exercise the right here conferred upon him. The fact that he is under arrest and confined in the county jail, awaiting the action of the grand jury, is not necessarily an obstacle, as he could appear by counsel in court before the grand jury were sworn, and thus protect his rights. The fact that he was unable to employ counsel is not a legal excuse for having failed to avail himself of this statutory privilege. The court has no power to appoint counsel until arraignment, after indictment found. Code Cr. Proc. § 308. It is then its duty to ask the defendant if he desires counsel, and, if he does, the assignment must be made. We have been cited to no case where it has been held that it is the duty of the court to advise every prisoner detained in jail, awaiting trial, that an opportunity will be afforded him, before the grand jury is sworn, to exercise his right of challenge to each individual grand juror. Certainly no such duty can be assumed in the absence of positive statutory provision. People v. Jewett, 3 Wend. 314, is a conclusive authority on this point. That case presents a state of facts as strongly in favor of a defendant as could well be imagined. The defendant was indicted before he knew that a charge of crime had been made against him, and it appeared affirmatively that as to one of the grand jurors a good ground of challenge existed. Notwithstanding these very persuasive facts, the court held that the challenge to the grand juror came too late when made after he was sworn and impaneled. Chief Justice Savage, writing in that case, said: "There are causes of challenge to grand jurors, and these may be urged by those accused, whether in prison or out on recognizance; and it is even said that a person wholly disinterested may, as an amicus curiæ, suggest that a grand juror is disqualified. But such objection, to be availing, must be made previous to the jury being impaneled and sworn. It has been urged upon us that the defendant, not having been apprised of any intended proceeding against him, not having been arrested on a criminal charge or required to enter into a recognizance to appear at the court where the bill of indictment was found, had not the opportunity to make his challenge; that now is his earliest day in court; and that he ought, therefore, to be permitted to avail himself of this defense. Although the force of this appeal is felt, I cannot yield to it, and consent that, after an indictment found, the party charged may urge an objection of this kind in avoidance of the indictment. The books are silent on the subject of such exception after indictment found, and, in the absence of authority, I am inclined to say, in consideration of the inconvenience and delay which would unavoidably ensue in the administration of criminal justice, was a challenge to a grand juror permitted to be made after he was sworn and impaneled, that the objection comes too late." This rule has been followed in many of the states. State v. Hamlin, 47 Conn. 95, 106, 36 Am. Rep. 54; Commonwealth v. Smith, 9 Mass. 107; Maher v. State of Minnesota, 3 Minn. 444 (Gil. 329); and numerous other cases. The states which allow this objection after indictment found are those where the old plea in abatement exists. In the case at bar, unlike People v. Jewett, supra, the defendant did not allege that he was prejudiced by reason of the disqualification of any particular grand juror. There is no charge of prejudice, or other legal ground of objection.

We are of opinion, both upon principle and authority, that the motion to dismiss the indictment on the ground that the defendant had been unlawfully deprived of his right to challenge a grand juror was properly denied. Assuming that the objection to the panel of grand jurors is properly before the court, notwithstanding the provision of the Code of Criminal Procedure that there is no challenge allowed to the panel or to the array, it rests upon the same ground that is urged in the challenge to the panel of trial jurors, and may be considered in that connection.

At the trial, after it had been suggested that no opportunity had been afforded the defendant to challenge any individual grand juror, and the court had overruled the objection, as already stated, the defendant's counsel filed a challenge in writing to the panel of trial jurors and the additional panel ordered to complete the jury, on the ground of a material departure, to the prejudice of the defendant, from the forms prescribed by the Code of Civil Procedure in respect to the drawing and return of the jury, and specified certain facts as constituting the ground of challenge. Those facts, stated briefly, were that the jurors were not selected in manner and form provided by certain sections of the Code of Civil Procedure which were cited, but were selected under the law of 1892, as amended in 1893, as quoted above, and constitute the special jury law for the county of Westchester; that it was claimed by the defendant that this special jury law is unconstitutional, as contravening article 3, § 18, of the Constitution of this state, which provides that the Legislature shall not pass a private or local bill for selecting, drawing, summoning, or impaneling grand or petit jurors. The counsel for the defendant then offered to prove by the commissioner of jurors in and for the county of Westchester, and by the county clerk of said county, that said trial jurors were not selected, drawn, and served in the manner and form prescribed and provided by the Code of Civil Procedure, but were so selected in the manner provided by chapter 491, p. 1016, of the Laws of 1892, and the amendments thereof. The counsel further offered to prove by the clerk of the Senate of the state of New York, and by the journals of the Senate and Assembly of the state of New York, and of the Legislature of the state of New York, for the years 1892 and 1893, and by the original acts themselves, that chapter 491, p. 1016, of the Laws of 1892, and the amendment thereof by chapter 269, p. 532, of the Laws of 1893, were neither of them reported to the Legislature by any commission or commissioners appointed pursuant to law to revise the statutes. It was also asked on the part of the defendant that the court take judicial notice that no commission or commissioners to revise the statutes existed in the years 1892 and 1893 in the state of New York. After the said challenge and offers to prove were read, the following occurred, according to the record:

"The Court: Well, produce your evidence. Counsel for Defendant: We have none here. The Court: There being no proof on the subject, I overrule the objection. Defendant's Counsel: I except.

"The jury was thereupon called and sworn, each juror being examined separately by each side, and each side expressing satisfaction with each juror and withdrawing all challenge to him before being sworn."

It thus appears that the fullest opportunity was afforded the defendant to sustain his challenge to the panel of trial jurors, and he failed to avail himself of it. Counsel must be presumed to know that a challenge which, if sustained, would postpone the trial until a legal panel could be obtained, is in its nature preliminary, and must be heard and determined at the threshold of the proceeding. We are of the opinion that the defendant must be deemed to have waived his challenge, under the circumstances.

We have the additional fact that the jury was thereupon called and sworn; that each juror was examined separately by each of the counsel, and both sides expressed satisfaction with each juror and withdrew all challenge to him before being sworn. This constitutes a second and clear waiver of the challenge to the panel.

As before intimated, if the defendant had at the time of the trial any right to attack the special jury law for Westchester county under his attempted challenge to the panel of grand jurors, the opportunity was afforded him at the same time when the challenge to the panel of trial jurors should have been tried. The law presumes the constitutionality of every statute until the contrary is made to appear. We therefore express no opinion as to the constitutionality of the special jury law for Westchester county, as the question is not presented at this time.

The defendant was indicted by a grand jury and tried by a trial jury selected from the citizens of Westchester county under the forms of law, and the presumption is that he has been fairly dealt with and accorded all of his constitutional rights. The right of the defendant which is said to have been invaded at this trial is shadowy, and, aside from all technical argument, does not appeal to the judicial sense of justice. The trial having thus proceeded under the forms of law, it is urged that the defendant's rights have been disregarded, notwithstanding he has failed to show any ground of legitimate challenge to a grand or trial juror.

We are satisfied that the legal questions in this case were properly disposed of in the court below, and that the judgment of conviction should be affirmed.

PARKER, C. J., and O'BRIEN, HAIGHT, VANN, CULLEN, and WERNER, JJ., concur.

Judgment of conviction affirmed.

(178 N. Y. 236)

HAWKINS et al. v. MAPES-REEVE CONST. CO. et al.

(Court of Appeals of New York. April 8, 1904.)

MUNICIPAL IMPROVEMENTS—MECHANIC'S LIEN—SERVICE OF NOTICE—PARTIES—NONJOINDER—ASSIGNMENT OF CAUSE OF ACTION.

1. Laws 1897, p. 520, c. 418, § 12, relating to public improvements, directs that notice of lien shall be filed with the head of the department having charge of the construction of any municipal improvement, or with the financial officer of the municipality. A notice of mechanic's lien against an addition to Gouverneur Hospital in the city of New York, authorized to be erected by the commissioners of the sinking fund (Laws 1894, p. 1751, c. 703, amended Laws 1895, p. 746, c. 399), was filed with the comptroller, who was not only the chief financial officer of the city, but was also a commissioner of the sinking fund. *Held*, in the absence of statute or evidence that there was a regular official head to that body, it was a proper service.

2. A plea of nonjoinder of proper parties defendant is insufficient where it does not point out the precise defect, or show that complete determination of the matter could not be had without the presence of an additional party.

3. A contract to erect a hospital was assigned conditionally, the assignment to become absolute on certain contingencies, which did not eventuate until after the assignor had brought an action on the contract. *Held*, that he could, under Code Civ. Proc. § 756, relating to procedure in case of a transfer of interest, continue the action unless the court directed the transferee to be substituted, or to join as a party.

Appeal from Supreme Court, Appellate Division, First Department.

Action by Frank B. Hawkins and others against the Mapes-Reeve Construction Company and the American Bonding & Trust Company of Baltimore City. From a judgment of the Appellate Division (81 N. Y. Supp. 794) affirming a judgment for plaintiffs, defendant American Bonding & Trust Company appeals. Affirmed.

William F. Kimber and Charles De Hart Brower, for appellant. Leo Everett and Charles M. Hough, for respondents.

WERNER, J. The plaintiffs, as subcontractors under the Mapes-Reeve Construction Company, agreed to furnish all the materials and labor for the iron and steel work that was to go into an addition to Gouverneur Hospital, in the city of New York, at the price of $13,400. It is conceded that this subcontract was never fully performed by the plaintiffs, but they claim that it was unjustifiably terminated by the Mapes-Reeves Construction Company, while the latter contends that the plaintiffs abandoned the work without cause. The plaintiffs filed a notice of lien, which was later discharged upon the giving of an undertaking for that purpose by the defendant American Bonding & Trust Company.

At Special Term it was held upon conflicting evidence that the Mapes-Reeve Company was at fault in refusing to make payments to plaintiffs as they became due, and in neglecting to provide them with the detail drawings necessary to enable them to complete the work. This finding of fact was followed by the legal conclusion that the plaintiffs were entitled to judgment for the sum of $2,963.15, with interest and costs. The judgment entered upon this decision was affirmed at the Appellate Division by a divided court. Having ascertained from the record that there is some evidence to support the findings of fact made at Special Term, we have reached the limit of our power to investigate the facts. The question whether there is any evidence to support a finding of fact is one of law reviewable by this court. When there is such evidence, the question is no longer one of law, and the decision of the courts below upon the facts is final, even though it may be erroneous. Ostrom v. Greene, 161 N. Y. 353, 55 N. E. 919. There are other questions of law presented for our consideration, however, which we have jurisdiction to review, and these we will briefly discuss.

1. The American Bonding & Trust Company, which alone has appealed from the judgment below, contends that there should have been no recovery against it because plaintiffs' notice of lien was improperly filed. At Special Term it was held that the lien was properly filed. At the Appellate Division the contrary view was taken, but the judgment for the plaintiffs was upheld (a) under section 3412 of the Code of Civil Procedure, which provides, in substance, that if a lienor shall fail for any reason to establish a valid lien he may recover judgment in an action to enforce or foreclose a mechanic's lien against any party to the action for any sum that he might recover in an action on contract; and (b) that the bond given by the appellant surety company was broad enough to secure the payment of such a judgment. In determining whether plaintiffs' notice of lien was properly filed, two considerations are to be borne in mind. The first is that the statute (chapter 703, p. 1751, Laws 1894, amended chapter 399, p. 746, Laws 1895) authorizing the addition to Gouverneur Hospital, for which the plaintiffs' labor and materials were furnished, does not clearly designate any board, body, or official as having charge of the work, and it is therefore difficult, if not impossible, to decide with whom the notice of lien was to be filed. The second is that the lien law is to be construed liberally to secure the beneficial interests and purposes thereof, and that a substantial compliance with its terms shall be sufficient for the validity of a lien and to give jurisdiction to the courts to enforce the same. Section 22, c. 418, p. 525, Laws 1897. Under the statute providing for the erection of an addition to Gouverneur Hospital, the commissioners of the sinking fund were authorized and directed, when required by the board of estimate and apportionment, to set apart a portion of Gouverneur Slip, and to erect thereon an addition to Gouverneur Hos-

pital. The commissioners of the sinking fund were empowered to employ an architect and to make contracts, but the work was to be done under the supervision of the superintendent of public works of the city of New York. The latter was to certify to the commissioners of the sinking fund any contractor's delay or abandonment of work, and any willful violation of the contract, and in such case the said commissioners were required to give notice to the sureties of the defaulting contractor, to the end that the work should either be properly and expeditiously proceeded with by the contractor, or completed by the commissioner of public works, with the consent of the commissioners of the sinking fund, according to the contingencies specified in the statute. Section 204 of the charter of New York City (Laws 1897, p. 63, c. 378) designates as commissioners of the sinking fund the mayor, comptroller, chamberlain, president of the council, and chairman of the finance committee of the board of aldermen, but it does not specify how the board of commissioners of the sinking fund shall be organized, and the only provision of the charter that seems to be germane to the subject is section 1541, which, in the absence of any other specific charter provision, permits each municipal board to choose a president, treasurer, and chief clerk or secretary. Section 12 of the lien law (chapter 418, p. 520, Laws 1897), relating to public improvements, directs that notice of lien shall be filed with the head of the department or bureau having charge of the construction of any municipal improvement, and with the financial officer of the municipality.

Plaintiffs' lien was filed with the comptroller, who is concededly the chief financial officer of the city, and with the president of the department of charities. As the department of charities seems to have had nothing whatever to do with the construction of this public work, it is obvious that the filing of a notice of lien with the president of that body was a nullity. But the comptroller, in addition to being the chief financial officer of the city, was also a member of the board of commissioners of the sinking fund, and, in the absence of statutory or record evidence that there was a regular official head to that body, we think service upon the comptroller as a member thereof was service upon the board. It is to be observed that the statutes of 1894 and 1895, authorizing the construction of the public improvement upon which plaintiffs' work was done, when read in connection with the section (12) of the lien law which specifies the method of serving a notice of lien upon a municipality, show that it is by no means clear just how a notice of lien is to be served in a case like the one at bar. Under these circumstances, and in view of the liberal construction of the lien law provided for in section 22 thereof, we think it must be held that the plaintiffs' notice of lien was properly filed, and to that extent we feel constrained to disagree with the learned Appellate Division. In this view of the case it is unnecessary to determine whether the court below properly invoked section 3412 of the Code of Civil Procedure in support of plaintiffs' judgment, or whether the bond of the appellant would be broad enough to secure the payment of the judgment herein if the lien were held to be invalid.

2. The appellant, in its supplemental answer to the complaint, pleaded a nonjoinder of proper parties defendant, and it now urges that the city of New York was a necessary party defendant. It is true that under subdivision 3 of section 3402 of the Code of Civil Procedure the city of New York, as owner of the property against which the lien was filed, was a necessary party defendant, but it does not follow that the omission to make it a party is fatal to the judgment. The answer does not point out the precise defect of parties, as seems to be required by sections 488, 490, and 498 of the Code of Civil Procedure, and it does not appear to have been brought to the attention of the court during the progress of the trial. Neither was it shown that the city of New York had any such interest in the trial that without its presence as a party a complete determination of the controversy could not be had, as was the case in Steinbach v. Prudential Ins. Co., 172 N. Y. 472, 65 N. E. 281, and under these circumstances we think the court below properly held that the appellant's plea of nonjoinder of parties was ineffectual.

3. The appellant makes the further objection that the plaintiffs are not the real parties in interest. This objection is pleaded in its answer, and is predicated upon the fact that prior to the filing of their lien the plaintiffs assigned their contract to the Phœnix Iron Company as collateral security for materials to be furnished by the latter to be used on the building against which the lien was subsequently filed. A contemporaneous agreement made between the plaintiffs and the Phœnix Iron Company shows that the assignment was to become absolute only upon the happening of certain contingencies which did not eventuate until after the commencement of this action, when the plaintiffs executed a further transfer to the same assignee of the cause of action set forth in the complaint. This brings the case within the purview of section 756 of the Code of Civil Procedure, which provides that, "in case of a transfer of interest or devolution of liability (pendente lite) the action may be continued by or against the original party," unless the court directs the transferee, etc., to be substituted or joined as a party.

The judgment should be affirmed, with costs.

PARKER, C. J., and GRAY, O'BRIEN, HAIGHT, MARTIN, and CULLEN, JJ., concur.

Judgment affirmed.

(178 N. Y. 242)

MADIGAN v. OCEANIC STEAM NAV. CO., Limited, et al.

(Court of Appeals of New York. April 26, 1904.)

INJURY TO EMPLOYÉ—FELLOW SERVANTS.

1. A stevedore working in the hold of a vessel until dark was injured by neglect of the foreman to light the lamps which the employer had provided, and which it was the duty of the foreman to light. *Held*, that the employer was not liable, such act not being within the personal duty of the employer, but within the line of a mere servant's duty, and a detail of the work in which the foreman and the employés were fellow servants.

Appeal from Supreme Court, Appellate Division, First Department.

Action by Mary Madigan, as administratrix of Patrick Madigan, deceased, against the Oceanic Steam Navigation Company, Limited, and another. From a judgment of the Appellate Division (81 N. Y. Supp. 705) reversing an order of the Trial Term setting aside a verdict for plaintiff, defendant navigation company appeals. Reversed.

Everett P. Wheeler and Clarence Bishop Smith, for appellant. Richard T. Greene, for respondent.

GRAY, J. The plaintiff's husband was employed by the defendant as one of a gang of stevedores, and, while engaged upon the work of transferring coal from a barge into the steamship Oceanic he was killed. The plaintiff has sued to recover damages for his death, charging that it was caused through the negligence of the defendant. The plaintiff obtained a verdict in her favor, but the trial court set it aside and ordered a new trial. The Appellate Division, reviewing this order upon an appeal, reversed it, and directed judgment to be entered for the plaintiff in accordance with the verdict rendered. In that determination the court was not unanimous, and, upon this appeal by the defendant, the sole question actually is whether it had fulfilled its whole duty to its employé with respect to providing a safe place for him in which to do his work. It was and is charged by the plaintiff that the defendant was negligent in the failure to supply lamps or lights to illuminate the interior of the coal barge where the deceased was stationed upon the occasion in question. That omission, as it appears from the opinion of the majority of the Appellate Division Justices, was regarded as having been the cause of the accident, and, because the coal foreman of the defendant was in charge of the work and represented the latter in that respect, his negligence in failing to provide the lights was to be attributed to the general employer.

The facts may be briefly stated. The coal barge lay between the steamship and the wharf, and a number of stevedores, of whom the deceased was one, were in the hold of the barge, engaged in shoveling coal into buckets, which were let down into the hold at the end of a rope or "fall." When they were filled, they would be hoisted out and up the side of the steamship. The captain of the barge stood upon the barge's deck, and, by the use of a guy rope attached to the "fall," he was able to control the rise of a bucket from, or its descent into, the hold. The importance of this was in the necessity of preventing the buckets from swinging to and fro and against the side of the vessel. Upon this occasion, work was commenced in the middle of the day, and was continued until after sunset, when the hold had become darkened. McDonald was the defendant's coal foreman, who employed and directed the other stevedores, and it came within his duties to get out lamps whenever the darkness made them necessary. He did not do so at this time, as he testified, because he "did not think it necessary." A bucket which had been filled with coal on the side of the hold furthest away from the steamship was being hoisted, when, from the failure of the barge's captain to properly secure the guy rope, it swung violently over and towards the steamship, striking the head of the deceased against a bolt projecting from the barge's side, and killing him. The barge's captain testified that it was too dark to enable him to see into the hold, and that he did not know the coal bucket was hooked on. As the case was submitted to the jury, it is clear that the verdict must have been reached upon the theory that the defendant was liable for the foreman's neglect to supply the lights.

It was not disputed that the defendant had provided lamps sufficient, and quite available to the foreman, for the men's use. They were in sheds on the wharf, and also upon the steamship, and if they were not used upon this occasion it was simply because, in the foreman's judgment, they were not required. I cannot agree with the court below that the omission or neglect of this foreman was chargeable to the defendant. That he was so far the alter ego of the master as to make the latter responsible for any failure to furnish a safe place to work in, or safe appliances to work with, may be readily admitted; but if, as to some detail of the undertaking, he was actually doing the work devolving upon a servant, the others took the risk of their fellow servant's performance. The defendant was not at fault in any of those general respects in which an employer is regarded as under obligations towards those whom he employs to work for him. The hold of the barge was a safe enough place to work in, the foreman was competent, and no complaint is made as to the machinery or appliances used in the work. Whether a master shall be held to be liable when the negligent act or omission to act was that of one of his servants, depends usually, if not, indeed, always, upon the character of the act. That is to say, if the specific act is one the doing of which can be properly and justly regarded as within the personal duties of the master, whose performance he has delegated to another, and not some act within the line of a mere servant's duty, then the master is properly chargeable with the results of a negligent performance or omission. When McDonald, the defendant's coal foreman, in the exercise of his judgment, omitted to get the lamps for the stevedores, which the defendant had been careful to provide, I think that it was the omission of a duty resting on the foreman as a fellow servant having that detail in charge. It was either for him to judge when the lamps were needed, or it was for the others to demand them if the place had become too dark to remain in at work. There is no evidence of their having made any request of the foreman; so that, if the conditions had become so changed as to render continuance in their work dangerous, they all erred in their judgment. As it was said in Kimmer v. Weber, 151 N. Y. 417, 45 N. E. 860, 56 Am. St. Rep. 630, where it was a question of sufficiently safe scaffolding put up under the instructions of a foreman by the workmen, "it was, at most, but an error of judgment on the part of the foreman with respect to a detail of the work in which the masons [in that case] were engaged. He concluded, as the workmen themselves did, that the place was safe, and, in determining that question, they were all co-servants." In Crispin v. Babbitt, 81 N. Y. 516, 37 Am. Rep. 521, the plaintiff, a laborer, was injured, while engaged with others in lifting the fly wheel off of an engine. The defendant in that case had intrusted the conduct of his business to a general manager, and he, upon the occasion in question, carelessly started the engine. It was held that, notwithstanding his position, he was not, in what he did, acting in the defendant's place. It was observed, in the opinion, that "a superintendent of a factory, although having power to employ men, or represent the master in other respects, is, in the management of the machinery, a fellow servant of the other operatives." In Geoghegan v. Atlas Steamship Company, 146 N. Y. 369, 40 N. E. 507, where it was claimed that the deceased had come to his death by reason of certain gangway doors in the side of the vessel having been carelessly left open, through which he had fallen, we held that the defendant was not liable for the failure of the officer whose duty it was to close the doors, and that the negligence which led to the result was that of a co-servant. These cases, and others which might be cited, rest upon the principle that the liability of the master does not depend upon the grade or the rank of the servant who represents him in the superintendence of the others in his employment, but the act which causes or results in an injury in the course of the work must be of a character which the master, as such, should perform, and not one which would be expected of a servant, as such. Here the defendant provided a supply of lamps for its servants, and they could, and should, have taken and used them when they were required. To get them was a mere detail of the work, which it was the foreman's duty, as one of a number of servants engaged in a common task, to execute.

I advise the reversal of the order of the Appellate Division, and that a new trial be had, with costs to abide the event.

PARKER, C. J., and O'BRIEN, BARTLETT, HAIGHT, and CULLEN, JJ., concur. MARTIN, J., concurs in result.

Order reversed, etc.

(178 N. Y. 274)

PEOPLE v. MILLS.

(Court of Appeals of New York. April 26, 1904.)

CRIMES—RECEIVING STATE PROPERTY—THEFT OF PUBLIC RECORDS—ESTOPPEL OF STATE—PRINCIPAL.

1. Where the property of the state is delivered to any one under any circumstances for the purpose of having him steal it, and he takes possession of it with intent to steal it, the attempt is a crime.

2. Defendant formed a plot to obtain possession of certain indictments, for the purpose of destroying them, by bribing the assistant district attorney, having them in his charge, to deliver them to him for a certain consideration. A third party, pretending to act for such district attorney, delivered them to him, and he took possession of them and walked away, whereupon he was arrested, and the indictments recovered. *Held*, that he was properly convicted, under Pen. Code, § 94, of an attempt to unlawfully remove documents from a public officer, and under section 531 of an attempt to commit grand larceny in the second degree.

3. Where a district attorney was informed of a plot on the part of defendant to obtain possession of certain indictments for the purpose of destroying them, and directed his employés to seemingly comply with the proposition of defendant in order to apprehend defendant in the commission of the crime, and the district attorney procured the indictments with the consent of the judge, and they were delivered to the defendant, it is no defense, on the ground that the object of the district attorney was not to detect crime, but to create a crime, and that defendant was innocent because he took the indictments with the consent of the state as represented by the district attorney, as such officer in such case exceeded his authority, and his acts were not those of the state, but were his individual acts, and did not estop the state from prosecuting and convicting the defendant.

4. Where defendant proposed a scheme by which he was to obtain possession of certain indictments for the purpose of destroying them, and under such scheme the indictments were actually removed from the files of the court, and delivered to him, he was a principal throughout the transaction, and if he took them from the person actually removing them either with or without his consent, he was guilty of a theft of public records.

O'Brien and Bartlett, JJ., dissenting.

Appeal from Supreme Court, Appellate Division, First Department.

George E. Mills was convicted of an attempt to commit grand larceny in the second degree and of an attempt to commit the crime of willfully removing public documents from the custody of the officer to whom they were conveyed by law. From an order of the Appellate Division (86 N. Y. Supp. 529) affirming the judgment, he appeals. Affirmed.

The indictment against the defendant contains two counts, each charging an attempt to violate a distinct section of the Penal Code; the first being founded on section 94, and the second on section 531. The facts appearing on the trial, as well stated by the Appellate Division, are as follows:

Richard C. Flower was a physician, and was also engaged in promoting certain mining interests. In connection with such enterprise he was indicted under six different indictments for alleged larcenies, and was also suspected of being implicated in the suspicious death of one Hagaman, which case the district attorney was investigating shortly prior to the offenses charged in the present indictment. Francis P. Garvan, an assistant district attorney of the county of New York, had special charge of the prosecution of the indictments against Flower, and also of the investigation of the death of Hagaman. The defendant was a lawyer, engaged in the practice of his profession in the city of New York with a son of Richard C. Flower, and he was also interested in various mining companies in connection with Dr. Flower and Andrew D. Meloy and others at the time when the indictments were found against Flower, and when he was being otherwise investigated, and he took a very lively interest in Dr. Flower's behalf.

It appeared from the testimony of Meloy: That he was president and a member of the board of directors of the Lone Pine Mining Company, of which board the defendant was a member. That on Saturday, March 28, 1903, at a directors' meeting of this mining company, the defendant called attention to the prosecution against Dr. Flower, and stated that it was having a bad effect upon the company. That he thought Garvan was persecuting Flower. That the ends of justice were not being promoted, and he expressed a wish that the directors should pass some resolution asking Garvan or the district attorney's office to discontinue the attack upon Flower. Such resolution, however, was neither adopted nor offered. On the next day Meloy testified that he received a telephone message from the defendant, asking him to meet him on Riverside drive, about Eighty-Fifth or Eighty-Sixth streets. That he met him there alone; had a conversation with him, in which he spoke of Flower's increasing difficulties, about his counsel, what they had done, and what his anxieties and fears were. He discussed Garvan and the latter's attitude to the case, and asked Meloy if he would not make an engagement with Garvan so that the defendant could see and have a talk with him, and see if the prosecutions could not be stopped; and there was some conversation about the money which had been paid for counsel, and that, if it were given to Garvan, it would accomplish greater results. The defendant finally said: "'I will not give Hart any money, or any lawyer. * * * I know the head of this thing, and I am going to give what money I give to Garvan. * * * What I want to do is to get in contact with Garvan, and I want you to do it for me.' * * * When he said he wanted to get in contact, I asked him if he knew what he was doing—what he was about. He said he thought he did. Then I said the same general remark—'Be careful.' At the end of the conversation I left Mr. Mills, and stated I would see Mr. Garvan the next day, and make an engagement." Meloy further testified that he asked the defendant why he did not get in touch with Garvan himself, and in reply the defendant stated, in substance, "that if he came himself, Mr. Garvan would be afraid, but that you could arrange it for him." Meloy then parted from the defendant with the understanding that he was to see Garvan, and make an appointment for him the next day. Meloy, however, took an entirely different course. The next day he consulted with his own counsel, telling him what had occurred. Thereupon his counsel and himself interviewed Garvan over the telephone, with the result that the three had a meeting in the afternoon, and the whole matter of the conversation was stated to Garvan, after which Mr. Jerome, the district attorney, was brought into the conference, and informed of what had taken place. Jerome testified that on the next day after the conference he communicated with Detective Sergeant Brindley, and gave him directions concerninig the case, as a result of which he was to put himself into communication with the defendant for the purpose of detecting him in the commission of any crime which he might commit or attempt to commit. Meloy had no communication with Brindley, but the latter called him up on the telephone for the purpose of making arrangements by which he could meet the defendant. Meloy then saw the defendant, and informed him that he had seen Garvan and made arrangements for him to meet Garvan's wardman, Brindley. The defendant demurred to this, stating that he wanted to meet Garvan. Meloy told him that Garvan would not do business with him directly, but that he would have to do it with Brindley, and thereupon the defendant consented to see him; and Meloy, in the defendant's presence, called up Brindley by telephone at the district attorney's office, and told him that the defendant would meet him. As a result of this, the defendant and Brindley met in the afternoon in Haan's restaurant, No. 11 Park Row, in the city of New York. After identifying each other, they went into one of the booths, when Mills stated that he had been instructed by Dr. Flower to have an interview with Garvan about the disposition of the charges against Flower. Brindley informed him that it was impossible for him to see Garvan, and defendant said: "Well, Dr. Flower is anxious for me to talk to Garvan, and I do not see why he does not want to talk to me just as lawyer to lawyer. That would be all right." And when informed that this was impossible, he said, "Well, if you can assure me that you will fulfill any contract or proposition that I make to you I am willing to talk with you." After some further conversation defendant stated: "That Dr. Flower was a fool to have let the matter go as far as it did, as the opportunity was presented to him when Mr. Garvan had him in his office for examination in the Hagaman matter; that this was his time for to make a settlement, instead of fighting it out; and that now he has engaged high-priced counsel, who would drag the case out so as to justify a large fee. * * * He would go to the fountainhead and settle the case. I asked him then, 'Well, what is it you want us to do?' He says, 'Well, these indictments that have been found against Dr. Flower, you can withdraw them and misplace them, lose them, or dispose of them in some way, or Mr. Garvan could go into court, and permit him to go into court on a demurrer, and have the indictments quashed.' I told him that I would see Mr. Garvan, and submit this to him, and let him know. He then said, 'Well, Mr. Garvan ought to be satisfied with this. The matter is not worth as much money now as it would have been to us if it had been disposed of before indictment and all of this publicity. Dr. Flower's business has suffered very much from this, and, of course, it is not worth the money it would have been before the publicity.' He said that as to the Hagaman matter 'Mr. Garvan could say that, after thorough examination of witnesses, and the autopsy, and the examination of the report of the physician and chemist, he had come to the conclusion that the death of Mr. Hagaman was caused by natural causes, and that this would relieve both Dr. Flower and his client, Mrs. Hagaman—that is, Mills' client—of this notoriety.' * * * He said he would have to see Dr. Flower so as to make the arrangements for the money; that Dr. Flower is an old bird at this game; has had twenty years' experience, and would be very particular about arranging these matters." After arranging that the defendant should be known thereafter as McChesney, the parties separated. This conversation was repeated by Brindley to Jerome, and thereupon Jerome applied to "a judge of" the court having the custody of the indictments, explained how he desired to use them, without, however, mentioning any name, and the "judge" permitted them to be taken from the files of the office, and Jerome delivered them to Brindley. In the afternoon of the next day the defendant telephoned Brindley at the district attorney's office that everything was all right; that he had seen Dr. Flower, and "that it would be a go." At 12 o'clock of that day Brindley and the defendant again met at Haan's restaurant, when the defendant asked, "'As to those indictments, what have you done?' I says, 'Well, pursuant to your suggestion of yesterday about these indictments, I have inquired as to what effect it would have, and find that there are copies in the district attorney's office of these indictments.' He says: 'Yes, that is right. By taking these indictments—the originals—the copies could be made demurrable, and Mr. Garvan could go into court, and with all apparent good faith fight our motion to demur on those indictments, and, of course, the judge would decide against him.' He says, 'But how do we know as to your good faith in those other matters that may come up in the future?' 'Well,' I says, 'You would have possession of the indictments then, and that would be evidence of good faith on our part.' He says, 'Yes, but I do not want those indictments. I will take them from you—buy them—and would go somewheres with you and destroy them.' I says, 'Well, I have withdrawn those indictments, have given no reason why I did, and have them with me;' and I showed them to him. He took them and examined them. After carefully examing them, he says, 'Well, there are only five indictments here, and there has been no indictment on the bribery charge. That makes that the easier to dispose of; one prisoner already having been discharged, it would be an easy matter for Mr. Garvan to have the other one discharged.' He said, 'I will have to see Dr. Flower to get the money, and will try to find him by five o'clock this afternoon.' I said, 'Well, that would be after banking hours, and would be rather late,' and he says, 'Well, I will have to try to find him somewheres.' I then said, 'Well, what amount did you want to pay for this service?' He says, 'Well, $1,500.' I says I thought that was rather cheap. He said, 'Well, I will make it $2,000, in this way: $1,500 to be paid to Mr. Garvan and $500 you and I will divide.'" Brindley consented to this, and after some further conversation the parties separated, agreeing to meet again later in the afternoon. Subsequently the defendant called Brindley over the telephone, stating that he could not make the arrangements for that day; would have to postpone it to the next. Brindley replied that it was a risky thing for him to keep the indictments out of the Court of General Sessions. "He said: 'Well, under no conditions put them back. Keep them out. It will be all right. You can make any excuse. Say you cannot find them, but keep them out, anyway.'" The parties had prior to this time agreed to refer to the indictments as "subpoenas," and the money as "additional evidence." A meeting was arranged for next day, at which time Brindley posted in Haan's restaurant other officers and persons to observe what transpired between him and the defendant. He met the defendant shortly after 1 o'clock at Haan's rathskeller, and after considerable conversation with respect to the Hagaman matter, and what might occur in the future with respect to complaints against Dr. Flower, defendant said: "'I have the money here, and we can do more business in the future.' He put his hand in his inside pocket, and withdrew an envelope—this one (indicating)—and passed it to me and said: 'Just count it. There is $1,500.' The envelope was open when he handed it to me. I took it from him—from his hand. I looked into it. It had 15 $100 bills in it. I counted them. They are there now." The envelope and money were then received in evidence. Defendant then said: "This is for Mr. Garvan. Give this to Mr. Garvan. You and Mr. Garvan can settle for this $1,500." He said, "Look out; be careful." Thereupon the defendant called attention to certain persons who were observing them, and Brindley told him they were all "grafters." He then gave to Brindley $250 more, and said, "The other $250 I have in my pocket." Brindley then produced the indictments, which the defendant examined, and finally suggested, as they were being watched, that they go upstairs. He picked up the indictments, placed them in his outside pocket, walked to the stairway leading to the café upstairs, when Brindley placed him under arrest. He was searched in the presence of other persons in the café, the indictments were found upon him, and he was taken to the station house. The defendant admitted that the indictments were found upon his person at the time of his arrest, and he did not deny but that he had meetings with Brindley, as testified to by the latter, or but that the money which was produced in court and introduced into evidence was given by him to Brindley at the place and time that the testimony established. The defendant's claim in answer thereto was that he and Brindley were engaged in buying up claims against Dr. Flower, and that in all the negotiations which he had with Brindley he was acting as the representative of Flower against creditors and their attorney, Mr. Hart, from whom he was to receive releases to be delivered to him by Brindley; but he admits that Brindley produced the indictments; told him what they were; that he looked at them, and subsequently put them in his pocket at the request of Brindley.

The jury found the defendant guilty upon both counts, and he was sentenced accordingly. Upon appeal to the Appellate Division the judgment was affirmed, one of the justices dissenting, and the defendant thereupon came to this court.

John R. Dos Passos, Benjamin S. Steinhardt, and Edmund F. Harding, for appellant. William Travers Jerome, Dist. Atty. (Robert C. Taylor, of counsel), for the People.

VANN, J. (after stating the facts). The indictments against Dr. Flower were records or documents filed in a public office under the authority of law. Code Cr. Proc. § 272; Code Civ. Proc. § 866. They were the property of the state, and a willful and unlawful removal of them constituted a crime under section 94 of the Penal Code. Any one who unlawfully obtained or appropriated them was guilty of grand larceny in the second degree, according to the provisions of another section of the same statute. Pen. Code, § 531. Whoever is guilty of violating either section may be convicted of an attempt to commit the offense specified therein, even if it appears on the trial that the crime was fully consummated, unless the court in its discretion discharges the jury, and directs the defendant to be tried for the crime itself, which was not done in the case before us. Code Cr. Proc. §§ 35, 685. The jury found the defendant guilty of an attempt both to remove and to steal the indictments, and after affirmance by the Appellate Division we are confined in our review to such questions as were raised by exceptions taken during the trial.

In view of the able and exhaustive opinion of the Appellate Division, the only question we feel called upon to consider is that raised by the challenge of the learned counsel for the appellant in the nature of a demurrer to the evidence. He claims that, even on the assumption that all the evidence for the prosecution is true, still the facts thus proved do not constitute the crime charged in either count of the indictment. His argument is that the object of the district attorney was not to detect, but to create, a crime; and that no crime was committed by the defendant in taking the indictments into his possession, because he took them with the consent of the state, as represented by the district attorney. The flaw in this argument is found in the fact that the records were the property of the state, not of the district attorney, and that the latter could not lawfully give them away, or permit them to be taken by the defendant. Purity of intention only could prevent the action of the district attorney from being a crime on his part. This is true also as to the detective, for, if either had in fact intended that the defendant should permanently remove the indictments, and steal, appropriate, or destroy them, he would have come within the statute. Neither of those officers represented the state in placing the records where the defendant could take them, but each was acting as an individual only. Neither had the right or power, as a public officer, to deliver them to the defendant, and, if either had acted with an evil purpose, his act would have been criminal in character. An act done with intent to commit a crime, and tending, but failing, to effect its commission, is an attempt to commit that crime. Pen. Code, § 34. Felonious intent alone is not enough, but there must be an overt act shown, in order to establish even an attempt. An overt act is one done to carry out the intention, and it must be such as would naturally effect that result, unless prevented by some extraneous cause. In People v. Bush, 4 Hill, 133, the prisoner solicited one Kinney to burn a barn, and gave him matches for the purpose, and it was held sufficient to warrant a conviction for attempt at arson, although the prisoner did not mean to be present at the commission of the offense, and Kinney did not intend to commit it. The furnishing of the matches was the overt act. If the defendant did anything with intent to steal the papers, which in the ordinary course of events, unless interfered with, would have resulted in the theft thereof, it was an overt act. People v. Sullivan, 173 N. Y. 122, 133, 65 N. E. 989, 93 Am. St. Rep. 582. Taking up the records, putting them in his pocket, and walking away with them was an overt act, because it was done with the intent to remove and appropriate them, and would ordinarily result in carrying that intention into effect. It was a trespass to take the indictments into his possession under the circumstances, for he did it, as the jury found, with the intention of stealing them. It was not necessary that the trespass should be accompanied with violence, as it was enough for him to secure the physical custody of the papers, and have it in his power to take them away and appropriate them, the same as if he had picked them up in the clerk's office. No more force would be required in the case supposed than in the case proved. The touch of a pickpocket is so light that it cannot be felt, yet the force is sufficient to constitute a trespass and an attempt to commit a crime, even if there is nothing in the pocket to steal. People v. Moran, 123 N. Y. 254, 25 N. E. 412, 10 L. R. A. 109, 20 Am. St. Rep. 732. As was said by the court in a late case: "It is now the established law, both in England and in this country, that the crime of attempting to commit larceny may be committed although there was no property to steal, and thus the full crime of larceny could not have been committed." People v. Gardner, 144 N. Y. 119, 125, 38 N. E. 1003, 1004, 28 L. R. A. 699, 43 Am. St. Rep. 741, and cases cited.

Knowing that he had no right to the indictments, and that the officers had no right to let him have them, when the defendant picked them up from the table and put them in his pocket animo furandi, the law presumes that the act was done vi et armis, for the amount of violence is not important. He removed the papers from the control of the real owner, and had them in his own control, so that the state could not have recovered possession without his consent or by forcibly taking them away from him, which was in fact done. The detective could only get them back if he and his assistants were strong enough, unless the defendant voluntarily gave them up. He had the same control of them that he had of his own pocketbook, for both were in his pocket, and neither could be taken from him except by the use of force. Temporary possession, though but for a moment, by one who intends to steal, is enough, and possession "is the having or holding or detention of property in one's power or command." Harrison v. People, 50 N. Y. 518, 10 Am. Rep. 517. As was said by Judge Folger in the case cited, quoting with approval from an old manuscript of a distinguished judge: "If every part of the thing is removed from the space which that part occupied, yet the whole thing is not removed from the whole space which the whole thing occupied, the asportation will be sufficient; so, drawing a sword partly out of its scabbard will constitute a complete asportavit." The defendant picked up the papers from the table; he held them in his hand; he put them in his pocket, and was walking away with them when he was arrested. In whose possession were they at that time, if not in his, and how did they get there unless by his unauthorized, physical interference with them? The district attorney did not authorize him to take them, for he could not, and the defendant knew that he could not. Neither the district attorney nor the detective stood for the state of New York in placing them where the defendant could get them, for no court or officer has that power under the law. The statute expressly prohibits a record or document "whereof a transcript duly certified may by law be read in evidence" from being "removed, by virtue of a subpœna duces tecum, from the office in which it is kept, except temporarily, by the clerk having it in custody, to a term or sitting of the court of which he is clerk, or by the officer having it in custody, to a term or sitting of a court or * * * referee held in the city or town where his office is situated." Where it is required at any other place for use as evidence, it may be removed by order of the court "entered in the minutes, specifying that the production of the original, instead of the transcript, is necessary." Code Civ. Proc. § 866. This is the only statute which confers any power on the court in relation to the subject, and clearly it did not authorize the court to allow the district attorney to take the indictments in question for the purpose of giving them away, even temporarily, or permitting them to be taken into possession by one who wanted to steal them. An order made for such a purpose would be void, but no order of the kind was actually made by the court, or "entered in the minutes." The district attorney told one of the judges, out of court, what he wanted of the indictments, and, to use his own words, "that I desired to keep them over night, but I did not want to go to the clerk's office about it, and that I did not want to do it without the consent of some judge, and he was the only judge in the building, and he consented."

While such consent gave some moral support to the district attorney, it added not a whit to his legal powers. The Code of Criminal Procedure requires that an indictment "must be filed with the clerk and remain in his office as a public record." Section 272. No one is authorized to take it away, except when it is needed as evidence, or in court upon the trial of the accused. We have recently held that a record made for the purpose of identifying a convict, and kept in the office of the superintendent of state prisons, could not be given away or surrendered, even after the person convicted had been acquitted upon a new trial granted through appeal. We declared that the record was beyond the control of the superintendent except for preservation and use, and that even the courts could not compel him to give it up without express authority from the Legislature. Molineux v. Collins, 177 N. Y. 395, 398, 69 N. E. 727. If the district attorney had had the indictments in his possession for use in court in prosecuting Dr. Flower, such possession would have been the possession of the state, for it would have been lawful, and in the line of his duty. When, however, he had them in his possession for the purpose of delivering them to the defendant, or letting him take them with intent to carry them away and destroy them, such possession was not that of the state, for the district attorney was not then acting in an authorized or official capacity, although it is conceded that he thought he was. As the defendant "proposed the scheme and put in motion the forces by which the indictments were actually removed from the files of the court and delivered to him," we agree with the Appellate Division that he was a principal throughout the transaction. Pen. Code, § 29; People v. Bliven, 112 N. Y. 79, 19 N. E. 638, 8 Am. St. Rep. 701; People v. Peckens, 153 N. Y. 576, 47 N. E. 883. However, even if he had not instigated the scheme pursuant to which the indictments were removed from the office of the clerk and brought where he could put his hands upon them, still, if he then took them into his possession with intent to steal them, knowing what they were and where they came from, he was guilty of the offense charged. It was unnecessary for him to remove them from the clerk's office, but was sufficient if he took them animo furandi from any place, or from any person, either with or without consent.

We shall not review the authorities cited on either side, for that duty has been so thoroughly discharged by the Appellate Division that we can throw no further light upon the subject. We merely state that an important distinction between this case and those relied upon by the appellant is found in the difference between public and private ownership of the property taken by the accused. In most cases some third person is injured by the crime, and is directly or indirectly the complainant, but in this case the state was, as it must be in all criminal cases, the prosecutor, and it was also the injured party, for its property was the subject of the attempt at larceny. If an individual owner voluntarily delivers his property to one who wishes to steal it, there is no trespass, but when the property of the state is delivered by any one, under any circumstances, to any person for the purpose of having him steal it, and he takes it into his possession with intent to steal it, there is a trespass, and the attempt is a crime. The state did not solicit or persuade or tempt the defendant, any more than it took his money when he handed it over to the detective. Neither did the district attorney, as such, but Mr. Jerome did, acting as an individual, with the best of motives, but without authority of law, and hence his action did not bind the state. While the courts neither adopt nor approve the action of the officers, which they hold was unauthorized, still they should not hesitate to punish the crime actually committed by the defendant. It is their duty to protect the innocent and punish the guilty. We are asked to protect the defendant, not because he is innocent, but because a zealous public officer exceeded his powers and held out a bait. The courts do not look to see who held out the bait, but to see who took it. When it was found that the defendant took into his possession the property of the state with intent to steal it, an offense against public justice was established, and he could not insist as a defense that he would not have committed the crime if he had not been tempted by a public officer whom he thought he had corrupted. He supposed he had bought the assistant district attorney when he handed over the money, but he knew he had not bought the state of New York, and hence that the assistant had no right to give him its property for the purpose of enabling him to steal it.

The judgment of conviction should be affirmed.

O'BRIEN, J. (dissenting). This case is sui generis. There is no case in this state that I have been able to find that is at all substantially similar. The cases cited in support of this conviction at the bar and in the courts below are well enough in their way, but they do not touch the vital question involved in the case. This will be seen upon an examination of the cases themselves in connection with the views herein expressed. After a careful examination of the record, the first thought that impresses the mind has been admirably expressed by an eminent judge of the highest court in the land in a famous case which has just been decided in that court: "Great cases, like hard cases, make bad law. For great cases are called great, not by reason of their real importance in shaping the law for the future, but because of some question of an immediate, overwhelming interest which appeals to the feelings and distorts the judgment. These immediate interests exercise a kind of hydraulic pressure, which makes what previously was clear seem doubtful, and before which even well-settled principles of law will bend." There is in this case, doubtless, something of immediate, overwhelming interest, which distorts the judgment and leads it away from the real principles that ought to control the decision.

The defendant was indicted and convicted for an attempt to steal six indictments that had been filed by the grand jury against a certain Dr. Flower. He, it seems, was a director, and manager of a mining corporation, and, in connection with his transactions concerning the stock of that corporation, he was indicted for stealing certain moneys that it is said he received upon a sale of the stock. The particular facts upon which the indictments rest are of no consequence. It is enough for us to know that they were presented by the grand jury in the usual course, and were on file in the proper office. The defendant is an attorney at law, and was a director in the same corporation, and was a friend of Flower. A man named Meloy was also a director, who had some quarrel or dispute with the defendant and Flower concerning the management of the corporation. He had some dispute or quarrel with the defendant in the corporate meetings, and was really an enemy of the defendant, though he professed to be a friend. The desire for revenge still nestled in his bosom, and that doubtless is a sufficient explanation for his conduct in the transaction which will be presently related. The transaction is a very remarkable one, and, although it appears at length and with considerable detail in the large record before us, it can be compressed into a very brief statement. In stating the case I will aim to give it the coloring which is most unfavorable to the defendant, and will wholly reject his own version of the transaction.

On or about the 29th of March, 1903, the defendant called up Meloy on the telephone, and asked him to meet him at a designated place in New York. This meeting took place, and Meloy testifies that the defendant made at that interview the following statement to him: The defendant said, in substance, that there had been a large amount of money spent for counsel in the Flower case, and that if the money had been given to the district attorney, or one of his deputies, the prosecution would have long since ceased, and the defendant suggested to Meloy that the latter make an engagement for an interview with an assistant district attorney. In other words, the defendant disclosed to Meloy, in plain words, a project to bribe the district attorney, or rather his assistant, to make way with the indictments, or to terminate the prosecution by some proceeding in court upon a demurrer. There can be no doubt whatever that the defendant entertained the design to terminate the prosecution upon these six indictments by bribery. The exact course to be followed was evidently not clear in his mind, and was to await further development. This, of course, was a project that shocks our sense of propriety, and arouses at once a prejudice against the defendant. It is the one thing in this case that distorts the judgment, and is liable to lead courts away from the legal question involved in the case. When the interview was finished, and Meloy and the defendant parted, it was agreed that Meloy was to see the assistant district attorney, and arrange an interview between the latter and the defendant. Here Meloy found his opportunity to get even with the defendant, and in that way settle their old quarrel. Instead of going to see the assistant, as he had led the defendant to believe, he went to his own lawyer, and disclosed to him the conversation and proposal which had been made by the defendant to him. He and his counsel then proceeded to call upon the assistant the same day, and informed him of the conversation that Meloy had had with the defendant. The assistant immediately asked Meloy and his counsel to accompany him to the office of the district attorney, where these four persons had an interview, and then, or perhaps at a subsequent one, a plan was arranged by which the district attorney agreed to obtain from the files of the court the six indictments which were pending against Flower, and to deliver them into the custody of a detective in his office, who would meet the defendant, with the indictments, and obtain from him a proposition for the delivery of them to the defendant upon payment of a certain sum, which the detective would represent would go to the assistant.

Subsequently to the interview which resulted in the foregoing plan, Meloy, acting under the instructions of the district attorney and of his own counsel, had another interview with the defendant, and informed him that it was impossible for the assistant to meet the defendant, but that the assistant had deputed a wardman or detective in the office, in whom he had confidence, to meet the defendant and receive from him his proposition; and it was through Meloy that the defendant and the detective finally connected with each other. When Meloy met the defendant, he concealed from the latter the fact that he had an interview with the district attorney, and that there was a plan on foot to entrap him. Subsequently the detective and the defendant connected with each other over the telephone, and, as a result of that connection, they met at a certain restaurant in the city at about 3 o'clock on the afternoon of the 31st day of March, 1903. In this interview the defendant told the detective that these indictments had been found against Dr. Flower, and that he could withdraw them and misplace them; and he suggested to the detective, who claimed to represent the district attorney's office, that he could withdraw them, misplace, lose, or dispose of them in some way, or the assistant could go into court or permit him to go into court on a demurrer and have the indictments quashed. All this resulted in a proposition by the detective to procure the indictments and deliver them to the defendant on payment of $1,750. On a subsequent interview at the same place the detective and the defendant met, and the former received the money, produced the indictments, handed them to the defendant, who put them in his pocket, and thereupon the detective and a policeman, who was outside the door, looking on, immediately arrested the defendant, and, of course, the detective took the indictments away from him, and here the heroic farce ended. The rest is judicial history.

It will be seen from this statement that all the defendant did was to disclose to Meloy his corrupt purpose to bribe the district attorney. That, of course, was bad enough, and he could have been arrested after the disclosure under the provisions of the Code for the prevention of crime, and could have been required to give security for his good behavior. Code Cr. Proc. §§ 82-90. It will be seen also that everything else in the transaction which subsequently took place was aided, induced, procured, and consummated by the state itself, acting through its officers and agents.

The six indictments in question were doubtless records within the meaning of the statute. The law requires that such records be filed with the clerk, and remain in his office as public records, not to be shown to any person other than a public officer until the defendant has been arrested. Code Cr. Proc. § 272. But the statute permits them to be removed by order of the court, specifying that the production of the original, instead of the transcript, is necessary. It must be assumed, and in fact it appears, that the district attorney procured the delivery of the indictments to him in compliance with law. No one suggests that he or any one else purloined or obtained them by any fraud or in any illegal way. Hence he had the lawful possession and custody of the records, and, as authorized agent, voluntarily delivered them to the defendant for a moment, intending all the time to take them back. In other words, the custodian of the papers, as they went into the pocket of the defendant, had a string tied to the package, which enabled him in a moment to resume the actual possession. There was not a moment of time when these records were not surrounded by the legal protection that they would have had if never removed from the proper office. There were two detectives looking on, and constructively, if not actually, they were in the possession of these papers all the time. There never was a time when the defendant had in any legal sense any dominion over them, or the opportunity to remove or destroy them. The statute declares that "a person is guilty of grand larceny in the second degree who, under circumstances not amounting to grand larceny in the first degree, * * * steals or unlawfully obtains or appropriates * * * a record of a court or officer, or a writing, instrument or record kept, filed or deposited according to law, with, or in keeping of any public office or officer." Pen. Code, § 531. It also declares that "an act, done with intent to commit a crime, and tending but failing to effect its commission, is an attempt to commit that crime." Pen. Code, § 34. Now, what act is imputable to the defendant, that was done with intent to steal the records? We know that he intended to bribe the district attorney. But the only thing done in the whole transaction by the defendant was to put the records in his pocket for a moment, after having them voluntarily handed to him by the detective, and they were immediately taken away from him. There was no intention on the part of the detective to do anything but to carry out a plan previously formed, to which the defendant was not a party, and under these circumstances there was not, in law, any delivery whatever. The crime charged would have been just as well supported if the defendant had done nothing more than to touch the papers with his little finger. He did nothing except what the state, acting through its officers and agents, wanted him to do—solicited, persuaded, tempted, and procured him to do—and I may add that the officers would have been grievously disappointed and chagrined, had the defendant acted otherwise than he did. And if he had refused to touch the papers he would have been just as guilty then of stealing, or of an attempt to steal, as he is now.

The defendant is charged in the indictment with having done something "against the peace of the people of the state of New York and their dignity." How far the peace of the state has been disturbed, or its dignity violated or insulted, will appear from what has already been stated. The state has taken advantage of a man with an evil and corrupt disposition—a man who was willing to commit a crime—and through its officers has tempted and procured him to put six indictments in his pocket, and then complains that its peace has been disturbed and its dignity violated. The question arises here whether this farce constitutes a criminal offense. There is no complainant or third person in this case against whom the injury was inflicted. There is nobody but the state itself and the defendant, and it seems to me that there could be no crime committed by the defendant in accepting the indictments, because it was with the full consent of the state. "Volenti non fit injuria." And herein this case differs widely from any other existing precedent. I have said that the state was an aggressive, voluntary actor in this transaction. The state was the owner and custodian of these indictments. It permitted them to be taken from the clerk's office by its laws and its courts, and to be placed in the custody of its prosecuting officer, and in all that he did with these records he represented the state. The state, existing only as an artificial and impalpable being, could not act without agents; and hence the district attorney, for all the purposes of this case, and for the purposes of the administration of criminal justice, is the agent of the state, and his acts are imputable to the state and to the people; and hence the delivery of the indictments to the defendant by authority of the district attorney was an absolute consent on the part of the state to the defendant to receive them. Hence the state, instead of seeking to redress a wrong which had ensued from a violation of the criminal law, evidenced by the defendant's threat to bribe one of its public officers, stopped to conspire to entice a man to commit a crime and become a criminal. The representative of the state took its records, and sought to make their voluntary delivery to the defendant a crime. This court has held that a process server, employed by a railroad company to subpœna witnesses to testify in a pending suit, represented the company, and acted within the scope of his duty and employment, when engaged in an attempt to bribe witnesses to testify falsely in the case; that, although an attempt to suborn witnesses was unlawful, yet the act of the agent bound the principal, and his unlawful act would be imputed to the corporation. Nowack v. Met. St. Ry. Co., 166 N. Y. 433, 60 N. E. 32, 54 L. R. A. 592, 82 Am. St. Rep. 691. In view of this decision, it is difficult to see upon what ground or for what reason it is asserted in this case that the district attorney's office did not represent the state, and that the acts of the detective, set in motion by the office, cannot be imputed to the state. If the public prosecutor and his detective did not represent the state, they did not represent the law; and, if they did not represent the law, they must have been using records of the criminal courts in eating houses and other public places in order to tempt the unwary.

I have said that there was no precedent in this state to uphold this judgment, and fortunately that is true. There are precedents that justify the state and its officers, when a crime has been committed, to entrap the perpetrator by acts, admissions, or circumstances, or, in other words, to procure evidence to convict a party of a crime with which he is charged. All the cases cited seem to be authorities of that character. I have no comment to make upon them, but I think it may be safely asserted that never before in this state have the courts been called upon to pass on a case where the crime was created by the act, advice, and procurement of the commonwealth. But while it is true that no prosecution like this has ever come before any of the courts of this state, our sister states have not been so fortunate.

The law upon the subject is well discussed in the case of State v. Hayes, 105 Mo. 76, 16 S. W. 514, 24 Am. St. Rep. 360. In that case the accused proposed to another to commit burglary of a storehouse. The other consented, or pretended to consent, but, like Meloy in this case, proceeded to inform the authorities, and then went with the accused to the storehouse, and entered it by raising a window with the assistance of the accused. He handed out a piece of bacon to the accused, who assisted him out of the building. The accused took the bacon, and was arrested while carrying it away; the whole transaction having previously been arranged with the authorities. It was held that the accused could not be convicted of either burglary or larceny.

In State v. Hull, 33 Or. 56, 54 Pac. 159, 72 Am. St. Rep. 694, the accused had been convicted of stealing cattle. It appeared, however, that a person employed by the owner to detect suspected thieves, of which the defendant was one, co-operated or pretended to co-operate with them or with the accused in planning and carrying out the larceny and asportation. It was held that it was not larceny, and the conviction was reversed. The case of People v. Collins, 53 Cal. 185, is to the same effect.

The principle at the bottom of all the cases is this, viz., that a person decoyed by others into the doing of some act that otherwise would be a crime is no criminal, in the eye of the law, unless the persons inducing or procuring him to do the act were themselves criminals, intending to commit the crime. Hence the defendant in this case committed no crime unless Meloy and the district attorney themselves intended to and did commit a crime. But that hypothesis is simply absurd.

In State v. Stickney, 53 Kan. 308, 36 Pac. 714, 42 Am. St. Rep. 284, the court said: "If Payne was employed by the owner to open the door and decoy the appellant within the building, and the entrance was with the consent of the owner, then certainly the appellant cannot be held responsible for a burglarious entry."

In Williams v. State, 55 Ga. 391, the court said: "It is difficult to see how a man may solicit another to commit a crime upon his property, and, when the act to which he was invited has been done, be heard to say that he did not consent to it. In the present case, but for the owner's incitement, through his agent, the accused may have repented of the contemplated wickedness before it had developed into act. It may have stopped at sin, without putting on the body of crime. To stimulate unlawful intentions, with the motive of bringing them to punishable maturity, is a dangerous practice. Much better is it to wait and see if they will not expire. Humanity is weak. Even strong men are sometimes unprepared to cope with temptation and resist encouragement to evil."

In People v. McCord, 76 Mich. 200, 42 N. W. 1106, the court said: "But our duty to public justice and decency requires us to dispose of the other views of the case. In some of its features, it is one of the most disgraceful instances of criminal contrivance to induce a man to commit a crime, in order to get him convicted, that has ever been before us. If the prisoner's statement is believed—and the court, in the latter part of the charge, seems to have assumed it was probable—he was not the active agent in the crime, but guilty of aiding and abetting Flint, and therefore only guilty if Flint was guilty. It would be absurd to hold Flint guilty of burglary. He did what he was expected to do, and had no such intent as would hold him responsible. It may be true that a person does not lose the character of an injured party by merely waiting and watching for expected developments. Possibly—but we do not care to decide this—leaving temptation in the way, without further inducement, will not destroy the guilt, in law, of the person tempted, although it is a diabolical business, which, if not punishable, probably ought to be. But it would be a disgrace to the law if a person who had taken active measures to persuade another to enter his premises and take his property can treat the taking as a crime, or qualify any of the acts done by invitation as criminal. What is authorized to be done is no wrong, in law, to the instigator."

In Love v. People, 160 Ill. 501, 43 N. E. 710, 32 L. R. A. 139, the court said: "Acts, otherwise criminal, done by a party against property at the instigation and by the encouragement of a detective, who acts in pursuance of a plan previously arranged with the owner of the property, do not constitute a crime. * * * If he could make the criminal, and induce the commission of the crime, and cause the arrest of the actor, or throw around him a web of circumstances that would lead to a conviction, it would redound to the glory of his chief and cause his advancement. With him the end justified the means, and the reputation of the agency to which he belonged and his own advancement were apparently his object. Such means and agents are more dangerous to the welfare of society than are the crimes they were intended to detect and the criminals they were to arrest. * * * Strong men are sometimes unprepared to cope with temptation and resist encouragement to evil when financially embarrassed and impoverished. A contemplated crime may never be developed into a consummated act. To stimulate unlawful intentions for the purpose and with the motive of bringing them to maturity, so the consequent crime may be punished, is a dangerous practice. It is safer law and sounder morals to hold, where one arranged to have a crime committed against his property or himself, and knows that an attempt is to be made to encourage others to commit the act by one acting in concert with such owner, that no crime is thus committed. The owner and his agent may wait passively for the would-be criminal to perpetrate the offense, and each and every part of it for himself, but they must not aid, encourage, or solicit him that they may seek to punish. After a careful consideration of the evidence in this record, and with a deliberate regard for the importance of the question under discussion, we are constrained to hold the evidence does not sustain this conviction. The judgment is reversed, and the defendant is ordered discharged."

In Connor v. People, 18 Colo. 373, 33 Pac. 159, 25 L. R. A. 341, 36 Am. St. Rep. 295, the court said: "In the case under consideration, the only evidence of the inception of the scheme to rob the express company is that of Holliday, who states that it was instigated by his superiors at St. Louis, and by him suggested to the plaintiffs in error. It further appears that before the consummation of the conspiracy the officers of the express company were informed of and consented to the scheme; hence, under the foregoing authorities, the prosecution cannot be sustained. We do not wish to be understood as intimating that the services of a detective cannot be legitimately employed in the discovery of the perpetrators of a crime that has been or is being committed; but we do say that when, in their zeal, or under a mistaken sense of duty, detectives suggest the commission of a crime, and instigate others to take part in its commission, in order to arrest them while in the act, although the purpose may be to capture old offenders, their conduct is not only reprehensible, but criminal, and ought to be rebuked, rather than encouraged, by the courts."

In O'Brien v. State, 6 Tex. App. 665, the court said: "When the officer first suggests his willingness to a person to accept a bribe to release a prisoner in his charge, and thereby originates the criminal intent, and apparently joins the defendant in a criminal act first suggested by the officer, merely to entrap the defendant, the case is not within the spirit of said article 307 of the Criminal Code."

In Commonwealth v. Bickings, 12 Pa. Dist. R. 206, the court said: "The liability of men to fall into crime by consulting their interests and passions is unfortunately great, without the stimulus of encouragement. No state, therefore, can safely adopt a policy by which crime is to be artificially propagated. * * * This is virtually the case of a detective who, by promising to perpetrate a crime, lures an innocent man into aiding and abetting it; the object being, not the perpetration of the crime, but the luring of the abettor. Such a proceeding is not a reality, but merely a tragical farce, in which the detective, masquerading as a criminal, captivates the unsophisticated defendant, and then, with mock heroics, denounces him."

These cases and many others that might be cited show very clearly the character of the prosecution disclosed by the record, as it is understood and treated in the criminal law. This court, in its indignation at the defendant's project to bribe a public officer, should not lose sight of its own duty and dignity. No court can afford to close its ears against reason, to ignore logic, and to brush aside legal principles, in order to put some miscreant for a few months in jail. We cannot affirm this judgment without adopting and approving all the acts and proceedings which enter into the judgment and form a part of it. I am not disposed to criticise the learned district attorney for doing what he supposed to be his duty. No doubt, he acted honestly. But this court has its own duty and responsibility. If the prosecuting officers of the state can tempt every evil-disposed person into overt criminal acts, and then prosecute them, there is an opportunity, doubtless, to fill the prisons to overflowing. But I think we ought not to approve of that at the expense of destroying fundamental maxims of the law.

We cannot affirm this judgment without holding that fraud does not vitiate every transaction. If it is committed by the state, through its officers, and for the purpose of procuring evil-disposed persons to manifest their corrupt intentions by overt acts, then, according to the judgment in this case, the fraud is not only lawful, but commendable. We cannot hold that the end always justifies the means. We cannot hold that it is more important that one evil-disposed person shall be put in prison than that ninety-nine innocent persons be acquitted. It is not the law yet that in criminal cases, where there is a doubt upon the law or the facts, the people, and not the accused, shall have the benefit of it. It is still law, at least in theory, that a person is to be presumed innocent until shown to be guilty. It seems to me that some or all of these fundamental maxims have been ignored in this case, and nothing has been seen except the evil purpose of the defendant to bribe a public officer. If this defendant is, in law, guilty of attempting to steal the papers that were handed to him by the detective, I have no comment to make upon the conduct of the officers who devised and carried out the plan. It may be that they might be considered public benefactors, as possessing the zeal and the vigor to punish evil intentions. But I am not prepared to make this court a party to the transaction by giving it approval, as it must logically, if this judgment is affirmed.

The argument of the learned court below in support of the conviction rests upon a single proposition, which I quote from the opinion: "Having proposed the scheme and set in motion the forces by which the indictments were actually removed from the files of the court and delivered to him, every act from the inception of the scheme to its final consummation by the delivery of the indictments was the act of the defendant, no matter by whom it was performed, and it constituted him a principal in the transaction." The fallacy of this proposition consists entirely in its application, since every one will admit that a party who employs or procures another to commit a crime is a principal. Whatever other persons, acting as his agents, do in furtherance of the crime, may be imputed to the one who set the forces in motion. No one questions this rule of law. But did the defendant set the district attorney and his staff in motion? Were they his instruments and agents in the scheme to steal the records? If so, they were criminals worse than the defendant, since they were the sworn officers of the law, and intrusted, for the time being, with the custody and safe-keeping of the records. Were they doing the defendant's work, and engaged in promoting and effectuating his evil purpose to bribe them? If the proposition quoted is correct as applied to this case, it logically follows that they were certainly guilty of all these things. But that is only a distorted view of the facts, since they were not acting for the defendant. They were not his agents in crime, and in no legal and proper sense did they represent the defendant. The whole scheme that was finally consummated in the saloon, when the detective succeeded in getting the records in the defendant's coat pocket for an instant of time, originated with themselves. There was not, and could not have been, any crime whatever, without the active aid, procurement, encouragement, and connivance of these public officers, and hence there was not, in law, any crime at all. There was an evil purpose in the defendant's mind, which was never carried out or consummated. The proposition of the learned court quoted above virtually and logically represents the district attorney's office as aiding the defendant, and therefore as an agency for the perpetration and promotion of crime. How much more reasonable, charitable, and just it would be to present the office and its occupants in the true light, namely, as representing the state and acting for it in all that was done! I should be surprised if the learned, able, and honest district attorney would desire to be represented as acting in any other capacity; and I will add it is much more complimentary to him to treat the transaction in the saloon, when the records were produced by his detective, as a mere farce or experiment, rather than a crime, which, if committed at all, was by his aid, advice, and procurement. It was not only harmless, but the whole performance was absolutely silly, since copies of the six indictments were in the district attorney's office, and the loss of the originals could not embarrass the prosecution in the least. The defendant, though a lawyer himself, evidently did not see what a silly project the whole scheme was, but certainly the district attorney, his assistant, and the detective must have known. The genius and vigilance that can convert evil thoughts into criminal acts might be admired, but on sober reflection no public officer can think it fair or proper to be represented as giving aid, advice, or assistance to an evil-disposed person, that may enable him to do, or appear to do, the things that constitute a crime. It is plain from the opinions that I have quoted from the courts of sister states that those tribunals entertain no such views of this transaction as those expressed by the learned court below in this case. These cases hold that such a transaction does not amount to any crime, and, in my opinion, they are the expression of good sense and sound law. That view is safer for the public, and much more charitable to the officers themselves. I would not give to them the character of agents carrying out the defendant's evil purpose, but rather as engaged in a harmless farce or experiment. The fundamental question in this case is plain and simple, and it is this: Can the state, through one of its own officers and agents, on learning that one of its citizens harbors criminal designs in his mind, and has a criminal inclination, enter upon a plan to tempt him, suggest to him what to do in order to accomplish his criminal purpose, take records from the files in pursuance of the plan, and deliver them for a sum of money previously agreed upon, all conceived and carried out in fraud for the very purpose of decoying the person into some criminal act in order to prosecute him for the same, upon the sole ground that its peace and dignity have by that act been insulted and violated? I have no hesitation in asserting that an act thus procured and manufactured cannot be a punishable crime, either in the domain of law, of morals, or of common sense.

It has been said, with perhaps much truth, that it is and always has been the natural disposition of mankind to reverence law more in its high abuses and summary movements than in its calm and constitutional energy, when it dispensed blessings with an unseen but liberal hand. Courts cannot inspire much respect for the majesty and dignity of law or the orderly administration of justice when they depart from sound and settled principles in order to crown with success the traps devised by public officers to decoy evil-minded persons into the commission of acts which under other circumstances would be criminal. When the state and its officers come into a court of justice, demanding the punishment of a person accused of crime, they ought to appear there with clean hands, and not as a part of the forces that procured the consummation of the unlawful act.

The highest and most enlightened court is liable to be misled by plausible and distorted arguments. But in this case the wayfaring man cannot err, since he has the force of reason and the light of authority to guide him. This judgment can be affirmed with the strong hand of power, but it is quite useless to try to cover it with a glamour of reason or law. The evil purpose of this defendant, never consummated, ought not to have any more influence over the question involved in this case than the smallest pebble on the shore over the turbulent and angry waves of the sea. I think the approval of this judgment is a bad precedent, since we cannot escape adopting acts and arguments that are only a virtual modification of the arguments in support of lynch law. It is not worth while for this court to become a party to this transaction for the sake of sending this defendant, who, so far as we know, is a bad man, to a prison for a few months.

There was a ruling made by the learned trial judge which seems to me should not be ignored. The people were permitted to prove that, about the time the transaction referred to took place, an assistant district attorney was engaged in investigating the cause of the death of a man named Hagaman. The assistant himself was put upon the stand, and he testified that the body had been exhumed; that an autopsy had been performed; that the record of the pathologist had been received; that the organs of the dead man had been preserved, and were in process of a chemical analysis by the expert; that Dr. Flower, supposed to know something about the conditions surrounding the death, had been examined, and the written statements taken; that the autopsy was held at Poughkeepsie where Hagaman was buried. All these things, he said, took place in January or February, previous to the transaction in question. The assistant testified that, as head of the homicide bureau, he had charge of the proceedings against Flower; that the matter had been submitted to the grand jury; and that the assistant had collected the evidence. Now, what all these matters had to do with the question before the court, which manifestly was whether the defendant stole or attempted to steal the indictments when he put them in his pocket for a moment in the saloon, it is utterly impossible to conceive. The defendant was not indicted for or charged with bribery, nor for any complicity or connection with the death of Hagaman. It seems that it was a subject that had been widely discussed in all the papers, and the name of Flower, the defendant's client, had been connected in some way with the matter. The evidence was all objected to by the defendant's counsel. The objections were overruled in every case, and exceptions taken. This evidence could serve only one purpose, and that was to present the defendant before the jury as an associate, friend, and counselor of a man who was suspected, if not accused, of murder. The ruling of the learned trial judge admitting this evidence against the defendant's exception and objection was manifestly prejudicial to the defendant's rights to a degree which is difficult to describe. If the defendant had been indicted for bribery or for an attempt to bribe the district attorney or his assistant, it is possible that this evidence could be justified, but a motive for the commission of one crime is not evidence in the prosecution for another and different offense. It seems to me that the ruling embodies a fatal error, and, even if the testimony was not as clearly incompetent on its face as it appears to be, the presumption is that it prejudiced the accused, under the settled rule of this court. People v. Koerner, 154 N. Y. 377, 48 N. E. 730; People v. Helmer, 154 N. Y. 603, 49 N. E. 249; Stokes v. People, 53 N. Y. 183, 13 Am. Rep. 492; Greene v. White, 37 N. Y. 405.

The judgment of conviction should be reversed, and a new trial granted.

BARTLETT, J. (dissenting). I concur in the result reached by Judge O'BRIEN.

It is argued that the error in the reasoning of counsel for the defendant consists in assuming that the district attorney and his detective represented the state of New York in the scheme devised in the district attorney's office to entrap the defendant. I deem this the crucial point in the case. The district attorney and his detective undoubtedly acted upon the theory that they were representing the state, and doing it a great service in bringing this defendant into a situation that would result in conviction, and, as they supposed, merited punishment. This was an unfortunate error of judgment. It is a violent assumption, under the circumstances, that the district attorney and his detective were acting as private citizens, and the state was not bound in any way by what they did. The state, as a legal entity, can only be represented by officers duly authorized to exercise certain of its powers resting in its absolute sovereignty. In the case at bar, according to the testimony of the people's witnesses, the district attorney was advised that the defendant had expressed the desire to one of these witnesses to bribe an assistant district attorney to withdraw, misplace, or lose the six indictments against Flower, or go into court and oppose a motion to quash the indictments in such a manner as to permit it to succeed. This wicked purpose to bribe an official, existing in the mind of the defendant, and communicated to a man whom he supposed was his friend, represents his extreme position at the time the district attorney was advised that one of his assistants might be improperly approached. No crime had been committed or attempted. It will be observed that, according to the people's witnesses, the intention lurking in the defendant's mind was bribery. He did not contemplate getting possession of the indictments himself; his idea being that the assistant district attorney, if capable of being bribed, might lose or misplace them, or defend in a half-hearted manner a motion made to quash them. At this juncture the scheme was devised in the district attorney's office of allowing one of its detectives to place himself in communication with the defendant, and assure him that he sustained such relations to the district attorney's office and assistant district attorney as would serve his purpose. This plan was carried out, and resulted in leading the defendant into the supposed commission of two entirely distinct crimes, to wit: (1) An attempt to commit the crime of willfully, etc., removing, etc., a public document, i. e., certain indictments, in violation of section 94 of the Penal Code; (2) the crime of attempted grand larceny in the second degree, by attempting to steal the aforesaid indictments. This was not a scheme or device to detect crime already committed, wherein secrecy and deception are often resorted to in order to bring the guilty to punishment, but it was a plan to entrap the defendant, who up to that time had commited no crime whatever, but was planning in his own mind a wicked scheme to bribe an assistant district attorney. In order to carry out the scheme of the district attorney, it required the exercise of the great power and discretion conferred upon him by law. The indictments in question were on file in the clerk's office, and no court or officer had the power, under the law, to remove them for the purposes contemplated by this scheme. Code Civ. Proc. § 866. This section permits records to be brought into court in the custody of a clerk when necessary, and, when they are required at any other place, they may be removed by order of the court, specifying that the production of the original instead of the transcript is necessary. The district attorney obtained this order of the court, and secured the possession of the indictments in question; giving his official receipt therefor. Nevertheless this defendant is indicted for removing filed documents from a public office and stealing the same. The indictments were removed from the files of a public office by the district attorney, and were in his official custody and control every moment of time until they were returned to the proper custodian, and the receipt given for the same taken up. The farce enacted in the saloon where this defendant was surrounded by the officers of the law shocks the sense of justice, and, if the state disapproves this mode of procedure, it should renounce its unsavory fruits. In order to reach the conclusion that the district attorney did not represent the state in devising and carrying out this scheme, we are compelled to regard him merely as the agent of the state, exceeding his authority in the premises. I am of opinion that this familiar principle of the law of agency has no application to this case. It is essential that the sovereignty of the state should be duly represented by its officials, and there is no valid reason why it should not be bound by the action of the district attorney when he commits a grave error of judgment. The argument that the district attorney and his detective did not represent the state in this prosecution permits the inference that if they did this conviction could not stand. It is contrary to public policy and sound reason, when a defendant is entrapped by the district attorney's office into the commission of a crime he did not originally contemplate, that the state should be able to say it will treat the alleged criminal precisely as if the crime for which he was indicted originated in his own wicked intention, unaided by the officials who claim to represent it and who deliberately induced him to act.

In the case of Love v. People, 160 Ill. 501, 43 N. E. 710, 32 L. R. A. 139, cited by defendant's counsel, the court held: "Burglary is not committed by those assisting a detective in entering a building and taking money from a safe in pursuance of a previously arranged plan between him and the owner, with the sole intent of entrapping the others into the apparent commission of a crime. Acts otherwise criminal, done by a party against property at the instigation and by the encouragement of a detective, who acts in pursuance of a plan previously arranged with the owner of the property, do not constitute a crime." Numerous cases laying down this same principle of law are cited from various states.

A sound public policy requires that the state of New York should be estopped, as is a private individual who seeks to induce a person by scheme or device to commit a crime. It well comports with the dignity of the state to say that it repudiates this action of its officials, and permits this defendant, although unworthy, to go free, because he stands convicted of a crime which he never would have attempted and could not have committed save by the assistance of those who on this occasion, however proper their motives, have misrepresented it.

I vote for reversal.

PARKER, C. J., and HAIGHT, CULLEN, and WERNER, JJ., concur with VANN, J. O'BRIEN and BARTLETT, JJ., read dissenting opinions.

Judgment of conviction affirmed.

(178 N. Y. 270)

PIERSON et al. v. SPEYER.

(Court of Appeals of New York. April 26, 1904.)

RIPARIAN RIGHTS—WATER OF STREAM—REASONABLE USE—INJUNCTION.

1. A riparian owner may use the water flowing in a natural stream over his premises for domestic purposes, and to furnish power to run machinery and to irrigate his land, when the amount so used is not out of proportion to the size of the stream, and create ponds for fish and small fowl, so long as they are not large enough to materially diminish, by evaporation, the quantity of water usually flowing in the stream.

2. An upper riparian owner built a dam over the stream in order to use the water for both ornamental and domestic purposes, and the lower riparian owner sought an injunction restraining him from in any manner interfering with the water of the stream so as to diminish its natural flow. The court found that by the act of the upper riparian owner a much larger surface of water was exposed to evaporation and absorption than otherwise would have been exposed, so as to deprive the lower riparian owners of the use of water to which they were entitled. *Held* not to authorize an injunction, in the absence of a finding that the use made by defendant was unreasonable under the circumstances.

Appeal from Supreme Court, Appellate Division, Second Department.

Action by Paul M. Pierson and others against James Speyer. From a judgment of the Appellate Division (81 N. Y. Supp. 636) affirming a judgment for plaintiffs, defendant appeals. Reversed.

Charles J. Fay and Darius E. Peck, for appellant. Smith Lent, for respondents.

HAIGHT, J. This action was brought to enjoin the defendant from intercepting the flow of water in a natural stream through his premises, or in any manner interfering with the same so as to diminish the natural flow of water therein through the plaintiffs' premises. The defendant was the upper riparian owner and the plaintiffs the lower owners of the stream in question. The plaintiffs had constructed a dam and reservoir by which they impounded the waters of the stream for the purpose of supplying water daily to the growing of roses, a business in which they were engaged. In the summer of 1899 the defendant constructed a dam across the stream upon his own premises, thereby creating a reservoir about 1½ acres in extent, and impounded the water therein for both ornamental and domestic purposes. The trial court found as a fact that by reason of the construction of the dam and reservoir by the defendant "a much larger surface of water is exposed to sun and air than otherwise would be exposed, and the increased evaporation and absorption caused the water to cease flowing to and over the plaintiffs' land, and deprived them of the use of water to which they were entitled." There was no finding of fact that the defendant's use of the water was unreasonable. The decision was in what is commonly designated the "long form," containing specific findings of fact and conclusions of law. Upon these findings a judgment was entered, in which the defendant "is enjoined and restrained from continuing or permitting to continue the dam erected by him herein described in said complaint," etc.

We think the judgment entered in this case was not authorized by the findings of fact made by the trial court. It is not pretended that the defendant made any unreasonable use of the water flowing through the stream upon his premises, that he diverted or polluted it, or that he decreased the amount of the flow other than by that which was caused from evaporation and absorption. A riparian owner is entitled to a reasonable use of the water flowing in a natural stream over his premises. He may use it for domestic purposes, both in his house and his barn, and may consume it for the support of his horses, his cattle, and his poultry. He may temporarily detain it by dams, in order to furnish power to run machinery and for the purpose of irrigation of his lands, when the amount used is reasonable, and is not out of proportion to the size of the stream. He may also construct ornamental ponds, and store them with fish, or use them for his geese, his ducks, or his swans, so long as the size of the ponds is not so large as to materially diminish, by evaporation and absorption, the quantity of water usually flowing in the stream. The rights of riparian owners have been the subject of recent consideration in this court in the case of Strobel v. Kerr Salt Co., 164 N. Y. 303–320, 58 N. E. 142, 147, 51 L. R. A. 687, 79 Am. St. Rep. 643, in which the authorities and text-writers upon the subject have been collected and cited. In that case Judge Vann states the general rule as follows: "A riparian owner is entitled to a reasonable use of the water flowing by his premises in a natural stream, as an incident to his ownership of the soil, and to have it transmitted to him without sensible alteration in quality or unreasonable diminution in quantity. While he does not own the running water, he has the right to a reasonable use of it as it passes by his land. As all other owners upon the same stream have the same right, the right of no one is absolute, but is qualified by the right of the others to have the stream substantially preserved in its natural size, flow, and purity, and to protection against material diversion or pollution. This is the common right of all, which must not be interfered with by any. The use of each must, therefore, be consistent with the rights of the others, and the maxim of sic utere tuo observed by all. The rule of the ancient common law is still in force—'Aqua currit et debet currere, ut currere solebat.' Consumption by watering cattle, temporary detention by dams in order to run machinery, irrigation when not out of proportion to the size of the stream, and some other familiar uses, although in fact a diversion of the water involving some loss, are not regarded as an unlawful diversion, but are allowed as a necessary incident to the use in order to effect the highest average benefit to all the riparian owners. As the enjoyment of each must be according to his opportunity, and the upper owner has the first chance, the lower owners must submit to such loss as is caused by reasonable use." See, also, Broom's Legal Maxims, p. *373; Pomeroy on Water Rights, §§ 7, 8; Cummings v. Barrett, 10 Cush. 186.

The defendant in this case, as we have seen, was the upper riparian owner. By reason thereof he had the right to the first reasonable use of the water flowing through the stream, taking into consideration the size and velocity thereof; and, in the absence of a finding that the use made by him of the water under the circumstances was unreasonable, there was no basis for the judgment that was entered herein.

It follows that the judgment should be reversed, and a new trial ordered, with costs to abide the event.

PARKER, C. J., and O'BRIEN, BARTLETT, VANN, CULLEN, and WERNER, JJ., concur.

Judgment reversed, etc.

(162 Ind. 696)

MOORE v. ZUMBRUM.*

(Supreme Court of Indiana. April 22, 1904.)

APPEAL—FAILURE OF APPELLEE TO ACT—REVERSAL.

1. Where for 10 months after the filing of appellant's brief no steps are taken by appellee, and no excuse for such conduct is offered, the judgment will be reversed.

Appeal from Circuit Court, Whitley County; J. W. Adair, Judge.

Action by Edward Zumbrum against Nathan B. Moore and others. From a judgment for plaintiff, defendant Moore appeals. Transferred from Appellate Court under section 1337u, Burns' Ann. St. 1901. Reversed.

W. E. Leonard and John W. Orndorf, for appellant.

DOWLING, J. This is an action by the appellee against the appellants for damages alleged to have been sustained by the appellee by reason of the negligence and unskillfulness of the appellants, who were physicians and surgeons, in their treatment of the appellee during an attack of illness. Issues were formed, and a trial by a jury resulted in a verdict in favor of the appellee for $1,500. A motion for a new trial was overruled, and judgment was rendered upon the verdict. Moore alone appeals, notice having been served upon his codefendant.

Errors are assigned upon the ruling of the court on demurrers to the several paragraphs of the complaint and on the motion for a new trial.

The record was filed in the Appellate Court April 2, 1903, and notices of the appeal were issued on the same day, and were served on the appellee. The cause was fully briefed by counsel for the appellant, and his briefs were filed with the clerk of this court June 19, 1903. Ten months have elapsed since the filing of the briefs for the appellant, but no steps of any kind have been taken in the case by the appellee. No brief has been filed in his behalf, and no excuse for not filing it has been shown. Under these circumstances, the silence and neglect of the appellee to take any steps in the cause, or to controvert any of the errors assigned, may be taken as a

¶ 1. See Appeal and Error, vol. 3, Cent. Dig. § 3106.
*Motion to modify mandate denied.

confession that they exist, and that the judgment should be reversed. The rule in such cases has been plainly stated in several decisions that the judgment may, in the discretion of the court, be reversed. Berkshire v. Caley, 157 Ind. 1, 60 N. E. 696; Neu v. Town of Bourbon, 157 Ind. 476, 62 N. E. 7; People's National Bank v. State ex rel., 159 Ind. 353, 65 N. E. 6.

Judgment reversed, with directions to the court to sustain the motion of the appellant Moore for a new trial as to him.

(162 Ind. 509)

KLEIN v. NUGENT GRAVEL CO.

(Supreme Court of Indiana. April 21, 1904.)

STREET IMPROVEMENT—REPORT OF CITY ENGINEER—ASSESSMENT—VALIDITY—COLLATERAL ATTACK.

1. Under Burns' Ann. St. 1901, § 4290, providing that the owners of lots bordering on a street shall be liable for their proportion of the cost of a street improvement in the ratio of the front line of their lots to the whole line of the improvement, an assessment for such improvement should be made against the owners of lots on both sides of the street, though the improvement is of only a part of the width of the street.

2. Under Burns' Ann. St. 1901, § 4293, providing that, when a street improvement has been made, the common council shall cause a final estimate of the cost to be made by the city engineer, and require him to report the number of front feet owned by respective owners on that part of the street improved, the report should state the number of front feet of the lots bordering on both sides of the street.

3. An assessment by a city council of the cost of improvement of part of the width of a street on the owners of lots immediately bordering the part improved, omitting those on the opposite side of the street, is void, and subject to collateral attack.

Appeal from Circuit Court, Gibson County; A. M. Welborn, Judge.

Action by the Nugent Gravel Company against Anthony J. Klein. From a judgment in favor of the plaintiff, defendant appeals. Reversed by Appellate Court (66 N. E. 486), and transferred under Burns' Ann. St. 1901, § 1337j. Reversed.

Ireland & Reister, for appellant. J. G. Owen and G. K. Denton, for appellee.

JORDAN, J. This cause was originally appealed to and decided by the Second Division of the Appellate Court, and was transferred under the provisions of the second subdivision of section 1337j, Burns' Ann. St. 1901, on the ground that the opinion contravened a ruling precedent of the Supreme Court.

As preliminary, it may be stated that the transfer was not ordered because we believed that, under the facts stated in the opinion of the Appellate Court, the judgment of reversal was not a correct result, but for the reason that some of the declarations or statements of legal principles contained in the court's opinion leading up to the ultimate conclusion contradicted ruling precedents or decisions of the Supreme Court. Especially may this be said to be true in respect to the holding in Adams v. City of Shelbyville, 154 Ind. 467, 57 N. E. 114, 49 L. R. A. 797, 77 Am. St. Rep. 484. The very object of the statute under which transfers from the Appellate to the Supreme Court are authorized upon application of the losing party is to enable the Supreme Court, when necessary, to control the statements or declarations of legal principles contained in the opinion of the Appellate Court in the particular case. Barnett v. Bryce, etc., Co., 157 Ind. 572, 62 N. E. 6.

This case was successfully prosecuted in the lower court by appellee to foreclose a street assessment lien against the property of appellant, arising out of the improvement of a public street in the city of Evansville, Ind., under the provisions of what is commonly known as the "Barrett Law." The assignment of errors is based upon the overruling of appellant's demurrer to the complaint, and denying his motion for a new trial. The facts disclosed by the complaint and established by the evidence are substantially as follows:

The common council of the city of Evansville on the 10th day of February, 1890, by a resolution duly adopted, ordered that Water street be improved from Ingle street to Fulton avenue, a distance of four blocks. Water street runs east and west, and the abutting real estate situated on the south side thereof is adjacent to the Ohio river. The street is not of uniform width. From the east terminus, running west for the distance of two blocks, it is 100 feet wide. Along the third block it is 40 feet wide, and along the fourth block the street varies from 60 to 100 feet in width. The resolution or ordinance adopted by the council provided that a strip or part of the street 28 feet wide on the north side thereof from the curb line should be improved. The sidewalk on the north side of the street is 12 feet wide, which, together with the 28 feet of the roadway ordered improved, made the improvement in question extend 40 feet from the property line on the north side of the street, and left a strip 60 feet in width on the south side of said street along the first and second blocks unimproved. A strip of the street 20 to 60 feet in width, situated on the south side, along the fourth block, was also left unimproved. Or in other words, the only part of the street which was improved, under the proceedings, the entire width thereof, was along the third block, counting from the east. Such steps appear to have been taken by the common council as resulted in a contract being let to appellee for making the improvement.

Among other things, the complaint avers and shows that, upon the completion of the work by appellee, the city engineer, by direction of the common council, made a final estimate of the total cost of the improvement, and filed his report, showing the following facts: (1) That the total cost of the improvement was $5,901.10. (2) That the average cost per running front foot of the whole length of the part of the street improved was $4.25. This average cost is shown to have been obtained by dividing the whole cost of the improvement by the length of the part of the street improved, which length was 1,388½ feet. (3) The name of each person owning property abutting on that part or side of the street improved, the name of appellant being one of the property owners stated in the report. (4) The number of front feet owned by the respective property owners, the number of feet owned by appellant being 106. (5) The amount of the total cost of the improvement due on each lot and parcel of ground abutting or bordering on the part or side of the street improved, which amount is shown to have been estimated and fixed by multiplying the average cost price per running front foot by the number of running front feet of the several lots and parcels of ground respectively abutting on the north side of said Water street in the first, second, and fourth blocks from the east. The amount apportioned by the engineer in his report to each lineal foot of property situated on said north side along each of these blocks was $4.25. The property on the opposite side of the street along the first, second, and fourth blocks, which did not immediately abut on the strip improved, was not assessed for the cost of the improvement. In the third block from the east, the abutting property on both sides of the street was assessed. The amount of the assessment for each foot of the several pieces of property in this block was obtained by multiplying the whole number of running front feet of each lot or parcel of ground on each side of the street for the entire length of the improvement by one-half the cost per running foot, or, in other words, the assessment made per running foot on the abutting property on each side of the street in this block was $2.12½, or one-half of $4.25, obtained in the manner hereinbefore stated. Appellant's property, as is shown, is situated on the north side of the street, in the first block from the east, fronting on said improvement, and the amount assessed against his property was estimated and arrived at by multiplying the number of front feet on that side owned by him, to wit, 106, by $4.25, which made the amount of his assessment $450.50; being the amount, together with interest and attorney's fees, sought to be recovered in this action. The report set forth a full description, together with the owner's name, of each lot and parcel of ground abutting immediately or bordering upon the strip or part of the street improved. The report of the engineer, containing the above facts, was presented to the council, and, after giving the required notice in regard to a hearing thereon, it accepted, approved, and concurred in the said report, and assessed against the property of appellant $4.25, the amount per foot as estimated and apportioned by the engineer in his report; and this amount was declared by the council to be the assessment against his property and other lots abutting on the north side of said street along blocks 1, 2, and 4 from the east. By the resolution under which the council ordered the improvement in question, it was provided "that the abutting real estate owners each be assessed and required to pay for all costs of said improvement in their proportion." In adopting and concurring in the report of the engineer, the common council made the estimate or assessment therein reported by the engineer its own assessment, and, under the circumstances, it must be considered as the act of the common council. Leeds v. Defrees, 157 Ind. 392, 61 N. E. 930.

Section 3 of the Barrett law, which is embraced in section 4290, Burns' Ann. St. 1901, provides that the cost of any street or alley improvement shall be ascertained according to the whole length of the street or alley, or the part thereof to be improved, per running foot, and the owner of lots or parts of lots bordering on such street or alley, or the part thereof to be improved, shall be liable to the city for their proportion of the cost in the ratio of the front line of their lots to the whole improvement line for street and alley improvements. Section 4293, Burns' Ann. St. 1901, provides that, when any such improvement has been made and completed according to the terms of the contract, the common council of such city shall cause a final estimate of the cost thereof to be made by the city engineer, and shall require him to report to it the following facts touching such improvement: (1) The total cost thereof; (2) the average cost per running front foot of the whole length of that part of the street or alley so improved; (3) the name of each property owner on that part of the street or alley so improved; (4) the number of front feet owned by the respective owners on that part of the street so improved; (5) the amount of such cost for improvement due upon each lot or parcel of ground bordering on said street or alley, which amount shall be ascertained and fixed by multiplying the average cost price per running front foot by the number of running front feet of the several lots or parcels of ground, respectively; (6) "a full description together with the owner's names of each lot or parcel of ground *bordering on said street so improved.*" (Our italics.) It is manifest, from the facts herein, that the engineer, in making his report to the council, disregarded in several respects the material provisions of section 4293, supra. The engineer, in his report, as well as the common council in approving and concurring therein, seems to have proceeded upon the theory that, under the circumstances, the property abutting on the south side of Water street, in the first, second, and fourth blocks from the eastern terminus of the improvement, was not subject or liable, under the law, to any assessment whatever for the cost of the improvement, for the reason that such property did not immediately abut or border upon the strip or part of the street improved on the north side. Upon this theory or assumption, the assessment made and reported to the council by the engineer, and concurred in by that body, was limited or confined for the entire length of the three blocks in question to the abutting property on the north side of the street; being the property which abutted immediately on the improved strip. It is evident that the council, by the method adopted in making the assessment, did not even attempt to comply with the requirements of sections 4290 and 4293, supra. The council, by its act in approving and adopting the assessment reported by the engineer, in effect, arbitrarily fixed a taxing district other than that prescribed by the statute. It is certainly evident that this action of the council was beyond the power conferred upon it by the statute, and therefore was illegal and void, and hence is open to a collateral attack. Adams v. City of Shelbyville, supra; Boyce v. Tuhey (at this term) 70 N. E. 531. The engineer, instead of reporting correctly to the council, as the law exacted, the entire frontage or running front feet on both sides of the street within the line of the improvement, reported only the frontage on the north side, which, as shown, was 1,388½ feet. It is manifest, if this constitutes the whole number of running front feet along the north side of the street for the entire length of the improvement, that the total frontage on both sides would be 2,777 feet, or double the number reported by the engineer. Consequently, under these circumstances, the average cost per running front foot of the total amount of the cost of the improvement would not be $4.25, as reported, but would be only about one-half that amount. In fact, it is shown by the report that all the abutting property on both sides of the street for the length of one block was assessed at $2.12½ per running front foot, instead of $4.25, as assessed against the property of appellant. If the assessment in question be tested by the prima facie rule or standard provided under the provisions of the Barrett law, as recognized by the decisions of this court, for measuring in the first instance the special benefits received by all the abutting property on both sides of the street along the line of the improvement, it is evident that the assessment as made is not in accordance with the requirements of the statute. Adams v. City of Shelbyville, supra; Hibben v. Smith, 158 Ind. 206, 62 N. E. 447.

It is clear that the method or mode adopted in making the assessment resulted in subjecting the property of appellant to an illegal assessment and burden. The question presented is not one of a mere irregularity upon the part of the engineer and common council in attempting to comply with the positive requirements of the statute. The facts present a case in which the council is clearly shown to have exceeded the power or authority with which it was invested. Its authority to levy an assessment against the property of appellant for the cost of the improvement was strictly statutory, and, in making it, no other method than that prescribed by the statute could be legally adopted. In fact, it was only by reason of the authority or power conferred by the statute upon the common council of the city of Evansville that it had any right in the particular case to levy an assessment and fasten a lien against the property of appellant. Such statutory power is to be strictly construed, and, before appellee could successfully enforce his lien in this action, he would be required to show that the assessment upon which it is based was made within the power of the council. Niklaus v. Conkling, 118 Ind. 289, 20 N. E. 797, and cases cited; Barber, etc., Co. v. Edgerton, 125 Ind. 455, 25 N. E. 436, and cases cited; Indianapolis, etc., Co. v. Capitol, etc., Co., 24 Ind. App. 114, 54 N. E. 1076; Elliott on Roads & Streets (2d Ed.) §§ 545, 549.

The fact that a part in width, only, of the roadway of the street was improved would not, under the law, exempt from the assessment of benefits the abutting property on the south side for the distance of three blocks, as shown, merely because such property did not immediately border on the improved strip. Indianapolis, etc., Ry. Co. v. Capitol, etc., Co., supra; City of Muscatine v. Chicago, etc., Ry. Co., 88 Iowa, 291, 55 N. W. 100; Morrison v. Hershire, 82 Iowa, 271.

The assessment in this case is the very foundation of the action. It is shown to be absolutely void, for the reason, as stated, that the common council, in making it, exceeded its statutory power or authority. Consequently no action thereon can be maintained by appellee. It may be suggested, however, that, under the circumstances, the proceedings of the common council in the matter of the improvement stand as though no assessment had been made against the property of appellant.

The judgment is reversed, and the cause remanded to the lower court, with directions to grant appellant a new trial and sustain the demurrer to the complaint.

(162 Ind. 526)

SHIPLEY v. SMITH.

(Supreme Court of Indiana. April 22, 1904.)

INFANTS—CONTRACTS — DISAFFIRMANCE — PLACING OTHER PARTY IN STATU QUO—INFANT MARRIED WOMAN — DISABILITY — EMANCIPATION.

1. On the disaffirmance of a contract, an infant is not bound to place the other party in statu quo.

¶ 1. See Infants, vol. 27, Cent. Dig. § 157.

2. All voidable contracts of an infant in reference to personalty may be avoided by the infant at any time during his minority, or on his arrival at full age.

3. A lease of real estate for years is personal estate.

4. A wife may, without the consent of her husband, make leases of her land for periods not longer than three years; such a lease not being an incumbrance or conveyance, within the statute which denies her power to incumber or convey her lands save by a deed in which her husband shall join.

5. Burns' Ann. St. 1901, § 2690 (Rev. St. 1881, § 2526; Horner's Ann. St. 1901, § 2526), provides that marriage of any female ward to a person of full age shall operate as a discharge of her guardianship, and that the guardian shall be authorized to account to the wife, with the assent of the husband. *Held*, that the statute does not emancipate an infant married woman, whose husband is of full age, from the disability of infancy, save in so far as such accounting is concerned, and hence, where an infant married woman, together with her adult husband, leased her lands for two years, and received rent for the first year during her minority, on arriving at her majority, at the beginning of the second year, she might disaffirm the lease, and take possession, without restoring the rent previously received.

Appeal from Circuit Court, Morgan County; Jno. C. Robinson, Special Judge.

Action by Harriet E. Smith against Jacob A. Shipley. From a judgment in favor of plaintiff, defendant appealed. Transferred from the Appellate Court under section 1337u, Burns' Ann. St. 1901 (Acts 1901, p. 590, c. 259). Affirmed.

J. E. Sedwick and Oscar Matthews, for appellant. C. G. Renner and J. C. McNutt, for appellee.

MONKS, J. Appellee brought this action against appellant to recover possession of real estate held by him under a lease executed by her when an infant, she having disaffirmed the same on her becoming 21 years of age. After issues were joined, a trial of said cause resulted in a verdict and judgment in favor of appellee for possession of said real estate and costs of suit.

The controlling question is, can a married woman, under 21 years of age, who, together with her husband, who is over 21 years of age, has executed a lease of her land for a period of 2 years, and received the first year's rent during her minority, upon arriving at the age of 21 years, a few days after the commencement of the second year of said lease, disaffirm the same, and recover possession of said real estate, without restoring or offering to restore the rent received for the first year? The trial court, by overruling the demurrer to the complaint and appellant's motion for a new trial, decided this question in the affirmative. If such decision was correct, the judgment must be affirmed; otherwise it must be reversed.

It is a general rule that the contracts of infants are voidable and may be disaffirmed, and it is not necessary, in order to give effect to such disaffirmance, that the other party be placed in statu quo. The infant is not bound to tender back the money or property he has received before suing for the value or possession of the property given by him to the adult. Upon the avoidance of a contract on account of infancy, the case stands as if none had been made. Carpenter v. Carpenter, 45 Ind. 142; Towell v. Pence, 47 Ind. 304; Indianapolis Chair Co. v. Wilcox, 59 Ind. 429, and cases cited; Ayers v. Burns, 87 Ind. 245, 44 Am. Rep. 759, and cases cited; Rice v. Boyer, 108 Ind. 472, 9 N. E. 420, 58 Am. Rep. 53, and cases cited; Clark v. Van Court, 100 Ind. 113, 50 Am. Rep. 774, and cases cited; Shirk v. Shultz, 113 Ind. 571, 578, 15 N. E. 12, and cases cited; House v. Alexander, 105 Ind. 109, 4 N. E. 891, 55 Am. Rep. 192; White v. Branch, 51 Ind. 210; Briggs v. McCabe, 27 Ind. 327, 89 Am. Dec. 503; Pitcher v. Laycock, 7 Ind. 398.

All voidable contracts by an infant in reference to personalty may be avoided by such infant at any time during his minority or on his arrival at full age. Indianapolis, etc., Co. v. Wilcox, 59 Ind. 433, and cases cited; Shirk v. Shultz, 113 Ind. 578, 15 N. E. 12, and cases cited; Clark v. Van Court, 100 Ind. 116, 50 Am. Rep. 774, and cases cited. It is held in this state that a lease of real estate for years is personal estate, and passes to the personal representative of the lessee, upon his death intestate, and not to his heirs. Smith v. Dodds, 35 Ind. 452, 456, 457, and authorities cited; Schee v. Wiseman, 79 Ind. 389, 392; Cunningham v. Baxley, 96 Ind. 367; Mark v. North, 155 Ind. 575, 577, 578, 57 N. E. 902. It has also been held "that a wife may, without the consent or participation of her husband, make leases of her land for periods not longer than three years; such a lease not being an incumbrance or conveyance, within the meaning of the statute which denies her 'power to encumber or convey such lands except by deed in which her husband shall join.' Pearcy v. Henley, 82 Ind. 129." Nash v. Berkmeir, 83 Ind. 536; Heal v. The Niagara, etc., Co., 150 Ind. 483, 50 N. E. 482.

It is insisted by appellant that by virtue of the statutes of this state which enlarge the power of married women to contract, and section 2690, Burns' Ann. St. 1901 (section 2526, Rev. St. 1881; section 2526, Horner's Ann. St. 1901), enacted in 1863, which provides that "the marriage of any female ward to a person of full age shall operate as a legal discharge of the guardianship, and the guardian shall be authorized to account to the wife with the assent of the husband;" an infant married woman whose husband is of full age is completely emancipated from the disability of infancy, and is bound by her contracts the same as if she were over 21 years of age. Statutes which confer upon married women the power to contract generally, or even to convey their separate real estate, with or without the consent of their husbands, do not remove the disabilities of infancy from an infant married woman. Such statutes simply remove the disability of coverture, and the disability of infancy of infant married women is the same as if such statutes were not in force. Craig v. Van Bebber, 18 Am. St. Rep. note pp. 584, 586, 638, and cases cited; Harrod v. Meyers, 21 Ark. 592, 76 Am. Dec. 409. Said section 2690, supra, does not purport to remove the disability of infancy from an infant married woman when her husband is over 21 years of age, but only terminates her guardianship, and authorizes her guardian to settle with the wife, with the assent of the husband. No power is given infant married women by said section to contract with any one for any purpose, except in making an accounting with her former guardian, which can be done only with the assent of her husband. With this exception, the disability of infancy is the same as if said section had never been passed.

It follows that the result reached by the final judgment in this case was correct. Judgment affirmed.

JORDAN, J., took no part in the decision of this cause.

(163 Ind. 244)

STATE ex rel. BEREE et al. v. SEELEY.[1]

(Supreme Court of Indiana. April 20, 1904.)

SCHOOL DISTRICTS—SCHOOLS—ABANDONMENT—STATUTES—DISCRETION OF TRUSTEE—FRAUD—PETITION FOR RE-ESTABLISHMENT.

1. Burns' Ann. St. 1901, § 5920f, provides that no township trustee shall abandon any district school until he shall have procured the consent of the majority of the legal voters, provided that it shall not apply to schools that have a daily attendance of 12 pupils or less. *Held* that, where a school has an attendance of less than 12 pupils, the closing of the school by a trustee in good faith is within his discretion, and not subject to revision by the courts.

2. Where, in proceedings to compel a trustee to reopen a school which he had caused to be closed, it appeared that when it was closed the attendance was 11 pupils, and that there were not sufficient funds to maintain all the schools for the full school year, and that the deficiency in the revenue was due to the failure of the trustee and his predecessor to make a sufficient levy, though a levy of the maximum tax would have produced a sufficient fund, and that 2 of the pupils had, prior to the closing, been transferred to another school at the request of their parents, there was nothing to show that the trustee did not act in good faith, or that he had been guilty of a fraudulent attempt to evade the limitation on his authority, by Burns' Ann. St. 1901, § 5920f.

3. Burns' Ann. St. 1901, § 5920f, provides that it shall be the duty of the trustee to re-establish any school on a petition of two-thirds of the legal voters. *Held*, that the provision for re-establishing a school does not apply where the trustee is authorized to close the school without the consent of the voters.

Appeal from Circuit Court, De Kalb County; F. M. Powers, Special Judge.

Proceedings by the state, on the relation of Adron Beree and others, against William Seeley, as trustee of a school township, to compel the reopening of a school. From a judgment in favor of respondent, relators appeal. Affirmed.

E. B. Dunten and P. V. Hoffman, for appellants. McBride & Denny, George L. Denny, and John W. Baxter, for appellee.

GILLETT, C. J. Relators instituted this proceeding to require appellee by mandate to re-establish a certain school in Newville township, De Kalb county. Upon request the lower court filed special findings of fact, together with its conclusions of law thereon. Such conclusions were adverse to appellants, and a judgment was entered pursuant thereto. The special findings, so far as it is necessary to state their substance here, show the following facts: Appellee, as trustee of said school township, closed said school, and transferred the pupils thereof to another school in said township, in April, 1902. The school which was closed was a good brick building, suitably equipped for conducting a common school. The school to which said pupils were transferred was a comfortable and commodious school building in which two teachers were employed, and with the usual facilities for conducting a district school. Previous to the closing of said former school, a number of the pupils thereof had been transferred by appellee to said latter school at the request of said pupils and of their parents, in order, as they claimed, to secure better advantages for study and instruction. At the time of closing the school in question the average daily attendance upon said school, as shown by the report of the teacher thereof, was only 11 pupils, and there were not sufficient funds available to maintain all of the schools of the township for the full school year. For these reasons appellee closed said school. At that time there were resident in said district 22 children of school age, 14 of whom were between 8 and 14 years of age, and required by law to attend school unless excused by sickness, and 8 of whom were between the ages of 14 and 21, and entitled to attend school. Two pupils residing in said district, and within a short distance of said schoolhouse, had been permitted by appellee to attend said other school, although it was a mile and one-half distant. The deficiency in the revenue for tuition was due to the failure of appellee and his predecessor to make a sufficient levy for tuition purposes. A levy of the maximum tuition tax authorized by law would have produced a tuition fund adequate for the maintenance of all the schools in said township for the full term of six months. All of the relators reside in said school district, and more than two miles from the schoolhouse in said other district. Their children, 10 in number, are all of school age. After the closing of said school appellee furnished a conveyance to and from said other school to such pupils resident in said district as lived more than two miles

[1] Rehearing denied.

from the school to which they had been transferred. All the other pupils of said district, except said children of relators, live within two miles of said other school, which is accessible to them by good public roads. Prior to the institution of this proceeding, more than two-thirds of the voters in said school district entitled to vote for township trustee in said township presented to appellee a petition requesting him to re-establish said school, which request he refused to grant.

In the administration of the affairs of the common schools many questions of expediency arise. In a matter of this kind a school officer who, in good faith, acts within the range of his discretion, is not liable to have his judgment revised by the courts. Braden v. McNutt, 114 Ind. 214, 16 N. E. 170; Tufts v. State ex rel., 119 Ind. 232, 21 N. E. 892; Crist v. Brownsville Tp., 10 Ind. 461. Prior to the act of March 7, 1901 (Acts 1901, p. 159, c. 97; section 5920f, Burns' Ann. St. 1901), it was for the township trustee to determine, subject to the right of appeal to the county superintendent, what schools should be maintained in his township. State ex rel. v. Wilson, 149 Ind. 253, 48 N. E. 1030; Davis v. Mendenhall, 150 Ind. 205, 49 N. E. 1048. The case before us does not present a state of circumstances which warrants us in interfering. We cannot presume, in the absence of a showing to that effect, that appellee has been guilty of a fraudulent attempt to evade the limitation put upon his authority by the act of 1901. The law makes no provision for the re-establishing of a school upon petition where the trustee is authorized to close the school without the consent of the voters.

Judgment affirmed.

(162 Ind. 504)

KEPLER v. RINEHART.

(Supreme Court of Indiana: April 19, 1904.)

APPEALS—STATUTES GOVERNING—CONSTRUCTION—PROSPECTIVE OPERATION.

1. The right of appeal is given by the law applicable thereto in force when the final judgment is rendered, and, unless it is evident from the terms of a statute which gives, modifies, or takes away the right of appeal that it was intended to have a retrospective effect, it has no application to cases in which final judgment was rendered prior to the time such act took effect.

2. Acts 1903, p. 281, c. 156, providing that no appeal "shall hereafter be taken" to the Supreme or Appellate Court in certain cases, but which extends the right of appeal in some instances, cannot be given a retrospective construction, so as to give an appeal from a final judgment rendered before the act took effect, which was not appealable for any purpose at the time the judgment was rendered.

Appeal from Circuit Court, Wayne County; H. C. Fox, Judge.

Action by Frank W. Rinehart against George T. Kepler. From a judgment of the circuit court affirming a justice's judgment for plaintiff, defendant appeals. Transferred from the Appellate Court under Burns' Ann. St. 1901, § 1337u. Dismissed.

Lynn E. Kepler, for appellant. Daniel W. Mason, for appellee.

MONKS, J. This action was commenced before a justice of the peace, and appealed to the court below, where a trial resulted in a judgment for $100 in favor of appellee on November 10, 1902. Appellee insists that said cause was not appealable when said final judgment was rendered, and no right to appeal the same was given by the act of 1903 (Acts 1903, p. 281, c. 156). Said cause, being within the jurisdiction of a justice of the peace, was not, when final judgment was rendered in the court below, appealable for any purpose, except, under section 1337h, Burns' Ann. St. 1901, to present the question of the validity of a franchise, or the validity of an ordinance of a municipal corporation, or the constitutionality of a statute, state or federal, or the proper construction of a statute or rights guarantied by the state or federal Constitution. Sections 1337f, 1337g, 1337h, Burns' Ann. St. 1901; sections 6, 7, 8, Acts 1901, p. 566, c. 247. No such question was presented in said cause, and it was not appealable at the time final judgment was rendered.

This appeal was perfected on April 28, 1903, after the taking effect of the act approved March 4, 1903 (Acts 1903, p. 281, c. 156), which provided that "no appeal shall hereafter be taken to the Supreme or Appellate Court in any civil case when the amount in controversy exclusive of interest and cost does not exceed $50, except as provided in section 8 [section 1337h, Burns' Ann. St. 1901; Acts 1901, p. 566, c. 247] of this act." As a general rule, the right of appeal is governed by the law applicable thereto in force when the final judgment is rendered, and, unless it is evident from the terms of a statute which gives, modifies, or takes away the right of appeal that it was intended to have a retrospective effect, it has no application to causes in which final judgment was rendered prior to the time such act took effect. 2 Cyc. 520, 521, and cases cited; Carr v. Miner, 40 Ill. 33; Rivers v. Cole, 38 Iowa, 677; City of Davenport v. Davenport, etc., R. Co., 37 Iowa, 624; Barrett v. Johnson, 4 Kan. 327; Owensboro, etc., R. Co. v. Barclay, 102 Ky. 16, 43 S. W. 177; White v. Blum, 4 Neb. 555; Ely v. Holton, 15 N. Y. 595; Rice v. Floyd, 1 N. Y. 608; Spaulding v. Kingsland, Id. 426; Yarborough v. Deshazo, 7 Grat. (Va.) 374; Pritchard v. Spencer, 2 Ind. 486; Rogers v. Rogers, 137 Ind. 151, 36 N. E. 895; Wilhite v. Hamrick, 92 Ind. 594; Maxwell v. Board, etc., 119 Ind. 20, 19 L. Ed. 617; Aurora, etc., Co. v. Holthouse, 7 Ind. 59; Pomeroy v. Beach, 149 Ind. 511, 49 N. E. 370. Said act of 1903 (Acts 1903, pp. 280, 281, c. 156), under which

¶ 1. See Appeal and Error, vol. 2, Cent. Dig. § 6.

this appeal was taken, in express words, is prospective only, and cannot be given a retrospective construction. It is clear, therefore, that said act of 1903 did not make any case appealable in which final judgment was rendered before it took effect, if not appealable for any purpose at the time said final judgment was rendered.

Appeal dismissed.

(162 Ind. 506)

CASTO v. EIGEMAN.

(Supreme Court of Indiana. April 21, 1904.)

JUDGMENT—MODIFICATION—RETAXATION OF COSTS—MOTION—SUFFICIENCY.

1. On appeal from a judgment denying a motion for a modification of a judgment dismissing the cause and awarding defendant costs, plaintiff is in no position to question the correctness of the proceedings in dismissing the action and rendering judgment for costs, he having made no motion for a new trial or to set aside the order dismissing the suit.

2. A judgment reciting, "It is therefore considered and adjudged by the court that this cause be dismissed, and that defendant recover from the plaintiff all costs herein expended," is the proper one to be entered on an order dismissing the action with costs to defendant.

3. Where a judgment dismissed the cause and awarded defendant "all costs herein expended," a motion by plaintiff for a modification of the judgment and a retaxation of costs was not the correct remedy if the object of it was to correct a supposed error in the taxation of costs, since "all costs herein expended" meant only such costs as were authorized and could properly be taxed in favor of defendant.

4. After the dismissal of a cause with costs to defendant, plaintiff moved for a retaxation on the ground that the fees for witnesses were not claimed until a subsequent term, and that plaintiff could not find the return of any subpœna for such witness. The motion was verified, and plaintiff filed with it a cert' 'ate of the clerk of the court stating the same facts. *Held*, that that part of the motion to retax the witness fees was so indefinite that it would be presumed, on appeal, that a judgment denying the motion was proper, since neither the verified motion nor the certificate of the clerk constituted evidence of the taxation and entry of witness fees on the proper feebook and record.

Appeal from Circuit Court, Dubois County; E. A. Ely, Judge.

Action by Jabez C. Casto against John G. Eigeman. From a judgment denying a motion to modify a judgment in favor of defendant and to retax costs, plaintiff appeals. Transferred from Appellate Court under section 1337u, Burns' Ann. St. 1901. Affirmed.

Josiah T. Walker, for appellant.

DOWLING, J. The appellant sued the appellee for damages on account of the breach of a contract in writing for the sale and conveyance of real estate. The cause was tried by a jury, and before the introduction of the evidence was finished, upon proof by the appellee of very gross misconduct of the appellant affecting the trial itself, all the attorneys for the appellant withdrew from his case, and the court, without objection on the part of the appellant, dismissed the suit at his costs. No motion to vacate the order of dismissal or to reinstate the action was made. The judgment was in these words: "It is therefore considered and adjudged by the court that this cause be dismissed, and that the defendant recover from the plaintiff all costs herein expended." Afterwards, at the same term of the court, the appellant asked for a modification of the judgment and a retaxation of the costs, and filed his motion therefor. No ground whatever for a modification of the judgment was stated, nor was the nature or extent of the proposed modification suggested. He alleged in his motion that the defendant's costs amounted to $270.60, and, without assigning any reason for such relief, he demanded that the whole of these be taxed against the defendant. It was further averred in the motion that the fees for witnesses for attendance at the October term, 1901, amounting to $76.05, "were not claimed or demanded by any of such witnesses until the 21st day of March, 1902, at a subsequent term of said court, viz., March term, 1902, and that he is unable to find the return of any subpœna for such witnesses." The motion was verified, and appellant filed with it a certificate of the clerk of the court stating substantially the same facts. The motion was overruled, and the appellant excepted. These proceedings and papers are brought into the record by a bill of exceptions. Error is assigned upon this ruling.

No objection having been made by the appellant to the order of the court dismissing his action, and no motion for a new trial, or to set aside the order dismissing the suit, appearing in the record, the appellant is not in a position to question the correctness of the proceedings of the court in dismissing the action and rendering judgment against him. The judgment is regular in form, and was the proper one to be entered upon such an order. No modification was shown to be necessary, nor was any change in its terms requested. If the object of the motion to modify was to correct a supposed error in the taxation of the costs, the appellant mistook his remedy. The judgment did not mention the amount of the costs, but was for "all costs herein expended." This meant only such costs as were authorized by law and could be properly taxed in favor of the defendant below. Wilson v. Jenkins, 147 Ind. 533, 46 N. E. 889; Mott v. State, 145 Ind. 353, 44 N. E. 548.

The part of the motion to retax the witness fees for the October term, 1901, because not claimed in time, is so indefinite that we must presume that the action of the court overruling it was correct. They may not have been "taxed" at all, or they may have been voluntarily paid by the appellant. The bill of exceptions states that on the hearing of the motion to retax the costs "no evidence was given or heard other than the verified motion itself, and the certificate of the clerk attached thereto." The latter was not a copy of any record, but a mere voluntary statement by the clerk. Neither of these constituted evidence of the taxation and entry of the witness fees on the proper feebook and record. The court may have considered the evidence insufficient for this reason. Section 466, Burns' Ann. St. 1901; Louisville, etc., R. Co. v. Palmer, 13 Ind. App. 161, 39 N. E. 881, 41 N. E. 400; Garn v. Working, 5 Ind. App. 14, 31 N. E. 821; Thompson v. Doty, 72 Ind. 336; Thompson v. Jacobs, 74 Ind. 598.

There is no error in the record. Judgment affirmed.

(162 Ind. 538)

AGER v. STATE ex rel. HEASTON, Drainage Com'r.

(Supreme Court of Indiana. April 28, 1904.)

DRAINS — CONSTRUCTION — BENEFITS—ASSESSMENT—DESCRIPTION OF LAND—CORRECTION—JURISDICTION—MOTION IN ARREST—FINDINGS.

1. Where the description of defendant's land sought to be assessed for the construction of a public drain was erroneous, the court had jurisdiction to correct such assessment after the filing and recording of the drainage commissioner's report in a suit to recover benefits assessed.

2. Though a landowner's motion in arrest of judgment in a suit to recover an assessment for benefits for the construction of a public drain, on the ground that the description of his lands in the report of the commissioner was too indefinite to sustain a judgment, presented no issue which such landowner was authorized to tender, it nevertheless amounted to an admission that there was a defect or error in the description, so that a decision denying the motion in arrest did not amount to a finding that the description was either correct or sufficient.

Appeal from Circuit Court, Wabash County; H. B. Shiveley, Judge.

Action by the state, on the relation of Benjamin Heaston, drainage commissioner, against Eugene Ager. From a judgment in favor of complainant, defendant appealed to the Appellate Court, which transferred the case to the Supreme Court under Burns' Ann. St. 1901, § 1337u. Affirmed.

B. M. Cobb, for appellant. Sayler & Sayler, for appellee.

DOWLING, J. It appears from the complaint that in a proceeding for the construction of a public drain mistakes were made by the drainage commissioner in his report in the description of two tracts of land owned by the appellant which were found to be benefited, and were assessed for their proportionate share of the expense of the improvement. The errors were not discovered by the commissioner until six years after the filing of the report in the office of the auditor and the recording of the same. The appellant had remonstrated against the construction of the drain on various grounds, and on the hearing before the board of commissioners had accurately described the particular parcels of his lands which would be benefited. The board dismissed the remonstrance, and he appealed to the circuit court, where the cause was again decided against him. While the drain was being constructed, the appellant stood by, and pointed out the places where he wished lateral drains constructed on his lands. They were constructed as he directed, and he continues to use and enjoy them. The descriptions of the lands set out in the report and assessment of benefits were as follows: "Eugene Eger, Pt. E. ½ of S. E. ¼ of N. E. ¼, Sec. 11, Tp. 27, R. 9, 15 Acres. Benefit, $120.00." "Eugene Eger, Pt. N. E. ¼ of S. W. ¼, Sec. 12, Tp. 27, R. 9, 12 Acres, $20.00." The correct and full descriptions of the lands intended to be assessed were these: "Fifteen acres off the entire north end of the east half of the southeast quarter of the northeast quarter of section 11, township 27 north, range 9 east," and "twelve acres off the north side of the northeast quarter of the southwest quarter of section 12, township 27 north, range 9 east." The relief demanded was that the description of each tract of appellant's land be corrected, that the appellee have judgment for the amounts of the benefits assessed, that the same be declared liens on said lands, that the lands so benefited be sold, etc. A demurrer to each paragraph of the complaint was overruled. The answer was in five paragraphs, the first being a general denial. Demurrers were sustained to the others. The cause was tried by the court, a special finding of facts was made and conclusions of law were stated thereon. A motion for judgment for the appellant on the finding was overruled. Each conclusion of law was excepted to, and a motion for a new trial was overruled. Error is assigned upon the several rulings on the demurrers, upon each conclusion of law, on the ruling on the motion for judgment on the special finding, and on the motion for a new trial.

The points made by counsel for appellant are that an assessment under the drainage act of 1893 must contain an accurate and sufficient description of each parcel of land intended to be charged with its proportion of cost of the improvement; that errors in the description of the lands assessed cannot be corrected after the filing and recording of the report of the drainage commissioner; and that in this case, objection to the description having been made by the appellant in the circuit court by motion in arrest of judgment because of such indefiniteness and uncertainty, and the motion decided against him, by this decision the description of his lands was held sufficiently certain, and that the matter of such description is therefore res adjudicata, and cannot be re-examined in this case. Neither the brief for the appellant nor that for the appellee states under what statute the proceedings to construct the drain in question were taken, but we infer that they were based upon sections 5655-5671, Burns' Ann. St. 1901, authorizing the construction of drains by the board of commissioners of any county upon the petition of one or more landowners whose lands will be affected by or assessed for the expense of the construction of such drain. The propositions relied upon by counsel for appellant are not sustained by the decisions of this court. The very reverse has been held to be the law. It has been said repeatedly that, when mistakes have occurred, there is no valid reason why the description should not be corrected and made accurate, so that the assessment may be enforced against the property actually benefited by the improvement. As the commissioner must file a complaint to enforce the assessment in a court of general jurisdiction, after due notice to the property owner, an opportunity for a full hearing upon all questions involved is afforded, and the court then renders a judgment upon the merits of the controversy. Justice requires that the land actually benefited should bear its proportion of the expense of the construction of the drain, and, where the court can ascertain the proper description of the land, it has the power to correct mistakes in the commissioners' report so that the assessment may be enforced, and, when properly invoked, the power ought to be exercised. The State ex rel. Ely v. Smith, 124 Ind. 302, 24 N. E. 331; Luzadder v. The State ex rel. 131 Ind. 598, 31 N. E. 453. These cases are conclusive upon the power of the court to correct such mistakes in the assessment.

Appellant's motion in arrest of judgment in the circuit court on the ground that the description of his lands in the report of the commissioner was too indefinite to sustain a judgment presented no issue which the appellant was authorized to tender. It did amount, however, to an admission of record that there was a defect or error in the description, and the decision on the motion was not a finding that the description was correct or sufficient. The admission was evidence in this action that the defects or errors existed. Miles v. Wingate, 6 Ind. 458; McNutt v. Dare, 8 Blackf. 35; Boots v. Canine, 94 Ind. 408; Railway Co. v. Evarts, 112 Ind. 533, 14 N. E. 309; Lux & Talbott Stone Co. v. Donaldson, 68 N. E. 1014, 161 Ind. —. It follows that there was no error in any of the rulings complained.

Judgment affirmed.

(163 Ind. 330)

CHRISTMAN v. HOWE et al.*

(Supreme Court of Indiana. April 27, 1904.)

CONTINUING TRESPASS—INJUNCTION—ADEQUATE REMEDY AT LAW.

1. Where plaintiff, who was the owner of a lot, and of the basement and first story of a building thereon, the upper story of which was owned by defendants, who also held a perpetual easement to maintain a stairway from the street to the second story, sued to enjoin defendants from erecting or maintaining under the stairs certain sewer, water and gas pipes for use in the second story of the building, on the theory that such pipes constituted a continuing trespass, but the real purpose of the action was to settle a disputed question of title to the real estate between the parties under the contract for the erection of the building, an injunction was properly denied; the evidence showing that the acts to be enjoined had been committed before the suit was tried, and as plaintiff had a complete and adequate remedy at law to recover damages, which would afford complete redress for the injury.

Appeal from Circuit Court, Miami County; J. T. Cox, Judge.

Suit by John Christman against Maurice S. Howe and others. From a judgment in favor of defendants, plaintiff appealed to the Appellate Court, which transferred the case to the Supreme Court, as authorized by Burns' Ann. St. 1901, § 1337u. Affirmed.

Alvah Taylor, A. H. Plummer, and W. G. Todd, for appellant. H. C. Pettit, for appellees.

JORDAN, J. Appellant on July 8, 1895, instituted this action to enjoin appellees from running gas, water, and sewage pipes from the second story of a certain brick building, situated on the following real estate: Twenty-five feet off the north end of lot No. 53 in the city of Wabash, Ind. The west part of these premises fronted on Wabash street, and the north line thereof abutted on Market street. The complaint, stripped of conclusions, etc., discloses the following facts: On November 10, 1863, appellant was the owner of the above real estate, and on that date he and one William S. Ludlow entered into a written contract, a copy of which was made a part of the complaint, whereby it was agreed between them to erect a two-story brick building on the said premises. The first story was to be erected and maintained by appellant, and the second story was to be erected and maintained by Ludlow. For the consideration, as recited in the contract, appellant covenanted as follows: "Doth covenant, as hereinafter set out, and bargain, sell and convey unto the said Ludlow, his heirs and assigns, the free and uninterrupted use, as long as the building hereinafter mentioned shall stand, on the following described real estate, situate in the county of Wabash and State of Indiana [describing it], to erect and maintain thereon, and use the same, the second story of the brick building to be erected on said part of said lot by the said Christman and Ludlow. Also, the free and uninterrupted use of space sufficient in the south side of said building to erect, maintain and use the same, the stairway 3½ feet in width in the clear, the stairway for said stairs to extend from the pavement in front of said building up to said room," etc. A supplemental contract executed by these parties on August 26, 1864, provided that "the said parties hereby agree that the said Ludlow,

¶ 1. See Injunction, vol. 27, Cent. Dig. § 16.
*Rehearing denied.

his heirs and assigns, shall have a perpetual right to erect and maintain a room in the second story over the lot mentioned in said instrument." Under the terms and provisions of this contract, appellant and Ludlow did erect a two-story brick building on said lot, and a stairway was constructed from Wabash street, on the south side of the lot, to the second story, and was 3½ feet wide in the clear. The first story and the basement of this building were occupied by appellant and his tenants up to the time of the commencement of this action. The upper or second story has been occupied by Ludlow and his grantees from the date of said contract until the institution of this action. In the year 1895 appellee Maurice S. Howe became the owner of said second story by purchase from the Masonic Lodge, the latter having purchased it from Ludlow. At the time Howe became the owner the second story consisted of one large room. This he partitioned so as to make five rooms, which he fitted up to rent as offices. It is charged in the complaint "that in the construction of said stairs no part of the first-story room was occupied or used, except so much as was necessary to erect said stairway." The complaint charges that on or about the 8th day of July, 1895, the defendant Maurice S. Howe wrongfully and without the license or consent of the plaintiff threatened and was at the commencement of this suit threatening to, and will if not restrained by the order of the court, run and construct water, gas, and sewer pipes from his said second-story room through the floor of said second story, about 10 inches beyond the landing of the stairs on said second floor, and into plaintiff's said first-story room, and against the south wall of said building, thence south along said south wall and underneath said stairway until the same reaches the floor of said first-story room; thence through said floor and into the basement; thence under said sidewalk adjoining the building into the mains of the respective kinds of pipe, to wit, water, gas, and sewer pipe mains. It is further charged that the weight of these pipes will weaken the stairs and walls of the building and that cutting the holes through the walls of said building, and fastening the pipes to the same, will impose excessive weight upon said stairs; that said acts will amount to and constitute a continual trespass upon the basement story of said building, and will continue to cause great damage to plaintiff, by reason of the careless and negligent overflow of water basins and closets in the said upper story, thereby flooding said first story; and that, by reason of the character of said injuries, plaintiff cannot be compensated in damages. The prayer of the complaint is that the defendants be forever restrained and enjoined from maintaining any pipes in the said building, and that they be required to permit the building to remain as it was prior to the wrongs threatened and complained of, and that plaintiff's title to the said first-story room, and the basement thereunder, and the space under said stairs, be forever quieted and put at rest. Appellant, after the commencement of the action, filed what is termed a second paragraph, or supplemental complaint, wherein it is alleged that, notwithstanding the commencement of this action, of which the defendant Howe had notice, the latter has proceeded, over the objections of plaintiff, and placed the pipes in question as he had threatened to do, and that his said acts in so doing amount to a continuing trespass on the basement story of said building, which causes damage to the plaintiff, by reason of negligently permitting the water mains and closets in the second story to overflow, and thereby flood the lower story of said building, etc. A temporary restraining order was granted upon the complaint, which was subsequently dissolved. A demurrer to the complaint was overruled, and the defendants answered in three paragraphs, the first of which was a general denial. The demurrer to the second and third paragraphs of the answer was overruled, and appellant replied by a general denial. A trial by the court upon the issues joined by the parties resulted in a finding in favor of the appellees, and, over appellant's motion for a new trial, judgment was rendered that he take nothing by his action. The errors assigned are based on the overruling of the demurrer to the second and third paragraphs of the answer, and denying appellant's motion for a new trial.

The theory of the complaint apparently is to enjoin appellees from putting gas, water, and sewage pipes from the second story underneath the stairway to the basement, and thereby connecting such pipes with the respective mains in the public street. The second and third paragraphs of the answer are but argumentative denials. The second sets up and relies on the contract referred to in the complaint, and alleges, among other things, the necessity of having the rooms situated on the second story supplied with gas, water, and sewage pipes, etc. The third alleges that the defendants are the owners of the free and uninterrupted use and enjoyment of the real estate described in plaintiff's complaint. It is averred that under the contract in question they are seised of a perpetual title to said real estate, without restriction. It is further alleged that, by the conveyance made by plaintiff in said contract, he conveyed to the defendants the free and uninterrupted use of a space sufficient on the south side of said building to erect, maintain, and use a stairway 3½ feet in width in the clear, and that the said lot upon which the said building is located is situated in the very center of the business part of the city of Wabash, and is surrounded by business properties, in all of which there is the common use of gas, water, sewage, and closets by means of similar pipes; that the second story of said building is adapted to and is equipped for suites of offices, and that the same cannot be used, rented, and enjoyed in the usual and ordinary manner prevailing in similar properties in said city without supply pipes for gas and water; that it is the desire of the defendant to avail himself of the necessities and conveniences of gas, water, and closets in the use and enjoyment of his said second story, and that it is absolutely necessary for him, in order to utilize in the usual and ordinary manner his said premises, and for himself and tenants as well, to have a supply of water and gas in his said premises and rooms, together with a sewage pipe to discharge sewage therefrom. It is further alleged that the stairway to said premises arises at the southwest part of the building on Wabash street, at an angle of about 40 degrees, and that for 32 years last past a space has been, by mutual agreement of all the owners of said buildings, set off the south side thereof, nearly its full depth, and 3½ feet wide, and partitioned from the remainder of said first story by a solid wall, with no openings except doorways; that at the west end thereof, and vertically below defendant's stairway, plaintiff has a cellar stairway; and that the space below the stairway is dark and unused, except as a passageway to the cellar and for stowage; the said stairway leading to the second story is solid and substantial, and rests upon a four-inch projection from the south wall of said brick building, and the north side of the stairway is securely held and supported by timbers of unusual strength and durability; that these defendants, in the use of gas, water, and sewage pipes, propose to use only so much of the first story, viz., a space about 6 by 10 inches square, inclosed by boxing immediately under and against the south end of the stairway from the lower rest to a point where it joins the floor above, and to connect the same at the lower end under the Wabash street doorsill 3 feet under ground, through the building foundation, with supply and discharge pipes in the streets; that the gas and water supply pipes are two inches, and the soil pipe is four inches; that all of these pipes are to be inclosed neatly and away from any possible use to which plaintiff's first story can be applied, viz., that is to say, in the said dark and unused cellar spaces between the two stairways, and 10 feet above the cellar stairway; that defendants cannot place said pipes outside said building, because of being subjected to freezing; that placing them in the place selected will cause the least obstruction; that neither of said pipes, nor the use thereof, can or will interfere in any way with the full use and enjoyment by plaintiff of the premises described in his complaint, and that the present use and enjoyment thereof, together with gas, water, and sewage therein, are absolutely necessary to the ordinary and usual enjoyment by the defendants of the second story, and that said pipes do not and will not in any manner weaken, destroy, or impair the present strength, durability, and condition of said building and its foundation; that defendants do not propose to cut any openings in said building, other than a small hole in the second floor, over the dark passageway, immediately below the top of said steps, and against the south wall, and an opening in the foundation wall under the Wabash street doorsill, three feet below said sill.

The facts alleged in each of these paragraphs, so far as the same were admissible, could have been introduced in evidence under the first paragraph of the answer, which, as previously stated, was the general denial. By reason of the conclusion reached in this case, we may dismiss the question as to whether these paragraphs of answer were sufficient to withstand appellant's demurrer. If it be conceded that, under the facts averred in the complaint, appellant is entitled to equitable relief by injunction, nevertheless a consideration of the evidence fully discloses that the finding and judgment of the court denying the injunction was a correct conclusion. The contract in pursuance of which the building was erected upon the real estate in question was introduced in evidence, and it was shown that the parties thereunder constructed a two-story brick building upon the real estate therein described, and that the appellant had used and enjoyed the lower story thereof, and appellees and their grantors had used and enjoyed the second story. The evidence discloses that the acts of appellees which appellant seeks to enjoin constituted nothing more, at the farthest, than a mere trespass. It is not proven that any great or irreparable damage will be sustained by him by reason of appellees placing and maintaining the gas and water supply pipes in controversy. They base their right or authority to place the pipes as they did on the ground that, under the contract in question, they were vested with the fee simple in and to the premises upon which the building is situated, to the extent, at least, that they may, in a reasonable and appropriate manner, by a proper plumbing, conduct from the public mains artificial gas and water pipes to the second story, and also in like manner conduct or run sewage pipes from the said story into the public sewer. There is evidence in the case to show that the only place which they can run or place these pipes on the south side of the building is under the stairway, to which they were given free and uninterrupted use by the provisions of the contract. They appear to have run two small water and gas supply pipes, and one four-inch soil or sewage pipe, from below under this stairway through a dark and unused closet or basement beneath up to the second story. These pipes appear to have been hung under the stairway by means of hooks fastened thereto, and the combined weight of the pipes for the entire length thereof was 180 pounds. They were incased in pine boxing, about 8 inches square, and it is shown that in no manner did they serve to weaken or affect the walls of appellant's lower story. It appears that they were necessary in order to supply the second story of the building with gas and water. This story had been partitioned off into five rooms, which were rented for office purposes. It is further shown that the acts which appellant sought to enjoin had been fully committed after the commencement of the action, but before the time of the trial. As previously stated, appellant, in his petition, prayed for an injunction, and that his title to the real estate and the basement of his story be quieted. The evidence apparently discloses that the very purpose of the action is to settle a disputed question in regard to the title or interest acquired by appellees, under the contract, in the realty upon which the building is situated. The law affords appellant an appropriate and adequate remedy for settling such a controversy. By the facts in the case, as shown by the evidence, the question is fully presented whether appellant is entitled to the interposition of a court of equity. Or, in other words, under the evidence, was he entitled to an injunction? That he is not is fully decided and settled in the appeal of Wabash Railroad Co. v. Engleman, 160 Ind. 329, 66 N. E. 892. In that case it is said: "Of course, the right to invoke the jurisdiction of a court of equity must depend upon the peculiar or particular facts in each case, and one of the questions to be decided is whether the legal remedy under the particular circumstances of the case is adequate, or, in other words, is such remedy as practicable and efficient to promote the interests of justice and its prompt administration as is the remedy in equity? * * * The authorities affirm that the inadequacy of the legal remedy is the very foundation or indispensable prerequisite for the interposition of a court of equity, for the plain or evident reason that, inasmuch as the law has provided a complete or adequate remedy for the redress of the particular wrong, therefore a court of chancery is not authorized to interpose its prerogative." As a general rule, in order to give a court of equity the right to interpose by injunction and prevent a wrong about to be committed against or upon the property of another, the threatened injury must be of such a character or nature as not to be susceptible of complete pecuniary compensation. In addition to this fact, the title or right of the complainant in and to the property in question must be admitted or established by legal adjudication. Wabash R. R. Co. v. Engleman, supra.

It follows that the judgment below was a correct result, and is therefore affirmed.

(162 Ind. 534)

McCRORY v. O'KEEFE, Treasurer.

(Supreme Court of Indiana. April 26, 1904.)

TAXATION — CREDITS—INDEBTEDNESS—DEDUCTION — DEMAND—TIME—INJUNCTION—GROUNDS—BURDEN OF PROOF.

1. In a suit to enjoin the collection of taxes the burden is on the complainant to allege and prove either that the property on which the taxes were assessed was not subject to taxation, or that the taxes had been paid.

2. Where property is taxable, the want of notice, or its insufficiency, or any other irregularity or informality in the assessment, does not entitle the owner of the property to an injunction restraining the collection of a tax levied thereon.

3. Under Burns' Ann. St. 1901, § 8411, providing that for the purposes of taxation personal property shall include all indebtedness due to inhabitants of the state above the amounts respectively owed by them, etc., where a taxpayer claimed a deduction of a bona fide indebtedness from credits sought to be listed for taxation at the time of notice given of its contemplated assessment as omitted property he was entitled to such deduction notwithstanding he failed to claim the same at the time he listed his property for the year for which it was alleged the credit subsequently taxed was omitted.

Appeal from Circuit Court, Marshall County; Harry Bernetha, Judge.

Action by Francis M. McCrory against William O'Keefe. From a judgment sustaining a demurrer to the complaint, plaintiff appealed to the Appellate Court, by which the case was transferred to the Supreme Court, as authorized by Burns' Ann. St. 1901, § 1337u. Reversed.

H. A. Logan, for appellant. Martindale & Stevens, for appellee.

MONKS, J. Appellant brought this suit against appellee, as treasurer of Marshall county, to enjoin the collection of certain taxes for the year 1900 assessed by the county assessor and placed on the tax duplicate by the county auditor as taxes on omitted property. The court sustained a demurrer for want of facts to the first and second paragraphs of the complaint and to the amended third and fourth paragraphs of the complaint. Final judgment against appellant. The errors assigned and not waived call in question the action of the court in sustaining the demurrer to each of said amended paragraphs of the complaint.

It appears from the amended third paragraph of complaint that the county assessor of Marshall county on December 30, 1902, after written notice to appellee and a hearing, listed and assessed a note secured by mortgage, held and owned by appellee on the 1st day of April, 1900, upon which there was due a balance of $1,500, at $1,500, as omitted property; that the auditor of said county placed the same on the tax duplicate for collection, and the treasurer is attempting to collect the same; that about eight months after the listing of appellee's property for taxation in the year 1900 the county assessor of said county, after notice to appellee and hearing, listed and assessed against him for said year on account of personal property $890 as omitted property, and the same was placed on the tax duplicate for 1900, and he paid the taxes thereon to the treasurer of said county. It is not alleged that said promissory note upon which there was a balance due of $1,500 on April 1, 1900, was ever listed and assessed for taxation for the year 1900, or that any tax was ever paid thereon for that year, nor that said promissory note was included in the omitted property assessed by the county assessor at $890 on December 30, 1900. As against appellant the presumption is that the county assessor on December 30, 1900, properly listed and assessed said promissory note for the year 1902 as omitted property, and that the same is properly on the tax duplicate in the hands of appellee, as the treasurer of said county, for collection.

One who seeks to enjoin the collection of taxes must show by allegation and proof either that the property upon which the taxes are assessed is not subject to taxation, or that said taxes have been paid. This rests upon the principle that a court of equity will not give any aid to one who seeks to avoid the payment of taxes upon taxable property. If the property is taxable, want of notice, or its insufficiency, or any other irregularity or informality, does not entitle the owner of the property to an injunction. Crowder v. Riggs, 153 Ind. 158, 161, 53 N. E. 1019, and cases cited; 1 Spelling on Injunctions (2d Ed.) § 645; High on Injunctions (3d Ed.) § 497. It is evident that the court did not err in sustaining the demurrer to the amended third paragraph of complaint.

The facts alleged in the amended fourth paragraph of complaint and admitted by the demurrer were that the county assessor, after notice and hearing, on December 30, 1902, listed and assessed a note secured by mortgage, held and owned by appellant on April 1, 1900, upon which there was then due a balance of $1,500, at $1,500, as omitted property, and that the same was placed on the tax duplicate for collection; that the said credit so listed and assessed was due and owing to appellant from one Jourdon; that on said 1st day of April, 1900, appellant was justly indebted to Nancy Rose in the sum of $1,500, evidenced by a promissory note secured by mortgage on real estate owned by appellant; that at the hearing before the county assessor he stated all of the foregoing facts, and demanded that the debt due from him to said Rose for $1,500 be deducted from the balance of $1,500 due him from said Jourdon, but the county assessor refused to make or allow said deduction on the ground that "he [appellant] had failed to take credit for the same when listing his property with the township assessor for the year 1900"; that prior to the time of the assessment complained of all the property of appellant had been assessed, and he had paid the taxes thereon, except only said $1,500 evidenced by said note and mortgage, and that he was not liable for any taxes thereon for the reason that he was entitled to a deduction for the same amount on account of his indebtedness to said Rose; that he disclosed all the facts alleged in regard to his said indebtedness and credits to the township assessor when listing his property in 1900, and to the county assessor at said hearing.

It is provided in section 8411, Burns' Ann. St. 1901: "For the purposes of taxation * * * personal property shall include all indebtedness due to inhabitants of this state above the amounts respectively owed by them whether such indebtedness is due from individuals or corporations public or private, and whether such debtors reside within or without the state." The form of schedule for the assessment of personal property enacted by the Legislature and in force since 1899 requires that the taxpayer's indebtedness, evidenced by promissory notes, for which he claims deduction from credits, should be itemized by giving the name of each person or persons to whom he is so indebted, the date of maturity of the same, and the amount. Unless the taxpayer itemizes his indebtedness as required by said schedule, he is not entitled to deduct the same from credits listed by him in said schedule. In this case, however, appellant did not list on the schedule filled out by him in the year 1900 said promissory notes on said Jourdon, for a balance due of $1,500, nor did he claim credit in said schedule for the $1,500 note he owed Nancy H. Rose. He did claim credit therefor at the hearing before the county assessor in December, 1902, when required to appear and show cause why said note on Jourdon for a balance of $1,500 should not be listed and assessed against him for taxation for the year 1900 as omitted property. If said claim for deduction was made at the time and place as alleged in said amended fourth paragraph of complaint, it should have been allowed, if the same was a bona fide indebtedness of appellant on April 1, 1900. Moore v. Hewitt, 147 Ind. 464, 46 N. E. 905; Florer v. Sheridan, 137 Ind. 28, 32, 36 N. E. 365, 23 L. R. A. 278. The Legislature no doubt has the power to provide that any person who fails to list any or all of his credits as required by said schedules (section 8463, Burns' Ann. St. 1901) should not be allowed any deduction for indebtedness, but no such law has been enacted. It follows that the court erred in sustaining appellee's demurrer to the amended fourth paragraph of complaint.

Judgment reversed, with instruction to overrule the demurrer to the amended fourth paragraph of complaint, and for further proceedings not inconsistent with this opinion.

(162 Ind. 554)

EATON v. STATE.

(Supreme Court of Indiana. April 29, 1904.)

INVOLUNTARY MANSLAUGHTER — INDICTMENT— UNLAWFUL ACT—POINTING WEAPON— ALLEGATION OF PURPOSE.

1. Burns' Ann. St. 1901, § 1981, provides that whoever wrongfully kills any human being without malice, involuntarily, but in the commission of some unlawful act, is guilty of manslaughter. *Held*, that an indictment must show that accused was engaged in the commission of some unlawful act from which the homicide resulted.

2. Burns' Ann. St. 1901, § 1981, provides that whoever unlawfully kills any human being without malice, involuntarily, but in the commission of some unlawful act, is guilty of manslaughter. Section 2073 provides that it shall be unlawful for any person over the age of 10 years, with or without malice, purposely to point or aim any pistol or other firearm, either empty or loaded, towards any other person. *Held*, that an indictment charging involuntary manslaughter because of the killing of deceased by accused while he was violating section 2073, by pointing and aiming a firearm at deceased, was insufficient for failing to employ the word "purposely," or any other word of equivalent import, in describing the conduct of accused.

Appeal from Circuit Court, Gibson County; O. M. Welborn, Judge.

Charles Eaton was convicted of involuntary manslaughter, and he appeals. Reversed.

W. E. Stilwell and Henry Kester, for appellant. Wm. Espenschied, C. W. Miller, Atty. Gen., W. C. Geake, C. C. Hadley, and L. G. Rothschild, for the State.

JORDAN, J. Appellant was tried upon an indictment and found guilty by a jury of having committed the crime of involuntary manslaughter. The jury found that his true age was 19 years. Over his motion for a new trial, he was sentenced by the court to be confined in the Indiana Reformatory Prison for a period of not less than 2 nor more than 21 years. From this judgment he appeals, and assigns as errors (1) that the court erred in overruling his motion to quash the indictment; (2) in overruling his motion for a new trial.

That part of the indictment charging the offense is as follows: "That one Charles Eaton, late of said county, on the 15th day of April, A. D. 1903, at said county and state aforesaid, did then and there unlawfully and feloniously, and without malice, express or implied, and involuntarily, kill one Lizzie Eaton, by then and there shooting her, the said Lizzie Eaton, in and upon the body, with a certain pistol loaded with gunpowder and leaden balls, which he, the said Charles Eaton, then and there had and held in his hand, while he, the said Charles Eaton, was then and there in the commission of an unlawful act, to wit, pointing and aiming a certain firearm, to wit, a pistol, at and toward the said Lizzie Eaton, he the said Charles Eaton being then and there over the age of ten (10) years, whereby, and by means of said unlawful pointing and aiming said pistol as aforesaid at the said Lizzie Eaton, said pistol was discharged at, against, and into the body of the said Lizzie Eaton, and did then and there mortally wound the said Lizzie Eaton, and of which wound so inflicted as aforesaid the said Lizzie Eaton then and there died, contrary," etc. Involuntary manslaughter is defined by our statute as follows: "Whoever unlawfully kills any human being without malice, express or implied, * * * involuntarily, but in the commission of some unlawful act, is guilty of manslaughter, and upon conviction thereof, shall be imprisoned in the State Prison not more than twenty-one years nor less than two years." Section 1981, Burns' Ann. St. 1901. To constitute a good charge of this crime, it is essential that it be shown in the indictment that the accused person was engaged in the commission of some unlawful act from which the homicide in question resulted. Willey v. State, 46 Ind. 363. The unlawful act in the commission of which it is claimed by counsel for the state appellant was engaged, and the one to which the indictment attributed the killing of the deceased, is defined by section 2073, Burns' Ann. St. 1901, as follows: "It shall be unlawful for any person over the age of ten years, with or without malice, purposely to point or aim any pistol, gun, revolver, or other firearm either loaded or empty, at or towards any other person, and any person so offending shall be guilty of an unlawful act, and upon conviction shall be fined in any sum not less than one nor more than five hundred dollars." The objection urged against the sufficiency of the indictment is that it fails to disclose that the accused was engaged in the commission of the unlawful act declared by this section of the statute, for the reason that neither the word "purposely," contained in the statute, nor any word of equivalent import or meaning, is employed in the indictment, in charging that he was in the commission of such unlawful act. Or in other words, his counsel contend that the gravamen of the offense described or defined by the section in question is that the pointing or aiming of the pistol must be purposely or intentionally done on the part of the accused person. In answer to this contention, counsel for the state say: "This contention is undoubtedly true so far as the word 'point' is concerned, yet the court will observe that the statute also contains the word 'aim,' with the reference to the use of any pistol, gun, revolver," etc. Therefore they argue that the absence of the word "purposely" does not render the pleading defective, because, in addition to the word "pointing," the word "aiming" is used. Counsel's position in this respect is wholly untenable. It will be seen that the statute declares it to be an unlawful act for any one over the age of 10 years "purposely to point or aim any pistol," etc. "Purposely," as therein used, means intentionally or designedly. Fahnestock v. State, 23 Ind. 231. The word "aim" is used in the disjunctive, and under such circumstances the statute may be violated by doing either or both of the forbidden acts. The person accused thereunder may be charged (1) with having purposely pointed the pistol at and towards another; (2) with having purposely aimed the weapon at and towards another; (3) with having purposely pointed and aimed the weapon at and towards another. See Gillett's Criminal Law (2d Ed.) § 679, and the form of an indictment therein given.

By the latter method of pleading but one offense would be charged, and upon conviction the violator would be subject to the penalty provided. Rosenbarger v. State, 154 Ind. 425, 56 N. E. 914.

The Legislature has made the qualifying word "purposely" a necessary ingredient of the crime defined by section 2073, supra, and hence it cannot be dispensed with in charging such offense, unless a word of equivalent import be used. Murder in the second degree is declared by our statute to be where one "purposely and maliciously * * * kills any human being." Certainly no one would contend that a charge of murder of the second degree would be sufficient where neither the word "purposely," nor language of an equivalent meaning, was employed by the pleader. Wherein, then, can it, in reason, be asserted that in charging the commission of the unlawful act defined by section 2073, supra, the pleading will be sufficient, although neither the word "purposely," nor one conveying the same meaning, is used? In Graham v. State, 8 Ind. App. 497, 35 N. E. 1109, the court had under consideration this same statute. In that appeal it was held that, to constitute the offense, the pointing of the weapon must be purposely done.

That the indictment in the case at bar is fatally defective for the reasons stated is certainly evident. Other objections are urged against it, but as to whether it is open to these we need not and do not determine.

It follows that the court erred in overruling the motion to quash, for which error the judgment is reversed, and the cause remanded, with instructions to the lower court to quash the indictment. The clerk will issue the proper order for the return of the prisoner to the sheriff of Gibson county.

(162 Ind. 517)

REPUBLIC IRON & STEEL CO. v. BERKES.

(Supreme Court of Indiana. April 22, 1904.)

MASTER AND SERVANT—INJURY—NEGLIGENCE—EVIDENCE—PRESUMPTION—APPEAL.

1. Evidence that a common laborer, who had placed a bar of iron between the jaws of shears which opened and shut at equal intervals about 20 times a minute, was suddenly commanded by his foreman to cut the bar in a different place, and, while attempting to remove the bar in obedience to the command, without knowledge of any danger, was injured, presented a case for the jury as to whether the foreman was negligent in giving the order.

2. Where a servant was obeying a specific order of the foreman, under whose control he had been placed by the master, he had the right to presume, in the absence of warning or notice to the contrary, that he would not thereby be subjected to injury.

3. Where there is evidence to sustain a judgment in every material respect, it will not be disturbed on appeal.

Appeal from Circuit Court, Lake County; W. C. McMahan, Judge.

Action by Charles Berkes against the Republic Iron & Steel Company. From a judgment in favor of the plaintiff, defendant appeals. Transferred from the Appellate Court under Burns' Ann. St. 1901, § 1337u. Affirmed.

Miller, Elam & Fesler and S. D. Miller, for appellant. A. F. Knotts, George Reiland, and F. M. Conroy, for appellee.

JORDAN, J. This action was prosecuted by appellee, as plaintiff below, to recover damages for personal injuries received while in the employ of appellant. A trial by jury resulted in a verdict in favor of appellee. Answers to numerous interrogatories were also returned by the jury along with their general verdict. Appellant, at the close of appellee's evidence, unsuccessfully moved the court to direct the jury to find in its favor. Its motion for a new trial was denied, and judgment was rendered in favor of appellee for the damages awarded by the jury.

The complaint, in substance, avers and sets up the following facts: On and prior to the 11th day of January, 1900, the date upon which appellee was injured, the defendant was a corporation incorporated under the laws of the state of Illinois. On that day and prior thereto it was engaged in the city of East Chicago, Lake county, Ind., in manufacturing iron and steel. Plaintiff was an employé of appellant, engaged in working as a common laborer in its mills and factory at said city, and at the time of receiving the injuries of which he complains, he was working in the line of his duty. Defendant, on employing him to work in its mills and factory, put him at work in cutting scrap iron into pieces by means of large iron shears operated in said factory. While engaged at this work the plaintiff was under the control and orders of one John Flack, who was the foreman of the defendant in the department of its factory where the plaintiff worked. Flack, as such foreman, had the right and authority from defendant to order and direct the plaintiff in regard to the work in which he was engaged, and plaintiff was required to conform to and obey the orders and directions of the said foreman. At the time of the accident the plaintiff and another person in the employ of the defendant were directed and required to cut into small pieces a long, crooked, and warped iron bar by means of the said shears provided by defendant for that

¶ 2. See Master and Servant, vol. 34, Cent. Dig. § 778.

purpose. Immediately prior to the injury received by plaintiff as hereinafter stated, he and his assistant had properly placed this bar of iron in the jaws or mouth of the shears, and had pushed it as far back as possible, in order that when the knives of the shears came together they would cut the iron into square pieces without turning the bar over. The jaws of these shears, it is alleged, "worked up and down at regular intervals." As plaintiff and his helper were in a proper manner placing the said bar in the shears, and just at the time the jaws thereof had commenced to descend upon the said iron bar, Flack, said foreman, then and there carelessly and negligently in a loud tone of voice and in a decisive and abrupt manner ordered and directed plaintiff and his helper not to cut the iron bar at the point where plaintiff was about to cut it, but to cut it at another point. The complaint then proceeds to charge that the foreman negligently and carelessly gave said command and order at a time when it was extremely dangerous for the plaintiff to undertake to obey it. The plaintiff at the time had no knowledge of such danger, and had no time to consider the result of obeying the order. The danger to which he was subjected, as alleged, in obeying the order in question consisted in necessitating him at that time to withdraw the iron bar from the mouth of the shears. In order to obey the command of the foreman and to prevent the bar from being cut at the point where he had directed it should not be cut the plaintiff had to quickly change the position of the bar in the mouth of the shears to comply with the command. But in his attempt to change the position of the bar in the mouth of the shears and to comply with the order given the shears closed down and cut the bar near the end of the shears, and in such a manner as to cause it to turn and rebound from the mouth thereof, and with much force to strike the left leg of the plaintiff, thereby severely injuring that limb. A particular statement of the character and permanency of the injury, and the suffering endured by the plaintiff, and the money which he expended in attempting to heal and cure his said injuries, are all set out in the complaint. The pleading then proceeds to repeat the charge that the injuries received by the plaintiff were occasioned solely by the negligence and carelessness of the foreman in giving the order in question, which the plaintiff was bound to obey and did obey, etc.

It is evident, under the facts alleged in the pleading, that appellee based his cause of action on the second clause of section 7083, Burns' Ann. St. 1901, which provides "that every railroad or other corporation * * * operating in this state shall be liable for damages for personal injuries suffered by any employé while in its service, * * * in the following cases: * * * Second, where such injury resulted from the negligence of any person in the service of such corporation, to whose order or direction the injured employé at the time of the injury was bound to conform and did conform." In fact, counsel for appellee contend that the complaint, under the facts, is sustained by this provision of the statute, which contention counsel for appellant apparently do not controvert. In respect to the construction of the clause of the section in question, see Louisville, etc., Ry. Co. v. Wagner, 153 Ind. 420, 53 N. E. 927; Thacker v. Chicago, etc., Ry. Co., 159 Ind. 82, 64 N. E. 605, 59 L. R. A. 792. A demurrer to the pleading was overruled, and appellant answered by the general denial. Counsel for appellant contend that the judgment below should be reversed on the grounds (1) that the evidence fails to establish any negligence on the part of appellant's foreman; (2) that the alleged negligence is not shown to have been the proximate cause of the injury received. Or, in other words, we are requested to adjudge that upon a consideration of all the evidence most favorable to appellee, together with all of the reasonable inferences which may be drawn therefrom, the jury should have found in favor of appellant. The evidence, to an extent, is conflicting, and it will serve no useful purpose to recite it all in detail. It may be said, however, that there is evidence to establish, among others, the following facts: Appellant at and prior to the accident in question was a corporation engaged in manufacturing iron and steel in the city of East Chicago, Lake county, Ind. One James Flack was the foreman in its factory, and as such he had control and supervision of its employés in the department in which appellee worked. On the 10th day of January, 1900, Flack, as such foreman, hired appellee to work for appellant in said factory, and on that day he put him to work in operating a pair of shears in cutting bars of scrap iron. Appellee was under the control of Flack, as foreman, and was required to conform to and obey his orders while at work. The accident by which appellee was injured occurred on the night of January 11, 1900. On the day before—January 10th, the day when appellee was put to work—he was furnished with a helper to aid him when he needed assistance. On the second day, or the night of the accident, it appears that he had not the same assistant that he had the day before, but a different employé. This helper, it appears, was a foreigner, and did not understand the English language. Of this fact the foreman appears to have had knowledge. Appellee, however, did not know this helper, nor did he know that he could not understand English. On the first day of appellee's employment it appears that he sheared a lot of crooked pieces of iron. The blades of the shears operated by appellee were 18 inches long, and when in operation its mouth or jaws went up and down about 20 times in the course of a minute. On the occasion of the accident in question, appellee, with the assistance of his helper, had shoved or placed a large, crooked iron bar as far back as he could in the mouth of the shears. This bar weighed 150 pounds, and was 8 feet long. The bar was crooked at one of its ends, the crook extending up some distance along the bar in the shape of the letter S. Just as appellee had placed this bar under the knives of the shears, and had it in a position to be cut, Flack, the foreman aforesaid, came up where appellee was at work, and very suddenly or hastily, and in an abrupt manner, said, "Don't cut that bar there; cut it in the center." In obedience to this order, appellee immediately began to remove the bar from the shears in order to place it so that it would be cut in the center, the point where the foreman had ordered him to cut it. It appears that it was necessary to remove the bar from the mouth of the shears in order to comply with the command of the foreman. As appellee was in the act of removing the bar, the shears came down and caught it, turning it down, and threw or flopped it over against appellee's leg, whereby he was severely and permanently injured. There is evidence to show that, had the bar been left where it was placed in the first instance by appellee, it would have been properly cut without any injury to him. It appears to have been the crooked part of the bar which turned over as the knives closed down upon it. Appellee had no notice or warning that in attempting to withdraw the bar as he did he would expose himself to any danger or injury. The proper way to feed or place a bar of iron like the one in question into the shears was to put it at the back part of the mouth as far back as it could be pushed. This appellee did. If it were placed into the shears obliquely, or into the front part of the jaws, the latter, under such circumstances, would have a tendency to twist the bar and throw it out. Appellee was in the line of his duty at the time of the accident, and was standing at the proper place in front of the machine, and in all respects, it appears, was in the exercise of due care under the circumstances. The special findings of the jury are in harmony with the general verdict.

The jury find, in answer to an interrogatory which there is evidence to support, that appellee could not have stopped the shears "while cutting the pieces of iron in question." The distance between the points of the lower and upper knives of the shears when open is about 12 inches. Counsel for appellee contend that under all of the evidence and circumstances in this case the question as to whether the foreman was guilty of negligence in giving the order was for the decision of the jury. The evidence, it is said, supports all of the facts necessary or material to entitle appellee to recover; therefore it is contended that this court is not authorized to find as a matter of law to the contrary. We concur in this view of the case. We are of the opinion that, when all of the evidence most favorable to appellee, together with all of the reasonable inferences which the jury might have drawn therefrom, is considered, we would not be warranted in finding that appellee had failed to establish the cause of action alleged in his complaint. That the evidence proves that the order in question was one within the scope of the foreman's authority, and that appellee, as the servant of appellant, was bound to obey it, cannot be seriously controverted. The jury, by their general verdict, impliedly find that the foreman, in giving the order, was guilty of negligence, and that this negligence was the proximate cause of the injury received by appellee. The latter is shown to have been an unskilled or common laborer in the service of appellant, receiving a compensation of 14 cents per hour, of all of which the foreman had knowledge. There is evidence to show that the foreman was aware of the quick movement up and down of the jaws of the shears, the size and shape of the bar, and the position in which it had been placed in the mouth of the machine ready for cutting. He gave an imperative order to appellee not to cut it at the point where the latter was intending, but to cut it in the center. From the evidence and all of the circumstances placed before the jurors they were justified in drawing therefrom the reasonable inference that the foreman, at the time he gave the order, knew that appellee, in complying therewith, would be compelled to quickly withdraw the bar from the jaws of the shears, and in so doing, if it failed to clear the moving jaws, it might be caught therein, and wrenched or twisted from the hands of appellee to his injury. The evidence may be said to be open not only to this inference, but to other inferences which reasonably and fairly tend to establish that giving the order in controversy was an act of negligence on the part of the foreman. It is apparent that, had the foreman desired, he could have readily shut off the power by which the shears were operated before he gave the order or direction to appellee.

Appellee's duty as the servant of appellant was to yield obedience to the orders of his superiors. In fact, it appears that he was obeying a specific order of the foreman, under whose control and authority he had been placed by the master. He had the right to presume, in the absence of warning or notice to the contrary, that in conforming to the order he would not be subjected to injury. Taylor v. Evansville, etc., R. Co., 121 Ind. 124, 22 N. E. 876, 6 L. R. A. 584, 16 Am. St. Rep. 372, and cases there cited. He was justified in presuming that the foreman would not give improper orders, and would not direct him to assume improper risks. In regard to a servant's right of action for injuries received in obeying a direct command or order, in addition to our own cases, see Eaves v. Atlantic, etc., Co., 176 Mass. 369, 57 N. E. 669; Stephens v.

Hannibal, etc., Ry. Co., 96 Mo. 207, 9 S. W. 598, 9 Am. St. Rep. 336; Illinois Steel Co. v. Schymanowiski, 162 Ill. 447, 44 N. E. 876; Long's Adm'r v. Illinois Central, etc., R. Co. (Ky.) 68 S. W. 1095, 58 L. R. A. 237. Eaves v. Atlantic, etc., Co., supra, was an action under the employer's liability act of Massachusetts, by an employé, for personal injuries sustained through an alleged negligent order given by the superintendent of the company, whereby the plaintiff was directed to start a pressing machine. In obeying this order she was injured by the presser coming down upon and crushing her fingers. The court, in its opinion in that case, said: "Talbot was a person whose principal duty was that of a superintendent; that as such superintendent he gave to the plaintiff the order to start up the machine; that at the time of the order he had reason to know that she might understand it as a command to try to ascertain by resuming her work whether the machine was all right; that she so understood it, and was justified in so understanding it; that, acting under that understanding, she attempted to resume her work; that while she was doing that, and in the exercise of due care, by reason of the violent and unusual shaking of the machine her hand was thrown from its usual place, and the presser came down upon her fingers and crushed them; and that, under the circumstances, the order was negligent. This would make a case for the plaintiff. * * * The jury must have found the facts to be as above stated." In the case at bar it appears that appellee was suddenly or hastily ordered, as shown, to cut the bar in the center. The foreman, as it appears, saw that appellee was about to cut it at what was testified to be the usual place for cutting such a bar. He ordered appellee, in effect at least, to change the position of the bar in the mouth of the machine in order to cut it at another point. In attempting to obey this order, no time, under the circumstances, appears to have been afforded to appellee to consider or reflect whether or not, in complying therewith, he would expose himself to injury or danger. The test of the foreman's negligence in the manner under the general rule applicable to other cases, is whether a person of ordinary prudence under the particular circumstances would have given the order. Labatt's Master and Servant, § 119.

Counsel for appellant argue that, if there is any negligence shown in the case, it must be charged to appellee's helper, who, it is said, did not co-operate with appellee in withdrawing the bar from the mouth of the shears. While it may be said that the order was given in the presence of appellee and his helper, it is shown, however, that the latter did not understand the English language, and did not understand what the order meant.

The case, on the question of negligence, cannot be said to fall within the operation of the rule which affirms that, where one inference only can be drawn from the undisputed evidence or facts, and where such inference can lead to but one result, then, under such circumstances, the question of negligence becomes one of law, and not of fact. It has been repeatedly affirmed by this court that its province upon appeal is to correct errors of law. The fact that the evidence in a particular case upon which the judgment of the lower court rests may be said to be weak or unsatisfactory is not available, for, if there is evidence to sustain the judgment in every material respect, we are not authorized to disturb it upon appeal. Lee v. State, 156 Ind. 541, 60 N. E. 299, and cases cited; Mead v. Burk, 156 Ind. 577, 60 N. E. 338. The jury, as previously stated, found that the negligence of the foreman was the proximate cause of the injury received by appellee. This finding is supported by the evidence. No other intervening cause can be said to have produced the injury. Louisville, etc., Ferry Co. v. Nolan, 135 Ind. 60, 34 N. E. 710.

Judgment affirmed.

GILLETT, C. J., did not participate in the decision of this case.

(43 Ind. App. 211)

CASE v. HURSH.[1]

(Appellate Court of Indiana, Division No. 1. April 26, 1904.)

PLEADING—DEMURRER—EVIDENCE AS AID TO PLEADING—REVERSIBLE ERROR.

1. A demurrer to a complaint in several paragraphs on the ground "that neither of said paragraphs states facts sufficient to constitute a cause of action" is not joint.

2. Evidence of a fact in the record on appeal is not to be regarded by the appellate tribunal in passing on a ruling on a demurrer.

3. A complaint was filed in three paragraphs, the first being on a note, the second for money loaned, and the third for work and labor done and performed. There was a genera verdict for plaintiff, without special findings in answer to interrogatories. The amount was larger than could have been recovered properly on the first paragraph alone. There was an answer in denial of each paragraph of complaint, an answer of payment, and an answer that the note was executed without consideration. There was also an answer of set-off to each of the claims in the complaint. *Held*, that the overruling of a demurrer to each paragraph of complaint, the first being admittedly insufficient in failing to set out the note, was reversible error, it being impossible to determine what sum, if any, entered into the amount of the verdict on the note.

Appeal from Superior Court, Allen County; O. N. Heaton, Judge.

Action by John C. Hursh against Emilius Case. From a judgment for plaintiff, defendant appeals. Reversed.

Breen & Morris, for appellant. Colerick, Larwill & Colerick, for appellee.

BLACK, J. The appellee's complaint contained three paragraphs seeking recovery; the first upon a promissory note, the second

[1] Rehearing denied. Transfer to Supreme Court denied.

for money loaned, and the third for work and labor done and performed. The appellant has assigned as error, and has presented for our consideration, the action of the court in overruling his demurrer to the first paragraph of the complaint, the one based upon a promissory note. This paragraph does not set out a copy of the note, and, though it is stated in the body of the pleading that a copy of the note "is filed herewith and made a part of this complaint," it does not otherwise appear from the record that a note, or a copy thereof, was filed as an exhibit. The paragraph in question not only does not disclose the form of the note, but also does not fully describe the contents thereof. It is admitted by the learned counsel for the appellee that because of this failure to set forth or exhibit the note, the first paragraph of the complaint was not sufficient on demurrer; but it is contended on behalf of the appellee that the demurrer to the complaint was directed against all the paragraphs thereof jointly, and not to each paragraph separately, and that there could be no available error in overruling it, as the sufficiency of some of the paragraphs is not questioned. The demurrer in the body thereof was in form as follows: "The defendant, Emilius Case, demurs to each paragraph of the plaintiff's complaint on the ground that neither of said paragraphs state facts sufficient to constitute a cause of action against him." This demurrer, we think, was sufficient to enable and to require the court to apply it to the paragraphs of the complaint distributively. It was addressed to each paragraph, and, though not in every respect conforming to grammatical rule, it attacked each paragraph on the ground that neither of them stated facts sufficient. The objection that it was joint cannot be sustained. See Terre Haute, etc., R. Co. v. Sherwood, 132 Ind. 129, 31 N. E. 781, 17 L. R. A. 339, 32 Am. St. Rep. 239; Mitchell v. Stinson, 80 Ind. 324; Indiana, etc., R. Co. v. Dailey, 110 Ind. 75, 10 N. E. 631; Funk v. Rentchler, 134 Ind. 68, 33 N. E. 364, 898; Baltimore, etc., R. Co. v. Little, 149 Ind. 167, 48 N. E. 862; Silvers v. Junction R. Co., 43 Ind. 435, and cases cited.

Again, it is pointed out by counsel that the note in suit was introduced in evidence, and is set forth in the bill of exceptions containing the evidence, in the record before us, and it is claimed that therefore the error in overruling the demurrer to the first paragraph of complaint is not available on behalf of the appellant. This claim cannot prevail, for in determining the question involved in such an assignment of error the evidence cannot be resorted to by this court in aid of the pleading. The evidence was introduced to enable the jury to find upon the facts in issue, and we may look to it in its entirety to ascertain whether or not it was sufficient to sustain the verdict, but evidence of a fact in the record on appeal is not to be regarded by the appellate tribunal, in passing upon a ruling on a demurrer to a pleading, as a fact established, but only as evidence; the province of determining what it proves belonging to the triors of the facts. If the existence of a fact has been specially found from the evidence by the court or the jury trying the facts, it may be said that such fact is to be regarded by the court on appeal as established for the purposes of the case other than in the investigation of the question whether the finding was sufficiently sustained by the evidence. We therefore cannot decide that an essential fact omitted in pleading existed because it appears in evidence. This conclusion has been many times stated in the published decisions.

The verdict in this case was general, without any special findings in answer to interrogatories. The amount was larger than could have been recovered properly on the first paragraph of the complaint alone. In the complaint it was alleged that the note provided for the payment of attorney's fees, but it does not appear from the complaint that any standard for determining the amount thereof was stated in the note. There was an answer in denial of each paragraph of the complaint, an answer of payment addressed to the whole complaint, and an answer that the note was executed without consideration. There was also an answer of set-off to all the claims in the complaint. It is plain that we cannot determine with proper certainty what sum, if any, entered into the amount of the verdict or ought to have been included therein, upon the note. We cannot say that the ruling upon the demurrer was harmless.

The other paragraphs of the complaint have not been examined by us with reference to their sufficiency, no question thereon having been suggested by counsel for the appellant in their briefs.

The judgment is reversed, with instruction to the court below to sustain the appellant's demurrer to the first paragraph of complaint.

(33 Ind. A. 92)

CITY OF HAMMOND v. WINSLOW.

(Appellate Court of Indiana, Division No. 1. April 27, 1904.)

MUNICIPAL CORPORATION — DEFECTIVE SIDEWALKS — PERSONAL INJURIES—COMPLAINT —ASSIGNMENT OF ERROR—SUFFICIENCY.

1. Where a complaint was filed in two paragraphs, to which separate demurrers were filed, but one paragraph was dismissed after the evidence was heard and before the finding, an assignment of error that the court erred in overruling appellant's demurrer to appellee's complaint presents the question of the ruling on the demurrer for review as against an objection that the assignment was joint, since so much of the demurrer as applied to the paragraph dismissed went out of the record with it.

2. A complaint in an action against a city for personal injuries, alleging that "at the time of the commission of the grievances hereinafter alleged," etc., and then setting out a defective condition of sidewalk as the cause of the injuries,

sufficiently shows the sidewalk was defective on the day plaintiff was injured, where the only date thereafter alleged was the date of the injury.

3. A complaint in an action against a city for personal injuries, the result of a fall from a defective sidewalk, because no barriers were maintained along the side of the walk, not averring that, had the guards been maintained, plaintiff would not have fallen, does not show that the alleged negligence of the city was proximate cause of the injury.

Appeal from Superior Court, Porter County; H. B. Tuthill, Judge.

Action by Harriet Winslow against the city of Hammond. From a judgment for plaintiff, defendant appeals. Reversed.

N. L. Agnew, Lawrence Becker, and V. S. Reiter, for appellant. F. N. Gavit, for appellee.

ROBINSON, J. Suit by appellee for personal injuries. Appellant demurred separately and severally to each of the two paragraphs of amended complaint, which was overruled. Answer in denial, trial by the court, finding for appellee, and, over appellant's motion for a new trial because the finding is not sustained by sufficient evidence and is contrary to law, judgment on the finding. After the evidence was heard, and before the finding, appellee dismissed the second paragraph of complaint.

It is first insisted that the first error assigned, "The court erred in overruling appellant's demurrer to appellee's amended complaint," presents no question for review. The demurrer was a separate and several demurrer to each paragraph, and the error assigned could be called "joint." But when appellee dismissed the second paragraph of amended complaint, such dismissal took out of the record all pleadings addressed to that paragraph. So much of the demurrer as applied to the second paragraph went out with the complaint. It is true the pleading left was the first paragraph of amended complaint; but, being the only paragraph, it was not necessary further to so designate it. Had the demurrer been joint, a different question might be presented by this assignment of error. But, when appellee dismissed the second paragraph, the case stood precisely as if but a single paragraph had been filed in the first instance. The question presented to this court is the same question presented to the trial court by the separate and several demurrer. Appellee voluntarily chose to have but a single paragraph of complaint, to which had been addressed a separate demurrer. The record in this particular stands as he himself has made it, and in the record thus made is a single paragraph of complaint, which paragraph only could we be asked to consider for any purpose. The demurrer asked the court to consider the sufficiency of each paragraph of the complaint separately. So far as concerns this court, the second paragraph having been dismissed, the only ruling the trial court made on the demurrer was overruling the demurrer to the amended complaint.

The complaint avers that "at the time of the commission of the grievances hereinafter alleged, and for two years prior thereto, defendant had carelessly and negligently and knowingly permitted a certain sidewalk on the public street in said city to be and remain in a dangerous condition for travel, in this: that the same was so constructed and maintained as to be four feet above the street thereunder and immediately adjoining the same, and thus causing a vertical drop of four feet from the side of said sidewalk to the street thereunder and along the side thereof, with no barriers, guards, railing, or protection of any kind to prevent persons stepping or falling off the same; that on the 6th day of May, 1901, and after the darkness of night had set in, and when it was dark, plaintiff was passing over said sidewalk as a foot passenger, and was unable to see the edge or any portion of said sidewalk on account of the darkness, and while so passing over said sidewalk, and using due care and caution, fell off the side of the same, and to the ground of the street along the side thereof," causing injuries which are described. The complaint is not open to the objection that it does not sufficiently show the sidewalk was defective on the day the appellee was injured. The words "at the time of the commission of the grievances hereinafter alleged" may reasonably be said to have reference to the only date thereafter alleged, which is the date of the injury. In Corporation of Bluffton v. Mathews, 92 Ind. 213, where the complaint averred that on the 24th day of October, 1881, the defect existed, and that appellee was injured on the —— day of ——, 1881, it was held that it was not shown the city was at fault when the injury occurred.

It is further argued that the complaint fails to show that the alleged negligence of the city was the proximate cause of the appellee's injury. The pleading is open to the objection that it shows no connection between the negligence charged and the injury, in the way of cause and effect. So far as informed by the complaint, might not the injury have occurred, just as it did occur, had there been no omission of duty on appellant's part? The complaint does not aver what caused the injury, nor does it aver facts from which it can be said that the injury must necessarily have occurred from the negligence charged. So far as disclosed, the walk was of uniform width, and the charge is that no guards or barriers were maintained along the side of the walk. It is left altogether to inference that, if guards had been maintained along the side, she would not have fallen. Under a number of rulings we think the complaint must be held insufficient. Corporation of Bluffton v. Mathews, supra; Pittsburgh, etc., R. Co. v. Conn, 104 Ind. 64, 3 N. E. 636; Baltimore, etc., R. Co. v. Young, 146 Ind. 374, 45 N. E. 479; Toledo, etc., Ry. Co. v. Beery (Ind. App.) 68 N. E. 702; Lake Erie, etc., R. Co. v. Mikesell, 23 Ind. App. 395, 55

N. E. 488; South Chicago, etc., R. Co. v. Moltrum, 26 Ind. App. 550, 60 N. E. 361; Ohio, etc., R. Co. v. Engrer, 4 Ind. App. 261, 30 N. E. 924; Harris v. Board, etc., 121 Ind. 299, 23 N. E. 92.

Judgment reversed.

(33 Ind. A. 316)

CLEVELAND, C., C. & ST. L. RY. CO. v. WASSON et al.[1]

(Appellate Court of Indiana. April 22, 1904.)

RAILROAD—INJURY TO ANIMALS ON TRACK—LOCOMOTIVE RUN BY TRESPASSER.

1. Burns' Ann. St. 1901, § 5313, providing that whenever any animal shall be killed or injured by the locomotives or cars on any railroad, whether they be run by the company, or by its lessee, assignee, receiver, or other person, the owner of the animal shall have a right of action against the company, does not render the company liable for such damages caused by a locomotive or car run by a trespasser.

On petition for rehearing. Petition overruled.

For former opinion, see 66 N. E. 1020.

HENLEY, C. J. By section 5313, Burns' Ann. St. 1901, it is provided, in effect, that whenever any animals shall have been killed or injured by the locomotives, cars, or carriages used on any railroad running in, into, or through the state, whether the same may be or may have been run and controlled by the company, or by its lessee, assignee, receiver, or other person, the owner of the animal so killed or injured shall have a right of action against the parties named in the statute. But this section of the statute, as we understand it, does not give to the party who has suffered the damage any new right, but merely affects the remedy; and under this section it is essential that the plaintiff show that the defendant, or some one for whose acts it is liable, caused the injury of which complaint is made. The complaint in the case at bar does not aver that the appellant caused the injury, and this counsel for appellee concede. We do not think that sections 5312 and 5313, Burns' Ann. St. 1901, when construed together, can be held to mean that a railroad corporation, or a lessee, assignee, receiver, or other person or corporation controlling or operating the railroad, can be held liable for damages occasioned by the killing of stock by a locomotive or car run and operated by a mere trespasser. The object of the statute was to give the claimant a right of action against one or all of the parties named therein, so that the claimant might not be compelled to inquire into the relative rights or liabilities of the parties, created by contract or arrangement between themselves. But as a matter of pleading, whichever party the claimant seeks to charge with the damages inflicted must be charged directly and positively with having caused the injury of which he complains. We believe the case of Wabash, etc., R. R. Co. v. Rooker, 90 Ind. 581, is controlling in the case at bar.

The petition for a rehearing is overruled.

COMSTOCK, WILEY, BLACK, and ROBINSON, JJ., concur. ROBY, J., absent.

[1] Transfer denied.

(34 Ind. A. 494)

HELLER v. DAILEY et al.†

(Appellate Court of Indiana, Division No. 1. April 22, 1904.)

APPEAL AND ERROR—SUBSEQUENT APPEAL—LAW OF THE CASE.

1. The law as announced on appeal by a court of last resort remains the law of the case through all its stages, whether right or wrong.

Appeal from Circuit Court, Wells County; J. W. Headington, Special Judge.

Action by Lemuel Heller against Michael Dailey and others. From a judgment for defendants, plaintiff appeals. Reversed.

For former opinion, see 63 N. E. 490.

Mock & Sons, for appellant. Dailey, Simmons & Dailey, for appellees.

HENLEY, C. J. Appellant commenced this action to collect rents alleged to be due on an oil and gas lease. Upon the former appeal in this case the judgment of the trial court was reversed, and the cause remanded, with instruction to sustain the demurrer to certain answers. For the opinion upon the former appeal, see Heller v. Dailey, 28 Ind. App. 555, 63 N. E. 490.

In the trial court, appellees filed an amended third, fourth, and fifth paragraph of answer. To each of these answers appellant addressed a demurrer, which the court overruled, and, appellant refusing to plead further, judgment was rendered on demurrer.

The alleged errors brought to the attention of this court relate to the action of the trial court in overruling appellant's demurrer to the third, fourth, and fifth paragraphs of answer. The answers filed by appellees are substantially alike, and contain the following allegations: That, pursuant to the terms and conditions of the lease mentioned in the complaint, appellees, prior to the time they sold and assigned said lease to the Capital Oil Company, drilled two oil wells on the premises therein described, which wells were drilled and completed within 120 days from the execution of the lease; that the wells so drilled produced large quantities of oil, and the appellant received and accepted the interest in the oil so produced, as was provided in the lease; that, prior to the expiration of 180 days from the date of the execution of the lease, appellees were attempting to sell the lease and the property placed by them on the leased premises to the Capital Oil Company, and that at said time said oil company, by its agent, William H. Dye, and these appellees, called upon appellant and informed him that appellee Dailey was about to sell and assign his lease to said oil com-

† Rehearing denied. Transfer denied.

pany, and that said lease would be sold and assigned to said oil company if appellant would agree to substitute the Capital Oil Company as the lessee in said lease, and release appellees from all liability under said lease that might accrue after such sale and transfer; that appellant then and there promised and agreed with appellees that, if they sold and transferred the lease and property owned by them to the Capital Oil Company, he would accept the Capital Oil Company as the lessee in said lease, and as his sole and only tenant under said lease, and would accept said company for the payment of all liabilities and rentals that might accrue thereunder, and that he would release appellees from all liabilities under and by virtue of said lease; that, in accordance with said contract and agreement, and in consideration of the promise and agreement of appellant to release appellees from any liability under the lease, appellees sold, conveyed, assigned, and transferred said lease and all property thereon to said Capital Oil Company, and said Capital Oil Company then and there took immediate and absolute possession of the land under said lease, and all the property thereon, all of which was done with the knowledge and consent and at the request of the appellant; that appellant then and thereafter accepted the Capital Oil Company as his sole and only tenant, and accepted the said company for the payment of all liabilities and rentals which afterward accrued under said lease, and the said oil company agreed with appellant and appellees to become the sole tenant of appellant, and to pay and discharge all the obligations, rentals, and liabilities arising under said lease, and to comply with all the terms of the said lease; that, after the sale and transfer by appellees of their interest in said lease to the Capital Oil Company, said company caused to be produced, and did produce, large quantities of oil from the wells drilled under said lease on appellant's land, and delivered the part of the oil due appellant under said lease to said appellant, which oil appellant at all times accepted. It is further averred that at the time the lease and the property thereon was so sold, assigned, and transferred to said Capital Oil Company, no rental was due thereon, but the same had been fully paid up to and including the date of said sale and transfer, and such rental had been accepted by appellant.

It was held by this court upon the former appeal that the answers were insufficient, because they attempted to plead a surrender; that a verbal surrender is ineffectual; and that a surrender by act and operation of law was not sufficiently alleged; the court saying: "It is generally established that the lessee, who, before his assignment of the lease to a third person, is bound by both the express and the implied covenants of the lease, continues after the assignment to be liable upon his express covenants therein, as if no assignment had been made, and that the assignee is liable to the lessor upon all the covenants which run with the land, for nonperformance thereof while the estate is in him, but is not liable for breaches of any covenants which occur before the assignment to him, or after his assignment to another; the liability of the lessee after his assignment resting in privity of contract; that of the assignee resting in privity of estate, and continuing only while such privity exists, though he remains, after his assignment to another, liable for breaches which he committed while he had the estate. If the assignee hold possession under the lease, or have immediate right to the possession, when any rent falls due, he will continue liable therefor, and will not escape such liability by his subsequent assignment; and this is true whether he became assignee by the act of the lessee or of the lessee's assignee, or by the act of the law, as by purchase at a sheriff's or receiver's sale. Fennell v. Guffey, 139 Pa. 341, 20 Atl. 1048; Aderhold v. Oil Well Supply Co., 158 Pa. 401, 28 Atl. 22; Edmonds v. Mounsey, 15 Ind. App. 399, 44 N. E. 196; Breckenridge v. Parott, 15 Ind. App. 411, 44 N. E. 66. The appellees Dailey and Eddington, who would thus be liable as lessees upon their express covenants in a mining lease for breaches thereof accruing after the assignment thereof by them, sought by their answers to show a surrender to the appellant. In none of the paragraphs was a written surrender shown. If we are correct in characterizing the written instrument as a grant of an interest in land, then, not being a lease for three years or less, and being necessarily in writing, it could not be surrendered in fact without a writing, whether classed as a grant of an incorporeal hereditament or as a lease; and therefore it cannot be held that any surrender in fact was properly pleaded. In the third paragraph of each answer it was sought to set up an agreement for a surrender between the lessor and the holders of the lease—one holding an interest therein as lessee, and therefore bound by privity of contract; the other having an interest by privity of estate as assignee—and, in consideration of such surrender, a release of the lessee 'and their assigns.' This pleading can only be regarded as an attempt to show a surrender in fact, and it must be held insufficient for such purpose."

We cannot see in what respect the amended answers constitute a different defense from that set up by the answers which were held insufficient in the former appeal in this case. Whether the contract here involved was a grant of an incorporeal hereditament or a lease of real estate for more than three years, it could not be surrendered by parol contract, though, if it were regarded as a lease for more than three years, it might be surrendered by operation of law. The opinion of this court upon the former appeal plainly indicates that the contract was the grant of an incorporeal hereditament, although it was shown that, if it was regarded as a lease for a term of more than three years, it could not be surrendered, except by writing or by operation of law; and it was expressly held that the contract could not, in any view, be regarded as a lease for three years or less. An incorporeal hereditament cannot be surrendered, except by written instrument. It cannot be surrendered by parol contract or by operation of law, and, notwithstanding what was said by this court in the former opinion concerning surrenders of leases for terms of more than three years, the contract under consideration was held to be a grant of an incorporeal hereditament, and one which could not be surrendered except by written instrument. The law as there stated must be regarded as controlling. The facts stated in the answers would not release appellees from liability under the contract. The law as announced by the court upon the former appeal of this case remains the law of the case through all its stages, whether right or wrong; and, under the rules of law as therein announced, the trial court ought to have sustained appellant's demurrer to the third, fourth, and fifth paragraphs of amended answer.

The judgment is reversed, with instructions to the trial court to sustain appellant's demurrer to each of the third, fourth, and fifth paragraphs of appellees' answer.

(34 Ind. App. 176)

BENNER v. MAGEE.[1]

(Appellate Court of Indiana, Division No. 2. April 22, 1904.)

AGENCY—COMMISSION—PENALTY.

1. Where a contract provided that an agent should receive 5 per cent. commission for selling stone in Indianapolis for certain parties, and should sell stone for no one else, a provision that he should receive 25 per cent. commission in addition for all sales by the principals directly, or through other parties, was not void as providing a penalty.

Appeal from Superior Court, Marion County; Vinson Carter, Judge.

Action by Adolphus A. Magee against William J. Benner. From a judgment in favor of plaintiff, defendant appeals. Reversed.

J. E. McCullough, for appellant. Wickens & Osborn and Gavin & Davis, for appellee.

COMSTOCK, J. This was an action by the appellee, who was the owner of a stone quarry in Decatur county, Ind., against the appellant, who acted as appellee's agent during the year 1898 for sale of stone at Indianapolis, for money alleged to have been received by appellant as such agent, and not accounted for; and a cross-action by appellant against appellee for money alleged to be due pursuant to the contract in which appellant was constituted such agent.

The first paragraph of the complaint sues for $363.76 and interest, alleged to have been collected by appellant as appellee's agent in the year 1898 from J. C. Veney, and not accounted for, for stone sold him. The second paragraph for the sum of $234.71, alleged to have been collected by appellant during said year as such agent, and not accounted for, for stone sold to W. H. Abbott. The third paragraph for money had and received by appellant for the use and benefit of appellee, naming the two items sued on, respectively, in the first and second paragraphs. The fourth paragraph for the same item and interest sued for in the first paragraph, but sets out in full the contract under which appellant was constituted and acted as agent. The fifth paragraph for the same item as the second, but also sets out said contract in full. The appellant answered by general denial and payment. Appellant also filed an amended cross-complaint in two paragraphs. To the first paragraph the court sustained a demurrer for want of facts, and overruled a demurrer on the same ground to the second. Issue was formed on the said second paragraph of the cross-complaint, and the court directed the jury to find for appellee in the sum of $600, and a verdict was returned for said amount. Appellant's motion for a new trial was overruled, and judgment rendered on the verdict. The errors assigned are the action of the court in sustaining appellee's demurrer to the first paragraph of the amended cross-complaint and in overruling's appellant's motion for a new trial.

The first paragraph of cross-complaint alleges the execution of contract on July 7, 1898, between the plaintiff and various other quarry owners and cross-complainant, by which cross-complainant, Benner, was to having during the year 1898 the exclusive agency for the sale of plaintiff's stone in the city of Indianapolis, which stone was to be sold at prices fixed in the contract, for which Benner was to receive 5 per cent. commission on the net amount sold—that is, on the amount sold less freight and other expenses—which 5 per cent. was to be in full payment of Benner's services. Plaintiff agreed to sell in Indianapolis only through Benner. It was further agreed in this contract that Benner should receive 25 per cent. commission on all curb, crossing, gutter, and marginal stone shipped during 1898 to Indianapolis by the plaintiff, where the same was sold or collections made by the plaintiff, or any person acting for him except said Benner. That at the time he entered into said contract he had an established agency and business in the city of Indianapolis for the sale of stone and other material, upon commission and otherwise, built up and established by long years of conducting and of attention to his said business. That at the time he entered into said contract the parties thereto other than himself required him to agree and contract with each one of them, and he did in said contract agree and contract with each one of

[1] Rehearing denied. Transfer to Supreme Court denied.

them, that he would sell stone for no other quarry owners or persons during said year than those mentioned in said contract; that he would sell at the prices mentioned in said contract only, unless those prices should be changed by a majority of said quarry owners giving this cross-complainant written instructions to that effect. Cross-complainant further avers that during said year 1898 Magee shipped to and sold in Indianapolis to various parties stone to the amount of $4,000, and that Benner has never received the 25 per cent. commission agreed on in said contract for said stone so sold, which commission of 25 per cent. on said $4,000—$1,000 —is now due and unpaid to cross-complainant. Wherefore he prays judgment against plaintiff for $1,000. The contract is made a part of the first and second paragraphs of the cross-complaint.

If the 25 per cent. commission provided for stone sold outside of the agency of Indianapolis was a penalty, the demurrer was properly sustained. If it is to be regarded as liquidated damages, the demurrer should have been overruled. The decisions intended to assist the courts in determining whether a sum named in contract is to be regarded as a penalty or as stipulated damages are very numerous, but they are for the most part a collection of special cases. The law laid down in Jaqua v. Headington, 114 Ind. 300, 16 N. E. 527, has been accepted and applied in later cases. It is in the following language: "Where the sum named is declared to be fixed as liquidated damages, is not greatly disproportionate to the loss that may result from a breach, and the damages are not measurable by any exact pecuniary standard, the sum designated will be deemed to be stipulated damages." Hale on Damages, at page 137, there states the rule: "Where damages can be easily and precisely determined by a definite pecuniary standard —as by proof of market values—but the parties have stipulated for a much larger sum, such sum will usually be held to be a penalty, for it is contended that the principle of compensation has been disregarded." Appellant agreed to sell only the stone from the quarries of the appellee and his co-contractors for 5 per cent., in connection with the other provision that he was to receive 25 per cent. commission on the stone sold outside his agency. The 25 per cent. commission was in addition to the 5 per cent., and doubtless influenced him in agreeing to accept a less commission for what he himself sold. The language of the contract is, "Said agent is also to receive 25 per cent. commission," etc. It is the language of compensation, rather than of penalty. The paragraph in question alleges that he had been building up his agency in 1897. His business for the year 1898 was, presumably, partially, at least, the outgrowth of his business established the preceding year. What that business would be, and the outlay in time and money attending it, would necessarily depend upon conditions not within the knowledge of the contracting parties. The profits, if any, to be derived therefrom, were at the time of the execution of the contract involved in uncertainty. Appellant's profits would, in a measure, depend upon the amount of business done. The advertisement which extensive business relations would give him was an element of value, difficult, of course, to ascertain, but it was doubtless influential in inducing appellant to enter into the contract. The parties, experienced in practical affairs, in view of all the facts elected to make certain in advance what otherwise was indefinite and unknown. Appellant obligated himself to sell only from the quarries of his principals at prices fixed by them, thus making himself entirely dependent upon appellee and his co-contractors for the supplies with which he was to deal. The policy of the law favors the enforcement of contracts not against public policy, entered into without fraud by parties competent to make them. Such is the contract before us. The language employed plainly, as we believe, provides for compensation, and not a penalty. There is nothing to indicate that the parties, when they executed it, had in contemplation the distinction between penalty and liquidated damages; and while their intention, or the name they might give the provision in question, would not necessarily control against its fair legal construction under the rules of law, it is proper to consider them. The 5 per cent. and the 25 per cent. commissions together constituted the consideration passing to appellant. We are of the opinion that the loss which might result to appellant cannot "be easily and precisely determined by definite pecuniary standard," nor can we say that the said per cent. fixed was greatly disproportionate to the loss. Questions raised by the motion for a new trial may not arise upon a second trial.

Judgment reversed, with instructions to overrule appellee's demurrer to the first paragraph of the cross-complaint.

ROBY, J. I concur in the result. The contract does not stipulate that appellee shall make no sales in Indianapolis other than by appellant. If it had done so, and if the breach averred were in making such sales directly or by other agents, then a fixed amount to be paid appellant because thereof might be a penalty or liquidated damages according to circumstances, but the breach set up is the failure of appellee to pay commissions according to his agreement, upon sales made in Indianapolis. The promise is a direct one and unless the contract is illegal should be performed. I do not think there is anything illegal in the agreement. Of course no question going to the manner of procurement or other affirmative defense based on matter of fact, can arise on a demurrer to the pleading.

The making of sales by appellee itself in Indianapolis, was contemplated by the contract and the rate of commission upon such sales was definitely fixed and so far as the law is concerned the parties must abide by the contract they themselves have made.

WILEY, P. J., concurs in result and in the concurring opinion.

(33 Ind. A. 86)

POPPY v. WALKER.

(Appellate Court of Indiana, Division No. 1. April 22, 1904.)

WILL—CONSTRUCTION—RIGHTS OF LEGATEE.

1. A testator directed that the proceeds of the sale of certain property should be paid to his daughter-in-law, to be held by her for life, and at her decease paid to her children, and that she should have the use, interest, and profits of the money or property for life, for her maintenance and support, and, if they were insufficient, she should have the right to use so much of the principal as might be reasonably necessary. *Held*, that the court properly directed the administrator to pay the sum to her unconditionally.

Appeal from Circuit Court, Noble County. Jos. W. Adair, Judge.

Proceedings in the matter of decedent's estate. From a judgment directing the administrator, George W. Poppy, to pay a certain sum unconditionally to Amelia Walker, the administrator appeals. Affirmed.

H. G. Zimmerman, for appellant. L. W. Welker, for appellee.

ROBINSON, J. A testator directed that the proceeds of the sale of certain property "shall be by my executor paid over to my daughter-in-law" (appellee), widow of a deceased son, "to be by her held and enjoyed during her natural lifetime, and at her decease, said sum or amount so paid over to her, shall be by my executor paid over to and vest" in two of the son's children named; that the daughter-in-law "shall have the use, interest, income and profits of said share of money or property so paid over or delivered to her for her life, for her maintenance and support and for the maintenance and support of her infant child Mabel, until the latter arrives at the age of twenty-one years; and I further direct that in case the said interest, income and profits shall be insufficient for said uses and purposes, that then she shall have the right to use so much of the principal of said share as may be reasonably necessary therefor." Upon filing his final report, the administrator with the will annexed paid to the clerk of the court the amount in his hands for distribution, including, as his report showed, the distributive share of appellee; and in his report he asked that the court order appellee to execute to the administrator her obligations with security for the return to him, or account to him by herself or personal representative, of the principal sum of such share at her decease, to be by him applied as the will directed; and that, in default thereof, the administrator be directed to invest the share and pay appellee the income thereof, and such portion of the principal as provided by the will. Upon exceptions filed by appellee, and a hearing, the court ordered the clerk to pay appellee her share unconditionally, and in other respects approved the report and discharged the administrator.

Conceding, without deciding, that the court's order is one from which the administrator might appeal, the order is right so far as the administrator is concerned. He was directed by the will to pay the money to appellee, not to some trustee for her sue, nor was it to be invested for her. The payment is to be made by him to her unconditionally, and she is not only to have the use and income of the principal for the support and maintenance of herself and child, but for such uses and purposes she may use such of the principal as may be reasonably necessary. What title she took is of no concern to the administrator, and need not here be discussed. When he made the payment as the will directs and is discharged by the court, his responsibility ends.

Judgment affirmed.

(33 Ind. A. 75)

HUNT et al. v. HINSHAW.

(Appellate Court of Indiana. Division No. 1. April 20, 1904.)

CLAIMS AGAINST ESTATES—SALE OF REAL ESTATE—WHEN AUTHORIZED—PETITION—SUFFICIENCY.

1. A debt secured by a mortgage on land executed subsequent to the execution of a will devising the land is a debt of the estate of the testator.

2. Burns' Ann. St. 1901, § 2743, provides that, in the absence of direction in testator's will for the payment of a mortgage on land devised the mortgage shall be discharged out of the part of the estate charged with the payment of debts, if any; otherwise out of any personal property undisposed of. Section 2739 declares that, if the personal estate is insufficient to pay the debts, the undevised real estate shall be first charged in exoneration of the real estate devised. Testator's will did not charge any part of the estate with the payment of debts. *Held* that, in order to sell devised lands for the discharge of a mortgage thereon, it must appear that the personalty not specifically bequeathed is insufficient to pay the debts, and that the testator left no undisposed of real estate, or that the undisposed of real estate is insufficient to pay the debts.

3. An averment, in a petition for the sale of land devised to pay a mortgage thereon, that there is no personal estate of testator to pay the same, as by the terms of the will all of the personalty was given to testator's wife, is insufficient to show that the personal estate is not subject to the payment of debts, as under Burns' Ann. St. 1901, § 2648, the personal estate descends to the heirs on the failure of the widow to elect within 90 days to take under the will.

Appeal from Circuit Court, Randolph County; Henry C. Fox, Special Judge.

Action by Eliza Hinshaw, administratrix of Absolom Hinshaw, deceased, against Mary

Hinshaw Hunt and others. From a judgment for plaintiff, defendants appeal. Reversed.

Engle, Caldwell & Parry, for appellants. Nichols & Carter, for appellee.

HENLEY, C. J. This was an action by appellee to procure an order of court to sell certain real estate to make assets to pay debts. The legatees and heirs of the deceased testator were made defendants. The trial court ordered the real estate sold as prayed in the petition. The only questions presented by the appeal arise upon the action of the trial court in overruling the separate demurrer of appellant Mary Hinshaw Hunt to the petition, and in sustaining the appellee's demurrer to the separate answer of said appellant. The averments of the petition show the date of the testator's death; the names of all the heirs and legatees; that the total value of the personal estate which has come to the knowledge or possession of the administratrix is $1,003.08; that by the terms of decedent's will all of the personal property was given to the widow; that all claims filed against said estate have been paid by the administratrix out of the sale of the personal property, except a mortgage debt of $1,000, filed as a claim against said estate, which claim is now pending and unpaid; that by reason of the fact that all the personal estate of decedent was given to his widow by the terms of the will, there is no personal estate with which to pay and discharge the said claim. The will is made a part of the petition. The part of the will which is material in the consideration of the question of the sufficiency of the petition is as follows:

"It is my will and desire that all my just debts and funeral expenses be first paid by my executor.

"Item First: I do will, devise and bequeath to my wife, Eliza Hinshaw, all the following described real estate, to have and to hold during her natural life, viz: The southeast quarter of northwest quarter and the north half of the east half of the southwest quarter, and ten (10) acres off of the southwest quarter of section fifteen (15) township nineteen (19) Range fifteen (15) east in Randolph county in the State of Indiana, estimated to contain ninety acres, more or less, being the same land I bought of Elwood Hinshaw, and after the death of my said wife, I bequeath the said above described land to my daughter Mary Hinshaw to have and to hold in fee simple forever.

"Item Second: I will, devise and bequeath to Columbus Hinshaw the following described real estate, to-wit: The south half of the southwest quarter and twenty-six (26) acres off of the south end of the Northeast quarter of the southwest quarter, of section fifteen (15) township nineteen (19) north, range fourteen (14) east, in Randolph county, Indiana, being one hundred and six (106) acres more or less, to have and to hold in fee simple forever, subject however to the payment of a rent or to the payment of the rents and profits on one-third part of said real estate to my said wife, Eliza, during her natural life time, and I do hereby charge said land with the payment of one-third part of the rents and profits of the same to my said wife, Eliza, during her natural life and I bequeath and will to my said wife, Eliza, the rents and profits of the one-third part of said real estate during her natural life time.

"Item Third: I do hereby will and bequeath to my said wife, Eliza Hinshaw, all my personal property, money and notes, which I may have at the time of my death, to have and to hold during her natural life time and to sell and convert any part or the whole of my said personal property into money as to her may seem best, and to use such part of the same as she may need in her support and after the death of my said wife, Eliza, I will, devise and bequeath all the remainder of said personal property, money, notes, and the proceeds of any part of the same, so converted to money, and all the interest accrued thereon and all personal property acquired from said money and personal property and from any investments made with the same, together with any unexpended and unused rents and profits of said land to my children and the descendants of such as may be dead, share and share alike."

The petition further avers that the testator, Absolom Hi: shaw, died on the 31st day of December, 1900, and that his said will was probated on the 3d day of January, 1901; that after the execution of said will, and on the 16th day of November, 1898, said testator mortgaged to the state of Indiana the following described real estate, viz., the southeast quarter of the northwest quarter and the northeast quarter of the southwest quarter of section 15, township 19, range 14 east, in Randolph county, Ind., to secure the payment of the debt to the state of Indiana in the sum of $1,000; that said real estate so mortgaged "is liable to sale to make assets for the payment of said mortgage debt"; that the probable value of said real estate, exclusive of the rights of the widow of decedent therein, is $2,500. The prayer of the petition is that the court order the sale of the mortgaged real estate, subject to the rights of the widow, for the purpose of discharging the mortgage lien. The testator, in his will, by its very first operative provision, said: "It is my will and desire that all my just debts and funeral expenses be first paid by my executor." No specific part or parcel of his estate was thereby charged with the payment of the debts, or with the payment of any particular part of the debts. This was the only reference made by the testator in his will to debts. It cannot be denied that the debt secured by the mortgage on the land devised to the appellant Hunt was one of the debts of the estate. By section 2743, Burns' Ann. St. 1901, it is provided: "Whenever any person shall have devised his estate or any part thereof, and any of his real estate subject to a mortgage, executed by such testator, shall descend to an heir or pass to a devisee, and no specific direction is given in the will for the payment of such mortgage, the same shall be discharged as follows: First. If such testator shall have charged any particular part of his estate, real or personal, with the payment of his debts, such mortgage shall be considered a part of his debts. Second. If the will contains no directions as to what part of the estate shall be taken for the payment of his debts, and any part of his personal estate shall be unbequeathed or undisposed of by his will, such mortgage shall be included among his debts, to be discharged out of such estate unbequeathed or undisposed of." By section 2739, Burns' Ann. St. 1901, it is provided that whenever the personal estate is insufficient to pay the debts of a testator, the real estate, if any, left undevised by the will, shall be first chargeable with the debts in exoneration, as far as possible, of the real estate that is devised, "unless it shall appear from the will that a different disposition of the assets for the payment of his debts was made by the testator." It is clearly apparent from the sections of the statute cited that, in order to sell devised lands for the discharge of testator's debts, two of the essential averments of the petition must be, first, that the personal property not specifically bequeathed is insufficient for the purpose of discharging the debts; second, that the testator left no real estate undisposed of by the will, or that the real estate undevised by the will is insufficient for the purpose of discharging the debts. In the case at bar the second requirement is entirely wanting. The petition is silent as to whether or not the testator died seised of any estate in lands which was not specifically disposed of. The averment of the petition that "there is no personal estate of said decedent to pay and discharge said claim, as by the terms of said will all of the personal estate of said decedent was given to said decedent's widow," is insufficient for the purpose of showing that the testator's personal estate was not subject to the payment of his debts. Its effect was merely to show that the testator, by the terms of his will, disposed of all his personal property. This the will itself disclosed. But the personal property in question was all bequeathed to the widow, who, in her administrative capacity, was the petitioner in the trial court and is the appellee here. Under section 2648, Burns' Ann. St. 1901, the provisions of which section relate to personal property, only, devised to a widow, she must signify whether or not she accepts the provisions of the will by taking affirmative action in manner and form and within the time prescribed by the statute. This election must be made within 90 days, and is a right personal to the widow, and can be exercised by no other person. If the widow fails to elect, the personal property descends to the heirs under the law of descent. Miller, Executor, v. Stephens, 158 Ind. 438, 63 N. E. 847. It appears from the petition that testator left personal property which went into the hands of the administratrix, and sufficient facts are not averred to relieve the personalty from being used to discharge the debts, one of which was the mortgage in question. The testator having directed the payment of all his debts in the opening clause of his will, and not having directed therein any specific part or parcel of his estate that should be applied to that purpose, we think sections 2739 and 2743, supra, control. The petition is fatally defective for the reasons stated.

Judgment reversed.

(33 Ind. A. 83)

LEONARD v. WOOD et al.

(Appellate Court of Indiana, Division No. 2. April 21, 1904.)

BOUNDARIES — DESCRIPTION IN MORTGAGE—SURVEY—MEANDER LINE OF RIVER—RIGHTS OF FORECLOSURE PURCHASER.

1. Evidence in ejectment by a mortgagor to recover from a foreclosure purchaser a tract between the surveyor's meandering of a river, inserted in the descriptive clause of the mortgage, and the river boundary as it existed after a change of course, examined in connection with the language of the mortgage, and *held* to show that the surveyor's line was not an independent boundary, but was merely a meander line of the river, so that a conveyance bounded by it was a conveyance bounded by the river.

2. The question whether a foreclosure purchaser takes land formed by accretion after a survey of the premises, which was inserted in the descriptive clause of the mortgage, depends on whether the line run by the surveyor was merely the meander line of the river or was an independent boundary.

Appeal from Circuit Court, Owen County; M. H. Parks, Judge.

Action by John M. Leonard against Lulu Wood and others. Judgment for defendants, and plaintiff appeals. Affirmed.

W. N. Pickerill and Jno. C. Robinson, for appellant. J. W. Pryor and Willis Hickam, for appellees.

ROBY, J. Action in ejectment by appellant. Cross-complaint by appellees to quiet title. Trial by the court. Finding and judgment against appellant on his complaint and for appellees on their cross-complaint.

John Franklin was, on November 9, 1875, the owner of certain real estate in Owen county, and on said day conveyed the same to appellant, describing it as bounded in part by White river. In 1876 appellant applied to a loan company for a loan to be secured by mortgage on said land. The agent of the company examined the land, and required appellant to have it surveyed, so that the description would show the actual amount of good land in the tract, the river being regarded as too indefinite. Appellant thereupon procured a survey to be made, and thereafter obtained the loan, executing a mortgage to secure it, in which the description given by the surveyor took the place of the general reference to the river. The description being in part as follows: "Thence 87 degrees 30' west 118 rods and 16 links to the left bank of White river; thence down stream with the meanderings thereof south, 34 degrees east, 40 rods; thence south, 67 degrees east, 19 rods; thence north, 80 degrees east, 25 rods; thence south, 45 degrees east, 23 rods; thence south, 27 degrees east, 28 rods; thence south 14 rods to the south line of said tract," etc. The appellees now have possession of the tract admittedly described, as well as that part in controversy, holding and claiming title to it all by virtue of a foreclosure of said mortgage. Since the execution of the mortgage the course of White river has changed, so that between the lines made by the surveyor and the river as it now runs there is a tract of from 35 to 40 acres of land. If the line run by the surveyor was merely the meander line of the river, a conveyance bounded by it was a conveyance bounded by the river (Sizer v. Logansport, 151 Ind. 626, 50 N. E. 377, 44 L. R. A. 814), and the land made by accretion belongs to appellees (Jefferies v. East Omaha, 134 U. S. 178, 33 L. Ed. 872, 10 Sup. Ct. 518; St. Clair County v. Lovingston, 90 U. S. 46, 23 L. Ed. 59). If the line was an independent one, the mortgagee's title would not extend beyond it, and the tract in controversy would belong to appellant, he not having parted with title to the strip between the line and the river.

The question is whether the judgment is sustained by evidence. The engineer who ran the line and furnished the description for the mortgage testified as follows: "I surveyed approximately where the river was. I surveyed down around the edge of the river. Some places might have been a rod or so, or two or three, and there was bars and sand in some places, and a high river bank. At the high river bank we kept as close as we could, and where it was feather edge we were not so particular. Q. What do you mean by a feather edge? A. An indefinite edge. Q. Do you mean to say that this distance and direction beginning from a point from which you reached on the left bank of the river down to where the distance starts out east is a following of the river's edge? A. Practically followed the river, this meandering is." The appellant's mortgage, after setting out the description by metes and bounds, concluded, "Making in all one hundred and seventeen and $^{53}/_{100}$ acres, and being all the land owned by the said John M. Leonard in said section twenty-one, township nine north, range four west, in the said county of Owen and state of Indiana, together with all the privileges and appurtenances thereunto belonging or in any wise appertaining, and all the estate, right, title, and interest of the parties of the first part in and to the same, and every part and parcel thereof." This language is consistent with appellees' contention that the line was run for the purpose of measuring the land owned by Leonard, and not for the purpose of establishing a boundary independent of the river. The strip between this land and the meander line was narrow and worthless. That Leonard did not intend to reserve it is a deduction that may be legitimately drawn from the language used in the mortgage, when taken in connection with the then existing conditions.

Appellant insists that the words, "thence down stream with the meanderings thereof," apply only to the clause immediately following, and cannot be applied to or carried forward to subsequent clauses contained in the deed. It is not necessary to consider the proposition except as it arises upon the facts herein involved, which include the clause quoted as to the intent to cover all land owned by the mortgagor in the section, the force of which is sufficient, in connection with the circumstances under which the survey was made, to justify the application of the phrase quoted to those lines running with the river.

Judgment affirmed.

(32 Ind. A. 644)

AMERICAN CAR & FOUNDRY CO. v. CLARK.

(Appellate Court of Indiana. April 5, 1904.)

INJURIES TO SERVANT—NEGLIGENCE—ASSUMPTION OF RISK—PLEADING—COMPLAINT—SUFFICIENCY — DEFENSES — ANSWER — HARMLESS ERROR—EVIDENCE—DAMAGES—INSTRUCTIONS.

1. A complaint in an action for injuries to a servant which alleged that plaintiff, while feeding wood to a woodworking machine, was injured, owing to the fact that the machine was not supplied with springs to hold the wood in proper position, was not defective for failing to allege that it was practicable to provide the springs.

2. The doctrine of assumption of obvious risks does not apply where a servant is ordered to do work out of the line and away from the place of the work he is hired to do.

3. Acts 1899, p. 231, c. 142 (Burns' Ann. St. 1901, § 7087i), makes it the duty of an owner of a manufacturing establishment to guard all gearing, etc. Held, that the doctrine of assumed risk does not apply in an action by a servant for injuries where the negligence counted on is a violation of the statute.

4. The mere fact that a servant works at a defective machine is not conclusive on the question of contributory negligence.

5. In an action for injuries to a servant, it is not necessary that defendant set up by answer that the risk on account of which the injury occurred was an assumed one, in order to receive the benefit of that fact.

6. Conflicting answers to interrogatories are fatal to a motion for judgment notwithstanding the general verdict.

7. In an action for injuries to a servant, evidence *held* insufficient to sustain a finding that

¶ 5. See Master and Servant, vol. 34, Cent. Dig. §§ 858, 868.

he was employed to work on a planing machine, and not in any other manner.

8. Where, in an action by a servant for injuries, there was no evidence as to the value of any medical services rendered him, or that any medicine or nursing was furnished, it was error to instruct that the jury might take into consideration, in awarding damages, expenses incurred for medical services, nursing, and medicine.

9. Burns' Ann. St. 1901, § 401, provides that no judgment shall be reversed for error which does not injuriously affect the adverse party; and section 670 provides that there shall be no reversal where it appears that the merits have been fairly tried. *Held* that, where the statute is invoked by an appellee, the record must be such as to show that the error complained of did not affect appellant's substantial rights.

10. It is to be presumed that the court, in charging the jury, correctly stated the law.

11. It is to be presumed that the jury followed the instructions of the court.

12. Where, in an action by a servant for injuries, the court instructed the jury, "You will consider expenses incurred for services of physicians, nursing, and medicine," but there was no evidence of such expenses, it could not be presumed that the jury considered only those matters shown by the evidence.

13. Where, in an action by a servant to recover for the loss of a part of two fingers, the verdict was for $1,500, it could not be said that an erroneous instruction that the jury should consider expenses of medical services, nursing, and medicine, when there was no evidence of such services, was harmless.

Appeal from Circuit Court, Clark County; James K. Marsh, Judge.

Action by Volta F. Clark against the American Car & Foundry Company. From a judgment in favor of plaintiff, defendant appeals. Reversed.

M. Z. Stannard, for appellant. G. H. Voigt, for appellee.

ROBY, J. Action by appellee. Verdict and judgment for $1,500. Complaint in three paragraphs. Verdict based on first and third. Separate demurrers thereto were overruled.

The facts set up in the first paragraph are substantially: That appellant is a manufacturer of cars at Clarksville, Clark county, Ind., and, in one of the departments of its plant, maintained and operated a machine called a "woodworker," used to cut wood into desired shapes, and for that purpose supplied with knives attached to a shaft, which, when the machine was operated, revolved, bringing said knives in contact with wood placed on a table and run over said knives, which said machine should have been supplied with springs to hold said wood in proper position as it was run over said knives, but appellant, well knowing that said machine was not supplied with such springs, negligently failed to provide them. That on January 28, 1902, appellee was employed by appellant to operate a planing mill, at said plant, and, under his contract, he was not required to perform any other or different service. That he operated said planing machine under said employment, and while so employed, on the 1st day of February, 1902, was directed and required by appellant to temporarily leave said employment and operate said woodworker, and in obedience to such direction he did temporarily leave said employment and engage in the operation of the woodworker. While so engaged he placed a piece of wood on the table, and proceeded to run it over said knives for the purpose of cutting it into desired shape, and while so engaged he was, by the absence of such springs, required to hold such wood in position with his hands as it passed over said knives, and, while so holding it, the same was by the operation of the machine suddenly turned thereby, causing one of his hands to come in contact with said knives, cutting off part of two fingers. That said injury was caused by appellant's act in directing him to leave his regular employment and engage in the operation of the woodworker, and its negligent failure to supply said machine with springs, as aforesaid. That, had it been so supplied, he would not have been required to hold said wood in position with his hands as it passed over said knives, and would not have been injured. That the work he was doing was different from, and more hazardous than, that he was employed to do, and was done at another place than that of his regular employment. All of which appellant knew. Wherefore, etc. The third paragraph differs from the first in the charge of negligence. It is averred that there was danger in operating the machine, as appellant knew, and that a guard could have been placed thereon without interference with the proper operation of the machine, which would have prevented any injury from said danger, but appellant, well knowing that it had not been done, then and there, and in violation of the statute, negligently failed to provide said machine with such guard, it being then and there without such guard, by reason of which appellee was injured, etc.

The complaint is skillfully drawn, and the briefs filed in this court by both parties are model ones.

The first paragraph is not defective in failing to aver that it was practicable to provide the springs which it is averred should have been provided and were negligently not provided. The absence of springs is not averred to have been unknown to appellee, nor to have constituted a latent or unobservable defect. The risk would therefore be an assumed risk, except for the further allegation as to the temporary change of employment. The doctrine of the assumption of obvious risks does not apply where the employé is ordered to do work out of the line and away from the place of the work he is hired to do, and is so engaged when injured. Clark, etc., v. Wright, 16 Ind. App. 630, 45 N. E. 817. The first paragraph therefore stated a cause of action.

The act of 1899 makes it the duty of an owner of a manufacturing establishment to protect the machines operating therein. "All vats, pans, saws, planers, cogs, gearing, belting, shafting, set screws and machinery of every description shall be guarded." Buehner v. Feulner (Ind. App.) 63 N. E. 240; Acts 1899, p. 231, c. 142 (Burns' Ann. St. 1901, § 7087i). The averments are that appellant negligently failed to perform the duty thus enjoined upon it, and are sufficient. The doctrine of assumed risk does not apply where the negligence counted upon is the violation of this positive and explicit statute. Monteith v. Kokomo (Ind. Sup.) 64 N. E. 610, 58 L. R. A. 944; Buehner v. Feulner, supra; Wortman v. Minnich, 28 Ind. App. 31, 62 N. E. 85; Davis Coal Co. v. Polland (Ind. Sup.) 62 N. E. 492, 92 Am. St. Rep. 319. In so far as Bodell v. Block Coal Co., 25 Ind. App. 654, 58 N. E. 856, holds otherwise, it has ceased to be authority. The facts averred do not include a description of the conduct of appellee at the time he was injured, and, in their absence, contributory negligence cannot be determined. It will not do to say that the mere fact that an employé works at a defective machine concludes the question of contributory negligence against him. The doctrine of assumed risk covers that phase. A man may be careful while working with a dangerous machine. "Assumption of risk is matter of contract. Contributory negligence is a question of conduct." Davis Coal Co. v. Pollard, 158 Ind. 607, 619, 62 N. E. 492, 497, 92 Am. St. Rep. 319. The complaint was not subject to the objection that contributory negligence affirmatively appeared therefrom, and the demurrers were properly overruled.

Appellant filed an answer to the first paragraph of complaint, in two paragraphs: First, a general denial; second, that the danger by reason of which appellee was injured was open and obvious, and therefore an assumed risk. A demurrer to the second paragraph of answer was sustained, and Umback v. Lake Shore, etc., 83 Ind. 191, is relied upon in support of the error assigned therein. In that case a demurrer was overruled to an answer similar to the one under consideration. The plaintiff could not have been injured thereby. It is not necessary, under our decisions, that the defendant set up by answer that the risk on account of which the injury complained of occurred was an assumed one, in order that he receive the benefit of that fact, and it was not error to sustain a demurrer to the second paragraph of answer.

Appellant's motion for judgment on the answers to interrogatories was overruled. It asserts that such action was erroneous, for the reason that it is disclosed by such answers that appellee's employment was not limited as averred in the first paragraph of his complaint. Without setting out the interrogatories and answers relied upon, it is sufficient to say that, according to an answer to one interrogatory, he was, at the time he was injured, engaged in other work than that he was employed to perform. Conflicting answers to interrogatories are fatal to a motion for judgment notwithstanding the general verdict.

What has heretofore been said upon the subject of contributory negligence applies to the motion for judgment, as well as to the ruling on the demurrer to the complaint. The facts considered in Buehner Chair Co. v. Feulner, 28 Ind. App. 479, 63 N. E. 239, were not limited to the character of the machine, and the exposure of all its parts to the operator's view, but included a failure to look while he was operating it, and the placing of his arm or hand under the bit, by which he was injured, without any necessity for so doing. The court did not err in overruling the motion for judgment.

The ninth assignment of error is that the court erred in overruling appellant's motion for a new trial. The motion questions the sufficiency of the evidence to sustain the verdict, and the action of the court in giving and refusing specified instructions. The theory of the first paragraph of the complaint is that appellee was employed to operate a planer, and that he was required by appellants to temporarily leave his regular employment and engage in the operation of a woodworker; the latter being a more hazardous occupation than that which he had contracted to perform. The evidence of the appellee—and there is none in the record more favorable to himself, nor conflicting with it—is that he was employed in the cabinet department of appellant's shop by the foreman of that department, who told him they were going "to start to work nights," and, if he wanted to, he could work, and that Mr. Walker would assign him. This conversation took place on Saturday, and on Monday he reported for work, and was told by the foreman to go to the new planer, which he did, working there eight or ten days. The night before he was injured, the night foreman said to him: "Clark, you run the woodworker. Dick Rouerk is off. He won't be here." Appellee ran the latter machine that night and was injured the next night. He worked the second night until about 2:30 a. m. "I wanted to run another machine—a sticker—but that would leave the woodworker standing idle." He had previous to the last employment worked at the planer three years, five or six feet distant from the woodworker, and was familiar with it. The evidence does not show that the appellee was employed to work at the planer. There was nothing in the contract relative to the machine at which he was to work. He was employed in the department, and might have been assigned by the foreman to the woodworker in the first instance, as he was in the last. The facts stated do not bring the case within the rule stated, nor within its reason, and the evidence was therefore insufficient to sustain the verdict upon the first paragraph of the complaint. The judgment therefore rests upon the third paragraph of complaint, and, it stating sufficient facts to constitute a cause of action, is not wholly unsupported by evidence as to any material allegation.

The ninth instruction given was as follows: "(9) In determining the amount of damages you will assess, if you find a verdict for the plaintiff, you *will* take into consideration the character, nature, and extent of his injuries, the pain and physical suffering and the mental anguish caused thereby, the loss of his services and value thereof, and *expenses incurred for services of physician and surgeon who attended and treated him, and for nursing and medicine,* and to what extent his ability to earn a livelihood has been impaired by reason of his injuries, and assess him such damages as will reasonably and *fully* compensate him for his injuries, not to exceed the amount asked for in the complaint." Objection is made to that part which is italicized. There was no evidence to the value of any services rendered to appellee by a physician or surgeon, or that any medicine was furnished or nursing done. Instructions should be pertinent to the evidence in the case. Adams v. Vanderbeck, 148 Ind. 99, 45 N. E. 645, 47 N. E. 24, 62 Am. St. Rep. 497; Blough v. Parry, 144 Ind. 463, 40 N. E. 70, 43 N. E. 560; Lake Erie Ry. v. Stick, 143 Ind. 466, 41 N. E. 365; Pelley v. Wills, 141 Ind. 688, 691, 41 N. E. 354; Lindley v. Sullivan, 133 Ind. 593, 32 N. E. 738, 33 N. E. 361; Summerlot v. Hamilton, 121 Ind. 87, 22 N. E. 973; Nicklaus v. Burns, 75 Ind. 93; Moore v. State, 65 Ind. 382; McMahon v. Flanders, 64 Ind. 334; Hill v. Newman, 47 Ind. 187; Hays v. Hynds, 28 Ind. 531; Ry. Co. v. Hoffbauer, 23 Ind. App. 614, 56 N. E. 54. "Instructions should be pertinent to the case. Juries are apt to assume, and are justified in assuming, that they are applicable." Hays v. Hynds, supra; Lindley v. Sullivan, supra; Blough v. Parry, supra. "Jurors are liable enough to consider matter outside the evidence without being led off in that direction by the court. Such practice is well calculated to confuse and mislead the jury." Nicklaus v. Burns, supra; Blough v. Parry, 144 Ind. 463, 471, 40 N. E. 70, 45 N. E. 560; McMahon v. Flanders, supra; Palmer v. Wright, 58 Ind. 486; Clem v. State, 31 Ind. 480; Swank v. Nichols' Adm'r, 24 Ind. 199; Wallace v. Morgan, 23 Ind. 399, 409; Delphi v. Lowery, 74 Ind. 527, 39 Am. Rep. 98; Durham v. Smith, 120 Ind. 468, 22 N. E. 333. "When the instructions are contradictory, and necessarily tend to confuse and mislead the jury, or when they are not applicable to the evidence, and are liable to have a like effect, the error canot be regarded as a harmless one." Summerlot v. Hamilton, 121 Ind. 91, 22 N. E. 973; Hill v. Newman, supra; McMahon v. Flanders, supra; Moore v. State, supra; Nichlaus v. Burns, supra; Evans v. Gallatine, 57 Ind. 367; Terry v. Shively, 64 Ind. 106; Machine Co. v. Reber, 66 Ind. 498. When it appears from the record that an erroneous instruction did not injuriously affect the rights of the complaining party, the judgment will not be reversed on account of its having been given. Haxton v. McClaren, 132 Ind. 247, 31 N. E. 48; Perry v. Makemson, 103 Ind. 300, 2 N. E. 713; Wolfe v. Pugh, 101 Ind. 293; Ry. Co. v. Darting, 6 Ind. App. 375, 33 N. E. 636; McCall v. Seevers, 5 Ind. 187; Stockton v. Stockton, 73 Ind. 510, 514; Lytton v. Baird, 95 Ind. 349, 357; Ry. Co. v. Falvey, 104 Ind. 409, 429, 3 N. E. 389, 4 N. E. 908. Section 401, Burns' Ann. St. 1901, provides that no judgment shall be reversed for error in the proceedings which does not injuriously affect the adverse party; section 670, that there shall be no reversal "where it shall appear to the court that the merits of the cause have been fairly tried and determined in the court below." It has been always held, where these provisions are invoked, that the record must be such as to show that the error complained of did not affect the appellant's substantial rights. Lafayette v. Ashby, 8 Ind. App. 214, 34 N. E. 238, 35 N. E. 516; Rush v. Thompson, 112 Ind. 158, 164, 13 N. E. 665; Lynch v. Bates, 139 Ind. 206, 38 N. E. 806; Kepler v. Conkling, 89 Ind. 392; Sessengut v. Posey, 67 Ind. 408, 33 Am. Rep. 98; Bissell v. Wert, 35 Ind. 54. When the court said to the jury that, in determining the amount of damages, "you will take into consideration * * * expenses incurred for services of physician and surgeon who attended and treated him, and for nursing and medicine, * * * and award him such damages as will reasonably and fully compensate him," it thereby, in peremptory phrase, directed that elements of damages be considered which had not been proven. In the absence of such proof, such elements ought not to have been taken into account, and the instruction was wrong. Chicago, etc., R. Co. v. Butler, 10 Ind. App. 259, 38 N. E. 1. It has been held that the absence of any evidence as to the existence of elements of damage rendered instructions similar to that under consideration harmless, where they included a direction to find from the evidence—a direction which was not included in the instruction under consideration. Ry. Co. v. Stein, 140 Ind. 61, 39 N. E. 246; Indianapolis v. Scott, 72 Ind. 196; Ry. Co. v. Falvey, 104 Ind. 409, 3 N. E. 389, 4 N. E. 908; Ry. Co. v. Carlson, 24 Ind. App. 559, 56 N. E. 251; Ry. Co. v. Hoffbauer, 23 Ind. App. 614, 56 N. E. 54. In so far as these cases are based upon their own particular facts, from which the harmlessness of the erroneous instructions appeared, their authority does not govern this case; and there is no room in this case to apply the presumption that the jury did not find anything except from the evidence, or consider any matter not shown by the evidence, for the reason that it is the duty of the court to state the law, and the duty of the jury to take it as stated. The presumption is that the law was correctly stated (section 542, subd. 5, Burns' Ann. St. 1901; Herron v. State, 17 Ind. App. 161, 46 N. E. 540), and that the instructions were followed by the jury (Walworth v. Readsboro, 24 Vt. 252; Pettibone v. Maclem, 45 Mich.

381, 8 N. W. 84; Stanton v. French, 91 Cal. 274, 27 Pac. 657, 25 Am. St. Rep. 174; Hackett v. Gas Co. [Com. Pl.] 26 N. Y. Supp. 11; Bank of Westfield v. Inman, 8 Ind. App. 239, 34 N. E. 21). This is nothing more than an application of the presumption of right action, to the benefit of which every court and officer is entitled. Board v. Heating Co., 128 Ind. 240, 27 N. E. 612, 12 L. R. A. 502; Parvin v. Wimberg, 130 Ind. 561, 30 N. E. 790, 15 L. R. A. 775, 30 Am. St. Rep. 254; Lawson's Presumptive Evidence, 67, 98. "It constitutes reversible error if inapplicable instructions tend to injure the complaining party." Robinson v. State, 152 Ind. 308, 53 N. E. 223; Stockton v. Stockton, 73 Ind. 510. "If an instruction is given concerning a fact or set of facts to which no evidence has been adduced, it will be reversible error, unless it clearly appears that the party affected was not harmed thereby." Haines v. State, 155 Ind. 118, 57 N. E. 705, and cases cited; Blashfield, Ins. To Juries, § 377. In the absence of an instruction which it is bound to follow, the jury will be presumed to have considered only those matters shown by the evidence, but this presumption must give way to the one above stated.

The verdict of $1,500, when considered with reference to the character and extent of the injury complained of, does not permit it to be said that the elements of damage erroneously stated in the ninth instruction were not taken into account. It is at least possible that the verdict was affected by speculation as to what was the probable value of such service as would probably be rendered necessary by injuries such as appellee received. The defendant is as much entitled to have damages assessed in accordance with the law as it is to have its original liability determined with reference thereto.

Other questions argued are not likely to arise in a retrial of the cause.

Judgment reversed and cause remanded, with instructions to sustain motion for new trial.

HENLEY, C. J., and WILEY, COMSTOCK, and BLACK, JJ., concur.

ROBINSON, J. I concur in the result. The doctrine announced in Bodell v. Block Coal Co., 25 Ind. App. 654, 58 N. E. 856, as to assumption of risk in such cases, was overruled by the Supreme Court in Davis Coal Co. v. Polland, 158 Ind. 607, 62 N. E. 492, 92 Am. St. Rep. 319.

(33 Ind. App. 57)

GOODWINE v. KELLEY et al.

(Appellate Court of Indiana, Division No. 2. April 19, 1904.)

CONTRACT FOR SALE OF REALTY—SPECIFIC PERFORMANCE — UNEQUAL CHARACTER — ACTION AT LAW FOR BREACH—MEASURE OF DAMAGES.

1. Plaintiffs contracted in writing with defendant to sell the latter a farm, the price to be paid by an immediate delivery to plaintiffs of a grocery, etc., by the payment of $1,625 on delivery of the deed, and by the giving of defendant's note for a like sum, due on a certain date, and secured by mortgage on the realty. Plaintiffs were to furnish an abstract of title as soon as it could reasonably be compiled, showing a title in them which defendant should deem sufficient and satisfactory, and were to convey by warranty deed. It was fairly inferable from the contract that plaintiffs did not own the land at the time it was executed. In the event of their failure to furnish an abstract, no provision was made for the return of the grocery, etc., or for compensation in lieu thereof. Had plaintiffs failed to obtain title, or if the title were incumbered, there was no provision in the contract under which specific performance against them could have been decreed. *Held*, that the contract was unequal, so that plaintiffs could not enforce specific performance thereof.

2. The vendor's legal remedy for a vendee's failure to perform an executory contract in writing for the sale of realty is an action for damages, and an action for the purchase price will not lie.

3. The measure of damages in a vendor's action for the vendee's breach of a written executory contract for the purchase of realty is the difference between the price fixed in the contract, and the fair cash value at the time of its breach, and the purchase price is not recoverable.

¶ 1. See Specific Performance, vol. 44, Cent. Dig. §§ 89, 152.

Appeal from Circuit Court, Putnam County; Presley O. Colliver, Judge.

Action by Charles A. Kelley and another against Blanche Goodwine. Judgment for plaintiffs, and defendant appeals. Reversed.

Moore Bros. and Henry H. Mathias, for appellant. B. F. Corwin and S. A. Hays, for appellees.

COMSTOCK, J. Appellees were plaintiffs below. The complaint was in two paragraphs. The first was withdrawn. The second alleged, in substance, that appellee Kelley, for the benefit of himself and co-appellee Hannah, on April 28, 1902, entered into a written contract with appellant by which appellees sold to the appellant a farm in Monroe township, Putnam county, Ind., which was known to the parties of said contract as the "Samuel H. Hillas Farm," and contained 159¾ acres. Possession of the farm was reserved until December 25, 1902. The agreed purchase price was $5,200, and to be paid in the following manner: (1) The appellant was to deliver immediately to the appellees her grocery, delivery wagon, horse, and harness, which she had in the city of Greencastle, which was to be taken as a part payment of $2,000 of the purchase price of the farm. (2) The sum of $1,625 was to be paid in cash upon the delivery of the deed. (3) The sum of $1,625 was to be evidenced by the appellant's note due December 25, 1902, and to be secured by mortgage upon the real estate. The appellees to furnish an abstract of title to the land as soon as it could reasonably be compiled, and to convey the real estate by a warranty deed. The plaintiff alleges that the contract of the parties was reduced to writing, and that the scrivener, in describing the farm, by mistake described it as being in range number 5 west, when in truth and in fact the farm was in range number 4 west, and that the parties to the contract signed the same with the understanding that it described the farm known as the "Samuel H. Hillas Farm," situate in Monroe township, Putnam county, Ind. The complaint further alleges a performance by the appellees of all of the conditions and agreements contained in the contract to be performed by them, and a delivery by the appellant to the appellees of the grocery, wagon, horse, and harness under the contract, and also alleges that an abstract of title and deed of general warranty for the land had been made and tendered to the appellant, and that she refused to accept the deed, and refused to make the cash payment, and refused to execute the note and mortgage. The relief which the complaint asks is that the contract be reformed by inserting a correct description, and that the appellees should have judgment for the sum of $1,625 due, and judgment for the further sum of $1,625 to become due on December 25, 1902, and a prayer that the judgment be decreed a lien upon the premises sold. A copy of the contract is filed with and made a part of the complaint. The appellant answered in two paragraphs, the first being in general denial. The second paragraph of the answer admitted the execution of the contract, but alleged that under the terms of the contract the real estate was to be conveyed free and clear of all incumbrances or liens, as shown by the abstract of title which was to be furnished, and that at the time the deed was tendered there was a tax lien against the property amounting to $17.59, as shown by the abstract of title. At the request of the appellant, and over the objection of the appellees, a jury was called. The jury returned a verdict for the appellees. The court, of its own motion, adopted the verdict of the jury as a finding of the amount due the appellees from the appellant; and found that the sums so found by the jury were for the balance of the unpaid purchase price of the real estate described in the appellees' complaint; that the appellees were entitled to have a vendor's lien on said real estate for the said sum of $1,625, now due, and for the further sum of $1,625 to become due December 25, 1902; that, if the said sums of money found due were not paid to the appellees before the 25th day of December, 1902, the said real estate ought to be sold, and the proceeds of such sale applied to the payment of the amounts so found due to appellees; that the allegations contained in the complaint are true; and that the contract mentioned in appellees' complaint ought to be reformed, and the mistake therein corrected, as in the appellees' complaint asked, and judgment rendered in accordance with said findings for said amounts, and ordered the reformation of said contract and the sale of the said real estate as prayed for in the complaint.

It will not be necessary to consider all the errors assigned in this appeal. Counsel differ as to the theory of the second paragraph of the complaint. Counsel for appellant state that it was formed on one theory, the issues made upon another, and the cause tried upon still another; that the court construed it, in passing upon the demurrer, as an action at law on the promise in the contract to pay the purchase price for the land in question, and not for specific performance. For appellees it is contended that the theory of the complaint was to recover an unpaid balance of the purchase money. It is the recognized rule that the theory of a pleading is to be determined from its controlling averments, and not by the name given it. It is also the rule that, when a complaint states facts sufficient to entitle a party to any relief, it is good against a demurrer. So that, if the complaint is good either for specific performance or to recover the balance of the purchase money, the demurrer was properly overruled. Coleman v. Floyd, 131 Ind. 330, 31 N. E. 75. Is it sufficient for specific performance? An executory contract will not be enforced unless it is perfectly fair, equal, and just in its terms and in the circumstances. 3 Pom. Eq. J. § 1405; R. R. Co. v. Bodenschatz-Bedford Stone Co., 141 Ind. 263, 39 N. E. 703, and cases cited. By the terms of the contract appellant was required to deliver to the appellees the stock of goods, wagon, and harness, and were to be immediately delivered to appellees, which appellees agreed to accept and did accept in payment of $2,000 of the purchase price of the land. Appellees were not required to execute a conveyance until after an abstract of title had been furnished appellant. In the event of the failure of appellees to furnish an abstract of title to the appellant, no provision is made in the contract for the return of the goods, horse, wagon, etc., or for compensation in lieu thereof. It may be fairly inferred from the contract that the land contracted to be sold was not owned by the appellees at the time of the execution of the contract. Had appellees failed to obtain title, or if the title was incumbered by lien, the contract contained no terms under which specific performance against appellees could have been decreed. Appellant, under such conditions, would have been limited to her remedy at law. The contract is unequal. "A less strong case is sufficient to defeat a suit for a specific performance than is requisite to obtain the remedy." Note 1 to section 1405, p. 2164, Pomeroy, supra. Other objections are made to the sufficiency of the complaint for specific performance which it is not necessary to notice.

Is the complaint good for the unpaid purchase money? There are two remedies for the failure to perform an executory contract in writing for the sale of real estate: (1) An action for damages for the breach of the contract; (2) for specific performance. 2 Ency.

P. & P. p. 398; 2 Beach on Con. § 878, p. 1092. An action at law will not lie on an executory contract in writing for the sale of real estate to recover the purchase price. Porter v. Travis, 40 Ind. 556. If we should concede that the action is not upon the executory contract, but is an action at law for breach of contract, a reversal is required, because the court instructed the jury that the measure of damages, if they found for appellees, would be the amount of the cash payment mentioned in such contract, with 6 per cent. interest thereon from June 13, 1902, and the amount of the payment to become due under such contract on December 25, 1902. This was error. The measure of damages in such a case is the difference between the price of the property as fixed in the contract and the fair cash value of the property at the time of the breach of the contract. Farmers', etc., v. Rector, 22 Ind. App. 102, 53 N. E. 297, and cases cited. The verdict and judgment were based upon said erroneous measure of damages.

Judgment reversed, with instructions to sustain the demurrer to the second paragraph of the complaint.

ROBY, J. (concurring). The contract between the parties stipulated that appellees should furnish an abstract of title as soon as could be reasonably done, it to be compiled by an abstracter to be approved by appellant, the same to show a title to said real estate in the "party of the first part which the party of the second part shall deem to be a sufficient and satisfactory title." I think the action is one to compel the specific performance of this contract, and I do not think the complaint sufficient, as against a demurrer for want of facts for the reason, in addition to those stated in the opinion, that it does not contain averments showing that the abstracter who made the abstract was approved by appellee, nor that the title shown thereby was deemed to be sufficient by her. New Telephone Co. v. Foley, 28 Ind. App. 418, 66 N. E. 56; Allen v. Pockwitz, 103 Cal. 85, 36 Pac. 1039, 42 Am. St. Rep. 99.

(34 Ind. App. 459)

PENNSYLVANIA CO. v. FERTIG.*

(Appellate Court of Indiana, Division No. 1. April 19, 1904.)

RAILROADS — CROSSING ACCIDENT CASE — COMPLAINT—ALLEGATIONS NEGATIVING CONTRIBUTORY NEGLIGENCE — EFFECT—DEFENDANT'S NEGLIGENCE — CONCLUSION — APPROACHING TRAIN — DUTY TO GIVE SIGNALS—PROXIMATE CAUSE — SPECIAL FINDINGS—INCONSISTENCY WITH GENERAL VERDICT.

1. Under Burns' Ann. St. 1901, § 359a, providing that in personal injury actions it shall not be necessary for plaintiff to plead want of contributory negligence, but the same shall be matter of defense, allegations in a complaint for personal injuries, negativing contributory negligence, will not cast the burden of proving its absence on the plaintiff.

2. An averment, in a complaint for personal injuries, that the injury complained of was received through and by defendant's negligence, which is not applied to any act or omission of the defendant stated in the same connection, or any preceding averments, is without effect.

3. The statutory duties imposed on railroad companies of keeping flagmen at railroad crossings, and of having trains give signals of their approach, are not merely to protect travelers from actual collision with passing trains, but also to afford opportunity to travelers in vehicles drawn by animals to secure them from taking fright at passing trains.

4. Where a complaint for personal injuries sustained in a railroad crossing accident alleges the company's failure to give the signals and warnings of the approach of a train as required by statute, it is not necessary to expressly describe such failure as negligence, it constituting negligence per se.

5. A complaint for personal injuries sustained in a railroad crossing accident alleged plaintiff's approach to the crossing in a vehicle drawn by a horse, the obstruction of his view of the track by intervening objects as he approached the crossing, the precipitous character of the descent on the opposite side of the track, and the approach of a train, without giving the statutory signals, which he did not discover until he was on the track. It also alleged that the only possible escape was to go forward quickly, which plaintiff did; that when his buggy left the track the locomotive barely missed it; and that his horse became frightened at the train, plunged forward rapidly and viciously, became unmanageable, upset his buggy, and threw him violently to the ground. *Held*, that the complaint showed that the company's negligence was the proximate cause of the injury.

6. Where, in a railroad crossing accident case, it is impossible to determine with accuracy from the special findings whether, when plaintiff was at any certain point in his approach to the crossing after having stopped, looked, and listened, he could have seen or heard the train, a general verdict for plaintiff will not be set aside.

Appeal from Circuit Court, Marshall County; A. C. Capron, Judge.

Action by David Fertig against the Pennsylvania Company. Judgment for plaintiff, and defendant appeals. Affirmed.

Zollars, Worden & Zollars and Saml. Parker, for appellant. Martindale & Stevens, for appellee.

BLACK, J. In the amended complaint of the appellee, a demurrer to which, for want of sufficient facts, was overruled, after preliminary averments, it was stated, in substance, that on, etc., the appellee and his wife were lawfully traveling in a buggy, drawn by a gentle horse, from their home in Marshall county to Plymouth, Ind., and went north on Fifth street, which crossed, within the city limits, the track of a railroad operated by the appellant; that the street extended north and south, and the railroad ran through the city northwesterly and southeasterly; that on the west side of the street, and the south side of the railway and near thereto, there were a number of dwelling houses, a grape arbor, trees, vines, outhouses and other buildings, which obstructed the view to the west, so that a person going north on the street south of the crossing could not see a train approaching from the west until

¶ 1. See Negligence, vol. 37, Cent. Dig. § 231.

*Rehearing denied. Transfer to Supreme Court denied.

it approached within 100 feet of the crossing; that at the crossing the railroad was built upon a high grade, and on the north side thereof, in the street, there was a steep and abrupt ascent, so that a vehicle drawn rapidly north, off the crossing, would leave the ground for some distance, and strike the earth with great force; that the appellee, on entering Fifth street, and when within 100 feet of the crossing, stopped his horse and looked and listened for an approaching train, and also requested his wife to look and listen for an approaching train, and after they had stopped and listened and looked for some moments, and hearing and seeing no train or locomotive, he started and drove on to the crossing, and on reaching the crossing he for the first time discovered an east-bound passenger train coming from the west at a high rate of speed and almost upon him, at which time his horse became frightened at the approach of the train, lunged forward rapidly and viciously, became unmanageable, upset his buggy, and appellee was violently thrown upon the ground, and as a result thereof his left leg was broken just below the hip joint, and he was otherwise bruised and injured, all of which occurred within 150 feet of the track at the crossing; that when appellee discovered the train approaching he was upon the track, and it was too late for him to turn back, and the only way possible for him to avoid being struck by the locomotive was to go forward as quickly as possible, which he did, and when his buggy left the railroad track the locomotive was so close that in passing it barely missed the hind wheels of his buggy. It was then alleged that appellant gave no warning or signal whatever on approaching the crossing, as is required by law, and there was no watchman or flagman stationed at the crossing, as by the ordinance of the city of Plymouth the appellant was then and there required to have; that the appellant, the railroad company, then and there carelessly and negligently approached the crossing with the passenger train, without sounding the whistle or ringing the bell when within 100 rods of the crossing, while approaching thereto, and without giving any warning of the approach thereto, as the law requires, and without having a flagman stationed at the crossing, as was then and there required by the ordinance of the city; that if appellant had not been negligent and careless in failing to sound the whistle and ring the bell as aforesaid, and in failing to have a flagman stationed at the crossing as required by said ordinance, in full force and effect at the time of the injury herein complained of, the appellee would have had warning of the approach of the train, and would not have driven on the crossing until after the train had passed, and would have avoided the injury complained of herein, which was received between the hours of 10 and 11 o'clock a. m., on the day before mentioned, through and by the negligence of the appellant, and without any fault or negligence on the part of the appellee. There were also allegations concerning the character and extent of the injury, and relating to the amount of the damages, for which judgment was demanded.

The pleader seems to have sought to follow precedents in vogue before the enactment of the statute of 1899, making it unnecessary for the plaintiff to plead or prove the want of contributory negligence on his part in such a case (section 359a, Burns' Ann. St. 1901), and the portions of the complaint introduced solely for such purpose are of no importance; notwithstanding such averments, the burden of proving contributory negligence of the plaintiff would rest upon the defendant. The averment, in the concluding portion of the complaint, that the injury complained of herein was received through and by the negligence of the defendant, without applying the averment to any act or omission of the appellant stated in the same connection or in the preceding averments, likewise did not add any material fact to those already stated, or impart any additional force to the preceding allegations. Ohio, etc., R. Co. v. Engrer, 4 Ind. App. 261, 30 N. E. 924; Cincinnati, etc., R. Co. v. Voght, 26 Ind. App. 665, 60 N. E. 797. It must be considered that the statutory duty of giving signals of the approach to a crossing, and the duty prescribed by an ordinance of keeping a flagman at a crossing, are duties imposed not merely for the protection of travelers from actual collision with passing trains, but also to afford opportunity to travelers in vehicles drawn by animals to secure them against taking fright at passing trains. The complaint shows failure on the part of the appellant to cause the giving of required signals and warnings of the approach of the train, and thereby shows omissions constituting negligence per se, it not being necessary to expressly designate or describe such failures as having been negligent. It is alleged that if the appellant had not been negligent and careless in failing to sound the whistle and to ring the bell, and in failing to have a flagman stationed at the crossing (the negligent omissions charged in the complaint), he would have had warning of the approach of the train, and would not have driven on the crossing (where he first discovered the train, and where the horse was frightened by the approach of the train) until after the train had passed, and would have avoided the injury complained of. We think the complaint must be regarded as showing that an injury was suffered which would not have occurred without negligence charged, and that the negligent omissions alleged constituted the cause of the injury. It is true that a person is not responsible for every injury which would not have occurred without some act or omission on his part; but if an act or omission constituted negligence, and an injury to one not chargeable with fault follows, of such a character that it might have been anticipated as a natural result of such negligence, and the particular injury would not have occurred without such negligence, then though other causes, whether wrongful or otherwise, contributed to the injury, the negligence without which the injury would not have occurred must be considered as contributing proximately thereto. Here the appellee alleged that if the appellant had not been negligent, as charged, he would have had warning, and would not have gone to the place of danger, and would have avoided the injury; and the negligence was such that it might have been anticipated, as a natural result thereof, that a person in the situation and condition of the appellee would have been induced thereby to go to such place, and would have been so injured. In Terre Haute, etc., R. Co. v. Brunker, 128 Ind. 542, 550, 26 N. E. 178, 180, it was said: "As between said railroad company and the approaching traveler, it induced him to approach to within an unsafe proximity of the crossing by failure to give the lawful signals, and the train is not lawfully there as against the traveler, without having first given the signal required by law before coming on the crossing." In Evansville, etc., R. Co. v. Krapf, 143 Ind. 647, 652, 36 N. E. 901, 902, it was said: "There is nothing in the first paragraph of complaint showing that the alleged resultant injury was produced by the use of the alleged defective drawbar and coupling appliances; that is, nothing to show that without such use the injury would not have occurred." In Ohio, etc., R. Co. v. Trowbridge, 126 Ind. 391, 395, 26 N. E. 64, 65, we find this language: "The principle underlying this doctrine is that there must be some connection between the effect and the cause—between the wrong and the injury. It is not necessary, however, that there should be a direct connection between the wrong and the injury; it is enough if it appears that but for the wrong no injury would have occurred, and that the injury was one which might have been anticipated." See, also, Chicago, etc., R. Co. v. Fenn, 3 Ind. App. 250, 29 N. E. 790; Louisville, etc., R. Co. v. Ousler, 15 Ind. App. 232, 36 N. E. 290; Baltimore, etc., R. Co. v. Musgrave, 24 Ind. App. 295, 55 N. E. 496; Palmer v. Inhabitants of Andover, 2 Cush. 600; Toms v. Whitby, 35 Up. Can. Q. B. 195. While the complaint is not in very good form, we hold it sufficient.

With the general verdict in favor of the appellee, the jury returned answers to a large number of interrogatories submitted by the parties, and the court overruled the appellant's motion for judgment in its favor upon these answers. In the numerous answers the jury specially found many facts in entire agreement with the general verdict, substantially in the language of the complaint, and we cannot regard it as worth the required space to set out all the special findings. It was found that there was no ordinance of the city requiring the keeping of a flagman at the crossing, and there was no flagman there, and the appellee knew before the accident that the appellant had no watchman or guard at the crossing. Therefore the negligence of the appellant on which the general verdict was based consisted in its failure to sound the whistle and to ring the bell, as required by law. Many of the interrogatories relate to the physical surroundings and to the facilities for discovering the approach of the train. There were a number of contradictory findings. It was found that the appellee, when at a point within 100 feet from the place where the railroad crossed the street, stopped his horse, and looked and listened for approaching trains on the railroad; also that he stopped and listened at a point about 125 feet south of the main track; that it was about 150 feet to the main track from a corner of the street on which he approached the railroad, and that over about 140 feet of this distance the horse moved at a trot. There were obstructions to the view on the west side of the street, south of the right of way of the appellant, preventing a person driving north on the street from seeing a train approaching from the west, consisting of buildings, grape arbor, apple tree, and shrubbery. In looking to the west up the tracks, there was nothing to obstruct the view after reaching the south line of the appellant's right of way, except an apple tree with grape vines thereon. This tree was about 66 feet west of the center of the street. A part of the top of the tree projected over the right of way. Its limbs extended over the right of way, so as to obstruct the view, 8 or 9 feet. The railroad ran 77 degrees north of west. The appellee knew that a passenger train coming from the west was due about the time he reached the crossing. There was a sounding of the whistle about three-fourths of a mile west, for another crossing, and some persons in the vicinity of the street on which he was traveling heard it.

There were a number of interrogatories and answers relating to the distances at which a train might be seen. Thus it was found that, at a point 43 feet south of the main track (which would be within the right of way), the appellee could have seen an approaching train at the distance of about 1500 feet, and that a person at intermediate points between such place and the main track could have seen the train about as far west as his sight could carry; and to questions asking if the appellee, when at a point 43 feet south of the center of the main track, and at a point 35 feet south thereof, could have seen the train approaching from the west, at a distance of at least 2,760 feet, if he had looked, and had ordinarily good eyesight, the jury answered that they thought he could. The train, consisting of a locomotive and tender and a number of cars, passed over a frog and switch about 350 feet west of the center of the crossing. The jury answered that when at a point 43 feet south of the main track the appellant might have heard the noise of the coming train, if he had listened and been of ordinarily good hearing. Also, to the question how far west of the street could he have heard the noise of the train, if he had listened at a point 43 feet south of the main track, if he had been of ordinarily good hearing, the jury answered, about 400 feet. To the question, did the train as it approached the crossing, make a natural rumbling noise, loud enough to be heard by persons of ordinary hearing, diligently listening, when on the street 100 feet or more from the railroad tracks? the jury answered, "Not real sure they could." Also to the question, could the appellee have heard the natural rumbling noise of the train before he reached the south line of the appellant's right of way, had he stopped and listened diligently? the jury answered, "Not real sure he could." The speed of the train as it passed was about 30 miles an hour.

We have sought to state the principal facts which seem to have been supposed to be important as furnishing a basis for the motion for judgment. A train running at the rate of 30 miles an hour runs 2,640 feet in one minute, or 44 feet in one second. It would run 1,500 feet in a little less than 35 seconds, and 2,760 feet in one minute and a little less than three seconds. The statute provides for warning by whistling, at a distance not more than 100 rods or less than 80 rods—that is, not more than 1,650 feet and not less than 1,320 feet—and by the continuous ringing of the bell from the time of sounding the whistle until the crossing is passed. There is no question, under the motion for judgment as to the negligence of the appellant, but the supposed ability of the appellee to protect himself against the consequences of the appellant's failure is urged against the general verdict. We are not informed by the special findings as to the speed at which the appellee advanced, except that his horse, 12 years old, proceeded at a trot. It is impossible to determine with accuracy, from the special findings, that when he was at any certain point, after he stopped, looked, and listened, he could have seen or heard the train before he did become aware of its approach when he was already on the crossing. It seems to us to be beyond our province to decide, against the jury and the trial court, that the appellee did not exercise reasonable care under the circumstances, the burden of which question was upon the appellant.

The overruling of the appellant's motion for a new trial is assigned as error. The evidence was such as to make the case one peculiarly for the jury, both upon the question as to the appellant's negligence and upon the question as to whether the appellee was at fault, and we cannot disturb the conclusion reached in the court below thereon.

Some objections raised in the examination of witnesses and the refusal of some instructions asked by the appellant are presented here, but, upon examination and consideration of these matters, we find nothing of sufficient importance for discussion. We do not find any available error in the record.

Judgment affirmed.

(33 Ind. A. 69)

EIKENBURY v. BURNS, Pros. Atty., et al.

(Appellate Court of Indiana, Division No. 1. April 20, 1904.)

DIVORCE—RECRIMINATION—EXAMINATION BY JUDGE.

1. A wife guilty of adultery, under Burns' Ann. St. 1901, § 1045, cannot obtain a divorce on the ground of abandonment by the husband.

2. On the trial of an action for divorce, where defendant does not appear, the trial judge has the right, and it is his duty, as representing the state, to elicit facts as to matrimonial offenses committed by plaintiff, and grant or withhold the decree accordingly.

Appeal from Circuit Court, Wells County; E. C. Vaughn, Judge.

Action for divorce by Josephine Eikenbury, in which action, on the default of defendant, John Burns, prosecuting attorney, appeared. From a judgment denying the divorce, plaintiff appeals. Affirmed.

Mock & Sons, for appellant.

ROBINSON, J. Appellant sued for divorce, averring in her petition, filed in September, 1901, that appellee, without cause, had abandoned appellant for more than two years; that he had failed to provide for appellant and their child for more than two years, and had been guilty of cruel and inhuman treatment. Notice was given appellee by publication, and after he was defaulted the prosecuting attorney was ruled to answer the complaint. The record does not show that any answer was filed, but the prosecutor appeared when the cause was submitted for trial. Upon the trial, in December, 1901, the residence of appellant was proven as the statute requires. Appellant testified that she was 26 years old, and was married to appellee in 1895; that they lived together until May, 1899, and that she had not lived or cohabited with him since that time; that he left her, and said nothing when he left; that she had not seen him since he left, and that, the last she heard from him, he was in the Philippine Islands; that she had one child as the issue of the marriage, born Christmas, 1899; that appellee was not present at the birth of the child, and has never seen it, and has made no provision for appellant or the child since he left in May, 1899. In answer to questions by the court, she testified that her husband never wrote to her, except in answer to her letters asking for money; that he never sent her any money; and that he gave her no reason for leaving. Appellant then rest-

¶ 1. See Divorce, vol. 17, Cent. Dig. §§ 192, 197.

ed her case, which was by the court continued for further hearing until the next term. On May 10, 1902, at the April term, appellant and her counsel and the prosecuting attorney being present, appellant, at the request of the court, was recalled, and asked by the court whether she and a man named were not then living together as husband and wife, and whether she was not then pregnant, all of which she denied. Afterward, on September 29, 1902, at the September term, the case was called for further hearing, and, as a part of the testimony in the case, it was admitted in open court by counsel for appellant "that the plaintiff had been delivered of a child, which was yet living, and that said child was born after the 10th day of May, 1902, and before July 1, 1902." The court denied appellant's petition, and rendered judgment against her for costs. To the questions asked appellant by the court, objection was made at the time on the ground that they were irrelevant, immaterial, not cross-examination, and not within the issues; there being no pleadings filed charging appellant with adultery. For the action of the court in asking appellant these questions, and that the decision of the court is not sustained by sufficient evidence and is contrary to law, a new trial was asked, which was overruled, and this ruling is assigned as error.

Marriage is not a civil contract, except in so far as the relation is based upon the agreement of the parties. It is true the statute (section 7289, Burns' Ann. St. 1901) declares marriage to be a civil contract, but the statute itself takes it out of the class of simple contracts by providing that it may be entered into by persons under age. The agreement to marry partakes of the nature of a civil contract, as upon its violation the injured party may recover damages. But the contract or agreement to marry, and the marriage relation itself, are by no means one and the same. When the agreement to marry has been executed in a legal marriage, the relation thus formed becomes much more than a mere civil contract. The rights and duties incident to this relation are from a source much higher than any contract of which the parties are capable, and can neither be restricted nor enlarged nor in any way controlled by any contract which the parties can make. The marriage executed, regulated as it is by law upon principles of public policy, is an institution of society in which the state is deeply concerned. The state itself regulates it, because the state has an interest in maintaining the family relation. "In every enlightened government," said the court in Noel v. Ewing, 9 Ind. 37, "it is pre-eminently the basis of civil institutions, and thus an object of the deepest public concern. * * * It is not a matter of mere pecuniary consideration. It is a great public institution, giving character to our whole civil policy." Watkins v. Watkins, 125 Ind. 163, 25 N. E. 175, 21 Am. St. Rep. 217, and cases cited; Hood v. State, 56 Ind. 263, 26 Am. Rep. 21; Maynard v. Hill, 125 U. S. 210, 8 Sup. Ct. 723, 31 L. Ed. 654; Cooley, Const. Lim. (6th Ed.) 128; Story, Confl. Laws (8th Ed.) § 108 et seq.; Rugh v. Ottenheimer, 6 Or. 231, 25 Am. Rep. 513; Wade v. Kalbfleisch, 58 N. Y. 282, 17 Am. Rep. 250; Adams v. Palmer, 51 Me. 481. And because marriage is declared to be a civil contract, it does not follow that a suit for divorce should be considered in the light of a civil action merely. It is a civil action in so far as the divorce act in itself fails to prescribe rules of procedure. If the divorce act is to be made effective, résort must be had to the Civil Code. But in so far only as recourse must be had to the rules of civil procedure is it a civil action. Powell v. Powell, 104 Ind. 18, 3 N. E. 639. As the marriage relation is of public concern, so divorce is of public concern. Public policy, good morals, the interests of society, all require that divorces shall be discouraged by the law, and that reconciliation should be effected if practicable or possible. The policy of the law in all Christian countries has been against divorce except for adultery. The doctrines of the ecclesiastical courts, which originally had jurisdiction in divorce cases, is yet recognized in some states so far as they are applicable and not in conflict with constitutional or statutory provisions or the general spirit of the laws. Wuest v. Wuest, 17 Nev. 217, 30 Pac. 886; Nogees v. Nogees, 7 Tex. 538, 58 Am. Dec. 78; J. G. v. H. G., 33 Md. 401, 3 Am. Rep. 183; Bauman v. Bauman, 18 Ark. 320, 68 Am. Dec. 171; Jeans v. Jeans, 2 Har. (Del.) 38. The Legislature declares the reasons for which divorces may be granted, and a party within the statute should be granted the relief there given. And while a divorce statute should not be construed in a spirit of improper liberality, nor with a view to defeat its ends, yet it should be construed strictly. All legislation upon the subject is based upon the idea that the marriage is indissoluble except for cause shown, and of the sufficiency of the cause the parties are not themselves to determine. Any tendency to regard marriage as a mere temporary arrangement of conscience, to be terminated upon some slight pretext through some formal proceeding, should be effectively disapproved in the interest of sound morals and public decency. Those who look upon marriage, as to its continuance and dissolution, as a contract merely, have wholly failed to appreciate this most important of all social institutions. Nor should they be led to believe that if marriages are entered into, and result in mismated and unhappy couples, the parties may have the relation terminated in some back-stairs, semi-secret proceeding, accelerated, perhaps, by a waiver of process, and in which little else is done than to judicially ratify an agreement previously made by the discontented parties. The matter of divorce is not one of private concern merely. When appellant filed her petition, three parties became interested—the husband, the wife, and the state. In certain divorce cases the law requires an appearance by a public officer, because of the interest the state has in preserving the purity of the institution of marriage. The trial judge, in the fullest sense, represents the state, when asked to dissolve the marriage relation. He has the right to know, not simply whether one party has broken a contract made with another, but he has the right to inquire of the parties themselves, the manner in which they have observed towards each other, and the community in which they lived, the obligations required of them by the state, and the motives prompting them in seeking a separation. He is asked to grant a remedy provided for an innocent party who has been wronged by the other. If both parties are equally guilty, he has the right to know it, because, if that be the fact, a decree of divorce should be denied.

The evidence of appellant as to abandonment shows the husband wholly unfit to be a husband, and this evidence, with the admission made, shows appellant guilty of a matrimonial offense, and wholly unfit to be a wife. In Alexander v. Alexander, 140 Ind. 555, 38 N. E. 855, the court quotes the following from Brown on Divorce: "Where each of the married parties has committed a matrimonial offense, which is a cause for divorce, so that, when one asks for this remedy, the other is equally entitled to the same, whether the offenses are the same or not, the court can grant the prayer of neither." The statute of this state provides that a party guilty of adultery cannot obtain a divorce on the ground of adultery. Section 1045, Burns' Ann. St. 1901. And upon the authority of Alexander v. Alexander, supra, a party guilty of adultery should not be granted a divorce on the ground of abandonment. The record shows appellant guilty of conduct that would be ground for divorce, and in such a case the court, on its own motion, should apply the principles of recrimination. And from the nature of the relation the trial judge was asked to dissolve, and the character of the remedy he was asked to grant, he not only had the right, but, representing the state, an interested party, it was his duty, to elicit the facts, and to grant or withhold a decree accordingly. See Mattox v. Mattox, 2 Ohio, 233, 15 Am. Dec. 547; Pierce v. Pierce, 3 Pick. 299, 15 Am. Dec. 210; Christianberry v. Christianberry, 3 Blackf. 202, 25 Am. Dec. 96; Armstrong v. Armstrong, 27 Ind. 186; Scott v. Scott, 17 Ind. 309; Hale v. Hale, 47 Tex. 336, 26 Am. Rep. 294; Wood v. Wood, 2 Paige, 108; Conant v. Conant, 10 Cal. 249, 70 Am. Dec. 717; Smith v. Smith, 4 Paige, 432, 27 Am. Dec. 75; Moores v. Moores, 16 N. J. Eq. 275; Knight v. Knight, 31 Iowa, 451; Stewart, Marriage & Divorce, § 314; Ribert v. Ribert, 39 Ala. 348; Wass v. Wass, 41 W. Va. 126, 23 S. E. 537.

Judgment affirmed.

CLEVELAND, C., C. & ST. L. RY. CO. v. OSGOOD.[1]

(Appellate Court of Indiana, Division No. 2. April 21, 1904.)

DEATH BY WRONGFUL ACT—ALIEN NEXT OF KIN—RIGHT OF RECOVERY.

1. Burns' Ann. St. 1901, § 285, providing that, where the death of one is caused by the wrongful act or omission of another, the personal representative may maintain an action therefor, the damages to inure to the exclusive benefit of the widow, etc., and the next of kin, to be distributed in the same manner as personal property, does not confer a right of action on the administrator for negligently occasioning the death of his intestate where the next of kin who would be entitled to the recovery are nonresident aliens.

Appeal from Superior Court, Marion County; Vinson Carter, Judge.

Action by Henry S. Osgood, as administrator, against the Cleveland, Cincinnati, Chicago & St. Louis Railway Company. Judgment for plaintiff, and defendant appeals. Reversed.

Elliott, Elliott & Littleton, for appellant. J. E. McCullough and H. H. Lee, for appellee.

WILEY, P. J. Appellee sued appellant to recover damages for the death of appellee's decedent, which was alleged to be the result of appellant's negligence. The complaint was in one paragraph, to which a demurrer was overruled. Answer in denial, trial by jury, verdict and judgment for appellee. With their general verdict, the jury found specially by answering certain interrogatories addressed to them. Appellant's motions for a new trial and for judgment upon the answers to interrogatories notwithstanding the general verdict were respectively overruled. All rulings adverse to appellant are assigned as errors.

Appellant does not rely for a reversal upon the overruling of its demurrer to the complaint, and counsel have not discussed its sufficiency. It is unnecessary, therefore, to set out the material averments of the complaint, and a brief statement of the manner in which the decedent met his death, as disclosed by the allegations of the complaint, will suffice.

It is charged that the decedent was an employé of appellant as assistant fireman, and was on one of appellant's locomotives in that capacity, and, while seated on the seat box in the cab of one of appellant's locomotives, he came in contact with a car in the switchyards at Indianapolis, which had carelessly and negligently been left in the nighttime so near the track upon which the locomotive in which he was riding was being run that it

[1] Transfer to Supreme Court denied. See 73 N. E. 285. Rehearing denied.

came in contact with the cab of the locomotive, and that in such collision the decedent was mangled and killed. The complaint further charges that the decedent left surviving him a widowed mother, with four infant children, who were dependent upon him for support.

The first question discussed by counsel is a new one in this jurisdiction, and involves the right of appellee to recover for the benefit of the deceased's mother and her infant children, who are aliens. It is earnestly and ably contended by counsel for appellant that an action for the death of a person cannot be maintained where the sole beneficiaries are aliens. Such right of action did not survive at common law, and it is only by virtue of the statute that it can be maintained under any circumstances. It is important, therefore, to look to the statute giving the right of action. Section 285, Burns' Ann. St. 1901, provides that, "where the death of one is caused by the wrongful act or omission of another, the personal representatives of the former may maintain an action therefor against the latter, if the former might have maintained an action, had he or she * * * lived, against the latter for an injury for the same act or omission. * * * The damages can not exceed ten thousand dollars; and must inure to the exclusive benefit of the widow or widower, * * * and children, if any, or next of kin, to be distributed in the same manner as personal property of the deceased." Before an action can be maintained under this statute, the plaintiff must bring himself clearly within its provisions. Thornburg v. American Co., 141 Ind. 443, 40 N. E. 1062, 50 Am. St. Rep. 334; Hilliker v. Citizens' St. Ry. Co., 152 Ind. 86, 52 N. E. 607; Wabash, etc., Ry. Co. v. Cregan, 23 Ind. App. 1, 54 N. E. 767. The evidence is without conflict that the deceased's mother was a widow, who is a resident of England; that she has four minor children residing with her; and that the deceased contributed to her support. If it is contemplated by the statute that its provisions are applicable to aliens, then appellee's right to recover, in this regard, is established. If not, then the judgment cannot be maintained.

As above suggested, the question is a new one, and there is a conflict of authority upon it. Courts which have held that such an action cannot be maintained for the benefit of nonresident aliens rest their decision upon the principle that the presumption is, in the absence of a clearly apparent intention to the contrary, that the lawmaking department of government does not design its statutes to operate beyond the territorial limits of its jurisdiction, and that, unless the "contrary be expressed or implied from the absolute necessity of the case, a legislature must be presumed to have intended by its enactments to regulate the rights which should subsist between its own subjects, and not to affect the rights of foreigners, whether by way of restriction or augmenting their natural rights." Cope v. Doherty, 4 Kay & J. 367; The Zollverein, 1 Swab. Admr. 96; Ex parte Blain, 12 Ch. Div. 522; Jeffreys v. Boosey, 4 H. L. Cas. 815; Rose v. Himely, 4 Cranch, 279, 2 L. Ed. 608. The statutes of this and other states giving a right of action for the wrongful death of a human being are patterned largely after Lord Campbell's act of 1846 (9 & 10 Vict. c. 93). That was the first act in the history of legislation conferring such right of action, and in that regard departing from the common law. It is important, therefore, to look to the construction placed upon the act by courts of England. A leading case is that of Adams v. British & Foreign Steamship Co., 2 Q. B. 430 (1898). In that case plaintiff's son was in the employment of appellee, and was killed, by its negligence, in a collision at sea. She was a Belgium subject, and prosecuted her action to recover damages for her son's death, and bottomed her right of action upon Lord Campbell's act. In the course of the decision the following language was used: "Independent of Lord Campbell's act, it was conceded that a representative of an alien killed by the negligence of a British subject on the high seas cannot maintain an action in this court. Now, Lord Campbell's act gives a new cause of action. This is decided by Lord Selbourne in the case of The Vera Cruz; but it is a principle of our law that acts of Parliament do not apply to aliens, at least if they be not temporarily in this country, unless the language of the statute expressly refers to them. In the case of The Zollverein, Dr. Lushington says: 'In looking to an act of Parliament, as to whether it is intended to apply to foreigners or not, I should always bear in mind the power of the British legislature, for it is never to be presumed, unless the words are so clear that there can by no possibility be a mistake, that the British legislature exceeded that power which, according to the law of the whole world, probably belonged to it. The power of this country is to legislate for its own subjects all over the world, and as to foreigners within its jurisdiction, but not farther.' Lord Esker, in Colquhoun v. Hedden, held that the proper construction to be put upon an act of Parliament is that Parliament was dealing only with such persons and things as are within the general words, and also within its jurisdiction. He used the following language: 'It seems to me that our Parliament ought not to deal in any way, either by regulation or otherwise, directly or indirectly, with any foreign person or thing which is outside its jurisdiction; and, unless it does so in express terms, so clear that their meaning is beyond doubt, the courts ought always to construe general words as applying only to persons and things which will answer the description, and which are also within the jurisdiction of Parliament.'" In Jeffreys v. Boosey, 4 H. L. Cas. 815, Jervis, C. J., said:

"Statutes must be understood, in general, to apply to those only who owe obedience to the laws, and whose interests it is the duty of the legislature to protect. Natural-born subjects and persons domiciled or resident within its kingdom owe obedience to the laws of the kingdom, and are within the benefits conferred by the legislature; but no duty can be imposed upon aliens abroad, and with them the legislature of this country has no concern, either to protect their interests or protect their rights." Recurring again to Adams v. British, etc., Co., supra, the court held that there was nothing in Lord Campbell's act to show that it was intended to apply for the benefit of foreigners not resident in England. Darling, J., said: "The intention of the legislature is to be collected from the statute, and I see no implied, and certainly no express, intention to give to foreigners out of the jurisdiction a right of action which even British subjects had not until the passing of 9 & 10 Vict. c. 93. * * * An act of Parliament is not an allocution addressed urbi et orbi."

We have examined all the English cases to which our attention has been called, or to which our research has led, and the courts of that country have uniformly adhered to the rule announced. As the right to maintain such an action as the one before us had its origin in the legislature of England, the construction placed upon the statute by the courts of that country, and the reasoning leading to such construction, should not be passed over lightly, but should receive due and careful consideration.

Turning to the construction of like statutes by our own courts, and the adjudications thereunder, we find a conflict of opinion which cannot be reconciled. The case of Deni v. Pennsylvania R. R. Co., 181 Pa. 525, 37 Atl. 558, 59 Am. St. Rep. 676, is in harmony with the English cases. The plaintiff in that case was a subject of Italy, and was domiciled there. Her son was killed while in the employment of the appellee, and the action was prosecuted to recover damages, under the statute, for the benefit of his mother, to whose support he contributed. In the decision of the case, the court said: "Our statute was not intended to confer upon nonresident aliens rights of action not conceded to them or to us by their own country, or to put burdens upon our citizens to be discharged for their benefit. It has no extraterritorial force, and the plaintiff is not within the purview of it. While it is possible that the language of the statute may admit of a construction which would include nonresident alien husbands, widows, children, and parents of the deceased, it is a construction so obviously opposed to the spirit and policy of the statute that we cannot adopt it. A nonresident defendant is not entitled to our exemption laws, although the language of these laws may admit of a construction which would include them. * * * In one respect, at least, our act of 1855 [the act giving right of action, etc.] resembles our exemption laws. It is intended primarily for the benefit of the family of which the deceased was a member. * * * We have a number of statutes which expressly confer rights upon aliens, but none which confer them by implication or inference. When the Legislature intends to concede to nonresident aliens the rights which our own citizens have, under and by virtue of the act of April 26, 1855 [P. L. 309], it will say so."

The most recent and possibly the best-considered case in which the question before us is involved is that of McMillan v. Spider Lake, etc., Co. (Sup. Ct. Wis.) 91 N. W. 979, 60 L. R. A. 589. In that case the party killed was a young man whose mother resided in Canada, and it was charged that he was her only support, and that he contributed thereto. All the cases pro and con, bearing upon the question, are collected and commented on, and, after reviewing all the authorities, the court reaches the conclusion that there could not be a recovery, under a statute quite similar to ours, for the benefit of a nonresident alien. Brannigal et al. v. Union Gold Mining Co., 93 Fed. (U. S. Cir. Ct. Dist. Colo.) 164, is in point. In that case it was held that nonresident aliens are not entitled to the benefit of the Colorado statute giving a right of action for death by wrongful act to the next of kin to the deceased, and cannot maintain an action therefor. It was suggested in the opinion that the statute did not give them the action as heirs of representatives; that the moneys recovered are not the estate of the person killed; that they are recovered by the persons designated by the statute, and not as a matter of inheritance from the deceased. In the case of Utah, etc., Co. v. Diamond, etc., Co., decided by the district court of the Second Judicial District of Utah, the question received a careful consideration. The case was appealed to the Supreme Court (73 Pac. 524), but that court did not pass upon the right to maintain the action for the benefit of nonresident aliens. Counsel for appellant, however, have favored us with copious extracts from a certified copy of the opinion of the district court; and, while it cannot be taken as authority, it is a well-considered case, and abounds in strong reasoning in support of the rule declared in England under Lord Campbell's act, and the cases in this country which have adhered to that rule. In the course of the opinion it was said: "The best reasoning is in favor of the proposition that the legislative enactments in our various states of the provisions of Lord Campbell's act giving a right of action to the heirs of a person whose death was caused by the wrongful or negligent act of another must be presumed to have been made for the benefit of our own residents and citizens, and not for the benefit of nonresident aliens, in whose welfare we are not specially interested, and whose support cannot likely fall upon our own citizens."

We do not deem it necessary to further comment upon the cases sustaining the doctrine first declared by the English courts in construing Lord Campbell's act, that such statutes did not apply to nonresident aliens. A brief review of the cases supporting a contrary rule may be instructive. There are two cases based upon the Massachusetts statute: Vetaloro v. Perkins et al. (C. C.) 101 Fed. 393, and Mulhall v. Fallon, 176 Mass. 266, 57 N. E. 386, 54 L. R. A. 934, 79 Am. St. Rep. 309. The first case was decided by the United States Circuit Court, District of Massachusetts. The statute upon which the action was founded is as follows: "Where an employé is instantly killed, or dies without conscious suffering, as the result of the negligence of an employer, or the negligence of any one for whose negligence the employer is liable under the provisions of this act, the widow of the deceased, or in case there is no widow, the next of kin, provided that such next of kin were at the time of the death of such an employé dependent upon the wages of such employé for support, may maintain an action for damages therefor and may recover in the same manner and to the same extent as if the death of the deceased had not been instantaneous, or as if the deceased had consciously suffered." Rev. Laws Mass. p. 932, c. 106, § 76. While the statute differs from ours, in that it applies only to the death of an employé, caused by the negligence of the employer, etc., the evident purpose of it was to give a right of action to certain designated persons who might survive the death of such employé. This is a special statute applying only to employés, yet it does not necessarily follow that it will admit of a more liberal construction than our own statute, which has a general application. The court held that the statute made no distinction between citizens and aliens, and that to exclude nonresident aliens from the right to maintain an action under the statute quoted would be to incorporate into it a restriction which it does not contain. Colt, J., said: "It is to refuse compensation to a certain class of persons for a real injury recognized by statute law. It is to relieve employers, with respect to some employés, from the exercise of due care in the employment of safe and suitable tools and machinery and competent superintendents. It is to offer an inducement to employers to give preference to aliens and to discriminate against citizens." The court then briefly reviews the argument and reasoning of the cases holding that the statute does not extend to nonresident aliens. Reference is made to Lord Campbell's act, and the learned judge suggests that the decisions denying the right of aliens to maintain such an action rest largely upon the proposition that no case can be found in which Lord Campbell's act has been extended to nonresident aliens, and that the act has no extraterritorial force. "This," the court says, "is hardly in accordance with the fact. A more correct statement, it seems to me, would be to say that the English courts have never questioned the right of a nonresident alien to maintain an action in the common-law courts under Lord Campbell's act." The case of Adams v. British, etc., Co., supra, was decided in July, 1891, and the case of Vetaloro v. Perkins, supra, was decided in April, 1900. It is apparent, therefore, that Mr. Justice Colt, in the latter case, was not aware of the decision in Vetaloro v. Perkins, or that he wholly ignored it. His attention was evidently not called to the English case, for otherwise he would not have made a statement so at variance with the fact that the "English courts have never questioned the right of a nonresident alien to maintain an action in the common-law courts under Lord Campbell's act." The ground of the decision in the Vetaloro Case is made manifest by this language of the court: "This whole act relating to the liability of employers is highly remedial. It was designed to benefit all employés. It has received, and should continue to receive, a liberal construction." The case of Mulhall v. Fallon, 176 Mass. 266, 57 N. E. 386, 54 L. R. A. 934, 79 Am. St. Rep. 309, was prosecuted under the same statute as the Vetaloro Case, and was decided a month later; and it was held that a nonresident alien mother could maintain an action for the wrongful death of her son, resulting from the imputed negligence of his employer. The court in that case cited the Adams Case, supra, and said: "But so far as the principle for which we cite the case is concerned, it is in accord with our own decisions; assuming that, like Lord Campbell's act, the statute was regarded as conferring a new right of action on the executor or administrator, and not as giving an action to the deceased which went to the executor by survival only." The court then points out that, while no duties can be imposed upon persons outside of the territorial jurisdiction of the Legislature, yet rights can be offered to such persons, and, if the power that governs them makes no objection, they may accept the proffered rights. As a concluding basis for the conclusion reached by the Supreme Court of Massachusetts, it is argued that the statute was enacted primarily as a penalty for the protection of life, and the penalty being payable to the heirs, the question of residence becomes immaterial. The other case cited and relied upon by appellee is that of Kellyville Coal Co. v. Petraytis, 195 Ill. 215, 63 N. E. 94, 88 Am. St. Rep. 191. That case arose under a special statute of Illinois relating to mines and miners. It provides that for injury to person or property occasioned by any willful violation of the act, or willful failure to comply with any of its provisions, a right of action shall accrue to the party injured, and, in case of loss of life by reason of such willful violation or failure as aforesaid, a right of action shall accrue to the widow and others (naming them) who were, before such loss of life, dependent for support upon the person or persons killed. The court there adopted the rule declared in Massachusetts, and based its decision upon it.

We must determine the question in controversy between these conflicting authorities. Reverting to the Mulhall Case, supra, we desire to notice some of the reasoning by which the court arrived at its conclusion. It may be true, as a general proposition, that, while a legislature cannot impose duties upon nonresident aliens, it may offer rights to them, yet it would seem to be a reasonable construction that, when a lawmaking body seeks to confer such rights, it would do so by express language, upon the undisputed proposition that such body legislates for the benefit of resident subjects, and that it is not designed that its acts should operate beyond the territorial limits of its jurisdiction. Under this rule, before it can be said that the statute operates for the benefit of nonresident aliens, we must read something into it which the Legislature did not insert. Again, under the Massachusetts statute, the right of action, unlike that under our statute, is put upon the ground of a right of action surviving for the benefit of the estate of the deceased, and is not treated as a new and independent cause of action, and so the Massachusetts statute requires the damages in such case to be assessed according to "the degree of culpability of the defendant." It is upon this basis that it is held that it is for the interest of employés, and for their protection, and in the nature of a penalty, no difference whether the beneficiaries may happen to be citizens or foreigners. And so it is with the Illinois statute, and in this respect, at least, they differ materially from ours. Marshall, C. J., in the case of Rose v. Himely, 4 Cranch, 240, at page 278, 2 L. Ed. 620, said: "It is conceded that the Legislature of every country is territorial; that, beyond its own territory, it can only affect its own citizens or subjects." Endlich on the Interpretation of Statutes lays down the rule that, in general, statutes must be understood as applying to those only who owe obedience to the Legislature which enacts them, and whose interests it is the duty of the Legislature to protect, and, as regards alien residents abroad, the Legislature has no concern to protect their interests. Endlich, Interp. St. § 109, and authorities cited. It is the law that, as the right to recover damages for the death of a human being is purely statutory, the statute must be strictly construed, and a party seeking to recover under such statute must bring himself clearly within its terms. If the person or persons for whom such benefit the action accrues does or do not exist, then no recovery can be had. McDonald v. Pittsburgh, etc., R. R. Co., 144 Ind. 459, 43 N. E. 447, 32 L. R. A. 309, 55 Am. St. Rep. 185. If a statute has no extraterritorial force, and the general rule stated by Endlich, supra, and supported by authority, is to govern, then the beneficiaries in this case do not come within the purview of the statute, and hence, so far as the right given by the statute is concerned, do not exist. If this is true, then, under the undisputed facts, no right of action survived appellee's decedent. We must go to the Parliament of England for the initial and pioneer act of legislation upon this subject, from which our own statute and that of our sister states is largely copied, and which in this regard changed the course of the common law. The courts of England have denied the right of nonresident aliens to claim the benefit of that statute, upon the sole ground that it was enacted for the protection and benefit of its own citizens and subjects, and did not confer any extraterritorial rights on subjects of other governments. Her course, under the rule declared, would deny to one of our citizens the right claimed and the remedy here sought for the benefit of one of its subjects. Why should we extend to one of her subjects a valuable right which she denies to one of our own citizens? The best solution to this inquiry is to abide by the law as declared by the courts of England upon the identical question with which we are here confronted. We think it is safe to anchor in the harbor she has prepared, for she first made and lighted the way.

These considerations lead to a reversal, and hence it is unnecessary to consider other questions presented by the record. The judgment is reversed, and the court below is directed to sustain appellant's motion for a new trial.

CHICAGO, I. & L. RY. CO. v. SOUTHERN INDIANA RY. CO.*

(Appellate Court of Indiana. April 6, 1904.)

RAILROADS — COMBINATIONS — RESTRAINT OF COMPETITION—ESTOPPEL TO DENY CORPORATE POWERS—CONTRACTS ILLEGAL IN PART—ENFORCEMENT.

1. A contract between competing railroad companies, whereby one of them agrees not to run any tracks to or from quarries connected with the road of the other company by switches, nor to make any demands for the use of the tracks of the latter company lending to the quarries for the shipment of stone therefrom, nor to interfere with or divert the benefits derived to the latter company from its connection and business with such quarries, the purpose of the contract as expressed therein being to preserve to the latter company the benefits acquired in the quarry business, is void, as creating a monopoly and destroying competition.

2. A combination between common carriers to prevent competition is prima facie illegal, and the parties thereto must establish the legality thereof before the courts will uphold it.

3. An agreement by a common carrier not to furnish sidings to stone quarries near its line is, like an agreement not to locate stations or de-

¶ 1. See Monopolies, vol. 35, Cent. Dig. § 12.

*Rehearing denied. Transfer to Supreme Court denied.

pots within prescribed limits, against public policy and void.

4. The principle that a corporation may not retain the benefits received under an ultra vires contract, and at the same time set up its own want of power to contract, is inapplicable to a contract which is illegal because prohibited by statute, or because contrary to public policy.

5. The courts will refuse aid in the enforcement of an executory contract which is illegal, and will leave the parties thereto where they place themselves in executing it in whole or in part.

6. Where the consideration of a contract is in part illegal, the courts, as a general rule, will not determine how much of the consideration is based on the illegal consideration, and enforce the contract as to the balance; but the whole contract will be deemed illegal, and enforcement thereof wholly refused.

7. Plaintiff, a railroad company, granted to defendant, another railroad company, the right to construct and operate its railroad across the tracks of plaintiff. Defendant agreed to furnish the materials and labor necessary therefor, and further agreed not to run any tracks to stone quarries connected with the road of plaintiff, nor to make any demands for the use of plaintiff's tracks leading to the quarries for shipment of stone therefrom. The contract between the parties expressly stated that the consideration for granting the privilege to defendant was defendant's covenant not to interfere with or divert the benefits derived by plaintiff from its connection and business with the quarries. *Held*, that the illegality of defendant's agreement not to interfere with plaintiff's business could not be separated from the valid portions of the contract, but the whole contract must be held illegal.

Black and Wiley, JJ., dissenting.

Appeal from Circuit Court, Lawrence County; W. H. Martin, Judge.

Action by the Chicago, Indianapolis & Louisville Railway Company against the Southern Indiana Railway Company. From a judgment rendered on sustaining demurrers to the complaint, plaintiff appeals. Affirmed.

E. C. Field, G. W. Kretzinger, and H. R. Kurrie, for appellant. F. M. Trissal and Brooks & Brooks, for appellee.

ROBY, J. Demurrers were sustained to each of the three paragraphs of appellant's complaint, and the correctness of such action is the question for decision.

A written contract, executed by the Louisville, New Albany & Chicago Railway Company as the party of the first part, and by the Evansville & Richmond Railway Company as party of the second part, is filed with each paragraph and forms the basis for the relief prayed, which in the first and second paragraphs is specific performance of the contract, and in the third judgment for the reasonable cost of constructing the interlocking switch specified therein. The averments are made that appellant succeeded to the rights of the Louisville, New Albany & Chicago Railway Company, and that appellee holds the title of the Evansville & Richmond Railway Company, and that the one has the right to enforce and the other is bound by the contract in question. This is not controverted, so that the rights of the parties will not be different from what they would be, had the agreement been between them originally, and the terms "first party" and "second party," when used in this opinion, will be used as applicable to appellant and appellee, respectively.

The contract made on July 29, 1889, in terms grants to the second party the right to construct and operate its railroad over and across the main track and switches owned by the first party at a designated distance north of the Bedford telegraph office upon certain specified conditions, which the second party bound itself to perform. The substance of these conditions was that the second party should furnish all materials and perform all labor necessary to raise a certain switch track belonging to the first party, to furnish all material and perform all labor incident to the construction and maintenance of the crossing, including an interlocking switch and signal system. In event that the first party should thereafter wish to construct additional tracks, it agreed to adapt its own tracks thereto and pay one-half of the expense of whatever else (frogs, signals, etc.) might be necessary to make the crossing safe. It was further stipulated that proper appliances were to be used in such improvement, and that employés performing service at said crossing should be subject to removal at the demand of the first party. The second party bound itself to hold the first party harmless from cost and damage resulting from the construction of the use of said crossing. The concluding clauses of the contract were of the tenor following:

"Sixth. The second party agrees not to run any track or tracks to or from any stone quarry which is connected with the road of the first party, by switches or tracks built thereto by said first party or under contract therefor, and will not make any demands for the use of said first party's tracks or switches leading to any such quarries, for the shipment of stone therefrom, the express purpose of this clause being to preserve the said party all rights and benefits now acquired in the business of such quarries; and it is hereby expressly understood and agreed that the consideration for granting the rights and privileges herein expressed to said second party is the covenant and agreement of said second party not in any manner, directly or indirectly, to interfere with or divert the benefits now derived or to be hereafter derived from said first party's connection and business with such quarries.

"Seventh. In consideration of making a Y connection, it is agreed between the parties hereto that, in case any party or parties require said first party to forward stone or other car-load freight to the line of the second company, it is agreed that the proportion of the through rate from any given quarry or station accruing to the party of the first part shall not be less than three cents per hundred (100) pounds."

By clause 6 the second party agreed not to

run any track into any stone quarry connected by switches or tracks with the road of first party, and not to demand the use of such tracks for the shipment of stone; "the express purpose of this clause being to preserve the said first party all rights and benefits now acquired in the business of such quarries." The concluding portion of the clause contains a further agreement by the second party not to "directly or indirectly interfere with or divert the benefits now derived or to be hereafter derived from said first party's connection and business with such quarries." This clause clearly states the purpose for which it is drawn. Its effect, and its intended effect, is to deprive a class of citizens engaged in a certain business of advantages that might accrue to them from the facilities afforded them for the shipment of their merchandise over a competing railroad. By this agreement the two railroad companies undertook to contract away the rights of third parties, without their knowledge, and in defiance of the public duty devolved upon such companies. That the contracting parties were conscious of the quality of such undertaking is indicated by the seventh clause of the contract, where, in case "any party or parties require said first party to forward stone * * * to the line of the second party," then, irrespective of distance, at least three cents per 100 pounds must be paid first party for its share of the through rate; a stipulation the effect of which is to deprive the shipper of the benefit of competition, should he demand that the second party discharge its public duty by furnishing transportation facilities to him.

The policy of the law is to prevent the creation of monopolies and to foster fair competition. Eel River v. State, 155 Ind. 433-457, 57 N. E. 388; Railroad v. Dohn, 153 Ind. 10, 53 N. E. 937, 45 L. R. A. 427, 74 Am. St. Rep. 274; State ex rel. v. Portland, etc., Oil Co., 153 Ind. 489, 53 N. E. 1089, 53 L. R. A. 413, 74 Am. St. Rep. 314; Board v. Railway, 50 Ind. 85; Elliott, § 359. "A contract between corporations charged with a public duty, such as that of common carriers, providing for the formation of a combination, having no other purpose than that of stifling competition, and providing means to accomplish that object, is illegal. The purpose to break down competition poisons the whole contract, and there is no antidote which will rescue it from legal death." Cleveland, etc., Ry. v. Closser, 126 Ind. 348-361, 26 N. E. 159, 9 L. R. A. 754, 22 Am. St. Rep. 593. The important thing to be secured was, the court declared in the case above cited, a sound and salutary general principle, and not merely cases with closely resembling facts. The principle declared, as heretofore quoted, accords with the necessities of commerce and development, and is supported by a vast volume of authority, including the following: L., N. A. & C. Ry. Co. v. Sumner, 106 Ind. 55-59, 5 N. E. 404, 55 Am. Rep. 719; St. Louis Ry. Co. v. Mathers, 71 Ill. 592, 22 Am. Rep. 122; Greenhood on Public Policy, p. 626; Kettle River Co. v. Eastern Ry., 43 N. W. 469, 6 L. R. A. 117; Trans. Co. v. Pipe Line Co., 22 W. Va. 626, 46 Am. Rep. 527.

It is contended in argument that it was competent to make the contract in question, in order to prevent destructive competition. There is no basis of fact justifying the proposition. A combination between common carriers to prevent competition is prima facie illegal. "The burden is on the carriers to remove the presumption, and until it is removed the agreement goes down before the presumption, and is held within the condemnation directed against all contracts violative of public policy." Cleveland, etc., Ry. v. Closser, 126 Ind. 360, 26 N. E. 159, 9 L. R. A. 754, 22 Am. St. Rep. 593; State ex rel. v. Portland Oil Co., supra. The appellee railroad company has power, by the provisions of the statute, to purchase, receive, and take such lands as may be necessary to the construction and maintenance of its railroad, stations, depots, and other accommodations necessary to accomplish the objects for which the corporation was created. Section 5153, Burns' Ann. St. 1901. The statute also makes it the duty of the railroad corporations to furnish sufficient accommodations for the transportation of all such persons and property as shall within a reasonable time previous thereto offer or be offered for transportation at the place of starting, at the junction of other railroads, and at sidings and stopping places established for receiving way passengers and freight. Section 5185, Burns' Ann. St. 1901. It has frequently been adjudged that contracts of a railroad company, by which it undertakes not to locate stations or depots within prescribed limits, are contrary to public policy and void. L., N. A. & C. Ry. v. Sumner, supra; Railroad v. Ryan, 11 Kan. 602, 15 Am. Rep. 357; Florida Cent. R. Co. v. Tavares, 31 Fla. 482, 13 South. 103, 20 L. R. A. 419, 34 Am. St. Rep. 30; Elkhart v. Cary, 98 Ind. 238, 49 Am. Rep. 746. The analogy between an agreement not to furnish facilities for transportation by the location of depots, and an agreement not to furnish facilities for transportation by the location of certain side tracks, is exact.

No question of the exercise of the right of eminent domain is involved in this appeal. It is not even shown that it would be necessary to condemn or purchase any land in order to reach the stone quarries, that are presumptively within reach of appellee's railroad. So far as facts are shown, its right of way may abut upon any number of quarries, in the output of which, not only the owners, but the purchasing public, are interested, both as to price and delivery. If sidings were in existence connecting appellee's railroad with such quarries, it would be bound to receive and transport freight there offered to it. To disable itself, by contract with a competing carrier, from constructing such siding, is something it cannot be allowed to do. The siding is as essential to the proprietor of the stone quarry, in the transportation of his commodity, as the station or depot is to him who wishes to take passage himself or to ship lighter merchandise. The agreement made by the second party to this contract, as specified in clause 6, is within the reason of the law and the authorities. It is therefore illegal.

Appellant, however, contends that, even if the contract be declared ultra vires, the second party to it, having acquired the right to cross its tracks, and having crossed them, will be required to make compensation, upon the established principle that a corporation may not retain the benefit received under ultra vires contract and at the same time set up its own want of power to contract. The difficulty with the application of this doctrine is that the undertaking is not ultra vires in the strict sense, but it is illegal and absolutely void. "The doctrine does not apply to contracts, where the same are forbidden by statute or are contrary to public policy." Franklin Nat'l Bank v. Whitehead, 149 Ind. 560-579, 49 N. E. 592, 39 L. R. A. 725, 63 Am. St. Rep. 302. "If a promise to do several acts is indivisible, and is in part illegal, it cannot be enforced as to that part which is legal, but the whole agreement is void." Clark, Contracts, p. 472. "Where the agreement consists of one promise, made upon several considerations, some of which are bad and some good, here, also, the promise is wholly void; for it is impossible to say whether the legal or the illegal portion of the consideration most affected the mind of the promisor, and induced him to promise." Clark, Contracts, p. 473. Where an action was brought upon a note, part of the consideration of which was an agreement that the makers should have the exclusive right to carry policies of marriage benefit insurance upon the payee and his intended wife, the contract was held to be entire and unenforceable. James v. Jellison, 94 Ind. 292, 48 Am. Rep. 151.

The authorities sustaining the propositions stated are too numerous to require citation. The doctrine is as thoroughly settled, and its principle is as wholesome, as any known to the law. Higham v. Harris, 108 Ind. 246, 8 N. E. 255; Ricketts v. Harvey, 106 Ind. 566, 6 N. E. 325; Rainbolt v. East, 56 Ind. 538, 26 Am. Rep. 40; Bishop, Contracts, 487. In Hunter v. Pfeiffer, 108 Ind. 197, 9 N. E. 124, an agreement was made by a number of parties to enter into a partnership in the construction of a public work. The plaintiff based his right to recover upon a breach of such contract of partnership. The action was apparently inoffensive, but facts were stated in the pleadings from which the court inferred that one of the reasons for making the partnership contract was a desire to prevent competition in bidding upon the public work. Recovery was refused. The opinion, written by Judge Mitchell, is most direct. It is said therein: "The whole purpose of the statute is to encourage open competition between responsible bidders, and any secret combination, call it partnership or anything else, the effect of which is to abate honest rivalry or fair competition, is to be condemned, as violative of public policy and void. No one can predicate an enforceable right upon such an agreement." Hunter v. Pfeiffer, 108 Ind. 200, 9 N. E. 126.

The appellant is seeking to enforce a contract illegal in itself. The law will refuse to lend its aid to that end. Executory, it will interfere at the suit of neither party; executed in whole or in part, it leaves the parties where they have placed themselves. Brewing Co. v. Hartman, 19 Ind. App. 603, 49 N. E. 864; Woodford v. Hamilton, 139 Ind. 481, 39 N. E. 47; Hutchins v. Weldin, 114 Ind. 80, 15 N. E. 804; Schmueckle v. Waters, 125 Ind. 265, 25 N. E. 281. It makes no difference that the whole consideration was not in itself illegal. In Kain v. Bare, 4 Ind. App. 440, 31 N. E. 205, the note in suit had been given for Bohemian oats, and the contract, calling for the sale of other oats, was held to be a gambling contract, and therefore illegal, as against public policy. This court then said: "The fact that the answer concedes the oats to have been of some value is used as an argument by appellant's counsel in favor of the position that, the consideration not being wholly illegal, the answer is but a partial response to the complaint, when it attempts to meet all, and is therefore bad. If the answer sought to avoid the contract on account of fraud, the appellant's position would be sound, as this court has decided. Regensburg v. Notestine, 2 Ind. App. 97, 27 N. E. 108. But where the entire contract is illegal and void, from public policy, the courts will not lend themselves to the enforcement of any part of it. Schmueckle v. Waters, supra."

If the action were brought by the appellee under the contract to enforce its rights to the crossing, questions involved would be presented exactly as in an action on a promissory note given in consideration of two agreements, one legal and one illegal, as in James v. Jellison, supra. No one could then say that the consideration for the contract, enforcement of which is asked, was not tainted, and no one could tell what part of the engagement depended upon the illegal part thereof. In Edwards Co. v. Jennings (Tex. Sup.) 35 S. W. 1053, the commissioners of a county granted an exclusive right to lay pipe, etc., in the streets of a town, and agreed to pay $3,500 in consideration of the erection of a waterworks system in said town. The grant of an exclusive franchise was, under the law of the state, illegal. The court refused to separate the parts of the consideration, saying that it was impossible to determine how much of the contractor's obligation was based upon the illegal part of the consideration. Does the fact that the crossing has been made, and that the action is to recover that part of the consideration not in itself illegal, render the contract divisible and enforceable? The answer, upon principle, is that neither divisibility nor illegality depend upon the form of the action, or which party happens to be plaintiff. The question, however, is settled by the authorities.

In Railroad v. Koons, 105 Ind. 507, 5 N. E. 549, a written contract was considered by which Koons conveyed to the railroad a right of way over his land; it agreeing in return to fence the right of way and also to build certain cattle guards. The action was brought to recover the reasonable cost of the fences, which, it was averred, the company had failed to build. The defense was that in a prior action Koons had recovered judgment for $40 on account of the failure of the company to build cattle guards. The Supreme Court held that the contract was entire and indivisible, and that, notwithstanding no recovery had been sought or had in the prior action on account of the failure to fence, there could be none in a latter one, in the absence of stipulations making the dates of performance separate and different. Railroad v. Koons, 105 Ind. 511, 5 N. E. 549.

The contract considered by the court in that case, the conclusion stated, and the reason therefor, render the case an authority in this one, and compel the conclusion that the contract now under consideration is an entire contract. Being entire for one purpose, it is entire for all purposes. When a mortgage secures two notes, one valid and one illegal, or a bill of goods consists of various items, a specific price being fixed to each item, and in other similar cases, a different rule applies; but in the case at bar it must be held, in the language of Judge Elliott: "If the promissory notes which constituted the cause of action upon which the plaintiff must recover, or not recover at all, were founded on an illegal consideration, then, no matter what the court may have instructed upon the subject of an executed consideration, the verdict is right. The defense which the answers to the interrogatories reveals renders a recovery by the plaintiff legally impossible. It cuts up his cause of action 'root and branch.' * * * The first instruction asked by appellant was properly refused. If the consideration of a promissory note is in part illegal and in part legal, and is indivisible, there can be no recovery upon the note."

The present action is one in which it is not only appropriate for the court to consider the contract made by these parties, but the duty of the court to the public, against whom the contract in question is directed, calls upon it to do so. That duty cannot be put aside until appellant comes into court asking that the illegal clause be enforced. The presumption is that it will not need ever to do this. It cannot be deferred until some quarryman or citizen institutes a proceeding to declare its invalidity. The fallacy of such an idea can in no way be so clearly exposed as by an illustration, extreme in terms, but equivalent in principle. Preliminary to the illustration it may be recalled that this court has declared: "It is now settled here that contracts which are void at common law, because they are against public policy, like contracts which are prohibited by statute, are illegal, as well as void. They are prohibited by law, because they are considered vicious, and it is not necessary to impose a penalty in order to render them illegal." Nave v. Wilson, 12 Ind. App. 43, 38 N. E. 878. If, in consideration of property conveyed or delivered, one should contract to pay money and commit crime, larceny, burglary, or robbery, would any enlightened conscience entertain the idea that the vendor could recover the money consideration in court, and that the illegality of the undertaking could only be set up when the crime was being consummated, and then by the unsuspecting victim?

If it were to be assumed that the contract in question contains no express stipulation preventing the separation of the valid from the illegal portion of the consideration, the principle stated by the authority heretofore cited would forbid the courts from making such division. The stipulations of the written contract make it impossible, in any view that might be taken. It is premised that the consideration of a written contract may be made contractual, and that it can then no more be varied than any other portion of the instrument. Penn. Co. v. Dolan, 6 Ind. App. 109, 32 N. E. 802, 51 Am. St. Rep. 289; Stewart v. Ry. Co., 141 Ind. 55, 40 N. E. 67. The intention of the parties controls. "Where the intention clearly appears from the words used, there is no need to go further; for in such a case the words must govern, or, as it is sometimes said, where there is no doubt, there is no room for construction." Clark, Contracts, p. 590. The intention is so potent that, where it appears that the parties intended the contract to be an entire one, such intention will control, and prevent its being considered as divisible, although it might so be regarded, in the absence of the contrary intention. A. & E. Ency. of Law, vol. 7, p. 95; Wooten v. Walters, 110 N. C. 251, 14 S. E. 734, 736; Loud v. Pomona, 153 U. S. 564, 14 Sup. Ct. 928, 38 L. Ed. 822; Southwell v. Beezley, 5 Or. 458. The contract under examination excludes the court from treating it as a divisible one. The parties deliberately carry and put the illegality into every portion thereof. The language used is: "It is expressly understood and agreed that the consideration for granting the rights and privileges herein expressed to said second party is the covenant and agreement of said second party not in any manner, directly or indirectly, to interfere with," etc. They thus say that the right to cross appellee's track was given in consideration of its undertaking not to compete with it for freight. What court will dispute them? Who will, in the face of this deliberately made agreement, say that the consideration for the right to cross was anything else? Regan v. First Nat'l Bank, 157 Ind. 623, 61 N. E. 575, 62 N. E. 701. It is but just to appellant's attorneys, who have argued this case with distinguished ability, to say that they have not suggested such action.

Probably an interlocker and signal systen ought to be constructed at this crossing. But that is not a question in this case.

This leads to an affirmance of the judgment.

HENLEY, C. J., and COMSTOCK and ROBINSON, JJ., concur. BLACK, J., dissents.

WILEY, J. (dissenting). I cannot concur in the opinion reached by the majority of my Associates, nor in the reasoning leading thereto. That I may fully express my views upon the legal questions involved, I deem it necessary to state fully the facts stated in the complaint.

In July, 1889, the Louisville, New Albany & Chicago Railway Company owned and operated a line of railway, running north and south in and through Lawrence county, Ind. At the city of Bedford, in said county, it maintained a station and telegraph office. At that time the Evansville & Richmond Railway Company was constructing a line of railroad in and through said county, running east and west. The latter company had to cross the former company's right of way and track, about 2,125 feet north of the former's telegraph office at Bedford. On the 29th day of July, 1889, the two companies entered into a written contract, by which the latter company bound itself to "put in and permanently maintain, protect, and operate an interlocking switch and signal system" at the intersection of the two roads. In that contract the Louisville, New Albany & Chicago Railway Company is designated as "party of the first part," and the Evansville Railway Company is designated as "party of the second part," and for convenience and brevity these terms will hereafter be used in this opinion where a reference to the two companies is necessary. By the terms of that contract the party of the first part granted to the party of the second part the right to construct and maintain its railroad over and across the main track, switches proper, and what was known as the "Blue Hole Switch," owned by the party of the first part. The crossing was to be on a grade with the road of the first party, and the point of crossing was designated. The terms upon which the grant to cross were given may be stated as follows:

The party of the second part was to furnish all material and perform all labor to raise the track, known as the "Blue Hole Switch" (which was a track connecting with the main line of the first party, extending to the Chicago & Bedford Stone Company), to a common grade or level with the main line, and to raise all bridges on said switch, so as to conform to such grade. The second party was to perform all labor incident to the construction and maintenance of said crossing, including crossing frogs, targets, signals, etc.; and, inasmuch as the grade at the point of crossing was heavy, and trains of the road of the first party could not be stopped at said crossing, the second party agreed to put in and permanently maintain, protect, and operate an interlocking switch and signal system, of a safe and approved kind, so as to enable the first party, without violation of law, to cross at said point without having to stop its trains. The first party at all times was to have priority of right to run its trains over said crossing of the same class, as against the right of trains of the second party. If the first party at any time wished to construct additional tracks at the point of intersection, the second party, at its own expense, was to adapt its own tracks to such additional tracks, and construct and maintain one-half of all necessary crossings, frogs, targets, signals, etc. All appliances, structures, fixtures, and instruments pertaining to said crossing, switches, and signals were to be of such design, pattern, quality, and construction as were necessary and safe in the opinion of the proper officers of the first party, and all persons employed by the second party to perform services at such crossing were to be subject to removal at the demand of the first party. The second party was to protect and save harmless the first party against all loss, damage, cost, or expense which might result, either in the construction, maintenance, or use of the crossing, or from the acts of any person who might be appointed to perform services by the second party at the crossing.

The sixth subdivision or clause of the contract is as follows: "Sixth. The second party agrees not to run any track or tracks to or from any stone quarry which is connected with the road of the first party by switches or tracks built thereto by said first party or under contract therefor, and will not make any demands for the use of said first party's tracks or switches leading to any such quarries for the shipment of stone therefrom, the express purpose of this clause being to preserve the said first party all rights and benefits now acquired in the business of such quarries; and it is hereby expressly understood and agreed that the consideration for granting the rights and privileges herein expressed to said second party is the covenant and agreement of said second party not in any manner, directly or indirectly, to interfere with or divert the benefits now derived or to be hereafter derived from said first party's connection and business with such quarries."

The seventh and last subdivision of the

contract is as follows: "Seventh. In consideration of making a Y connection, it is agreed between the parties hereto that, in case any party or parties require said first party to forward stone or other car-load freight to the line of the second party, it is agreed that the proposition of the through rate from any given quarry or station accruing to the party of the first part shall not be less than three cents per hundred (100) pounds."

The interlocking switch provided for in the contract has never been constructed.

This action was brought by appellant, as successor to the Louisville, New Albany & Chicago Railway Company, against appellee, the successor to the Evansville & Richmond Railway Company, upon that contract. The complaint is in three paragraphs, to each of which a separate demurrer was sustained. Appellant, assuming that each paragraph of complaint was impregnable to a successful assault of a demurrer, stood upon the ruling thereon, and declined to plead over. From a judgment against it for costs, it prosecuted this appeal, and by its assignment affirms that sustaining the demurrer to its complaint was error.

In each paragraph of the complaint it is averred that in 1897 appellant became the owner of all the rights and property of the Louisville, New Albany & Chicago Railway Company; that on July 29, 1889, its predecessor entered into the contract above specified with the Evansville & Richmond Railway Company; that said last-named company was incorporated under the laws of Indiana for the purpose of owning and operating a railway from Elnora, in Daviess county, to the city of Richmond, and to construct said road, it was necessary to cross the line of road of the Louisville, New Albany & Chicago Railway Company in the city of Bedford, and that said contract was entered into for the purpose of securing a right to make said crossing; that at the time of the execution of said contract the Evansville & Richmond Company had not completed its road, and had done no construction on the right of way or tracks of appellant's predecessor; that said company had no interest in said right of way or tracks, or right to cross the same, and entered into said contract for the sole purpose of securing said right. Each paragraph contains the following averment: "That the said Evansville & Richmond Railway Company took possession of said easement and right of way under said contract; that the only consideration received or promised for the granting of said easement and right to cross said right of way and railroad was the covenant expressed in said contract to do and perform the matters and things therein set forth;" that, acting under the right given by said contract, the said Evansville & Richmond Railway Company entered upon said right of way and tracks, and constructed its superstructure, laid its steel, and completed its railway across the same, and while it continued to own said railway it so occupied said crossing and tracks. It is further averred that the Evansville & Richmond Railway Company, to secure certain bonds, executed its mortgage on its railway property, but at the time of the execution of said mortgage it had not constructed its railway at said point of crossing, and it did not then have any right to or interest in the property of appellant's predecessor, or right to cross such right of way or tracks, and that said right to so cross was not secured until long afterwards, and by the said contract alone; that said Evansville & Richmond Railway Company defaulted in the payment of said mortgage debts, and on this account said mortgages were foreclosed and all of its rights and property sold to pay said indebtedness; that at said sales the Evansville & Richmond Railway Company became the purchaser of said rights and property; that its name was changed to the Southern Indiana Railway Company, the appellee herein; that since said purchase the Evansville & Richmond Railway Company continued to own and operate said railway rights and franchises; that the corporate name thereof was afterwards changed to the Southern Indiana Railway Company, and since said change in name appellee has continued to own and operate said line of railroad and rights and franchises of its predecessor company, and has "continually occupied the said crossing, and has asserted the right and title to said easement under and by virtue of the title acquired at said foreclosure sales, and not otherwise." Each paragraph contains the following averments: "The Southern Indiana Railway Company obtained and took the right and title which the said Evansville & Richmond Railway Company acquired in and to said easement in said right of way crossing, and has ever since held the same, and has always asserted its legal right to do so under said agreement, and by no other source of title." All three paragraphs aver that on account of the steep grade on appellant's road at and near the point of crossing, which is averred to be 57 feet to the mile, it is very difficult, and at times impossible, to stop its south-bound trains before reaching said crossing; that in running its trains northward it is necessary to run at a rapid rate of speed, in order to obtain sufficient momentum to enable an engine to draw the trains up and over the grade; that on account thereof there has been and will continue to be great danger of collision, which would involve great loss of life and property; that if said interlocking switch is installed it will be impossible for trains and engines to collide on said roads at said crossing, and all danger to life and property would be thereby avoided. Each paragraph also avers that said contracting party, and its successor, the appellee, have failed and neglected to perform the conditions of said contract on their part. The second paragraph differs from the first and third, in that, in addition to all of said general averments, it alleges that, pending the receivership and foreclosure proceedings against the Evansville & Richmond Railway Company, the Louisville, New Albany & Chicago Railway Company intervened, and asked that performance of said contract be required, and that, before the trustees of the bondholders of the said Evansville & Richmond Railway Company or the appellee acquired any interest in said property under said sale, they had actual and constructive notice of said contract and its terms and provisions. The prayer of the first and second paragraphs of complaint is that appellee be required to construct and maintain the interlocking switch provided for in the contract sued on. The prayer of the third paragraph is for $5,500 damages, which appellant avers it has sustained by reason of the failure to perform the contract, and that amount would be required to construct, etc., said interlocking switch.

Counsel for appellee directed the major part of their argument against the sufficiency of the complaint, on the theory that the contract sued on is ultra vires and void. This contention is based upon the sixth subdivision of the contract, which we have above quoted, which it is averred places an inhibition on the party of the second part from running any track or tracks to or from any stone quarry which was connected with the road of the first party. It is urged that such an inhibition is against public policy, and therefore the contract cannot be enforced. The right of one railroad to cross another is a recognized right, and public policy and the general interests of the public require it. That right is regulated by statute in this jurisdiction. Section 3903, subd. 6, Horner's Ann. St. 1901; section 5153, subd. 6, Burns' Ann. St. 1901. Provision is made that, in case one railroad company desires to cross the right of way and tracks of another and the two companies cannot "agree as to the amount of compensation to be made therefor, or the point or manner of such crossings or connections, the same shall be ascertained and determined by commissioners," etc. Section 5154, Burns' Ann. St. 1901. Section 3904, Horner's Ann. St. 1901, provides that, "where it becomes necessary for the track of one railroad company to cross the track of another railroad company, the company owning the road last constructed at such crossing shall, unless otherwise agreed to between such companies, be at the expense of constructing such crossing in a manner to be convenient and safe for both companies." In the absence of a contract to the contrary, when such crossing is constructed, the statute (section 3905, Burns' Ann. St. 1901) makes it the duty of each company to maintain and keep in repair its own track, so as at all times to provide a ready, safe, and convenient crossing of all locomotives or trains passing on either road at such point.

Independent of any statutory provisions, I have no doubt of the right of two railroad companies to contract between themselves upon what terms and conditions whose line of road is last constructed may cross the other. Possessing such right, it carries with it the additional right to contract as to the kind and character of the crossing, the terms thereof, and fix the burden by which it shall be maintained. This right, it must be understood, cannot be exercised to the detriment of the public, nor in contravention of public policy. Having a right to so contract, it is the duty of the courts to enforce such contracts, if they are in all things valid. It must be kept in mind that, where two railroads intersect or cross, the one last constructed does not acquire any title to the right of way, property, and track of the original road, but only acquires an easement therein. In the case I am now considering there is no doubt but what the two original contracting companies had a right to contract between themselves whereby the "party of the second part" bound itself to construct and maintain at the point of crossing an interlocking switch. By entering into the contract, the "party of the first part" parted with a valuable right, in that by crossing its tracks the latter company would, to some extent at least, interfere with the free and uninterrupted use of its property, which it previously enjoyed. By virtue of the terms of the contract the "party of the second part" acquired and enjoyed all the rights and benefits thereby conferred upon it. The appellee here is now enjoying such rights and benefits by succession.

If, under the contract, appellee's predecessor acquired an easement, and of this there can be no doubt, then the first question for determination is: Did such easement pass to appellee? The complaint avers that appellant succeeded to all rights, privileges, property, and contracts of the Louisville, New Albany & Chicago Railway Company, and that appellee, in the foreclosure proceedings and purchase thereunder, acquired all the rights, privileges, property, etc., of the Evansville & Richmond Railway Company. It is hard to conceive, from a legal or equitable standpoint, how under such conditions and circumstances either of the succeeding companies could acquire all the beneficial rights, privileges, property, etc., of their predecessors, and be relieved of all their burdens. By the terms of the contract, appellee's predecessor acquired a right of way over and across the private property of the Louisville, New Albany & Chicago Railway Company. Thus by the contract a covenant was created, which covenant runs with the use of such way, and, under the authorities, is binding upon the appellee, which succeeded to the rights, etc., of one of the contracting parties. Dayton, etc., Ry. v. Lewton, 20 Ohio St. 401; Midland Ry. v. Fisher, 125 Ind. 19, 24 N. E. 756, 8 L. R. A. 604, 21 Am. St. Rep. 189; Lake Erie Ry. v. Priest, 131 Ind. 413, 416, 31 N. E. 77; Toledo, St. L. & K. C. R. Co. v. Cosand, 6 Ind. App. 222, 224, 33 N. E. 251; L. E. Ry. v. Griffin, 25 Ind. App. 138, 142, 53 N. E. 1042, 57 N. E. 722. Appellee cannot assert its right to exercise the beneficial privileges given by the contract, and at the same time repudiate its covenants. It enjoys its easement to cross appellant's tracks, side tracks, and right of way, and unless there is something in the contract itself to exempt it from performance, as, for instance, the contract is ultra vires, then it is bound to perform. To permit it to retain its rights and privileges, and repudiate its burdensome obligations—its covenants—would be antagonistic to the broad and wholesome principles of equity, and shock good conscience. Louisville, etc., Ry. Co. v. Power, 119 Ind. 269, 272, 21 N. E. 751; Bloomfield Ry. Co. v. Grace, 112 Ind. 128, 13 N. E. 680; Lake Erie, etc., Ry. Co. v. Griffin, 107 Ind. 464, 8 N. E. 451; Midland Ry. Co. v. Fisher, supra; Joy v. St. Louis, 138 U. S. 1, 11 Sup. Ct. 243, 34 L. Ed. 843. See, also, Brannon v. May, 42 Ind. 92; Hazlett v. Sinclair, 76 Ind. 488, 40 Am. Rep. 254.

The question of controlling influence, and the one possibly fraught with the greatest difficulty, is that raised by appellee—that by reason of the sixth clause or subdivision of the contract it is ultra vires. Under the facts pleaded, it can only be held to be ultra vires upon two grounds: First, that the contract was prohibited by statute; or, second, that it is against public policy. It is certain that there was no statutory inhibition forbidding the contract, and hence, if ultra vires, it is because it was against public policy. In this connection, it is well to consider, first, the power of two corporations to enter into contracts. Generally speaking, there is no question but what they possess such power. The contracting parties here, therefore, had the right and authority to agree between themselves that "the party of the second part" might cross the right of way and tracks of "the party of the first part." The statute above cited specifically creates such right. The right to contract implies the right to fix the terms of the contract. The contract is now an executed one, viz., the appellee is in full enjoyment of all the rights and privileges granted to its predecessor, and to which it succeeded. While it continues in the enjoyment of such rights and privileges, and in the possession and use of the easement thus granted to it, can it in equity deny the validity of the contract?

For the purposes of the determination of this question, let it be conceded that the contract was ultra vires. When this contract was executed "the party of the second part" had no right to any part of appellant's right of way, over which to effect a crossing, except a statutory right. It did not proceed under the statute, but selected its remedy by contract. Under that contract it took possession, and still retains and enjoys possession. If inquiry should be made of appellee by what right it crosses appellant's right of way and tracks, and thus occupies the same, it would have to answer that it was by reason of the right acquired by the contract. In Louisville, etc., Ry. Co. v. Power, supra, appellant was occupying its right of way under a deed, and it sought to deny its validity because no grantee was named therein. It was held that, holding the land under the deed as it did, it was bound to perform its contract to fence its right of way. In Midland Ry. Co. v. Fisher, supra, it was held that one who takes a privilege in land to which a burden is annexed has no right to claim the privilege and deny the responsibility of the burden; that a party who acquires such a privilege acquires it subject to the conditions and burdens bound up with it, and must, if he asserts a right to the privilege, bear the burden which the contract creating the privilege brought into existence. The court said: "The one he cannot have at the expense of the other." The case of Nashua, etc., Ry. Co. v. Boston, etc., Ry. Co. (C. C.) 19 Fed. 804, was where the two companies entered into a pooling agreement. While acting under the agreement, one company received money to which the other was entitled. In an action to recover for the money so received, the defendant interposed the defense that the contract was invalid. It was held that, though the pooling contract was not within the corporate powers of the two companies, it could afford no defense to the Boston Company, when called upon to restore to the plaintiff the sum received in excess of its due. The decision was based upon the proposition that the contract had been fully executed, and the defendant had availed itself of all the benefits to be derived from it, and was therefore estopped from denying its validity. The case of Central Trust Co. v. Ohio Central Ry. Co. (C. C.) 23 Fed. 306, also involved rights growing out of a pooling contract. It was held that, whether the contract was legal or not, the question was whether one party, who had received all the expected benefits to be derived from it, should account for the fruits of its performance, which by its terms belonged to another, and which, contrary to its terms, it retained. The equitable rule was there enforced, requiring an accounting.

The case of Joy v. St. Louis, supra, is supportive of the principle of law now under consideration. In that case the city of St. Louis gave two railway companies the right to construct a track through one of its parks. The agreement provided that other roads should use the track upon specific and equitable terms. Such use was granted to avoid cutting up the park by other roads. In an action to enforce that part of the agreement by one of the roads, a defense was predicated upon the proposition that the city had no right to impose such terms. In deciding the question the court said: "In order to obtain the right of way through the park, the Kansas City Company subjected itself to the condition imposed by paragraph 9 of the tripartite agreement, and it is right that that company and its successors should be held to a strict compliance with its covenant. The appellants, although enjoying the benefit of the $40,000 expended by the park commissioners, and of the right of way through the park, deny their liability under the agreement, without offering to return to the grantors the property obtained by the agreement. Under such circumstances these parties cannot be heard to allege that the agreement was against the policy of the law." In Warren v. Jones, 51 Me. 146, one of the parties sold to the other his factory and "all his trade and customers." The purchaser brought an action against the seller to prevent him from entering into the same business in violation of his contract. The seller contended that the contract was in restraint of trade, and hence was against public policy. The court tersely disposed of the question by declaring that the contract was not against the policy of the law, and, even if it was, the defendant could not profit by it and at the same time retain the consideration. The following cases are in point and illustrative of the question we are now considering. We cite them without comment: Manchester Ry. Co. v. Concord Ry. Co., 66 N. H. 100, 20 Atl. 383, 9 L. R. A. 689, 49 Am. St. Rep. 582; Brooks v. Martin, 2 Wall. 70, 17 L. Ed. 732; Wiggins Ferry Co. v. Chicago, etc., Ry. Co., 73 Mo. 389, 39 Am. Rep. 519.

The term "ultra vires," in its literal sense, means beyond the power or capacity of a corporation, company or person. This must be understood to mean lawful authority. Am. & Eng. Encyc. of Law, vol. 27 (1st Ed.) 352; Century Dict.; Brown's Law Dict.; Anderson's Law Dict. In modern jurisprudence, the defense of ultra vires is very generally regarded by the courts as an ungracious and odious one, and it now seems to be firmly settled that neither party to the contract can avail himself of such defense, when the contract has been fully performed by the other party, and he has received the full benefit of the performance of the contract. If an action cannot be brought directly upon the contract, either equity will grant relief, or an action in some other form will lie. Am. & Eng. Encyc. of Law, vol. 27, p. 360; Whitney Arms Co. v. Barlow, 63 N. Y. 62, 20 Am. Rep. 504. It has been declared that, generally speaking, the rule of ultra vires prevails in full force only where the contracts of corporations remain wholly executory. Thompson v. Lambert, 44 Iowa, 239. Dealings of corporations, which, on their face or according to their apparent import, are within the powers granted, are not to be considered as illegal or unauthorized, without some evidence tending to show that they are of such a character. In the absence of proof, there is no presumption that the law has been violated. Am. & Eng. Encyc. of Law, vol. 27, p. 355; Chautauqua County Bank v. Risley, 19 N. Y. 371, 75 Am. Dec. 347; Allegheny City v. McClurkan, 14 Pa. 81; Mitchell v. Rome Ry. Co., 17 Ga. 574; Oxford Iron Co. v. Spradley, 46 Ala. 98; Downing v. Mt. Washington, etc., Co., 40 N. H. 230; Union Water Co. v. Murphy's Flat Fluming Co., 22 Cal. 621. In the case of Bissell v. Michigan Southern and Northern Indiana Railroad Companies, 22 N. Y. 258, the rule was declared that when a corporation received the consideration of its contract, although it might be unauthorized, and a restitution would not do complete justice, the remedy of the other party is not confined to a suit in disaffirmance of the contract, but may be directly upon it, and would be enforced under any circumstances of controlling equity.

There are numerous authorities holding that the ground upon which the defense of ultra vires is most generally excluded is that of estoppel; and this, of course, is on the basis that the corporation, having received the fruits of the contract, should not be permitted to plead want of power in the corporation and thus escape liability. This principle is fully discussed in volume 27, Am. & Eng. Encyc. of Law, p. 361, and numerous authorities are collected and cited. In the contract before us, it must be kept in mind that the contract was fully executed on the part of one of the contracting parties. By it the other party got all that it bargained for, and is still enjoying its fruits. The Supreme Court of Colorado has held that, where a corporation has received the benefit of a contract, it may not deny its validity. Denver Fire Ins. Co. v. McClelland, 9 Colo. 11-21, 9 Pac. 771, 59 Am. Rep. 134. And so there is a distinction between ultra vires contracts purely executory and those fully executed on one side. Such distinction is founded in reason and good conscience. Where the contract has been fully performed by one of the parties, the infraction of the law has already taken place, which eliminates all questions of public policy, and allows the courts to deal with the contract upon equitable principles. Pennsylvania Ry. Co. v. St. Louis, etc., Ry. Co., 118 U. S. 290, 6 Sup. Ct. 1094, 30 L. Ed. 83; St. Louis, etc., Ry. Co. v. Terre Haute, etc., Ry. Co., 145 U. S. 393, 12 Sup. Ct. 953, 36 L. Ed. 748; Thomas v. West Jersey, etc., Ry. Co., 101 U. S. 71, 25 L. Ed. 950; Mallory v. Hanaur Oil Works, 86 Tenn. 598, 8 S. W. 396; Darst v. Gale, 83 Ill. 137; Bradley v. Ballard, 55 Ill. 413, 8 Am. Rep. 656.

Where one railroad corporation used the roadbed, rolling stock, and equipments of another, it was held that it could not set up the defense of ultra vires to a bill in equity by the latter for an accounting and returning of the property. Manchester, etc., Ry. Co. v. Concord, etc., Ry. Co., supra.

The language of the court in that case is so forceful and clear that we quote the following: "The defense set up is so repugnant to the natural sense of justice, so contrary to good faith and fair dealing, and so opposed to the weight of modern authority, that it need only be said that, in equity at least, neither party to a transaction ultra vires simply will be heard to allege its invalidity while retaining its fruits. However the contractual powers of the defendant may be limited under its charter, there is no limitation of its power to make restitution to the other party, whose money or property it has obtained through an unauthorized contract; nor, as a corporation, is it exempted from the common obligation to do justice which binds individuals, for this duty rests upon all persons alike, whether natural or artificial." See Memphis, etc., Ry. Co. v. Dow (C. C.) 19 Fed. 388; Brown v. Atchison, 39 Kan. 37, 17 Pac. 465, 7 Am. St. Rep. 515; Manville v. Belden Mining Co. (C. C.) 17 Fed. 425; Union Lines, etc., Co. v. Boston, etc., Co., 147 U. S. 431, 13 Sup. Ct. 396, 37 L. Ed. 23; Buford v. Keokuk Co., 69 Mo. 611. In Bedford, etc, Ry. Co. v. McDonald, 17 Ind. App. 492, 46 N. E. 1022, 60 Am. St. Rep. 172, it was held that where a private corporation has entered into a contract, not immoral in itself and not forbidden by any statute, and it has been in good faith fully performed by the other party, the corporation will not be heard on the plea of ultra vires. Thompson's Corp. § 6026. Prima facie all contracts of corporations, public or private, are valid. and it is incumbent on those who impeach them to show that they are invalid. Smith v. Board, 6 Ind. App. 153, 33 N. E. 243.

If there was any doubt about the correct meaning and interpretation of clause 6 of the contract, it is clarified by the seventh. It is there provided that, in consideration of making a Y connection, "it is agreed between the parties that, in case any party or parties require said first party to forward stone or other car-load freight to the line of the second party, it is agreed that the proportion of the through freight from any given quarry or station accruing to the party of the first part shall not be less than three cents per hundred (100) pounds." Thus it appears that under the contract appellee had access to all such quarries, and was entitled to receive, upon a fixed consideration, freight therefrom to be shipped over its lines. By the terms of the contract appellant was bound to deliver the freight to it. In this regard the rights of the public are protected. It affirmatively appears from the contract itself that the switches or spurs referred to were additional facilities for handling freight. There was a separate one for each quarry or customer. The duty of common carriers in regard to receiving freight for transportation is fixed by statute. Section 5185, Burns' Ann. St. 1901. Railroad companies are not required to go off of their lines to get freight for transportation. They have filled the measure of their statutory duty to the public, in that regard, when they have established and continue to maintain fixed places and ordinarily convenient accommodations for receiving and discharging freight. The statute does not impose upon a railway company the duty of establishing a station at any particular place, except at crossings, and they are only required to receive freight at the places established for that purpose. See People v. Railway Co., 104 N. Y. 58, 9 N. E. 856, 58 Am. Rep. 484; Northern Pac. Ry. Co. v. Washington, 142 U. S. 492, 12 Sup. Ct. 283, 35 L. Ed. 1092; State v. Kansas City, etc., Ry. Co. (Ala.) 25 South. 126; State v. Des Moines, etc., Ry. Co. (Iowa) 54 N. W. 461; Florida Central Ry. Co. v. State (Fla.) 13 South. 103, 20 L. R. A. 419, 34 Am. St. Rep. 30. In Louisville, etc., Ry. Co. v. Flanagan, 113 Ind. 488, 14 N. E. 370, 3 Am. St. Rep. 674, it was held that a railroad company was not liable for failing to furnish cars, and for not transporting goods, unless goods are offered at a regular depot, or other usual or designated place for receiving freight. 3 Wood, Ry. Law, 1580. It logically follows, from what I have said and the authorities, that a railroad company owes no duty to a shipper or the public to receive freight at any place, other than that provided for that purpose. An able and exhaustive discussion of the question now under consideration will be found in the following cases: Atchison, etc., Ry. Co. v. Denver, etc., Ry. Co., 110 U. S. 667-682, 4 Sup. Ct. 185, 28 L. Ed. 291; Missouri, etc., Ry. Co. v. Carter (Tex. Sup.) 68 S. W. 159.

But, if that clause of the contract which seeks to prohibit the junior company from running any switches or spurs to stone quarries with which the senior company was then connected, etc., is invalid, as being against public policy and in restraint of trade, does it necessarily follow that it vitiates the entire contract? If that provision of the contract is void, then no inhibition is placed upon appellee from connecting its line of road with such stone quarries by switches. If that provision can be eliminated without destroying the contract, then the remaining provisions may be enforced. Aside from the consideration expressed in that provision, a valuable consideration moved to the junior company in its acquirement of the right to cross the senior company's tracks and right of way. By agreeing to let it so cross, it was relieved from proceeding under the statute; also from the assessment of damages and the payment thereof. A valuable consideration passed to the senior company, in that the junior company agreed to construct, equip, and maintain an interlocking switch, so as to permit the uninterrupted and safe running of its trains over the crossing. These considerations were both legal and valuable, so that, if the consideration expressed in the sixth clause of the contract was illegal, there is sufficient and valid consideration in other provisions to support the contract. It is the law that, where valid and illegal considerations in the same contract are susceptible of division or distinction, that part of the consideration which is legal may be enforced. Pierce v. Pierce, 17 Ind. App. 107, 46 N. E. 480; Emshwiler, Adm'r, v. Tyner, 21 Ind. App. 347, 52 N. E. 459, 69 Am. St. Rep. 360. The recent case of Trentman v. Wahrenburg, 30 Ind. App. 304, 65 N. E. 1057, is directly in point. That was an action on a contract, where the defense interposed was that it was void because it was in restraint of trade. The court said: "But if appellee's contention should be sustained, which it cannot, still, as the complaint does not aver that this part of the contract has been violated, the contract being divisible, that part of it which is legal could be enforced." Quoting from Oregon Steam Nav. Co. v. Winsor, 87 U. S. 64, 22 L. Ed. 315, continuing, it is said: "It is laid down by Chitty as a result of the cases, and his authorities support the statement, that agreements in restraint of trade, whether under seal or not, are divisible; and accordingly it has been held that when such an agreement contains a stipulation which is capable of being construed divisibly, and one part thereof is void as being in restraint of trade, whilst the other is not, the court will give effect to the latter, and will not hold the agreement void altogether."

So, if it be conceded that clause 6 of the contract is invalid, all of its other provisions are valid; and, as that which is valid is divisible from that which is invalid, if in fact it is, the valid provisions may be enforced. And it is worthy of remark, in this connection, to say that appellant is only seeking to enforce that provision of the contract about which there is no question as to its validity. This action is to enforce that part of the contract by which the junior company agreed to construct and maintain an interlocking switch. It is not, and could not, in law or reason, be contended that the two companies could not make that agreement. That agreement rests upon a sufficient consideration. In this action no right or benefit is claimed or asserted under subdivision 6 of the contract. As it must be conceded that the provision of the contract here sought to be enforced is valid, the fact that some other provision, which no effort to enforce is made or claimed, which as asserted by appellee is invalid, and as the contract may stand, regardless of such asserted invalid provision, relief should be given, to the end that that part of the contract which is valid could be enforced, and the rights and equities of the parties preserved. City of Valparaiso v. Valparaiso, etc., 30 Ind. App. 316, 65 N. E. 1063.

In the case of Hitchcock v. City of Galveston, 96 U. S. 341, 24 L. Ed. 659, is a very able discussion of the question we are now considering. That action grew out of a contract between appellant and appellee, by which the former agreed to improve and pave certain streets, and the latter agreed to make payment in certain bonds. The contention of the appellee was that the city had no right to issue bonds for that purpose, and that therefore the whole contract was inoperative and void. It was held that, if the city had no authority to issue bonds, it did not follow that the contract was wholly illegal and void, or that the plaintiff had no right under it. The court said: "They are not suing upon the bonds, and it is not necessary to their success that they should assert the validity of those instruments. It is enough for them that the city council have power to enter into a contract for the improvement of the sidewalks; that such a contract was made with them; that under it they have proceeded to furnish materials and do work, as well as to assume liabilities; that the city has received, and now enjoys, the benefit of what they have done and furnished; that for these things the city promised to pay; and that, after having received the benefit of the contract, the city has broken it. It matters not that the promise was to pay in a manner not authorized by law. * * * The contract between the parties is in force, so far as it is lawful. * * * Having received benefits at the expense of the other contracting party, it cannot object that it was not empowered to perform what it promised in return in the mode in which it promised to perform."

The case of Nebraska City v. Gas Co., 9 Neb. 339, 2 N. W. 870, was where the appellee sued appellant to recover the contract price of gas furnished the city for a certain month. The city defended on the ground that the contract contained certain illegal provisions respecting the exemption of property from taxation, etc. It was held that, admitting that in the particulars designated the city authorities exceeded their powers, which was not decided, that would be no defense to the action; that under the charter they were authorized to contract for lighting the streets with gas, and to bind the city for the price agreed upon; and that, so long as the city voluntarily received gaslight under the provisions of the contract, it could not resist payment of the agreed price simply because of the alleged illegal promises as to the particular fund from which the money should be drawn. The court said: "The consideration for these promises being entirely legal, and the price agreed upon being payable, if not otherwise, out of the general fund, these objectionable provisions may, if necessary, be rejected, and the rest of the contract permitted to stand, especially where, as here, the city has received the consideration for which the promises were made. Chitty, Cont. § 674. If the city were resisting a tax levied in violation of this agreement, or if they were endeavoring to compel payment of a gas bill out of the sinking fund, the argument of counsel for the city in this behalf would be entitled to great weight; but under the issues in this case we deem it altogether inapplicable." Argenti v. City of San Francisco, 16 Cal. 255, 264; City of Brenham v. Water Co. (Tex. Sup.) 4 S. W. 143; Dodge v. City of Council Bluffs, 57 Iowa, 560, 10 N. W. 886; Maher v. City of Chicago, 38 Ill. 266.

This is not an action to enforce any right under the sixth subdivision of the contract, but to secure to appellant the consideration moving to it in the promise to construct, etc., an interlocking switch. In other words, it is an action to require appellee to do that which it agreed to do, and which it has an unquestioned right to bind itself to do. It will be time to consider any question that may arise affecting the rights of the parties or the public, as fixed by the sixth subdivision of the contract, when that question is presented. It is not before us now. That clause of the contract may be eliminated, and the contract be enforced as to the immediate rights of the parties under it. It is far more important to protect life and property by requiring appellee to comply with its contract to erect and maintain an interlocking switch, and more to the interest of the public, than is it to seek the aid of courts to annul a part of the contract under which the complaining party is not seeking redress, but by which it secured all the rights it desired and still continues to enjoy such rights. In Russel v. Pittsburgh, etc., Ry. Co., 157 Ind. 305, 61 N. E. 678, 55 L. R. A. 253, 87 Am. St. Rep. 214, the court quoted approvingly from Baltimore, etc., Ry. Co. v. Voight, 176 U. S. 498, 20 Sup. Ct. 385, 44 L. Ed. 560, the following: "It must not be forgotten that the right of private contract is no small part of the liberty of the citizen, and that the usual and most important functions of courts of justice is rather to maintain and enforce contracts than to enable parties thereto to escape from their obligation on the pretext of public policy, unless it clearly appears that they contravene public right or the public welfare."

One who seeks to put restraint upon the freedom of contracts must make it plainly and obviously clear that the contract in question is void. Payne v. Terre Haute, etc., Ry. Co., 157 Ind. 616, 62 N. E. 472, 56 L. R. A. 472. Common honesty, good conscience, and well-settled principles of equity demand that appellee should perform the burdens of its contract while it continues to enjoy the benefits and fruits derived from it.

The judgment should be reversed, and the court below be directed to overrule the demurrer to each paragraph of the complaint.

(178 N. Y. 310)

AUSTIN v. BARTLETT.

(Court of Appeals of New York. April 26, 1904.)

EVIDENCE—DECLARATIONS—RES GESTÆ.

1. Plaintiff sued to recover for injuries caused by a vicious dog alleged to belong to defendant, and the ownership of the dog was in issue. *Held*, that self-serving declarations made after the injury by plaintiff, in the absence of defendant, that it was his dog, and not that of his tenant, which frightened her horse, are inadmissible as part of the res gestæ.

2. In an action for injuries received, caused by an attack of a vicious dog belonging to defendant, evidence that, after the injuries, defendant did not call on plaintiff, is inadmissible; its only object being to arouse the prejudice of the jury.

Appeal from Supreme Court, Appellate Division, Fourth Department.

Action by Lena G. Austin against Rush Bartlett. From a judgment of the Appellate Division modifying a judgment for plaintiff (73 N. Y. Supp. 156), defendant appeals. Reversed.

See 77 N. Y. Supp. 1121.

William Kernan and Charles D. Thomas, for appellant. P. C. J. De Angelis, for respondent.

VANN, J. The plaintiff alleged in her complaint that on and for a long time prior to the 4th of September, 1889, the defendant kept on his farm in the town of Winfield, Herkimer county, a savage dog, which, to his knowledge, was accustomed to rush out and bite horses passing along on the public highway. At about sundown on the day last named, while she was driving on the street in front of the defendant's residence, said dog flew out and bit her horse, causing him to run away and throw her out, whereby she was seriously injured. The defendant denied every allegation of the complaint, and alleged that the plaintiff, when slightly injured by an accident for which he was not responsible, aggravated her injuries by voluntarily submitting to treatment by unskillful and unprofessional attendants. There was much evidence to support the allegations of the complaint, and some tending to show that the dog which bit the horse belonged to one Henry Hinckley, a tenant of the defendant, who resided about 65 rods from him, but on the same farm. The question as to the ownership of the dog that did the mischief was submitted to the jury, with the other questions in the case, and a verdict was rendered in favor of the plaintiff for the sum of $8,000. Upon appeal the Appellate Division reversed the judgment, and ordered a new trial, unless the plaintiff should stipulate to reduce the recovery to $4,000, in which event it was directed that the judgment should be affirmed, without costs of the appeal to either party. The plaintiff filed a stipulation accordingly, whereupon the judgment, as thus modified, was unanimously affirmed, and the defendant, after obtaining permission, came here.

During the trial much evidence was received, subject to objection and exception on the part of the defendant, and two of the rulings involve reversible error:

1. It appeared that the horse, after he was frightened by the dog, ran into the barnyard of the defendant, where the plaintiff was thrown out and injured. Shortly after the accident she led her horse home, a distance of about 120 rods, and put him in the stable. At this time she did not suppose her injuries were serious, and, missing her pocketbook, she procured a lantern, as it was then dark, and, about 30 minutes after the accident, went back to the place where it occurred. She found the pocketbook, and was walking home, when Henry Hinckley overtook her, and walked along with her as far as his house. She testified that during this walk she blew out her lantern, withdrew to the shelter of some trees, pulled down her stocking, and examined her knee to see if it was hurt. Mr. Hinckley was called for the defendant, and on his direct examination, after giving other evidence, denied this story of the plaintiff, but he did not swear to any conversation that he had with her during the walk. On his cross-examination, however, the plaintiff went into the conversation, and called for his version of what was said between herself and the witness in relation to which dog frightened the horse. His account was unsatisfactory, as the counsel for the plaintiff called her in rebuttal to contradict him, and, subject to objection and exception, she was allowed to state her own declarations, as well as those of Hinckley, in relation to the two dogs, their habits, etc. Some of these declarations had been received without objection, when the defendant moved "to strike out of the record what Hinckley has said about his dog, or the habits of Bartlett's dog or of any dogs." The court thereupon remarked: "I think that will have to be stricken out. I will leave in the case a statement of whether he inquired whether his dog was engaged in it, or not, and that she said it was not." Exception was taken by the defendant's counsel. Subject to the objection that the evidence was immaterial and incompetent, and that the declaration could not affect the defendant, the plaintiff was allowed, under exception, to testify as follows: "Q. Did Hinckley say to you that, 'If my dog was there, I will kill him?' A. Yes, sir. Q. When, did he say? A. He said he would kill him that night; he would not keep him another day. Q. Did you reply to him, 'You need not kill your dog, because he did not do it?' A. Yes, sir; he was not there." The defendant also moved to strike out these questions and answers, but the court refused, and he again excepted. This evidence was received, as the trial justice remarked, "not on the ground that his declarations are competent against your man, but simply as a contradiction of Hinckley." Assuming that the court could properly have refused to strike out the evidence received without objection, leaving the defendant to protect himself by a request to charge upon the subject, since the motion was entertained, a part of the evidence struck out, and the rest allowed to stand, there was a distinct ruling that the portion remaining in the case was competent for the consideration of the jury. The exceptions taken to this ruling, and to the allowance of the questions subsequently objected to, raised the question whether evidence of declarations made in the absence of the defendant was competent against him. This evidence was not competent for the purpose of contradicting Hinckley, because he had not testified upon the subject at the instance of the defendant, but only on the cross-examination of the plaintiff, who thus made him her own witness to that extent. Kay v. Metropolitan Street Ry. Co., 163 N. Y. 447, 451, 57 N. E. 751. It is a general rule that statements made in the absence of a party by one who did not speak by his authority are incompetent. Self-serving declarations made by the plaintiff when the defendant was not present to the effect that it was his dog, and not Hinckley's, that frightened the plaintiff's horse, were a mere narrative of a past transaction, inadmissible as part of the res gestæ or for any purpose. As this court once said: "The res gestæ, speaking generally, was the accident. These declarations were no part of that; were not made at the same time, or so nearly contemporaneous with it as to characterize it or throw any light upon it. They are purely narrative, giving an account of a transaction not partly past, but wholly past and completed." Waldele v. N. Y. C. & H. R. R. R. Co., 95 N. Y. 274, 278, 47 Am. Rep. 41. What was said during the walk in no wise qualified or characterized what was done, for it related to a different subject. What was done by the plaintiff was competent evidence for the defendant, as an act bearing upon the extent of her injuries. What was said either by her or by Hinckley related to the cause of the injury, and had no connection with the extent thereof. The defendant, by showing what was done, did not open the plaintiff's mouth so that she could testify to what was said upon a wholly different subject in the absence of the defendant. Martin v. N. Y., N. H. & Hartford R. R. Co., 103 N. Y. 626, 9 N. E. 505; Sherman v. D., L. & W. R. R. Co., 106 N. Y. 542, 546, 13 N. E. 616, 617. In the case last cited the court said: "It is perfectly evident that the conversation about which the brakeman was interrogated on his cross-examination was a conversation after the accident had happened, and was aimed at drawing out a statement from the witness as to how the accident had occurred or what caused it, and whose fault it was. That evidence was plainly inadmissible against the defendant. * * * The evidence being in its nature inadmissible,

the plaintiff could not obtain the benefit of it by cross-examining the brakeman in regard to it, and, upon his denying it, seek to prove it by another witness under the guise of contradicting the brakeman." The ownership of the dog that attacked the plaintiff's horse was a contested question of fact which was submitted to the jury, and declarations made so soon after the accident, when the recollection was fresh and mistake improbable, "must have had weight with them in determining that question." They naturally tended to induce the jury to believe that the source of the trouble was not Hinckley's dog, but the defendant's, and we cannot assume that the evidence was harmless, or that it had no material effect upon the verdict.

2. After the defendant had testified and had left the witness stand, he was recalled by the plaintiff for further cross-examination, and was asked how soon after the accident he learned that she was hurt. Subject to objection and exception, he answered that it was 10 or 12 days. He was then asked: "Did you ever call upon her?" This was objected to as incompetent and immaterial, but the objection was overruled, an exception taken, and the defendant answered: "No, sir; I was never inside the house but once." Whether the defendant acted in a neighborly way, or not, toward the plaintiff after her misfortune, had no bearing upon the cause or effect of the injury, and was clearly inadmissible for any purpose. It furnished no lawful aid to the jury, but was calculated to lead them away from the issues, and to arouse in their minds sympathy for the plaintiff and prejudice against the defendant. Prejudice and sympathy are dangerous elements in a lawsuit, and evidence having as its sole object or effect an appeal to either is condemned by the courts. We recently reversed a judgment because evidence was received as to the number and needs of the relatives of a decedent killed, as it was alleged, by the negligence of the defendant, although they were not entitled to any part of the recovery. Lipp v. Otis Bros. & Co., 161 N. Y. 559, 56 N. E. 79. In another negligence case we reversed because a photograph of the deceased was received in evidence, thus introducing a personal element for the consideration of the jury. Smith v. Lehigh Valley R. R. Co., 177 N. Y. 379, 69 N. E. 729, 70 N. E. 1. Courts should be particularly careful to protect the rights of defendants in actions for personal injuries alleged to have been caused by negligence, because juries so frequently find negligence on insufficient grounds, when the plaintiff has sustained a severe injury, and their sympathies are awakened by suffering and misfortune. Whether the plaintiff's counsel made eloquent comments upon the unneighborly conduct of the defendant or not, the evidence was received, and it was the duty of the jury to consider it, the same as the other evidence in the case, yet how could they consider it without doing the defendant an injustice? We cannot say that it did no harm, when the jury found a verdict for an amount twice as large as the judges of the Appellate Division, with their control of the facts, thought was reasonable.

The judgment should be reversed, and a new trial granted, with costs to abide the event.

PARKER, C. J., and O'BRIEN, BARTLETT, CULLEN, and WERNER, JJ., concur. HAIGHT, J., absent.

Judgment reversed, etc.

(178 N. Y. 347)

GILLESPIE v. BROOKLYN HEIGHTS R. CO.

(Court of Appeals of New York. April 26, 1904.)

CARRIERS—MISCONDUCT OF EMPLOYÉS—LIABILITY—DAMAGES.

1. A street railway company is liable to a passenger for an injury to his feelings because of insulting language used by a conductor.

2. In an action against a railroad to recover for injuries to feelings, caused by insulting language of conductor, the jury may consider the humiliation and injury to the feelings, but not any injury to the character resulting therefrom.

3. Where a passenger on a street car tendered the conductor an amount more than the fare, and asked for a transfer, and, after the conductor had attended to another passenger, demanded her change, whereupon the conductor in an abusive manner refused to return any change, but called the passenger a deadbeat and swindler, a directed verdict for plaintiff for the amount of the change as the extent of the carrier's liability is reversible error.

Parker, C. J., and Gray and O'Brien, JJ., dissenting.

Appeal from Supreme Court, Appellate Division, Second Department.

Action by Elizabeth S. Gillespie against the Brooklyn Heights Railroad Company. From a judgment of the Appellate Division (81 N. Y. Supp. 1127) affirming a judgment for defendant, plaintiff appeals. Reversed.

On the 26th of December, 1900, the plaintiff, who was a practicing physician, boarded one of the defendant's cars at the corner of Nostrand avenue and Fulton street at about 10:20 in the morning. As to what thereafter occurred the plaintiff testified: "I know who the conductor was on that car; Conductor Wright. He came to collect my fare just a few minutes after I got on the car. I gave him a twenty-five cent piece, and said to him, 'A transfer, please, to Reid avenue.' Just at that moment a lady on the opposite side called to him. He crossed, and he went to punch a transfer, and I thought it was mine, and I said to him, 'Please don't do that until I speak with you.' He paid no attention. After he gave the lady her transfer, I said to him: 'Won't you please come here? I wish

¶ 1. See Carriers, vol. 9, Cent. Dig. § 1121.

to speak to you about the transfer?' So he came across very growly and roughly, and wanted to know, 'What is the matter with yes?' I said, 'Won't you please tell me—I don't know much about those streets away up here—which would be the nearest, Reid avenue or Sumner avenue, to Stuyvesant avenue.' He said, 'We don't have any Reid avenue transfers; we transfer at Sumner avenue.' 'Well,' I said then, 'I thank you; please give me a transfer for Sumner avenue and my change;' and he actually hollowed at me, 'What change?' I said, 'The money I gave you, twenty-five cents; and I want my change;' and he put his hands in his pocket, and he pulled out a whole handful of pennies or nickels. He said, 'Do you see any twenty-five cents there?' He said: 'It is the likes of ye. You are a deadbeat. You are a swindler. I know the likes of ye.' He said, 'You didn't give me twenty-five cents.' The lady that sat next to me set the conductor right. She said to him, 'I am sure, sir, she gave you a quarter of a dollar; I saw her give it to you;' and he turned. 'Well, perhaps you are a friend of hers.' Then he said that deadbeats like me, he knew that every day they were traveling on the cars; he knew the swindlers and the deadbeats. 'But you can't deadbeat me. I know you. You belong to them;' and he said then, 'Why, only here the other day I had just such a woman as you trying to deadbeat me out of money;' and I said, 'I want my change, and I don't want such insolence.' Then he walked back, and two gentlemen got on the car, and he called the attention of those gentlemen to me, and said, pointing to me— I went to the door, and he was telling them how I was trying to swindle him. 'But,' he said, 'I know them. They are all deadbeats. She can't beat me.' I said to him, 'Look here, sir; I know President Rossiter, and I shall make a complaint of you;' and he came over close to me. He said, 'Ah, the likes of you,' he said. 'You couldn't make a complaint to President Rossiter,' he said. 'I have been on this road too long for you to have any authority with him; no, no.' 'Well,' I said, 'I shall tell him,' and I went back and sat down." The plaintiff further and in substance testified that she noticed that there was a smell of whisky in the conductor's breath; that he did not give her her change at all; that he gave her no transfer; that he said nothing except merely that he had nothing to do with her, and that "I was a deadbeat and a swindler." She then testified as to her efforts to see President Rossiter; that when she reached his office she was about four miles from home; that she walked that distance because she had no money with which to pay her fare; that she became sick, was confined to the bed for two days, and as to its effect upon her business. All this evidence was undisputed. At the close of the plaintiff's case the defendant made a motion for a dismissal of the complaint, and the court said: "The allegation of the complaint is that it was done maliciously by the servant of the corporation, so that takes it out of the action against the corporation anyway, so far as the slander part of it is concerned. The only question now is whether she is entitled to recover the amount that she paid for the fare." The plaintiff claimed she was entitled to recover more. The court thereupon said: "On the testimony as it stands they [the company] did receive it. It is uncontradicted now that they did receive it. I think I will direct a verdict for the twenty cents if you [referring to the defendant's counsel] want to." The plaintiff excepted to the direction of a verdict, and asked to go to the jury "upon the facts in the case, upon the wrong and the wrongful detention of this woman's money, and the suffering occasioned by it," and the court directed a verdict for the plaintiff for 20 cents, and held that that was the extent to which the railroad company was liable, and that "the other damages, if any have grown out of it, are not the proximate result of the act of the conductor." The verdict was directed with the consent of the defendant's counsel.

Melville J. France and James D. Bell, for appellant. I. R. Oeland and George D. Yeomans, for respondent.

MARTIN, J. (after stating the facts). The principal, and practically the only, question involved upon this appeal is whether the plaintiff was entitled to recover for the tort or breach of contract proved an amount in excess of the sum she actually overpaid the defendant's conductor. Confessedly, the plaintiff was a passenger on the defendant's car, and entitled to be carried over its road. That at the time of this occurrence the relation of carrier and passenger existed between the defendant and the plaintiff is not denied. The latter gave the conductor a quarter of a dollar from which to take her fare. He received it, but did not return her the 20 cents change to which she was entitled. She subsequently asked him for it, when he, in an abusive and impudent manner, not only refused to pay it, but also grossly insulted her by calling her a deadbeat and a swindler, and by the use of other insulting and improper language, even after a fellow passenger had informed him that she had given him the amount she claimed. In this case there was obviously a breach of the defendant's contract and of its duty to its passenger. It was its duty to receive any coin or bill not in excess of the amount permitted to be tendered for fare on its car under its rules and regulations, and to make the change, and return it to the plaintiff, or person tendering the money for the fare. That certainly must have been a part of the contract entered into by the defendant, and the refusal of the conductor to return her change was a tortious act upon his part, performed by him while acting in the line of his duty as the defendant's servant. To that extent, at least, the contract between the parties was broken, and as an incident to and accompanying that breach the language and tortious acts complained of were employed and performed by the defendant's conductor.

This brings us to the precise question whether, in an action to recover damages for the breach of that contract and for the tortious acts of the conductor in relation thereto, the conduct of such employé and his treatment of the plaintiff at the time may be considered upon the question of damages, and in aggravation thereof. That the plaintiff suffered insult and indignity at the hands of the conductor, and was treated disrespectfully and indecorously by him under such circumstances as to occasion mental suffering, humiliation, wounded pride, and disgrace, there can be little doubt. At least the jury might have so found upon the evidence before them. This question was treated on the argument as a novel one, and as requiring the establishment of a new principle of law to enable the plaintiff to recover damages in excess of the amount retained by the defendant's conductor which rightfully belonged to her. In that we think counsel were at fault, and that the right to such a recovery is established beyond question, as will be seen by the authorities which we shall presently consider. The consideration of this general question involves two propositions. The first relates to the duties of carriers to their passengers, and the second to the rule of damages when there has been a breach of such duty. The relation between a carrier and its passenger is more than a mere contract relation, as it may exist in the absence of any contract whatsoever. Any person rightfully on the cars of a railroad company is entitled to protection by the carrier, and any breach of its duty in that respect is in the nature of a tort, and recovery may be had in an action of tort as well as for a breach of the contract. 2 Sedgwick on Damages, 637. In considering the duties of carriers to their passengers, we find that the elementary writers have often discussed this question, and that it has frequently been the subject of judicial consideration. Thus, in Booth on Street Railways, § 372, it is said: "The contract on the part of the company is to safely carry its passengers, and to compensate them for all unlawful and tortious injuries inflicted by its servants. It calls for safe carriage, for safe and respectful treatment from the carrier's servants, and for immunity from assaults by them, or by other persons, if it can be prevented by them. No matter what the motive is which incites the servant of the carrier to commit an improper act towards the passenger during the existence of the relation, the master is liable for the act and its natural and legitimate consequences. Hence it is responsible for the insulting conduct of its servants, which stops short of actual violence." In Hutchinson on Carriers, §§ 595, 596, the rule is stated as follows: "The passenger is entitled not only to every precaution which can be used by the carrier for his personal safety, but also to respectful treatment from him and his servants. From the moment the relation commences, as has been seen, the passenger is, in a great measure, under the protection of the carrier, even from the violent conduct of other passengers, or of strangers who may be temporarily upon his conveyance. * * * The carrier's obligation is to carry his passenger safely and properly, and to treat him respectfully; and, if he intrusts the performance of this duty to his servants, the law holds him responsible for the manner in which they execute the trust. The law seems to be now well settled that the carrier is obliged to protect his passenger from violence and insult from whatever source arising. He is not regarded as an insurer of his passenger's safety against every possible source of danger, but he is bound to use all such reasonable precautions as human judgment and foresight are capable of to make his passenger's journey safe and comfortable. He must not only protect his passenger against the violence and insults of strangers and co-passengers, but, a fortiori, against the violence and insults of his own servants. If this duty to the passenger is not performed, if this protection is not furnished, but, on the contrary, the passenger is assaulted and insulted through the negligence or willful misconduct of the carrier's servant, the carrier is necessarily responsible. And it seems to us it would be cause of profound regret if the law were otherwise. The carrier selects his own servants, and can discharge them when he pleases, and it is but reasonable that he should be responsible for the manner in which they execute their trust." In Thompson on Negligence, § 3186, the learned writer, after stating the foregoing rule, adds: "The carrier is liable absolutely, as an insurer, for the protection of the passenger against assaults and insults at the hands of his own servants, because he contracts to carry the passenger safely and to give him decent treatment en route. Hence, an unlawful assault or an insult to a passenger by his servant is a violation of his contract by the very person whom he has employed to carry it out. The intendment of the law is that he contracts absolutely to protect his passenger against the misconduct of his own servants whom he employs to execute the contract of carriage. The duty of the carrier to protect the passenger during the transit from the assaults and insults of his own servants being a duty of an absolute nature, the usual distinctions which attend the doctrine of respondeat superior cut little or no figure in the case." Again, in Schouler on Bailments, § 644, it is said: "Nor is it only good treatment from fellow passengers and from strangers coming upon the car, vessel, or vehicle that each passenger is entitled to, but he should be well treated by the passenger carrier himself, and all whom such carrier employs in and about the vehicle in the course of the journey. If the general doctrine of master and servant may be said to apply here, it applies with a very strong bias against the master, even where the servant's acts appear to be aggressive, wanton, malicious, and, so to speak, such as one's strict contract of service or agency does not readily imply. Such is the general contruction, so long as the offensive words and acts of a conductor, * * * or other such servant complained of, were said or committed in the usual line of duty, while, for instance, scrutinizing tickets and determining the right to travel, excluding offenders and trespassers, and enforcing, or pretending to enforce, the carrier's rules aboard the vehicle; and this whether the transportation of passengers be by land or water."

Having thus considered a portion of the elementary authorities relating to this question, we will now consider a few of the many decided cases relating to the same subject. In Chamberlain v. Chandler, 3 Mason, 242, 245, Fed. Cas. No. 2,575, Judge Story, who delivered the opinion of the court, in discussing the duties, relations, and responsibilities which arise between the carrier and passenger, said: "In respect to passengers, the case of the master is one of peculiar responsibility and delicacy. Their contract with him is not for mere shiproom and personal existence on board, but for reasonable food, comforts, necessaries, and kindness. It is a stipulation, not for toleration merely, but for respectful treatment, for that decency of demeanor which constitutes the charm of social life, for that attention which mitigates evils without reluctance, and that promptitude which administers aid to distress. In respect to females it proceeds yet farther; it includes an implied stipulation against general obscenity, that immodesty of approach which borders on lasciviousness, and against that wanton disregard of the feelings which aggravates every evil, and endeavors by the excitement of terror and cool malignancy of conduct to inflict torture upon susceptible minds. * * * It is intimated that all these acts, though wrong in morals, are yet acts which the law does not punish; that if the person is untouched, if the acts do not amount to an assault and battery, they are not to be redressed. The law looks on them as unworthy of its cognizance. The master is at liberty to inflict the most severe mental sufferings in the most tyrannical manner, and yet, if he withholds a blow, the victim may be crushed by his unkindness. He commits nothing within the reach of civil jurisprudence. My opinion is that the law involves no such absurdity. It is rational and just. It gives compensation for mental sufferings occasioned by acts of wanton injustice, equally whether they operate by way of direct or of consequential injuries. In each case the contract of the passengers for the voyage is, in substance, violated; and the wrong is to be redressed as a cause of damage." In Knoxville Traction Company v. Lane, 103 Tenn. 376, 53 S. W. 557, 46 L. R. A. 549, it was held that an electric street railway company was liable in damages to a passenger for the injury to his feelings by the indecent and insulting language of its employé, upon the ground, not of tort or negligence, but of breach of its contract that obligates the carrier not only to transport the passenger but to guaranty him respectful and courteous treatment, and to protect him from violence and insult from strangers and from its own employés; that as to the latter, the obligation of its contract is absolute; and that it selects its agents to perform its contract, and the carrier, and not the passenger, must assume the responsibility for the acts and conduct of such agents. In Cole v. Atlanta & West Point R. R. Co., 102 Ga. 474, 477, 31 S. E. 107, it was held that it was the unquestionable duty of a railroad company to protect a passenger against insult or injury from its conductor, and that the unprovoked use by a conductor to a passenger of opprobrious words and abusive language tending to humiliate the passenger or subject him to mortification gives to the latter a right of action against the company. In that case it was said: "The carrier's liability is not confined to assaults committed by its servants, but it extends also to insults, threats, and other disrespectful conduct." In Goddard v. Grand Trunk R. R. Co., 57 Me. 202, 213, 2 Am. Rep. 39, it was held that a common carrier of passengers is responsible for the misconduct of his servant towards a passenger. In that case Walton, J., delivering the opinion of the court, said: "The carrier's obligation is to carry his passenger safely and properly, and to treat him respectfully, and, if he intrusts the performance of this duty to his servants, the law holds him responsible for the manner in which they execute the trust. The law seems to be now well settled that the carrier is obliged to protect his passenger from violence and insult, from whatever source arising. * * * He must not only protect his passenger against the violence and insults of strangers and co-passengers, but, a fortiori, against the violence and insults of his own servants. If this duty to the passenger is not performed, if this protection is not furnished, but, on the contrary, the passenger is assaulted and insulted, through the negligence or the willful misconduct of the carrier's servant, the carrier is necessarily responsible"—citing Howe v. Newmarch, 12 Allen, 55; Moore v. Railroad, 4 Gray, 465, 64 Am. Dec. 83; Seymour v. Greenwood, 7 Hurl. & Nor. 354; Railroad v. Finney, 10 Wis. 388; Railroad v. Vandiver, 42 Pa. 365, 82 Am. Dec. 520; Railroad v. Derby, 14 How. (U. S.) 468, 14 L. Ed. 502;

Railway v. Hinds, 53 Pa. 512, 91 Am. Dec. 224; Flint v. Transportation Co., 34 Conn. 554, Fed. Cas. No. 4,873; Landreaux v. Bell, 5 La. [O. S.] 275; Railroad v. Blocher, 27 Md. 277. The decision in Southern Kansas R. R. Co. v. Hinsdale, 38 Kan. 507, 16 Pac. 937, was to the effect that where a conductor, in ejecting a person from a train, uses insulting or abusive language, such person may recover damages therefor on account of the injury to his feelings, but cannot, in an action for damages for his expulsion, also receive damages because the words used tended to bring him into ignominy and disgrace. So, in Craker v. Chicago & N. W. R. R. Co., 36 Wis. 657, 17 Am. Rep. 504, it was held that a railroad company is bound to protect female passengers on its trains from all indecent approach or assault; and where a conductor on the company's train makes an assault the company is liable for compensatory damages. In Bryan v. Chicago, R. I. & P. R. R. Co., 63 Iowa, 464, 19 N. W. 295, it was also held that an action by a passenger on the defendant's road would lie for injuries sustained from insolent, abusive, and offensive words spoken to her by the conductor. In McGinness v. Mo. Pac. Ry. Co., 21 Mo. App. 399, the decision of the United States court in Chamberlain v. Chandler was followed, and the discussion of the court in that case closely followed the discussion by Judge Story. In Spohn v. Missouri Pacific Railway Co., 87 Mo. 74, the court held that the company was liable to its passengers for any violence or insult from others while the relation of carrier and passenger existed. See, also, Malecek v. Tower Grove & Lafayette R. R. Co., 57 Mo. 17; Lou. & Nash. R. R. Co. v. Ballard, 85 Ky. 307, 3 S. W. 530, 7 Am. St. Rep. 600; Winnegar's Administrator v. Cent. Pass. Ry. Co., 85 Ky. 547, 4 S. W. 237; Sherley v. Billings, 8 Bush, 147, 8 Am. Rep. 451; Eads v. Metropolitan St. Ry. Co., 43 Mo. App. 536; Block v. Bannerman, 10 La. Ann. 1; and Coppin v. Braithwaite, 8 Jurist, pt. 1, 875. The duties arising between a carrier and passenger have been several times discussed in this state, as in Stewart v. Brooklyn & Crosstown R. R. Co., 90 N. Y. 588, 590, 43 Am. Rep. 185, where it was said: "By the defendant's contract with the plaintiff, it had undertaken to carry him safely and to treat him respectfully; and while a common carrier does not undertake to insure against injury from every possible danger, he does undertake to protect the passenger against any injury arising from the negligence or willful misconduct of its servants while engaged in performing a duty which the carrier owes to the passenger. * * * 'The carrier's obligation is to carry his passenger safely and properly, and to treat him respectfully, and, if he intrusts this duty to his servants, the law holds him responsible for the manner in which they execute the trust.'" The court then quoted with approval the decision in Nieto v. Clark, 1 Cliff. 145, 149, Fed. Cas. No. 10,262, where it was said: "In respect to female passengers, the contract proceeds yet further, and includes an implied stipulation that they shall be protected against obscene conduct, lascivious behavior, and every immodest and libidinous approach. * * * A common carrier undertakes absolutely to protect his passengers against the misconduct of their own servants engaged in executing the contract." Subsequently, in Dwinelle v. N. Y. C. & H. R. R. R. Co., 120 N. Y. 117, 125, 24 N. E. 319, 8 L. R. A. 224, 17 Am. St. Rep. 611, the same doctrine was held, and the foregoing portion of the opinion in the Stewart Case was quoted and reaffirmed by this court. It was then added: "These and numerous other cases hold that, no matter what the motive is which incites the servant of the carrier to commit an unlawful or improper act toward the passenger during the existence of the relation of carrier and passenger, the carrier is liable for the act and its natural and legitimate consequences." Again, in Palmeri v. Manhattan R. Co., 133 N. Y. 261, 266, 30 N. E. 1001, 16 L. R. A. 136, 28 Am. St. Rep. 632, it was held that the corporation is liable for the acts of injury and insult by an employé, although in departure from the authority conferred or implied, if they occur in the course of the employment. In that case the employé alleged that the plaintiff was a counterfeiter and a common prostitute, placed his hand upon her, and detained her for a while, but let her go without having her arrested. The action was to recover damages for unlawful imprisonment, accompanied by the words alleged to have been spoken. This court held she was entitled to recover. The judge then said: "Though injury and insult are acts in departure from the authority conferred or implied, nevertheless, as they occur in the course of the employment, the master becomes responsible for the wrong committed."

The foregoing authorities render it manifest that the defendant was not only liable to the plaintiff for the money wrongfully retained by its conductor, but also for any injury she suffered from the insulting and abusive language and treatment received at his hands.

This brings us to the consideration of the elements of damages in such a case, and what may be considered in determining their amount. Among the elements of compensatory damages for such an injury are the humiliation and injury to her feelings which the plaintiff suffered by reason of the insulting and abusive language and treatment she received, not, however, including any injury to her character resulting therefrom. She was entitled to recover only such compensatory damages as she sustained by reason of the humiliation and injury to her feelings, not including punitive or exemplary damages. "Damages given on the footing of humiliation, mortification, mental suffering, etc., are compensatory, and not exemplary, damages. They are given because of the suffering to which the passenger has been wrongfully subjected by the carrier. The quantum of this suffering may not, and generally does not, depend at all upon the mental condition of the carrier's servant, whether he acted honestly or dishonestly, with or without malice. But, whatever view is taken of this question, it is clear that, where the expulsion is made in consequence of a mistake of another agent of the carrier—as in a case where a previous conductor erroneously punched the transfer check which he gave to the passenger so as to read 2:40 p. m. instead of 3:40 p. m., and, in addition to this, the expulsion was accompanied by insulting remarks made to the passenger in the presence of others, damages may be given, founded on the humiliation and injury to the feelings of the passenger." Thompson on Negligence, § 3288. The same doctrine is laid down in Joyce on Damages, § 354. In Hamilton v. Third Ave. R. R. Co., 53 N. Y. 25, where a passenger was ejected by the conductor, who honestly supposed the fare had not been paid, and no unnecessary force was used, it was held that the act of the defendant's servant, being unlawful, rendered the defendant liable for compensatory damages, including compensation for loss of time, the fare upon another car, and a suitable recompense for the injury done to the plaintiff's feelings. In Eddy v. Syracuse Rapid Transit R. Co., 50 App. Div. 109, 63 N. Y. Supp. 645, it was held that, where the plaintiff entered a car believing that his transfer was valid, and was not negligent in failing to discover that it had been punched erroneously, he was there lawfully, and entitled to recover compensatory damages, including the indignity, humiliation, and injury to his feelings by the remarks of the conductor and his wrongful ejection from the car. In Miller v. King, 84 Hun, 308, 310, 32 N. Y. Supp. 332, it was held that the conductor had no right to eject the plaintiff; that his action in doing so was unlawful, and that the plaintiff was entitled to damages for the indignity and humiliation suffered thereby. See, also, Sedgwick on Damages, § 865. In Jacobs v. Third Ave. R. R. Co., 71 App. Div. 199, 202, 75 N. Y. Supp. 679, it was held that the plaintiff was entitled to recover compensatory damages, which embraced loss of time, the amount which the plaintiff was obliged to pay for passage upon another car, and injury done to his feelings by reason of the indignity which he wrongfully suffered. The same doctrine was held in Ray v. Cortland & Homer Traction Co., 19 App. Div. 530, 534, 46 N. Y. Supp. 521. See, also, Pullman's Palace Car Co. v. King, 99 Fed. 381, 382, 39 C. C. A. 573. In Shepard v. Chicago, R. I. & P. R. R. Co., 77 Iowa, 54, 41 N. W. 564, the court charged the jury: "When a passenger is wrongfully compelled to leave a train and suffer insult and abuse, the law does not exactly measure his damages, but it authorizes the jury to consider the injured feelings of the party, the indignity endured, the humiliation, wounded pride, mental suffering, and the like, and to allow such sum as the jury may say is right;" and it was held that his instruction was not subject to the objection that it authorized an allowance of exemplary damages, because damages may properly be allowed for mental suffering caused by indignity and outrage, and such damages are compensatory, and not exemplary. In Craker v. Chicago & N. W. R. R. Co., 36 Wis. 657, 17 Am. Rep. 504, it was held that in actions for personal torts the compensatory damages which may be recovered of the principal for the agent's act include not merely the plaintiff's pecuniary loss, but also compensation for mental suffering, and that in awarding compensatory damages in such cases no distinction is to be made between other forms of mental suffering and that which consists in a sense of wrong or insult arising from an act really or apparently dictated by a spirit of willful injustice, or by a deliberate intention to vex, degrade, or insult. In Cole v. Atlanta & West Point R. R. Co., 102 Ga. 474, 479, 31 S. E. 107, it was held that, even where there was no actual assault, but the company has failed in its duty to protect its passenger from insult, abuse, and ill treatment, the plaintiff is entitled to recover damages for the pain and mortification of being publicly denounced as a deadbeat, and in that case it was said: "While this was a wanton act of commission by a servant of the company, it was also a negligent omission on the part of its servants to perform towards the plaintiff a duty imposed by law upon their master." Humiliation and indignity are elements of actual damages, and these may arise from a sense of injury and outraged rights in being ejected from a railroad train without regard to the manner in which the ejection was effected, though only done through mistake. Louisville & Nashville R. R. Co. v. Hine, 121 Ala. 234, 25 South. 857. Where unnecessary violence was used in ejecting a passenger from a train, he is entitled to damages for the direct consequences of the wrong, including as well physical pain as mental suffering resulting from accompanying insults, if any. Texas Pacific R. R. Co. v. James, 82 Tex. 306, 18 S. W. 589, 15 L. R. A. 347. A conductor of a railroad company represents the company in the discharge of his functions, and being in the line of his duty in collecting the fare or taking up tickets, the corporation is liable for any abuse of his authority, whether of omission or commission. In that case the court charged that "in estimating damages they might take into consideration the indignity, insult, and injury to plaintiff's feelings by being publicly expelled," and it was held proper. S. K. R. R. Co. v. Rice, 38 Kan. 398, 16 Pac. 817, 5 Am.

St. Rep. 766. Damages may be properly allowed for mental suffering caused by indignity and outrage, whether connected with physical suffering or not; and such damages are compensatory, and not exemplary. Shepard v. Chicago, R. I. & P. R. R. Co., 77 Iowa, 54, 41 N. W. 564. Where the plaintiff, holding a ticket, was wrongfully threatened with expulsion from the cars, charged with attempting to ride without paying therefor, and paid his fare rather than to be ejected, it was held that he was entitled to recover damages for the humiliation suffered and indignity done him by such action on the part of the conductor. Penn. Co. v. Bray, 125 Ind. 229, 25 N. E. 439. Where a passenger is expelled from a train, and without fault on his part, he may recover more than nominal damages, although he has suffered no pecuniary loss or received actual injury to the person by reason of such expulsion; and the jury, in estimating the damages, may consider not only the annoyance, vexation, delay, and risk to which the person was subjected, but also the indignity done him by the mere fact of his expulsion. Chicago & Alton R. R. Co. v. Flagg, 43 Ill. 364, 92 Am. Dec. 133. A person wrongfully ejected from a train is entitled to recover such damages as he may have sustained by the delay occasioned by the expulsion, and all the additional expenses necessarily incurred thereby, as well as reasonable damages for the indignity to which he was subjected in being expelled from the train. Penn. R. R. Co. v. Connell, 127 Ill. 419, 20 N. E. 89. Where there was a wrongful expulsion of a passenger from the car, although unaccompanied by any physical force or violence, it is actionable, and in such a case the sense of wrong suffered and the feeling of humiliation and disgrace engendered is an actual damage for which the injured party may recover compensation, such damages being compensatory, and not exemplary. Willson v. Northern Pacific R. R. Co., 5 Wash. 621, 32 Pac. 468, 34 Pac. 146. See, also, G. C. & S. F. R. R. Co. v. Copeland, 17 Tex. Civ. App. 55, 42 S. W. 239; Railroad Co. v. Goben, 15 Ind. App. 123, 42 N. E. 1116, 43 N. E. 890; Cooper v. Mullins, 30 Ga. 146, 76 Am. Dec. 638; Railroad Co. v. Deloney, 65 Ark. 177, 45 S. W. 351, 67 Am. St. Rep. 913; Railroad Company v. Dickerson, 4 Kan. App. 345, 45 Pac. 975.

After this somewhat extended review of the authorities bearing upon the subject, we are led irresistibly to the conclusion that the defendant is liable for the insulting and abusive treatment the plaintiff received at the hands of its servant, that she is entitled to recover compensatory damages for the humiliation and injury to her feelings occasioned thereby, and that the trial court erred in directing a verdict for the plaintiff for 20 cents only, and in refusing to submit the case to the jury.

The judgments of the Appellate Division and trial court should be reversed, and a new trial granted, with costs to abide the event.

GRAY, J. (dissenting). I dissent, because I think it is extending unduly the doctrine of a common carrier's liability in making it answerable in damages for the slanderous words spoken by one of its agents.

BARTLETT, HAIGHT, and CULLEN, JJ., concur with MARTIN, J. PARKER, C. J., and O'BRIEN, J., concur with GRAY, J.

Judgments reversed, etc.

(178 N. Y. 339)

BRAUER v. OCEANIC STEAM NAV. CO., Limited.

(Court of Appeals of New York. April 26, 1904.)

STATUTE OF FRAUDS—PLEADING—WRITTEN CONTRACT—EVIDENCE.

1. Where plaintiff sues to recover for the breach of an alleged written contract, and defendant denies the execution of such contract, it authorizes defendant, on proof by plaintiff of an oral contract, to object that such contract was within the statute of frauds by a motion to dismiss or to direct a verdict.

2. Where, after certain oral negotiations, telegraphic correspondence followed, and purported to ratify a proposed agreement, but omitted several important parts thereof, it is not a valid written contract, binding upon the parties, on which an action for an alleged breach can be founded.

Appeal from Supreme Court, Appellate Division, First Department.

Action by William W. Brauer against the Oceanic Steam Navigation Company, Limited. From a judgment of the Appellate Division overruling plaintiff's exceptions, and denying a motion for new trial, and directing judgment for defendant (82 N. Y. Supp. 1095), plaintiff appeals. Affirmed.

Lyman E. Warren and Ira D. Warren, for appellant. Everett P. Wheeler, for respondent.

CULLEN, J. The action was brought to recover damages for the breach of an alleged written contract whereby the defendant agreed to let to the plaintiff the cattle space in all its steamships plying between the city of New York and the city of Liverpool for the purpose of transporting cattle thereon from December 1, 1897, to the 30th day of November, 1898, in consideration whereof the plaintiff agreed to pay 42s. 6d. sterling per head. The defendant denied making the agreement. The defendant is the owner of what is commonly known as the White Star Line. In October, 1897, the plaintiff called on the defendant's agent in the city of New York, and applied for the exclusive control of the facilities of the de-

¶ 1. See Frauds, Statute of, vol. 23, Cent. Dig. §§ 371, 372.

fendant's steamers for the transportation of cattle for the period of one year. He stated to the agent that he had already secured an option on the American Transport Line for the same service for a similar period, that he was acting as broker for the people interested in the cattle market in England, and that, to make the plan or scheme of the plaintiff and his associates successful, it was necessary that he should have control of the cattle transportation of both lines. Thereupon negotiations were had concerning the terms and conditions of the proposed contract, which included a number of details, such as the length of notice to be given to the plaintiff of the proposed time of sailing of any steamer; the sum for which the cattle should be insured by the defendant; the erection of stalls; the carriage of the necessary feed for the cattle; the transportation of men to attend the cattle, and their return to this country; demurrage for any delay in the sailing of the vessel caused by the shipper; compensation to the plaintiff in case, after notice given, there should be delay in sailing; and other incidents to which it is unnecessary to specifically refer. According to the plaintiff's testimony, in these oral negotiations all the details and conditions necessary to a contract were agreed upon, except the price to be paid for the transportation of the cattle, and the payment of brokerage for the charter party. As to these matters the agent stated that he would telegraph to his principals in Europe before giving the plaintiff a definite answer. In this state of the negotiations, the plaintiff went to Chicago, and while he was there the following telegraphic correspondence passed between the parties:

"New York, Oct. 25th, 1897. W. W. Brauer, Auditorium Annex, Chicago: Am ready to close all White Star steamers carrying cattle December 1st, 1897, to November 30th, 1898, inclusive, 42/6 insured. Maximum numbers our call subject to your giving satisfactory guarantee, Liverpool, November 15th, but decline positively, pay brokerage subject to reply by noon to-morrow (Tuesday). [Signed] H. Maitland Kersey."

"Dated Chicago, Ill., Oct. 26. To H. Maitland Kersey, White Star Line, Broadway: Accept your proposition, confirm closing your boats for one year. Brauer."

"Dated New York, Oct. 26. To W. W. Brauer, Aud. Annex: Message received. Consider space closed. H. Maitland Kersey."

On the plaintiff's return to the city of New York, a few days after this correspondence, he called on the defendant's agent, and the latter prepared a written contract for the plaintiff to sign. Plaintiff declined to execute the proposed contract, claiming that its terms varied substantially from those agreed upon in the conversations between the parties. Defendant's agent insisted he must sign that, or the negotiations would terminate. The plaintiff persisted in his refusal, and thereupon the defendant repudiated any obligation in the matter. Thereafter the plaintiff brought this action for damages for the defendant's breach of contract. At the close of the evidence the learned trial judge, in obedience to a decision of the Appellate Division made on a previous appeal in the action, dismissed the complaint on the ground that no completed contract had been entered into by the parties. This disposition of the case has been affirmed by the Appellate Division, and an appeal is now taken to this court.

We very much doubt whether the ground on which the decisions of the courts below have proceeded can be sustained. If oral negotiations of the parties were sufficient to establish a binding contract, we are inclined to the view that under the plaintiff's testimony the case would have been for the jury. He testified to an agreement upon all details sufficient to constitute a working contract. It is true that both parties expected that subsequently a formal written contract should be executed. But such an expectation or intent did not abrogate the force of the previous agreement as an obligatory contract. Pratt v. Hudson R. R. R. Co., 21 N. Y. 305; Sanders v. Pottlitzer Bros. F. Co., 144 N. Y. 209, 39 N. E. 75, 29 L. R. A. 431, 43 Am. St. Rep. 757; Raubitschek v. Blank, 80 N. Y. 480. This doctrine the learned Appellate Division fully conceded, but was of opinion that some of the terms of the agreement remained unsettled. This, as already said, could not be so held as a matter of law, but, on the evidence, presented a question of fact for the jury. It is unnecessary, however, to pursue the discussion, as we think the alleged agreement, which was not to be performed within the term of one year, was void under the statute of frauds.

It is urged that the defendant is not in a position to raise this objection, the statute not having been pleaded. Ever since the decision in Crane v. Powell, 139 N. Y. 379, 34 N. E. 911, the law has been settled in this state—whatever uncertainty there may have been on the subject before that—that, to avail himself of the defense of the statute of frauds, the defendant must, in a proper case, plead the statute. It is to be borne in mind, however, that in the case now before us the plaintiff declared on a written contract, and "the statute concerns oral contracts only. Written contracts, of whatever nature, are untouched by its provisions." Browne on Frauds, § 344a. It is difficult to see how the defendant could plead that a written contract was not reduced to writing, nor any note or memorandum thereof made in writing. If it be possible for such a plea to be true, it can only be true in the sense that it charges that the written contract was not made at all. This, however, the defendant has sufficiently pleaded, for it has specifically denied the allegation of the complaint that a written contract was executed. Proof by the plaintiff of an oral contract, instead of a written contract, did not constitute any such variance as required the court on the trial to dismiss the complaint. It did not change the cause of action, and, if necessary, the court could have amended the complaint to conform to the facts proved. But the extension of such a favor to the plaintiff could not in any respect deprive the defendant of its rights. Therefore, when the oral contract was proved, either in lieu or in support of the written one declared on in the complaint, the defendant could properly raise the objection of the statute by a motion to dismiss or for the direction of a verdict.

Personally I should incline to the view that he telegrams between the parties are not sufciently definite to enable a court to spell ut a complete contract of any kind. The eneral rule is held by this court to be "that note or memorandum sufficient to take a ontract out of the operation of the statute ' frauds must state the whole contract with asonable certainty, so that the substance ereof may be made to appear from the recd itself, without regard to parol evidence." 'ard v. Hasbrouck, 169 N. Y. 407, 62 N. E. 4. In Drake v. Seaman, 97 N. Y. 230, a itten memorandum signed by the defendt, and accepted in writing by the plaintiff, ich stated the understanding between the rties to be that the plaintiff was to be paid .000 for the first year, $2,500 for the second r, and, provided the increased sales warted it, $3,000, was insufficient to take the e without the statute, because it did not ress what the plaintiff was to do in coneration of such payments. In Mentz v. wwitter, 122 N. Y. 491, 25 N. E. 1044, 11 L. A. 97, 19 Am. St. Rep. 514, a memorandum the contract of sale was held insufficient ause the name of the vendee did not apr therein. At the same time parol evice is admissible to explain the meaning of racters, marks, and technical terms used particular business, which are unintellie to persons not acquainted therewith, re they occur in a written instrument. a v. Fiedler, 12 N. Y. 40, 62 Am. Dec. 130. the circumstances surrounding the paralso may be shown to explain its mean- Hagan v. Domestic Sewing Machine Co., un, 73. Both the cases cited arose under statute of frauds. But in neither did the l testimony which was held admissible ist of oral negotiations between the parbut related to the circumstances of the es, and the meaning in the trade of techterms. The parol testimony in this case sts almost exclusively of the oral negons. The number and capacity of the e Star steamers, their sailing days, that plied from New York to Liverpool, were cts properly proved by parol to explain eaning of the defendant's first telegram, of October 25th. I am by no means so that "42/6" meant 42s. 6d. sterling ead was proved by competent testimo- There was no proof of a usage in the that rates for transporting cattle were fixed in shillings and pence by the head. The explanation depends entirely on the conversations between the parties, and in this respect differs from Dana v. Fiedler. What was to be the nature or subject-matter of the guaranty mentioned in the telegram can be explained only by similar testimony. However, I shall not attempt to further analyze the various conditions of the telegrams. Such an analysis might well provoke differences of opinion among ourselves, and is unnecessary, as the plaintiff does not stand on the terms of the telegrams alone, as constituting a complete contract. It is conceded that no reference whatever, direct or indirect, is to be found in the telegrams to some most important conditions of what the plaintiff contends to have been the real contract. The plaintiff was to have six days' notice of the time of the departure of the steamers, and twelve hours' notice of the time when the cattle would be required to be alongside of the steamer. This was a matter of moment, for the plaintiff's purchases of cattle were to be made in Chicago, and the cattle transported from Chicago to New York in time to properly pass the government inspection before being shipped on the vessels. In connection with this, there were further provisions for delay or demurrage for which either party might be responsible. If the defendant failed to transport the plaintiff's cattle at the time specified, it was obliged to pay 50 cents a head per day for every day the shipment was detained, while, if the plaintiff detained the boat by failure to have his cattle ready for shipment, he was to pay, according to his testimony, £80 per day as demurrage; according to the defendant's testimony, £90 per day. It was on these very provisions that the negotiations between the parties were ruptured. The defendant, in its proposed written contract, inserted £90 as the daily demurrage, and provided that the defendant might, at its election, sail its boats at the time fixed for their departure, without waiting for the plaintiff's cattle, in which case the plaintiff should pay the freight, as if the cattle had been shipped. It also excluded from its liability to pay for the expense of keeping detained cattle where the delay was caused by latent defects in the machinery or hull of the vessel, strikes, or labor stoppage. The plaintiff refused absolutely to accede to these conditions, but insisted on the terms of what he declares to have been the oral agreement between the parties. Therefore, if the telegrams are to be construed as constituting a contract between the parties, complete and exclusive in its terms, the plaintiff, by its repudiation, was just as much guilty of a breach as the defendant. Both parties equally contended that there were provisions additional and beyond those contained in the correspondence. There are provisions as to other matters, essential parts of the real contract, on which the telegrams are silent. The defendant was to transport free of cost one man to every 25 head to take charge of the cattle, and to return free of cost such men to this country. The stalls on the ships were to be erected by the shipper. The shipper was to supply the feed, which was to be carried by the vessels free of charge, but excess of feed beyond that used, which might be sold in England, was to be paid for as freight. In fact, the learned counsel for the appellant, in his brief, enumerates many conditions of what he contends to have been the completed contract of the parties, none of which is to be found in the telegraphic correspondence. There is no evidence that these are governed by custom in the trade, and can be implied as incidents to the contract, but they rest solely in the alleged oral agreement. Therefore, within the well-settled rules of law, the agreement for the breach of which the plaintiff seeks to recover was not valid and binding on the defendant. May v. Thomson, L. R. [20 Ch. D.] 705; Winn v. Bull, L. R. [7 Ch. D.] 29.

The judgment appealed from should be affirmed, with costs.

PARKER, C. J., and O'BRIEN, BARTLETT, HAIGHT, VANN, and WERNER, JJ., concur.

Judgment affirmed.

(178 N. Y. 325)

WESTERN UNION TELEGRAPH CO. v. ELECTRIC LIGHT & POWER CO. OF SYRACUSE et al.

(Court of Appeals of New York. April 26, 1904.)

INJUNCTION—FRANCHISES—SUBWAYS UNDER CITY STREETS—REMEDY AT LAW.

1. Where plaintiff sued to restrain defendant from maintaining a street subway in close proximity to plaintiff's subway, previously constructed, and to compel defendant to remove its lines therefrom, but did not allege in its complaint that defendant was insolvent or that a multiplicity of suits would result, a judgment denying the injunction, but directing that defendant should indemnify plaintiff for any injuries it might suffer through the trespass by the execution of a bond, was erroneous, as an adjudication that an action in equity was unnecessary, as plaintiff had a sufficient remedy at law.

2. Where the common council of a city granted a corporation a right to construct a subway below the surface of the street, and provided that such franchise should not be deemed to give such company any exclusive right to the street for such subway, and reserved to the city all rights not specifically given, such company cannot object because the city thereafter gave another company a right to locate its subway so close to plaintiff's subway as to cause expense in making repairs, if such subsequent location was not an unreasonable interference with plaintiff's rights.

O'Brien, Bartlett, and Haight, JJ., dissenting.

Appeal from Supreme Court, Appellate Division, Fourth Department.

Action by the Western Union Telegraph Company against the Electric Light & Power Company of Syracuse and others. From a judgment of the Appellate Division affirming a judgment for plaintiff (81 N. Y. Supp. 1147), defendant electric light and power company appeals. Reversed.

William P. Goodelle, for appellant. Charles P. Ryan, for respondent.

VANN, J. This is a controversy between two underground occupants of a public street in the city of Syracuse, each having a franchise granted by the common council. The plaintiff's franchise, which is the earlier in date, permitted it to construct a subway or conduit under certain streets, and to place wires therein "necessary in the operation and conduct" of its telegraph business, according to plans and specifications to be approved by the commissioner of public works or the common council. Among the many conditions and limitations of the grant was the provision that no "exclusive franchise to use the streets and public places of the city, or any of them, for a subway, or for any other purpose," should be deemed to be conferred upon the plaintiff, and that "all rights and privileges not herein specifically given are expressly reserved by the common council." Under this permit the plaintiff constructed a subway, which consists of a structure 16 inches high and 9 inches wide, laid a few feet below the surface of the streets. It contains six wooden ducts, one of which, as required by the grant, is for the exclusive use of the city, and is controlled by it accordingly.

Subsequently the common council, upon similar conditions, gave the defendant a franchise to construct a subway to conduct and distribute "electricity for light, heat or power for public or private use." The defendant built its line in some of the streets already occupied by the subway of the plaintiff. Its structure, 26 inches wide by 17 inches high, was located, as the franchise provided, by the commissioner of public works, and in some instances was placed above and parallel to the line of the plaintiff, and at a distance of but 1 or 2 feet therefrom. On the south side the two structures are bounded by the same vertical line, but on the north side the defendant's subway projects about 17 inches over that of the plaintiff. In one locality, for a distance of about 420 feet, if the earth beneath the defendant's subway were removed, it could not sustain itself, for it is not self-supporting except in sections four feet long, and artificial support would be necessary in order to repair the plaintiff's line or remove a duct therefrom. At this point the street contains many substructures, including a sewer, water and gas mains, other subways, and the like, while on the surface there is a double-track street railroad. On the side of the street selected, the unoccupied space where the defendant's subway could have been located without interfering with any substructure is about 3 feet wide, and is just south of and between plaintiff's subway and a water main. On the other side of the street there was also unoccupied space, which was certain, however, to be needed in the future.

While the defendant was constructing its work the plaintiff protested against the location selected, and some delay resulted; but finally the defendant placed its subway, pursuant to its franchise, in the exact situation and position directed by the commissioner of public works. After the defendant had completed its line, the plaintiff, with no allegation of insolvency in its complaint, or that a multiplicity of suits would result, brought this action to restrain the defendant from using or maintaining its subway as located in the street in question, and to compel it to remove its line therefrom. The theory of the complaint is that the location of the defendant's subway interferes with access to the subway of the plaintiff for the purpose of making repairs, and that it will "necessarily cause great inconvenience and expense." The trial court did not grant an injunction, but required the defendant and the city of Syracuse, which was joined as a defendant, but for some reason did not defend, within 30 days after entry of judgment and notice thereof, to execute a bond in the penalty of $5,000, with two sureties, to "indemnify the plaintiff * * * against any loss, damage, or expense which it or its successors may sustain by reason of the location" of the defendant's line, and restraining both defendants from using the subway or placing any wires therein during said period of 30 days. The Appellate Division unanimously affirmed the judgment, and the Syracuse Electric Light & Power Company appealed to this court.

The question presented for review is whether, upon the facts alleged in the complaint, and those found by the trial judge, the court had power to grant the relief provided by its judgment.

The object of the action was to restrain an alleged trespass, which is not permitted except under peculiar circumstances not shown to exist in this case. The result of the action was an adjudication, in effect, that a resort to equity was unnecessary, because the requirement of a bond to indemnify against damages shows that there was an adequate remedy at law through the recovery of damages as compensation. Thus the court, sitting as a court of equity, awarded nothing but what could be had in an action at law, except to provide security that the damages when admeasured at law would be paid. An action at law would be required to recover any damages under the bond, and the same damages could be recovered to the same amount in an action at law without a bond. The court adjudged that the structure of the defendant was unlawful, and that it might result in damages to the plaintiff in the future, but the only relief awarded was to require the defendant to secure the payment of such damages if they should accrue. It did not grant an injunction provided the defendants should not execute a bond, but issued an absolute command requiring the two corporations—one a city of the second class—to furnish security for all time to come that, if damages should result from the defendant's illegal action, they would be paid. This adjudication necessarily involved, as a part thereof, that the recovery of damages was an adequate remedy, and hence that an action in equity was unnecessary.

While I think the judgment should be reversed upon the ground already stated, there are other considerations which should not be lost sight of, for they involve the welfare of the public in all municipal corporations. Space beneath the surface of streets in our large cities is becoming more valuable every year for the purpose of conducting water, heat, and light to the dwellings of the inhabitants, as well as for the construction of sewers, underground railroads, subway lines, pneumatic tubes, and other agencies of great public utility. The existence of surface railroads frequently renders access to the various structures beneath the streets more or less difficult, and makes it undesirable that subways or other structures should be located under the tracks. It is in view of such circumstances and possibilities that a franchise granted by a city permitting a corporation to place some structure beneath the surface of the streets is to be considered and construed. When, therefore, the common council, in granting a franchise to the plaintiff, provided that nothing therein contained should be deemed to give it "any exclusive franchise to use the streets for a subway or for any other purpose," and reserving all rights and privileges not specifically given, it did not empower the plaintiff to dictate what other structures should be located beneath the street, or where they should be placed. All that the plaintiff can lawfully demand is that its structure shall not be unreasonably interfered with. This is involved in the terms of its grant, when construed in the light of all the facts. It cannot keep out other structures, even if their construction involves expense and inconvenience to itself. It cannot say there shall be no subway above, beneath, or on either side of its own, for that right the city reserved, and doubtless it would have been reserved by implication if it had not been reserved expressly. The franchise "is to be construed in the interest of the public, and hence in favor of the grantor, and not, as in ordinary cases, in favor of the grantee." Trustees of Southampton v. Jessup, 162 N. Y. 122, 127, 56 N. E. 538, 539; Syracuse Water Co. v. City of Syracuse, 116 N. Y. 167, 178, 22 N. E. 381, 5 L. R. A. 546. The plaintiff took nothing by its grant but what was expressly given, or necessarily involved in what was expressly given. There is nothing in its franchise to prevent the city from laying a subway on any side of the plaintiff's subway, and immediately adjoining it, or from authorizing some other corporation to do it. If the city, which has control of the streets both above and below the surface, sees fit to economize space with reference to the wants of the future, it has a right to do so, and for this purpose to place, or authorize another corporation to place, conduit lines so near that of the plaintiff as to make access somewhat inconvenient and expensive. The city cannot destroy the plaintiff's line, nor prevent reasonable access to it, but it is not obliged to consult the mere convenience of the plaintiff, nor study to save it from expense, to the detriment of the public. In other words, the plaintiff may make a reasonable, but not an unreasonable, use of the right granted. While the city could not grant to another the right to use the same space occupied by the plaintiff's line, it could authorize the use of any other space, provided access to the line was left open, even if it was less convenient and more expensive.

The defendant's subway does not interfere with the operation of the plaintiff's line in any way, as there is the same convenience of access for that purpose as before. When, however, repairs or changes become necessary, it cannot reach its structure by digging down directly thereto, but must dig down by the side, and make a deeper excavation. If the repairs should require the removal of the earth between its line and that of the plaintiff for a distance exceeding four feet, it would be necessary for it to notify the defendant to support its line while the repairs were in progress, or else to support it at its own expense. This is the extent of the interference with the plaintiff's subway by the location of the defendant's line. It simply involves a slight increase of expense in order to reach the plaintiff's structure for the purpose of making repairs.

The charter of the city of Syracuse, in force when the franchises in question were granted, provided that the common council should have power "to require that telegraph, telephone or electric light wires or cables, or other appliances for conducting electricity, except trolley and feed wires, poles and fixtures used in operating street railroads, and the poles thereof heretofore erected in any street, alley or public ground * * * be removed from overhead in such street, alley or public ground, or any part thereof, within a reasonable time, not less than three months after the enactment of such ordinance. * * * No company, corporation or individual shall place its wires and electrical conductors in conduits under the surface of the streets, alleys or public grounds in such manner as to unnecessarily interfere with the use of such street, alley, or public grounds, or local improvements of any character or with the sewers or water or gas mains or branches thereof, nor without first obtaining the consent of the common council, subject to such regulations and restrictions as the common council may by ordinance make, or impose, in respect thereto, for the benefit of the public, the city or its citizens, and under the direction and supervision of the commissioner of public works. * * * And any company, corporation or individual so placing its wires under ground in any street, alley or public ground of said city, shall, upon notice from the city, or any of its departments that a local improvement or sewer or water main, or branch thereof, is to be constructed in such manner as will necessitate the moving or altering of the conduit or conduits, by said individual, company or corporation, move or alter the same at its own expense so as to permit the construction of the improvement where ordered, and should any person, company or corporation omit to comply with such notice, the conduit or conduits may be altered or moved by the city, and the cost and expense thereof recovered from such individual, company or corporation; to regulate the erection of telegraph, electric light and telephone poles, wires, cables and other electrical conductors," and require them to "be placed underground, subject to such restrictions and regulations as it may make by general ordinance, but nothing in this section contained shall affect any grant or consent heretofore made or given pursuant to general laws, as to any matter provided for in and by such grant or consent." Laws 1893, p. 1132, c. 531, § 2, amending section 22 of the Revised Charter.

This statute is part of the franchise granted to either party to this action, and is to be construed in connection therewith. It shows that the city has control of the subject, and that the plaintiff accepted its franchise subject to the right of the city to grant similar franchises to other corporations, and subject to the right of the commissioner of public works to locate the position of any new structure beneath the surface of the street. The question is not before us whether the commissioner selected the best possible location for the defendant's line, but simply whether he exercised his power in a reasonable way. The law made it his duty to determine the location, not the duty of the court. The statute gave him discretionary power in the premises, which is not subject to judicial control, "except in extraordinary and exceptional instances of gross abuse." Dillon, Municipal Corporations, § 832; High on Injunctions, §§ 1240, 1270.

I think that when the franchise of the plaintiff is construed in connection with the city charter in force when it was granted, and in the light of facts relating to the use of the street then existing or in reasonable contemplation by the parties, the commissioner of public works had the right to locate the plaintiff's line where it now is, and that the courts have no power to adjudge that location unlawful, under the circumstances of this case.

I vote for reversal and a new trial; costs to abide event.

O'BRIEN, J. (dissenting). The plaintiff brought this action for the purpose of restraining the Syracuse Electric Light & Power Company, the city, and its commissioner of public works, from interfering with the underground subway constructed by the plaintiff for the wires and appliances of its business operations. The controversy is really between the plaintiff, a telegraph company, and the defendant, an electric light company. There is practically no dispute about the facts, and they appear in the record at great length and with much detail. The trial court did not grant the relief demanded by the plaintiff, which was the removal of the subway of the electric light company at a certain point in the street from the present location, which is directly over the plaintiff's subway; and it is found as a fact that the construction and existence of the defendant's subway injures the rights and property of the plaintiff, and is really an unlawful interference therewith. The controlling facts in the case may be stated very briefly as follows:

On the 19th day of June, 1893, the city of Syracuse granted to the plaintiff a franchise or authority to construct and operate a subway, with necessary conduits and appliances, and to maintain therein its wires and cables necessary for the conduct of its business under the surface of certain streets named, within the corporate limits of the city, subject to certain terms and conditions therein contained. One of these conditions was that the plaintiff should furnish, for the use of the city, one of the ducts in said subway, and subsidiary ducts and branches to be reserved to the exclusive use of the city, to be used for its own wires, without compensation to the plaintiff. This was the consideration which the city received for the privilege of permitting the plaintiff to use the streets for the purposes of its subway. Subsequently the plaintiff was permitted to construct a subway in other streets than those named in the original franchise. The plaintiff accepted the franchise, and in the year 1896, at a large cost, constructed the subway under various streets in the city; and it included the duct for the city, which was also constructed as required by the terms of the franchise, and the city has since exercised control over the same. The plaintiff's subway was laid in a trench several feet beneath the surface of the streets, and consisted of six wooden ducts, laid two side by side, and three in height, each duct being 4½ inches square, with planking above and below, making a structure 16 inches high and 9 inches wide.

On the 6th day of June, 1898, the defendant, a private corporation, secured from the city a franchise to construct a subway under the streets, through which to conduct electricity for heat, light, and power. It appears that at a certain point in one of the streets, for a distance of 420 feet, the subway of the electric light company is laid parallel with, and directly above and overlapping, the plaintiff's subway; the distance between the bottom of the defendant's and the top of the plaintiff's subway varying from 1 foot to a little over 2 feet.

The court found that the subway of the defendant was not self-supporting; that, in case the earth is removed from around or under it, it is incapable of sustaining its own weight for a greater distance than 4 feet; that no repairs or changes can be made in the plaintiff's subway without first sustaining the defendant's subway by artificial means; that, in order to remove any duct from plaintiff's subway, an excavation of at least 12 feet must be made; that, in order to gain access to or make repairs upon plaintiff's subway, it will be necessary to tunnel under the subway of the defendant; that accidents often occur in and about structures of the character of these subways, making it frequently necessary to gain access to them, and the ducts therein contained, for the purpose of enlarging, inspection, repairs, and removing obstructions, and for remedying disturbances resulting from the settling of the ground, breaking of other substructures, and other causes, and in such event it becomes necessary to excavate from the surface of the street down to and around the subways, and remove the ducts therefrom, and that the maintenance of appellant's subway as built will result in loss, damage, and expense to the plaintiff.

It appears that, while the subway of the defendant was in process of construction, the plaintiff notified it and the city of the danger to the plaintiff's rights that would exist in consequence of locating the defendant's subway directly over that of the plaintiff, and the plaintiff made an objection to the projected work, both to the city and to the electric light company, but after some negotiation and delay the defendant proceeded with the construction of its subway according to the original plans. The franchise granted by the city to the plaintiff, and which the latter accepted, constituted a contract between the plaintiff and the city, which could not be affected or changed by one of the parties to it without the consent of the other. When the plaintiff, with the permission of the city, accepted the conditions of the grant and completed its subway, the structure underneath the surface of the street was property which could not be invaded or interfered with any more than any other corporate property which the plaintiff possessed. Neither the defendant the electric light company, nor the city acting through its commissioner of public works, had the right, for the purpose of constructing the defendant's subway, to interfere with or impair the free and unobstructed use by the plaintiff of the subway constructed by it under the franchise granted. The city had the undoubted right subsequently to grant a similar franchise to the defendant, but it had no right to locate the place where the same was to be constructed in such a way as to interfere with or injure the structure of the plaintiff. The city, in granting the franchise to the plaintiff, attached to it a condition reserving to itself the right to use one of the plaintiff's ducts for its own purposes, and this consideration furnishes an additional reason, if such is required, why the plaintiff's rights, as granted, cannot be disturbed.

We think that such an interference with the plaintiff's property rights, threatened or consummated, constitutes, under the circumstances of this case, a sufficient ground for the interference of a court of equity by injunction. It is quite true that the plaintiff has not yet, so far as appears, sustained any damage by reason of the facts complained of; but a court of equity will grant relief preventive in character when satisfied that such interference, although in the nature of a trespass, will injure the plaintiff's property and interfere with its lawful operations, which are affected by a public interest.

The difficulty in this case, if any, consists in the form of the judgment, or rather the character of the relief which was given to the plaintiff at the trial. The court did not direct the defendant to remove its structure or change its location, but determined that, for the plaintiff's protection, it should execute and deliver to it a bond in the sum of $5,000 as indemnity to the plaintiff against any loss, damage, or expense which it might sustain by reason of the construction and maintenance of the defendant's subway, and restraining the use of the subway until the filing of the bond. The city has not appealed from the judgment, and, so far as the record discloses, it has acquiesced in the judgment, which requires it to become a party to the bond. It may be, as suggested, that the city has no power to enter into any such arrangement, but this court has nothing to do with that question so long as the city itself does not complain. It is quite clear that the defendant the electric light company has no right to complain of the judgment in that respect. We think that, upon the facts found in this case, the court had jurisdiction to direct the removal of the defendant's subway, for the reason that it was an invasion of and menace to the plaintiff's right of enjoyment of the privileges secured to it by the franchise. The findings of fact fully disclose the difficulties and obstructions which the defendant's subway would constitute to the free enjoyment by the plaintiff of its property rights in the underground structure. It is quite likely that by the lapse of time the defendant would acquire a right by prescription to maintain its structure where it is, however inconvenient, dangerous, or damaging it might prove to be to the plaintiff, and in such cases a court of equity will interfere in order to prevent an unlawful invasion ripening into a legal right. Amsterdam Knitting Co. v. Dean, 162 N. Y. 278, 56 N. E. 757.

The judgment, in effect, requires the defendant to indemnify the plaintiff against damages that may arise from a future trespass, and in this respect the relief granted is doubtless exceptional and peculiar. It appears that before the case came to trial the street at the point in question had been regulated and paved at the expense of the property owners, and the court doubtless hesitated before granting the drastic relief which the plaintiff demanded; that is, to have the subway entirely removed to some other part of the street. Instead of decreeing that to be done, it granted a measure of relief more liberal to the defendant, compliance with which would be cheaper and more convenient. We are not prepared to say that the court was without power to grant the relief specified in the judgment. At all events, it does not seem to us that the defendant has any right to complain because it is simply required to give a bond of indemnity, rather than change the location of its subway. When a court of equity obtains jurisdiction of a case, it may grant such relief as the nature of the case may require, and in some cases it may award damages, as in an action at law, when such a course is necessary in order to do complete justice. Whatever may be said as to the outcome of this controversy expressed in the judgment, it does not appear to us to be unjust to the defendant, or to constitute any real ground of complaint.

The judgment should be affirmed, with costs.

PARKER, C. J., and MARTIN and WERNER, JJ., concur with VANN, J. BARTLETT and HAIGHT, JJ., concur with O'BRIEN, JJ.

Judgment reversed, etc.

(178 N. Y. 316)

MURRAY et al. v. MILLER et al.

(Court of Appeals of New York. April 26, 1904.)

WILL—DEVISE IN TRUST—VALIDITY—POWER IN TRUST.

1. Testator died in 1876, and devised the remainder of his estate after the death of his widow to the person who should then be known by an unincorporated ecclesiastical body as its treasurer, in trust for the benefit of such body, providing that, if at such time there should be no treasurer, then to the presiding officer at the last meeting of such body upon the same trust. *Held* invalid, because when the will took effect an unincorporated association was incompetent to take by devise, and a trust for an indefinite beneficiary was void; Laws 1893, p. 1748, c. 701, providing that devises otherwise valid shall

no longer be deemed invalid by indefiniteness or uncertainty of beneficiaries, not applying to such devise, it not being retroactive in its effect.

2. A devise of an estate to a person who shall be known at the death of the life tenant as treasurer of an unincorporated ecclesiastical body, in trust, to apply to the use of such body, is invalid, as unlawfully suspending the power of alienation.

3. A devise of the remainder of an estate after the death of testator's widow to the then treasurer of an unincorporated ecclesiastical body is not valid as a power in trust on the ground that at the death of the testator his real property descended to his heirs at law, subject to the widow's life estate, and subject to be divested on the death of the widow, which occurred in 1895, by the exercise of the power, and that the beneficiary had then acquired capacity to take by virtue of Laws 1893, p. 1748, c. 701, authorizing devises otherwise valid to be no longer held invalid because of indefiniteness or uncertainty of beneficiaries, since, such attempted trust being unlawful at the time of testator's death, in 1876, the power in trust would be also invalid, and the beneficiary could take under neither.

Appeal from Supreme Court, Appellate Division, First Department.

Submission of controversy, under Code Civ. Proc. § 1279, between William Murray and others and Walter T. Miller and others. From a judgment of the Appellate Division in favor of plaintiffs (83 N. Y. Supp. 591), defendants appeal. Affirmed.

James Fraser died on the 14th day of June, 1876, seised of the real property described in the record, and left a will dated the 3d day of December, 1862, which was admitted to probate on the 11th day of January, 1877, the material parts of which, disposing of his residuary estate, are as follows:

"I give, devise and bequeath to my beloved wife, Jessie, all my estate, real and personal, of which I may die seized or possessed, or to which I may then be entitled, for the term of her natural life. I authorize her to invest and collect and reinvest any and all of the personal estate in such manner as she may deem proper, without responsibility to any one, and to use and enjoy the income thereof.

"I give the remainder of all my real estate and the residue of my personal estate, at her death, to the person who shall then be known and recognized by the unincorporated ecclesiastical body now calling itself and known by the style of 'The Synod of the Reformed Presbyterian Church in North America' as its treasurer, in trust, to apply the same to the uses and for the benefit of such ecclesiastical body; and if at the time of the death of my wife there shall be no person known and recognized as its treasurer, then to the person who was at the last preceding meeting of such ecclesiastical body known and recognized as its presiding officer, by whatever name he may have been known, upon the same trust."

Upon the death of the testator, his widow, Jessie Fraser, entered into possession and enjoyment of the property, and so continued until her death on April 5, 1895. The widow, Jessie Fraser, also left a will, dated in November, 1877, by which her entire estate was given to the "Trustees of the Synod of the Reformed Presbyterian Church of North America," a corporation formed under the laws of Pennsylvania. Upon the death of Jessie Fraser the corporation above named went into possession of the property described in the record, and collected the rents thereof until May 9, 1899, when John T. Morton, as treasurer and trustee of the Synod of the Reformed Presbyterian Church of North America, the unincorporated association named as beneficiary in the will of James Fraser, conveyed said premises to Walter T. Miller for the expressed consideration of $28,000, and took back a purchase-money mortgage for $26,000. The unincorporated association above referred to was formed in 1809. The corporation above named was incorporated in 1871. Both were in existence at the time of the death of James Fraser, as separate and distinct organizations, and both so continued down to the time of the submission of this controversy.

James Fraser left, him surviving, as his heirs at law, a niece, Elizabeth Murray, who died in 1879 without issue, and whose only heir at law was Robert Murray, a nephew of James Fraser, who died in 1899, leaving the defendant Catharine Murray as his widow, and the plaintiffs as his heirs at law. The plaintiffs, as heirs at law of their father, now deceased, are therefore the heirs at law of James Fraser, and as such they claim title to the real estate described in the record, subject to their mother's dower, on the ground that the provisions of the will of James Fraser purporting to create a trust or power in trust for the benefit of said unincorporated association are void.

Upon an agreed statement of facts, the material parts of which are above recited, the controversy between the plaintiffs and the defendants was submitted to the Appellate Division, where it was decided that the plaintiffs were entitled to recover the real estate referred to, with damages for its detention.

Augustus C. Brown, for appellants. Benjamin N. Cardozo and Moses Esberg, for respondents.

WERNER, J. (after stating the facts). As disclosed by the foregoing statement of facts, this controversy arises over the title to certain real property in the city of New York, of which James Fraser died seised, and which he attempted to dispose of by his will. The respondents, consisting of the plaintiffs and their mother, the defendant Catharine Murray, assert the invalidity of this testamentary disposition, and, as heirs at law and dowress, respectively, claim title and possession to the lands in question. The appellants, with the exception of the corporation above named, are variously interested as trustee, beneficiary, purchaser, and tenants, respectively; and they rely upon the will as creating a valid power in trust, under which they defend their claims. The defendant corporation, known as the "Trustees of the Synod of the Reformed Presbyterian Church of North America," has no legal interest in this controversy, it being conceded by appellants' counsel that it is not the beneficiary named in the will of James Fraser, and that its interference with the real property mentioned was not only ill-advised, but wholly unauthorized. With this brief explanatory statement of the nature of the controversy, and the relation thereto of the several parties, we come to the consideration of the above-quoted testamentary provision, upon the construction of which this issue depends.

That the testator, James Fraser, intended to create an express trust for the benefit of the unincorporated association known as "The Synod of the Reformed Presbyterian Church of North America," and that he failed in the attempt, is clear to a demonstration. Indeed, the appellants now concede that this testamentary disposition is invalid as a trust, but they contend that it is valid as a power in trust. In the light of this concession, we need refer to the attempted trust only for the purpose of disclosing the effect of its invalidity upon the alleged power in trust. The will was executed in 1862, the testator died in 1876, and probate was effected in 1877. The beneficiary of the attempted trust was then, and has ever since been, an unincorporated association, whose constituent membership was transitory and fluctuating. As the law of this state then stood, an unincorporated association was incompetent to take by devise. Owen v. Miss. Soc. M. E. Church, 14 N. Y. 380, 67 Am. Dec. 160; White v. Howard, 46 N. Y. 160; People v. Powers, 147 N. Y. 104, 41 N. E. 432, 35 L. R. A. 502; Fairchild v. Edson, 154 N. Y. 205, 48 N. E. 541, 61 Am. St. Rep. 609. And a trust for an indefinite or uncertain beneficiary was void. Levy v. Levy, 33 N. Y. 107; Bascom v. Albertson, 34 N. Y. 584; Prichard v. Thompson, 95 N. Y. 76, 47 Am. Rep. 9; Holland v. Alcock, 108 N. Y. 312, 16 N. E. 305, 2 Am. St. Rep. 420; Read v. Williams, 125 N. Y. 560, 26 N. E. 730, 21 Am. St. Rep. 748; Tilden v. Green, 130 N. Y. 29, 28 N. E. 880, 14 L. R. A. 33, 27 Am. St. Rep. 487. The law in this respect was changed in 1893, to the extent of providing that devises, etc., otherwise valid, should no longer be deemed invalid by reason of indefiniteness or uncertainty of beneficiaries. Laws 1893, p. 1748, c. 701. But that does not help the appellants at bar, even though the trust estate here sought to be created be held to be future and expectant, since it is legally deemed to have come into being, if at all, at the death of the testator. Section 54, Real Property Law (Laws 1896, p. 568, c. 547). And as the statute of 1893 is not retroactive in its operation (People v. Powers, supra), the trust falls under the condemnation of the law in existence at the time of its attempted creation.

The gift is also void as a trust, because it either unlawfully suspends the power of alienation of real estate and the absolute ownership of personal property, or, on the other hand, because it is a mere passive trust, which fails for the reason that there is no cestui que trust competent to take. The devise is to the treasurer of the unincorporated association, "in trust, to apply the same to the uses and for the benefit of such ecclesiastical body." If this provision is to be construed as a direction to apply rents and income, or even corpus and principal, from time to time, according to the needs of the "ecclesiastical body," it offends the law against perpetuities, because the application of interest and income only necessarily involves a never-ending trust. If corpus or principal is also to be applied "to the uses and for the benefit of such ecclesiastical body," such uses may never require the total consumption of corpus or principal, or at least may not consume the same within the statutory period, and therefore the result will be the same. The time for which the alienation of real property and the absolute ownership of personal property may be suspended can no more be extended by a trust than by the limitation of a strictly legal estate. Levy v. Levy, supra; Adams v. Perry, 43 N. Y. 487; Cottman v. Grace, 112 N. Y. 299, 19 N. E. 839, 3 L. R. A. 145; Cruikshank v. Home for Friendless, 113 N. Y. 337, 21 N. E. 64, 4 L. R. A. 140.

When we turn from this aspect of the testamentary disposition to the only other view in which it can be regarded as a trust, namely, as a trust to take and apply the whole corpus of the estate to the use of the beneficiary, immediately upon the death of the life tenant, then we have a trust for a purpose not authorized by statute, and it becomes eo instanti a passive trust, under which title ordinarily vests directly in the beneficiary (Real Property Law, § 73), but in the case at bar vested in the testator's heirs at law, because, as above stated, the beneficiary was not competent to take.

This brings us to the contention of the appellants that, even though the testamentary provision is invalid as a trust, it is nevertheless valid as a power in trust. It is said that upon the death of the testator his real property descended to his heirs at law subject to the widow's life estate, and subject to be divested by the execution of the power, and, as this power was not to be executed until the death of the widow, which occurred in 1895, the beneficiary had then acquired capacity to take by virtue of the enabling statute of 1893. A power is defined to be "an authority to do an act in relation to real property * * * which the owner, granting * * * the power, might himself lawfully perform." Real Property Law, § 111. The statutes classify powers as general and special, beneficial and in trust. A special power is declared to be in trust where a person or class of persons, other than the grantee, is designated as entitled to any benefit from the disposition or charge authorized by the power. Real Property Law, § 118. A valid power arises by operation of law where an express trust is attempted to be created for a purpose which is lawful, but is not authorized by our statutes. In such a case the trust fails, but, if it directs or authorizes the performance of any act which may be lawfully performed under a power, it is valid as a power in trust. Real Property Law, § 79. The difficulty with the power in trust asserted by the appellants is that it is not for a lawful purpose, but is as unlawful as the trust itself, and must fail for the same reasons. When the testator died it was, as we have seen, impossible to create a valid trust in perpetuity, or for an uncertain and indefinite beneficiary for any purpose. These legal limitations which then hedged about the creation of trust estates quite as effectually prohibited the power to give as the capacity to take. If the attempted trust was unlawful because it contravened the statute of perpetuities, the asserted power in trust is equally so, because the act sought to be performed under the power is the very act forbidden by the statute. Garvey v. McDevitt, 72 N. Y. 556; Dana v. Murray, 122 N. Y. 604, 26 N. E. 21. Were the sole objection to the trust that its purpose, although lawful in itself, is not one for which the law authorizes an express trust, then it could be held good as a power in trust; but, as neither trust nor power can be executed without violating the law as it existed at the time of the testator's death, there can no more be a valid power than there could be a valid trust. Chaplin on Trusts & Powers, p. 441. Counsel for the appellants argues that the question is primarily and only one of capacity in the beneficiary to take the gift, and that, when this testamentary provision is considered as a power instead of a trust, its validity depends upon the law in force at the time of its execution, rather than at the time of its creation; and from this premise he goes on to the conclusion that the statute of 1893 had made it possible for the beneficiary to take in 1895 what it was incapable of taking in 1877.

The difficulty with this contention is that it ignores (1) that provision of the Revised Statutes (1 Rev. St. [1st Ed.] p. 737, pt. 2, c. 1, tit. 2) which declares that "no estate or interest can be given or limited to any person, by an instrument in execution of a power, which such person would not have been capable of taking, under the instrument by which the power was granted"; and (2) the vested constitutional property rights of the heirs at law, which could not be affected by a subsequently enacted statute. In other words, as the beneficiary could not take under the trust attempted to be raised by the will, so it could not take under an alleged power in execution of the trust; and, as both trust and power were absolutely void in their inception, the rights of the heirs at law then and there became vested, and could not be divested by any law thereafter enacted. This view of the case renders it superfluous to discuss the questions whether, without regard to the statute which saves as a power that which fails as a trust, a power may be implied from the language of the will, or whether the remainder limited upon the life estate was future and contingent, or immediate and vested, subject to the life estate, for in either event the result would be the same so far as the respondents are concerned. There being no valid trust or power in trust, the rights of the latter became vested upon the death of the testator, subject to the widow's life estate.

For the same reasons, we refrain from discussing the cases cited by appellants' counsel in which, under testamentary gifts to person of a designated class, questions have arisen as to the rights of those born into the class after the death of the testator, or the cases in which absolute gifts in remainder or in trust have been made for the benefit of charitable institutions in case they should acquire corporate existence and capacity after the death of the testator, either within a specified time, or before the expiration of a supervening life estate. None of these cases are applicable to the facts before us.

The judgment of the Appellate Division should be affirmed, with costs.

PARKER, C. J., and O'BRIEN, BARTLETT, HAIGHT, VANN, and CULLEN, JJ., concur.

Judgment affirmed.

(178 N. Y. 364)

JOHNSON v. COLE et al.

(Court of Appeals of New York. April 26, 1904.)

EVIDENCE—DECLARATIONS—RES GESTÆ.

1. Where, in partition, one of the issues is as to whether transfers of property by a mother before her death to the defendants were absolute gifts, or advancements, declarations of the mother made some time after these transfers that they were gifts are inadmissible.

2. Evidence as to statements by a father at the time he gave to his daughter a certificate of deposit, before the death of her mother, that he did this in his own behalf, and not in that of his wife, is admissible as part of the res gestæ.

Appeal from Supreme Court, Appellate Division, Fourth Department.

Action by Mary L. Johnson against Charles S. Cole and others. From a judgment of the Appellate Division (78 N. Y. Supp. 489) affirming an interlocutory judgment entered on the report of a referee, directing the sale of certain lands, certain of the defendants appeal. Reversed.

This appeal was allowed and the following questions certified by order of the Appellate Division:

"First. In an action for partition of real estate of a decedent, who died intestate, among the heirs of said decedent, in which action is also litigated the question whether certain real and personal property transferred by the decedent in her lifetime to two of the defendants, who are heirs at law and next of kin of said decedent, should be charged against them severally as advancements, may evidence be given in behalf of such defendants, upon the trial of said action, of statements made by the decedent, to a person not a party to the action, subsequent to such transfers, tending to show that such transfers were made as absolute gifts, and not by way of advancement, when such statements are offered to be proven by competent and qualified witnesses, and is the exclusion of such evidence error?

"Second. In an action such as described in the first above question, where it is claimed by plaintiff that the decedent in her lifetime gave one of the defendants certain money, which plaintiff claims was so given by said decedent by way of advancement to said defendant as her heir and next of kin, and should be charged as such against said defendant, and which money the said defendant claims was given her by the husband of the decedent, and not by or in behalf of the decedent, the undisputed evidence showing that the said money was personally delivered to said defendant by said decedent's husband, not in the presence of the decedent, the plaintiff claiming that in making such delivery said husband acted as agent of said decedent to make the alleged advancement, which claim was contested upon the trial by said defendant, who claimed that the said transfer of said money to her was a gift from said decedent's husband personally to said defendant, may the defendant prove upon the trial of said action what the said husband said, at the time he so delivered said money to said defendant, upon the subject of giving it to said defendant, and that he, the said husband, said, when he so delivered said money to said defendant, that it was a present from him, and had nothing to do with the decedent? And is the exclusion of such evidence error?"

Elmer E. Charles, for appellants. Frank W. Brown, for respondent.

BARTLETT, J. (after stating the facts). The learned Appellate Division, with a divided court, has determined both questions of law involved in the above questions in favor of the plaintiff.

The plaintiff, Mary L. Johnson, and the defendants (other than the defendant Ida M. Cole, the wife of the defendant Charles S. Cole) are the only children and heirs at law of Lucia A. Cole, who died intestate, leaving the real estate which is the subject of this action in partition. The intestate was also the owner of personal property of the value of $5,500 over and above her debts and the expenses of administration.

The intestate transferred in her lifetime to her children certain property, and the question was litigated before the referee whether these transfers were an absolute gift, or an advancement that could be charged against the share of a child in the final distribution of the estate. The children of the intestate offered to show by her declarations made some time after these transfers that they were gifts, and not advancements. The referee refused to admit these declarations, and the first question presented to us is whether they were competent, and does the exclusion of them present reversible error. We have been cited to no case in this court where the question has been decided. The courts in the various states have divided on this question, and there is authority in the decisions of several jurisdictions in favor of admitting these declarations. In a number of the states these transfers of property to children in the lifetime of a parent are required to be evidenced by a writing showing whether they are gifts or advancements. We regard such legislation as very desirable, and as safeguarding the interests of all parties connected with such transfers of property. We consider the admission of such declarations as fraught with great danger, and opening the door for fraudulent evidence tending to defeat the intention of parents who can no longer be heard in their own behalf. We do not intimate that any such fraudulent intention is disclosed in this case, but apply our remarks to the general situation. It is, of course, unfortunate that by the enforcement of this rule absolute gifts may have to yield to the presumption that such transfers of property are deemed advancements. If the situation presented requires a remedy, the appeal should be made to the Legislature, and not to the courts. We therefore answer the first question in the negative.

The second question arises out of the following facts: During the lifetime of the intestate, Chester A. Cole, her husband, and also the father of the defendant Emma J. Owen, called upon his daughter, and presented her with a certificate of deposit for $500. The material question growing out of this transaction is whether Chester A. Cole, in presenting the certificate of deposit to his daughter, acted as the agent of his wife, or for himself as principal. The daughter took the stand in her own behalf, and testified as follows: "The talk between me and my father, when he gave me the certificate of deposit was— He said, 'Well, Emma, you are away behind.' He says, 'I have not done anything much for you,' and he said, 'Here is a little something;' and I took it, and, when I saw how much it was, I was delighted, and thanked him for it." At a subsequent hearing, Charles Owen, the husband of Emma, testified: "I remember the time when Mr. Cole delivered to my wife a certificate of deposit for $500. That was about a year, or such a matter, before his death—I think, in 1892; somewhere along there. It was delivered to her at her house where we live—the Paddock place. When he gave it to her, he came and handed it to her, and said: 'Here is something for you. I have never given you anything, and I want to make you a present of this, and I want you to understand it is from me, and has nothing to do with your mother.' " Thereafter the defendant, Emma J. Owen, again took the stand, and was asked this question: "At the time your father, Chester A. Cole, gave you the certificate of deposit for $500, did he say to you that this was a present from him, and had nothing to do with your mother?" Objected to by plaintiff. Objection sustained, and defendant excepted. While the ground of this objection now insisted upon was not spread upon the record, it is presented by the form of the second question submitted for answer. The respondent seeks to justify the exclusion of this evidence on the ground that declarations of an agent are not competent to charge a principal upon proof merely that the relation of principal and agent existed at the time when the declarations were made. Something more must be shown. It must further appear that the agent, at the time the declarations were made, was engaged in executing the authority conferred upon him, and that the declarations related to and were connected with the business then depending, so that they constituted a part of the res gestæ. It is argued that, if Chester A. Cole was acting as his wife's agent, these declarations were outside of his agency, or, as in this case disclaiming the agency, were not competent, but were mere hearsay, and could not bind Mrs. Cole or her estate. If he was not acting as agent for his wife, but on his own account, then his declarations to his daughter were immaterial and hearsay. The one question involved in this phase of the case was whether Chester A. Cole was acting in his own behalf, or as agent of his wife. It follows that whatever occurred at the interview, when he handed the certificate of deposit to his daughter is material, as a part of the res gestæ. The principle of agency invoked by the respondent has no application to the situation here presented. We are therefore of opinion that it was competent for the defendant Emma J. Owen to prove what Chester A. Cole said at the time of delivering to her the certificate of deposit; also that the exclusion of such evidence was reversible error. We therefore answer the second question in the affirmative.

The judgment appealed from and the interlocutory judgment entered upon the report of the referee should be reversed, with costs to the appellants in all the courts to abide the event.

PARKER, C. J., and O'BRIEN, HAIGHT, VANN, CULLEN, and WERNER, JJ., concur.

Judgment reversed, etc.

(162 Ind. 558)

MUNCIE PULP CO. v. DAVIS.

(Supreme Court of Indiana. April 29, 1904.)

SERVANTS' INJURIES — EMPLOYERS' LIABILITY ACT — NEGLIGENCE OF SUPERINTENDENT — PLEADING — NECESSARY ALLEGATIONS — APPEAL—ANSWERS TO INTERROGATORIES—CONSIDERATION.

1. Under Burns' Ann. St. 1901, § 7083, subd. 2, making corporations liable for injuries suffered by employés, and resulting from the negligence of any person in the service of the corporation, to whose order or direction the injured employé was bound, and did conform, the negligence which gives a cause of action is that of a servant who has authority to give the order or direction which the injured servant was obeying at the time of the injury.

2. The characterization of an act of omission as negligent will not supply the want of averments of fact from which the existence of a duty to exercise care is shown to exist.

3. The giving of a proper command by a superior servant does not in every instance impose on him the duty of protecting the servant commanded while the latter is executing the order.

4. A complaint for a servant's injuries, under Burns' Ann. St. 1901, § 7083, subd. 2, making corporations liable for servants' injuries resulting from the negligence of a superior servant, to whose order the injured servant was bound to, and did, conform, which alleged that the superior failed and "omitted to keep said valves closed, and carelessly and negligently permitted the same to be left open by the employés of defendant corporation," is insufficient, in that it fails to allege that there was any duty on the part of the servant, under the terms or practice of his employment, to keep the valves closed.

5. The Supreme Court cannot consider an answer to an interrogatory submitted to the jury, stating on what paragraph of the complaint their verdict is based.

Appeal from Circuit Court, Delaware County; J. G. Leffler, Judge.

Action by Frank K. Davis against the Muncie Pulp Company. From a judgment for plaintiff, defendant appeals. Transferred from the Appellate Court, under Burns' Ann. St. 1901, § 1337u. Reversed.

Thompson & Thompson, for appellant. Gregory, Silverburg & Lotz, for appellee.

GILLETT, C. J. This action was instituted by appellee to recover for an injury to his person. The complaint was in three paragraphs. Appellant unsuccessfully demurred to each of said paragraphs, and then filed answer by way of general denial. Appellee recovered a verdict, on which judgment was rendered. The record has been so framed as to present the sufficiency of each paragraph of complaint as against said demurrer.

Some statement, as to said first paragraph, must be made as a basis for the opinion which is to follow; but, in the making of such statement, we shall endeavor to show the character of said paragraph with reference to the objections urged against it, rather than to make an abridged exhibit of all its averments. It appears from said paragraph that at the time of appellee's injury, January 7, 1902, appellant, a corporation, engaged in the manufacture of pulp, had in its factory two batteries of boilers, with a fire box beneath each of said boilers; that it was necessary to clean said boilers by steam and hot water every three or four hours; that for that purpose said batteries were encircled by what is termed a "blow line"; that opposite each boiler there was an individual line extending from said blow line through the fire box and into said boiler; that there was a valve on each of said individual lines, whereby the steam and hot water could be shut out of it. It further appears from said paragraph that appellee, a pipe fitter in the employ of appellant, was injured by the steam and hot water being turned on in said blow line while he was making a repair to the system by the replacing of a pipe in the fire box of furnace No. 7, and that appellee was doing said work pursuant to the order of appellant's boiler superintendent, one Thornburg, to whose order appellee, under his contract with appellant, was bound to conform, and was conforming at the time of his injury. It is alleged that appellant and said Thornburg and a number of appellee's co-employés knew of said order, and had full knowledge of appellee's dangerous position while he was working in said fire box. It does not appear who turned the steam and hot water into the blow line, but it is alleged that the valve in the pipe leading to said furnace was "negligently, carelessly, and wrongfully left open by the defendant corporation, its employés, and the said Thornburg, without any knowledge or fault of the plaintiff, so that when the steam was turned into said blow line the full force thereof was negligently, carelessly, and wrongfully rushed and forced into the fire box, where plaintiff was then and there working, and upon and against his body, and that the said Thornburg failed, neglected, and omitted to keep said valves closed, and carelessly and negligently permitted the same to be left open by the employés of the defendant corporation, without any fault, knowledge, or notice on the part of the plaintiff." After alleging the nature of appellee's injuries, it is charged in said paragraph that all of such injuries were caused "by reason of the said carelessness, negligence, and acts and omissions of the defendant corporation, through its employés, agents, and servants, and through the said negligent and careless acts and omissions of the said Thornburg."

Counsel for appellee do not claim that the paragraph of complaint in question states facts sufficient to create a liability at common law, but they claim that said paragraph states a cause of action under the employers' liability act (section 7083 et seq., Burns' Ann. St. 1901). Appellant's counsel, on the other hand, limit their argument as to said paragraph to a discussion as to whether the facts therein alleged bring the case within the terms of said act. In view of the manner in which the case has been presented, we shall assume that the sufficiency of the paragraph is to be judged by the standard indicated.

The particular contention of counsel for appellee is that a cause of action is stated in said paragraph under the second subdivision of the first section of said act. The portions of said section thus brought into review are as follows: "That every railroad or other corporation, except municipal, operating in this state, shall be liable in damages for personal injury suffered by any employé while in its service the employé so injured being in the exercise of due care and diligence, in the following cases: * * * Second. When such injury resulted from the negligence of any person in the service of such corporation, to whose order or direction the injured employé at the time of the injury was bound to conform, and did conform." It is to be observed that it is not alleged in said paragraph that it was negligent to give the order to make the repairs in said firebox. Construing the pleading most strongly against the pleader, we are warranted in indulging the assumption that the order was one which it was proper to give. We do not wish to be understood as intimating that it is required, under said subdivision, that the original order should have been negligently given. Our present purpose is to point out the fact that what is complained of occurred after the giving of said order; that is, leaving the valve in the pipe leading from the blow line to the fire box of boiler No. 7 open, and in failing to keep said valve closed. The charge that appellant and appellee's co-employés, other than Thornburg, were guilty of said omissions, indicates that the pleader did not have a very clear idea of the effect of the subdivision of the statute under consideration. The principal purpose of the employers' liability act was to put limitations on the co-servant rule, by providing for a liability upon the part of the master, in certain circumstances, for the negligence of certain classes of servants. Baltimore, etc., R. Co. v. Little, 149 Ind. 167, 48 N. E. 862; Thacker v. Chicago, etc., R. Co., 159 Ind. 82, 64 N. E. 605, 59 L. R. A. 792; Pittsburgh, etc., R. Co. v. Gipe, 160 Ind. 360, 65 N. E. 1034. It is clear that the negligence which gives a cause of action under the second subdivision of the first section of the act is the negligence of the servant who had the authority to give the order or direction which the person complaining was pursuing at the time of the injury. But as the paragraph in question also alleges that Thornburg was negligent in the particulars mentioned, we need not discuss the effect of a charge that appellant and appellee's co-employés were also negligent.

The question arises, however, whether the paragraph in question is not insufficient for the reason that it fails to show that a duty devolved upon Thornburg to exercise care for the safety of appellee. In Faris v. Hoberg, 134 Ind. 269, 33 N. E. 1028, 39 Am. St. Rep. 261, this court, speaking by Hackney, J., said: "In every case involving actionable negligence, there are necessarily three elements essential to its existence: (1) The existence of a duty on the part of the defendant to protect the plaintiff from the injury of which he complains; (2) a failure by the defendant to perform that duty; (3) an injury to the plaintiff from such failure of the defendant. When these elements are brought together, they unitedly constitute actionable negligence. The absence of any one of these elements renders a complaint bad, or the evidence insufficient." See, also, Evansville, etc., R. Co. r. Griffin, 100 Ind. 221, 50 Am. Rep. 783; Lousville, etc., R. Co. v. Sandford, 117 Ind. 265, 19 N. E. 770; Daugherty v. Herzog, 145 Ind. 225, 44 N. E. 457, 32 L. R. A. 837, 57 Am. St. Rep. 204; American, etc., Co. v. Hullinger (on ehearing, Ind. Sup.) 69 N. E. 460; Black, aw & Prac. in Accident Cases, § 138. In a leading the characterization of an act or mission as negligent causes that word to ake on a technical significance, but such a harge will not supply averments of fact from hich the existence of a duty to exercise care s shown to have existed. It cannot be said o be a proposition of law that the giving of proper command by a superior servant in very instance imposes upon him the duty of rotecting the servant commanded while the tter is engaged in the execution of the order. See Southern Indiana R. Co. v. Martin, 60 Ind. 280, 66 N. E. 886. In respect to the eping of the valve in said individual line osed, there is no allegation that such was e duty of Thornburg under the terms or the actice of his employment. He was not the aster, and he was not, in the absence of ecial circumstances, called on to look after e details of the work. For the reason sugsted, the demurrer to said paragraph should ve been sustained.

We are not authorized to consider an aner to an interrogatory submitted to the ju- stating on what paragraph of the comint the verdict is based. Clear Creek one Co. v. Dearmin, 160 Ind. 162, 66 N. E.); Consolidated Stone Co. v. Morgan, 160 l. 241, 66 N. E. 696; Farmers' Ins. Co. v. avis (at this term) 70 N. E. 518; Salemdford Stone Co. v. Hilt, 26 Ind. App. 543, N. E. 97. It cannot be determined wheththe verdict of the jury was founded on the t paragraph of complaint, and therefore judgment must be reversed.

Appellant's counsel further contend that the second and third paragraphs of complaint are insufficient. The questions which are presented concerning these paragraphs are of a technical character, and will doubtless be obviated by amendment. In view of this, and of the further fact that the general principles governing the liability of the master to his servant are well settled, we have concluded that we are not warranted in prolonging this opinion to the extent necessary to pass upon said paragraphs.

Judgment reversed, with an instruction to the trial court to sustain the demurrer to the first paragraph of complaint, and to grant leave to the parties to reframe the issues.

(162 Ind. 542)

STATE v. HARRISON.

(Supreme Court of Indiana. April 29, 1904.)

INTOXICATING LIQUORS—PLACE OF SALE—GRANTING OF LICENSE—EFFECT.

1. Paved alleys, 16 feet wide, passing through the middle of a block, are not streets or highways, within Burns' Ann. St. 1901, § 7283d, prohibiting the sale of intoxicating liquors by virtue of a license in any room, unless it is arranged either with window or glass door, or so that the whole of it may be in view from the street or highway.

2. Under Burns' Ann. St. 1901, § 7283d, providing that any room where intoxicating liquors are sold by virtue of a license shall be so arranged that the whole of it may be in view from the street or highway, and providing for revoking of the license, as a part of the judgment of the court, on the second or third conviction for violation of this requirement, the granting of a license does not adjudicate that the room described in the application is located on a street.

Appeal from Circuit Court, Hamilton County; Jno. F. Neal, Judge.

James E. Harrison was tried and acquitted of selling intoxicating liquors in a room not located on a street or highway, and the state appeals. Appeal sustained.

Chas. W. Miller, L. G. Rothschild, C. C. Hadley, and W. C. Geake, for the State. Kane & Kane, Shirts & Fertig, and Baker & Daniels, for appellee.

GILLETT, C. J. This was a prosecution for a violation of section 4, Acts 1895, p. 248 (section 7283d, Burns' Ann. St. 1901). Appellee was tried and acquitted, and the state appeals, under section 1955, Burns' Ann. St. 1901. The questions reserved are based on the giving and the refusal of certain instructions. These instructions present the following questions: (1) Whether the room in which appellee was conducting the business of selling intoxicating liquor at retail under the license laws of this state was located upon a street or highway, within the meaning of section 7283d, supra; and (2) whether the order of the board of commissioners in issuing a license to sell intoxicating liquor in such room, the proceeding being regular on its face, is a defense to this prosecution.

We shall consider these questions in the order in which they are suggested.

1. The evidence shows the following state of facts: Block 15 of the city of Noblesville is bounded on the north by Connor street, on the east by Ninth street, on the south by Maple avenue, and on the west by Eighth street. All of said streets are 66 feet wide, except Maple avenue, which is 49½ feet wide. There are two ways, each 16½ feet wide, running at right angles through, and intersecting each other at the center of, said block. On the petition of the owners of the abutting property, the common council of said city designated said last-mentioned ways as Court street and O'Brien street, respectively. There are no sidewalks along said ways, but they are paved with brick; the improvement having been made upon proceedings had by said common council. Various kinds of business are conducted in the property abutting upon said paved ways. Whether such places of business face upon either of said ways does not appear. Said ways are open to and used by the public as public ways, both for travel in vehicles and on foot. The conditions indicated respecting said ways have existed since a time prior to the time that appellee applied for and received a license as hereinafter stated. In 1901 appellee erected a building at the southwest angle of said intersection, with a ground floor room having doors and windows facing upon each of said ways. The evidence further shows that appellee received a license in the year 1901 to sell intoxicating liquors in said room, that the proceeding to obtain such license was regular on its face, and that he made the sale in question during the time for which said license was granted. Section 7283d, supra, is as follows: "Any room where intoxicating liquors are sold by virtue of a license issued under the law of the state of Indiana, for the sale of spirituous, vinous, malt or other intoxicating liquors in less quantities than a quart at a time, with permission to drink the same upon the premises, shall be situated upon the ground floor or basement of the building where the same are sold, and in a room fronting the street or highway upon which such building is situated, and said room shall be so arranged, either with window or glass door, as that the whole of said room may be in view from the street or highway, and no blinds, screens or obstructions to the view shall be arranged, erected or placed so as to prevent the entire view of said room from the street or highway upon which the same is situated during such days and hours when the sales of such liquors are prohibited by law. Upon conviction for the violation of this or either of the foregoing sections of this act, the defendant shall be fined in any sum not less than $10 nor more than $100, to which may be added imprisonment in the county jail not exceeding ninety days and in case of the conviction for the second offense, either upon a plea of guilty or conviction upon trial thereof, in any circuit, superior, criminal, justice or police court of Indiana, as a part of the judgment, the court may make an order revoking the license of the person convicted, which said judgment shall have the effect to completely annul and set aside such license, and all privileges and rights under the same. And upon the third conviction or plea of guilty entered, the court rendering judgment thereon shall annul and set aside such license and all privileges and rights under the same." The term "highway" is generic, comprehending, in its broadest sense, every public way, from an alley to a railroad or a navigable river. It will not be contended, however, that the Legislature used said term in an unrestricted sense. The word "street" has been defined as "a public way or road, whether paved or unpaved, in a village, town or city, ordinarily including a sidewalk or sidewalks and a roadway, and having houses or town lots on one or both sides; a main way, in distinction from a lane or alley." Century Dictionary, tit. "Street." See Stroud's Judicial Dictionary, same title. The practice has grown up in the legislation of this state of referring to rural ways as highways, as distinguished from streets, the thoroughfares of cities and towns. Common Council v. Croas, 7 Ind. 9; City of Lafayette v. Jenners, 10 Ind. 70; Debolt v. Carter, 31 Ind. 355; Lake Shore, etc., R. Co. v. Town of Whiting (Ind. Sup.) 67 N. E. 933. Ways like those in question are too narrow to be used extensively by travelers in vehicles, and, if so used, they would be unsafe for persons on foot. Said ways answer the description of alleys in every particular in which they are described, and their character is shown by their relation to the streets surrounding said block. Elliott, Roads & Streets, § 23. We know judicially that alleys are almost wholly used for local convenience. They are not thoroughfares, and during Sundays and the late hours of the night—at times when the provisions of the statute might be efficacious to prevent unlawful sales of intoxicating liquors—the travel along such ways, for all ordinary purposes, is practically nil. As the title of the act of 1895 indicates, the purpose of the law was "to better regulate and restrict the sale" of intoxicating liquors. Section 4 of the enactment contains a number of regulations which are referable to such expressed purpose, and as their efficacy in cities and towns depends largely upon such places of business being located upon the general ways of travel therein—streets, in the ordinary sense of the term—the conclusion cannot be escaped that the word "street" was used in such sense in said section. It is clear that the action of the common council in designating the ways in question as streets did not constitute them such in fact.

2. The granting of a license to sell intoxicating liquors does not adjudicate that the

room described in the application was located upon a street. Under the law the question of the place is not one which the board is called on to adjudicate upon, although it should, of course, refuse to grant a license to sell at a place not located upon a street or a highway, as the issuing of such a license would not protect the applicant, and as no use could be made of it except to violate the law. If, however, a license issues, the applicant is bound to take notice of the limitations upon his right which said section 4 contains. That section provides that "any room where intoxicating liquors are sold by virtue of a license issued under the law of the state of Indiana * * * shall be so arranged * * * that the whole of said room may be in view from the street or highway upon which the same is situated. * * * Upon conviction for a violation of this or either of the foregoing sections of this act, the defendant shall be fined," etc. In the latter part of the section, provision is made for the revoking of the license, as a part of the judgment of the court, upon a second or a third conviction. Under said section the offense consists in the failure to arrange a room "where intoxicating liquors are sold by virtue of a license" so that the whole of the room may be in view of the street or highway upon which the room is situated. In Hipes v. State, 18 Ind. App. 426, 48 N. E. 12, it was said: "The offense is not complete when a person has received his license to sell liquor, and has opened a room for that purpose not located as the law provides. The statute is intended to prevent the sale of liquors in a room not located as provided by statute. * * * The purpose of this statute is to regulate the sale of intoxicating liquor, and, although a person may hold a license to sell, and have a stock of liquors in a room not located as required, yet until he makes a sale in such room he has not violated the statute." The case from which we just quoted was cited by this court as authority upon the construction of said section 4 in Gates v. Haw, 150 Ind. 370, 50 N. E. 299. It is as definitely required, under the language of said section, that there should have been a license granted to sell in a particular room, as it is that there should have been a sale therein, to constitute the keeping of such room in a manner contrary to the provisions of the section an offense. As said section only undertakes to regulate the conduct of the business of licensed vendors of intoxicants, it follows that a holding that the granting of a license constitutes an adjudication as to the proper location of the room would work a destruction of an important part of the section, and, further, to so hold would require us to discard the provisions of said statute relative to the revoking of the license as a part of the punishment. A license is not a contract. It is a mere permission, which may not only be changed or annulled by statute, but can only be enjoyed upon the terms prescribed by the lawmaking power. State v. Gerhardt, 145 Ind. 439, 44 N. E. 469, 33 L. R. A. 313. When so understood, there is no incongruity in the holding that a license to sell intoxicating liquors at a particular place cannot be exercised except as the location of the place complies with the requirement of law. The licensee must take notice that such requirement is a factor that the granting of the license has in no wise canceled.

The appeal of the state is sustained.

(162 Ind. 548)

SCOTT et ux. v. HAYES et al.

(Supreme Court of Indiana. April 29, 1904.)

MUNICIPAL CORPORATIONS — STREET IMPROVEMENT BONDS—ACTION BY OWNERS—RIGHT TO SUE—BARRETT LAW—PLEADING AND PROOF—INTEREST—ATTORNEY'S FEE.

1. Owners of street improvement bonds issued under the Barrett law (Burns' Ann. St. 1894, § 4296) are by sections 4290 and 4294 expressly authorized to sue thereon, and to enforce collection by foreclosure or otherwise.

2. No resolution of the city council is necessary to authorize the owners of street improvement bonds issued under the Barrett law (Burns' Ann. St. 1894, § 4296) to bring an action to enforce the lien of the assessments.

3. A demand on the city issuing street improvement bonds under the Barrett law (Burns' Ann. St. 1894, § 4296), by the owners, to pay or to collect the bonds, is not necessary, before the owners are entitled to maintain a suit to enforce the lien of the assessments.

4. Prior to 1893 the benefit of the Barrett law (Burns' Ann. St. 1894, § 4296) was limited by section 4294 to assessments exceeding the sum of $50. Acts 1893, p. 283, c. 123 (Burns' Ann. St. 1894, § 4295), extended the benefits to lot owners whose assessment on any one lot was $50 or less, "provided they shall execute the stipulation waiving objections on account of illegality or irregularities in the proceedings of assessment as now required by law in cases of assessments exceeding $50." Section 4294 required the waiver of objections, and an agreement to pay the assessments. *Held*, that an objection that section 4295 so changed the law as not to require an agreement to pay is untenable.

5. No proof of an averment in a complaint by owners of street improvement bonds issued under the Barrett law (Burns' Ann. St. 1894, § 4296) that the city issuing the bonds failed and refused to pay the amount of assessments is necessary, in an action to enforce the lien of the assessments.

6. Where an ordinance, in directing the issuance of street improvement bonds under the Barrett law (Burns' Ann. St. 1894, § 4296), named the rate of interest they were to bear, there was a sufficient compliance with section 4294, authorizing the city council to fix the rate of interest.

7. Under the Barrett law (Burns' Ann. St. 1894, §§ 4294, 4297), authorizing the allowance of an attorney's fee in an action to enforce the lien of assessments for street improvements, an attorney's fee is properly included in the judgment.

Appeal from Superior Court, Howard County; Hiram Brownlee, Judge.

Action by William J. Hayes and others against Enos A. Scott and wife. From a judgment for plaintiffs, defendants appeal. Transferred from the Appellate Court under Burns' Ann. St. 1901, § 1337u. Affirmed.

Bell & Purdum and B. C. Moon, for appellants. C. O. Willits and W. R. Voorhis, for appellees.

DOWLING, J. The appellees were the owners of certain street improvement bonds issued by the city of Kokomo under section 4296, Burns' Ann. St. 1894, part of the act generally known as the "Barrett Law," and the amendments thereof for the purpose of anticipating the collection of assessments. The appellant owned six lots bordering upon the part of the street improved, and, in consideration of the privilege of paying his assessment in 10 annual installments, he executed the agreement provided for by the statute; waiving all illegality and irregularity in the proceedings, and expressly promising to pay the sum of the assessments. He failed to make such payments, and this action was brought by the appellee to enforce the lien of the assessment against the said lots, and to recover a personal judgment against the appellant for any deficiency in case the lots did not sell for enough to pay the amount of the assessment, interest, attorney's fees, and costs. A demurrer to the complaint was overruled. The defendants, Scott and wife, filed an answer in three paragraphs, the first of which was a general denial, the second a plea of payment, and the third addressed to so much of the complaint only as sought the recovery of attorney's fees and penalties; denying that the defendants agreed to pay such fees and penalties, and averring that they promised to pay the assessments with interest and nothing more. The defendant Enos A. Scott filed a separate answer of want of consideration for his promise to pay the assessments. Replies in denial. Trial by the court, and finding for the plaintiff. Motion by appellant Enos A. Scott for a new trial, overruled. Judgment on finding. Separate motions to modify the judgment by striking out each part thereof declaring a personal liability of Enos A. Scott for the assessment, the interest, and the attorney's fees. These motions were overruled. Error is assigned upon all these rulings.

The first objection taken to the complaint is that no default of the city of Kokomo in collecting the assessments is averred; and, second, that it does not appear that a resolution was passed by the common council authorizing the plaintiff to bring this action.

The bonds in question were issued under section 4296, Burns' Ann. St. 1894, for the purpose of anticipating the collection of the assessments for the improvement. Sections 4290 and 4294 authorized the owner of such bonds to sue upon the same, and to enforce their collection by foreclosure or otherwise. No resolution of the council was necessary, nor was it requisite, before suit, that a demand should be made upon the city to pay or to collect such bonds. Marten v. Wills, [illegible] Ind. 153, 60 N. E. 1021. Section 4297, [illegible]s' Ann. St. 1894, provides that the certificates and bonds therein named shall transfer to the contractor and his assigns all the right and interest of such city or town in and to every such assessment, and the lien thereby created against the property of such owners assessed as shall avail themselves of the provisions of the act to have their assessments paid in installments. It further declares that such certificates or bonds shall authorize such contractor and his assigns to receive, sue for, and collect every such assessment embraced in any such certificate or bond by or through any of the methods provided by law for the collection of assessments for local improvements, including the provisions of the statute under consideration. The section contains the further provision that if the city or town shall fail, neglect, or refuse to pay said certificates or bonds, or to promptly collect any of such assessments when due, the owner of any of such certificates or bonds may proceed in his own name to collect such assessment, and foreclose the lien thereof in any court of competent jurisdiction, and that he shall recover, in addition to the amount of such bonds or certificates and the interest thereon, a reasonable attorney's fee, together with the costs of such suit. It would seem that this section applies more particularly to cases where the certificates or bonds are issued directly to the contractor; but, if it can be construed, in connection with the other sections of the statute, to include a case where the bonds are issued by the city, under section 4296, in anticipation of the collection of the assessments, then it expressly authorizes the owner of the bonds to sue in his own name in any court of competent jurisdiction, and the averment of the complaint that the city of Kokomo "failed and refused to pay said past-due bonds and interest coupons" brought the claim of the plaintiff within the very terms of this section.

The next point made by counsel for appellant is that by the amendment of March 3, 1893 (Acts 1893, p. 283, c. 123, § 1; Burns' Ann. St. 1894, § 4295), the form of the written stipulation waiving objections to the proceedings on account of irregularity or illegality was so changed that it was not required to contain a promise to pay the assessments, and therefore that so much of the agreement signed by the appellant, Scott, as amounted to a promise to pay the assessment, was not authorized by law, and was void for want of consideration. Section 2 of the act of March 6, 1891 (Acts 1891, p. 323, c. 118; Burns' Ann. St. 1894, § 4294), contained this provision: "Should any one of such assessments exceed the sum of fifty dollars, then if the owner of the lot or parcel of land against which said assessment is made may, if he within two weeks after the making of such assessment shall promise and agree in writing * * * in consideration of the right to pay his or their assessment or respective assessments in installments that they will not make any objections to illegality or irregularity as to their respective assessments, and will pay the same, with interest thereon at the rate of not exceeding six per centum per annum as shall by ordinance or resolution of the common council of such city * * * be prescribed and required, he or they shall have the benefit of paying said assessments in ten annual installments as hereinafter provided." (Sic.) This part of section 2 was extended March 8, 1893 (Acts 1893, p. 288, c. 123; Burns' Ann. St. 1894, § 4295), as follows: "Section 1. That the privilege now granted by law to persons assessed for the construction of street or alley improvements, or sewers, to pay the same in ten years in installments, if such assessment exceed fifty dollars upon any one lot shall be extended to all persons without regard to the sum assessed: provided they shall execute the stipulation waiving objections on account of illegality or irregularities in the proceedings of assessment, as now required by law in cases of assessments exceeding fifty dollars." The sole and evident purpose of the later act was to extend the benefit of the former statute to lot owners whose assessment upon any one lot was $50 or less. There was no intention to change the conditions on which the privilege of paying the assessment in 10 annual installments depended. The reference to "the stipulation waiving objections on account of illegality or irregularities in the proceedings" was made only for the identification of that part of the section amended. The "stipulation waiving illegality or irregularities in the proceedings required by law" expressly provided, as one of its conditions, that the lot owner should promise to pay the assessment; and the privilege of paying in 10 annual installments was extended to all persons, without regard to the sum assessed, upon the same terms as that privilege was previously offered to lot owners whose assessment exceeded $50 on a lot.

In support of the motion for a new trial, counsel say that there was no proof that the city failed or refused to pay the amount of the assessments. None was required. The failure of the city to pay was not a condition precedent, but constituted a situation in which a suit would be necessary. Payment was a defense. The allegation was strictly formal, and it sufficiently appeared from the proceedings that the assessments had not been paid. Lewis v. Albertson, 23 Ind. App. 147, 53 N. E. 1071.

Another point made by counsel is that the court erred in allowing interest on the assessment. They contend that as the common council did not fix a rate of interest, as it was authorized to do by section 4294, Burns' Ann. St. 1894, no interest was chargeable upon the assessments. But by the ordinance directing the issuing of the improvement bonds, 6 per cent. per annum was named as the rate of interest they were to bear. This was a compliance with the statute requiring the common council to establish the rate on all unpaid installments. When the instrument of waiver is filed, and 10 years' time is given for the payment of the assessment, the bonds are the evidence of the claim against the lots, and of the rate of interest to be paid, if any has been fixed. Burns' Ann. St. 1894, § 4294.

The last point made is that an attorney's fee was improperly included in the judgment. Such fee was authorized by sections 4294, 4297, Burns' Ann. St. 1894. That part of these sections does not seem to have been repealed by any later acts. As soon as the waiver was signed and delivered, the city had the right to issue the improvement bonds. The bonds, when issued, transferred to the owner all rights of the city under the same, and among these was the right to recover a reasonable attorney's fee in an action to enforce the lien of the assessments. Burns' Ann. St. 1894, §§ 4294, 4296, 4297; Indiana Bond Company v. Jameson, 24 Ind. App. 8, 11, 56 N. E. 37; Pittsburgh, etc., Co. v. Fish, 158 Ind. 525, 529, 63 N. E. 454.

The statute is to be read and treated as a whole, and its various sections are to be so construed, if possible, that all may stand. The object of the law was to enable cities and towns to make necessary improvements of their public streets and alleys; to charge the property abutting thereon with the cost of such improvements; to enable lot owners to pay in 10 annual installments, if they wished to do so, and complied with the conditions of the statute; to secure the payment of the cost of the improvements, first, from the abutting property, and, second, from the owner who signed the waiver and promised to pay the same; and in the event of a failure of the lot owner to pay his proportionate share of the cost of the improvement, and the prosecution of a suit to collect the claim and enforce the lien, to subject the delinquent lot owner to all the expenses of such delay and legal proceedings, including interest and a reasonable attorney's fee. Porter v. City of Tipton, 141 Ind. 347, 40 N. E. 802.

We find no error in the record, and we think the judgment of the court is just and equitable in every respect. Judgment affirmed.

(162 Ind. 530)

TOMLINSON v. TOMLINSON.

(Supreme Court of Indiana. April 26, 1904.)

VENDOR AND PURCHASER — CONVEYANCE IN CONSIDERATION OF SUPPORT — FRAUD — SUIT FOR RECONVEYANCE — COMPLAINT — ALLEGATIONS — SUFFICIENCY — NEW TRIAL AS OF RIGHT.

1. In a suit to set aside a conveyance of land made in consideration of support for life, the complaint alleged that plaintiff had for several years been sick, and easily susceptible to persuasions of others, and that defendant, knowing her enfeebled condition, and his great influence

over her, and corruptly intending to defraud her, proposed to support her for life in consideration of a conveyance, and that she was overcome by such persuasions, and believed that his promises would be kept. *Held*, that the allegations of the complaint relative to the fraud were sufficient.

2. Where, in a suit to set aside a conveyance of land made in consideration of plaintiff's future support, the complaint alleged that; after the conveyance, plaintiff went to live with defendant, and that soon thereafter defendant, by a course of inhuman treatment, drove plaintiff from the house, the allegations as to defendant's conduct sufficiently showed such an abandonment of his contract, as against an assault on the complaint made for the first time on appeal, as to have rendered an allegation of a demand for performance unnecessary.

3. A complaint in a suit to set aside a conveyance made in consideration of future support by defendant, on the ground that defendant had refused to perform his contract, was insufficient, where it alleged neither a re-entry, nor demand for possession.

4. The unsuccessful party in a suit to annul a conveyance and revest title in the owner, who had been induced to part with it by imposition and fraud, is entitled to a new trial, under Burns' Ann. St. 1901, § 1076, relative to ejectment, and giving the unsuccessful party a new trial as a matter of right.

5. Burns' Ann. St. 1901, § 1076, relative to ejectment, and giving the unsuccessful party a new trial as a matter of right, is mandatory, and, in a case within the statute, the court has no discretion whatever.

Appeal from Circuit Court, Wells County; E. C. Vaughn, Judge.

Suit by Eliza Tomlinson against William H. Tomlinson. From a judgment in favor of plaintiff, defendant appealed. Transferred from the Appellate Court under section 1337u, Burns' Ann. St. 1901. Reversed.

John Q. Cline and W. H. Eichhorn, for appellant. Watkins & Morgan and Daily, Simmons & Daily, for appellee.

HADLEY, J. Appellee sued appellant, who is her son, to annul a deed of conveyance of real estate, and to quiet her title. The complaint is in a single paragraph, and as nearly as we are able to make out, in substance avers that the plaintiff, being the owner in fee of certain lands, for several years had been sick and enfeebled in body and mind, and thereby easily susceptible to the influence and persuasions of others, and the defendant, knowing the enfeebled condition of his mother, and the great influence he had over her, as her son, corruptly intending to defraud her out of her farm, invited her to come and live and make her home with him, and proposed to and promised her, if she would convey to him 40 acres of land, he would support and maintain her, in sickness and in health, the remainder of her natural life. The plaintiff, being overcome by the persuasions and importunities of the defendant, and believing his promises would be kept, and that he would give her a comfortable home with him and supply all her personal wants, and relying thereon, did, in consideration thereof, execute to the defendant a deed conveying to him a certain described 40 acres of land. The only consideration for the deed was defendant's promise to provide for the plaintiff during the remainder of her life. After the conveyance, plaintiff went to live with the defendant on the farm conveyed in pursuance of the agreement, and soon thereafter the defendant, by a course of inhuman and unnatural treatment, drove the plaintiff from his house. Wherefore she asks that the deed be set aside, and her title quieted to said real estate. Appellant demurred to the complaint, but pending the demurrer, and without a decision thereon, filed his answer and went to trial. There was a finding for appellee, and, over appellant's motion for a venire de novo and a new trial, judgment was rendered against him.

1. It is assigned here as independent error that the complaint does not state facts sufficient to constitute a cause of action. The points made against the complaint are (1) that the acts constituting the fraud and undue influence are not sufficiently stated; (2) that no demand for performance, and (3) no re-entry for condition broken, is averred. A first assault upon a complaint in this court will be successful when it appears that the pleading is destitute of averment of some fact which is absolutely necessary to support the judgment. Shoemaker v. Williamson, 156 Ind. 384, 59 N. E. 1051; Taylor v. Johnson, 113 Ind. 164, 15 N. E. 238. In this complaint the allegations of fraud are general, and there is no averment of a demand for performance or of a re-entry upon the premises before the action was commenced. Ordinarily, in a case like this, both these absent averments are essential to a good complaint. With respect to the demand for performance, see Schuff v. Ransom, 79 Ind. 458; Cory v. Cory, 86 Ind. 567, 573; Lindsey v. Lindsey, 45 Ind. 552, 567. But such a demand may be dispensed with when it is made to appear that the defendant has renounced his contract, and given the plaintiff notice of his refusal to perform. It is sufficiently shown by a refusal that a demand would be unavailing, and the law does not require a useless thing. Richter v. Richter, 111 Ind. 456, 461, 12 N. E. 698; Burns v. Fox, 113 Ind. 205, 14 N. E. 541; Harshman v. Mitchell, 117 Ind. 312, 20 N. E. 228; Denlar v. Hile, 123 Ind. 68, 24 N. E. 170; Horner v. Clark, 27 Ind. App. 6, 13, 60 N. E. 732. The allegations of the complaint relating to imposition and fraud, though unskillfully pleaded, are sufficient, within the doctrine laid down in the very similar case of Sherrin v. Flinn, 155 Ind. 422, 58 N. E. 549; and the allegation that the defendant, by a course of inhuman and unnatural treatment, drove the plaintiff from his house, though general and in the nature of a conclusion, as against an assault upon the complaint for the first time in this court, we think, is sufficient to charge the defendant with an abandonment of his contract. He had contracted to maintain and keep his mother at his house during the remainder of her life, and to drive her away, which implies coercion, is wholly

4. See New Trial, vol. 37, Cent. Dig. § 351.

inconsistent with intended performance. But we know of no case wherein it has been held that an action to enforce a forfeiture for breach of a condition subsequent may be maintained without a re-entry upon the premises, or a demand for possession, which, under our present law, is its equivalent, has been first made and refused. Clark v. Holton, 57 Ind. 564; Cory v. Cory, 86 Ind. 567, 578. A breach does not of itself devest the grantee's title. The grantor may prefer his damages, rather than a restoration of his title, and, if he elects the latter remedy, it has been uniformly held he must signify it by a previous re-entry, or by that which is tantamount thereto. Preston v. Bosworth, 153 Ind. 458, 55 N. E. 224, 74 Am. St. Rep. 313, and cases cited. The total absence of averment of re-entry or of previous demand for possession renders the complaint inadequate to support the judgment, and it is therefore null.

2. On December 30, 1902, the court having overruled appellant's motion for a venire de novo and for a new trial for cause, final judgment was thereupon rendered annulling the plaintiff's deed, and quieting her title to the real estate in controversy. On February 27, 1903, appellant filed his statutory bond, which was approved by the court, and thereupon moved for a new trial as of right, under section 1076, Burns' Ann. St. 1901. The motion was overruled, and the new trial as of right denied, to which an exception was properly reserved. This was error. The action is not an ordinary one to set aside a fraudulent conveyance for the benefit of creditors, but one to annul a conveyance and revest the title in an owner who had been induced to part with it by imposition and fraud. The title was necessarily adjudicated, and the case brought within the operation of said section 1076. McKittrick v. Glenn, 116 Ind. 27, 18 N. E. 388; Warburton v. Crouch, 108 Ind. 83, 8 N. E. 634; College v. Wilkinson, 89 Ind. 23. The statute providing for a new trial as a matter of right is mandatory, and in a proper case the court has no discretion. Anderson v. Anderson, 128 Ind. 254, 27 N. E. 724.

Judgment reversed and cause remanded, with leave to amend the complaint.

(162 Ind. 494)

HALL et al. v. BREYFOGLE.

(Supreme Court of Indiana. April 19, 1904.)

DEDICATION — DEFECTIVE INSTRUMENT—ADOPTION BY PROPRIETORS — ACCEPTANCE—MANNER—IMPLIED ACCEPTANCE—RIGHTS OF PUBLIC—RIGHTS OF PROPRIETORS—STREETS—OBSTRUCTIONS—NUISANCES—OPENING—INJUNCTION—GROUNDS.

1. Under Burns' Ann. St. 1901, § 4412, providing that a donation noted as such on the plat of the town wherein such donation may have been made shall be considered a general warranty to the donee for the purposes intended by the donor, the making of a plat of a town, or of an addition thereto, upon which streets, alleys, lots, and blocks are noted as such, and the recording of such plat and sale of lots as designated thereon, operates as an irrevocable dedication to the public of all streets and alleys so marked on such plat, so far as purchasers of lots are concerned.

2. The acts of proprietors in recognizing an unauthorized and invalid plat recorded on the proper public record, and selling lots or blocks in reference thereto, and as marked thereon, is an adoption of such plat so far as to constitute a dedication to the public of the streets and alleys indicated thereon, which is effectual as to lot purchasers.

3. Acceptance by the public of a dedication may be manifested by some formal act of the public authorities, or implied from their improving or repairing the property dedicated, or from any other act with respect to such property that clearly indicates an assumption of jurisdiction and dominion over the same.

4. The failure of a municipal corporation to open an improved part of a new street does not operate as a rejection of the part not opened or improved.

5. Since a dedication is to the public, and not to the municipality, which latter holds merely as a trustee, and cannot surrender the grant except as provided by statute, nor lose the same by the negligence of its officers, title by prescription cannot be acquired by adverse possession of land dedicated to the public for streets and alleys, in the laying off or platting of a town or addition.

6. A material obstruction to a public street is per se a public nuisance, and, as against the author, may be abated at any time.

7. The purchaser of a lot in a platted district acquires a vested right in the easement of the streets, not only in front of his purchase, but in all the streets of the platted district designated as such on the plat, and the right to have them all kept open.

8. Acts of a municipality in extending its corporate limits to embrace an addition platted in due form, designated as an addition to the town, and acknowledged before the recorder, and in causing a sidewalk to be improved for the whole length of a street in such addition, and in keeping certain streets in repair for a number of years, and in directing the opening and improvement of three streets, sufficiently showed an acceptance of the dedication of the addition.

9. Where a plat, though irregular and void as to the landowners, was, after being recorded, adopted by them, every part and portion of the land platted being sold and conveyed by them to other parties according to the plat, and not according to any governmental subdivision, a purchaser of particular lots designated on such plat could not both claim title to the center of streets designated as such in the plat and at the same time deny that they were streets.

10. Where a dedication has been accepted by a town on behalf of the public by assumption of jurisdiction and acts of dominion, it may proceed with the occupation and use thereof as public convenience requires.

11. An allegation in a complaint that defendant town, if not restrained, will collect in side ditches a large amount of storm water, and cast the same in a flood on plaintiff's premises, is not ground for enjoining the town from opening streets under an ordinance, as it will be presumed that the officers, in carrying out the improvement, will do their duty, and perform the work in a skillful manner, so as not to injure plaintiff's premises.

Appeal from Circuit Court, Lake County; A. C. Capron, Special Judge.

Action by Louis V. Breyfogle against Thomas H. Hall and others. From a judgment for plaintiff, defendants appeal. Reversed.

¶ 2. See Dedication, vol. 15, Cent. Dig. § 46.

Fancher & Pattee, for appellants. A. J. Bruce and J. Frank Meeker, for appellee.

HADLEY, J. Injunction to restrain appellant town from opening and improving certain alleged streets, and to prevent the flooding of appellee's land with storm water. The facts shown exclusively by public records and uncontradicted are these: In 1855 one Smith, being the owner of certain lands adjacent to the town of Crown Point, platted the same into lots of 10 acres each, which he designated and recorded in the recorder's office of Lake county as "Smith's Addition of Outlots to the Town of Crown Point." Said lots were numbered from 1 to 16, inclusive. November 16, 1870, John M. Scott was the owner by mesne conveyances from Smith of all that part of said outlot 2 lying east of the Centerville road, and the north half of said outlot 3, and Mary Boyd a like owner from Smith of the south half of said outlot 3. On said November 16, 1870, William M. Boyd, husband of Mary Boyd, acknowledged before the recorder of the county a plat of all of said outlot 3 and all of 2 lying east of the Centerville road; said plat covering the property (but not so stated) then owned by John M. Scott and Mary Boyd, which plat was designated as "Summit Addition to the Town of Crown Point," and was marked into numbered and dimensioned lots, blocks, and streets as shown by the following diagram:

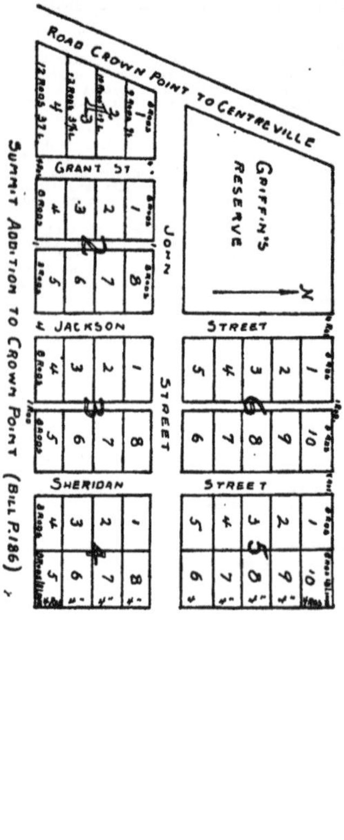

Said plat was placed of record in the recorder's office of the county. That noted on the plat as Griffin's Reserve, and blocks 1, 2, 5, and 6, was the land owned by Scott, and that noted as blocks 3 and 4 was that owned by Mary Boyd. After the making and recording of said last-named plat, to wit, June 15, 1881, Mary Boyd and husband conveyed said blocks 3 and 4 to one Andrews by warranty deed describing the same as follows: "The south half of lot 3 in Smith's Addition of Outlots to the Town of Crown Point, which is known as blocks 3 and 4 in Summit Addition to the Town of Crown Point." These two blocks are now owned by the Chicago & Erie Railroad Company, it deriving title by mesne conveyances from Andrews by same description. After the recording of the plat of Summit Addition, to wit, August 27, 1886, John M. Scott conveyed by mortgage a part of his lands covered by said plat, describing the same as follows: "All of blocks 1 and 2; all of block 5, except lots 5 and 6; and all of block 6 except that part deeded to the Chicago & Atlantic Railroad Company for right of way. All as marked and laid down on the recorded plat of Summit Addition to the Town of Crown Point." The mortgage was foreclosed, and the premises sold by the sheriff under same description, and on April 12, 1898, the appellee accepted the sheriff's deed conveying to him said premises under the identical description. Also, on September 20, 1894, appellee purchased and accepted by mesne conveyance from Scott another portion of said premises under the following description: "Griffin's Reserve, as marked and laid down on the recorded plat of Summit Addition to the Town of Crown Point," and on January 11, 1898, by a like mesne conveyance from Scott, the remainder of the premises in controversy, under the following description: "Lots numbered 5 and 6, in block 5, in Summit Addition to Crown Point in Lake County, Indiana." The platted territory was taken up in the tax duplicate, and taxed as lots and blocks in Summit Addition. Summit Addition, at some indefinite time, was embraced within the corporation limits of the town of Crown Point. Grant street, as noted, was but a northern extension of a street of that name running through the town, and on October 1, 1883, the trustees of the town by proper ordinance caused an improvement at the expense of the abutting property owners of the east sidewalk of Grant street from Foote to the north line of John street, which improvement extended the full length of Grant street in Summit Addition; and the entire length of Grant street, and that part of John street, in Summit Addition, lying west of Grant street, have been worked by the town for an indefinite period, not less than two years before the commencement of this suit. John street east of Grant street, and all of Jackson and Sheridan streets in Summit Addition, have been inclosed and used by appellee and his grantors for 30 years. On July 8, 1902, the trustees of the town passed an ordinance for the opening and improvement of the streets in Summit Addition, for public use and convenience, to the full width as marked and laid down in the recorded plat thereof, and directing the marshal to cause all obstructions to be removed, and said streets opened and put in condition for public use as fixed and shown by said recorded plat. On October 7, 1902, the town marshal served written notice upon appellee that he would on October 9th, by order of the trustees, open John street the full length through Summit and Railroad Addition, and did about the time indicated enter and was engaged in the construction of a center grade and side ditches, when stopped by a restraining order issued upon appellee's complaint filed October 13, 1902. The storm water that may be collected in the side ditches of streets of said town and in those to be constructed in Summit Addition can be successfully and conveniently dispatched by the construction of an adequate ditch eastwardly along the south side of John street to the intersection of a public drain in Indiana avenue.

These facts, shown by the pleadings and uncontradicted record evidence, present for decision the single question: Is appellee entitled thereunder to injunction against appellant town preventing it from opening and improving for public use the streets in Summit Addition? Certain fundamental and well settled principles must be given effect.

1. The making of a plat of a town, or of an addition thereto, upon which streets, alleys, lots, and blocks are noted as such, and the recording of such plat, and sale of lots as designated thereon, operates as an irrevocable dedication to the public of all streets and alleys so marked on such plat so far as purchasers of lots are concerned. Section 4412, Burns' Ann. St. 1901; Woodruff Place v. Raschig, 147 Ind. 517, 46 N. E. 990; Rhodes v. Brightwood, 145 Ind. 21, 43 N. E. 942; Fowler v. Linguist, 138 Ind. 566, 37 N. E. 792; Wolfe v. Sullivan, 133 Ind. 331, 32 N. E. 1017; Miller v. Indianapolis, 123 Ind. 196, 24 N. E. 228.

2. The acts of proprietors in recognizing an unauthorized and invalid plat, recorded upon the proper public record, and selling lots or blocks in reference thereto and as marked thereon, is an adoption of such plat so far as to constitute a dedication to the public of the streets and alleys indicated thereon, which is effectual as to lot purchasers. Town of Woodruff v. Raschig, 147 Ind. 517, 46 N. E. 990; Miller v. Indianapolis, 123 Ind. 196, 24 N. E. 228; Indianapolis v. Kingsbury, 101 Ind. 200, 51 Am. Rep. 749; Thompson v. Maloney (Ill.) 65 N. E. 236, 239; Russell v. City of Lincoln (Ill.) 65 N. E. 1083.

3. Acceptance by the public of a dedication may be manifested by some formal act of the public authorities, or implied from the latter's improving or repairing the same, or from any other act with respect to the subject-matter that clearly indicates an assumption of jurisdiction and dominion over the same. Ross v. Thompson, 78 Ind. 90, 96; Summers v. State, 51 Ind. 201; Strunk v. Pritchett, 27 Ind. App. 582, 586, 61 N. E. 973; Elliott, Roads & Streets (2d Ed.) § 152. And the failure of a municipal corporation to open and improve part of a new street does not operate as a rejection of the part not opened or improved. Sims v. Frankfort, 79 Ind. 456; 9 Am. & Eng. Ency. of Law (2d Ed.) pp. 50, 56, and authorities cited.

4. Title by prescription cannot be acquired by adverse possession of land dedicated to the public for streets and alleys in the laying off or the platting of a town or an addition thereto. Such a dedication is to the public, and not to the municipality. The latter holds as trustee, and cannot surrender the grant, except as the statute provides, nor lose the same by the negligence or laches of its officers. Sims v. Frankfort, 79 Ind. 446; Collett v. Board, 119 Ind. 27, 32, 21 N. E. 329, 4 L. R. A. 321; Wolfe v. Sullivan, 133 Ind. 331, 334, 32 N. E. 1017; Cheek v. Aurora, 92 Ind. 107.

5. A material obstruction to a public street is per se a public nuisance, and as against the author may be abated at any time. Valparaiso v. Bozarth, 153 Ind. 536, 55 N. E. 439, 47 L. R. A. 487, and cases cited.

6. The purchaser of a lot in a platted district acquires a vested right in the easement of the streets, not only in the street in front of his purchase, but in all the streets of the platted district designated as such on the plat, and the right to have them all kept open. Wolfe v. Sullivan, 133 Ind. 331, 334, 32 N. E. 1017; Indianapolis v. Kingsbury, 101 Ind. 200, 51 Am. Rep. 749, and cases collected on page 212. Giving force to these principles, a solution of the question is not difficult. The plat of Summit Addition was in due form. It was marked into regular lots and blocks. The lots and blocks were numbered in the usual consecutive order, and dimensioned, and each block was bounded by a regular, narrow strip of ground, marked respectively, "John Street," "Grant Street," "Jackson Street," and "Sheridan Street." It was acknowledged before the recorder, and in terms announced that it was a plat of an addition to the town of Crown Point. As an evidence of approval of the addition and of acceptance of the dedication, the town extended its corporation limits to embrace Summit Addition, thus assuming jurisdiction over the territory and all its highways; not only over those established, but over those granted and not opened. Railway Company v. Town of Whiting (Ind. Sup.; last term) 67 N. E. 933. And in 1883, more than 10 years before appellee acquired any interest in the territory, the town, by ordinance and due process of law, caused the east sidewalk of Grant street to be improved for its full

length in Summit Addition (the street crossings at the expense of the town), and for an indefinite number of years the town authorities worked and kept in repair at public expense all of Grant street, and all that part of John street lying west of Grant. The evidence also shows that appellee complained to the officers of the imperfect manner in which such repairs were kept up. It also appears that three months before this suit was commenced the town by ordinance directed its marshal to open and improve all of John street remaining unimproved, together with Jackson and Sheridan streets, and had about completed the grading of John street when this suit was commenced. Under the authorities referred to, these acts of jurisdiction and dominion sufficiently show an acceptance by the public.

There is still another reason equally as conclusive against appellee's right to recover. The plat, though irregular and void as to the landowners, was, after being recorded, adopted by them, and every part and parcel of the land platted was sold and conveyed by them to other parties according to the plat, and not according to any governmental subdivision. Every vestige of title appellee has in the district is derived through, and by the terms of, the plat. Every purchase, and every deed he has received, conveys to him particular lots or squares of land of fixed and certain dimensions, as marked and laid down on the recorded plat of Summit Addition. He has no deed which purports to convey to him any right or title in the strips called streets, and, unless they are streets, dedicated as such by the proprietors, he has no title or interest in them, and hence no standing in court to resist their invasion. It is only upon the assumption that the strips are public streets, impliedly granted by the owners, as appurtenances to the lots, that appellee may claim to the center of them. To deny them being streets is to repudiate his title in them, and to claim title is to assert that they are public streets.

The fact that parts of all the streets but Grant have been inclosed and occupied by appellee and his grantors for 30 years does not strengthen the former's claim. As we have seen, the dedication or grant was to the public, and, appellee being a citizen, and member of the public, it cannot be said that his possession was inconsistent with the possession of the public, nor that the lapse of time, under the facts of this case, ripened into a title. As a remote grantee of part of the lots in Summit Addition, appellee is the owner in fee to the center of the streets in front of his lots, that portion within the street limits being subject to the superior right of the public to use it as a highway. In this use appellee has a right in common with all the other owners of lots in the addition, and he can no more deprive them of their right in the street than they can deprive him of his. Coburn v. New Telephone Co., 156 Ind. 90, 59 N. E. 324. It is shown that there are 16 lots in said addition, comprising all of blocks 3 and 4, and abutting on John, Jackson, and Sheridan streets, which are owned by another.

But we rest the decision upon broader grounds. The dedication having been accepted by the town of Crown Point on behalf of the public by assuming jurisdiction and acts of dominion over it, it may proceed with the occupation and use as public convenience requires. "Whenever a new town (or addition) is laid out, it is not expected that all the streets and parks will be needed by the public at once. Acceptance by use and improvement whenever the growth of the town demands it will be sufficient." 9 Am. & Eng. Ency. of Law (2d Ed.) p. 50, and authorities collated; Cason v. Lebanon, 153 Ind. 567, 55 N. E. 768.

The averments of the third paragraph of complaint that the town, if not restrained, will collect in side ditches a large amount of storm water, and cast the same in a flood on appellee's premises, presents no ground for equitable interference. It is shown in the same paragraph that appellants are proceeding under an ordinance. The ordinance calls for the opening and improvement of the streets in Summit Addition for public use. How the storm water that may be collected in the side ditches shall be disposed of is not prescribed. The order for opening and improvement implies that it shall be done in a proper and skillful manner. It is presumed that officers will do their duty (Valparaiso v. Hagen, 153 Ind. 337, 344, 54 N. E. 1062, 48 L. R. A. 707, 74 Am. St. Rep. 305), and, if they do, and construct an adequate ditch along the south side of John street to intersect the public drain in Indiana avenue, the flood water collected will be successfully carried away without damage to appellee.

The case presents no ground for injunction. Sufficient facts are embraced in what purports to be a special finding to make it apparent that no benefit could result to appellee from a retrial. The judgment is therefore reversed, with instructions to restate the conclusion of law in accordance with this opinion, and to render thereon the proper judgment.

GILLETT, C. J., did not participate in the decision of this case.

(33 Ind. A. 88)

CRUMP v. DAVIS.

(Appellate Court of Indiana, Division No. 2. April 26, 1904.)

CARRIERS—INJURIES TO PASSENGER—INSTRUCTIONS—NEGLIGENCE.

1. In an action against the owner of a street railway for injuries received while alighting from a car, the mere fact that the car was mov-

ing when plaintiff alighted did not make the question of her negligence in attempting to alight one of law.

2. In a personal injury action against an individual owning a street railway, it was not error to charge that, although not a corporation, defendant, being a common carrier, was under the same obligation to provide for the safety of passengers as a corporation carrier.

3. After stopping a stre· ; car to allow passengers to alight, it is the duty of the persons in charge of the car to ascertain before starting it that no passenger is in the act of alighting, and it is not sufficient that the car is operated in the usual manner.

4. Carriers of passengers must exercise the highest practicable degree of care for the safety of their passengers, and a failure to do so is actionable negligence.

5. It is not negligence per se for a passenger to fail to take hold of the hand rail in alighting from a street car.

Appeal from Circuit Court, Johnson County; W. J. Buckingham, Judge.

Action by Harriet Davis against John S. Crump. From a judgment for plaintiff, defendant appeals. Affirmed.

James F. Cox, Robt. M. Miller, Henry Barnett, Wm. E. Deupree, and D. E. Slack, for appellant. W. A. Johnson, W. J. Buck, and C. S. Baker, for appellee.

ROBY, J. Appellee recovered judgment against appellant for $1,000, from which he appeals. The case was tried three times; the first two trials resulting in disagreements of the jury, and the last one as stated. Errors argued are covered by the assignment that the court erred in overruling the motion for a new trial.

The complaint is in two paragraphs. It is averred that appellant on February 17, 1899, owned and operated a street railway in the city of Columbus, Bartholomew county, Ind.; that appellee on said day, at 8:30 p. m., took passage on one of his cars, paid her fare, and asked the agent and servant in charge to stop the car at Sycamore street, as she wished there to alight. It is averred that when the car arrived at Sycamore street it was stopped, and she notified of the fact; that she proceeded at once to leave the car, and was in the act of stepping to the ground, when the said agent and servant negligently started the car with a sudden jerk, throwing and injuring her. The negligence charged in the second paragraph is that the car was negligently started, in a manner sudden and unexpected to her, before she had reasonable time to alight. The stubbornly contested question of fact in the case was whether the car was started while she was attempting to alight, or whether she attempted to get off before it stopped. The evidence was conflicting. Appellee testified that the motorman nodded to her to get off, and that, when she started to do so, the car was stopped. The motorman testified that he shut off the current in order to turn a switch as he approached the street, and that he afterward turned it on with sufficient force to carry the car across the street, and a little by the usual place of stopping; that the car did not stop until after appellee had been thrown; and that he did not announce the street to her.

So far as the negligence of appellee in attempting to alight as she did is concerned, that was a question for the jury. The mere fact that the car was moving does not make the question one of law for the court. Conner v. Railway Co., 105 Ind. 62, 67, 4 N. E. 441, 55 Am. Rep. 177; Railway v. Spahr, 7 Ind. App. 23, 33 N. E. 446. The verdict finds, however, within the allegations of the complaint, that, when she started to alight, the car had stopped; and, there being evidence to support it, there is no necessity of considering the relative duties of the parties in connection with the act of alighting from a moving car.

In the thirteenth instruction the jury were told that, although not a corporation, the appellant, being a common carrier, was under the same obligation to provide for the safety of passengers as a corporation carrier. The instruction is said to "simply make an odious comparison." The law has no varying standard of duty for common carriers. The trial judge knew the attitude assumed in argument by the attorneys for either side. For all that appears, the instruction may have been necessary to avoid the exoneration of appellant from liability incident to an occupation selected by himself. There was no error in giving it.

The fifteenth instruction given was as follows: "The law requires the employés of street railways to do more than to stop reasonably long enough for passengers to safely alight from cars. They are bound and required to ascertain and know that no passenger is in the act of alighting from the car before putting it in motion again. If an employé fails in that respect, then such failure is imputed to his employer, and is actionable negligence on the part of the employer, and it is no excuse for the employé or his employer to show that the car on the particular occasion was operated in the usual manner." The instruction stated the law. Anderson v. Ry. Co., 12 Ind. App. 194, 38 N. E. 1109; 1 Fetter, pp. 177, 178, § 72; Booth, Ry. L. § 349; 3 Thompson, Neg. (2d Ed.) 3519–3520; Ry. Co. v. Hoffbauer, 23 Ind. App. 614, 620, 56 N. E. 54; Ry. Co. v. Harman, 147 U. S. 571, 13 Sup. Ct. 557, 37 L. Ed. 284; Ry. Co. v. Burt, 9 South. 410, 18 L. R. A. 95.

The fourteenth instruction was as follows: "The law requires of carriers of passengers that they exercise not only ordinary care, but that they exercise the highest practicable degree and kind of care, for the safety of their passengers, and any failure in this respect constitutes actionable negligence." The instruction accords with the law stated in Ry. Co. v. Hoffbauer, supra; Ry. Co. v.

¶ 3. See Carriers, vol. 9, Cent. Dig. § 1228½.

Snyder, 20 N. E. 284, 3 L. R. A. 434, 10 Am. St. Rep. 60; Ry. Co. v. Sheeks, 155 Ind. 74, 56 N. E. 434; 4 Elliott on Ry. 1585.

Appellant complains of the refusal of the court to give an instruction requested by him in terms as follows: "If there were hand rails on the car, or on the platform of the car, which plaintiff could have held to until she reached the ground, and if the plaintiff stepped from said platform the distance of 17 or 18 inches to the ground without holding to said hand rail or hand rails or any other object to support herself as she left said car, then, in that event, I instruct you that she was guilty of contributory negligence, and your verdict should be for the defendant." The instruction selected one of the facts connected with appellee's conduct, and ignored the others. The question of negligence was for the jury to determine in view of all the circumstances under which she acted. It is not negligence per se for a passenger to fail to take hold of the hand rail in alighting from a street car. 3 Thompson, Neg. (2d Ed.) p. 949, § 3589; p. 953, note 516; p. 895, note 216; Schaefer v. Central. etc., Ry. Co. (Sup.) 61 N. Y. Supp. 806; Neslie v. Second, etc., Ry. Co., 113 Pa. 300, 6 Atl. 72; Martin v. Ry. Co. (Sup.) 38 N. Y. Supp. 220; McDonald v. Ry. Co., 116 N. Y. 546, 22 N. E. 1068, 15 Am. St. Rep. 437.

The appellant had a fair trial. The rulings of the court in every instance gave him all to which he was entitled. A number of the rulings were of such a character as to require a reversal, had the verdict been otherwise than it is. The instructions, taken as a whole, were correct. The judgment is affirmed.

WILEY, P. J., concurs in result.

(34 Ind. App. 541)

AVERY v. NORDYKE & MARMON CO.[1]

(Appellate Court of Indiana. April 28, 1904.)

SERVANT'S INJURIES — ASSUMPTION OF RISK—KNOWLEDGE OF DEFECT — APPRECIATION OF DANGER — QUESTIONS FOR JURY—EVIDENCE—ADMISSIBILITY—APPEAL—HARMLESS ERROR—BILLS OF EXCEPTION — SUFFICIENCY — CONFLICTING STATEMENTS — VERDICT—ANSWERS TO INTERROGATORIES — SUFFICIENCY—STATEMENTS OF CONCLUSIONS.

1. The Appellate Court cannot disregard a bill of exceptions because the statement of evidence therein contained is in narrative form.

2. The statement in a bill of exceptions as to the dates of trial controls, where there is a discrepancy between it and the record made by the clerk.

3. It is not necessary that the evidence incorporated in a bill of exceptions should be transcribed by the official stenographer.

4. Where a bill of exceptions recites, "this was all the evidence given in the case," and does not on its face show that other evidence was introduced, it is sufficient, although part of the testimony of one witness set out in the bill reads, "I did not notice any difference between that rick and others, in the mode of piling, etc.," ut the abbreviation would be treated as having en used by the witness.

5. What shall be contained in a bill of exceptions is a matter exclusively for the determination of the trial judge.

6. Under Burns' Ann. St. 1901, § 661, providing that on the request of appellant the clerk shall forthwith deliver or transmit to the clerk of the Supreme Court the transcript of the record, or so much thereof as appellant directs, where appellant directs the clerk to make out a transcript, without giving specific directions as to any particular part of the record, it is the duty of the clerk to make out and deliver or transmit a complete transcript.

7. By Acts 1903, p. 340, c. 193, § 7, an original bill of exceptions, containing the evidence, constitutes and is considered a part of the transcript.

8. Where instructions are incorporated in the bill of exceptions, it is not necessary for the trial judge to sign marginal exceptions thereon.

9. Only such grounds of objection to evidence as are presented to the trial court can be insisted upon on appeal.

10. In an action for a servant's injuries, where plaintiff's witness testified that he told the foreman that a pile of pig iron on ricks looked dangerous, and also testified on cross-examination that before he went to the foreman he remarked that it looked dangerous, it was proper for defendant to call and interrogate one of the men with whom witness was working as to whether witness said anything to him about the rick looking dangerous or liable to fall.

11. In order to create an implied contract on the part of a servant to assume a risk arising from an open and obvious danger, it is essential that the employé both knew and appreciated the danger, and knowledge does not necessarily embrace the required appreciation.

12. Where an obvious defect is such that there is no room for diverse inferences with regard to knowledge and appreciation of danger by an injured employé, assumption of risk becomes a question for the court, but where there is room for such diverse inferences the question is for the jury.

13. Where a servant saw or should have seen the defects in a pile of iron, and appreciated the danger of the falling of the same, the fact that his duties did not relate to the department of the employer's work which had to do with the piling of the iron did not prevent the application to him of the doctrine of assumed risk.

14. In an action for a servant's injuries, caused by the falling over of a pile of pig iron on him, whether plaintiff assumed the risk *held*, under the evidence, a question for the jury.

15. In an action for a servant's injuries, where the jury, in answering interrogatories, made no finding negativing a specific act of negligence charged in the complaint, and which there was evidence tending to establish, error in refusing an instruction on the question of assumed risk could not be treated as harmless.

16. Where a complaint for a servant's injuries does not charge the employment of inexperienced or incompetent men, a finding that the men were competent is not within the issues, nor open to consideration in disposing of the appeal.

17. Statements in answer to interrogatories submitted to the jury that work was carefully done, and that the men engaged therein exercised ordinary and reasonable care, are conclusions, and not to be considered in disposing of an appeal.

18. In an action for a servant's injuries, caused by the falling of a rick of pig iron, general comparisons with other ricks which did not fall are irrelevant.

19. An answer to an interrogatory submitted to the jury in an action for a servant's injuries, that defendant did not know that the rick which fell was dangerous, is not the equivalent of a finding of facts showing reasonable care to make the place where the servant was working safe.

¶ 11. See Master and Servant, vol. 34, Cent. Dig. § 575.

[1] Rehearing denied. Appeal dismissed, 73 N. E. 119. Appeal to Supreme Court denied.

Appeal from Superior Court, Marion County; Vinson Carter, Judge.

Action by George R. Avery against the Nordyke & Marmon Company. From a judgment for defendant, plaintiff appeals. Reversed.

Wymond J. Beckett and Henry M. Dowling, for appellant. E. E. Stevenson and E. H. Knight, for appellee.

ROBY, J. Action to recover damages for personal injury. The amended complaint was in one paragraph. Its averments, summarized, are to the effect that the defendant corporation is a manufacturer of milling machinery in Indianapolis; that on August 24, 1900, appellant was working for it in its factory, cleaning or smoothing the rough places off of milling machinery; that this was his chief duty, and that, to perform it, he was required by appellee to place said machinery or castings upon a truck which ran into said factory, and such truck was then run out of the building into appellee's yard, where it was the custom and appellant's duty to clean and smooth the castings while thereon; that on said day appellant was working at his usual and customary duties in cleaning and smoothing castings upon said truck in said yard, without negligence on his part; that appellee had negligently piled or caused to be piled near said track and appellant's working place pig iron in ricks parallel with said track, and near thereto; that said iron had been piled too near said track, too high, and in an unsubstantial and negligent manner, making said ricks dangerous and likely to fall, thereby rendering appellant's working place dangerous; that appellant was engaged at his work as aforesaid, with his back to said ricks, and in said place as aforesaid, without fault on his part, and without knowledge that they would fall on him and injure him, but said appellee knew, or ought to have known, that said ricks of pig iron would fall on and injure him; that on said day appellant was working, cleaning castings, in his usual place, and that by the negligence of the appellee the rick of pig iron fell on him, to his damage, etc. The issue was formed by a general denial, trial and verdict for appellee, motion for new trial overruled, and judgment rendered on the verdict.

The error assigned is in overruling the motion for a new trial. In support of the assignment, appellant has argued questions relating to the admission of evidence, the giving of certain instructions, and the refusal to give others requested. Preliminary to the consideration of these, it must be determined whether the bill of exceptions containing the evidence and the bill of exceptions containing the instructions are in the record.

The bill purporting to contain the evidence was duly signed by the trial judge, duly filed, and certified to this court. The statement therein contained is in narrative form. We are not authorized to disregard it for that reason. Weakley v. Wolf, 148 Ind. 208, 47 N. E. 466; Grisell v. Noel, 9 Ind. App. 251, 36 N. E. 452.

The bill states that the evidence was introduced on the 29th of January, 1902. The clerk's transcript shows that the trial was had on the 23d, 24th, 27th, 28th, and 29th days of January, 1902. The statement of the bill of exceptions as to dates controls where there is a discrepancy between it and the record made by the clerk. Alley v. State, 76 Ind. 94, 95; Railway v. Adams, 112 Ind. 302, 303, 14 N. E. 80; Ewbank's Manual, § 84, p. 47.

The evidence, as incorporated in the bill, does not purport to have been transcribed by the official reporter. It is not necessary that it should be so transcribed. Adams v. State, 156 Ind. 596-600, 59 N. E. 24; Tombaugh v. Grogg, 156 Ind. 356-358, 59 N. E. 1060.

A part of the testimony of one witness is set out in the bill as follows: "I did not notice any difference between that rick and others, in the mode of piling, etc." It is argued that this shows affirmatively that all of the evidence is not in the record. The answer purports to be that of the witness, and the abbreviation must be treated as having been used by him. The bill recites, "This was all the evidence given in the case." It does not on its face show that other evidence was introduced, and it is therefore sufficient. Ewbank's Pl. & Pr. §§ 48, 54.

Appellee filed written objections to the bill of exceptions before it was signed and filed; giving therein specific reasons, supported by affidavit, why, in its opinion, the bill should not be authenticated. Such objection was overruled, and is shown by the bill of exceptions presented by appellee. What shall be contained in the bill is a matter exclusively for the trial judge to determine. Jelley v. Roberts, 50 Ind. 1.

The rulings upon the various objections made as aforesaid do not authorize this court to disregard the bill as settled. Appellant, by præcipe, directed the clerk to make out a transcript for appellee. No specific directions as to any particular part of the record were given, and it thereby became the duty of the clerk to make out and deliver or transmit a complete transcript. Section 661, Burns' Ann. St. 1901; Barnes v. Pelham, 18 Ind. App. 166-168, 47 N. E. 648.

The original bill of exceptions containing the evidence constitutes and is considered a part of the transcript. Acts 1903, p. 340, c. 193, § 7.

The certificate of the clerk was in due and regular form. Acts 1903, p. 340, c. 193, § 7.

The instructions having been incorporated in the bill of exceptions, it was not necessary for the trial judge to sign marginal exceptions thereon. Moore v. Combs, 24 Ind. App. 464, 56 N. E. 35, cited and relied upon by appellee, does not control. Ayres v. Blevins, 28 Ind. App. 101, 62 N. E. 305.

The bills of exceptions are properly a part of the record.

The appellant, when injured, was engaged in cleaning a casting which was on a truck standing in the usual and proper place. He received his orders from one Linneman, boss of the department in which he was employed. Appellee's employés, working under the direction of the foreman of the "piling gang," a distinct department of its business, on the day before, had been piling pig iron in ricks 28 inches south of and along the track upon which said truck and castings stood at the time of the accident complained of. On the morning of the accident, such work was resumed. Appellant was not subject to the orders of the boss of the said piling gang. The separate pieces of pig iron so piled were from 6 inches to 2½ feet long, and 3 or 4 inches in diameter, and were rough on the sides and ends. The particular rick that fell upon appellant was piled to a height of from 7 to 8 feet. It had just been completed, and a new one begun, when it fell. Properly piled, the rick would have been safe, and the fact that this one fell indicated that it was not piled right. There was a conflict in the evidence relative to the foreman's knowledge that it was dangerous. A witness called by appellant, who was one of the gang that piled the iron, testified that the rick looked dangerous and quivered whenever a piece of iron was thrown upon it, and that 30 minutes before it fell, he told the foreman in charge that the pile looked dangerous. On cross-examination he was asked if he said anything to the men he was working with about the pile looking dangerous. He answered: "Yes; before I went to see Foggleson [the foreman], I made the remark that it looked dangerous, and that I would go and see him." Thereafter appellee called one of the men with whom the witness was working, and asked whether said first-named witness said anything to him about the rick looking dangerous or liable to fall. Appellant contends that his objection to this question should have been sustained, stating the proposition that a witness cannot be impeached upon immaterial and collateral matters testified to by him upon cross-examination. The objection to the testimony stated at the trial was based upon other grounds than these argued, i. e., that notice to the witness would not be notice to the defendant; that the evidence was incompetent, immaterial, and irrelevant. Only such grounds of objection to the admission of evidence as are presented to the trial court can be insisted upon in this court. Everitt v. Paper Co., 25 Ind. App. 287, 57 N. E. 281. There was, however, no error in admitting the evidence. It was competent to prove what the witness did with reference to conveying notice of the dangerous character of the rick to the foreman, appellee's representative. Where it is competent to prove the act, it is competent to prove the statement accompanying it, as part of the res gestæ of such act. McConnell v. Hannah, 96 Ind. 102; Boone v. Wallace, 18 Ind. 82-85; Creighton v. Hoppis, 99 Ind. 369-371. The testimony elicited upon direct examination tended to show that the witness conveyed notice to the foreman of the defect. It being relevant to prove what he said upon the subject, and what he did in the respect indicated, all that he did and said at the time became relevant. The legal proposition stated by appellant is abstractly correct, as shown by the authorities cited, but it is not applicable to the facts.

The ninth instruction given to the jury was as follows: "When a servant engages in the employment of a master, he thereby assumes all such risks of injury as are incidental and necessarily attend and attach to the kind of work for which he was employed. He also assumes all dangers and risks as are open, obvious, and apparent, or which, by the exercise of reasonable and ordinary care, he would have ascertained and known of. The meaning of this doctrine of assumption of risk amounts to this: That when a servant engages in an employment which is necessarily attended with some risk or danger, or if while he is engaged in such employment he becomes aware of danger or risks, although not incident to the employment in which he is engaged, or that such dangers are so apparent that he ought to observe and know of the same if he had used ordinary care, and, with such knowledge or means of knowledge, he continues on in his work, and is injured by reason of any such dangers above named, then for such injuries the servant would not be entitled to recover." By the eleventh instruction given, the questions as to whether there was "any defect or danger in the place where plaintiff was required to work," "whether such danger, if any, was incident to the employment," and "whether the danger or defect was known and obvious," were submitted to the jury. Appellant requested that the jury be instructed as follows: "The rule that a servant assumes such risks of his employment as are apparent or incidental to it is to be considered in connection with the more general principle which requires that the master shall provide for the safety of his servants. It is a question for you to determine, under the facts of this case, whether the risks or danger, if any, to the plaintiff's working place, were visible, palpable, incident to the particular service, or should have been discovered by the plaintiff in the exercise of ordinary care. An agreement on the part of the servant to assume the risks of danger to his working place cannot be conclusively presumed from mere knowledge of its existence. It is only where the person injured, knowing and appreciating the danger, voluntarily encounters it, that such knowledge is a defense. The knowledge, however, is a material fact, if it exists, for your consideration, in determining whether, under all the circumstances, the plaintiff assumed the risk, or was guilty of contributory negligence." The instruction refused is based upon and follows the language of the opinion in City of Ft. Wayne v. Christie, 156 Ind. 172, 176, 59 N. E. 385. It is conceded that "it is not enough that a servant should know of a defect alone, for his experience or ignorance may be such that the risk or danger attending such defect would not be understood, and therefore not known to him. He must know of the danger, and, once knowing it, he is charged with all the risks springing from knowledge thus obtained. It would be a travesty on justice, indeed, to permit a servant to escape this rule of law by claiming that, although he knew the danger, yet he did not appreciate it. He might properly assert that he knew of the defect, but did not appreciate the danger therefrom." The instructions given are not so clear in distinguishing knowledge of defect and knowledge of danger as the above-quoted extract from the very exhaustive and able argument made by appellee's counsel, but, although the instructions given be considered as a correct exposition of the law, so far as they go, the exception to the one refused presents the question involved in appellant's proposition. The doctrine of assumed risk depends upon an implied contract created, in the case of obvious danger, from the voluntary act of the employé in continuing in the service. Wortman v. Minich, 28 Ind. App. 31, 62 N. E. 85; Davis Coal Co. v. Polland, 158 Ind. 615, 62 N. E. 492, 92 Am. St. Rep. 319. There can be no room for implying such contract except where the employé acts in view of the danger to which he is subjected. Where he is an infant, or otherwise lacking in discretion or judgment, there can never be any doubt but that he must be shown to have appreciated the danger, before he can be charged with assumption of the risk arising therefrom: and this, too, although the facts brought to his knowledge are sufficient to have warned one of ordinary capacity. Mullin v. Horseshoe Co., 105 Cal. 77, 38 Pac. 535. The principle is stated in a recent text-book as follows: "The plaintiff is presumed to possess ordinary knowledge, and to exercise care to discover what such intelligence would enable him to know and appreciate. And as he is required to apply this grade of intelligence to the investigation of the risks of the employment which he undertakes, so he is required to draw upon whatever of special knowledge or experience he may have. Dangers that would not be heeded by persons unused to factories would become apparent to one who had had years of experience at different shops, and so dangers of machinery that might not be apparent to him may be obvious to a skilled mechanic or engineer. Each, according to the degree of skill, experience, or knowledge in the business he possesses, must exercise due care to discover what dangers surround him." Dresser on Emp. Liab. § 95, pp. 435, 436. The requirement that the employé does or should appreciate the danger to which he is subjected is essential to a contract for assumption of the risk arising from the existence of an obvious defect. Where the risk assumed is incident to the occupation, the acceptance of the employment creates the contract. The risk, because of which appellant was injured, was not incidental to his employment, and whether he would be permitted to set up his nonappreciation of such a danger is not, therefore, decided; the decision being limited by the facts of the case to danger assumed because of its being open and obvious. In Ferren v. Old Colony Ry. Co., 143 Mass. 197, 9 N. E. 608, the plaintiff was of mature age, and had been in the railroad company's service about seven years as a blacksmith. His contract did not contemplate work outside of the shop. In compliance with the direction of his foreman, he went with others into the yard to move a car. He was caught between the side of the car and the wall, and was crushed. He had not been before between the car track and the corner of the building at the place where he was injured, although he had never refused to help move cars. The Supreme Court of Massachusetts, in affirming the judgment in his favor, said: "Of course, he could see that the space was narrow, but it would seem that neither he nor the others who were pushing on the same side of the car with himself understood that it was too narrow to allow them to pass through in safety. That was his mistake. Seeing the situation in a general way, he took hold among the others, and tried to pass through what proved to be too narrow a place for him. He did not rightly estimate the possibility or extent of the peril to which he was exposing himself. Though he could see the position of the car and of the building, it might nevertheless be found by a jury that he did not appreciate, and in the exercise of due care was not bound to appreciate, the danger. If, under the circumstances stated, he was called upon by the foreman to assist in this work, which was outside of the work which he was employed to do, and in the place where he had not before done such work, and, if the peril was not obvious to him, he failed to take notice that the space between the car and the building was too narrow for him to pass through in safety, and he did not discover the danger until it was too late to save himself, we cannot say that he must be held to have assumed the risk. The case is close, but the evidence is sufficient to be submitted to the jury, upon the question of whether he was in the exercise of due care." In Roth v. Pacific Co. (Or.) 22 Pac. 842, the employé was a laborer injured while passing from one place to another in a factory by a rapidly revolving shaft with projecting set screws. The court said: "But it is to be borne in mind that there is a difference between a knowledge of the facts, and a knowledge of the risks which they involve. One may know the facts, and yet not understand the risks. * * * It is not so much a question whether the party injured has a knowledge of all the facts in his situation, but whether he is aware of the danger that threatens him. * * * So that in a case like the present, where the evidence is conflicting as to whether or not decedent had knowledge of the risk to which he is exposed, the question is pre-eminently for the jury." "Sometimes the circumstances may show, as a matter of law, that the risk is understood and appreciated, and then they may present in that particular a question for the jury." Fitzgerald v. Paper Co., 155 Mass. 155, 29 N. E. 464, 31 Am. St. Rep. 537; Mahoney v. Dore, 155 Mass. 513, 30 N. E. 366; Russell v. M. & St. L. Ry., 32 Minn. 234, 20 N. W. 147. "One does not voluntarily assume a risk, within the meaning of the law that debars recovery, when he merely knows that there is some danger, without appreciating the danger." Mundle v. Hill Mfg. Co., 86 Me. 400, 405, 30 Atl. 16. The principles declared in the cases cited are recognized by the following text-books: Sherman & Redfield on Neg. (5th Ed.) vol. 1, § 215, p. 371; Dresser, Emp. Liab. Acts, pp. 397, 436; Bailey's Per. Inj. Relating to Master and Servant, vol. 1, §§ 841, 844. That it is essential, to create an implied contract to assume a risk arising from the open and obvious character of the danger, that the employé both know and appreciate the danger, has recently been so often declared by the Supreme Court that we do not feel at liberty to hold otherwise, nor to hold that knowledge embraces and includes the appreciation required. Ft. Wayne v. Christie, supra; Consolidated Stone Co. v. Summit, 152 Ind. 297–303, 53 N. E. 235; Wright v. Chicago, 160 Ind. 583–590, 66 N. E. 454; Railroad v. Lee, 29 Ind. App. 480, 64 N. E. 675; Chicago v. Richards, 28 Ind. App. 46, 61 N. E. 18. The liability of confusing the terms "defect" and "danger," as used in the instructions given, in view of the evidence, rendered it proper that the distinction made by the instruction refused should have been expressed to the jury.

The evidence does not show that the plaintiff was of inferior intelligence or tender age. Being of ordinary capacity and intelligence, evidence that he did not know all the danger which he ought to have seen and appreciated would amount to nothing. "But when a man experienced testifies that he did not know of the risk, the courts cannot as readily say that he could have seen it, had he looked, and the jury must decide the conflict of fact and inference." Dresser's Emp. Liab. § 95, p. 437. There are, however, other facts than those relating to the incapacity of the party injured justifying the inference that the danger arising from a known defect, or an opportunity to know a given defect, was not appreciated by the employé. In Ft. Wayne v. Christie, supra, the employé was of mature age, and injured while digging a trench. In Consolidated Stone Co. v. Summit, supra, the appellee was a derrick hand. In Wright v. Chicago, supra, in R. R. v. Lee, and in Chicago v. Richards the persons injured were brakemen, and presumably of full age and capacity.

Where the obvious defect is such that there is no room for diverse inference with regard to the knowledge and appreciation of the danger thereof by the injured employé, assumption of the risk becomes a question for the court, exactly as any other question of fact with regard to which the evidence is uncontroverted. Where there is room for diverse inference, the question is one for the jury. It becomes necessary in the case at bar to determine whether there was any evidence authorizing the submission to the jury of the question presented by the instruction refused. If so, the plaintiff was entitled to a full statement of the law applicable to the hypothesis of fact maintained by him. The evidence of the plaintiff herein was in part as follows: "I was employed at the works of the defendant. * * * While with defendant I cleaned castings. The cleaning was done in the yard on a tramway between the chipping room and the turntable in good weather. In bad weather I worked inside the chipping room. I had been working on mill frames several weeks before I got hurt, and at defendant's works. * * * John Linneman, the straw boss, ordered the men out into the yard to do their chipping. Linneman ordered me out on the tramway when the weather was good. A crane raised the mill frames onto the truck. Then two to four men pushed the trucks and frames out onto the tramway. The truck thus pushed out was always left between the chipping room and the turntable. * * * It took all morning to clean one mill frame. * * * After they were cleaned, we took them into the machine shop, if they were needed there, or piled them in the yard. * * * I was cleaning a mill frame when I was injured. I was in the yard on the tramway about six feet from the turntable. The casting was on a truck which was eighteen inches high, three and a half or four feet wide, and four to six feet long. It was made of wood and iron. The top was wooden, and about two inches thick. It was narrower one way than the other, being about three feet wide by two. It was made in the foundry, raised by a crane, and let down on a truck which three or four men pushed out on the tramway. The trucks were always taken out about fifteen or twenty minutes before seven o'clock in the morning and put on the tramway. Two or three men pushed them out. The truck I was working on when I was injured was setting where it was when the accident happened. When I went to work in the morning I could not move it alone. * * * I put my feet on the truck and cleaned the inside of the castings. Then I cut the rough places off with a chisel and emery stone. Then I sat on the truck; took the chisel in my left hand and a hammer in my right. My face was always toward the casting. I was all the time looking backwards, and cleaning under the flaring part of the casting. I was cleaning the east end of the casting when I was hurt, and my face was towards the west. There was nobody working on the pig iron when I began work that morning. The pile that fell on me was then three or four feet high. Chalmers Grabtree and James K. Greenwood worked on the pig iron later. I did not notice the pig iron. I did not know it was likely to fall, and was never notified that it was dangerous when piled seven or eight feet high. The pile that fell was three or four feet from the truck. There had never been any pig iron piled so near the working place as that before. Pulley rims were piled there for a long time, and these were taken away and the pig iron put in their place. * * * I do not know how the pile was when it fell, and remember nothing about the accident. The first I knew, I was in the City Hospital. This was the second day after the accident. * * * My injuries were a hole in the back of my head, my face skinned, my left collar bone displaced, my right arm stiff, my hip cut, my leg cut and scabbed, my testicle bursted out so that it had to be sewed up, my right leg and knee crushed, and my spine injured." It does not appear from the testimony of any witness that the plaintiff had actual knowledge of the danger to which he was subjected by the defectively piled iron, or that he had knowledge of the defects therein. The utmost that can be said is that he might, by an examination, have discovered them. The circumstances are such as to admit of different inferences. If he saw or should have seen the defects in the iron piled, and appreciated the danger therefrom, the fact that his duties did not relate to that department of his employer's work will not prevent the application of the doctrine of assumed risk to him. Whether he ought to have seen the defect, in the exercise of reasonable care, depends to a large degree upon the circumstances in which he was placed. The evidence shows that he knew the iron was piled near the track where he was working. That fact alone is not sufficient, as a matter of law, within the principle announced by the cases cited, to charge him with the assumption of risk arising from the defective piling thereof. If he knew or ought to have known and appreciated the risk incurred by continuing in his work, he cannot recover. The question was one for the jury, and, in view of the undisputed facts as to his knowledge of the iron being piled near the track, the nature of the defect of such piles, and his asserted ignorance of the danger arising therefrom, the instruction requested was a proper one.

The complaint counts upon negligence in the following particulars: (1) Piling pig iron along and too near the track upon which plaintiff was working; (2) piling said iron too high; (3) piling the said iron in unsubstantial ricks; (4) piling said iron in a negligent manner, making said ricks dangerous and likely to fall upon him. The jury, in answer to interrogatories, found that the men engaged in piling the pig iron were experienced in doing that kind of work, and were ordinarily careful and competent men; that the men piled the pig iron carefully, and as it had ordinarily been piled in defendant's yard; that the men piling the iron had been told by their foreman to pile it carefully; that the defendant did not, before the rick fell, know that it was dangerous; that the men thought the rick was safe before it fell; that the rick had been piled in the same manner as other ricks, and to the same height; that the defendant had found by experience that it was safe to pile pig iron to a height of seven or eight feet in the manner the ricks that fell were piled; that the defendant exercised ordinary and reasonable care in inspecting the rick that fell. There is no finding whatever negativing the negligence charged in piling the iron too near the track. The facts thus exhibited are not sufficient to establish appellee's freedom from negligence, and thereby render harmless error in refusing an instruction relative to the question of assumed risk. There was no charge in the complaint that inexperienced or incompetent men were employed. The finding upon that point is not, therefore, within the issues, and cannot be considered. Elliott, App. Prac. §§ 766, 767; Bowlus v. Phenix Ins. Co., 133 Ind. 106, 32 N. E. 319, 20 L. R. A. 400. The statements that the work was carefully done are conclusions, and cannot be considered. "Care" and "carefulness" are antonyms for "neglect" and "negligence." That negligence is a conclusion of law has been often enough decided. Railroad v. Spencer, 98 Ind. 194; Railroad v. Burger, 124 Ind. 279, 24 N. E. 981. That the men piling the iron exercised ordinary and reasonable care is also a conclusion of law. Conner v. Ry. Co., 105 Ind. 62, 4 N. E. 441, 55 Am. Rep. 177; Town v. Wakley, 149 Ind. 69, 48 N. E. 637; Railroad v. Spencer, supra. The negligence charged in piling the rick that fell depends upon the manner in which it was piled. The interrogatories are silent upon that point. The question to be determined cannot be influenced by evidence of facts not connected therewith. Such facts are not relevant. General comparisons with other ricks which did not fall cannot be made. Washington v. McCormick, 19 Ind. App. 665, 49 N. E. 1085; Gas Co. v. Ins. Co., 23 Ind. App. 305, 53 N. E. 485. That the appellee did not know that the rick was dangerous is not equivalent to a finding of facts showing reasonable care to make the place where its employé was working safe. There is no charge of willfulness in the case, and what the men thought about the safety of the rick does not appear to be in issue.

For error in refusing the instruction requested, the judgment is reversed, and the cause remanded, with instructions to sustain motion for new trial and for further proceedings.

(70 Oh. St. 57)

MOONEY v. PURPUS et al.

(Supreme Court of Ohio. April 12, 1904.)

WILLS—RESIDUARY BEQUEST—LAWFUL HEIRS.

1. Where a testator bequeaths his residuary estate to his lawful heirs, without other or further designation as to who are intended as his beneficiaries, and by his will directs that such residuum "shall be equally divided amongst my lawful heirs, share and share alike," *held*, that all persons who at the time of the testator's death answer the description, his "lawful heirs," are entitled to share in such residuary estate, regardless of the degree of their relationship to the testator; and, in the distribution of said estate, such heirs take per capita, and not per stirpes.

(Syllabus by the Court.)

Error to Circuit Court, Auglaize County.

Action by Edward Purpus, executor of Frank Koehl, against D. F. Mooney and others. From a decree of the circuit court, Mooney brings error. Reversed.

Petition was filed in the court of common pleas of Auglaize county by the defendant in error, Edward Purpus, as executor of the will of Frank Koehl, deceased, praying for a construction of said will, and asking the advice and direction of said court how, properly, to execute and administer his trust under the provisions of said will. The will contained the following provisions:

"First. My will is that all my just debts and funeral expenses shall be paid out of my estate as soon after my decease as shall be found convenient.

"Second. I give, devise and bequeath tr my son, Pearl Koehl, the corner lot and building, situate on the corner of Spring and Main streets with the lot extending to Front street whereon the stable building, to be his forever, after my decease, except the lot and brick building whereon at present a drug store and department store is in with the lot belonging to the same is hereby devised and bequeathed to my daughter, Emma Federspiel, to be hers forever after my decease.

"Third. I bequeath and devise to my daughter, Emma Federspiel, and my son, Pearl Koehl, all personal property now contained in the corner building, Spring and Main streets, to be theirs forever, share and share alike.

"Fourth. Whatever there remains after my decease shall be equally divided amongst my lawful heirs, share and share alike."

Upon the hearing of the case in the court of common pleas, that court made and entered the following decree:

"The court further finds that the correct and lawful construction of said will of said Frank Koehl, Sr., deceased, is as follows, to wit:

"First. That Philip Pearl Koehl and Emma Federspiel are among the residuary legatees, and each share equal with all the other such legatees in the residuum of said estate, under item 4 of said last will and testament of said Frank Koehl, Sr., deceased.

"Second. That the bequests of personal property contained in the building at the corner of Spring and Main streets, in St. Marys, Ohio, bequeaths all tangible personal property therein contained, including the money, to Philip Pearl Koehl and Emma Federspiel, but does not bequeath to them the notes, mortgages, certificates of stock, accounts, credits, and other evidences of indebtedness or the property they represent, but that these go into the residuum of testator's estate, and should be disposed of as directed in the fourth item of the will.

"Third. That Emil Henry Koehl and Louisa Maria Koehl, under item 4 of said last will and testament, take per capita, and not per stirpes.

"Fourth. The court further finds that items 1 and 2 of said last will and testament are plain and unambiguous, and need no construction or interpretation.

"It is therefore ordered, adjudged, and decreed that Edward Purpus, as executor of said last will and testament of Frank Koehl, Sr., deceased, be governed in the administration of said estate, and in making distribution thereof, by the terms of the provisions of said last will and testament, and the construction placed thereon as hereinbefore set out."

An appeal was taken from this decree to the circuit court of Auglaize county, where a like construction was by that court given the provisions of said will, except as to item 4 thereof. As to item 4 the circuit court found and held that under and by the provisions thereof Emil Henry Koehl and Louisa Maria Koehl, who were grandchildren of said testator, took per stirpes, and not per capita, and ordered and decreed that distribution be made accordingly. To obtain a reversal of this order and decree of the circuit court, plaintiff in error, as guardian of said Emil Henry Koehl and Louisa Maria Koehl, prosecutes this proceeding in error. Other facts are stated in the opinion.

D. F. Mooney and E. B. Kinkead, for plaintiff in error. Koenig & Koenig, for defendants in error.

CREW, J. (after stating the facts). The only item in the will of Frank Koehl about which there is any controversy in this case is item 4. The language of this item is as follows: "Whatever there remains after my decease shall be equally divided amongst my lawful heirs, share and share alike." At the time of his death the testator, Frank Koehl, left survivng him as his sole and only heirs at law, his five children, who are defendants in error here, viz.: Frank Koehl, Jr., Emma Federspiel, Catharine Walters, Maggie Boesche, and Pearl Koehl, and his two grandchildren, Emil Henry Koehl and Louisa Maria Koehl, plaintiffs in error, who were children of Louis Koehl, a son of said testator, who died more than eight years prior to the execution of said will. The question presented here for determination is whether, under the provisions of said item 4 of the will of Frank Koehl, the residuum of his estate thereby disposed of is to be distributed among his "lawful heirs," the children and grandchildren above named, in equal portions, and one-seventh part thereof given to each, or whether such residuum is to be divided into six equal parts, and one-sixth given to each of the five children of testator, and the remaining sixth to his two grandchildren. In other words, is the distribution of said residuum, under item 4, to be made per stirpes or per capita? It was contended in the courts below, and is the contention of defendants in error here, that where a testator bequeaths his estate, or the residuum thereof, to his heirs, or as in this case, to his "lawful heirs," without other or further designation, and without naming them, thereby making necessary a resort to the statutes of descent and distribution in order to ascertain and determine who shall take under the will, that such devisees or legatees, when so ascertained, will take only in the proportion designated and prescribed by the statutes of descent and distribution, and, if not of equal degree, they will take by right of representation, or per stirpes, and not per capita. That such is the general rule, in the absence of any specific direction by testator as to how or in what proportion each shall take, would seem, from the authorities, to be well settled. Richards v. Miller, 62 Ill. 417; Daggett v. Slack et al., 8 Metc. (Mass.) 450; West v. Rassman, 135 Ind. 278, 34 N. E. 991; Woodward v. James, 115 N. Y. 346, 22 N. E. 150; Eyer v. Beck, 70 Mich. 179, 38 N. W. 20; Conklin v. Davis, 63 Conn. 377, 28 Atl. 537; Kirkpatrick v. Kirkpatrick, 197 Ill. 144, 64 N. E. 267; Mattison v. Tanfield, 3 Beav. 131. But this rule, resting as it does upon the presumption, that, because the testator has made necessary a resort to the statute in order to determine who his donees are, therefore he also intended that the statute should govern and control as to the proportion each should take, can have no application to a case like the one at bar, where the testator has in clear and specific language prescribed and directed how such division shall be made as between those whom he has designated as his beneficiaries, viz., "equally, share and share alike." Having so declared and directed, nothing is left for inference or presumption as to the mode of distribution, and division must be made as directed by the testator. By item 4 of his will, the testator, Frank Koehl, gives the residue of his estate to a "class," which in terms he therein designates by the general description, his "lawful heirs." This being the only designation or description of those who were intended as beneficiaries under this clause of the will, of necessity resort must be had to the statute, in order to determine who are the legal heirs of the testator, within the meaning of this clause. In a technical or strict legal sense, neither the children nor grandchildren of testator were at the time of the making of this will his heirs. "Nemo est hæres viventis." But by reference to the statute we find that all of them, both children and grandchildren, are, within the purview and meaning of the statute, his "lawful heirs," inasmuch as, without the will, all would be entitled, by inheritance, to share in the distribution of his estate. All, then, being beneficiaries under item 4 of this will, it only remains to ascertain their respective interests, and to determine the share to which each is entitled, upon a distribution of the residuum of testator's estate disposed of by this item of the will; and this must be ascertained and determined, if it may be, according to the intention of the testator, as disclosed by the language of the will itself. In thus ascertaining the intention of testator, effect must be given to every word of the testamentary clause under consideration, without rejecting any of them, if this can be done by a reasonable construction, not inconsistent with the manifest intent and purpose of said testator, apparent from the whole will, taken together. Guided, then, by this rule of construction, and there being nothing found elsewhere in said will to limit, control, or vary the direction given by testator in item 4 as to the method of distribution and division of the residuum of his estate, the intention of the testator as to the manner in which such division should be made, and as to the share each should take, would, from the language employed by him in directing such division, seem entirely clear. By the phrase "my lawful heirs," testator describes the objects of his bounty, and designates who are to be his beneficiaries; and by the words "equally, share and share alike," he defines and points out the manner in which they are to take the estate comprehended by the gift. If, as contended by counsel for defendants in error, the testator had meant that both the persons who were to take and the manner of division should be governed by, and should be in accordance with, the statutes of descent and distribution, and as if he had died intestate, then item 4 of his will was entirely useless, for in that case the same persons would take, and in the same manner, as if he had died leaving no will. Testator does not say that the persons designated as beneficiaries are to take in the same manner, and in like proportions, as though he should die intestate, but, on the contrary, after describing those who are to be the objects of his bounty by the general designation "my lawful heirs," which includes both children and grandchildren, he, in clear and specific language, directs that division shall be made amongst them "equally, share and share alike." Primarily, the object of making a will is to direct another and different mode of distribution of the testator's estate from that marked out by the law of descent. That Frank Koehl made a will is a circumstance tending to show that he intended thereby to make provision for his heirs different from that which the law would make. And the fact that he made a will is a fact that weighs against such construction of the provision of item 4 of this will as is here contended for by counsel for defendants in error, because, if the construction for which they contend is to prevail, it would, at most, only accomplish that which the law itself would effect in the absence of any such clause or provision, and it makes the insertion in this will of item 4 an idle and useless act on the part of the testator. There being nothing in this will to suggest or require a different conclusion, we must presume and conclude that the testator, Frank Koehl, had a purpose and object in employing the particular language he did employ in item 4, and, from the language therein used by him, we think this intention is clear and unmistakable. By the use of the phrase "my lawful heirs" he manifestly intended that all those persons who would be his heirs under the statute of descent, in case of his intestacy, should be his beneficiaries, and should take the residuum of his estate. And by the use of the words "equally, share and share alike," he just as clearly evidenced the intention that they should not take such residuum in the manner prescribed by the statute, but should take it equally, share and share alike, as directed by his will. By reference to the statute, we ascertain who are to take under item 4, and, by the plain provisions of the will itself, we are told how they are to take; that is, "equally, share and share alike," per capita, and not per stirpes. Huston v. Crook, 38 Ohio St. 328; McKelvey v. McKelvey, 43 Ohio St. 213, 1 N. E. 594; Bisson et al. v. W. S. R. R. Co. et al., 143 N. Y. 125, 38 N. E. 104; Ramsey v. Stephenson, 34 Or. 408, 56 Pac. 520, 57 Pac. 195; Walker et al. v. Webster et al., 95 Va. 377, 28 S. E. 570; Dowding v. Smith, 3 Beav. 541; Butler v. Stratton, 3 Brown's Chancery Rep. 367; Page on Wills, § 554; Richards v. Miller, 62 Ill. 417.

We are of opinion that the circuit court erred in holding that the residuum of the estate of the testator, Frank Koehl, should, under item 4 of his will, be distributed per stirpes, and not per capita, and for such error the decree of the circuit court, in so far as it orders and directs distribution and division of the property disposed of by said item 4 to be made per stirpes, and not per capita, is reversed, and judgment will be entered for the plaintiff in error in accordance with this opinion. Reversed and judgment for plaintiff in error.

SPEAR, C. J., and DAVIS, SHAUCK, PRICE, and SUMMERS, JJ., concur.

(70 Oh. St. 92)

THOMAS v. BOARD OF TRUSTEES OF OHIO STATE UNIVERSITY et al.

(Supreme Court of Ohio. April 12, 1904.)

DEVISE TO EDUCATIONAL INSTITUTION—IN CASE DEVISE FAILS—TESTATOR EMPOWERS ONLY LINEAL DESCENDANT TO RATIFY DEVISE—DESCENDANT DEEDS TO DEVISEE—SECTION 5915, REV. ST.—CONSTRUCTION OF WILLS.

1. A testator having devised to an educational institution, and, in case such devise should fail or be held void for any cause, then to the children of his two brothers, and having in a codicil authorized, empowered, and requested his daughter, who was his only lineal descendant, to ratify and confirm the devise to the institution, declaring that, "in case she complies" with this request, the devises and bequests over to the children of the testator's brothers "are revoked," and the testator having died within a year from the making of the will, so that the devise to the institution became invalid by virtue of section 5915, Rev. St., and the daughter having executed the power by a deed to the institution, the children of the testator's brothers take nothing under the will. Board of Trustees of Ohio State University v. Folsom et al., 47 N. E. 581, 56 Ohio St. 701, approved and followed.

2. The power and authority by the testator conferred upon his daughter and heir at law is not a devise in trust to or for such institution, but is a naked power to appoint to a designated object, and is not rendered invalid by section 5915, Rev. St.

3. A deed of confirmation expressly purporting to execute such power, and conveying the property which had been devised, is operative to invest the grantees with a full and perfect title to the property therein described.

(Syllabus by the Court.)

Error to Circuit Court, Pickaway County.

Action by John G. Haas and Daniel Haas against Charlotte G. Page, the board of trustees of the Ohio State University, and others. Judgment for defendants, and Maria F. Thomas, one of the defendants, brings error. Affirmed.

This is another phase of the same controversy which appears in the case of Board of Trustees of Ohio State University v. Folsom et al., 56 Ohio St. 701, 47 N. E. 581. This action was begun by John G. Haas and Daniel Haas, as trustees under the last will and testament of Henry F. Page, deceased, against Charlotte G. Page, the widow of the testator, the board of trustees of the Ohio State University, the plaintiff in error, Maria F. Thomas, Charles J. Folsom, Ellen Gill, Henry P. Folsom, Clarence H. Folsom et al.; the object and purpose of said action being to obtain an interpleader between the said defendants in respect to their claims under the will and codicils thereto of Henry F. Page, and a certain deed made by Isabel Page, his daughter, as hereinafter stated, and to determine the rights of the said defendants thereunder. The last will and testament of Henry F. Page, late of Pickaway county, contained, among other things, the following:

"V. I give and devise to the Ohio State University to be invested as the endowment fund, in fee simple and absolutely, all the residue, rest and remainder of my real estate and personal property in Ohio, Illinois, or elsewhere. This devise shall include lands or personal property acquired hereafter, or acquired under Item 7.

"VI. If the devise and bequests contained in the last clause shall fail or be held void for any cause, then I give and devise the real and personal estate described in said clause number five (5) to the children and legal representatives of my brother, Charles Folsom, and of George Folsom, deceased, in fee simple and absolutely.

"VII. By the words rest and residue and remainder, in clause five, is meant all my real and personal property, subject to the life estate and interest given to my wife and daughter."

Also a codicil containing the following:

"II. The object and intention of the devise in my will to the children of George Folsom, deceased, and to the children of Charles Folsom, was that in case of my death within a year from the date of my will and the consequent failure of the bequest and devise to the Ohio State University, the said children should take the property, but not that they should have the same in any other event.

"I now provide and declare that my said daughter is fully authorized and empowered to ratify and confirm said devise and bequest to the said university in case of my death within a year from the date of said will, and she is desired and requested by me to do so.

"In case she complies with this request the devises and bequests to the said children of George Folsom and Charles Folsom are hereby revoked."

The said daughter of Henry F. Page, Isabel Page, executed the power conferred in the said will and codicil by a deed of confirmation, in which the material parts are as follows:

"Now, therefore, I, the said Isabel Page, the daughter and only issue of the said Henry F. Page, the said testator, in execution of the authority and power conferred upon and vested in me by said testator in and by the first of said codicils, to ratify and confirm the said devise and bequest to the Ohio State University contained in said will and the said first codicil, and in consideration of the premises and of the sum of one dollar to me paid by the Board of Trustees of the Ohio State University, the receipt whereof is hereby acknowledged, do hereby ratify and confirm said devise and bequest to the said Ohio State University, and do hereby convey unto the Board of Trustees of the Ohio State University, and the successors and assigns of said board forever, in trust for the use and benefit of said university, to be invested as the endowment fund, all the property, real and personal, devised and bequeathed by said testator to the said Ohio State University in and by his said will and codicils, the same being all the residue, rest and remainder of the real estate and personal property in Ohio or elsewhere of which said testator died seized," etc.

After executing the said deed Isabel Page, who was the daughter and only lineal descendant of Henry F. Page, died, leaving her mother, Charlotte G. Page, claiming to be her only heir at law. The plaintiff in error claims an interest in the lands devised to the board of trustees of the Ohio State University by virtue of the said will of Henry F. Page, and also claims by inheritance from him through the said Isabel Page. Charlotte G. Page afterwards, on or about January 17, 1898, by deed of that date, released and quitclaimed to the board of trustees of the Ohio State University all of the real estate of the testator, Henry F. Page, in Ohio and Illinois, subject to her life estate therein.

This suit was heard in the court of common pleas of Pickaway county, and was dismissed for the reason that the court was of opinion that it had no jurisdiction to try the issues therein presented. An appeal was taken to the circuit court by the board of trustees of the Ohio State University, and upon the hearing in the circuit court the findings and adjudication of that court were in favor of the board of trustees of the Ohio State University. A motion for new trial was made by Maria F. Thomas, which was overruled, and she files her petition in error in this court to reverse the judgment of the circuit court.

H. J. Booth and Abernethy & Folsom, for plaintiff in error. Harrison, Olds & Henderson and Lawrence Maxwell, Jr., for board of trustees of Ohio State University. Sater & Sater, for George Folsom.

DAVIS, J. (after stating the facts). The counsel have elaborately argued several technical questions relating to the jurisdiction and procedure in the courts below. As to these matters, it is sufficient to say that we are of the opinion that the circuit court had jurisdiction, not only of the subject-matter, but of all necessary parties, and in sufficiently proper form, to determine all the issues in the case.

The circuit court found and adjudged that the title to the lands in controversy had been adjudicated in favor of the defendants in error the board of trustees of the Ohio

State University by the Circuit Court of the United States and the circuit court of the state of Illinois, although the decree of the former court had been appealed from, and a proceeding in error had been instituted to review the decree of the latter court; and for that reason the court declined to pass "upon the question as to what was the operation and effect of the deed of confirmation by Isabel Page, made on the 5th day of December, 1891, as shown by the record." Whether the court below was right or wrong in this conclusion is immaterial now, for the view which we take of the real controversy between the parties disposes of the whole case.

In Board of Trustees of Ohio State University v. Folsom et al., 56 Ohio St. 701, 47 N. E. 581, construing the same will which we are now considering, it was held by this court that the children of the testator's brothers take nothing under the provisions of the will, because the devise over to them is not made to depend upon the validity of the ratification of the devise and conveyance to the trustees of the university, but is defeated by the fact that it was made. Their rights were made determinable upon a condition which has happened, and therefore, whatever may be the state of the title to the property as between the trustees of the university and the children of the testator's brothers as heirs of the testator's daughter, it is clear that they cannot take as devisees under the will. There has been suggested to us no sufficient reason for receding from that position. It follows that if the deed of confirmation which was made by Isabel Page after her father's death was ineffectual to invest the trustees of the university with the title, and Isabel Page died seised of the property in question as an estate of inheritance, then the children of the testator's brothers are entitled as her heirs. It is therefore apparent that the material questions to be now determined are, first, was the instrument which was executed by Isabel Page operative and effective to vest the estate in the board of trustees of the Ohio State University under the will? and, second, if the estate passed to Isabel Page as intestate property of her father, then was it conveyed by the instrument which she executed to the board of trustees of the Ohio State University? If either or both of these questions must be answered in the affirmative, the judgment of the circuit court must be upheld, regardless of the reasoning upon which it was founded.

The Revised Statutes of Ohio (section 5915) provide: "If any testator die, leaving issue of his body, or an adopted child, living, or the legal representatives of either, and the will of such testator give, devise or bequeath the estate of such testator, or any part thereof, to any benevolent, religious, educational, or charitable purpose, * * * or to any person in trust for any of such purposes, * * * whether such trust appears on the face of the instrument * * * or not; such will as to such gift, devise or bequest shall be invalid unless such will shall have been executed according to law, at least one year prior to the decease of such testator." It is obvious that this statute does not make the act of giving, devising, or bequeathing property an illegal act, for the same gift, devise, or bequest which is declared to be invalid if the testator shall die within one year from the execution of his will may become valid if the testator shall live one year or more after making the will. In other words, the devise or bequest may be valid or invalid according to the lapse of time. It is therefore apparent that this statute is intended to operate merely as a limitation upon the testator's power of disposition, for the protection of the heir against improvident wills or wills made under undue influence. Being such a limitation, the statute is to be strictly construed. Theobald et al. v. Fugman et al., per Spear, J., 64 Ohio St. 473, 481, 60 N. E. 606; McGlade's Appeal, 99 Pa. 339, 343. And being such a limitation, and no contrary principle of right or of public policy being involved, the person for whose benefit it is made may waive or relinquish it. This statute declares invalid only gifts, devises, and bequests directly to or in trust for the purposes named. The will which we are now considering devises directly to the board of trustees of the Ohio State University, and, recognizing the possibility that it might be defeated by his death within a year, the testator devises over to the children of his brothers; and later, by a codicil, without revoking this direct devise to the trustees of the university, he "authorized and empowered" his daughter, who was his only child and heir at law, "to ratify and confirm said devise and bequest" in case it should fail by reason of his death within a year, and "she is desired and requested" to do so, and he further declares that "in case she complies with this request the devises and bequests to the said children of George Folsom and Charles Folsom, are hereby revoked." She did comply with his request, and the devises and bequests to the children of George Folsom and Charles Folsom were thereby revoked, as this court has heretofore decided, and still so holds. There now being "no other disposition made of the property in the will" (Patton v. Patton, 39 Ohio St. 590), it descended immediately to the heir, if her act of appointment, ratification, or confirmation was ineffectual; and can there be any reasonable doubt that she might voluntarily relinquish the estate thus cast upon her, or that she might waive the protection which the statute gave to her?

There was no trust in this will. The estate was not devised to Isabel to hold in trust for the trustees of the university, nor in trust to convey to them. The remainder in the estate was not devised to her at all. The testator conferred upon her the naked power to appoint the remainder to the designated object. He imposed no conditions as to the manner of executing the power. He only asked that his wishes might be carried out. He did not attempt the futile project of compelling a conveyance to the devisees whom he had selected. The donee was merely "empowered," and he left it entirely optional with her whether she would carry out his purpose—his deliberate and stubborn purpose, it seems. The context clearly shows that Isabel was at liberty to do as she might choose in regard to carrying out the testator's wishes in regard to the devise to the trustees of the university. The mere use of the precatory words "desire" and "request" will not be sufficient to create an enforceable trust, or a power in the nature of a trust, when the context clearly shows that the testator's intention was the contrary. "No authoritative case ever laid it down that there could be any other ground for deducing a trust or condition than the intention of the testator as shown by the will, taken as a whole, though no doubt in older cases that intention was sometimes inferred on insufficient grounds." In re Williams (1897) 2 Ch. D. 28. It does not matter that a degree of confidence is reposed in the donee by the testator, for, so long as it appears that the execution of the power is not obligatory, and it is left entirely to the discretion of the donee, no trust arises. Meredith v. Heneage, 1 Sim. 543; Williams v. Williams, 1 Sim. N. S. 358; Toms v. Owen (C. C.) 52 Fed. 417; Spooner v. Lovejoy, 108 Mass. 529; Huskisson v. Bridge, 4 De G. & Sm. 245; Eaton v. Watts, 4 Law Rep. Eq. 151.

It is manifest that this testator, who was himself a competent lawyer, fully understood the scope and effect of the statute; and it cannot be presumed that he would defeat the purpose which he so obviously had in mind by an attempt to create a trust. Indeed, it is clear, upon all considerations, that he did not intend to create a trust, and studiously endeavored to avoid doing so. The authorities above cited, and the numerous authorities cited by the counsel for the defendants in error, fully sustain the contention that the will of Henry F. Page conferred upon his daughter the naked power to appoint the remainder of his estate to the board of trustees of the Ohio State University, in her discretion; and in our construction of section 5915, Rev. St., that is not prohibited by either the letter or the spirit of the statute.

But it is argued that the testator could not empower his daughter to do that which he could not lawfully do himself. We have already called attention to the fact that the mere act of making a will for a benevolent or charitable purpose is not unlawful, and that such act is only made invalid for the protection of the heir when it occurs within a year prior to the decease of the testator; and counsel seem to overlook the other fact that in this instance the power to ratify and confirm necessarily implies a deed confirming and conveying the property to the appointee, for the donee of the power is authorized to appoint only after the devise and bequests to the trustees of the university "shall fail or be held void for any cause." A will might not suffice, because an appointment by will might fail in the same way, but she could sanction, carry out, and make sure his desire by a conveyance, and it would seem that she could fully execute the power in no other way. Now, can anybody doubt that the testator could have lawfully conveyed the property to the trustees of the university? If yea, then this argument falls to the ground, because this power was to be executed, and was executed, by a conveyance.

As we have already remarked, the testator did not prescribe the mode in which the donee should execute the power. The form in which she should "ratify and confirm said devise and bequest," as well as the execution of the power itself, was left to her discretion. It seems to have been deliberately and carefully drawn; and in view of the fact that the children of George Folsom and Charles Folsom do not take under the will, and of the fact that, if the exercise of the power of appointment should for any reason fail in its purpose, the property would pass to the donee herself, as intestate property, we have no trouble with the dual form of the instrument by which she executed the power. It may be construed as an execution of the power granted in the will, or as an original conveyance, or both, and it is operative to invest the board of trustees of the Ohio State University with a full and perfect title to the property therein described. But if, by reason of mistake, accident, or ignorance, the power was defectively executed, it is within the power of the court in this case to make it effectual. "Whenever a man, having power over an estate, whether of ownership or not, in discharge of his moral or natural obligations, shows an intention to execute such power, the court will operate upon the conscience of the heir or other person benefited by the default to make him perfect this intention." Chapman v. Gibson, 3 Brown, Ch. 229; Barr v. Hatch, 3 Ohio, 527; Bispham, Eq. §§ 193, 195.

There is an ultra refinement of logic in the contention that Isabel Page could not make and deliver a deed of confirmation under the power conferred in the will, and a deed of conveyance in the same instrument, delivered in the same instant of time. It would be unprofitable to discuss this point at length. Upon the death of the testator within 12 months from the date of the will, the property devised and bequeathed to the trustees of the university immediately vested in the children of his brothers, subject to be divested by appointment to the trustees by the donee of the power. Patton v. Patton, 39 Ohio St. 590; Trustees of University v. Folsom et al., 56 Ohio St. 701, 47 N. E. 581. From the death of the testator, it was a future, contingent estate in Isabel Page, which might be made absolute by appointment to the object designated by the testator, which would determine the interests of the children of the testator's brothers (Board of Trustees, etc., v. Folsom, 56 Ohio St. 701, 47 N. E. 581), and by the failure of the appointment by reason of invalidity or for any other reason. This future contingent interest she might convey. Thompson's Lessee v. Hoop, 6 Ohio St. 480. And if it became absolute thereafter, the title would relate back to the time of the conveyance.

The judgment of the circuit court is affirmed.

SPEAR, C. J., and SHAUCK, PRICE, and CREW, JJ., concur.

(70 Ohio St. 88)

CINCINNATI, H. & D. RY. CO. v. BAILEY.

(Supreme Court of Ohio. April 12, 1904.)

PETITION IN ERROR—FAILURE TO SUBSCRIBE—AMENDMENT.

1. Section 5114, Rev. St. 1892, providing for the amendment of "any pleading, process or proceeding," is applicable to proceedings in error; and, if a petition in error has been filed within the time limited for that purpose, the plaintiff and his counsel having, by mistake, omitted to subscribe it, it may, under favor of this section, be amended by subscribing it after the expiration of such time.

(Syllabus by the Court.)

Error to Circuit Court, Putnam County.

Action by John P. Bailey against the Cincinnati, Hamilton & Dayton Railway Company. Judgment for plaintiff, and defendant brings error. Reversed.

In the court of common pleas the defendant in error instituted an action against the railway company, and, upon the trial of the issues of fact joined, recovered a judgment against it. The company, within the time limited by the statute, took proper steps to have a bill of exceptions made a part of the record, and filed its petition in error in the circuit court for the reversal of the judgment of the court of common pleas for errors specifically assigned. By mistake and inadvertence the petition in error was not signed at the bottom thereof by the company, its counsel, or any one representing it. There was, however, indorsed upon it the following waiver of process and entry of appearance: "I, the defendant in error, hereby waive the issuing and service of process, and enter my appearance in the above-entitled cause in the circuit court of Putnam county, Ohio. John P. Bailey, defendant in error. May 17, 1902." Thereupon, after the expiration of the time limited for filing the petition in error, the defendant in error filed a motion "to strike from the files of the court the paper styled a 'petition in error.'" The company thereupon filed a motion for leave to amend its petition in error by subscribing the same, and with its motion filed an affidavit by its counsel who had charge of the preparation and filing of the petition in error, showing that by mere mistake and inadvertence the waiver of summons had been obtained upon what was intended to be an office copy, and that it had been filed instead of the petition which had been signed. These motions came on for hearing in the circuit court, and on October 29, 1902, that court overruled the motion of the company for leave to amend the petition in error by signing it, and sustained the motion to strike it from the files. The rulings upon these motions are here assigned as grounds for reversing the judgment of the circuit court.

R. D. Marshall and Watts & Moore, for plaintiff in error. Handy & Unverferth and D. M. Bailey, for defendant in error.

SHAUCK, J. (after stating the facts). It will be necessary to consider but one of the reasons assigned by counsel for the plaintiff in error in support of the conclusion that the judgment of the circuit court is erroneous. The question first in order and importance is, did the circuit court err in refusing leave to the plaintiff in error to amend its petition in error by subscribing it? It has long been recognized that, with respect to questions of practice in reviewing courts, they are, in the absence of statutory provisions specially applicable, determined by the provisions of the Code of Civil Procedure with respect to similar questions arising in original cases. The case of Smetters v. Rainey, 14 Ohio St. 288, was determined by such analogy. The case, though adversely criticized in other respects, has in this respect always been followed with approval. It was so approved in Robinson v. Orr et al., 16 Ohio St. 289, where the subject is sufficiently discussed, and in numerous other cases.

Is the amendment proposed by the motion for leave to amend within the established rules with respect to the general subject of amendments? The legislation upon the subject is found in section 5114, Rev. St. 1892, that: "The court may, before or after judgment, in furtherance of justice, and on such terms as may be proper, amend any pleading, process, or proceeding, by adding or striking out the name of any party, or by correcting a mistake in the name of a party, or a mistake in any other respect, or by inserting other allegations material to the case, or, when the amendment does not change substantially the claim or defense, by conforming the pleading or proceeding to the facts proved; and when an action or proceeding fails to conform to the provisions of this title, the court may permit the same to be made conformable thereto, by amendment." We have not been favored with a process of reasoning by which it is supposed that a proceeding in error may be excepted from the provisions of the statute which provides generally for the amendment of proceedings. The section has been under consideration many times, and in Irwin v. Bank, 6 Ohio St. 81, it was held applicable to an appellate proceeding, and to authorize the correction of a substantial defect in such proceeding, if it results from mistake, and the correction would be made in furtherance of justice. The express terms of the statute defining the amendment which may be made authorize the addition of a name. To the suggestion that the case presented nothing to amend, it is sufficient to say that it has already been decided that an unsigned petition is a petition. Conn v. Rhodes, 26 Ohio St. 644. Since the section authorizes the amendment of proceedings with respect to substantial defects, no inference against the right to amend can be drawn from the dismissal of petitions substantially defective, when no application was made for leave to amend. It seems, therefore, that all suggestions urged in support of the action of the court on the motion for leave to amend have been clearly answered by the decided cases.

It seems important to observe that the tendency of recent legislation and attendant adjudication is toward, and not from, the view that proceedings in error are not to be regarded with less favor than other remedial proceedings.

Judgment reversed.

SPEAR, C. J., and DAVIS, PRICE, CREW, and SUMMERS, JJ., concur.

(209 Ill. 405)

BROSSEAU v. LOWY et al.

(Supreme Court of Illinois. April 20, 1904.)

MORTGAGES—ASSUMPTION BY GRANTEE—ADMISSIBILITY OF PAROL EVIDENCE—TRANSFER AFTER DISCHARGE—INQUIRY BY PURCHASER—CONTRACT FOR HUSBAND'S BENEFIT—HUSBAND'S AGENCY.

1. A husband who is the agent of his wife, having full power and authority to bind her in all matters, may pledge her securities for his own benefit so as to bind her.

2. Evidence in a foreclosure suit examined, and *held* sufficient to show that a grantee of mortgaged property assumed the indebtedness by including it in the purchase money to be paid by her.

3. Where a grantee of mortgaged property, who has assumed the indebtedness, executes a second note to secure an extension of time, the first note and mortgage being held as collateral security therefor, and then pays the second note, receiving the first note and mortgage uncanceled, the transaction amounts to a satisfaction of the latter evidences of indebtedness.

4. The holder of a note secured by a mortgage, who, without the mortgagor's knowledge, extends time to a grantee who assumed the indebtedness, and who also releases sufficient of the land to satisfy the debt, thereby discharges the mortgagor from all liability—even that of surety.

5. Where a grantee of mortgaged property agrees to pay the indebtedness as a part of the purchase money, it is an assumption thereof, though the indebtedness is not mentioned in the deed, and there is no express or formal contract in regard thereto.

6. Parol evidence is admissible to show that a grantee of mortgaged property assumed the indebtedness, though it was not mentioned in the deed, which contained full covenants of warranty.

7. It is the duty of the assignee of a trust deed to inquire of the maker thereof as to the status of the debt.

8. Where one who has conveyed land with warranty, which is subject to a mortgage, afterwards takes an assignment of the mortgage, it is thereby discharged, and a lien cannot be preserved by its transfer to a third person.

Appeal from Appellate Court, First District.

Suit by Haiman Lowy and others against Zenophile P. Brosseau. From a judgment of the Appellate Court (110 Ill. App. 16) reversing a decree giving priority to a mortgage held by defendant, Brosseau, he appeals. Affirmed.

The question presented by this suit is the determination of the priority of two certain mortgages or trust deeds. The suit was brought June 20, 1900, by the appellee Haiman Lowy in the circuit court of Cook county to foreclose a trust deed executed by George Gillespie to Anton Boenert, as trustee, to secure the payment of three promissory notes, aggregating $8,000, executed by said Gillespie, payable to his own order, and by him indorsed, dated February 15, 1896, and all payable on or before February 15, 1899, which said notes and trust deed were the property of Auguste Boenert, wife of said Anton Boenert, who pledged them to said Lowy as collateral security for a loan of $6,000 made by said Lowy to Anton Boenert on April 30, 1896. The other party contesting for priority of his mortgage is Zenophile P. Brosseau, appellant here, who is the holder of a promissory note executed by one William Ziese on August 23, 1878, payable to his own order, and by him indorsed, and secured by a trust deed to George Coombs, as trustee, duly acknowledged and recorded on August 27, 1878, which said Ziese trust deed incumbers the same property as the trust deed subsequently executed by George Gillespie, above referred to.

The history of these two trust deeds, and the notes secured by them, may be briefly stated, as follows: August 23, 1878, Anton Boenert, being the owner of the east half of the southeast quarter of section 12, sold and conveyed it to William Ziese, his brother-in-law. August 26, 1878, Ziese executed the note and trust deed now held by Brosseau to secure a loan of $1,500 made to him by George Coombs, the trustee in the said deed, as agent for one Brander. March 30, 1883, Ziese and wife sold their equity in said land to Auguste Boenert for $1,200; nothing

¶ 7. See Mortgages, vol. 35, Cent. Dig. § 686.

being said in the deed of conveyance about the trust deed theretofore executed by Ziese, and the lien thereunder. July 10, 1890, Coombs released the northeast quarter of the southeast quarter of said section from said trust deed, and on November 18, 1891, he also released the south half of the southeast quarter of the southeast quarter of said section from said trust deed; both releases being made at the instigation and request of Anton Boenert. The Ziese note was executed August 26, 1878. It was for $1,500, and was payable in three years. On it are numerous indorsements of interest paid, and extensions of time for payment, all said to be in the handwriting of Anton Boenert, but not signed by any one. Finally, in February, 1893, as a condition for further extending time of payment of the Ziese note, which was still in the possession of Coombs, as agent, Auguste Boenert was required to give a gold note, running for two years, for the indebtedness, and Coombs still retained the Ziese note and trust deed as collateral security for the payment of the gold note. July 21, 1895, Auguste Boenert and husband conveyed, by warranty deed, the remaining 20 acres not released from the Ziese mortgage (being the premises in controversy) to George Gillespie, which deed was filed for record February 21, 1896. February 15, 1896, Gillespie and wife executed the notes and trust deed now held by appellee Lowy, and on April 30, 1896, Anton Boenert gave the Gillespie notes and trust deed to Lowy as collateral security for the above-mentioned loan of $6,000. May 13, 1896, Auguste Boenert paid the gold note given to Coombs, and she received from him the Ziese note and trust deed, uncanceled. On February 24, 1898, the said $1,500 Ziese note, being then in the possession of Auguste Boenert, was sold by her for $1,250 to the appellant, Brosseau. Neither the deed from Ziese to Auguste Boenert, nor the deed from Auguste Boenert to Gillespie, makes mention of the Ziese mortgage or trust deed.

The evidence in this case was taken before a master in chancery, and was, under stipulation, read upon the hearing below. The trial court gave priority to the lien of the Ziese mortgage, which secures the note held by the appellant, Brosseau; but on appeal to the Appellate Court the decree of the circuit court was reversed, and an order entered remanding the cause to the circuit court, with directions to that court to give the appellee Lowy, holder of the Gillespie notes and mortgage, a first lien, and the appellant, Brosseau, a second lien.

Samson & Wilcox, for appellant. Consider H. Willett, for appellees.

RICKS, J. (after stating the facts). Appellant contends that the transfer of the Gillespie notes and trust deed in question by Anton Boenert to appellee Lowy as security was without the knowledge or authority of Auguste Boenert, who seems to have been the owner. On the part of appellee Lowy it is contended that such action on the part of Anton Boenert was with the authority and as the agent of his wife, Auguste, and there is evidence in the record to support such contention. The trial court, in the opinion attached to appellant's brief, and based on the same evidence here presented, also states: "The proof also tends to show that Anton Boenert was the agent of his wife, having full power and authority to bind her in all matters." The Appellate Court has also accepted such conclusion, and we are satisfied to concur therein. If, then, as stated by the trial court, "Anton Boenert was the general agent of his wife, having full power and authority to bind her in all matters," the transfer of the notes and trust deed to appellee, as security, by Anton Boenert, though his wife may have been the legal owner of the same, was binding upon her; and we cannot sustain the insistence of appellant that the transfer in question, being for the benefit of Anton Boenert, was therefore not binding upon his wife.

The question next remains to be considered, what effect did the purchase of the land from Ziese by Auguste Boenert, and her subsequent conduct in reference thereto, have upon the Ziese note and trust deed? It is contended by appellee, and was so held by the Appellate Court, that the Ziese $1,500 note, secured by the trust deed to Coombs, which incumbered 80 acres, of which the 20 acres subsequently incumbered by the trust deed now held by appellee Lowy form a part, constituted a part of the consideration for said purchase. The evidence would seem to leave no doubt of the correctness of this contention. Ziese and Boenert both testified that only $1,200 in cash was paid to Ziese for the conveyance to Auguste Boenert. Ziese stated, when asked who was to pay his $1,500 note: "Not me. The man that followed me was to pay it. The mortgage stays on the farm until the farm was sold to somebody else." He also stated that he was never asked to pay the note, or to pay the interest thereon, after he sold the farm; that he knew nothing about the extensions of time or changes as to the interest, which, with the payments of interest, were indorsed on the note. When asked if he was to pay his note after such sale, he answered: "I could not pay the $1,500. I don't own the land. I guess the owner of the land has to pay." And in reply to the further inquiry if he paid it, he replied, "No." Anton Boenert testified that Ziese said to him, "If you or your wife, or whoever buys the property, gives me so much for my equity, I will convey the property and go to Dakota," and that the consideration in the deed was $8,000, because the land was then considered worth $100 per acre. The cash payment and the Ziese note together would make but $2,700. How the difference between this amount and the consideration named in the deed was made up, if it was made up at all, the record does not disclose.

The facts connected with the execution of the two release deeds also tend strongly to show that Auguste was to pay the Ziese note, as a part of the purchase price, in the purchase of the land from Ziese. Ziese was not consulted, and had no knowledge of their execution. The release deeds, being for sufficient land to pay the note, released Ziese of all personal liability. After Mrs. Boenert received the Ziese deed, she paid the interest on the Ziese note to Coombs; and finally, in order to procure a still further extension of the Ziese note, the Boenerts, on February 28, 1893, gave Coombs a gold note for $1,500, due in two years, and after the giving of that note no interest was paid on the Ziese note, but it was still held by Coombs as collateral security for the gold note; and finally, when the gold note was paid by Mrs. Boenert, in 1896, the Ziese note was surrendered to her. The loan of the $6,000 from Lowy was obtained April 30, 1896, just a few days before the gold note was paid, and it is likely it was from this source that the money was obtained to pay off the gold note.

The conduct of Mrs. Boenert and the testimony of Anton Boenert and Ziese seem conclusively to indicate that Mrs. Boenert was to pay the Ziese $1,500 note as a part of the purchase price of the equity of Ziese; and if, then, we accept such to be the fact, and also that Mrs. Boenert assumed the incumbrance on the land by her thus purchased, the land became the primary fund for the payment of said incumbrance, and when Mrs. Boenert purchased the Ziese note the incumbrance was discharged. Lilly v. Palmer, 51 Ill. 331; Drury v. Holden, 121 Ill. 130, 13 N. E. 547, and cases cited. The Ziese note and incumbrance, by the surrender of the said note to Mrs. Boenert, the legal owner of the fee, were discharged; and it was impossible, by any manner or form of transfer, as to third parties, to keep the same alive. In the case at bar, Coombs, the trustee in the trust deed, at the solicitation and request of one or both the Boenerts, and without the knowledge of the mortgagor, Ziese, not only extended the time of payment of the indebtedness, but released more than enough of the land covered by the trust deed necessary to make good the entire debt. So the mortgagor must have been released, even as to the liability of a surety, which relation he might otherwise have held.

The rule to be extracted from the numerous holdings of the courts upon this subject is that, where the amount of the mortgage is to be paid as a part of the purchase money, it is an assumption of the debt (Torrey v. Thayer, 37 N. J. Law, 344), and that precise and formal words are unnecessary to impose upon a grantee an engagement to pay off a mortgage, but the inquiry is as to the intention of the parties (Collins v. Rowe, 1 Abb. N. C. 99). In Drury v. Holden, supra, this court said (page 137, 121 Ill., and page 548, 13 N. E.): "It is well established that, when a party purchases premises which are incumbered to secure the payment of indebtedness, and assumes the payment of the indebtedness as a part of the purchase money, the premises purchased are in his hands a primary fund for the payment of the debt, and it is his duty to pay it.' Lilly v. Palmer, 51 Ill. 331; Russell v. Pistor, 7 N. Y. 171 [57 Am. Dec. 509]. And the rule is the same, although there be no assumption of payment of the indebtedness, if the purchase be made expressly subject to the incumbrance, and the amount of the indebtedness thereby secured is included in, and forms a part of, the consideration of the conveyance. Lilly v. Palmer, supra; Comstock v. Hitt, 37 Ill. 542; Fowler v. Fay, 62 Ill. 375; Russell v. Pistor, supra; Ferris v. Crawford, 2 Denio, 598." In Winans v. Wilkie, 41 Mich. 264, 1 N. W. 1049, it was held that if a grantee of mortgaged premises assumes the incumbrance, and afterwards takes an assignment of the mortgage, he extinguishes the debt, and cannot afterwards give any right to foreclose the mortgage by assigning it. In Carlton v. Jackson, 121 Mass. 592, it was held that when an incumbrance is paid by one whose duty it was, by contract or otherwise, to pay it, such payment effected a release or discharge of the debt, and it could not thereafter be kept alive for any purpose.

The appellant, however, contends that inasmuch as Ziese conveyed his equity to Auguste Boenert "by a warranty deed, with full covenants, and nothing was said about the payment of incumbrances," oral evidence showing that the grantee, Auguste Boenert, assumed the incumbrance, was incompetent. The rule of this court is against this contention. In Drury v. Holden, supra, it is stated (page 137, 121 Ill., and page 548, 13 N. E.): "It is said the deed from Daggett to Drury contained full covenants of warranty, to which there was no exception; that thereby Drury's grantor covenanted that he would warrant and defend the lots conveyed against the holders of all incumbrances. The covenants extended only to what was conveyed, and that was not the lots absolutely, but the lots subject to the incumbrance." And on page 138, 121 Ill., and page 549, 13 N. E.: "It is objected that oral evidence was inadmissible to show that the amount of the incumbrances was deducted from the amount of the purchase price, and allowed to Drury. The evidence, being in regard to what constituted the consideration of the deed to Drury, and that the amount of the incumbrances was included in and formed a part of the consideration, was clearly competent, under the rule which permits parol evidence upon such subject of the consideration of a deed." In Lloyd v. Sandusky, 203 Ill. 621, 68 N. E. 154, after referring with approval to the case above quoted, we said (page 631, 203 Ill., and page 157, 68 N. E.): "Whenever the question has come before this court, it has been uniformly held that the statement of the amount of the consideration and acknowledgment of its receipt in the deed were formal recitals—their only operation, in law, being to prevent a resulting trust—and that they might be explained, varied, and contradicted by parol evidence."

It may be contended that the application of the views above expressed, and to deny the appellant the relief he seeks, will operate with much harshness as to him; but such condition could only result from his neglect to attend to what was manifestly his duty, and against such negligence equity does not afford relief. It was appellant's duty, as the assignee of a trust deed, if he wished to protect himself, to have inquired of the maker thereof as to the status of the debt. Had he done so, he would have learned sufficient to have put him on his guard. The position of appellee is entirely different. He took the notes pledged to him under representations that they were purchase-money notes, and the trust deed securing them was a first lien on the premises, and further inquiry would have developed the fact that the Ziese note had been surrendered by Coombs, the trustee under the Ziese trust deed, the same having been duly paid; and the fact that said note had been surrendered to Auguste Boenert, the purchaser from Ziese, and owner of the fee in the premises conveyed, who subsequently conveyed the same to Gillespie by warranty deed, would have justified the legal conclusion that then, even if Auguste Boenert had received an assignment of the Ziese mortgage, and the same was uncanceled, such assignment must inure to the benefit of her grantee, and under no hypothesis or theory could Auguste Boenert again sell the said Ziese note and mortgage, and invest the purchaser with any prior or superior lien upon the land, as against another holding a valid lien thereon. The rule applicable in such case is stated in Jones on Mortgages, § 867, as follows: "When one who has conveyed land with warranty, which is subject to a mortgage, whether made by him or by another, afterwards takes an assignment of such mortgage, he holds it for the benefit of the person to whom he has granted the land, and the mortgage is in fact discharged by coming into his hands. Even if he should assign it to one who in good faith pays full consideration for it, the purchaser would acquire no lien upon the land." And in Pomeroy's Equity Jurisprudence, vol. 2, note to section 798, it is also stated: "If a person who has conveyed land with a covenant warranting against incumbrances afterwards pays off or takes an assignment of a mortgage upon the premises, the same becomes extinguished. He cannot keep it alive as a subsisting lien, for to do so would be a direct violation of his covenant"—which rule is supported by ample authorities there cited.

Applying the well-recognized rules of law that are applicable to the facts appearing in the case at bar, we are of the opinion that the relief prayed for by appellant was properly denied; and, being of such opinion on the points already considered, it is not necessary that we discuss the other defenses insisted upon by appellee.

In this case it is not insisted upon as error to have given appellant, Brosseau, the holder of the Ziese mortgage, a second lien, by any other person than appellant himself, who alone assigned errors upon the judgment of the Appellate Court, and whose only contention is that his lien should be first instead of second. We therefore deem it unnecessary to enter into a review of the authorities as to the right of Brosseau to have a second lien.

The judgment of the Appellate Court will therefore be affirmed. Judgment affirmed.

(209 Ill. 496)

HURSEN v. HURSEN.

(Supreme Court of Illinois. April 20, 1904.)

COURTS — APPEAL—FREEHOLD—JURISDICTION—STATUTES.

1. Where the bill in an action by a husband against his wife to set aside a conveyance of real estate from him to her prior to their marriage treats the deed as an absolute conveyance, and asks that it be declared null and void, and the record shows that it was treated by the parties as a conveyance of land, a claim by appellant, on appeal from an order of the Appellate Court dismissing the appeal to that court on the ground that a freehold was involved, that the deed was in fact a mortgage given to secure his wife in her property rights, and was not intended to, and in fact did not, convey to her the fee, and consequently that no freehold was involved, is untenable.

2. The necessary result of a decree in an action by a husband to set aside, on the ground of fraud and conspiracy, a conveyance of land to his wife prior to their marriage, involves a freehold; and hence an appeal from the circuit to the appellate court is properly dismissed, under Hurd's Rev. St. 1901, c. 37, par. 25, declaring that the Appellate Courts shall not exercise appellate jurisdiction where a freehold is involved.

Appeal from Appellate Court, First District.

Suit by Patrick Hursen against Margaret Hursen. From an order of the Appellate Court (110 Ill. App. 345) dismissing the appeal, plaintiff appeals. Affirmed.

F. S. Baird, for appellant. Benedict J. Short, for appellee.

WILKIN, J. Appellant filed his bill in the circuit court of Cook county against appellee, his wife, to set aside a certain deed of conveyance from him to her upon the ground of fraud and conspiracy. The bill alleges that appellant was a widower, and proposed marriage to appellee, which she accepted, provided he would make her certain presents. He then charges that appellee, previous to her marriage with him, conspired with her sister and other persons to him unknown, to obtain from him certain real estate described in the bill, and that she fraudulently, with the intent to cheat and defraud him out of said premises, entered into marriage relations with him, meaning and intending thereby to secure from him as many presents and as much property as possible and then refuse to live with him, and that, in furtherance of such conspiracy, she did marry him, and did obtain from him a deed to said property, and afterward refused to live with him. The bill avers that said deed is a cloud upon his title, and prays that it be declared null and void and canceled of record. Appellee, in her answer, denied the alleged fraud set up in the bill, and averred that the property was agreed to be, and was, conveyed by appellant to her in settlement of property rights between them before their marriage. Upon a hearing before the chancellor on bill, answer, replication, and evidence, the bill was dismissed for want of equity at the cost of appellant. From that order an appeal was prayed to the Appellate Court, where the appeal was dismissed upon the ground that a freehold was involved, and that the appeal should have been taken directly to this court, from which order of dismissal this further appeal has been prosecuted.

It is now claimed by appellant that the deed to appellee was in fact a mortgage given to secure her in her property rights, and was not intended to, and in fact did not, convey to her the fee of the premises in question, and consequently no freehold was involved. This contention, however, is not sustained by the record. The conveyance is by warranty deed absolute upon its face. It was treated by the parties as a conveyance of land, not as a security or mortgage upon land. The bill, as filed, treats the deed as an absolute conveyance, and not as a mortgage, and asks that it be canceled and declared null and void. A freehold, within the meaning of the statute, is involved in a case where the necessary result of the judgment or decree is that one party gains and the other loses an estate in land, or where the title to the estate is so put in issue by the pleadings that the determination of the case necessarily involves a decision of that issue, and by the terms of the statute in all such cases an appeal lies directly from the trial court to this court. Hurd's Rev. St. 1901, c. 37, par. 25; Nevitt v. Woodburn, 175 Ill. 376, 51 N. E. 593. The necessary result of the decree below involves the fee of the land. Therefore a freehold was involved, and the appeal should have been taken directly to this court.

The affirmance of the order of the Appellate Court dismissing the appeal disposes of the case so far as this court is concerned, but, in considering that question, it has become necessary to examine the evidence offered before the court; and we are impressed with the fact that it wholly fails to support the allegations of the bill charging fraud and conspiracy, and that the chancellor committed no error in dismissing the same at the complainant's cost. However, we can only affirm the judgment of the Appellate Court. Judgment affirmed.

(209 Ill. 402)

BROWN v. ILLINOIS, I. & M. RY. CO.

(Supreme Court of Illinois. April 20, 1904.)

EMINENT DOMAIN — CONDEMNATION PROCEEDINGS — DAMAGES — EVIDENCE—REBUTTAL—PREJUDICIAL ERROR—INCOMPETENT EVIDENCE—EVIDENCE STRICKEN OUT—ADEQUACY OF DAMAGES—REVISION ON APPEAL.

1. In condemnation proceedings, where the evidence is evenly divided, two sets of witnesses fixing the value of the land and taken at widely different amounts, the verdict, when within the range of the testimony, will not be disturbed as inadequate.

2. In condemnation proceedings, evidence as to the cost to the railroad of filling up and improving the land to make it suitable for its purposes is incompetent.

3. In condemnation proceedings, the admission of incompetent evidence as to the cost to the railroad of filling up and improving the land for its purposes could not be held prejudicial, where the verdict was for about three times as much as the petitioner's witnesses testified the land was worth, and the evidence showed that it was used for pasture only, that it was low and marshy and subject to overflow, and that its rental value was very small.

4. In condemnation proceedings, where a witness for respondent testified that the land was worth from $600 to $700 per acre, and gave as the basis of his opinion that he understood that another piece of land in the neighborhood sold on foreclosure for between $300 and $400 per acre, it was proper for petitioner to introduce in rebuttal the master's certificate on the foreclosure, showing that the land sold for about $63 per acre.

5. Where improper evidence is stricken out by the court, its introduction will not constitute reversible error, unless it appears that the jury were influenced by reason thereof.

Appeal from Kane County Court; M. C. Southworth, Judge.

Condemnation proceedings by the Illinois, Iowa & Minnesota Railway Company against Charles E. Brown. From the judgment fixing his compensation for land taken, respondent appeals. Affirmed.

Sears & Smith, for appellant. Murphy & Alschuler, for appellee.

RICKS, J. On the 18th day of August, 1903, appellee filed its petition in the county court of Kane county, under the eminent domain act, to condemn a part of block 1 in Hercules Park Addition to the city of Aurora; there being about 12.7 acres sought to be taken by the petitioner. No claim is made for damages to land not taken. After the jury were impaneled and sworn to try the case, they made a personal inspection of the premises sought to be condemned, and, after such inspection, evidence was introduced by both appellant and appellee as to the value of the said premises; and, after being properly instructed, the jury returned a verdict fixing the compensation to be paid appellant for the land taken at $2,000. Judgment was entered on the verdict, from which respondent appeals to this court.

There are no instructions complained of, and no questions of law presented, except the objection to certain evidence introduced by the petitioner.

It is also claimed by appellant that the verdict is inadequate, but it is not disputed by him that the compensation awarded by the jury is within the range of values as testified to on the trial; six witnesses having testified for appellee, fixing the value of the tract designated at from $45 to $75 per acre, and six witnesses testified for appellant, fixing the value at from $400 to $900 per acre. We have repeatedly held that when there is a conflict in the evidence, and the jury view the premises, a verdict will not be disturbed, unless it is manifestly against the weight of all the evidence introduced in the case. Here the evidence is apparently evenly divided, two sets of witnesses fixing the value at widely different amounts; and, under the circumstances, the verdict will not be disturbed on the ground that the allowance is too small.

Upon the trial of the case the petitioner introduced evidence to show that the property in question was very low and marshy, and that it would cost to exceed $29,000 to fill it up to a level with the land on either side, to make it accessible to the uses for which it was sought to be put by appellee. The evidence as to the cost of filling up and improving the land to make it suitable for the purposes for which appellee desired the same was not competent evidence, but, unless it appears that the jury were misled by such evidence, the verdict ought not to be disturbed. The evidence shows that the land was used by appellant for pasture only, and was low and marshy, and subject to overflow; that its rental value did not exceed $3 per acre; and that it was not a profitable piece of land, so far as any income was derived from it by appellant. And the verdict being for about three times as much as the witnesses for the petitioner testified the land was worth, we cannot say that the jury were prejudiced or influenced by reason of such evidence, inasmuch as appellant has apparently received just compensation, taking into consideration the uses to which he has devoted the land, and the uses to which it was adapted.

It is also insisted by appellant that a master's certificate offered in evidence, showing what other property sold for in the neighborhood of this property, was not proper evidence. But the record shows that a witness for appellant testified on his direct examination that he considered the land in question was worth from $600 to $700 per acre, and on cross-examination gave as the basis of his opinion that he understood the piece of land described in the master's certificate, on a foreclosure, sold for between $300 and $400 per acre. The master's certificate was proper evidence to rebut this evidence, showing that the land, under the foreclosure, sold for about $63 per acre; and, apparently, being introduced for this purpose, we are unable to say that it was error.

Other evidence introduced by the petitioner is complained of, but, inasmuch as it was stricken out by the court, we are unable to see how appellant could be seriously injured by reason of its introduction, as, where improper evidence is stricken out by the court, it will not be reversible error, unless it appears that the jury were influenced by reason of the introduction of the same.

Finding no reversible error, the judgment of the county court of Kane county will be affirmed. Judgment affirmed.

(209 Ill. 376)

SMYTHE'S ESTATE et al. v. EVANS.

(Supreme Court of Illinois. April 20, 1904.)

CONTRACTS — VALIDITY — PUBLIC POLICY—ADMINISTRATION OF ESTATES—CLAIMS—EVIDENCE—INSTRUCTIONS.

1. A contract between the engineer having the supervision of the construction of a plant and the contractor under contract for the construction thereof, stipulating that the engineer shall share in the profits of the contractor realized from the construction of the plant, is contrary to public policy and void.

2. Where a corporation let a contract for the construction of a plant under the supervision of its engineer, a contract between the engineer and the contractor stipulating that the former shall share in the profits realized from the construction of the plant will not be enforced, though the contract between the corporation and the contractor has been fully performed, unless the corporation, acting through its board of directors, expressly agreed that the engineer might make the contract, or unless the corporation, through the same authority, expressly ratified the act of the engineer.

3. An instruction, in an action on a contract giving plaintiff a share in the profits realized by defendant's intestate in the construction of a plant, that there could be no recovery unless it appeared that the intestate received as profits some "certain, definite, and fixed amount," was misleading, as conveying the idea that there could be no recovery unless the evidence fixed the exact amount which the intestate received.

4. A person who is to be paid for his services a share of the profits realized by another in a venture in which the services are to be rendered is not the latter's partner.

5. A requested instruction containing a correct statement of the law applicable to the case, but preceded by an erroneous abstract proposition, is properly refused.

6. A credit of a payment contained in the statement of a claim filed in the probate court against the estate of a decedent is no evidence of payment by the decedent.

7. In proceedings for the allowance of a claim against the estate of a decedent it appeared that

¶ 4. See Partnership, vol. 38, Cent. Dig. §§ 22, 43.

the claimant, as administrator of the estate, had, prior to the filing of the claim, filed an inventory of the estate and an account current showing disbursements sufficient to reduce the assets below the amount of the claim. The probate court had, prior to the filing of the claim, entered two orders for the distribution of the estate. Both orders recited that they were made on the petition of the administrator. *Held*, that the inventory, the account current, and the orders were admissible in evidence as tending to show that the claim was invalid.

8. The orders of the probate court should be preceded by the petitions on which they were based, or, if the petitions could not be found, proof of their contents should be given before the admission of the orders.

9. In an action on a contract to recover a share of the profits realized by a contractor in the construction of a plant, the books of the contractor pertaining to the construction of the plant are competent evidence.

10. In an action on a contract to recover a share of the profits realized by a contractor in the construction of a plant an expert accountant may show the jury the results of footings, etc., but cannot state the amount of the profits, that being a conclusion which is for the jury to determine.

Appeal from Appellate Court, First District.

Proceedings in the probate court fo. the allowance of a claim of Charles H. Evans against the estate of Andrew E. Smythe, deceased. From a judgment of the Appellate Court (108 Ill. App. 145) affirming a judgment of the circuit court in favor of the claimant rendered on appeal from an order of the probate court disallowing the claim, the estate of the deceased and his sole heir appeal. Reversed.

Appellee, on September 21, 1899, filed his claim for $125.000 in the probate court of Cook county against the estate of Andrew E. Smythe, deceased. That court, after hearing the evidence, entered an order disallowing the claim. Evans appealed to the circuit court of Cook county, where the case was tried before a jury, and a verdict was rendered in favor of appellee for $82,760.97. Motions for a new trial and in arrest of judgment were respectively overruled by the court, and judgment was rendered upon the verdict. Appellants appealed to the Appellate Court for the First District, where the judgment of the circuit court was affirmed, and they now appeal to this court.

Charles H. Evans, the appellee, was the administrator of the estate of Andrew E. Smythe at the time this claim was filed in the probate court, and that court appointed John T. Richards to defend said estate against this claim. Margaretta M. Smith is the sole heir and distributee of said estate, and joins in the appeal to this court. The claim of appellee, on which he obtained judgment below, is for one-half of the profits realized by deceased under a contract for the construction of a gas plant in the city of Chicago for the Universal Gas Company, of that city. The contract was made on March 14, 1895, between the gas company and Smythe, and provided that the plant should be constructed under the supervision of Evans, appellee, as engineer, who should pass upon the sufficiency of the work done under the contract. Smythe was to receive $1,177,000 for the work. which was to be completed by March 5, 1897, and payments were to be made from time to time upon the certificate of Evans to the amount of 85 per cent. of the value of the work done, 15 per cent. of the contract price to be withheld until the work was completed and accepted. On October 14, 1895, Smythe assigned the contract for the construction of this gas plant to the Continental Contract Company, a corporation with a capital stock of $100,000, of which Smythe owned all but $200 of the stock. Afterwards C. H. Randle acquired one-half of all the stock, and Smythe continued the owner of one-half. Evans superintended the construction of the gas plant, inspected material, received and passed on the bids of subcontractors, and ordered payments by the Continental Contract Company to the subcontractors as the work progressed, and contends that Smythe agreed to pay him one-half of the profits received by him (Smythe) from the construction of the gas plant for rendering these services, as Evans was an expert in the business of constructing plants of this character, while Smythe was not specially skilled in such work. The evidence also tends to prove that Smythe, or the Continental Contract Company, had a superintendent of construction by the name of Tibbets, whose duty it was to see that the work was properly constructed by the subcontractors, and, in general, to perform for the Continental Contract Company the duties of superintendent. Appellants contend that any supervision exercised by the claimant was in his capacity as engineer for the gas company. According to appellee, the net profits to the Continental Contract Company from this work amounted to $451,043.90, of which Smythe, as owner of one-half the capital stock of the company, was entitled to $225,521.95, and Evans, in his claim filed below, gives Smythe credit for $30,000 paid to him on account.

Appellants offered no evidence except the inventory and report of appellee, as administrator, and two orders for partial distribution, entered by the probate court of Cook county in Smythe's estate, to all of which objections were sustained. Appellants, both at the close of the evidence for the claimant and at the conclusion of all the evidence, asked the court to instruct the jury to find the issues for the estate, but the court refused to give such instructions. Appellants deny the existence of any contract between appellee and Smythe, but aver that, if cne existed, as claimed by appellee, the same was contrary to public policy, and void, because inconsistent with the duties which appellee, in his capacity as engineer for the Universal Gas Company, owed to that corporation. Appellants also insist that there is no evidence showing that Smythe received any profits from the work; that the circuit court erred in refusing to give instructions numbered 7, 8, 9, and 10, offered by appellants, and in giving instruction numbered 2 for appellee, and that the court erred in refusing to admit in evidence the inventory, report, and orders for partial distribution, offered by appellants.

John T. Richards, for appellant Smythe's Estate. Jesse A. & Henry R. Baldwin, for appellant Smith. Kretzinger, Gallagher & Rooney, for appellee.

SCOTT, J. (after stating the facts). A contract for the erection of a gas plant was made between the Universal Gas Company, as party of the first part, and Andrew E. Smythe, as party of the second part, and provides that it is "to be built and constructed under the supervision of C. H. Evans, engineer, and, in case of his death, removal, or disability, then under such other engineer as may be designated by said party of the first part, which said engineer shall pass upon the sufficiency of the work done under said contract. The workmanship and material to be first-class in all respects, and the work to be done to the satisfaction and acceptance of the engineer in charge." And one of the questions in the case is, did Evans act as engineer for the gas company, as contemplated by the parties to the foregoing contract at the time it was executed?

It appears from the testimony of Joseph Dawson, a civil engineer and draftsman, that in 1895 and 1896 he was employed by the Universal Gas Company in preparing the detail plans for the erection of this plant, that Evans gave him instructions in reference to this work, and that Evans was engineer of the Universal Gas Company and in the employ of that company while the witness was there. The evidence therefore at least tends to show that Charles H. Evans, the claimant, was the engineer in charge of the work for the Universal Gas Company, whose duty it was to pass upon the sufficiency of the work done under the contract, and who had to be satisfied by Smythe that the workmanship and material were first-class in all respects. If, as he now contends, he was also in the employ of Smythe, the contractor, and entitled to receive from Smythe one-half of the profits realized by the latter from the contract, then he was in a position where absolute loyalty to the interests of his employer, the Universal Gas Company, would bring him in conflict with his own interests as the employé of Smythe, because in the latter capacity it would advance his own interests to accept, as a compliance with the contract, workmanship and material of a cheaper grade than first-class, for the reason that Smythe's profits, and consequently his own compensation, would thereby be increased.

In the case of Gilman, Clinton & Springfield Railroad Co. v. Kelly, 77 Ill. 426, where a bill was filed by a stockholder in the railroad company charging that certain directors thereof had become stockholders in another corporation, the Morgan Improvement Company, and that the railroad company had made a contract for the construction of certain work with the improvement company under which work had been done, and asking that the contract be declared fraudulent in law and void, and requiring the directors who were stockholders of the improvement company to surrender to the railroad company the profits they had realized from the construction contract, this court held that the relief sought should be granted. It will be perceived that the case closely approaches the case at bar. Here the claimant was an agent of the corporation, as the evidence tends to show, while in the Kelly Case the persons charged with improper conduct were directors of the corporation. It is not believed that this is an essential difference. One man cannot serve two masters with reference to any matter where their interests are adverse, and it matters not, where one of those masters be a corporation, whether the servant be a director or agent. His duty to his master is none the less imperative.

In the case to which we have just referred we used this language (page 434): "It may be added, the rule stands on the obligation which a party owes to himself and his principal that forbids him to assume a position which would ordinarily excite a conflict between his individual interest and a faithful discharge of his fiduciary duties. It operates to restrain all agents or trustees, public or private. The inquiry is not whether the contract the trustee has made is the best that could have been made for the cestui que trust, or whether it is fraudulent in fact. So strictly is this principle adhered to that no question is allowed to be raised as to fairness of the contract. The principle has a broader scope. The law has absolutely inhibited the agent or trustee from placing himself in a position where his own private interests would naturally tend to make him neglectful of his obligations to his principal, or where his position would afford him an opportunity to speculate in the trust property." In Aberdeen Railway Co. v. Blaikie, 1 MacQueen (H. L.) 461, it is said: "A corporate body can only act by agents, and it is, of course, the duty of those agents so to act as best to promote the interests of those corporations whose affairs they are conducting. Such agents have duties to discharge of a fiduciary nature towards their principal, and it is a rule of universal application that no one having such duties to discharge shall be allowed to enter into engagements in which he has or can have a personal interest conflicting, or which position may conflict, with the interests of those whom he is bound to protect." To the same effect are Story on Agency, § 211; Higgins v. Lansingh, 154 Ill. 301, 40 N. E. 362; Young v. Trainor, 158 Ill. 428, 42 N. E. 139; Hafner v. Herron, 165 Ill. 242, 46 N. E. 211; Meyer v. Hanchett, 43 Wis. 247; Rice v. Davis, 136 Pa. 439, 20 Atl. 513, 20 Am. St. Rep. 931; Bell v. McConnell, 37 Ohio St. 396, 41 Am. Rep. 528; Lum v. McEwen, 56 Minn. 278, 57 N. W. 662; Farnsworth v. Hemmer, 1 Allen, 494, 79 Am. Dec. 756. These cases proceed upon the ground that such a contract made by the agent of one party to serve another with whom the first employer is dealing is contrary to public policy where the interests of the employers which are involved are adverse.

Appellee suggests, however, that here the contract between the corporation and Smythe has been fully performed, and, as the corporation has not in any wise interfered or objected to the existence or enforcement of the contract which it is claimed existed between Evans and Smythe, Smythe cannot interpose its illegality in a suit brought to compel him to divide the ill-gotten gains. Cases are cited from Georgia and California which seem to support this position. Counsel also refer to to the case of Brooks v. Martin, 2 Wall. 70, 17 L. Ed. 732, which we think not in point. That was a case where a partnership had been formed for the purpose of buying from soldiers of the United States then returning from the Mexican war their claims for bounty land or scrip before the land warrants or scrip were issued by the government—a traffic prohibited by statute. The suit was to compel a division of profits among the partners. It is to be observed that neither of the partners owed any obligation of a fiduciary character to the persons from whom the property was purchased and from which the profits were realized, and in that respect the case is distinguishable from this one.

The great weight of authority is that, where a party comes into court seeking to enforce a contract which is against public policy, or is prohibited by public law, the court will refuse to aid either party, and will leave them where they have placed themselves; and in refusing to enforce such contracts the court does not act for the benefit, or for the preservation of the alleged rights, of either party, but in the maintenance of its own dignity, the public good, and the laws of the state. Wright v. Cudahy, 168 Ill. 86, 48 N. E. 39; Crichfield v. Bermudez Paving Co., 174 Ill. 466, 51 N. E. 552, 42 L. R. A. 347; Young v. Trainor, supra; Hafner v. Herron, supra; Meyer v. Hanchett, supra; Bell v. McConnell, supra; Lynch v. Fallon, 11 R. I. 311, 23 Am. Rep. 458; Raisin v. Clark, 41 Md. 158, 20 Am. Rep. 66; Oscanyan v. Winchester Repeating Arms Co., 103 U. S. 261, 26 L. Ed. 539; Findlay v. Pertz, 66 Fed. 427, 13 C. C. A. 559; Holman v. Johnson, 1 Cowp. 341; Lum v. McEwen, supra. Nor will the fact, if it be a fact, that both parties knew of the double employment, enable Evans to recover. Before he can recover from Smythe it must appear from a preponderance of the evidence that the Universal Gas Company, acting through or by the authority of its board of directors, expressly agreed that he should enter into the contract with Smythe, or that, after the contract with Smythe had been made, the gas company was made aware of all the material facts, and then, through or by the authority of its board of directors, acquiesced and expressly ratified the act of its agent, Evans, in entering into that agreement. 1 Am. & Eng. Ency. of Law (2d Ed.) p. 1113; Gilman, Clinton & Springfield Railroad Co. v. Kelly, supra; Meyer v. Hanchett, supra; Rice v. Davis, supra; Raisin v. Clark, supra; Lynch v. Fallon, supra; Bollman v. Loomis, 41 Conn. 581; Capener v. Hogan, 40 Ohio St. 203; Everhart v. Searle, 71 Pa. 256; Bell v. McConnell, supra. The case of Tewksbury v. Spruance, 75 Ill. 187, to which we are referred by appellee, is not in conflict with this statement of the law. There agents were employed to purchase wheat, and it was held that they could not turn over to their principal wheat held by the agents, even if they charged no more than the market price, unless they disclosed the fact to the principal. If the fact was so disclosed, and the principal accepted the wheat, of course there could be no ground of complaint.

It follows that instruction No. 2, given on the part of appellee, is wrong, in that it advises the jury that Evans may recover if the Universal Gas Company knew of the contract with Smythe, "and with such knowledge, did not object." The law requires more than knowledge and a failure to object. It requires either approval of the contract at or before the time it was entered into with Smythe, or ratification of the act of the agent, with full knowledge of all material facts after it was entered into.

Appellants complain of the refusal of instructions numbered 7, 8, 9, and 10. The seventh is to the effect that there can be no recovery unless it appears from the evidence that Smythe received, as profits from said contract, some "certain, definite, and fixed amount." We think this instruction was apt to mislead the jury by conveying to them the idea that there could be no recovery unless the evidence fixed the exact amount which Smythe received. If the claimant was entitled to recover, on his theory of the case he could recover one-half of whatever amount Smythe received, and to entitle him to recover it was not necessary the evidence should fix with absolute certainty the amount of profits received by Smythe; that is, if it were shown that Smythe received as profits some indefinite amount, which, however, was shown to be in excess of $100,000, then the claimant, if entitled to recover one-half thereof, would be entitled to recover $50,000, even though the evidence did not fix the exact amount of profits received by Smythe.

The eighth instruction proceeds on the theory that if the jury find, from the evidence, that there was a partnership between Evans and Smythe, then there can be no recovery in this suit unless there was a settlement of the partnership affairs in the lifetime of Smythe. There was nothing in the evidence on which to base this instruction. Claimant's contention was that he was to be paid for his services one-half of Smythe's profits. This would not make them partners. Burton v. Goodspeed, 69 Ill. 237.

The latter part of the ninth instruction is that, "if you should find, from the evidence herein, that the claimant, Charles H. Evans, was the superintendent or engineer of the Universal Gas Company at the time of the performance or carrying out of the contract for the construction of a gas plant for the said company, and that the said Charles H. Evans was, by his agreement with the contractor for the said work, to receive a portion of the profits which said contractor was to receive or might derive out of the said contract, then that the said law relating to public policy would bar the said Evans from recovering upon his said contract for the recovery of the said profits or any part or portion thereof, and that in such case your verdict must be for the estate of Andrew E. Smythe," and as quoted lays down the law correctly; but it was preceded by an abstract proposition of law, in the first part of the instruction, in reference to an agent placing himself in a position where his position would afford him an opportunity to speculate in trust property—wholly inapplicable here—and the instruction was therefore properly refused.

The tenth contained the same vice as the seventh.

As the case must be submitted to another jury, we deem it proper to pass on three questions arising in reference to the admissibility of evidence. Appellee argues, and it is stated in the opinion of the Appellate Court, that "Smythe paid Evans $30,000 on account, pursuant to the terms of their contract." Evans, in the statement of his claim filed in the probate court, gives credit for the sum of $30,000 paid him by Smythe in the lifetime of the latter. There is no other evidence of such a payment, and it is scarcely necessary to say that this is not evidence against appellants.

The appellants offered the inventory in the estate of Smythe, filed by Evans on December 7, 1897, and an account current made by the claimant as administrator of the estate of Smythe, filed in the probate court of Cook county on February 27, 1900, which showed disbursements prior to the filing of this claim which would reduce the available assets in the hands of the administrator, as we understand, to some amount between $55,000 and $60,000, which is less than the amount of this claim. They also offered in evidence certified copies of two orders of distribution in Smythe's estate entered in the probate court one on October 12, 1897, and the other on December 22, 1897, both of which recite that they are made upon the petition of the administrator. The first directs the disbursement of $20,000 to the heir at law. The second orders the investment of $2,000 and the distribution of $10,000 to the heir at law, the order for the distribution to the heir at law in each instance reciting that it be made provided that the sum specified be not necessary for the purposes of administration, and the report shows payments to the heir at law in excess of $20,000 prior to the time when appellee's claim was filed in the probate court. These transactions, unexplained, are inconsistent with the existence of a claim in favor of the administrator for $82,000. The natural thing for an administrator to do would be to keep in his hands sufficient funds to meet the known liabilities of the estate. The account current which was offered in evidence, and which appears in the transcript, shows that Evans entered upon the administration of this estate at least as early as October 12, 1897. He did not file his claim until September 21, 1899. He says by his counsel in this case that the mere fact that he did not object "to the entry of two orders for payment to the heirs of sums that should have been retained to apply to his claim is not evidence against his claim," from which we understand there is no question but that it appears from the offered documents that he made such distribution to the heir at law that the assets in his hands were thereby reduced to an amount insufficient to meet his own claim if allowed.

In the case of Johnson v. Gillett, 52 Ill. 358, where an administrator asserted that he had paid and satisfied all the claims against the estate except a claim in his own favor, which he filed against the estate, and averred that he had, in the payment of such other claims, exhausted the personal estate, this court said (page 361): "It is the acknowledged duty of all courts, when the claims of an administrator are preferred against an estate he represents, that all matters pertaining to it and to the administration of the estate should be closely scrutinized. Such is the relation he bears to the estate, and to all the parties interested in it, that courts can hardly be too careful and scrutinizing, so that the true facts and the real condition of the estate and the acts and doings of the administrator can be readily seen and easily comprehended by those in interest." We think the court should have received in evidence the inventory, the account current, and the orders. The latter, however, should be preceded by the petitions upon which they were based, if such petitions are in existence; and if they are not in existence, or cannot be found, then proof of their contents, if it is to be had, should be made before the admission of the orders.

Harry Flyton was bookkeeper for the Continental Contract Company. The books of that corporation pertaining to the construction of this gas plant have never been closed, so as to show the amount of profits realized. Flyton made a statement from the books, and was permitted, over objection, to testify, after refreshing his memory from that statement, what the amount of the profits was. Appellants' brief does not present the matter so that we can understand precisely what was done in the court below. These books were competent evidence. It is also proper, for the convenience of the jury, to take the evidence of a bookkeeper, accountant, or other person skilled in work of that character, to show the footing of a column of figures, or to show the result of any calculation from a complicated set of figures which cannot be readily carried in mind by the jury, where the calculation is purely mathematical. In making these figures from these books the only thing which it was proper to show by Flyton was the footings or other results obtained, in figures. His statement, based upon his examination of the books, that the profits were a certain sum, is a conclusion, and inadmissible. It is for the jury to ascertain from the evidence what profits were received by Smythe, if any.

The judgments of the Appellate and circuit courts will be reversed, and the cause remanded to the circuit court for further proceedings in conformity with the views herein expressed.

Reversed and remanded.

(209 Ill. 448)

GLOS v. PATTERSON.

(Supreme Court of Illinois. April 20, 1904.)

EJECTMENT — TRIAL—PLEAS DENYING POSSESSION—TIME OF PRESENTATION—PREJUDICIAL ERROR — DEMAND — NECESSITY—DEFENDANTS NOT IN POSSESSION — EVIDENCE — LOST INSTRUMENTS—ABSTRACTS OF TITLE.

1. In ejectment one made a party defendant under section 6 of the ejectment act (Hurd's Rev. St. 1901, c. 45), as one not in possession of the premises, and who, on the trial, was not claimed to have been in possession, was not injured by the denial of his motion for leave to file a verified plea denying possession.

2. In ejectment a motion for leave to file a verified plea denying possession is not presented in time, when not made until the case is called for trial, and without excuse offered for failure to present it sooner.

3. Under Hurd's Rev. St. 1901, c. 116, § 29, providing that when a party shall testify or make affidavit that the originals of deeds relating to land are lost, such party may offer, as evidence, any abstract of title or letterpress copies thereof, made in the ordinary course of business, prior to such loss, and any extracts or minutes which were at the date of loss in the possession of persons engaged in the business of making abstracts of title for hire, affidavits showing the loss of original deeds and records by fire, and memoranda which were stated by the affidavits to be true copies of abstracts of title, and of books of original entry, and of minutes taken from books and indices, in the possession of a title and trust company, were properly admitted in evidence, although the history of the memoranda or the correctness of the copies was not shown.

4. One not in possession of premises, but made a party to an ejectment because of a claim of interest in the premises by reason of tax deeds, could not complain that no demand for possession had been made on the defendant in possession.

5. In ejectment, where the declaration alleged that on a certain date defendant entered into possession of the premises, and unlawfully withheld the same from plaintiff, and such defendant defaulted, thereby confessing the allegations of the declaration, it was unnecessary, on the trial against a codefendant not in possession, to prove a demand for possession made on the defaulting defendant.

Appeal from Circuit Court, Cook County; F. A. Smith, Judge.

Action by Catherine Patterson against Adam S. Glos and another. From a judgment for plaintiff, defendant Glos appeals. Affirmed.

See 68 N. E. 443.

Enoch J. Price, for appellant. William Gibson and F. W. Becker, for appellee.

WILKIN, J. On November 9, 1898, appellee brought suit in ejectment in the circuit court of Cook county against George Lotz and Adam S. Glos to recover possession of lot 24, block 11, in the city of Chicago. A trial by jury on July 22, 1901, resulted in a judgment for the plaintiff for possession of the premises, from which an appeal was prosecuted to this court, and the judgment below was affirmed. See 204 Ill. 540, 68 N. E. 443. Within a year after the entry of that judgment the defendant Glos paid the costs and took a new trial under the statute. A jury being waived, a trial was had before the court, and judgment again rendered on December 31, 1902, in favor of the plaintiff, and the defendant again appeals.

A statement of the facts of the case will be found in our former opinion (Glos v. Patterson, 204 Ill. 540, 68 N. E. 443); also the questions then presented for our decision.

At the beginning of the trial upon which the judgment now appealed from was rendered, defendant entered a motion for leave to file a verified plea denying possession, which was overruled by the court, and renewed at the close of all the evidence, and again denied. It is insisted by counsel for appellant that such a plea was proper in order to make the issues conform to the proof. It is impossible to see what injury could have resulted to the defendant on account of the absence of such a plea. He was made a party defendant under section 6 of the ejectment act (Hurd's Rev. St. 1901, c. 45), as one not in possession of the premises sued for, and it was not claimed or pretended upon the trial that he was, or ever had been, in possession. What purpose, then, would his plea have served denying possession? Neither was the plea presented in apt time, the motion not being made until the case was called for trial, and no excuse offered for the failure to present it sooner. Phenix Ins. Co. v. Stocks, 149 Ill. 319, 36 N. E. 408.

On the trial plaintiff attempted to show a connected paper title derived from the government, but, except one certified copy from the general land office, all the links in her chain of title prior to the fire of 1871 were shown by an affidavit of William Gibson as to the loss of the original deeds and the destruction by fire of the original records, followed by two affidavits of Henry H. Handy, one having an annexed memorandum which the affidavit stated was a true copy of an abstract of title in the possession of the Title Guarantee & Trust Company, and another affidavit having an annexed memorandum which the affidavit stated was a true copy from a book of original entry formerly belonging to Jones & Sellars, and now in the possession of the Title Guarantee & Trust Company. There was also an affidavit, with memorandum attached, made by Harrison B. Riley, which stated that the memorandum was a true copy of an abstract and minutes taken from books and indices formerly belonging to Chase Bros. and Shortall & Hoard, etc., now in the possession of the Title Guarantee & Trust Company. No evidence was offered to show the history of these memoranda or the correctness of the copies, and appellant claims that the preliminary proofs, as made, were insufficient, under the statute, to admit the secondary evidence.

Section 29, c. 116, Hurd's Rev. St. 1901, p. 1429, provides, in substance, that whenever, upon the trial of any suit, any party, or his agent or attorney, shall, orally in court or by affidavit filed, testify and state under oath that the originals of any deeds or records relating to any land or title in controversy are lost or destroyed, or are not within the power of the party to produce the same, it shall be lawful for such party to offer as evidence any abstract of title or letterpress copy thereof made in the ordinary course of business prior to such loss or destruction, and it shall also be lawful for any such party to offer extracts or minutes which were at the date of such destruction or loss in the possession of persons then engaged in the business of making abstracts of title for others for hire. We think the affidavits offered in evidence as to the destruction of the deeds and records, and the letterpress copies as offered, were in substantial compliance with this statute, and the court committed no error in admitting them. Russell v. Mandell, 73 Ill. 136; Miller v. Shaw, 103 Ill. 277; Chicago & Alton Railroad Co. v. Keegan, 152 Ill. 413, 39 N. E. 33; Cooney v. Booth Packing Co., 169 Ill. 370, 48 N. E. 406.

It is next insisted by the appellant that the judgment below was erroneously entered, for the reason that no demand for possession was made upon Lotz before the commencement of the suit. This point was passed upon in the former case (204 Ill. 540, 68 N. E. 443), and what we there said applies to this appeal, not as res judicata, but because the question was there decided, and nothing is here shown to question the correctness of that decision. The declaration alleges that on the 9th day of November, 1898, Lotz entered into possession of said premises and unlawfully withheld from the plaintiff the same. To this declaration Lotz permitted his default to be entered, thus confessing the allegations of the declaration as true. The appellant was only made a party defendant because he claimed some title or interest in the premises by reason of his tax deeds. It was admitted in the record that he was not in possession and had never been in possession, and had never made any attempt to get in possession. Therefore the question of the possession of Lotz, and any demand that might have been made upon him, in no way affected the title or interest of appellant, and he therefore was in no position to make any complaint that a demand was not made upon Lotz, even if such demand had been necessary under the pleadings in the case. As the record now stands, no demand was necessary upon Lotz, and for this reason the appellant has no cause for complaint.

We find no reversible error in the record, and the judgment of the circuit court will be affirmed. Judgment affirmed.

(178 N. Y. 391)

VALENTINE v. HEALEY et al.

(Court of Appeals of New York. May 3, 1904.)

TENANTS IN COMMON—HOLDING OVER—LIABILITIES.

1. A tenant in common can, in opposition to his co-tenant, permit a firm of which he is a member, and which had a lease of the premises for a year, to continue in possession temporarily without subjecting it to the liabilities of an ordinary tenant holding over.

Parker, C. J., and O'Brien, J., dissenting.

Appeal from Supreme Court, Appellate Division, First Department.

Action by Henry C. Valentine against Warren M. Healey and others. From a judgment of the Appellate Division (79 N. Y. Supp. 1149) reversing a judgment in favor of defendants, they appeal. Reversed.

Elihu Root and Robert Thorne, for appellants. John Notman, for respondent.

CULLEN, J. The action was brought to recover a quarter's rent of certain premises in the city of New York, owned by the plaintiff and the defendant Healey as tenants in common, the plaintiff owning three-quarters and the defendant Healey one-quarter. In May, 1891, the plaintiff and Healey by a written lease demised the premises to a firm composed of said Healey and the defendant Zabriskie for the term of one year at the annual rent of $8,500, payable quarterly, with the privilege to the defendants of continuing the lease for two years more upon giving notice in writing to the owners on or before February 1, 1892. Notice to renew was not given. The relations between the plaintiff and Healey were unfriendly. On April 29, 1892, Healey & Co. wrote two letters, one to the plaintiff and one to the defendant Healey, informing each that, as indicated by their failure to exercise the option reserved in the lease, they did not intend to renew it. They further stated that, understanding the premises had not been rented for the coming year, they would be pleased to occupy the same for a few weeks from the 1st of May paying a pro rata rent for such use and occupation. On the following day the plaintiff replied in writing: "You have been already informed that I would renew the lease of the factory for one year at the same rent as in the present lease, but would not let it for a shorter period. As your letter only repeats your request for a few weeks occupancy from May first, my answer repeats my refusal to grant it. Yours truly, Henry C. Valentine." The defendant Healey replied to the letter of Healey & Co. as follows: "You are at liberty to continue to occupy the premises at a pro rata rent for the period of such occupancy. This privilege is accorded you only with the understanding and agreement that such occupancy is to be terminated on a week's notice from either party, in order that we may take advantage of any opportunity that may offer to rent the premises for the entire year. Very truly, Warren M. Healey." Other correspondence was had between the parties, the details of which are not necessary to the disposition of this case. The defendants continued to occupy the premises for some weeks after the expiration of the lease, and then removed from the premises. The learned judge at Trial Term dismissed the complaint on the authority of the decision of this court on a previous appeal in the action, reported in 158 N. Y., at page 369, 52 N. E. 1097, 43 L. R. A. 667. The Appellate Division, by a divided court, reversed the judgment and ordered a new trial. From that order this appeal is taken.

We are of opinion that the disposition of this case is necessarily controlled by our previous decision. The theory on which the action is brought is that, where a tenant remains in possession after the termination of his lease, the landlord may, at his option, hold him as a tenant for another year upon the terms of the prior lease, and that such is the general rule there is no doubt. Haynes v. Aldrich, 133 N. Y. 287, 31 N. E. 94, 28 Am. St. Rep. 636. But on the previous appeal this court held, through Haight, J., who wrote the prevailing opinion, that the general rule does not apply to a case where the tenant holding over is a tenant in common owning an interest in the premises. It is true that the opinion proceeded also on the further ground that as it appeared that the written lease was executed by the defendant Healey alone (which is now shown not to be the fact), it might be assumed that he was the agent for the plaintiff, and was authorized to treat with the defendants as to the terms on which they might remain in possession of the premises. This latter ground is now wholly eliminated, for it appears that the plaintiff refused to consent to the defendants remaining in possession of the premises unless the same were taken for another year. But the two grounds on which the judgment of the court was based were entirely independent, and the fact that in the present record one of the legal propositions determined is no longer applicable in no way affects the determination of the other.

It must be now assumed that Healey, in authorizing his firm to remain in possession of the premises, acted in direct opposition to the will of his co-tenant, the plaintiff, and the only question presented is whether, by his title as tenant in common, he had power to suffer the firm to remain in possession without subjecting it to the liabilities that ordinarily obtain where a tenant holds over. This question was decided by the courts of this state as early as McKay v. Mumford, 10 Wend. 351. There the plaintiffs and E. Mumford, one of the defendants, were tenants in common of a grist mill, each owning one moiety. The plaintiffs leased their half of the mill to the defendants, their co-tenant

E. Mumford and one W. Mumford, for the term of nine months. The defendants remained in occupation of the whole mill after the expiration of the lease, and the action was brought to recover for use and occupation the amount reserved as rent in the lease. It was there held that such continuance in possession by a tenant in common or under the authority of a tenant in common did not operate as a renewal of the lease at the election of his co-tenant. It was there said by Judge Nelson: "The fact of his [a tenant in common] not leaving possession does not authorize the inference that he still intends to hold under the lease; on the contrary, the presumption is that he holds under his own title, which gives him a right to the possession and enjoyment of the whole estate, liable, however, to account to his co-tenant at law. This presumption of possession by virtue of his own title may undoubtedly be rebutted, and then he would hold, as to the moiety of his co-tenant, as any other tenant, and subject to the same rules at law. But evidence that E. Mumford intended or avowed his intention to hold in defiance of the plaintiffs and in exclusion of their rights does not rebut the presumption that he holds under his own title; it confirms it. * * * There should be evidence showing, either expressly or impliedly, a recognition of the holding after the term as tenant to the plaintiffs, or, in other words, an intention to hold under the agreement or with the assent of the plaintiffs, and not merely a possession entirely consistent with his common-law rights." In principle the case cited is on all fours with the one before us. There, as here, the tenants who it was claimed held over were not only the co-tenants of the lessors, but also a third party, the partner of the co-tenant, and the possession retained was that of the whole premises. If there be any difference between the two cases it lies in this: that in the McKay Case the lease was only of the undivided share of the lessor, which the tenant never offered to surrender to his lessor at the expiration of the demised term, while here the lease was of the whole property, executed by both the tenants in common. If the difference in circumstances justifies any distinction in principle, that distinction would operate in favor of the defendants, for Healey could be under no obligation to surrender his undivided fourth to the plaintiff. The authority of McKay v. Mumford has never been impaired by any subsequent decision in this state, but, on the contrary, the case itself was approved by this court on the previous appeal in this action. It has been recognized as a correct exposition of the law in Rockwell v. Luck, 32 Wis. 71, and in Freeman on Cotenancy, § 258, and we are referred to no authority in this country to the contrary. It may be that in the present case the action of the defendant Healey has been prejudicial to the interests of his co-tenant, the plaintiff, though there is no proof of that in the present record, as the owners seem to have been unable to lease the premises to any third party, and the defendant Healey remains liable to account for any profit he has reaped by the use of the property in excess of his share. If, however, such be the fact, it is one of the unfortunate results of common ownership of property. An obstinate or hostile tenant in common may subject his co-tenants to inconvenience and often loss. If so, there is always open a remedy to the co-tenants—an action may be brought for the partition of the common property. But we do not see how the plaintiff can succeed in this case without overturning the settled rules of law regulating the tenure of property by tenants in common.

The order of the Appellate Division should be reversed, and the judgment of the trial court affirmed, with costs.

O'BRIEN, J. (dissenting). In this case the plaintiff was the owner of three-fourths of the demised premises. The defendant Healey was the owner of the other fourth, and a member of the firm that went into possession of the premises under a written lease, agreeing to pay a stipulated rent, three-fourths of it to the plaintiff, and to surrender possession of the premises at the expiration of the term. The legal question presented is this: Can the defendant Healey's firm, after having entered as tenants under the lease, upon the authority of a letter from him written before the expiration of the demised term, remain in possession of the demised premises after the expiration of the term indefinitely without payment of rent, and without incurring the legal obligation arising out of the relation of landlord and tenant to be liable for rent for another year? Of course, it is elementary law that a tenant for a year who holds over after the expiration of the term becomes a tenant for another year at the option of the landlord. But it is said that the presence of Healey, the co-tenant in the firm or legal entity which became tenant under the lease, changes this rule, and that during the existence of the lease he has the power to extend the right of possession indefinitely, and that, too, without any obligation to pay any rent whatever. It is argued that this court on a former appeal decided just that proposition, and hence we are bound to decide in the same way now upon the principle of stare decisis. I do not think that this court has ever decided any such proposition, and, if it is law at all, it will have to be promulgated now for the first time.

A brief review of the history of this case will show very clearly that this statement is correct. This case first came before the Appellate Court nearly 10 years ago. Valentine v. Healey, 86 Hun, 259, 33 N. Y. Supp. 246. That was an appeal to the General

Term from a decision of the trial court dismissing the complaint. It was held that the cases in this court establish the rule that where a tenant in common is in exclusive possession of the common property *by virtue of his own title* he is not liable for rent to his co-tenant. But it was also held that this rule did not apply to this case, inasmuch as Healey was not *in exclusive possession as owner*, but was merely a member of a firm that was in possession as tenant under a lease. It will be seen that this proposition has never been questioned in this court. The judgment, having been unanimously reversed, came before the Appellate Division again. Valentine v. Healey, 1 App. Div. 502, 37 N. Y. Supp. 287. The plaintiff had recovered upon the second trial, and on appeal the judgment was unanimously affirmed, and in the opinion the court said: "The letter written by Healey was a consent that the lessees might hold over, as desired by them, and, if he had the power to bind the plaintiff by such consent, then the ordinary legal effect of the holding over was avoided, and this action cannot be maintained. It is not claimed that the plaintiff had any knowledge of this correspondence. The lease by its terms made the rent payable to each of the tenants in common according to their respective interests in the property. Healey was not authorized to act for plaintiff as his agent or otherwise, and the consent could not be operative as plaintiff's consent in any way. The only theory upon which it can be claimed that this consent of Healey's avoided the legal effect of the holding over is that he was a tenant in common with plaintiff as owner of the property, and, being such tenant in common, he could give his firm the right, outside of the lease, to remain in the occupancy of the property. At the time this consent was given, however, he was, as we have seen, *not in possession or occupancy as owner*, but merely as a tenant under the lease as a member of his firm. Such was the relation assumed by him and his firm in taking the lease, and they could not change this relation *during the term* so as to affect the plaintiff's rights under the lease without his knowledge or consent." From that decision an appeal was taken to this court. Valentine v. Healey, 158 N. Y. 369, 52 N. E. 1097, 43 L. R. A. 667. On reading the prevailing opinion of this court on that appeal it will be seen that none of the vital propositions that had been decided by the appellate courts below were questioned or overruled in any particular. After referring to the case of McKay v. Mumford, 10 Wend. 351, and the principle there decided, the court said: "This rule was recognized by the General Term in this case. 86 Hun, 259, 33 N. Y. Supp. 246. But that court distinguished that case from this. Healey is not the sole lessee. The lease ran to a firm of which he was a member. *In this respect the cases are distinguishable*, but we fail to see why Healey, *at the termination of the lease*, may not assume his authority over the premises as an owner and a tenant in common. As such tenant in common he had the right to take and occupy the whole of the premises *and preserve them from waste or injury* so long as he did not interfere with the right of his co-tenant to also occupy the premises." It is clearly apparent, so far, that there was not the slightest conflict between this court and the appellate courts below that had previously passed upon the case. But the learned judge who wrote the opinion in this court on that occasion went still farther, and stated this proposition: "There is another view of the case which we think may properly be adopted. It may be and doubtless is the law that a tenant in common cannot bind a co-tenant without his consent by a contract or a lease with reference to the property of which they are the owners." It is very clear that that is precisely what Healey attempted to do as disclosed by the record now before us. Before the demised term had expired, and while his firm was in under a lease, without any surrender of the lease, he wrote a letter to his firm giving it permission to hold over indefinitely. I think it may be safely asserted that there is nothing in the opinion of this court on the former appeal that in the least supports any such contention. In fact, just the contrary appears from the above quotations in the opinion. I am not able to find anything in it to sustain the proposition now asserted—that Healey, as a member of his firm, while in possession under the lease and before its expiration, could write a letter to his firm giving them permission to remain in possession indefinitely without any obligation to pay rent, and thus bind the plaintiff. If there is anything of that kind in the opinion, I confess I have not been able to understand it. In quoting the language of the opinions I should observe that the italics are my own.

From this review of the judicial history of this case, it seems to me that neither this court nor any other court ever decided the propositions now asserted in the prevailing opinion. The truth is, and that is perfectly plain from the record, that when this case was here on the former appeal it was reversed upon two questions which did not involve the merits at all. These questions were, first, that inasmuch as plaintiff's signature did not appear upon the printed copy of the lease contained in the record, then it might be presumed that Healey executed the lease for the plaintiff as his agent, and so acted as his agent throughout; second, that, being such agent to make the lease, he had authority also, as agent for the plaintiff, to bind him by giving the firm permission to remain in possession after the expiration of the demised term, and that, as such permission was evidenced by the letter which was excluded at the trial, the ruling in that respect was erroneous. It is now admitted on all sides that both of these questions have disappeared from the case, and hence the reason for the former decision of this court has disappeared also. When this case came here on the former appeal the appellate court below had decided twice that this case was not within the principle of McKay v. Mumford, supra. This court did not question the correctness of that proposition; on the contrary, it acquiesced in it, and went still farther, and stated the proposition quoted, and which, if followed now, would require an affirmance of the judgment; and I think it ought to be affirmed, since the equity and justice, and, as it seems to me, the law of the case, were on the side of the plaintiff.

GRAY, HAIGHT, and MARTIN, JJ., concur with CULLEN, J. PARKER, C. J., concurs with O'BRIEN, J. WERNER, J., absent.

Order reversed, etc.

(178 N. Y. 381)

NEW YORK LIFE INS. CO. v. CASEY et al.

(Court of Appeals of New York. April 26, 1904.)

MORTGAGE — EXTENSION—EVIDENCE—RELEASE OF SURETY.

1. The mere receipt from the grantee of mortgaged premises by the mortgagee of interest 3 days in advance is no evidence of a valid extension of the time of payment of the mortgage, where there is no proof of any agreement for such extension, and 2½ of the 3 days were legal holidays.

2. Evidence that a mortgagee directed an increase in the rate of interest, which the grantee of the mortgaged premises thereafter voluntarily paid, is insufficient, in the absence of any other evidence, to show a valid agreement between the mortgagee and the grantee to change the rate without the knowledge or consent of the surety, so as to discharge him.

Werner, Bartlett, and Martin, JJ., dissenting.

Appeal from Supreme Court, Appellate Division, Third Department.

Action by the New York Life Insurance Company against John Casey and others. From a judgment of the Appellate Division (81 N. Y. Supp. 1) reversing, as to John Casey, a judgment in favor of plaintiff, plaintiff appeals. Reversed.

This action was commenced to foreclose a mortgage executed by the defendant John Casey to the plaintiff to secure the payment of his bond for the sum of $24,000, and covering certain real property situated in the city of New York. The bond was to become due on April 5, 1902, and bore interest at the rate of 5 per cent. per annum, payable on the 1st days of January and July. Casey conveyed the mortgaged premises, subject to the mortgage, to one Friedberg, who in turn conveyed them to one Nordenschild. In September, 1893, while Nordenschild was the owner of the property, the finance committee of the plaintiff directed that the rate of interest on the bond and mortgage should be increased to 6 per cent. on and after October 1, 1893. On December 29, 1893, Nordenschild paid to the plaintiff the interest from July, 1893, to January 1, 1894, at the rate of 5 per cent. from July to October, and at the rate of 6 per cent. from October 1st to January 1st. It is admitted that the increase in the rate of interest and the payment of such increase were made without the knowledge or consent of the defendant Casey. It was also admitted that the value of the mortgaged property in 1893 was equal to the amount of the mortgage and accrued interest. On December 15, 1893, the rate of interest was ordered to be restored to the original rate of 5 per cent. from January 1, 1894.

The trial court found "that there was no agreement on the part of the plaintiff to change the rate of interest, or to extend the time of payment of the bond and mortgage, and that the fact that plaintiff accepted a different rate of interest than that provided in the bond and mortgage does not prove an agreement to change the rate of interest, and that no consideration for such an agreement was shown." Judgment was directed in favor of the plaintiff, and that judgment, on appeal to the Appellate Division in the First Department, has been reversed as to the defendant Casey. The order of reversal being silent as to its grounds, the determination of that learned court must be presumed to have been upon the law solely.

Andrew Hamilton, for appellant. Jacob Steinhardt, for respondent.

GRAY, J. (after stating the facts). This appeal presents the question whether the defendant Casey, standing as surety for the payment of the mortgage debt, was discharged from his liability upon his bond by the transactions which took place between the plaintiff and Nordenschild. If such was their effect, of course a judgment for any deficiency arising upon a sale of the mortgaged premises could not be entered against him, as was the case here. The finding of fact by the trial court was that there was no agreement on the part of the plaintiff to change the rate of interest upon, or to extend the time of payment of, the bond. With respect to so much of the question as turns upon the existence of any agreement by the plaintiff to extend the time of payment, I concur with what was said below by the dissenting justices, through Mr. Justice INGRAHAM, and with what is said by Judge WERNER in his opinion, and I shall not continue that discussion. I agree with the view that there was, in the evidence, sufficient to sustain the finding that no such agreement was made out, and therefore that it was error for the Appellate Division to reverse upon such a ground.

But I am also of the opinion that the reversal by the court below cannot be sustained upon the other ground—that there was an agreement to change the rate of interest, whereby Casey's liability was discharged. The finding of fact is to the contrary, and to affect its conclusiveness, upon this review by us of the order of the Appellate Division, we have nothing in the findings of the decision of the trial court, unless it be found in the language that "the fact that plaintiff accepted a different rate of interest than that provided in the bond and mortgage does not prove an agreement to change the rate of interest." It is not pretended that there was any evidence of the making of such an agreement, other than in the action of the plaintiff's finance committee in ordering an increase in the rate of interest during the six-months interest period from July to January, to be paid from October 1st, and in the payment by the owner of the mortgaged property of the increased rate for the last three months of that interest period. Does that prove any agreement, and, if it should be considered as tending to prove one, what sufficient consideration was there? It is clear that an agreement which was unenforceable for want of any consideration would not discharge the surety. The plaintiff did not bind itself to do anything in consideration of receiving an increased interest, and the defendant does not appear to have received any benefit. There were no mutual promises disclosed. If Nordenschild chose to pay more than the bond and mortgage obligated him to pay in the way of interest, that would not discharge Casey, if there was no valid agreement changing the contractual obligation. The court is not to imply some agreement merely because there was a consideration upon which one might have rested. The agreement which was to affect the principal contract must be proved clearly. The plaintiff might have covenanted with Nordenschild to extend the time of payment, or might have granted some indulgence, upon such a consideration; but it did not do so, and that is what the trial court found as a fact. I am quite unable to agree in the view that the action of the plaintiff's finance committee and the voluntary payment by the debtor, under the circumstances disclosed, furnished the facts for an inference of an agreement. The debtor was not bound to pay at the increased rate for the three months of the interest period, and he came under no apparent obligation to pay it thereafter. As matter of fact, the action of the finance committee appears to have been annulled, and the fixed contract rate re-established for the ensuing interest period.

For the reasons stated, I think that the reversal of the judgment of the trial court was erroneous, and I advise that the judgment of the Appellate Division should be reversed, and that the judgment of the Special Term should be affirmed, with costs to the appellant in this court and in the Appellate Division.

WERNER, J. (dissenting). Upon this appeal it must be presumed that the judgment entered upon the decision of the trial court was reversed upon the law and not upon the facts. Code Civ. Proc. § 1338. As none of the rulings upon evidence are presented for our consideration, and as the trial court's conclusions of law are clearly supported by the facts found, the only question that survives for our decision is whether any material finding of fact is without evidence to support it. Nat. Harrow Co. v. Bement & Sons, 163 N. Y. 505, 57 N. E. 764.

The learned Appellate Division seems to have based its decision upon two grounds: (1) That the acceptance by the plaintiff of the interest upon the bond and mortgage for the last half of the year 1893, three days before such interest was due, constituted an agreement to extend the time of payment of the mortgage, which extension worked a discharge of the respondent Casey from his liability on the bond. (2) That the receipt by the plaintiff of an increased rate of interest without the knowledge or consent of Casey was such a variation of the terms of the contract of suretyship assumed by the latter as to accomplish the same result.

In respect to the first question the trial court found as a fact that there was no agreement on the part of the plaintiff to extend the time of payment of the bond and mortgage. If there was any evidence to sustain this finding, the Appellate Division erred in reversing it as a matter of law. It is the settled law of this state that any extension of the mortgage debt by the creditor, without the knowledge or consent of the bondsman, releases the latter to the extent of the value of the land. Murray v. Marshall, 94 N. Y. 611; Antisdel v. Williamson, 165 N. Y. 372. And this is true although it suspends the right of action but a single day. Place v. McIlvain, 38 N. Y. 96, 99, 97 Am. Dec. 777; Ducker v. Rapp, 67 N. Y. 464, 472. But to effect this result there must be a valid agreement, express or implied, between the creditor and the principal debtor. Powers v. Silberstein, 108 N. Y. 169, 15 N. E. 185; Cary v. White, 52 N. Y. 138. The facts relating to this question are that on December 29, 1893, three days before it was due, the interest on the mortgage was paid to and received by the defendant. In that year December 29th fell on Friday, so that the day of payment was followed by a legal half holiday, one Sunday, and a full legal holiday, the latter being the day on which the interest was due. The respondent gave no evidence of any express agreement to extend the time or to forbear the collection of the debt during the days mentioned. The receipt by the plaintiff's auditor of the interest on December 29th is relied upon as of itself constituting an agreement to extend the time of payment, or to forbear the enforcement of the debt. Upon this subject Brandt on Suretyship (2d Ed. 352) says: "The general rule is that the reception of interest in advance upon a note is prima facie evidence of a binding contract to forbear and delay the time of payment, and no suit can be maintained against the maker during the period for which the interest has been paid unless the right to sue is reserved by the agreement of the parties. The payment of interest in advance is not of itself a contract to delay, but is evidence of such contract, and while this evidence may be rebutted, yet in the absence of any rebutting evidence it becomes conclusive." The rule as thus laid down seems to be supported by the great weight of authority in this country. Hitchcock v. Frackelton, 116 Mich. 487, 491, 74 N. W. 720; Warner v. Campbell, 26 Ill. 282; N. H. Savs. Bank v. Ela, 11 N. H. 335; Same v. Colcord, 15 N. H. 119, 124, 41 Am. Dec. 685; Crosby v. Wyatt, 10 N. H. 318; People's Bank v. Pearsons, 30 Vt. 711; Batavian Bank v. McDonald, 77 Wis. 486, 500, 46 N. W. 902; Hollingsworth v. Tomlinson, 108 N. C. 245, 12 S. E. 989; Scott v. Safford, 37 Ga. 384; First Nat. Bank of Springfield v. Leavitt, 65 Mo. 562; Am. Bank v. Love, 62 Mo. App. 378; Union Bank v. McClung, 9 Humph. (Tenn.) 98. In some states it is held that the taking of interest in advance is not only prima facie evidence of an agreement to forbear, but is conclusive evidence of such an agreement. Gardner v. Gardner, 23 S. C. 588; Preston v. Henning, 6 Bush (Ky.) 556; Jarvis v. Hyatt, 43 Ind. 163; Hamilton v. Winterrowd, Id. 393; Woodburn v. Carter, 50 Ind. 376; Starrett v. Burkhalter, 86 Ind. 439. In other jurisdictions there has been a disposition to hold that the taking of interest in advance is not evidence of an agreement to extend the time of payment. Agricultural Bank v. Bishop, 6 Gray, 317; Blackstone Bank v. Hill, 10 Pick. 129; Oxford Bank v. Lewis, 8 Pick. 457; Haydenville Savs. Bank v. Parsons, 138 Mass. 53; Mariners' Bank v. Abbott, 28 Me. 280; Freeman's Bank v. Rollins, 13 Me. 202.

We think the rule first adverted to, and supported by a great preponderance of authority, is just and sound. The taking of interest in advance may properly be regarded as prima facie evidence of an agreement to extend the time of payment, which may be rebutted by other facts and circumstances. Applying this rule to the case at bar, it will be seen that only three days intervened between the payment of the interest and the date when it was due. The first was a legal half holiday, the second was a full legal holiday, and the third, on which interest was due, was also a legal holiday. Nothing was said about an extension of time, and the circumstances which indicate that there was no intention to extend the time of payment are, to say the least, quite as strong as those relied upon to show that such an intention existed. Taking all the evidence together, we cannot say that there were no circumstances to rebut the presumption arising from the acceptance of the interest by the plaintiff three days in advance. It was, therefore, a question of fact whether such an extension was intended, and we think the Appellate Division erred in reversing this finding of fact as a matter of law. The case of Wakefield Bank v. Truesdell, 55 Barb. 602, is in entire accord with our view, for in that case the General Term of the Supreme Court affirmed the decision of a referee who had found that the evidence disclosed an intention on the part of the plaintiff to extend the time of payment.

The second question we are called upon to consider is whether the increase in the rate of interest from 5 per cent. to 6 per cent. for the last three months of the year of 1893, under the direction of the finance committee of the plaintiff, and received and accepted by the plaintiff, was such a variance of the terms of the contract entered into by the defendant Casey on his bond as to discharge him from any liability thereon. The trial court found that the acceptance by the plaintiff of a different rate of interest than that provided in the bond and mortgage did not prove an agreement to change the rate of interest, and that no consideration for such an agreement was shown. The learned Appellate Division held that the change in the rate constituted a valid, executed agreement to change the rate of interest, which discharged Casey from his liability. The bond in suit provided that the interest should be payable semiannually at 5 per cent. "until the principal sum be paid." "When the contract provides that the interest shall be at a specified rate until the principal be paid, then the contract rate governs until payment of the principal, or until the contract is merged in a judgment." O'Brien v. Young, 95 N. Y. 428, 47 Am. Rep. 64. If, then, there was a valid agreement for the alteration of the provisions of the bond in respect to the rate of interest, by increasing the amount thereof, a greater burden was placed upon the owner of the land, and the bondsman was thereby discharged. Antisdel v. Williamson, 165 N. Y. 372, 59 N. E. 207; Murray v. Marshall, 94 N. Y. 611; Page v. Krekey, 137 N. Y. 307, 33 N. E. 311, 21 L. R. A. 409, 33 Am. St. Rep. 731; Paine v. Jones, 76 N. Y. 274.

It is conceded that the rate of interest was increased by order of the finance committee of the plaintiff, that the plaintiff accepted and retained the interest at the increased rate, and that the then owner of the land paid the increased rate, thus acquiescing in the change. These facts, we think, clearly disclose an executed agreement entered into by the plaintiff with the owner for a change in the rate of interest. The appellant urges that there was no consideration shown for such agreement. With the amount of the increased interest in its coffers, the plaintiff cannot be heard now to say that there was no consideration for such an agreement. We think the Appellate Division properly held that the only inference to be drawn from the facts upon this branch of the case was that the plaintiff intended to and did change the rate of interest by increasing it 1 per cent., and that the owner of the land acquiesced in such change by paying the increase. In Dewey v. Reed, 40 Barb. 16, the holder and maker of a promissory note, by agreement with the maker and without the knowledge or consent of the surety, changed the note so that the interest should be payable semiannually instead of at the date of maturity, and it was held such a material alteration as to release the surety. In Harsh v. Klepper, 28 Ohio St. 200, the interest on a note was increased 1 per cent., and the surety was exonerated from liability thereby. To the same effect is Warrington v. Early, 2 El. & Bl. 763. The appellant cites the case of Merritt v. Youmans, 21 App. Div. 256, 47 N. Y. Supp. 664, as sustaining his contention; but there the interest was reduced 1 per cent. instead of being increased, and, as was said in the similar case of Cambridge Savs. Bank v. Hyde, 131 Mass. 77, 79, 41 Am. Rep. 193, "if the change in the original contract from its nature is beneficial to the surety, or if it is self-evident that it cannot prejudice him, the surety is not discharged"—citing Smith v. United States, 2 Wall. 219, 17 L. Ed. 788; Appleton v. Parker, 15 Gray, 173; General Steam Navigation Co. v. Rolt, 6 C. B. (N. S.) 550; Bowmaker v. Moore, 7 Price, 223; Holme v. Brunskill, 3 Q. B. D. 495. So far as the cases of Offutt v. Glass, 4 Bush (Ky.) 486, and Eaton v. Waite, 66 Me. 221, are in conflict with the views herein expressed, we do not deem it wise to follow them.

We think the learned Appellate Division properly reversed the finding of the trial court upon the second ground, as a matter of law, and its reversal should therefore be affirmed.

PARKER, C. J., and HAIGHT and VANN, JJ., concur with GRAY, J. MARTIN, J., concurs with WERNER, J., and BARTLETT, J., concurs, also, on the ground that there was an unlawful extension, and also that there was a valid agreement changing the rate of interest and discharging the surety.

Judgment reversed, etc.

(178 N. Y. 400)

PEOPLE v. LOOMIS.

(Court of Appeals of New York. May 3, 1904.)

CRIMINAL LAW—CONFESSION—OTHER CRIMES—ADMISSIBILITY.

1. Where defendant, charged with burglary and larceny, confesses his guilt, and in the same conversation admits his guilt of another burglary not charged in the indictment, that portion of the confession is incompetent where there is no legal connection between the latter burglary and the crimes with which he is charged, and the prosecution could prove his confession as to the crimes charged without also proving what he had said as to such other crime.

2. Where a confession is coupled with extenuating statements, the whole of the conversation in which the confession is made may be given, though each part of the conversation is so interwoven with every other part that a confession of the crime charged cannot be shown without admitting evidence of a confession of another crime, and the confession necessarily relates to another crime.

Appeal from Supreme Court, Appellate Division, Third Department.

Augustus Loomis was convicted of burglary, and from a judgment of the Appellate Division (78 N. Y. S. 578) affirming the conviction, he appeals. Reversed.

G. P. Pudney, for appellant. M. H. Kiley, Dist. Atty., for respondent.

WERNER, J. The defendant appeals from a judgment affirming his conviction under both counts of an indictment charging him with the crimes of burglary and larceny, alleged to have been committed on the 17th day of September, 1898, in the town of Eaton and county of Madison. There is no controversy over the fact that the crimes of burglary and larceny were committed by some one, at or about the time stated in the indictment, upon certain premises owned by John E. Smith & Son in the town and county named. The question that was vigorously contested upon the trial was whether the defendant was one of the perpetrators of these crimes, and upon this issue a jury has found the defendant guilty.

There are many exceptions to rulings in receiving and rejecting evidence that are now relied upon by the defendant as presenting sufficient grounds for the reversal of this judgment. A careful examination of the record has led us to the conclusion that the only exception in the case which we cannot disregard as technical and unsubstantial under section 542 of the Code of Civil Procedure is the one relating to defendant's alleged confession of a crime not charged in the indictment. Upon the direct case for the prosecution, a witness named Vosburg was permitted to testify that the defendant confessed that he was one of the perpetrators of the burglary and larceny charged in the indictment, as well as a burglary committed upon the premises of one Mrs. Lewis. The evidence relating to the Lewis burglary was given in response to a direct question asked by the district attorney, and was objected to by defendant's counsel as incompetent, improper, and immaterial, because it tended to prove a separate and distinct crime not charged in the indictment. The district attorney contends that the evidence of the defendant's confession of complicity in the Lewis burglary was competent, not only because it was part of the conversation in which he confessed his guilt of the crimes charged in the indictment, but because the crimes confessed were part of a series of crimes said to have been committed by the defendant, in concert with others, pursuant to a common plan or scheme. Counsel for the defendant, on the other hand, relies upon the general rule that evidence of one crime is inadmissible to prove guilt of another and wholly distinct crime. This general rule is so thoroughly settled and so commonly understood that without discussion thereof we pass at once to the consideration of the circumstances which, it is claimed, except the case at bar from its operation.

It is said that a series of burglaries and larcenies had been committed in the county of Madison and vicinity, at about the same time as the crimes charged in the indictment, by a "gang" of which the defendant was a member, and that evidence of all or any of these crimes was therefore competent to establish the defendant's guilt of the crimes charged. The difficulty with this contention is that it is not borne out by the facts of record. Beyond the reference to the Lewis burglary in the defendant's alleged confession to Vosburg, there is nothing in the evidence to justify the assertion of the learned district attorney that other burglaries had been committed in that neighborhood, or that the finger of suspicion was pointed at the defendant in connection therewith. Nor is there any evidence that the burglary and larceny charged in the indictment were in the slightest degree connected with the Lewis burglary. It may be that the stolen goods recovered by the officers of the law were identified as belonging to different owners, and, while that may prove that several burglaries or larcenies had been committed, it does not establish such a connection between these separate crimes as to make evidence of one competent upon the trial of another. If A. steals a horse from one person, and a cow from another, the fact that both animals are found in the thief's possession does not make it competent to prove that the accused was guilty of stealing the cow by showing that he stole the horse. That is precisely the logic applicable to the case at bar. The burglary and larceny charged in the indictment, and the Lewis burglary, are entirely separate and distinct crimes, and yet proof of one is relied upon in part to secure a conviction of the other. The case of Hope v. People, 83 N. Y. 418, 38 Am. Rep. 460, cited for the prosecution, not only illustrates the principle which justifies the reception of evidence tending to prove a crime not charged, if it is relevant and material upon the one that is charged, but it also serves to show the utter misapplication of the principle to the case at bar. In the Hope Case the plaintiff in error was tried upon an indictment charging him with robbery in the first degree. The robbery was committed by a band of masked men, who took from the janitor of a bank the key thereof, and immediately thereafter burglarized the bank. It was held that proof of the burglary was competent, because it tended to show (1) that the robbery was part of a prior scheme to rob the bank, to which the accused was a party, and (2) that the evidence tended to show that the same persons who were identified as having participated in the burglary were also guilty of the robbery. In the case at bar there is evidence of two distinct burglaries having no connection of time, place, or circumstance, and no relation to each other except that the defendant is said to have been engaged in the commission of both. The contrast between the Hope Case and the case at bar is so marked that further discussion or citation of authority upon this point seems superfluous.

It is further claimed by the learned district attorney that Vosburg's narration of defendant's confession of the Lewis burglary was competent, because it was a part of the same conversation in which defendant admitted his connection with the crimes charged in the indictment, and Abbott's Criminal Trial Brief, p. 452, and State v. Underwood, 75 Mo. 236, are cited as authority for this contention. Abbott, in the work referred to, says: "If the accused, in the same conversation or communication, confessed not only the crime charged, but another offense also, the confession of the offense charged is not thereby rendered inadmissible, but, if that part be competent, the prosecution has a right to prove the whole." It is to be noted, however, that the authorities cited by the learned author very materially qualify his broad assertion. In State v. Underwood, supra, the charge was murder in the first degree. The prosecution was permitted to show that the accused had said that certain marks upon his pistol indicated the number of men he had killed, and one of the marks was for the deceased. This cogent and connected evidence does not, as it seems to us, support the broad dictum in the opinion, to the effect that the confession of a homicide and another crime in the same conversation makes evidence of both competent, and it will be observed, moreover, that the court in that case took occasion to add that "it was impossible to separate that portion of the conversation of the prisoner relating to the particular offense from that portion of the conversation relating to another offense." Another case cited by Abbott is Gore v. State, 162 Ill. 259, 44 N. E. 500, but there it was distinctly held that a "confession by the accused of a crime other than that charged in the indictment, while not admissible as a substantive fact, may, when not separable from a competent confession, go to the jury, under cautionary directions from the court." It is also clear that the authorities referred to in State v. Underwood, supra, do not support the contention made for the prosecution in the case at bar. In Barbour's work on Criminal Law (volume 2, p. 462), the learned author says: "In all cases the whole of the confession should be given in evidence, for it is a general rule that the whole of the account which a party gives of a transaction must be taken together, and his admission of a fact disadvantageous to himself shall not be received without receiving at the same time his contemporaneous assertion of a fact favorable to him, not merely as evidence that he made such assertion, but admissible evidence of the matter thus alleged by him, in his defense." To the same effect are Greenleaf on Evidence, vol. 1, § 218, Rex v. Cleeves, 4 Car. & Payne N. C. 354, and State v. Carlisle, 57 Mo. 102.

Thus we see that in three classes of cases it may be necessary or proper to take as evidence the whole of a conversation in which a defendant confesses his guilt of the crime charged, although that confession may constitute only a part of such conversation. The first class embraces those cases in which the confession of guilt is coupled with exculpatory or extenuating statements. The second class includes those cases in which a confession, relevant and competent as to the crime charged, is not rendered inadmissible because it also necessarily relates to another crime. In the third class are the cases in which each part of a conversation is so essentially interwoven with every other part that a confession of the crime charged cannot be proven without admitting evidence of the whole transaction; but in such a case the extraneous matter, if it tends to incriminate the defendant, should not be taken as substantive fact, and should only go to the jury under cautionary instructions from the court.

The mere statement of these exceptions to the general rule, that evidence of one crime may not be used to establish guilt of another, very clearly indicates that the case at bar does not fall within either of them. There was no legal connection between the Lewis burglary and the crimes charged in the indictment. Nor was there anything in the nature of the conversation between Vosburg and the defendant which rendered it impossible to prove the latter's alleged confession of the crimes charged without also proving what he said about the Lewis burglary. On the contrary, a simple statement from the district attorney that he desired only that portion of the conversation which related to the crimes charged would have eliminated everything else without the slightest injury to his case. Not only was this salutary and necessary precaution wholly omitted, but in the most explicit language the district attorney directly called forth the forbidden evidence, and the court received it, notwithstanding the proper objection and exception of defendant's counsel. We cannot say that the error thus committed did not affect the substantial rights of the defendant. It may be that he would have been convicted without the evidence of his confession of the Lewis burglary, but it is enough to say that it may also have been sufficient to resolve against him any reasonable doubt that might previously have been entertained as to his guilt.

The judgment of conviction herein should be reversed, and a new trial granted.

PARKER, C. J., and O'BRIEN, BARTLETT, HAIGHT, VANN, and CULLEN, JJ., concur.

Judgment of conviction reversed, etc.

(178 N. Y. 416)

In re ANDERSEN.

(Court of Appeals of New York. May 10, 1904.)

HIGHWAYS—CHANGE OF GRADE—DAMAGES TO ABUTTING OWNER—CONSTITUTIONALITY OF STATUTE—REVIEW ON APPEAL.

1. Laws 1903, p. 1396, c. 610, relating to damages for change of grade of a highway "in any town in which a highway has been or hereafter shall be repaired," gives an abutting owner on a street, the grade of which has been changed before the passage of the act, a right to recover for damages caused thereby.

2. The Court of Appeals will not consider the constitutionality of a statute where objection is not raised below.

Appeal from Supreme Court, Appellate Division, Second Department.

In the matter of the petition of Kirstine M. Andersen for the appointment of commissioners to assess damages from a change of grade in the town of Eastchester. From an order of the Appellate Division (87 N. Y. Supp. 24) reversing an order of the Special Term appointing commissioners, petitioner appeals. Reversed.

This proceeding involves the construction of chapter 610, p. 1396, of the Laws of 1903, which amends the highway law by inserting therein a new section, known as section 11a, which reads as follows: "Sec. 11a. Damages for change of grade. In any town in which a highway has been or hereafter shall be repaired, graded and macadamized from curb to curb by the authorities of the town in accordance with the provisions of section sixty-nine of chapter six hundred and eighty-six of the Laws of eighteen hundred and ninety-two, the owner or owners of the land adjacent to the said highway shall be entitled to recover from the town the damage resulting from any change of grade. A person claiming damages from such change of grade must present to the town board of such town a verified claim therefor. The board may agree with such owner upon the amount of damages to be allowed him. If no agreement be made within thirty days after the presentation of the claim, the person presenting it may apply to the supreme court for the appointment of three commis-

¶ 2. See Appeal and Error, vol. 3, Cent. Dig. § 1037.

sioners to determine the compensation to which he is entitled. Notice of the application must be served upon the supervisor of the town at least ten days before the hearing thereof. All proceedings subsequent to the appointment of commissioners shall be taken in accordance with the provisions of the condemnation law so far as applicable. Such town board, or such commissioners, shall, in determining the compensation, consider the fair value of the work done, or necessary to be done, in order to place the claimants' lands, or buildings, or both, in the same relation to the changed grade as they stood to the former grade, and make awards accordingly, except that said board or said commissioners may make an allowance for benefits derived by the claimant from such improvement. The amount agreed upon for such damages, or the award therefor together with the costs, if any allowed to the claimant, shall be a charge against such town and the supervisor shall pay the same, if there be sufficient funds in his hands available, and if not, the town board shall borrow money for the payment thereof, or issue certificates of indebtedness therefor."

Alfred E. Smith, for appellant. Isaac N. Mills and Henry W. Smith, for respondents.

BARTLETT, J. (after stating the facts). The petitioner herein, Kirstine M. Andersen, applied to the Special Term for the appointment of three commissioners under Laws 1903, p. 1396, c. 610, above quoted, to determine the compensation to which she was entitled by reason of change of grade in a public street opposite her premises in the town of Eastchester, Westchester county. The Special Term found, in substance, that the town of Eastchester is and had been a municipal corporation prior to the month of March, 1901; that Jefferson Place, in said town, prior to the month of March, 1901, was and since has been a public highway; that in and about the said month the lawful authorities of the town, in accordance with the provisions of section 69, p. 1761, c. 686, of the Laws of 1892, caused this avenue, the same being then a public highway, to be repaired, graded, and macadamized from curb to curb, and in doing the work raised the surface thereof about four feet, thereby changing the grade in front of petitioner's premises; that the petitioner at the time was the owner of the premises, and still owns the plot of land fronting on the avenue, and a dwelling house was erected thereon; that this work damaged petitioner's premises; that on the 25th of May, 1903, the petitioner presented to the town board of said town a verified claim for damages, and thereafter, and on or about the 1st day of June, 1903, the claim was rejected; that more than 30 days elapsed between the date of the presentation of the claim and the commencement of this proceeding; that the claim remained wholly unpaid; that due notice of the presentation of the petition was served upon the supervisor of the town of Eastchester. The conclusions of law were, in substance, that the work done in front of petitioner's premises was in law a change of grade as contemplated by the act in question, and that the petitioner was entitled to have three commissioners appointed as prayed for. The law of 1903 refers to grading, etc., done by the authorities of a town in accordance with the provisions of Laws 1892, p. 1761, c. 686, § 69. This is chapter 18 of the General Laws, known as the "County Law," and section 69 thereof authorizes a town to borrow money for various purposes, and among others to lay out, widen, grade, or macadamize highways of a town. We have in the case before us the express finding that the work of repairing, grading, and macadamizing from curb to curb of the highway in question was done by the lawful authorities of the town in accordance with the said act of 1892. The learned Appellate Division reversed the order of the Special Term, on the ground that the law of 1903 is not intended by its terms to be retroactive, and should not be construed to permit a recovery of damages in the case presented by the petitioner herein.

It is pointed out in the opinion that it is in general true that no statute shall be construed to have a retrospective operation without express words to that effect, either by an enumeration of the cases in which the act is to have such retrospective operation or by words which can have no meaning unless such construction is adopted. People v. Supervisors of Columbia County, 10 Wend. 363. There is no doubt concerning these general propositions of law, and it is also true that it is the settled law of this state that a change of grade in a public highway or street imposes no liability on the part of a town or municipality except as provided by statute. Radcliff's Executors v. Mayor, etc., of Brooklyn, 4 N. Y. 195, 53 Am. Dec. 357; Talbot v. N. Y. & Harlem R. R. Co., 151 N. Y. 155, 45 N. E. 382, and cases there cited. We are, however, unable to agree with the construction placed upon the act of 1903 by the Appellate Division, as, in our opinion, the statute bears upon its face the expressed intention of the Legislature to make it retroactive. It reads: "In any town in which a highway has been or hereafter shall be repaired, graded and macadamized from curb to curb by the authorities of the town in accordance with the provisions of section sixty-nine of chapter six hundred and eighty-six of the Laws of eighteen hundred and ninety-two, the owner or owners of the land adjacent to the said highway shall be entitled to recover from the town the damage resulting from any change of grade." The remainder of this section provides the mode of procedure thereunder, and is immaterial in determining this question of retroactive effect.

It is difficult to conceive of language more plainly indicating the intention of the Legislature to render a statute retroactive than is here employed. The learned counsel for the respondent makes the point that the statute of 1903 is unconstitutional in two respects, viz., in that it undertakes to make a gratuity of the moneys of the town; and, second, it takes the funds of the town without due process of law, and for other than town purposes. There is nothing to advise us that these constitutional questions were raised either at the Special Term or in the Appellate Division. It is well settled that, unless the constitutional question is raised in the court of first instance, it will not be considered here. Dodge v. Cornelius, 168 N. Y. 242, 61 N. E. 244, and cases there cited. It was stated on the argument that the act of 1903 is ill-advised legislation, and calculated to open the door to many claims that may have arisen throughout the state since the enactment of the county law in 1892. This suggestion should be addressed to the Legislature, and not to the court.

The order of the Appellate Division should be reversed, and the order of the Special Term affirmed, with costs to the petitioner in all the courts.

PARKER, C. J., and GRAY, O'BRIEN, HAIGHT, VANN, and WERNER, JJ., concur.

Order reversed, etc.

(178 N. Y. 377)

KLINE v. ABRAHAM et al.

(Court of Appeals of New York. April 26, 1904.)

INJURY TO EMPLOYÉ—ASSUMPTON OF RISK.

1. Where a clerk was perfectly familiar with the slippery condition of the marble steps in the building in which she worked, she assumed the risk of their condition, and could not recover for injuries received from slipping on them.

Appeal from Supreme Court, Appellate Division, Second Department.

Action by Josephine Kline against Abraham Abraham and others. Judgment for plaintiff. From a judgment of the Appellate Division affirming the same (81 N. Y. Supp. 1132), defendants appeal. Reversed.

Frank Verner Johnson, for appellants. Thomas F. Magner, for respondent.

HAIGHT, J. This action was brought to recover damages for personal injuries sustained by the plaintiff while in the employ of the defendants in their dry goods store in the borough of Brooklyn on the 13th day of April, 1898. The defendants had recently constructed a new stairway with marble steps leading from the first floor of their building to the basement. The new stairway was opened for use by the public some time in December, 1897, and was thereafter extensively used by the patrons of the defendants and by their employés. The plaintiff was an assistant cashier, and up to the time of her injuries had been engaged in the discharge of her duties as such at the glove counter in the defendants' store, situated near the top of the stairway, which she had been in the habit of using going up and down twice each day to the cashier's office. At the time of the accident she was going down the stairway to turn over the money she had collected to the cashier, having her cash box under one arm and a stamp for marking receipts in the other hand. She had descended the stairway as far as the square landing five or six steps from the foot without having hold of the railing, and then in stepping from the landing to the next step her feet slipped, causing her to fall, and receive an injury to the rudimentary bones at the end of the spinal column. Upon the trial the testimony of the plaintiff's witnesses was to the effect that the marble steps were "slippery as ice," "smooth as glass," and "highly polished." While on the part of the defendants it was shown that the marble steps had been rubbed down with pumice stone, making a smooth, but not a polished, surface, and that such is the recognized and customary finish in general use in buildings where marble is used for steps or floors. It further appeared on behalf of the plaintiff that several persons had previously slipped upon these stairs. While on behalf of the defendants it was shown that only seven persons had been reported as having slipped upon the stairs; that they were used extensively by the patrons and employés of the defendants, about 2,000 persons going up and down the stairs daily; that the defendants were engaged in the conduct of a large retail store, which was daily thronged with customers, and that accidents of various kinds were of common occurrence; that they kept a book, in which was entered an account of the accidents as they occurred, and that the number ranged from 500 to 600 during a year. It further appeared that the defendants had under advisement the supplying of rubber treads to be placed upon the marble steps, and that an estimate of the expense had been called for, but that such treads had not, at the time of the accident, been adopted. At the conclusion of the plaintiff's evidence the defendants asked for a dismissal of the complaint upon the ground that the evidence did not show that the plaintiff was free from negligence contributing to the accident, that no negligence had been shown on behalf of the defendants, and that the condition of the stairs was open, obvious, and apparent to the plaintiff, and was a part of the risk of her employment. This was denied, and an exception was taken by the defendants. At

¶ 1. See Master and Servant, vol. 34, Cent. Dig. § 584.

the close of the case the same motion was renewed, with like result. We think the motion should have been granted.

Marble, in the construction of public buildings, large fireproof hotels, and stores upon the floors and stairways, has been in common use for many years. The surface is smooth, and a person walking thereon is required to use care to avoid slipping. The same is equally true with reference to floors and stairs constructed of hard wood, especially where the surface has been polished, as in the case of many of our more expensive private residences; but heretofore the construction of such floors or stairways has not been considered to be dangerous, unlawful, or a nuisance. It has not been generally understood that a master, charged with the duty of furnishing a safe place for his servant to work, failed in his obligation by reason of his having supplied marble stairs. In this case, as we have seen, the plaintiff was perfectly familiar with these stairs. She had been up and down the staircase at least twice daily, and must have known of its condition. It was an open, visible structure having no latent, hidden, or unseen defects. It is not pretended that there was any foreign substance upon the steps to make them more slippery. If they were slippery by reason of their smoothness or polish, that fact was as apparent to her as it was to her employers. She knew that the steps were not covered with rubber treads, carpets, or other material, and we think the risk incidental to their use was assumed by her. Sweeney v. Berlin & Jones Envelope Co., 101 N. Y. 520, 5 N. E. 358, 54 Am. Rep. 722; Gibson v. Erie Ry. Co., 63 N. Y. 452, 20 Am. Rep. 552; De Forest v. Jewett, 88 N. Y. 264; Maltbie v. Belden, 167 N. Y. 307, 312, 60 N. E. 645, 54 L. R. A. 52; and see authorities there cited.

The judgment of the Appellate Division and that of the trial court should be reversed, and a new trial granted, with costs to abide the event.

PARKER, C. J., and O'BRIEN, BARTLETT, VANN, CULLEN, and WERNER, JJ., concur.

Judgment reversed, etc.

(178 N. Y. 421)

In re MAYOR, ETC., OF CITY OF NEW YORK.

(Court of Appeals of New York. May 10, 1904.)

ACQUISITION OF LAND FOR STREET—REPORT OF COMMISSIONERS—SUFFICIENCY.

1. Greater N. Y. Charter (Laws 1897, p. 347, c. 378) § 980, provides that the commissioners of estimate and assessment shall in no case assess any real estate more than one-half of the value of such property as valued by them. *Held* not to require the commissioners in a proceeding to acquire title to lands for street purposes to state in their report the specific valuation of the different properties assessed, and a statement that in no case have they exceeded in the assessments for benefits one-half the value of the lot assessed, taken in connection with the tabulated statements of the specific assessments on the property assessed by them in their report, is sufficient.

Appeal from Supreme Court, Appellate Division, First Department.

Application of the mayor, aldermen, and commonalty of the city of New York as to acquiring title to Whitlock avenue. From an order of the Appellate Division (85 N. Y. Supp. 650) reversing an order of the Special Term confirming the report of commissioners of estimate and assessment of property belonging to John B. Simpson, Jr., and others, as executors, etc., the city of New York appeals. Reversed.

John J. Delany, Corp. Counsel (Theodore Connoly, John P. Dunn, and Thomas C. Blake, of counsel), for appellant. Barclay E. V. McCarty and Jared G. Baldwin, Jr., for respondents.

GRAY, J. In this proceeding to acquire the title to lands for street-opening purposes in the city of New York, the commissioners of estimate and assessment presented a report which stated specifically their estimates of awards for damages and of assessments for benefits upon the various properties described, but which did not state specifically their valuations of the different properties assessed for benefits. As to such valuations this statement, only, was contained in their report: "We further report that in no case have we exceeded in our assessment for benefits one-half of the value of the lot assessed as valued by us." Objection was made to the confirmation of their report, but the objection was overruled, and the report was confirmed by the court at Special Term. Upon appeal to the Appellate Division, in the First Department, the order of confirmation was reversed, and the report of the commissioners was sent back to them. Leave, however, has been given by the Appellate Division to appeal to this court, and the following questions of law were certified for our review, viz.: First. Are the commissioners of estimate and assessment in this proceeding required by the following provisions of section 980 of the Greater New York charter (Laws 1897, p. 347, c. 378), to wit, "The said commissioners shall in no case assess any house, lot, improved or unimproved lands more than one-half the value of such house, lot, improved or unimproved lands as valued by them," in addition to the statement of the specific assessments on every lot assessed by them, to state the specific valuations which they have placed upon such parcel assessed? Second. Was the following statement in the commissioners' report, to wit, "We further report that in no case have we exceeded in our assessments for benefit one-half the value of the lot assessed, as valued by us," takes in connection with the tabulated statement of the specific assessments on the properties assessed by them in their report, a sufficient compliance with the provisions of section 980 of the Greater New York charter?

The learned Justices of the Appellate Division divided in opinion upon the question of the sufficiency of the report; the majority of them holding that the commissioners had not complied with the provisions of section 980, in that they had failed to state the specific valuations which they had placed on each piece of property assessed. That section, in the feature discussed, was amendatory of the provision of the former consolidation act, which limited the commissioners, in assessing for benefit, to one-half the value of the property assessed, as valued by the general tax assessing officers of the city. The effect of the amendment was to make the rule of valuation uniform, in establishing as a basis for the estimates of an award for damage and of an assessment for benefit the market value of the property as ascertained by the commissioners.

The report of the commissioners is in substantial compliance with the requirement of the statute. While it is true, in order to justify the assessment, that the report must show that the commissioners have kept within the limit imposed as to its amount, it does contain their statement that in no case had they exceeded in their assessment for benefit one-half the value of the property as valued by them. Having stated, specifically, in figures, the assessment upon each piece of property, it followed necessarily that they had previously valued the property; and that their valuation should have been stated in the general language used in the report, instead of specifically upon the schedule of assessments, is immaterial. The statute does not, in terms, require the report to contain any statement of specific valuations; and while it might be a more convenient arrangement, as a matter of form, that the figures of valuations should accompany the figures of assessments, it cannot be said that there was a fundamental defect, invalidating the exercise of the power conferred. While the statement of the commissioners as to their valuation may be characterized, in a sense, as a conclusion, it was nevertheless their statement, in effect, that their valuation in each case was at least double the assessment levied. Section 985 of the Greater New York charter, which prescribes what the report of the commissioners is to contain, does not appear to require the commissioners to give the valuation of the property assessed; and that is a reason, taken in connection with the general language of section 980, for our holding the form of report in this case to have been sufficient.

The first question certified should be answered in the negative; the second question certified should be answered in the affirmative; and therefore the order appealed from should be reversed, and that of the Special Term should be affirmed, with costs in this court and in the Appellate Division to the appellants.

PARKER, C. J., and O'BRIEN, BARTLETT, HAIGHT, VANN, and WERNER, JJ., concur.

Order reversed, etc.

(178 N. Y. 407)

STANDARD TRUST CO. v. NEW YORK CENT. & H. R. R. CO. et al.

(Court of Appeals of New York. May 8, 1904.)

EXTRA ALLOWANCE—REVIEW BY APPELLATE COURT—QUESTION OF LAW.

1. The question whether the trial court has the power to grant an additional allowance is a question of law reviewable in the Court of Appeals.

2. Code Civ. Proc. § 3253, authorizing the court to grant an additional allowance where the action is difficult and extraordinary, does not authorize such an allowance in an action for personal injuries, where the answer is withdrawn under a stipulation, and the only question for the court is the amount of the damages, and no difficult questions of law are involved.

Appeal from Supreme Court, Appellate Division, Second Department.

Action by the Standard Trust Company, executor of Alfred M. Perrin, deceased, against the New York Central & Hudson River Railroad Company and others. From so much of a judgment of the Appellate Division (84 N. Y. Supp. 1147) as affirms that part of a judgment in favor of plaintiff which includes an additional allowance of $2,000 to plaintiff's attorney, defendants appeal. Reversed.

John F. Brennan and Charles C. Paulding, for appellants. Paul E. De Fere, J. Addison Young, and William A. Moore, for respondent.

HAIGHT, J. This action was brought to recover damages for negligently causing the death of the plaintiff's testator, which resulted from a collision between trains in the Park avenue tunnel in the city of New York. The trial of this action succeeded that of a number of other similar actions based upon the same collision. Upon the commencement of the trial it was stipulated on the part of the attorneys for the defendant that the accident which resulted in the death of the plaintiff's testator was caused by the negligence of the employés of the defendant, and without contributory negligence on the part of the decedent. After this stipulation was entered upon the minutes, the trial proceeded for the purpose of determining the amount of damages that the plaintiff had suffered, resulting in a verdict of the jury for the sum of $75,000. To this the trial court

¶ 2. See Costs, vol. 13, Cent. Dig. § 624.

awarded the plaintiff's attorney an additional allowance of $2,000.

It is contended on behalf of the respondent that this court has no power to review the judgment as to the additional allowance, for the reason that such allowance was discretionary with the trial court. It is quite true that this court has no power to review discretionary orders, and consequently, in so far as the trial court had the power to grant an additional allowance, its exercise of such power is not subject to review here; but the question as to whether the trial court had the power or authority to grant any additional allowance is a question of law subject to review in this court. This was expressly held in the case of Hanover F. Ins. Co. v. Germania F. Ins. Co., 138 N. Y. 252, 33 N. E. 1065, and in Conaughty v. Saratoga County Bank, 92 N. Y. 401. We are thus brought to a consideration of the provisions of section 3253 of the Code of Civil Procedure. It, among other things, provides that "in a difficult and extraordinary case (where a defense has been interposed in an action) * * * the court may also, in its discretion, award to any party a further sum," not exceeding 5 per centum, etc. It will be observed that, under the provisions of this statute, the case must be both difficult and extraordinary, and also that it must be a case in which there was a defense interposed. If the case lacks either of these three requirements it is not brought within the provisions of the Code, and consequently the court would have no power to make an additional allowance. In the case under consideration it appears that an answer had been interposed, but under the stipulation read upon the trial the answer was in effect withdrawn, so that the only question left for the determination of the court was the amount that should be assessed as damages. Had timely notice of this stipulation been given to the plaintiff, it could not well have been contended that the case had a defense necessitating a trial. It is, however, contended on behalf of the respondent that it did not know that it was the intention of the defendant to stipulate that it was liable for the damages suffered, and that consequently the plaintiff had to prepare the case for trial upon the question of defendant's liability. For the purposes of this case we shall assume, but without so deciding, that the respondent's contention makes a difference, and that the case is to be treated as one in which the answer had not been withdrawn or the liability of the defendant admitted. We are then brought to a consideration of the meaning of the words "difficult and extraordinary." We think these are words of limitation, and that the practice of making an additional allowance in every case cannot be sanctioned. In construing this phrase we must give to the words "difficult and extraordinary" their usual and accepted meaning. A general rule specifying the precise limitation that they impose upon the power of courts to grant an additional allowance may be difficult to formulate, but their application to the facts of a particular case when presented is not troublesome. A negligence case may arise which may be so difficult and extraordinary as to bring it within the provisions of the statute, but ordinarily they are neither difficult nor extraordinary. Indeed, they are the most common and numerous of any class of cases which we have in court. In the case under consideration the death of the testator was caused from a collision between two trains under circumstances in which negligence would be presumed on the part of the employés of the defendant upon showing the fact of the collision. There was no difficult question of law to be examined or considered, or trouble with reference to making the necessary proof, and we think the case was not one in which the trial court had the power to grant any additional allowance whatever. It follows that so much of the judgment as is appealed from should be reversed, with costs.

PARKER, C. J., and O'BRIEN, BARTLETT, VANN, and WERNER, JJ., concur. GRAY, J., not sitting.

Judgment accordingly.

(187 N. Y. 411)

PEOPLE ex rel. BERLINGER v. WELLS et al.

(Court of Appeals of New York. May 3, 1904.)

APPEAL—REVIEW—REVERSAL—MANDAMUS—RETURN.

1. Where the return to the Court of Appeals shows such irregularity of practice as to amount to a mistrial, the orders of both courts below will be reversed.

2. When an issue of fact is joined by the filing of a return to an alternative writ of mandamus, the proceedings on the facts or on the law are, under Code Civ. Proc. § 2082, in all respects the same as in an action, except as otherwise expressly prescribed by the Code, and under section 2083 an issue of fact on an alternative writ of mandamus must be tried by a jury, unless a jury trial is waived. *Held*, that where issues of fact were tried without a jury, but at the close of the evidence counsel for defendant moved for direction of a verdict, and the motion was denied, and the trial justice then gave his reasons, and defendant's counsel moved to set aside "the finding of fact" and for a new trial, and the motion was denied, and thereafter the court filed certain findings, but there was no conclusion of law or direction for a judgment, and exceptions were filed, and the Appellate Division held that the paper signed by the trial justice was a decision of all the issues of fact, and the record showed that such Division had a right to reverse on the ground that the facts were against the evidence, but their opinion did not so state, so as to compel the presumption that the reversal was on the law, and there is no error of law, the judgment must be reversed.

Appeal from Supreme Court, Appellate Division, First Department.

Application by the state, on the relation of Henry Berlinger, for a writ of mandamus to James L. Wells and others, composing the board of taxes and assessments of the city of New York, to reinstate relator as chief clerk in the department. From an order of the Appellate Division (83 N. Y. Supp. 376) reversing an order of the Special Term granting the motion, plaintiff appeals. Reversed.

A. J. Skinner, George P. Heimberger, and Henry S. J. Flynn, for appellant. John J. Delany, Corp. Counsel (Theodore Connoly and William B. Crowell, of counsel), for respondents.

VANN, J. In August, 1898, the relator was appointed chief clerk of the board of taxes and assessments of the city of New York, and assigned to the borough of Manhattan. He assumed the office and performed its duties until May 1, 1902, when he was discharged by said board, without a hearing or an opportunity for explanation. No charges were preferred against him, and no reason for his removal was entered in the records of the board. By the return of the respondents to an alternative writ of mandamus granted to review their action in thus removing the relator, several issues of fact were raised bearing upon the question whether he was a regular clerk and not subject to summary removal, or was in a confidential position with reference to the commissioners and could be discharged without presentation of charges or expression of reasons. By consent of both parties the issues of fact were tried before the court without a jury, but upon the theory that the trial justice was acting, as he announced, "as if there were a jury present." The "case containing exceptions" is entitled: "Trial Term, Part First; Before Hon. Justice Leventritt and a jury." At the close of the evidence the counsel for the defendants moved for the direction of a verdict in their favor, but the motion was denied, and an exception taken. The trial justice then gave his reasons for deciding in favor of the relator, and thereupon the defendants' counsel, after stating, without dissent from any one, that this announcement "appears in place of a verdict," moved "to set aside the finding of fact, * * * and for a new trial under section 999 of the Code." The motion was denied, and an exception was taken, but no order was entered. The court subsequently prepared and signed a paper entitled "Findings," which, after certain recitals, was as follows:

"First. I find that the relator was a regular clerk, and did not occupy a confidential position. That the duties he was required to perform were not secret. That the relations which existed between him and the respondents were not those of trust and confidence. That none of the duties primarily resting on the respondents were delegated to the relator. That there was no assumption of any financial responsibility in connection with the position the relator occupied, and that the performance of relator's duties did not involve any of the elements necessary to make his position confidential.

"Second. I find a general verdict in favor of the relator and against the respondents on all the questions of fact raised by the mandamus herein and the return thereto."

There was no conclusion of law or direction for judgment, and the paper contained nothing, aside from the recital as to the time and place of trial, except as stated. Exceptions were filed by the defendants "to the decision or findings of fact made and signed herein by," etc. Upon all the papers and proceedings, including "the finding of fact of the Hon. David Leventritt, Justice of the Supreme Court," the relator moved at Special Term for a peremptory writ of mandamus, and from the order granting said motion the defendants appealed to the Appellate Division. Upon the hearing of the appeal the order was reversed, and the motion for a peremptory writ was denied, but no new trial was granted, and the order of reversal did not state that the facts had been reviewed or that the order of the Special Term was reversed upon a question of fact.

When an issue is joined by the filing of a return to an alternative writ of mandamus, the proceedings, "upon the facts or upon the law, are, in all respects, the same as in an action," except as otherwise expressly prescribed by the Code. Code Civ. Proc. § 2082. "The writ, the return, and the demurrer are deemed to be pleadings in an action," and the final order a final judgment which may be entered and docketed as such. Id. "An issue of fact, joined upon an alternative writ of mandamus, must be tried by a jury, as if it was an issue joined in an action * * * unless a jury trial is waived, or a reference is directed by consent of parties." Section 2083. Owing to the anomalous practice pursued at the Trial Term, such confusion has arisen that a review upon the merits is impossible without a departure from established precedents. The learned judges of the Appellate Division held that the trial was before the court without a jury, and that the paper signed by the trial justice was a decision by the court of the whole issues of fact. According to their opinion, which forms no part of the record, they reversed upon a question of fact, yet, as they did not say so in their order, the statute compels us to presume that the reversal was upon questions of law only. Code Civ. Proc. § 1338. An examination of the record discloses no error of law, as distinguished from an error in practice, but it also shows that the Appellate Division had the right to reverse upon the ground that the facts were found against the weight of evidence. If they had stated in their order that they reversed for this reason, we could not review their determination. Therefore, upon the theory that the facts were found by the court, as such, we should be compelled to reverse the order of the Appellate Division and restore that of the Special Term, because there is no error of law disclosed by the record, and we are compelled to presume that the reversal was not founded upon the facts. Hinckel v. Stevens, 165 N. Y. 171, 58 N. E. 879; Spence v. Ham, 163 N. Y. 220, 57 N. E. 412, 51 L. R. A. 238. On the other hand, if the decision is to be treated as the verdict of a jury, which was clearly the understanding of the parties at the trial, we are met by a difficulty of a like nature. Henavie v. N. Y. C. & H. R. R. Co., 154 N. Y. 278, 48 N. E. 525. After a trial before a jury the facts cannot be reviewed upon an appeal simply from the judgment, but a motion for a new trial must be made, an order entered, and an appeal taken from the order. Collier v. Collins, 172 N. Y. 99, 64 N. E. 787. While such a motion was made and denied in this case, no order was entered, and of course no appeal from such an order was taken to the Appellate Division. That court, therefore, upon this theory of the trial, was without jurisdiction to review the facts, and was confined to questions of law, of which there was none to justify a reversal.

In the effort to settle the facts in an informal way, the practice pursued was so irregular as to amount to a mistrial. The parties regarded the trial as before a jury, while the Appellate Division regarded it as before the court. By the final action of the trial justice it was treated as in the nature of both, for he found the facts as a judge and a verdict as a jury. The case was moved at a Trial Term, and a jury was in attendance, but none was impaneled. While the trial proceeded as if a jury were present, no verdict was even in form directed, and there was no effort to make the record appear as if a verdict had been rendered by a jury, as is sometimes done by consent. A court never finds a verdict, although it may direct one. The evidence of a verdict is the entry thereof in the minutes of the clerk; but no such entry was made in this case. The evidence of a decision of an action by the court is a paper signed by the trial judge stating the facts found or the conclusion reached and the relief awarded. The paper signed in this case stated certain facts as found, and then found "a general verdict in favor of the relator." It is impossible to clearly determine what this nondescript dish is, for it is part fish and part fowl, and hence we conclude that the trial was irregular and illegal. As the proceedings to review vary with the nature of the trial, confusion in the practice upon the appeal was almost inevitable, and the only way to avoid injustice is to reverse the orders of both courts below and direct a trial—for none has yet been had that the law can recognize—with costs to abide event.

PARKER, C. J., and GRAY, O'BRIEN, BARTLETT, HAIGHT, and WERNER, JJ., concur.

Orders reversed, etc.

(187 N. Y. 369)

GENERAL ELECTRIC CO. v. NATIONAL CONTRACTING CO.

(Court of Appeals of New York. April 26, 1904.)

SALES—ORAL MODIFICATION OF WRITTEN CONTRACT—ESTOPPEL—EVIDENCE—REFUSAL TO ACCEPT GOODS—RESALE BY SELLER—LIABILITY OF BUYER.

1. A written contract of sale may be modified as to time of performance by consent of the parties, notwithstanding the contract provides that no modification thereof shall be binding unless in writing.

2. Where a written contract of sale, providing that no modification thereof should be binding unless in writing, was, by consent of the parties and for their convenience, modified as to the time of performance, and defendant permitted plaintiff to go on with the work after the time specified in the contract, he is estopped from setting up the defense of nonperformance as to time.

3. An exception by defendant to certain testimony admitted in proceedings before a referee before the pleadings were amended is not available on appeal where the amendment obviated all objection to the testimony.

4. The seller of machinery to be delivered and installed at a specified time may, on refusal of the purchaser to accept or pay for the same, sell it at public auction, and recover from the original purchaser the price thereof, after deducting the amount received at the auction sale and the cost of installing the machinery, together with interest on such balance from the time of the purchaser's default.

Appeal from Supreme Court, Appellate Division, Third Department.

Action by the General Electric Company against the National Contracting Company for breach of contract. From a judgment of the Appellate Division (83 N. Y. Supp. 1106) affirming a judgment for plaintiff on report of a referee, defendant appeals. Affirmed.

L. Laflin Kellogg and Alfred C. Petté, for appellant. Richard Lockhart Hand, Edgar T. Brackett, and James O. Carr, for respondent.

O'BRIEN, J. Both parties to this action are domestic corporations. The plaintiff is extensively engaged in the manufacture and sale of all kinds of electrical appliances and apparatus, and the defendant, as its name indicates, is a contracting company. On the 15th day of June, 1900, they entered into a written contract whereby the plaintiff agreed to manufacture, deliver on board the cars and install for the defendant certain electric machinery and appliances, for which the defendant agreed to pay $65,000—one-third cash

¶ 4. See Sales, vol. 43, Cent. Dig. §§ 915, 924, 126.

on delivery, one-third in 30 days thereafter, and the balance in 60 days. In this action the plaintiff sought to recover damages for the defendant's alleged breach of this contract, and it had judgment upon the trial before the referee, which has been unanimously affirmed by the learned court below. The referee's findings of fact, which appear at length in the record, must, therefore, be treated as conclusive. The machinery and appliances that the plaintiff contracted to make and deliver to the defendant are described in the written contract and specifications in great detail, and the names or character of the articles need not be referred to, since there is no question raised, so far as the record discloses, that they are not in accordance with the contract. By the terms of the agreement, as originally made, a part of the property was to be delivered on January 1, 1901, and a part on the 1st of February following, and it is admitted on all sides that no delivery was made on these days, and out of this fact arises the principal question of law involved in the case. But the learned referee has found that time was not of the essence of the contract, and that by mutual verbal agreement between the parties the time of delivery was extended, and the defendant waived performance on these days. He has also found that on the 15th day of April, 1901, the plaintiff had boxed and packed all the various articles described in the contract, and delivered all on board the cars at its place of business within the time provided by the agreement as extended by the verbal conferences between the parties above referred to, and that the defendant refused to receive or pay for the property, and thereby was and is in default of performance. The written contract contained an express provision as follows: "No modification of this accepted agreement shall be binding upon the parties hereto or either of them unless such modification shall be in writing duly accepted by the purchaser and approved by an executive officer of the company." If it was legally possible for the parties to extend the time of performance fixed by the written agreement otherwise than by writing, it is quite apparent that they have done so as matter of fact, and herein lies the principal contention on the part of the defendant in support of this appeal.

It is found that, at the time of making the contract, it was understood by both of the parties and known to the plaintiff that the machinery and apparatus to be manufactured, mentioned and described in the agreement, were for the Hudson River Water Power Company, a corporation located at, or having a place of business and for the installment of such machinery and manufactured articles at, Spier's Falls, on the Hudson river, and that before the 1st day of January, 1901, when the first articles were to be delivered under the contract, it was known to both parties that differences had arisen between the defendant and the power company of such moment that it was apparently certain that, if the machinery and apparatus mentioned and described in the contract should be completed and furnished for delivery, the same would not be accepted from the defendant by the power company. But notwithstanding the differences between the defendant and the power company, there was no abandonment of the contract between the plaintiff and the defendant, nor any request by the defendant to be relieved from the contract. It is found that conferences were had between the representatives of the plaintiff and the representatives of the defendant with reference to the fulfillment of the contract as it had been modified, and the result of such conferences was that it was understood by and between the parties that a literal fulfillment by the plaintiff of the contract was not necessary in so far as the matter of time was involved. The findings are substantially to the effect that, inasmuch as there was doubt about the power company taking the property from the defendant, neither party to this action was particular as to the time of delivery, and hence the verbal arrangement for delivery at a later day than was stipulated in the written contract. It seems that the plaintiff could have manufactured and delivered the articles embraced in the contract within the time specified in the writing, and would have done so except for the attitude of the defendant, which led the plaintiff to believe that delivery on the days mentioned was not necessary. It is quite apparent that since there was some difficulty or misunderstanding between the defendant and the power company, which was ultimately to receive the property as a part of its plant, the delay on the part of the plaintiff in pushing the manufacture and delivery was not unreasonable, and that it acted in entire good faith.

We think that, under these circumstances, the defendant cannot escape responsibility on the ground that the extension of the time of performance by the plaintiff was not in writing. That was a stipulation which the parties, for their mutual convenience, could have waived or disregarded. According to the findings of fact, a situation had arisen between the defendant and the power company that had not been foreseen at the time of the execution of the contract, and it would seem to be only reasonable to say that the parties to this contract could have accommodated themselves to this new situation without writing. Dunn v. Steubing, 120 N. Y. 232, 24 N. E. 315; Thomson v. Poor, 147 N. Y. 402, 42 N. E. 13; Homer v. Guardian Mut. L. Ins. Co., 67 N. Y. 478; Quick v. Wheeler, 78 N. Y. 300. The defendant could, no doubt, have insisted upon strict performance of the contract according to the written instrument, and, had it assumed that position, the plaintiff would then know where it stood; but the defendant permitted the plaintiff to go on with the work after the specified date, and indeed was willing that it should do so, and hence we think it is estopped to claim that this was not performance of the contract. Excuse for nonperformance by the plaintiff on the precise day is not the plaintiff's position, but it insists that it is a case of performance because the defendant is estopped, under the circumstances of the case, to deny it. Gallagher v. Nichols, 60 N. Y. 438, 448; Smith v. Wetmore, 167 N. Y. 234, 60 N. E. 419. It is undoubtedly true that in many cases of mercantile contracts time is of the essence. There are numerous authorities which may be cited in support of that proposition. But this was a contract to manufacture and deliver goods at a specified day in the future, and the time of delivery was changed in the interest and for the accommodation of both parties. It was, therefore, in the power of the parties to change the terms of the contract by parol as to time. It is found that they did actually make the change, and the defendant, under the circumstances of the case, is estopped from setting up the defense of nonperformance as to time.

The trial of the action proceeded for several days under the original complaint, which alleged that the time of performance had been duly extended to March 1st. The learned referee admitted testimony, under defendant's objection and exception, tending to prove by parol that the time of performance had been further extended in the conferences between the parties after the date specified in the contract. It is claimed that the admission of this testimony was error. It is not necessary to decide whether or not it was strictly admissible under the original complaint, since it appears that on the trial the referee permitted the plaintiff, upon terms, to amend the complaint. A new and amended complaint was then actually served in the case, and the defendant served an amended answer, in which a counterclaim was set up in addition to the matter originally pleaded. Therefore, if the testimony was not admissible under the original complaint, it certainly was admissible under the amended complaint, and so we think the amendment of the pleadings thus had obviated all objection to the testimony, and hence the exceptions are not now available. The referee had power to permit the amendments, and, the pleading having thus been made sufficient to cover the testimony, the objection disappears. Nat. Bank of Deposit v. Rogers, 166 N. Y. 380, 59 N. E. 922; Nichols v. Scranton Steel Co., 137 N. Y. 471, 33 N. E. 561; Smith v. Rathbun, 75 N. Y. 122; Smith v. Wetmore, supra.

It appears that, in the month of August following the refusal of the defendant to receive the property or pay for it, the plaintiff, upon public notice, sold the property at auction for something over $30,000. This it had the right to do. There is no question for this court with reference to the fairness of the sale. The defendant having refused to receive the appliances, the right of the plaintiff to make a fair sale cannot well be questioned. It was a part of the plaintiff's contract to install the machinery and to wire the plant, but inasmuch as the defendant refused to receive the property, and since there was no plant provided in which it could be installed, the plaintiff is not at fault in that respect. The referee deducted from the recovery the sum which it would cost the plaintiff to perform in that respect, and hence the defendant has no ground of complaint. We think that interest was properly included in the recovery from the time of the defendant's default. The price of the property was fixed by the contract. The deductions in favor of the defendant on account of the sum received at the sale, and the allowance in consequence of being relieved from the expense of installing the appliances and wiring the plant, and some other matters embraced in the referee's report, when taken from the purchase prices, represents the damages which the plaintiff is entitled to recover. We think they were liquidated in the sense that the plaintiff was entitled to interest. Van Rensselaer v. Jewett, 2 N. Y. 135, 51 Am. Dec. 275; De Lavallette v. Wendt, 75 N. Y. 579, 582, 31 Am. Rep. 494; Mygatt v. Wilcox, 45 N. Y. 306, 6 Am. Rep. 90; McMahon v. N. Y. & Erie R. R. Co., 20 N. Y. 463; Gray v. Central R. R. Co. of N. J., 157 N. Y. 483, 52 N. E. 555.

We think that the record presents no error of law sufficient to warrant any interference with the judgment, and so it must be affirmed, with costs.

PARKER, C. J., and VANN, BARTLETT, HAIGHT, CULLEN, and WERNER, JJ., concur.

Judgment affirmed.

(185 Mass. 543)

CASHIN v. NEW YORK, N. H. & H. R. CO.

(Supreme Judicial Court of Massachusetts. Plymouth. May 18, 1904.)

PERSONAL INJURIES—DAMAGES—EVIDENCE—EXCLAMATIONS OF PAIN—MENTAL CONDITION—HOSPITAL RECORDS — WITNESSES—EXAMINATION—UNRESPONSIVE ANSWERS—REMEDY.

1. On the issue of damages for personal injuries resulting in melancholia, testimony of plaintiff's wife that she had heard him say that, if he did not have children, he would commit suicide, was admissible as a verbal act tending to show plaintiff's mental condition.

2. In an action for damages for personal injuries, testimony showing exclamations of present pain is admissible, although it carries with it an idea of similar past pain, in which case, however, it is not to be considered as any evidence of such past pain.

3. Where a question and a part of the answer are proper, counsel desiring to object to any part

¶ 2. See Evidence, vol. 20, Cent. Dig. §§ 381, 382.

of the answer as beyond the scope of the question should move to strike out such part as not responsive, and if he does not do so he cannot assign as ground of exception the irresponsiveness of such part.

4. In an action for personal injuries, hospital records, not kept under any requirement of law, and hence not public records, are not admissible in evidence, unless supported by the testimony of the one who made them, if such person is still alive and capable of being produced to testify.

Exceptions from Superior Court, Plymouth County; Robt. O. Harris, Judge.

Tort for personal injuries by one Cashin against the New York, New Haven & Hartford Railroad Company. There was a verdict for plaintiff, and defendant excepts. Affirmed.

Sherman L. Whipple and Knight & Brewster, for plaintiff. Frederick S. Hall, for defendant.

HAMMOND, J. One of the claims made in behalf of the plaintiff was that the accident had caused serious mental injury, resulting, among other things, in melancholia. As bearing upon his mental condition in that respect, the testimony of the wife that she had heard him say "if he didn't have children he would commit suicide" was plainly admissible. It was a verbal act, which tended to show the mental condition. Lane v. Moore, 151 Mass. 87, 23 N. E. 828, 21 Am. St. Rep. 430; Hayes v. Pitts-Kimball Co., 183 Mass. 262, 263, 67 N. E. 249, and cases cited. It is suggested in the defendant's brief that this was a private statement by a husband to his wife; but no such suggestion was made at the trial, and there is nothing in the record to show that the statement was part of a private conversation.

The question put to the witness Barnes, so far as it sought to show exclamations of present pain, was admissible. After a colloquy between counsel on each side and the court, in which counsel for the plaintiff expressly disclaimed any purpose except to show expressions or ejaculations of present pain, and expressly told the witness that, if the plaintiff said "he was sorry his head did ache, or that he wished he could go back where he was before," the witness "need not put that in," the court said, in substance, that the witness might answer the question so far as it called for any statement as to a then alleged existing pain and condition. The whole colloquy shows that the question called only for ejaculations of pain, and that the court admitted it solely for that purpose. The witness, however, with a perversity which it may be argued was not due to ignorance on his part as to the proper scope of the question—a kind of perversity quite common where a witness whose sympathies are enlisted has something which he wants to say very much—answered the question in a very objectionable manner; and in direct opposition to the instructions given him by the counsel who called him. That part of the answer which ends with the word "headaches," when taken in connection with the statement that at the time of the exclamation the plaintiff had his hands upon his head, may be regarded as an exclamation and ejaculation of present pain. And it is none the less so even if it also carries an idea of similar past pain. So far as it was an ejaculation of present pain, it was admissible, and was therefore rightly admitted; but it was not to be considered as any evidence whatever of similar prior pain. The rest of the answer was inadmissible. Since the question and a part of the answer were admissible, it was the duty of the counsel for the defendant, if he desired to object to any part of the answer as going beyond the proper scope of the question, to call the attention of the court to that fact by moving to strike out the part of the answer which was not responsive. Inasmuch as he did not take that course, the court and opposing counsel were warranted in assuming that he relied upon his general objection to the question, and not upon any specific objection to the answer, and that he regarded the whole answer as responsive, and within the proper scope of the question. Under these circumstances, he must stand upon the general objection to the question, and upon that matter the fact that some portion of the answer not responsive to the question was admitted is not material. It is to be assumed that in the instructions to the jury the proper bearing and scope of the answer was stated to the jury.

In the case of the books which were offered as records of the respective hospitals, it was not contended that, as to either institution, the records were kept under any requirement of law. They were, therefore, not public records, and were not admissible, unless supported by the testimony of the one who made them, if that person were still alive and capable of being produced to testify. Kennedy v. Doyle, 10 Allen, 161, 165. See, also, Townsend v. Pepperell, 99 Mass. 40, where the record was admitted evidently upon the doctrine that, it being more than 30 years old, there was no need to show the death of the person who made it. In the present case the court may well have found upon the evidence as to each hospital, both that the records were imperfect, and that there was no reason to suppose that the writers could not be produced. The records upon such a finding were properly excluded.

Exceptions overruled.

(185 Mass. 507)

D. O. HAYNES & CO. v. NYE.

(Supreme Judicial Court of Massachusetts. Bristol. May 18, 1904.)

ADVERTISING CONTRACT — BREACH — REMEDY— DAMAGES—JURY QUESTION—BURDEN OF PROOF.

1. The refusal to prepare or furnish an advertisement to be inserted in a newspaper is a breach of a contract with the publishers to insert an advertisement.

2. Where a contract to advertise in a newspaper, the advertisement to be changed at will, is breached by the failure to prepare or furnish an advertisement to be inserted, whereupon the publisher uses, over the advertiser's objection, copy previously furnished, the remedy of the publisher is an action for damages, and not for the contract price.

3. In an action to recover damages for breach of a contract to advertise in a newspaper the burden is on the publisher to establish the amount of his damages.

4. Though there is evidence in an action to recover damages for breach of a contract for advertising that the damage to plaintiff was the contract price, the question is one for the jury, where there were circumstances from which the jury might have found that the damage was something less than the contract price.

Exception from Superior Court, Bristol County; Fredk. Lawton, Judge.

Action by D. O. Haynes & Co. against William F. Nye. From a finding for plaintiff, defendant brings exceptions. Exceptions sustained.

Mayhew R. Hitch, for plaintiff. J. L. Gillingham, for defendant.

KNOWLTON, C. J. The plaintiff corporation is the proprietor of a newspaper called the New York Commercial, published in the city of New York, and it made a contract in writing with the defendant as follows:

"$300.00 New Bedford, October 25, 1900.

"D. O. Haynes and Company, Publishers, New York: Please insert our advertisement in the New York Commercial, to occupy a space of four inches, and to be inserted one time a week for twelve months, beginning with issue of December to January first, 1900, for which I agree to pay you three hundred dollars in monthly payments.

"Name William F. Nye

"Full address, New Bedford, Mass.

"Business, oil manufacturer.

"Agent, J. E. Sullivan."

The plaintiff at the time accepted the order through its agent, Sullivan, who forwarded to it the writing, and it entered upon the performance of the contract. The defendant was a dealer in oils, and it was understood that he could change the advertisement or copy at any time, as often as he chose. Sullivan had with him a copy of an advertisement which the defendant previously had published in another newspaper, and he told the defendant that he could send such copy as he desired to have published, and, if no copy was received before the time for publication, the plaintiff would publish the copy which the agent had with him. The defendant had previously told the agent that he did not wish to have that advertisement published, as he did not then have for sale some of the articles mentioned in it. Before the first publication of the advertisement the defendant notified the plaintiff by letter not to publish the advertisement, and he failed to furnish the plaintiff any copy for publication, although often requested to do so. The plaintiff published this advertisement for nine months, against repeated objections by the defendant. The declaration is in three counts—the first to recover damages for the breach of the contract, the second to recover the contract price for the performance of the contract, and the third upon an account annexed.

The defendant asked the court to rule "that the plaintiff had no claim against defendant except by virtue of the contract, and had no right to furnish copy for advertisement, and its only remedy was for damages for the breach of the contract." Also, "that the publication of the copy supplied by it against the protest of the defendant was not such a substantial performance of the contract on the part of the plaintiff as would entitle it to recover for such publication." The judge declined to give these instructions, but instructed the jury that "if, after the defendant's refusal to furnish an advertisement, the plaintiff did, in good faith, go ahead, and do the best they could to carry out the contract, then they are entitled to recover compensation for it." In another part of the charge he said: "The measure of that damage is, at all events, compensation for the advertisement for the number of times that it was inserted in the paper. * * * He is entitled to recover twenty-five dollars for nine months, and he is entitled to recover that, if he is entitled to recover anything, with interest from the date of the writ. * * * The simple question is whether that contract was made or not. * * * That is the sole and only question." The jury returned a verdict for the amount claimed and interest.

Under the contract the plaintiff was to "insert our advertisement"; that is, the defendant's advertisement. The defendant impliedly agreed to prepare an advertisement to be inserted. On the undisputed facts the contract was broken by the defendant before the first publication, and he persistently refused to perform it, and repeatedly forbade the plaintiff's attempts at performance afterwards. He is liable to the plaintiff in damages for the breach, and these damages may include the profits that the plaintiff might have made under the contract. His refusal to furnish an advertisement to be published, or to consent to the publication of the former advertisement, put it out of the power of the plaintiff to perform the contract, and its only ground of recovery is the breach for which it should be awarded damages. There was evidence that the damage to the plaintiff would be the contract price, and this would have warranted the jury in assessing damages accordingly. But the burden was on the plaintiff to establish its damages, and the jury were not bound to believe this evidence, or to disregard the circumstances from which they might have found that the damage was something less than the contract price. On this part of the case there was error in instructing the jury as matter of law as to the amount of the damages.

It has been suggested in argument that the contract may be interpreted as an agreement to reserve space for an advertisement of the defendant which he might fill in any proper way. If this had been the contract, the plaintiff might have left the space blank, or might have designated it properly as space reserved for the defendant, and have recovered for a performance of the contract; but it would not be performance of such a contract to persist, against the defendant's orders, in printing an advertisement which he did not want, and which represented him as having goods for sale which he did not have.

Exceptions sustained.

(185 Mass. 547)

MOONEY v. EDISON ELECTRIC ILLUMINATING LIGHT CO. et al.

(Supreme Judicial Court of Massachusetts. Suffolk. May 18, 1904.)

TORTS—JOINT TORT FEASORS.

1. Private corporations, through whose negligence a highway becomes charged with electricity, and a city which negligently suffers the highway to remain thus charged, are not joint tort feasors, and cannot be sued as such.

Appeal from Superior Court, Suffolk County.

Action by Matthew Mooney against the Edison Electric Illuminating Light Company and others. From a judgment for defendants on demurrer to the declaration, plaintiff appeals. Affirmed.

Thos. F. Meehan, for appellant. Saml. M. Child, for respondents.

HAMMOND, J. The plaintiff seeks to hold the two private corporations upon the ground that by their negligence the highway became charged with electricity, and the city of Boston upon the ground that it negligently suffered the highway to remain thus charged. As against the first two the liability rests solely upon the common law; as against the city, solely upon the statute. The private corporations had nothing to do with the negligence charged against the city, and the city had nothing to do with the negligence charged against the private corporations. The liability of the city depends upon statutory conditions, and is limited in amount, while the liability of the other defendants depends upon conditions entirely different, and is measured only by the amount of damages suffered by the plaintiff. As between the defendants, the liability of the private corporations is primary, that of the city secondary; and the city, in case of a recovery against it, could maintain an action against these other defendants to recover what it paid. Boston v. Coon, 175 Mass. 283, 56 N. E. 287, and cases cited. From these considerations it is plain that neither in fact nor in legal intendment are these defendants joint tort feasors. They therefore cannot be held as such, and the declaration is bad. For cases illustrative of the principle involved, see Parsons v. Winchell, 5 Cush. 592, 52 Am. Dec. 745; Mulchey v. Methodist Religious Society, 125 Mass. 487; Ridley v. Knox, 138 Mass. 83; Dutton v. Lansdowne Borough, 198 Pa. 563, 48 Atl. 494, 53 L. R. A. 469, 82 Am. St. Rep. 814.

Demurrer sustained.

(185 Mass. 496)

CARTER v. BOSTON TOWBOAT CO.

(Supreme Judicial Court of Massachusetts. Suffolk. May 17, 1904.)

SERVANT'S INJURIES—NEGLIGENCE—CONTRIBUTORY NEGLIGENCE—QUESTION FOR JURY.

1. In an action for injuries to a servant engaged in placing a pump being hoisted over the side of a wharf on the deck of a lighter, the question of contributory negligence *held*, under the evidence, one for the jury.

2. In an action for injuries to a servant engaged in placing a pump being hoisted over the side of a wharf on the deck of a lighter, the question of defendant's negligence *held*, under the evidence, one for the jury.

Exceptions from Supreme Judicial Court, Suffolk County.

Tort for personal injuries by one Carter against the Boston Towboat Company. There was a verdict for plaintiff, and defendant excepted. Exceptions overruled.

J. J. Feely, for plaintiff. John Lowell and Geo. McClure Sargent, for defendant.

HAMMOND, J. The evidence would have warranted the jury in finding that, by reason of the action of iron rust and salt water, some portion of the fiber of the sling had become weakened by rust, so that the sling was not strong enough to do the work expected of it, and was therefore defective; that by the exercise of reasonable care this should have been known to those persons to whom the duty of the defendant as to providing safe and proper appliances had been intrusted; that as to this particular sling the plaintiff was not such a person; that it did not sufficiently appear that within the reasonable reach of the servants there were slings of the requisite strength which might have been used in this job; that the plaintiff believed, and had no reason to believe to the contrary. that the sling was strong enough to hold the pump; that in trying to turn the pump as it came over towards the lighter of which he had charge he was in the performance of a duty; that he was reasonably careful in doing it; and that the accident was due to no negligence on his part, but solely to the breaking of the sling. Upon such findings the jury might properly come to the conclusion that the plaintiff, while in the exercise of due care, was injured by the failure of the defendant to see that due care was exercised to provide safe and proper appliances for its workmen, and, inasmuch as the risk of a failure to perform this duty was not on the plaintiff, they could properly hold the defendant answerable for the consequences. See Graham v. Badger, 164 Mass. 47, 41 N. E. 61; Moynihan v. Hills Co., 146 Mass. 586, 16 N. E. 574, 4 Am. St. Rep. 348; Haskell v. Cape Ann Anchor Works, 178 Mass. 486, 59 N. E. 1113; Boucher v. Robeson Mills, 182 Mass. 502, 65 N. E. 819. The case differs materially from Kilroy v. Foss, 161 Mass. 138, 36 N. E. 746, upon which, as to the question of due care of the plaintiff, the defendant strongly relies. In that case the plaintiff was caring for the tag rope at the end of a derrick boom used to guide the descending load to its place on the ground, and had room to keep clear of the load as it was lowered onto the ground. The load consisted of stone to be used in erecting a building, and was being unloaded from a cart by a hand derrick. It is stated in the bill of exceptions that the plaintiff testified that by means of the derrick boom and the tag rope "one would be enabled to guide stone at a distance, and stand away from it while it was suspended from the derrick boom, and that he knew these were the purposes for which the tag rope was used." In the case at bar it was the plaintiff's duty to place the pump on the deck of the lighter as it was hoisted over the side of the wharf and lowered onto the deck by men other than his crew. The jury were warranted in finding that neither the plaintiff nor any of his crew had anything to do with shackling on the sling, hoisting the pump, or lowering it onto the deck. Their duty was confined to placing it as it was lowered. One of his crew, George V. Ashland, called as a witness by the defendant, was tending the forward guy on the pump as it was lowered away to the deck, and he was told by the plaintiff not to "slack it too much." The pump had to be turned so as to be fore and aft with the lighter as it came over the side of the lighter, "in order to lower the pump any more," and the plaintiff was turning it, when "the sling broke, and he found himself underneath the pump." The plaintiff had to put his hands on the pump. He was not tending the tag rope of a derrick boom. The wharf gang had not hitched on a guy by which the plaintiff could turn the pump. He had to take hold of the pump. There is no direct evidence that he was under the pump farther than was necessary. The pump was coming over the side of the wharf, and was being lowered onto the deck. The plaintiff was on the deck. He was necessarily lower than the pump. It does not appear that he got unnecessarily under it. "He found himself underneath it" after it fell. It may be that he was on the after end of the pump, and that Ashland had been keeping the forward guy taut, and so had been keeping the pump from swinging forward, and that he slacked up, and it swung aft over the plaintiff, and fell on him. In the opinion of the majority of the court, the questions of the due care of the plaintiff and the negligence of the defendant were properly left to the jury. No error in law was committed in the admission of the questions put to the expert Miles and of the answers thereto.

Exceptions overruled.

(186 Mass. 487)

MARTIN v. MERCHANTS' & MINERS' TRANSP. CO.

(Supreme Judicial Court of Massachusetts. Suffolk. May 17, 1904.)

MASTER—INJURY TO SERVANT—EMPLOYERS' LIABILITY ACT — CONTRIBUTORY NEGLIGENCE — OBVIOUS DANGER—CAUSE OF ACCIDENT—JURY QUESTIONS.

1. In an action for personal injuries, predicated on the employers' liability act, the question whether plaintiff was in the exercise of due care at the time of his injury *held*, under the evidence, to be a question for the jury.

2. Whether the danger from a defective implement with which a servant was working at the time of injury was an obvious one, *held*, under the evidence, to be a question for the jury.

3. Whether the defective condition of an implement with which a servant was working was the sole cause of accident, *held*, under the evidence, to be a question for the jury.

Exceptions from Superior Court, Suffolk County, Edgar J. Sherman, Judge.

Action by one Martin against the Merchants' & Miners' Transportation Company. Verdict for plaintiff, and defendant brings exceptions. Exceptions overruled.

James E. Cotter and Thos. F. McAnarney, for plaintiff. G. C. Dickson, F. Peabody, and A. N. Williams, for defendant.

LORING, J. This is an action by an employé under the employers' liability act for negligence of a person acting as superintendent for the defendant. There was a count at common law, but a verdict for the defendant was directed on that count, and the case is here on an exception to the ruling allowing the jury to find for the plaintiff on the count under the statute.

The plaintiff, with other employés, was engaged in unloading the defendant's steamer Gloucester. The Gloucester arrived at her wharf at 12:30 p. m., July 13th. The work of unloading began without delay, and was continued without interruption. The accident to the plaintiff happened about 4 a. m.

on the following morning. The plaintiff was at work at hatchway No. 1. The cargo at this and the other hatchways was unloaded by means of a stationary crane and fall. At the end of the fall were a pair of sister hooks. A load was made up in the hold of the steamer, to be hoisted out by rolling the piece or pieces of which it was to be constituted onto a rope sling about 14 feet long, or by passing the sling around them or it. The sling was then brought up or around the load, one end being passed through the bight at the other end of it, and, when the fall came down, was hitched onto one of the sister hooks by a double back hitch. Word was then given to hoist, and the load went up. As the fall came down, a sling for the next load was thrown down, and, while the bale was going up, it was the duty of one of the gang to pick up the second sling. About two hours before the accident to the plaintiff, one of the sister hooks in use at this hatchway caught in the coaming of the hatchway as the load went up, and was thereby somewhat straightened. The double back hitch should be made above the shoulder made by the curved shape of the hook. There was testimony by witnesses found to be experts that, when the hook in question was straightened, it was not safe to make a hitch on it. For lack of a shoulder on the hook, the hitch might slip. When the hook in question was straightened, one of the employés called out to Wilson, who, it is admitted, "was a superintendent within the meaning of" the employers' liability act, to "take the hook off or some one will get hurt"; but Wilson replied, "Go on with your work, and never mind." This is the negligence of the superintendent relied on by the plaintiff. Two gangs of three men each worked at each hatchway—one on the inshore, and the other on the offshore, side of the hold. As a load went up, it was the duty of the head of the gang who made up that load to pick up the sling for the next load. The plaintiff was the head of the inshore gang at the hatchway in question, and it was his duty to pick up the sling. As the prior load made up by the plaintiff's gang was going up, the plaintiff "reached over" to pick up the sling for the next load; the sling "was on the keelson"; the hitch slipped, and the load fell on the plaintiff, causing the injuries here complained of.

These four questions were submitted to the jury, all of which were answered in the affirmative: "First. Was the plaintiff in the exercise of due care? Second. Was the fact that one of the sister hooks was partially straightened called to the attention of Wilson, the superintendent, before the accident? Third. Did Nelson and Wilson consult over the matter concerning the hook or the danger, and then did they say, 'Go on with the hooks'? Fourth. Was the use of the partially straightened hook the sole cause of the injury to the plaintiff?"

The defendant's first contention is that the jury were not warranted in finding that the plaintiff was in the exercise of due care. Its argument is that "there was no cause for hurry on Martin's part, and he could have picked up the sling when they were hooking on on the offshore side, when the fall was coming down into the hold, when they were unhooking the bale on deck, or when he was getting ready to hook onto his load." But the evidence warranted the jury in looking on these suggestions as academic, and in finding that the plaintiff's duty was to hurry; that the only time he was given to pick up the sling on which the next load was to be rolled was as the previous bale was going up. If not done then, it was not done when it should have been done to insure a prompt unloading. If the ascending load swung over the place where the sling to be picked up fell when thrown down, the jury were warranted in finding that it became the plaintiff's duty to go under the ascending load and pick it up. The case comes within Carter v. Boston Towboat Co., 70 N. E. 933, and not within Kilroy v. Foss, 161 Mass. 138, 36 N. E. 746, for the reasons stated in the opinion in the first of these two cases. In this connection see Hackett v. Middlesex Mfg. Co., 101 Mass. 101; Spicer v. South Boston Iron Co., 138 Mass. 426; Graham v. Badger, 164 Mass. 42, 41 N. E. 61; Haskell v. Cape Ann Anchor Works, 178 Mass. 485, 59 N. E. 1113; Pierce v. Arnold Print Works, 182 Mass. 260, 65 N. E. 368.

The defendant's next contention is that the danger from the straightened hook was an obvious one. It appeared from the evidence that it was the plaintiff's duty to make the hitch for the loads of the inshore gang, and that he had made all the hitches during the night in question except the hitch of the load which fell. The defendant contends that, when the plaintiff had been making hitches on this pair of sister hooks for two hours after the one in question had been straightened, he must have become aware of its condition. It was in evidence that, when the fall comes down, the head of the gang making up the load reaches out and catches hold of either hook, and makes the hitch on one of them, and that both hooks cannot be used. But the plaintiff testified that he "had been using the hooks continuously all that night, whichever came handiest, without noticing that there was anything wrong with them." There was evidence that there was not much light in the hold of the steamer that night. The jury were warranted in believing this testimony.

Neither do we think the defendant's next exception well taken. In our opinion, the finding that the straightened condition of the hook was the sole cause of the accident was not guesswork, but was warranted by the evidence. The fact that many of the loads made up by the inshore gang during the two hours which elapsed after the hook was straightened must be taken to have been made on the defective hook, and yet went up safely, does not show that the condition of the hook was not the cause of the accident. The evidence showed that each gang sent up 40 or 50 loads an hour. If this hook was used half the time, it carried up 40 or 50 loads after it was straightened. But a hitch, to be safe, must bind; it is not enough that it may bind. For that reason the fact that hitches on this hook did bind for some 40 or 50 times does not preclude a finding that the expert who testified that it was not safe to make a hitch on a straightened hook was right, and that the straightened hook was the sole cause of this injury. Freeman testified that the hitch in question was made by him, and was "a good double back hitch."

In the opinion of a majority of the court, the entry must be, exceptions overruled.

(185 Mass. 539)

TOWN OF WRENTHAM v. FALES.

(Supreme Judicial Court of Massachusetts. Norfolk. May 18, 1904.)

PUBLIC SCHOOLS—CHILDREN OF NEIGHBORING TOWN—ATTENDANCE—CONTRACT TO PAY FOR TUITION — LEGALITY — CONSENT OF SCHOOL COMMITTEE—REPEAL OF STATUTE.

1. Under St. 1894, p. 609, c. 498, § 8, providing that children may attend schools in cities and towns other than those in which their parents or guardians reside, children whose parents reside in one town in the state may attend school in another town.

2. Under St. 1894, p. 609, c. 498, § 8, providing that children may, with the consent of the school committee first obtained, attend schools in cities and towns other than those of their parents' residence, the committee whose consent is to be obtained is that of the town in which the school is located, and not that of the town in which the parents reside.

3. An express contract by a parent residing in one town to pay for the tuition of his children at a public school in another town is enforceable, though St. 1894, p. 609, c. 498, § 8, authorizing children whose parents reside in one town to attend school in another town, provides that "when a child resides in a city or town different from that of the residence of the parent or guardian, for the sole purpose of attending school there," the parent or guardian shall be liable for tuition.

4. Where children whose parents reside in one town were legally placed in the schools of another town under St. 1894, p. 609, c. 498, § 8, their parent expressly contracting to pay for their tuition, the fact that such statute was repealed by St. 1898, p. 465, c. 496, § 36, without a saving clause, during the period of their attendance, would not relieve the parent from liability for subsequent tuition.

Appeal from the Superior Court, Norfolk County.

Action by the town of Wrentham against one Fales. Judgment for plaintiff, and defendant appeals. Judgment entered for plaintiff.

Henry E. Ruggles, for appellant. E. J. Whitaker, for appellee.

HAMMOND, J. The defendant, a resident of the town of Norfolk, applied to the school committee of Wrentham for permission to have his children admitted to the public schools of the latter town, and upon his express promise to pay for such schooling permission was granted, and the children attended the schools for many weeks. After having received in full the benefit for which he thus agreed to pay, the defendant declines to pay upon the ground that the contract was invalid, in that the town could not legally enter into it. The chief question here is whether the defense of illegality is well taken.

"The laws of this commonwealth for the establishment and maintenance of public schools are designed to provide schools in each town or district for the benefit of the inhabitants thereof, and not for the benefit of residents in other towns or districts. It is only in a few exceptional cases specified by statute that the inhabitants of one town can send their children to the public school in any other town; and, except in such cases and upon such conditions as are thus provided by law, towns have no authority to open their schools to children of the inhabitants of other towns. If they do receive children from other towns in violation of law, they cannot maintain any action against the parents of such children for their tuition, even if there is an express contract to pay it. Such a contract, being founded upon illegality, cannot be enforced." Morton, J., in Haverhill v. Gale, 103 Mass. 104, 105. Both parties concede these general principles, but the plaintiffs contend that this case falls within the provisions of St. 1894, p. 609, c. 498, § 8. The question reduced to its lowest terms therefore is whether this section covers this case. It is as follows: "Children may, with the consent of the school committee first obtained, attend schools in cities and towns other than those in which their parents or guardians reside; but when a child resides in a city or town different from that of the residence of the parent or guardian, for the sole purpose of attending school there, the parent or guardian of such child shall be liable to pay such city or town for tuition, a sum equal to the average expense per scholar for the period during which the child so attends." The contention of the plaintiff, is that the first part of this section authorizes the school committee of any town to permit the children of another town within this state to attend school in the former, and that, such being the case, a special contract between such school committee and the parent of the children that he shall pay for such schooling contemplates no violation of law, and is not illegal. The contention of the defendant is, first, that the statute does not authorize the children of one town to attend the schools of another town; second, that, even if it does, the school committee of the town in which the parent resides, and not that in which the child attends school, is the one whose consent must first be obtained; and, third, that it clearly appears from the reading of the whole section that liability to pay attaches only in a case where "the child resides in a city or town different from that of the residence of his parent or guardian for the sole purpose of attending school there." The language of the first part of the statute is very broad, and, we think, covers the case of children whose parents reside in this commonwealth. In Haverhill v. Gale, ubi supra, the defendant resided in the state of New Hampshire, and the case was decided in his favor upon the ground that the section upon which the plaintiff there relied, which, so far as material to this point, was like St. 1894, p. 609, c. 498, § 8, the one now under consideration, was "to be construed in connection with the system of legislation of which it forms a part, and applies only to the children of parents who reside within the commonwealth." We think it plain also that the school committee whose consent is required must be that of the town in which is situated the school which the child desires to attend. The interpretation for which the defendant contends would subject the schools of any one town to a liability to be overrun by children residing in adjoining towns at the will of the various school committees of such adjoining towns, and would seriously interfere with the supervision of the schools of a town by its own school committee. Such a view of the statute is inconsistent with the general policy that the schools of any one town shall be under the supervision of the school committee of that town, is unreasonable, and is not to be adopted except upon the clearest expression of legislative intention to that effect. It follows that the children of the defendant were legally in the schools of Wrentham, so long, at least, as this statute stood.

As to the third contention of the defendant—that a liability to pay attaches only in the case where "the child resides in a city or town different from that of his parent or guardian for the sole purpose of attending school there"—it is to be noted that the liability to enforce which this suit is brought is not one imposed by statute, but one arising out of an express contract of the defendant. Even if the statute imposed no liability upon the defendant, an express contract upon his part is not thereby necessarily illegal. The question is not whether the statute imposes upon him a liability, but whether it permits him to impose one upon himself. The contract, as we have seen, under which he sent his children to school, contemplated no violation of law. The school committee of Wrentham made it possible for the defendant to send his children to the schools of that town under the law, and hence, so far as appears, there is no illegality in the contract.

It is further urged by the defendant that, even if the contract was valid, no action can now be maintained upon it, because the statute which we have been considering was repealed by St. 1898, p. 465, c. 496, § 36, and there was no saving clause; and he relies upon the principle that, where a statutory right of action is given, the repeal of the statute without a saving clause destroys the right. But this principle is not applicable. The right of action in this case does not depend upon a statute, but upon an express contract of the defendant, and therefore is to be enforced under the rules applicable generally to contracts.

It is also urged that, after the repealing statute of St. 1898, p. 465, c. 496, the children were not legally in the schools of Wrentham, and the defendant cannot legally be held for the time after that statute went into effect. We have not found it necessary to consider this point, because under the stipulation of the parties it does not seem open to the defendant in this court.

As we are of opinion that "the plaintiff is entitled to recover," judgment in accordance with the terms of the stipulation is to be entered for the plaintiff in the sum of $140.96, with interest from the date of the writ; and it is so ordered.

(185 Mass. 463)

WALKER ICE CO. v. AMERICAN STEEL & WIRE CO.

(Supreme Judicial Court of Massachusetts. Worcester. May 17, 1904.)

ICE—RIGHT TO TAKE FROM POND—LEASE—HOLDING OVER AFTER TERM—DESTRUCTION OF CROP—LEASE OF WATER FOR MANUFACTURING PURPOSES — CONSTRUCTION — ADMISSIBILITY OF EVIDENCE—VARYING WRITTEN INSTRUMENT—CONDUCT OF PARTIES.

1. A lease for a round sum of premises on the shores of a pond, "to be used for a dwelling house and other buildings for the ice business," and providing that the lessor leases to the lessee the right to cut and take ice from the pond, and that the lessee, in addition to the rent, shall deliver to the lessor as much ice as shall be required for two families during the lease, annexes the right to take ice to the leased premises as an easement or profit à prendre.

2. Where tenants hold over after the term of a written lease has expired, they are in as tenants at will, with all the rights which had been annexed to the premises, including the right to take ice from an adjacent pond.

3. Changes in the personnel of a tenant partnership, and its change from a partnership to a corporation, acquiesced to by the lessor, do not terminate a tenancy at will, there being no interruption of occupancy.

4. The owner of a pond leased it to a manufacturing company, "to be used for flowage purposes only * * *, with the exclusive right to flow, store and use water in said pond." The lease reserved to the lessor, his heirs, etc., "the exclusive right to cut, harvest, sell and store for sale ice from pond as at present exercised by W. & Co." The right to take ice from the pond was annexed to a tenancy at will of

¶ 2. See Landlord and Tenant, vol. 32, Cent. Dig. § 410.

premises adjoining the pond held by the W. Ice Co., which was the successor of W. & Co. *Held*, that any right given the manufacturing company to turn in and store hot water in the pond was subject to the right of the ice company to cut and take ice.

5. The owner of a pond leased it to a manufacturing company, which used the water for steam and condensing purposes, the lease reciting that the pond was "to be used for flowage purposes only * * *, with the exclusive right to flow, store and use water in said pond." The lease contained a reservation of the right to take ice from the pond. The pond was originally established for manufacturing purposes, and the cutting and taking of ice was an incidental matter. *Held*, that the manufacturing company had no right to turn in and store hot water in the pond.

6. The lease of a pond reserved to the lessor, "for himself, his heirs, executors, administrators and assigns," the right to harvest ice therein. *Held*, that a tenant at will, to whose estate the right to take ice was already annexed, was an assign within the terms of the lease, though the reservation was in the nature of an exception rather than an implied grant.

7. In a suit by the tenants of conflicting estates, evidence of conversations between the lessor and one tenant is admissible to show the terms and conditions of his tenancy and what was included therein.

8. One who is not a party to a written contract may introduce parol evidence to vary its terms.

9. Where the terms of the lease of a pond to a manufacturing company do not confer the right on the lessee to turn in and store hot water, evidence in its behalf that such act was reasonable and necessary to the operation of its plant, and that for 25 years the process of condensing and returning water to the source of supply had been a recognized method of operating steam plants, is properly excluded.

10. The owner of a pond leased premises adjacent thereto, to be used for buildings for the ice business "as at the present time." The lease also included the right to cut and take ice from the pond "as is done at this time." Later he leased other premises adjoining the pond, together with the pond itself, to a manufacturing company, reserving the right to harvest ice therefrom "as heretofore." A renewal of this lease contained the same reservation "as at present exercised by W. & Co." *Held*, that evidence that the manufacturing company for years past had discharged hot water into the pond when the lessees of the ice buildings were cutting ice was inadmissible to explain the meaning of the phrases "as at present exercised," "as heretofore," and "as is done at this time."

11. The conduct of tenants holding conflicting estates, of which the landlord is not cognizant, is not admissible to affect a construction of the lease of one of them.

Loring, Hammond, and Braley, JJ., dissenting.

Exception from Superior Court, Worcester County; Francis H. Gaskill, Judge.

Action by the Walker Ice Company against the American Steel & Wire Company. Verdict for plaintiff, and defendant excepts. Exceptions overruled.

Arthur P. Rugg and William C. Mellish, for plaintiff. Herbert Parker and George A. Gaskill, for defendant.

MORTON, J. This is an action of tort to recover damages for the alleged destruction by the defendants of a crop of ice on Salisbury Pond, in Worcester, which the plaintiff was preparing to harvest. There was a verdict for the plaintiff, and the case is here on exceptions by the defendants to the admission and exclusion of evidence, and to the instructions that were given and refused. The plaintiff contended that the ice was destroyed by the turning into the pond by the defendants of hot water from its condensers. The defendants admitted turning in hot water, but denied that the destruction of the ice was caused thereby. The verdict must, however, be taken to settle this issue against them.

Salisbury Pond is an artificial pond. It and the premises on the shore occupied by the plaintiff and its predecessors formerly belonged to Stephen Salisbury, Sr., and on his death, in 1884, passed to his son, Stephen Salisbury, Jr., the present owner. The pond was originally established and is principally used to furnish water for manufacturing purposes. But for upwards of 30 years the plaintiff and its predecessors, first as tenants of Stephen Salisbury, Sr., and then of the son, have occupied the premises on the shore of the pond for the ice business, and have cut and taken ice from the pond in connection therewith. Formerly this tenancy was under written leases. The last written lease that was put in evidence by the plaintiff was one from Stephen Salisbury, Sr., to Benjamin Walker, in 1878, for five years. Upon its expiration it was extended in writing for three years more upon the same terms and conditions. The extension expired in 1886, and since then the plaintiff and its predecessors have occupied the premises and cut and taken ice upon the same terms and conditions as contained in the lease of 1878, except that each was to give the other six months' notice of an intention to terminate the tenancy. The lease of 1878 bounded the premises in part on the shore of the pond, and provided that "the premises are to be used for a dwelling house, and other buildings for the ice business as at the present time." It also contained a provision that the "said Salisbury doth also lease to the said Walker the right to cut and take ice from Salisbury's Pond as is done at this time during the term of this lease," and a further provision that, in addition to the stipulated rent, the lessee should "deliver to the lessor as much ice as should be required for two families during the term of this lease as is done at this time." The plaintiff has paid the rent, and has done all the other things required. As we construe this lease, it demised the premises on the shore of the pond, with the privilege of cutting and taking ice as appurtenant thereto. The rent reserved was not apportioned between the premises and the right to cut and take ice, but consisted of a round sum, and this, taken in connection with the situation of the premises on the shore of the pond, and the provision that they were to be used for the ice business, renders the construction which we have given to it the only reasonable one. See Huntington v. Asher, 96 N. Y. 604

48 Am. Rep. 652. Strictly speaking, a right to cut and take ice is perhaps more in the nature of a profit à prendre than an easement, though it comes within the definition of an easement which was given by Chief Justice Shaw in Ritger v. Parker, 8 Cush. 145, 147, 54 Am. Dec. 744, and which was quoted with approval by the court in Owen v. Field, 102 Mass. 90, 108. But whether regarded as an easement or as a profit à prendre, the right was capable of being annexed to the premises which were demised (see Huntington v. Asher, supra), and must be considered, we think, according to the true construction of the lease, as having been so annexed. Upon the termination of the written lease the occupancy did not cease, but the relation of landlord and tenant continued between Mr. Salisbury and the parties in possession, the only difference being that, instead of being in under a written lease and for a fixed time, they were in by parol and as tenants at will. In holding over, whether by mutual consent and agreement or otherwise, they held the same premises with all the rights and privileges that had been annexed to them, and upon the terms and conditions as specified in the written lease, except so far as modified by mutual arrangement. Dimock v. Van Bergen, 12 Allen, 551; Weston v. Weston, 102 Mass. 514, 518; Webber v. Shearman, 3 Hill, 547. They were not in any sense licensees, but were tenants at will. And if the landlord had deprived them of the right to cut and take ice, it would have constituted a substantial interference with their right of quiet enjoyment, if not an eviction. Brown v. Holyoke Water Power Co., 152 Mass. 463, 25 N. E. 966, 23 Am. St. Rep. 844; Case v. Minot, 158 Mass. 577, 33 N. E. 700, 22 L. R. A. 536. The occupation has been a continuous one since the expiration of the lease, and the successive changes rendered necessary by death and the taking in of new partners, and the change from a partnership to a corporation, have not interrupted the tenancy, and have all been agreed to by Mr. Salisbury. If the case had stopped here, there can be no doubt, we think, that the plaintiff had such possession of the ice that the defendants would be liable for the damage done in causing its destruction by turning hot water into the pond.

But the case does not stop here. The defendant claims under a written lease from Mr. Salisbury, of what it asserts is the pond and the land under it, to the Washburn & Moen Manufacturing Company, to whose rights it is admitted that the defendant has succeeded; and it contends that under this lease it had the right to turn in hot water, and that if the plaintiff has a right to cut and take ice, which it denies, the right is subject to its right to flow, store, and use the water of the pond for manufacturing purposes. It also contends—and this is the ground on which it denies the plaintiff's right to cut and take ice—that the plaintiff derives any right or privilege that it has to cut and take ice from the reservation to Mr. Salisbury contained in the lease, that that created an easement in gross in favor of Mr. Salisbury which could only pass by grant, and that, having no grant, the plaintiff was only a licensee, and, not having reduced the ice to possession at the time when it was destroyed, has no cause of action against the defendant. This renders it necessary to consider the lease under which the defendant claims. If the construction contended for by the defendants is correct, it is manifest that the conclusion for which they contend must follow. But we do not think that the construction for which they contend is correct.

Omitting what is not essential in the consideration of the case before us, what was demised by the lease to the Washburn & Moen Company was "that tract of land lying on the westerly side of said Grove street as shown on plan recorded herewith * * * comprising the area known as Salisbury Pond, to be used for flowage purposes only, * * * with the exclusive right to flow, store and use water in said pond by means of its dam and flashboards at a height," etc. Later in the lease is the following reservation: "The said lessor for himself, his heirs, executors, administrators and assigns reserves the exclusive right to cut, harvest, sell and store for sale ice from Salisbury Pond as at present exercised by B. Walker & Co. during the lease and its extension." The lease was dated January 31, 1890, and for 25 years from July 1, 1888. There had been an earlier lease from Mr. Salisbury, Sr., to the Washburn & Moen Company, which was offered in evidence by the defendant, and excluded, subject to its exception. This lease was dated the 1st day of July, 1868, and expired on the same day as that under which the defendant now claims took effect. What was demised by that lease was "all the water in Salisbury Pond on the north side of Grove Street * * * to be used for manufacturing purposes * * * subject to the reservation hereinafter expressed." The reservation, so far as material, was as follows: "The said Salisbury reserves to himself his heirs and assigns during the term of this lease the right to take ice from the pond as heretofore." The Washburn & Moen Company was and is a large manufacturing establishment which the defendant operates, and the water is used for steam and condensing purposes.

The first question is whether the defendants had the right under their lease to turn hot water into the pond, as it is found that they did. We do not think that they had. No doubt, if Mr. Salisbury had seen fit to do so, he could have leased the pond and the land under it to the Washburn & Moen Company, or to the defendants, so as to give them the right to turn in hot water, and have made the right to cut and take ice subject thereto, leaving the plaintiff and its predecessors to such remedy, if any, as they might have against him. But it does not seem to us that he has done so. The lease contains an express reservation to himself, his heirs and assigns, of the right to cut and take ice as at present exercised by B. Walker & Co. The earlier lease that was offered and excluded contained a similar reservation. The effect of these reservations is to rebut any intention on his part to give the Washburn & Moen Company a right in the waters of the pond, or in the pond itself, superior to the right to cut and take ice. And the reference to B. Walker & Co., though that was not the style of the firm then carrying on the ice business, which was the Walker Ice Company, a successor to B. Walker & Co., shows plainly, it seems to us, a purpose on his part to protect the rights of those in occupation of the premises on the shore of the pond, and engaged in cutting and taking ice, from interference therewith on the part of the Washburn & Moen Company, and to make the rights demised to that company in the waters of the pond subject to the right to cut and take ice. The reservation is in the nature of an exception, and should be so construed. Hamlin v. N. Y. & N. E. R. R., 160 Mass. 459, 36 N. E. 200. Even if, therefore, the lease gave to the defendants the right to turn in and store hot water, we think that the right was subject to the plaintiff's right to cut and take ice.

But we do not think that there is anything in the lease or the circumstances under which it was executed which gave to the Washburn & Moen Company the right to turn in and store hot water, though, no doubt, it might do so, so long as nobody interested objected. The lease demised the pond and the land under it for flowage purposes only, with the exclusive right to flow, store, and use the water as high as a certain bolt. There is nothing, in terms at least, which gives the right to turn in and store hot water, and we think that the rights that are given have reference to water in its natural condition, as it comes in the ordinary course of nature, from the ponds and streams in which it has gathered, to and is held back by the dam to the height prescribed. This is the natural construction, particularly of the right of flowage, and there is nothing to show that the language was used in any other sense or should receive a different construction. The fact that the defendant was and is a manufacturing establishment, and used the water for steam and condensing purposes, does not show, and has no tendency to show, that the lease should be construed so as to give it the right to turn in and store the water used for steam and condensing purposes. Neither does the fact that the pond was originally established to furnish water for manufacturing purposes, and that the cutting and taking of ice was an incidental matter, show that the lease should be so construed. The question is one of construction. And, with these facts before them, and all that might be properly inferred as to their knowledge respecting what was done in steam plants operated as that of the Washburn & Moen Company was, and what was or might be reasonable and necessary for its operation and economical running in the way of turning back water when the supply was short, the parties have seen fit to use language whose only reasonable construction is that it applies to water in its natural condition, and does not include the right to turn in and store water that has been used for steam and condensing purposes. The question is not what is necessary and proper for the economical running of a steam plant where water is used for condensing purposes, or what, under certain circumstances, it may be necessary and proper to do in the way of returning water to the pond or the source of supply to keep up the plant in operation, but whether the language which the parties have used in the lease can or should be so construed as to include the right to turn hot water into and store it in the pond, and, for reasons which we have given, we are of opinion that it cannot and should not be so construed. With the consequences of what we think is the true construction, we have, of course, nothing to do. The Washburn & Moen Company should have provided for them in the lease if it anticipated them, and if it did not anticipate them it is not for the court to supply the omission. However great his necessity, one riparian owner would have no right to foul the water of a stream, or turn in hot water to the injury of another riparian owner (Merrifield v. Lombard, 13 Allen, 16, 90 Am. Dec. 172; Mason v. Hills, 3 B. & A. 1), and we cannot think that under a lease of a pond and the land under it for flowage purposes only, with the exclusive right in the lessee to flow, store, and use the water held back by the dam, the lessee would have any greater right to interfere with the natural condition of the water as against one having the right to cut and take ice from the pond. If the rule that doubtful words are to be taken most strongly against the grantor has any application to a case like this, which we do not concede, it being a case of an indenture, and not between the parties to the instrument, nevertheless the words are to be interpreted according to their natural meaning and effect as applied to the subject-matter (Simonds v. Wellington, 10 Cush. 313), and, so interpreted in the case before us, the lease does not, it seems to us, include the right to turn in and store hot water in the pond.

The view which we have taken as to the purpose and effect of the reservation renders it unnecessary to consider further the contention of the defendants that the reservation operated to create an easement in gross in favor of Mr. Salisbury, and that the easement so created is the source of the plaintiff's right, if it has any, to cut and take ice. But we do not see how an easement, in gross or otherwise, can be acquired by the owner of the fee in his own land.

It follows from what we have said that the defendants' first and second requests, that on the pleadings and the evidence the plaintiff was not entitled to recover, were rightly refused. So, also, we think were the other requests. What we have said disposes of them all, except the twelfth, without considering them seriatim. They were all, except the twelfth, based, in one form or another, upon the contention that the defendant had an exclusive right in and to the waters of the pond, or that the plaintiff's right, if it had any, was subordinate to that of the defendant, and that the defendant had the right to use the pond and the waters thereof in such manner as was reasonably necessary for the purpose of carrying on its business, even though the result was to prevent the plaintiff from taking ice. These contentions are manifestly inconsistent with the construction which we have given to the lease, and with the views which we have expressed as to the rights of the parties. The twelfth request was properly refused. It assumed that the suspension, if there was one, was temporary, and was in the nature of the suspension of a right which the defendant had to turn in hot water. To have given it would have been misleading.

We see no error in the instructions that were given. The plaintiff could fairly be said to be an assign within the meaning of the reservation, as the court instructed the jury (Metcalfe v. Westaway, 17 C. B. N. S. 658), though, as we have already said, the reservation was in the nature of an exception of the right to cut and take ice which remained in the possession of Mr. Salisbury and his tenants, rather than an implied grant of an easement of the right to cut and take ice.

There remain the questions of evidence, which we proceed to take up so far as relied upon and argued by the defendant, treating the others as waived.

1. Conversations between the Messrs. Salisbury, father and son, and Mr. White, the treasurer of the plaintiff, and for many years a tenant of the premises, and the predecessor of the plaintiff, were admitted, against the objections and exceptions of the defendant. We think that they were properly admitted for the purpose of showing that the plaintiff was occupying the premises as tenant at will, and what was included in, and the terms and conditions of, the tenancy. The plaintiff claimed adversely to the lease to the Washburn & Moen Company, and the objection that the evidence tended to vary the written contract contained in that lease has no force. The plaintiff had a right to show the terms and conditions, and nature and extent, of its occupancy.

2. The defendant offered to show that the condensing process was reasonably necessary for the proper operating of a steam plant; that for 25 years the process of condensing under certain conditions and returning water to the source of supply had been a recognized method of operating steam plants, and was reasonably necessary; that there were conditions, where the supply of water was limited, when the return of water to the pond to be cooled and used over again became absolutely necessary to the economical running of the plant and to keep it in operation; and that by reason of the condition of the water in the pond in December, 1899, and January, 1900, it was necessary, in order to run the steam plant in its mill, to turn back into the pond water which otherwise would have been wasted. This offer of evidence was excluded, and we think rightly. It may be doubtful whether the defendant was harmed by the exclusion. It had been allowed to introduce, by cross-examination of one of plaintiff's witnesses and by the direct testimony of one of its own, evidence tending to show that condensing was a proper and necessary way to gain most efficiency for the engines, that the method of condensing employed at its mill was a long-established system and was necessary for economy in running any steam plant, and that it was necessary to turn back water into the pond in December, 1899, and January, 1900, to render the condensing system feasible. The testimony that was offered and excluded was the same in substance as that which was thus admitted without objection. We do not see, therefore, as we have already said, how the defendant was harmed by the exclusion. Furthermore, although the testimony was offered for the purpose of affecting the construction of the lease under which the defendant claims, there was no offer to show that Mr. Salisbury was cognizant, at the time when he executed the lease, of what may be termed the state of the art. But, assuming that he was cognizant of the facts that the defendant offered to show in regard to the condensing process, and what it was or might be necessary or proper to do in turning back water, the conclusive answer to the contention that the evidence should have been admitted is, as already observed, that with these facts before them the parties saw fit to use language the natural and reasonable construction of which not only does not include the right to turn back hot water into the pond, but excludes it.

3. Still further, the defendant offered to show, as bearing on the construction of the lease, that warm water had been discharged into the pond in years past by the Washburn & Moen Company when the plaintiff's predecessors were cutting ice. The evidence was excluded. It would seem that in this instance, also, the defendant was not harmed by the exclusion, since evidence to the same effect had been previously introduced by it, without objection, on the cross-examination

of one of the plaintiff's witnesses. But in regard to this evidence, as well as that just considered, the defendant contends that it was admissible to aid in interpreting the phrase "as at present exercised by B. Walker & Co." used in the reservation in the lease of 1890, and the phrase "as heretofore" similarly used in the reservation in the prior lease to the Washburn & Moen Company, and the phrase "as is done at this time" in the lease of 1878 to Benjamin Walker. But there is nothing to show that those phrases had any reference to the condition of things offered to be shown, or any relation thereto in any way. The obvious purpose and effect of the language referred to, when considered in connection with the rest of the provisions in which they are found, was to secure to Mr. Salisbury and his tenants the full and unrestricted right to cut and take ice. Furthermore, the uncontradicted testimony showed that, when requested to do so by the plaintiff or its predecessors, in order to enable them to gather the ice, the Washburn & Moen Company ceased to turn in hot water till the ice had been gathered and they had been notified thereof, which was a recognition of the plaintiff's right rather than an assertion of their own. And, lastly, so far as the evidence that was excluded related to a course of conduct, it was the conduct, not of the parties to the lease, but of the plaintiff and defendant, and it does not appear that Mr. Salisbury was cognizant of it, and it was therefore inadmissible to affect the construction of the lease.

4. The defendant offered in evidence the prior lease from Mr. Salisbury to the Washburn & Moen Company, and it was excluded, subject to its exception. We do not see how the defendant was harmed by its exclusion. If it had been admitted, it could not, for reasons already given, have possibly affected the result.

The remaining exceptions to the admission and exclusion of evidence have not been argued, and we treat them as waived.

For these reasons, a majority of the court think that the exceptions should be overruled. So ordered.

LORING, J. (dissenting). I am unable to concur in the opinion in this case.

This is an action by the plaintiff, claiming to be "lessee at will" of the exclusive privilege of cutting ice on Salisbury Pond, to recover damages caused to a sheet of ice which had formed on the pond, and which the plaintiff had prepared for cutting and was about to cut, by hot water turned into the pond by the defendant on January 8 and 9, 1900. Salisbury Pond is an artificial body of water which was made by damming up the waters of several brooks about the year 1840. The land under the pond and the water rights in the pond were owned by Stephen Salisbury, the elder, until he died, in 1884, and then passed to his son, Stephen Salisbury, the younger, who has since then been the owner of them. It appeared, on the one hand, that by a lease dated in January, 1890, Stephen Salisbury, the younger, demised to the Washburn & Moen Manufacturing Company, among other things, "that tract of land lying on the westerly side of Grove Street, as shown on a plan recorded herewith, containing as per plan one million ninety-three thousand seven hundred (1,093,700) square feet, comprising the area known as Salisbury Pond, to be used for flowage purposes only, * * * with the exclusive right to flow, store, and use water in said pond by means of its dam and flashboards at a height" stated. The term created by this lease began July 1, 1888, and ended July 30, 1913, and it was admitted that the rights of the Washburn & Moen Company under it had passed to the defendant. The Washburn & Moen Company had been in possession for 20 years prior to July 1, 1888, under a lease made in 1868 by Stephen Salisbury, Sr., and had a somewhat similar right to use the waters of Salisbury Pond. This earlier lease was offered in evidence by the defendant, and excluded. On the other hand, it appeared that it had been the practice to cut ice on Salisbury Pond from early times, the date when this practice began not being given. Stephen Salisbury, Jr., testified that "father used to cut ice himself before Walker and Sweetser cut it there. Then ice was cut by Walker and Sweetser, then by Benjamin Walker." And it appeared from other testimony that Benjamin Walker was cutting ice there as early as 1870, then by Benjamin Walker & Co., and then by a partnership known as the Walker Ice Company, and finally by the plaintiff corporation, which was organized in 1899. In 1878, Stephen Salisbury, the elder, by an indenture of lease, demised to Benjamin Walker a tract of land bordering on the pond, "the premises to be used for a dwelling-house and other buildings for the ice business," and also "the right to cut and take ice from Salisbury's Pond, as is done at this time, during the term of this lease." This lease expired in 1883, and was extended until 1886, and finally expired at that time. Since then the successors in the business of Benjamin Walker have repeatedly tried to get a written lease from the owner of the pond, Stephen Salisbury, the younger, but without success. He has, however, agreed with them by word of mouth that they might hold on the terms of the lease of 1878. There is no pretense that the lease of 1878 has been assigned by Benjamin Walker to his successors in business, or that it has been kept alive by extensions. The practice of cutting ice on the pond has been carried on continuously down to the day when the ice was destroyed by the hot water turned into the pond in January, 1900. There was evidence that the hot water complained of came from the condensers of the defendant's engines, and was turned into the pond in December, 1899, and from then until February 3, 1900, and that this was done in place of its being turned into the sewers, as had been done immediately before, because the waters of the pond were very low at that time. The defendant offered to show that "during the past twenty-five years the process of condensing under certain conditions and returning water to the source of supply has been a recognized method of operating steam plants, and is reasonably necessary." Before this evidence was offered, the plaintiff's witness, Stephen Salisbury, the younger, had testified that "Salisbury Pond is an artificial pond constructed for manufacturing purposes," and that "the plant of the Washburn & Moen Company has been a steam plant, and the water has been largely used to generate steam," and that at that time, i. e., about 1870, "Washburn & Moen, or their predecessors, used the waters for manufacturing purposes, and the pond has been so used from 1840." As I have already said, the Washburn & Moen Company were in possession of the same premises under a lease from Stephen Salisbury, Sr., for 20 years prior to the date when the lease in question, dated January, 1890, went into effect, and that that lease was offered in evidence and excluded. Had that lease been admitted in evidence, it would have appeared, in connection with this testimony of Stephen Salisbury, the younger, that for a period of 32 years before the time of the grievances here complained of the Washburn & Moen Company, and its successor and assignee, the defendant corporation, had been in the possession of a steam plant, with a right to use the waters of this pond for generating steam to run its plant. In my opinion, under the facts in evidence, the lease dated January, 1890, must be construed in the same way as if it had been stated therein that the waters of Salisbury Pond could be used by the lessee to generate steam in running its steam plant situated on the borders thereof, and on this point I do not understand there is any difference of opinion between my Brethren and myself.

It is plain to me that, in determining whether, as matter of construction, the right to turn back water from its condensing engines is given by a lease of water to be used in generating steam to operate a manufacturing plant run by steam, the court cannot refuse to consider evidence that "during the past twenty-five years [which includes 12½ years under the lease and 12½ years prior thereto] the process of condensing under certain conditions and returning water to the source of supply has been a recognized method of operating steam plants, and is reasonably necessary." It is so plain to my mind that nothing can be added to the statement of it.

The defendant also offered to show by one Allen what had taken place in the past in the matter of discharging warm water into Salisbury Pond from the condensers of the steam plant which is now owned by the defendant and was then owned by the Washburn & Moen Manufacturing Company. Allen testified that he had been in business in Worcester since 1870; that he had lived near the pond all his life, and was familiar with it; and that he had seen the discharge of warm water from the condensing engine into the waters of the pond in years past. He was then asked to state what he had observed in that regard. This was objected to, and, on being asked how the question was relevant, the defendant's counsel stated, "if it is a fact that at an earlier time the predecessors of this plaintiff were cutting ice in that pond, and when their rights, as I assume, must be referred to some extent to the conditions formerly obtained—if at that time it appears that this condensing process of the discharge of warm water direct into that pond existed, I claim it to be material and important on one fact as determining the measure of the assumed right of the plaintiff." It had appeared in evidence before this offer of proof was made that for 30 years prior to 1900—that is to say, from 1870 to 1900—there had been a pipe which took hot water from the condensers of the defendant's engines and carried it into Salisbury Pond; that this pipe was disconnected in 1890, after being in operation for 20 years, from 1870 to 1890, and remained disconnected for the next 9 years, until the winter of 1899-1900 (that is, until the time of the grievances here complained of) when this old pipe was reconnected, and another pipe, and afterwards a trough, were put in, which also took the water from the condensers into the pond.

The first ground on which evidence is admissible of what took place in the matter of the discharge of warm water from this old pipe from 1870 to 1890 is the fact that by the terms of the agreement between Stephen Salisbury, Jr., and the plaintiff, that was the measure of the right to cut ice which Stephen Salisbury, Jr., gave to the plaintiff. By the terms of the oral agreement between the plaintiff corporation and Stephen Salisbury, the younger, the right which he gave to it to cut ice was the right given in the written lease between Stephen Salisbury, Sr., and Benjamin Walker, in 1878, and the right given to Benjamin Walker by that lease was "to cut and take ice from Salisbury Pond as is done at this time." It further appeared that the rights given by Stephen Salisbury, the younger, by word of mouth to the plaintiff's predecessors in business, was also that given in the lease to B. Walker. The lease to B. Walker was in existence from 1878 to 1886; the period during which the old pipe was in operation was from 1870 to 1890. That is to say, the old pipe was in operation eight years before the written lease to Benjamin Walker, during the time in which that lease was in operation and for 14 years after it expired, during which the right given by word of mouth was the right to cut ice, as was done when the lease to B. Walker was executed. I am unable to understand why the defendant was not at liberty to show what was done in the matter of discharging warm water into the pond during these 30 years, which include the whole term of the lease to Benjamin Walker, 8 years before it began, and 14 years after its expiration, when the measure of the right which Stephen Salisbury gave to the plaintiff was the right given to Benjamin Walker by the written lease, and the right given to Benjamin Walker was "the right to cut ice as is done at this time." Not only is this evidence admissible on the ground that this is all Mr. Salisbury undertook to give to the plaintiff, but it is also admissible, in my opinion, on the ground that it is all Mr. Salisbury had to give. All the right to cut ice which Mr. Salisbury had after the lease dated January, 1890, was the right reserved to him under the reservation in that deed, and the terms of that reservation were "to cut, harvest, sell or store for sale ice from Salisbury Pond, as at present exercised." The old pipe was not disconnected until 1890; this lease, though dated January, 1890, went into operation July 1, 1888. I think it was competent to prove what was done during the first year and a half of this lease, and for the years immediately before it began, in the matter of discharging warm water into the pond, because by the terms of the lease the right reserved to Mr. Salisbury was to cut ice "as at present exercised." Moreover, I think it was competent to prove what was done by the parties in the matter of discharging warm water into the pond prior to the lease and for the first 1½ years of the lease as the contemporaneous acts of the parties giving a construction to the lease. In this connection the defendant offered to show "that by reason of the state of the water and the supply in Salisbury Pond in December, 1899, and January, 1900, it was necessary to turn back water, which otherwise might have been wasted, into Salisbury Pond, in order to run the steam plant in the mill." It had previously appeared in evidence that the water in Salisbury Pond at that time was lower than it ever had been within the memory of man, and that 7,500,000 gallons were taken out of the pond daily by the defendant in generating steam, and 2,950,000 gallons of hot water put back; that this continued until February 3, 1900, when, owing to heavy rains which occurred at the end of January, "the water in the pond was high enough then to run the mill without turning it [the hot water] back into the pond," in the words of one of the plaintiff's own witnesses. This offer of evidence was made to complete the defendant's offer of proof. If the defendant had a right to use the waters of the pond to generate steam, and if returning hot water from the condensers is a recognized method of operating steam plants, it was incumbent upon the defendant to show that in the case at bar it was necessary for it, under the circumstances existing, to return the hot water into the pond in order to keep its steam plant in operation.

Neither can I concur in the disposition made in the opinion of the contention that, by the true construction of the lease dated January, 1890, apart from the evidence I have already dealt with, the defendant had no right to turn hot water from the condensers into the pond. It is stated, as a reason for this conclusion, that the right to cut ice reserved to Mr. Salisbury in that lease operated by way of exception, under the doctrine peculiar to Massachusetts, acted upon in Hamlin v. New York & New England R. R. Co., 160 Mass. 459, 36 N. E. 200, and under consideration in Simpson v. Boston & Maine R. R. Co., 176 Mass. 359, 57 N. E. 674. But in determining whether the right retained by a grantor is superior to the grant or subordinate to it, it makes no difference whether the deed by which an easement is retained in the grantor operates by way of exception or by way of a grant back from the grantee, which is usually spoken of as a "reservation." The correlative rights of an abutter on a railroad and of the railroad company in a private way over the railroad location are precisely the same whether the deed retaining in the abutter a right to use the private way operates by way of exception or by way of reservation. The general rule of construction is equally applicable in both cases that a deed shall be construed against the grantor (Ashley v. Pease, 18 Pick. 268, 275; Palmer v. Evangelical Society, 166 Mass. 143, 43 N. E. 1028), and that what is retained by the grantor shall be construed so as not to be repugnant to the grant (Pynchon v. Stearns, 11 Metc. 304, 45 Am. Dec. 207; Id., 11 Metc. 312, 45 Am. Dec. 210; Dexter v. Manley, 4 Cush. 14; Corbin v. Healy, 20 Pick. 514). The complainant's own witness, Stephen Salisbury, Jr., testified, without objection, that "cutting ice" was "always an incident to the use of the water for manufacturing purposes." The conclusion reached by the court is directly in the teeth of this evidence, which was admitted by both parties without objection, and thereby became evidence in the case, although, had it not been for that, it would have been incompetent. Damon v. Carrol, 163 Mass. 404, 40 N. E. 185; Boyle v. Columbian Fireproofing Co., 182 Mass. 93, 99, 64 N. E. 726.

Whether in this case there was a right to turn hot water into the pond is a question which, in the absence of the evidence offered, is not ripe for decision. But in my opinion there is a fatal objection to the maintenance of this action by the plaintiff in any event, and that objection is that the plaintiff had no right to cut ice, but was a mere licensee. I understand that in the case at bar it is conceded that the plaintiff corporation did not become tenant at will of the land under the pond, but that the land under the pond, during the term of the lease to the Washburn & Moen Company, dated January, 1890, was either the land of Mr. Salisbury or the land of the defendant, who had succeeded to the estate of the lessee under that lease. I also understand it to be conceded that no right of property in the cutting of ice in water flowing this land, which at the time was, as I have said, the land either of Mr. Salisbury or of the defendant, vested in the plaintiff corporation by virtue of the parol agreement between it and Mr. Salisbury proprio vigore, and that this is so because the right to cut ice under these circumstances is an incorporeal right in the land of some one other than the plaintiff, and this agreement was not under seal. And I further understand that the plaintiff's right to cut ice is made out on the ground that that right had become appurtenant to the land (of which the plaintiff became tenant at will under an oral agreement), and passed to the plaintiff as appurtenant to that parcel of land. I understand further that the way in which it is made out that this right to cut ice had become appurtenant to this parcel of land, of which the plaintiff was a tenant at will, was because it was made appurtenant to it in the lease of 1878, which finally expired in 1886, and because since then the practice of cutting ice on the pond in connection with the parcel of land of which the plaintiff was the tenant at will has de facto continued without a break.

The right to cut ice created by the lease to B. Walker dated October, 1878, terminated on the final expiration of that lease in 1886, and the proposition is this: If A. owns an icehouse and the land under it, and also a pond, and for a great number of years ice has been in fact cut on the pond to fill the icehouse, and A. lets the icehouse and the land under it by word of mouth, a right to cut ice on land which under the lease continues to be the land of the lessor passes to the tenant at will as appurtenant to the land. From that proposition I must dissent. The right to cut ice is not appurtenant to the land on which the icehouse stands, in the case put above and in the case at bar, because during all the years in question both have been owned by the same person, and occupied by him or by his tenants. What is meant by a right passing as appurtenant to a parcel of land which is demised is that an incorporeal easement or right in the land of a third person has been granted to the owner of the land demised as appurtenant to that land, and that this right in land of a third person passes to the tenant as appurtenant to the land demised; and that where both the parcel of land demised and the parcel of land subject to the right in question—that is to say, both the dominant and servient estates—are owned by the same person, there can be no right in the one parcel appurtenant to the other parcel, however they have been used in fact, and no matter how long that use may have continued. In other words, the continued use of what would be an incorporeal right, were the two parcels owned by different persons, however long continued, does not bring into being a right over one parcel appurtenant to the other parcel. It has been held in England since the time of Elizabeth to the present day that, where the dominant and servient tenements have come into the ownership of one person, an old servitude to which one of those tenements had been subject prior thereto, and which was then appurtenant to the other tenement, is extinguished by the unity of ownership, and is not continued by a de facto continuance of the old use, and does not pass by a conveyance of what was formerly the dominant estate with appurtenances thereto belonging. Saunders v. Oliff, Moore, 467; Grymes v. Peacock, Buls. 17; Whalley v. Thompson, 1 B. & P. 371; Clements v. Lambert, 1 Taunt. 205; Barlow v. Rhodes, 1 Cr. & M. 439; Plant v. James, 5 B. & Ad. 791.

If a de facto use in one parcel of land in connection with another parcel of land, when both are owned by the same person, makes the use of the first parcel appurtenant to the second parcel, the right in question in each of the above cases would have passed under the conveyances with "appurtenances." Take, for example, the case of Plant v. James. There a way from the highway had in fact always been used to and from a parcel of land called "Park Hall" over a parcel of land called "Woodseaves." Park Hall was owned by two persons in common, and Woodseaves, the land over which this way was laid, was also owned by the same tenants in common. A partition was made by deed, and Park Hall was conveyed to the defendant with appurtenances, and Woodseaves was conveyed to the other tenant. It was held that no right of way over Woodseaves lot passed to the grantee of Park Hall. To pass a right which is de facto in use, but which is not de jure a right, the grant must contain words which will revive or recreate an easement of the same kind as the old easement which formerly existed, but which had been extinguished by the unity of ownership, and words equivalent to these are sufficient for that purpose: "Together with all rights commonly used or enjoyed with the granted premises." See, Bailey v. Great Western R. R. Co., L. R. 26 Ch. 434, and cases there cited.

It follows that in the case at bar, there being nothing more than a parol agreement, the plaintiff had no right to cut ice; he was nothing more than a licensee. It is also plain that a licensee, even while his license is unrevoked, has no right of action if the property upon which he has a license is injured or destroyed by a stranger. A license gives no right to the property in respect of which the license is given; it goes no further than to excuse what would otherwise be a trespass. So long ago as 1673 it was laid down by Chief Justice Vaughan in the Exchequer Chamber that "a dispensation or license properly passeth no interest nor alters or transfers property in anything, but it makes an action lawful which without it has been unlawful." Thomas v. Lowell, Vaughan, 330, 351. And this has been cited with approval in England in Murckett v. Hill, 5 Bing. N. C. 694, 707, and in Heap v. Hartley, 42 Ch. D. 461, 468. The same has been laid down in this commonwealth in Clapp v. Boston, 133 Mass. 367. In that case, the petitioner had placed an hydraulic ram in a well dug by him on land of one Lewis, by Lewis' license. The defendant, in taking a water supply under St. 1872, p. 127, c. 177, took some of the petitioner's land, and "lawfully flowed the land of Lewis where the ram and well were, so that the ram would not work, and the petitioner was thereby deprived of the use of the water at his house and barn." It was held that the petitioner could have no compensation for this loss, not on the ground that his license was revocable, and had been revoked by the defendant, but on the ground that the license from Lewis "gave the petitioner no estate or right in the land. It was a permission by the owner which excused acts done under it, which without it would be unlawful." Where A. owns a parcel of land covered with water, and gives B. a license to cut ice on the water, the land and the ice forming on the water continue to be A.'s, and if any injury is done to either it is an injury suffered by A. on his property, and he alone can sue for it. All that B. has is a dispensation which excuses him from being a trespasser if he cuts ice on A.'s land. He has no right of property in the ice, and therefore has no standing in court to complain that it is injured. The cases of Balcom v. McQuesten, 65 N. H. 81, 17 Atl. 638, and Ottawa Gas Light Co. v. Thompson, 39 Ill. 598, are direct authorities to the effect that a licensee, even while his license is unrevoked, has no right of action for injury to the property in question; and, to the same effect, see Holford v. Bailey, 8 Q. B. 426, 446; Clark v. Close, 43 Iowa, 92.

It may seem hard that the plaintiff, who had secured a right to cut ice, so far as an oral contract founded on a valuable consideration could give it to him, and who had gone to the expense of preparing to cut the ice, should have no remedy for the destruction of the ice by the defendant turning hot water into the pond, which, for the purposes of his discussion, I assume it had no right to do. But the hardship is of the plaintiff's own making. It is a rule of our law that no right in the land of another can be acquired [without] a grant under seal. The plaintiff chose to go to the expenditures he was at in the premises without securing a right to cut ice. It is no more a hardship to apply that elementary rule of law than it would be to hold that a grantee under a conveyance of land, made by word of mouth, and without more, gets no title, although he has paid for the land. The real question of hardship is this: Is it wise to require a seal to make a valid grant of an incorporeal right in land which remains the grantor's? I myself think that it would be unwise to allow a valid grant of such a right to be made by word of mouth. Whether wise or not, it is the rule of the common law, and until altered by the Legislature must be enforced by the courts.

To state my view of this case summarily, it is this: The land under Salisbury Pond became the land of the lessee by virtue of the lease dated January, 1890, during the term thereby created, although the lessee was restricted in the use it could make of the water flowing over the land and of the land itself. The lessor, during the term of this lease, had an easement in gross in the land under the pond (which, during the continuance of the lease, was the land of the defendant) to cut ice on the pond, and that this easement did not pass to the plaintiff because the agreement between the plaintiff and defendant was by word of mouth, and an easement can no more be transferred than it can be created, even for a term of years, except by a grant under seal. Duke of Somerset v. Fogwell, 5 B. & C. 875; Mayfield v. Robinson, 7 Q. B. 486, see pp. 489, 490; Wood v. Leadbitter, 13 M. & W. 838, 842, 843. See, also, Bird v. Great Eastern Ry., 19 C. B. N. S. 268, 286; Bird v. Higginson, 2 A. & E. 697; Roffey v. Henderson, 17 Q. B. 574; Taylor on Evidence (9th Ed.) §§ 973, 974; Hall, Profits à Prendre, 36-38; Goddard on Easements, 359. A valid contract, even one based on a valid consideration, does not convey a right of property in an easement; all that it does is to give a right of action against the other party to the contract in case he fails to perform his obligation under the contract, as was laid down in McCrea v. Marsh, 12 Gray, 211, 213, 71 Am. Dec. 745, and was subsequently held in Kerrison v. Smith (1897) 2 Q. B. 445. Therefore, it is of no consequence whether this contract is or is not within the statute of frauds, as to which see Cole v. Hadley, 162 Mass. 579, 39 N. E. 279; McManus v. Cook, 35 Ch. Div. 681; Webber v. Lee, L. R. 9 Q. B. D. 315; Duke of Sutherland v. Heathcote (1892) 1 Ch. 475; Ferrell v. Ferrell, 1 Baxt. 329. Whatever may be the rights of the plaintiff against Mr. Salisbury in contract, the ice was Mr. Salisbury's ice, and for an injury to it no one but the owner, Mr. Salisbury, can sue.

For these reasons I think that the entry should be: Exceptions sustained.

Mr. Justice HAMMOND and Mr. Justice BRALEY authorize me to state that they concur in this dissent.

(33 Ind. App. 106)

PHŒNIX INS. CO. OF BROOKLYN, N. Y., v. McATEE.

(Appellate Court of Indiana, Division No. 2. April 29, 1904.)

FIRE INSURANCE — ACTION AGAINST FOREIGN COMPANY—LOCALITY OF ORGANIZATION—COMPLAINT — SUFFICIENCY — ANSWER—ALLEGATIONS OF FRAUD—EVIDENCE—MATERIALITY.

1. In an action on a policy issued by a foreign insurance company, in which the title of the cause and the policy sued on designated the defendant as the "Phœnix Insurance Company of Brooklyn, New York," there was a sufficient allegation as to the state under whose laws defendant was organized.

2. Where the complaint in an action against an insurance company set out the issuance of a fire policy, the ownership of the property, its destruction by fire, and that the parties disagreed as to the amount of the loss, and thereafter alleged that, in accordance with the terms of the policy, appraisers were appointed, who made an award fixing the amount of loss, and a recovery of this amount was sought, a demurrer on the ground that the action was on the policy, while the complaint showed that the loss was settled by arbitration and award, was properly overruled.

3. In an action on an insurance policy, a paragraph of the answer alleging that plaintiff committed fraud in making certain false statements contained in the plans and specifications sworn to by plaintiff, but in support of which no copy of the specifications was filed, stated no defense.

4. In an action on an insurance policy, a paragraph of the answer alleging that plaintiff swore falsely in the specifications furnished by him, but averring no fact showing fraud, stated no defense.

5. In an action on a fire policy, it is proper to allow plaintiff to testify that he was the owner of the insured building.

6. In an action on a fire policy, in which there was no question of fraud or misrepresentation, evidence that insured had stated that he had learned that he "had a firebug" as a tenant, and would have to increase his insurance, and did so, was immaterial.

7. In an action on a fire policy, it was proper to allow insured to testify as to the nature of the fixtures insured, and their value at the time of the fire.

Appeal from Circuit Court, Greene County; O. B. Harris, Judge.

Action by Benjamin F. McAtee against the Phœnix Insurance Company of Brooklyn, N. Y. From a judgment for plaintiff, defendant appeals. Affirmed.

Jno. S. Bays and Lee F. Bays, for appellant. C. D. Hunt, for appellee.

COMSTOCK, J. The complaint upon which this cause was tried alleges that appellee was on the 20th day of October, 1901, the owner in fee simple of certain real estate in Farmersburg, Ind., and a certain brick building situate thereon, together with fixtures for lighting, counters, shelving, and store furniture therein, and that he was the owner of all such property on the 22d day of November, 1901, at which time the same was wholly destroyed by fire; that on said last-named date appellant, in consideration of the sum of $15 paid by appellee to appellant, issued to appellee its policy of insurance, insuring the said property against loss and damage by fire in the sum of $1,500; that by the terms of said policy it was expressly provided that the loss, if any, should be made payable to the Ft. Harrison Savings Association, of Terre Haute, Ind., a corporation duly organized under the statutes of the state of Indiana, as the interest of said association might appear, as mortgagee, according to the terms and conditions of a mortgage clause attached to and made a part of said policy, in the interest of said building, savings, and loan association; that on the 24th day of November, 1901, plaintiff gave defendant due notice and proof of said fire and loss, and plaintiff further says that he has duly performed on his part all the conditions of said policy of insurance incumbent upon him by the terms thereof; that said defendant insurance company, in response to said notice, sent its duly authorized agent to said town of Farmersburg, which agent viewed and inspected said loss; that by the terms of said policy it was, among other things, provided that, in the event of a disagreement as to the amount of the loss, the same would be ascertained by two competent, disinterested appraisers, the insured and said company each selecting one, and the two so chosen first should select a competent and disinterested umpire, and said appraisers should then estimate and appraise the loss according to the plans specified in said policy; that said plaintiff and defendant did disagree upon the amount of said loss, and, pursuant to said policy, on the 22d day of April, 1902, said plaintiff demanded the payment of said loss, and said plaintiff and defendant each, in accordance with the provisions of said policy, chose an appraiser, and said appraisers chose an umpire, and thereupon made an award of the amount of loss under said policy, and reported the same to plaintiff and defendant; that said award was fixed by said appraisers at the sum of $1,325, as the amount of loss upon said building; that said award of said appraisers was made in writing as provided in said policy, and duly signed and executed by the plaintiff and defendant; that said building was worth $2,000, and so destroyed by fire on the 20th day of April, 1902; that the plaintiff demanded of said defendant the payment of said insurance; that on the 17th day of October, 1902, the said defendant paid to the said Ft. Harrison Savings Association the full amount of its said mortgage claim due under said policy, to wit, the sum of $514; and that the said Ft. Harrison Savings Association has no further interest in said policy. "There remains due and wholly unpaid to plaintiff on this policy the sum of $986, with interest from the 22d day of November, 1901. A copy of said policy, with the said indorsement of said savings association thereon, is made a part of the complaint, and said award of said arbitrators is filed herewith as a part hereof, and marked 'Exhibit B.' Wherefore," etc.

The defendant answered in five paragraphs. The first is a general denial. No question is raised upon the second and fourth. The third alleges that "it is one of the conditions of the policy in suit that in case 'of any fraud or false swearing by the insured touching any matters relating to this insurance or the subject thereof, whether before or after a loss,' this entire policy shall be void. And the defendant says that the plaintiff did so swear falsely, or did so commit fraud by falsely swearing that a part of the glass in the building destroyed was double-strength plate glass, which sworn statement was wholly false and untrue. Said false swearing is contained in the plans and specifications sworn to by plaintiff, which is attached hereto, and marked 'Exhibit ——;' said specifications touching any matter relating to this insurance or the subject thereof. Wherefore defendant claims that the entire policy in suit is wholly void and of no force and effect, and that said plaintiff should not recover thereon." The fifth paragraph is as follows:

"That one of the conditions of the policy in suit is, 'This entire policy shall be void in case of any fraud or false swearing by the insured touching any matter relating to this insurance or the subject thereof, whether before or after loss.' And defendant avers that the insured—the plaintiff in this case—did so swear falsely in the specifications furnished by him under the conditions of the policy in suit, which specifications were sworn to by the plaintiff, and which were touching matters relating to the insurance, or subjects thereof. That said false swearing by the plaintiff was with the intention of defrauding the defendant, and to the injury of the defendant. Wherefore the defendant asks that the entire policy in the suit be declared wholly void."

The cause was put at issue, and upon proper request the court made a special finding of facts, stated conclusions of law, and rendered judgment thereon in favor of plaintiff for $827. The alleged errors were the overruling of appellant's demurrer to the amended complaint, the sustaining the demurrer to the third and fifth paragraphs of appellant's answer, and overruling appellant's motion for a new trial.

Two objections are made to the complaint: First, that, the appellant being a foreign insurance company, the complaint should set forth the state under whose laws it was organized. Citing section 380 of Ostrander on Fire Insurance. In the title of the cause the defendant is named as the "Phœnix Insurance Company of Brooklyn, New York." In the policy appellant designates itself by the same name. Its title imports that it is a corporation. That it is a foreign corporation only appears from its name, and its domicile appears from the same allegation. If the allegation is essential, which we do not concede, it, in effect, appears.

The remaining objection to the complaint is that "the action is on the policy, when the complaint shows that the loss was settled by the arbitrators as provided in the policy, and an award made." The complaint avers that the insurer and the insured disagreed upon the amount of the loss, and that, in accordance with the terms of the policy, the appraisers were appointed, and an award fixing the amount of loss upon the building at $1,325. The averments with reference to the issuing of the policy, the ownership of the property, its destruction by fire, and the disagreement as to the amount of the loss were necessary averments leading up to the appointment of the appraisers. Both the policy and the award were made exhibits to the complaint, and the amount sought to be recovered is that fixed by the award. The demurrer to the complaint was properly overruled.

The third paragraph of answer avers that appellee committed fraud in making certain "false statements contained in the plans and specifications sworn to by plaintiff which is attached hereto and marked 'Exhibit ——.'" But a copy of said specifications is not filed with the answer. The fifth paragraph of answer also charges that appellee swore falsely in the specifications furnished by him, but avers no facts showing fraud. Neither of these paragraphs stated a defense to the complaint. Curry v. Keyser, 30 Ind. 214.

The first four reasons for a new trial are that the decision and finding of the court are not sustained by sufficient evidence. The findings show that appellee had an insurance policy on his building issued by appellant company; that it was destroyed by fire while the policy was in force, and while he was the owner thereof; that notice was given by appellee and received by the appellant, and, in response to said notice, appellant sent its agent who viewed the premises. (Whether he was the officer or agent named in the policy, or some other representative of the company, made no difference, since appellant, in response to said notice, sent its agent who viewed the premises.) Specifications were furnished by appellee as required by the policy, and subsequently appellant asked for an appraisement, and an appraisement was had as to the amount of the loss. There is evidence to support each finding.

It is claimed that the court erred in permitting appellee to state, while testifying in his own behalf, that he was the owner of the building in controversy.

In this there was no error. It is further urged that the court erred in refusing to permit the defendant to ask the plaintiff upon cross-examination the following question: "I will ask you furthermore if it is not a fact that you stated soon after Mr. French was occupying your premises at Farmersburg that you learned that you had a firebug in there (meaning your storehouse), and that you guessed you would have to increase your insurance, and did increase it $500 afterwards?" It appears from the evidence that appellee's building at the time of the issuance was occupied by a tenant as a drug store. Under the issues, there was no question of fraud or misrepresentation, and the evidence was immaterial. It is also claimed that the court erred in permitting plaintiff to testify as to the value of the fixtures insured at the time of the fire, and to show what fixtures he had in the building before it was consumed by fire, and their value. We find no error.

Judgment affirmed.

(70 Oh. St. 46)

ELECTRIC ST. R. CO. v. HAMLET OF NORTH BEND (two cases).

(Supreme Court of Ohio. April 12, 1904.)

STREET RAILROADS — HAMLETS—CONSTRUCTION OF ROAD IN STREET—CONSENT OF HAMLET.

1. Hamlets in existence at the time the Municipal Code of 1902 went into effect were municipal corporations, and thereafter, if they had a population of less than 5,000 at the last federal census, they are villages; and a street railway company is without authority to construct its road on or above their streets or roads without their consent.

(Syllabus by the Court.)

Error to Circuit Court, Hamilton County.

Action by the Hamlet of North Bend against the Electric Street Railroad Company for an injunction. An order dissolving a temporary injunction was set aside on appeal to the circuit court, and plaintiff brings error. Affirmed.

Shepherd & Shaffer and Peck, Shaffer & Peck, for plaintiff in error. Stanley Struble and Dempsey & Fridman, for defendant in error.

SUMMERS, J. These cases—the Cincinnati, Lawrenceburg & Aurora Electric Street Railroad Co. v. The Hamlet of North Bend and Patrick Farrell, and the Cincinnati, Lawrenceburg & Aurora Electric Street Railroad Co. v. The Hamlet of North Bend—present the same question. One was a suit to enjoin the defendant below, a street railroad corporation engaged in constructing a road between Cincinnati, Ohio, and Aurora, Ind., and through the hamlet of North Bend, from constructing its road over, along, and upon certain streets therein; and the other to enjoin the company from constructing an elevated road from its power house to the Ohio river over and above one of the streets of said hamlet without its consent. In each case a temporary injunction was allowed, and subsequently dissolved, and appeals were taken to the circuit court from the order of dissolution. On appeal the circuit court stated the following conclusions of fact, as summarized by counsel for defendants in error: "(1) The plaintiff the hamlet of North Bend, some years prior to October 22, 1902, was organized as a hamlet under the statutes then in force relating to the subject. (2) Its officers were three trustees, each of whom had been elected and qualified for a term of three years; a clerk and treasurer, elected and qualified for a term of two years; and a marshal and supervisor, elected and qualified for a term of one year. (3) The population of the hamlet, according to the federal census of 1900, was 532. (4) The Secretary of State, in his proclamation made November 17, 1902, under section 2 of the new Municipal Code, included North Bend as a municipal corporation having a population of less than 5,000. (5) North Bend has no other officers except such hamlet trustees, clerk, treasurer, marshal, and supervisor. (6) North Bend has taken no steps to organize as a village (not refused to organize as a village, as counsel for plaintiff in error have it in their brief). (7) The finding in each case as to the grievances, which need not be stated here at length. (8) The said electric street railroad company has pending before the county commissioners of Hamilton county an application for authority to construct its railroad within the limits of North Bend. (9) The said electric street railroad company does not intend to, nor claims the right to, make such construction without the authority from said county commissioners. (10) This application has not been acted upon by the county commissioners, who are awaiting a decision by the courts on the question of their jurisdiction over the streets in question, and will not be acted upon by them until this question is decided. (11) The said electric street railroad company has not procured in the one case, nor procured or attempted to procure in the other case, from the hamlet of North Bend, authority either to construct its railroad across the streets of said hamlet or to construct said bridge over the one particular street before mentioned. (12) The reason for this failure to procure, or to attempt to procure, such authority from said hamlet, is that said electric street railroad company is advised and claims that there is no such municipal corporation under the laws of Ohio as the hamlet of North Bend." That court should have found also that the defendant, in the event permission was granted to it by the county commissioners, intended to proceed with the construction of its road above and across the streets of the hamlet as averred; but it is perhaps immaterial, as the case proceeded in that court and has been argued in this on that assumption. The circuit court concluded as matter of law that the plaintiff was at the time of the commencement of the suits a village, and as such had capacity to bring them, and that its title in the actions should be amended by substituting the word "village" for "hamlet," and that it was entitled to the relief prayed for, and it ordered and decreed that the order setting aside and dissolving the restraining order and temporary injunction should be superseded and set aside, and that the restraining order and temporary injunction should be continued, and remanded the suits for further proceedings. These proceedings in error are prosecuted to reverse the order and decree of the circuit court.

The contention of counsel for plaintiff in error, briefly stated, is that section 231 of the new Municipal Code (96 Ohio Laws, p. 96), repealed sections 1550 and 1552, Rev. St., creating hamlets and conferring powers upon them, and that on and after the first Monday of May, 1903, municipalities ceased to exist as hamlets, and that they became either villages by electing village officers or unincorporated villages by failure to elect, and that, inasmuch as the municipality of North Bend failed to elect, the county commissioners, under section 29 of the new Municipal Code, have authority to grant permission to the defendant to construct its road above and on the streets of said municipality. In support of this principal contention it is argued that hamlets had no existence under the Constitution, that instrument recognizing only cities and villages; and that to hold that corporations organized as hamlets became villages under the new Code, but that such of them as failed to elect village officers may continue through their hamlet officers to exercise the powers of hamlets, would make the Code to that extent unconstitutional for want of uniform operation. By the act of May 3, 1852, "to provide for the organization of cities and incorporated villages" (50 Ohio Laws, p. 223), it is provided:

"Section 1. That all corporations which existed when the present constitution took effect, for the purposes of municipal government, either general or special, and described or denominated in any law then in force, as cities, towns, villages, or special road districts, shall be, and they are hereby organized into cities, and incorporated villages, with the territorial limits to them respectively prescribed, or belonging, in manner following: All such municipal corporations, as in any such law are denominated cities, shall be deemed cities; and those denominated towns, villages, or special road districts, shall be deemed incorporated villages; to be respectively governed as cities, or incorporated villages, and in case of the latter, for general or special purposes, as provided in this act."

"Sec. 19. All municipal corporations organized, or to be organized under this act, except incorporated villages for special purposes, shall have the general powers and privileges, and be subject to the rules and restrictions granted and prescribed in the twenty succeeding sections of this act."

"Sec. 40. In respect to the exercise of certain corporate powers, and to the number, character, powers and duties of certain officers, municipal corporations are, and shall be divided into the classes following: Cities of the first, and cities of the second class; incorporated villages, and incorporated villages for special purposes."

Section 44 provided that the corporate authority of incorporated villages organized or to be organized under this act for the special purposes of being a road district shall be vested in three trustees; that they should appoint a clerk, and might appoint a supervisor and such other officers or agents as might be necessary, and by proper bylaws and ordinances prescribe the duties and compensation of the officers so appointed; and by section 45 the trustees were given exclusive supervision and control of all public roads, streets, and alleys, sewers and drains within the limits of such special road districts, and they had no other powers except such as were necessary to carry into execution those above enumerated, and they were invested with no general municipal power. By chapter 5 of the Municipal Code of 1869 (66 Ohio Laws, p. 145), municipal powers in addition to those above enumerated were conferred upon incorporated villages for special purposes. By the act of May 14, 1878 (75 Ohio Laws, p. 161), to amend, revise, and consolidate the statutes relating to municipal corporations, for the purpose of incorporating them in the revision of the statutes of 1880, municipal corporations were divided into cities, villages, and hamlets. Cities were divided into two classes and into seven grades, villages into two grades, and corporations organized as incorporated villages for special purposes were named hamlets. But what's in a name? They still had the same offices and the same powers, and no other, as when called "incorporated villages for special purposes"; so that, if it be conceded that the Constitution admits of cities and villages only as municipal corporations, it would follow that they were villages still, and the only question presented would be the one of classification. That question it is not necessary to determine. By the first act passed in compliance with the mandate of the Constitution to provide for the organization of cities and villages by general laws, cities and villages were classified, and for more than 50 years the power to do so was recognized by repeated decisions of this court, and, if it should be affirmed that the power exists, but became impossible of exercise because of its abuses, or should be conceded that it does not and did not exist, still, on the plainest principles of public policy, the validity of classification such as this ought to be assumed until transition under the new Code is effected.

Assuming, then, that the hamlet of North Bend had a constitutional existence, the question arises, how is it affected by the repealing sections of the new Code, and the fact that it failed to elect village officers as provided by the new Code? Was its life taken; or was it permitted to live, but in a state of suspended animation; or may its officers perform their duties, and thus enable it still to perform its functions as an agency of the state? Section 231 of the new Code provides: "For the purpose of carrying into effect the powers and duties conferred and imposed upon present councils, boards of legislation, or other legislative bodies, by the provisions of this act, and for the purpose of conducting the first election to be held in every municipality hereunder, and of preparing for the change in the organization of municipalities herein provided for, this act shall take effect from and after the fifteenth day of November, 1902; and for all other purposes this act, and every portion of the same, including the repeal of existing laws, shall take effect on the first Monday in May, 1903, and the following sections of the Revised Statutes of Ohio are hereby repealed." Then follow in the enumeration of laws repealed section 1550, Rev. St., defining hamlets; section 1551, Rev. St., providing that a hamlet shall not be organized until its territory, embraces 50 electors, and that it shall not be advanced to a village until it attains a population of 200; and section 1552, Rev. St., providing that "municipal corporations, now or hereafter organized, are bodies politic and corporate, under the name of the city of ——, the village of ——, or the hamlet of ——, as the case may be; and as such they may sue and be sued, contract and be contracted with," etc.

If section 231 was the only one to be considered, it might be that the municipality of North Bend would be without authority to sue; but it would not follow that it is an unincorporated village within the meaning of section 29 of the new Code, and that thereunder the county commissioners have authority to grant the right to construct a street railway within the limits of North Bend. It was an incorporated municipality, and, whatever might be necessary for it to do to exercise the powers of a village, it was not necessary that it be incorporated. It was the hamlet and is the village of North Bend. But section 231 is not the only section. The whole Code must be considered. Section 213 provides that all officers in any municipal corporation "shall remain in their respective offices and employments and continue to perform the several duties thereof under existing laws, and receive the compensation therefor until their successors are chosen or appointed and qualified or until removed by the proper authority in accordance with the provisions of this act." Section 214 provides: "All by-laws, ordinances and resolutions heretofore lawfully passed or adopted by the council, board of legislation or other legislative body in any municipal corporation, and not inconsistent with this act, shall remain in force until duly altered or repealed." Looking to these sections, as well as to section 231, it is manifest that the officers in office and whose successors were not elected or appointed when the new Code went into effect remained in those offices, and not only remained, but by the new Code itself are expressly enjoined to "continue to perform the several duties thereof under existing laws" until their successors are chosen or appointed and qualified. Under the Code the name of this municipality was changed to the "village of North Bend," and by section 7 it was given power to sue, and the fact that it was mistaken in its name does not affect the suit. In State v. Village of Perrysburg, 14 Ohio St. 472, 482, Brinkerhoff, C. J., speaking of the effect of the act of May 3, 1852, "to provide for the organization of cities and villages" (50 Ohio Laws, p. 223), supra, says: "Does the consequence follow, as claimed by the defendant that all preexisting municipal corporations were 'wiped out of existence,' and all prior acts granting to them special powers or privileges became thereupon inoperative, or were, by force of this general act, repealed? We are unable to arrive at such a conclusion. Neither the corporate existence nor the corporate identity of the municipal corporations of the state were affected by the general act for the organization of cities and villages. Some of them took, under its operation, a different legal designation—as incorporated villages, instead of towns. The particular mode of their organization was somewhat changed, and their powers, privileges, rights, and duties were restricted, enlarged, or modified; but their territorial limits remained the same as before; legal obligations incurred by or to them remained unchanged; and their corporate identity was no more affected by a reorganization under the general law than is the personal identity of a feme sole by marriage, in virtue of which her name is changed, and her powers, privileges, rights, and duties are, in law, enlarged, restricted, or modified. The corporate life of the village of Perrysburg was a continuation of the life of the town of Perrysburg. It was a continuation; not an annihilation and a re-creation."

It was stated in oral argument that the failure of this municipality to elect officers under the new Code was not because of any hostility to it, but because of uncertainty as to the intention of the Legislature. Chapter 2, div. 2, tit. 12, §§ 1553–1571a, Rev. St., inclusive, providing for the organization of hamlets, and chapter 1, div. 3, tit. 12, §§ 1648–1654, Rev. St., inclusive, prescribing the officers of hamlets and some of their powers and duties, and conferring broad municipal powers upon hamlets, are not repealed by the Code. The reason is not apparent. It may be doubt existed whether hamlets were municipal corporations. Incorporated villages for special purposes originally were not, though so classified. See comment of Ranney, J., in Street Railway v. Cumminsville, 14 Ohio St. 523, 541. But, as we have already seen, they were invested with municipal powers by the Code of 1869, and by the act of 1878 were named "hamlets," and were properly classified as municipal corporations, and given general municipal powers; and it is evident from the legislation and decisions since the Constitution, as well as from the manifest purpose of section 6, art. 13, of the Constitution, directing the General Assembly to provide for the organization of cities and incorporated villages by general laws, that all municipal corporations are comprised by its terms, and that outside of the system so provided there is not room for a corporation having general municipal powers. Being a municipal corporation, the hamlet of North Bend became the village of North Bend, and, while its hamlet officers may continue to perform their duties until their successors are elected and qualified, there is no power in the village either of election or appointment to fill these offices. The village cannot go on as a hamlet, but must sooner or later elect village officers, or be incapable of exercising municipal powers; and want of uniformity in the operation of the law is not apparent.

The order and decree of the circuit court in each case is affirmed.

SPEAR, C. J., and DAVIS, SHAUCK, PRICE, and CREW, JJ., concur.

(70 Oh. St. 36)

JONES v. STATE.

(Supreme Court of Ohio. April 12, 1904.)

ARSON—BURNING INSURED BUILDING.

1. It is not essential to the crime defined by section 6832, Rev. St., which makes it a crime to maliciously burn any building of the value of $50, the same being his own property, and insured against loss or damage by fire, with the intent to prejudice the insurer, that the building be the sole property of the person who burns it, or that the value of his property in it be $50; it is sufficient that he has an estate in it, and that the building be of the value of $50; and an indictment charging the building as of the value of more than $50 and as the property of the accused is, in respect of those elements of the crime, sufficient.

(Syllabus by the Court.)

Edwin Jones was convicted of maliciously burning a building, and moves for leave to file petition in error. Motion overruled.

Charles C. Bow and O. C. Volkmore, for plaintiff in error. Robert H. Day, for the State.

SUMMERS, J. The plaintiff in error was indicted by the grand jury of Stark county for burning a building, his own property, with intent to prejudice the insurer. The crime was described in the indictment in the following language: "Did unlawfully, willfully, and maliciously burn a certain building, to wit, a building used as a storehouse by Robert Legg, of the value of more than fifty dollars, the property of the said Edwin Jones and Mary Jones, with intent in so doing to prejudice, damage and defraud the German Fire Insurance Co. of the city of Pittsburg, Pennsylvania, the insurer of said property, which said building used as a storehouse by said Robert Legg, the property of said Edwin Jones and Mary Jones, was then and there insured against loss or damage by fire unto the said Edwin Jones and Mary Jones in the sum of $1,000 by the said the German Fire Insurance Co. of the city of Pittsburg, Pennsylvania, by a contract and policy of insurance duly executed by and between the said the German Fire Insurance Co. of the city of Pittsburg, Pennsylvania, and the said Edwin Jones and Mary Jones therefor." The statute (section 6832, Rev. St.) is as follows: "Whoever maliciously burns or sets fire to any dwelling house, kitchen, smokehouse, shop, office, barn, stable, storehouse, warehouse, stillhouse, mill, pottery, or any other building, of the value of fifty dollars, or any goods, wares, merchandise, or other chattels, of the value of fifty dollars, the same being his own property, and insured against loss or damage by fire, with intent to prejudice the insurer, shall be imprisoned in the penitentiary not more than twenty years." A motion to quash and a general demurrer were filed and overruled. The defendant entered a plea of guilty, and then filed a motion in arrest of judgment, which was overruled, and he was sentenced to three years in the penitentiary. The circuit court affirmed the judgment of the court of common pleas, and a motion is made for leave to file a petition in error in this court.

By the motions and the demurrer it was sought to question the sufficiency of the indictment on two grounds: First, that it appears upon the face of the indictment that the plaintiff is not the owner of the property; and, second, that it does not appear that the plaintiff's interest in the property is of the value of $50. At common law arson is the malicious burning of another's house. "It is an offense against the security of the habitation, rather than the property. So that by 'another's house' is meant another's to occupy; consequently, at common law, one cannot commit arson of his own house, even when it is insured." 2 Bishop's New Criminal Law, §§ 8, 12; Snyder v. People, 26 Mich. 106, 12 Am. Rep. 302. Our arson statute reads as follows (section 6831, Rev. St.): "Whoever maliciously burns, or attempts to burn, any dwelling house, kitchen, smokehouse, shop, office, barn, stable, storehouse, warehouse, railroad coach or car, malthouse, stillhouse, mill, pottery or any other building, the property of another person or any church, meeting house, courthouse, workhouse, schoolhouse, jail or the Ohio penitentiary, or any shop, storehouse or building within the inclosed walls thereof, or any other public building, or any ship or other water craft, or any toll bridge or any part thereof, erected across any river, wholly or partly within this state, or any other bridge erected across any of the waters within this state, or sets fire to or attempts to set fire to anything in or near to any such building, coach or car, water craft or bridge, with intent to burn the same, shall, if the value of any such building, coach or car, water craft or bridge, burned, attempted or intended to be burned, is fifty dollars or more, be imprisoned in the penitentiary not more than twenty years, or if the value is less than that sum, be fined not more than $200, or imprisoned not more than thirty days, or both." This section, while extending the offense of arson at common law, also comprised it, and, as we shall see, was interpreted in the light of the principles of the common law, and did not make it an offense to burn one's own building; hence the reason for section 6832, Rev. St., making it an offense for one to burn a building his own property, of the value of $50, with intent to prejudice the insurer. The crime under the latter section is a different crime than that under the former. The former is a crime against property, while the essence of the latter is the burning of property with the intent specified. Under the former a person is guilty if he maliciously burn the property of another whether or not it was also with the intent to prejudice, and he is not guilty thereunder for burning his own property, even if it be with the intent to defraud the insurer; while under the latter he is guilty if he burn his own property with the intent to prejudice the insurer, but not for the burning of the property of another. The reason for inserting the words "the same being his own property" in the latter section is not apparent unless it be that it was assumed that, if it was not his own property, he would be guilty under the first section. Whether or not this is so we are not called upon to determine. In Commonwealth v. Makely, 131 Mass. 421, it is ruled: "An indictment on Gen. St., c. 161, § 1, for burning the dwelling house of another, is not sustained by proof that the defendant burned the house by the owner's procurement, to enable him to obtain money from an insurer." The punishment for the two crimes is substantially the same, and it might have been better, as is done in some states, to omit the words, "the same being his own property," since the gravamen of the crime is the burning of a building of the value of $50 with the intent to defraud. But, whatever the reason, it is evident that the latter, being the later enactment, is to be interpreted in the light of the former.

In Allen v. State, 10 Ohio St. 287, William C. Herron was indicted for arson in burning a warehouse described as "of the value of $500, there situate, the property of the Four Mile Valley Railroad Co., a body corporate, duly incorporated by the laws of the state of Ohio; said warehouse then and there being in the possession and occupancy of one Simeon Allen, under a temporary lease of said warehouse from said Four Mile Valley Railroad Co. to said Simeon Allen." Judge Thurman, long a distinguished judge of this court, was counsel for the accused, and contended that the indictment did not charge Allen with arson, for the reason that, Allen being the lessee in possession of the building, it was his property, and not the property of another person, within the meaning of the statute; and he said (page 295): "Again, if the tenant in possession is not the owner of the property, within the meaning of the act, who is? There may be various estates in the same property, all existing at the same time, to wit, estates at will, for years, for life, in fee, estates in possession, remainder, reversion. Very frequently out of an estate for years—ex gra., for ninety-nine years—divers estates for smaller terms are created by subletting. Now, if the tenant in possession is not to be deemed the owner, which of the various tenants for years, for life, in fee, remaindermen, or reversioners is to be deemed the owner? The indictment must aver that the building was the property of some other person that the incendiary, and must name such other person. Which of the various persons, interested as above, shall it name?" The court ruled that the warehouse was the property of another person within the meaning of the statute. In the opinion (page 302), Sutliff, J., says: "Our statute against the burning of buildings is not confined to the common-law offense of arson or felonious burning. It seems to comprehend that kind of burning which, at common law, constituted merely a high misdemeanor, as well as those which were arson, or felonies, at common law. The description of the offenses as well as the grade of punishment, extending, as it does, from one to twenty years, seems to indicate this to have been the object of the statute; and that our statute was meant to embrace the case of a tenant willfully and maliciously burning buildings the property of another, of which he was the tenant or in possession. * * * But we think, upon sound reason and undoubted principles of law, derived from analogies as well as from the language of the statute, it is sufficient to aver the property to be that of the general owner, as well as to aver it to be the property of the special owner or tenant. And, there being no legal or reasonable objection to so comprehensive a rule, we think that consideration of public convenience and a furtherance of the ends of justice recommend its adoption; and especially so, inasmuch as no contrary rule has ever, to our knowledge, been adopted in the courts of this state." In Indiana (Garrett v. The State, 109 Ind. 527, 10 N. E. 570), under a statute that (page 529, 109 Ind., page 571, 10 N. E.): "Whoever wilfully and maliciously burns or attempts to burn any dwelling house or other building, finished or unfinished, occupied or unoccupied, whether the building be used or intended for a dwelling house or for any other purpose; * * * the property so burned being of the value of twenty dollars or upwards, and being the property of another, * * * is guilty of arson, and, upon conviction thereof, shall be imprisoned in the state prison not more than twenty-one years nor less than one year, and fined not exceeding double the value of the property destroyed"—it was held that: "If a man unlawfully, feloniously, willfully, and maliciously sets fire to and burns the dwelling house of his wife, wherein she permits him to live with her as her husband, he is guilty of arson, though he may have furnished the money to build the house." And Howk, J., says (page 531, 109 Ind., page 572, 10 N. E.): "It will be readily seen from an examination of section 1927, supra [Rev. St. Ind. 1881], that arson, as defined in our statute, is a different offense, in many respects, from arson at the common law. Arson, as defined in our statute, is an offense against the property, as well as the possession; and the question of occupancy or nonoccupancy, habitation or nonhabitation, of or in the property, as we have seen, becomes and is an immaterial question, in view of the statutory definition of the offense." "At common law a mere tenant at sufferance could not commit arson of the house whereof he was such tenant, nor a tenant from year to year, or from month to month, or for any time, however short, or as mortgagor in possession, though the mortgage divested him of the legal title." 2 Bishop's New Criminal Law, § 13. But it seems there must have been an estate in the house, for a servant dwelling in a building in the possession of the master was guilty of the offense if he maliciously burned it. And so any one maliciously burning a house in which another had an estate was guilty of burning the house of another person. In B. & O. Railroad Co. v. Walker, 45 Ohio St. 577, 16 N. E. 475, it was necessary to determine the meaning of the words "companies owning the tracks," and Williams, J. (page 585, 45 Ohio St., page 480, 16 N. E.), says: "An owner is not necessarily one owning the fee simple, or one having in the property the highest estate it will admit of. One having a lesser estate may be an owner; and, indeed, there may be different estates in the same property vested in different persons, and each be an owner thereof. In the construction of statutes to ascertain the proper meaning of such terms regard must be had to their various provisions, and such effect given them as these provisions clearly indicate they were intended to have, and as will render the statute operative." And then he cites several instances, to which may be added The Sun Fire Office of London v. Clark, 53 Ohio St. 414, 424, 42 N. E. 248, 38 L. R. A. 562. In Jackson v. Parker, 9 Cow. 73, 81, Savage, C. J., says: "The term 'estate' is very comprehensive, and signifies the quantity of interest which a person has, from absolute ownership down to naked possession. It is the possession of lands which renders them valuable, and the quantity of interest is determined by the duration and extent of the right of possession. 'Real estate,' therefore, includes every possible interest in lands, except a mere chattel interest." And in State v. Lyon, 12 Conn. 487, under a statute which enacts that "every person who shall wilfully burn, being the property of another, any ship," etc., "shall be guilty of arson," Huntington, J., says (page 489): "To constitute an offense under this statute, the building must be the property of another. It is not, indeed, required that the absolute title or entire interest should be in the person named in the information as the party injured; for such a possession, as gives a special property, while it exists, is sufficient. It is essential to the crime of arson at common law that the burning should be of the house or outhouse of another; and in indictments or informations for that offense, as well as for the one of which this prisoner was convicted, it is necessary to aver ownership in another, and to prove the averment as laid. It is important to enable the defendant to prepare his defense, and to plead autrefois acquit or autrefois convict to another prosecution for the same offense." If the contention of counsel for plaintiff in error is sound, then the assured could not have been held for arson, for the building was not exclusively the property of another person, but partly his own. Nor is the soundness of the conclusion reached less certain by the fact, if it be conceded, that the accused might have been prosecuted under either or both sections. Bishop's New Criminal Law, § 778.

The contention that section 7224, Rev. St., settles the question here presented is not sound. That section provides: "When an offense is committed upon, or in relation to, any property belonging to partners or joint owners, the indictment for such offense shall be deemed sufficient if it allege the ownership of such property to be in such partnership by its firm name, or in any one or more of such partners or owners, without naming all of them; and in all indictments under section sixty-eight hundred and fifty-nine it shall not be necessary to allege that the will, codicil, or other instrument is the property of any person, or is of any value." But this is a rule of pleading, and not of substantive law. When the purpose of averring ownership is merely to identify the crime, and to enable the accused in any subsequent prosecution to plead former acquittal or conviction, that section applies; but the question here is not whose is the property? but is it averred that the building is the property of the accused? for, if not, no crime is charged.

The objection that it is not charged that his property in the building is of the value of $50 is not well taken. Within the letter of the statute the crime consists in burning a building of the value of $50 with intent to prejudice the insurer. It is immaterial how little is the value of his property in the building. The insurance money he could obtain would not be more than the value of his property, and, the smaller his interest, the less should be the temptation and the greater the offense. In Elliott v. The State, 30 Ohio St. 318, 323, Johnson, J., says: "Is the indictment defective in not stating that the barn was insured for at least fifty dollars? We think not. By the statute above cited (74 Ohio Laws, p. 248, § 2; section 6832, Rev. St.) the value of the property insured, and not the amount of insurance thereon, must be fifty dollars. The amount that the insurer would be defrauded is not a material element of the crime, but the value of the property burned should be of the value of fifty dollars."

Motion overruled.

SPEAR, C. J., and DAVIS, SHAUCK, PRICE, and CREW, JJ., concur.

(70 Oh. St. 121)

CAREY v. STATE.

(Supreme Court of Ohio. April 12, 1904.)

INTOXICATING LIQUORS — ELECTION — CRIMINAL PROSECUTION — JURY TRIAL — PUNISHMENT.

1. Sections 4364-20a, 4364-20b, Rev. St., which provide for an election in any municipality to determine whether or not the sale of intoxicating liquors as a beverage within the limits of such municipality shall be prohibited, and prescribes punishment for violations of said act where such sales are so prohibited, apply to hamlets as the same existed in this state prior to the adoption of the Municipal Code, October 22, 1902.

2. The term "offense," as used in the last-named section, is the equivalent of conviction. Hence an affidavit for prosecution under said act which charges three separate sales to different persons on the same day, but does not allege a previous conviction, is in legal effect a charge of a first offense only, and the party so charged is not entitled to be tried by a jury.

3. The maximum fine provided by the act for the first offense being $200 only, a fine of $300 is in such case excessive and erroneous.

(Syllabus by the Court.)

Error to Circuit Court, Cuyahoga County.

One Carey was convicted of unlawfully selling intoxicating liquors, and brings error. Reversed.

The plaintiff in error was tried before the mayor of the village of Bedford, in Cuyahoga county, upon a charge of violating section 4364-20b, Rev. St., popularly known as the "Beal Law." The affidavit on which the prosecution was founded embraced three counts, each charging an unlawful sale of intoxicating liquor to be used as a beverage on July 22, 1903, to three separate purchasers. The sales were averred to have occurred at the village of Lakewood, Cuyahoga county. It appeared in evidence that Lakewood, prior to May 4, 1903, was a municipality known as a hamlet, and that on November 24, 1902, upon a vote of the qualified electors of the hamlet held under the statute referred to, a majority of said electors voted against the sale in the municipality of intoxicating liquor as a beverage. On the appearance of the accused he interposed a motion to dismiss on the grounds of want of jurisdiction of the person and of the subject-matter, and of the insufficiency in law of the affidavit; also a certificate of prejudice. This motion being overruled, and the affidavit ignored, accused demanded that the action be tried to a jury. This demand was overruled, and the trial proceeded. Record proof of the election in the hamlet of Lakewood was offered by the state, and admitted over the objection and exception of defendant. The state offered testimony as to the sales, the defendant offered testimony in contradiction, the state gave rebuttal evidence, and the cause was submitted on briefs by counsel. At the conclusion of the state's testimony a motion was interposed to dismiss the case, which was overruled. After consideration the court found the defendant guilty as charged, and sentenced him to pay a fine of $300, being $100 on each count, and to pay costs of prosecution, and to stand committed to the workhouse of the city of Cleveland until fine and costs should be paid. Error being prosecuted to the court of common pleas, the judgment of the mayor was affirmed, and, that judgment being affirmed by the circuit court, the defendant below brings error to this court.

Vernon H. Burke and Clifford B. Haskins, for plaintiff in error. G. N. Shaver, Charles A. Niman, and W. B. Wheeler, for the State.

PER CURIAM. A number of grounds of error are urged, which will be considered seriatim.

1. As to the mayor's jurisdiction. It is insisted that the mayor of the village of Bedford could have no jurisdiction over an offense committed in the village of Lakewood, and if the claim of jurisdiction is believed to be based on section 1536-876, Bates' Ann. St., then that section is in conflict with article 4, § 10, of the Constitution. The clause referred to provides that "the judges other than those provided in this Constitution shall be elected by the electors of the judicial district for which they may be created." The point is not well taken. Section 18 of the same article provides that "the several judges of the Supreme Court * * * and of such other courts as may be created, shall respectively have and exercise such

power and jurisdiction, at chambers or otherwise, as may be directed by law." It is apparent that the provision of section 10, art. 4, applies to the district for election purposes, and does not affect the matter of jurisdiction, power to provide which is specifically given to the General Assembly by section 18. Steamboat Northern Indiana v. Milliken, 7 Ohio St. 383; State v. Peters, 67 Ohio St. 494, 66 N. E. 521.

2. The affidavit of prejudice. This proposition of error is based on section 550, Rev. St. 1892. This section applies to judges of the court of common pleas. It has no application whatever to mayors, nor is there, so far as we are aware, any provision of like character which affects mayors. The affidavit of prejudice was properly ignored.

3. Joinder of counts. The law in Ohio is well settled. There was no error in overruling the motion to require the state to elect. Bailey v. State, 4 Ohio St. 440; Eldredge v. State, 37 Ohio St. 191; State v. Bailey, 50 Ohio St. 636, 36 N. E. 233.

4. The demand for a jury. This demand was made upon the claim that, as there were three counts in the affidavit, there were three separate offenses charged, and, inasmuch as a party on conviction of a third offense may be imprisoned as part of the sentence, he would be entitled to be tried by a jury. This claim rests upon a misconception of the statute. The term "offense" in the statute embraces the entire charge, though there may be a number of counts. The provision as to punishment is that the convicted party shall "be fined not more than two hundred dollars nor less than fifty dollars for the first offense, and shall for a second offense be fined not more than five hundred dollars nor less than one hundred dollars, and for any subsequent offense be fined not less than two hundred dollars and be imprisoned not more than sixty days and not less than ten days." The manifest purpose is to increase the penalty for offenses after the first because the party has persisted in violating the law. With this purpose in mind, it seems clear that the term "second offense" means second conviction. Hence, as this was the first trial for the violation of the law, there could be no imprisonment as part of the sentence, and the party was not, therefore, entitled to a jury.

5. The objection to the admission of record evidence respecting the election in the hamlet of Lakewood presents the question whether the statute (sections 4364-20a, 4364-20b, Rev. St.) which makes provision for such election applies to hamlets. We are of opinion that its terms are broad enough to embrace hamlets. The opening clause covers in plain terms "any municipal corporation." By the provision of statute then in force, a hamlet was a municipal corporation. It is true that the statute uses the term "council" as the governing body, and the term "mayor" as the executive; yet in hamlets there were trustees who stood to the hamlet as the council stands to the village or city, and the president of the board of trustees stood to the hamlet as the mayor stands to the village or city. The statute is a police regulation enacted in the interest of good order in municipalities, and should receive a reasonable construction. No reason exists for such a regulation in a village which would not equally apply to a hamlet, and the terms of the statute, except in the particulars named, are broad, and clearly include all municipalities. This conclusion is in accord with the holding of the Circuit Court of the Eighth Circuit in Re Annexation of Territory to Township of Newburgh, 8 Cir. Ct. Dec. 24, 15 Ohio Cir. Ct. R. 78, and in State ex rel. Keeler v. Wagar, 10 Cir. Ct. Dec. 160, 19 Ohio Cir. Ct. R. 149.

6. Complaint is made that the rulings of the mayor respecting the cross-examination of some of the state's witnesses worked prejudice to the defendant, in that he was prevented from showing interest on the part of such witnesses in the event of prosecution. The extent to which cross-examination may be conducted is usually a matter of discretion on the part of the trial court. The questions refused were mainly repetitions of questions which had been put in another form and answered. We fail to discover that the discretion was abused, or that the limit placed on the cross-examination was an unreasonable one. We find no prejudicial error in the rulings as to testimony.

7. It is further contended that the trial court erred in not dismissing the complaint at the conclusion of the state's testimony because the case was rested by the state on the uncorroborated testimony of private detectives in the employ of the Anti-Saloon League. It is true that the testimony of hired detectives should be received with caution and carefully scrutinized, but it is not, as matter of law, error for the court to found a conviction upon such testimony. The sufficiency of the evidence in this case has passed the scrutiny of the common pleas and the circuit court, and it is not important that it be further discussed here.

8. The sentence. It is insisted that it was excessive. We think this point is well taken. For reasons stated under paragraph 4, the conviction which resulted was the first conviction. For this the maximum fine provided by the statute is $200. The sentence of $300 being excessive, the judgment of sentence will be reversed, and the cause remanded for resentence, in conformity with the direction herein.

Judgments of the circuit court and the court of common pleas and of the mayor's court reversed, and cause remanded to the latter court for sentence.

SPEAR, C. J., and DAVIS, SHAUCK, PRICE, CREW, and SUMMERS, JJ., concur.

(70 Oh. St. 67)

HUMPHREYS et al. v. STATE et al.

(Supreme Court of Ohio. March 22, 1904.)

COLLATERAL INHERITANCE TAX—BEQUEST TO CHARITABLE INSTITUTION — CONSTITUTIONAL LAW—APPEAL—NOTICE OF INTENTION—UNDERTAKING.

1. Where the probate court, in the settlement of the estate of a decedent, determines the liability of a devise, legacy, bequest, or inheritance to pay a collateral inheritance tax, under the provisions of section 2731-1, Rev. St., appeal may be taken by either party to the controversy regarding the tax from the judgment of the probate court to the court of common pleas, as authorized by section 2731-13, Rev. St.; and where the state, or the prosecuting attorney in behalf of the state, takes the appeal, it may be done without giving an undertaking for such appeal, and without filing the written notice of an intention to appeal provided for in section 6408, Rev. St. The appeal may be perfected by either party according to the provisions of sections 6411 and 5227, Rev. St.

2. Boards and societies and auxiliaries thereto, which are incorporated and organized under the laws of other states, for "purposes of purely public charity or other exclusively public purposes," are not "institutions" of that class in this state within the meaning of the latter clause of section 2731-1, Rev. St.; and where they are entitled to receive property within the jurisdiction of this state by deed of gift, bequest, or devise, such gift, bequest, or devise is liable to a collateral inheritance tax as provided in said section, although some of the charitable work, operations, and enterprises of the institutions so incorporated and organized are carried on within this state.

3. The statute so construed is not obnoxious to the second section of our Bill of Rights, nor to the fourteenth amendment to the Constitution of the United States.

(Syllabus by the Court.)

Error to Circuit Court, Hamilton County.

Petition by John E. Humphreys, executor of the estate of Isabella Brown, deceased, to determine the liability of certain legacies to inheritance tax. A judgment by the common pleas court, on appeal from probate court, finding legacies to certain religious societies and boards liable to such tax, was affirmed by the circuit court, and the executor and said legatees bring error. Affirmed.

On July 9, 1888, Isabella Brown, a resident of Cincinnati, duly executed her last will and testament, in which she made some bequests to her sister, Mrs. Atkins, to a nephew, Meredith Atkins, and other bequests to Mrs. Gass, of Camden, N. J., in trust, with provision therein that the income arising from the money so bequeathed should be paid to two nieces, Harriet and Mary Gass, until each should arrive at the age of 32 years, when the principal sum should be paid them equally. The testator bequeathed to the American Bible Society the sum of $5,000, to the American Tract Society $5,000, and to the American Sunday School Union $2,000. Bequests were also made to certain missionary societies and other benevolent religious organizations, which are named separately in the will, and which are also plaintiffs in error. This will was admitted to probate on September 19, 1899, and John E. Humphreys, executor, who was, by the terms of a codicil to the will, appointed executor, entered upon the execution of the trust. In progress of the settlement of the estate a question arose in the probate court concerning the payment of an inheritance tax on the several legacies made by the will to the various religious societies and boards, and the executor, Humphreys, submitted to the probate court his petition to have the matter determined. The prosecuting attorney of Hamilton county appeared in behalf of the state, and contended that each of said legacies was subject to a collateral inheritance tax. After hearing, that court decided that no inheritance tax is payable on any of the legacies to the religious societies and boards, and ordered the executor to distribute the estate accordingly. The prosecuting attorney gave notice of appeal from so much of said order as finds that an inheritance tax is not payable upon the legacies to the American Bible Society and the several other religious societies and boards, naming each in the notice. The appeal was filed in the court of common pleas, where a motion was made by the appellees to dismiss the appeal on the ground that no appeal bond had been given, nor was written notice of intention to appeal filed, and on the general ground that appellant had not otherwise complied with the law for such appeals. The court of common pleas overruled the motion, and the appellees excepted. The case was then heard on the merits, and the court found and adjudged that each of said legacies is liable to a tax of 5 per centum of the amount of such legacies, with interest thereon from August 25, 1900. A motion for new trial was overruled, a bill of exceptions taken embracing the evidence adduced at the hearing, and the case was taken on error to the circuit court, where the judgment of the court of common pleas was affirmed. Error is prosecuted in this court to reverse the judgments of the circuit and common pleas courts. Additional facts appear in the opinion.

Lawrence Maxwell, Jr., John E. Humphreys, and Joseph S. Graydon, for plaintiffs in error. Hoffheimer, Morris & Sawyer, for defendants in error.

PRICE, J. (after stating the facts). It is said in the opening of the brief for plaintiffs in error that this proceeding involves two questions of law: "(1) Whether the appeal from the probate court to the court of common pleas was duly taken; (2) whether the legacies are taxable."

1. The right to appeal in cases like the present is conferred by section 2731-13, Rev. St., which is: "The court of probate, having either principal or auxiliary jurisdiction of the settlement of the estate of the decedent, shall have jurisdiction to hear and determine all questions in relation to said tax

that may arise, affecting any devise, legacy or inheritance under this act, subject to appeal as in other cases, and the prosecuting attorney shall represent the interests of the state in any such proceedings." It is claimed for plaintiffs in error that the words "subject to appeal as in other cases" mean that the remedy of appeal must be exercised according to the general rule provided for appeal from the probate to the court of common pleas, which is found in section 6408, Rev. St. That section provides, in substance, that the person desiring to take an appeal shall, within 20 days after the making of the order, decision, or decree from which he desires to appeal, give a written undertaking * * * to the adverse party, with one or more sufficient sureties, to be approved by the probate judge, and conditioned, etc. But when the person appealing * * * is a party in a fiduciary capacity, in which he has given bond within this state, and he appeals in the interest of the trust, he shall not be required to give bond, but shall be allowed the appeal by giving written notice to the court of his intention to appeal within the time limited for giving bond. It is conceded in this case that no bond was given by either the state or by the prosecuting attorney in behalf of the state, and it is manifest on the record that the only notice of appeal was given by journal entry as follows: "The prosecuting attorney gives notice of appeal from so much of said order as finds that an inheritance tax is not payable upon the legacies to the following legatees, viz., American Bible Society," et al., naming each of the other religious societies and boards receiving legacies. But is the mode of appeal governed by section 6408, Rev. St.? In such a proceeding before the probate court it cannot be correctly stated that either the state or the prosecuting attorney acts in a fiduciary capacity. On the contrary, the state is a sovereign, and such is its relation to the controversy. It is provided in section 213, Rev. St.: "No undertaking or security is required on behalf of the state or of any officer thereof in the prosecution or defense of any action, writ, or proceeding; nor is it necessary to verify the pleadings on the part of the state or any officer thereof in any such action, writ, or proceeding." It is under this section that the state or its officer is relieved from giving bond for an appeal, and not under section 6408, supra; and, the state or the prosecuting attorney not sustaining a fiduciary relation to the proceeding, the notice of appeal in behalf of the state need not be in writing, as provided in the latter section, for it is only where that relation exists that such written notice is required under its provisions. We are of opinion that section 6411 of the same chapter and title furnishes the guide in this case. "The provisions of law governing civil proceedings in the court of common pleas shall, so far as applicable, govern like proceedings in the probate court, when there is no provision on the subject in this title." We have seen that the other provisions of the title do not apply to this class of proceedings. We therefore look to the manner of appeal from the court of common pleas as found in section 5227, Rev. St., which is: "A party desiring to appeal his cause to the circuit court, shall, within three days after the judgment or order is entered, enter on the records notice of such intention. * * *" This was the law at the time of the appeal in this case. Notice of intention to appeal was entered on the records of the probate court in conformity with the above rule, and we think it is sufficient. The appeal was properly sustained.

2. Whether the legacies are subject to the collateral inheritance tax depends on the construction of section 2731-1, Rev. St. The statute in its present form was enacted April 6, 1900. See 94 Ohio Laws, p. 101. This act provides in part: "That all property within the jurisdiction of this state, and any interests therein, whether belonging to inhabitants of this state or not, and whether tangible or intangible, which shall pass by will or by the intestate laws of this state, or by deed, grant, sale or gift, made or intended to take effect in possession or enjoyment after the death of the grantor, to any person in trust or otherwise, other than to or for the use of the father, mother, husband, wife, brother, sister, niece, nephew, lineal descendant, adopted child, * * * or the lineal descendants of any adopted child, the wife or widow of a son, the husband of the daughter of a decedent, shall be liable to a tax of five per centum of its value, above the sum of two hundred dollars, seventy-five per centum of such tax to be for the use of the state, and twenty-five per centum for the use of the county wherein the same is collected. * * * But the provisions of this act shall not apply to property, or interests in property, transmitted to the state of Ohio under the intestate laws of this state, or embraced in any bequest, devise, transfer or conveyance to, or for the use of the state of Ohio, or to or for the use of any municipal corporation or other political subdivision of said state for exclusively public purposes, or public institutions of learning, or to or for the use of, any institution in said state for purposes of purely public charity or other exclusively public purposes; and the property, or interests in property so transmitted or embraced in any such devise, bequest, transfer or conveyance is hereby declared to be exempt from all inheritance and other taxes, while used exclusively for any of said purposes." The words in the exemption clause, "to or for the use of any institution in said state for purposes of purely public charity or other exclusively public purposes," are the subject of the present controversy. The first lines of

the act are comprehensive, and would embrace the legacies named, and subject them to the inheritance tax, unless they are saved by the above exemption clause. Therefore counsel have discussed, and we are called upon to consider, the scope of the language quoted when applied to the facts of the present case. What are the material facts? It is shown by the record that all the legatee societies and boards who are plaintiffs in error, save the Woman's Home Missionary Society, are incorporated in states other than Ohio; and while they are not organizations for profits, but for the purpose of advancing the cause of religion and dispensing charity, they are, nevertheless, foreign corporations. Some were chartered under the laws of New York, and others under the laws of Pennsylvania. The Woman's Home Missionary Society is an auxiliary to the Board of Home Missions, and the Woman's Foreign Missionary Society is auxiliary to the Board of Foreign Missions. The parent of all these societies and boards seems to be the General Assembly of the Presbyterian Church in America, incorporated in another state, which is the central and supreme authority; and where the subordinate societies and boards became incorporated it was done under the direction of the general assembly. The American Tract Society has colporteurs in almost, if not all, the states of the Union, and other agencies for the distribution of religious literature. The aim of the American Bible Society is the distribution of the Holy Scriptures, translated into numerous languages, among the people generally, and especially among the destitute and needy classes. While foreign corporations, or auxiliaries thereto, it is true that the work laid out for each board and society is carried on in all the states through local and subordinate agencies; and it may be admitted that theirs are works of charity in the broad sense, that the uplifting of men, women, and children to the standard of life taught in the Scriptures is, indeed, a work of charity, the greatest of the three Christian graces. The funds to carry forward these religious enterprises under the various names and organizations are raised by church and other collections and largely aided by devises and legacies. The testatrix, Isabella Brown, no doubt was a devout member of the Presbyterian Church, and of her bounty she liberally gave to these several societies and boards, believing they could best employ her gifts in advancing the cause of the church of her choice.

The work of the Board of Missions for Freedmen lies mostly in our southern states. But it must be stated as a fact appearing in the record that, while legatees who are plaintiffs in error through auxiliary and subordinate agencies are diligent in every state of the Union, the higher authority to which they must account resides beyond the jurisdiction of this state, and hence the question recurs, are they "institutions in this state for purposes of purely public charity, or other exclusively public purposes?" We are urged to conclude that, because the work of these societies and boards is in progress, in greater or less degree, and their influence felt, in this state through the various subordinate agencies employed, the institutions themselves are in this state within the meaning of the statute. If this is true of Ohio, it is true of every other state, and we have these institutions not only in the state where they are chartered, but omnipresent, and in all the states; in other words, they would, as institutions, exist in any state where any of their charitable or religious enterprises are projected and carried on, no matter in what degree. Such a construction of the facts and the law, we think, is not permissible, if the statute is valid, of which we shall speak later in this opinion. It seems to be true that some of these societies and boards have an office in Ohio in charge of a representative, the better to conduct the affairs of that church agency. So also have railway, insurance, telegraph, telephone, and other foreign corporations; but that is to further their business enterprises. Such companies are not "institutions in this state" because they have traffic and conduct business here. They are still corporations and institutions of the state where chartered and organized. Learned counsel for plaintiffs in error ask in their brief: "Where are these institutions if not in Ohio? Where were the institutions before charters were granted? for they were in existence long prior to the dates of the charters." It is perhaps true that these institutions now operating under charters may have had another form of existence prior to the date of the charters, but in the wisdom of the general assembly of the church it was decided to organize them under charters, and it selected the state under whose laws it should be done. It is not a new proposition that the home of the corporation is the state of its incorporation, and when so incorporated under the laws of a state selected for that purpose it has also selected its abiding place, and no longer can be recognized as homeless, or as abiding in every state where they have agencies carrying forward their work of benevolence and charity. We think this view is abundantly supported by the authorities. The will of Mrs. Brown, who was a resident of Cincinnati, gave no directions to her executor or her legatees as to the place where the money should be expended, nor does it undertake to control the time or place of the expenditure. Once in the possession of these institutions, it may be disbursed as they deem proper, and all of it may be disbursed in communities beyond our borders. So we do not find that we are adopting a narrow construction of our statute if it appears that it undertakes to tax the right of the foreign, though charitable, institutions, to receive and so absolutely control the disposition of property owned by the testatrix in this state. We think these legatees are not "institutions in this state" within the meaning of the statute.

The doctrine we maintain is happily expressed by Justice Field in Paul v. Virginia, 8 Wall. 181, 19 L. Ed. 357, as follows: "Now, a grant of corporate existence is a grant of special privileges to the corporators, enabling them to act for certain designated purposes as a single individual, and exempting them (unless otherwise specially provided) from individual liability. The corporation, being the mere creation of local law, can have no legal existence beyond the limits of the sovereignty where created. As said by this court in Bank of Augusta v. Earle [13 Pet. 519, 10 L. Ed. 274]: 'It must dwell in the place of its creation, and cannot migrate to another sovereignty.' The recognition of its existence even in other states, and the enforcement of its contracts made therein, depend purely upon the comity of those states—a comity which is never extended where the existence of the corporation or the exercise of its powers are prejudicial to their interests or repugnant to their policy. * * * They may exclude the foreign corporation entirely; they may restrict its business to particular localities, or they may exact such security for the performance of its contracts with its citizens as, in their judgment, will best promote the public interest. The whole matter rests in their discretion." Again, in speaking of the assent of the other states to transact business within their borders, the learned justice adds "that such assent may be granted upon such terms and conditions as those states may think proper to impose." We have from this high authority a definition of the situs of corporations and their relation to states other than where chartered, and we find no distinction in this respect between business corporations and those not for profit, or for religious or charitable purposes. Quotation from other authorities we think superfluous, and it seems clear that these charitable and religious institutions, being corporations foreign to this state, are not "institutions in this state," and are therefore not within the exemption provided in the inheritance statutes.

Applying the doctrine in a practical manner, we have numerous decisions, many of which are cited in the brief for defendants in error. We will occupy space in citing and discussing but few of them, and only such as may serve as fairly representative of the many others. In People v. The Seaman's Friend Society, 87 Ill. 246, it appears that the society was incorporated under the laws of Ohio. It had a building in Chicago in charge of a superintendent, where seamen, dockmen, were solicited to meet for religious and moral instruction, and lodging was provided for needy cases. The object of the society, as declared in the act of incorporation, is "for disseminating moral and religious instruction, and other charities, among sailors and laborers doing business on our western waters." This institution resisted the collection of a tax on the Chicago premises on the ground that, being a place where charity is dispensed, it was exempt. The court, on page 249, say: "But if a broader construction could be given to the statute, and it could be held to embrace all institutions that dispense charity, whether public or private, and the property used exclusively for that purpose, there is still a valid reason why the property in this case is not exempt from its just proportion of taxation. The statute must, in any event, be understood to have exclusive reference to institutions or corporations created by the laws of this state, and not to foreign corporations that may choose to locate branches in this state. It is only by the comity that exists between states that foreign corporations are permitted to transact in this state the business for which they were created. The General Assembly has manifested no intention to relieve the property situated in this state, belonging to such corporations, no matter what their objects may be, whether charitable or otherwise, from the burdens of taxation." We further illustrate the application of the statute by reference to another leading case, decided by the Court of Appeals of New York: Matter of Estate of Prime, Deceased, 136 N. Y. 347, 32 N. E. 1091, 18 L. R. A. 713. Prime, a resident of that state, died in the city of New York on April 7, 1891, leaving a will disposing of real and personal property. He gave legacies to collateral relatives, and also to two foreign corporations—the American Board of Commissioners for Foreign Missions and the Presbyterian Board of Relief for Disabled Ministers. The taxing authorities exacted a collateral inheritance tax on the legacies to those corporations as well as on the legacies to the collateral heirs. These legatees appealed, and the controversy finally reached the Court of Appeals. Other questions were in the case as to the condition of the statutes of that state upon the subject, which are not relevant here, and they are omitted. We quote from the able opinion of Andrews, C. J., as follows: "The claim that the test of liability of foreign corporations to a legacy tax is the liability of a domestic corporation of the same character to the payment of such tax, and that, if one is exempt, the other is exempt also, has, we think, no foundation. In both cases the question is the same—has the statute made the legacy taxable? * * * The argument that gifts for the promotion of charity, education, and religion should be encouraged and should not be diminished by exactions of the state, presents a moral and political, rather than a judicial, question. It is the duty of courts in the interpretation of statutes to declare the law as it is, and the interests of society are best subserved by a close adherence by courts to what they find to be their plain meaning, neither narrowing the application on one hand nor extending the meaning on the other to meet a case not specified, which may be within the reason of the law. * * * It is the policy of society to encourage benevolence and charity. But it is not the proper function of a state to go outside its own limits, and devote its resources to support the cause of religion, education, or missions for the benefit of mankind at large." The opinion from which the above is quoted was unanimous. The same court had before it another inheritance tax case, which is found in Matter of Balleis, 144 N. Y. 132, 38 N. E. 1007, where the Prime Case was considered, and its principles unanimously approved. It was held that: "A statute of a state granting powers and privileges to corporations must, in the absence of plain indications to the contrary, be held to apply only to corporations created by the state, and over which it has the power of visitation and control. The Legislature in such cases is dealing with its own creations, whose rights and obligations it may limit, define, and control." The Prime Case was considered as a valuable authority in United States v. Perkins, 163 U. S. 625, 16 Sup. Ct. 1073, 41 L. Ed. 287, and it is quoted from, as we have done, with approval, and adds, as found on page 629, 163 U. S., page 1075, 16 Sup. Ct., 41 L. Ed. 287: "Such a tax [inheritance tax] was also held by this court to be free from any constitutional objection in Mager v. Grima, 8 How. 490-493 [12 L. Ed. 1168], Mr. Justice Taney remarking that: 'The law in question is nothing more than an exercise of the power, which every state and sovereignty possesses, of regulating the manner and terms within which property, real and personal, within its dominion, may be transferred by last will and testament or by inheritance, and of prescribing who shall and who shall not be capable of taking it. * * * If a state may deny the privilege altogether, it follows that when it grants it it may annex to the grant any conditions which it supposes to be required by its interests or policy.' We think that it follows from this that the act in question is not open to the objection that it is an attempt to tax the property of the United States (a legatee of personal property), since the tax is imposed upon the legacy before it reaches the hands of the government. The legacy becomes the property of the United States only after it has suffered a diminution to the amount of the tax, and it is only upon this condition that the Legislature assents to a bequest of it." The same doctrine is found in Eidman v. Martinez, 184 U. S. 578, 22 Sup. Ct. 515, 46 L. Ed. 697; Horn Silver Mining Co. v. New York, 143 U. S. 305, 12 Sup. Ct. 403, 36 L. Ed. 164.

From the foregoing cases we see that the exemptions of charitable institutions would relate only to domestic institutions of that class, even if the words "in the state" had been omitted from the statute. It is not a tax upon property, but upon the right to receive property and have it transferred. Our statute does not impose the tax upon the property directly, because it provides that "all administrators, executors and trustees * * * shall be liable for all such taxes, with lawful interest, as hereinafter provided. * * *"

However, it is argued that our construction of the statute places it in conflict with section 2 of our Bill of Rights, and also in conflict with the fourteenth amendment to the Constitution of the United States. We will consider these guaranties together. That part of section 2 of our Bill of Rights which is germane to the argument is: "And no special privileges or immunities shall ever be granted, that may not be altered, revoked, or repealed by the General Assembly." That portion of the so-called fourteenth amendment to the Constitution of the United States which is pertinent now is: "No state shall make or enforce any law which shall abridge the privileges or immunities of citizens of the United States; * * * nor deny to any person the equal protection of the laws." Very much that we have already said and quoted bears upon the interposition of these provisions, and we still fail to see how the statute under consideration discriminates against the institutions complaining here. Section 2 of the Bill of Rights interdicts the conferring special privileges and immunities beyond the power of the General Assembly to alter, revoke, or repeal. There is nothing occult or mysterious about this language in our declaration of fundamental principles. Our Constitution was adopted by the people of Ohio as their charter of rights and restraints, and it is not charged with the care of nonresident persons or corporations; and the statute in question creates no privileges or immunities in favor of charitable institutions within the state which the General Assembly may not alter, revoke, or repeal; and surely it is competent for it to exempt the property of institutions, corporations, which it has created, which property is devoted to purely religious or charitable purposes. There are no Ohio institutions here complaining of any discrimination against them. Nor do we see any help for plaintiffs in error in the fourteenth amendment to our federal Constitution. The statute we are considering does not abridge the privileges or immunities of citizens of other states, nor does it deny to any person the equal protection of the laws. Within the meaning of this clause a foreign corporation is not a citizen, and cannot invoke its protection. By judicial construction of the Constitution of the United States and the federal judiciary act, a corporation is a citizen, for the purposes of federal jurisdiction, of the state by which its charter has been granted, and this without reference to the residence of the members or shareholders who compose the corporation. When a corporation charter d by or created under the laws of a foreign state is sued in a state court, it may remove the cause to the Circuit Court of the United States in like manner as a nonresident citizen may, without regard to residence of its members or shareholders. But it is a settled principle of constitutional law that a corporation is not a citizen within the meaning of that clause of the Constitution of the United States which declares that "the citizens of each state shall be entitled to all privileges and immunities of citizens of the several states." 10 Cyc. 150; Ducat v. Chicago, 48 Ill. 172, 95 Am. Dec. 529; Tatem v. Wright, 23 N. J. Law, 429; Ducat v. Chicago, 10 Wall. 410, 19 L. Ed. 972. In Pembina Consolidated Silver Mining & Milling Co. v. Pennsylvania, 125 U. S. 181, 8 Sup. Ct. 737, 31 L. Ed. 650, the Supreme Court of the United States says in the syllabus: "Corporations are not citizens within the meaning of the clause of the Constitution declaring that the citizens of each state shall be entitled to all privileges and immunities of citizens in the several states. Article 4, § 2, cl. 1. A private corporation is included under the designation of 'person' in the fourteenth amendment to the Constitution (section 1). The provisions in the fourteenth amendment to the Constitution (section 1) 'that no state shall deny to any person within its jurisdiction the equal protection of the laws,' do not prohibit a state from requiring for the admission within its limits of a corporation of another state such conditions as it chooses." This doctrine was fully reviewed and indorsed in Horn Silver Mining Co. v. New York State, 143 U. S. 305, 12 Sup. Ct. 403, 36 L. Ed. 164. It seems unnecessary to cite other decisions by state courts, since the highest tribunal in the land has thus expounded these constitutional provisions.

There is another reason why the alleged discriminations against nonresident institutions is without foundation. The Legislature has the right, in laying taxes, to classify corporations, as has been done in this state in recent years, and which has been upheld by this court as within the constitutional power of the General Assembly. Railroad companies are reached by one mode of appraisal and assessment for taxes; telegraph, telephone, and express companies by other methods; and more private corporations by still another mode. No discriminations can be tolerated in favor of or against one of the corporations of the same class; but there is no valid objection in the fact that one class is required to share in the common burden of taxation in a different way—even in a different degree—from those in other classes. Lee, Treas., v. Sturges, 46 Ohio St. 153, 19 N. E. 560; Hagerty v. The State ex rel., 55 Ohio St. 613, 45 N. E. 1046. If resident corporations, the creatures of our own laws, cannot justly complain of such classification, how can foreign corporations be heard to find fault, when they may be subjected to any reasonable condition for their admission to operate in this state, and even may be excluded altogether, unless engaged in interstate commerce?

The judgment of the lower court is sound, and it is affirmed. Judgment affirmed.

SPEAR, C. J., and DAVIS, SHAUCK, CREW, and SUMMERS, JJ., concur.

(178 N. Y. 451)

WILLIS v. McKINNON et al.

(Court of Appeals of New York. May 17, 1904.)

ACTION TO RECOVER REALTY—DAMAGES—CONSTRUCTION OF STATUTE.

1. Code Civ. Proc. §§ 1496, 1497, provide that in an action to recover real property plaintiff may, in a proper case, recover damages for withholding the property, which damages shall include the rents and profits, and the value of the use and occupation thereof. Section 1531 authorizes plaintiff to recover as damages the rents and profits, or the value of the use and occupation of the real property recovered, for a term not exceeding six years. *Held*, that in such an action plaintiff could recover damages for wrongfully withholding the property for six years before the commencement of the action, and also for the time that elapses after and before the final trial and judgment, and is not limited by section 1531 to a recovery for a term not exceeding six years immediately preceding the commencement of the action.

Appeal from Supreme Court, Appellate Division, Third Department.

Action by John C. Willis against Frank H. McKinnon and another. From a judgment of the Appellate Division of the Supreme Court (79 N. Y. Supp. 936) affirming a judgment for plaintiff entered on a decision of the court at a Trial Term, defendants appeal. Affirmed.

James R. Baumes and William H. Johnson, for appellants. Charles L. Andrus and John C. Willis, for respondent.

MARTIN, J. We are of the opinion that this appeal cannot be sustained. The action was to recover the possession of real property, and damages for wrongfully withholding the same. While numerous questions are presented and were discussed upon the argument and in the briefs of counsel, we are satisfied they were properly disposed of by the court below, and that but a single question need be considered by this court, which relates to the damages the plaintiff was allowed for the wrongful withholding of the property. Upon that question there was a division of opinion in the court below. The majority held that the plaintiff was entitled to recover for six years before

¶ 1. See Ejectment, vol. 17, Cent. Dig. § 443.

the commencement of the action, and also during its pendency, while the minority was of the opinion that he was entitled to recover for the period of six years only, with interest until the termination of the action. We agree with the opinion of the majority in that respect. Indeed, we should affirm the judgment without opinion, but for the fact that the question as to the length of time for which a plaintiff in such an action is entitled to recover damages has never been clearly and distinctly settled by this court. Thus the sole question to be determined is whether the plaintiff was entitled to recover damages for wrongfully withholding the property in suit for six years before the commencement of the action, and also for the time that elapsed after and before the final trial and judgment, or whether the period for which such a recovery could be had is absolutely limited to six years.

Although, under the various statutes relating to the subject which have previously existed in this state, different rules seem to have been applied, and the decisions under such statutes have been inharmonious, yet we do not think it would be profitable to review or attempt to harmonize them, as it is manifest that some at least are in direct conflict. The existing statutes relating to this subject are now contained in the Code of Civil Procedure. By sections 1496 and 1497 it is provided that in an action to recover real property, or the possession thereof, the plaintiff may demand in his complaint, and in a proper case recover, damages for withholding the property, which include the rents and profits, or the value of the use and occupation thereof. Thus, under these provisions, the right to recover damages for withholding the property may be made a part of the original complaint in an action to recover real property, so that, when commenced, the action is not only to recover possession of real property, but also to recover damages for withholding it. Such was not the case under previous statutes, where a judgment for ejectment must precede either an action of trespass to recover the damages for withholding the possession, or a suggestion to recover damages therefor. Under those statutes the right of action for damages arose subsequently to the judgment for the recovery of the property, and could be enforced either by an action or by a suggestion under which a trial of that question might be had. Thus, under the previous statutes and the procedure provided therein, it is obvious that no action or proceeding for damages could be said to have been commenced or to be pending until the termination of the action for the possession of the property, and hence the situation was the same as it would be in an action to recover damages for withholding the possession commenced after the determination of the action of ejectment. When the Legislature provided that a claim for damages could be enforced in and as a part of an action of ejectment, and that such claim might form a part of the relief demanded in the original complaint, it enabled a party to join what had hitherto been separate rights of action, one accruing after the determination of the other. Under these provisions it became quite evident that the Legislature intended to provide what might be recovered as of the time when the action was commenced, namely, the possession of the real property, and also existing damages for withholding the same.

But it is insisted that section 1531 of the Code of Civil Procedure limits the right to recover damages for withholding the property to a term not exceeding six years. That section, so far as material, is: "In an action, brought as prescribed in this article, the plaintiff, where he recovers judgment for the property, or possession of the property, is entitled to recover, as damages, the rents and profits, or the value of the use and occupation, of the real property recovered, for a term not exceeding six years." Was it the purpose of that section to absolutely limit the right of recovery for damages for withholding real property to the period of six years, without regard to the time when the final judgment was rendered? We think not. It seems but reasonable to suppose that the intention of the Legislature was that that period of limitation should apply only to the cause of action, set up in the plaintiff's complaint, existing at the commencement of the action; that it related directly to the recovery which might be had under the complaint as of the time the action was commenced, and that it has no application to such damages for use and occupation as might accrue subsequently to the commencement of the action and before the final determination thereof. It may be observed in this connection that ordinarily, at least, the various statutes of limitation relate to a time before commencement of action, and we can discover no reason to believe that a different time was intended by the provisions of section 1531. When these sections are all construed together, we find that under sections 1496 and 1497, in an action to recover real property, the plaintiff may demand in his complaint, and recover, damages for withholding it, including the rents and profits, or the value of the use and occupation thereof. In these provisions there is no limitation as to time, but the plaintiff may recover all the damages which he has sustained by reason of such withholding, so that, independently of section 1531, he would be entitled to recover for all the actual damages he had sustained thereby up to the time of the trial of the action, except as it might be controlled by the general statute of limitations if this special limitation had not been enacted. We think the purpose of the limitation could not have been to limit the recovery at the conclusion of the trial, but only to limit the amount for which the action might be brought for damages which had been suffered before it was commenced. It relates to the cause of action when commenced, and not to the amount of the final recovery. The purpose of this statute could not have been to arbitrarily determine the length of time for which a plaintiff could recover at the close of a long and protracted litigation, without regard to his own acts or rights at that time, or to deprive him of his plain and just rights by reason of a situation which he neither created nor could avoid, and for which the wrongful and dilatory acts of the defendants might alone be responsible. We think the plain purpose of this statute was to limit the plaintiff's right to recover, during the time he had slept upon his rights, to the period of six years before the commencement of the action, thus avoiding any question as to limitation in such an action, under the general statute limiting the time for the commencement of an action, and that after the action was commenced he was entitled to recover, in addition to six years before the commencement of the action, if the wrongful withholding had continued for that time, for any period of time which elapsed during the pendency thereof.

Obviously, the purpose of the provision that in an action of ejectment the plaintiff might insert a claim for damages for withholding the possession of the property was twofold: (1) To enable the plaintiff to avoid a multiplicity of actions, and (2) to enable him to recover the full amount of damages he had sustained for the whole time during which he was deprived of the use of his property, except only the portion as to which he had slept upon his rights for more than six years before action. Its purpose in that regard was to carry into effect the spirit and object of the general statute of limitations. It was intended merely as a statute of repose, to prevent the enforcement of his rights for a period before the action was commenced longer than he could if it had been a direct action to recover such damages. It is upon the theory that the plaintiff is entitled to recover damages for withholding the possession of real property during the pendency of a litigation in regard to the title or possession thereof, that a defendant in such an action to stay the enforcement of the judgment is required, on appeal, to give an undertaking to pay the value of the use and occupation of the premises, if in his possession or under his control.

If these views are correct, it follows that the plaintiff was entitled to recover damages, not only for six years before the commencement of the action, but also the damages which accrued during its pendency and until its final determination. That such was the intention of the Legislature we have no doubt. Any other construction would produce such glaring injustice and inequitable results as to render it quite impossible to suppose that such was the intent or purpose of the statute. If the construction contended for by the appellants were to obtain, then a defendant might be able, by dilatory action upon his part as to the trial, by unnecessary appeal, and by taking a new trial under the statute, to obtain for the use of the premises a sum largely in excess of their value, even after deducting the damages for withholding the property for the period of six years without having the slightest right to such possession and use, thus placing a premium upon unnecessary delay. We cannot believe that such an absurd result was intended. "Statutes will be construed in the most beneficial way which their language will permit, to prevent absurdity, hardship, or injustice." Sutherland on Statutory Construction, § 324. Where, as in this case, the withholding is wrongful, the claim for damages is in the nature of a claim for a tort, and the question is, how much the plaintiff was actually damaged on the day of the trial by the defendant's wrongful act, which was continuous to that period. And the same considerations of convenience and propriety should here control as in other cases where a recovery in one action is permitted in order to prevent unnecessary litigation by multiplicity of suits. The judgment should, as it may well do in a case like this, settle and determine the rights of the parties as to the entire subject of the litigation, so that, if acquiesced in, no further controversy would remain. Vandevoort v. Gould, 36 N. Y. 639, 646. The measure of damages in a case like this is that which would obtain in assumpsit for use and occupation. Holmes v. Davis, 19 N. Y. 488. We are of the opinion that in actions for the recovery of real property, like actions for the recovery of the possession of personal property, where the property has a usable value, the value of its use during the time of its detention is a proper item of damages. Allen v. Fox, 51 N. Y. 562, 10 Am. Rep. 641.

These considerations lead us to the conclusion that the words "for the term not exceeding six years," when read in connection with the other provisions of the statute, should be construed as relating to a term not exceeding six years prior to the commencement of the action.

The judgment should be affirmed, with costs.

GRAY, J. I vote for the affirmance of this judgment. The case of Clason v. Baldwin, 129 N. Y. 183, 29 N. E. 226, did not present the question for our decision which this case now presents. There the plaintiff recovered a verdict which, in addition to awarding possession of the premises, awarded a sum of money as the rental value of the premises from the commencement of the action to the day of trial. The General Term reversed as to the recovery of those damages, and when the case came to this court we reinstated the judgment as it had been. The Code sections discussed in the opinion were 1496 and 1497, and it was with reference to them that it was observed that a recovery of damages for withholding possession could not be had for a time prior to the commencement of the action. That question was not actually raised, the plaintiff in the case claiming only that the judgment upon the verdict as rendered was right. The demand in the present action is to recover damages for a time prior to its commencement, and, as to the extent of that right, I think that section 1531 of the Code should be construed as applying.

PARKER, C. J., and O'BRIEN, BARTLETT, VANN, and CULLEN, JJ., concur.

Judgment affirmed.

(178 N. Y. 425)

PEOPLE ex rel. McPIKE v. VAN DE CARR, Warden.

(Court of Appeals of New York. May 17, 1904.)

NATIONAL FLAG—USE FOR ADVERTISING PURPOSES—STATUTE—CONSTITUTIONALITY—DUE PROCESS OF LAW.

1. Pen. Code, § 640, subd. 16, as amended by Laws 1903, p. 572, c. 272, provides that any person who shall place or cause to be placed any word, figure, mark, picture, or design, etc., or any advertisement of any nature, upon any flag, standard, color, or ensign of the United States or state flag of this state, or who shall expose to public view, manufacture, "sell, expose for sale, give away or have in possession for sale or to give away, or for use for any purpose, any article or substance," being an article of merchandise or a receptacle of merchandise upon which "shall have been printed, painted, attached or otherwise placed" a representation of any such flag, standard, etc., to advertise, call attention to, decorate, mark, or distinguish the article or substance on which so placed, shall be deemed guilty of a misdemeanor. *Held* that, in so far as the statute applies to articles manufactured and in existence when it was lawful to manufacture them and have them in possession, it violates Const. art. 1, § 6, declaring that no person shall be "deprived of life, liberty or property without due process of law; nor shall private property be taken for public use without just compensation."

Appeal from Supreme Court, Appellate Division, First Department.

Application by the people, on the relation of Jacob H. McPike, against John E. Van De Carr, as warden of the City Prison of the city of New York, for a writ of habeas corpus. An order of the Special Term dismissing the writ and remanding the relator to custody was reversed by the Appellate Division of the Supreme Court (86 N. Y. Supp. 644), and defendant appeals. Affirmed.

John McPike, the relator, sued out a writ of habeas corpus to review a judgment of conviction rendered against him for violating chapter 272, p. 572, Laws 1903, entitled "An act to amend section six hundred and forty of the Penal Code, relative to the desecration, mutilation or improper use of the flag of the United States, or of this state." The statute is as follows: "Any person who, in any manner, for exhibition or display, shall place or cause to be placed, any word, figure, mark, picture, design, drawing or any advertisement, of any nature, upon any flag, standard, color or ensign of the United States or state flag of this state or ensign, or shall expose or cause to be exposed to public view any such flag, standard, color or ensign, upon which shall be printed, painted, or otherwise placed, or to which shall be attached, appended, affixed, or annexed, any word, figure, mark, picture, design, or drawing, or any advertisement of any nature, or who shall expose to public view, manufacture, sell, expose for sale, give away, or have in possession for sale, or to give away, or for use for any purpose, any article, or substance, being an article of merchandise, or a receptacle of merchandise upon which shall have been printed, painted, attached, or otherwise placed, a representation of any such flag, standard, color, or ensign, to advertise, call attention to, decorate, mark, or distinguish, the article, or substance, on which so placed, or who shall publicly mutilate, deface, defile, or defy, trample upon, or cast contempt, either by words or act, upon any such flag, standard, color, or ensign, shall be deemed guilty of a misdemeanor, and shall be punished by a fine not exceeding one hundred dollars or by imprisonment for not more than thirty days, or both, in the discretion of the court. The words flag, standard, color, or ensign, as used in this subdivision or section, shall include any flag, standard, color, ensign, or any picture or representation, of either thereof, made of any substance, or represented on any substance, and of any size, evidently purporting to be, either of, said flag, standard, color or ensign, of the United States of America, or a picture or a representation, of either thereof, upon which shall be shown the colors, the stars, and the stripes, in any number of either thereof, or by which the person seeing the same, without deliberation may believe the same to represent the flag, colors, standard, or ensign, of the United States of America. This subdivision and section shall not apply to any act permitted by the statutes of the United States of America or by the United States army and navy regulations, nor shall it be construed to apply to a newspaper, periodical, book, pamphlet, circular, certificate, diploma, warrant or commission of appointment to office, ornamental picture, article of jewelry, or stationery for use in correspondence, on any of which shall be printed, painted or placed, said flag, disconnected from any advertisement."

William Travers Jerome, Dist. Atty. (Howard S. Gans, of counsel), for appellant. Louis Marshall, for respondent.

PARKER, C. J. (after stating the facts). The Constitution of this state vests the legislative power in the Senate and Assembly, and subjects it to certain important limitations, one of which is that no person shall be "deprived of life, liberty or property without due process of law; nor shall private property be taken for public use without just compensation." Const. art. 1, § 6. In Wynehamer v. People, 13 N. Y. 378, Wynehamer was convicted of selling liquors contrary to a statute entitled "An act for the prevention of intemperance, pauperism and crime." This court holds in that case that, if the statute was limited in its operation to the sale of liquors manufactured or imported after the act took effect, it would be valid; but, as the act goes further, and substantially destroys the property in intoxicating liquors owned and possessed by persons within the state when the act took effect, it offends against the constitutional provisions quoted supra, and is void, and may not be sustained in respect to any liquor, whether existing at the time the act took effect or acquired subsequently. This case and its doctrine is referred to with approval in Matter of Townsend, 39 N. Y. 171, 180, and again very recently in People v. Orange County Road Const. Co., 175 N. Y. 84, 93, 67 N. E. 129. It is settled in this state, therefore, that a statute which attempts to destroy an existing property right is void.

The statute under which McPike was convicted provides that: "Any person, who in any manner, for exhibition or display, shall place or cause to be placed any word, figure, mark, picture, design, drawing or any advertisement, of any nature, upon any flag, standard, color or ensign of the United States or state flag of this state or ensign, * * * or who shall expose to public view, manufacture, sell, expose for sale, give away, or have in possession for sale, or to give away, or for use for any purpose, any article, or substance, being an article of merchandise, or a receptacle of merchandise upon which shall have been printed, painted, attached, or otherwise placed, a representation of any such flag, standard, color, or ensign, to advertise, call attention to, decorate, mark, or distinguish the article, or substance, on which so placed, * * * shall be deemed guilty of a misdemeanor. * * *" The statute in express terms, therefore, applies as well to articles manufactured and in existence when it was lawful to manufacture them and have them in possession as to those thereafter manufactured or acquired. It attempts, therefore, to destroy existing property rights, and, whether the value thereof be much or little, the Legislature is powerless to effectuate such a result. It follows that so much of the statute as precedes the provision affecting those who "shall publicly mutilate, deface, defile, or defy, trample upon, or cast contempt, either by words or act, upon any such flag, standard, color or ensign" is void. It was under that portion of the statute which we hold the Constitution prohibits that McPike was convicted, and it follows that the order of the Appellate Division should be affirmed.

GRAY, O'BRIEN, HAIGHT, MARTIN, CULLEN, and WERNER, JJ., concur.

Order affirmed.

(178 N. Y. 429)

PEOPLE v. BURNESS.

(Court of Appeals of New York. May 17, 1904.)

MURDER—SUFFICIENCY OF EVIDENCE.

1. In a prosecution for murder, evidence examined, and *held* sufficient, apart from defendant's confession, to support a verdict convicting him of murder in the first degree.

Appeal from Kings County Court.

Frank H. Burness was convicted of murder in the first degree, and appeals. Affirmed.

Edmund F. Driggs, for appellant. John F. Clarke, Dist. Atty. (Robert H. Elder, of counsel), for the People.

PARKER, C. J. Understanding that it was to be used against him, defendant, before trial, made a voluntary written confession, and upon this trial testified to facts which, if true, establish that he committed the crime of murder in the first degree. He admits that he had worked for Capt. Townsend, the murdered man, and that they had a dispute about wages; that, learning that Townsend's schooner was in port, defendant went from New Haven to New York intending to find Townsend and kill him if he refused to pay him; that defendant bought a revolver and cartridges, and located the schooner at a Brooklyn dock; that on November 12, 1903, about noon, he went aboard, and found Townsend, with the mate, the steward, and one Sorenson, on deck; that he demanded of Townsend the amount he claimed, and was refused; that Townsend went down into the forward cabin; that after some conversation with Sorenson defendant followed Townsend, and again demanded the money; that Townsend again refused; that as he turned away defendant shot him several times, and killed him; that Townsend tried to escape by the after companionway, which was closed; that defendant reloaded his revolver to defend himself if attacked while leaving the schooner; that he went away without interference; and that he pawned the revolver.

Under section 395, Code Cr. Proc., before a man who has confessed a crime may be convicted, there must be "additional proof that the crime charged has been committed." But proof of the finding of a body with marks of violence upon it, supplemented by a defendant's confession of guilt, is sufficient for conviction, as the meaning of the Code is that there must be some other evidence of the corpus delicti besides the confession. People v. Deacons, 109 N. Y. 374, 377, 16 N. E. 676. In this case, however, there is not only ample corroboration of every fact in defendant's confession—he not being contradicted in even the most trivial detail—but there is also abundant evidence apart from his confession to support the verdict rendered by the jury. It appears by uncontradicted evidence of other witnesses that defendant claimed to have a grievance against Townsend; that he had been looking for him diligently; that he came aboard the schooner, and demanded payment of his claim from Townsend; that he then appeared calm and unexcited; that Townsend refused to pay him, but that there was no anger shown on either side, and nothing apparent in the conversation to excite it; that Townsend descended to the forward cabin, and defendant, still appearing cool and calm, remained a few minutes on deck, conversing in a desultory way with Sorenson; that Townsend was then alone in the cabin, which could only be entered by the forward companionway, the only other entrance being fastened; that defendant descended to the cabin through the forward companionway, and was alone with Townsend about four minutes, during which time no noise was heard except by Sorenson, who thought he heard two shots, but not distinctly enough to make him certain; that Townsend was shot from behind several times, as the doctor who examined the body showed conclusively; that Townsend endeavored to escape by the after companionway, which was closed, as shown by the position in which the body was found; that defendant reloaded his revolver, as proved by the box of cartridges left on the table with the paper in which they had been wrapped and by the empty shells on the floor; that defendant returned to the deck coolly and deliberately, and left the boat; that he afterward pawned the revolver; that immediately on defendant's departure the dead body was discovered; and that there was no disorder in the cabin, and nothing else to indicate that there had been any struggle there.

The testimony we have epitomized here would, without defendant's confession, justify the jury in reaching the conclusion that defendant, without excuse, unjustifiably and with deliberation and premeditation shot and killed Capt. Townsend. And this evidence is, of course, strengthened by the confession of defendant, which corroborates it in every detail.

The judgment of conviction should be affirmed.

GRAY, O'BRIEN, BARTLETT, MARTIN, VANN, and CULLEN, JJ., concur.

Judgment of conviction affirmed.

(178 N. Y. 433)

PEOPLE ex rel. COMMERCIAL CABLE CO. v. MORGAN, Comptroller.

(Court of Appeals of New York. May 17, 1904.)

TAXATION — CORPORATIONS — FRANCHISE TAX—CAPITAL STOCK — UNITED STATES BONDS—STOCK OF OTHER CORPORATIONS—REVIEW ON APPEAL—QUESTION OF LAW.

1. A question of law reviewable by the Court of Appeals is presented by an order of the Appellate Division reversing a determination of the State Comptroller in the assessment of a franchise tax, not as to the amount of property held by a corporation within the state, but as to the character of a part thereof.

2. In the Corporation Tax Law, § 182, Laws 1896, p. 856, c. 908, providing that every corporation organized under the law of the state shall pay an annual tax computed on the basis of the amount of its capital stock employed within the state, the term "capital stock," does not mean the share stock held by individuals, but the actual capital which it represents so employed.

3. Construing the term "capital stock," as used in Corporation Tax Law, § 182, Laws 1896, p. 856, c. 908, to mean the actual capital which it represents, employed in the state, United States bonds should, in the absence of proof that they were bought by the corporation with its surplus, be treated as capital, and as part of the basis upon which the franchise tax is to be computed.

4. Under Corporation Tax Law, § 182, Laws 1896, p. 856, c. 908, requiring every corporation organized under the laws of the state to pay an annual tax, computed on the basis of the amount of its capital stock employed within the state, stocks of other corporations held by a corporation sought to be taxed on its franchise are considered as "capital stock" employed in the state; and the fact that such corporation not only owns the entire stock of another corporation, but has also acquired all of its assets, property, and privileges, except its corporate franchises and some nonassignable contracts, does not exempt such stock from the operation of the rule, on the ground that the ownership thereof is merged in the ownership of the assets and privileges represented by it, and that it is therefore of no value, where the corporation has never been dissolved, retains its corporate franchise, and remains a going concern.

Gray and O'Brien, JJ., dissenting.

Appeal from Supreme Court, Appellate Division, Third Department.

Certiorari by the people, on the relation of the Commercial Cable Company, against William J. Morgan, as Comptroller of the State of New York, to review a revision of a franchise tax assessed against relator. From an order of the Appellate Division of the Supreme Court (83 N. Y. Supp. 998) modifying, and affirming as modified, the determination of the Comptroller, both parties appeal. Reversed.

The relator is a domestic corporation owning and operating a system of cable and telegraph lines extending from this state into other states and countries. Its authorized capital stock is $10,000,000, upon which it paid in 1897 a dividend of 8 per cent. Its aggregate assets were $31,414,469.21, of which $13,162,068.33 were concededly employed without the state. The basis for the tax was originally fixed by the Comptroller at $5,483,-860, capital stock employed in this state, upon which the tax was fixed at $10,967.72, but upon a hearing for revision the amount of capital stock employed in this state was reduced to $4,500,000, upon which the tax was cut down to $9,000. Upon appeal from this decision of the Comptroller, the Appellate Division of the Third Department still further reduced the amount of capital stock employed in this state to $1,104,691.92, upon which the tax was fixed at $2,209.38, and from the order entered upon that decision both parties appeal to this court. The relator contends that of its aggregate assets of about thirty-one millions, at least twenty-nine millions are employed without the state, leaving approximately two millions within the state, the larger portion of which is not capital stock or capital employed within this state in any such sense as to furnish a basis for taxation. This contention is sought to be fortified by various combinations of figures set forth at great length in the relator's brief. The learned Attorney General presents other schedules of figures, from which it is argued that the relator has at least twenty-nine millions of assets employed within this state.

Edmund L. Cole, for relator. John Cunneen, Atty. Gen. (William H. Wood, on the brief), for defendant.

WERNER, J. (after stating the facts). If we had the right to review the facts in proceedings to revise and readjust franchise taxes, the case at bar would present some embarrassing questions that evidently perplexed the Comptroller and the Appellate Division. As our jurisdiction is limited, however, to the review of questions of law, we must take the facts as established by the record. The Comptroller decided, in the first instance, that the relator's capital stock to the extent of $5,483,860 was employed within this state, and upon this basis he fixed the relator's franchise tax at $10,967.72. The relator then applied for a revision and readjustment of this tax, and the Comptroller, under the power conferred upon him by section 195 of the Corporation Tax Law, Laws 1896, p. 864, c. 908, reviewed his first decision, reducing the amount of relator's capital stock held to be employed within this state to $4,500,000, and cutting down the tax to $9,000. This decision by the Comptroller, based upon sufficient evidence, has the effect of a judgment rendered by a court, and his return is conclusive upon this appeal (People ex rel. Roebling's Sons Co. v. Wemple, 138 N. Y. 586, 34 N. E. 386), unless the facts upon which his conclusions are based were reversed by the Appellate Division. Upon consulting the order of the Appellate Division, we find that it reduces the amount of relator's capital stock employed in this state from $4,500,000 to $1,104,691.92. In many cases such a reduction would necessarily involve a reversal of the Comptroller's decision upon questions of fact, but in the case at bar it clearly appears from the order itself that the conclusion of the Appellate Division was reached, not because the Comptroller erred in holding that capital stock was employed here when in fact it was employed elsewhere, but because he held that property owned by the relator, and concededly within this state, was not capital stock or capital that was a proper basis for taxation. In other words, the Appellate Division differed from the Comptroller, not as to the amount of the relator's property held within this state, but as to the character of a part of it. This presents a legal conclusion that is reviewable by this court.

According to the relator's own showing, its New York assets in 1897 were West Shore Railroad bonds, $107,125; Commercial Union Telegraph stock, $33,945; United States bonds, $158,125; New York Times bonds, $9,000; New York Central & Hudson River Railroad bonds, $775,779.25; Commercial Cable Building bonds, $250,000; United States bonds, $228,500; bank balances, $163,215.36; real estate, Postal Telegraph lines, $140,000; real estate, Commercial Cable lines, $84,505; bills and accounts receivable, Cable and Postal lines, $311,931.26; supply stores, $52,-904.30. These items make an aggregate valuation of $2,315,330.17. In addition to the foregoing properties, the relator was the owner of 107,750 shares of the capital stock of the Postal Telegraph Cable Company, of the face value of $10,775,000, all of which was in this state under circumstances that will be more fully stated later on. The Comptroller's decision does not set forth the items from which he computed the amount of relator's capital stock employed within this state, but it is evident that if the assets above enumerated, which were concededly within this state, are to be regarded as capital stock or capital employed therein, the relator has no just cause for complaint, since the amount upon which its tax was based is considerably less than the sum which might properly have been fixed as the basis of taxation. The Appellate Division held that the bonds of the West Shore Railroad Company, of the New York Times, of the New York Central & Hudson River Railroad Company, and of the United States were neither capital stock nor capital, but simply investments, and therefore not taxable. No reference is made in the order of the Appellate Division to the stock of the Postal Telegraph Cable Company, above referred to, but, as it is excluded from the schedule of assets held to be a proper basis for taxation, it is obvious that it was regarded as not belonging to that class. As we view the case, it presents for our review three questions of law: (1) What is the meaning to be given to the term "capital stock," as used in section 182 of the corporation tax law? (2) Are the railroad bonds, the United States bonds, and the New York Times bonds held by the relator to be considered as part of its capital stock employed within this state under that section? (3) Is the capital stock of the Postal Telegraph Cable Company held by the relator to be considered as part of its capital stock employed within this state under that section? These questions, together with the subsidiary considerations which they involve, we will proceed to discuss in the order in which they are stated.

Section 182 of the corporation tax law (page 856) provides that: "Every corporation, joint stock company or association incorporated, organized or formed under, by or pursuant to law in this state, shall pay to the state treasurer annually, an annual tax to be computed upon the basis of the amount of its capital stock employed within this state, and upon each dollar of such amount, at the rate of one-quarter of a mill for each one per centum of dividends made and declared upon its capital stock during each year ending with the thirty-first day of October, if the dividends amount to six or more than six per centum upon the par value of such capital stock. If such dividend or dividends amount to less than six per centum on the par value of the capital stock, the tax shall be at the rate of one and one-half mills upon such portion of the capital stock at par as the amount of capital employed within this state bears to the entire capital of the corporation." It is apparent, of course, that this section applies to two classes of corporations. In the first class are those that declare and pay dividends of 6 per cent. or more upon their capital stock, and in the second class are those that declare and pay dividends of less than six per cent. upon their capital stock. The tax upon corporations in the first class is "to be computed upon the basis of the amount of its capital stock employed within this state," while the tax upon corporations in the second class is "upon such portion of the capital stock at par as the amount of capital employed within this state bears to the entire capital of the corporation." It will be observed that in either case the tax can only be based upon the capital stock employed in this state, although the methods for ascertaining the amount thereof are different. If the share stock were the basis for the tax, as distinguished from the assets representing capital, then this difference in method might be very material, for in one case it would be competent for the Comptroller to fix the amount of capital stock within this state without reference to the amount or location of capital, while in the other case the presence of share stock within the state would furnish a basis for taxation only to the extent of the capital employed here. But if, on the other hand, the actual capital employed in this state, not exceeding the authorized capital stock, is the basis upon which the tax is to be computed, then, notwithstanding the difference in rate, it is in both cases based upon the same thing, namely, the amount of capital employed within this state. And, if the tax is to be computed upon that basis, the rule of proportion, practically agreed upon by the respective counsel, but discarded by the Appellate Division, is simply a rule of confusion. This is a simple fact which no amount of statutory verbiage can obscure, and which no divergence in methods can change. What, then, is the basis upon which the tax is to be computed? Is it the share stock held by individuals, or is it the capital held by the corporation? The tax is upon the corporation. It would seem to follow that the amount of the tax is to be measured by something that the corporation owns. A franchise stock corporation owns three things: (1) Its capital, existing in money or property; (2) its surplus, if any; (3) its franchise. The franchise is the thing taxed, and the tax is "computed upon the basis of the amount of its capital stock employed within the state." The share stock, or, in other words, the paper certificates held and owned by individuals, are not employed within this state. It is the capital represented by such certificates that is so employed. The total share stock of a domestic corporation may be held by nonresidents, and yet all of its capital may be employed within the state. In such a case there would be absolutely no basis for taxation, unless the capital of the corporation, instead of the share stock held by its members, is the thing upon which the tax is to be computed. In construing this section of the corporation tax law, the authorized issue of the share stock of a corporation needs to be considered only as fixing the limit beyond which a corporate franchise cannot be taxed in a case where all of the corporate capital is employed within this state. This court has held that the term "capital stock," as used in statutes similar to the one under consideration, means, not share stock, but the property of the corporation contributed by its stockholders, or otherwise obtained by it, to the extent required in its charter. Williams v. West. Union Tel. Co., 93 N. Y. 162. The expression "capital stock" is often loosely used in speech, and sometimes in statutory phraseology, to denote capital and nothing more. State v. Morristown Fire Ins. Co., 23 N. J. Law, 195. In Burrall v. Bushwick R. R. Co., 75 N. Y. 211, capital stock was defined as "money or property which is put in a single corporate fund by those who, by subscription therefor, become members of a corporate body." "Capital stock" and "capital" are practically the equivalent of each other when considered as a basis for a franchise tax.

The second question to be considered is whether the bonds of the United States, and of the railroads above mentioned, and of the New York Times, held by the relator within this state, are to be treated as capital employed within this state, and therefore as a part of the basis upon which the relator's francise tax is to be computed. If these bonds were purchased with capital, as distinguished from surplus, they furnish a proper basis for taxation (People ex rel. Edison El. Light Co. v. Campbell, 138 N. Y. 543, 34 N. E. 370, 20 L. R. A. 453); and so, if they were bought with surplus, they are not a basis for taxation (People ex rel. United Verde Copper Co. v. Roberts, 156 N. Y. 585, 51 N. E. 293). The Comptroller has included these bonds in the list of assets that represent capital for the purpose of franchise taxation. There is nothing to show that they were bought with surplus. The relator does, it is true, claim that they were bought with surplus, but its contention is founded upon nothing more than an argument to the effect that, because it has more assets than share stock, there must be a presumption that capital would be invested in properties relating to its business, while surplus would naturally be invested in safe interest-bearing securities. We can indulge in no such presumption, but, if we could, it would be of no avail as against the Comptroller's decision, which should not be disturbed unless clearly erroneous. People ex rel. American C. & D. Co. v. Wemple, 129 N. Y. 558, 29 N. E. 812.

The third question that remains to be considered is whether the stock of the Postal Telegraph Cable Company held by the relator is a proper element in the basis for taxation. Stocks of other corporations held by a corporation sought to be taxed upon its franchise fall within the same rules that govern the bonds above referred to. People ex rel. Edison El. Light Co. v. Campbell, supra, and People ex rel. U. V. Copper Co. v. Roberts, supra. The recital of a few facts relating to the acquisition of the Postal Telegraph Cable Company's stock by the relator will enable us to determine whether there was anything in that transaction to take it out of the operation of the general rule. The relator not only acquired all of the share stock of the Postal Telegraph Cable Company, but all of its assets, property, and privileges, except its corporate franchise and some nonassignable contracts. The relator issued bonds in payment of the property and rights thus acquired by it, and then deposited with a trust company, to whom the bonds were turned over for collection, the stock of the Postal Telegraph Cable Company as collateral security to the bonds. Upon these facts the relator contends, in effect, that its ownership of the stock was merged in the ownership of the assets and privileges represented by it, and was therefore of no value. The difficulty with this contention is that the Postal Telegraph Cable Company is, in a legal sense, as much of a corporation as it ever was. The holder or holders of its stock can at any time pursue the business for which it was organized. The corporation has never been dissolved, and it still retains its corporate franchise. That its stock has not ceased to have life and value is very cogently shown by the deposit thereof as collateral security to relator's bonds. To some extent the tangible property and equipment of the Postal Telegraph Cable Company acquired by the relator is used by the latter in the name of the former and under its franchise. It seems clear, therefore, that the stock of the Postal Telegraph Cable Company held by the relator should be regarded as capital employed within this state, and is a proper item in the sum total upon which the relator's franchise tax should be computed.

This view of the larger features of this case renders it unnecessary to discuss some of the incidental matters, which in other aspects might have had an important bearing upon the result, and leads to the conclusion that the order of the Appellate Division should be reversed and the revised decision of the Comptroller affirmed, with costs to Comptroller.

PARKER, C. J., and BARTLETT, HAIGHT, and VANN, JJ., concur. GRAY and O'BRIEN, JJ., dissent.

Order reversed, etc.

(178 N. Y. 442)

UNITED STATES TRUST CO. OF NEW YORK et al. v. SOHER et al.

(Court of Appeals of New York. May 17, 1904.)

WILLS — CONSTRUCTION — TRUSTS—VALIDITY—ACCUMULATIONS—DISTRIBUTION—STATUTE.

1. Testator, after making certain specific bequests, one of which was to his minor son, to be paid on his coming of age, devised and bequeathed the residue of his estate to his executors in trust, giving them power to sell the property, and directing them to invest the proceeds thereof, and from the income to pay a fixed sum annually to each of his two sons during the life of each. *Held*, that the trust created for the payment of annuities to the sons was valid.

2. The will further provided that, on the death of either of the sons, one-half of the trust estate, including the accumulations of income, if any, should be distributed among the children of each deceased son or the issue of any such deceased child that should then survive; or, in case such deceased son should die without leaving any lawful children or the issue of any deceased child surviving, the trustee should in that event, deliver the property and accumulations to his brother in case he should then survive, or, in case of his death, to his lawful children, or their issue in case of their decease. Decedent left a large estate producing an income which, after paying the annuities directed to be paid to the sons, left a large annual surplus. *Held*, that the contemplated accumulation of the surplus income for the benefit of decedent's grandchildren was invalid under the statutes relating to accumulations (Real Property Law, §§ 51, 53, Laws 1896, p. 568, c. 547, and Personal Property Law, § 4, Laws 1897, p. 508, c. 417), since neither of decedent's sons was married at the time of decedent's death, and consequently there were no grandchildren in being for whom the surplus could be accumulated.

3. Real Property Law, § 53, Laws 1896, p. 568, c. 547, provides that, where there is no valid direction for the accumulation of rents

and profits, they shall belong to the persons presumptively entitled to the next eventual estate. *Held*, that the statute had no application under the provisions of the will in question, since there were no grandchildren in being to whom, as persons entitled to the next eventual estate, the surplus could be paid; and since the court, having no authority to indulge a presumption as to which of the brothers would survive, could not determine which one would be entitled to the estate, the surplus should be distributed between the sons as in case of intestacy, each taking one-half of the surplus as heir at law or next of kin of his father.

Appeal from Supreme Court, Appellate Division, First Department.

Bill by the United States Trust Company of New York and another, as trustees under the will of Andrew Soher, deceased, against Le Roy Soher and another, for the construction of the will. A judgment of the Special Term on a referee's report was modified, and affirmed as modified, by the Appellate Division of the Supreme Court (85 N. Y. Supp. 266), and defendants appeal. Affirmed.

Peter B. Olney, for appellant Le Roy Soher. Thomas N. Rhinelander, for appellant Rodney Soher. Edward M. Sheldon and Charles A. Desbon, for respondents.

HAIGHT, J. The question brought up for review involves the construction of the will of Andrew Soher, who died on the 9th day of February, 1901, in the city of New York, leaving the will in question, which has been duly admitted to probate by the surrogate of that county. He left, him surviving, as his only next of kin and heirs at law, two sons, Le Roy, born in January, 1882, and Rodney, born in November, 1893. The testator, by his will, after making certain specific bequests, among which was one to Rodney of $15,000 upon his becoming 21 years of age, devised and bequeathed all the residue and remainder of his estate, real and personal, to his executors in trust, giving them a power of sale as to his real and personal property, and directing them to invest the proceeds and to apply the income by paying an annuity to each of his sons, varying in amount, but specifically fixed for each year until the amount reached $6,000 per year for Le Roy and $9,000 per year for Rodney, and thereafter such sums were payable yearly during the life of each. Upon the death of either of the sons, one-half of the trust estate, including the accumulations of income, if any, was directed to be distributed among the children of such deceased son or the issue of any such deceased child that should then survive; or, in case such deceased son should die without leaving any lawful child or the issue of any deceased child him surviving, then in that event the trustees were directed to deliver the same over to his brother in case he should then survive, or, in case of his death, to his lawful children, or their issue in case of their decease. The testator left a large estate, consisting of real and personal property, which produced an annual income of upwards of $50,000, which, after paying the annuities directed to be paid to the sons, has thus far left a surplus exceeding $40,000 per year.

We fully concur with the learned Appellate Division in the conclusions which it has reached, to the effect that the trust created by the will is valid; that but one trust was created; and that the implied or contemplated accumulation of the surplus income for the benefit of the grandchildren is in violation of the statute. As to the legacy payable to Rodney upon his becoming of age, we have had some doubt as to whether it was payable out of the principal or income, but, under the view which we take of the will, it makes but little difference to the parties, and we have finally concluded to approve of the conclusions reached by the Appellate Division that it should be paid out of the income, if sufficient. There is but one question in the case which we propose to discuss, and that arises out of the disposition that should be made of the surplus income.

Sections 51 and 53 of the real property law (chapter 547, p. 568, Laws 1896) provide as follows:

"All directions for the accumulation of the rents and profits of real property, except such as are allowed by statute, shall be void. An accumulation of rents and profits of real property, for the benefit of one or more persons, may be directed by any will or deed sufficient to pass real property as follows: 1. If such accumulation be directed to commence on the creation of the estate out of which the rents and profits are to arise, it must be made for the benefit of one or more minors then in being; and terminate at or before the expiration of their minority. 2. If such accumulation be directed to commence at any time subsequent to the creation of the estate out of which the rents and profits are to arise, it must commence within the time permitted, by the provisions of this article, for the vesting of future estates, and during the minority of the beneficiaries, and shall terminate at or before the expiration of such minority. 3. If in either case such direction be for a longer term than during the minority of the beneficiaries it shall be void only as to the time beyond such minority." Section 51.

"When, in consequence of a valid limitation of an expectant estate, there is a suspension of the power of alienation, or of the ownership, during the continuance of which the rents and profits are undisposed of, and no valid direction for their accumulation is given, such rents and profits shall belong to the persons presumptively entitled to the next eventual estate." Section 53.

Section 4 of the personal property law (chapter 417, p. 508, Laws 1897) contains substantially the same provisions as that incorporated in section 51 of the real property law. It will be observed that under the statute, whether it be real property or personal property, the accumulation of income or profits, in order to be valid, must be for the benefit of one or more minors then in being. Under the will, as we have seen, there has been no disposition of the surplus profits except in the clauses in which provision is made that, upon the death of one of the sons, the one-half of the trust estate, consisting of the residue and remainder, including one-half of all the profits and accumulations, shall be paid over and distributed to the children of such deceased son. It was, therefore, evidently intended that the surplus profits should accumulate during the lifetime of the sons for the benefit of their children, and such accumulation is not limited to the period within the minority of such children. While an accumulation for the benefit of an unborn child, which commences after its birth and terminates during its minority, is lawful, the statute does not permit an accumulation for the benefit of an unborn child where the accumulation is to commence before its birth. Manice v. Manice, 43 N. Y. 303, 376; Haxtun v. Corse, 2 Barb. Ch. 518; Kilpatrick v. Johnson, 15 N. Y. 322. Neither of the testator's sons, at the time of the trial, had married, and consequently there were no grandchildren in being for whom the surplus could be accumulated. Its accumulation, therefore, was unauthorized and illegal, and it follows that it must be disposed of in accordance with the provisions of the statute.

Under the real property law, to which we have called attention, the surplus income is required to be paid over to the persons who are "presumptively entitled to the next eventual estate." In order to determine who are the persons entitled to the next eventual estate, we must examine the provisions of the will, to which we have already referred. It, in substance, provides that, upon the death of one of the sons, one-half of the estate, including the surplus, is to be distributed among his children. The children of the sons are the persons, therefore, first entitled to the next eventual estate created by the will. The accumulation being illegal, the grandchildren, who would be entitled to receive the rents and profits when the period of accumulation ends, are permitted to anticipate the event which is to terminate the accumulation, and to take at once the rents and profits which are undisposed of. Manice v. Manice, 43 N. Y. 385. But, as we have seen, there are no grandchildren in being, and consequently the surplus undisposed of cannot be paid over to them. Under the will, the next estate created, after that to the grandchildren, is the one providing for the delivery of such estate, in the absence of grandchildren, to the surviving brother. Under this provision the claim is made that the sons of the testator are themselves entitled to the next eventual estate; that, in case of the death of Le Roy without children his share goes to Rodney, and in case of Rodney's death without children, his share goes to Le Roy; and that, therefore, the surplus should be evenly divided between them. While this construction of the statute at first seems reasonable, there are obstacles in the way which cause us to hesitate about adopting it. It is quite evident that the testator intended to provide for his sons out of his estate upon substantially an equal basis. It appears that his relation with them before his death was of the most cordial character, and, while he provided an annuity for one of the sons some larger than to the other, he had advanced to the other before his death the sum of $28,000. It appears that Le Roy is of marriageable age. Indeed, it was stated upon the argument of this appeal that he had already married. Rodney is still an infant 10 years of age. Should a child be born to Le Roy, then it might be claimed, under this construction of the statute, that the child so born, instead of Rodney, the brother, would take Le Roy's portion of the surplus, while Le Roy himself would still continue to take Rodney's portion, thus giving to Le Roy and his family the entire surplus arising from the estate until Rodney arrives at marriageable age, is married, and has children of his own, and that then his children would take the surplus, leaving him during life dependent only upon the annuity provided by the will. It is difficult to believe that the testator ever intended or contemplated such an unequal disposition of his estate. But there is another difficulty with reference to the adoption of this construction of the statute, and that is that under the will the brothers take from each other. The survivor alone is given his deceased brother's share, so that the surviving brother would be the person presumptively entitled to the next eventual estate. But we are given no authority to determine or to indulge a presumption as to which of these brothers will survive the other, and cannot, therefore, before the happening of that event, ascertain which will be entitled to the estate. In the case of Phelps' Exr. v. Pond, 23 N. Y. 69, 84, Selden, J., after discussing the applicability of this statute to the next eventual estate created by the will in that case, says: "The case cannot, therefore, in any view be brought within the provisions of the statute, and hence if, after deducting the payments for any year from the income of that year, a surplus of income should remain, that surplus would belong, not to the residuary legatees, but to the next of kin. In England income unlawfully accumulated goes to the heirs or next of kin as in cases of intestacy. 1 Jarman on Wills (5th Ed.) 312. Such would be the rule in this country were it not for the statute to which we have referred. Cochrane v. Schell, 140 N. Y. 516, 539, 35 N. E. 971. If, therefore, the provisions of the will do not bring the case within the provisions of this statute, the surplus must be disposed of either under the statute of descents or of distribution. The statute does not say the ultimate, but the next eventual, estate. Manice v. Manice, 43 N. Y. 385. There are no grandchildren in being that can take the next eventual estate, and the provision with reference to the brothers is not only the ultimate estate, but we have no power to determine which brother will be the survivor of the other and be entitled to take. It therefore follows that section 58 of the real property law does not apply to the provisions of the will in this case, and consequently the surplus should be distributed between the sons as in case of intestacy, each taking one-half of the surplus as the heir at law or next of kin of his father. We have discussed this question upon the assumption that the disposition of the surplus income derived from the personal property was the same as that derived from the real estate. It has been so held in Cook v. Lowry, 95 N. Y. 103-108; Mills v. Husson, 140 N. Y. 99-104, 35 N. E. 422.

The judgment in this case reserves the question as to the manner of the distribution of the surplus after the birth of grandchildren. We consequently have considered the question of the distribution of the surplus, only, during the period that intervenes between the death of the testator and the birth of grandchildren. While we may differ in the reasons given, the result reached by us is the same as that by the Appellate Division.

The judgment should therefore be affirmed, with costs to all of the parties appearing in this court, payable out of the surplus moneys of the estate.

PARKER, C. J., and GRAY, MARTIN, VANN, and WERNER, JJ., concur. BARTLETT, J., votes for affirmance on the grounds stated in the opinion of the Appellate Division.

Judgment affirmed.

(178 N. Y. 458)

GOLOB v. PASINSKY.

(Court of Appeals of New York. May 17, 1904.)

LANDLORD AND TENANT—DEFECTIVE PREMISES—INJURY TO TENANT—ACTION FOR DAMAGES—PLEADING.

1. In an action by a tenant against his landlord to recover for injuries received from the fall of a ceiling, the complaint alleged that defendant reserved to himself the control of the roof and ceilings in the building and apartment occupied by plaintiff, and that, by reason of the landlord's negligence in permitting the roof of such building and the ceiling of the apartment occupied by plaintiff to be and remain in a dangerous condition, the plaster from the ceiling in one of the rooms fell and struck plaintiff on the head, causing the injuries complained of. *Held*, that the complaint stated a cause of action, though it did not show how the defective condition of the roof caused the ceiling to fall, this being a matter of proof, and not of pleading.

Parker, C. J., and Gray and Vann, JJ., dissenting.

Appeal from Supreme Court, Appellate Division, First Department.

Action by Rosa Golob against Henry Pasinky to recover for personal injuries. From a judgment of the Appellate Division of the Supreme Court (81 N. Y. Supp. 1127), affirming a final judgment dismissing the complaint, plaintiff appeals. Reversed, and judgment of Special Term affirmed.

Theodore B. Chancellor and Abraham Gruber, for appellant. Alvin C. Cass and Carl Schurz Petrasch, for respondent.

CULLEN, J. The action is for personal injuries. The complaint alleges that the defendant was the owner of a tenement house, in the city of New York, divided into separate apartments, one of which, on the upper floor, was rented by the plaintiff's husband, and occupied by him and his family. It further alleges "that the defendant had and reserved to himself control of the roof and ceilings in said building, and apartments therein, as well as other parts and portions of said building, during all the times herein mentioned." It is also charged that the defendant negligently suffered the roof of the said building, and the ceilings in the plaintiff's apartment, to become and remain in so defective and dangerous condition that, "by reason of the carelessness and negligence on the part of the defendant in permitting the roof of said building and the ceilings of said apartment to be and remain in a dangerous condition as aforesaid, a large piece of plaster or other substance from the ceiling in one of the rooms in said apartment occupied by plaintiff fell and struck plaintiff on the head and back." To this complaint the defendant demurred on the ground that it did not state facts sufficient to constitute a cause of action. The learned judge at Special Term overruled the demurrer, holding that, while there was no sufficient connection pleaded between the condition of the roof and the falling of the ceiling, the allegation that the defendant reserved control of the ceiling was sufficient to render him responsible for its condition. The Appellate Division reversed the judgment below on the ground that the liability of the landlord for a breach of his covenant to repair was simply ex contractu for the cost of the necessary repairs, and not ex delicto for injuries inflicted thereby on the tenant or third parties. Schick v Fleischhauer, 26 App. Div. 210, 49 N. Y. Supp. 962. The learned court conceded the rule which imposes liability on landlords for negligence in maintaining the stairs, halls, and ways of passage over which they retain control and which are used in common by the various tenants (Dollard v. Roberts, 130 N. Y. 269, 29 N. E. 104, 14 L. R. A. 238; Looney v.

McLean, 129 Mass. 33, 37 Am. Rep. 295), but held that, as the ceiling was a part of the demised premises, the rule did not apply to the present case.

It will thus be seen that the difference of opinion in this case relates not so much to the rules governing the liability of landlords of apartment houses for defects in their condition, as it does to the proper construction of the plaintiff's pleading. Doubtless the demise of an apartment includes a demise of the ceilings therein, and in such a case the liability of the defendant would be governed by the ordinary rule which obtains between landlord and tenant. But the plaintiff expressly alleges that the defendant "had and reserved to himself control of the roof and ceilings in said building, and apartments therein." This is an allegation of fact, not that the defendant covenanted to repair the roof of the building and the ceilings, but that he reserved to himself control of the same; in other words, that they did not constitute a part of the demised premises. It may be very improbable that a landlord reserved or excepted the ceiling of an apartment from a demise of the apartment, but, unless it can be said that such a reservation is impossible as a matter of law, I do not see how the effect of the plain and specific allegation of the complaint in this respect can be avoided. But, however this may be, there is no such difficulty with the reservation of the roof. As a matter of common custom and practice in apartment houses, it is not demised to any particular tenant, but possession and control is retained by the landlord. Nor, so far as the pleading is concerned, do we see any break in the chain of causation between the negligence of the defendant in respect to the condition of the roof and the injury to the plaintiff. The case of Allinger v. McKeown, 30 Misc. Rep. 275, 63 N. Y. Supp. 221, and Id., 50 App. Div. 628, 64 N. Y. Supp. 1131, cited by the learned trial judge, is not in point. There the action was for personal injuries. It was alleged that a dumb-waiter or elevator in common use by all the tenants was negligently suffered to become out of repair, and that while the plaintiff was at the shaft, without any fault on her part, the waiter fell and injured her. The defect of the pleading in that case lay here: It did not aver that the fall of the elevator was occasioned by the defective condition in which it was allowed to remain by the defendant, and for all that was stated in the complaint it might have fallen from the independent act of some third party to which its defective condition did not contribute. Logically the objection is well founded, and had it been taken by demurrer, when pleadings are to be scanned with some strictness, it should have prevailed. But as it was raised only on the trial after proof given, it seems a little liberality by way of permitting an amendment to the complaint might well have been extended to the plaintiff. There is no such defect in the complaint before us. The allegation is explicit that by the negligence of the defendant the roof was permitted to become dangerous and out of repair, and that by the dangerous condition caused by the negligence of the defendant the plaster of the ceiling fell and injured the plaintiff. How the defective condition of the roof caused the ceiling to fall was a matter of proof, not of pleading.

The judgment of the Appellate Division should be reversed, with costs in all the courts, and that of the Special Term affirmed, with leave to the defendant, on payment of costs, to withdraw demurrer and serve answer.

O'BRIEN, BARTLETT, and MARTIN, JJ., concur. PARKER, C. J., and GRAY and VANN, JJ., dissent on opinion of PATTERSON, J., below.

Judgment reversed, etc.

(70 Oh. St. 113)

CINCINNATI, H. & D. RY. CO. v. WACHTER.

(Supreme Court of Ohio. April 12, 1904.)

RAILROADS—GRANT OF RIGHT OF WAY—RIGHTS RETAINED BY GRANTOR—RIGHT TO PRIVATE CROSSING—LIMITATIONS.

1. An instrument of writing, by which the absolute owner of a tract of land consisting of 20 acres or more, releases to a steam railroad company a right of way 100 feet in width and passing through said lands, leaving a portion thereof on each side of said right of way, conveys an easement in the land for railroad purposes, leaving the fee, subject to such servitude, in the general owner.

2. Among the rights not granted, but remaining in the vendor and incident to his title in fee, is a right to a private crossing over such right of way, where the same is necessary for the convenient use of his two parcels of land lying on each side, provided the same can be constructed and used without unreasonably interfering with the use of the right of way by the company for railroad purposes.

3. The possession of the right of way by the railroad company for railroad purposes is not adverse to the rights remaining in the owner of the fee. Hence the right to a crossing is not barred by the statute of limitations of 21 years; and a plea of the statute, which alleges that "neither the plaintiff nor any predecessor in title ever used any easement to cross said right of way, or any private crossing, farm crossing, way of necessity, or way reserved by implication over said right of way during said time," does not constitute a defense to a suit brought by the landowner to enjoin the company from interfering with him in the construction and use of such crossing.

(Syllabus by the Court.)

Error to Circuit Court, Lucas County.

Action by Clara F. Wachter against the Cincinnati, Hamilton & Dayton Railway Company for an injunction. Judgment for plaintiff was affirmed by the circuit court, and defendant brings error. Affirmed.

¶ 1. See Railroads, vol. 41, Cent. Dig. § 163.

B. A. Hayes, for plaintiff in error. Frank G. Crane, for defendant in error.

SPEAR, C. J. The defendant in error, Clara F. Wachter, is the owner in fee of a tract of about 20 acres of land, lying partly in the county of Wood and partly in the county of Lucas. The railroad of the plaintiff in error passes through that portion of the land which is situate in Wood county; its right of way extending in an easterly and westerly direction, and being 100 feet in width. The parties derive their rights from a common source of title, viz., Gabriel Crane, father of defendant in error. The conveyance from Gabriel Crane, under which the company claims, was executed March 20, 1854, to the predecessor of the present company, which immediately took possession, and which it enjoyed without interruption as a right of way of a steam railroad until in the year 1863, when all its rights passed to the plaintiff in error, which company has had like possession and use since. The conveyance by Gabriel Crane is entitled "Release of Right of Way." It is recited in the release on the part of said Crane that, for the consideration of $1,200 "and the advantages which may or will result to the public in general and myself in particular by the construction of the Dayton & Michigan Railroad, as now surveyed or as the same may be finally located, and for the purpose of facilitating the construction and completion of said work, do hereby, for myself, my heirs, executors, administrators, and assigns, release, relinquish, and forever quitclaim to the president and directors of the Dayton & Michigan Railroad Company the right of way for so much of said railroad as may pass through the following described pieces, parcels, or lots of land, to wit: [Here follows description.] Said right of way to be one hundred feet wide, to extend across the two pieces and parcels of land above described. And I hereby further release and relinquish to the president and directors of the Dayton & Michigan Railroad Company all damages, right of damages, actions, and causes of action, whatever, which I may sustain or be entitled to, by reason of anything connected with or consequent upon the location or construction of said work, or the repairing thereof, when finally established or completed." There is no reservation of any kind expressed in the release. The right of way has been, during all of the time since the completion of the road in the year 1854, used in the operation of a railroad, passenger trains running daily in both directions at a high rate of speed, also freight trains at the usual rate, and for switching cars, and for no other purpose. A fence has been maintained since about the year 1867 on the southeast line of the strip, in which there has been no opening by gate, or bars, or otherwise. No crossing has at any time been constructed across said strip, nor has it ever been possible. Plaintiff cannot use a crossing in a public street, road, lane, or highway, in passing from her land on one side of the defendant's railroad to that on the other side without great inconvenience. The plaintiff has occasion to cross the railroad at the point designated in her petition only during the daytime, and the number of trains passing, except switch trains, is about 14 during that time. The plaintiff has fulfilled all the requirements of the statute as to notice and demand. Other facts appear in the record, but they are not regarded as essential to an understanding of the legal questions involved.

Upon this state of facts was the plaintiff below entitled to the relief prayed for? A large portion of the briefs of counsel is taken up with a discussion of the constitutionality of sections 3327, 3328, Rev. St., which provide when private crossings must be built, and when the landowner may build at the company's expense; it being claimed on the part of the plaintiff in error that those sections undertake to authorize in effect the taking of private property for private purposes, and to deprive an owner of his property without due process of law, and are therefore in conflict with the first clause of section 19 of article 1 of our Constitution, and with the third clause of the first section of the fourteenth amendment to the Constitution of the United States. But, as we view the case, it is unnecessary to consider this question (the plaintiff below not asking that the crossing be made at the company's expense), and a disposition of it is properly postponed until a case arises in which a decision of it becomes necessary.

Independent of the statute what are the respective rights of the parties? The right of way of the company is an easement. Washb. on E. & S. 4. It is, using exact language, a servitude imposed as a burden on the land. The conveyance from Crane in terms specifies that it is a "release of a right of way," and no question is made, and we presume none can be, that the right thus granted is not different from, nor greater than, that which would result from an appropriation proceeding under the statute. Platt v. Penna. Co., 43 Ohio St. 228, 1 N. E. 420; Clarke v. R. L. & N. E. R. Co., 18 Barb. 350. An easement implies necessarily a fee in another, and it follows that it is a right, by reason of such ownership, to use the land for a special purpose, and one not inconsistent with the general property in the land of the owner of the fee; his property rights, however, to be exercised in such way as not to unreasonably interfere with the special use for which the easement was acquired. Bouvier's Law Dic. 631; Clark v. Glidden, 60 Vt. 702, 15 Atl. 358. That special purpose is, in the present case, the construction and operation of a steam railroad. The corporation has taken and holds the property by virtue of its power of eminent domain, and the purpose must necessarily be a public purpose; else there would be no power under the Constitution to clothe the corporation with such right. Adopting the language of Ranney, J., in Giesy v. C., W. & Z. R. R. Co., 4 Ohio St. 308, the private owner has yielded "the use of his property only to the public, and just so much, and no more, as will answer their purposes; the corporation being a mere trustee of the interest for their use, with no power to divert it to any other purpose, or to hold it one moment longer than it is made to serve the uses for which it was appropriated." It cannot be assumed that it was the purpose of the vendor in selling, or of the vendee in buying, that any estate different from that which the company was by its charter authorized to acquire and use, would be conferred upon the company. No reservation of a right to a crossing, it is true, was expressed in the release. But none was necessary. From the character of the paper, and the relation of the parties, and the nature of the transaction, such reservation springs out of the contract and is implied in law. Hence the construction of a crossing is not a taking of the property of another. It is but the enforcement of a right not granted, but remaining in the vendor. Nor does the paragraph of the release releasing damages which might arise by reason of the location or construction or repair of the work qualify, or in any way affect, this legal conclusion. The action is not one for damages.

It is insisted in argument that the case presented a question of common-law way of necessity, and Meredith v. Frank, 56 Ohio St. 479, 47 N. E. 656, is cited to the proposition that one cannot derogate from his grant. But the conveyance about which the court was speaking in the case cited was a deed in fee simple purporting to convey all the grantor's interest, and to clothe the grantee with an unqualified and absolute title to the land. The general rule, as stated, is recognized in the above case, and is conceded, but we have an essentially different case. The claim of the plaintiff below does not derogate from the release of Gabriel Crane, but is entirely consistent with it.

The statute of limitations of 21 years is pleaded, and is insisted upon. It is true that more than 21 years have elapsed since the plaintiff in error went into possession, and that no demand for a crossing was made until the commencement of suit below. But there is, as we think, a complete answer to that claim in the fact that the possession of the corporation was not adverse. It was, on the other hand, enjoyed for the purpose of an easement only, and such use is entirely consistent with the continued ownership and right of the owner of the fee. It is true, also, that a fence was constructed, without gate or other opening in it, some 35 years since on the southeast line of the right of way. This was, however, after the enactment of the fencing statute of March 25, 1859 (Laws 1859, p. 62), and is clearly referable to the compulsory duty by that statute enjoined, and does not indicate a claim of adverse possession. It is manifest that the plea of the statute, if good, goes to every right of the owner of the fee. If it can be successfully urged against a right to a crossing, it can by the same line of reasoning prevail against the right of reversion in case of abandonment. It is not good against either. There was, therefore, presented to the trial court the issue as a question of fact whether or not the demand of the plaintiff for a right to construct a private crossing was a reasonable exercise of her rights as owner of the fee. The court necessarily had to consider all the circumstances, and determine from a consideration of the whole case whether the maintaining of her claim would unreasonably interfere with the business of the company in operating its road. If it did, a denial of the prayer of the petition would follow; if it did not, a decree granting the prayer would be proper. The court reached the latter conclusion, and we accept it as settling the question of fact, and, as a consequence, the rights of the parties.

The case is here treated somewhat briefly, and in the form of statement, rather than argument and extended citation of authorities, because it has seemed to us that its determination rests upon the application of simple, elementary principles, well settled in this state; also, from the further fact that all the essential propositions were disposed of by this court adversely to the claim of plaintiff in error in Railroad Co. v. Mitchell & Rowland Lumber Co., 59 Ohio St. 607, 54 N. E. 1107, in which case the judgment of the circuit court of Lucas county, affirming that of the common pleas, was affirmed, without, however, passing on the validity of the statute. The original case will be found reported in Mitchell & Rowland Lumber Co. v. Railway Co., 6 Dec. 135, 8 Ohio N. P. 231.

The judgment of the circuit court will be affirmed.

SHAUCK, CREW, and SUMMERS, JJ., concur.

(163 Ind. 642)

GLENDENNING v. SUPERIOR OIL CO. et al.

(Supreme Court of Indiana. May 13, 1904.)

MORTGAGE FORECLOSURE—SALE OF PROPERTY BY CERTIFICATE HOLDER—ESTOPPEL.

1. At sale on foreclosure of a mortgage on lands, oil wells, and other oil-producing structures thereon, plaintiff became the purchaser, and received a certificate of purchase. Before receiving a deed of the property, plaintiff, who was in full and absolute possession, sold to defendant, with the participation and approval of the mortgagor, all the right, title, and interest of plaintiff in and to the oil under the land, together with the wells and other oil-producing structures, and put defendant in unqualified possession. *Held* that, if plaintiff's title was not complete at the time of the sale, it was nevertheless sufficient to estop him, having re-

ceived and retained the purchase price, to reclaim the property after obtaining a sheriff's deed.

Appeal from Circuit Court, Jay County; John M. Smith, Judge.

Action by Joseph Glendenning against the Superior Oil Company and others. Judgment for defendants. Plaintiff appeals. Transferred from Appellate Court under section 1337u, Burns' Ann. St. 1901. Affirmed.

F. H. Snyder, for appellant. Dailey, Simmons & Dailey, for appellees.

HADLEY, J. The Logansport Oil Company owned 40 acres of land in Jay county. It had constructed and had in operation on the land four oil wells. The wells were of a class known in oil fields as "water wells"; that is, wells in which the inpour of salt water required constant pumping to recover oil, and the continuous services of an attendant, known as a "pumper." Prior to February, 1899, said real estate and oil-producing structures thereon, consisting of wells, buildings, engines, boilers, pipes, tanks, belts, and other machinery, were sold by the sheriff on a decretal order of foreclosure to one Neely, and on February 16, 1899, Neely, for value, assigned the certificate of purchase to appellant, who received and took the absolute and undisputed possession of all said land, oil wells, structures, and machinery. On the next day after his purchase of the certificate, to wit, February 17th, the Superior Oil Company (appellee), upon the solicitation of appellant and the Logansport Oil Company, the mortgagor, bought said oil plant of appellant, under the following agreement:

"State of Indiana, Adams County, ss: For value received the undersigned Joseph Glendenning of said county, do hereby sell, assign, transfer and set over to the Superior Oil Company, a corporation, all right, title, and interest of said Joseph Glendenning in and to the oil and gas in and under the following described real estate in Jay county, State of Indiana, to-wit: the south west quarter of the north west quarter of section two (2) in township twenty-four (24) north, range thirteen east, together with all engines, boilers, pipes, tanks, belts, oil wells and such buildings as have been erected especially for the production of oil, and all tools, machinery and personal property used in the production and pumping of oil, and now on said land.

"In Witness Whereof, the said Joseph Glendenning has hereunto set his hand and seal this 17th day of February, 1899.

"Joseph Glendenning. [Seal.]

"State of Indiana, Adams County, ss.: Personally appeared before me, William Drew, a Notary Public within and for said county, the above named Joseph Glendenning, who acknowledged the execution of the above assignment.

"Witness my name and Notarial Seal.

"William Drew, Notary Public."

Upon the execution of said agreement appellee paid appellant as the consideration for said purchase $1,400 cash, and thereupon appellant put appellee in the full and complete possession of all said wells and oil-producing structures and appliances. In a few days thereafter, to wit, March 6, 1899, appellant demanded and received from the sheriff, by virtue of said certificate of purchase, a deed conveying to him the title to said mortgaged premises. At the time of said foreclosure and sale, and at the time of the sale of said oil plant by appellant to appellee (February 17, 1899), the said wells were, and continued to the commencement of this suit (April 14, 1900), to produce a large amount of oil. Appellant, who was the plaintiff below, brought this action for possession of said premises, for mesne profits, and for waste in taking and removing from the premises 500 barrels of oil, and made the Superior Oil Company, James Hardison, and Earl Weist, defendants. The defendant Oil Company answered ownership and rightful possession of the oil plant as above set forth, and disclaimer of possession, or claim of right of possession, to the premises further than was awarded by the plaintiff and is absolutely necessary to the enjoyment of its right to mine the oil thereunder. The defendant Weist answered that he is the company's pumper in charge of the wells, is the servant of the company, and has no possession of the premises except that he manages the pumps and resides in the dwelling house that was erected on the premises for that purpose and is a part of the oil plant. The answer of the defendant Hardison is that he is the manager of the defendant oil company, and has never had or claimed any possession on his own account, or in any other way or manner than as manager for appellee. Appellant's demurrer to the separate answers having been overruled, he refused to plead further, and judgment was rendered against him for costs. The only question presented is the sufficiency of the answers, which were substantially identical.

The question, in a nutshell, is, can appellant repudiate his contract, keep the $1,400 he received for the gas plant, and dispossess appellee of the property and rights conveyed? Appellant contends that, because he held only the sheriff's certificate of purchase for the property on February 17th, nothing passed to appellee oil company by the contract of that date, and that the title he subsequently acquired by the sheriff's deed did not inure to appellee's benefit. We deem it unprofitable to enter upon a discussion of the legal force of a certificate of purchase, or the relative rights of the holder and one entitled to redeem in the class of property involved, as we are invited to do, for, whatever might be said upon these subjects, certain simple and fundamental principles would at last be found controlling.

A demurrer admits the truth of all facts

pleaded. It is alleged in the oil company's answer that it purchased the oil plant of appellant upon the request of the mortgagor, the person entitled to redeem; that at the time of the sale appellant was in full and absolute possession, and put appellee in unqualified possession pursuant to the contract. The right of property and the right to sell the same was at the time exclusively vested in the Logansport Oil Company, mortgagor, and appellant, as holder of the certificate of purchase. The sale to appellee was made with the participation and approval of both. The contract recites the sale and transfer to appellee oil company of all the right, title, and interest of appellant in and to all the oil and gas under the described 40 acres, together with all the engines, boilers, pipes, tanks, belts, oil wells, and such buildings as have been erected for the production of oil, and all tools, machinery, and personal property used in the production and pumping of oil, and now on the land. At the moment the contract was executed, appellant at least had such a right and interest in the property as two weeks later, without any additional act or consideration on his part, ripened into such an estate as entitled him to demand and receive a conveyance of the absolute legal title. And, if his title was not complete at the time of the sale, it was, as to him, with the price in his pocket, sufficient to estop him from reclaiming it.

The answer of appellee Weist alleges that he is the pumper in charge of said wells, as the servant of the oil company, and has no possession of the premises, except that he operates the pumps and resides in the house constructed on the land as a part of the oil plant.

The answer of Hardison avers that he has no possession of the land, and no interest in the property, except as manager of appellee Superior Oil Company.

We think both these answers were good as against a demurrer.

We find no error in the record. Judgment affirmed.

(162 Ind. 584)

HOOP v. AFFLECK et al.

(Supreme Court of Indiana. May 10, 1904.)

INTOXICATING LIQUORS—CONSTITUTIONAL LAW—PRIVILEGES AND IMMUNITIES—JUDICIAL POWER—APPLICATION FOR LICENSE—REMONSTRANCE.

1. Burns' Ann. St. 1901, § 7283i, providing that, if a remonstrance signed by a majority of the voters of a township be filed against the granting of an application for a liquor license, no such license shall be granted, is not violative of Const. art. 7, § 1, providing that all judicial power shall be vested in a supreme and circuit and such other courts as the General Assembly may establish.

2. Const. art. 1, § 23, declares that there shall not be granted to any citizen or class privileges or immunities which, on the same terms, shall not be equally open to all citizens. The Nicholson Law, Act 1895, p. 251, c. 127, § 9, Burns' Ann. St. 1901, § 7283i, provides that if, on an application for a license to sell liquor, a majority of the voters of the township filed a remonstrance, no application shall be granted. *Held*, that the fact that the name of each person affixed to a remonstrance was signed by one person, in pursuance of authority vested in him by a power of attorney executed by all those whose names appeared, did not render the operation of section 7283i violative of the Constitution, on the ground that the applicant did not have an equal chance of success with an applicant confronted by a personally signed remonstrance.

Appeal from Circuit Court, Marion County; H. C. Allen, Judge.

Application by James Hoop for a license to sell intoxicating liquors in the town of Acton. From a judgment of the circuit court sustaining the action of the board of commissioners in refusing to strike a remonstrance from the files, the applicant appeals. Affirmed.

Baker & Daniels and Evans Woolen, for appellant. C. J. Orbison and Eli F. Ritter, for appellee.

HADLEY, J. The appellant filed with the board of commissioners of Marion county his application for a license to sell intoxicating liquors in the town of Acton. There was timely filed with the auditor a remonstrance against the issuance of a license to the appellant, signed by divers legal voters of the township. The name of each person affixed to the remonstrance was signed by S. L. Arnold, in pursuance of authority vested in him by a written power of attorney executed conjointly, but severally, by all the persons whose names appeared to the remonstrance. Appellant's motion to strike said remonstrance from the files was overruled. The board, having considered the same and found it contained the signatures of 72 more than a majority of all the legal voters of the township, thereupon refused to consider appellant's application for license. Whereupon appellant appealed to the Marion circuit court, and upon a trial therein there was a finding and judgment against him for costs, from which latter judgment this appeal is prosecuted.

The judgment of the lower court is assailed upon the ground that section 9, c. 127, p. 251 of the act of 1895, commonly known as the "Nicholson Law," being section 7283i, Burns' Ann. St. 1901, contravenes section 1, art. 7, and section 23, art. 1, of the state Constitution. It is argued that the power of voters to defeat an application for license by filing a remonstrance under said section 7283i amounts to the clothing of a class of citizens with judicial power, in violation of section 1, art. 7, of the Constitution, which provides that all judicial power shall be vested in a supreme, circuit, and such other courts as the General Assembly may establish. The power to confer or defeat jurisdiction is legislative, and not judicial. The board of commissioners, being a creature of the Legislature, has only such judicial power or jurisdiction as that body has seen proper to give, and may exercise that given only upon the terms and conditions prescribed. Under the Nicholson law the board of commissioners is empowered, as a court, to take cognizance of an application for license. If it finds that proper notice has been given, it must then take up the question of a remonstrance. If it is found that one has been timely filed, it then becomes its duty, under the law, to inquire and decide whether such remonstrance is in proper form and substance, and executed by a majority of the legal voters of the particular district. The authority to inquire and decide is both judicial power and jurisdiction. If it is found that the remonstrance is in due form and adequately signed, the finding, ipso facto, defeats the further jurisdiction of the board in the same sense that an affirmative finding on a plea in abatement will defeat jurisdiction. The execution and presentation of a remonstrance is in no sense the exercise of judicial power. It amounts to nothing more than the proving or establishing of a fact, as against which the General Assembly has said the commissioners shall have no power to proceed. State v. Gerhardt, 145 Ind. 439, 44 N. E. 469, 33 L. R. A. 313; Cochell v. Reynolds, 156 Ind. 14, 58 N. E. 1029; Ludwig v. Cory, 158 Ind. 582, 64 N. E. 14.

We decided in Boomershine v. Uline, 159 Ind. 500, 65 N. E. 513, that section 9 does not grant special privileges in violation of section 23, art. 1, of the Constitution, since all applicants are subject to the same conditions; but it is here contended that the applicant who is confronted with a remonstrance signed by an omnibus power of attorney, as in this case, has not an equal chance of success with an applicant confronted by a personally signed remonstrance; that the former's opportunity to secure a hearing is less, and the trouble and expense to which he is subjected by reason of unfairness and fraud of remonstrators is greater, than the applicant who must contest against remonstrances personally signed, and thus all applicants are not on an equal footing, or enjoy equal privileges and immunities under the law. Legislation must reach a much higher state of perfection than it has attained, or is likely to attain, before it will secure to disputing litigants under its provisions perfect equality of fairness, and under the present state of legislative liability to err, and difficulty in suppressing craftiness in contending litigants, we must hold the Constitution, satisfied with a law framed in such terms as grant to all citizens equal privileges and immunities upon the same terms, upon the assumption that all proceedings under it will be fairly and impartially conducted. We are not informed by the record, and we do not know as a matter of law, that the applicant confronted by a remonstrance signed by an omnibus power of attorney has an unequal chance with the applicant who contests against a remonstrance personally signed.

Judgment affirmed.

(162 Ind. 567)

UNION TRACTION CO. OF INDIANA v. FORST.

(Supreme Court of Indiana. May 10, 1904.)

APPEAL—CONFESSION OF ERRORS—FAILURE OF APPELLEE TO FILE BRIEF—REVERSAL.

1. Where appellant advances much argument and cites many authorities to establish its assignment of error, and asserts that the question presented was one which has not been decided by either the Supreme or the Appellate Court, and for over 10 months after the filing of appellant's brief appellee fails to file any brief or to offer any excuse for his neglect, he will be deemed to have confessed the error assigned by appellant, and the judgment will be reversed for his neglect.

Appeal from Circuit Court, Huntington County; J. C. Branyan, Judge.

Action by the Union Traction Company of Indiana against Alfred Forst, as executor of the last will and testament of S. Forst, deceased. From a judgment for defendant, plaintiff appeals. Transferred from the Appellate Court under Burns' Ann. St. 1901, § 1337u. Reversed.

J. A. Van Osdol and Spencer & Branyan, for appellant.

JORDAN, J. Appellant prosecuted this action in the lower court to set aside the probate of the last will and testament of Sarah Forst, and to revoke and cancel letters testamentary issued therein to appellee, Alfred Forst. Appellee demurred to the complaint upon two grounds: (1) Want of capacity of the plaintiff to sue; (2) insufficiency of facts. The court appears to have sustained the demurrer upon both grounds, and, upon appellant's refusal to further plead, judgment was rendered against it on demurrer. The transcript was filed on March 28, 1903, and the cause was submitted on April 27th. Appellant filed its brief on June 25, 1903. Ten months and over have elapsed since that date, but appellee has wholly failed to file any brief or to offer any excuse for his neglect.

Much argument is advanced and many authorities cited by counsel for appellant to establish the assignment that the court erred in sustaining the demurrer to its complaint. Its counsel assert that the question presented is one which has not been decided either by this or the Appellate Court. By reason of the failure of appellee to file a brief in the appeal, we are left wholly unaided, so far as he is concerned, in the determination of the questions presented. His neglect, therefore, under the circumstances, must be deemed to be a confession of the error assigned by ap-

¶ 1. See Appeal and Error, vol. 3, Cent. Dig. § 3110.

pellant, and accordingly operates to reverse the judgment. Berkshire v. Caley, 157 Ind. 1, 60 N. E. 696; Neu v. Town of Bourbon, 157 Ind. 476, 62 N. E. 7; People's Nat. Bank, etc., v. State, 159 Ind. 353, 65 N. E. 6; Moore v. Zumbrum (at this term) 70 N. E. 800. See, also, authorities cited in 3 American Digest (Century Ed.) col. 938, § 3110.

Without considering the questions presented, the judgment below is reversed, and the ruling on demurrer vacated at the cost of appellee, without prejudice to either party, and the cause is remanded to the lower court for further proceedings.

(162 Ind. 568)

BROOKS, Clerk, et al., v. STATE ex rel. SINGER.

(Supreme Court of Indiana. May 11, 1904.)

STATES — MEMBERS OF LEGISLATURE — APPORTIONMENT—CONSTITUTIONALITY OF STATUTE—JUDICIAL QUESTION—RIGHT TO MAINTAIN ACTION—PARTIES DEFENDANT.

1. Whether the discretion in apportioning Senators and Representatives vested in the Legislature has been abused by being exercised in defiance of the constitutional limitations thereon is a judicial question.

2. A male inhabitant of the state, over the age of 21, may sue to test the constitutionality of a statute apportioning Senators and Representatives, though the wrong complained of does not exist in his own senatorial or representative district.

3. The only defendants necessary to an action to test the constitutionality of an act apportioning Senators and Representatives are the clerk, sheriff, and auditor of the county in which the suit is brought.

4. Acts 1903, p. 358, c. 206, apportioning Senators and Representatives in an unnecessarily unequal manner, violates Const. §§ 2-6, providing that the Senate shall not exceed 50, nor the House of Representatives 100, members, who shall be chosen by the electors of the representative counties or districts into which the state may from time to time be divided; that the General Assembly shall every 6 years cause an enumeration to be made of all the male inhabitants over 21 years old; that the number of Senators and Representatives shall be apportioned among the several counties according to the number of such inhabitants; and that a senatorial or representative district, where including more than one county, shall be composed of contiguous counties, and no county, for senatorial apportionment, shall ever be divided.

Appeal from Circuit Court, Ripley County; Willard New, Judge.

Mandamus by the state of Indiana, on the relation of James Singer, against Absalom J. Brooks and others. From a judgment awarding a peremptory writ, respondents appeal. Affirmed.

R. A. Cregmile and W. C. Mitchell, for appellants. S. M. Ralston, Dan Simms, Nicholas Cornett, A. G. Smith, J. W. Kern, T. P. Davis, G. V. Menzies, M. A. Ryan, Lincoln Dixon, and Bernard Korbly, for the State.

DOWLING, J. This suit was brought in the name of the state, on the relation of James Singer, who is described in the complaint as a resident of Ripley county, and a qualified voter thereof, against the clerk, sheriff, and auditor of Ripley county, for an alternative writ of mandate requiring each of these officers to show cause why he should not be compelled to perform the duties imposed upon him by law in regard to the election of Senators and Representatives to be held on Tuesday, November 8, 1904, under the act of February 25, 1897, fixing the number of Senators and Representatives to the General Assembly of the state of Indiana, and to apportion the same among the several counties of this state. Acts 1897, p. 65, c. 51. The real purpose of the action was to obtain a decision of this court upon the question of the constitutionality of the apportionment act of 1903 (Acts 1903, p. 358, c. 206). The appellants, who were the defendants below, waived the issuing and service of the alternative writ, and demurred to the complaint. Their demurrer was overruled, and, upon their failure to plead further, judgment was rendered on the demurrer in favor of the appellee. From that judgment the defendants below appeal, and the error assigned is the ruling on the demurrer.

The complaint alleges that the plaintiff is a resident, a citizen, and a voter of Ripley county, and that the three persons named as defendants are, respectively, the clerk of the circuit court, and the sheriff and auditor of said Ripley county; that, by the act of the General Assembly of the state of Indiana approved February 25, 1897, it was provided that the General Assembly of said state should consist of 50 Senators and 100 Representatives, and, among other things, that the county of Ripley should constitute a representative district; that an election for members of the General Assembly of said state will be held on Tuesday, November 8, 1904, and that under the said act one Representative should be elected in the representative district composed of the said county of Ripley; that the relator made a demand on the defendant Absalom J. Brooks, clerk of the circuit court of said county of Ripley, more than 20 days before the said election, that said clerk should certify to the sheriff of said Ripley county that one Representative in the said representative district composed of said Ripley county is to be elected; that said relator also made a demand upon the defendant Henry Voss, sheriff of said county, that he, as such sheriff, should give 15 days' notice of the election of such Representative at said general election, by posting at the usual places of holding elections in his said county a copy of the certificates of said election so demanded by the relator to be issued by the clerk of said county when the same should be received by said sheriff, and by one publication thereof in a newspaper of general circulation in his said county, if any there be, and that the said sheriff should also deliver a copy of said certificate to the township trustee of each township within said county;

that the said relator had made a demand upon the defendant Nicholas Volz, auditor of said county, that he should make out and cause to be delivered to the duly appointed inspectors of election for the several precincts of said county, at least 10 days prior to the time of holding said general election, a suitable number of blank forms, pollbooks, and election returns, with proper captions, forms of oaths, certificates, and tally papers, to be used by the election officers of said precincts at said election to properly register, certify, and return the votes cast for the election of said Representative, but that each of said officers wholly refused and refuses to comply with such demand, claiming and asserting that the said act of February 25, 1897, expired by limitation, because enacted prior to the enumeration of the male inhabitants of the state of Indiana, over the age of 21 years, taken pursuant to law in the year 1901 (Laws 1901, p. 525, c. 227), and that the same was repealed by an act fixing the number of Senators and Representatives to the General Assembly of this state, and to apportion the same among the several counties of this state, approved March 9, 1903, and that said officers give out and threaten that they will proceed to perform their said duties according to said last-named act alone; that the said act of March 9, 1903, is in conflict with the fourth and fifth sections of article 4 of the Constitution of the state of Indiana, for the reasons that in the year 1901 an enumeration of the male inhabitants of said state, over the age of 21 years, was taken under the authority and by the direction of the General Assembly, as required by the Constitution (the enumeration referred to is then set out in the complaint, the total being 694,346); that it became the duty of the General Assembly at its session next following such enumeration, to wit, the sixty-third regular session, to fix the number of Senators, not exceeding 50, and Representatives, not exceeding 100, and apportion them among the several counties according to the number of male inhabitants above 21 years of age, as shown by said enumeration, and that at said session the said General Assembly did attempt to discharge its duty under the Constitution by passing the said act of March 9, 1903; that, in apportioning the Senators and Representatives upon the basis of the enumeration of 1901, each senatorial district should have contained 13,886 male inhabitants above the age of 21 years, as nearly as reasonably possible, and that each representative district should have contained 6,943 male inhabitants above the age of 21 years, as nearly as reasonably possible (the apportionment made by the act of 1903 is next set out); that by said act of March 9, 1903, 46 counties are formed into 20 districts, to each of which 1 Senator is apportioned; that 10 of said districts, composed of 28 counties, contained, by said enumeration of 1901, 159,767 male inhabitants above the age of 21 years, while the other 10 of said districts, composed of 18 counties, contained, by said enumeration, only 117,369 such inhabitants; that no other senatorial representation is given by said act to any of the counties contained in said first-mentioned districts, and that by such apportionment the senatorial representation of 42,389 male inhabitants above the age of 21 years of said districts, being 3 Senators, with a fraction over, of 470, is wrongfully denied to the counties contained in said 10 districts, and is given to said counties contained in said 10 districts, whereby their representation, which should be but 8 Senators, is increased to 10, and the representation of the counties contained in the first mentioned 10 districts is reduced to 10, when of right it should be 11. The names of the counties composing the said 20 senatorial districts are next set out, with the number of male inhabitants above 21 years of age in each district, as shown by said enumeration, with the excess of such inhabitants in each of the first 10 districts over each of those in the second-mentioned 10 districts. The complaint then charges that by the act of March 9, 1903, the counties of Switzerland, Ohio, Dearborn, and Franklin, whose male inhabitants over the age of 21 years, according to the said enumeration, was 15,652, being more than the senatorial unit, and which by reason thereof were entitled to have one Senator apportioned to them, were denied such Senator, and were united with the county of Union for the election of one Senator, the district so constituted having an excess over the senatorial unit of 3,889; that by the said act of March 9, 1903, the counties of Ohio, Dearborn, Franklin, and Union, whose male inhabitants over the age of 21 years, by said enumeration, were 14,345, being more than the senatorial unit, and which by reason thereof were entitled to have one Senator apportioned to them, were denied such Senator, and were united with the county of Switzerland for the election of one Senator, such district having an excess of 3,829; that included in the second-mentioned districts are 5 districts, each of which is given a Senator, although each of said districts lacks more than 2,000 inhabitants of possessing the senatorial unit, while the counties of Switzerland, Ohio, Dearborn, and Franklin, which themselves possessed 1,766 more than the unit of a Senator, are denied a Senator; that said 5 districts, and 2 other districts not heretofore named, are given Senators by said act of March 9, 1903, while each of said districts lacks the senatorial unit, as follows (the names of the counties comprising these seven districts are set out, with the deficiency in each district); that Wayne county, which is contiguous to Union, is given a Senator, although lacking the 2,599 inhabitants necessary to constitute the senatorial unit; that by said act of March 9, 1903, 40 counties are formed into 26 districts, to each of which one

Representative is apportioned; that such districts, as far as composed of counties entitled to any representation therein, are made up of counties otherwise wholly unrepresented in the apportionment for Representatives, and counties having an excess over the representative unit, which excess is otherwise represented, and is alone entitled to representation in said districts; that 13 of said districts, composed of 24 counties, contained, according to said enumeration of 1901, 109,314 male inhabitants over the age of 21 years, who have no representation for Representatives in the General Assembly under said act, except the 13 Representatives apportioned to said districts, while the other 13 of said districts, composed of 16 counties, contained, according to said enumeration, only 75,000 such male inhabitants otherwise unrepresented, by reason of which apportionment 34,308 male inhabitants over the age of 21 years, in said first-mentioned districts, who are entitled to 15 Representatives, with a fraction of 5,169 of the representative unit, are entirely deprived of such representation, and 2 of such Representatives are given, without right, to the second group of 13 districts, whereby their representation is increased to 13, whereas, of right, it should be only 10, and that of the first group of districts is reduced to 13, whereas, of right, it should be 15; that said 26 districts are composed of the following named counties, respectively (here follows a list of the counties, one county from each district being given, and set the one under the other, with the number of the male inhabitants over 21 years of age in each). The complaint then in general terms charges that in many other respects and instances the act of 1903 fails and omits to apportion the Senators and Representatives in the manner required by the Constitution. It is alleged that, by reason of these violations of the Constitution by and through the act of March 9, 1903, the constitutional rights of the relator as a citizen and an elector are impaired, abridged, and violated. The complaint concludes with a prayer for an alternative writ of mandate requiring the defendants, the clerk, sheriff, and auditor, to show cause why they should not be compelled by the order of the court to make the certificates, give the notices, and perform the other duties enjoined upon them in connection with the general election of November 8, 1904, agreeably to the provisions of the act of 1897, and not under the act of 1903.

The previous decisions of this court in similar cases have firmly settled many of the questions arising in this case, and it will not be necessary to enter upon an extended discussion of the principles by which we must be guided in determining the present controversy.

The rules of the Constitution which regulate the apportionment of representation are

The Senate shall not exceed fifty, nor the House of Representatives one hundred members; and they shall be chosen by the electors of the respective counties or districts into which the state may, from time to time, be divided."

"Sec. 4. The General Assembly shall, at its second session after the adoption of this Constitution, and every six years thereafter, cause an enumeration to be made of all the male inhabitants over the age of twenty-one years.

"Sec. 5. The number of Senators and Representatives shall, at the session next following each period of making such enumeration, be fixed by law, and apportioned among the several counties according to the number of male inhabitants above twenty-one years of age in each. * * *

"Sec. 6. A senatorial or representative district, where more than one county shall constitute a district, shall be composed of contiguous counties; and no county, for senatorial apportionment, shall ever be divided."

It has been said by this court that it was the intention of the constitutional convention to secure to the electors of the state, by section 6, supra, an equal voice, as nearly as possible, in the selection of those who should make the laws by which they were to be governed. The General Assembly has no discretion to make an apportionment in disregard of the enumeration provided for by the Constitution. The districting of the state for the apportionment of Senators and Representatives must proceed upon the basis of the enumeration of the male inhabitants over the age of 21 years, and it should be so adjusted as to secure to each voter of the state, as nearly as practicable, an equal voice with every other voter in the state in the choice of Senators and Representatives. The provisions of the Constitution on this subject are of the highest importance, and they are mandatory upon the Legislature. While it is true that exact equality among the voters of the state cannot be secured, it can be approximated, and the Constitution requires that it shall be approximated in every instance as nearly as practicable. The formation of districts containing large fractions unrepresented, where it is possible to avoid it, and the over-representation of other districts, are forbidden by the rule which requires an approximation to equality in the representation of the districts. The General Assembly has much discretion in the disposition of the fractions of the unit of representation, but that discretion must be exercised within the limitations of the Constitution. If it is abused, and the validity of an apportionment act is brought into dispute, the question becomes a judicial one, and the courts have the right to determine whether that discretion has been exercised according to the restrictions put upon it by the Constitution. Parker v. State ex rel. Powell, 133 Ind. 178, 32 N. E. 836, 33 N. E. 119, 18 L. R. A. 567; Denney v. State ex rel. Basler, 144 Ind. 503, 42 N. E. 929, 31 L. R. A. 726; Fesler v. Brayton, 145 Ind. 71, 44 N. E. 37, 32 L. R. A. 578. See, also, 2 Am. & Eng. Ency. of Law, p. 480, and notes; State v. Cunningham, 83 Wis. 90, 53 N. W. 35, 17 L. R. A. 145, 35 Am. St. Rep. 29; Board of Supervisors v. Blacker, 92 Mich. 638, 52 N. W. 951, 16 L. R. A. 432; Van Bokkelen v. Canaday, 73 N. C. 198, 21 Am. Rep. 465; Baird v. Kings County, 138 N. Y. 95, 33 N. E. 827, 20 L. R. A. 81; Smith v. St. Lawrence County, 148 N. Y. 187, 42 N. E. 592.

We entertain no doubt of the right of the relator to maintain this action. Every male inhabitant of the state, over the age of 21 years at the time the last preceding enumeration of such inhabitants was taken, has a direct interest in the constitutional apportionment of Senators and Representatives throughout the state; and if, by an apportionment act, his rights in this respect are denied or impaired, he may obtain redress by proper action in the courts. It is not requisite to his right to sue that the wrong complained of should exist in his own senatorial or representative district. Overrepresentation in other districts, or the denial of fair representation, is just as injurious to the political rights of any portion of the male inhabitants over 21 years of age, aggrieved thereby, as if these inequalities were found in their own district. Hamilton, Auditor, v. State ex rel., 3 Ind. 452; Board v. State, 86 Ind. 8; Parker v. State ex rel. Powell, 133 Ind. 178, 32 N. E. 836, 33 N. E. 119, 18 L. R. A. 567; Denney v. State ex rel. Basler, 144 Ind. 503, 42 N. E. 929, 31 L. R. A. 726; State v. Sovereign, 17 Neb. 173, 22 N. W. 353; State v. Brown, 38 Ohio St. 344; State v. Tanzey, 49 Ohio St. 656, 32 N. E. 750; Landes v. Walls, 160 Ind. 216, 221, 66 N. E. 679.

It is perfectly clear that it was not necessary to make defendants to the action any other persons than the clerk, sheriff, and auditor of the county in which the suit was brought. Parker v. State ex rel. Powell, 133 Ind. 178, 32 N. E. 836, 33 N. E. 119, 18 L. R. A. 567; Denney v. State ex rel. Basler, 144 Ind. 503, 42 N. E. 929, 31 L. R. A. 726.

The first general inquiry in this case is whether the General Assembly, by the act of March 9, 1903, did apportion the number of Senators and Representatives among the several counties according to the number of male inhabitants above 21 years of age in each, as shown by the enumeration taken in 1901. In the very nature of things, some inequalities were unavoidable, but are there others which might and should have been excluded? Are any of these deviations from the unit of representation so pronounced as to give to one or more districts a larger representation than they are entitled to have, under the Constitution, or to deprive others of the full number of Senators and Representatives authorized by the number of male inhabitants above the age of 21 years within their bounds. The duty of the General Assembly in making the apportionment is plainly stated in the Constitution. Exact equality of representation according to the enumeration of all the inhabitants entitled to be represented is admitted to be unattainable. But this difficulty cannot excuse or render lawful an apportionment which widely and unnecessarily departs from the constitutional principles upon which every such distribution of Senators and Representatives should rest. An apportionment which gives, and is intended to give, to one political party or another, a decided and unfair advantage in the election of members of the General Assembly, where such disparity can be avoided, must for that reason be condemned. In the consideration of such statutes, the courts can regard with no favor a law which designedly disfranchises any portion of the male inhabitants of the state over the age of 21 years, or deprives them of that fair proportion of representation which the Constitution declares they shall have.

The number of male inhabitants of the counties of Switzerland, Ohio, Dearborn, and Franklin, over the age of 21 years, as shown by the enumeration of 1901, was 15,652; being 1,766 more than the senatorial unit of 13,886. The act of March 9, 1903, failed to apportion a Senator to these counties, but the county of Union was added to make up a senatorial district, which then contained an excess of 3,889. An examination of the map of the counties of the state in connection with the enumeration made under the act of 1901 discloses that this inequality was not an unavoidable one, but that senatorial districts could readily have been formed of contiguous counties which would have conformed much more closely to the rule of the Constitution. It also appears that the county of Wayne was given a Senator, although it lacked 2,599 inhabitants of the senatorial unit, and that the county of Union, which was contiguous to it, was attached to the counties of Switzerland, Ohio, Dearborn, and Franklin, which already contained more than the unit. Again, while the five counties of Switzerland, Ohio, Dearborn, Franklin, and Union, with 17,775 male inhabitants over the age of 21 years, are given one Senator by the act of March 9, 1903, the counties of La Grange and Noble, with only 10,787 such inhabitants, have one Senator; Rush, Fayette, and Shelby counties, with 17,111 such inhabitants, have one Senator; and Lake county, with 11,162 such inhabitants, has one also; Miami and Howard counties, with 16,009 such inhabitants, have but one Senator, and Wayne county, with only 11,287 such inhabitants, has one; Jefferson, Jennings, and Ripley counties, with 15,831 such inhabitants, have one Senator; and the county of Tippecanoe, with but 11,762 such inhabitants, also has one Senator; Montgomery and Parke counties, with 15,829 such inhabitants, have one Senator, and Lawrence and Monroe counties, with but 11,661 such inhabitants, also have one Senator. It is not necessary that we should go farther. The inequalities in the apportionment which we have mentioned cannot be explained on the ground that they were inevitable, or defended upon the pretense that they were approximately just. These instances are sufficient to compel this court to declare that the act of March 9, 1903, does not conform to the requirements of the Constitution, and that it is void.

The court did not err in overruling the demurrer to the complaint, and its judgment is affirmed.

(162 Ind. 580)

STATE ex rel. MOORE v. BOARD OF COM'RS OF CLINTON COUNTY et al.

(Supreme Court of Indiana. May 11, 1904.)

RAILROAD AID TAX—BOARD OF COMMISSIONERS—ENFORCEMENT—INJUNCTION—MANDAMUS.

1. Mandamus will not lie to compel a board of county commissioners to order the collection of a railroad aid tax which it has been enjoined from enforcing, especially where the personnel of the board has changed since the injunction was granted on default.

On rehearing. Denied.

For former opinions, see 68 N. E. 295, 70 N. E. 373.

GILLETT, C. J. The fact that we have modified our original mandate by ordering a reversal upon two of the cross-assignments of error while the cause was before us on appellees' petition for a rehearing has resulted in appellant seeking a rehearing. In the brief of appellant's counsel a number of cases are cited to the effect that, after a court of law has rendered a judgment in a cause over which it has jurisdiction, and is proceeding to enforce its judgment, it will not permit its authority to grant relief to be defeated by an injunction against an officer. In each of such cases, with the exception of Savage v. Sternberg, 19 Wash. 679, 54 Pac. 611, 67 Am. St. Rep. 751, the prior judgment was in full force, and the question was presented by the effort of the court rendering such judgment to collect it. In some of such cases a mandate had become necessary, as the judgment could not be collected by execution; but the writs were not new suits, and were in aid of a jurisdiction which had previously attached. This was clearly pointed out in United States v. Council of Keokuk, 6 Wall. 514, 18 L. Ed. 933, which is one of the cases upon which counsel for appellant rely. In Savage v. Sternberg, supra, it was assumed that the proceeding in equity was void as against the plaintiff in the subsequent mandate proceeding, since he was not a party, and on that ground the court assumed to criticise the cases in which it had been held that an officer will not be required by mandate to do an act which he has been expressly enjoined from doing. We have shown that, whatever may be the effect of such a decree as the answers under consideration set up, it was not void as to the officers who were made defendants in said action. The order was valid not only as to them, but also as to their successors in office.

We appreciate the force of the authorities cited by counsel for appellant which deny to an officer any shelter from a decree rendered against him alone, as against what might be likened to proceedings supplemental to execution in the court which not only originally had, but still retains, jurisdiction over the cause; but we deny the application of such authorities here. When the judgment of the White circuit court was adjudged on appeal to be a nullity as against the board of commissioners, the auditor, and the treasurer, that adjudication became the law of the case. As a result, the White circuit court lost all authority to enforce its judgment. It required a new and independent proceeding, instituted in another court, to enforce said judgment; and, since it had been adjudged a nullity as to said officers, the injunction decree became, in effect, the prior order. For this reason we think that the facts of this case are not such as to bring it within the doctrine of the line of cases relied on by appellant's counsel relative to the attempted arrest of proceedings at law by injunction against a ministerial officer.

It is urged upon our consideration that the recognition of the doctrine that mandamus will not ordinarily lie to enforce the performance of an act which the officer has been enjoined from doing will lead to collusive attempts to evade the performance of public duties by means of injunction decrees obtained upon default. It is always to be understood that each case is decided on appeal upon its own particular facts, and it is therefore to be understood that what we decide in this case is limited to its own facts. We do not doubt the propriety of applying such doctrine here, since all of the officers who were parties to said injunction suit are now out of office. Their successors, although bound by the decree, are not to be charged with laches in failing to defend. As to the officers defaulted, the fact that their own laches had brought them between two fires might be a controlling element, if there were no other remedy, in prompting the issuance of the peremptory writ. In a case like this, however, where the relator has sinned away his opportunity to proceed against such officers by delaying the institution of this proceeding for nearly five years after the rendition of said decree, the matter has a different aspect. The present officers, who have not been guilty of any default, ought not, at their peril, to be compelled to answer for contempt of the authority of the court that granted the injunction. While it may be possible that they might purge themselves by proof of the facts, yet said court, having the prior jurisdiction, would naturally be disposed to use its power to prevent the officers from persevering in a course which would work the entire undoing of the decree, and in an internecine controversy between courts making conflicting demands upon the same officers, it is probable that, although entirely innocent, they would be burdened with expense and harassed with anxiety, if not actually punished for contempt, before the matter could be disposed of. The fact that the issuance of the final writ would work confusion and injustice affords a sufficient reason, in view of relator's delay, for the refusal of the writ.

After further consideration, and in the light of the brief of counsel for appellant upon the question as to the sufficiency of said answers, we are still of the opinion that they stated facts in bar of the issuance of the peremptory writ.

Appellant's petition for a rehearing is overruled.

(162 Ind. 646)

CLEVELAND, C., C. & ST. L. RY. CO. v. MILES.

(Supreme Court of Indiana. May 13, 1904.)

RAILROADS—STREET CROSSING ACCIDENT—NEGLIGENCE—INJURY TO INFANT—CONTRIBUTORY NEGLIGENCE—ACTION BY PARENT—LOSS OF SERVICES — AMENDMENT OF COMPLAINT—DISCRETION—REFILING—INSTRUCTIONS.

1. A railroad company which, in a populous city, runs a locomotive and car along a track across a street at 30 miles an hour without warning signal, while at the same time a long train of freight cars is running on a parallel track in the opposite direction, obstructing the view and drowning the noise of the locomotive and car for a pedestrian waiting to cross, and who, crossing behind the freight train, is struck by the locomotive, is guilty of negligence.

2. A complaint for the wrongful death of an infant by a locomotive at a street crossing, which alleges that decedent was waiting to cross the railroad tracks as soon as a freight train moving in the opposite direction from the locomotive, and obscuring the view and drowning the noise thereof, should move off of the crossing, and that as soon as this happened decedent started to cross the track, without notice or warning of the approach of the locomotive, and without fault or carelessness on his part, when he was injured, etc., does not exhibit contributory negligence rendering it demurrable.

3. In an action by a parent for the wrongful death of his infant son, in which the complaint alleges the relationship, that the child was 11 years old, healthy and strong, that plaintiff was entitled to his services, care, and custody, and that he was killed by the defendant's negligence, to the damage of plaintiff in the sum of $10,000, it is not an abuse of discretion (under Burns' Ann. St. 1901, § 397, providing that amendments after answer shall be by leave of court, and section 390, providing that the court may at any time, in its discretion, direct any material allegation to be inserted to conform the pleadings to the facts proved, when the amendment does not substantially change the claim) to permit an amendment, after argument begun, alleging that, by reason of the death of the child, plaintiff was deprived of its services from the time of its death until it would have arrived at 21 years, which would have been of the value of $10,000; the evidence fully authorizing the averment, and no further evidence being given under it.

4. The refusal to require plaintiff to refile his complaint after amendment is not ground for reversal, where defendant is permitted to file a demurrer to the amended pleading.

5. Under Burns' Ann. St. 1901, § 359a, providing that in personal injury actions it shall not be necessary for plaintiff to allege and prove the want of contributory negligence, but that it shall be a matter of defense, it is not error to instruct that the burden of proving contributory negligence is on defendant, and that he must prove the fact by a fair preponderance of the evidence, where the court adds that the fact need not be established by defendant's evidence, but it is sufficient if it is made to appear by a preponderance of all the evidence in the case.

6. A railroad company owes the duty to a pedestrian at a street crossing to give timely warning of the approach of a train, though there is no statute or ordinance requiring signals to be given at street crossings.

7. In an action by a parent for the wrongful death of his infant son, it is proper to instruct that he could not recover the value of the child's services independent of the expense of caring for and maintaining him during minority.

8. In an action against a railroad company for negligently killing plaintiff's infant son at a street crossing, it is proper to instruct that the care which the law requires a child to exercise is according to his maturity, experience, and capacity, and is to be determined by the jury on all the facts of the particular case.

Appeal from Superior Court, Marion County; Jas. M. Leathers, Judge.

Action by James H. Miles against the Cleveland, Cincinnati, Chicago & St. Louis Railway Company. Judgment for plaintiff and defendant appeals. Affirmed. Transferred from Appellate Court under section 1337u, Burns' Ann. St. 1901.

Elliott, Elliott & Littleton, for appellant.
Kealing & Hugg, for appellee.

DOWLING, J. The infant son of the appellee was run over and killed April 10, 1901, at a street crossing in the city of Indianapolis, on the east track of the Indianapolis Union Railway Company, by a locomotive and car owned by the appellant, and then and there being run by it on said track. This action was brought by the father against both companies to recover damages for the injury to and death of his child. On the trial, upon a peremptory instruction by the court, the jury returned a verdict in favor of the Indianapolis Union Railway Company, and thereafter the cause proceeded against the appellant alone.

The complaint was in two paragraphs, and the first alleged that the negligence of the appellant consisted in running its locomotive, drawing a caboose, over and along one of two parallel tracks nine feet distant from each other, and over and across their intersection with Morris street, one of the public streets of said city, at a reckless and dangerous rate of speed, to wit, 30 miles per hour, while a long train of freight cars was running in the opposite direction on the other track, completely shutting out of view

¶ 6. See Railroads, vol. 41, Cent. Dig. § 1005.

said locomotive and car, and drowning the noise thereof; that the appellant failed to give to the decedent notice of the approach of said locomotive and car by ringing the bell or sounding the whistle on said locomotive, and that the watchman at said intersection, employed and kept there by the Indianapolis Union Railway Company, did not warn the decedent of the approach of the said locomotive and car, as it was his duty under his employment to do; that appellant's son, with other persons, was waiting on the sidewalk on Morris street, just west of the west track, to cross over said tracks to a point immediately east of the east track so soon as said train on the west track should move off of said crossing; that the said moving freight train on said west track, going south, prevented appellant's son from seeing the approaching locomotive and car coming north on the east track, and that the noise made by it prevented him from hearing the approach of said locomotive and car; that, as soon as the north end of the said freight train had moved far enough south to enable appellant's son to cross the west track, he started to do so, without notice or warning of the approach of the said locomotive and car on the east track, and without fault or carelessness on his part, when the appellant carelessly and negligently ran its said locomotive and car at a dangerous rate of speed, to wit, 30 miles per hour, and without any signal of its approach, against and upon appellant's son, wounding and injuring him so that in one hour he died. It was also alleged, in connection with the charge of negligence on the part of the appellant, that the said railroad crossing was in a thickly settled part of the city of Indianapolis, and was much used by travelers on foot and in vehicles. The second paragraph of the complaint was similar to the first, but contained the additional averment that the train which struck and killed the child was being run at a high rate of speed, to wit, 30 miles per hour, in violation of an ordinance of the city of Indianapolis of March 12, 1866, limiting the speed of trains within the city to four miles per hour. No question is made as to the other and merely formal averments of the complaint, and it is not necessary to set them out. A demurrer to each paragraph of the complaint for want of sufficient facts was overruled, the appellant filed its answer in denial, and the cause was submitted to the jury for trial. After all the evidence was given, written requests for instructions filed, and a part of the argument heard, the court, on motion of the appellee, and over the objection and exception of the appellant, permitted the appellee to amend each paragraph of his complaint by inserting these words: "That by reason of the death of said Harry Walden Miles, caused by the negligent acts of the defendant as aforesaid, he, the plaintiff, was deprived of the services of his said son from the time of his death, as aforesaid, to the time he would have arrived at the age of twenty-one years, which services the plaintiff alleges were, and would have been, of the value of ten thousand ($10,000) dollars to him." The appellant then moved that the appellee be required to file his complaint as an amended complaint, which motion was overruled. Appellant next demurred to each paragraph of the complaint as amended. These demurrers were overruled. A verdict was returned for the appellee, and, over a motion by appellant for a new trial, judgment was rendered on the verdict. All these rulings of the court on the demurrers and motions are assigned for error.

Does the complaint contain a sufficient charge of actionable negligence on the part of the appellant? If so, was the child of the appellee guilty of contributory fault? It is well settled that, where one or more railroad tracks cross a public street of a city in a populous neighborhood, greater vigilance and care on the part of the company to avoid injuring persons using the street are required than at ordinary highway crossings in the country, or in sparsely settled and unfrequented places. In this, as in other cases, the degree of care to be exercised by the company must be commensurate with the dangers of the particular situation created by its use of the street. It may have the right to occupy the street with its tracks, and to use them for the purpose of moving its locomotives, cars, and trains, but it has no exclusive right to the use of the street, and the law imposes upon it, as upon all other persons, the duty of using its property in such manner as not to injure others who are themselves lawfully using the street and crossing. The running of locomotives and trains at a high rate of speed over street crossings in a city, even where the ordinary signals or the statutory warnings are given, may constitute negligence, and render the company liable for injuries occasioned thereby. And, where no signals are required by statute, a failure to give reasonable notice and warning of the approach of a locomotive by ringing the bell or sounding the whistle may subject the company to liability, where a traveler at the crossing is injured without contributory fault on his part. If the dangers of the situation require it, extraordinary precautions must be taken by the company to protect the public from injuries likely to occur at such crossing. Neither the ringing of the locomotive bell, nor the sounding of the whistle, nor the maintenance of a flagman at a street crossing is sufficient of itself to exonerate the railroad company from responsibility for an accident and injury resulting from the high and dangerous speed of the train, if these precautions were inadequate to render the public reasonably safe and secure in the lawful and careful use of the street. In such cases, if grade crossings are maintained, a material reduction of the speed of the train, or the erection and maintenance of safety gates, or other like measures, may be the only means, or the most reasonable and available means, by which the persons lawfully and carefully using the street may be sufficiently protected against accident. At such crossings, where there are two or more tracks parallel with each other and only a few feet apart, the risk of accident is greatly increased, and it is necessarily dangerous to a very high degree to run two trains in opposite directions on the parallel tracks at the same time, the one entirely hiding the other from the view of passengers waiting to cross the tracks and drowning the noise of the farther train.

The Chicago, etc., R. Co. v. Boggs, 101 Ind. 522, 51 Am. Rep. 761, is a strong case, and is very much in point. There one train followed another so closely on the same track that the noise of the first train drowned the signals of the train following it, and a traveler was struck and seriously injured by the second train. Upon this branch of the case the court said: "It may be laid down as settled law that the omission to give the signals required by the statute constitutes culpable negligence, and that such signals are intended to warn travelers in lawful use of the highway of approaching trains. As this is settled law, positively declared by statute, the railroad company cannot disobey it without incurring liability to a traveler who is injured without fault on his part contributing to the injury. Nor can the company by its own wrong render unavailing the signals required by law. If it runs one train so close upon another that there is no time to give the warning in the manner prescribed by law, it is guilty of negligence. It is obvious that the object of the statute would be defeated if one train could be run so close upon another as that the noise and rumble of the leading train would drown the signals of the train following it. Railroad companies have no greater rights to the crossing than the traveler, except the right to priority in passing, and they have no right to do any act that will mislead a traveler and expose him to needless danger. * * * There are many cases holding that if a railroad company creates an appearance of safety, and a traveler, influenced by the appearance, enters upon the track and is injured, he may maintain an action for injuries resulting from the negligence. * * * This principle applies here, and is, indeed, essentially the same as that declared in the cases we have referred to. It certainly is negligence to create an appearance of safety where there is, in fact, danger, and such a false appearance is created when one train follows another so closely as not to allow time for giving the signals prescribed by statute. * * * If the traveler can, by the exercise of ordinary prudence, discern and avoid the danger, he must, of course, do so, but this by no means proves that the wrongful act of the railroad company does not constitute negligence. * * * We think the court did right in this case in instructing the jury that if the view of the track from the highway was obstructed so that a train could not be seen, and the appellant ran a train so close behind another as not to allow time for the statutory signals to be given, the railroad company was guilty of negligence."

Indianapolis Union Railway Company v. Neubaucher, 16 Ind. App. 21, 43 N. E. 576, 44 N. E. 669, is still more closely analogous to the present case, the accident having occurred in precisely the same manner on the parallel tracks of the same company. The law was thus stated by the court: "A feature of the negligence charged, or, perhaps, more correctly speaking, a reason for the requirement of special precautionary measures, was the running of trains so closely together on the tracks as to cause the noises made by such running to prevent a person attempting to cross from hearing the distinct sound of the approaching train, or its signals. To permit such noises and the passing of trains at such short intervals was not necessarily negligence, but it necessarily created additional danger to the pedestrian who might desire to cross, and brought with it the necessary requirement of providing such signals of warning as would be sure to apprise travelers over the crossing of the approach of trains."

Louisville, etc., Ry. Co. v. Rush, 127 Ind. 545, 26 N. E. 1010, has many features in common with the case before us.

These decisions seem to be well supported by the authorities. Broom's Leg. Max. 365; Heaven v. Pender, 11 Q. B. D. 503; Hill v. Portland, etc., R. Co., 55 Me. 438, 92 Am. Dec. 601; Louisville, etc., Ry. Co. v. Rush, 127 Ind. 545, 26 N. E. 1010; Chicago, etc., R. R. Co. v. Spilker, 134 Ind. 380, 33 N. E. 280, 34 N. E. 218; 7 A. & E. Ency. Law (2d Ed.) 405, and notes; Indianapolis, etc., Ry. Co. v. Wilson, 134 Ind. 95, 33 N. E. 793; Louisville, etc., Ry. Co. v. Sears, 11 Ind. App. 654, 38 N. E. 837; Pennsylvania Co. v. McCaffrey, 139 Ind. 430, 38 N. E. 67, 29 L. R. A. 104.

In the case before us the crossing was in a city, and the statute requiring a whistle to be blown when the train was 80 rods from the crossing did not apply. But it was no less the duty of the appellant to give to travelers approaching its tracks reasonable warning of the coming of the train on the east track. As it was hidden from sight by the train on the west track, and as that train completely drowned the noise made by it, the appellant was negligent in running the train on the east track so close to the train on the west track that these results followed.

The complaint alleges that appellant's child was 11 years of age. The only care which could be required from him was such as he could reasonably be expected to exercise, his age, intelligence, and experience being considered. Nothing in the complaint authorizes the inference that he failed to use such care. Under the allegations of the complaint it was a question for the jury whether he did so. Atchison, etc., R. Co. v. Hardy, 94 Fed. 294, 37 C. C. A. 359; Steele v. Northern, etc., R. Co., 21 Wash. 287, 57 Pac. 820; Davidson v. Lake Shore, etc., R. Co., 179 Pa. 227, 36 Atl. 291. We are of the opinion that the complaint was sufficient to withstand a demurrer, and that the court did not err in so deciding.

At the close of the evidence, and after the case had been argued by the attorneys for the Indianapolis Union Railway Company, the court permitted the appellee to amend each paragraph of the complaint by inserting an allegation that by the death of his son the appellee was deprived of his services, which were of the value of $10,000. The complaint would probably have been sufficient without this averment. It already contained allegations of the relationship of the appellee to the child, that the latter resided with the appellee, that he was 11 years old, healthy and strong, that the appellee was entitled to his services, care, and custody, and that he was killed by the negligence of the appellant, to the damage of the appellee $10,000. Although the allegation "that the plaintiff thereby lost and was deprived of the services and assistance of" the child or wife injured was generally inserted in declarations at common law in actions by the father, master, or husband, yet it seems to be rather a conclusion from the other facts pleaded than a material averment of an independent fact, and we have found no case where a declaration was held bad on general demurrer because of its omission. 2 Chitty, Pl. 855, 856. In the present case the evidence already before the jury fully authorized the addition of the averment, and no further evidence was given under it. Such amendments are very much under the control of the court, and we think there was no abuse of judicial discretion in permitting the amendment to be made. Sections 397, 399, Burns' Ann. St. 1901; Citizens' Bank v. Adams, 91 Ind. 280; City of Huntington v. Folk, 154 Ind. 91, 54 N. E. 759. The appellant did not show by affidavit that it was in any way prejudiced by the amendment, nor ask for a continuance because of it. Section 397, Burns' Ann. St. 1901; The Toledo, etc., R. R. Co. v. Stephenson, Trustee, etc., 131 Ind. 203, 30 N. E. 1082. The refusal of the court to require the appellee to file his complaint after the addition of the averment of the loss of the services of his son did not constitute reversible error. The court permitted the appellant to file a demurrer to each paragraph after the amendment, so that the question of the sufficiency of the pleading was again raised, and the benefit of exceptions to the rulings thereon was fully saved to appellant. The amendment did not in any way impair the complaint, and, as we have held that the pleading was sufficient before the amendment, it is not necessary to add anything to our previous statement of our reasons for so regarding it. The demurrers to the paragraphs as amended were properly overruled.

The last error assigned is the overruling of the motion for a new trial. There is little or no controversy concerning the facts. Whether the appellant was or was not negligent in running its trains on the parallel tracks, and whether it adopted reasonable precautions to prevent accidents to travelers who were using the street at the crossing, were questions of fact for the jury. So, also, was the question in regard to the care to be exercised by a child 11 years of age suddenly placed in such a situation of danger and confusion by the negligent and wrongful conduct of the railroad company. The evidence as to the negligence of the appellant and the absence of contributory fault on the part of the child was sufficient to sustain the verdict in these particulars, and we do not feel authorized to set it aside. This case is readily distinguishable from Oleson v. Lake Shore, etc., R. Co., 143 Ind. 405, 42 N. E. 736, 32 L. R. A. 149, and the cases therein cited, both as to the particular circumstances and conditions under which the injury occurred, and the fact that in this case the person injured was a child and not an adult.

Objection is made by counsel for appellant to the 4th, 8th, 18th, and 19th instructions given by the court, and to the refusal of the court to give the 2d, 3d, 6th, 7th, 10th, 11th, and 14th instructions asked for by appellant. The supposed error in the fourth instruction was that it stated that the burden of proving that the appellee's son was guilty of contributory negligence, if there was such negligence, was upon the appellant, and that the appellant must prove that fact by a fair preponderance of the evidence. Had this been all that was said upon the subject, the instruction would have been incorrect. But it was not all. The jury were fully and clearly instructed that such fact need not be established by the evidence introduced by the appellant, but that it would be sufficient if it was made to appear by a preponderance of the evidence given in the case, whether by the appellant or by the appellee. The direction of the court upon this branch of the case was so plain, emphatic, and unmistakable in its meaning that we cannot believe that it was misunderstood by the jury, or that they were misled by it to the injury of the appellant. It was strictly correct to inform the jury that contributory negligence was a matter of defense, and that it might be proved under the answer of general denial. The statement that the appellant must prove that fact by a fair preponderance of the evidence was, in other parts of the instructions, so modified and explained that it could not mislead the jury, and was therefore harmless. Acts 1899, p. 58; section 359a, Burns' Ann. St. 1901; Indianapolis St. R. Co. v. Taylor, 158 Ind. 274, 279, 280, 63 N. E. 456. It may be added that the whole of the evidence, taken together, authorized the jury to find, as already observed, that the appellee's son was not guilty of contributory negligence, but that he exercised such care as could be required from him, his age, intelligence, and experience considered.

The eighth instruction properly stated that it was the duty of the appellant "to give timely warning of the approach of a train." This it was bound to do, whether there was a statute or ordinance requiring signals to be given at the street crossing, or otherwise. It was a measure of care which the law exacted, and failure to exercise it at such a crossing as was shown to exist in this case would have been negligence on the part of the railroad company. The Chicago, etc., R. Co. v. Boggs, 101 Ind. 522, supra; Indianapolis Union Ry. Co. v. Neubaucher, 16 Ind. App. 21, supra; Louisville, etc., Ry. Co. v. Rusk, 127 Ind. 545, 26 N. E. 1010.

The eighteenth instruction, in regard to the measure of damages in this case, was not materially defective or misleading. The jury were informed by it that the appellee could not recover "the value of such services independent of the expense of caring for and maintaining the son during minority."

The nineteenth instruction contains an accurate statement of the law regarding the care to be exercised by children of tender years in situations of peril. The court very properly told the jury that the care which the law requires a child to exercise is according to his maturity, experience, and capacity, and that it is to be determined by the jury upon the proof of all the facts of the particular case. The court did not assume that the appellee's son was of any particular age, although the undisputed evidence would have justified it in stating that he was an infant aged 11 years. If the language used concerning the degree of care to be exercised by an infant was not technically exact, there is not the slightest probability that the jury were misled by any failure of the court to observe the nice distinction pointed out by counsel between degree of care and quantum of care.

The instructions asked by the appellant and refused by the court need not be set out or considered in detail. Some of them were entirely at variance with the views expressed in this opinion; the others related to subjects on which the jury had been properly and sufficiently advised by the court.

We do not find in the amount of damages assessed for the loss of the services of appellee's son any indication of unfairness, prejudice, or passion. There is no exact standard by which the value of the services of a minor son from the age of 11 years to the age of 21 years can be measured, and, as this boy was already earning money, we cannot say that it was improbable that he would have continued to do so, and that his earnings would have increased from year to year until he attained his majority.

Our conclusion is that the court did not err in overruling the motion for a new trial. We find no error in the record. Judgment affirmed.

(33 Ind. App. 521)

CITY OF BLUFFTON et al. v. MILLER.[1]

(Appellate Court of Indiana, Division No. 1. May 12, 1904.)

MUNICIPAL CORPORATIONS — IMPROVEMENTS — STATUTES — VALIDITY OF ORDINANCE — DESCRIPTION OF IMPROVEMENT—CONTRACT—DELEGATION OF POWERS TO CITY ENGINEER—EQUITY.

1. Where a municipality, in assessing property for a public improvement, attempts some other method than that provided by statute, or exceeds the authority given, it is without jurisdiction to that extent, and its acts are void.

2. Where a city has entered into a contract for the making of a public improvement, which contract is beyond the scope of its municipal power, a property owner affected by the improvement is entitled to an injunction to restrain the carrying out of the contract.

3. Acts 1901, p. 534, c. 231 (Burns' Ann. St. 1901, § 3623a), relative to municipal improvements, provides that the common council desiring to make a street improvement shall order the same by the adoption of a resolution, stating the kind, location, etc., thereof, and that any property owner whose lands shall be assessed may remonstrate, and if the remonstrance is signed by two-thirds of the property owners residing on the lots abutting on the improvement, and representing two-thirds of the number of lineal feet of the improvement, all proceedings shall be abandoned. *Held*, that a resolution for the improvement of a street by paving the roadway between the curbs with either sheet asphalt or brick paving blocks or with bituminous macadam was unauthorized as not a compliance with the statutory requirement that the "kind" of improvement shall be specified.

4. Inasmuch as Burns' Ann. St. 1901, § 3508, relative to street improvements, and requiring the city engineer to prepare plans and specifications, gives him no authority to determine the character of the improvement or the materials to be used, a contract for a street improvement which left the character of the improvement, and the nature of some of the materials to be used, to the determination of the engineer, was invalid.

Appeal from Circuit Court, Wells County; James P. Hale, Special Judge.

Suit by Charles M. Miller against the city of Bluffton and another to enjoin the carrying out of a contract for a street improvement. From a judgment overruling demurrers to the complaint, defendants appeal. Affirmed.

C. E. Sturgis, J. H. C. Smith, and Elliott, Elliott & Littleton, for appellants. Wilson & Townley, Dailey, Simmons & Dailey, and W. H. Eichhorn, for appellee.

¶ 2. See Injunction, vol. 12, Cent. Dig. § 158.
[1] Rehearing denied.

ROBINSON, J. Suit by appellee, an abutting property owner, against appellant city and a contractor, to enjoin the carrying out of a contract for a street improvement. Demurrers to each of the two paragraphs of complaint were overruled, and, appellants refusing to plead further, the court rendered judgment against them for costs, and decreed a perpetual injunction.

It is first argued that this is a collateral attack, and cannot be sustained unless the proceedings are void for want of jurisdiction, and that, as a remedy by remonstrance and also by appeal is given, injunction will not lie. The authority to assess abutting property for a street improvement is purely statutory, and such statutes are to be strictly construed. The manner in which the statute provides the assessment shall be made is the measure of the city's power to make it. Whether this power has been exercised as the statute directs, presents a question in its nature jurisdictional. If the municipality attempts some other method other than that provided by the statute, or goes beyond the authority given, to that extent it is without jurisdiction and its acts are void. In such cases it is undertaking the exercise of an unauthorized power, which equity will enjoin. If mandatory provisions of the statute or charter have been disregarded in an ordinance, and a contract beyond the scope of municipal power entered into, the ordinance and contract are illegal, and an assessment made upon property through such proceedings would be illegal. It cannot be said that the remedy at law in such cases is as adequate or efficient as the remedy by injunction. It has been held, time and time again, that where statutes grant a municipality power to impose a burden upon private property, requiring the doing of some particular thing, in its nature jurisdictional, as a condition precedent to the right to impose such burden, the failure to do the thing required renders the proceeding void. If the act of the municipality is void because of a want of power to do the thing attempted, it is void because of a want of jurisdiction. See Sackett v. City of New Albany, 88 Ind. 473, 45 Am. Rep. 467; Barber Co. v. Edgerton, 125 Ind. 461, 25 N. E. 436; Board v. Gillies, 138 Ind. 667, 38 N. E. 40; Wickwire v. Elkhart, 144 Ind. 305, 43 N. E. 216; Case v. Johnson, 91 Ind. 477; Lowe v. Lawrenceburg, etc., Co. (Ind. Sup.) 69 N. E. 148; Spring Steel Co. v. City of Anderson (Ind. App.) 69 N. E. 404; Cleveland, etc., Ry. v. Jones, 20 Ind. App. 87, 50 N. E. 319; Adams v. Shelbyville, 154 Ind. 467, 495, 57 N. E. 114, 49 L. R. A. 797, 77 Am. St. Rep. 484; City of Fort Wayne v. Shoaff, 106 Ind. 66, 5 N. E. 403; Goring v. McTaggart, 92 Ind. 200; City of Delphi v. Startzman, 104 Ind. 343, 3 N. E. 937; 2 Dillon, Mun. Corp. (4th Ed.) §§ 908, 914; Smith, Mun. Corp. § 1242.

In Watson v. Sutherland, 5 Wall. 74, 18 L. Ed. 580, the rule is stated: "It is not enough that there is a remedy at law; it must be plain and adequate, or, in other words, as practical and efficient to the ends of justice and its prompt administration as the remedy in equity." This principle has been approved in this state in a number of cases. See Hart v. Hildebrandt, 30 Ind. App. 415, 66 N. E. 173, and cases cited; Meyer v. Boonville (Ind. Sup.) 70 N. E. 146; Dillon Mun. Corp. (4th Ed.) § 914. It is no longer necessary in this state that a plaintiff should show by averment and proof that he will suffer irreparable injury. In 3 Pomeroy's Equity (2d Ed.) § 1357, the author says: "Judges have been brought to see and acknowledge—contrary to the opinion held by Chancellor Kent—that the common-law theory of not interfering with persons until they shall have actually committed a wrong is fundamentally erroneous, and that a remedy which prevents a threatened wrong is in its essential nature better than a remedy which permits the wrong to be done and then attempts to pay for it by the pecuniary damages which a jury may assess." See Xenia Real Estate Co. v. Macy, 147 Ind. 568, 47 N. E. 147; Champ v. Kendrick, 130 Ind. 549, 30 N. E. 787; Bishop v. Moorman, 98 Ind. 1, 49 Am. Rep. 731.

The proceedings of the council leading up to and including the contract are questioned first upon the ground that the declaratory resolution and notice for bids failed to specify the kind of improvement and invite competitive bidding thereon. In the original resolution, and in the notice inviting bids, the street was to be improved by paving the roadway between the curbs with either sheet asphalt pavement upon a concrete foundation, or brick paving blocks upon a concrete foundation, or with bituminous macadam, as the council should determine after receiving the bids. The statute provides that the common council, desiring to make a street improvement, "shall order the same by the adoption of a resolution declaring such improvement to be necessary, and stating the kind, size, location and terminal points thereof, and fixing a date upon which bids will be received for the construction of said improvement." It is further provided that the council shall open the bids upon the date fixed and award the contract, that it may take the bids under advisement, and may reject any and all bids, and that any property owner whose lands shall be assessed for the improvement may remonstrate "against said improvement at any time before the letting of the contract," and if the remonstrance "is signed by two-thirds of the property owners, residing upon the lots abutting on such improvement, and representing two-thirds of the number of lineal feet of such improvement, then all further proceedings shall be abandoned." Acts 1901, p. 534, c. 231 (Burns' Ann. St. 1901, § 3623a). This statute manifestly was intended to and does curtail the power formerly given to city councils in making street improvements on their own motion. For the first time abutting property owners who are to pay for the improvement are given the right to defeat the kind of improvement the council proposes to make. This gives to the declaratory resolution and notice an importance which it did not before possess. The statute does not require that the abutting owners shall state any reasons for objecting to the kind of improvement proposed, but, if the number mentioned object to the particular kind before the contract is let, the matter is at an end. The property owners have the right to know at the outset the kind of improvement selected. If they remonstrate, they must do it before the contract is let. The declaratory resolution states that the street is to be improved in one of three ways as the council shall determine after receiving bids. The acceptance of some particular bid and the letting of the contract may be practically one and the same act. If effect is to be given the language used in the section, it cannot be said that the "kind of improvement" means that the improvement should be described as the paving of a roadway, the construction of a sidewalk, and the like. The statute means that the council shall state in the declaratory resolution, not only that the improvement is necessary, but shall state the nature and character of the improvement. The council is to secure definite bids for a particular kind of work. It is a matter of common knowledge that there are various kinds of street improvements, and the statute does not say that the council shall state a number of kinds of improvements, one of which, after bids are received, may be selected, but it directs that the declaratory resolution shall state the kind of improvement, and shall fix a date upon which bids will be received for the construction of that improvement. After the kind of improvement has been selected and property owners given an opportunity to be heard, bids are to be asked and the contract let. The power possessed by the council is whatever the statute gives it. The mode prescribed excludes all others. Any method adopted other than that named in the statute is void, because there is no power to adopt it. A method actually adopted might bring as good or better results than the one provided. But that is not the question. The only question is, what method has the Legislature prescribed, and has the council followed that method? It is purely a question of power. The Legislature has delegated to the council the power to charge the property of individuals with the expense of the improvement, and the steps to be taken are not merely directory, but are mandatory, and are to be strictly pursued. The property owner may insist upon the observance of every statutory requirement which will in the least tend to his protection. An order for a street improvement "is in some respects," said the court in Merrill v. Abbott, 62 Ind. 549, "analogous to a judicial act, and ought clearly and explicitly to prescribe what it authorizes to be done as regards the contemplated improvement to which it is intended to apply."

If the council may designate more than one kind of improvement, it may designate all kinds. We do not think it can be said that the competitive bidding contemplated by the statute would necessarily be secured where bids are invited on various kinds of improvements. In such a case the bidders would not be put on terms of perfect equality, because they would not be bidding on the same proposition on the same terms. It is true the contract is to be let to the best bidder, not necessarily the lowest, but the bid accepted is to be the best bid, not merely for the improvement of the street, but the best bid for improving the street in the manner already designated by the council. Such a plan could result in injury to the property holder. In Wickwire v. City of Elkhart, 144 Ind. 305, 43 N. E. 216, the court approved the following: "It is, however, the duty of the courts to resolve doubts against the validity of the exercise of the authority wherever there is any substantial deviation at all, and to restrain proceedings, in cases where there is not an exact compliance with the statute, only when it clearly and unmistakably appears that no possible injury has resulted to the landowner, or could result to him." See Helms v. Bell, 155 Ind. 502, 58 N. E. 707; Coggeshall v. City of Des Moines, 78 Iowa, 235, 41 N. W. 617, 42 N. W. 650; Fones Bros. Co. v. Erb, 54 Ark. 645, 17 S. W. 7, 13 L. R. A. 353; Wrought Iron Bridge Co. v. Board, 19 Ind. App. 672, 48 N. E. 1050; Mazet v. City of Pittsburgh, 137 Pa. 548, 20 Atl. 693; Fairbanks v. City of North Bend (Neb.) 94 N. W. 537; Ricketson v. Milwaukee (Wis.) 81 N. W. 864, 47 L. R. A. 685; Kneeland v. Milwaukee, 18 Wis. 413; Wells v. Burnham, 20 Wis. 112; Kneeland v. Furlong, 20 Wis. 437.

In Connersville v. Merrill, 14 Ind. App. 303, 42 N. E. 1112, cited by counsel for appellant, the general character of the walk was to be of stone, and bids were invited on three different kinds of stone. One set of specifications would, no doubt, have been sufficient. The only question raised was as to the uncertainty with reference to the bidding, and it was there held that the property holder "had the benefit of competition on each brand or special kind of the general material to be used." This language, we think, distinguishes that case from the case at bar, where there was no general material specified, but the materials in the kinds of improvement designated were entirely different. Moreover, the act of 1901 gives the landholder a right with reference to the kind of improvement which he did not have under the act in force in the above case, and the statute should be construed to make this new right effective.

The proceedings of the council are questioned also on the ground that certain powers and duties were unlawfully delegated to the city civil engineer. In the specifications for a bituminous macadam street, which specifications are made a part of the contract entered into for the improvement, it is provided, among other things, that on top of a certain foundation "shall be sprinkled a thin layer of Warren's No. 1 semi-liquid composition, same to be fluid enough to unite with the cold stone, or some other preparation of coal tar, free from petroleum or other foreign substance and of equal and uniform density and quality, same to be determined by the city engineer. Over this shall be spread, by pouring, a heavy coating of Warren's No. 24 'Puritan Brand' hard macadam bituminous cement or other preparation of coal tar, free from petroleum or other foreign substances, and of equal uniform density and quality, same to be determined by the city engineer." Upon the above foundation is to be a wearing surface, "which shall be two inches thick and composed of carefully selected and very hard limestone, or other hard stone, acceptable to the city engineer, and gravel ranging in size from one inch in diameter to an impalpable powder mixed with sand, and containing all sizes and grades, * * * the stone and sand shall be heated * * * not higher than 300 degrees Fahrenheit, it shall then be thoroughly mixed by machinery with Warren's Puritan brand No. 19 bituminous macadam composition or some other preparation of coal tar, free from petroleum or other foreign substances and of equal and uniform density and quality, same to be determined by the city engineer, * * * the amount of said composition to be used shall be 9 per cent. to 18 per cent. by weight; the exact proportion of materials will depend upon the character of materials, the location, grade and traffic of the street. * * * After the rolling of the wearing surface there should be spread a thin coating of Warren's quick drying bituminous flush coat composition or some other preparation of coal tar free from petroleum or other foreign substance and of equal and uniform density and quality, same to be determined by the city engineer. * * * Before the final rolling shall take place, a slight coating of coarse sand or finely crushed screenings shall be sprinkled on the pavement, the screenings may be increased in size if ordered by the engineer. * * * On side hills, where ordered by the engineer, there may be rolled into the surface a thin layer of stone chips." Bidders proposing to use other brands of material than those mentioned in the specifications should file samples with the engineer at least three days before the letting, "or such bids will not be read or considered, nor will they be considered unless the same are approved by the engineer and common council." The statute gives to the engineer no authority whatever to determine the character of the improvement, or to determine the materials to be used. He prepares plans and specifications for public improvements when directed to do so by the council (Burns' Ann. St. 1901, § 3508), but these plans and specifications become a part of the contract which the city makes for the improvement, and are with reference to the kind of improvement and materials to be used as determined by the council. It is not a delegation of power to leave to the engineer the execution of a work which the council has ordered to be done in a particular way. But the power to determine that an improvement shall be made, or the manner in which it shall be made, is a public power conferred by the Legislature on the legislative department of the municipal government, and cannot be delegated to any officer or any other department, but must be exercised in strict conformity with the statute conferring the power. The Legislature evidently intended to place the responsibility of determining the plan of the improvement upon the common council. As the expenses of the improvement are to be paid by the property owners, the power to make the improvement is a power of taxation, and a court is not authorized to say that such sovereign authority may be exercised by any officer or officers except those whom the statute in terms designates. The council was without authority to delegate to the engineer the power to select any of the materials to be used in making the improvement, but it attempted to do this when it delegated to him the power to order used at his discretion these various Warren's compounds or other compounds of equal density or quality. It is the duty of the council to determine the nature of the improvement to be made. Nor is there any authority for giving the engineer a voice in the letting of the contract. The statute plainly directs that when the bids are received the council shall let the contract to the best bidder. Selecting the kind of material to be used cannot be said to be a matter of detail which may be left to the engineer, nor can it be said that selecting the material is a ministerial duty. In Smith v. Duncan, 77 Ind. 92, an ordinance provided that a pavement should be of wooden blocks, "but," said the court, "of what wood the blocks shall be, how they shall be laid, to what grade, and every minutia of the work, is left to be determined by the engineer. The law does not contemplate the delegation of such powers to that officer." See Thompson v. Schermerhorn, 6 N. Y. 92, 55 Am. Dec. 386; California Imp. Co. v. Reynolds, 123 Cal. 88, 55 Pac. 802; Hydes v. Joyes, 67 Ky. 464, 96 Am. Dec. 311; McCrowell v. City of Bristol, 89 Va. 652, 16 S. E. 867, 20 L. R. A. 653; Bolton v. Gilleran, 105 Cal. 244, 38 Pac. 881, 45 Am. St. Rep. 33; City of St. Louis v. Clemens, 43 Mo. 395; Birdsall v. Clark, 73 N. Y. 73, 29 Am. Rep. 105; City of Indianapolis v. Lawyer, 38 Ind. 348; Dillon, Mun. Corp. (4th Ed.) §§ 96, 779; Smith, Mun. Corp. § 564.

In Hitchcock v. Galveston, 96 U. S. 341, 24 L. Ed. 659, the council directed the pavements to be constructed of one or the other of several materials, and gave abutting lot owners the privilege of selecting the kind, and reserving to the chairman of their committee authority to select in case the lot owners failed. The council having provided for the work and for the bidding, the execution of a contract on behalf of the city for doing the work was a ministerial act which the council might direct should be performed by the mayor and chairman of the committee on streets and alleys. It is there stated that a municipality may do its ministerial work by agents, and that there was no unlawful delegation of power, "but," said the court, "if there had been, the contract was ratified by the council after it was made."

Counsel cite also the case of Mayor v. Stewart, 92 Md. 535, 48 Atl. 165, where the council had selected asphalt as the material with which the street was to be paved, and permitted the engineer to use vitrified brick in lieu of asphalt in the gutters, and upon such other portions of the street as in his judgment might be necessary or advisable; but the council had designated both materials by ordinance, and the only discretion given the engineer was to use one in preference to the other at particular places. In that case it is held that "the power to determine what material should be used in paving a street is a legislative power, and cannot be transferred by the city council to any one else." In the case at bar we do not think it can be said that the discretion given the engineer was, "with respect to the details of doing the work, 'necessary discretion in a workman employed to do a work,'" as stated in the above case.

In Ray v. City of Jeffersonville, 90 Ind. 567, the statute expressly imposed upon the engineer the duty of making the assessments in certain cases, and the case is to be distinguished from the case of Smith v. Duncan, 77 Ind. 92. In Taber v. Grafmiller, 109 Ind. 206, 9 N. E. 721, the council ordered that certain sidewalks "be graded to a width of ten feet, and paved with brick to a width of six feet," and that "said improvement shall be made under the supervision and to the satisfaction of the city civil engineer, and in accordance with plans and specifications" on file in the engineer's office, and that the engineer should set the proper stakes. It was held there was no delegation of authority, that there was a "specification of the nature of the work," that the resolution clearly implied that there was an existing grade previously established, that the specification that the pavement should be of brick was sufficiently certain, as "the just and reasonable implication is that the brick shall be paving brick of the kind ordinarily used." We do not understand that this case overrules Smith v. Duncan, 77 Ind. 92, or that there is any conflict in the views announced in the two cases.

In Swift v. City of St. Louis (Mo. Sup.) 79 S. W. 172, the board of public improvements gave notice that on a certain day it would consider the improvement of a street with either one of four kinds of material specified, and afterwards recommended to the municipal assembly an ordinance for the improvement with bituminous macadam. A contract was made under the ordinance. The specifications of material to be used were certain compositions known as "Warren's Puritan Brands," but no power was given the engineer in that case to use any other composition which he might think equally as good.

We think the proceedings of the council were invalid because of the failure of the resolution and notice to specify the kind of improvement contemplated, and because certain powers were unlawfully delegated to the civil engineer.

Judgment affirmed.

(33 Ind. A. 124)

TERRE HAUTE ELECTRIC CO. v. WATSON.

(Appellate Court of Indiana, Division No. 2. May 10, 1904.)

JURORS — CHALLENGES—PERMANENT INJURIES —PLEADING SPECIAL DAMAGES—CROSS-EXAMINATION.

1. Overruling a challenge to a juror for cause is not ground for reversal, the juror having been excused on a peremptory challenge, and it not appearing that the party exhausted his peremptory challenges.

2. Averment in a complaint that plaintiff's injuries are permanent, and will leave him in a crippled condition for life, is sufficient to admit evidence of impairment of earning capacity.

3. Questions calculated to test witness' knowledge of cars, to enable the jury to weigh his testimony given in chief that the car was in perfect order the night before the accident, are proper on cross-examination.

Appeal from Circuit Court, Clay County; P. O. Colliver, Judge.

Action by Thomas Watson against the Terre Haute Electric Company. Judgment for plaintiff. Defendant appeals. Affirmed.

A. W. Knight, for appellant. Coffey & McGregor, for appellee.

COMSTOCK, J. Appellee recovered in the court below a verdict and judgment thereon in the sum of $1,000 for personal injuries alleged to have been sustained on account of a collision between one of appellant's street cars, in which he was riding as a passenger, and a switching train on the Terre Haute & Indianapolis Railroad Company. The cause was put at issue by general denial. The only error relied on for reversal is the

¶ 2. See Damages, vol. 15, Cent. Dig. § 443.

overruling of appellant's motion for a new trial. The first reason set out in said motion which is discussed is the third, and is the overruling of defendant's challenge for cause to one Archer, a juror called on the trial of the cause. Said juror on his voir dire answered as follows: "Q. Have you, Mr. Archer, any prejudice against this street car company? A. I think I have. Q. I will ask you if your prejudice against the street car company is such as would prevent you from giving the defendant a fair and impartial trial in this case according to the law and the evidence? A. No, sir. Q. Do you think you could fairly and impartially try the case as if you had no prejudice against this company? A. Yes. Q. On what grounds are you prejudiced against the defendant? A. On account of the strike. Q. Have you any prejudice against the company in this case? A. No, sir." Defendant's counsel, in objecting, said: "I challenge the juror for cause for the reason that in answer to a question by the attorney for the defendant he states that he is prejudiced against the defendant." The court overruled the challenge made by defendant, to which defendant excepted, and counsel for defendant excused Mr. Archer. The defendant thereupon objected to the competency of said Archer to serve as a juror, and stated to the court, as ground for challenge, that said Archer had stated in answer to a question by defendant's counsel that he was prejudiced against the defendant, but the court overruled the defendant's challenge, to which ruling the defendant at the time excepted, and then peremptorily challenged and excused said juror. The decisions all recognize the principle "that the object of the law is to procure impartial and unbiased persons for jurors." Juries should be devoid of prejudice. Upon this plain proposition we cite a few Indiana cases: Keiser v. Lines, 57 Ind. 431; Fletcher v. Crist, 139 Ind. 126, 38 N. E. 472; Chandler v. Ruebelt, 83 Ind. 139; Stoots v. State, 108 Ind. 415, 9 N. E. 380; Brown v. State, 70 Ind. 576; Elliot, C. J., in Pearcy v. Ins. Co., 111 Ind. 61, 12 N. E. 98, 60 Am. Rep. 673; Block v. State, 100 Ind. 357. Conceding, without deciding, that the court erred in holding the juror qualified, were the substantial rights of appellant prejudiced by the action of the court? Only errors affecting the substantial rights of litigants are cause for reversal. Horner's Ann. St. § 398. Archer did not sit as a juror. A jury was subsequently selected, and it does not appear that appellant's peremptory challenges were exhausted. It is contended by appellant that the peremptory challenge did not cure the error of the court in overruling the challenge for cause. Brown v. State, supra, and Fletcher v. Crist, supra, are cited in support of this claim. These cases so hold, but in Siberry v. State, 149 Ind. 684, 39 N. E. 936, Brown v. State is expressly overruled, and Fletcher v. Crist, supra, is modified so far as it follows and recognizes Brown v. State, supra. We quote from Siberry v. State: "As long as he had accepted the jury without having exhausted his peremptory challenges, the error, if error it was, of forcing him to use two of his peremptory challenges to get rid of the two alleged incompetent jurors, did no harm, and hence will be disregarded by the express terms of the statute." Upon the subject of reversal of judgment for harmless error, see, also, Union Mutual Life Ins. Co. v. Buchanan, 100 Ind. 63; McGee v. State, 103 Ind. 444, 3 N. E. 139; Walling v. Burgess, 122 Ind. 299, 22 N. E. 419, 23 N. E. 1076, 7 L. R. A. 481; Rinehart v. Niles, 3 Ind. App. 553, 30 N. E. 1, and cases cited.

During the trial the plaintiff was asked how much money he was able to earn before he received his injury. Defendant objected on the ground that the evidence thus sought to be elicited tended to establish special damages not prayed for in the complaint, and, not being alleged, it was error to admit evidence thereof.

The complaint alleges that plaintiff's "injuries are permanent, and will leave him in a crippled condition for life." An averment of permanent disability is, as a rule, sufficient to admit evidence of impairment of earning capacity. Watson on Damages for Personal Injuries, 639, 640; Morgan v. Kendall, 124 Ind. 454, 24 N. E. 143, 9 L. R. A. 445. See, also, Logansport v. Justice, 74 Ind. 378, 39 Am. Rep. 79; C., C., C. & St. L. Ry. Co. v. Gray, 148 Ind. 266, 46 N. E. 675. The purpose of alleging special damages is to give notice thereof that the adverse party may be prepared to meet them. The allegations of the complaint are sufficient for that purpose.

It is further contended that the cross-examination of appellant's witness Henry Kerney was contrary to the established rules of procedure, and injurious to the appellant. This witness was the car inspector of appellant. He testified on direct examination that the car upon which the appellee was riding at the time of the injury was inspected by him on the night before the injury, and was in perfect order. On cross-examination he testified that he was an expert not only in examining cars, but in their operation. All the questions about which the appellant complains were calculated to test his knowledge of cars to enable the jury to weigh his testimony given in chief when he said this particular car was in perfect order on the night before the injury. This was proper cross-examination. Boyle v. State, 105 Ind. 4[illegible], 5 N. E. 203, 55 Am. Rep. 218; Hyland v. M[illegible]ner, 99 Ind. 308; Wachstetter v. State, [illegible] Ind. 290, 50 Am. Rep. 94. The extent to which the cross-examination may go is largely in the discretion of the trial court, and a judgment will not be reversed unless the court abused such discretion to the injury of the party complaining. City of South end v. Hardy, 98 Ind. 577, 49 Am. Rep.)2; Besette v. State, 101 Ind. 85.

We have considered all the questions dis- ıssed.

Judgment affirmed.

Ind. A. 138)

ꞮDIANAPOLIS ST. RY. CO. v. BORDENCHECKER.

Appellate Court of Indiana, Division No. 2. May 12, 1904.)

REET RAILWAYS — CHILDREN ON STREETS — NEGLIGENCE — CONTRIBUTORY NEGLIGENCE— PERSONS NON SUI JURIS — PRESUMPTIONS — BURDEN OF PROOF — TRIAL — OVERRULING CHALLENGES—HARMLESS ERROR.

1. An infant 2½ years old is too young to be gligent himself, or have the negligence of hers imputed to him.

2. In an action against a street railroad for juries to a child on the street, the burden of owing negligence is on plaintiff.

3. Negligence, like any other fact, may be oven by direct or circumstantial evidence, d reasonable inferences may be drawn by the ry from the facts proven.

4. The fact that a street car was not stopped ıtil its rear end had reached a point beyond ɛ place of collision, variously estimated to ve been from three rods to 160 feet, is evince tending to show a high rate of speed.

5. Servants in charge of a street car have no ht to assume, as in case of an adult, that a ild 2½ years of age, approaching the car, will rn back from impending peril.

6. The question whether or not a motorman a street car sounded the gong before the car uck plaintiff is for the jury, though the conting evidence is direct on the one hand and rely negative on the other.

7. In an action against a street railway for iuries to a child 2¼ years of age, who collidwith a car, evidence *held* sufficient to supt a finding of defendant's negligence.

8. Where a party in a civil as well as in a minal case accepts the jury without having hausted his peremptory challenges, error, if y, in forcing him to use peremptory chalges, is harmless.

Appeal from Superior Court, Marion Coun- Vinson Carter, Judge.

Action by William Bordenchecker, by next end, against the Indianapolis Street Rail- y Company. From a judgment for plain- ', defendant appeals. Affirmed.

Ŧ. Winter and W. H. Latta, for appellant. E. Fenstermacher and W. W. Caffrey, appellee.

ƆOMSTOCK, J. Appellee, an infant, by next friend, sued appellant to recover nages for personal injuries. The comint was in two paragraphs. The first ırges that at the time plaintiff received injuries the defendant had laid tracks l was engaged in operating a street railу upon the streets of Indianapolis; that intiff was on one of its tracks, and on acnt of his youth could not realize the dan- ; that defendant could have seen plain- more than 1,500 feet, and by using or- ary care could have stopped the car before striking plaintiff, but that the defendant negligently ran its car against him without giving warning of its approach, and inflicted the injuries of which he complains. The charging part of the second paragraph differs from the first in alleging that plaintiff, instead of standing on, was standing within one foot of, the defendant's track at the time of the collision. A demurrer to each paragraph of the complaint was overruled. The cause was put at issue by general denial, and trial by jury, and resulted in a verdict and judgment in favor of appellee for $300. The overruling of appellant's motion for a new trial is relied upon for a reversal of the judgment.

The first reason for a new trial discussed is that the verdict is not sustained by sufficient evidence, and for that reason is contrary to law. The plaintiff, as shown by the evidence, was 2½ years old, too young to be negligent himself or to have the negligence of others imputed to him. If, therefore, there is evidence fairly tending to show that appellant's negligence caused plaintiff's injuries, this court cannot disturb the judgment for the reason for a new trial under consideration. The evidence shows that the accident occurred on Tenth street, a street in the city of Indianapolis, running east and west, and over which appellant maintains a double track. Said street at the place of collision is intersected by the following streets: Brookside avenue, from the north at an angle; Highland and Stilwell streets from the south. The street is 35 feet wide from curb to curb. The distance from the curb to the first rail of the south track is 10 feet and to the first rail of the second track is 20 feet. The view of the track from said place of collision is unobstructed for a distance of a mile. On the day of the accident the mother of the plaintiff sent him and his sister, whose age is not given, but who is spoken of as a little girl, to a grocery on the corner of Highland avenue for a loaf of bread. The home of the children was on Brookside avenue, to which they were returning when the plaintiff received his injuries. Appellee introduced no witness who saw the collision. Ida Geiger, a witness in behalf of appellee, testified in part as follows: "In October, 1901, I was living on Brookside avenue. A child was injured on Tenth street during that month about twenty minutes of twelve, noon. I went to the drug store, and saw a child coming from McLane's grocery at the corner of Highland avenue and Tenth street. That is a short distance—hardly a half square—from Brookside avenue. When I saw the child he was coming from the grocery; just leaving the sidewalk; almost between the first track going east; almost ready to step onto the track. He was going north. I was going south. His little sister was with him, and they had a loaf of bread in their arms. I spoke to them. I saw a car

5. See Street Railroads, vol. 44, Cent. Dig. § 202.

approaching, probably a block away, coming from the city. I went to a meat market at the corner of Stilwell street at the south side of Tenth, and the next I saw of the little boy was after the car had struck him. I remained in the meat market a few moments, and when I came out the car had stopped, and I saw the motorman or conductor picking up a child quite a distance back of the car. * * * The boy lay almost three rods back of the car. * * * I heard no gong sounded. When I got there, the motorman had the child in his arms. The motorman said it was a narrow escape for both of them. When I passed the children, the little girl was about one step in front of the boy. * * * I did not see the car hit the child. * * * The bakery is at Highland avenue. When I saw the children they were coming from the bakery. * * * I did not see them come out of the bakery. I saw them leave the sidewalk. They were between the curb and the track in the roadway. They were going diagonally in the direction of Brookside avenue, northwest, and I was going southwest." Daisy McLane testified as follows: "I have a grocery at the corner of Tenth street and Highland avenue. The plaintiff came in the grocery and got a loaf of bread just before the accident. Their home is northwest of my store. I saw the car pass the door just after they left. I do not remember of hearing the gong. After the car went by, I went out, and the plaintiff was in front of the drug store near the track." There was no evidence as to the speed of the car. No one connected with appellant corporation as agent or employé testified. Appellant introduced but one witness. He testified that appellee left the sidewalk, and immediately began to run diagonally in the direction of the track, passing over a distance of approximately 20 feet; that at the time the child began to run towards the track the car was 65 feet from the place of collision; that as soon as plaintiff started to run in the direction of the track the motorman began sounding his gong, and appeared to be arranging the brake—that is, going through movements like he was applying the brake (the witness could not see the brake); and continued his efforts to stop the car until the child had been struck by the car, after which said witness did "not look at the actions of the motorman." He also testified that the plaintiff ran against the side of the car about five feet from the front end of the car proper and three feet from the ground. Appellant insists that the testimony of this witness clearly exonerates appellant from fault. The burden of showing appellant's negligence was upon appellee. The negligence of the adverse party is not presumed in favor of one upon whom the burden rests of establishing it, but, like any other fact, it may be proven by direct or circumstantial evidence. Juries are warranted, too, in drawing reasonable inferences from facts proven. The car was a small closed car, and therefore might be promptly stopped, if not running at a high rate of speed. At a distance of a block away the motorman could have seen the plaintiff moving toward and apparently about to cross the track. The facts do not show a case of a child standing by the track without evidence of an intention to cross. It cannot be presumed that a child of plaintiff's age will exercise discretion or caution. There was evidence from which the jury could reasonably conclude that the motorman, in the exercise of ordinary care, could have seen the appellee and stopped the car in time to have avoided the collision. The fact that the car was not stopped until its rear end had reached a point beyond the place of collision, variously shown by the evidence to have been from 3 rods to 160 feet, is evidence tending to show a high rate of speed. Negligence has been ascribed to the running of an electric car over a crossing at a high rate of speed, or without having the car under control, and using proper means to stop it if occasion requires. 2 Thompson, Con. Neg. § 1397. Appellant's servants had no right to assume, as in the case of an adult, that plaintiff would turn back from an impending peril. Elwood v. Ross, 26 Ind. App. 258, 58 N. E. 535.

It was for the jury to pass upon a conflict of evidence as to whether or not the motorman sounded the gong before the accident—a conflict raised by direct and by negative evidence, but still a conflict. The presumption is that they found the failure of appellant to give warning in accordance with the averments of the complaint. We cannot say that the finding that appellant was negligent is without the support of evidence.

Other reasons set out in the motion for a new trial are that the court erred in overruling the challenge of the defendant to the jurors Pierson and Martin. Section 1450a, Burns' Ann. St. 1901, is as follows: "Additional jurors in certain counties.—1. That in counties having a population of over one hundred and fifty thousand according to the last preceding United States census, and in which there is a circuit court, and a superior court having more than one judge, the clerk shall whenever he shall draw one or more petit juries for such courts or either of them, draw twelve additional jurors in the same manner as regular petit jurors are drawn for such courts, and such twelve additional jurors shall be and remain during the term for which said juries are drawn, as special talesmen subject to call to the jury in any or either of said courts. When the regular panel shall have been exhausted in any or either of said courts, or is insufficient from any cause, the bailiff shall call such special talesmen to fill such jury, and bystanders shall not be called until said detail of special talesmen shall have been exhausted, and when any member of any regular panel in any or either of said courts shall be challenged off of said panel for any reason, such juror shall take his place among said special talesmen and may be called for service on the jury in any other one of the said courts: provided, that the provisions of this act shall not be construed so as to apply to, alter or repeal the laws of Indiana providing for special juries, for juries by agreement, or struck juries or for special venires, and service as such special talesmen shall not be cause for challenge during the term for which they are drawn." In the cause before us the defendant challenged two jurors who had been called by the judge, and who, after being so called, had not only served in the room in which they were called, but had also served in the circuit court. They were challenged upon the ground that they had served on a jury in the county within a year, and the challenge was overruled, and thereupon the appellant challenged the jurors peremptorily. It is claimed that this was error under section 1450a, supra, and sections 1450, 1451, 1, and 529 of Burns' Ann. St. 1901. Error to warrant a reversal of a judgment must be harmful. Appellant accepted the jury without having exhausted its peremptory challenges. "As long as he had accepted the jury without having exhausted his peremptory challenges, the error, if error it was, of forcing him to use two of his peremptory challenges to get rid of the two alleged incompetent jurors, did no harm, and herein will be disregarded by the express terms of the statute." Siberry v. The State, 149 Ind. 684, 39 N. E. 936; Terre Haute, etc., Co. v. Watson (present term of this court) 70 N. E. 993. Counsel for appellant admit that there are cases in this state in which it has been held that the error in overruling a challenge for cause is harmless if the complaining party has peremptory challenges unexhausted; but note that the rule was announced in criminal cases, in which the party has the right to a large number of peremptory challenges, and in all of which cases the party had more than one peremptory challenge remaining at the time the jury was selected and sworn. The rule has also been made to apply to civil cases. Fletcher v. Crist, 139 Ind. 121, 38 N. E. 472, recognizing a different rule, was in Siberry v. State, supra, modified to conform to the opinion in the case last named. Apart from the modification of the opinion in Fletcher v. Crist, supra, we see no stronger reason for the application of the rule in a criminal than in a civil cause.

Judgment affirmed.

(Ind. A. 120)

MacMILLAN et al. v. CLEMENTS et al.

(Appellate Court of Indiana, Division No. 2. May 10, 1904.)

S — MORTGAGES — LIMITATIONS—PAYMENT OF INTEREST—EQUITY—BILL—PARTIES —DEMURRER.

In an action for the foreclosure of a mortgage and other equitable relief, the bill is not defective for failure to join parties in interest as parties defendant who are joined as complainants to the bill.

2. A payment of interest on a note constitutes a sufficient acknowledgment or promise to pay to toll the statute of limitations.

3. Where a sufficient payment on a note secured by mortgage was made to take the note out of the statute of limitations, such payment was effective to prevent the mortgage securing the debt from being barred.

Appeal from Circuit Court, Jackson County; T. B. Buskirk, Judge.

Action by Heloise MacMillan and others against James S. Clements and others. From a judgment in favor of defendants, plaintiffs appeal. Reversed.

O. H. Montgomery and W. T. Branaman, for appellants. Long & Long and Elliott, Elliott & Littleton, for appellees.

WILEY, P. J. The appellants, who were plaintiffs below, sued the appellees upon a note and to foreclose a mortgage on real estate. It is averred in the complaint that on the 6th day of April, 1873, one Samuel Gillespie, who has since died, and the appellee Sarah T. Gillespie, by their promissory note promised to pay Mary J. Gillespie, three years after date, $1,000, with interest at the rate of 6 per cent. per annum; that said note is due and remains unpaid; that at the time of the execution of the said note said Samuel Gillespie and Sarah T. Gillespie executed a mortgage on certain real estate to secure the payment thereof, which said mortgage was duly recorded; that on the 14th day of November, 1874, the said Mary J. Gillespie died testate, the owner of said note and mortgage; that by the terms of her will the Pennsylvania Company for Insurance on Lives and Granting Annuities was made executor of her last will and testament and trustee thereunder of said Mary J. Gillespie, with full power to have, hold, manage, and control her entire estate in trust until the death of said Samuel Gillespie: that said company duly qualified, and assumed the duties as said executor and trustee, and as such held, controlled, and managed said note and mortgage in trust until the death of said Samuel Gillespie; that by the terms and provisions of the last will and testament the children of the said Samuel Gillespie living, and the children living of such of his children as might be dead at his death, became the absolute owners of said note and mortgage; that said Samuel Gillespie died on the 6th day of December, 1899; that said executor and trustee collected of and from the makers of said note the interest thereon annually until the 6th day of September, 1899; that said Samuel Gillespie, at his death, left surviving him only three children, who are the plaintiffs in this action; that the makers of said note, from the date thereof, annually made a payment of $60 thereon each and every year until the 6th day

¶ 1. See Limitation of Actions, vol. 33, Cent. Dig. § 633.

of September, 1899, on which date the last of said payments was made by them; that on the 8th day of April, 1900, pursuant to the terms and provisions of said last will and testament, and in compliance with the decree of court in settlement of said trust, said executor and trustee assigned, by written assignment, said note and mortgage to the plaintiffs in this action, and indorsed said note to them by writing on the back thereof, and delivered said note and mortgage to them on that date. The complaint further avers that since the execution and recordation of said mortgage the appellee James S. Clements has purchased, and now claims some interest in, said mortgaged premises by virtue of sheriff and tax sales, all of which are subsequent, junior, and inferior to said mortgage of appellants; that the appellee Carrie Clements is the wife of the appellee James S. Clements, and that they are made parties to this action so that they may be required to assert any interest to such mortgaged premises that they or either of them have, or claim to have; that at the time said mortgage was executed the mortgagors owned only the west one-third of the real estate embraced in the mortgage, and by mistake in the written description in said mortgage it was made to describe the west two-thirds of said real estate, and that said mortgagors intended only to mortgage the west one-third thereof. The defendants each separately demurred to the complaint upon two grounds: (1) That there was a defect of parties defendant, in that Heloise MacMillan, Pink G. Holmes, and Mary G. Trohs are necessary parties defendant; and (2) that the amended complaint did not state facts sufficient to constitute a cause of action. These demurrers were sustained, and, the appellants refusing to plead further, judgment was entered against them for costs.

The demurrer on account of a defect of parties defendant is not well taken, for the persons named as being necessary parties defendant were the plaintiffs below and appellants here. The question presented by the facts pleaded is this: Does the payment of interest on a promissory note postpone the running of the statute of limitations? That question is answered by the authorities in this state, for it has been held that payment of principal and payment of interest stand upon the same footing as affecting the limitation of action. Payment is regarded as an acknowledgment of an existing obligation, and from such acknowledgment a promise to pay may be implied. Whether payment be a part of the principal or the interest, it is an acknowledgment of an existing indebtedness, from which the promise to pay will be implied. Brudi v. Trentman, 16 Ind. App. 512, 44 N. E. 932; Koontz v. Hammond, 21 Ind. App. 76, 51 N. E. 506; Meitzler v. Todd et al., 12 Ind. App. 381, 39 N. E. 1046, 54 Am. St. Rep. 531; Conwell v. Buchanan, 7 Blackf. 537. As was said in the case first cited, "Each payment starts the statute afresh from its date." The obligation being thus kept alive, the next inquiry is, is a mortgage securing its payment revived and kept alive as a security? It is the law that a payment upon a note secured by mortgage, if sufficient to take the note out of the operation of the statute of limitations, will have a like effect upon the mortgage, and, so long as any part of the debt remains unpaid, and not barred, the lien of the mortgage continues unimpaired. Bottles et al. v. Miller, 112 Ind. 584, 14 N. E. 728; Hibernian Banking Ass'n v. Commercial Nat. Bank (Ill.) 41 N. E. 919; Ewell v. Daggs, 108 U. S. 143, 2 Sup. Ct. 408, 27 L. Ed. 682; Schifferstein v. Allison, 123 Ill. 662, 15 N. E. 275. By the averment of the complaint the payors of the note and mortgagors paid the interest on the note up to September 6, 1899. This revived the debt, and the statute of limitations would commence to run from that date, and under the authorities neither the note nor mortgage is barred by the statute of limitations. The amended complaint was sufficient to withstand a demurrer.

The judgment is reversed, and the court below is directed to overrule the demurrer to the amended complaint.

(33 Ind. A. 400)

CLEVELAND, C., C. & ST. L. RY. CO. v. LINDSEY.[1]

(Appellate Court of Indiana. May 11, 1904.)

APPEAL—REHEARING—GROUNDS—BRIEFS.

1. Under Supreme and Appellate Court Rules 22, 23 (55 N. E. vi), regulating the form and contents of briefs on appeal, a rehearing will not be granted on a point not made or referred to in the original briefs.

On rehearing. Denied.

For former opinion, see 70 N. E. 283.

PER CURIAM. A rehearing is asked in this cause upon a point not made nor referred to in the original briefs. Under rules 22 and 23 of this court (55 N. E. vi) it is not permitted to raise such alleged error.

Petition overruled.

ROBY, J. (concurring). The complaint was in five paragraphs. Separate demurrers to each of them were overruled, and the ruling was excepted to. The record entry made is as follows: "And the court, being sufficiently advised, now overrules the demurrer to the amended complaint herein, to which ruling of the court the defendant at the time excepts." I concur in overruling the petition for a rehearing, and place my assent upon the ground that the exception taken is as broad as the ruling, and applies to each paragraph of the complaint. If it does not do so, the trial judge ought to have made five separate entries of his action, in order that appellant be enabled to pursue its rights by separate exceptions, all of which involves an absurdity, which I do not think the law requires.

[1] Transfer denied.

(33 Ind. App. 329)

SEXTON v. GOODWINE et al.

(Appellate Court of Indiana, Division No. 1. May 10, 1904.)

INTOXICATING LIQUORS — LICENSE — REMONSTRANCE—WITHDRAWAL OF NAMES—TIME.

1. A remonstrant against the granting of a liquor license cannot revoke his signature unless his right to withdraw is exercised prior to the first of the three days provided for the filing of the remonstrance.

On rehearing. Denied.

For former opinion, see 68 N. E. 929.

ROBINSON, J. Appellant's counsel earnestly insist upon a rehearing and the argument rests upon the following in Ludwig v. Cory, 158 Ind. 582, 64 N. E. 14: "The rights of voters remonstrating through the agency of another, or any of them, to entirely revoke or modify the power conferred upon their agent before the remonstrance is filed, must be conceded; and their further right, after the filing of the remonstrance, and before the beginning of the three-days limitation, of any or all such remonstrators, to withdraw their names from the document, as held in State v. Gerhardt, 145 Ind. 439 [44 N. E. 469, 33 L. R. A. 313]; White v. Prifogle, 146 Ind. 64 [44 N. E. 926], and Sutherland v. McKinney, 146 Ind. 611 [45 N. E. 1048], must also be granted." It will be noticed that in the Ludwig Case the right of remonstrators to withdraw was not directly in issue, but that the above language was used in considering the nature of the right exercised by a person signing a remonstrance, either in person or through an attorney in fact. In the Gerhardt Case was this question: "Has a remonstrant, after the expiration of the time within which a remonstrance may be filed, the absolute right without cause to withdraw from it, leaving the remonstrance, which theretofore had contained sufficient remonstrants to defeat the granting of the license, insufficient on account of the withdrawal of the signatures to accomplish the result?" After stating that this question must be answered in the negative, the court said: "Until the beginning of this three-days period, *whether the remonstrance has been placed on file or not*, any remonstrator must be deemed to have an absolute right, by some affirmative act of his own, to withdraw his name from such remonstrance. But, if this right is not exercised prior to the beginning of the first day of this three-days period, it no longer exists." (Our italics.) This language states a general rule with reference to withdrawals, and is plain. We cannot agree with the statement of counsel that, if anything can be said to be contained in the above language supporting appellee's position, it must be admitted to be obiter. We think the language used by the court is plain, and that it applies to the case at bar. The remonstrance in the case at bar could be filed on Friday (Flynn v. Taylor, 145 Ind. 533, 44 N. E. 540), but the Gerhardt Case plainly holds that the right to withdraw did not exist after the beginning of Friday.

Petition overruled.

¶ 1. See Intoxicating Liquors, vol. 29, Cent. Dig. § 67.

(33 Ind. App. 532)

MUNCIE PULP CO. v. KOONTZ.[1]

(Appellate Court of Indiana. May 11, 1904.)

WATERS AND WATER COURSES—RIPARIAN PROPRIETORS — RIGHTS — REASONABLE USE OF STREAM—INJURY TO LOWER PROPRIETOR—UNREASONABLE USE—HARMLESS ERROR—CONSIDERATION OF SPECIAL FINDINGS—RULINGS ON DEMURRER—TRIAL BY JURY.

1. In an action for damages for past injuries and for an injunction, where it was not claimed that the complaint did not show a cause of action for damages, and the only issue submitted was that of the past injury, and no equitable relief was included in the judgment, error in overruling a demurrer to the complaint for failure to state a cause of action for the injunction was harmless.

2. In an action for damages for past injuries and for an injunction, where the court, in its instructions, did not submit to the jury any questions except those relating to the action at law, and the only relief given by the judgment was an award of damages in accordance with the verdict, the action of the court in overruling a motion for a trial by the court without a jury is not available as error.

3. Riparian owners, both upper and lower, have the right to a reasonable use of a natural stream for manufacturing and for domestic and agricultural purposes; and so long as the use by an upper proprietor is reasonable the lower proprietor has no remedy for an impure condition of the water caused by such use, but if the impure condition of the water, or other substantial interference with the equal right of the lower proprietor, results from an unreasonable use by the upper proprietor, the latter is liable to the lower proprietor in damages.

4. Whether or not the discharge of waste or impure matter into a stream by an upper riparian proprietor is a reasonable use of the stream is a question of fact for the jury.

5. In examining instructions for the purpose of determining whether or not the giving thereof constituted reversible error, an appellate court may properly consider the apparent effect of the instructions on the jury by referring to the special findings in answer to interrogatories.

Appeal from Circuit Court, Henry County; W. O. Barnard, Judge.

Action by J. Harve Koontz against the Muncie Pulp Company. From a judgment for plaintiff, defendant appeals. Transferred from the Supreme Court. Affirmed.

Ryan & Ryan and A. W. Brady, for appellant. Forkner & Forkner, for appellee.

BLACK, J. This cause was transferred from the Supreme Court, having been commenced in the Delaware circuit court, from which the venue was changed to the court below. It was an action brought by the appellee, as the owner of lands which he used for agricultural purposes and as a place of residence, to recover damages for past injuries caused by the pollution of an ancient natural stream named "Buck Creek," which

[1] Rehearing denied.

bordered upon a portion of the lands and ran through another portion thereof, the pollution being caused by the discharge into the stream, some miles above the appellee's lands, of deleterious matter from the appellant's pulp mill, and also to obtain an injunction restraining the appellant from discharging the refuse matter from its factory. A demurrer to the complaint for the want of sufficient facts having been overruled, a number of paragraphs of answer and a reply were filed, and the cause was tried by jury, the court having overruled the motion of the appellant that the issues be tried by the court without the intervention of a jury, on the alleged ground that the cause was a suit for injunction in which the relief asked by way of damages was merely incidental to the relief asked by way of injunction, and that the cause was one which, prior to June 18, 1852, was of exclusive equitable jurisdiction. The jury returned a general verdict for the appellee, and assessed his damages at $1,600. The jury also returned special findings in answer to interrogatories submitted, by which special findings it was shown, amongst other things, that the amount awarded by the verdict was assessed as damages for the six years preceding the commencement of the action, for depreciation in the value of the use of the appellant's real estate, and for discomfort or inconvenience caused to the appellant. The appellant's motion for a new trial having been overruled, the court rendered an ordinary judgment at law in favor of the appellee against the appellant for the amount so awarded as damages by the general verdict and costs.

The objections urged in the brief for the appellant against the complaint all relate to the question as to its sufficiency as a complaint for equitable relief by way of injunction. No matter having been decided by the jury except the issue as to the past injury, and the amount of damages to which the appellee was entitled for that injury, and no equitable relief being included in the judgment, which related solely to relief at law pursuant to the verdict, and it not being claimed that the complaint did not show a cause of action for damages for injury already accrued, we would not be authorized to treat the ruling on demurrer as reversible error merely because, though showing a cause of action at law, it did not also show facts sufficient for the additional equitable relief sought. The cause of action at law was not dependent for its existence upon the existence also of grounds for an injunction, and as the court, in its instructions, did not submit to the jury any question except those relating to the issue at law, and the only relief given by the judgment was the award of damages in accordance with the verdict, there could be no available error in overruling the appellant's motion for a trial by the court without a jury.

Counsel for the appellant assail the sixth instruction to the jury, as follows: "If you find from the evidence that the defendant, at the time this suit was brought, was, and had been for several years prior thereto, the owner and operator of a pulp mill situated near said stream, and was and has been during said time engaged in manufacturing pulp at its said mill from wood, by use of certain processes, appliances, and certain chemicals; that the plaintiff was at the time, and had been for many years, the owner and in possession of the lands described in plaintiff's complaint; that said lands were situated on said stream, some miles below the situation of said pulp mill, and the said stream ran through or bordered upon the same; that the defendant took its water supply from said stream above its said mill, and returned the same, or a portion thereof not consumed, into said stream below its said factory; that said water so returned to said stream by the defendant, if any, was caused or permitted by the defendant to be polluted or charged with chemicals, lime, or other substances, and to flow into said stream so charged, to any extent, and the same flowing down to the plaintiff's lands worked any injury to the plaintiff or his property—the defendant would be liable for any injury that the plaintiff suffered by reason thereof." In another instruction, to which the appellant excepted—the eleventh—the court told the jury that the owner of land through which a natural water course runs has a right to make reasonable use of the stream for manufacturing purposes, and may, in the exercise of such reasonable right, cast waste matter into the stream, if he does not thereby cause injury to the owners of lands along the stream. It is undoubtedly true that the appellant, being a riparian owner, had the right to a reasonable use of the natural stream for manufacturing purposes; and it is no less true that the appellee, a lower riparian proprietor, had the right to a reasonable use for his own benefit of the natural stream for domestic and agricultural purposes; and the upper proprietor had no right by the unreasonable use of the stream, though beneficial for himself, to deprive the lower proprietor, to any measurable extent, of what should be regarded, under all the circumstances, as a reasonable use by him for domestic and agricultural purposes. So far as an impure condition of the water of a natural stream as it comes to a riparian owner results from a reasonable use of the stream by an upper proprietor in accordance with the common right of all riparian owners to the use of the stream, the lower proprietor has no remedy; but the right of the lower proprietor to have the water come to him in its natural condition is subject only to the right of the upper proprietor to make what, under the circumstances, may properly be regarded as a reasonable use of the stream. The property in the water "should be limited to a reasonable use or consumption, against the rights of other riparian proprietors." The

State v. Pottmeyer, 33 Ind. 402, 5 Am. Rep. 224. It is true that the lower proprietor can recover damages for the use made by the upper proprietor only where the latter has made some unreasonable use, which wholly deprives the former of his right, or practically in some perceptible and substantial degree diminishes or impairs the equal and common right of the lower proprietor. Cummings v. Barrett, 10 Cush. 186, quoted in The State v. Pottmeyer, supra. Whether or not the throwing or discharging of waste or impure matter into the stream, in a given case, would be a reasonable use of the stream, has been held to be a question of fact to be determined by the jury. Barnard v. Sherley, 135 Ind. 547, 559, 34 N. E. 600, 35 N. E. 117, 24 L. R. A. 568, 41 Am. St. Rep. 454; Hayes v. Waldron, 44 N. H. 580, 84 Am. Dec. 105. In Snow v. Parsons, 28 Vt. 459, 67 Am. Dec. 723, it was said concerning the use of water in streams: "The reasonableness of such use must determine the right, and this must depend upon the extent of detriment to the riparian proprietors below. If it essentially impairs the use below, then it is unreasonable and unlawful, unless it is a thing altogether indispensable to any beneficial use at every point on the stream." In Hayes v. Waldron, supra, it was said: "So, in respect to the size and character of the stream, it being obvious that an amount of diminution or pollution which would be insignificant in a large stream might in a small one be wholly destructive to the common right. So, also, in determining the reasonableness of suffering the manufacturer's waste to pass off in the current, much depends upon the use to which the stream below can be applied—whether as a mere highway alone, for purposes of manufacture requiring pure water, or for the supply of an aqueduct to a large city, as in case of the Croton river; and in respect to the lands below adjacent to the river the character of the banks—whether they are usually overflowed or not in high water—should be considered."

It might well be that in a given case an injunction would not lie to prevent the carrying on of a business because not materially and essentially injurious to the plaintiff, where, however, there might be a recovery of damages at law for minor inconveniences. See Bowen v. Mauzy, 117 Ind. 258, 19 N. E. 526; Barnard v. Sherley, 135 Ind. 547, 558, 34 N. E. 600, 35 N. E. 117, 24 L. R. A. 568, 41 Am. St. Rep. 454; Muncie Pulp Co. v. Martin, 23 Ind. App. 558, 562, 55 N. E. 796, and cases cited. In the case last named this court said: "No doubt merely slight injury to the water of a stream by pollution, which results from a reasonable use of it, is not actionable; but pollution which substantially impairs its value for the ordinary uses of life, or renders it to a measurable degree unfit for domestic purposes, or which, by causing offensive or unwholesome odors or vapors to arise, impairs the comfortable or the beneficial enjoyment of property in its vicinity, is a nuisance, and as such is actionable." We also said in that case: "The necessary results of conducting a lawful business may constitute a nuisance, and there may be a recovery of damages to the extent of the sensible injury caused thereby, because one must so use his own as not to injure another." The following language, used in that case, is applicable to the case at bar: "The case before us is not one wherein the defendant is charged with making some lawful natural use of his real property, or one wherein he is charged with producing damage by an occasional or temporary action in the preparation or adaptation by necessary and usual means of his real property to a lawful use; but it is one wherein he is charged with continuously doing that which diminishes the lawful use of the property of the plaintiffs, and thereby injures them materially, the injurious acts not pertaining to the development or use of the natural resources of the defendant's real property." See, also, Western Paper Co. v. Pope, 155 Ind. 394, 57 N. E. 719, 56 L. R. A. 899; Indianapolis Water Co. v. Am. Straw Board Co. (C. C.) 53 Fed. 970.

In the seventh instruction the court told the jury that the action, so far as it was addressed to the jury, was one for damages on account of creating and continuing a nuisance as alleged in the complaint; and the court then gave the jury as the statutory definition of a nuisance the following: "Whatever is injurious to health, or indecent or offensive to the senses, or an obstruction to the free use of property, so as essentially to interfere with the comfortable enjoyment of life or property, is a nuisance, and the subject of an action." The business of the appellant, by conducting which the stream is polluted to the detriment of lower proprietors, however many persons may constitute the corporation, and however many persons may have profitable employment in assisting in carrying on the business, and however great may be the output of the manufactory, and however large the profit therefrom, is, in its nature, not a business in which the general interest of the public as such is involved, or one located where public necessity requires it to be, or one the location of which is fixed by nature, and which, therefore, cannot be conducted elsewhere; but is a business of a private nature, the location of which was determined by the question of the convenience of its proprietors, the manufactory having been established and conducted, not for the development of the natural resources of the land owned by the proprietors in the neighborhood of the stream, or in or by way of the ordinary use of the land, but, on the contrary, essentially for the benefit of the proprietors alone through the profits of the manufacture of a salable product of such a character that, while the manufacture thereof requires the use and pollution of quantities of comparatively pure water, yet it is not necessary that such manufacture be carried on, if at all, in the locality where it is conducted, to the injury of the appellee in the way described in the complaint. In examining instructions given to the jury for the purpose of determining whether or not the giving thereof constituted reversible error, the appellate tribunal may properly consider the apparent effect of the instructions upon the jury by referring to the special findings in answer to interrogatories. We thus find in the record before us that the jury specially found that in each of the six years immediately preceding the commencement of the action, except the last year, the appellee was awarded $267, and that for the last year he was awarded $265, one half of the amount awarded for each year being damages for depreciation in the value of the use of the appellee's real estate during the year and the other half damages for discomfort or inconvenience caused to the appellee during the year. The answers of the jury also showed the modes in which the injuries were inflicted, the acts of the appellant which produced them, substantially as stated in the complaint. It thus sufficiently appears in the record that the use made by the appellant of the stream was found to be not reasonable, and that the damage inflicted by the unreasonable use was not slight, or insignificant, or inappreciable, but was substantial, measurable, and great. It cannot be supposed that the instructions in question were understood and applied by the jury to the wrongful detriment of the appellant, or that they constituted reversible error.

Other matters relating to the trial are mentioned in appellant's brief, the discussion of which does not seem to be necessary. The case appears to have been fairly tried and determined.

Judgment affirmed.

(34 Ind. App. 295)

BUNYAN v. REED et al.*

(Appellate Court of Indiana, Division No. 1. May 11, 1904.)

BENEFICIAL ASSOCIATIONS—RIGHTS OF BENEFICIARY—VESTED RIGHT—REGULATIONS OF ORDER.

1. A beneficiary acquires no vested right to the benefits that are to accrue to him on the death of a member of a mutual benefit association until such death occurs, and the member may exercise his power of appointment without any restriction other than such as may be imposed by the organic law or the rules and regulations of the association.

2. A law of a mutual benefit association provided that in the event of the death of one or more of the beneficiaries, if no other disposition should be made, the benefit, in case of death of the member, should be paid in full to the surviving beneficiaries, each sharing pro rata. A member designated as beneficiaries three persons, one of whom had been made beneficiary in order to secure a debt due him from the member, and such beneficiary died before the death of the member. *Held*, that the other beneficiaries took the entire fund, the heirs of the deceased beneficiary having no interest therein.

¶ 1. See Insurance, vol. 28, Cent. Dig. §§ 1948, 1949.

*Rehearing denied. Transfer to Supreme Court denied.

Appeal from Circuit Court, Noble County; Joseph W. Adair, Judge.

Action by Rebecca B. Bunyan, as administratrix of the estate of James R. Bunyan, deceased, against the National Union, Catherine E. Reed, and others. From the judgment plaintiff appeals, and defendants Reed and another assign cross-errors. Reversed.

L. H. Wrigley and Marshall, McNagny & Clugston, for appellant. R. P. Barr, E. V. Strong, and A. A. Chapin, for appellees.

HENLEY, C. J. The appellant, Rebecca B. Bunyan, as administratrix of the estate of her deceased husband, James R. Bunyan, commenced this action against the National Union, an incorporated, fraternal, beneficiary association organized under the laws of the state of Ohio, and Catherine E. Reed, Helen M. Ostrander, George B. Bunyan, Walter W. Bunyan, James R. Bunyan, Jr., and George B. Bunyan, as executor of the will of William Bunyan, deceased. The purpose of the action was to enforce a claim upon a benefit fund of $3,000, which was promised to be paid to her said husband as beneficiary under the benefit certificate issued by the said National Union upon the life of William Bunyan, who was a brother of the said James R. Bunyan, deceased. Aside from the National Union, the other defendants were made parties to answer as to their interests, if any, in the said fund of $3,000. The National Union, by a proper pleading, admitted its liability to pay the sum of $3,000, but showed that conflicting claims were being made by other parties to the suit with reference to said fund, and that it could not with safety to itself pay the fund to either of the claimants, and asked to be allowed to pay the $3,000 into court, and be discharged from further liability on account thereof, and leave to the court the matter of determining to whom the money should be distributed. Afterward, and before the trial of the cause, the said National Union paid the full $3,000 into court, and was discharged from further liability. The defendants, other than Reed and Ostrander, filed a cross-complaint, setting up their claim to the fund in dispute, and the defendants Reed and Ostrander also filed a cross-complaint, setting up their claim to the fund. The demurrer filed by appellees Reed and Ostrander to each paragraph of appellant's complaint was overruled. The cross-complaint of appellees Reed and Ostrander was held insufficient. Various answers were filed by which the issues were closed, and the cause was submitted for trial to the court, with the request for a special finding of facts.

We do not think it necessary to make any further statement here of the issues, because we are convinced that the judgment of the trial court must be reversed upon the cross-errors assigned by appellees Reed and Ostrander. We regard each paragraph of appellant's complaint as wholly insufficient for the relief demanded, and as showing upon its face that the fund in question legally belongs with the appellees Reed and Ostrander. The two paragraphs of complaint are not materially different. They aver that the National Union is a fraternal, beneficiary association incorporated under the laws of the state of Ohio in 1881, and engaged in the business of insuring lives of its members by issuing to them benefit certificates, promising to pay death benefits to be realized from assessments upon the members; that prior to February 20, 1886, a subordinate council, called "Kendallville Council, No. 192," was established at Kendallville, Noble county, Ind., which council is still in existence, and that agencies of this character are the means by which the said National Union transacts its business; that one William Bunyan, prior to February 20, 1886, became a member of said Kendallville Council and of the National Union, and at his death was a member thereof in good standing; that on said last-mentioned date the National Union executed to William Bunyan a benefit certificate of $5,000, payable to his wife, Cornelia Bunyan, as beneficiary, which certificate remained in force until February 23, 1901. Cornelia Bunyan died December 21, 1900, and the said William thereafter until his death remained unmarried, childless, and having no living parents; that it was one of the laws of said National Union that members may, at any time, surrender their benefit certificates, and cause new ones to be issued payable to different beneficiaries than those originally named; that for more than 30 years prior to February 23, 1901, William Bunyan and his brother, James R. Bunyan, Sr., appellant's decedent, were engaged as partners, under the firm name of W. & J. R. Bunyan, in conducting a drug store at Kendallville; that prior to said February 23d the said William was, and acknowledged himself to be, indebted to James R. in the sum of $3,000, and for such indebtedness the said William desired to give security, and after the death of the said Cornelia Bunyan, and prior to February 23, 1901, it was agreed between the brothers that, to secure to James R. the payment of said indebtedness, William should surrender his existing certificate in the National Union, and have issued to him a new certificate, in which James R. should be named as beneficiary in the sum of $3,000, and that the promise of the said National Union in such certificate to pay to said James R. the $3,000 should be the security to him for the payment of said indebtedness; that in pursuance of this agreement the said William, complying in all respects with the laws of said National Union, did on February 23, 1901, surrender his existing certificate, and the National Union executed to him a new certificate for $5,000, in which the beneficiaries and the amount to be paid each of them were as follows: "The National Union hereby promises and agrees to pay out of the benefit fund to James R. Bunyan $3000, brother, Catherine E. Reed, sister, $1000 and Helen M. Ostrander, sister, $1000, Five Thousand Dollars." This new and substituted certificate was properly executed and delivered to William Bunyan, to retain the possession of the same until his death.

It is further averred that in July, 1901, James R. sold and conveyed to William his interest in the firm property and business, and in connection with such sale there was had between the partners a settlement of the partnership affairs; that no part of the $3,000 indebtedness, and none of the matters and transactions had in which the same arose, were included in the settlement, or adjusted or settled therein, but the same was properly omitted and excluded therefrom, both parties relying upon the faith of the arrangement previously made in said benefit certificate for the payment of said $3,000 debt; that both William Bunyan and James R. Bunyan performed each and every condition in said substituted certificate to be by them performed; that James R. Bunyan died in Noble county, Ind., intestate, August 26, 1901, leaving as his only heirs at law his widow, the appellant, Rebecca B. Bunyan, and his three sons, George B. Bunyan, Walter W. Bunyan, and James R. Bunyan, Jr.; that afterward, to wit, on August 31, 1902, William Bunyan, the holder of the benefit certificate issued by said National Union, died, leaving as his only heirs at law his two sisters, the appellees Reed and Ostrander, and his three nephews, the sons of James R. Bunyan, heretofore named as such; that among the laws of the said National Union in force when the benefit certificate was issued to William Bunyan, and ever since in force, are the following, known as sections 6 and 7 of law 38 of said National Union:

"Sec. 6. In the event of the death of one or more of the beneficiaries selected by the member before the decease of such member, if no other or further disposition thereof be made in accordance with the laws of the order by the member in case of death the benefit shall be paid in full to the surviving beneficiary or beneficiaries, each sharing pro rata, unless otherwise provided in the benefit certificate.

"Sec. 7. In the event of the death of all the beneficiaries selected by the member before the decease of such member, if no other or further disposition thereof be made, the benefit shall be paid to the heirs of the deceased member, and if no person or persons shall be entitled to receive such benefit by the laws of the order it shall revert to the benefit fund."

It is further averred that the appellees Reed and Ostrander, and each of them, claim that as surviving beneficiaries they are entitled to the whole of said benefit of $3,000, to the exclusion of the appellant, and that each of said appellees Reed and Ostrander claim that as the heir of William Bunyan she is entitled to and has rights and interests in said fund superior to any right of appellant therein; that the appellants George B., Walter W., and James R. Bunyan, and each of them, claim some interest in said fund as heirs of William Bunyan.

The prayer of the complaint is that the indebtedness of $3,000 alleged to exist against William Bunyan and in favor of the estate of James R. Bunyan, deceased, be declared to be a lien upon the fund in question, and that it be ordered paid to the appellant as administratrix of the estate of James R. Bunyan, deceased.

The benefit to be paid by the beneficiary certificate issued to William Bunyan was $5,000, and by his said certificate three beneficiaries were named. The division of the $5,000 into three sums payable to different persons and in different amounts did not in any way sever the certificate. It was one benefit, and one benefit certificate for $5,000. The object of this action is to hold the $3,000, not as the property and in behalf of a beneficiary who could have been legally designated as such by the act under which the National Union was incorporated or by its rules and by-laws, but to recover it as a creditor who obtained a vested interest in so much of the fund as would secure his debt, and who was as such creditor designated a beneficiary. It appears upon the face of the complaint that James R. Bunyan, named as beneficiary to the amount of $3,000, died prior to the death of the insured. It is a settled rule of law in this state, supported by the great weight of authority, that a beneficiary acquires no vested right to the benefits that are to accrue to him upon the death of a member of a mutual benefit association until such death occurs, and that the member may exercise the power of appointment without the consent of such beneficiary, and without any restriction other than such as may be imposed by organic law or the rules and regulations of the association. Masonic Mutual, etc., v. Burkhart, 110 Ind. 189, 10 N. E. 79, 11 N. E. 449; Miller v. Bowman, 119 Ind. 448, 21 N. E. 1094, 5 L. R. A. 95; Appeal of Beatty, 122 Pa. 428, 15 Atl. 861; Beatty v. Supreme, etc., 154 Pa. 484, 25 Atl. 644; Lamont v. Grand Lodge, etc. (C. C.) 31 Fed. 177; Knights of Honor v. Watson, 64 N. H. 517, 15 Atl. 125; Metropolitan Life Ins. Co. v. O'Brien, 92 Mich. 584, 52 N. W. 1012; Sabin v. Phinney, 134 N. Y. 423, 31 N. E. 1087, 30 Am. St. Rep. 681; Eastman v. Provident Mutual, etc., Ass'n (N. H.) 20 Cent. Law J. 266; Richmond v. Johnson, 28 Minn. 447, 10 N. W. 596; Gambs v. Insurance Co., 50 Mo. 44; Kerman v. Howard, 23 Wis. 108; Splawn v. Chew, 60 Tex. 532; Ballou v. Gile, 50 Wis. 614, 7 N. W. 561; May on Ins. § 392.

In Richmond v. Johnson, supra, Charles H. Richmond was the holder of a benefit certificate in which his wife was named as the beneficiary. She died shortly before her husband. Upon the death of the husband the question arose as to whether the money due under the certificate should be paid to the administrator of the deceased wife, or be distributed under the rules and regulations of the association. The court said: "Here is not an ordinary contract of insurance made between an insurance company and another person, the rights of the parties to be determined exclusively by the policy. The rights of Charles H. Richmond, and of any one claiming through him, depended, not on the certificate only, but rather on his membership in the association, and such rights were defined and controlled by its constitution and by-laws. So far as the provisions of the constitution and by-laws are shown by the admitted statements of the complaint and by the certificate, the members are the beneficiaries entitled to the benefits of the fund, provided with the right at all times to hold, dispose of, and control said benefit at all times. With the right at all times to hold, dispose of, and control, his mere designation of some person to receive the benefit would be revocable. It would not prevent his subsequently designating some other person to receive it. While, in case of his death without having revoked his appointment of his wife, she would have been entitled to receive the benefit, yet during his life, because of the power of revocation, all that she had was a mere expectancy, dependent upon his will and pleasure. That expectancy was not property, not estate. The expectancy terminated when she died, and did not pass to her administrator."

The Supreme Court of Texas in Splawn v. Chew, supra, in holding that a beneficiary took no vested interest in a benefit certificate of the kind we are here considering, said: "Every one insured by reason of membership in such a company is charged with a knowledge of its constitution and by-laws, bound by their requirements, and entitled to the rights and privileges conferred by them. May on Insurance, § 552; Coles v. Insurance Co., 18 Iowa, 425. The present order did not issue policies as do ordinary insurance companies, but delivered to the insured a benefit certificate, which, together with the positive regulations of the order, evidenced the contract between the member and the company, so far as the insurance was concerned. * * * The provision of article 3, § 2, of its by-laws, is as follows: 'Applicants shall enter upon their application the name or names of the members of their family or those dependent upon them, to whom they desire their benefit paid, and the same shall be entered in the benefit certificate by the supreme secretary, subject to such future disposal of the benefit among their dependents as they thereafter direct.' The clear import of the section is to place the certificate entirely under control of the member, so far as the selection of the beneficiaries is concerned. He may direct at any time that the money shall be paid to persons different from those named or contemplated in the certificate, provided they are persons dependent upon him. So far from vesting an irrevocable right in the original beneficiaries, it vests no right whatever which the insured cannot by the very terms of the contract revoke and amend. They have no perfect or vested right in the certificate until the insured dies without divesting its benefits in favor of other dependents, and he alone is to determine which of these dependents is entitled to the insurance money. Hence all the rules of law for the construction of ordinary policies, so far as they refer to the indefeasible rights of beneficiaries accruing previously to the death of the insured, have no application to this case, being contrary to the express provisions of the contract."

The holder of a benefit certificate takes it subject to, and with notice of, all the reasonable rules, by-laws, and regulations of the association issuing it. It is a contract between the holder and the association, restricted only by the rules and regulations of the association and the law under which it was organized. Masonic Mutual, etc., Society v. Burkhart, supra. The very contingency which has here happened is completely provided for by section 6 of law 38 of the association which issued the benefit certificate to William Bunyan. James R. Bunyan, a beneficiary to the extent of $3,000, in a benefit certificate calling for $5,000, in which two other beneficiaries were named for $1,000 each, died before the death of the insured. Under the plain terms of the rule governing this contract, which appears in the complaint, the $3,000 should be paid "to the surviving beneficiary or beneficiaries, each sharing pro rata." James Bunyan had no vested interest in the funds to be paid upon the death of his brother unless he survived him. He had nothing but a mere expectancy, which, by the very terms of the benefit certificate under which has personal representative is claiming, would be defeated by his death prior to the death of his brother. Masonic, etc., Association v. Burkhart, supra. The benefit certificate declares upon its face that it is subject to the laws of the association. We think we have fully shown that under the decisions of our Supreme Court these rules must govern. It thus appears upon the face of the complaint that neither James R. Bunyan nor his heirs acquired any interest in the fund arising from the benefit certificate held by William Bunyan, the said James R. having died prior to the death of William.

The judgment is reversed upon the cross-errors assigned by appellees Reed and Ostrander, with instruction to the trial court to sustain the demurrer of appellees Reed and Ostrander to each paragraph of the complaint, and for further proceedings not inconsistent with this opinion.

(33 Ind. A. 149)

MALEY v. CLARK et al.

(Appellate Court of Indiana, Division No. 1. May 13, 1904.)

MUNICIPAL CORPORATIONS — STREET IMPROVEMENTS — REMONSTRANCE — SUFFICIENCY —SIGNERS—STATUTES—CONSTRUCTION.

1. Acts 1901, p. 534, c. 231 (Burns' Ann. St. 1901, § 3623a), provides that, if the remonstrance against a street improvement "is signed by two-thirds of the property owners, residing upon the lots abutting on such improvement, and representing two-thirds of the number of lineal feet of such improvement, then all further proceedings shall be abandoned." *Held*, that the persons whose signatures can make the remonstrance peremptory must be two-thirds of those property owners who reside upon lots which abut on the improvement, and who also represent two-thirds of the number of lineal feet of the improvement, the word "residing" and the words "and representing" relating equally to the preceding "two-thirds of the property owners"; and hence, where the remonstrators owned more than two-thirds of the lineal feet abutting on the improvement and were more than two-thirds of the property owners residing on the real estate abutting on the improvement, but the remonstrators who resided on their lots did not own or represent two-thirds of the lineal feet, the remonstrance was insufficient.

Appeal from Circuit Court, Fayette County; F. S. Swift, Judge.

Suit by Thomas Maley against Thomas J. Clark and others, as mayor and members of the common council of Connersville, to enjoin the awarding of a contract for a street improvement. From a judgment sustaining a demurrer to the complaint, complainant appeals. Affirmed.

McKee, Little & Frost and Reuben & Conner, for appellant. L. L. Broaddus, for appellee.

BLACK, J. The appellant, in his complaint against the appellees, who were the mayor and the members of the common council of Connersville, a city of less than 10,000 inhabitants, sought to enjoin the appellees from awarding a contract for the improvement of a certain portion of one of the streets of the city, the appellant, the owner of a lot on which he resided adjoining the portion of the street to be improved, and other lot owners having remonstrated against the improvement. The complaint showed that the common council had voted to accept the bid of a person named for the making of the improvement, but that the city had not yet entered into a contract therefor. It was shown by averments of facts, amongst other things, that prior to the acceptance of the bid the remonstrance was filed with the clerk of the city, and, by order of the mayor, was read before the council, and that the remonstrators owned more than two-thirds of the lineal feet of the real estate abutting upon the part of the street to be improved, and that the remonstrators were more than two-thirds of the property owners residing upon the real estate abutting upon the proposed improvement, but that the remonstrators who thus resided upon their respective lots abutting upon the proposed improvement did not own or represent two-thirds of the lineal feet of all the real estate abutting upon the proposed improvement. The court sustained a demurrer to the complaint for want of sufficient facts, and the correctness of the ruling depends upon the proper construction of the second proviso of section 1 of the act of March 11, 1901, Acts 1901, p. 534, c. 231 (section 3623a, Burns' Ann. St. 1901), which proviso reads as follows: "Provided, that nothing herein contained, shall prevent any property owner, whose lands shall be assessed for the improvement of any street, to remonstrate against said improvement at any time before the letting of the contract, and if the remonstrance is signed by two-thirds of the property owners, residing upon the lots abutting on such improvement, and representing two-thirds of the number of lineal feet of such improvement, then all further proceedings shall be abandoned."

It is contended on behalf of the appellant "that all that is necessary to make the remonstrance effectual is that it be signed by the requisite two-thirds of the property owners residing on abutting lots, and that the signers to said remonstrance shall represent two-thirds of the number of lineal feet of such improvement." The statute recognizes a right to remonstrate as belonging to any property owner whose lands shall be assessed for the improvement; but the Legislature has left the consideration of the remonstrance and the determination thereon to the common council, by which the remonstrance is to be regarded as advisory, unless a specified combination of incidents characterizes the remonstrance, the existence of which renders the remonstrance peremptory, through the command of the Legislature that all further proceedings shall be abandoned. The remonstrance is of such peremptory character if it "is signed by two-thirds of the property owners, residing upon lots abutting on such improvement, and representing two-thirds of the number of lineal feet of such improvement." The persons whose signatures can make the remonstrance peremptory must be two-thirds of those property owners who reside upon lots which abut on the improvement, and who also represent two-thirds of the number of lineal feet of the improvement. The word "residing" and the words "and representing" relate equally to the preceding "two-thirds of the property owners," and there is no other antecedent to which they can be referred.

No doubt, by interpolating but a few words, we might give the language of the statute the meaning for which the appellant contends, but the language of the Legislature is capable of definite meaning, and there is no occasion for such interpolation in order to give expression to the intention of the lawmaking branch of the government. It is not for us to reconstruct the statute upon a supposition that the Legislature could not have intended to make it so difficult as the language of the statute indicates to deprive the common council of the discretionary power, otherwise contemplated, of proceeding with the improvement, notwithstanding the remonstrance of property owners whose lands would be assessed for the improvement. If it may be claimed that the punctuation lends plausibility to the argument of the appellant, and tends to militate against the construction adopted by the court below, it must be admitted that the proviso, taken as a whole, indicates want of due care in its preparation, not only in the employment of some inappropriate words, but also in the adoption of loose and manifestly improper punctuation. Besides, punctuation, though useful for purposes of construction in exceptional instances, is in general a fallible standard. It is never allowed to control the sense of the language used. It may sometimes aid in determining between different constructions equally consistent with the rules of grammar and the ordinary meaning of the words employed, but the words used by the Legislature are to be considered first, and if they convey a clear, definite, and sensible meaning, without ambiguity, that meaning cannot be enlarged, restricted, or perverted by the punctuation. The words of the statute must be allowed their natural and ordinary effect, without regard to the punctuation. It is not permissible to make the construction of a statute dependent upon punctuation, where there is no ambiguity other than that created by the punctuation itself. Black, Interp. of Laws, 185. The legitimate meaning of the words of the statute in the order in which they are placed is that, in order to be peremptory, the remonstrance must be signed by two-thirds of those property owners whose lands will be assessed, who have certain qualifications, consisting both of residing upon lots abutting on the improvement and of representing two-thirds of the number of lineal feet of the improvement, and to give the punctuation such effect as to permit it to change this legitimate meaning into one adverse to the construction given to the statute by the court below does not seem to be permissible.

Judgment affirmed.

(33 Ind. A. 123)

PITTSBURG, C., C. & ST. L. RY. CO. v. MILLER.

(Appellate Court of Indiana, Division No. 2. May 11, 1904.)

CARRIERS—INJURY TO ALIGHTING PASSENGER—CONTRIBUTORY NEGLIGENCE.

1. A complaint for injuries to a passenger, alleging that he alighted from a moving train on a dark, stormy night, and slipped on the wet platform, shows contributory negligence, the only excuse stated being that the station had been called; that the train appeared to have

stopped; that the action of the brakeman in going down in front of plaintiff led him to believe the train had stopped; that, on account of the absence of all lights and the failure of the brakeman to have his lantern with him on the platform, plaintiff was unable to see whether the train had stopped, but believed it had; and that, the train being closely coupled together and moving noiselessly on a smooth track, the darkness led him to believe it had stopped.

Appeal from Circuit Court, Floyd County; E. G. Henry, Judge pro tem.

Action by William L. Miller against the Pittsburg, Cincinnati, Chicago & St. Louis Railway Company. Judgment for plaintiff. Defendant appeals. Reversed.

M. Z. Stannard and McIntyre & James, for appellant. C. L. & H. E. Jewett, for appellee.

ROBY, J. Action for damages on account of personal injuries. Judgment, $2,750.

Appellee was a passenger on one of appellant's passenger trains running between New Albany and Jeffersonville. He desired to alight at Ninth street station in the former city, to which point he had purchased his ticket. No question is made as to the sufficiency of the complaint, in so far as appellant's negligence is concerned. It is averred: That said station was reached about five minutes before 11 o'clock p. m. on January 29, 1901. That the night was dark and stormy, much rain having fallen, rendering appellant's platform slippery and unsafe. That there was no light at said platform, and it was impossible to see the same when alighting upon it. As the train neared Ninth street, the brakeman announced said station, and the air brakes were applied for the purpose of stopping at the platform. The brakeman thereupon went out of the door and down the steps to the platform, but did not take his lighted lantern, with which he might have lighted up said steps so that plaintiff could have safely left the car. The conductor did not go out of the car, but remained within, retaining in his possession both his own lantern and that of the brakeman. Appellee, when the station was announced, went forward to the front door of the car in which he was riding, and looked down at said platform for the purpose of alighting thereon. The further averments of the complaint are as follows: "Said train at the time appeared to have stopped, and the action of the said brakeman in going down in front of the plaintiff led plaintiff to believe that said train had stopped at said platform. On account of the darkness and the failure to have any lights at said platform, and the failure of said brakeman to have his lantern with him upon said platform, the plaintiff was unable to see whether said train had actually stopped, but he believed that the same had stopped, and he could safely alight on said platform. The plaintiff avers that thereupon, using due care, he stepped from the steps of said car to said platform, but because of the wet and slippery condition of the platform, and the fact that said train was still moving, he was at once thrown violently to said platform, injuring, wounding, and bruising him in and upon his body, back, and sides, permanently disabling him. The plaintiff avers that at the time he stepped from said train, although said train appeared to have stopped, said train was in fact slowly moving, but, being closely coupled together and moving noiselessly upon a smooth track in the darkness, plaintiff was led to believe that said train had stopped. After plaintiff stepped upon said platform and was thrown down, as aforesaid, said train continued to run for a distance of about 10 feet, and required a second application of the brakes to bring the same to a full stop, because of the negligent failure of those in charge of the locomotive and engine to apply said brakes to a sufficient extent when the same were first applied. Plaintiff says that by reason of being so thrown to the platform of the defendant and bruised and hurt, as aforesaid, he has been permanently injured, etc., wherefore," etc.

While various acts of negligence upon the part of appellant are charged, it is made to affirmatively appear that the fact that the train was moving at the time appellee alighted contributed to cause the injury complained of. If the complaint shows that appellee was himself in fault in leaving the train as he did, then the demurrer to the complaint should have been sustained. The pleading discloses that appellee voluntarily alighted from a moving train. Such act was not necessarily negligent. Whether it was negligent or not depended upon attendant conditions. The question was for the jury unless the conditions disclosed are such as to exclude the inference of nonnegligence, in which case it was for the court. Harris v. P., C., C. & St. L. (Ind. App.) 70 N. E. 407; Ry. Co. v. Crunk, 119 Ind. 553, 21 N. E. 31, 12 Am. St. Rep. 443; Carr v. Ry. Co., 21 L. R. A. 354, notes; Distler v. Ry. Co. (N. Y.) 45 N. E. 937, 35 L. R. A. 762; Watkins v. Ry. Co. (Ala.) 24 South. 392, 43 L. R. A. 297.

The averments of the complaint show that appellee, when he alighted, supposed the train was standing still. It is not averred that it was prudent for him to leave the train when in motion, as he did; the contrary, indeed, is shown. It is inferable, as against the pleading, that, had he known the train was in motion, he would not have then left it; certainly not in manner as he did. He says, as an excuse, that the train "appeared" to have stopped—an averment that, in view of the difference in appearance between moving and stationary bodies, must mean that it appeared to him, in the light of such attention as he gave the matter, to have stopped. The announcement of

¶ 1. See Carriers, vol. 9, Cent. Dig. § 1291.

the station by the brakeman was not an invitation for passengers to alight before the train was brought to a standstill. England v. Ry. Co., 158 Mass. 490, 27 N. E. 1; Fetter, Carr. of Pass. § 58. It is a general proposition deducible from the authorities that to get off a passenger train before it is brought to a standstill at the station is contributory negligence. An exception arises when the act is induced by the company through its agents. Appellee, in order to avail himself of the exception, has averred that the train was closely coupled together, and moving noiselessly upon a smooth track in the darkness. No invitation to leave the moving train can be inferred from such fact. That because of the absence of a light at the platform he was unable to see whether the train had stopped or not, but that he believed that it had stopped. Why he so believed, in view of the fact that he was unable to see, is not stated. A belief without reasonable basis, acted upon to the believer's detriment, does not ordinarily furnish a right of action. He also avers that the action of the brakeman in going down in front of him led him to believe that the train had stopped, and the "failure of the brakeman to have his lantern with him upon said platform." If this means that the brakeman stepped from the car to the station platform, it is manifest that appellee, being able to see him, must have been able to have known that the train was in motion, while if it means that the brakeman remained standing on the platform of the forward car, such attitude was not consistent with a present invitation to alight.

The complaint discloses that appellee voluntarily left the train, without reason, while it was in motion, under circumstances that rendered such action dangerous to him, as he should have known, and the demurrer to it should, therefore, have been sustained. England v. Ry. Co., supra; Ry. Co. v. Massengill, 15 Lea, 328; Secor v. Ry. Co. (C. C.) 10 Fed. 15; Brown v. N. Y. Ry. Co. (Mass.) 63 N. E. 939, 940. Its facts differentiate this case from those in which the train is not stopped a sufficient time to allow the passenger to leave it, and also from those in which he is invited or directed by the trainmen to alight, and also from those in which the passenger's action is affected by his tender age or other incapacity.

Judgment reversed, and cause remanded, with instructions to sustain the demurrer to the complaint.

(33 Ind. A. 119)

GUERNSEY'S ESTATE v. PENNINGTON.

(Appellate Court of Indiana, Division No. 1. May 10, 1904.)

PARTIES — ESTATE OF DECEDENT—REPRESENTATIVE.

1. The estate of a decedent cannot be a party to an action without some representative.

Appeal from Circuit Court, Lake County; H. S. Barr, Special Judge.

Suit between William Pennington and the estate of Chester Guernsey. From the judgment, the estate appeals. Appeal dismissed.

J. Frank Meeker, for appellant. J. Kopelke, for appellee.

HENLEY, C. J. Appellee has moved to dismiss this appeal, for the reasons that the record fails to show that the appeal is prosecuted by any proper person, and that the assignment of errors does not contain the full names of the parties.

Appellee's objection is well taken. It is a well-established rule in the courts of appeal in this state that the estate of a dead man cannot be a party to an action without some representative. To this effect are the following decisions: Peden's Estate v. Noland, 45 Ind. 354; Estate of Wells v. Wells, 71 Ind. 509; Estate of Thomas v. Service, 90 Ind. 128; Dunn v. Estate of Evans, 28 Ind. App. 448, 63 N. E. 36; and in the recent case of Whistler v. Whistler (Ind. Sup.) 67 N. E. 984, the same rule was announced, and the cases heretofore mentioned were cited with approval.

The appeal is dismissed.

(186 Mass. 99)

BEATTY v. WEED et al.
LYDON v. SAME.

(Supreme Judicial Court of Massachusetts. Middlesex. May 20, 1904.)

INJURIES TO SERVANT—NEGLIGENCE—ACTS OF FELLOW SERVANTS.

1. Where defendant was engaged in superintending the demolition of a building, and during his absence for an hour the workmen departed from the plan of work which he was pursuing, and, to facilitate the work battered a pier of the building with an iron pipe, so that the building fell down in a heap and injured plaintiff, another workman, the negligence, if any, was that of plaintiff's fellow servants, and defendant was not responsible therefor.

Exceptions from Superior Court, Middlesex County; Chas. A. De Courcy, Judge.

Tort for personal injuries by one Beatty and by one Lydon against one Weed and others. There were verdicts for plaintiffs, and defendant Weed excepted. Exceptions sustained.

Francis P. Curran and John P. Feeney, for plaintiffs. David T. Montague and Wade Keyes, for defendant Weed.

HAMMOND, J. The question is whether the evidence warranted the verdict against Weed. It appears that he was engaged in superintending the demolition of a boiler house. This was a brick building running east and west, 28 feet long, 22 feet wide, with brick sides and end walls, and an arched brick roof supported by a brick wall running lengthwise through the building from the ground up to the arch. The thickness of the outside walls was 12 inches and of the center wall eight inches. The arch roof was 8 inches thick, being composed of two layers of brick, set edgewise in cement. Iron stay rods, 2 or 3 feet apart, ran crosswise of the building, through the side and center walls, their ends projecting through the side walls and through a strip of iron upon the outside of the building, to which iron the rods were firmly held by nuts. The southeast corner of the building was supported by a brick pier, there being two doors next to the pier, one on the south side and one on the east side of the building. On the morning of the accident the plaintiffs, with several other men, were set to work by Weed to demolish the building. The plaintiffs first knocked out a portion of the west end, and then, by Weed's orders, went upon the northerly half of the adjoining part of the roof, and began to break that in by hammers, working easterly. While doing this, they stood upon the roof, and the bricks, as they were knocked off, fell inside the building. They continued this work several hours, until 12 o'clock, when they stopped one-half hour for dinner. Upon the easterly end of the building similar work was being done by some of the other men. Only a few feet of the roof, however, had been removed at either end when all the workmen stopped for dinner. While the men were engaged in this work, the defendant Weed, as was his custom, left the premises a few minutes before 12, to go to dinner, and returned in an hour. While he was gone, the accident occurred. The plaintiff's evidence tended to show that at half past 12 the men all resumed work at their respective places. Shortly after resuming, three of the men at work at the easterly end came to the conclusion that there was a more expeditious method of demolishing the structure than that adopted by Weed, whereupon they looked around, and finally found "somewhere on the grounds" a heavy iron pipe about 15 feet long, and, using this as a battering ram against the pier at the southeast corner of the building, speedily demonstrated the accuracy of their theory. The pier being knocked away, down came the whole building in a heap, and the plaintiffs were hurt.

We think that there was no evidence of negligence on the part of Weed. It is plain that the accident was not due to any fault in the plan of demolition adopted by Weed, but to the action of the fellow servants of the plaintiffs in departing from that plan. He had the right to assume that during the short time in which the work would go on in his absence the general directions which he had given would be followed, and we do not think that his failure to anticipate so ambitious and unusual an attempt on the part of his workmen to facilitate the work and shorten the job can be regarded as negligence. Whatever negligence there was was that of the fellow servants of the plaintiffs.

Exceptions sustained.

(186 Mass. 89)

OTIS CO. v. LUDLOW MFG. CO. et al.

(Supreme Judicial Court of Massachusetts. Suffolk. May 20, 1904.)

DAMS—PRIORITY OF APPROPRIATION OF SITES—RIGHTS OF UPPER AND LOWER OWNERS—EMINENT DOMAIN — COMPENSATION—AGREEMENT AS TO DAMS.

1. One who first appropriates water power by beginning the erection of a dam, whether he be the upper or lower owner, and not the one who first completes his dam, has the superior right under Pub. St. 1882, c. 190, § 2, providing that no dam shall be erected to the injury of a mill lawfully existing either above or below it, nor to the injury of a mill site on the same stream on which a mill or mill dam has been lawfully erected and used, nor shall a mill dam be erected to the injury of any such mill site which has been occupied by the owner thereof, if he, within a reasonable time after commencing such occupation, completes and puts in operation a mill for the working of which the water of such stream is applied.

2. The restriction on the use of a mill site declared by Pub. St. 1882, c. 190, § 2, where another mill site has been previously appropriated, is not a taking under the right of eminent domain.

3. The statutory provision for compensation for damages for interference by Pub. St. 1882, c. 190, § 2, with the right at common law of an owner of a mill site where another such site on the stream has been previously appropriated, is adequate to meet such constitutional requirements as are applicable to a statute of the kind.

4. Plaintiff and M., in connection with proposed conveyances of land on a river, one from plaintiff to M., the other from M. to plaintiff, each agreed with the other not to construct dams of more than a certain height. *Held* that, the agreement having reference only to the lands then owned by them and those which would come to them under the proposed conveyances, the acquisition by defendant from M. of land covered by the agreement did not affect defendant's right to erect a dam on other land owned by it.

Case Reserved from Superior Court, Suffolk County; Francis A. Gaskill, Judge.

Suit by the Otis Company against the Ludlow Manufacturing Company and another for injunction. Case reserved and reported for consideration of the full court. Bill dismissed.

Boyd B. Jones and Chas. L. Gardner, for plaintiff. Wm. H. Brooks, James B. Carroll, and Walter S. Robinson, for defendant.

KNOWLTON, C. J. The plaintiff, a riparian proprietor upon the Chicopee river, has lately built across the stream a dam 19.29 feet high and 353 feet long, with a length upon the rollway of 210 feet. Its expenditure for this development of power was $271,000. The water power is used to generate electricity, which is conducted about three-quarters of a mile up the stream to the plaintiff's factory at Three Rivers, in Palmer, and there applied to the plaintiff's motors. This factory previously had been run in part by water power taken from the river further up, and in part by steam power. The first-mentioned defendant, the Ludlow Manufacturing Company, which will hereinafter be called "the defendant," is also a riparian proprietor upon the river, and at a point two miles below the plaintiff's dam it has lately built a dam whose height is 51 feet, whose length is 880 feet, and the length of whose rollway is 300 feet. The defendant's expenditure for this development of power was $800,000. This dam was built to enable the defendant to generate electricity to be conducted about four miles down the stream to furnish additional power for use at the defendant's old factories and at a new one in Ludlow. The defendant's dam sets back water upon the plaintiff's dam in such a way as very greatly to diminish the water power there, and this bill is brought to enjoin the defendant from maintaining the dam and setting back the water.

The defendant became the owner in fee, in 1891, of certain land which includes the site of this present dam and the accompanying structures. In 1894, and again in 1898, it employed an engineer to take levels and make surveys, plans, and soundings along and upon the property, for the purpose of determining whether or not it was practicable to erect a mill dam upon the site of the dam since completed, and he did the work for which he was employed. In January, 1899, the defendant employed one Ball, a civil and hydraulic engineer of experience, and the contract with him recited that the defendant had determined to erect a mill dam on this site, and required him to proceed immediately to make surveys, cross-sectionings, soundings, plans, and estimates necessary for the erection of the dam, with raceways, canals and other structures, and to do such other things as might be necessary for the proper development of the water power on this mill site. Immediately thereafter the defendant determined upon the present height and present site of the dam. Ball, and the defendant's other agents and employés, commenced without delay the work of preparation for building the dam and other structures and making said development, and they prosecuted it and the work of construction of the dam and other structures, continuously and with due diligence, to the completion thereof within a reasonable time. The actual work of building the dam was begun on August 3, 1899, with the commencement of the construction of the tailrace, and within a reasonable time after making this beginning the defendant completed the dam, with all its appurtenances, and all the transmission lines and mechanism for the utilization of the water power in connection with a new mill which it had built near its other mills at Ludlow, and in connection with the other mills previously constructed, for the working of which this power was to be used. This work was completed and the power was ready to be utilized on October 16, 1901, and the mills were put in operation with the power, but the use of it was suspended by the bringing of this suit. On the 4th day of April, 1900, the plaintiff determined to build a dam at the site of its present dam, and then began its preparatory work therefor, and prosecuted this work with due diligence until the 11th day of August, 1900, when it began the work of excavating for the foundations of its dam, and from this latter date it continuously prosecuted the work of construction with due diligence to the completion within a reasonable time of its dam and all appurtenances necessary for the utilization of the power. This work was completed on July 1, 1901. Each part of the work of building its dam, the preliminary, the preparatory, and the permanent work, was begun by the defendant before the corresponding part of the work of building the plaintiff's dam was begun by the plaintiff. The plaintiff's dam was completed first.

The principal question in the case is, What is the construction of the mill act as applied to these facts? Pub. St. 1882, c. 190, § 2 (Rev. Laws, c. 196, § 2) is as follows: "No such dam shall be erected to the injury of a mill lawfully existing either above or below it, nor to the injury of a mill site on the same stream on which a mill or mill dam has been lawfully erected and used, unless the right to maintain the mill on such last mentioned site has been lost or defeated by abandonment or otherwise; nor shall a mill dam be hereafter erected or raised to the injury of any such mill site which has been occupied by the owner thereof, if such owner, within a reasonable time after commencing such occupation, completes and puts in operation a mill, for the working of which the water of such stream is applied," etc.

The plaintiff contends that the defendant has violated that part of the statute which forbids the erection of a dam to the injury of an existing mill site on which a mill dam has been lawfully erected, and the defendant contends that the erection of the plaintiff's dam was a violation of that part of the statute which forbids the erection of a mill dam to the injury of a mill site which has been occupied by the owner thereof, when the owner, within a reasonable time after commencing such occupation, completes and puts in operation a mill, for the working of which the water of such stream is applied. The statute was enacted for the regulation of the rights of property owners upon streams adapted to use for the supply of power. The framers of it recognized the fact that such property, in many cases, could not be used judiciously by an owner for a short distance along the stream, without affecting the property of other owners above and below, and preventing a like use of the stream for mill sites on other land. An enforcement by riparian proprietors of their rights at common law would often make it impossible for any of them to use water power effectively. Therefore their personal interests, as well as the interests of the public, call for legislation modifying the common law, and regulating the rights of owners of this peculiar kind of property. Our mill act is intended to meet this requirement in a way to promote the development of water power from streams for the benefit of individual owners, no less than for that of the general public. Lowell v. Boston, 111 Mass. 454-464, 15 Am. Rep. 39. The framers of the statute foresaw the possibility of a desire of two riparian proprietors owning lands near together on the same stream, each to establish a mill on his own land, when an advantageous use of the water for power would make it impracticable to maintain a mill in more than one of the two places. It was proper to provide for such cases by statute. Accordingly, we have the provision last above quoted. This is, in substance, that, as between riparian proprietors so situated, priority of appropriation shall give the better right. The Legislature might have established a different rule. If the time of completion of a mill had been adopted as the time which should determine precedence in the right to use the water, there would have been an inducement to owners to engage in a race to see which could first get the water upon his wheel. In different ways the results of such a rule would have been harmful. The rule prescribed by the statute calls for an actual appropriation of the site to use for the development of water power, followed by a completion of the work and the actual use of the water within a reasonable time. This is substantially the construction which was put upon St. 1795, p. 443, c. 74, in the case of Bigelow v. Newell, 10 Pick. 348, although that statute contained no special provision touching this subject. Rev. St. 1882, c. 116, § 2, was in different language from the former act, and contained a prohibition of the erection of a dam to the injury of any mill site on the same stream. Under this statute the case of Baird v. Wells, 22 Pick. 312, was decided, in which it was held that the Revised Statutes had changed the law, and that the remedy of one who had begun his mill, but had not finished it until after another mill interfering with his had been completed, was by an assessment of damage under the mill act. Thereupon the Legislature passed St. 1841, p. 346, c. 18, which is found in almost identical language in that part of Pub. St. 1882, c. 190, § 2, on which the present defendant relies. This enactment restored the rule stated in Bigelow v. Newell, 10 Pick. 348, which was held to have been changed by Rev. St. 1882, c. 116, § 2. Storm v. Manchaug Company, 13 Allen, 10-15. That this is the true construction of this statute is further indicated by the language used in other cases. Dean v. Colt, 99 Mass. 486, 487; Fitch v. Stevens, 4 Metc. 426-428. See, also, Washburn on Easements (4th Ed.) 467, 468. For general discussion of the law, see Fuller v. Chicopee Manufacturing Company, 16 Gray, 43; Fiske v. Framingham Manufacturing Company, 12 Pick. 68; Fitch v. Stevens, 4 Metc. 426; Cary v. Daniels, 8 Metc. 466, 41 Am. Dec. 532; Gould v. Boston Duck Company, 13 Gray, 442; Smith v. Agawam Canal Company, 2 Allen, 355, 356.

The plaintiff contends that the language of the statute on which the defendant relies applies only to owners on the stream below, and forbids their building a dam to the injury of an upper proprietor who has appropriated the power by beginning to build a dam which he completes within a reasonable time and uses in connection with a mill, and that it does not apply to an owner on the stream above, who completes a dam, and seeks to have it remain with the outflow from the tailrace undisturbed by backwater from the dam of one who in like manner had previously appropriated the power at a point below. We are of opinion that this would be too narrow a construction of the provision. The building of a dam by an upper proprietor, for which he claims the common-law right of a riparian owner to have the water flow down the stream without obstruction, would, if the claim were valid, be a great injury to the property of a proprietor below who had previously appropriated the power, but had been unable to complete his dam as soon as the upper dam was completed. In such a case, if the upper dam were protected as lawfully built under the mill act, in reference to a right to have the water flow freely away from it for the creation of power, the injury would be as great as it would be if a dam were built below which set back water upon a previously appropriated mill site above. The result would be that which is sought by the plaintiff in the present case, namely, a requirement that the dam below should be lowered so as not to set back water upon the upper mill. The reason for the enactment of the statute seems to require us to hold it applicable to a proper appropriation of water power in a stream, whether above or below the place where another subsequently begins to build, with the hope of preceding the other in the completion of his work. This is in accordance with decisions in other states under similar statutes. Miller v. Troost, 14 Minn. 365-369 (Gil. 282); Kelly v. Natoma Water Company, 6 Cal. 105; Kimball v. Gearhart, 12 Cal. 27; Irwin v. Straight, 18 Nev. 436, 4 Pac. 1215.

The plaintiff contends that the statute so construed is unconstitutional. We do not deem it necessary to consider at length the constitutionality of this statute. It has often been considered and discussed in previous decisions, and it has uniformly been affirmed. It is urged that the provision for the payment of damages is inadequate. This argument is founded mainly on an assumption that there is a taking of property under the right of eminent domain: but whatever may be the interference with the use of neighboring property by an appropriation of a mill site, it is not a taking under the right of eminent domain. Murdock v. Stickney, 8

Cush. 113; Hazen v. Essex Company, 12 Cush. 475; Lowell v. Boston, 111 Mass. 454-464, 15 Am. Rep. 39; Turner v. Nye, 154 Mass. 579, 28 N. E. 1048, 14 L. R. A. 487; Head v. Amoskeag Manufacturing Company, 113 U. S. 9, 5 Sup. Ct. 441, 28 L. Ed. 889. It is unnecessary to determine, in this case, what constitutional rights one has, in reference to damages for an interference by statute with his right at common law to use the water of a stream without obstruction, where such interference is permitted, in the regulation of the rights of different owners, as necessary to an advantageous use of the power; nor is it important now to decide what principles will hereafter be applied in assessing the damages of the present plaintiff, in view of existing conditions. It is enough to say that in our opinion the provision for compensation for damages is adequate to meet such constitutional requirements as are applicable to a statute of this kind. Even in cases arising under statutes which authorize an exercise of the right of eminent domain, it has been held that similar provisions are sufficient to satisfy the language of the Constitution. Boston & Roxbury Corporation v. Newman, 12 Pick. 467, 23 Am. Dec. 622; Brickett v. Haverhill Aqueduct Company, 142 Mass. 394, 8 N. E. 119.

The plaintiff contends that the defendant was precluded from erecting a dam which would interfere with the right to use water power secured to the plaintiff, as between it and one Metcalf, by a parol contract in writing with Metcalf, made on September 26, 1882, but not recorded. This agreement was made in connection with a proposed conveyance from Metcalf to the plaintiff of certain land on the river, and a proposed contemporaneous conveyance from the plaintiff to Metcalf of other land. In it each agreed with the other not to construct a dam for the development of his or its power which should afford more than a prescribed number of feet fall that represented the extent of the power that was allowed to each, namely, 19.65 feet fall to the plaintiff and 21.32 feet fall to Metcalf. Conveyances of land were subsequently made by each to the other, in pursuance of this agreement, and Metcalf afterwards conveyed his land to the Ludlow Cordage Company, a corporation which holds it, as the master has found, for the benefit of the defendant as the equitable owner. The master also found that the defendant procured the sale from Metcalf to the Ludlow Cordage Company for its benefit, with full knowledge of this agreement.

We need not determine the effect of this contract in all particulars, for if we should assume, in favor of the plaintiff, that it was not merely a personal contract with Metcalf, but one which binds subsequent purchasers of his land who take with notice of it, we are of opinion that it is of no effect in the present case. It was an agreement made in reference to the use of the lands then owned by the respective parties, and of those which would come to them subsequently through the proposed conveyances. If a purchaser of either lot, with notice of the agreement, would be bound not to use it in violation of the agreement, it does not follow that such a purchaser would be deprived of his right to use other lands, which he might chance to own, in any lawful way. The land on which the defendant's dam was erected is nearly two miles further down the stream than the land which Metcalf owned, to which the agreement pertains. The dam was erected under the mill act, by virtue of the defendant's right as a riparian proprietor at the point where the mill site was established. The agreement was either a mere personal contract of Metcalf, or it was a contract connected with his land, which, in equity, would follow the land in the possession of a subsequent owner who took it with notice. If it follows the land, it has no effect upon the rights of the defendant as the owner of other land below. The ruling of the master on this part of the case was right.

Bill dismissed, with costs.

(185 Mass. 555)

BOARDMAN v. HANKS.

(Supreme Judicial Court of Massachusetts. Suffolk. May 19, 1904.)

PRINCIPAL AND AGENT — COMPENSATION OF AGENT—PROCUREMENT OF OPTION TO PURCHASE PROPERTY.

1. One not employed to purchase property, but simply to procure an option, and whose employer did not avail himself of the services rendered to make the purchase, was only entitled to reasonable compensation for the services rendered in procuring the option, and not to the same compensation to which he would have been entitled had he been employed to purchase the property.

Exceptions from Superior Court, Suffolk County; Albert Mason, Judge.

Action by one Boardman against one Hanks. Judgment for plaintiff, and he excepts. Exceptions overruled.

H. E. Bolles, Charles H. Tyler, and Olcott O. Partridge, for plaintiff. H. E. Warner and P. L. Stackpole, for defendant.

MORTON, J. This is an action by a broker against his principal to recover commissions. The declaration contained 10 counts, and alleged an employment of the plaintiff by the defendant to effect a purchase and sale of certain real estate called "Misery Island," at the mouth of Salem Harbor, and that he effected such purchase and sale, and also that he was employed by the defendant to obtain an option for the purchase and sale, and did so. The case was heard by the court without a jury. The court found "that the defendant did not employ the plaintiff in any capacity whatever to purchase or sell the real estate,

* * * nor did the plaintiff buy or sell said real estate, nor did any services of the plaintiff in relation thereto bring about any purchase or sale of said real estate." The court also found that the plaintiff was employed as a real estate broker by the defendant to obtain from one Mason an option for the purchase of said real estate for the sum of $100,000, and that the plaintiff procured the option, for which $1,000 was paid, and subsequently, at the request of the defendant, procured an extension of the option for $500, but that no purchase or sale resulted from the option. The court further found that there was no agreement as to the plaintiff's compensation for obtaining the option, other than that implied by law from the employment, and, in effect, ruled that the plaintiff was entitled to reasonable compensation, and that reasonable compensation would be 2½ per cent. on the value of the option which the court found was $1,500. The court accordingly found and ordered judgment for the plaintiff for the sum of $37.50. The plaintiff duly excepted.

We think that the ruling was right. If the plaintiff had been employed by the defendant to purchase the property, and had procured, as he did, from the owner, or the person representing him, a valid and binding agreement to sell, and the defendant had for any reason declined to go on with the transaction and complete the purchase, it is clear that the plaintiff would have been entitled to his commission. Fitzpatrick v. Gilson, 176 Mass. 477, 57 N. E. 1000. So, if the plaintiff had been employed by the defendant to procure an option as incident to a negotiation for a contemplated purchase, and had done so, and the defendant had availed himself of the services rendered by the plaintiff in procuring the option to purchase the property, we cannot doubt that the plaintiff would have been entitled to compensation for the purchase thus effected. But neither one of these things happened in this case. The plaintiff was not employed by the defendant to purchase the property, but simply to get an option, and the defendant did not avail himself of services rendered by the plaintiff in procuring an option, as an incident in negotiations for a purchase, to make the purchase. The option gave the defendant the right to purchase the property or not, as he saw fit. He decided not to purchase, as he had a right to do, and as the plaintiff understood that he might do when he undertook to procure the option. We see no ground on which it can be held that the plaintiff is entitled to the same compensation to which he would have been entitled if he had been employed to purchase the property. In that case the situation would have been an entirely different one. What the plaintiff was entitled to was reasonable compensation for the services rendered in procuring the option, and the court so ruled, and must be deemed so to have found.

Exceptions overruled.

(185 Mass. 526)

MASSACHUSETTS BREWERIES CO. v. HILLS.

(Supreme Judicial Court of Massachusetts. Suffolk. May 18, 1904.)

PRINCIPAL AND AGENT — WHAT CONSTITUTES AGENCY—CONVEYANCE OF BUSINESS ON TRUST.

1. A liquor dealer conveyed his property to a trustee, to secure moneys advanced by breweries to enable him to pay his license fee. The trust instrument described his business as his own, he agreeing therein to conduct it in an orderly manner, subject to the direction of the trustee, covenanting with the trustee and his successor that he would give it his whole time and best efforts, and would account to the trustee at least once a week for all moneys, less a stipulated salary. The conveyance was declared to be "as collateral security for the payment of my debts and the performance by me of the covenants hereinafter contained." The trustee or his successor was authorized to sell the good will, stock in trade, and license on becoming satisfied that the dealer was losing money in the business, or on the breach of any of his covenants. After the execution of the instrument the liquor dealer continued to buy and pay for the goods, and the trustee never ordered any of them, nor was he consulted in reference thereto, nor did he pay nor was he charged with the bills. *Held*, that the liquor dealer was not constituted the agent of the trustee or his successor, so as to render the latter liable for debts contracted by the dealer in the conduct of the business.

Appeal from Superior Court, Suffolk County.

Action by the Massachusetts Breweries Company against one Hills. From a judgment for defendant, plaintiff appeals. Affirmed.

I. R. Clark, for plaintiff. Geo. E. Hills, for defendant.

MORTON, J. This is an action to recover for beer and ale alleged to have been sold by the plaintiff to the defendant. The defendant filed a declaration in set-off. The case was heard in the superior court upon agreed facts, and the court found for the defendant on the plaintiff's declaration, and for the plaintiff on the declaration in set-off. The plaintiff appealed.

From the agreed facts it appears that one Marotta and one Stucke were carrying on the business of licensed liquor dealers in Boston, under the style of Frank Marotta & Co., under licenses granted by the police board of Boston. Stucke had no interest in the licenses or the business, but was an employé of the American Brewing Company, till that company with others was consolidated into the Massachusetts Breweries Company, when he became an employé of the Breweries Company. In May, 1900, Marotta was largely indebted to various persons, firms, and corporations, including the American Brewing Company, the Roessle Brewery, and the Continental Brewing Company, and was unable to pay for the licenses which were granted to the firm of Frank Marotta & Co. for the year beginning May 1, 1900. Thereupon the three companies expressed a willingness to advance the funds necessary to pay for the licenses, upon being secured therefor, and the sealed instrument of May 14, 1900, was accordingly executed, and delivered by Marotta to Niles, and the companies advanced the funds necessary to pay for the licenses. Niles accepted the conveyance and the trusts therein contained, upon the express agreement that he could retire at any time by assigning the property upon the same trusts to some suitable person, and the acceptance of the trusts by such person, and that he should not be personally liable for any of his acts done under the conveyance, except for willful default and neglect. On the 15th of November, 1900, Niles executed to the defendant an instrument by which the defendant succeeded to all the right, title, and interest of Niles in the premises. The defendant accepted the conveyance, and the trusts therein referred to, upon the same terms and conditions as Niles had accepted them.

The plaintiff contends that the effect of these conveyances was to constitute Marotta the agent of the defendant, and to make the defendant personally liable for the goods bought by Marotta in carrying on the business after the execution of the instrument of May 14, 1900. But it seems to us plain that the scope and effect of that instrument was to convey the property therein described to Niles, and his successor in the trust, as collateral security for Marotta's debts, including the sums advanced by the three brewing companies to pay for the licenses, and upon the trusts therein set forth, and to constitute Niles and his successor mortgagee and trustee, and not the proprietor of the business. The business is spoken of throughout the instrument as Marotta's business, and he agrees to conduct it in an orderly and economical manner, subject to the directions of the trustee. He covenants with Niles and his successor that he will give his "whole time and attention and best efforts to carrying on my said business carefully and economically under his [the trustee's] direction," that he will pay for all purchases in cash as far as possible, that he will keep accurate books of account, and that he will account to said Niles at least once a week for all moneys received or paid out by him, less a salary of $25 a week. It is manifest that the accounting is to be to Niles, or his successor, as trustee, and not as the owner of the business; the provision as to salary being a prudent arrangement for all concerned. The conveyance is expressly declared to be "as collateral security for the payment of my debts in the order hereinafter named, and the performance by me of the covenants hereinafter contained to be by me performed." Then follows a statement of the order in which payment is to be made. The trustee or his successor is authorized "to sell at public auction or private sale, and without notice to me, all my said personal property, good will, stock in trade, and licenses, upon becoming satisfied that I am losing money in my business, or upon my making a breach of any of the covenants hereinafter contained to be by me performed"—which is inconsistent with ownership on the part of the defendant or Niles. The whole tenor of the instrument is at variance with the view that Marotta was the defendant's agent, and so also, so far as appears, is the conduct of the parties. For aught that appears, Marotta bought and paid for the goods. Neither the defendant nor Niles, so far as appears, ever ordered any goods, or were consulted in the ordering of any, or paid any of the bills. There is nothing to show that the goods were charged to them, or that bills were made out to them, or that credit was given to any one except Marotta. We see no ground on which it can be fairly contended that Marotta was the agent of the defendant or of Niles. In the case of Sartwell v. Frost, 122 Mass. 184, it distinctly appeared that the defendants were carrying on the business, and that the purchasers of the goods were their agents.

Judgment affirmed.

(186 Mass. 87)

HIGGINS v. SHEPARD et al.

(Supreme Judicial Court of Massachusetts. Suffolk. May 20, 1904.)

MASTER AND SERVANT—TERM OF EMPLOYMENT—ACTION ON CONTRACT — EVIDENCE — MATERIALITY—PREJUDICIAL ERROR—INSTRUCTIONS.

1. Where, in an action involving the issue whether plaintiff was hired for a term of one year or for an indefinite term, one of the defendants testified that his firm never made contracts with their employés for an absolute term, evidence as to whether another defendant had testified in another court that plaintiff's predecessor in the business in which he was hired had a contract for a year was immaterial.

2. Where, on the issue whether plaintiff was hired for a term of one year or for an indefinite term, one of the defendants answered the question as to whether he had testified in another court that plaintiff's predecessor in the business in which he was hired had a contract for a year, "I don't know. I may have," and subsequently testified that plaintiff's predecessor was not hired for any definite term, the error in overruling the objection to the question was not prejudicial.

3. In the absence of exceptions to instructions, the court will assume that the jury were fully and properly instructed.

Exceptions from Superior Court, Suffolk County; Frederick Lawton, Judge.

Action on contract by one Higgins against one Shepard and others. There was a verdict for plaintiff, and defendants bring exceptions. Exceptions overruled.

Robt. Levi, for plaintiff. John J. Higgins, for defendants.

HAMMOND, J. So far as respects the question of liability, the only matter really

¶ 2. See Appeal and Error, vol. 3, Cent. Dig. § 1523.

in dispute was whether the plaintiff was hired for an absolute term of one year or for an indefinite term. After Shepard, one of the defendants, had testified on cross-examination that his firm never made with their employés contracts for an absolute term, Cole, another defendant, was asked upon cross-examination whether he had not testified in another court that Mr. Murphy, the predecessor of the plaintiff in the business for which she was hired, "had a contract for a year." The defendants seasonably objected to this question, on the ground that it was immaterial. The objection was overruled, and, subject to the exception of the defendants, the witness was allowed to answer, "I don't know. I may have."

As this evidence was immaterial to the issue, it was inadmissible. But the rule is that the admission of such evidence furnishes no ground of exception unless it be prejudicial to the excepting party. It will be observed that the answer was a statement, in substance, that the witness did not know whether he had testified in another court that Murphy was hired for a year; and the phrase "I may have" was not necessarily, or even probably, intended as a statement that his best recollection was that he had so testified, but rather that he had no recollection whatever about it. In fine, the answer seems to be a statement that he did not know and had no recollection about his former testimony. Moreover, on further cross-examination he testified positively that Murphy was not hired for any definite term. No exceptions were taken to the instructions under which the case was submitted to the jury, and while, in the charge, no allusion was made to the evidence excepted to, we must assume that the jury were fully and properly instructed. Under the circumstances it is not made to appear that the defendants were prejudiced by the answer of the witness Cole.

Exceptions overruled.

(185 Mass. 535)

GLOUCESTER WATER SUPPLY CO. v. CITY OF GLOUCESTER.

(Supreme Judicial Court of Massachusetts. Essex. May 18, 1904.)

COURT COMMISSIONERS — COMPENSATION—STATUTE—CONSTRUCTION—COSTS—PAYMENT—EFFECT.

1. Under Rev. Laws, p. 1485, c. 165, § 54, providing that whenever commissioners are appointed by the courts to hear parties, assess damages, and make an award the court shall award reasonable compensation to the commissioners, to be paid by the county in which they are appointed, and not to be taxed in the bill of costs, there is no power in the commissioners or the court to award compensation to them to be paid by either of the parties, in the absence of a special contract.

2. The payment of costs in advance, including compensation to court commissioners, does not alter the legal status of an award by them of compensation to themselves.

3. Where commissioners were appointed in a case, the rescript in which from the full court to the county court was not sent in until June 19, 1901, prior to which time it could not be known whether the report of the commissioners would be sustained, it was a case pending, within St. 1901, p. 280, c. 366 (Rev. Laws, p. 1485, c. 165), providing for an award to court commissioners by the court for their compensation, and that it shall apply to pending cases, the act taking effect May 3, 1901.

Proceedings for the taking of the property of the Gloucester Water Supply Company by the city of Gloucester. From a decree in which the commissioners awarded themselves compensation, an appeal was taken. Reversed.

Robt. M. Morse, for petitioner. A. E. Pillsbury and C. A. Russell, for respondent.

KNOWLTON, C. J. Commissioners were appointed under St. 1895, p. 508, c. 451, to award compensation for the taking of the Gloucester Water Supply Company's property by the respondent. The questions before us relate to the power of these commissioners, under existing legislation, to fix their own compensation to be paid by the parties under their award. The statute now in force, embodied in Rev. Laws, p. 1485, c. 165, § 54, took effect May 3, 1901, and was first enacted in St. 1901, p. 280, c. 366, as follows:

"Whenever, upon a petition for the assessment of damages or any other proceeding authorized by law, one or more commissioners are appointed by the Supreme Judicial Court or by the superior court to hear parties, assess damages, and make an award to be returned into court, the court shall award reasonable compensation to each of such commissioners, to be paid by the county in which they are appointed, and not to be taxed in the bill of costs of either party to the action.

"Sec. 2. This act shall apply to pending cases as well as to those hereafter begun, and shall take effect upon its passage."

This statute covers the whole subject of the compensation of commissioners appointed for such purposes, and it leaves in the commissioners no power to award any compensation to themselves to be paid by either of the parties, and in the court no power to make an order or decree for the payment of any such compensation by any party to the proceeding. Boston Belting Co. v. Boston, 183 Mass. 261, 67 N. E. 428. It provides fully for the compensation of such commissioners, to be paid from the treasury of the county. Of course, it does not affect the validity of contracts made by commissioners in their private capacity with parties to such proceedings. If parties choose to make special contracts with commissioners in regard to their compensation, these contracts are enforceable. But in the absence of such contracts there is no way in which commissioners or the court can compel a party to pay any part of the commissioner's compensation. By its terms the statute is made applicable to pending cases. In every sense the present case was pending when the act was passed. The rescript from the full court to the county court was not sent until June 19, 1901, a month and a half after the passage of this act. Until then it was not known whether the report of the commissioners would be sustained upon the principal questions raised at the hearing. The whole matter was before the court, and the case might have been recommitted to the commissioners for a rehearing upon important substantive questions. In a special sense it was pending upon the questions relating to the compensation of the commissioners, for their report was attacked in this particular, and was sent back for further hearing before a single justice. The case is still pending, for not only was their original award as to compensation subject to rejection or revision by the court, but it was found by the single justice, who has since heard the case, to be improper and erroneous, as it plainly was. By the decree appealed from, which is now before us, the case was recommitted to the commissioners for a further hearing as to their compensation. The payment of costs in advance, including compensation to the commissioners, which we understand was made by the petitioner, did not change the legal status of the award on the subject of compensation. Boston Belting Co. v. Boston, 183 Mass. 261, 67 N. E. 428. Presumably it was made provisionally, subject to the action of the court upon the validity and legal effect of this part of the award. It seems plain that this was a pending case, which comes within the express terms of the statute.

These commissioners were officers of the court, appointed under a special statute, and they were not, by virtue of their appointment, in contractual relations with either of the parties. The most that they could ultimately expect under the existing practice was that the court, by proper orders, if necessary, would make provision for their reasonable compensation. If no statute were passed, they might expect that this compensation would come from the parties under an order of the court. In Newburyport Water Co. v. Newburyport, 168 Mass. 541-556, 47 N. E. 533, it was decided before the enactment of this statute that such commissioners had power to award costs; but in that case there was no question as to the amount of the commissioners' charges, and it was not intimated that they could arbitrarily fix their own pay, or that, in any event, they had a right to payment of anything more than a reasonable compensation. If there was a dispute about it, the amount to be paid them would be fixed by the court. The present statute simply provides a different source from which their payment is to come. It does not affect the amount of it in the least. Nor can it be said that this kind of provision is in any sense improper or inadequate. Payment from the county treasury is as certain as any future payment can be. The commissioners cannot object that this mode of payment is provided, instead of that which might have been adopted at the common law. In the absence of contract, and as officers of the court, they had no right to have their compensation from the parties, if the Legislature saw fit to say that they should be paid from the public treasury.

St. 1899, p. 509, c. 458, which went into effect on June 2, 1899, more than a year before the commissioners filed their report, and which applied to pending cases, was substantially like the act which we have been considering, except that the reasonable compensation which might be allowed was limited to $15 per day. As it was superseded by St. 1901, p. 280, c. 366, we need not consider its application to the present case.

Decree reversed.

(185 Mass. 549)

BOWDEN v. MARLBOROUGH ELECTRIC MACHINE & LAMP CO.

(Supreme Judicial Court of Massachusetts. Middlesex. May 18, 1904.)

INJURIES TO SERVANT—NEGLIGENCE—FAILURE TO INSTRUCT SERVANT.

1. In an action for injuries to a young and inexperienced servant put to work at a wire-cutting machine, evidence *held* sufficient to justify a finding of negligence in failing to sufficiently instruct plaintiff as to the operation of the machine.

Exceptions from Superior Court, Middlesex County; Wm. B. Stevens, Judge.

Tort for personal injuries by one Bowden against the Marlborough Electric Machine & Lamp Company. There was a verdict for plaintiff, and defendant excepted. Exceptions overruled.

J. J. Shaughnessy, for plaintiff. Chas. F. Choate, Jr., for defendant.

KNOWLTON, C. J. The plaintiff was injured by catching her fingers in revolving cogwheels on a machine in the defendant's factory, and she sues to recover for her injury. The only question argued is whether there was evidence of negligence on the part of the defendant.

The plaintiff was a girl of 15 years of age, and there was evidence that she was immature for her years. She was set to work on a machine which was used to cut platinum wire. On the back of the machine, opposite where she sat at her work, a large and a small cogwheel were geared together, and she might have seen them as she was moving about the machine. In different parts of her testimony she made conflicting statements as to whether she noticed the small cogwheel. She began to work on Thursday afternoon, and was injured on Saturday. The machine was stopped by pressing a lever which moved back a clutch and disconnected the power. One Miss McCarty, who worked on the machine, instructed her how to start and stop it, and the plaintiff testified that she was told to take hold of the large wheel with her hand, after pressing with a file on the lever, and thus to stop it. This wheel, which was about a foot in diameter, revolved at about the height of her head, the upper part moving backward from her face. She testified that Miss McCarty was accustomed to take hold of it with her hand to stop it, after pressing the lever, as it would not stop at once when the power was disconnected. On Saturday Miss McCarty went away, and the plaintiff, being alone at the machine, pressed with the file to stop it, and then took hold of the rim of the wheel, and her hand was carried over the top and down into the gearing on the back side, nearly on a level with the axis of the wheel. It seems that her pressure on the lever did not draw back the clutch far enough to disconnect the power.

The only question is whether the jury might find the instructions given her insufficient or misleading to such a degree as to leave her unreasonably exposed to danger. In this respect, did the defendant neglect the duty which it owed her as a young and inexperienced person? The question is not free from difficulty, but we are of opinion that there was evidence for the plaintiff proper for the consideration of the jury. She probably had no appreciation of the risk of a failure completely to draw back the clutch by the pressure of the file on the lever, and of the risk that in taking hold of the rim of the large wheel she would encounter enough power to carry her hand entirely over to the back side of the machine and bring her fingers into the gearing. It was not a kind of danger that would be likely to suggest itself to a young and unintelligent and inexperienced person. Miss McCarty represented the defendant in giving the plaintiff instructions, and we are of opinion that the jury might find, on the plaintiff's evidence, that she ought to have known that further instructions were needed. Wheeler v. Wason Mfg. Co., 135 Mass. 294; De Costa v. Hargraves Mills, 170 Mass. 375, 49 N. E. 735; Joyce v. American Writing Paper Co., 184 Mass. 230, 68 N. E. 213.

Exceptions overruled.

(185 Mass. 551)

COMMONWEALTH v. ALEXANDER.

(Supreme Judicial Court of Massachusetts. Suffolk. May 19, 1904.)

SUNDAY—GIVING OF ENTERTAINMENTS—RELIGIOUS SOCIETIES—CRIMINAL STATUTES—CONSTRUCTION.

1. A corporation, the business of which is expressed in its charter as the establishment and maintenance of a synagogue for worship in accordance with the principles of the Hebraic religion, and for such other charitable and religious objects as the corporation may deem advisable, is a religious and also a charitable society, within the meaning of Rev. Laws, c. 98, § 2, forbidding the conduct of a play or public diversion on Sunday, other than entertainments given by religious or charitable societies.

2. Under Rev. Laws, c. 98, § 2, relative to Sabbath breaking, but which permits the giving on Sunday of an entertainment by a religious or charitable society, the proceeds of which, if any, are to be devoted exclusively to a charitable or religious purpose, it is not necessary that the entire gross receipts of the entertainment be devoted to a charitable purpose, but the word "proceeds" means the net returns after the payment of necessary expenses incidental to the entertainment.

3. Management of an entertainment, such as is permitted by Rev. Laws, c. 98, § 2, which, while prohibiting the management of plays or public diversions on Sunday, allows the giving of an entertainment by a religious or charitable society, does not subject the manager to criminal punishment.

4. Rev. Laws, c. 98, § 2, prohibiting the holding of plays or public diversions on Sunday, excepting entertainments given by a religious or charitable society, the proceeds of which are to be devoted exclusively to a charitable or religious purpose, and subjecting persons violating its provisions to a fine, is a criminal statute, to be strictly construed, and its language cannot be extended or enlarged so as to create an offense not included therein.

Simon Alexander was convicted of a violation of the statute in relation to the observance of the Lord's Day, and excepts. Verdict set aside.

John P. Leahy, for defendant. John D. McLaughlin, Second Asst. Dist. Atty., for the Commonwealth.

KNOWLTON, C. J. This is a criminal complaint brought under Rev. Laws, c. 98, § 2, for a violation of the statute in relation to the observance of the Lord's Day. This section is as follows: "Whoever, on the Lord's Day, keeps open his shop, warehouse or workhouse, or does any manner of labor, business or work, except works of necessity and charity, or takes part in any sport, game, play or public diversion, except a concert of sacred music or an entertainment given by a religious or charitable society the proceeds of which, if any, are to be devoted exclusively to a charitable or religious purpose, shall be punished by a fine of not more than fifty dollars for each offence; and the proprietor, manager or person in charge of such game, sport, play or public diversion, except as aforesaid, shall be punished by a fine not less than fifty nor more than five hundred dollars for each offence." The Congregation Beth Israel is a corporation organized under general laws for religious purposes, and having its place of worship in Cambridge. Its purpose, according to its charter, is "the establishment and maintenance of a synagogue for the public worship of God in accordance with the principles and doctrines of the Hebraic religion, and for such other charitable, benevolent and religious objects as the corporation may from time to time deem advisable." The corporation received a license from the selectmen of Revere "to conduct a charitable entertainment at Crescent Garden Boulevard on Sunday afternoon and evening, August 9, 1903." A committee of four members was appointed, by vote of the corporation, to take charge of the entertainment, and the defendant was made chairman of the committee. On this Sunday the defendant was in charge of the entertainment, which was given under the auspices of the corporation, and which consisted of songs, and other features commonly known as "vaudeville." The public was admitted to the entertainment, an admission fee was charged, and the total receipts were taken by the committee. Incidental expenses for the performers, lights, attendance, and other things were paid by the committee, and the balance was retained and paid to the corporation. Upon these facts the defendant asked the court to rule that he was entitled to an acquittal as matter of law, and the question before us arises upon the refusal of the judge to give this ruling.

The only charge in the complaint is that the defendant "was the person in charge of a certain public diversion, to wit, a theatrical performance, given on said day," etc. The statute above quoted is the only one which he is charged with having violated. The only question is whether he was within the exception. The report states that this was an entertainment given by the religious society referred to. It is not contended, and it cannot successfully be contended, that the corporation is not a religious society within the meaning of the exception. According to the terms of its charter, it is both a religious and charitable society, and, if it is either, it is within the language of the exception. The balance of receipts above expenses was paid over to the corporation which gave the entertainment, and the only proper inference is that it was to be devoted exclusively to the purposes of the corporation, which were religious and charitable. The district attorney, in his brief, says: "It is not contended, however, by the commonwealth that in the case at bar the intent of the defendant was other than to devote the surplus to a religious purpose, to wit, the purposes of the church which he represented." The principal argument for the commonwealth is that the term "proceeds" in the statute means the entire gross receipts, and that the exception cannot avail a religious or charitable society in any case where any part of the money received, however small, is used for the payment of any expense incidental to the entertainment. We think that this is too narrow a construction of the statute, and that if adopted it would defeat the purpose of the Legislature in reference to such societies. Probably there is hardly any entertainment given by a religious or charitable society in which there is not some payment for expenses. We think the meaning of the word "proceeds" is that which finally results or proceeds from the entertainment, taking into account not only that which is received, but that which is incidentally and properly paid out. The proceeds are the net returns after the payment of necessary expenses.

The proof shows that the defendant is within the exception of the statute in every particular. Management of an entertainment, such as is referred to in the exception, does not subject a person to punishment. There is no statute that makes a manager of such an entertainment an offender. This is a criminal law, and criminal statutes are to be construed strictly. The court cannot extend or enlarge a statute to create an offense which is not created by the language of the enactment. Doubtless the Legislature did not intend to open a door for the giving of theatrical performances for the diversion of the public on the Lord's Day. Probably no one thought it possible that a religious or charitable society would give such an entertainment to obtain money for a charitable or religious use. It was doubtless supposed that the provisions adopted in the exception were a sufficient safeguard against the giving of improper entertainments on Sunday. So the statute excepts all entertainments given by a religious or charitable society the proceeds of which are to be devoted exclusively to a charitable or religious purpose. There may be religious or charitable societies that do not object to an entertainment of vaudeville on secular days, if they object to them on holy days. There may be religious societies according to whose belief and observance Sunday is a secular day. Persons of such a belief are referred to in Rev. Laws, c. 98, § 4.

The exception which we have been discussing, and which is referred to again in similar language in Rev. Laws, c. 98, § 5, and in chapter 102, § 172, was not stated in terms sufficiently guarded to accomplish the probable purpose of the Legislature. But this does not enable the court to amend the statute by declaring that certain kinds of entertainments may be given and that certain others are prohibited. The remedy, if any is needed, must come from the Legislature. In the opinion of a majority of the court, the entry must be:

Verdict set aside.

(185 Mass. 567)

WOOD v. TOWN OF WESTPORT.

(Supreme Judicial Court of Massachusetts. Bristol. May 19, 1904.)

DEATH—CONTRIBUTORY NEGLIGENCE—EVIDENCE.

1. In an action for death from an injury received on a public highway, where it appeared that decedent had driven, on a very dark night, over a bank wall between the highway

and a mill where he had worked for years, evidence of his declaration that he "was driving easy, but it was darker than hell," and conflicting evidence as to whether he had been drinking before the accident, was insufficient to justify a finding that he was in the exercise of due care.

2. In an action for death resulting from the decedent's driving over an unguarded bank wall near a highway, where evidence was introduced to show that about the time of the accident a witness was driving along the highway, and that it was very dark, and that his horse jumped out sideways and a team went by like a shot, it was a question of fact for the court, in determining the admissibility of the evidence, whether the other circumstances of the case made this one material in determining whether the decedent had used due care.

Exceptions from Superior Court, Bristol County; Jabez Fox, Judge.

Action by one Wood, administratrix, against the town of Westport. Verdict for defendant, and plaintiff excepts. Exceptions overruled.

J. W. & C. R. Cummings, for plaintiff. Jennings, Morton & Brayton, for defendant.

KNOWLTON, C. J. This is an action to recover for an injury received by the plaintiff's intestate upon a public highway in the defendant town. The first count is founded on his conscious suffering after the injury, before his death, and the second is for his death. A verdict was ordered for the defendant, and the plaintiff excepted.

The place of the accident was near a certain building belonging to the Westport Manufacturing Company, called "Mill No. 2," and sometimes the "Star Mill," and sometimes the "Forge Mill." The "Forge Road," so-called, runs past this mill in a direction nearly north and south, on the easterly side of it. The mill is about 220 feet long and 40 feet wide, running north and south. The road is laid out 40 feet wide, and is macadamized through the traveled part 16 feet wide. Just before the road reaches the mill, going south, is a bridge over the stream, and just to the east of the bridge the water falls over a dam and runs under the bridge, in an easterly direction. In front of the mill the macadamized road, coming southward from the bridge, curves slightly to the left, so that at the south end of the mill it runs a little to the east of south. The mill sits back to the west of the road, so that there is a distance of 35 feet between it and the nearest part of the macadam at the northerly end of the mill, and a distance of 33 feet, as given by the maker of the plan and the defendant's witnesses, at the south end of the mill, and of 23 feet at that point, as estimated by the plaintiff's witnesses. From the southerly front corner of the mill is a bank wall extending to the east 20 feet, towards the macadam, and from that point another wall running a little to the southeast 11 feet, not quite parallel to the line of the road, and from this last point another wall running south 50 or 60 feet, with a railing upon it, constructed by the town. There is no railing upon the first two walls, and the land in front of the mill north of the wall is on a level with the top of the wall. The land southerly and westerly of this wall is much lower, the depth being 11 feet from the top of the wall at the corner of the mill, and 5 feet at the easterly end of the wall. This lowland to the south and west was covered by scrub trees and bushes, and was referred to as the "ditch" or "swamp." The accident happened on Sunday, January 26, 1902, on a very dark and somewhat rainy evening. About a quarter after 9 o'clock on that evening some persons walking on the road a short distance south of the mill heard a noise in the bushes below, which on investigation proved to be made by the horse and wagon of the defendant's intestate. The intestate was found lying, seriously injured, about seven feet from the wall which is along the road, and seven to eight feet from the wall which is at right angles to the road. The horse and wagon were further along in a southwest direction. There were wheel tracks south of the wall which runs from the mill to the street, beginning at about seven feet from the corner where the walls come together, and there was a space of about seven feet southerly of the first-mentioned wall where there were no wheel tracks. No wheel tracks were discovered above the wall. The theory of the plaintiff is that her husband, while driving southerly along the road, by reason of the darkness passed out of the traveled part of the way and drove over the wall which leads from the corner of the mill towards the road. The two walls on which there is no railing were built by the manufacturing company, and except for the macadam, which was laid 2 or 3 years before the accident, the premises have been in the same condition nearly 30 years. The plaintiff's intestate had been employed by the manufacturing company many years, working some of the time as a teamster about the Forge Mill and their other mills. He lived about a mile from the place of the accident, and was thoroughly familiar with the situation. There was no testimony as to how the accident happened, and this can only be inferred from the conditions subsequently discovered.

We will not consider the question whether there was negligence on the part of the defendant in the mode of constructing the road, for we are of opinion that there was no evidence of care on the part of the plaintiff's intestate. The plaintiff testified, on cross-examination: "That on the Sunday of his accident her husband first went driving about 3 o'clock in the afternoon, and took her little boy with him; that he returned about half past 7; that he was not under the influence of liquor; that he came to the house and wanted her to go out with him; that it was then dark; that he drove for her to come, and she didn't go; that she didn't wish to go, and that her husband took the horse out of the wagon, and it didn't want to go into the barn, and her husband said he guessed he would give it another little drive, and perhaps it would go in then; that he tried to persuade it to go in, and it wouldn't go; that her husband whipped the horse to try to make him go into the barn, and she went out and tried to stop her husband; that she told her husband to hitch the horse outside and let it stand, but didn't remember what he replied; that she didn't think she asked him to stop whipping the horse; that there were two persons present who were as near as she was to the horse; that one of them tried to get the horse into the barn, and her husband told him to go to hell; that she didn't know what else took place; that she came away then; that she didn't hear her husband say he would kill the horse or the horse would kill him; that after the man tried to get the horse to go into the barn, and her husband had told him to go to hell, she didn't know what happened; that she didn't stay out; that she went into the house and didn't come out again; that her husband drove up to the door and asked her to go to ride; that she didn't go, and that she didn't see or hear more after she went in; that she didn't say to her husband that he was too drunk; that her husband had not been drinking; that it was about 8 o'clock; that she told him (her husband) that she guessed she wouldn't go to ride, but gave no reason for not going; that the horse was then acting all right, and that when her husband was whipping it the horse did nothing bad; he kind of danced around a little, but wouldn't go into the stable, and didn't go into the stable until they brought him back; that it was the stable he was usually kept in." Four other witnesses, two of them were present on the occasion of which the plaintiff testified, and another of whom rode with the plaintiff's intestate a while on Sunday afternoon, gave testimony which tended to show that he was under the influence of intoxicating liquor, and three of them testified directly that they noticed signs of his having been drinking. These were the only witnesses who testified to having seen him that Sunday afternoon or evening. Two declarations of the plaintiff's intestate were in evidence. One witness said, "I asked him if the horse was getting away from him and he says, 'No, I was driving easy, but it was darker than hell.'" Another testified "that he went into Mr. Wood's room and asked how it happened, and Mr. Wood said that he had got dumped into the ditch, down at the forge." It appeared that the mill was generally called the "forge." Except the single expression of the plaintiff's intestate first quoted, there is nothing but conjecture to guide us on the question whether he was exercising any care. That expression has no reference to the subject on which particular care was necessary. Taken in connection with the question to which it was an answer, it simply indicated that the horse was not running away, and that he was not going very fast. The testimony in regard to the darkness of the evening was undisputed, and this fact called for special care in driving, to avoid going out of the road. No prudent person, under such conditions, would think of driving otherwise than very slowly, taking all possible precautions to keep from getting off the traveled road. But the fact that the tracks of the wheels nearest to the wall were seven or eight feet south of it indicates that he went over pretty rapidly. The deceased knew that if he swerved to the right in passing the mill he would drive into the millyard, and if he kept on would drive over the wall. If he was attentive he could not fail to know when he was passing the mill, for the sound of the wooden bridge in passing over it and the sound of the water falling over the dam would tell him that he was within a few feet of the mill. If he couldn't see where he was going, he was bound to use care proportional to the danger. But there is nothing to show that he used any care.

If we resort to probabilities, his conduct that afternoon and evening does not indicate that he was acting prudently. His wife testified that on this winter day he went out driving at about 3 o'clock, taking his little boy with him, and did not return until half past 7, and that he then almost immediately went out again on this very dark night, trying to have her go with him. In addition to what the plaintiff said, two witnesses testified to his whipping the horse and swearing when he was trying to get him into the stable. According to one of them he said, "I will get that horse tired so he will come back so he will go in," and after that said, "he would die or the horse would die—something like that." Both these witnesses said he seemed to be under the influence of liquor. In the absence of any evidence that he was taking precautions against driving out of the road into the millyard and driving over the wall, the jury could not find affirmatively that he was in the exercise of due care.

The only remaining exception was to the admission of the testimony of the witness Hawes that about 7 o'clock that evening, as he was driving along on the Forge Road, not far from where the plaintiff's intestate lived, it was very dark; his "horse jumped right out and went sideways, * * * and a team went by just like a shot." Whether the other circumstances of the case made this circumstance of any significance for consideration in connection with the plaintiff's claim as to her husband's due care was a question of fact to be determined by the presiding justice in passing upon the admissibility of the testimony. Unless the person who went by was the plaintiff's intestate, it was of no consequence. We are of opinion that the probabilities, depending upon a variety of facts, were such as to leave the admission or exclusion of the evidence within the discretion of the presiding justice.

Exceptions overruled.

(185 Mass. 522)

MULLIN v. BOSTON ELEVATED RY. CO. (two cases).

(Supreme Judicial Court of Massachusetts. Suffolk. May 18, 1904.)

CARRIERS — STREET RAILWAY PASSENGER — INJURY IN COLLISION—NEGLIGENCE—EXTENT OF INJURY — ADMISSIBILITY OF EVIDENCE — INJURY TO OTHER PASSENGERS—PLAINTIFF'S FAMILY HISTORY—HARMLESS ERROR.

1. In an action by a street car passenger for injuries received in a collision, the court, sitting without a jury, found on sufficient evidence that the tracks were wet and slippery, by reason of which, and notwithstanding all reasonable and proper efforts by the motorman of the colliding car, in applying brakes, etc., the car slid on the rails, and the fender came in contact with that of the car in which plaintiff was; and that the force of the impact did not injure the fender or woodwork of either car, nor were other passengers affected beyond the sensation of a jar. *Held*, that a judgment for defendant, based on an absence of negligence, was proper, notwithstanding the motorman on cross-examination had testified that he "took the risk"; it being for the court to say what the motorman meant by that statement, and whether, under the circumstances, it was negligence for him to take the risk.

2. In an action for personal injuries, which plaintiff testified had resulted in fainting fits, which she had never before had, evidence for defendant that three years before the accident she was subject to fainting spells, was competent.

3. In an action by a street car passenger for injuries in a collision, evidence as to whether other passengers were injured was competent, as tending to establish the force of the impact, which bore on the question of the motorman's negligence.

4. In an action for personal injuries engendering nervous troubles, allowing questions to be put to plaintiff's attending physician as to whether he had got from her or others any of her family history as to nervous disorders, was not ground for reversal where the witness answered that he never did.

Exceptions from Superior Court, Suffolk County; Henry K. Braley, Judge.

Action by Winifred Mullin against the Boston Elevated Railway Company and by her husband, Michael Mullin, against the same defendant. The actions were tried together, judgment rendered for defendant in each, and plaintiffs except. Exceptions overruled.

E. B. Callender and E. M. Shanley, for plaintiffs. Geo. H. Mellen, for defendant.

MORTON, J. These two actions were tried and argued together. The first is an action by the female plaintiff, whom we shall speak of as the "plaintiff," for injuries alleged to have been sustained while a passenger on one of the defendant's open cars in July, 1900. The second is by the husband for the loss of services. The cases were tried by the court without a jury, and the court found for the defendant in each case. It was admitted that the plaintiff was in the exercise of due care. The cases are here on exceptions by the plaintiffs to certain rulings in regard to the admission of evidence, and to the refusal to adopt certain instructions that were requested.

We think that the rulings were right. The plaintiff was seated in the car so that she faced towards the rear. There had been a rain, and the tracks were somewhat wet and slippery. Another car approached on the same tracks from the rear, and "by reason," as the court found, "of the moisture on the rails, notwithstanding all reasonable and proper efforts used by the motorman in applying the brakes and using the power, the car slid on the rails, and * * * the fender * * * came in contact with the fender of the car in which the plaintiff was seated." The court further found as follows: "The force of the impact did not cause any injury to the fender or woodwork of either car; neither were any other passengers, so far as the evidence showed, affected by such impact beyond the sensation of a jar on the part of those who were seated in the car with the plaintiff. The plaintiff, a person whose health had been somewhat impaired by previous nervous difficulties, disclosed by the evidence, seeing the car approaching, and anticipating that there would be a collision, * * * reached out her right hand, took hold of the stanchion at the end of the seat, swooned, and fell to the floor. Such fall was not caused by the impact of the cars, but was the result of the fainting at the anticipated collision, the fainting fit being caused by fright." The court also found that, as a result of the fall, she sustained certain bruises of a superficial nature, and thereafter suffered serious nervous prostration, caused by the shock and the nervous fright. In view of these findings, which were warranted by the evidence, we do not see how it can be said that there was negligence on the part of the defendant. Whether, if there was, it could be said that the plaintiff's injuries were due to it, need not be considered. See Warren v. Boston & Maine R. R., 163 Mass. 484, 40 N. E. 895; Spade v. Lynn & Boston R. R., 168 Mass. 285, 47 N. E. 88, 38 L. R. A. 512, 60 Am. St. Rep. 393; Gannon v. N. Y., N. H. & H. R. R., 173 Mass. 40, 52 N. E. 1075, 43 L. R. A. 833; Berard v. B. & A. R. R., 177 Mass. 179, 58 N. E. 586. The plaintiff relies on a statement by the motorman made during the course of his cross-examination that he took the risk. But it was for the court to say what he meant by that statement, and whether, under the circumstances, it was negligent for him to take the risk, and it must be held that the court has found that it was not.

The evidence that three years before the accident the plaintiff was subject to fainting spells was competent to contradict her statement that she had never been subject to fainting fits before the accident, and as furnishing some ground for questioning the truth of her claim that the fainting fits to which she testified that she was subject were caused by the accident.

Quite a number of the passengers on the car with the plaintiff were called as witnesses by the plaintiff and defendant, and against the objection of the plaintiff the defendant was allowed to show by them that none of them received any injury as a result of the collision, and it did not appear that any person besides the plaintiff was injured. The force with which the cars came together had a bearing upon the question of the alleged negligence of the motorman. One way of judging of the force was by its effect upon the cars and passengers, and it was competent for the defendant to show not only that no injury was done to the cars, but to inquire of the passengers who were witnesses whether any of them received any injury. If none of them did, that fact would have an important bearing on the force with which the cars came together and on the motorman's alleged negligence.

If the questions that were allowed to be put to the witness who had been the attending physician of the plaintiff whether he got from the plaintiff, or from any one else in her presence, any of her family history concerning her mother's physical condition or mental or nervous condition, and her sister's, were improperly admitted, on which we express no opinion, nevertheless no harm was done as the witness answered that he never did.

We have considered the exceptions so far as relied on by the plaintiffs in their brief, and we treat the others as waived. The result is that the exceptions must be overruled.

So ordered.

(185 Mass. 500)

OLDS et al. v. CITY TRUST, SAFE-DEPOSIT & SURETY CO.

(Supreme Judicial Court of Massachusetts. Hampshire. May 18, 1904.)

ACTION ON BOND—PRINCIPAL AND SURETY—CORPORATIONS — DISSOLUTION — JURISDICTION — PRESUMPTIONS—AGREED FACTS—BOND—VALIDITY—ESTOPPEL.

1. The surety of a bond given to dissolve an attachment is estopped to assert the invalidity of the bond, where it appears that it was intended by the giving of the bond to induce plaintiffs to abandon their attempt to appropriate to the payment of their demand then in suit a debt owing by an alleged trustee of the attachment debtor, and that it did have that result, to the legal detriment of plaintiffs.

2. The obligee in a bond given to dissolve an attachment is not required to exhaust security collateral to the demand on which the attachment proceeding was being prosecuted, before taking judgment against the surety in an action to enforce the bond.

3. Rev. Laws, c. 109, § 53, providing that every corporation whose corporate existence is terminated shall nevertheless be continued as a body corporate for three years after the time when it would have been so terminated, for the purpose of prosecuting and defending suits, does not apply to foreign corporations.

4. The dissolution of a corporation is a peculiar function which resides primarily in the Legislature, and is conferred on courts only by explicit legislative authority.

5. Where the dissolution of a foreign corporation which was a party to an action in Massachusetts is agreed to have been decreed, by a court of general jurisdiction in the state of its domicile, after the institution of the action and before judgment therein, whether the court had jurisdiction to dissolve it is a question of fact for the trial court in Massachusetts.

6. There is no presumption that the statutes of another state give the courts thereof power to dissolve a corporation domiciled there.

7. In an action against a surety on the bond of a foreign corporation, given to dissolve an attachment of a debt due the corporation, there were agreed facts that the corporation, after the institution of the action in which the bond was given, and before judgment therein, had been decreed to be dissolved by a court of general jurisdiction in the state of its domicile, and that the court could have provided in its decree for the continuance in the name of the corporation of suits then pending by and against it, but did not so provide. *Held*, that it does not follow, as an inevitable inference from the facts, that the court had jurisdiction to decree a dissolution of the corporation.

¶ 1. See Principal and Surety, vol. 40, Cent. Dig. § 675.

Appeal from Superior Court, Hampshire County; Elisha B. Maynard, Judge.

Action by one Olds and another against the City Trust, Safe-Deposit & Surety Company. From a judgment for plaintiffs, defendant appeals. Affirmed.

Wm. G. Bassett and Edw. L. Shaw, for appellant. John B. O'Donnell and E. Henry Hyde, for appellees.

BARKER, J. The plaintiffs, Olds and Whipple, on November 11, 1896, brought an action of contract in the superior court in Hampshire county against the Mapes Reeve Construction Company by a writ the ad damnum of which was $10,000, and in which one De Witt Smith, alleged therein to be commorant of Northampton, was named as trustee of the defendant, with goods, effects, and credits of the defendant in his hands to that amount. The alleged trustee answered that he was not a citizen or resident of Massachusetts, that he had no place of business therein, and that he had no goods, effects, or credits of the defendants in his hands, except that the construction company had brought an action against him seeking to establish a certain disputed claim, and to establish a lien therefor upon certain real estate belonging to him in Northampton, submitting himself to examination, and asking to be discharged, and for his costs. The construction company, on January 11, 1897, entered a general appearance, and filed an answer denying each and every material allegation in the writ and declaration. This being the situation of the case in court at the October sitting in 1898, the construction company filed a motion, alleging that there was an attachment of its property on mesne process in the suit, by the summoning therein of the alleged trustee, to the amount of $10,000, and that the same was excessive, and asking for a reduction of the attachment. At the same sitting, by consent and by order of the court, the attachment was reduced to $4,500. Thereupon, on or about November 16, 1898, the construction company, as principal, and the City Trust, Safe-Deposit & Surety Company of Philadelphia, the defendant in the present suit, as surety, gave to the plaintiffs a joint and several bond for the sum of $4,500, reciting the attachment, and stating that the construction company desired to dissolve it according to law. The present action is brought to recover from the surety upon this bond. One condition of the bond, among others not now material, is that, if the construction company shall, within 30 days after the final judgment in the action in which the attachment was made, pay to the plaintiffs the amount, if any, which they shall recover in the action, the obligation of the bond shall be void. Thereafter the action was referred to an auditor, and such other proceedings were had therein that on December 3, 1900, judgment for the plaintiff was entered therein, by consent, for $4,354.13 damages, and $94.33 costs, and on this judgment execution issued on December 5, 1900. The construction company refusing to pay the judgment, demand was made on the surety company to pay it or to satisfy the execution, and on March 1, 1901, this suit was brought against it on the bond of November 16, 1898. The action was heard upon an agreed statement of facts by the superior court, sitting without a jury, in June, 1903, and after a finding for the plaintiffs in the sum of $5,157 damages, filed on August 10, 1893, the defendant appealed to this court, a judgment for the plaintiffs upon the finding having been entered in the superior court as of August 10, 1893.

1. The first contention of the defendant is that the bond was neither a good statutory bond nor a good common-law bond, and that therefore it is invalid. In support of this contention it is urged that there was no attachment, because the alleged trustee answered in such a way as to discharge himself. But his answer was not an absolute denial of funds. It in substance admitted that the construction company contended that he owed it a debt for which it was prosecuting a suit against him in which the company sought to establish a lien for its debt upon his land in Northampton. One of the agreed facts is that when the service was made on the alleged trustee he was indebted to the construction company in a sum greater than the amount of the judgment which the plaintiffs recovered against that company, and that he paid the company his debt after the bond now in suit was filed. When the bond was offered it was still open to the plaintiff to file interrogatories to the alleged trustee upon all matters stated in his answer, and if he had answered truly it would have appeared that when summoned as trustee he was largely indebted to the construction company. It cannot now be assumed that, if compelled to answer interrogatories as an alleged trustee, he would not have made statements upon which he would have been charged, and the debt due from him to the construction company held and applied under the process to the extinguishment of the plaintiffs' demand. In consequence of the filing of the bond the alleged trustee was subjected to no further proceedings in the suit, and the plaintiff was left to rely wholly on the bond. The short answer to the contention that the bond is invalid is that, it having been given under such circumstances, it is not open to the defendant, when sued upon it, to contend that there was no attachment. It was intended to induce the plaintiffs to abandon their attempt to appropriate to the payment of their demand then in suit a debt owing by the alleged trustee to the construction company, and it did have that result, to the legal detriment of the plaintiff. All the elements of an estoppel are present. See Stiff v. Ashton, 155 Mass. 139, 29 N. E. 208.

2. The defendant contends that its position as one of the obligors of the bond was merely that of a guarantor of the solvency of the construction company and of one Reeve, who, when the bond was given, was indorser on promissory notes given by that company to the plaintiff as collateral to the demand on which the suit was being prosecuted. But the contract entered into by the defendant was an explicit undertaking to pay the plaintiff $4,500, unless the construction company should pay a judgment within 30 days after it might be rendered. It would be absurd to hold that the surety on a bond given to dissolve an attachment could require the obligee to exhaust any collateral security which he might hold before taking judgment in the suit in which the bond was given. If, as we do not intimate, such an obligor has any concern with the action of his obligee as to collateral, or as to other remedies which may be open to the obligee as against the defendant whose property is to be freed from the attachment, it can be no more than a right to subrogation on payment of his bond, and in no event can it be more than an equitable defense to a suit upon his bond. The agreed facts show that the notes held as collateral were in existence and maturing when the bond was given, and that they never were renewed. While the agreed facts state that Reeve testifies that when the notes matured he was solvent and able to pay them, and that he thereafter became insolvent and unable to pay them, it is not a conclusion of law from

that statement that he was ever solvent, or that any suit against him on the notes would have brought in money to the plaintiff. It is plain that the court which heard the case on the agreed facts was not bound in law to find for the defendant because of the collateral notes or the plaintiff's conduct with reference to them.

8. The remaining contention is that the judgment against the construction company was void because that corporation was dissolved before the judgment was entered. The corporation was one organized under the general laws of the state of New York. Upon a petition of its directors for a voluntary dissolution, an order was entered in the Supreme Court of New York on November 13, 1899, appointing a receiver, and another order, making the appointment permanent and purporting to dissolve the corporation, was entered on May 4, 1900. The only statement in the agreed facts as to the law of New York is that the court could have provided in its decree purporting to dissolve the corporation for the continuance in its name of suits then pending by and against it, and did not so provide. Neither of these orders was brought to the attention of the superior court, and no proceedings were taken to enforce them here. There seems to have been a studied attempt to keep the plaintiff in this suit, and the courts in which this suit was pending, in ignorance of the dissolution proceedings. The original suit against the construction company was sent to an auditor, who filed his report in favor of the plaintiff in May, 1899. The New York decree purporting to dissolve the construction company was entered on May 4, 1900. The Massachusetts suit was tried by the court without a jury in June, 1900, and a finding filed in August, 1900. The plaintiff took exceptions to the full court, which were argued in October, 1900, a rescript was sent down October 20, 1900, and judgment was entered by agreement in December, 1900. The attorney for the surety company in the present action was attorney for the construction company in the original action. One Kimber of New York, attorney, assisted in the defense of the construction company in the original action from beginning to end, and is assisting the surety company in the same capacity in the present action. This same Kimber presented, in November, 1899, the petition in the New York court for the dissolution of the construction company, and it was upon his motion that the dissolution was decreed on May 4, 1900. After this decree, and without giving notice of it to the Massachusetts courts, this same Kimber allowed the Massachusetts attorney who had appeared for the defense up to that time to appear for the construction company and to try the case for it before the superior court in June, 1900, and then to argue the exceptions for the construction company in October, 1900, and then to agree to a judgment against the construction company in December, 1900. The plaintiffs contend that the provisions of our statute relating to corporations whose charters have expired, or whose corporate existence has been terminated in any other manner, originally enacted in St. 1819, c. 43, and now found in Rev. Laws, c. 109, § 53, kept the construction company in existence as a body corporate in Massachusetts for three years from May 4, 1900. Whether similar statutes should be held to apply to corporations created by any other sovereignty than that by which the statutes are enacted has been more or less discussed, and with results which have varied in different jurisdictions. See Fitts v. National Life Association, 130 Ala. 413, 30 South. 374; Marion Phosphate Co. v. Perry, 74 Fed. 425, 20 C. C. A. 490, 33 L. R. A. 252; Stetson v. City Bank of New Orleans, 2 Ohio St. 167, and 12 Ohio St. 577; Life Association of America v. Fassett, 102 Ill. 315; Rodgers v. Adriatic Ins. Co., 148 N. Y. 34, 42 N. E. 515; Hammond v. National Life Association (Sup.) 69 N. Y. Supp. 585, and 168 N. Y. 262, 61 N. E. 244. We are of the opinion that our own statutes referred to were intended by the Legislature to apply only to our own domestic corporations. At the same time we are not ready to concede that, after the dissolution of a foreign corporation by the sovereignty by which it was created, its creditors in this state cannot in some way, by proceedings in equity or otherwise, take advantage of the former corporate life, through our own courts, so far as to avail themselves of assets in this state, and we do not now determine whether there was, even if there was, a complete dissolution of the construction company in New York on May 4, 1900. The present case was heard by the lower court upon agreed facts. Since it was agreed that a decree purporting to dissolve the construction company was entered in the Supreme Court of New York on May 4, 1900, the finding for the plaintiffs implies a finding that the decree of dissolution was void. The court which entered it was a court of general jurisdiction; but the dissolution of a corporation is a peculiar function, which resides primarily in the Legislature, and is conferred upon courts only by explicit legislative authority. Folger v. Columbian Insurance Co., 99 Mass. 267, 96 Am. Dec. 747. Therefore the decree of dissolution was void, unless jurisdiction to enter it had been conferred upon the Supreme Court of New York by some statute law of that state. Therefore it was a question of fact for the lower court in the present case whether jurisdiction to dissolve the construction company had been given to the New York court by a statute of that state. The agreed statement of facts does not contain a clause that the court may draw inferences of fact from the facts and evidence stated, and therefore neither the inferior court in the first instance, nor this court upon the appeal, had or has the right to found its judgment upon any disputable inferences of fact. Old Colony Railroad v. Wilder, 137 Mass.

536, 538; Gallagher v. Hathaway Mfg. Co., 169 Mass. 578, 48 N. E. 844. Unless upon the facts stated, "with the inevitable inferences, or, in other words, such inferences as the law draws from them," jurisdiction to dissolve the corporation appeared, neither the inferior court nor this court can infer such jurisdiction, nor find that the construction company was in fact dissolved. It is not an inevitable inference which the law draws conclusively from the entry of a judgment by a court of general jurisdiction that the court which entered it had jurisdiction of the cause, or to give all the relief which by its decree it purported to give. Nor is there any presumption in Massachusetts that the statutes of New York give power to any court of New York to dissolve a corporation. See Kelley v. Kelley, 161 Mass. 111, 112, 36 N. E. 837, 25 L. R. A. 806, 42 Am. St. Rep. 389. Therefore the precise question is whether it was an inevitable inference from the agreed facts that the New York court had jurisdiction to decree a dissolution of the corporation on May 4, 1900, and then did make a decree, not only purporting to dissolve the construction company, but which in law and fact actually then extinguished totally its life. In our opinion no such inevitable inference is drawn by the law from the facts stated, and therefore neither the lower court, nor this court upon the appeal, was precluded from finding that the judgment entered against the construction company after the date of the decree purporting to dissolve it was a valid judgment.

Judgment for plaintiff affirmed.

(185 Mass. 576)

DOLAN v. BOOTT COTTON MILLS.

(Supreme Judicial Court of Massachusetts. Middlesex. May 19, 1904.)

TRIAL—LIST OF JURY CASES—NOTICE—TIME FOR FILING—EXTENSION—MASTER AND SERVANT—DEFECTIVE MACHINERY—UNCOVERED GEARING—CUSTOM IN OTHER MILLS—ADMISSIBILITY OF EVIDENCE — NEGLIGENCE—INADEQUATE INSTRUCTIONS TO SERVANT — SUFFICIENCY OF EVIDENCE.

1. Under Rev. Laws, c. 173, § 56, providing that a case may be entered on the list of those to be tried by jury within such time after the parties are at issue as the court may by general or special order direct, and rule 18 of the superior court, providing that notice of a desire for a jury trial shall be filed not later than 10 days after the time allowed for filing the answer or plea, unless the court by special order shall extend the time, it is within the power of the court to make such special order, though the time prescribed by the general order has already expired.

2. In a servant's action for injuries from the uncovered gearing of a machine, in which it was undisputed that such gearing was sometimes covered and sometimes uncovered on different machines, and that the defendant had other machines of the same kind on which it was covered, it was within the discretion of the trial court to exclude a question put by defendant to its overseer as to whether he knew what the fact was about gears of this kind in different mills being operated without covers; there being nothing to show that the witness' knowledge extended further than his observance of the practice in particular mills.

3. Evidence in an action by a servant for injuries from the uncovered gearing of a machine *held* to sustain a finding of the master's negligence in failing to give sufficient instructions, and in giving misleading instructions.

Exceptions from Superior Court, Middlesex County; John A. Aiken, Judge.

Action by one Dolan, an infant, by her next friend, against the Boott Cotton Mills. Verdict for plaintiff, and defendant excepts. Exceptions overruled.

Francis W. Qua, for plaintiff. F. E. Dunbar, for defendant.

KNOWLTON, C. J. The question raised by the first bill of exceptions is whether it was in the power of the court, under Rev. Laws, c. 173, § 56, and rule 18 of the superior court, after the expiration of 10 days from the filing of the answer, to make a special order permitting the plaintiff to put the case on the list of cases to be tried by a jury. That part of the statute which is applicable allows the entry of an action upon this list "within such time after the parties are at issue as the court may by general or special order direct." The general order of the superior court is found in rule 18 of the common-law rules, which provides that notice of a desire for a trial by jury shall be filed "not later than ten days after the time allowed for filing the answer or plea, * * * unless the court by special order shall extend the time." It is plain that the statute contemplates the making of a general order by the court, with power to make a special order in any particular case, as well after the expiration of the time prescribed by the general order as before it. Indeed, if the time prescribed by the general order had not expired, there would ordinarily be no need of a special order. Unless the court by this rule has limited the power given it by the statute, the special order referred to in the rule must be held to include authority to extend the time after its expiration as well as before. While there is force in the argument that the word "extend," used in reference to a period of time, seems to imply the existence of an unexpired portion of the period, there are other opposing considerations applicable to this case which we deem of more weight. In the first place, the court would hardly be expected, by a rule in regard to procedure, to deprive itself of power conferred by the statute to give relief from accidents, and to permit the correction of mistakes. Whether it would have constitutional authority to do so, in a matter relating to the right of trial by jury, is a question which we need not now consider. Under this statute, the rule of the court at that time being expressed in language different from the present rule, this court said in Bailey v. Joy, 132 Mass. 356, that it was within the discretion of the court after the expiration of 10 days to refuse a motion for a trial by jury, and plainly implied that it was within the power of the court to allow it. The case of Cleverly v. O'Connell, 156 Mass. 88, 30 N. E. 88, arose when the twenty-second common-law rule of the superior court, of the edition of 1886, was in force, which ends with the words "unless the court shall by special order restrict or extend the time." These words are certainly as favorable to the defendant's contention as those of the present rule. In that case Chief Justice Field said in the opinion: "After the time provided for filing such a notice by the general rule of the court has elapsed, it is in the discretion of the court * * * to grant or deny to any party the right to file the notice required by the statute." This language was not necessary to the decision, and may be regarded as a dictum. But the case of Haynes v. Saunders, 11 Cush. 537, is a direct adjudication involving the meaning of the word "extend" in a statute, which in this particular is almost identical with the rule of court before us. It was held that the court had power to allow the filing of an affidavit of merits upon a motion made after the expiration of the prescribed time, the statute giving express authority to extend the time. The statute in regard to the filing of exceptions and giving of notice to counsel (Rev. Laws, c. 173, § 106) is materially different. Its intended effect is that on the expiration of the prescribed time the parties shall know definitely whether the decision excepted to stands, or whether it is subject to revision by a higher court. Barstow v. Marsh, 4 Gray, 165; Com. v. Greenlaw, 119 Mass. 208; Conway v. Callahan, 121 Mass. 165; Purcell v. Boston, Halifax, etc., Steamship Company Line, 151 Mass. 158, 23 N. E. 834. We are of opinion that it was within the discretion of the court to make the order permitting a trial by jury.

The exceptions taken at the trial present, first, a question of evidence. The plaintiff was injured by having her fingers caught in the gearing of a fly frame—a kind of spinning machine in the defendant's cotton mill. This gearing was uncovered. One Rice, a witness called by the defendant, testified that he had been an overseer of carding in the defendant's mills for 19 years. This question was put to him by the defendant: "I will ask you, Mr. Rice, if you know what the fact is about gears of this kind, in different mills, being operated without these covers." On objection of the plaintiff, and subject to the defendant's exception, the witness was not permitted to answer. On the question whether the use of a particular machine or appliance by a defendant is negligent, a jury may properly consider all facts that throw light upon it. The possibility and the ease or difficulty of procuring something different which is safer and better are important facts bearing upon it. That something safer has been invented and is in common use is ordinarily a fact of considerable significance. Evidence of this kind is often received in such cases. Wheeler v. Wason Manufacturing Company, 135 Mass. 294; Myers v. Hudson Iron Company, 150 Mass. 125, 22 N. E. 631, 15 Am. St. Rep. 176; Veginan v. Morse, 160 Mass. 143, 35 N. E. 451; McCarthy v. Boston Duck Company, 165 Mass. 165, 42 N. E. 568; McMahon v. McHale, 174 Mass. 320-325, 54 N. E. 854. On the other hand, there is danger that the introduction of such evidence will lead to collateral inquiries which will becloud the main issue. For this reason, much is properly left to the discretion of the presiding judge in determining when it is best to receive such evidence. Veginan v. Morse, ubi supra; McCarthy v. Boston Duck Company, 165 Mass. 165-169, 42 N. E. 568; Ford v. Mt. Tom Sulphite Company, 172 Mass. 544-546, 52 N. E. 1065, 48 L. R. A. 96. Especially is this so if the question relates to the methods of particular persons or in particular places. McCarthy v. Boston Duck Company, ubi supra. It is also to be noted that the methods adopted by certain persons or in certain places, or even the common usage of a small class of persons engaged in a particular business, is not to be made a standard by which the defendant's conduct is to be judged in reference to care. Veginan v. Morse, 160 Mass. 143-148, 35 N. E. 451; Ford v. Mt. Tom Sulphite Company, 172 Mass. 544-546, 52 N. E. 1065, 48 L. R. A. 96. In Hill v. Winsor, 118 Mass. 251-259, Mr. Justice Colt said in the opinion: "There is no rule of law which exempts one from the consequences of his negligent conduct, upon proof that he proceeded in the usual manner, and took the usual course pursued by parties similarly situated, although he was without notice that he could not safely do so. The defendants cannot protect themselves by proving the careless practices of others," etc. It is conceivable that the persons engaged in a certain business, comprising but a small class working in a narrow range, may have adopted generally a method which ordinary persons, of different callings and with a broader view, would generally condemn as careless. Such a method is not the standard by which one is to be judged, although, if it can easily be proved, it is competent evidence for a jury, in some kinds of cases, on the question whether he exercised due care.

In actions against towns for accidents upon highways, and in other similar cases, such evidence is excluded, chiefly because it relates to methods of dealing with external conditions which differ greatly in different cases, and which cannot be understood without opening unprofitable collateral inquiries. Perhaps another reason for its exclusion in the early cases was that, under the law prior to St. 1877, p. 630, c. 234, the liability of cities and towns depended upon a failure to maintain the way at a required standard of safety, rather than upon a failure to use reasonable care and diligence. Hinckley v. Barnstable, 109 Mass. 126; Bailey v. New Haven & Northampton Company, 107 Mass. 496; Craven v. Mayers, 165 Mass. 271, 42 N. E. 1131. In the present case it appeared as an undisputed fact that upon different machines this gearing was sometimes covered and sometimes uncovered, and that the defendant had other machines of the same kind on which it was covered. So far as appears, an answer to the question would have added nothing to the facts which were not in controversy. At all events, there is nothing to show that the knowledge of the witness extended further than his observation of the practice in certain particular mills, and the ruling falls within the decision in McCarthy v. Boston Duck Company, 165 Mass. 165-169, 42 N. E. 568, and other similar cases, in which the exclusion of such questions was held to be within the discretion of the presiding judge.

There was evidence that the defendant was negligent in failing to give the plaintiff sufficient instructions, and in giving her misleading instructions. The plaintiff was a girl 14 years of age, who had just begun to work in the defendant's mill as a bobbin girl. She had never before worked outside of her home, and she had no knowledge of machinery. She worked three weeks upon a machine, and it had been a part of her duty to clean the machine. The gearing on this machine was covered. She was then taken to another room, and put to work under another girl upon a machine like the first, except that the part of the gearing by which she was injured was left uncovered. There was evidence that she was told to clean this machine, without being given any instructions or warning as to this part of the gearing. After she had worked upon it three days, the accident happened. The evidence tended to show that it was not safe to clean this part of the gearing on this machine when it was in motion, and that the girl in charge of it, under whom the plaintiff was working, had been accustomed to stop the machine and clean this part herself. The plaintiff's testimony tended to show that, under the directions given her, she supposed, and was warranted in supposing, that it was her duty to clean this gearing, as well as other parts of the machine, while it was in motion. The judge rightly declined to rule that there was no evidence to warrant a verdict for the plaintiff. The other requests for instructions, so far as they correctly state propositions of law, were sufficiently covered by the charge.

Exceptions overruled.

(185 Mass. 492)

GORDON v. RICHARDSON.

(Supreme Judicial Court of Massachusetts. Suffolk. May 17, 1904.)

LEASES—RELIEF FROM FORFEITURE—FAILURE TO PAY TAXES—APPEAL.

1. While relief may be had from forfeiture of a lessee's estate for failure to pay rent, relief will not be granted from forfeiture for breach of covenant to pay taxes, where the landlord's estate has been sold to pay the tax; at least, where accident or mistake on the lessee's part is not shown.

2. On appeal from a decree dismissing the bill, there being no statement of facts found or rulings made, the decree, so far as it involves matters of fact, will stand, unless it appears by the evidence, allowing for the court's right to discredit testimony, to be clearly erroneous.

3. One bringing suit in equity for relief from a forfeiture at law may not claim there was no forfeiture at law.

¶ 1. See Landlord and Tenant, vol. 32, Cent. Dig. § 342.

Appeal from Superior Court, Suffolk County.

Suit by Albert L. Gordon against Alice G. Richardson. Bill dismissed, and plaintiff appeals. Affirmed.

Chas. R. Darling, for appellant. Harvey N. Shepard, for respondent.

LORING, J. The ground on which a tenant gets relief in equity from the forfeiture of his estate for a failure to pay rent is that in equity the landlord's right of re-entry is given as security for the payment of the rent, and on the rent being paid the very thing is done for which the security was given; and, although the payment in that case is made after it is due, on interest being paid compensation is made for the delay in performance, and on compensation being made relief is given. Peachy v. Somerset, 1 Stra. 447; Hill v. Barclay, 16 Ves. 402, and 18 Ves. 56; Reynolds v. Pitt, 19 Ves. 134; Howard v. Fanshawe [1895] 2 Ch. 589. The Massachusetts cases are Atkins v. Chilson, 11 Metc. 112; Sanborn v. Woodman, 5 Cush. 36. See, also, in this connection, Stone v. Ellis, 9 Cush. 95; Hancock v. Carlton, 6 Gray, 39, explained in Mactier v. Osborn, 146 Mass. 399, 402, 15 N. E. 641, 4 Am. St. Rep. 323.

But that does not cover the case before us. In this case the defendant entered for breach of the covenant to pay taxes, as well as for breach of the covenant to pay rent. When he exercised his right of re-entry in September, 1902, not only was the tax for 1900 not paid, but the estate of the defendant had been sold because of the plaintiff's failure to pay this tax as he had agreed to do. The defendant's estate had been sold to pay this tax in the June preceding the September when the defendant entered on the estate. The thing here in question secured by the right of re-entry not only has not been performed, but it cannot now be performed. The tax for 1900 has been paid, and no longer can be paid by the plaintiff. The tax was paid to the collector by the application thereto of the proceeds of the tax sale. There is a right to redeem this tax title, but the tax has been paid, and the thing secured by the landlord's right of reentry can no longer be performed by the tenant. By the very terms of the covenant secured by the forfeiture, any performance of it is at an end, and that is the end of the plaintiff's application for relief from the forfeiture in the case at bar.

Moreover, if it were permissible to look beyond the terms of the covenant here in question to what might be termed its true nature and substance, the plaintiff would gain nothing. If you look behind its terms, the real substance and nature of a covenant to pay taxes assessed on the demised premises is to protect and hold harmless the landlord's estate. When the breach of the covenant has reached the stage where the landlord's estate is sold to pay the taxes which the tenant should have paid, where the stage has been reached that through the default of the tenant a paramount outstanding title has come into existence, we have a breach of covenant for which the plaintiff fails to show that compensation can be made. We have a breach of a covenant, like the breach of a covenant to insure or repair, where equity does not ordinarily grant relief against forfeiture of the tenant's estate. Mactier v. Osborn, 146 Mass. 399, 402, 15 N. E. 641, 4 Am. St. Rep. 323. Hill v. Barclay, 16 Ves. 402, and 18 Ves. 56 (overruling Lord Erskine's opinion in Sanders v. Pope, 12 Ves. 282, which never went to decree, page 294); Reynolds v. Pitt, 19 Ves. 134; Bracebridge v. Buckley, 2 Price, 200; Green v. Bridges, 4 Sim. 96. Lord Erskine's opinion in Sanders v. Pope was in effect that the forfeiture of a leasehold estate for breach of a collateral covenant stood on the same ground at common law as that on which the forfeiture of a bond stands under St. 8 & 9 Wm. III, c. 11, § 8, which (as Baron Parke said in Beckham v. Drake, 2 H. L. 579, 629) "in effect makes the bond a security only for the damages really sustained." But that view did not prevail. It is settled that in case of waste (Peachy v. Somerset, 1 Stra. 447), in case of a breach of a covenant to make repairs (Hill v. Barclay, 16 Ves. 402, and 18 Ves. 56; Bracebridge v. Buckley, 2 Price, 200), and in case of the breach of a covenant to insure (Reynolds v. Pitt, 19 Ves. 134; Green v. Bridges, 4 Sim. 96), it being impossible for the tenant to show affirmatively that compensation can be made, relief ordinarily will not be given. It was this which C. Allen, J., had in mind in Lundin v. Schoeffel, 167 Mass. 465, 469, 45 N. E. 933, when he said of the case then before the court that it "was not like a case where the omission caused a present injury or increase of risk to the lessors, as in the case of waste, nonrepair, or noninsurance." The lack of recent cases in England is owing to the fact that relief is given by statute in case of covenants other than the covenant to pay rent. St. 22 & 23 Vict. c. 35, § 4, authorized relief in case of the breach of a covenant to insure, and St. 44 & 45 Vict. c. 41, § 14, in case of all other covenants except the covenant to pay rent (see clause 8 of section 14), in case of which a bill must be brought within six months from the execution putting the landlord in possession, by force of St. 4 Geo. II, c. 28. It is settled that, if a bill is brought within the time allowed for relief against a forfeiture for breach of a covenant to pay rent, the relief is given at common law. Howard v. Fanshawe [1895] 2 Ch. 589; Stanhope v. Haworth, 3 T. L. R. 34. As to the purpose of St. 4 Geo. II, c. 28, see Lord Mansfield in Doe v. Lewis, 1 Burr. 614, 619, and Wigram, V. C., in Bowser v. Colby, 1 Hare, 109, 125.

From what has been said, it is apparent that we are not prepared to go so far as the Court of Appeals went in its opinion in Giles v. Austin, 62 N. Y. 486, 493. The facts in that case are stated in 6 Jones & S. 215, and it appears that the failure to pay the taxes in that case was through accident and mistake.

There is, however, jurisdiction to relieve against a forfeiture for breach of collateral covenants, if the breach came through accident or mistake. This was established in this commonwealth in Mactier v. Osborn, 146 Mass. 399, 15 N. E. 641, 4 Am. St. Rep. 323, following the suggestion of Lord Eldon in Hill v. Barclay, 18 Ves. 56, 62, affirmed in Bamford v. Creasy, 3 Giff. 675, 680, and Bargent v. Thomson, 4 Giff. 473. If it be assumed in favor of the plaintiff that he could have relief here on proving that it was through an accident or a mistake on his part that the nonpayment of the 1900 taxes went to a sale, the decree must be affirmed. The case comes here by appeal from a decree dismissing the bill. The evidence is before us, but there is no statement of facts found or of rulings made. The decree, so far as it involves matters of fact, is to stand, unless it appears by the evidence to be clearly erroneous. Brown v. Brown, 174 Mass. 197, 54 N. E. 522, 75 Am. St. Rep. 303; Dickinson v. Todd, 172 Mass. 184, 51 N. E. 976; Edwards-Hall Co. v. Dresser, 168 Mass. 136, 46 N. E. 420; Lundin v. Schoeffel, 167 Mass. 165, 45 N. E. 933. See, also, Blossom v. Negus, 182 Mass. 515, 65 N. E. 846. It is enough that the presiding judge who saw the plaintiff on the stand may not have given credit to the excuse which he made, namely, that the sale for the 1900 tax was made earlier than usual. So far as the case depends upon a finding of fact, the decree must be affirmed.

We have not considered the plaintiff's argument that there was no forfeiture of the lease. We are of opinion that, in a bill in equity to be relieved from a forfeiture at law, it is not open to him to make the contention that there is no forfeiture at law. Such a case comes within Pitkin v. Springfield, 112 Mass. 309, in which it was held that, in a petition for compensation for land taken, it was not open to contend that the statute providing for the taking was unconstitutional, or that the taking was invalid. See, also, in this connection, Smith v. Valence, 1 Rep. Ch. 90. The case of Boston &

Maine Railroad v. Graham, 179 Mass. 62, 60 N. E. 405, stands on its special circumstances. Whether the plaintiff could have attacked the forfeiture at law and filed this bill in case he was unsuccessful at law (see Moore v. Sanford, 151 Mass. 285, 24 N. E. 323, 7 L. R. A. 151), or must in such a case make his election in the first instance, it is not necessary to consider.

Decree affirmed.

(185 Mass. 533)

DONOVAN v. LYNN & B. R. CO.

(Supreme Judicial Court of Massachusetts. Suffolk. May 18, 1904.)

STREET RAILROADS—INJURY AT CROSSING—CONTRIBUTORY NEGLIGENCE.

1. Where the street car by which plaintiff was injured was well lighted, so it could be seen 150 to 300 feet, and was only 10 feet away when she stepped on the track, and made sufficient noise in the setting of brakes to attract attention, she was guilty of contributory negligence, barring recovery for her injury.

Exceptions from Superior Court, Suffolk County; Henry N. Sheldon, Judge.

Action by one Donovan against the Lynn & Boston Railroad Company. To a ruling that plaintiff could not recover, and a direction of a verdict for defendant, plaintiff excepts. Exceptions overruled.

Michael F. Phelan and Edward E. Reardon, for plaintiff. Henry F. Hurlbut and Damon E. Hall, for defendant.

MORTON, J. This is an action of tort to recover for personal injuries caused by the plaintiff's being struck by one of the defendant's cars as she was crossing Chelsea street, in Charlestown, on the evening of July 8, 1899. At the close of the plaintiff's evidence, the court ruled that she could not recover, and directed a verdict for the defendant. The case is here on the plaintiff's exceptions to this ruling and direction.

We think that the ruling was right, and that the plaintiff was not in the exercise of due care. The accident happened at about 11 o'clock in the evening, and the plaintiff was struck by the car just as she was in the act of stepping onto the track. The night was misty and rainy. The plaintiff lived near by, and was familiar with the street and the running of the cars. She was on her way to a store to purchase some meat. She testified that as she came to the crossing she looked around, and saw that a car was just about as far as Gray street; that she "just gave a look around, and saw another car coming from City Square, quite a distance away, also going towards Chelsea"; that she "walked along the crossing, and * * * was struck by a car coming along from Chelsea and going towards City Square"; that she "did not see any car coming from Chelsea; did not hear any gong nor any car." But the uncontradicted testimony of her own witnesses showed that the car which struck her was well lighted, and, notwithstanding that the night was misty and raining, could be seen from 150 to 300 feet away. It also showed that the car was only 10 feet away when she stepped onto the track, and that the noise made by the motorman in putting on the brakes was sufficient to attract attention. The distance from the curbing to the track on which she was in the act of stepping when struck was 17½ feet, and her own statement on cross-examination was that she "stepped down onto the crosswalk and walked right across on the crossing, and was struck"; that she "walked kind of fast," and all she "noticed was the car which the last time" she "saw it was at Gray street, and the other car some distance away from me, coming out from City Square"; and that she paid no attention to anything, except that she was going to some store. If she looked as she stepped onto the cross-walk, it would seem to have been done so hastily and carelessly as to give her no information as to the actual situation on which she was justified in relying, and she passed over the distance between the sidewalk and the track on which the car was approaching, and stepped onto the track, almost in front of the car, without, so far as appears, taking any further precaution to guard against accident. It is true that there is no absolute rule of law that requires that a person should look and listen before crossing an electric street railway track. Robbins v. Springfield St. Ry. Co. (Mass.) 42 N. E. 334. But the circumstances may be such that a failure to look or listen will be conclusive evidence of a want of due care. Hall v. West End St. Ry., 168 Mass. 461, 47 N. E. 124; Kelly v. Wakefield, etc., St. Ry., 175 Mass. 331, 56 N. E. 285. In the present case, we think, as already observed, that the circumstances show that the plaintiff was not in the exercise of due care.

Exceptions overruled.

¶ 1. See Street Railroads, vol. 44, Cent. Dig. §§ 207, 208.

(186 Mass. 67)

McCARTHY v. PEACH.

(Supreme Judicial Court of Massachusetts. Suffolk. May 20, 1904.)

EVIDENCE—TELEPHONE CONVERSATIONS—QUESTIONS FOR JURY.

1. Testimony of a witness, who was present in the room with plaintiff while the latter was telephoning to defendant, as to what witness heard plaintiff say during the course of the conversation, was admissible, to show the conversation, although the witness had no personal knowledge as to whom plaintiff was talking with, and did not hear anything that defendant said, and did not know that defendant heard anything that plaintiff said; plaintiff testifying that the conversation was with defendant.

2. In an action on a contract, the question whether a certain telephone conversation between plaintiff and defendant took place as alleged, or was fictitious, was one for the jury.

Exceptions from Superior Court, Suffolk County; Wm. Cushing Wait, Judge.

Action by Charles J. McCarthy against John Peach. Verdict for plaintiff, and defendant excepted. Exceptions overruled.

Cutler & James, for plaintiff. Edwin C. Jenney, for defendant.

MORTON, J. This is an action to recover a balance alleged to be due to the plaintiff from the defendant for services rendered in securing a customer for an express business in Salem. There was a verdict for the plaintiff, and the case is here on the defendant's exceptions.

The only question is whether a witness was properly allowed to testify to what he heard the plaintiff say as a part of an alleged conversation with the defendant over the telephone; the plaintiff being in Boston, and the defendant in Chelsea, and the witness being in the presence and hearing of the plaintiff. The witness had no personal knowledge with whom the plaintiff was talking, and did not hear anything that was alleged to have been said by the defendant, and did not know that the defendant heard anything that the plaintiff said. At the argument of the case it was admitted by counsel for the defendant that the plaintiff testified that the conversation was with the defendant. We think that the evidence was rightly admitted. The analogies furnished by conversations between parties through an interpreter and conversations in a loud tone by one party and a whisper by the other are not altogether complete. In such cases a third party who testifies to more or less of the conversation, as the case may be, is in the presence of the persons whose conversation he undertakes to repeat, and therefore has personal knowledge in respect to the parties to the conversation, though he may not have or understand all that is said by the principals. In the present case the witness had no personal knowledge as to the identity of the other party to the alleged conversation, or that there was any other party, or, if there was, that he heard what the plaintiff purported to say to him. It is not contended that the mere fact that the conversation was over a telephone rendered what the witness testified to incompetent. Lord Electric Co. v. Morrill, 178 Mass. 304, 59 N. E. 807. The evidence that was admitted cannot be regarded as hearsay evidence, or declarations made by the plaintiff in his own interest, simply because the witness did not know of his own knowledge that the other party to the alleged conversation was the defendant, or that there was any other party, or that the defendant heard what purported to be said to him. If the alleged conversation took place as the plaintiff testified that it did, then what the plaintiff said was admissible as a part of it. Whether it did take place as alleged, or was fictitious, was a question of fact for the jury. It could not be ruled, as matter of law, that there was no evidence of a conversation between the plaintiff and defendant of which what was testified to by the witness constituted a part. See Miles v. Andrews, 153 Ill. 267, 38 N. E. 644; Sullivan v. Kuykendall, 82 Ky. 483, 56 Am. Rep. 901; Oskamp v. Gadsden, 35 Neb. 7, 52 N. W. 718, 17 L. R. A. 440, 37 Am. St. Rep. 428; Wolfe v. Missouri Pacific Ry. Co., 97 Mo. 473, 11 S. W. 49, 3 L. R. A. 539, 10 Am. St. Rep. 331.

Exceptions overruled.

(186 Mass. 54)

CITY OF CAMBRIDGE v. HANSCOM et al.

(Supreme Judicial Court of Massachusetts. Suffolk. May 20, 1904.)

SUBROGATION—TORTS — INDEMNITY—ENFORCEMENT—CITY SOLICITORS—INDEPENDENT EMPLOYMENT—COMPENSATION.

1. Where judgments for tort were obtained against a city in such a manner as to give it a recovery over against a water board representing the commonwealth, or against contractors acting under contract with the water board—such contractors being the parties ultimately liable—and the commonwealth paid the judgment, it was subrogated to the rights of the city against the contractors; and the city could enforce the commonwealth's right of subrogation in an action against the contractors for the use of the commonwealth, although the judgments were never paid by the city, but by the commonwealth directly to the judgment creditors.

2. Where a city solicitor, receiving from the city a stated compensation for his services, but being under no obligation not to engage in individual practice, was retained by the commonwealth to conduct the defense of a suit against the city, the defense of which was assumed by the commonwealth, and was paid by the commonwealth for his services, the city, being under no obligation to pay him for such services, could not maintain an action, on the theory of subrogation, to recover the amount paid by the commonwealth for its own use, or for the use of the commonwealth, against the persons who were ultimately liable for the amount of the judgment recovered in the action against it.

Appeal from Superior Court, Suffolk County.

Action by the city of Cambridge, for the benefit of the commonwealth of Massachusetts, against Harvey A. A. Hanscom and others. From a judgment for plaintiff, defendants appeal. Reversed.

The facts are that in August, 1897, two persons were injured on a public highway in Cambridge, and recovered judgments against the city and against the defendants in this action. The judgments were enforced against the city only, but they were so obtained that payment was actually made by the commonwealth. The defendants in this case were acting under contract with the metropolitan water board, which employed Mr. Pevey to defend the actions brought against the city on the refusal of the defendants to assume their defense. Mr. Pevey at the time was solicitor of the city of Cambridge, receiving for his services a stated compensation. In this case he was authorized to act, and was directed by one of the Attorney General's assistants. Other facts necessary to an understanding of the case sufficiently appear in the opinion.

Geo. W. Buck, for appellants. Ralph A. Stewart, Asst. Atty. Gen., for appellee.

HAMMOND, J. The judgments against the city of Cambridge established its liability, and there rested upon it the duty of paying them. If it had paid them, then, upon the agreed facts, it would have had a right to recover either against the metropolitan water board, representing the commonwealth, or against the defendants. If it had proceeded against the defendants, and had recovered from them, that would end the matter, because the latter had no right of indemnity against any one. If it had proceeded against the water board, representing the commonwealth, then the latter, upon paying, would have had an action of indemnity against the defendants, because, as between the defendants and the board, the former were ultimately liable; and, under the well-established principles of subrogation, the commonwealth would have been subrogated to the rights of the city against the defendants. Hart v. Western Railroad, 13 Metc. 99, 46 Am. Dec. 719; Wall v. Mason, 102 Mass. 313, 316.

It is urged, however, by the defendants, that the city met with no loss, because the judgments were paid, not by it, but by the commonwealth. But this manner of payment can make no difference. To hold that the rights of the commonwealth were unfavorably affected by its payment of the judgments, instead of waiting for the city to pay, and then paying the city, is to lose sight of the substance of the transaction. The city of Cambridge was under the weight of the liability established by the judgments, and was called upon to discharge them. It was the duty of the commonwealth to relieve the city from that load. The money was paid by it, not in the discharge of any duty due from it to the judgment creditors, but in the discharge of its duty to indemnify and protect the city, and the simple fact that the payment was made directly to the judgment creditors cannot make the transaction any the less one of indemnity. So far, therefore, as respects the amount of the judgments, the commonwealth is subrogated to the right of the plaintiff against the defendants.

But as to the counsel fee of $1,000 paid by the commonwealth to Mr. Pevey, the case is different. It is plain, upon the agreed facts, that the commonwealth assumed the defense of the cases, and hired Mr. Pevey as its counsel, and that the above sum was paid to him as such, and not as city solicitor of Cambridge. It is true that he was the general solicitor of Cambridge, which paid him an annual salary, but he was not under the exclusive employ of the city. He had the right to engage in business outside of, and in addition to, his work as city solicitor, and such always had been the custom on the part of all those who ever had held the office. Under these circumstances he was employed by the commonwealth. It is the same as though some other person than he had been employed. The city of Cambridge never was under any obligation to him or to anybody else to pay this fee. This sum was not, nor was it ever intended to be, any part of the money to be paid by the city to him as city solicitor, and in paying it the commonwealth discharged no obligation or liability of the city. If it be said that, in so far as Mr. Pevey acted as city solicitor in these cases, it may be assumed that a part of his official salary went to pay for these services, the answer is that this fee does not cover what he did as city solicitor, but what he did as counsel for the commonwealth, under his employment as such. Since the city never paid this fee, and never was under any obligation, contingent or absolute, to pay it, the doctrine of subrogation is not applicable, and the city cannot maintain an action to recover it for its own use, or for that of any other party. "There can be no subrogation unless there is something to be subrogated to." Morton, J., in Skinner v. Tirrell, 159 Mass. 474, 34 N. E. 692, 21 L. R. A. 673, 38 Am. St. Rep. 447.

Judgment reversed and case remanded to superior court, with instructions to enter judgment only for the amounts paid on the judgments, with interest.

(186 Mass. 31)

TAFT v. SMITH et al.

(Supreme Judicial Court of Massachusetts. Franklin. May 20, 1904.)

TRUSTS—MANAGEMENT OF TRUST ESTATE—TRUSTEE'S GOOD FAITH—SOUND DISCRETION—WRONGFUL ACT—RESULTING LOSS.

1. A trustee, in making investments, and in the general management of the trust, is held only to good faith and sound discretion, and is not liable for the consequences of an error in judgment, unless the error is such as to show either that he acted in bad faith, or failed to exercise sound discretion.

2. Whether a trustee, in making an investment of the trust fund, acted in good faith and exercised sound discretion, must be determined with reference to the situation at the time the investment was made, and not in the light of subsequent events which could not have been reasonably anticipated.

3. A trustee held a farm subject to a mortgage of $1,300. By order of the probate court it was sold for $4,300, including the first mortgage. The purchaser paid the trustee $1,000 in

cash and gave his note for $2,000, payable in annual sums of $100, secured by a mortgage on the property subject to the prior mortgage of $1,300. The trustee had no reason to anticipate that the value of the property would depreciate to any appreciable extent, but in seven years it depreciated 50 per cent., due to general causes applicable to the whole neighborhood. *Held* not to show that the trustee did not exercise sound discretion in making the loan.

4. While, as a general rule, a trustee should not invest in second mortgages, it cannot be said that under every circumstance such an investment is inconsistent with sound discretion.

5. A trustee was a creditor of an insolvent. The debt was secured by a mortgage on real estate. The trustee and assignee in insolvency joined in making a sale of the property mortgaged without complying with Gen. St. 1860, c. 118, § 27, requiring such sale to be made under the supervision of the court, and hence the trustee could not prove against the estate of the insolvent the balance due. It did not appear that the assignee had any property belonging to the insolvent's estate. *Held* that, though the trustee could not plead ignorance of the law in justification of his wrongful act, he was not liable, as no loss was shown to have resulted therefrom.

Report from Superior Court, Franklin County; John A. Aiken, Judge.

Bill in equity by one Taft against one Smith, executor of Geo. R. Smith, deceased, and others, for accounting of Geo. R. Smith as guardian of Esther Wright and as trustee of Sophia Wright. On report from the superior court. Bill dismissed.

Henry J. Field and Archibald D. Flower, for plaintiff. Burt H. Winn and Lamb & Lawler, for respondents.

HAMMOND, J. All exceptions to the form of the proceedings having been waived by the defendant, the case is before us on the master's report; and the first question arising on the merits is whether the investment in the second mortgage was improper. It has long been the rule in this commonwealth that in making investments, as well as in the general management of the trust, a trustee is held only to good faith and sound discretion, and hence that he cannot be held for the consequences of an error in judgment, unless the error is such as to show either that he acted in bad faith or failed to exercise sound discretion. Harvard College v. Amory, 9 Pick. 446; Pine v. White, 175 Mass. 585, 590, 56 N. E. 967. The master having found that the trustee acted in good faith, the real question upon this branch of the case is whether he failed to use sound discretion. Of course, this question should be determined with reference to the situation at the time the investment was made, and not in the light of subsequent events which could not have been reasonably anticipated. The trust fund was small, and not only the income, but such portion of the principal as might be necessary, might be expended for the support of the cestuis que trust for life; and it seems quite apparent from the master's report that at the time of the sale of the real estate the personal property in the trust had been exhausted, and that good management required that the real estate should be sold for the purpose in part of paying outstanding claims for which the trust fund was ultimately liable. The real estate consisted chiefly of a farm, subject to a mortgage to the amount of $1,300. By authority of the probate court the property was sold to one Martin at a valuation of $4,300, including the first mortgage. This left $3,000 due to the trust; and Martin paid $1,000 in cash, and in payment of the balance gave his note for $2,000, payable in annual sums of $100 each, with interest at the rate of 7 per cent. per annum. Martin also assumed and agreed to pay the second mortgage. The trustee was a farmer, having owned and occupied for many years a farm which was situated about a mile distant from the Wright farm, both being on the same road. He was one of the selectmen of the town, and had settled several estates. From the glimpses we get of him, he evidently was a sturdy New England yeoman of the best type. By the sale he had received $1,000 in cash, and had as security for the balance of the purchase money of $2,000 what he had just sold for $3,000 to a bona fide purchaser, who, we infer, bought the farm for the purpose of occupying it himself as a farmer. The trustee was familiar with the farm and its value for farming purposes. It is true that his security was subject to a prior mortgage, but he might well have thought that, in view of its size, whether absolute or relative, there was nothing to be feared from that. In this he seems to have been right, for the trouble in this case is due in no respect to the existence of the first mortgage. The farm was not on some lonely, unfrequented road, but was on the main street in the town. So far as appears, the trustee had no reason to anticipate that the value of the property would decrease to any appreciable extent, much less to the extraordinary degree of 50 per cent. in seven years. Moreover, the mortgage provided for the annual payment of $100 a year on the principal. It is to be noted also that the depreciation does not seem to have been due to any mismanagement of this particular farm, but to general causes applicable to the whole neighborhood, and not foreseen at the time of the sale. We are aware that in several cases in other states it has been stated that a trustee should not invest in second mortgages. While we accept that as a principle generally to be applied, we cannot accept it as an absolute, ironclad rule. After all, the true rule is whether, under the circumstances, sound discretion was exercised; and it cannot be said that under every conceivable practical set of circumstances an investment in a second mortgage is inconsistent with sound discretion. In view of the nature and size of the trust, taken in connection with the provision that from time to time some portion of the principal might be expended as required for the support of the cestuis que trust for life, and in view also of the small size of the first mortgage, either absolute or relative to the value of the whole estate, of the character and size of the farm, and of the improbability that its value would so far depreciate as to result in loss on the mortgage, we cannot say that, acting in the light which he had, the trustee did not exercise sound discretion in making the loan. Nor did he violate the terms of his license.

The next question is whether the trust fund is shown to have suffered any loss by the manner in which the trustee undertook to realize upon the note and mortgage of Martin at the time of the insolvency of the latter. It appears from the report of the master that the trustee and the assignee of Martin's estate agreed to join in making a sale of the land subject to the first mortgage, the proceeds of the sale to be indorsed on the note. The land was accordingly sold for the sum of $800, which sum was indorsed upon the note, and then the trustee undertook to prove against Martin's estate in insolvency the balance due, amounting to $1,-281.29. The assignee made no objection, but on the objection of Martin, the debtor, the court rejected the claim on the ground that, the sale not having been made under the supervision of the court, the right to prove against the estate for the balance due was lost. Gen. St. 1860, c. 118, § 27. See Smith v. Warner, 133 Mass. 71. As to this matter, it is found by the master that the trustee acted in good faith, and that it did not appear that the assignee had any property in his hands belonging to the estate of Martin. Under these circumstances, even if it be assumed that the trustee, although acting in good faith, could not successfully plead his ignorance of the law as a justifiable excuse (Pierce v. Prescott, 128 Mass. 140), it is not shown that the estate suffered by the loss of the right to prove the balance of the note. No loss being shown by this act, there is no occasion to consider it further.

The result to which we have come upon these questions renders it unnecessary to pass upon the validity of the conveyances of his private property made by the trustee to the defendant as set out in the bill.

Bill dismissed.

(186 Mass. 7)

CADIGAN v. CRABTREE.

(Supreme Judicial Court of Massachusetts. Suffolk. May 20, 1904.)

PRINCIPAL AND AGENT—REAL ESTATE BROKERS—DISCHARGE—RIGHT TO COMMISSIONS.

1. The relation between a real estate broker and the owner of property who employs him is primarily that of principal and agent, and by employing the broker the owner does not bind himself to give the broker even a reasonable time within which to produce a tenant or purchaser, or bind himself not to change his mind as to the use or disposition of his property, and, when acting in good faith, may so change his intention, and thereby discharge the broker, at any time.

2. In the absence of any custom or usage to the contrary, the right of a real estate broker to work for a commission, as well as his right to impose any obligation on his principa by reason of holding himself ready to proceed as agent, ends upon his discharge by the principal, acting in good faith, no matter what may be the stage of negotiations between the broker and a prospective customer, provided the broker has not yet succeeded in securing a customer ready and willing to accede to the principal's terms.

1. See Brokers, vol. 8, Cent. Dig. § 11.

Exceptions from Supreme Judicial Court, Suffolk County; Wm. Caleb Loring, Judge.

Action by one Cadigan against one Crabtree. Verdict for plaintiff, and defendant excepts. Exceptions sustained.

Whipple, Sears & Ogden, for plaintiff. Frank Paul, for defendant.

HAMMOND, J. This is an action by a real estate broker to recover a commission upon a lease. So far as material to the question before us, the evidence for the plaintiff, taken in the light most favorable to him, tended to show the following facts: About November 1, 1898, the defendant employed the plaintiff to procure a tenant for certain real estate owned by her. He saw several persons on the matter, among whom were one Gould and one Mann. With the latter, negotiations were soon begun which finally resulted in an agreement as to terms, and in the preparation of some papers. The Mann lease, however, "fell through" on December 20, 1898, because the person who was to become the surety for the tenant changed his mind and withdrew. Directly after this the plaintiff renewed his negotiations with Gould, and within a day or two told the defendant that he thought he could get a good tenant, mentioning Gould, whom he said he would "see right away," and she said to him, "All right; go ahead." On December 22d, the plaintiff had an interview with Gould and Pollo, who were acting together, showed them certain plans, told them what the terms of the Mann lease were, and said that those were the only terms on which the property could be hired. They said they would think it over. The plaintiff reported this interview to Gilman, the general agent of the defendant, who said he would see what could be done. In two or three days, Gilman said he could not get the defendant to decide to do anything at that time. On the 1st or 2d of January the defendant and the plaintiff, according to his testimony, had an interview in which the plaintiff told the defendant about his talks with Gould, and that the latter was satisfied with the terms of the Mann lease. The defendant said, in substance, that she had decided not to lease, but to sell. "She would not talk lease at all." The plaintiff did not see the defendant again. He wrote to her two or three times between January 2d and February 8th, the substance of the letters being that he could not sell the property for the price named by her, and that she had better lease it; mentioning Gould and Pollo. She replied on February 8th that the property was "for sale only." Meanwhile the plaintiff saw Gould and Pollo every little while, and talked with them about the defendant. By letter dated March 3d, the defendant informed the plaintiff that she had withdrawn the property from the market for sale, had decided to lease it, and had placed it in the hands of Mr. Fitzpatrick, as her sole agent, who alone had authority to negotiate for her. Up to the time the plaintiff received this letter of March 3d, he never had heard that any other broker was having anything to do with the business of leasing the property, and during this whole time he was ready and willing to act as a broker in carrying on negotiations for the lease to Gould and Pollo. Neither Gould nor Pollo, acting together or separately, ever agreed with the plaintiff to take the lease, nor did either of them authorize the plaintiff to convey to the defendant an offer. The negotiations never reached that point. On December 28th or 29th the plaintiff, at the order of the defendant, acting through Gilman, took down his sign from the estate. On December 20, 1898, the day the negotiations for the Mann lease ended, the defendant met one Fitzpatrick, a real estate broker, who also had been talking with Gould for several months about hiring the property. In this interview Fitzpatrick spoke of Gould and Pollo as persons who would be good tenants, and asked the defendant to give them a lease, but she declined to consider the question of leasing the property; and she continued in this frame of mind until March 3d, when, after discussion with Fitzpatrick as to whether to sell or lease, she finally again changed her mind, and placed the property in his hands as her sole agent to lease. This was her first employment of Fitzpatrick. On March 12th she saw Gould for the first time, and on March 16th the lease was made to him and Pollo. It was not contended by the plaintiff that the defendant, in deciding not to lease, acted in bad faith. It is to be noted also that the testimony was conflicting as to whether the plaintiff had the interview with the defendant between December 20th and January 2d, as to which he testified. The defendant testified that no such interview took place, and that, after the conclusion of the negotiations as to the Mann lease on December 20th she did not see or have any communication with the plaintiff until the interview in January. The jury might have believed the plaintiff, however, and we have assumed that they did.

The case was tried upon the third and fourth counts of the declaration. At the close of the evidence the court ordered a verdict for the defendant on the third count. As to the fourth count, the court ruled that the jury would not be warranted in finding for the plaintiff upon the ground "that the plaintiff was the predominating, efficient cause of the lease given by the defendant to Gould and Pollo, and that his services brought about the making of that lease." The court further ruled that the terms of the Mann lease, so called, "were not substantially the same as the terms of the lease * * * to Gould and Pollo, and that the action could not be maintained upon the fourth count, in so far as a finding for the plaintiff involved a finding that said leases were substantially alike in their terms." The court, however, declined to rule, as requested by the defendant, that the action could not be maintained upon this count, and then submitted the case to the jury upon it, upon instructions to which no exceptions were taken.

The question is whether the court erred in refusing to order a verdict for the defendant upon the fourth count. The principle upon which the case was submitted to the jury was stated by the court in the following language: "If the owner of property employs a broker to find a customer for him, and the broker introduces to the principal a person who he says is willing to negotiate, and if the principal and the customer enter into negotiations, and, while these negotiations are going on, they are suspended, or for the time, at any rate, ended by the principal, and not by the customer, and afterwards the principal should close the trade with that customer, the broker is entitled to his commission. I say 'if afterwards the principal should close the trade with that customer,' and I say 'if the negotiations are ended or suspended by the principal, and not by the customer.' It is not enough that the broker gives the name of John Smith or Henry Jones, and afterwards the principal should, through the negotiations of another broker, close a trade with John Smith or Henry Jones. The broker cannot entitle himself to a commission by simply having given the name of John Smith or Henry Jones. If he does not do anything more than that, he is not entitled to a commission. Even if he names them as customers—if he reports that to his principal—it is not enough. The matter has got to go further. It must result in negotiations between the customer and the principal after the customer has been introduced by the broker. If negotiations begin, and, before they have resulted in a refusal by the principal of the customer's terms, they are suspended, merely, and are subsequently resumed—I am putting a case where the negotiations are begun, and are suspended by the principal without having come to a definite conclusion, because they cannot trade at that time, and afterwards the principal trades with that customer—a commission is due the broker. If, however, the negotiations are ended by the customer making an offer which is refused, then that ends that introduction, so far as the question of a broker's commission is concerned. For instance, in this case, you will remember that in November Mr. Cadigan brought an offer. It was stated by Mr. Gould that he would not give any more than a sum then named, and that this statement was not a definite offer, but Mr. Cadigan brought it as an offer to the defendant. I think it was $25,000 a year, and the owner to make all the repairs. Miss Crabtree refused definitely to take that offer. That ended that as a transaction in which Gould and Pollo were Cadigan's customer. If the transaction stopped there, and nothing more happened, and then later Miss Crabtree made a trade, that would not entitle the plaintiff to a commission." Having thus stated and illustrated this principle, the court proceeded to state that "the question of efficient cause has nothing to do with" the case, and, after having called the attention of the jury to the conflict of evidence, to which reference has hereinbefore been made, as to whether, after the Mann lease fell through, there was any interview between the defendant and the plaintiff in which she told him to go ahead with his attempts to procure a tenant, finally left the case to the jury in this concrete form: "If, after the Mann lease fell through, negotiations were in fact begun, with the defendant's knowledge and approval, by Mr. Cadigan, and if the negotiations went so far that they could be really said to be negotiations, and if, after the naming of a customer, they were suspended by the defendant, and she afterward made a trade with that same customer with whom the plaintiff had talked, then you will find for the plaintiff. If you find that negotiations went on, and the defendant did not know of them, or if you find that the negotiations did not go on at all, you will find for the defendant; but if you find that they did go on, with the defendant's knowledge and approval, you will find for the plaintiff." The evidence clearly shows that even if, after the Mann lease fell through, the defendant still employed the plaintiff as a broker to effect a lease, the authority was revoked on January 2d. Both parties testify as to this, and the plaintiff does not contend that thereafterwards he was ever given authority to act in the matter. The authority was revoked because the defendant had really and in good faith abandoned her intention to lease, and she notified the plaintiff of that fact. While the plaintiff was acting under her authority he had not effected a lease. More than two months elapsed after the revocation of the plaintiff's authority before one was effected. It is also to be noted that there was no proof of any usage or custom. The jury therefore were allowed to find for the plaintiff, under the conditions stated in the last paragraph of the charge, even if the termination of the employment of the plaintiff and of the negotiations was caused by the defendant's bona fide change in her intention, and also irrespective of the question whether he was the efficient cause of the lease, and in the absence of any usage or custom. We think that the proposition as thus laid down is too broad. The relation between the defendant and the plaintiff was primarily that of principal and agent, and, as has been decided in this very case as reported in 179 Mass. 474, 61 N. E. 37, 55 L. R. A. 77, 88 Am. St. Rep. 397, the defendant had the right to discharge the plaintiff at any time. When the defendant applied to the plaintiff to secure his services, she did not bind herself to give him even a reasonable time within which to produce a tenant. Cadigan v. Crabtree, ubi supra. Much less did she bind herself that she would not change her mind as to the use or disposition of her property. In deciding not to lease, and in discharging him for that reason, she violated no right of the plaintiff. Under the general laws of agency, his rights were fixed at the time of his discharge, provided she acted in good faith. At that time the plaintiff's efforts had been unavailing, and he had not earned his commission. He did not earn it by anything he did afterwards. It is not even shown that under the doctrine of efficient cause, as this term is understood when used in this connection, he earned a commission. His right to work for a commission, as well as his right to impose any obligation upon the defendant by reason of holding himself ready to proceed as her agent, ended upon his discharge, she acting in good faith. Such a view is sustained by the general law of agency, and, in the absence of proof of any custom or usage to the contrary, must be applicable to this form of agency. And on principle this must be so, no matter what may be the stage of the negotiations, from the simple introduction of the customer to the nearly completed ending, provided always that the broker has not succeeded in securing the customer ready and willing to accede to the terms of the principal. As applicable to this case, we adopt the following statement of the principle as found in Sibbald v. Bethlehem Iron Co., 83 N. Y. 378, 38 Am. Rep. 441: "If, in the midst of negotiations instituted by the broker, and which were plainly and evidently approaching success, the seller should revoke the authority of the broker, with the view of concluding the bargain without his aid, and avoiding the payment of commissions about to be earned, it might well be said that the due performance of his obligation by the broker was purposely prevented by the principal. But if the latter acts in good faith, not seeking to escape the payment of commissions, but moved fairly by a view of his own interest, he has the absolute right, before a bargain is made, while negotiations remain unsuccessful, before commissions are earned, to revoke the broker's authority; and the latter cannot thereafter claim compensation for a sale made by the principal, even though it be to a customer with whom the broker unsuccessfully negotiated, and even though, to some extent, the seller might justly be said to have availed himself of the fruits of the broker's labor."

This case is to be distinguished from the class of cases in which the relation of agency has not been terminated, as well as from the class where it has been terminated in bad faith. The case is also to be distinguished from those in which there is proof of a custom or usage, as in Loud v. Hall, 106 Mass. 404. On principle, then, the proposition upon which the case was submitted, as above stated, is too broad. The authorities also seem to be against it. See, as bearing upon the question, Leonard v. Eldridge, 184 Mass. 594, 69 N. E. 337; Bailey v. Smith, 103 Ala. 641, 15 South. 900; Fairchild v. Cunningham, 84 Minn. 521, 88 N. W. 15; Wylie v. Marine National Bank, 61 N. Y. 415; Sibbald v. Bethlehem Iron Co., 83 N. Y. 378, 38 Am. Rep. 441; Alden v. Earle (Super. N. Y.) 4 N. Y. Supp. 548; Gillett v. Corum, 5 Kan. 608; Livezy v. Miller, 61 Md. 337; Stedman v. Richardson, 100 Ky. 79, 37 S. W. 259; Earp v. Cummins, 54 Pa. 394, 93 Am. Dec. 718, cited by Gray, C. J., in Ward v. Fletcher, 124 Mass. 224; Uphoff v. Ulrich, 2 Ill. App. 399; Abbott v. Hunt, 129 N. C. 403, 40 S. E. 119. See, also, contra, Gottschalk v. Jennings, 1 La. Ann. 5, 45 Am. Dec. 70, which seems to be in conflict with the general weight of authority.

We are of opinion that the jury should have been instructed, as requested by the defendant, that upon all the evidence the jury would not be warranted in returning a verdict for the plaintiff upon the fourth count. Exceptions sustained.

(186 Mass. 25)

SELLS v. DELGADO et al.

(Supreme Judicial Court of Massachusetts. Norfolk. May 20, 1904.)

TRUSTS—DISCLAIMER OF TRUSTEE—SUBSTITUTION BY COURT—POWERS OF SUBSTITUTED TRUSTEE—DISCRETIONARY POWERS—PERSONAL LIMITATION—TRANSMISSION.

1. Where a power is given in a will or deed by words that clearly indicate that the donor placed special confidence in the donee, so that the element of personal choice is found, such power must be exercised by the person or persons thus selected, and ordinarily is not transmissible.

2. A person named as a trustee in a will is not obliged to accept and execute the trust, but may expressly decline to serve; and where he never qualifies as a trustee under a will, though he has been duly appointed as executor thereunder, he will be deemed by his conduct to have disclaimed the office of trustee.

3. Where a trustee designated in a will declines to serve, or fails to qualify as such, a court having jurisdiction of the probate of the will, or vested with general equity jurisdiction, will, upon application of those interested as beneficiaries or otherwise, appoint a trustee to administer the trust as if none had been originally named.

4. A power conferred on trustees in a will to distribute the property at a certain time if in their judgment it is prudent and for the welfare of the beneficiaries, is not a mere detached naked authority purely discretionary with the trustees, and which may be exercised at their pleasure, but is blended with the trust to which it attaches.

5. A will in which testatrix provided that the bulk of her estate should be divided into two equal parts, which should be held in trust for the benefit of her children, and further provided that when either child attained the age of 25 years, the property might be distributed, and the trust wholly or partially determined, if in the judgment of the trustees "or the survivor of them" it would be for the welfare of the children, did not confer a purely personal power of distribution, restricted in its exercise to the trustees named, but rather conferred the power of distribution on whomsoever should be appointed to administer the trust.

6. Under Rev. Laws, c. 147, §§ 5, 6, providing that where a trustee under a written instrument declines to serve, or resigns, or is removed, the new trustee appointed in his place under a trust similar to that created by the will shall have and exercise the same powers, rights, and duties as if he had been originally appointed, a discretionary power given to trustees named in a will to distribute the estate at a certain time if it shall seem best to them, and which is not strictly limited by its terms to the first trustees, devolves on their successor appointed to fill the office, who, when acting honestly, may either execute the power or refuse to execute it, in his discretion.

¶ 1. See Powers, vol. 40, Cent. Dig. §§ 79, 96.

Case Reserved from Supreme Judicial Court, Norfolk County; John W. Hammond, Judge.

Petition for instructions by Elijah W. Sells, trustee under the will of Ella A. Delgado, deceased, against Philip Mario Delgado and others. Case reserved in the Supreme Judicial Court for the consideration of the full court. Decree rendered.

J. Mott Hallowell and Moses, Morris & Westervelt, for respondents. W. H. Lewis and John L. Dyer, for respondent Philip Mario Delgado.

BRALEY, J. The general rule at law is that where a power is created and given in a will or deed by words that clearly indicate that the donor of the power placed special confidence in the donee, so that the element of personal choice or selection is found, then the exercise of such a power must be confined to and exercised by the person or persons thus selected, and ordinarily is not transmissible. Richardson v. Morey et al., 18 Pick. 181, 187; Shelton v. Homer et al., 5 Metc. 462, 465; Tainter v. Clark, 13 Metc. 220, 226; Greenough v. Welles, 10 Cush. 571, 575; White v. Ditson, 140 Mass. 351, 359, 4 N. E. 606, 54 Am. Rep. 473.

Among other questions raised it becomes important to first determine whether the trustees named in the will of the testatrix come within this rule. She provided that the bulk of her estate should be divided into "two equal parts or shares," and respectively held in trust for the sole use and benefit of her children, the income arising therefrom to be paid to them with rights of survivorship as to principal and income not now material to the decision of the case. The further provision appears that when either attained the age of 25 years, if, in the judgment of the trustees, or the survivor of them, it was prudent and for their welfare, the property then might be distributed, and that part coming to each paid, and the trust wholly or partially determined. In the fifth clause, which created the trust, she does not speak of the trustees by name, but they are referred to as "my * * * trustees hereinafter named, or the survivor of them." In the sixth clause they are spoken of by name, and appointed trustees to execute the trust created in the preceding clause. The language used by her is apt to express her purpose; and to them she confided discretionary powers in the management of the trust estate, and it was provided that, in case of the death of one, the survivor succeeded to all the authority possessed by both. An examination of the record discloses the fact that of the original trustees one has died, and, though they were duly appointed executors, yet they never qualified as trustees, and must be held by their conduct to have disclaimed the office. But a person named as trustee in a will or other instrument is not obliged to accept and execute the trust. He may expressly decline to serve, or, by his failure to act, or to take such steps as may be required legally to qualify him for his office, may leave it completely unexecuted, and, if his conduct was conclusive, then it would follow that the trust itself would fail for want of a trustee to carry it into effect. This is not permitted, and under such conditions a court having jurisdiction of the probate of the will, or vested with general equity jurisdiction, will, upon application of those interested as beneficiaries or otherwise, appoint a trustee or trustees to administer the trust as if none had been originally named or appointed. Bowditch v. Banuelos et al., 1 Gray, 220; Atty. Gen. v. Barbour, 121 Mass. 568, 574; Carruth v. Carruth, 148 Mass. 431, 19 N. E. 369. For it is a familiar maxim in equity that a trust shall not be allowed to fail for want of a trustee, and in a case like that under consideration the power conferred is not a mere detached naked authority purely discretionary with them, which may be exercised at their pleasure, but is blended with the trust to which it attaches. Gibbs v. Marsh, 2 Metc. 243, 251; Leeds v. Wakefield et al., 10 Gray, 514, 517. A different construction would cause a serious impairment of the full design of the testatrix, and leave it imperfectly executed. Although the receipt of the income is assured, yet it may be equally, if not more, advantageous to the beneficiaries to call for a distribution of the principal to be made under the provisions of the will, and it might be a great hardship to either if deprived of this privilege because it was found to be limited to the persons named. That she did not intend such a result is shown not only by her purpose that her children, if found competent, were to be permitted, when of mature age, to receive the principal, but also in the use by her of the comprehensive phrase, "my trustees, or the survivor of them"; and, if it had been a part of the general plan to limit such a power to those originally selected, then she would have used words to make plain such a limitation. It may therefore be inferred that her intention was not to restrict its exercise to those named, but rather to confer it on whomsoever should be appointed to administer the trust.

At the time when her will was admitted to probate, it had been the settled law of this state for 75 years that when a trustee under a written instrument declines to serve, or resigns, or is removed, a new trustee appointed in his place under a trust similar to that created by this will shall have and exercise the same powers, rights, and duties as the original trustee, and by force of law, on such appointment being made, the estate vests in him as if he had been primarily designated. St. 1817, p. 649, c. 190, § 40; Rev. St. c. 69, §§ 7, 8; Gen. St. c. 100, § 9; Pub. St. c. 141, §§ 5, 6; Rev. Laws, c. 147, §§ 5, 6; Richardson v. Morey et al., ubi supra; Nugent v. Cloon, 117 Mass. 219, 221; Bradford v. Monks, 132 Mass. 405; Wemyss v. White, 159 Mass. 484, 34 N. E. 718; Stanwood v. Stanwood, 179 Mass. 223, 60 N. E. 584. See, also, Chase v. Davis, 65 Me. 102; In Goods of Woodfall, L. R. 3 P. 108 (where, under similar statutory provisions, a like result was reached). Compare Leggett v. Hunter, 19 N. Y. 445. The object of this provision of the statute is to remove any doubt as to the authority of trustees to act who may from any cause take the place of, and are substituted for, those named in the instrument; and by the act of succession the trust itself is not in any way impaired or narrowed, but is kept alive and fully executed. If a power of the nature under discussion has been given, but which is not strictly limited by its terms to the first trustees by name, then those who succeed them, by the operation of the statute, become clothed with a like authority; and they may, when acting honestly, either execute the power or refuse to exercise the discretion left open to their personal judgment. Weymss v. White, ubi supra; Stanwood v. Stanwood, ubi supra. It must therefore be held that the petitioner, under his appointment by the probate court, has succeeded to all the powers and duties originally conferred, and possesses the right to determine whether the trust estate shall now be divided according to the provisions of the will.

No occasion is found which requires a consideration of the question that might arise whether a trustee vested with such powers, but who refuses to exercise them, could be compelled by a court of equity to take action, for the petitioner states in his petition that, in his opinion and judgment, he considers "it advantageous, prudent, and desirable" that Marina Elena Parke, one of the beneficiaries, who is within the preliminary condition as to age, should now receive her share of the property. Eldridge v. Heard, 106 Mass. 579; Proctor et al. v. Heyer et al., 122 Mass. 525. Because there is a bare possibility that she and her children may not survive him, her brother Philip Mario Delgado, who, though of age, is not yet 25 years old, and has become insane, by his guardian ad litem opposes the granting of the petition on the ground already discussed; but the will confers on the trustees, or the survivor of them, the right to determine, after either of the beneficiaries has reached the age of 25 years, when, in his judgment, the event shall happen upon which distribution of the property shall be made, and for the reasons stated the present trustee can, in his discretion, pay over to the daughter of the testatrix one-half of the entire trust estate.

Decree accordingly.

(186 Mass. 44)

NATIONAL MACHINE & TOOL CO. v. STANDARD SHOE MACHINERY CO.

(Supreme Judicial Court of Massachusetts. Suffolk. May 20, 1904.)

ASSESSMENT OF DAMAGES—INQUEST—ISSUES—FINDINGS—EXCEPTIONS—REVIEW.

1. Where defendant did not take specific exceptions to the findings of an assessor appointed to assess plaintiff's damages, and did not request that so much of the evidence as bore on the points covered by the exceptions be reported to the court, such exceptions could not be reviewed on an order denying a motion to recommit the report to the assessor.

2. Where it had been previously determined that defendant was liable to plaintiff on the claim sued on, the question of liability could not be again raised at a hearing before an assessor appointed to assess damages, or by a request for a ruling by the court on a motion for a new trial.

Exceptions from Superior Court, Suffolk County; Franklin G. Fessenden, Judge.

Action by the National Machine & Tool Company against the Standard Shoe Machinery Company. The case was sent to an assessor to assess plaintiff's damages and report his findings to the court, and to an order denying a motion to recommit the assessor's report defendant excepts. Overruled.

W. N. Buffum and Burton E. Eames, for plaintiff. Elder & Whitman, James Thomas Pugh, and H. Ware Barnum, for defendant.

HAMMOND, J. 1. The motion to recommit the report to the assessor was addressed to the discretion of the judge, and is not subject to exception or appeal. If the defendant desired the findings of the assessor to be reviewed by the superior court, he should have taken specific objections to them, and have requested so much of the evidence to be reported as bore upon the points covered by the exceptions. If this had been done, these questions could have been brought to this court. Carew v. Stubbs, 161 Mass. 294, 37 N. E. 171, and cases cited.

2. It does not appear that there was any error in law in overruling the motion for a new trial. The question of the liability of the defendant had been already determined against the defendant (181 Mass. 275, 63 N. E. 900), and it was not open to the defendant to raise that question at the hearing before the assessor, or by request for ruling by the court on a motion for a new trial. Paddock v. Commercial Ins. Co., 104 Mass. 521.

3. The court had the power to order judgment upon the report of the assessor, and no error in law appears. Carew v. Stubbs, ubi supra, and cases cited.

The result is that the exceptions are overruled, and the order for judgment from which the defendant appealed is affirmed. So ordered.

(186 Mass. 47)

HOFNAUER v. R. H. WHITE CO.

(Supreme Judicial Court of Massachusetts. Suffolk. May 20, 1904.)

MASTER AND SERVANT—INJURIES TO SERVANT—NEGLIGENCE—RES IPSA LOQUITUR—ASSUMED RISK—WARNING.

1. Where plaintiff, a saleswoman in a store, was injured by the falling of a medicine chest from an inclining, and therefore defective, shelf, evidence that three months before the time of the accident a chest fell from the shelf was insufficient to establish defendant's negligence, without proof of the circumstances surrounding the occurrence; tending to show that the chest fell solely by reason of the inclination of the shelf, and not from some other independent cause.

2. While plaintiff, a saleswoman in a store, was injured by the falling of a medicine chest from a shelf which was slightly inclined at one end, and there was nothing to show that the inclination of the shelf affected the stability of the other chests resting thereon, the mere fact that the chest fell was insufficient to establish defendant's negligence in providing an insecure place for such chest, without proof that other causes did not operate to produce the fall.

3. Where plaintiff had been employed in a store as saleswoman for more than two years, and a part of her duty was to show prospective purchasers certain medicine chests stored on a shelf, one of the ends of which was slightly inclined, which condition was open and obvious, and continued to be so down to the time plaintiff was injured by the fall of one of the chests from the shelf, plaintiff assumed the risk of such injury, and was not entitled to recover.

4. A master is not bound to inform his servant of a danger with which she must be held to have been previously acquainted by reason of the fact that it was open and obvious.

¶ 4. See Master and Servant, vol. 34, Cent. Dig. §§ 308, 310.

Exceptions from Superior Court, Suffolk County; Edward B. Pierce, Judge.

Action by one Hofnauer against the R. H. White Company. Judgment in favor of defendant, and plaintiff brings exceptions. Overruled.

Jas. E. Young and John J. Scott, for plaintiff. John Lowell and Jas. A. Lowell, for defendant.

BRALEY, J. This is an action of tort brought by the plaintiff to recover damages for personal injuries suffered by her while in the employment of the defendant as a saleswoman, for which she had been working at the time of the accident during a period of more than two years. It appears to have been a part of her duty to show those who might become purchasers certain medicine chests that were placed on a shelf which was of a width of 2½ feet, and of the total length of 60 feet, while its height from the floor was 5½ feet; and when in position on the side of the room it was supported by posts about 12 feet apart, but one of its ends extended for about 3 feet beyond the last post. As the plaintiff was standing near this end, in the performance of her usual duties, one of these chests fell, struck her person, and caused the injuries of which she complains. The uncontradicted evidence shows that, about three months before the time when the plaintiff was hurt, a similar chest had fallen from the same part of the shelf, and that there was a perceptible slant of two or three inches in that end of it, which continued from that time to the day of the accident, and could have been clearly seen by the plaintiff. It further appeared in evidence that during the time of the plaintiff's service, and when the first chest fell, a person by the name of Muir was present, and that his duty was "to sign slips and tell us what to do if there was anything out of order around the place," and he also gave direction from time to time to the persons employed in the department. He was subsequently succeeded by one Bott, who was charged with like duties; but it does not appear that either was intrusted with any care or control of the premises, or that it was the duty of either to see that the appliances and instrumentalities that may have been furnished by the company were kept in good order and condition, and were reasonably suitable for use.

Under a declaration which contained three counts—one at common law, for an improperly constructed shelf, that was in a dangerous and defective condition; one under the employer's liability act, for a "defect in the condition of the ways and works used in the business of the defendant" (Rev. Laws, p. 1, c. 106, § 71), and which in each instance had not been remedied, owing to its negligence; and one declaring on the negligence of some person in the service of the defendant, and who was intrusted with exercising superintendence, which was his sole or principal duty—it was ruled at the trial in the superior court that the plaintiff could not recover, and, a verdict having been ordered and returned in favor of the defendant, the plaintiff brings her case here upon exceptions.

If it be conceded that the plaintiff was in the exercise of due care, it is still incumbent upon her to show some act of negligence on the part of the defendant, and in order to do this she first relies on the fact that a chest fell from the shelf three months before the time of the accident. But if we give to this incident every possible probative force, it does not tend to prove the fact in issue, for the circumstances surrounding its fall are not disclosed, and there is no evidence that it was caused solely by the inclination of the shelf; and, for aught that appears, its fall may have been attributable to the carelessness of an employé in not replacing it securely after it had been taken down and shown to customers.

The plaintiff, however, relies on the additional fact that on the day of the accident the chest itself fell, as supplying sufficient proof to require a submission of the case to the jury, under the familiar principle that where an accident is of such an unusual character it can be said that it would not have happened except for the fault of the defendant, and for this reason it may fairly be inferred that it would not have occurred here but for its negligence, if not otherwise explained. The mere inclination of the shelf does not seem to have affected the stability of the other chests, which apparently remained in place after being once put in position; and it cannot be said that, under the circumstances disclosed, where chests were being taken off, and put back if not sold, in the ordinary course of business, because one of them happened to fall the doctrine invoked becomes applicable, and that such an occurrence was of so uncommon a character that of itself it furnished evidence of negligence on the part of the defendant. Pinney v. Hall, 156 Mass. 225, 30 N. E. 1016. If there were other causes besides the fact of the fall of the chest itself that may have produced such a result, the plaintiff is obliged to go further, and eliminate them, by showing that they did not operate; but, instead of doing this, she is content to rest her case upon the bald statement of fact that the chest fell, and nothing more. But the incline of the shelf from a level surface is shown to have been only from two to three inches at the end, and less than three feet from the post by which at that point it was supported; and it cannot be said that, in a shelf of this length and width, this was so unusual as to lead to the inference of negligence, or that this condition alone caused the chest to fall, for here, again, it may have been placed so insecurely by the acts of a fellow servant that, from some cause not disclosed, it fell.

It is not necessary, however, to rest the

decision of the case on these two counts solely on this ground, for there is another answer to the plaintiff's contention, as it may be inferred that at the time she entered the service of the defendant the shelf was a part of its establishment where she was to work, and there is no dispute, on the evidence, that the condition of the shelf was not open and obvious, and continued to be down to the time when she was injured. Under such conditions, as there was no concealed danger, she must be held to have assumed any risk of the nature disclosed, and this alone is sufficient to prevent her recovery. O'Maley v. South Boston Gaslight Co., 158 Mass. 135, 32 N. E. 1119, 47 L. R. A. 161; Lamson v. American Axe & Tool Co., 177 Mass. 144, 58 N. E. 585, 83 Am. St. Rep. 267; Langley v. Wheelock, 181 Mass. 474, 63 N. E. 944.

An extended discussion of the remaining count is not required, as the person alleged to have been acting as superintendent at the time of the accident is not shown to have been intrusted with the duty either of the construction or repair of the shelf, and there is no claim that he set the plaintiff at work in a place where the chest would be likely to fall upon her. Fitzgerald v. Boston & Albany Railroad Co., 156 Mass. 293, 295, 31 N. E. 7. Besides, there was no duty resting upon him to inform her of a danger with which she must be held to have been previously acquainted. Perry v. Old Colony Railroad Co., 164 Mass. 296, 300, 41 N. E. 289.

Exceptions overruled.

(185 Mass. 563)

FOTTLER v. MOSELEY.

(Supreme Judicial Court of Massachusetts. Suffolk. May 19, 1904.)

FRAUD — BROKERS — REPRESENTATIONS—RELIANCE ON REPRESENTATIONS — HOLDING CORPORATE STOCK—DECLINE IN VALUE.

1. Where plaintiff was induced by the fraudulent representations of a stockbroker to cancel an order to sell certain stock, and to retain it until it depreciated in value, the broker was liable, though the depreciation was caused by the embezzlement of an officer of the corporation, which was not contemplated by the broker.

Exceptions from Superior Court, Suffolk County; Edgar J. Sherman, Judge.

Action by John Fottler, Jr., against Charles W. Moseley. Judgment for defendant, and plaintiff brings exceptions. Exceptions sustained.

Nason & Proctor, for plaintiff. Benj. L. M. Tower and Ernest O. Hiler, for defendant.

KNOWLTON, C. J. The parties and the court seem to have assumed that the evidence was such as to warrant a verdict for the plaintiff, under the law stated at the previous decision of this case, reported in 179 Mass. 295, 60 N. E. 788, if the diminution in the selling price of the stock came from common causes. The defendant's contention is that the embezzlement of an officer of a corporation, being an unlawful act of a third person, should be treated as a new and independent cause of the loss, not contemplated by the defendant, for which he is not liable. To create a liability, it is never necessary that a wrongdoer should contemplate the particulars of the injury from his wrongful act, nor the precise way in which the damages will be inflicted. He need not expect even that damage will result at all, if he does that which is unlawful, and which involves a risk of injury. An embezzler is criminally liable, notwithstanding that he expects to return the money appropriated after having used it. If the defendant fraudulently induced the plaintiff to refrain from selling his stock when he was about to sell it, he did him a wrong; and a natural consequence of the wrong, for which he was liable, was the possibility of loss from diminution in the value of the stock from any one of numerous causes. Most, if not all, of the causes which would be likely to affect the value of the stock, would be acts of third persons, or at least conditions for which neither the plaintiff nor the defendant would be primarily responsible. Acts of the officers, honest or dishonest, in the management of the corporation, would be among the most common causes of a change in value. The defendant, if he fraudulently induced the plaintiff to keep his stock, took the risk of all such changes. The loss to the plaintiff from the fraud is as direct and proximate, if he was induced to hold his stock until an embezzlement was discovered, as if the value had been diminished by a fire which destroyed a large part of the property of the corporation, or by the unexpected bankruptcy of a debtor who owed the corporation a large sum. Neither the plaintiff nor the defendant would be presumed to have contemplated all the particulars of the risk of diminution in value for which the defendant made himself liable by his fraudulent representations. It would be unjust to the plaintiff in such a case, and impracticable, to enter upon an inquiry as to the cause of the fall in value, if the plaintiff suffered from the fall wholly by reason of the defendant's fraud. The risk of a fall, from whatever cause, is presumed to have been contemplated by the defendant when he falsely and fraudulently induced the plaintiff to retain his stock.

We do not intimate that these circumstances, as well as others, may not properly be considered in determining whether the plaintiff was acting under the inducement of the fraudulent representations in continuing to hold the stock up to the time of the discovery of the embezzlement. The false representations may or may not have ceased to operate as an inducement as to the disposition of his stock before that time. Of course, there can be no recovery except for the direct results of the fraud. But if the case is so far established that the plaintiff, immediately upon the discovery of the embezzlement, was entitled to recover on the ground that he was then holding the stock in reliance upon the fraudulent statements, and if the great diminution in value came while he was so holding it, the fact that this diminution was brought about by the embezzlement of an officer leaves the plaintiff's right no less than if it had come from an ordinary loss.

Exceptions sustained.

(209 Ill. 504)

McMULLEN et al. v. REYNOLDS.*

(Supreme Court of Illinois. April 20, 1904.)

PARTITION — SOLICITOR'S FEES—LIABILITY OF DEFENDANTS—AMOUNT OF FEES—EVIDENCE.

1. On a hearing to determine the reasonable value of the attorney's fees to be awarded complainant's solicitor in a partition suit, plaintiff's witnesses testified that $5,000 was a reasonable fee, while defendant's witnesses fixed the usual and customary charges in such cases to be from $200 to $350. Thereupon the court called in three members of the bar, and stated the case to them, and asked them to report their conclusions as to what would be a reasonable attorney's fee in the case, and, on their reporting that $2,000 would be a reasonable fee, allowed that sum. *Held* that, the members of the committee not having been sworn, their report was incompetent evidence, and the allowance will be set aside.

2. In fixing the value of the services of complainant's solicitor in partition, the court has no right to refer that matter to members of the bar called in on the court's own motion.

3. Under Partition Act, § 40 (Hurd's Rev. St. 1899, p. 1259), providing that the court may apportion the costs, including a reasonable solicitor's fee, that fee should be taxed like other costs, and judgment therefor should not be rendered in favor of the solicitor in his own name.

4. Under Hurd's Rev. St. 1899, § 40, p. 1259, declaring that in partition, when the rights and interests of all the parties are properly set forth in the petition, the court shall apportion the costs, including a reasonable solicitor's fee, unless defendants, or some one of them, shall interpose a good and substantial defense, in which case they shall recover their costs against the complainant, defendants in partition cannot be charged with any portion of complainant's solicitor's fees where the proceeding is not amicable, and complainant's solicitor represents complainant alone, in a manner hostile to defendants, requiring them to employ a solicitor to protect their interests.

Appeal from Appellate Court, First District.

Bill by Elizabeth Keogh against Mary A. McMullen and others, in which Frank P. Reynolds was allowed a certain sum as solicitor's fees. From a portion of the decree allowing such solicitor's fees, defendants appealed to the Appellate Court, and, from a judgment of that court (105 Ill. App. 386) affirming judgment below, defendants appeal. Reversed.

This was a bill in chancery filed in the circuit court of Cook county by Elizabeth Keogh against Mary A. McMullen, John H. McMullen, Agnes E. Ducey, and William T. McMullen for the partition of certain real estate located in said county. An answer and replication were filed, and the case was referred to a master to take proofs, and, his report coming in, a decree was entered finding that Elizabeth Keogh, Mary A. McMullen, John H. McMullen, and William T. McMullen were each the owners of the equal undivided one-sixth part of said real estate, and that Agnes E. Ducey was the owner of the equal undivided two-sixths part, of said real estate, and commissioners were appointed to divide and allot the real estate among the parties. The commissioners appraised the real estate at $72,500, and made a division and partition thereof among the parties, and filed a report of such division and allotment, which was approved and confirmed by the court; and thereupon the court fixed the solicitor's fee of Frank P. Reynolds, the complainant's solicitor, at the sum of $1,999.98, and provided that each of the parties who owned a one-sixth part of the real estate should pay $333.33, and that Agnes E. Ducey, who owned the two-sixths part thereof, should pay $666.66 thereof to said Reynolds within 10 days from the date of the entry of the decree, which sums were made a lien upon the shares allotted to the parties, respectively, and in default of such payment the decree provided execution should issue in favor of Reynolds, and against the several parties to the suit, for the amount found due from each of them to him. An appeal from so much of said decree as relates to the solicitor's fee was prosecuted to the Appellate Court for the First District by Mary A. McMullen, Agnes E. Ducey, and William T. McMullen, where the decree of the circuit court was affirmed, and they have prosecuted a further appeal to this court.

Frank E. Makeel and Thomas E. D. Bradley, for appellants. William Slack, for appellee.

HAND, C. J. (after stating the facts). It is first contended that the court considered improper evidence in fixing the amount of the solicitor's fee. The complainant called six attorneys, who testified they were engaged in the active practice of law in the county of Cook, that they were acquainted with the usual and customary fees of solicitors in partition suits in said county, and that $5,000 was a reasonable solicitor's fee in said case. The defendants called four attorneys, who testified that a reasonable solicitor's fee in said case, according to the usual and customary charges made by attorneys in Cook county in such cases, in their judgment, would be from $200 to $350. The judge, after hearing said testimony, expressed doubt as to what course of action

---

*Rehearing denied June 8, 1904.

he should pursue, and, upon his own motion, called before the court three members of the Cook county bar, and made or caused to be made to them a statement of the facts of the case—that is, the character and extent of the services performed, the value of the real estate to be partitioned, the length of time the case had been pending, the condition of the title to the property to be divided, and the number of parties to the suit —and requested said attorneys to retire and confer together upon the subject of the amount that should be allowed as a solicitor's fee in the case, and to report their conclusions to the court. The committee so appointed retired, and, after conferring together, returned into court and reported that, in their opinion, $2,000 would be a reasonable solicitor's fee. The court thereupon fixed the solicitor's fee at the sum suggested by the committee, less two cents, which amount it was necessary to eliminate from their report, that the amount allowed might be apportioned equally between the parties to the suit. The gentlemen called by the court on its own motion were not sworn.

While it is the general rule in chancery cases, where the hearing is before the court without a jury, that the court will be presumed to have disregarded incompetent evidence, and to have based its decision upon the competent evidence in the case, and, if there is sufficient competent evidence to support its decree, the fact that incompetent evidence has been admitted will not constitute reversible error, that rule does not apply when there is no competent evidence in the record to support the decree, and it is apparent the court did consider incompetent evidence, and base its decree thereon. In other words, if it appear that the decree cannot be sustained unless incompetent evidence be considered, the decree will be reversed. Yarde v. Yarde, 187 Ill. 636, 58 N. E. 000. The evidence of the complainant was to the effect that a reasonable solicitor's fee was $5,000, while that of the defendants was that a reasonable solicitor's fee would not exceed $350. In this great divergence of opinion, it is apparent that the court adopted the report of the committee, and incorporated the finding of the committee into its decree. This was clearly error. The court had no more power to submit for decision to the gentlemen called before it the question of the amount to be allowed as a solicitor's fee, than it would have had power to submit to the committee the question whether or not a solicitor's fee for any amount, under the law, could properly be allowed. While the court may doubtless take into consideration, in connection with the testimony offered, its own knowledge upon the subject of the value of solicitor's fees in partition and similar suits (Culver v. Allen Medical Ass'n, 206 Ill. 40, 69 N. E. 53), still the parties to a suit have the right to have the question determined by the court upon sworn testimony, which the court should weigh in view of its own knowledge and experience, and which testimony must be preserved in the record by a certificate of evidence to entitle a party to have the question reviewed upon appeal or writ of error (Goodwillie v. Millimann, 56 Ill. 523; Albright v. Smith, 68 Ill. 181; Spring v. Collector of the City of Olney, 78 Ill. 101; Metheny v. Bohn, 164 Ill. 495, 45 N. E. 1011); and parties cannot be required to submit to the determination of committees, or other bodies extrajudicial in character, the amount that shall be allowed as solicitor's fees and paid by them in partition suits or other similar suits to which they are parties. The action of the court in calling before it said committee, and in submitting to the committee for decision a matter which it alone had the power to determine upon sworn testimony, and the basing of its decree thereon, was reversible error.

It is next contended that it was error to enter judgment and order execution for the solicitor's fee in favor of the solicitor instead of the complainant. The principle is fundamental that it is erroneous to enter judgment and order execution for costs in favor of one not a party to the suit unless express authority for so doing is given by statute. Lilly v. Shaw, 59 Ill. 72; Wallace v. Espy, 68 Ill. 143; 5 Ency. of Pl. & Pr. 148. It is clear that section 40 of the partition act (Hurd's Rev. St. 1899, p. 1259), which provides that the court may apportion the costs, including a reasonable solicitor's fee, contemplates that the solicitor's fee, when allowed in that class of cases, shall be taxed like the other taxable costs in the case, and that a judgment therefor shall not be rendered in favor of the solicitor, with the right to take out execution in his own name. In the Lilly Case, supra, on page 78, it was said: "Besides the irregularities pointed out, there is still another. The $1,200 allowance was not made as costs taxed in the cause, but appellees were introduced as new parties into the record upon mere motion. That sum was allowed to them by name, and they would be entitled to execution in their favor if the order were allowed to stand. The order making such allowance must be reversed." In Habberton v. Habberton, 156 Ill. 444, 41 N. E. 222, the question presented here was not raised; and that case does not sustain the position that the judgment for the solicitor's fee was properly rendered in favor of the solicitor, with the right to have execution in his name to enforce the collection thereof. The judgment is therefore not in proper form, and, under the authority of the Lilly Case, should be reversed.

It is also contended that the court erred in taxing any part of the solicitor's fee allowed in the case against the appellants, and that is the main question presented for consideration by this appeal, as the other errors complained of will not arise on another hearing, while that question goes to the right to tax the complainant's solicitor's fee as costs in any amount, and apportion the same among the parties in interest.

It appears that James McMullen died seised of a considerable estate; that he left, him surviving, six children—the five heretofore named, three of whom were nonresidents of the state of Illinois, and Alice Atkinson, who conveyed her interest in the property sought to be partitioned to her sister Agnes E. Ducey before the bill was filed; that a portion of the real estate of which James McMullen died seised was apportioned, by agreement, between his children, but that they were unable to agree as to a partition of the real estate covered by this bill; that the bill set out the rights and interests of all the parties in interest correctly; that the defendants, in their answer, admitted that James McMullen, deceased, the father of the complainant and defendants, died seised of the said real estate, and that the complainant was entitled to the one-sixth part thereof, and to have partition thereof, and stated the defendants were willing to have their interests set off jointly, and not severally, to them. The defendants appeared by their solicitor before the master, and there made the same admissions, and the report of the master was based mainly upon the admissions contained in the answer of the defendants and those of their solicitor made before the master. The real estate sought to be divided consisted of 50 acres of unimproved property occupied by a golf club as lessee, and a block of houses located in the city of Chicago, which were occupied by 14 tenants; that one commissioner was selected upon the suggestion of complainant, and one upon the suggestion of the defendants, and one by the court; that the parties at various times endeavored to agree upon the portion of the real estate that should be set off and allotted to the complainant, and, with that end in view, conferred with the commissioners through their solicitors, and the commissioners on one or more occasions conferred directly with the parties; that at all of said conferences Reynolds represented the complainant; that, after the commissioners had agreed upon the amount which should be allotted to complainant, Reynolds endeavored to induce them to change said allotment, and give to complainant a larger portion of said real estate than the commissioner had determined to allot to her, or than was subsequently allotted to her.

The statute providing for the allowance of solicitor's fees in partition suits reads as follows: "In all proceedings for the partition of real estate, when the rights and interests of all the parties in interest are properly set forth in the petition or bill, the court shall apportion the costs, including the reasonable solicitor's fee, among the parties in interest in the suit, so that each party shall pay his or her equitable portion thereof, unless the defendants, or some one of them, shall interpose a good and substantial defense to said bill or petition. In such case the party or parties making such substantial defense shall recover their costs against the complainant according to equity." Hurd's Rev. St. 1899, § 40, p. 1259.

It is the contention of appellee that as the bill filed by the complainant properly set forth the rights and interests of all the parties in interest, and no good and substantial defense to the bill was interposed by any of the defendants, the court was required by the statute to make an allowance for the reasonable solicitor's fee of the complainant, and apportion the same among the parties to the suit as costs, regardless of whether it was equitable the defendants should pay a portion of said solicitor's fee or not. We do not agree with such contention. Anterior to the passage of the act of 1889, above set forth, it had been uniformly held by this court, under statutes authorizing the court to apportion the costs in partition suits, including reasonable solicitor's fees, among the parties, so that each party should pay his equitable share thereof; that no allowance could be made in a contested case where the solicitor for complainant conducted the case in a manner hostile to the defendants, and by reason thereof it was necessary for the defendants to employ counsel to protect their interests. In Strawn v. Strawn, 46 Ill. 412, the circuit court taxed as costs against the defendants their share of the sum of $3,600 as a fee to the solicitors of the complainants. On page 414 the court said: "The proceeding was not an amicable one. The defendants appeared by their own solicitors, as they had the right to do; and why they should be required to assist in paying the counsel of complainants, we do not perceive. Here was a great estate to be divided, and if the parties could not agree upon a division, and litigation became necessary, each was entitled to have his interests protected in court by counsel of his own selection; and one party cannot, under our practice, be compelled to pay the fees of the other." In Kilgour v. Crawford, 51 Ill. 249, the court allowed $100 as fees to the counsel for complainants, and directed the same to be taxed as costs, pro rata, against all the parties, pursuant to the act of 1869 (Laws 1869, p. 368). This court, on page 253, said: "The terms of that law are not mandatory. It merely provides that 'it shall be lawful for the court to order that a reasonable fee be allowed,' etc.; the provision being restricted to proceedings in partition and the assignment of dower. Where the proceedings are amicable, and the parties defendant do not deem it necessary to employ counsel to protect their interests, it is proper that the power given by this law should be exercised, as all the parties have the benefit of the partition. But where the defendants deem it necessary to employ counsel in order to protect their interests, and secure a just partition or an equitable assignment of dower, we can see no reason why they should be required not only to pay the fees of their own counsel, but also a part of the fees of adverse counsel. This is not done in other legal proceedings, in some of which it might be done with much more propriety—as when, for example, a defendant is resisting the payment of an honest debt. In these partition proceedings the defendants have generally been guilty of no default or wrong. In many cases there are minor heirs or married women, which circumstance renders legal proceedings unavoidable; and, even when there are not, the mere fact that the joint owners have not been able to agree upon a partition is no reason why the defendants should be made to pay the counsel of complainants. We are satisfied the act should be construed as intending the taxation of counsel fees only in cases where the proceedings are amicable."

In Lilly v. Shaw, supra, the court allowed the complainant's solicitors a fee of $1,200. In disposing of that question, on page 77 of the opinion, it was said: "But, aside from all other questions, the case was not within the purview of the statute of 1869. In Kilgour v. Crawford, 51 Ill. 249, it was held that the act should be construed as intending the taxation of counsel fees only in cases where the proceedings are amicable. It does not affect the question that this was begun as an amicable suit, when it immediately developed into the ordinary case of adverse parties. The court surely could not have intended to allow appellees—two of the three solicitors who filed the petition—the enormous sum of $1,200 for merely filing the petition. If he did not, then the order is to compel appellants to pay for the services of counsel whose principal efforts were on behalf of the opposite party and against them. It would be a novel addition to the quantum meruit count for professional services to go into our formbooks, running thus: 'For the work, labor, and professional services of plaintiff, as an attorney at law, done and performed as such attorney in a certain suit lately pending,' etc., 'of A. B. against the said defendant, at the request of, for and in behalf of, the said A. B.' The principle of such a count would be precisely the same as that of the allowance in question. It, no doubt, has happened that the services of attorneys at law, rendered upon the retainer of one party, were of great value to the opposite party, but it appears from the record that the services of appellees were not of that kind. They were evidently bestowed with zeal, ability, and effect against appellants. The statute in question was not designed as an instrument of injustice, or to throw the rights of parties into confusion. Why are appellees any more entitled to such an allowance than the solicitors for appellants?"

In Stunz v. Stunz, 131 Ill. 210, 23 N. E. 407, the court allowed a solicitor's fee of $200. This court, on page 220, 131 Ill., and page 409, 23 N. E., said: "It is patent upon the face of the record that the entire proceeding was conducted with unfairness toward the wards and in the interest of the widow. The proceeding, as conducted, was not an amicable suit instituted for the benefit of the wards, but was hostile to their interests. Such fees may be allowed when the suit is an amicable one, for the reason that therein the solicitors represent the interests of all the parties alike. It would be grossly unjust to compel these children to pay the fees of the solicitor of the widow, who alone represented her interest, and who so conducted the proceeding as to produce the unconscionable result already indicated."

It will be observed the statute now in force provides "the court shall apportion the costs, including the reasonable solicitor's fee, among the parties in interest in the suit so that each party shall pay his or her equitable portion thereof." It would seem clear, therefore, under the terms of the statute, if it would be inequitable for the defendants to pay any portion of the complainant's solicitor's fee, that such fee should not be taxed as costs and apportioned against them; and if it was inequitable, prior to the passage of the act of 1889, to require defendants to pay a part of complainant's solicitor's fee where the solicitor of complainant represented only the complainant's interest, and assumed an attitude hostile in its character toward the defendants, whereby it became necessary for them to employ counsel in order to protect their interests, and to obtain a just partition of their lands, we see no reason why the rule should be different under the act of 1889—that is, if it was inequitable, under such circumstances, to allow a solicitor's fee prior to the act of 1889, why it is not equally inequitable to allow a solicitor's fee, under such circumstances, subsequent to the passage of that act—and such has been the holding of this court.

In Hartwell v. De Vault, 159 Ill. 325, 42 N. E. 789, the complainant sought to have his solicitor's fees taxed as costs, and apportioned between the parties in interest. The appellant had neglected to make two of the tenants in common with her parties defendant, and the proceedings were not amicable, but were hotly contested by the parties. The court, on page 336, 159 Ill., and page 793, 42 N. E., said: "The statute provides that, in all proceedings for the partition of real estate, where the rights and interests of all the parties are properly set forth in the petition or bill, the court shall apportion the costs, including the reasonable solicitor's fee, among the parties in interest in the suit," etc. 3 Starr & C. Ann. St. 1896, c. 30, p. 935. We have held, in regard to this statute, that where the proceedings are not amicable, and the defendants deem it necessary to employ counsel in order to protect their interests, and secure a just partition or an equitable assignment of dower, they should not be required to pay the fees of adverse counsel as well as of their own counsel."

In Metheny v. Bohn, supra, on page 499, 164 Ill., and page 1012, 45 N. E., it was said: "Prior to this amendment [the amendment of 1889] it was uniformly held, under statutes which authorized the court to apportion the costs, including reasonable solicitor's fees, among the parties to the proceeding, so that each party should pay his equitable portion thereof, that no allowance could be made in a contested suit where the solicitor for the complainant conducted the proceeding against the interest of the defendants, and they were required to employ counsel to represent such interest. It was considered equitable that each should contribute to the fee of complainant's solicitor only in cases where he represented all interests in an amicable proceeding. By the amended section, the apportionment is still to be such that each party shall only pay his or her equitable portion of the fee. * * * The section of the statute in question was considered in Hartwell v. De Vault, 159 Ill. 325, 42 N. E. 789, and the same rule prevailing under the former statute was reasserted. In that case the complainant, in her original bill, had not stated the names and interests of all parties, but had afterward amended her bill so as to state them. This omission was connected with the fact that the proceeding was hotly contested by the parties, and the latter fact was given as one of the reasons for refusing an allowance of a solicitor's fee."

Here the parties were unable to agree upon a division of the real estate. It was valuable, and consisted of both vacant and improved property. Three of the defendants were nonresidents of the state. The solicitor of the complainant was employed by her, and was actively engaged in endeavoring to further her interests before the commissioners by increasing the amount of the estate which should be allotted to her, the effect of which would be to lessen the portion which would be allotted to the defendants, and endeavored to have taxed as costs a solicitor's fee of $5,000, five-sixths of which he sought to have made a charge in his favor upon the estate of the defendants. The attitude of the complainant and her solicitor toward the defendants appears to have been hostile from the commencement of the suit, and the record justifies the conclusion it was necessary for the defendants to be represented by their own counsel, in order that their rights might be protected, and they obtain a just partition of their lands. While in a proper case the statute permitting a solicitor's fee to be taxed as costs and apportioned among the parties in interest is a wholesome law, in many cases, if recklessly applied by the courts, it would work a great hardship. The fact that an answer is filed or a frivolous defense interposed should not be allowed to defeat the operation of the statute, if the bill or petition sets forth the rights and interests of the parties correctly. Walker v. Tink, 159 Ill. 323, 42 N. E. 773. Still, when the court can see that it is necessary for the defendants to have counsel to protect their interests and to insure a just partition of their estate, and that the solicitor of the complainant represents alone the interests of the complainant, and that it would be inequitable to require the defendants to pay their own counsel, and contribute toward the payment of complainant's counsel also, the court should not tax complainant's solicitor's fee as costs, and apportion the same among the parties in interest in the suit.

We are of the opinion the court erred in taxing the complainant's solicitor's fee as costs, and apportioning a part thereof against the defendants.

The judgment of the Appellate Court and the decree of the circuit court will be reversed, and the cause remanded to the circuit court for further proceedings in accordance with the views herein expressed. Reversed and remanded.

(209 Ill. 517)

GLOS et ux. v. GLEASON.*

(Supreme Court of Illinois. April 20, 1904.)

TAXATION — DEEDS — VALIDITY—SUITS TO REMOVE CLOUD — EVIDENCE OF TITLE—SUFFICIENCY—TENDER—PERSON TO WHOM MADE—RECORD TITLE HOLDER — EQUITY PRACTICE—REFERENCE TO MASTER — TRIAL CALENDAR—NOTICE—COSTS ON APPEAL—ADDITIONAL ABSTRACT.

1. In a suit to remove a cloud from title, it is not necessary for complainant to prove title with the same strictness as in an action of ejectment; and proof showing that, at the time the bill was filed, complainant was in the possession of the property, claiming in good faith to be the owner thereof, under a deed conveying the same to him, is sufficient, where the only cloud which complainant seeks to remove is a tax deed.

2. Under Hurd's Rev. St. 1901, c. 120, § 194, requiring the county clerk, on the day advertised for a tax sale, to make a certificate, to be entered on the record, reciting the correctness of the record and the rendition of judgment, a tax deed based on a sale advertised for August 1st was invalid where the certificate was made on July 13th.

3. A tender of the amount paid at a tax sale, with subsequent taxes, interests, and costs, made to the record holder of a tax title previous to the filing of a bill for the removal of a cloud, and kept good by a payment into court on filing the bill, was sufficient to absolve complainant from liability for costs, although defendant had conveyed the property to his wife, who was later made a party defendant by supplemental bill; the deed to her not having been recorded.

4. In a suit to set aside a tax deed as a cloud on title, it was unnecessary to refer the cause to a master to ascertain the amount due as redemption money.

5. In the absence of a rule of court or a statute requiring it, notice need not be given to defendant of the placing of a cause on the trial calendar.

6. Appellee may recover costs of printing an additional abstract, the necessity of which is made to appear.

*Rehearing denied June 8, 1904.

Appeal from Circuit Court, Cook County; Abner Smith, Judge.

Bill in equity by F. G. Gleason against Jacob Glos and wife. From a decree for complainant, defendants appeal. Affirmed.

On January 20, 1902, appellee filed a bill in the circuit court of Cook county against appellant Jacob Glos to set aside a tax deed to certain lots in the city of Chicago, as being a cloud upon appellee's title to the lots; said deed having been issued by the county clerk of Cook county to Glos. Subsequent to the filing of the bill a deed from Jacob Glos to his wife, Emma J. Glos, dated January 2, 1902, and acknowledged on January 20, 1902, conveying an undivided one-half interest in said lots, was filed for record in the recorder's office of said county; and on February 12, 1902, appellee filed a supplemental bill in the circuit court, making Emma J. Glos a party defendant, and praying that her deed to the lots in question be set aside as a cloud upon appellee's title. Both defendants answered, denying that appellee is the owner of the said lots, and averring ownership in the defendants by virtue of the deeds referred to; denying that the tax deed to Jacob Glos is void, as alleged in the bill; denying that a tender had been made to Jacob Glos, as claimed by appellee in his bill; and denying that appellee is entitled to the relief prayed for. A replication was filed to these answers, and the cause was heard in open court before the presiding judge thereof. The court rendered a decree finding that the material allegations of the bill were true; that complainant therein is the owner in fee simple of the lots described in the bill, and was in the actual and exclusive possession of the same at and before the filing of the bill herein; that the tax deed to Jacob Glos is invalid, and that the deed to Emma J. Glos was filed subsequent to the commencement of this suit, and is also invalid as against the complainant; that both deeds are clouds upon the complainant's title to the lots; and the decree therefore orders the same canceled and removed of record. It also finds that a tender was made to Jacob Glos prior to the commencement of the suit, and orders that he pay the costs of this proceeding, but that Emma J. Glos recover no costs. Both defendants appeal from the decree to this court.

The evidence shows that in 1897 appellee obtained a quitclaim deed to these lots, which was recorded in the recorder's office of Cook county on June 28, 1898; that his grantor, Marie A. Kennicott, had paid the taxes on these lots from 1891 up to 1898, when they were sold for taxes to Jacob Glos; that appellee had caused a fence to be erected, inclosing these lots; and that a sidewalk had been laid in front of them. The taxes assessed for the year 1897 remaining unpaid on said lots, judgment was entered against the same by the county court of Cook county on July 11, 1898, and the lots were advertised to be sold for taxes on August 1, 1898. The certificate of the clerk required by section 194 of chapter 120 of Hurd's Revised Statutes of 1901 was made on July 13, 1898, instead of on August 1, 1898. The sale of lands for delinquent taxes opened on August 1, 1898, as advertised, and on September 14, 1898, the lots in question were sold to appellant Jacob Glos for the sum of $34.15, and a certificate of sale was issued to him. He also paid the taxes for the ensuing year, amounting to $28.50. On June 21, 1901, the lots remaining unredeemed from said tax sale, Jacob Glos applied to the county clerk of Cook county for a deed, and thereupon filed a notice, with its certificate of publication, which notice had been published from May 23, 1900, to June 6, 1900, and which notified Mary Kennicott, Mary E. Kennicott, and the unknown owners of, and persons interested in, said lots, that the time for redemption would expire on September 14, 1900, and also filed two affidavits—one made by himself, and the other made by his agent, Timke—in which it was stated that each had made diligent search and inquiry for the said Mary Kennicott and Mary E. Kennicott, and the unknown owners of and persons interested in said lots, and that affiants had not been able to find any of them in said county. The bill charges that the statements in the affidavits are untrue; that Gleason has resided in the city of Chicago for more than 20 years, and is and has been for a long time well known in Cook county; that his deed to said lots appeared on the records in the recorder's office of said county; that his name, together with his address—both business and residence—has for a long time appeared in the Chicago directories, and that it appeared in the directory which was in use in the city of Chicago during the year 1900; that he could have been easily found in the city of Chicago at any and all times during the year 1900 by making ordinary search and inquiry for him, and that no notice of purchase or any other kind of notice was served by Glos, or any one acting for him, upon complainant; and that complainant received no such notice in any way. Shortly before filing the bill herein, and on the same day, the attorney and agent for Gleason tendered to Jacob Glos the sum of $75, which was refused, and that amount was deposited with the clerk when the suit was commenced, and was found by the court to be the sum due Jacob Glos, and ordered paid to him.

Jacob Glos, pro se. John R. O'Connor, for appellant Emma J. Glos. Alexander S. Bradley, for appellee.

SCOTT, J. (after stating the facts). It is urged that the proof does not show that complainant was the owner of the real estate described in the bill. We have frequently held that, in a suit to remove a cloud from the title, it is not necessary for the complainant to prove title with the same strictness as in an action of ejectment. Glos v. Randolph, 138 Ill. 268, 27 N. E. 941; Pease v. Sanderson, 188 Ill. 597, 59 N. E. 425; Glos v. Boettcher, 193 Ill. 534, 61 N. E. 1017. The proof in this case shows that, at the time the bill was filed, complainant was in the possession of the property, claiming in good faith to be the owner thereof, under a deed conveying the same to him. This is sufficient proof of title where the only cloud which complainant seeks to remove is a tax deed. The evidence here is sufficient to sustain the finding in the decree that the complainant is the owner of the property.

The sale upon which the deed involved herein is based was advertised for August 1, 1898. Section 194 of chapter 120 of Hurd's Revised Statutes of 1901, requires that, "on the day advertised for sale, the county clerk * * * shall make a certificate, to be entered" on the record, following the order of the court, that such record is correct, and that judgment was rendered upon the property therein mentioned for taxes, etc. This certificate was made by the clerk in this instance on July 13, 1898, instead of on August 1st of that year. The tax deed is therefore invalid. Glos v. Randolph, supra.

On the day the bill herein was filed, January 20, 1902, but prior to the filing thereof, complainant tendered to Jacob Glos $75 in payment of the amount paid at the tax sale, subsequent taxes, interest, and costs, which was slightly in excess of the amount due to Glos under section 224 of chapter 120 of Hurd's Revised Statutes of 1901. The tender was not accepted. Complainant at 2 o'clock on the same day filed his bill, and kept the tender good by paying the same to the clerk. Thereafter, on the same day, appellant Emma J. Glos, wife of appellant Jacob Glos, filed for record a quitclaim deed from Jacob Glos, conveying to her an undivided one-half of the premises described in the bill. This deed is dated January 2, 1902, and acknowledged before one Timke, the agent of Jacob Glos, on January 20, 1902. Later, Emma J. Glos was made a party defendant by supplemental bill. Under these circumstances, it is urged that the tender was not made to the proper parties, and that it was erroneous to render a decree for costs against Jacob Glos, and to leave Emma J. Glos to pay her own costs. The tender was made to the person who by the record was shown to be the holder of the tax title. Complainant had no notice, constructive or otherwise, that Jacob Glos had conveyed to Emma J. Glos. To hold, under such circumstances, that he must make a tender to her, or be liable for costs, would virtually deprive him of the right of making a tender before bringing suit. The grantee in such a deed, who is not in possession, can protect himself from any injurious consequences from the rule here applied by promptly recording his deed upon its delivery to him.

It is also assigned as error that the cause should have been referred to a master for the purpose of ascertaining the amount due as redemption money. Under the authority of Glos v. Boettcher, supra, this was unnecessary.

Emma J. Glos insists that no notice was given to her of this cause being placed on the trial calendar in the court below. For that reason, she moved to strike the cause from that calendar, and assigns the denial of her motion as error. The record does not disclose any rule of court showing necessity for such notice, and there is no statute requiring it. The error is therefore not well assigned.

Appellee has filed an additional abstract in this court, and moves that the cost thereof be taxed herein. The necessity for this additional abstract appears, and the motion will be allowed.

The decree of the circuit court will be affirmed. Decree affirmed.

(209 Ill. 483)

CRAVER v. ACME HARVESTER CO.*

(Supreme Court of Illinois. April 20, 1904.)

INTERMEDIATE APPEAL—FACTS FOUND BY APPELLATE COURT — CONCLUSIVENESS — SUBSEQUENT APPEAL — REVIEW — SCOPE—JUDGMENT.

1. Under Practice Act, § 87 (Hurd's Rev. St. 1899, p. 1296), providing that the judgment of the Appellate Court is final as to all matters of fact, where such court found the facts different from those found by the trial court, and incorporated the findings in its judgment, the only open inquiry on a further appeal to the Supreme Court was whether the law was properly applied to the facts as so found.

2. Where, in an action to recover the price of the good will of a business, the Appellate Court found that plaintiff did not own and did not sell or transfer such good will, and that defendant did not undertake and promise to pay plaintiff therefor, a judgment that plaintiff was not entitled to recover was a proper application of the law to the facts.

Appeal from Appellate Court, First District.

Action by Charles F. Craver against the Acme Harvester Company. From a judgment in favor of plaintiff, reversed by the Appellate Court (110 Ill. App. 413), plaintiff appeals. Affirmed.

Archibald Cattell and George P. Cary, for appellant. Defrees, Brace & Ritter, for appellee.

CARTWRIGHT, J. Charles F. Craver, appellant, brought this suit in the superior court of Cook county against the Acme Harvester Company, appellee, and W. H. Binnian. The suit was discontinued as to Binnian, and there was a judgment against the appellee for $20,750 and costs. The appellee appealed to the Appellate Court for the First District, and the branch of that court reversed the judgment and entered a judgment in favor of appellant against appellee for

*Rehearing denied June 8, 1904.

$750, which was not in controversy, and had been admitted to be due appellant. The determination of the cause in the Appellate Court resulted from finding the facts different from the finding of the superior court, and the Appellate Court recited in the final judgment a finding of facts, as provided by statute. From the judgment of the Appellate Court, the appellant prosecuted this appeal.

The suit was brought to recover the purchase price or value of the good will and business which the plaintiff alleged that he controlled and transferred to the defendant. The amended declaration contained four special counts. The first count alleged that the defendant, being desirous of purchasing the good will and business controlled by plaintiff, entered into negotiations with him for that purpose; that he agreed to turn over to defendant said good will and business, and to enter into defendant's employ; that defendant promised to pay him $75,000 for the good will and business, and a salary of $500 per month; and that he complied with the terms of the contract on his part. The second count alleged that plaintiff had been engaged in the manufacture and sale of agricultural implements for harvesting grain in the western portion of the United States and the various republics of South America; that his name was well known in the South American republics as a maker of such machines, and he had personally acquired and controlled the business therein to the amount of $200,000 per annum, which he was able to, and did, take with him to whatever firm or corporation he was engaged with; and that, in pursuance of negotiations, he made a written proposition to defendant to engage in its service, and turn over, as far as he was able, the South American business, and if, at the close of the season of 1900, the season had been a fairly good one, and proper efforts had been put forth by defendant to complete and sell machines being manufactured at the plant of the Harvester King Company, the good will and assets of which defendant was purchasing, then, if the South American business should amount to $200,000 or more, there should be issued to plaintiff shares of capital stock of defendant equal to one-half the profits arising from said purchase made by defendant from the Harvester King Company, and for the conduct of the business for the season, but not to exceed $150,000, and if the total sales for South America should amount to less than $200,000, and the crop conditions in the United States made it impossible to sell all the machines contemplated, plaintiff would accept stock to the amount of $100.000 or $75,000 in cash, at his option, for the good will and South American trade, so far as his efforts could make the transfer complete, and also for his influence in the United States, and in addition a salary of $500 per month for his services. It was then averred that defendant accepted the proposition, and that plaintiff performed his part of the contract. The third count alleged that plaintiff was possessed of certain trade and good will in the sale of harvesting machinery, derived from the sale of the same to certain exporting houses in New York and London, which trade and good will were of the value of $100,000; that plaintiff offered to turn over to defendant, so far as he was able, said trade and good will for $75,000, which defendand undertook and promised to pay him; and that he performed the contract on his part. The fourth count alleged that the plaintiff was possessed of certain trade and good will for the sale of harvesting machinery to certain exporters in New York and London; that he made the written proposition set out in the second count; that defendant accepted the proposition, and promised, in consideration of such trade and good will, to pay plaintiff $75,000; and that plaintiff transferred such trade and good will so far as his efforts could make the transfer complete. The declaration also contained the common counts, and the defendant pleaded the general issue and the statute of limitations.

There was no evidence tending to prove any express contract for the sale or purchase of the good will or business, as alleged in the special counts. In January, 1900, plaintiff was employed by the Harvester King Company, a corporation engaged in the manufacture of harvesters and headers at Harvey, Ill. That company had been manufacturing a header which was largely sold for the South American trade, and the business had originated many years before with a firm of which plaintiff was a partner. The machines were sold to John Dunn, Son & Co., of New York, and they were shipped to the Argentine Republic. The business had been quite large, and at one time as many as 2,100 headers were sold to John Dunn, Son & Co., of New York, in one year. In January the Harvester King Company concluded to close out its business, and plaintiff was given an option on the entire property, capital stock, and assets, at $87,000, subject to the debts. He sought for a purchaser, and negotiated a sale to the defendant, for which he was paid a commission of $5,000. He then claimed to own and control the South American business individually, and sent a letter to defendant containing a proposition substantially as stated in the declaration. The defendant declined the proposition in a letter, and offered a salary of $400 per month. Upon receipt of the letter declining his proposition, plaintiff telegraphed defendant that he considered its proposition an insult, and resigned his position with defendant. During the negotiations the defendant was corresponding with John Dunn, Son & Co. for orders for the South American trade. That company was anxious to have plaintiff employed by defendant, and plaintiff endeavored to prevent the defendant from obtaining the order unless it acquiesced in his proposition. After his resignation he did what he could to prevent defendant from obtaining the business, but defendant did receive an order for 500 machines. It was agreed at the trial that the defendant was indebted to the plaintiff in the sum of $750 for his services from February 8 to March 16, 1900, at the rate of $500 per month, which was the amount for which the Appellate Court entered judgment. The judgment in the superior court was recovered on an alleged implied contract of the defendant to pay the value of the good will and business. Plaintiff claimed that he owned the South American trade as his own property, and that he sold it to defendant and transferred it as far as he was able, while defendant contended that it purchased the good will and business when it purchased the stock and property of the Harvester King Company.

The finding of facts by the Appellate Court, incorporated in its judgment, is as follows: "The court finds that appellee did not own and did not sell and transfer to appellant the good will, trade, and patronage of the South American trade, so far as he was able, and that appellant did not undertake and promise to pay appellee therefor." The appellee mentioned in said finding is the appellant in this appeal, and the appellant therein mentioned is the appellee in this court.

Under section 87 of the practice act, the judgment of the Appellate Court is final and conclusive as to all matters of fact. Hurd's Rev. St. 1899, p. 1296. The only inquiry in this court is whether the law was properly applied to the facts as found and recited in the finding. Jones v. Fortune, 128 Ill. 518, 21 N. E. 523; Hancock v. Singer Mfg. Co., 174 Ill. 503, 51 N. E. 820; Coker v. Wabash Railroad Co., 183 Ill. 223, 55 N. E. 693. There can be no doubt that the judgment in this case was a proper application of the law to the facts as found. If the plaintiff did not own, and did not sell and transfer to the defendant, the good will, trade, and patronage of the South American trade, so far as he was able, and the defendant did not undertake and promise to pay plaintiff therefor, there could be no recovery of the purchase price or value under any count of the declaration.

The judgment of the Appellate Court is affirmed. Judgment affirmed.

(209 Ill. 595)

LASH v. LASH et al.*

(Supreme Court of Illinois. April 20, 1904.)

WILLS — CONSTRUCTION—EQUITABLE CONVERSION—EFFECT—EXECUTORS—POWER OF SALE —TITLE TO PROPERTY—LAPSED LEGACIES.

1. Where a will directs the sale of lands and the division of the proceeds among designated persons, the executor is charged by law with the duty of applying the fund produced by the sale to the payment directed to be made by the will, and is vested by implication of law with the power to sell the land, although not expressly authorized by the will.

2. A will in unequivocal terms gave testator's widow a life estate in certain property, and provided that at her death the property should be sold and the proceeds divided among testator's children in specified proportions. The concluding sentence provided that the executor should "have the use of the above-described lands for one year free of rent, and is to have one year after my decease to sell the lands, and charge no fee for settling up the estate." *Held*, that the testator's evident intention was to give his widow a life estate, and after her death to give the executor a year's use of the land for compensation, at the expiration of which time he was to sell the same; and as the insertion of the word "wife's" between "my" and "decease" would have made that intention clear, and such word was evidently omitted by mistake, it would be supplied by the court to effectuate the testator's intention.

3. A direction in a will that lands should be sold after the death of testator's wife, and the proceeds of sale be divided among testator's children in proportions varying from those fixed by the statute of descent, effected an equitable conversion of the land into money, and the bequests of the proceeds of sale would be regarded as bequests of personal property, and not as devises of interests in the land.

4. The concurrent action of all the legatees is necessary in order to make a valid election to take real estate ordered by the will to be sold, instead of the bequests of money arising from the sale as provided in the will.

5. The conversion of land into money is to be deemed as having been effected at the time of testator's death, although the sale of the land is to be postponed until after the death of a life tenant.

6. Where an executor is charged with the positive duty of selling the fee-simple title to land after the death of the widow and dividing the proceeds among certain legatees, he becomes a trustee, and by implication of law takes by the will such estate in the land as is necessary to enable him to sell and convey it, and therefore the remainder in fee passes to him, and not to the heirs at law.

7. Under the express provisions of 2 Starr & C. Ann. St. 1896, c. 39, § 11, where a devisee or legatee, being a child or grandchild of the testator, dies without issue before the death of the testator, the legacy is treated as intestate property.

8. Where a will provides for the sale of land and division of the proceeds among testator's children, the death of one of the children without issue does not work a failure of the conversion of the land into money, but the lapsed bequest to such deceased child goes to those entitled to take as intestate personal property, or in the form of money; no contrary intent appearing from the context of the will.

9. A transaction between a legatee and the executor, by which the former assigns to the latter his bequest of the portion of the proceeds of a sale of real property directed by the will to be made, does not defeat the intention of the testator that such sale should be made, or prevent the operation of the equitable doctrine of conversion.

Appeal from Circuit Court, McLean County; C. D. Meyers, Judge.

Bill for partition by James A. Lash against William E. Lash, and others. From a decree dismissing the bill, complainant appeals. Affirmed.

Louis Fitz Henry and D. D. Donahue, for appellant. Welty, Sterling & Whitmore, for appellees.

---

*Rehearing denied June 8, 1904.

¶ 5. See Conversion, vol. 11, Cent. Dig. § 44.

BOGGS, J. Isaac Lash, of McLean county, departed this life May 13, 1902, seised of the title to the W. ½ of the E. ½ of section 27, and the W. ½ of the N. E. ¼ of section 31, in township 23 N., range 2 E. of the third principal meridian, in said county. He left his last will and testament, which reads as follows:

"I, Isaac Lash, of the city of Bloomington, in the county of McLean and state of Illinois, aged eighty-one (81) years, being of sound and disposing mind and memory, do hereby make, publish and declare this instrument to be my last will and testament. That is to say, after the payment of my debts and funeral expenses I give and devise to my beloved wife, Anna Lash, all those tracts or parcels of land described as the west half of the east half of section No. twenty-seven (27), also the west half of the north-east quarter of section No. thirty-four (34), all being in township No. twenty-three (23), north, range two (2), east of the third principal meridian, situate in the county of McLean and state of Illinois. To have and to hold, together with the rents and profits thereof, during her natural life, and at her death the above described lands shall be sold and the proceeds thereof shall be divided as follows between my heirs, to wit: To my daughter Eliza Jane Lash I give the sum of $1,000. To my son James A. Lash I give the sum of $1,000. The balance of the proceeds of the sale of the foregoing described lands shall be divided equally between my six (6) children, to wit: Martha Ann Lash, Levi A. Lash, David N. Lash, Mary E. Orendorf (formerly Mary E. Lash), Frank O. Lash and William E. Lash, save and except Martha Ann Lash is to have $600 out of my estate over and above her equal share with the other five heirs. The sum of $1,000 is to be deducted from Mary E. Orendorf's share and to be equally divided between Martha Ann Lash, Levi A. Lash, David N. Lash, Frank O. Lash and William E. Lash, I having to pay $1,000 for Mary E. Orendorf as guardian. I give all my personal property to my beloved wife, Anna Lash. I hereby appoint William E. Lash, of McLean county, Illinois, executor of this instrument without bond, hereby revoking all former wills by me made. My executor shall have the use of the above described lands for one year free of rent, and is to have one year after my decease to sell the lands, and charge no fee for settling up the estate."

On the 1st day of July, 1903, the appellant filed this his bill in chancery, in which, as amended, he alleged the execution and probate of the will; that the testator was his father, and that certain of the appellees herein were the other heirs at law of the testator; that Martha Ann Lash, a daughter of the testator, and one of the persons entitled under the will to a portion of the proceeds arising from the sale of the land, departed this life after the execution of the will and before the death of the testator; that the true construction of the will is, to quote from the bill, "that the said lands were to be sold and the proceeds divided among the testator's children, providing that the said wife died within the space of one year after the testator's death, but that the said wife did not die within the space of one year, and that the power of sale and gifts were contingent upon the death of the said wife within the space of one year after the death of the testator, and the said power of sale and gifts, being contingent upon the death of the said wife within one year after the testator's death, failed, and neither the gifts and power of sale ever vested"; that the provisions of the will as to the said Martha Ann Lash, deceased, lapsed by reason of her death prior to the death of the testator; and that, as the legal effect thereof, the interest of Martha Ann in said lands became intestate property, and descended, as land, to the heirs at law of the testator, of whom one was the appellant. The bill also alleged that on June 28, 1902, Frank O. Lash conveyed all his right, title, and interest in the land, under the will of Isaac Lash, to William E. Lash, the executor and the possessor of the power of sale, and that the grantor warranted all his interest in said land to the grantee, and the deed expressly covenanted "that in the event of the sale of the said land by the executor of the will of Isaac Lash, deceased, or otherwise, the said grantee shall take all the proceeds arising from the grantor's interest." The bill also averred that by reason of errors, omissions, and misdescriptions in conveyances in the chain of title to the lands, different persons (some 75 in number, who were also named and made parties defendant to the bill) had apparent interests in the title to the land. The prayer of the bill was that a decree should be entered finding the title in fee to the lands to be in the heirs at law of the said testator as tenants in common, and ordering that the title thereto should be quieted and the lands be partitioned and allotted in severalty to said complainant and the other heirs at law of the testator, in accordance with their rights and interests under the statute of descent as such heirs at law and tenants in common. A general demurrer to the bill was sustained, and a decree entered dismissing the bill for want of equity, at the cost of the appellant. From this decree the appellant has prosecuted this appeal.

We think the demurrer was properly sustained. It is very clear from a consideration of the will that it was the intention of the testator that the land should not descend as land to his heirs at law. He caused it to be set down plainly and explicitly in his will that his wife should have the use and benefit of the land during her natural life, and that after the death of his wife the land should be sold, and the proceeds paid to his sons and daughters, not in the proportions in which it would descend under the statute of descent, but in amounts and proportions as fixed upon by himself and specified in the will. The direction that the land shall be sold is positive and absolute, the only restriction being that the sale should not be made until after the death of his widow. The testator did not contemplate that in any contingency his heirs at law, or any of them, would succeed to the title to the land. The testator did not in express terms confer power on the executor to sell the land, but the executor was charged by law with the duty of applying the fund produced by the sale of the land to the payment of the amounts ordered by the will to be paid therefrom to the appellant and the other persons designated in the will to receive it, and power to sell the land vested in the executor by implication of law. 11 Am. & Eng. Ency. of Law, 1046; Williams on Executors, p. 413; Rankin v. Rankin, 36 Ill. 293, 87 Am. Dec. 205. Moreover, there is an express recognition that the executor possessed such power, to be found in the provisions of the concluding sentence of the will. This final sentence of the will was incorporated therein for the purpose of nominating an executor and for providing the compensation to be paid to such executor, and in it is to be found the language on which the appellant bases the contention that the power of the executor to sell the land and convert it into personalty for distribution as such was contingent upon the death of the wife of the testator within one year after the testator's death. In this clause of the will it is provided that the executor, as his compensation for his services in that capacity, shall have the use of the lands of which the testator died seised for one year free of rent, and then follows this provision, "and is to have one year after my decease to sell the lands."

Aside from this quotation, the intention of the testator, to be collected from the context of the will in all of its parts, is clear. It was that his wife should have the use, benefit, and control of the lands during her natural life, and that at her death the land should be sold and the proceeds applied by the executor as directed in the will. Of this there can be no room for debate or doubt. It is manifest it was not intended to abrogate this intent and change the whole purpose of the will by the clause appointing the executor and providing for his compensation. The testator, having decided to appoint his son William E. Lash executor of the will, and to pay such executor for his services by giving him the use of the land for one year without rent, in view of the former provisions of the will that the widow should have the use of the land until her death and that the land should be sold at the death of his widow, found it necessary to add a provision that would secure to his executor such use of the land for one year after the death of the widow and before a sale should be made. In attempting to accomplish this object the testator, after declaring the executor should have the use of the lands for one year free from rent, used the phrase, "and is to have one year after my decease to sell the lands." It is beyond question the language thus employed did not accurately or correctly express his meaning. It is unmistakable, when the whole will is considered together, and the plan and scope thereof disclosed, that he intended that his executor should have one year after the death of his (testator's) wife in which to use the land before selling the same, and in consideration of which use the executor was to "charge no fee for settling up the estate," and therefore was not to be required to sell the land until the expiration of the period of one year after the death of the wife of the testator. What the testator intended to express by that portion of the will from which the quotation is made was that his executor should have one year after the decease of his (testator's) wife in which to use and sell the land, and such intent would have been clearly expressed if the word "wife's" had been inserted between the word "my" and the word "decease" in the sentence hereinbefore quoted. It is, we think, clear that word was omitted in drafting the will. The ambiguity or apparent inconsistency arising on the face of the will is plainly ascribable to the omission of that word. It may therefore be supplied by the court in order to effectuate the intention of the testator as gathered from the context of the will. 2 Jarman on Wills, c. 16, *486, 60; 29 Am. & Eng. Ency. of Law, 372. The express direction of the testator that the lands should be sold after the death of his wife, and the proceeds of such sale divided among appellant and other of the children of the testator, not in the proportions in which they would inherit under the statute of descent, but in amounts or in proportions as fixed upon by himself and specified in the will, effected an equitable conversion of the land into money, and the bequests of the proceeds of the sale to the appellant and other legatees are to be regarded by the courts as bequests of personal property, and not as devises of interests in the land. Baker v. Copenbarger, 15 Ill. 103, 58 Am. Dec. 600; Crerar v. Williams, 145 Ill. 625, 34 N. E. 467, 21 L. R. A. 454; In re Matter of Corrington, 124 Ill. 363, 16 N. E. 252; Dorsey v. Dodson, 203 Ill. 32, 67 N. E. 395.

The effect of an election on the part of legatees to take the real estate ordered to be sold, instead of bequests of money arising from the sale thereof, is not here involved, for the reason, in instances in which such election may be made, the concurrent action of all the legatees thereto is necessary. Jennings v. Smith, 29 Ill. 116; Strode v. McCormick, 158 Ill. 142, 41 N. E. 1091. Here the conversion of the land into money is to be considered as having been effected at the time of the death of the testator. Wurts'

Ex'rs v. Page, 19 N. J. Eq. 365, and Dodge v. Pond, 23 N. Y. 69; both cases being also cited with approval in In re Matter of Corrington, supra. That the sale of the land was to be postponed until after the death of the life tenant had no effect to prevent a conversion. 7 Am. & Eng. Ency. of Law (2d Ed.) 468. The executor became also a trustee, and as such was charged with the positive, absolute, and unconditional duty to sell the fee-simple title to the land to the purchaser at the sale to be made after the death of the widow. The trustee, therefore, by implication of law, acquired by the will such estate in the land as was necessary to enable him to sell and convey it. Ebey v. Adams, 135 Ill. 80, 25 N. E. 1013, 10 L. R. A. 162; Lawrence v. Lawrence, 181 Ill. 248, 54 N. E. 918. The exigency of the trust required the title to the remainder in fee should pass to and vest in the executor in trust, and such estate therefore vested in the trustee. The appellant did not, as an heir at law of the testator, succeed to any estate whatever in the land. Jennings v. Smith, supra. The bequest to the appellant of the sum of $1,000 of the proceeds of the sale of the land was a bequest of personalty, and did not invest him with any estate of freehold in the land itself. Nevitt v. Woodburn, 175 Ill. 376, 51 N. E. 593.

Martha Ann Lash having died without issue before the death of the testator, the bequest to her of a portion of the proceeds arising from the sale of the lands lapsed, and under the provisions of section 11 of chapter 39, entitled "Descent," 2 Starr & C. Ann. St. 1896, p. 1433, is to be considered and treated in all respects as intestate property. But the sale of the land by the executor was essential to the purposes of the will, notwithstanding the fact that one of the persons, entitled under the will to take a portion of the proceeds of the sale of the land as a bequest had died during the lifetime of the testator, and that for that reason such bequest lapsed. The necessity for the conversion of the land into money remained, notwithstanding the lapsing of one of the bequests to be satisfied by such conversion. The death of Martha Ann Lash did not work a failure of the conversion of the land into money, such conversion being necessary to satisfy other purposes of the will. In such cases the lapsed bequest goes to those entitled to take as intestate personal property or in the form of money, no contrary intent appearing from the context of the will. Dorsey v. Dodson, supra. The appellant did not acquire any estate or interest in the land by reason of the death of Martha Ann Lash and the lapsing of the bequest to her.

Though it is alleged in the bill that Frank O. Lash conveyed to William E. Lash, the executor, an interest in the land, it appears from the further allegations of the bill that the instrument called a conveyance was so qualified by an express covenant therein incorporated that it constituted nothing more than an assignment of the bequest of that portion of the proceeds of the sale of the land which Frank O. Lash would be entitled to receive under the will. The transaction between Frank O. Lash and the executor could not operate to defeat the intention of the testator or prevent the operation of the equitable doctrine of conversion.

The appellant, not having any interest in the land, had no standing as complainant in a bill for partition or to quiet title to the land, and the demurrer to the bill was properly sustained. The decree is affirmed.

Decree affirmed.

(210 Ill. 70)

COMMONWEALTH ELECTRIC CO. v. MELVILLE.*

(Supreme Court of Illinois. April 20, 1904.)

NEGLIGENCE — ELECTRIC WIRES—INSUFFICIENT INSULATION — OCCUPATION OF STREET WITH WIRES—INJURIES—SUFFICIENCY OF EVIDENCE —APPEAL—QUESTIONS OPEN TO REVIEW.

1. On appeal from a judgment of the Appellate Court by the party who was appellant there, the Supreme Court will not consider an error, assigned on the record of the trial court, which was not presented by appellant to the Appellate Court.

2. On appeal by defendant, in an action for injuries, from a judgment of the Appellate Court, appellant assigned as error the action of the circuit court in overruling appellant's motion for a peremptory instruction in his favor, and it appeared, from an examination of the brief of appellant in the Appellate Court, that he there urged that there was no evidence tending to prove negligence on his part or the exercise of due care by plaintiff, and such question was argued in the Supreme Court under the assignment. *Held*, that the assignment would be considered by the Supreme Court.

3. An electric company, acting under authority of a city ordinance, placed an electric cable beneath a sidewalk, and, while the sidewalk was several feet above the surface of the ground, there was, owing to the curbing, no access from the street to the space under the sidewalk: but there was access to such space from the abutting lot, the rear of which opened into an alley. Fire broke out under the sidewalk, owing to the "grounding" of the electric current, and plaintiff, a boy, went under the sidewalk from the lot, and was injured by coming accidentally in contact with the cable, which was insufficiently insulated. It appeared that boys were in the habit of playing on the lot and going under the sidewalk, without objection from the lot owner or the city. *Held*, in an action against the electric company for the injury, that the relation of the boy to defendant was not that of a trespasser or licensee.

4. Plaintiff having come in contact with the cable, owing to his having slipped and caught hold of it, a contention that plaintiff became a trespasser, when he laid his hand on the wire, by virtue of his act in touching it, was without merit; plaintiff's act having been an accident.

5. An electric company, by virtue of a city ordinance, maintained an electric cable under a sidewalk in a city; and in an action for injuries sustained by a boy, who, going under a sidewalk, accidentally came in contact with the cable, it appeared that the cable had been in use from 8 to 14 years, that in some places the insulation was defective, that the cable had been

*Rehearing denied June 8, 1904.

out of repair on several occasions near the place where the accident happened, that the wire had on many occasions been grounded, that the effect of such condition was to send a current along the lead covering of the cable, and that the wire carried 2,000 volts of electricity. *Held*, that the evidence tended to show a lack of ordinary care on the part of defendant.

6. In an action against an electric company for injuries to a boy, owing to his having come in contact with an insufficiently insulated electric cable maintained under a sidewalk, the question of plaintiff's contributory negligence *held* one for the jury.

7. An electric company, acting under authority of a city ordinance, placed an electric cable beneath a sidewalk, and, while the sidewalk was several feet above the surface of the ground, there was, owing to the curbing, no access from the street to the space under the sidewalk; but there was access to such space from the abutting lot, the rear of which opened into an alley. Fire broke out under the sidewalk, owing to the "grounding" of the electric current, and plaintiff, a boy, went under the sidewalk from the lot, and was injured by coming accidentally in contact with the cable, which was defectively insulated. It appeared that boys were in the habit of playing in the lot and going under the sidewalk, without objection from the lot owner or the city. *Held*, that the doctrine of traps was not applicable.

8. The doctrine of attractive nuisances was not applicable.

Appeal from Appellate Court, First District.

Action by David Melville against the Commonwealth Electric Company. From a judgment of the Appellate Court (110 Ill. App. 242), affirming a judgment in favor of plaintiff, defendant appeals. Affirmed.

This is an appeal from a judgment of the Appellate Court for the First District, affirming a judgment for $3,500 rendered against appellant in the circuit court of Cook county as damages for a personal injury sustained by David Melville, the appellee. The injury was caused by contact with an electric wire or cable, belonging to the defendant, which had been placed underneath a wooden sidewalk on Ogden avenue, in the city of Chicago. This sidewalk passes in front of a vacant lot. On one side of the lot is a building used for a barber shop, and on the other side is a building referred to as a "brick building." The sidewalk in front of these premises is about five feet above the ground over which it is built. The surface of the vacant lot is almost on a level with the ground under the sidewalk, and the surface of the street is a little lower than that of the lot. The sidewalk is nine or ten feet in width. The curbstone extends from the surface of the street up to the outer edge of the sidewalk, and separates the space below the sidewalk from the street. The space in front of the barber shop and that in front of the brick building are inclosed on all sides, and are used for storing coal. Both are separated from that in front of the vacant lot by wooden partitions. The space in front of the lot is not inclosed on the side next to the lot, and there is nothing to prevent a person on the lot from going under the sidewalk. There is no fence at the back of the lot, which opens on an alley. In front of the lot, extending up from the inner edge of the sidewalk, is a billboard about 20 feet in height. There is a space of from 2 to 3 feet between the sidewalk and the bottom of the billboard, so that a person seeking access to the lot from the street would have to crawl through the space between the sidewalk and the billboard. The electric wire or cable of the defendant was fastened to the under part of the sidewalk, and lay either alongside or on top of the curbstone, or stone wall which separates this space from the street.

On October 22, 1900, this wire became out of order, and the electricity escaping from it set fire to the lower part of the sidewalk to which it was fastened, causing smoke to come up between the boards of the sidewalk in front of the barber shop and for quite a distance along the block, but not in front of the vacant lot. This attracted a considerable number of men and boys, among them the plaintiff, who was a boy 14 years of age. The cause of the smoke had not been discovered when appellee, in company with two other boys, crawled through the space between the sidewalk and billboard, dropped down to the lot, and from there went under the sidewalk over to the farther side, next to the curbstone or stone wall. Plaintiff's two companions looked through a hole in the partition which separated the space in front of the lot from that in front of the barber shop, and saw the sidewalk on fire where the wire or cable was attached to it in front of the shop. Plaintiff then attempted to look through the hole, but in some way slipped, threw his right hand up, and caught hold of the wire, which at that place sagged down from the sidewalk several inches, thereby receiving a shock which rendered him unconscious, and the wire burned his hand to such an extent that its usefulness is greatly impaired and the hand is permanently injured.

The evidence for the plaintiff tends to show that this cable consisted, first, of a copper wire which carried the electricity. This was inclosed by the insulating material, and the whole was covered with lead, except at the joints, where the wire and insulation were incased by another insulating material. When new, the cable had an outside covering of jute. This had worn off or decayed in many places, leaving the lead, which is a conductor of electricity, exposed. A "ground," as that term is used by electrical experts, is occasioned by a defect or break in the insulation, which permits the current to escape from the copper wire to the lead covering, and from there to the earth. In such instances the current is carried along the cable by the lead, and communicated to anything with which the lead comes in contact. The evidence also tends to show that this cable had been "grounded" in the vicinity of the accident on several occasions shortly prior to the time of the injury; that it had been in use for a period of from 8 to 14 years; that the wire in the circuit of which it was a part had frequently been repaired by removing pieces of the cable and replacing them with new cable, but that portions of the cable as originally placed were still in use on the circuit; that a short distance from the place where the injury occurred the circuit had been out of order about two weeks before October 22d; that at that time there was a "ground" on the circuit, and defendant's employés, in attempting to locate the trouble, had gone under the sidewalk in front of the vacant lot; and that on the day preceding the injury to the plaintiff the wire was out of order under the sidewalk in front of the adjoining lot. The evidence further tends to show that the vacant lot had been used by children of the neighborhood as a playground for a considerable period prior to October 22, 1900; that children often went under the sidewalk from the lot when playing games, and sometimes for shelter from the sun or rain.

The declaration, as originally filed, consisted of three counts. Afterwards four additional counts were filed. At the close of plaintiff's evidence, and again at the close of all the evidence in the case, the defendant moved the court to give to the jury an instruction to find the defendant not guilty, and at the same time offered an instruction which directed the jury to return such verdict. The court overruled the motion and refused the instruction in each instance. The errors assigned and urged by appellant for a reversal of the cause are: First, that no count of the declaration states a cause of action; and, second, that the court should have given the peremptory instruction.

F. J. Canty and R. J. Folonie, for appellant. Ela, Grover & Graves, for appellee.

SCOTT, J. (after stating the facts). It is urged that the declaration herein does not state a cause of action. This question arose in the circuit court upon a motion in arrest of judgment. Appellee, upon leave obtained in this court, has filed here a certified copy of the brief and argument of appellant which was filed in the Appellate Court. It appears therefrom that in that court the insufficiency of the declaration was not suggested; but it is said that, where a declaration omits to aver a material fact essential to a valid cause of action, the judgment will be reversed, although no question is made below. It is unnecessary to discuss this proposition, as the authorities cited in support thereof do not apply in a court of review, where the question is pending on appeal from or writ of error to an intermediate court, which is likewise a court of review. We can only determine whether the Appellate Court decided correctly. National Bank v. Le Moyne, 127 Ill. 253, 20 N. E. 45. In doing this it is manifest we can consider no matters except those which were presented to that court. Sherwood v. Illinois Trust & Savings Bank, 195 Ill. 112, 62 N. E. 835, 88 Am. St. Rep. 183. We will not consider an error assigned on the record of the court of original jurisdiction which was not presented by appellant's brief to the Appellate Court, where the same party is the appellant here.

Appellant assigns as error the action of the circuit court in overruling its motion for a peremptory instruction at the conclusion of all the evidence, and appellee insists that this alleged error was not presented in the Appellate Court. We find, on examination of the brief filed by the electric company in that court, that it was there urged that there was no evidence tending to prove negligence on the part of the defendant or the exercise of due care by the plaintiff; and, as this is the question which appellant argues under this assignment in this court, we think it proper for our consideration.

It is earnestly insisted on the part of the electric company that the relation of the plaintiff to the defendant was that of trespasser or licensee, and that, consequently, the defendant was not liable, unless the injury to the plaintiff resulted from some willful or wanton act of the defendant. We think this a misapprehension. The only right the electric company had under the ordinance was a right to place its wire under the sidewalk. It was entitled to permanently occupy no more space for that purpose than was necessary for the wire and any devices used to protect the wire and to keep persons from coming in contact therewith. It had no right or permission to occupy the whole of the space under the sidewalk where the accident occurred. It appears that there was nothing to prevent access from the alley in the rear to the lot fronting on this space; that boys were in the habit of playing on that lot, and passing into this space under the sidewalk to shelter themselves from rain or sun, or for any other purpose that occurred to them; and that this was done without objection from the owner of the lot or the city, and on the occasion of this accident the plaintiff went under this sidewalk in company with three other boys, one of whom, at least, had been in the habit of playing on the lot. It is manifest that it was not the purpose of the city that the public should have access to and use this space as it did the space above the sidewalk. If, however, the curb, which was at the outer edge of this sidewalk and prevented access to the space from the street, had not been there, there could be no question but that the public would have had the same right to pass under this sidewalk from the street that they would have to pass under a stairway or platform of a station of an elevated railway located in the street. There the public has, and exercises, the right to pass over the same portion of the street on two different levels, and it seems apparent that the public would have the same right to pass upon this space, where they came upon it from an abutting lot, in the absence of objection from the lot owner. Plaintiff was, therefore, rightfully in this space, and he was not there by the leave or license of the defendant. The same rule does not apply to him as applies to one who goes upon the property of another, whether with or without permission. He was not upon property either owned or controlled by the defendant.

It is then urged that he became a trespasser when he laid his hand upon the wire, by virtue of his act in touching the wire without the permission of the owner thereof; and Hector v. Boston Electric Light Co., 161 Mass. 558, 37 N. E. 773, 25 L. R. A. 554, is referred to in support of this position. In that case the plaintiff received the injury while upon the roof of a building where he had no right, and where he was neither invited nor licensed to be. The distinction is apparent. Plaintiff's act in taking hold of the wire was an accident. The injury resulted from that accident, and, while it may be conceded that he had no right to take hold of the wire, the question still remains, who was responsible for the injury that resulted from his accidental contact with that wire? So far as being in the space under the sidewalk was concerned, plaintiff had the same right to be there that the defendant had; but he could not rightfully interfere with the property of the defendant, or occupy the space already pre-empted by it. Appellant urges that the rights of the parties to be in this space were not equal, for the reason that it was there in pursuance of the terms of an ordinance and could not be summarily ejected, as the plaintiff, perhaps, might be. This is wholly immaterial. The question is, not how long either party had the right to remain, but what right they had to be there at the instant of the accident.

The evidence tends to prove that the electric cable passing along under this sidewalk had been in use from 8 to 14 years; that in some places the insulation was defective; that the cable had been out of repair on several occasions near the place where this accident occurred; that the wire had on frequent occasions prior to this accident been "grounded" in the vicinity where this trouble occurred; that the effect of that condition is to send a current of electricity along and on the lead covering of the cable; that, when a "ground" would occur, the lead on the outside of the cable would be electrified from the "ground," in each direction to a place where there would be another "ground," or a point in the cable where the current would be broken or stopped by a different covering used at the joints. This was a high-tension wire, carrying 2,000 volts of electricity, and the lead covering, when so electrified, would severely shock and burn any human being coming in contact therewith. Electricity is a subtle and powerful agent. Ordinary care, exercised by those who make a business of using it for profit, to prevent injury to others therefrom, requires much greater precaution in its use than where the element used is of a less dangerous character. As there is greater danger and hazard in the use of electricity, there must be a corresponding exercise of skill and attention, for the purpose of avoiding injury to another, to constitute what the law terms "ordinary care." The care must be commensurate with the danger. 10 Am. & Eng. Ency. of Law (2d Ed.) p. 873; Alton Illuminating Co. v. Foulds, 190 Ill. 367, 60 N. E. 537; Perham v. Portland General Electric Co., 33 Or. 451, 53 Pac. 14, 24, 40 L. R. A. 799, 72 Am. St. Rep. 730; Haynes v. Raleigh Gas Co., 114 N. C. 203, 19 S. E. 344, 26 L. R. A. 810, 41 Am. St. Rep. 786; McLaughlin v. Louisville Electric Light Co., 100 Ky. 173, 37 S. W. 851, 34 L. R. A. 812; Ennis v. Receiver, 87 Hun, 355, 34 N. Y. Supp. 379. We are of the opinion that the appellant's failure to use some device to guard its wires in this space under this sidewalk, so that no person could inadvertently touch the cable, tended to show a lack of ordinary care.

It is urged, however, that the plaintiff was guilty of contributory negligence, as a matter of law, in going under the sidewalk; and we are referred to the case of Heimann v. Kinnare, 190 Ill. 156, 60 N. E. 215, 52 L. R. A. 652, 83 Am. St. Rep. 123. This is a case where a boy lost his life by drowning. A small pond was partly filled with water, and the water was partly covered with ice; there being an open space of water around the edge of the ice. For the purpose of ascertaining if the ice thereon was strong, he ran down an incline leading to the water, jumped over the open water upon the edge of the ice, and ran out toward the middle of the pond, where the ice gave way and he was drowned. He knew, before going there, that the water was beyond his depth. He had knowledge of the danger consequent on the breaking of the ice. In the case at bar the plaintiff did not know that the wire in question was under the sidewalk, and did not know that there was danger there of the kind he encountered. He was attracted to this place by fire in the vicinity, occasioned by the "grounding" of this wire. At the place where the accident occurred he was not near enough to the fire so occasioned to be in danger from the fire itself, and while negligence cannot be attributed to the defendant for a failure to correct the difficulty which had resulted in the wire being "grounded" on this occasion, as it does not appear that it either had or ought to have had notice that the wire was so grounded," still it was natural for the boy to gratify his curiosity by going into this space for the purpose of looking at the fire, and in so doing he went where he had a right to go, and where he had no reason to anticipate any serious danger. The question of contributory negligence was one for the jury.

We do not think the doctrine of traps, or that of attractive nuisances, applicable. No other errors have been discussed. The judgment of the Appellate Court will be affirmed.

Judgment affirmed.

(209 Ill. 627)

WELLS v. O'HARE.*

(Supreme Court of Illinois. April 20, 1904.)

MASTER AND SERVANT—SERVANT'S INJURIES—FELLOW SERVANT'S NEGLIGENCE—CARE REQUIRED OF MASTER—INSTRUCTIONS—TRIAL—ABSENCE OF JUDGE DURING ARGUMENT—PROPRIETY.

1. In an action for the death of a contractor's employé, caused by the fall of a brick down an elevator shaft in a building in process of construction, plaintiff's theory being that the brick, which had been placed under a plank, was drawn into the shaft in the removal of the plank by another employé, it was proper to instruct that, as a matter of law, the negligence of a fellow servant is one of the risks assumed by a servant, and if the jury believe that the injury in this case was caused solely by the negligent act of a fellow servant they should find for defendant.

2. It was error to instruct that the ordinary risk of employment meant such risks as are usual and ordinary in the employment, after the employer has taken reasonable care to discover and prevent them; since the jury were thus misled into understanding that defendant would be liable unless he had taken reasonable care to discover that decedent would be exposed to danger because of the acts of the other employé, and had taken reasonable care to prevent the act or omission occasioning decedent's death.

3. If objection to the judge's absence from the courtroom during the argument of a case to the jury is seasonably made and properly presented such conduct should be regarded as fatal error, except where, in a civil case or misdemeanor, it plainly appears to the reviewing court that the cause of the objecting party was not prejudiced by what occurred during the judge's absence.

Appeal from Appellate Court, First District.

Action by Thomas J. O'Hare, as administrator of the estate of Michael Corbett, deceased, against A. E. Wells. From a judgment of the Appellate Court affirming a judgment for plaintiff (110 Ill. App. 7), defendant appeals. Reversed.

O. W. Dynes, for appellant. Alexander Sullivan (Francis J. Woolley, of counsel), for appellee.

BOGGS, J. This is an appeal from a judgment of the Appellate Court for the First District affirming a judgment in the sum of $2,500 entered in the circuit court of Cook county against the appellant and in favor of the appellee, as administrator of the estate of Michael Corbett, deceased. The declaration was in case, and claimed damages for the wrongful death of plaintiff's intestate by the alleged negligent act of defendant, and averred "that the defendant, regardless of his duty in the premises, carelessly and negligently threw or caused to fall from a great height, to wit, forty feet above where the plaintiff was then and there lawfully prosecuting his labor, in the exercise of all due care and caution for his own safety, some hard substance, to wit, a brick, down to and upon said deceased, whereby and by means whereof the death of the said Michael Corbett was then and there caused."

At the time of the accident the deceased was a common laborer in the employ of appellant, Wells, who was a general contractor in the city of Chicago, and had the contract for the mason work on a nine-story brick building located in said city. For the purpose of carrying the brick and mortar to the different stories or floors as the building went up, a temporary devise such as is used by builders, called a "hoist," was put in, which consisted of two rough elevator platforms traveling up and down in vertical shafts, one platform counter-balancing the other, so that when one was at the bottom of the shaft the other was at the top. The cable attached to either platform passed over sheaves at the top, and was operated by steam power, and was so arranged that it could be adjusted to the various floors; that is, when it was needed to hoist material to the second floor the platforms ascended to that floor and no farther, and as the work progressed to the third floor the cables were again lengthened so that they would extend to the fourth floor, and so on with each succeeding floor. On the day prior to the accident the mason work on the eighth floor had been completed, and it became necessary to adjust the hoist to the ninth floor. In order to do so, one of the platforms was drawn up to that floor, and a plank placed under it to support it, and after the cable had been adjusted the plank was left under the platform until the next morning. An employé of the defendant, named Sullivan, was engaged in operating the hoist at the top, and on the night before the accident the foreman ordered him to put the plank under the platform to keep it in position while the cables were being adjusted. In doing so he placed one or more bricks under the south end of the plank in order to level it up. These bricks rested on a tile floor about level with the edge of the shaft, some two feet from its south edge or side. At the time of the accident the foreman of appellant ordered Corbett, the deceased, to assist at the bottom of the shaft in pulling the cable, the object being to raise the platform above so the plank could be removed. Corbett, in obedience to the order, with one or two other employés, stepped into the shaft, took hold of the cable, and pulled down on it, while Sullivan above took hold of the end of the plank and pulled it out. At the same time a brick fell from some point above,

---

*Rehearing denied June 8, 1904.

¶ 3. See Trial, vol. 46, Cent. Dig. § 32.

striking the deceased on the head, inflicting a fatal wound. Plaintiff's theory of the case, on the evidence, is that the brick which fell from above causing the injury was caused to fall through the negligent act of the employé, Sullivan, in this: that he negligently omitted to take the brick from under the plank before attempting to draw the plank from across the elevator shaft, and that Sullivan, in removing the plank, drew or "scraped" the brick which was under it into the shaft, from whence it fell to the bottom and struck and killed Corbett. There was no direct proof that the brick was caused to fall by Sullivan.

It was insisted by counsel for the appellant that, even conceding that the plaintiff's intestate lost his life through the negligent act of Sullivan, still the appellant was not liable because the relation existing between the deceased and Sullivan at that time was that of fellow servants, and that the deceased assumed the risk and danger of receiving an injury through the negligence of those with whom he should be engaged at work as a fellow servant. The declaration did not allege that Sullivan caused the brick to fall, and there is no averment therein that Sullivan was incompetent or that the appellant was guilty of any negligence in employing him, nor did anything appear in the proof tending to show that Sullivan was incompetent. A declaration to recover for negligence must allege the negligence or omission relied upon to give the right to recover. If the alleged negligence on which recovery of damages is sought is that an employer negligently employed an incompetent fellow servant, the declaration should so aver. 13 Ency. of Pl. & Pr. 899. On this branch of the case the issue, then, was whether the relation of fellow servant existed between the deceased and Sullivan. The evidence was such that the Appellate Court was moved to declare in its opinion that whether these workmen were fellow servants was "a matter of very grave doubt," and this view is, in our opinion, the most favorable to the cause of the appellee that could be drawn from the testimony. In a case so close on the facts it is indispensable to the maintenance of the verdict and judgment that the instructions given to the jury relative to the legal principles involved in the determination of the issue should be free from any inaccurate direction which may have influenced the jury improperly against the appellant.

At the request of the appellant the court gave to the jury the following instruction: "The court instructs the jury that, as a matter of law, the negligence of a fellow servant is one of the risks of the employment assumed by a servant, and if you believe, from the evidence, that the injury to the deceased in this case was caused solely by the negligent act of a fellow servant, then it is your duty to find the defendant, A. E. Wells, not guilty."

Under the pleadings and proof in the case this instruction correctly stated the rule of law as to the risks assumed by the deceased. In Chicago, Burlington & Quincy Railroad Co. v. Avery, 109 Ill. 314, we said (page 322): "The negligence of fellow servants is one of the ordinary perils of the service which one takes the hazard of in entering into any employment." In Toledo, Wabash & Western Railway Co. v. Durkin, 76 Ill. 395, we said page 397): An employé "undertakes to run all the ordinary risks incident to the employment, including his own negligence or unskillfulness; and this includes the risk of occasional negligence or unskillfulness of his fellow servants engaged in the same line of duty, or incident thereto, provided such fellow servants are competent and skillful to discharge the duty assigned them." That such risk is assumed by an employé is declared in 12 Am. & Eng. Ency. of Law (2d Ed.) 902, on the authority of many judicial decisions cited in note 4.

But we think the appellant has just ground to complain the jury were not permitted to guide their deliberations by this instruction or to apply the principle there announced to the evidence produced in the cause. At the request of the appellee the court gave to the jury a further instruction relative to the assumption by the deceased of the usual and ordinary risks of his employment, which cast upon the appellant, as the common master, a greater burden of diligence than the law required of him, and imposed upon him an obligation to take precautions beyond any duty legally devolving upon him. The instruction referred to read as follows: "The jury are instructed that the terms 'ordinary risks or hazards of deceased's employment,' as used in these instructions, mean such risks as are usual and ordinary in such employment after the employer has taken reasonable care to discover and prevent such risks."

The theory upon which the appellee sought a verdict was that Sullivan, when attempting to remove the plank on which the elevator had rested on the eighth floor, negligently omitted to take from beneath it the brick which he had on the evening before placed under the plank, and that in removing the plank he scraped or drew the brick into the shaft, and it fell from thence to the bottom of the shaft, and struck and killed the deceased. If Sullivan was a fellow servant of the deceased, the verdict of the jury, under the pleadings and proof, should have been for the appellant, for the reason the law did not require the appellant to answer for the negligence of a fellow servant of the deceased, there being neither allegation nor proof that the master had not exercised ordinary care in selecting Sullivan for the work he was engaged in doing; or, in other words, the rule of law is that the deceased assumed the danger of injury caused by any negligence of Sullivan as one of the risks of his employment, and should look to Sullivan, and not the common employer of both, for any damages arising from the negligence of Sullivan. The jury would, however, understand from the instruction so given at the request of the appellee, that though Sullivan and the deceased were fellow servants, yet the deceased did not assume the risk of receiving injury because of the alleged negligent omission of Sullivan to take away the brick before attempting to draw away the plank from across the shaft, unless it appeared in the proof that the appellant had taken steps to discover that the brick had been left under the plank, and had taken some precautions to prevent the brick from being dragged into the shaft in an effort to remove the plank. The requirement of the instruction given for the appellee, that the employer should be required to take "reasonable care to discover and prevent such risk," could convey no other meaning to the minds of the jurors. This is to make the common master liable for the negligent acts of the fellow servant of one who is injured unless the master can show he could not have anticipated that the fellow servant would be guilty of the negligent act or omission, and could not, by some reasonable precaution, have prevented the doing of the negligent act or compelled the performance of the omitted duty. If the master has performed his own duty toward his servant he is not responsible for the injuries arising wholly from the negligence of a fellow servant of the injured servant. One of the duties which the master owes to an employé is to use ordinary or reasonable care and diligence to select and retain in his employ such other servants as are competent. In Illinois Central Railroad Co. v. Cox, 21 Ill. 20, 71 Am. Dec. 298, we said (page 26, 21 Ill., 71 Am. Dec. 298): "We think the doctrine established by these cases the correct doctrine. It is right and proper that one servant should not recover against the common master for the carelessness of his fellow servant, provided competent servants have been selected by the master." In Consolidated Coal Co. v. Haenni, 146 Ill. 614, 35 N. E. 162, we said (page 622, 146 Ill., and page 164, 35 N. E.): "Among the risks incident to the business which the servant is understood to take upon himself by the contract of hiring are those arising from the careless or wrongful acts of fellow servants. Wood on Law of Master and Servant, § 427. But the assumption by the servant of risks resulting from the negligence of his fellow servants is subject to the implied undertaking of the master that he will use all reasonable care to furnish safe premises, machinery, and appliances, and to employ competent and prudent co-employés. Pittsburg, Cincinnati & St. Louis Railway Co. v. Adams, 105 Ind. 151, 5 N. E. 187; Wood on Law of Master & Servant, §§ 329, 416." In Western Stone Co. v. Whalen, 151 Ill. 472, 38 N. E. 241, 42 Am. St. Rep. 244, we said (page 484, 151 Ill., and page 244, 38 N. E., 42 Am. St. Rep. 244): "The servant, upon entering the employment, is held to assume the natural and ordinary risks incident to the business in which he engages, and impliedly contracts that the master shall not be liable for injuries consequent upon the negligence of a fellow servant in the employment of whom the master has exercised due and proper care." In 12 Am. & Eng. Ency. of Law (2d Ed.; p. 897) the rule is stated as follows: "Where the master uses due diligence in the selection of competent and trusty servants, and furnishes them with suitable means to perform the service in which he employs them, he is not answerable, where there is no countervailing statute, to one of them for an injury received by him in consequence of the carelessness of another while both are engaged in the same service." It was therefore plainly erroneous to say to the jury, as, in effect, did the instruction under consideration, that the appellee could recover for the injury occasioned by the negligent act of Sullivan, even though the deceased and Sullivan were fellow servants, unless the appellant, the common master of both, had taken reasonable care to discover that the deceased would be exposed to the danger of receiving injury because of the acts of Sullivan, and had taken reasonable care to "prevent" the negligent act or omission of Sullivan which occasioned the death of the deceased.

Counsel for appellee cite cases in which this court has applied the doctrine that an employé does not assume all risks that are incident to his employment, but only such as are usual, ordinary, and remain incident after the master has taken reasonable care to prevent or remove them. It is the duty of the employer to take reasonable measures of prevention to obviate the danger of injury to servants from risks that are incident to the employment. In the cases cited the negligence charged was the failure of the master to take those measures of precaution which were reasonably required to obviate the risk of injury to the servant from dangers incident to the employment, as in Chicago & Alton Railroad Co. v. House, 172 Ill. 601, 50 N. E. 151, where the railway, the employer, had negligently removed and ceased to longer provide a switch light, the maintenance whereof constituted a reasonable provision against the dangers incident to the employment which caused the injury; and in Alton Paving Brick Co. v. Hudson, 176 Ill. 270, 52 N. E. 256, where the master failed to advise an inexperienced servant of the existence of a risk incident to the employment and particularly hazardous, of which the master had knowledge and the servant had not; and in City of La Salle v. Kostka, 190 Ill. 130, 60 N. E. 72, where the servant was injured by the caving in upon him of the banks of a sewer, a danger incident to his employment, but which the city could have obviated by the exercise of reasonable care in bracing or shoring the walls or banks of the sewer. In these cases we held, and in other like cases have uniformly held, that the servant did not assume a risk incident to his employment if the master, by the exercise of reasonable care for the safety of his workmen, could have prevented or removed or lessened the risk. The issue presented to the jury in the case at bar was whether the appellee was injured through the negligence of a fellow servant. Such a risk was incidental to his employment. It could be obviated, or at least lessened, by the exercise of care on the part of the master to the end that only competent fellow servants should be employed to labor with the deceased, and therefore the duty was cast upon the appellant to take reasonable precaution to employ none but competent workmen. There was no contention the appellant was negligent in this regard, and it was error to mislead the jury to understand, as did the instruction, that it further devolved upon the master, as a legal duty, to discover and prevent the alleged negligent act or omission of a competent fellow servant of the deceased.

The appellant presents a serious objection to a matter of procedure in the trial court. While counsel for the appellee was making his closing argument to the jury, counsel for the appellant interrupted him with the objection that there was no evidence of the alleged facts which counsel for the appellee was stating in his argument. It was then discovered that the judge was not in his seat or in the courtroom. One of the counsel for the appellee requested the bailiff "to call the court." The bailiff replied, "The judge is not in his room." Counsel for appellee asked counsel for appellant if he should suspend, and counsel for appellant said he did not ask that, but wanted to save an exception to the improper statements in the argument. Counsel for the appellee then proceeded in the absence of the court, and, in the opinion of counsel for the appellant, soon after indulged in a repetition of the other alleged improper statements, and counsel for the appellant again objected, and a colloquy occurred between counsel with reference to the matter. Subsequently the judge returned, but how soon thereafter is not shown by the record. The cause was submitted to the jury without further objection on the part of the appellant.

In Meredeth v. People, 84 Ill. 479, during the argument of the case the judge absented himself from the courtroom to attend to other judicial duties, his position on the bench being occupied by a member of the bar. This was a criminal proceeding, but in the course of an opinion reversing the judgment because of the conduct of the judge we said (page 482): "Serious misconduct, it is insisted, was permitted in the presence of the jury hurtful to the cause of defendant; but whether that is so or not, the absence of the judge from the courtroom, engaged in other judicial labors, for a part of two days, in a trial of this magnitude, cannot be justified on any principle or for any cause. It is not allowable in a trial involving only mere property interests, much less in a case where the life of a human being depends upon the issue." It is the duty of the presiding judge of a trial court to preside in a judicial capacity during all of the time of the trial of a civil case. In Meredeth v. People, supra, we said the argument of the cause is as much a part of the trial as the hearing of the evidence. Whether the fact that the judge so absented himself during a portion of the time of the trial of this case shall be deemed fatal error, working, within itself, a reversal of the judgment, need not be here decided, for the reason there is a conflict of authorities as to the necessary effect of such action by a judge (21 Ency. of Pl. & Pr. 977); and the views of the members of this court are not in harmony on the question, and the decision thereof is not necessary to be here made, as the verdict and judgment in the case will be reversed for the error in giving the instruction hereinbefore noted. We feel impelled to say such a practice merits the most emphatic disapproval, even in such cases, if any there be, where, under the circumstances of the instance, it should be held not fatal error. The absence of the trial judge during the course of a trial, civil as well as criminal, not only opens the way for, but invites, abuses and misconduct that may obstruct and defeat a fair and impartial hearing and decision of the case and pervert the administration of the law to injustice, and such conduct on the part of the judge is always detrimental to the decorum and dignity of a judicial tribunal. If the presiding judge finds it necessary to absent himself from the court when a trial is in progress, he should suspend all judicial proceedings until he has returned. The evils likely to follow any departure from this rule are so obvious and grievous that if objection thereto is seasonably made and properly presented it should be regarded a fatal error, except when, in a civil case or misdemeanor, it shall plainly appear to the reviewing court that the cause of the complaining party was not prejudiced by what occurred in the court during the absence of the judge.

The judgment of the circuit court and that of the Appellate Court will each be reversed, and the cause will be remanded to the circuit court for further proceedings not inconsistent with this opinion.

Reversed and remanded.

(210 Ill. 66)

BIXLER v. SUMMERFIELD et al.*

(Supreme Court of Illinois. April 20, 1904.)

CORPORATIONS — MINORITY STOCKHOLDER — RIGHTS—ACTION—MISAPPROPRIATION OF FUNDS—ULTRA VIRES.

1. The decision of the Supreme Court on appeal from an order dismissing a bill on demur-

*Rehearing denied June 8, 1904.

rer, reversing the order, establishes the bill's sufficiency, and on a second trial the only question is whether the facts shown by the evidence sustain the allegations of the bill.

2. In a suit by a minority stockholder in a corporation against the owner of the majority of the stock for misappropriation of the funds of the corporation because it paid to himself and wife unreasonable and fraudulent sums for salaries, evidence examined, and *held* to fail to show that the salaries paid were excessive.

3. In a suit by a minority stockholder in a corporation against the owner of the majority of the stock for loaning the funds of the corporation contrary to its charter, it appeared that the majority stockholder loaned small sums out of the corporate funds contrary to the charter; that the loans were secured and were repaid with interest; that all of the loans were made while the minority stockholder was an officer of the corporation; and that on his objection to the loans, made after his leaving the corporation's employment, steps were taken to collect the money loaned. *Held* insufficient to warrant the granting of relief to the minority stockholder.

4. In a suit by a minority stockholder in a corporation against the owner of the majority of the stock, based on the ground that the corporation purchased and held real estate in violation of the statute, it appeared that the corporation purchased a half acre of land for $300, and held the title thereto for about two years, contrary to the statute; that, as soon as complaint was made as to the holding of the land, the directors authorized the sale thereof, and the president sold it at a profit of $10. *Held* not to warrant the dissolution of the corporation.

Appeal from Circuit Court, Cook County; Richard Tuthill, Judge.

Suit by Samuel J. Bixler against Nelson G. Summerfield and another. From a decree dismissing the bill, plaintiff appeals. Affirmed.

See 62 N. E. 849.

Wm. Hindley and Ernest Severy, for appellant. A. W. Brickwood, for appellees.

RICKS, J. This suit was before us at a previous term, an appeal being prosecuted by appellant from a decretal order dismissing the bill on demurrer thereto. The decree was reversed, and the cause remanded for further proceedings in accordance with the views expressed in the former opinion of this court, reported in 195 Ill. 147, 62 N. E. 849, to which reference is made for a more complete statement of the facts. In the former appeal the question presented was whether the allegations of the bill set up a cause of action sufficient to require an answer, the demurrer admitting the facts as alleged. The reversal by this court established the fact of the bill's sufficiency, and now the only question presented is whether the facts established by the evidence sustain the allegations of the bill and warrant the relief prayed for by complainant. The trial court in the present case was of the opinion that the evidence did not warrant the relief prayed, and entered a decree dismissing the bill.

The main allegations in the bill are: First, that the company paid unreasonable and fraudulent sums for salaries; second, the loaning of the funds of the company, contrary to its charter; third, the adding to the business the manufacture of goods, against the provisions of its charter; and, fourth, the purchase and holding of real estate in violation of the statute. The company, as organized, was known as the "Story Finishing Company," and at the time of incorporation its capital stock was $15,000, which was divided into 300 shares, each representing a face value of $50, and at the time of filing the amended bill the appellee Nelson G. Summerfield owned and controlled 241 shares of the stock, the appellant, Bixler, owned 58 shares, and Sophia H. Hoff 1 share. There is no allegation in the bill that the corporation is insolvent, but, on the contrary, the assets are stated to be $16,196.83, and the liabilities, excepting capital stock, are stated to be $241.13. The company was organized in April, 1893, and at the time of its organization appellee Summerfield, John T. Story, and the appellant appear to have been the organizers. Appellant, Bixler, was elected director and secretary, his duties being the keeping of the books of the company, and, when not engaged on the books of the company, doing other work; and for the services thus rendered he received the sum of $15 per week, and from 1896 to 1897 was president of the company. The evidence also discloses that he remained in the employ of the company until about the 1st of November, 1900, when he quit, and established a business of his own similar to that of the Story Finishing Company, and in January, 1901, filed the bill in this case.

The first question being in reference to excessive salaries, the record discloses that appellant, as secretary, received $15 per week; John T. Story, one of the organizers, who was elected president, received $25 per week; and appellee N. G. Summerfield was elected vice president, treasurer, and general manager, and received $25 per week. The salaries so remained until a meeting of the board of directors in August, 1895, when it became necessary, by reason of the company's financial embarrassment, to reduce the salaries, and a resolution of the board was adopted fixing appellant's salary at $12 per week and Summerfield's and Story's salaries at $5 per week for the term of 18 months, or until the company's debts were paid. Shortly after this time Story quit the company, selling his interest to Summerfield, and at the election of officers in 1897 Summerfield, having control of a majority of the stock, elected himself president and general manager, fixing his salary at $25 per week, and elected A. E. Summerfield secretary; but it does not appear from the evidence that any salary was fixed for the secretary, but the evidence discloses that she received as wages from $3.50 to $7 per week, and that she worked in the factory the same as other employés. Appellant's salary remained the same until he quit working for the company. In October, 1900, the treasury showed considerable surplus, and the salary of the president, Summerfield, was fixed at $35 per week, and in December of the same year the board, by resolution, fixed his salary at $50 per week, which amount he was receiving at the time of filing the bill in this suit. The evidence discloses that Summerfield devoted his whole time and attention to the company's business, working early and late, and making no extra charges for overtime, and the book value of the stock has increased from $15 per share to $55 per share, and that the profits of the company for the year 1900 alone, in excess of all expenses, was $3,400. From a review of the evidence we find there is a conflict as to what the services of appellee Summerfield were reasonably worth. Upon an average for the whole time from 1893 to 1900 the salary of Summerfield did not exceed $20 per week, and the fact that the stock had more than trebled in value would seem to indicate that the management of the corporation was very skillful, and we are not prepared to say, under such circumstances, that the services of those in control and by whose management this state of affairs had been brought about, particularly Summerfield, were exorbitantly high.

It is also complained that Mrs. Summerfield, wife of N. G. Summerfield, was receiving $25 per week for the performance of work for which only from $3.50 to $5 per week had been allowed. The evidence, however, shows that Mrs. Summerfield took a very active interest in the business of the company, and materially aided in building up and managing the business of the company; and, as the witnesses differed as to what said services were reasonably worth, we cannot say that the amount paid for the same was manifestly too high.

It is next contended that appellee Summerfield made various loans out of the funds of the company, contrary to its charter; but the record discloses that all of such loans were for small sums, and that security was taken for same; that all were repaid, with interest, and that at no time was there loaned to exceed $400; that all of said loans were made while appellant was an officer and in the employment of the company, and it was not until after appellant quit such employment that he made any objection to the loans thus made, and as soon as objection was made the company took steps to and did collect all the money loaned by it.

It is next contended that the company purchased a half acre of land in the suburbs of the city of Chicago, paying therefor the sum of $300, and held the title to the same for about two years, contrary to the statute. It is claimed by Summerfield that the purchase was made for a factory site. Whether this fact be regarded as established or not is wholly immaterial, for the undisputed evidence shows that as soon as complaint was made as to the holding of this property, a resolution was passed by the board of directors' authorizing the sale of said land, and the same was disposed of by the president of the company at a profit of $10.

It will thus be seen from the foregoing that the stock of the appellee company was not impaired in value by any misappropriation of the corporate funds, but it had been greatly enhanced by the management of those in its control. We think the evidence wholly fails to establish the allegations of complainant's bill, and the action of the circuit court in dismissing said bill was proper, and the same will be affirmed.

Decree affirmed.

(209 Ill. 468)

KOENIG v. DOHM et al.*

(Supreme Court of Illinois. April 20, 1904.)

STATUTE OF FRAUDS—NECESSITY OF PLEADING—SUFFICIENCY OF PLEADING—CONTRACTS FOR SALE OF LAND—AUTHORITY OF AGENT—SIGNATURE OF PERSON CHARGED—ESTOPPEL TO PLEAD—PART PERFORMANCE—PAYMENT OF PURCHASE MONEY.

1. Where a contract violates the statute of frauds, it is merely voidable, and may be enforced as made, unless the defense is taken advantage of either by demurrer, plea, or answer.

2. Answers to a bill for specific performance, alleging that defendant's wife, when she signed an alleged contract for the sale of the property described in the bill, had no authority in writing from defendant, nor memoranda thereof, for the sale of the property, and alleging that defendant did not authorize his wife, or any other person, either orally or in writing, to make any bargain for the sale of the property, sufficiently plead the statute of frauds (2 Starr & C. Ann. St. 1896 [2d Ed.] p. 1997), which provides that no action shall be brought to charge any person on a contract for the sale of lands, unless such contract, or some memorandum or note thereof, shall be made in writing, signed by the party to be charged, or some other person authorized in writing.

3. A mere indorsement of the name of the owner of property on the check given by a prospective purchaser for earnest money is not a compliance with the statute of frauds (2 Starr & C. Ann. St. 1896 [2d Ed.] p. 1997).

4. The payment of a small portion of the purchase money is not a sufficient part performance of a contract for the sale of real estate to take the same out of the statute of frauds.

5. The fact that the owner of property stated to a prospective purchaser that he could call on his wife and mother-in-law, and, if they were satisfied, the contract for the sale of the property could be signed for him by his wife, but without making any representation that his wife had any written authority from him to sign the contract, or any false and fraudulent representation, did not raise an equitable estoppel such as to preclude the owner from pleading the statute of frauds to a suit for the specific performance of a contract, signed by his wife, for the sale of the property.

6. Notice, actual or constructive, of a contract for the sale of land, void under the statute of frauds, does not prevent the person having such notice from becoming a purchaser of the property from the original owner.

---

*Rehearing denied June 8, 1904.

¶ 4. See Frauds, Statute of, vol. 23, Cent. Dig. §§ 311, 312.

Appeal from Superior Court, Cook County; Jesse Holdom, Judge.

Bill for specific performance by Mathias Koenig against William Dohm and others. From a decree dismissing the bill, complainant appeals. Affirmed.

This is a bill, originally filed on March 20, 1902, and subsequently amended on October 14, 1902, in the superior court of Cook county, by the appellant against the appellees, William Dohm, Augusta J. Dohm, Thekla Schwartz, William Schwertfeger, and Peter Van Vlissingen, to enforce the specific performance of a contract for the sale of the premises, hereinafter described as 1111 Lincoln avenue, in Chicago, by William Dohm and Augusta J. Dohm, his wife; to enforce a verbal agreement by said Schwartz, as second mortgagee, with appellant to release her mortgage lien; to remove a subsequent contract and warranty deed executed to said Schwertfeger, as subsequent purchaser or grantee from Dohm, as clouds upon appellant's title; and to obtain from said Van Vlissingen, trustee named in two trust deeds upon the property, written releases thereof. Answers were filed to the bill by the defendants, and the cause was referred to the master to take the testimony and report his conclusions. Testimony was taken before the master, and returned by him with his reports. The master made two reports, in the first of which he found that the appellant was not entitled to the specific performance prayed for, and recommended a dismissal of the bill for want of equity. Subsequently the master made a supplementary report, wherein he reached an opposite conclusion from that announced in his original report, and recommended therein a decree of specific performance, substantially as prayed for in the bill. Objections and exceptions were filed to the master's reports, and on December 8, 1902, upon a hearing of the cause, the court sustained the exceptions filed to the amended report of the master, and dismissed the bill at appellant's cost for want of equity. From the decree so dismissing the bill for the want of equity, the present appeal is prosecuted.

The material facts are substantially as follows: On January 30, 1902, and theretofore, the defendant below, William Dohm, was the owner in fee of the real estate described in the bill as follows, to wit: "Lot 3 in block 10, in Gross' North Addition to Chicago, in the southeast quarter of section 19, township 40 north, range 14, east of the third principal meridian, also known and described as No. 1111 Lincoln avenue, city of Chicago, together with the improvements." Augusta J. Dohm is the wife of William Dohm, and Thekla Schwartz is the mother of Augusta J. Dohm, and they live together. Said Schwertfeger had been a tenant of the premises here in controversy for some nine years, and had carried on the butcher's business there during that period. The complainant below, appellant here, Mathias Koenig, is also a butcher, and for several years carried on that business at 1101 Lincoln avenue. On January 30, 1902, the premises in question were incumbered as follows: One trust deed, dated May 7, 1897, to said Van Vlissingen, as trustee, to secure a promissory note of even date for $3,000; trust deed, dated June 15, 1897, to said Van Vlissingen, as trustee, to secure a note for $3,000, of even date, both notes payable in five years from date; and a third trust deed, dated June 20, 1900, to secure a note for $401, maturing in three years. The latter trust deed was released and satisfied of record when this bill was filed on March 20, 1902. Van Vlissingen held the first note of May 7, 1897, and Thekla Schwartz held the second note of June 15, 1897.

On January 30, 1902, William Dohm and Koenig made a verbal arrangement, by the terms of which Koenig was to pay Dohm $5,650 for said premises, upon condition that the price should be satisfactory to Mrs. Schwartz, the holder of the second incumbrance, it being understood that she would release a part of her debt in order to permit the sale of the property at the price named. At that time, it is agreed, William Dohm was bankrupt. William Dohm and his wife and mother-in-law were desirous of disposing of the premises in order to pay the liens thereon, except the lien of Mrs. Schwartz, and, as to that, to obtain as much of it as possible, and use the proceeds in re-establishing Dohm in business. On said January 30th, it was arranged between Koenig and Dohm that Koenig should call at Dohm's house on the next afternoon, and, if Mrs. Schwartz should be then satisfied with the price of $5,650, Koenig should enter into an agreement for the purchase of the premises for that sum. Dohm said that his wife could sign the contract for him as his agent. On January 31, 1902, which was Friday, Koenig and Mrs. Dohm and Mrs. Schwartz agreed to the purchase and sale of the premises, and an agreement in writing was entered into between the parties, dated January 31, 1902, signed by Koenig, and to which Mrs. Dohm signed the name of her husband, William Dohm, and her own name as his agent. By the terms of this written agreement Dohm and his wife agreed to convey said premises in fee, clear of all incumbrances, by a warranty deed to Koenig, together with the improvements, and Koenig thereby agreed to pay Dohm and his wife the sum of $5,650—$500 upon the signing of the agreement, and $5,150 upon the delivery of a good and sufficient warranty deed. Upon the execution and delivery of the contract, Koenig delivered to Mrs. Dohm a check for $500, payable to the order of William Dohm, upon the First National Bank of Chicago, signed by said Koenig, which check was on the evening of January 31st delivered to Dohm, and then, or upon the morning of February 1st, indorsed by Dohm. On February 1st the check was cashed and collected by Mrs. Dohm, and the money received by her and deposited in a safety-vault box. When the contract was made, Mrs. Schwartz agreed that she would accept and receive in full payment of her second mortgage the sum of $2,000. Koenig and Mrs. Schwartz and the Dohms, with others, met again on Monday, February 3d, and the Dohms and Mrs. Schwartz claimed that Koenig had misrepresented to Mrs. Schwartz and Mrs. Dohm the price which Dohm had agreed to take for the premises. On Tuesday, February 4th, Koenig and his attorney called upon John Pfeiffer, Dohm's attorney, to obtain the abstract of title for examination, and Pfeiffer then informed them that a real estate agent was making claims for commissions. Thereupon Koenig, through his attorney, agreed to pay an additional $50 to defray the expense of contesting said commission claim. The abstract of title was delivered to Koenig's attorney, and by him returned the next day with his opinion. The opinion was received by Pfeiffer, with the promise that he would immediately cure the objections therein stated. From February 5 until March 10, 1902, Koenig's attorney frequently communicated with Dohm's attorney, and requested him to settle the objections and complete the contract. None of the objections were removed prior to March 10, 1902. Koenig had no notice of Schwertfeger's intentions to purchase the premises until March 10, 1902, when he learned that Schwertfeger was negotiating for their purchase. Schwertfeger had actual notice on February 5, 1902, and thereafter on February 17, 1902, of the contract for the sale of the premises to Koenig. On the latter date Koenig told Schwertfeger that he had bought the property, and requested him to pay the rents to him, which, however, Schwertfeger did not do. On March 10, 1902, Pfeiffer informed Koenig's attorney that Mrs. Schwartz had withdrawn her consent to the sale of the property, and insisted upon the payment in full of her mortgage. On March 10, 1902, Mr. and Mrs. Dohm entered into an agreement with Schwertfeger for the sale of the premises to him for $6,-00, and, on March 14, 1902, delivered to him their warranty deed. Koenig served notice on March 12, 1902, on the Dohms and Mrs. Schwartz, of a demand for specific performance of the contract of January 31, 1902, but after March 10, 1902, they refused to carry out said contract. Koenig has always been ready, willing, and able to carry out the contract on his part. Koenig has paid two small sums on account of taxes upon the premises. Koenig tendered to Mr. and Mrs. Dohm and Mrs. Schwartz in lawful currency $5,250, which tender was refused by them. At the hearing before the master Mr. and Mrs. Dohm and Mrs. Schwartz tendered and offered to Koenig the $500 paid by him as earnest money, which was refused by him. The liens upon the premises, except the first trust deed and $1,000 on the trust deed held by Mrs. Schwartz, have been paid by Dohm.

Matthew J. Huss and Bernhardt J. Frank, for appellant. Hanlon & Pfeiffer, for appellees.

MAGRUDER, J. (after stating the facts). Appellee Augusta J. Dohm, the wife of appellee William Dohm—the latter being the owner of the real estate in controversy—had no authority in writing to sign her husband's name to the written contract for the sale of the premises to the appellant, Mathias Koenig. The main defense made by the appellees against the specific performance of the contract in question is that Mrs. Dohm, acting as agent for her husband, William Dohm, had no such written authority, and that therefore the contract was void under the statute of frauds. Hence the material question to be determined is whether the defense thus set up is a good one under the facts of this case.

First. It is first insisted by the appellant that the statute of frauds was not properly set up as a defense in the answer or answers. Where a contract is alleged to be invalid as being in violation of the statute of frauds, it is merely voidable, and may be enforced as made, unless the defendant takes advantage of the statute by setting it up as a defense, either by demurrer, plea, or answer. McClure v. Otrich, 118 Ill. 320, 8 N. E. 784; Esmay v. Gorton, 18 Ill. 483. But in pleading the statute of frauds it is not necessary to make an express reference to the statute by its title or otherwise. It is enough to state facts sufficient to show that the defendant seeks the protection of the statute, and the plea or answer setting up the statute should expressly aver that the contract or authority to make the contract was not in writing. Schoonmaker v. Plummer, 139 Ill. 612, 29 N. E. 1114; 9 Ency. of Pl. & Pr. pp. 713, 715; Wright v. Raftree, 181 Ill. 464, 54 N. E. 998. We think that in the original and amended answers in this case the statute of frauds is sufficiently pleaded to enable the appellees to avail themselves of its provisions. Section 2 of the statute of frauds provides that "no action shall be brought to charge any person upon any contract for the sales of lands * * * unless such contract or some memorandum or note thereof shall be in writing, and signed by the party to be charged therewith, or some other person, thereunto by him lawfully authorized in writing, signed by such party." 2 Starr & C. Ann. St. 1896 (2d Ed.) p. 1997. The original answer of the appellee William Dohm, filed herein on May 3, 1902, contains the following allegation: "That he has offered to return said $500 to Koenig, and notified him that he made no such bargain or agreement, nor did he authorize his wife, or Thekla Schwartz, or any other person, either orally or in writing, to make any bargain for the sale of the said real estate, but that Koenig declined and refused to accept the

$500." The amended answer of appellee William Dohm, filed on August 27, 1902, contains the following allegation: "That this defendant's wife, when she signed the said alleged contract for the sale of the property described in the bill, had no authority in writing from this defendant, nor memoranda thereof for the sale of said property." While the statute of frauds is not expressly referred to in the above-quoted allegations of the answers, yet the language used negatives the existence of the fact required by the statute of frauds. The requirement of the statute is that the "contract or some memorandum or note thereof shall be in writing and signed by the party to be charged therewith, or some other person thereunto by him lawfully authorized in writing, signed by such party." The person here signing the contract as agent for the owner, William Dohm, was Augusta J. Dohm, his wife, and it is stated, in substance, that she was not authorized by him in writing to make any contract for the sale of the land in question. To be sure, the word "bargain" is used, but that word is broad enough in its meaning to include "contract." The word "bargain" is defined in Webster's Dictionary as "an agreement between parties concerning the sale of property; or a contract, by which one party binds himself to transfer the right to some property for a consideration, and the other party binds himself to receive the property and pay the consideration." "Bargain" is also there defined as "an agreement or stipulation of any kind."

Second. As has already been stated, there is no evidence to show, nor, indeed, is any claim made by the appellant, that Mrs. Dohm had any authority in writing to sign a contract for the sale of the property in question. It is true that, when the written contract made with appellant was signed by Mrs. Dohm, the appellant handed to her a check, payable to the order of William Dohm, and on the evening of the day on which the check was received, or on the morning of the next day thereafter, the appellee William Dohm indorsed the check. His indorsement, however, of his name upon the back of the check was no such note or memorandum in writing as is required by the statute. In Kopp v. Reiter, 146 Ill. 437, 34 N. E. 942, 22 L. R. A. 273, 37 Am. St. Rep. 156, where it appeared that the husband of the owner of a lot made a written contract for the sale of it without any written authority from his wife, and where it appeared that the purchaser made a payment of earnest money, amounting to $250, it was held that a deed to the purchaser, afterwards signed by the wife, which made no reference to the contract, and failed to express its terms, and which she deposited with her husband to be delivered on certain conditions, but which was destroyed without delivery, could not be regarded as such a memorandum or note of the original contract as to take the case out of the statute of frauds. In Kopp v. Reiter, supra, the authorities were reviewed, and it was there held that, while no form of language is necessary in order to determine what sort of writing is sufficient to meet the requirements of the statute, if only the intention can be gathered, and that any kind of writing from a solemn deed down to mere hasty notes or memoranda in books, papers, or letters would suffice, yet "that the writings, notes, or memoranda must contain on their face, or by reference to others, the names of the parties, vendor and vendee, a sufficiently clear and explicit description of the property to render it capable of being identified from other property of like kind, together with the terms, conditions (if there be any), and price to be paid, or other consideration to be given; and such writing, note, or memorandum must be signed by the party to be charged, or, if signed by an agent, the authority of such agent must be in writing, signed by the party to be charged, and the contract or memorandum or note thereof made by the agent must also be in writing, and signed by him." It was also further held in that case that where a deed, executed by an owner of land and not delivered, is held to be a sufficient memorandum of a contract of sale under the statute, it will be found to contain or refer to the terms and conditions of the contract. It cannot be said that the mere indorsement of the name of William Dohm, the owner, upon the check given for the earnest money, complies with the requirements of the statute as thus set forth. See, also, Browne on the Statute of Frauds (5th Ed.) 354b.

Third. The mere fact that the appellant, Koenig, paid the sum of $500 as earnest money, and that the same was accepted by the appellee Dohm, is not sufficient to take the case out of the statute of frauds. The $500 was a part, and only a small part, of the purchase money agreed to be paid. It has been decided by this court that an oral sale of real estate may be taken out of the statute of frauds "by a payment of the purchase money, being let into possession, and the making of lasting and valuable improvements." Wright v. Raftree, 181 Ill. 464, 54 N. E. 998; Holmes v. Holmes, 44 Ill. 168; Ferbrache v. Ferbrache, 110 Ill. 210; Pond v. Sheean, 132 Ill. 312, 23 N. E. 1018, 8 L. R. A. 414. But whether or not it is necessary to go to the length of requiring all of these acts, to wit, payment of the purchase money, possession, and valuable improvements, in order to constitute such a part performance of the contract as to justify a decree for specific performance, it is certainly true that a payment of the purchase money alone, without either possession or improvements, is not such a part performance as to take the case out of the statute.

In Temple v. Johnson, 71 Ill. 13, referring to the general rule stated by Story in his work on Equitable Jurisprudence, we said:

"He says that, although formerly a payment of the purchase money was considered a sufficient part performance to take the case out of the statute, the rule is now otherwise settled, and in this he is fully sustained by the adjudged cases, both in the British and American courts." What was said upon this subject in Temple v. Johnson, supra, was subsequently approved in the case of Pond v. Sheean, 132 Ill. 312, 23 N. E. 1018, 8 L. R. A. 414. See, also, Gorham v. Dodge, 122 Ill. 528, 14 N. E. 44; Morrison v. Herrick, 130 Ill. 631, 22 N. E. 537. In the case at bar, appellant did not take possession of the premises under the oral contract, nor make any improvement thereon. If, as is held in the cases cited, a court of equity will not decree the specific performance of a parol agreement to convey land where the purchaser has merely paid the purchase money, without going into possession under the contract, it certainly cannot be held that his payment of a small part of the purchase money is a sufficient part performance to take the case out of the statute.

Fourth. Appellant, however, in support of his contention that he is entitled to a decree for specific performance in this case, invokes the doctrine of equitable estoppel. It is claimed that the appellee Dohm made false and fraudulent representations to Koenig as to his wife's authority to execute the contract, and that, inasmuch as appellant paid the earnest money and received the abstracts of title for examination in reliance upon these alleged false and fraudulent representations, appellee Dohm is estopped from denying the validity of the contract. There are cases which hold that verbal sales of land are taken out of the statute of frauds by an application of the doctrine of equitable estoppel. But, where this doctrine is applied, it is for the purpose of preventing the statute of frauds from being used for the perpetration of the frauds the statute was designed to prevent. Mills v. Graves, 38 Ill. 455, 87 Am. Dec. 314. There must, however, be something more than the moral wrong of refusing to be bound by a verbal agreement. A man who makes an oral contract to sell land and violates his agreement, and relies upon the statute of frauds in order to justify himself in its nonperformance, may be guilty of a wrong in the domain of morals, but not of such a fraud as relieves against the application of the statute. In his work on Specific Performance of Contracts, Pomeroy (page 202) says: "There must be some positive act of contrivance, deceit, false representation, or concealment on the part of the defendant, by which the plaintiff is prevented from insisting upon or obtaining a written contract, or is induced to accept or rely upon a parol agreement in place of that required by the statute." We can see no reason why it should be regarded as any greater wrong in point of morals for a man to refuse to carry out a contract to sell or convey land, made by an agent having only verbal authority, than to refuse to perform an oral contract for the sale or conveyance of land, made by himself without the intervention of any agent.

We see nothing in the facts presented by the present record which justifies the appellant in invoking the doctrine of equitable estoppel, for the reason that there is nothing which shows any positive act of fraud or false representation on the part of Dohm. He stated to Koenig that the latter should call upon his wife and mother-in-law, and that, if they were satisfied, the contract could be signed for him by his wife. Dohm was a butcher, and was obliged to be at his work during the whole of the day. The testimony shows that he went to his work as early in the morning as 4 o'clock, and was therefore unable to spend the time to attend to such a matter of business as this. He accordingly directed the appellant to go to his home and see his wife and mother-in-law, and stated to him that, if they were satisfied, a contract could be made out, and his wife could sign it for him (Koenig). He made no representation that his wife had any written authority from him to sign a contract. If his statement amounted to a representation that she had authority to sign a contract, it cannot be regarded, in view of the language used, as anything more than a statement that she had oral authority from him to sign it. In the absence of false and fraudulent representation on the part of Dohm, the doctrine of equitable estoppel, in order to relieve against the statute of frauds, has no application here. As is well said by Pomeroy in his work on Specific Performance of Contracts, p. 202: "The moral wrong in refusing to be bound by a verbal agreement, because it does not comply with the statute, is not the fraud intended by this equitable principle; if it were, the statute would be rendered entirely nugatory."

Fifth. Some stress is laid upon the fact that Schwertfeger, when he took his contract and deed from appellees, had notice of the previous contract made with the appellant. The proof does show that he had such notice, but, in view of what has been said, it makes no difference whether he had notice or not. Notice, actual or constructive, of a contract which is void under the statute of frauds, will not prevent the person having such notice from becoming a purchaser of the property from the original owner. Where the owner may lawfully refuse to perform a contract, he may lawfully sell and convey to another, and, by so doing, repudiate the contract, and the purchaser from him will not be affected by the prior sale rendered void by the statute of frauds. Van Cloostere v. Logan, 149 Ill. 588, 36 N. E. 946; Wright v. Raftree, 181 Ill. 464, 54 N. E. 998.

We are of the opinion, for the reasons above stated, that the statute of frauds was correctly treated by the court below as a defense against the specific performance of the contract here involved. Accordingly, there was no error in the decree dismissing the bill for want of equity, and that decree is affirmed.

Decree affirmed.

(209 Ill. 550)

KNIGHTS TEMPLAR & MASONS' LIFE INDEMNITY CO. v. CRAYTON et al.*

(Supreme Court of Illinois. April 20, 1904.)

LIFE INSURANCE—POLICY—STIPULATIONS—CONSTRUCTION — PROOFS OF DEATH—SUFFICIENCY — DEFENSES—SUICIDE—BURDEN OF PROOF — EVIDENCE — ADMISSIBILITY — ERRORS — WAIVER.

1. A defendant offering evidence after the court's denial of a motion for a verdict made after the close of plaintiff's case waives his right to insist on the error, if any, in denying the motion.

2. The error in denying defendant's motion for a verdict, not being insisted on in the motion for a new trial, cannot be reviewed on appeal.

3. Evidence in an action on a policy stipulating that it should be void in case of the self-destruction of the insured, whether voluntary or involuntary, sane or insane, examined, and *held* not to show self-destruction on the part of the insured.

4. A guardian of beneficiaries in a life policy has no authority, without an express order of the court, to compromise the claim and accept a settlement for less than the full payment; Starr & C. Ann. St. 1896, c. 64, § 17, authorizing a guardian to compound his ward's claim with the approbation of the court.

5. A life policy provided that the insurer would pay to the beneficiaries $5,000 if the insured died from any cause other than suicide, and also the assessments that the insured had paid under the policy. On the death of the insured the guardian of the beneficiaries furnished proofs of death. The insurer, claiming that the insured committed suicide, paid to the guardian the amount of the assessments which were payable, though the insured committed suicide. *Held*, the guardian's release of further liability on receiving the amount of the assessments paid was without consideration, and did not prevent a collection of the face of the policy if the assured did not commit suicide.

6. The beneficiaries in the policy were not estopped from claiming the face of the policy by accepting from their guardian, as they attained their majority, their share in the amount paid by the insurer to the guardian.

7. A stipulation in a policy, declared to be void if insured commits suicide, that the claimant thereunder shall make satisfactory proof of death of the insured, does not mean that such proof shall be made as shall in all cases satisfy the insurer of the cause of death, but the insurer is only entitled to reasonable proof of the fact of death and reasonable proof as to the cause of death; and such proof, when the cause of death becomes a question, is not binding on the insurer or claimant.

8. The provision in a life policy that all claims under it shall be made in 6 months after insured's death is sufficiently complied with by furnishing, within 30 days after death, proof of death, to which the insurer made no objection, together with a statement that the guardian of the beneficiaries was authorized to receive the full amount of the insurance.

9. A policy designating specifically the beneficiaries and the sums to be paid, and stipulating that the same shall be paid within 60 days after proof of death—the assessments paid by the assured to be repaid without interest—but containing no statement with reference to interest on the face of the policy, is a contract for the payment of money, within Hurd's Rev. St. 1901, c. 74, § 2; and hence the insurer is liable for interest at the legal rate on the face of the policy from 60 days after proof of death.

10. In an action on a policy stipulating that it shall be void if the assured commits suicide, the insurer has the burden of proving self-destruction, though the proofs of death tend to show that the death was suicidal, and, in the absence of proof of cause of death, natural or accidental causes will be presumed, and, if the jury are unable to determine the cause of death, they cannot find that it was suicidal.

11. In an action on a policy stipulating that it shall be void if the assured commits suicide, the verdict of the coroner's jury in the inquest over the remains of assured is admissible, but the testimony of the witnesses at the inquest is inadmissible for any purpose other than contradiction.

12. Where, in an action on a life policy by the beneficiaries, one of the beneficiaries, who had testified at the coroner's inquest over the remains of the assured, was a witness at the trial, the insurer might use his deposition before the coroner for the purpose of impeachment.

13. An infant cannot himself make, or authorize any one for him to make, admissions against his interest.

14. A statement of the guardian of the infant beneficiaries in a policy rendered void on the assured committing suicide, that the immediate cause of death of the assured was supposed suicide, cannot be treated as an admission as against the beneficiaries.

15. It is not error to refuse instructions covered by instructions given by the court.

*Rehearing denied June 8, 1904.

¶ 4. See Guardian and Ward, vol. 25, Cent. Dig. § 147.

Appeal from Appellate Court, Second District.

Action by Frank L. Crayton and others against the Knights Templar & Masons' Life Indemnity Company. From a judgment of the Appellate Court (110 Ill. App. 648) affirming a judgment for plaintiffs, defendant appeals. Affirmed.

Jack, Irwin, Jack & Danforth, Ward & Graydon, and Jay H. Magoon, for appellant. Clark Varnum, W. A. Foster, and L. C. McMurtrie, for appellees.

RICKS, J. This is an appeal from a judgment of the Appellate Court affirming a judgment of the circuit court of Marshall county in an action of assumpsit by the appellees against the appellant upon a certificate of membership issued to John Crayton, the father of appellees, providing for the payment to appellees of the sum of $5,000, and of the money paid on the policy in assessments, within 60 days after notice and the receipt of satisfactory proofs of death of the said John Crayton.

The policy provided that in case of self-destruction of the holder of the policy, whether voluntary or involuntary, sane or insane, the policy should become null and void, so far as the same related to benefits, but that the company would pay the widow and heirs or devisees such an amount as the holder should have paid to the company in assessments on the same, without interest. The certificate of membership was issued to said John Crayton on the 1st day of April, 1886, upon his application, and was payable, specifically, to Frank L., Laura, and Margaret J. Crayton, the appellees and beneficiaries therein named. The insured came to his death on the 31st day of July, 1891, by means of a gunshot wound through the head, and his death was either suicidal or accidental. A coroner's inquest was held on the day of the death of the insured, and the verdict of the jury was that the deceased came to his death "by means of a rifleball shot through his head by his own hands, from a Winchester rifle; * * * said wound having been inflicted with suicidal intent, while laboring under a fit of insanity." On the 8th day of August, 1891, Ellen C. Crayton, the mother of appellees, was appointed their guardian. At that time the ages of appellees were as follows: Frank L. Crayton, 17 years; Laura Crayton, 16 years; and Margaret J., commonly called Josephine, 13 years. Notice of the death was immediately given to appellant, and blanks for making proof of death, together with instructions as to what was required by appellant in making such proof, were forwarded to the guardian. By the instructions the claimant was required to state by what title she made her claim; to furnish a certificate of the attending physician; the certificate of a householder, the undertaker, and, in case of suicide or sudden death, a certified copy of the verdict, and of the evidence on which such verdict was based, before the coroner. About the 12th of August, 1891, the proofs, as required, were completed and sent to the appellant, and the receipt of such proofs was acknowledged by the appellant. In the statement of the guardian making such proof, the following, among other things, appeared:

"Number, date, and amount of policy. No. 2,174; date, September 7, 1886; $5,000.

"(a) In what capacity or by what title do you make complaint? (a) Guardian for Frank, Laura, and Josephine Crayton.

"(b) Are you legally entitled to receive the entire amount payable on the policy? (b) Yes.

"(a) Remote cause of death? (a) Supposed sunstroke some two or three years ago.

"(c) Immediate cause of death? (c) Supposed suicide."

Upon the receipt of the proofs of death, appellant notified the guardian that the case was one of suicide, and that the only liability of appellant, under the policy, was for the amount of assessments paid upon the policy, exclusive of interest, which was stated to be $179, and on January 24, 1892, pursuant to an agreement between Ellen C. Crayton, as the guardian of appellees, and appellant, paid to such guardian $179. The payment was made by draft or check drawn by appellant's president and manager upon the appellant company, payable to the order of Ellen C. Crayton, guardian, and contained the following: "Being payment in full of all demands under policy No. 2,174, on the life of John Crayton, deceased." Upon receipt of this check or draft, the guardian surrendered up the policy or certificate of insurance, and indorsed thereon a receipt, which purported to be "in full of all claims under the within policy."

The declaration consists of a special count and the common counts. The special count is upon the policy in hæc verba, and alleges the death of the insured on the 31st day of July, 1891; that appellees were the beneficiaries under the policy; that the insured performed the conditions of the policy required of him; and that appellant was furnished with satisfactory proof of death.

Eleven pleas were filed. A demurrer was sustained to the second, fourth, and fifth pleas, and, as error is not assigned upon this, it need not be further noticed. The first plea was the general issue; the third, that the assured committed suicide or perished by self-destruction, voluntary or involuntary, while sane or insane; the sixth, that the plaintiffs did not make claim for benefits under said policy within six months after death of the assured, as is provided by the policy, constitution, and by-laws; the seventh is the 10-years statute of limitations; the eighth, fraud and misrepresentation in obtaining the certificate of membership sued on; the ninth, settlement and release; the tenth, settlement and nondisaffirmance by the plaintiff; and the eleventh, ratification of the settlement by the plaintiffs. Replications were filed to the pleas, and upon a trial before a jury a verdict was rendered for appellees for $7,457.50. A motion for new trial was made by appellants and overruled, and judgment entered on the verdict.

Just prior to entering upon the trial in the court below, appellant asked leave to file four additional pleas, which was denied by the court; and, though error is assigned upon the action of the court, no error is pointed out or insisted upon by appellant in its brief and argument, and the same need not be further adverted to.

The only errors urged for our consideration relate to the giving and refusing of instructions.

At the close of the plaintiffs' evidence the appellant requested the court to give, and offered, an instruction directing a verdict in its favor. This instruction was refused, and at the close of all the evidence was again offered. As appellant, after the close of plaintiffs' evidence, offered evidence on its part, it thereby made a submission of the case upon the whole evidence, and waived its right to insist upon the error, if any, in refusing the peremptory instruction at the close of the plaintiffs' evidence. West Chicago Street Railroad Co. v. McCallum, 169 Ill. 240, 48 N. E. 424. It also appears that this error was not insisted upon in the motion for a new trial, and cannot now be relied upon for that reason. Illinois Central Railroad Co. v. Johnson, 191 Ill. 594, 61 N. E. 334; Brewer & Hoffman Brewing Co. v. Boddie, 162 Ill. 346, 44 N. E. 819.

We are called upon to determine whether the peremptory instruction should have been given at the close of all the evidence. We have examined the evidence carefully, and are impressed with the résumé of it given by the Appellate Court in its opinion, which is as follows: "The main question is whether John Crayton committed suicide. We have read the evidence on this subject in the record itself, and have endeavored to give it careful consideration. There were circumstances proved from which the inference of suicide might be drawn. Deceased was killed by a bullet which entered near the center of his forehead and passed out near the rim of his hat on the back of his head. The shooting took place on his barn floor, between 11 a. m. and noon. His body was found lying on the floor, with his head to the east, and with his Winchester rifle between or near his legs, pointing to the southeast. His rifle contained only an exploded shell. A pine stick lay near him, which defendant asks us to infer he used in firing the gun. Deceased had suffered from a sunstroke some years before, and since then had been moody, excitable, and peculiar, and his family and neighbors doubted his sanity. During the forenoon of his death he had spoken harshly to his son about being out late at night. On the other hand, it does not appear that he had ever expressed or indicated any suicidal purpose or intent. He went to the barn about eleven o'clock that forenoon for the expressed purpose of cleaning his rifle. He called for certain apparatus he had for that purpose, and caused his children to search the house for it. When they could not find it, he said he would go to the barn and use a wire for a ramrod; meaning in cleaning his gun. His body was found in front of and close to his workbench in the barn, in front of a window, and with the big barn doors open towards the house. Pieces of cloth and other suitable apparatus for cleaning the gun were on the bench. All the cartridges but this one were on the bench. The exploded shell in the gun bore the marks of a knife. A common jackknife was stuck in the bench. Deceased had on his boots, and could not have fired the gun with his feet. It was shown that kindling wood was often split at that place, and that there were quite a number of pine sticks lying near where deceased fell; thus weakening the inference that deceased had been using the stick which defendant's witness described as lying near his body. There was no discoloration by powder or by burning about the head of deceased. Experiments were made during the trial by firing cartridges of the same make and size out of the same gun at a heavy cardboard paper—one where the muzzle of the rifle was held close to, and almost in contact with, the cardboard, and others at six, twelve, twenty-four, and thirty inches distance therefrom. These papers were identified and put in evidence. Though objection was made and exception preserved by defendant, yet that exception, as already suggested, is not argued in defendant's opening brief, and it is therefore waived, and the case stands here as if that proof had been received without objection. But though the bill of exceptions recites these cardboards were admitted in evidence, they are omitted from it. In this condition of the record, we think it fair to assume they tended to show that, where the muzzle was near the cardboard, the latter bore indications of discoloration by powder or burning, and tended to show that the muzzle of this rifle was not near the head of John Crayton when the rifle was discharged. If the muzzle was two or three feet from Crayton's head when the rifle was discharged, this might well be considered * * * as tending to indicate the discharge was accidental and not intentional. Deceased may have intentionally killed himself. On the other hand, he may have gone to the barn solely to clean the rifle, and, in his preparations to clean it, may have got together the cleaning apparatus found on the bench, and removed from the rifle the cartridges found on the bench; may have tried to remove the last cartridge, and had difficulty in doing so, and used the knife upon it in an unsuccessful effort to get it out, and thereby made the marks found upon the exploded shell, and then stuck the knife in the bench, and may then have done something else with the rifle, carelessly, in an effort to loosen the remaining shell, and in so doing unintentionally discharged the gun, with the fatal result. The burden of proving intentional self-destruction was upon defendant. In our opinion, the language of the policy with reference to self-destruction, 'whether voluntary or involuntary, sane or insane,' does not apply here if the gun was accidentally discharged while being handled by Crayton, if he had no intention of discharging it or no intention of hitting himself." This statement and review of the facts we adopt, and from it are satisfied that the court did not err in refusing the peremptory instruction.

It is suggested, however, that the Appellate Court, in its review and consideration of the instruction above mentioned, failed to consider certain matters that were material to the case, and that the appellees should have proved, but failed to prove, that the assured paid assessments under his policy according to its terms. We are unable to see how this question can arise, when it is expressly stipulated in the record that the amount of the assessments paid by the assured was $179, and appellant at all times admitted its liability to that extent, and bases its defense mainly upon the theory that the acceptance by the guardian of the assessments paid by the assured was a settlement of all claims and a bar to this action. Nor was the supposed settlement made with the guardian a bar to this action. No authority was given by the probate court or county court to the guardian to compound or release the claim due the appellees, as her wards, or any part of it. The matter was not brought to the attention of the court until the year 1900, when the guardian made a report. The guardian had no personal interest in the policy, or the funds arising from the same, and could not, upon any theory of which we are advised, make any settlement with the appellant for less than full payment without the express order of the court appointing her, from which its approbation of her purpose to compound should appear. Starr & C. Ann. St. 1896, c. 64, par. 17; Hayes v. Massachusetts Mutual Life Ins. Co., 125 Ill. 626, 18 N. E. 322, 1 L. R. A. 303.

The policy in this case provides that appellant will pay to appellees, as beneficiaries, $5,000, if John Crayton dies from any other cause than suicide, and also pay all assessments that he paid under said policy. If, then, the assured did not die a suicide, as the trial and appellate courts have found he did not, appellant owed and should have paid to appellees, or their legal guardian, upon receipt of notice and proof of death, or within 60 days thereafter, both sums; that is, the $5,000, and the $179 paid in assessments. That it received notice and proof of death promptly, and that the proofs were satisfactory to it, cannot, under this record, be questioned. By its supposed settlement with the guardian, it paid her one of the sums that it owed to her. There was no question about that amount being due, and the payment of it could not, in any sense, be said to be a settlement of anything. It was simply payment of a sum of money due. At the time of that settlement, if John Crayton was not a suicide, $5,000 still remained due to appellees, and was not paid within 60 days from the receipt of notice and proof of death. By the payment of a portion of a whole debt, or by the payment of one of two entire debts, the appellant could not, by any stipulation made with the guardian, be released from its liability to pay the entire debt thus owing, and the release relied upon was ineffectual because there was no consideration for it. Hart v. Strong, 183 Ill. 349, 55 N. E. 629; Jaffray v. Davis, 11 L. R. A. 711, note; Tyler v. Odd Fellows' Mutual Relief Ass'n, 145 Mass. 134, 13 N. E. 360. The case last cited is quite similar to the one at bar, and fully sustains appellees' position in all its substantial phases.

Nor were appellees estopped by the acceptance from their guardian, as they attained their majority, of their respective proportionate shares of the $179 so received by the guardian. There was no element of estoppel present. Appellant had in no manner changed its position. Under a claim advanced by itself, it was enabled to effect a supposed settlement with the guardian by paying her one of the sums due. It did not, as in the case of Tyler v. Odd Fellows' Mutual Relief Ass'n, supra, pay the other sum to any one, but held it under the claim that it was not liable to pay it to any one. And the claim that the sum now sued for was not demanded within six months is hardly worthy of consideration. The giving of the notice of death and making the required proof thereof was all the demand that was necessary. The appellant undertook to pay these sums of money upon notice and proof of death, and it had these, and made no question about them. The question was as to the cause of death, and upon that question it attempted to effect a settlement with one who had no authority to make such settlement. Had appellees been adults, and themselves received the $179 paid by appellant, they would have only received one of the sums due them, and would not have been precluded by any supposed settlement or release from insisting upon the other sum now sought to be recovered in this suit. Such being the case, the fact that after they attained their majority they received from their guardian their proportionate shares of the money of these assessments received by her can no more operate as an estoppel or be treated as a ratification by them, or have other or greater effect, than if the settlement had been made by them with appellant directly.

The provision of the policy that the claimant should make satisfactory proof of death cannot be held to mean that such proof should be made as should in all cases satisfy the insuring company of the cause of the death. In the present case it appears that, although the guardian complied with all the requirements made by appellant in making the proof of death, appellant was not satisfied that the death was or was not the result of suicide, but saw fit to urge upon the guardian that the proof showed it a case of suicide, and insisted upon a settlement upon that basis, and now insists that such a settlement was made. The appellant was entitled to have satisfactory proof that the insured was dead, and to demand of the beneficiaries, or those representing them, to adduce reasonable proof of that fact, and also reasonable proof as to the cause of death, but neither the appellant nor the beneficiaries were bound by such proof when the cause of death became a question. Although the proof was satisfactory as formally establishing the death, appellant had the right to refuse to pay upon the ground that the insured came to his death by willful self-destruction, and to put appellees to their action to recover. Instead of doing so, it took the position that its liability was limited to that of the assessments paid, and procured a supposed settlement. Had the proof of death stated explicitly that the immediate cause of death was suicide, which it did not, but stated that it was supposed suicide, the appellees would not have been bound thereby. Nor would the guardian, who made the statement, if she had been the beneficiary, been estopped to deny upon the trial that death was due to suicide, but could have shown the contrary. Knights of Maccabees of the World v. Stensland, 206 Ill. 124, 68 N. E. 1098.

The provision in the policy that all claims under it shall be made within 6 months was sufficiently complied with in less than 30 days after death, to which objections were not made, and the statement of the guardian of the beneficiaries that she was authorized to receive the full amount of the insurance was presented to appellant.

It is complained that the jury were instructed that, if they found for appellees, they should find for $5,000, with interest at 5 per cent. from 60 days after proofs of death were given to appellant. By the policy, which was the contract, and which was complete in all its parts, designating specifically the beneficiaries and the sums to be paid, it was provided that the assessments paid by the insured should be paid to the beneficiaries without interest, but no such provision was made as to the principal sum. Appellant has cited cases supporting its contention, but in all the cases so cited it will be found that the written contract was not complete, but that the contract rested partly in parol, and required evidence to determine who were the beneficiaries under it, or the amount of the insurance, or to establish some other material part of the contract, or was in cases where, by the policy, interest was not to be paid. The amount of the assessments had been agreed upon and paid before suit, and the principal beneficial sum sued for was certain and payable to persons whose identity was fixed in the contract, within 60 days from the receipt of notice and proofs of death, and was, within our statute, a contract for the payment of money; and the instruction was proper. Hurd's Rev. St. 1901, c. 74, § 2; Massachusetts Mutual Life Ins. Co. v. Robinson, 98 Ill. 324.

The cases relied upon by appellant are Conductors' Benefit Ass'n v. Loomis, 142 Ill. 560, 32 N. E. 424; Conductors' Benefit Ass'n v. Tucker, 157 Ill. 194, 42 N. E. 398, 44 N. E. 286; and West Chicago Alcohol Works v. Sheer, 104 Ill. 586. The last case cited is simply authority for the proposition that interest is not allowed unless the contract is in writing, and for a sum certain. In Conductors' Benefit Ass'n v. Loomis, supra, the entire policy or certificate consisted of four lines, outside of the date and signatures of the officers, and merely stated that Loomis was a member of the association. By the rules of the association, certain persons named in its by-laws were appointed as beneficiaries of the members, and certain benefits were to be paid to such beneficiaries upon the death of the member; but the policy neither pointed out who the beneficiary was, nor what was to be paid him, and it was necessary by parol evidence to ascertain both these matters, and this court held that the contract was an oral one. The Tucker Case, supra, arises over a certificate precisely like that in the Loomis Case, and the same reason and rule apply. We do not regard either of these cases as authority for the proposition contended for, when applied to the policy in the case at bar.

It was proper to instruct the jury that the burden of proof was upon appellant to show that the assured came to his death by self-destruction, and that, in the absence of proof of the cause of death, natural or accidental causes will be presumed, and that, if the jury were unable to determine the cause of death, they were not authorized to find it was from self-destruction; and the fact that the proofs of death tended to show that the death was suicidal did not change the rule or shift the burden. Knights of Maccabees of the World v. Stensland, 206 Ill. 124, 68 N. E. 1098.

On the trial of the cause, appellees did not offer any evidence of proofs of death, but simply introduced testimony showing that proofs had been made, sent to and received by appellant, and acted upon by it. Appellant did introduce the proofs of death, and all the papers attached thereto, which were admitted over objections of appellees. The court instructed the jury that neither the proofs of death, nor the papers attached thereto, except the verdict of the coroner's jury, should be considered by them in determining the cause of death. It is urged by appellant that this instruction is wrong in two respects: That the papers attached to the proofs of death all became competent evidence to be considered by the jury in determining the cause of death, and particularly the testimony taken before the coroner's jury, which, it is urged, formed a part of the inquisition, and, under the former decisions of this court, as found in United States Life Ins. Co. v. Vocke, 129 Ill. 557, 22 N. E. 467, 6 L. R. A. 65, Pyle v. Pyle, 158 Ill. 289, 41 N. E. 999, Grand Lodge I. O. M. A. v. Wieting, 168 Ill. 408, 48 N. E. 59, 61 Am. St. Rep. 123, and other cases cited, should have been considered by the jury, in connection with the verdict of the coroner's jury, in determining that question. In this we think counsel for appellant are in error. This court has never held that the depositions taken at a coroner's inquest were competent evidence in such cases, but, on the contrary, in Pittsburg, Cincinnati & St. Louis Railway Co. v. McGrath, 115 Ill. 172, 3 N. E. 439, we held they were incompetent, and subsequently, in the Vocke Case, supra, and other cases following it, held that the verdict was competent, and gave to it somewhat the dignity of a court proceeding; but the depositions, which are mere ex parte statements, would seem, upon principle, to be incompetent for any purpose other than contradiction.

It is said that one of the appellees (Frank L. Crayton) testified at the inquisition, and that his deposition was among those attached, and that the deposition should have been considered in connection with his testimony, or that his testimony contained in the deposition should have been treated as his admission. He was a witness upon the trial of this case, and appellant was afforded ample opportunity to cross-examine him; and if, in his testimony in the trial, he stated the matters differently than they were stated in his deposition, appellant had the right to use the deposition to show that fact, and break the force of his evidence. This was not done, and no reason exists for holding that his deposition should have been considered by the jury as his admission. It may be further suggested that by mere admission infants are not bound. They can neither make them, nor authorize any other person to make them for them. Where guardians are appointed, it is their duty to conserve and protect the interests of their wards; but it is neither their duty, nor have they authority, to make admissions that will be adverse to their interests. 15 Am. & Eng. Ency. of Law (2d Ed.) 71; Cochran v. McDowell, 15 Ill. 10. And so the further contention of appellant that the statement of the guardian, in her affidavit making proof of death, that the immediate cause of death was supposed suicide, should have been treated as an admission of that fact, cannot be sustained.

Numerous other questions are made, upon instructions that were given and refused, but what we have stated above covers all that seems to be material as to any that were given, and those that were refused were properly refused, because such of them as stated correct propositions of law applicable to the case were covered by other given instructions containing the same proposition.

From a careful review of the case we are satisfied that appellant was accorded a fair and impartial trial, and that the instructions, as a series, fairly and fully presented the law of the case to the jury.

The judgment of the Appellate Court is right, and is affirmed. Judgment affirmed.

(209 Ill. 607)

MARKHAM et al. v. KATZENSTEIN et al.*

(Supreme Court of Illinois. April 20, 1904.)

TRUST — EVIDENCE — SUFFICIENCY — ANSWER —STATUTE OF FRAUDS.

1. In a suit to declare a trust in real estate which defendant refused to convey to complainants, testimony of complainants that defendant agreed to buy the land at a time when complainants no longer had any interest in it, and gave his note, mortgage, and money for the purchase of it, taking a deed to himself, and agreeing to hold it in trust (as claimed by complainants) until they should pay the purchase price, with 7 per cent. interest, no time being fixed within which the money was to be paid by complainants, and no manner of payment agreed on, is insufficient to show that defendant's purchase was impressed with a trust in any form.

2. In a suit to declare a trust in real estate under an alleged parol agreement, defendant answered, alleging that it is provided in the statute of frauds that no action shall be brought whereby to charge any person upon any contract for the sale of any lands, tenements, or hereditaments, or any interest in and concerning the same, unless the agreement upon which such action should be brought, or some memoranda or note in writing, shall be signed by the party to be charged therewith, or some other person thereunto by him lawfully authorized in writing and signed by such party. *Held*, that the answer, while substantially using the language of the second section of the statute of frauds, is broad enough to entitle the defendant to the benefit of the ninth, or any, section of the statute coming reasonably within the language of the answer.

Appeal from Circuit Court, McDonough County; G. W. Thompson, Judge.

Suit by Levi H. Markham and others against Joseph Katzenstein and another. From a decree for defendants, complainants appeal. Affirmed.

This is a bill filed in the circuit court of McDonough county by appellants, and, as amended, sets up the following facts: That the complainant Sarah Markham is the widow, and the complainants Levi M., William, and Dwight Markham are the sons, of Dr. Levi Markham; that on July 1, 1878, Dr. Levi Markham died testate; that prior to his death he, together with his wife, mortgaged the premises in controversy, being 160 acres of land in McDonough county, to one Ira T. Smith, and in 1886 the mortgage was foreclosed in the United States Circuit Court for the Southern District of Illinois, and that said Smith became the purchaser at the master's sale, the consideration in the certificate of purchase being $4,460.20; that the land was of much greater value than the amount of the mortgage debt; that the complainants were about to sell their equity of redemption in the land to one Harvey Langsford, formerly of said county, but since deceased, and that said Langsford had offered to buy the land and pay to complainants about $3,000 for their equity of redemption; that one Joseph Katzenstein at the time stated to complainants that if they would not redeem said premises, but would permit Smith to obtain a deed to said premises under said sale, then the said Smith would execute a deed to said Katzenstein, and that he (the said Katzenstein) would then deed said premises to complainants whenever complainants would pay the said Katzenstein the amount paid by him to the said Smith, together with interest thereon at the rate of 7 per cent. per annum from the date of said payment by Katzenstein to Smith until complainants should pay said Katzenstein said amount, and that complainants should retain possession of the premises until such redemption; that complainants then and

*Rehearing denied June 8, 1904.

there agreed with Katzenstein that they would accept said proposition, and that in pursuance of said agreement complainants did not redeem said premises; that on the 13th day of February, 1888, the master in chancery of said court made and executed a deed of conveyance of said premises to the said Ira T. Smith, and on the 5th day of April, 1888, Smith made and executed, for the purported consideration of $6,400, his deed of conveyance to the said Joseph Katzenstein, and that said Katzenstein then and there agreed with complainants to hold said premises as proposed by him and as stated above; that complainants have retained possession of said premises and made lasting and valuable improvements, and that Katzenstein now claims to be the owner in fee simple of said premises and refuses to convey the premises to complainants; that complainants are willing and ready to pay said Katzenstein the money due him by the terms of the agreement. The bill prays that an accounting may be taken, under the terms of the agreement, with the said Katzenstein; that he may be decreed to convey said premises to complainants upon their paying to him the amount found by the court to be due him, and for such other and further relief as equity may require, etc.

Joseph Katzenstein answered, denying all the material allegations of complainants' bill, and setting up the following, being under section 2 of the statute of frauds: "Defendant further states that it is provided in and by the statute of frauds and perjuries of this state that no action shall be brought whereby to charge any person upon any contract for the sale of any lands, tenements, and hereditaments, or any interest in and concerning the same, unless the agreement upon which such action should be brought, or some memoranda or note in writing, shall be signed by the party to be charged therewith, or some other persons thereunto by him lawfully authorized in writing and signed by such party; and this defendant further states that he did not enter into any writing signed by him, and did not and has not in writing authorized anybody to enter into the alleged contract for him, and states that there is no such contract in writing; and this defendant insists upon said statute, and claims the same benefit as if he had pleaded the same." He further sets up that if the complainants had any such contract, as alleged, to purchase said premises, they have been guilty of laches, etc., and denies the complainants are entitled to the relief prayed.

Upon a trial of the cause before the chancellor a decree was entered dismissing the bill, from which decree an appeal was prayed and allowed to this court. Two sets of briefs are filed by the attorneys in this case on behalf of appellants—one by Switzer & Meloan, and the other by Hon. Joseph N. Carter, as counsel. The argument of Messrs. Switzer & Meloan is apparently on the theory that the bill is for a specific performance of a contract, while, on the other hand, it is argued by Joseph N. Carter that the alleged agreement creates a trust, and that the defendant Katzenstein holds the land in trust, because of procuring it to be conveyed to him by fraudulent means, etc. A reply brief is filed, which is signed by both sets of attorneys for complainants, and it is therein insisted that the facts as alleged in the bill set up a trust, and the theory is abandoned that the deed to Katzenstein was intended as a mortgage or that the bill is for specific performance; but it is admitted that some of the testimony would tend to support such an allegation, as well as one of trust, and it is insisted that the trust is either an implied trust or an express trust, and that, even if there is no contract in writing, they have a right to show an express trust by parol evidence.

Switzer & Meloan (Joseph N. Carter, of counsel), for appellants. T. J. Sparks and Sherman, Tunnicliff & Gumbart, for appellees.

RICKS, J. (after stating the facts). Appellants in their bill proceed upon the theory that Smith, the purchaser at the foreclosure sale, held a certificate of purchase of the land in question calling for $4,460.20; that the land was of much greater value than the amount called for by the certificate; that complainants had an equity of redemption, and were offered by one Langsford $3,000 for that equity; and that Katzenstein, being apprised of the offer of Langsford, stated to complainants that if they would not sell their equity to Langsford, but would permit a deed to issue to Smith, and cause Smith to execute a deed to him (Katzenstein), the latter would hold the property in question in trust for appellants, who, upon the payment of the amount paid by Katzenstein, with 7 per cent. interest, should have a deed from Katzenstein for the land. The uncontradicted evidence is that at the time appellants first saw Katzenstein the time of redemption had expired, and Smith, the purchaser at the foreclosure sale, who was the mortgagee in the mortgage under which the sale was had, had obtained a deed to the premises. It is also shown beyond controversy that at the time appellants approached Katzenstein with a view of interesting him in this property, or at any time during the negotiations between appellants and Katzenstein, the proposal of Langsford to purchase appellants' interests in the property was in no manner mentioned or brought to Katzenstein's knowledge; but, on the contrary, the evidence shows that, when appellants sought Katzenstein and endeavored to get him to take the property, they stated that they had been negotiating with one Haines; that appellants had tried to arrange with Smith by which they might lease the lands from him, but Smith declined making a lease, saying that he preferred to and intended to sell the land; that appellants endeavored to get Haines to purchase the land, in order that they might lease the same from him, but that Haines, after considering the matter, declined to purchase the land and lease it to appellants. The evidence further discloses that at the time appellants first talked with Katzenstein about the land they informed him that Smith demanded $6,400 for it, and that he would take half the purchase money down and a mortgage upon the land to secure the balance. Katzenstein thereupon wrote Smith, offering $6,200 for the land, which Smith declined, but renewed his statement that he would take $6,400 upon the terms above mentioned. Katzenstein then borrowed from his brother $3,000, and applied that, together with $400 which he himself had, upon the purchase of the land and gave a mortgage to Smith for $3,000 of the purchase price. As soon as Katzenstein had obtained his deed to the land appellants proposed to purchase it, and Katzenstein offered to sell it to them if they would pay him $1,000 more than he had paid. This appellants declined to do, and thereupon a lease was executed to Levi M. Markham, one of the appellants, which was in writing and for the land in question, at the annual rental of $680. This lease was not found, and is not in evidence, but its execution is admitted; and that appellant Levi M. Markham, who lived upon the land, with all the other appellants as part of the family, acted upon and paid the rent for at least three years under this lease, no question is made. On September 3, 1891, Katzenstein made to Levi M. Markham another lease, in writing, for the same land from March 1, 1892, to March 1, 1893, at an annual rental of $720, and the evidence shows that appellants held under this lease from that time to 1898 and paid rent according to its terms. By this latter lease the tenant was to keep the fences and appurtenances in repair at his own expense. In the years 1895 and 1896 the rent was in arrear, and Katzenstein served notice upon Levi M. Markham, and brought forcible detainer under the statute for failure to pay rent. The suit of 1895, upon the day set for trial, was continued, and afterwards dismissed, and the suit of 1896 went to judgment, but the evidence shows that both of these suits were settled by Markham paying the rent and paying Katzenstein's lawyer his fee and the costs of the court. In April, 1898, another lease was executed between Katzenstein and appellant Levi M. Markham for the same premises for the rental of $720, containing a condition that on failure of the tenant to pay the rent when due, $80 should be added to the rent. The Markhams held under this lease until February, 1902, when a lease between Katzenstein and William Markham and Levi M. Markham was prepared, and was taken by appellants to their home to sign and return, and was kept by them, but not returned. By this lease the rental was fixed at $800, and the undisputed evidence is that after the making of it, and up to the time of the bringing of this suit, the Markhams, as tenants, paid rent according to the terms of this unsigned lease.

The matters relied upon by appellants to overcome the unquestioned facts above stated are, first, the testimony of appellants Sarah Markham and her son, Levi M., to the effect that they were together when they had the first interview with Katzenstein in reference to this transaction, and that Katzenstein there agreed that he would furnish the money and take the title from Smith, and hold the title in trust for appellants, and that upon the payment by the latter to Katzenstein of the amount paid by him, and 7 per cent. interest, the appellants should have a deed from Katzenstein to the land. These two witnesses testified to a conversation, both before and after obtaining the deed from Smith, to the effect above stated. This conversation is absolutely denied by Katzenstein and by one Jacobs, who was a clerk in Katzenstein's store at the time the transaction took place. Katzenstein says, and is corroborated by Jacobs in the statement, that appellant Sarah Markham alone came to the store to see him and get him to purchase the land in controversy, and proposed to him to purchase it and hold it for appellants, and permit them to pay him the amount he had paid and 7 per cent., interest, and redeem the land, but that Katzenstein positively refused to go into such transaction, and stated that, if he bought the land at all, he would buy it for himself, and that, if the appellants wished to occupy it as tenants and would pay the rent, they could do so, and that Mrs. Markham then expressed the desire that Katzenstein should go ahead and purchase the land, and they would become his tenants and try to pay the rent. Appellants further rely upon alleged declarations of Katzenstein, made to numerous persons during the period between the time of the purchase of the land by Katzenstein and the bringing of the suit, that appellants were to have the land whenever they paid for it, and remarks of similar import; but a careful review of the record shows that these remarks were of such equivocal character and made under such conditions and surroundings that little weight can be attributed to them. Appellants further rely upon what they allege to be a part performance, in that they have, as they say, paid the interest according to the agreement, paid taxes, and placed permanent and valuable improvements upon the land. With reference to the payment of interest, it must be said, under the facts in this record, such a claim is exceedingly weak. The interest on $6,400 would be $448, and $100 per year for taxes would be an excessive amount, and upon this basis, by the first lease, appellants paid $132 in excess of interest and taxes; and by the second lease, under which they paid $720 a year, they paid $172 in excess; and by the last lease they were paying at the rate of $252 in excess of interest and taxes; and the evidence shows that they at no time paid any part of the taxes. The taxes were always and regularly paid by Katzenstein.

Appellants who were not parties to the leases attempt to say that they had no knowledge of the existence of the leases, and that they thought they were holding under the original agreement as testified to by them. This testimony cannot be credited or believed by any reasonable mind, in the light of all the evidence. Two of the sons, William and Levi, were adults at the time of this purchase by Katzenstein. Dwight, another of the sons, was a minor, then of the age of 16 or 18 years. By their father's will this land was devised to these three boys. The widow, Sarah, was to occupy and control it until Dwight should become of age, and then the three boys were to take the land and pay to their sisters certain sums of money, made charges upon the land. William was in debt, and executions were hanging over him at the time of the first lease; and it is evident that the lease was made to Levi M. in order that the farm might be conducted and the crops be undisturbed by the creditors of William. They all lived upon the land together and in the same house, and the undisputed evidence is that practically all the crops were sold or disposed of in the name of Katzenstein; and to say that for 13 or 14 years this course of business could be kept up by a family of ordinary intelligence, without each member being apprised of the way the business was being conducted, would be to unreasonably tax credulity. The improvements testified to were the building of a summer kitchen at a cost of $30; the building of a barn, the material of which cost $100, outside of what was gotten off of the farm itself; building a string of fence between the farm in question and an adjoining farm, and the planting of some fruit trees. As we have seen, the lease of 1891 required that Levi M. Markham should keep up the fence and appurtenances at his own cost. The evidence shows that there was an old stable upon the premises, which had practically rotted down, and some material was gotten on the farm, and $100 worth of lumber bought, and in the course of two or three years a stable or barn was built. Levi Markham testified that the total value of the improvements placed by him on the farm was from $500 to $600; but the items of the improvements as shown by him amount to but little more than half of that amount, and the evidence tends to show that $300 or $400 would be a high estimate of the value of the improvements, taking their first cost.

Levi M. Markham and Sarah Markham both testified that, immediately after Katzenstein obtained his deed to the land, they wanted him to enter into a writing by which he would agree that, upon the payment to him by them of the amount paid by him and 7 per cent. interest, they should have a deed to the land, and that he declined to do this unless they would pay him $1,000 in excess of the amount he had paid, and that they refused to pay that amount. Appellants further claim that they are supported in their contentions by the fact that the land was worth from $1,600 to $3,000 more at the time Katzenstein purchased it than he gave for it, and they have offered evidence which tends very strongly, so far as testimony and opinions of people can do, to show that it was worth anywhere from $1,000 to $3,000 more than Katzenstein paid for it. This evidence would have very great weight, were it not for the fact that the record shows, beyond question, that the deed was made to Smith in February, 1888. His certificate of purchase only required the payment of $4,460.20 and interest to enable appellants to redeem from that sale. The deed was taken reasonably promptly after the time of redemption had expired. Within a few months, then, of the time Smith did get his deed for this land for $5,000 or less, a redemption could have been made from the sale to Smith; and, if this land were worth as much more as the witnesses testified and as appellants now claim, it is indeed remarkable that they could find no one who would furnish the money and enable them to redeem the land, taking it as security, and the fact that they did not and could not find any one who would furnish the money to redeem from the sale, when it was only $4,460.20 and interest, tends to controvert their position and contention now, that Katzenstein would pay $6,400 for the land, borrow $3,000 with which to do so, give a mortgage upon the land for the amount remaining unpaid, and give appellants the opportunity to redeem upon the terms they claim he did.

If the case stated in the bill had been established by the evidence, there would be no question of the right of appellants to relief. A constructive trust would then be established under the rule announced in Lantry v. Lantry, 51 Ill. 458, 2 Am. Rep. 310; Biggins v. Biggins, 133 Ill. 211, 24 N. E. 516, and Fischbeck v. Gross, 112 Ill. 208. It is entirely clear that neither the bill nor the evidence tends to establish a resulting trust, as no part of the purchase money was ever paid by appellants. As we view the evidence, it wholly fails to support the allegations of the bill. Instead of appellants having an equity in the property at the time of the alleged agreement with Katzenstein, the equity had been swept away, and Smith, the purchaser at the mortgage sale, had a good and valid deed, conveying absolute title; and instead of the evidence supporting the allegation of the bill that Langsford was about to redeem the property from the sale and give appellants $3,000 for their equity, and that Katzenstein, with a knowledge of that offer, had induced appellants to decline the offer of Langsford and accept the offer they impute to him, the evidence distinctly shows that in the first place there was no equity for which Langsford could pay $3,000, and in the next place there was no communication to Katzenstein of any offer on the part of Langsford or any negotiations between him and appellants, and instead of appellants paying interest, as they allege, they paid rent for the lands, the rents increasing as the value of the lands increased. It is a well-known fact that since 1888 money has been more plentiful, and interest has, in the main, decreased, and yet, upon the theory that appellants were paying interest on $6,400 at 7 per cent., every lease that was made was for a practical increase of every annual payment. According to appellants' own testimony, the case was simply one in which Katzenstein agreed to buy land in which appellants no longer had any interest, giving his note and mortgage and money for the purchase of it, taking a deed to himself, and agreeing to hold it in trust, as appellants claim, until they should pay the purchase price, with 7 per cent. interest. No time was fixed within which the money should be paid, and no manner of payment agreed upon. From such a transaction as this, can it be said that a trust arises in any form? We think not. There must be some relation existing between the parties, and the party claiming the benefit of the trust must bear such a relation to the property out of which the trust is supposed to arise, that, taking into consideration the relations of the parties claiming the benefit of the trust to the property itself and the agreement of the party who shall stand in the position of a trustee, to permit the latter to deny the trust or refuse to perform its conditions would be more than a mere moral wrong, but would amount to legal fraud.

Mr. Pomeroy, in his work on Equity, after discussing the conditions under which trusts ex maleficio arise, says: "The foregoing cases should be carefully distinguished from those in which there is a mere verbal promise to purchase and convey land. In order that the doctrine of trusts ex maleficio with respect to land may be enforced under any circumstances, there must be something more than a mere verbal promise, however unequivocal; otherwise, the statute of frauds would be virtually abrogated. There must be an element of positive fraud accompanying the promise, and by means of which the acquisition of the legal title is wrongfully consummated. Equity does not pretend to enforce verbal promises in the face of the statute. It endeavors to prevent and punish fraud by taking from the wrongdoer the fruits of his deceit, and it accomplishes this object by its beneficial and far-reaching doctrine of constructive trusts." 2 Pomeroy's Eq. Jur. § 1056. In Lantry v. Lantry, supra, it is said (page 465): "If A. voluntarily conveys land to B., the latter having taken no measures to procure the conveyance, but accepting it and verbally promising to hold the property in trust for C., the case falls within the statute, and chancery will not enforce the parol promise. But if A. was intending to convey the land directly to C., and B. interposed and advised A. not to convey directly to C., but to convey to him, promising, if A. would do so, he (B.) would hold the land in trust for C., chancery will lend its aid to enforce the trust, upon the ground that B. obtained the title by fraud and imposition upon A." To the same effect are Biggins v. Biggins, supra; Stevenson v. Crapnell, 114 Ill. 19, 28 N. E. 379; Gruhn v. Richardson, 128 Ill. 178, 21 N. E. 18; Levy v. Brush, 45 N. Y. 589; Wheeler v. Reynolds, 66 N. Y. 228.

There is no diversity of opinion that a mere parol agreement for the conveyance of land is void, both at law and in equity; but, where it appears that the agreement was the result of the fraud of a person holding the land and refusing to convey, equity, upon the ground of fraud, assumes jurisdiction and grants relief. Wheeler v. Reynolds, supra. It is said, however, that a verbal agreement to convey land is good, and may be enforced, unless the statute of frauds is pleaded or relied upon, and that the appellee Katzenstein, in the case at bar, has pleaded the wrong section of the statute; and it is asserted that he has pleaded the second section of the statute, when he should have pleaded the ninth section, which is said, and appears by the said statute, to relate more particularly to trusts. It must be first said that appellants have not made the case stated in their bill, but have sought to make another case. It is so well established by the laws of this state, that the rule is no longer questioned, that in order to have relief in equity the proof must establish the case made by the bill; and though a case may be shown by the evidence which, if alleged in the bill, would have entitled the party to relief, still the relief cannot be granted where the allegations of the bill will not support it, and this bill could well have been dismissed upon the ground that the case sought to be made by the evidence was not the case alleged in the bill.

Nor do we think the contention that appellee Katzenstein should not have the benefit of the statute of frauds because section 2, instead of section 9, was pleaded, should be sustained. The whole agreement relied upon here, and tending to support which there is any evidence, is a parol agreement to convey land, in which, as we think, there is such absence of fraud as fails to create the relation of the parties that of a trust relation. Section 9 of the statute of frauds is: "All declarations or creations of trusts or confidences of any lands, tenements or hereditaments, shall be manifested and proved by some writing signed by the party who is by law enabled to declare such trust, or by his last will in writing; or else they shall be utterly void and of no effect: provided, that resulting trusts or trusts created by construction, implication or operation of law, need not be in writing, and the same may be proved by parol." The only class of trusts to which the statute does not apply, as expressly provided by its terms, are resulting trusts. The answer of Katzenstein states: "It is provided in and by the statute of frauds and perjuries of this state that no action shall be brought whereby to charge any person upon any contract for the sale of any lands, tenements, or hereditaments, or any interest in and concerning the same, unless the agreement upon which such action should be brought, or some memoranda or note in writing, shall be signed by the party to be charged therewith, or some other person thereunto by him lawfully authorized in writing and signed by such party; and this defendant further states that he did not enter into any writing signed by him, and did not and has not in writing authorized anybody to enter into the alleged contract for him; and states that there is no such contract in writing; and this defendant insists upon said statute, and claims the same benefit as if he had pleaded the same." We think the language used in the answer, while it is substantially the language of the second clause of the statute of frauds, is broad enough to cover the rights insisted upon in this case, whether they should be construed to be rights arising from a trust, or otherwise. No particular section is designated by the answer, but the defendant therein states the legal effect of the statute of frauds, and advises the court that he relies upon that statute, and it is our opinion that such a plea or statement in the answer is sufficiently broad to entitle the defendant to the benefit of any section of the statute coming reasonably within the language of the plea or answer. Bogardus v. Trinity Church, 4 Paige, 197.

It is also insisted in the answer that appellants were guilty of laches, and under the evidence in this case and in view of all the circumstances as shown, if the decree in question had been predicated upon laches alone, we would not have felt at liberty to disturb it.

A careful consideration of this record leads us to the conclusion that the decree of the circuit court dismissing appellants' bill was right, and should be, and is, affirmed.

Decree affirmed.

(209 Ill. 528)

WEARE COMMISSION CO. v. PEOPLE.*

(Supreme Court of Illinois. April 20, 1904.)

GAMING—GRAIN OPTIONS—UNLAWFUL PLACES—STATUTES—CONSTRUCTION—CONSTITUTIONALITY—POLICE POWER—INTENTION.

1. 1 Starr & C. Ann. St. 1896, c. 38, par. 262, provides that it shall be unlawful for any corporation to keep or cause to be kept within the state any bucket-shop or office wherein is conducted or permitted the pretended buying or selling of grain, on margins or otherwise, without any intention of receiving or paying for the property so bought, or of delivering the property so sold, or wherein is conducted or permitted the pretended buying or selling of such property on margins, or when the party buying or offering to buy does not intend actually to receive the same, if purchased, or to deliver the same, if sold. *Held*, that Hurd's Rev. St. 1899, c. 38, par. 280, defining a criminal offense as a violation of a public law, in the commission of which there shall be a union of act and intention, or criminal negligence, did not require proof that the keeper of a commission office participated in the intention of a customer to purchase grain unlawfully in order to sustain a conviction for unlawfully keeping a place prohibited by the statute; it being sufficient that the place was kept where such unlawful purchases and sales were in fact permitted.

2. Defendant corporation opened a broker's office at P., and placed the same in charge of F. Grain quotations were sent to F. by telegraph, and by him posted for the information of customers. F. received orders from two customers for the purchase of grain on margins for future delivery, one of whom, however, stated to F. that he intended actually to receive the grain. F. sent the orders to defendant at C., by which the grain was purchased in its own name on the Board of Trade, according to the Board of Trade rules, after which defendant sent to the customers a bill of sale showing the purchases and the persons from whom the grain was bought, also containing a statement that the customer contemplated actual delivery. The grain, however, was never delivered, the customers both selling out at a profit before the option matured, for which they received credit from defendant; and both testified that they did not intend to keep the grain until the maturity of the option, one of them, at least, being wholly unable to pay for the grain purchased. The sales were made through the office in charge of F., under a rule of the Board of Trade authorizing settlement in that manner before the maturity of the option. *Held*, that such transactions were speculative merely, and sustained a conviction of defendant for keeping a place for the pretended buying or selling of grain, in violation of 1 Starr & C. Ann. St. 1896, c. 38, par. 262.

3. 1 Starr & C. Ann. St. 1896, c. 38, par. 262, prohibiting any person from keeping any bucket-shop or place for the pretended purchase and sale of grain on margins, where delivery of the grain purchased is not intended, is not limited to bucket-shops and bucket-shopping, but includes all places wherein gambling in grain is permitted or conducted in any form.

4. Where defendant corporation, located in C., opened an office at P., and placed the same in charge of an agent, who received orders for the pretended purchase of grain on margins, which he sent to defendant at C., by which the orders were filled on the Board of Trade in its own name, notice of which was sent by defendant direct to the customers at P., who subsequently closed their trades before the maturity of their options through the same office at P., defendant's violation of 1 Starr & C. Ann. St. 1896, c. 38, par. 262, prohibiting the keeping of any place for the pretended purchase and sale of grain, by such transactions, occurred at P., where such office was maintained.

5. 1 Starr & C. Ann. St. 1896, c. 38, par. 262, prohibiting the keeping of any place for the pretended purchase and sale of grain on margins where actual delivery is not intended, is a proper exercise of the state's police power, and is not in violation of Const. U. S. Amend. 14.

Error to Appellate Court, First District.

The Weare Commission Company was convicted of unlawfully keeping an office where-

*Rehearing denied June 8, 1904.

in there was permitted the pretended buying of grain on margins without any intention of receiving the grain so bought, which conviction was affirmed by the Appellate Court, from which defendant brings error. Affirmed.

This is an indictment against the plaintiff in error, returned on January 9, 1903, into the circuit court of Bureau county by the grand jury of that county, charging that the plaintiff in error, a corporation, on the 20th day of September, 1901, "and on divers other dates and times between that day and the finding of this indictment, in the city of Princeton, in the said county of Bureau and state aforesaid, did unlawfully keep an office wherein there was then and there permitted the pretended buying of grain on margins without any intention of receiving the grain so bought, contrary to the form of the statute," etc. The charge in the indictment against the plaintiff in error, as above quoted, was embodied in the fifth count of the indictment; and the plaintiff in error was convicted under section 1 of an act entitled "An act to suppress bucket-shops, and gambling in stocks, bonds, petroleum, cotton, grain, provisions, and other produce," in force July 1, 1887. 1 Starr & C. Ann. St. 1896, c. 38, pars. 262-265. Sections 1, 2 and 4 of this act of 1887 are set forth in Soby v. People, 134 Ill. 66, 25 N. E. 109. A motion to quash the indictment was denied, and plaintiff in error pleaded not guilty, and, a jury being waived, the cause was tried before the court without a jury, and the court adjudged plaintiff in error guilty, and imposed a fine of $200. From the judgment of conviction, so entered by the circuit court, an appeal was taken to the Appellate Court, and the Appellate Court, holding that, although an appeal does not lie in a criminal case, yet where the people do not move to dismiss, but file briefs, as was done here, the Appellate Court is at liberty to treat the case as if pending on a writ of error, disposed of the case accordingly, in accordance with decisions made by it in Ferrias v. People, 71 Ill. App. 559, and cases there cited, and Reddish v. People, 83 Ill. App. 63, and thereupon affirmed the judgment of the trial court. The present writ of error is sued out for the purpose of reviewing the judgment of affirmance so entered by the Appellate Court.

The case was tried upon a written stipulation of facts, which were agreed by the parties to be taken as true, with leave to either party to introduce such further evidence as might be competent. The only evidence introduced by the people, besides that embodied in said stipulation, was the testimony of two witnesses, Theodore Kruse and Thomas Cecil, who were customers of the plaintiff in error at its office in Princeton. The plaintiff in error, defendant below, introduced no testimony, except certain rules and by-laws of the Board of Trade of the city of Chicago, being a statement of the objects of the association—sections 8, 9, 10, and 11 of rule 4; sections 1 and 2 of rule 14; sections 1 and 2 of rule 22; and sections 1 and 2 of rule 23. At the close of the evidence the plaintiff in error moved the court to find it not guilty, on the ground that the evidence was, as matter of law, insufficient to justify its conviction; it also moved that the court exclude from its consideration the evidence offered on behalf of the people, on the ground that the conviction of the plaintiff in error under the evidence would be in violation of the fourteenth amendment of the Constitution of the United States; and it further moved the court to find it not guilty, on the ground that its conviction under the evidence would be in violation of said fourteenth amendment to the federal Constitution—all of which motions the trial court overruled, and to such rulings the plaintiff in error excepted. The plaintiff in error also requested the court to hold as law in the decision of the case three written propositions, which were marked "Refused" by the court.

So much of the facts as are not stated in the opinion were thus stated by the Appellate Court in its opinion deciding this case:

"Defendant is a corporation engaged in the commission business, and has its principal office in Chicago. On February 6, 1902, it opened a branch office at Princeton, and placed it in charge of F. E. Flower as its agent, and said office was conducted by Flower for defendant during the period covered by the indictment. The prices at which grain and other commodities were selling on the Chicago Board of Trade were from time to time communicated by telegraph to the branch office, and there displayed on a blackboard to inform defendant's customers of such prices, with a view to enabling defendant to obtain business from said customers. Flower received orders from defendant's customers at Princeton for the purchase or sale of grain, etc., and transmitted said orders by telegraph to the defendant at Chicago. Defendant received the orders at Chicago, and executed them in its own name upon the Chicago Board of Trade, and reported the transactions by telegraph to its agent at Princeton, and he reported the transactions verbally to the customers. Defendant also mailed to each customer a report upon a printed blank, filled out with the details of the transaction. Each such report contained the following printed statement: 'It is distinctly understood and agreed to by you that actual delivery of property herein mentioned is contemplated.' When a customer gave an order to defendant's agent at Princeton for the purchase or sale of grain, he was required to deposit a margin of not less than two cents per bushel on the amount of grain so ordered bought or sold. If the market changed against the customer, he was required to furnish an additional margin. If he refused, defendant would dispose of the grain so bought or sold, and charge the customer with the loss or credit him with the profit. The customer also had the right to order a sale of property purchased, or a purchase of property sold, on his account, and was charged with the loss or credited with the profit of the transaction. Section 8 of rule 4 of the rules of the Chicago Board of Trade provided for the expulsion from that body of any member who should knowingly execute any order for any one 'dealing in differences on the fluctuations in the market price of any commodity without a bona fide purchase and sale of property for an actual delivery.' Section 2 of rule 23 of said rules is as follows: 'In case any property contracted for future delivery is not received and paid for when properly tendered, it shall be the duty of the seller, in order to establish any claim on the purchaser, to sell it on the market at any time during the next twenty-four hours, at his discretion, after such default shall have been made, notifying the purchaser within one hour of such sale; and any loss resulting to the seller shall be paid by the party in default.'

"Kruse and Cecil were witnesses for the prosecution. Kruse bought at defendant's Princeton office, in December, 1902, 1,000 bushels of wheat at about 70 cents per bushel for May delivery, and put up $30 as a margin, or 3 cents per bushel. He did not receive any wheat, but sold out at a profit through defendant before the day for delivery. Afterwards he bought another 1,000 bushels of wheat at 77 cents per bushel, also for May delivery, and paid $30 as a margin, and also sold that wheat at a profit before the day for delivery. He testified that, when Flower sold him this wheat, he said, 'Now, your intention is to take this wheat if they deliver it to you?' and that he answered, 'Yes, sir.' He received reports of these purchases from the Chicago house of defendant on blanks like those above described. He testified he bought with the intention of taking the wheat, if he stayed with it till delivery day came, but that he did not intend to do that, and take the wheat. He had had other like transactions through other parties, and always sold out before the time for delivery. At the time of the transactions with defendant he was worth about $300. Cecil bought 5,000 bushels of oats, put up a margin of $150 or $200, received a like statement from the Chicago house, received no grain, and sold out in 30 or 60 days. He testified he was unable to say positively what his intentions were as to actually receiving the grain or selling it at a profit, but on cross-examination he said he owned a farm of over 500 acres, and could have made use of the grain if he had had it."

Henry S. Robbins, for plaintiff in error. H. J. Hamlin, Atty. Gen., Ora H. Porter, State's Atty., and Geo. B. Gillespie, Asst. Atty. Gen., for the People.

MAGRUDER, J. (after stating the facts). The questions of law presented by this record are substantially the same questions which were decided by this court in the case of Soby v. People, 134 Ill. 66, 25 N. E. 109. But it is stated by the learned counsel for the plaintiff in error that the object in presenting the present case to this court is to bring the construction of the act of 1887 again to the attention of the court, "in the hope that the decision in the Soby Case may be more accurately confined to its facts, and a further construction of the statute may be had, which, while not impairing at all its efficacy to accomplish the purposes sought in its enactment, will not work * * * unjust consequences to legitimate traders."

First. Section 1 of the act of 1887, referred to in the statement preceding this opinion, provides "that it shall be unlawful for any corporation * * * or person to keep or cause to be kept within this state any bucketshop, office, store or other place, wherein is conducted or permitted the pretended buying or selling of * * * grain, provisions or other produce, either on margins or otherwise, without any intention of receiving and paying for the property so bought, or of delivering the property so sold; or wherein is conducted or permitted the pretended buying or selling of such property on margins; or when the party buying any of such property, or offering to buy the same, does not intend actually to receive the same if purchased, or to deliver the same if sold; and the keeping of all such places is hereby prohibited." 1 Starr & C. Ann. St. 1896, p. 1304, c. 38, par. 262. By the fifth count in the indictment, under which the conviction here sought to be reviewed was secured, it is charged against the plaintiff in error that on September 20, 1901, and on divers other dates and times between that day and the finding of this indictment, in the city of Princeton, in Bureau county, it "did unlawfully keep an office wherein there was then and there permitted the pretended buying of grain on margins without any intention of receiving the grain so bought."

As explained in the statement of the facts preceding this opinion, and as set forth in paragraph 5 of the written stipulation between the parties as to the facts, plaintiff in error kept a branch office in the city of Princeton, and employed one F. E. Flower there as its agent. When a customer wished to buy grain for future delivery, he would give his order for such purchase, either in writing, or orally, or by telephone, to Flower, and would deposit with Flower, as the agent of plaintiff in error, a margin of not less than two cents per bushel on the grain so desired to be bought, to secure plaintiff in error against loss by reason of the execution of the order. Flower would thereupon send an order by telegraph to plaintiff in error at Chicago, and thereupon the plaintiff in error would buy on the Chicago Board of

Trade the amount of grain so ordered to be bought by such customer. The purchase would always be made in the name of the plaintiff in error, in accordance with the rules and regulations of the Board of Trade, and plaintiff in error would enter the transaction in the account kept by it with such customer. Additional margins would from time to time be required from the customer by plaintiff in error, in case, by reason of the fall in the market price of the grain bought, such additional margins were necessary to protect plaintiff in error against loss by reason of the execution of the order; but otherwise additional margins would not be required. All purchases of grain made by plaintiff in error for its customers were reported by it to its agent in Princeton by telegraph, and he reported the transactions verbally to the customers. Plaintiff in error also reported all such purchases from its Chicago office directly to its customers upon printed blanks, showing the quantity, the date, the time of delivery, the commodity purchased, the price, the name of the seller, and the name and address of the customer. At the bottom of these blanks was a notice that the plaintiff in error reserved the right, without further notice, to close the above contracts at any time, when in its judgment funds on hand were not sufficient for marginal purposes. Paragraph 5 of the written stipulation in regard to the facts also provided as follows: "The customer also had the right at any time to order any property which had been purchased or sold on his account to be sold or purchased, in which case, if the purchase and sale or sale and purchase resulted in a loss, he would be charged with the loss; but, if it resulted in a profit, he would be credited with the profit in his account with the defendant." The charge here made against the plaintiff in error related to the buying of grain; but the same method, under the stipulation and the rules and the evidence, would apply in case the transaction was a selling, instead of a buying, of grain.

The offense charged against the plaintiff in error is that of keeping an office in Princeton wherein is permitted the pretended buying of grain without any intention of receiving and paying for it. It is insisted by counsel for plaintiff in error that the intention of the customer or purchaser to buy the grain without any intention of receiving it, but with the intention of selling it upon a rise in the market price, and thereby making the difference between the contract and the market prices, may not be known or communicated to, or participated in, by the keeper of the place, and that such keeper ought not to be punished for the unlawful intention of his customer, unless he is a party to that intention and participates in it. It is assumed, in support of this contention, that proof of the intention of the party giving the order for the purchase or sale of the grain is treated as being sufficient to convict the person who keeps the place, without reference to what the intention of the latter may be. Counsel refers to and quotes the provision of the Criminal Code which provides that "a criminal offense consists in a violation of a public law, in the commission of which there shall be a union, or joint operation, of act and intention, or criminal negligence." Hurd's Rev. St. 1899, c. 38, par. 280. The objection thus made by counsel would seem to relate rather to the extent and amount of proof required to show a participation of the keeper of the place in the intention of the customer, rather than to an absence altogether of such intention on the part of the keeper. In Soby v. People, supra, we said (page 73, 134 Ill., and page 111, 25 N. E.): "Under this provision of the act, the keeper of such office or place, etc., cannot shield himself from criminal responsibility behind the fact that he made no inquiry of his customers. The statute is preventive in its character, and is aimed at the keeping of places where gambling in grain is permitted. The keeper must know that the transaction is not gambling, or in good faith have just reason to believe that the buying or selling is not within the intended prohibition of the statute." Again, in that case it was said: "The Legislature have, as they might, rendered it unnecessary to show the intention of the keeper of the office, or place, to bring the transaction within the prohibition of the statute." The statute presumes, and the decision thus criticised presumes, that, where a man keeps a place where gambling in grain is permitted, he must necessarily intend to permit it; otherwise, he would not keep the place, where it is carried on by other parties. The testimony in this record shows no instances where there were any legitimate transactions in grain; that is to say, purchases or sales of grain, wherein there was actual delivery of the grain. All the transactions taking place at the office in Princeton, so far as they are shown by the proof in the record, were transactions where grain was ordered to be delivered in the future, and then sold out upon a rise in the market before the day of delivery arrived. Where such transactions are carried on in the office of a particular person, and with his aid and concurrence, a presumption of his knowledge of what is going on is made by the law, without any requirement of proof on the part of the people or prosecution.

It has been held, in reference to transactions of the kind here under consideration, that the question of intention is a question for the jury, to be determined by a consideration of all the evidence. Pope v. Hanke, 155 Ill. 617, 40 N. E. 839, 28 L. R. A. 568; Jamieson v. Wallace, 167 Ill. 388, 47 N. E. 762, 59 Am. St. Rep. 302. In their opinion, deciding this case, the Appellate Court say: "We have carefully read all this testimony from the record, and are satisfied these parties did not intend to receive the grain, or to pay anything therefor except the margins, but only to speculate on the price, and that Flower knew it." We are satisfied that this statement of the Appellate Court is correct, and that, if it is necessary to establish a participation of the plaintiff in error in the illegal intention of the customer, not only the actual transactions which occurred, but the method in which the business was done, and the rules in pursuance of which such business was carried on, necessarily suggest the conclusion that there was a participation in the illegal intent on the part of plaintiff in error, or keeper of the place. When the customer came into the office at Princeton and gave Flower an order to purchase grain, Flower telegraphed that order to plaintiff in error in Chicago. The margin, which was put up by the customer when he gave the order, was left in the hands of Flower, the agent. When plaintiff in error purchased the grain in Chicago, it purchased it in its own name. Under the rules of the Board of Trade itself, plaintiff in error was required to make the purchase in its own name. Under the rules, or by the mode of doing business as set forth in the agreed statement of facts, the customer had the right at any time to order the property, which had been purchased or sold on his account, to be sold or purchased. When he gave the order that the grain purchased by him should be sold, he gave that order to Flower, or to the plaintiff in error in Chicago. Kruse testifies that he bought 1,000 bushels of wheat at about 70 cents per bushel, and put up a margin of $30, or 3 cents per bushel, and that he sold out the grain, and made a profit, without waiting for the time for its delivery to arrive. His evidence also shows that he did not intend to wait until the time of delivery before selling the grain, if there should be a rise in the market. He also says that, when he sold it, he "sold it through the same office he bought it of"; that is to say, when there was a rise in the market, and he made up his mind to sell in order to make the difference between the contract price and the market price, he ordered the sale to be made through the plaintiff in error, or its agent at Princeton. Now, when the plaintiff in error bought the grain for Kruse upon the mere deposit of a margin, and without the payment of the whole of the purchase money, and when it, under the direction of Kruse, sold the grain before the time of delivery arrived, it certainly knew that there was a mere speculation on the part of Kruse in differences. Flower was certainly aware of the fact that Kruse, instead of waiting until the time of delivery should arrive, was selling out before such time of delivery, because the sale was made through plaintiff in error itself, or Flower, its agent.

Parties are always presumed to intend the natural consequences of their acts. When Kruse gave the order for the purchase of the grain, and made his deposit, and then, as soon as there was a rise in the market price, sold out the grain, the presumption is that he intended, when he first made the purchase, to sell out as soon as there was a rise; and when the plaintiff in error, or its agent, aided him in the transaction, and helped him to carry out the transaction in this illegal way, it is idle to say that the plaintiff in error did not know what the intention of Kruse was. Two purchases of grain were made by Kruse; each purchase, as we understand the evidence, being of 1,000 bushels of wheat. Kruse states in his testimony that he was worth only about $300, and, this being so, he would not have been able in all probability to have paid for the grain, if he had waited until the time of the delivery, and the delivery of the grain had been tendered to him. "The question of intention is a question for the jury, or for the court, to be determined by a consideration of all the evidence. * * * The intention of the parties in such cases may be determined from the nature of the transaction and from the manner and method of carrying on the business. * * * An examination of the authorities * * * will show that the intention of the parties may be determined from a variety of circumstances. Among these circumstances, besides the mode of dealing between the parties, is the pecuniary ability of the party purchasing. If the purchases of a party, as ordered through a broker, are larger in amount than he is able to pay for, it is a strong circumstance indicating that there was no intention of receiving the property, but rather an intention to settle the difference between the market price and the contract price. Such intention may be also inferred where the party making the purchase never calls upon the party ordering the purchase for the purchase money, but only for margins. It makes no difference whether the real intention is formally expressed in words or not, if the facts and circumstances in proof show that it was the real understanding that there should be no actual purchase and no delivery or acceptance of the property involved in the contract, but merely an adjustment of damages upon differences." Jamieson v. Wallace, supra.

Under the testimony in this case, it is conclusively shown that plaintiff in error kept an office in Princeton where these illegal purchases or operations of gambling in grain were carried on. Plaintiff in error cannot relieve itself of responsibility upon the ground that it acted merely as an agent for its customers in these unlawful transactions. In Pearce v. Foote, 113 Ill. 228, 55 Am. Rep. 414, we said: "There is and can be no such thing as agency in the perpetration of crimes or misdemeanors, or, indeed, in the doing of any unlawful act. All persons actively participating are principals." "If parties to speculative dealings intend merely to gamble in the rise and fall of prices, and the broker is privy to the unlawful design of the parties, and brings them together for the very purpose of entering into an illegal agreement, he is particeps criminis." 8 Am. & Eng. Ency. of Law (1st Ed.) pp. 1011, 1012. If actual delivery was contemplated in all the transactions and operations carried on in this branch office at Princeton, why was it made known to the customers that they could at any time free themselves from their agreements to receive and pay for the grain when the date for delivery should arrive, by selling out before the day of such delivery upon a rise in the market? The rules governing the purchases and sales were such that the purchaser might at any time close out his deal, and adjust it on the basis of the difference between the purchase price and the market price at the time of closing it out; and thus they tend to show that the grain was not purchased for actual delivery.

It is to be noted, also, that Kruse and Cecil, who purchased grain through this office, and the other customers of the office, became responsible to no one except plaintiff in error for the purchase price. They did not deal directly with the seller of the grain, but dealt only with the plaintiff in error, or its agent in Princeton. The fact that the printed circular sent to customers contained a statement to the effect that "it is distinctly understood and agreed to by you that actual delivery of property herein mentioned is contemplated," and the fact that Flower, the agent, asked Kruse, when the latter gave his order for the purchase of grain, if it was his intention to take the wheat, if they should deliver it to him, did not necessarily show that the parties contemplated an actual delivery. These preliminary precautions were unusual; and it was said in Central Stock Exchange v. Board of Trade, 196 Ill. 396, 63 N. E. 740: "The requiring a party who purchased or sold to sign a contract to accept or make delivery is an unusual circumstance, and not at all necessary in a bona fide transaction; the law in such case being that the party selling is bound to deliver and the party purchasing is bound to accept delivery. Therefore the purpose of such a contract must have been something other than the securing of a legal right." Again, in speaking of the rules of the Board of Trade, it was said in Pardridge v. Cutler, 168 Ill. 504, 48 N. E. 125: "No one can be found to deny that parties can gamble in differences under these rules as easily as to do a legitimate business, and it was wholly immaterial that the rules provided for legitimate methods."

Counsel contends that the object of the act of 1887 was merely to suppress bucket-shops and bucket-shopping. But it was held in Soby v. People, supra, that the act was intended to go further, and to suppress all places wherein was conducted or permitted gambling in grain or produce in any form. It makes no difference whether the places or offices where such gambling is conducted are the offices of commission merchants, or members of the Board of Trade of Chicago, or not. In Soby v. People, supra, we said (page 72, 134 Ill., and page 111, 25 N. E.): "It is a matter of common notoriety that, notwithstanding the highly penal character of the statute of 1874, the evil it was aimed at continued to increase with wonderful rapidity throughout the state, and until in almost every city or town of any considerable importance commission houses, offices, or agencies were established, in which the great bulk of the business transacted was the making of contracts which, while legitimate upon their face, were in fact mere gambling transactions, which were never allowed to mature, but were uniformly adjusted before maturity upon differences in market price, and without any actual delivery of the articles which were the subject-matters of such pretended contracts. To remedy the mischief, the Legislature, satisfied of the futility of attempting to suppress gambling in grain and other commodities by striking merely at the gambling contracts themselves and the parties entering into such contracts, has sought by the statute of 1887 to suppress all bucket-shops, offices, stores, or other places wherein gambling in grain or other commodities is conducted or permitted. * * * It is apparent from the whole act, from the title to the concluding sentence, that the purpose and object of the Legislature was to suppress the evil of gambling in produce."

We concur in the following statement, made by the Appellate Court in their opinion deciding this case: "The act of Flower in asking Kruse if he intended to take the grain, and the act of defendant in printing in each statement it issued language purporting to bind the customer to the proposition that, in making the deal, he contemplated an actual delivery, were unusual precautions. In ordinary transactions of the purchase and sale of personal property, such care would not be taken; for the law binds the seller to deliver and the purchaser to receive the property. The purpose of these precautions seems to have been to give an outward appearance of an intention to deliver and receive the property, where the actual intention was well understood by the parties to be that margins only should be advanced, and that the trades should be settled by the payment of differences without any delivery. * * * It is obvious Kruse had no use for 1,000 bushels of wheat, nor the means to pay for it. Cecil states no facts to give reasonable color to his testimony that he could use 5,000 bushels of oats on his farm. Both Kruse and Cecil had traded in this manner before with other houses."

Second. It is claimed on the part of the plaintiff in error that the crime, if any, was committed in Chicago, instead of Princeton. We do not think that this contention can be maintained. The only contract or agreement which either of the witnesses in this case made was so made in the office of the plaintiff in error in Princeton. The market quotations were there posted upon the blackboard, and were there made known to the customers. The orders for the purchase or sale of grain were given in the office at Princeton. All margins that were put up were paid in the office at Princeton. The agent of the plaintiff in error at Princeton and the customer met each other in the office at that place. No grain was ever purchased by either Kruse or Cecil on the Board of Trade in their names. The only difference between the case of Soby v. People, supra, and the case at bar is that, in the former case, the agent of the firm which was doing the business on the Board of Trade was indicted, while in the case at bar the principal was indicted. Although the deal was carried out on the Chicago Board of Trade, as was done here, yet in the Soby Case the conviction was sustained in the county where the orders were given, and where the margins were paid, and where the office was kept.

Third. The point, made by the counsel for plaintiff in error, that this law is unconstitutional, as being in contravention of the fourteenth amendment of the Constitution of the United States, is fully answered by the cases of Booth v. People, 186 Ill. 43, 57 N. E. 798, 50 L. R. A. 762, 78 Am. St. Rep. 229, and Booth v. Illinois, 184 U. S. 425, 22 Sup. Ct. 425, 46 L. Ed. 623. In Booth v. People, supra, this court held that laws for the suppression of all forms of gambling have, without exception, been regarded by the courts and law writers as a proper exercise of the police power of the state. The doctrine of Booth v. People, supra, was approved of by the Supreme Court of the United States in Booth v. Illinois, supra. In the latter case it was held that the Legislature of Illinois did not transcend the limits of constitutional authority when it enacted the statute against options, known as section 130 of the Criminal Code of Illinois, and it was there said: "We cannot say, from any facts judicially known to the court, or from the evidence in this case, that the prohibition of options to sell grain at a future time has, in itself, no reasonable relation to the suppression of gambling grain contracts, in respect of which the parties contemplate only a settlement on the basis of differences in the contract and market prices. * * * It must be assumed that the Legislature was of opinion that an effectual mode to suppress gambling grain contracts was to declare illegal all options to sell or buy at a future time. The court is unable to say that the means employed were not appropriate to the end sought to be attained, and which it was competent for the state to accomplish." We see no reason why the same reasons for holding the act in regard to options constitutional do not apply to the act of 1887, under which the present conviction was had.

We are of the opinion that there was no error in the judgment of the lower courts. Accordingly, the judgment of the Appellate Court is affirmed.

Judgment affirmed.

(210 Ill. 50)

WOLF v. HOPE et al.*

(Supreme Court of Illinois. April 20, 1904.)

CITY COURTS—JURISDICTION—JUDGES—MUNICIPAL OFFICERS — SALARIES—INCREASE—CITY COUNCIL—INJUNCTION — PARTIES — APPEAL —RECORD—IMPEACHMENT—AMENDMENT.

1. Where a transcript on appeal shows that a final decree has been entered, such transcript imports absolute verity, and cannot be impeached by affidavits that no final decree has been filed, in support of a motion to dismiss the appeal on such ground.

2. Where, after appeal from a decree, it was discovered that the record in the trial court was erroneous, in that a judgment was entered of record which had not been actually pronounced by the judge, the correct practice is to apply to the trial court to have the record amended, and apply to the Supreme Court for a continuance until the application for amendment in the trial court can be heard, and the amendment, if made, shown on appeal by an additional transcript.

3. Where a bill to restrain the payment of salary of a judge of a city court clearly showed that the cause involved the validity of a statute and the construction of the Constitution, an appeal from an order sustaining a demurrer to the bill was properly taken directly to the Supreme Court, though there was no express statement in the bill that the statute in question was unconstitutional.

4. A bill by a taxpayer to restrain members of a city council from voting salary to the judge of a city court at an alleged illegal rate properly joined all the members of such council as defendants, though it alleged that a minority had uniformly voted against such allowance, since, after the salary was allowed, it constituted the act of the council acting as a unit, whether the vote was unanimous or by a bare majority.

5. Const. art. 6, § 1, provides that the judicial powers shall be vested in one Supreme Court, circuit courts, county courts, justices of the peace, police magistrates, and such courts as may be created by law in and for cities and incorporated towns. Hurd's Rev. St. 1899, c. 37, § 240, provides for the organization of city courts, to have concurrent jurisdiction with circuit courts within the city in all civil cases, and also in criminal cases, except treason and murder, and in appeals from justices of the peace in such city; and section 244 provides that the judges of such city courts shall be elected by the voters of the city in the same manner as city officers; that they shall hold office for the term of four years, and be vested with the same power and perform the same duties as circuit judges; that when a vacancy occurs, if the unexpired term exceeds one year, it shall be filled at a special election, called by the same authority by which such elections are held, but, if the vacancy is for less than a year, it shall be filled by the Governor. *Held*, that the judges of the city courts are municipal, and not state, officers, within Const. art. 9, § 11, providing that the fees, salary, or compensation of no municipal officer elected or appointed for a definite term shall be increased or diminished during such term.

6. Since, under Hurd's Rev. St. 1899, c. 37, § 240, fixing the jurisdiction of city courts, such jurisdiction is territorially limited to the cities

*Rehearing denied June 8, 1904.

in which such courts are established, and they have no jurisdiction in prosecutions for murder and treason, such courts are "inferior courts of record," within Hurd's Rev. St. 1899, c. 53, § 5, providing that judges of inferior courts of record in towns and cities shall receive, in lieu of all other fees, perquisites, and benefits whatsoever, in cities and towns having a population of more than 5,000 inhabitants, $1,500, to be paid out of the city or town treasury.

7. Hurd's Rev. St. 1901, c. 37, § 262, changing the salaries to be paid to judges of city courts, applies only to judges whose terms of office began on or after the date the act took effect.

Appeal from Circuit Court, Madison County; P. McWilliams, Judge.

Bill by Valentine Wolf against Alexander W. Hope and others. From a decree sustaining a demurrer to the bill, complainant appeals. Reversed.

This is an appeal from a decree of the circuit court of Madison county, sustaining a demurrer to a bill for an injunction, dismissing the bill, which was filed by Valentine Wolf, a citizen and taxpayer of the city of Alton, and dissolving a temporary injunction which restrained Alexander W. Hope, as judge of the city court of the city of Alton, from receiving, and various officers of said city from allowing and paying to said Hope, as judge, any sum as salary in excess of $1,500 per annum. It appears from the bill that the city of Alton has a population of 15,000; that a city court in and for that city had been established many years prior to July 1, 1901; that on Tuesday, March 5, 1901, Alexander W. Hope was elected judge of that court, and on March 12, 1901, qualified and was commissioned by the Governor of the state as judge of that court for a term of four years from and after March 12, 1901; that his lawful salary on March 12, 1901, was $1,500 per annum, which was to be paid out of the treasury of the city, and which compensation could not be increased or diminished during his term of office, and that he is not entitled to receive any salary in excess thereof; that for several months after his election and commission as such judge he received his salary on the basis of $1,500 per annum; that beginning with the month of August, 1901, he presented bills to the city council for, and received, salary at the rate of $2,000 per annum, or $166.66 per month, being $41.66 in excess of his lawful salary, and being the rate fixed by the act of May, 1901, hereinafter mentioned; that he solicited the opinion of the Attorney General of the state of Illinois as to whether or not the judge of a city court in the state of Illinois, elected, qualified, and commissioned prior to July 1, 1901, was entitled to an increase of salary during the term for which he was elected, under and by virtue of an act in relation to courts of record in cities, approved May 10, 1901 (Laws 1901, p. 136; Hurd's Rev. St. 1901, c. 37, § 262), and was advised by said Attorney General, under date of June 28, 1901, that such judge was not entitled to such increase, and the letter of the Attorney General is set out at length in the bill; that on September 9, 1902, Judge Hope addressed to the city council a written communication containing the following:

"To the Honorable Mayor and City Council:

"Gentlemen—The condition which exists and has existed for several months in the city council, created by five aldermen, who entered that body with the avowed purpose and have formed a conspiracy to resist the operation of the law fixing the salary of the judge of city court, is a remarkable spectacle, stating it mildly, in this country of law. These five members were not satisfied with voting against the salary in the teeth of the opinion of the corporation counsel, in view of which they might have conceded that there was a chance for an honest difference of opinion as to the validity of this law; but they did not do this. This would not serve their lawless purpose. On the contrary, they sought to intimidate the nine other aldermen, and prevent them from voting for the law. They made threats of indictments against them, and these aldermen, and certain newspapers acting with them, put in false statements regarding their position and reflecting upon their official character, because these nine aldermen would not enter a conspiracy to defeat the law. This state of affairs is an outrage, and will not be permitted to continue any longer. I have determined to call a halt on these lawbreakers. Therefore I send this communication to the city council, to inform you, especially these five members, of their official duty, and the penalty for a failure to perform it, and the law against a conspiracy to do an unlawful act; also to notify these aldermen, and certain newspapers acting with them, that I will protect the nine aldermen doing their official duty, obeying their official oaths, and respecting the law from any further attacks on their official character. To accomplish this object I shall not hesitate to resort to the harshest measures. 'Patience has ceased to be a virtue' with you. The last Legislature passed a city court law, entitled 'Courts of Record in and for Cities.' Chapter 37, Hurd's Rev. St. Ill. 1901, par. 262, § 23, is as follows: 'The judges of said courts shall receive an annual salary in cities having more than 8,000 inhabitants and less than 25,000 inhabitants, the sum of two thousand ($2,000) dollars.'"

The letter then contains the substance of certain other sections of the statute, and continues:

"This city court law, in force July 1, 1901, is the only law on the statute books relating to city courts in the state of Illinois under which any judge of such courts can receive any salary or any city court can exercise any power or jurisdiction. All other laws or parts of law were repealed by this law. This is the law for city councils, for these five aldermen, and every other public officer in the state. The excuse made by these aldermen for obstructing the law, which conceals their real purpose and deceives no one, is that the law is unconstitutional. This is a question for the court; not for city councils, or the members thereof. There were about one hundred lawyers in the House and Senate of the Legislature that passed this law, and the Governor that signed it was a lawyer himself. How strange it seems that they were so ignorant of the Constitution, and those five aldermen are so wise about it. Mark what the Supreme Court of the state of Illinois said to a public officer, cited for a failure to perform his official duty and obey the law, when he answered that the law was unconstitutional. People v. Salomon, 54 Ill. 45."

Here the letter sets out at considerable length the opinion of this court in the Salomon Case, and section 27 of the act on cities and villages, and sections 46 and 208 of the Criminal Code (Hurd's Rev. St. 1901, c. 38, §§ 46, 208), which provide penalties for malfeasance and misfeasance by municipal officers and for conspiracy to do an illegal act, and then continues:

"These aldermen may be prosecuted and convicted under any and all of the above sections of the criminal statutes. The five members of the city council whose misconduct is under discussion are Messrs. Giberson, Noonan, Gregory, Yager, and Wegener. They entered the city council with the avowed purpose and formed a conspiracy to nullify that part of the city court act that fixes the salary of the judge thereof. They have resorted to all kinds of means and threats, even of indictment, to prevent the other aldermen from voting for the salary of the judge of such court. They, and certain newspapers acting with them, have attacked and circulated false statements reflecting upon the official character of the aldermen who followed the path of duty marked out by law and refused to depart from it. This unseemly performance has been kept up by them, without abatement, at every meeting of the city council for many months. Therefore take notice, the above-named members of the city council, that your unlawful acts must cease. I propose to protect from any further attacks from you, or the newspapers acting with you, the nine aldermen who did their official duty and obeyed their official oaths when they voted for the salary of the judge of the city court, while you violated your official duty and your official oaths when you voted against it. I tell you in plain words, that you cannot misunderstand, that you can no longer pursue your lawless course. If you attempt it, you will be prosecuted to the fullest extent of the law. You pose as reformers in the city council, without any character to support the role. You claim you are trying to find lawbreakers and punish them. We have found five lawbreakers in your persons. If you make it necessary, we will commence and punish you first. It is up to you now.

"Respectfully, Alex. W. Hope."

The bill avers that the tendency of the letter is to interfere with the members of the city council in the performance of their duty, and further avers that unless an injunction is issued, without notice, the city council will, on October 14, 1902, again allow the salary of the defendant, Judge Hope, in an excessive amount, and the same will be paid in due course thereafter by the city comptroller and the city treasurer; that notice has not been given, because the time intervening prior to the meeting of the council is so short that it will not admit of the delay which would be occasioned by giving the notice. Alexander W. Hope, the aldermen (14 in number), the mayor, the city treasurer, and the city comptroller were made defendants. The bill was filed on October 13, 1902, and a temporary injunction issued restraining Judge Hope from receiving, and the city authorities from paying, any salary at a rate in excess of $1,500 per annum. The five aldermen specifically named in the letter of appellee, Judge Hope, filed an answer admitting the material averments of the bill, and stating that they had never voted for the allowance of any salary in excess of $1,500 per annum, and did not expect to do so. The remaining defendants filed demurrers, on the ground, first, that there is no equity in the bill; second, parties defendant are improperly joined; third, it is not shown by the bill or affidavits attached that rights of complainant will be unduly prejudiced if the injunction is not issued without notice. Judge Hope made an application for a change of venue on the ground of the prejudice, as alleged by him, of each and every of the circuit judges in and for the circuit in which the county of Madison is situated. Thereupon the demurrer was heard by Hon. Paul McWilliams, judge of the city court of the city of Litchfield, presiding as judge of the circuit court of Madison county, upon the request of one of the judges of the latter court, and at the January term of that court the decree above mentioned was entered, and the complainant appeals to this court. The order allowing the appeal continues the temporary injunction in force.

Burton & Wheeler, for appellant. B. H. Canby, B. J. O'Neill, C. W. Terry, and L. B. Washburn, for appellees.

SCOTT, J. (after stating the facts). A preliminary question is presented by a motion to dismiss the appeal, based upon two grounds; the first being that no final decree has ever been entered by the circuit court in this cause. It is sought to make this fact appear by affidavits filed here. The transcript of the record herein shows a final decree. The record, as exhibited to us by the transcript, imports absolute verity. For the purpose of disposing of the cause in this court, it is the sole, conclusive, and unimpeachable evidence of the proceedings in the lower court. 3 Cyc. p. 152; Chicago, Burlington & Quincy Railroad Co. v. Lee, 68 Ill. 576. Where the record of the court below is erroneous, in that a judgment or decree has been entered of record which was not actually pronounced by the judge, the correct practice is to apply to the court below, upon proper notice, to have the record amended; and where it is made to appear in this court, when the cause is pending here, that it is probable such an amendment should be made in the court below, the cause will be continued in this court, when justice requires, until application can be heard for an amendment of the record in the court below, and until the amendment, if made, can be shown here by an additional transcript. Bergen v. Riggs, 40 Ill. 61, 89 Am. Dec. 335; Shipley v. Spencer, 40 Ill. 105. But such a mistake in entering the decree or judgment below is not a ground for dismissing the appeal, and affidavits showing such a mistake will only be considered in this court, when filed in support of a motion for a continuance which has been made in due time, for the purpose of permitting the court below to pass on the application of the complaining party.

The other ground upon which the motion to dismiss is based is that the court has no jurisdiction of this appeal, because it is taken directly from the circuit court to this court. The position of appellees is that the appeal should have been to the Appellate Court, and that the validity of a statute or a construction of the Constitution is not involved, for the reason that it is not expressly stated in the bill herein that section 23 of the act approved May 10, 1901 (Acts 1901, p. 136), which is section 262 of chapter 37 of Hurd's Revised Statutes of 1901, is unconstitutional or invalid; and in support of this position we are referred to Beach v. Peabody, 188 Ill. 75, 58 N. E. 679, Chicago General Railway Co. v. Sellers, 191 Ill. 524, 61 N. E. 495; Pearce v. Vittum, 193 Ill. 192, 61 N. E. 1116, and Cleveland, Cincinnati, Chicago & St. Louis Railway Co. v. McGrath, 195 Ill. 104, 62 N. E. 782. An examination of these cases shows that they do not go to this extent. They hold that a case cannot be brought by appeal or writ of error directly to this court from the trial court, on the ground that it involves the validity of a statute or a construction of the Constitution, unless the record shows that such question was in some way presented to the trial court for its decision. An inspection of this bill clearly shows that the cause involves the validity of a statute and a construction of the Constitution. This gives this court jurisdiction, without an express statement in the bill that the statute in question is unconstitutional. The motion to dismiss the appeal is therefore overruled.

It is urged that there is a misjoinder of defendants, for the reason that five aldermen who had persistently voted against paying the increased salary are made defendants, and that as the bill does not charge that they were doing any illegal act, or threatening to do an illegal act, they should not have been joined with the nine aldermen who were charged with doing an illegal act in voting the increased compensation. Whenever the bill of Judge Hope for his salary, which was presented monthly, was allowed, the act of allowing it became the act of the entire city council, whether the bill was allowed by unanimous vote, or by a mere majority of one; and if any of the aldermen were proper parties defendant to this suit, it was lawful, in enjoining that body, to enjoin each and every alderman. A city council is a unit. It cannot be divided into two or more parts, and one part restrained from the performance of functions which can be performed only by the entire body.

Another ground of demurrer is that the injunction was issued without notice, and without any averment in bill or affidavit that the rights of the complainant would be unduly prejudiced if the injunction was not issued without notice. This question is not raised by a demurrer. The averment said to be lacking might be omitted entirely from the bill, and contained in an affidavit filed therewith. It is manifest that a bill is not demurrable because it does not contain an averment which the statute provides it may contain, but which, under the statute, it need not contain. Under such circumstances it is not material to the cause stated by the bill. It is therefore unnecessary to determine whether. under the allegations of the bill, notice should have been given.

The question arising upon the merits is, can the salary of a judge of a city court, elected and commissioned in March, 1901, for a period of four years from the 12th day of that month, be increased during his term of office by virtue of an act approved May 10, 1901, and in force July 1, 1901, or is such increase prohibited by the Constitution of the state? By the provisions of sections 7, 16, and 25 of article 6, section 21 of article 4, section 23 of article 5, and section 10 of article 10, Constitution of 1870, it is provided that the salaries or compensation of judges of the Supreme Court, judges of the circuit courts, judges of the superior court and the state's attorney of Cook county, members of the General Assembly, the executive officers of the state, including officers of all the public institutions of the state, and county officers, shall not be increased or diminished during the terms of such officers; and section 11 of article 9 of the Constitution provides: "The fees, salary or compensation of no municipal officer who is elected or appointed for a definite term of office shall be increased or diminished during such term." The purpose of the constitutional convention evidently was to provide that the salary of no public officer holding place for a definite period under the laws of this state should be increased or diminished during his term of office; but it is urged that the judge of a city court is not within any clause of the Constitution prohibiting an increase or decrease of salary during the term, and that, therefore, the Legislature had the power to make a change in the salary attached to that office during the term of the incumbent thereof.

City courts were erected under section 1 of article 6 of the present Constitution, which reads as follows: "The judicial powers, except as in this article is otherwise provided, shall be vested in one Supreme Court, circuit courts, county courts, justices of the peace, police magistrates, and such courts as may be created by law in and for cities and incorporated towns." Under this provision of the Constitution the Legislature in 1874 provided as follows: "The several courts of record now existing in and for cities, and such as may hereafter be established by law, in and for any city in this state, shall severally be styled 'the city court of [name of city],' and shall have concurrent jurisdiction with the circuit courts within the city in which the same may be, in all civil cases, and in all criminal cases except treason and murder, and in appeals from justices of the peace in said city; and the course of proceedings and practice in such courts shall be the same as in the circuit courts, so far as may be." Hurd's Rev. St. 1899, c. 37, § 240. This section continued in force until July 1, 1901. Section 244 of the same act provided that the judges of such courts should be elected by the qualified voters of the said city in the same manner that the city officers are elected, and shall hold office for the term of four years, and until their successors are elected and qualified; that they shall qualify and be commissioned in the same manner, and be vested with the same powers, and perform the same duties, as circuit judges. Where a vacancy occurs, if the unexpired term exceeds one year, it shall be filled at a special election called by the same authority by which other city elections are called. If the unexpired term does not exceed one year, the vacancy shall be filled by appointment by the Governor.

Judges of city courts are not specifically mentioned in the Constitution, and it is earnestly insisted that they are not municipal officers, within the meaning of section 11 of article 9 of the Constitution, but that they are state officers, because commissioned by the Governor, and because their duties pertain to the state at large and to the general public. In our judgment this position is at variance with the law as stated by this court in the case of County of Cook v. Sennott, 136 Ill. 314, 26 N. E. 491, where it is held that the clerk of the probate court of Cook county is a municipal officer. He is an officer of a court of greater territorial jurisdiction than a city court, and which, as well as a city court, has jurisdiction of affairs which pertain to the state at large and to the general public. Hurd's Rev. St. 1901, c. 37, § 220. He is commissioned by the Governor. Section 229, Id. The fact that the judge of a city court has the power to interchange with and perform the duties of judges of circuit, superior, county, and probate courts throughout the state is without significance. County judges have a like power to exchange with each other throughout the state, but it would scarcely be contended that they thereby become state officers. We are unable to perceive any distinction that will enable us to hold that the judge of a city court is not a municipal officer, while holding that the clerk of a probate court is a municipal officer.

The provisions of the Constitution other than article 9 provided that the salaries of certain officers, including all the state officers, and all officers holding places under the executive department of the state for a definite term, should not be increased or diminished during their term. In our judgment the provision quoted from section 11 of article 9 of the Constitution was intended to include all officers, not specifically mentioned in other provisions of the Constitution, occupying offices created by the laws of the state in and for any of the political subdivisions of the state, and within the meaning of that section the judge of a city court is a municipal officer.

It is further urged, however, that prior to July 1, 1901, there was no law in this state fixing the salary of judges of city courts, and that the act of May, 1901, fixing the salary, was, therefore, a valid exercise of power, as it did not increase or diminish the salary during the term, and that all judges of city courts throughout the state were entitled to compensation at the rate fixed by that act from and after July 1, 1901, even though their terms of office had commenced prior to that time. Section 8 of chapter 53 of Hurd's Rev. St. 1899, which is the "Fees and Salaries Act," fixes the salaries of judges of the circuit court and of the superior court of Cook county. Section 4 of that act provides the method by which such salaries shall be paid. Section 5 contains the following: "Judges of inferior courts of record in towns and cities shall be allowed, and receive in lieu of, all other fees, perquisites or benefits whatsoever, in cities or towns having a population not exceeding five thousand (5,000) inhabitants, five hundred dollars ($500), and in cities or towns having more than five thousand (5,000) inhabitants, fifteen hundred dollars ($1,500), to be paid out of the city or town treasury: provided, that in cities having a population of one hundred thousand (100,-000) or more, the city or common council may give such additional compensation, to be paid out of the city or town treasury, to the judge or judges of such court, as shall be deemed reasonable, not exceeding a sum sufficient to make the entire salary five thousand dollars ($5,000), which additional compensation shall be fixed prior to the election of such judge or judges, and shall be provided for in the annual appropriation ordinance of each year, and shall not be increased or diminished during the term of office of such judge or judges."

The argument is that a city court is not an inferior court of record. Section 1 of article 5 of the Constitution of 1848 provided as follows: "The judicial power of this state shall be and is hereby vested in one Supreme Court, in circuit courts, in county courts, and in justices of the peace: provided, that inferior local courts, of civil and criminal jurisdiction, may be established by the General Assembly in the cities of this state, but such courts shall have a uniform organization and jurisdiction in such cities." Under the proviso to this section of that Constitution, various local courts were created by the Legislature in cities of the state, and it is to be observed that the clause of the Constitution just quoted denominates them as "inferior" courts. For the purpose of preventing inconvenience that might otherwise arise from the alterations and amendments of the organic law of the state, the Constitution of 1870 continued these local courts in existence by section 5 of the schedule, which is a part of that document and which reads as follows: "All existing courts which are not in this Constitution specifically enumerated, shall continue in existence and exercise their present jurisdiction until otherwise provided by law." Hurd's Rev. St. 1901, p. 75. Under that section such local courts continued in existence until July 1, 1874, when they were superseded by or merged into the city courts under and by virtue of the act on city courts, which became effective on that day, and the first section of which is section 240 of chapter 37 of Hurd's Revised Statutes of 1899.

It will be observed that the fees and salaries act was originally approved March 29, 1872, and in force July 1, 1872, and the conclusion of the appellees is that the term "inferior courts of record," in section 5 of that act, therefore, has reference only to the inferior local courts which existed under the Constitution of 1848, and which were still in existence at the time of the passage of the fees and salaries act in 1872, and consequently should not be held to apply to the judge of a city court, which belongs to a class of courts not then in existence, and not aptly described by the language of section 5. This section, as originally passed, did not contain the proviso which it now contains, and which is herein above set forth. Hurd's Rev. St. 1874, c. 53, § 5. In 1877, after the passage of the city court act, section 5, supra, was amended by re-enacting the entire section with the proviso inserted therein. The proviso authorizes the city council to increase the salary "to the judge or judges of such court." The term "such court" refers to the first part of the section, and means one of the "inferior courts of record." As there were no courts in existence to which this proviso could apply when it was enacted in 1877, or to which section 5 as re-enacted in that year could apply, except city courts, we think it apparent that the Legislature, by the enactment of the proviso, made the language of section 5 applicable to city courts, even had it not been so applicable prior to that time; otherwise, the enactment of the proviso was a useless thing.

Further, section 5 of the fees and salaries act, as passed in 1872, fixed the salaries of "judges of inferior courts of record in towns and cities." Section 1 of article 5 of the Constitution of 1848 did not authorize the creation of courts of record "in towns." The only authority contained in that section of that Constitution for the creation of inferior local courts required that they be established "in the cities of this state." Section 1 of article 6 of the Constitution of 1870, on the other hand, authorized the establishment of "such courts as may be created by law in and for cities and incorporated towns." It follows, therefore, that in enacting section 5 of the fees and salaries act of 1872 the Legislature must have had in contemplation judges of courts that might thereafter be erected under section 1 of article 6 of the Constitution of 1870, as well as judges of "inferior local" courts which had been organized under the Constitution of 1848 and which were then still in existence.

Disregarding, however, the reasoning consequent upon a consideration of the enactment of the proviso in section 5 of chapter 53 of Hurd's Revised Statutes of 1901, and a comparison of the language of that section with the language of the sections from the Constitutions of 1848 and 1870 last above referred to, we would still incline to the view that judges of city courts are within the language of section 5 as originally enacted. The term "inferior courts of record," as contained in that section, designates courts of record inferior to the circuit court and the superior court of Cook county; and while the city court is not an inferior court, in the sense that an appeal lies from that court either to the circuit or superior court, still it was inferior, as it existed in March, 1901, so far as its original jurisdiction was concerned—that is, it did not have jurisdiction of murder or treason. It was not a court of unlimited, general jurisdiction, as are the circuit court and the superior court; nor is the extent of the territory throughout which it may exercise its jurisdiction as great as that throughout which may be exercised the jurisdiction of the circuit or superior court. In these respects it is an inferior court, and the judge thereof is a "judge of an inferior court of record," within the meaning of section 5 of the fees and salaries act.

We therefore hold that it was not within the power of the Legislature to increase or diminish the salary of the judge of a city court during the term for which said judge was elected, and that section 262 of chapter 37 of Hurd's Revised Statutes of 1901 applies only to judges of the city courts whose terms of office begin on or after July 1, 1901. The decree of the circuit court will be reversed, and the cause remanded, with directions to that court to overrule the demurrer, and to grant leave to appellees to answer or plead, if they shall move for such leave. The temporary injunction will continue in force until the further order of the circuit court.

Reversed and remanded, with directions.

(209 Ill. 488)

DADY v. CONDIT.*

(Supreme Court of Illinois. April 20, 1904.)

VENDOR AND PURCHASER—CONTRACTS—BREACH BY VENDOR—DAMAGES—EVIDENCE—SALES OF OTHER PROPERTY — ELEMENTS—BOOM CONDITIONS — ADAPTABILITY TO PARTICULAR PURPOSES — INSTRUCTIONS — APPEAL — PREJUDICIAL ERROR—INTEREST.

1. In an action for breach of a contract to sell land located in the vicinity of a town which was undergoing a boom, testimony that at the time of the breach of the contract the lands had a cash market value for subdivision purposes, and that by reason of the developments at that time taking place and expected to take place there was a greatly increased demand for all property in the vicinity, was admissible to show the cash market value of the land on the date of the breach.

2. In an action for breach of a contract to sell land, evidence of the sales of similar land in the same vicinity was admissible on the issue of the market value of the land at the time of the breach, though such sales were made partly on time, where the deferred payments bore 6 per cent. interest.

3. The facts that the purchasers in such other sales did not in all cases pay the actual amount agreed upon, and that a number of years afterwards the vendors disposed of their mortgages at a discount, could be shown to militate against the weight of the evidence, but did not show that the sales failed, so as to render it inadmissible.

4. The fact that the location and quality of such other lands was not precisely the same as the land in dispute, and that the parcels varied in distance from the town, the proximity of which gave them their value, did not render such evidence inadmissible.

5. In an action for breach of a contract to sell land, where evidence of sales of other land in the vicinity is introduced, a broad latitude should be allowed in cross-examination of witnesses as to such sales.

6. In an action for breach of a contract to sell land, the sole question on the issue of damages is the determination of the cash market value of the land on the date of the breach, irrespective of whether the conditions which fixed the market price on that date were permanent or not.

7. In an action for breach of a contract to sell land, an instruction that the market value of land is the highest price which it will bring in cash on the open market, and that if, by reason of the conditions existing on the day of the breach, the land would then have sold for more than the plaintiff agreed to pay for it, the jury should take such increased value into consideration in arriving at the value of the land, no matter whether the conditions then existing were permanent or temporary, could not have misled the jury where a subsequent instruction told them that the cash market value of the land on the day of the breach was not the market value under peculiar circumstances, and on very favorable terms, but was a sum for which the land could be sold at public auction where the owner was not obliged to sell and purchasers were willing to buy.

8. In an action for the breach of a contract to sell land, an instruction that if there was a demand for property in the vicinity of that in dispute on the date of the breach, in consequence of which the land had a market value above the price which plaintiff agreed to pay for it, the jury would take such increased value into consideration, was not subject to the criticism of allowing the jury to take into consideration the increased value of the land, even though the increased value might not equal the contract price.

9. In an action for breach of a contract to sell land, an instruction allowing the jury to take into consideration on the issue of value the "supposed" adaptability of the land to subdivision and sale in lots, was not objectionable.

10. In an action for breach of a contract to sell land, a charge directing the consideration of the jury to the question of whether certain improvements were expected in the town near which the land was located was proper, though the word "expected" was not qualified by the word "reasonably," for the increased valuation resulting from such expectation was a proper item of damage, whether the expectation was well founded or not.

11. In an action for breach of a contract to sell land, an instruction that the jury might take into consideration other sales of similar property made near the date of the breach in determining the market value of the land on that date was not incomplete in failing "to state certain elements which should be taken into consideration in connection with sales."

12. A charge that a preponderance of evidence on any point at issue is sufficient to justify a verdict for the side on which the preponderance exists could not have misled the jury into believing that there would have to be a preponderance of evidence in favor of defendant in order to find for him, where in other instructions the jury were informed that plaintiff could not recover unless he established his claim by a preponderance of the evidence, and the jury were specifically instructed that the burden of proof rested on plaintiff to establish by a preponderance of the evidence every material allegation and fact necessary to a recovery.

13. In an action for breach of a contract to sell land, a charge that a preponderance of evidence on any point is sufficient to justify a verdict for the side on which the preponderance exists, is not prejudicial where the only point at issue is the value of the land on the date of the breach.

14. In an action for breach of a contract to sell land, the jury could consider the increased value of the land by reason of the fact that it was believed to be adaptable to subdivision, and therefore actually had a higher cash market value, though it was not actually subdivided or actually adapted to subdivision.

15. In an action for breach of a contract to sell land the jury should determine the cash market value of the land on the day of the breach by what it would have sold for at the time on the market for cash, or its equivalent.

16. In an action for breach of a contract to sell land, a charge that the jury should fix the actual cash market value of the land on the day of the breach, and should consider its fair cash value if sold in the market under ordinary circumstances, or under the circumstances then existing, was not open to the objection of allowing the jury to consider peculiar circumstances and very favorable terms, increasing the land to much more than its fair cash value.

17. In an action for breach of a contract to sell land, a charge that plaintiff was in any event

*Rehearing denied June 8, 1904.

entitled to nominal damages, whereas defendant had in fact made a tender of costs and $1, was not prejudicial where the jury found large actual damages.

18. Where there is no marked inconsistency, one instruction may supplement another, and the jury are presumed, in making up their verdict, to have considered the instructions as a whole.

19. In an action for breach of a contract to sell land, where the damages were not so certain or definite that defendant could, without the verdict of a jury, have known how much he was liable for, plaintiff was properly denied interest from the date of the breach to the date of his verdict.

Appeal from Appellate Court, Second District.

Action by James M. Condit against Robert Dady. From a judgment of the Appellate Court affirming a judgment for plaintiff, defendant appeals. Affirmed.

This suit has been submitted to this court before for review. Its history can be obtained from an examination of 163 Ill. 511, 45 N. E. 224, affirming the judgment of the Appellate Court reported in 56 Ill. App. 545, and the further opinion of this court reported in 188 Ill. 234, 58 N. E. 900, reversing the judgment of the Appellate Court reported in 87 Ill. App. 250.

The controversy out of which the present suit arose, as well as the other prolonged litigation between the same parties, relates to a certain written contract between them, entered into at Milwaukee, January 14, 1891, wherein appellant agreed to sell to appellee a quarter section of land at $150 per acre, located near the city of Waukegan. Appellee paid nothing down, but was to have paid $500 upon the delivery of an abstract, and, in case he paid $3,000 more on or before August 1, 1891, and gave a mortgage securing the balance of the purchase money, he was to be entitled to a deed. The contract is set out in full in the opinion of this court in 163 Ill. 511, 45 N. E. 224. Appellee made a tender of performance of the various preliminaries required of him by said contract, but appellant failed and refused to carry out his part of the said contract; so on the 10th of August, 1891, Condit commenced suit against Dady, appellant, in the circuit court of Lake county, for damages for breach of the contract. On the 23d of April, 1893, Dady filed his bill in equity in the same court against Condit to set aside the said contract on the grounds of fraud and want of delivery, and to enjoin the suit at law. A temporary injunction was issued enjoining the suit at law. On the hearing of the chancery suit the circuit court found in favor of Condit on the ground of fraud, but in favor of Dady on the ground of want of delivery, entering a decree setting aside the contract as null and void, and perpetually enjoining suit upon it. On appeal to the Appellate Court the decree of the circuit court was reversed, with directions that the injunction be dissolved, and that said bill be dismissed for want of equity. From that judgment Dady took an appeal to this court, where the judgment of the Appellate Court was affirmed. Thereupon the case was again redocketed in the circuit court, but the suit was afterwards dismissed by Condit, who, on November 22, 1897, brought the present suit. This suit has been tried three times. On the first trial the plaintiff obtained a verdict for $4,920, which amount being unsatisfactory to him, he requested and was granted a new trial. On the second trial the plaintiff secured a verdict for $15,000, but, under compulsion, remitted $3,000, and judgment was given for $12,000. From this judgment the defendant took an appeal to the Appellate Court, where said judgment was affirmed, but on further appeal to this court was reversed. On the third trial plaintiff obtained a verdict for $16,000, for which amount judgment was entered, but the defendant took an appeal to the Appellate Court, where, on the ground that the verdict was excessive, the plaintiff was required to remit half of his judgment or submit to a reversal of the case. A remittitur for the amount indicated having been filed, the judgment for $8,000 was affirmed, from which defendant prosecutes this further appeal.

The principal grounds urged for a reversal relate to the competency of certain evidence and the correctness of certain instructions. The only question before the jury in this case was the amount of substantial damages due appellee, nominal damages being admitted.

Eddy, Haley & Wetten (Clyde A. Morrison, of counsel), for appellant. Hoyne, O'Connor & Hoyne (John L. Griffith and Elam L. Clarke, of counsel), for appellee.

RICKS, J. (after stating the facts). Appellant first insists that there was error in the trial of this case by "allowing incompetent evidence to be introduced by the appellee as to the value of the land for speculative purposes and future uses under altered conditions which might or might not arise." We have examined the evidence referred to, and, under the circumstances of this case, are of the opinion that its admission was proper. The land in question was in the vicinity of Waukegan. At the time of the execution of the contract out of which this litigation arises, and for several years thereafter, and until the depression of 1893, Waukegan and the surrounding district was experiencing a boom occasioned by rumors that the Washburn & Moen Manufacturing Company and other concerns were about to establish factories there, and the above-mentioned factory, and many others, were, in fact, so established, and as a result the population of Waukegan was greatly increased, and from the early part of 1891 until the panic of 1893 there was great activity in the sale of real estate in said district. As a result of these conditions the evidence clearly shows there was a great demand for land adjacent to and surrounding Waukegan

¶ 19. See Interest, vol. 29, Cent. Dig. § 35.

for subdivision and lot purposes, and the cash market value of said lands was greatly enhanced in price. The lands in question here were farm lands, and for such use, it is contended, were worth but about $50 or $60 per acre; but numerous witnesses offered by appellee testified that by reason of the existence of the conditions above mentioned the lands in question on August 1, 1891, had a fair cash market value of from $300 to $500 per acre. The plaintiff had a right to show that at the time of the breach of the contract the lands had a cash market value for subdivision purposes, and numerous witnesses testified to this fact. The evidence of these witnesses was supplemented by an actual view of the premises by the jury. The testimony of numerous witnesses for appellee was to the effect that by reason of the developments at that time taking place and expected to take place in Waukegan there was a greatly increased demand for all property in that vicinity. This testimony was proper for the purpose of showing the cash market value of the land in question on August 1, 1891. South Park Com'rs v. Dunlevy, 91 Ill. 49.

Counsel for appellant seem, however, to insist that this testimony related solely to speculative and prospective valuation and of an imaginative character, which has never, in fact, materialized, and was therefore incompetent. Appellant relies upon that class of cases which hold that in estimating the value of lands remote, uncertain, imaginary, and speculative uses cannot be shown. We do not, however, regard those cases as in point here. The rule established by such cases is well recognized, and not to be disturbed, but there is a broad distinction, which appellant's argument does not seem to recognize, between the value which the expectation of changes or improvements may give to land and the value which changes or improvements, when actually made, may add to land. The cases relied upon by appellant do not hold that, if the expectation of changes or improvements does actually affect the cash market value of land sold in the open market, such value is not a proper basis for the estimation of damages.

The theory on which this case was tried was that appellant was under contract to convey to appellee land on August 1, 1891; that he broke his contract, and was liable to appellee for the excess, if any, above the contract price which appellee could have obtained for such land in the open market, when sold for cash, on the day of such breach. It is conceded that the said land on said day, if used only for farm purposes, was not worth more than, or scarcely half of, the contract price. But appellee, if the lands were conveyed to him according to the contract, was under no obligation to continue their use for farm purposes. It was his privilege to buy and sell and derive a profit on his contract, if he could. The testimony offered was to the effect that appellee, had he been permitted to sell in the open market, for cash, could have, on said August 1, 1891, derived a certain profit, thus giving the jury a basis on which to estimate his damages. It is not uncommon for the price which real estate will bring in the open market to be affected more or less by the expectation of changed conditions in the neighborhood of the property; and in this case, so far as the cash market value of the land was affected by such expected change, the appellee was entitled to show by the evidence and have the benefit thereof. Cobb v. Boston, 112 Mass. 181; Moulton v. Newburyport Water Co., 137 Mass. 163; Sanitary District v. Loughran, 160 Ill. 362, 43 N. E. 359.

Appellant next assigns as error that appellee was permitted to introduce, as claimed, incompetent evidence "of alleged sales of other lands which were not actual sales for cash, but were on time, some of which completely failed," and also introduced "evidence of sales of dissimilar property with better locations and more desirable." In those sales which are said to have been on time, part only of the purchase price was deferred, and such deferred payments bore 6 per cent. interest; and, while the point to be arrived at by the jury was the actual cash value of the land in controversy at a certain time, we think that evidence of other sales of the character testified to might furnish some criterion valuable to the jury in fixing such cash value; and such evidence would also furnish a means of testing the value and weight to be given the testimony of appellee's witnesses who swore as to the actual cash value of the land. If evidence were to be excluded of all sales every cent of which was not cash, the door would practically be closed as to the evidence of other sales, and such evidence, when of similar land in the same community, has always been regarded as the most satisfactory. We think the evidence as to the other sales was clearly competent, but, of course, the value of such evidence was for the jury, and appellant had the right, by cross-examination, to elicit all the unfavorable facts connected with such sales, and thus minimize, as much as he could, the weight of such evidence.

The contention of appellant that such sales, or some of them, failed, is based on the fact that the purchasers did not in all cases pay the actual amount agreed upon, and a number of years after the transaction the vendors disposed of their mortgages at a discount. We concede this might be shown so as to militate against the weight properly to be accorded such evidence, but it can hardly be said that the sales failed. There is nothing very peculiar or strange in the fact that the holder of a mortgage disposes of it at a discount. But, however this may be regarded, it is disclosed by the evidence in this case that, taking into consideration the discount testified to, still the vendors in the sales testified about received more, without including the interest, than was the evident valuation placed by the jury on the land here in question.

It is objected, however, that the sales testified to were of lands dissimilar in quality and location to the land involved in the contract. We do not think the evidence shows such dissimilarity as to support this objection. The lands were all in the vicinity of Waukegan. As a matter of fact, the location and quality of all could not be precisely the same. The relative distances from the principal parts of the city had probably as much to do as any other factor in varying the price, and this fact could easily be and was made to appear by the evidence. We regard the evidence as conclusively showing that there was, as to the lands testified about, a general similarity in location, character, and adaptability, and we think the evidence was competent to go to the jury to assist them, in connection with the other facts and circumstances in the case, in determining the question presented to them. St. Louis, Vandalia & Terre Haute Railroad Co. v. Haller, 82 Ill. 208.

It is next insisted that there was an undue restriction in the cross-examination of appellant's witnesses as to the value of certain lands testified about, and that a given sale had failed. Relative to these questions it was proper to allow a broad latitude in the cross-examination, but we have examined so much of these objections as is urged in the brief of appellant's counsel, and find the objections are untenable.

It is insisted in appellant's brief that the court improperly denied him the right to introduce evidence as to the fair cash market value of the land a reasonable time before and after August 1, 1891. We regard appellant's rights as not having been improperly sacrificed in the respect mentioned.

Appellant next urges upon our consideration alleged improper remarks of the trial court during the progress of the trial. These remarks were made in the course of a controversy with appellant's counsel in regard to the execution of the contract, the court insisting that, as it was admitted that there was a contract and breach, it was useless to take up time quibbling about the execution of the contract, or to go over matters that were already settled; and a review of the case satisfies us that the court properly stated the issues, and committed no error as to the point in question.

Appellant next insists upon numerous alleged errors as to instructions. The principal objection urged as to the first instruction is that it directs the jury to estimate the land at its market value on August 1, 1891, no matter whether such rise in value was permanent or temporary. The sole question before the jury was the determination of the cash market value of the land on August 1, 1891—the day of the breach—and, if such value was greater than the contract price, then the excess furnished the jury a definite basis on which to estimate appellee's damages. As stated when this case was formerly before this court (Dady v. Condit, 188 Ill. 234, 58 N. E. 900): "The measure of damages was the increased value, if any, of the premises at the time of the breach [August 1, 1891] above the contract price." The main point in the objection to this instruction seems to be that it was error to confine the jury, in their estimation of the value of the land, to the particular day of the breach, and to advise them that it made no difference whether the conditions which fixed the market price of the land on that particular day were permanent or not. It was not wrong thus to advise the jury. As already stated, it was the market value of the land on a particular day that the jury were charged with the duty of estimating, and we cannot see how error could arise from admonishing them that they were not to be governed by the conditions of the market prior or subsequent to the day stated. If they were to be controlled by the variations of the market, and the market proved to be unsteady through a long period, as with some commodities might very likely be the case, we are unable to see how the jury could arrive at any definite conclusion; and the very necessity of the case would seem to require the limitation that is complained of in this instruction. In our judgment the point urged by appellant is not well taken.

The seventh instruction told the jury "that the market value of land is the highest price which it will bring in cash on the open market," and then also told the jury that if, by reason of the conditions existing on August 1, 1891, the land in controversy would then have sold in the open market, for cash, for more than Condit agreed to pay for it, the jury should take such increased value into consideration in arriving at the value of the land at that time, no matter whether the conditions then existing were permanent or temporary. This instruction, appellant insists, told the jury that the "market value of the land is the highest price which the land will bring in the market, regardless of the causes that contribute to its value," and is therefore bad, and is also objectionable for the same error imputed to the first instruction. This latter objection has already been considered. In support of appellant's contention as to the first objection, it is insisted that this instruction is substantially the same as the seventh instruction condemned by this court on the former trial. What was there said is as follows: "The seventh instruction tells the jury 'that the market value of land is the highest price which the land will bring in the market, regardless of the causes that contribute to its value.' This is an incorrect definition. * * * Lands may bring in the market, under peculiar circumstances and on very favorable terms, much more than their fair cash value." We think there is a clear distinction between the instruction here presented and the one referred to on the former trial. The present instruction defines market value as the highest price obtainable in the open market for cash, and thus eliminates the objection stated in the opinion as to the former instruction. Having properly defined market value, the instruction then simply tells the jury that if the market value, as thus defined, of the lands on August 1, 1891, was more than the contract price, then such increased value should be taken into consideration by the jury, which was proper. By appellant's fifteenth instruction the jury were told that "the cash market value on August 1, 1891, of the tract of land in controversy in this case, is not the market value under peculiar circumstances and on very favorable terms, but is the sum for which the land could be sold at public auction, where the owner is not obliged to sell and there are purchasers willing to buy." With so favorable an instruction in behalf of appellant we do not think the jury could have been misled by the instruction above complained of.

The third instruction for appellee was as follows: "If the jury believe from the evidence that there was a demand for acreage property in and about Waukegan on August 1, 1891, for purposes of subdivision and sale in lots, and that the land in controversy was at that time supposed to be adapted to subdivision and sale in lots, and in consequence of its supposed adaptability to such subdivision and sale in lots had a market value above the price which the plaintiff, Condit, agreed to pay for it, the jury must take into consideration such increased value above such contract price, whether such demand for acreage property, if any, was permanent or temporary, and whether, if the land in controversy had been subdivided, there would have been at that time any demand for the lots thereof or not." The objection that this instruction is substantially the same as the eighth instruction, which was condemned by this court on the former trial, is unfounded. The fault found to the previous instruction was as follows: "Even if the land was increased in value by a boom, that added value could in no way enter into the consideration of the jury 'in estimating the damages in the case,' unless the increased value made it worth more in the market on August 1, 1891, than the contract price—$150 per acre." The instruction condemned provided that if the land had an increased value by reason of a boom, etc., the jury were to take such into consideration, even though the increased value might not equal the contract price. The present instruction is not subject to such criticism. The word "supposed," in the instruction, is also objected to, but we think the objection is without merit. If land is supposed to be suitable for a particular purpose, and by reason of such supposed adaptability commands a higher price when sold in the open market, for cash, than it otherwise would, such greater value is to be taken into consideration when estimating the value of the land. Calumet River Railway Co. v. Moore, 124 Ill. 329, 15 N. E. 764.

Appellee's fourth instruction contains the expression, "If the jury believe from the evidence that certain improvements were expected in and about Waukegan on August 1, 1891," etc., and it is objected that in this instruction the word "expected" is not qualified by the word "reasonably." In our judgment, this qualification was not necessary in this particular case. Nor do we regard our holding as in conflict with the cases cited by appellant. Those were condemnation cases, and the point made in them was that in estimating the damages, if the lands claimed to be actually adapted to some other purpose than the present use and sought to be condemned might be considered reasonably adapted to such other certain use, or if there was reasonable chance or probability of such changed conditions, and such reasonable adaptability or chance of change affected the actual market value of the lands at the time in question, then these contingencies were proper to be considered by the jury in determining the value of the land. In the present case certain improvements were expected in the vicinity of the lands in question, and according to the evidence such expectation did actually increase the value of the lands, and people were willing to pay more for them, when sold in the open market for cash, than they otherwise would; and we think the only just and legal rule to apply under such circumstances is, that such increased valuation was proper to be considered by the jury in estimating the value of the land, no matter whether such expectations were well founded or not.

By the fifth instruction the jury were told that "the price for which the land would have sold on the 1st day of August, 1891, is to be taken as its market value at that time, without regard to its present value, or its value at any time since the said 1st day of August, 1891." It is insisted by appellant that this instruction is wrong, and that it was the duty of the jury, in determining the value of the land on the 1st day of August, 1891, to consider its value before and after the 1st day of August, 1891, within reasonable limits; and the case of Springer v. City of Chicago, 135 Ill. 552, 26 N. E. 514, 12 L. R. A. 609, is cited in support of this contention. We think the objection is not well taken, and for reasons already stated in this opinion. The case cited is not in point. In that case the recovery of damages occasioned by the construction of a viaduct was involved, and it was held the measure of damages was the difference between the market value of the property before and after the improvement. But the case at bar is different. Here the measure of damages, as previously stated, was "the increase of the value, if any, of the premises at the time of the breach [August 1, 1891]. above the contract price," and the sole point before the jury was the determination of the value on the day mentioned, not their value before or after that time.

By the eighth instruction the jury were told that if they believed that sales of similar property in the neighborhood on or about August 1, 1891, had been made, they might take such sales into consideration in determining the market value in controversy on that date. This instruction is objected to as being incomplete, and that "it fails to state certain elements which should be taken into consideration in connection with sales." We fail to see wherein this instruction is erroneous. Sales of similar property in the vicinity were competent evidence, and any difference in the terms of such sales and the one being investigated was a circumstance to be taken into consideration in weighing such evidence.

By the ninth instruction the jury were told that they were sworn to decide the case according to the evidence, and that "a preponderance of the evidence on any point at issue is sufficient to justify a verdict for the side on which the preponderance exists." It is objected to this instruction that under it there would have to be a preponderance of the evidence in favor of the defendant in order to find for him. We do not think the jury could have been so misled, for several other instructions informed the jury that the plaintiff could not recover unless he established his claim by a preponderance of the evidence. By the nineteenth instruction for appellant the jury were told that the "burden of proof rests upon the plaintiff to establish, by a preponderance of the evidence, every material allegation and fact necessary to a recovery in the case." The instruction is further objected to on the ground that by it the jury are told that, if they find a preponderance of evidence on any point in the case, that is sufficient to justify a verdict for the side on which the preponderance exists. While this language is not technically correct, yet no harm could have resulted therefrom, for there was really but one point before the jury, which was the value of the land on August 1, 1891.

Appellant next objects to the court's modification of his seventeenth instruction. This modification was proper, for, as offered, the instruction directed the jury not to consider the value of the land in controversy for the purpose of subdivision unless it was either actually subdivided or actually adapted to the purpose of subdivision. This is not the law. If the land was believed to be adapted to subdivision, and by reason of such supposition actually had a higher cash market value, such increased value was proper to be considered by the jury. The instruction told the jury that in considering the value of the land they "could consider its fair cash market value on the date aforesaid, and that value is to be determined by what it would have sold for at that time on the market for cash or its equivalent, so far as such fact is shown by the evidence." In this, we think, the jury were correctly advised.

Defendant's eighteenth instruction, as modified and given, was as follows: "The jury are instructed that in determining the value of the one hundred and sixty acre tract of land involved in this case they are to fix the actual cash market value of said land on August 1, 1891; and you are further instructed that you are not to consider the price which the land would sell for under special or extraordinary circumstances not existing at the time, but its fair cash value if sold in the market under ordinary circumstances, or under the circumstances then existing, for cash, and not on time, and assuming that the owner is willing to sell and the purchaser is willing to buy." This instruction is objected to as having been directly condemned by this court in its former opinion in this case. Dady v. Condit, 188 Ill. 234, 58 N. E. 900. We do not regard this instruction as substantially the same as the instruction referred to and previously condemned. The latter instruction was condemned because it stated that "the market value of land is the highest price which the land will bring in the market, regardless of the causes that contribute to its value," and it was said that this rule as to market value is incorrect, as "lands may bring in the market, under peculiar circumstances, and on very favorable terms, much more than their fair cash value." This objection does not appear in the instruction given in the present case, but here the jury are expressly told that they are to "fix the actual cash market value of said land on August 1, 1891," and to consider "its fair cash value if sold in the market under ordinary circumstances, or under the circumstances then existing, for cash, and not on time, and assuming that the owner is willing to sell and the purchaser is willing to buy."

Appellant's nineteenth instruction, as modified, is objected to because the jury were told that the plaintiff was, in any event, entitled to nominal damages, and it is said in behalf of appellant that he had made a tender of the costs and $1, so, unless the jury should find greater damages than $1, then the verdict should have been for defendant. It is useless to discuss this contention, for it is evident the defendant was not injured by the defect, if any, here claimed, since the jury did find that the damages were in fact much more than $1, and it is unnecessary to discuss how the verdict should have been if the damages found had been for $1 or less.

On a review of the whole case we think defendant's instructions were as favorable to him as they legally could have been, and, even if there are minor inaccuracies in appellee's instructions, the same were so supplemented by other instructions that we think the jury could not have been misled. We do not, however, wish to be understood as holding that a palpable error in one instruction will be obviated by another instruction where the two are clearly variant, but simply that, where there is no marked inconsistency, one instruction may supplement another, and the jury are presumed, in making up their verdict, to have considered the instructions as a whole.

We think no such error has intervened in this case as would warrant a reversal of the present judgment. The case has already been tried three times, each succeeding verdict being for appellee, and being for a greater amount than the preceding. By the Appellate Court the last verdict was cut in two, thus relieving appellant of half the liability imposed upon him by the trial court. We feel that appellant was given a fair trial, and are not disposed to prolong this litigation because of slight inaccuracies or technical objections.

Appellee insists that the Appellate Court erred in not allowing interest on the amount found due him from August 1, 1891, to the time of the verdict, but we think there was no error in this respect. The damages due appellee for the breach of the contract were not so certain or definite that appellant could, without the verdict of a jury, know how much he was liable for, and the case does not come within the provisions of the statute for the allowance of damages. Harvey v. Hamilton, 155 Ill. 377, 40 N. E. 592; Brownell Improvement Co. v. Critchfield, 197 Ill. 61, 64 N. E. 332.

The judgment of the Appellate Court will be affirmed. Judgment affirmed.

MEMORANDUM DECISIONS.

ABRAHAM, Respondent, v. BURSTEIN et al., Appellants. (Court of Appeals of New York. April 8, 1904.) Appeal from a judgment of the Appellate Division of the Supreme Court in the First Judicial Department (82 App. Div. 631, 81 N. Y. Supp. 937), entered May 18, 1903, affirming a judgment in favor of plaintiff entered upon a verdict and an order denying a motion for a new trial. Louis Burstein and Jacob Mylburn Schoenfeld, for appellants. Francis A. McCloskey, for respondent.

PER CURIAM. Judgment affirmed, with costs.

PARKER, C. J., and GRAY, O'BRIEN, BARTLETT, HAIGHT, MARTIN, and CULLEN, JJ., concur.

ALLEN, Respondent, v. LESTER et al., Appellants. (Court of Appeals of New York. March 1, 1904.) Appeal from a judgment of the Appellate Division of the Supreme Court in the Fourth Judicial Department (81 App. Div. 376, 80 N. Y. Supp. 1053), entered April 8, 1903, affirming a judgment in favor of plaintiff entered upon a decision of the court on trial at an Equity Term. Levant D. Lester, for appellants. Daniel W. Allen and Herbert B. Butterfield, for respondent.

PER CURIAM. Judgment affirmed, with costs.

PARKER, C. J., and GRAY, O'BRIEN, HAIGHT, MARTIN, VANN, and CULLEN, JJ., concur.

AMERICAN CASUALTY INS. CO. OF ONEONTA, Appellant, v. GREEN, Respondent. (Court of Appeals of New York. April 5, 1904.) Appeal from a judgment of the Appellate Division of the Supreme Court in the Third Judicial Department (70 App. Div. 267, 75 N. Y. Supp. 407), entered March 10, 1902, affirming a judgment in favor of defendant entered upon the report of a referee. T. B. Merchant and L. M. Merchant, for appellant. James T. Rogers, for respondent.

PER CURIAM. Judgment affirmed, with costs.

PARKER, C. J., and GRAY, O'BRIEN, HAIGHT, MARTIN, CULLEN, and WERNER, JJ., concur.

ANDREWS, Respondent, v. WESTERN NEW YORK & P. RY. CO., Appellant. (Court of Appeals of New York. May 17, 1904.) Appeal from a judgment of the Appellate Division of the Supreme Court in the Fourth Judicial Department (79 App. Div. 646, 80 N. Y. Supp. 1129), entered February 7, 1903, affirming a judgment in favor of plaintiff entered upon a verdict and an order denying a motion for a new trial. C. S. Cary, for appellant. J. H. Waring, for respondent.

PER CURIAM. Judgment affirmed, with costs.

PARKER, C. J., and GRAY, O'BRIEN, BARTLETT, and VANN, JJ., concur. WERNER, J., dissents. HAIGHT, J., not voting.

ARTHUR, Respondent, v. SIRE, Appellant. (Court of Appeals of New York. May 17, 1904.) Appeal from an order of the Appellate Division of the Supreme Court in the First Judicial Department (87 App. Div. 633, 84 N. Y. Supp. 1117), entered December 2, 1903, which affirmed an order of Special Term made pursuant to section 1947 of the Code of Civil Procedure. Franklin Bien, for appellant. William A. Keener and Leon Laski, for respondent.

PER CURIAM. Appeal dismissed, with costs.

PARKER, C. J., and GRAY, O'BRIEN, BARTLETT, HAIGHT, VANN, and WERNER, JJ., concur.

In re BAKER'S ESTATE. (Court of Appeals of New York. March 29, 1904.) Appeal from an order of the Appellate Division of the Supreme Court in the Fourth Judicial Department (83 App. Div. 530, 82 N. Y. Supp. 390), made May 5, 1903, which affirmed a decree of the Monroe county Surrogate's Court exempting a part of the estate of Henry B. Baker, deceased, from the payment of a transfer tax. William T. Plumb, for appellant. Charles M. Williams, for respondent.

PER CURIAM. Order affirmed, with costs, on opinion below.

PARKER, C. J., and GRAY, O'BRIEN, HAIGHT, MARTIN, CULLEN, and WERNER, JJ., concur.

BATES, Respondent, v. HOLBROOK et al., Appellants. (Court of Appeals of New York.

March 22, 1904.) Motion to dismiss an appeal from a judgment of the Appellate Division of the Supreme Court in the First Judicial Department entered January 26, 1904 (85 N. Y. Supp. 673), affirming a judgment in favor of plaintiff entered upon the report of a referee appointed to assess damages after the affirmance by the Court of Appeals (171 N. Y. 470, 64 N. E. 181) of an order of the Appellate Division reversing a judgment in favor of defendants (73 N. Y. Supp. 417), entered upon a dismissal of the complaint by the court on trial at Special Term (83 N. Y. Supp. 929), and granting a new trial and a direction for judgment absolute in favor of plaintiff. The motion was made upon the grounds that the appeal was improperly brought and was not authorized. Charles F. Brown, for the motion. F. E. Smith, opposed. No opinion. Motion granted, and appeal dismissed, with costs and $10 costs of motion.

BEALS et al., Appellants, v. FIDELITY & DEPOSIT CO. OF MARYLAND, Respondent, et al. (Court of Appeals of New York. April 5, 1904.) Appeal from an order of the Appellate Division of the Supreme Court in the Fourth Judicial Department (76 App. Div. 526, 78 N. Y. Supp. 584), entered November 29, 1902, reversing a judgment in favor of plaintiffs entered upon a verdict directed by the court and granting a new trial. August Becker, for appellants. Thomas C. Burke, for respondent.

PER CURIAM. Order affirmed, and judgment absolute ordered for defendant on the stipulation, with costs.

PARKER, C. J., and GRAY, O'BRIEN, BARTLETT, HAIGHT, MARTIN, and CULLEN, JJ., concur.

BELL, Respondent, v. MANHEIM et al., Appellants. (Court of Appeals of New York. April 26, 1904.) Appeal from a judgment of the Appellate Division of the Supreme Court in the First Judicial Department (84 App. Div. 641, 82 N. Y. Supp. 1094), entered June 10, 1903, affirming a judgment in favor of plaintiff entered upon a verdict and an order denying a motion for a new trial. Jacob Manheim, for appellants. Alfred R. Bunnell, for respondent.

PER CURIAM. Judgment affirmed, with costs.

PARKER, C. J., and GRAY, BARTLETT, HAIGHT, MARTIN, VANN, and WERNER, JJ., concur.

BENJAMIN et al. v. AMERICAN FIRE INS. CO. OF PHILADELPHIA et al. (Court of Appeals of New York. March 1, 1904.) Appeal from a judgment of the Appellate Division of the Supreme Court in the Second Judicial Department (80 App. Div. 631, 80 N. Y. Supp. 1130), entered February 25, 1903, affirming a judgment in favor of plaintiffs and defendant Diven, entered upon a verdict directed by the court. Michael H. Cardozo, for appellant. William B. Ellison and Arnold L. Davis, for respondents Benjamin and others. William W. Dewhurst, for respondent Diven.

PER CURIAM. Judgment affirmed, with costs, on opinion below.

PARKER, C. J., and GRAY, O'BRIEN, HAIGHT, MARTIN, VANN, and CULLEN, JJ., concur.

BENJAMIN et al. v. GREENWICH INS. CO. OF CITY OF NEW YORK et al. (Court of Appeal of New York. March 1, 1904.) Appeal from a judgment of the Appellate Division of the Supreme Court in the Second Judicial Department (80 App. Div. 631, 80 N. Y. Supp. 1130), entered February 25, 1903, affirming a judgment in favor of plaintiffs and defendant Diven, entered upon a verdict directed by the court. Michael H. Cardozo, for appellant Greenwich Ins. Co. William B. Ellison and Arnold L. Davis, for respondents Benjamin and others. William W. Dewhurst, for respondent Diven.

PER CURIAM. Judgment affirmed, with costs, on opinion below.

PARKER, C. J., and GRAY, O'BRIEN, HAIGHT, MARTIN, VANN, and CULLEN, JJ., concur.

BENJAMIN et al. v. INSURANCE CO. OF NORTH AMERICA et al. (Court of Appeals of New York. March 1, 1904.) Appeal from a judgment of the Appellate Division of the Supreme Court in the Second Judicial Department (80 App. Div. 631, 80 N. Y. Supp. 1130), entered February 25, 1903, affirming a judgment in favor of plaintiffs and defendant Diven, entered upon a verdict directed by the court. Michael H. Cardozo, for appellant. William B. Ellison and Arnold L. Davis, for respondents Benjamin and others. William W. Dewhurst, for respondent Diven.

PER CURIAM. Judgment affirmed, with costs, on opinion below.

PARKER, C. J., and GRAY, O'BRIEN, HAIGHT, MARTIN, VANN, and CULLEN, JJ., concur.

BENJAMIN et al. v. PALATINE INS. CO., Limited, of LONDON, ENGLAND, et al. (Court of Appeals of New York. March 1, 1904.) Appeal from a judgment of the Appellate Division of the Supreme Court in the Second Judicial Department (80 App. Div. 260, 80 N. Y. Supp. 256), entered February 25, 1903, affirming a judgment in favor of plaintiffs and defendant Diven, entered upon a verdict directed by the court. John Notman, for appellant. William B. Ellison and Arnold L. Davis, for respondents Benjamin and others. William W. Dewhurst, for respondent Diven.

PER CURIAM. Judgment affirmed, with costs, on opinion below.

PARKER, C. J., and GRAY, O'BRIEN, HAIGHT, MARTIN, VANN, and CULLEN, JJ., concur.

BERBERICH, Respondent, v. SYRACUSE RAPID TRANSIT RY. CO., Appellant. (Court of Appeals of New York. April 8, 1904.) Appeal from a judgment of the Appellate Division of the Supreme Court in the Fourth Judicial Department (84 App. Div. 632, 82 N. Y. Supp. 1004), entered May 14, 1903, affirming a judgment in favor of plaintiff entered upon a verdict and an order denying a motion for a new trial. Charles E. Spencer, for appellant. Frank C. Sargent, for respondent.

PER CURIAM. Judgment affirmed, with costs.

PARKER, C. J., and GRAY, O'BRIEN, BARTLETT, HAIGHT, MARTIN, and CULLEN, JJ., concur.

BINGHAM, Respondent, v. HENDRIX et al., Appellants. (Court of Appeals of New York. April 26, 1904.) Appeal from a judgment of the Appellate Division of the Supreme Court in the Fourth Judicial Department (79 App. Div. 644, 80 N. Y. Supp. 1130), entered January 19, 1903, affirming a judgment of the Monroe County Court in favor of plaintiff entered upon a decision of the court on trial without a jury. William W. Webb, for appellants. John H. Hopkins, for respondent.

PER CURIAM. Judgment affirmed, with costs.

PARKER, C. J., and BARTLETT, HAIGHT, VANN, CULLEN, and WERNER, JJ., concur. O'BRIEN, J., not voting.

BLUMENBERG PRESS, Appellant, v. MUTUAL MERCANTILE AGENCY, Respondent. (Court of Appeals of New York. May 3, 1904.) No opinion. Motion for reargument denied, with $10 costs. See 177 N. Y. 362, 69 N. E. 641.

BOLSTER, Respondent, v. ITHACA ST. RY. CO., Appellant. (Court of Appeals of New York. March 4, 1904.) Appeal from an order of the Appellate Division of the Supreme Court in the Third Judicial Department (79 App. Div. 239, 79 N. Y. Supp. 597), entered January 21, 1903, reversing a judgment in favor of defendant entered upon a dismissal of the complaint by the court at a Trial Term and granting a new trial. E. A. Denton, for appellant. Myron N. Tompkins, for respondent.

PER CURIAM. Order affirmed, and judgment absolute ordered for plaintiff on the stipulation, with costs.

PARKER, C. J., and GRAY, HAIGHT, MARTIN, VANN, CULLEN, and WERNER, JJ., concur.

BOSSERT et al., Respondents, v. POERSCHKE, Appellant. (Court of Appeals of New York. March 4, 1904.) Appeal from a judgment of the Appellate Division of the Supreme Court in the Second Judicial Department (80 App. Div. 641, 81 N. Y. Supp. 1119), entered March 16, 1903, affirming a judgment in favor of plaintiffs entered upon the report of a referee. Jacob Fromme, for appellant. J. Stewart Ross and Frank Obernier, for respondents.

PER CURIAM. Judgment affirmed, with costs.

PARKER, C. J., and HAIGHT, MARTIN, VANN, CULLEN, and WERNER, JJ., concur. GRAY, J., absent.

BRISTOL, Respondent, v. MENTE et al., Appellants. (Court of Appeals of New York. April 26, 1904.) Appeal from a judgment of the Appellate Division of the Supreme Court in the Second Judicial Department (79 App. Div. 67, 80 N. Y. Supp. 52), entered February 11, 1903, affirming a judgment in favor of plaintiff entered upon a verdict and an order denying a motion for a new trial. Dean Emery and Frederic R. Kellogg, for appellants. William D. Sawyer and Henry P. Driggs, for respondent.

PER CURIAM. Judgment affirmed, with costs.

PARKER, C. J., and O'BRIEN, BARTLETT, VANN, and WERNER, JJ., concur. HAIGHT and CULLEN, JJ., dissent.

BRONNER, Appellant, v. FULLER et al., Respondents. (Court of Appeals of New York. April 26, 1904.) Appeal from a judgment of the Appellate Division of the Supreme Court in the Fourth Judicial Department (79 App. Div. 645, 80 N. Y. Supp. 1131), entered March 6, 1903, affirming a judgment in favor of defendants entered upon a decision of the court on trial at Special Term. Frank Hopkins, for appellant. V. K. Kellogg, for respondents.

PER CURIAM. Judgment affirmed, with costs.

PARKER, C. J., and O'BRIEN, BARTLETT, HAIGHT, VANN, CULLEN, and WERNER, JJ., concur.

BROOKLYN HILLS IMP. CO., Appellant, v. NEW YORK & R. B. RY. CO., Respondent. (Court of Appeals of New York. April 26, 1904.) Appeal from a judgment of the Appellate Division of the Supreme Court in the Second Judicial Department (80 App. Div. 508, 81 N. Y. Supp. 187), entered April 6, 1903, affirming a judgment for costs in favor of defendant, entered upon a verdict for nominal damages in favor of plaintiff, and an order denying a motion for a new trial. John H. Corwin, for appellant. Edward M. Shepard, Joseph F. Keany, and William J. Kelly, for respondent.

PER CURIAM. Judgment affirmed, with costs.

GRAY, BARTLETT, HAIGHT, MARTIN, VANN, and WERNER, JJ., concur. PARKER, C. J., not voting.

BROOKLYN & R. B. R. CO., Appellant, v. LONG ISLAND R. CO. et al., Respondents. (Court of Appeals of New York. April 26, 1904.) Appeal from an order of the Appellate Division of the Supreme Court in the Second Judicial Department (72 App. Div. 496, 76 N. Y. Supp. 777), entered May 29, 1902, reversing a judgment in favor of plaintiff entered upon a decision of the court on trial at Special Term and granting a new trial. Augustus Van Wyck, George W. Wingate, and Charles W. Church, Jr., for appellant. Edward M. Shepard and Joseph F. Keany, for respondents.

PER CURIAM. Appeal dismissed, with costs.

PARKER, C. J., and GRAY, BARTLETT, HAIGHT, MARTIN, VANN, and WERNER, JJ., concur.

CALEDONIA SPRINGS ICE CO., Respondent, v. FOREST, Appellant. (Court of Appeals of New York. March 29, 1904.) Appeal from a judgment of the Appellate Division of the Supreme Court in the Fourth Judicial Department (81 App. Div. 654, 81 N. Y. Supp. 1120), entered March 16, 1903, affirming a judgment in favor of plaintiff entered upon a verdict and the report of a referee. Merton E. Lewis, for appellant. George D. Reed, for respondent.

PER CURIAM. Judgment affirmed, with costs.

O'BRIEN, BARTLETT, HAIGHT, VANN, CULLEN, and WERNER, JJ., concur. PARKER, C. J., absent.

CHISHOLM, Respondent, v. TOPLITZ, Appellant. (Court of Appeals of New York. April 26, 1904.) Appeal from a judgment of the Appellate Division of the Supreme Court in the First Judicial Department (82 App. Div. 346, 82 N. Y. Supp. 1081), entered May 18, 1903, affirming a judgment in favor of plaintiff entered upon a decision of the court at a Trial Term without a jury. Richard L. Sweezy, for appellant. William H. Van Benschoeten and John M. Bowers, for respondent.

PER CURIAM. Judgment affirmed, with costs, on opinion below.

PARKER, C. J., and BARTLETT, HAIGHT, VANN, CULLEN, and WERNER, JJ., concur. O'BRIEN, J., not voting.

CITY OF BUFFALO, Appellant, v. DELAWARE, L. & W. R. CO., Respondent. (Court of Appeals of New York. March 16, 1904.) Appeal from so much of a judgment of the Appellate Division of the Supreme Court in the Fourth Judicial Department (68 App. Div. 488, 74 N. Y. Supp. 843), entered February 19, 1902, as affirmed a judgment in favor of defendant entered upon a decision of the court on trial at Special Term. Charles L. Feldman, for appellant. John G. Milburn, for respondent.

PER CURIAM. Judgment affirmed, with costs.

PARKER, C. J., and GRAY, O'BRIEN, BARTLETT, and VANN, JJ., concur. MARTIN and WERNER, JJ., absent.

CITY OF NEW YORK, Respondent, v. UNITED STATES TRUST CO. OF NEW YORK, Appellant, et al. (Court of Appeals of New York. March 4, 1904.) Appeal from a judgment of the Appellate Division of the Supreme Court in the First Judicial Department (78 App. Div. 366, 79 N. Y. Supp. 1010), entered February 6, 1903, which affirmed a judgment of Special Term impressing a trust upon certain moneys in the hands of the appellant herein belonging to the estate of Louis J. Jordan, deceased. Edward W. Sheldon and George L. Shearer, for appellant. John J. Delany, Corp. Counsel (Theodore Connoly and Charles A. O'Neil, of counsel), for respondent.

PER CURIAM. Judgment affirmed, with costs.

PARKER, C. J., and GRAY, O'BRIEN, HAIGHT, MARTIN, VANN, and CULLEN, JJ., concur.

CLARK, Appellant, v. CROSS, Respondent. (Court of Appeals of New York. May 17, 1904.) Appeal from a judgment of the Appellate Division of the Supreme Court in the Fourth Judicial Department (77 App. Div. 632, 79 N. Y. Supp. 1129), entered November 26, 1902, upon an order affirming a judgment in favor of defendant entered upon a verdict and an order denying a motion for a new trial. James A. Ward, for appellant. Thomas Burns, for respondent.

PER CURIAM. Order affirmed, with costs.

PARKER, C. J., and GRAY, BARTLETT, HAIGHT, VANN, and WERNER, JJ., concur. O'BRIEN, J., not voting.

CLARK, Appellant, v. RUMSEY et al., Respondents. (Court of Appeals of New York. April 26, 1904.) Appeal from an order of the Appellate Division of the Supreme Court in the Fourth Judicial Department (59 App. Div. 435, 69 N. Y. Supp. 102), entered March 27, 1901, reversing a judgment in favor of plaintiff entered upon a decision of the court at a Trial Term without a jury and granting a new trial. John E. Pound, for appellant. Ansley Wilcox, for respondents.

PER CURIAM. Appeal dismissed, with costs.

PARKER, C. J., and GRAY, BARTLETT, HAIGHT, MARTIN, VANN, and WERNER, JJ., concur.

COMSTOCK, Respondent, v. GOFF, Appellant. (Court of Appeals of New York. March 15, 1904.) Appeal from a judgment of the Appellate Division of the Supreme Court in the Fourth Judicial Department (79 App. Div. 645, 80 N. Y. Supp. 1182), entered February 2, 1903, affirming a judgment in favor of plaintiff entered upon a verdict directed by the court and an order denying a motion for a new trial. Frank M. Goff, for appellant. Nelson E. Spencer, for respondent.

PER CURIAM. Judgment affirmed, with costs.

O'BRIEN, BARTLETT, HAIGHT, VANN, CULLEN, and WERNER, JJ., concur. PARKER, C. J., absent.

CONSTABLE et al., Appellants, v. ROSENER, Respondent. (Court of Appeals of New York. April 8, 1904.) Appeal from a judgment of the Appellate Division of the Supreme Court in the First Judicial Department (82 App. Div. 155, 81 N. Y. Supp. 376), entered April 16, 1903, upon an order which reversed an order of the Appellate Term reversing a judgment of the Municipal Court of the City of New York in favor of defendant, and affirmed said Municipal Court judgment. Jesse S. Epstein and Mark H. Ellison, for appellants. William H. Maginnis, for respondent.

PER CURIAM. Judgment affirmed, with costs, on opinion below.

PARKER, C. J., and GRAY, O'BRIEN, BARTLETT, HAIGHT, MARTIN, and CULLEN, JJ., concur.

CORWIN, Respondent, v. ERIE R. CO., Appellant. (Court of Appeals of New York. April 8, 1904.) Appeal from a judgment of the Appellate Division of the Supreme Court in the Second Judicial Department (84 App. Div. 555, 82 N. Y. Supp. 753), entered June 13, 1903, affirming a judgment in favor of plaintiff entered upon a decision of the court on trial at Special Term. Henry Bacon, John J. Beattie, and Joseph Merritt, for appellant. John C. R. Taylor, for respondent.

PER CURIAM. Judgment affirmed, with costs.

PARKER, C. J., and GRAY, O'BRIEN, BARTLETT, HAIGHT, MARTIN, and CULLEN, JJ., concur.

CORWIN, Respondent, v. ERIE R. CO., Appellant. (Court of Appeals of New York. May 3, 1904.) No opinion. Motion for reargument denied, with $10 costs. See 178 N. Y. —, ubi supra.

COVERLY et al., Appellants, v. TERMINAL WAREHOUSE CO., Respondent. (Court of Appeals of New York. April 26, 1904.) Appeal from a judgment of the Appellate Division of the Supreme Court in the First Judicial Department (85 App. Div. 488, 83 N. Y. Supp. 369), entered July 29, 1903, affirming a judgment in favor of defendant entered upon a verdict directed by the court. Wallace MacFarlane and Everett Masten, for appellants. John M. Bowers, for respondent.

PER CURIAM. Judgment affirmed, with costs.

PARKER, C. J., and O'BRIEN, BARTLETT, HAIGHT, VANN, CULLEN, and WERNER, JJ., concur.

DE COPPET et al., Respondents v. NEW YORK CENT. & H. R. R. CO. et al., Appellants. (Court of Appeals of New York. May 3, 1904.) Appeal from so much of a judgment of the Appellate Division of the Supreme Court in the Second Judicial Department (88 App. Div. 615, 84 N. Y. Supp. 1123), entered November 24, 1903, as affirms that part of a judgment in favor of plaintiffs which includes an additional allowance of $2,000 to the plaintiffs' attorney. John F. Brennan and Charles C.

Paulding, for appellants. Willard Parker Butler and Edwin T. Rice, for respondents.

PER CURIAM. Judgment, so far as appealed from, reversed, with costs, on opinion in Standard Trust Co. v. N. Y. C. & H. R. R. R. Co., 178 N. Y. —, 70 N. E. 925.

PARKER, C. J., and O'BRIEN, BARTLETT, VANN, and WERNER, JJ., concur. GRAY, J., not sitting.

DEVANEY, Respondent, v. DEGNON-McLEAN CONST. CO., Appellant. (Court of Appeals of New York. May 20, 1904.) Appeal from a judgment of the Appellate Division of the Supreme Court in the Second Judicial Department (79 App. Div. 62, 79 N. Y. Supp. 1050), entered January 26, 1903, affirming a judgment in favor of plaintiff entered upon a verdict and an order denying a motion for a new trial. L. Sidney Carrère, for appellant. George W. Roderick, for respondent.

PER CURIAM. Judgment affirmed, with costs.

PARKER, C. J., and GRAY, VANN, and WERNER, JJ., concur. O'BRIEN, J., not voting. BARTLETT, J., dissents. HAIGHT, J., absent.

DUNN, Sheriff, Respondent, v. NATIONAL SURETY CO., Appellant. (Court of Appeals of New York. March 4, 1904.) Appeal from a judgment of the Appellate Division of the Supreme Court in the First Judicial Department (80 App. Div. 605, 80 N. Y. Supp. 744), entered March 16, 1903, affirming a judgment in favor of plaintiff entered upon a verdict and an order denying a motion for a new trial. Charles E. Hughes and Arthur C. Rounds, for appellant. Philip J. Britt, for respondent.

PER CURIAM. Judgment affirmed, with costs.

PARKER, C. J., and HAIGHT, MARTIN, VANN, and WERNER, JJ., concur. GRAY and CULLEN, JJ., dissent.

EAGLE IRON WORKS, Respondent, v. FARLEY, Appellant. (Court of Appeals of New York. April 26, 1904.) Appeal from a judgment of the Appellate Division of the Supreme Court in the Second Judicial Department (83 App. Div. 82, 82 N. Y. Supp. 503), entered June 3, 1903, affirming a judgment in favor of plaintiff entered upon a decision of the court on trial at Special Term. Paul Eugene Jones, for appellant. I. N. Sievwright, for respondent.

PER CURIAM. Judgment affirmed, with costs.

PARKER, C. J., and GRAY, BARTLETT, HAIGHT, MARTIN, VANN, and WERNER, JJ., concur.

FARRELL, Respondent, v. MANHATTAN RY. CO. et al., Appellants. (Court of Appeals of New York. April 26, 1904.) Appeal from a judgment of the Appellate Division of the Supreme Court in the First Judicial Department (83 App. Div. 393, 82 N. Y. Supp. 334), entered May 25, 1903, affirming a judgment in favor of plaintiff entered upon a decision of the court on trial at Special Term. Sherrill Babcock, Julien T. Davies, and Charles A. Gardiner, for appellants. Edwin M. Felt and Leo C. Dessar, for respondent.

PER CURIAM. Judgment affirmed, with costs.

PARKER, C. J., and GRAY, BARTLETT, HAIGHT, MARTIN, VANN, and WERNER, JJ., concur.

FASY et al., Respondents, v. INTERNATIONAL NAV. CO., Appellant. (Court of Appeals of New York. March 1, 1904.) Appeal from a judgment of the Appellate Division of the Supreme Court in the First Judicial Department (77 App. Div. 469, 79 N. Y. Supp. 1103), entered January 2, 1903, affirming a judgment in favor of plaintiffs entered upon a verdict directed by the court and an order denying a motion for a new trial. Henry Galbraith Ward and Norman B. Beecher, for appellant. Joseph P. Osborne, for respondents.

PER CURIAM. Judgment affirmed, with costs.

PARKER, C. J., and GRAY, O'BRIEN, HAIGHT, MARTIN, VANN, and CULLEN, JJ., concur.

FORD, Appellant, v. BOARD OF SUP'RS OF DELAWARE COUNTY, Respondent. (Court of Appeals of New York. May 17, 1904.) Appeal from an order of the Appellate Division of the Supreme Court in the Third Judicial Department (92 App. Div. 119, 87 N. Y. Supp. 407), entered March 21, 1904, which affirmed an order of Special Term denying a motion for a peremptory writ of mandamus to compel defendant to audit a claim of relator. Charles L. Pashley, for appellant. George A. Fisher, for respondent.

PER CURIAM. Appeal dismissed, with costs.

PARKER, C. J., and GRAY, O'BRIEN, BARTLETT, HAIGHT, VANN, and WERNER, JJ., concur.

FORSYTH, Appellant, v. GAUNTLETT et al., Respondents. (Court of Appeals of New York. April 26, 1904.) Appeal from a judgment of the Appellate Division of the Supreme Court in the Third Judicial Department (79 App. Div. 642, 80 N. Y. Supp. 1135), entered February 9, 1903, affirming a judgment in favor of defendant entered upon a dismissal of the complaint by the court on trial at Special Term. M. S. Lynch, for appellant. William Nelson Noble, for respondents.

PER CURIAM. Judgment affirmed, with costs.

PARKER, C. J., and GRAY, BARTLETT, HAIGHT, MARTIN, VANN, and WERNER, JJ., concur.

FOWLER, Appellant, v. MANHEIMER, Respondent. (Court of Appeals of New York. April 5, 1904.) Appeal from a judgment of the Appellate Division of the Supreme Court in the First Judicial Department (70 App. Div. 56, 75 N. Y. Supp. 17), entered March 22, 1902, affirming a judgment in favor of defendant entered upon a dismissal of the complaint by the court on trial at Special Term. Abel E. Blackmar, for appellant. Samson Lachman and Theodore Baumeister, for respondent.

PER CURIAM. Judgment affirmed, with costs.

PARKER, C. J., and GRAY, O'BRIEN, HAIGHT, MARTIN, CULLEN, and WERNER, JJ., concur.

GEORGE BORGFELDT & CO., Appellant, v. O'NEILL et al., Respondents. (Court of Appeals of New York. March 1, 1904.) Appeal from a judgment of the Appellate Division of the Supreme Court in the First Judicial Department (81 App. Div. 636, 81 N. Y. Supp. 1119), entered March 31, 1903, affirming a judgment in favor of defendants, entered upon a dismissal of the complaint by the court at a Trial Term without a jury. James Dunne, for appellant. Isaac Fromme and Edward W. S. Johnston, for respondents.

PER CURIAM. Judgment affirmed, with costs.

PARKER, C. J., and GRAY, O'BRIEN, HAIGHT, MARTIN, VANN, and CULLEN, JJ., concur.

GERMAN-AMERICAN BANK OF TONAWANDA, Appellant, v. SCHWINGER, Respondent. (Court of Appeals of New York. March 29, 1904.) Appeal from a judgment, entered October 8, 1902, upon an order of the Appellate Division of the Supreme Court in the Fourth Judicial Department (75 App. Div. 393, 78 N. Y. Supp. 38), overruling plaintiff's exceptions, ordered to be heard in the first instance by the Appellate Division, denying a motion for a new trial and directing judgment for defendant upon the verdict. Richard Crowley, for appellant. Nathaniel Norton, for respondent.

PER CURIAM. Judgment affirmed, with costs.

PARKER, C. J., and O'BRIEN, BARTLETT, MARTIN, VANN, and WERNER, JJ., concur. GRAY, J., absent.

GILLOON, Clerk of Municipal Court, Respondent, v. WOOD, Appellant. (Court of Appeals of New York. March 29, 1904.) Appeal from an order of the Appellate Division of the Supreme Court in the First Judicial Department (86 N. Y. Supp. 1135), entered February 27, 1904, which affirmed an order of Special Term requiring the appellant herein to deliver to the respondent all the books and papers appertaining to the office of clerk of the Municipal Court of the City of New York for the Twelfth district, borough of Manhattan. Henry A. Forster and Robert C. McCormick, for appellant. Louis W. Stotesbury, for respondent.

PER CURIAM. Order affirmed, with costs.

PARKER, C. J., and GRAY, O'BRIEN, HAIGHT, MARTIN, CULLEN, and WERNER, JJ., concur.

In re GOETZ et al. (Court of Appeals of New York. May 10, 1904.) Appeal from an order of the Appellate Division of the Supreme Court in the First Judicial Department (87 App. Div. 631, 84 N. Y. Supp. 1127), entered November 12, 1903, which affirmed a decree of the New York county Surrogate's Court settling the accounts of the executors and trustees herein. Thomas F. Byrne, for appellants. William H. Hamilton, for respondents.

PER CURIAM. Order affirmed, with costs.

GRAY, O'BRIEN, BARTLETT, HAIGHT, VANN, and WERNER, JJ., concur. PARKER, C. J., not voting.

GRIGGS, Appellant, v. GRIGGS, Respondent. (Court of Appeals of New York. March 29, 1904.) Appeal from a judgment of the Appellate Division of the Supreme Court in the Second Judicial Department (80 App. Div. 339, 80 N. Y. Supp. 724), entered March 17, 1903, affirming a judgment in favor of defendant entered upon a dismissal of the complaint by the court at a Trial Term and an order denying a motion for a new trial. Edward W. S. Johnston and Howard Thornton, for appellant. James G. Graham and A. H. F. Seeger, for respondent.

PER CURIAM. Judgment affirmed, with costs.

O'BRIEN, BARTLETT, HAIGHT, VANN, CULLEN, and WERNER, JJ., concur. PARKER, C. J., absent.

HADDOCK, Respondent, v. HADDOCK, Appellant. (Court of Appeals of New York. March 15, 1904.) Appeal from a judgment of the Appellate Division of the Supreme Court in the First Judicial Department (76 App. Div. 620, 79 N. Y. Supp. 1133), entered December 5, 1902, affirming a judgment in favor of plaintiff entered upon the report of a referee. Charles W. Fuller and William H. Willits, for appellant. Henry B. B. Stapler and William T. Tomlinson, for respondent.

PER CURIAM. Judgment affirmed, with costs.

PARKER, C. J., and GRAY, O'BRIEN, BARTLETT, MARTIN, VANN, and WERNER, JJ., concur.

HAGAN, Appellant, v. WARD et al., Respondents. (Court of Appeals of New York. March 15, 1904.) Appeal from a judgment of the Appellate Division of the Supreme Court in the First Judicial Department (86 App. Div. 620, 83 N. Y. Supp. 436), entered July 22, 1903, affirming a judgment in favor of defendants entered upon a dismissal of the complaint by the court on trial at Special Term. Albert Stickney and Everett V. Abbott, for appellant. Elihu Root and George P. Hotaling, for respondents.

PER CURIAM. In Hagan v. Sone, 174 N. Y. 317, 66 N. E. 973, the trial court directed a verdict for the defendant, upon which judgment was entered and affirmed by the Appellate Division. On appeal this court held that when evidence is given of such a character that different inferences may fairly and reasonably be drawn from it, the fact must be determined by the jury. In the case before us the trial judge, on evidence of a similar character, has decided the issues in favor of the defendants, upon which decision judgment was entered and affirmed by the Appellate Division. The facts as thus settled are binding on this court. The judgment should be affirmed, with costs to defendant Sone. Judgment affirmed.

PARKER, C. J., and GRAY, O'BRIEN, BARTLETT, MARTIN, VANN, and WERNER, JJ., concur.

HAGAN, Appellant, v. WARD et al., Respondents. (Court of Appeals of New York. April 8, 1904.) No opinion. Motion for reargument denied, with $10 costs. See 178 N. Y. —, ubi supra.

HARMS, Respondent, v. HORGAN et al., Appellants. (Court of Appeals of New York. March 22, 1904.) Appeal from a judgment of the Appellate Division of the Supreme Court in the First Judicial Department (82 App. Div. 636, 81 N. Y. Supp. 1128), entered May 7, 1903, affirming a judgment in favor of plaintiff entered upon the report of a referee. Joseph E. Bullen, for appellants. Edward Browne, for respondent.

PER CURIAM. Judgment affirmed, with costs.

O'BRIEN, BARTLETT, HAIGHT, VANN, CULLEN, and WERNER, JJ., concur. PARKER, C. J., absent.

HENDRICK et al., Appellants, v. PATTERSON, Respondent, et al. (Court of Appeals of New York. April 5, 1904.) Appeal from a judgment of the Appellate Division of the Supreme Court in the Third Judicial Department (61 App. Div. 616, 70 N. Y. Supp. 1140), entered May 17, 1901, affirming a judgment in favor of defendant entered upon a dismissal of the complaint by the court on trial at Special Term. John Conboy, for appellants. E. H. Neary, for respondent.

PER CURIAM. Judgment affirmed, with costs.

PARKER, C. J., and GRAY, HAIGHT, MARTIN, CULLEN and WERNER, JJ., concur. O'BRIEN, J., not voting.

HERMAN, Appellant, v. DANIELS, Respondent. (Court of Appeals of New York. May 10, 1904.) Motion to dismiss an appeal from a judgment of the Appellate Division of the Supreme Court in the First Judicial Department (87 N. Y. Supp. 1130), entered April 13, 1904, affirming a judgment in favor of defendant entered upon a dismissal of the complaint by the court on trial at Special Term. The motion was made upon the grounds that the findings of fact were unanimously affirmed by the Appellate Division, and there was no question of law involved of sufficient doubt as to require its review by the Court of Appeals. George S. Daniels, for the motion. Herbert J. Hindes, opposed. No opinion. Motion granted, and appeal dismissed, with costs and $10 costs of motion.

HERNE, Respondent, v. LIEBLER et al., Appellants. (Court of Appeals of New York. April 26, 1904.) Appeal from a judgment, entered June 11, 1903, upon an order of the Appellate Division of the Supreme Court in the First Judicial Department (84 App. Div. 641, 82 N. Y. Supp. 1102), which affirmed an order of Special Term granting an injunction restraining defendants from producing a certain play. Howe & Hummel, for appellants. Max D. Josephson, for respondent.

PER CURIAM. Judgment affirmed, with costs.

PARKER, C. J., and O'BRIEN, BARTLETT, HAIGHT, VANN, CULLEN, and WERNER, JJ., concur.

HERNE, Respondent, v. LIEBLER et al., Appellants. (Court of Appeals of New York. April 26, 1904.) Appeal from a judgment of the Appellate Division of the Supreme Court in the First Judicial Department (84 App. Div. 641, 82 N. Y. Supp. 1102), entered June 11, 1903, affirming a judgment in favor of plaintiff entered upon a verdict directed by the court. Howe & Hummel, for appellants. Max D. Josephson, for respondent.

PER CURIAM. Judgment affirmed, with costs.

PARKER, C. J., and O'BRIEN, BARTLETT, HAIGHT, VANN, CULLEN, and WERNER, JJ., concur.

HILTZ, Respondent, v. FOWLER, Appellant. (Court of Appeals of New York. April 26, 1904.) Appeal from a judgment of the Appellate Division of the Supreme Court in the Second Judicial Department (83 App. Div. 634, 81 N. Y. Supp. 1129), entered June 25, 1903, affirming a judgment of the Westchester County Court in favor of plaintiff entered upon a verdict and an order denying a motion for a new trial. William Riley, for appellant. Charles A. Van Auken and William S. Beers, for respondent.

PER CURIAM. Judgment affirmed, with costs.

PARKER, C. J., and GRAY, BARTLETT, HAIGHT, MARTIN, VANN, and WERNER, JJ., concur.

HOLLAND TRUST CO., Appellant, v. SUTHERLAND, Respondent. (Court of Appeals of New York. March 22, 1904.) No opinion. Motion for reargument denied, with $10 costs. See 177 N. Y. 327, 69 N. E. 647.

HOPPER, Respondent, v. EMPIRE CITY SUBWAY CO., Limited, Appellant. (Court of Appeals of New York. April 8, 1904.) Appeal from a judgment of the Appellate Division of the Supreme Court in the First Judicial Department (78 App. Div. 637, 79 N. Y. Supp. 907), entered January 24, 1903, affirming a judgment in favor of plaintiff entered upon a verdict and an order denying a motion for a new trial. Henry A. Powell, for appellant. Moses Weinman and Abraham Benedict, for respondent.

PER CURIAM. Judgment affirmed, with costs.

PARKER, C. J., and GRAY, O'BRIEN, BARTLETT, HAIGHT, MARTIN, and CULLEN, JJ., concur.

HUDSON RIVER WATER POWER CO., Appellant, v. GLENS FALLS GAS & ELECTRIC LIGHT CO., Respondent, et al. (Court of Appeals of New York. May 10, 1904.) Appeal, by permission, from a judgment entered February 3, 1904, upon an order of the Appellate Division of the Supreme Court in the Third Judicial Department (90 App. Div. 513, 85 N. Y. Supp. 577), which reversed an interlocutory judgment of Special Term sustaining a demurrer to a counterclaim and overruled said demurrer. The following question was certified: "Does the counterclaim set forth in the amended answer of the defendant Glens Falls Gas & Electric Light Company state facts sufficient to constitute a cause of action?" Richard Lockhart Hand and Henry W. Williams, for appellant. Howard Taylor, for respondent Glens Falls Gas & Electric Light Co.

PER CURIAM. Question certified answered in the affirmative, and interlocutory judgment affirmed, with costs, with leave to serve reply within 20 days.

PARKER, C. J., and GRAY, HAIGHT, VANN, and WERNER, JJ., concur. O'BRIEN and BARTLETT, JJ., dissent.

INSURANCE PRESS, Appellant, v. MONTAUK FIRE DETECTING WIRE CO. et al., Respondents. (Court of Appeals of New York. May 20, 1904.) Appeal from a judgment of the Appellate Division of the Supreme Court in the First Judicial Department (83 App. Div. 239, 82 N. Y. Supp. 104), entered May 18, 1903, affirming a judgment in favor of defendants entered upon a dismissal of the complaint by the court at Special Term. A. Walker Otis, for appellant. Theodore B. Chancellor, William M. K. Olcott, Henderson Peck, Irving L. Ernst, and Henry L. Washburn, for respondents.

PER CURIAM. Judgment affirmed, with costs.

GRAY, O'BRIEN, BARTLETT, MARTIN, VANN, and CULLEN, JJ., concur. PARKER, C. J., not voting.

IZZO, Respondent, v. LUDINGTON, Appellant. (Court of Appeals of New York. May 20, 1904.) Appeal from a judgment of the Appellate Division of the Supreme Court in the Third Judicial Department (79 App. Div. 272, 79 N. Y. Supp. 744), entered January 19, 1903, affirming a judgment in favor of plaintiff entered upon a verdict and an order denying a motion for a new trial. Clarence W. McKay, for appellant. Robert O. Bascom, for respondent.

PER CURIAM. Judgment affirmed, with costs.

PARKER, C. J., and GRAY, O'BRIEN, BARTLETT, MARTIN, VANN, and CULLEN, JJ., concur.

JACKSON, Appellant, v. VOLKENING, Respondent. (Court of Appeals of New York. March 16, 1904.) Appeal from an order of the Appellate Division of the Supreme Court in the First Judicial Department (81 App. Div. 36, 80 N. Y. Supp. 1102), entered March 19, 1903, reversing a judgment in favor of plaintiff entered upon a verdict directed by the court and granting a new trial. Frederick Hulse and Ernest F. Eidlitz, for appellant. Carlisle Norwood, for respondent.

PER CURIAM. Order affirmed, and judgment absolute ordered for defendant on the stipulation, with costs.

O'BRIEN, BARTLETT, HAIGHT, VANN, CULLEN, and WERNER, JJ., concur. PARKER, C. J., absent.

JONES, Respondent, v. CITY OF BUFFALO, Appellant. (Court of Appeals of New York. May 3, 1904.) No opinion. Motion for reargument denied, with $10 costs. See 178 N. Y. 45, 70 N. E. 99.

KAMINSKI, Respondent, v. SCHEFER et al., Appellants. (Court of Appeals of New York. March 22, 1904.) Appeal from a judgment of the Appellate Division of the Supreme Court in the First Judicial Department (78 App. Div. 644, 80 N. Y. Supp. 1138), entered February 5, 1903, affirming a judgment in favor of plaintiff entered upon a verdict directed by the court and an order denying a motion for a new trial. Alexander Blumenstiel, for appellants. Otto Horwitz, for respondent.

PER CURIAM. Judgment affirmed, with costs.

O'BRIEN, BARTLETT, HAIGHT, VANN, CULLEN and WERNER, JJ., concur. PARKER, C. J., absent.

KIRKWOOD, Appellant, v. SMITH, Respondent, et al. (Court of Appeals of New York. April 5, 1904.) Appeal from a judgment of the Appellate Division of the Supreme Court in the Second Judicial Department (82 App. Div. 411, 81 N. Y. Supp. 891), entered April 28, 1903, affirming a judgment in favor of defendant entered upon a dismissal of the complaint by the court on trial at Special Term. Edward J. McCrossin, for appellant. Charles De Hart Brower and William R. Hill, for respondent Smith.

PER CURIAM. Judgment affirmed, with costs.

PARKER, C. J., and GRAY, O'BRIEN, BARTLETT, HAIGHT, MARTIN, and CULLEN, JJ., concur.

KIRSOP, Respondent, v. MUTUAL LIFE INS. CO., Appellant. (Court of Appeals of New York. April 28, 1904.) Appeal from an order of the Appellate Division of the Supreme Court in the First Judicial Department (87 App. Div. 170, 84 N. Y. Supp. 95), entered November 5, 1903, which reversed an order of Special Term granting a motion to interplead a claimant of the proceeds of a policy of life insurance issued by the defendant. Charles E. Hotchkiss, Julien T. Davies, and Garrard Glenn, for appellant. Benjamin E. De Groot, for respondent.

PER CURIAM. Appeal dismissed, with costs.

PARKER, C. J., and GRAY, O'BRIEN, BARTLETT, HAIGHT, VANN, and WERNER, JJ., concur.

KRAUSE, Respondent, v. RUTHERFORD et al., Appellants. (Court of Appeals of New York. April 5, 1904.) Appeal from a judgment of the Appellate Division of the Supreme Court in the Third Judicial Department (81 App. Div. 341, 81 N. Y. Supp. 465), entered March 18, 1903, affirming a judgment in favor of plaintiff entered upon a decision of the court at a Trial Term. E. H. Hanford and E. A. Mackey, for appellants. George W. Youmans and Frederick W. Youmans, for respondent.

PER CURIAM. Judgment affirmed, with costs.

PARKER, C. J., and GRAY, O'BRIEN, BARTLETT, HAIGHT, MARTIN, and CULLEN, JJ., concur.

LANDUSKY, Respondent, v. BEIRNE, Appellant. (Court of Appeals of New York. March 4, 1904.) Appeal from a judgment of the Appellate Division of the Supreme Court in the Second Judicial Department (80 App. Div. 272, 80 N. Y. Supp. 238), entered February 20, 1903, affirming a judgment in favor of plaintiff entered upon a decision of the court on trial at Special Term. Lewis E. Carr and W. A. Parshall, for appellant. Frank Lybolt, for respondent.

PER CURIAM. Judgment affirmed, with costs, on opinion below.

GRAY, O'BRIEN, HAIGHT, MARTIN, VANN, and CULLEN, JJ., concur. PARKER, C. J., absent.

LANE, Respondent, v. BROOKLYN HEIGHTS R. CO., Appellant. (Court of Appeals of New York. May 20, 1904.) Appeal from a judgment of the Appellate Division of the Supreme Court in the Second Judicial Department (85 App. Div. 85, 82 N. Y. Supp. 1057), entered June 22, 1903, affirming a judgment in favor of plaintiff entered upon a verdict and an order denying a motion for a new trial. I. R. Oeland and George D. Yeomans, for appellant. James C. Cropsey, for respondent.

PER CURIAM. Judgment affirmed, with costs.

O'BRIEN, BARTLETT, MARTIN, VANN, and CULLEN, JJ., concur. PARKER, C. J., and GRAY, J., not voting.

LEEDS, Respondent, v. NEW YORK TELEPHONE CO., Appellant. (Court of Appeals of New York. May 3, 1904.) No opinion. Motion for reargument denied, with $10 costs. See 178 N. Y. 118, 70 N. E. 219.

LEVY, Respondent, v. LAFOUNTAIN et al., Appellants. (Court of Appeals of New York. March 15, 1904.) Appeal from a judgment of the Appellate Division of the Supreme Court in the Third Judicial Department (81 App. Div. 636, 81 N. Y. Supp. 468), entered March 20, 1903, affirming a judgment in favor of plaintiff entered upon a decision of the court at a Trial Term without a jury. S. L. Wheeler, for appellants. John B. Riley, for respondent.

PER CURIAM. Judgment affirmed, with costs.

PARKER, C. J., and GRAY, O'BRIEN, BARTLETT, MARTIN, VANN, and WERNER, JJ., concur.

LITTLE, Appellant, v. THIRD AVE. R. CO., Respondent. (Court of Appeals of New York. April 8, 1904.) Appeal from a judgment of the Appellate Division of the Supreme Court in the First Judicial Department (83 App. Div. 330, 82 N. Y. Supp. 55), entered June 12, 1903, affirming a judgment in favor of defendant entered upon a dismissal of the complaint by the court at a Trial Term. Jacob Fromme, for appellant. Charles F. Brown, Bayard H. Ames and Henry A. Robinson, for respondent.

PER CURIAM. Judgment affirmed, with costs.

PARKER, C. J., and GRAY, O'BRIEN, BARTLETT, HAIGHT, MARTIN, and CULLEN, JJ., concur.

LONG ISLAND LOAN & TRUST CO., Respondent, v. LONG ISLAND CITY & N. R. CO. et al., Appellants. (Court of Appeals of New York. April 18, 1904.) Appeal from a judgment of the Appellate Division of the Supreme Court in the Second Judicial Department (85 App. Div. 36, 82 N. Y. Supp. 644), entered June 13, 1903, affirming a judgment in favor of plaintiff entered upon a verdict. I. R. Oeland, William E. Stewart and George F. Hickey, for appellants. Melvin G. Palliser, Roger S. Baldwin and William M. Ingraham, for respondent.

PER CURIAM. Judgment affirmed, with costs, on opinion below.

PARKER, C. J., and GRAY, O'BRIEN, BARTLETT, HAIGHT, MARTIN, and CULLEN, JJ., concur.

LURMAN, Appellant, v. JARVIE et al., Respondents. (Court of Appeals of New York. March 15, 1904.) Appeal from a judgment of the Appellate Division of the Supreme Court in the First Judicial Department (82 App. Div. 37, 81 N. Y. Supp. 468), entered April 24, 1903, affirming a judgment in favor of defendants entered upon a dismissal of the complaint by the court at a Trial Term. Charles Stewart Davison, for appellant. Edward M. Shepard, for respondents.

PER CURIAM. Judgment affirmed, with costs.

O'BRIEN, BARTLETT, HAIGHT, VANN, CULLEN, and WERNER, JJ., concur. PARKER, C. J., absent.

In re McELHENY. (Court of Appeals of New York. May 10, 1904.) Appeal from an order of the Appellate Division of the Supreme Court in the First Judicial Department (91 App. Div. 131, 86 N. Y. Supp. 326), entered February 18, 1904, which reversed an order of Special Term confirming the report of a referee disallowing a claim of the respondent herein. William M. Bennett, for appellant. Willard Parker Butler and Sanford Robinson, for respondent.

PER CURIAM. Order affirmed, with costs.

PARKER, C. J., and GRAY, O'BRIEN, BARTLETT, HAIGHT, VANN, and WERNER, JJ., concur.

McNALLY, Respondent, v. PROVIDENCE WASHINGTON INS. CO., Appellant. (Court of Appeals of New York. March 1, 1904.) Appeal from a judgment of the Appellate Division of the Supreme Court in the Third Judicial Department (81 App. Div. 645, 81 N. Y. Supp. 1134), entered March 16, 1903, affirming judgment in favor of plaintiff entered upon decision of the court on trial at Special Term. Leroy S. Gove and James J. Macklin, for appellant. W. N. Gill, for respondent.

PER CURIAM. Judgment affirmed, with costs.

PARKER, C. J., and GRAY, O'BRIEN, HAIGHT, MARTIN, VANN, and CULLEN, JJ., concur.

MAHER v. HOME INS. CO. OF NEW YORK. (Court of Appeals of New York. April 8, 1904.) Cross-appeals from a judgment of the Appellate Division of the Supreme Court in the Third Judicial Department (76 App. Div. 622, 79 N. Y. Supp. 1137), entered January 16, 1903, reversing a judgment in favor of defendant entered upon a dismissal of the complaint by the court at a Trial Term without a jury and directing judgment for plaintiff in a specified sum. Louis Silberman, for plaintiff. Franklin M. Danaher, for defendant.

PER CURIAM. Judgment affirmed, with costs.

PARKER, C. J., and GRAY, BARTLETT, HAIGHT, and MARTIN, JJ., concur. O'BRIEN and CULLEN, JJ., dissent.

In re MAITLAND. (Court of Appeals of New York. May 10, 1904.) Appeal from an order of the Appellate Division of the Supreme Court in the First Judicial Department (81 App. Div. 633, 81 N. Y. Supp. 19), made April 6, 1903, which modified and affirmed as modified a decree of the New York county Surrogate's Court passing the accounts of Thomas A. Maitland, as trustee under the will of Sarah Parish Dillon, deceased. Judson S. Landon, Paul N. Turner, and J. Edward Ackley, for appellant. Albert Stickney, Charles I. McBurney, Edward D. O'Brien, J. Allison Kelly, and Charles M. Hough, for respondents.

PER CURIAM. Order affirmed, with costs.

PARKER, C. J., and GRAY, O'BRIEN, BARTLETT, HAIGHT, VANN, and WERNER, JJ., concur.

MALONEY, Respondent, v. MARTIN, Appellant, et al. (Court of Appeals of New York. March 4, 1904.) Appeal from a judgment of the Appellate Division of the Supreme Court in the Fourth Judicial Department (81 App. Div. 432, 80 N. Y. Supp. 763), entered March 17, 1903, affirming a judgment in favor of plaintiff entered upon a verdict and an order denying a motion for a new trial. Frank J. Hone, for appellant. P. Chamberlain and J. S. Keenan, for respondent.

PER CURIAM. Judgment affirmed, with costs.

GRAY, O'BRIEN, HAIGHT, MARTIN, VANN, and CULLEN, JJ., concur. PARKER, C. J., absent.

MAXWELL v. WHITAKER et al. (Court of Appeals of New York. April 28, 1904.) Motion to dismiss an appeal from a judgment of the Appellate Division of the Supreme Court in the First Judicial Department (90 App. Div. 606, 85 N. Y. Supp. 1138), entered January 19, 1904, affirming a judgment in favor of plaintiff and defendants respondents entered upon the report of a referee. The motion was made upon the grounds that the decision of the Appellate Division was unanimous, and there were no questions of law involved requiring review by the Court of Appeals. Eustace Conway, for the motion. W. C. Prime, opposed. No opinion. Motion denied, with $10 costs.

MENDIZABAL, Respondent, v. NEW YORK CENT. & H. R. R. CO., Appellant.

(Court of Appeals of New York. May 17, 1904.) Motion to dismiss an appeal from a judgment of the Appellate Division of the Supreme Court in the Second Judicial Department (89 App. Div. 386, 85 N. Y. Supp. 896), entered January 11, 1904, affirming a judgment in favor of plaintiff entered upon a verdict and an order denying a motion for a new trial. The motion was made upon the ground that the judgment of affirmance having been unanimous the Court of Appeals had no jurisdiction to entertain the appeal. Cornelius O'Connor, for the motion. Charles C. Paulding, opposed. No opinion. Motion granted, and appeal dismissed, with costs, and $10 costs of motion.

MICHEL, Respondent, v. FRICK CO., Appellant. (Court of Appeals of New York. March 22, 1904.) Appeal from a judgment of the Appellate Division of the Supreme Court in the Second Judicial Department (80 App. Div. 634, 81 N. Y. Supp. 1135), entered March 24, 1903, affirming a judgment in favor of plaintiff entered upon a verdict and an order denying a motion for a new trial. Tallmadge W. Foster, for appellant. William Van Wyck, for respondent.

PER CURIAM. Judgment affirmed, with costs.

O'BRIEN, BARTLETT, HAIGHT, VANN, CULLEN, and WERNER, JJ., concur. PARKER, C. J., absent.

MITCHELL, Respondent, v. DOETSCH, Appellant. (Court of Appeals of New York. March 1, 1904.) Appeal from a judgment of the Appellate Division of the Supreme Court in the Third Judicial Department (81 App. Div. 646, 81 N. Y. Supp. 1136), entered April 15, 1903, modifying and affirming as modified a judgment in favor of plaintiff entered upon a verdict. James I. Curtis and T. F. Bush, for appellant. John F. Anderson and Frank S. Anderson, for respondent.

PER CURIAM. Judgment affirmed, with costs.

PARKER, C. J., and GRAY, O'BRIEN, HAIGHT, MARTIN, VANN, and CULLEN, JJ., concur.

MORGAN et al., Respondents, v. MERCHANTS' CO-OPERATIVE FIRE INS. ASS'N OF CENTRAL NEW YORK, Appellant. (Court of Appeals of New York. April 26, 1904.) Appeal from a judgment of the Appellate Division of the Supreme Court in the Fourth Judicial Department (70 App. Div. 623, 75 N. Y. Supp. 1129), entered March 29, 1902, affirming a judgment in favor of plaintiffs entered upon a verdict directed by the court and an order denying a motion for a new trial. J. W. Rayhill, for appellant. P. C. J. De Angelis, for respondents.

PER CURIAM. Judgment affirmed, with costs.

PARKER, C. J., and O'BRIEN, BARTLETT, HAIGHT, VANN, CULLEN, and WERNER, JJ., concur.

MURRAY et al., Respondents, v. MILLER et al., Appellants. (Court of Appeals of New York. April 26, 1904.) Appeal from a judgment of the Appellate Division of the Supreme Court in the First Judicial Department (86 App. Div. 623, 83 N. Y. Supp. 1111), entered July 23, 1903, in favor of plaintiffs, upon the submission of a controversy under section 1279 of the Code of Civil Procedure. Augustus C. Brown, for appellants. Benjamin N. Cardozo and Moses Esberg, for respondents.

PER CURIAM. Judgment affirmed, with costs, on opinion in Murray v. Miller, 178 N. Y. 316, 70 N. E. 870.

MUTUAL LIFE INS. CO. OF NEW YORK, Respondent, v. CROUCH et al., Appellants. (Court of Appeals of New York. April 28, 1904.) Motion to dismiss an appeal from a judgment of the Appellate Division of the Supreme Court in the Fourth Judicial Department (90 App. Div. 610, 85 N. Y. Supp. 1139), entered January 7, 1904, affirming a judgment in favor of plaintiff entered upon a decision of the court on trial at an Equity Term. The motion was made upon the grounds that the Court of Appeals had no jurisdiction to entertain the appeal; the decision of the Appellate Division having been unanimous, there being no question of law to be reviewed, the exceptions being frivolous, and the appeal taken for the purpose of delay only. Henry G. Danforth, for the motion. Horace G. Pierce, opposed. No opinion. Motion granted, and appeal dismissed, with costs, and $10 costs of motion.

NATIONAL BANK OF RONDOUT, Respondent, v. BYRNES, Appellant, et al. (Court of Appeals of New York. March 16, 1904.) Appeal from a judgment of the Appellate Division of the Supreme Court in the Third Judicial Department (84 App. Div. 100, 82 N. Y. Supp. 497), entered May 11, 1903, affirming a judgment in favor of plaintiff entered upon a verdict and an order denying a motion for a new trial. Edward C. Conway and J. Stewart Ross, for appellant. Howard Chipp, for respondent.

PER CURIAM. Judgment affirmed, with costs.

O'BRIEN, BARTLETT, HAIGHT, VANN, CULLEN, and WERNER, JJ., concur. PARKER, C. J., absent.

NICHOLS, Respondent, v. PHŒNIX INS. CO. OF HARTFORD, Appellant. (Court of Appeals of New York. March 1, 1904.) Appeal from a judgment of the Appellate Division of the Supreme Court in the Fourth Judicial Department (77 App. Div. 632, 79 N. Y. Supp. 1139), entered December 1, 1902, affirming a judgment in favor of plaintiff entered upon a verdict and an order denying a motion for a new trial. Carey D. Davie and Hudson Ansley, for appellant. Moses Shire, for respondent.

PER CURIAM. Judgment affirmed, with costs.

PARKER, C. J., and GRAY, O'BRIEN, HAIGHT, MARTIN, VANN, and CULLEN, JJ., concur.

In re NORTON et al. (Court of Appeals of New York. May 3, 1904.) Appeal from an order of the Appellate Division of the Supreme Court in the First Judicial Department (92 App. Div. 462, 87 N. Y. Supp. 128), entered March 15, 1904, which affirmed an order of the New York county Surrogate's Court permitting the compromise of a claim against the estate of George F. Gilman, deceased. Raphael J. Moses, for appellant. John J. Crawford, Lincoln McCormack, and T. S. Ormiston, for respondents.

PER CURIAM. We approve of the opinion below, in so far as it holds that the surrogate had jurisdiction to authorize the administrators to compromise the claim of Hall against the estate. As to the wisdom of authorizing a compromise, that involves a discretion of the court below which we have no power to review. Order affirmed, with costs.

PARKER, C. J., and GRAY, BARTLETT, HAIGHT, VANN, and WERNER, JJ., concur. O'BRIEN, J., not voting.

OCORR & RUGG CO., Respondent, v. CITY OF LITTLE FALLS, Appellant, et al. (Court of Appeals of New York. May 20, 1904.) Appeal from a judgment of the Appellate Division of the Supreme Court in the Fourth Judicial Department (77 App. Div. 592, 79 N. Y. Supp. 251), entered December 19, 1902, affirming a judgment in favor of plaintiff entered upon the report of a referee. A. M. Mills and S. H. Newberry, for appellant. John D. Lynn, for respondent.

PER CURIAM. Judgment affirmed, with costs.

PARKER, C. J., and GRAY, O'BRIEN, BARTLETT, MARTIN, VANN, and CULLEN, JJ., concur.

O'SULLIVAN, Appellant, v. KNOX, Respondent. (Court of Appeals of New York. March 22, 1904.) Appeal from a judgment of the Appellate Division of the Supreme Court in the Fourth Judicial Department (81 App. Div. 438, 80 N. Y. Supp. 848), entered March 17, 1903, affirming a judgment in favor of defendant entered upon a dismissal of the complaint upon the merits by the court at a Trial Term. Theodore E. Hancock, for appellant. Fred. Linus Carroll, for respondent.

PER CURIAM. Judgment modified by striking out the words "on the merits," and, as modified, affirmed, without costs of this appeal to either party.

O'BRIEN, BARTLETT, HAIGHT, VANN, CULLEN, and WERNER, JJ., concur. PARKER, C. J., absent.

PAYNE, Respondent, v. WILLIAMS, Appellant. (Court of Appeals of New York. April 8, 1904.) Appeal from a judgment of the Appellate Division of the Supreme Court in the First Judicial Department (83 App. Div. 388, 82 N. Y. Supp. 284), entered June 1, 1903, affirming a judgment in favor of plaintiff entered upon a verdict and an order denying a motion for a new trial. Richard T. Greene, for appellant. Jacob Marks, for respondent.

PER CURIAM. Judgment affirmed, with costs.

PARKER, C. J., and GRAY, O'BRIEN, BARTLETT, HAIGHT, MARTIN, and CULLEN, JJ., concur.

PERRY, Respondent, v. LEVENSON et al., Appellants. (Court of Appeals of New York. March 15, 1904.) Appeal from a judgment of the Appellate Division of the Supreme Court in the First Judicial Department (82 App. Div. 94, 81 N. Y. Supp. 586), entered April 16, 1903, affirming a judgment in favor of plaintiff entered upon the report of a referee. Edward W. S. Johnston and Benno Loewy, for appellants. George W. Wager, for respondent.

PER CURIAM. Judgment affirmed, with costs.

O'BRIEN, BARTLETT, HAIGHT, VANN, CULLEN, and WERNER, JJ., concur. PARKER, C. J., absent.

PERTH AMBOY MUT. LOAN, HOMESTEAD & BUILDING ASS'N, Respondent, v. CHAPMAN, Appellant. (Court of Appeals of New York. March 15, 1904.) Appeal from a judgment entered March 19, 1903, upon an order of the Appellate Division of the Supreme Court in the First Judicial Department (80 App. Div. 556, 81 N. Y. Supp. 38), overruling defendant's exceptions, ordered to be heard in the first instance by the Appellate Division, denying a motion for a new trial and directing judgment for the plaintiff on the verdict. Clarence F. Birdseye, for appellant. Edward S. Savage, for respondent.

PER CURIAM. Judgment affirmed, with costs, on opinion below.

O'BRIEN, BARTLETT, HAIGHT, VANN, and CULLEN, JJ., concur. PARKER, C. J., and WERNER, J., absent.

PEOPLE, Appellant, v. CALABUR, Respondent. (Court of Appeals of New York. May 3, 1904.) Motion to dismiss an appeal from an order of the Appellate Division of the Supreme Court in the Second Judicial Department (91 App. Div. 529, 87 N. Y. Supp. 121), entered March 11, 1904, which reversed a judgment of the Kings County Court, entered upon a verdict convicting the defendant of the crime of assault in the first degree, and granted a new trial. The motion was made upon the grounds that the Appellate Division reversed the judgment of conviction as a matter of discretion, and that, therefore, no questions of law are presented which the Court of Appeals has jurisdiction to review. Francis L. Carrao, for the motion. John F. Clark, Dist. Atty. (Robert H. Roy, of counsel), opposed. No opinion. Motion denied.

PEOPLE, Respondent, v. McCUE, Appellant. (Court of Appeals of New York. April 5, 1904.) Appeal from an order of the Appellate Division of the Supreme Court in the Second Judicial Department (87 App. Div. 72, 83 N. Y. Supp. 1088), made October 9, 1903, which affirmed a judgment of the Westchester County Court, entered upon a verdict convicting the defendant of the crime of pool selling. John F. Brennan, for appellant. J. Addison Young, for the People.

PER CURIAM. Judgment of conviction affirmed.

PARKER, C. J., and GRAY, O'BRIEN, HAIGHT, MARTIN, CULLEN, and WERNER, JJ., concur.

PEOPLE, Respondent, v. ST. JOHN, Appellant. (Court of Appeals of New York. May 17, 1904.) Appeal from an order of the Appellate Division of the Supreme Court in the Fourth Judicial Department (89 App. Div. 617, 85 N. Y. Supp. 1140), entered December 17, 1903, overruling defendant's exceptions, ordered to be heard in the first instance by the Appellate Division, denying a motion for a new trial and directing judgment for the plaintiff upon a verdict directed by the trial court. William Brennan, Jr., for appellant. John Cunneen, Atty. Gen. (Thomas C. Burke, of counsel), for the People.

PER CURIAM. Order affirmed, with costs.

PARKER, C. J., and GRAY, BARTLETT, HAIGHT, VANN, and WERNER, JJ., concur. O'BRIEN, J., not voting.

PEOPLE, Respondent, v. SHARKEY, Appellant. (Court of Appeals of New York. April 5, 1904.) Appeal from an order of the Appellate Division of the Supreme Court in the First Judicial Department (87 App. Div. 532, 84 N. Y. Supp. 780), entered November 20, 1903, affirming a judgment entered at a Trial Term upon a verdict convicting the defendant of the crime of manslaughter in the second degree. Henry W. Unger and Abraham Levy, for appellant. William Travers Jerome, Dist.

Atty. (Robert C. Taylor, of counsel), for the People.

PER CURIAM. Judgment of conviction affirmed.

PARKER, C. J., and GRAY, O'BRIEN, BARTLETT, HAIGHT, MARTIN, and CULLEN, JJ., concur.

PEOPLE, Respondent, v. WALKER, Appellant. (Court of Appeals of New York. March 22, 1904.) Appeal from an order of the Appellate Division of the Supreme Court in the First Judicial Department (85 App. Div. 556, 83 N. Y. Supp. 372), made July 7, 1903, which affirmed a judgment of the Court of General Sessions in the county of New York convicting the defendant of the crime of grand larceny in the first degree. Charles E. Le Barbier, for appellant. William Travers Jerome, Dist. Atty. (Robert C. Taylor, of counsel), for the People.

PER CURIAM. Judgment of conviction affirmed.

O'BRIEN, BARTLETT, HAIGHT, VANN, CULLEN, and WERNER, JJ., concur. PARKER, C. J., absent.

PEOPLE, Respondent, v. WHITE, Appellant. (Court of Appeals of New York. April 8, 1904.) Appeal from an order of the Appellate Division of the Supreme Court in the Fourth Judicial Department (88 App. Div. 620, 84 N. Y. Supp. 1140), entered November 24, 1903, which affirmed a judgment of the Cayuga County Court entered upon a verdict convicting the defendant of a violation of the liquor tax law. Amasa J. Parker and Dudley K. Wilcox, for appellant. Harry T. Dayton, Dist. Atty. (Albert H. Clark, of counsel), for the People.

PER CURIAM. Judgment of conviction affirmed.

PARKER, C. J., and GRAY, BARTLETT, HAIGHT, MARTIN, and CULLEN, JJ., concur. O'BRIEN, J., not voting.

PEOPLE, Respondent, v. WITTENBERG, Appellant. (Court of Appeals of New York. March 22, 1904.) Appeal from an order of the Appellate Division of the Supreme Court in the First Judicial Department (84 App. Div. 641, 82 N. Y. Supp. 1110), entered June 12, 1903, which affirmed a judgment of the Court of General Sessions in the county of New York convicting the defendant of the crime of playing policy. F. V. S. Oliver and James Oliver, for appellant. William Travers Jerome, Dist. Atty. (Robert C. Taylor, of counsel), for the People.

PER CURIAM. Judgment of conviction affirmed.

O'BRIEN, BARTLETT, HAIGHT, VANN, CULLEN, and WERNER, JJ., concur. PARKER, C. J., absent.

PEOPLE ex rel. ACRITELLI et al., Respondents, v. GROUT, City Comptroller, Appellant. (Court of Appeals of New York. March 1, 1904.) Appeal from an order of the Appellate Division of the Supreme Court in the First Judicial Department (87 App. Div. 193, 84 N. Y. Supp. 97), entered October 29, 1903, which affirmed an order of Special Term granting a motion for a peremptory writ of mandamus to compel defendant to pay to relator an amount awarded to an attorney for his services on the trial of an indictment for murder, and duly assigned by him to such relator. John J. Delany, Corp. Counsel (Theodore Connoly, of counsel), for appellant. Cæsar B. F. Barra, for respondents.

PER CURIAM. Order affirmed, with costs, on prevailing opinion below.

PARKER, C. J., and GRAY, O'BRIEN, HAIGHT, MARTIN, VANN, and CULLEN, JJ., concur.

PEOPLE ex rel. BREWSTER, Appellant, v. OLD GUARD OF CITY OF NEW YORK et al., Respondents. (Court of Appeals of New York. March 29, 1904.) Appeal from an order of the Appellate Division of the Supreme Court in the First Judicial Department (87 App. Div. 478, 84 N. Y. Supp. 766), entered December 21, 1903, which reversed an order of Special Term granting a motion for a peremptory writ of mandamus to compel defendants to restore relator to membership in the Old Guard of the City of New York. Oscar B. Thomas, for appellant. Asa Bird Gardiner, for respondents.

PER CURIAM. Order affirmed, with costs.

PARKER, C. J., and GRAY, O'BRIEN, HAIGHT, MARTIN, CULLEN, and WERNER, JJ., concur.

PEOPLE ex rel. BROOKLYN UNION ELEVATED R. CO., Appellant, v. KNIGHT, State Comptroller, Respondent. (Court of Appeals of New York. March 29, 1904.) Appeal from an order of the Appellate Division of the Supreme Court in the Third Judicial Department (85 App. Div. 623, 83 N. Y. Supp. 1114), entered August 5, 1903, which affirmed a determination of the defendant assessing a franchise tax upon the relator. Charles A. Collin, for appellant. John Cunneen, Atty. Gen. (William H. Wood, on the brief), for respondent.

PER CURIAM. Order affirmed, with costs.

PARKER, C. J., and HAIGHT, MARTIN, CULLEN, and WERNER, JJ., concur. GRAY and O'BRIEN, JJ., dissent.

PEOPLE ex rel. COMMISSIONER OF PUBLIC CHARITIES OF CITY OF NEW YORK, Respondent, v. THOMPSON, Appellant. (Court of Appeals of New York. April 26, 1904.) Appeal from an order of the Appellate Division of the Supreme Court in the First Judicial Department (87 App. Div. 633, 84 N. Y. Supp. 1140), entered November 20, 1903, which affirmed an order of the Court of General Sessions of the city of New York modifying, and affirming as modified, an order of a city magistrate adjudging defendant to be a disorderly person. Alexander Rosenthal, for appellant. John J. Delany, Corp. Counsel (Theodore Connoly and Herman Steifel, of counsel), for respondent.

PER CURIAM. Order affirmed, without costs.

PARKER, C. J., and GRAY, BARTLETT, HAIGHT, MARTIN, VANN, and WERNER, JJ., concur.

PEOPLE ex rel. CONEY ISLAND & G. RY. CO., Appellant, v. KNIGHT, State Comptroller, Respondent. (Court of Appeals of New York. March 29, 1904.) Appeal from an order of the Appellate Division of the Supreme Court in the Third Judicial Department (85 App. Div. 623, 83 N. Y. Supp. 1114), entered August 5, 1903, which affirmed a determination of the defendant assessing a franchise tax upon the relator. Charles A. Collin, for appellant. John Cunneen, Atty. Gen. (William H. Wood, on the brief), for respondent.

PER CURIAM. Order affirmed, with costs.

PARKER, C. J., and HAIGHT, MARTIN, CULLEN, and WERNER, JJ., concur. GRAY and O'BRIEN, JJ., dissent.

PEOPLE ex rel. COX, Appellant, v. GREENE, Police Com'r, Respondent. (Court of Appeals of New York. May 10, 1904.) Appeal from an order of the Appellate Division of the Supreme Court in the First Judicial Department (89 App. Div. 613, 85 N. Y. Supp. 1142), made December 11, 1903, which dismissed a writ of certiorari to review the proceedings of the defendant in dismissing the relator from the police force of the city of New York and affirmed such proceedings. Charles L. Hoffman and Henry A. Friedman, for appellant. John J. Delany, Corp. Counsel (Theodore Connoly and Terence Farley, of counsel), for respondent.

PER CURIAM. Order affirmed, with costs.

PARKER, C. J., and GRAY, O'BRIEN, BARTLETT, HAIGHT, VANN, and WERNER, JJ., concur.

PEOPLE ex rel. DALY, Appellant, v. GREENE, Police Com'r, Respondent. (Court of Appeals of New York. May 17, 1904.) Appeal from an order of the Appellate Division of the Supreme Court in the First Judicial Department (91 App. Div. 58, 86 N. Y. Supp. 322), entered February 13, 1904, which dismissed a writ of certiorari to review the proceedings of the defendant in reducing the relator from the grade of detective sergeant to that of patrolman in the police department of the city of New York and affirmed such proceedings. William C. De Witt and James F. Lynch, for appellant. John J. Delany, Corp. Counsel (Theodore Connoly and Terence Farley, of counsel), for respondent.

PER CURIAM. Order affirmed, with costs.

PARKER, C. J., and GRAY, O'BRIEN, BARTLETT, HAIGHT, VANN, and WERNER, JJ., concur.

PEOPLE ex rel. DAY, Appellant, v. GREENE, Police Com'r, et al., Respondents. (Court of Appeals of New York. May 10, 1904.) Appeal from an order of the Appellate Division of the Supreme Court in the First Judicial Department (90 App. Div. 606, 85 N. Y. Supp. 1142), entered January 14, 1904, which dismissed a writ of certiorari to review the proceedings of the defendants in dismissing the relator from the police force of the city of New York and affirmed such proceedings. Robert L. Redfield, for appellant. John J. Delany, Corp. Counsel (Theodore Connoly and Terence Farley, of counsel), for respondents.

PER CURIAM. Order affirmed, with costs.

PARKER, C. J., and GRAY, O'BRIEN, BARTLETT, HAIGHT, VANN, and WERNER, JJ., concur.

PEOPLE ex rel. DUFOUR et al., Appellants, v. WELLS et al., Tax Com'rs, Respondents. (Court of Appeals of New York. Feb. 23, 1904.) Appeal from an order of the Appellate Division of the Supreme Court in the First Judicial Department (85 App. Div. 440, 82 N. Y. Supp. 866, 83 N. Y. Supp. 387), entered July 13, 1903, which reversed an order of Special Term denying a motion to quash a writ of certiorari to review an assessment for taxation of personal property of relators and granted such motion. Edmund L. Cole, for appellants. John J. Delany, Corp. Counsel (George S. Coleman, James M. Ward, and E. Crosby Kindleberger, of counsel), for respondents.

PER CURIAM. Order affirmed, with costs.

GRAY, HAIGHT, MARTIN, VANN, and CULLEN, JJ., concur. PARKER, C. J., and O'BRIEN, J., dissent.

PEOPLE ex rel. EDISON ELECTRIC ILLUMINATING CO. OF BROOKLYN, Respondent, v. FEITNER et al., Tax Com'rs, Appellants. (Court of Appeals of New York. March 29, 1904.) Appeal by permission from an order of the Appellate Division of the Supreme Court in the First Judicial Department (86 App. Div. 46, 83 N. Y. Supp. 1114), entered November 7, 1903, which reversed an order of Special Term quashing a writ of certiorari to review the action of the defendants in assessing property of the relator for the purpose of taxation. The following question was certified: "Was the following written application, presented to the commissioners of taxes and assessments of the city of New York: 'To the Commissioners of Taxes and Assessments: The undersigned, the Edison Electric Illuminating Company of Brooklyn, represents that it is the owner of real estate in various parts of the borough of Brooklyn, consisting of foundations, substructures, superstructures, conduits, pipes, wires, cables, and connections of the said company. It finds that the same has been assessed on the assessment roll of 1899 at a valuation of $905,000, whereas the same should not have been, in its judgment, valued at more than $500,000 to be in proportion to the assessed value of similar property, and in accordance with the fair marketable value thereof. The said system, comprising the electric system of distribution of your petitioner, whereby it distributes electric light and power throughout the said borough, is being superseded by different systems of electric distribution. The entire system has been deteriorated and damaged by the action of stray currents in the ground not owned or controlled by your petitioner, causing a deterioration in the said system by a process known as electrolysis. Much of the system has been in the ground for many years, and is worth but a part of its original cost. The present cost price of similar material is much less at the present time than it was when said system was put in. Your petitioner therefore asks that the said assessment may be reduced to the amount stated. Dated Brooklyn, City of New York, April 29, 1899. Edison Electric Illuminating Company of Brooklyn, by Royal C. Peabody, Vice President'—sufficient to sustain a writ of certiorari under the general tax law and the Greater New York charter to review the assessment of real estate upon the ground of overvaluation?" John J. Delany, Corp. Counsel (George S. Coleman and David Rumsey, of counsel), for appellants. Charles A. Collin, for respondent.

PER CURIAM. Order affirmed, with costs, and question certified answered in the affirmative.

PARKER, C. J., and GRAY, O'BRIEN, HAIGHT, MARTIN, CULLEN, and WERNER, JJ., concur.

PEOPLE ex rel. ERNEST OCHS, Incorporated, Appellant, v. HILLIARD, Special Deputy Excise Com'r, Respondent. (Court of Appeals of New York. April 5, 1904.) Appeal from an order of the Appellate Division of the Supreme Court in the First Judicial Department (81 App. Div. 71, 80 N. Y. Supp. 792), entered March 17, 1903, which affirmed an order of Special Term denying an application for a peremptory writ of mandamus to compel defendant to cancel a liquor tax certificate and issue rebate receipts and dismissing an alternative writ theretofore allowed. Moses Weinman, for appellant. Herbert H. Kellogg, for respondent.

PER CURIAM. Order affirmed, with costs.

PARKER, C. J., and GRAY, O'BRIEN, BARTLETT, HAIGHT, MARTIN, and CULLEN, JJ., concur.

PEOPLE ex rel. LEFFERTS, Respondent, v. McCLELLAN et al., Board of Estimate and Apportionment, Appellants. (Court of Appeals of New York. May 17, 1904.) Appeal from an order of the Appellate Division of the Supreme Court in the Second Judicial Department (87 N. Y. Supp. 1145), entered March 19, 1904, which affirmed an order of Special Term granting a motion for a peremptory writ of mandamus to compel defendants to act on a resolution for a local improvement. John J. Delany, Corp. Counsel (James D. Bell, of counsel), for appellants. George E. Waldo and De Witt V. D. Reilly, for respondent.

PER CURIAM. Order affirmed, with costs.

PARKER, C. J., and GRAY, O'BRIEN, BARTLETT, HAIGHT, VANN, and WERNER, JJ., concur.

PEOPLE ex rel. MANHATTAN LIFE INS. CO., Appellant, v. WELLS et al., Tax Com'rs, Respondents. (Court of Appeals of New York. May 10, 1904.) Appeal from an order of the Appellate Division of the Supreme Court in the First Judicial Department (91 App. Div. 44, 86 N. Y. Supp. 456), entered February 11, 1904, which affirmed an order of Special Term quashing a writ of certiorari to review an assessment upon real property of relator. Benjamin F. Tracy and M. F. Neville, for appellant. John J. Delany, Corp. Counsel (Theodore Connoly and David Rumsey, of counsel), for respondents.

PER CURIAM. Order affirmed, with costs, on opinion below.

GRAY, HAIGHT, VANN, and WERNER, JJ., concur. PARKER, C. J., and BARTLETT, J., dissent. O'BRIEN, J., not voting.

PEOPLE ex rel. MISSIONARY SISTERS OF THIRD ORDER OF ST. FRANCIS, Respondent, v. REILLY et al., Town Assessors, Appellants. (Court of Appeals of New York. May 10, 1904.) Appeal from an order of the Appellate Division of the Supreme Court in the Second Judicial Department (85 App. Div. 71, 83 N. Y. Supp. 39), entered September 28, 1903, which affirmed orders of Special Term vacating assessments for taxation of real property of relator. William Vanamee, for appellants. Michael J. Scanlan, for respondent.

PER CURIAM. Order affirmed, with costs.

PARKER, C. J., and GRAY, O'BRIEN, BARTLETT, HAIGHT, VANN, and WERNER, JJ., concur.

PEOPLE ex rel. NELSON, Appellant, v. MARSH et al., Drainage Com'rs, et al., Respondents. (Court of Appeals of New York. May 17, 1904.) Appeal from an order of the Appellate Division of the Supreme Court in the Second Judicial Department (82 App. Div. 571, 81 N. Y. Supp. 579), entered May 4, 1903, which affirmed an order of a Trial Term denying a motion for a peremptory writ of mandamus to compel the defendant commissioners to levy an assessment for the payment of certain drainage bonds. John R. Dos Passos, John Murray Mitchell, Samuel W. Bower, and Edmund F. Harding, for appellant. John J. Delany, Corp. Counsel (Theodore Connoly and George L. Sterling, of counsel), for respondent city of New York. George J. Greenfield, for respondent commissioners.

PER CURIAM. Order affirmed, with costs.

GRAY, BARTLETT, VANN, and WERNER, JJ., concur. PARKER, C. J., and O'BRIEN, J., not voting. HAIGHT, J., absent.

PEOPLE ex rel. NASSAU ELECTRIC R. CO., Appellant, v. KNIGHT, State Comptroller, Respondent. (Court of Appeals of New York. March 29, 1904.) Appeal from an order of the Appellate Division of the Supreme Court in the Third Judicial Department (85 App. Div. 623, 83 N. Y. Supp. 1115), entered August 5, 1903, which affirmed a determination of the defendant assessing a franchise tax upon the relator. Charles A. Collin, for appellant. John Cunneen, Atty. Gen. (William H. Wood, on the brief), for respondent.

PER CURIAM. Order affirmed, with costs.

PARKER, C. J., and HAIGHT, MARTIN, CULLEN, and WERNER, JJ., concur. GRAY and O'BRIEN, JJ., dissent.

PEOPLE ex rel. TOWN OF COLESVILLE, Appellant, v. DELAWARE & H. CO., Respondent. (Court of Appeals of New York. March 22, 1904.) No opinion. Motion for reargument denied, with $10 costs. See 177 N. Y. 337, 69 N. E. 651.

PEOPLE ex rel. WESTERN ELECTRIC CO., Appellant, v. MILLER, State Comptroller, Respondent. (Court of Appeals of New York. March 29, 1904.) Appeal from an order of the Appellate Division of the Supreme Court in the Third Judicial Department (90 App. Div. 618, 85 N. Y. Supp. 1143), entered January 15, 1904, which affirmed a determination of the defendant assessing certain taxes upon the relator for the year ending October 31, 1901. Edwin T. Rice, for appellant. John Cunneen, Atty. Gen. (William H. Wood, on the brief), for respondent.

PER CURIAM. Order affirmed, with costs.

PARKER, C. J., and GRAY, HAIGHT, MARTIN, CULLEN, and WERNER, JJ., concur. O'BRIEN, J., not voting.

POERSCHKE, Respondent, v. HOROWITZ et al., Appellants. (Court of Appeals of New York. April 26, 1904.) Appeal from a judgment of the Appellate Division of the Supreme Court in the First Judicial Department (84 App. Div. 443, 82 N. Y. Supp. 742), entered July 21, 1903, modifying, and affirming as modified, a judgment in favor of plaintiff entered upon a decision of the court on trial at Special Term. Jacob Manheim, for appellants. William R. Hill, for respondent.

PER CURIAM. Judgment affirmed, with costs.

PARKER, C. J., and O'BRIEN, BARTLETT, HAIGHT, VANN, CULLEN, and WERNER, JJ., concur.

POTTER, Appellant, v. HODGMAN, Respondent, et al. (Court of Appeals of New York. April 5, 1904.) Appeal from an order of the Appellate Division of the Supreme Court in the Third Judicial Department (81 App. Div. 233, 80 N. Y. Supp. 1056), entered March 17, 1903, reversing a judgment in favor of plaintiff entered upon a decision of the court at a Trial Term without a jury and granting a new trial. Edgar T. Brackett and Robert O. Bascom, for appellant. C. H. Sturges and Edgar Hull, for respondent.

PER CURIAM. Order affirmed, and judgment absolute ordered for defendant on the stipulation, with costs, on opinion below.

PARKER, C. J., and GRAY, O'BRIEN, HAIGHT, MARTIN, CULLEN, and WERNER, JJ., concur.

POWELL, Appellant, v. HARRISON et al., Respondents. (Court of Appeals of New York. March 22, 1904.) Motion to dismiss an appeal from an order of the Appellate Division of the Supreme Court in the Third Judicial Department (88 App. Div. 228, 85 N. Y. Supp. 452), entered November 27, 1903, which affirmed an order of Special Term vacating an order of reference and an order of distribution in surplus money proceedings. The motion was made upon the ground that the order attempted to be appealed from is not appealable to the Court of Appeals. Alexander D. Falck, for the motion. J. John Hassett, opposed. No opinion. Motion granted, and appeal dismissed, with costs, and $10 costs of motion, on the ground that, while the proceeding is a special one, the order is not a final order.

PRESCOTT et al., Respondents, v. LE CONTE et al., Appellants. (Court of Appeals of New York. April 8, 1904.) Appeal from a judgment of the Appellate Division of the Supreme Court in the First Judicial Department (83 App. Div. 482, 82 N. Y. Supp. 411), entered May 28, 1903, affirming a judgment in favor of plaintiffs entered upon a verdict and an order denying a motion for a new trial. Robert E. Deyo, for appellants. Herbert J. Hindes, for respondents.

PER CURIAM. Judgment affirmed, with costs.

PARKER, C. J., and GRAY, O'BRIEN, BARTLETT, HAIGHT, MARTIN, and CULLEN, JJ., concur.

PRIEST, Respondent, v. GUMPRECHT et al., Appellants. (Court of Appeals of New York. April 26, 1904.) Appeal from a judgment of the Appellate Division of the Supreme Court in the First Judicial Department (81 App. Div. 631, 80 N. Y. Supp. 759), entered March 11, 1903, affirming a judgment in favor of plaintiff entered upon a decision of the court on trial at Special Term. Wayland E. Benjamin, for appellants. Charles A. Decker, for respondent.

PER CURIAM. Judgment affirmed, with costs.

PARKER, C. J., and GRAY, BARTLETT, HAIGHT, MARTIN, VANN, and WERNER, JJ., concur.

RAILWAY ADVERTISING CO., Respondent, v. STANDARD ROCK CANDY CO., Appellant. (Court of Appeals of New York. March 29, 1904.) Appeal from a judgment of the Appellate Division of the Supreme Court in the Second Judicial Department (83 App. Div. 191, 83 N. Y. Supp. 338), entered June 1, 1903, affirming a judgment in favor of plaintiff entered upon a decision of the court at a Trial Term without a jury. Frank Barker, for appellant. M. S. Guiterman, for respondent.

PER CURIAM. Judgment affirmed, with costs.

O'BRIEN, HAIGHT, VANN, CULLEN, and WERNER, JJ., concur. PARKER, C. J., absent. BARTLETT, J., taking no part.

RANGER, Appellant, v. THALMANN et al., Respondents. (Court of Appeals of New York. March 29, 1904.) Appeal, by permission, from a judgment entered June 19, 1903, upon an order of the Appellate Division of the Supreme Court in the First Judicial Department (84 App. Div. 341, 82 N. Y. Supp. 846), which reversed an interlocutory judgment of Special Term overruling a demurrer to the complaint. The following is the question certified: "Does the amended complaint herein state facts sufficient to constitute a cause of action?" Thomas D. Adams and Arthur C. Palmer, for appellant. Edwin C. Hoyt and Henry G. Wiley, for respondents.

PER CURIAM. Judgment affirmed, with costs, on opinion below, and question certified answered in the negative.

PARKER, C. J., and GRAY, O'BRIEN, HAIGHT, MARTIN, CULLEN, and WERNER, JJ., concur.

ROGERS et al. v. SMITH et al. (Court of Appeals of New York. March 1, 1904.) Appeal from a judgment of the Appellate Division of the Supreme Court in the Third Judicial Department (75 App. Div. 141, 77 N. Y. Supp. 392), entered December 12, 1902, affirming an interlocutory judgment of Special Term directing the sale of certain real estate to pay legacies. J. Sanford Potter, B. G. Higley, and Charles R. Paris, for appellants. Archibald S. Derby and Grenville M. Ingalsbe, for respondents.

PER CURIAM. Judgment affirmed, with costs.

PARKER, C. J., and GRAY, O'BRIEN, HAIGHT, MARTIN, VANN, and CULLEN, JJ., concur.

ST. JAMES CO., Respondent, v. SECURITY TRUST & LIFE INS. CO., Appellant. (Court of Appeals of New York. March 15, 1904.) Appeal from a judgment of the Appellate Division of the Supreme Court in the First Judicial Department (82 App. Div. 242, 81 N. Y. Supp. 739), entered May 11, 1903, affirming a judgment in favor of plaintiff entered upon the report of a referee. Jacob Halstead, for appellant. L. Laflin Kellogg and Alfred C. Petté, for respondent.

PER CURIAM. Judgment affirmed, with costs.

PARKER, C. J., and O'BRIEN, BARTLETT, HAIGHT, VANN, CULLEN, and WERNER, JJ., concur.

SANDERS v. CARLEY et al. (Court of Appeals of New York. May 20, 1904.) Cross-appeals from a judgment of the Appellate Division of the Supreme Court in the Second Judicial Department (83 App. Div. 193, 83 N. Y. Supp. 106), entered June 4, 1903, affirming a judgment of a Trial Term determining the ownership of a certain plot of land in the borough of Brooklyn. Robert Goeller and Joseph H. Mahan, for plaintiff. James A. Sheehan, Stephen M. Hoye, and Edward L. Somerville, for defendants.

PER CURIAM. Judgment affirmed, without costs.

PARKER, C. J., and GRAY, O'BRIEN, BARTLETT, MARTIN, VANN, and CULLEN, JJ., concur.

SCHLIMBACH, Respondent, v. McLEAN, Appellant. (Court of Appeals of New York. April 26, 1904.) Appeal from a judgment of the Appellate Division of the Supreme Court in the Second Judicial Department (83 App. Div. 157, 82 N. Y. Supp. 516), entered June 5, 1903, affirming a judgment in favor of plaintiff entered upon the report of a referee. Albert Ritchie, for appellant. Lucius L. Gilbert, for respondent.

PER CURIAM. Judgment affirmed, with costs.

PARKER, C. J., and O'BRIEN, BARTLETT, HAIGHT, VANN, CULLEN, and WERNER, JJ., concur.

SECURITY TRUST CO. OF ROCHESTER, Respondent, v. WELLS, FARGO & CO. EXPRESS, Appellant. (Court of Appeals of New York. May 20, 1904.) Appeal from a judgment of the Appellate Division of the Supreme Court in the Fourth Judicial Department (81 App. Div. 426, 80 N. Y. Supp. 830), entered March 20, 1903, affirming a judgment in favor of plaintiff entered upon a verdict directed by the court and an order denying a motion for a new trial. James M. E. O'Grady, for appellant. Edward Harris, for respondent.

PER CURIAM. Judgment affirmed, with costs, on opinion below.

PARKER, C. J., and O'BRIEN, BARTLETT, MARTIN, VANN, and CULLEN, JJ., concur. GRAY, J., not voting.

SHAFFER, Respondent, v. ALEXANDER et al., Appellants. (Court of Appeals of New York. May 20, 1904.) Appeal from a judgment of the Appellate Division of the Supreme Court in the Third Judicial Department (81 App. Div. 546, 81 N. Y. Supp. 1143), entered March 28, 1903, affirming a judgment in favor of plaintiff entered upon a decision of the court on trial at Special Term. Myron N. Tompkins, for appellants. J. T. Newman and Charles H. Blood, for respondent.

PER CURIAM. Judgment affirmed, with costs.

PARKER, C. J., and GRAY, O'BRIEN, BARTLETT, MARTIN, VANN, and CULLEN, JJ., concur.

SHANLEY, Appellant, v. KOEHLER, Respondent. (Court of Appeals of New York. March 15, 1904.) Appeal from a judgment of the Appellate Division of the Supreme Court in the First Judicial Department (80 App. Div. 566, 80 N. Y. Supp. 679), entered March 13, 1903, affirming a judgment in favor of defendant entered upon a dismissal of the complaint by the court on trial at Special Term. Michael Kirtland and John Conville, for appellant. Arnold Charles Weil, for respondent.

PER CURIAM. Judgment affirmed, with costs.

PARKER, C. J., and GRAY, O'BRIEN, BARTLETT, MARTIN, VANN, and WERNER, JJ., concur.

SMITH et al., Appellants, v. FIRTH et al., Respondents. (Court of Appeals of New York. March 22, 1904.) Appeal from a judgment of the Appellate Division of the Supreme Court in the Second Judicial Department (72 App. Div. 631, 76 N. Y. Supp. 1063), entered May 17, 1902, affirming a judgment in favor of defendants entered upon a dismissal of the complaint by the court on trial at Special Term. Ambrose G. Todd and George B. Class, for appellants. George M. Baker and Alexander H. Van Cott, for respondents.

PER CURIAM. Judgment affirmed, with costs.

O'BRIEN, BARTLETT, HAIGHT, VANN, CULLEN, and WERNER, JJ., concur. PARKER, C. J., absent.

SPENCE, Respondent, v. METROPOLITAN ST. RY. CO., Appellant, et al. (Court of Appeals of New York. March 22, 1904.) Appeal from a judgment of the Appellate Division of the Supreme Court in the First Judicial Department (82 App. Div. 636, 81 N. Y. Supp. 1144), entered May 5, 1903, affirming a judgment in favor of plaintiff entered upon a verdict and an order denying a motion for a new trial. Bayard H. Ames, Charles F. Brown, Arthur Ofner, and Henry A. Robinson, for appellant Metropolitan St. Ry. Co. William H. H. Ely and Luther Shafer, for respondent.

PER CURIAM. Judgment affirmed, with costs.

O'BRIEN, BARTLETT, HAIGHT, VANN, CULLEN, and WERNER, JJ., concur. PARKER, C. J., absent.

SPOSATO, Appellant, v. CITY OF NEW YORK, Respondent. (Court of Appeals of New York. April 5, 1904.) Appeal from a judgment of the Appellate Division of the Supreme Court in the Second Judicial Department (75 App. Div. 304, 78 N. Y. Supp. 168), entered October 15, 1902, affirming a judgment in favor of defendant entered upon a dismissal of the complaint by the court at a Trial Term. George Wallace, for appellant. John J. Delany, Corp. Counsel (James D. Bell, of counsel), for respondent.

PER CURIAM. Judgment affirmed, with costs.

PARKER, C. J., and GRAY, O'BRIEN, BARTLETT, HAIGHT, MARTIN, and CULLEN, JJ., concur.

SPRAGUE, Appellant, v. CITY OF NEW YORK, Respondent. (Court of Appeals of New York. April 5, 1904.) Appeal from a judgment of the Appellate Division of the Supreme Court in the Second Judicial Department (74 App. Div. 625, 77 N. Y. Supp. 1140), entered July 9, 1902, affirming a judgment in favor of defendant entered upon a decision of the court on trial at Special Term. George Wallace, for appellant. John J. Delany, Corp. Counsel (James D. Bell and Richard B. Greenwood, of counsel), for respondent.

PER CURIAM. Judgment affirmed, with costs.

PARKER, C. J., and GRAY, O'BRIEN, HAIGHT, MARTIN, and CULLEN, JJ., concur. BARTLETT, J., not voting.

STAATS et al., Appellants, v. STORM et al., Respondents. (Court of Appeals of New York. March 1, 1904.) No opinion. Motion to amend remittitur granted, and remittitur amended by providing for a bill of costs to respondents represented by separate counsel in this court who argued the appeal either orally or by printed brief. See 177 N. Y. —, 69 N. E. 1131.

STRAUS et al., Respondents, v. AMERICAN PUBLISHERS' ASS'N et al., Appellants. (Court of Appeals of New York. March 22, 1904.) No opinion. Motion to return remittitur granted, and the clerk of the Supreme Court is requested to return the remittitur in this action to this court, to the end that the same may be so amended as to give leave to the defendants herein to withdraw their demurrers to the complaint and to serve answers, without costs of motion. See 177 N. Y. 473, 69 N. E. 1107.

STREETS, Appellant, v. GRAND TRUNK RY. Co. et al., Respondents. (Court of Appeals of New York. March 4, 1904.) Appeal from a judgment, entered December 11, 1902, upon an order of the Appellate Division of the Supreme Court in the Fourth Judicial Department (76 App. Div. 480, 78 N. Y. Supp. 729), overruling plaintiff's exceptions ordered to be heard in the first instance by the Appellate Division, denying a motion for a new trial and directing judgment for defendants. John Cunneen, for appellant. William L. Marcy, Adel-bert Moot, and Charles A. Pooley, for respondents.

PER CURIAM. Judgment affirmed, with costs.

PARKER, C. J., and HAIGHT, MARTIN, VANN, CULLEN, and WERNER, JJ., concur. GRAY, J., not sitting.

STROMBERG, Respondent, v. TRIBUNE ASS'N, Appellant. (Court of Appeals of New York. May 10, 1904.) Appeal, by permission, from an order of the Appellate Division of the Supreme Court of the First Judicial Department (88 App. Div. 589, 85 N. Y. Supp. 259), entered December 18, 1903, which affirmed an interlocutory judgment of Special Term overruling a demurrer to the complaint. The following question was certified: "Does the amended complaint in this action state facts sufficient to constitute a cause of action in favor of plaintiff herein, against the defendant herein?" Henry W. Sackett, for appellant. Max D. Steuer, for respondent.

PER CURIAM. Question certified answered in the affirmative, and interlocutory judgment affirmed, with costs, with leave to defendant to answer within 20 days, on opinion of INGRAHAM, J., below.

GRAY, O'BRIEN, VANN, and WERNER, JJ., concur. PARKER, C. J., and BARTLETT and HAIGHT, JJ., dissent.

STROWGER et al., Respondents, v. AMERICAN BONDING & TRUST CO. OF BALTIMORE CITY et al., Appellants. (Court of Appeals of New York. March 4, 1904.) Appeal from a judgment, entered February 10, 1903, upon an order of the Appellate Division of the Supreme Court in the Fourth Judicial Department (79 App. Div. 644, 80 N. Y. Supp. 1149), overruling defendant's exceptions, ordered to be heard in the first instance by the Appellate Division, denying a motion for a new trial and directing judgment for plaintiffs upon the verdict. Nathaniel Foote, for appellants. Walter S. Hubbell, for respondents.

PER CURIAM. Judgment affirmed, with costs.

PARKER, C. J., and GRAY, MARTIN, VANN, CULLEN, and WERNER, JJ., concur. HAIGHT, J., absent.

STUDEMAN, Appellant, v. BECKER, Respondent. (Court of Appeals of New York. May 10, 1904.) Motion to dismiss an appeal from an order of the Appellate Division of the Supreme Court in the Fourth Judicial Department (90 App. Div. 612, 85 N. Y. Supp. 1148), entered January 28, 1904, which affirmed an order of Special Term denying a motion to amend a judgment. The motion was made upon the ground that the appeal was unauthorized. Elton D. Warner, for the motion. Thomas H. Larkins, opposed. No opinion. Motion granted, and appeal dismissed, with costs, and $10 costs of motion.

TAFT, Respondent, v. LITTLE, Appellant. (Court of Appeals of New York. April 8, 1904.) No opinion. Motion for reargument denied, with $10 costs. See 178 N. Y. 127, 70 N. E. 211.

TANENBAUM, Respondent, v. EISEMAN et al., Appellants. SAME v. LEVY et al. (Court of Appeals of New York. April 26, 1904.) Appeals from judgments of the Appellate Division of the Supreme Court in the First Judicial Department (83 App. Div. 639, 82 N. Y. Supp. 76; 83 App. Div. 319, 82 N. Y. Supp. 171), entered June 4, 1903, modifying, and affirming as modified, judgments in favor of plaintiff entered upon verdicts directed by the court and affirming orders denying motions for new trials. A. Blumenstiel, for appellants. Ernest Hall and Mayer L. Halff, for respondent.

PER CURIAM. Judgments affirmed, with costs.

PARKER, C. J., and GRAY, BARTLETT, HAIGHT, MARTIN, VANN, and WERNER, JJ., concur.

In re TOTTEN. (Court of Appeals of New York. April 28, 1904.) Motion to dismiss an appeal from an order of the Appellate Division of the Supreme Court in the Second Judicial Department (89 App. Div. 368, 85 N. Y. Supp. 928), made December 30, 1903, which reversed a decree of the Kings County Surrogate's Court rejecting claims of the respondent herein against the estate of Fanny A. Lattan, deceased. The motion was made upon the grounds that there were no questions involved which the Court of Appeals could review, the appeal being frivolous and taken for delay only. R. L. Maynard, for the motion. Benjamin F. Tracy, opposed.

PER CURIAM. Motion denied, with $10 costs.

TOULMIN, Respondent, v. LADOW, Appellant. (Court of Appeals of New York. April 8, 1904.) Appeal from a judgment of the Appellate Division of the Supreme Court in the Third Judicial Department (84 App. Div. 636, 81 N. Y. Supp. 1145), entered May 8, 1903, affirming a judgment in favor of plaintiff entered upon the report of a referee. Frederick W. Cameron, for appellant. Marcus T. Hun, for respondent.

PER CURIAM. Judgment affirmed, with costs.

PARKER, C. J., and GRAY, O'BRIEN, BARTLETT, HAIGHT, MARTIN, and CULLEN, JJ., concur.

TOWN OF SMITHTOWN, Respondent, v. MILLER, Appellant. (Court of Appeals of New York. May 20, 1904.) Appeal from a judgment of the Appellate Division of the Supreme Court in the Second Judicial Department (75 App. Div. 309, 78 N. Y. Supp. 178), entered October 16, 1902, affirming a judgment in favor of plaintiff entered upon a verdict and an order denying a motion for a new trial. W. P. Knapp, for appellant. Rowland Miles, for respondent.

PER CURIAM. Judgment affirmed, with costs.

PARKER, C. J., and GRAY, O'BRIEN, BARTLETT, MARTIN, VANN, and CULLEN, JJ., concur.

TURNER et al., Appellants, v. PENDERGAST et al., Respondents. (Court of Appeals of New York. May 3, 1904.) Motion to dismiss an appeal from a judgment of the Appellate Division of the Supreme Court in the Fourth Judicial Department (86 App. Div. 172, 83 N. Y. Supp. 1013), entered July 23, 1903, affirming a judgment in favor of defendants entered upon a dismissal of the complaint by the court on trial at Special Term. The motion was made upon the grounds that the decision of the Appellate Division was unanimous, and that there were no questions of law to review; the exceptions being frivolous. S. M. Lindsley, for the motion. William Townsend, opposed. No opinion. Motion denied, without costs.

UNITED PRESS, Respondent, v. A. S. ABELL CO. et al., Defendants. (Court of Appeals of New York. March 29, 1904.) Appeal from a judgment of the Appellate Division of the Supreme Court in the first judicial department (79 App. Div. 550, 80 N. Y. Supp. 454), entered March 16, 1903, modifying and affirming as modified a judgment in favor of plaintiff entered upon a verdict and affirming an order denying a motion for a new trial. Austen G. Fox and Henry T. Fay, for appellant Agnus. William C. Davis, for respondent.

PER CURIAM. Judgment affirmed, with costs.

PARKER, C. J., and GRAY, HAIGHT, MARTIN, CULLEN, and WERNER, JJ., concur. O'BRIEN, J., not voting.

UNIVERSAL TRUST CO., Respondent, v. LENT, Appellant, et al. (Court of Appeals of New York. March 15, 1904.) Appeal from a judgment of the Appellate Division of the Supreme Court in the Second Judicial Department (83 App. Div. 634, 81 N. Y. Supp. 1145), entered May 9, 1903, affirming a judgment in favor of plaintiff entered upon a decision of the court on trial at Special Term. T. M. Tyng, for appellant Lent. George E. Waldo, for respondent.

PER CURIAM. Judgment affirmed, with costs.

PARKER, C. J., and O'BRIEN, BARTLETT, MARTIN, VANN, and WERNER, JJ., concur. GRAY, J., absent.

VINCENT, Respondent, v. ALDEN, Appellant. (Court of Appeals of New York. March 22, 1904.) No opinion. Motion for reargument denied, with $10 costs. See 177 N. Y. 545, 69 N. E. 1132.

WALSH, Respondent, v. NEW YORK & Q. C. RY. CO., Appellant. (Court of Appeals of New York. April 18, 1904.) Appeal from a judgment of the Appellate Division of the Supreme Court in the Second Judicial Department (80 App. Div. 316, 80 N. Y. Supp. 767), entered March 16, 1903, affirming a judgment in favor of plaintiff entered upon a verdict and an order denying a motion for a new trial. I. R. Oeland and William E. Stewart, for appellant. S. S. Whitehouse, for respondent.

PER CURIAM. Judgment affirmed, with costs.

O'BRIEN, BARTLETT, HAIGHT, MARTIN, and CULLEN, JJ., concur. PARKER, C. J., and GRAY, J., dissent.

WARNER v. HOUSE et al. (Court of Appeals of New York. April 28, 1904.) Motion to dismiss an appeal from an order of the Appellate Division of the Supreme Court in the Fourth Judicial Department (90 App. Div. 611, 85 N. Y. Supp. 1150), made January 5, 1904, which affirmed an order of a Trial Term setting aside a verdict in favor of defendant and granting a new trial. The motion was made upon the ground that the order appealed from was not appealable to the Court of Appeals. Alexander H. Cowie, for the motion. Costello, Welch & Costello, opposed. No opinion. Motion granted, and appeal dismissed, with costs, and $10 costs of motion.

WEAVER, Appellant, v. WEAVER, Respondent. (Court of Appeals of New York. May 20, 1904.) Appeal from a judgment of the Appellate Division of the Supreme Court in the Fourth Judicial Department (74 App. Div. 591, 77 N. Y. Supp. 568), entered July 29, 1902, affirming a judgment in favor of defendant entered upon a dismissal of the complaint by the court on trial at Special Term. Charles Van Voorhis, for appellant. Percival De W. Oviatt, for respondent.

PER CURIAM. Judgment affirmed, with costs.

PARKER, C. J., and GRAY, O'BRIEN, BARTLETT, MARTIN, VANN, and CULLEN, JJ., concur.

WESTERFIELD et al., Appellants, v. ROGERS et al., Respondents. (Court of Appeals of New York. March 22, 1904.) No opinion. Motion to amend remittitur granted, and the clerk of the Supreme Court requested to return the remittitur in this action to this court, to the end that the same may be amended, so that the judgment of the Appellate Division (71 N. Y. Supp. 401) shall be reversed, and the judgment entered on the report of the referee modified by inserting schedule B of the referee's report, and, as so modified, affirmed. See 174 N. Y. 230, 66 N. E. 813; 175 N. Y. 499, 67 N. E. 1091.

WHEELER CONDENSER & ENGINEERING CO., Respondent, v. R. G. PACKARD CO., Appellant. (Court of Appeals of New York. March 29, 1904.) Appeal from a judgment of the Appellate Division of the Supreme Court in the First Judicial Department (83 App. Div. 288, 82 N. Y. Supp. 165), entered May 18, 1903, affirming a judgment in favor of plaintiff entered upon a verdict directed by the court. C. D. Rust, for appellant. Norman W. Kerngood, for respondent.

PER CURIAM. Judgment affirmed, with costs, and 10 per cent. damages, under section 3251 of the Code of Civil Procedure.

O'BRIEN, BARTLETT, HAIGHT, VANN, CULLEN, and WERNER, JJ., concur. PARKER, C. J., absent.

YORKVILLE BANK v. HENRY ZELTNER BREWING CO. et al. (Court of Appeals of New York. March 29, 1904.) Appeal from an order of the Appellate Division of the Supreme Court in the First Judicial Department (80 App. Div. 578, 80 N. Y. Supp. 839), entered March 21, 1903, which reversed an order of Special Term denying a motion to vacate and set aside a judgment theretofore entered in this action, the execution issued thereon, and a levy made under said execution, and granted such motion. Louis Marshall, Moses Weinman, and Abraham Benedict, for appellant. Henry A. Forster, for respondent Sutherland.

PER CURIAM. Appeal dismissed, with costs.

PARKER, C. J., and GRAY, O'BRIEN, HAIGHT, MARTIN, CULLEN, and WERNER, JJ., concur.

CLARK v. CITY OF CHICAGO. (Supreme Court of Illinois. April 20, 1904.) Appeal from Cook County Court; O. N. Carter, Judge. Action by the city of Chicago against Robert C. Clark, trustee. From a judgment for the city, defendant appeals. Reversed. Eugene H. Garnett (Gwynn Garnett and Joseph H. Fitch, of counsel), for appellant. Robert Redfield and Frank Johnston, Jr. (Edgar Bronson Tolman, Corp. Counsel, of counsel), for appellee.

PER CURIAM. This appeal is prosecuted from a judgment of the county court of Cook county overruling appellant's objections and confirming a special assessment against the property of appellant. The only issue was upon the legal objections, and only one of them is involved here. It appears that the record of the first resolution of the board of local improvements in this proceeding refers to the engineer's estimate in the following language: "The estimate of the cost of such improvement made by the engineer of the board being $887,000, which said estimate is hereby made a part hereof by reference." No other mention of the estimate is found in any part of the record, the evidence showing that the estimate was filed in the vault used by the board and was open for inspection. It will thus be seen that the question here presented is upon the same legal objection, and identical with the question considered in the case of Kilgallen v. City of Chicago, 206 Ill. 557, 69 N. E. 586, wherein it is held that a like objection to the one made in this case should have been sustained. That case is conclusive of the question here presented, and the judgment of the county court will be reversed, and the cause remanded. Reversed and remanded.

McDONALD et al. v. HOLDOM. (Supreme Court of Illinois. Feb. 17, 1904.) Appeal from Appellate Court, First District. Action by Jesse Holdom against Michael C. McDonald and others. From a judgment of the Appellate Court (108 Ill. App. 449), reversing an order of the circuit court, defendants appeal. Affirmed.

PER CURIAM. This is an appeal from a judgment of the Appellate Court for the First District reversing an order of the circuit court of Cook county, remanding the cause and directing a judgment in the lower court. This suit is between the same parties, involves precisely the same questions, was heard in the two lower courts on precisely the same proofs and with the same results, as the case of McDonald v. Holdom, 69 N. E. 21, in which a judgment of affirmance has been entered in this court at the present term. The order of the circuit court in that case directed the satisfaction of a judgment in that court, recovered by appellee against appellants on an appeal bond given by appellants upon an appeal from the Appellate Court to this court in earlier litigation between the parties. The order of the circuit court in this case directed the satisfaction of a judgment in that court, recovered by appellee against appellant on an appeal bond given by appellants upon the appeal from the circuit court to the Appellate Court in the former suit. A full statement of the facts relating to both cases will be found in McDonald v. Holdom, supra. For the reasons assigned in the opinion in that case, the judgment of the Appellate Court under review in this case must be affirmed. Judgment affirmed.

CARR et al. v. DIAMOND PLATE GLASS CO. et al. (Supreme Court of Indiana. March 29, 1904.) Appeal from Superior Court, Howard County; Hiram Brownlee, Judge. Action by Sarah J. Carr and others against the Diamond Plate Glass Company. From a judgment for defendant, plaintiffs appeal. Transferred from the Appellate Court, under section 1337u, Burns' Ann. St. 1901. Reversed. B. C. Moon, for appellants. Bell & Perdum and Blacklidge, Shirley & Wolf, for appellee.

HADLEY, J. Contract for exploring for gas. Suit to recover stipulated sum for delay in drilling a well and damage for failure to furnish free gas. The complaint in this case and the contract sued on are in all respects, except as to dates and amounts, like those involved in Hancock v. Diamond Plate Glass Co. (decided February 16, 1904) 70 N. E. 149, and, as in the latter case, the only question involved in this is the sufficiency of the complaint. For reasons stated in the Hancock Case, the judgment in this case is reversed, with instructions to overrule the demurrer to the amended complaint.

NORTHWESTERN MUT. LIFE INS. CO. v. McKEEN et al. (Supreme Court of Indiana. April 1, 1904.) Appeal from Circuit Court, Vigo County; Jas. E. Piety, Judge. Action by William R. McKeen and others against the Northwestern Mutual Life Insurance Company. From a judgment in favor of plaintiffs, defendant appeals. Transferred from the Appellate Court under Acts 1901, p. 567, § 10, cl. 3 (Burns' Ann. St. 1901, 1337j). Affirmed. B. V. Marshall and Baker & Daniels, for appellant. McNutt & McNutt, for appellees.

MONKS, J. The questions presented by this appeal are substantially the same as those decided in Northwestern Mutual Life Insurance Company v. Kate Kidder (this term) 70 N. E. 489. Upon the authority of that case, the judgment of the trial court is affirmed.

CLAYPOOL et al. v. STEIN. (Appellate Court of Indiana. May 10, 1904.) Appeal from Superior Court, Marion County; Jno. L. McMaster, Judge. Action between Edward F. Claypool and others and Theodore Stein, trustee, etc. From a judgment in favor of the latter, the former appeal. Reversed. Jno. W. Claypool, Daniel Wait Howe, and Russell T. Byers, for appellants. Florea & Seidensticker and Wilson & Townley, for appellee.

PER CURIAM. The questions involved in this appeal are in principle the same as those presented in Claypool v. German Fire Insurance Company (March 9, 1904) 70 N. E. 281. Upon the authority of that case, the judgment herein is reversed, and the cause is remanded, with instructions to restate the conclusions of law and exclude from the amount for which appellee is awarded priority the sum of $221.44, expended or retained as expenses incident to the loan.

COFFINBERRY v. McCLELLAN et al.[1] (Appellate Court of Indiana. Feb. 19, 1904.) Appeal from Circuit Court, De Kalb County; C. W. Watkins, Special Judge. Action between Elizabeth K. Coffinberry and Elizabeth A. McClellan, as executrix, and others. From a judgment in favor of the latter, the former appeals. Transferred to Supreme Court on division of judges. Fraser & Isham and J. E. & J. H. Rose, for appellant. F. S. Roby and Zollars, Worden & Zollars, for appellees.

PER CURIAM. This cause coming up for determination by the First Division, and the three judges of such division having failed to concur in the result, and the cause having been submitted to the entire court, and one of the judges being disqualified to sit in the case, and four of the remaining judges having failed to concur in the result, the cause is transferred to the Supreme Court, under section 1337o, Burns' Ann. St. 1901.

CURLESS v. DIAMOND PLATE GLASS CO. (Appellate Court of Indiana, Division No. 1. April 21, 1904.) Appeal from Circuit Court, Howard County; J. F. Elliott, Judge. Action by Clarinda Curless against the Diamond Plate Glass Company. From a judgment overruling a demurrer to the third paragraph of the answer, plaintiff appeals. Reversed. B. C. Moon, for appellant. Bell & Purdum and Blacklidge, Shirley & Wolf, for appellee.

BLACK, J. Upon the authority of Hancock v. Diamond Plate Glass Company, 70 N. E. 149, decided by the Supreme Court of Indiana February 16, 1904, the judgment herein is reversed, and the cause is remanded, with instruction to sustain the demurrer of the appellant to the third paragraph of the answer by the appellees.

ECHELBARGER v. DIAMOND PLATE GLASS CO. (Appellate Court of Indiana, Division No. 1. April 21, 1904.) Appeal from Circuit Court, Howard County; J. F. Elliott,

[1] Transferred to Supreme Court, 73 N. E. 97.

Judge. Action by Francis M. Echelbarger against the Diamond Plate Glass Company. From a judgment overruling a demurrer to the third and fourth paragraphs of the answer, plaintiff appeals. Reversed. B. C. Moon, for appellant. Bell & Purdum and Blacklidge, Shirley & Wolf, for appellee.

BLACK, J. Upon the authority of Hancock v. Diamond Plate Glass Co., 70 N. E. 149, decided by the Supreme Court of Indiana February 16, 1904, the judgment herein is reversed, and the cause is remanded, with instruction to sustain the appellant's demurrer to the third and fourth paragraphs of the answer of the appellees.

FREEMAN et al. v. DIAMOND PLATE GLASS CO. et al. (Appellate Court of Indiana, Division No. 1. April 1, 1904.) Appeal from Superior Court, Howard County; B. F. Harness, Judge. Action by Anna Freeman and others against the Diamond Plate Glass Company and others. Judgment for defendants, and plaintiffs appeal. Reversed. B. C. Moon, for appellants. Bell & Purdum and Blacklidge, Shirley & Wolf, for appellees.

HENLEY, C. J. The questions involved in this appeal are in all respects similar to the questions decided by the Supreme Court of this state in the case of Hancock v. Diamond Plate Glass Company (decided at November term, 1903) 70 N. E. 149; and upon the authority of that case this case is reversed. We are of the opinion that justice will best be subserved by granting a new trial in this case. The judgment is therefore reversed, and a new trial ordered.

STATE ex rel. STUART et al. v. SCHMIDT et al.* (Appellate Court of Indiana. Division No. 2. March 8, 1904.) Appeal from Circuit Court, Marion County; H. C. Allen, Judge. Action by the state of Indiana, on the relation of Romus F. Stuart and another, against William H. Schmidt and others. Judgment for defendants, and relators appeal. Affirmed. See the companion case of State ex rel. Stuart v. Holt, 70 N. E. 387. Pliny W. Bartholomew, for appellants. Hawkins & Smith and Wilson & Townley, for appellees.

ROBY, J. The "State of Indiana ex rel. Romus F. Stuart and Romus F. Stuart" instituted this suit against William H. Schmidt and his several sureties, upon two official bonds executed by him as treasurer of Marion county, covering terms beginning, respectively, September 3, 1895 and 1897. The amended complaint is in two paragraphs, in each of which a money judgment is prayed on account of specific facts set up. The board of commissioners and the auditor of Marion county were made defendants; it being alleged against them that they, knowing the facts, refused to institute the action, and had, as plaintiffs were informed and believed, executed a receipt and made a pretended settlement with Schmidt. To the complaint demurrers were sustained. Appellants refused to plead further, and appeal from the judgment of the court thereupon rendered. The special grounds of demurrer stated were that the plaintiffs had no legal capacity to sue, that there was a defect of parties, that the complaint did not state facts sufficient to constitute a cause of action, and that no breach of the bond averred in the complaint stated facts sufficient to constitute a cause of action. The questions argued as to the appellants' right to maintain this action are decided adversely to appellees' contention in Zuelly v. Casper (Ind. Sup.) 67 N. E. 103. This action was, like that one, instituted for the benefit of the county by a citizen and taxpayer thereof. The absence of a special injury different from that suffered by the general public was insisted upon in that case, as in this one. Following the prior decision, we hold that the grounds of demurrer, exclusive of those questioning the sufficiency of fact, were not well taken. This action is brought upon official bond. In the Zuelly Case suit was brought against the officer to recover money alleged to have been wrongfully appropriated by him. The statute is that "actions upon official bonds and bonds payable to the state shall be brought in the name of the state of Indiana upon the relation of the party interested." Burns' Ann. St. 1901, § 253; State v. Wright, 8 Blackf. 65. The logic of the decisions holding that the individual taxpayer may maintain an action for the benefit of the county requires that he be recognized as a proper relator in a suit on an official bond, when the officers upon whom the duty to act as relator primarily rests refuse to act or are parties to the wrongful acts counted upon as a breach of the bond. The complaint avers that the treasurer and principal in the bond in suit, during his two terms, collected interest on time warrants, loaned public moneys and received interest thereon, and collected delinquent tax collection fees, and refused and refuses to account for any part of the sums so received, and that he was paid his salary without having refunded fees collected by him, as required by the fee and salary act of 1895. For the purpose of this opinion, in view of the result reached, it is sufficient to say that the complaint states facts sufficient to constitute a cause of action upon the officer's official bond in favor of the state of Indiana on relation of a proper person, which we hold an individual taxpayer, under the averments relative to the attitude of the county officers, to be. The action is brought by the "State of Indiana on relation of Romus F. Stuart." The amended complaint begins as follows: "The plaintiffs herein, the state of Indiana ex rel. Romus F. Stuart and Romus F. Stuart, by Pliny W. Bartholomew, their attorney, complain of the defendants, and for cause of action allege: That Romus F. Stuart is a resident taxpayer and freeholder of Marion county, Indiana, and has so been for ten years last past, and has paid his taxes into the treasury of Marion county, Indiana, all of said time, including the taxes of 1899, and first installment of 1900. That as such resident taxpayer he has an interest in all money paid into, paid out, and belonging to the treasury of Marion county, Indiana, during the years 1895, 1896, 1897, 1898, and 1899, in common and jointly with all taxpayers of Marion county, Indiana. That the number of resident taxpayers of Marion county, Indiana, is more than fifty thousand, making it impracticable for them to join the plaintiffs herein as coplaintiffs. Therefore the plaintiffs bring this action for their own, on behalf of and for the benefit of all the taxpayers of Marion county, Indiana, and in trust for the county of Marion, Indiana. That a part of the money sued for in the plaintiffs' complaint herein belongs to plaintiffs as such taxpayers, and was held and placed in the hands of William H. Schmidt, treasurer of Marion county, Indiana, as custodian for plaintiffs and all taxpayers of Marion county, Indiana, as by the law in such cases made and provided, and for their use and benefit." It is well settled that an individual cannot in his own name as plaintiff maintain an action upon an official bond. Neal v. State, 49 Ind. 51; Yater v. State, 58 Ind. 299. Nor can an action upon an official bond payable to the state be jointly maintained by a proper and an improper relator. Neal v. State, 49 Ind. 51; Elliott v. Pontius, 136 Ind. 653, 35 N. E. 562, 36 N. E. 421, and cases cited. A complaint must proceed upon some definite theory, and upon that theory it must state a cause of action in favor of all who join as plaintiffs. Gas Co. v. Spaugh, 17 Ind. App. 683, 46 N. E. 691; Martin v. Davis, 82 Ind. 38, 41; Fatman v. Leet, 41 Ind. 133; Peters v. Guthrie, 119 Ind. 44, 20 N. E. 536. If a complaint states one cause of action

*Rehearing denied April 19, 1904.

in favor of one plaintiff and another in favor of another plaintiff, but does not state the same cause of action in favor of both, it is insufficient on demurrer for want of facts. Smith v. Roseboom, 10 Ind. App. 129, 37 N. E. 559. The question for decision is not alone whether the complaint states a good cause of action in favor of Mr. Stuart in his individual capacity, but whether it states the same cause of action in his favor as is stated in favor of the state of Indiana ex rel., etc. The assignment of error is entitled as the amended complaint. It begins as follows: "Now comes the state of Indiana on relation of Romus F. Stuart and Romus F. Stuart, appellants, and says." The action, as hereinbefore stated, is founded upon two official bonds, breaches of which are set up. Whatever might be said of Mr. Stuart's right to maintain a suit in his own name to recover from the officer for the benefit of the county, as was done in the Zuelly Case, it cannot be said that he has any individual right to recover on the bond in his own name. When the taxpayer is permitted, under special conditions, to act as relator, he has been placed in a position to enable him to fully guard the public interest. There is an averment in this complaint as follows: "That the plaintiffs herein have been put to great labor and expense in the preparation and prosecution of this cause, and in the employment of legal counsel herein. That a reasonable compensation to remunerate them in the premises is a sum of money equal to 25 per cent. of whatever moneys may be recovered in final settlement and adjudication of this cause." The relator in such a proceeding as this is entitled to reasonable fees and charges out of the fund recovered through his effort. Kimble v. Board (Ind. App.) 66 N. E. 1023. This fact does not give him an individual claim against the officer or his sureties. His claim is against the fund recovered, and in no wise affects the recovery. It is not founded upon the bond. It is not necessary to consider when or in what form such relator may present his claim. The averment quoted does not make the pleading good. We fully agree with the learned counsel for appellants "that all power comes from and abides in the people; that whatever is right, true, and honest for and in behalf of the people must be done by their trustees and agents in the conduct of their affairs; that the courts should, so far as possible, protect the people in their property rights, and secure to them their own." But it is equally true that regular methods of procedure are essential to the security of public and private rights. No rule is here enforced against appellants which has not been long settled and repeatedly declared. The complaint was once amended in the trial court, and opportunity existed for further amendment. Courts consider causes as they are presented. The amended complaint does not state any cause of action upon this bond in favor of Mr. Stuart individually, and the demurrer was properly sustained. Judgment affirmed.

YEOMANS et al. v. HEATH et al. (Supreme Judicial Court of Massachusetts. Suffolk. Feb. 26, 1904.) Appeal from Superior Court, Suffolk County; L. Le B. Holmes, Judge. Action by Edward S. Yeomans and others against Frank Heath and others. From a judgment for plaintiffs, defendants appeal. Judgment for the defendants. Joseph Cavanagh, for appellants. Wm. Henri Irish, for appellees.

KNOWLTON, C. J. The case as stated in the agreed statement of facts and in the plaintiffs' declaration is within St. 1890, p. 479, c. 437, but is not within the law as amended by St. 1901, p. 391, c. 459. This amendment deprived the plaintiffs of the right of recovery which they previously had. The case is covered by the decision in Wilson v. Head et al. (Mass.) 69 N. E. 317. Assuming, as we must for the purpose of this decision, that the agreed statement of facts correctly presents the case, the entry should be: Judgment for the defendants.

ANDERSON v. RAILWAY CO. (No. 7,614.) (Supreme Court of Ohio. March 3, 1903.) Error to Circuit Court, Franklin County. Thomas E. Powell, for plaintiff in error. Watson, Burr & Livesay, for defendant in error.

PER CURIAM. Judgment affirmed.

BURKET, C. J., and DAVIS, SHAUCK, PRICE, and CREW, JJ., concur.

ÆTNA LIFE INS. CO. v. HANNER. (No. 8,181.) (Supreme Court of Ohio. Jan. 5, 1904.) Error to Circuit Court, Lucas County. James, Beverstock & Donahey and James, Millard & Powell, for plaintiff in error. Kinney & Newton, for defendant in error.

PER CURIAM. Judgment affirmed.

BURKET, C. J., and SPEAR and CREW, JJ., concur.

BAKER v. LAMKIN et al. (No. 7,678.) (Supreme Court of Ohio. March 3, 1903.) Error to Circuit Court, Huron County. S. M. Young, for plaintiff in error. Andrews Bros., for defendants in error.

PER CURIAM. Judgment affirmed.

BURKET, C. J., and DAVIS and PRICE, JJ., concur.

BALTIMORE & O. R. CO. v. MILLER. (No. 7,988.) (Supreme Court of Ohio. Oct. 6, 1903.) Error to Circuit Court, Richland County. J. H. Collins and Cummings, McBride & Wolfe, for plaintiff in error. H. T. Manner and J. M. Reed, for defendant in error.

PER CURIAM. Judgment affirmed.

BURKET, C. J., and SPEAR, DAVIS, SHAUCK, PRICE, and CREW, JJ., concur.

BANK et al. v. GRANGER. (No. 7,985.) (Supreme Court of Ohio. June 16, 1903.) Error to Circuit Court, Hamilton County. Charles W. Baker, for plaintiffs in error. Foraker, Outcalt, Granger & Prior and Burch & Johnson, for defendants in error.

PER CURIAM. Judgment of the circuit court reversed, and that of the common pleas affirmed.

BURKET, C. J., and SPEAR, DAVIS, SHAUCK, and PRICE, JJ., concur.

BANK v. MAUMEE CYCLE CO. et al. (No. 7,750.) (Supreme Court of Ohio. April 21, 1903.) Error to Circuit Court, Lucas County. Smith & Beckwith and R. S. Holbrook, for plaintiff in error. Seney & Johnson and Doyle & Lewis, for defendants in error.

PER CURIAM. Judgment affirmed.

BURKET, C. J., and SPEAR and DAVIS, JJ., concur as to releasing stockholders from liability for debts incurred after transfer of their stock. BURKET, C. J., and DAVIS and PRICE, JJ., concur as to distribution of fund. SPEAR, SHAUCK, and CREW, JJ., dissent as to said distribution.

BARBER et al. v. COFFMAN. (No. 8,183.) (Supreme Court of Ohio. Dec. 15, 1903.) Error to Circuit Court, Franklin County. T. J.

uncan and Eugene Lane, for plaintiffs in er-r. Thomas H. Clark, for defendant in error.

PER CURIAM. Judgment affirmed.

SPEAR, SHAUCK, and CREW, JJ., con-r.

BARRETT v. CITY OF CLEVELAND. ;o. 7,559.) (Supreme Court of Ohio. March 1903.) Error to Circuit Court, Cuyahoga ounty. Ingersoll & Clum, for plaintiff in er-r. M. W. Beacom and Babcock, Payer, Gage Carey, for defendant in error.

PER CURIAM. Judgment affirmed.

BURKET, C. J., and DAVIS and PRICE, ., concur.

BATES v. DUBBS. (No. 7,821.) (Supreme ourt of Ohio. March 31, 1903.) Error to ircuit Court, Columbiana County. W. S. mmons, for plaintiff in error. A. W. Taylor nd L. P. Metzger, for defendant in error.

PER CURIAM. Judgment affirmed.

SPEAR, SHAUCK, and CREW, JJ., con-ur.

BAXTER et al. v. HEWITT et al. (No. .884.) (Supreme Court of Ohio. Oct. 13, 903.) Error to Circuit Court, Richland Coun-y. Brucker & Cummins, for plaintiffs in er-or. Jenner & Weldon, for defendants in error.

PER CURIAM. Judgment affirmed.

BURKET, C. J., and DAVIS and PRICE, J., concur.

BEALL et al. v. CITY OF MARTINS FER-RY et al. (No. 7,747.) (Supreme Court of Ohio. April 21, 1903.) Error to Circuit Court, Belmont County. S. W. Boyd, F. R. Sedgwick, and H. G. Pratt, for plaintiffs in error. C. L. Weems and George Cooke, for defendants in error.

PER CURIAM. Judgment affirmed.

BURKET, C. J., and SPEAR, DAVIS, and SHAUCK, JJ., concur.

BENNET & CO. v. RAILWAY CO. (No. 8,233.) (Supreme Court of Ohio. April 21, 1903.) Error to Circuit Court, Franklin Coun-y. J. H. Collins, for plaintiffs in error. Mer-ick & Tompkins and T. J. Duncan, for de-fendant in error.

PER CURIAM. Judgment affirmed.

BURKET, C. J., and DAVIS and PRICE, JJ., concur.

BERDAN & CO. v. RAILWAY CO. (No. 7,736.) (Supreme Court of Ohio. March 24, 1903.) Error to Circuit Court, Lucas County. Ralph S. Holbrook, for plaintiff in error. Swayne, Hayes & Tyler, for defendant in error.

PER CURIAM. Judgment affirmed.

BURKET, C. J., and DAVIS, SHAUCK, PRICE, and CREW, JJ., concur.

BICK v. REITER. (No. 7,991.) (Supreme Court of Ohio. Oct. 27, 1903.) Error to Circuit Court, Franklin County. Donaldson & Tussing, for plaintiff in error. Edward L. Taylor, Jr., Augustus T. Seymour, and Karl T. Weber, for defendant in error.

PER CURIAM. Judgment affirmed.

BURKET, C. J., and DAVIS and PRICE, JJ., concur.

BOARD OF EDUCATION v. STATE ex rel. MORGANSTERN. (No. 8,239.) (Supreme Court of Ohio. June 9, 1903.) Error to Circuit Court, Trumbull County. T. H. Gillmer and E. E. Roberts, for plaintiff in error. Charles Fillius, for defendant in error.

PER CURIAM. Judgment affirmed.

BURKET, C. J., and SPEAR, DAVIS, SHAUCK, PRICE, and CREW, JJ., concur.

BOARD OF EDUCATION v. STATE ex rel. PARKE. (No. 8,240.) (Supreme Court of Ohio. June 9, 1903.) T. H. Gillmer and E. E. Roberts, for plaintiff in error. Charles Fillius, for defendant in error.

PER CURIAM. Judgment affirmed.

BURKET, C. J., and SPEAR, DAVIS, SHAUCK, PRICE, and CREW, JJ., concur.

BODE v. KECK et al. (No. 8,012.) (Supreme Court of Ohio. Nov. 10, 1903.) Error to Circuit Court, Hamilton County. Goebel & Bettinger, for plaintiff in error. Jones & James, for defendants in error.

PER CURIAM. Judgment of the circuit court reversed, and judgment of the court of common pleas affirmed.

SPEAR, DAVIS, SHAUCK, and PRICE, JJ., concur.

BOGEN et al. v. CINCINNATI UNION STOCKYARDS CO. (No. 7,670.) (Supreme Court of Ohio. March 10, 1903.) Error to Superior Court of Cincinnati. John C. Healy, for plaintiffs in error. William Worthington, Follett & Kelley, Peck, Shaffer & Peck, and Dennis F. Cash, for defendant in error.

PER CURIAM. Judgment affirmed.

BURKET, C. J., and SPEAR, DAVIS, SHAUCK, PRICE, and CREW, JJ., concur.

BOGEN et al. v. CINCINNATI UNION STOCKYARDS CO. (No. 7,671.) (Supreme Court of Ohio. March 10, 1903.) Error to Superior Court of Cincinnati. John C. Healy, for plaintiffs in error. William Worthington, Follett & Kelley, Peck, Shaffer & Peck, and Dennis F. Cash, for defendant in error.

PER CURIAM. Judgment affirmed.

BURKET, C. J., and SPEAR, DAVIS, SHAUCK, PRICE, and CREW, JJ., concur.

BOWLUS v. CABLE. (No. 8,187.) (Supreme Court of Ohio. Dec. 15, 1903.) Error to Circuit Court, Lucas County. D. R. Austin and G. Harmon, for plaintiff in error. O. S. Brumback and C. A. Thatcher, for defendant in error.

PER CURIAM. Judgment affirmed.

SPEAR, SHAUCK, and CREW, JJ., concur.

BRAUCHER et al. v. BRAUCHER. (No. 7,645.) (Supreme Court of Ohio. March 10, 1903.) Error to Circuit Court, Stark County. Day, Lynch & Day and A. Pomerene, for plaintiffs in error. Sterling & Braucher, for defendant in error.

PER CURIAM. Judgment affirmed.

BURKET, C. J., and DAVIS and PRICE, JJ., concur.

BRETZ et al. v. MOORE. (No. 8,227.) (Supreme Court of Ohio. Jan. 19, 1904.) Error to Circuit Court, Sandusky County. Edmund B.

King and George H. Withey, for plaintiffs in error. Richards & Heffner, for defendant in error.

PER CURIAM. Judgment affirmed.

SPEAR, SHAUCK, and CREW, JJ., concur.

BREYMAN et al. v. WILTSIE. (No. 7,625.) (Supreme Court of Ohio. March 3, 1903.) Error to Circuit Court, Lucas County. B. A. Hayes, for plaintiff in error. G. F. Wells, for defendant in error.

PER CURIAM. Judgment affirmed.

BURKET, C. J., and DAVIS and PRICE, JJ., concur.

BRITSCH v. BRITSCH et al. (No. 7,965.) (Supreme Court of Ohio. Dec. 18, 1903.) Error to Circuit Court, Marion County. Copeland & Bartram, for plaintiff in error. J. W. Jacoby and Hoke W. Donithen, for defendants in error.

PER CURIAM. Judgment affirmed.

BURKET, C. J., and SPEAR, DAVIS, SHAUCK, PRICE, and CREW, JJ., concur.

BURCKHARDT v. GREENE. (No. 7,859.) (Supreme Court of Ohio. May 5, 1903.) Error to Circuit Court, Hamilton County. Goebel & Bettinger, for plaintiff in error. Galvin & Galvin, for defendant in error.

PER CURIAM. Judgment affirmed.

BURKET, C. J., and DAVIS and PRICE, JJ., concur.

BURKHART v. FIELDS. (No. 7,709.) (Supreme Court of Ohio. March 17, 1903.) Error to Circuit Court, Lorain County. L. B. Fauver and A. R. Webber, for plaintiff in error. E. G. Johnson and Thompson & Glitsch, for defendant in error.

PER CURIAM. Judgment affirmed.

BURKET, C. J., and DAVIS and PRICE, JJ., concur.

BURNS-BOWE BANKING CO. v. JORDAN et al. (No. 7,998.) (Supreme Court of Ohio. June 25, 1903.) Error to Circuit Court, Cuyahoga County. Hart & Canfield, for plaintiff in error. Noble, Pinney & Willard and James M. Jones, for defendants in error.

PER CURIAM. Judgment affirmed.

SPEAR, SHAUCK, and CREW, JJ., concur.

CALHOUN v. SIMMONS. (No. 7,772.) (Supreme Court of Ohio. April 14, 1903.) Error to Circuit Court, Madison County. M. S. Murray and John A. Lincoln, for plaintiff in error. Selwyn N. Owen, T. E. Powell, and R. H. McCloud, for defendant in error.

PER CURIAM. Judgment affirmed, there not being enough of the record printed to raise the question argued.

BURKET, C. J., and SPEAR, DAVIS, SHAUCK, PRICE, and CREW, JJ., concur.

CAMERON v. LAYMON. (No. 7,732.) (Supreme Court of Ohio. March 24, 1903.) Error to Circuit Court, Montgomery County. Kreitzer & Kreitzer, for plaintiff in error. Gottschall, Crawford & Limbert, for defendant in error.

PER CURIAM. Judgment reversed as per journal entry.

BURKET, C. J., and SPEAR, SHAUCK, PRICE, and CREW, JJ., concur.

CAMPBELL et al. v. CONRAD. (No. 7,655.) (Supreme Court of Ohio. March 17, 1903.) Error to Circuit Court, Licking County. S. M. Hunter and A. A. Stasel, for plaintiffs in error. Kibler & Kibler, for defendant in error.

PER CURIAM. Judgment affirmed.

BURKET, C. J., and DAVIS, SHAUCK, PRICE, and CREW, JJ., concur.

CARENO v. STATE. (No. 8,179.) (Supreme Court of Ohio. Dec. 8, 1903.) Error to Circuit Court, Summit County. Wilcox & Grant and W. A. Spencer, for plaintiff in error. H. M. Hagelbarger, Pros. Atty., and Allen, Waters & Andress, for the State.

PER CURIAM. Judgment affirmed.

SPEAR, SHAUCK, and CREW, JJ., concur.

CENTRAL TRUST CO. et al. v. COOPER. (No. 7,570.) (Supreme Court of Ohio. Feb. 24, 1903.) Error to Circuit Court, Allen County. Harmon, Colston, Goldsmith & Hoadly, Doyle & Lewis and Leopold Wallach, for plaintiffs in error. Wheeler & Brice, Becker & Becker, Richie, Leland & Roby, C. B. Adgate, and Cable & Parmenter, for defendant in error.

PER CURIAM. Judgment affirmed.

BURKET, C. J., and SPEAR, PRICE, and CREW, JJ., concur.

CENTRAL TRUST CO. et al. v. MANHATTAN TRUST CO. (No. 7,566.) (Supreme Court of Ohio. Feb. 24, 1903.) Error to Circuit Court, Allen County. Harmon, Colston, Goldsmith & Hoadly, Doyle & Lewis, and Leopold Wallach, for plaintiffs in error. Wheeler & Brice, Becker & Becker, Richie, Leland & Roby, C. B. Adgate, and Cable & Parmenter, for defendants in error.

PER CURIAM. Judgment affirmed.

BURKET, C. J., and SPEAR, PRICE, and CREW, JJ., concur.

CENTRAL TRUST CO. et al. v. PARK BROS. et al. (No. 7,567.) (Supreme Court of Ohio. Feb. 24, 1903.) Error to Circuit Court, Allen County. Harmon, Colston, Goldsmith & Hoadly, Doyle & Lewis, and Leopold Wallach, for plaintiffs in error. Wheeler & Brice, Becker & Becker, Richie, Leland & Roby, C. B. Adgate, and Cable & Parmenter, for defendants in error.

PER CURIAM. Judgment affirmed.

BURKET, C. J., and SPEAR, PRICE, and CREW, JJ., concur.

CENTRAL TRUST CO. et al. v. SNYDER. (No. 7,568.) (Supreme Court of Ohio. Feb. 24, 1903.) Error to Circuit Court, Allen County. Harmon, Colston, Goldsmith & Hoadly, Doyle & Lewis, and Leopold Wallach, for plaintiffs in error. Wheeler & Brice, Becker & Becker, Richie, Leland & Roby, C. B. Adgate, and Cable & Parmenter, for defendants in error.

PER CURIAM. Judgment affirmed.

BURKET, C. J., and SPEAR, PRICE, and CREW, JJ., concur.

CENTRAL TRUST CO. et al. v. SPARGUR & CO. (No. 7,569.) (Supreme Court of Ohio. Feb. 24, 1903.) Error to Circuit Court, Allen County. Harmon, Colston, Goldsmith & Hoadly, Doyle & Lewis, and Leopold Wallach, for plaintiffs in error. Wheeler & Brice, Becker &

Becker, Richie, Leland & Roby, C. B. Adgate, and Cable & Parmenter, for defendants in error.

PER CURIAM. Judgment affirmed.

BURKET, C. J., and SPEAR, PRICE, and CREW, JJ., concur.

CHENEY v. BANK. (No. 7,782.) (Supreme Court of Ohio. April 21, 1903.) Error to Circuit Court, Lucas County. Seney & Johnson, for plaintiff in error. Smith & Beckwith, for defendant in error.

PER CURIAM. Judgment affirmed.

BURKET, C. J., and SPEAR, DAVIS, SHAUCK, PRICE, and CREW, JJ., concur.

CINCINNATI, H. & D. RY. CO. v. CITY OF LIMA. (No. 7,812.) (Supreme Court of Ohio. Sept. 29, 1903.) Error to Circuit Court, Allen County. R. D. Marshall, I. R. Longsworth, and A. McL. Marshall, for plaintiff in error. Wheeler & Bentley and D. C. Henderson, for defendant in error.

PER CURIAM. Judgment affirmed.

BURKET, C. J., and DAVIS and CREW, JJ., concur.

CINCINNATI, P., B. S. & P. PACKET CO. v. BAY et al. (No. 8,002.) (Supreme Court of Ohio. June 25, 1903.) Error to Circuit Court, Lawrence County. Stephens & Lincoln and Julius L. Anderson, for plaintiff in error. Lawrence Maxwell, Jr., and J. O. Yates, for defendants in error.

PER CURIAM. Judgment vacated, and cause remanded to the circuit court, with direction to consider bill of exceptions.

BURKET, C. J., and SPEAR, DAVIS, SHAUCK, PRICE, and CREW, JJ., concur.

CINCINNATI UNION STOCKYARDS CO. v. MONTGOMERY et al. (No. 7,669.) (Supreme Court of Ohio. March 10, 1903.) Error to Superior Court of Cincinnati. William Worthington, Follett & Keeley, Peck, Shaffer & Peck, and Dennis F. Cash, for plaintiff in error. Harmon, Colston, Goldsmith and Hoadly and John C. Healy, for defendants in error.

PER CURIAM. Judgment affirmed.

BURKET, C. J., and SPEAR, DAVIS, SHAUCK, PRICE, and CREW, JJ., concur.

CITY OF CINCINNATI et al. v. KORF. (No. 8,338.) (Supreme Court of Ohio. Oct. 20, 1903.) Error to Circuit Court, Hamilton County. C. J. Hunt and Albert H. Morrill, for plaintiffs in error. Theo. Horstman and G. H. Kattenhorn, for defendant in error.

PER CURIAM. Judgment reversed on authority of Shoemaker v. Cincinnati, 68 Ohio St. 603, 68 N. E. 1.

BURKET, C. J., and SPEAR, SHAUCK, PRICE, DAVIS, and CREW, JJ., concur.

CITY OF CINCINNATI et al. v. SHOEMAKER et al. (No. 7,950.) (Supreme Court of Ohio. June 23, 1903.) Error to Circuit Court, Hamilton County. Charles J. Hunt and Albert H. Morrill, Corp. Counsel, for plaintiffs in error. Wilby & Wald and Charles E. Tenney, for defendants in error.

PER CURIAM. Judgment affirmed.

BURKET, C. J., and SPEAR, DAVIS, PRICE, and CREW, JJ., concur.

CITY OF CLEVELAND v. ETZENSPERGER & ORSCHAK. (No. 7,942.) (Supreme Court of Ohio. Dec. 1, 1903.) Error to Circuit Court, Cuyahoga County. M. W. Beacom and Baker, Payer, Gage & Carey, for plaintiff in error. Poppleton, Billman & Billman, for defendant in error.

PER CURIAM. Judgment of the circuit court affirmed.

BURKET, C. J., and SPEAR, PRICE, and CREW, JJ., concur.

CITY OF LIMA et al. v. BAXTER. (No. 7,879.) (Supreme Court of Ohio. May 19, 1903.) Error to Circuit Court, Allen County. Wheeler & Bentley and D. C. Henderson, for plaintiffs in error. Motter, Mackenzie & Weadock, for defendant in error.

PER CURIAM. Judgment affirmed, on authority of City of Dayton v. Beauman, 66 Ohio St. 379, 64 N. E. 433.

BURKET, C. J., and SPEAR, DAVIS, SHAUCK, and CREW, JJ., concur.

CITY OF MARTINS FERRY v. RATCLIFF et al. (No. 7,938.) (Supreme Court of Ohio. April 28, 1903.) Error to Circuit Court, Belmont County. George Cooke and C. L. Weems, for plaintiff in error. L. J. C. Drennen, for defendants in error.

PER CURIAM. Judgments of the courts below reversed, demurrer to the answer overruled, and cause remanded to the court of common pleas for further proceedings according to law.

BURKET, C. J., and SPEAR, DAVIS, and SHAUCK, JJ., concur.

CITY OF TOLEDO v. OLDER. (No. 8,222.) (Supreme Court of Ohio. Oct. 13, 1903.) Error to Circuit Court, Lucas County. Denman & Friedman, for plaintiff in error. P. C. Prentiss and Seney & Johnson, for defendant in error.

PER CURIAM. Judgment affirmed.

SPEAR, SHAUCK, and CREW, JJ., concur.

CITY OF TOLEDO v. RADBONE. (No. 7,801.) (Supreme Court of Ohio. March 24, 1903.) Error to Circuit Court, Lucas County. Moses R. Brailey and Charles K. Friedman, for plaintiff in error. Frank H. Geer and King & Tracy, for defendant in error.

PER CURIAM. Judgment affirmed.

SPEAR, SHAUCK, and CREW, JJ., concur.

CLEVELAND CO-OPERATIVE STOVE CO. v. MEHLING. (No. 7,508.) (Supreme Court of Ohio. March 3, 1903.) Error to Circuit Court, Cuyahoga County. Wilcox & Friend and Henderson & Quail, for plaintiff in error. Weed & Meals, for defendant in error.

PER CURIAM. Judgment affirmed.

SPEAR, SHAUCK, and CREW, JJ., concur.

COLBY v. CITY OF TOLEDO et al. (No. 7,730.) (Supreme Court of Ohio. April 21, 1903.) Error to Circuit Court, Lucas County. Kinney & Newton, Smith & Beckwith, G. W. Kinney, and Alexander L. Smith, for plaintiff in error. King & Tracy and Brown, Geddes & Bodman, for defendants in error.

PER CURIAM. Judgment affirmed.

BURKET, C. J., and SPEAR, DAVIS, SHAUCK, PRICE, and CREW, JJ., concur.

COLLINS v. RAILWAY CO. (No. 7,956.) (Supreme Court of Ohio. March 10, 1903.) Error to Circuit Court, Marion County. Charles

F. Garberson, for plaintiff in error. J. T. Dye, S. O. Bayless and Mouser & Quigley, for defendant in error.

PER CURIAM. Judgment affirmed.

BURKET, C. J., and SHAUCK and PRICE, JJ., concur.

COMMERCIAL BANK v. UNION CENT. LIFE INS. CO. (No. 8,242.) (Supreme Court of Ohio. Feb. 2, 1904.) Error to Circuit Court, Seneca County. McCauley & Weller, for plaintiff in error. Noble, Keppel & Noble and Robert Ramsey, for defendant in error.

PER CURIAM. Judgment affirmed.

SPEAR, SHAUCK, and CREW, JJ., concur.

CONNER v. CONNER. (No. 7,863.) (Supreme Court of Ohio. Oct. 13, 1903.) Error to Circuit Court, Guernsey County. J. H. Mackey and J. A. Troette, for plaintiff in error. Fred L. Rosemond, for defendant in error.

PER CURIAM. Judgment affirmed.

BURKET, C. J., and SPEAR, DAVIS, SHAUCK, PRICE, and CREW, JJ., concur.

CONTINENTAL INS. CO. v. DRACKETT et al. (No. 7,691.) (Supreme Court of Ohio. March 3, 1903.) Error to Circuit Court, Cuyahoga County. C. W. Fuller, for plaintiff in error. Moffett & Hawley, J. W. Taylor and T. H. Garry, for defendants in error.

PER CURIAM. Judgment affirmed.

BURKET, C. J., and DAVIS and PRICE, JJ., concur.

COOPER v. REITER. (No. 7,990.) (Supreme Court of Ohio. Oct. 27, 1903.) Error to Circuit Court, Franklin County. Donaldson & Tussing, for plaintiff in error. Edward L. Taylor, Jr., Augustus T. Seymour, and Karl T. Weber, for defendant in error.

PER CURIAM. Judgment affirmed.

BURKET, C. J., and DAVIS and PRICE, JJ., concur.

CORBET v. FENT et al. (No. 8,130.) (Supreme Court of Ohio. Nov. 24, 1903.) Error to Circuit Court, Putnam County. Baily & Baily and Ben L. Griffiths, for plaintiff in error. Watts & Moore and Creamer & Creamer, for defendants in error.

PER CURIAM. Judgment affirmed.

SPEAR, SHAUCK, and CREW, JJ., concur.

COUNCIL OF CITY OF DEFIANCE v. STATE ex rel. CHAPMAN et al. (No. 8,166.) (Supreme Court of Ohio. June 23, 1903.) Error to Circuit Court, Defiance County. F. L. Hay, City Sol., and J. M. Sheets, for plaintiff in error. Ansberry & Farrell, for defendants in error.

PER CURIAM. Judgment of the circuit court and of common pleas reversed, and petition of plaintiff below dismissed, for the reason that mandamus is not proper remedy; the plaintiff having an adequate remedy at law.

BURKET, C. J., and DAVIS, SHAUCK, PRICE, and CREW, JJ., concur.

COVINGTON STONE & MARBLE CO. v. SAWYER. (No. 7,653.) (Supreme Court of Ohio. March 17, 1903.) Error to Circuit Court, Hamilton County. Robertson & Buchwalter and Robert C. Pugh, for plaintiff in error. Edward M. Ballard, for defendant in error.

PER CURIAM. Judgment affirmed.

BURKET, C. J., and DAVIS and PRICE, JJ., concur.

COWEN et al. v. LANEHART. (No. 7,888.) (Supreme Court of Ohio. May 19, 1903.) Error to Circuit Court, Richland County. J. H. Collins and Cummings, McBride & Wolfe, for plaintiffs in error. Andrew Stevenson and Jenner & Weldon, for defendant in error.

PER CURIAM. Judgment affirmed.

BURKET, C. J., and SPEAR, SHAUCK, PRICE, and CREW, JJ., concur.

COX v. CITY OF LANCASTER. (No. 8,236.) (Supreme Court of Ohio. Feb. 2, 1904.) Error to Circuit Court, Fairfield County. C. D. Martin and M. A. Daugherty, for plaintiff in error. A. W. Mithoff, City Sol., and G. E. Martin, for defendant in error.

PER CURIAM. Judgment affirmed.

SPEAR, SHAUCK, and PRICE, JJ., concur.

CRAWFORD v. AMERICAN MISSIONARY ASS'N et al. (No. 7,767.) (Supreme Court of Ohio. May 12, 1903.) Error to Circuit Court, Lucas County. Charles G. Wilson and E. F. Bacon, for plaintiff in error. Rhoades & Rhoades, for defendants in error.

PER CURIAM. Judgment affirmed.

SPEAR, SHAUCK, and CREW, JJ., concur.

CULLOM v. CITY OF CINCINNATI. (No. 7,978.) (Supreme Court of Ohio. Nov. 10, 1903.) Error to Circuit Court, Hamilton County. Edward M. Ballard, for plaintiff in error. Charles J. Hunt, John V. Campbell, and Albert H. Morrill, for defendant in error.

PER CURIAM. Judgment affirmed.

BURKET, C. J., and DAVIS and PRICE, JJ., concur.

DAVID v. BRIGHT. (No. 7,755.) (Supreme Court of Ohio. April 21, 1903.) Error to Circuit Court, Hancock County. Phelps & David, W. W. Chapman and L. A. Carabin, for plaintiff in error. George F. Pendleton and W. F. Brickman, for defendant in error.

PER CURIAM. Judgment affirmed.

BURKET, C. J., and SPEAR, SHAUCK, PRICE, and CREW, JJ., concur.

DICKMAN v. STATE. (No. 7,874.) (Supreme Court of Ohio. June 25, 1903.) Error to Circuit Court, Allen County. Ridenour & Halfhill, for plaintiff in error. John M. Sheets, Atty. Gen., and William Klinger, Pros. Atty., for the State.

PER CURIAM. Judgment affirmed.

SPEAR, PRICE, and CREW, JJ., concur.

DICKSON v. TOM et al. (No. 8,080.) (Supreme Court of Ohio. Oct. 27, 1903.) Error to Circuit Court, Muskingum County. S. M. Winn and John C. Bassett, Jr., for plaintiff in error. Frank H. Southard, for defendants in error.

PER CURIAM. Judgment affirmed.

SPEAR, SHAUCK, and CREW, JJ., concur.

DR. J. L. STEPHENS REMEDY CO. v. BUNYAN. (No. 7,698.) (Supreme Court of Ohio. March 10, 1903.) Error to Circuit

Court, Warren County. Eltzroth & Maple and John E. Bruce, for plaintiff in error. Runyan & Stanley and Brandon & Burr, for defendant in error.

PER CURIAM. Judgment affirmed.

BURKET, C. J., and DAVIS and PRICE, JJ., concur.

DOVEL v. DOVEL et al. (No. 8,224.) (Supreme Court of Ohio. Jan. 26, 1904.) Error to Circuit Court, Fairfield County. W. H. Lane, C. W. McCleery and A. J. Dovel, for plaintiff in error. C. D. Martin, M. A. Daugherty, L. B. Tussing, T. H. Dolson, and G. E. Martin, for defendants in error.

PER CURIAM. Judgment affirmed, on authority of Ryan v. Rothweiler, 50 Ohio St. 595, 35 N. E. 679.

SPEAR, DAVIS, SHAUCK, PRICE, and CREW, JJ., concur.

DOWD v. CASSILLY et al. (No. 7,752.) (Supreme Court of Ohio. March 24, 1903.) Error to Circuit Court, Hamilton County. Bates & Meyer and Campbell & Clendening, for plaintiff in error. Stephens & Lincoln and Harmon, Colston, Goldsmith & Hoadly, for defendants in error.

PER CURIAM. Judgment affirmed.

SPEAR, SHAUCK, and CREW, JJ., concur.

DOWNING v. RAILWAY CO. (No. 7,546.) (Supreme Court of Ohio. Feb. 24, 1903.) Error to Circuit Court, Cuyahoga County. William J. Starkweather and John H. Smart, for plaintiff in error. A. T. Ingersoll, for defendant in error.

PER CURIAM. Judgment affirmed.

BURKET, C. J., and DAVIS, SHAUCK, PRICE, and CREW, JJ., concur.

DOYLE v. CINCINNATI, H. & D. RY. CO. (No. 8,199.) (Supreme Court of Ohio. Oct. 13, 1903.) Error to Circuit Court, Jackson County. E. C. Powell and J. K. McClung, for plaintiff in error. R. D. Marshall, A. E. Jacobs, and A. McL. Marshall, for defendant in error.

PER CURIAM. Judgment affirmed.

BURKET, C. J., and DAVIS and PRICE, JJ., concur.

DRAKE et al. v. STATE. (No. 8,324.) (Supreme Court of Ohio. Nov. 24, 1903.) Error to Circuit Court, Union County. W. T. Hoopes, Geo. B. Okey, and Edw. L. Hyneman, for plaintiffs in error. J. M. Sheets, Atty. Gen., and J. L. Cameron, for the State.

PER CURIAM. Judgment affirmed.

BURKET, C. J., and SPEAR, DAVIS, SHAUCK, PRICE, and CREW, JJ., concur.

EARLEY v. EARLEY et al. (No. 7,995.) (Supreme Court of Ohio. Dec. 15, 1903.) Error to Circuit Court, Mahoning County. W. M. Roach and Jones & Anderson and A. W. Jones, for plaintiff in error. Murray & Koonce, Jared Huxley, and D. D. Aitken, for defendants in error.

PER CURIAM. Judgment affirmed.

BURKET, C. J., and DAVIS, SHAUCK, PRICE, and CREW, JJ., concur.

ECLIPSE STOVE CO. v. KINER. (No. 8,264.) (Supreme Court of Ohio. Oct. 20, 1903.) Error to Circuit Court, Richland County. Cummings, McBride & Wolfe, for plaintiff in error. Kerr & La Dow, for defendant in error.

PER CURIAM. Judgment affirmed.

BURKET, C. J., and DAVIS and PRICE, JJ., concur.

EDIS v. BUTLER. (No. 7,607.) (Supreme Court of Ohio. Feb. 17, 1903.) Error to Circuit Court, Cuyahoga County. Hart, Canfield & Callaghan, for plaintiff in error. M. W. Beacom, Charles Y. Stocker, W. B. Wheeler, A. V. Taylor, and Babcock, Payer, Gage & Carey, for defendant in error.

PER CURIAM. Judgment affirmed.

SPEAR, SHAUCK, and CREW, JJ., concur.

EDWARDS et al. v. AVONDALE LOAN & BUILDING CO. (No. 7,521.) (Supreme Court of Ohio. March 3, 1903.) Error to Superior Court of Cincinnati. Charles W. Baker, for plaintiffs in error. Foraker, Putcalt, Granger & Prior and John D. De Witt, for defendant in error.

PER CURIAM. Judgment affirmed.

BURKET, C. J., and DAVIS and PRICE, JJ., concur.

ELLIS v. VILLAGE OF HARVEYSBURG. (No. 7,633.) (Supreme Court of Ohio. Feb. 24, 1903.) Error to Circuit Court, Warren County. Frank Brandon and George A. Burr, for plaintiff in error. Miles & Clevenger, for defendant in error.

PER CURIAM. Judgment affirmed.

SPEAR, SHAUCK, and CREW, JJ., concur.

EUREKA FIRE & MARINE INS. CO. et al. v. GRAY. (No. 8,032.) (Supreme Court of Ohio. Oct. 20, 1903.) Error to Circuit Court, Ashtabula County. Hoyt & Munsell, for plaintiffs in error. Edward P. Hall and Perry & Roberts, for defendant in error.

PER CURIAM. Judgment affirmed.

SPEAR, SHAUCK, and CREW, JJ., concur.

EVANS v. STATE. (No. 7,775.) (Supreme Court of Ohio. April 21, 1903.) Error to Circuit Court, Lucas County. D. H. Commanger and H. S. Commanger, for plaintiff in error. Charles E. Sumner, for the State.

PER CURIAM. Judgment affirmed.

BURKET, C. J., and SPEAR, DAVIS, SHAUCK, PRICE, and CREW, JJ., concur.

FAUROT v. NORTON et al. (No. 7,892.) (Supreme Court of Ohio. June 9, 1903.) Error to Circuit Court, Defiance County. J. M. Dawson, for plaintiff in error. Harris, Cameron & Shaw, Squire, Sanders & Dempsey, Winn & Hay, Kline, Carr, Tolles & Goff, Swayne, Hayes & Tyler, S. T. Sutphen, Elizer G. Johnson, Virgil P. Kline, and T. H. Bushnell, for defendants in error.

PER CURIAM. Judgment affirmed.

BURKET, C. J., and SPEAR, DAVIS, SHAUCK, and CREW, JJ., concur.

FAUROT v. WOODLAND AVE. SAVINGS & LOAN CO. et al. (No. 8,078.) (Supreme Court of Ohio. Oct. 20, 1903.) Error to Circuit Court, Defiance County. J. M. Dawson, for plaintiff in error. Kline, Carr, Tolles & Goff, for defendants in error.

PER CURIAM. Judgment affirmed.

SPEAR, SHAUCK, and CREW, JJ., concur.

FINDLAY, FT. W. & W. RY. CO. v. KINDELL. (No. 7,961.) (Supreme Court of Ohio. Dec. 8, 1903.) Error to Circuit Court, Hancock County. H. F. Burket and Watts & Moore, for plaintiff in error. John Poe and Cable & Parmenter, for defendant in error.

PER CURIAM. Judgment affirmed, on authority of B. & O. Ry. Co. v. Glenn, 66 Ohio St. 395, 64 N. E. 438.

SPEAR, DAVIS, SHAUCK, PRICE, and CREW, JJ., concur.

FIRE ASSUR. CO. v. PLATO et al. (No. 7,810.) (Supreme Court of Ohio. April 21, 1903.) Error to Circuit Court, Lorain County. Thomas Bates, F. M. Stevens, and E. G. Johnson, for plaintiff in error. H. G. Redington and Weber & Metcalf, for defendants in error.

PER CURIAM. Judgment affirmed.

BURKET, C. J., and DAVIS and PRICE, JJ., concur.

FIRE INS. CO. v. BALBIAN. (No. 7,823.) (Supreme Court of Ohio. April 28, 1903.) Error to Circuit Court, Seneca County. Thomas A. Logan, for plaintiff in error. Bunn & Royer, for defendant in error.

PER CURIAM. Judgment affirmed.

BURKET, C. J., and DAVIS and PRICE, JJ., concur.

FIRE INS. CO. v. BALBIAN et al. (No. 7,824.) (Supreme Court of Ohio. April 28, 1903.) Error to Circuit Court, Seneca County. Thomas A. Logan, for plaintiff in error. Bunn & Royer, for defendants in error.

PER CURIAM. Judgment affirmed.

BURKET, C. J., and DAVIS and PRICE, JJ., concur.

FLEMING et al. v. DWYER. (No. 7,957.) (Supreme Court of Ohio. Dec. 18, 1903.) Error to Circuit Court, Montgomery County. Wright & Ozias, for plaintiffs in error. Craighead & Craighead, for defendant in error.

PER CURIAM. Judgment affirmed.

BURKET, C. J., and SPEAR, DAVIS, SHAUCK, PRICE, and CREW, JJ., concur.

FOXHEVER v. ORDER OF RED CROSS et al. (No. 7,831.) (Supreme Court of Ohio. May 12, 1903.) Error to Circuit Court, Lucas County. Orville S. Brumback and Charles A. Thatcher, for plaintiff in error. Kohn & Northup, for defendants in error.

PER CURIAM. Judgment affirmed.

SPEAR, SHAUCK, and CREW, JJ., concur.

FREY v. STEWART. (No. 8,092.) (Supreme Court of Ohio. Dec. 15, 1903.) Error to Circuit Court, Clark County. Keifer & Keifer, for plaintiff in error. Stafford & Arthur and Bowman & Bowman, for defendant in error.

PER CURIAM. Judgment affirmed.

SHAUCK, PRICE, and CREW, JJ., concur. BURKET, C. J., and SPEAR and DAVIS, JJ., dissent.

GARY v. BANK. (No. 7,763.) (Supreme Court of Ohio. June 16, 1903.) Error to Circuit Court, Hancock County. M. B. Gary and J. A. & E. V. Bope, for plaintiff in error. Blackford & Blackford, for defendant in error.

PER CURIAM. Judgment of the circuit court reversed, and judgment in favor of plaintiff in error as per entry, on authority of Rouse v. Bank, 46 Ohio St. 493, 22 N. E. 293, 5 L. R. A. 378, 15 Am. St. Rep. 644.

BURKET, C. J., and SPEAR, DAVIS, SHAUCK, and PRICE, JJ., concur.

GERMAN FIRE INS. CO. v. YATES. (No. 8,168.) (Supreme Court of Ohio. Nov. 24, 1903.) Error to Circuit Court, Lawrence County. Johnson & Corn, for plaintiff in error. J. O. Yates, for defendant in error.

PER CURIAM. Judgment affirmed.

SPEAR, SHAUCK, and CREW, JJ., concur.

GIBSONBURG BANKING CO. v. LORAIN COUNTY BANKING CO. (No. 7,706.) (Supreme Court of Ohio. March 17, 1903.) Error to Circuit Court, Sandusky County. Hunt & De Ran and Lester Wilson, for plaintiff in error. Andrews Bros., for defendant in error.

PER CURIAM. Judgment affirmed.

SPEAR, SHAUCK, and CREW, JJ., concur.

GILL v. WRIGHT. (No. 7,242.) (Supreme Court of Ohio. March 24, 1903.) Error to Circuit Court, Fairfield County. C. W. McCleery, for plaintiff in error. Carl Norpell and M. A. Daugherty, for defendant in error.

PER CURIAM. Judgment affirmed.

BURKET, C. J., and DAVIS and PRICE, JJ., concur.

GILLEN v. CITY OF WARREN. (No. 7,840.) (Supreme Court of Ohio. April 21, 1903.) Error to Circuit Court, Trumbull County. E. B. Taylor and E. E. Roberts, for plaintiff in error. Charles M. Wilkins and T. H. Gillmer, for defendant in error.

PER CURIAM. Judgment affirmed.

BURKET, C. J., and DAVIS, PRICE, and CREW, JJ., concur.

GOODWIN et al. v. WHITE. (No. 7,865.) (Supreme Court of Ohio. Sept. 22, 1903.) Error to Circuit Court, Clark County. Frank W. Geiger and Hagan & Kunkle, for plaintiffs in error. John C. Bassett, for defendant in error.

PER CURIAM. Judgment affirmed.

BURKET, C. J., and SPEAR, DAVIS, SHAUCK, PRICE, and CREW, JJ., concur.

GRAHAM v. RAILWAY CO. (No. 8,375.) (Supreme Court of Ohio. May 5, 1903.) Error to Circuit Court, Cuyahoga County. C. N. Sheldon, for plaintiff in error. E. A. Foote, for defendant in error.

PER CURIAM. Judgment affirmed, under rule 19.

BURKET, C. J., and DAVIS and PRICE, JJ., concur.

GRANT v. GRANT et al. (No. 7,996.) (Supreme Court of Ohio. May 19, 1903.) Error to Circuit Court, Sandusky County. Van Horn & Mead and Meek, Dudrow & Worst, for plaintiff in error. Hunt & De Ran, for defendants in error.

PER CURIAM. Judgment affirmed.

SPEAR, SHAUCK, and CREW, JJ., concur.

RESSMAN v. BRUNING. (No. 7,827.) preme Court of Ohio. May 5, 1903.) Er- to Circuit Court, Lucas County. J. S. rtman, for plaintiff in error. Southard & ithard and Rhoades & Rhoades, for defendant error.

ER CURIAM. Judgment affirmed.

URKET, C. J., and DAVIS and PRICE, , concur.

RIMES v. McCULLOUGH et al. (No. 8,- .) (Supreme Court of Ohio. June 23, 1903.) or to Circuit Court, Adams County. Kin- d, Merwine & Schumacher, for plaintiff in or. A. C. Blair, for defendants in error.

ER CURIAM. Judgment affirmed.

AVIS, SHAUCK, and PRICE, JJ., concur. RKET, C. J., dissents.

ROVES v. SELSOR. (No. 7,690.) (Su- me Court of Ohio. March 17, 1903.) Error Circuit Court, Fayette County. Van Deman Chaffin, for plaintiff in error. Humphrey es, for defendant in error.

ER CURIAM. Judgment vacated, on the hority of Falconer v. Martin, 66 Ohio St. , 64 N. E. 430, and cause remanded to the uit court, with directions to overrule the tion to dismiss, and sustain the motion for ve to file perfect transcript, and for further ceedings according to law.

URKET, C. J., and SPEAR, DAVIS, AUCK, PRICE, and CREW, JJ., concur.

WYN v. DONSON. (No. 7,835.) (Supreme urt of Ohio. April 28, 1903.) Error to Cir- t Court, Van Wert County. Glenn & Allen, plaintiff in error. Saltzgaber & Hoke, for endant in error.

ER CURIAM. Judgment affirmed, on au- rity of Raudabaugh v. Hart, 61 Ohio St. 73, N. E. 214, 76 Am. St. Rep. 361.

URKET, C. J., and DAVIS and PRICE, ., concur.

IAINES v. BALLINGER et al. (No. 7,795.) preme Court of Ohio. March 31, 1903.) ror to Circuit Court, Union County. J. L. meron and Robert McCrory, for plaintiff in or. Piper, Porter & Porter, for defendants error.

PER CURIAM. Judgment affirmed.

BURKET, C. J., and DAVIS and PRICE, ., concur.

HALKER v. TRUSTEES OF OTTAWA . (No. 7,829.) (Supreme Court of Ohio. t. 6, 1903.) Error to Circuit Court, Putnam unty. Bailey & Bailey, for plaintiff in error. raman & Malone, for defendants in error.

PER CURIAM. Judgment affirmed.

BURKET, C. J., and SPEAR, SHAUCK, RICE, and CREW, JJ., concur.

HAMILTON COUNTY COM'RS v. FAS- LD. (No. 7,828.) (Supreme Court of Ohio. t. 13, 1903.) Error to Circuit Court, Hamil- n County. G. C. Wilson, Co. Sol., and O. J. sgrave and O. B. Jones, Asst. Co. Sols., for aintiff in error. J. J. Glidden, J. R. Von ggern, and Cormany & Cormany, for defend- t in error.

PER CURIAM. Judgment affirmed.

BURKET, C. J., and SPEAR and CREW, ., concur.

HAMILTON, G. & C. TRACTION CO. v. DUEMER. (No. 8,052.) (Supreme Court of Ohio. Oct. 27, 1903.) Error to Circuit Court, Butler County. Burch & Johnson and John W. Warrington, for plaintiff in error. Shepherd & Shaffer, for defendant in error.

PER CURIAM. Judgment affirmed.

BURKET, C. J., and DAVIS and PRICE, JJ., concur.

HAMM v. WILSON et al. (No. 7,973.) (Supreme Court of Ohio. Oct. 27, 1903.) Error to Circuit Court, Ross County. John Logan, Seymour Cunningham and F. P. Hinton, for plaintiff in error. H. W. Woodrow, for defendants in error.

PER CURIAM. Judgment affirmed.

BURKET, C. J., and DAVIS and PRICE, JJ., concur.

HASKELL v. BRODHEAD. (No. 8,010.) (Supreme Court of Ohio. Nov. 10, 1903.) Error to Circuit Court, Franklin County. H. M. Daugherty, D. B. Sharp, and Bailey & Bailey, for plaintiff in error. Thomas E. Powell, for defendant in error.

PER CURIAM. Judgment affirmed.

BURKET, C. J., and DAVIS, PRICE, and CREW, JJ., concur.

HASTINGS v. LUCAS COUNTY COM'RS. (No. 8,255.) (Supreme Court of Ohio. Dec. 18, 1903.) Error to Circuit Court, Lucas County. B. A. Hayes, for plaintiff in error. Sumner & Tucker and C. W. Everett, for defendants in error.

PER CURIAM. Judgments of the circuit court and of the court of common pleas reversed, demurrer overruled, and cause remanded for further proceedings.

BURKET, C. J., and SPEAR, DAVIS, SHAUCK, PRICE, and CREW, JJ., concur.

HAVOURD v. WAGNER et al. (No. 7,- 676.) (Supreme Court of Ohio. March 17, 1903.) Error to Circuit Court, Hancock County. Ross & Kinder, for plaintiff in error. Blackford & Blackford, for defendants in error.

PER CURIAM. Judgment affirmed.

DAVIS, SHAUCK, and CREW, JJ., concur.

HAYES et al. v. BOARD OF EDUCATION. (No. 7,745.) (Supreme Court of Ohio. March 24, 1903.) Error to Circuit Court, Cuyahoga County. Henderson & Quail, for plaintiffs in error. M. W. Beacom and Baker, Payer, Gage & Carey, for defendant in error.

PER CURIAM. Judgment affirmed.

BURKET, C. J., and DAVIS and PRICE, JJ., concur.

HEAD v. CHESBROUGH. (No. 8,048.) (Supreme Court of Ohio. Oct. 20, 1903.) Error to Circuit Court, Lucas County. King & Tracy, for plaintiff in error. Clayton W. Everett, for defendant in error.

PER CURIAM. Judgment affirmed.

SPEAR, SHAUCK, and CREW, JJ., concur.

HENRY v. FRANKS et al. (No. 8,003.) (Supreme Court of Ohio. Oct. 20, 1903.) Error to Circuit Court, Wood County. Baldwin & Harrington and S. P. Harrison, for plaintiff in error. James O. Troup, for defendants in error.

PER CURIAM. Judgment affirmed.

BURKET, C. J., and DAVIS and PRICE, JJ., concur.

HICKS v. WEIR. (No. 8,038.) (Supreme Court of Ohio. Oct. 20, 1903.) Error to Circuit Court, Hamilton County. Campbell & Clendening, for plaintiff in error. Lawrence Maxwell, Jr., and Judson Harmon, for defendant in error.

PER CURIAM. Judgment affirmed.

SPEAR, SHAUCK, and CREW, JJ., concur.

HIGGINS' ESTATE et al. v. HOLMES. (No. 7,618.) (Supreme Court of Ohio. Feb. 17, 1903.) Error to Circuit Court, Franklin County. Thomas E. Powell, for plaintiffs in error. James T. Holmes, Jr., for defendant in error.

PER CURIAM. Judgment vacated, on authority of Falconer v. Martin et al., 66 Ohio St. 352, 64 N. E. 430, and cause remanded to the circuit court, with direction to overrule the motion to dismiss, and to sustain the motion to file perfect transcript, and for further proceedings according to law.

BURKET, C. J., and SPEAR, DAVIS, SHAUCK, PRICE, and CREW, JJ., concur.

HINCHMAN et al. v. MEAD et al. (No. 7,496.) (Supreme Court of Ohio. April 21, 1903.) Error to Circuit Court, Hamilton County. Ernst, Cassatt & McDougall and Alfred C. Cassatt, for plaintiffs in error. Foraker, Outcalt, Granger & Prior and George M. Eichelberger, for defendants in error.

PER CURIAM. Judgment affirmed as per journal entry.

BURKET, C. J., and SPEAR, PRICE, and CREW, JJ., concur.

HEDRICK et al. v. GILBERT et al. (No. 7,839.) (Supreme Court of Ohio. April 21, 1903.) Error to Circuit Court, Mercer County. Robert L. Mattingly, for plaintiffs in error. Cable & Parmenter and Marsh & Loree, for defendants in error.

PER CURIAM. Judgment affirmed.

BURKET, C. J., and SPEAR, DAVIS, SHAUCK, PRICE, and CREW, JJ., concur.

HELLER v. CASS et al. (No. 7,981.) (Supreme Court of Ohio. May 12, 1903.) Error to Circuit Court, Putnam County. Watts & Moore, Brown, Geddes & Bodman, and Swayne, Hayes & Tyler, for plaintiff in error. Bailey & Bailey and Harvey Scribner, for defendants in error.

PER CURIAM. Judgment affirmed.

BURKET, C. J., and DAVIS, SHAUCK, PRICE, and CREW, JJ., concur.

HELVIE v. TROY BUGGY WORKS CO. (No. 7,640.) (Supreme Court of Ohio. March 10, 1903.) Error to Circuit Court, Miami County. Addison F. Broomhall and Walter E. Robinson, for plaintiff in error. Thomas & Thomas and Long & Kyle, for defendant in error.

PER CURIAM. Judgment affirmed.

BURKET, C. J., and DAVIS and PRICE, JJ., concur.

HERBERT v. INSURANCE CO. (No. 7,808.) (Supreme Court of Ohio. March 24, 1903.) Error to Circuit Court, Lucas County. Marshall & Fraser, for plaintiff in error. Smith & Baker, for defendant in error.

PER CURIAM. Judgment affirmed.

SPEAR, SHAUCK, and CREW, JJ., concur.

HOFFHINE v. GOLDSBERRY et al. (No. 7,943.) (Supreme Court of Ohio. Jan. 5, 1904.) Error to Circuit Court, Ross County. John C. Entrekin, John P. Phillips, and Lyle S. Evans, for plaintiff in error. John W. Goldsberry, for defendants in error.

PER CURIAM. Judgment affirmed.

BURKET, C. J., and DAVIS, SHAUCK, and CREW, JJ., concur.

HOLLENBECK v. ZUCK. (No. 7,606.) (Supreme Court of Ohio. March 3, 1903.) Error to Circuit Court, Hardin County. Smick & Hoge, for plaintiff in error. Johnson & Johnson, for defendant in error.

PER CURIAM. Judgment affirmed.

SPEAR, SHAUCK, and CREW, JJ., concur.

HOWLE v. PRUDENTIAL INS. CO. (No. 7,628.) (Supreme Court of Ohio. March 10, 1903.) Error to Circuit Court, Cuyahoga County. Hart, Canfield & Callaghan, for plaintiff in error. Meyer & Mooney, for defendant in error.

PER CURIAM. Judgment affirmed.

BURKET, C. J., and DAVIS and PRICE, JJ., concur.

HUBER v. HUBER. (No. 7,855.) (Supreme Court of Ohio. May 5, 1903.) Error to Circuit Court, Wood County. Peter Emslie, for plaintiff in error. J. E. Shatzel, for defendant in error.

PER CURIAM. Judgment affirmed.

BURKET, C. J., and DAVIS and PRICE, JJ., concur.

HUFFMAN v. PIERCE et al. (No. 7,902.) (Supreme Court of Ohio. May 12, 1903.) Error to Circuit Court, Preblé County. I. E. Craig, for plaintiff in error. Alex. F. Hume, F. G. Shuey, and Davis Pierce, for defendants in error.

PER CURIAM. Judgment affirmed.

BURKET, C. J., and DAVIS and PRICE, JJ., concur.

HUMPHREYS MFG. CO. v. KENNEDY. (No. 7,959.) (Supreme Court of Ohio. Dec. 8, 1903.) Error to Circuit Court, Richland County. Kerr & La Dow, for plaintiff in error. Cummings, McBride & Wolfe and Bricker & Workman, for defendant in error.

PER CURIAM. Judgment of the circuit court reversed, and that of the common pleas affirmed.

SPEAR, DAVIS, SHAUCK, PRICE, and CREW, JJ., concur.

HUNT v. McCURDY. (No. 7,905.) (Supreme Court of Ohio. May 12, 1903.) Error to Circuit Court, Miami County. Davy, Campbell & St. John, for plaintiff in error. A. F. Broomhall, for defendant in error.

PER CURIAM. Judgment affirmed.

BURKET, C. J., and DAVIS and CREW, JJ., concur.

HUTCHINS et al. v. SENEY et al. (No. 8,193.) (Supreme Court of Ohio. Jan. 12, 1904.) Error to Circuit Court, Hancock County. A. G. Fuller, for plaintiffs in error. Henry W. Seney, for defendants in error.

PER CURIAM. Judgment affirmed.

SPEAR, SHAUCK, and CREW, JJ., concur.

HUTSON COAL CO. v. WELTY et al. (No. 7,909.) (Supreme Court of Ohio. May 12, 1903.) Error to Circuit Court, Portage County. T. H. Johnson, E. T. Hamilton, and W. J. Beckley, for plaintiff in error. I. T. Siddall, for defendants in error.

PER CURIAM. Judgment as to the petition in error affirmed, and judgment as to the cross-petition in error reversed, and judgment in favor of cross-petition in error.

BURKET, C. J., and SPEAR, DAVIS, SHAUCK, PRICE, and CREW, JJ., concur.

ILGENFRITZ v. LOHMAN et al. (No. 7,915.) (Supreme Court of Ohio. May 19, 1903.) Error to Circuit Court, Mahoning County. S. L. Clark and R. B. Murray, for plaintiff in error. A. J. Woolf and William A. Maline, for defendants in error.

PER CURIAM. Judgment affirmed.

BURKET, C. J., and DAVIS and PRICE, JJ., concur.

INNIS v. RAILWAY CO. (No. 8,234.) (Supreme Court of Ohio. April 21, 1903.) Error to Circuit Court, Franklin County. J. H. Collins, for plaintiff in error. Merrick & Tompkins and T. J. Duncan, for defendant in error.

PER CURIAM. Judgment affirmed.

BURKET, C. J., and DAVIS and PRICE, JJ., concur.

INSURANCE CO. v. BROWN. (No. 7,579.) (Supreme Court of Ohio. March 3, 1903.) Error to Circuit Court, Ashtabula County. Will G. Gunther and Theodore Hall & Son, for plaintiff in error. J. T. Herrington and H. E. Starkey, for defendant in error.

PER CURIAM. Judgment affirmed.

BURKET, C. J., and SPEAR, PRICE, and CREW, JJ., concur.

INSURANCE CO. v. BURKE. (No. 7,720.) (Supreme Court of Ohio. March 24, 1903.) Error to Circuit Court, Fairfield County. Maxwell & Ramsey, for plaintiff in error. M. A. Daugherty, for defendant in error.

PER CURIAM. Judgment affirmed.

BURKET, C. J., and SPEAR and PRICE, JJ., concur.

INSURANCE CO. v. EDMONDS. (No. 7,971.) (Supreme Court of Ohio. June 25, 1903.) Error to Circuit Court, Cuyahoga County. C. W. Fuller and R. H. Patchin, for plaintiff in error. Alex. H. Martin and O. C. Pinney, for defendant in error.

PER CURIAM. Judgment affirmed.

SPEAR, PRICE, and CREW, JJ., concur.

INSURANCE CO. v. DUNLAP. (No. 7,578.) (Supreme Court of Ohio. Feb. 24, 1903.) Error to Circuit Court, Franklin County. Thomas B. Paxton and J. W. Mooney, for plaintiff in error. Booth, Keating, Peters & Butler and M. R. Patterson, for defendant in error.

PER CURIAM. Judgment affirmed.

BURKET, C. J., and SPEAR, DAVIS, SHAUCK, PRICE, and CREW, JJ., concur.

INSURANCE CO. v. MUELLER. (No. 7,522.) (Supreme Court of Ohio. March 31, 1903.) Error to Circuit Court, Hamilton County. Maxwell & Ramsey, Robert Ramsey, and W. W. Ramsey, for plaintiff in error. Gorman & Thompson, for defendant in error.

PER CURIAM. Judgment affirmed.

BURKET, C. J., and DAVIS, SHAUCK, and CREW, JJ., concur.

INSURANCE CO. v. STRONG. (No. 7,847.) (Supreme Court of Ohio. April 28, 1903.) Error to Circuit Court, Wood County. Stephens & Lincoln, Datus R. Jones, and Charles H. Stephens, for plaintiff in error. James O. Troup, for defendant in error.

PER CURIAM. Judgment affirmed.

SPEAR, SHAUCK, and CREW, JJ., concur.

ISENNAGLE v. BURKE. (No. 7,714.) (Supreme Court of Ohio. March 17, 1903.) Error to Circuit Court, Ross County. John C. Entrekin and Robert W. Manly, for plaintiff in error. Seymour Cunningham, for defendant in error.

PER CURIAM. Judgment affirmed.

BURKET, C. J., and DAVIS and PRICE, JJ., concur.

ISRAEL et al. v. METHAM. (No. 7,718.) (Supreme Court of Ohio. March 24, 1903.) Error to Circuit Court, Knox County. J. B. Waight, Critchfield & Devin and Bert Voorhees, for plaintiffs in error. E. W. James and J. B. Graham, for defendant in error.

PER CURIAM. Judgment affirmed.

BURKET, C. J., and DAVIS and PRICE, JJ., concur.

JACKMAN v. CITY OF TOLEDO. (No. 8,099.) (Supreme Court of Ohio. Oct. 27, 1903.) Error to Circuit Court, Lucas County. Southard & Southard and Chas. F. Watts, for plaintiff in error. J. M. Sheets, Atty. Gen., M. R. Brailey, City Sol., and Frank M. Sala, Sp. Counsel, for defendant in error.

PER CURIAM. Judgment affirmed.

SPEAR, SHAUCK, and CREW, JJ., concur.

JACKMAN et al. v. JACKMAN. (No. 8,073.) (Supreme Court of Ohio. Oct. 27, 1903.) Error to Circuit Court, Cuyahoga County. Foran & McTighe, J. J. McCormick, and Brinsmade & Armstrong, for plaintiffs in error. Dawley & Meals and James M. & Walter F. Brown, for defendant in error.

PER CURIAM. Judgment affirmed.

BURKET, C. J., and DAVIS and PRICE, JJ., concur. SPEAR, SHAUCK, and CREW, JJ., dissent.

JARMUSCH v. OTIS IRON & STEEL CO. (No. 7,968.) (Supreme Court of Ohio. May 12, 1903.) Error to Circuit Court, Cuyahoga County. Herman Preusser, for plaintiff in error. Squires, Sanders & Dempsey, for defendant in error.

PER CURIAM. Judgment affirmed.

SPEAR, SHAUCK, and CREW, JJ., concur.

JENKINS v. EMRICH et al. (No. 7,710.) (Supreme Court of Ohio. March 17, 1903.) Error to Circuit Court, Ottawa County. George E. Reiter and H. L. Peeke, for plaintiff in error. King & Guerin, for defendants in error.

PER CURIAM. Judgment affirmed.

BURKET, C. J., and DAVIS and PRICE, JJ., concur.

JOHNS v. CLEVELAND, C., C. & ST. L. RY. CO. (No. 7,924.) (Supreme Court of Ohio. Sept. 29, 1903.) Error to Circuit Court, Cuyahoga County. John O. Winship, for plaintiff in error. E. A. Foote, for defendant in error.

PER CURIAM. Judgment affirmed.

SPEAR, DAVIS, SHAUCK, PRICE, and CREW, JJ., concur.

JOHNSON v. JOHNSON. (No. 7,849.) (Supreme Court of Ohio, May 5, 1903.) Error to Circuit Court, Belmont County. Fred L. Rosemond, for plaintiff in error. Wells & Sheppard and Petty & Crew, for defendant in error.

PER CURIAM. Judgment affirmed.

BURKET, C. J., and SPEAR and PRICE, JJ., concur.

JONES, Auditor, et al. v. BRITTON. (No. 8,369.) (Supreme Court of Ohio. Dec. 15, 1903.) Error to Circuit Court, Franklin County. Cyrus Huling and Taylor, Seymour, Webber & King, for plaintiffs in error. C. T. Clark, Rogers & Rogers, Chas. Kinney, F. Rathmell, E. E. Corwin, M. E. Thrailkill, and H. J. Ossing, for defendant in error.

PER CURIAM. Judgment of the circuit court reversed, injunction dissolved, and petition of plaintiff below dismissed.

BURKET, C. J., and DAVIS, SHAUCK, PRICE, and CREW, JJ., concur.

JONES, Auditor, et al. v. BRITTON. (No. 8,370.) (Supreme Court of Ohio. Dec. 15, 1903.) Error to Circuit Court, Franklin County. Cyrus Huling and Taylor, Seymour, Webber & King, for plaintiffs in error. C. T. Clark, Rogers & Rogers, Chas. Kinney, F. Rathmell, E. E. Corwin, M. E. Thrailkill, and H. J. Ossing, for defendant in error.

PER CURIAM. Judgment of the circuit court reversed, injunction dissolved, and petition of plaintiff below dismissed.

BURKET, C. J., and DAVIS, SHAUCK, PRICE, and CREW, JJ., concur.

JONES v. JONES. (No. 8,185.) (Supreme Court of Ohio. Sept. 29, 1903.) Error to Circuit Court, Scioto County. Nelson W. Evans and Frank W. Moulton, for plaintiff in error. James S. Thomas and Bannon & Bannon, for defendant in error.

PER CURIAM. Judgment affirmed.

BURKET, C. J., and SPEAR, DAVIS, SHAUCK, PRICE, and CREW, JJ., concur.

JONES v. JONES. (No. 8,186.) (Supreme Court of Ohio. Sept. 29, 1903.) Error to Circuit Court, Scioto County. Nelson W. Evans and Frank W. Moulton, for plaintiff in error. James S. Thomas and Bannon & Bannon, for defendant in error.

PER CURIAM. Judgment affirmed.

BURKET, C. J., and SPEAR, DAVIS, SHAUCK, PRICE, and CREW, JJ., concur.

JONES v. JONES et al. (No. 8,228.) (Supreme Court of Ohio. Oct. 13, 1903.) Error to Circuit Court, Butler County. E. W. Kittredge, Andrews & Morey, and Shotts & Millikin, for plaintiff in error. Alex. F. Hume, for defendant in error.

PER CURIAM. Judgment affirmed.

BURKET, C. J., and DAVIS, SHAUCK, and PRICE, JJ., concur.

KARNS v. KARNS et al. (No. 7,862.) (Supreme Court of Ohio. May 5, 1903.) Error to Circuit Court, Mercer County. Mauk & Jackson, for plaintiff in error. A. D. Marsh and John W. Loree, for defendants in error.

PER CURIAM. Judgment affirmed.

BURKET, C. J., and DAVIS and PRICE, JJ., concur.

KIMERLINE, Auditor, v. STATE ex rel. SEARS et al. (No. 7,743.) (Supreme Court of Ohio. March 24, 1903.) Error to Circuit Court, Crawford County. Finley & Gallinger, for plaintiff in error. Harris & Sears, for defendants in error.

PER CURIAM. Judgment affirmed.

SPEAR, SHAUCK, and CREW, JJ., concur.

KING v. MELIA. (No. 7,648.) (Supreme Court of Ohio. March 24, 1903.) Error to Circuit Court, Mahoning County. Jones & Anderson, for plaintiff in error. E. H. Moore and J. P. Wilson, for defendant in error.

PER CURIAM. Judgment affirmed.

BURKET, C. J., and SPEAR and PRICE, JJ., concur on the ground that there is no error in the judgment below, and all concur in the judgment of affirmance on the ground that there is no compliance with that part of section 6711, Rev. St. 1892, which requires so much of the record to be reviewed as will show the error complained of to be printed.

KING et al. v. TOLEDO LOAN CO. et al. (No. 8,020.) (Supreme Court of Ohio. Oct. 20, 1903.) Error to Circuit Court, Lucas County. A. W. Eckert and John A. King, for plaintiffs in error. King & Tracy and Samuel N. Young, for defendants in error.

PER CURIAM. Judgment affirmed.

BURKET, C. J., and DAVIS and PRICE, JJ., concur.

KNEDLER et al. v. DOSTER. (No. 8,015.) (Supreme Court of Ohio. Jan. 19, 1904.) Error to Circuit Court, Fayette County. Gregg, Patton & Gregg and Post & Reid, for plaintiffs in error. H. H. Sanderson, for defendant in error.

PER CURIAM. Judgment affirmed, on authority of Banning v. Gotshall, 62 Ohio St. 210, 56 N. E. 1030.

BURKET, C. J., and DAVIS and PRICE, JJ., concur.

KNOWLTON v. POND. (No. 7,650.) (Supreme Court of Ohio. Feb. 17, 1903.) Error to Circuit Court, Licking County. A. A. Stasel, for plaintiff in error. Kibler & Kibler and David M. Keller, for defendant in error.

PER CURIAM. Judgment affirmed.

BURKET, C. J., and DAVIS and PRICE, JJ., concur.

KNOX v. CARR et al. (No. 8,217.) (Supreme Court of Ohio. Jan. 26, 1904.) Error to Circuit Court, Greene County. Geo. Arthur, Horace L. Smith, and John B. Knox, for plaintiff in error. Charles L. Spencer and Charles H. Kyle, for defendants in error.

PER CURIAM. Judgment affirmed.

SPEAR, DAVIS, SHAUCK, PRICE, and CREW, JJ., concur.

KOTTE v. CREED et al. (No. 7,910.) (Supreme Court of Ohio. May 19, 1903.) Error to Superior Court of Cincinnati. Charles W. Baker, for plaintiff in error. Alfred B. Benedict, for defendants in error.

PER CURIAM. Judgment affirmed.

BURKET, C. J., and DAVIS and PRICE, JJ., concur.

LAKE SHORE & M. S. RY. CO. v. HOTCHKISS. (No. 8,371.) (Supreme Court of Ohio. Dec. 1, 1903.) Error to Circuit Court, Cuyahoga County. Brewer, Cook & McGowan, for plaintiff in error. Kline, Carr, Tolles & Goff, for defendant in error.

PER CURIAM. Judgment affirmed.

BURKET, C. J., and SPEAR, DAVIS, SHAUCK, PRICE, and CREW, JJ., concur.

LEICK v. SANFORD. (No. 7,786.) (Supreme Court of Ohio. March 31, 1903.) Error to Circuit Court, Cuyahoga County. Beavis & Johnson, for plaintiff in error. W. H. Boyd, for defendant in error.

PER CURIAM. Judgment affirmed.

BURKET, C. J., and DAVIS and PRICE, JJ., concur.

LIMA ELECTRIC LIGHT & POWER CO. v. ANTRIM. (No. 8,022.) (Supreme Court of Ohio. Dec. 1, 1903.) Error to Circuit Court, Allen County. Richie & Richie and W. H. Leete, for plaintiff in error. Motter, Mackenzie & Weadock and Goeke & Hoskins, for defendant in error.

PER CURIAM. Judgment affirmed.

BURKET, C. J., and SPEAR, DAVIS, SHAUCK, PRICE, and CREW, JJ., concur.

LINKE v. WALCUTT et al. (No. 7,819.) (Supreme Court of Ohio. Sept. 22, 1903.) Error to Circuit Court, Franklin County. J. D. Sullivan, for plaintiff in error. Frank Rathmell and A. H. Johnson, for defendants in error.

PER CURIAM. Judgment affirmed.

SPEAR, DAVIS, SHAUCK, PRICE, and CREW, JJ., concur.

LEONARD v. BANK. (No. 7,816.) (Supreme Court of Ohio. June 9, 1903.) Error to Circuit Court, Lorain County. Johnston & Leonard, for plaintiff in error. W. B. Thompson and Geo. L. Glitsch, for defendant in error.

PER CURIAM. Judgment affirmed.

BURKET, C. J., and SHAUCK and CREW, JJ., concur.

LEWIS, Auditor, v. STATE ex rel. HARRIS. (No. 8,426.) (Supreme Court of Ohio. Feb. 2, 1904.) Error to Circuit Court, Hamilton County. Ampt, Ireton, Collins & Schoenle, for plaintiff in error. Dan Thew Wright, for defendant in error.

PER CURIAM. Judgment reversed, on authority of Lewis, Auditor, v. Kramer, 69 Ohio St. 473, 69 N. E. 980.

SPEAR, DAVIS, SHAUCK, and PRICE, JJ., concur.

LIFE INS. CO. v. HOWLE. (No. 7,992.) (Supreme Court of Ohio. May 12, 1903.) Error to Circuit Court, Cuyahoga County. C. L. Hotze, for plaintiff in error. Hart & Canfield and W. S. Kerruish, for defendant in error.

PER CURIAM. Judgment affirmed.

SPEAR, SHAUCK, and CREW, JJ., concur.

LONGANECKER et al. v. DARKE COUNTY COM'RS et al. (No. 8,203.) (Supreme Court of Ohio. Dec. 1, 1903.) Error to Circuit Court, Darke County. Martin B. Trainor, for plaintiffs in error. Meeker & Gaskill and Anderson, Bowman & Anderson, for defendants in error.

PER CURIAM. Judgment affirmed.

BURKET, C. J., and SHAUCK and PRICE, JJ., concur.

LUEBBERT v. VAN PELT et al. (No. 7,704.) (Supreme Court of Ohio. March 10, 1903.) Error to Circuit Court, Hamilton County. Closs & Luebbert, for plaintiff in error. A. J. Cunningham, for defendants in error.

PER CURIAM. Judgment affirmed.

BURKET, C. J., and SPEAR, DAVIS, SHAUCK, PRICE, and CREW, JJ., concur.

LUHRIG COAL CO. v. ALLISON. (No. 7,997.) (Supreme Court of Ohio. Dec. 8, 1903.) Error to Circuit Court, Athens County. Burch & Johnson, W. E. Peters and Grosvenor, Jones & Worstell, for plaintiff in error. Lawrence T. Neal and Jewett & Wood, for defendant in error.

PER CURIAM. Judgment affirmed.

SPEAR, SHAUCK, PRICE, and CREW, JJ., concur.

McCAMMON et al. v. COOPER et al. (No. 8,238.) (Supreme Court of Ohio. Jan. 5, 1904.) Error to Circuit Court, Hamilton County. Harlan Cleveland and Bromwell & Bruce, for plaintiffs in error. Harmon, Colston, Goldsmith & Hoadly, for defendants in error.

PER CURIAM. Judgment affirmed, on authority of McCammon et al. v. Cooper, Trustee, 69 Ohio St. 366, 69 N. E. 658.

SPEAR, DAVIS, SHAUCK, and PRICE, JJ., concur.

McGILLIN v. VIETOR et al. (No. 7,787.) (Supreme Court of Ohio. March 31, 1903.) Error to Circuit Court, Mahoning County. George F. Arrel and Foran, McTighe & Baker, for plaintiff in error. Jones & Anderson, T.

H. Gilmer, James E. Walsh, and M. C. McNab, for defendants in error.

PER CURIAM. Judgment affirmed.

BURKET, C. J., and DAVIS and PRICE, JJ., concur.

MADDEN et al. v. STATE ex rel. FISHER et al. (No. 7,785.) (Supreme Court of Ohio. March 31, 1903.) Error to Circuit Court, Greene County. C. W. Whitmer, for plaintiffs in error. William F. Orr and Marcus Shoup, for defendants in error.

PER CURIAM. Judgment affirmed.

BURKET, C. J., and DAVIS and PRICE, JJ., concur.

MATHIAS v. WILLARD. (No. 7,657.) (Supreme Court of Ohio. March 3, 1903.) Error to Circuit Court, Tuscarawas County. Richards & McCullough, for plaintiff in error. E. M. Bailey and E. S. Douthitt, for defendant in error.

PER CURIAM. Judgment modified as per journal entry.

BURKET, C. J., and SPEAR, DAVIS, and CREW, JJ., concur.

MEEHAN v. CITY OF CINCINNATI. (No. 7,832.) (Supreme Court of Ohio. April 14, 1903.) Error to Circuit Court, Hamilton County. John Weld Peck and H. J. Power, for plaintiff in error. Charles J. Hunt and Wade H. Ellis, for defendant in error.

PER CURIAM. Judgment affirmed.

SPEAR, SHAUCK, and CREW, JJ., concur.

MICHIGAN MUT. LIFE INS. CO. v. EAST SIDE LUMBER CO. et al. (No. 8,248.) (Supreme Court of Ohio. Feb. 2, 1904.) Error to Circuit Court, Lucas County. E. R. Guiney and G. W. Kinney, for plaintiff in error. C. W. Everett, N. O. Winter, Chas. E. Longwell, Clem V. Wagner, and Griffin & Conklin, for defendants in error.

PER CURIAM. Judgment affirmed.

DAVIS, SHAUCK, PRICE, and CREW, JJ., concur.

MIDLAND NAT. BANK v. LONG et al. (No. 8,198.) (Supreme Court of Ohio. Jan. 19, 1904.) Error to Circuit Court, Fayette County. Post & Reid, for plaintiff in error. Mills Gardner, Rogers & Dempsey, and Creamer & Creamer, for defendants in error.

PER CURIAM. Judgment affirmed.

SPEAR, SHAUCK, and CREW, JJ., concur.

MILTON et al. v. JONES et al. (No. 7,729.) (Supreme Court of Ohio. March 24, 1903.) Error to Circuit Court, Monroe County. Hamilton & Matz and C. L. Weems, for plaintiffs in error. A. D. Follett, F. L. Blackmarr, and J. P. Spriggs & Son, for defendants in error.

PER CURIAM. Judgment affirmed.

BURKET, C. J., and DAVIS and PRICE, JJ., concur.

MISCHLER v. WHITEMAN et al. (No. 7,930.) (Supreme Court of Ohio. May 12, 1903.) Error to Circuit Court, Brown County. Parker & Waters and J. W. Tarbell, for plaintiff in error. Rufus L. Fite, for defendants in error.

PER CURIAM. Judgment affirmed, on authority of Cleveland Trust Co. et al. v. Lander, Treasurer, 62 Ohio St. 266, 56 N. E. 1036.

BURKET, C. J., and DAVIS and PRICE, JJ., concur.

MITCHELL et al. v. TUCKER et al. (No. 7,986.) (Supreme Court of Ohio. Dec. 8, 1903.) Error to Circuit Court, Lucas County. Charles A. Thatcher, for plaintiffs in error. Clayton W. Everett, for defendants in error.

PER CURIAM. Judgment affirmed on two grounds: (1) That the plaintiff in error has failed to print the record of the judgment complained of; (2) that, if it were printed, it would fail to show any error of the circuit court.

SPEAR, DAVIS, SHAUCK, and CREW, JJ., concur.

MORRISON v. BARRON et al. (No. 7,638.) (Supreme Court of Ohio. March 3, 1903.) Error to Circuit Court, Franklin County. Pugh & Pugh and F. B. Hoffman, for plaintiff in error. Dyer, Williams & Stouffer and Taylor, Seymour & Webber, for defendants in error.

PER CURIAM. Judgment affirmed.

BURKET, C. J., and SPEAR, DAVIS, SHAUCK, PRICE, and CREW, JJ., concur.

MURDOCK-WEST CO. v. LOGAN et al. (No. 7,999.) (Supreme Court of Ohio. Oct. 13, 1903.) Error to Circuit Court, Washington County. McConica & Dwiggins and C. C. Middleswart, for plaintiff in error. A. D. Follett, A. L. Weil, and C. M. Thorp, for defendants in error.

PER CURIAM. Judgment affirmed.

SHAUCK, PRICE, and CREW, JJ., concur. BURKE, C. J., and DAVIS, J., dissent.

MURRAY v. CITY OF CINCINNATI. (No. 7,972.) (Supreme Court of Ohio. March 3, 1903.) Error to Circuit Court, Hamilton County. Edward M. Ballard, for plaintiff in error. Charles Hunt, John V. Campbell, and Albert H. Morrill, Corp. Counsel, for defendant in error.

PER CURIAM. Judgment affirmed.

BURKET, C. J., and DAVIS, SHAUCK, and CREW, JJ., concur.

MYERS v. WEBER et al. (No. 8,047.) (Supreme Court of Ohio. Oct. 27, 1903.) Error to Circuit Court, Williams County. Boothman & Newcomer and Conway & Duffey, for plaintiff in error. John M. Killits, for defendants in error.

PER CURIAM. Judgment affirmed.

BURKET, C. J., and DAVIS, SHAUCK, PRICE, and CREW, JJ., concur.

NATIONAL LIFE INS. CO. v. HANNER. (No. 8,180.) (Supreme Court of Ohio. Jan. 5, 1904.) Error to Circuit Court, Lucas County. Doyle & Lewis, for plaintiff in error. Kinney & Newton, for defendant in error.

PER CURIAM. Judgment affirmed.

BURKET, C. J., and SPEAR and CREW, JJ., concur.

NATIONAL STEEL CO. v. LINN. (No. 8,374.) (Supreme Court of Ohio. Jan. 5, 1904.) Error to Circuit Court, Jefferson County. P. P. Lewis, for plaintiff in error. D. M. Gruber, for defendant in error.

PER CURIAM. Judgment of the circuit court reversed, and that of the common pleas affirmed.

BURKET, C. J., and DAVIS, SHAUCK, and CREW, JJ., concur.

NATIONAL SURETY CO. v. PECK-WILLIAMSON HEATING & VENTILATING CO. (No. 7,844.) (Supreme Court of Ohio. April 21, 1903.) Error to Circuit Court, Hamilton County. Paxton & Warrington, C. S. Bowman and Wilson & Wilson, for plaintiff in error. Harmon, Colston, Goldsmith & Hoadly, C. B. Matthews, and Ernst, Cassatt & McDougall, for defendant in error.

PER CURIAM. Judgment affirmed.

BURKET, C. J., and SPEAR, DAVIS, SHAUCK, PRICE, and CREW, JJ., concur.

NATIONAL TUBE CO. v. EASTERN TUBE CO. et al. (No. 8,115.) (Supreme Court of Ohio. Dec. 8, 1903.) Error to Circuit Court, Muskingum County. Garfield, Garfield & Howe and Sullivan & Cromwell, for plaintiff in error. Frank A. Durban, for defendants in error.

PER CURIAM. Judgment affirmed.

SPEAR, DAVIS, SHAUCK, PRICE, and CREW, JJ., concur.

NEWPORT & C. BRIDGE CO. v. JUTTE et al. (No. 7,514.) (Supreme Court of Ohio. April 14, 1903.) Error to Circuit Court, Hamilton County. Maxwell & Ramsey, Robert Ramsey, and W. W. Ramsey, for plaintiff in error. Stephens & Lincoln and Charles H. Stephens, for defendants in error.

PER CURIAM. Judgment affirmed.

BURKET, C. J., and DAVIS, SHAUCK, PRICE, and CREW, JJ., concur.

NIXON v. RAILROAD CO. (No. 7,575.) (Supreme Court of Ohio. Feb. 24, 1903.) Error to Circuit Court, Cuyahoga County. Johnson & Hackney, for plaintiff in error. Ford, Snyder, Henry & McGraw, for defendant in error.

PER CURIAM. Judgment affirmed.

BURKET, C. J., and DAVIS, SHAUCK, PRICE, and CREW, JJ., concur.

NORTHWESTERN NAT. INS. CO. v. GREEN. (No. 8,009.) (Supreme Court of Ohio. Jan. 19, 1904.) Error to Circuit Court, Ashtabula County. Hoyt & Munsell, for plaintiff in error. Charles Lawyer and Perry & Roberts, for defendant in error.

PER CURIAM. Judgment affirmed.

BURKET, C. J., and DAVIS and PRICE, JJ., concur.

OAK LOAN & BUILDING CO. v. FLETCHER et al. (No. 7,310.) (Supreme Court of Ohio. March 31, 1903.) Error to Superior Court of Cincinnati. Coppock, Hammel & Coppock, for plaintiff in error. Maxwell & Ramsey and Franklin T. Cahill, for defendants in error.

PER CURIAM. Judgment affirmed.

BURKET, C. J., and SPEAR, DAVIS, SHAUCK, PRICE, and CREW, JJ., concur.

OGLEVIE et al. v. MILLER et al. (No. 8,028.) (Supreme Court of Ohio. June 16, 1903.) Error to Circuit Court, Knox County. J. B. Graham and J. B. Waight, for plaintiff in error. Cooper & Moore and McIntire & McIntire, for defendants in error.

PER CURIAM. Judgment affirmed.

BURKET, C. J., and SPEAR, SHAUCK, PRICE, and CREW, JJ., concur.

OHIO NAT. SMOKE CONSUMER CO. v. PRATT. (No. 7,643.) (Supreme Court of Ohio. Feb. 17, 1903.) Error to Circuit Court, Cuyahoga County. Hessenmueller & Bemis, for plaintiff in error. Frank C. Phillips, for defendant in error.

PER CURIAM. Judgment affirmed.

BURKET, C. J., and DAVIS and PRICE, JJ., concur.

OHIO & P. COAL CO. v. HOUSE. (No. 7,807.) (Supreme Court of Ohio. Nov. 17, 1903.) Error to Circuit Court, Columbiana County. Billingsley & Clark, for plaintiff in error. P. M. Smith, L. C. Moore, and Potts & Moore, for defendant in error.

PER CURIAM. Judgment of the circuit court reversed, and that of the common pleas affirmed.

BURKET, C. J., and DAVIS, SHAUCK, PRICE, and CREW, JJ., concur.

O'MALLEY v. TRUSTEES et al. (No. 7,894.) (Supreme Court of Ohio. May 5, 1903.) Error to Superior Court of Cincinnati. Coppock, Hammel & Coppock, for plaintiff in error. Thornton M. Hinkle, for defendants in error.

PER CURIAM. Judgment affirmed.

SPEAR, SHAUCK, and CREW, JJ., concur.

PADDOCK, HODGE & CO. v. RAILWAY CO. (No. 7,618.) (Supreme Court of Ohio. March 3, 1903.) Error to Circuit Court, Lucas County. Porter Paddock, for plaintiffs in error. Bowman & Bowman and Doyle & Lewis, for defendant in error.

PER CURIAM. Judgment affirmed.

BURKET, C. J., and DAVIS and PRICE, JJ., concur.

PARKER v. TOWNSEND. (No. 7,781.) (Supreme Court of Ohio. March 24, 1903.) Error to Circuit Court, Huron County. Harlon L. Stewart, for plaintiff in error. Andrews Bros., for defendant in error.

PER CURIAM. Judgment affirmed.

BURKET, C. J., and DAVIS and PRICE, JJ., concur.

PATRICK v. FOGLE. (No. 7,659.) (Supreme Court of Ohio. March 3, 1903.) Error to Circuit Court, Cuyahoga County. Weed & Miller, for plaintiff in error. John O. Winship, for defendant in error.

PER CURIAM. Judgment affirmed.

BURKET, C. J., and SPEAR, DAVIS, SHAUCK, PRICE, and CREW, JJ., concur.

PATTISON et al. v. TAYLOR. (No. 7,663.) (Supreme Court of Ohio. March 10, 1903.) Error to Circuit Court, Hamilton County. C. Hammond Avery and Harper & Allen, for plaintiffs in error. R. De V. Carroll, for defendant in error.

PER CURIAM. Judgment affirmed.

BURKET, C. J., and SPEAR, DAVIS, and PRICE, JJ., concur.

PEARSON v. YOUNT et al. (No. 7,680.) (Supreme Court of Ohio. March 3, 1903.) Error to Circuit Court, Miami County. Gilbert & Shipman, for plaintiff in error. Long & Kyle and B. F. Hershey, for defendants in error.

PER CURIAM. Judgment affirmed.

BURKET, C. J., and DAVIS and PRICE, JJ., concur.

PENNSYLVANIA CO. v. STATE ex rel. GALLINGER. (No. 8,336.) (Supreme Court of Ohio. Oct. 6, 1903.) Error to Circuit Court, Crawford County. Wheeler & Bentley, for plaintiff in error. Finley & Gallinger, for defendant in error.

PER CURIAM. Judgment reversed, demurrer to answer overruled, demurrer to petition sustained, and petition dismissed, on authority of the P., C., C. & St. L. Ry. Co. v. Cox, 55 Ohio St. 497, 45 N. E. 641, 35 L. R. A. 507, and State ex rel. v. The P. C., C. & St. L. Ry. Co., 68 Ohio St. 9, 67 N. E. 93.

BURKET, C. J., and SPEAR, DAVIS, SHAUCK, PRICE, and CREW, JJ., concur.

PEOPLE'S BUILDING, LOAN & SAVINGS ASS'N v. CUNNINGHAM. (No. 7,728.) (Supreme Court of Ohio. March 17, 1903.) Error to Circuit Court, Sandusky County. Chester M. Elliott, Richards & Heffner, Kinney & O'Farrell, and John B. Stahl, for plaintiff in error. Hunt & DeRan, for defendants in error.

PER CURIAM. Judgment affirmed. Cross-petition in error dismissed for want of jurisdiction.

SPEAR, SHAUCK, and CREW, JJ., concur.

PEOPLE'S BUILDING, LOAN & SAVINGS ASS'N v. FRONIZER et al. (No. 7,727.) (Supreme Court of Ohio. March 17, 1903.) Error to Circuit Court, Sandusky County. Chester M. Elliott, Richards & Heffner, Kinney & O'Farrell, and John B. Stahl, for plaintiff in error. Hunt & DeRan, for defendants in error.

PER CURIAM. Judgment affirmed.

SPEAR, SHAUCK, and CREW, JJ., concur.

PEOPLE'S BUILDING, LOAN & SAVINGS ASS'N v. KNOX. (No. 7,725.) (Supreme Court of Ohio. March 17, 1903.) Error to Circuit Court, Sandusky County. Chester M. Elliott, Richards & Heffner, Kinney & O'Farrell, and John B. Stahl, for plaintiff in error. Jesse Vickery, for defendant in error.

PER CURIAM. Judgment affirmed.

SPEAR, SHAUCK, and CREW, JJ., concur.

PEOPLE'S BUILDING, LOAN & SAVINGS ASS'N v. MAXWELL et al. (No. 7,729.) (Supreme Court of Ohio. March 17, 1903.) Error to Circuit Court, Sandusky County. Chester M. Elliott, Richards & Heffner, Kinney & O'Farrell, and John B. Stahl, for plaintiff in error. Hunt & DeRan, for defendants in error.

PER CURIAM. Judgment affirmed. Cross-petition in error dismissed for want of jurisdiction.

SPEAR, SHAUCK, and CREW, JJ., concur.

PEOPLE'S BUILDING, LOAN & SAVINGS ASS'N v. ZIMMERMAN et al. (No. 7,726.) (Supreme Court of Ohio. March 17, 1903.) Error to Circuit Court, Sandusky County. Chester M. Elliott, Richards & Heffner, Kinney & O'Farrell, and John B. Stahl, for plaintiff in error. Love & Culbert, for defendants in error.

PER CURIAM. Judgment affirmed.

SPEAR, SHAUCK, and CREW, JJ., concur.

POLSDORFER v. BRUON. (No. 7,896.) (Supreme Court of Ohio. May 12, 1903.) Error to Circuit Court, Putnam County. Krauss & Eastman and Bailey & Bailey, for plaintiff in error. Leasure & Powell and Watts & Moore, for defendant in error.

PER CURIAM. Judgment affirmed.

BURKET, C. J., and DAVIS and PRICE, JJ., concur.

PRIDDY v. BEATTY et al. (No. 7,722.) (Supreme Court of Ohio. May 12, 1903.) Error to Circuit Court, Hancock County. George F. Pendleton, John Poe, and John E. Beatty, for plaintiff in error. Axline & Betts and E. T. Dunn, for defendants in error.

PER CURIAM. Judgment affirmed.

SPEAR, SHAUCK, and CREW, JJ., concur.

PULTNEY FOUNDRY & ENGINEERING CO. et al. v. BANK et al. (No. 7,806.) (Supreme Court of Ohio. March 10, 1903.) Error to Circuit Court, Mahoning County. Arrel, McVey & Robinson and Jones & Anderson, for plaintiffs in error. T. W. Sanderson, J. P. Wilson, Johnston & Calvin, and Norris, Jackson & Rose, for defendants in error.

PER CURIAM. Judgment affirmed.

BURKET, C. J., and DAVIS, SHAUCK, PRICE, and CREW, JJ., concur.

RAILROAD CO. v. BUTLER. (No. 8,016.) (Supreme Court of Ohio. March 3, 1903.) Error to Circuit Court, Lucas County. E. D. Potter, Ashley Pond, and Henry Russell, for plaintiff in error. Hamilton & Kirby and Cole, Whitlock & Cooper, for defendant in error.

PER CURIAM. Judgment affirmed.

BURKET, C. J., and DAVIS and PRICE, JJ., concur.

RAILROAD CO. v. RUBLE. (No. 8,024.) (Supreme Court of Ohio. March 24, 1903.) Error to Circuit Court, Allen County. John B. Cockrum, Richie & Richie, and W. H. Leete, for plaintiff in error. Ridenour & Hafhill, for defendant in error.

PER CURIAM. Judgment affirmed.

BURKET, C. J., and SPEAR, PRICE, and CREW, JJ., concur.

RAILWAY CO. v. HAM. (No. 8,095.) (Supreme Court of Ohio. June 9, 1903.) Error to Circuit Court, Fulton County. E. D. Potter, Geo. C. Greene, and F. J. Jerome, for plaintiff in error. Ham, Ham & Ham and Handy & Handy, for defendant in error.

PER CURIAM. Judgment of the circuit court reversed, and that of the common pleas affirmed.

BURKET, C. J., and DAVIS, SHAUCK, and CREW, JJ., concur.

RAILWAY CO. v. POTTER. (No. 7,494.) (Supreme Court of Ohio. March 3, 1903.) Error to Circuit Court, Butler County. Shotts & Millikin and R. D. Marshall, for plaintiff in error. Alex. F. Hume and C. J. Smith, for defendant in error.

PER CURIAM. Judgment affirmed.

SPEAR, SHAUCK, and CREW, JJ., concur.

RAILWAY CO. v. TAYLOR. (No. 8,173.) (Supreme Court of Ohio. June 16, 1903.) Error to Circuit Court, Franklin County. Merrick, Tompkins & Godown, for plaintiff in error. T. E. Powell, C. C. Snyder, and W. J. Ford, for defendant in error.

PER CURIAM. Judgment affirmed.

SPEAR, SHAUCK, and CREW, JJ., concur.

RASCHE v. VARWIG et al. (No. 7,984.) (Supreme Court of Ohio. June 16, 1903.) Error to Circuit Court, Hamilton County. L. H. Pummill and W. G. Williams, for plaintiff in error. Louis J. Dolle and Alfred B. Benedict, for defendants in error.

PER CURIAM. Judgment affirmed.

SPEAR, SHAUCK, and CREW, JJ., concur.

RAYMER v. GENDRON. (No. 8,191.) (Supreme Court of Ohio. Jan. 12, 1904.) Error to Circuit Court, Lucas County. O. S. Brumback and C. A. Thatcher, for plaintiff in error. Smith & Baker, for defendant in error.

PER CURIAM. Judgment affirmed.

BURKET, C. J., and DAVIS and CREW, JJ., concur.

READ v. TERHUNE et al. (No. 7,908.) (Supreme Court of Ohio. May 5, 1903.) Error to Circuit Court, Lucas County. W. H. A. Read, for plaintiff in error. King & Tracy, for defendants in error.

PER CURIAM. Judgment affirmed.

SPEAR, SHAUCK, and CREW, JJ., concur.

RECTOR v. CITY DEPOSIT BANK CO. (No. 8,162.) (Supreme Court of Ohio. Nov. 24, 1903.) Error to Circuit Court, Franklin County. Pugh & Pugh, Thomas E. Steele, and Fred C. Rector, for plaintiff in error. Outhwaite, Linn & Thurman, for defendant in error.

PER CURIAM. Judgment affirmed.

BURKET, C. J., and SPEAR, DAVIS, SHAUCK, and CREW, JJ., concur.

RECTOR v. COMMERCIAL NAT. BANK. (No. 8,161.) (Supreme Court of Ohio. Nov. 24, 1903.) Error to Circuit Court, Franklin County. Pugh & Pugh and Thomas E. Steele, for plaintiff in error. F. F. D. Albery, for defendant in error.

PER CURIAM. Judgment affirmed.

BURKET, C. J., and DAVIS and SHAUCK, JJ., concur. PRICE, J., dissents.

REILY v. WHITEMAN et al. (No. 8,065.) (Supreme Court of Ohio. Oct. 20, 1903.) Error to Circuit Court, Hamilton County. Johnson & Levy, for plaintiff in error. Coffey, Mallon, Mills & Vordenberg, for defendants in error.

PER CURIAM. Judgments of the circuit court and of the common pleas court reversed, and cause remanded, on authority of Yetzer v. Thoman, 17 Ohio St. 130, 91 Am. Dec. 222, and McAllister v. Hartzell, 60 Ohio St. 69, 53 N. E. 715.

BURKET, C. J., and SPEAR, DAVIS, SHAUCK, PRICE, and CREW, JJ., concur.

RANNELLS et al. v. BENTLEY et al. (No. 7,685.) (Supreme Court of Ohio. March 10, 1903.) Error to Circuit Court, Clinton County. James M. Morton and D. B. Van Pelt, for plaintiffs in error. J. M. Kirk and Telfair & Telfair, for defendants in error.

PER CURIAM. Judgment affirmed.

BURKET, C. J., and DAVIS and PRICE, JJ., concur.

RICKETTS v. BROWN. (No. 8,021.) (Supreme Court of Ohio. Jan. 12, 1904.) Error to Circuit Court, Hamilton County. Horstman & Horstman and G. H. Kattenhorn, for plaintiff in error. W. A. Hicks, for defendant in error.

PER CURIAM. Judgment affirmed.

BURKET, C. J., and DAVIS and PRICE, JJ., concur.

RINEHART v. REED et al. (No. 7,705.) (Supreme Court of Ohio. March 17, 1903.) Error to Circuit Court, Jefferson County. J. C. Bigger and D. M. Bruber, for plaintiff in error. Erskine & Erskine, for defendants in error.

PER CURIAM. Judgment affirmed.

BURKET, C. J., and DAVIS and PRICE, JJ., concur.

RISSLER et al. v. EDWARDS. (No. 8,004.) (Supreme Court of Ohio. Jan. 19, 1904.) Error to Circuit Court, Richland County. Twitchell & Hartman, for plaintiffs in error. Douglass & Mengert, for defendant in error.

PER CURIAM. Judgment affirmed.

BURKET, C. J., and SPEAR, DAVIS, SHAUCK, PRICE, and CREW, JJ., concur.

RISSLER et al. v. KELLER. (No. 8,005.) (Supreme Court of Ohio. Jan. 19, 1904.) Error to Circuit Court, Richland County. Twitchell & Hartman, for plaintiffs in error. Douglass & Mengert, for defendant in error.

PER CURIAM. Judgment affirmed.

BURKET, C. J., and SPEAR, DAVIS, SHAUCK, PRICE, and CREW, JJ., concur.

RUNYON & DICKSEID v. KIRK-CHRISTY CO. (No. 7,611.) (Supreme Court of Ohio. March 10, 1903.) Error to Circuit Court, Lawrence County. A. R. Johnson and E. E. Corn, for plaintiffs in error. White, Johnson, McCaslin & Cannon, John Hamilton, and Phillips & Phillips, for defendant in error.

PER CURIAM. Judgment affirmed.

BURKET, C. J., and SPEAR, DAVIS, PRICE, and CREW, JJ., concur.

SATER et al. v. ROBBINS et al. (No. 8,026.) (Supreme Court of Ohio. Nov. 24, 1903.) Error to Circuit Court, Hamilton County. Milton Sater and Follett, Kelley & Follett, for plaintiffs in error. Paxton & Warrington, for defendants in error.

PER CURIAM. Judgment affirmed.

BURKET, C. J., and SPEAR, DAVIS, SHAUCK, PRICE, and CREW, JJ., concur.

SAUER v. SAUER. (No. 7,934.) (Supreme Court of Ohio. Oct. 13, 1903.) Error to Circuit Court, Hamilton County. Heilker & Heilker and Ellis B. Gregg, for plaintiff in error. P. H. Kumler and Walter A. De Camp, for defendant in error.

PER CURIAM. Judgment affirmed, on authority of Pretzinger v. Pretzinger, 45 Ohio St. 452, 15 N. E. 471, 4 Am. St. Rep. 542.

SPEAR, SHAUCK, and CREW, JJ., concur.

SCARBOROUGH et al. v. GIBSON et al. (No. 8,463.) (Supreme Court of Ohio. Feb. 2, 1904.) Error to Superior Court of Cincinnati. F. O. Suire, A. B. Benedict, and Outcalt & Foraker, for plaintiff in error. Ampt, Ireton, Collins & Schoenle, for defendants in error.

PER CURIAM. Judgment affirmed.

SHAUCK, PRICE, and CREW, JJ., concur.

SCHMIDT et al. v. WUNKER. (No. 7,923.) (Supreme Court of Ohio. May 19, 1903.) Error to Circuit Court, Hamilton County. Chris. Von Seggern and Conner & Walker, for plaintiffs in error. Goebel & Bettinger, for defendant in error.

PER CURIAM. Judgment affirmed.

BURKET, C. J., and DAVIS and PRICE, JJ., concur.

SCHULTZ et al. v. SCHROEDER et al. (No. 7,741.) (Supreme Court of Ohio. March 31, 1903.) Error to Circuit Court, Cuyahoga County. Sanders & Wilson, for plaintiffs in error. H. T. Cowin and Alexander Hadden, for defendants in error.

PER CURIAM. Judgment affirmed.

SPEAR, SHAUCK, and CREW, JJ., concur.

SCHROEDER v. PHILLIPS. (No. 7,967.) (Supreme Court of Ohio. Jan. 5, 1904.) Error to Circuit Court, Cuyahoga County. Beavis & Johnson, for plaintiff in error. Foran, McTighe & Baker and C. C. Lones, for defendant in error.

PER CURIAM. Judgment affirmed.

BURKET, C. J., and SPEAR, DAVIS, SHAUCK, PRICE, and CREW, JJ., concur.

SHAFFER v. FATE. (No. 7,674.) (Supreme Court of Ohio. Feb. 17, 1903.) Error to Circuit Court, Huron County. Laser & Huston, for plaintiff in error. Donnel & Marriott, F. D. Gunsaullus, and Andrews Bros., for defendant in error.

PER CURIAM. Judgment affirmed, on the ground that the contract was not part of petition, and not printed in bill of exceptions, and is therefore not before this court for consideration.

BURKET, C. J., and DAVIS and PRICE, JJ., concur.

SHARON SAVINGS & LOAN ASS'N v. KATON et al. (No. 7,646.) (Supreme Court of Ohio. March 3, 1903.) Error to Circuit Court, Butler County. J. C. Smith and Slayback & Harr, for plaintiff in error. M. O. Burns and Gorman & Thompson, for defendants in error.

PER CURIAM. Judgment affirmed.

SPEAR, SHAUCK, and CREW, JJ., concur.

SHAW v. FRENCH et al. (No. 8,249.) (Supreme Court of Ohio. Nov. 24, 1903.) Error to Circuit Court, Hamilton County. Charles W. Baker, for plaintiff in error. Ampt, Ireton, Collins & Schoenle, Co. Sols., for defendants in error.

PER CURIAM. Judgment affirmed.

BURKET, C. J., and SPEAR, DAVIS, SHAUCK, PRICE, and CREW, JJ., concur.

SHERMAN et al. v. CAMPBELL et al. (No. 7,846.) (Supreme Court of Ohio. April 21, 1903.) Error to Circuit Court, Sandusky County. Hunt & De Ran, for plaintiff in error. Finefrock & Garver, W. W. Campbell, and L. J. Turley, for defendants in error.

PER CURIAM. Judgment affirmed.

SPEAR, SHAUCK, and CREW, JJ., concur.

SHRADER v. DOWNER et al. (No. 8,106.) (Supreme Court of Ohio. Oct. 20, 1903.) Error to Circuit Court, Licking County. C. & C. H. Follett, for plaintiff in error. Samuel M. Hunter and John M. Swartz, for defendant in error.

PER CURIAM. Judgment affirmed.

BURKET, C. J., and DAVIS and PRICE, JJ., concur.

SKINNER v. STATE et al. (No. 7,842.) (Supreme Court of Ohio. June 23, 1903.) Error to Circuit Court, Jackson County. R. H. Jones, for plaintiff in error. A. E. Jacobs, Pros. Atty., for defendants in error.

PER CURIAM. Judgment affirmed.

SPEAR, SHAUCK, and CREW, JJ., concur.

SMITH et al. v. VERWOHLT et al. (No. 7,864.) (Supreme Court of Ohio. May 5, 1903.) Error to Circuit Court, Jefferson County. P. M. Smith and A. G. Smith, for plaintiffs in error. Beatrice M. Kelley, Erskine & Erskine, D. M. Gruber, and J. C. Bigger, for defendants in error.

PER CURIAM. Judgment affirmed.

BURKET, C. J., and DAVIS, SHAUCK, and CREW, JJ., concur.

SNYDER v. COATES. (No. 7,762.) (Supreme Court of Ohio. Nov. 24, 1903.) Error to Circuit Court, Hancock County. Geo. F. Pendleton, for plaintiff in error. Blackford & Blackford, for defendant in error.

PER CURIAM. Judgment affirmed.

SPEAR, SHAUCK, and CREW, JJ., concur.

SPURRIER v. MARTIN et al. (No. 7,926.) (Supreme Court of Ohio. Sept. 29, 1903.) Error to Circuit Court, Morgan County. Kennedy & Tannehill and Barry & Finley, for plaintiff in error. Chas. H. Fouts and M. E. Danford, for defendants in error.

PER CURIAM. Judgment of the circuit court reversed, and that of the common pleas affirmed.

SPEAR, DAVIS, SHAUCK, and PRICE, JJ., concur. CREW, J., not sitting.

STATE v. BAILEY. (No. 7,951.) (Supreme Court of Ohio. Nov. 17, 1903.) Error to Circuit Court, Pickaway County. Irvin F. Snyder, for the State. Chris. A. Weldon, for defendant in error.

PER CURIAM. Judgment affirmed.

BURKET, C. J., and SPEAR, DAVIS, SHAUCK, PRICE, and CREW, JJ., concur.

STATE v. BISHOP et al. (No. 7,949.) (Supreme Court of Ohio. Nov. 17, 1903.) Exceptions from Court of Common Pleas, Butler County. Warren Gard, Pros. Atty., for the State. John F. Neilan and Allen Andrews, for defendants in error.

PER CURIAM. Exceptions overruled. Fees to counsel, $75.

BURKET, C. J., and SPEAR, DAVIS, SHAUCK, PRICE, and CREW, JJ., concur.

STATE v. BOWERS. (No. 7,974.) (Supreme Court of Ohio. Dec. 8, 1903.) Exceptions from Court of Common Pleas, Stark County. J. M. Sheets, Atty. Gen., and Robert H. Day, Pros. Atty., for the State. James Sterling, for defendant in error.

PER CURIAM. Exceptions overruled. A fee of $50 allowed to James Sterling, Esq., counsel, to be paid from the treasury of Stark county.

SPEAR, DAVIS, SHAUCK, PRICE, and CREW, JJ., concur.

STATE v. COSNER. (No. 8,241.) (Supreme Court of Ohio. May 12, 1903.) Error to Circuit Court, Richland County. W. H. Bowers, for the State. W. F. Voegele, Jr., for defendant in error.

PER CURIAM. Judgment affirmed.

BURKET, C. J., and DAVIS and PRICE, JJ., concur.

STATE v. COMMERCIAL BANK. (No. 8,-201.) (Supeme Court of Ohio. Jan. 26, 1904.) Error to Circuit Court, Jackson County. Elmer C. Powell, for the State. J. M. McGillivray, for defendant in error.

PER CURIAM. Judgment affirmed.

BURKET, C. J., and SPEAR, DAVIS, SHAUCK, PRICE, and CREW, JJ., concur.

STATE v. ELLIS. (No. 8,384.) (Supreme Court of Ohio. June 16, 1903.) Error to Circuit Court, Mahoning County. W. R. Graham, Pros. Atty., for the State. Frank Jacobs, for defendant in error.

PER CURIAM. Judgment of the circuit court reversed, and that of the common pleas affirmed, on authority of State v. Allen, 68 Ohio St. 516, 67 N. E. 1053.

BURKET, C. J., and SPEAR, DAVIS, SHAUCK, PRICE, and CREW, JJ., concur.

STATE v. HOOD. (No. 7,877.) (Supreme Court of Ohio. May 19, 1903.) Error to Circuit Court, Guernsey County. James Joyce, for the State. Thomas E. Steele and G. D. Dugan, for defendant in error.

PER CURIAM. Judgment of the circuit court reversed, and that of the common pleas affirmed.

BURKET, C. J., and SPEAR, DAVIS, SHAUCK, and CREW, JJ., concur.

STATE v. SHELL. (No. 7,837.) (Supreme Court of Ohio. Oct. 13, 1903.) Error to Circuit Court, Perry County. J. M. Sheets, Atty. Gen., J. E. Todd, and S. W. Bennet, for the State. Kibler & Kibler, for defendant in error.

PER CURIAM. Judgment affirmed.

BURKET, C. J., and DAVIS, PRICE, and CREW, JJ., concur.

STATE v. TOLEDO RY. & TERMINAL CO. (No. 8,419.) (Supreme Court of Ohio. November 10, 1903.) Error to Circuit Court, Lucas County. B. A. Hayes, for the State. J. K. Hamilton, Clarence Brown, and King & Tracy, for defendant in error.

PER CURIAM. Judgment affirmed.

BURKET, C. J., and SPEAR, DAVIS, SHAUCK, and PRICE, JJ., concur.

STATE ex rel. BIRCH v. CLAPSADDLE et al. (No. 7,857.) (Supreme Court of Ohio. May 5, 1903.) Error to Circuit Court, Columbiana County. P. M. Smith and W. F. Jones, for plaintiff in error. Potts & Moore, for defendants in error.

PER CURIAM. Judgment affirmed.

BURKET, C. J., and DAVIS and PRICE, JJ., concur.

STATE ex rel. COLE v. ADAMS, Auditor. (No. 7,852.) (Supreme Court of Ohio. Sept. 22, 1903.) Error to Circuit Court, Columbiana County. E. B. Dillon and L. P. Metzger, for plaintiff in error. J. H. Brookes, for defendant in error.

PER CURIAM. Judgment affirmed.

BURKET, C. J., and SHAUCK, PRICE, and CREW, JJ., concur.

STATE ex rel. LLOYD v. DOLLISON, Sheriff. (No. 8,109.) (Supreme Court of Ohio. March 24, 1903.) Error to Circuit Court, Guernsey County. R. M. Nevin, James Joyce, and F. S. Monnett, for plaintiff in error. W. B. Wheeler, A. L. Stevens, L. D. Lilly, J. M. Sheets, and A. V. Taylor, for defendant in error.

PER CURIAM. Judgment affirmed.

BURKET, C. J., and SPEAR, DAVIS, SHAUCK, PRICE, and CREW, JJ., concur.

STATE ex rel. McKINZIE v. HYMAN. (No. 7,713.) (Supreme Court of Ohio. March 17, 1903.) Error to Circuit Court, Cuyahoga County. J. H. Hardy and Noble, Pinney & Willard, for plaintiff in error. M. W. Beacom and Babcock, Payer, Gage & Carey, for defendant in error.

PER CURIAM. Judgment affirmed.

BURKET, C. J., and DAVIS and PRICE, JJ., concur.

STATE ex rel. MOFFATT v. GOTCHELL. (No. 8,514.) (Supreme Court of Ohio. June 25, 1903.) Mandamus. F. A. Jeffers, for plaintiff. Mallory & Sears, for defendants.

PER CURIAM. Demurrer to petition overruled, and peremptory writ of mandamus awarded.

BURKET, C. J., and SPEAR, DAVIS, SHAUCK, and CREW, JJ., concur.

STATE ex rel. O'BRIEN v. YAPLE, Mayor, et al. (No. 7,952.) (Supreme Court of Ohio. June 16, 1903.) Error to Circuit Court, Ross County. Charles R. Doll, for plaintiff in error. Wallace D. Yaple and James A. Cahill, for defendants in error.

PER CURIAM. Judgment affirmed.

SPEAR, SHAUCK, and CREW, JJ., concur.

STATE ex rel. SHEETS, Atty. Gen., v. CINCINNATI & E. ELECTRIC RY. CO. (No. 8,096.) (Supreme Court of Ohio. Sept. 29, 1903.) Quo Warranto. J. M. Sheets, Atty. Gen., G. H. Jones, Asst. Atty. Gen., and F. C. Rector, for plaintiff in error. E. G. Kinkead and H. M. Daugherty, for defendants in error.

PER CURIAM. Demurrer to supplemental answer overruled, and petition dismissed, on the ground that quo warranto is not the proper remedy. State ex rel. v. Railroad Co., 50 Ohio St. 239, 33 N. E. 1051.

BURKET, C. J., and SPEAR, DAVIS, SHAUCK, PRICE, and CREW, JJ., concur.

STATE ex rel. SUDBOROUGH v. McKENNEY et al. (No. 7,853.) (Supreme Court of Ohio. April 28, 1903.) Error to Circuit Court, Cuyahoga County. Samuel Doefler, for plaintiff in error. John G. White and Clifford A. Neff, for defendants in error.

PER CURIAM. Judgment reversed, demurrer to reply overruled, and cause remanded for further proceedings as per journal entry.

BURKET, C. J., and SPEAR, DAVIS, SHAUCK, PRICE, and CREW, JJ., concur.

STATE ex rel. WILLIS v. HIGGINS et al. (No. 7,838.) (Supreme Court of Ohio. Dec. 1, 1903.) Error to Circuit Court, Jackson County. Elmer C. Powell, for plaintiff in error. John T. Moore, John Harper, S. F. White, and Hogan & McFarland, for defendants in error.

PER CURIAM. Judgment affirmed.

BURKET, C. J., and SPEAR, DAVIS, PRICE, and CREW, JJ., concur.

STATE NAT. BANK v. WILLIAMS. (No. 8,188.) (Supreme Court of Ohio. Jan. 12, 1904.) Error to Circuit Court, Cuyahoga County. Brewer, Cook & McGowan, for plaintiff in error. Johnson & Dunlap, for defendant in error.

PER CURIAM. Judgment affirmed.

SPEAR, DAVIS, SHAUCK, PRICE, and CREW, JJ., concur.

STEVENSON v. PIQUA HOSIERY CO. (No. 7,916.) (Supreme Court of Ohio. May 5, 1903.) Error to Circuit Court, Miami County. Long & Kyle, for plaintiff in error. Robert J. Smith, for defendant in error.

PER CURIAM. Judgment affirmed.

BURKET, C. J., and DAVIS and PRICE, JJ., concur.

STEWART et al. v. TURNER et al. (No. 7,962.) (Supreme Court of Ohio. June 23, 1903.) Error to Circuit Court, Guernsey County. J. B. Ferguson, for plaintiffs in error. J. W. Smallwood and R. T. Scott, for defendants in error.

PER CURIAM. Judgment of the circuit court reversed, and that of the common pleas affirmed.

BURKET, C. J., and SPEAR, DAVIS, SHAUCK, PRICE, and CREW, JJ., concur.

STOCKER et al. v. VILLAGE OF ARCANUM. (No. 7,811.) (Supreme Court of Ohio. April 21, 1903.) Error to Circuit Court, Darke County. Martin B. Trainor and Kirk Hoffman, for plaintiffs in error. Meeker & Gaskill, for defendants in error.

PER CURIAM. Judgment affirmed, on authority of Comstock v. Nelsonville, 61 Ohio St. 288, 56 N. E. 15, and Findlay v. Pendleton, 62 Ohio St. 80, 56 N. E. 649.

BURKET, C. J., and SPEAR, DAVIS, SHAUCK, PRICE, and CREW, JJ., concur.

STRAUB et al. v. SOUTH ZANESVILLE SEWER PIPE & BRICK CO. (No. 7,711.) (Supreme Court of Ohio. March 24, 1903.) Error to Circuit Court, Seneca County. Alex. Kiskadden, for plaintiffs in error. S. M. Winn and Kelly & Merrill, for defendant in error.

PER CURIAM. Judgment affirmed.

SPEAR, SHAUCK, and CREW, JJ., concur.

STREIT v. OUTCALT et al. (No. 8,244.) (Supreme Court of Ohio. Feb. 2, 1904.) Error to Circuit Court, Hamilton County. Burch & Johnson, for plaintiff in error. Philip Roettinger, Harper & Allen, and M. C. Slutes, for defendants in error.

PER CURIAM. Judgment affirmed.

DAVIS, SHAUCK, PRICE, and CREW, JJ., concur.

STROUSE et al. v. STROUSE et al. (No. 7,715.) (Supreme Court of Ohio. March 31, 1903.) Error to Circuit Court, Seneca County. Brewer & Brewer and N. L. Brewer, for plaintiffs in error. Lutes & Lutes and Geo. E. Schroth, for defendants in error.

PER CURIAM. Judgment affirmed.

BURKET, C. J., and SPEAR, DAVIS, SHAUCK, PRICE, and CREW, JJ., concur.

SUBURBAN BUILDING & LOAN ASS'N v. PUGH. (No. 7,891.) (Supreme Court of Ohio. June 16, 1903.) Error to Superior Court of Cincinnati. Benjamin F. Ehrman, for plaintiff in error. Cohen & Mack, for defendant in error.

PER CURIAM. Judgment affirmed.

BURKET, C. J., and SPEAR, SHAUCK, PRICE, and CREW, JJ., concur.

SULLIVAN et al. v. BURGER et al. (No. 7,929.) (Supreme Court of Ohio. Sept. 29, 1903.) Error to Circuit Court, Hamilton County. Shay & Cogan, for plaintiffs in error. Goebel & Bettinger, for defendants in error.

PER CURIAM. Judgment affirmed.

BURKET, C. J., and SPEAR, DAVIS, SHAUCK, PRICE, and CREW, JJ., concur.

SWART v. HURON DOCK CO. et al. (No. 8,403.) (Supreme Court of Ohio. Jan. 19, 1904.) Error to Circuit Court, Erie County. C. A. Thatcher and W. B. Starbird, for plaintiff in error. Wickham & Wickham, for defendants in error.

PER CURIAM. Judgment affirmed, on authority of Busby v. Finn, 1 Ohio St. 409, the map and blue print being filed with the bill of exceptions, and so described as to leave no doubt of their identity, and the same are therefore held to be a part of the bill of exceptions.

BURKET, C. J., and DAVIS, SHAUCK, PRICE, and CREW, JJ., concur.

TEEPLE v. JOHNSON. (No. 7,843.) (Supreme Court of Ohio. June 25, 1903.) Error to Circuit Court, Summit County. S. G. Rogers and L. S. Pardee, for plaintiff in error. H. C. Sanford and Tibbals & Frank, for defendant in error.

PER CURIAM. Judgment affirmed.

SPEAR, SHAUCK, and CREW, JJ., concur.

THATCHER v. KIRKPATRICK et al. (No. 7,966.) (Supreme Court of Ohio. Dec. 18, 1903.) Error to Circuit Court, Clark County. D. F. Reinoehl and L. F. Young, for plaintiff in error. C. C. Kirkpatrick and Hagan & Kunkle, for defendants in error.

PER CURIAM. Judgment affirmed.

BURKET, C. J., and SPEAR, DAVIS, SHAUCK, PRICE, and CREW, JJ., concur.

THOMAS v. W. J. GAWNE CO. (No. 8,622.) (Supreme Court of Ohio. Dec. 8, 1903.) Error to Circuit Court, Hamilton County. Harrison & Aston, for plaintiff in error. Cohen & Mack, for defendant in error.

PER CURIAM. Judgment affirmed, on authority of B. & O. R. R. Co. v. Fulton, 59 Ohio St. 575, 53 N. E. 265, 44 L. R. A. 520.

SPEAR, DAVIS, SHAUCK, PRICE, and CREW, JJ., concur.

TILTON v. KIMBALL. (No. 7,665.) (Supreme Court of Ohio. March 10, 1903.) Error to Circuit Court, Butler County. Alex. F. Hume, Frank Brandon, and George A. Burr, for plaintiff in error. Morey, Andrews & Morey, for defendant in error.

PER CURIAM. Judgment affirmed.

SPEAR, SHAUCK, and CREW, JJ., concur.

TRAVELERS' INS. CO. v. ROSCH. (No. 8,132.) (Supreme Court of Ohio. Dec. 8, 1903.) Error to Circuit Court, Lorain County. Hoyt, Dustin & Kelley, for plaintiff in error. Metcalf & Cinniger, for defendant in error.

PER CURIAM. Judgment affirmed.

SPEAR, SHAUCK, PRICE, and CREW, JJ., concur.

TROY CARRIAGE CO. et al. v. BANK et al. (No. 7,906.) (Supreme Court of Ohio. May 5, 1903.) Error to Circuit Court, Miami County. Davey, Campbell & St. John, for plaintiffs in error. Gilbert & Shipman, for defendants in error.

PER CURIAM. Judgment affirmed, on authority of Henkle v. Salem Mfg. Co., 39 Ohio St. 547, and Holcomb, Adm'r v. Gibson, 58 Ohio St. 710, 51 N. E. 1098.

SPEAR, SHAUCK, and CREW, JJ., concur.

TRUDGEN v. DAY et al. (No. 7,507.) (Supreme Court of Ohio. March 3, 1903.) Error to Circuit Court, Hamilton County. Thomas L. Michie and Joel C. Clore, for plaintiff in error. Goebel & Bettinger, for defendants in error.

PER CURIAM. Judgment affirmed.

SPEAR, SHAUCK, and CREW, JJ., concur.

TURPIN v. HAGERTY, Recorder. (No. 7,932.) (Supreme Court of Ohio. Sept. 29, 1903.) Error to Circuit Court, Hamilton County. Goebel & Bettinger, for plaintiff in error. J. Shroder and S. B. Deal, for defendant in error.

PER CURIAM. Judgment affirmed.

BURKET, C. J., and SPEAR, DAVIS, SHAUCK, PRICE, and CREW, JJ., concur.

TWINING v. CUSAC. (No. 7,716.) (Supreme Court of Ohio. March 17, 1903.) Error to Circuit Court, Hancock County. Phelps & David and Marion G. Foster, for plaintiff in error. John Poe, for defendant in error.

PER CURIAM. Judgment affirmed.

SPEAR, SHAUCK, and CREW, JJ., concur.

UMBRAUGH et al. v. FAST. (No. 7,687.) (Supreme Court of Ohio. March 17, 1903.) Error to Circuit Court, Ashland County. Clem. P. Winbigler, for plaintiffs in error. Nicol & Boffenmyer and Welty & Albaugh, for defendant in error.

PER CURIAM. Judgment reversed, and judgment for plaintiffs in error. Grounds stated in journal entry.

BURKET, C. J., and SPEAR, DAVIS, SHAUCK, PRICE, and CREW, JJ., concur.

UNION SAV. BANK & TRUST CO. v. CENTRAL TRUST & SAFE DEPOSIT CO. et al. (No. 7,953.) (Supreme Court of Ohio. Dec. 1, 1903.) Error to Circuit Court, Hamilton County. Howard Douglass and Geo. W. Harding, for plaintiff in error. Charles B. Wilby, for defendants in error.

PER CURIAM. Judgment affirmed.

SPEAR, DAVIS, SHAUCK, PRICE, and CREW, JJ., concur.

UNITED STATES FIDELITY & GUARANTY CO. v. DRUCKER. (No. 7,724.) (Supreme Court of Ohio. March 24, 1903.) Error to Circuit Court, Cuyahoga County. A. A. Stearns, for plaintiff in error. Brewer, Cook & McGowan, for defendant in error.

PER CURIAM. Judgment affirmed.

BURKET, C. J., and DAVIS and PRICE, JJ., concur.

VILLAGE OF MT. GILEAD v. HAYDEN. (No. 8,284.) (Supreme Court of Ohio. Dec. 15, 1903.) Error to Circuit Court, Morrow County. Benjamin Olds, for plaintiff in error. James, Millard & Powell, J. E. Ladd, and Harlan & Wood, for defendant in error.

PER CURIAM. Judgment affirmed.

BURKET, C. J., and DAVIS and PRICE, JJ., concur.

VILLAGE OF NEW LEXINGTON v. ROSE. (No. 7,887.) (Supreme Court of Ohio. May 5, 1903.) Error to Circuit Court, Perry County. Tom D. Binckley and L. A. Tussing, for plaintiff in error. H. D. Cochran, J. A. Ivers, and Donahue & Spencer, for defendant in error.

PER CURIAM. Judgment affirmed.

BURKET, C. J., and DAVIS and PRICE, JJ., concur.

VILLAGE OF MINERAL CITY v. RAILROAD CO. (No. 7,644.) (Supreme Court of Ohio. March 17, 1903.) Error to Circuit Court, Tuscarawas County. Richards & McCullough, for plaintiff in error. Carey & Mullins, for defendant in error.

PER CURIAM. Judgment affirmed.

BURKET, C. J., and DAVIS and PRICE, JJ., concur.

VILLAGE OF PERRYSBURG v. BUCKHOUSE. (No. 8,008.) (Supreme Court of Ohio. Jan. 12, 1904.) Error to Circuit Court, Wood County. Baldwin & Harrington, for plaintiff in error. James, Beverstock & Donahey, for defendant in error.

PER CURIAM. Judgment of the circuit court reversed, and that of the common pleas affirmed.

BURKET, C. J., and SPEAR, DAVIS, SHAUCK, PRICE, and CREW, JJ., concur.

VINTON v. STAUT. (No. 7,667.) (Supreme Court of Ohio. March 17, 1903.) Error to Circuit Court, Tuscarawas County. Neely & Patrick, for plaintiff in error. J. H. Mitchell, for defendant in error.

PER CURIAM. Judgment affirmed.

SPEAR, SHAUCK, and CREW, JJ., concur.

WADE v. BROWN. (No. 7,656.) (Supreme Court of Ohio. March 3, 1903.) Error to Circuit Court, Butler County. Shotts & Milliken, for plaintiff in error. Edward H. Jones and Morey, Andrews & Morey, for defendant in error.

PER CURIAM. Judgment affirmed.

SPEAR, SHAUCK, and CREW, JJ., concur.

WADSWORTH SALT CO. v. RAILROAD CO. et al. (No. 7,814.) (Supreme Court of Ohio. April 28, 1903.) Error to Circuit Court, Medina County. Grant & Sieber, for plaintiff in error. Tibbals & Frank, for defendants in error.

PER CURIAM. Cause dismissed for want of jurisdiction, it not appearing that more than $300 is involved in the judgment sought to be reversed.

BURKET, C. J., and DAVIS and PRICE, JJ., concur.

WALTERS v. KEENAN et al. (No. 7,703.) (Supreme Court of Ohio. March 17, 1903.) Error to Circuit Court, Hancock County. Phelps & Davis, for plaintiff in error. John Sheridan, for defendants in error.

PER CURIAM. Judgment affirmed.

SPEAR, SHAUCK, and CREW, JJ., concur.

WALTON v. CITY OF TOLEDO. (No. 8,098.) (Supreme Court of Ohio. Oct. 27, 1903.) Error to Circuit Court, Lucas County. Southard & Southard and Chas. F. Watts, for plaintiff in error. J. M. Sheets, Atty. Gen., M. R. Brailey, City Sol., and Frank M. Sala, Sp. Counsel, for defendant in error.

PER CURIAM. Judgment affirmed.

SPEAR, SHAUCK, and CREW, JJ., concur.

WARD v. CLEVELAND TRUST CO. et al. (No. 7,919.) (Supreme Court of Ohio. May 19, 1903.) Error to Circuit Court, Cuyahoga County. H. W. Ward, for plaintiff in error. Garfield, Garfield & Howe, for defendants in error.

PER CURIAM. Judgment affirmed.

BURKET, C. J., and DAVIS and PRICE, JJ., concur.

WASHBURN et al. v. WASHBURN et al. (No. 7,721.) (Supreme Court of Ohio. April 21, 1903.) Error to Circuit Court, Pike County. John P. Phillips, John A. Eylar, and Stephen D. McLaughlin, for plaintiffs in error. Seney & Johnson and James A. Douglas, for defendants in error.

PER CURIAM. Judgment of dismissal set aside and vacated, and judgment of the circuit court affirmed.

BURKET, C. J., and DAVIS and PRICE, JJ., concur.

WASSON v. SECOR et al. (No. 7,622.) (Supreme Court of Ohio. March 3, 1903.) Error to Circuit Court, Lucas County. B. F. Reno, for plaintiff in error. King & Tracy, H. C. Rorick, Ray & Cordill, Delphey & Corbett, J. R. Calder, B. F. Reno, Southard & Southard, T. J. McDonnell, and Smith & Baker, for defendants in error.

PER CURIAM. Judgment affirmed, as per stipulations in Spear v. Walbridge et al. (No. 7,621) 67 N. E. 1101, and order of priority to be same as in that case.

BURKET, C. J., and SPEAR, DAVIS, SHAUCK, PRICE, and CREW, JJ., concur.

WEATHERHEAD v. CULBERTSON. (No. 7,610.) (Supreme Court of Ohio. March 3, 1903.) Error to Circuit Court, Miami County. Long & Kyle and H. H. Williams, for plaintiff in error. John W. Morris and A. F. Broomhall, for defendant in error.

PER CURIAM. Judgment affirmed.

BURKET, C. J., and DAVIS and PRICE, JJ., concur.

WEHRMANN v. KNIGHTS TEMPLARS' & MASONIC MUT. AID ASS'N et al. (No. 7,980.) (Supreme Court of Ohio. Nov. 24, 1903.) Error to Circuit Court, Hamilton County. Kelley & Hauck, for plaintiff in error. Robertson & Buchwalter, for defendants in error.

PER CURIAM. Judgments of the lower courts reversed, and judgment for plaintiff in error, on authority of State National Bank v. Esterly, Receiver, 69 Ohio St. 24, 68 N. E. 582.

BURKET, C. J., and SPEAR, DAVIS, and PRICE, JJ., concur.

WELCH et al. v. ATWOOD. (No. 7,765.) (Supreme Court of Ohio. March 24, 1903.) Error to Circuit Court, Stark County. A. A. Thayer and C. C. Bow, for plaintiffs in error. John H. White and Charles C. Upham, for defendant in error.

PER CURIAM. Judgment affirmed.

BURKET, C. J., and DAVIS and PRICE, JJ., concur.

WELLSTON COAL CO. v. SMITH. (No. 8,204.) (Supreme Court of Ohio. Oct. 13, 1903.) Error to Circuit Court, Jackson County. J. M. McGillivray, for plaintiff in error. E. C. Powell, C. C. McCormick, and E. E. Eubanks, for defendant in error.

PER CURIAM. Judgment affirmed.

BURKET, C. J., and DAVIS and PRICE, JJ., concur.

WERTS v. FIRE & MARINE INS. CO. (No. 7,818.) (Supreme Court of Ohio. April 21, 1903.) Error to Circuit Court, Miami County. Gilbert & Shipman, for plaintiff in error. J. H. Cabell, Cabell & Freiberg, and A. F. Broomhall, for defendant in error.

PER CURIAM. Judgment affirmed.

BURKET, C. J., and SPEAR, DAVIS, SHAUCK, PRICE, and CREW, JJ., concur.

WEST v. KNOPPENBERGER. (No. 7,833.) (Supreme Court of Ohio. April 14, 1903.) Error to Circuit Court, Auglaize County. Jesse Stephens, Stueve & Connaughton, and Sumner & Tucker, for plaintiff in error. Layton & Son, D. F. Mooney, and Goeke & Hoskins, for defendant in error.

PER CURIAM. Judgment vacated, and cause remanded to the circuit court for further proceedings, as per journal entry.

BURKET, C. J., and SPEAR, DAVIS, SHAUCK, PRICE, and CREW, JJ., concur.

WESTERN STAR PUB. CO. v. DECHANT. (No. 7,813.) (Supreme Court of Ohio. March 31, 1903.) Error to Circuit Court, Warren County. Frank Brandon and George A. Burr, for plaintiff in error. John E. Smith and W. C. Thompson, for defendant in error.

PER CURIAM. Judgment affirmed.

SPEAR, SHAUCK, and CREW, JJ., concur.

WHITE v. CHERRY. (No. 8,007.) (Supreme Court of Ohio. June 9, 1903.) Error to Circuit Court, Hancock County. L. Howard Jones, for plaintiff in error. C. B. Dwiggins and H. Walter Doty, for defendant in error.

PER CURIAM. Judgment affirmed.

BURKET, C. J., and DAVIS and SHAUCK, JJ., concur.

WICK BANKING & TRUST CO. v. WARNER. (No. 8,077.) (Supreme Court of Ohio. April 14, 1903.) Error to Circuit Court, Cuyahoga County. E. T. Hamilton and William M. Raynolds, for plaintiff in error. O. C. Pinney and A. A. Stearns, for defendant in error.

PER CURIAM. Judgment affirmed.

BURKET, C. J., and SPEAR, DAVIS, SHAUCK, PRICE, and CREW, JJ., concur.

WICKER et al. v. MESSINGER et al. (No. 7,748.) (Supreme Court of Ohio. April 14, 1903.) Error to Circuit Court, Lucas County. B. A. Hayes, for plaintiffs in error. King & Tracy, for defendants in error.

PER CURIAM. Judgment modified, and remanded to the court of common pleas for entry of proper final judgment.

BURKET, C. J., and SPEAR, DAVIS, PRICE, and CREW, JJ., concur.

WILLIAMS v. STATE. (No. 8,036.) (Supreme Court of Ohio. Jan. 12, 1904.) Error to Circuit Court, Lucas County. Chittenden & Chittenden and C. W. F. Kirkley, for plaintiff in error. J. M. Sheets, Atty. Gen., and W. F. Brown, for the State.

PER CURIAM. Judgment affirmed.

BURKET, C. J., and DAVIS and PRICE, JJ., concur.

WINKLEMAN v. BOARD OF TRUSTEES. (No. 7,536.) (Supreme Court of Ohio. Feb. 17, 1903.) Error to Circuit Court, Putnam County. Bailey & Bailey, for plaintiff in error. Straman & Malone, for defendant in error.

PER CURIAM. Judgment affirmed.

BURKET, C. J., and SPEAR, DAVIS, SHAUCK, PRICE, and CREW, JJ., concur.

WINLAND v. STATE ex rel. ZITZMAN et al. (No. 7,954.) (Supreme Court of Ohio. Dec. 8, 1903.) Error to Circuit Court, Monroe County. Hamilton & Matz, for plaintiff in error. Mallory & Sears, W. E. Moore, F. A. Jeffers, E. L. Lynch, and F. W. Ketterer, for defendants in error.

PER CURIAM. Judgment affirmed. Cross-petition not considered because not printed.

SPEAR, DAVIS, SHAUCK, PRICE, and CREW, JJ., concur.

WOLF et al. v. HAPNER. (No. 7,878.) (Supreme Court of Ohio. May 5, 1903.) Error to Circuit Court, Preble County. King & Lowry, for plaintiffs in error. Risinger & Risinger, for defendant in error.

PER CURIAM. Judgment affirmed.

BURKET, C. J., and DAVIS and PRICE, JJ., concur.

WORST et al. v. NICOL. (No. 7,649.) (Supreme Court of Ohio. March 3, 1903.) Error to Circuit Court, Ashland County. Frank Taggart and Frank S. Patterson, for plaintiffs in error. John W. Albaugh and Nicol & Boffenmyer, for defendant in error.

PER CURIAM. Judgment affirmed.

BURKET, C. J., and DAVIS and PRICE, JJ., concur.

YEISER v. RAILWAY CO. (No. 7,761.) (Supreme Court of Ohio. April 21, 1903.) Error to Circuit Court, Warren County. George S. Baily, for plaintiff in error. Foraker, Outcalt, Granger & Prior and J. A. Runyan, for defendant in error.

PER CURIAM. Judgment affirmed, for the reason that the judgment of the court of common pleas was reversed by the circuit court for the reason that it was against the weight of the evidence.

BURKET, C. J., and SPEAR, DAVIS, SHAUCK, PRICE, and CREW, JJ., concur.

YODER v. BEVARD et al. (No. 8,508.) (Supreme Court of Ohio. Dec. 18, 1903.) Error to Circuit Court, Wayne County. W. F. Kean and A. B. Metz, for plaintiff in error. M. L. Smyser, for defendants in error.

PER CURIAM. Judgment affirmed.

BURKET, C. J., and SPEAR, DAVIS, SHAUCK, PRICE, and CREW, JJ., concur.

END OF CASES IN VOL. 70.

Lightning Source UK Ltd.
Milton Keynes UK
UKHW020020181218
334174UK00006B/133/P

9 780260 700339